AMERICAN
LIBRARY LAWS

AMERICAN
LIBRARY LAWS

Fifth Edition

ALEX LADENSON, J.D., Ph.D.
Editor

CHICAGO

American Library Association

1983

Library of Congress Cataloging in Publication Data
Main entry under title:

American library laws.

Includes index.
1. Library legislation—United States.   I. Ladenson, Alex, 1907–
II. American Library Association.
KF4315.A3   1983   344.73'092   83-21543
ISBN 0-8389-0400-9   347.30492

—————————————— **To Inez** ——————————————

For her keen interest,
warm encouragement
and deep inspiration

—

Foreword

The fifth edition of *American Library Laws* is a complete revision of all the basic general library laws enacted by the state and federal governments. The present volume, with minor exceptions, contains the laws in effect as of December 31, 1982.

As in the previous editions, the material has been arranged either by type of library or by subject. Under these broad headings, the individual sections are usually arranged in numerical order by code section number. The citation appearing underneath each heading refers to the code or compilation from which the laws have been reprinted. At the end of each individual section is a reference to the official source of the law.

This volume has been produced by the same method, a combination of photocopy from official codes and statutory compilations and of offset printing, that was employed in the publications of the third edition. It is a pleasure for the editor to express his deep appreciation to the following law publishers for granting permission to reproduce the text of the new or amended laws: W. H. Anderson Co., Cincinnati, OH, Bobbs-Merrill Co., Indianapolis, Ind.; Callaghan & Co., Chicago, Ill.; The Harrison Co., Atlanta, Ga.; The Lawyers Cooperative Publishing Co., Rochester, New York; The Michie Co., Charlottesville, Va.; Oxford Publishing Co., Oxford New Hampshire; Allen Smith Co., Indianapolis, Ind.; Edward Thompson Co., Brooklyn, N.Y; Vernon Law Book Co., Kansas City, Mo.; and West Publishing Co., St. Paul, Minn.

I wish to express my deep appreciation to William J. Powers, Jr., Executive Librarian, Cook County Law Library, and Stephen F. Czike, Executive Librarian, Chicago Bar Association, for making the volumes available for photocopying.

I owe a special debt of gratitude to Mrs. Genevieve O. Blechschmidt for her assistance in preparing the manuscript for the printer.

Alex Ladenson

Contents

I. FEDERAL GOVERNMENT

II. THE STATES

CONTENTS

III. TERRITORIES AND DEPENDENCIES

PART I
THE FEDERAL GOVERNMENT

LIBRARY OF CONGRESS

JOINT COMMITTEE ON THE LIBRARY

(United States Code Annotated, 1982, Title 2, s.132a, 132b, 133.)

§ 132a. Appropriations for increase of general library   The unexpended balance of any sums appropriated by Congress for the increase of the general library, together with such sums as may be appropriated to the same purpose, shall be laid out under the direction of the joint committee of Congress on the Library. R.S. § 82; Feb. 7, 1902, No. 5, 32 Stat. 735; Aug. 2, 1946, c. 753, Title II, § 223, 60 Stat. 838.

§ 132b. Joint Committee on the Library

The Joint Committee of Congress on the Library shall, on and after January 3, 1947, consist of the chairman and four members of the Committee on Rules and Administration of the Senate and the chairman and four members of the Committee on House Administration of the House of Representatives. Aug. 2, 1946, c. 753, Title II, § 223, 60 Stat. 838.

§ 133. Joint Committee during recess of Congress

The portion of the Joint Committee of Congress on the Library on the part of the Senate remaining in office as Senators shall during the recess of Congress exercise the powers and discharge the duties conferred by law upon the Joint Committee of Congress on the Library.
As amended Aug. 2, 1946, c. 753, Title II, § 223, 60 Stat. 838.

DEPARTMENTS

(United States Code Annotated, 1982, Title 2, s.132, 131, 134, 135, 137, 137c, 138.)

§ 132. Departments of Library

The Library of Congress shall be arranged in two departments, a general library and a law library.
R.S. § 81.

3

§ 131. Collections composing Library

The Library of Congress, composed of the books, maps, and other publications which on December 1, 1873 remained in existence, from the collections theretofore united under authority of law and those added from time to time by purchase, exchange, donation, reservation from publications ordered by Congress, acquisition of material under the copyright law, and otherwise, shall be preserved in the Library Building. The law library shall be preserved in the Capitol in the rooms which were on July 4, 1872 appropriated to its use, and in such others as may hereafter be assigned thereto.

As amended Oct. 19, 1976, Pub.L. 94–553, Title I, § 105(g), 90 Stat. 2600.

§ 134. Incidental expenses of law library

The incidental expenses of the law library shall be paid out of the appropriations for the Library of Congress.

R.S. § 83.

§ 135. Purchase of books for law library

The Librarian shall make the purchases of books for the law library, under the direction of and pursuant to the catalogue furnished him by the Chief Justice of the Supreme Court.

R.S. § 84.

§ 137. Use and regulation of law library

The justices of the Supreme Court shall have free access to the law library; and they are authorized to make regulations, not inconsistent with law, for the use of the same during the sittings of the court. But such regulations shall not restrict any person authorized to take books from the Library from having access to the law library, or using the books therein in the same manner as he may be entitled to use the books of the general Library.

R.S. § 95.

§ 137c. Withdrawal of books from Library of Congress

The chief judge and associate judges of the United States Court of Appeals for the District of Columbia and the chief judge and associate judges of the United States District Court for the District of Columbia are authorized to use and take books from the Library of Congress in the same manner and subject to the same regulations as justices of the Supreme Court of the United States. Joint Res. No. 9, Jan. 27, 1894, 28 Stat. 577; June 7, 1934, c. 426, 48 Stat. 926; June 25, 1936, c. 804, 49 Stat. 1921; June 25, 1948, c. 646, § 32(a), (b), 62 Stat. 991; May 24, 1949, c. 139, § 127, 63 Stat. 107.

§ 138. Law library open, when

The law library shall be kept open every day so long as either House of Congress is in session.

July 11, 1888, c. 615, § 1, 25 Stat. 262.

PERSONNEL

(United States Code Annotated, 1982, Title 2, s.136, 136a, 136a-1, 139, 140.)

§ 136. Librarian of Congress; appointment; rules and regulations

The Librarian of Congress shall be appointed by the President, by and

with the advice and consent of the Senate. He shall make rules and regulations for the government of the Library.
Feb. 19, 1897, c. 265, § 1, 29 Stat. 544, 546, amended June 6, 1972, Pub. L. 92–310, Title II, § 220(f), 86 Stat. 204.

§ 136a. Librarian of Congress; compensation

The compensation of the Librarian of Congress shall be at an annual rate which is equal to the rate for positions at level IV of the Executive Schedule.
Pub.L. 88–426, Title II, § 203(c), Aug. 14, 1964, 78 Stat. 415, amended Pub.L. 90–206, Title II, §§ 219(2), 225(h), Dec. 16, 1967, 81 Stat. 639, 644; Pub.L. 94–82, Title II, § 204(b), Aug. 9, 1975, 89 Stat. 421.

§ 136a—1. Deputy Librarian of Congress; compensation

The compensation of the Deputy Librarian of Congress shall be at an annual rate which is equal to the rate for positions at level V of the Executive Schedule.
Pub.L. 88–426, Title II, § 203(d), Aug. 14, 1964, 78 Stat. 415, amended Pub.L. 90–206, Title II, § 219(3), 225(h), Dec. 16, 1967, 81 Stat. 639, 644; Pub.L. 94–82, Title II, § 204(b), Aug. 9, 1975, 89 Stat. 421.

§ 139. Report of Librarian of Congress

The Librarian of Congress shall make to Congress not later than April 1, a report for the preceding fiscal year, as to the affairs of the Library of Congress, including the copyright business, and said report shall also include a detailed statement of all receipts and expenditures on account of the Library and said copyright business.
As amended Apr. 21, 1976, Pub.L. 94–273, § 30, 90 Stat. 380.

§ 140. Employees; fitness

All persons employed in and about said Library of Congress under the Librarian shall be appointed solely with reference to their fitness for their particular duties.
Feb. 19, 1897, c. 265, § 1, 29 Stat. 545; June 29, 1922, c. 251, § 1, 42 Stat. 715.

FISCAL OPERATIONS

(United States Code Annotated, 1982, Title 2, s.142a-142f,
143a, 143b.)

§ 142a. Office of administrative assistant and disbursing officer in Library of Congress abolished; transfer of duties to appointee of Librarian

From and after June 10, 1928, the office of administrative assistant and disbursing officer of the Library of Congress, created by section 142 of this title, is abolished and thereafter the duties required to be performed by the administrative assistant and disbursing officer shall be performed, under the direction of the Librarian of Congress, by such persons as the Librarian may appoint for those purposes.
May 11, 1928, c. 521, 45 Stat. 497, amended June 6, 1972, Pub.L. 92–310, Title II, § 220(h), 86 Stat. 205.

§ 142b. Certifying officers of the Library of Congress; accountability; relief by Comptroller General

On and after June 13, 1957, each officer and employee of the Library of Congress, including the Copyright Office, who has been duly autho-

rized in writing by the Librarian of Congress to certify vouchers for payment from appropriations and funds, shall (1) be held responsible for the existence and correctness of the facts recited in the certificate or otherwise stated on the voucher or its supporting papers and for the legality of the proposed payment under the appropriation or fund involved; (2) Repealed; (3) be held responsible and accountable for the correctness of the computations of certified vouchers; and (4) be held accountable for and required to make good to the United States the amount of any illegal, improper, or incorrect payment resulting from any false, inaccurate, or misleading certificate made by him, as well as for any payment prohibited by law or which did not represent a legal obligation under the appropriation or fund involved: *Provided*, That the Comptroller General of the United States may, at his discretion, relieve such certifying officer or employee of liability for any payment otherwise proper whenever he finds (1) that the certification was based on official records and that such certifying officer or employee did not know, and by reasonable diligence and inquiry could not have ascertained, the actual facts, or (2) that the obligation was incurred in good faith, that the payment was not contrary to any statutory provision specifically prohibiting payments of the character involved, and the United States has received value for such payment: *Provided further*, That the Comptroller General shall relieve such certifying officer or employee of liability for an overpayment for transportation services made to any common carrier covered by section 244 of Title 31, whenever he finds that the overpayment occurred solely because the administrative examination made prior to payment of the transportation bill did not include a verification of transportation rates, freight classifications, or land grant deductions.
Pub.L. 85–53, § 1, June 13, 1957, 71 Stat. 81, amended Pub.L. 92–310, Title II, § 220(k), June 6, 1972, 86 Stat. 205.

§ 142c. Same; enforcement of liability

The liability of these certifying officers or employees shall be enforced in the same manner and to the same extent as now provided by law with respect to enforcement of the liability of disbursing and other accountable officers; and they shall have the right to apply for and obtain a decision by the Comptroller General on any question of law involved in a payment on any vouchers presented to them for certification. Pub.L. 85—53, § 2, June 13, 1957, 71 Stat. 81.

§ 142d. Disbursing officer of the Library of Congress; disbursements in accordance with voucher; examination of vouchers; liability

The disbursing officer of the Library of Congress shall (1) disburse moneys of the Library of Congress only upon, and in strict accordance with, vouchers duly certified by the Librarian of Congress or by an officer or employee of the Library of Congress duly authorized in writing by the Librarian to certify such vouchers; (2) make such examination of vouchers as may be necessary to ascertain whether they are in proper form, and duly certified and approved; and (3) be held accountable accordingly: *Provided*, That the disbursing officer shall not be held accountable or responsible for any illegal, improper, or incorrect payment resulting from any false, inaccurate, or misleading certificate, the responsibility for which, under section 142b of this title, is imposed upon a certifying officer or employee of the Library of Congress. Pub.L. 85—53, § 3, June 13, 1957, 71 Stat. 81.

§ 142e. Congressional Budget Office; computation and disbursement of basic pay by Library of Congress

From and after January 1, 1976, the Disbursing Officer of the Library of Congress is authorized to disburse funds appropriated for the Congressional Budget Office, and the Library of Congress shall provide financial management support to the Congressional Budget Office as may be required and mutually agreed to by the Librarian of Congress and the Director of the Congressional Budget Office. The Library of Congress is further authorized to compute and disburse the basic pay of all personnel of the Congressional Budget Office pursuant to the provisions of section 5504 of Title 5, except the Director, who as head of an agency, shall have pay computed and disbursed pursuant to the provisions of section 5505 of Title 5.

All vouchers certified for payment by duly authorized certifying officers of the Library of Congress shall be supported with a certification by an officer or employee of the Congressional Budget Office duly authorized in writing by the Director of the Congressional Budget Office to certify payments from appropriations of the Congressional Budget Office. The Congressional Budget Office certifying officers shall (1) be held responsible for the existence and correctness of the facts recited in the certificate or otherwise stated on the voucher or its supporting paper and the legality of the proposed payment under the appropriation or fund involved, (2) be held responsible and accountable for the correctness of the computations of certifications made, and (3) be held accountable for and required to make good to the United States the amount of any illegal, improper, or incorrect payment resulting from any false, inaccurate, or misleading certificate made by him, as well as for any payment prohibited by law which did not represent a legal obligation under the appropriation or fund involved: *Provided*, That the Comptroller General of the United States, may at his discretion, relieve such certifying officer or employee of liability for any payment otherwise proper whenever he finds (1) that the certification was based on official records and that such certifying officer or employee did not know, and by reasonable diligence and inquiry could not have ascertained the actual facts, or (2) that the obligation was incurred in good faith, that the payment was not contrary to any statutory provision specifically prohibiting payments of the character involved, and the United States has received value for such payment: *Provided further*, That the Comptroller General shall relieve such certifying officer or employee of liability for an overpayment for transportation services made to any common carrier covered by section 244 of Title 31, whenever he finds that the overpayment occurred solely because the administrative examination made prior to payment of the transportation bill did not include a verification of transportation rates, freight classifications, or land grant deductions.

The Disbursing Officer of the Library of Congress shall not be held accountable or responsible for any illegal, improper, or incorrect payment resulting from any false, inaccurate, or misleading certificate, the responsibility for which is imposed upon a certifying officer or employee of the Congressional Budget Office.

Pub.L. 96–536, § 101(c), Dec. 16. 1980, 94 Stat. 3167.

§ 142f. Office of Technology Assessment; disbursement of funds, computation and disbursement of basic pay, and provision of financial management support by Library of Congress

From and after October 1, 1981, the Disbursing Officer of the Library of Congress is authorized to disburse funds appropriated for the Office of Technology Assessment, and the Library of Congress shall provide financial management support to the Office of Technology Assessment as may be required and mutually agreed to by the Librarian of Congress and the Director of the Office of Technology Assessment. The Library of Congress is further authorized to compute and disburse the basic pay of all personnel of the Office of Technology Assessment pursuant to the provisions of section 5504 of Title 5.

All vouchers certified for payment by duly authorized certifying officers of the Library of Congress shall be supported with a certification by an officer or employee of the Office of Technology Assessment duly authorized in writing by the Director of the Office of Technology Assessment to certify payments from appropriations of the Office of Technology Assessment. The Office of Technology Assessment certifying officers shall (1) be held responsible for the existence and correctness of the facts recited in the certificate or otherwise stated on the voucher or its supporting paper and the legality of the proposed payment under the appropriation or fund involved, (2) be held responsible and accountable for the correctness of the computations of certifications made, and (3) be held accountable for and required to make good to the United States the amount of any illegal, improper, or incorrect payment resulting from any false, inaccurate, or misleading certificate made by him, as well as for any payment prohibited by law which did not represent a legal obligation under the appropriation or fund involved: *Provided*, That the Comptroller General of the United States may, at his discretion, relieve such certifying officer or employee of liability for any payment otherwise proper whenever he finds (1) that the certification was based on official records and that such certifying officer or employee did not know, and by reasonable diligence and inquiry could not have ascertained the actual facts, or (2) that the obligation was incurred in good faith, that the payment was not contrary to any statutory provision specifically prohibiting payments of the character involved, and the United States has received value for such payment: *Provided further*, That the Comptroller General shall relieve such certifying officer or employee of liability for an overpayment for transportation services made to any common carrier covered by section 244 of Title 31, whenever he finds that the overpayment occurred solely because of the administrative examination made prior to payment of the transportation bill did not include a verification of transportation rates, freight classifications, or land grant deductions.

The Disbursing Officer of the Library of Congress shall not be held accountable or responsible for any illegal, improper, or incorrect payment resulting from any false, inaccurate, or misleading certificate, the responsibility for which is imposed upon a certifying officer or employee of the Office of Technology Assessment.

Pub.L. 97–51, § 101(c), Oct. 1, 1981, 95 Stat. 959.

§ 143a.   Disbursement of funds

From and after October 1, 1978, funds available to the Library of Congress may be expended to reimburse the Department of State for medical services rendered to employees of the Library of Congress stationed abroad and for contracting on behalf of and hiring alien employees for the Library of Congress under compensation plans comparable to those authorized by section 889 of Title 22; for purchase or hire of passenger motor vehicles; for payment of travel, storage and transportation of household goods, and transportation and per diem expenses for families enroute (not to exceed twenty-four); for benefits comparable to those payable under sections 1136(9), 1136(11), and 1156, respectively, of Title 22; and travel benefits comparable with those which are now or hereafter may be granted single employees of the Agency for International Development, including single Foreign Service personnel assigned to A.I.D. projects, by the Administrator of the Agency for International Development—or his designee —under the authority of section 2396(b) of Title 22; subject to such rules and regulations as may be issued by the Librarian of Congress.

Pub.L. 96–536, § 101(c), Dec. 16, 1980, 94 Stat. 3167.

§ 143b.   Payments in advance for subscriptions or other charges

From and after October 1, 1980, payments in advance for subscriptions

or other charges for bibliographical data, publications, materials in any other form, and services may be made by the Librarian of Congress whenever he determines it to be more prompt, efficient, or economical to do so in the interest of carrying out required Library programs.
Pub.L. 96–536, § 101(c), Dec. 16, 1980, 94 Stat. 3167.

BUILDINGS AND GROUNDS

(United States Code Annotated, 1982, Title 2, s.141, 143, 167, 167a-167j.)

§ 141. Duties of Architect of the Capitol and Librarian of Congress

The Architect of the Capitol shall have charge of all structural work at the Library Building and on the grounds, including all necessary repairs, the operation, maintenance, and repair of the mechanical plant and elevators, the care and maintenance of the grounds, and the purchasing of all equipment other than office equipment. The employees required for the performance of the foregoing duties shall be appointed by the Architect of the Capitol. All other duties on June 29, 1922, required to be performed by the Superintendent of the Library Building and Grounds shall be performed under the direction of the Librarian of Congress, who shall appoint the employees necessary therefor. The Librarian of Congress shall provide for the purchase and supply of office equipment and furniture for library purposes.
As amended June 12, 1970, Pub.L. 91–280, 84 Stat. 309.

§ 143. Appropriations for Library Building and Grounds

All appropriations made to the Architect of the Capitol on account of the Library Building and Grounds shall be disbursed for that purpose in the same manner as other appropriations under his control.
June 29, 1922, c. 251, § 3, 42 Stat. 715.

§ 167. Buildings and grounds; designation of employees as special policemen

(a) The Librarian of Congress may designate employees of the Library of Congress as special policemen for duty in connection with the policing of the Library of Congress buildings and grounds and adjacent streets and shall fix their rates of basic pay as follows:

    (1) Private GS–7—step one through five;
    (2) Sergeant GS–8—step one through five;
    (3) Lieutenant GS–9—step one through five;
    (4) Senior Lieutenant GS–10—step one through five; and
    (5) Captain GS–11—step one through seven.

(b) The Librarian of Congress may apply the provisions of subchapter V of chapter 55 of Title 5 to members of special police force of the Library of Congress.
Aug. 4, 1950, c. 561, § 1, 64 Stat. 411, amended Oct. 21, 1968, Pub.L. 90–610, § 1, 82 Stat. 1201; Dec. 5, 1973, Pub.L. 93–175, § 1, 87 Stat. 693.

§ 167a. Same; public use

Public travel in and occupancy of the Library of Congress grounds is restricted to the sidewalks and other paved surfaces. Aug. 4, 1950, c. 561, § 2, 64 Stat. 411.

§ 167b. Same; sale of articles; signs; solicitation

It shall be unlawful to offer or expose any article for sale in the Library of Congress buildings or grounds; to display any sign, placard, or other form of advertisement therein; or to solicit fares, alms, subscriptions, or contributions therein. Aug. 4, 1950, c. 561, § 3, 64 Stat. 411.

§ 167c. Same; injuries to property

It shall be unlawful to step or climb upon, remove, or in any way injure any statue, seat, wall fountain, or other erection or achitectural feature, or any tree, shrub, plant, or turf in the Library of Congress buildings or grounds. Aug. 4, 1950, c. 561, § 4, 64 Stat. 411.

§ 167d. Same; firearms or fireworks; speeches; objectionable language

It shall be unlawful to discharge any firearm, firework or explosive, set fire to any combustible, make any harangue or oration, or utter loud, threatening, or abusive language in the Library of Congress buildings or grounds. Aug. 4, 1950, c. 561, § 5, 64 Stat. 411.

§ 167e. Same; parades or assemblages; display of flags

It shall be unlawful to parade, stand, or move in processions or assemblages in the Library of Congress buildings or grounds, or to display therein any flag, banner, or device designed or adapted to bring into public notice any party, organization, or movement. Aug. 4, 1950, c. 561, § 6, 64 Stat. 411.

§ 167f. Same; additional regulations; publication; effective date

(a) In addition to the restrictions and requirements specified in sections 167a–167e of this title, the Librarian of Congress may prescribe such regulations as may be deemed necessary for the adequate protection of the Library of Congress buildings and grounds and of persons and property therein, and for the maintenance of suitable order and decorum within the Library of Congress buildings and grounds.

(b) All regulations promulgated under the authority of this section shall be printed in one or more of the daily newspapers published in the District of Columbia, and shall not become effective until the expiration of ten days after the date of such publication. Aug. 4, 1950, c. 561, § 7, 64 Stat. 411.

§ 167g. Same; prosecution and punishment of offenses

Whoever violates any provision of sections 167a–167e of this title, or of any regulation prescribed under section 167f of this title, shall be fined not more than $100 or imprisoned not more than sixty days, or both, prosecution for such offenses to be had in the municipal court for the District of Columbia, upon information by the United States attorney or any of his assistants: *Provided,* That in any case where, in the commission of any such offense, public property is damaged in an amount exceeding $100, the period of imprisonment for the offense may be not more than five years. Aug. 4, 1950, c. 561, § 8, 64 Stat. 412.

§ 167h. Same; jurisdiction of police

The special police provided for in section 167 of this title shall have the power, within the Library of Congress buildings and grounds and adjacent streets, to enforce and make arrests for violations of any provision of sections 167a–167e of this title, of any regulation prescribed under section 167f of this title, or of any law of the United States, any law of the District of Columbia, or of any State, or any regulation promulgated pursuant thereto: *Provided,* That the Metropolitan Police force of the District of Columbia are authorized to make arrests within the Library of Congress buildings and grounds for any violations of any such laws or regulations, but such authority shall not be construed as authorizing the Metropolitan Police force, except with the consent or upon the request of the Librarian of Congress or his assistants, to enter the Library of Congress buildings to make arrests in response to complaints or to serve warrants or to patrol the Library of Congress buildings or grounds.

Aug. 4, 1950, c. 561, § 9, 64 Stat. 412, amended Dec. 24, 1973, Pub.L. 93-198, Title VII, § 739(g)(9), 87 Stat. 829.

§ 167i. Same; suspension of prohibitions against use of grounds

In order to permit the observance of authorized ceremonies within the Library of Congress buildings and grounds, the Librarian of Congress may suspend for such occasions so much of the prohibitions contained in sections 167a–167e of this title as may be necessary for the occasion, but only if responsible officers shall have been appointed, and arrangements determined which are adequate, in the judgment of the Librarian, for the maintenance of suitable order and decorum in the proceedings, and for the protection of the Library buildings and grounds and of persons and property therein. Aug. 4, 1950, c. 561, § 10, 64 Stat. 412.

§ 167j. Same; area comprising—Metes and bounds

(a) For the purposes of sections 167–167j of this title the Library of Congress grounds shall be held to extend to the line of the face of the east curb of First Street Southeast, between B Street Southeast and East Capitol Street; to the line of the face of the south curb of East Capitol Street, between First Street Southeast and Second Street Southeast; to the line of the face of the west curb of Second Street Southeast, between East Capitol Street and B Street Southeast; to the line of the face of the north curb of B Street Southeast, between First Street Southeast and Second Street Southeast; and to the line of the face of the east curb of Second Street Southeast, between Pennsylvania Avenue Southeast and the north side of the alley separating the Library Annex Building and the Folger Shakespeare Library; to the line of the north side of the same alley, between Second Street Southeast and Third Street Southeast; to the line of the face of the west curb of Third Street Southeast, between the north side of the same alley and B Street Southeast; to the line of the face of the north curb of B Street Southeast, between Third Street Southeast and Pennsylvania Avenue Southeast; to the line of the face of the northeast curb of Pennsylvania Avenue Southeast, between B Street Southeast and Second Street Southeast.

Library of Congress buildings and grounds

(b) For the purposes of sections 167 to 167j of this title, the term "Library of Congress buildings and grounds" shall include (1) the whole or any part of any building or structure which is occupied under lease or otherwise by the Library of Congress and is subject to supervision and control by the Librarian of Congress, (2) the land upon which there is situated any building or structure which is occupied wholly by the Library of Congress, and (3) any subway or enclosed passageway connecting two or more buildings or structures occupied in whole or in part by the Library of Congress.

Aug. 4, 1950, c. 561, § 11, 64 Stat. 412, amended June 17, 1970, Pub.L. 91–281, 84 Stat. 309.

PUBLICATIONS

(United States Code Annotated, 1982, Title 2, s.150, 164, 164a, 165, 168-168d.)

§ 150. Sale of copies of card indexes and other publications

The Librarian of Congress is hereby authorized to furnish to such in-

stitutions or individuals as may desire to buy them, such copies of the
card indexes and other publications of the Library as may not be required
for its ordinary transactions, and charge for the same a price which will
cover their cost and ten per centum added, and all moneys received by
him shall be deposited in the Treasury and shall be credited to the appropriation for necessary expenses for the preparation and distribution of
catalog cards and other publications of the Library.
As amended Aug. 5, 1977, Pub.L. 95-94, Title IV, § 405(a), 91 Stat. 682.

§ 164. Index and digest of State legislation; preparation. The Librarian of Congress is authorized and directed to prepare biennially an
index to the legislation of the States of the United States enacted during
the biennium, together with a supplemental digest of the more important
legislation of the period. Feb. 10, 1927, c. 99, § 1, 44 Stat. 1066; Feb.
28, 1929, c. 367, § 1, 45 Stat. 1398.

§ 164a. Same; official distribution. The Librarian of Congress is directed to have the indexes and digests authorized by section 164 of this
title printed and bound for official distribution only. Feb. 28, 1929, c.
367, § 1, 45 Stat. 1398.

§ 165. Appropriation for biennial index. There is authorized to
be appropriated annually for carrying out the provisions of section 164
of this title the sum of $30,000, to remain available until expended. Feb.
10, 1927, c. 99, § 2, 44 Stat. 1066.

**§ 168. Constitution of the United States; preparation and publication
of revised edition; annotations; supplements; decennial editions and
supplements**
The Librarian of Congress shall have prepared—
    (1) a hardbound revised edition of the Constitution of the United
States of America—Analysis and Interpretation, published as Senate
Document Numbered 39, Eighty-eighth Congress (referred to hereinafter as the "Constitution Annotated"), which shall contain annotations of decisions of the Supreme Court of the United States
through the end of the October 1971 term of the Supreme Court,
construing provisions of the Constitution;
    (2) upon the completion of each of the October 1973, October
1975, October 1977, and October 1979 terms of the Supreme Court,
a cumulative pocket-part supplement to the hardbound revised edition of the Constitution Annotated prepared pursuant to clause (1),
which shall contain cumulative annotations of all such decisions
rendered by the Supreme Court after the end of the October 1971
term;
    (3) upon the completion of the October 1981 term of the Su-
preme Court, and upon the completion of each tenth October term
of the Supreme Court thereafter, a hardbound decennial revised
edition of the Constitution Annotated, which shall contain annotations of all decisions theretofore rendered by the Supreme Court
construing provisions of the Constitution; and
    (4) upon the completion of the October 1983 term of the Su-
preme Court, and upon the completion of each subsequent October
term of the Supreme Court beginning in an odd-numbered year
(the final digit of which is not a 1), a cumulative pocket-part supplement to the most recent hardbound decennial revised edition of
the Constitution Annotated, which shall contain cumulative annota-

tions of all such decisions rendered by the Supreme Court which were not included in that hardbound decennial revised edition of the Constitution Annotated.

Pub.L. 91–589, § 1, Dec. 24, 1970, 84 Stat. 1586.

§ 168a. Same; printing as Senate documents

All hardbound revised editions and all cumulative pocket-part supplements shall be printed as Senate documents.

Pub.L. 91–589, § 2, Dec. 24, 1970, 84 Stat. 1586.

§ 168b. Same; printing of additional copies; distribution

There shall be printed four thousand eight hundred and seventy additional copies of the hardbound revised editions prepared pursuant to clause (1) of section 168 of this title and of all cumulative pocket-part supplements thereto, of which two thousand six hundred and thirty-four copies shall be for the use of the House of Representatives, one thousand two hundred and thirty-six copies shall be for the use of the Senate, and one thousand copies shall be for the use of the Joint Committee on Printing. All Members of the Congress, Vice Presidents of the United States, and Delegates and Resident Commissioners, newly elected subsequent to the issuance of the hardbound revised edition prepared pursuant to such clause and prior to the first hardbound decennial revised edition, who did not receive a copy of the edition prepared pursuant to such clause, shall, upon timely request, receive one copy of such edition and the then current cumulative pocket-part supplement and any further supplements thereto. All Members of the Congress, Vice Presidents of the United States, and Delegates and Resident Commissioners, no longer serving after the issuance of the hardbound revised edition prepared pursuant to such clause and who received such edition, may receive one copy of each cumulative pocket-part supplement thereto upon timely request.

Pub.L. 91–589, § 3, Dec. 24, 1970, 84 Stat. 1586.

§ 168c. Same; printing and distribution of decennial editions and supplements

Additional copies of each hardbound decennial revised edition and of the cumulative pocket-part supplements thereto shall be printed and distributed in accordance with the provisions of any concurrent resolution hereafter adopted with respect thereto.

Pub.L. 91–589, § 4, Dec. 24, 1970, 84 Stat. 1587.

§ 168d. Same; authorization of appropriations

There are authorized to be appropriated such sums, to remain available until expended, as may be necessary to carry out the provisions of sections 168 to 168d of this title.

Pub.L. 91–589, § 5, Dec. 24, 1970, 84 Stat. 1587.

DEPOSIT OF PUBLICATIONS

(United States Code Annotated, 1982, Title 44, s.1718, 1719, 1318, Title 20, s.105.)

§ 1718. Distribution of Government publications to the Library of Congress

There shall be printed and furnished to the Library of Congress for official use in the District of Columbia, and for international exchange as provided by section 1719 of this title, not to exceed one hundred and fifty copies of:

> House documents and reports, bound;
>
> Senate documents and reports, bound;
>
> Senate and House journals, bound;
>
> public bills and resolutions;
>
> the United States Code and supplements, bound; and
>
> all other publications and maps which are printed, or otherwise reproduced, under authority of law, upon the requisition of a Congressional committee, executive department, bureau, independent office, establishment, commission, or officer of the Government.

Confidential matter, blank forms, and circular letters not of a public character shall be excepted.

In addition, there shall be delivered as printed to the Library of Congress:

> ten copies of each House document and report, unbound;
>
> ten copies of each Senate document and report, unbound; and
>
> ten copies of each private bill and resolution and fifty copies of the laws in slip form.

Pub.L. 90–620, Oct. 22, 1968, 82 Stat. 1282.

§ 1719. International exchange of Government publications

For the purpose of more fully carrying into effect the convention concluded at Brussels on March 15, 1886, and proclaimed by the President of the United States on January 15, 1889, there shall be supplied to the Library of Congress not to exceed one hundred and twenty-five copies each of all Government publications, including the daily and bound copies of the Congressional Record, for distribution, through the Smithsonian Institution, to foreign governments which agree to send to the United States similar publications of their governments for delivery to the Library of Congress.

Pub.L. 90–620, Oct. 22, 1968, 82 Stat. 1282.

§ 1318. Geological Survey: classes and sizes of publications; report of mineral resources; number of copies; reprints; distribution

The publications of the Geological Survey shall consist of the annual report of the Director, which shall be confined to one volume of royal octavo size; monographs, of quarto size; professional papers, of quarto size; bulletins, of ordinary octavo size; water-supply and irrigation papers, of ordinary octavo size; and maps, folios, and atlases required by law.

*   *   *

The Director of the Geological Survey shall transmit to the Library of Congress two copies of every report of the bureau as soon as the first delivery to the Survey is made, in addition to those received by the Library of Congress under any other law.

Pub.L. 90–620, Oct. 22, 1968, 82 Stat. 1268.

§ 105.   Books for Library of Congress

The distribution of embossed books manufactured by the American Printing House for the Blind at Louisville, Kentucky, out of the income of the fund provided by sections 101, 102 and 104 of this title, shall include one copy of every book so manufactured to be deposited in the Library of Congress at Washington.

Mar. 4, 1913, c. 142, § 1, 37 Stat. 748.

THE BLIND AND PHYSICALLY HANDICAPPED
(United States Code Annotated, 1982, Title 2, s.135a, 135a-1, 135b.)

§ 135a.   Books and sound-reproduction records for blind and other physically handicapped residents;   annual appropriations;   purchases

There is authorized to be appropriated annually to the Library of Congress, in addition to appropriations otherwise made to said Library, such sums for expenditure under the direction of the Librarian of Congress as may be necessary to provide books published either in raised characters, on sound-reproduction recordings or in any other form, and for purchase, maintenance, and replacement of reproducers for such sound-reproduction recordings, for the use of the blind and for other physically handicapped residents of the United States, including the several States, Territories, insular possessions, and the District of Columbia, all of which books, recordings, and reproducers will remain the property of the Library of Congress but will be loaned to blind and to other physically handicapped readers certified by competent authority as unable to read normal printed material as a result of physical limitations, under regulations prescribed by the Librarian of Congress for this service.   In the purchase of books in either raised characters or in sound-reproduction recordings the Librarian of Congress, without reference to the provisions of section 5 of Title 41, shall give preference to nonprofit-making institutions or agencies whose activities are primarily concerned with the blind and with other physically handicapped persons, in all cases where the prices or bids submitted by such institutions or agencies are, by said Librarian, under all the circumstances and needs involved, determined to be fair and reasonable.   Mar. 3, 1931, c. 400, § 1, 46 Stat. 1487, amended Mar. 4, 1933, c. 279, 47 Stat. 1570;   June 14, 1935, 7, 1939, c. 191, 53 Stat. 812;   June 6, 1940, c. 255, 54 Stat. 245;   Oct. c. 242, § 1, 49 Stat. 374;   April 23, 1937, c. 125, § 1, 50 Stat. 72;   June 1, 1942, c. 575, § 1, 56 Stat. 764;   June 13, 1944, c. 246, § 1, 58 Stat. 276;   Aug. 8, 1946, c. 868, § 1, 60 Stat. 908;   July 3, 1952, c. 566, 66 Stat. 326;   Sept. 7, 1957, Pub.L. 85–308, § 1, 71 Stat. 630;   July 30, 1966, Pub.L. 89–522, § 1, 80 Stat. 330.

§ 135a—1.   Library of musical scores, instructional texts, and other specialized materials for use of blind persons or other physically handicapped residents;   authorization of appropriations

(a) The Librarian of Congress shall establish and maintain a library of musical scores, instructional texts, and other specialized materials for the use of the blind and for other physically handicapped residents of the United States and its possessions in furthering their educational, vocational, and cultural opportunities in the field of music. Such scores, texts, and materials shall be made available on a loan basis under regulations developed by the Librarian or his designee in consultation with persons, organizations, and agencies engaged in work for the blind and for other physically handicapped persons.

(b) There are authorized to be appropriated such amounts as may be necessary to carry out the provisions of this section. Pub.L. 87–765, Oct. 9, 1962, 76 Stat. 763, amended Pub.L. 89–522, § 2, July 30, 1966, 80 Stat. 331.

§ 135b. Local and regional centers; preference to blind and other physically handicapped veterans; rules and regulations; authorization of appropriations

(a) The Librarian of Congress may contract or otherwise arrange with such public or other nonprofit libraries, agencies, or organizations as he may deem appropriate to serve as local or regional centers for the circulation of (1) books, recordings, and reproducers referred to in section 135a of this title, and (2) musical scores, instructional texts, and other specialized materials referred to in section 135a—1 of this title, under such conditions and regulations as he may prescribe. In the lending of such books, recordings, reproducers, musical scores, instructional texts, and other specialized materials, preference shall at all times be given to the needs of the blind and of the other physically handicapped persons who have been honorably discharged from the Armed Forces of the United States.

(b) There are authorized to be appropriated such sums as may be necessary to carry out the purposes of this section. Mar. 3, 1931, c. 400, § 2, 46 Stat. 1487, amended July 30, 1966, Pub.L. 89–522, § 1, 80 Stat. 330.

CONGRESSIONAL RESEARCH SERVICE
(United States Code Annotated, 1982, Title 2, s.166.)

§ 166. Congressional Research Service—Redesignation of Legislative Reference Service

(a) The Legislative Reference Service in the Library of Congress is hereby continued as a separate department in the Library of Congress and is redesignated the "Congressional Research Service."

Functions and objectives

(b) It is the policy of Congress that—

(1) the Librarian of Congress, shall, in every possible way, encourage, assist, and promote the Congressional Research Service in—

(A) rendering to Congress the most effective and efficient service,

(B) responding most expeditiously, effectively, and efficiently to the special needs of Congress, and

(C) discharging its reponsibilities to Congress;

and

(2) the Librarian of Congress shall grant and accord to the Congressional Research Service complete research independence and the maximum practicable administrative independence consistent with these objectives.

Appointment and compensation of Director, Deputy Director, and other necessary personnel; minimum grade for Senior Specialists; placement in grades GS–16, 17, and 18 of Specialists and Senior Specialists; appointment without regard to civil service laws and political affiliation and on basis of fitness to perform duties

(c) (1) After consultation with the Joint Committee on the Library, the Librarian of Congress shall appoint the Director of the Congressional Research Service. The basic pay of the Director shall be at a per annum rate equal to the rate of basic pay provided for level V of the Executive Schedule contained in section 5316 of Title 5.

(2) The Librarian of Congress, upon the recommendation of the Director, shall appoint a Deputy Director of the Congressional Research Service and all other necessary personnel thereof. The basic pay of the Deputy Director shall be fixed in accordance wtih chapter 51 (relating to classification) and subchapter III (relating to General Schedule pay rates) of chapter 53 of Title 5, but without regard to section 5108(a) of such title. The basic pay of all other necessary personnel of the Congressional Research Service shall be fixed in accordance with chapter 51 (relating to classification) and subchapter III (relating to General Schedule pay rates) of chapter 53 of Title 5, except that—

(A) the grade of Senior Specialist in each field within the purview of subsection (e) of this section shall not be less than the highest grade in the executive branch of the Government to which research analysts and consultants, without supervisory responsibility, are currently assigned; and

(B) the positions of Specialist and Senior Specialist in the Congressional Research Service may be placed in GS–16, 17, and 18 of the General Schedule of section 5332 of Title 5, without regard to section 5108(a) of such title, subject to the prior approval of the Joint Committee on the Library, of the placement of each such position in any of such grades.

(3) Each appointment made under paragraphs (1) and (2) of this subsection and subsection (e) of this section shall be without regard to the civil service laws, without regard to political affiliation, and solely on the basis of fitness to perform the duties of the position.

Duties of Service; assistance to congressional committees; list of terminating programs and subjects for analysis; legislative data, studies, etc.; information research; digest of bills, preparation; legislation, purpose and effect, and preparation of memoranda; information and research capability, development

(d) It shall be the duty of the Congressional Research Service, without partisan bias—

(1) upon request, to advise and assist any committee of the Senate or House of Representatives and any joint committee of Congress in the analysis, appraisal, and evaluation of legislative proposals within that committee's jurisdiction, or of recommendations submitted to Congress, by the President or any executive agency, so as to assist the committee in—

(A) determining the advisability of enacting such proposals;

(B) estimating the probable results of such proposals and alternatives thereto; and

(C) evaluating alternative methods for accomplishing those results;

and, by providing such other research and analytical services as the committee considers appropriate for these purposes, otherwise to assist in furnishing a basis for the proper evaluation and determination of legislative proposals and recommendations generally; and in the performance of this duty the Service shall have authority, when so authorized by a committee and acting as the agent of that committee, to request of any department or agency of the United States the production of such books, records, correspondence, memoranda, papers, and documents as the Service considers necessary, and such department or agency of the United States shall comply with such request; and, further, in the performance of this and any other relevant duty, the Service shall maintain continuous liaison with all committees;

(2) to make available to each committee of the Senate and House of Representatives and each joint committee of the two Houses, at the opening of a new Congress, a list of programs and activities being carried out under existing law scheduled to terminate during the current Congress, which are within the jurisdiction of the committee;

(3) to make available to each committee of the Senate and House of Representatives and each joint committee of the two Houses, at the opening of a new Congress, a list of subjects and policy areas which the committee might profitably analyze in depth;

(4) upon request, or upon its own initiative in anticipation of requests, to collect, classify, and analyze in the form of studies, reports, compilations, digests, bulletins, indexes, translations, and otherwise, data having a bearing on legislation, and to make such data available and serviceable to committees and Members of the Senate and House of Representatives and joint committees of Congress;

(5) upon request, or upon its own initiative in anticipation of requests, to prepare and provide information, research, and reference materials and services to committees and Members of the Senate and House of Representatives and joint committees of Congress to assist them in their legislative and representative functions;

(6) to prepare summaries and digests of bills and resolutions of a public general nature introduced in the Senate or House of Representatives;

(7) upon request made by any committee or Member of the Congress, to prepare and transmit to such committee or Member a concise memorandum with respect to one or more legislative measures upon which hearings by any committee of the Congress have been announced, which memorandum shall contain a statement of the purpose and effect of each such measure, a description of other relevant measures of similar purpose or effect previously introduced in the Congress, and a recitation of all action taken theretofore by or within the Congress with respect to each such other measure; and

(8) to develop and maintain an information and research capability, to include Senior Specialists, Specialists, other employees, and consultants, as necessary, to perform the functions provided for in this subsection.

Specialists and Senior Specialists; appointment; fields of appointment

(e) The Librarian of Congress is authorized to appoint in the Congressional Research Service, upon the recommendation of the Director, Specialists and Senior Specialists in the following broad fields:

(1) agriculture;
(2) American government and public administration;
(3) American public law;
(4) conservation;
(5) education;
(6) engineering and public works;
(7) housing;
(8) industrial organization and corporation finance;
(9) international affairs;
(10) international trade and economic geography;
(11) labor and employment;
(12) mineral economics;

(13) money and banking;

(14) national defense;

(15) price economics;

(16) science;

(17) social welfare;

(18) taxation and fiscal policy;

(19) technology;

(20) transportation and communications;

(21) urban affairs;

(22) veterans' affairs; and

(23) such other broad fields as the Director may consider appropriate.

Such Specialists and Senior Specialists, together with such other employees of the Congressional Research Service as may be necessary, shall be available for special work with the committees and Members of the Senate and House of Representatives and the joint committees of Congress for any of the purposes of subsection (d) of this section.

Duties of Director; establishment and change of research and reference divisions or other organizational units, or both

(f) The Director is authorized—

(1) to classify, organize, arrange, group, and divide, from time to time, as he considers advisable, the requests for advice, assistance, and other services submitted to the Congressional Research Service by committees and Members of the Senate and House of Representatives and joint committees of Congress, into such classes and categories as he considers necessary to—

(A) expedite and facilitate the handling of the individual requests submitted by Members of the Senate and House of Representatives,

(B) promote efficiency in the performance of services for committees of the Senate and House of Representatives and joint committees of Congress, and

(C) provide a basis for the efficient performance by the Congressional Research Service of its legislative research and related functions generally,

and

(2) to establish and change, from time to time, as he considers advisable, within the Congressional Research Service, such research and reference divisions or other organizational units, or both, as he considers necessary to accomplish the purposes of this section.

Budget estimates

(g) In order to facilitate the study, consideration, evaluation, and determination by the Congress of the budget requirements of the Congressional Research Service for each fiscal year, the Librarian of Congress shall receive from the Director and submit, for inclusion in the Budget of the United States Government, the budget estimates of the Congressional Research Service which shall be prepared separately by the Director in detail for each fiscal year as a separate item of the budget estimates of the Library of Congress for such fiscal year.

Experts or consultants, individual or organizational, and persons and organizations with specialized knowledge; procurement of temporary or intermittent assistance; contracts, nonpersonal and personal service; advertisement requirements inapplicable; end product; pay; travel time

(h) (1) The Director of the Congressional Research Service may procure the temporary or intermittent assistance of individual experts or consultants (including stenographic reporters) and of persons learned in particular or specialized fields of knowledge—

(A) by nonpersonal service contract, without regard to any provision of law requiring advertising for contract bids, with the individual expert, consultant, or other person concerned, as an independent contractor, for the furnishing by him to the Congressional

Research Service of a written study, treatise, theme, discourse, dissertation, thesis, summary, advisory opinion, or other end product; or

(B) by employment (for a period of not more than one year) in the Congressional Research Service of the individual expert, consultant, or other person concerned, by personal service contract or otherwise, without regard to the position classification laws, at a rate of pay not in excess of the per diem equivalent of the highest rate of basic pay then currently in effect for the General Schedule of section 5332 of Title 5, including payment of such rate for necessary travel time.

(2) The Director of the Congressional Research Service may procure by contract, without regard to any provision of law requiring advertising for contract bids, the temporary (for respective periods not in excess of one year) or intermittent assistance of educational, research, or other organizations of experts and consultants (including stenographic reporters) and of educational, research, and other organizations of persons learned in particular or specialized fields of knowledge.

Special report to Joint Committee on the Library

(i) The Director of the Congressional Research Service shall prepare and file with the Joint Committee on the Library at the beginning of each regular session of Congress a separate and special report covering, in summary and in detail, all phases of activity of the Congressional Research Service for the immediately preceding fiscal year.

Authorization of appropriations

(j) There are hereby authorized to be appropriated to the Congressional Research Service each fiscal year such sums as may be necessary to carry on the work of the Service.

Aug. 2, 1946, c. 753, Title II, § 203, 60 Stat. 836, amended Oct. 28, 1949, c. 782, Title II, § 1106(a), 63 Stat. 972; Oct. 26, 1970, Pub.L. 91–510, Title III, § 321(a), 84 Stat. 1181.

LIBRARY OF CONGRESS
TRUST FUND BOARD

(United States Code Annotated, 1982, Title 2, s.154-163.)

§ 154. Library of Congress Trust Fund Board; members; quorum; seal; rules and regulations

A board is hereby created and established, to be known as the Library of Congress Trust Fund Board (hereinafter referred to as the board), which shall consist of the Secretary of the Treasury (or an Assistant Secretary designated in writing by the Secretary of the Treasury), the chairman of the Joint Committee on the Library, the Librarian of Congress, and two persons appointed by the President for a term of five years each (the first appointments being for three and five years, respectively). Three members of the board shall constitute a quorum for the transaction of business, and the board shall have an official seal, which shall be judicially noticed. The board may adopt rules and regulations in regard to its procedure and the conduct of its business.

As amended May 12, 1978, Pub.L. 95–277, 92 Stat. 236.

§ 155. Same; expenses

No compensation shall be paid to the members of the board for their services as such members, but they shall be reimbursed for the expenses necessarily incurred by them, out of the income from the fund or funds in connection with which such expenses are incurred. The voucher of

the chairman of the board shall be sufficient evidence that the expenses are properly allowable. Any expenses of the board, including the cost of its seal, not properly chargeable to the income of any trust fund held by it, shall be estimated for in the annual estimates of the librarian for the maintenance of the Library of Congress.
Mar. 3, 1925, c. 423, § 1, 43 Stat. 1107.

§ 156. Same; gifts, etc., to

The Board is authorized to accept, receive, hold, and administer such gifts, bequests, or devises of property for the benefit of, or in connection with, the Library, its collections, or its service, as may be approved by the Board and by the Joint Committee on the Library. Mar. 3, 1925, c. 423, § 2, formerly § 1, 43 Stat. 1107, renumbered Apr. 13, 1936, c. 213, 49 Stat. 1205.

§ 157. Same; trust funds; management of

The moneys or securities composing the trust funds given or bequeathed to the board shall be receipted for by the Secretary of the Treasury, who shall invest, reinvest, or retain investments as the board may from time to time determine. The income as and when collected shall be deposited with the Treasurer of the United States, who shall enter it in a special account to the credit of the Library of Congress and subject to disbursement by the librarian for the purposes in each case specified; and the Treasurer of the United States is authorized to honor the requisitions of the librarian made in such manner and in accordance with such regulations as the Treasurer may from time to time prescribe: *Provided, however,* That the board is not authorized to engage in any business nor to exercise any voting privilege which may be incidental to securities in its hands, nor shall the board make any investments that could not lawfully be made by a trust company in the District of Columbia, except that it may make any investments directly authorized by the instrument of gift, and may retain any investments accepted by it.
Mar. 3, 1925, c. 423, § 2, formerly § 1, 43 Stat. 1107, renumbered Apr. 13, 1936, c. 213, 49 Stat. 1205.

§ 158. Same; deposits with Treasurer of United States

Should any gift or bequest so provide, the board may deposit the principal sum, in cash, with the Treasurer of the United States as a permanent loan to the United States Treasury, and the Treasurer shall thereafter credit such deposit with interest at a rate which is the higher of the rate of 4 per centum per annum or a rate which is 0.25 percentage points less than a rate determined by the Secretary of the Treasury, taking into consideration the current average market yield on outstanding long-term marketable obligations of the United States, adjusted to the nearest one-eighth of 1 per centum, payable semiannually, such interest, as income, being subject to disbursement by the Librarian of Congress for the purposes specified: *Provided, however,* That the total of such principal sums at any time so held by the Treasurer under this authorization shall not exceed the sum of $5,000,000.
Mar. 3, 1925, c. 423, § 2, formerly § 1, 43 Stat. 1107, renumbered Apr. 13, 1936, c. 213, 49 Stat. 1205, and amended June 23, 1936, c. 734, 49 Stat. 1894; July 3, 1962, Pub.L. 87–522, 76 Stat. 135; May 22, 1976, Pub.L. 94–289, 90 Stat. 521.

§ 159. Same; perpetual succession; suits by or against

The board shall have perpetual succession, with all the usual powers and obligations of a trustee, including the power to sell, except as herein limited, in respect of all property, moneys, or securities which shall be conveyed, transferred, assigned, bequeathed, delivered, or paid over to it for the purposes above specified. The board may be sued in the United States District Court for the District of Columbia, which is given jurisdiction of such suits, for the purpose of enforcing the provisions of any trust accepted by it. As amended Jan. 27, 1926, c. 6, § 1, 44 Stat. 2; June 25, 1936, c. 804, 49 Stat. 1921; June 25, 1948, c. 646, § 32(a), 62 Stat. 991; May 24, 1949, c. 139, § 127, 63 Stat. 107.

§ 160.   Same; gifts, etc., to Library not affected

Nothing in sections 154 to 162 and 163 of this title shall be construed as prohibiting or restricting the Librarian of Congress from accepting in the name of the United States gifts or bequests of money for immediate disbursement in the interest of the Library, its collections, or its service. Such gifts or bequests, after acceptance by the librarian, shall be paid by the donor or his representative to the Treasurer of the United States, whose receipts shall be their acquittance. The Treasurer of the United States shall enter them in a special account to the credit of the Library of Congress and subject to disbursement by the librarian for the purposes in each case specified.

Mar. 3, 1925, c. 423, § 4, 43 Stat. 1108.

§ 161.   Same; gifts, etc., exempt from Federal taxes

Gifts or bequests or devises to or for the benefit of the Library of Congress, including those to the board, and the income therefrom, shall be exempt from all Federal taxes, including all taxes levied by the District of Columbia. As amended Oct. 2, 1942, c. 576, 56 Stat. 765.

§ 162.   Same; employees; compensation

Employees of the Library of Congress who perform special functions for the performance of which funds have been entrusted to the board or the librarian, or in connection with cooperative undertakings in which the Library of Congress is engaged, shall not be subject to section 66 of Title 5; and section 3105 of Title 5 shall not apply to any additional compensation so paid to such employees. Mar. 3, 1925, c. 423, § 6, 43 Stat. 1108; Jan. 27, 1926, c. 6, § 2, 44 Stat. 2; Aug. 19, 1964, Pub.L. 88–448, Title IV, § 401(j), 78 Stat. 491.

§ 162a.   Same; gross salary of employees

Here after the gross salary of any position in the Library which is augmented by payment of an honorarium from other than appropriated funds under terms of section 162 of this title shall not exceed an amount, which when combined with such honorarium, will exceed the maximum salary provided in chapter 51 and subchapter III of chapter 53 of Title 5. June 22, 1949, c. 235, § 101, 63 Stat. 226.

§ 163.   Same; report to Congress

The board shall submit to the Congress an annual report of the moneys or securities received and held by it and of its operations.

Mar. 3, 1925, c. 423, § 7, 43 Stat. 1108.

CENTER FOR THE BOOK

(United States Code Annotated, 1982, Title 2, s.171-175.)

§ 171.   Congressional declaration of findings and purpose

The Congress hereby finds and declares—

(1) that the Congress of the United States on April 24, 1800,

established for itself a library of the Congress;

(2) that in 1815, the Congress purchased the personal library of the third President of the United States which contained materials on every science known to man and described such a collection as a "substratum of a great national library";

(3) that the Congress of the United States in recognition of the importance of printing and its impact on America purchased the Gutenberg Bible in 1930 for the Nation for placement in the Library of Congress;

(4) that the Congress of the United States has through statute and appropriations made this library accessible to any member of the public;

(5) that this collection of books and other library materials has now become one of the greatest libraries in civilization;

(6) that the book and the printed word have had the most profound influence on American civilization and learning and have been the very foundation on which our democratic principles have survived through our two hundred-year history;

(7) that in the year 1977, the Congress of the United States assembled hereby declares its reaffirmation of the importance of the printed word and the book and recognizes the importance of a Center for the Book to the continued study and development of written record as central to our understanding of ourselves and our world.

It is therefore the purpose of sections 171 to 175 of this title to establish a Center for the Book in the Library of Congress to provide a program for the investigation of the transmission of human knowledge and to heighten public interest in the role of books and printing in the diffusion of this knowledge.

Pub.L. 95–129, § 1, Oct. 13, 1977, 91 Stat. 1151.

§ 172. Definitions

As used in sections 171 to 175 of this title

(1) the term Center means the Center for the Book;

(2) the term Librarian means the Librarian of Congress.

Pub.L. 95–129, § 2, Oct. 13, 1977, 91 Stat. 1151.

§ 173. Establishment of Center

There is hereby established in the Library of Congress a Center for the Book.

The Center shall be under the direction of the Librarian of Congress.

Pub.L. 95–129, § 3, Oct. 13, 1977, 91 Stat. 1151.

§ 174. Function of Center

The Librarian through the Center shall stimulate public interest and research in the role of the book in the diffusion of knowledge through such activities as a visiting scholar program accompanied by lectures, exhibits, publications, and any other related activities.

Pub.L. 95–129, § 4, Oct. 13, 1977, 91 Stat. 1152.

§ 175. Administrative provisions

The Librarian of Congress, in carrying out the Center's functions, is authorized to—

(1) prescribe such regulations as he deems necessary;

(2) receive money and other property donated, bequeathed, or devised for the purposes of the Center, and to use, sell, or otherwise dispose of such property for the purposes of carrying out the Center's functions, without reference to Federal disposal statutes; and

(3) accept and utilize the services of voluntary and noncompen-

sated personnel and reimburse them for travel expenses, including per diem, as authorized by section 5703 of Title 5.
Pub.L. 95–129, § 5, Oct. 13, 1977, 91 Stat. 1152.

AMERICAN TELEVISION AND RADIO ARCHIVES
(United States Code Annotated, 1982, Title 2, s.170)

§ 170. American Television and Radio Archives—Establishment and maintenance in Library of Congress; purpose; determination of composition, cataloging, indexing and availability by Librarian

(a) The Librarian of Congress (hereinafter referred to as the "Librarian") shall establish and maintain in the Library of Congress a library to be known as the American Television and Radio Archives (hereinafter referred to as the "Archives"). The purpose of the Archives shall be to preserve a permanent record of the television and radio programs which are the heritage of the people of the United States and to provide access to such programs to historians and scholars without encouraging or causing copyright infringement.

(1) The Librarian, after consultation with interested organizations and individuals, shall determine and place in the Archives such copies and phonorecords of television and radio programs transmitted to the public in the United States and in other countries which are of present or potential public or cultural interest, historical significance, cognitive value, or otherwise worthy of preservation, including copies and phonorecords of published and unpublished transmission programs—

(A) acquired in accordance with sections 407 and 408 of Title 17 as amended by the first section of this Act; and

(B) transferred from the existing collections of the Library of Congress; and

(C) given to or exchanged with the Archives by other libraries, archives, organizations, and individuals; and

(D) purchased from the owner thereof.

(2) The Librarian shall maintain and publish appropriate catalogs and indexes of the collections of the Archives, and shall make such collections available for study and research under the conditions prescribed under this section.

Reproduction, compilation, and distribution for research of regularly scheduled newscasts or on-the-spot coverage of news events by Librarian; promulgation of regulations

(b) Notwithstanding the provisions of section 106 of Title 17 as amended by the first section of this Act, the Librarian is authorized with respect to a transmission program which consists of a regularly scheduled newscast or on-the-spot coverage of news events and, under standards and conditions that the Librarian shall prescribe by regulation—

(1) to reproduce a fixation of such a program, in the same or another tangible form, for the purposes of preservation or security or for distribution under the conditions of clause (3) of this subsection; and

(2) to compile, without abridgment or any other editing, portions of such fixations according to subject matter, and to reproduce such compilations for the purpose of clause (1) of this subsection; and

(3) to distribute a reproduction made under clause (1) or (2) of this subsection—

(A) by loan to a person engaged in research; and

(B) for deposit in a library or archives which meets the requirements of section 108(a) of Title 17 as amended by the first section of this Act, in either case for use only in research and not for further reproduction or performance.

Liability for copyright infringement by Librarian or any employee of Librarian

(c) The Librarian or any employee of the Library who is acting under the authority of this section shall not be liable in any action for copyright infringement committed by any other person unless the Librarian or such employee knowingly participated in the act of infringement committed by such person. Nothing in this section shall be construed to excuse or limit liability under Title 17 as amended by the first section of this Act for any act not authorized by that title or this section, or for any act performed by a person not authorized to act under that title or this section.

Short title

(d) This section may be cited as the "American Television and Radio Archives Act".

Pub.L. 94-553, Title I, § 113, Oct. 19, 1976, 90 Stat. 2602.

COPYRIGHT

(United States Code Annotated, Title 17, s.101, 106-108, 117, 407, 504, 602, 701-710.)

§ 101. Definitions

As used in this title, the following terms and their variant forms mean the following:

An "anonymous work" is a work on the copies or phonorecords of which no natural person is identified as author.

"Audiovisual works" are works that consist of a series of related images which are intrinsically intended to be shown by the use of machines or devices such as projectors, viewers, or electronic equipment, together with accompanying sounds, if any, regardless of the nature of the material objects, such as films or tapes, in which the works are embodied.

The "best edition" of a work is the edition, published in the United States at any time before the date of deposit, that the Library of Congress determines to be most suitable for its purposes.

A person's "children" are that person's immediate offspring, whether legitimate or not, and any children legally adopted by that person.

A "collective work" is a work, such as a periodical issue, anthology, or encyclopedia, in which a number of contributions, constituting separate and independent works in themselves, are assembled into a collective whole.

A "compilation" is a work formed by the collection and assembling of preexisting materials or of data that are selected, coordinated, or arranged in such a way that the resulting work as a whole constitutes an original work of authorship. The term "compilation" includes collective works.

"Copies" are material objects, other than phonorecords, in which a work is fixed by any method now known or later developed, and from which the work can be perceived, reproduced, or otherwise communicated, either directly or with the aid of a machine or device. The term "copies" includes the material object, other than a phonorecord, in which the work is first fixed.

"Copyright owner", with respect to any one of the exclusive rights comprised in a copyright, refers to the owner of that particular right.

A work is "created" when it is fixed in a copy or phonorecord for the first time; where a work is prepared over a period of time, the portion of it that has been fixed at any particular time constitutes the work as of that time, and where the work has been prepared in different versions, each version constitutes a separate work.

A "derivative work" is a work based upon one or more preexisting works, such as a translation, musical arrangement, dramatization, fictionalization, motion picture version, sound recording, art reproduction, abridgment, condensation, or any other form in which a work may be recast, transformed, or adapted. A work consisting of editorial revisions, annotations, elaborations, or other modifications which, as a whole, represent an original work of authorship, is a "derivative work".

A "device", "machine", or "process" is one now known or later developed.

To "display" a work means to show a copy of it, either directly or by means of a film, slide, television image, or any other device or process or, in the case of a motion picture or other audiovisual work, to show individual images nonsequentially.

A work is "fixed" in a tangible medium of expression when its embodiment in a copy or phonorecord, by or under the authority of the author, is sufficiently permanent or stable to permit it to be perceived, reproduced, or otherwise communicated for a period of more than transitory duration. A work consisting of sounds, images, or both, that are being transmitted, is "fixed" for purposes of this title if a fixation of the work is being made simultaneously with its transmission.

The terms "including" and "such as" are illustrative and not limitative.

A "joint work" is a work prepared by two or more authors with the intention that their contributions be merged into inseparable or interdependent parts of a unitary whole.

"Literary works" are works, other than audiovisual works, expressed in words, numbers, or other verbal or numerical symbols or indicia, regardless of the nature of the material objects, such as books, periodicals, manuscripts, phonorecords, film, tapes, disks, or cards, in which they are embodied.

"Motion pictures" are audiovisual works consisting of a series of related images which, when shown in succession, impart an impression of motion, together with accompanying sounds, if any.

To "perform" a work means to recite, render, play, dance, or act it, either directly or by means of any device or process or, in the case of a motion picture or other audiovisual work, to show its images in any sequence or to make the sounds accompanying it audible.

"Phonorecords" are material objects in which sounds, other than those accompanying a motion picture or other audiovisual work, are fixed by any method now known or later developed, and from which the sounds can be perceived, reproduced, or otherwise communicated, either directly or with the aid of a machine or device. The term "phonorecords" includes the material object in which the sounds are first fixed.

"Pictorial, graphic, and sculptural works" include two-dimensional and three-dimensional works of fine, graphic, and applied art, photographs, prints and art reproductions, maps, globes, charts, technical drawings, diagrams, and models. Such works shall include works of artistic craftsmanship insofar as their form but not their mechanical or utilitarian aspects are concerned; the design of a useful article, as defined in this section, shall be considered a pictorial, graphic, or sculptural work only if, and only to the extent that, such design incorporates pictorial, graphic, or sculptural features that can be identified separately from, and are capable of existing independently of, the utilitarian aspects of the article.

A "pseudonymous work" is a work on the copies or phonorecords of which the author is identified under a fictitious name.

"Publication" is the distribution of copies or phonorecords of a work to the public by sale or other transfer of ownership, or by rental, lease, or lending. The offering to distribute copies or phonorecords to a group of persons for purposes of further distribution, public performance, or public display, constitutes publication. A public performance or display of a work does not of itself constitute publication.

To perform or display a work "publicly" means—

(1) to perform or display it at a place open to the public or at any place where a substantial number of persons outside of a normal circle of a family and its social acquaintances is gathered; or

(2) to transmit or otherwise communicate a performance or display of the work to a place specified by clause (1) or to the public, by means of any device or process, whether the members of the public capable of receiving the perform-

ance or display receive it in the same place or in separate places and at the same time or at different times.

"Sound recordings" are works that result from the fixation of a series of musical, spoken, or other sounds, but not including the sounds accompanying a motion picture or other audiovisual work, regardless of the nature of the material objects, such as disks, tapes, or other phonorecords, in which they are embodied.

"State" includes the District of Columbia and the Commonwealth of Puerto Rico, and any territories to which this title is made applicable by an Act of Congress.

A "transfer of copyright ownership" is an assignment, mortgage, exclusive license, or any other conveyance, alienation, or hypothecation of a copyright or of any of the exclusive rights comprised in a copyright, whether or not it is limited in time or place of effect, but not including a nonexclusive license.

A "transmission program" is a body of material that, as an aggregate, has been produced for the sole purpose of transmission to the public in sequence and as a unit.

To "transmit" a performance or display is to communicate it by any device or process whereby images or sounds are received beyond the place from which they are sent.

The "United States", when used in a geographical sense, comprises the several States, the District of Columbia and the Commonwealth of Puerto Rico, and the organized territories under the jurisdiction of the United States Government.

A "useful article" is an article having an intrinsic utilitarian function that is not merely to portray the appearance of the article or to convey information. An article that is normally a part of a useful article is considered a "useful article".

The author's "widow" or "widower" is the author's surviving spouse under the law of the author's domicile at the time of his or her death, whether or not the spouse has later remarried.

A "work of the United States Government" is a work prepared by an officer or employee of the United States Government as part of that person's official duties.

A "work made for hire" is—

(1) a work prepared by an employee within the scope of his or her employment; or

(2) a work specially ordered or commissioned for use as a contribution to a collective work, as a part of a motion picture or other audiovisual work, as a translation, as a supplementary work, as a compilation, as an instructional text, as a test, as answer material for a test, or as an atlas, if the parties expressly agree in a written instrument signed by them that the work shall be considered a work made for hire. For the purpose of the foregoing sentence, a "supplementary work" is a work prepared for publication

as a secondary adjunct to a work by another author for the purpose of introducing, concluding, illustrating, explaining, revising, commenting upon, or assisting in the use of the other work, such as forewords, afterwords, pictorial illustrations, maps, charts, tables, editorial notes, musical arrangements, answer material for tests, bibliographies, appendixes, and indexes, and an "instructional text" is a literary, pictorial, or graphic work prepared for publication and with the purpose of use in systematic instructional activities.

Pub.L. 94–553, Title I, § 101, Oct. 19, 1976, 90 Stat. 2541.

§ 106. Exclusive rights in copyrighted works

Subject to sections 107 through 118, the owner of copyright under this title has the exclusive rights to do and to authorize any of the following:

(1) to reproduce the copyrighted work in copies or phonorecords;

(2) to prepare derivative works based upon the copyrighted work;

(3) to distribute copies or phonorecords of the copyrighted work to the public by sale or other transfer of ownership, or by rental, lease, or lending;

(4) in the case of literary, musical, dramatic, and choreographic works, pantomimes, and motion pictures and other audiovisual works, to perform the copyrighted work publicly; and

(5) in the case of literary, musical, dramatic, and choreographic works, pantomimes, and pictorial, graphic, or sculptural works, including the individual images of a motion picture or other audiovisual work, to display the copyrighted work publicly.

Pub.L. 94–553, Title I, § 101, Oct. 19, 1976, 90 Stat. 2546.

§ 107. Limitations on exclusive rights: Fair use

Notwithstanding the provisions of section 106, the fair use of a copyrighted work, including such use by reproduction in copies or phonorecords or by any other means specified by that section, for purposes such as criticism, comment, news reporting, teaching (including multiple copies for classroom use), scholarship, or research, is not an infringement of copyright. In determining whether the use made of a work in any particular case is a fair use the factors to be considered shall include—

(1) the purpose and character of the use, including whether such use is of a commercial nature or is for nonprofit educational purposes;

(2) the nature of the copyrighted work;

(3) the amount and substantiality of the portion used in relation to the copyrighted work as a whole; and

(4) the effect of the use upon the potential market for or value of the copyrighted work.

Pub.L. 94–553, Title I, § 101, Oct. 19, 1976, 90 Stat. 2546.

§ 108.   Limitations on exclusive rights: Reproduction by libraries and archives

(a) Notwithstanding the provisions of section 106, it is not an infringement of copyright for a library or archives, or any of its employees acting within the scope of their employment, to reproduce no more than one copy or phonorecord of a work, or to distribute such copy or phonorecord, under the conditions specified by this section, if—

(1) the reproduction or distribution is made without any purpose of direct or indirect commercial advantage;

(2) the collections of the library or archives are (i) open to the public, or (ii) available not only to researchers affiliated with the library or archives or with the institution of which it is a part, but also to other persons doing research in a specialized field; and

(3) the reproduction or distribution of the work includes a notice of copyright.

(b) The rights of reproduction and distribution under this section apply to a copy or phonorecord of an unpublished work duplicated in facsimile form solely for purposes of preservation and security or for deposit for research use in another library or archives of the type described by clause (2) of subsection (a), if the copy or phonorecord reproduced is currently in the collections of the library or archives.

(c) The right of reproduction under this section applies to a copy or phonorecord of a published work duplicated in facsimile form solely for the purpose of replacement of a copy or phonorecord that is damaged, deteriorating, lost, or stolen, if the library or archives has, after a reasonable effort, determined that an unused replacement cannot be obtained at a fair price.

(d) The rights of reproduction and distribution under this section apply to a copy, made from the collection of a library or archives where the user makes his or her request or from that of another library or archives, of no more than one article or other contribution to a copyrighted collection or periodical issue, or to a copy or phonorecord of a small part of any other copyrighted work, if—

(1) the copy or phonorecord becomes the property of the user, and the library or archives has had no notice that the copy or phonorecord would be used for any purpose other than private study, scholarship, or research; and

(2) the library or archives displays prominently, at the place where orders are accepted, and includes on its order form, a warning of copyright in accordance with requirements that the Register of Copyrights shall prescribe by regulation.

(e) The rights of reproduction and distribution under this section apply to the entire work, or to a substantial part of it, made from the collection of a library or archives where the user makes his or her request or from that of another library or archives, if the library or archives has first determined, on the basis of a reasonable investigation, that a copy or phonorecord of the copyrighted work cannot be obtained at a pair price, if—

(1) the copy or phonorecord becomes the property of the user, and the library or archives has had no notice that the copy or phonorecord would be used for any purpose other than private study, scholarship, or research; and

(2) the library or archives displays prominently, at the place where orders are accepted, and includes on its order form, a warning of copyright in accordance with requirements that the Register of Copyrights shall prescribe by regulation.

(f) Nothing in this section—

(1) shall be construed to impose liability for copyright infringement upon a library or archives or its employees for the unsupervised use of reproducing equipment located on its premises: *Provided*, That such equipment displays a notice that the making of a copy may be subject to the copyright law;

(2) excuses a person who uses such reproducing equipment or who requests a copy or phonorecord under subsection (d) from liability for copyright infringement for any such act, or for any later use of such copy or phonorecord, if it exceeds fair use as provided by section 107;

(3) shall be construed to limit the reproduction and distribution by lending of a limited number of copies and excerpts by a library or archives of an audiovisual news program, subject to clauses (1), (2), and (3) of subsection (a); or

(4) in any way affects the right of fair use as provided by section 107, or any contractual obligations assumed at any time by the library or archives when it obtained a copy or phonorecord of a work in its collections.

(g) The rights of reproduction and distribution under this section extend to the isolated and unrelated reproduction or distribution of a single copy or phonorecord of the same material on separate occasions, but do not extend to cases where the library or archives, or its employee—

(1) is aware or has substantial reason to believe that it is engaging in the related or concerted reproduction or distribution

of multiple copies or phonorecords of the same material, whether made on one occasion or over a period of time, and whether intended for aggregate use by one or more individuals or for separate use by the individual members of a group; or

(2) engages in the systematic reproduction or distribution of single or multiple copies or phonorecords of material described in subsection (d): *Provided*, That nothing in this cause prevents a library or archives from participating in interlibrary arrangements that do not have, as their purpose or effect, that the library or archives receiving such copies or phonorecords for distribution does so in such aggregate quantities as to substitute for a subscription to or purchase of such work.

(h) The rights of reproduction and distribution under this section do not apply to a musical work, a pictorial, graphic or sculptural work, or a motion picture or other audiovisual work other than an audiovisual work dealing with news, except that no such limitation shall apply with respect to rights granted by subsections (b) and (c), or with respect to pictorial or graphic works published as illustrations, diagrams, or similar adjuncts to works of which copies are reproduced or distributed in accordance with subsections (d) and (e).

(i) Five years from the effective date of this Act, and at five-year intervals thereafter, the Register of Copyrights, after consulting with representatives of authors, book and periodical publishers, and other owners of copyrighted materials, and with representatives of library users and librarians, shall submit to the Congress a report setting forth the extent to which this section has achieved the intended statutory balancing of the rights of creators, and the needs of users. The report should also describe any problems that may have arisen, and present legislative or other recommendations, if warranted.

Pub.L. 94–553, Title I, § 101, Oct. 19, 1976, 90 Stat. 2546.

§ 117.   Scope of exclusive rights: Use in conjunction with computers and similar information systems

Notwithstanding the provisions of sections 106 through 116 and 118, this title does not afford to the owner of copyright in a work any greater or lesser rights with respect to the use of the work in conjunction with automatic systems capable of storing, processing, retrieving, or transferring information, or in conjunction with any similar device, machine, or process, than those afforded to works under the law, whether title 17 or the common law or statutes of a State, in effect on December 31, 1977, as held applicable and construed by a court in an action brought under this title.

Pub.L. 94–553, Title I, § 101, Oct. 19, 1976, 90 Stat. 2565.

§ 407. Deposit of copies or phonorecords for Library of Congress

(a) Except as provided by subsection (c), and subject to the provisions of subsection (e), the owner of copyright or of the exclusive right of publication in a work published with notice of copyright in the United States shall deposit, within three months after the date of such publication—

(1) two complete copies of the best edition; or

(2) if the work is a sound recording, two complete phonorecords of the best edition, together with any printed or other visually perceptible material published with such phonorecords.

Neither the deposit requirements of this subsection nor the acquisition provisions of subsection (e) are conditions of copyright protection.

(b) The required copies or phonorecords shall be deposited in the Copyright Office for the use or disposition of the Library of Congress. The Register of Copyrights shall, when requested by the depositor and upon payment of the fee prescribed by section 708, issue a receipt for the deposit.

(c) The Register of Copyrights may by regulation exempt any categories of material from the deposit requirements of this section, or require deposit of only one copy or phonorecord with respect to any categories. Such regulations shall provide either for complete exemption from the deposit requirements of this section, or for alternative forms of deposit aimed at providing a satisfactory archival record of a work without imposing practical or financial hardships on the depositor, where the individual author is the owner of copyright in a pictorial, graphic, or sculptural work and (i) less than five copies of the work have been published, or (ii) the work has been published in a limited edition consisting of numbered copies, the monetary value of which would make the mandatory deposit of two copies of the best edition of the work burdensome, unfair, or unreasonable.

(d) At any time after publication of a work as provided by subsection (a), the Register of Copyrights may make written demand for the required deposit on any of the persons obligated to make the deposit under subsection (a). Unless deposit is made within three months after the demand is received, the person or persons on whom the demand was made are liable—

(1) to a fine of not more than $250 for each work; and

(2) to pay into a specially designated fund in the Library of Congress the total retail price of the copies or phonorecords demanded, or, if no retail price has been fixed, the reasonable cost of the Library of Congress of acquiring them; and

(3) to pay a fine of $2,500, in addition to any fine or liability imposed under clauses (1) and (2), if such person willfully or repeatedly fails or refuses to comply with such a demand.

(e) With respect to transmission programs that have been fixed and transmitted to the public in the United States but have not been published, the Register of Copyrights shall, after consulting with the Librarian of Congress and other interested organizations and officials, establish regulations governing the acquisition, through deposit or otherwise, of copies or phonorecords of such programs for the collections of the Library of Congress.

(1) The Librarian of Congress shall be permitted, under the standards and conditions set forth in such regulations, to make a fixation of a transmission program directly from a transmission to the public, and to reproduce one copy or phonorecord from such fixation for archival purposes.

(2) Such regulations shall also provide standards and procedures by which the Register of Copyrights may make written demand, upon the owner of the right of transmission in the United States, for the deposit of a copy or phonorecord of a specific transmission program. Such deposit may, at the option of the owner of the right of transmission in the United States, be accomplished by gift, by loan for purposes of reproduction, or by sale at a price not to exceed the cost of reproducing and supplying the copy or phonorecord. The regulations established under this clause shall provide reasonable periods of not less than three months for compliance with a demand, and shall allow for extensions of such periods and adjustments in the scope of the demand or the methods for fulfilling it, as reasonably warranted by the circumstances. Willful failure or refusal to comply with the conditions prescribed by such regulations shall subject the owner of the right of transmission in the United States to liability for an amount, not to exceed the cost of reproducing and supplying the copy or phonorecord in question, to be paid into a specially designated fund in the Library of Congress.

(3) Nothing in this subsection shall be construed to require the making or retention, for purposes of deposit, of any copy or phonorecord of an unpublished transmission program, the transmission of which occurs before the receipt of a specific written demand as provided by clause (2).

(4) No activity undertaken in compliance with regulations prescribed under clauses (1) or (2) of this subsection shall result in liability if intended solely to assist in the acquisition of copies or phonorecords under this subsection.

Pub.L. 94–553, Title I, § 101, Oct. 19, 1976, 90 Stat. 2579.

§ 504. Remedies for infringement: Damages and profits

(a) In General.—Except as otherwise provided by this title, an infringer of copyright is liable for either—

(1) the copyright owner's actual damages and any additional

profits of the infringer, as provided by subsection (b); or

(2) statutory damages, as provided by subsection (c).

(b) Actual Damages and Profits.—The copyright owner is entitled to recover the actual damages suffered by him or her as a result of the infringement, and any profits of the infringer that are attributable to the infringement and are not taken into account in computing the actual damages. In establishing the infringer's profits, the copyright owner is required to present proof only of the infringer's gross revenue, and the infringer is required to prove his or her deductible expenses and the elements of profit attributable to factors other than the copyrighted work.

(c) Statutory Damages.—

(1) Except as provided by clause (2) of this subsection, the copyright owner may elect, at any time before final judgment is rendered, to recover, instead of actual damages and profits, an award of statutory damages for all infringements involved in the action, with respect to any one work, for which any one infringer is liable individually, or for which any two or more infringers are liable jointly and severally, in a sum of not less than $250 or more than $10,000 as the court considers just. For the purposes of this subsection, all the parts of a compilation or derivative work constitute one work.

(2) In a case where the copyright owner sustains the burden of proving, and the court finds, that infringement was committed willfully, the court in its discretion may increase the award of statutory damages to a sum of not more than $50,000. In a case where the infringer sustains the burden of proving, and the court finds, that such infringer was not aware and had no reason to believe that his or her acts constituted an infringement of copyright, the court it[1] its discretion may reduce the award of statutory damages to a sum of not less than $100. The court shall remit statutory damages in any case where an infringer believed and had reasonable grounds for believing that his or her use of the copyrighted work was a fair use under section 107, if the infringer was: (i) an employee or agent of a nonprofit educational institution, library, or archives acting within the scope of his or her employment who, or such institution, library, or archives itself, which infringed by reproducing the work in copies or phonorecords; or (ii) a public broadcasting entity which or a person who, as a regular part of the nonprofit activities of a public broadcasting entity (as defined in subsection (g) of section 118) infringed by performing a published nondramatic literary work or by reproducing a transmission program embodying a performance of such a work.

Pub.L. 94–553, Title I, § 101, Oct. 19, 1976, 90 Stat. 2585.

[1] So in original. Probably should read "in".

§ 602. Infringing importation of copies or phonorecords

(a) Importation into the United States, without the authority of the owner of copyright under this title, of copies or phonorecords of a work that have been acquired outside the United States is an infringement of the exclusive right to distribute copies of phonorecords under section 106, actionable under section 501. This subsection does not apply to—

(1) importation of copies or phonorecords under the authority or for the use of the Government of the United States or of any State or political subdivision of a State, but not including copies or phonorecords for use in schools, or copies of any audiovisual work imported for purposes other than archival use;

(2) importation, for the private use of the importer and not for distribution, by any person with respect to no more than one copy or phonorecord of any one work at any one time, or by any person arriving from outside the United States with respect to copies or phonorecords forming part of such person's personal baggage; or

(3) importation by or for an organization operated for scholarly, educational, or religious purposes and not for private gain, with respect to no more than one copy of an audiovisual work solely for its archival purposes, and no more than five copies or phonorecords of any other work for its library lending or archival purposes, unless the importation of such copies or phonorecords is part of an activity consisting of systematic reproduction or distribution, engaged in by such organization in violation of the provisions of section 108(g)(2).

(b) In a case where the making of the copies or phonorecords would have constituted an infringement of copyright if this title had been applicable, their importation is prohibited. In a case where the copies or phonorecords were lawfully made, the United States Customs Service has no authority to prevent their importation unless the provisions of section 601 are applicable. In either case, the Secretary of the Treasury is authorized to prescribe, by regulation, a procedure under which any person claiming an interest in the copyright in a particular work may, upon payment of a specified fee, be entitled to notification by the Customs Service of the importation of articles that appear to be copies or phonorecords of the work.

Pub.L. 94–553, Title I, § 101, Oct. 19, 1976, 90 Stat. 2589.

§ 701. The Copyright Office: General responsibilities and organization

(a) All administrative functions and duties under this title, except as otherwise specified, are the responsibility of the Register of Copyrights as director of the Copyright Office of the Library of

Congress. The Register of Copyrights, together with the subordinate officers and employees of the Copyright Office, shall be appointed by the Librarian of Congress, and shall act under the Librarian's general direction and supervision.

(b) The Register of Copyrights shall adopt a seal to be used on and after January 1, 1978, to authenticate all certified documents issued by the Copyright Office.

(c) The Register of Copyrights shall make an annual report to the Librarian of Congress of the work and accomplishments of the Copyright Office during the previous fiscal year. The annual report of the Register of Copyrights shall be published separately and as a part of the annual report of the Librarian of Congress.

(d) Except as provided by section 706(b) and the regulations issued thereunder, all actions taken by the Register of Copyrights under this title are subject to the provisions of the Administrative Procedure Act of June 11, 1946, as amended (c. 324, 60 Stat. 237, title 5, United States Code, Chapter 5, Subchapter II and Chapter 7). Pub.L. 94–553, Title I, § 101, Oct. 19, 1976, 90 Stat. 2591.

§ 702. Copyright Office regulations

The Register of Copyrights is authorized to establish regulations not inconsistent with law for the administration of the functions and duties made the responsibility of the Register under this title. All regulations established by the Register under this title are subject to the approval of the Librarian of Congress. Pub.L. 94–553, Title I, § 101, Oct. 19, 1976, 90 Stat. 2591.

§ 703. Effective date of actions in Copyright Office

In any case in which time limits are prescribed under this title for the performance of an action in the Copyright Office, and in which the last day of the prescribed period falls on a Saturday, Sunday, holiday, or other nonbusiness day within the District of Columbia or the Federal Government, the action may be taken on the next succeeding business day, and is effective as of the date when the period expired. Pub.L. 94–553, Title I, § 101, Oct. 19, 1976, 90 Stat. 2591.

§ 704. Retention and disposition of articles deposited in Copyright Office

(a) Upon their deposit in the Copyright Office under sections 407 and 408, all copies, phonorecords, and identifying material, including those deposited in connection with claims that have been refused registration, are the property of the United States Government.

(b) In the case of published works, all copies, phonorecords, and identifying material deposited are available to the Library of Congress for its collections, or for exchange or transfer to any other library. In the case of unpublished works, the Library is entitled, under regulations that the Register of Copyrights shall prescribe, to select any deposits for its collections or for transfer to the National Archives of the United States or to a Federal records center, as defined in section 2901 of title 44.

(c) The Register of Copyrights is authorized, for specific or general categories of works, to make a facsimile reproduction of all or any part of the material deposited under section 408, and to make such reproduction a part of the Copyright Office records of the registration, before transferring such material to the Library of Congress as provided by subsection (b), or before destroying or otherwise disposing of such material as provided by subsection (d).

(d) Deposits not selected by the Library under subsection (b), or identifying portions or reproductions of them, shall be retained under the control of the Copyright Office, including retention in Government storage facilities, for the longest period considered practicable and desirable by the Register of Copyrights and the Librarian of Congress. After that period it is within the joint discretion of the Register and the Librarian to order their destruction or other disposition; but, in the case of unpublished works, no deposit shall be knowingly or intentionally destroyed or otherwise disposed of during its term of copyright unless a facsimile reproduction of the entire deposit has been made a part of the Copyright Office records as provided by subsection (c).

(e) The depositor of copies, phonorecords, or identifying material under section 408, or the copyright owner of record, may request retention, under the control of the Copyright Office, of one or more of such articles for the full term of copyright in the work. The Register of Copyrights shall prescribe, by regulation, the conditions under which such requests are to be made and granted, and shall fix the fee to be charged under section 708(a)(11) if the request is granted.

Pub.L. 94–553, Title I, § 101, Oct. 19, 1976, 90 Stat. 2591.

§ 705. Copyright Office records: Preparation, maintenance, public inspection, and searching

(a) The Register of Copyrights shall provide and keep in the Copyright Office records of all deposits, registrations, recordations, and other actions taken under this title, and shall prepare indexes of all such records.

(b) Such records and indexes, as well as the articles deposited in connection with completed copyright registrations and retained under the control of the Copyright Office, shall be open to public inspection.

(c) Upon request and payment of the fee specified by section 708, the Copyright Office shall make a search of its public records, indexes, and deposits, and shall furnish a report of the information they disclose with respect to any particular deposits, registrations, or recorded documents.

Pub.L. 94–553, Title I, § 101, Oct. 19, 1976, 90 Stat. 2592.

§ 706. Copies of Copyright Office records

(a) Copies may be made of any public records or indexes of the Copyright Office; additional certificates of copyright registration and copies of any public records or indexes may be furnished upon request and payment of the fees specified by section 708.

(b) Copies or reproductions of deposited articles retained under the control of the Copyright Office shall be authorized or furnished only under the conditions specified by the Copyright Office regulations.

Pub.L. 94–553, Title I, § 101, Oct. 19, 1976, 90 Stat. 2592.

§ 707. Copyright Office forms and publications

(a) **Catalog of Copyright Entries.**—The Register of Copyrights shall compile and publish at periodic intervals catalogs of all copyright registrations. These catalogs shall be divided into parts in accordance with the various classes of works, and the Register has discretion to determine, on the basis of practicability and usefulness, the form and frequency of publication of each particular part.

(b) **Other Publications.**—The Register shall furnish, free of charge upon request, application forms for copyright registration and general informational material in connection with the functions of the Copyright Office. The Register also has the authority to publish compilations of information, bibliographies, and other material he or she considers to be of value to the public.

(c) **Distribution of Publications.**—All publications of the Copyright Office shall be furnished to depository libraries as specified under section 1905 of title 44, and, aside from those furnished free of charge, shall be offered for sale to the public at prices based on the cost of reproduction and distribution.

Pub.L. 94–553, Title I, § 101, Oct. 19, 1976, 90 Stat. 2592.

§ 708. Copyright Office fees

(a) The following fees shall be paid to the Register of Copyrights:

(1) for the registration of a copyright claim or a supplementary registration under section 408, including the issuance of a certificate of registration, $10;

(2) for the registration of a claim to renewal of a subsisting copyright in its first term under section 304(a), including the

issuance of a certificate of registration, $6;

(3) for the issuance of a receipt for a deposit under section 407, $2;

(4) for the recordation, as provided by section 205, of a transfer of copyright ownership or other document of six pages or less, covering no more than one title, $10; for each page over six and each title over one, 50 cents additional;

(5) for the filing, under section 115(b), of a notice of intention to make phonorecords, $6;

(6) for the recordation, under section 302(c), of a statement revealing the identity of an author of an anonymous or pseudonymous work, or for the recordation, under section 302(d), of a statement relating to the death of an author, $10 for a document of six pages or less, covering no more than one title; for each page over six and for each title over one, $1 additional;

(7) for the issuance, under section 601, of an import statement, $3;

(8) for the issuance, under section 706, of an additional certificate of registration, $4;

(9) for the issuance of any other certification, $4; the Register of Copyrights has discretion, on the basis of their cost, to fix the fees for preparing copies of Copyright Office records, whether they are to be certified or not;

(10) for the making and reporting of a search as provided by section 705, and for any related services, $10 for each hour or fraction of an hour consumed;

(11) for any other special services requiring a substantial amount of time or expense, such fees as the Register of Copyrights may fix on the basis of the cost of providing the service.

(b) The fees prescribed by or under this section are applicable to the United States Government and any of its agencies, employees, or officers, but the Register of Copyrights has discretion to waive the requirement of this subsection in occasional or isolated cases involving relatively small amounts.

(c) All fees received under this section shall be deposited by the Register of Copyrights in the Treasury of the United States and shall be credited to the appropriation for necessary expenses of the Copyright Office. The Register may, in accordance with regulations that he or she shall prescribe, refund any sum paid by mistake or in excess of the fee required by this section; however, before making a refund in any case involving a refusal to register a claim under section 410(b), the Register may deduct all or any part of the prescribed registration fee to cover the reasonable administrative costs of processing the claim.

Pub.L. 94–553, Title I, § 101, Oct. 19, 1976, 90 Stat. 2593; Pub.L. 95–94, Title IV, § 406(b), Aug. 5, 1977, 91 Stat. 682.

§ 709. Delay in delivery caused by disruption of postal or other services

In any case in which the Register of Copyrights determines, on the basis of such evidence as the Register may by regulation require, that a deposit, application, fee, or any other material to be delivered to the Copyright Office by a particular date, would have been received in the Copyright Office in due time except for a general disruption or suspension of postal or other transportation or communications services, the actual receipt of such material in the Copyright Office within one month after the date on which the Register determines that the disruption or suspension of such services has terminated, shall be considered timely.

Pub.L. 94–553, Title I, § 101, Oct. 19, 1976, 90 Stat. 2594.

§ 710. Reproduction for use of the blind and physically handicapped: Voluntary licensing forms and procedures

The Register of Copyrights shall, after consultation with the Chief of the Division for the Blind and Physically Handicapped and other appropriate officials of the Library of Congress, establish by regulation standardized forms and procedures by which, at the time applications covering certain specified categories of nondramatic literary works are submitted for registration under section 408 of this title, the copyright owner may voluntarily grant to the Library of Congress a license to reproduce the copyrighted work by means of Braille or similar tactile symbols, or by fixation of a reading of the work in a phonorecord, or both, and to distribute the resulting copies or phonorecords solely for the use of the blind and physically handicapped and under limited conditions to be specified in the standardized forms.

Pub.L. 94–553, Title I, § 101, Oct. 19, 1976, 90 Stat. 2594.

MISCELLANEOUS PROVISIONS
(United States Code Annotated, Title 2, s.144-146, 149, 150-153, 169, 601, Title 7, s.1703, Title 22, s.614.)

§ 144. Copies of Statutes at Large

Ten of the copies of the Statutes at Large, published by Little, Brown & Co., which were deposited in the Library prior to February 5, 1859, shall be retained by the librarian for the use of the justices of the Supreme Court, during the terms of court.
R.S. § 96.

§ 145. Copies of Journals and Documents

Two copies of the Journals and Documents, and of each book printed by either House of Congress, bound as provided in section 116 of Title 44, shall be deposited in the Library. R.S. § 97; Jan. 12, 1895, c. 23, § 86, 28 Stat. 622.

§ 145a. Periodical binding of printed hearings of committee testimony

The Librarian of the Library of Congress is authorized and directed to have bound at the end of each session of Congress the printed hearings of testimony taken by each committee of the Congress at the preceding session. Aug. 2, 1946, c. 753, Title I, § 141, 60 Stat. 834.

§ 146. Deposit of Journals of Senate and House

Twenty-five copies of the public Journals of the Senate, and of the House of Representatives, shall be deposited in the Library of the United States, at the seat of government, to be delivered to Members of Congress during any session, and to all other persons authorized by law to use the books in the Library, upon their application to the librarian, and giving their responsible receipts for the same, in like manner as for other books. R.S. § 98.

§ 149. Transfer of books to other libraries

The Librarian of Congress may from time to time transfer to other governmental libraries within the District of Columbia, including the Public Library, books and material in the possession of the Library of Congress in his judgment no longer necessary to its uses, but in the judgment of the custodians of such other collections likely to be useful to them, and may dispose of or destroy such material as has become useless: *Provided,* That no records of the Federal Government shall be transferred, disposed of, or destroyed under the authority granted in this section. As amended Oct. 25, 1951, c. 562, § 4(1), 65 Stat. 640.

§ 151. Smithsonian Library

The library collected by the Smithsonian Institution under the provisions of the Act of August 10, 1846, chapter 25, and removed from the building of that institution, with the consent of the Regents thereof, to the Library of Congress, shall, while there deposited, be subject to the same regulations as the Library of Congress, except as hereinafter provided. R.S. § 99.

§ 152. Same; how kept and used

The Smithsonian Institution shall have the use of the library referred to in section 151 of this title in like manner as before its removal. All the books, maps, and charts of the Smithsonian Library shall be properly cared for and preserved in like manner as are those of the Congressional Library; from which the Smithsonian Library shall not be removed except on reimbursement by the Smithsonian Institution to the Treasury of the United States of expenses incurred in binding and in taking care of the same, or upon such terms and conditions as shall be mutually agreed upon by Congress and the Regents of the Institution. R.S. § 100.

§ 153. Control of Library of House of Representatives

The library of the House of Representatives shall be under the control and direction of the Librarian of Congress, who shall provide all needful books of reference therefor. The librarian, two assistant librarians, and assistant in the library, shall be appointed by the Clerk of the House, with the approval of the Speaker of the House of Representatives. No removals shall be made from the said positions except for cause reported to and approved by the Committee on Rules. Mar. 3, 1901, c. 830, § 1, 31 Stat. 964.

§ 169. Positions in Library of Congress exempt from citizenship requirement

Not to exceed fifteen positions in the Library of Congress may be exempt from the provisions of appropriation Acts concerning the employment of aliens during the current fiscal year, but the Librarian shall not make any appointment to any such position until he has ascertained that he cannot secure for such appointments a person in any of the categories specified in such provisions who possesses the special qualifications for the particular position and also otherwise meets the general requirements for employment in the Library of Congress. Pub.L. 94–440, Title VIII, § 802, Oct. 1, 1976, 90 Stat. 1457.

§ 601. Establishment

(a) In general.—

(1) There is established an office of the Congress to be known as the Congressional Budget Office (hereinafter in this chapter referred to as the "Office"). The Office shall be headed by a Director; and there shall be a Deputy Director who shall perform such duties as may be assigned to him by the Director and, during the absence or incapacity of the Director or during a vacancy in that office, shall act as Director.

* * *

(e) Relationship to other agencies of Congress.—In carrying out the duties and functions of the Office, and for the purpose of coordinating the operations of the Office with those of other congressional agencies with a view to utilizing most effectively the information, services, and capabilities of all such agencies in carrying out the various responsibilities assigned to each, the Director is authorized to obtain information, data, estimates, and statistics developed by the General Accounting Office, the Library of Congress, and the Office of Technology Assessment, and (upon agreement with them) to utilize their services, facilities, and personnel with or without reimbursement. The Comptroller General, the Librarian of Congress, and the Technology Assessment Board are authorized to provide the Office with the information, data, estimates, and statistics, and the services, facilities, and personnel, referred to in the preceding sentence.

Pub.L. 93–344, Title II, § 201, July 12, 1974, 88 Stat. 302.

§ 1704. Purposes for which foreign currencies may be used

Notwithstanding any other provision of law, the President may use or enter into agreements with foreign countries or international organizations to use the foreign currencies, including principal and interest from loan repayments, which accrue in connection with sales for foreign currencies under agreements for such sales entered into prior to January 1, 1972, for one or more of the following purposes:

(a) For payment of United States obligations (including obligations entered into pursuant to other legislation);

(b) For carrying out programs of United States Government agencies to—

* * *

(2) finance with not less than 2 per centum of the total sales proceeds received each year in each country activities to assist international educational and cultural exchange and to provide for the strengthening of the resources of American schools, colleges, universities, and other public

and nonprofit private educational agencies for international studies and research under the programs authorized by title VI of the National Defense Education Act, the Mutual Educational and Cultural Exchange Act of 1961, the International Education Act of 1966, the Higher Education Act of 1965, the Elementary and Secondary Education Act of 1965, the National Foundation on the Arts and the Humanities Act of 1965, and the Public Broadcasting Act of 1967;

* * *

(5) finance under the direction of the Librarian of Congress, in consultation with the National Science Foundation and other interested agencies, (A) programs outside the United States for the analysis and evaluation of foreign books, periodicals, and other materials to determine whether they would provide information of technical or scientific significance in the United States and whether such books, periodicals, and other materials are of cultural or educational significance, (B) the registry, indexing, binding, reproduction, cataloging, abstracting, translating, and dissemination of books, periodicals, and related materials determined to have such significance; and (C) the acquisition of such books, periodicals, and other materials and the deposit thereof in libraries and research centers in the United States specializing in the areas to which they relate;

As amended Dec. 20, 1975, Pub.L. 94–161, Title II, § 204, 89 Stat. 852; Aug. 14, 1979, Pub.L. 96–53, Title I, § 121, 93 Stat. 366; Dec. 29, 1981, Pub.L. 97–113, Title IV, §§ 401(5), 402, 95 Stat. 1537.

§ 614. Filing and labeling of political propaganda

Copies to Attorney General; statement as to places, times, and extent of transmission

(a) Every person within the United States who is an agent of a foreign principal and required to register under the provisions of this subchapter and who transmits or causes to be transmitted in the United States mails or by any means or instrumentality of interstate or foreign commerce any political propaganda for or in the interests of such foreign principal (i) in the form of prints, or (ii) in any other form which is reasonably adapted to being, or which he believes will be, or which he intends to be, disseminated or circulated among two or more persons shall, not later than forty-eight hours after the beginning of the transmittal thereof, file with the Attorney General two copies thereof and a statement, duly signed by or on behalf of such agent, setting forth full information as to the places, times, and extent of such transmittal.

* * *

(d) For purposes of the Library of Congress, other than for public distribution, the Secretary of the Treasury and the Postmaster

General are authorized, upon the request of the Librarian of Congress, to forward to the Library of Congress fifty copies, or as many fewer thereof as are available, of all foreign prints determined to be prohibited entry under the provisions of section 1305 of Title 19 and of all foreign prints excluded from the mails under authority of section 1717 of Title 18.

Notwithstanding the provisions of section 1305 of Title 19 and of section 1717 of Title 18, the Secretary of the Treasury is authorized to permit the entry and the Postmaster General is authorized to permit the transmittal in the mails of foreign prints imported for governmental purposes by authority or for the use of the United States or for the use of the Library of Congress.

June 8, 1938, c. 327, § 4, 52 Stat. 632; Aug. 7, 1939, c. 521, § 3, 53 Stat. 1246; Apr. 29, 1942, c. 263, § 1, 56 Stat. 255; July 4, 1966, Pub. L. 89–486, § 4, 80 Stat. 246.

LIBRARIES OF THE
EXECUTIVE DEPARTMENTS

NATIONAL AGRICULTURAL LIBRARY

(United States Code Annotated, Title 7, s.2204, 2206, 2223, 2239,
2242, 2244, 2264, 2265, 2328, 2331.)

§ 2204. General duties of Secretary; advisory functions; research and development

(a) The Secretary of Agriculture shall procure and preserve .all information concerning agriculture, rural development, aquaculture, and human nutrition which he can obtain by means of books and correspondence, and by practical and scientific experiments, accurate records of which experiments shall be kept in his office, by the collection of statistics, and by any other appropriate means within his power; he shall collect new and valuable seeds and plants; shall test, by cultivation, the value of such of them as may require such tests; shall propagate such as may be worthy of propagation; and shall distribute them among agriculturists; and he shall advise the President, other members of his Cabinet, and the Congress on policies and programs designed to improve the quality of life for people living in the rural and nonmetropolitan regions of the Nation.

(b) The Secretary is authorized to initiate or expand research and development efforts related to solution of problems of rural water supply, rural sewage and solid waste management, rural housing, rural industrialization, and technology appropriate to small- and moderate-sized family farming operations, and any other problem that the Secretary may determine has an effect upon the economic development or the quality of life in rural areas.

As amended Pub.L. 94–273, § 7(4), Apr. 21, 1976, 90 Stat. 378; Pub.L. 95–113, Title XV, § 1502(b), Sept. 29, 1977, 91 Stat. 1021; Pub.L. 96–355, § 5, Sept. 24, 1980, 94 Stat. 1174.

§ 2206. Custody of property and records

The Secretary of Agriculture shall have charge, in the building and premises appropriated to the department, of the library, furniture, fixtures, records, and other property appertaining to it, or acquired for use in its business.

R.S. § 525.

§ 2223. Same; from and to library and bureaus and offices

Employees of the library may be temporarily detailed by the Secretary of Agriculture for library service in the bureaus and offices of the department, and employees of the bureaus and offices of the department engaged in library work may also be temporarily detailed to the library.

Mar. 4, 1911, c. 238, 36 Stat. 1261.

§ 2238.   Use of field work funds for purchase of arms and ammunition

Funds available for field work in the Department of Agriculture may be used for the purchase of arms and ammunition whenever the individual purchase does not exceed $50, and for individual purchases exceeding $50, when such arms and ammunition cannot advantageously be supplied by the Secretary of the Army pursuant to section 61 of Title 50.

§ 2239.   Use of funds for purchase of scientific and technical articles

Funds available to the Department of Agriculture may be used for the purchase of scientific and technical articles.

Sept. 6, 1950, c. 896, ch. VI, Title IV, § 406, 64 Stat. 679; Sept. 23, 1950, c. 1010, § 6, 64 Stat. 986.

§ 2242.   Sale of copies of card index of publications

The Secretary of Agriculture may furnish to such institutions or individuals as may care to buy them, copies of the card index of the publications of the department and of other agricultural literature prepared by the library, and charge for the same a price covering the additional expense involved in the preparation of these copies. He may furnish to such institutions or individuals as may care to buy them copies of the card index of agricultural literature prepared by the Office of Experiment Stations, and charge for the same a price covering the additional expense involved in the preparation of these copies, the money received from such sales to be deposited in the Treasury of the United States as miscellaneous receipts. He may furnish to such institutions or individuals as may care to buy them copies of the card index of agricultural literature prepared by the Department of Agriculture in connection with its administration of the Act of March second, eighteen hundred and eighty-seven, and the Act of March sixteenth, nineteen hundred and six, and the Acts amendatory of and supplementary thereto, and charge for the same a price covering the additional expenses involved in the preparation of these copies, the money received from such sales to be deposited in the Treasury of the United States as miscellaneous receipts.

May 23, 1908, c. 192, 35 Stat. 264, 266; Mar. 4, 1915, c. 144, 38 Stat. 1109.

§ 2244.   Manufacture and sale of copies of bibliographies, photographic reproductions of books, and library supplies

The Secretary of Agriculture is authorized to make copies of bibliographies prepared by the Department library, microfilm and other photographic reproductions of books and other library materials in the Department and sell such bibliographies and reproductions at such prices (not less than estimated total cost of furnishing same) as he may determine, the money received from such sales to be deposited in the Treasury to the credit of the applicable appropriation current at the time the materials are furnished or payment therefor is received.

Sept. 21, 1944, c. 412, Title VII, § 708, 58 Stat. 742.

§ 2264.   National Agricultural Library;   acceptance of gifts, bequests, or devises;   conditional gifts

The Secretary of Agriculture is hereby authorized to accept, receive, hold, and administer on behalf of the United States gifts, bequests, or devises of real and personal property made unconditionally for the benefit of the National Agricultural Library or for the carrying out of any of its functions.   Conditional gifts may be accepted and used in accordance with their provisions provided that no gift may be accepted which is conditioned on any expenditure not to be met therefrom or from the income thereof unless such expenditure has been approved by Act of Congress.

Pub.L. 91–591, § 2, Dec. 28, 1970, 84 Stat. 1588.

§ 2265.   Deposit of money accepted for benefit of National Agricultural Library;   disbursement

Any gift of money accepted pursuant to the authority granted in section 2264 of this title, or the net proceeds from the liquidation of any other property so accepted, or the proceeds of any insurance on any gift property not used for its restoration shall be deposited in the Treasury of the United States for credit to a separate account and shall be disbursed upon order of the Secretary of Agriculture.

Pub.L. 91–591, § 3, Dec. 28, 1970, 84 Stat. 1588

§ 2328.   Library

The Secretary shall maintain a library of scientific and other works and periodicals, both foreign and domestic, in the Plant Variety Protection Office to aid the officers in the discharge of their duties.

Pub.L. 91–577, Title I, § 8, Dec. 24, 1970, 84 Stat. 1543.

§ 2331.   Copies for public libraries

The Secretary may supply printed copies of specifications, drawings, and photographs of protected plant varieties to public libraries in the United States which shall maintain such copies for the use of the public.

Pub.L. 91–577, Title I, § 11, Dec. 24, 1970, 84 Stat. 1544.

DEPARTMENT OF COMMERCE LIBRARY
(United States Code Annotated, Title 15, s.1518, 1151-1157,
Title 44, s.1307.)

§ 1518.   Custody of buildings; officers transferred

The Secretary of Commerce shall have charge, in the buildings or premises occupied by or appropriated to the Department of Commerce, of the library, furniture, fixtures, records, and other property pertaining to it or acquired for use in its business; and he shall be allowed to expend for periodicals and the purposes of the library, and for the rental of appropriate quarters for the accommodation of the Department of Commerce within the District of Columbia, and for all other incidental expenses, such sums as Congress may provide from time to time.   Where any office, bureau, or branch of the public service transferred to the Department of Commerce is occupying rented buildings or premises, it may still continue to do so until other suitable quarters are provided for its use.   All officers, clerks, and employees employed on February 14, 1903, in or by any of the bureaus, offices, departments, or branches of the public service transferred to the Department of Commerce are each and all transferred to said department, except where otherwise provided by law.   All laws prescribing the work and defining the duties of the several bureaus, offices, departments, or branches of the public service transferred to and made a part of the Department of Commerce shall, so far as the same are not in conflict with the provisions of this Act, remain in full force and effect until otherwise provided by law.

(Feb. 14, 1903, c. 552, § 9, 32 Stat. 829.)

§ 1151.   Purpose of chapter

The purpose of this chapter is to make the results of technological research and development more readily available to industry and business, and to the general public, by clarifying and defining the functions and responsibilities of the Department of Commerce as a central clearinghouse for technical information which is useful to American industry and business.

(Sept. 9, 1950, c. 936, § 1, 64 Stat. 823.)

§ 1152.   Clearinghouse for technical information; removal of security classification

The Secretary of Commerce (hereinafter referred to as the "Secretary") is directed to establish and maintain within the Department of Commerce a clearinghouse for the collection and dissemination of scientific, technical, and engineering information, and to this end to take such steps as he may deem necessary and desirable—

(a) To search for, collect, classify, coordinate, integrate, record, and catalog such information from whatever sources, foreign and domestic, that may be available;

(b) To make such information available to industry and business, to State and local governments, to other agencies of the Federal Government, and to the general public, through the preparation of abstracts, digests, translations, bibliographies, indexes, and microfilm and other reproductions, for distribution either directly or by utilization of business, trade, technical, and scientific publications and services;

(c) To effect, within the limits of his authority as now or hereafter defined by law, and with the consent of competent authority, the removal of restrictions on the dissemination of scientific and technical data in cases where consideration of national security permit the release of such data for the benefit of industry and business.

(Sept. 9, 1950, c. 936, § 2, 64 Stat. 823.)

§ 1153. Rules, regulations, and fees

The Secretary is authorized to make, amend, and rescind such orders, rules, and regulations as he may deem necessary to carry out the provisions of this chapter, and to establish, from time to time, a schedule or schedules of reasonable fees or charges for services performed or for documents or other publications furnished under this chapter.

It is the policy of this chapter, to the fullest extent feasible and consistent with the objectives of this chapter, that each of the services and functions provided herein shall be self-sustaining or self-liquidating and that the general public shall not bear the cost of publications and other services which are for the special use and benefit of private groups and individuals; but nothing herein shall be construed to require the levying of fees or charges for services performed or publications furnished to any agency or instrumentality of the Federal Government, or for publications which are distributed pursuant to reciprocal arrangements for the exchange of information or which are otherwise issued primarily for the general benefit of the public.

(Sept. 9, 1950, c. 936, § 3, 64 Stat. 823; Sept. 25, 1970, Pub.L. 91–412, § 3(e), 84 Stat. 864).

§ 1154. Reference of data to armed services and other government agencies

The Secretary is directed to refer to the armed services all scientific or technical information, coming to his attention, which he deems to have an immediate or potential practical military value or significance, and to refer to the heads of other Government agencies such scientific or technical information as relates to activities within the primary responsibility of such agencies.

(Sept. 9, 1950, c. 936, § 4, 64 Stat. 824).

§ 1155. General standards and limitations; preservation of security classification

Notwithstanding any other provision of this chapter, the Secretary shall respect and preserve the security classification of any scientific or technical information, data, patents, inventions, or discoveries in, or coming into, the possession or control of the Department of Commerce, the classified status of which the President or his designee or designees certify as being essential in the interest of national defense, and nothing in this chapter shall be construed as modifying or limiting any other statute relating to the classification of information for reasons of national defense or security.

(Sept. 9, 1950, c. 936, § 5, 64 Stat. 824).

§ 1156. Use of existing facilities

(a) The Secretary may utilize any personnel, facilities, bureaus, agencies, boards, administrations, offices, or other instrumentalities of the Department of Commerce which he may require to carry out the purposes of this chapter.

(b) The Secretary is authorized to call upon other departments and independent establishments and agencies of the Government to provide, with their consent, such available services, facilities, or other cooperation as he shall deem necessary or helpful in carrying out the provisions of this chapter, and he is directed to utilize existing facilities to the full extent deemed feasible.

(Sept. 9, 1950, c. 936, § 6, 64 Stat. 824.)

§ 1157. Relation to other provisions

Nothing in this chapter shall be construed to repeal or amend any other legislation pertaining to the Department of Commerce or its component offices or bureaus.

(Sept. 9, 1950, c. 936, § 7, 64 Stat. 824.)

§ 1307. Environmental Science Service Administration: charts; sale and distribution

(a) The charts published by the Environmental Science Service Administration shall be sold at cost of paper and printing as nearly as practicable. The price to the public shall include all expenses incurred in actual reproduction of the charts after the original cartography, such as photography, opaquing, platemaking, press time and bindery operations; the full postage rates, according to the rates for postal services used; and any additional cost factors considered appropriate by the Secretary such as overhead and administrative expenses allocable to the production of the charts and related reference materials. The cost of basic surveys and geodetic work done may not be included in the price of the charts and reference materials. The Secretary of Commerce shall publish the prices at which charts and reference materials are sold to the public at least once each calendar year.

(b) There may not be free distribution of charts except to the departments and officers of the United States requiring them for public use; and a number of copies of each sheet, not to exceed three hundred, to be presented to such foreign governments, libraries, and scientific associations, and institutions of learning as the Secretary of Commerce directs; but on the order of Senators and Representatives not to exceed one hundred copies to each may be distributed through the Environmental Science Service Administration.

Pub.L. 90–620, Oct. 22, 1968, 82 Stat. 1266.

Patent Office Library
(United States Code Annotated, Title 35, s.8, 13.)

§ 8. Library
The Commissioner shall maintain a library of scientific and other works and periodicals, both foreign and domestic, in the Patent and Trademark Office to aid the officers in the discharge of their duties.

As amended Jan. 2, 1975, Pub.L. 93–596, § 1, 88 Stat. 1949.

§ 13. Copies of patents for public libraries

The Commissioner may supply printed copies of specifications and drawings of patents to public libraries in the United States which shall maintain such copies for the use of the public, at the rate for each year's issue established for this purpose in section 41(a) 9 of this title. July 19, 1952, c. 950, § 1, 66 Stat. 794.

DEPARTMENT OF INTERIOR LIBRARY
(United States Code Annotated, Title 43, s.1467.)

§ 1467. Working capital fund; establishment; uses; reimbursement
There is established a working capital fund of $300,000, to be available without fiscal year limitation, for expenses necessary for the maintenance and operation of (1) a central reproduction service; (2) communication services; (3) a central supply service for stationery, supplies, equipment, blank forms, and miscellaneous materials, for which adequate stocks may be maintained to meet in whole or in part requirements of the bureaus and offices of the Department in the city of Washington and elsewhere; (4) a central library service; (5) health services; and (6) such other similar service functions as the Secretary determines may be performed more advantageously on a reimbursable basis. Said fund shall be reimbursed from available funds of bureaus, offices, and agencies for which services are performed at rates which will return in full all expenses of operation, including reserves for accrued annual leave and depreciation of equipment.

Sept. 6, 1950, c. 896, ch. VII, Title I, § 101, 64 Stat. 680.

Geological Survey Library
(United States Code Annotated, Title 43, s.36, 36a, 41, 42, 1320.)

§ 36. Purchase of books

The purchase of professional and scientific books and periodicals needed for statistical purposes by the scientific divisions of the United States Geological Survey is hereby authorized to be made and paid for out of appropriations made for the said Survey. June 28, 1902, c. 1301, § 1, 32 Stat. 455.

§ 36a. Acquisition of scientific or technical books, maps, etc. for library

The Director of the Geological Survey, under the general supervision of the Secretary of the Interior, is authorized to acquire for the United States, by gift or devise, scientific or technical books, manuscripts, maps, and related materials, and to deposit the same in the library of the Geological Survey for reference and use as authorized by law. May 14, 1940, c. 190, 54 Stat. 212.

§ 41. Publications and reports; preparation and sale

Except as otherwise provided in section 260 of Title 44, the publications of the Geological Survey shall consist of geological and economic maps illustrating the resources and classification of the lands, and reports upon general and economic geology and paleontology. All special memoirs and reports of said survey shall be issued in uniform quarto series if deemed necessary by the director, but otherwise in ordinary octavos. Three thousand copies of each shall be published for scientific exchanges and for sale at the price of publication, and all literary and cartographic materials received in exchange shall be the property of the United States and form a part of the library of the organization; and the money resulting from the sale of such publications shall be covered into the Treasury of the United States, under the direction of the Secretary of the Interior. Mar. 3, 1879, c. 182, § 1, 20 Stat. 394; May 16, 1902, No. 22, 32 Stat. 741; Aug. 7, 1946, c. 770, § 1(10), 60 Stat. 867.

§ 42. Distribution of maps and atlases, etc.

The Director of the Geological Survey is authorized and directed, on the approval of the Secretary of the Interior, to dispose of the topographic and geologic maps and atlases of the United States, made and published by the Geological Survey, at such prices and under such regulations as may from time to time be fixed by him and approved by the Secretary of the Interior; and a number of copies of each map or atlas, not exceeding five hundred, shall be distributed gratuitously among foreign governments and departments of our own Government to literary and scientific associations, and to such educational institutions or libraries as may be designated by the Director of the Survey and approved by the Secretary of the Interior. After June 7, 1924, the distribution of geological publications to libraries designated as special depositaries of such publications shall be discontinued. Feb. 18, 1897, No. 13, § 1, 29 Stat. 701; June 7, 1924, c. 303, 43 Stat. 592.

§ 1320. Geological Survey: distribution of publications to public libraries

The Director of the Geological Survey shall distribute to public libraries that have not already received them copies of sale publications on hand at the expiration of five years after date of delivery to the Survey document room, excepting a reserve number not to exceed two hundred copies.

Pub.L. 90–620, Oct. 22, 1968, 82 Stat. 1269.

DEPARTMENT OF LABOR
(United States Code Annotated, Title 29, s.558.)

§ 558. Library, records, etc., of Department

The Secretary of Labor shall have charge in the buildings or premises occupied by or appropriated to the Department of Labor, of the library, furniture, fixtures, records, and other property pertaining to it or acquired for use in its business. He shall be allowed to expend for periodicals and the purposes of the library and for rental of appropriate quarters for the accommodation of the Department of Labor within the District of Columbia, and for all other incidental expenses, such sums as Congress may provide from time to time.

Mar. 4, 1913, c. 141, § 6, 37 Stat. 738.

MISCELLANEOUS PROVISIONS
(United States Code Annotated, Title 44, s.1103, 1123.)

§ 1103. Certificate of necessity; estimate of cost

When a department, the Supreme Court, the Court of Claims, or the Library of Congress requires printing or binding to be done, it shall certify that it is necessary for the public service. The Public Printer shall then furnish an estimate of cost by principal items, after which requisitions may be made upon him for the printing or binding by the head of the department, the Clerk of the Supreme Court, chief judge of the Court of Claims, or the Librarian of Congress, respectively. The Public Printer shall place the cost to the debit of the department in its annual appropriation for printing and binding.

Pub.L. 90–620, Oct. 22, 1968, 82 Stat. 1261.

§ 1123. Binding materials; bookbinding for libraries

Binding for the departments of the Government shall be done in plain sheep or cloth, except that record and account books may be bound in Russia leather, sheep fleshers, and skivers, when authorized by the head of a department. The libraries of the several departments, the Library of Congress, the libraries of the Surgeon General's Office, the Patent Office, and the Naval Observatory may have books for the exclusive use of these libraries bound in half Turkey, or material no more expensive.

Pub.L. 90–620, Oct. 22, 1968, 82 Stat. 1264.

NATIONAL LIBRARY
OF MEDICINE

(United States Code Annotated, 1982, Title 42, s.275 to 280a-1.)

§ 275.   Congressional declaration of purpose; establishment

In order to assist the advancement of medical and related sciences, and to aid the dissemination and exchange of scientific and other information important to the progress of medicine and to the public health, there is established in the Public Health Service a National Library of Medicine (hereinafter referred to in this part as the "Library").

(July 1, 1944, c. 373, Title III, § 381, formerly § 371, as added Aug. 3, 1956, c. 907, § 1, 70 Stat. 960, and renumbered Mar. 13, 1970, Pub.L. 91–212, § 10(a)(3), 84 Stat. 66.)

§ 276.   Functions of Secretary

Acquisition, organization, etc., of materials

(a) The Secretary, through the Library and subject to the provisions of subsection (c) of this section, shall—

(1) acquire and preserve books, periodicals, prints, films, recordings, and other library materials pertinent to medicine;

(2) organize the materials specified in clause (1) of this subsection by appropriate cataloging, indexing, and bibliographical listing;

(3) publish and make available the catalogs, indexes, and bibliographies referred to in clause (2) of this subsection;

(4) make available, through loans, photographic or other copying procedures or otherwise, such materials in the Library as he deems appropriate;

(5) provide reference and research assistance; and

(6) engage in such other activities in furtherance of the purposes of this part as he deems appropriate and the Library's resources permit.

Exchange, destruction, or disposal of unneeded materials

(b) The Secretary may exchange, destroy, or otherwise dispose of any books, periodicals, films, and other library materials not needed for the permanent use of the Library.

Rules for public access to materials

(c) The Secretary is authorized, after obtaining the advice and recommendations of the Board (established under section 277 of this title), to prescribe rules under which the Library will provide copies of its publications or materials, or will make available its facilities for research or its bibliographic, reference, or other services, to public and private agencies and organizations, institutions, and individuals. Such rules may provide for making available such publications, materials, facilities, or services (1) without charge as a public service, or (2) upon a loan, exchange, or charge basis, or (3) in appropriate circumstances, under contract arrangements made with a public or other nonprofit agency, organization, or institution.

(July 1, 1944, c. 373, Title III, § 382, formerly § 372, as added Aug. 3, 1956, c. 907, § 1, 70 Stat. 960, and renumbered and amended Mar. 13, 1970, Pub.L. 91–212, § 10 (a)(3), (b)(1), (d)(1), 84 Stat. 66, 67; Nov. 18, 1971, Pub.L. 92–157, Title III, § 301 (d)(1), 85 Stat. 463.)

§ 277.   Board of Regents

Establishment; composition; appointment of members; Chairman; executive secretary

(a) There is established in the Public Health Service a Board of Regents of the National Library of Medicine (referred to in this part as the "Board") consisting of the Surgeons General of the Public Health Service, the Army, the Navy, and the Air Force, the Chief Medical Director of the Department of Medicine and Surgery of the Veterans' Administration, the Assistant Director for Biological and Medical Sciences of the National Science Foundation, and the Librarian of Congress, all of whom shall be ex officio members and ten members appointed by the Secretary. The ten appointed members shall be selected from among leaders in the various fields of the fundamental sciences, medicine, dentistry, public health, hospital administration, pharmacology, or scientific or medical library work, or in public affairs. At least six of the appointed members shall be selected from among leaders in the fields of medical, dental, or public health research or education. The Board shall annually elect one of the appointed members to serve as Chairman until the next election. The Secretary shall designate a member of the Library staff to act as executive secretary of the Board.

Duties of Board; annual report of Secretary

(b) It shall be the duty of the Board to advise, consult with, and make recommendations to the Secretary on important matters of policy in regard to the Library, including such matters as the acquisition of materials for the Library, the scope, content and organization of the Library's services, and the rules under which its materials, publications, facilities, and services shall be made available to various kinds of users, and the Secretary shall include in his annual report to the Congress a statement covering the recommendations made by the Board and the disposition thereof. The Secretary is authorized to use the services of any member or members of the Board in connection with matters related to the work of the Library, for such periods, in addition to conference periods, as he may determine.

Terms of office; vacancies; reappointment

(c) Each appointed member of the Board shall hold office for a term of four years, except that (A) any member appointed to fill a vacancy occurring prior to the expiration of the term for which his predecessor was appointed shall be appointed for the remainder of such term, and (B) the terms of the members first taking office after August 3, 1956, shall expire as follows: three at the end of four years after August 3, 1956, three at the end of three years after August 3, 1956, two at the end of two years after August 3, 1956, and two at the end of one year after August 3, 1956, as designated by the Secretary at the time of appointment. None of the appointed members shall be eligible for reappointment within one year after the end of his preceding term.

(July 1, 1944, c. 373, Title III, § 383, formerly § 373, as added Aug. 3, 1956, c. 907, § 1, 70 Stat. 960, amended Oct. 22, 1965, Pub.L. 89–291, § 4, 79 Stat. 1067, and renumbered and amended Mar. 13, 1970, Pub.L. 91–212, § 10(a)(3), (d)(1), 84 Stat. 66, 67; Oct. 30, 1970, Pub.L. 91–515, Title VI, § 601(b)(2), 84 Stat. 1311; Nov. 18, 1971, Pub.L. 92–157, Title III, § 301(d)(2), 85 Stat. 464; Nov. 9, 1978, Pub.L. 95–622, Title II, § 212, 92 Stat. 3421.)

§ 278. Acceptance and administration of gifts; establishment of memorials

The provisions of section 219 of this title shall be applicable to the acceptance and administration of gifts made for the benefit of the Library or for carrying out any of its functions, and the Board shall make recommendations to the Secretary of Health and Human Services relating to establishment within the Library of suitable memorials to the donors.

(July 1, 1944, c. 373, Title III, § 384, formerly § 374, as added Aug. 3, 1956, c. 907, § 1, 70 Stat. 961, and renumbered and amended Mar. 13, 1970, Pub.L. 91–212, § 10(a)(3), (d)(1), 84 Stat. 66, 67; Oct. 17, 1979, Pub.L. 96–88, Title V, § 509(b), 93 Stat. 695.)

§ 279. Definitions

For purposes of this part the terms "medicine" and "medical" shall, except when used in section 277 of this title, be understood to include preventive and therapeutic medicine, dentistry, pharmacy, hospitalization, nursing, public health, and the fundamental sciences related thereto, and other related fields of study, research, or activity.

(July 1, 1944, c. 373, Title III, § 385, formerly § 375, as added Aug. 3, 1956, c. 907, § 1, 70 Stat. 962, and renumbered and amended Mar. 13, 1970, Pub.L. 91–212, § 10 (a)(3), (b)(2), 84 Stat. 66.)

§ 280. Library facilities

There are authorized to be appropriated sums sufficient for the erection and equipment of suitable and adequate buildings and facilities for use of the Library in carrying out the provisions of this part. The Administrator of General Services is authorized to acquire, by purchase, condemnation, donation, or otherwise, a suitable site or sites, selected by the Secretary in accordance with the direction of the Board, for such buildings and facilities and to erect thereon, furnish, and equip such buildings and facilities. The sums authorized in this section to be appropriated shall include the cost of preparation of drawings and specifications, supervision of construction, and other administrative expenses incident to the work. The Administrator of General Services shall prepare the plans and specifications, make all necessary contracts, and supervise construction.

(July 1, 1944, c. 373, Title III, § 386, formerly § 376, as added Aug. 3, 1956, c. 907, § 1, 70 Stat. 962, and renumbered and amended Mar. 13, 1970, Pub.L. 91–212, § 10 (a)(3), (d)(1), 84 Stat. 66, 67; Nov. 18, 1971, Pub.L. 92–157, Title III, § 301(d)(3), 85 Stat. 464.)

§ 280a.   Transfer of Armed Forces Medical Library

All civilian personnel, equipment, library collections, other personal property, records, and unexpended balances of appropriations, allocations, and other funds (available or to be made available), which the Director of the Office of Management and Budget shall determine to relate primarily to the functions of the Armed Forces Medical Library, are transferred to the Service for use in the administration and operation of this part. Such transfer of property, funds, and personnel, and the other provisions of this part, shall become effective on the first day, occurring not less than thirty days after August 3, 1956, which the Director of the Office of Management and Budget determines to be practicable.

(July 1, 1944, c. 373, Title III, § 387, formerly § 377, as added Aug. 3, 1956, c. 907, § 1, 70 Stat. 962, amended 1970 Reorg.Plan No. 2, § 102, eff. July 1, 1970, 35 F.R. 7959, 84 Stat. 2085, and renumbered Mar. 13, 1970, Pub.L. 91–212, § 10(a)(3), 84 Stat. 66.)

§ 280a–1.   Regional branches

(a) Whenever the Secretary, with the advice of the Board, determines that—

> (1) in any geographic area of the United States, there is no regional medical library adequate to serve such area;

> (2) under the criteria prescribed in section 280b–8 of this title, there is a need for a regional medical library to serve such area; and

> (3) because there is located in such area no medical library which, under the provisions of section 280b–8 of this title, can feasibly be developed into a regional medical library adequate to serve such area,

he is authorized to establish, as a branch of the National Library of Medicine, a regional medical library to serve the needs of such area.

(b) For the purpose of establishing branches of the National Library of Medicine under this section, there are hereby authorized to be appropriated for each fiscal year, beginning with the fiscal year ending June 30, 1966, and ending with the fiscal year ending June 30, 1970, such sums, not to exceed $2,000,000 for any fiscal year, as may be necessary. Sums appropriated pursuant to this section for any fiscal year shall remain available until expended.

(July 1, 1944, c. 373, Title III, § 388, formerly § 378, as added Oct. 22, 1965, Pub. L. 89–291, § 3, 79 Stat. 1067, and renumberd and amended Mar. 13, 1970, Pub.L. 91–212, § 10(a)(3), (d)(1), 84 Stat. 66, 67; Nov. 18, 1971, Pub.L. 92–157, Title III, § 301(d)(4), 85 Stat. 464.)

DISTRICT OF COLUMBIA PUBLIC LIBRARY

(District of Columbia Code Annotated, 1982, s.37-101 to 37-110.)

§ 37-101. Public library established; Mayor authorized to accept gifts.

A free public library is hereby established and shall be maintained in the District of Columbia, which shall be the property of the said District and a supplement of the public educational system of said District. Said library shall consist of a central library and such number of branch libraries so located and so supported as to furnish books and other printed matter and information service convenient to the homes and offices of all residents of the said District. All actions relating to such library, or for the recovery of any penalties lawfully established in relation thereto, shall be brought in the name of the District of Columbia, and the Mayor of the said District is authorized on behalf of said District to accept and take title to all gifts, bequests, and devises for the purpose of aiding in the maintenance or endowment of said library; and the Mayor of said District is further authorized to receive, as component parts of said library, collections of books and other publications that may be transferred to him. (June 3, 1896, 29 Stat. 244, ch. 315, § 1; Apr. 1, 1926, 44 Stat. 229, ch. 98, § 1; 1973 Ed., § 37-101.)

§ 37-102. Branch libraries.

In order to make the said library an effective supplement of the public educational system of the said District and to furnish the system of branch libraries provided for in § 37-101, the Board of Library Trustees, hereinafter provided, is authorized to enter into agreements with the Board of Education of the said District for the establishment and maintenance of branch libraries in suitable rooms in such public-school buildings of the said District as will supplement the central library and branch libraries in separate buildings. The Board of Library Trustees, hereinafter provided, is authorized within the limits of appropriations first made therefor, to rent suitable buildings or parts of buildings for use as branch libraries and distributing stations. (June 3, 1896, 29 Stat. 244, ch. 315, § 2; Apr. 1, 1926, 44 Stat. 229, ch. 98, § 2; 1973 Ed., § 37-102.)

§ 37-103. Persons entitled to use of library; deposit of fees.

All persons who are permanent or temporary residents of the District of

Columbia shall be entitled to the privileges of the District of Columbia Public Library including the use of books and other materials, as a lending or circulating library, subject to rules and regulations established by the Board of Library Trustees. For purposes of this section, persons living outside of the District of Columbia but having regular business or employment or attending school in the District of Columbia shall also be deemed temporary residents of the District of Columbia. Persons residing in jurisdictions outside of the District of Columbia but within the Washington Metropolitan Area (the Washington Metropolitan Area means the Standard Metropolitan Statistical Area (SMSA)) who do not qualify as temporary residents in the manner described above may obtain a free library user's card from the District of Columbia Public Library: Provided, that the jurisdiction in which such person resides permits District of Columbia residents to obtain a free library user's card from the public library in that jurisdiction. Any person residing in the Washington Metropolitan Area who does not qualify under any of the conditions stated above for the free library user's card may obtain a library user's card from the District of Columbia Public Library upon payment of a fee to be fixed by the Board of Library Trustees. (June 3, 1896, 29 Stat. 244, ch. 315, § 3; Apr. 1, 1926, 44 Stat. 229, ch. 98, § 3; 1973 Ed., § 37-103; Mar. 3, 1979, D.C. Law 2-131, § 2, 25 DCR 3487.)

§ 37-104. Board of Trustees — Appointment and tenure.

The said library shall be in charge of a Board of Library Trustees, who shall purchase the books, magazines, and newspapers and procure the necessary appendages for such library. The said Board of Trustees shall be composed of 9 members, each of whom shall be a taxpayer in the District of Columbia, and shall serve without compensation. They shall be appointed by the Mayor of the District of Columbia and shall hold office for 6 years. Any vacancy occurring in said Board shall be filled by the District Mayor. Said Board shall have power to provide such regulations for its organization and government as it may deem necessary. (June 3, 1896, 29 Stat. 244, ch. 315, § 4; Apr. 1, 1926, 44 Stat. 229, ch. 98, § 4; 1973 Ed., § 37-104.)

§ 37-105. Same — Duties; deposit of fines; appointment of librarian; annual report.

The said Board shall have power to provide for the proper care and preservation of said library, to prescribe rules for taking and returning books, to fix, assess, and collect fines and penalties for the loss or injury to books, and for the retention of books beyond the period fixed by library regulations, and to establish all other needful rules and regulations for the management of the library as the said board shall deem proper. All fines and penalties so collected shall after June 30, 1927, be paid weekly to the Collector of Taxes of the District of Columbia for deposit in the Treasury of the United States to the credit of said District of Columbia. The said Board of Trustees shall appoint a librarian to have the care and superintendence of said library, in accordance with the provisions of the District of Columbia Government Comprehensive Merit Personnel Act of 1978 (D.C. Code, § 1-601.1 et seq.), who shall be responsible to the Board of Trustees for the impartial enforcement of all rules and regulations lawfully established in relation to the library. The said librarian shall appoint such assistants as the Board shall deem necessary for the proper conduct of the library in accordance with the provisions of subchapter VIII of Chapter 6 of Title 1. The said Board of Library Trustees shall make an annual report to the Mayor of the District of Columbia relative to the management of the said library. (June 3, 1896, 29 Stat. 244, ch. 315, § 5; Apr. 1, 1926, 44 Stat. 230, ch. 98, § 5; 1973 Ed., § 37-105; Mar. 3, 1979, D.C. Law 2-139, § 3205(jjj), 25 DCR 5740.)

§ 37-106. Mayor authorized to seek appropriations for library expenses.

Said Mayor of the said District is authorized to include in his annual estimates for appropriation such sums as he may deem necessary for the proper maintenance of said library, including branches, for the purchase of land for sites for library buildings, and for the erection and enlargement of necessary library buildings. (June 3, 1896, ch. 315, § 6; Apr. 1, 1926, 44 Stat. 230, ch. 98, § 6; 1973 Ed., § 37-106.)

§ 37-106.1. Purchase and sale of library-related items; use of profits.

The Board shall have power to purchase and sell library-related items, including, but not limited to: Film catalogs and other publications of the library; publications and items of special interest commemorating individuals and events connected with the library; and promotional items and souvenirs such as book tote bags, pens, notebooks, and postcards. Any profits realized shall be used to purchase books and other publications. (Oct. 8, 1981, D.C. Law 4-38, § 2, 28 DCR 3389.)

§ 37-107. Takoma Park branch — Hours.

The Takoma Park branch shall be kept open at least 7 hours per day on the same week days as the free public library shall be open to the public. (Mar. 4, 1913, 37 Stat. 943, ch. 150, § 1; 1973 Ed., § 37-107.)

§ 37-108. Same — Appropriation.

The appropriation for the expenses of the Takoma Park branch of the public library shall not exceed in any 1 year the sum of 10 per centum of the total costs of such branch library building. (Apr. 4, 1910, 36 Stat. 290, ch. 141; 1973 Ed., § 37-108.)

§ 37-109. Transfer of miscellaneous books to District public library.

Any books of a miscellaneous character no longer required for the use of any executive department, or bureau, or commission of the government, and not deemed an advisable addition to the Library of Congress, shall, if appropriate to the uses of the free public library of the District of Columbia, subject to applicable regulations under the Federal Property and Administrative Services Act of 1949, as amended, be turned over to that library for general use as a part thereof. (Feb. 25, 1903, 32 Stat. 865, ch. 755, § 1; Oct. 31, 1951, 65 Stat. 706, ch. 654, § 2(1); 1973 Ed., § 37-109.)

§ 37-110. Depository of Government publications.

The Public Library of the District of Columbia is hereby constituted a designated depository of governmental publications, and the Superintendent of Documents shall supply to such library 1 copy of each such publication, in the same form as supplied to other designated depositories. (Sept. 28, 1943, 57 Stat. 568, ch. 243; 1973 Ed., § 37-111.)

District of Columbia library laws are reprinted from DISTRICT OF COLUMBIA CODE ANNOTATED published by The Michie Co., Charlottesville, Virginia.

LIBRARY SERVICES AND CONSTRUCTION ACT

(United States Code Annotated, 1982, Title 20, s.351 to 355e-2, 361-364.)

§ 351. Declaration of policy

(a) It is the purpose of this chapter to assist the States in the extension and improvement of public library services in areas of the States which are without such services or in which such services are inadequate, and with public library construction, and in the improvement of such other State library services as library services for physically handicapped, institutionalized, and disadvantaged persons, in strengthening State library administrative agencies, in promoting interlibrary cooperation among all types of libraries, and in strengthening major urban resource libraries.

As amended Oct. 7, 1977, Pub.L. 95–123, § 4(a), 91 Stat. 1095.

(b) Nothing in this chapter shall be construed to interfere with State and local initiative and responsibility in the conduct of library services. The administration of libraries, the selection of personnel and library books and materials, and, insofar as consistent with the purposes of this chapter, the determination of the best uses of the funds provided under this chapter shall be reserved to the States and their local subdivisions.

June 19, 1956, c. 407, § 2, 70 Stat. 293; Feb. 11, 1964, Pub.L. 88–269, § 1(a)(1), 78 Stat. 11; July 19, 1966, Pub.L. 89–511, § 2, 80 Stat. 313; Dec. 30, 1970, Pub.L. 91–600, § 2(b), 84 Stat. 1660.

§ 351a. Definitions

The following definitions shall apply to this chapter:

(1) "Commissioner" means the Commissioner of Education.

(2) "Construction" includes construction of new buildings and acquisition, expansion, remodeling, and alteration of existing buildings, and initial equipment of any such buildings, or any combination of such activities (including architects' fees and the cost of acquisition of land). For the purposes of this paragraph, the term "equipment" includes machinery, utilities, and built-in equipment and any necessary enclosures or structures to house them; and such term includes all other items necessary for the functioning of a particular facility as a facility for the provision of library services.

(3) "Library service" means the performance of all activities of a library relating to the collection and organization of library materi-

als and to making the materials and information of a library available to a clientele.

(4) "Library services for the physically handicapped" means the providing of library services, through public or other nonprofit libraries, agencies, or organizations, to physically handicapped persons (including the blind and other visually handicapped) certified by competent authority as unable to read or to use conventional printed materials as a result of physical limitations.

(5) "Public library" means a library that serves free of charge all residents of a community, district, or region, and receives its financial support in whole or in part from public funds. Such term also includes a research library, which, for the purposes of this sentence, means a library which—

(A) makes its services available to the public free of charge;

(B) has extensive collections of books, manuscripts, and other materials suitable for scholarly research which are not available to the public through public libraries;

(C) engages in the dissemination of humanistic knowledge through services to readers, fellowships, educational and cultural programs, publication of significant research, and other activities; and

(D) is not an integral part of an institution of higher education.

(6) "Public library services" means library services furnished by a public library free of charge.

(7) "State" means a State, the District of Columbia, the Commonwealth of Puerto Rico, Guam, American Samoa, the Virgin Islands, or the Trust Territory of the Pacific Islands.

(8) "State Advisory Council on Libraries" means an advisory council for the purposes of clause (3) of section 351d(a) of this title which shall—

(A) be broadly representative of the public, school, academic, special, and institutional libraries, and libraries serving the handicapped, in the State and of persons using such libraries, including disadvantaged persons within the State;

(B) advise the State library administrative agency on the development of, and policy matters arising in the administration of, the State plan; and

(C) assist the State library administrative agency in the evaluation of activities assisted under this chapter;

(9) "State institutional library services" means the providing of books and other library materials, and of library services, to (A) inmates, patients, or residents of penal institutions, reformatories, residential training schools, orphanages, or general or special insti-

tutions or hospitals operated or substantially supported by the State, or (B) students in residential schools for the physically handicapped (including mentally retarded, hard of hearing, deaf, speech impaired, visually handicapped, seriously emotionally disturbed, crippled, or other health impaired persons who by reason thereof require special education) operated or substantially supported by the State.

(10) "State library administrative agency" means the official agency of a State charged by law of that State with the extension and development of public library services throughout the State, which has adequate authority under law of the State to administer State plans in accordance with the provisions of this chapter.

(11) "Basic State plan" means the document which gives assurances that the officially designated State library administrative agency has the fiscal and legal authority and capability to administer all aspects of this chapter; provides assurances for establishing the State's policies, priorities, criteria, and procedures necessary to the implementation of all programs under provisions of this chapter; and submits copies for approval as required by regulations promulgated by the Commissioner.

(12) "Long-range program" means the comprehensive five-year program which identifies a State's library needs and sets forth the activities to be taken toward meeting the identified needs supported with the assistance of Federal funds made available under this chapter. Such long-range programs shall be developed by the State library administrative agency and shall specify the State's policies, criteria, priorities, and procedures consistent with this chapter as required by the regulations promulgated by the Commissioner and shall be updated as library progress requires.

(13) "Annual program" means the projects which are developed and submitted to describe the specific activities to be carried out annually toward achieving fulfillment of the long-range program. These annual programs shall be submitted in such detail as required by regulations promulgated by the Commissioner.

June 19, 1956, c. 407, § 3, as added Dec. 30, 1970, Pub.L. 91–600, § 2(b), 84 Stat. 1660, and amended Oct. 19, 1973, Pub.L. 93–133, § 4(a), 87 Stat. 466.

(14) "Major urban resource library" means any public library located in a city having a population of 100,000 or more individuals, as determined by the Commissioner.
These annual programs shall be submitted in such detail as required by regulations promulgated by the Commissioner.
As amended Oct. 7, 1977, Pub.L. 95–123, § 4(b), 91 Stat. 1095.

§ 351b. Authorization of appropriations; availability of appropriations

(a) For the purpose of carrying out the provisions of this chapter the following sums are authorized to be appropriated:

(1) For the purpose of making grants to States for library services as provided in subchapter I of this chapter, there are authorized to be appropriated $112,000,000 for the fiscal year ending June 30, 1972, $117,600,000 for the fiscal year ending June 30, 1973, $123,500,000 for the fiscal year ending June 30, 1974, $129,-675,000 for the fiscal year ending June 30, 1975, $137,150,000 for the fiscal year ending June 30, 1976, $110,000,000 for fiscal year 1978, $140,000,000 for fiscal year 1979, and $150,000,000 for fiscal year 1980 and each of the two succeeding fiscal years.

(2) For the purpose of making grants to States for public library construction, as provided in subchapter II of this chapter, there are authorized to be appropriated $80,000,000 for the fiscal year ending June 30, 1972, $84,000,000 for the fiscal year ending June 30, 1973, $88,000,000 for the fiscal year ending June 30, 1974, $92,500,000 for the fiscal year ending June 30, 1975, $97,-000,000 for the fiscal year ending June 30, 1976, and such sums as may be necessary for fiscal year 1978 through fiscal year 1981, and $97,000,000 for fiscal year 1982.

(3) For the purpose of making grants to States to enable them to carry out interlibrary cooperation programs authorized by subchapter III of this chapter, there are hereby authorized to be appropriated $15,000,000 for the fiscal year ending June 30, 1972, $15,750,000 for the fiscal year ending June 30, 1973, $16,500,000 for the fiscal year ending June 30, 1974, $17,300,000, for the fiscal year ending June 30, 1975, $18,200,000 for the fiscal year ending June 30, 1976, $15,000,000 for fiscal year 1978, and $20,000,000 for fiscal year 1979 and each of the three succeeding fiscal years.

(4) For the purpose of making grants to States to enable them to carry out public library service programs for older persons authorized by subchapter IV of this chapter, there are authorized to be appropriated such sums as may be necessary for each fiscal year ending prior to October 1, 1982.

As amended Oct. 7, 1977, Pub.L. 95–123, § 2, 91 Stat. 1095.

(b) Notwithstanding any other provision of law, unless enacted in express limitation of the provisions of this subsection, any sums appropriated pursuant to subsection (a) of this section shall (1), in the case of sums appropriated pursuant to paragraphs (1) and (3) thereof, be available for obligation and expenditure for the period of time specified in the Act making such appropriation, and (2), in the case of sums appropriated pursuant to paragraph (2) thereof, subject to regulations of the Commissioner promulgated in carrying out the provisions of section 351c(b) of this title, be available for obligation and expenditure for the year specified in the Appropriation Act and for the next succeeding year.

June 19, 1956, c. 407, § 4, as added Dec. 30, 1970, Pub.L. 91–600, § 2(b), 84 Stat. 1662, and amended May 3, 1973, Pub.L. 93–29, Title VIII, § 801(b), 87 Stat. 58.

§ 351c.   Allotments to States; minimum allotment; population basis for distribution of remaining funds; reallotment

(a)(1) From the sums appropriated pursuant to paragraph (1),

(2), (3), or (4) of section 351b(a) of this title for any fiscal year, the Commissioner shall allot the minimum allotment, as determined under paragraph (3) of this subsection, to each State. Any sums remaining after minimum allotments have been made shall be allotted in the manner set forth in paragraph (2) of this subsection.

(2) From the remainder of any sums appropriated pursuant to paragraph (1), (2), (3), or (4) of section 351b(a) of this title for any fiscal year, the Commissioner shall allot to each State such part of such remainder as the population of the State bears to the population of all the States.

(3) For the purposes of this subsection, the "minimum allotment" shall be—

(A) with respect to appropriations for the purposes of subchapter I of this chapter, $200,000 for each State, except that it shall be $40,000 in the case of Guam, American Samoa, the Virgin Islands, and the Trust Territory of the Pacific Islands;

(B) with respect to appropriations for the purposes of subchapter II of this chapter, $100,000 for each State, except that it shall be $20,000 in the case of Guam, American Samoa, the Virgin Islands, and the Trust Territory of the Pacific Islands;

(C) with respect to appropriations for the purposes of subchapter III of this chapter, $40,000 for each State, except that it shall be $10,000 in the case of Guam, American Samoa, the Virgin Islands, and the Trust Territory of the Pacific Islands; and

(D) with respect to appropriations for the purposes of subchapter IV of this chapter, $40,000 for each State, except that it shall be $10,000 in the case of Guam, American Samoa, the Virgin Islands, and the Trust Territory of the Pacific Islands.

If the sums appropriated pursuant to paragraph (1), (2), (3), or (4) of section 351b(a) of this title for any fiscal year are insufficient to fully satisfy the aggregate of the minimum allotments for that purpose, each of such minimum allotments shall be reduced ratably.

(4) The population of each State and of all the States shall be determined by the Commissioner on the basis of the most recent satisfactory data available to him.

(5) There is hereby authorized for the purpose of evaluation (directly or by grants or contracts) of programs authorized by this chapter, such sums as Congress may deem necessary for any fiscal year.

(b) The amount of any State's allotment under subsection (a) of this section for any fiscal year from any appropriation made pursuant to paragraph (1), (2), (3), or (4) of section 351b(a) of this title which the Commissioner deems will not be required for the period and the purpose for which such allotment is available for carrying out the State's annual program shall be available for reallotment from time to time on such dates during such year as the Commissioner shall fix. Such amount shall be available for reallotment to other States in proportion to the original allotments for such year to such States under subsection (a) of this section but with such proportionate amount for any of such other State being reduced to the extent that it exceeds the amount which the Commissioner estimates the State needs and will be able to use for such period of time for which the original allotments were made and the total of such reductions shall be similarly reallotted among the States not suffering such a reduction. Any amount reallotted to a State under this subsection for any fiscal year shall be deemed to be a part of its allotment for such year pursuant to subsection (a) of this section.

June 19, 1956, c. 407, § 5, as added Dec. 30, 1970, Pub.L. 91–600, § 2(b), 84 Stat. 1662, and amended May 3, 1973, Pub.L. 93–29, Title VIII, § 801(c), 87 Stat. 58.

§ 351d. State plans and programs—Prerequisites for allotment of basic State plan in effect, submission of annual program, and establishment of State Advisory Council on Libraries

(a) Any State desiring to receive its allotment for any purpose under this chapter for any fiscal year shall (1) have in effect for such fiscal year a basic State plan as defined in section 351a(11) of this title and meeting the requirements set forth in subsection (b) of this section, (2) submit an annual program as defined in section 351a(13) of this title for the purposes for which allotments are desired, meeting the appropriate requirements set forth in subchapters I, II, III, and IV of this chapter, and shall submit (no later than July 1, 1972) a long-range program as defined in section 351a(12) of this title for carrying out the purposes of this chapter as specified in subsection (d) of this section, and (3) establish a State Advisory Council on Libraries which meets the requirements of section 351a(8) of this title.

Provisions of plan

(b) A basic State plan under this chapter shall—

(1) provide for the administration, or supervision of the administration, of the programs authorized by this chapter by the State library administrative agency;

(2) provide that any funds paid to the State in accordance with a long-range program and an annual program shall be expended solely for the purposes for which funds have been authorized and appropriated and that such fiscal control and fund accounting procedures have been adopted as may be necessary

to assure proper disbursement of, and account for, Federal funds paid to the State (including any such funds paid by the State to any other agency) under this chapter;

(3) provide satisfactory assurance that the State agency administering the plan (A) will make such reports, in such form and containing such information, as the Commissioner may reasonably require to carry out his functions under this chapter and to determine the extent to which funds provided under this chapter have been effective in carrying out its purposes, including reports of evaluations made under the State plans, and (B) will keep such records and afford such access thereto as the Commissioner may find necessary to assure the correctness and verification of such reports; and

(4) set forth the criteria to be used in determining the adequacy of public library services in geographical areas and for groups of persons in the State, including criteria designed to assure that priority will be given to programs or projects which serve urban and rural areas with high concentrations of low-income families, and to programs and projects which serve areas with high concentrations of persons of limited English-speaking ability (as defined in section 880b–1(a) of this title).

As amended Aug. 21, 1974, Pub.L. 93–380, Title VIII, § 841(b), 88 Stat. 609.

Approval of basic State plan by Commissioner

(c)(1) The Commissioner shall not approve any basic State plan pursuant to this chapter for any fiscal year unless—

(A) the plan fulfills the conditions specified in section 351a(11) of this title and subsection (b) of this section and the appropriate subchapters of this chapter;

(B) he has made specific findings as to the compliance of such plan with requirements of this chapter and he is satisfied that adequate procedures are subscribed to therein insure that any assurances and provisions of such plan will be carried out.

(2) The State plan shall be made public as finally approved.

(3) The Commissioner shall not finally disapprove any basic State plan submitted pursuant to subsection (a)(1) of this section, or any modification thereof, without first affording the State reasonable notice and opportunity for hearing.

Long-range State programs; development; provisions

(d) The long-range program of any State for carrying out the purposes of this chapter shall be developed in consultation with the Commissioner and shall—

(1) set forth a program under which the funds received by the State under the programs authorized by this chapter will be used to carry out a long-range program of library services and

construction covering a period of not less than three nor more than five years;

(2) be annually reviewed and revised in accordance with changing needs for assistance under this chapter and the results of the evaluation and surveys of the State library administrative agency;

(3) set forth policies and procedures (A) for the periodic evaluation of the effectiveness of programs and projects supported under this chapter, and (B) for appropriate dissemination of the results of such evaluations and other information pertaining to such programs or projects; and

(4) set forth effective policies and procedures for the coordination of programs and projects supported under this chapter with library programs and projects operated by institutions of higher education or local elementary or secondary schools and with other public or private library services programs.

Such program shall be developed with advice of the State advisory council and in consultation with the Commissioner and shall be made public as it is finally adopted.

Termination or limitation of payments to States by Commissioner; procedure; grounds

(e) Whenever the Commissioner, after reasonable notice and opportunity for hearing to the State agency administering a program submitted under this chapter, finds—

(1) that the program has been so changed that it no longer complies with the provisions of this chapter, or

(2) that in the administration of the program there is a failure to comply substantially with any such provisions or with any assurance or other provision contained in the basic State plan,

then, until he is satisfied that there is no longer any such failure to comply, after appropriate notice to such State agency, he shall make no further payments to the State under this chapter or shall limit payments to programs or projects under, or parts of, the programs not affected by the failure, or shall require that payments by such State agency under this chapter shall be limited to local or other public library agencies not affected by the failure.

Judicial review of Commissioner's final actions; procedure

(f)(1) If any State is dissatisfied with the Commissioner's final action with respect to the approval of a plan submitted under this chapter or with his final action under subsection (e) of this section such State may, within sixty days after notice of such action, file with the United States court of appeals for the circuit in which such State is located a petition for review of that action. A copy of the petition shall be forthwith transmitted by the clerk of the court to the Commissioner. The Commissioner thereupon shall file in the court the record of the proceedings on which he based his action as provided in section 2112 of Title 28.

(2) The findings of fact by the Commissioner, if supported by substantial evidence, shall be conclusive; but the court, for good cause shown, may remand the case to the Commissioner to take further evidence, and the Commissioner may thereupon take new or modified findings of fact and may modify his previous action, and shall certify to the court the record of further proceedings.

(3) The court shall have jurisdiction to affirm the action of the Commissioner or to set it aside, in whole or in part. The judgment of the court shall be subject to review by the Supreme Court of the United States upon certiorari or certification as provided in section 1254 of Title 28.

June 19, 1956, c. 407, § 6, as added Dec. 30, 1970, Pub.L. 91–600, § 2(b), 84 Stat. 1663, and amended May 3, 1973, Pub.L. 93–29, Title VIII, § 801(c), 87 Stat. 59.

§ 351e.   Payments to States; prerequisites; Federal share; promulgation by Commissioner of Federal share

(a) From the allotments available therefor under section 351c of this title from appropriations pursuant to paragraph (1), (2), (3), or (4) of section 351b(a) of this title, the Commissioner shall pay to each State which has a basic State plan approved under section 351d(a)(1) of this title, an annual program and a long-range program as defined in section 351a(12) and (13) of this title an amount equal to the Federal share of the total sums expended by the State and its political subdivisions in carrying out such plan, except that no payments shall be made from appropriations pursuant to such paragraph (1) for the purposes of subchapter I of this chapter to any State (other than the Trust Territory of the Pacific Islands) for any fiscal year unless the Commissioner determines that—

(1) there will be available for expenditure under the programs from State and local sources during the fiscal year for which the allotment is made—

(A) sums sufficient to enable the State to receive for the purpose of carrying out the programs payments in an amount not less than the minimum allotment for that State for the purpose, and

(B) not less than the total amount actually expended, in the areas covered by the programs for such year, for the purposes of such programs from such sources in the second preceding fiscal year; and

(2) there will be available for expenditure for the purposes of the programs from State sources during the fiscal year for

which the allotment is made not less than the total amount actually expended for such purposes from such sources in the second preceding fiscal year.

(b)(1) For the purpose of this section, the "Federal share" for any State shall be, except as is provided otherwise in subchapter III and subchapter IV of this chapter, 100 per centum less the State percentage, and the State percentage shall be that percentage which bears the same ratio to 50 per centum as the per capita income of such State bears to the per capita income of all the States (excluding Puerto Rico, Guam, American Samoa, the Virgin Islands, and the Trust Territory of the Pacific Islands), except that (A) the Federal share shall in no case be more than 66 per centum, or less than 33 per centum, and (B) the Federal share for Puerto Rico, Guam, American Samoa, and the Virgin Islands shall be 66 per centum, and (C) the Federal share for the Trust Territory of the Pacific Islands shall be 100 per centum.

(2) The "Federal share" for each State shall be promulgated by the Commissioner within sixty days after the beginning of the fiscal year ending June 30, 1971, and of every second fiscal year thereafter, on the basis of the average per capita incomes of each of the States and of all the States (excluding Puerto Rico, Guam, American Samoa, the Virgin Islands, and the Trust Territory of the Pacific Islands), for the three most recent consecutive years for which satisfactory data are available to him from the Department of Commerce. Such promulgation shall be conclusive for each of the two fiscal years begining after the promulgation.

June 19, 1956, c. 407, § 7, as added Dec. 30, 1970, Pub.L. 91–600, § 2(b), 84 Stat. 1665, and amended May 3, 1973, Pub.L. 93–29, Title VIII, § 801(d), 87 Stat. 59.

§ 351f. Administrative costs

The amount expended by any State, from an allotment received under this chapter for any fiscal year, for administrative costs in connection with any program or activity carried out by such State under this chapter shall be matched by such State from funds other than Federal funds.

June 19, 1956, c. 407, § 8, as added Oct. 7, 1977, Pub.L. 95–123, § 3 (a), 91 Stat. 1095.

§ 352. Grants to States for public library services

The Commissioner shall carry out a program of making grants from sums appropriated pursuant to section 351b(a)(1) of this title to States which have had approved basic State plans under section 351d of this title and have submitted annual programs under section 354 of this title for the extension of public library services to areas without such services and the improvement of such services in areas in which such services are inadequate, for making library services more accessible to persons who, by reason of distance, residence, or physical handicap, or other disadvantage, are unable to receive the benefits of public library services regularly made available to the public, for adapting public library services to meet particular needs of persons within the States, for improving and strengthening library administrative agencies, and in strengthening major urban resource libraries.

As amended Oct. 7, 1977, Pub.L. 95–123, § 4(c), 91 Stat. 1096.

§ 353. Uses of Federal funds—Development of programs and projects to extend library services to physically handicapped, disadvantaged areas, etc.; expanding services of major urban resource libraries; limitation on grants

(a) Funds appropriated pursuant to paragraph (1) of section 351b (a) of this title shall be available for grants to States from allotments under section 351c(a) of this title for the purpose of paying the Federal share of the cost of carrying out State plans submitted and approved under sections 351d and 354 of this title. Except as is provided in subsection (b) of this section, grants to States under this subchapter may be used solely—

> (1) for planning for, and taking other steps leading to the development of, programs and projects designed to extend and improve library services, as provided in clause (2);
> (2) for (A) extending public library services to geographical areas and groups of persons without such services and improving such services in such areas and for such groups as may have inadequate public library services; and (B) establishing, expanding, and operating programs and projects to provide (i) State institutional library services, (ii) library services to the physically handicapped, and (iii) library services for the disadvantaged in urban and rural areas; and (C) strengthening metropolitan public libraries which serve as national or regional resource centers; and
> (3) for supporting and expanding library services of major urban resource libraries which, because of the value of the collections of such libraries to individual users and to other libraries, need special assistance to furnish services at a level required to meet the demands made for such services.

No grant may be made under clause (3) of this subsection unless the major urban resource library provides services to users throughout the regional area in which such library is located.

Payment of costs of administering State plans, planning for and evaluation of library services, dissemination of information concerning library services, etc.; increase capacity of State library administrative agencies

(b) Subject to the provisions of section 351f of this title such limitations and criteria as the Commissioner shall establish by regulation, grants to States under this subchapter may be used (1) to pay the cost of administering the State plans submitted and approved under this chapter (including obtaining the services of consultants), statewide planning for and evaluation of library services, dissemination of information concerning library services, and the activities of such advisory groups and panels as may be necessary to assist the State library administrative agency in carrying out its functions under this subchapter, and (2) for strengthening the capacity of State library administrative agencies for meeting the needs of the people of the States.

Reservation of allotments

(c)(1) Subject to such criteria as the Commissioner shall establish by regulation, in any fiscal year in which sums appropriated pursuant to paragraph (1) of section 351b(a) of this title exceed $60,000,000, each State which is subject to the provisions of this subsection shall reserve that portion of the allotment of each State attributable to the amount in excess of $60,000,000 in that fiscal year in the manner required in paragraph (2).

(2)(A) In each State having one or more cities with a population of 100,000 or more individuals, as determined by the Commissioner, and in which the aggregate population of such cities does not exceed 50 percent of the total population of the State, the portion of the excess amount specified in paragraph (1) shall be reserved for the purposes described in subsection (a)(3) of this section in accordance with clause (2) of section 354 of this title in an amount which bears the same ratio to the total of such excess amount as the aggregate population of such cities bears to the total population of such State.

(B) In each State having one or more cities with a population of 100,000 or more individuals, as determined by the Commissioner, and in which the aggregate population of such cities exceeds 50 percent of the total population of the State, 50 percent of the excess amount specified in paragraph (1) shall be reserved for the purposes described in subsection (a)(3) in accordance with clause (2) of section 354 of this title.

(C) Any State which does not include any city with a population of 100,000 or more individuals, as determined by the Commissioner, shall not be subject to the provisions of this subsection.
As amended Oct. 7, 1977, Pub.L. 95–123, §§ 3(b), 4(d), (e), 91 Stat. 1095, 1096.

§ 354. Annual State program for library services; submission; contents; limitation on reduction of funds

Any State desiring to receive a grant from its allotment for the purposes of this subchapter for any fiscal year shall, in addition to having had submitted, and having had approved, a basic State plan under section 351d of this title, submit for that fiscal year an annual program for library services. Such program shall be submitted at such time, in such form, and contain such information as the Commissioner may require by regulation, and shall—

(1) set forth a program, subject to clause (2) of this section, for the year submitted under which funds paid to the State from appropriations pursuant to paragraph (1) of section 351b(a) of this title for that year will be used, consistent with its long-range program, solely for the purposes set forth in section 353 of this title;

(2) set forth a program for the year submitted under which the amount reserved by the State under section 353(c) of this title, if applicable, will be used for the purposes set forth in clause (3) of section 353(a) of this title;

(3) set forth the criteria used in allocating such funds among such purposes, which criteria shall insure that the State will expend from Federal, State, and local sources an amount not less than the amount expended by the State from such sources for State institutional library services, and library services to the physically handicapped during the second fiscal year preceding the fiscal year for which the determination is made;

(4) include such information, policies, and procedures as will assure that the activities to be carried out during that year are consistent with the long-range program; and

(5) include an extension of the long-range program, taking into consideration the results of evaluations.

No State shall, in carrying out the provisions of clause (2) of this section, reduce the amount paid to an urban resource library below the amount that such library received in the year preceding the year for which the determination is made under such clause (2).
As amended Oct. 7, 1977, Pub.L. 95–123, §§ 4(f), 5, 91 Stat. 1096, 1097.

§ 355a. Grants to States for public library construction

The Commissioner shall carry out a program of making grants to States which have had approved a basic State plan under section 351d of this title and have submitted a long-range program and submit annually appropriately updated programs under section 355c of this title for the construction of public libraries.

June 19, 1956, c. 407, Title II, § 201, as added Feb. 11, 1964, Pub.L. 88–269, § 7(a), 78 Stat. 13, and amended July 19, 1966, Pub.L. 89–511, § 6, 80 Stat. 313; Dec. 30, 1970, Pub.L. 91–600, § 2(b), 84 Stat. 1668.

§ 355b. Payment of Federal share; uses of Federal funds

Funds appropriated pursuant to paragraph (2) of section 351b(a) of this title shall be available for grants to States from allotments under section 351c(a) of this title for the purpose of paying the Federal share of the cost of construction projects carried under State plans. Such grants shall be used solely for the construction of public libraries for the remodeling of public libraries necessary to meet standards adopted pursuant to the Act of August 12, 1968, commonly known as the Architectural Barriers Act of 1968, and for remodeling designed to conserve energy in the operation of public libraries under approved State plans.

As amended Oct. 7, 1977, Pub.L. 95–123, § 6, 91 Stat. 1097.

§ 355c. Annual State program for construction of public libraries; submission; contents

Any State desiring to receive a grant from its allotment for the purpose of this subchapter for any fiscal year shall, in addition to having submitted, and having had approved, a basic State plan under section 351d of this title, submit such projects as the State may approve and are consistent with its long-range program.

Such projects shall be submitted at such time and contain such information as the Commissioner may require by regulation and shall—

(1) for the year submitted under which funds are paid to the State from appropriations pursuant to paragraph (2) of section 351b(a) of this title for that year, be used, consistent with the State's long-range program, for the construction of public libraries in areas of the State which are without the library facilities necessary to provide adequate library services;

(2) follow the criteria, policies, and procedures for the approval of applications for the construction of public library facilities under the long-range program;

(3) follow policies and procedures which will insure that every local or other public agency whose application for funds under the plan with respect to a project for construction of public library facilities is denied will be given an opportunity for a hearing before the State library administrative agency;

(4) include an extension of the long-range program taking into consideration the results of evaluations.

June 19, 1956, c. 407, Title II, § 203, as added Feb. 11, 1964, Pub.L. 88–269, § 7(a), 78 Stat. 13, and amended Apr. 13, 1970, Pub.L. 91–230, Title IV, § 401(g)(3), 84 Stat. 174; Dec. 30, 1970, Pub.L. 91–600, § 2(b), 84 Stat. 1668.

§ 355e.   Grants to States for interlibrary cooperation programs

The Commissioner shall carry out a program of making grants to States which have an approved basic State plan under section 351d of this title and have submitted a long-range program and an annual program under section 355e–2 of this title for interlibrary cooperation programs.

June 19, 1956, c. 407, Title III, § 301, as added July 19, 1966, Pub.L. 89–511, § 9, 80 Stat. 314, and amended Dec. 30, 1970, Pub.L. 91–600, § 2(b), 84 Stat. 1668.

§ 355e-1.   Payment of Federal share; uses of Federal funds; amount

(a) Funds appropriated pursuant to paragraph (3) of section 351b(a) of this title shall be available for grants to States from allotments under paragraphs (1) and (3) of section 351c(a) of this title for the purpose of carrying out the Federal share of the cost of carrying out State plans submitted and approved under section 355e–2 of this title. Such grants shall be used (1) for planning for, and taking other steps leading to the development of, cooperative library networks; and (2) for establishing, expanding, and operating local, regional, and interstate cooperative networks of libraries, which provide for the systematic and effective coordination of the resources of school, public, academic, and special libraries and information centers for improved supplementary services for the special clientele served by each type of library or center.

(b) For the purposes of this subchapter, the Federal share shall be 100 per centum of the cost of carrying out the State plan.

June 19, 1956, c. 407, Title III, § 302, as added and amended July 19, 1966, Pub.L. 89–511, §§ 9, 12(a), 80 Stat. 314, 318; Dec. 30, 1970, Pub.L. 91–600, § 2(b), 84 Stat. 1669.

§ 355e-2.   Annual State program for interlibrary cooperation; submission; contents

Any State desiring to receive a grant from its allotment for the purposes of this subchapter for any fiscal year shall, in addition to having submitted, and having had approved, a basic State plan under section 351d of this title, submit for that fiscal year an annual

program for interlibrary cooperation. Such program shall be submitted at such time, in such form, and contain such information as
the Commissioner may require by regulation and shall—

> (1) set forth a program for the year submitted under which
> funds paid to the State from appropriations pursuant to para-
> graph (3) of section 351b(a) of this title will be used, consist-
> ent with its long-range program for the purposes set forth in
> section 355e–1 of this title,

> (2) include an extension of the long-range program taking
> into consideration the results of evaluations.

June 19, 1956, c. 407, Title III, § 303, as added July 19, 1966, Pub.L.
89–511, § 9, 80 Stat. 314, and amended Nov. 24, 1967, Pub.L. 90–154,
§ 1, 81 Stat. 509; Dec. 30, 1970, Pub.L. 91–600, § 2(b), 84 Stat. 1669.

§ 361. Grants to States for older readers services

The Commissioner shall carry out a program of making grants to
States which have an approved basic State plan under section 351d
of this title and have submitted a long-range program and an annual program under section 363 of this title for library services for
older persons.

June 19, 1956, c. 407, Title IV, § 401, as added May 3, 1973, Pub.L.
93–29, Title VIII, § 801(a), 87 Stat. 57.

§ 362. Uses of Federal funds; Federal share

(a) Funds appropriated pursuant to paragraph (4) of section
351b(a) of this title shall be available for grants to States from allotments under section 351c(a) of this title for the purpose of carrying out the Federal share of the cost of carrying out State plans
submitted and approved under section 363 of this title. Such grants
shall be used for (1) the training of librarians to work with the elderly; (2) the conduct of special library programs for the elderly; (3)
the purchase of special library materials for use by the elderly; (4)
the payment of salaries for elderly persons who wish to work in libraries as assistants on programs for the elderly; (5) the provision
of in-home visits by librarians and other library personnel to the elderly; (6) the establishment of outreach programs to notify the elderly of library services available to them; and (7) the furnishing
of transportation to enable the elderly to have access to library
services.

(b) For the purposes of this subchapter, the Federal share shall
be 100 per centum of the cost of carrying out the State plan.

June 19, 1956, c. 407, Title IV, § 402, as added May 3, 1973, Pub.L.
93–29, Title VIII, § 801(a), 87 Stat. 57.

§ 363. State annual program for library services for the elderly

Any State desiring to receive a grant from its allotment for the

purposes of this subchapter for any fiscal year shall, in addition to
having submitted, and having had approved, a basic State plan under section 351d of this title, submit for that fiscal year an annual
program for library services for older persons. Such program shall
be submitted at such time, in such form, and contain such information as the Commissioner may require by regulation and shall—

(1) set forth a program for the year submitted under which
funds paid to the State from appropriations pursuant to paragraph (4) of section 351b(a) of this title will be used, consistent with its long-range program for the purposes set forth in
section 362 of this title, and

(2) include an extension of the long-range program taking
into consideration the results of evaluations.

June 19, 1956, c. 407, Title IV, § 403, as added May 3, 1973, Pub.L.
93–29, Title VIII, § 801(a), 87 Stat. 58.

§ 364. Administrative coordination with programs for older Americans

In carrying out the program authorized by this subchapter, the
Commissioner shall consult with the Commissioner of the Administration on Aging and the Director of ACTION for the purpose of coordinating where practicable, the programs assisted under this subchapter with the programs assisted under the Older Americans Act
of 1965.

June 19, 1956, c. 407, Title IV, § 404, as added May 3, 1973, Pub.L.
93–29, Title VIII, § 801(a), 87 Stat. 58.

HIGHER EDUCATION ACT

(United States Code Annotated, 1982, Title 20, s.1021, 1022, 1029, 1031-1034, 1041, 1042.)

§ 1021. Authorizing provisions

Congressional declaration of purpose

(a) The Secretary shall carry out a program to assist—

(1) institutions of higher education in the acquisition of library resources, including law library resources, and in the establishment and maintenance of networks for sharing library resources in accordance with part A;

(2) in the training of persons in librarianship and to encourage research and development relating to the improvement of libraries (including the promotion of economical and efficient information delivery, cooperative efforts, and developmental projects) in accordance with part B;

(3) the Nation's major research libraries, in maintaining and strengthening their collections, and in making their holdings available to other libraries whose users have need for research materials, in accordance with part C; and

(4) the establishment of a National Periodical System Corporation, in accordance with part D.

Authorization of appropriations

(b)(1)(A) There are authorized to be appropriated to carry out part A $10,000,000 for the fiscal year 1981, $30,000,000 for the fiscal year 1982 and for each of the two succeeding fiscal years, and $35,000,000 for the fiscal year 1985.

(B) There are authorized to be appropriated to carry out part B $10,000,000 for the fiscal year 1981, $30,000,000 for the fiscal year 1982 and for each of the two succeeding fiscal years, and $35,000,000 for the fiscal year 1985.

(C) There are authorized to be appropriated to carry out part C $10,000,000 for the fiscal year 1981, $15,000,000 for the fiscal year 1982 and each of the three succeeding fiscal years.

(2) Notwithstanding paragraph (1), no funds are authorized to be appropriated for part D unless the appropriation for each of parts A, B, and C equals or exceeds the amount appropriated for each such part, respectively, for fiscal year 1979.

Sectarian instruction; religious worship; divinity schools or departments

(c) No grant may be made under this subchapter for books, periodicals, documents, or other related materials to be used for sectarian instruction or religious worship, or primarily in connection with any part of the program of a school or department of divinity.

Pub.L. 89–329, Title II, § 201, as added Pub.L. 96–374, Title II, § 201, Oct. 3, 1980, 94 Stat. 1383.

§ 1022. Notification of State agency

Each institution of higher education which receives a grant under this

subchapter shall annually inform the State agency designated pursuant
to section 1143 of this title of its activities under this subchapter.
Pub.L. 89–329, Title II, § 202, as added Pub.L. 96–374, Title II, § 201,
Oct. 3, 1980, 94 Stat. 1384.

§ 1029. Resource development grants

Grant authority; $10,000 maximum

(a) From the amount appropriated for this part, the Secretary shall
make grants to institutions of higher education or combinations thereof
(and to each branch of an institution which is located in a community
different from that in which its parent institution is located), and to
other public and private nonprofit library institutions whose primary function is to provide library and information services to institutions of higher education on a formal, cooperative basis. The amount of a resource
development grant under this section shall not exceed $10,000.

Application for grant

(b) A grant under this part may be made only if the application provides—
>   (1) information about the institution and its library resources
>   as prescribed by the Secretary in regulations;
>   (2) satisfactory assurance that the applicant will expend, for all
>   library material expenditures (exclusive of construction) during the
>   fiscal year for which the grant is sought, from funds other than funds
>   received under this part, an amount not less than the average an-
>   nual aggregate amount or the average amount per full-time equiva-
>   lent student it expended for such purposes during the two fiscal years
>   preceding the fiscal year for which assistance is sought under this
>   part;
>   (3) for such fiscal control and fund accounting procedures as are
>   necessary to assure proper disbursement of and accounting for Fed-
>   eral funds paid to the applicant under this part; and
>   (4) for making such reports as the Secretary may require and for
>   keeping such records and for affording such access thereto as the
>   Secretary deems necessary to assure the correctness and verification
>   of such reports.

Waiver of assurance requirement in very unusual circumstances

(c) If the Secretary determines, in accordance with regulations, that
there are very unusual circumstances which prevent the applicant from
making the assurance required by subsection (b)(2) of this section, the
requirement for such assurance may be waived. For purposes of this
subsection, the term "very unusual circumstances" means theft, vandalism,
fire, flood, earthquake, or other occurrence which may temporarily reduce the level of expenditures for library materials and total library purposes, or which resulted in unusually high expenditures for library materials and total library purposes.

Allowable uses for grant funds

(d) Grants under this part may be used only for books, periodicals,
documents, magnetic tapes, phonographic records, audiovisual materials,
and other related library materials (including necessary binding) and for
the establishment and maintenance networks for sharing library resources
with other institutions of higher education.
Pub.L. 89–329, Title II, § 211, as added Pub.L. 96–374, Title II, § 201,
Oct. 3, 1980, 94 Stat. 1384.

§ 1031. Grant authority

From the amount appropriated for this part, the Secretary shall make

grants in accordance with sections 1032, 1033, and 1034 of this title. Of such amount, one-third shall be available for the purposes of each such section.
Pub.L. 89–329, Title II, § 221, as added Pub.L. 96–374, Title II, § 201, Oct. 3, 1980, 94 Stat. 1385.

§ 1032. Library career training

Allowable uses of grant funds

(a) The Secretary shall make grants to, and contracts with, institutions of higher education and library organizations or agencies to assist them in training persons in librarianship. Such grants or contracts may be used by such institutions, library organizations, or agencies (1) to assist in covering the cost of courses of training or study (including short term or regular session institutes), (2) to establish and maintain fellowships or traineeships with stipends (including allowances for travel, subsistence, and other expenses) for fellows and others undergoing training and their dependents, not in excess of such maximum amounts as may be determined by the Secretary, and (3) to establish, develop, or expand programs of library and information science, including new techniques of information transfer and communication technology.

Fellowships and traineeships

(b) Not less than 50 per centum of the grants made under this section shall be for the purpose of establishing and maintaining fellowships or traineeships under subsection (a)(2) of this section.
Pub.L. 89–329, Title II, § 222, as added Pub.L. 96–374, Title II, § 201, Oct. 3, 1980, 94 Stat. 1385.

§ 1033. Research and demonstrations

The Secretary is authorized to make grants to, and contracts with, institutions of higher education and other public or private agencies, institutions, and organizations for research and demonstration projects related to the improvement of libraries, training in librarianship, and information technology, and for the dissemination of information derived from such projects.
Pub.L. 89–329, Title II, § 223, as added Pub.L. 96–374, Title II, § 201, Oct. 3, 1980, 94 Stat. 1385.

§ 1034. Special purpose grants

Grant authority; allowable uses of grant funds

(a) The Secretary is authorized to make special purpose grants to (1) institutions of higher education to meet special national or regional needs in the library or information sciences, (2) combinations of institutions of higher education which demonstrate a need for special assistance in establishing and strengthening joint-use library facilities, resources, or equipment, (3) other public and private nonprofit library institutions which provide library and information services to institutions of higher education on a formal, cooperative basis for the purpose of establishing, developing, or expanding programs or projects that improve their services, and (4) institutions of higher education which demonstrate a need for special assistance to develop or expand programs or projects that will service the communities in which the institutions are located.

Application for grant; requisite assurances

(b) A grant under this section may be made only if the application therefor (whether by an individual institution or a combination of institutions) is approved by the Secretary on the basis of criteria prescribed in regulations and provides satisfactory assurance that (1) the applicant will expend during the fiscal year for which the grant is sought (from funds other than funds received under this subchapter), for the same purpose as such grant, an amount from such other sources equal to not less than one-third of such grant, and (2) the applicant will expend during such fiscal year from such other sources for all library purposes (exclusive of construction) an amount not less than the average annual amount it expended for such purposes during the two fiscal years preceding the fiscal year for which the grant is sought under this section.

Pub.L. 89–329, Title II, § 224, as added Pub.L. 96–374, Title II, § 201, Oct. 3, 1980, 94 Stat. 1385.

§ 1041. Eligibility for assistance

Grant authority

(a)(1) From the amount appropriated for this part, the Secretary shall make grants to institutions with major research libraries.

(2) For the purposes of this part, the term "major research library" means a public or private nonprofit institution (including the library resources of an institution of higher education), an independent research library, or a State or other public library, having a library collection which is available to qualified users and which—

(A) makes a significant contribution to higher education and research;

(B) is broadly based and is recognized as having national or international significance for scholarly research;

(C) is of a unique nature, and contains material not widely available; and

(D) is in substantial demand by researchers and scholars not connected with that institution.

Grants as precluding resource development grants or special purpose grants

(b) No institution receiving a grant under this part for any fiscal year may receive a grant under section 1029 or 1034 of this title for that year.

Pub.L. 89–329, Title II, § 231, as added Pub.L. 96–374, Title II, § 201, Oct. 3, 1980, 94 Stat. 1386.

§ 1042. Geographical distribution of grants

In making grants under this part, the Secretary shall endeavor to achieve broad and equitable geographical distribution throughout the Nation.

Pub.L. 89–329, Title II, § 232, as added Pub.L. 96–374, Title II, § 201, Oct. 3, 1980, 94 Stat. 1386.

NATIONAL PERIODICAL SYSTEM

(United States Code Annotated, Title 20, s.1047-1047j.)

§ 1047. Congressional declaration of purpose

It is the purpose of this part to assess the feasibility and advisability of, and, if feasible and advisable, prepare a design for a national periodical system to serve as a national periodical resource by contributing to the preservation of periodical materials and by providing access to a comprehensive collection of periodical literature to public and private libraries throughout the United States.

Pub.L. 89–329, Title II, § 241, as added Pub.L. 96–374, Title II, § 201, Oct. 3, 1980, 94 Stat. 1386.

§ 1047a. Establishment of National Periodical System Corporation

There is established a nonprofit corporation, to be known as the National Periodical System Corporation, which shall not be considered an agency or establishment of the United States Government. The Corporation shall be subject to the provisions of this part, and to the extent consistent with this chapter, to the laws of the jurisdiction where incorporated.

Pub.L. 89–329, Title II, § 242, as added Pub.L. 96–374, Title II, § 201, Oct. 3, 1980, 94 Stat. 1387.

§ 1047b. Functions of National Periodical System Corporation

Feasibility, advisability, and design of document delivery system

(a) The Corporation shall assess the feasibility and advisability of a national system and, if feasible and advisable, design such a system to provide reliable and timely document delivery from a comprehensive collection of periodical literature. A design may be implemented by the Corporation only in accordance with the provisions of section 1047g of this title.

Requisite features of system

(b) Any design for a national periodical system shall include provisions for such system to—

(1) acquire current and past issues of periodicals, and to preserve and maintain a dedicated collection of such documents;

(2) provide information on periodicals to which the system can insure access, including those circulated from private sector sources, and coöperate in efforts to improve bibliographic and physical access to periodicals;

(3) make such periodicals available through libraries, by loan, photoreproduction or other means;

(4) coöperate with and participate in international borrowing and lending activities as may be appropriate for such purposes;

(5) ensure that copyright owners who do not wish to participate in such system are not required to participate;

(6) ensure that copyright fees are fixed by the copyright owners

for any reproduction or dissemination of a document delivered through the system;

(7) complement and not duplicate activities in the private sector to provide access to periodical literature;

(8) ensure, to the maximum extent feasible, that such system not adversely affect the publication and distribution of current periodicals, particularly scholarly periodicals of small circulation; and

(9) ensure coordination with existing programs to distribute periodical literature, including programs of regional libraries and programs of interlibrary loan and library networks.

Role of Corporation in system

(c) Any design shall include provisions for the role, if any, of the Corporation in the governance, administration, and operation of the system.

Cost estimate for each fiscal year

(d) Any design shall be accompanied by an estimate of the cost for each fiscal year of carrying out the system proposed in the design.

Pub.L. 89–329, Title II, § 243, as added Pub.L. 96–374, Title II, § 201, Oct. 3, 1980, 94 Stat. 1387.

§ 1047c. Board of Directors of National Periodical System Corporation

Membership

(a) The Corporation shall have a Board of Directors, consisting of fifteen members, including fourteen members appointed by the President, by and with the advice and consent of the Senate, and the Director of the Corporation.

Appointment

(b) The members of the Board appointed by the President shall be equitably representative of the needs and interests of the Government, academic and research communities, libraries, publishers, the information community, authors, and the public. Except for the initial Board of Directors, the members shall be appointed after consultation with the Board.

Directors as incorporators of Corporation

(c) The members of the initial Board of Directors shall serve as incorporators and shall take whatever actions are necessary to establish the Corporation under the laws of the jurisdiction in which it is incorporated.

Term of office

(d) The term of office for each member of the Board (other than the Director) shall be two years except that any member appointed to fill a vacancy occurring prior to the expiration of the term for which his predecessor was appointed shall be appointed for the remainder of such term. Notwithstanding the preceding provisions of this paragraph, a member whose term has expired may serve until his successor has taken office.

Compensation

(e)(1) The members of the Board shall not, by reason of membership, be deemed employees of the United States. Except as provided in paragraph (2), members shall, while engaged in activities of the Board, be entitled to receive compensation at the rate equal to the daily rate prescribed for grade GS–18 of the General Schedule under section 5332 of Title 5 for each day and, while away from their homes or regular place of business, may be allowed travel expenses.

(2) Members of the Corporation who are full-time officers and employees of the United States shall receive no additional pay, allowances, or benefits by reason of their service on the Corporation.

Quorum

(f) Eight members of the Board shall constitute a quorum.

Chairman

(g) The Board shall elect annually one of its members to serve as the Chairman.

Meetings

(h) The Board shall meet annually or at the call of the Chairman or a majority of its members.

Pub.L. 89–329, Title II, § 244, as added Pub.L. 96–374, Title II, § 201, Oct. 3, 1980, 94 Stat. 1387.

§ 1047d. Director and staff of National Periodical System Corporation

Appointment and function of Director

(a) The Corporation shall have a Director, and such other officers as appointed by the Board for the terms and at rates of compensation fixed by the Board. The Director shall manage the operations of the Corporation, subject to such rules as may be prescribed by the Board.

Appointment and pay of personnel

(b) Subject to such rules as may be prescribed by the Board, the Director may appoint and fix the pay of personnel and may procure temporary and intermittent services.

Pub.L. 89–329, Title II, § 245, as added Pub.L. 96–374, Title II, § 201, Oct. 3, 1980, 94 Stat. 1388.

§ 1047e. Nonprofit nature of National Periodical System Corporation

Stock; dividends

(a) The Corporation shall have no power to issue any shares of stock, or to declare or pay any dividends.

Corporation income and assets

(b) No part of the incomes or assets of the Corporation shall inure to the benefit of any director, officer, employee, or any other individual except as salary or reasonable compensation for services.

Tax exempt status

(c) The National Periodical System Corporation shall be exempt from taxation now or hereafter imposed by the United States, or any territory or possession thereof, or by any State, county, municipality, or local taxing authority.

Pub.L. 89–329, Title II, § 246, as added Pub.L. 96–374, Title II, § 201, Oct. 3, 1980, 94 Stat. 1388.

§ 1047f. Authority of National Periodical System Corporation

Authorized corporate functions

(a) The Corporation is authorized to—

(1) obtain grants from and to make contracts with individuals and with private, State, and Federal agencies, organizations, and institutions;

(2) conduct its business, carry on its operations, and have officers and exercise the power granted by this section in any State without regard to any qualification or similar statute in any State;

(3) lease, purchase, or otherwise acquire, own, hold, improve, use or otherwise deal in and with any property (real, personal, or mixed), or any interest therein, wherever situated;

(4) sell, convey, mortgage, pledge, lease, exchange, and otherwise dispose of its property and assets; and

(5) enter into contracts, execute instruments, incur liabilities, and do all things as are necessary or incidental to the proper management of its affairs and the proper conduct of its business.

Usual corporate powers

(b) To carry out its functions and to engage in the activities described in subsection (a) of this section, the Corporation shall have the usual powers conferred upon a nonprofit corporation by the jurisdiction in which the Corporation is incorporated.

Use of United States mails; administrative support services

(c) The Corporation may use the United States mails in the same manner and under the same conditions as departments and agencies of the United States. The Administrator of General Services shall provide to the Corporation on a reimbursable basis such administrative support services as the Corporation may request.

Gifts, bequests, and devises of property

(d) The Corporation is authorized to accept, hold, administer, and use gifts, bequests, and devises of property, both real and personal, for the purpose of aiding or facilitating the authority of the Corporation pursuant to section 1047b of this title. For the purpose of Federal income, estate, and gift taxes, property accepted by the National Periodical System Corporation shall be a gift, bequest, or devise to the United States.

Open meetings

(e) The Corporation shall be subject to the provisions of section 552b of Title 5.
Pub.L. 89–329, Title II, § 247, as added Pub.L. 96–374, Title II, § 201, Oct. 3, 1980, 94 Stat. 1388.

§ 1047g. Implementation of System design; Congressional joint resolution of approval

Any design established under this part shall be submitted to the Congress not later than December 31, 1981, and may not be implemented until the design is approved in whole or in part by enactment of a joint resolution of the Congress approving such design.
Pub.L. 89–329, Title II, § 248, as added Pub.L. 96–374, Title II, § 201, Oct. 3, 1980, 94 Stat. 1389.

§ 1047h. Copyrights

Nothing in this part shall be considered to amend, affect, or redefine the provisions of Title 17, relating to copyrights.
Pub.L. 89–329, Title II, § 249, as added Pub.L. 96–374, Title II, § 201, Oct. 3, 1980, 94 Stat. 1389.

§ 1047i. Definitions

As used in this part—

(1) the term "access" means the ability to identify, locate, and

obtain a specific item (generally a periodical article), and includes both bibliographic access (the ability to identify a specific item from its description) and physical access to materials (the ability to obtain the text of an item in an appropriate form, such as visual, audio, or printed formats);

(2) the term "Board" means the Board of Directors of the National Periodical System Corporation;

(3) the term "comprehensive collection" means a collection of periodical titles which will provide access to approximately 90 per centum of the requests received, except that such titles need not all be physically located in the same place;

(4) the term "copyright owner" means the owner of any one of the exclusive rights comprised in a copyright;

(5) the term "Corporation" means the National Periodical System Corporation established under this part;

(6) the term "dedicated collection" means a collection of periodicals maintained for the sole purpose of assuring the provision of permanent physical access;

(7) the term "document" means any portion or the entire issue of a periodical;

(8) the term "periodical" means a publication consisting of issues in a continuous series under the same title published at regular or irregular intervals, over an indefinite period, individual issues in the series being numbered consecutively or each issue being dated; and

(9) the term "private sector" means nongovernmental, nonprofit, and for-profit organizations.

Pub.L. 89–329, Title II, § 250, as added Pub.L. 96–374, Title II, § 201, Oct. 3, 1980, 94 Stat. 1389.

§ 1047j. Authorization of appropriations

(a) There are authorized to be appropriated, for the purpose of carrying out this part, $750,000 for each of fiscal years 1981 and 1982, and such sums as may be necessary for each of the fiscal years 1983, 1984, and 1985.

(b) In any fiscal year after the joint resolution described in section 1047g of this title is enacted, there are authorized to be appropriated such additional sums as may be necessary to implement an approved design for any such fiscal year ending prior to October 1, 1985.

Pub.L 89–329, Title II, § 251, as added Pub.L. 96–374, Title II, § 201, Oct. 3, 1980, 94 Stat. 1390.

MEDICAL LIBRARY
ASSISTANCE ACT

(United States Code Annotated, 1982, Title 42, s.280b to 280b-2,
280b-4, 280b-5, 280b-7 to 280b-11.)

§ 280b. Congressional findings and declaration of policy

Finding of lack of growth in facilities for dissemination of knowledge

(a) The Congress hereby finds and declares that (1) the unprecedented expansion of knowledge in the health sciences within the past two decades has brought about a massive growth in the quantity, and major changes in the nature of, biomedical information, materials, and publications; (2) there has not been a corresponding growth in the facilities and techniques necessary adequately to coordinate and disseminate among health scientists and practitioners the ever-increasing volume of knowledge and information which has been developed in the health science field; (3) much of the value of the ever-increasing volume of knowledge and information which has been, and continues to be, developed in the health science field will be lost unless proper measures are taken in the immediate future to develop facilities and techniques necessary to collect, preserve, store, process, retrieve, and facilitate the dissemination and utilization of, such knowledge and information.

Statement of policy to assist in distribution and utilization of information

(b) It is therefore the policy of this part to—

(1) assist in the training of medical librarians and other information specialists in the health sciences;

(2) assist, through grants to physicians and other practitioners in the sciences related to health, to scientists, and to public or nonprofit private institutions on behalf of such physicians, other practitioners, and scientists, in the compilation of existing, and the creation of additional, written matter which will facilitate the distribution and utilization of knowledge and information relating to scientific, social, and cultural advancements in sciences related to health;

(3) assist in the conduct of research, investigations, and demonstrations in the field of medical library science and related activities, and in the development of new techniques, systems, and equipment for processing, storing, retrieving, and distributing information in the sciences related to health;

(4) assist in establishing, expanding, and improving the basic re-

sources of medical libraries and related facilities;

(5) assist in the development of a national system of regional medical libraries each of which would have facilities of sufficient depth and scope to supplement the services of other medical libraries within the region served by it; and

(6) provide financial support to biomedical scientific publications.

Authorization of appropriations

(c) For the purpose of grants and contracts under sections 280b–3, 280b–4, 280b–5, 280b–7, and 280b–8 of this title, there are authorized to be appropriated $17,500,000 for the fiscal year ending June 30, 1975, $20,000,000 for the fiscal year ending June 30, 1976, $14,600,000 for the fiscal year ending September 30, 1978, $15,000,000 for the fiscal year ending September 30, 1979, $16,500,000 for the fiscal year ending September 30, 1980, $18,500,000 for the fiscal year ending September 30, 1981, and $7,500,000 for the fiscal year ending September 30, 1982.

(July 1, 1944, c. 373, Title III, § 390, as added Oct. 22, 1965, Pub.L. 89–291, § 2, 79 Stat. 1059, and amended Mar. 13, 1970, Pub.L. 91–212, §§ 4(b), 5(b), 6(b), 84 Stat. 64, 65; July 23, 1974, Pub.L. 93–353, Title II, §§ 201(a), 202(a), 88 Stat. 371, 372; Aug. 1, 1977, Pub.L. 95–83, Title II, § 202, 91 Stat. 386; Nov. 9, 1978, Pub.L. 95–622, Title II, § 211, 92 Stat. 3420; Aug. 13, 1981, Pub.L. 97–35, Title IX, § 925 (a), 95 Stat. 569.)

§ 280b–1. Definitions

As used in this part—

(1) the term "sciences related to health" includes medicine, osteopathy, dentistry, and public health, and fundamental and applied sciences when related thereto;

(2) the terms "National Medical Libraries Assistance Advisory Board" and "Board" mean the Board of Regents of the National Library of Medicine established under section 277(a) of this title; and

(3) the term "medical library" means a library related to the sciences related to health.

(July 1, 1944, c. 373, Title III, § 391, as added Oct. 22, 1965, Pub.L. 89–291, § 2, 79 Stat. 1059, and amended Mar. 13, 1970, Pub.L. 91–212, § 10(b)(3), 84 Stat. 66; July 23, 1974, Pub.L. 93–353, Title II, § 202(b), 88 Stat. 372.

§ 280b–2. National Medical Libraries Assistance Advisory Board

Composition

(a) The Board of Regents of the National Library of Medicine established pursuant to section 277(a) of this title shall, in addition to its functions prescribed under section 277 of this title, constitute and serve as the National Medical Libraries Assistance Advisory Board (hereinafter in this part referred to as the "Board").

Functions

(b) The Board shall advise and assist the Secretary in the preparation of general regulations and with respect to policy matters arising in the administration of this part.

Authorization to use services of members for periods in addition to conference periods

(c) The Secretary is authorized to use the services of any member or members of the Board, in connection with matters related to the administration of this part, for such periods, in addition to conference periods, as he may determine.

Compensation; travel expenses

(d) Appointed members of the Board who are not otherwise in the employ of the United States, while attending conferences of the Board or otherwise serving at the request of the Secretary in connection with the administration of this part, shall be entitled to receive compensation, per diem in lieu of subsistence, and travel expenses in the same manner and under the same conditions as that prescribed under section 277(d) of this title, when attending conferences, traveling, or serving at the request of the Secretary in connection with the administration of Part I of this subchapter.

(July 1, 1944, c. 373, Title III, § 392, as added Oct. 22, 1965, Pub.L. 89–291, § 2, 79 Stat. 1060, and amended Mar. 13, 1970, Pub.L. 91–212, § 10(b)(4), (d)(2)(A), 84 Stat. 66, 67; July 23, 1974, Pub.L. 93–353, Title II, § 202(c), 88 Stat. 372.

§ 280b–4.   Grants for training in medical library sciences

(a) To carry out the purposes of section 280b(b)(1) of this title, the Secretary shall make grants—

(1) to individuals to enable them to accept traineeships and fellowships leading to postbaccalaureate academic degrees in the field of medical library science, in related fields pertaining to sciences related to health, or in the field of the communication of information;

(2) to individuals who are librarians or specialists in information on sciences relating to health, to enable them to undergo intensive training or retraining so as to attain greater competence in their occupations (including competence in the fields of automatic data processing and retrieval);

(3) to assist appropriate public and private nonprofit institutions in developing, expanding, and improving, training programs in library science and the field of communications of information pertaining to sciences relating to health; and

(4) to assist in the establishment of internship programs in established medical libraries meeting standards which the Secretary shall prescribe.

(b) Payment pursuant to grants made under this section may be made in advance or by way of reimbursement and in such installments as the Secretary shall prescribe by regulations after consultation with the Board.

(July 1, 1944, c. 373, Title III, § 393, formerly § 394, as added Oct. 22, 1965, Pub. L. 89–291, § 2, 79 Stat. 1062, amended Mar. 13, 1970, Pub.L. 91–212, §§ 2(b), 10 (d)(2)(A), 84 Stat. 63, 67; June 18, 1973, Pub.L. 93–45, Title I, § 107(a), 87 Stat. 92, and renumbered and amended July 23, 1974, Pub.L. 93–353, Title II, §§ 203(a), 204, 88 Stat. 372, 373.

§ 280b–5. Assistance for special scientific projects, and research and development in medical library science and related fields

Grants for compilation or writing of contributions relating to advancements in sciences related to health

(a) To carry out the purposes of section 280b(b)(2) of this title, the Secretary shall make grants to physicians and other practitioners in the sciences related to health, to scientists, and to public or nonprofit private institutions on behalf of such physicians, other practitioners, and scientists for the compilation of existing, or writing of original, contributions relating to scientific, social, or cultural, advancements in sciences related to health. In making such grants, the Secretary shall make appropriate arrangements whereby the facilities of the National Library of Medicine and the facilities of libraries of public and private nonprofit institutions of higher learning may be made available in connection with the projects for which such grants are made.

Grants for special projects in medical library science and related fields

(b) To carry out the purposes of section 280b(b)(3) of this title, the Secretary shall make grants to appropriate public or private nonprofit institutions and enter into contracts with appropriate persons, for purposes of carrying out projects of research, investigations, and demonstrations in the field of medical library science and related activities and for the development of new techniques, systems and equipment for processing, storing, retrieving, and distributing information pertaining to sciences related to health.

Manner of payment; regulations

(c) Payment pursuant to grants made under this section may be in advance or by way of reimbursement and in such installments as the Secretary shall prescribe by regulations after consultation with the Board.

(July 1, 1944, c. 373, Title III, § 394, formerly § 395, as added Oct. 22, 1965, Pub. L. 89–291, § 2, 79 Stat. 1062, amended Mar. 13, 1970, Pub.L. 91–212, §§ 2(c), (d), 4(a), 5(a), 10(c)(1)(A), (B), (2)(A)–(C), (d)(2)(A), 84 Stat. 63, 64, 66, 67; June 18, 1973, Pub.L. 93–45, Title I, § 107(b), (c), 87 Stat. 92, and renumbered and amended July 23, 1974, Pub.L. 93–353, Title II, §§ 203(b), 204, 88 Stat. 372, 373.)

§ 280b–7. Grants for establishing, expanding, and improving basic medical library or related resources

Uses for which grants may be employed

(a) To carry out the purposes of section 280b(b)(4) of this title, the Secretary shall make grants of money, materials, or both, to public or private nonprofit medical libraries and related scientific communication instrumentalties for the purpose of establishing, expanding, and improving their basic medical library or related resources. The uses for which grants so made may be employed include, but are not limited to, the following: (1) acquisition of books, journals, photographs, motion picture and other films, and other similar materials, (2) cataloging, binding, and other services and procedures for processing library resource materials for use by those who are served by the library or related instrumentality, and (3) acquisition of duplication devices, facsimile equipment, film projectors, recording equipment, and other equipment to facilitate the use of the resources of the library or related instrumentality by those who are served by it, and (4) introduction of new technologies in medical librarianship.

Computation of amount of grant; factors considered in determining scope of services provided by library; maximum amount of grant

(b)(1) The amount of any grant under this section to any medical library or related instrumentality shall be determined by the Secretary on the basis of the scope of library or related services provided by such library or instrumentality in relation to the population and purposes served by it. In making a determination of the scope of services served by any medical library or related instrumentality, the Secretary shall take into account the following factors—

(A) the number of graduate and undergraduate students making use of the resources of such library or instrumentality;

(B) the number of physicians and other practitioners in the sciences related to health utilizing the resources of such library or instrumentality;

(C) the type of supportive staffs, if any, available to such library or instrumentality;

(D) the type, size, and qualifications of the faculty of any school with which such library or instrumentality is affiliated;

(E) the staff of any hospital or hospitals or of any clinic or clinics with which such library or instrumentality is affiliated; and

(F) the geographic area served by such library or instrumentality and the availability, within such area, of medical library or related services provided by other libraries or related instrumentalities.

(2) In no case shall any grant under this section to a medical library or related instrumentality for any fiscal year exceed $200,000; and grants to such medical libraries or related instrumentalities shall be in such amounts as the Secretary may by regulation prescribe with a view to assuring adequate continuing financial support for such libraries or instrumentalities from other sources during and after the period for which Federal assistance is provided.

(July 1, 1944, c. 373, Title III, § 395, formerly § 397, as added Oct. 22, 1965, Pub. L. 89–291, § 2, 79 Stat. 1063, renumbered § 396 and amended Mar. 13, 1970, Pub. L. 91–212, §§ 2(e), 6(a)(1), (2), 10(c)(3), (d)(2)(A), 84 Stat. 63, 64, 67; June 18, 1973, Pub.L. 93–45, Title I, § 107(d), 87 Stat. 92, and renumbered § 395 and amended July 23, 1974, Pub.L. 93–353, Title II, §§ 203(c), 204, 88 Stat. 372, 373.)

§ 280b–8. Grants for establishment of regional medical libraries

Grants to public or private nonprofit medical libraries

(a) To carry out the purposes of section 280b(b)(5) of this title, the Secretary, with the advice of the Board, shall make grants to existing public or private nonprofit medical libraries so as to enable each of them to serve as the regional medical library for the geographical area in which it is located.

Uses for which grants may be employed

(b) The uses for which grants made under this section may be employed include, but are not limited to, the following—

(1) acquisition of books, journals, and other similar materials;

(2) cataloging, binding, and other procedures for processing library resource materials for use by those who are served by the library;

(3) acquisition of duplicating devices and other equipment to facilitate the use of the resources of the library by those who are served by it;

(4) acquisition of mechanisms and employment of personnel for the speedy transmission of materials for the regional library to local libraries in the geographic area served by the regional library; and

(5) planning for services and activities under this section.

Conditions prerequisite; priorities

(c)(1) Grants under this section shall be made only to medical libraries which agree (A) to modify and increase their library resources, and to supplement the resources of cooperating libraries in the region, so as to be able to provide adequate supportive services to all libraries in the region as well as to individual users of library services, (B) to provide free loan services to qualified users, and make available photoduplicated or facsimile copies of biomedical materials which qualified requesters may retain.

(2) The Secretary, in awarding grants under this section, shall give priority to medical libraries having the greatest potential of fulfilling the needs for regional medical libraries. In determining the priority to be assigned to any medical library, he shall consider—

(A) the adequacy of the library (in terms of collections, personnel, equipment, and other facilities) as a basis for a regional medical library; and

(B) the size and nature of the population to be served in the region in which the library is located.

Maximum amount of grants

(d) Grants under this section for basic resource materials to a library may not exceed 50 per centum of the library's annual operating expense (exclusive of Federal financial assistance under this part) for the preceding year; or in case of the first year in which the library receives a grant under this section for basic resource materials, 50 per centum of its average annual operating expenses over the past three years (or if it had been in operation for less than three years, its annual operating expenses determined by the Secretary in accordance with regulations prescribed by him).

Payments

(e) Payment pursuant to grants made under this section may be made in advance or by way of reimbursement and in such installments as the Secretary shall prescribe by regulations after consultation with the Board.

Authority to contract; limitations

(f) The Secretary may also carry out the purposes of this section through contracts, and such contracts shall be subject to the same limitations as are provided in this section for grants.

(July 1, 1944, c. 373, Title III, § 396, formerly § 398, as added Oct. 22, 1965, Pub. L. 89–291, § 2, 79 Stat. 1065, renumbered § 397 and amended Mar. 13, 1970, Pub. L. 91–212, §§ 2(f), 7, 10(c)(3), (d)(2)(A), 84 Stat. 63, 65, 67; June 18, 1973, Pub.L. 93–45, Title I, § 107(e), 87 Stat. 92, and renumbered § 396 and amended July 23, 1974, Pub.L. 93–353, Title II, §§ 202(e), (f), 203(d)(1), 204, 88 Stat. 372, 373.)

§ 280b–9. Grants to provide support for biomedical scientific publications

Purpose of grants

(a) To carry out the purposes of section 280b(b)(6) of this title, the Secretary, with the advice of the Board, shall make grants to, and enter into appropriate contracts with, public or private nonprofit institutions of higher education and individual scientists for the purpose of supporting biomedical scientific publications of a nonprofit nature and to procure the compilation, writing, editing, and publication of reviews, abstracts, indices, handbooks, bibliographies, and related matter pertaining to scientific works and scientific developments.

Duration

(b) Grants under this section in support of any single periodical publication may not be made for more than three years, except in those cases in which the Secretary determines that further support is necessary to carry out the purposes of this section.

Payments

(c) Payment pursuant to grants made under this section may be made in advance or by way of reimbursement and in such installments as the Secretary shall prescribe by regulations after consultation with the Board.

(July 1, 1944, c. 373, Title III, § 397, formerly § 399, as added Oct. 22, 1965, Pub. L. 89–291, § 2, 79 Stat. 1066, renumbered § 398 and amended Mar. 13, 1970, Pub. L. 91–212, §§ 2(g), 8, 10(c)(3), (d)(2)(A), 84 Stat. 63, 65, 67; June 18, 1973, Pub.L. 93–45, Title I, § 107(f), 87 Stat. 92, and renumbered § 397 and amended July 23, 1974, Pub.L. 93–353, Title II, §§ 203(e), 204, 88 Stat. 372, 373.)

§ 280b–10. Continuing availability of appropriated funds

Funds appropriated to carry out any of the purposes of this part for any fiscal year shall remain available for such purposes for the fiscal year immediately following the fiscal year for which they were appropriated.

(July 1, 1944, c. 373, Title III, § 398, formerly § 399a, as added Oct. 22, 1965, Pub. L. 89–291, § 2, 79 Stat. 1066, renumbered § 399, Mar. 13, 1970, Pub.L. 91–212, § 10(c)(3), 84 Stat. 67, and renumbered § 398, July 23, 1974, Pub.L. 93–353, Title II, § 204, 88 Stat. 373.)

§ 280b–11. Records and audit

(a) Each recipient of a grant under this part shall keep such records as the Secretary shall prescribe, including records which fully disclose the amount and disposition by such recipient of the proceeds of such grant, the total cost of the project or undertaking in connection with which such grant is given or used, and the amount of that portion of the cost of the project or undertaking supplied by other sources, and such other records as will facilitate an effective audit.

(b) The Secretary of Health and Human Services and the Comptroller General of the United States, or any of their duly authorized representatives, shall have access for the purpose of audit and examination to any books, documents, papers, and records of such recipients that are pertinent to any grant received under the provisions of this part.

(July 1, 1944, c. 373, Title III, § 399, formerly § 399b, as added Oct. 22, 1965, Pub. L. 89–291, § 2, 79 Stat. 1066, renumbered § 399a and amended Mar. 13, 1970, Pub. L. 91–212, § 10(c)(3), (d)(2)(A), 84 Stat. 67, renumbered § 399, July 23, 1974, Pub. L. 93–353, Title II, § 204, 88 Stat. 373, and amended Oct. 17, 1979, Pub.L. 96–88, Title V, § 509(b), 93 Stat. 695.)

NATIONAL COMMISSION ON LIBRARIES
AND INFORMATION SCIENCE

(United States Code Annotated, 1982, Title 20, s.1501-1506.)

§ 1501. Congressional statement of policy

The Congress hereby affirms that library and information services adequate to meet the needs of the people of the United States are essential to achieve national goals and to utilize most effectively the Nation's educational resources and that the Federal Government will cooperate with State and local governments and public and private agencies in assuring optimum provision of such services.

Pub.L. 91–345, § 2, July 20, 1970, 84 Stat. 440.

§ 1502. Establishment; administrative services

(a) There is hereby established as an independent agency within the executive branch, a National Commission on Libraries and Information Science (hereinafter referred to as the "Commission").

(b) The Department of Health, Education, and Welfare shall provide the Commission with necessary administrative services (including those related to budgeting, accounting, financial reporting, personnel, and procurement) for which payment shall be made in advance, or by reimbursement, from funds of the Commission and such amounts as may be agreed upon by the Commission and the Secretary of Health, Education, and Welfare.

Pub.L. 91–345, § 3, July 20, 1970, 84 Stat. 440.

§ 1503. Contributions

The Commission shall have authority to accept in the name of the United States grants, gifts, or bequests of money for immediate disbursement in furtherance of the functions of the Commission. Such grants, gifts, or bequests, after acceptance by the Commission, shall be paid by the donor or his representative to the Treasurer of the United States whose receipts shall be their acquittance. The Treasurer of the United States shall enter them in a special account to the credit of the Commission for the purposes in each case specified.

Pub.L. 91–345, § 4, July 20, 1970, 84 Stat. 441.

§ 1504.   Functions and powers

Advice to President and Congress; studies and surveys; plans; annual report

(a) The Commission shall have the primary responsibility for developing or recommending overall plans for, and advising the appropriate governments and agencies on, the policy set forth in section 1501 of this title. In carrying out that responsibility, the Commission shall—

(1) advise the President and the Congress on the implementation of national policy by such statements, presentations, and reports as it deems appropriate;

(2) conduct studies, surveys, and analyses of the library and informational needs of the Nation, including the special library and informational needs of rural areas, of economically, socially, or culturally deprived persons, and of elderly persons, and the means by which these needs may be met through information centers, through the libraries of elementary and secondary schools and institutions of higher education, and through public, research, special, and other types of libraries;

(3) appraise the adequacies and deficiencies of current library and information resources and services and evaluate the effectiveness of current library and information science programs;

(4) develop overall plans for meeting national library and informational needs and for the coordination of activities at the Federal, State, and local levels, taking into consideration all of the library and informational resources of the Nation to meet those needs;

(5) be authorized to advise Federal, State, local, and private agencies regarding library and information sciences;

(6) promote research and development activities which will extend and improve the Nation's library and information-handling capability as essential links in the national communications networks;

(7) submit to the President and the Congress (not later than January 31 of each year) a report on its activities during the preceding fiscal year; and

(8) make and publish such additional reports as it deems to be necessary, including, but not limited to, reports of consultants, transcripts of testimony, summary reports, and reports of other Commission findings, studies, and recommendations.

Contract authority

(b) The Commission is authorized to contract with Federal agencies and other public and private agencies to carry out any of its functions under subsection (a) of this section and to publish and disseminate such reports, findings, studies, and records as it deems appropriate.

Hearings

(c) The Commission is further authorized to conduct such hearings at such times and places as it deems appropriate for carrying out the purposes of this chapter.

Cooperation with other agencies

(d) The heads of all Federal agencies are, to the extent not prohibited by law, directed to cooperate with the Commission in carrying out the purposes of this chapter.

Pub.L. 91–345, § 5, July 20, 1970, 84 Stat. 441; Pub.L. 93–29, Title VIII, § 802(a), May 3, 1973, 87 Stat. 59.

§ 1505. Membership

Appointment; terms of office; Chairman; vacancies

(a) The Commission shall be composed of the Librarian of Congress and fourteen members appointed by the President, by and with the advice and consent of the Senate. Five members of the Commission shall be professional librarians or information specialists, and the remainder shall be persons having special competence or interest in the needs of our society for library and information services, at least one of whom shall be knowledgeable with respect to the technological aspects of library and information services and sciences, and at least one other of whom shall be knowledgeable with respect to the library and information service and science needs of the elderly. One of the members of the Commission shall be designated by the President as Chairman of the Commission. The terms of office of the appointive members of the Commission shall be five years, except that (1) the terms of office of the members first appointed shall commence on July 20, 1970, and shall expire two at the end of one year, three at the end of two years, three at the end of three years, three at the end of four years, and three at the end of five years, as designated by the President at the time of appointment, and (2) a member appointed to fill a vacancy occurring prior to the expiration of the term for which his predecessor was appointed shall be appointed only for the remainder of such term.

Compensation; travel expenses

(b) Members of the Commission who are not in the regular full-time employ of the United States shall, while attending meetings or conferences of the Commission or otherwise engaged in the business of the Commission, be entitled to receive compensation at a rate fixed by the Chairman, but not exceeding the rate specified at the time of such service for grade GS–18 in section 5332 of Title 5, including traveltime, and while so serving on the business of the Commission away from their homes or regular places of business, they may be allowed travel expenses, including per diem in lieu of subsistence, as authorized by section 5703 of Title 5 for persons employed intermittently in the Government service.

Professional and technical personnel

(c)(1) The Commission is authorized to appoint, without regard to the provisions of Title 5 covering appointments in the competitive service, such professional and technical personnel as may be necessary to enable it to carry out its function under this chapter.

(2) The Commission may procure, without regard to the civil service or classification laws, temporary and intermittent services of such personnel as is necessary to the extent authorized by section 3109 of Title 5, but at rates not to exceed the rate specified at the time of such service for grade GS–18 in section 5332 of Title 5, including traveltime, and while so serving on the business of the Commission away from their homes or regular places of business they may be allowed travel expenses, including per diem in lieu of subsistence, as authorized by section 5703 of Title 5 for persons employed intermittently in the Government service.

Pub.L. 91–345, § 6, July 20, 1970, 84 Stat. 442; Pub.L. 93–29, Title VIII, § 802(b), May 3, 1973, 87 Stat. 59.

§ 1506. Authorization of appropriations

There are hereby authorized to be appropriated $500,000 for the fiscal year ending June 30, 1970, and $750,000 for the fiscal year ending June 30, 1971, and for each succeeding year, for the purpose of carrying out the provisions of this chapter.

Pub.L. 91–345, § 7, July 20, 1970, 84 Stat. 442.

DEPOSIT AND DISTRIBUTION
OF PUBLIC DOCUMENTS

GENERAL PROVISIONS
(United States Code Annotated, 1982, Title 44, s.1702, 1705,
1707, 1708, 1710, 1711, 1720, 730.)

§ 1702. Superintendent of Documents; sale of documents

The Public Printer shall appoint a competent person to act as Superintendent of Documents who shall be under the control of the Public Printer.

When an officer of the Government having in his charge documents published for sale desires to be relieved of them, he may turn them over to the Superintendent of Documents, who shall receive and sell them under this section. Moneys received from the sale of documents shall be returned to the Public Printer on the first day of each month and be covered into the Treasury monthly.

The Superintendent of Documents shall also report monthly to the Public Printer the number of documents received by him and the disposition made of them. He shall have general supervision of the distribution of all public documents, and to his custody shall be committed all documents subject to distribution, excepting those printed for the special official use of the executive departments, which shall be delivered to the departments, and those printed for the use of the two Houses of Congress, which shall be delivered to the Senate Service Department and House of Representatives Publications Distribution Service and distributed or delivered ready for distribution to Members upon their order by the superintendents of the Senate Service Department and House Publications Distribution Service, respectively.

Pub.L. 90–620, Oct. 22, 1968, 82 Stat. 1279.

§ 1705. Printing additional copies for sale to public; regulations

The Public Printer shall print additional copies of a Government publication, not confidential in character, required for sale to the public by the Superintendent of Documents, subject to regulation by the Joint Committee on Printing and without interference with the prompt execution of printing for the Government.

Pub.L. 90–620, Oct. 22, 1968, 82 Stat. 1279.

§ 1707. Reprinting of documents required for sale

The Superintendent of Documents may order reprinted, from time to time, public documents required for sale, subject to the approval of the Secretary or head of the department in which the public document originated. The appropriation for printing and binding shall be reimbursed for the cost of reprints from the moneys received by the Superintendent of Documents from the sale of public documents.

Pub.L. 90–620, Oct. 22, 1968, 82 Stat. 1280.

§ 1708. Prices for sales copies of publications; crediting of receipts; resale by dealers; sales agents

The price at which additional copies of Government publications are offered for sale to the public by the Superintendent of Documents shall be based on the cost as determined by the Public Printer plus 50 percent. A discount of not to exceed 25 percent may be allowed to book dealers and quantity purchasers, but the printing may not interfere with prompt execution of work for the Government. Receipts from general sales of publications in excess of the total costs and expenses incurred in connection with the publication and sale thereof, as determined by the Public Printer, shall be deposited in the Treasury of the United States to the credit of miscellaneous receipts.

As amended Pub.L. 95–94, Title IV, § 409(a), Aug. 5, 1977, 91 Stat. 683.

The Superintendent of Documents may prescribe terms and conditions under which he authorizes the resale of Government publications by book dealers, and he may designate any Government officer his agent for the sale of Government publications under regulations agreed upon by the Superintendent of Documents and the head of the respective department or establishment of the Government.

Pub.L. 90–620, Oct. 22, 1968, 82 Stat. 1280.

§ 1710.   Index of documents: number and distribution

The Superintendent of Documents, at the close of each regular session of Congress, shall prepare and publish a comprehensive index of public documents, upon a plan approved by the Joint Committee on Printing. The Public Printer shall, immediately upon its publication, deliver to him a copy of every document printed by the Government Printing Office. The head of each executive department, independent agency and establishment of the Government shall deliver to him a copy of every document issued or published by the department, bureau, or office not confidential in character. He shall also prepare and print in one volume a consolidated index of Congressional documents, and shall index single volumes of documents as the Joint Committee on Printing directs. Two thousand copies each of the comprehensive index and of the consolidated index shall be printed and bound in addition to the usual number, two hundred for the Senate, eight hundred for the House of Representatives and one thousand for distribution by the Superintendent of Documents.

Pub.L. 90–620, Oct. 22, 1968, 82 Stat. 1280.

§ 1711.   Catalog of Government publications

On the first day of each month the Superintendent of Documents shall prepare a catalog of Government publications which shall show the documents printed during the preceding month, where obtainable, and the price. Two thousand copies of the catalog shall be printed in pamphlet form for distribution.

Pub.L. 90–620, Oct. 22, 1968, 82 Stat. 1280.

§ 1720.   Documents not needed by departments to be turned over to Superintendent of Documents

Public documents accumulating in the several executive departments, bureaus, and offices, not needed for official use, shall be turned over to the Superintendent of Documents annually for distribution or sale.

Pub.L. 90–620, Oct. 22, 1968, 82 Stat. 1282.

§ 730.   Distribution of documents to Members of Congress

When, in the division among Senators, and Representatives, of documents printed for the use of Congress there is an apportionment to each or either House in round numbers, the Public Printer may not deliver the full number so accredited at the Senate Service Department and House of Representatives Publications Distribution Service, but only the largest multiple of the number constituting the full membership of that House, including the Secretary and Sergeant at Arms of the Senate and Clerk, Sergeant at Arms, and Doorkeeper of the House, which is contained in the round numbers thus accredited to that House, so that the number delivered divides evenly and without remainder among the Members of the House to which they are delivered; and the remainder of the documents thus resulting shall be turned over to the Superintendent of Documents, to be distributed by him, first, to public and school libraries for the purpose of completing broken sets; second, to public and school libraries that have not been supplied with any portions of the sets, and, lastly, by sale to other persons; the libraries to be named to him by Senators and Representatives; and in this distribution the Superintendent of Documents, as far as practicable, shall make an equal allowance to each Senator and Representative.

Pub.L. 90–620, Oct. 22, 1968, 82 Stat. 1253.

DEPOSITORY LIBRARIES
(United States Code Annotated, 1982, Title 44, s.1901-1916, 738.)

§ 1901.   Definition of Government publication

"Government publication" as used in this chapter, means informational matter which is published as an individual document at Government expense, or as required by law.

Pub.L. 90–620, Oct. 22, 1968, 82 Stat. 1283.

§ 1902. Availability of Government publications through Superintendent of Documents; lists of publications not ordered from Government Printing Office

Government publications, except those determined by their issuing components to be required for official use only or for strictly administrative or operational purposes which have no public interest or educational value and publications classified for reasons of national security, shall be made available to depository libraries through the facilities of the Superintendent of Documents for public information. Each component of the Government shall furnish the Superintendent of Documents a list of such publications it issued during the previous month, that were obtained from sources other than the Government Printing Office.

Pub.L. 90–620, Oct. 22, 1968, 82 Stat. 1283.

§ 1903. Distribution of publications to depositories; notice to Government components; cost of printing and binding

Upon request of the Superintendent of Documents, components of the Government ordering the printing of publications shall either increase or decrease the number of copies of publications furnished for distribution to designated depository libraries and State libraries so that the number of copies delivered to the Superintendent of Documents is equal to the number of libraries on the list. The number thus delivered may not be restricted by any statutory limitation in force on August 9, 1962. Copies of publications furnished the Superintendent of Documents for distribution to designated depository libraries shall include—

the journals of the Senate and House of Representatives;

all publications, not confidential in character, printed upon the requisition of a congressional committee;

Senate and House public bills and resolutions; and

reports on private bills, concurrent or simple resolutions; but not so-called cooperative publications which must necessarily be sold in order to be self-sustaining.

The Superintendent of Documents shall currently inform the components of the Government ordering printing of publications as to the number of copies of their publications required for distribution to depository libraries. The cost of printing and binding those publications distributed to depository libraries obtained elsewhere than from the Government Printing Office, shall be borne by components of the Government responsible for their issuance; those requisitioned from the Government Printing Office shall be charged to appropriations provided the Superintendent of Documents for that purpose.

Pub.L. 90–620, Oct. 22, 1968, 82 Stat. 1283.

§ 1904. Classified list of Government publications for selection by depositories

The Superintendent of Documents shall currently issue a classified list of Government publications in suitable form, containing annotations of contents and listed by item identification numbers to facilitate the selection of only those publications needed by depository libraries. The selected publications shall be distributed to depository libraries in accordance with regulations of the Superintendent of Documents, as long as they fulfill the conditions provided by law.

Pub.L. 90–620, Oct. 22, 1968, 82 Stat. 1284.

§ 1905. Distribution to depositories; designation of additional libraries; justification; authorization for certain designations

The Government publications selected from lists prepared by the Superintendent of Documents, and when requested from him, shall be distributed to depository libraries specifically designated by law and to libraries designated by Senators, Representatives, and the Resident Commissioner from Puerto Rico, by the Commissioner of the District of Columbia, and by the Governors of Guam, American Samoa, and the Virgin Islands, respectively. Additional libraries within areas served by Representatives or the Resident Commissioner from Puerto Rico may be designated by them to receive Government publications to the extent that the total number of libraries designated by them does not exceed two within each area. Not more than two additional libraries within a State may be designated by each Senator from the State. Before an additional library within a State, congressional district or the Commonwealth of Puerto Rico is designated as a depository for Government publications, the head of that library shall furnish his Senator, Representative, or the Resident Commissioner from Puerto Rico, as the case may be, with justification of the necessity for the additional designation. The justification, which shall also include a certification as to the need for the additional depository library designation, shall be signed by the head of every existing depository library within the congressional district or the Commonwealth of Puerto Rico or by the head of the library authority of the State or the Commonwealth of Puerto Rico, within which the additional depository library is to be located. The justification for additional depository library designations shall be transmitted to the Superintendent of Documents by the Senator, Representative, or the Resident Commissioner from Puerto Rico, as the case may be. The Commissioner of the District of Columbia may designate two depository libraries in the District of Columbia, the Governor of Guam and the Governor of American Samoa may each designate one depository library in Guam and American Samoa, respectively, and the Governor of the Virgin Islands may designate one depository library on the island of Saint Thomas and one on the island of Saint Croix.

Pub.L. 90–620, Oct. 22, 1968, 82 Stat. 1284.

§ 1906.   Land-grant colleges constituted depositories

Land-grant colleges are constituted depositories to receive Government publications subject to the depository laws.

Pub.L. 90–620, Oct. 22, 1968, 82 Stat. 1284.

§ 1907.   Libraries of executive departments, service academies, and independent agencies constituted depositories; certifications of need; disposal of unwanted publications

The libraries of the executive departments, of the United States Military Academy, of the United States Naval Academy, of the United States Air Force Academy, of the United States Coast Guard Academy, and of the United States Merchant Marine Academy are designated depositories of Government publications. A depository library within each independent agency may be designated upon certification of need by the head of the independent agency to the Superintendent of Documents. Additional depository libraries within executive departments and independent agencies may be designated to receive Government publications to the extent that the number so designated does not exceed the number of major bureaus or divisions of the departments and independent agencies. These designations may be made only after certification by the head of each executive department or independent agency to the Superintendent of Documents as to the justifiable need for additional depository libraries. Depository libraries within executive departments and independent agencies may dispose of unwanted Government publications after first offering them to the Library of Congress and the Archivist of the United States.

Pub.L. 90–620, Oct. 22, 1968, 82 Stat. 1285.

§ 1908.   American Antiquarian Society to receive certain publications

One copy of the public journals of the Senate and of the House of Representatives, and of the documents published under the orders of the Senate and House of Representatives, respectively, shall be transmitted to the Executive of the Commonwealth of Massachusetts for the use and benefit of the American Antiquarian Society of the Commonwealth.

Pub.L. 90–620, Oct. 22, 1968, 82 Stat. 1285.

§ 1909.   Requirements of depository libraries; reports on conditions; investigations; termination; replacement

Only a library able to provide custody and service for depository materials and located in an area where it can best serve the public need, and within an area not already adequately served by existing depository libraries may be designated by Senators, Representatives, the Resident Commissioner from Puerto Rico, the Commissioner of the District of Columbia, or the Governors of Guam, American Samoa, or the Virgin Islands as a depository of Government publications. The designated depository libraries shall report to the Superintendent of Documents at least every two years concerning their condition.

The Superintendent of Documents shall make first hand investigation of conditions for which need is indicated and include the results of investigations in his annual report. When he ascertains that the number of books in a depository library is below ten thousand, other than Government publications, or it has ceased to be maintained so as to be accessible to the public, or that the Government publications which have been furnished the library have not been properly maintained, he shall delete the library from the list of depository libraries if the library fails to correct the unsatisfactory conditions within six months. The Representative or the Resident Commissioner from Puerto Rico in whose area the library is located or the Senator who made the designation, or a successor of the Senator, and, in the case of a library in the District of Columbia, the Commissioner of the District of Columbia, and, in the case of a library in Guam, American Samoa, or the Virgin Islands, the Governor, shall be notified and shall then be authorized to designate another library within the area served by him, which shall meet the conditions herein required, but which may not be in excess of the number of depository libraries authorized by law within the State, district, territory, or the Commonwealth of Puerto Rico, as the case may be.

Pub.L. 90–620, Oct. 22, 1968, 82 Stat. 1285.

§ 1910.   Designations of replacement depositories; limitations on numbers; conditions

The designation of a library to replace a depository library, other than a depository library specifically designated by law, may be made only within the limitations on total numbers specified by section 1905 of this title, and only when the library to be replaced ceases to exist, or when the library voluntarily relinquishes its depository status, or when the Superintendent of Documents determines that it no longer fulfills the conditions provided by law for depository libraries.

Pub.L. 90–620, Oct. 22, 1968, 82 Stat. 1286.

§ 1911.   Free use of Government publications in depositories; disposal of unwanted publications

Depository libraries shall make Government publications available for the free use of the general public, and may dispose of them after retention for five years under section 1912 of this title, if the depository library is served by a regional depository library. Depository libraries not served by a regional depository library, or that are regional depository libraries themselves, shall retain Government publications permanently in either printed form or in micro-facsimile form, except superseded publications or those issued later in bound form which may be discarded as authorized by the Superintendent of Documents.

Pub.L. 90–620, Oct. 22, 1968, 82 Stat. 1286.

§ 1912. Regional depositories; designation; functions; disposal of publications

Not more than two depository libraries in each State and the Commonwealth of Puerto Rico may be designated as regional depositories, and shall receive from the Superintendent of Documents copies of all new and revised Government publications authorized for distribution to depository libraries. Designation of regional depository libraries may be made by a Senator or the Resident Commissioner from Puerto Rico within the areas served by them, after approval by the head of the library authority of the State or the Commonwealth of Puerto Rico, as the case may be, who shall first ascertain from the head of the library to be so designated that the library will, in addition to fulfilling the requirements for depository libraries, retain at least one copy of all Government publications either in printed or microfacsimile form (except those authorized to be discarded by the Superintendent of Documents); and within the region served will provide interlibrary loan, reference service, and assistance for depository libraries in the disposal of unwanted Government publications. The agreement to function as a regional depository library shall be transmitted to the Superintendent of Documents by the Senator or the Resident Commissioner from Puerto Rico when the designation is made.

The libraries designated as regional depositories may permit depository libraries, within the areas served by them, to dispose of Government publications which they have retained for five years after first offering them to other depository libraries within their area, then to other libraries.

Pub.L. 90–620, Oct. 22, 1968, 82 Stat. 1286.

§ 1913. Appropriations for supplying depository libraries; restriction

Appropriations available for the Office of Superintendent of Documents may not be used to supply depository libraries documents, books, or other printed matter not requested by them, and their requests shall be subject to approval by the Superintendent of Documents.

Pub.L. 90–620, Oct. 22, 1968, 82 Stat. 1286.

§ 1914. Implementation of depository library program by Public Printer

The Public Printer, with the approval of the Joint Committee on Printing, as provided by section 103 of this title, may use any measures he considers necessary for the economical and practical implementation of this chapter.

Pub.L. 90–620, Oct. 22, 1968, 82 Stat. 1287.

§ 1915. Highest State appellate court libraries as depository libraries

Upon the request of the highest appellate court of a State, the Public Printer is authorized to designate the library of that court as a depository library. The provisions of section 1911 of this title shall not apply to any library so designated.

Added Pub.L. 92–368, § 1(a), Aug. 10, 1972, 86 Stat. 507.

§ 1916. Designation of libraries of accredited law schools as depository libraries

(a) Upon the request of any accredited law school, the Public Printer shall designate the library of such law school as a depository library. The Public Printer may not make such designation unless he determines that the library involved meets the requirements of this chapter, other than those requirements of the first undesignated paragraph of section 1909 of this title which relate to the location of such library.

(b) For purposes of this section, the term "accredited law school" means any law school which is accredited by a nationally recognized accrediting agency or association approved by the Commissioner of Education for such purpose or accredited by the highest appellate court of the State in which the law school is located.

Added Pub.L. 95–261, § 1, Apr. 17, 1978, 92 Stat. 199.

§ 738.　Binding of publications for distribution to libraries

The Public Printer shall supply the Superintendent of Documents with sufficient copies of publications distributed in unbound form, to be bound and distributed to the State libraries and other designated depositories for their permanent files. Every publication of sufficient size on any one subject shall be bound separately and receive the title suggested by the subject of the volume, and the others shall be distributed in unbound form as soon as printed. The library edition, as well as all other bound sets of congressional numbered documents and reports, shall be arranged in volumes and bound in the manner directed by the Joint Committee on Printing.

Pub.L. 90–620, Oct. 22, 1968, 82 Stat. 1254.

CONGRESSIONAL RECORD
(United States Code Annotated, 1982, Title 44, s.906.)

§ 906. Congressional Record: gratuitous copies; delivery

The Public Printer shall furnish the Congressional Record only as follows:

　　of the bound edition—

　　　　*　　*　　*

　　to the Library of Congress for official use in Washington, District of Columbia, and for international exchange, as provided by sections 1718 and 1719 of this title, not to exceed one hundred and forty-five copies of the daily, five semimonthly copies, and one hundred and fifty bound copies;

to the library of the Senate, three copies of the daily, two semi-monthly copies, and not to exceed fifteen bound copies;

to the library of the House of Representatives, five copies of the daily, two semimonthly copies, and not to exceed twenty-eight bound copies, of which eight copies may be bound in the style and manner approved by the Joint Committee on Printing;

to the library of the Supreme Court of the United States, two copies of the daily, two semimonthly copies, and not to exceed five bound copies;

to the library of each United States Court of Appeals, each United States District Court, the United States Court of Claims, the United States Court of Customs and Patent Appeals, the United States Court of International Trade, the Tax Court of the United States, and the United States Court of Military Appeals, upon request to the Public Printer, one copy of the daily, one semimonthly copy, and one bound copy;

to the Public Printer for official use, not to exceed seventy-five copies of the daily, ten semimonthly copies, and two bound copies;

to the Director of the Botanic Garden, two copies of the daily and one semimonthly copy;

to the Archivist of the United States, five copies of the daily, two semimonthly copies, and two bound copies;

to the library of each executive department, independent office, and establishment of the Government in the District of Columbia, except those designated as depository libraries, and to the libraries of the municipal government of the District of Columbia, the Naval Observatory, and the Smithsonian Institution, each, two copies of the daily, one semimonthly copy, and one bound copy;

*   *   *

to the Superintendent of Documents, as many daily and bound copies as may be required for distribution to depository libraries;

As amended Pub.L. 91–276, June 12, 1970, 84 Stat. 303; Pub.L. 92–373, Aug. 10, 1972, 86 Stat. 528; Pub.L. 93–314, § 1(b), June 8, 1974, 88 Stat. 239; Pub.L. 95–94, Title IV, § 407(a), Aug. 5, 1977, 91 Stat. 683; Pub.L. 96–417, Title VI, § 601(11), Oct. 10, 1980, 94 Stat. 1744.

HOUSE AND SENATE DOCUMENTS
(United States Code Annotated, 1982, Title 44, s.701.)

§ 701.   "Usual number" of documents and reports; distribution of House and Senate documents and reports; binding; reports on private bills; number of copies printed; distribution

(a) The order by either House of Congress to print a document or report shall signify the "usual number" of copies for binding and distribution among those entitled to receive them. A greater number may not be printed unless ordered by either House, or as provided by this section. When a special number of a document or report is ordered printed, the usual number shall also be printed, unless already ordered.

(b) The "usual number" of documents and reports shall be one thousand six hundred and eighty-two copies, which shall be printed at one time and distributed as follows:

Of the House documents and reports, unbound—to the Senate document room, one hundred and fifty copies; to the office of the Secretary of the Senate, ten copies; to the House document room, not to exceed five hundred copies; to the office of the Clerk of the House of Representatives, twenty copies; to the Library of Congress, ten copies, as provided by section 1718 of this title.

Of the Senate documents and reports, unbound—to the Senate document room, two hundred and twenty copies; office of the Secretary of the Senate, ten copies; to the House document room, not to exceed five hundred copies; to the Clerk's office of the House of Representatives, ten copies; to the Library of Congress, ten copies, as provided by section 1718 of this title.

(c) Of the number printed, the Public Printer shall bind a sufficient number of copies for distribution as follows:

Of the House documents and reports, bound—to the Senate library, fifteen copies; to the Library of Congress, not to exceed one hundred and fifty copies, as provided by section 1718 of this title; to the House of Representatives library, fifteen copies; to the Superintendent of Documents, as many copies as are required for distribution to the State libraries and designated depositories.

Of the Senate documents and reports, bound—to the Senate library, fifteen copies; to the Library of Congress, copies as provided by sections 1718 and 1719 of this title; to the House of Representatives library, fifteen copies; to the Superintendent of Documents, as many copies as may be required for distribution to State libraries and designated depositories. In binding documents the Public Printer shall give precedence to those that are to be distributed to libraries and to designated depositories. But a State library or designated depository entitled to documents that may prefer to have its documents in unbound form, may do so by notifying the Superintendent of Documents to that effect prior to the convening of each Congress.

(d) The usual number of reports on private bills, concurrent or simple resolutions, may not be printed. Instead there shall be printed of each Senate report on a private bill, simple or concurrent resolution, in addition to those required to be furnished the Library of Congress, three hundred and forty-five copies, which shall be distributed as follows: to the Senate document room, two hundred and twenty copies; to the Secretary of the Senate, fifteen copies; to the House document room, one hundred copies; to the Superintendent of Documents, ten copies; and of each House report on a private bill, simple or concurrent resolution, in addition to those for the Library of Congress, two hundred and sixty copies, which shall be distributed as follows: to the Senate document room, one hundred and thirty-five copies; to the Secretary of the Senate, fifteen copies; to the House document room, one hundred copies; to the Superintendent of Documents, ten copies.

This section does not prevent the binding of all Senate and House reports in the reserve volumes bound for and delivered to the Senate and House libraries, nor abridge the right of the Vice President, Senators, Representatives, Resident Commissioner, Secretary of the Senate, and Clerk of the House to have bound in half morocco, or material not more expensive, one copy of every public document to which he may be entitled. At least twelve copies of each report on bills for the payment or adjudication of claims against the Government shall be kept on file in the Senate document room.

Pub.L. 90–620, Oct. 22, 1968, 82 Stat. 1246.

HOUSE AND SENATE JOURNALS
(United States Code Annotated, 1982, Title 44, s.713.)

§ 713.   Journals of Houses of Congress

There shall be printed of the Journals of the Senate and House of Representatives eight hundred and twenty-two copies, which shall be distributed as follows:

> to the Senate document room, ninety copies for distribution to Senators, and twenty-five additional copies;

> to the Senate library, ten copies;

> to the House document room, three hundred and sixty copies for distribution to Members, and twenty-five additional copies;

> to the Department of State, four copies;

> to the Superintendent of Documents, one hundred and forty-four copies to be distributed to three libraries in each of the States to be designated by the Superintendent of Documents;

> to the Court of Claims, two copies; and

> to the library of the House of Representatives, ten copies.

The remaining number of the Journals of the Senate and House of Representatives, consisting of twenty-five copies, shall be furnished to the Secretary of the Senate and the Clerk of the House of Representatives, respectively, as the necessities of their respective offices require, as rapidly as signatures are completed for distribution.

Pub.L. 90–620, Oct. 22, 1968, 82 Stat. 1249.

ARCHIVAL ADMINISTRATION

(United States Code Annotated, 1982, Title 44, s.2101-2114.)

§ 2101.   Definitions

As used in sections 2103–2113 of this title—

"Presidential archival depository" means an institution operated by the United States to house and preserve the papers and books of a President or former President of the United States, together with other historical materials belonging to a President or former President of the United States, or related to his papers or to the events of his official or personal life;

"historical materials" including books, correspondence, documents, papers, pamphlets, works of art, models, pictures, photographs, plats, maps, films, motion pictures, sound recordings, and other objects or materials having historical or commemorative value.

Pub.L. 90–620, Oct. 22, 1968, 82 Stat. 1287.

§ 2102.   Archivist of the United States

The Administrator of General Services shall appoint the Archivist of the United States.

Pub.L. 90–620, Oct. 22, 1968, 82 Stat. 1287.

§ 2103.   Acceptance of records for historical preservation

When it appears to the Administrator of General Services to be in the public interest, he may—

(1) accept for deposit with the National Archives of the United States the records of a Federal agency or of the Congress determined by the Archivist of the United States to have sufficient historical or other value to warrant their continued preservation by the United States Government;

(2) direct and effect the transfer to the National Archives of the United States of records of a Federal agency that have been in existence for more than thirty years and determined by the Archivist of the United States to have sufficient historical or other value to warrant their continued preservation by the United States Government, unless the head of the agency which has custody of them certifies in writing to the Administrator that they must be retained in his custody for use in the conduct of the regular current business of the agency;

(3) direct and effect, with the approval of the head of the originating agency, or if the existence of the agency has been terminated, then with the approval of his successor in function,

112

if any, the transfer of records deposited or approved for deposit with the National Archives of the United States to public or educational institutions or associations; title to the records to remain vested in the United States unless otherwise authorized by Congress; and

(4) **transfer** materials from private sources authorized to be received **by** the Administrator by section 2107 of this title.

As amended Pub.L. 94–575, § 4(a), Oct. 21, 1976, 90 Stat. 2727; Pub.L. 95–416, § 1(a), Oct. 5, 1978, 92 Stat. 915.

§ 2104. Responsibility for custody, use, and withdrawal of records

(a) The Administrator of General Services shall be responsible for the custody, use, and withdrawal of records transferred to him. When records, the use of which is subject to statutory limitations and restrictions, are so transferred, permissive and restrictive statutory provisions with respect to the examination and use of records applicable to the head of the agency from which the records were transferred or to employees of that agency are applicable to the Administrator, the Archivist of the United States, and to the employees of the General Services Administration, respectively. Except as provided in subsection (b) of this section, when the head of a Federal agency states, in writing, restrictions that appear to him to be necessary or desirable in the public interest with respect to the use or examination of records being considered for transfer from his custody to the Administrator of General Services, the Administrator shall, if he concurs, and in consultation with the Archivist of the United States, impose such restrictions on the records so transferred, and may not relax or remove such restrictions without the written concurrence of the head of the agency from which the material was transferred, or of his successor in function, if any. In the event that a Federal agency is terminated and there is no successor in function, the Administrator is authorized to relax, remove, or impose restrictions on such agency's records when he determines that such action is in the public interest. Statutory and other restrictions referred to in this subsection shall remain in force until the records have been in existence for thirty years unless the Administrator of General Services by order, having consulted with the Archivist and the head of the transferring Federal agency or his successor in function, determines, with respect to specific bodies of records, that for reasons consistent with standards established in relevant statutory law, such restrictions shall remain in force for a longer period. Restriction on the use or examination of records deposited with the National Archives of the United States imposed by section 3 of the National Archives Act, approved June 19, 1934, shall continue in force regardless of the expiration of the tenure of office of the official who imposed them but may be removed or relaxed by the Administrator with the concurrence in writing of the head of the agency from which material was transferred or of his successor in function, if any.

(b) With regard to the census and survey records of the Bureau of the Census containing data identifying individuals enumerated in population censuses, any release pursuant to this section of such identifying information contained in such records shall be made by the Administrator of General Services pursuant to the specifications and agreements set forth in the exchange of correspondence on or about the date of October 10, 1952, between the Director of the Bureau of the Census and the Archivist of the United States, together with all amendments thereto, now or hereafter entered into between the Director of the Bureau of the Census and the Archivist of the United States. Such amendments, if any, shall be published in the Register.

As amended Pub.L. 95–416, § 1(b), Oct. 5, 1978, 92 Stat. 915.

§ 2105.   Preservation, arrangement, duplication, exhibition of records

The Administrator of General Services shall provide for the preservation, arrangement, repair and rehabilitation, duplication and reproduction (including microcopy publications), description, and exhibition of records or other documentary material transferred to him as may be needful or appropriate, including the preparation and publication of inventories, indexes, catalogs, and other finding aids or guides to facilitate their use.   He may also prepare guides and other finding aids to Federal records and, when approved by the National Historical Publications Commission, publish such historical works and collections of sources as seem appropriate for printing or otherwise recording at the public expense.

Pub.L. 90–620, Oct. 22, 1968, 82 Stat. 1288.

§ 2106.   Servicing records

The Administrator of General Services shall provide and maintain facilities he considers necessary or desirable for servicing records in his custody that are not exempt from examination by statutory or other restrictions.

Pub.L. 90–620, Oct. 22, 1968, 82 Stat. 1288.

§ 2107.   Material accepted for deposit

When the Administrator of General Services considers it to be in the public interest he may accept for deposit—

(1) the papers and other historical materials of a President or former President of the United States, or other official or former official of the Government, and other papers relating to and contemporary with a President or former President of the United States, subject to restrictions agreeable to the Administrator as to their use; and

(2) documents, including motion-picture films, still pictures, and sound recordings, from private sources that are appropriate for preservation by the Government as evidence of its organization, functions, policies, decisions, procedures, and transactions.

This section shall not apply in the case of any Presidential records which are subject to the provisions of chapter 22 of this title.

As amended Pub.L. 95–591, § 2(b)(2), Nov. 4, 1978, 92 Stat. 2528.

§ 2108.   Presidential archival depository

(a) When the Administrator of General Services considers it to be in the public interest he may accept, for and in the name of the United States, land, buildings, and equipment offered as a gift to the United States for the purposes of creating a Presidential archival depository, and take title to the land, buildings, and equipment on behalf of the United States, and maintain, operate, and protect them as a Presidential archival depository, and as part of the national archives system;   and make agreements, upon terms and conditions he considers proper, with a State, political subdivision, university, institution of higher learning, institute, or foundation to use as a Presidential archival depository land, buildings, and equipment of the State, subdivision, university, or other organization, to be made available by it without transfer of title to the United States, and maintain, operate, and protect the depository as a part of the national archives system.

The Administrator shall submit a report in writing on a proposed Presidential archival depository to the President of the Senate and the Speaker of the House of Representatives, and include—

a description of the land, buildings, and equipment offered as a gift or to be made available without transfer of title;

a statement of the terms of the proposed agreement, if any;

a general description of the types of papers, documents, or other historical materials proposed to be deposited in the Presidential archival depository so to be created, and of the terms of the proposed deposit;

a statement of the additional improvements and equipment, if any, necessary to the satisfactory operation of the depository, together with an estimate of the cost; and

an estimate of the annual cost to the United States of maintaining, operating, and protecting the depository.

The Administrator may not take title to land, buildings, and equipment or make an agreement, until the expiration of the first period of 60 calendar days of continuous session of the Congress following the date on which the report is transmitted, computed as follows:

Continuity of session is broken only by an adjournment sine die, but the days on which either House is not in session because of an adjournment of more than three days to a day certain are excluded.

(b) When the Administrator considers it to be in the public interest, he may deposit in a Presidential archival depository papers, documents, or other historical materials accepted under section 2107 of this title, or Federal records appropriate for preservation.

(c) When the Administrator considers it to be in the public interest, he may exercise, with respect to papers, documents, or other historical materials deposited under this section, or otherwise, in a Presidential archival depository, all the functions and responsibilities otherwise vested in him pertaining to Federal records or other documentary materials in his custody or under his control. The Administrator, in negotiating for the deposit of Presidential historical materials, shall take steps to secure to the Government, as far as possible, the right to have continuous and permanent possession of the materials. Papers, documents, or other historical materials accepted and deposited under section 2107 of this title and this section are subject to restrictions as to their availability and use stated in writing by the donors or depositors, including the restriction that they shall be kept in a Presidential archival depository. The restrictions shall be respected for the period stated, or until revoked or terminated by the donors or depositors or by persons legally qualified to act on their behalf. Subject to the restrictions, the Administrator may dispose by sale, exchange, or otherwise, of papers, documents, or other materials which the Archivist determines to have no permanent value or historical interest or to be surplus to the needs of a Presidential archival depository. Only the first two sentences of this subsection shall apply to Presidential records as defined in section 2201(2) of this title.

As amended Pub.L. 94–575, § 4(a), Oct. 21, 1976, 90 Stat. 2727; Pub.L. 95–591, § 2(b)(3), Nov. 4, 1978, 92 Stat. 2528.

(d) When the Administrator considers it to be in the public interest, he may cooperate with and assist a university, institution of higher learning, institute, foundation, or other organization or qualified individual to further or to conduct study or research in historical materials deposited in a Presidential archival depository.

(e) When the Administrator considers it to be in the public interest, he may charge and collect reasonable fees for the privilege of visiting and viewing exhibit rooms or museum space in a Presidential archival depository.

(f) When the Administrator considers it to be in the public interest, he may provide reasonable office space in a Presidential archival depository for the personal use of a former President of the United States.

(g) When the Administrator considers it be in the public interest, he may accept gifts or bequests of money or other property for the purpose of maintaining, operating, protecting, or improving a Presidential archival depository. The proceeds of gifts or bequests, together with the proceeds from fees or from sales of historical materials, copies or reproductions, catalogs, or other items, having to do with a Presidential archival depository, shall be paid into the National Archives Trust Fund to be held, administered, and expended for the benefit and in the interest of the Presidential archival depository in connection with which they were received, including administrative and custodial expenses as the Administrator determines.

Pub.L. 90–620, Oct. 22, 1968, 82 Stat. 1289.

§ 2109.   Depository for agreements between States

The Administrator of General Services may receive duplicate originals or authenticated copies of agreements or compacts entered into under the Constitution and laws of the United States, between States of the Union, and take necessary actions for their preservation and servicing.

Pub.L. 90–620, Oct. 22, 1968, 82 Stat. 1290.

§ 2110.   Preservation of motion-picture films, still pictures, and sound recordings

The Administrator of General Services may make and preserve motion-picture films, still pictures, and sound recordings pertaining to and illustrative of the historical development of the United States Government and its activities, and provide for preparing, editing, titling, scoring, processing, duplicating, reproducing, exhibiting, and releasing for non-profit educational purposes, motion-picture films, still pictures, and sound recordings in his custody.

Pub.L. 90–620, Oct. 22, 1968, 82 Stat. 1290.

§ 2111. Reports; correction of violations

(a) When the Administrator of General Services considers it necessary, he may obtain reports from Federal agencies on their activities under chapters 21, 25, 27, 29, 31, and 33 of this title.

(b) When the Administrator finds that a provision of chapter 21, 25, 27, 29, 31, or 33 of this title has been or is being violated, he shall inform in writing the head of the agency concerned of the violation and make recommendations for its correction. Unless corrective measures satisfactory to the Administrator are inaugurated within a reasonable time, the Administrator shall submit a written report of the matter to the President and the Congress.

As amended Pub.L. 94–575, § 4(b), Oct. 21, 1976, 90 Stat. 2727.

§ 2112. Legal status of reproductions; official seal; fees for copies and reproductions

(a) When records that are required by statute to be retained indefinitely have been reproduced by photographic, microphotographic, or other processes, in accordance with standards established by the Administrator of General Services the indefinite retention by the photographic, microphotographic, or other reproductions constitutes compliance with the statutory requirement for the indefinite retention of the original records. The reproductions, as well as reproductions made under regulations to carry out chapters 21, 29, 31, and 33 of this title, shall have the same legal status as the originals.

As amended Pub.L. 94–575, § 4(b), Oct. 21, 1976, 90 Stat. 2727.

(b) There shall be an official seal for the National Archives of the United States which shall be judicially noticed. When a copy or reproduction, furnished under this section, is authenticated by the official seal and certified by the Administrator, the copy or reproduction shall be admitted in evidence equally with the original from which it was made.

(c) The Administrator may charge a fee not in excess of 10 percent above the costs or expenses for making or authenticating copies or reproductions of materials transferred to his custody. Fees shall be paid into, administered, and expended as a part of the National Archives Trust Fund. He may not charge for making or authenticating copies or reproductions of materials for official use by the United States Government. Reimbursement may be accepted to cover the cost of furnishing copies or reproductions that could not otherwise be furnished.

Pub.L. 90–620, Oct. 22, 1968, 82 Stat. 1291.

§ 2113. Limitation on liability

When letters and other intellectual productions (exclusive of patented material, published works under copyright protection, and unpublished works for which copyright registration has been made) come into the custody or possession of the Administrator of General Services, the United States or its agents are not liable for infringement of copyright or analogous rights **arising** out of use of the materials for display, inspection, research, **reproduction,** or other purposes.

As amended **Pub.L.** 94–553, § 105(b), Oct. 19, 1976, 90 Stat. 2599.

§ 2114. Records of Congress

The Secretary of the Senate and the Clerk of the House of Representatives, acting jointly, shall obtain at the close of each Congress all the noncurrent records of the Congress and of each congressional committee and transfer them to the General Services Administration for preservation, subject to the orders of the Senate or the House of Representatives, respectively.

Pub.L. 90–620, Oct. 22, 1968, 82 Stat. 1291.

RECORDS MANAGEMENT

(United States Code Annotated, 1982, Title 44, s.2901-2909,
3101-3107,3301-3303a, 3308-3324.)

§ 2901. Definitions

As used in this chapter, and chapters 21, 25, 27, 31, and 33 of this title—

(1) the term "records" has the meaning given it by section 3301 of this title;

(2) the term "records management" means the planning, controlling, directing, organizing, training, promoting, and other managerial activities involved with respect to records creation, records maintenance and use, and records disposition;

(3) the term "records creation" means the production or reproduction of any record;

(4) the term "records maintenance and use" means any activity involving—

(A) location of records of a Federal agency;

(B) storage, retrieval, and handling of records kept at office file locations by or for a Federal agency;

(C) processing of mail by a Federal agency; or

(D) selection and utilization of equipment and supplies associated with records and copying;

(5) the term "records disposition" means any activity with respect to—

(A) disposal of temporary records no longer necessary for the conduct of business by destruction or donation;

(B) transfer of records to Federal agency storage facilities or records centers;

(C) transfer to the National Archives of the United States of records determined to have sufficient historical or other value to warrant continued preservation; or

(D) transfer of records from one Federal agency to any other Federal agency;

(6) the term "records center" means an establishment maintained and operated by the Administrator or by another Federal agency primarily for the storage, servicing, security, and processing of records which need to be preserved for varying periods of time and need not be retained in office equipment or space;

(7) the term "records management study" means an investigation and analysis of any Federal agency records, or records management practices or programs (whether manual or automated), with a view toward rendering findings and recommendations with respect thereto;

(8) the term "inspection" means reviewing any Federal agency's records or records management practices or programs with respect to effectiveness and compliance with records management laws and making necessary recommendations for correction or improvement of records management;

(9) the term "servicing" means making available for use information in records and other materials in the custody of the Administrator, or in a records center—

119

(A) by furnishing the records or other materials, or information from them, or copies or reproductions thereof, to any Federal agency for official use, or to the public; or

(B) by making and furnishing authenticated or unauthenticated copies or reproductions of the records or other materials;

(10) the term "unauthenticated copies" means exact copies or reproductions of records or other materials that are not certified as such under seal and that need not be legally accepted as evidence;

(11) the term "National Archives of the United States" means those official records which have been determined by the Archivist of the United States to have sufficient historical or other value to warrant their continued preservation by the Federal Government, and which have been accepted by the Administrator for deposit in his custody;

(12) the term "Administrator" means the Administrator of General Services;

(13) the terms "executive agency" and "Federal agency" shall have the meanings given such terms by subsections (a) and (b), respectively, of section 3 of the Federal Property and Administrative Services Act of 1949 (40 U.S.C. 472(a) and (b)).

Added Pub.L. 94–575, § 2(a)(1), Oct. 21, 1976, 90 Stat. 2723.

§ 2902.   Objectives of records management

It is the purpose of this chapter, and chapters 21, 31, and 33 of this title, to require the establishment of standards and procedures to assure efficient and effective records management. Such records management standards and procedures shall seek to implement the following goals:

(1) Accurate and complete documentation of the policies and transactions of the Federal Government.

(2) Control of the quantity and quality of records produced by the Federal Government.

(3) Establishment and maintenance of mechanisms of control with respect to records creation in order to prevent the creation of unnecessary records and with respect to the effective and economical operations of an agency.

(4) Simplification of the activities, systems, and processes of records creation and of records maintenance and use.

(5) Judicious preservation and disposal of records.

(6) Direction of continuing attention on records from their initial creation to their final disposition, with particular emphasis on the prevention of unnecessary Federal paperwork.

(7) Establishment and maintenance of such other systems or techniques as the Administrator considers necessary to carry out the purposes of this chapter, and chapters 21, 31, and 33 of this title.

Added Pub.L. 94–575, § 2(a)(1), Oct. 21, 1976, 90 Stat. 2724.

§ 2903.   Custody and control of property

The Administrator shall have immediate custody and control of the National Archives Building and its contents, and may design, construct, purchase, lease, maintain, operate, protect, and improve buildings used by him for the storage of records of Federal agencies in the District of Columbia and elsewhere.

Pub.L. 90–620, Oct. 22, 1968, 82 Stat. 1296.

§ 2904.   General responsibilities of Administrator·

The Administrator shall provide guidance and assistance to Federal agencies with respect to records creation, records maintenance and use, and records disposition. In providing such guidance and assistance, the Administrator shall have responsibility to—

(1) promote economy and efficiency in the selection and utilization of space, staff, equipment, and supplies for records management;

(2) promulgate standards, procedures, and guidelines with respect to records management and records management studies;

(3) conduct research with respect to the improvement of records management practices and programs;

(4) serve as a clearinghouse for information with respect to records management and as a central source for reference and training materials with respect to records management;

(5) establish such interagency committees and boards as may be necessary to provide an exchange of information among Federal agencies with respect to records management;

(6) disseminate information with respect to technological development in records management;

(7) direct the continuing attention of Federal agencies and the Congress on the burden placed on the Federal Government by unnecessary paperwork, and on the need for adequate policies governing records creation, maintenance and use, and disposition;

(8) conduct records management studies and, in his discretion, designate the heads of executive agencies to conduct records management studies with respect to establishing systems and techniques designed to save time and effort in records management, with particular attention given to standards and procedures governing records creation;

(9) conduct inspections or records management studies which involve a review of the programs and practices of more than one Federal agency and which examine interaction among and relationships between Federal agencies with respect to records and records management; and

(10) report to the appropriate oversight and appropriations committees of the Congress and to the Director of the Office of Management and Budget annually and at such other times as the Administrator deems desirable (A) on the results of activities conducted pursuant to paragraphs (1) through (9) of this section, (B) on evaluations of responses by Federal agencies to any recommendations resulting from inspections or studies conducted under paragraphs (8) and (9) of this section, and (C) to the extent practicable, estimates of costs to the Federal Government resulting from the failure of agencies to implement such recommendations.

Added Pub.L. 94–575, § 2(a)(2), Oct. 21, 1976, 90 Stat. 2725, and amended Pub.L. 96–511, § 2(c)(1), Dec. 11, 1980, 94 Stat. 2825.

§ 2905. Establishment of standards for selective retention of records; security measures

(a) The Administrator of General Services shall establish standards for the selective retention of records of continuing value, and assist Federal agencies in applying the standards to records in their custody. He shall notify the head of a Federal agency of any actual, impending, or threatened unlawful removal, defacing, alteration, or destruction of records in the custody of the agency that shall come to his attention, and assist the head of the agency in initiating action through the Attorney General for the recovery of records unlawfully removed and for other redress provided by law.

(b) The Administrator of General Services shall assist the Administrator for the Office of Information and Regulatory Affairs in conducting studies and developing standards relating to record retention requirements imposed on the public and on State and local governments by Federal agencies.

As amended Pub.L. 96–511, § 2(c)(2), Dec. 11, 1980, 94 Stat. 2825.

§ 2906. Inspection of agency records

(a)(1) In carrying out his duties and responsibilities under this chapter, the Administrator of General Services or his designee may inspect the records or the records management practices and programs of any Federal agency solely for the purpose of rendering recommendations for the improvement of records management practices and programs. Officers and employees of such agencies shall cooperate fully in such inspections, subject to the provisions of paragraphs (2) and (3) of this subsection.

(2) Records, the use of which is restricted by law or for reasons of national security or the public interest, shall be inspected, in accordance with regulations promulgated by the Administrator, subject to the approval of the head of the agency concerned or of the President.

(3) If the Administrator or his designee inspects a record, as provided in this subsection, which is contained in a system of records which is subject to section 552a of title 5, such record shall be—

　　(A) maintained by the Administrator or his designee as a record contained in a system of records; or

　　(B) deemed to be a record contained in a system of records for purposes of subsections (b), (c), and (i) of section 552a of title 5.

(b) In conducting the inspection of agency records provided for in subsection (a) of this section, the Administrator or his designee shall, in addition to complying with the provisions of law cited in subsection (a)(3), comply with all other Federal laws and be subject to the sanctions provided therein.

Added Pub.L. 94–575, § 2(a)(3), Oct. 21, 1976, 90 Stat. 2725.

§ 2907. Records centers and centralized microfilming services

The Administrator may establish, maintain, and operate records centers and centralized microfilming services for Federal agencies.

Added Pub.L. 94–575, § 2(a)(3), Oct. 21, 1976, 90 Stat. 2726.

§ 2908. Regulations

Subject to applicable law, the Administrator of General Services shall promulgate regulations governing the transfer of records from the custody of one executive agency to that of another.

Pub.L. 90–620, Oct. 22, 1968, 82 Stat. 1297.

§ 2909. Retention of records

The Administrator of General Services may empower a Federal agency, upon the submission of evidence of need, to retain records for a longer period than that specified in disposal schedules; and, in accordance with regulations promulgated by him, may withdraw disposal authorizations covering records listed in disposal schedules.

As amended Pub.L. 91–287, § 4, June 23, 1970, 84 Stat. 322.

§ 3101. Records management by agency heads; general duties

The head of each Federal agency shall make and preserve records containing adequate and proper documentation of the organization, functions, policies, decisions, procedures, and essential transactions of the agency and designed to furnish the information necessary to protect the legal and financial rights of the Government and of persons directly affected by the agency's activities.

Pub.L. 90–620, Oct. 22, 1968, 82 Stat. 1297.

§ 3102.   Establishment of program of management

The head of each Federal agency shall establish and maintain an active, continuing program for the economical and efficient management of the records of the agency.   The program, among other things, shall provide for

(1) effective controls over the creation and over the maintenance and use of records in the conduct of current business;

(2) cooperation with the Administrator of General Services in applying standards, procedures, and techniques designed to improve the management of records, promote the maintenance and security of records deemed appropriate for preservation, and facilitate the segregation and disposal of records of temporary value;   and

(3) compliance with sections 2101–2113, 2501–2507, 2701, 2901–2909, and 3101–3107, of this title and the regulations issued under them.

As amended Pub.L. 94–575, § 3(a)(1), (2), Oct. 21, 1976, 90 Stat. 2726.

§ 3103.   Transfer of records to records centers

When the head of a Federal agency determines that such action may affect substantial economies or increased operating efficiency, he shall provide for the transfer of records to a records center maintained and operated by the Administrator, or, when approved by the Administrator, to a center maintained and operated by the head of the Federal agency.

Added Pub.L. 94–575, § 3(a)(3), Oct. 21, 1976, 90 Stat. 2726.

§ 3104.   Certifications and determinations on transferred records

An official of the Government who is authorized to certify to facts on the basis of records in his custody, may certify to facts on the basis of records that have been transferred by him or his predecessors to the Administrator of General Services, and may authorize the Administrator to certify to facts and to make administrative determinations on the basis of records transferred to the Administrator, notwithstanding any other law.

Pub.L. 90–620, Oct. 22, 1968, 82 Stat. 1298.

§ 3105.   Safeguards

The head of each Federal agency shall establish safeguards against the removal or loss of records he determines to be necessary and required by regulations of the Administrator of General Services.   Safeguards shall include making it known to officials and employees of the agency—

(1) that records in the custody of the agency are not to be alienated or destroyed except in accordance with sections 3301–3314 of this title, and

(2) the penalties provided by law for the unlawful removal or destruction of records.

Pub.L. 90–620, Oct. 22, 1968, 82 Stat. 1298.

§ 3106. Unlawful removal, destruction of records

The head of each Federal agency shall notify the Administrator of General Services of any actual, impending, or threatened unlawful removal, defacing, alteration, or destruction of records in the custody of the agency of which he is the head that shall come to his attention, and with the assistance of the Administrator shall initiate action through the Attorney General for the recovery of records he knows or has reason to believe have been unlawfully removed from his agency, or from another Federal agency whose records have been transferred to his legal custody.

Pub.L. 90–620, Oct. 22, 1968, 82 Stat. 1298.

§ 3107. Authority of Comptroller General

Chapters 21, 25, 27, 29, and 31 of this title do not limit the authority of the Comptroller General of the United States with respect to prescribing accounting systems, forms, and procedures, or lessen the responsibility of collecting and disbursing officers for rendition of their accounts for settlement by the General Accounting Office.

As amended Pub.L. 94–575, § 3(a)(4), Oct. 21, 1976, 90 Stat. 2726.

§ 3301. Definition of records

As used in this chapter, "records" includes all books, papers, maps, photographs, machine readable materials, or other documentary materials, regardless of physical form or characteristics, made or received by an agency of the United States Government under Federal law or in connection with the transaction of public business and preserved or appropriate for preservation by that agency or its legitimate successor as evidence of the organization, functions, policies, decisions, procedures, operations, or other activities of the Government or because of the informational value of data in them. Library and museum material made or acquired and preserved solely for reference or exhibition purposes, extra copies of documents preserved only for convenience of reference, and stocks of publications and of processed documents are not included.

As amended Pub.L. 94–575, § 4(c)(2), Oct. 21, 1976, 90 Stat. 2727.

§ 3302. Regulations covering lists of records for disposal, procedure for disposal, and standards for reproduction

The Administrator of General Services shall promulgate regulations, not inconsistent with this chapter, establishing—

(1) procedures for the compiling and submitting to him of lists and schedules of records proposed for disposal,

(2) procedures for the disposal of records authorized for disposal, and

(3) standards for the reproduction of records by photographic or microphotographic processes with a view to the disposal of the original records.

As amended Pub.L. 94–575, § 4(c)(1), Oct. 21, 1976, 90 Stat. 2727.

§ 3303. Lists and schedules of records to be submitted to Administrator of General Services by head of each Government agency

The head of each agency of the United States Government shall submit to the Administrator of General Services, under regulations promulgated as provided by section 3302 of this title—

(1) lists of any records in the custody of the agency that have been photographed or microphotographed under the regulations and that, as a consequence, do not appear to have sufficient value to warrant their further preservation by the Government;

(2) lists of other records in the custody of the agency not needed by it in the transaction of its current business and that do not appear to have sufficient administrative, legal, research, or other value to warrant their further preservation by the Government; and

(3) schedules proposing the disposal after the lapse of specified periods of time of records of a specified form or character that either have accumulated in the custody of the agency or may accumulate after the submission of the schedules and apparently will not after the lapse of the period specified have sufficient administrative, legal, research, or other value to warrant their further preservation by the Government.

Pub.L. 90–620, Oct. 22, 1968, 82 Stat. 1299.

§ 3303a. Examination by Administrator of General Services of lists and schedules of records lacking preservation value; disposal of records

(a) The Administrator of General Services shall examine the lists and schedules submitted to him under section 3303 of this title. If the Administrator determines that any of the records listed in a list or schedule submitted to him do not, or will not after the lapse of the period specified, have sufficient administrative, legal, research, or other value to warrant their continued preservation by the Government, he may—

(1) notify the agency to that effect; and

(2) empower the agency to dispose of those records in accordance with regulations promulgated under section 3302 of this title.

(b) Authorizations granted under lists and schedules submitted to the Administrator under section 3303 of this title, and schedules promulgated by the Administrator under subsection (d) of this section, shall be mandatory, subject to section 2909 of this title. As between an authorization granted under lists and schedules submitted to the Administrator under section 3303 of this title and an authorization contained in a schedule promulgated under subsection (d) of this section, application of the authorization providing for the shorter retention period shall be required, subject to section 2909 of this title.

(c) The Administrator may request advice and counsel from the Committee on Rules and Administration of the Senate and the Committee on House Administration of the House of Representatives with respect to the disposal of any particular records under this chapter whenever he considers that—

(1) those particular records may be of special interest to the Congress; or

(2) consultation with the Congress regarding the disposal of those particular records is in the public interest.

However, this subsection does not require the Administrator to request such advice and counsel as a regular procedure in the general disposal of records under this chapter.

(d) The Administrator shall promulgate schedules authorizing the disposal, after the lapse of specified periods of time, of records of a specified form or character common to several or all agencies if such records will not, at the end of the periods specified, have sufficient administrative, legal, research, or other value to warrant their further preservation by the United States Government. A Federal agency may request changes in such schedules for its records pursuant to section 2909 of this title.

(e) The Administrator may approve and effect the disposal of records that are in his legal custody, provided that records that had been in the custody of another existing agency may not be disposed of without the written consent of the head of the agency.

(f) The Administrator shall make an annual report to the Congress concerning the disposal of records under this chapter, including general descriptions of the types of records disposed of and such other information as he considers appropriate to keep the Congress fully informed regarding the disposal of records under this chapter.
Added Pub.L. 91–287, § 1, June 23, 1970, 84 Stat. 320, and amended Pub. L. 95–440, § 1, Oct. 10, 1978, 92 Stat. 1063.

§ 3308.   Disposal of similar records where prior disposal was authorized

When it appears to the Administrator of General Services that an agency has in its custody, or is accumulating, records of the same form or character as those of the same agency previously authorized to be disposed of, he may empower the head of the agency to dispose of the records, after they have been in existence a specified period of time, in accordance with regulations promulgated under section 3302 of this title and without listing or scheduling them.
As amended Pub.L. 91–287, § 2(a), June 23, 1970, 84 Stat. 321.

§ 3309.   Preservation of claims of Government until settled in General Accounting Office; disposal authorized upon written approval of Comptroller General

Records pertaining to claims and demands by or against the Government of the United States or to accounts in which the Government of the United States is concerned, either as debtor or creditor, may not be disposed of by the head of an agency under authorization granted under this chapter, until the claims, demands, and accounts have been settled and adjusted in the General Accounting Office, except upon the written approval of the Comptroller General of the United States.
As amended Pub.L. 91–287, § 2(b), June 23, 1970, 84 Stat. 321.

§ 3310.   Disposal of records constituting menace to health, life, or property

When the Administrator of General Services and the head of the agency that has custody of them jointly determine that records in the custody of an agency of the United States Government are a continuing menace to human health or life or to property, the Administrator shall eliminate the menace immediately by any method he considers necessary. When records in the custody of the Administrator are disposed of under this section, the Administrator shall report their disposal to the agency from which they were transferred.

Pub.L. 90–620, Oct. 22, 1968, 82 Stat. 1301.

§ 3311. Destruction of records outside continental United States in time of war or when hostile action seems imminent; written report to Administrator of General Services

During a state of war between the United States and another nation, or when hostile action by a foreign power appears imminent, the head of an agency of the United States Government may authorize the destruction of records in his legal custody situated in a military or naval establishment, ship, or other depository outside the territorial limits of continental United States—

(1) the retention of which would be prejudicial to the interests of the United States or

(2) which occupy space urgently needed for military purposes and are, in his opinion, without sufficient administrative, legal, research, or other value to warrant their continued preservation.

Within six months after their disposal, the official who directed the disposal shall submit a written report to the Administrator of General Services in which he shall describe the character of the records and state when and where he disposed of them.

Pub.L. 90–620, Oct. 22, 1968, 82 Stat. 1301.

§ 3312. Photographs or microphotographs of records considered as originals; certified reproductions admissible in evidence

Photographs or microphotographs of records made in compliance with regulations under section 3302 of this title shall have the same effect as the originals and shall be treated as originals for the purpose of their admissibility in evidence. Certified or authenticated reproductions of the photographs or microphotographs shall be admitted in evidence equally with the original photographs or microphotographs.

Pub.L. 90–620, Oct. 22, 1968, 82 Stat. 1302.

§ 3313. Moneys from sale of records payable into the Treasury

Money derived by agencies of the Government from the sale of records disposed of under this chapter shall be paid into the Treasury of the United States unless otherwise required by law.

Pub.L. 90–620, Oct. 22, 1968, 82 Stat. 1302.

§ 3314. Procedures for disposal of records exclusive

The procedures prescribed by this chapter are exclusive, and records of the United States Government may not be alienated or destroyed except under this chapter.

Pub.L. 90–620, Oct. 22, 1968, 82 Stat. 1302.

§ 3315. Definitions

For purposes of this section and section 3316 through section 3324 of this title—

(1) the term "Federal official" means any individual holding the office of President or Vice President of the United States, or Senator or Representative in, or Delegate or Resident Commissioner to, the Congress of the United States, or any officer of the executive, judicial, or legislative branch of the Federal Government;

(2) the term "Commission" means the National Study Commission on Records and Documents of Federal Officials; and

(3) the term "records and documents" shall include handwritten and typewritten documents, motion pictures, television tapes and recordings, magnetic tapes, automated data processing documentation in various forms, and other records that reveal the history of the Nation.

Added Pub.L. 93–526, Title II, § 202, Dec. 19, 1974, 88 Stat. 1698.

§ 3316. Establishment of Commission

There is established a commission to be known as the National Study Commission on Records and Documents of Federal Officials.

Added Pub.L. 93–526, Title II, § 202, Dec. 19, 1974, 88 Stat. 1699.

§ 3317. Duties of Commission

It shall be the duty of the Commission to study problems and questions with respect to the control, disposition, and preservation of records and documents produced by or on behalf of Federal officials, with a view toward the development of appropriate legislative recommendations and other recommendations regarding appropriate rules and procedures with respect to such control, disposition, and preservation. Such study shall include consideration of—

(1) whether the historical practice regarding the records and documents produced by or on behalf of Presidents of the United States should be rejected or accepted and whether such practice should be made applicable with respect to all Federal officials;

(2) the relationship of the findings of the Commission to the provisions of chapter 19 of this title, section 2101 through section 2108 of this title, and other Federal laws relating to the control, disposition, and preservation of records and documents of Federal officials;

(3) whether the findings of the Commission should affect the control, disposition, and preservation of records and documents of agencies within the Executive Office of the President created for short-term purposes by the President;

(4) the recordkeeping procedures of the White House Office, with a view toward establishing means to determine which records and documents are produced by or on behalf of the President;

(5) the nature of rules and procedures which should apply to the control, disposition, and preservation of records and documents produced by Presidential task forces, commissions, and boards;

(6) criteria which may be used generally in determining the scope of materials which should be considered to be the records and documents of Members of the Congress;

(7) the privacy interests of individuals whose communications with Federal officials, and with task forces, commissions, and boards, are a part of the records and documents produced by such officials, task forces, commissions, and boards; and

(8) any other problems, questions, or issues which the Commission considers relevant to carrying out its duties under section 3315 through section 3324 of this title.

Added Pub.L. 93–526, Title II, § 202, Dec. 19, 1974, 88 Stat. 1699.

§ 3318. Membership

(a)(1) The Commission shall be composed of seventeen members as follows:

(A) one Member of the House of Representatives appointed by the Speaker of the House upon recommendation made by the majority leader of the House;

(B) one Member of the House of Representatives appointed by the Speaker of the House upon recommendation made by the minority leader of the House;

(C) one Member of the Senate appointed by the President pro tempore of the Senate upon recommendation made by the majority leader of the Senate;

(D) one Member of the Senate appointed by the President pro tempore of the Senate upon recommendation made by the minority leader of the Senate;

(E) one member of the Federal judiciary appointed by the Chief Justice of the United States;

(F) one person employed by the Executive Office of the President or the White House Office, appointed by the President;

(G) three appointed by the President, by and with the advice and consent of the Senate, from persons who are not officers or employees of any government and who are specially qualified to serve on the Commission by virtue of their education, training, or experience;

(H) one representative of the Department of State, appointed by the Secretary of State;

(I) one representative of the Department of Defense, appointed by the Secretary of Defense;

(J) one representative of the Department of Justice, appointed by the Attorney General;

(K) the Administrator of General Services (or his delegate);

(L) the Librarian of Congress;

(M) one member of the American Historical Association, appointed by the counsel of such Association;

(N) one member of the Society of American Archivists, appointed by such Society; and

(O) one member of the Organization of American Historians, appointed by such Organization.

(2) No more than two members appointed under paragraph (1)(G) may be of the same political party.

(b) A vacancy in the Commission shall be filled in the manner in which the original appointment was made.

(c) If any member of the Commission who was appointed to the Commission as a Member of the Congress leave such office, or if any member of the Commission who was appointed from persons who are not officers or employees of any government becomes an officer or employee of a government, he may continue as a member of the Commission for no longer than the sixty-day period beginning on the date he leaves such office or becomes such an officer or employee, as the case may be.

(d) Members shall be appointed for the life of the Commission.

(e)(1) Members of the Commission shall serve without pay.

(2) While away from their homes or regular places of business in the performance of services for the Commission, members of the Commission shall be allowed travel expenses in the same manner as persons employed intermittently in the service of the Federal Government are allowed expenses under section 5703 of title 5, United States Code, except that per diem in lieu of subsistence shall be paid only to those members of the Commission who are not full-time officers or employees of the United States or Members of the Congress.

(f) The Chairman of the Commission shall be designated by the President from among members appointed under subsection (a)(1)(G).

(g) The Commission shall meet at the call of the Chairman or a majority of its members.

Added Pub.L. 93–526, Title II, § 202, Dec. 19, 1974, 88 Stat. 1699, and amended Pub.L. 94–261, 1(a), Apr. 11, 1976, 90 Stat. 326.

§ 3319. Director and staff; experts and consultants

(a) The Commission shall appoint a Director who shall be paid at a rate not to exceed the rate of basic pay in effect for level V of the Executive Schedule (5 U.S.C. 5316).

(b) The Commission may appoint and fix the pay of such additional personnel as it deems necessary.

(c)(1) The Commission may procure temporary and intermittent services to the same extent as is authorized by section 3109(b) of title 5, United States Code, but at rates for individuals not to exceed the daily equivalent of the annual rate of basic pay in effect for grade GS–15 of the General Schedule (5 U.S.C. 5332).

(2) In procuring services under this subsection, the Commission shall seek to obtain the advice and assistance of constitutional scholars and members of the historical, archival, and journalistic professions.

(d) Upon request of the Commission, the head of any Federal agency is authorized to detail, on a reimbursable basis, any of the personnel of such agency to the Commission to assist it in carrying out its duties under sections 3315 through 3324 of this title.

Added Pub.L. 93–526, Title II, § 202, Dec. 19, 1974, 88 Stat. 1701.

§ 3320. Powers of Commission

(a) The Commission may, for the purpose of carrying out its duties under sections 3315 through 3324 of this title, hold such hearings. sit and act at such times and places, take such testimony, and receive such evidence, as the Commission may deem desirable.

(b) When so authorized by the Commission, any member or agent of the Commission may take any action which the Commission is authorized to take by this section.

(c) The Commission may secure directly from any department or agency of the United States information necessary to enable the Commission to carry out its duties under section 3315 through section 3324 of this title. Upon request of the Chairman of the Commission, the head of such department or agency shall furnish such information to the Commission.

Added Pub.L. 93–526, Title II, § 202, Dec. 19, 1974, 88 Stat. 1701.

§ 3321. Support services

(a) The Administrator of General Services shall provide to the Commission on a reimbursable basis such administrative support services and assistance as the Commission may request.

(b) The Archivist of the United States shall provide to the Commission on a reimbursable basis such technical and expert advice, consultation, and support assistance as the Commission may request.

Added Pub.L. 93–526, Title II, § 202, Dec. 19, 1974, 88 Stat. 1701.

§ 3322. Report

The Commission shall transmit to the President and to each House of the Congress a report not later than March 31, 1977. Such report shall contain a detailed statement of the findings and conclusions of the Commission, together with its recommendations for such legislation, administrative actions, and other actions, as it deems appropriate.

Added Pub.L. 93–526, Title II, § 202, Dec. 19, 1974, 88 Stat. 1701, and amended Pub.L. 94–261, § 1(b), Apr. 11, 1976, 90 Stat. 326.

§ 3323. Termination

The Commission shall cease to exist sixty days after transmitting its report under section 3322 of this title.

Added Pub.L. 93–526, Title II, § 202, Dec. 19, 1974, 88 Stat. 1701.

§ 3324. Authorization of appropriations

There is authorized to be appropriated such sums as may be necessary to carry out section 3315 through section 3324 of this title.

Added Pub.L. 93–526, Title II, § 202, Dec. 19, 1974, 88 Stat. 1701.

PRESIDENTIAL RECORDS

(United States Code Annotated, 1982, Title 44, s.2201-2207.)

§ 2201. **Definitions**

As used in this chapter—

(1) The term "documentary material" means all books, correspondence, memorandums, documents, papers, pamphlets, works of art, models, pictures, photographs, plats, maps, films, and motion pictures, including, but not limited to, audio, audiovisual, or other electronic or mechanical recordations.

(2) The term "Presidential records" means documentary materials, or any reasonably segregable portion thereof, created or received by the President, his immediate staff, or a unit or individual of the Executive Office of the President whose function is to advise and assist the President, in the course of conducting activities which relate to or have an effect upon the carrying out of the constitutional, statutory, or other official or ceremonial duties of the President. Such term—

(A) includes any documentary materials relating to the political activities of the President or members of his staff, but only if such activities relate to or have a direct effect upon the carrying out of constitutional, statutory, or other official or ceremonial duties of the President; but

(B) does not include any documentary materials that are (i) official records of an agency (as defined in section 552(e) of title 5, United States Code); (ii) personal records; (iii) stocks of publications and stationery; or (iv) extra copies of documents produced only for convenience of reference, when such copies are clearly so identified.

(3) The term "personal records" means all documentary materials, or any reasonably segregable portion theof,[1] of a purely private or nonpublic character which do not relate to or have an effect upon the carrying out of the constitutional, statutory, or other official or ceremonial duties of the President. Such term includes—

(A) diaries, journals, or other personal notes serving as the functional equivalent of a diary or journal which are not prepared or utilized for, or circulated or communicated in the course of, transacting Government business;

(B) materials relating to private political associations, and having no relation to or direct effect upon the carrying out of constitutional, statutory, or other official or ceremonial duties of the President; and

(C) materials relating exclusively to the President's own election to the office of the Presidency; and materials directly relating to the election of a particular individual or individuals to Federal, State, or local office, which have no relation to or direct effect upon the carrying out of constitutional, statutory, or other official or ceremonial duties of the President.

(4) The term "Archivist" means the Archivist of the United States.

[1] So in original.

(5) The term "former President", when used with respect to Presidential records, means the former President during whose term or terms of office such Presidential records were created.
Added Pub.L. 95–591, § 2(a), Nov. 4, 1978, 92 Stat. 2523.

§ 2202. Ownership of Presidential records

The United States shall reserve and retain complete ownership, possession, and control of Presidential records; and such records shall be administered in accordance with the provisions of this chapter.
Added Pub.L. 95–591, § 2(a), Nov. 4, 1978, 92 Stat. 2524.

§ 2203. Management and custody of Presidential records

(a) Through the implementation of records management controls and other necessary actions, the President shall take all such steps as may be necessary to assure that the activities, deliberations, decisions, and policies that reflect the performance of his constitutional, statutory, or other official or ceremonial duties are adequately documented and that such records are maintained as Presidential records pursuant to the requirements of this section and other provisions of law.

(b) Documentary materials produced or received by the President, his staff, or units or individuals in the Executive Office of the President the function of which is to advise and assist the President, shall, to the extent practicable, be categorized as Presidential records or personal records upon their creation or receipt and be filed separately.

(c) During his term of office, the President may dispose of those of his Presidential records that no longer have administrative, historical, informational, or evidentiary value if—

(1) the President obtains the views, in writing, of the Archivist concerning the proposed disposal of such Presidential records; and

(2) the Archivist states that he does not intend to take any action under subsection (e) of this section.

(d) In the event the Archivist notifies the President under subsection (c) that he does intend to take action under subsection (e), the President may dispose of such Presidential records if copies of the disposal schedule are submitted to the appropriate Congressional Committees at least 60 calendar days of continuous session of Congress in advance of the proposed disposal date. For the purpose of this section, continuity of session is broken only by an adjournment of Congress sine die, and the days on which either House is not in session because of an adjournment of more than three days to a day certain are excluded in the computation of the days in which Congress is in continuous session.

(e) The Archivist shall request the advice of the Committee on Rules and Administration and the Committee on Governmental Affairs of the Senate and the Committee on House Administration and the Committee on Government Operations of the House of Representatives with respect to any proposed disposal of Presidential records whenever he considers that—

(1) these particular records may be of special interest to the Congress; or

(2) consultation with the Congress regarding the disposal of these particular records is in the public interest.

(f)(1) Upon the conclusion of a President's term of office, or if a President serves consecutive terms upon the conclusion of the last term, the Archivist of the United States shall assume responsibility for the custody, control, and preservation of, and access to, the Presidential records of that President. The Archivist shall have an affirmative duty to make such records available to the public as rapidly and completely as possible consistent with the provisions of this Act.

(2) The Archivist shall deposit all such Presidential records in a

Presidential archival depository or another archival facility operated by the United States. The Archivist is authorized to designate, after consultation with the former President, a director at each depository or facility, who shall be responsible for the care and preservation of such records.

(3) The Archivist is authorized to dispose of such Presidential records which he has appraised and determined to have insufficient administrative, historical, informational, or evidentiary value to warrant their continued preservation. Notice of such disposal shall be published in the Federal Register at least 60 days in advance of the proposed disposal date. Publication of such notice shall constitute a final agency action for purposes of review under chapter 7 of title 5, United States Code.

Added Pub.L. 95–591, § 2(a), Nov. 4, 1978, 92 Stat. 2524.

§ 2204. Restrictions on access to Presidential records

(a) Prior to the conclusion of his term of office or last consecutive term of office, as the case may be, the President shall specify durations, not to exceed 12 years, for which access shall be restricted with respect to information, in a Presidential record, within one or more of the following categories:

(1)(A) specifically authorized under criteria established by an Executive order to be kept secret in the interest of national defense or foreign policy and (B) in fact properly classified pursuant to such Executive order;

(2) relating to appointments to Federal office;

(3) specifically exempted from disclosure by statute (other than sections 552 and 552b of title 5, United States Code), provided that such statute (A) requires that the material be withheld from the public in such a manner as to leave no discretion on the issue, or (B) establishes particular criteria for withholding or refers to particular types of material to be withheld;

(4) trade secrets and commercial or financial information obtained from a person and privileged or confidential;

(5) confidential communications requesting or submitting advice, between the President and his advisers, or between such advisers; or

(6) personnel and medical files and similar files the disclosure of which would constitute a clearly unwarranted invasion of personal privacy.

(b)(1) Any Presidential record or reasonably segregable portion thereof containing information within a category restricted by the President under subsection (a) shall be so designated by the Archivist and access thereto shall be restricted until the earlier of—

(A)(i) the date on which the former President waives the restriction on disclosure of such record, or

(ii) the expiration of the duration specified under subsection (a) for the category of information on the basis of which access to such record has been restricted; or

(B) upon a determination by the Archivist that such record or reasonably segregable portion thereof, or of any significant element or aspect of the information contained in such record or reasonably segregable portion thereof, has been placed in the public domain through publication by the former President, or his agents.

(2) Any such record which does not contain information within a category restricted by the President under subsection (a), or contains information within such a category for which the duration of restricted access has expired, shall be exempt from the provisions of subsection (c) until the earlier of—

(A) the date which is 5 years after the date on which the Archivist obtains custody of such record pursuant to section 2203(d)(1); or

(B) the date on which the Archivist completes the processing and organization of such records or integral file segment thereof.

(3) During the period of restricted access specified pursuant to subsection (b)(1), the determination whether access to a Presidential record or reasonably segregable portion thereof shall be restricted shall be made by the Archivist, in his discretion, after consultation with the former President, and, during such period, such determinations shall not be subject to judicial review, except as provided in subsection (e) of this section. The Archivist shall establish procedures whereby any person denied access to a Presidential record because such record is restricted pursuant to a determination made under this paragraph, may file an administrative appeal of such determination. Such procedures shall provide for a written determination by the Archivist or his designee, within 30 working days after receipt of such an appeal, setting forth the basis for such determination.

(c)(1) Subject to the limitations on access imposed pursuant to subsections (a) and (b), Presidential records shall be administered in accordance with section 552 of title 5, United States Code, except that paragraph (b)(5) of that section shall not be available for purposes of withholding any Presidential record, and for the purposes of such section such records shall be deemed to be records of the National Archives and Records Service of the General Services Administration. Access to such records shall be granted on nondiscriminatory terms.

(2) Nothing in this Act shall be construed to confirm, limit, or expand any constitutionally-based privilege which may be available to an incumbent or former President.

(d) Upon the death or disability of a President or former President, any discretion or authority the President or former President may have had under this chapter shall be exercised by the Archivist unless otherwise previously provided by the President or former President in a written notice to the Archivist.

(e) The United States District Court for the District of Columbia shall have jurisdiction over any action initiated by the former President asserting that a determination made by the Archivist violates the former President's rights or privileges.

Added Pub.L. 95–591, § 2(a), Nov. 4, 1978, 92 Stat. 2525.

§ 2205. Exceptions to restricted access

Notwithstanding any restrictions on access imposed pursuant to section 2204—

(1) the Archivist and persons employed by the National Archives and Records Service of the General Services Administration who are engaged in the performance of normal archival work shall be permitted access to Presidential records in the custody of the Archivist;

(2) subject to any rights, defenses, or privileges which the United States or any agency or person may invoke, Presidential records shall be made available—

(A) pursuant to subpena or other judicial process issued by a court of competent jurisdiction for the purposes of any civil or criminal investigation or proceeding;

(B) to an incumbent President if such records contain information that is needed for the conduct of current business of his office and that is not otherwise available; and

(C) to either House of Congress, or, to the extent of matter within its jurisdiction, to any committee or subcommittee thereof if such records contain information that is needed for the conduct of its business and that is not otherwise available; and

(3) the Presidential records of a former President shall be available to such former President or his designated representative.

Added Pub.L. 95–591, § 2(a), Nov. 4, 1978, 92 Stat. 2527.

§ 2206. Regulations

The Archivist shall promulgate in accordance with section 553 of title 5, United States Code, regulations necessary to carry out the provisions of this chapter. Such regulations shall include—

(1) provisions for advance public notice and description of any Presidential records scheduled for disposal pursuant to section 2203 (f)(3);

(2) provisions for providing notice to the former President when materials to which access would otherwise be restricted pursuant to section 2204(a) are to be made available in accordance with section 2205(2);

(3) provisions for notice by the Archivist to the former President when the disclosure of particular documents may adversely affect any rights and privileges which the former President may have; and

(4) provisions for establishing procedures for consultation between the Archivist and appropriate Federal agencies regarding materials which may be subject to section 552(b)(7) of title 5, United States Code.

Added Pub.L. 95–591, § 2(a), Nov. 4, 1978, 92 Stat. 2527.

§ 2207. Vice-Presidential records

Vice-Presidential records shall be subject to the provisions of this chapter in the same manner as Presidential records. The duties and responsibilities of the Vice President, with respect to Vice-Presidential records, shall be the same as the duties and responsibilities of the President under this chapter with respect to Presidential records. The authority of the Archivist with respect to Vice-Presidential records shall be the same as the authority of the Archivist under this chapter with respect to Presidential records, except that the Archivist may, when the Archivist determines that it is in the public interest, enter into an agreement for the deposit of Vice-Presidential records in a non-Federal archival depository. Nothing in this chapter shall be construed to authorize the establishment of separate archival depositories for such Vice-Presidential records.

Added Pub.L. 95–591, § 2(a), Nov. 4, 1978, 92 Stat. 2527.

NATIONAL HISTORICAL PUBLICATIONS AND RECORDS COMMISSION

(United States Code Annotated, 1982, Title 24, s.2501-2507.)

§ 2501. Creation; composition; appointment and tenure

The National Historical Publications and Records Commission shall consist of the Archivist of the United States (or an alternate designated by him), who shall be Chairman; the Librarian of Congress (or an alternate designated by him); one Senator to be appointed, for a term of four years, by the President of the Senate; one Representative to be appointed, for a term of two years, by the Speaker of the House of Representatives; one member of the judicial branch of the Government to be appointed, for a term of four years, by the Chief Justice of the United States; one representative of the Department of State to be appointed, for a term of four years, by the Secretary of State; one representative of the Department of Defense to be appointed, for a term of four years, by the Secretary of Defense; two members of the American Historical Association to be appointed for terms of four years by the council of the Association; two members of the Organization of American Historians to be appointed for terms of four years by the Executive Board of the Organization, one of whom shall be appointed for an initial term of two years, and whose successors shall each serve four years; two members of the Society of American Archivists to be appointed, for terms of four years, by the Society of American Archivists; two members of the American Association for State and Local History to be appointed, for terms of four years, by the American Association for State and Local History; and two other members outstanding in the fields of the social or physical sciences to be appointed for terms of four years by the President of the United States.

The Commission shall meet annually and on call of the Chairman.

The authority of the Administrator of General Services under section 754 of title 40 to regroup, transfer, and distribute functions within the General Services Administration does not extend to the Commission or its functions.

As amended Pub.L. 92–546, § 1(a), Oct. 25, 1972, 86 Stat. 1155; Pub.L. 93–536, § 1(b), Dec. 22, 1974, 88 Stat. 1735; Pub.L. 96–98, § 2(b), Nov. 1, 1979, 93 Stat. 731.

§ 2502. Vacancies

A person appointed to fill a vacancy in the membership of the Commission shall be appointed only for the unexpired term of the member whom he succeeds, and his appointment shall be made in the same manner as the appointment of his predecessor.

Pub.L. 90–620, Oct. 22, 1968, 82 Stat. 1294.

§ 2503. Executive director; editorial and clerical staff; reimbursement of members for transportation expenses; honorarium

The Commission may appoint, without reference to chapter 51 of title 5, an executive director and such editorial and clerical staff as it determines to be necessary. Members of the Commission who represent a branch or agency of the Government shall serve as members of the Commission without additional compensation. All members of the Commission shall be reimbursed for transportation expenses incurred in attending meetings of the Commission, and members other than those who represent a branch or agency of the Government of the United States shall receive a per diem allowance in lieu of subsistence, as authorized by section 5703 of title 5, United States Code, for individuals in the Government serving without pay.

As amended Pub.L. 92–546, § 1(b), Oct. 25, 1972, 86 Stat. 1155; Pub.L. 96–98, § 2(a), Nov. 1, 1979, 93 Stat. 731.

§ 2504. Duties; authorization of grants for collection, reproduction, and publication of documentary historical source material

(a) The Commission shall make plans, estimates, and recommendations for historical works and collections of sources, it considers appropriate for printing or otherwise recording at the public expense. It shall also cooperate with and encourage appropriate Federal, State, and local agencies and nongovernmental institutions, societies, and individuals in collecting and preserving and, when it considers it desirable, in editing and publishing the papers of outstanding citizens of the United States, and other documents as may be important for an understanding and appreciation of the history of the United States. The Administrator of General Services may, within the limits of available appropriated and donated funds, make allocations to Federal agencies, and grants to State and local agencies and to non-profit organizations and institutions, for the collecting, describing, preserving and compiling, and publishing (including microfilming and other forms of reproduction) of documentary sources significant to the history of the United States. Before making allocations and grants, the Administrator should seek the advice and recommendations of the National Historical Publications Commission. The Chairman of the Commission shall transmit to the Administrator from time to time, and at least annually, plans, estimates, and recommendations approved by the Commission.

(b) There is hereby authorized to be appropriated to the General Services Administration for the fiscal year ending September 30, 1981, an amount not to exceed $4,000,000 for the purposes specified in subsection (a) of this section: *Provided,* That such appropriations shall be available until expended when so provided in appropriation Acts.

As amended Pub.L. 92–546, § 1(c), Oct. 25, 1972, 86 Stat. 1155; Pub.L. 93–536, § 1(c), Dec. 22, 1974, 88 Stat. 1735; Pub.L. 96–98, § 1, Nov. 1, 1979, 93 Stat. 731.

§ 2505. Special advisory committees; membership; reimbursement

The Commission may establish special advisory committees to consult with and make recommendations to it, from among the leading historians, political scientists, archivists, librarians, and other specialists of the Nation. Members of special advisory committees shall be reimbursed for transportation and other expenses on the same basis as members of the Commission.

Pub.L. 90–620, Oct. 22, 1968, 82 Stat. 1294.

§ 2506. Records to be kept by grantees

(a) Each recipient of grant assistance under section 2504 of this title shall keep such records as the Administrator of General Services prescribes, including records which fully disclose the amount and disposition by the recipient of the proceeds of the grants, the total cost of the project or undertaking in connection with which funds are given or used, and the amount of that portion of the cost of the project or undertaking supplied by other sources, and any other records as will facilitate an effective audit.

(b) The Administrator and the Comptroller General of the United States or their authorized representatives shall have access for the purposes of audit and examination to books, documents, papers, and

§ 2507.   Report to Congress

The Administrator of General Services shall make an annual report to the Congress concerning projects undertaken and carried out under section 2504 of this title, including detailed information concerning the receipt and use of all appropriated and donated funds made available to him.

Pub.L. 90–620, Oct. 22, 1968, 82 Stat. 1295.

FEDERAL INFORMATION POLICY

(United States Code Annotated, 1982, Title 44, s.3501-3520.)

§ 3501. Purpose

The purpose of this chapter is—

(1) to minimize the Federal paperwork burden for individuals, small businesses, State and local governments, and other persons;

(2) to minimize the cost to the Federal Government of collecting, maintaining, using, and disseminating information;

(3) to maximize the usefulness of information collected by the Federal Government;

(4) to coordinate, integrate and, to the extent practicable and appropriate, make uniform Federal information policies and practices;

(5) to ensure that automatic data processing and telecommunications technologies are acquired and used by the Federal Government in a manner which improves service delivery and program management, increases productivity, reduces waste and fraud, and, wherever practicable and appropriate, reduces the information processing burden for the Federal Government and for persons who provide information to the Federal Government; and

(6) to ensure that the collection, maintenance, use and dissemination of information by the Federal Government is consistent with applicable laws relating to confidentiality, including section 552a of title 5, United States Code, known as the Privacy Act.

Added Pub.L. 96–511, § 2(a), Dec. 11, 1980, 94 Stat. 2812.

§ 3502. Definitions

As used in this chapter—

(1) the term "agency" means any executive department, military department, Government corporation, Government controlled corporation, or other establishment in the executive branch of the Government (including the Executive Office of the President), or any independent regulatory agency, but does not include the General Accounting Office, Federal Election Commission, the governments of the District of Columbia and of the territories and possessions of the United States, and their various subdivisions, or Government-owned contractor-operated facilities including laboratories engaged in national defense research and production activities;

(2) the terms "automatic data processing," "automatic data processing equipment," and "telecommunications" do not include any data processing or telecommunications system or equipment, the function, operation or use of which—

(A) involves intelligence activities;

(B) involves cryptologic activities related to national security;

(C) involves the direct command and control of military forces;

(D) involves equipment which is an integral part of a weapon or weapons system; or

(E) is critical to the direct fulfillment of military or intelligence missions, provided that this exclusion shall not include automatic data processing or telecommunications equipment used for routine administrative and business applications such as payroll, finance, logistics, and personnel management;

(3) the term "burden" means the time, effort, or financial resources expended by persons to provide information to a Federal agency;

(4) the term "collection of information" means the obtaining or soliciting of facts or opinions by an agency through the use of written report forms, application forms, schedules, questionnaires, reporting or recordkeeping requirements, or other similar methods calling for either—

(A) answers to identical questions posed to, or identical reporting or recordkeeping requirements imposed on, ten or more persons, other than agencies, instrumentalities, or employees of the United States; or

(B) answers to questions posed to agencies, instrumentalities, or employees of the United States which are to be used for general statistical purposes;

(5) the term "data element" means a distinct piece of information such as a name, term, number, abbreviation, or symbol;

(6) the term "data element dictionary" means a system containing standard and uniform definitions and cross references for commonly used data elements;

(7) the term "data profile" means a synopsis of the questions contained in an information collection request and the official name of the request, the location of information obtained or to be obtained through the request, a description of any compilations, analyses, or reports derived or to be derived from such information, any record retention requirements associated with the request, the agency responsible for the request, the statute authorizing the request, and any other information necessary to identify, obtain, or use the data contained in such information;

(8) the term "Director" means the Director of the Office of Management and Budget;

(9) the term "directory of information resources" means a catalog of information collection requests, containing a data profile for each request;

(10) the term "independent regulatory agency" means the Board of Governors of the Federal Reserve System, the Civil Aeronautics Board, the Commodity Futures Trading Commission, the Consumer Product Safety Commission, the Federal Communications Commission, the Federal Deposit Insurance Corporation, the Federal Energy Regulatory Commission, the Federal Home Loan Bank Board, the Federal Maritime Commission, the Federal Trade Commission, the Interstate Commerce Commission, the Mine Enforcement Safety and Health Review Commission, the National Labor Relations Board, the Nuclear Regulatory Commission, the Occupational Safety and Health Review Commission, the Postal Rate Commission, the Securities and Exchange Commission, and any other similar agency designated by statute as a Federal independent regulatory agency or commission:

(11) the term "information collection request" means a written report form, application form, schedule, questionnaire, reporting or recordkeeping requirement, or other similar method calling for the collection of information;

(12) the term "information referral service" means the function that assists officials and persons in obtaining access to the Federal Information Locator System;

(13) the term "information systems" means management information systems;

(14) the term "person" means an individual, partnership, association, corporation, business trust, or legal representative, an organized group of individuals, a State, territorial, or local government or branch thereof, or a political subdivision of a State, territory, or local government or a branch of a political subdivision;

(15) the term "practical utility" means the ability of an agency to use information it collects, particularly the capability to process such information in a timely and useful fashion; and

(16) the term "recordkeeping requirement" means a requirement imposed by an agency on persons to maintain specified records.

Added Pub.L. 96–511, § 2(a), Dec. 11, 1980, 94 Stat. 2813.

§ 3503. Office of Information and Regulatory Affairs

(a) There is established in the Office of Management and Budget an office to be known as the Office of Information and Regulatory Affairs.

(b) There shall be at the head of the Office an Administrator who shall be appointed by, and who shall report directly to, the Director. The Director shall delegate to the Administrator the authority to administer all functions under this chapter, except that any such delegation shall not relieve the Director of responsibility for the administration of such functions. The Administrator shall serve as principal adviser to the Director on Federal information policy.

Added Pub.L. 96–511, § 2(a), Dec. 11, 1980, 94 Stat. 2814.

§ 3504. Authority and functions of Director

(a) The Director shall develop and implement Federal information policies, principles, standards, and guidelines and shall provide direction and oversee the review and approval of information collection requests, the reduction of the paperwork burden, Federal statistical activities, records management activities, privacy of records, interagency sharing of information, and acquisition and use of automatic data processing telecommunications, and other technology for managing information resources. The authority under this section shall be exercised consistent with applicable law.

(b) The general information policy functions of the Director shall include—

(1) developing and implementing uniform and consistent information resources management policies and overseeing the development of information management principles, standards, and guidelines and promoting their use;

(2) initiating and reviewing proposals for changes in legislation, regulations, and agency procedures to improve information practices, and informing the President and the Congress on the progress made therein;

(3) coordinating, through the review of budget proposals and as otherwise provided in this section, agency information practices;

(4) promoting, through the use of the Federal Information Locator System, the review of budget proposals and other methods, greater sharing of information by agencies;

(5) evaluating agency information management practices to determine their adequacy and efficiency, and to determine compliance of such practices with the policies, principles, standards, and guidelines promulgated by the Director; and

(6) overseeing planning for, and conduct of research with respect

to, Federal collection, processing, storage, transmission, and use of information.

(c) The information collection request clearance and other paperwork control functions of the Director shall include—

(1) reviewing and approving information collection requests proposed by agencies;

(2) determining whether the collection of information by an agency is necessary for the proper performance of the functions of the agency, including whether the information will have practical utility for the agency;

(3) ensuring that all information collection requests—

(A) are inventoried, display a control number and, when appropriate, an expiration date;

(B) indicate the request is in accordance with the clearance requirements of section 3507; and

(C) contain a statement to inform the person receiving the request why the information is being collected, how it is to be used, and whether responses to the request are voluntary, required to obtain a benefit, or mandatory;

(4) designating as appropriate, in accordance with section 3509, a collection agency to obtain information for two or more agencies;

(5) setting goals for reduction of the burdens of Federal information collection requests;

(6) overseeing action on the recommendations of the Commission on Federal Paperwork; and

(7) designing and operating, in accordance with section 3511, the Federal Information Locator System.

(d) The statistical policy and coordination functions of the Director shall include—

(1) developing long range plans for the improved performance of Federal statistical activities and programs;

(2) coordinating, through the review of budget proposals and as otherwise provided in this section, the functions of the Federal Government with respect to gathering, interpreting, and disseminating statistics and statistical information;

(3) developing and implementing Government-wide policies, principles, standards, and guidelines concerning statistical collection procedures and methods, statistical data classifications, and statistical information presentation and dissemination; and

(4) evaluating statistical program performance and agency compliance with Government-wide policies, principles, standards, and guidelines.

(e) The records management functions of the Director shall include—

(1) providing advice and assistance to the Administrator of General Services in order to promote coordination in the administration of chapters 29, 31, and 33 of this title with the information policies, principles, standards, and guidelines established under this chapter;

(2) reviewing compliance by agencies with the requirements of chapters 29, 31, and 33 of this title and with regulations promulgated by the Administrator of General Services thereunder; and

(3) coordinating records management policies and programs with related information programs such as information collection, statistics, automatic data processing and telecommunications, and similar activities.

(f) The privacy functions of the Director shall include—

(1) developing and implementing policies, principles, standards, and guidelines on information disclosure and confidentiality, and on safeguarding the security of information collected or maintained by or on behalf of agencies;

(2) providing agencies with advice and guidance about informa-

tion security, restriction, exchange, and disclosure; and

(3) monitoring compliance with section 552a of title 5, United States Code, and related information management laws.

(g) The Federal automatic data processing and telecommunications functions of the Director shall include—

(1) developing and implementing policies, principles, standards, and guidelines for automatic data processing and telecommunications functions and activities of the Federal Government, and overseeing the establishment of standards under section 111(f) of the Federal Property and Administrative Services Act of 1949;

(2) monitoring the effectiveness of, and compliance with, directives issued pursuant to sections 110 and 111 of such Act of 1949 and reviewing proposed determinations under section 111(g) of such Act;

(3) providing advice and guidance on the acquisition and use of automatic data processing and telecommunications equipment, and coordinating, through the review of budget proposals and other methods, agency proposals for acquisition and use of such equipment;

(4) promoting the use of automatic data processing and telecommunications equipment by the Federal Government to improve the effectiveness of the use and dissemination of data in the operation of Federal programs; and

(5) initiating and reviewing proposals for changes in legislation, regulations, and agency procedures to improve automatic data processing and telecommunications practices, and informing the President and the Congress of the progress made therein.

(h)(1) As soon as practicable, but no later than publication of a notice of proposed rulemaking in the Federal Register, each agency shall forward to the Director a copy of any proposed rule which contains a collection of information requirement and upon request, information necessary to make the determination required pursuant to this section.

(2) Within sixty days after the notice of proposed rulemaking is published in the Federal Register, the Director may file public comments pursuant to the standards set forth in section 3508 on the collection of information requirement contained in the proposed rule.

(3) When a final rule is published in the Federal Register, the agency shall explain how any collection of information requirement contained in the final rule responds to the comments, if any, filed by the Director or the public, or explain why it rejected those comments.

(4) The Director has no authority to disapprove any collection of information requirement specifically contained in an agency rule, if he has received notice and failed to comment on the rule within sixty days of the notice of proposed rulemaking.

(5) Nothing in this section prevents the Director, in his discretion—

(A) from disapproving any information collection request which was not specifically required by an agency rule;

(B) from disapproving any collection of information requirement contained in an agency rule, if the agency failed to comply with the requirements of paragraph (1) of this subsection; or

(C) from disapproving any collection of information requirement contained in a final agency rule, if the Director finds within sixty days of the publication of the final rule that the agency's response to his comments filed pursuant to paragraph (2) of this subsection was unreasonable.

(D) from disapproving any collection of information requirement where the Director determines that the agency has substantially modified in the final rule the collection of information requirement contained in the proposed rule where the agency has not given the Director the information required in paragraph (1), with respect to the modified collection of information requirement, at least sixty days before the issuance of the final rule.

(6) The Director shall make publicly available any decision to disapprove a collection of information requirement contained in an agency rule, together with the reasons for such decision.

(7) The authority of the Director under this subsection is subject to the provisions of section 3507(c).

(8) This subsection shall apply only when an agency publishes a notice of proposed rulemaking and requests public comments.

(9) There shall be no judicial review of any kind of the Director's decision to approve or not to act upon a collection of information requirement contained in an agency rule.

Added Pub.L. 96–511, § 2(a), Dec. 11, 1980, 94 Stat. 2815.

§ 3505. Assignment of tasks and deadlines

In carrying out the functions under this chapter, the Director shall—

(1) upon enactment of this Act—

(A) set a goal to reduce the then existing burden of Federal collections of information by 15 per centum by October 1, 1982; and

(B) for the year following, set a goal to reduce the burden which existed upon enactment by an additional 10 per centum;

(2) within one year after the effective date of this Act—

(A) establish standards and requirements for agency audits of all major information systems and assign responsibility for conducting Government-wide or multiagency audits, except the Director shall not assign such responsibility for the audit of major information systems used for the conduct of criminal investigations or intelligence activities as defined in section 4–206 of Executive Order 12036, issued January 24, 1978, or successor orders, or for cryptologic activities that are communications security activities;

(B) establish the Federal Information Locator System;

(C) identify areas of duplication in information collection requests and develop a schedule and methods for eliminating duplication;

(D) develop a proposal to augment the Federal Information Locator System to include data profiles of major information holdings of agencies (used in the conduct of their operations) which are not otherwise required by this chapter to be included in the System; and

(E) identify initiatives which may achieve a 10 per centum reduction in the burden of Federal collections of information associated with the administration of Federal grant programs; and

(3) within two years after the effective date of this Act—

(A) establish a schedule and a management control system to ensure that practices and programs of information handling disciplines, including records management, are appropriately integrated with the information policies mandated by this chapter;

(B) identifying initiatives to improve productivity in Federal operations using information processing technology;

(C) develop a program to (i) enforce Federal information processing standards, particularly software language standards, at all Federal installations; and (ii) revitalize the standards development program established pursuant to section 759(f)(2) of title 40, United States Code, separating it from peripheral technical assistance functions and directing it to the most productive areas;

(D) complete action on recommendations of the Commission on Federal Paperwork by implementing, implementing with modification or rejecting such recommendations including, where necessary, development of legislation to implement such recommendations;

(E) develop, in consultation with the Administrator of General Services, a five-year plan for meeting the automatic data processing and telecommunications needs of the Federal Government in accordance with the requirements of section 111 of the Federal Property and Administrative Services Act of 1949 (40 U.S.C. 759) and the purposes of this chapter; and

(F) submit to the President and the Congress legislative proposals to remove inconsistencies in laws and practices involving privacy, confidentiality, and disclosure of information.

Added Pub.L. 96–511, § 2(a), Dec. 11, 1980, 94 Stat. 2818.

§ 3506. Federal agency responsibilities

(a) Each agency shall be responsible for carrying out its information management activities in an efficient, effective, and economical manner, and for complying with the information policies, principles, standards, and guidelines prescribed by the Director.

(b) The head of each agency shall designate, within three months after the effective date of this Act, a senior official or, in the case of military departments, and the Office of the Secretary of Defense, officials who report directly to such agency head to carry out the responsibilities of the agency under this chapter. If more than one official is appointed for the military departments the respective duties of the officials shall be clearly delineated.

(c) Each agency shall—

(1) systematically inventory its major information systems and periodically review its information management activities, including planning, budgeting, organizing, directing, training, promoting, controlling, and other managerial activities involving the collection, use, and dissemination of information;

(2) ensure its information systems do not overlap each other or duplicate the systems of other agencies;

(3) develop procedures for assessing the paperwork and reporting burden of proposed legislation affecting such agency;

(4) assign to the official designated under subsection (b) the responsibility for the conduct of and accountability for any acquisitions made pursuant to a delegation of authority under section 111 of the Federal Property and Administrative Services Act of 1949 (40 U.S.C. 759); and

(5) ensure that information collection requests required by law or to obtain a benefit, and submitted to nine or fewer persons, contain a statement to inform the person receiving the request that the request is not subject to the requirements of section 3507 of this chapter.

(d) The head of each agency shall establish such procedures as necessary to ensure the compliance of the agency with the requirements of the Federal Information Locator System, including necessary screening and compliance activities.

Added Pub.L. 96–511, § 2(a), Dec. 11, 1980, 94 Stat. 2819.

§ 3507. Public information collection activities—Submission to Director; approval and delegation

(a) An agency shall not conduct or sponsor the collection of information unless, in advance of the adoption or revision of the request for collection of such information—

(1) the agency has taken actions, including consultation with the Director, to—

(A) eliminate, through the use of the Federal Information Locator System and other means, information collections which seek to obtain information available from another source within the Federal Government;

(B) reduce to the extent practicable and appropriate the burden on persons who will provide information to the agency; and

(C) formulate plans for tabulating the information in a manner which will enhance its usefulness to other agencies and to the public;

(2) the agency (A) has submitted to the Director the proposed information collection request, copies of pertinent regulations and other related materials as the Director may specify, and an explanation of actions taken to carry out paragraph (1) of this subsection, and (B) has prepared a notice to be published in the Federal Register stating that the agency has made such submission; and

(3) the Director has approved the proposed information collection request, or the period for review of information collection requests by the Director provided under subsection (b) has elapsed.

(b) The Director shall, within sixty days of receipt of a proposed information collection request, notify the agency involved of the decision to approve or disapprove the request and shall make such decisions publicly available. If the Director determines that a request submitted for review cannot be reviewed within sixty days, the Director may, after notice to the agency involved, extend the review period for an additional thirty days. If the Director does not notify the agency of an extension, denial, or approval within sixty days (or, if the Director has extended the review period for an additional thirty days and does not notify the agency of a denial or approval within the time of the extension), a control number shall be assigned without further delay, the approval may be inferred, and the agency may collect the information for not more than one year.

(c) Any disapproval by the Director, in whole or in part, of a proposed information collection request of an independent regulatory agency, or an exercise of authority under section 3504(h) or 3509 concerning such an agency, may be voided, if the agency by a majority vote of its members overrides the Director's disapproval or exercise of authority. The agency shall certify each override to the Director, shall explain the reasons for exercising the override authority. Where the override concerns an information collection request, the Director shall without further delay assign a control number to such request, and such override shall be valid for a period of three years.

(d) The Director may not approve an information collection request for a period in excess of three years.

(e) If the Director finds that a senior official of an agency designated pursuant to section 3506(b) is sufficiently independent of program responsibility to evaluate fairly whether proposed information collection requests should be approved and has sufficient resources to carry out this responsibility effectively, the Director may, by rule in accordance with the notice and comment provisions of chapter 5 of title 5, United States Code, delegate to such official the authority to approve proposed requests in specific program areas, for specific purposes, or for all agency purposes. A delegation by the Director under this section shall not preclude the Director from reviewing individual information collection requests if the Director determines that circumstances warrant such a review. The

Director shall retain authority to revoke such delegations, both in general and with regard to any specific matter. In acting for the Director, any official to whom approval authority has been delegated under this section shall comply fully with the rules and regulations promulgated by the Director.

(f) An agency shall not engage in a collection of information without obtaining from the Director a control number to be displayed upon the information collection request.

(g) If an agency head determines a collection of information (1) is needed prior to the expiration of the sixty-day period for the review of information collection requests established pursuant to subsection (b), (2) is essential to the mission of the agency, and (3) the agency cannot reasonably comply with the provisions of this chapter within such sixty-day period because (A) public harm will result if normal clearance procedures are followed, or (B) an unanticipated event has occurred and the use of normal clearance procedures will prevent or disrupt the collection of information related to the event or will cause a statutory deadline to be missed, the agency head may request the Director to authorize such collection of information prior to expiration of such sixty-day period. The Director shall approve or disapprove any such authorization request within the time requested by the agency head and, if approved, shall assign the information collection request a control number. Any collection of information conducted pursuant to this subsection may be conducted without compliance with the provisions of this chapter for a maximum of ninety days after the date on which the Director received the request to authorize such collection.

Added Pub.L. 96–511, § 2(a), Dec. 11, 1980, 94 Stat. 2819.

§ 3508. Determination of necessity for information; hearing

Before approving a proposed information collection request, the Director shall determine whether the collection of information by an agency is necessary for the proper performance of the functions of the agency, including whether the information will have practical utility. Before making a determination the Director may give the agency and other interested persons an opportunity to be heard or to submit statements in writing. To the extent, if any, that the Director determines that the collection of information by an agency is unnecessary, for any reason, the agency may not engage in the collection of the information.

Added Pub.L. 96–511, § 2(a), Dec. 11, 1980, 94 Stat. 2821.

§ 3509. Designation of central collection agency

The Director may designate a central collection agency to obtain information for two or more agencies if the Director determines that the needs of such agencies for information will be adequately served by a single collection agency, and such sharing of data is not inconsistent with any applicable law. In such cases the Director shall prescribe (with reference to the collection of information) the duties and functions of the collection agency so designated and of the agencies for which it is to act as agent (including reimbursement for costs). While the designation is in effect, an agency covered by it may not obtain for itself information which it is the duty of the collection agency to obtain. The Director may modify the designation from time to time as circumstances require. The authority herein is subject to the provisions of section 3507(c) of this chapter.

Added Pub.L. 96–511, § 2(a), Dec. 11, 1980, 94 Stat. 2821.

§ 3510. Cooperation of agencies in making information available

(a) The Director may direct an agency to make available to another agency, or an agency may make available to another agency, information obtained pursuant to an information collection request if the disclosure is not inconsistent with any applicable law.

(b) If information obtained by an agency is released by that agency to another agency, all the provisions of law (including penalties which relate to the unlawful disclosure of information) apply to the officers and employees of the agency to which information is released to the same extent and in the same manner as the provisions apply to the officers and employees of the agency which originally obtained the information. The officers and employees of the agency to which the information is released, in addition, shall be subject to the same provisions of law, including penalties, relating to the unlawful disclosure of information as if the information had been collected directly by that agency.

Added Pub.L. 96–511, § 2(a), Dec. 11, 1980, 94 Stat. 2822.

§ 3511. Establishment and operation of Federal Information Locator System

(a) There is established in the Office of Information and Regulatory Affairs a Federal Information Locator System (hereafter in this section referred to as the "System") which shall be composed of a directory of information resources, a data element dictionary, and an information referral service. The System shall serve as the authoritative register of all information collection requests.

(b) In designing and operating the System, the Director shall—

(1) design and operate an indexing system for the System;

(2) require the head of each agency to prepare in a form specified by the Director, and to submit to the Director for inclusion in the System, a data profile for each information collection request of such agency;

(3) compare data profiles for proposed information collection requests against existing profiles in the System, and make available the results of such comparison to—

(A) agency officials who are planning new information collection activities; and

(B) on request, members of the general public; and

(4) ensure that no actual data, except descriptive data profiles necessary to identify duplicative data or to locate information, are contained within the System.

Added Pub.L. 96–511, § 2(a), Dec. 11, 1980, 94 Stat. 2822.

§ 3512. Public protection

Notwithstanding any other provision of law, no person shall be subject to any penalty for failing to maintain or provide information to any agency if the information collection request involved was made after December 31, 1981, and does not display a current control number assigned by the Director, or fails to state that such request is not subject to this chapter.

§ 3513. Director review of agency activities; reporting; agency response

(a) The Director shall, with the advice and assistance of the Administrator of General Services, selectively review, at least once every three years, the information management activities of each agency to ascertain their adequacy and efficiency. In evaluating the adequacy and efficiency of such activities, the Director shall pay particular attention to whether the agency has complied with section 3506.

(b) The Director shall report the results of the reviews to the appropriate agency head, the House Committee on Government Operations, the Senate Committee on Governmental Affairs, the House and Senate Committees on Appropriations, and the committees of the Congress having jurisdiction over legislation relating to the operations of the agency involved.

(c) Each agency which receives a report pursuant to subsection (b) shall, within sixty days after receipt of such report, prepare and transmit to the Director, the House Committee on Government Operations, the Senate Committee on Governmental Affairs, the House and Senate Committees on Appropriations, and the committees of the Congress having jurisdiction over legislation relating to the operations of the agency, a written statement responding to the Director's report, including a description of any measures taken to alleviate or remove any problems or deficiencies identified in such report.

Added Pub.L. 96–511, § 2(a), Dec. 11, 1980, 94 Stat. 2822.

§ 3514. Responsiveness to Congress

(a) The Director shall keep the Congress and its committees fully and currently informed of the major activities under this chapter, and shall submit a report thereon to the President of the Senate and the Speaker of the House of Representatives annually and at such other times as the Director determines necessary. The Director shall include in any such report—

(1) proposals for legislative action needed to improve Federal information management, including, with respect to information collection, recommendations to reduce the burden on individuals, small businesses, State and local governments, and other persons;

(2) a compilation of legislative impediments to the collection of information which the Director concludes that an agency needs but does not have authority to collect;

(3) an analysis by agency, and by categories the Director finds useful and practicable, describing the estimated reporting hours required of persons by information collection requests, including to the extent practicable the direct budgetary costs of the agencies and identification of statutes and regulations which impose the greatest number of reporting hours;

(4) a summary of accomplishments and planned initiatives to reduce burdens of Federal information collection requests;

(5) a tabulation of areas of duplication in agency information collection requests identified during the preceding year and efforts made to preclude the collection of duplicate information, including designations of central collection agencies;

(6) a list of each instance in which an agency engaged in the collection of information under the authority of section 3507(g) and an identification of each agency involved;

(7) a list of all violations of provisions of this chapter and rules, regulations, guidelines, policies, and procedures issued pursuant to this chapter; and

(8) with respect to recommendations of the Commission on Federal Paperwork—

(A) a description of the specific actions taken on or planned for each recommendation;

(B) a target date for implementing each recommendation accepted but not implemented; and

(C) an explanation of the reasons for any delay in completing action on such recommendations.

(b) The preparation of any report required by this section shall not increase the collection of information burden on persons outside the Federal Government.

Added Pub.L. 96–511, § 2(a), Dec. 11, 1980, 94 Stat. 2823.

§ 3515. Administrative powers

Upon the request of the Director, each agency (other than an independent regulatory agency) shall, to the extent practicable, make its services, personnel, and facilities available to the Director for the performance of functions under this chapter.
Added Pub.L. 96–511, § 2(a), Dec. 11, 1980, 94 Stat. 2824.

§ 3516. Rules and regulations

The Director shall promulgate rules, regulations, or procedures necessary to exercise the authority provided by this chapter.
Added Pub.L. 96–511, § 2(a), Dec. 11, 1980, 94 Stat. 2824.

§ 3517. Consultation with other agencies and the public

In development of information policies, plans, rules, regulations, procedures, and guidelines and in reviewing information collection requests, the Director shall provide interested agencies and persons early and meaningful opportunity to comment.
Added Pub.L. 96–511, § 2(a), Dec. 11, 1980, 94 Stat. 2824.

§ 3518. Effect on existing laws and regulations

(a) Except as otherwise provided in this chapter, the authority of an agency under any other law to prescribe policies, rules, regulations, and procedures for Federal information activities is subject to the authority conferred on the Director by this chapter.

(b) Nothing in this chapter shall be deemed to affect or reduce the authority of the Secretary of Commerce or the Director of the Office of Management and Budget pursuant to Reorganization Plan No. 1 of 1977 (as amended) and Executive order, relating to telecommunications and information policy, procurement and management of telecommunications and information systems, spectrum use, and related matters.

(c)(1) Except as provided in paragraph (2), this chapter does not apply to the collection of information—

(A) during the conduct of a Federal criminal investigation or prosecution, or during the disposition of a particular criminal matter;

(B) during the conduct of (i) a civil action to which the United States or any official or agency thereof is a party or (ii) an administrative action or investigation involving an agency against specific individuals or entities;

(C) by compulsory process pursuant to the Antitrust Civil Process Act and section 13 of the Federal Trade Commission Improvements Act of 1980; or

(D) during the conduct of intelligence activities as defined in section 4–206 of Executive Order 12036, issued January 24, 1978, or successor orders, or during the conduct of cryptologic activities that are communications security activities.

(2) This chapter applies to the collection of information during the conduct of general investigations (other than information collected in an antitrust investigation to the extent provided in subparagraph (C) of paragraph (1)) undertaken with reference to a category of individuals or entities such as a class of licensees or an entire industry.

(d) Nothing in this chapter shall be interpreted as increasing or decreasing the authority conferred by Public Law 89–306 on the Administrator of the General Services Administration, the Secretary of Commerce, or the Director of the Office of Management and Budget.

(e) Nothing in this chapter shall be interpreted as increasing or decreasing the authority of the President, the Office of Management and Budget or the Director thereof, under the laws of the United States, with respect to the substantive policies and programs of departments, agencies and offices, including the substantive authority of any Federal agency to enforce the civil rights laws.

Added Pub.L. 96–511, § 2(a), Dec. 11, 1980, 94 Stat. 2824.

§ 3519. Access to information

Under the conditions and procedures prescribed in section 313 of the Budget and Accounting Act of 1921, as amended, the Director and personnel in the Office of Information and Regulatory Affairs shall furnish such information as the Comptroller General may require for the discharge of his responsibilities. For this purpose, the Comptroller General or representatives thereof shall have access to all books, documents, papers and records of the Office.

Added Pub.L. 96–511, § 2(a), Dec. 11, 1980, 94 Stat. 2825.

§ 3520. Authorization of appropriations

There are hereby authorized to be appropriated to carry out the provisions of this chapter, and for no other purpose, sums—

(1) not to exceed $8,000,000 for the fiscal year ending September 30, 1981;

(2) not to exceed $8,500,000 for the fiscal year ending September 30, 1982; and

(3) not to exceed $9,000,000 for the fiscal year ending September 30, 1983.

Added Pub.L. 96–511, § 2(a), Dec. 11, 1980, 94 Stat. 2825.

MISCELLANEOUS PROVISIONS

GENERAL
(United States Code Annotated, 1982, Title 31, s.174, Title 15, s.13c,
Title 36, s.973, Title 20, s.91, 103, Title 16, s.4070.)

§ 174. Impressions of portraits

The Secretary of the Treasury, at the request of a Senator, Representative, or Delegate in Congress, the head of a department or bureau, art association, or library, may furnish impressions from any portrait or vignette which is now, or may be a part of the engraved stock of the Bureau of Engraving and Printing, at such rates and under such conditions as he may deem necessary to protect the public interests. Dec. 22, 1879, c. 2, 21 Stat. 59.

§ 13c. Exemption of non-profit institutions from price discrimination provisions

Nothing in sections 13–13b and 21a of this title, shall apply to purchases of their supplies for their own use by schools, colleges, universities, public libraries, churches, hospitals, and charitable institutions not operated for profit. May 26, 1938, c. 283, 52 Stat. 446.

§ 973. Purposes of corporation [Agricultural Hall of Fame]

The purposes of the corporation shall be:

*   *   *

(E)   To establish and maintain a library and museum for the collection and preservation for posterity of agricultural tools, implements, machines, vehicles, pictures, paintings, books, papers, documents, data, relics, mementos, artifacts, and other items and things relating to agriculture.

Pub.L. 86–680, § 3, Aug. 31, 1960, 74 Stat.

§ 91.   Literary and scientific collections accessible to investigators and students

The facilities for study research and illustration in the Government departments and in the following and any other governmental collections now existing or hereafter to be established in the city of Washington for the promotion of knowledge shall be accessible, under such rules and restrictions as the officers in charge of each department or collection may prescribe, subject to such authority as is now or may hereafter be permitted by law, to the scientific investigators and to duly qualified individuals, students and graduates of any institution of learning in the several States and Territories and the District of Columbia, to wit:

One. Of the Library of Congress.
Two. Of the National Museum.
Three. Of the Patent Office.
Four. Of the Office of Education.
Five. Of the Bureau of Ethnology.
Six. Of the Army Medical Museum.
Seven. Of the Department of Agriculture.
Eight. Of the Fish and Wildlife Service.
Nine. Of the Botanic Gardens.
Ten. Of the Coast and Geodetic Survey.
Eleven. Of the Geological Survey.
Twelve. Of the Naval Observatory.
Thirteen. Of the Zoological Park.
Fourteen. Of the Government Printing Office.

Apr. 12, 1892, No. 8, 27 Stat. 395; Mar. 3, 1901, c. 831, § 1, 31 Stat. 1039; May 14, 1928, c. 551, § 1, 45 Stat. 531; 1939 Reorg.Plan No. II, § 4(e), eff. July 1, 1939, 4 F.R. 2731, 53 Stat. 1433; 1940 Reorg. Plan No. III, § 3, eff. June 30, 1940, 5 F.R. 2108, 54 Stat. 1232.

§ 103.   Publications for National Library for the Blind

Two copies of each of the publications printed by the American Printing House for the Blind shall be furnished free of charge to the National Library for the Blind located at 1729 H Street Northwest, Washington, District of Columbia.

Nov. 4, 1919, c. 93, § 1, 41 Stat. 332.

§ 407o.   Construction of buildings; acceptance of donations

The Secretary of the Interior, in his discretion, is authorized to construct upon a portion of the land described in section 407m of this title, or upon other land that may be donated for such purpose, which property he is authorized to accept, such offices and administration buildings as he may deem advisable, together with a suitable auditorium for the interpretation of the historical features of the national historical park. The Secretary of the Interior is also authorized to accept donations of property of national historical significance located in the city of Philadelphia which the Secretary may deem proper for administration as part of the Independence National Historical Park. Any property donated for the purposes of this section shall become a part of the park, following its establishment, upon acceptance by the United States of title to such donated property. The Secretary of the Interior is authorized to permit the American Philosophical Society, a nonprofit corporation, without cost to the United States, to construct, operate, and maintain in the park a building to be located on approximately the original site of historic Library Hall to house the library of the American Philosophical Society and any additions to said library, such permission to be granted the society pursuant to a lease, contract, or authorization without charge, on such terms and conditions as may be approved by the Secretary and accepted by the society, and for such length of time as the society shall continue to use the said building for the housing, display, and use of a library and scientific and historical collections: *Provided*, That the plans for the construction of the building and any additions thereto shall be approved by the Secretary of the Interior. June 28, 1948, c. 687, § 3, 62 Stat. 1062; July 10, 1952, c. 653, § 2, 66 Stat. 575.

LIBRARIES OF SENATE AND
HOUSE OF REPRESENTATIVES

(United States Code Annotated, 1982, Title 2, s.145, 146, 153,
Title 44, s.727, 741, 737, Title 40, s.190.)

§ 145. Copies of Journals and Documents

Two copies of the Journals and Documents, and of each book printed by either House of Congress, bound as provided in section 116 of title 44, shall be deposited in the Library. R.S. § 97; Jan. 12, 1895, c. 23, § 86, 28 Stat. 622.

§ 146. Deposit of Journals of Senate and House.

Twenty-five copies of the public Journals of the Senate, and of the House of Representatives, shall be deposited in the Library of the United States, at the seat of government, to be delivered to Members of Congress during any session, and to all other persons authorized by law to use the books in the Library, upon their application to the librarian, and giving their responsible receipts for the same, in like manner as for other books. (R. S. § 98.)

§ 153. Control of Library of House of Representatives.

The library of the House of Representatives shall be under the control and direction of the Librarian of Congress, who shall provide all needful books of reference therefor. The librarian, two assistant librarians, and assistant in the library, shall be appointed by the Clerk of the House, with the approval of the Speaker of the House of Representatives. No removals shall be made from the said positions except for cause reported to and approved by the Committee on Rules. (Mar.

§ 727.   Committee reports: indexing and binding

The Secretary of the Senate and the Clerk of the House of Representatives shall procure and file for the use of their respective House copies of all reports made by committees, and at the close of each session of Congress shall have the reports indexed and bound, one copy to be deposited in the library of each House and one copy in the committee from which the report emanates.   Pub.L. 90–620, Oct. 22, 1968, 82 Stat. 1252.

§ 741.   Disposition of documents stored at Capitol

The Secretary and Sergeant at Arms of the Senate and the Clerk and Doorkeeper of the House of Representatives, at the convening in regular session of each successive Congress shall cause an invoice to be made of public documents stored in and about the Capitol, other than those belonging to the quota of Members of Congress, to the Library of Congress and the Senate and House libraries and document rooms. The superintendents of the Senate Service Department and House of Representatives Publications Distribution Service shall put the documents to the credit of Senators and Representatives in quantities equal in the number of volumes and as nearly as possible in value, to each Member of Congress, and the documents shall be distributed upon the orders of Senators and Representatives, each of whom shall be supplied by the superintendents of the Senate Service Department and House of Representatives Publications Distribution Service with a list of the number and character of the publications thus put to his credit, but before apportionment is made copies of any of these documents desired for the use of a committee of either House shall be delivered to the chairman of the committee.

Four copies of leather-bound documents shall be reserved and carefully stored, to be used in supplying deficiencies in the Senate and House libraries caused by wear or loss.

Pub.L. 90–620, Oct. 22, 1968, 82 Stat. 1255.

§ 737.   Binding for Senate library

The Secretary of the Senate may make requisition upon the Public Printer for the binding for the Senate library of books he considers necessary, at a cost not to exceed $200 per year.

Pub.L. 90–620, Oct. 22, 1968, 82 Stat. 1254.

§ 190b.   Location of reference library for Senate and House of Representatives

The rooms and space recently occupied by the Library of Congress in the Capitol building shall be divided into three stories, the third story of which shall be fitted up and used for a reference library for the Senate and House of Representatives, and that portion of the other two stories north of a line drawn east and west through the center of the Rotunda shall be used for such purpose as may be designated by the Senate of the United States, and that portion of the first and second stories south of said line shall be used for such

purpose as may be designated by the House of Representatives.
June 6, 1900, No. 33, 31 Stat. 719.

POSTAL REGULATIONS AFFECTING LIBRARIES
(United States Code Annotated, 1982, Title 39, s.3204, 3403-3405.)

§ 3204. Restrictions on use of penalty mail

(a) Except as otherwise provided in this section, an officer, executive department, or independent establishment of the Government of the United States may not mail, as penalty mail, any article or document unless—

(1) a request therefor has been previously received by the department or establishment; or

(2) its mailings is required by law.

(b) Subsection (a) of this section does not prohibit the mailing, as penalty mail, by an officer, executive department, or independent agency of—

* * *

(8) articles or documents to educational institutions or public libraries, or to Federal, State, or other public authorities.
Pub.L. 91–375, Aug. 12, 1970, 84 Stat. 752.

§ 3403. Matter for blind and other handicapped persons

(a) The matter described in subsection (b) of this section (other than matter mailed under section 3404 of this title) may be mailed free of postage, if—

(1) the matter is for the use of the blind or other persons who cannot use or read conventionally printed material because of a physical impairment and who are certified by competent authority as unable to read normal reading material in accordance with the provisions of sections 135a and 135b of title 2;

(2) no charge, or rental, subscription, or other fee, is required for such matter or a charge, or rental, subscription, or other fee is required for such matter not in excess of the cost thereof;

(3) the matter may be opened by the Postal Service for inspection; and

(4) the matter contains no advertising.

(b) The free mailing privilege provided by subsection (a) of this section is extended to—

(1) reading matter and musical scores;

(2) sound reproductions;

(3) paper, records, tapes, and other material for the production of reading matter, musical scores, or sound reproductions;

(4) reproducers or parts thereof, for sound reproductions; and

(5) braille writers, typewriters, educational or other materials or devices, or parts thereof, used for writing by, or specifically designed or adapted for use of, a blind person or a person having a physical impairment as described in subsection (a)(1) of this section.

Pub.L. 91–375, Aug. 12, 1970, 84 Stat. 757.

§ 3404. Unsealed letters sent by blind or physically handicapped persons

Unsealed letters sent by a blind person or a person having a physical impairment, as described in section 3403(a)(1) of this title, in raised characters or sightsaving type, or in the form of sound recordings, may be mailed free of postage.

Pub.L. 91–375, Aug. 12, 1970, 84 Stat. 758.

§ 3405. Markings

All matter relating to blind or other handicapped persons mailed under section 3403 or 3404 of this title, shall bear the words "Free Matter for the Blind or Handicapped", or words to that effect specified by the Postal Service, in the upper right-hand corner of the address area.

Pub.L. 91–375, Aug. 12, 1970, 84 Stat. 758.

COURT LIBRARIES
(United States Code Annotated, 1982, Title 28, s.674, 672, 713, 832,
Title 26, 7472.)

§ 674. Librarian

(a) The Supreme Court may appoint a librarian, whose salary it shall fix, and who shall be subject to removal by the Court.

(b) The librarian shall, with the approval of the Chief Justice, appoint necessary assistants and fix their compensation and make rules governing the use of the library.

(c) He shall select and acquire by purchase, gift, bequest, or exchange, such books, pamphlets, periodicals, microfilm and other processed copy as may be required by the Court for its official use and for the reasonable needs of its bar.

(d) The librarian shall certify to the marshal for payment vouchers covering expenditures for the purchase of such books and other material, and for binding, rebinding and repairing the same.
As amended June 6, 1972, Pub.L. 92–310, Title II, § 206(d), 86 Stat. 203.

§ 672. Marshal

(a) The Supreme Court may appoint a marshal, who shall be subject to removal by the Court, and may fix his compensation.

    *   *   *

c) The marshal shall: * * *

(5) Disburse funds appropriated for the purchase of books, pamphlets, periodicals and other publications, and for their repair, binding, and rebinding, upon vouchers certified by the librarian of the Court; June 25, 1948, c. 646, 62 Stat. 918.

§ 713. Criers, bailiffs and messengers

(a) Each court of appeals may appoint a librarian and necessary library assistants who shall be subject to removal by the court.

*   *   * June 25, 1948, c. 646, 62 Stat. 920, as amended May 24, 1949, c. 139, § 75, 63 Stat. 100.

§ 832. Marshal

The Court of Customs and Patent Appeals may appoint a marshal who shall serve within the District of Columbia and shall be subject to removal by the court.

He shall attend the court at its sessions, and shall serve and execute all process and orders issuing from it. He shall purchase books and supplies, supervise the library and perform such other duties as the court may direct. Under regulations prescribed by the Director of the Administrative Office of the United States Courts, he shall pay the salaries of judges, officers, and employees of the court and disburse funds appropriated for the expenses of the court.

United States marshals for other districts where sessions of the court are held shall serve as marshals of the court. June 25, 1948, c. 646, 62 Stat. 924, as amended May 24, 1949, c. 139, § 76, 63 Stat. 101.

§ 7472. Expenditures

The Tax Court is authorized to make such expenditures (including expenditures for personal services and rent at the seat of Government and elsewhere, and for law books, books of reference, and periodicals), as may be necessary efficiently to execute the functions vested in the Tax Court. All expenditures of the Tax Court shall be allowed and paid, out of any moneys appropriated for purposes of the Tax Court, upon presentation of itemized vouchers therefor signed by the certifying officer designated by the chief judge. Aug. 16, 1954, 9:45 a.m., E.D.T., c. 736, 68A Stat. 888.

EDUCATIONAL EXCHANGE PROGRAMS
(United States Code Annotated, Title 22, s.1447, 1448, 2174.)

§ 1447. Books and materials

The Director is authorized to provide for interchanges between the United States and other countries of books and periodicals, including government publications, for the translation of such writings, and for the preparation, distribution, and interchange of other educational materials.

Jan. 27, 1948, c. 36, Title II, § 202, 62 Stat. 7; 1977 Reorg.Plan No. 2, § 7(a)(1), 42 F.R. 62461, 91 Stat. 1637.

§ 1448. Assistance to certain institutions abroad founded or sponsored by United States citizens

The Director is authorized to provide for assistance to schools, libraries, and community centers abroad, founded or sponsored by citizens of the United States, and serving as demonstration centers for methods and practices employed in the United States. In assisting any such schools, however, the Director shall exercise no control over their educational policies and shall in no case furnish assistance of any character which is not in keeping with the free democratic principles and the established foreign policy of the United States.

Jan. 27, 1948, c. 36, Title II, § 203, 62 Stat. 7; 1977 Reorg.Plan No. 2, § 7(a)(1), 42 F.R. 62461, 91 Stat. 1637.

§ 2174. American schools, libraries and hospital centers abroad

Assistance for schools and libraries

(a) The President is authorized to furnish assistance, on such terms and conditions as he may specify, to schools and libraries outside the United States founded or sponsored by United States citizens and serving as study and demonstration centers for ideas and practices of the United States.

Assistance for hospital centers

(b) The President is authorized, notwithstanding the provisions of the Mutual Defense Assistance Control Act of 1951, to furnish assistance, on such terms and conditions as he may specify, to institutions referred to in subsection (a) of this section, and to hospital centers for medical education and research outside the United States, founded or sponsored by United States citizens.

Authorization of appropriations

(c) To carry out the purposes of this section, there are authorized to be appropriated to the President $25,000,000 for the fiscal year 1979, which amount is authorized to remain available until expended.

Pediatric plastic and reconstructive surgery centers

(d) Notwithstanding the provisions of subsection (b) of this section, funds appropriated under this section may be used for assistance to centers for pediatric plastic and reconstructive surgery established by Children's Medical Relief International, except that assistance may not be furnished for the domestic operations of any such center located in the United States, its territories or possessions.   Pub.L. 95–424, Title I, § 114, Oct. 6, 1978, 92 Stat. 950.

SMITHSONIAN INSTITUTION
(United States Code Annotated, Title 20, s.46, 50, 51.)

§ 46.   Duties of secretary

The secretary of the Board of Regents shall take charge of the building and property of the institution, and shall, under their direction, make a fair and accurate record of all their proceedings, to be preserved in the institution until no longer needed in conducting current business; and shall also discharge the duties of librarian and of keeper of the museum, and may, with the consent of the Board of Regents, employ assistants. R.S. § 5583; Oct. 25, 1951, c. 562, § 2(4), 65 Stat. 639.

§ 50.   Reception and arrangement of specimens and objects of art

*   *   *   The minerals, books, manuscripts, and other property of James Smithson, which have been received by the Government of the United States, shall be preserved separate and apart from other property of the institution. R.S. § 5586.

§ 51.   Library

The Regents shall make, from the interest of the fund, an appropriation, not exceeding an average of $25,000 annually, for the gradual formation of a library composed of valuable works pertaining to all departments of human knowledge. R.S. § 5587.

FRANKLIN D. ROOSEVELT LIBRARY
(United States Statutes at Large, 1939, Vol. 53, Part 2, Chap. 324.)

[CHAPTER 324]

JOINT RESOLUTION
To provide for the establishment and maintenance of the Franklin D. Roosevelt Library, and for other purposes.

Resolved by the Senate and House of Representatives of the United States of America in Congress assembled,

TITLE I—DEFINITIONS

SECTION 1. As used in this joint resolution—
(a) The term "donor" means Franklin D. Roosevelt.
(b) The term "historical material" includes books, correspondence, papers, pamphlets, works of art, models, pictures, photographs, plats,

maps, and other similar material.

(c) The term "Board" means the Trustees of the Franklin D. Roosevelt Library.

TITLE II—FRANKLIN D. ROOSEVELT LIBRARY

SEC. 201. The Archivist of the United States is authorized to accept for and in the name of the United States from the donor, or from such person or persons as shall be empowered to act for the donor, title to a tract of land consisting of an area of twelve acres, more or less, of the Hyde Park estate of the donor and his family, located on the New York-Albany Post Road, in the town of Hyde Park, Dutchess County, State of New York; such area to be selected and carved out of the said estate by the donor and to be utilized as a site for the Franklin D. Roosevelt Library provided for in this title.

SEC. 202. The Archivist is authorized to permit the Franklin D. Roosevelt Library, Incorporated, a New York corporation organized for that purpose, to construct on the area referred to in section 201 of this title a building, or buildings, to be designated as the Franklin D. Roosevelt Library, and to landscape the grounds within the said area. Such project shall be carried out in accordance with plans and specifications approved by the Archivist. The Federal Works Administration is authorized to permit the facilities and personnel of the Public Building Administration to be utilized in the preparation of plans for and in the construction and equipping of the project: *Provided*, That the Franklin D. Roosevelt Library, Incorporated, shall enter into an arrangement satisfactory to the Secretary of the Treasury to reimburse the said Public Building Administration for the costs and expenses incurred for such purposes, as determined by the Federal Works Administration.

SEC. 203. Upon the completion of the project authorized in section 202 of this title, the Archivist shall accept for the Franklin D. Roosevelt Library, as a gift from the donor, such collection of historical material as shall be donated by the donor. The Archivist may also acquire for the said Library from other sources, by gift, purchase, or loan, historical books related to and other historical material contemporary with and related to the historical material acquired from the donor. The historical material acquired under this section shall be permanently housed in the Franklin D. Roosevelt Library: *Provided*, That the Archivist may temporarily remove any of such material from the said Library when he deems it to be necessary: *And provided further*, That the Archivist may dispose of any duplicate printed material in the said Library by sale or exchange, and, with the approval of the National Archives Council, may dispose of by sale, exchange, or otherwise any material in the said Library which appears to have no permanent value or historical interest. The proceeds of any sale made under this section shall be paid into the special account provided for in subsection (d) of section 205 of this title, to be held, administered, and expended in accordance with the provisions of that subsection.

SEC. 204. The faith of the United States is pledged that, upon the construction of the Franklin D. Roosevelt Library and the acquisition from the donor of the collection of historical material in accordance with the terms of this title, the United States will provide such funds as may be necessary for the upkeep of the said Library and the administrative expenses and costs of operation thereof, including the preservation and care of historical material acquired under this title, so that the said Library shall be at all times properly maintained.

SEC. 205. (a) A Board to be known as the Trustees of the Franklin D. Roosevelt Library is hereby established. The Archivist and the Secretary of the Treasury shall be ex officio members, and the Archivist shall be chairman of the Board. There shall also be five members of the Board appointed by the President for life, but the President may remove any such member for cause. Vacancies on the Board shall be filled by the President. Membership on the Board shall not be deemed to be an office within the meaning of the Constitution and statutes of the United States.

(b) No compensation shall be paid to the members of the Board for their services as such members, but they shall be allowed their necessary expenses incurred in the discharge of their duties under this title. The certificate of the chairman of the Board shall be sufficient evidence that the expenses are properly allowable.

(c) The Board is hereby authorized to accept and receive gifts and bequests of personal property and to hold and administer the same as trust funds for the benefit of the Franklin D. Roosevelt Library. The moneys or securities composing trust funds given or bequeathed to the Board shall be receipted for by the Secretary of the Treasury who shall invest, reinvest, and retain investments as the Board may from time to time determine: *Provided, however,* That the Board is not authorized to engage in any business nor to exercise any voting privilege which may be incidental to securities in such trust funds, nor shall the Secretary of the Treasury make any investments for the account of the Board which could not lawfully be made by a trust company in the District of Columbia, except that he may make any investment directly authorized by the instrument of gift under which the funds to be invested are derived, and may retain any investments accepted by the Board.

(d) The income from any trust funds held by the Board, as and when collected, shall be deposited with the Treasurer of the United States who shall enter it in a special account to the credit of the Franklin D. Roosevelt Library and subject to disbursement by the Archivist, except where otherwise restricted by the instrument of gift, in the purchase of equipment for the Franklin D. Roosevelt Library; in the preparation and publication of guides, inventories, calendars, and textual reproduction of material in the said Library; and in the purchase, under section 203 of this title, of historical material for the said Library. The Archivist may make sales of any publications authorized by this section at a price which will cover their cost and 10 per centum added, and all moneys received from such sales shall be paid into, administered, and expended as a part of the special account herein provided for.

(e) Unless otherwise restricted by the instrument of gift, the Board, by resolution duly adopted, may authorize the Archivist to use the principal of any gift or bequest made to it for any of the purposes mentioned in subsection (d) hereof.

(f) The Board shall have all the usual powers of a trustee in respect to all funds administered by it, but the members of the Board shall not be personally liable, except for misfeasance. In the administration of such trust funds the actions of the Board, including any payments made or authorized to be made by it from such funds, shall not be subject to review or attack except in an action brought in the

United States District Court for the District of Columbia, which is hereby given jurisdiction of such suits, for the purpose of enforcing the provision of any trust accepted by the Board.

Sec. 206. The Commissioner of Public Buildings shall be responsible for the care, maintenance, and protection of the buildings and grounds of the Franklin D. Roosevelt Library in the same manner and to the same extent as he is responsible for the National Archives Building in the District of Columbia. Except as provided in the preceding sentence, the immediate custody and control of the Franklin D. Roosevelt Library, and such other buildings, grounds, and equipment as may from time to time become a part thereof, and their contents shall be vested in the Archivist of the United States, and he is authorized to appoint and prescribe the duties of such officers and employees, including clerical assistance for the Board, as may be necessary for the execution of the functions vested in him by this title.

Sec. 207. The Archivist shall prescribe regulations governing the arrangement, custody, protection, and use of the historical material acquired under this title; and, subject to such regulations, such material shall be available to the public free of charge: *Provided*, That the Archivist is authorized to charge and collect, under regulations prescribed by him, a fee not in excess of 25 cents per person for the privilege of visiting and viewing the exhibit rooms or museum portion of the said Library; and any funds so derived shall be paid by the Archivist into the special account provided for in subsection (d) of section 205 of this title, to be held, administered, and expended under the provisions of that subsection.

Sec. 208. The Archivist shall make to the Congress, at the beginning of each regular session, a report for the preceding fiscal year as to the Franklin D. Roosevelt Library. Such report shall include a detailed statement of all accessions, all dispositions of historical material, and all receipts and expenditures on account of the said Library.

Sec. 209. The costs incurred by the Archivist in carrying out the duties placed upon him by this title, including the expenses of the members of the Board and the costs of the Board's necessary clerical assistance, shall be paid out of the appropriations for The National Archives Establishment as other costs and expenses of The National Archives Establishment are paid; and such sums as may be necessary for such purposes are hereby authorized to be appropriated.

TITLE III—FRANKLIN D. ROOSEVELT RESIDENCE

Sec. 301. The head of any executive department, pursuant to agreement between him and the donor, may accept for and in the name of the United States from the donor, or from such person or persons as shall be empowered to act for the donor, title to any part or parts of the said Hyde Park estate of the donor and his family which shall be donated to the United States for use in connection with any designated function of the Government administered in such department. The title to any such property may be accepted under this section notwithstanding that it may be subject to the life estate of the donor or of any other person or persons now living: *Provided*, That during the continuance of any life estate reserved therein no expense to the United States in connection with the ordinary maintenance of the property so acquired shall be incurred: *Provided further*, That the acceptance hereunder by the United States of the title to property in which any life estate is reserved shall not during the existence of such life estate exempt the property, except to the extent provided in section 304 of this title, from taxation by the town of Hyde Park, Dutchess County, or the State of New York as other real property in the said town, county, or State is taxed under the applicable laws relating to taxation of real property.

SEC. 302. Upon the expiration of all life estates reserved in any property acquired under this title for use in connection with a designated function of the Government, or, if no life estate is reserved, immediately upon the acceptance of title thereto, the head of the department administering the said function shall assume jurisdiction and control over the property so acquired and administer it for the purpose designated, subject to the applicable provisions of law.

SEC. 303. The right is reserved in the Congress to take such action and to make such changes, modifications, alterations, and improvements in connection with and upon any property acquired under this title, during or after the expiration of any life estate reserved therein, as the Congress shall deem proper and necessary to protect and preserve the same; but neither the improvements so made nor any increase in the value of the property by reason thereof shall be subject to taxation during the existence of any life estate reserved in the property.

Approved, July 18, 1939.

Federal library laws are reprinted, with minor exceptions, from UNITED STATES CODE ANNOTATED published by West Publishing Co., St. Paul, Minnesota and Edward Thompson Co., Brooklyn, New York.

PART II
THE STATES

ALABAMA

PUBLIC LIBRARY SERVICE
(Code of Alabama, 1982, s.41-8-1 to 41-8-8.)

§ 41-8-1. Creation; chief objective.

In order to aid in the development of higher ideals of citizenship and the enlargement of opportunity for culture and recreation and in order to afford an additional means for the further upbuilding of the educational facilities of the state, there shall be a public library service, which shall be known as the Alabama public library service and shall have as its chief objective the development of a cooperative system of providing books and library service for the various municipalities and counties of the state. (Acts 1939, No. 171, p. 297; Code 1940, T. 55, § 278; Acts 1959, No. 600, p. 1488.)

§ 41-8-2. Executive board generally.

The executive board of the Alabama public library service shall consist of five members appointed by the governor. Such members shall be qualified electors of the state and shall have resided in the state for five years next preceding their appointment. Appointments shall be for five years, and all vacancies, including expired and unexpired terms, shall be filled by the governor by appointment. Members of the executive board shall be allowed $10.00 per day, not to exceed 20 days per year, plus travel expenses pursuant to article 2 of chapter 7 of Title 36 of this Code. It shall be the duty and power of the executive board to conduct the affairs of the public library service, to administer the funds received from the treasury that are allocated to the public library service and to be responsible for the program and for such other activities as would naturally be administered by such an executive board. (Acts 1939, No. 171, p. 297; Code 1940, T. 55, § 279; Acts 1959, No. 600, p. 1488.)

§ 41-8-3. Election of officers of executive board; director of public library service and assistants.

The members of the executive board shall elect from its membership a chairman and vice-chairman.

The board shall appoint a director. The director shall be a graduate of an accredited library school who shall have had a minimum of three years of library experience in an administrative capacity or shall be a college graduate with a master's degree with a major in library science who shall have had a minimum of five years of library experience in an administrative capacity. The director shall not be a member of the executive board and shall serve at the pleasure of the board. All other members of the staff of the service shall be appointed by the executive board on the nomination of the director and shall be subject to the provisions of the state merit system law. The director shall keep a record of the proceedings of the board, shall keep accurate accounts of all financial transactions of the service, shall have charge of its work in organizing new libraries and improving those already established and in general perform such duties as may from time to time be assigned by the executive board. (Acts 1939, No. 171, p. 297; Code 1940, T. 55, § 281; Acts 1959, No. 600, p. 1488.)

§ 41-8-4. Annual report of executive board to governor.

The executive board shall make an annual report to the governor. The report shall show public library conditions and progress in Alabama and a statement of the expenses and activities of the public library service. These annual reports shall be printed as other annual reports of the state departments and shall be distributed by the board or the director thereof. (Acts 1939, No. 171, p. 297; Code 1940, T. 55, § 282; Acts 1959, No. 600, p. 1488.)

§ 41-8-5. Powers and duties of public library service generally.

The Alabama public library service shall give advice to all free public, regional, municipal and county libraries and to all communities in the state which may propose to establish public libraries, in the manner provided in this article, as to the best means of establishing and administering such public library service, selecting and cataloging books and other details of library management and may send any of its staff to aid in organizing such libraries or to assist in the improvement of those already established. The service may advise as to the proper qualifications of librarians of free public, regional, municipal and county libraries and shall perform such other services consistent with and in furtherance of the purpose of this article as shall from time to time appear feasible. Moreover, the service shall advise as to arrangements as provided in section 11-90-4, by which local governmental agencies may combine in the establishment of joint units of library service. The service may receive and shall administer all funds, books or other property from whatever source, under such conditions as may be deemed necessary in order to carry out the purpose of this article; and, by the use of such means and methods as circumstances warrant, the service may acquire and operate traveling libraries and circulate or loan such books and libraries among communities, libraries, library associations, social and civic clubs and organizations and other public agencies and institutions under such conditions and rules as the board deems necessary in order to protect the interests of the state and to increase the efficiency and promote the extension of public library service throughout the state. (Acts 1939, No. 171, p. 297; Code 1940, T. 55, § 280; Acts 1959, No. 600, p. 1488.)

§ 41-8-6. Scholarships and grants in field of library service.

The executive board of the Alabama public library service may, upon such terms and conditions as it may fix, award scholarships or grants in the field of library science on the graduate or undergraduate level to persons of high integrity whom it may select to the extent that funds are available therefor from funds not otherwise obligated which are available to the Alabama public library service in accordance with the state plan provided for by United States Public Law 597, approved June 19, 1965, the "Library Services Act," as now exists or is hereafter amended or replaced. (Acts 1961, No. 812, p. 1188, § 1.)

§ 41-8-7. Service to obtain reports from public libraries.

(a) The Alabama public library service shall each year obtain from all free public libraries in the state of Alabama reports showing the conditions, growth, development and conduct of said libraries. This provision shall not apply to the libraries of the supreme court of Alabama, the department of archives and history or school libraries aided and supervised by the department of education and the libraries of institutions of higher learning.

(b) All libraries, other than private libraries, in this state, including all free public or subscription libraries or libraries maintained by institutions, societies, colleges, institutes or schools shall make both regular and special reports to the Alabama public library service as may be called for and in accordance with such regulations as may be prescribed by the service. (Acts 1915, No. 693, p. 745; Code 1923, § 1400; Acts 1939, No. 171, p. 297; Code 1940, T. 55, §§ 257, 283; Acts 1959, No. 600, p. 1488.)

§ 41-8-8. Applicability and effect of article.

This article shall in no way affect the administration and supervision of public school libraries which have been or may hereafter be established by aid through the department of education, except by agreement, nor shall this article affect in any way the administration and supervision of public school libraries under the control of any city or county board of education, except by agreement; nor shall it, except by agreement, affect or apply to libraries of institutions of higher learning nor to free public libraries in counties where a city having a population of not less than 65,000 already maintains a free public library. (Acts 1939, No. 171, p. 297; Code 1940, T. 55, § 284.)

INTERSTATE LIBRARY COMPACT
(Code of Alabama, 1982, s.41-8-20 to 41-8-25.)

§ 41-8-20. "State library agency" defined.

As used in the compact, "state library agency" with reference to this state means the Alabama public library service. (Acts 1973, No. 1121, p. 1884, § 3.)

§ 41-8-21. Enactment of compact; form.

The Interstate Library Compact is hereby enacted into law and entered into by this state with all states legally joining therein in the form substantially as follows:

INTERSTATE LIBRARY COMPACT.

Article I. Policy and Purpose.

Because the desire for the services provided by libraries transcends governmental boundaries and can most effectively be satisfied by giving such services to communities and people regardless of jurisdictional lines, it is the policy of the states party to this compact to cooperate and share their responsibilities; to authorize cooperation and sharing with respect to those types of library facilities and services which can be more economically or efficiently developed and maintained on a cooperative basis and to authorize cooperation and sharing among localities, states and others in providing joint or cooperative library services in areas where the distribution of population or of existing and potential library resources makes the provision of library service on an interstate basis the most effective way of providing adequate and efficient service.

Article II. Definitions.

As used in this compact:

(a) "Public library agency" means any unit or agency of local or state government operating or having power to operate a library.

(b) "Private library agency" means any nongovernmental entity which operates or assumes a legal obligation to operate a library.

(c) "Library agreement" means a contract establishing an interstate library district pursuant to this compact or providing for the joint or cooperative furnishing of library services.

Article III. Interstate Library Districts.

(a) Any one or more public library agencies in a party state in cooperation with any public library agency or agencies in one or more other party states may establish and maintain an interstate library district. Subject to the provisions of this compact and any other laws of the party states which pursuant hereto remain applicable, such district may establish, maintain and operate some or all of the library facilities and services for the area concerned in accordance with the terms of a library agreement therefor. Any private library agency or agencies within an interstate library district may cooperate therewith, assume duties, responsibilities and obligations thereto and receive benefits therefrom as provided in any library agreement to which such agency or agencies become party.

(b) Within an interstate library district and as provided by a library agreement, the performance of library functions may be undertaken on a joint or cooperative basis or may be undertaken by means of one or more arrangements between or among public or private library agencies for the extension of library privileges to the use of facilities or services operated or rendered by one or more of the individual library agencies.

(c) If a library agreement provides for joint establishment, maintenance or operation of library facilities or services by an interstate library district, such district shall have power to do any one or more of the following in accordance with such library agreement:

1. Undertake, administer and participate in programs or arrangements for securing, lending or servicing of books and other publications, any other materials suitable to be kept or made available by libraries and library equipment or for the dissemination of information about libraries, the value and significance of particular items therein and the use thereof.

2. Accept for any of its purposes under this compact any and all donations and grants of money, equipment, supplies, materials and services (conditional or otherwise) from any state or the United States or any subdivision or agency thereof, or interstate agency, or from any institution, person, firm or corporation, and receive, utilize and dispose of the same.

3. Operate mobile library units or equipment for the purpose of rendering bookmobile service within the district.

4. Employ professional, technical, clerical and other personnel and fix terms of employment, compensation and other appropriate benefits and, where desirable, provide for the inservice training of such personnel.

5. Acquire, hold and dispose of any real or personal property or any interest or interests therein as may be appropriate to the rendering of library service.

6. Construct, maintain and operate a library, including any appropriate branches thereof.

7. Do such other things as may be incidental to or appropriate for the carrying out of any of the foregoing powers.

Article IV. Interstate Library Districts, Governing Board.

(a) An interstate library district which establishes, maintains or operates any facilities or services in its own right shall have a governing board which shall direct the affairs of the district and act for it in all matters relating to its business. Each participating public library agency in the district shall be represented on the governing board, which shall be organized and conduct its business in accordance with provisions therefor in the library agreement. But in no event shall a governing board meet less often than twice a year.

(b) Any private library agency or agencies party to a library agreement establishing an interstate library district may be represented on or advise with the governing board of the district in such manner as the library agreement may provide.

Article V. State Library Agency Cooperation.

Any two or more state library agencies of two or more of the party states may undertake and conduct joint or cooperative library programs, render joint or cooperative library services and enter into and perform arrangements for the cooperative or joint acquisition, use, housing and disposition of items or collections of materials which, by reason of expense, rarity, specialized nature or infrequency of demand therefor would be appropriate for central collection and shared use. Any such programs, services or arrangements may include provision for the exercise on a cooperative or joint basis of any power exercisable by an interstate library district and an agreement embodying any such program, service or arrangement shall contain provisions covering the subjects detailed in Article VI of this compact for interstate library agreements.

Article VI. Library Agreement.

(a) In order to provide for any joint or cooperative undertaking pursuant to this compact, public and private library agencies may enter into library agreements. Any agreement executed pursuant to the provisions of this compact shall, as among the parties to the agreement:

(1) Detail the specific nature of the services, programs, facilities, arrangements or properties to which it is applicable.

(2) Provide for the allocation of costs and other financial responsibilities.

(3) Specify the respective rights, duties, obligations and liabilities of the parties.

(4) Set forth the terms and conditions for duration, renewal, termination, abrogation, disposal of joint or common property, if any, and all other matters which may be appropriate to the proper effectuation and performance of the agreement.

(b) No public or private library agency shall undertake to exercise itself, or jointly with any other library agency, by means of a library agreement any power prohibited to such agency by the constitution or statutes of its state.

(c) No library agreement shall become effective until filed with the compact administrator of each state involved and approved in accordance with Article VII of this compact.

Article VII. Approval of Library Agreements.

(a) Every library agreement made pursuant to this compact shall, prior to and as a condition precedent to its entry into force, be submitted to the attorney general of each state in which a public library agency party thereto is situated, who shall determine whether the agreement is in proper form and compatible with the laws of his state. The attorneys general shall approve any agreement submitted to them unless they shall find that it does not meet the conditions set forth herein and shall detail in writing addressed to the governing bodies of the public library agencies concerned the specific respects in which the proposed agreement fails to meet the requirements of law. Failure to disapprove an agreement submitted hereunder within 90 days of its submission shall constitute approval thereof.

(b) In the event that a library agreement made pursuant to this compact shall deal in whole or in part with the provision of services or facilities with regard to which an officer or agency of the state government has constitutional or statutory powers of control, the agreement shall, as a condition precedent to its entry into force, be submitted to the state officer or agency having such power of control and shall be approved or disapproved by him or it as to all matters within his or its jurisdiction in the same manner subject to the same requirements governing the action of the attorneys general pursuant to paragraph (a) of this article. This requirement of submission and approval shall be in addition to and not in substitution for the requirement of submission to and approval by the attorneys general.

Article VIII. Other Laws Applicable.

Nothing in this compact or in any library agreement shall be construed to supersede, alter or otherwise impair any obligation imposed on any library by otherwise applicable law, nor to authorize the transfer or disposition of any property held in trust by a library agency in a manner contrary to the terms of such trust.

Article IX. Appropriations and Aid.

(a) Any public library agency party to a library agreement may appropriate funds to the interstate library district established thereby in the same manner and to the same extent as to a library wholly maintained by it and, subject to the laws of the state in which such public library agency is situated, may pledge its credit in support of an interstate library district established by the agreement.

(b) Subject to the provisions of the library agreement pursuant to which it functions and the laws of the states in which such district is situated, an interstate library district may claim and receive any state and federal aid which may be available to library agencies.

Article X. Compact Administrator.

Each state shall designate a compact administrator with whom copies of all library agreements to which this state or any public library agency thereof is party shall be filed. The administrator shall have such other powers as may be conferred upon him by the laws of his state and may consult and cooperate with the compact administrators of other party states and take such steps as may effectuate the purposes of this compact. If the laws of a party state so provide, such state may designate one or more deputy compact administrators in addition to its compact administrator.

Article XI. Entry Into Force and Withdrawal.

(a) This compact shall enter into force and effect immediately upon its enactment into law by any two states. Thereafter, it shall enter into force and effect as to any other state upon the enactment thereof by such state.

(b) This compact shall continue in force with respect to a party state and remain binding upon such state until six months after such state has given notice to each other party state of the repeal thereof. Such withdrawal shall not be construed to relieve any party to a library agreement entered into pursuant to this compact from any obligation of that agreement prior to the end of its duration as provided therein.

Article XII. Construction and Severability.

This compact shall be liberally construed so as to effectuate the purposes thereof. The provisions of this compact shall be severable; and, if any phrase, clause, sentence or provision of this compact is declared to be contrary to the constitution of any party state or of the United States or the applicability thereof to any government, agency, person or circumstance is held invalid, the validity of the remainder of this compact and the applicability thereof to any government, agency, person or circumstance shall not be affected thereby. If this compact shall be held contrary to the constitution of any state party thereto, the compact shall remain in full force and effect as to the remaining states and in full force and effect as to the state affected as to all severable matters. (Acts 1973, No. 1121, p. 1884, § 1.)

§ 41-8-22. Compact administrator; deputy contract administrators.

The director of the Alabama public library service shall be the compact administrator pursuant to Article X of the compact. The director of the Alabama public library service may appoint one or more deputy compact administrators pursuant to said article. (Acts 1973, No. 1121, p. 1884, § 5.)

§ 41-8-23. Restrictions as to entry into library agreements for construction or maintenance of libraries, etc., by counties, municipalities, etc.

No county, municipality or other political subdivision of this state shall be party to a library agreement which provides for the construction or maintenance of a library pursuant to Article III, subdivision (c) 7 of the compact nor pledge its credit in support of such a library or contribute to the capital financing thereof, except after compliance with any laws applicable to such counties, municipalities or other political subdivisions relating to or governing capital outlays and the pledging of credit. (Acts 1973, No. 1121, p. 1884, § 2.)

§ 41-8-24. State aid to interstate library districts lying partly within state; application for and receipt of federal aid by such districts.

(a) An interstate library district lying partly within this state may claim and be entitled to receive state aid in support of any of its functions to the same extent and in the same manner as such functions are eligible for support when carried on by entities wholly within this state. For the purposes of computing and apportioning state aid to an interstate library district, this state will consider that portion of the area which lies within this state as an independent entity for the performance of the aided function or functions and compute and apportion the aid accordingly.

(b) Subject to any applicable laws of this state, such a district also may apply for and be entitled to receive any federal aid for which it may be eligible. (Acts 1973, No. 1121, p. 1884, § 4.)

§ 41-8-25. Sending and receipt of notices required in event of withdrawal from compact.

In the event of withdrawal from the compact the governor shall send and receive any notices required by Article XI (b) of the compact. (Acts 1973, No. 1121, p. 1884, § 6.)

DEPARTMENT OF ARCHIVES AND HISTORY
(Code of Alabama, 1982, s.41-6-1 to 41-6-15.)

§ 41-6-1. Establishment; location.

There shall be a department of archives and history, to be located at Montgomery. (Code 1907, § 793; Code 1923, § 1398; Code 1940, T. 55, § 255.)

§ 41-6-2. Objects and purposes.

(a) The objects and purposes of the department are:

(1) The care and custody of official archives;

(2) The collection of materials bearing upon the history of the state and of the territory included therein from the earliest times;

(3) The completion and publication of the state's official records and other historical materials;

(4) The diffusion of knowledge in reference to the history and resources of the state;

(5) The encouragement of historical work and research;

(6) The encouragement of and assistance in the establishment of public school libraries and in the improvement and strengthening of those already in existence; and

(7) The provision of advice and assistance to libraries and library workers in library administration, methods and economy.

(b) The department shall bring together and arrange for ready consultation a reference collection of materials for the use of members of the legislature, state officers and others on all subjects which may, from time to time, be deemed of public interest and importance to the people of the state.

(c) The department shall perform such other acts and requirements as may be enjoined by law. (Code 1907, § 794; Code 1923, § 1399; Code 1940, T. 55, § 256.)

§ 41-6-3. Board of trustees of department — Composition.

Said department shall be under the control of a board of trustees, one from each congressional district. (Code 1907, § 795; Acts 1923, No. 40, p. 23; Code 1923, § 1401; Code 1940, T. 55, § 258.)

§ 41-6-4. Same — Vacancies; terms of office; meetings; officers; compensation; powers and duties generally.

The said board shall fill all vacancies occurring therein, whether by expiration of term of service or by death or resignation, but the names of all newly elected members shall be communicated to the next ensuing regular session of the state senate for confirmation; and, in case it shall reject any of the said newly elected trustees, it shall proceed forthwith to fill the vacancy or vacancies by an election.

All trustees appointed to succeed the present members or their successors, whose terms shall have fully expired, shall serve for a term of six years, and appointees to fill vacancies by death or resignation shall only serve out the unexpired terms of their predecessors.

The board shall hold at the state capitol at least one regular meeting during every year and as many special meetings as may be necessary, and at said meeting a majority of the trustees shall constitute a quorum. The governor of the state shall be a member of said board, and he shall, as far as possible, lend every encouragement to the success and upbuilding thereof. The director shall be the secretary of the board. The trustees shall receive no compensation for their services.

The board may adopt rules for its own government and also for the government of the department, may elect a director and may provide for the selection or appointment of other officials or employees as may be authorized, may provide for the publication of historical material pertaining to the state under the supervision of the director, may have the direction and control of the marking of historical sites or houses and the exploration of prehistoric and Indian mounds and other remains existing in the state, may control and expend such appropriations as may be made for the maintenance of the department and may do and perform such other acts and things as may be necessary to carry out the true intent and purposes of this article. (Code 1907, § 796; Code 1923, § 1402; Code 1940, T. 55, § 259.)

§ 41-6-5. Director — Election; term of office.

The department shall be under the immediate management and control of a director, to be elected by the board of trustees, whose term of office shall be six years and until his successor is elected and qualified. (Code 1907, § 797; Code 1923, § 1403; Code 1940, T. 55, § 260.)

§ 41-6-6. Same — Oath of office; director to be commissioned.

The director shall take an oath of office as other public officials and shall be commissioned in like manner. (Code 1907, § 798; Code 1923, § 1404; Code 1940, T. 55, § 261.)

§ 41-6-7. Same — Salary.

The director shall receive an annual salary to be fixed in accordance with the provisions of section 36-6-6, which shall be payable as the salaries of other state officers are paid. (Code 1907, § 804; Acts 1923, No. 600, p. 789; Code 1923, § 1411; Acts 1933, Ex. Sess., No. 138, p. 124; Acts 1935, No. 373, p. 792; Acts 1939, No. 435, p. 582; Code 1940, T. 55, § 268; Acts 1943, No. 396, p. 364; Acts 1953, No. 594, p. 846.)

§ 41-6-8. Same — Powers, functions and duties generally.

The powers, functions and duties of the director of the department of archives and history shall be as follows:

(1) To control and direct the work and operations of the department of archives and history;

(2) To administer the state official archives;

(3) To prepare the Alabama official and statistical register;

(4) To diffuse knowledge in reference to the history and resources of the state;

(5) To administer all military records for historical purposes;

(6) To administer the state's historical library and to collect and administer historical portraits and museums;

(7) To collect, organize and preserve noncurrent county records for historical purposes;

(8) To edit the Alabama Historical Quarterly and other historical publications;

(9) To distribute state official reports;

(10) To designate and describe historic spots in Alabama for monumental purposes;

(11) To have custody and supervision, under the direction of the director of finance, of the Alabama memorial building; and

(12) To perform any and all other powers, functions and duties as may now or hereafter be placed upon the director of the department of archives and history. (Code 1907, § 799; Code 1923, § 1405; Acts 1939, No. 435, p. 582; Code 1940, T. 55, § 262.)

§ 41-6-9. Clerical assistants in department.

Subject to the provisions of the state merit system, there may be employed in the department of archives and history such number of curators, clerks, librarians, stenographers, statisticians and other employees as are necessary to carry out the functions and duties of the department. (Code 1907, § 809; Acts 1923, No. 600, p. 789; Code 1923, § 1417; Acts 1933, Ex. Sess., No. 138, p. 124; Acts 1939, No. 58, p. 68; Code 1940, T. 55, § 270.)

§ 41-6-10. Surrender by state, county, etc., officials of books, records, etc., not in current use to department for permanent preservation.

Any state, county or other official may, in his discretion, turn over to the department for permanent preservation therein any official books, records, documents, original papers, newspaper files and printed books not in current use in his offices. (Code 1907, § 800; Code 1923, § 1406; Code 1940, T. 55, § 263.)

§ 41-6-11. Provision of certified copies of books, records, etc., surrendered to department.

When books, records, documents, original papers and newspaper files have been surrendered in accordance with section 41-6-10, copies therefrom shall be made and certified by the director upon the application of any person interested, which certificate shall have all the force and effect as if made by the officer originally in the custody of them and for which the same fees shall be charged, to be collected in advance. (Code 1907, § 801; Code 1923, § 1407; Code 1940, T. 55, § 264.)

§ 41-6-12. Provision of official publications, etc., of commissions, bureaus, boards, etc., to department; disposition of same by department.

In addition to the number of copies of any report or other official publication of any executive office, department, commission, bureau, board and state institution now or which may hereafter be authorized by law, except the reports of the supreme court, the court of civil appeals, the court of criminal appeals and the acts and journals of the legislature, the state printer or other person printing such report or document shall print 250 additional copies for the use of the department of archives and history, to be held for free distribution and exchange with state libraries, public libraries, institutions and individuals in Alabama and elsewhere. (Acts 1915, No. 679, p. 738; Code 1923, § 1408; Code 1940, T. 55, § 265.)

§ 41-6-13. Collection, etc., of data as to Alabama soldiers in war between states.

The department shall make special effort to collect data in reference to soldiers from Alabama in the war between the states, both from the department of defense and also from private individuals, and to cause the same to be prepared for publication as speedily as possible. (Code 1907, § 803; Code 1923, § 1410; Code 1940, T. 55, § 267.)

§ 41-6-14. Statistical register.

(a) An official and statistical register of the state of Alabama shall be compiled every two years by the director to contain:

(1) Brief sketches of the several state officials, the members of congress from Alabama, the supreme court judges and the members of the senate and house of representatives of the state of Alabama;

(2) Rosters of all state and county officials;

(3) Lists of all state institutions with officials;

(4) State and county population and election statistics; and

(5) Miscellaneous statistics.

(b) Said register shall be published in an edition of 1,000 copies for free distribution, the printing and binding to be paid for as other printing and binding. (Code 1907, § 802; Code 1923, § 1409; Code 1940, T. 55, § 266.)

§ 41-6-15. Historical quarterly.

One thousand copies of the Alabama Historical Quarterly shall be published each quarter. The said quarterly shall be edited by the director of the department of archives and history and shall be supplied gratis to public officials, public and high school libraries and, upon call, to any responsible person in the interest of propagating facts about the history of the state. (Acts 1939, No. 583, p. 953; Code 1940, T. 55, § 271.)

Endowment Fund

(Code of Alabama, 1982, s.41-6-30 to 41-6-34.)

§ 41-6-30. Gifts or donations of money to department of archives and history to be deposited in state treasury to credit of department.

Unless otherwise provided, in accordance with section 41-6-50, whenever any gift or donation of money from any source is made to the department of archives and history of this state, the same must be deposited in the state treasury for the use of said department as provided in this article. (Acts 1943, No. 454, p. 416, § 1.)

§ 41-6-31. Endowment fund established; composition; expenditure; investment of fund.

The principal amount of such gift or donation shall be set aside by the state

treasurer in a special fund designated: "Endowment Fund — Department of
Archives and History," and moneys so deposited shall constitute an endowment
fund for said department. In no event shall more than 10 percent of the amount
remaining in said fund be expended in any one fiscal year. The director of finance
shall invest or reinvest from time to time, at his discretion and with the approval
of the governor, all or any part or portion of said fund in such bonds as are
authorized by the laws of Alabama governing investments in bonds by domestic
life insurance companies, and the interest thereon shall be paid to said
department by the state treasurer upon a requisition signed by the director of
said department and approved by the governor. (Acts 1943, No. 454, p. 416, §
2.)

§ 41-6-32. Interest accruing, earned or paid from investment of fund appropriated to department; expenditure thereof.

The interest accrued, earned or paid as the result of investment of said
endowment fund is hereby appropriated to said department of archives and
history and shall be used by said department only for such purposes as its
trustees may specify and the governor approve; provided, however, that no
expenditure of such funds may be made or approved by said board of trustees
unless it is for the purpose of acquiring rare and valuable articles, property or
materials or acquiring, marking and preserving or maintaining historical
locations or spots within the state of Alabama. (Acts 1943, No. 454, p. 416, § 3.)

§ 41-6-33. Lease, sale, etc., of gifts or donations of real property authorized; disposition of proceeds from sale or rent.

Should any gift or donation to said department be in the form of real property
it may be leased, rented or sold in the discretion of said board of trustees, but
the sum received as rent or the amount received as the purchase price, in the
event of sale, must be deposited to the credit of said endowment fund, and such
sum shall remain intact as a part of the principal amount of such endowment
fund, and the interest received from the investment thereof shall be paid in the
same manner as provided in this article for the payment of interest on other
moneys deposited to the credit of said endowment fund. (Acts 1943, No. 454, p.
416, § 4.)

§ 41-6-34. Perpetuation or memorialization of names of certain donors.

Should any gift or donation by any person amount in value to as much as
$5,000.00, said board of trustees is hereby authorized to perpetuate or
memorialize the name of the persons making such gift or donation by
designating any property or project or material or program acquired or carried
on by proceeds derived from said endowment fund with appropriate
nomenclature. (Acts 1943, No. 454, p. 416, § 5.)

Memorial Fund
(Code of Alabama, 1982, s.41-6-50 to 41-6-53.)

§ 41-6-50. Establishment; certain gifts or donations of money to be deposited in state treasury in said fund.

Whenever any gift or donation of money to the department of archives and history is in an amount not exceeding $100.00 or whenever the donor thereof, regardless of the amount of the gift, requests that such gift be used for a specified purpose and such purpose is a purpose approved by the board of trustees of such department and whenever the donor designates the gift as a memorial gift, such money shall be deposited in the state treasury in a special fund designated "Memorial Fund — Department of Archives and History," which fund is hereby established. (Acts 1967, No. 522, p. 1252, § 1.)

§ 41-6-51. Disposition and expenditure of fund.

Such part of the fund as is derived from gifts for a designated purpose shall be used and expended by the director of the department of archives and history in accordance with the terms of the gift. The remainder of the fund shall be used and expended by the director in accordance with such policies as may be established by the board of trustees, and, at each regular meeting of the board of trustees, the director shall report all such expenditures made since the next preceding regular meeting. (Acts 1967, No. 522, p. 1252, § 2.)

§ 41-6-52. Identification of item or purpose for which gift expended where gift designated in memory of specified person.

When a gift is designated as a gift in memory of a specified person, then the item or purpose for which such gift is expended shall be identified as a memorial to such designated person. (Acts 1967, No. 522, p. 1252, § 3.)

§ 41-6-53. Gifts deemed gifts to state; deduction of amount of gift for income tax purposes.

Every gift to the department of archives and history payable into the fund, whether or not the use thereof is prescribed by the donor or the gift is designated as a memorial to a specified person, shall be deemed a gift to the state of Alabama. The donor in computing his net income for state income tax purposes for the year in which he makes the gift may deduct the amount of the gift from his gross income as authorized in section 40-18-15. (Acts 1967, No. 522, p. 1252, § 4.)

Public Records
(Code of Alabama, 1982, s.41-13-1, 41-13-4, 41-13,5, 41-13-40 to 41-13-44.)

§ 41-13-1. Public records defined.

As used in this article, the term "public records" shall include all written, typed or printed books, papers, letters, documents and maps made or received in pursuance of law by the public officers of the state, counties, municipalities and other subdivisions of government in the transactions of public business and shall also include any record authorized to be made by any law of this state belonging or pertaining to any court of record or any other public record authorized by law or any paper, pleading, exhibit or other writing filed with, in or by any such court, office or officer. (Acts 1945, No. 293, p. 486, § 1.)

§ 41-13-4. Assistance of public officials in preserving, filing, etc., of public records by department of archives and history.

The department of archives and history may examine into the condition of public records and shall at the request of the custodian thereof give advice and assistance to any public official in the solution of his problems of preserving, filing and making available the public records in his custody. (Acts 1945, No. 293, p. 486, § 5.)

§ 41-13-5. Destruction, etc., of public records having no significance, importance or value.

Any public records, books, papers, newspapers, files, printed books, manuscripts or other public records which have no significance, importance or value may, upon the advice and recommendation of the custodian thereof and upon the further advice, recommendation and consent of the state or county records commission be destroyed or otherwise disposed of. The state and county records commissions are hereby authorized and empowered to make such orders, rules, and regulations as may be necessary or proper to carry the provisions of this section into effect. (Acts 1945, No. 293, p. 486, § 3.)

§ 41-13-40. Photographing or microphotographing of records, books, files, etc.; admissibility in evidence, etc., of photographs, microfilms, etc.

The head of any office, court, commission, board, institution, department or agency of the state or of any political subdivision thereof may cause any record, document, plat, court file, book, map, paper, or writing made, acquired or received as required by law to be photographed or microphotographed on plate or film. Such photographs, microfilms or prints made therefrom, when duly authenticated by the custodian thereof, shall have the same force and effect at law as the original record or of a record made by any other legally authorized means and may be offered in like manner and shall be received in evidence in any court where such original record or record made by other legally authorized means could have been so introduced and received; provided, that the provisions of this article shall not apply to the state department of pensions and security, the state health department, the state board of health, the state department of industrial relations or to any other office, court, commission, board, institution, department or agency of the state which is otherwise authorized by law to provide for the photographing or microphotographing of its records. (Acts 1955, No. 565, p. 1226, § 1.)

§ 41-13-41. Photographing or microphotographing of state centralized in department of archives and history; charges for photographing or microphotographing.

The photographing or microphotographing of public records, except the public records of counties, municipalities and other political subdivisions of the state of Alabama, shall be centralized in the department of archives and history. The department of archives and history is authorized to charge any office, court, commission, board, institution, department or agency of the state for the photographing or microphotographing of public records belonging to that office, court, commission, board, institution, department or agency. Such charge shall be on a cost basis. (Acts 1955, No. 565, p. 1226, § 2.)

§ 41-13-42. Purchase or lease of photographic or microphotographic equipment and supplies by department of archives and history authorized; appropriation of funds therefor.

The department of archives and history is hereby authorized to purchase or lease photographic or microphotographic equipment and supplies necessary to carry out the duties prescribed in this article.

There is hereby appropriated out of the general fund of the state an amount sufficient to cover the cost of purchase or lease of such equipment and supplies, such appropriation to be released only upon the approval of the governor. (Acts 1955, No. 565, p. 1226, § 4.)

§ 41-13-43. Appropriation of funds by counties or municipalities for photographing or microphotographing of public records authorized.

The county commission of any county or municipality may appropriate an amount sufficient to cover the cost of photographing or microphotographing the public records belonging to that county or municipality. (Acts 1955, No. 565, p. 1226, § 3.)

§ 41-13-44. State and county officials, etc., not to destroy, etc., public records until microfilmed copies processed and checked for accuracy.

No state or county official or employee shall destroy, dispose of or cause to be destroyed or disposed of any public record that has been microfilmed under the provisions of this article until the microfilm copy has been processed and checked with the original for accuracy. (Acts 1955, No. 565, p. 1226, § 9.)

COUNTY AND MUNICIPAL LIBRARIES
(Code of Alabama, 1982, s.11-90-1 to 11-90-4, 16-11-23.)

§ 11-90-1. Powers of counties and municipalities as to establishment and maintenance of free public libraries generally.

The county commissions of the counties of this state and municipalities, through their governing bodies, may establish and maintain or aid in establishing and maintaining free public libraries for the use of the citizens of the respective counties or municipalities, either separately or in connection with public schools, and to that end may accept gifts, donations and bequests of land, buildings or money therefor and may make appropriations from the county or municipal treasury in support thereof in such sums as they may deem proper. (Acts 1920, Ex. Sess., No. 93, p. 146; Code 1923, § 1545; Acts 1939, No. 198, p. 350; Code 1940, T. 55, § 285.)

§ 11-90-2. Library boards — Composition; appointment and terms of members; vacancies in office.

The government and supervision of such libraries shall be vested in a library board consisting of five members who shall be appointed by the county commission or the governing body of the municipality. The terms of membership on the library board, as first appointed, for one member shall be for one year, for the second member shall be for two years, for the third member shall be for three years, and for the remaining two members the terms shall be for four years. After the first term, all appointments shall be for four years. The county commission or governing body shall fill all vacancies including expired and unexpired terms. Members of the library board shall serve without compensation. (Acts 1919, No. 763, p. 1124; Code 1923, § 1546; Acts 1939, No. 199, p. 351; Code 1940, T. 55, § 286.)

§ 11-90-3. Same — Powers and duties.

(a) The library board shall have full power and authority to:
   (1) Control the expenditure of all funds received or appropriated for such libraries;
   (2) Erect or rent buildings to cost not in excess of the funds available to it;
   (3) Purchase books and equipment;
   (4) Provide a system of library service to be made easily available to all citizens of the county or municipality through central library, branches, stations, book truck service or other appropriate means;
   (5) Elect a librarian and other employees; and
   (6) Manage and control the said library in order to carry out the full intent and purpose of this chapter.
(b) A careful and complete record and set of books shall be kept by the library board, showing the proceedings of their several meetings and the receipts and disbursements in detail of all funds.

(c) In counties where a city having a population of not less than 65,000 already maintains a free public library, a separate county library board need not be appointed, and the county libraries and the appropriations authorized shall be administered by the governing board of such free public library on such terms as may be agreed upon between the county commission and the said governing board. (Acts 1919, No. 763, p. 1124; Code 1923, § 1547; Acts 1939, No. 200, p. 351; Code 1940, T. 55, § 287.)

§ 11-90-4. Establishment and maintenance of joint library service.

In lieu of establishing or maintaining free public libraries exclusively for a single county or municipality in the manner provided in this chapter, the library board of any county or municipality free public library may contract, in behalf of the political unit represented by such local library board, to and with the library board of another political unit or governmental agency or instrumentality with respect to the establishment or maintenance of joint library service upon such terms as may be agreed upon by the several contracting parties. Where there is no existing public library, the power thus to contract shall vest in the county commission of the county or the governing body of the municipality. Included in the power conferred is the determination of the basis and personnel of representation of the local political units on the joint library board administering the joint library service established under this section. Such board, when appointed, shall have the powers and duties granted by this chapter to county or municipal library boards. County and municipal library boards or joint library boards shall have the power to cooperate with all state and federal agencies and institutions in furtherance of the purpose of this chapter, and all municipal, county and joint library boards shall from time to time submit such records and reports as may be required by the public library service; provided, that nothing in this section shall be so construed as to infringe upon any municipal charter provisions governing the administration of existing free public libraries. (Acts 1919, No. 763, p. 1124; Code 1923, § 1548; Acts 1939, No. 201, p. 352; Code 1940, T. 55, § 288.)

§ 16-11-23. Libraries and special schools established and maintained.

The city board of education shall have the right to establish and maintain, or aid in establishing and maintaining, public libraries, either separately or in connection with the public schools, and also special schools for backward, defective, truant or incorrigible children, day or night schools for adult illiterates and for the Americanization of foreigners and part-time continuation classes. (School Code 1927, § 215; Code 1940, T. 52, § 173.)

PUBLIC LIBRARY AUTHORITIES
(Code of Alabama, 1982, s.11-57-1 to 11-57-26.)

§ 11-57-1. Definitions.

The following words and phrases, whenever used in this chapter, shall have the following respective meanings, unless the context clearly indicates otherwise:

(1) AUTHORITY. A corporation organized pursuant to the provisions of this chapter.

(2) BOARD. The board of directors of the authority.

(3) BOND. Any bond issued under the provisions of this chapter, including refunding bonds.

(4) COUNTY. That county in which the certificate of incorporation of the authority shall be filed for record.

(5) COUPON. Any interest coupon evidencing an installment of interest payable with respect to a bond.

(6) FISCAL YEAR. A fiscal year of the municipality.

(7) GOVERNING BODY. The council, board of commissioners or other like body in which the legislative functions of the municipality are vested by law.

(8) INDENTURE. A mortgage, an indenture of mortgage, deed of trust or trust indenture executed by the authority as security for any bonds.

(9) LEASE AGREEMENT. Any agreement of lease respecting the project or any part thereof which is made pursuant to the provisions of this chapter.

(10) MUNICIPALITY. That incorporated city or town in the state which authorized the organization of the authority.

(11) PROJECT. One or more buildings located or to be located within the municipality or within its police jurisdiction and designed for use as a public library, branch library and related public library facilities and any equipment and lands necessary therefor.

(12) STATE. The state of Alabama. (Acts 1961, No. 895, p. 1407, § 2; Acts 1961, Ex. Sess., No. 289, p. 2335, § 2.)

§ 11-57-2. Legislative intent; construction of chapter generally.

(a) It is the intention of the legislature by the passage of this chapter to empower each incorporated municipality in the state to authorize the incorporation of one or more public corporations as political subdivisions of the state for the purpose of providing public library facilities for lease to and use by the municipality, to invest each corporation organized under this chapter with all powers that may be necessary to enable it to accomplish such purposes, including the power to lease its properties and to issue interest-bearing revenue bonds and to grant to each such municipality power to rent such public library facilities on a year to year basis.

(b) This chapter shall be liberally construed in conformity with the said intent. (Acts 1961, No. 895, p. 1407, § 1; Acts 1961, Ex. Sess., No. 289, p. 2335, § 1.)

§ 11-57-3. Application for authority to form corporation; adoption of resolution by governing body authorizing incorporation; procedure for incorporation generally.

Whenever any number of natural persons, not less than three, shall file with the governing body an application in writing for permission to incorporate a public corporation under the provisions of this chapter, if it shall be made to appear to the governing body that each of the said persons is a duly qualified elector of and property owner in the municipality; and, if the governing body shall duly adopt a resolution wherein it shall be declared that it will be wise, expedient and necessary that such a public corporation be formed and that the persons filing such application shall be authorized to proceed to form such public corporation, then the said persons shall become the incorporators of and shall proceed to incorporate the authority in the manner provided in this chapter.

No corporation shall be formed under this chapter unless the application provided for in this section shall be made and unless the resolution provided for in this section shall be adopted. (Acts 1961, No. 895, p. 1407, § 3; Acts 1961, Ex. Sess., No. 289, p. 2335, § 3.)

§ 11-57-4. Certificate of incorporation — Contents; execution and acknowledgment; approval by governing body.

(a) The certificate of incorporation of the authority shall state:

(1) The name and address of each of the incorporators and a statement that each of them is a duly qualified elector of and property owner in the municipality;

(2) The name of the corporation (which shall be "The Public Library Authority of the (City or Town) of . . . ." or some other name of a similar import);

(3) The location of its principal office, which shall be in the municipality;

(4) The number of directors (which shall be three or a multiple of three); and

(5) Any other matter relating to the authority that the incorporators may choose to insert and which shall not be inconsistent with this chapter or with the laws of the state.

(b) The certificate of incorporation shall be signed and acknowledged by each of the incorporators before an officer authorized by the laws of the state to take acknowledgments of deeds.

(c) The form and contents of the certificate of incorporation must be submitted to the governing body for its approval, which shall be evidenced by a resolution duly entered upon the minutes of the governing body. (Acts 1961, No. 895, p. 1407, § 4; Acts 1961, Ex. Sess., No. 289, p. 2335, § 4.)

§ 11-57-5. Same — Filing and recordation.

The certificate of incorporation, having attached thereto a certified copy of the resolution provided for in section 11-57-3 and a certificate by the secretary of state that the name proposed for the authority is not identical with that of any other corporation in the state or so nearly similar thereto as to lead to confusion and uncertainty, shall be filed in the office of the judge of probate of any county in which any portion of the municipality is located, who shall forthwith receive and record the same.

When such certificate of incorporation and attached documents have been so filed, the authority referred to therein shall come into existence and shall constitute a public corporation and a political subdivision of the state under the name set forth in such certificate of incorporation, whereupon the authority shall be vested with the rights and powers granted in this chapter. (Acts 1961, No. 895, p. 1407, § 5; Acts 1961, Ex. Sess., No. 289, p. 2335, § 5.)

§ 11-57-6. Board of directors; record of proceedings of board.

The authority shall have a board of directors composed of the number of directors provided in the certificate of incorporation. All powers of the authority shall be exercised by the board or pursuant to its authorization. The directors shall be residents of the municipality and shall be elected by the governing body for staggered terms of office as follows: the first term of one third of the directors shall be two years; the first term of the second one third of the directors shall be four years and the first term of the remaining one third of the directors shall be six years. Upon the expiration of the initial term of each director, each subsequent term shall be six years. If any director resigns, dies, becomes incapable of acting as a director or ceases to reside in the municipality, the governing body shall elect a successor to serve for the unexpired portion of his term of office. Directors shall be eligible to succeed themselves in office. No director shall be an officer of the state or of the municipality. A majority of the members of the board shall constitute a quorum for the transaction of business. No vacancy in the membership of the board shall impair the right of a quorum to exercise all the powers and duties of the authority. The members of the board and the officers of the authority shall serve without compensation, except that they may be reimbursed for actual expenses incurred in and about the performance of their duties.

All resolutions adopted by the board shall constitute actions of the authority, and all proceedings of the board shall be reduced to writing and signed by the secretary of the authority and shall be recorded in a well-bound book. Copies of such proceedings, when certified by the secretary of the authority, under the seal of the authority, shall be received in all courts as prima facie evidence of the matters and things therein certified. (Acts 1961, No. 895, p. 1407, § 6; Acts 1961, Ex. Sess., No. 289, p. 2335, § 6.)

§ 11-57-7. Officers.

The officers of the authority shall consist of a president, a vice-president, a secretary, a treasurer and such other officers as the board shall deem necessary to accomplish the purposes for which the authority was organized. The offices of secretary and treasurer may but need not be held by the same person. The president and vice-president of the authority shall be elected by the board from its membership. The secretary, the treasurer and any other officers of the authority who may but need not be members of the board shall also be elected by the board. (Acts 1961, No. 895, p. 1407, § 7; Acts 1961, Ex. Sess., No. 289, p. 2335, § 7.)

§ 11-57-8. Powers — Generally.

The authority shall have the following powers and capacities, among others specified in this chapter, together with all powers incidental thereto or necessary to the discharge thereof:

(1) To have succession by its corporate name until dissolved as provided in this chapter;

(2) To sue others and to prosecute civil actions;

(3) To be sued by others in any form of litigation other than an action ex delicto and to defend any litigation brought against it;

(4) To have and use a corporate seal and to alter the same at pleasure;

(5) To adopt and alter bylaws for the regulation and conduct of its affairs and business;

(6) To acquire, whether by purchase, gift, lease, devise or otherwise, property of every description which the board may deem necessary or desirable to the acquisition, construction, reconstruction, improvement, enlargement, equipment, operation or maintenance of a project and to hold title thereto;

(7) To construct, enlarge, improve, equip, maintain and operate one or more projects;

(8) To borrow money for any of its corporate purposes and to sell and issue in evidence of such borrowing its interest-bearing revenue bonds as provided in this chapter;

(9) To sell and issue refunding revenue bonds;

(10) To secure any of its bonds by pledge and indenture as provided in this chapter;

(11) To appoint, employ and compensate such agents, architects and legal counsel as the business of the authority may require;

(12) To provide for such insurance as the board may deem advisable;

(13) To invest any of its funds pending need therefor as provided in this chapter;

(14) To contract, lease and make lease agreements respecting its properties or any thereof as provided in this chapter; and

(15) To sell and convey any of its properties that may have become obsolete or worn out or that may no longer be needed or useful in connection with or in the operation of any project; provided, that it shall not have the power to sell or convey any project substantially as a whole except as provided in this chapter. (Acts 1961, No. 895, p. 1407, § 8; Acts 1961, Ex. Sess., No. 289, p. 2335, § 8.)

§ 11-57-9. Same — Eminent domain.

The authority shall have the same power of eminent domain as is vested by law in the municipality, which power shall be exercised in the same manner and under the same conditions as are provided by law for the exercise of the power of eminent domain by the municipality. (Acts 1961, No. 895, p. 1407, § 9; Acts 1961, Ex. Sess., No. 289, p. 2335, § 9.)

§ 11-57-10. Leasing of projects.

The authority and the municipality are hereby respectively authorized to enter into one or more lease agreements with each other whereunder one or more projects or any part thereof shall be leased by the authority to the municipality. No such lease agreement shall be for a term longer than the then current fiscal year in which it is made. Any such lease agreement made, however, may contain a grant to the municipality of successive options to renew such lease agreement, on the conditions specified therein, for additional terms, but no such additional term shall be for a period longer than the fiscal year in which such renewal shall be made. The lease agreement may contain provisions as to the method by which such renewal may be effected. The obligation on the part of the municipality to pay the rental required to be paid and to perform the agreements on the part of the municipality required to be performed during any fiscal year during which the lease agreement is in effect shall constitute a general obligation of the municipality, and the municipality is authorized to pledge its full faith and credit for the payment of such rental and the performance of such agreements; provided, that the rental required to be paid and the agreements required to be performed by the municipality under the lease agreement during any fiscal year during which the lease agreement is in effect shall be payable solely out of the current revenues of the municipality for such fiscal year. Any lease agreement may contain such covenants as shall not be inconsistent with this chapter. The rental required to be paid and the agreements required to be performed by the municipality under the provisions of the lease agreement shall never create an indebtedness of the municipality within the meaning of section 225 of the Constitution of the state.

If any space available for rent in any project which shall have been leased in whole or in part to the municipality should become vacant after acquisition or construction of the project by the authority, then until such time as all such vacant space shall have been filled or rented neither the municipality nor any officer, department or agency thereof shall thereafter enter into any rental agreement or renew any then existing rental agreement for other space in or about the municipality to be used for the same purposes for which such vacant space in the project is capable of being used. (Acts 1961, No. 895, p. 1407, § 10; Acts 1961, Ex. Sess., No. 289, p. 2335, § 10.)

§ 11-57-11. Bonds — Authority for issuance; security for payment of principal and interest generally; form, terms, denominations, etc.; sale, redemption, etc.

The authority is empowered at any time and from time to time to sell and issue its revenue bonds for the purpose of providing funds to acquire, construct, improve, enlarge, complete and equip one or more projects and for payment of obligations incurred for any such purpose. The principal of and interest on any such bonds shall be payable solely out of the revenues derived from the project with respect to which such bonds were issued.

Any bonds of the authority may be delivered by it at any time and from time to time, shall be in such form and denominations and of such tenor and maturities, shall bear such rate or rates of interest, payable and evidenced in such manner, may contain provisions for redemption prior to maturity and may contain other provisions not inconsistent with this chapter as may be provided by the resolution of the board whereunder such bonds are authorized to be issued; provided, that no bond of the authority shall have a specified maturity date later than 30 years after its date. Each bond of the authority having a specified maturity date more than 10 years after its date shall be made subject to redemption at the option of the authority at the end of the tenth year after its date and on any interest payment date thereafter under such terms and conditions as may be provided in the resolution under which such bond is authorized to be issued.

Bonds of the authority may be sold at either public or private sale in such manner and at such time or times as may be determined by the board to be most advantageous to the authority.

Bonds issued by the authority shall not be general obligations of the authority but shall be payable solely out of the revenues derived from the project with respect to which such bonds were issued. (Acts 1961, No. 895, p. 1407, § 11; Acts 1961, Ex. Sess., No. 289, p. 2335, § 11.)

§ 11-57-12. Same — Recital as to authority for issuance; notice of resolution authorizing issuance of bonds; limitation period for actions, etc., as to validity of proceedings for issuance of bonds, etc.

(a) Any resolution authorizing any bonds under this chapter shall contain a recital that they are issued pursuant to the provisions of this chapter, which recital shall be conclusive evidence that said bonds have been duly authorized pursuant to the provisions of this chapter, notwithstanding the provisions of any other law now in force or hereafter enacted or amended.

(b) Upon the adoption by the board of any resolution providing for the issuance of bonds, the authority may, in its discretion, cause to be published once a week for two consecutive weeks in a newspaper then published in the municipality or, if there is no newspaper then published in the municipality, then in a newspaper published or circulated in the county, a notice in substantially the following form (with any appropriate changes and with the blanks being properly filled in): "..........., a public corporation and a political subdivision of the state of Alabama, has authorized the issuance of $...... principal amount of bonds of the said authority to be dated ...... for purposes authorized in the act of the legislature of Alabama under which the said authority was organized, and has entered into a lease with the (city or town) of .... respecting the project described therein and pledged said lease and the rentals payable thereunder as security for said bonds. Any civil action or proceeding questioning the validity of the said bonds, or the pledge and the indenture to secure the same, or the said lease, must be commenced within 20 days after the first publication of this notice.

"................

"By ....

Its president"

(c) Any civil action or proceeding in any court to set aside or question the validity of the proceedings for the issuance of the bonds referred to in said notice or to contest the validity of any such bonds or the validity of the lease agreement pledged therefor or the validity of the indenture must be commenced within 20 days after the first publication of such notice. After the expiration of the said period no right of action or defense questioning or attacking the validity of the said proceedings or of the said bonds or the lease agreement or the indenture shall be asserted nor shall the validity of the said proceedings, bonds, lease agreement or indenture be open to question in any court on any ground whatsoever except in a civil action or proceeding commenced within said period. (Acts 1961, No. 895, p. 1407, § 23; Acts 1961, Ex. Sess., No. 289, p. 2335, § 23.)

§ 11-57-13. Same — Execution and delivery.

The bonds of the authority shall be signed by either its president or its vice-president as shall be provided in the resolution under which the bonds shall be issued, and the seal of the authority shall be affixed to the bonds and attested by its secretary; provided, that a facsimile of the signature of one, but not both, of the officers whose signatures will appear on the bonds may be imprinted or otherwise reproduced on any of the bonds in lieu of his manually signing the same; provided further, that a facsimile of the seal of the authority may be imprinted or otherwise reproduced on any of the bonds in lieu of being manually affixed thereto. Any interest coupons applicable to the bonds shall be signed either manually by or with a facsimile of the signature of either the president or the vice-president of the authority as shall be provided in the resolution under which the bonds shall be issued.

If, after any of the bonds or interest coupons thereunto appertaining shall be so signed, whether manually or by facsimile, any such officer shall for any reason vacate his office, the bonds and interest coupons so signed may nevertheless be delivered at any time thereafter as the act and deed of the authority. (Acts 1961, No. 895, p. 1407, § 13; Acts 1961, Ex. Sess., No. 289, p. 2335, § 23.)

§ 11-57-14. Same — Negotiability.

All bonds issued by the authority, while not registered, shall be construed to be negotiable instruments even though they are payable from a limited source. All coupons applicable to any bonds issued by the authority, while the applicable bonds are not registered as to both principal and interest, shall likewise be construed to be negotiable instruments although payable from a limited source. (Acts 1961, No. 895, p. 1407, § 19; Acts 1961, Ex. Sess., No. 289, p. 2335, § 19.)

§ 11-57-15. Same — Security for payment of principal and interest.

The principal of and the interest on the bonds shall be secured by a pledge of the revenues out of which the bonds shall be made payable by an assignment or pledge of the lease agreement covering the project from which revenues so pledged shall be derived and by a pledge of the rental from such project and may be secured by a nonforeclosable indenture covering the project.

The trustee under any indenture may be a trust company or bank having trust powers, whether located within or without the state. The indenture may contain any agreements and provisions customarily contained in instruments securing evidences of indebtedness, including, without limiting the generality of the foregoing, provisions respecting the collection, segregation and application of the rental from any project covered by such indenture, the terms to be incorporated in the lease agreement respecting the project, the maintenance and insurance of the project, the creation and maintenance of special funds from the rental of the project and the rights and remedies available in the event of default to the holders of the bonds or the trustee under the indenture as the board shall deem advisable and shall not be in conflict with the provisions of this chapter; provided, that in making any such agreements or provisions the authority shall not have the power to obligate itself except with respect to the project and the application of the revenues therefrom. The indenture may contain provisions regarding the rights of any trustee thereunder and the holders of the bonds and coupons and may contain provisions restricting the individual rights of action of the holders of the bonds and coupons. (Acts 1961, No. 895, p. 1407, § 14; Acts 1961, Ex. Sess., No. 289, p. 2335, § 14.)

§ 11-57-16. Same — Disposition of proceeds from sale.

(a) The proceeds derived from the sale of any bonds sold by the authority, other than refunding bonds, shall be used only to pay the cost of acquiring, constructing, improving, enlarging and equipping one or more projects as may be provided in the proceedings in which the bonds are authorized to be issued.

(b) Such cost, which shall be paid from the proceeds derived from the sale of bonds, shall be deemed to include the following:

(1) The cost of acquiring any land forming a part of the project;

(2) The cost of the labor, materials and supplies used in any such construction, improvement or enlargement, including architect's and engineer's fees and the cost of preparing contract documents and advertising for bids;

(3) The purchase price of and the cost of installing equipment for the project;

(4) The cost of landscaping the lands forming a part of the project and of constructing and installing roads, sidewalks, curbs, gutters, utilities and parking places in connection therewith;

(5) Legal, fiscal and recording fees and expenses incurred in connection with any such acquisition and construction and with the authorization, sale and issuance of the bonds issued in connection with the project; and

(6) Interest on the bonds for a reasonable period prior to the commencement of the construction of the project and during the period that is estimated will

be required for such construction and for a period of not more than six months after the completion of such construction.

(c) If any proceeds derived from the sale of the bonds remain undisbursed after completion of the work and payment of all costs and expenses in connection with the project with respect to which the bonds are issued, such balance shall be applied toward the retirement of the bonds. The proceeds derived from the sale of any refunding bonds shall be used only for the purposes for which the refunding bonds were authorized to be issued. (Acts 1961, No. 895, p. 1407, § 15; Acts 1961, Ex. Sess., No. 289, p. 2335, § 15.)

§ 11-57-17. Refunding bonds.

The authority may at any time and from time to time sell and issue its refunding revenue bonds for the purpose of refunding the principal of and interest on any matured or unmatured bonds of the authority at the time outstanding and for the payment of any expenses incurred in connection with such refunding and any premium necessary to be paid to redeem or retire the bonds so to be refunded. Any such refunding may be effected either by sale of refunding bonds and the application of the proceeds thereof to payment, redemption or retirement of the bonds to be refunded thereby, by exchange of the refunding bonds for the bonds or interest coupons to be refunded thereby or by any combination thereof; provided, that the holders of any bonds or coupons so to be refunded shall not be compelled without their consent to surrender their bonds or coupons for payment or exchange prior to the date on which they may be paid or redeemed by the authority under their respective provisions. Any refunding bonds of the authority shall be payable solely from the revenues out of which the bonds or coupons to be refunded thereby were payable.

All provisions of this chapter pertaining to bonds of the authority that are not inconsistent with the provisions of this section shall, to the extent applicable, also apply to refunding bonds issued by the authority. (Acts 1961, No. 895, p. 1407, § 12; Acts 1961, Ex. Sess., No. 289, p. 2335, § 12.)

§ 11-57-18. Investment in bonds — By municipalities.

The governing body is authorized in its discretion to invest in bonds of the authority any idle or surplus money held in the treasury of the municipality which is not otherwise earmarked or pledged. (Acts 1961, No. 895, p. 1407, § 22; Acts 1961, Ex. Sess., No. 289, p. 2335, § 22.)

§ 11-57-19. Same — By executors, savings banks, insurance companies, etc.

Bonds issued under the provisions of this chapter are hereby made legal investments for savings banks and insurance companies organized under the laws of the state. Unless otherwise directed by the court having jurisdiction thereof or the document that is the source of authority, a trustee, executor, administrator, guardian or one acting in any other fiduciary capacity may, in addition to any other investment powers conferred by law and with the exercise of reasonable business prudence, invest trust funds in bonds of the authority. (Acts 1961, No. 895, p. 1407, § 21; Acts 1961, Ex. Sess., No. 289, p. 2335, § 21.)

§ 11-57-20. Remedies upon default on bonds, lease agreements, etc.

(a) *In event of default on the bonds.* — If there should be any default in the payment of the principal of or interest on any bonds issued under this chapter, then the holder of any of the bonds and of any of the interest coupons applicable thereto and the trustee under any indenture, or any one or more of them, may by mandamus, injunction or other proceedings compel performance of all duties of the officers and directors of the authority with respect to the use of funds for the payment of the bonds and for the performance of the agreements of the authority contained in the proceedings under which they were issued, shall be entitled to a judgment against the authority for the principal of and interest on the bonds so in default and, regardless of the sufficiency of the security for the bonds in default and as a matter of right, shall be entitled to the appointment of a receiver to make lease agreements respecting the project out of whose revenues the bonds so in default are payable and fix and collect rents therefor and to operate, administer and maintain the project as a public library facility with all powers of a receiver in the exercise of any of said functions. The income derived from any lease agreement made and any operation of the project carried on by any such receiver shall be expended in accordance with the provisions of the proceedings under which the bonds were authorized to be issued and the orders of the court by which such receiver is appointed.

(b) *In event of default in lease agreement, etc.* — If there should be any default by the municipality in the payment of any installment of rent or in the performance of any agreement required to be made or performed by the municipality under the provisions of any lease agreement, the authority and the trustee under any indenture, or either of them, may by mandamus, injunction or other proceedings compel performance by the officials of the municipality of their duties respecting the payment of the rentals required to be paid and performance of the agreements on the part of the municipality required to be performed under any such lease agreement, and shall be entitled to a judgment against the municipality for all monetary payments required to be made by the municipality under the provisions of such lease agreement with respect to which the municipality is then in default.

(c) *Remedies cumulative.* — The remedies specified in subsections (a) and (b) of this section shall be cumulative to all other remedies which may otherwise be available for the benefit of the holders of the bonds and the coupons applicable thereto; provided, that any indenture shall not be subject to foreclosure and shall not be construed so as to authorize the sale of any project covered thereby or any part thereof in satisfaction of the bonds secured thereby. (Acts 1961, No. 895, p. 1407, § 16; Acts 1961, Ex. Sess., No. 289, p. 2335, § 16.)

§ 11-57-21. Liability of state or municipalities on bonds and obligations of authorities.

All obligations incurred by the authority and all bonds issued by it shall be solely and exclusively an obligation of the authority and shall not create an obligation or debt of the state of Alabama or of the municipality. (Acts 1961, No. 895, p. 1407, § 20; Acts 1961, Ex. Sess., No. 289, p. 2335, § 20.)

§ 11-57-22. Investment of funds of authorities.

Any portion of the principal proceeds derived from the sale of the bonds which the board may determine is not presently needed for any of the purposes for which the bonds are authorized to be issued and any other moneys of the authority which the board may determine will not be presently needed by the authority may, on order of the board, be invested in any securities that are direct obligations of the United States of America or the principal of and interest on which are unconditionally and irrevocably guaranteed by the United States of America. Any securities in which any such investment is made may, at any time and from time to time on order of the board, be sold or otherwise converted into cash. The income derived from any such investments shall be disbursed on order of the board for any purpose for which the authority may lawfully expend funds. (Acts 1961, No. 895, p. 1407, § 17; Acts 1961, Ex. Sess., No. 289, p. 2335, § 17.)

§ 11-57-23. Conveyances of property to authorities by municipalities.

The municipality is hereby authorized to transfer and convey to the authority, with or without the payment of monetary consideration therefor, any property that may immediately preceding such conveyance be owned by the municipality, whether or not such property is necessary for the conduct of the governmental or other public functions of the municipality; provided, that such conveyance shall be authorized by a resolution duly adopted by the governing body prior to the conveyance. Such resolution shall be published one time, at least five days before such transfer is consummated, in a newspaper published in the municipality or, if there is no newspaper then published in the municipality, then in a newspaper published or circulated in the county. (Acts 1961, No. 895, p. 1407, § 24; Acts 1961, Ex. Sess., No. 289, p. 2335, § 24.)

§ 11-57-24. Authority and procedure for dissolution of authorities; vesting of title to assets or properties thereof in municipalities upon dissolution; formation of authorities not to prevent subsequent formation of other authorities by same municipalities.

(a) At any time when the authority does not have any bonds outstanding, the board may adopt a resolution, which shall be duly entered upon its minutes, declaring that the authority shall be dissolved. Upon the filing for record of a certified copy of said resolution in the office of the judge of probate of the county, the authority shall thereupon stand dissolved; and, in the event that it owned any assets or property at the time of its dissolution, the title to all its assets and property shall thereupon vest in the municipality. In the event the authority shall at any time have outstanding bonds issued hereunder payable out of the revenues of different projects, then as and when the principal of and interest on all bonds payable from the revenues derived from any project shall have been paid in full, title to the project with respect to which the bonds so paid in full have been paid shall thereupon vest in the municipality, but such vesting of title in the municipality shall not affect the title of the authority to any other project the revenues from which are pledged to the payment of any other bonds then outstanding.

(b) The formation of one or more public corporations under the provisions of this chapter shall not prevent the subsequent formation under this chapter of other public corporations pursuant to permission granted by the same municipality. (Acts 1961, No. 895, p. 1407, § 25; Acts 1961, Ex. Sess., No. 289, p. 2335, § 25.)

§ 11-57-25. Exemption from taxation of properties, bonds, etc.

The properties of the authority and the income therefrom, all lease agreements made by the authority, all bonds issued by the authority and the coupons applicable thereto and the income therefrom and all indentures executed with respect thereto shall be forever exempt from any and all taxation in the state of Alabama. (Acts 1961, No. 895, p. 1407, § 18; Acts 1961, Ex. Sess., No. 289, p. 2335, § 18.)

§ 11-57-26. Construction of chapter.

This chapter shall not be construed as a restriction or limitation upon any power, right or remedy which any municipality or any corporation now in existence or hereafter formed may have in the absence hereof and shall be construed as cumulative and independent thereof. (Acts 1961, No. 895, p. 1407, § 26; Acts 1961, Ex. Sess., No. 289, p. 2335, § 26.)

SCHOOL LIBRARIES
(Code of Alabama, 1982, s.16-21-1 to 16-21-23.)

§ 16-21-1. County may appropriate funds for school libraries.

The county commission or board of education in any county is hereby authorized to appropriate funds to any public school under the control of the county board of education and to any county high school for the purpose of establishing, maintaining, enlarging or improving public libraries in such schools. (School Code 1927, § 391; Code 1940, T. 52, § 376.)

§ 16-21-2. Library books and equipment.

The state superintendent of education, with the advice of the director of the department of archives and history, shall compile and publish a carefully selected and annotated list of books from which the libraries herein provided shall be chosen, and he shall also adopt and publish rules and regulations for the choice of books, their use, preservation and circulation, the erection of book-shelves or bookcases, the equipment of library rooms or buildings and the training of librarians or custodians for the libraries. The selection shall be as nearly as possible representative of the whole field of literature, and maximum prices for purchase shall be indicated. (School Code 1927, § 394; Code 1940, T. 52, § 377.)

§ 16-21-3. Circulating libraries.

Any county board of education may in lieu of granting separate libraries for each school establish a system of circulating libraries, said libraries to be purchased under the same conditions and in keeping with the plan set out in the previous sections of this chapter by the county superintendent of education. Such circulating libraries shall be available for use in the public schools of the county under rules and regulations prescribed by the county board of education with the approval of the state board of education. (School Code 1927, § 397; Code 1940, T. 52, § 380.)

SUPREME COURT LIBRARY
(Code of Alabama, 1982, s.12-2-151 to 12-2-160.)

§ 12-2-151. Designation of marshal as state law librarian, etc.; discharge of duties of office generally.

The marshal of the supreme court shall be the state law librarian and shall be the director of the supreme court and state law library, and shall also be marshal and librarian of the court of criminal appeals and court of civil appeals, and shall, in discharging the duties of his office, obey such rules and regulations as may be prescribed by the justices. (Code 1867, § 671; Code 1876, § 582; Code 1886, § 688; Code 1896, § 3848; Code 1907, § 5974; Code 1923, § 10310; Code 1940, T. 13, § 75.)

§ 12-2-152. Entry of appointment of marshal on minutes of court; oath.

The appointment of the marshal must be entered on the minutes of the court; and, before receiving any compensation, he must make oath before one of the justices that he will faithfully discharge his duties as marshal and librarian and that he will, to the best of his ability, preserve the libraries from loss and injury. (Code 1852, § 576; Code 1867, § 673; Code 1876, § 584; Code 1886, § 690; Code 1896, § 3850; Code 1907, § 5976; Code 1923, § 10312; Code 1940, T. 13, § 77.)

§ 12-2-153. Bond.

Before entering upon the duties of his office, the marshal and librarian shall execute to the state of Alabama a bond, to be approved by the governor, in the amount of $5,000.00, for the faithful performance of his duties. (Acts 1943, No. 122, p. 123; Acts 1961, Ex. Sess., No. 208, p. 2190.)

§ 12-2-154. Salary.

The salary of the marshal and librarian of the supreme court and state law library shall be fixed under the provisions of the merit system at the maximum paid to attorneys in the classified service and shall be payable out of the treasury as the salaries of other state officers are paid. (Code 1852, § 577; Code 1867, § 675; Code 1876, § 596; Code 1886, § 692; Code 1896, § 3852; Code 1907, § 5978; Acts 1919, No. 606, p. 854; Code 1923, § 10314; Acts 1933, Ex. Sess., No. 138, p. 124; Acts 1939, No. 416, p. 557; Code 1940, T. 13, § 78; Acts 1967, No. 389, p. 977.)

§ 12-2-155. Deputy marshals, assistant librarian, clerk and other employees — Appointment.

The marshal and librarian, subject to the approval of the justices, is authorized to designate or appoint the necessary deputy marshals, an assistant librarian, a clerk IV in the unclassified service and such other employees under the provisions of the merit system as are necessary for the performance of his duties. (Code 1886, § 686; Code 1896, § 3846; Code 1907, § 5972; Code 1923, § 10308; Code 1940, T. 13, § 79; Acts 1967, No. 726, p. 1561.)

§ 12-2-156. Same — Salaries.

The salaries of the persons designated or appointed pursuant to section 12-2-155 shall be fixed under the provisions of the merit system, and they shall be paid as are other state employees. (Code 1886, § 687; Code 1896, § 3847; Code 1907, § 5973; Acts 1923, No. 600, p. 789; Code 1923, § 10309; Acts 1933, Ex. Sess., No. 138, p. 124; Acts 1939, No. 58, p. 68; Code 1940, T. 13, § 80.)

§ 12-2-157. Library fund.

The library fund of the supreme court and state law library shall consist of funds appropriated by the legislature, fees collected under the provision of law and moneys collected from the sale of copies, books and other materials or received from donations, gifts, grants and funds other than those appropriated. Expenditures out of this fund shall be made by the state law librarian for the use and benefit of the appellate courts under the direction of the justices. (Code 1852, § 592; Code 1867, § 691; Code 1876, §§ 587, 603; Code 1886, § 693; Code 1896, § 3853; Code 1907, § 5979; Code 1923, § 10315; Code 1940, T. 13, § 81.)

§ 12-2-158. Use of library fund for purchase of law books for office of attorney general.

The marshal and librarian may use, in the purchase of law books for the office of the attorney general, so much of the library fund as the justices may from time to time direct. (Code 1896, § 3855; Code 1907, § 5981; Code 1923, § 10317; Code 1940, T. 13, § 83.)

§ 12-2-159. Library tax.

For the maintenance of the supreme court library there shall be taxed in each civil case decided by the supreme court or the courts of appeals on appeal the sum of $5.00, which must be taxed and collected as other costs in the case and, when collected, must be paid by the clerk to the marshal and librarian, by whom it must be disbursed on the order of the justices. (Code 1886, § 694; Code 1896, § 3854; Code 1907, § 5980; Code 1923, § 10316; Code 1940, T. 13, § 82.)

§ 12-2-160. Justices to make rules for preservation and protection of libraries.

The justices of the supreme court must make such rules as they deem necessary for the preservation and protection of the libraries. (Code 1867, § 672; Code 1876, § 583; Code 1886, § 689; Code 1896, § 3849; Code 1907, § 5975; Code 1923, § 10311; Code 1940, T. 13, § 76.)

COUNTY LAW LIBRARIES
(Code of Alabama, 1982, s.11-25-1 to 11-25-12.)

§ 11-25-1. Authorized; power to appropriate space and funds; filing of resolutions.

The governing body of each county by resolution thereof shall have the power to establish and maintain a county law library for each courthouse in their respective counties for the use and benefit of the county and state officials, court system and the public; and shall have the power to appropriate and set aside for the establishment, maintenance and support of said libraries, such space and funds as it shall deem necessary and appropriate. All resolutions setting up county law libraries shall be filed in the probate office of the county where located and with the administrative director of courts. (Acts 1979, No. 79-751, p. 1336, § 1.)

§ 11-25-2. Existing libraries; alternative method of establishing libraries; successors to property, funds, etc.

The governing body of each county having county law libraries under existing laws on August 8, 1979, may come under the provisions of this chapter by resolution thereof, upon the request of the presiding circuit judge, and the filing of a copy of said resolution with the secretary of state and the administrative director of courts. This is an alternative method to the local act method of establishing county law libraries and a county may elect at any time to use either method but may not have a county law library under both methods at the same time. All county law libraries established under the provisions of this chapter shall become owners and successors to all property, funds and obligations of their predecessors and all property and funds subsequently acquired by the county law libraries. (Acts 1979, No. 79-751, p. 1336, § 2.)

§ 11-25-3. County to furnish space and utilities for libraries; supplement budget.

In return for the county law libraries serving the legal materials needs of the county and court officials and of the citizens of the county, the county governing body may furnish adequate space and utilities for law libraries established under the provisions of this chapter and may supplement the book and materials budget if it considers such to be needed. (Acts 1979, No. 79-751, p. 1336, § 3.)

§ 11-25-4. Municipalities authorized to appropriate funds or property.

Municipal governing bodies may appropriate funds or property to the county law libraries in consideration of said libraries making their facilities and holdings available to the citizens of the municipalities. (Acts 1979, No. 79-751, p. 1336, § 4.)

§ 11-25-5. Judge authorized to appoint law librarian or custodian.

Upon the establishment of a county law library, or the continuance of a present county law library under the provisions of this chapter, the presiding judge of the circuit, or a district or circuit judge designated by him, may appoint a full or part time county law librarian or custodian. (Acts 1979, No. 79-751, p. 1336, § 5.)

§ 11-25-6. Administration of library; appointment of advisory committee.

The presiding circuit judge for the county or county law librarian if one exists, shall administer the county law library and shall disburse the library funds, and shall appoint such librarians and assistants as are necessary for the proper operation of the library. The presiding judge of the circuit shall appoint an advisory committee to the county law library. (Acts 1979, No. 79-751, p. 1336, § 6.)

§ 11-25-7. County law library fund; audit, use, etc.; purchases exempt from taxes.

Upon the establishment of a county law library under the provisions of this chapter each county shall have and maintain a separate fund known as the county law library fund and may have a separate law library fund for each law library in the county. The county law library funds shall consist of funds appropriated by the state, county or municipal governments, funds collected under the provisions of law, proceeds from the sale of copies, books and other materials, or received from donations, gifts, grants and funds other than those appropriated, and shall be audited as county funds are audited. Said fund may be used to match grants for library purposes. Library funds may be used to pay library personnel. All purchases by or on behalf of such library shall be exempt from all state of Alabama, county or municipal sales, use or other similar taxes. (Acts 1979, No. 79-751, p. 1336, § 7.)

§ 11-25-8. Power to receive gifts, exchange books, etc.; furnish services to county and court officials without cost.

County law libraries shall have the power to receive gifts, grants, and to exchange books and materials with other libraries and may furnish the legal needs of books, materials, and copies to the county officials and circuit, probate and district court officials at no cost. (Acts 1979, No. 79-751, p. 1336, § 8.)

§ 11-25-9. Library fee as court cost; disposition.

For the support and maintenance of county law libraries established under the provisions of this chapter a library fee of two dollars shall be paid in all causes and cases of whatever nature in the district and circuit courts of the various counties wherein this law is in effect, to be collected as other court costs are collected and paid at the same time as docket or filing fees are paid. Said library fees shall be paid in all proceedings wherein a docket or filing fee is paid. All of the funds collected under the provisions of this section shall be transmitted to the proper county law library fund by the tenth of each month following their collection. (Acts 1979, No. 79-751, p. 1336, § 9.)

§ 11-25-10. Libraries to receive state acts and Code.

County law libraries shall be on the distribution list of the secretary of state to receive one set each of the acts of Alabama and the Code of Alabama and the supplements thereto. (Acts 1979, No. 79-751, p. 1336, § 10.)

§ 11-25-11. Network of law libraries.

The county law libraries are a part of a network of law libraries with the state-supported law libraries, and the non-state-supported law libraries on a voluntary basis, for their mutual benefit. (Acts 1979, No. 79-751, p. 1336, § 11.)

§ 11-25-12. Authority to transfer, lend, etc., books, materials, etc.

The state, counties and state agencies have the authority to transfer, sell, give or lend books, property and materials to the county law libraries; and said county law libraries have the authority to transfer books, property and materials to the state, counties and state agencies, and to other county law libraries in the state on a voluntary basis. (Acts 1979, No. 79-751, p. 1336, § 12.)

LIBRARY SERVICE FOR THE HANDICAPPED
(Code of Alabama, 1982, s.21-1-15.)

§ 21-1-15. Department of adult blind and deaf established; appropriations; operation of library service.

There shall be at the Alabama Institute for Deaf and Blind a separate department of adult blind and deaf. Legislative appropriations for the department shall be made separate and apart from the legislative appropriations made for the support and operation of the institute. The department shall have authority to establish and to operate a library service for blind, visually handicapped, deaf or severely handicapped persons, and the department is hereby designated as the official agency to operate a regional library for the blind, visually handicapped, deaf and severely handicapped. (Acts 1939, No. 467, p. 680; Code 1940, T. 52, § 528; Acts 1969, No. 425, p. 829, § 1.)

Alabama library laws are reprinted from the CODE OF ALABAMA published by The Michie Co., Charlottesville, Virginia.

ALASKA

STATE LIBRARY AND HISTORICAL LIBRARY
(Alaska Statutes, 1982, s.14.56.010 to 14.56.080.)

Sec. 14.56.010. Department of Education to govern library. The Department of Education shall manage and have complete charge of all of the property contained in the institutions known as the state library and state historical library. The state library and state historical library shall be maintained in the state capital. (§ 57 ch 98 SLA 1966; am § 1 ch 192 SLA 1968)

Sec. 14.56.020. Powers of Department of Education. The department shall

(1) stimulate and encourage citizens' participation in the development and improvement of library facilities; and

(2) establish policies, plans, and procedures of the department, and promulgate reasonable regulations and orders, with penalties, as may be required. (§ 57 ch 98 SLA 1966)

Sec. 14.56.030. State library duties. The department shall undertake state library functions which will benefit the state and its citizens, including:

(1) coordinate library services of the state with other educational services and agencies to increase effectiveness and eliminate duplication;

(2) provide reference library service to state and other public officials;

(3) provide library services and administer state and other grants-in-aid to public libraries to supplement and improve their services, the grants to be paid from funds appropriated for that purpose, or from other funds available for that purpose;

(4) provide library service directly to areas in which there is not sufficient population or local revenue to support independent library units;

(5) distribute financial aid to public libraries for extension of library

service to surrounding areas and to improve inadequate local library service under regulations promulgated by the department;

(6) offer consultant service on library matters to state and municipal libraries, community libraries, school libraries, and libraries in unincorporated communities;

(7) serve as a depository for state and federal publications concerning Alaska;

(8) apply for, receive, and spend federal, state, or private funds available for library purposes;

(9) record and distribute the election pamphlet provided for by AS 15.57 to libraries throughout the state for use by blind voters. (§ 57 ch 98 SLA 1966; am § 1 ch 10 SLA 1975)

Sec. 14.56.040. Application for grant-in-aid. An association desiring to receive the benefits of §§ 20 — 60 of this chapter shall file a copy of its articles of incorporation and bylaws with the department, and shall file an annual report with the department listing the members of its library board and an accurate record of money spent on the purchase of books and periodicals. A copy of these records shall be sent to the department at the close of each fiscal year. (§ 57 ch 98 SLA 1966)

Sec. 14.56.050. Payment of grant-in-aid. An association that, during a fiscal year, has complied with §§ 20 — 60 of this chapter and the regulations promulgated by the department under it, is entitled to receive the authorized amount of aid. Payment of the grant-in-aid is on a reimbursement basis upon the presentation by the association of paid invoices listing the authors and titles of books and periodicals purchased. No payment made for the purchase of any books of a religious or sectarian nature, or for other property except books and periodicals shall be counted as part of the sums for which reimbursement may be claimed under §§ 20 — 60 of this chapter. (§ 57 ch 98 SLA 1966)

Sec. 14.56.060. Limitation on grant-in-aid. The state shall provide assistance to any association incorporated under the laws of the state, for the purpose of maintaining public libraries, to the extent of paying to the association a sum equal to the sum which the association spends in purchasing books and periodicals for public libraries in the state, not exceeding $250 in one year to each association, in accordance with the rules of the department. (§ 57 ch 98 SLA 1966)

Sec. 14.56.065. Public library construction grants. (a) The director of the division of state libraries shall administer a program providing for grants to municipalities in the state for the construction and equipping of libraries. To be eligible for a grant under this section a municipality shall provide not less than 40 per cent of the total cost of the project for which funds are granted. The department shall administer the funds under this section and shall adopt regulations necessary to carry out the purposes of this section.

(b) In this section "municipality" means a city or organized borough of any class. (§ 1 ch 100 SLA 1970)

Sec. 14.56.080. Historical library duties. The department shall

(1) collect, catalog, and preserve an Alaska collection consisting of books, laws, pamphlets, periodicals, manuscripts, microreproductions, audiovisual materials, etc.;

(2) serve as a depository for state and federal historical publications concerning Alaska;

(3) acquire, catalog, and maintain private papers and manuscripts relative to Alaska which are adjudged worthy of preservation for reference and research purposes;

(4) perform other functions necessary to the operation of a historical library. (§ 57 ch 98 SLA 1966; am § 2 ch 191 SLA 1970)

STATE AID
Library Assistance Grants
(Alaska Statutes, 1982, s.14.56.300 to 14.56.340.)

Sec. 14.56.300. Library assistance grant fund. There is established in the department a library assistance grant fund. From legislative appropriations to the fund, the department shall make grants to eligible libraries for public library operations or for interlibrary cooperation or for both. (§ 1 ch 36 SLA 1981)

Sec. 14.56.310. Eligibility. (a) Libraries eligible for grants under AS 14.56.300 are:

(1) public libraries operated by municipalities or by public library nonprofit corporations; and

(2) libraries sharing resources or providing services to other libraries.

(b) A library described in (a) (1) of this section is eligible for a public library assistance grant. A library described in either (a) (1) or (2) of this section is eligible for an interlibrary cooperation assistance grant. (§ 1 ch 36 SLA 1981)

Sec. 14.56.320. Applications. An eligible library may apply to the department for a grant under AS 14.56.300 — 14.56.340 in accordance with regulations adopted by the board. (§ 1 ch 36 SLA 1981)

Sec. 14.56.330. Limitations. (a) A public library assistance grant under AS 14.56.300 — 14.56.340 may not exceed $10,000 for each local public library service outlet in any one fiscal year. However, no amount over $5,000 may be granted unless it is equally matched by local money.

(b) State money granted to a library under AS 14.56.300 — 14.56.340 may not be used to supplant local money equal to local expenditures for that library in fiscal year 1980, as adjusted annually by the commissioner to conform approximately to changes in the United States Department of Labor Bureau of Labor Statistics consumer price index for Anchorage, Alaska. A library that uses state money to supplant local money forfeits eligibility for grants under AS 14.56.300 — 14.56.340 for two years. (§ 1 ch 36 SLA 1981)

Sec. 14.56.340. Regulations. The board shall adopt regulations necessary to carry out the purposes of AS 14.56.300 — 14.56.330. (§ 1 ch 36 SLA 1981)

Rural Community Libraries
(Alaska Statutes, 1982, s.14.56.200 to 14.56.240.)

Sec. 14.56.200. Grants for constructing and equipping libraries. The division of state libraries shall administer a program providing for grants to rural communities for constructing and equipping community libraries according to the provisions of §§ 210 — 240 of this chapter. (§ 1 ch 42 SLA 1970)

Sec. 14.56.210. Application for grants. (a) A rural community desiring to receive the benefits of the grants provided for in § 200 of this chapter shall apply to the division of state libraries. If the rural community is within a borough with areawide library powers, the borough may apply on behalf of the community.

(b) To be eligible for a grant under §§ 200 — 240 of this chapter, the applicant shall provide not less than 10 per cent of the total cost of the project for which the funds are granted. The remaining percentage shall be provided by the state. The matching share of the applicant may be in the form of money, land, services, or other items acceptable to the division of state libraries. Satisfactory assurance of the continuation of library services shall be included as part of the application. (§ 1 ch 42 SLA 1970)

Sec. 14.56.220. Ownership of facility. Title to a library constructed under §§ 200 — 240 of this chapter shall be in the applicant unless the applicant is an unincorporated city, in which case the state shall retain title until the time of any subsequent incorporation. (§ 1 ch 42 SLA 1970)

Sec. 14.56.230. Regulations. The division of state libraries shall adopt regulations necessary to carry out the purposes of §§ 200 — 240 of this chapter. (§ 1 ch 42 SLA 1970)

Sec. 14.56.240. "Rural community" defined. In §§ 200 — 230 of this chapter, "rural community" means any community except a first class city of over 2,000 population. (§ 1 ch 42 SLA 1970; am § 27 ch 53 SLA 1973)

STATE LIBRARY DISTRIBUTION AND DATA ACCESS CENTER
(Alaska Statutes, 1982, s.14.56.090 to 14.56.180.)

Sec. 14.56.090. State library distribution and data access center established. There is established in the state library the state library distribution and data access center. (§ 1 ch 2 SLA 1970; am § 2 ch 27 SLA 1979)

Sec. 14.56.100. Duties of center. The center shall, in cooperation with federal, municipal, and private data collection and research efforts, promote the establishment of an orderly depository library and data index distribution and access system. (§ 1 ch 2 SLA 1970; am § 3 ch 27 SLA 1979)

Sec. 14.56.120. Deposit of publications and research data. (a) Each state agency shall deposit, upon release, at least four copies of each of its state publications in the center. Additional copies of each publication may be requested by the center for deposit in quantities necessary to meet the needs of the depository library system and to provide inter-library service to those libraries not having depository status.

(b) Each state agency shall notify the center of the creation of all data published or compiled by or for it at public expense and provide for its accessibility through the center, unless the data is protected by the constitutional right to privacy or is of a type stated by law to be confidential or the agency is otherwise prohibited by law from doing so.

(c) The center is also a depository for publications of municipalities and regional educational attendance areas, including surveys and studies produced by a municipality or regional educational attendance area or produced for it on contract. Four copies of each publication produced for a municipality or regional educational attendance area may be deposited with the center for record and distribution purposes.

(d) Each municipality or regional educational attendance area may notify the center of the creation of all data published or compiled by or for it at public expense and provide for its accessibility through the center, unless the data is protected by the constitutional right to privacy or is of a type stated by law to be confidential or the municipality or regional educational attendance area is otherwise prohibited by law from doing so.

(e) When a research project or study is conducted for a person by a state agency, a municipality, or a regional educational attendance area, even though no state funding is involved, the state agency, municipality or regional educational attendance area shall request that person for permission to make copies of its final report available to the center under AS 14.56.090 — 14.56.180. If permission is granted, the report shall be deposited with the center. (§ 1 ch 2 SLA 1970; am § 4 ch 27 SLA 1979)

Sec. 14.56.123. Liaison with center. Each state agency shall and each municipality and regional educational attendance area may designate one of its employees to be responsible for depositing the materials and information specified in AS 14.56.120. (§ 5 ch 27 SLA 1979)

Sec. 14.56.125. Summaries and indices. (a) Upon notification of the creation of data under AS 14.56.120, a state agency shall and a municipality or regional educational attendance area may prepare an abstract or summary of it.

(b) The center shall prepare and keep current an index of all publications and data abstracts or summaries on file and shall publish and distribute that index regularly to contracting depository libraries and to other Alaska libraries upon request. (§ 5 ch 27 SLA 1979)

Sec. 14.56.130. Other documents required of state agencies. Upon the request of the center, a state agency shall furnish the center with a complete list of its current state publications, data published or compiled by or for it at public expense, and a copy of its mailing or exchange lists. However, data which is protected by the constitutional right to privacy or is of a type stated by law to be confidential or which the agency is otherwise prohibited by law from distributing may not be furnished to the center. (§ 1 ch 2 SLA 1970; am § 6 ch 27 SLA 1979)

Sec. 14.56.135. Efficiency and computerization. The center shall, to the extent practicable, avoid duplication, coordinate its activities with other state agencies charged with record-keeping functions, and employ computerization to compile or organize research data and other materials. (§ 7 ch 27 SLA 1979)

Sec. 14.56.150. Depository library contracts. The center may enter into depository contracts with municipal, regional educational attendance area, university or community college libraries, public library associations, state library agencies, the Library of Congress, and other state and federal library systems. The requirements for eligibility to contract as a depository library shall be established by the Department of Education upon the recommendation of the state librarian and shall include and take into consideration the type of library, its ability to preserve publications or data and to make them available for public use, and the geographical location of the library for ease of access to residents in all areas of the state. (§ 1 ch 2 SLA 1970; am § 8 ch 27 SLA 1979)

Sec. 14.56.170. Distribution of state publications and research data. The center may not engage in general public distribution of either (1) state publications or lists of publications or (2) the index of publications and research data. However, unless expressly prohibited by law, the center shall make available to any person, upon request and under procedures established by it, publications, summaries, research data, indices, and other materials in its possession. Reasonable fees for reproduction or printing costs and for mailing and distribution of materials may be charged by the center. (§ 1 ch 2 SLA 1970; am § 9 ch 27 SLA 1979)

Sec. 14.56.180. Definitions. In AS 14.56.090 — 14.56.180, unless the context otherwise requires,

(1) "center" means the state library distribution and data access center;

(2) "state agency" includes state departments, divisions, agencies, boards, associations, commissions, corporations and offices, and the University of Alaska and its affiliated research institutes;

(3) "municipal" and "municipality" includes cities and organized boroughs of every class, including municipalities unified under AS 29.68.240 — 29.68.440;

(4) "state publication" includes any official document, compilation, journal, bill, law, resolution, bluebook, statute, code, register, pamphlet, list, book, report, study, hearing transcript, leaflet, order, regulation, directory, periodical or magazine issued or contracted for by a state agency determined by the state librarian to be appropriate for retention in the center;

(5) "research data" or "data" means a representation of facts, concepts or instructions in a formalized manner suitable for communication, interpretation, or processing by humans or by automatic means which was prepared to serve as a basis for reasoning, calculation.

discussion or decision and which is determined appropriate for indexing by the state librarian. (§ 1 ch 2 SLA 1970; am § 10 ch 27 SLA 1979)

PUBLIC RECORDS
(Alaska Statutes, 1982, s.40.21.010 to 40.21.150.)

Sec. 40.21.010. Purpose. The purpose of this chapter is to provide for the orderly management of current state and local public records and to preserve noncurrent public records of permanent value for study and research. (§ 1 ch 191 SLA 1970)

Sec. 40.21.020. Archival and records management program creation and administration. There is established in the Department of Administration the Alaska State Archives. The department shall establish and administer a state archives and records management program. To implement the program and head the Alaska State Archives, the department shall create the position of state archivist, and shall appoint as state archivist a person qualified by special training or experience in archival or historical work. The state archivist shall be the official custodian of the archival resources of the state. (§ 1 ch 191 SLA 1970)

Sec. 40.21.030. Duties of the state archivist. (a) In order to carry out the archival program, the state archivist shall:

(1) negotiate for, acquire and receive public records of permanent value including public records of the state and political subdivisions of the state and of defunct public agencies;

(2) establish and operate a state archival depository which shall provide for the preservation, arrangement, repair, rehabilitation, duplication, reproduction, description and exhibition of permanent public records or other documentary material transferred to, or acquired by the state archivist;

(3) review and approve all agency records retention schedules to identify and to insure the preservation of those records having parmanent value;

(4) make permanent records under his supervision, other than those required by AS 09.25.120 to be kept confidential, available for public use at reasonable times;

(5) make available to any person for a reasonable fee copies of archival material under AS 09.25.120;

(6) adopt a seal for official use and for certification of record copies which copies shall have the same force and effect as if made by the original custodian of the records;

(7) negotiate payment for the acquisition of public records with the possessor of them;

(8) if negotiations under (7) of this subsection are unsuccessful or if the person in possession of the public records is unwilling to enter into those negotiations, arrange with the person in possession for the microfilming of the records;

(9) accept gifts, bequests and endowments for purposes consistent with the objectives of this chapter;

(10) prepare inventories, indexes, catalogs, and other finding aids or guides to facilitate the use of the archives;

(11) accept documents, including motion picture film, still pictures and sound recordings, that are appropriate for preservation by the state as evidence of its organization, functions, policies, decisions, procedures and transactions.

(b) In order to carry out the records management program, the state archivist shall

(1) analyze, develop and coordinate the standards and procedures for record making and current record keeping;

(2) insure the maintenance and security of records;

(3) initiate action to recover state records removed without authorization;

(4) establish and operate state records centers for the purposes of accepting, servicing, storing and protecting state records which must be preserved for varying periods of time but which are not needed for the transaction of current business;

(5) transfer records considered to have permanent value to the state archives;

(6) institute and maintain a training and information program in all phases of the management of current records for all state agencies;

(7) make continuing surveys of paperwork operations and recommend improvements in current records management practices, including the use of space, equipment and supplies;

(8) initiate programs for improving the management of correspondence, forms, reports and directives as integral parts of the overall records management program;

(9) provide centralized microfilm service for state agencies as determined to be necessary by the department;

(10) establish standards for the preparation of records retention schedules providing for the retention of state records of permanent value and for the prompt and orderly disposition of state records no longer possessing administrative, legal, or historical value to warrant their retention;

(11) receive records retention schedules from the agencies and submit them to the attorney general for review and approval;

(12) obtain from agencies reports which are required for the administration of the program. (§ 1 ch 191 SLA 1970)

Sec. 40.21.040. Gifts, bequests or endowments of money. Gifts, bequests or endowments of money shall be deposited in a separate account in the general fund and may be invested in a manner not inconsistent with the investment of other state funds. Proceeds of invested funds shall be used to carry out the purposes for which the money was given. (§ 1 ch 191 SLA 1970)

Sec. 40.21.050. Regulations. The department shall adopt regulations necessary to carry out the purposes of this chapter. (§ 1 ch 191 SLA 1970)

Sec. 40.21.060. Duties of chief executive officers of state agencies. The chief executive officer of each state agency shall

(1) make and preserve public records containing adequate and proper documentation of the organization, functions, policies, decisions, procedures and essential transactions of the agency, and designed to furnish the information necessary to protect the legal and financial rights of the state and of persons directly affected by the agency's activities;

(2) establish and maintain an active, continuing program for the efficient management of the records of the agency under the procedures prescribed by the Department of Administration, including effective controls over the creation, maintenance and use of records in the conduct of current business;

(3) submit to the Department of Administration, in accordance with the standards established by it, records retention schedules proposing the length of time which records having administrative, legal or historical value shall be retained;

(4) apply the provisions of approved records retention schedules to insure the orderly disposition of state records including transfer to a state records center;

(5) identify, segregate and protect records vital to the continuing operation of an agency in the event of natural, man-made or war-caused disaster;

(6) cooperate with the Department of Administration in conducting surveys made by it under the provisions of this chapter;

(7) establish safeguards against unauthorized or unlawful removal or loss of state records;

(8) comply with the regulations, standards and procedures relating to records management and archives established by the Department of Administration;

(9) appoint a records officer who shall act as a liaison between the Department of Administration and the agency on all matters relating to the records management program. (§ 1 ch 191 SLA 1970)

Sec. 40.21.070. Records management for local records. The governing body of each political subdivision of the state shall promote the principles of efficient records management for local public records kept in accordance with state law. The governing body shall, as far as practical, follow the program established for the management of state records. The department shall, upon request of the governing body of a political subdivision, provide advice and assistance in the establishment of a local records management program. (§ 1 ch 191 SLA 1970)

Sec. 40.21.080. Disposal of public records by political sub division. An official of a political subdivision of the state having in his legal custody public records which are considered by him to be without legal or administrative value or historical interest may compile lists of these records sufficiently detailed to identify them and submit the lists to the governing body of the political subdivision. The governing body may authorize the disposal and the method of disposal of the records in the list that it finds to be without legal or administrative value or historical interest. The governing body may also, upon request of the legal custodian of the records, authorize in advance the periodic disposal of routine records that the governing body considers to have no legal, administrative, or historical value. After receipt of written authorization from the governing body, the legal custodian of the records may dispose of the records. The legal custodian shall file in the office from which the records were drawn a descriptive list of the records disposed of and a record of the disposal itself. Copies of these documents shall be transmitted to the governing body which shall file and preserve them. (§ 1 ch 191 SLA 1970)

Sec. 40.21.090. Transfer of public records of political subdivision to department. The governing body of a political subdivision of the state may authorize the transfer to the department of records which have legal, administrative, or historical value but which are not required for the transaction of current business. The official of the political subdivision having custody of the records shall prepare a list describing the records transferred in sufficient detail to identify them. Copies of the list shall be filed with the department and with the public corporation or political subdivision transferring the records. The department shall acknowledge receipt of the list. Listed records approved by the department for transfer may be transferred to a records center designated by the department. The records center shall transfer any permanent records to the archives. Records transferred remain the property of the political subdivision. The department is the legal custodian of records in its possession. (§ 1 ch 191 SLA 1970)

Sec. 40.21.100. Assistance to legislative and judicial branches. Upon request, the department shall assist in the establishment of records management programs in the legislative and judicial branches of the state government and shall provide program services similar to those available to the executive branch of state government. (§ 1 ch 191 SLA 1970)

Sec. 40.21.110. Care of records. Except for public records lawfully in the possession of a person other than the state, public records of existing or defunct agencies of the state, territorial and Russian governments in Alaska are the property of the state and shall be created, maintained, preserved, stored, transferred, destroyed or disposed of, and otherwise managed in accordance with the provisions of this chapter. Records shall be delivered by outgoing officials and employees to their successors, and may not be removed, destroyed or disposed of, except as provided in this chapter. (§ 1 ch 191 SLA 1970)

Sec. 40.21.120. Standards of clarity, accuracy, and permanency of copies or reproductions of public records. When a public officer performing duties under this chapter is required or authorized by law to record, copy, recopy, or replace any public record, he may do so by photostatic, photographic, microphotographic, microfilm or other mechanical process which produces a clear, accurate and permanent copy or reproduction of the original record, in accordance with the latest standards approved for the reproduction of permanent records by the department. (§ 1 ch 191 SLA 1970)

Sec. 40.21.130. Alteration and replacement of public records. An original public record which is worn or damaged may be replaced by a reproduction made in accordance with this chapter. Certification by the agency having custody of the record that the replacement is a true and correct copy of the original shall appear at the end of the reproduction. When original public records are photographed or otherwise mechanically reproduced under the provisions of this chapter and the photographic or other mechanical reproductions are placed in conveniently accessible files and provisions made for preserving and using them, the original records from which they were made may be destroyed only with the approval of the state archivist. (§ 1 ch 191 SLA 1970)

Sec. 40.21.140. Use of copies and replacements as evidence. Reproductions or replacements of records made under this chapter are considered original records for all purposes and are admissible in evidence as original records. (§ 1 ch 191 SLA 1970)

Sec. 40.21.150. Definitions. In this chapter, unless the context otherwise requires,

(1) "agency" or "state agency" means a department, office, agency, state board, commission, public corporation or other organizational unit of or created under the executive branch of the state government; the term does not include the University of Alaska;

(2) "archives" means

(A) the noncurrent records of a state agency or political subdivision of the state preserved, after appraisal, because of their value; also referred to as archival material or archival holdings; or

(B) the agency responsible for selecting, preserving and making available archival material; also referred to as an archival agency; or

(C) the building or part of a building where archival material is located; also referred to as an archival depository;

(3) "department" means the Department of Administration;

(4) "local record" means a public record of a city or borough of any class, villages, district, authority or other political subdivision unless the record is designated or treated as a state record under state law;

(5) "record" means any document, paper, book, letter, drawing, map, plat, photo, photographic file, motion picture film, microfilm, microphotograph, exhibit, magnetic or paper tape, punched card, or other document of any other material. regardless of physical form or characteristic, developed or received under law or in connection with the transaction of official business and preserved or appropriate for preservation by an agency or political subdivision, as evidence of the organization, function, policies, decisions, procedures, operations or other activities of the state or political subdivision or because of the informational value in them; the term does not include library and museum material developed or acquired and preserved solely for reference, historical or exhibition purposes, extra copies of documents preserved solely for convenience of reference, or stocks of publications and processed documents;

(6) "records center" means a records depository in the department for the storage and disposition of noncurrent records;

(7) "state record" means a record of a department, office, commission, board, public corporation, or other agency of the state government, including a record of the legislature or a court and any other record designated or treated as a public record under state law. (§ 1 ch 191 SLA 1970)

MISCELLANEOUS PROVISIONS
(Alaska Statutes, 1982, s.24.05.135, 29.48.030, 44.27.020.)

Sec. 24.05.135. Record of proceedings. (a) All floor sessions of each house shall be electronically recorded. However, each house may suspend this recording requirement by concurrence of two-thirds of its members when there is an equipment failure or when no recording equipment is available as a result of a natural disaster or other exigency.

(b) The legislature shall provide by uniform joint rule for the recording or reporting of committee session proceedings.

(c) As the tapes, spools, or other recording devices are filled, or as reports are completed, they shall be transferred to the state library for placement in the state archives. Reproductions shall be placed in a centrally located public library in Juneau, Anchorage and Fairbanks, until one year after adjournment of the legislative session recorded. The division of libraries shall supply reproductions of electronic recordings at cost to any person requesting them. (§ 1 ch 12 SLA 1975)

Sec. 29.48.030. Municipal facilities and services. (a) A municipality may exercise the powers necessary to provide the following public facilities and services:

*   *   *

(14) libraries, visual or performing arts centers, or museums;

*   *   *

(§ 2 ch 118 SLA 1972; am § 3 ch 215 SLA 1975; am § 4 ch 78 SLA 1978; am § 5 ch 62 SLA 1979)

Sec. 44.27.020. Duties of department. The Department of Education shall

(1) administer the state's program of education at the elementary, secondary, and adult levels, including, but not limited to, programs of vocational education and training, vocational rehabilitation, library services, correspondence courses, adult basic education, and fire-service training, but not including degree programs of postsecondary education;

(2) administer the historical library;

(3) plan, finance and operate related school and educational activities and facilities. (§ 11 ch 64 SLA 1959; am § 77 ch 69 SLA 1970; am § 5 ch 86 SLA 1979)

Alaska library laws are reprinted from ALASKA STATUTES published by The Michie Co., Charlottesville, Virginia.

ARIZONA

DEPARTMENT OF LIBRARY, ARCHIVES
AND PUBLIC RECORDS

(Arizona Revised Statutes Annotated, 1982, s.41-1331 to 41-1353, 41-2366.)

§ 41-1331. Divisions of department of library, archives and public records

A. There shall be a department of the legislative branch known as the department of library, archives and public records which shall include the library division, the records management division, the library extension service division and the division of Arizona history and archives.

B. Notwithstanding the provisions of § 41-771, the provisions of articles 5 and 6 of chapter 4 of this title shall apply to all positions within the department of library, archives and public records, except the library, archives and public records director. Added by Laws 1976, Ch. 104, § 6.

§ 41-1332. Board of library, archives and public records; appointment of director

A. There is established a board of library, archives and public records composed of the president of the senate, speaker of the house of representatives and one member of the senate appointed by the president of the senate and one member of the house of representatives appointed by the speaker of the house of representatives.

B. Meetings of the board shall be held at the call of the chairman. The speaker of the house of representatives shall serve as chairman in even-numbered years and the president of the senate shall serve as chairman in odd-numbered years.

C. The board shall exercise general supervision over the department of library, archives and public records and shall appoint the director of the department of library, archives and public records. The director shall serve at the pleasure of the board. Added by Laws 1976, Ch. 104, § 6.

§ 41-1334. Compensation of director

The compensation of the director of the department of library, archives and public records shall be as determined by the board. Added by Laws 1976, Ch. 104, § 6.

§ 41-1335. Powers and duties of director of library, archives and public records

A. The director of the department of library, archives and public records shall:

1. Establish rules and regulations for the use of books or other materials in the custody of the department and for the removal of books from the library, including assessment of reasonable penalties for failure to return books when due. The proceeds from the assessment of reasonable penalties shall be transmitted to the state treasurer for the credit of the department, and such monies shall be used only for the purchase of other books or materials.

2. Sell or exchange undesired duplicate copies of books, or books not of value for the purposes of the library, or photographic reproductions of departmental holdings, and remit the proceeds to the state treasurer for credit to the department fund which shall be used for the purchase of other books or materials.

3. Bring actions for the recovery of books, or for three times the value thereof, against any persons having them in their possession or who are responsible therefor, and who have failed or refused to return them upon demand. If a book is one of a set the value thereof may be deemed the value of the entire set.

4. Certify copies from books, documents or other archival or public records which have been deposited in the custody of the department. The fee for such certification shall be the same as prescribed for the certification of records by the secretary of state. Such certificates shall have the same force and effect as if made by the officer originally in charge of such record.

5. Arrange with the federal government, other states and foreign countries for a system of exchange of official state reports and publications, session laws, statutes, legislative journals and supreme court reports. Except for statutes and official supplements of the statutes which shall be purchased directly by the department and distributed, the department shall make requisition upon the secretary of state, the president of the senate, the speaker of the house of representatives, the heads of departments and all officers and agents of the state for the number of copies of official publications the department needs for such exchange, and it shall be the duty of the officers to supply them.

6. Supply one copy of each official compilation or revision of the laws and annually one official supplement thereof to each public library in this state that applies therefor.

7. Make an annual report for submission to the legislature on the condition of the department, its activities and the disposition of monies expended for its maintenance and transmit a copy thereof to the governor.

8. Appoint librarians and assistants necessary to perform the duties of the department and assign their duties.

B. The director of the department of library, archives and public records may:

1. Enter into contracts to establish a depository system and an exchange program with any municipal, county or regional public library, state college or state university library and out-of-state research libraries. Except for statutes and official supplements of the statutes which shall be purchased directly by the department and distributed, the department shall make requisition upon the secretary of state, the heads of departments and all officers and agents of the state for the number of copies of official publications the department needs for the depository system and any exchange programs established pursuant to this subsection and it shall be the duty of the officers to supply them.

2. Cooperate with the legislative council in carrying out § 41-1304, subsection B.

3. Establish and operate a state capitol museum for public educational purposes.
Added by Laws 1976, Ch. 104, § 6. Amended by Laws 1977, Ch. 20, § 9, eff. April 26, 1977; Laws 1981, Ch. 286, § 8.

§ 41-1336. State library administrative agency

A. The department of library, archives and public records is the state library administrative agency, and the director of the department of library, archives and public records may accept, on behalf of the state, any allocation of money or materials made by the federal government for library purposes, any appropriations of state funds for the extension and improvement of statewide library service or any bequests, grants or gifts to the department for such purpose, and administer all of them under rules and regulations he prescribes, not inconsistent with the conditions of the allocation, appropriation, bequest, grant or gift.

B. All monies received as provided by this section shall be deposited in the state treasury and disbursed in the manner prescribed for the disbursement of state funds, but shall not be subject to § 35–190, relating to lapsing appropriations.

Added by Laws 1976, Ch. 104, § 6.

§ 41–1337. Library division; library extension service division

A. The library division shall include:

1. A law library.

2. A government unit containing works on political science, economics, sociology and all subjects pertaining to the theory and practice of government.

3. An American history and biography unit.

4. A mineralogy and geology unit.

5. A genealogy unit.

6. A documents unit containing reports and other publications of the federal and state governments.

7. A general reference unit.

8. Other units the director deems advisable.

B. The library extension service division shall:

1. Prepare a plan for statewide public library service including a supplementary service to libraries of books, other printed materials and audiovisual materials, and a direct service to individuals and groups of books, pamphlets and visual materials. Such plan shall be put into effect to the extent made practicable by available facilities.

2. Encourage and assist the development of library services in state institutions.

3. Compile statistics and other data relating to libraries and library services, and disseminate them by newspaper, radio, bulletins or other means.

4. Give professional advice and assistance in the establishment and operation of county free libraries, municipal libraries, or any combinations thereof, and to joint ventures of public and private or nonprofit libraries in this state which make library information available to the public and which request such professional advice and assistance.

5. Develop library service for the blind and physically handicapped through state and regional centers.

6. Perform all other duties necessary or appropriate to the development of statewide library service.

Added by Laws 1976, Ch. 104, § 6.

§ 41–1338. Arizona history and archives division

The Arizona history and archives division shall contain:

1. All available works, books, newspaper files, pamphlets, papers, manuscripts, documents, magazines and newspaper articles, maps, pictures, items and materials pertaining to or bearing upon the history of Arizona.

2. Copies of current official reports, public documents and publications of state, county and municipal officers, departments, boards, commissions, agencies and institutions, and public archives. To permit compliance with this paragraph it is the duty of all public officers required by law to make written reports to the governor, or to the governing officer or body of a county, city or town, to provide the department of

library, archives and public records, for filing in the Arizona history and archives division, with copies of such reports except those that are confidential.
Added by Laws 1976, Ch. 104, § 6.

§ 41-1339. Depository of official archives

A. The Arizona history and archives division is the central depository of all official books, records and documents not in current use of the various state officers and departments of the state, the counties and incorporated cities and towns, which materials constitute the state archives. The state archives shall be carefully kept and preserved, classified, catalogued and made available for inspection under rules the director of the department of library, archives and public records prescribes.

B. The library extension service division shall:

1. Prepare a plan for statewide public library service including a supplementary service to libraries of books, other printed materials and audiovisual materials, and a direct service to individuals and groups of books, pamphlets and visual materials. Such plan shall be put into effect to the extent made practicable by available facilities.

2. Encourage and assist the development of library services in state institutions.

3. Compile statistics and other data relating to libraries and library services, and disseminate them by newspaper, radio, bulletins or other means.

4. Give professional advice and assistance in the establishment and operation of county free libraries, municipal libraries, or any combinations thereof, and to joint ventures of public and private or nonprofit libraries in this state which make library information available to the public and which request such professional advice and assistance.

5. Develop library service for the blind and physically handicapped through state and regional centers.

6. Perform all other duties necessary or appropriate to the development of statewide library service.
Added by Laws 1976, Ch. 104, § 6.

§ 41-1338. Arizona history and archives division

The Arizona history and archives division shall contain:

1. All available works, books, newspaper files, pamphlets, papers, manuscripts, documents, magazines and newspaper articles, maps, pictures, items and materials pertaining to or bearing upon the history of Arizona.

2. Copies of current official reports, public documents and publications of state, county and municipal officers, departments, boards, commissions, agencies and institutions, and public archives. To permit compliance with this paragraph it is the duty of all public officers required by law to make written reports to the governor, or to the governing officer or body of a county, city or town, to provide the department of library, archives and public records, for filing in the Arizona history and archives division, with copies of such reports except those that are confidential.
Added by Laws 1976, Ch. 104, § 6.

§ 41-1339. Depository of official archives

A. The Arizona history and archives division is the central depository of all official books, records and documents not in current use of the various state officers and departments of the state, the counties and incorporated cities and towns, which materials constitute the state archives. The state archives shall be carefully kept and preserved, classified, catalogued and made available for inspection under rules the director of the department of library, archives and public records prescribes.

B. State officers in possession of official state or territorial archives shall deposit such with the director of the department of library, archives and public records.

C. Any county, municipal or other public official may in his discretion, deposit

with the Arizona history and archives division for permanent preservation therein official books, records, documents and original papers not in current use.
Added by Laws 1976, Ch. 104, § 6.

§ 41–1340. Historical records

The Arizona history and archives division shall:

1. Collect from the files of old newspapers, court records, church records, private collections and other sources, data treating upon the history of the state.

2. Accept loans or gifts of rare volumes, manuscripts, maps, pictures and other articles or things of historical value.

3. Classify, edit, annotate and publish from time to time records considered of public interest.

4. Encourage the proper marking of points of historical importance.

5. Systematically stimulate historical research and encourage the study of Arizona history.
Added by Laws 1976, Ch. 104, § 6.

§ 41–1341. Public records division

The public records division shall:

1. Receive and safely retain official copies of all enactments of the legislature.

2. Prepare a record of all official acts of the governor.

3. Receive and retain official copies of all written opinions of the supreme court or any intermediate court of appeals.

4. Record in proper books all conveyances made to the state, except conveyances made under the revenue laws of lands sold for taxes.

5. Receive and record in proper books the official bonds of all state officers, and keep the original on file with the section.

6. Record the names of all persons who have been certified to the governor as having received at any election the highest number of votes for any office.

7. Receive and record a certified copy of the rules and regulations of any agency or department.

8. Retain any books, records, deeds, papers and other material deposited in the department.

9. Furnish on request to any person paying the fees therefor, a certified copy of all or any part of any law, record or other instrument filed in the office.

10. Keep a record of all fees charged and monies collected, with the date, name of payer and the nature of the service involved.
Added by Laws 1976, Ch. 104, § 6.

§ 41–1342. Reproduction of archives and public records

A. For purposes of preservation, reduction of volume and efficiency of administration, the Arizona history and archives division and the public records division are authorized to reproduce by photography, microphotography or other standard method of reproduction on film, public records in their custody, whether obsolete or current, or any archival records or historical material subject to deposit in the state archives or desired for filing therein, and classify, catalogue and index such records for convenient reference.

B. A photographic reproduction of a public record, the negative or film of which is certified by the person in charge of such reproduction as being an exact replica of the original, and by the director of the department of library, archives and public records as being a record deposited in the department of library, archives and public records is admissible in evidence in all courts, and in hearings before any officer, board or commission having jurisdiction or authority to conduct such hearings, in like manner as the original.
Added by Laws 1976, Ch. 104, § 6.

§ 41-1343. Access to public records

The director of the department of library, archives and public records, in person or through a deputy, has the right of reasonable access to all nonconfidential public records in the state, or any public office of the state of Arizona or any county, city, municipality, district or political subdivision thereof, because of the historical and research value of data contained therein, with a view to securing their safety and determining their need for preservation or disposal.
Added by Laws 1976, Ch. 104, § 6.

§ 41-1344. Disagreement as to value of records

If the department of library, archives and public records determines, after consultation with the historical advisory commission, attorney general and auditor general, that any records in the custody of a public officer, other than a public officer of a county, municipality, district or other political subdivision, are of no legal, administrative, historical or other value, and the public officer having custody of the records or from whose office the records originated disagrees with the determination and opposes disposal of the records, the department may request the governor to make his determination as to whether the records should be disposed of in the interests of conservation of space, economy or safety.
Added by Laws 1976, Ch. 104, § 6.

§ 41-1345. Public records, powers and duties of director

A. The director of the department of library, archives and public records shall administer the public records management section and be responsible for the preservation of public records. In addition to other powers and duties, the director of the department of library, archives and public records shall:

1. Establish standards, procedures and techniques for effective management of records.

2. Make continuing surveys of paper work operations and recommend improvements in current record management practices including the use of space, equipment and supplies employed in creating, maintaining, storing and servicing of records.

3. Establish standards for the preparation of schedules providing for the retention of records of continuing value and for the prompt and orderly disposal of records no longer possessing sufficient administrative, legal or fiscal value to warrant their further keeping.

4. Establish criteria for designation of essential records within the following general categories:

(a) Records containing information necessary to the operations of government in the emergency created by a disaster.

(b) Records containing information necessary to protect the rights and interests of persons or to establish and affirm the powers and duties of governments in the resumption of operations after a disaster.

5. Reproduce or cause to be reproduced essential records and prescribe the place and manner of their safekeeping.

6. Obtain such reports from agencies as are required for the administration of this program.

7. Request transmittal, pursuant to § 41-1348, subsection B, paragraph 1, of the originals of records reproduced by agencies of the state or its political subdivisions pursuant to § 41-1348 or certified negatives or films of such originals, or both, if in his judgment such records may be of historical or other value.

B. Upon request, the director of the department of library, archives and public records shall assist and advise in the establishment of records management programs in the legislative and judicial branches of the state and shall, as required by them, provide program services similar to those available to the executive branch of state government pursuant to the provisions of this article.
Added by Laws 1976, Ch. 104, § 6.

§ 41-1346. State and local public records management

A. The head of each state and local agency shall:

1. Establish and maintain an active, continuing program for the economical and efficient management of the public records of the agency.

2. Make and maintain records containing adequate and proper documentation of the organization, functions, policies, decisions, procedures and essential transactions of the agency designed to furnish information to protect the rights of the state and of persons directly affected by the agency's activities.

3. Submit to the director of the department of library, archives and public records, in accordance with established standards, schedules proposing the length of time each record series warrants retention for administrative, legal or fiscal purposes after it has been received by the agency. Also, submit a list of public records in the agency's custody that are not needed in the transaction of current business and that are not considered to have sufficient administrative, legal or fiscal value to warrant their inclusion in established disposal schedules.

4. Submit to the director of the department of library, archives and public records lists of all essential public records in the custody of the agency.

5. Cooperate with the director of the department of library, archives and public records in the conduct of surveys.

6. Comply with rules, regulations, standards and procedures issued by the director of the department of library, archives and public records.

B. The governing body of each county, city, town, or other political subdivision, shall promote the principles of efficient record management for local public records. Such governing body shall, as far as practicable, follow the program established for the management of state records. The director of the department of library, archives and public records shall, upon request of the governing body, provide advice and assistance in the establishment of a local public records management program.

Added by Laws 1976, Ch. 104, § 6.

§ 41-1347. Preservation of public records

A. All records made or received by public officials of this state in the course of their public duties are the property of the state. Except as provided in this article, the director of the department of library, archives and public records and every other custodian of public records shall carefully protect and preserve the records from deterioration, mutilation, loss or destruction and, when advisable, shall cause them to be properly repaired and renovated. All paper, ink and other materials used in public offices for the purpose of permanent records shall be of durable quality.

B. Records shall not be destroyed or otherwise disposed of by any agency of the state, unless it is determined by the department that the record has no further administrative, legal, fiscal, research or historical value. The original of any record reproduced pursuant to the provisions of § 41-1348 may be determined by the department to have no further administrative, legal, fiscal, research or historical value.

Added by Laws 1976, Ch. 104, § 6.

§ 41-1348. Reproduction and destruction of records by agencies of the state and political subdivisions; programs; approval; procedures

Text of amendment conditioned on compliance with Federal Voting Rights Act

A. Each agency of the state or any of its political subdivisions may implement a program for the reproduction by photography, microphotography or other standard method of reproduction on film of records in its custody, whether obsolete or current, and classify, catalogue and index such records for convenient reference. Such agency, prior to the institution of any such program of reproduction, shall obtain approval from the director of the department of library, archives and public records of the types of records to be so reproduced and of the methods of reproduction and storage and the equipment which the agency proposes to use in connection with such reproduction.

B. The head of such agency, that has an approved program for the reproduction of records, that desires to reproduce specific records in its custody shall designate an employee who shall be in charge of such reproduction and who shall:

1. Give notice in writing to the director of the department of library, archives and public records that such agency intends to reproduce records in its custody. This notice shall describe with specificity the records to be reproduced. The director shall have thirty days after receipt of such notice within which to request in writing either or both of the following:

(a) That any or all of such original records be transmitted to him for disposition in accordance with § 41–1349 immediately after the process of reproduction is completed.

(b) That a negative or film of the reproduced records, certified as being an exact replica of the original, be transmitted to him for disposition in accordance with § 41–1349.

2. Not less than thirty days after receipt by the director of the notice provided in paragraph 1 of this subsection:

(a) Certify the negative or film of the reproduced records as being an exact replica of the original and promptly seal and store at least one certified, original negative of each microphotographic film in such manner and place as will reasonably assure its preservation indefinitely against loss, theft, defacement or destruction, and transmit one such certified negative or film to the assistant director if requested.

(b) Transmit immediately to the director the original records requested.

(c) If the reproduced record is a record of an original document that would have been open to public inspection, maintain for the use of the public a microphotographic film print or copy of each such record so destroyed, together with a mechanical device by which such film may be conveniently examined or reproduced.

C. A photographic reproduction of any record reproduced pursuant to this section, the negative or film of which has been certified by the person in charge of such reproduction as being an exact replica of the original, and which has been certified by the appropriate officer or employee as being a record on file with the agency, shall be admissible in evidence in all courts and in hearings before any officer, board or commission having jurisdiction or authority to conduct such hearings, in like manner as the original. This subsection shall not be construed to permit disclosure in any proceeding of any such reproduced record if the original would have been protected from disclosure by any other provision of law.

D. The provisions of this section shall not be applicable to permit destruction of current original affidavits of registration as that term is used in § 16–163.
Added by Laws 1976, Ch. 104, § 6. Amended by Laws 1979, Ch. 209, § 21.

§ 41–1349. Duties of department relating to historical value

A. The department of library, archives and public records shall:

1. With approval of the attorney general and auditor general, determine whether public records presented to it are of legal, administrative, historical or other value.

2. Dispose of records determined to be of no legal, administrative, historical or other value.

3. Accept those records deemed by a public officer having custody thereof to be unnecessary for the transaction of the business of his office and deemed to be of legal, administrative, historical or other value.

B. All public records of any public office, upon the termination of the existence and functions of the office, shall be checked by the department of library, archives and public records and either disposed of or transferred to the custody of the department, in accordance with the procedure of this article. If a public office is terminated or reduced by the transfer of its powers and duties to another office or to other offices, its appropriate public records shall pass with the powers and duties transferred.

Added by Laws 1976, Ch. 104, § 6.

§ 41-1350. Definition of records

In this chapter, unless the context otherwise requires, "records" means all books, papers, maps, photographs, or other documentary materials, regardless of physical form or characteristics, including microphotographic film prints or copies of such items reproduced pursuant to § 41-1348, made or received by any governmental agency in pursuance of law or in connection with the transaction of public business and preserved or appropriate for preservation by the agency or its legitimate successor as evidence of the organization, functions, policies, decisions, procedures, operations, or other activities of the government, or because of the informational and historical value of data contained therein. Library or museum material made or acquired solely for reference or exhibition purposes, extra copies of documents preserved only for convenience of reference, and stocks of publications or documents intended for sale or distribution to interested persons, are not included within the definition of "records" as used in this chapter.

Added by Laws 1976, Ch. 104, § 6.

§ 41-1351. Determination of value; disposition

Every public officer who has public records in his custody shall consult periodically with the department of library, archives and public records and the department shall determine whether the records in question are of legal, administrative, historical or other value. Those records determined to be of no legal, administrative, historical or other value shall be disposed of by such method as the department may specify. A list of all records so disposed of, together with a statement signed by the director of the department of library, archives and public records certifying compliance with this article, shall be filed and preserved in the office from which the records were drawn and in the files of the department of library, archives and public records.

Added by Laws 1976, Ch. 104, § 6.

§ 41-1352. Historical advisory commission; membership; expenses

A. There shall be an historical advisory commission appointed by the director of the department of library, archives and public records. The commission membership of not less than ten nor more than twenty members shall consist of professional historians, librarians, or persons otherwise associated with the encouragement of research, writing or teaching Arizona history.

B. Members shall serve without compensation but those employed by the state shall be reimbursed for travel and subsistence by the department or agency they represent.

Added by Laws 1976, Ch. 104, § 6.

§ 41-1353. Review and transfer of certain historic property; exemption; definition

A. An agency shall notify the board of library, archives and public records on forms prescribed by the board if the agency has or acquires furniture, equipment or other personal property which is forty or more years of age or of known historical interest, including property escheated to the state under title 12, chapter 7, article 5.

B. The board may authorize a person to inspect the personal property reported under subsection A of this section and recommend to the board whether the personal property is of an historic interest or value as would in the public interest require it to be made available permanently for placement on public display in any restored executive, legislative or judicial facility or museum area.

C. If the board determines the personal property should be made available for display purposes it shall provide written notice to the agency requesting prompt transfer of the personal property to the department of library, archives and public records.

D. An agency may apply to the board for an exemption from the transfer required under subsection C by filing a prompt written response to the board stating:

1. The length of time the agency has used the personal property.

2. Why the value of the personal property to the agency is greater than the educational and historic value in displaying the personal property.

3. What harm the agency would suffer if the personal property is transferred to the department.

4. That the use of federal monies in the initial acquisition of the personal property legally precludes its transfer to the board.

E. The board shall grant an exemption to a requested property transfer if it finds that the transfer of the property would result in significant cost or disruption to the agency which would outweigh the educational and historic value in displaying the property.

F. In this section "agency" means any branch, department, commission, board or other unit of the state organization which receives, disburses or expends state monies or incurs obligations against this state.

Added by Laws 1981, Ch. 286, § 9.

§ 41–2366. Schedule for termination July 1, 1990

Text as amended by Laws 1981, Ch. 225, § 9

A. The following agencies shall terminate on July 1, 1990:

*   *   *

14. The department of library, archives, and public records, including the activities and functions of the library and archives board and director and the historical advisory commission and the board of library examiners.

Added as § 41–2261, subsec. F by Laws 1978, Ch. 210, § 1. Renumbered as § 41–2366. Amended by Laws 1979, Ch. 48, § 5; Laws 1980, 4th S.S., Ch. 1, § 25, eff. June 12, 1980; Laws 1981, Ch. 225, § 9.

DISTRIBUTION OF PUBLIC DOCUMENTS

(Arizona Revised Statutes Annotated, 1982, s.41-123,12-108.)

§ 41–123. Distribution of statutes and journals

A. Immediately after publication of the statutes, and upon receipt of an official compilation or revision of the laws or an official supplement thereof, copies of which are supplied him by law for distribution, the secretary of state shall supply one copy thereof to:

1. Each judge and the clerk of the United States district court for the district of Arizona, and the United States attorney and United States marshal for that district.

2. Each senator and representative in congress from this state.

B. The secretary of state shall sell to the director of the department of library, archives and public records for the purpose of exchange with other states, territories, the United States and foreign countries, such number of copies of the statutes and official supplements of the statutes as the director requisitions, in accordance with section 41–1335.

C. The secretary of state shall supply to the president of the senate and the speaker of the house of representatives such number of copies of the statutes and official supplements of the statutes as such officers shall request for distribution as provided by section 41–1177.

Amended by Laws 1976, Ch. 104, § 19; Laws 1976, Ch. 161, § 6, eff. June 27, 1976.

§ 12-108. Reports of decisions; contract for publication; distribution of reports by secretary of state; cost of publication

A. The supreme court may contract with the person who agrees to publish and sell the report of decisions on terms most advantageous to the state. Such contractor shall agree to publish and deliver to the secretary of state at the contract price the number of volumes as the secretary of state may require.

B. The secretary of state shall deliver the volumes as follows:

1. To the department of library, archives and public records the number of copies necessary for its use and for exchange with the libraries of other states and countries.

2. To the law library of the University of Arizona the number of copies necessary for its use and for exchange with the law libraries of other states and countries.

3. To the law library of Arizona State University the number of copies necessary for its use and for exchange with the law libraries of other states and countries.

4. To each supreme court justice, court of appeals judge, superior court judge, the clerk of each court and county attorney and the reporter of decisions of the supreme court, one copy.

5. To the law library of each county, two copies.

6. To the department of law, thirty copies.

7. To the corporation commission, two copies.

8. To the industrial commission, seven copies.

9. To the department of public safety, two copies.

C. Upon application and subject to legislative appropriation, the secretary of state shall deliver one volume each to all other agencies, boards, commissions and departments of the state. Upon a showing of need, the secretary of state may deliver additional volumes to a state agency, board, commission or department of the state.

D. Copies of reports delivered to a person on account of the office held by such person remain the property of this state and shall have stamped or written on them the name of the office and shall be kept for the use of the office.

E. The cost of publishing reports of decisions shall be paid from the appropriation for the supreme court.

Amended by Laws 1980, Ch. 107, § 2.

COUNTY LIBRARIES
(Arizona Revised Statutes Annotated, 1982, s.11-901 to 11-906,
11-908 to 11-916.)

§ 11-901. Establishment and maintenance of libraries

The board of supervisors may establish and maintain, within the county, a county free library in the manner and with the powers prescribed in this article.   § 1, Ch. 39, L. '29; 17-1501, C. '39.

§ 11-902. Area served by library system; notice of proposed establishment of library

A. The board of supervisors may establish at the county seat a county free library for that part of the county lying outside of incorporated cities and towns maintaining free public libraries, and for all such cities and towns within the county as may elect to become a part of, or to participate in, the county free library system, as provided in this article.

B. At least once each week for three successive weeks prior to taking action upon the establishment of the county free library, the board shall publish in the county notice of such contemplated action, giving therein the date and time of the meeting at which the action is proposed to be taken.   § 2, Ch. 39, L. '29; 17-1502, C. '39.

§ 11-903. City or town joining or withdrawing from county library system

A. After the establishment of a free county library as provided in this article, the governing body of any incorporated city or town in the county maintaining a free public library, may notify the board of supervisors that the city or town desires to become a part of the county free library system, and thereafter the city or town shall be a part thereof and its inhabitants shall be entitled to the benefits of the county free library, and the property within the city or town shall be subject to taxes levied for county free library purposes.

B. The governing body of an incorporated city or town in the county may at any time notify the board that the city or town no longer desires to be a part of the county free library system, and thereafter the city or town shall cease to participate in the benefits of the county free library, and the property located in the city or town shall not be subject to taxes for county free library purposes.

C. The governing body of an incorporated town or city shall publish once each week for three successive weeks, prior either to giving or to withdrawing such notice, notice of its contemplated action in a newspaper of general circulation in the city or town, designated by the governing body, giving therein the date, place and time of the meeting at which such action is proposed to be taken.

§ 3, Ch. 39, L. '29 ; 17–1503, C. '39.

§ 11-904. Contracts for city or town library to assume function of county free library; termination

Instead of establishing a separate county free library, the board of supervisors may enter into a contract under the provisions of this section with the board of library trustees or other authority in charge of the free public library of an incorporated city or town, and the board of library trustees or other authority in charge may make such a contract. The contract may provide that the free public library of the incorporated city or town shall assume the functions of a county free library within the county, including incorporated cities and towns therein. The board of supervisors may pay annually into the library fund of the incorporated city or town such sum as is agreed upon. Either party may terminate the contract by giving six months notice of intention to do so.

§ 4, Ch. 39, L. '29 ; 17–1504, C. '39.

§ 11-905. Contracts between counties for use of library

A. The board of supervisors of a county in which a county free library has been established under the provisions of this article, may enter into contracts with the board of supervisors of any other county to secure to the residents of the other county such privileges of the county free library as may by the contract be agreed upon, and upon such consideration as may be expressed in the contract, which shall be paid into the county free library fund. Thereafter the inhabitants of the other county shall have such privileges of the county free library as may be agreed upon by the contract.

B. The board of supervisors of the county may enter into a contract with the board of supervisors of another county in which a county free library has been established under the provisions of this article, as provided in this section, and may levy a library tax, as provided in this article, for the purpose of carrying out the contract, but the making of the contract shall not bar the board of supervisors of the county during the continuance of the contract from establishing a county free library therein under the provisions of this article if one is not already established therein. Upon the establishment of such a county free library the contract may be terminated upon such terms as may be agreed upon by the parties thereto, or it may continue for the term thereof.

§ 5, Ch. 39, L. '29 ; 17–1505, C. '39.

§ 11–906. Board of library examiners; membership; compensation; powers and duties

A. The board of library examiners shall consist of the director of the department of library, archives and public records, who shall be ex officio chairman, the librarian of the university of Arizona and the librarian of the Phoenix public library. The members of the board shall receive no compensation for their services except actual and necessary travel expenses which shall be paid from the general fund.

B. The board shall pass upon the qualifications of persons desiring to become county librarians, and may, in writing, adopt rules and regulations not inconsistent with law for its government and to carry out the purposes of this article.

As amended Laws 1976, Ch. 104, § 11.   § 6, Ch. 39, L. '29; 17–1506, C. '39.

§ 11–908. County librarian; term

A. Upon establishment of a county free library, the board of supervisors shall appoint a county librarian, who shall hold office for a term of four years. The librarian may be removed at any time for cause after a hearing by the board.

B. No person shall be eligible for appointment to the office of county librarian unless prior to appointment he has received from the board of library examiners a certificate of qualification for the office.
                                              § 7, Ch. 39, L. '29; 17–1507, C. '39.

§ 11–909. General supervision; branch libraries; employees

A. The county free library shall be under the general supervision of the board of supervisors, which may make general rules and regulations regarding the policy of the county free library, and establish, upon recommendation of the county librarian, branches and stations throughout the county which may be located in incorporated or unincorporated cities and towns when deemed advisable.

B. The board may determine the number and kind of employees of the library, and may appoint and dismiss such employees upon recommendation of the county librarian. An employee shall not be removed except for cause, and in case a removal is made upon the ground that the services of the employee are no longer required, the removed employee shall have the first right to be restored to employment when such services are again required, but the board may at the time of employing an employee, and upon the recommendation of the county librarian, enter into an agreement that the employee be employed for a definite time only.

C.   All employees of the county free library whose duties require special training in library work shall be classified in grades to be established by the county librarian, with the advice and approval of the board of library examiners, according to the duties required of them, experience in library work and other qualifications for the service required.   Before appointment to a position in classified service, the candidate shall pass an examination appropriate to the position sought, satisfactory to the county librarian, and disclose a satisfactory experience in library work.   Work in approved library schools or libraries, or certificates issued by the board of library examiners, may be accepted by the county librarian in lieu of such examination.

D.   The county librarian may accept as apprentices, without compensation, persons possessing personal qualifications satisfactory to him and may dismiss them at any time if in his judgment their work is not satisfactory.   § 8, Ch. 39, L. '29 ; 17–1508, C. '39.

§ 11–910.   Supervision by director of department of library, archives and public records; annual convention of county librarians

A.   All county free libraries established under the provisions of this article shall be under the general supervision of the director of the department of library, archives and public records who shall, either personally or by one of his assistants, periodically visit the libraries and inquire into their condition.   The actual and necessary expenses of the visits shall be paid from the state library fund.

B.   The director shall annually call a convention of county librarians to convene at such time and place as he deems most convenient for the discussion of questions pertaining to supervision and administration of the county free libraries, the laws relating thereto and such other subjects affecting the welfare and interest of the libraries as are proper.

C.   It is the duty of all county librarians to attend and take part in the proceedings of the convention.

As amended Laws 1976, Ch. 104, § 12.   § 10, Ch. 39, L. '29 ; 17–1510, C. '39.

§ 11–911.   Reports by county librarian

The county librarian shall, on or before July 31 of each year, report to the board of supervisors and to the director of the department of library, archives and public records on the condition of the county free library for the year ending June 30 preceding. The report shall, in addition to other matters deemed expedient by the county librarian, contain such statistical and other information deemed desirable by the director. For this purpose the director may send to the county librarians instructions or question blanks so as to obtain the material for a comparative study of library conditions in the state.

As amended Laws 1976, Ch. 104, § 13.   § 11, Ch. 39, L. '29; 17–1511, C. '39.

§ 11–912. Tax levies

A. The board of supervisors, after a county free library is established, shall annually levy in the same manner and at the same time as other county primary property taxes are levied, and in addition to all other taxes, a mill tax sufficient to insure the payment of salaries, maintenance and upkeep and other necessary expenses of the county free library system. The tax shall be levied and collected upon all property in the county outside incorporated cities and towns maintaining free public libraries, and upon all property within incorporated cities and towns which have elected to become a part of the county free library system as provided in this article. The fund raised by the tax levy shall be used for the purpose of purchasing periodicals, books, records and other supplies, and for purchasing property for establishing and maintaining the county free library.

B. All laws applicable to the collection of county taxes shall apply to the collection of the tax provided for in this section.

Amended by Laws 1981, Ch. 317, § 4.

§ 11–913. County free library fund; custody

Funds of the county free library, whether derived from taxation or otherwise, shall be deposited with the county treasurer. They shall constitute a separate fund, called the county free library fund, and shall be used for the county free library. Each claim against the county free library fund shall be authorized and approved by the county librarian or, in his absence from the county, by his assistant. Claims shall be approved and paid in the same manner as other claims against the county.

§ 12, Ch. 39, L. '29; 17–1512, C. '39, in part.

§ 11–914. Gift, bequest or devise to county free library; title to property

A. The board of supervisors may receive, on behalf of the county, any gift, bequest or devise for the county free library, or for any branch or subdivision thereof.

B. The title to the property used by the county free library shall be vested in the county.

§ 12, Ch. 39, L. '29; 17–1512, C. '39, in part.

§ 11-915. Bonds; issuance

Bonds of the county to acquire and equip a county free library building and to purchase land therefor may be issued in the manner now provided by law for the issuance of county bonds.

§ 12, Ch. 39, L. '29; 17–1512, C. '39, in part.

§ 11-916. Dissolution of library

A.   After a county free library has been established, it may be dissolved in the same manner it was established.

B.   At least once each week for three consecutive weeks prior to taking such action, the board of supervisors shall publish in a newspaper designated by them and published in the county, notice of the contemplated action, stating the date and time of the meeting at which the contemplated action is proposed to be taken.

§ 13, Ch. 39, L. '29; 17–1513, C. '39.

MUNICIPAL LIBRARIES
(Arizona Revised Statutes Annotated, 1982, s.9-411 to 9-420.)

§ 9-411. Tax levy for library purposes

A city or town may levy annually, in addition to all other taxes, a tax not to exceed one and one-half mills on the assessed value of all property in the city or town, exclusive of the valuation of property exempt from taxation, for the purpose of establishing and maintaining therein free public libraries and reading rooms, for purchasing books, journals and other publications, and erecting and maintaining such buildings as may be necessary therefor.

§ 522, R.S. '01; § 1925, R.S. '13 am., § 1, Ch. 106, L. '19; § 444, R.C. '28; am., '53.

§ 1, Ch. 41, L. '41; § 1, Ch. 29, L. '45: § 1, Ch. 18, L. '53; 16–1201, C. '39 Supp. '53.

§ 9-412. Receipt of gifts for library

Cities or town may receive, hold or dispose of gifts made to them for library purposes and may apply them in a manner which will best promote the uses of the library, subject to the terms of the gift.

§ 523, R.S. '01; § 1926, R.S. '13; § 445, R.C. '28; 16–1202, C. '39.

§ 9-413. Library fund

All money received for library purposes, whether by taxation or otherwise, shall belong to and be designated as the library fund, shall be paid into the city or town treasury, kept separate and apart from other funds, and shall be drawn therefrom as provided in this article, but only for purposes therein authorized.

§ 524, R.S. '01; § 1927, R.S. '13; § 446, R.C. '28; 16–1203, C. '39.

§ 9-414. Trustees; terms; compensation

A. The governing body of a city or town may appoint residents of the city or town as trustees of its library.

B. In cities or towns of less than three thousand inhabitants there may be six trustees, and in other cities or towns there may be nine trustees. Trustees shall hold office for three years from July 1 in the year of their appointment, unless sooner removed for good cause.

C. Upon the first appointment of trustees in a city or town, they shall, at their first meeting, divide themselves by lot into three classes, one third to serve for one year, one third to serve for two years, and one third to serve for three years.

D. The office shall be honorary and without compensation.

§§ 526, 527, R.S. '01; §§ 1929, 1930, R. S. '13, am., § 2, Ch. 106, L. '19, § 447, R. C. '28; 16-1204, C. '39.

§ 9-415. Trustees; organization; appointment of librarian

A. The trustees shall have charge of the library and all library property. They shall meet for business purposes on the first Tuesday of each month, and at such other times as they shall appoint, at a place to be provided for the purpose. They may elect from their body a president and secretary, and may adopt an official seal. The secretary shall keep a full statement and account of all property, receipts and expenditures, and a record of the proceedings of the board.

B. The trustees may appoint a librarian.

As amended Laws 1975, Ch. 39, § 1.　　§ 528, R.S. '01; § 1931, R.S. '13; § 448, R.C. '28; 16-1205, C. '39.

§ 9-416. Powers of trustees

The trustees, by a majority vote of their members recorded in the minutes with the ayes and nays at length, may:

1. Make and enforce all rules, regulations and by-laws necessary for the administration and government of the library and all library property.

2. Exercise and administer any trust declared or created for the library or reading room.

3. Define the powers and prescribe the duties of officers and elect and remove at will officers and assistants.

4. Purchase necessary books, journals, publications and other personal property.

5. Order the drawing and payment, upon properly authenticated

vouchers, certified by the president and secretary, of money out of the library fund for any liability authorized.

6. Fix the salary of the librarian.

7. By and with the consent and approval of the governing body of the city or town, purchase real property and erect and equip buildings as may be necessary for the library and reading rooms.

§ 529, R.S. '01; § 1932, R.S. '13; § 449, R.C. '28; 16–1206, C. '39.

§ 9-417.   Audit and payment of claims

The warrant of the trustees, when made and authenticated as provided in § 9–416, shall be verified and audited by the auditing officer, and paid by the treasurer of the city or town from the library fund.

§ 530, R.S. '01; § 1933, R.S. '13; § 450, R.C. '28; 16–1207, C. '39.

§ 9-418.   Annual reports by trustees

A. The trustees, on or before the first Monday of July of each year, shall make a report to the governing body of the city or town containing:

1. A full statement of all property and money received, where derived and how used and expended.

2. The number of books, journals and other publications on hand, the number added by gift, purchase or otherwise during the year, the number lost or missing and the number and kind of those loaned.

3. Such other statistics, information and suggestions as may be of general interest.

B. A financial report, showing all receipts and disbursements of money, shall be made by the secretary of the board of trustees, verified by oath.

§ 531, R.S. '01; § 1934, R.S. '13; § 451, R.C. '28; 16–1208, C. '39.

§ 9-419.   Regulation of library use; use of land for library

A. A city or town in which a public library is established may pass ordinances for the protection of the library and library property, and imposing penalties for punishment of persons committing injury to the library or its property or books, or for failure to return a book or other library property.

B. The city or town may grant, donate or authorize the use of land belonging to the city or town, or dedicated to public use therein, for the purpose of erecting and maintaining a building to be used only for a public library and reading room.

§ 532, R.S. '01; § 1935, R.S. '13; § 452, R.C. '28; 16–1209, C. '39.

§ 9-420. Contracts between city or town and department; expenditure of public funds

The governing body of a city or town having a free library, or a library established under this article, may enter into a contract with the department of library, archives and public records to provide supervision by the department of expenditures of all funds involved in financing a library service or construction project when any portion thereof is allocated by the federal government.

Added Laws 1965, Ch. 47, § 1. As amended Laws 1976, Ch. 104, § 7.

SCHOOL LIBRARIES
(Arizona Revised Statutes Annotated, 1982, s.15-362.)

§ 15-362. Libraries; powers and duties; authority to contract with a county free library or other public library

A. The governing board of a school district may establish and maintain libraries. Such libraries shall be under control of the board. The board shall be accountable for the care of the libraries, but it may appoint district librarians, or it may put the libraries under direct charge of a teacher or other qualified person. When requested, the board shall report on the libraries to the county school superintendent on forms supplied by the superintendent of public instruction.

B. The governing board shall:

1. Enforce the rules prescribed for government of school libraries.

2. Exclude from school libraries all books, publications and papers of a sectarian, partisan or denominational character.

C. A district library shall be free to all pupils of suitable age who attend the school. Residents of the district may become entitled to library privileges by payment of fees and compliance with regulations prescribed by the board. The governing board may enter into a contract or agreement with the proper authorities of a county free library or other public library possessing facilities for rendering the desired service for the procurement of reference or other library books or the extension services of such library. The amount so expended shall not exceed two per cent of the total school district budget for the school year during which the services are utilized.

Added by Laws 1981, Ch. 1, § 2, eff. Jan. 23, 1981.

COUNTY LAW LIBRARIES
(Arizona Revised Statutes Annotated, 1982, s.12-305.)

§ 12-305.   Law library fund

A. Effective July 1, 1976 there shall be set apart to a county law library fund twenty-five per cent of the first twenty thousand dollars and ten per cent of all amounts above twenty thousand dollars of all fees collected by the clerk of the superior court in each county. The fees set apart to any county law library fund shall be deposited to such fund on a monthly basis.

B. The county law library fund shall be used for the purchase of books for a county law library under the direction of a judge of the superior court in and for the county. The monies in the fund shall be paid out only upon the order of the judge directed to the county treasurer.

C. When the county law library fund at the close of the fiscal year exceeds three thousand dollars, the board of supervisors may by resolution adopted by vote of the members, and with the concurrence of the judge of the superior court in and for the county, transfer the surplus of the fund in the excess of three thousand dollars to a fund known as the building repair fund. Monies so transferred shall be expended only for additions, alterations and repairs to the court house. The fund shall be subject to provisions of law relating to advertising and calling for bids.

Amended by Laws 1961, Ch. 103, § 2; Laws 1965, Ch. 62, § 1, eff. April 10, 1965; Laws 1976, Ch. 15, § 4, eff. May 7, 1976; Laws 1980, 2nd S.S., Ch. 8, § 13, eff. July 1, 1981.

TAX EXEMPTION
(Arizona Revised Statutes Annotated, 1982, s.42-271.)

Arizona library laws are reprinted from ARIZONA REVISED STATUTES ANNOTATED published by West Publishing Co., St. Paul, Minnesota.

ARKANSAS

STATE LIBRARY
(Arkansas Statutes Annotated, 1982, s.6-301 to 6-307.)

6-301. State library — State librarian — State library board — State library commission abolished. — [1] [a] There is hereby created and established within the Department of Education a division to be known as the Arkansas State Library, which shall function within the Department of Education in the same manner as provided by agencies transferred to the principal department of government being a "type one [1] transfer" under the provisions of Section 1 of Act 38 of 1971 [§ 5-901], and which shall be adequately funded and properly housed in a designated building at the seat of State Government.

[(b)] The Arkansas State Library shall be headed by a State Librarian, to be appointed by the State Library Board, and shall serve for such time and for such terms as the State Library Board may prescribe. The State Librarian shall be a person of good professional standing and reputation, holding at least a Master's Degree from an American Library Association accredited graduate school of Library Science, and shall have had experience in library administration in academic, public, school, and/or special libraries. The State Librarian shall serve as executive secretary of the State Library Board, but without a vote thereon, and shall attend all of the Board meetings and keep records thereof. The State Librarian shall have charge of the work of the State Library, and shall perform such other duties as the State Library Board may prescribe. On the effective date [July 1, 1979] of this Act, the Executive Secretary and Librarian of the Arkansas Library Commission shall become the State Librarian.

[2](a) There is hereby created the State Library Board, hereinafter

referred to as the "Board," to consist of seven (7) members, to be appointed by the Governor subject to confirmation by the Arkansas Senate. One member of the Board shall be appointed from each of the four Congressional Districts of this State in existence on the effective date of this Act, and three (3) members shall be selected from the State at-large, provided, that no more than two (2) members of the Board shall be appointed from any one Congressional District.

(b) The members of the Board shall be appointed by the Governor for reasons of their interest in libraries and statewide library development.

(c) The Arkansas Library Commission is hereby abolished, and not less than four (4) of the members serving on the Library Commission on the effective date [July 1, 1979] of this Act shall be appointed by the Governor to serve on the Board first appointed under the provisions of this Act [§§ 6-301 — 6-307]. The Governor shall designate the term that each of the seven original members of the Board shall serve so that there will be staggered terms of one [1], two [2], three [3], four [4], five [5], six [6], and seven [7] years, and so that the term of one [1] of the members of such Board shall expire each year. After the selection of the initial Board and the designation of their respective terms by the Governor, all successor members appointed to the Board shall serve terms of seven [7] years and until their successors are appointed and qualified, provided, that vacancies occurring on the Board due to death, resignation, or other reason shall be filled by appointment of the Governor for the remainder of the unexpired portion of the term in the same manner as for the initial appointment.

(d) Members of the Board shall receive per diem at the rate of forty-five dollars ($45.00) per day in attending Board meetings or in performing other services required of members in their official capacity as a member of said Board, and in addition thereto, shall be entitled to mileage at the rate provided by law for official travel of State employees for each mile in traveling from their place of residence to meetings of the Board and return, or in attending to other authorized business of the Board. [Acts 1979, No. 489, §§ 1, 2, p. 1017.]

6-302. Meetings of board — Quorum. — The Board shall meet at such place or places and shall keep such records as it may deem to be appropriate. The Board shall select annually a Chairman and such other officers as it deems necessary, and shall adopt policies and bylaws governing its meetings, the conduct of its business, and the business of the State Library. A majority of its members shall constitute a quorum for the transaction of business, and all business transacted by the Board shall be by majority vote of its members. [Acts 1979, No. 489, § 3, p. 1017.]

6-303. Powers and duties of the library. — The State Library shall, within the limitations of facilities and funds provided therefor:

(1) acquire by purchase, exchange, gift, grant, or donation, books and other library materials, and catalog and maintain the same and make the same available for reference and research use of the public, the public officials and employees of this State and its political subdivisions under such rules and regulations established by the Board as may be reasonably necessary to govern the use and preservation thereof;

(2) establish and maintain a collection of books and library materials of and pertaining to Arkansas, its people, resources and history, and maintain the same as a separate section within the State Library;

(3) assist communities, libraries, schools, colleges, universities, study and civic clubs and groups, charitable and penal institutions, State agencies and departments, county and municipal governments, and any other institutions, agencies and individuals with books, information, library materials and services as needed;

(4) direct the establishment and development of county and regional library systems and programs, devise and implement a certification plan for public librarians, and assist in the design and building of public library facilities;

(5) conduct courses of library instruction, hold library institutes in various parts of the State and encourage the recruitment and training of library personnel in any suitable manner;

(6) cooperate with the Department of Education and the Department of Higher Education in devising plans for the development of libraries, in aiding librarians in their administration, in certification policies, and in formulating rules and regulations for their use;

(7) receive gifts of library materials, money and property, both real and personal, to be held in trust, subject to the terms of donation for purposes of this Act [§§ 6-301 — 6-307];

(8) shall be the official State Library agency designated to administer State and federal programs of aid to libraries and undertake such other activities and services as will further statewide development of libraries and library systems through interlibrary, interagency, and interstate cooperation to secure efficient, effective library service for all Arkansans;

(9) cooperate with the various officers, departments, and agencies of State government in pooling and sharing library materials and programs to the end that duplication of such services and facilities shall be minimized and maximum utilization may be made of the library services and resources of this State; in furtherance of which the State Library may enter into contracts or agreements with State officers, departments, and agencies for the providing of special library services where needed, and under the terms of such contract or agreement may provide for the method of financing special costs incurred by the State Library in furnishing and maintaining such special library services;

(10) operate and maintain a collection of multi-media materials to complement book collections, and establish reasonable rules and regulations for

the use and preservation thereof;

(11) provide specialized services to the blind and physically handicapped under a cooperative plan with the Library of Congress, National Library Service for the blind and physically handicapped; and

(12) perform all other functions and services that are common to the purposes and objectives of a State Library. [Acts 1979, No. 489, § 4, p. 1017.]

6-304. State historical materials and archives — Placement in state library. — The State Library, acting through the Board, is hereby authorized to enter into necessary agreements with the Arkansas History Commission with respect to an overall plan and design to assure that the functions and materials of the State Library and the History Commission may be convenient to the public and public officials of this State, and to its political subdivisions, and that unnecessary duplication of services and facilities be minimized. In addition, the State Library is authorized to enter into contracts and agreements with the Secretary of State for the custody, storage, cataloging, or display of any books, records, documents, or other papers in the custody of the Secretary of State, in the State Library or State Archives, under such terms and conditions as may be mutually agreed to by the parties, and to accept custody and control over any books, records, and documents which the Secretary of State is now required by law to keep or maintain in his official files or volumes, if the Secretary of State shall: (1) determine that such records could be properly cataloged, stored, and preserved in the State Library or State Archives, and (2) the Governor agrees in writing for the transfer of the books, records, and documents from the office of the Secretary of State to the State Library or State Archives, in accordance with the terms of the agreement made in writing signed by the Secretary of State and the State Librarian or the State Historian for the custody, cataloging, preservation, and care of such records. [Acts 1979, No. 489, § 5, p. 1017.]

6-305. State library to cooperate with other libraries. — The State Library shall cooperate with the public and private libraries in the State of Arkansas, and may enter into necessary agreements with libraries in other states and the Library of Congress for the sharing of library books, documents, facilities or services under such terms and conditions as the State Library Board shall determine to be within the scope and services of the State Library and in keeping with the State's library programs.

The State Library shall obtain reports from all libraries and each year report the condition, growth, development, and manner of development of such libraries and such other facts and statistics as may be of public interest, and shall include a summary thereof in its biennial report, which shall be filed with the Governor and the presiding officer of each house of the General Assembly. [Acts 1979, No. 489, § 6, p. 1017.]

6-306. Library commission's property and powers transferred to state library and library board. — All library materials, furniture, equipment, supplies, materials, books, records, and other property, both real and personal, of the Arkansas Library Commission are hereby transferred to the State Library, to be preserved and used in the State Library in such manner as the Board may determine to be in the best interest of the State Library. All powers and duties heretofore vested by law in the Arkansas Library Commission, not otherwise specifically repealed by this Act [§§ 6-301 — 6-307] or inconsistent with the provisions of this Act are hereby transferred and shall hereafter be performed by the State Library, acting under the direction and policies of the Board. [Acts 1979, No. 489, § 7, p. 1017.]

6-307. Federal documents depository — State and local publications clearinghouse — Definitions. — (a) The Arkansas State Library shall serve as the State's regional depository library for federal documents and shall become the official depository for State and local documents. The Arkansas State Library shall create and maintain a State and Local Government Publications Clearinghouse. All State agencies, including the General Assembly and its committees, constitutional officers, and any department, division, bureau, board, commission, or agency of the State of Arkansas, and all local governments, including cities of the first and second class and incorporated towns, and counties, and all boards, commissions or agencies thereof, shall furnish to the State Library, upon release, a specified number of copies of each of its State or local publications, to enable the State Publications Clearinghouse to meet the needs of the Depository Library System and to provide library loan services to those libraries without depository status. Such distribution will be required only if sufficient funds are appropriated for the printing of these materials by the agencies, boards, and commissions, and for the distribution thereof by the Arkansas State Library to depository libraries.

For the purposes of this Act [§§ 6-301 — 6-307], the expression "State publication" and/or "local publication" shall include any document issued or printed by any State agency or local government which may be released for such distribution, but does not include:

(i.) the bound volumes of the printed Acts of each of the sessions of the General Assembly of the State of Arkansas;

(ii.) the bound volumes of the Arkansas Supreme Court Reports;

(iii.) printed copies of the Arkansas Statutes, 1947, annotated, or pocket part supplements thereto;

(iv.) any other printed document which may be obtained from the office of the Secretary of State upon the payment of a charge or fee therefor;

(v.) correspondence and intraoffice or interoffice or agency communication [communications] or document [documents] which are not of vital interest to the public;

(vi.) publications of State or local agencies intended or designed to be of limited distribution to meet the requirements of educational, cultural, scientific, professional, or similar use of a limited or restricted purpose, and which are not designed for general distribution; and similarly, other publications or printed documents which are prepared to meet the limited distribution requirements of a governmental grant or use, which are not intended for general distribution, shall also be deemed exempt from the provisions of this Act unless funds have been provided for printing of a quantity of such publication [publications] sufficient for distribution, provided, that a depository copy of each such document noted in subsections (i.), (ii.), (iii.), and (vi.) shall be made available to the State Library.

(b) The State Library shall make rules and regulations as may be necessary to carry out the purposes of the State Publications Clearinghouse.

(c) The Arkansas State Library may enter into depository agreements with any city, county, district, regional, town, school, college, or university library in this State. The State Library shall establish standards for eligibility as a depository library under this Section. Such standards may include and take into account:

(i.) the type of library;

(ii.) its ability to preserve such publications and to make them available for public use; and

(iii.) its geographical location, in order to assure that the publications are conveniently accessible to residents in all areas of the State.

(d) Each State and local agency printing or duplicating publications of the type which are to be made available to the State Publications Clearinghouse shall, if sufficient funds are available therefor, print or duplicate fifty (50) additional copies or such lesser number as may be requested by the State Library, for deposit with the State Publications Clearinghouse of the State Library for distribution to established depository libraries or interstate library exchange. Provided, however, that if a State agency or a local governmental agency does not have sufficient funds or resources available to furnish said fifty [50] copies to the State Publications Clearinghouse of the State Library, they shall notify the State Library and deliver to the State Publications Clearinghouse three (3) copies of each publication to be maintained in the State Library, to be indexed and made available on loan to participating libraries through the interlibrary loan services of the State Library.

(e) The State Publications Clearinghouse of the State Library shall publish, at least quarterly and more frequently if funds are available, and upon request, distribute to all State agencies and contracting depository libraries a list of State publications.

(f) Nothing in this Act shall be construed to repeal, amend, modify, or affect the status of the General Library of the University of Arkansas at Fayetteville as a depository of State, city, and county documents under the provisions of Act 170 of 1947 [§§ 14-431, 14-432], nor shall this Act repeal, amend, modify, or affect the powers of the General Library of the University of Arkansas at Fayetteville, or the library of each of the State-supported institutions of higher learning to be a selective or partial depository of State, city, and county documents under the provisions of Act 163 of 1971 [§§ 14-440 — 14-442]. Provided, however, that the State Library is hereby authorized to enter into contracts or agreements with the General Library of the University of Arkansas at Fayetteville and the library of each of the State supported institutions of higher learning in this State to provide through the State Publications Clearinghouse any of the clearinghouse, exchange, depository or selective or partial depository duties or functions of any of said libraries, or to provide depository library services in behalf of any of said libraries that may be mutually agreed to by the State Library and the General Library of the University of Arkansas at Fayetteville or one of the several institutions of higher learning of this State.

All powers, functions, and duties to be performed by the Secretary of State under the provisions of Act 163 of 1971 [§§ 14-440 — 14-442] are hereby transferred to, and shall hereafter be performed by, the Arkansas State Library. [Acts 1979, No. 489, § 8, p. 1017.]

INTERSTATE LIBRARY COMPACT
(Arkansas Statutes Annotated, 1982, s.6-310 to 6-315.)

6-310. Interstate library compact enacted. — The Interstate Library Compact is hereby enacted into law and entered into by this State with all states legally joining therein and in the form substantially as follows:

INTERSTATE LIBRARY COMPACT

Article I. Policy and Purpose. Because the desire for the services provided by libraries transcends governmental boundaries and can most effectively be satisfied by giving such services to communities and people regardless of jurisdictional lines, it is the policy of the states party to this compact to cooperate and share their responsibilities; to authorize cooperation and sharing with respect to those types of library facilities and services which can be more economically or efficiently developed and maintained on a cooperative basis, and to authorize cooperation and sharing among localities, states and others in providing joint or cooperative library services in areas where the distribution of population or of existing and potential library resources make the provisions of library service on an interstate basis the most effective way of providing adequate and efficient service.

Article II. Definitions. As used in this compact: (a) "Public library agency" means any unit or agency of local or state government operating or having power to operate a library.

(b) "Private library agency" means any nongovernmental entity which operates or assumes a legal obligation to operate a library.

(c) "Library agreement" means a contract establishing an interstate library district pursuant to this compact or providing for the joint or cooperative furnishing of library services.

Article III. Interstate Library Districts. (a) Any one or more public library agencies in a party state in cooperation with any public library agency or agencies in one or more other party states may establish and maintain an interstate library district. Subject to the provisions of this compact and any other laws of the party states which pursuant hereto remain applicable, such district may establish, maintain and operate some or all of the library facilities and services for the area concerned in accordance with the terms of a library agreement therefor. Any private library agency or agencies within an interstate library district may cooperate therewith, assume duties, responsibilities and obligations thereto, and receive benefits therefrom as provided in any library agreement to which such agency or agencies become party.

(b) Within an interstate library district, and as provided by a library agreement, the performance of library functions may be undertaken on a joint or cooperative basis or may be undertaken by means of one or more arrangements between or among public or private library agencies for the extension of library privileges to the use of facilities or services operated or rendered by one or more of the individual library agencies.

(c) If a library agreement provides for joint estalishment [establishment], maintenance or operation of library facilities or services by an interstate library district, such district shall have power to do any one or more of the following in accordance with such library agreement:

1. Undertake, administer and participate in programs or arrangements for securing, lending or servicing of books and other publications, any other materials suitable to be kept or made available by libraries, library equipment or for the dissemination of information about libraries, the value and significance of particular items therein, and the use thereof.

2. Accept for any of its purposes under this compact any and all donations, and grants of money, equipment, supplies, materials, and services (conditional or otherwise), from any state or the United States or any subdivision or agency thereof, or interstate agency, or from any institution, person, firm or corporation, and receive, utilize and dispose of the same.

3. Operate mobile library units or equipment for the purpose of rendering bookmobile service within the district.

4. Employ professional, technical, clerical and other personnel, and fix terms of employment, compensation, and other appropriate benefits; and where desirable, provide for the in-service training of such personnel.

5. Sue and be sued in any court of competent jurisdiction.

6. Acquire, hold, and dispose of any real or personal property or any interest or interests therein as may be appropriate to the rendering of library service.

7. Construct, maintain and operate a library, including any appropriate branches thereof.

8. Do such other things as may be incidental to or appropriate for the carrying out of any of the foregoing powers.

Article IV. Interstate Library Districts, Governing Board. (a) An interstate library district which establishes, maintains or operates any facilities or services in its own right shall have a governing board which shall direct the affairs of the district and act for it in all matters relating to its business. Each participating public library agency in the district shall be represented on the governing board which shall be organized and conduct its business in accordance with provision therefor in the library agreement. But in no event shall a governing board meet less often than twice a year.

(b) Any private library agency or agencies party to a library agreement establishing an interstate library district may be represented on or advise with the governing board of the district in such manner as the library agreement may provide.

Article V. State Library Agency Cooperation. Any two or more state library agencies of two or more of the party states may undertake and conduct joint or cooperative library programs, render joint or cooperative library services, and enter into and perform arrangements for the cooperative or joint acquisition, use, housing and disposition of items or collections of materials which, by reason of expense, rarity, specialized nature, or infrequency of demand therefor would be appropriate for central collection and shared use. Any such programs, services or arrangements may include provision for the exercise on a cooperative or joint basis of any power exercisable by an interstate library district and an agreement embodying any such program, service or arrangement shall contain provision covering the subjects detailed in Article VI of this compact for interstate library agreements.

Article VI. Library Agreements. (a) In order to provide for any joint or cooperative undertaking pursuant to this compact, public and private library agencies may enter into library agreements. Any agreement executed pursuant to the provisions of this compact shall, as among the parties to the agreement:

1. Detail the specific nature of the services, programs, facilities, arrangements or properties to which it is applicable.

2. Provide for the allocation of costs and other financial responsibilities.

3. Specify the respective rights, duties, obligations and liabilities of the parties.

4. Set forth the terms and conditions for duration, renewal, termination, abrogation, disposal of joint or common property, if any, and all other matters which may be appropriate to the proper effectuation and performance of the agreement.

(b) No public or private library agency shall undertake to exercise itself, or jointly with any other library agency, by means of a library agreement any power prohibited to such agency by the constitution or statutes of its state.

(c) No library agreement shall become effective until filed with the compact administrator of each state involved, and approved in accordance with Article VII of this compact.

Article VII. Approval of Library Agreements. (a) Every library agreement made pursuant to this compact shall, prior to and as a condition precedent to its entry into force, be submitted to the attorney general of each state in which a public library agency party thereto is situated, who shall determine whether the agreement is in proper form and compatible with the laws of his state. The attorneys general shall approve any agreement submitted to them unless they shall find that it does not meet the conditions set forth herein and shall detail in writing addressed to the governing bodies of the public library agencies concerned the specific respects in which the proposed agreement fails to meet the requirements of law. Failure to disapprove an agreement submitted hereunder within ninety days of its submission shall constitute approval thereof.

(b) In the event that a library agreement made pursuant to this compact shall deal in whole or in part with the provision of services or facilities with regard to which an officer or agency of the state government has constitutional or statutory powers of control, the agreement shall, as a condition precedent to its entry into force, be submitted to the state officer or agency having such power of control and shall be approved or disapproved by him or it as to all matters within his or its jurisdiction in the same manner and subject to the same requirements governing the action of the attorneys general pursuant to paragraph (a) of this article. This requirement of submission and approval shall be in addition to and not in substitution for the requirement of submission to and approval by the Attorneys General.

Article VIII. Other Laws Applicable. Nothing in this compact or in any library agreement shall be construed to supersede, alter or otherwise impair any obligation imposed on any library by otherwise applicable law, nor to authorize the transfer or dispose of any property held in trust by a library agency in a manner contrary to the terms of such trust.

Article IX. Appropriations and Aid. (a) Any public library agency party to a library agreement may appropriate funds to the interstate library district established thereby in the same manner and to the same extent as to a library wholly maintained by it and, subject to the laws of the state in which such public library agency is situated, may pledge its credit in support of an interstate library district established by the agreement.

(b) Subject to the provisions of the library agreement pursuant to which it functions and the laws of the states in which such district is situated, an interstate library district may claim and receive any state and federal aid which may be available to library agencies.

Article X. Compact Administrator. Each state shall designate a compact administrator with whom copies of all library agreements to which his state or any public library agency thereof is party shall be filed. The administrator shall have such other powers as may be conferred upon him by the laws of his state and may consult and cooperate with the compact administrators of other party states and take such steps as may effectuate the purposes of this compact. If the laws of a party state so provide, such state may designate one or more deputy compact administrators in addition to its compact administrator.

Article XI. Entry Into Force and Withdrawal. (a) This compact shall enter into force and effect immediately upon its enactment into law by any two states. Thereafter, it shall enter into force and effect as to any other state upon the enactment thereof by such state.

(b) This compact shall continue in force with respect to a party state and remain binding upon such state until six months after such state has given notice to each other party state of the repeal thereof. Such withdrawal shall not be construed to relieve any party to a library agreement entered into pursuant to this compact from any obligation of that agreement prior to the end of its duration as provided therein.

Article XII. Construction and Severability. This compact shall be liberally construed so as to effectuate the purposes thereof. The provisions of this compact shall be severable and if any phrase, clause, sentence or provision of this compact is declared to be contrary to the constitution of any party state or of the United States or the applicability thereof to any government, agency, person or circumstance is held invalid, the validity of the remainder of this compact and the applicability thereof to any government, agency, person or circumstance shall not be affected thereby. If this compact shall be held contrary to the constitution of any state party thereto, the compact shall remain in full force and effect as to the remaining states and in full force and effect as to the state affected as to all severable matters. [Acts 1967, No. 419, § 1, p. 964.]

6-311. Compliance with Constitution and laws required — Approval by library commission. — No county, city, town or combination thereof acting as a regional library district of this State shall be party to a library agreement which provides for the construction or maintenance of a library pursuant to Article III, subdivision (c-7) of the compact, nor pledge its credit in support of such a library, or contribute to the capital financing thereof, except after compliance with the constitution of this State and any laws applicable to such county, city, town or combination thereof relating to or governing capital outlays and the pledging of credit and after submitting such plan to the Arkansas Library Commission for approval thereof. [Acts 1967, No. 419, § 2, p. 964.]

6-312. "State library agency" defined. — As used in this compact, "state library agency," with reference to this State, means the Arkansas Library Commission. [Acts 1967, No. 419, § 3, p. 964.]

6-313. Interstate library districts included. — An interstate library district lying partly within this State may claim to be entitled to receive state aid in support of its functions to the same extent and in the same manner as such functions are eligible for support when carried on by entities wholly within this State. For the purposes of computing and apportioning state aid to an interstate library district, this State will consider that portion of the area which lies within this State as an independent entity for the performance of the aided function or functions and compute and apportion the aid accordingly. Subject to any applicable laws of this State, such a district also may apply for and be entitled to receive any federal aid for which it may be eligible. [Acts 1967, No. 419, § 4, p. 964.]

6-314. Compact administrator — Deputy compact administrators — Appointment. — The Governor shall appoint an officer of this State who shall be the compact administrator pursuant to Article X of the compact. The Governor shall also appoint one or more deputy compact administrator(s) pursuant to said article. [Acts 1967, No. 419, § 5, p. 964.]

6-315. Notices required by compact. — In the event of withdrawal from the compact the Governor shall send and receive any notices required by Article XI (b) of the compact. [Acts 1967, No. 419, § 6, p. 964.]

DISTRIBUTION OF PUBLIC DOCUMENTS
(Arkansas Statutes Annotated, 1982, s.14-422 to 14-434.)

14-422. Distribution of Supreme Court reports—County library— Circuit clerk to turn over books to successor—Penalty—Annual check by state comptroller—Liability of clerk and bondsmen—Replacement of missing books.—The Secretary of State shall furnish the Clerk of the Circuit Court of each County, the Circuit Judge, and the Chancery Judge of each District, with a set of Reports (not including the first forty-seven (47) volumes) of the decisions of the Supreme Court of Arkansas, and shall furnish said persons and each prosecuting attorney in this State, the forthcoming volumes of said Reports, one (1) copy each, as same shall be published and bound. He shall also furnish two hundred (200) copies of each volume of the Reports of the State Supreme Court, hereafter published to the Clerk of the Supreme Court to be sold by him, the money to be placed to the credit of the Arkansas Supreme Court Library Fund to be used in building up the Supreme Court library. He shall also furnish each Judge of the Supreme Court of Arkansas two (2) copies of the Supreme Court Reports published hereafter, taking receipts therefor. He shall also furnish two (2) copies of each volume of the Arkansas Reports to the Attorney General's office as soon as they are published, and shall not furnish anyone else free copies of said Reports. The several Clerks of the Circuit Courts of the State of Arkansas shall be furnished with one [1] full set of the Reports (not including the first forty-seven (47) volumes) of the decisions of the Supreme Court of Arkansas and shall keep the same in good order, and the County Judge of each County shall furnish a room or other suitable place therefor convenient for the Circuit Clerk, County officials and Circuit

Court at or near the Circuit Court room or in the Circuit Clerk's office, and said Circuit Clerk shall be in full and complete custody of said Reports and shall turn them over to his successor in office, and upon failure to do so he shall be fined in any sum not less than five (5) times the worth of the volumes which he has failed to turn over. All officers and officials receiving sets and volumes of the Arkansas Supreme Court Reports shall turn same over to their successors in office. Immediately after the effective date [June 11, 1941] of this Act, the Director of Administration shall check the reports in the office of the Chancery Clerks, Circuit Clerks and County Clerks of the State of Arkansas that have previously been issued to said officials, and shall assemble from such books as he shall find one (1) complete set in the office of each Circuit Clerk or county legal library, and shall cause any excess volumes to be returned to the office of the Secretary of State. If the Director of Administration shall not find sufficient books in each county to complete one [1] full set of Arkansas Supreme Court Reports, he shall so certify in writing to the Secretary of State, who shall then make available to said county library sufficient volumes of the Arkansas Supreme Court Reports to make said set complete, not including the first forty-seven (47) volumes of the Arkansas Supreme Court Reports. It shall be the duty of the Director of Administration to make a check of the County libraries once a year and report his findings to the Secretary of State; also, it shall be the duty of the Director of Administration to check the Arkansas Supreme Court Reports of each outgoing Circuit Clerk, and his findings shall be binding and shall be filed with the Secretary of State. When said county library is set up, the Director of Administration shall have placed on each volume the following statement: "This book is the property of the State of Arkansas."

The Circuit Clerk and his bondsmen shall be personally liable and responsible for the safekeeping of said Reports and no volume shall be loaned or removed, and said Clerk shall, out of his personal funds, replace any volumes found missing by the Director of Administration so that at all times one (1) full set, not including the first forty-seven (47) volumes, of the Reports of the decisions of the Arkansas Supreme Court shall be available in each county in the State of Arkansas for the general use of the courts, county officials and attorneys. [Acts 1941, No. 413, § 1, p. 1187; 1971, No. 322, § 1, p. 809.]

14-423. Each county seat furnished with set of reports.—In counties where there are more than one [1] county seat, each county seat shall be furnished with a set of the Arkansas Supreme Court Reports, and section 1 [§ 14-422] hereof shall apply to each county seat. [Acts 1941, No. 413, § 2, p. 1187.]

14-424. Destruction of county library—Replacement.—If the reports of the Supreme Court shall be destroyed in the county library in any county in this state by causes not within the control of the Circuit Clerk, the Comptroller of the State of Arkansas shall so ascertain, and shall certify to the Secretary of State a new set of the Arkansas Supreme Court Reports, or the missing volume or volumes, not including the first forty-seven [47] volumes. [Acts 1941, No. 413, § 4, p. 1187.]

14-425. Number of copies of reports to be retained by secretary of state.—The whole number of Reports [in the office of the Secretary of State] shall not be reduced below the number of three [3] copies of each volume. [Act July 18, 1868, No. 33, § 3, p. 110; C. & M. Dig., § 4417; Pope's Dig., § 5432.]

14-426. Expense of distribution.—The Secretary of State shall be authorized to draw upon the contingent fund of his office for the payment of the necessary expense incurred by transmitting said reports to the respective officers entitled to receive the same. [Act Jan. 12, 1853, § 3, p. 202; C. & M. Dig., § 4409; Pope's Dig., § 5424.]

14-427. Exchange of books with other states and countries—Furnishing books to federal courts and Library of Congress.—The Secretary of State is hereby authorized to exchange with other States and countries the Reports of the Supreme Court, Acts of the Legislature of the State of Arkansas, when bound and ready for distribution, and Digests of the Statutes, when revised and published, that extend to this State similar courtesies; also to furnish, upon demand, to the Federal Courts of Arkansas the current Digest of the Statutes of Arkansas, the Acts of the Legislature and the Reports of the Supreme Court of the State beginning wih volume 126.

The Secretary of State is further authorized to distribute to the Library of Congress the Acts of the Legislature of the State of Arkansas, Digests of the Statutes and reports of the Supreme Court after the same have been published or after they may be hereafter published, and all other publications of any sort by the State of Arkansas or any Department or Agency thereof, provided that the Secretary of State shall not distribute to said Library of Congress more than eight [8] copies of such Acts, Digests, Reports and other publications, and provided, that in no event shall any number be so distributed to said Library of Congress until said Library shall agree to furnish to the State of Arkansas for the use of the Supreme Court Library, a like number of the copies of all similar publications made by the United States Government. [Acts 1921, No. 207, § 3, p. 274; 1937, No. 209, § 1, p. 767; Pope's Dig., § 5435.]

14-428. General library of University of Arkansas designated as state depository.—The General Library of the University of Arkansas [shall] be designated as an official state depository of all public documents published by or under the authority of the state or any division thereof. [Acts 1947, No. 170, § 1, p. 398.]

14-429. Publications furnished to library of University of Arkansas—Exchange of documents.—Each department or division of the State under whose jurisdiction any document is issued is hereby authorized and directed to send to the General Library of the University of Arkansas at Fayetteville twenty [20] copies of all such documents or publications, provided that this requirement may be waived or the number of copies required reduced upon instructions of the University Librarian to the state printing clerk and the state agency issuing the publication.. These documents shall comprise all printed, mimeographed or other near-print publications, including proceedings of constitutional conventions, Senate and House Journals, Acts of the General Assembly,

Revised statutes, Constitutions, Statutes at Large, Digests, Codes, Supreme Court Reports, of all department reports of the State government, publications of all state supported institutions, miscellaneous publications, reports of investigations of impeachment trials, and sundry documents. Copies required for public use shall remain on permanent deposit in the General Library of the University of Arkansas in convenient form accessible to the public. Copies not required by the University libraries may be used by the University Librarian for exchange for needed publications of other states. Provided, that only three [3] copies of all mimeographed or near-print publications, other than annual or biennial reports, shall be sent to the University Library unless other copies are specifically requested by the Librarian. [Acts 1947, No. 170, § 2, p. 398; 1955, No. 379, § 1, p. 924.]

14-430. Affidavit showing delivery to library required before printing account paid.—No account for printing of any documents as provided for in section 2 [§ 14-429] shall be approved and no warrants or voucher checks shall be issued therefor until the Auditor's State Printing Clerk is furnished by the disbursing officer with an affidavit certifying to delivery to said library of copies of publications as provided for. [Acts 1947, No. 170, § 3, p. 398.]

14-431. County and municipal governments to send copies of publications to university.—Each department or division of government of municipalities and counties under whose jurisdiction any printed or processed book, pamphlet or report or other publication is issued at the expense of a municipal corporation or of a county, or of a county and city, is hereby directed to send two [2] copies of each such publication to the General Library of the University of Arkansas for inclusion in said depository. [Acts 1947, No. 170, § 4, p. 398.]

14-432. Act cumulative.—This act [§§ 14-428—14-432] is cumulative to and shall not repeal Sections 12236 to 12242 [§§ 6-201—6-204, 6-207, 6-208], inclusive, of Pope's Digest of the Statutes of Arkansas. [Acts 1947, No. 170, § 5, p. 398.]

14-433. Federal publications to be furnished university library.—The Secretary of State is further directed to send to the library of the University a copy of all publications of the Federal government, where there are duplicate copies in the State Library. This shall include the Congressional Globe, Congressional Record, executive documents, departmental and commercial reports, and any Federal documents. [Act Mar. 10, 1905. No. 80, § 3, p. 201; C. & M. Dig.. § 4405; Pope's Dig., § 5420.]

14-434. Distribution of reports and proceedings of legislature to Law Library Association, Inc., Shelby County, Tennessee.—The Secretary of State is also directed to deliver to said [Law Library] Association [Inc., of Shelby County, Tennessee], as a donation and without charge, as same are published, all volumes of the Reports of the Arkansas Supreme Court and all volumes of the proceedings of the General Assembly of this State. [Acts 1937, No. 97, § 2, p. 368; Pope's Dig.. § 5440.]

COUNTY LIBRARIES

(Arkansas Constitution, Amendment No. 38, 3.1-4;
Arkansas Statutes Annotated, 1982, 17-1001 to 14-1011.)

Sec. 1. Petition for tax levy—Election.—Whenever 100 or more tax paying electors of any county shall file a petition in the County Court asking that an annual tax on real and personal property be levied for the purpose of maintaining a public county library or a county library service or system and shall specify a rate of taxation not exceeding one mill on the dollar, the question as to whether said tax shall be levied shall be submitted to the qualified electors of such county at a general county election. Such petition must be filed at least thirty days prior to the election at which it will be submitted to the voters. The ballot shall be in substantially the following form:

FOR a_____mill tax on real and personal property to be used for maintenance of a public county library or county library service or system.

AGAINST a_____mill tax on real and personal property to be used for maintenance of a public county library or county library service or system.

Sec. 2. Result of election—Certification—Record—Tax levy—Funds —Disbursement.—The election commissioners shall certify to the County Judge the result of the vote. The County Judge shall cause the result of the election to be entered of record in the County Court. The result so entered shall be conclusive unless attacked in the courts within thirty days. If a majority of the qualified electors voting on the question at such election vote in favor of the specified tax, then it shall thereafter be continually levied and collected as other general taxes of such county are levied and collected; provided, however, that such tax shall not be levied against any real or personal property which is taxed for the maintenance of a city library, pursuant to the provisions of Amendment No. 30; and no voter residing within such city shall be entitled to vote on the question as to whether county tax shall be levied. The proceeds of any tax voted for the maintenance of a county public library or county library service or system shall be segregated by the county officials and used only for that purpose. Such funds shall be held in the custody of the County Treasurer. No claim against said funds shall be approved by the County Court unless first approved by the County Library Board, if there is a county Library Board functioning under Act 244 of 1927 [§§ 17-1001—17-1011], or similar legislation.

Sec. 3. Raising, reducing or abolishing tax—Petition and election.— Whenever 100 or more tax paying electors of any county having library tax in force shall file a petition in the County Court asking that such tax be raised, reduced or abolished, the question shall be submitted to the qualified electors at a general county election. Such petition must be filed at least thirty days prior to the election at which it will be submitted to the voters. The ballot shall follow, as far as practicable, the form set forth in Section 1 hereof. The result shall be certified and entered of record shall be conclusive unless attacked in the courts within thirty days. The tax shall be lowered, raised or abolished, as the case may be, according to the majority of qualified electors voting on the question at such election; provided, however, that it shall not be raised to more than one mill on the dollar. If lowered or raised, the revised tax shall thereafter be continually levied and collected and proceeds used in the manner and for the purposes as provided in Section 2 hereof.

Sec. 4. Co-ordination of county with city library.—Nothing herein shall be construed as preventing the co-ordination of the services of a city public library and county public library, or the co-ordination of the services of libraries of different counties.

17-1001. County courts may establish libraries.—The county courts of the several counties shall have power and authority to establish, maintain and operate county free libraries in the manner and with the functions prescribed in this act [§§ 17-1001—17-1011], and counties may appropriate money for said purposes.

The county court shall also have the power to establish in cooperation with another county or other counties, a joint free library for the benefit of the cooperating counties.

Establishment of said county libraries shall be evidenced by a regular order of the county court to be duly recorded, and appropriations for the establishment and maintenance thereof shall be in the manner prescribed by law for expenditures by counties. [Acts 1927, No. 244, § 1, p. 831; Pope's Dig., § 2629.]

17-1002. County free library fund — Custody. — All funds of the county free library shall be in the custody of the county treasurer and shall constitute a separate fund to be known as the County Free Library Fund. No claim against such fund shall be approved by the county court until acted upon by the County Library Board, if such board has been created, and payment authorized by said board. Such claim [claims] when certified as valid claims by the board shall be acted upon as all other claims against the county. Funds received by the county free library by gift, bequest, devise, or donation shall remain in the custody of the County Library Board, if such board has been created, and shall be used by it for the establishment, maintenance and operation of the county library. [Acts 1927, No. 244, § 2, p. 831; Pope's Dig., § 2630; 1981, No. 49, § 1, p. —.]

17-1003. County library board—Members—Term—Election of county librarian.—County free libraries established under this act [§§ 17-1001—17-1011] shall be under the control of a board of six [6] members to be appointed by the county court, to be known as the county library board. The members of said board shall be appointed for a term of three [3] years each, but the first appointments hereunder shall be so arranged that the terms of two [2] members of said board shall expire each year. The county court may therefore in establishing said board, appoint two [2] members for a term of one [1] year, two [2] members for a term of two [2] years, and two [2] members for a term of three [3] years, all appointments thereafter to be for a term of three [3] years. Said board shall have full charge of the county library systems established hereunder and shall elect a county librarian. [Acts 1927, No. 244, § 3, p. 831; Pope's Dig., § 2631.]

17-1004. Qualification of librarian — Duties. — No person shall be appointed to the office of County Librarian unless prior to appointment he shall have received from the State Library Board a certificate of qualification for the office, which must be filed with the County Clerk before any salary claims may be honored. The County Librarian shall conduct the library according to the most approved county library methods, and shall attend all State Library Association meetings. [Acts 1927, No. 244, § 4, p. 831; Pope's Dig., § 2632.]

17-1005. State library board—Members—Meetings.—The State Library Board shall consist of the Librarian of the Arkansas Library Commission who shall be ex-officio chairman of the Board, the President of the State Teachers' College who shall be ex-officio member, and the President of the State Library Association, who shall be ex-officio member. The members of said State Library Board'shall receive no compensation for their services except the actual and necessary traveling expenses which shall be paid out of the appropriation for the Arkansas Library Commission.

Said Board shall arrange for such meetings as may be necessary for the discharge of duties hereinafter set out. [Acts 1927, No. 244, § 5, p. 831; Pope's Dig., § 2633; Acts 1951, No. 300, § 1, p. 702.]

17-1006. Location of county library—Service throughout county.— The County Library shall be located at the county seat and the County Court shall provide suitable quarters in the Courthouse if requested by the County Library Board.

The said board and the County Librarian shall give service to all parts of the county through such branch libraries, deposit stations and other extension methods, as in their judgment should be established. [Acts 1927, No. 244, § 6, p. 831; Pope's Dig., § 2634.]

17-1007. Duties of county library board—Salaries and expenses— Annual report of librarian.—The County Library Board shall fix the salary of the County Librarian, shall appoint the necessary assistants on the recommendation of the County Librarian, and shall have full authority for directing the expenditures of the funds appropriated for the purpose of this Act [§§ 17-1001—17-1011]. They shall allow all actual and necessary traveling expenses. The librarian shall render an annual report to the County Library Board and to the Arkansas Library Commission and such other reports as the County Board may require. [Acts 1927, No. 244, § 7, p. 831; Pope's Dig., § 2635; Acts 1951, No. 300, § 2, p. 702.]

17-1008. Gifts, bequests and devises—Title vests in county.—The County Library Board is authorized and empowered to receive on behalf of the County, any gift, bequest or devise for the County Free Library or any branch or subdivision thereof, and shall use and administer such gifts in accordance with the terms imposed thereon. The title to all property belonging to the County Free Library shall be vested in the County. [Acts 1927, No. 244, § 8, p. 831; Pope's Dig., § 2636.]

17-1009. Cooperation with municipal library facilities.—The County Library Board shall have authority to enter into contract with municipalities having library facilities approved by the Arkansas Library Commission whereby free county library service may be rendered throughout the county, and the expenses of maintaining such joint municipal and county library service shall be apportioned in such manner as may be jointly agreed upon by the municipal authorities and the County Library Board. The librarian of such library must hold county library certificate. Said Board shall have authority to take over municipal library property upon proper action by municipal authorities and any municipality of this state may make its library facilities a part of the County Free Library system by appropriate action. [Acts 1927, No. 244, § 9, p. 831; Pope's Dig., § 2637; Acts 1951, No. 300, § 3, p. 702.]

17-1010. Adjoining counties may act jointly.—Two [2] or more adjacent counties may by proper order of the County Courts enter into agreements for joint free library service under the terms of this act [§§ 17-1001—17-1011]. In such cases, the affairs of the joint library system shall be administered by agreements of the Boards in the respective counties and the property to be used jointly by said counties shall not be withdrawn except in accordance with the terms of such agreements as may be entered into or with the consent of the other counties. [Acts 1927, No. 244, § 10, p. 831; Pope's Dig., § 2638.]

17-1011. Apportionment of expenses of joint library service.—The expenses of conducting such joint library service may be apportioned by agreement and all claims arising out of the joint library agreement shall constitute valid claims against the respective counties to be acted upon as herein provided for, in the case of a single county free library service. [Acts 1927, No. 244, § 11, p. 831; Pope's Dig., § 2639.]

MUNICIPAL LIBRARIES
(Arkansas Constitution, Amendment No. 34, s.1-4;
Arkansas Statutes Annotated, 1982, s.19-3201 to s.19-3211.)

Sec. 1. Petition for tax levy—Election.—Whenever 100 or more taxpaying electors of any city, having a population of not less than 5,000, shall file a petition with the Mayor asking that an annual tax on real and personal property be levied for the purpose of maintaining a public city library and shall specify a rate of taxation not exceeding one mill on the dollar, the question as to whether such tax shall be levied shall be submitted to the qualified electors of such city at a general city election. Such petition must be filed at least thirty days prior to the election at which it will be submitted to the voters. The ballot shall be in substantially the following form:

For a ———— mill tax on real and personal property to be used for maintenance of a public city library.

Against a ———— mill tax on real and personal property to be used for maintenance of a public city library.

Sec. 2. Result of election—Certification and proclamation—Tax levy.—The Election Commissioners shall certify to the Mayor the result of the vote, and if a majority of the qualified electors voting on the question at such election vote in favor of the specified tax, then it shall thereafter be continually levied and collected as other general taxes of such city are levied and collected. The result of the election shall be proclaimed by the Mayor. The result so proclaimed shall be conclusive unless attacked in the courts within thirty days. The proceeds of any tax voted for the maintenance of a city public library shall be segregated by the city officials and used only for that purpose.

Sec. 3. Raising, reducing or abolishing tax—Petition and election.— Whenever 100 or more taxpaying electors of any city having a library tax in force shall file a petition with the Mayor asking that such tax be raised, reduced or abolished, the question shall be submitted to the qualified electors at a general city election. Such petition must be filed at least thirty days prior to the election at which it will be submitted to the voters. The ballot shall follow, as far as practicable, the form set forth in Section 1 hereof. The result shall be certified and proclaimed, as provided in Section 2 hereof, and the result as proclaimed shall be conclusive unless attacked in the courts within thirty days. The tax shall be lowered, raised or abolished, as the case may be, according to the majority of the qualified electors voting on the question of such election; provided, however, that it shall not be raised to more than one mill on the dollar. If lowered or raised, the revised tax shall thereafter be continually levied and collected and the proceeds used in the manner and for the purposes as provided for in Section 2 hereof.

Sec. 4. Co-ordination of city with county library.—Nothing herein shall be construed as preventing a co-ordination of the services of a city public library and a county public library.

19-3201. **Establishment of libraries and reading rooms—Appropriation—Petition for establishment—Election.—A.** The city council of properly constituted municipal authorities may maintain a public library or reading room for the use and benefit of the inhabitants of such city. When such a library or reading room has been established, the city council or properly constituted municipal authorities may allot, for library purposes, a maximum appropriation of one-half mill from the revenue derived from all real and personal property within the city limits to be used exclusively for the maintenance of such library or reading room.

B. In cities of the first class, on petition of five per cent [5%] of the voters praying for the establishment of a public library, the city council or properly constituted municipal authorities shall, within thirty [30] days after the filing of such petition, call an election to be held within sixty [60] days thereafter. Such election shall be advertised and conducted as special elections are required by law to be. The ballots shall be marked "For Public Library," "Against Public Library." If a majority of the electors voting at such election vote in favor of the establishment of such a library, it shall be the duty of such city council or properly constituted municipal authorities immediately to establish a public library and continue to maintain it, in accordance with the provisions of section 1 [this section] hereof. [Acts 1931, No. 177, § 1, p. 607; Pope's Dig., § 9590.]

19-3202. Appointment of board of trustees—Oath.—When any city council shall have decided to establish and maintain a public library under this act [§§ 19-3201—19-3209], the mayor of such city shall, with the approval of the city council, appoint a board of five [5] trustees for the same, chosen from the citizens at large with reference to their fitness for such office. Said trustees shall receive no compensation for their services and shall, before entering upon the duties of their office, make oath or affirmation before some judicial officer to discharge the duties enjoined on them. [Acts 1931, No. 177, § 2, p. 607; Pope's Dig., § 9591.]

19-3203. Term of office—Vacancies.—Two [2] trustees shall hold office for two [2] years, two [2] for four [4] years and one [1] for six [6] years from the first day of January following their appointment in each case. At the first meeting they shall cast lots for their respective terms, reporting the result of such lot to the council. All subsequent terms shall be for six [6] years. The removal of any trustee permanently from the city, or his absence from four [4] consecutive meetings of the board, without due explanation of absence, shall render his office as trustee as vacant. Vacancies on the board shall be filled by the mayor with the approval of the city council. [Acts 1931, No. 177, § 3, p. 607; Pope's Dig., § 9592.]

19-3204. Organization of board of trustees.—Said trustees shall, immediately after their appointment, meet and organize by the election of one of their number as president. and by the election of such other officers as they may deem necessary. They shall make and adopt such by-laws, rules and regulations for their own guidance as they see fit. They shall meet once a month, and oftener if necessary, for the transaction of business. [Acts 1931, No. 177, § 4, p. 607; Pope's Dig., § 9593.]

19-3205. Power of trustees—Appointment of librarian and employees. —All money received for library purposes, whether by taxation or otherwise, shall belong to and be designated as the library fund, and shall be paid into the city treasury, and kept separate and apart from other funds, of such city, and drawn upon by the proper officers of said library upon the properly authenticated vouchers of the library board.

Said board shall have exclusive control of the expenditures of all moneys collected to the credit of the library fund, and of the construction of any library building, and the supervision, care and custody of the grounds, rooms or buildings constructed, leased or set apart for that purpose.

Said board shall have the power to purchase or lease ground, or to purchase, lease, erect and occupy an appropriate building or buildings for the use of said library. When a building erected or purchased by the board is not adapted to its purpose or needs, the board may remodel or reconstruct such building. Said board may also sell or otherwise dispose of any real or personal property that it deems no longer necessary or useful for library purposes.

Said board shall have the power to appoint a librarian qualified by education, training, experience and personality, who shall serve at the will of the board. They shall have power to appoint necessary assistants and other members of the staff, basing their appointment on the recommendation of the librarian.

Said board shall have the power to make necessary rules and regulations for administering the library, and shall make provisions for representation at library conventions. [Acts 1931, No. 177, § 5, p. 607; Pope's Dig., § 9594.]

19-3205.1. Use of surplus funds—Authority to match federal funds. —The Governing Board of any city or county public library is hereby authorized to use any surplus funds available in the operating or maintenance account of said public library for matching federal or other funds available therefor in financing necessary expansions or improvements of any such public library. Before using any of said funds for the purposes of this Act [Section], the governing board of the city or county public library shall adopt a resolution setting forth the amount of said funds to be used, the purposes for which the same are to be used, the amount of matching funds to be derived by the use of such funds, the nature of the expansions or improvements to be made, and said resolution shall include a declaration that the use of such funds will not jeopardize any existing program of the city or county public library, and that the same are not needed for any existing or anticipated maintenance or operating purpose of the library. The governing board of any city or county library using funds as authorized in this Act [Section] is hereby authorized to enter into contracts or agreements necessary to accomplish the purposes of this Act [Section], and with respect thereto, the governing board is authorized to accept gifts, grants or donations of property, both real and personal, from the federal government or from any person, firm or corporation to be used for the purposes of the expansion or improvement of the public library. [Acts 1965, No. 402, § 1, p. 1377.]

19-3206. Contracts for library services outside of city.—Said board may extend the privilege and use of such library and reading rooms to persons residing outside the city upon such terms and conditions as said board may from time to time by its regulations prescribe. Said board may also contract for library service with the county quorum court or with the municipal authorities of a neighboring city, town or village, or with school authorities. [Acts 1931, No. 177, § 6, p. 607; Pope's Dig., § 9595.]

19-3207. Donations for benefit of library.—Any person desiring to make donations of money, personal or real estate, for the benefit of such library, shall have the right to vest the title to the money or real estate so donated in the board of trustees created under this act [§§ 19-3201— 19-3209], to be held and controlled by such board, when accepted, according to the terms of the deed, gift, devise or bequest of such property; and as to such property the said board shall be held and considered trustees. [Acts 1931, No. 177, § 7, p. 607; Pope's Dig., § 9596.]

19-3208. Injuries to library property—Punishment.—The city council of said city shall have power to pass ordinances imposing suitable penalties for the punishment of persons committing injury upon library grounds or property thereof, or for injury or failure to return any book, periodical or property belonging to the library. Said board of trustees may refuse the use of the library to such offenders. [Acts 1931, No. 177, § 8, p. 607; Pope's Dig., § 9597.]

19-3209. Report of trustees.—At the end of each fiscal year, the board of trustees shall present a report of the condition of the trust to the city council. This report shall be verified under oath by the secretary of some responsible person. It shall contain (a) an itemized statement of the various sums of money received from the library fund and other sources; (b) a statement of the number of books and periodicals available for use, and the number and character thereof circulated; (c) a statement of the real and personal property received by devise, bequest, purchase, gift or otherwise; (d) a statement of the character of any extension of library service which may have been undertaken; (e) a statement of the financial requirements of the library for the ensuing year; (f) any other statistics, information or suggestions that might be of interest. A copy of this report shall be filed with the Arkansas Library Commission. [Acts 1931, No. 177, § 9, p. 607; Pope's Dig., § 9598; Acts 1951, No. 299, § 1, p. 701.]

19-3210. Joint maintenance with other cities.—When any city council of a city of the first class shall have decided to establish and maintain a public library under the terms of Act 177, Acts of the General Assembly of Arkansas, 1931, (Sections 19-3201 to 19-3209, inclusive, Arkansas Statutes, 1947), the Board of Trustees for such library appointed pursuant to such Act in fulfilling the purposes of said Act may contract with the municipal authorities of a neighboring city within this State or without this State if the city limits of such neighboring city so without this State extend to the State line of this State and are contiguous to the city limits of such city of the first class within this State, whereby a common library for the residents of both may be established and maintained by both such cities and providing for the division of the total cost of establishing, maintaining and operating the same between such cities, even though such library be located without this State; provided, however, that such contract shall become effective only from and after its ratification by a majority of the elected members of the city council of such city of the first class. [Acts 1951, No. 36, § 1, p. 66.]

19-3211. Joint library deemed a public city library.—Any such library when so established and operated shall be a public city library for all the intents and purposes of said Act 177 of the Acts of the General Assembly of the State of Arkansas, 1931, and of Amendment 30 to the Constitution of this State. [Acts 1951, No. 36, § 2, p. 66.]

SUPREME COURT LIBRARY

(Arkansas Statutes Annotated, 1982, s.22-232 to 22-240.)

22-232. Duties of clerk with respect to library.—The clerk of the Supreme Court, (for the time being, shall be the librarian, whose compensation shall be such as said court, shall from time to time, prescribe, payable out of any money in his hands for the use of the library, and) whose duty it shall be to take charge of, and keep all books by this act [§§ 22-232, 22-234—22-238] directed to be placed in his custody, and to take charge of, and expend, under the directions of the Supreme Court, all moneys appropriated or collected under the provisions of this act for the increase of said library and paying the expenses thereof, and who shall, before entering upon the duties of his office give bond to the

By unanimous vote of the justices, the Arkansas Supreme Court is hereby authorized and empowered at any time or times hereafter to dispose of any books, magazines, papers, or files, which may be in the library or in the clerk's office, and which may be found by said court to be no longer useful. [Acts 1957, No. 67, § 1, p. 228.]

22-240. Method of disposition.—The said disposition may be by sale, gift, or burning, as the said justices may determine. If the disposition is by sale, then the proceeds shall be placed in the library fund of the Arkansas Supreme Court. [Acts 1957, No. 67, § 2, p. 228.]

COUNTY LAW LIBRARIES
(Arkansas Statutes Annotated, 1982, s.25.504 to 25.511.)

25-504. County law library authorized. — Any county of this State is hereby authorized to own, operate and maintain a county law library and, in connection therewith, to own, buy, sell, lend, borrow, receive bequests and donations of, and otherwise deal in and contract concerning such books, volumes, treatises, pamphlets and other educational materials useful for the purpose of legal education and to use therefor any available funds including proceeds of the court costs levied and collected pursuant to the provisions of this Act [§§ 25-504 — 25-508]. [Acts 1971, No. 284, § 1, p. 659.]

25-505. Levy of costs — Amount of levy — Collection and disposition — County law library book fund. — In addition to all other costs now or as may hereafter be provided by law, effective upon the entry of an implementing order of the county court in accordance with the provisions of Section 3 [§ 25-506] hereof, there shall be levied and collected in each county for which an implementing county court order is entered, as costs, the following:

(1) From each defendant upon each judgment of conviction, plea of guilty or nolo contendere or forfeiture for failure to appear, in felony and in misdemeanor cases as follows, to-wit:

(a) In the Circuit Court, the sum of $1.00.
(b) In the Municipal Court, the sum of $1.00.
(c) In the Police Court, the sum of $1.00.
(d) In the Mayor's Court, the sum of $1.00.
(e) In the Justice of the Peace Court, the sum of $1.00.

(2) In civil cases as follows:

(a) In the Circuit Court, the sum of $1.00.
(b) In the Chancery Court, the sum of $1.00.
(c) In the Probate Court, the sum of $1.00.
(d) In the Municipal Court, the sum of $1.00.
(e) In the Mayor's Court, the sum of $1.00.
(f) In the Justice of the Peace Court, the sum of $1.00.

All Circuit Clerks, Chancery Clerks, County and Probate Clerks, Municipal Clerks, Sheriffs, or other officers who are now or who may hereafter be charged by law with collection of other costs in such cases are hereby required under the same penalties of law to collect the costs levied pursuant to the provisions of this Act [§§ 25-504 — 25-508], and no officer of any court may make a separate remission of the additional costs levied pursuant to the provisions of this Act. Such costs shall be collected at the time and in the manner as are other costs in such cases.

No county or municipality shall be liable for payment of the costs provided for by this Act in any instance in which they are not collected.

All collections from costs levied pursuant to the provisions of this Act shall forthwith be paid over by the collecting officer to the County Treasurer and by him credited on his records to a fund to be designated and known as the "County Law Library Book Fund." The said Book Fund shall be used for no other purposes than those provided in this Act and expenditures therefrom shall not require appropriation by the Quorum Court. [Acts 1971, No. 284, § 2, p. 659; 1975, No. 589, § 1, p. 1624.]

25-506. Conditions precedent to levy and collection of costs — Resolution of bar association — Implementing order. — The costs levied pursuant to the provisions of this Act [§§ 25-504 — 25-508] shall not be levied and collected unless there has been filed with the county court of a county a resolution of the county bar association (or, in counties where there is no county bar association, a resolution of the regional bar association which includes that county), signed by the president and attested by the secretary of such bar association, requesting the levying and collecting of the costs levied pursuant to the provisions of this Act. After receipt of such resolution, the county court may enter an order (the "implementing order") levying the costs levied pursuant to the provisions of this Act and directing their collection. [Acts 1971, No. 284, § 3, p. 659.]

25-507. Law library board — Establishment — Composition — Qualifications, appointment and terms of members — Duties. — A county law library established pursuant to this Act [§§ 25-504 — 25-508] shall be under the control of a county law library board of not less than three (3) nor more than five (5) persons, who shall be practicing attorneys residing in the county, and who shall be appointed by the county court from attorneys nominated by the county bar association, or, in counties where there is no county bar association, by a regional bar association which includes that county. Provided, in any county in which there are fewer than three (3) practicing attorneys, the board shall be composed of not less than three (3) nor more than five (5) persons including the practicing attorney or attorneys in the county together with one or more additional persons who are legal residents and qualified electors of the county, appointed by the county court. Members of the board shall be appointed for a term of five (5) years, but the initial appointments shall be so arranged that the terms of each member initially appointed expire in succeeding years. The board shall have charge of the operation and maintenance of the county law library and the custody and care of its property, and shall direct the expenditure of funds derived for law library purposes under this Act, and any other funds received by the county, or the board, for the use of the law library. [Acts 1971, No. 284, § 4, p. 659; 1977, No. 89, § 1, p. 40.]

25-508. Authority of board. — The Board, subject to approval of the county court, is hereby authorized, in implementation of the purposes of this Act [§§ 25-504 — 25-508], to enter into agreements with any person, including other public bodies, in this State pertaining to the operation and maintenance of a county law library. Without limiting the generality of the foregoing, agreements entered into pursuant to the provisions hereof may contain provisions making available to any institution of higher learning the county law library, and related facilities, and the books, volumes, treatises, pamphlets and other educational materials located therein, authorizing the institution to maintain, locate and relocate (in the county law library), select, replace, supervise the use of, buy, sell, lend, borrow, receive bequests and donations of, and otherwise deal in and contract concerning, such books, volumes, treatises, pamphlets and other educational materials, and providing for the operation, maintenance and supervision of the county law library, and related facilities, for the benefit of the institution, the county, judges and attorneys, and the public. Such agreements may make available to the institution all or a portion of the collections of the costs levied pursuant to the provisions of this Act, for the purpose of performing the obligations of the institution thereunder. [Acts 1971, No. 284, § 5, p. 659.]

25-509. North central Arkansas regional law library established. — There is hereby created the North Central Arkansas Regional Law Library to serve the counties of Fulton, Sharp and Izard. The county law libraries of said counties and their respective boards are hereby abolished. All assets and liabilities of such libraries are transferred to the North Central Arkansas Regional Law Library. [Acts 1979, No. 572, § 1, p. 1166.]

25-510. Library board. — The North Central Arkansas Regional Law Library shall be under the control of a board consisting of six [6] members who shall be practicing attorneys residing in the counties served by the library. The county judges of Fulton, Sharp and Izard Counties shall each appoint two [2] members from a list of attorneys nominated by the county bar association, or if no county bar association exist [exists], by a regional bar association which includes that county. Members of the Board shall be appointed for six [6] year terms, except that the terms of the initial Board members shall be determined by lot so that the term of one [1] member expires every year. The Board shall elect one [1] of its members to serve as treasurer and such person shall be bonded in accordance with Act 338 of 1955 [§§ 13-401 — 13-412], as amended. The treasurer shall be responsible for the deposit of funds collected and payment of debts incurred by the Board. [Acts 1979, No. 572, § 2, p. 1166.]

25-511. Powers of board. — The Board is authorized to designate the location of the library and own, buy, sell, lend, borrow, receive bequests and donations of and otherwise deal in and contract concerning such books, volumes, treatises, pamphlets and other educational materials useful for the purpose of legal education, and use therefor any available funds including proceeds of the court costs levied and collected pursuant to Act 284 of 1971 [§§ 25-504 — 25-508], as amended.

The Board shall direct the expenditure of all funds received by it for the use of the law library. The treasurer of the Board is authorized to maintain a bank account in a depository for all funds collected hereunder and for payment of all purchases made pursuant to this Act and the Board shall be subject to audit by the Legislative Joint Auditing Committee.

The Board is authorized to enter into agreements with any person or organization, including other public bodies, pertaining to the operation and maintenance of a regional law library. [Acts 1979, No. 572, § 3, p. 1166.]

TAX EXEMPTION
(Arkansas Constitution, Art. 16, s.5.)

Arkansas library laws are reprinted from ARKANSAS STATUTES ANNOTATED published by Bobbs-Merrill Co., Indianapolis, Indiana.

CALIFORNIA

STATE LIBRARY

(West's Annotated California Codes, Education Code, 1982,
s.19300-19334, 12130.)

§ 19300. Legislative declaration

The Legislature hereby declares that it is in the interest of the people and of the state that there be a general diffusion of knowledge and intelligence through the establishment and operation of public libraries. Such diffusion is a matter of general concern inasmuch as it is the duty of the state to provide encouragement to the voluntary lifelong learning of the people of the state.

The Legislature further declares that the public library is a supplement to the formal system of free public education, and a source of information and inspiration to persons of all ages, and a resource for continuing education and reeducation beyond the years of formal education, and as such deserves adequate financial support from government at all levels.

(Stats.1976, c. 1010, § 2, operative April 30, 1977.)

§ 19301. Division of Libraries

There is in the Department of Education the Division of Libraries.

(Stats.1976, c. 1010, § 2, operative April 30, 1977.)

§ 19302. State Librarian

The division shall be in charge of a chief who shall be a technically trained librarian and shall be known as the "State Librarian."

(Stats.1976, c. 1010, § 2, operative April 30, 1977.)

§ 19303. Appointment

The State Librarian shall be appointed by and hold office at the pleasure of the Governor, subject to confirmation by the Senate.

(Stats.1976, c. 1010, § 2, operative April 30, 1977.)

§ 19304. Duties of State Librarian

The State Librarian shall administer the State Library in accordance with law and such regulations as may be adopted by the State Board of Education, which board shall determine all policies for the conduct of the State Library.

(Stats.1976, c. 1010, § 2, operative April 30, 1977.)

§ 19305. Attendance at library

The State Librarian shall be in attendance at the library during office hours.

(Stats.1976, c. 1010, § 2, operative April 30, 1977.)

§ 19306. Appointment of assistant

The State Librarian may appoint an assistant who shall be a civil executive officer.

(Stats.1976, c. 1010, § 2, operative April 30, 1977.)

§ 19320. Powers and duties of Department of Education

The Department of Education may:

(a) Make rules and regulations, not inconsistent with law, for its government and for the government of the State Library.

(b) Authorize the librarian to appoint such other assistants as are necessary.

(c) Sell or exchange duplicate copies of books.

(d) Keep in order and repair the books and property in the library.

(e) Prescribe rules and regulations permitting persons other than Members of the Legislature and other state officers to have the use of books from the library.

(f) Collect and preserve statistics and other information pertaining to libraries, which shall be available to other libraries within the state applying for the information.

(g) Establish, in its discretion, deposit stations in various parts of the state, under the control of an officer or employee of the State Library. No book shall be kept permanently away from the main library, which may be required for official use. Books and other library materials from public libraries of the state may be accepted for deposit, under agreements entered into by the State Librarian and the public libraries concerned, whereby materials which should be preserved but are rarely used in the region may be stored and made available for use under the same conditions that apply to materials in the State Library.

(h) Collect, preserve, and disseminate information regarding the history of the state.

(i) Serve as regional library for the blind, in cooperation with the Library of Congress.

(j) Give advisory, consultive, and technical assistance with respect to public libraries to librarians and library authorities, and assist all other authorities, state and local, in assuming their full responsibility for library services.

(k) Serve as the central reference and research library for the departments of state government and maintain adequate legislative reference and research library services for the Legislature.

(l) Acquire, organize and supply books and other library informational and reference materials to supplement the collections of other public libraries of the state with the more technical, scientific and scholarly works, to the end that through an established interlibrary loan system, the people of the state shall have access to the full range of reference and informational materials.

(m) Make studies and surveys of public library needs and adopt rules and regulations for the allocation of federal funds to public libraries.

(n) Contract, at its discretion, with other public libraries in the state to give public services of the types referred to in subdivisions (g) and (l) of this section, when service by contract appears to be a needed supplement to the facilities and services carried on directly by the State Library.

(Stats.1976, c. 1010, § 2, operative April 30, 1977.)

§ 19321. Additional powers and duties of Department of Education

The Department of Education shall also:

(a) Purchase books, maps, engravings, paintings, and furniture for the library.

(b) Number and stamp all books and maps belonging to the library, and keep a catalog thereof.

(c) Have bound all books and papers that require binding.

(d) Keep a register of all books and property added to the library, and of the cost thereof.

(e) Keep a register of all books taken from the library.

(Stats.1976, c. 1010, § 2, operative April 30, 1977.)

§ 19322. Library services

The Department of Education may:

(a) Contract with counties, cities, or districts within this state, agencies of the state, and agencies of the United States government for the purpose of providing library services.

(b) Establish and operate library service centers.

(Stats.1976, c. 1010, § 2, operative April 30, 1977.)

§ 19323. Tape recordings of books, etc., to blind persons

The State Librarian shall make available on a loan basis to legally blind persons, or to persons who are visually or physically handicapped to such an extent that they are unable to read conventional printed materials, in the state tape recordings of books and other related materials. The tape recordings shall be selected by the State Library on the same basis as the State Library's general program for providing library materials to legally blind readers.

(Stats.1976, c. 1010, § 2, operative April 30, 1977.)

§ 19324. Duplication of braille materials

The State Librarian may duplicate any braille book master, other than textbook masters, presented by any legally blind person directly to the State Librarian for duplication. The State Librarian may duplicate any braille book master, other than textbook masters, presented by any other person or agency directly to the State Librarian for duplication.

(Stats.1976, c. 1010, § 2, operative April 30, 1977.)

§ 19330. Withdrawal of books by state officers

Books may be taken from the library by the Members of the Legislature and by other state officers at any time.

(Stats.1976, c. 1010, § 2, operative April 30, 1977.)

§ 19331. Failure to return books

The Controller, when notified by the Department of Education that any officer or employee of the state for whom he draws a warrant for salary has failed to return any book taken by him, or for which he has given an order, within the time prescribed by the rules, or the time within which it was agreed to be returned, and which notice shall give the value of the book, shall, after first informing the officer or employee of the notice, upon failure by him to return the book, deduct from the warrant for the salary of the officer or employee, twice the value of the book, and place the amount deducted in the General Fund.

(Stats.1976, c. 1010, § 2, operative April 30, 1977.)

§ 19332. Purchase of duplicate

In case of the neglect or refusal on the part of any officer or employee of the state to return a book for which he has given an order or a receipt or has in his possession, the Department of Education may purchase for the library a duplicate of the book, and notify the Controller of the purchase, together with the cost of the book. Upon the receipt of the notice from the department, the Controller shall deduct twice the cost of the duplicate book from the warrant for the salary of the officer or employee, and place the amount deducted in the General Fund.

(Stats.1976, c. 1010, § 2, operative April 30, 1977.)

§ 19333. Suit for the recovery of book, or three times its value

The Department of Education may bring suit in its official capacity for the recovery of any book, or for three times the value thereof, together with costs of suit, against any person who has the book in his possession or who is responsible therefor. If the department has purchased a duplicate of any book, it may bring suit for three times the amount expended for the duplicate, together with costs of suit.

(Stats.1976, c. 1010, § 2, operative April 30, 1977.)

§ 19334. Liability of person who injures or fails to return books

Every person who injures or fails to return any book taken is liable in three times its value.

(Stats.1976, c. 1010, § 2, operative April 30, 1977.)

§ 12130. Acceptance, receipt and administration of federal aid to public libraries

The State Department of Education is hereby named and designated as the proper state agency to accept, receive and administer any and all funds, moneys or library materials, granted, furnished, provided, appropriated, dedicated or made available by the United States or any of its departments, commissions, boards, bureaus or agencies for the purpose of giving aid to public libraries in the State of California.

(Stats.1976, c. 1010, § 2, operative April 30, 1977.)

LIBRARY SERVICES ACT
(West's Annotated California Codes, Education Act, 1982, s.18700-18767.)

§ 18700. Short title

This chapter shall be known as the California Library Services Act.

(Added by Stats.1977, c. 1255, § 2.)

§ 18701. Legislative declaration

The Legislature finds and declares that it is in the interest of the people of the state to insure that all people have free and convenient access to all library resources and services that might enrich their lives, regardless of where they live or of the tax base of their local government.

This finding is based on the recognition that:

(a) The public library is a primary source of information, recreation, and education to persons of all ages, any location or any economic circumstance.

(b) The expansion of knowledge and the increasing complexity of our society create needs for materials and information which go beyond the ability of any one library to provide.

(c) The public libraries of California are supported primarily by local taxes. The ability of local governments to provide adequate service is dependent on the taxable wealth of each local jurisdiction and varies widely throughout the state.

(d) Public libraries are unable to bear the greater costs of meeting the exceptional needs of many residents, including the handicapped, non-English and limited English-speaking persons, those who are confined to home or in an institution, and those who are economically disadvantaged.

(e) The effective sharing of resources and services among the libraries of California requires an ongoing commitment by the state to compensate libraries for services beyond their clientele.

(f) The sharing of services and resources is most efficient when a common data base is available to provide information on where materials can be found.

(Added by Stats.1977, c. 1255, § 2.)

§ 18702. Legislative intent

It is the intent of the Legislature to provide all residents with the opportunity to obtain from their public libraries needed materials and informational services by facilitating access to the resources of all libraries in this state.

This policy shall be accomplished by assisting public libraries to improve service to the underserved of all ages, and by enabling public libraries to provide their users with the services and resources of all libraries in this state.

(Added by Stats.1977, c. 1255, § 2.)

§ 18703. Legislative policy

In adopting this chapter, the Legislature declares that its policy shall be:

(a) To reaffirm the principle of local control of the government and administration of public libraries, and to affirm that the provisions of this chapter apply only to libraries authorized by their jurisdictions to apply to participate in the programs authorized by this act.

(b) To require no library, as a condition for receiving funds or services under this chapter, to acquire or exclude any specific book, periodical, film, recording, picture, or other material, or any specific equipment, or to acquire or exclude any classification of books or other material by author, subject matter, or type.

(c) To encourage adequate financing of libraries from local sources, with state aid to be furnished to supplement, not supplant, local funds.

(d) To encourage service to the underserved of all ages.

(e) To encourage and enable the sharing of resources between libraries.

(f) To reimburse equitably any participating library for services it provides beyond its jurisdiction if a public library, or, if not a public library, beyond its normal clientele.

(g) To ensure public participation in carrying out the intent of this act.

(Added by Stats.1977, c. 1255, § 2.)

§ 18710. Definitions

As used in this chapter, unless the context otherwise indicates or unless specific exception is made:

(a) "Academic library" means a library established and maintained by a college or university to meet the needs of its students and faculty, and others by agreement.

(b) "Act" means the California Library Services Act.

(c) "Cooperative Library System" means a public library system which consists of two or more jurisdictions entering into a written agreement to implement a regional program in accordance with this chapter, and which, as of the effective date of this chapter, was designated a library system under the Public Library Services Act of 1963 or was a successor to such a library system.

(d) "Direct loan" means the lending of a book or other item directly to a borrower.

(e) "Equal access" means the right of the residents of jurisdictions which are members of a Cooperative Library System to use on an equal basis with one another the services and loan privileges of any and all other members of the same system.

(f) "Independent public library" means a public library not a member of a system.

(g) "Interlibrary loan" means the lending of a book or other item from one library to another as the result of a user request for the item.

(h) "Interlibrary reference" means the providing of information by one library or reference center to another library or reference center as the result of a user request for the information.

(i) "Jurisdiction" means a county, city and county, city, or any district which is authorized by law to provide public library services and which operates a public library.

(j) "Libraries for institutionalized persons" means libraries maintained by institutions for the purpose of serving their resident populations.

(k) "Net imbalance" means the disproportionate cost incurred under universal borrowing or equal access when a library directly lends a greater number of items to users from outside its jurisdiction than its residents directly borrow from libraries of other jurisdictions.

(l) "Public library" means a library, or two or more libraries, which is operated by a single public jurisdiction and which serves its residents free of charge.

(m) "School library" means an organized collection of printed and audiovisual materials which (a) is administered as a unit, (b) is located in a designated place, and (c) makes printed, audiovisual, and other materials as well as necessary equipment and services of a staff accessible to elementary and secondary school students and teachers.

(n) "Single Library System" means a library system which consists of a single jurisdiction and which, as of the effective date of this act, was designated as a library system under the Public Library Services Act of 1963.

(o) "Special library" means one maintained by an association, government service, research institution, learned society, professional association, museum, business firm, industrial enterprise, chamber of commerce, or other organized group, the greater part of their collections being in a specific field or subject, e. g. natural sciences, economics, engineering, law, history.

(p) "Special Services Programs" means a project establishing or improving service to the underserved of all ages.

(q) "State board" means the California Library Services Board.

(r) "System" includes both Cooperative Library Systems and Single Library Systems.

(s) "Underserved" means any population segment with exceptional service needs not adequately met by traditional library service patterns; including, but not limited to, those persons who are geographically isolated, economically disadvantaged, functionally illiterate, of non-English-speaking or limited English-speaking ability, shut-in, institutionalized, or handicapped.

(t) "Universal borrowing" means the extension by a public library of its direct loan privileges to the eligible borrowers of all other public libraries.

(Added by Stats.1977, c. 1255, § 2.)

§ 18720. California Library Services Board; establishment

There is hereby established in the state government the California Library Services Board, to consist of 13 members. The governor shall appoint nine members of the state board. Three of the governor's appointments shall be representative of laypersons, one of whom shall represent the handicapped, one representing limited and non-English speaking persons, and one representing economically disadvantaged persons.

The governor shall also appoint six members of the board, each of whom shall represent one of the following categories: school libraries, libraries for institutionalized persons, public library trustees or commissioners, public libraries, special libraries, and academic libraries.

The Legislature shall appoint the remaining four public members from persons who are not representative of categories mentioned in this section. Two shall be appointed by the Senate Rules Committee and two shall be appointed by the Speaker of the Assembly.

(Added by Stats.1977, c. 1255, § 2.)

§ 18721. Term of members

Initial appointments to the board shall be made in the following manner:

(1) The Governor shall appoint five members for a two-year term, and four members for a four-year term.

(2) The Senate Rules Committee shall appoint one member for a two-year term, and one member for a four-year term.

(3) The Speaker of the Assembly shall appoint one member for a two-year term, and one member for a four-year term.

Initial appointments to the California Library Services Board shall become effective on January 10, 1978. All subsequent terms of office of members of the state board shall be four years, and will begin on January 1 of the year in which the respective terms are to start.

(Added by Stats.1977, c. 1255, § 2.)

§ 18722. Validation of board's acts

The concurrence of seven members of the state board shall be necessary to the validity of any of its acts.

(Added by Stats.1977, c. 1255, § 2.)

§ 18723. Compensation of members

Members of the state board shall serve without pay. They shall receive their actual and necessary traveling expenses while on official business.

(Added by Stats.1977, c. 1255, § 2.)

§ 18724. Duties of the board

The duties of the state board shall be to adopt rules, regulations, and general policies for the implementation of this chapter. In addition, the state board, consistent with the terms and provisions of this chapter, shall have the following powers and duties:

(a) To direct the State Librarian in the administration of this chapter.

(b) To review for its approval all annual proposals submitted under this chapter.

(c) To annually submit budget proposals as part of the annual budget of the Department of Education.

(d) To expend the funds appropriated for the purpose of implementing the provisions of this chapter.

(e) To require * * * participating libraries and systems to prepare and submit any reports and information which are necessary to carry out the provisions of this chapter, and to prescribe the form and manner for providing such reports and information.

(f) To develop formulas for the equitable allocation of reimbursements under Sections 18731, 18743, 18744, and 18765. Such formulas shall be submitted to the Department of Finance for approval.

(g) * * * To require that any public library participating in programs authorized by this chapter provide access to its bibliographic records and materials location information consistent with the legislative policy of encouraging the sharing of resources between libraries.

(Amended by Stats.1978, c. 331, p. 680, § 2, urgency, eff. June 30, 1978; Stats.1979, c. 395, p. 1470, § 1, urgency, eff. July 27, 1979.)

Asterisks * * * Indicate deletions by amendment

(h) To require that any public library participating in programs authorized by this chapter provide access to its bibliographic records and materials location information consistent with the legislative policy of encouraging the sharing of resources between libraries.

(Added by Stats.1977, c. 1255, § 2.)

§ 18725.   State Advisory Council on Libraries

The state board shall serve as the State Advisory Council on Libraries for the purpose of meeting the requirements of the federal Library Services and Construction Act.

(Added by Stats.1977, c. 1255, § 2.)

§ 18726.   State Librarian; chief executive officer

The State Librarian shall be the chief executive officer of the state board for purposes of this chapter and shall:

(a) Make such reports and recommendations as may be required by the state board.

(b) Administer the provisions of this chapter.

(c) Review all claims to insure programmatic and technical compliance with the provisions of this chapter.

(Added by Stats.1977, c. 1255, § 2.)

§ 18730.   Applications for special services programs

Any public library or combination of public libraries may submit proposals to the state board for Special Services Programs within the service area. Applications shall identify the needs of the target service group, assess the capacity of the applicant library or libraries to respond to those needs, and shall identify the activities and timelines necessary to achieve those objectives. Funds may be expended for the development of collections to meet the needs of the underserved, together with the employment or retraining of staff necessary to properly utilize the collections, and to provide appropriate services to the underserved.

(Stats.1976, c. 1010, § 2, operative April 30, 1977. Added by Stats.1977, c. 1255, § 2.)

§ 18731.   Universal borrowing

Any California public library may participate in universal borrowing. Public libraries participating in universal borrowing may not exclude the residents of any jurisdiction maintaining a public library. Public libraries which incur a net imbalance shall be reimbursed for the handling costs of the net loans according to the allocation formula developed pursuant to subdivision (g) of Section 18724. Reimbursement shall be incurred only for imbalances between:

(a) System member libraries and independent public libraries.

(b) Independent public libraries with each other.

(c) Member libraries of one system with member libraries of other systems.

(Added by Stats.1977, c. 1255, § 2.)

§ 18732.   Consolidation of two or more jurisdictions into a single library agency; establishment grants

If two or more public library jurisdictions wish to consolidate their libraries into a single library agency, an establishment grant in the annual maximum amount of twenty-thousand dollars ($20,000) shall be made to the newly consolidated library jurisdiction for each of two years, provided that notice of such consolidation is filed with the State Librarian within one year * * * after the consolidation.
(Amended by Stats.1979, c. 395, p. 1471, § 2, urgency, eff. July 27, 1979.)

Asterisks * * * Indicate deletions by amendment

Underline Indicates changes or additions by amendment

§ 18740.   Formation of library systems

A library system, eligible for funds under this article, may consist of the following systems:

(a) A library system which, as of the effective date of this act, was designated a system under the Public Library Services Act of 1963.

(b) A library system in which two or more systems consolidate to form a library system.

(c) A library system which is formed by adding independent public library jurisdictions to an existing system.

(d) A library system formed by any combination of the above.

(Added by Stats.1977, c. 1255, § 2.)

§ 18741.   Annual reference allowance

(a) Each system described in Section 18740 shall receive an annual allowance for the improvement and maintenance of coordinated reference service support to the members of the system. The allowance for the first fiscal year following the effective date of this chapter shall be equal to three cents ($0.03) per capita, plus two thousand dollars ($2,000) for each member jurisdiction. Following the effective date of this chapter, if there occurs a consolidation among individual public libraries which, as of the effective date of this chapter, are members of a system, the per member allowance to the system shall continue at the same level as if the consolidation had not taken place.

(b) After identifying the needs of the underserved, each system shall use a fair and equitable portion of its reference allowance to improve the system's reference service to its underserved population through appropriate collection development, provision of reference specialists, and staff training. Funds for the reference grant may also be used for general and specialized reference collection development, employment of reference specialists, and system-wide reference training.

(Added by Stats.1977, c. 1255, § 2.)

§ 18742.   System-wide applications for Special Services Programs

Any system may apply to the state board for funds for Special Service Programs on a system-wide basis. Proposals shall identify the needs of the target service group, assess the capacity of the applicant system to respond to those needs, and shall identify the activities and timelines necessary to achieve those objectives. Systems may also apply for funds for other system-wide programs, but such programs shall include a component for serving the underserved on a system-wide basis.

(Added by Stats.1977, c. 1255, § 2.)

§ 18743.   Equal access to all residents of the system

Each member library of a Cooperative Library System shall provide equal access to all residents of the area served by the system. Member libraries which incur a net imbalance shall be reimbursed through the system for the handling costs of the net loans according to the allocation formula developed pursuant to subdivision (g) of Section 18724.

(Added by Stats.1977, c. 1255, § 2.)

§ 18744. Interlibrary loans

Each member library of a Cooperative Library System shall be reimbursed through the system to cover handling costs, excluding communication and delivery costs, of each interlibrary loan between member libraries of the system according to the allocation formula developed pursuant to subdivision (g) of Section 18724.

(Added by Stats.1977, c. 1255, § 2.)

§ 18745. Intrasystem communications and delivery

Each Cooperative Library System shall annually apply to the state board for funds for intrasystem communications and delivery. Proposals shall be based upon the most cost-effective methods of exchanging materials and information among the member libraries.

(Added by Stats.1977, c. 1255, § 2.)

§ 18746. Funds for planning, coordination and evaluation of overall systemwide services

Each Cooperative Library System shall annually apply to the state board for funds for planning, coordination, and evaluation of the overall systemwide services authorized by this chapter.

(Added by Stats.1977, c. 1255, § 2.)

§ 18747. Administrative Council

(a) Each Cooperative Library System shall establish an Administrative Council whose membership consists of the head librarians of each jurisdiction in the system. Duties of the Administrative Council shall include general administrative responsibility for the system, adopting a system plan of service, and submitting annual proposals to the state board for implementation of the provisions of this article.

(b) Each Cooperative Library System shall establish an advisory board consisting of as many members as there are member jurisdictions of the system. The governing body of each member jurisdiction shall appoint one member to the advisory board from among its residents.

(Added by Stats.1977, c. 1255, § 2.)

§ 18748.   Advisory board; appointment of members

Each Single Library System shall establish an advisory board consisting of at least five members to be appointed by the governing body of the jurisdiction.

(Added by Stats.1977, c. 1255, § 2.)

§ 18749.   Advisory board; terms of members

The term of any member of a system advisory board shall be for two years, and each member shall serve no more than two consecutive terms. Staggered terms shall be established by drawing of lots at the first meeting of the advisory board so that a simple majority of the members shall initially serve a two-year term, and the remainder initially a one-year term.

The appointing jurisdiction shall ensure that members of a system advisory board are representative of the public-at-large and of the underserved residents in the system service area.

(Added by Stats.1977, c. 1255, § 2.)

§ 18750.   Advisory board; duties

The duties of each system advisory board shall include, but are not limited to, the following:

(a) Assisting the Administrative Council in the development of the system plan of service.

(b) Advising the Administrative Council on the need for services and programs.

(c) Assisting in the evaluation of the services provided by the system.

(Added by Stats.1977, c. 1255, § 2.)

§ 18751.   System consolidation grant

When any system or systems consolidate, a grant of ten thousand dollars ($10,000) for each of the two years following the consolidation shall be made to the newly consolidated system.

(Added by Stats.1977, c. 1255, § 2.)

§ 18752.   Jurisdiction joining already existing system; grant

When jurisdictions, not previously a member of any system, join an existing system, a grant shall be made to such a system as follows:

(a) If the jursidiction joins in the first fiscal year after the effective date of this chapter, the award shall be five thousand dollars ($5,000) for each of the two succeeding years.

(b) If the jurisdiction joins in the second fiscal year after the effective date of this chapter, the award shall be for four thousand dollars ($4,000) for each of the two succeeding years.

(c) If the jurisdiction joins in the third fiscal year after the effective date of this chapter, the award shall be three thousand dollars ($3,000) for each of the two succeeding years.

(d) If the jurisdiction joins in the fourth fiscal year after the effective date of this chapter, the award shall be two thousand dollars ($2,000) for each of the two succeeding years.

(e) If the jurisdiction joins in the fifth fiscal year after the effective date of this chapter, the award shall be one thousand dollars ($1,000) for each of the two succeeding years.

(f) Grants made pursuant to this section shall terminate at the end of the fifth fiscal year following the effective date of this chapter.

(Added by Stats.1977, c. 1255, § 2.)

§ 18760. State reference centers; establishment

The state board shall establish and administer two or more state reference centers. The centers shall be responsible for answering reference requests that cannot be met by systems and libraries participating in the programs authorized by this chapter.

(Added by Stats.1977, c. 1255, § 2.)

§ 18761. State reference centers; services

Each reference center established by the state shall provide statewide service. Such service shall include the handling of reference requests that cannot be met locally and regionally.

(Added by Stats.1977, c. 1255, § 2.)

§ 18762. State reference centers; reciprocal or contractual agreements

Each reference center established pursuant to Section 18760 may enter into reciprocal or contractual agreements with libraries or any other information source for the purpose of making available their materials and informational services for the benefit of the library users of this state. Each California public library participating in any program under this chapter shall make materials and services available, as needed, to state reference centers.

(Added by Stats.1977, c. 1255, § 2.)

§ 18763.   State reference centers; budget

The budget of any reference center established pursuant to Section 18760 may include funds for the general operations of such centers, including funds for collection development and use.

(Added by Stats.1977, c. 1255, § 2.)

§ 18764.   State reference centers; collections relevant to economically disadvantaged and non-English-speaking persons

The state board shall designate one or more of the reference centers established pursuant to Section 18760 as a repository for collections specially relevant to economically disadvantaged persons and non-English-speaking persons.

(Added by Stats.1977, c. 1255, § 2.)

§ 18765.   State interlibrary loan program; reimbursement

Each California library eligible to be reimbursed under this section for participation in the statewide interlibrary loan program shall be reimbursed according to the allocation formula developed pursuant to subdivision (g) of Section 18724 to cover the handling costs of each interlibrary loan whenever the borrowing library is a public library, except for the interlibrary loans made between members of a cooperative library system as provided in Section 18744. Libraries eligible for interlibrary loan reimbursement under this section shall include public libraries, libraries operated by public schools or school districts, libraries operated by public colleges or universities, libraries operated by public agencies for institutionalized persons, and libraries operated by nonprofit private educational or research institutions. Loans to eligible libraries by public libraries shall also be reimbursed according to the allocation formula developed pursuant to subdivision (g) of Section 18724.

(Added by Stats.1977, c. 1255, § 2.)

§ 18766.   Statewide communications and delivery network

The state board shall establish and maintain a statewide communications and delivery network between and among systems, state reference centers, independent public libraries and all other libraries participating in the programs authorized by this act.

(Added by Stats.1977, c. 1255, § 2.)

§ 18767. Computerized data base; bibliographic records and location of materials
The state board shall establish and maintain a computerized data base of bibliographic records and locations of all materials acquired by public libraries in this state, for the purpose of carrying out the legislative policy of enabling libraries to share resources efficiently.
(Added by Stats.1978, c. 331, p. 680, § 1, urgency, eff. June 30, 1978.)

CONSERVATION EDUCATION SERVICE
(West's Annotated California Codes, Education Act, 1982, s.8722, 8730-8733.)

§ 8722. Additional powers and duties

The Conservation Education Service shall have the following additional powers and duties:

• • •

(5) To establish and maintain a central library and repository for conservation education materials pursuant to Article 3 (commencing with Section 8730) of this chapter.

(Stats.1976, c. 1010, § 2, operative April 30, 1977.)

§ 8730. Central library and repository

There is in the Department of Education a Central Library and Repository for conservation education materials. Such materials may be developed by private conservation groups, by industry, and by professional, scientific, and governmental sources.

(Stats.1976, c. 1010, § 2, operative April 30, 1977.)

§ 8731. Purpose

The purpose of the library shall be to serve as a master source of materials for the Conservation Education Service, public school districts, county superintendents of schools, and any regional conservation education centers which may be established.

(Stats.1976, c. 1010, § 2, operative April 30, 1977.)

§ 8732. Department's duties in establishing library

The department shall, in establishing the library, explore new methods in data processing, new library procedures, and new means

for distributing materials to local school districts, county superintendents of schools, and any regional conservation education centers
which may be established.

(Stats.1976, c. 1010, § 2, operative April 30, 1977.)

§ 8733. Additional duties

The library shall thoroughly evaluate new materials for validity,
pertinence, objectivity, and usefulness, and shall advise the state
board in the adoption of textbooks in regard to meeting the requirements for conservation education.

(Stats.1976, c. 1010, § 2, operative April 30, 1977.)

DISTRIBUTION OF PUBLIC DOCUMENTS
(West's Annotated California Codes, Government Code, 1982,
s.14900-14912, 9742, 9791, 12240-12241, 50110.)

§ 14900. State policy; distribution of state publications to libraries

It is the policy of the State of California to make freely available
to its inhabitants all state publications by distribution to libraries
throughout the state, subject to the assumption by such libraries of
the responsibilities of keeping such documents readily accessible for
use, and of rendering assistance in their use to qualified patrons without charge.

(Added by Stats.1965, c. 371, p. 1563, § 179.)

§ 14901. Library stock room; copies for state archivist; disposi-tion of remaining copies

To the end that the policy specified in Section 14900 may be effectively carried out, the State Printer shall print a sufficient number
of copies of each state publication as determined by the State Librarian in accordance with Sections 14901, 14903, 14904, 14905.1, and
14907, not to exceed three hundred fifty (350), unless the Department of General Services with the advice of the State Librarian determines that a greater number is necessary in order to meet the requirements for deposit in a "library stockroom" (to be maintained by
the State Printer for that purpose) for distribution to libraries as
hereinafter provided, except that of legislative bills, daily journals,
and daily or weekly histories, not more than one hundred fifty (150)
copies shall be printed for such deposit and distribution, and of publications not printed by the State Printer, the department, commission
or other agency concerned shall print one hundred (100) copies for

such distribution. An additional two (2) copies of each state publication as selected by the State Archivist shall be printed and delivered to the State Archivist by the State Printer or the department, commission, or other agency concerned, and all remaining copies in excess of two (2) copies heretofore received shall be distributed to interested parties without charge or destroyed. The cost of printing, publishing, and distributing such copies shall be fixed and charged pursuant to Section 14866.

(Added by Stats.1965, c. 371, p. 1563, § 179. Amended by Stats.1965, c. 1825, p. 4214, § 1; Stats.1972, c. 616, p. 1085, § 1; Stats.1976, c. 1038, p. 4648, § 2, operative July 1, 1977.)

§ 14902. Definitions

"State publication" or "publication" as herein employed is defined to include any document, compilation, journal, law, resolution, Blue Book, statute, code, register, pamphlet, list, book, report, memorandum, hearing, legislative bill, leaflet, order, regulation, directory, periodical or magazine issued by the state, the Legislature, constitutional officers, or any department, commission or other agency thereof or prepared for the state by private individual or organization and issued in print, and "print" is defined to include all forms of duplicating other than by the use of carbon paper. The publications of the University of California, however, and intraoffice or interoffice publications and forms shall not be included.

(Added by Stats.1965, c. 371, p. 1564, § 179. Amended by Stats.1972, c. 616, p. 1085, § 2.)

§ 14903. Forwarding to state and university libraries; exchange copies

As soon as practicable after deposit of the copies in the library stockroom, the State Printer shall forward of each publication other than the legislative bills, daily journals and daily or weekly histories, fifty (50) copies to the State Library at Sacramento, twenty-five (25) copies each to the University of California libraries at Berkeley and Los Angeles, and fifty (50) copies to the California State Colleges, to be allocated among the libraries thereof as directed by the Trustees of the California State Colleges. Such copies in excess of the number required for the institutions themselves, may be used for exchanges with other institutions or with agencies of other states and countries.

(Added by Stats.1965, c. 371, p. 1564, § 179. Amended by Stats.1965, c. 1825, p. 4214, § 2.)

§ **14904.**   Distribution to complete and selective depositories; distribution to other libraries on request

The copies remaining in the library stockroom, including the legislative bills, daily journals, and daily or weekly histories, shall be distributed as soon as practicable by the State Printer first one copy each to the libraries which are on his mailing list as "complete depositories," second one copy each to the libraries which are on his mailing list as "selective depositories," and third the balance to any libraries which may write for a copy or copies. Publications not printed by the State Printer shall be distributed by the issuing department, commission or other agency as soon as practicable after printing, first to all "complete depositories," and second to "selective depositories," designated by the Department of General Services.

(Added by Stats.1965, c. 371, p. 1564, § 179.)

§ **14905.**   Designation of libraries as complete or selective depositories; conditions

To be placed on the mailing list as a "complete depository" or as a "selective depository," a library must contract with the Department of General Services to provide adequate facilities for the storage and use of the publications, and must agree to render reasonable service without charge to qualified patrons in the use of the publications. A library designated as a "complete depository" shall be sent one copy of every state publication, while a library designated as a "selective depository" shall be sent one copy of each publication of the type or issuing agency it selects.

(Added by Stats.1965, c. 371, p. 1564, § 179.)

§ **14905.1.**   Exchange of publications

The California State Library may enter into agreements with the appropriate state agencies of each of the 49 other states of the United States of America, to establish a program for the exchange of publications of legislative service agencies, other than publications of the Joint Legislative Audit Committee and of the Joint Legislative Budget Committee. The California legislative reports to be exchanged shall be selected by the State Librarian after consultation with, and subject to the approval of, the Joint Committee on Legislative Organization. The legislative research reports received from other states in exchange shall be made available by the California State Library to the California Legislature.

Prior to designation as an exchange agency, the state agency shall agree to provide adequate facilities for the storage and use of the publications, and must agree to render reasonable service in the use of the publications without charge to the legislature of that state and other qualified patrons.

The California State Library shall notify the appropriate state agency of each of the other states of the provisions of this section.

The additional number of copies of publications, not to exceed 100, needed to implement the program shall be printed or otherwise duplicated. The State Printer and the state legislative agencies upon notification of the need shall provide the designated number of publications.

(Added by Stats.1965, c. 1232, p. 3085, § 2.)

§ 14906. Designation of libraries as complete or selective depositories; eligibility; consideration of applications

Any municipal or county free library, any state college or state university library, the library of any incorporated college or university in this state, and the State Library, may contract as above provided. Applications are to be considered in the order of their receipt by the Department of General Services.

(Added by Stats.1965, c. 371, p. 1565, § 179.)

§ 14907. Law libraries; designation as complete or selective depositories

Upon application, county law libraries, the law libraries of any law school approved by the State Bar of California, the Supreme Court Library, and the law libraries of the Department of Justice and the law library of the Continuing Education of the Bar of the University of California Extension may contract as provided in Section 14905 to become a selective or complete depository library.

(Added by Stats.1965, c. 371, p. 1565, § 179.)

§ 14908. Disregard of proximity to another depository in selection of law library as depository

Because of the specialized service rendered the citizens of this state through assistance in the administration of justice, proximity to another depository library shall be disregarded in the selection of a law library as a depository of legal materials.

(Added by Stats.1965, c. 371, p. 1565, § 179.)

§ 14909. Basic documents

Maintenance of basic general documents shall not be required of law library depositories, but basic legal documents shall be maintained by them. Such basic legal documents shall include legislative bills, legislative committee hearings and reports, legislative journals, statutes, administrative reports, California Administrative Code and Register, annual reports of state agencies and other legal materials published by the state, where obtainable through the agency preparing same.

(Added by Stats.1965, c. 371, p. 1565, § 179.)

§ 14910. Monthly or quarterly lists of publications; annual cumulative list

To facilitate the distribution of state publications, the State Library shall issue monthly or quarterly a complete list of state publications issued during the immediately preceding month or quarter, such lists to be cumulated and printed at the end of each calendar year. All state departments, commissions and other agencies shall, upon request, supply information to the State Library for the preparation of the monthly or quarterly lists and the annual cumulative lists.

(Added by Stats.1965, c. 371, p. 1565, § 179. Amended by Stats.1976, c. 1038, p. 4649, § 3, operative July 1, 1977.)

§ 14911. Mailing lists; annual correction

Whenever any state agency maintains a mailing list of public officials or other persons to whom publications or other printed matter is sent without charge, the state agency shall correct its mailing list and verify its accuracy at least once each year. This shall be done by addressing an appropriate post card or letter to each person on the mailing list. The name of any person who does not respond to such letter or post card, or who indicates that he does not desire to receive such publications or printed matter, shall be removed from the mailing lists. The responses of those desiring to be on the mailing list shall be retained by these agencies for one year.

(Added by Stats.1965, c. 371, p. 1565, § 179.)

§ 14912. Number of copies of statutes

Notwithstanding any other provision of this article, the number of copies of statutes distributed to an authorized recipient shall not exceed the number requested by such recipient, or the number authorized by this article, whichever is the lesser.

(Added by Stats.1970, c. 72, p. 86, § 2, eff. April 30, 1970.)

§ 9742. Distribution

The manual shall be distributed as follows:

(a) To each Senator and Assemblyman as determined by the Rules Committee of the respective houses.

(b) Each elective state officer, one copy.

(c) The State Library, five copies.

(d) Each free public library in the state, one copy.

(e) The Congressional Library at Washington, D. C., five copies.

(Added by Stats.1945, c. 111, p. 425, § 1. Amended by Stats.1973, c. 7, p. 12, § 20, eff. March 13, 1973.)

§ 9791. Distributees; number of copies

The laws, resolutions and journals of the Legislature shall be distributed by the Department of General Services as follows:

(a) To the Library of Congress, two copies.

(b) To the Governor, Lieutenant Governor, each Member of the Legislature, the Secretary of the Senate, the Chief Clerk of the Assembly, and the Legislative Auditor, one copy each.

(c) To the State Library, 60 copies or as many more as the State Librarian may require for exchange purposes, and to each county law library, one copy.

(d) To the Attorney General, six copies, and as many additional copies as may be requested, not exceeding the number necessary to supply each Assistant Attorney General, and each Deputy Attorney General with one copy of each.

(e) To the Legislative Counsel Bureau, as many copies as may be requested, not exceeding the number necessary to supply one copy of each for the use of the Legislative Counsel and each Deputy Legislative Counsel.

(f) To the State Supreme Court, 11 copies and as many additional copies as may be requested not to exceed four copies.

(Added by Stats.1945, c. 111, p. 427, § 1. Amended by Stats.1945, c. 1403, p. 2655, § 4; Stats.1947, c. 182, p. 742, § 2; Stats.1965, c. 371, p. 1518, § 107; Stats.1965, c. 592, p. 1927, § 1; Stats.1971, c. 272, p. 572, § 1; Stats. 1973, c. 7, p. 12, § 22, eff. March 13, 1973.)

§ 12240. Duty to compile, publish, and distribute

Whenever an appropriation is made by the Legislature for the purpose, the Secretary of State shall compile, publish, and distribute a roster of the State and local public officials of California.

(Added by Stats.1945, c. 111, p. 454, § 3.)

§ 12241.   Printing and distribution

The Secretary of State shall cause the roster to be printed and shall distribute copies free of charge, as follows: To the Governor, 50 copies; to the Lieutenant Governor, 30 copies; to each member of the Senate and to each member of the Assembly, 30 copies; to each elective State officer, each head of a State department, each county clerk, each public library upon request, each Governor and each Secretary of State of a State of the United States, one copy. The remaining copies may be distributed, singly and free of charge to any person requesting them.

(Added by Stats.1945, c. 111, p. 454, § 3.)

§ 50110. Publications; Copies for state library and university; preservation

The legislative body, and each office, officer, or employee of a local agency shall furnish the clerk three copies of each printed, mimeographed, or processed book, pamphlet, report, bulletin, or other publication issued by them at the expense of the local agency. The clerk shall send one copy of each publication to the State Library at Sacramento, the * * * <u>Institute of Governmental Studies</u> of the University of California at Berkeley, and the * * * <u>Public Affairs Service</u> of the University of California at Los Angeles, to be preserved for reference use in those institutions.

(Amended by Stats.1974, c. 544, p. 1252, § 18.)

Asterisks * * * indicate deletions by amendment

<u>Underline</u> **indicates changes or additions by amendment**

STATE ARCHIVES
(West's Annotated California Codes, Government Code, 1982,
s-12220–12233.)

§ 12220.   Item, definition

As used in this article, "item" includes but is not limited to any paper, document, book, map, or other type of record.

(Added by Stats.1945, c. 111, p. 453, § 3.)

§ 12221.   Custodian

The Secretary of State is the custodian of the public archives of the State.

(Added by Stats.1945, c. 111, p. 453, § 3.)

§ 12222.   Vaults

The Secretary of State shall maintain and properly equip safe and secure vaults for the preservation, indexing, and use of the archives.

(Added by Stats.1945, c. 111, p. 453, § 3.)

§ 12223. Required items

The Secretary of State shall receive into the archives any item that is required by law to be delivered to or filed with him.

(Added by Stats.1945, c. 111, p. 453, § 3.)

§ 12224. Items of historical value; items from state agencies

The Secretary of State may receive into the archives any item that he deems to be of historical value and shall receive into the archives any other item from a state agency if directed to do so by the Department of General Services.

(Added by Stats.1945, c. 111, p. 453, § 3. Amended by Stats.1965, c. 371, p. 1527, § 139.)

§ 12225. Return of items to state agencies

With the approval of the Department of General Services, the Secretary of State may at any time return to the state agency from which it was received any item in the archives which he does not deem to be of historical value.

(Added by Stats.1945, c. 111, p. 453, § 3. Amended by Stats.1965, c. 371, p. 1527, § 140.)

§ 12226. Official items transferred by county or city

With the consent of the Secretary of State, the governing body of a county or city may by order or resolution direct the transfer to the Secretary of State for inclusion in the State archives of official items it deems have historic interest or value, and which are in the custody of any officer of the county or city. Accurate copies of the transferred items shall be substituted for the originals when the governing body deems necessary.

(Added by Stats.1945, c. 111, p. 453, § 3.)

§ 12227. Preservation, indexing, availability for use

The Keeper of the Archives is responsible for the preservation and indexing of material deposited in the State archives, and shall make the material readily available for use.

(Added by Stats.1945, c. 111, p. 454, § 3.)

§ 12228. Receipts for material received

The Keeper of the Archives shall give an appropriate receipt for all material received by him as a part of the archives.

(Added by Stats.1945, c. 111, p. 454, § 3.)

§ 12229.   Maintenance of items in active file

The Secretary of State may maintain any item in an active file in his office for such time as he deems proper before transferring it to the archives.

(Added by Stats.1945, c. 111, p. 454, § 3.)

§ 12230.   Document preservation shop and indexing section; establishment; exhibitions

The Secretary of State shall establish a Document Preservation Shop and an Indexing Section to facilitate the preservation and indexing of the archives. He shall also prepare exhibitions of documentary materials from the archives to be displayed in the State Capitol Building.

(Added by Stats.1965, c. 1632, p. 3727, § 1.)

§ 12231.   Consultations with, and consideration to recommendations of, California Heritage Preservation Commission

In carrying out the provisions of this article, the Secretary of State shall consult with and give consideration to the recommendations of the California Heritage Preservation Commission, which for such purpose shall serve in an advisory capacity to the Secretary of State.

(Added by Stats.1965, c. 1632, p. 3727, § 2.)

§ 12232.   County historical records commission; utilization of state commission and library by secretary to coordinate activities

The Secretary of State shall utilize the California Heritage Preservation Commission and the California State Library to advise, encourage, and coordinate the activities of the county historical records commissions, either designated or appointed by the county boards of supervisors pursuant to Section 26490. The chairman or his designate of each county historical records commission may attend an annual meeting with the named state representatives, at state expense, to receive advice in the preservation of local government archives and public library collections of historical materials.

(Added by Stats.1974, c. 59, p. 128, § 1.)

§ 12233.   Governmental history documentation project; contract

The Secretary of State may contract with the Regents of the

University of California for the Regional Oral History Office of the Bancroft Library to conduct a governmental history documentation project to provide through the use of oral history techniques a continuing documentation of California's legislative and executive history from and after the year 1925. The contract shall require the Regional Oral History Office of the Bancroft Library to work in conjunction with other oral history programs affiliated with a public or private nonprofit college, university, or historical society located in California and to provide for the participation of other persons having expertise in California state government. The contract shall require the Regional Oral History Office of the Bancroft Library to submit an annual report to the Legislature on the governmental documentation project.

(Added by Stats.1979, c. 536, § 2, operative July 1, 1980.)

STATE RECORDS
(West's Annotated California Codes, Government Code, 1982, s.14740-14770.)

§ 14740. California records act

This chapter shall be known as the "State Records Management Act."

(Added by Stats.1965, c. 371, p. 1549, § 179.)

§ 14741. "Record" or "records" defined

As used in this chapter "record" or "records" means all papers, maps, exhibits, magnetic or paper tapes, photographic films and prints, punched cards, and other documents produced, received, owned or used by an agency, regardless of physical form or characteristics. Library and museum materials made or acquired and preserved solely for reference or exhibition purposes, and stocks of publications and of processed documents are not included within the definition of the term "record" or "records" as used in this chapter.

(Added by Stats.1965, c. 371, p. 1549, § 179.)

§ 14745. Records management program

The director shall establish and administer in the executive branch of state government a records management program, which will apply efficient and economical management methods to the creation, utilization, maintenance, retention, preservation, and disposal of state records.

(Added by Stats.1965, c. 371, p. 1550, § 179.)

§ 14746.   Duties of director

The duties of the director shall include but not be limited to:

(a) Establishing standards, procedures, and techniques for effective management of records.

(b) Providing appropriate protection for records designated by state agencies, with the concurrence of the director, as essential to the functioning of state government in the event of a major disaster.

(c) Obtaining from agencies reports required for the administration of the program.

(Added by Stats.1965, c. 371, p. 1550, § 179. Amended by Stats.1967, c. 640, p. 1989, § 1.)

§ 14750.   Agency records; compliance with rules and regulations

The head of each agency shall:

(a) Establish and maintain an active, continuing program for the economical and efficient management of the records of the agency.

(b) Determine, with the concurrence of the director, records essential to the functioning of state government in the event of a major disaster.

(c) Comply with the rules, regulations, standards and procedures issued by the director.

(Added by Stats.1965, c. 371, p. 1550, § 179.)

§ 14755.   Preservation of records having value

(a) No record shall be destroyed or otherwise disposed of by any agency of the state, unless it is determined by the director that the record has no further administrative, legal, or fiscal value and the Secretary of State has determined that the record is inappropriate for preservation in the State Archives.

(b) The director shall not authorize the destruction of any record subject to audit until he has determined that the audit has been performed.

(Added by Stats.1965, c. 371, p. 1550, § 179.)

§ 14756.   Microfilmed and photographically reproduced records; standards; certification

The public records of any state agency may be microfilmed or otherwise photographically reproduced and certified on the written authorization of the head of the agency. The microfilming or photographic reproduction must meet the standard specification of the United States Bureau of Standards.

The certification of each such reproduction or set of reproductions shall be in accordance with the standards, or have the approval, of the Attorney General. The certification shall contain a statement of the identity, description, and disposition or location of the records reproduced, the date, reason, and authorization for such reproduction, and such other information as the Attorney General requires.

Such certified photographic reproductions shall be deemed to be original public records for all purposes, including introduction in courts of law and state agencies.

(Added by Stats.1965, c. 371, p. 1550, § 179.)

§ 14760.   Report to governor

The director shall, through the Secretary of the Agriculture and Services Agency, make an annual written report to the Governor. The report shall describe the status and progress of programs established pursuant to this chapter and shall include the recommendations of the director for improvements in the management of records in the state government.

(Added by Stats.1965, c. 371, p. 1551, § 179.   Amended by Stats.1969, c. 138, p. 319, § 117, eff. Sept. 11, 1969.)

§ 14765.   Transfers; personnel

All persons, other than temporary employees, serving in the state civil service and employed by the Secretary of State in the Central Record Depository, shall remain in the state civil service and are hereby transferred to the Department of General Services. The status, positions, and rights of such persons shall not be affected by their transfer and shall continue to be retained by them pursuant to the State Civil Service Act.

(Added by Stats.1965, c. 371, p. 1551, § 179.)

§ 14766.   Transfers; equipment and records

All equipment and records in the Central Record Depository in the office of the Secretary of State are transferred to the Department of General Services.

(Added by Stats.1965, c. 371, p. 1551, § 179.)

§ 14767.   Record centers; purposes

The director shall establish, maintain and operate record centers for the storage, processing, and servicing of records for state agencies pending their deposit with the Archives of the State of California or their disposition in any other manner authorized by law.

(Added by Stats.1965, c. 371, p. 1551, § 179.)

§ 14768. Operative date of article

This article shall become operative on January 1, 1967.

(Added by Stats.1965, c. 371, p. 1551, § 179.)

§ 14770. Reproduction of public record plant

(a) As used in this section:

(1) "Acquire" includes acquisition by gift, purchase, lease, eminent domain, or otherwise.

(2) "Public record plant" means the plant, or any part thereof, or any record therein, of any person engaged in the business of searching or publishing public records or insuring or guaranteeing titles to real property, including copies of public records and abstracts or memoranda taken from public records, which is owned by or in the possession of such person or which is used by him in his business.

(b) If public records of any state agency have been lost or destroyed by conflagration or other public calamity, the director may acquire the right to reproduce such portion of a public record plant as is necessary for the purpose of restoring or replacing the records or their substance.

(Added by Stats.1975, c. 1240, p. 3166, § 28, operative July 1, 1976.)

COUNTY LIBRARIES

(West's Annotated California Codes, Education Code, 1982, s.19100-19180; Government Code, 1982, s.26150, 26151, 25351, 25210.78-25210.78i.)

§ 19100. Power to establish and maintain

The boards of supervisors of the several counties may establish and maintain, within their respective counties, county free libraries pursuant to this chapter.

(Stats.1976, c. 1010, § 2, operative April 30, 1977.)

§ 19101. Establishment at the county seat or elsewhere in the county

The board of supervisors of any county may establish at the county seat or elsewhere in the county, a county free library for that part of the county lying outside of cities maintaining free public libraries, and outside of library districts maintaining district libraries, and for all such additional portions of the county as may elect to become a part of, or to participate in, the county free library system as provided in this chapter.

(Stats.1976, c. 1010, § 2, operative April 30, 1977.)

§ 19102.   Publication of notice of contemplated action

At least once a week for two successive weeks prior to taking any action, the board of supervisors shall publish, in a newspaper designated by it and published in the county, notice of the contemplated action, giving the date of the meeting at which the action is proposed to be taken.

(Stats.1976, c. 1010, § 2, operative April 30, 1977.)

§ 19103.   Participation by city or library districts in the county library system

After the establishment of a county free library, the board of trustees, common council, or other legislative body of any city in the county maintaining a free public library, or the board of trustees of any library district maintaining a district library, may notify the board of supervisors that the city or library district desires to become a part of the county free library system. Thereafter the city or library district shall be a part of the system and its inhabitants shall be entitled to the benefits of the county free library, and the property within the city or library district shall be liable to taxes levied for county free library purposes.

(Stats.1976, c. 1010, § 2, operative April 30, 1977.)

§ 19104.   Withdrawal of city or library district from county library system

The board of trustees, common council, or other legislative body of any city or the board of trustees of any library district may on or before January 1st of any year, notify the board of supervisors that the city or library district no longer desires to be a part of the county free library system. The notice shall be accompanied by a statement complying with the requirements of Chapter 8 (commencing with Section 54900) of Part 1 of Division 2 of Title 5 of the Government Code. The clerk of the board of supervisors shall file the statement with the county assessor and the State Board of Equalization. Thereafter the city or library district shall cease to participate in the benefits of the county free library, and the property situated in the city or library district shall not be liable to taxes for county free library purposes.

(Stats.1976, c. 1010, § 2, operative April 30, 1977.)

§ 19105.   Effective date of withdrawal

If the notice is given after January 1st of any year, the property situated in the city or library district shall be liable to taxes for county free library purposes during the immediately succeeding year, and the notice shall not be effective until the next succeeding year, and library service shall be rendered in the city or library district during the year for which taxes are levied for library purposes in the city or library district.

(Stats.1976, c. 1010, § 2, operative April 30, 1977.)

§ 19106.   Publication of notice of contemplated participation in, or withdrawal from county library system

Before any board of trustees, common council, or other legislative body of any city, or the board of trustees of any library district gives notice that the city or library district desires to become a part of the county free library system, or gives notice of withdrawal from the system, the board of trustees, common council, or other legislative body of the city or the board of trustees of the library district shall publish at least once a week for two successive weeks prior to the giving of either notice, in a newspaper designated by the board of trustees, common council, or other legislative body of the city or the board of library trustees of the library district, and circulating throughout the city or library district, notice of the contemplated action, giving the date and the place of the meeting at which the contemplated action is proposed to be taken.

(Stats.1976, c. 1010, § 2, operative April 30, 1977.)

§ 19107.   Contracts with cities

The board of supervisors of any county in which a county free library has been established may enter into contracts with any city maintaining a free public library, and any such city, through its board of trustees or other legislative body, may enter into contracts with the county to secure to the residents of the city the same privileges of the county free library as are granted to, or enjoyed by, the residents of the county outside of the city, or such privileges as are agreed upon in the contract, upon such consideration named in the contract as is agreed upon, to be paid into the county free library fund. Thereupon the residents of the city shall have the same privileges with regard to the county free library as the residents of the county outside of the city, or such privileges as are agreed upon by the contract.

(Stats.1976, c. 1010, § 2, operative April 30, 1977.)

§ 19108.   Contracts with other counties

The board of supervisors of any county in which a county free library has been established may enter into a contract with the board of supervisors of any other county to secure to the residents of the other county such privileges of the county free library as are agreed upon by the contract and upon such considerations as are agreed upon in the contract to be paid into the county free library fund. Thereupon the inhabitants of the other county shall have such privileges of the county free library as are agreed upon by the contract.

(Stats.1976, c. 1010, § 2, operative April 30, 1977.)

§ 19109.   Library tax to carry out contract

The board of supervisors of any county may enter into a contract with the board of supervisors of another county in which a county free library has been established, and may levy a library tax, for the purpose of carrying out the contract.

(Stats.1976, c. 1010, § 2, operative April 30, 1977.)

§ 19110.   Contracts with other counties for services of single librarian; residence of appointee

The board of supervisors of any county may contract with the board of supervisors of any other county or two or more other counties to provide for the services of a single qualified librarian to serve simultaneously as the county librarian of each county.

When so appointed the county librarian shall be required to establish a residence in but one of the counties in which he is appointed.

(Stats.1976, c. 1010, § 2, operative April 30, 1977.)

§ 19111.   Termination of contract upon the establishment of county library

The making of the contract shall not bar the board of supervisors of the county during the continuance of the contract from establishing a county free library under the provisions of this chapter if none is already established. Upon the establishment of any county free library, the contract may be terminated upon such terms as may be agreed upon by the parties thereto, or may continue for the term thereof.

(Stats.1976, c. 1010, § 2, operative April 30, 1977.)

§ 19112.   Contract that city library assume functions of county library

Instead of establishing a separate county free library, the board

of supervisors may enter into a contract with the board of library
trustees or other authority in charge of the free public library of any
city and the board of library trustees, or other authority in charge of
the free public library, may make such a contract. The contract may
provide that the free public library of the city shall assume the functions of a county free library within the county with which the contract is made, including cities in the county. The board of supervisors
may agree to pay annually into the library fund of the city such sum
as may be agreed upon. Either party to the contract may terminate
the contract by giving six months' notice of intention to do so.

(Stats.1976, c. 1010, § 2, operative April 30, 1977.)

§ 19113.   Disestablishment of county library

After a county free library has been established, it may be disestablished in the same manner as it was established. At least once a
week for two successive weeks prior to taking any action, the board
of supervisors shall publish, in a newspaper designated by them, and
published in the county, notice of the contemplated action, giving
therein the date of the meeting at which the contemplated action is
proposed to be taken.

(Stats.1976, c. 1010, § 2, operative April 30, 1977.)

§ 19114.   Annexation of territory by municipal corporation not served by county library

Whenever any of the territory being served by a county free library is annexed to, or otherwise included within, any municipal corporation not served by the county free library, the board of supervisors of the county shall order the county free library to continue to
serve the territory annexed to, or otherwise included within the municipality, until the end of the fiscal year or years for which a tax
has been levied upon the property of the annexed territory for the
support of the county free library.

(Stats.1976, c. 1010, § 2, operative April 30, 1977.)

§ 19115.   Use of library by nonresidents of territory taxed for library purposes

The board of supervisors may establish a reasonable fee to be
collected from persons who desire to participate in the services and
benefits of the county free library and who are not residents of the
territory in the county which is liable for taxes for county free library purposes. In establishing the fee, the board may also prescribe
such regulations or limitations applicable to the use of the county

free library by such persons as may reasonably be necessary.
(Stats.1976, c. 1010, § 2, operative April 30, 1977.)

§ 19140. Appointment of county librarian

Upon the establishment of a county free library, the board of supervisors shall appoint a county librarian.
(Stats.1976, c. 1010, § 2, operative April 30, 1977.)

§ 19141. Civil service

If any county adopts a civil service system or a limited civil service system for county officers and employees, the county librarian shall be entitled to the benefits of such civil service system.

This section does not limit any powers conferred on any county by charter.
(Stats.1976, c. 1010, § 2, operative April 30, 1977.)

§ 19142. Certificate of qualification

No person is eligible to the office of county librarian unless prior to his appointment, he has received from the board of library examiners a certificate of qualification for the office.
(Stats.1976, c. 1010, § 2, operative April 30, 1977.)

§ 19143. Residence

At the time of his appointment, the county librarian need not be a resident of the county nor a citizen of the State of California.
(Stats.1976, c. 1010, § 2, operative April 30, 1977.)

§ 19145. Oath and bond

The county librarian shall, prior to entering upon his duties, file the usual oath, and he shall be required to file an official bond in an amount determined by the board of supervisors, unless he is covered by a master bond pursuant to Section 1481 of the Government Code.
(Stats.1976, c. 1010, § 2, operative April 30, 1977.)

§ 19144. Eligibility of persons of either sex

Persons of either sex are eligible to certification for the office of county librarian.
(Stats.1976, c. 1010, § 2, operative April 30, 1977.)

§ 19146. Duties

The county librarian shall, subject to the general rules adopted by the board of supervisors, build up and manage, according to accepted principles of library management, a library for the use of the people of the county, and shall determine what books and other library equipment shall be purchased.

(Stats.1976, c. 1010, § 2, operative April 30, 1977.)

§ 19147.   Payment of salary

The salary of the county librarians shall be paid by each of the counties in equal monthly installments, at the same time and in the same manner and out of the same fund as the salaries of other county officers are paid.

(Stats.1976, c. 1010, § 2, operative April 30, 1977.)

§ 19148.   Payment of salary in county with more than 400,000 population

The board of supervisors of a county over 400,000 population, as determined by the 1960 decennial census, maintaining a county free library may provide that the salary of the county librarian be paid from the same fund used for maintaining and operating the county free library..

Nothing in this section shall be construed as modifying the status of the county librarian as a county official pursuant to Section 24000 of the Government Code.

(Stats.1976, c. 1010, § 2, operative April 30, 1977.)

§ 19149.   Traveling expenses

The county librarian and his assistant shall be allowed actual and necessary traveling expenses incurred on the business of the office.

(Stats.1976, c. 1010, § 2, operative April 30, 1977.)

§ 19150.   Certificate of qualification for acting librarian

Except when the county librarian is temporarily absent, no person shall serve in the position of county librarian under the title of acting county librarian, or assistant librarian in charge, or any other such title, unless the person has received from the Board of Library Examiners a certificate of qualification for the position of county librarian.

In the event qualified candidates for the position of the county librarian cannot be found, the county supervisors shall secure a written permission from the Board of Library Examiners to appoint an unqualified person to the position. This written permission may be granted by the library examiners for a period of time up to but not exceeding one year. The examiners may from time to time in their discretion renew the permit.

The provisions of this section shall not apply to the present appointment or reappointment of any person serving on September 11, 1957, in any position which is in lieu of the position of county librarian.

(Stats.1976, c. 1010, § 2, operative April 30, 1977.)

§ 19160. Powers and duties of board of supervisors

The county free library is under the general supervision of the board of supervisors, which may:

(a) Make general rules and regulations regarding the policy of the county free library.

(b) Establish, upon the recommendation of the county librarian, branches and stations throughout the county and may locate the branches and stations in cities wherever deemed advisable.

(c) Determine the number and kind of employees of the library.

(d) Appoint and dismiss the employees upon the recommendation of the county librarian.

(Stats.1976, c. 1010, § 2, operative April 30, 1977.)

§ 19161. Removal of employees

No employee shall be removed except for cause.

(Stats.1976, c. 1010, § 2, operative April 30, 1977.)

§ 19162. Re-employment right

If any removal is made upon the ground that the services of the employee are no longer required, the removed employee shall have the first right to be restored to the employment when his services are again required.

(Stats.1976, c. 1010, § 2, operative April 30, 1977.)

§ 19163. Employment for definite time

The board of supervisors may, at the time of appointing any employee, and upon the recommendation of the county librarian, enter into an agreement that the employee is employed for a definite time only.

(Stats.1976, c. 1010, § 2, operative April 30, 1977.)

§ 19164. Grading of employees

All employees of the county free library whose duties require special training in library work shall be graded in grades established by the county librarian, with the advice and approval of the State Librarian, according to the duties required of them, experience in library work and other qualifications for the service required.

(Stats.1976, c. 1010, § 2, operative April 30, 1977.)

§ 19165. Appointment to position in graded service

Before appointment to a position in the graded service, the candidate shall pass an examination appropriate to the position sought, satisfactory to the county librarian, and show a satisfactory experience in library work. Work in approved library schools or libraries, or certificates issued by the Board of Library Examiners, may be accepted by the county librarian in lieu of such examination.

(Stats.1976, c. 1010, § 2, operative April 30, 1977.)

§ 19166. Apprentices

The county librarian may accept as apprentices, without compensation, candidates possessing personal qualifications satisfactory to him and may dismiss them at any time if in his judgment their work is not satisfactory to him.

(Stats.1976, c. 1010, § 2, operative April 30, 1977.)

§ 19167. Supervision by State Librarian

The county free libraries are under the general supervision of the State Librarian, who shall from time to time, either personally or by one of his assistants, visit the county free libraries and inquire into their condition. The actual and necessary expenses of the visits shall be paid out of the moneys appropriated for the support of the Division of Libraries.

(Stats.1976, c. 1010, § 2, operative April 30, 1977.)

§ 19168. Annual convention by county librarians

The State Librarian shall annually call a convention of county librarians, to assemble at such time and place as he deems most convenient, for the discussion of questions pertaining to the supervision and administration of the county free libraries, the laws relating thereto, and such other subjects affecting the welfare and interest of the county free libraries as are properly brought before it. All county librarians shall attend and take part in the proceedings of the convention. The actual and necessary expenses of the county librarians attending the convention shall be paid out of the county free library fund.

(Stats.1976, c. 1010, § 2, operative April 30, 1977.)

§ 19169. Annual report of county librarian

The county librarian shall, on or before August 31st, in each year, report to the board of supervisors and to the State Librarian on the condition of the county free library, for the year ending June 30th preceding. The reports shall, in addition to other matters deemed expedient by the county librarian, contain such statistical and other information as is deemed desirable by the State Librarian. For this purpose the State Librarian may send to the several county librarians instructions or question blanks so as to obtain the material for a comparative study of library conditions in the state.

(Stats.1976, c. 1010, § 2, operative April 30, 1977.)

§ 19171. Allocations of federal funds

The county board of supervisors of any county may in its discretion allocate and appropriate any funds received by the county under the State and Local Fiscal Assistance Act of 1972 (Public Law 92–512) for the purpose of establishing, maintaining, and purchasing property for the county free library.

(Stats.1976, c. 1010, § 2, operative April 30, 1977.)

§ 19172. Tax for district not part of system

In counties wherein a union high school library district, maintaining a district free public library was established prior to June 30, 1912, and such district has not elected to become a part of the county free library system, the board of supervisors may levy a tax in such amount as may be necessary upon all the property in the county outside of cities maintaining free public libraries, union high school library districts maintaining district free public libraries and outside of library districts maintaining district libraries, and upon all property within cities and library districts, which have elected to become a part of any county free library system, for the purpose of acquiring sites for, and constructing, leasing, building, rebuilding, furnishing, refurnishing, or repairing county free library buildings. In all other counties, county bonds may be issued, in the manner prescribed in Article 1 (commencing with Section 29900) of Chapter 6 of Division 3 of Title 3 of the Government Code, for the erection and equipment of county free library buildings and the purchase of land therefor.

(Stats.1976, c. 1010, § 2, operative April 30, 1977.)

§ 19173. Creation of special taxing zones

The board of supervisors may create special taxing zones within the territory of the county subject to taxation for county free library purposes for the purpose of levying special taxes within the zones when it is found by the board that the territory within the zones require special services or special facilities in addition to those provided generally by the county free library system and that the special tax levy is commensurate with the special benefits to be provided in the zones.

Taxes levied pursuant to this section, together with taxes levied pursuant to Section 19170, shall not exceed the higher of the limit provided by Section 19170 or the applicable provisions of Section 2263 of the Revenue and Taxation Code.

(Stats.1976, c. 1010, § 2, operative April 30, 1977.)

§ 19174.   Receipt of gifts, bequests or devises

The board of supervisors may receive, on behalf of the county, any gift, bequest, or devise for the county free library, or for any branch or subdivision of the library.

(Stats.1976, c. 1010, § 2, operative April 30, 1977.)

§ 19174.5   County general fund; use

Notwithstanding any other provision of law, funds from the county general fund may be used to support the county free library.

(Added by Stats.1978, c. 331, p. 681, § 3, urgency, eff. June 30, 1978.)

§ 19175.   Property, collection of taxes, and funds

The title to all property belonging to the county free library is vested in the county. All laws applicable to the collection of county taxes shall apply to the collection of the taxes provided in Sections 19170 and 19172. All moneys of the county free library, whether derived from taxation or otherwise, shall be in the custody of the county treasurer.

(Stats.1976, c. 1010, § 2, operative April 30, 1977.)

§ 19176.   Claims against the county free library fund

Each claim against the county free library fund shall be authorized and approved by the county librarian, or in his absence from the county by his assistant. It shall then be acted upon in the same manner as other claims against the county.

(Stats.1976, c. 1010, § 2, operative April 30, 1977.)

§ 19177.   Contracts or agreements with county law libraries

In any county of this state where a law library exists under the provisions of Chapter 5 (commencing with Section 6300) of Division

3 of the Business and Professions Code, the board of supervisors of the county may enter into contracts, or agreements with the board of law library trustees of the law library for the cooperation of the law library and the county free library, and, in that connection, may contract or agree with the board of law library trustees of the law library that the county librarian and other employees of the county free library perform the duties required to be done or performed by the officers and employees of the law library for a compensation to be named in the contract or agreement, and to be paid into the county free library fund.

(Stats.1976, c. 1010, § 2, operative April 30; 1977.)

§ 19178. School and teachers' libraries

The board of supervisors may accept on behalf of the county free library, all books and other property of school libraries and of the teachers' library, and may manage and maintain them as a part of the county free library.

(Stats.1976, c. 1010, § 2, operative April 30, 1977.)

§ 19179. Application of chapter to prior county libraries and to contracts between counties and cities

Any county library which was established and existed on April 26, 1911, under the provisions of an act entitled "an act to provide county library systems," approved April 12, 1909, is continued under the provisions of this chapter and shall be considered the same as if established under the provisions of this chapter. If a contract has been entered into between any county board of supervisors and any city pursuant to this article, the contract shall continue in force, and the provisions of Section 19112 shall be applicable thereto, until the establishment and equipment of a county free library under the provisions of this chapter, unless sooner terminated.

(Stats.1976, c. 1010, § 2, operative April 30, 1977.)

§ 19180. Financing of buildings for county free library purposes

The board of supervisors of any county in which there has been established a county free library which does not serve the entire county may, on behalf of the county free library, construct, build, repair or refurnish buildings to be used for county free library purposes, payment for which may be made from the general fund of the county. If payment is made from the county's general fund, the county auditor shall each fiscal year thereafter transfer from the county free library fund to the county's general fund as a prior claim against the county free library fund for as many years as are determined by the board of supervisors but not to exceed 20, an equal annual installment in such amount that over the designated period of years the entire payment from the county's general fund will be completely repaid. Payment of the costs of the construction of a county free library building may also be made from the employees retirement fund of a retirement system established under the authority of the County Employees Retirement Law of 1937 as an investment of that fund and under the conditions specified in that law.

(Stats.1976, c. 1010, § 2, operative April 30, 1977.)

§ 26150. County free libraries

County free libraries may be constructed, leased, built, rebuilt, furnished, refurnished, or repaired pursuant to the Education Code, or pursuant to this part; provided that, in counties wherein a union high school library district maintaining a district free public library was established prior to June 30, 1912, county free libraries shall be constructed, leased, built, rebuilt, furnished, refurnished or repaired pursuant to Section 27264 of the Education Code until such time as the union high school library district elects to become a part of the county free library system. (Added Stats.1947, c. 424, p. 1137, § 1, as amended Stats.1951, c. 1681, p. 3878, § 2; Stats.1968, c. 449, p. ——, § 50.)

§ 26151. Library service at county institutions

The board of supervisors may provide library service at charitable, detention, and penal institutions of the county under its supervision and control, and may also provide to officers and employees of county departments such library service as is required in the performance of their duties. Such service shall be rendered through the county free library and the cost is a charge upon the county payable out of the general fund. (Added Stats.1947, c. 424, p. 1137, § 1.)

§ 25351. Construction and repair of buildings

The board may construct, lease, build, rebuild, furnish, refurnish, or repair buildings for a hospital, almshouse, courthouse, jail, historical museum, aquarium, library, art gallery, art institute, exposition building for exhibiting and advertising farming, mining, manufacturing, livestock raising, and other resources of the county, stadium, coliseum, sports arena, or sports pavilion or other building for holding sports events, athletic contests, contests of skill, exhibition, spectacles and other public meetings, and such other public buildings as are necessary to carry out the work of the county government. Library buildings shall be constructed, built, repaired or refurnished only from taxes levied upon property which is a part of the county free library system as defined in Chapter 2, Division 20 of the Education Code. (Added Stats.1947, c. 424, p. 1115, § 1, as amended Stats.1951, c. 1681, p. 3878,

§ 1; Stats.1955, c. 327, p. 779, § 1; Stats.1957, c. 1266, p. 2570, § 1; Stats.1968, c. 449, p. —, § 43.)

§ 25210.78 Establishment and maintenance

The board of supervisors of any county is authorized to establish and maintain, pursuant to the provisions of this chapter, extended library facilities and services within any county service area established for that purpose. (Added Stats.1957, c. 617, p. 1828, § 2.)

§ 25210.78a Definition

As used in this chapter, "extended library facilities and services" means the acquisition or improvement of sites for library buildings, the construction, alteration, repair, or maintenance of library buildings, or the acquisition, repair or maintenance of furniture or equipment, except books, for library buildings, or all or any combination thereof. (Added Stats.1957, c. 617, p. 1828, § 2.)

§ 25210.78b Specification of facilities and services; extent of work; designation of manager

If extended library facilities and services are to be established and maintained within any county service area, the board of supervisors may on or before April 1st of each year, by resolution, specify the extended library facilities and services to be established and maintained at the expense of county service area funds within the county service area and the extent of the work to be done in connection therewith during the next succeeding fiscal year. The board shall also designate the county officer whose duty it shall be to maintain, operate, manage and control such facilities and perform such work, subject to the direction of the board of supervisors. (Added Stats.1957, c. 617, p. 1828, § 2.)

§ 25210.78ba Determination of cost; tax levy

If extended library facilities and services are to be established and maintained within any county service area the board of supervisors may at the time it adopts its final budget for the county determine the nature, extent and cost of such extended library facilities and services to be provided at the expense of county service area funds within the area during the fiscal year for which the final budget of the county is adopted. In the event that the board of supervisors elects to and does determine the nature, extent and cost of providing such extended library facilities and services pursuant to this section, the provisions of Sections 25210.78b, 25210.78c, 25210.78d and 25210.78e shall be inapplicable to any such determinations and the board of supervisors shall fix, levy and collect taxes therefor within the area in the same manner and at the same time as other county taxes are fixed, levied and collected. (Added Stats.1967, c. 680, p. 2049, § 5.)

§ 25210.78c   Estimate of cost

On or before July 10th of each year, as the board of supervisors directs, the officer designated by the board of supervisors for that purpose, shall file with the board of supervisors and the county auditor an estimate accompanied by such supporting data as the board of supervisors may require, of the cost of providing the extended library facilities and services determined upon by the resolution of the board of supervisors. The estimate shall show the amount of money required for general fund purposes and for salary fund purposes. (Added Stats.1957, c. 617, p. 1828, § 2.)

§ 25210.78d   Adoption or revision of estimate; fixing amount of funds required

The board of supervisors shall either adopt or revise the estimate and the estimate as finally approved by the board of supervisors shall fix the amount of money required for the purpose of providing, pursuant to this chapter, extended library facilities and services in the area for the next succeeding fiscal year and no other budgetary requirements for such extended library facilities and services shall be deemed applicable to the area. (Added Stats.1957, c. 617, p. 1828, § 2.).

§ 25210.78e   Rate of tax

Each year at the time the board of supervisors fixes and levies taxes for county purposes it shall also fix the rates of county service area taxes and shall levy the taxes upon all taxable property within the area. The rate shall be such as will produce, after due allowance for delinquency as fixed by the board, the amount found by deducting from the estimate, finally approved by the board, the amount of estimated revenue from other sources of the county service area during the fiscal year and any available surplus. (Added Stats.1957, c. 617, p. 1828, § 2.)

§ 25210.78f   Levy and collection of tax; time; manner; deposit

The tax for extended library facilities and services shall be annually levied and collected by the same officers and at the same time and in the same manner as other county taxes are levied and collected. All collections shall be paid into the county treasury to the credit of the county service area. (Added Stats.1957, c. 617, p. 1829, § 2.)

§ 25210.78g   Transfer of funds; reimbursement of county general fund and salary fund

From time to time during the fiscal year as determined by the board of supervisors, the board of supervisors shall order the transfer from the funds in the county treasury standing to the credit of the county service area of an amount found by the board of supervisors to be sufficient to reimburse the county general fund and the county salary fund for the expenditures made therefrom in providing extended library facilities and services in the area.   (Added Stats.1957, c. 617, p. 1829, § 2.)

§ 25210.78h   Property exempt from taxation

Any property included in a county service area which is also included in a district organized and existing under Chapter 4 (commencing at Section 27501), 5 (commencing at Section 27751), or 6 (commencing at Section 28001) of Division 20 of the Education Code shall be exempt from taxation under this chapter and none of the funds raised by taxation upon the county service area for the purpose of providing extended library facilities and services shall be expended within the area included in such a district.   (Added Stats.1957, c. 617, p. 1829, § 2, as amended Stats.1968, c. 449, p. ——, § 42.)

§ 25210.78i   Use of county sales and use tax revenues

Any of the revenues received by a county under a sales and use tax adopted by the board of supervisors in accordance with the provisions of Part 1.5 (commencing at Section 7200) of Division 2 of the Revenue and Taxation Code attributable to either the sale of tangible personal property at retail within the unincorporated area of such county or the storage, use or other consumption of tangible personal property in such unincorporated area if such property is purchased for the storage, use or other consumption in such unincorporated area, may be used for the establishment and maintenance of extended library facilities and services within a county service area established pursuant to this article. (Added Stats.1959, c. 632, p. 2610, § 1.)

MUNICIPAL LIBRARIES
(West's Annotated California Codes, Education Code, 1982, s.18900-18965.)

§ 18900.   Establishment by legislative body

The common council, board of trustees, or other legislative body of any city in the state may, and upon being requested to do so by one-fourth of the electors of the municipal corporation in the manner provided in this article, shall, by ordinance, establish in and for the municipality a public library if there is none already established therein.

(Stats.1976, c. 1010, § 2, operative April 30, 1977.)

§ 18901.   Petition of electors

The request may be by a single petition, or by several petitions. The several petitions shall be substantially in the same form. The single petition, or several petitions in the aggregate, shall have, the signatures of the requisite number of electors.

(Stats.1976, c. 1010, § 2, operative April 30, 1977.)

§ 18910.   Appointment of board of trustees

The public library shall be managed by a board of library trustees, consisting of five members, to be appointed by the mayor, president of the board of trustees, or other executive head of the municipality, with the consent of the legislative body of the municipality.

(Stats.1976, c. 1010, § 2, operative April 30, 1977.)

§ 18911.   Term of office and compensation

The trustees shall hold office for three years. The members of the first board appointed shall so classify themselves by lot that one of their number shall go out of office at the end of the current fiscal year, two at the end of one year thereafter, and two at the end of two years thereafter.

The legislative body of the municipality may, by ordinance, provide for the compensation of such trustees; provided that the respective compensation for such trustees shall not exceed fifty dollars ($50) per month.

(Stats.1976, c. 1010, § 2, operative April 30, 1977.)

§ 18912.   Eligibility of men and women

Men and women are equally eligible to appointment as trustees.

(Stats.1976, c. 1010, § 2, operative April 30, 1977.)

§ 18913.   Vacancies

Vacancies shall be filled by appointment for the unexpired term in the same manner as the original appointments are made.

(Stats.1976, c. 1010, § 2, operative April 30, 1977.)

§ 18914.   Monthly meetings

Boards of library trustees shall meet at least once a month at such times and places as they may fix by resolution.

(Stats.1976, c. 1010, § 2, operative April 30, 1977.)

§ 18915.   Special meetings

Special meetings may be called at any time by three trustees, by written notice served upon each member at least three hours before the time specified for the proposed meeting.

(Stats.1976, c. 1010, § 2, operative April 30, 1977.)

§ 18916.   Quorum

A majority of the board shall constitute a quorum for the transaction of business.

(Stats.1976, c. 1010, § 2, operative April 30, 1977.)

§ 18917.   President

The board shall appoint one of its number president, who shall serve for one year and until his successor is appointed, and in his absence shall select a president pro tem.

(Stats.1976, c. 1010, § 2, operative April 30, 1977.)

§ 18918.   Record of proceedings

The board shall cause a proper record of its proceedings to be kept.

(Stats.1976, c. 1010, § 2, operative April 30, 1977.)

§ 18919.   Rules, regulations and by-laws

The board of library trustees may make and enforce all rules, regulations, and bylaws necessary for the administration, government, and protection of the libraries under its management, and all property belonging thereto.

(Stats.1976, c. 1010, § 2, operative April 30, 1977.)

§ 18920.   Administration of trusts; receipt, holdings and disposal of property

The board of library trustees may administer any trust declared or created for the library, and receive by gift, devise, or bequest and hold in trust or otherwise, property situated in this state or elsewhere, and where not otherwise provided, dispose of the property for the benefit of the library.

(Stats.1976, c. 1010, § 2, operative April 30, 1977.)

§ 18921.   Officers and employees

The board of library trustees may prescribe the duties and powers of the librarian, secretary, and other officers and employees of the library; determine the number of and appoint all officers and employees, and fix their compensation. The officers and employees shall hold their officers or positions at the pleasure of the board.

(Stats.1976, c. 1010, § 2, operative April 30, 1977.)

§ 18922.   Purchase of personal property

The board of library trustees may purchase necessary books, journals, publications, and other personal property.

(Stats.1976, c. 1010, § 2, operative April 30, 1977.)

§ 18923.   Purchase of real property, and erection of rental and equipment of buildings or rooms

The board of library trustees may purchase real property, and

erect or rent and equip, such buildings or rooms, as may be necessary, when in its judgment a suitable building, or portion thereof, has
not been provided by the legislative body of the municipality for the
library.

(Stats.1976, c. 1010, § 2, operative April 30, 1977.)

§ 18924.   State publications

The board of library trustees may request the appropriate state
officials to furnish the library with copies of any and all reports,
laws, and other publications of the state not otherwise disposed of by
law.

(Stats.1976, c. 1010, § 2, operative April 30, 1977.)

§ 18925.   Borrowing from, lending to, and exchanging with other libraries; nonresident borrowing

The board of library trustees may borrow books from, lend books
to, and exchange books with other libraries, and may allow nonresidents to borrow books upon such conditions as the board may prescribe.

(Stats.1976, c. 1010, § 2, operative April 30, 1977.)

§ 18926.   Incidental powers of board

The board of library trustees may do and perform any and all
other acts and things necessary or proper to carry out the provisions
of this chapter.

(Stats.1976, c. 1010, § 2, operative April 30, 1977.)

§ 18927.   Annual report to legislative body and to State Librarian

The board of library trustees, or if there is no board of trustees,
then the administrative head of the library shall, on or before August
31st, in each year, report to the legislative body of the municipality
and to the State Librarian on the condition of the library, for the
year ending the 30th day of June preceding. The reports shall, in addition to other matters deemed expedient by the board of trustees or
administrative head of the library, contain such statistical and other
information as is deemed desirable by the State Librarian. For this
purpose the State Librarian may send to the several boards of trustees or administrative heads of the library instructions or question
blanks so as to obtain the material for a comparative study of library
conditions in the state.

(Stats.1976, c. 1010, § 2, operative April 30, 1977.)

§ 18951.   Library fund

All money acquired by gift, devise, bequest, or otherwise, for the purposes of the library, shall be apportioned to a fund to be designated the library fund, and shall be applied to the purposes authorized in this chapter.

(Stats.1976, c. 1010, § 2, operative April 30, 1977. Amended by Stats.1977, c. 309, § 1.1, urgency, eff. July 8, 1977.)

§ 18952. Safety, preservation, and application of fund not payable into treasury

If payment into the treasury is inconsistent with the conditions or terms of any gift, devise, or bequest, the board shall provide for the safety and preservation of the fund, and the application thereof to the use of the library, in accordance with the terms and conditions of the gift, devise, or bequest.

(Stats.1976, c. 1010, § 2, operative April 30, 1977.)

§ 18953. Payments from the library fund

Payments from the fund shall be made upon warrants issued after due audit by, and an order from, the library trustees. The warrants shall be signed by the president and secretary of the board of library trustees. The treasurer of the municipality shall pay such warrants without any further order or warrant from any other authority.

(Stats.1976, c. 1010, § 2, operative April 30, 1977.)

§ 18960. Library free to inhabitants; violations of rules, regulations or by-laws

Every library established pursuant to this chapter shall be forever free to the inhabitants and nonresident taxpayers of the municipality, subject always to such rules, regulations, and bylaws as may be made by boards of library trustees. Any person who violates any rule, regulations, or bylaw may be fined or excluded from the privileges of the library.

(Stats.1976, c. 1010, § 2, operative April 30, 1977.)

§ 18961. Contracts with neighboring municipalities or county

The board of library trustees and the legislative body of any neighboring municipality or the board of supervisors of the county in which the public library is situated, may contract for lending the books of the library to residents of the county or neighboring municipality, upon a reasonable compensation to be paid by the county or neighboring municipality.

(Stats.1976, c. 1010, § 2, operative April 30, 1977.)

§ 18962.   Title to property

The title to all property acquired for the purposes of the library, when not inconsistent with the terms of its acquisition, or otherwise designated, vests in the municipality in which the library is situated, and in the name of the municipal corporation may be sued for and defended by action at law or otherwise.

(Stats.1976, c. 1010, § 2, operative April 30, 1977.)

§ 18963.   Application of chapter to prior municipal libraries and libraries governed by city charter

Any municipal library which was established and existed on June 11, 1909, under the provisions of an act entitled "An act to establish free public libraries and reading rooms," approved April 26, 1880, is continued under the provisions of this chapter and shall be considered the same as if established under the provisions of this chapter. This chapter has no application to any library established or governed by a city charter, and any city charter is in no manner affected by this chapter.

(Stats.1976, c. 1010, § 2, operative April 30, 1977.)

§ 18964.   Disestablishment of library

Any ordinance establishing a library adopted pursuant to this chapter shall be repealed by the body which adopted it upon being requested to do so by 51 percent of the electors of the municipal corporation, as shown by the great register. Upon the repeal of the ordinance the library is disestablished in the municipal corporation.

(Stats.1976, c. 1010, § 2, operative April 30, 1977.)

§ 18965.   Government of public library services upon consolidation

Whenever the governing bodies of two or more cities or counties consolidate their existing public library services, as a joint exercise of powers under Chapter 5 (commencing with Section 6500), Division 7, Title 1 of the Government Code, and the ownership or management of the cities' and counties' library facilities and other library assets are turned over to a newly formed joint agency, any boards of public library trustees existing prior to the consolidation, may be dissolved by ordinance.

(Stats.1976, c. 1010, § 2, operative April 30, 1977.)

DISTRICT LIBRARIES

(West's Annotated California Codes, Education Code, 1982,
s.19400-19532.)

§ 19400. Organization and powers of district

A library district may be organized, as provided in this chapter. The library district may establish, equip, and maintain a public library for the dissemination of knowledge of the arts, sciences, and general literature and may exercise the powers granted or necessarily implied pursuant to this chapter.

(Stats.1976, c. 1010, § 2, operative April 30, 1977.)

§ 19401. Territory includable in district

The library district may include incorporated or unincorporated territory, or both, in any one or more counties, so long as the territory of the district consists of contiguous parcels and the territory of no city is divided.

(Stats.1976, c. 1010, § 2, operative April 30, 1977.)

§ 19402. Petition to form district

Whenever the formation of a library district is desired, a petition which may consist of any number of instruments, may be presented at a regular meeting of the board of supervisors of the county in which is located the largest proportionate value of the lands within the proposed district as shown by the last equalized county assessment roll. The board of supervisors to whom the petition is presented is designated in this chapter as the supervising board of supervisors.

(Stats.1976, c. 1010, § 2, operative April 30, 1977.)

§ 19403. Qualifications of signers and number required

The petition shall be signed by registered voters residing within the proposed library district equal in number to at least 5 percent of the number of votes cast in the territory comprising the proposed district at the last preceding general state election at which a Governor was elected.

(Stats.1976, c. 1010, § 2, operative April 30, 1977.)

§ 19404. Proceedings for filing and hearing

The proceedings for the filing and hearing of the petition are governed and controlled by the provisions of Sections 58032, 58033, 58034, 58060, and 58061 of the Government Code.

(Stats.1976, c. 1010, § 2, operative April 30, 1977.)

§ 19405. Proceedings for final hearing

The proceedings for final hearing of the petition and the formation of the district are governed and controlled by the provisions of Article 4 (commencing with Section 58090), Article 5 (commencing with Section 58130), and Article 7 (commencing with Section 58200) of Chapter 1 of Title 6 of the Government Code.

(Stats.1976, c. 1010, § 2, operative April 30, 1977.)

§ 19406. Written protests

On the filing of written protests by registered voters residing in the proposed district equal in number to at least 50 percent of the number of votes cast in the territory comprising the proposed district at the last preceding general state election at which a Governor was elected, the proceeding for the formation of the district shall be terminated as provided in Sections 58103 and 58104 of the Government Code.

(Stats.1976, c. 1010, § 2, operative April 30, 1977.)

§ 19407. Organization of districts in more than one county

No library district including territory in more than one county shall be organized under this chapter without the concurrent consent by resolution of each board of supervisors involved, as well as the consent of the governing body of each city to be included.

(Stats.1976, c. 1010, § 2, operative April 30, 1977.)

§ 19420. Appointment and number of trustees

Within 30 days after the filing with the Secretary of State of the resolution declaring the organization of the district, a board of three library trustees shall be appointed for the district. The board shall consist of one trustee to be appointed from each unit, in the case of any unincorporated territory by the board of supervisors and in the case of a city by the governing body thereof.

If a board thus appointed would consist of more than three members, the supervising board of supervisors shall appoint three library trustees from the district at large.

If the board thus appointed consists of less than three members, the supervising board of supervisors shall appoint from the district at large enough additional members to make a board of three trustees.

As used in this section, "unit" means all unincorporated territory in the district which lies in a single county and also means each city in the district.

(Stats.1976, c. 1010, § 2, operative April 30, 1977.)

§ 19421. Designation of governing board

The governing board of the district shall be called "the Board of Library Trustees of _____ Library District" (inserting the name of the particular district).

(Stats.1976, c. 1010, § 2, operative 30, 1977.)

§ 19422. Term of office

The trustee shall hold office for the term of four years beginning on the * * * <u>last Friday in November</u> next succeeding their appointment or election. * * *

(Amended by Stats.1978, c. 1376, p. 4561, § 4.)

§ 19423. Classification of members of first board

The first board of library trustees appointed or elected in a district shall at their first meeting so classify themselves by lot that their terms shall expire: one on the * * * <u>last Friday in November</u> of the first odd-numbered calendar year next succeeding his appointment or election, and two on the * * * <u>last Friday in November</u> of the second succeeding odd-numbered calendar year.

(Amended by Stats.1978, c. 1376, p. 4561, § 5.)

§ 19424. Organization of board

At its first meeting called after the original appointment of the board, and annually thereafter at its first meeting called after the * * * <u>last Friday in November</u> in odd-numbered years, the board shall organize by electing one of its number president, and another one of its number secretary. They shall serve as such for one year or until their successors are elected and qualified.

(Amended by Stats.1978, c. 1376, p. 4561, § 6.)

Asterisks * * * indicate deletions by amendment
<u>Underline</u> indicates changes or additions by amendment

§ 19425. Record of proceedings and filing of certificate of establishment

The board shall cause a proper record of its proceedings to be kept, and at the first meeting of the board of trustees of the library district, it shall immediately cause to be made out and filed with the Department of Education at Sacramento a certificate showing that the library district has been established, with the date thereof, the names of the trustees, and the officers of the board chosen for the current fiscal year.

(Stats.1976, c. 1010, § 2, operative April 30, 1977.)

§ 19426. Vacancies

A vacancy in the board of library trustees shall be filled for the unexpired term by appointment of the supervising board of supervisors.

(Stats.1976, c. 1010, § 2, operative April 30, 1977.)

§ 19427. Holding office until successor is elected and qualified

Each library trustee shall hold office until his successor is elected and qualified.

(Stats.1976, c. 1010, § 2, operative April 30, 1977.)

§ 19428. Monthly meetings

The board of library trustees shall meet at least once a month, at such time and place as it may fix by resolution.

(Stats.1976, c. 1010, § 2, operative April 30, 1977.)

§ 19429. Special meetings

Special meetings may be called at any time by two trustees, by written notices served upon each member at least 12 hours before the time specified for the meeting.

(Stats.1976, c. 1010, § 2, operative April 30, 1977.)

§ 19430. Quorum

Two members constitute a quorum for the transaction of business.

(Stats.1976, c. 1010, § 2, operative April 30, 1977.)

§ 19460. Rules, regulations, and by-laws

The board of library trustees shall make and enforce all rules, regulations, and bylaws necessary for the administration, government, and protection of the library under its management, and all property belonging to the district.

(Stats.1976, c. 1010, § 2, operative April 30, 1977.)

§ 19461. Administration of trust; receipt holding and disposal of property

The board of library trustees shall administer any trust declared or created for the library, and received by gift, devise, or bequest, and hold in trust or otherwise, property situated in this state or elsewhere, and where not otherwise provided, dispose of the property for the benefit of the library.

(Stats.1976, c. 1010, § 2, operative April 30, 1977.)

§ 19462. Officers and employees

The board of library trustees shall prescribe the duties and powers of the librarian, secretary, and other officers and employees of the library, determine the number of and appoint all officers and em-

ployees, and fix their compensation. The officers and employees shall hold their offices and positions at the pleasure of the board.
(Stats.1976, c. 1010, § 2, operative April 30, 1977.)

§ 19463. Purchase of personal property

The board of library trustees shall purchase necessary books, journals, publications, and other personal property.
(Stats.1976, c. 1010, § 2, operative April 30, 1977.)

§ 19464. Purchase of real property and erection or rental and equipment of buildings or rooms

The board of library trustees shall purchase real property, and erect or rent and equip, such buildings or rooms, as in its judgment are necessary properly to carry out the provisions of this chapter.
(Stats.1976, c. 1010, § 2, operative April 30, 1977.)

§ 19465. State publications

The board of library trustees shall require the Secretary of State and other state officials to furnish the library with copies of any and all reports, laws, and other publications of the state not otherwise disposed of by law.
(Stats.1976, c. 1010, § 2, operative April 30, 1977.)

§ 19466. Borrowing from, lending to, and exchanging with other libraries; nonresident borrowing

The board of library trustees shall borrow books from, lend books to, and exchange books with other libraries, and may allow nonresidents of the district to borrow books upon such conditions as the board may prescribe.
(Stats.1976, c. 1010, § 2, operative April 30, 1977.)

§ 19467. Incidental powers of board

The board of library trustees shall borrow money, give security therefor, purchase on contract, and do and perform any and all other acts and things necessary or proper to carry out the provisions of this chapter.
(Stats.1976, c. 1010, § 2, operative April 30, 1977.)

§ 19468. Annual report to State Librarian

The board of library trustees shall file, through the librarian, on or before the last day of August of each year, a report with the State

Librarian at Sacramento giving the condition of its library and the number of volumes contained therein on the 30th day of June preceding. The report shall, in addition to other matters deemed expedient by the board of trustees or the district librarian, contain such statistical and other information as is deemed desirable by the State Librarian. For this purpose the State Librarian may send to the several district librarians instructions or question blanks so as to obtain the material for a comparative study of library conditions in the state.

(Stats.1976, c. 1010, § 2, operative April 30, 1977.)

§ 19469. Hours open for public use

The board of library trustees shall designate the hours during which the library shall be open for the use of the public. All public libraries established under this chapter shall be open for the use of the public during every day in the year.

(Stats.1976, c. 1010, § 2, operative April 30, 1977.)

§ 19470. Annual estimate of costs

Annually, at least 15 days before the first day of the month in which county taxes are levied, the board of library trustees of each library district shall furnish to the board of supervisors of the county in which the district or any part thereof is situated, an estimate in writing of the amount of money necessary for all purposes required under this chapter during the next ensuing fiscal year.

(Stats.1976, c. 1010, § 2, operative April 30, 1977.)

§ 19471. Levy of special tax

Each board of supervisors in which any part of the district is situated shall thereupon levy a special tax upon all taxable property of the county lying within the district sufficient in amount to maintain the district.

(Stats.1976, c. 1010, § 2, operative April 30, 1977.)

§ 19472. Maximum rate of tax

The tax shall in no case exceed the rate of fifteen cents ($0.15) on each one hundred dollars ($100) of the assessed valuation of all taxable property within the district, but it may be in addition to all other taxes allowed by law to be levied upon the property.

(Stats.1976, c. 1010, § 2, operative April 30, 1977.)

§ 19473. Library district fund

The tax shall be computed, entered upon the tax rolls, and collected in the same manner as county taxes are computed, entered, and collected. All money collected shall be paid into the county treasury to the credit of the particular library district fund and shall be paid out on the order of the district board, signed by the president and secretary.

(Stats.1976, c. 1010, § 2, operative April 30, 1977.)

§ 19474. Taxes in districts in more than one county

If the district embraces territory lying in more than one county, the amount estimated shall be ratably apportioned among the several counties in the district in proportion to the exact value of the property in the several counties included within the district as shown upon the last equalized assessment rolls of the counties. The estimates apportioned to the several counties shall be rendered to the respective boards of supervisors, and the tax shall be levied and collected by the officials of the counties upon the property of the district lying in each county.

(Stats.1976, c. 1010, § 2, operative April 30, 1977.)

§ 19475. Deposit of money to credit of library fund

All money acquired by gift, devise, bequest, or otherwise, for the purposes of the library, shall be paid into the county treasury to the credit of the library fund of the district, subject only to the order of the library trustees of the district.

(Stats.1976, c. 1010, § 2, operative April 30, 1977.)

§ 19476. Safety, preservation, and application of fund not payable into treasury

If the payment into the treasury is inconsistent with the terms or conditions of any gift, devise, or bequest, the board of library trustees shall provide for the safety and preservation of the fund, and the application thereof to the use of the library, in accordance with the terms and conditions of the gift, devise, or bequest.

(Stats.1976, c. 1010, § 2, operative April 30, 1977.)

§ 19477. Warrants

Upon the receipt by the county auditor of an order of the library trustees of the district, he shall issue his warrant upon the county treasurer for the amount stated in the order.

(Stats.1976, c. 1010, § 2, operative April 30, 1977.)

§ 19478. Nonpayment for want of funds

When any warrant is presented to the treasurer for payment and it is not paid for want of funds, the treasurer shall endorse thereon "not paid for want of funds" with the date of presentation and sign his name thereto, and from that time the warrant bears interest at the rate of 6 percent per annum until it is paid or until funds are available for its payment and the county treasurer gives notice to the warrant holder that funds are available for the payment. The giving of the notice is deemed complete upon deposit thereof in the United States mail in a sealed envelope addressed to the warrant holder at his address given by him at the time of presentation of the warrant to the treasurer, with postage thereon fully prepaid and registered.

(Stats.1976, c. 1010, § 2, operative April 30, 1977.)

§ 19479.   Library free to inhabitants; violation of rules, regulations and by-laws

Every library established under this chapter shall be forever free to the inhabitants and nonresident taxpayers of the library district, subject always to such rules, regulations, and bylaws as may be made by the board of library trustees. For violation of any rule, regulation, or bylaw a person may be fined or excluded from the privileges of the library.

(Stats.1976, c. 1010, § 2, operative April 30, 1977.)

§ 19480.   Title to property

The title to all property acquired for the purposes of the library, when not inconsistent with the terms of its acquisition, or not otherwise designated, vests in the district in which the library is or is to be situated.

(Stats.1976, c. 1010, § 2, operative April 30, 1977.)

§ 19481.   Designation of district

Every library district shall be designated by the name and style of _____ Library District (using the name of the district) of _____ County (using the name of the county or counties in which the district is situated). In that name the trustees may sue and be sued, and may hold and convey property for the use and benefit of the district. A number shall not be used as a part of the designation of any library district.

(Stats.1976, c. 1010, § 2, operative April 30, 1977.)

§ 19482.   Contracts with other libraries

The board of library trustees and the boards of trustees of neighboring library districts, or the governing bodies of neighboring cities, or boards of supervisors of counties in which public libraries are situated, may contract to lend the books of libraries created under this chapter to residents of the counties, neighboring cities, or library districts, upon a reasonable compensation to be paid by the counties, neighboring cities, or library districts.

(Stats.1976, c. 1010, § 2, operative April 30, 1977.)

§ 19483. Property liable to taxation for county free library

Anything in Sections 19100 to 19179, inclusive, to the contrary, notwithstanding, the property in any library district created under this chapter subsequent to the establishment of a county free library is subject to taxation for county free library purposes as though the library district had not been created.

(Stats.1976, c. 1010, § 2, operative April 30, 1977.)

§ 19500. Claims for money or damages

All claims for money or damages against the district are governed by Part 3 (commencing with Section 900) and Part 4 (commencing with Section 940) of Division 3.6 of Title 1 of the Government Code except as provided therein, or by other statutes or regulations expressly applicable thereto.

(Stats.1976, c. 1010, § 2, operative April 30, 1977.)

§ 19510. Biennial election of trustees

An election shall be held biennially in each library district for the election of one or more library trustees who shall hold office for four years beginning on the * * * last Friday in November next succeeding his election. This election shall be held in the district on the same day as the school district election as specified in Section 5000 in the odd-numbered years. Trustees shall be nominated in the manner prescribed in Section 5012.
(Amended by Stats.1978, c. 1376, p. 4561, § 7.)

§ 19511. Electors qualified to vote

To be qualified to vote at any library district election a person shall be * * * registered to vote in the library district, * * * at least * * * 29 days before the election.
(Amended by Stats.1978, c. 1376, p. 4561, § 8.)

§ 19514. Appointment of nominee, or any qualified voter if no person nominated

If pursuant to Section * * * 5327 a district election is not held, the board of supervisors of the county in which the district, or the largest part thereof in area, is situated shall at its next regular meeting appoint to the positions of trustee those persons nominated, and such persons shall qualify, take office, and serve exactly as if elected at a general district election. If no person has been nominated, the board of supervisors shall appoint any qualified voter of the district to the position.
(Amended by Stats.1979, c. 334, p. 1193, § 15, urgency, eff. July 27, 1979.)

Asterisks * * * Indicate deletions by amendment
Underline indicates changes or additions by amendment

§ 19515.   Provisions governing notices and elections

Except as otherwise provided in this article, Chapter 3 (commencing with Section 5300) of Part 4 of this division shall govern and control the conduct of elections pursuant to this chapter.

(Stats.1976, c. 1010, § 2, operative April 30, 1977. Amended by Stats.1977, c. 36, § 81, urgency, eff. April 29, 1977, operative April 30, 1977.)

§ 19520.   Calling election and submission of questions as to issuance and sale of bonds

The board of trustees of any library district may, when in their judgment it is deemed advisable, and shall, upon a petition of 50 or more taxpayers and residents of the library district, call an election and submit to the electors of the district, the proposition of whether the bonds of the district will be issued and sold for the purpose of raising money for any or all of the following:

(a) The purchase of suitable lots.

(b) Procuring plans and specifications and erecting a suitable building.

(c) Furnishing and equipping the building and fencing and ornamenting the grounds, for the accommodation of the public library.

(d) Any or all of the purposes of this chapter.

(e) Liquidating any indebtedness incurred for the purposes.

(f) Refunding any outstanding valid indebtedness, evidenced by bonds or warrants of the district.

(Stats.1976, c. 1010, § 2, operative April 30, 1977.)

§ 19521.   Bond election

The bond election shall be called and conducted and the results thereof canvassed, returned, and declared in the manner provided in Chapter 3 (commencing with Section 5300) of Part 4 of this division.

(Stats.1976, c. 1010, § 2, operative April 30, 1977. Amended by Stats.1977, c. 36, § 82, urgency, eff. April 29, 1977, operative April 30, 1977.)

§ 19522.   Contents of resolution calling election

The board of trustees shall set forth in the resolution calling for a bond election the amount and denomination of the bonds, the rate of interest, and the number of years that all or any part of the bonds are to run.

(Stats.1976, c. 1010, § 2, operative April 30, 1977. Amended by Stats.1977, c. 36, § 83, urgency, eff. April 29, 1977, operative April 30, 1977.)

§ 19523. Method of voting

Voting shall be by ballot, without reference to the general election law in regard to form of ballot, or manner of voting, except that the words to appear on the ballot shall be "Bonds—Yes," and "Bonds —No." Persons voting at the bond election shall put a cross (+) upon their ballots, with pencil or ink, after the words "Bonds—Yes," or "Bonds—No," as the case may be, to indicate whether they have voted for or against the issuance of the bonds.

(Stats.1976, c. 1010, § 2, operative April 30, 1977.)

§ 19524. Favorable vote

The board of library trustees shall meet on the seventh day after the election, at 8 o'clock p. m., and canvass the returns. If it appears that two-thirds of the votes cast at the election were cast in favor of issuing the bonds, the board shall enter the fact upon its minutes and shall certify all the proceedings to the supervising board of supervisors. Thereupon the board of supervisors shall issue the bonds of the district, in the number and amount provided in the proceedings, and the district shall be named on the bonds. The bonds shall be paid out of the building fund of the district.

The money for the redemption of the bonds and the payment of interest thereon shall be raised by taxation upon the taxable property in the district.

(Stats.1976, c. 1010, § 2, operative April 30, 1977.)

§ 19525. Limitation on total amount of bonds issued

The total amount of bonds issued shall not exceed 5 percent of the * * * assessed value of the property of the district, prior to the 1980–81 fiscal year and shall not exceed 1.25 percent of the assessed value of the district beginning after the 1981–82 fiscal year, as shown by the last equalized assessment roll of the county or counties in which the district is situated.
(Amended by Stats.1980, c. 1208, p. ——, § 30.)

Asterisks * * * indicate deletions by amendment

Underline indicates changes or additions by amendment

§ 19526. Form and term of bonds

The supervising board of supervisors by an order entered upon its minutes shall prescribe the form of the bonds and of the interest coupons attached thereto, and shall fix the time when the whole or any part of the principal of the bonds shall be payable, which shall not be more than 40 years from the date thereof.

(Stats.1976, c. 1010, § 2, operative April 30, 1977.)

§ 19527.   Maximum interest and sale price of bonds; proceeds of sale

The bonds shall not bear a greater amount of interest than 6 percent, to be payable annually or semiannually. The bonds shall be sold in the manner prescribed by the board of supervisors, but for not less than par, and the proceeds of the sale thereof shall be deposited in the county treasury to the credit of the building fund of the library district, and shall be drawn out for the purposes for which the bonds were issued as other library money is drawn out.

(Stats.1976, c. 1010, § 2, operative April 30, 1977.)

§ 19528.   Tax levy for interest and redemption

The board of supervisors of each county in which any part of the district is situated, at the time of making the levy of taxes for county purposes, shall levy a tax for that year upon the taxable property in the district, at the equalized assessed value thereof for that year, for the interest and redemption of the bonds. The tax shall not be less than sufficient to pay the interest of the bonds for that year, and such portion of the principal as is to become due during the year. In any event the tax shall be high enough to raise, annually, for the first half of the term the bonds are to run, a sufficient sum to pay the interest thereon, and during the balance of the term, high enough to pay the annual interest and to pay, annually, a proportion of the principal of the bonds equal to a sum produced by taking the whole amount of the bonds outstanding and dividing it by the number of years the bonds then have to run.

(Stats.1976, c. 1010, § 2, operative April 30, 1977.)

§ 19529.   Deposit and use of money collected

All money levied, when collected, shall be paid into the county treasury to the credit of the library district, and shall be used for the payment of principal and interest on the bonds, and for no other purpose. The principal and interest on the bonds shall be paid by the county treasurer, upon the warrant of the county auditor, out of the fund provided therefor. The county auditor shall cancel and file with the county treasurer the bonds and coupons as rapidly as they are paid.

(Stats.1976, c. 1010, § 2, operative April 30, 1977.)

§ 19530.   Petition for withdrawal and cancellation of unsold bonds

Whenever any bonds issued under this article remain unsold for the period of six months after having been offered for sale in the manner prescribed by the supervising board of supervisors, the board of trustees of the library district for or on account of which the bonds were issued, or of any library district composed wholly or partly of territory which, at the time of holding the election authorizing the issuance of the bonds, was embraced within the district for or on account of which the bonds were issued, may petition the supervising board of supervisors to cause the unsold bonds to be withdrawn from the market and canceled.

(Stats.1976, c. 1010, § 2, operative April 30, 1977.)

§ 19531. Notice of hearing on petition

Upon receiving the petition, signed by a majority of the members of the board of trustees, the supervising board of supervisors shall fix a time for hearing the petition, which shall be not more than 30 days thereafter, and shall cause a notice, stating the time and place of hearing, and the object of the petition in general terms, to be published as provided in this chapter.

(Stats.1976, c. 1010, § 2, operative April 30, 1977.)

§ 19532. Hearing and order for cancellation

At the time and place designated in the notice for hearing the petition, or at any subsequent time to which the hearing is postponed, the supervising board of supervisors shall hear any reasons that are submitted for or against the granting of the petition, and if they deem it for the best interests of the library district named in the petition that the unsold bonds be canceled, they shall make and enter an order in the minutes of their proceedings that the unsold bonds be canceled. Thereupon the bonds, and the vote by which they were authorized to be issued, shall cease to be of any validity whatever.

(Stats.1976, c. 1010, § 2, operative April 30, 1977.)

DISTRICT LIBRARIES IN INCORPORATED TOWNS AND VILLAGES

(West's Annotated California Codes, Education Code, 1982, s.19600-19734.)

§ 19600. Authority to establish, equip and maintain library and museum

Any unincorporated town or village of this state may establish, equip, and maintain a public library for the dissemination of knowledge of the arts, sciences, and general literature, in accordance with this chapter. Any unincorporated town or village of this state may also establish, equip, and maintain a public museum in accordance with this chapter.

(Amended by Stats.1978, c. 988, p. 3052, § 2.)

Underline indicates changes or additions by amendment

§ 19601.   Petition and election for formation of a district

Upon the application, by petition, of 50 or more taxpayers and residents of any unincorporated town or village to the board of supervisors in the county in which the town or village is located, praying for the formation of a library district, and setting forth the boundaries of the proposed district, the board of supervisors shall, within 10 days after receiving the petition, by resolution, order that an election be held in the proposed district for the determination of the question and shall appoint three qualified electors of the proposed district to conduct the election.

(Stats.1976, c. 1010, § 2, operative April 30, 1977.)

§ 19602.   Election notice

The election shall be called by posting notice in three of the most public places in the proposed library district, and by publication in a daily or weekly paper, if there is one, at least once a week for not less than 15 days. The notices shall specify the time, place, and the purposes of the election, and the hours during which the polls will be kept open.

(Stats.1976, c. 1010, § 2, operative April 30, 1977.)

§ 19603.   Transmittal of notification of election call; action by local agency formation commission

Within five days after the district formation election has been called, the legislative body which has called the election shall transmit, by registered mail, a written notification of the election call to the executive officer of the local agency formation commission of the county or principal county in which the territory or major portion of the territory of the proposed district is located. Such written notice shall include the name and a description of the proposed district, and may be in the form of a certified copy of the resolution adopted by the legislative body calling the district formation election.

The executive officer, within five days after being notified that a district formation election has been called, shall submit to the commission, for its approval or modification, an impartial analysis of the proposed district formation.

The impartial analysis shall not exceed 500 words in length and shall include a specific description of the boundaries of the district proposed to be formed.

The local agency formation commission, within five days after the receipt of the executive officer's analysis, shall approve or modify the analysis and submit it to the officials in charge of conducting the district formation election.

(Stats.1976, c. 1010, § 2, operative April 30, 1977.)

§ 19604.   Filing of arguments for and against district formation

The board of supervisors or any member or members of the board authorized by the board, or any individual voter or bona fide association of citizens entitled to vote on the district formation proposition, or any combination of such voters and associations of citizens, may file a written argument for or a written argument against the proposed district formation.

Arguments shall not exceed 300 words in length and shall be filed with the officials in charge of conducting the election not less than 54 days prior to the date of the district formation election.

(Stats.1976, c. 1010, § 2, operative April 30, 1977.)

§ 19605.   Selection of arguments; preferences, priorities

If more than one argument for or more than one argument against the proposed district formation is filed with the election officials within the time prescribed, such election officials shall select one of the arguments for printing and distribution to the voters.

In selecting the arguments, the election officials shall give preference and priority in the order named to the arguments of the following:

(a) The board of supervisors or any member or members of the board authorized by the board.

(b) Individual voters or bona fide associations of citizens or a combination of such voters and associations.

(Stats.1976, c. 1010, § 2, operative April 30, 1977.)

§ 19606.   Ballot pamphlet

The officials in charge of conducting the election shall cause a ballot pamphlet concerning the district formation proposition to be voted on to be printed and mailed to each voter entitled to vote on the district formation question.

The ballot pamphlet shall contain the following in the order prescribed:

(a) The complete text of the proposition.

(b) The impartial analysis of the proposition prepared by the local agency formation commission.

(c) The argument for the proposed district formation.

(d) The argument against the proposed district formation.

The election officials shall mail a ballot pamphlet to each voter entitled to vote in the district formation election at least 10 days prior to the date of the election. Such a ballot pamphlet is "official matter" within the meaning of Section 10010 of the Elections Code.

(Stats.1976, c. 1010, § 2, operative April 30, 1977. Amended by Stats.1977, c. 1205, § 20.5.)

§ 19607. Hours for polls to be open

In districts with a population of 10,000 or over, the polls shall be opened at 8 o'clock a. m., and kept open until 7 o'clock p. m., and in districts where the population is less than 10,000, the polls shall not be opened before 1 o'clock p. m., and shall be kept open not less than six hours.

(Stats.1976, c. 1010, § 2, operative April 30, 1977.)

§ 19608. Conduct of election

The election shall be conducted in accordance with the general election laws of this state, where applicable, without reference to form of ballot or manner of voting, except that the ballots shall contain the words, "For library district," and the voter shall write or print after the words on his ballot the word "Yes," or the word "No."

(Stats.1976, c. 1010, § 2, operative April 30, 1977.)

§ 19609. Electors entitled to vote

Every qualified elector, resident within the proposed district for the period requisite to enable him to vote at a general election, shall be entitled to vote at the election.

(Stats.1976, c. 1010, § 2, operative April 30, 1977.)

§ 19610. Report of election results

The election officers shall report the result of the election to the board of supervisors within five days after the election.

(Stats.1976, c. 1010, § 2, operative April 30, 1977.)

§ 19611. Establishment of district; appointment and qualifications of board of library trustees

If a majority of the votes at the election is in favor of a library district, the board of supervisors shall by resolution, establish the library district, and shall appoint five trustees, who shall be qualified electors and residents within the limits of the district, to be known as a board of library trustees of the town or village for which they are appointed.

(Stats.1976, c. 1010, § 2, operative April 30, 1977.)

§ 19612. Filling of vacancies

Vacancies shall be filled by the board of supervisors by appointment for the unexpired term.

(Stats.1976, c. 1010, § 2, operative April 30, 1977.)

§ 19613. Unfavorable vote

If a majority of the votes cast is against a library district, the board of supervisors shall, by order, so declare, and no other proceedings shall be taken in relation thereto until the expiration of one year from the date of presentation of the petition.

(Stats.1976, c. 1010, § 2, operative April 30, 1977.)

§ 19614. Entries in minutes of board of supervisors

The fact of the presentation of the petition, and the order establishing the library district and making the appointment of the five library trustees, shall be entered in the minutes of the board of supervisors and shall be conclusive evidence of the due presentation of a proper petition, and that each of the petitioners was, at the time of signature and presentation of the petition, a taxpayer and resident of the proposed district, and of the fact and regularity of all prior proceedings of every kind and nature provided for by this article and of the existence and validity of the district.

(Stats.1976, c. 1010, § 2, operative April 30, 1977.)

§ 19640. Monthly meetings of board of library trustees

The board of library trustees shall meet at least once a month, at such time and place as it may fix by resolution.

(Stats.1976, c. 1010, § 2, operative April 30, 1977.)

§ 19641. Special meetings

Special meetings may be called at any time by three trustees, by written notices served upon each member at least 12 hours before the time specified for the meeting.

(Stats.1976, c. 1010, § 2, operative April 30, 1977.)

§ 19642. Quorum

Three members constitute a quorum for the transaction of business.

(Stats.1976, c. 1010, § 2, operative April 30, 1977.)

§ 19643.   Organization of board

At its first meeting held after the general district election the board shall organize by electing one of its number president, and another one of its number secretary. They shall serve as such for one year or until their successors are elected and qualified.

(Stats.1976, c. 1010, § 2, operative April 30, 1977.)

§ 19644.   Record of proceedings and filing of certificate of establishment

The board shall cause a proper record of its proceedings to be kept, and at the first meeting of the board of trustees, it shall immediately cause to be made out and filed with the Department of Education at Sacramento a certificate showing that the library has been established, with the date thereof, the names of the trustees, and the officers of the board chosen for the current fiscal year.

(Stats.1976, c. 1010, § 2, operative April 30, 1977.)

§ 19645.   Rules, regulations and bylaws

The board of library trustees shall make and enforce all rules, regulations, and bylaws necessary for the administration, government, and protection of the library under its management, and all property belonging to it.

(Stats.1976, c. 1010, § 2, operative April 30, 1977.)

§ 19646.   Administration of trusts, receipts, holdings and disposal of property

The board of library trustees shall administer any trust declared or created for the library, and receive by gift, devise, or bequest, and hold in trust or otherwise, property situated in this state or elsewhere, and where not otherwise provided, dispose of the property for the benefit of the library.

(Stats.1976, c. 1010, § 2, operative April 30, 1977.)

§ 19647.   Officers and employees

The board of library trustees shall prescribe the duties and powers of the librarian, secretary, and other officers and employees of the library, determine the number of and appoint all officers and employees, and fix their compensation. The officers and employees shall hold their offices and positions at the pleasure of the board.

(Stats.1976, c. 1010, § 2, operative April 30, 1977.)

§ 19648. Purchase of personal property

The board of library trustees shall purchase necessary books, journals, publications, and other personal property.

(Stats.1976, c. 1010, § 2, operative April 30, 1977.)

§ 19649. Purchase of real property, and erection or rental and equipment of building or rooms

The board of library trustees shall also purchase such real property, and erect or rent and equip, such building or rooms, as in its judgment is necessary to properly carry out the provisions of this chapter.

(Stats.1976, c. 1010, § 2, operative April 30, 1977.)

§ 19650. State publications

The board of library trustees may request the appropriate state officials to furnish the library with copies of any and all reports, laws, and other publications of the state not otherwise disposed of by law.

(Stats.1976, c. 1010, § 2, operative April 30, 1977.)

§ 19651. Borrowing from, lending to, and exchanging with other libraries; nonresident borrowing.

The board of library trustees shall borrow books from, lend books to, and exchange books with other libraries. It shall allow nonresidents to borrow books upon such conditions as it may prescribe.

(Stats.1976, c. 1010, § 2, operative April 30, 1977.)

§ 19652. Incidental power of board

The board of library trustees shall do and perform any and all other acts and things necessary or proper to carry out the provisions of this chapter.

(Stats.1976, c. 1010, § 2, operative April 30, 1977.)

§ 19653. Annual report to State Librarian

The board of library trustees shall file, through the librarian, on or before the last day in the month of August of each year, a report with the State Librarian at Sacramento giving the condition of the library and the number of volumes contained therein on the 30th day of June preceding. The report shall, in addition to other matters deemed expedient by the board of trustees or the librarian, contain such statistical and other information as is deemed desirable by the State Librarian. For this purpose the State Librarian may send to the several district librarians instructions or question blanks so as to obtain the material for a comparative study of library conditions in the state.

(Stats.1976, c. 1010, § 2, operative April 30, 1977.)

§ 19654.   Hours open to public

The board of library trustees shall designate the hours during which the library is open for the use of the public. All public libraries established under this chapter shall be open for the use of the public during every day in the year except on such legal holidays as may be determined by the board of library trustees.

(Stats.1976, c. 1010, § 2, operative April 30, 1977.)

§ 19655.   Annual estimate of costs

In any library district formed under the provisions of this chapter, which maintains a public library, or which has petitioned for and been granted permission to establish, and intends to maintain a public library in accordance with this chapter, the board of library trustees shall furnish to the board of supervisors of the county in which the library district is situated, each and every year, on or before the first day of September, an estimate of the cost of any or all of the following:

(a) Leasing temporary quarters.

(b) Purchasing a suitable lot.

(c) Procuring plans and specifications and erecting a suitable building.

(d) Furnishing and equipping the building and fencing and ornamenting the grounds, for the accommodation of the public library.

(e) Conducting and maintaining the library for the ensuing fiscal year.

(Stats.1976, c. 1010, § 2, operative April 30, 1977.)

§ 19656.   Board elections

The board of library trustees may, when in its judgment it is deemed advisable, and upon the petition of 50 or more taxpayers residing within the library district shall, call an election and submit to the electors of the library district the question of whether the bonds of the library district shall be issued and sold for any or all the purposes of this chapter.

(Stats.1976, c. 1010, § 2, operative April 30, 1977.)

§ 19657.   Special tax levy

When the estimate has been submitted to the board of supervisors, the board of supervisors shall, at the time of levying county taxes, levy a special tax upon all of the taxable property within the limits of the library district, sufficient in amount to maintain the public library, or to purchase the site, erect and equip the building, improve the grounds or building, or for any or all of the purposes of this chapter. The taxes shall be computed, entered upon the tax roll, and collected in the same manner as other taxes are computed, entered, and collected.

(Stats.1976, c. 1010, § 2, operative April 30, 1977.)

§ 19658.   Library and safety, preservation and application of fund not payable to treasury

The revenue derived from the tax, together with all money acquired by gift, devise, bequest, or otherwise, for the purposes of the library, shall be paid into the county treasury, to the credit of the library fund of the district in which the tax is collected, subject only to the order of the library trustees of the district. If payment into the treasury is inconsistent with the terms or conditions of any gift, devise, or bequest, the board of library trustees shall provide for the safety and preservation of the fund, and the application thereof to the use of the library, in accordance with the terms and conditions of the gift, devise, or bequest.

(Stats.1976, c. 1010, § 2, operative April 30, 1977.)

§ 19660.   Nonpayment of warrants

When any warrant is presented to the treasurer for payment and it is not paid for want of funds the treasurer shall endorse thereon "not paid for want of funds" with the date of presentation and sign his name thereto and from that time the warrant bears interest at the rate of 6 percent per annum until it is paid or until funds are available for its payment and the county treasurer gives notice to the warrant holder that funds are available for payment. The giving of the notice is deemed complete upon deposit thereof in the United States mail in a sealed envelope addressed to the warrant holder at his address given by him at the time of presentation of the warrant to the treasurer, with postage thereon fully prepaid and registered.

(Stats.1976, c. 1010, § 2, operative April 30, 1977.)

§ 19659.   Warrants

Upon the receipt by the county auditor of an order of the library trustees of the district he shall issue his warrant upon the county treasurer for the amount stated in the order.

(Stats.1976, c. 1010, § 2, operative April 30, 1977.)

§ 19661. Library free to inhabitants; violations of rules, regulations or bylaws

Every library established under this chapter shall be forever free to the inhabitants and nonresident taxpayers of the library district, subject always to such rules, regulations, and bylaws as may be made by the board of library trustees. For any violation of the rules, regulations, or bylaws a person may be fined or excluded from the privileges of the library.

(Stats.1976, c. 1010, § 2, operative April 30, 1977.)

§ 19662. Contracts with other libraries

Boards of library trustees and the boards of trustees of neighboring library districts, or the legislative bodies of neighboring municipalities, or boards of supervisors of the counties in which public libraries are situated, may contract to lend the books of the libraries to residents of the counties or neighboring municipalities, or library districts, upon a reasonable compensation to be paid by the counties, neighboring municipalities, or library districts.

(Stats.1976, c. 1010, § 2, operative April 30, 1977.)

§ 19663. Title to property

The title to all property acquired for the purposes of the libraries, when not inconsistent with the terms of its acquisition, or not otherwise designated, vests in the district in which libraries are, or are to be situated.

(Stats.1976, c. 1010, § 2, operative April 30, 1977.)

§ 19664. Designation of district

Every library district shall be designated by the name and style of _____ Library District, (using the name of the district), of _____ County, (using the name of the county in which the district is situated). In that name the trustees may sue and be sued, and may hold and convey property for the use and benefit of the district. A number shall not be used as a part of the designation of any library district.

(Stats.1976, c. 1010, § 2, operative April 30, 1977.)

§ 19670. Power to establish; board of museum trustees

The board of library trustees may vote to establish a public museum in the library district and to constitute the board of library trustees as the board of museum

trustees for the purposes of managing such museum in accordance with the provisions of this chapter.
(Added by Stats.1978, c. 988, p. 3052, § 3.)

§ 19690.   Claims for moneys or damages

All claims for money or damages against the district are governed by Part 3 (commencing with Section 900) and Part 4 (commencing with Section 940) of Division 3.6 of Title 1 of the Government Code except as provided therein, or by other statutes or regulations expressly applicable thereto.

(Stats.1976, c. 1010, § 2, operative April 30, 1977.)

§ 19700. Conduct of elections; terms of trustees

(a) Except as otherwise provided in this article, the Uniform District Election Law (Part 3 (commencing with Section 23500) of Division 14 of the Elections Code) shall govern and control the conduct of elections pursuant to this chapter. Elections shall be held biennially in the district on the same day as the school district election as specified in Section 5000 in the odd-numbered years.

(b) The trustees shall hold office for the term of four years beginning on the * * * last Friday in November next succeeding their appointment or election.
* * *

(c) The members of the first board of library trustees appointed or elected in a district shall, at their first meeting, so classify themselves by lot that their terms shall expire: two on the * * * last Friday in November of the first odd-numbered calendar year next succeeding their appointment or election, and three on the * * * last Friday in November of the second succeeding odd-numbered calendar year.
(Amended by Stats.1978, c. 1376, p. 4561, § 9.)

§ 19701.   Number of trustees

The number of library trustees for any library district established under the provisions of this chapter is five.

(Stats.1976, c. 1010, § 2, operative April 30, 1977.)

§ 19702. Eligibility to vote

Every * * * person who is registered to vote in the library district * * * where the election is held at least * * * 29 days before the election, may vote at the election.
(Added by Stats.1978, c. 1376, p. 4562, § 10.)

Asterisks * * * indicate deletions by amendment

Underline indicates changes or additions by amendment

§ 19720.   Calling election and submission of questions as to issuance and sale of bonds

The board of trustees of any library district may, when in their judgment it is deemed advisable, and shall upon a petition of 50 or more taxpayers and residents of the library district, call an election and submit to the electors of the district the question of whether the

bonds of the district shall be issued and sold for the purpose of raising money for any or all of the following:

(a) The purchase of suitable lots.

(b) Procuring plans and specifications and erecting a suitable
building.

(c) Furnishing and equipping the building, and fencing and ornamenting the grounds, for the accommodation of the public library.

(d) Any or all of the purposes of this chapter.

(e) Liquidating any indebtedness incurred for the purposes.

(f) Refunding any outstanding valid indebtedness, evidenced by
bonds or warrants of the district.

(Stats.1976, c. 1010, § 2, operative April 30, 1977.)

§ 19721.   Notice of election

The election shall be called by posting notices, signed by the
board, in three of the most public places in the district, for not less
than 20 days before the election, and by publishing the notice not less
than once a week for three successive weeks in a newspaper published
in the district if there is one, or if there is none, in a newspaper published in the county.

(Stats.1976, c. 1010, § 2, operative April 30, 1977.)

§ 19722.   Contents of notice

The notice shall contain:

(a) Time and place of holding the election.

(b) The names of inspectors and judges to conduct the election.

(c) The hours during the day in which the polls will be open.

(d) The amount and denomination of the bonds, the rate of interest, and the number of years, not exceeding 40, the whole or any
part of the bonds are to be run.

(Stats.1976, c. 1010, § 2, operative April 30, 1977.)

§ 19723.   Conduct of election

The election shall be conducted in accordance with the provisions
relating to the election of trustees, insofar as they are applicable to
the election for bonds.

(Stats.1976, c. 1010, § 2, operative April 30, 1977.)

§ 19724.   Method of voting

Voting shall be by ballot without reference to the general election law in regard to form of ballot, or manner of voting, except that the words to appear on the ballot shall be, "Bonds—Yes," and "Bonds —No." Persons voting at the bond election shall put a cross (+) upon their ballots, with pencil or ink, after the words, "Bonds—Yes," or "Bonds—No," as the case may be, to indicate whether they have voted for or against the issuance of the bonds. The ballot shall be handed by the elector voting to the inspector, who shall then, in his presence, deposit the ballot in the ballot box, and the judges shall enter the elector's name on poll list.

(Stats.1976, c. 1010, § 2, operative April 30, 1977.)

§ 19725. Favorable vote

On the seventh day after the election, at 8 o'clock p. m., the returns having been made to the board of trustees, the board shall meet and canvass the returns, and if it appears that more than one-half of the votes cast at the election are in favor of issuing the bonds, then the board shall cause an entry of the fact to be made upon its minutes and shall certify to the board of supervisors, all the proceedings had in the premises. Thereupon the board of supervisors shall issue the bonds of the district, to the number and amount provided in the proceedings, payable out of the building fund of the district, naming the district.

(Stats.1976, c. 1010, § 2, operative April 30, 1977.)

§ 19726. Taxation for redemption and payment of interest

The money shall be raised by taxation upon the taxable property in the district, for the redemption of the bonds and the payment of the interest thereon.

(Stats.1976, c. 1010, § 2, operative April 30, 1977.)

§ 19727. Limitation on total amount of bonds issued

The total amount of bonds issued shall not exceed 5 percent of the taxable property of the district, as shown by the last equalized assessment book of the county.

(Stats.1976, c. 1010, § 2, operative April 30, 1977.)

§ 19728. Form of bonds and coupons; time when principal payable

The board of supervisors by an order entered upon its minutes shall prescribe the form of the bonds and of the interest coupons attached thereto, and shall fix the time when the whole or any part of the principal of the bonds shall be payable, which shall not be more than 40 years from the date thereof.

(Stats.1976, c. 1010, § 2, operative April 30, 1977.)

§ 19729.   Maximum interest and sale price of bonds; proceeds of sale

The bonds shall not bear a greater amount of interest than 6 percent, to be payable annually or semiannually. The bonds shall be sold in the manner prescribed by the board of supervisors, but for not less than par, and the proceeds of the sale thereof shall be deposited in the county treasury to the credit of the building fund of the library district, and shall be drawn out for the purposes for which the bonds were issued as other library moneys are drawn out.

(Stats.1976, c. 1010, § 2, operative April 30, 1977.)

§ 19730.   Tax levy for interest and redemption

The board of supervisors, at the time of making the levy of taxes for county purposes, shall levy a tax for that year upon the taxable property in the district, at the equalized assessed value thereof for that year, for the interest and redemption of the bonds. The tax shall not be less than sufficient to pay the interest of the bonds for that year, and such portion of the principal as is to become due during the year. In any event the tax shall be high enough to raise, annually, for the first half of the term the bonds have to run, a sufficient sum to pay the interest thereon, and during the balance of the term, high enough to pay the annual interest and to pay, annually, a proportion of the principal of the bonds equal to a sum produced by taking the whole amount of the bonds outstanding and dividing it by the number of years the bonds then have to run.

(Stats.1976, c. 1010, § 2, operative April 30, 1977.)

§ 19731.   Deposit and use of money collected

All money levied, when collected, shall be paid into the county treasury to the credit of the library district, and shall be used for the payment of principal and interest on the bonds, and for no other purpose. The principal and interest on the bonds shall be paid by the county treasurer, upon the warrant of the county auditor, out of the fund provided therefor. The county auditor shall cancel and file with the county treasurer the bonds and coupons as rapidly as they are paid.

(Stats.1976, c. 1010, § 2, operative April 30, 1977.)

§ 19732. Petition for withdrawal and cancellation of unsold bonds

Whenever any bonds issued under this article remain unsold for the period of six months after having been offered for sale in the manner prescribed by the board of supervisors, the board of trustees of the library district for or on account of which the bonds were issued, or of any library district composed wholly or partly of territory which, at the time of holding the election authorizing the issuance of the bonds, was embraced within the district for or an account of which the bonds were issued, may petition the board of supervisors to cause the unsold bonds to be withdrawn from market and canceled.

(Stats.1976, c. 1010, § 2, operative April 30, 1977.)

§ 19733. Notice of hearing on petition

Upon receiving the petition, signed by a majority of the members of the board of trustees, the supervisors shall fix a time for hearing the petition, which shall be not more than 30 days thereafter, and shall cause a notice, stating the time and place of hearing, and the object of the petition in general terms, to be published for 10 days prior to the day of hearing, in some newspaper published in the library district, if there is one, and if there is no newspaper published in the library district, then in a newspaper published at the county seat of the county in which the library district or part thereof is situated.

(Stats.1976, c. 1010, § 2, operative April 30, 1977.)

§ 19734. Hearing and order for cancellation

At the time and place designated in the notice for hearing the petition, or at any subsequent time to which the hearing is postponed, the supervisors shall hear any reasons that are submitted for or against the granting of the petition, and if they deem it for the best interests of the library district that the unsold bonds be canceled, they shall make and enter an order in the minutes of their proceedings that the unsold bonds be canceled. Thereupon the bonds, and the vote by which they were authorized to be issued, shall cease to be of any validity whatever.

(Stats.1976, c. 1010, § 2, operative April 30, 1977.)

SCHOOL DISTRICT LIBRARIES
(West's Annotated California Codes, Education Code, 1982,
s.18300-18571.)

§ 18300. "Trustees" and "library trustees"

"Trustees," or "library trustees" as used in this chapter mean the regularly elected union high school trustees who reside within the library district.

(Stats.1976, c. 1010, § 2, operative April 30, 1977.)

§ 18301.　"Library," "library district," and "library districts"

"Library," "library district," or "library districts" as used in this chapter mean "union high school library district."

(Stats.1976, c. 1010, § 2, operative April 30, 1977.)

§ 18310.　Establishment of library district in unified district

For the purposes of this chapter a unified school district has all of the powers and duties of a union high school district. A library district may be formed upon the application of 50 or more taxpayers and residents of any unified district, and after an election, in the manner prescribed by this chapter for the formation of a library district upon the application of taxpayers and residents of a union high school district. If the requisite number of votes cast at the election are in favor of a unified school district library district the board of supervisors shall by resolution establish the library district and place the district in the control of the governing board of the unified school district.

(Stats.1976, c. 1010, § 2, operative April 30, 1977.)

§ 18311.　Definitions

As used in this chapter the words "union high school district" mean union high school district or unified school district and the words "union high school" mean union high school or unified school district. Whenever the provisions of this chapter are being exercised by, or are being made applicable in, a unified school district, the words "union high school district" and "union high school" shall be deemed to mean unified school district.

(Stats.1976, c. 1010, § 2, operative April 30, 1977.)

§ 18312.　Unified school district library district

If there are formed substantially within the territory of a union high school library district two or more unified school districts, the library district shall become a unified school district library district which shall be governed by the governing board of the unified school district whose territory includes the largest portion of the territory of the library district.

(Stats.1976, c. 1010, § 2, operative April 30, 1977.)

§ 18320.　Authority to establish library

Any union high school district may establish, equip. and maintain a public library for the dissemination of knowledge of the arts, sciences, and general literature, in accordance with this chapter.

(Stats.1976, c. 1010, § 2, operative April 30, 1977.)

§ 18321. Title to property

The title to all property acquired for the purposes of the library, when not inconsistent with the terms of its acquisition, or not otherwise designated, vests in the district in which the library is, or is to be, situated.

(Stats.1976, c. 1010, § 2, operative April 30, 1977.)

§ 18322. Library free to inhabitants; violation of rules, regulations and by-laws

Every union high school library established under this chapter shall be forever free to the inhabitants and nonresident taxpayers of the library district, subject always to such rules, regulations, and by-laws as may be made by the board of library trustees. For violations of any rule, regulation, or bylaw a person may be fined or excluded from the privileges of the library.

(Stats.1976, c. 1010, § 2, operative April 30, 1977.)

§ 18330. Petition and election

Upon the application by petition of 50 or more taxpayers and residents of any union high school district to the board of supervisors in the county in which the union high school district is located, praying for the formation of a library district, and setting forth the boundaries of the proposed district, the board of supervisors shall, within 10 days after receiving the petition, by resolution, order that an election be held in the proposed district for the determination of the question and shall appoint three qualified electors thereof to conduct the election.

(Stats.1976, c. 1010, § 2, operative April 30, 1977.)

§ 18331. Election notices

The election shall be called by posting notices in three of the most public places in the proposed library district, and by publication in a daily or weekly paper therein, if there is one, at least once a week for not less than 15 days. The notices shall specify the time, place, and the purpose of the election, and the hours during which the polls will be kept open.

(Stats.1976, c. 1010, § 2, operative April 30, 1977.)

§ 18332. Hours for polls to be open

In districts with a population of 10,000 or over, the polls shall be opened at 8 o'clock a. m. and kept open until 7 o'clock p. m., and in districts where the population is less than 10,000, the polls shall not be opened before 1 o'clock p. m. and shall be kept open not less than six hours.

(Stats.1976, c. 1010, § 2, operative April 30, 1977.)

§ 18333.   Conduct of election

The election shall be conducted in accordance with the general election laws of this state, where applicable, without reference to form of ballot or manner of voting, except that the ballots shall contain the words, "For Union High School Library District." The voter shall write or print after the words on his ballot the word "Yes" or the word "No."

(Stats.1976, c. 1010, § 2, operative April 30, 1977.)

§ 18334.   Electors entitled to vote

Every qualified elector, resident within the proposed district for the period requisite to enable him to vote at a general election, shall be entitled to vote at the election.

(Stats.1976, c. 1010, § 2, operative April 30, 1977.)

§ 18335.   Report of election results

The election officers shall report the result of the election to the board of supervisors within five days subsequent to the holding thereof.

(Stats.1976, c. 1010, § 2, operative April 30, 1977.)

§ 18336.   Establishment of district

If two-thirds of the votes cast at the election are in favor of a union high school library district, the board of supervisors shall, by resolution, establish the library district, and place the district in the control of the governing board of the union high school district.

(Stats.1976, c. 1010, § 2, operative April 30, 1977.)

§ 18337.   Unfavorable vote

If more than one-third of the votes cast in the election is against a library district, the board of supervisors shall, by order, so declare and no other proceedings shall be taken in relation thereto until the expiration of one year from the date of presentation of the petition.

(Stats.1976, c. 1010, § 2, operative April 30, 1977.)

§ 18338.   Proceedings entered in the minutes of the board of supervisors

The fact of the presentation of the petition and the order establishing the library district shall be entered on the minutes of the board of supervisors, and shall be conclusive evidence of the due presentation of a proper petition, and that each of the petitioners was, at the time of signature and presentation of the petition a taxpayer and resident of the proposed district, and of the fact and regularity of all prior proceedings of every kind and nature provided for by this article, and of the existence and validity of the district.

(Stats.1976, c. 1010, § 2, operative April 30, 1977.)

§ 18339. Designation of district

Every library district shall be designated by the name and style of "_____ Library District (using the name of the district) of _____ County (using the name of the county in which the district is situated)." A number shall not be used as a part of the designation of any library district.

(Stats.1976, c. 1010, § 2, operative April 30, 1977.)

§ 18340. Suits, and holding and conveying property in name of district

In the name of the library district, the governing board may sue and be sued, and may hold and convey property for the use and benefit of the district.

(Stats.1976, c. 1010, § 2, operative April 30, 1977.)

§ 18341. Term of trustees

The trustees in whose control the library district has been placed shall severally hold office during the term for which they have been elected as trustees of the union high school district.

(Stats.1976, c. 1010, § 2, operative April 30, 1977.)

§ 18370. Election upon question of dissolution

The district may at any time be dissolved if two-thirds of the votes cast at an election called by the library trustees upon the question of dissolution are in favor of the dissolution.

(Stats.1976, c. 1010, § 2, operative April 30, 1977.)

§ 18371. Calling and conduct of election

The election shall be called and conducted in the same manner as other elections of the district.

(Stats.1976, c. 1010, § 2, operative April 30, 1977.)

§ 18372. Vesting of property upon dissolution

Upon dissolution, the property of the district shall vest in any

union high school district in which the library is situated.
(Stats.1976, c. 1010, § 2, operative April 30, 1977.)

§ 18373. Effect of dissolution on bonded indebtedness

If at the time of the election to dissolve the district, there is any outstanding bonded indebtedness of the district, the vote to dissolve the district shall dissolve it for all purposes excepting only the levy and collection of taxes for the payment of the indebtedness. From the time the district is dissolved until the bonded indebtedness, with the interest thereon, is fully paid, satisfied, and discharged, the board of supervisors is ex officio the library board of the district. The board shall levy such taxes and perform such other acts as are necessary in order to raise money for the payment of the indebtedness and the interest thereon.

(Stats.1976, c. 1010, § 2, operative April 30, 1977.)

§ 18380. Monthly meetings

The boards of library trustees shall meet at least once a month, at such time and place as it may fix by resolution.

(Stats.1976, c. 1010, § 2, operative April 30, 1977.)

§ 18381. Special meetings

Special meetings may be called at any time by two trustees, by written notices served upon each member at least 12 hours before the time specified for the meeting.

(Stats.1976, c. 1010, § 2, operative April 30, 1977.)

§ 18382. Quorum

Three members constitute a quorum for the transaction of business.

(Stats.1976, c. 1010, § 2, operative April 30, 1977.)

§ 18383. Organizational meeting; terms of members

The board shall hold an annual organizational meeting. In a year in which a regular election for board members is conducted, the meeting shall be held on a day within a 15-day period that commences with the date upon which a board member elected at that election takes office. Organizational meetings in years in which no such regular election for board members is conducted shall be held during the same 15-day period on the calendar. At each of such meetings, the board shall elect one of its number president, and another one of its number secretary. They shall serve as such for one year or until their successors are elected and qualified.

(Stats.1976, c. 1010, § 2, operative April 30, 1977.

§ 18384. Record of proceedings

The board shall cause a proper record of its proceedings to be kept.

(Stats.1976, c. 1010, § 2, operative April 30, 1977.)

§ 18385. Certificate of establishment

At the first meeting of the board of trustees of any library district formed under this chapter it shall immediately cause to be made out and filed with the Department of Education at Sacramento a certificate showing that the library has been established, with the date thereof, the names of the trustees, and the officers of the board chosen for the current fiscal year.

(Stats.1976, c. 1010, § 2, operative April 30, 1977.)

§ 18400. Rules, regulations, and by-laws

The board of library trustees shall make and enforce all rules, regulations, and bylaws necessary for the administration, government, and protection of the library under its management, and all property belonging to the library.

(Stats.1976, c. 1010, § 2, operative April 30, 1977.)

§ 18401. Administration of trust; receipt holding, and disposal of property

The board of library trustees shall administer any trust declared or created for the library and receive by gift, devise, or bequest, and hold in trust or otherwise, property situated in this state or elsewhere, and where not otherwise provided, dispose of the property for the benefit of the library.

(Stats.1976, c. 1010, § 2, operative April 30, 1977.)

§ 18402. Officers and employees

The board of library trustees shall prescribe the duties and powers of the librarian, secretary, and other officers and employees of the library, determine the number of and appoint all officers and employees, and fix their compensation. The officers and employees shall hold their offices and positions at the pleasure of the boards.

(Stats.1976, c. 1010, § 2, operative April 30, 1977.)

§ 18403. Purchase of personal property

The board of library trustees shall purchase necessary books, journals, publications, and other personal property.

(Stats.1976, c. 1010, § 2, operative April 30, 1977.)

§ 18404. Purchase of real property and erection or rental and equipment of buildings or rooms

The board of library trustees shall purchase such real property, and erect or rent and equip such buildings or rooms, as in its judgment are necessary to properly carry out the provisions of this chapter.

(Stats.1976, c. 1010, § 2, operative April 30, 1977.)

§ 18405. State publications

The board of library trustees may request the appropriate state officials to furnish the library with copies of any and all reports, laws, and other publications of the state not otherwise disposed of by law.

(Stats.1976, c. 1010, § 2, operative April 30, 1977.)

§ 18406. Borrowing from, lending to, and exchanging with other libraries; nonresident borrowing

The board of library trustees shall borrow books from, lend books to, and exchange books with other libraries, and shall allow nonresidents to borrow books upon such conditions as it may prescribe.

(Stats.1976, c. 1010, § 2, operative April 30, 1977.)

§ 18407. Incidental powers of board

The board of library trustees shall do and perform any and all other acts and things necessary or proper to carry out the provisions of this chapter.

(Stats.1976, c. 1010, § 2, operative April 30, 1977.)

§ 18408. Annual report to State Librarian

The board of library trustees shall file through the librarian on or before the last day in August of each year, a report with the State Librarian at Sacramento, giving the condition of its library and the number of volumes contained therein on the 30th day of June preceding. The report shall, in addition to other matters deemed expedient by the board of trustees or the district librarian, contain such statistical and other information as is deemed desirable by the State Librarian. For this purpose the State Librarian may send to the several district librarians instructions or question blanks so as to obtain the material for a comparative study of library conditions in the state.

(Stats.1976, c. 1010, § 2, operative April 30, 1977.)

§ 18409. Hours

The board of library trustees shall designate the hours during which the library will be open for the use of the public.

(Stats.1976, c. 1010, § 2, operative April 30, 1977.)

§ 18410. Library to be open at reasonable times

All public libraries established under this chapter shall be open for the use of the public at all reasonable times.

(Stats.1976, c. 1010, § 2, operative April 30, 1977.)

§ 18411. Contracts with other libraries

Boards of library trustees and the boards of trustees of neighboring library districts, or the legislative bodies of neighboring municipalities, or boards of supervisors of the counties in which public libraries are situated, may contract to lend the books of the libraries to residents of the counties, neighboring municipalities, or library districts, upon a reasonable compensation to be paid by the counties, neighboring municipalities, or library districts.

(Stats.1976, c. 1010, § 2, operative April 30, 1977.)

§ 18440. Appointment of library commission

A board of library trustees may appoint, by resolution or other order entered in the minutes of the board of library trustees, a library commission consisting of five members to manage and operate the library or libraries of the district. Before any board of library trustees appoints a library commission as provided herein, the board of library trustees shall hold at least one public hearing on the matter of the creation of a library commission; notice of such hearing shall be given by publication pursuant to Section 6066 of the Government Code, in a newspaper designated by the board of library trustees and circulated throughout the district, and by posting of the notice in three public places in the district at least 15 days prior to the date of the public hearing.

(Stats.1976, c. 1010, § 2, operative April 30, 1977.)

§ 18441. Terms of members

The members of the library commission shall hold office for three years from the first day of July next succeeding their appointment and until their successors are appointed and qualified, and shall serve without compensation.

(Stats.1976, c. 1010, § 2, operative April 30, 1977.)

§ 18442.   Classification

The members of the first commission appointed shall be so classified by the board of library trustees at the time of their appointment that the term of office of one of the members shall expire on the first day of July one year after the first day of July next succeeding his appointment, two at the end of one additional year thereafter, and two at the end of two additional years thereafter.

(Stats.1976, c. 1010, § 2, operative April 30, 1977.)

§ 18443.   Vacancies

Vacancies shall be filled by the board of library trustees by appointment for the unexpired term.

(Stats.1976, c. 1010, § 2, operative April 30, 1977.)

§ 18444.   Meetings

Within 30 days after their first appointment, and whenever vacancies in any office may occur and are filled, the commission shall meet and organize as a commission, electing a president and a secretary from their number, after which they may transact business. The commission shall meet at least once a month at such time and place as they may fix by resolution.   Regular and special meetings shall be called and conducted as prescribed in Chapter 9 (commencing with Section 54950), Part 1, Division 2, Title 5 of the Government Code.

(Stats.1976, c. 1010, § 2, operative April 30, 1977.)

§ 18445.   Quorum

A majority of the commission shall constitute a quorum for the transaction of business.

(Stats.1976, c. 1010, § 2, operative April 30, 1977.)

§ 18446.   Effective action

The commission shall act only by resolution or motion.   A majority vote of the members of the commission is required on each action taken, and the vote thereon shall be recorded.

(Stats.1976, c. 1010, § 2, operative April 30, 1977.)

§ 18447.   Record of proceedings

The commission shall cause a proper record of its proceedings to be kept and maintained.

(Stats.1976, c. 1010, § 2, operative April 30, 1977.)

§ 18448. Traveling and incidental expenses

Members of the commission may be allowed actual necessary traveling and incidental expenses incurred in the performance of official business of the district as approved by the commission.

(Stats.1976, c. 1010, § 2, operative April 30, 1977.)

§ 18449. Powers and duties

The commission shall do and perform any and all powers and duties authorized or required of the board of library trustees in Article 7 (commencing with Section 18400) of this chapter with the exception of Section 18411, provided that the consent of the board of library trustees shall be necessary before the commission may dispose of property pursuant to Section 18401 and before the purchase, erection, rental, and equipment of buildings or rooms pursuant to Section 18404.

(Stats.1976, c. 1010, § 2, operative April 30, 1977.)

§ 18450. Warrant on county treasurer

Upon the receipt by the county auditor of an order of the library commission of the district, he shall issue his warrant upon the county treasurer for the amount stated in the order if sufficient funds be on deposit in the account of the district with the county treasurer.

(Stats.1976, c. 1010, § 2, operative April 30, 1977.)

§ 18451. Budget

Annually, and on or before the first day of June of each and every year, the commission shall submit or cause to be submitted to the board of library trustees its proposed budget for the operating and maintaining of the library or libraries of the district for the ensuing fiscal year. The proposed budget shall include an estimate of the cost of any or all of the following:

(a) Leasing of temporary quarters;

(b) Purchasing of suitable real property;

(c) Procuring plans and specifications, and erecting a suitable building or buildings;

(d) Furnishing and equipping the library building, and fencing and ornamenting the grounds for the accommodation of the public library.

(Stats.1976, c. 1010, § 2, operative April 30, 1977.)

§ 18452. Dissolution of commission

The board of library trustees may dissolve the library commission created under the provisions of this article effective as of the 30th day of June next succeeding. Before taking action to dissolve a library commission, the board of library trustees shall hold at least one public hearing on the matter; notice of such hearing shall be given by publication pursuant to Section 6066 of the Government Code, in a newspaper designated by the board of library trustees and circulated throughout the district, and by posting of the notice in three public places in the district at least 15 days prior to the date of the public hearing.

(Stats.1976, c. 1010, § 2, operative April 30, 1977.)

§ 18480.   Annual estimate of costs

In any library district formed under this chapter which maintains a public library, or which has petitioned for and has been granted permission to establish, and intends to maintain, a public library in accordance with this chapter, the board of library trustees shall furnish to the board of supervisors of the county in which the library district is situated, each and every year, on or before the first day of September, an estimate of the cost of any or all of the following:

(a) Leasing temporary quarters.

(b) Purchasing a suitable lot.

(c) Procuring plans and specifications and erecting a suitable building.

(d) Furnishing and equipping the building, and fencing and ornamenting the grounds for the accommodation of the public library.

(e) Conducting and maintaining the library for the ensuing fiscal year.

(Stats.1976, c. 1010, § 2, operative April 30, 1977.)

§ 18490.   Levy of special tax

When the estimate provided for in Section 18480 has been submitted to the board of supervisors of any county in which a library district has been established, the board of supervisors shall, at the time of levying county taxes, levy a special tax upon all taxable property within the limits of the library district.

(Stats.1976, c. 1010, § 2, operative April 30, 1977.)

§ 18491.   Amount of levy

The tax levied shall be sufficient in amount to maintain the union high school library, or to purchase the site, erect and equip the building, improve the grounds or building, or for any or all of the purposes enumerated in Section 18480.

(Stats.1976, c. 1010, § 2, operative April 30, 1977.)

§ 18492. Computation, entry, and collection

The taxes levied shall be computed, entered upon the tax roll, and collected in the same manner as other taxes are computed, entered, and collected.

(Stats.1976, c. 1010, § 2, operative April 30, 1977.)

§ 18493. Library fund

The revenue derived from the tax, together with all money acquired by gift, devise, bequest, or otherwise for the purposes of the library, shall be paid into the county treasury to the credit of the library fund of the district in which the tax was collected, subject only to the order of the library trustees of the district.

(Stats.1976, c. 1010, § 2, operative April 30, 1977.)

§ 18494. Safety, preservation, and application of fund not payable into treasury

If the payment into the treasury is inconsistent with the terms or conditions of any gift, devise, or bequest, the board of library trustees shall provide for the safety and preservation of the fund, and the application thereof to the use of the library, in accordance with the terms and conditions of the gift, devise, or bequest.

(Stats.1976, c. 1010, § 2, operative April 30, 1977.)

§ 18500. Claims for money or damages

All claims for money or damages against the district are governed by Part 3 (commencing with Section 900) and Part 4 (commencing with Section 940) of Division 3.6 of Title 1 of the Government Code except as provided therein, or by other statutes or regulations expressly applicable thereto.

(Stats.1976, c. 1010, § 2, operative April 30, 1977.)

§ 18510. Calling election and submission of question as to issuance and sale of bonds

The board of trustees of any union high school library district may, when in its judgment it is deemed advisable, and shall upon a petition of 50 or more taxpayers and residents of the library district, call an election and submit to the electors of the district the proposition of whether the bonds of the district shall be issued and sold for the purpose of raising money for any or all of the following purposes:

(a) The purchase of suitable lots.

(b) Procuring plans and specifications and erecting a suitable building.

(c) Furnishing and equipping the building and fencing and ornamenting the grounds, for the accommodation of the union high school library.

(d) Any or all of the purposes of this chapter.

(e) Liquidating any indebtedness incurred for the purposes.

(f) Refunding any outstanding valid indebtedness evidenced by bonds or warrants of the district.

(Stats.1976, c. 1010, § 2, operative April 30, 1977.)

§ 18511. Costs included in determining the amount of bonds to be issued and sold

In determining the amount of bonds to be issued and sold, the board of trustees may include:

(a) Legal or other fees incidental to or connected with the authorization, issuance and sale of the bonds.

(b) The costs of printing the bonds and other costs and expenses incidental to or connected with the authorization, issuance and sale of the bonds.

If such a determination is made, the proceeds of the sale of the bonds may be used to pay such costs and fees.

(Stats.1976, c. 1010, § 2, operative April 30, 1977.)

§ 18512. Hours for polls to be open

The hours during which the polls shall be opened at the election shall be as established by the board, but in no event for less than nine hours.

(Stats.1976, c. 1010, § 2, operative April 30, 1977.)

§ 18513. Method of voting

Voting shall be by ballot, without reference to the general election law in regard to form of ballot or manner of voting, except that the words to appear on the ballot shall be "Bonds—Yes" and "Bonds—No." Persons voting at the bond election shall put a cross (+) upon their ballot with pencil or ink, after the words "Bonds—Yes" or "Bonds—No," as the case may be, to indicate whether they have voted for or against the issuance of the bonds. The ballot shall be handed by the elector voting to the inspector, who shall then, in his presence, deposit it in the ballot box, and the judges shall enter the elector's name on the poll list.

(Stats.1976, c. 1010, § 2, operative April 30, 1977.)

§ 18514. Canvass of returns

On the seventh day after the election, at 8 o'clock p. m., the returns having been made to the board of trustees, the board shall meet and canvass the returns.

(Stats.1976, c. 1010, § 2, operative April 30, 1977.)

§ 18515. Favorable vote

If it appears that two-thirds of the votes cast at the election are in favor of issuing the bonds, the board shall cause an entry of the fact to be made upon its minutes and shall certify to the board of supervisors of the county all the proceedings had in the premises.

(Stats.1976, c. 1010, § 2, operative April 30, 1977.)

§ 18516. Notice of election

Notice of election shall be given substantially in the manner and for the time provided in Section 18331.

(Stats.1976, c. 1010, § 2, operative April 30, 1977.)

§ 18517. Consolidation with other election

Any election called pursuant to this article may be consolidated with any other election pursuant to the provisions of Chapter 4 (commencing with Section 23300) of Part 2 of Division 14 of the Elections Code. In such event, the provisions of law governing such other election with respect to the manner of marking ballots and hours of elections shall apply.

(Stats.1976, c. 1010, § 2, operative April 30, 1977. Amended by Stats.1977, c. 1205, § 20.)

§ 18518. Taxpayers' substantial rights affected to invalidate election

No error, irregularity, or omission which does not affect the substantial rights of the taxpayers within the district or the electors voting at any election at which bonds of any district are authorized to be issued shall invalidate the election or any bonds authorized by such election.

(Stats.1976, c. 1010, § 2, operative April 30, 1977.)

§ 18530. Issuance of bonds

After the provisions of Sections 18510 to 18515, inclusive, have been complied with, the board of supervisors shall issue the bonds of the district, to the number and amount provided in the proceedings, payable out of the building fund of the district, naming it, and the money shall be raised by taxation upon the taxable property in the district, for the redemption of the bonds and the payment of the interest thereon.

(Stats.1976, c. 1010, § 2, operative April 30, 1977.)

§ 18531.   Limitation on total amount of bonds issued

The total amount of bonds issued, shall not exceed 5 percent of the taxable property of the district, as shown by the last equalized assessment book of the county.

(Stats.1976, c. 1010, § 2, operative April 30, 1977.)

§ 18532.   Interest

The bonds shall not bear a rate of interest greater than 8 percent, payable annually or semiannually.

(Stats.1976, c. 1010, § 2, operative April 30, 1977.)

§ 18533.   Form of bonds and interest coupons

The board of supervisors by an order entered upon its minutes shall prescribe the form of the bonds and of the interest coupons attached thereto.

(Stats.1976, c. 1010, § 2, operative April 30, 1977.)

§ 18534.   Time of payment

The board of supervisors by an order entered upon its minutes shall fix the time when the whole or any part of the principal of the bonds will be payable, which shall not be more than 40 years from the date thereof.

(Stats.1976, c. 1010, § 2, operative April 30, 1977.)

§ 18534.3.   Division into series bonds

The board of supervisors may divide the principal amount of any issue into two or more series and fix different dates for the bonds of each series.   The bonds of one series may be made payable at different times from those of any other series.

(Added by Stats.1977, c. 36, § 408, urgency, eff. April 29, 1977, operative April 30, 1977.)

§ 18534.5.   Redemption prior to maturity

The board of supervisors may provide for redemption of bonds before maturity at prices determined by it.   A bond shall not be subject to call or redemption prior to maturity unless it contains a recital to that effect.

(Added by Stats.1977, c. 36, § 409, urgency, eff. April 29, 1977, operative April 30, 1977.)

§ 18535.   Sale of bonds

The bonds shall be sold in the manner prescribed by the board of supervisors, but for not less than 95 percent of par.

(Stats.1976, c. 1010, § 2, operative April 30, 1977. Amended by Stats.1977, c. 36, § 74, urgency, eff. April 29, 1977, operative April 30, 1977.)

§ 18536. Deposits and withdrawal of proceeds

The proceeds of the sale of the bonds shall be deposited in the county treasury to the credit of the building fund of the library district, and shall be drawn out for the purposes for which the bonds were issued as other library money is drawn out.

(Stats.1976, c. 1010, § 2, operative April 30, 1977.)

§ 18550. Petition for withdrawal and cancellation of unsold bonds

Whenever any bonds issued under the provisions of this chapter remain unsold for the period of six months after having been offered for sale in the manner prescribed by the board of supervisors, the board of trustees of the library district for or on account of which the bonds were issued, or of any library district composed wholly or partly of territory which, at the time of holding the election authorizing the issuance of the bonds, was embraced within the district for or on account of which the bonds were issued, may petition the board of supervisors to cause the unsold bonds to be withdrawn from market and canceled.

(Stats.1976, c. 1010, § 2, operative April 30, 1977.)

§ 18551. Notice of hearing on petition

Upon receiving the petition, signed by a majority of the members of the board of trustees, the supervisors shall fix a time for hearing the petition, which shall not be more than 30 days thereafter, and shall cause a notice, stating the time and place of hearing, and the object of the petition in general terms, to be published for 10 days prior to the day of hearing in a newspaper published in the library district, if there is one, and if there is no newspaper published in the library district, then in a newspaper published at the county seat of the county in which the library district or part thereof is situated.

(Stats.1976, c. 1010, § 2, operative April 30, 1977.)

§ 18552. Hearing and order for cancellation

At the time and place designated in the notice for hearing the petition, or at any subsequent time to which the hearing may be postponed, the supervisors shall hear any reasons that may be submitted for or against the granting of the petition, and if they deem it for the best interests of the library district named in the petition that the unsold bonds be canceled, they shall make and enter an order in the minutes of their proceedings that the unsold bonds be canceled.

(Stats.1976, c. 1010, § 2, operative April 30, 1977.)

§ 18553.   Effect of cancellation order

Thereupon the bonds and the vote by which they were authorized to be issued, shall cease to be of any validity whatever.

(Stats.1976, c. 1010, § 2, operative April 30, 1977.)

§ 18555.   Issuance of unsold bonds

When the board of trustees of the library district determines that the purpose and object of the bonds has been accomplished, it may request the board of supervisors to cause any unsold bonds to be issued and sold and the proceeds thereof used for any or all of the purposes set forth in Section 18510.

(Added by Stats.1977, c. 36, § 410, urgency, eff. April 29, 1977, operative April 30, 1977.)

§ 18556.   Notice of hearing

Upon receiving the request, signed by a majority of the members of the board of trustees, the supervisors shall fix a time for hearing the request, which shall not be more than 30 days thereafter, and shall cause a notice, stating the time and place of hearing, and the object of the request in general terms, to be published for 10 days prior to the day of hearing in a newspaper published in the library district, if there is one, and if there is no newspaper published in the library district, then in a newspaper published at the county seat of the county in which the library district or part thereof is situated.

(Added by Stats.1977, c. 36, § 410, urgency, eff. April 29, 1977, operative April 30, 1977.)

§ 18557.   Hearing and granting request

At the time and place designated in the notice for hearing the request, or at any subsequent time to which the hearing may be postponed, the supervisors shall hear any reasons that may be submitted for or against the granting of the request. If, before the conclusion of the hearing, a petition signed by registered voters within the district equal to not less than 10 percent of the vote cast within the boundaries of the district for all candidates for governor at the last gubernatorial election requesting an election is not filed, the board of supervisors may, if they determine it to be for the best interests of the library district, grant the request. In such event, they shall make and enter an order in the minutes of their proceedings that the unsold bonds shall be sold and the proceeds used for the purposes specified in the request.

(Added by Stats.1977, c. 36, § 410, urgency, eff. April 29, 1977, operative April 30, 1977.)

§ 18558.   Submission to voters

In the event a petition, as set forth in Section 18557, is filed, the board of supervisors shall not grant the request without first submitting the question to the voters in the same manner and with the same effect as provided for a referendum by the electors of a district pursuant to Section 5200 of the Elections Code.

(Added by Stats.1977, c. 36, § 410, urgency, eff. April 29, 1977, operative April 30, 1977.)

§ 18560.   Tax levy

The board of supervisors, at the time of making a levy of taxes for county purposes, shall levy a tax for that year upon the taxable property in the district, at the equalized assessed value thereof for that year, for the interest and redemption of the bonds.

(Stats.1976, c. 1010, § 2, operative April 30, 1977.)

§ 18561.   Amount of tax

The tax shall not be less than sufficient to pay the interest of the bonds for that year, and such portion of the principal as is to become due during the year.   In any event the tax shall be high enough to raise, annually, for the first half of the term the bonds have to run, a sufficient sum to pay the interest thereon, and, during the balance of the term, high enough to pay the annual interest, and to pay annually, a proportion of the principal of the bonds equal to a sum produced by taking the whole amount of the bonds outstanding and dividing it by the number of years the bonds then have to run.

(Stats.1976, c. 1010, § 2, operative April 30, 1977.)

§ 18562.   Deposit and use of money collected

All money levied, when collected, shall be paid into the county treasury to the credit of the library district, and be used for the payment of principal and interest on the bonds, and for no other purpose.

(Stats.1976, c. 1010, § 2, operative April 30, 1977.)

§ 18570.   Payment of principal and interest

The principal and interest on the bonds shall be paid by the county treasurer, upon the warrant of the county auditor, out of the fund provided therefor.

(Stats.1976, c. 1010, § 2, operative April 30, 1977.)

§ 18571.   Cancellation of bonds

The county auditor shall cancel and file with the county treasurer the bonds and coupons as rapidly as they are paid.

(Stats.1976, c. 1010, § 2, operative April 30, 1977.)

SCHOOL LIBRARIES
(West's Annotated California Codes, Education Code, 1982,
s.18100-18172, 1770-1775.)

§ 18100.   School library services required

The governing board of each school district or community college district shall provide school library services for the pupils and teachers of the district by establishing and maintaining school libraries or by contractual arrangements with another public agency.

(Stats.1976, c. 1010, § 2, operative April 30, 1977.)

§ 18101.   Standards

The State Board of Education shall adopt standards, rules and regulations for school library services.

The Board of Governors of the California Community Colleges shall adopt standards, rules, and regulations for school library services for community colleges.

(Stats.1976, c. 1010, § 2, operative April 30, 1977.)

§ 18102.   Establishment and maintenance

Libraries may be established and maintained under the control of the governing board of any school district or community college district.

(Stats.1976, c. 1010, § 2, operative April 30, 1977.)

§ 18103.   Libraries open to teachers and pupils

The libraries shall be open to the use of the teachers and the pupils of the school district or community college district during the schoolday.   In addition, the libraries may be open at such other hours, including evenings and Saturdays, as the governing board may determine.   Libraries open to serve students during evening and Saturday hours shall be under the supervision of certificated personnel. Certificated personnel employed to perform full-time services in an elementary, junior high, or high school during the regular schoolday, may supervise, but shall not without their consent be required to supervise, a school library on evenings or Saturdays.   If such a person agrees to supervise the school library during Saturday or evening hours, he shall be compensated in the amounts determined by the governing board of the district as indicated on the salary schedule.

(Stats.1976, c. 1010, § 2, operative April 30, 1977.).

§ 18110. Adoption of book lists and other library materials

County boards of education may adopt lists of books and other library materials for districts not employing a superintendent of schools or a librarian for full time. The lists may be distributed to all school districts or community college districts in a county for use in the selection of books and other library materials.

(Stats.1976, c. 1010, § 2, operative April 30, 1977.)

§ 18111. Exclusion of books by governing board

The governing board of any school district or community college district may exclude from schools and school libraries all books, publications, or papers of a sectarian, partisan, or denominational character.

(Stats.1976, c. 1010, § 2, operative April 30, 1977.)

§ 18120. Appointment and qualification of district librarian

The governing board of a school district or community college district maintaining its own library or libraries may appoint a librarian or librarians to staff such libraries provided they qualify as librarians pursuant to Section 44868 or 87435.

(Stats.1976, c. 1010, § 2, operative April 30, 1977.)

§ 18121. Rules and regulations

The governing board of a school district or community college district is accountable for the proper care and preservation of the school libraries of the district, and may make all necessary rules and regulations not provided for by the State Board of Education, or the Superintendent of Public Instruction, or the board of governors and not inconsistent therewith.

(Stats.1976, c. 1010, § 2, operative April 30, 1977.)

§ 18122. Annual report by governing board to Department of Education

The governing board of a school district shall, on or before August 31st, in each year, report to the State Department of Education or the board of governors as appropriate, on the condition of school libraries, for the year ending June 30th preceding. The report shall, in addition to other matters deemed expedient by the governing board or the librarians, contain such statistical and other information as is deemed desirable by the State Department of Education or the board of governors. For this purpose the State Department of Education or the board of governors may send to the several districts under their supervision, instructions or question blanks so as to obtain the material for a comparative study of library conditions in the state.

(Stats.1976, c. 1010, § 2, operative April 30, 1977.)

§ 18130. Contract with county library

Whenever the county in which a district is situated maintains a county library, the governing board of any school district or community college district may agree with the proper authorities of the county to contract for the provision of school library services by the county library. Either the governing board of the school district or community college district or the governing body of the county library may initiate proceedings for the provision of library services for the schools of the district. Such agreements shall be reviewed annually by contracting parties.

(Stats.1976, c. 1010, § 2, operative April 30, 1977.)

§ 18131. Purchase of books by school districts

Notwithstanding any other section of this article to the contrary, school districts or community college districts may purchase textbooks, reference books, periodicals, and other publications approved by any board authorized to adopt such materials in addition to those furnished by the county library.

(Stats.1976, c. 1010, § 2, operative April 30, 1977.)

§ 18132. Use of transferred funds

All funds transferred to a county library pursuant to this article shall be used by the county library only for: (a) the acquisition of such books and other materials as are adopted by the body authorized to adopt courses of study for the school districts or community college districts which have entered into an agreement for the provision of school library services by the county library, and (b) the care and distribution of the books and other materials to schools which are eligible to receive school library services from the county library.

(Stats.1976, c. 1010, § 2, operative April 30, 1977.)

§ 18133. Disposal of books and materials

The county librarian may (a) at his discretion dispose of books and other materials no longer fit for service, and (b) with the approval of the county board of education dispose of any books or other materials no longer needed by the course of study.

(Stats.1976, c. 1010, § 2, operative April 30, 1977.)

§ 18134. Agreement with city

In any city conducting a public library owned and managed by the city, the governing board of any school district or community college district may enter into an arrangement with the governing body of the public library of the city similar to the arrangement authorized by this article between the governing boards of any school district or community college district and the county library.

(Stats.1976, c. 1010, § 2, operative April 30, 1977.)

§ 18135. Transfer of fund

Whenever an agreement is made that school library services will be provided by a city, or county library, the county, or city and county, or city superintendent of schools may draw a warrant for the whole amount stipulated in the agreement, payable to the proper authorities of the library, upon the filing with him of a copy of the resolution of the governing board of the district embodying the agreement made with the library. The copy shall be duly certified as correct by the clerk of the district or other proper officer.

(Stats.1976, c. 1010, § 2, operative April 30, 1977.)

§ 18136. High school district agreement with county for use of county free library

The governing board of any high school district lying wholly or partly within a county maintaining a county free library may enter into a contract or agreement with the board of supervisors of the county by which the high school district may secure the advantages of the county free library upon such terms and conditions as are fixed in the contract or agreement.

(Stats.1976, c. 1010, § 2, operative April 30, 1977.)

§ 18137. Care of property

Whenever the governing board of a school district or community college district enters into an agreement with a county or city library for school library services the district shall provide for the care and custody of and assume responsibility for the books and other property delivered to it subject to the rules and regulations of the county or city library and the terms of the agreement.

(Stats.1976, c. 1010, § 2, operative April 30, 1977.)

§ 18138. Termination of affiliation

With the consent of the county superintendent of schools the governing board of the school district or community college district may agree with the proper authorities of the county or city to terminate the affiliation of the district with the county or city library. Either the governing board of the school district or community college district or the governing body of the county library may initiate termination proceedings. The proceedings shall be terminated prior to the first day of February of the school year in which begun and may provide for either:

(a) The complete withdrawal of affiliation effective on the first day of July next succeeding, or

(b) A gradual withdrawal over a period of not to exceed three years beginning on the first day of July next succeeding the termination of proceedings.

The governing board of the school district or community college district shall enter into a written agreement with the proper authorities of the city or county providing for the terms of the gradual withdrawal, including the period to be covered, not to exceed three years, the amount of payment for each year, and the amount of service to be rendered.

Unless otherwise provided in the withdrawal agreement, the books purchased by a district during the period of the withdrawal become the property of the district.

All books purchased by a district shall be approved by the body authorized to adopt courses of study for the school districts or community college districts of the county.

(Stats.1976, c. 1010, § 2, operative April 30, 1977.)

§ 18139.   Proceedings for termination of library services

With the consent of the county board of education, in those counties in which the county superintendent of schools performs library services for the school library of any district, the governing board of the school district or community college district may agree with the proper authorities of the county to terminate the affiliation of the district with the county superintendent of schools with respect to library services. The proceedings shall be terminated prior to the first day of February of the school year in which begun and may provide for either:

(a) The complete withdrawal of affiliation effective on the first day of July next succeeding, or

(b) A gradual withdrawal over a period of not to exceed five years beginning on the first day of July next succeeding the termination of proceedings.

The county board of education shall adopt rules and regulations governing such a gradual withdrawal, including the period to be covered, not to exceed five years, the amount of payment for each year, and the amount of service to be rendered. The terms of such gradual withdrawal shall comply with such rules and regulations.

(Stats.1976, c. 1010, § 2, operative April 30, 1977.)

§ 18170. Expenditure of library fund

The governing board of any school district or community college district shall expend the library fund, together with such money as is added thereto by donation, in the purchase of school apparatus and books for a school library, including books for supplementary work.
(Stats.1976, c. 1010, § 2, operative April 30, 1977.)

§ 18171. Itemized bill required

No warrant shall be drawn by the superintendent of schools upon the order of any governing board of any school district or community college district against the library fund of any district unless the order is accompanied by an itemized bill, showing the books and apparatus, and the price of each in payment of which the order is drawn, and unless the books and apparatus, except in the case of library books and apparatus purchased by a district employing a district superintendent of schools or a school librarian for full time, have been adopted by the county, city, or city and county board of education.
(Stats.1976, c. 1010, § 2, operative April 30, 1977.)

§ 18172. Approval required prior to purchase

All orders of the governing board of any school district or community college district for books or apparatus shall in every case be submitted to the superintendent of schools of the county, city, or city and county, respectively, for his approval, before the books or apparatus shall be purchased.
(Stats.1976, c. 1010, § 2, operative April 30, 1977.)

§ 1770. Provision of library services

(a) The county superintendent of schools may, with the approval of the board of supervisors and the county board of education, agree with the county librarian to take over all existing contracts for supplementary books and other material adopted for the course of study between the school districts or community college districts and the county librarian entered into pursuant to the provisions of Sections 18130 to 18139, inclusive. Thereafter the county superintendent of schools shall generally perform such library services for the school districts or community college districts as were theretofore performed by the county library.

(b) After the above agreement has been entered into, the governing board of any district which had not yet joined the county library may enter into an agreement with the county superintendent of schools for the performance of school library services upon such terms and conditions as are fixed in the contracts or agreements.

(c) Whenever the county superintendent of schools performs school library services for any district, the provisions of Sections 18130 to 18139, inclusive, so far as applicable, shall control. The county superintendent shall employ a librarian holding a valid credential authorizing services as a librarian issued by the State Board of Education or Commission for Teacher Preparation and Licensing. He shall also employ such assistants as may be necessary to carry on this service. The cost of the salaries of such librarian and assistants, and the other necessary expenses of maintenance of the library, including necessary supplies, equipment, and books, may be paid from the county school service fund.

(Stats.1976, c. 1010, § 2, operative April 30, 1977.)

§ 1771. Establishment and maintenance of county school library service

(a) The county superintendent of schools of any county in which no county library is maintained may, with the approval of the county board of education, establish and maintain a county school library service for such elementary school districts of the county as elect to participate in such service.

(b) Upon the governing board of any elementary school district electing to participate in such service, the governing board of the district shall enter into an agreement with the county superintendent of schools, and the provisions of Sections 18130 to 18139, inclusive, shall control and be applicable in the same manner as they apply to a school district which enters into an agreement for school library services from the county library.

(c) The county superintendent of schools shall have the same powers, duties, responsibilities, and jurisdiction with respect to the furnishing and performance of library services to elementary school districts which have elected to participate in the county school library service as may be exercised by a county library with respect to school library services.

(d) Whenever the county superintendent of schools establishes and maintains a county school library service pursuant to subdivision (a) of this section, he shall employ a librarian holding a valid credential authorizing service as a school librarian issued by the State Board of Education or Commission for Teacher Preparation and Licensing.

(e) The county superintendents of schools of two more contiguous counties which have established county school library services under the provisions of this section may cooperate with each other and to that end may enter into agreements with each other, and may do any and all things necessary or convenient to aid and cooperate in carrying out the provisions of this section.

(Stats.1976, c. 1010, § 2, operative April 30, 1977.)

§ 1772. Transfer of funds to purchase books

The county superintendent of schools may, with the approval of the county board of education, agree with the proper authorities of the county to transfer funds from the county school service fund to the county library for the purchase of such books and other materials as are adopted by the body authorized to adopt courses of study for the school districts of this county.

(Stats.1976, c. 1010, § 2, operative April 30, 1977.)

§ 1773. Agreement to provide school library services in emergency elementary schools

The county superintendent of schools of any county maintaining one or more emergency elementary schools may, if the county maintains a county library, enter into an agreement with the proper authorities of the county to provide school library services in each of the schools under such terms and conditions as may be agreed upon. The agreement may, among other matters, provide for the payment by the county superintendent of schools to the proper authorities for the use of the county library from the county school service fund of such money at such times as may be agreed upon. All money transferred shall be used solely by the authorities of the county library for the purchase of books and other materials as may be adopted by the county board of education and for the care and distribution of such books and other materials to the schools.

(Stats.1976, c. 1010, § 2, operative April 30, 1977.)

§ 1774. Establishment and operation of county teachers' library

(a) The county superintendent of schools may establish a county teachers' library and expend from the county school service fund such amounts as are necessary for the purchase of books therefor and for the payment of the necessary expenses of maintenance thereof.

(b) If there is a county library in any county, the county superintendent of schools may enter into an agreement with the county library for the transfer to it of all books and other property belonging to the county teachers' library and may order such sums to be transferred from the county school service fund as are necessary for expenditure for the purchase and maintenance of books of professional interest to teachers. Thereupon the teachers' library shall be administered as a part of the county library.

(Stats.1976, c. 1010, § 2, operative April 30, 1977.)

§ 1775. Annual report to State Department of Education

Whenever the county superintendent of schools assumes responsibility for the establishment of a library or the performance of library services pursuant to this article, the county superintendent shall, on or before August 31st, in each year, report to the State Department of Education on the condition of the libraries under his supervision, for the year ending June 30th preceding. The reports of the superintendent shall, in addition to other matters deemed expedient by the librarian and the superintendent, contain such statistical and other information as is deemed desirable by the State Department of Education. For this purpose the State Department of Education may send to the several county superintendents or librarians instructions or question blanks so as to obtain the material for a comparative study of library conditions in the state.

(Stats.1976, c. 1010, § 2, operative April 30, 1977.)

COUNTY LAW LIBRARIES

(West's Annotated California Codes, Business and Professional
Code, 1982, s.6300-6365.)

§ 6300. Existence of boards in counties

There is in each county of this State a board of law library trustees, which governs the law library established for the county under the provisions of this chapter.

(Added by Stats.1941, c. 452, p. 1742, § 1.)

§ 6301. Constitution of boards

A board of law library trustees is constituted as follows:

(a) In a county where there are no more than three judges of the superior court, each of such judges is ex officio a trustee; in a county where there are more than three judges of the superior court, the judges of the court shall elect three of their number to serve as trustees. However, where there are no more than three judges of the superior court, the judges may at their option select only one of their number to serve as a trustee, and in such event they shall appoint two additional trustees who are members of the bar of the county.

Any judge who is an ex officio or elected member may at his option designate a member of the bar of the county to act for him as trustee.

(b) In a county * * * with no more than two municipal and justice courts * * * the judges of such court or courts shall elect one of their number to serve as trustee. In a county * * * with three or more municipal and justice courts * * * the judges of such courts may elect two of their number to serve as trustees.

(c) The chairman of the board of supervisors is ex officio a trustee, but the board of supervisors at the request of the chairman may appoint a member of the bar of the county or any other member of the board of supervisors of the county to serve as trustee in place of said chairman. The appointment of the person selected in lieu of the chairman of the board of supervisors shall expire when a new chairman of the board of supervisors is selected, and such appointment shall not be subject to the provisions of Section 6302.

(d) The board of supervisors shall appoint as many additional trustees, who are members of the bar of the county, as may be necessary to constitute a board of * * * six members in any county where the municipal <u>and justice</u> courts have elected one member, or of seven members in any county where the municipal <u>and justice</u> courts have elected two members to serve as trustees.

(Amended by Stats.1977, c. 1257, p. 4754, § 1, urgency, eff. Oct. 3, 1977.)

§ 6301.5 Board of not less than three members in certain counties

In any county in which * * * there is no county bar association, if the board of supervisors determines that there is not a sufficient number of members of the State Bar <u>residing, and</u> with their principal places of office for the practice of law, in the county eligible for appointment to the board of library trustees by the board of supervisors pursuant to subdivision (d) of Section 6301 for the constitution of a * * * <u>six-member or seven-member</u> board of library trustees, the board of library trustees may consist of not less than three members.

(Amended by Stats.1977, c. 1257, p. 4754, § 2, urgency, eff. Oct. 3, 1977.)

Asterisks * * * indicate deletions by amendment

<u>Underline</u> **indicates changes or additions by amendment**

§ 6302.   Appointments of trustees

Appointments of trustees which are to be made by the board of supervisors of the county shall be made at the first meeting of the board of supervisors after the establishment of a law library in the county, the appointees to serve until the first meeting of the board of supervisors in the succeeding January. The board shall, at any such meeting in each succeeding January, appoint such trustees to serve for the term of one year.

(Added by Stats.1941, c. 452, p. 1742, § 1.)

§ 6303.   Compensation of trustee

The office of trustee is honorary, without salary or other compensation.

(Added by Stats.1941, c. 452, p. 1742, § 1.)

§ 6304.   Meetings of trustees

Each board of law library trustees shall meet regularly each month on such day as it shall appoint, but if it appoint no day, it shall meet on the first Tuesday after the first Saturday of each month, and any board may meet at such other times as it may appoint, at a place to be designated for that purpose. The president of the board may call a special meeting at any time for the transaction of necessary business. A majority of the members constitutes a quorum for business, and an affirmative vote of a majority of the members is required to exercise the powers of the board.

(Added by Stats.1941, c. 452, p. 1743, § 1. Amended by Stats.1943, c. 776, p. 2557, § 1; Stats.1945, c. 1113, p. 2122, § 1.)

§ 6305.   Removal of trustees; vacancies

A board of law library trustees may remove any trustee, except an ex officio trustee, who neglects to attend or who absents himself from the meetings of the board, and may fill all vacancies that from any cause occur in the board.

(Added by Stats.1941, c. 452, p. 1743, § 1.)

§ 6306.   President of board

Each board shall appoint one of its number as president.

(Added by Stats.1941, c. 452, p. 1743, § 1.)

§ 6307.   Secretary; records; seal

Each board shall elect a secretary, who shall keep a full statement and account of all property, money, receipts and expenditures, and shall keep a record and full minutes in writing, with the ayes and noes at length, of all proceedings of the board.

The secretary may certify to such proceedings, or any part thereof, under his hand, verified by an official seal adopted and provided by the board for that purpose.

(Added by Stats.1941, c. 452, p. 1743, § 1.)

§ 6320.   Disposition of moneys

All money collected for the law library in each county, must be deposited with the treasurer of the county, who must keep the same separate and apart in a trust fund or trust account, to be disbursed by the board of law library trustees. Money may be disbursed only as in this chapter provided, and only for the purposes herein authorized.

Whenever a law library and a board of trustees to govern the same, is in existence under the provisions of any law, other than the law superseded by this chapter, in any county, or city and county, in this State, money so collected shall be paid into the hands of those, and in the manner, provided by such law.

(Added by Stats.1941, c. 452, p. 1743, § 1. Amended by Stats.1941, c. 453, p. 1747, § 1; Stats.1943, c. 776, p. 2557, § 2; Stats.1961, c. 396, p. 1453, § 20.)

§ 6321.   Filing fee

On the commencement in, or the removal to, the superior court of any county in this State, of any civil action, proceeding, or appeal, and on the commencement in, or removal to, the municipal court or justice court in any county, of any civil action or proceeding, the party instituting such proceeding, or filing the first papers, shall pay to the clerk of the court, for the law library, on filing the first papers, the sum of one dollar ($1) as costs, in addition to the fees fixed by law.

(Added by Stats.1941, c. 452, p. 1743, § 1. Amended by Stats.1955, c. 1117, p. 2113, § 1.)

§ 6322. First appearance fee

Thereafter, any defendant, respondent, adverse party, or intervening party, on his first appearance in a superior, or municipal, or justice court, or any number of such defendants, respondents, or parties, appearing jointly, shall pay to the clerk of the court, for the law library, the sum of one dollar ($1) as costs, in addition to the fees fixed by law.
(Amended by Stats.1977, c. 1257, p. 4755, § 3, urgency, eff. Oct. 3, 1977.)

§ 6322.1 Increase of fees; effective date

(a) Except in counties containing a population of 4,000,000 and over, the board of supervisors of any county may increase the costs provided in Section 6321 and 6322 to not more than * * * twelve dollars ($12) for each event therein described whenever it shall determine that the increase is necessary to defray the expenses of the law library.

(b) In counties containing a population of 4,000,000 and over, the board of law library trustees may increase the costs provided in Sections 6321 and 6322 to not more than five dollars ($5) for each event therein described whenever it shall determine that the increase is necessary to defray the expenses of the law library.

(c) Notwithstanding the provisions of any other section, any increase or decrease in costs of law library fees in any county shall not be effective until January 1 of the year next following adoption by the board of supervisors or the law library board of trustees of such increase or decrease.
(Amended by Stats.1974, c. 647, p. 1510, § 1; Stats.1980, c. 64, p. —, § 1.)

§ 6323. Costs; exemptions

Such costs shall not be collected, however, in small claims courts, nor shall they be collected * * * on the filing of a petition for letters of adoption, or the filing of a disclaimer.
(Amended by Stats.1977, c. 1257, p. 4755, § 4, urgency, eff. Jan. 3, 1977.)

Asterisks * * * indicate deletions by amendment
Underline indicates changes or additions by amendment

§ 6324. Additional payments to fund

The board of supervisors of any county may set apart from the fees collected by the county clerk, sums not exceeding one thousand two hundred dollars ($1,200) in any one fiscal year, to be paid by the county clerk into the law library fund in addition to the moneys otherwise provided to be deposited in that fund by law. The board of supervisors may also appropriate from the county treasury for law library purposes such additional sums as may in their discretion appear proper. When so paid into the law library fund, such sums shall constitute a part of the fund and be used for the same purposes.

(Added by Stats.1941, c. 452, p. 1744, § 1. Amended by Stats.1941, c. 453, p. 1748, § 4.)

§ 6325. Orders and demands; auditing, payment and record

The orders and demands of the trustees of the law library, when

duly made and authenticated as hereinafter provided, shall be verified and audited by the auditing officer, and paid by the treasurer of
the county out of the law library fund. Full entry and record shall
be kept as in other cases.

(Added by Stats.1941, c. 452, p. 1744, § 1.)

§ 6326.　Revolving fund

A revolving fund of not more than　*　*　*　two thousand five hundred dollars
($2,500) may be established from money in the law library fund, by resolution of
the board of law library trustees, for expenditures of not exceeding one hundred
fifty dollars ($150) each for purposes for which the law library fund may lawfully
be expended. The board shall prescribe the procedure by which money may be
drawn from the revolving fund, the records to be kept, and the manner in which
reimbursements shall be made to the revolving fund by demand and order from
the law library fund. All or any part of the money in the revolving fund may be
deposited in a commercial account in a bank, subject to payments of not exceeding
*　*　*　one hundred fifty dollars ($150) each by check on the signature of the
secretary or any other person or persons designated by the board.
(Amended by Stats.1980, c. 64, p. ——, § 2.)

Asterisks　*　*　*　Indicate deletions by amendment

Underline indicates changes or additions by amendment

§ 6340.　Duty to maintain library.　Each board of law library
trustees shall establish and maintain a law library at the county seat
of the county in which it is appointed and may lease suitable quarters
therefor or construct quarters pursuant to the provisions of this chapter, and may provide leased or constructed quarters with suitable
furniture and utility services.　(Added Stats.1941, c. 452, p. 1744, § 1,
as amended Stats.1959, c. 1076, p. 3138, § 1.)

§ 6341.　Branch libraries

Any board of law library trustees may establish and maintain a
branch of the law library in any city in the county, other than the
county seat, in which a session of the superior court or of a municipal court is held, or in which a municipal court has been authorized
by statute but has not yet begun to operate. In any city constituting
the county seat, any board of law library trustees may establish and
maintain a branch of the law library at any location therein where
four or more judges of the municipal court are designated to hold
sessions more than 10 miles distant from the principal office of the
municipal court. In any city and county any board of law library
trustees may establish and maintain branches of the law library. A
branch is in all respects a part of the law library and is governed accordingly.

(Added by Stats.1941, c. 452, p. 1744, § 1. Amended by Stats.1949, c. 809, p.
1553, § 1; Stats.1959, c. 739, p. 2728, § 1; Stats.1961, c. 803, p. 2068, § 1.)

§ 6342. Powers of trustees; disposition of fund

A board of law library trustees may order the drawing and payment, upon properly authenticated vouchers, duly certified by the president and secretary, of money from out of the law library fund, for any liability or expenditure herein authorized, and generally do all that may be necessary to carry into effect the provisions of this chapter.

(Added by Stats.1941, c. 452, p. 1744, § 1.)

§ 6343. Rules, regulations and by-laws; expenditures

A board may make and enforce all rules, regulations, and by-laws necessary for the administration, government, and protection of the law library, and of all property belonging thereto, or that may be loaned, devised, bequeathed, or donated to it. A board may make expenditures for the suitable maintenance, repair, protection and insurance against loss of such property, both real and personal.

(Added by Stats.1941, c. 452, p. 1744, § 1. Amended by Stats.1941, c. 453, p. 1748, § 6.)

§ 6344. Books and other property

A board may purchase books, journals, other publications, and other personal property. It may dispose of obsolete or duplicate books, and other unneeded or unusable property.

(Added by Stats.1941, c. 452, p. 1744, § 1. Amended by Stats.1945, c. 1113, p. 2122, § 2.)

§ 6345. Librarian and subordinates

A board may appoint a librarian and define the powers and prescribe the duties of any officers, determine the number, and elect all necessary subordinate officers and assistants, and at its pleasure remove any officer or assistant.

For the purpose of facilitating the recruitment of professional and technically trained persons to fill positions for which there is a shortage of qualified applicants, a board may authorize payment of all or a part of the reasonable travel expense of applicants who are called for interview and all or part of the reasonable travel and moving expense of persons who change their place of residence to accept employment with the law library.

(Added by Stats.1941, c. 452, p. 1744, § 2. Amended by Stats.1963, c. 39, p. 648, § 1.)

§ 6346. Salaries; bonds

A board shall fix the salaries of the secretary, librarian, and other officers and assistants, and may require a bond of any officer or assistant, in such sum as it may fix. The premium on any such bond given by an authorized surety company may be paid from the law library fund.

(Added by Stats.1941, c. 452, p. 1745. Amended by Stats.1941, c. 453, p. 1749, § 7.)

§ 6346.5   Membership in state employees' retirement system

A board of law library trustees may contract with the Board of Administration of the State Employees' Retirement System, to make all or any of the officers or employees of the law library members of the system.

(Added by Stats.1943, c. 948, p. 2819, § 1.)

§ 6346.6   Election for membership in county system; contributions

As an alternative to Section 6346.5, a board of law library trustees may, with the consent of the board of administration of the applicable retirement system, elect to make all or any of the officers or employees of the law library members of the retirement system which covers the officers and employees of the county in which the law library is established and to have the law library officers and employees deemed to be county employees for purposes of that retirement system. In the event of such an election, the employer contributions on behalf of the covered law library officers and employees shall be made from law library funds.

(Added by Stats.1981, c. 156, p. ——, § 1.)

§ 6347.   Contracts with law library associations

A board may contract with any law library association to make use of its library as a public law library, under proper rules and regulations to be prescribed by the board, either by lease or such other contracts as may best carry into effect the purposes of this chapter.

(Added by Stats.1941, c. 452, p. 1745, § 1.)

§ 6348.   Building or quarters for library

A board may expend surplus funds in excess of ten thousand dollars ($10,000) under its control, not necessary for use to maintain the law library, to acquire or lease real property and erect thereon a library building to house the law library. In the alternative, a board of law library trustees may appropriate from such surplus funds in excess of ten thousand dollars ($10,000), so much as in the discretion of said board may be necessary to obtain adequate quarters for the law library in any building hereafter erected by the board of supervisors of the county in which the law library is maintained. The moneys so appropriated shall not be more than the proportion of the total cost of such building which the space allotted to the law library bears to the total usable space in the building. The moneys so appropriated may be transferred to the board of supervisors of the county for use in erecting the building, or may be paid directly on contracts for the erection thereof made by the board of supervisors.

(Added by Stats.1941, c. 452, p. 1745, § 1.   Amended by Stats.1965, c. 1069, p. 2714, § 1.)

§ 6348.1   Terms and conditions as to quarters; use of state, county or city land

An appropriation to obtain quarters for the law library in a building to be erected by the board of supervisors of the county, may be made subject to such terms and conditions, including approval of plans and specifications, and regarding maintenance and use of the quarters, as may be mutually agreed upon by the board of law library trustees and the board of supervisors.

Where a board of law library trustees determines to erect a library building to house the law library, the State of California or the county or the city in which the building is to be located, may set apart and dedicate or lease land owned by any of them for the permanent use of the building and access thereto.

(Added by Stats.1945, c. 1113, p. 2122, § 3.   Amended by Stats.1965, c. 1069, p. 2715, § 2.)

§ 6348.2   Borrowing for library building

When a board of law library trustees in any county having a population in excess of two million determines to erect a library building to house the law library, it may borrow money for that purpose and repay the loan from its future income.   The board may borrow the money from any person, or private or public agency, or corporation, in an amount not exceeding half of the funds of the board allocated to the construction of the building, upon such terms as may be agreed upon by the board and the lender and approved by resolution of the board of supervisors of the county.

(Added by Stats.1949, c. 1123, p. 2024, § 1.)

§ 6348.3   Courtrooms and offices in library building; lease thereof

A library building erected to house the law library may include not more than four courtrooms with offices in connection therewith, offices for use of a county bar association, and an office for a notary public and public stenographer, which courtrooms and offices the board of law library trustees may lease, the income to be deposited in the law library fund.

(Added by Stats.1941, c. 453, p. 1749, § 8.   Amended by Stats.1965, c. 1069, p. 2715, § 3;   Stats.1967, c. 68, p. 967, § 1.)

§ 6348.4   Sale of realty

Real property acquired by a board other than by dedication, may

be sold by the board to the State of California or to any governmental agency, the proceeds to be deposited in the law library fund.
(Added by Stats.1949, c. 1123, p. 2025, § 2.)

§ 6348.5   Investment of surplus funds

A board of law library trustees may invest surplus funds, with the approval of the county treasurer, in excess of one hundred thousand dollars ($100,000) or of the average annual expenditures of the library for the four fiscal years immediately preceding the investment, whichever is lesser, in bonds of the government of the United States or of this State. Bonds so purchased may be sold at any time in the discretion of the board. In computing average annual expenditures for the purposes of this section, capital expenditures for the purchase of real property and construction of a library building shall not be included.
(Added by Stats.1941, c. 453, p. 1749, § 9.   Amended by Stats.1957, c. 1296, p. 2615, § 1; Stats.1963, c. 39, p. 648, § 2.)

§ 6348.6   Counties with population of 400,000 to 700,000; contracts with board of supervisors

In any county having a population of 400,000 but less than 700,-000, a board of law library trustees may contract with the board of supervisors of the county upon such terms as may be mutually agreeable for the construction by the board of supervisors of a law library building or any part thereof or for quarters in a building to be erected by the board of supervisors. Such agreement may be made subject to such terms and conditions including approval of plans and specifications, regarding the furnishing and equipping of the building or quarters, and regarding maintenance and use of the quarters, as may be mutually agreed upon by the board of law library trustees and the board of supervisors. Such contract may provide that the board of law library trustees shall make payments to the board of supervisors out of future income in payment for constructing or furnishing or equipping such law library building or part thereof or such quarters in a building. Any contract heretofore executed by a board of law library trustees and a board of supervisors, which, if executed subsequent to the effective date of this section would be valid, is hereby ratified and validated.
(Added by Stats.1957, c. 138, p. 733, § 1.)

§ 6349.   Annual report by trustees

Each board of law library trustees, on or before the 15th day of August of each year, shall make an annual report to the board of supervisors of the county in which the law library is maintained, for the preceding fiscal year ending on the 30th day of June. A copy of the report shall be filed with the auditor of the county.

The report shall give the condition of their trust, with full statements of all their property and money received, whence derived, how used and expended, the number of books, periodicals and other publications on hand, the number added by purchase, gift, or otherwise during the year, the number lost or missing, and such other information as might be of interest.

(Added by Stats.1941, c. 452, p. 1745, § 1. Amended by Stats.1970, c. 38, p. 58, § 1; Stats.1970, c. 40, p. 59, § 1.)

§ 6350. Financial report by secretary

A financial report, showing all receipts and disbursements of money, shall be made by the secretary, duly verified by his oath, at the same time that the report of the board is made.

(Added by Stats.1941, c. 452, p. 1745, § 1.)

§ 6360. Use of library; charges

A law library established under the provisions of this chapter shall be free to the judiciary, to State and county officials, to members of the State Bar, and to all residents of the county, for the examination of books and other publications at the library or its branches.

The board of law library trustees may permit the removal of such books and other publications from the library and its branches as it considers proper, subject to such rules, and, in its discretion, the giving of such security, as it may provide to insure the safekeeping and prompt return thereof, but no security shall be required of members of the judiciary or county officials. The board may provide for the levying of fines and charges for violation of the rules, and may make charges to cover the cost of special services, such as the making of photocopies of pages of library books, and messenger service.

The board of law library trustees may require persons other than members of the judiciary, county officials, and members of the bar resident in the county, to pay such dues as the board may fix for the privilege of removing books and other publications from the library.

(Added by Stats.1941, c. 452, p. 1745, § 1. Amended by Stats.1941, c. 453, p. 1749, § 10.)

§ 6361. Quarters and facilities

The board of supervisors of the county in which the law library is established shall provide sufficient quarters for the use of the li-

brary upon request of the board of law library trustees, except that
the board of supervisors need not provide such quarters when the
board of law library trustees determines it has sufficient funds, over
and above those necessary for operation and maintenance expenses,
to provide its own quarters. Such provision may include, with the
room or rooms provided, suitable furniture, window shades, floor cov-
erings, lighting, heat and telephone and janitor service.

(Added by Stats.1941, c. 452, p. 1746, § 1. Amended by Stats.1943, c. 206,
p. 1096, § 1; Stats.1959, c. 1076, p. 3138, § 2.)

§ 6362.5   Information by state librarian regarding newly pub-
lished materials

The State Librarian shall periodically supply to each law library
established under the provisions of this chapter, and requesting the
same, information regarding newly published materials to aid such libraries in their selection of new materials.

(Added by Stats.1965, c. 1385, p. 3307, § 1.)

§ 6363.   Effect of chapter as to existing libraries

Whenever a law library, and a board of trustees to govern the
same, is in existence under the provisions of any law, other than the
law superseded by this chapter, in any county, or city and county, in
this State, this chapter shall not be considered a repeal of any legislation under which such library was established and is now governed,
but shall be deemed to confer upon such library the benefits of Sections 6321, 6322, 6322.1, 6326, 6341, 6345, 6346, 6346.5, and 6347.

(Added by Stats.1941, c. 452, p. 1746, § 1. Amended by Stats.1941, c. 453,
p. 1750, § 11; Stats.1949, c. 810, p. 1554, § 1; Stats.1955, c. 1786, p. 3295,
§ 1.)

§ 6364.   Discretion to make chapter applicable

It is discretionary with the board of supervisors of any county to
provide by ordinance for the application of the provisions of this chapter to the county.

(Added by Stats.1941, c. 452, p. 1746, § 1.)

§ 6365.   Discontinuance of library

Whenever the board of supervisors in any county in this State in
which there is but one judge of the superior court, which board shall
have adopted the provisions of this chapter and established a law library, desire to discontinue such law library, they shall by ordinance
declare their intention so to do, and shall provide in such ordinance
that the books already in the library shall be transferred to and kept
in the chambers of the judge of the superior court of such county.

All moneys on hand in the law library fund of such county shall be by the same ordinance transferred to the school fund of such county, and the office of member of the board of law library trustees of such law library shall be abolished. After such an ordinance takes effect, the county clerk of such county shall not collect the fees and costs provided for the law library.

(Added by Stats.1941, c. 452, p. 1746, § 1. Amended by Stats.1945, c. 1113, p. 2122, § 4.)

MISCELLANEOUS PROVISIONS

(West's Annotated California Codes, Education Code, 1982,
19325, 19900, 19901, 19902, 19910, 19911; Government Code, 1982, s.6254.)

§ 19325. Toll-free telephone service; regional libraries for the blind and handicapped; rules and regulations

There is hereby appropriated from the General Fund the sum of fifteen thousand dollars ($15,000) to the Division of Libraries in the State Department of Education for the purpose of providing toll-free telephone services during the 1978–79 fiscal year for registered patrons of the federally designated regional libraries for the blind and physically handicapped, in order to enable such persons to have direct patron access to library services.

The State Librarian shall administer these funds and shall adopt regulations governing their use by federally designated regional libraries for the blind and physically handicapped.

(Added by Stats.1978, c. 606, p. 2045, § 1.)

§ 19900. Authority to deposit newspaper files

The board of supervisors of any county may authorize the county recorder to deposit with any free public library maintained at the county seat, or with the State Library, such newspaper files, or portions thereof, as may be in the custody of the recorder by virtue of Chapter 110 of the Statutes of 1862, relating to the purchase and preservation of newspapers, or by virtue of any other act.

(Stats.1976, c. 1010, § 2, operative April 30, 1977.)

§ 19901. Agreement for preservation, care and accessibility of files

Before making the deposit, the board of supervisors shall obtain from the board of trustees or authorities in charge of the free public library, or the Department of Education, or the board of governors, as the case may be, an agreement that it will properly preserve and care for the newspaper files, and make them accessible to the public.

(Stats.1976, c. 1010, § 2, operative April 30, 1977.)

§ 19902. Deposit in State Library

The board of supervisors of any county may authorize the boards of trustees or other authorities in charge of any free public library with which newspaper files have been deposited in accordance with Section 19900 to deposit the newspaper files with the State Library.

(Stats.1976, c. 1010, § 2, operative April 30, 1977.)

§ 19910.   Malicious cutting, tearing, defacing, breaking, or injuring

Any person who maliciously cuts, tears, defaces, breaks, or injures any book, map, chart, picture, engraving, statue, coin, model, apparatus, or other work of literature, art, mechanics, or object of curiosity, deposited in any public library, gallery, museum, collection, fair, or exhibition, is guilty of a misdemeanor.

The parent or guardian of a minor who willfully and maliciously commits any act within the scope of this section shall be liable for all damages so caused by the minor.

(Stats.1976, c. 1010, § 2, operative April 30, 1977.)

§ 19911.   Willful detention of property

Any person who willfully detains any book, newspaper, magazine, pamphlet, manuscript, or other property belonging to any public or incorporated library, reading room, museum, or other educational institution, for 30 days after notice in writing to return the article or property, given after the expiration of the time for which by the rules of the institution the article or property may be kept, is guilty of a misdemeanor.

The parent or guardian of a minor who willfully and maliciously commits any act within the scope of this section shall be liable for all damages so caused by the minor.

(Stats.1976, c. 1010, § 2, operative April 30, 1977.)

§ 6254.   Exemption of particular records

Except as provided in Section 6254.7, nothing in this chapter shall be construed to require disclosure of records that are any of the following:

*   *   *

(j) Library circulation records kept for the purpose of identifying the borrower of items available in libraries, and library and museum materials made or acquired and presented solely for reference or exhibition purposes. The exemption in this subdivision shall not apply to records of fines imposed on such borrowers.

This section shall become operative on January 1, 1982.
(Added by Stats.1981, c. 684, p. ——, § 1.5, urgency, eff. Sept. 23, 1981, operative Jan. 1, 1982.)

California library laws are reprinted from WEST'S ANNOTATED CALIFORNIA CODES published by West Publishing Co., St. Paul, Minnesota.

COLORADO

COLORADO LIBRARY LAW
(Colorado Revised Statutes, 1982, s.24-90-101 to 24-90-118.)

24-90-101. Short title. This part 1 shall be known and may be cited as the "Colorado Library Law"

Source: R & RE, L. 79, p. 983, § 1; amended, L. 80, p. 619, § 3.

24-90-102. Legislative declaration. The general assembly hereby declares that it is the policy of this state, as a part of its provision for public education, to promote the establishment and development of all types of publicly-supported free library service throughout the state to ensure equal access to information without regard to age, physical or mental health, place of residence, or economic status, to aid in the establishment and improvement of library programs, to improve and update the skills of persons employed in libraries through continuing education activities, and to promote and coordinate the sharing of resources among libraries in Colorado and the dissemination of information regarding the availability of library services.

Source: R & RE, L. 79, p. 983, § 1.

24-90-103. Definitions. As used in this article, unless the context otherwise requires:

(1) "Governmental unit" means any county, city, city and county, town, or school district of the state of Colorado.

(2) "Legislative body" means the body authorized to determine the amount of taxes to be levied in a governmental unit.

(3) "Library district" means a public library established and maintained by two or more governmental units or parts thereof, which may include but is not limited to a multicounty library.

(4) "Library network" means a number of libraries or other organizations cooperatively interconnected by communication links or channels which can be used for the exchange or transfer of materials and information.

(5) "Publicly-supported library" means a library supported principally with money derived from taxation and includes the following:

(a) Academic libraries operated by a publicly-supported college, university, community college, or junior college primarily for the use of its students and faculty;

(b) Joint libraries operated jointly by two or more agencies which could operate any publicly-supported library;

(c) Public libraries, supported in whole or in part with money derived from taxation, which are for the free use of the public, including county and municipal libraries and libraries operated by an Indian tribe having a reservation in this state;

(d) School libraries maintained by a school district for the use of its students and staff as well as for the general public under such regulations as the school district directors may prescribe;

(e) Special libraries operated by a publicly-supported association, agency, or other group primarily for the use of its specialized clientele.

(6) "Qualified elector" means a person who is qualified to vote at general elections in this state.

(7) "Regional library service system" means an organization of publicly-supported libraries established to provide cooperative interlibrary services within a designated geographical area.

(8) "Resource centers" means libraries designated through contractual arrangements with the state library to provide specialized, statewide library services.

(9) "State library" means the state library created pursuant to section 24-90-104.

Source: R & RE, L. 79, p. 983, § 1.

24-90-104. State library created - administration. (1) The state library is hereby created as a division of the department of education, and its operation is declared to be an essential administrative function of the state government.

(2) The commissioner of education, as ex officio state librarian, has charge and direction of the state library, but may delegate to the assistant commissioner in charge of the state library any or all of the powers given to the state librarian in this article for such periods and under such restrictions as he sees fit, upon approval of the state board of education.

(3) The commissioner of education shall appoint an assistant commissioner, office of library services, in accordance with the provisions of section 13 of article XII of the state constitution. Said assistant commissioner shall have at least a master's degree from a library school accredited by the American library association and shall have at least seven years of progressively responsible library experience, five of which shall have been in administrative positions.

Source: R & RE, L. 79, p. 984, § 1.

24-90-105. Powers and duties of state librarian. (1) The state librarian has the following powers and duties with respect to the state library:

(a) (I) To make reasonable rules and regulations for the administration of the provisions of this part 1; for the use of state library materials; for the purchase, control, and use of books and other resources; and for the establishment, maintenance, and operation of libraries maintained by the state in correctional institutions, medical and mental hospitals, youth facilities, home and training schools, psychiatric centers, nursing homes, and community care centers.

(II) Rules or regulations promulgated under provisions of this part 1 shall be subject to sections 24-4-103 (8) (c) and (8) (d) and 24-4-108.

(b) To appoint all professional and clerical help in the state library, subject to the provisions of section 13 of article XII of the state constitution;

(c) To furnish or contract for the furnishing of library or information services to state officials and departments;

(d) To furnish or contract for the furnishing of library service to correctional, residential, and medical institutions operated by the state;

(e) To furnish or contract for the furnishing of library services to the blind and physically handicapped, including persons who cannot use printed materials in their conventional format;

(f) To contract for the furnishing of library resources to ensure equal access to information for all Coloradans;

(g) To coordinate programs and activities of the regional library service systems, as provided by section 24-90-115;

(h) To provide for the collection, analysis, publication, and distribution of statistics and information relevant to the operation of the state library and all other types of libraries in the state. Publications circulated in quantity outside the executive branch shall be issued in accordance with fiscal rules promulgated by the controller pursuant to the provisions of section 24-30-208.

(i) To conduct or contract for research projects necessary to the development of long-range planning for effective library programs in the state;

(j) To contract for the lending of books and other resources to publicly-supported libraries and institutions;

(k) To report to the state board of education at such times and on such matters as the board may require.

(l) To accept gifts and bequests of money or property, and, subject to the terms of any gift or bequest and to applicable provisions of law, to hold in trust, invest, or sell any gift or bequest of money or property, and to use either the principal or interest or the proceeds of sale for programs or purposes specified in the gift or bequest as approved by the state board of education. The use of gifts and bequests shall be subject to audit by the state auditor or his designee. The principal of any gift or bequest and the interest received thereon from investment shall be available for use by the state library in addition to any funds appropriated by the general assembly. The acceptance of any gift or bequest under this paragraph (l) shall not commit the state to any expenditure of state funds.

(2) The state librarian has the following powers and duties with respect to other publicly-supported libraries in the state:

(a) To further library development and encourage contractual and cooperative relations to enhance resource sharing among all types of libraries and agencies throughout the state;

(b) To serve as the agency of the state to receive and administer state or federal funds which may be appropriated to further library development within the state upon approval of the state board of education; except that this paragraph (b) shall not preclude other governmental units, including, but not limited to, municipalities, counties, a city and county, and library districts, from applying for, receiving, or administering such state or federal funds;

(c) To develop regulations under which state grants are distributed for assisting in the establishment, improvement, or enlargement of libraries or regional library service systems and to develop all necessary procedures to comply with federal regulations under which such grants are distributed for assisting in the establishment, improvement, or enlargement of libraries;

(d) To provide for the supplying of consultative assistance and information to all types of publicly-supported libraries in the state through field visits, conferences, institutes, correspondence, statistical information, and publications and to do any and all things he may reasonably be expected to do to promote and advance library services;

(e) To cooperate with local legislative bodies, library boards, library advisory committees, appropriate professional associations, and other groups in the development and improvement of libraries throughout the state.

Source: R & RE, L. 79, p. 985, § 1; (1) (a) amended, L. 80, pp. 619, 788, § § 4, 22; (1) (l) added, L. 81, p. 1253, § 1.

24-90-106. Establishment of public libraries. Any governmental unit of the state of Colorado has the power to establish and maintain a public library under the provisions of this part 1, either by itself or in cooperation with one or more other governmental units; except that the legislative body of any governmental unit which maintains a public library within the territory to be served by a county library or a library district may decide not to participate in said county library or library district.

Source: R & RE, L. 79, p. 986, § 1; amended, L. 80, p. 619, § 5.

24-90-107. Method of establishment. (1) A public library may be established for a governmental unit either by the legislative body of said governmental unit on its own initiative or upon petition of one hundred qualified electors residing in the governmental unit to the legislative body of such governmental unit.

(2) If establishment of a public library is by petition of qualified electors, petitions shall be addressed to the legislative body of the governmental unit and shall request the establishment of a public library. Upon receipt of such petition, the legislative body for the governmental unit shall submit the question of the establishment of a public library to a vote of the qualified electors residing in said unit at the next municipal election held thereafter, in the case of a city or town, or the next general election held thereafter, in the case of a library district or county, if such petition has been received by such legislative body more than ninety days preceding such election. If a majority of the electors voting on the question vote in favor of the establishment of a public library, the legislative body shall forthwith establish such public library and provide for its financial support beginning with the next succeed-

ing tax year.

(3) A joint library may be established by the legislative bodies of the participating governmental units through contract.

Source: R & RE, L. 79, p. 986, § 1.

24-90-108. Board of trustees. (1) The management and control of any library established or operated under the provisions of this part 1 shall be vested in a board of not fewer than five nor more than seven trustees.

(2) (a) In cities and towns the trustees shall be appointed by the mayor with the consent of the legislative body.

(b) In counties the trustees shall be appointed by the board of county commissioners.

(c) In library districts the trustees shall be appointed in the manner set forth in section 24-90-110 (4) (a).

(d) In school districts the trustees shall be appointed by the school board.

(3) (a) The first appointments of such boards of trustees shall be for terms of one, two, three, four, and five years respectively if there are five trustees, one for each of such terms except the five-year term for which two shall be appointed if there are six trustees, and one for each of such terms except the four-year and five-year terms for each of which two shall be appointed if there are seven trustees. Thereafter a trustee shall be appointed annually to serve for five years.

(b) Vacancies shall be filled for the remainder of the unexpired term as soon as possible in the manner in which trustees are regularly chosen.

(4) A trustee shall not receive a salary nor other compensation for services as a trustee, but necessary traveling and subsistence expenses actually incurred may be paid from the public library fund.

(5) A library trustee may be removed only by a majority vote of the appointing legislative body, but only upon a showing of good cause.

(6) The board of trustees, immediately after their appointment, shall meet and organize by the election of a president and a secretary and such other officers as deemed necessary.

Source: R & RE, L. 79, p. 987, § 1; (1) amended, L. 80, p. 619, § 6.

24-90-109. Powers and duties of board of trustees. (1) The board of trustees shall:

(a) Adopt such bylaws, rules, and regulations for its own guidance and for the government of the library as it deems expedient;

(b) Have supervision, care, and custody of all property of the library, including rooms or buildings constructed, leased, or set apart therefor;

(c) Employ a librarian and, upon the librarian's recommendation, employ such other employees as may be necessary, prescribe their duties, and fix their compensation;

(d) Submit annually a budget as required by law and certify to the legislative body of the governmental unit which the library serves the sums necessary to maintain and operate the library during the ensuing year;

(e) Have exclusive control of the disbursement of the finances of the library;

(f)   Accept such gifts of money or property for library purposes as it deems expedient;

(g)   Hold and acquire land by gift, lease, or purchase for library purposes;

(h)   Lease, purchase, or erect any appropriate building for library purposes and acquire such other property as may be needed therefor;

(i)   Sell, assign, transfer, or convey any property of the library, whether real or personal, which may not be needed within the foreseeable future for any purpose authorized by law, upon such terms and conditions as it may approve, and lease any such property, pending sale thereof, under an agreement of lease, with or without an option to purchase the same. The board, prior to the conveyance of such property, shall make a finding that the property may not be needed within the foreseeable future for library purposes, but no such finding shall be necessary if the property is sold or conveyed to a state agency or political subdivision of this state.

(j)   Borrow funds for library purposes by means of a contractual short-term loan when moneys are not currently available but will be in the future. Such loan shall not exceed the amount of immediately anticipated revenues and such loan shall be liquidated within six months.

(k)   Authorize the bonding of persons entrusted with library funds;

(l)   Submit financial records for audit as required by the legislative body of the appropriate governmental unit;

(m)   Authorize the purchase of library materials and equipment on the recommendation of the librarian;

(n)   Hold title to property given to or for the use or benefit of the library, to be used according to the terms of the gift;

(o)   Do all other acts necessary for the orderly and efficient management and control of the library.

(2)   At the close of each year, the board of trustees of every public library shall make a report to the legislative body of the appropriate governmental unit showing the condition of its trust during the year, the sums of money expended and the purposes of the expenditures, the number of books and periodicals on hand, the number added during the year, the number retired, the number loaned out, and such other statistics and information and such suggestions as it deems of public interest. A copy of this report shall be filed with the state librarian.

(3)   The board of trustees of a public library or the governing board of any other publicly-supported library, under such rules and regulations as it may deem necessary and upon such terms and conditions as may be agreed upon may allow nonresidents of the governmental unit which the library serves to use such library's materials and equipment and may make exchanges of books and other materials with any other library, either permanently or temporarily.

Source: R & RE, L. 79, p. 987, § 1.

24-90-110.   Establishment of library districts - merger of public library - board of trustees. (1) (a)   A library district may be established by the legislative bodies of two or more governmental units, each proceeding to adopt a resolution or an ordinance to that effect or by petition of one hundred qualified electors residing within the proposed library district addressed to the legislative body of the governmental unit in the proposed library district having the largest population according to the most recent federal census. The petition shall contain a general description of the boundaries of the proposed library district with such certainty as to enable a property owner to determine whether or not his property is within the proposed district. At the time of filing the petition a bond shall be filed with said legislative body sufficient to pay all expenses connected with the organization of the library district if organization is not effected. Said legislative body shall provide for an election to be conducted as provided in section 24-90-107 (2). If organization is effected, the district shall reimburse the legislative body holding the election for expenses incurred in holding the election.

(b) The library districts shall be supported by and shall serve all unincorporated areas and all municipal corporations not operating their own public libraries within the territorial limits of the governmental units comprising the district.

(2) Any governmental unit maintaining a public library may merge its library with the library district by agreement of its legislative body and the board of trustees of the library district. Any library district established pursuant to this section may be dissolved by resolution of the legislative bodies of the governmental units comprising such district.

(3) Whenever the board of county commissioners of any county decides that only a part of the territory of the county which is not already served by a public library shall join in establishing a library district, the board may levy a tax on that part of the county for the support of said library district.

(4) (a) The legislative bodies of the governmental units creating a library district shall each appoint two of their members to a committee which shall appoint not fewer than five nor more than seven members of the board of trustees of the library district in the same manner as prescribed in section 24-90-108 (3). Trustee appointments shall be ratified by each of the respective legislative bodies.

(b) The board of trustees of a library district shall have management and control of any library district established or operated pursuant to this section, shall be governed by the provisions of section 24-90-108 (4) and (5), and shall have the same powers and duties as other boards of trustees of libraries as prescribed in section 24-90-109.

Source: R & RE, L. 79, p. 988, § 1.

24-90-111. Participation by established library. When a county library or library district has been established, the legislative body of any governmental unit in such county or library district maintaining a public library may decide, with the concurrence of the board of trustees of its library, to participate in the county library or library district while retaining title to its own property, continuing its own board of library trustees, and levying its own taxes for library purposes; or, by a vote as authorized by section 24-90-107 (2), a governmental unit may transfer, conditionally or otherwise, the ownership and control of its library, with all or any part of its property, to another governmental unit which is providing or will provide free library services in the territory of the former, and the trustees and legislative body making the transfer shall thereafter be relieved of responsibility pertaining to the property transferred.

Source: R & RE, L. 79, p. 989, § 1.

24-90-112. Tax support - elections. (1) (a) (I) The legislative body of any incorporated city or town is hereby authorized to levy a tax of not more than one and one-half mills for municipal libraries upon real and personal property for the establishment and maintenance of a public library.

(II) The board of county commissioners of any of the several counties is hereby authorized to levy a tax of not more than one and one-half mills for county libraries and library districts upon real and personal property for the establishment and maintenance of county libraries and library districts.

(b) The legislative body for the specified governmental unit shall submit the question of any increase in the existing maximum tax levy to not more than two and one-half mills for the establishment and maintenance of public libraries to a vote of the qualified electors residing in said unit at the next municipal election held thereafter in the case of a city or town or at the next general election held thereafter in the case of a county or library district. Each elector voting at said election and desirous of voting for or against said question shall cast his vote as provided by law either "Yes" or "No" on the proposition: "Shall the legislative body of (name of incorporated city or town, county, or library district) be authorized to increase the maximum tax levy from (existing maximum tax levy) to not more than (desired maximum tax levy) for the establishment and maintenance of public libraries?". The votes cast for the adoption or rejection of said question shall be canvassed and the result determined in the manner provided by law.

(2) The treasurer of the governmental unit in which such library is located or, if a library district has been established embracing parts or all of more than one county, the treasurer of the county containing the largest valuation for assessment of property for tax purposes of the said district shall be the custodian of the moneys for the library, whether derived from taxation, gift, or otherwise. The moneys shall be credited to a special fund in the office of said treasurer to be known as the public library fund. The fund shall be used only for library purposes and shall be expended only upon warrants signed by the president of the board of trustees or his designee.

Source: R & RE, L. 79, p. 990, § 1.

24-90-113. Contract to receive library service. In lieu of establishment of an independent public library, the legislative body of a governmental unit may contract to receive library service from an existing public library, the board of trustees of which has reciprocal power to contract to render the service. Any school district may contract for library service from any existing public library, such service to be paid from funds available to the school district for library purposes.

Source: R & RE, L. 79, p. 990, § 1.

24-90-114. Abolishment of libraries. A library established or maintained pursuant to this part 1 may be abolished only by vote of the qualified electors of the governmental unit in which the library is located, taken in the manner prescribed in section 24-90-107 (2) for a vote to establish a library. If a library is abolished, the materials and equipment belonging to it shall be disposed of as the legislative body of the governmental unit directs. Disposition of school district libraries that have been abolished shall be accomplished as provided by law.

Source: R & RE, L. 79, p. 990, § 1; amended, L. 80, p. 620, § 7.

24-90-115.   Regional library service system - governing board. (1) (a) The board of trustees of any public library or library district or the governing board of any publicly-supported library may participate in a regional library service system to provide cooperative services under a plan, including an organizational structure submitted to the state librarian and approved by the state board of education. The organizational structure of each regional library service system shall include a governing board.

(b)   The state board of education shall adopt rules and regulations, in accordance with article 4 of this title, relating to the establishment, governance, operation, and withdrawal of regional library service systems.

(2)   The governing board of a regional library service system shall consist of at least one representative of each type of library participating in the system. The governing board shall be appointed by a system membership council comprised of one representative of each system member.

(3) (a)   The governing board of each regional library service system has the right to exercise all powers vested in a board of trustees pursuant to section 24-90-109; except that such a governing board shall not hold or acquire title to land or buildings. The operation of regional library service systems shall be in accordance with rules and regulations established by the state board of education. Nothing pertaining to the organization or operation of a regional library service system shall be construed to infringe upon the autonomy of the board of trustees of a public library or the governing board of any publicly-supported library.

(b)   The governing board of each regional library service system shall submit annual plans and budgets under regulations established by the state librarian as provided in section 24-90-105 (1) (a).

(4)   Before withdrawing from a regional library service system, any participating library shall be required to fulfill all outstanding obligations for that fiscal year. Withdrawal shall be accomplished pursuant to rules and regulations established by the state board of education.

(5)   If the need for a regional library service system ceases to exist, the membership council thereof may, by a two-thirds vote of its members, declare its intent to dissolve the organization and file with the state library a plan for effecting such dissolution, which shall be carried out upon approval by the state board of education.

Source: R & RE, L. 79, p. 991, § 1.

24-90-116.   Existing libraries to comply. Any public library established on or after July 1, 1979, shall be established as provided in this part 1. Every public library which has been established prior to said date under provisions of state law shall be considered as established under this part 1, and the board of trustees and the legislative body of the governmental unit in which the library is located shall proceed forthwith to make such changes as may be necessary to effect a compliance with the terms of this part 1. Every contract existing prior to July 1, 1979, for library service shall continue in force and be subject to this part 1 until the contract is terminated or a public library is established by the governmental unit for which the service was engaged.

Source: R & RE, L. 79, p. 991, § 1; amended, L. 80, p. 620, § 8.

24-90-117. Theft or mutilation of library property. Any person who takes, without complying with the appropriate check-out procedures, or who willfully retains any property belonging to any publicly-supported library for thirty days after receiving notice in writing to return the same, given after the expiration of the time that by the rules of such institution such property may be kept, or who mutilates such property commits a class 3 misdemeanor and shall be punished as provided in section 18-1-106, C.R.S. 1973.

Source: R & RE, L. 79, p. 991, § 1.

24-90-118. Colorado libraries automated catalog project. (1) The general assembly declares that there shall be developed and established by the Colorado state library, in cooperation with the research libraries within Colorado, an automated catalog system, which shall be available for use by all publicly or privately supported libraries in Colorado. The system shall be compatible with the library of congress automated cataloging system, including federal standards for machine-readable cataloging, which will become effective on January 1, 1981.

(2) By October 15, 1979, the Colorado state library, in cooperation with the research libraries within Colorado, shall submit to the general assembly a project plan for a centralized automated catalog system based upon a feasibility study, which shall be available for use by all publicly and privately supported libraries in Colorado and shall be compatible with the library of congress automated cataloging system and cataloging standards. Such a plan shall include a provision for future funding by participating libraries through user fees.

(3) By February 15, 1980, the Colorado state library, in cooperation with the research libraries within Colorado, shall submit a progress report to the general assembly on the implementation of this section.

Source: Added, L. 79, p. 993, § 1.

INTERSTATE LIBRARY COMPACT
(Colorado Revised Statutes, 1982, s.24-60-1501 to 24-60-1507.)

24-60-1501. Compact approved and ratified. The general assembly hereby approves and ratifies and the governor shall enter into a compact on behalf of the state of Colorado with any of the United States or other jurisdictions legally joining therein in the form substantially as follows:

INTERSTATE LIBRARY COMPACT

ARTICLE I

Policy and Purpose

Because the desire for the services provided by libraries transcends governmental boundaries and can most effectively be satisfied by giving such services to communities and people regardless of jurisdictional lines, it is the policy of the states party to this compact to cooperate and share their responsibilities; to authorize cooperation and sharing with respect to those types of library facilities and services which can be more economically or efficiently developed and maintained on a cooperative basis, and to authorize cooperation and sharing among localities, states and others in providing joint or cooperative library services in areas where the distribution of population or of existing and potential library resources make the provision of library service on an interstate basis the most effective way of providing adequate and efficient service.

ARTICLE II

Definitions

As used in this compact:

(a) "Public library agency" means any unit or agency of local or state government operating or having power to operate a library.

(b) "Private library agency" means any nongovernmental entity which operates or assumes a legal obligation to operate a library.

(c) "Library agreement" means a contract establishing an interstate library district pursuant to this compact or providing for the joint or cooperative furnishing of library services.

ARTICLE III

Interstate Library Districts

(a) Any one or more public library agencies in a party state in cooperation with any public library agency or agencies in one or more other party states may establish and maintain an interstate library district. Subject to the provisions of this compact and any other laws of the party states which pursuant hereto remain applicable, such district may establish, maintain and operate some or all of the library facilities and services for the area concerned in accordance with the terms of a library agreement therefor. Any private library agency or agencies within an interstate library district may cooperate therewith, assume duties, responsibilities and obligations thereto, and receive benefits therefrom as provided in any library agreement to which such agency or agencies become party.

(b) Within an interstate library district, and as provided by a library agreement, the performance of library functions may be undertaken on a joint or cooperative basis or may be undertaken by means of one or more arrangements between or among public or private library agencies for the extension of library privileges to the use of facilities or services operated or rendered by one or more of the individual library agencies.

(c) If a library agreement provides for joint establishment, maintenance or operation of library facilities or services by an interstate library district,

such district shall have power to do any one or more of the following in
accordance with such library agreement:

1. Undertake, administer and participate in programs or arrangements for
securing, lending or servicing of books and other publications, any other
materials suitable to be kept or made available by libraries, library equipment
or for the dissemination of information from libraries, the value and significance of particular items therein, and the use thereof.

2. Accept for any of its purposes under this compact any and all donations,
and grants of money, equipment, supplies, materials, and services, (conditional or otherwise), from any state or the United States or any subdivision
or agency thereof, or interstate agency, or from any institution, person, firm
or corporation, and receive, utilize and dispose of the same.

3. Operate mobile library units or equipment for the purpose of rendering
bookmobile service within the district.

4. Employ professional, technical, clerical and other personnel, and fix
terms of employment, compensation and other appropriate benefits; and
where desirable, provide for the inservice training of such personnel.

5. Sue and be sued in any court of competent jurisdiction.

6. Acquire, hold, and dispose of any real or personal property or any interest or interests therein as may be appropriate to the rendering of library
service.

7. Construct, maintain and operate a library, including any appropriate
branches thereof.

8. Do such other things as may be incidental to or appropriate for the carrying out of any of the foregoing powers.

ARTICLE IV

Interstate Library Districts, Governing Board

(a)   An interstate library district which establishes, maintains or operates
any facilities or services in its own right shall have a governing board which
shall direct the affairs of the district and act for it in all matters relating
to its business. Each participating public library agency in the district shall
be represented on the governing board which shall be organized and conduct
its business in accordance with provision therefor in the library agreement.
But in no event shall a governing board meet less often than twice a year.

(b)   Any private library agency or agencies party to a library agreement
establishing an interstate library district may be represented on or advise with
the governing board of the district in such manner as the library agreement
may provide.

ARTICLE V

State Library Agency Cooperation

Any two or more state library agencies of two or more of the party states
may undertake and conduct joint or cooperative library programs, render
joint or cooperative library services, and enter into and perform arrangements
for the cooperative or joint acquisition, use, housing and disposition of items
or collections of materials which, by reason of expense, rarity, specialized
nature, or infrequency of demand therefor would be appropriate for central
collection and shared use. Any such programs, services or arrangements may

include provision for the exercise on a cooperative or joint basis of any power exercisable by an interstate library district and an agreement embodying any such program, service or arrangement shall contain provisions covering the subjects detailed in Article VI of this compact for interstate library agreements.

ARTICLE VI

Library Agreements

(a) In order to provide for any joint or cooperative undertaking pursuant to this compact, public and private library agencies may enter into library agreements. Any agreement executed pursuant to the provisions of this compact shall, as among the parties to the agreement:

1. Detail the specific nature of the services, programs, facilities, arrangements or properties to which it is applicable.

2. Provide for the allocation of costs and other financial responsibilities.

3. Specify the respective rights, duties, obligations and liabilities of the parties.

4. Set forth the terms and conditions for duration, renewal, termination, abrogation, disposal of joint or common property, if any, and all other matters which may be appropriate to the proper effectuation and performance of the agreement.

(b) No public or private library agency shall undertake to exercise itself, or jointly with any other library agency, by means of a library agreement any power prohibited to such agency by the constitution or statutes of its state.

(c) No library agreement shall become effective until filed with the compact administrator of each state involved, and approved in accordance with Article VII of this compact.

ARTICLE VII

Approval of Library Agreements

(a) Every library agreement made pursuant to this compact shall, prior to and as a condition precedent to its entry into force, be submitted to the attorney general of each state in which a public library agency party thereto is situated, who shall determine whether the agreement is in proper form and compatible with the laws of his state. The attorneys general shall approve any agreement submitted to them unless they shall find that it does not meet the conditions set forth herein and shall detail in writing addressed to the governing bodies of the public library agencies concerned the specific respects in which the proposed agreement fails to meet the requirements of law. Failure to disapprove an agreement submitted hereunder within ninety days of its submission shall constitute approval thereof.

(b) In the event that a library agreement made pursuant to this compact shall deal in whole or in part with the provision of services or facilities with regard to which an officer or agency of the state government has constitutional or statutory powers of control, the agreement shall, as a condition precedent to its entry into force, be submitted to the state officer or agency having such power of control and shall be approved or disapproved by him or it as to all matters within his or its jurisdiction in the same manner and subject to the same requirements governing the action of the attorneys general pursuant to paragraph (a) of this article. This requirement of submission and approval shall be in addition to and not in substitution for the requirement of submission to and approval by the attorneys general.

ARTICLE VIII

Other Laws Applicable

Nothing in this compact or in any library agreement shall be construed to supersede, alter or otherwise impair any obligation imposed on any library by otherwise applicable law, nor to authorize the transfer or disposition of any property held in trust by a library agency in a manner contrary to the terms of such trust.

ARTICLE IX

Appropriations and Aid

(a) Any public library agency party to a library agreement may appropriate funds to the interstate library district established thereby in the same manner and to the same extent as to a library wholly maintained by it and, subject to the laws of the state in which such public library agency is situated, may pledge its credit in support of an interstate library district established by the agreement.

(b) Subject to the provisions of the library agreement pursuant to which it functions and the laws of the states in which such district is situated, an interstate library district may claim and receive any state and federal aid which may be available to library agencies.

ARTICLE X

Compact Administrator

Each state shall designate a compact administrator with whom copies of all library agreements to which his state or any public library agency thereof is party shall be filed. The administrator shall have such other powers as may be conferred upon him by the laws of his state and may consult and cooperate with the compact administrators of other party states and take such steps as may effectuate the purposes of this compact. If the laws of a party state so provide, such state may designate one or more deputy compact administrators in addition to its compact administrator.

ARTICLE XI

Entry Into Force and Withdrawal

(a) This compact shall enter into force and effect immediately upon its enactment into law by any two states. Thereafter, it shall enter into force and effect as to any other state upon the enactment thereof by such state.

(b) This compact shall continue in force with respect to a party state and remain binding upon such state until six months after such state has given notice to each other party state of the repeal thereof. Such withdrawal shall not be construed to relieve any party to a library agreement entered into pursuant to this compact from any obligation of that agreement prior to the end of its duration as provided therein.

ARTICLE XII

Construction and Severability

This compact shall be liberally construed so as to effectuate the purposes thereof. The provisions of this compact shall be severable and if any phrase, clause, sentence or provision of this compact is declared to be contrary to the constitution of any party state or of the United States or the applicability thereof to any government, agency, person or circumstance is held invalid, the validity of the remainder of this compact and the applicability thereof to any government, agency, person or circumstance shall not be affected thereby. If this compact shall be held contrary to the constitution of any state party thereto, the compact shall remain in full force and effect as to the remaining states and in full force and effect as to the state affected as to all severable matters.

Source: L. 69, p. 552, § 1; C.R.S. 1963, § 74-16-1.

24-60-1502. Limitations on interstate library districts. (1) No interstate library district agreement shall be entered into by any public library agency in this state pursuant to article III (a) of the compact without first obtaining the approval thereof by any county or regional library district included in whole or in part in such proposed interstate library district, so as to eliminate duplication of library services.

(2) In lieu of an interstate library district, any county or regional library district in this state may enter into a contract with one or more similar public library agencies or governmental entities in one or more other party states for the furnishing of library services by or for such county or library district in this state.

Source: L. 69, p. 556, § 1; C.R.S. 1963, § 74-16-2.

24-60-1503. State political subdivisions to comply with laws. No political subdivision of this state shall be party to a library agreement which provides for the construction or maintenance of a library pursuant to article III (c) 7. of the compact, or pledge its credit in support of such a library, or contribute to the capital financing thereof except after compliance with any laws applicable to such political subdivision, including but not limited to those relating to or governing capital expenditures, the pledging of credit, and the appropriation of public moneys to nonpublic persons and organizations.

Source: L. 69, p. 556, § 1; C.R.S. 1963, § 74-16-3.

24-60-1504. State library agency. As used in the compact, "state library agency", with reference to this state, means the commissioner of education.

Source: L. 69, p. 557, § 1; C.R.S. 1963, § 74-16-4.

24-60-1505. State aid to library district located partly within state. An interstate library district lying partly within this state may claim and be entitled to receive state aid in support of any of its functions to the same extent and in the same manner as such functions are eligible for support when carried on by entities wholly within the state. For the purposes of computing and apportioning state aid to an interstate library district, this state shall consider that portion of the area of the interstate library district which lies within this state as an independent entity for the performance of the function to be aided, as well as the proportion of services rendered this state and compute and apportion the aid accordingly. Subject to any applicable laws of this state, such a district also may apply for and be eligible to receive any federal aid for which it may be eligible.

Source: L. 69, p. 557, § 1; C.R.S. 1963, § 74-16-5.

24-60-1506. Commissioner of education to administer compact. The commissioner of education shall be the compact administrator pursuant to article X of the compact, and the deputy compact administrator shall be the deputy state librarian.

Source: L. 69, p. 557, § 1; C.R.S. 1963, § 74-16-6.

24-60-1507. Withdrawal from compact. In the event of withdrawal from the compact, the governor shall send and receive any notices required by article XI (b) of the compact.

Source: L. 69, p. 557, § 1; C.R.S. 1963, § 74-16-7.

STATE PUBLICATIONS DEPOSITORY
AND DISTRIBUTION CENTER
(Colorado Revised Statutes, 1982, s.24-90-201 to 24-90-208.)

24-90-201. Establishment of a state publications depository and distribution center. There is hereby established a state publications depository and distribution center. Such center shall be a section of the state library. Its operation is declared to be an essential administrative function of the state government.

Source: Added, L. 80, p. 617, § 1.

24-90-202. Definitions. As used in this part 2, unless the context otherwise requires:

(1) "Center" means the state publications depository and distribution center.

(2) "Depository library" means a library designated to collect, maintain, and make available to the general public state agency publications.

(3) "State agency" means every state office, whether legislative, executive, or judicial, and all of its respective officers, departments, divisions, bureaus, boards, commissions, and committees, all state-supported colleges and universities which are defined as state institutions of higher education, and other agencies which expend state-appropriated funds.

(4) "State publication" means any printed or duplicated material, regardless of format or purpose, which is produced, purchased for distribution, or authorized by any state agency, including any document, compilation, journal, law, resolution, bluebook, statute, code, register, contract and grant

report, pamphlet, list, microphotographic form, audiovisual material, book, proceedings, report, public memorandum, hearing, legislative bill, leaflet, order, rule, regulation, directory, periodical, magazine, or newsletter, with the exception of correspondence, interoffice memoranda, or those items detailed by section 24-72-204.

Source: Added, L. 80, p. 617, § 1.

24-90-203. Purposes - direction - rules and regulations. (1) The purposes of the center are to collect, distribute, and make available to the public state publications. Public access to such publications may be accomplished by use of depository library facilities throughout the state.

(2) The center shall be under the direction of the state librarian.

(3) Adoption of such rules and regulations as are necessary or appropriate to accomplish the provisions of this part 2 shall be the responsibility of the state board of education after such rules are submitted to and approved by the committee on legal services. No rule or regulation shall deny public access during normal working hours to the state publications enumerated in this part 2.

Source: Added, L. 80, p. 618, § 1.

24-90-204. Deposits of state publications. Every state agency shall, upon publication, deposit at least four copies of each of its state publications (with the exception of audiovisual materials) with the center. One copy of each such audiovisual material shall be deposited with the center. The center may require additional copies of certain state publications to be deposited when designated by the state librarian as being required to fulfill the purposes of this part 2.

Source: Added, L. 80, p. 618, § 1.

24-90-205. Publication lists to be furnished by state agencies. Upon request by the state librarian, each state agency shall furnish the center with a complete list of its current state publications.

Source: Added, L. 80, p. 618, § 1.

24-90-206. Depository library agreements - requirements. The center may enter into depository agreements with any state agency or public library or with out-of-state research libraries and other state libraries. The number of depository libraries shall not exceed thirty. The requirements for eligibility to become and continue as a depository shall be established by the state library. The standards shall include and take into consideration population, the type of library or agency, ability to preserve such publications and to make them available for public use, and such geographic locations as will make the publications conveniently accessible to residents in all areas of the state.

Source: Added, L. 80, p. 618, § 1.

24-90-207.   Index of state publications. The center shall quarterly publish an index to state publications and distribute it to depository libraries and certain other libraries and state agencies as designated by the state librarian.

Source: Added, L. 80, p. 618, § 1.

24-90-208.   State publications distribution. The center shall distribute state publications, in microfiche, paper copy, or other format where appropriate, to depository libraries. The state librarian may make additional distributions in accordance with agreements with appropriate state agencies.

Source: Added, L. 80, p. 618, § 1.

STATE ARCHIVES AND PUBLIC RECORDS
(Colorado Revised Statutes, 1982, s.24-80-101 to 24.80-112.)

24-80-101.   Definitions. As used in this part 1, unless the context otherwise requires:

(1)   "Records" means all books, papers, maps, photographs, or other documentary materials, regardless of physical form or characteristics, made or received by any governmental agency in pursuance of law or in connection with the transaction of public business and preserved or appropriate for preservation by the agency or its legitimate successor as evidence of the organization, functions, policies, decisions, procedures, operations, or other activities of the government or because of the value of the official governmental data contained therein. As used in this part 1, the following are excluded from the definition of records:

(a)   Materials preserved or appropriate for preservation because of the value of the data contained therein other than that of an official governmental nature or because of the historical value of the materials themselves;

(b)   Library books, pamphlets, newspapers, or museum material made, acquired, or preserved for reference, historical, or exhibition purposes;

(c)   Private papers, manuscripts, letters, diaries, pictures, biographies, books, and maps, including materials and collections previously owned by persons other than the state or any political subdivision thereof and transferred by them to the state historical society;

(d)   Extra copies of publications or duplicated documents preserved for convenience of reference;

(e)   Stocks of publications.

Source: L. 51, p. 777, § 1; CSA, C. 154, § 18(10); CRS 53, § 131-3-1; L. 59, p. 742, § 3; C.R.S. 1963, § 131-3-1.

24-80-102.   Division created - personnel - duties. (1)   The division of state archives and public records, referred to in this part 1 as the "division", shall be a division of the department of administration. The division shall succeed to all records of the state of Colorado or any political subdivision thereof, as the same are defined in section 24-80-101. Except as provided in subsections (5), (6), and (7) of this section, the division shall be the official custodian and trustee for the state of all public records of whatever kind which are transferred to it under this part 1 from any public office of the state or any political subdivision thereof.

(2) The chief administrative officer of the division shall be the state archivist who shall be professionally qualified and who shall be appointed by the governor subject to the provisions and exemptions of section 13 of article XII of the state constitution.

(3) The state archivist shall be responsible for the proper administration of public records under this part 1. It is his duty to determine and direct the administrative and technical procedures of the division. He shall study the problems of preservation and disposition of records as defined in section 24-80-101 and based on such study shall formulate and put into effect, to the extent authorized by law, within the division or otherwise, such program as he deems advisable or necessary for public records conservation by the state of Colorado or political subdivisions thereof.

(4) To effectuate the purposes of this part 1, the governor may direct any department, division, board, bureau, commission, institution, or agency of the state, or any political subdivision thereof, to designate a records liaison officer to cooperate with and assist and advise the state archivist in the performance of the duties and functions of the division and to provide such other assistance and data as will enable the division properly to carry out its activities and effectuate the purposes of this part 1.

(5) Items in the present care, custody, and trusteeship of the state archivist which are not records as defined by section 24-80-101, because of their historical, library, or museum interest or value, shall be retained by the state historical society, and items which are not records which are in the future proposed for disposition under the provisions of this part 1, but determined to be of historical, library, or museum interest or value, shall be transferred to the state historical society with its consent in accordance with provisions set forth in section 24-80-104.

(6) The state historical society, qualified students, and scholars approved by the society or the state archivist and other appropriate persons shall have the right of reasonable access to all records in the custody of the state archivist for purposes of historical reference, research, and information, and the state historical society shall have the privilege of museum display of original historical records or facsimiles thereof, subject to provisions of section 24-80-106. Copies of records, as defined in section 24-80-101, having historical, library, or museum interest or value shall be furnished to the state historical society by the state archivist upon request of the society in accordance with provisions of sections 24-80-103 and 24-80-107.

(7) In the event of disagreement between the state historical society and the division as to the custody of any records as defined in section 24-80-101, the governor with the advice of the attorney general shall make final and conclusive determination, and order and direct custody accordingly.

(8) The state archivist shall prepare and transmit annually, in the form and manner prescribed by the controller pursuant to the provisions of section 24-30-208 a report accounting to the governor and the general assembly for the efficient discharge of all responsibilities assigned by law or directive to the division.

(9) Publications of the division circulated in quantity outside the executive branch shall be issued in accordance with fiscal rules promulgated by the controller pursuant to the provisions of section 24-30-208.

Source: L. 51, p. 777, § 2; CSA, C. 154, § 18(11); CRS 53, § 131-3-2; L. 59, p. 742, § 2; C.R.S. 1963, § 131-3-2; L. 64, p. 174, § 147; L. 68, p. 101, § § 57, 58.

24-80-103. Determination of value - disposition. Every public officer who has public records in his custody shall consult periodically with the state archivist of the division of state archives and public records and the attorney general of the state, and such three officers shall determine whether the records in question are of legal, administrative, or historical value. Those records unanimously determined to be of no legal, administrative, or historical value shall be disposed of by such method as such three officers may specify. A list of all records so disposed of, together with a statement certifying compliance with this part 1, signed by these three officers, shall be filed and preserved in the office from which the records were drawn and in the files of the state archivist. Public records in the custody of the state archivist may be disposed of upon a similar determination by the attorney general, the state archivist, and the head of the agency from which the records were received, or its legal successor.

Source: L. 51, p. 778, § 3; CSA, C. 154, § 18(12); CRS 53, § 131-3-3; C.R.S. 1963, § 131-3-3.

24-80-104. Transfer of records to archives. Those records deemed by the public officer having custody thereof to be unnecessary for the transaction of the business of his office and yet deemed by the attorney general or the state archivist to be of legal, administrative, or historical value may be transferred, with the consent of the state archivist, to the custody of the division of state archives and public records. A list of all records so transferred, together with a statement certifying compliance with this part 1, signed by such three officers, shall be preserved in the files of the office from which the records were drawn and in the files of the said division.

Source: L. 51, p. 778, § 4; CSA, C. 154, § 18(13); CRS 53, § 131-3-4; C.R.S. 1963, § 131-3-4.

24-80-105. Disposal of records. All public records of any public office, upon the termination of the existence and functions of that office, shall be checked by the state archivist and the attorney general and either disposed of or transferred to the custody of the division, in accordance with the procedure of this part 1 and the findings of such two officers. When a public office is terminated or reduced by the transfer of its powers and duties to another office or to other offices, its appropriate public records shall pass with the powers and duties so transferred.

Source: L. 51, p. 778, § 5; CSA, C. 154, § 18(14); CRS 53, § 131-3-5; C.R.S. 1963, § 131-3-5.

24-80-106. Protection of records. The division of state archives and public records and every other custodian of public records shall carefully protect and preserve them from deterioration, mutilation, loss, or destruction and, whenever advisable, shall cause them to be properly repaired and renovated.

All paper, ink, and other materials used in public offices for the purpose of permanent records shall be of durable quality.

Source: L. 51, p. 778, § 6; CSA, C. 154, § 18(15); CRS 53, § 131-3-6; C.R.S. 1963, § 131-3-6.

24-80-107. Reproduction on film - evidence. (1) Any public officer of the state or any county, city, municipality, district, or legal subdivision thereof may cause any or all records, papers, or documents kept by him to be photographed, microphotographed, or reproduced on film. Such photographic film shall comply with the minimum standards of quality approved for permanent photographic records by the national bureau of standards, and the device used to reproduce such records on such film shall be one which accurately reproduces the original thereof in all details. Such photographs, microphotographs, or photographic film shall be deemed to be original records for all purposes, including introduction in evidence in all courts or administrative agencies. A transcript, exemplification, or certified copy thereof, for all purposes recited in this section, shall be deemed to be a transcript, exemplification, or certified copy of the original.

(2) Whenever such photographs, microphotographs, or reproductions on film properly certified are placed in conveniently accessible files and provisions made for preserving, examining, and using the same, any such public officer may cause the original records from which the photographs or microphotographs have been made, or any part thereof, to be disposed of according to methods prescribed by sections 24-80-103 to 24-80-106. Such copies shall be certified by their custodian as true copies of the originals before the originals are destroyed or lost, and the copies so certified shall have the same force and effect as the originals. Copies of public records transferred from the office of their origin to the division, when certified by the state archivist or the assistant archivist, shall have the same legal force and effect as if certified by the original custodian of the records.

Source: L. 51, p. 779, § 7; CSA, C. 154, § 18(16); CRS 53, § 131-3-7; C.R.S. 1963, § 131-3-7.

24-80-108. Access to public records. The state archivist of the division of state archives and public records, in person or through a deputy, shall have the right of reasonable access to all nonconfidential public records in the state, or any public office of the state of Colorado, or any county, city, municipality, district, or political subdivision thereof, because of the historical and research value of data contained therein, with a view to securing their safety and determining their need for preservation or disposal.

Source: L. 51, p. 779, § 8; CSA, C. 154, § 18(17); CRS 53, § 131-3-8; C.R.S. 1963, § 131-3-8.

24-80-109. Records may be replevined. On behalf of the state and the division of state archives and public records, the attorney general may replevin any public records which were formerly part of the records or files of any public office of the territory or state of Colorado.

Source: L. 51, p. 779, § 9; CSA, C. 154, § 18(18); CRS 53, § 131-3-9; C.R.S. 1963, § 131-3-9.

24-80-110. Disagreement as to value of records. In the event the attorney general and the state archivist determine that any records in the custody of a public officer including the state archivist, but not those in the custody of a public officer of any county, city, municipality, district, or political subdivision thereof, are of no legal, administrative, or, subject to section 24-80-211 (1) (b), historical value, but the public officer having custody of said records or from whose office records originated fails to agree with such determination or refuses to dispose of said records, the attorney general and the state archivist may request the governor to make his determination as to whether said records should be disposed of in the interests of conservation of space, economy, or safety.

Source: L. 51, p. 780, § 10; CSA, C. 154, § 18(19); CRS 53, § 131-3-10; C.R.S. 1963, § 131-3-10; L. 64, pm 174, § 148.

24-80-111. Microfilm revolving fund. (1)   There is hereby appropriated out of any moneys in the state treasury not otherwise appropriated, the sum of not to exceed ten thousand dollars to the division of state archives and public records to establish a revolving fund for acquisition of microfilm stock and photographic supplies and for other related expenses and to pay personal services and state payments to the retirement fund for personnel engaged exclusively in work directly relating to the records microfilming program of the state.

(2)   The total amount of cash, accounts receivable, microfilm, and photographic stocks shall not exceed the total amount of ten thousand dollars. The amount allocated shall not be used for the payment of any operating expenses of the division except as outlined in subsection (1) of this section.

(3)   Charges made by the division to other agencies for records, microfilming, or related photographic work done under the program shall be at two percent above actual cost for the purpose of repaying the general fund the amount originally allocated to it on July 1, 1959. Any future surplus after repayment has been made to the general fund and after absorbing inventory losses or other nonchargeable expenses shall be transferred to the general fund as of June 30 of each year, so that the total amount of the revolving fund shall remain at ten thousand dollars.

Source: L. 59, p. 747, § 1; CRS 53, § 131-3-11; C.R.S. 1963, § 131-3-11.

24-80-112. Nonaffect of act. Sections 24-80-101, 24-80-102, and 24-80-211 shall in no way affect sections 24-80-104 to 24-80-110.

Source: L. 59, p. 744, § 5; CRS 53, § 131-3-12; C.R.S. 1963, § 131-3-12.

STATE HISTORICAL SOCIETY
(Colorado Revised Statues, 1982, s.24-80-201 to 24-80-213.)

24-80-201. Society an educational institution. The state historical society, an incorporated organization, is hereby declared to be one of the educational institutions of the state of Colorado.

Source: L. 15, h. 440, § 1; C. L. § 8225; CSA, C. 154, § 8; CRS 53, § 131-1-1; C.R.S. 1963, § 131-1-1.

24-80-202. Trustee for state - exchange duplicates - lending materials. Except as otherwise provided in part 1 of this article, the society shall be the trustee of the state and as such shall faithfully expend and apply all money received from the state to the uses and purposes directed by law, and shall hold its present and future collections and property for the state, and shall not sell, mortgage, transfer, or dispose of in any manner or remove from the Colorado state museum any article thereof, or part of the same, without authority of law. This shall not prevent the sale or exchange of any duplicates which the society may have or obtain, the loan for reasonable periods of time of materials or exhibits to responsible borrowers under adequate safeguards, or the transfer to other educational institutions of the state of property not deemed applicable to the purposes of the society.

Source: L. 15, p. 440, § 2; C. L. § 8226; CSA, C. 154, § 9; CRS 53, § 131-1-2; C.R.S. 1963, § 131-1-2; L. 71, p. 1219, § 1.

24-80-203. Report - publications. (1) The president of the society shall prepare and transmit annually, in the form and manner prescribed by the controller pursuant to the provisions of section 24-30-208, a report accounting to the governor and the general assembly for the efficient discharge of all responsibilities assigned by law or directive to the society.

(2) Publications of the society circulated in quantity outside the executive branch shall be issued in accordance with fiscal rules promulgated by the controller pursuant to the provisions of section 24-30-208.

Source: R & RE, L. 64, p. 173, § 145; C.R.S. 1963, § 131-1-3.

24-80-204. Employees. The board of directors of the society shall appoint its employees and fix their salaries, subject to the provisions and exemptions of section 13 of article XII of the state constitution; but for the purposes of this part 2, all officers, curators, assistant curators, and teachers of the society, so designated by the board of directors, are hereby declared, as a matter of legislative determination, to be officers and teachers in an educational institution and therefore not under the state personnel system.

Source: L. 15, p. 441, § 4; C. L. § 8228; CSA, C. 154, § 11; CRS 53, § 131-1-4; C.R.S. 1963, § 131-1-4; L. 64, p. 109, § 2.

24-80-205. Disposition of duplicate specimens - loans authorized. (1) Whenever the state historical society possesses natural history books, specimens, and documents which are duplicates of or similar to others possessed by the society or which are considered useless by the board of directors for the history of the state or more useful for exchange, the society is authorized to return such books or the material to the donors, to government departments, or to state institutions, to loan or deposit with its branch societies or exchange for other similar material, or otherwise to dispose of same as provided by law.

(2) The state historical society is authorized to loan, for reasonable periods of time, materials and exhibits possessed by the society to responsible

borrowers under adequate safeguards.

Source: L. 19, p. 662, § 1; C. L. § 8229; CSA, C. 154, § 12; CRS 53, § 131-1-5; C.R.S. 1963, § 131-1-5; L. 71, p. 1219, § 2.

24-80-206. Society to accept gifts. The state historical society is hereby authorized to accept and receive gifts and donations to carry out and promote the objects and purposes of the society.

Source: L. 21, p. 740, § 1; C. L. § 8230; CSA, C. 154, § 13; CRS 53, § 131-1-6; C.R.S. 1963, § 131-1-6.

24-80-207. Purpose of donations. Donations of moneys, securities, or other property may be made to and for the sole use of any one or more of the departments or bureaus of the society, and donations so made shall be kept in a separate fund for the use of such department.

Source: L. 21, p. 740, § 2; C. L. § 8231; CSA, C. 154, § 14; CRS 53, § 131-1-7; C.R.S. 1963, § 131-1-7.

24-80-208. Donations providing conditions on use. Donations made with the provision that the interest or income only therefrom shall be used by the society, if accepted, shall be received by the society, and the intent of the donor with reference to the same shall be observed and carried out, and the principal of said gift, if money, and such other funds as are available shall be invested by the state treasurer as state custodian of those funds, and the interest or income therefrom shall be available for the society for the purposes given.

Source: L. 21, p. 740, § 3; C. L. § 8232; CSA, C. 154, § 15; CRS 53, § 131-1-8; C.R.S. 1963, § 131-1-8.

24-80-209. Title to property - disbursement of revenues. The title to all property acquired by the society by gift, purchase, or otherwise shall absolutely vest in and belong to the state of Colorado when accepted or received by the society, and all moneys or securities received by it, whether from gifts, sale of duplicate or undesired books, specimens, documents, exhibits, or other properties, sale of microfilms or other copies, publication or sale of books, magazines, postcards, pamphlets, maps, or other materials, admissions, dues, operation or rental of concessions or facilities, rendering of services, or from any other source shall be held by the state treasurer as custodian separate and apart from other funds and may be withdrawn from his custody for the purposes and under the control of the society, only upon the issuance of vouchers signed by the president or vice-president and treasurer or secretary of the society and upon warrants drawn against such funds by the controller.

Source: L. 21, p. 741, § 4; C. L. § 8233; CSA, C. 154, § 16; L. 47, p. 820, § 1; CRS 53, § 131-1-9; C.R.S. 1963, § 131-1-9.

24-80-210. Collections classed and catalogued. Collections of a scientific or historical nature shall be properly classed and catalogued and shall be at all reasonable hours open for public inspection and examination but under such rules and regulations as shall be prescribed or adopted by said society.

Source: L. 05, p. 356, § 2; R. S. 08, § 6117; C. L. § 8223; CSA, C. 154, § 6; CRS 53, § 131-1-10; C.R.S. 1963, § 131-1-10.

24-80-211. Society and division. (1) The state historical society shall continue as an educational institution of the state, considered as a division of the department of higher education for the purpose of determining the order of its appropriation; except that:

(a) The division of state archives and public records shall be a division of the department of administration of the state government, separate and apart from the state historical society;

(b) The state archivist shall consult with the state historical society with respect to the proposed destruction under part 1 of this article of any documentary, library, or museum materials, whether or not defined in section 24-80-101 as records, and shall not consent to the destruction of any such materials determined by the state historical society to be of historical value; and

(c) The installation of any museum display or exhibition of historical materials in the division of state archives and public records shall be with the guidance and counsel of the state historical society.

Source: L. 59, p. 741, § 1; CRS 53, § 131-1-11; C.R.S. 1963, § 131-1-11.

24-80-212. Transfer of mineral exhibits and documents. On July 1, 1959, there shall be transferred from the bureau of mines of the state of Colorado to the state historical society that certain mineral exhibit presently maintained by the bureau of mines in the Colorado state museum building, together with all mineral and other collections, specimens, exhibits, displays, records, documents, cases, and other materials pertaining to said exhibits and all collections and exhibits subordinate thereto. The said exhibit shall be and remain from the date of such transfer part of the general collections of the state historical society as described in this part 2, subject to the obligations and powers of the state historical society as set forth in this part 2. That portion of the Colorado state museum building now occupied by the said exhibit shall be transferred on July 1, 1959 to the occupancy and control of the state historical society.

Source: L. 59, p. 745, § 1; CRS 53, § 131-1-12; C.R.S. 1963, § 131-1-12.

24-80-213. Assistance from educational institutions. At the request of the state historical society, officials of the bureau of mines of the state of Colorado, the Colorado school of mines, the university of Colorado, and other state educational institutions shall consult with the state historical society and shall assist and advise the society concerning the technical aspects, maintenance, display, and utilization of any part or all of the mineral exhibit described in section 24-80-212.

Source: L. 59, p. 745, § 1; CRS 53, § 131-1-13; C.R.S. 1963, § 131-1-13.

SUPREME COURT LIBRARY
(Colorado Revised Statutes, 1982, s.13-2-116 to 13-2-121,
13-2-125, 13-2-126.)

13-2-116. Disposition of law books. (1) The state librarian and all other officers who receive for public use from any other state or territory, or any officer thereof, or any other person any books of judicial reports or public statutes or any other books of law shall forthwith cause one copy of such books or statutes, and all of such books of reports, and other books of law to be deposited in the library of the supreme court, there to remain.

(2) The supreme court librarian shall furnish the supreme court annually, as the court may direct, a report designating any such copies of judicial reports, statutes, or books of law which, in the librarian's opinion, can be properly removed from the supreme court library and disposed of.

(3) The supreme court may take action pursuant to such report by ordering any copies of such judicial reports, statutes, or books of law designated therein disposed of in such manner as it shall determine.

Source: G. L. § 2623; G. S. § 3242; R. S. 08, § 1428; L. 11, p. 488, § 1; C. L. § 5640; CSA, C. 46, § 34; CRS 53, § 37-2-17; L. 57, p. 317, § 1; C.R.S. 1963, § 37-2-15.

13-2-117. Librarian to have charge of library. The librarian of the supreme court, under the direction of the court, shall have custody of the books pertaining to the library of the supreme court.

Source: G. L. § 2621; G. S. § 3240; not in R. S. 08; C. L. § 5641; CSA, C. 46, § 35; L. 37, p. 495, § 1; CRS 53, § 37-2-18; C.R.S. 1963, § 37-2-16.

13-2-118. Duties of librarian. It is the duty of the librarian to keep his office open every day in the year, Saturdays, Sundays, and holidays excepted, from eight-thirty a.m. until five p.m. of each day, so that the public may have access to the library, under such rules and regulations as the supreme court may prescribe.

Source: G. L. § 2622; G. S. § 3241; R. S. 08, § 1429; C. L. § 5642; CSA, C. 46, § 36; CRS 53, § 37-2-19; C.R.S. 1963, § 37-2-17.

13-2-119. Disposition of fees. At the end of each month all fees collected by the clerk of the supreme court during said month, including fees for admission to the bar, shall be deposited by him with the state treasurer, by whom the same shall be kept separate and apart from all other funds in his hands.

Source: L. 07, p. 594, § 1; R. S. 08, § 1430; L. 19, p. 680, § 1; C. L. § 5643; CSA, C. 46, § 37; CRS 53, § 37-2-20; C.R.S. 1963, § 37-2-18.

13-2-120. Supreme court library fund. The funds so set apart, together with the balance of the fund now in the state treasurer's hands and designated as the "supreme court library fund", shall be known as the "supreme court library fund", and the supreme court is authorized to use said fund for the following purposes: First, for the purchase of books for the supreme court library; second, for paying the expenses of binding briefs and other documents for use in said library; third, for the purchase and maintenance of bookcases, catalogues, furniture, fixtures, and other equipment for said library. Until this section is expressly repealed or amended, neither said fund nor any part thereof shall be used or appropriated for any other purpose whatsoever.

Source: L. 07, p. 594, § 1; R. S. 08, § 1430; L. 19, p. 680, § 2; C. L. § 5644; CSA, C. 46, § 38; CRS 53, § 37-2-21; C.R.S. 1963, § 37-2-19.

13-2-121. Manner of disbursement. The state controller is authorized to draw warrants upon said fund, from time to time upon certificate, of the sums required for the purposes specified in section 13-2-120 under the signature of the chief justice or a majority of the judges of the supreme court, and the state treasurer is directed to pay the same out of said fund.

Source: L. 07, p. 594, § 1; R. S. 08, § 1430; L. 19, p. 681, § 3; C. L. § 5645; CSA, C. 46, § 39; CRS 53, § 37-2-22; C.R.S. 1963, § 37-2-20.

13-2-125. Purchase, distribution, and sale of reports. (1) Upon the publication of each volume of said reports, the secretary of state shall be responsible for purchasing, through the state purchasing agent, as many copies as are required to meet the needs of the state and the public.

(2) The secretary of state is responsible for distribution of the reports without charge, and for record-keeping with reference thereto, as follows:

(a) State and territorial libraries, as directed by the librarian of the supreme court;

(b) The library of congress and of the United States supreme court;

(c) The attorney general and secretary of state of Colorado, and officials of the executive branch as required;

(d) District attorneys and judges of Colorado courts of record;

(e) The justices and reporter of the Colorado supreme court;

(f) The law library of the university of Colorado, and the library of any other accredited law school in Colorado;

(g) Copies for use in the supreme court library and by the general assembly;

(h) Copies to be used for exchange purposes in the maintenance of the supreme court library, as directed by the librarian of the supreme court;

(i) Office of revisor of statutes.

(3) All copies distributed to offices and agencies of the state of Colorado are at all times the property of the state and not the personal property of the incumbents of the respective offices, and shall be so marked as the property of the state. This shall not apply to the justices and reporter of the supreme court as to volumes prepared during their tenure of office.

(4) The secretary of state shall also sell the reports of the supreme court to the public at a price which is set at the cost of the report, plus a twenty-

five percent markup for handling. The proceeds from the sale of these reports to the public shall be deposited in the general fund.

Source: L. 1891, p. 371, § 7; R. S. 08, § 1438; C. L. § 5653; L. 27, p. 680, § 1; CSA, C. 46, § 46; L. 37, p. 495, § 2; CRS 53, § 37-2-30; L. 63, p. 269, § 3; C.R.S. 1963, § 37-2-24.

13-2-126. Reports and session laws furnished. (1) The secretary of state or whoever may be by law the legal custodian of publications of the state of Colorado is directed to furnish to the law library of the university of Colorado, free of charge from existing stocks if feasible, and in any event as such publications are from time to time issued:

(a) Thirty copies each of the reports of the supreme court of the state of Colorado; and

(b) Fifty copies each of the session laws, and of any published regulations and decisions of the various administrative agencies of the state of Colorado; and

(c) Five copies each of the Colorado yearbook; and

(d) Two copies each of published legislative journals, published opinions and reports of the attorney general, and printed briefs and abstracts of record of the supreme court of Colorado.

(2) The law library is authorized to exchange any or all of the above publications for like publications of other jurisdictions.

Source: L. 15, p. 482, § 1; C. L. § 5655; CSA, C. 46, § 48; L. 49, p. 338, § 1; CRS 53, § 37-2-32; C.R.S. 1963, § 37-2-25.

MISCELLANEOUS PROVISIONS
(Colorado Revised Statutes, 1982, s.39-3-101;
Constitution of Colorado, Art. IV, s.20.)

39-3-101. Exempt property. (1) The following shall be exempt from general taxation under the provisions of articles 1 to 13 of this title:

* * *

(d) Public libraries and the property, real and personal, of the state and its political subdivisions;

Source: R & RE, L. 64, p. 680, § 1; C.R.S. 1963, § 137-2-1; L. 67, pp. 946, 1077, 1082, § § 7, 1, 2, 1; L. 69, pp. 1116, 1117, § § 1, 1; L. 70, p. 381, § 14.

Section 20. State librarian. The superintendent of public instruction shall be ex officio state librarian.

Colorado library laws are reprinted from COLORADO REVISED STATUTES published by Bradford-Robinson Printing Co., Denver, Colorado.

CONNECTICUT

STATE LIBRARY

(Connecticut General Statutes Annotated, 1982,
s.11-1 to 11-9a.)

§ 11–1. Appointment and duties of board

(a) The state library board shall consist of the chief justice of the supreme court or his designee, the chief court administrator or his designee, the commissioner of education and five electors to be appointed by the governor for terms of five years from July first in the year of their appointment. The governor shall fill any vacancy in the office of an appointed member for the unexpired portion of the term. The chief justice may designate any judge of the supreme court to serve in his place.

(b) Said board may elect annually a chairman from its members to serve a term of one year from his election or until his successor is elected. Said chairman shall represent the board in certifying such actions as the board may approve. The board may designate the state librarian to act as its administrative officer with the authority to sign contracts approved by the board.

(c) Said board shall have charge of the state library and supreme court building and the grounds connected therewith, and shall appoint a state librarian and a state historian. Except when specifically prohibited by the conditions, if any, upon which a gift was created or by a conditional sales agreement, said board is authorized to sell, trade or otherwise dispose of any unwanted duplicate, out-of-date or irrelevant materials within the collections of the state library, provided that the monetary proceeds of such a transaction, if any, shall be deemed to be funds from private sources, and as such funds, shall be held in the manner prescribed by section 4–31 for use in furthering any purpose said board considers to be in harmony with the original purpose of the gift or purchase of such materials. Said board shall engage in planning for statewide library service, other than for school libraries, and for the establishment of a research center to facilitate the most effective use of materials in public, university, professional and industrial libraries and may take such action as is necessary to secure maximum state participation in federal aid for public libraries, for scholarships for students of library science and for cooperative library projects. Said board shall establish an interagency library planning committee to aid the board in such planning, which committee shall be composed of not less than fifteen and not more than twenty on a regional or statewide basis. Members of said planning committee shall serve without compensation or reimbursement of expenses. Said board may, by regulation, establish standards for principal public libraries and procedures ty-five members, of whom twenty per cent shall be persons who use library services and of whom eighty per cent shall represent established agencies or associations concerned with the provision of, or planning for, library services for naming such libraries and periodically review the same. To carry out its duties under the general statutes, said board may make contracts, subject to the approval of the attorney general and to any appropriations made for such purpose or the availability of other public or private funds.

(d) The state library board shall be within the department of education for administrative purposes only.

(1976, P.A. 76-436, §§ 10a, 473, eff. July 1, 1978; 1977, P.A. 77-614, §§ 302, 308, eff. Jan. 1, 1979; 1979, P.A. 79-610, § 44, eff. Oct. 1, 1979.)

§ 11-1a. Programs of statewide library service. Toll free telephone service

(a) The state library board may institute and conduct programs of statewide library service which may include, but need not be limited to, (1) a cataloging and processing service to be available to libraries, (2) the creation and maintenance of current and retrospective union catalogs of books, union lists of serials and similar cooperative listings of library materials, (3) a program of coordinated acquisitions, storage and deposit of library materials, (4) the support and encouragement of the transfer, as loans or copies, of library materials between libraries and to nonresident library patrons, (5) the provision of suitable high-speed communications facilities, (6) the creation and maintenance of bibliographic and regional reference centers, (7) the provision of travelling collections of library materials and of book examination centers, and (8) the provision of a publicity and public relations service for libraries.

(b) The state library board shall create and maintain one or more library research centers which shall utilize any appropriate sources of information, both within and outside of the state, to meet the needs of those making inquiries.

(c) The state library board shall maintain a system of law libraries at specified locations within the state. The tier I libraries in Bridgeport and New Haven shall be open to the public all day Monday to Friday, inclusive.

(d) The state library board shall cooperate with and assist the judicial department in maintaining the collections of judges.

(e) The state library board is authorized to expend an amount not in excess of forty-five hundred dollars annually to maintain books in New London, an amount not in excess of forty-five hundred dollars annually to maintain books in Danbury and an amount not in excess of three thousand dollars annually to maintain books in Willimantic, provided the state library board determines that staffing is not necessary at the tier II library in Norwich and provided further library facilities and staff are maintained at the locations at Willimantic, Danbury and New London without additional expense to the state.

(1969, P.A. 245, § 2, eff. May 23, 1969; 1973, P.A. 73–645, § 3, eff. July 1, 1973; 1975, P.A. 75–316, § 2; 1976, P.A. 76–368, § 3, eff. July 1, 1976.)

§ 11–1b. Regulations re statewide library service

The state library board shall promulgate regulations to implement the provisions of sections 11–1a, 11–24b and 11–31a.

(1973, P.A. 73–645, § 4, eff. July 1, 1973; 1975, P.A. 75–316, § 3.)

§ 11–2. Powers and duties of state librarian

The state library shall maintain a division of reader services and a division of library development. The state librarian, with the approval of the state library board, may appoint an associate state librarian as the administrative head of each of said divisions. Such associate librarians and members of the staff of the state library employed in positions requiring graduation from a library school shall be members of the unclassified service. The state librarian shall have charge, under the state library board, of the state library and supreme court building and the grounds connected therewith. He may purchase for the state library such books as the state library board directs or authorizes. He is authorized and directed to distribute copies of the files of each act favorably reported by any committee of the general assembly and printed in the files to each high school and university in the state, upon request. He may cause to be located and permanently identified the graves of all soldiers, sailors and marines, veterans of any war in which the colony of Connecticut or the United States of America has been or may be engaged, who are buried within the limits of this state. The state library board sha l report biennially to the general assembly.

(1980, P.A. 80–36, § 1, eff. July 1, 1980.)

§ 11–2a. Receipt of federal funds

The state librarian is empowered, subject to the provisions of the general statutes, to receive any federal funds made available to the state for purposes of programs under his jurisdiction and to expend such funds for the purpose or purposes for which they are made available. The state treasurer shall be the custodian of such funds.

(1972, P.A. 139.)

§ 11–3. Transfer of books to college libraries

The state librarian is authorized, from time to time, under the direction of the state library board, to transfer for an indefinite period, to the libraries of Yale University or any other university or college in the state, any duplicates or other books or pamphlets not in current use.

(1949 Rev., § 1631; 1975, P.A. 75–316, § 5.)

§ 11–4. Preservation of official documents in state library

Any official of the state or of any town, or any other official, may turn over to the state librarian, with his consent, for permanent preservation in the state library, any official books, records, documents, original papers or files, not in current use in his office, taking a receipt therefor, which shall be recorded; and such official may, in like manner, turn over to the state librarian, with his consent, for use of the state, any printed books, records, documents or reports not in current use in his office. Except as provided in section 11–5, nothing herein shall be construed to allow the removal of any books or records affecting the title to any estate, real or personal, within the jurisdiction of the official having custody of such records. The state librarian shall embody in his report to the governor a general list of all such books, records, documents or papers so received and, upon the request of any person entitled thereto, shall furnish a certified copy of any such record, document or paper, and such certified copy shall be entitled to the same weight as evidence as though certified by the authority by whom such record, document or paper was deposited with said librarian.

(1949 Rev., § 1633; 1959, P.A. 152, § 24.)

§ 11–4a. Temporary commissions to file reports with librarian

Each temporary commission or committee appointed by the governor or the general assembly, or both, and required to report its findings and recommendations, shall file with the state librarian as many copies of such report as the commission or committee and the librarian jointly deem appropriate and shall file any extra copies with the clerks of the senate and house of representatives.

(1959, P.A. 419.)

§ 11–4b. Furnishing of legislative materials to law libraries

The state library shall mail to each law library, established pursuant to chapter 189, a copy of each of the following legislative materials as they become available: Photo offset copies of each bill; bulletins; calendars; journals; file copies; engrossed copies, and the legislative record and index.

(1963, P.A. 264.)

§ 11–5. Preservation and reproduction of land and probate records

The town clerk of any town and the judge of any probate district, respectively, may deliver to the state librarian, with his consent, for preservation in the state library, any volume of land or probate records in his official custody, the age or condition of

which renders its continued use by the public inadvisable, and such clerk or judge shall take a receipt therefor, which shall be recorded in the records of such town or probate district. The state librarian shall, within a reasonable time after receiving any such volume, make a photostat copy of its contents and shall certify that such contents are correct and complete, and such certificate shall be included in such photostat copy. Such certified photostat copy shall be substantially bound, shall match the current volumes of land records of such town or probate records of such probate district so far as practicable, and shall be delivered to the town clerk or judge of probate from whom the original volume was received. Such town clerk or judge of probate is authorized to issue certified copies from such certified photostat volume of any instrument or other matter contained therein and such certified copies shall be admissible in evidence in the same manner and entitled to the same weight as copies made and certified from the original volume. The state librarian is authorized to issue certified copies of any instrument or other matter contained in any such volume, which certified copies shall be admissible in evidence in the same manner and entitled to the same weight as copies made and certified by the official from whom such volume was received.
(1949 Rev., § 1634.)

§ 11-6. Department of war records

The state library shall maintain a department of war records, which shall collect, classify, index and install in the library all available material relating to Connecticut participation, public or private, in the first and second world wars and thus establish a permanent and accessible record of their extent and character, such record to be as complete and comprehensive as possible and to cover not only the activities of the state, its subdivisions and agencies, but also of Connecticut agencies of the federal government, of organizations of private persons and of those individuals who were direct participants in said wars, whether as soldiers, sailors, aviators or otherwise. Said department shall be under the management and control of a committee consisting of eight or more members of which the state librarian shall be a member and its chairman and executive head. The remaining members of the committee shall be appointed by the state librarian with the approval of the state library board. They shall serve without compensation except that their necessary expenses incurred in the performance of their duties shall be paid. Whenever the appropriations made by the general assembly for the purpose of carrying on the work of said department prove insufficient, the governor shall, from time to time, make such further appropriations as may be reasonably needed for that purpose.

(1949 Rev., § 1635; 1975, P.A. 75–316, § 6.)

§ 11-7. Purchase of copies of town records

The comptroller shall purchase, at an expense not exceeding one thousand dollars per annum, one hundred bound copies of the printed records of any town which meet with the approval of the state librarian as to form, accuracy and workmanship, the cost of such printed records not to exceed one cent per page, including index. Such copies shall be deposited with the state librarian for purposes of exchange and distribution.

(1949 Rev., § 1636.)

§ 11–8. Department of archives and records administration. Public records administrator

The state library shall maintain a department of archives and records administration. The state librarian shall, subject to the provisions of chapter 67, appoint an assistant, who shall be the public records administrator and head of the department of archives and records administration. Under the direction of the state librarian he shall: Preserve and administer such public archives as are deposited in the state library; carry out a records management program for all state agencies within the executive department, and for all towns, cities, boroughs, districts and other political subdivisions of the state, including the probate districts, pursuant to the provisions of section 11–8a; supervise the operation of state records centers; provide photoduplication and microfilming service and document repair and restoration service for state and local records; approve security storage facilities, within or without the state, or establish and operate such facilities within the state, for the safe storage of original public records or security copies thereof; and carry out a program for the identification and preservation of essential records of the state and of its political subdivisions. He shall, with the approval of the state librarian, and in accordance with the provisions of chapter 54, adopt regulations for the creation and preservation of the records of the several towns, cities, boroughs and districts, including probate districts, of the state. Such regulations shall establish the physical characteristics required for papers, inks, typewriter ribbons, carbon papers, loose-leaf binders, photographic films or other supplies and materials, including photographic or other processes for recording documents, used in the creation of public records; and the design, construction and degree of fire resistance required for safes, cabinets, vaults and file rooms in which public records are housed. He shall ascertain from time to time whether the provisions of the general statutes and of such regulations relating to the recording, filing, indexing, maintenance and disposition of such records are being carried out. He may order any person having the care and custody of such records to comply with such statutes or with such regulations. He shall send a copy of such order to the chief administrative officer of the town, city, borough or district to which the records relate. The order shall specify the time within which it shall be complied with; and, in setting such time, he shall take into consideration the availability of facilities or equipment or the need for the construction or purchase thereof. The state librarian may cause the enforcement of any such order by application to the superior court, or to any judge thereof if said court is not then sitting, to issue an appropriate decree or process, which application shall be brought and the proceedings thereon conducted by the attorney general. The public records administrator shall report annually to the state librarian. All powers, functions and duties assigned by any provision of the general statutes to the examiner of public records are hereby transferred to the public records administrator.

(1977, P.A. 77-614, § 121, eff. Oct. 1, 1977; 1980, P.A. 80-338, § 4.)

§ 11-8a. Records management program. Retention and destruction of records. Centralized microcopying service

The state librarian shall be responsible for developing and directing a records management program for the books, records, papers and documents of all state agencies within the executive department, with the approval of the commissioner of administrative services, and for the books, records, papers and documents of the several towns, cities, boroughs, districts and other political subdivisions of the state including the probate districts, which program shall be implemented by the department of archives and records administration of the state library. In the performance of his duties pursuant to this section the state librarian shall consult with the attorney general, the probate court administrator and the chief executive officers of the Connecticut Town Clerks Association and the Municipal Finance Officers Association of Connecticut, or their duly appointed representatives. The state librarian may require each such state agency, or each political subdivision of the state, including each probate district, to inventory all books, records, papers and documents under its jurisdiction and to submit to him for approval retention schedules for all such books, records, papers and documents, or he may undertake such inventories and establish such retention schedules, based on the administrative need of retaining such books, records, papers and documents within agency offices or in suitable records centers. If the public records administrator determines that certain books, records, papers and documents which have no further administrative, fiscal or legal usefulness are of historical value to the state, the state librarian shall direct that they be transferred to the state library. If the state librarian determines that such books, records, papers and documents are of no administrative, fiscal, legal value, and the public records administrator determines that they are of no historical value to the state, the state librarian shall approve their disposal, whereupon the head of the state agency or political subdivision shall dispose of them as directed by the state librarian. Each agency head, and each local official concerned, shall notify the state librarian of any changes in the administrative requirements for the retention of any book, record, paper or document subsequent to the approval of retention schedules by the state librarian. The state librarian may establish and carry out a program of inventorying, repairing and microcopying for the security of those records of political subdivisions of the state which he determines to have permanent value; and he may provide safe storage for the security of such microcopies of such records.

(1980, P.A. 80-338, § 1.)

§ 11-9. Appropriations to the Connecticut Historical Society

The comptroller is authorized to draw his orders upon the treasurer in equal quarterly instalments in favor of the treasurer of the Connecticut Historical Society in such sums as may be appropriated to enable said society to classify and catalogue its collection of printed and manuscript material, to bind and arrange the same in a suitable and convenient manner, to mount, frame or otherwise suitably prepare its portraits, plates, engravings, lithographs, sketches, maps and surveys, to properly arrange for permanent exhibition its collection of articles in its museum and archaeological department, to publish its roll of soldiers who served in the revolutionary and colonial wars not heretofore printed, and to do such other work as may be necessary to preserve such documentary and historical matter in its possession as is in a perishable condition, and is intended for the use and benefit of the public. When such appropriations are made, said society shall deposit in the state library three hundred copies of each catalogue, report or other work published by said society pursuant to the provisions of this section, and the state librarian shall distribute or dispose of the same as other publications are distributed under state authority.

(1949 Rev., § 1676.)

§ 11-9a. Appointment and duties of cooperating library service unit review board

(a) For the purposes of this section, a "library service unit" means an entity providing library and information service from an organized body of recorded knowledge which may be in the form of books, periodicals, audio or video recordings on film, disc or tape; machine-stored information or knowledge preserved in any other recorded form, and which service was created and continues to exist for the purpose of transmitting such knowledge to mankind.

(b) The state library board shall appoint a fifteen member cooperating library service unit review board, representing special, school, academic and public library interests and existing regional cooperating library service units. Such review board shall establish criteria for, and encourage the formation of, a system of regional cooperating library service units and shall report its recommendations annually to the state library board and the joint standing committee on education of the general assembly. The members of the cooperating library service unit review board shall serve without compensation or reimbursement of expenses.

(1975, P.A. 75-363.)

STATE AID
(Connecticut General Statutes Annotated, 1982,
s.11-24a to 11-25.)

§ 11-24a. Definitions

As used in section 11-24(b):

(a) "Board" means state library board.

(b) "Public library" means any library which provides library services to any members of the public by means of central facilities, branch facilities or bookmobiles and which is at least partially supported by town taxation.

(c) "Principal public library" means any public library or the state library which has been so designated as follows: Any town may, in accordance with the regulations of the board, enter an agreement with any public library whereby such library agrees to provide library services without charge to the residents of such town on terms mutually acceptable to the parties. A town may designate only one library as its principal public library, but any public library may serve as a principal public library for more than one town.

(d) "Local funds" means moneys received by a public library from any source, public or private, except state or federal grants.

(e) "General library purposes" means all functions of a public library except the purchasing of land or the construction, alteration or remodeling of buildings.

(f) "Base period operational funds" means the sum of local funds authorized and expended by a public library in its first fiscal year ending after July 1, 1967, plus the amount of the state grant made to such library during the state fiscal year beginning July 1, 1967.

(1967, P.A. 590, § 2; 1975, P.A. 75-316, § 12.)

§ 11-24b. Grants to public libraries. Statewide library services

(a) On the order of the state library board the comptroller shall pay in the first year of the biennium beginning July 1, 1969, and each year thereafter (1) to each public library one thousand dollars, (2) to each principal public library twelve hundred dollars per town which such library serves as a designated principal public library and (3) to each principal public library which serves as such for a town or towns with a total population of over ten thousand persons according to the latest United States census as proportionately modified annually by the figures promulgated by the bureau of vital statistics of the Connecticut department of health for the immediately preceding year an additional amount which represents a portion of the remainder of the appropriation for grants to libraries under subdivisions (1) and (2) of this section which bears the same ratio to

such remainder as the population served by such library bears to
the total population served by such principal public libraries,
subject to the appropriation therefor and provided each such library has filed with the board an affidavit certifying that in its
fiscal year next preceding the year for which a grant is sought
such library expended authorized local funds for general library
purposes equal to or in excess of the base period operational
funds as defined in section 11–24a. In each year in which the
authorization and expenditures are less than the base period operational funds, the grant awarded to such library shall be one
dollar for each dollar of local funds authorized and expended by
that library in excess of the local funds expended by it in its
first fiscal year ending after July 1, 1967, but not more than one
thousand dollars in the case of a public library or twelve hundred dollars in the case of a principal public library. In no case
shall the state grant payable to any one library in any one year
under this subsection exceed one-half of the local funds expended
by it in its preceding fiscal year. Any appropriation for grants
under this section shall be divided equally for use in each year
in the period for which such appropriation is made.

(b) Any library offering statewide library services may
claim and be entitled to receive state aid for net services rendered to nonresidents, provided such library files with the state
library board a record of the number of items loaned to nonresidents of the town or towns which it normally serves not later
than thirty days after January first and July first of each year.
On the order of the state library board the comptroller shall pay
to such library an amount which bears the same ratio to one-
half of the total appropriation for such grants in a fiscal year as
the net services rendered to nonresidents by such library bears
to the total volume or net services rendered to nonresidents in libraries throughout the state. Such payments are to be used exclusively to defray costs incurred by such library in extending
its services to nonresidents. No portion of such grant may be
used for general library purposes nor may any portion of such
grant revert to the general fund of the town or towns normally
served by such library. For purposes of this section, "net services rendered to nonresidents" shall mean the library services,
based on the number of items loaned, rendered to nonresidents of
town or towns normally served by such library in excess of the
library service rendered to residents of such town or towns by
other libraries.

(1967, P.A. 590, §§ 3, 4; 1969, P.A. 579, § 1, eff. July 1, 1969; 1973,

P.A. 73–572; 1973, P.A. 73–645, § 2, eff. July 1, 1973; 1975, P.A. 75–316, § 13.)

§ 11–24c. Construction cost grants. Priority list

The state library board shall make construction grants to public libraries established pursuant to this chapter the board shall: (1) Establish criteria for the purpose of developing a priority listing of all construction projects and (2) grant an amount equal to one-third of the total construction cost, not to exceed two hundred thousand dollars for each approved project within the limits of the available appropriation for such projects. In the event that the appropriation is insufficient to fund projects as provided above, projects remaining on the priority list shall be included in the priority listing for the next fiscal year. Each application for such grant shall be filed on or before September first, annually, on forms to be prescribed by said board.

(1980, P.A. 80–400, § 1, eff. Oct. 1, 1981.)

§ 11–25. Reports by libraries

The libraries established under the provisions of this chapter, and any free public library receiving a state appropriation, shall annually make a report to the state library board.

(1949 Rev., § 1663; 1965, P.A. 490, § 8, eff. July 1, 1965; 1975, P.A. 75–316, § 15.)

INTERSTATE LIBRARY COMPACT
(Connecticut General Statutes Annotated, 1982, s.11-38 to 11-43.)

§ 11–38. Compact

The interstate library compact is hereby enacted into law and entered into by this state with all states legally joining therein in the form substantially as follows:

INTERSTATE LIBRARY COMPACT
Article I. Policy and Purpose

Because the desire for the services provided by libraries transcends governmental boundaries and can most effectively be satisfied by giving such services to communities and people regardless of jurisdictional lines, it is the policy of the states party to this compact to cooperate and share their responsibilities; to authorize cooperation and sharing with respect to those types of library facilities and services which can be more economically or efficiently developed and maintained on a cooperative basis, and to authorize cooperation and sharing among localities, states and others in providing joint or cooperative library services in areas where the distribution of population or of existing and potential library resources make the provision of library service on an interstate basis the most effective way of providing adequate and efficient service.

Article II. Definitions

As used in this compact:

(a) "Public library agency" means any unit or agency of local or state government operating or having power to operate a library.

(b) "Private library agency" means any non-governmental entity which operates or assumes a legal obligation to operate a library.

(c) "Library agreement" means a contract establishing an interstate library district pursuant to this compact or providing for the joint or cooperative furnishing of library services.

Article III. Interstate Library Districts

(a) Any one or more public library agencies in a party state in cooperation with any public library agency or agencies in one or more other party states may establish and maintain an interstate library district. Subject to the provisions of this compact and any other laws of the party states which pursuant hereto remain applicable, such district may establish, maintain and operate some or all of the library facilities and services for the area concerned in accordance with the terms of a library agreement therefor. Any private library agency or agencies within an interstate library district may cooperate therewith, assume duties, responsibilities and obligations thereto, and receive benefits therefrom as provided in any library agreement to which such agency or agencies become party.

(b) Within an interstate library district, and as provided by library agreement, the performance of library functions may be undertaken on a joint or cooperative basis or may be undertaken by means of one or more arrangements between or among public or private library agencies for the extension of library privileges to the use of facilities or services operated or rendered by one or more of the individual agencies.

(c) If a library agreement provides for joint establishment, maintenance or operation of library facilities or services by an interstate library district, such district shall have power to do any one or more of the following in accordance with such library agreement:

1. Undertake, administer and participate in programs or arrangements for securing, lending or servicing of books and other publications, any other materials suitable to be kept or

made available by libraries, library equipment or for the dissemination of information about libraries, the value and significance of particular items therein, and the use thereof.

2. Accept for any of its purposes under this compact any and all donations, and grants of money, equipment, supplies, materials, and services (conditional or otherwise), from any state or the United States or any subdivision or agency thereof, or interstate agency, or from any institution, person, firm or corporation, and receive, utilize and dispose of the same.

3. Operate mobile library units or equipment for the purpose of rendering bookmobile service within the district.

4. Employ professional, technical, clerical and other personnel and fix terms of employment, compensation and other appropriate benefits; and where desirable, provide for the inservice training of such personnel.

5. Sue and be sued in any court of competent jurisdiction.

6. Acquire, hold, and dispose of any real or personal property or any interest or interests therein as may be appropriate to the rendering of library service.

7. Construct, maintain and operate a library, including any appropriate branches thereof.

8. Do such other things as may be incidental to or appropriate for the carrying out of any of the foregoing powers.

Article IV.   Interstate Library Districts, Governing Board

(a) An interstate library district which establishes, maintains or operates any facilities or services in its own right shall have a governing board which shall direct the affairs of the district and act for it in all matters relating to its business. Each participating public library agency in the district shall be represented on the governing board which shall be organized and conduct its business in accordance with provision therefor in the library agreement. But in no event shall a governing board meet less often than twice a year.

(b) Any private library agency or agencies party to a library agreement establishing an interstate library district may be represented on or advise with the governing board of the district in such manner as the library agreement may provide.

Article V.   State Library Agency Cooperation

Any two or more state library agencies of two or more of the party states may undertake and conduct joint or cooperative library programs, render joint or cooperative library services, and enter into and perform arrangements for the cooperative or joint acquisition, use, housing and disposition of items or collections of materials which, by reason of expense, rarity, specialized nature, or infrequency of demand therefor would be appropriate for central collection and shared use. Any such programs, services or arrangements may include provision for the exercise on a cooperative or joint basis of any power exercisable by an interstate library district and an agreement embodying any such program, service or arrangement shall contain provisions covering the subjects detailed in article VI of this compact for interstate library agreements.

Article VI.   Library Agreements

(a) In order to provide for any joint or cooperative undertaking pursuant to this compact, public and private library agencies may enter into library agreements. Any agreement executed pursuant to the provisions of this compact shall, as among the parties to the agreement:

1.   Detail the specific nature of the services, programs, facilities, arrangements or properties to which it is applicable.

2.   Provide for the allocation of costs and other financial responsibilities.

3.   Specify the respective rights, duties, obligations and liabilities of the parties.

4.   Set forth the terms and conditions for duration, renewal, termination, abrogation, disposal of joint or common property, if any, and all other matters which may be appropriate to the proper effectuation and performance of the agreement.

(b) No public or private library agency shall undertake to exercise itself, or jointly with any other library agency, by means of a library agreement any power prohibited to such agency by the constitution or statutes of its state.

(c) No library agreement shall become effective until filed with the compact administrator of each state involved, and approved in accordance with article VII of this compact.

Article VII.   Approval of Library Agreements

(a) Every library agreement made pursuant to this compact shall, prior to and as a condition precedent to its entry into force, be submitted to the attorney general of each state in which a public library agency party thereto is situated, who shall determine whether the agreement is in proper form and compatible with the laws of his state. The attorneys general shall approve any agreement submitted to them unless they shall find that it does not meet the conditions set forth herein and shall detail in writing addressed to the governing bodies of the public library agencies concerned the specific respects in which the proposed agreement fails to meet the requirements of law. Failure to disapprove an agreement submitted hereunder within ninety (90) days of its submission shall constitute approval thereof.

(b) In the event that a library agreement made pursuant to this compact shall deal in whole or in part with the provision of services or facilities with regard to which an officer or agency of the state government has constitutional or statutory powers of control, the agreement shall, as a condition precedent to its entry into force, be submitted to the state officer or agency having such power of control and shall be approved or disapproved by him or it as to all matters within his or its jurisdiction in the same manner and subject to the same requirements governing the action of the attorneys general pursuant to paragraph (a) of this article. This requirement of submission and approval shall be in addition to and not in substitution for the requirement of submission to an approval by the attorneys general.

Article VIII. Other Laws Applicable

Nothing in this compact or in any library agreement shall be construed to supersede, alter or otherwise impair any obligation imposed on any library by otherwise applicable law, nor to authorize the transfer or disposition of any property held in trust by a library agency in a manner contrary to the terms of such trust.

Article IX. Appropriations and Aid

(a) Any public library agency party to a library agreement may appropriate funds to the interstate library district established thereby in the same manner and to the same extent as to a library wholly maintained by it and, subject to the laws of the state in which such public library agency is situated, may pledge its credit in support of an interstate library district established by the agreement.

(b) Subject to the provisions of the library agreement pursuant to which it functions and the laws of the states in which such district is situated, an interstate library district may claim and receive any state and federal aid which may be available to library agencies.

Article X. Compact Administrator

Each state shall designate a compact administrator with

whom copies of all library agreements to which his state or any public library agency thereof is party shall be filed. The administrator shall have such other powers as may be conferred upon him by the laws of his state and may consult and cooperate with the compact administrators of other party states and take such steps as may effectuate the purposes of this compact. If the laws of a party state so provide, such state may designate one or more deputy compact administrators in addition to its compact administrator.

Article XI.   Entry into Force and Withdrawal

(a) This compact shall enter into force and effect immediately upon its enactment into law by any two (2) states. Thereafter, it shall enter into force and effect as to any other state upon the enactment thereof by such state.

(b) This compact shall continue in force with respect to a party state and remain binding upon such state until six (6) months after such state has given notice to each other party state of the repeal thereof. Such withdrawal shall not be construed to relieve any party to a library agreement entered into pursuant to this compact from any obligation of that agreement prior to the end of its duration as provided therein.

Article XII.   Construction and Severability

This compact shall be liberally construed so as to effectuate the purposes thereof. The provisions of this compact shall be severable and if any phrase, clause, sentence or provision of this compact is declared to be contrary to the constitution of any party state or of the United States or the applicability thereof to any government, agency, person or circumstance is held invalid, the validity of the remainder of this compact and the applicability thereof to any government, agency, person or circumstance shall not be affected thereby. If this compact shall be held contrary to the constitution of any state party thereto, the compact shall remain in full force and effect as to the remaining states and in full force and effect as to the state affected as to all severable matters.

(1967, P.A. 278, § 1.)

§ 11-39.   Municipal participation

No town, city, borough or other political subdivision of this state shall be party to a library agreement which provides for the construction or maintenance of a library pursuant to article III, subdivision (c-7) of the compact, or pledge its credit in support of such a library, or contribute to the capital financing thereof, except after compliance with any laws applicable to such towns, cities, boroughs or political subdivisions relating to or governing capital outlays and the pledging of credit.

(1967, P.A. 278, § 2.)

§ 11-40. State library agency defined

As used in the compact, "state library agency," with reference to this state, means the Connecticut state library, or an agency approved by the state librarian.

(1967, P.A. 278, § 3.)

§ 11-41. State aid for interstate library districts

An interstate library district lying partly within this state may claim and be entitled to receive state aid in support of any of its functions to the same extent and in the same manner as such functions are eligible for support when carried on by entities wholly within this state. For the purposes of computing and apportioning state aid to interstate library districts hereinafter to be created, this state will consider that portion of the area which lies within this state as an independent entity for the performance of the aided function or functions and compute and apportion the aid accordingly. Subject to any applicable laws of this state, such a district also may apply for and be entitled to receive any federal aid for which it may be eligible.

(1967, P.A. 278, § 4.)

§ 11-42. Compact administrator

The Connecticut state librarian shall be the compact administrator pursuant to article X of the compact. An associate state librarian may be deputy compact administrator.

(1967, P.A. 278, § 5.)

§ 11-43. Notices on withdrawal

In the event of withdrawal from the compact the state librarian shall send and receive any notices required by article XI(b) of the compact.

(1967, P.A. 278, § 6.)

DISTRIBUTION OF PUBLIC DOCUMENTS

(Connecticut General Statutes Annotated, 1982, s.2-23, 2-27, 2-49, 2-61, 3-86, 3-90, 7-148a, 11-9b to 11-9d.)

§ 2-23. Copies of legislative bills and resolutions; records and

index. Furnishing of legislative publications to public and municipalities

The joint committee on legislative management shall provide by contract, purchase or lease a photo-offset process for the reproduction of copies of each bill and each resolution proposing an amendment to the constitution and other substantive resolution introduced in both houses in number sufficient to supply the needs of the legislature and the public. Such reproduction shall be under the supervision of the clerks of the senate and the house. To carry out the provisions of this section, said committee is authorized to hire necessary personnel and acquire supplies and equipment. The joint committee on legislative management shall set aside in the state capitol a room for use as a legislative bill room for distribution of copies under the supervision of the clerks of the senate and house. The clerks of the senate and house shall, during each session of the general assembly, keep copies of all bills and resolutions reproduced as above provided, in such room, for the convenience of the members of the legislature and the public. A file of such bills and resolutions and the records of hearings of committees and the proceedings of each house, suitably indexed, shall be kept in the state library for public inspection, and the clerks of the senate and house shall furnish copies of such bills and resolutions for this purpose. The state librarian is authorized to hire not more than two additional employees and to secure supplies and equipment necessary to make said index. Copies of bills and resolutions printed after favorable report by a committee or the amendment on the third reading, i. e., files, not needed by members of the general assembly or for other official use shall be delivered to the legislative bill room for distribution. After adjournment of the general assembly, distribution of such bills, resolutions and files shall be made from the office of the clerks. To carry out the provisions of this section, said clerks are authorized to hire additional employees for distribution of such copies. The public may obtain copies of bills, resolutions, journals, bulletins, legislative indexes and other legislative publications by calling for the same at the state capitol, provided the clerks may, in their discretion, limit the number of copies to be furnished to any one person and may, with the approval of the committee, fix reasonable charges for furnishing copies in quantities which the clerks believe cannot be furnished free of charge without undue expense to the state. The clerks shall, at the request of the chief executive officer of any town, city or borough, send by first class mail one copy of each legislative bulletin and of the legislative record index to such office of such municipality as such chief executive officer shall designate. Copies of engrossed bills and resolutions shall be distributed from the office of the legislative commissioners.

(1973, P.A. 73-394; 1978, P.A. 78-237, § 1, eff. July 1, 1978; 1979, P.A. 79-631, § 25.)

§ 2-27. Printing and distribution of file bills

Copies of each bill for an act reported favorably by a committee shall be printed in sufficient numbers, as determined by the clerks of the house and senate, for use by the general assembly, and copies of all such bills of a private nature, except for grants or payments of claims, shall be so printed at the expense of the parties applying therefor before being finally considered. A greater number of copies of any bill shall be printed upon order of either legislative commissioner. Seven copies of each printed bill shall be reserved for the use of the secretary of the state and he shall bind and distribute volumes thereof as follows:

One to the state library, one to the law library of Yale University, one to the library of The University of Connecticut and one to the law library of The University of Connecticut, one to the Wesleyan University library, one to the Library of Congress and one to the library of the University of Bridgeport.

(1949 Rev., § 32; 1957, P.A. 368; 1957, P.A. 627; 1959, P.A. 478 § 1; 1961, P.A. 285, § 1.)

§ 2–61. Distribution of revised statutes and supplements, public and special acts

The secretary of the state shall deliver five hundred copies of the revised statutes, of each supplement to the general statutes and of each revised volume thereof and three hundred fifty copies of each volume of the public acts and special acts to the state library for its general purposes and for exchange with other states and libraries, and four hundred copies of the revised statutes, of each supplement, of each revised volume and of each volume of the public acts, and such additional number of each as the executive secretary of the judicial department certifies as necessary, for the use of any of the state-maintained courts, and one hundred fifty copies of each volume of the special acts to said executive secretary for distribution to state-maintained courts, and, to the several departments, agencies and institutions of the executive branch of the state government, as many copies of the revised statutes, of each supplement, of each revised volume and of each of the volumes of public acts and special acts as they require for the performance of their duties. He shall send free of charge one copy of the revised statutes, of each supplement to the general statutes, of each revised volume thereof and of each of the volumes of public acts and special acts to the governor, lieutenant governor, treasurer, secretary of the state, attorney general, comptroller, adjutant general, each sheriff, each town clerk, each probate court, the police department of each municipality having a regularly organized police force, each assistant to the attorney general, and each county law library; and he shall supply free of charge one copy of the revised statutes to each member of the general assembly at the first session in which he serves as a member and, at each session in which he serves, one copy of each revised volume thereof and of each supplement not previously supplied to him, such distribution of the statutes and supplements to be made within thirty days after the election or reelection of such member, and, following each session at which he serves, one volume of each of the public acts and special acts passed at such session; and to the clerks of the house and senate, each, one copy of the revised statutes, of each revised volume thereof, of each supplement and one volume of each of the public acts and special acts for use in the clerks' office.

(1973, P.A. 73–679, § 4, eff. July 1, 1973; 1975, P.A. 75–537, § 14, eff. July 1, 1975; 1977, P.A. 77–614, § 19, eff. Oct. 1, 1977; 1980, P.A. 80–232.)

§ 3–86. Legislative acts and documents to each free public library

The secretary may send a copy of the laws passed by the general assembly at each session, together with the legislative documents and journals, to each free public library which desires them. (1949 Rev., § 1677.)

§ 3–90. Register and manual

The secretary shall, annually, prepare and publish a register and manual that shall give a complete list of the state, county and town officers, of the judges of all courts and of the officials attending thereon. The population, railroad and postal facilities and other items of general interest concerning each town shall also be given in such book, and such other information in relation to state departments, state institutions and other matters of public concern as the secretary deems desirable. Twenty-eight thousand three hundred twenty-four copies of the state register and manual shall be published each year and distributed as follows: Twenty-five hundred copies to the state board of education to be distributed by it to the public schools of this state; eight hundred and fifty copies to the state librarian for exchange with other states and foreign countries and public libraries and one copy to each state officer, judge and clerk of each court in the state, except courts of probate, each senator and representative in congress from this state, each judge of probate, state's attorney, sheriff, town clerk, mayor of a city and warden of a borough. Two copies shall be sent to each senator and two copies to each representative and the residue, after retaining a sufficient number for distribution to the state departments, commissions and boards and, in the discretion of the secretary, to other parties than those herein enumerated, shall be transmitted directly to the town clerks of the several towns in proportion to their population, except that no town shall receive fewer than five copies, to be distributed as such towns may direct. The maximum number of copies of the state register and manual authorized to be published under the provisions of this section may be reduced in any specified year and the number of copies to be distributed to the various agencies and officers may be varied but not increased at the discretion of the secretary as the actual need therefor requires.

(1976, P.A. 76–434, § 1, eff. July 1, 1976.)

§ 7–148a. Compilations of ordinances and special acts; supplements

Each town, city and borough in this state shall print and publish all amendments to its ordinances, all new ordinances and all special acts adopted after June 1, 1962, on or before March first of each even-numbered year as a cumulative supplement to the compilation of its ordinances and special acts. Such compilation and all supplements thereto shall be available for sale to the public at the office of the clerk or other similar office in such municipality at a reasonable cost to be determined by such municipality and a copy of each such compilation and supplement shall be deposited by the clerk of the municipality in the office of the secretary of the state, in the state library, in each bar library in the judicial district in which such municipality is located and in the courthouse library of the court nearest to such municipality. If any town, city or borough fails to comply with the provisions of this section, the secretary of the state shall provide for the original compilation and publication of such ordinances and special acts or of any supplement thereto and such town, city or borough shall be liable for the cost of such compilation and publication.

(1974, P.A. 74–183, § 175, eff. Dec. 31, 1974; 1976, P.A. 76–436, § 155, eff. July 1, 1978; 1978, P.A. 78–280, § 1, eff. July 1, 1978.)

§ 11–9b. Definitions

As used in this section and sections 11–9c and 11–9d:

(a) "State publications" means all publications printed or purchased for distribution by a state agency, or any other agency supported wholly or in part by state funds;

(b) "Printed" means all forms of printing and duplicating, regardless of format or purpose, with the exception of correspondence and interoffice memoranda;

(c) "State agency" means every state office, officer, department, division, bureau, board and commission, permanent or temporary in nature, whether legislative, executive or judicial, and any subdivisions of each, including state-supported institutions of higher education;

(d) "Depository library" means the designated library for collecting, maintaining and making available to the general public Connecticut state agency publications.

(1977, P.A. 77–561, § 1.)

§ 11–9c. Administration of state publications collection and depository library system

The state library shall administer a Connecticut state publications collection and a depository library system. The state library shall: (1) Establish and administer, with the approval of the state library board, such rules and regulations as may be deemed necessary to carry out the provisions of sections 11–9b to 11–9d, inclusive; (2) develop and maintain standards for depository libraries, including ascertaining their geographical distribution, with the approval of the state library board; (3) enter into depository contracts with libraries that meet the standards for eligibility established by the state library; (4) annually advise designated staff in each agency, required by section 11–9d, of the number of copies of publications needed for distribution; (5) receive from state agencies on or about publication date the specified number of copies of each publication; (6) retain sufficient copies in the Connecticut state library for preservation, reference and interlibrary loan purposes; (7) distribute two copies of each publication to the Library of Congress and one copy to an additional national or regional research library designated by the state library; (8) distribute copies of publications to depository libraries within the state in accordance with the terms of their depository contracts and to libraries outside the state in accordance with any agreements entered into for the exchange of state publications and (9) publish at least monthly and distribute to depository and other libraries in Connecticut, other state libraries, to state legislators and state agencies and libraries, upon request, an official indexed list of Connecticut state publications with an annual cumulated index.

(1977, P.A. 77–561, § 2.)

§ 11–9d. State agencies to supply publications to state library; designation of staff

(a) Designated staff in each state agency shall be responsible for supplying the publications of that agency to the state library. Each such agency shall notify the state library of the identity of such designated staff within thirty days after October 1, 1977, and upon any change of personnel. Said staff shall supply the state library annually or upon request with a complete list of the agency's current publications.

(b) Every state agency shall, upon publication, deposit a sufficient number of copies of each of its publications with the state library to meet the needs of the depository library system.

(1977, P.A. 77–561, § 3.)

MUNICIPAL LIBRARIES

(Connecticut General Statutes Annotated, 1982,
s.11-20 to 11-37, 9-185, 9-207.)

§ 11-20. Establishment. Gifts. Pensions

Any town, city, borough, fire district or incorporated school district may, by ordinance, establish a public library and may

expend such sums of money as may be necessary to purchase
land for a suitable site and to provide and maintain such suitable
rooms or buildings as may be necessary for such library or for
any library which is the property of any corporation without
capital stock or for any public library established in such municipality, provided the use of such library shall be free to its inhabitants under such regulations as its directors or trustees prescribe.   Any such municipality may receive, hold and manage
any devise, bequest or gift for the establishment, increase or
maintenance of any such library within its limits and may retire
with a pension or other reward any employee of any such library.

(1949 Rev., § 1657; 1957, P.A. 13, § 67.)

§ 11–21. Directors

In the absence of any other provision therefor, the management of the public library in any municipality, fire district or incorporated school district
which has established such library under the provisions of section 11–20 shall
be vested in a board of directors, consisting of a number divisible by three to
be elected in the manner provided in section 9–207. Such board may make
bylaws for its government and shall have exclusive right to expend all money
appropriated by such municipality for any such library.

(1979, P.A. 79–363, § 31.)

§ 11–22.   Expenses. Town clerk may deposit books

The officer designated by the directors or trustees of any
such library shall draw his order on the treasurer of any such
municipality for such sums as may be necessary to pay the expense of such library, but such sums shall not exceed in the aggregate the amount appropriated by any such municipality for
such library. Any town clerk may deposit in any such library
within his town any books, other than records, placed in his custody.

(1949 Rev., § 1658.)

§ 11–23.   State librarian to advise and assist libraries

The state librarian, with the approval of the state library
board, shall give to communities advice and assistance in the
organization, establishment and administration of free public
libraries, shall extend to the free public libraries, and to the librarian or director of any public library, aid in selecting and
cataloguing books and in library management. Said librarian
is authorized to purchase and arrange books and pictures to be
loaned to such public libraries, school libraries, associations and
individuals and other libraries as said librarian, with the approval of the state library board, may select. Said librarian

may give advice and assistance to libraries in the correctional
and charitable institutions of the state, subject to such rules and
regulations as the directors of such institutions may make.

(1949 Rev., § 1660; 1949 Supp. § 177a; 1955 Supp. § 1021d; 1965,
P.A. 490, § 3, eff. July 1, 1965; 1975, P.A. 75–316, § 9.)

§ 11-23a. Library service center in Middlesex and Wind-
ham-Tolland areas

The state library board shall maintain a library service center in the Middlesex county area and in the Windham-Tolland
county area, to serve the public libraries and public schools in
each of said areas. The board of directors of each local public
library and the board of education of each local public school
which desires to receive supplementary library services may designate a representative to serve on an advisory board of governors for the library service center in the area wherein is located
such public library or public school.

(1959, P.A. 581, § 1; 1965, P.A. 490, § 6, eff. July 1, 1965; 1975, P.A.
75–316, § 10.)

§ 11-23b. Library service centers for public libraries and
public schools

The state library board may establish and maintain library
service centers to provide supplementary books and related library materials and services to public libraries and to public
schools.

(1955 Supp. § 885d; Rev.1958, § 10–28; 1965, P.A. 490, § 5, eff.
July 1, 1965; 1975, P.A. 75–316, § 11.)

§ 11-26. Librarians' certificates

The state library board may, in accordance with such regulations as it provides, grant certificates to librarians in the public libraries of the state.

(1949 Rev., § 1664; 1965, P.A. 490, § 9, eff. July 1, 1965; 1975, P.A.
75–316, § 16.)

§ 11-27. Library fund

All moneys collected or received in payment for library
service contracted for and rendered shall be placed in the treasury of the town, city, borough, fire district or school district
for which such service was rendered, to the credit of its library
fund. The moneys in such fund shall be kept separate from other moneys and shall be withdrawn only by authorized officials,

upon authenticated vouchers of the directors or trustees of the public library which provides such service.

(1949 Rev., § 1668.)

§ 11-28.　Merger of library facilities

The directors or trustees of two or more public libraries may, with the approval of the towns in which such libraries are situated, contract for the merger, in whole or in part, of the facilities of such libraries.

(1949 Rev., § 1666.)

§ 11-29.　Transfer of employees

Members of the regular staff of any free public library may be transferred to one of its contract libraries, either on a temporary or a permanent basis, without affecting their status on the library payroll or their right to promotion, because of any town ordinance or regulation as to residence. The directors or trustees of any free public library may employ any person in a branch established in another town than that in which such library is located, without complying with any civil service or residence ordinance of either of such towns; but no such employee shall be transferred to a library within either of such towns which has civil service or residence ordinances.

(1949 Rev., § 1667.)

§ 11-30.　Contracts for library service

Any state agency, municipality, taxing district or public or private library may contract with any other state agency, municipality, taxing district or public or private library to provide or secure such library services as may be agreed upon, which services may include, but need not be limited to, (1) the lending of books and related library materials, (2) the establishment of branch libraries, depositories or bookmobile service and (3) co-operative purchasing and processing of books, recordings, films and related library materials.

(1949 Rev., § 1665; 1953 Supp. § 834c; 1955 Supp. § 1024d; 1957, P.A. 121, § 1; 1959, P.A. 489, § 1.)

§ 11-31.　Regional library service

Any town, city, borough, fire district or school district may raise money by taxation and make appropriations for defraying the expense of contract or regional library service, and shall be subject to the duties and entitled to the benefits prescribed by this chapter relating to free public libraries in towns or other municipalities.

(1949 Rev., § 1669.)

§ 11-31a. Statewide library service

The libraries established under the provisions of this chapter, and any library within the state which provides free public library services to the residents of one or more towns and which receives a part or all of its financial support from tax income or public solicitation or by contract with said town or towns, may extend their services to all residents of the state under the same rules and regulations they may have adopted or may in the future adopt governing the provision of library services to the residents of the town in which they lie, except that they may place restrictions on loans to nonresidents of said town or of such town or towns served by contract with respect to motion pictures, framed pictures and statuary. Any person presenting a valid library card, issued by any public library in the state or by the state library, shall be entitled to such service. A card shall be deemed valid when it contains (1) the name of the issuing library, (2) the name of the person to whom it was issued, or, if a family card, the name of the head of the family, and (3) a future expiration date.

(1973, P.A. 73-645, § 1, eff. July 1, 1973.)

§ 11-32. City council may establish and maintain a public library

The city council of any city may establish and maintain a public library and reading room, together with such kindred apartments and facilities as the council approves; and may levy a tax not to exceed two mills on the dollar annually on all taxable property of the city. Such tax shall be levied and collected as other taxes, and shall be known as the "library fund." Such library and reading room shall be free to the use of the inhabitants of the city, subject to such reasonable rules and regulations as the board of directors may adopt in order to render the use of the library and reading room of the greatest benefit. Such board may exclude from the use of such library and reading room any person who wilfully violates such rules, and may extend its privileges to persons residing in this state outside the city upon such terms and conditions as it may prescribe.

(1949 Rev., § 1670; 1973, P.A. 73-261, § 1, eff. May 16, 1973.)

§ 11-33. Powers and duties of directors in cities. Gifts

When any city council has decided to establish and maintain

a public library and reading room, the mayor of such city shall, with the approval of the council, appoint a board of nine directors. Not more than one member of the city council shall be a member of said board. The directors shall, immediately after their appointment, meet and organize by the election of one of their number as president and by the election of such other officers as they deem necessary. They shall make and adopt bylaws, rules and regulations for the government of the library and reading room and shall have exclusive control of the expenditure of all moneys collected to the credit of the library fund, and of the construction of any library building, and of the supervision, care and custody of the grounds, rooms or buildings constructed, leased, given or set apart for that purpose; provided all moneys collected and received for such purpose shall be placed in the treasury of such city, to the credit of its library fund, and shall be kept separate from other moneys of the city and shall be drawn upon by the proper officers of the city, upon duly authenticated vouchers of the directors. Such board may purchase, lease or accept grounds, and erect, lease or occupy an appropriate building or buildings, for the use of such library, appoint a librarian and all necessary assistants and fix their compensation. Any person desiring to make a gift for the benefit of such library may vest the title to such donation in the board of directors to be held and controlled according to the terms of the gift of such property; and such board shall be special trustee thereof.

(1949 Rev., § 1671.)

§ 11-34. Report by directors

The board of directors shall make, on or before the second Monday of June, an annual report to the city council for the year ending the first of June, stating the various sums of money received from the library fund and other sources and how such moneys have been expended; the number of books and periodicals on hand; the number added, by purchase, gift or otherwise, during the year; the number lost or missing; the number of visitors attending; the number of books loaned and the general character of such books, and such other statistics, information and suggestions as it deems of general interest. All such portions of such report as relate to the receipt and expenditure of money, as well as the number of books on hand, books lost or missing and books purchased, shall be verified by affidavit.

(1949 Rev., § 1672.)

§ 11-35. Penalties for injuries

The city council of such city may pass ordinances imposing

suitable penalties for damaging the grounds or other property of such library and for damaging or failing to return any book belonging to such library. . Each librarian or board of directors, having charge or control of such library or property, shall post in one or more conspicuous places connected therewith a printed copy of this section.

(1949 Rev., § 1673.)

§ 11-36. Town or borough tax

When fifty electors of any town or borough present a petition to the clerk of such town or borough, asking that an annual tax be levied for the establishment and maintenance of a free public library and reading room in such town or borough, and specify in their petition a rate of taxation, not to exceed three mills on the dollar, such clerk shall, in the next legal notice of the regular municipal election in such town or borough, give notice that at such election the question of an annual tax for the maintenance of a library is to be voted upon in the manner prescribed in section 9–369. The designation of such question on the voting machine ballot label shall be "For a . . . . . . mill tax for a free public library and reading room, YES" and "For a . . . . . . mill tax for a free public library and reading room, NO." Such notice and such designation of the question on the voting machine ballot label shall specify the rate of taxation mentioned in such petition. If, upon the official determination of the result of such vote, it appears that a majority of all the votes upon such question are in approval of such question, the tax specified in such notice shall be levied and collected in the same manner as other general taxes of such town or borough and shall be known as the "library fund." Such tax may afterwards be lessened or increased within the three-mill limit, or made to cease, in case the electors of any such town or borough so determine by a majority vote at any regular municipal election held therein, in the manner hereinbefore prescribed for voting upon such question; and the corporate authorities of such town or borough may exercise the same powers relative to free public libraries and reading rooms as are conferred upon the corporate authorities of cities.

(1949 Rev., § 1674; 1953 Supp. § 836c; 1955 Supp. § 1026d.)

§ 11-37. Directors' compensation

No director of any free public library and reading room, established under the provisions of this chapter in any town, city, borough, school district or fire district, shall receive any com-

pensation for any services rendered as such director.
(1949 Rev., § 1675.)

§ 9–185. Municipal officers

Unless otherwise provided by special act or charter, assessors, members of boards of tax review, selectmen, town clerks, town treasurers, agents of the town deposit fund, collectors of taxes, constables, registrars of voters, members of boards of education and library directors shall be elected, provided any town may, by ordinance, provide for the appointment, by its chief executive authority, of a constable or constables in lieu of constables to be elected under section 9–200. Unless otherwise provided by special act or charter, all other town officers shall be appointed as provided by law and, if no other provision for their appointment is made by law, then by (1) the chief executive officer of such municipality, or (2) where the legislative body is a town meeting, by the board of selectmen, or (3) by such other appointing authority as a town may by ordinance provide, and except that, if a board of finance is established under the provisions of section 7–340, the members thereof shall be elected as provided in section 9–202 and except that assessors may be elected or appointed under the provisions of section 9–198. Any town may, by a vote of its legislative body, determine the number of its officers and prescribe the mode by which they shall be voted for at subsequent elections.
(1973, P.A. 73–655, § 1; 1976, P.A. 76–173, § 2; 1977, P.A. 77–578, § 1, eff. Oct. 1, 1977.)

§ 9–207. Library directors

Any municipality, after establishing a library under the provisions of sections 11–20 and 11–21 shall at the first regular municipal election after the establishment of such library, elect one-third of the directors to hold office until the next such election, one-third until the second such election and one-third until the third such election, and, at all such elections of such municipality thereafter, one-third of the directors shall be elected to hold office for six years.
(1976, P.A. 76–173, § 11.)

INTERLOCAL AGREEMENTS
(Connecticut General Statutes Annotated, 1982, s.7-339b.)

§ 7–339b. Subjects of interlocal agreements

(a) Any public agency of this state may enter into interlocal agreements with any public agency or agencies of this state or any other state or states providing for any of the following:

(1) The exchange, furnishing or providing by one or more of the contracting public agencies to one or more of the other contracting public agencies, or the furnishing or providing for the joint use or benefit of the several contracting public agencies, of services, personnel, facilities, equipment or any other property or resources for any one or more of the following purposes or uses: Fire prevention and fire fighting; police protection and police services; supply of water, gas or electricity; garbage collection and disposal; sewer lines and sewage treatment and disposal; refuse collection and disposal, and establishment or use of public dumps; storm drainage; establishment or use of airports or landing fields;   public entertainment and amusement; establishment or use of parks, public gardens, gymnasiums, playgrounds, swimming pools, community centers, recreation centers or other recreational areas or facilities; establishment and preservation of open spac-

es; control of air and water pollution; planning services; engineering services; lighting; ambulance service; fire and police radio and communication systems; hospital service; public health services; mental health services; establishment or care of cemeteries; library or bookmobile services; suppression or control of plant and animal pests or diseases; flood control; water conservation; public shade tree protection services; traffic services; transportation services; redevelopment services, and publicizing the advantages of the region.

(2) The establishment of an interlocal advisory board or boards to recommend programs and policies for cooperative or uniform action in any fields of activity permitted or authorized hereunder for each contracting public agency, and from time to time to advise with the appropriate officials of the contracting public agencies in respect to such programs, policies or fields of activity.

(3) The establishment and maintenance of interlocal employees or officers of the contracting public agencies for the purpose of administering or assisting in any of the undertakings contemplated by subdivision (1) hereof or for the purpose of performing services for an interlocal advisory board as authorized by subdivision (2) hereof. Such employees or officers, if not continuing in or eligible for the merit system, insurance and pension benefits and status of employment with a contracting public agency, may continue in such status or be made eligible therefor if the interlocal agreement contains appropriate provisions to this effect. An interlocal advisory board may enter into an agreement with the federal secretary of health, education and welfare to provide old age and survivors insurance coverage to employees of such board.

(b) Nothing contained in sections 7–339a to 7–339*l*, inclusive, shall be construed to authorize or permit any public agency of this state to receive, obtain, furnish or provide services, facilities, personnel, equipment or any other property or resources, or to engage in or perform any function or activity by means of an interlocal agreement, if it does not have constitutional or statutory power or authorization to receive, obtain, furnish or provide the same or substantially similar services, facilities, personnel, equipment, other property or resources, or to engage in or perform the same or a substantially similar function or activity on its own account.
(1961, P.A. 429, § 2; 1967, P.A. 516, § 2.)

LAW LIBRARIES
(Connecticut General Statutes Annotated, 1982,
s.11-10a, 11-10b, 11-19a to 11-19d.)

§ 11-10a. Retirement of librarians

Upon certification by the bar library committee, any librarian of a law library existing under the provisions of section 11–19b may retire after thirty years of service, and shall thereafter receive an annual pension equal to two per cent of his average annual salary for each year of such service based on the five highest paid years of service, payable in monthly instalments; provided any such librarian having less than thirty years' service on October 1, 1960, shall not be granted such a pension but shall be eligible for membership in the state employees' retirement system, subject to such terms and conditions as to service credit and contributions to the retirement fund as the state employees' retirement commission determines. This section shall not apply to any librarian who is a member of the municipal employees' retirement system or who is receiving a pension under the provisions of any special act.

(1959, P.A. 427; 1973, P.A. 73–471, § 2, eff. July 1, 1973.)

§ 11–10b.   Budget

The state library board shall include in its budget recommendations to the governor and the general assembly such amounts as are required for such state law libraries to provide the services for which they exist.

(1973, P.A. 73–471, § 3, eff. July 1, 1973; 1975, P.A. 75–316, § 8; 1975, P.A. 75–479, § 24, eff. July 1, 1975; 1975, P.A. 75–567, § 76, eff. July 1, 1975; 1976, P.A. 76–368, § 5, eff. July 1, 1976.)

§ 11–19a.   System of law libraries

(a) There shall be a system of law libraries within the state, under the supervision of the state library board. Such libraries shall be arranged in a tier system according to the extent of potential use. Tier I libraries shall be located in Hartford, Bridgeport and New Haven. Tier II libraries shall be located in Stamford, Waterbury and Norwich. Tier III libraries shall be located in Litchfield, Rockville, Putnam and Middletown.

(b) The law library in Hartford shall be located in the state library building, except that a limited reference collection shall be maintained in the superior court building in Hartford.

(1976, P.A. 76–368, § 1, eff. July 1, 1976.)

§ 11–19b.   Law library use and regulation

Each such library shall be for the use of the courts and citizens of the state, subject to such regulations as may be prescribed by the state library board, with the advice of the law library advisory committee.
(1977, P.A. 77–452, § 2, eff. July 1, 1978.)

§ 11–19c.   Law library advisory committee

There shall be a state law library advisory committee consisting of nine members, two of whom shall be members of the public appointed by the governor, five of whom shall be attorneys-at-law authorized to practice in the courts of this state, appointed by the president of the state bar association, two of whom shall be judges of the superior court which judges shall be appointed by the chief justice. Said committee shall advise the state library board on all matters of operation of the law libraries system.
(1977, P.A. 77–452, § 1, eff. July 1, 1978.)

§ 11–19d.   Long term leases of law books to bar associations

The state library board shall, upon request of any local bar association, enter into a long-term agreement with such association for the leasing of books within the area in which such association is located, which prior to July 1, 1976, were in law libraries belonging to the state and which the state no longer maintains. Such lease shall be for one dollar per year. (1977, P.A. 77–270.)

SCHOOL LIBRARIES
(Connecticut General Statutes Annotated, 1982,
s.10-28a, 10-221.)

§ 10–221. Boards of education to prescribe rules

Boards of education shall prescribe rules for the management, studies, classification and discipline of the public schools and, subject to the control of the state board of education, the textbooks to be used; shall make rules for the control, within their respective jurisdictions, of school library media centers and approve the selection of books and other educational media therefor, and shall approve plans for public school buildings and superintend any high or graded school in the manner specified in this title.

(1978, P.A. 78–218, § 146; 1980, P.A. 80–32, § 2, eff. July 1, 1980.)

§ 10–28a. Advice and assistance to school library media centers

The state board of education shall give to communities advice and assistance in the organization, establishment and administration of school library media centers, shall extend to school library media centers, and to the media specialist and teachers of any public school, aid in selecting and organizing library media center collections and in management of library media services and may, for the purposes of this section, visit and evaluate library media centers organized under the provisions of section 10–221, and make recommendations for their improvement. Said board is authorized to purchase and organize books and other educational media to be loaned to such school library media centers, associations and individuals as the board may select.

(1980, P.A. 80–32, § 1, eff. July 1, 1980.)

MISCELLANEOUS PROVISIONS
(Connecticut General Statutes Annotated, 1982,
s.33-264g, 5-198.)

§ 33–264g. Receipt of funds by ecclesiastical societies, cemetery associations and library associations

Any ecclesiastical society which is not a religious society as defined in section 33–264a or which is not an ecclesiastical society under part II of this chapter and any cemetery association or library association organized for mutual or public benefit and not for the purpose of deriving financial profit from the operations thereof, shall have the power to receive and hold funds in any amount derived by gift or devise, provided the uses of any such fund and of the income therefrom are, by the terms of such gift or devise, limited to the purposes for which such ecclesiastical society, cemetery association or library association was organized.

(1969, P.A. 314, § 7.)

§ 5–198. Positions exempt from classified service

The offices and positions filled by the following-described incumbents shall be exempt from the classified service:

*   *   *

(g) All superintendents or wardens of state institutions, the state librarian, the president of The University of Connecticut and any other commissioner or administrative head of a state department or institution who is appointed by a board or commission responsible by statute for the administration of such department or institution;

(h) The state historian appointed by the state library board;

*   *   *

(t) Librarians employed by the state board of education or any constituent unit of the state system of higher education;

(1975, P.A. 75–316, § 18; 1976, P.A. 76–254, § 2, eff. June 4, 1976; 1977, P.A. 77–573, § 22, eff. Aug. 1, 1977; 1979, P.A. 79–621, §§ 3 to 5, eff. July 1, 1979.)

Connecticut library laws are reprinted from CONNECTICUT GENERAL STATUTES ANNOTATED published by West Publishing Co., St. Paul, Minnesota.

DELAWARE

STATE LIBRARY AGENCY
(Delaware Code Annotated, 1982, s.29-8603, 29-8610, 29-8611.)

§ 8603. Powers, duties and functions of the Secretary.

The Secretary shall have the following powers, duties and functions:

(1) To supervise, direct and account for the administration and operation of the Department, its divisions, subdivisions, offices, functions and employees;

(2) To appoint and fix the salary of, with the written approval of the Governor, the following division directors and office heads, who may be removed from office by the Secretary with the written approval of the Governor and who shall have such powers, duties and functions in the administration and operation of the Department as may be assigned by the Secretary:

* * *

c. A State Librarian who shall be a graduate of a school accredited by the American Library Association;
(29 Del. C. 1953. § 8603; 57 Del. Laws, c. 583, § 1; 57 Del. Laws, c. 679, § 7D; 59 Del. Laws, c. 480, § 3.)

§ 8610. Powers and duties of the Department relating to library services.

(a) The powers and duties of the Department relating to library services shall be:

(1) To provide information, resource materials and library services to state agencies, state and local governmental units and their subdivisions and, in the Department's discretion, to organizations in need of library services;

445

(2) To coordinate library services of the several counties in order to assure to every Delaware citizen free and equal access to services, resources and guidance in the use of such for continuing self-educational, political, cultural, economic, recreational and intellectual enrichment;

(3) To receive, accept, administer and expend any money, materials or other aid granted, appropriated or otherwise provided by local, state or federal governments, or by any source, public or private, in accordance with the terms thereof, and for the purposes provided hereinafter;

(4) To foster the recruitment, development and maximum utilization of library personnel throughout the state;

(5) To encourage broad community participation in library development, program planning and the implementation of such plans;

(6) To establish and promote cooperation among all types of libraries at all service levels;

(7) To ensure the state's compatibility to and reciprocity within a national information resources network;

(8) To provide access to a complete collection of current documents published by state government and a comprehensive collection of current local, state and federal documents of interest to the state;

(9) To stimulate every Delaware citizen to fully utilize the state's cultural resource materials and to maintain the individual's right of access to those materials;

(10) To offer resources which supplement and reinforce local libraries;

(11) To collect, compile, research, publish and disseminate information, including statistics, affecting the efficient operation of the state's library system;

(12) To recommend legislation to achieve meaningful statewide library development and use;

(13) To establish, interpret and administer standards of effective library services;

(14) To enter into contracts and agreements to provide or to obtain library services and materials;

(15) To perform all other activities pertinent to the organizational function of library services.

(b) Every state agency shall provide and deposit with the Department sufficient copies of all publications issued by such agencies for the purpose of making accessible to Delaware and other citizens resource materials published at the expense of the State. The Administrator of Libraries shall recommend the number of copies required for deposit, consistent with state interests. From time to time listing of such documents received under the terms of this section shall be published. (29 Del. C. 1953, § 8610; 57 Del. Laws, c. 583, § 1; 59 Del. Laws, c. 480, § 4.)

§ 8611. Council on Libraries.

(a) There is hereby established the Council on Libraries.

(b) The Council on Libraries shall serve in an advisory capacity to the Department and shall consider matters relating to libraries and library standards throughout the State and such other matters as may be referred to it by the Governor, the Secretary of the Department or the General Assembly. The Council on Libraries may study, research, plan and make advisory recommendations to the Governor, the Secretary of the Department or the General Assembly on matters it deems appropriate to provide the best possible library service in Delaware.

(c) The Council on Libraries shall be composed of 2 members who shall be elected annually by each County Library Advisory Board and who shall serve at its pleasure and 7 members appointed by the Governor. Of the 7 members appointed by the Governor, 3 members shall be appointed for a term of 1 year, 2 members shall be appointed for a term of 2 years and 2 members shall be appointed for a term of 3 years; at no time shall there be more than a bare majority representation of 1 major political party, but any person who declines to state his political affiliation shall be considered eligible for appointment as a member; and after the initial appointments, all terms shall be for 3 years. No member shall be appointed for more than 2 consecutive terms. The Chairman of the Council shall be chosen by the members of the Council from among its members and shall serve in that capacity for a term of 1 year and shall be eligible for reelection.

(d) Members of the Council on Libraries shall serve without compensation, except that they may be reimbursed for reasonable and necessary expenses incident to their duties.

(e) A vacancy prior to the expiration of the term of a member of the Council on Libraries shall be filled only for the remainder of that term. (29 Del. C. 1953, § 8611; 57 Del. Laws, c. 583, § 1; 59 Del. Laws, c. 480, § 5.)

PUBLIC ARCHIVES AND RECORDS
(Delaware Code Annotated, 1982, s.29-501 to 29-505, 29-507, 29-521 to 29-536.)

§ 501. General duties of the Department of State.

The Department of State, hereinafter referred to in this chapter as the "Department," shall be responsible for the care and preservation of all noncurrent public records of historical value of this State or any political subdivision thereof, which are now in or may hereafter come into the possession of the Department; the preservation of all other public records by conducting a public records administration program for the transfer of semicurrent records to records centers (subject to available space, staff, equipment and other facilities); and the operation of a centralized microfilming program, at the full cost of such goods and services, in accordance with § 6531 of this title. (29 Del. C. 1953, § 3301; 57 Del. Laws, c. 608, §§ 1A, 1B; 61 Del. Laws, c. 457, § 1.)

§ 502. Hall of Records; classification and cataloguing of records.

The Department shall occupy exclusively the rooms in the Hall of Records in

Dover. All books, records, documents and papers of historical or public interest, the custody of which is given to the Department, as in this chapter provided, shall be kept in the rooms of the Hall of Records and shall be classified and catalogued for reference. (23 Del. Laws, c. 77, § 3; 26 Del. Laws, c. 82; Code 1915, § 976; 40 Del. Laws, c. 105, § 1; Code 1935, § 1088; 42 Del. Laws, c. 96, § 2; 29 Del. C. 1953, § 3303; 57 Del. Laws, c. 608, § 1B.)

§ 503. Agents and assistants.

The Department may employ such agents or assistants as it may deem necessary for the purpose of carrying out the duties imposed upon it by this chapter. (23 Del. Laws, c. 77; 26 Del. Laws, c. 82; Code 1915, § 975; 40 Del. Laws, c. 105, § 1; Code 1935, § 1087; 29 Del. C. 1953, § 3304; 57 Del. Laws, c. 608, § 1B.)

§ 504. Publications; sale and distribution.

The Department, from time to time as it may deem advisable, may publish any records, documents and papers within its custody, or abstracts and calendars of the same or pamphlets, brochures and books pertaining to the records, documents and papers or relating in general to the history of the State or the annual reports to the Governor concerning the work of the Department. Such publications may be distributed gratis by the Department in such numbers as the requirements of its exchange list with state, university and other public libraries or historical societies may, in the discretion of the Department, necessitate. Copies of publications may be sold by the Department to the general public for such price per copy as the Department may determine. (23 Del. Laws, c. 77; 26 Del. Laws, c. 82; 27 Del. Laws, c. 100; Code 1915, § 977; 40 Del. Laws, c. 105, § 1; Code 1935, § 1089; 42 Del. Laws, c. 96, § 3; 29 Del. C. 1953, § 3306; 57 Del. Laws, c. 608, § 1B.)

§ 505. Disposition of proceeds.

The proceeds from the sale of publications, accompanied by a detailed statement, shall be paid to the Secretary of Finance for the General Fund. (23 Del. Laws, c. 77; 27 Del. Laws, c. 100; Code 1915, § 977; 40 Del. Laws, c. 105, § 1; Code 1935, § 1089; 42 Del. Laws, c. 77, §§ 1, 2; 42 Del. Laws, c. 96, § 3; 29 Del. C. 1953, § 3307; 57 Del. Laws, c. 608, § 1D.)

§ 507. Acquisition of public documents.

All agencies, departments, boards or commissions of this State or of any county or incorporated municipality thereof shall deposit with the Department of State 2 copies of the best edition of each publication issued. These publications are to be retained for reference and research purposes.

The Department of State shall have the authority to determine whether or not any of said publications lack sufficient information for retention as research materials, and it may request the publishing agency to discontinue depositing such publications with the Department. (29 Del. C. 1953, § 3309; 51 Del. Laws, c. 207; 57 Del. Laws, c. 608, §§ 1B, 1E, 1F.)

§ 521. Transfer of records to Hall of Records and records centers; penalty for refusal.

(a) The Department may select and transfer to the Hall of Records such noncurrent books, records, manuscripts, documents, maps and papers which it deems to be of an historical or public interest and which now are, or shall hereafter be, in the custody of any public official of this State or any political subdivision thereof.

(b) The Department may select and transfer to its records centers those semicurrent records of this State or of a county or an incorporated municipality which qualify under the terms of the Department's public records administration program.

(c) Subsections (a) and (b) of this section shall not be construed to apply to deed record books in the offices of the recorders of the counties of this State, except that transfer of such deed records may be made under § 9615 of Title 9.

(d) Whoever, being a public official, refuses to relinquish possession of public records as described in subsection (a) of this section that may be in his custody as such official shall be fined not less than $100 nor more than $500. (23 Del. Laws, c. 77, § 1; 26 Del. Laws, c. 82; 27 Del. Laws, c. 100, § 2; Code 1915, § 972; 40 Del. Laws, c. 105, § 1; Code 1935, § 1084; 45 Del. Laws, c. 91; 29 Del. C. 1953, § 3321; 52 Del. Laws, c. 86, § 2; 57 Del. Laws, c. 608, § 1B.)

§ 522. Transfer of records upon termination of state agencies.

All books, records, documents, maps and papers of historic or public interest which are in or shall come into the possession of any state department, board, commission or agency shall, upon the termination of such department, board, commission or agency, be transferred to the custody of the Department of State, provided that such transfer is consistent with any such termination. (41 Del. Laws, c. 93; 28 Del. C. 1953, § 3322; 57 Del. Laws, c. 608, § 1G.)

§ 523. Preservation of plans of state buildings.

The Department shall obtain a copy of all plans for future state buildings and file same in the Hall of Records, there to be kept and catalogued for future reference. (Code 1935, § 1084; 42 Del. Laws, c. 95; 29 Del. C. 1953, § 3323; 57 Del. Laws, c. 608, § 1B.)

§ 524. Deposit of deeds to state-owned property with Department.

All state departments, commissions, agencies, institutions and special school districts shall deposit with the Department of State for preservation and safekeeping the original deeds to all state-owned property. The Department of State shall give a receipt for each deed received in its custody and may exempt from this section such Department of Transportation deeds which are in constant use for administrative purposes. (Code 1935, § 1086A; 46 Del. Laws, c. 103, § 1; 29 Del. C. 1953, § 3324; 57 Del. Laws, c. 608, §§ 1B, 1E, 1H.)

§ 525. Duty of public officials to consult Department of State before repairing records.

To provide for the better preservation of public records, all public officials of this State or any political subdivision thereof shall consult with the Department of State regarding proper methods and materials before undertaking the repair or restoration of any public records, documents or papers whatsoever. (Code 1935, § 1086B; 46 Del. Laws, c. 103, § 2; 29 Del. C. 1953, § 3325; 57 Del. Laws, c. 608, § 1E.)

§ 526. Failure to comply with § 524, 525 or 529; penalty.

Failure to comply with § 524, 525 or 529 of this title shall be presumptive evidence of guilt, and whoever, being a public official, is convicted for such failure shall be fined not more than $100. (Code 1935, § 1086B; 46 Del. Laws, c. 103, § 2; 29 Del. C. 1953, § 3326.)

§ 527. Disposition of public records by state, county and municipal officers and agencies; definition of public records.

(a) All books, records, documents and papers of historic or public interest, which are in the possession of state boards or state commissions and which are not in current use, shall be transferred to the custody of the Department of State.

(b) No officer of any court, department, board, commission or agency of this State or of any county or incorporated municipality therein, shall destroy, sell or otherwise dispose of any public record or printed public document or official correspondence in his care or custody or under his control or which are no longer in current use without first having advised the Department of State of their nature and obtained its written consent.

(c) Whoever violates subsection (b) of this section shall be fined not less than $100 nor more than $500.

(d) As used in this section and other statutes appertaining thereto, the words "public records" mean any written or printed book, document or paper, map or plan which is the property of any court, department, board, commission or agency of this State or of any county or incorporated municipality therein and in or on which any entry has been made or is required to be made by law or which any officer or employee of this State or of a county or an incorporated municipality has received or is required to receive for recording or filing. (38 Del. Laws, c. 50; Code 1935, § 1090A; 41 Del. Laws, c. 92; 29 Del. C. 1953, § 3327; 57 Del. Laws, c. 608, § 1B.)

§ 528. Acquisition and custody of federal records; access by federal employees.

(a) The Department may acquire and take into its protective custody such public records in the custody of the government of the United States as may relate to the State. The provisions of this section have particular reference to the selective service records pertaining to Delaware, but early naturalizations, court proceedings and similar records may be acquired at the discretion of the Department or its qualified agent.

(b) Agents of the Federal Bureau of Investigation are assured access to such federal records which may be transferred under this section and the Department of State shall grant access to such records to other qualified federal employees upon presentation of proper identification. (Code 1935, § 1086C; 46 Del. Laws, c. 159, § 1; 29 Del. C. 1953, § 3328; 57 Del. Laws, c. 608, §§ 1B, 1E, 1I.)

§ 529. Inspection by Department of books, documents, etc., in possession of custodians of public records.

For the purpose of this chapter all custodians of public records of this State or of any political subdivision thereof shall, upon the request of the Department, afford to it all proper and reasonable access to and examination of all books, records, documents and papers of a public nature in their custody. (23 Del. Laws, c. 77, § 4; 26 Del. Laws, c. 82; Code 1915, § 974; 40 Del. Laws, c. 104, § 3; 40 Del. Laws, c. 105; Code 1935, §§ 1086, 6276; 29 Del. C. 1953, § 3329; 57 Del. Laws, c. 608, § 1B.)

§ 530. Reproduction by photographing records; expenses.

(a) The Department may make reproductions, by photographic process, of records in the custody of the Department, of those required by law to be copied and of such subjects as the Department may be requested to reproduce.

(b) All disbursements made by the Department for expenses pertaining to the work of photographic reproduction shall be paid by the Secretary of Finance out of moneys deposited with him from fees received by the Department for photographic reproductions to the credit of the Department in the General Fund upon vouchers issued by the proper officers designated by the Department and approved by the Auditor of Accounts. (Code 1935, § 1090B; 42 Del. Laws, c. 96, § 4; 29 Del. C. 1953, § 3330; 57 Del. Laws, c. 608, §§ 1B, 1J.)

§ 531. Destruction of original records after photographic copies made.

Whenever any agency, department, board or commission of this State or of any county or incorporated municipality thereof shall have photographed, photocopied or microphotographed all or any part of the records kept by it or under its control in a manner and on film that complies with the standard of quality approved for permanent photographic records by the Department, and whenever such photographs, photocopies or microphotographs shall be placed in adequately accessible containers and provision made for preserving, examining and using the same, the head of such agency, department, board or commission may, with the approval of the Department of State, cause the original records from which the photographs, photocopies or microphotographs have been made, or any part thereof, to be disposed of as the law provides. (44 Del. Laws, c. 74, § 1; 29 Del. C. 1953, § 3331; 57 Del. Laws, c. 608, §§ 1B, 1E.)

§ 532. Admissibility of photographic copies of records in evidence.

Photographs, photocopies or microphotographs of any record photographed, photocopied or microphotographed as provided in this subchapter shall have the same force and effect as the originals thereof would have had and shall be treated as originals for the purpose of their admissibility in evidence. Certified or authenticated copies of such photographs, photocopies or microphotographs or enlargements thereof shall be admitted in evidence equally with the original photographs, photocopies or microphotographs. (44 Del. Laws, c. 74, § 2; 29 Del. C. 1953, § 3332.)

§ 533. Standards for paper and ink used for public records.

All custodians of public books of record or registries of this State or any county or incorporated municipality therein whose duty it shall be to record or cause to be recorded papers or documents required by law to be recorded shall not use or permit to be used, for recording purposes, any book or paper which is not of a standard mill brand with dated watermark, nor shall any such custodian use or permit to be used for the recording any ink which is not of a standard quality. (40 Del. Laws, c. 104, § 1; Code 1935, § 6274; 29 Del. C. 1953, § 3333.)

§ 534. Determination of standards for books, paper and ink by Department.

The standard of the quality of book, paper and ink shall be determined by the Department.

The Department shall furnish each of the custodians a list of not less than 4 makes or brands of such standard books or papers and inks manufactured by different and separate concerns. No make or brand of paper and ink shall be designated by the Department unless it shall have the written approval, as to quality, of a reliable testing agency, which shall have examined such makes and brands as may be submitted to it by the Department. (40 Del. Laws, c. 104, § 2; Code 1935, § 6275; 44 Del. Laws, c. 75; 29 Del. C. 1953, § 3334; 57 Del. Laws, c. 608, § 1B.)

§ 535. Certified copies of records delivered to Department for preservation.

The Department of State may issue certified copies of any instrument or record or other matter contained in any volume, delivered by a recorder or register of wills to the Department for preservation, which certified copies shall be admissible in evidence in any court of justice in the same manner and entitled to the same weight as certified copies made by the official from whose office such volume was received. (37 Del. Laws, c. 110; Code 1935, § 1563; 29 Del. C. 1953, § 3335; 57 Del. Laws, c. 608, §§ 1B, 1E.)

§ 536. Penalty for using nonstandard books, paper or ink.

Whoever, being a custodian, uses or causes or permits to be used any book, paper or ink other than in the manner provided in this chapter is guilty of malfeasance in office and shall be fined not more than $100. (40 Del. Laws, c. 104, § 4; Code 1935, § 6277; 29 Del. C. 1953, § 3336.)

DISTRIBUTION OF PUBLIC DOCUMENTS
(Delaware Code Annotated, 1982, s.10-1962, 14-5310, 29-1123, s.29-1124.)

§ 1962. Distribution of judicial reports.

(a) The Secretary of State, upon the receipt of published legal reports, shall retain one copy in his office; shall send one copy to each judge of each state, county or municipal court, and to each justice of the peace; and shall distribute copies to such agencies and public officials of this State as show a need for them. He shall also transmit one copy to each of the following: The Library of Congress, the University of Delaware Library, the Delaware State College Library, the Historical Society of Delaware, the Wilmington Institute Free Library and to each public law library within this State, 2 copies each.

(b) The copies delivered to the judges and justices of the peace and state offices shall belong to their respective offices and shall be delivered to their successors in office. (10 Del. C. 1953, § 1962; 55 Del. Laws, c. 384, § 7; 56 Del. Laws, c. 421.)

§ 5310. Copies of public documents for University library.

The Secretary of State shall transmit to the University library a copy of all public documents of which he may receive duplicates, whenever the same shall not have been already appropriated. (Code 1852, § 791; 13 Del. Laws, c. 513, § 9; Code 1915, § 2342; 32 Del. Laws, c. 166, § 1; Code 1935, § 2784; 14 Del. C. 1953, § 5310.)

§ 1123. Free distribution with libraries.

The Director of the Legislative Council or his designee shall transmit a copy of the Session Laws and a copy of the journal of each House as soon after the books are published as practical to each of the following: The Library of Congress, the Historical Society of Delaware, the Wilmington Institute Free Library and to public law libraries within the State, 2 copies each. No agency except a public law library shall be entitled to receive gratis more than 1 copy of each book from the State, from whatever source received. (59 Del. Laws, c. 253, § 12.)

§ 1124. Exchanging.

The Director of the Legislative Council or his designee in conjunction with the State Law Library in Kent County shall forward a copy of the Session Laws and the legislative journals published by or under the authority of the State to each state, territory or district of the United States which exchanges its books with the State Law Library in Kent County and may exchange books with any province of Canada and foreign country that exchanges its books with the State Law Library in Kent County. In the event that any state, territory, district, province or country does not exchange Session Laws and legislative journals published by it or under its authority or does not exchange a book or set of books equivalent to sets of books published by the State, then the Director may refuse to transmit to such state, territory, district, province or country such books of the State as the Director of the Legislative Council or his designee may also exchange books of the State for books of equal value received from other sources. (59 Del. Laws, c. 253, § 12.)

COUNTY LIBRARIES

(Delaware Code Annotated, 1982, s.9-801 to 9-819.)

§ 801. Creation of county library agency; powers of county library administrator.

(a) The government of each county shall create a library agency as a part of the executive branch of county government and, in accordance therewith, shall have the power:

(1) To establish and administer a county library system offering to residents of the county access to services and resources and guidance in their use. Each county may create a countywide library system offering free and equal access to such services and resources to every resident of the county, or each county may create library districts within the county

supported by taxes levied upon real property within said districts as provided for in this chapter providing that county residents who are not residents of a library district shall have access to such library district's services and resources upon payment of a fee set by ordinance of the county;

(2) To receive, by taxation or otherwise, accept, administer and expend any money, materials or other aid granted, appropriated or otherwise provided by local, state or federal governments, or by any source, public or private, in accordance with the terms thereof, for the purposes provided in this chapter;

(3) To perform all other activities pertinent to the organizational function of the library agency.

(b) The county executive or president of levy court, whichever applies, upon the approval of the county library advisory board, may appoint a county library administrator who shall be referred to as county librarian and who shall be the administrator of the county library agency. (59 Del. Laws, c. 480, § 2; 60 Del. Laws, c. 162, § 1.)

§ 802. County library advisory board.

There is hereby created in each county a county library advisory board which:

(1) Shall serve in an advisory capacity to the county library administrator and the county library agency;

(2) Shall bring local library needs to their attention and shall recommend to them means for implementation of an effective county library system;

(3) May, through its members on the Council on Libraries, bring library matters to the attention of the Administrator of State Library Services. (59 Del. Laws, c. 480, § 2.)

§ 803. Authority to establish systems.

Kent County may establish a countywide library system or 1 or more district library systems by ordinance after public hearing held after 10 days' notice published once in a newspaper of general circulation in the County. In the event a district library is created said ordinance shall also create a library commission for each library district to advise the Levy Court on the operation of the district library. This power includes the power to acquire real estate by purchase, gift or devise. (60 Del. Laws, c. 162, § 2.)

§ 804. Payment of costs of countywide library system.

In the event that a countywide library system is established in Kent County, the cost of establishment, maintenance, operation and all other costs thereof shall be paid from the general fund of the County out of general county tax proceeds. (60 Del. Laws, c. 162, § 2.)

§ 805. Library districts — Establishment; budget.

Should Kent County elect to establish 1 or more library districts within the County, the County shall levy and raise by taxation a special district library tax for the purpose of the establishment of such a library in each district, and for the maintenance and increase and support of the library such sum of money as is annually approved in a budget for such purpose by the county governing body, said budget to be adopted at the same time the annual county budget is adopted. A library district may be created and a tax raised pursuant to this subchapter to raise funds to pay the Sussex or New Castle County government a contract fee to allow residents of said Kent County district the privilege of using a library located in Sussex or New Castle Counties. (60 Del. Laws, c. 162, § 2.)

§ 806. Same — Tax rate.

After the district library budget or budgets have been adopted, the Kent County Levy Court shall fix a district library tax rate or rates based upon the most recent assessment made by them of the real property located in each district sufficient to raise the amount determined to be raised in the budget for each county library district. (60 Del. Laws, c. 162, § 2.)

§ 807. Same — Tax levy.

After the Kent County Levy Court has fixed the district library tax rate or rates, it shall levy the district library tax or taxes on the real property located within each library district according to such tax rate or rates applied to the most recent assessment list in the County. The district library tax or taxes shall be in addition to and levied at the same time as the annual county tax. (60 Del. Laws, c. 162, § 2.)

§ 808. Same — Delivery of duplicate assessment list.

Promptly after levying the district library tax or taxes the Kent County Levy Court shall deliver to the Receiver of Taxes and County Treasurer, for his use in collecting the taxes, the duplicate assessment list for each library district as prepared and furnished to the county government by the Board of Assessment. (60 Del. Laws, c. 162, § 2.)

§ 809. Same — Tax collection warrant.

(a) At the time of delivery of the duplicate assessment lists to the Receiver of Taxes and County Treasurer there shall be attached to each list a tax collection warrant which shall be executed in the manner and substantially in the form prescribed by subsections (b) and (c) of this section.

(b) Each warrant shall be dated as of the date on which the taxes referred to therein were levied and shall be signed by at least 2 elected officials of the

Kent County Levy Court and sealed with the seal of the County and attested by the Clerk of the Peace.

(c) The warrants shall be substantially in the following form:

STATE OF DELAWARE }
                              } SS.
KENT COUNTY }

To the Receiver of Taxes and County Treasurer of Kent County, greetings:

We command you that you collect from the persons named in the duplicate assessment list annexed hereto, for their library district taxes payable to Kent County for the year beginning July first next, ... percent as a rate upon every one hundred dollars on the amount of their respective assessments; and if any person named in the annexed duplicate assessment list shall not pay his tax after you have demanded payment, we command you in such case that you collect the tax, or the part thereof remaining unpaid, with lawful costs, in the manner prescribed by law. And we further command you that you pay the amount which, according to this warrant and the annexed duplicate assessment list you are required to collect, in the manner and within the times appointed by law in this behalf. Hereof fail not at your peril.

Given at Dover by the order of Kent County, under the hands of us, members of said county governing body, the . . . . . day of . . . ., A.D. . . . . .

Seal of Office of the }
Clerk of Peace   }   . . . .
                                          . . . .
                                                  Commissioners
                              ATTEST: . . . .
                                          Clerk of the Peace

(60 Del. Laws, c. 162, § 2.)

§ 810. Same — Collection of library district taxes; lien on real property.

Thereafter the district library tax or taxes shall be collected by the Receiver of Taxes and County Treasurer at the same time and in the same manner as the annual general county tax is collected according to Title 9, Chapters 86 and 87, and shall be a lien on real property within the county library district or districts the same as the annual county tax levy according to Title 9, Chapters 86 and 87. (60 Del. Laws, c. 162, § 2.)

§ 811. General borrowing power.

Under the circumstances and conditions set forth in this subchapter, money may be borrowed by Kent County in aid of any public library in the County now or hereafter established whether a countywide or district library. (60 Del. Laws, c. 162, § 2.)

§ 812. Adoption of resolution.

The Kent County Levy Court shall adopt a resolution to the effect that it deems it advisable that a specified sum of money be borrowed for some specified purpose or purposes and whether the borrowing is to be for a countywide or district library. (60 Del. Laws, c. 162, § 2.)

§ 813. Submission of resolution to voters.

The Kent County Levy Court shall submit the question of the approval or rejection of the resolution to the residents of the library district, 18 years of age or older, at a special referendum called for the purpose or to the residents, 18 years of age or older, of the County as a whole if the borrowing is for a countywide library. (60 Del. Laws, c. 162, § 2.)

§ 814. Notice of resolution; publication; form.

The Kent County Levy Court shall give notice that the resolution will be submitted to the voters. Such notice shall be given by publication in 2 issues of a newspaper of general circulation in Kent County and by printed advertisements posted in at least 5 public places in the district at least 10 days prior to the date of the special referendum at which the resolution will be submitted to the voters. The notice shall state the substance of the resolution, and the day, hour and place that it will be submitted to the voters. (60 Del. Laws, c. 162, § 2.)

§ 815. Election ballot.

The Kent County Levy Court shall appoint the persons to conduct the election. The polls shall remain open at least 4 hours. All residents of the County, 18 years of age or older, shall be entitled to vote at such election if the borrowing is for a countywide library. If the borrowing is for a district library only the residents of the library district, 18 years of age or older, shall be entitled to vote. The voting shall be by ballot on which shall be written or printed the words "for the resolution in aid of the library" or "against the resolution in aid of the library." (60 Del. Laws, c. 162, § 2.)

§ 816. Results of election.

If a majority of the votes cast be for the resolution in aid of the library, authority to borrow the amount of money specified in the resolution shall be deemed to be thereby conferred. If a majority of the votes cast be against the resolution in aid of the library, the money shall not be borrowed. (60 Del. Laws, c. 162, § 2.)

§ 817. Bonds — Issuance; form.

If the results of the election be for the resolution in aid of the library, the Kent County Levy Court shall borrow the amount specified in the resolution and for this purpose may issue a bond or bonds for the amount. Such bond or bonds shall be in such form and denomination, shall bear such date and be at such rate of interest without limitation which may be determined by resolution of the Kent County Levy Court and shall mature at such time or times as the Kent County Levy Court determines. Any bond issued shall be signed by the President of the Kent County Levy Court and attested by the Clerk of Peace, and shall be sealed with the county seal. The faith and credit of Kent County shall be deemed to be pledged by every bond issued under this subchapter. (60 Del. Laws, c. 162, § 2.)

§ 818. Same — Payment of interest and principal; sinking fund.

Whenever any bond or bonds have been issued under this subchapter, the Kent County Levy Court shall annually raise by levy and taxation a sum sufficient for the payment of the interest on the amount or amounts borrowed and shall likewise raise from time to time by levy and taxation such sum or sums as shall be necessary to establish a sinking fund for the payment of the debt secured by the bond or bonds at or before the maturity thereof. The sums authorized to be raised for interest and for a sinking fund shall be raised in the same manner as the county library tax is raised and shall be in addition to all sums authorized to be raised by the County by any other statute. If the improvement for which bonds are sold are for the benefit of a library district, only the real property in that library district shall be taxed. (60 Del. Laws, c. 162, § 2.)

§ 819. Same — Assumption of existing library district bonds.

In the event any district library commission created pursuant to Chapter 71 of Title 14 conveys any property to the Kent County Levy Court for which bonds are outstanding, the Kent County Levy Court shall assume all obligations of said bonds if the property is used for a countywide library system but if the property is used for a district library system the cost of paying interest and principal on said bonds shall be included in the annual tax levy on real property in that district only. (60 Del. Laws, c. 162, § 2.)

NEW CASTLE COUNTY LIBRARY
(Delaware Code Annotated, 1982, s.9-1562.)

§ 1562. New Castle County libraries; Wilmington Institute.

(a) The county government of New Castle County may appropriate public moneys toward the maintenance and support of free public libraries for the use of the residents of New Castle County and for all purposes incident thereto.

(b) The Wilmington Institute, a corporation of the State, may administer a free library for the use of the residents of New Castle County outside of the

City of Wilmington, and may perform all functions incident thereto, such functions to be in addition to those now devolving upon the Wilmington Institute under existing laws and to be paid for with other funds than those received from the City of Wilmington.

(c) The county government of New Castle County and the Wilmington Institute may enter into continuous contracts, pursuant to resolutions of their respective bodies, with each other and with other persons or corporations, whether public or private, respecting payments of money to be made toward the maintenance and support of a free library for the use of the residents of New Castle County outside the City of Wilmington.

(d) The county government of New Castle County may construct and equip free public libraries in New Castle Hundred and Millcreek Hundred of New Castle County and for said purpose, may acquire land by purchase or gift and may enter into contracts for the construction and equipping of such public libraries in New Castle County outside of the City of Wilmington. The county government may enter into contracts with the Wilmington Institute for the operation and maintenance and support of the said public library.

(e) For the purpose of providing funds for the acquisition of land and construction and equipping of the public library provided in subsection (d) of this section, the county government of New Castle County may borrow money upon the faith and credit of New Castle County by issuing bonds notwithstanding any limitation prescribed by this chapter or any other law.

(1) The bonds shall bear interest at such rates, may be in 1 or more series, may bear such dates, may mature at such times not exceeding 20 years from their respective dates, may be payable in such medium of payment, at such place or places, may carry such registration privileges, may be subject to such terms of redemption, may be executed in such manner, may contain such terms, covenants and conditions, and may be in such form, either coupon or registered, as the resolution or subsequent resolutions provide.

(2) The bonds shall be sold at public sale upon sealed proposals after at least 10 days notice published at least once in a newspaper published in the City of Wilmington. Any of the bonds may be sold at private sale to the United States of America or any agency, instrumentality or corporation thereof, at not less than par.

(3) Pending the preparation of the definitive bonds, interim receipts or certificates in such form and with such provisions as the county government determines may be issued to the purchasers of bonds sold pursuant to this subsection.

(4) The rate of interest may be determined in advance of sale, or the bonds may be offered for sale at a rate of interest to be fixed by the successful bidder for such bonds.

(5) Bonds bearing the signatures of officers in office on the date of the signing thereof shall be valid and binding obligations notwithstanding that

before the delivery thereof and payment therefor any or all the persons whose signatures appear thereon have ceased to be officers of the County.

(6) The validity of the bonds shall not be dependent on nor affected by the validity or regularity of any proceeding relating to the matters authorized by subsection (d) of this section. The resolution authorizing the bonds may provide that the bonds shall contain a recital that they are issued pursuant to this chapter, which recital shall be conclusive evidence of their validity and of the regularity of their issuance.

(7) The faith and credit of the County are pledged to the payment of any bonds issued by the County under this section. The county government shall annually appropriate to the payment of such bonds and the interest thereon the amounts required to pay such bonds and interest as the same become due and payable. Notwithstanding the provisions of any other law the county government may levy an ad valorem tax, with limitation as to rate or amount, upon all property taxable by the County to raise the moneys necessary to meet any such appropriation. (36 Del. Laws, c. 112, §§ 1-3; Code 1935, § 1177; 41 Del. Laws, c. 109, § 1; 45 Del. Laws, c. 107, § 1; 47 Del. Laws, c. 79, § 1; 9 Del. C. 1953, § 1562; 49 Del. Laws, c. 95; 51 Del. Laws, c. 19; 52 Del. Laws, c. 250; 54 Del. Laws, c. 146; 54 Del. Laws, c. 210; 55 Del. Laws, c. 85, § 7N; 56 Del. Laws, c. 23.)

SCHOOL DISTRICT LIBRARIES
(Delaware Code Annotated, 1982, s.14-7101 to 14-7108.)

§ 7101. District library commissions requesting exemption.

Any district library commission, heretofore established to administer and supervise a free public library established by a school district pursuant to this chapter that requests and qualifies for exemption from subsections (a) and (b) of § 6, Chapter 480, Volume 59, Laws of Delaware, on or before August 31, 1975, shall continue in existence and subject to this chapter shall be empowered to administer and supervise the free public library in its district. (60 Del. Laws, c. 285, § 1.)

§ 7102. Appointment, term, etc., of district library commission.

Each district library commission shall be composed of 5 members who are residents of the school district in which the public library is established. The 5 members serving on any such district library commission as of July 1, 1975, shall continue in office until the expiration of the terms for which they were appointed. Upon the expiration of the term of any member, his successor shall be appointed by the Resident Judge of the Superior Court of the State for the county in which the school district is located for a term of 5 years. In case a district is located partly in each of 2 counties, the appointments to fill vacancies caused by expiration of a term shall be made alternately from the 2 counties by the Resident Judge of the county in which the greater number of residents of the school district reside. Appointment to fill an unexpired term is not to be considered a complete term. Each member shall hold office until his successor is appointed and qualified. Any vacancy in the membership of the commission shall be filled by the Resident Judge for the unexpired portion of the 5 year term. (60 Del. Laws, c. 285, § 1.)

§ 7103. Election of officers; meetings; failure to hold or attend meetings.

A district library commission shall annually, from its members, elect a president, secretary and treasurer. The secretary and treasurer may be one and the same person. The district library commission shall meet at least quarterly in each year. Failure to hold 4 formal meetings shall, at the option of the county library advisory board, necessitate the appointment of a new district library commission as provided in § 7102 of this title. The district library commission may adopt a rule that the failure of any member to attend a specified number of meetings of the district library commission shall create a vacancy in the office of such member. (60 Del. Laws, c. 285, § 1.)

§ 7104. Librarian and other employees.

The district library commission shall select a librarian and other employees necessary for the proper conduct of the library. The district library commission may fix the compensation of its employees. (60 Del. Laws, c. 285, § 1.)

§ 7105. Powers of district library commission.

(a) The district library commission shall have the custody and management of the library and all property owned or leased, or donated, relating thereto. All money, from whatever source, shall be placed in the care and custody of the commission to be expended or retained by the commission for and in behalf of the library.

(b) The district library commission may procure and maintain suitable quarters for the library; purchase or accept donations or gifts of printed matter; employ employees; and shall have such further and additional powers as may be necessary for the foundation and establishment, and the support and maintenance of a library.

(c) The district library commission shall have the power to take and hold in the name of the district library commission real and personal property by deed, devise, bequest, gift, grant or otherwise, except by eminent domain, and to alien, sell, transfer and dispose thereof as an occasion may require, and the proceeds realized therefrom may be reinvested in other property, funds or securities for the benefit of the district library.

(d) The district library commission shall have the power to enter into contracts for any library service with any other library, business or with any governmental unit.

(e) All deeds of real estate and bills of sale and contracts shall be executed on behalf of the district library commission by the president and secretary of the district library commission. (60 Del. Laws, c. 285, § 1.)

§ 7106. Reports.

(a) The district library commission shall make a detailed report to the county library advisory board annually of all its receipts and expenditures, and of all the property of the district in its care and custody, including a statement of any unexpended balance of money and of any bequests or donations in behalf of the district, and of any sum or sums received from the county or other governmental unit, with such recommendations as are deemed desirable.

(b) The district library commission shall also make such reports as may be requested by other governmental units. (60 Del. Laws, c. 285, § 1.)

§ 7107. Rules and regulations.

The district library commission may make such rules and regulations for the conduct of the persons employed by it, and for the care and use of the books, newspapers, magazines, reviews and other media in the library by the persons using the library, and also concerning the conduct and deportment of all persons while in or about the library or reading room, as the commission shall or may from time to time deem proper and advisable. The use of the library and reading rooms or the contents thereof for library purposes shall be free to any citizen of the State. The rules and regulations made by the commission may be enforced by a suitable penalty including fines as may be set by the commission. (60 Del. Laws, c. 285, § 1.)

§ 7108. Consolidated districts.

A district library commission located in a consolidated school district and responsible for the operation of more than 1 library may request the Resident Judge to appoint separate library commissions for each library in that district. Upon written request from the consolidated district library commission, the Resident Judge will make the number of appointments necessary to establish individual commissions for those libraries hitherto served by a consolidated commission, using those members currently serving on the consolidated commission as representatives of their library as nuclei for the new commissions. Upon such appointment of separate district library commissions the consolidated district library commissions shall cease to exist. (60 Del. Laws, c. 285, § 1.)

LAW LIBRARIES
(Delaware Code Annotated, 1982, s.10-1941, 19-1942.)

§ 1941. Control and supervision of law libraries.

The law library in each county maintained for the use of the judges of the courts shall be under the control and supervision respectively of the judges of the Court of Chancery and of the Superior Court residing in the county, who are empowered from time to time to purchase such law books as shall be necessary for the maintenance of the library. The judges residing in New Castle County are authorized to employ a librarian for the law library of New Castle County at such compensation as shall from time to time be fixed by the judges. The judges residing in Sussex County, if and when they shall determine that a librarian is required in the Sussex County library, are likewise authorized to employ one at such compensation as they may fix from time to time. The judges residing in Kent County, if and when they shall determine that a librarian is required in the Kent County library, are likewise authorized to employ one at such compensation as they may fix from time to time.

The payment of bills for the purchase and rebinding of law books, and other necessary expenses, including compensation of the librarian, shall, to the extent that other sources of income, if any, are insufficient, be made by the State Treasurer out of funds regularly appropriated for the operation of said law libraries. (26 Del. Laws, c. 266, §§ 1-4; 27 Del. Laws, c. 283; Code 1915, § 3802; 28 Del. Laws, c. 235; Code 1935, § 4314; 10 Del. C. 1953, § 1942; 50 Del. Laws, c. 72, § 2; 51 Del. Laws, c. 133, § 1.)

§ 1942. Law library in Kent County as official law library for State.

The law library in Kent County is designated as the official law library of the State. Any law books, statutes, legal periodicals, or other legal material suitable for a state law library received by the State on an exchange basis or on any other basis and not specifically acquired by or for some other subdivision of the State shall be deposited in the law library in Kent County. (10 Del. C. 1953, § 1943; 51 Del. Laws, c. 133, § 2.)

LIBRARY SERVICE TO THE BLIND
(Delaware Code Annotated, 1982, s.31-2116.)

§ 2116. Contracts for library services.

The Commission may contract with any public library for that library to render library service to the blind throughout the State and the Commission may reasonably compensate such public library for the cost of the service it renders under such contract. (31 Del. C. 1953, § 2117; 53 Del. Laws, c. 367.)

Delaware library laws are reprinted from DELAWARE CODE ANNOTATED published by The Mitchie Co., Charlottsville, Virginia.

FLORIDA

STATE LIBRARY

(Florida Statutes Annotated, 1982, s.257.01-257.06, 257.08, 257.12.)

20.10   Department of State

There is created a Department of State.

(1) The head of the Department of State is the Secretary of State.

(2) The following divisions of the Department of State are established:

(a) Divisions of Elections.

(b) Division of Archives, History and Records Management.

(c) Division of Corporations.

(d) Division of Library Services.

(e) Division of Licensing.

(f) Division of Cultural Affairs.

(g) Division of Administration.

Laws 1969, c. 69–106, § 10, eff. July 1, 1969. Amended by Laws 1970, c. 70–329, § 1, eff. July 1, 1970; Laws 1971, c. 71–355, § 3, eff. June 27, 1971; Laws 1974, c. 74–272, § 1, eff. July 1, 1974; Laws 1975, c. 75–22, § 15, eff. July 1, 1975; Laws 1977, c. 77–122, §§ 1 to 3, eff. Aug. 2, 1977; Laws 1979, c. 79–164, § 3, eff. Aug. 5, 1979; Laws 1980, c. 80–391, § 1, eff. July 9, 1980.

257.01   State Library; creation; administration

There is created and established the State Library which shall be located at the capital. The State Library shall be administered by the Division of Library Services of the Department of State.

Amended by Laws 1981, c. 81–68, § 1, eff. Oct. 1, 1981.

257.02   State Library Council

(1) There shall be a State Library Council to advise the Division of Library Services. The council shall consist of seven members who shall be appointed by the Secretary of State. Initially, the secretary shall appoint two members for terms of 4 years, two members for terms of 3 years, two members for terms of 2 years, and one member for a term of 1 year. Thereafter, members shall be appointed for 4-year terms. A vacancy shall be filled for the period of the unexpired term.

(2) Members of the council shall serve without compensation or honorarium but shall be entitled to receive reimbursement for per diem and traveling expenses as provided in s. 112.061. The council shall meet at the call of its chairman, at the request of a majority of its membership, at the request of the division, or at such times as may be prescribed by its rules.

(3) The Secretary of State may, in making appointments, consult the Florida Library Association and related organizations for suggestions as to persons having special knowledge and interest concerning libraries. Amended by Laws 1981, c. 81-68, § 2, eff. Oct. 1, 1981.

257.031 Organization of council; appointment of state librarian

(1) The officers of the state library council shall be a chairman, elected from the members thereof, and a secretary, who shall be librarian of the state library and who shall be a person trained in modern library methods, not a member of the council. The state librarian shall be appointed by the department of state and shall serve as the director of the division of state library services of the department of state. The department of state may, in making the appointment of state librarian, consult the members of the state library council.

(2) The state librarian shall:

(a) Keep a record of the proceedings of the council;

(b) Keep an accurate account of the division's financial transactions;

(c) Have charge of the work of the division in organizing new libraries and improving those already established; and

(d) In general, perform such duties as may, from time to time, be assigned to him by the department of state.

Laws 1970, c. 70-439, § 1.
Laws 1970, c. 70-250, § 4.

257.04 Publications, etc., received to constitute part of state library; powers and duties of division

(1) All books, pictures, documents, publications, and manuscripts received through gifts, purchase, or exchange, or on deposit from any source for the use of the state, shall constitute a part of the state library, and shall be placed therein for the use of the public, under the control of the Division of Library Services of the Department of State. The division may receive gifts of money, books or other property which may be used or held for the purpose or purposes given; and may purchase books, periodicals, furniture and equipment as it deems necessary to promote the efficient operation of the service it is expected to render the public.

(2) The division may, upon request, give aid and assistance, financial, advisory, or otherwise, to all school, state institutional, free, and public libraries, and to all communities in the state which may propose to establish libraries, as to the best means of establishing and administering libraries, selecting and cataloging books, and other details of library management.

(3) The division shall maintain a library for state officials and employees, especially of informational material pertaining to the phases of their work, and provide for them material for general reading and study.

(4) The division shall maintain and provide research and information services for all state agencies.

(5) The division shall make all necessary arrangements to provide library services to the blind and physically handicapped persons of the state.

(6) The division may issue printed material, such as lists and circulars of information, and in the publication thereof may cooperate with state library commissions and libraries of other states in order to secure the more economical administration of the work for which it is formed. It may conduct courses of library instruction and hold librarians' institutes in various parts of the state.

(7) The division shall perform such other services and engage in any other activity, not contrary to law, that it may think appropriate in the development of library service to state government, to the libraries and library profession of the state, and to the citizens of the state. Laws 1974, c. 74-228, § 3.

257.05 Copies of reports of state departments furnished division

(1) A "public document" as referred to in this section shall be defined as any annual, biennial, regular or special report or publication of which at least five hundred copies are printed and which may be subject to distribution to the public.

(2) Each and every state official, state department, state board, state court or state agency of any kind, issuing public documents shall furnish the division of library services of the department of state twenty-five copies of each of those public documents, as issued, for deposit in and distribution by the division. However, if the division shall so request, as many as twenty-five additional copies of each public document shall be supplied to it.

(3) It shall be the duty of the division to:

(a) Designate university, college and public libraries as depositories for public documents;

(b) Provide a system of distribution of the copies furnished to it under subsection (2) to such depositories;

(c) Publish a periodic bibliography of the publications of the state. The division is authorized to exchange copies of public documents for those of other states, territories and countries. Depositories receiving public documents under this section shall keep them in a convenient form accessible to the public.

(4) The division shall also be furnished by any state official, department or agency having charge of their distribution, as issued, bound journals of each house of the legislature; acts of the legislature, both local or special and general; annotated acts of the legislature; and revisions and compilations of the Laws of Florida. The number of copies furnished shall be determined by requests of the division, which number in no case shall exceed twenty-five copies of the particular publication and, in the case of legislative acts, annotated legislative acts, and revisions and compilations of the laws, not more than two copies.

(5) In any case in which any state official, state department, state board, state court, or state agency of any class or kind has more than ten copies of any one kind of publication from time to time heretofore issued, he or it shall, upon request of the division, supply said division with one copy of each such publication for deposit in the state library. Laws 1973, c. 73–305, § 1.

257.06 Annual report of division

The division of library services of the department of state shall, prior to March 1 of each year, make a report to the governor, which report shall show the condition of the state library and library conditions and progress in Florida and shall contain a detailed statement of the expenses of the division. This report, when printed, shall be presented to the legislature and distributed by the division. This report and other printing and binding for the division shall be printed under the same regulations as other reports of the executive officers of the state.

Laws 1973, c. 73–305, § 1.

257.08 Division to submit budget to legislature for appropriations

To carry out the provisions of this chapter, the division shall

submit to the department of state its budget for maintenance as a basis for appropriations. Laws 1969, c. 69–353, § 21.
Laws 1969, c. 69–106, §§ 10, 35.

257.12 Division of library services authorized to accept, etc., federal funds

(1) The division of library services of the department of state is authorized to accept, receive, administer and expend any moneys, materials or any other aid granted, appropriated, or made available by the United States or any of its agencies for the purpose of giving aid to libraries and providing educational library service in the state.

(2) The division is authorized to file any accounts required by federal law or regulation with reference to receiving and administering all such moneys, materials, and other aid for said purposes; provided, however, that the acceptance of such moneys, materials, and other aid shall not deprive the state from complete control and supervision of its library.

Laws 1969, c. 69–353, § 21.
Laws 1969, c. 69–106, §§ 10, 35.

STATE AID
(Florida Statutes Annotated, 1982, s.257.13-257.25.)

257.13 Definitions; §§ 257.14–257.25

The following terms, when used in §§ 257.14–257.25 or the rules, regulations and orders made pursuant hereto, shall be construed, respectively:

(1) "Population" means the latest reliable annual estimate of midyear population made by some state agency which is approved by the division of library services of the department of state.

(2) "Library unit" means all libraries operating under a single administration in any given area of the state wherein there is county participation.

(3) "Municipal library" means any library operated by a municipality the services of which are available to the entire county and which meets minimum standards established by the division of library services. Any municipal library, as defined by this subsection, shall be considered a library unit for the purposes of subsection (2), except that the provisions of this subsection shall not apply with respect to § 257.20. Laws 1972, c. 72–353, § 1.

257.14 Division of library services; rules and regulations

The division of library services may make all necessary and

reasonable rules and regulations to carry out the provisions of §§ 257.13–257.25.   Laws 1969, c. 69–353, § 21.
                                                  Laws 1969, c. 69–106, §§ 10, 35.

257.15   Division of library services; standards

The division of library services shall establish reasonable and pertinent operating standards for public libraries under which counties maintaining a free library, free library service by contract or municipal libraries shall be eligible to receive state moneys.   Laws 1972, c. 72–353, § 2.

257.16   Reports

All library units receiving grants under §§ 257.13–257.25 shall file with the division of library services on or before December 1 of each year a financial report on its operations and furnish the said division with such other information as said division may require.   Laws 1969, c. 69–353, § 21.
                                                  Laws 1969, c. 69–106, §§ 10, 35.

257.17   Operating grants

Any county which establishes or maintains a free library or which gives or receives free library service by contract with a municipality or nonprofit library corporation or association within said county, or any municipality which establishes or maintains a free library, shall be eligible to receive an annual operating grant of not more than 25 percent of all local funds expended during the preceding fiscal year by said county, by said municipality, or by said county and municipality or nonprofit library corporation or association, for the operation and maintenance of a library unit. Any county which joins with one or more counties to maintain a free library or contracts with another county or with a municipality in another county to receive free library service shall be eligible to receive an annual operating grant of not more than 25 percent of the local funds which said county expended during the preceding fiscal year for the operation and maintenance of a jointly maintained free library unit or free library service. No county or municipality shall be eligible to receive a grant unless the total operating budget of the library unit is at least twenty thousand dollars. Counties or municipalities establishing free public library service for the first time may submit a certified copy of their appropriation for library service, and their eligibility to receive an operating grant shall be based upon said appropriation.   Laws 1973, c. 73–138, § 1.

257.18   Equalization grants

Any county or municipality qualifying for an operating grant in which the appropriation for the library unit from all local sources is equivalent to the yield of a one-mill county tax or one dollar per capita, whichever is less, and whose equalization factor is less than one dollar, shall be eligible to receive an equalization grant computed by multiplying the population of the county by the difference between one dollar and the equalization factor. The equalization formula shall be computed annually for each county by the division based upon the ratio of each county's contribution to the state full value of assessment of property to the actual contribution to actual assessment of the state. The level of assessment of property for each county shall be determined by the state agency authorized by law, which shall certify the results of such determination to the division. During the initial year that this formula is used to compute the grants, no participating county will receive less equalization money than it received pursuant to the formula employed in fiscal 1972–1973.

Laws 1973, c. 73–138, § 2.

257.19   Establishment grants

Grants for the establishment or extension of library service may be paid for one year only to any county joining a regional library or to two or more counties forming a regional library or to any county contracting with a municipal library having a municipal budget of over twenty thousand dollars. An establishment grant shall equal, and be in addition to, the total grant (operating and equalization) to which a county is otherwise entitled, provided that no establishment grant shall exceed fifty thousand dollars. For the purposes of this section, § 257.21 shall not be applicable.

Laws 1973, c. 73–138, § 3.

257.191   Construction grants

The division of library services is authorized to accept and administer library construction moneys appropriated to it and shall allocate such appropriation to municipal, county, and regional libraries in the form of library construction grants on a matching basis. The local matching portion shall be no less than 50 percent. The division shall establish regulations for the administration of library construction grants and promulgate them pursuant to § 257.14. For the purposes of this section, § 257.21 shall not be applicable.

Laws 1973, c. 73–138, § 4.

257.192   Program grants

The division of state library services is authorized to accept and administer appropriations for library program grants and

to make such grants in accordance with the Florida long-range
program for library services.   Laws 1973, c. 73–138, § 5.

257.20   Determination of municipal fiscal year

Where county and municipal fiscal years do not coincide, the
municipal appropriation for the municipal fiscal year ending
during the county fiscal year for which grants are given shall be
used for calculating the grant.   Laws 1961, c. 61–402, § 8.

257.21   Maximum grants allowable

Any reduction in grants because of insufficient funds shall be
prorated on the basis of maximum grants allowable.

                                                    Laws 1961, c. 61–402, § 9.

257.22   Division of library services; allocation of funds

The moneys herein appropriated, and any moneys that may be
hereafter appropriated for use by counties or municipalities
maintaining a free library or free library service, shall be administered and allocated by the division of library services in
the manner prescribed by law. On or before November 1, for
the current year, and on or before November 1 of each year
thereafter, the division shall certify to the comptroller the
amount to be paid to each county or municipality, and the comptroller shall issue warrants to the respective boards of county
commissioners or chief municipal executive authorities for the
amount so allocated.   Laws 1972, c. 72–353, § 5.

257.23   Application for grant

(1) The board of county commissioners of any county desiring to receive a grant under the provisions of §§ 257.13–257.25
shall apply therefor to the division of library services on or before October 1, for the current year, and on or before October 1,
of each year thereafter, on a form to be provided by said division. In said application, which shall be signed by the chairman
of the board of county commissioners and attested by the clerk
of the circuit court, the board of county commissioners shall
agree to observe the standards established by the division as authorized in § 257.15, shall certify the annual tax income and the
rate of tax or the annual appropriation for the free library or
free library service, and shall furnish such other pertinent information as the division may require.

(2) The chief municipal executive authority of any municipality desiring to receive a grant under the provisions of §§ 257.-

13–257.25 shall apply therefor to the division of library services on or before October 1 for the current year, and on or before October 1 of each year thereafter, on a form to be provided by the division. In the application, which shall be signed by the chief municipal executive officer and attested to by the clerk of the circuit court, the chief municipal executive authority shall agree to observe the standards established by the division, as authorized in § 257.15, certify the annual tax income and the rate of tax or the annual appropriation for the free library, and furnish such other pertinent information as the division may require.

Laws 1972, c. 72–353, § 6.

257.24 Use of funds

State funds allocated to any county or municipality for a free library or free library service shall be expended only for library purposes in the manner prescribed by the division of library services. Such funds shall not be expended for the purchase or construction of a library building or library quarters, except such funds specifically appropriated for construction purposes as provided in this chapter.

Laws 1973, c. 73–138, § 6.

257.25 Free library service

The service of books in libraries receiving state funds shall be free and shall be made available to all persons living in areas taxed for library purposes.

Laws 1972, c. 72–353, § 7.

INTERSTATE LIBRARY COMPACT
(Florida Statutes Annotated, 1982, s.257.28-257.33.)

257.28 Compact

The Interstate Library Compact is hereby enacted into law and entered into by this state with all states legally joining therein in the form substantially as follows:

INTERSTATE LIBRARY COMPACT

The contracting states solemnly agree that:

Article I

Because the desire for the services provided by libraries transcends governmental boundaries and can most effectively be satisfied by giving such services to communities and people regardless of jurisdictional lines, it is the policy of the states party to this compact to cooperate and share their responsibilities; to authorize cooperation and sharing with respect to those types of library facilities and services which can be more economically or efficiently developed and maintained on a cooperative basis; and to authorize cooperation and sharing among localities, states and others in providing joint or cooperative library services in areas where the distribution of population or of existing and potential library resources make the provision of library service on an interstate basis the most effective way of providing adequate and efficient service.

Article II

As used in this compact:

(a) "Public library agency" means any unit or agency of a local or state government operating or having power to operate a library.

(b) "Private library agency" means any nongovernmental entity which operates or assumes a legal obligation to operate a library.

(c) "Library agreement" means a contract establishing an interstate library district pursuant to this compact or providing for the joint or cooperative furnishing of library services.

Article III

(a) Any one or more public library agencies in a party state in cooperation with any public library agency or agencies in one or more other party states may establish and maintain an interstate library district. Subject to the provisions of this compact and any other laws of the party states which pursuant hereto remain applicable, such district may establish, maintain and operate some or all of the library facilities and services for the area concerned in accordance with the terms of a library agreement therefor. Any private library agency or agencies within an interstate library district may cooperate therewith, assume duties, responsibilities and obligations thereto, and receive benefits therefrom as provided in any library agreement to which such agency or agencies become party.

(b) Within an interstate library district, and as provided by a library agreement, the performance of library functions may be undertaken on a joint or cooperative basis or may be undertaken by means of one or more arrangements between or among public or private library agencies for the extension of library privileges to the use of facilities or services operated or rendered by one or more of the individual library agencies.

(c) If a library agreement provides for joint establishment, maintenance or operation of library facilities or services by an interstate library district, such district shall have power to do any one or more of the following in accordance with such library agreement:

1. Undertake, administer and participate in programs or arrangements for securing, lending or servicing of books and other publications, any other materials suitable to be kept or made available by libraries, library equipment or for the dissemination of information about libraries, the value and significance of particular items therein, and the use thereof.

2. Accept for any of its purposes under this compact any and all donations, and grants of money, equipment, supplies, materials, and services, (conditional or otherwise), from any state or the United States or any subdivision or agency thereof, or interstate agency, or from any institution, person, firm or corporation, and receive, utilize and dispose of the same.

3. Operate mobile library units or equipment for the purpose of rendering bookmobile service within the district.

4. Employ professional, technical, clerical and other personnel and fix terms of employment, compensation, and other appropriate benefits; and where desirable, provide for the in-service training of such personnel.

5. Sue and be sued in any court of competent jurisdiction.

6. Acquire, hold, and dispose of any real or personal property or any interest or interests therein as may be appropriate to the rendering of library service.

7. Construct, maintain and operate a library, including any appropriate branches thereof.

8. Do such other things as may be incidental to or appropriate for the carrying out of any of the foregoing powers.

Article IV

(a) An interstate library district which establishes, maintains or operates any facilities or services in its own right shall have a governing board which shall direct the affairs of the district and act for it in all matters relating to its business. Each participating public library agency in the district shall be represented on the governing board which shall be organized and conduct its business in accordance with provision therefor in the library agreement. But in no event shall a governing board meet less often than twice a year.

(b) Any private library agency or agencies party to a library agreement establishing an interstate library district may be represented on or advise with the governing board of the district in such manner as the library agreement may provide.

Article V

Any two or more state library agencies of two or more of the party states may undertake and conduct joint or cooperative library programs, render joint or cooperative library services, and enter into and perform arrangements for the cooperative or joint acquisition, use, housing and disposition of items or collections of materials which, by reason of expense, rarity, specialized nature, or infrequency of demand therefor would be appropriated for central collection and shared use. Any such programs, services or arrangements may include provision for the exercise on a cooperative or joint basis of any power exercisable by an interstate library district and an agreement embodying any such program, service, or arrangement shall contain provisions covering the subjects detailed in Article VI of this compact for interstate library agreements.

Article VI

(a) In order to provide for any joint or cooperative undertaking pursuant to this compact, public and private library agencies may enter into library agreements. Any agreement executed pursuant to the provisions of this compact shall, as among the parties to the agreement:

1. Detail the specific nature of the services, programs, facilities, arrangements or properties to which it is applicable.

2. Provide for the allocation of costs and other financial responsibilities.

3. Specify the respective rights, duties, obligations and liabilities of the parties.

4. Set forth the terms and conditions for duration, renewal, termination, abrogation, disposal of joint or common property, if any, and all other matters which may be appropriate to the proper effectuation and performance of the agreement.

(b) No public or private library agency shall undertake to exercise itself, or jointly with any other library agency, by means of a library agreement any power prohibited to such agency by the constitution or statutes of its state.

(c) No library agreement shall become effective until filed with the compact administrator of each state involved, and approved in accordance with Article VII of this compact.

Article VII

(a) Every library agreement made pursuant to this compact

shall, prior to and as a condition precedent to its entry into force, be submitted to the attorney general of each state in which a public library agency party thereto is situated, who shall determine whether the agreement is in proper form and compatible with the laws of his state. The attorneys general shall approve any agreement submitted to them unless they shall find that it does not meet the conditions set forth herein and shall detail in writing addressed to the governing bodies of the public library agencies concerned the specific respects in which the proposed agreement fails to meet the requirements of law. Failure to disapprove an agreement submitted hereunder within ninety days of its submission shall constitute approval thereof.

(b) In the event that a library agreement made pursuant to this compact shall deal in whole or in part with the provision of services or facilities with regard to which an officer or agency of the state government has constitutional or statutory powers of control, the agreement shall, as a condition precedent to its entry into force, be submitted to the state officer or agency having such power of control and shall be approved or disapproved by him or it as to all matters within his or its jurisdiction in the same manner and subject to the same requirements governing the action of the attorneys general pursuant to paragraph (a) of this article. This requirement of submission and approval shall be in addition to and not in substitution for the requirement of submission to an approval by the attorneys general.

Article VIII

Nothing in this compact or in any library agreement shall be construed to supersede, alter or otherwise impair any obligation imposed on any library by otherwise applicable law, nor to authorize the transfer or disposition of any property held in trust by a library agency in a manner contrary to the terms of such trust.

Article IX

(a) Any public library agency party to a library agreement may appropriate funds to the interstate library district established thereby in the same manner and to the same extent as to a library wholly maintained by it and, subject to the laws of the state in which such public library agency is situated, may pledge its credit in support of an interstate library district established by the agreement.

(b) Subject to the provisions of the library agreement pursuant to which it functions and the laws of the states in which such district is situated, an interstate library district may claim and receive any state and federal aid which may be available to library agencies.

Article X

Each state shall designate a compact administrator with whom copies of all library agreements to which his state or any public library agency thereof is party shall be filed. The administrator shall have such other powers as may be conferred upon him by the laws of his state and may consult and cooperate with the compact administrators of other party states and take such steps as may effectuate the purposes of this compact. If the laws of a party state so provide, such state may designate one or more deputy compact administrators in addition to its compact administrator.

Article XI

(a) This compact shall enter into force and effect immediately upon its enactment into law by any two states. Thereafter, it shall enter into force and effect as to any other state upon the enactment thereof by such state.

(b) This compact shall continue in force with respect to a party state and remain binding upon such state until six months after such state has given notice to each other party state of the repeal thereof. Such withdrawals shall not be construed to relieve any party to a library agreement entered into pursuant to this compact from any obligation of that agreement prior to the end of its duration as provided therein.

Article XII

This compact shall be liberally construed so as to effectuate the purposes thereof. The provisions of this compact shall be severable and if any phrase, clause, sentence or provision of this compact is declared to be contrary to the constitution of any party state or of the United States or the applicability thereof to any government, agency, person or circumstance is held invalid, the validity of the remainder of this compact and the applicability thereof to any government, agency, person or circumstance shall not be affected thereby. If this compact shall be held contrary to the constitution of any state party thereto, the compact shall remain in full force and effect as to the remaining states and in full force and effect as to the state affected as to all severable matters.   Laws 1972, c. 72–157, § 1.

257.29   Compliance with local laws

No city, town, county, library system, library district, or other political subdivision of this state shall be party to a library agreement which provides for the construction or maintenance of a library pursuant to Art. III, subdivision (c)7. of the compact, pledge its credit in support of such a library, or contribute to the capital financing thereof except after compliance with any laws applicable to such cities, towns, counties, library systems, library districts, or other political subdivisions relating to or governing capital outlay and the pledging of credit.

Laws 1972, c. 72–157, § 2.

257.30   State library agency

As used in the compact, "state library agency," with reference to this state, means Florida state library or agency designated by the secretary of state.

Laws 1972, c. 72–157, § 3.

257.31   Appropriations

An interstate library district lying partly within this state may claim and be entitled to receive state aid in support of any of its functions to the same extent and in the same manner as such functions are eligible for support when carried on by entities wholly within this state. For the purposes of computing and apportioning state aid to interstate library districts hereinafter to be created, this state will consider that portion of the area which lies within this state as an independent entity for the performance of the aided function or functions and compute and apportion the aid accordingly. Subject to any applicable laws of this state, such a district also may apply for and be entitled to receive any federal aid for which it may be eligible.

Laws 1972, c. 72–157, § 4.

257.32   Compact administrator

The secretary of state shall be the compact administrator pursuant to Art. X of the compact. The secretary of state may appoint a deputy compact administrator pursuant to said article.

Laws 1972, c. 72–157, § 5.

257.33   Notices

In the event of withdrawal from the compact, the secretary of state shall send and receive any notices required by Art. XI(b) of the compact.

Laws 1972, c. 72–157, § 6.

DISTRIBUTION OF PUBLIC DOCUMENTS
(Florida Statutes Annotated, 1982, s.283.22-283.25.)

283.22   Public documents; university libraries

The general library of each institution in the university system shall be entitled to receive copies of reports of state officials, departments, institutions and all other state documents published by the state. Each officer of the state empowered by law to distribute such public documents is hereby authorized to transmit without charge, except for payment of shipping costs, the number of copies of each public document desired upon requisition from the librarian. It is made the duty of the library to keep public documents in convenient form accessible to the public. The library under rules formulated by the board of regents is authorized to exchange documents for those of other states, territories and countries.   Laws 1967, c. 67–223, § 2.

283.23   Law libraries of certain colleges designated as state legal depositories

(1) The law libraries of the University of Florida, Florida State University, Stetson University, Nova University, and University of Miami are designated as state legal depositories.
Amended by Laws 1979, c. 79–313, § 1, eff. June 29, 1979.

(2) Each officer of the state empowered by law to distribute legal publications is authorized to transmit, upon payment of shipping costs or cash on delivery, to the state legal depositories copies of such publications as requested. However, the number of copies of each of the general and special laws shall be limited to eight copies to each of the state legal depositories; the number of each of the volumes of the Florida Statutes and supplements shall be up to a maximum computed on the basis of one set for every ten students enrolled during the school year, based upon the average enrollment as certified by the registrar; and the number of house and senate journals shall be limited to one copy of each to each state legal depository.

(3) It is made the duty of the librarian of any depository to keep all public documents in convenient form accessible to the public.

(4) The libraries of all community colleges approved by the state board of education under § 230.752, shall be designated as state depositories for Florida Statutes and supplements published by or under the authority of the state; provided that these depositories may each receive one copy of each volume upon request, without charge except for payment of shipping costs.

       Laws 1973, c. 73–333, § 89.

283.24 Public printing; copies to Library of Congress

Any state official or state agency, board, commission, or institution having charge of publications hereinafter named, is hereby authorized and directed to furnish the library of congress in Washington, D. C., upon requisition from the library of congress, not to exceed three copies, of the journals of both houses of the legislature, volumes of the supreme court reports, volumes of periodic reports of cabinet officers, and copies of reports, studies, maps or other publications by official boards or institutions of Florida, from time to time, as such are published and are available for public distribution.   Laws 1973, c. 73–305, § 1.

283.25 Distribution of session laws

(1) Copies of session laws of each session of the legislature shall be distributed free by the committee as follows:

(a) As many copies as the governor, the supreme court, the district courts of appeal, and the department of legal affairs may require for official use.

(b) One copy as requested by each agency of the government of the United States, not to exceed a total of ten copies. A maximum of three copies shall be sent to the library of congress in Washington, D. C., on requisition of the library.

(c) A maximum of five copies upon request to each institution in the state university system, University of Miami, and Stetson University; two copies to the University of Tampa, Florida Southern College, and Rollins College, to be mailed to the president of each institution upon request.

(d) Such copies to each of the several cabinet members of this state (other than the governor and the attorney general); all duly constituted state departments, agencies, boards, commissions, and institutions; the supreme court of the United States; and the United States circuit court of appeals for the fifth circuit; as they shall request for official use, the maximum number to be determined by the committee.

(e) One copy to each member of the Florida Senate and House of Representatives of each current session of the Legislature; the Secretary of the Senate and the Clerk of the House of each current session of the Legislature; the judges of the courts of record, including the county court judges; the prosecuting attorneys and their assistants of the courts of record; the clerks of the courts of record; the public defenders in each judicial circuit; each member of the Congress of the United States from this state; each of the judges, marshals, clerks, and district attorneys of the district courts of the United States within this state, and the county law libraries; and, upon request, to the following county officers in each county: The sheriff, the property appraiser, the tax collector, the superintendent of schools, the supervisor of elections, and the board of county commissioners.

Amended by Laws 1977, c. 77–102, § 1, eff. Aug. 2, 1977.

(2) The committee may exchange Florida Statutes and session laws for copies of statutes and session laws of other states, not exceeding four copies of each to any one state. The copies so procured by exchange shall be deposited in the supreme court library, the attorney general's library, the University of Florida law library, and the Florida State University law library, the same to become a part of the respective libraries.

(3) Prior to October 1, 1970, the department of state shall take inventory of all officially published Laws of Florida, and the books and records previously kept by it shall be transferred to the committee. However, five sets may be reserved by the department of state for reference purposes. The committee may, after a period of ten years, take inventory of said books and may destroy obsolete volumes over ten years old, reserving five sets for reference purposes. A reasonable number of each volume shall be reserved for sale at a price to be set by the committee. Moneys received shall be deposited in the state treasury and credited to the appropriation for legislative expense.

Laws 1973, c. 73–334, § 22.

ARCHIVES AND RECORDS MANAGEMENT
(Florida Statutes Annotated, 1982, s.267.011-267.051, 267.10, 119.031-119.110.)

267.011 Short title

This act shall be known as the Florida Archives and History Act.

Laws 1967, c. 67–50, § 1.

267.021 Definitions

For the purpose of this act:

(1) "Division" shall mean the division of archives, history and records management of the department of state.

(2) "Public record" or "public records" shall mean all documents, papers, letters, maps, books, tapes, photographs, films, sound recordings, or other material regardless of physical form or characteristics made or received pursuant to law or ordinance or in connection with the transaction of official business by any agency.

(3) "Agency" shall mean any state, county, or municipal officer, department, division, board, bureau, commission, or other separate unit of government created or established by law.

(4) "Florida state archives" shall mean an establishment maintained by the division for the preservation of those public

records and other papers that have been determined by the division to have sufficient historical or other value to warrant their continued preservation by the state and have been accepted by the division for deposit in its custody.

(5) "Records center" shall mean an establishment maintained by the division primarily for the storage, processing, servicing, and security of public records that must be retained for varying periods of time but need not be retained in an agency's office equipment or space.

(6) "Historic sites and properties" shall mean real or personal property of historical value.

Laws 1971, c. 71–377, § 72.

267.031 Division of Archives, History and Records Management

(1) The Division of Archives, History and Records Management shall be organized into as many bureaus as deemed necessary by the division for the proper discharge of its duties and responsibilities under this chapter. The division may employ a chief to administer each such bureau and may prescribe such qualifications of training and experience for each such bureau chief as may be required to perform the duties of the chief and carry out the programs of the division.
Amended by Laws 1981, c. 81–173, § 1, eff. July 1, 1981.

(2) (a) The secretary of state is hereby authorized to appoint advisory councils to provide professional and technical assistance to the division. The councils shall consist of not less than five nor more than nine members, and such appointments shall consist of persons who are qualified by training and experience and possessed of proven interest in the specific area of responsibility and endeavor involved.

(b) The chairman of each of said councils shall be elected by a majority of the members of the council and shall serve for two years. If a vacancy occurs in the office of chairman before the expiration of his term, a chairman shall be elected by a majority of the members of the council to serve the unexpired term of such vacated office.

(c) It shall be the duty of any of the advisory councils appointed hereunder to provide professional and technical assistance to the division as to all matters pertaining to the duties and responsibilities of the division in the administration of the provisions of this chapter. Members of the councils shall serve without pay, but shall be entitled to reimbursement for their necessary travel expenses incurred in carrying out their official duties, as provided by § 112.061.

(3) The division may employ a director of the division and shall establish his qualifications. The director shall act as the agent of the division in coordinating, directing, and administering the activities and responsibilities of the division. The division may employ other employees as deemed necessary for the performance of its duties under this chapter.

(4) The division shall adopt such rules as deemed necessary to carry out its duties and responsibilities under this chapter, which rules shall be binding on all agencies and persons affected thereby. The willful violation of any of the rules and regulations adopted by the division shall constitute a misdemeanor.
Amended by Laws 1981, c. 81–173, § 1, eff. July 1, 1981.

(5) The division may make and enter into all contracts and agreements with other agencies, organizations, associations, corporations and individuals, or federal agencies as it may determine are necessary, expedient, or incidental to the performance of its duties or the execution of its powers under this chapter.

(6) The division may accept gifts, grants, bequests, loans, and endowments for purposes not inconsistent with its responsibilities under this chapter.

(7) All law enforcement agencies and offices are hereby authorized and directed to assist the division in carrying out its duties under this chapter. Laws 1973, c. 73–280, § 1.

267.041 Office of the director

(1) It shall be the duty and responsibility of the office of the director to render all services required by the division and the several bureaus that can be advantageously and effectively centralized. The office shall perform such other functions and duties as the division may direct.
Amended by Laws 1981, c. 81–173, § 2, eff. July 1, 1981.

(2) The director shall supervise, direct, and coordinate the activities of the division and its bureaus. Laws 1969, c. 69–106, §§ 10, 35.

267.042 Florida State Archives

(1) It is the duty and responsibility of the division to:

(a) Organize and administer the Florida State Archives.

(b) Preserve and administer such records as shall be transferred to its custody; accept arrange, and preserve them, according to approved archival practices, and permit them, at reasonable times and under the supervision of the division, to be inspected, examined, and copied, except that any record placed in the keeping of the division under special terms or conditions restricting its use shall be made accessible only in accordance with such terms and conditions.

(c) Assist the records and information management program in the determination of retention values for records.

(d) Cooperate with and assist insofar as practicable state institutions, departments, agencies, counties, municipalities, and individuals engaged in activities in the field of state archives, manuscripts, and history and accept from any person any paper, book, record or 1 similar material which in the judgment of the division warrants preservation in the state archives.

(e) Provide a public research room where, under rules established by the division, the materials in the state archives may be studied.

(f) Conduct, promote, and encourage research in Florida history, government, and culture and maintain a program of information, assistance, coordination, and guidance for public officials, educational institutions, libraries, the scholarly community, and the general public engaged in such research.

(g) Cooperate with and, insofar as practicable, assist agencies, libraries, institutions, and individuals in projects designed to preserve original source materials relating to Florida history, government, and culture and prepare and publish handbooks, guides, indexes, and other literature directed toward encouraging the preservation and use of the state's documentary resources.

(h) Encourage and initiate efforts to preserve, collect, process, transcribe, index, and research the oral history of Florida government.

(i) Assist and cooperate with the records and information management program in the training and information program described in s. 267.051(1)(f).

(2) Any agency is authorized and empowered to turn over to the division any record no longer in current official use. The division, in its discretion, is authorized to accept such record and, having done so, shall provide for its administration and preservation as herein provided and, upon acceptance, shall be considered the legal custodian of such record.

(3) Title to any record transferred to the Florida State Archives, as authorized in this chapter, shall be vested in the division.

(4) The division shall make certified copies under seal of any record transferred to it upon the application of any person, and said certificates shall have the same force and effect as if made by the agency from which the record was received. The division may charge a fee for this service based upon the cost of service.

(5) The division may establish and maintain as part of the state archives a Florida State Photographic Collection. The division shall:

(a) Acquire, identify, appraise, arrange, index, restore, and preserve photographs, motion pictures, drawings and other iconographic material considered appropriate for preservation.

(b) Initiate appropriate action to acquire, identify, preserve, recover, and restore photographs, motion pictures, and other iconographic material considered appropriate for preservation.

(c) Provide for an index to the historical photographic holdings of the Florida State Photographic Collection and the State of Florida.
Any use or reproduction of material deposited with the Florida State Photographic Collection shall be allowed pursuant to the provisions of paragraph (1)(b) and subsection (4) provided that appropriate credit for its use is given.

(6) The division shall promulgate such rules as necessary to implement the provisions of this act.
Added Laws 1981, c. 81–173, § 3, eff. July 1, 1981.

267.051 Records and information management
(1) It is the duty and responsibility of the division to:

(a) Establish and administer a records management program, including the operation of a records center or centers directed to the application of efficient and economical management methods relating to the creation, utilization, maintenance, retention, preservation, and disposal of records.

(b) Analyze, develop, establish, and coordinate standards, procedures, and techniques of recordmaking and recordkeeping.

(c) Ensure the maintenance and security of records which are deemed appropriate for preservation.

(d) Establish safeguards against unauthorized or unlawful removal or loss of records.

(e) Initiate appropriate action to recover records removed unlawfully or without authorization.

(f) Institute and maintain a training and information program in all phases of records and information management to bring approved and current practices, methods, procedures, and devices for the efficient and economical management of records to the attention of all agencies.

(g) Provide a centralized program of microfilming for the benefit of all agencies.

(h) Make continuous surveys of recordkeeping operations.

(i) Recommend improvements in current records management practices, including the use of space, equipment, supplies, and personnel in creating, maintaining, and servicing records.

(j) Establish and maintain a program in cooperation with each agency for the selection and preservation of records considered essential to the operation of government and to the protection of the rights and privileges of citizens.

(k) Make, or have made, preservation duplicates, or designate existing copies as preservation duplicates, to be preserved in the place and manner of safekeeping as prescribed by the division.

(2)(a) All records transferred to the division may be held by it in a records center or centers, to be designated by it, for such time as in its judgment retention therein is deemed necessary. At such time as it is established by the division, such records as are determined by it as having historical or other value warranting continued preservation shall be transferred to the Florida State Archives.

(b) Title to any record detained in any records center shall remain in the agency transferring such record to the division.

(c) When a record held in a records center is eligible for destruction, the division shall notify, in writing, by certified mail, the agency which transferred the record. The agency shall have 90 days from receipt of that notice to respond requesting continued retention or authorizing destruction or disposal of the record. If the agency does not respond within that time, title to the record shall pass to the division.

(d) The Florida State Records Center may charge fees for supplies and services, including, but not limited to, shipping containers, pickup, delivery, reference, and storage. Fees shall be based upon the actual cost of the supplies and services and shall be deposited in the operating trust fund.

(3) Any preservation duplicate of any record made pursuant to this chapter shall have the same force and effect for all purposes as the original record. A transcript, exemplification, or certified copy of such preservation duplicate shall be deemed, for all purposes, to be a transcript, exemplification, or certified copy of the original record.

(4) It is the duty of each agency to:

(a) Cooperate with the division in complying with the provisions of this chapter and designate a records management liaison officer.

(b) Establish and maintain an active and continuing program for the economical and efficient management of records.

(5) Each agency shall submit to the division in accordance with the rules of the division a list or schedule of records in its custody that are not needed in the transaction of current business and that do not have sufficient administrative, legal, or fiscal significance to warrant further retention by the agency. Such records shall, in the discretion of the division, be transferred to it for further retention and preservation, as herein provided, or may be destroyed upon its approval.

(6) No record shall be destroyed or disposed of by any agency unless approval of the division is first obtained. The division shall adopt reasonable rules not inconsistent with this chapter which shall be binding on all agencies relating to the destruction and disposal of records. Such rules shall provide but not be limited to:

(a) Procedures for complying and submitting to the division lists and schedules of records proposed for disposal.

(b) Procedures for the physical destruction or other disposal of records.

(c) Standards for the reproduction of records for security or with a view to the disposal of the original record.
Amended by Laws 1981, c. 81–173, § 4, eff. July 1, 1981.

267.10 Legislative intent

In enacting this law, the legislature is cognizant of the fact that there may be instances where an agency may be microfilming and destroying public records or performing other records management programs, pursuant to local or special acts; the legislature is further aware that it may not be possible to implement this chapter in its entirety immediately upon its enactment and it is not the legislative intent by this chapter to disrupt the orderly microfilming and destruction of public records pursuant to such local or special acts above referred to; provided, however, that such agencies make no further disposition of public records without approval of the division of archives, history and records management of the department of state pursuant to such rules and regulations as it may establish. Laws 1969, c. 69–106, §§ 10, 35.

119.031 Keeping records in safe places; copying or repairing certified copies

Insofar as practicable, custodians of public records shall keep them in fireproof and waterproof safes, vaults or rooms fitted with noncombustible materials and in such arrangement as to be easily accessible for convenient use. All public records should be kept in the buildings in which they are ordinarily used. Record books should be copied or repaired, renovated or rebound if worn, mutilated, damaged or difficult to read. Whenever any state, county or municipal records are in need of repair, restoration or rebinding, the head of such state agency, department, board or commission, the board of county commissioners of such county or the governing body of such municipality may authorize that the records in need of repair, restoration or rebinding be removed from the building or office in which such records are ordinarily kept for the length of time required to repair, restore or rebind them. Any public official who causes a record book to be copied shall attest it and shall certify on oath that it is an accurate copy of the original book. The copy shall then have the force and effect of the original. Laws 1967, c. 67–125, § 3.

119.041 Destruction of records regulated

No public official may mutilate, destroy, sell, loan or otherwise dispose of any public record without the consent of the division of archives, history and records management of the department of state.
Laws 1969, c. 69–106, §§ 10, 35.

119.05　Disposition of records at end of official's term

Whoever has the custody of any public records shall, at the expiration of his term of office, deliver to his successor, or if there be none, to the division of archives, history and records management of the department of state, all records, books, writings, letters and documents kept or received by him in the transaction of his official business.　　　　　　　　Laws 1969, c. 69–106, §§ 10, 35.

119.06　Demanding custody

Whoever is entitled to the custody of public records shall demand them from any person having illegal possession of them, who shall forthwith deliver the same to him.　Any person unlawfully possessing public records shall upon demand of any person and within ten days deliver such records to their lawful custodian unless just cause exists for failing to deliver such records.
　　　　　　　　Laws 1967, c. 67–125, § 6.

119.07　Inspection and examination of records; exemptions

(1) Every person having custody of public records shall permit them to be inspected and examined at reasonable times and under his supervision by any person, and he shall furnish certified copies thereof on payment of fees as prescribed by law.

(2) (a) All public records which presently are deemed by law to be confidential or which are prohibited from being inspected by the public, whether provided by general or special acts of the legislature or which may hereafter be so provided, shall be exempt from the provisions of this section.

(b) All public records referred to in §§ 794.03, 198.09, 199.222, 658.10(1), 624.319(3), (4), 624.311(2), and 63.181, are hereby exempt from the provisions of this section.
　　　　　　　　Laws 1967, c. 67–125, § 7.

119.08　Photographing public records

(1) In all cases where the public or any person interested has a right to inspect or take extracts or make copies from any public record, instruments or documents, any person shall hereafter have the right of access to said records, documents or instruments for the purpose of making photographs of the same while in the possession, custody and control of the lawful custodian thereof, or his authorized deputy.

(2) Such work shall be done under the supervision of the lawful custodian of the said records, who shall have the right to adopt and enforce reasonable rules governing the said work. Said work shall, where possible, be done in the room where the

said records, documents or instruments are by law kept, but if the same in the judgment of the lawful custodian of the said records, documents or instruments be impossible or impracticable, then the said work shall be done in such other room or place as nearly adjacent to the room where the said records, documents and instruments are kept as determined by the lawful custodian thereof.

(3) Where the providing of another room or place is necessary, the expense of providing the same shall be paid by the person desiring to photograph the said records, instruments or documents. While the said work hereinbefore mentioned is in progress, the lawful custodian of said records may charge the person desiring to make the said photographs for the services of a deputy of the lawful custodian of said records, documents or instruments to supervise the same, or for the services of the said lawful custodian of the same in so doing at a rate of compensation to be agreed upon by the person desiring to make the said photographs and the custodian of the said records, documents or instruments, or in case the same fail to agree as to the said charge, then by the lawful custodian thereof.

Laws 1967, c. 67–125, § 8.

119.09 Assistance of the division of archives, history and records management of the department of state

The division of archives, history and records management of the department of state shall have the right to examine into the condition of public records and shall give advice and assistance to public officials in the solution of their problems of preserving, creating, filing and making available the public records in their custody. When requested by the division, public officials shall assist the division in the preparation of an inclusive inventory of public records in their custody to which shall be attached a schedule, approved by the head of the governmental unit or agency having custody of the records and the division, establishing a time period for the retention or disposal of each series of records. Upon the completion of the inventory and schedule, the division shall (subject to the availability of necessary space, staff and other facilities for such purposes) make available space in its records center for the filing of semicurrent records so scheduled and in its archives for noncurrent records of permanent value and shall render such other assistance as needed, including the microfilming of records so scheduled.

Laws 1969, c. 69–106, §§ 10, 35.

119.10 Violation of chapter a misdemeanor

Any person willfully and knowingly violating any of the pro-

visions of this chapter shall be guilty of a misdemeanor of the
first degree, punishable as provided in § 775.082 or § 775.083.

Laws 1971, c. 71–136, § 74.

SCHOOL LIBRARIES

(Florida Statutes Annotated, 1982, s.230.23, 230.33, 231.15, 233.30.)

230.23 Powers and duties of school board

The school board, acting as a board, shall exercise all powers and perform
all duties listed below:

*   *   *

(7) Courses of study and other instructional aids.—Provide adequate instructional aids for all children as follows and in accordance with the requirements of chapter 233.

*   *   *

(d) *School library media services; establishment and maintenance.*—Establish and maintain school library media centers, or school library media centers open to the public, and, in addition thereto, such traveling or circulating
libraries as may be needed for the proper operation of the district school
system. Establish and maintain a program of school library media services
for all public school students which shall be designed to ensure effective use
of available resources and to avoid unnecessary duplication and shall include,
but not be limited to, basic skills development, instructional design, media collection development, media program management, media production, staff
development, and consultation and information services.

Amended by Laws 1978, c. 78–423, § 15, eff. July 1, 1978; Laws 1979, c. 79–
151, § 1, eff. July 1, 1979.

230.33 Duties and responsibilities of superintendent

The superintendent shall exercise all powers and perform all duties listed
below and elsewhere in the law; provided, that in so doing he shall advise
and counsel with the school board. The recommendations, nominations, proposals, and reports required by law and rule to be made to the school board
by the superintendent shall be either recorded in the minutes or shall be
made in writing, noted in the minutes, and filed in the public records of the
board. It shall be presumed that, in the absence of the record required in
this paragraph, the recommendations, nominations, and proposals required of
the superintendent were not contrary to the action taken by the school board
in such matters.

*   *   *

(9) Courses of study and other instructional aids.—Recommend such plans
for improving, providing, distributing, accounting for, and caring for textbooks and other instructional aids as will result in general improvement of
the district school system, as prescribed in chapter 233 and including the following:

(a) *Courses of study.*—Prepare and recommend for adoption, after consultation with teachers and principals and after considering any suggestions which
may have been submitted by patrons of the schools, courses of study for use
in the schools of the district needed to supplement those prescribed by the
state board.

(b) *Textbooks.*—Require that all textbooks and library books furnished by
the state and needed in the district are properly requisitioned, distributed, accounted for, stored, cared for, and used; and recommend such additional text-

books or library books as may be needed.

(c) *Other instructional aids.*—Recommend plans for providing and facilitate the provision and proper use of such other teaching accessories and aids as are needed.

(d) *School library media services; establishment and maintenance.*—Recommend plans for establishing and maintaining school library media centers, or school library media centers open to the public, and, in addition thereto, such circulating or traveling libraries as are needed for the proper operation of the district school system. Recommend plans for the establishment and maintenance of a program of school library media services for all public school students. The school library media services program shall be designed to insure effective use of available resources and to avoid unnecessary duplication and shall include, but not be limited to, basic skills development, instructional design, media collection development, media program management, media production, staff development, and consultation and information services.

Amended by Laws 1978, c. 78–423, § 16, eff. July 1, 1978; Laws 1979, c. 79–256, § 2, eff. Oct. 1, 1979; Laws 1980, c. 80–295, § 6, eff. July 1, 1980; Laws 1981, c. 81–103, § 2, eff. June 22, 1981; Laws 1981, c. 81–247, § 2, eff. July 1, 1981.

231.15 Positions for which certificates required

The State Board of Education shall have authority to classify school services and to prescribe regulations in accordance with which the regular, temporary, part-time, and substitute certificates shall be issued by the Department of Education to school employees who meet the standards prescribed by such regulations for their class of service. Each person employed or occupying a position as school supervisor, helping teacher, principal, teacher, or school librarian, or other position in which the employee serves in an instructional capacity, in any public school of any district of this state shall hold the certificate required by law and by regulations of the state board in fulfilling the requirements of the law for the type of service rendered. However, the state board shall adopt regulations authorizing school boards to employ selected noncertificated personnel to provide instructional services in the individual's field of speciality or to assist instructional staff members as teacher aids. Each person employed as a school nurse shall hold a license to practice nursing in the state, and each person employed as a school physician shall hold a license to practice medicine in the state.

Amended by Laws 1980, c. 80–325, § 5; Laws 1980, c. 80–378, § 1.

233.30 School board cooperative libraries

Each school board may, at its discretion, make contracts or agreements with county or community groups or organizations for a cooperative program or programs of library establishment, maintenance, and use, and all such contracts or agreements with county or community groups or organizations shall provide that such cooperative school and county or school and community libraries shall be established on public school property and shall continue under the supervision and control of such school board; and such part of the costs therefor as may, by contract or agreement, be properly chargeable to such school board shall be defrayed out of available district general school funds or, under limitations prescribed by law, other funds which may be or may become available for such purposes.　　　　Laws 1969, c. 69–300, § 1

LAW LIBRARIES
(Florida Statutes Annotated, 1982, s.25.341, 25.351,
25.361, 28.241, 35.28.)

25.341   Library of supreme court, custodian

The library of the supreme court shall be in custody of the librarian appointed by the court, who shall be subject to its direction.   Laws 1957, c. 57–274, § 1.

25.351   Acquisition of books

Books for the library of the supreme court may be acquired:

(1) **By purchase.**—As the supreme court shall direct.

(2) **By exchange.**—Such number of reports, statutes and journals as shall be obtained by the chief justice upon his request from the secretary of state shall be exchanged by the librarian with appropriate authorities of the United States and other states and territories for corresponding numbers of their reports.   Laws 1957, c. 57–274, § 1.

25.361   Obtaining state publications for exchange purposes

The supreme court is hereby authorized, for the purpose of making exchanges, to obtain copies of the report of the decisions of the supreme court and district courts of appeal, any of the Florida session laws, the Florida Statutes, or any other publication of the state available for distribution and exchange for any book or publication needed for use in the supreme court library.
                                          Laws 1957, c. 57–274, § 1.

28.241   Filing charges for trial and appellate proceedings

(1) The party instituting any civil action, suit, or proceeding in the circuit court shall pay to the clerk of said court a service charge of $20 in all cases in which there are not more than five defendants, and an additional service charge of $1 for each defendant in excess of five. An additional service charge of $5 shall be paid by the party seeking each severance that is granted. An additional service charge of $2 shall be paid to the clerk for each civil action filed, such charge to be remitted by the clerk to the State Treasurer for deposit into the General Revenue Fund unallocated. Service charges in excess of those herein fixed may be imposed by the governing authority of the county by ordinance, or by special or local law, and such excess shall be expended as provided by such ordinance or any special or local law, now or hereafter in force, in providing and maintaining facilities, including a law library, for the use of the courts of the county wherein the service charges are collected or for a legal aid program in such county. Postal charges incurred by the clerk of the circuit court in making service by certified or registered mail on defendants or other parties shall be paid by the party at whose instance service is made. That part of the within fixed or allowable service charges which is not by local or special law applied to the special purposes shall constitute the total service charges of the clerk of said court for all services performed by him in civil actions, suits, or proceedings.

(2) The clerk of the circuit court of any county in the state who operates his office from fees and service charges collected, as opposed to budgeted allocations from county general revenue, shall be paid by the county as service charges for all services to be performed by him in any criminal or juvenile action or proceeding in said court, in lieu of all other service charges heretofore charged, except as hereinafter provided, the sum of $20 for each defendant or juvenile. However, in cases involving capital punishment the charge shall be $25. In any county where a law creates a law library fund or other special fund, this charge may be increased for that purpose by a special or local law or an ordinance.

(3) Upon the institution of any appellate proceeding from any inferior court to the circuit court of any such county or from the circuit court to an appellate court of the state, the clerk shall charge and collect from the party or parties instituting such appellate proceedings a service charge of $25 for filing a notice of appeal from an inferior court and $10 for filing a notice of appeal to a higher court.

(4) Nothing in this section shall be construed to include the service charges required by law for the clerk as provided in s. 28.24 and other sections of the Florida Statutes.

(5) This section shall not apply to any suit or proceeding pending on July 1, 1790.

Amended by Laws 1974, c. 74-154, § 1, eff. June 11, 1974; Laws 1975, c. 75-124, § 4, eff. July 1, 1975; Laws 1977, c. 77-174, § 1, eff. Aug. 2, 1977; Laws 1977, c. 77-284, § 3, eff. Oct. 1, 1977.

35.28 District courts of appeal libraries

The library of each of the district courts of appeal and its custodian shall be provided for by rule of the supreme court. Payment for books, equipment, supplies, and quarters as provided for in such rules shall be paid from funds appropriated for the district courts, on requisition drawn as provided by law.

Laws 1957, c. 57-248, § 1.

MISCELLANEOUS PROVISIONS
(Florida Statutes Annotated, 1982, s.125.01, 257.261.)

125.01 Powers and duties

(1) The legislative and governing body of a county shall have the power to carry on county government. To the extent not inconsistent with general or special law, this power shall include, but shall not be restricted to, the power to:

* * *

(f) Provide parks, preserves, playgrounds, recreation areas, libraries, museums, historical commissions, and other recreation and cultural facilities and programs;   Laws 1971, c. 71-14, § 1.

257.261 Library registration and circulation records

All registration and circulation records of every public library, except statistical reports of registration and circulation, shall be confidential information. Except in accordance with proper judicial order, no person shall make known in any manner any information contained in such records. As used in this section, the term "registration records" includes any information which a library requires a patron to provide in order to become eligible to borrow books and other materials, and the term "circulation records" includes all information which identifies the patrons borrowing particular books and other materials. Any person violating the provisions of this section is guilty of a misdemeanor of the second degree, punishable as provided in s. 775.082, s. 775.083, or s. 775.084.

Laws 1978, c. 78–81, § 1, eff. Oct. 1, 1978.

Florida library laws are reprinted from FLORIDA STATUTES ANNOTATED published by The Harrison Co., Atlanta, Ga. and West Publishing Co., St. Paul, Minn.

GEORGIA

STATE LIBRARY
(Code of Georgia Annotated, 1982, s.101-101 to 101-105.)

101-101 Terms defined

For the purpose of Title 101 of the Code of Georgia of 1933, as amended, the following words as used therein, unless the context thereof clearly indicates otherwise, shall be construed to have the following meanings:

a. Librarian shall mean the State Librarian whose duties are set forth herein and in Chapter 101-2.

b. Library shall mean the State Library provided for in this Chapter.

c. Public documents shall mean the reports, bulletins and other publications of the several State departments and institutions of the Executive Branch of Government, exclusive of the reports of the Supreme Court and the Court of Appeals, the journals of the House and the Senate, and the session laws enacted by the General Assembly of Georgia.

d. Reports or court reports shall mean the bound volumes of the official reports of the decisions of the Supreme Court and of the Court of Appeals, and as the word reports is further defined in subsection b. of section 90-201.

e. Journals shall mean the bound volumes of the journals of the House and the Senate.

f. Laws shall mean the bound volumes of the Georgia session laws.

g. Publisher shall mean the State Publisher as defined in subsection c. of section 90-201.

h. Reporter shall mean the Reporter of the Supreme Court and Court of Appeals as defined in subsection a. of section 90-201.
(Acts 1975, pp. 741, 743.)

101-102 Library; incorporated into and maintained as division of State Law Department; located at seat of State government under supervision of Attorney General; when open

The library is hereby incorporated into and made a division of the State Law Department. The Attorney General shall keep and maintain under his supervision the library which shall be located in a building at the seat of State government and which shall be open to the general public Mondays through Fridays during the hours of 9:00 A.M. to 4:00 P.M., legally prevailing time, legal holidays excepted. The Attorney General shall have authority to provide for the library to be opened during such additional days and hours as he deems either necessary or proper.

(Acts 1975, pp. 741, 744.)

101-103 Librarian and library employees; employment, term, qualifications, compensation, removal, retirement benefits

The Attorney General shall appoint a librarian for such periods of time as he deems advisable. The librarian so appointed shall be a duly certified librarian, according to the provisions of Chapter 84-22 and of rules and regulations pursuant thereto, or an attorney-at-law. The librarian shall be responsible to the Attorney General and shall furnish such information and reports as the Attorney General shall require. The Attorney General shall appoint such library employees for such periods of time as he shall deem necessary for the proper functioning of the library. The Attorney General shall set the compensation of the librarian and all library employees, all of whom shall be removable by the appointing authority. The librarian and library employees shall be employees of the State Law Department and shall be covered as such by the Employees' Retirement System of Georgia.

(Acts 1975, pp. 741, 774.)

101-104 Same; duties; gifts to library

The librarian shall keep in sound condition all books and other library materials entrusted to his care and custody, he shall prepare and maintain an index to such books and materials which shall be revised without unnecessary delay from time to time, as the circumstances may require. The librarian is authorized to accept in behalf of the State gifts of books and other library materials.

(Acts 1975, pp. 741, 744.)

101-105 Same; disposition of books and other library materials

The librarian may transfer books and other library holdings of archival quality, including the public documents, reports, journals and laws defined in section 101-101, to the State Archives. Books, public documents and other library holdings which have become obsolete or surplus to the needs of the library, and defective or worn out volumes of the reports, journals and laws may, as the circumstances warrant, be either sold, destroyed or otherwise disposed of by the librarian with the approval in writing of the Attorney General.   (Acts 1975, pp. 741, 745.)

STATE PUBLIC LIBRARY SERVICE
(Code of Georgia Annotated, 1982, s.32-2604 to 32-2607, 32-625a.)

32-2604 State Library Commission abolished; transfer of functions and services to State Board of Education

The State Library Commission is hereby abolished and the functions and services heretofore exercised and performed by it shall be hereafter exercised and performed by the State Board of Education.
(Acts 1943, p. 385.)

32-2605 Duties of State Board of Education relating to libraries; employment of staff; expenses

The State Board of Education shall give aid, advice and counsel to all libraries and communities which may propose to establish libraries as to the best means of establishing and administering them, the selection of books, cataloging and other details of library management, and shall exercise supervision over all public libraries, and shall endeavor to improve libraries already established. The State Board may also conduct a book-lending and information service for the benefit of the citizens of the State, free of cost except postage. The board is also authorized to purchase for such purposes books, periodicals and other instructional materials. The board may also employ the necessary professional and clerical staff, upon the recommendation of the State Superintendent of Schools, to carry on the work as herein stated, and pay their necessary traveling expenses while engaged in such work.
(Acts 1943, p. 385.)

32-2606 Acceptance of gifts by board. Reports of libraries. Policy as to library service stated

The State Board shall have authority to accept gifts of books, money or other property from any public or private source, including the Federal Government, and shall have authority to perform any and all functions necessary to carry out the intention and purposes of this law [§§ 32-2604 through 32-2607]. All public libraries in the State shall submit reports annually to the State Board. It is hereby declared to be the policy of the State as a part of the provisions for public education to promote the establishment and development of public library service throughout the State.
(Acts 1943, pp. 385, 386.)

32-2607 Funds for public library services

The funds now appropriated or otherwise available to the State Library Commission for the carrying on of said work are hereby transferred to the State Board of Education. In order to effectuate the purposes of this law [§§ 32-2604 through 32-2607] there shall be made available to the State Board of Education whatever funds may be duly allocated to it by the proper authority, either by specific appropriation or otherwise as now provided by law, and the said State Board of Education shall be authorized to disburse such funds to public libraries serving persons of all ages through legally constituted municipal library boards and/or to the other legally constituted local library boards as may now or hereafter be established by law. Said State Board of Education shall, by virtue hereof, use such funds for the purpose of aiding and supplementing the establishment and development of public library services.
(Acts 1943, pp. 385, 386.)

32-626a Public libraries

(a) The State Board of Education shall annually determine and request of the

General Assembly the amount of funds needed for county and regional public libraries of the State. This request shall include, but not be limited to, funds to provide library books and materials, salaries and travel for professional librarians, capital outlay for public library construction, and maintenance and operation. The amount for library books and materials shall be not less than 35 cents per person. Funds for the purpose of paying the salaries of librarians allotted shall be in accordance with regulations established by the State Board and the State minimum salary schedule for teachers and other certificated professional personnel. Public library funds shall be apportioned to county and regional public libraries in proportion to the area and population to be served by such libraries in accordance with regulations and minimum public library requirements prescribed by the State Board. All such funds shall be distributed directly to the regional or county library boards.

(b) The State Board of Education shall further make adequate provisions for staff, supplies, services, and facilities to operate and maintain special media equipment to meet the library needs of Georgia's blind and handicapped citizens.

(c) The State Board of Education shall further provide the staff, materials, equipment, and supplies to provide a book lending and information service to all county and regional public libraries in the State and to coordinate interlibrary cooperation and interchange of materials and information among all types of libraries.

(d) The State Board of Education is further authorized and empowered as the sole agency to receive Federal funds allotted to Georgia under Acts of Congress appropriating Federal funds for public libraries.

(e) The State Board of Education shall adopt policies and regulations to implement this section.

(Acts 1974, pp. 1045, 1064; 1975, pp. 539, 552.)

INTERSTATE LIBRARY COMPACT
(Code of Georgia Annotated, 1982, s.32-2701a to 32-2718a.)

32-2701a Compact enacted
The "Interstate Library Compact" is hereby enacted into law and entered into with all other jurisdictions legally joining therein in the form substantially as follows:

(Acts 1972, p. 872.)

INTERSTATE LIBRARY COMPACT

32-2702a Article I. Policy and purpose
Because the desire for the services provided by libraries transcends governmental boundaries and can most effectively be satisfied by giving such services to communities and people regardless of jurisdictional lines, it is the policy of the States party to this compact to cooperate and share their responsibilities; to authorize cooperation and sharing with respect to those types of library facilities and services which can be more economically or efficiently developed and maintained on a cooperative basis, and to authorize cooperation and sharing among localities, States and others in providing joint or cooperative library services in areas where the distribution of population or of existing and potential library resources make the provision of library service on an interstate basis the most effective way of providing adequate and efficient service.

(Acts 1972, pp. 872, 873.)

32-2703a Article II. Definitions

As used in this compact:

(a) "Public library agency" means any unit or agency of local or state government operating or having power to operate a library.

(b) "Private library agency" means any nongovernmental entity which operates or assumes a legal obligation to operate a library.

(c) "Library agreement" means a contract establishing an interstate library district pursuant to this compact or providing for the joint or cooperative furnishing of library services. (Acts 1972, pp. 870, 873.)

32-2704a Article III. Interstate library districts

(a) Any one or more public library agencies in a party State in cooperation with any public library agency or agencies in one or more other party States may establish and maintain an interstate library district. Subject to the provisions of this compact and any other laws of the party States which pursuant hereto remain applicable, such district may establish, maintain and operate some or all of the library facilities and services for the area concerned in accordance with the terms of a library agreement therefor. Any private library agency or agencies within an interstate library district may cooperate therewith, assume duties, responsibilities and obligations thereto, and receive benefits therefrom as provided in any library agreement to which such agency or agencies become party.

(b) Within an interstate library district, and as provided by a library agreement, the performance of library functions may be undertaken on a joint or cooperative basis or may be undertaken by means of one or more arrangements between or among public or private library agencies for the extension of library privileges to the use of facilities or services operated or rendered by one or more of the individual library agencies.

(c) If a library agreement provides for joint establishment, maintenance or operation of library facilities or services by an interstate library district, such district shall have power to do any one or more of the following in accordance with such library agreement:

1. Undertake, administer and participate in programs or arrangements for securing, lending or servicing of books and other publications, any other materials suitable to be kept or made available by libraries, library equipment or for the dissemination of information about libraries, the value and significance of particular items therein, and the use thereof.

2. Accept for any of its purposes under this compact any and all donations, and grants of money, equipment, supplies, materials, and services, (conditional or otherwise), from any State or the United States or any subdivision or agency thereof, or interstate agency, or from any institution, person, firm or corporation, and receive, utilize and dispose of the same.

3. Operate mobile library units or equipment for the purpose of rendering bookmobile service within the district.

4. Employ professional, technical, clerical and other personnel, and fix terms of employment, compensation and other appropriate benefits; and where desirable, provide for the in-service training of such personnel.

5. Sue and be sued in any court of competent jurisdiction.

6. Acquire, hold, and dispose of any real or personal property or any interest or interests therein as may be appropriate to the rendering of library service.

7. Construct, maintain and operate a library, including any appropriate branches thereof.

8. Do such other things as may be incidental to or appropriate for the carrying out of any of the foregoing powers. (Acts 1972, pp. 872, 873.)

32-2705a Article IV. Interstate library districts, governing board

(a) An interstate library district which establishes, maintains or operates any facilities or services in its own right shall have a governing board which shall direct the affairs of the district and act for it in all matters relating to its business. Each participating public library agency in the district shall be represented on the governing board which shall be organized and conduct its business in accordance with provisions therefor in the library agreement. But in no event shall a governing board meet less often than twice a year.

(b) Any private library agency or agencies party to a library agreement establishing an interstate library district may be represented on or advise with the governing board of the district in such manner as the library agreement may provide.

(Acts 1972, pp. 872, 875.)

32-2706a Article V. State library agency cooperation

Any two or more State library agencies of two or more of the party States may undertake and conduct joint or cooperative library programs, render joint or cooperative library services, and enter into and perform arrangements for the cooperative or joint acquisition, use, housing and disposition of items or collections of materials which, by reason of expense, rarity, specialized nature, or infrequency of demand therefor would be appropriate for central collection and shared use. Any such programs, services or arrangements may include provision for the exercise on a cooperative or joint basis of any power exercisable by an interstate library district and an agreement embodying any such program, service or arrangement shall contain provisions covering the subjects detailed in Article VI [§ 32-2707a] of this compact for interstate library agreements.

(Acts 1972, pp. 872, 875.)

32-2707a Article VI. Library agreements

(a) In order to provide for any joint or cooperative undertaking pursuant to this compact, public and private library agencies may enter into library agreements. Any agreement executed pursuant to the provisions of this compact shall, as among the parties to the agreement:

1. Detail the specific nature of the services, programs, facilities, arrangements or properties to which it is applicable.

2. Provide for the allocation of costs and other financial responsibilities.

3. Specify the respective rights, duties, obligations and liabilities of the parties.

4. Set forth the terms and conditions for duration, renewal, termination, abrogation, disposal of joint or common property, if any, and all other matters which may be appropriate to the proper effectuation and performance of the agreement.

(b) No public or private library agency shall undertake to exercise itself, or jointly with any other library agency, by means of a library agreement any power prohibited to such agency by the constitution or statutes of its State.

(c) No library agreement shall become effective until filed with the compact administrator of each State involved, and approved in accordance with Article VII [§ 32-2708a] of this compact.

(Acts 1972, pp. 872, 876.)

32-2708a Article VII. Approval of library agreements

(a) Every library agreement made pursuant to this compact shall, prior to and as a condition precedent to its entry into force, be submitted to the Attorney General of each State in which a public library agency party thereto is situated, who shall determine whether the agreement is in proper form and compatible with the laws of his State. The attorneys general shall approve any agreement submitted to them unless they shall find that it does not meet the conditions set forth herein and shall detail in writing addressed to the governing bodies of the public library agencies concerned the specific respects in which the proposed agreement fails to meet the requirements of law. Failure to disapprove an agreement submitted hereunder within 90 days of its submission shall constitute approval thereof.

(b) In the event that a library agreement made pursuant to this compact shall deal in whole or in part with the provision of services of facilities with regard to which an officer or agency of the State government has constitutional or statutory powers of control, the agreement shall, as a condition precedent to its entry into force, be submitted to the State officer or agency having such power of control and shall be approved or disapproved by him or it as to all matters within his or its jurisdiction in the same manner and subject to the same requirements governing the action of the Attorneys General pursuant to paragraph (a) of this Article. This requirement of submission and approval shall be in addition to and not in substitution for the requirement of submission to and approval by the Attorneys General.

(Acts 1972, pp. 872, 877.)

32-2709a Article VIII. Other laws applicable

Nothing in this compact or in any library agreement shall be construed to supersede, alter or otherwise impair any obligation imposed on any library by otherwise applicable law, nor to authorize the transfer or disposition of any property held in trust by a library agency in a manner contrary to the terms of such trust.

(Acts 1972, pp. 872, 877.)

32-2710a Article IX. Appropriations and aid

(a) Any public library agency party to a library agreement may appropriate funds to the interstate library district established thereby in the same manner and to the same extent as to a library wholly maintained by it and, subject to the laws of the State in which such public library agency is situated, may pledge its credit in support of an interstate library district established by the agreement.

(b) Subject to the provisions of the library agreement pursuant to which it functions and the laws of the States in which such district is situated, an interstate library district may claim and receive any State and Federal aid which may be available to library agencies.

(Acts 1972, pp. 872, 878.)

32-2711a Article X. Compact administrator

Each State shall designate a compact administrator with whom copies of all library agreements to which his State or any public library agency thereof is party shall be filed. The administrator shall have such other powers as may be conferred upon him by the laws of his State and may consult and cooperate with the compact administrators of other party States and take such steps as may effectuate the purposes of this compact. If the laws of a party state so provide, such State may designate one or more deputy compact administrators in addition to its compact administrator.

(Acts 1972, pp. 872, 878.)

32-2712a Article XI. Entry into force and withdrawal

(a) This compact shall enter into force and effect immediately upon its enactment into law by any two States. Thereafter, it shall enter into force and effect as to any other State upon the enactment thereof by such State.

(b) This compact shall continue in force with respect to a party State and remain binding upon such State until six months after such State has given notice to each other party State of the repeal thereof. Such withdrawal shall not be construed to relieve any party to a library agreement entered into pursuant to this compact from any obligation of that agreement prior to the end of its duration as provided therein.

(Acts 1972, pp. 872, 878.)

32-2713a Article XII. Construction and severability

This compact shall be liberally construed so as to effectuate the purposes thereof. The provisions of this compact shall be severable and if any phrase, clause, sentence or provisions of this compact is declared to be contrary to the constitution of any party state or of the United States or the applicability thereof to any government, agency, person or circumstance is held invalid, the validity of the remainder of this compact and the applicability thereof to any government, agency, person or circumstance shall not be affected thereby. If this compact shall be held contrary to the constitution of any State party thereto, the compact shall remain in full force and effect as to the remaining States and in full force and effect as to the State affected as to all severable matters.

(Acts 1972, pp. 872, 879.)

32-2714a Limitations

No municipality, county, or other political subdivision of this State shall be a party to a library agreement which provides for the construction or maintenance of a library pursuant to Article III, subdivision (c-7) of the compact [§ 32-2704a], nor pledge its credit in support of such a library, or contribute to the capital financing thereof, except after compliance with any laws applicable to such municipalities, counties, or political subdivisions relating to or governing capital outlay and the pledging of credit.

(Acts 1972, pp. 872. 879.)

32-2715a "State library agency" defined

As used in the compact, "State library agency," with reference to this State, means the Public Library Service Unit of the Georgia Department of Education.

(Acts 1972, pp. 872, 879.)

32-2716a Interstate library districts lying partly within this State

An interstate library district lying partly within this State may claim and be entitled to receive State aid in support of any of its functions to the same extent and in the same manner as such functions are eligible for support when carried on by entities wholly within this State. For the purposes of computing and apportioning State aid to an interstate library district, this State will consider that portion of the area which lies within this State as an independent entity for the performance of the aided function or functions and compute and apportion the aid accordingly. Subject to any applicable laws of this State, such a district also may apply for and be entitled to receive any Federal aid for which it may be eligible.

(Acts 1972, pp. 872, 879.)

32-2717a Appointment of compact administrator

The State Superintendent of Schools shall appoint an officer of this State who shall be the compact administrator pursuant to Article X of the compact [§ 32-2711a]. The State Superintendent of Schools shall also appoint one or more deputy compact administrators pursuant to said Article.

(Acts 1972, pp. 872, 880.)

32-2718a Withdrawal of the compact

In the event of withdrawal of the compact the State Superintendent of Schools shall send and receive any notices required by Article XI (b) of the compact [§ 32-2712a]. (Acts 1972, pp. 872, 880.)

CERTIFICATION OF LIBRARIANS
(Code of Georgia Annotated, 1982, s.84-2201 to 84-2210.)

84-2201 State Board for Certification of Librarians; creation, membership, and appointment

A State Board for the Certification of Librarians is hereby created to consist of five persons, four of whom shall be appointed by the Governor from a list of seven persons nominated by the Executive Board of the Georgia Library Association. The other member shall be the Director of Public Library Services of the State Department of Education who shall serve as an ex-officio member of said board.
(Acts 1937, p. 245; 1978, p. 918, eff. March 14, 1978.)

84-2202 Same; terms of office

The terms of all members first appointed under this Chapter shall begin on the 1st day of July, 1937, but the terms of the members appointed by the Governor shall expire as follows: December 31, 1937, December 31, 1938, December 31, 1939, and December 31, 1940. The respective terms of the appointed members shall be determined by lot. Upon the expiration of the terms of members first appointed, their successors shall be appointed by the Governor from a list of seven persons nominated by the Executive Board of the Georgia Library Association for a term of five years. The term of the Director of Public Library Services of the State Department of Education shall be coextensive with the term of office in this position.
(Acts 1937, p. 245; 1978, p. 918, eff. March 14, 1978.)

84-2203 Same; compensation; expenses

Members of the board shall receive no compensation for their services, except actual and necessary traveling expenses incurred in attending meetings.
(Acts 1937, p. 245.)

84-2203.1 Same; additional member

Effective July 1, 1980, the State Board for the Certification of Librarians shall, in addition to the members provided for above, consist of a sixth member who shall be appointed by the Governor from the public at large and shall have no connection whatsoever to the library profession. The initial term for the additional member provided for by this section shall expire December 31, 1984, and, thereafter, the Governor shall appoint successors for a term of five years.
(Acts 1980, pp. 1075, 1076, eff. July 1, 1980.)

84-2204 Same; vacancies

Should a vacancy occur upon said board the Governor shall appoint a member for the unexpired term in the same manner as in the case of original appointees.
(Acts 1937, pp. 245, 246.)

84-2205 Same; jurisdiction of Joint-Secretary, State Examining Boards

The same jurisdiction, duties, powers, and authority which the Joint-Secretary, State Examining Boards, has with reference to other examining boards is hereby conferred upon him with respect to the State Board for the Certification of Librarians.
(Acts 1937, pp. 245, 246.)

84-2206 Certificates; grades; examinations

The board shall have authority to establish grades of certificates for librarians, to prescribe and hold examinations, or require submission of credentials to establish the qualifications of those seeking certificates as librarians, and to issue certificates of librarianship to qualified persons in accordance with such rules and regulations as it may prescribe.

(Acts 1937, pp. 245, 246.)

84-2207 Only licensed librarians to be employed; exceptions

From and after January 1, 1938, any public library serving a political subdivision or subdivisions having over 5,000 population according to the last official Federal census and every library operated by the State or its authority, including libraries of institutions of higher learning, shall not employ in the position of librarian or full time professional assistant in the library as defined by this board, a person who does not hold a librarian's certificate issued by the board. No public funds shall be paid to any library failing to comply with the provisions of this Chapter: Provided, however, that nothing in this Chapter shall apply to law libraries of counties and/or cities, or to libraries of public elementary and high schools.

(Acts 1937, pp. 245, 246.)

84-2208 Applications for certificates; fees; renewals; duplicate certificates

All applicants for a librarian's certificate shall file an application with the Joint-Secretary, State Examining Boards, accompanied by a fee which shall be set by the board, and said joint secretary shall remit the same to the State treasury, such fees shall be used only for the purpose of carrying out the provisions of this Chapter and payment of the necessary expenses contemplated under Chapter 84-1. All certificates issued under this Chapter will expire every two years on the 31st day of December beginning in 1979 unless a renewal fee to be set by the board is paid. Anyone not renewing his certificate by December 31 of each odd-numbered year may renew his expired certificate by paying all back fees plus a penalty to be set by the board.

Any certified librarian requesting a duplicate certificate shall be charged a fee as shall be set by the board.

(Acts 1937, pp. 245, 246; 1978, pp. 918, 919; 1980, p. 489, eff. March 20, 1980.)

84-2208 Applications for certificates; fees

All applicants for a librarian's certificate shall file an application with the Joint-Secretary, State Examining Boards, accompanied by a fee which shall be set by the board, and said Joint-Secretary shall remit the same to the State treasury, such fees shall be used only for the purpose of carrying out the provisions of this Chapter and payment of the necessary expenses contemplated under Chapter 84-1.

(Acts 1937, pp. 245, 246; 1978, pp. 918, 919, eff. March 14, 1978.)

84-2209 Librarians employed not affected

This Chapter shall not be construed to affect any librarian or full time assistant librarian in his or her present position. Such librarians as are now in service shall

be entitled to receive a certificate in accordance with their qualifications for positions now held without examination, upon payment of the prescribed fee, and such certificate so issued shall be a life certificate.
(Acts 1937, pp. 245, 247.)

84-2210 Libraries not supported by public funds
The board may issue certificates to qualified persons who are serving in libraries not supported by public funds.
(Acts 1937, pp. 245, 247.)

DISTRIBUTION OF PUBLIC DOCUMENTS
(Code of Georgia Annotated, 1982, s.101-201 to 101-205,
s.90-301 to 90-307.)

101-201 Reports of certain officers to be filed with librarian
The Governor and all of the officers who are, or may be, required to make reports to the General Assembly, shall furnish the librarian with at least three copies of each of said reports, and he shall have one copy of each report bound and preserved in the library for public use, the remaining copies to be held in reserve.
(Acts 1975, pp. 741, 745.)

101-202 State institutions, public libraries, and public schools to be supplied
Such of the State institutions, public libraries and public schools of Georgia, and such other institutions of learning as maintain libraries and desire to receive them, shall be supplied free of charge by the librarian with copies of public documents when available.
(Acts 1975, pp. 741, 745.)

101-203 Librarian as exchange officer
The librarian shall be the exchange officer of Georgia for the purpose of a regular exchange between this and other states of public documents, and the several state departments and institutions are required to deposit with the librarian for that purpose at least 50 copies of each of their public documents. The Attorney General, at his discretion, may order the librarian to exchange copies of public documents, court reports, journals of the House and of the Senate, and Georgia session laws with the proper authorities of foreign governments on whatever basis he deems advisable and in the public interest.

Each department and institution within the executive branch of State government shall make a report on or before December 1 of each year to the State Librarian containing a list by title of all public documents published or issued by such department or institution during the preceding State of Georgia fiscal year. The report shall also contain a statement noting the frequency of publication of each such public document. The State Librarian may disseminate copies of the lists, of such parts thereof, in such form as the State Librarian, in his or her discretion, deems shall best serve the public interest.
(Acts 1975, pp. 741, 745; 1978, pp. 2288, 2289, eff. April 11, 1978.)

101-204 Exchange of court reports with other States

The librarian shall establish and maintain with other States, through the proper authorities, the exchange of copies of reports for the reports of their appellate tribunals.

(Acts 1975, pp. 741, 746.)

101-205 Distribution and sale of copies of laws and journals; procedures in connection therewith

The librarian shall make distribution of the bound volumes of laws and journals. Volumes distributed to members of the General Assembly, to libraries, to institutions of learning, or to agencies outside the State of Georgia shall become the property of the recipient. All volumes distributed within the State of Georgia to the State or to any of its subordinate departments, agencies, or political subdivisions, or to public officers or to public employees within the State, other than members of the General Assembly, shall be the property of the appropriate public officer or employee during his term of office or employment, shall be turned over to his successor, and the librarian shall take and retain a receipt from each such public officer or employee acknowledging this fact. The librarian shall at all times use the most economical method of shipment consistent with the safety and security of the volumes. The librarian shall make the following distributions:

a. Georgia Session Laws

Administrative Office of the Courts	one set
Court of Appeals, Georgia	13 sets

(which number may be increased upon written order from the Chief Judge to the librarian.)

Clerk, House of Representatives	five sets
General Assembly (each member)	one set
General Assembly Fiscal Officer	one set
House Judiciary Committee	one set
Georgia Institute of Technology	one set
House Majority Leader	one set
House Minority Leader	one set
Law Department, State (other than State Library)	31 sets

(which number may be increased upon written order of the Attorney General.)

Legislative Budget Analyst	one set
Legislative Counsel	15 sets

(which number may be increased upon written order of the Legislative Counsel.)

Library, State Exchange Program:	
Each foreign government authority participating	one set
Each State participating	one set
Shelving	two sets
Newly created superior court circuits or judgeships	as appropriate

Whenever a new superior court circuit or a new judgeship within a circuit shall be created, if the officer entitled to session laws shall notify the librarian in writing of his assumption of office, the librarian shall add his position to those to receive future laws. Older laws may also be supplied, where available, at the discretion of the Attorney General.

Judge of the probate court (each county)   three sets
The three sets shall be distributed by the judge as follows: One set to be retained for his own use; one set to be issued to the county attorney; one set to be placed in the county law library, if any. If no library is maintained, to be retained in the judge's office for use of the general public.

President of Senate   one set
Recipients not named herein but named on the librarian's distribution list as of the date of his last distribution of the laws next preceding the effective date of this Chapter. Librarian, upon receipt of written order from the Attorney General so to do, shall add such of the names as the Attorney General shall direct to his listing of distributees to receive future laws. (each)   one set

President Pro Tem of Senate   one set
Secretary of the Senate   three sets
Secretary of State   eight sets
Senate Judiciary Committee   one set
Speaker of the House   one set
State Departments and agencies needing session laws shall notify the librarian in writing of their needs. Such requests may be filled in whole or in part as may be directed by the Attorney General.   as appropriate

Superior courts
Clerks (each)   one set
District attorneys (each)   one set
Judges (each)   one set
Supreme Court of Georgia   12 sets
(which number may be increased upon written order from the Chief Justice to the librarian.)

University of Georgia   52 sets
United States Courts
Court of Appeals, 5th Circuit   one set
District Courts, Georgia   six sets
Supreme Court   one set
(which numbers may be enlarged or diminished upon written order from the Attorney General.)

b. Journals of the House and Senate.
Administrative Services, Department of   one set
Archives, State   one set
Augusta College   one set
Clerk, House of Representatives   three sets
Court of Appeals, Georgia   as requested by the Chief Judge

Georgia Institute of Technology   one set

Georgia State University	one set
Historical Society, Georgia	one set
House Judiciary Committee	one set
House Majority Leader	one set
House Minority Leader	one set
Human Resources, State Department of	two sets
Law Department, State (other than State Library)	two sets

(which number may be increased by order of the Attorney General.)

Legislative Counsel	five sets

(which number may be increased upon written order of the Legislative Counsel.)

Legislative Fiscal Officer	nine sets
Library, State Exchange Program:	
Each foreign government authority participating	one set
Each State participating	one set
Shelving	two sets
Judge of the probate court (each county)	one set
President of Senate	one set
President Pro Tem of Senate	one set

Recipients not named herein but named on the librarian's distribution list as of the date of his last distribution of the journals next preceding the effective date of this Chapter. Librarian, upon receipt of written order from Attorney General so to do, shall add such of the names as the Attorney General shall direct to his listing of distributees to receive future

journals. (each)	one set
Secretary of State	two sets
Secretary of the Senate	four Senate sets and two House sets
Senate Judiciary Committee	one set
Speaker of the House	one set
State Departments and agencies	as appropriate

needing House and Senate Journals shall notify the librarian in writing of their needs. Such requests may be filled in whole or in part as may be directed by the Attorney General.

Supreme Court of Georgia	as requested by the Chief Justice
University of Georgia	seven sets

c. The librarian shall receive from the Secretary of State the laws and journals which shall be handled in accordance with this section. He shall reserve 50 copies each of the laws and of the journals for three years after their receipt by him. After three years he shall hold in reserve 25 copies of each of the laws and journals. Copies of the laws and journals in excess of the required reserve and not needed for purposes of distribution or exchange may be sold by the librarian at a price not less than the actual cost according to information supplied by the Secretary of State. The librarian may add to the price reasonable costs of handling and shipping, and all proceeds of such sales shall be paid to the State.

d. If any member of the General Assembly wishes to receive a copy of the House or Senate journals, or both, such member shall notify, in writing, the librarian on a form provided by the librarian. Upon receiving such written notification, the librarian shall distribute journals to the member in accordance with the request made therefor by such written notification.

(Acts 1975, pp. 741, 746; 1981, p. 818, eff. April 7, 1981.)

90-301 Citation

This Chapter shall be known and may be cited as "The Georgia Government Documents Act."

(Acts 1971, p. 216.)

90-302 Definitions

The following words and terms used in this Chapter shall be given the meanings hereinafter prescribed unless the context indicates otherwise.

(a) "Advisory council" shall mean the Advisory Council on Georgia Government Documents.

(b) "State agency" shall mean any State department, board, bureau, commission, Authority, council, committee and any other State agency or instrumentality.

(c) "Government document" shall mean any written material produced for dissemination to the public by any State agency; any written material which is required by law to be published or disseminated to the public by any State agency; any written material the publication or distribution of which involves, or may involve, the expenditure of State funds or the funds of any State agency; and any other written material which the advisory council may include, or exclude, as a Government document pursuant to authorization herein provided.

(Acts 1971, p. 216.)

90-303 The advisory council

(a) There is hereby created the Advisory Council on Georgia Government Documents to be composed of seven members as follows: one member of the Senate appointed by the President of the Senate from among those Senators who are members of the Legislative Services Committee; one member of the House of Representatives appointed by the Speaker of the House from among those Representatives who are members of the Legislative Services Committee; the Secretary of State; the State Auditor; the Legislative Counsel; the State Librarian and the President of the Georgia Library Association.

(b) The advisory council shall organize as soon as practicable after the organization of the General Assembly in each biennium and shall function in the manner of a legislative committee. The expenses of the advisory council shall be funded as if it were a subcommittee of the Legislative Services Committee, and the Legislative Services Committee shall approve the payment of such expenses. The State Treasurer is hereby authorized and directed to provide for the payment of such expenses authorized by the Legislative Services Committee from funds appropriated or otherwise available to the legislative branch of Government.

(c) When the General Assembly is not in session, the legislative members of the advisory council shall receive the expense and mileage allowance provided by law for legislative members of interim committees for each day of attendance at meetings of the advisory council. The expenses incurred thereby shall be paid from funds appropriated or otherwise available to the legislative branch of government. The members who are State officials shall be reimbursed for the expenses incurred by them as members of the advisory council in the same manner and from the same funds as they are reimbursed for expenses incurred by them in the performance of their official duties. The remaining member shall be reimbursed for expenses incurred by him as a member of the advisory council and for travel expenses incurred by him in attending meetings of the advisory council in the same manner as State employees from funds appropriated or otherwise available to the legislative branch of Government.

(Acts 1971, pp. 216, 217.)

90-304 Responsibility of the advisory council

It shall be the responsibility of the advisory council to establish, maintain and oversee a system of officially designated Georgia Government Documents and thereby obtain, by the exercise of the authority herein prescribed, maximum efficiency, economy and usefulness in the publication, compilation, distribution and preservation of the materials herein defined as Government documents. The advisory council shall have no authority with respect to the content of Government documents and shall not be authorized to designate any person or firm as the official printer or printers of Government documents.

(Acts 1971, pp. 216, 218.)

90-305 Authority of the advisory council

(a) The advisory council shall have authority to establish classifications of Government documents and to prescribe for each classification uniform standards of style, composition and format, including the method of printing or reproduction, binding, page size, weight of paper, type face, type size and similar matters.

(b) The advisory council shall have the authority to exempt from the application of this Chapter, or any part hereof, the Government documents produced or published by a State agency solely for its internal official use, or those produced or published for strictly administrative operational or promotional purposes in which, in the judgment of the advisory council, the general public has no substantial interest and in which there is no substantial educational value.

(c) The advisory council may require of each State agency a report on each Government document produced, published or distributed by it, including its distribution list. The advisory council may make recommendations to any State agency concerning the expansion or curtailment of the distribution list of any Government document. If the recommendation of the advisory council is to curtail a distribution list, and if the recommendation is not given effect by the State agency, these facts shall be reported to the Legislative Services Committee and shall also be noted by the State Auditor in his audit of the State agency.

(d) In connection with the distribution of Government documents, the advisory council may provide for the designation of educational institutions, public or private, as general or special depositories of Government documents and provide for the distribution of Government documents to these depositories under such rules and regulations as will insure maximum usefulness to the students of this State and the general public. The advisory council may revoke the depository designation in any case of noncompliance with its rules and regulations, or where the Government documents are being used for private purposes, or where the public interest has been neglected or disregarded.

(e) The advisory council shall have authority to provide for the distribution of Government documents without charge or cost. However, the advisory council shall have authority to make a charge or charges for Government documents, not in excess of the cost of printing and distribution when in its judgment there is reason to do so in the interest of maximum economy, efficiency and usefulness. All monies received from such charges shall be paid into the general fund of the State treasury.

(Acts 1971, pp. 216, 218.)

90-306 Authority inapplicable

The authority granted under section 90-305(a) shall not apply to:

(1) The Georgia Reports and the Court of Appeals Reports.

(2) The House or Senate Journals.

(3) The annual session laws of the General Assembly.

(4) The publications required of the Secretary of State under the Georgia Administrative Procedure Act [Title 3A].

(5) The publication of any bulletin, newsletter or gazette disseminating current information relative to developments within a State agency or information of current interest to a particular constituency of a State agency.
(Acts 1971, pp. 216, 219.)

90-307 Compliance with standards
When the advisory council has established standards for a particular classification of Government documents and communicated them to the various State agencies, it shall be the duty of each State agency to comply with the standards applicable to the Government documents produced, published or distributed within the scope of its activity and any expenditures for the production, publication, or distribution of Government documents which are not in compliance with the applicable standards or other directives of the advisory council shall be disallowed by the State Auditor as a legitimate expenditure of public funds.
(Acts 1971, pp. 216, 220.)

DEPARTMENT OF ARCHIVES AND HISTORY
(Code of Georgia Annotated, 1982, s.40-802, 40-801c to 40-814c.)

40-802 Objects and purposes
The objects and purposes of the department shall be to:

(a) Insure the retention and preservation of the records of any State or local agency with historical and research value by providing for the application of modern and efficient methods to the creation, utilization, maintenance, retention, preservation and disposal of records.

(b) Provide an archival and records depository in which to assemble and maintain the official archives and other inactive records of the State not in current and common use.

(c) Collect from the files of old newspapers, court records, church records, private collections, and other sources, data of all kinds bearing upon the history of the State.

(d) Secure from private individuals, either by loan or gift, rare volumes, manuscripts, documents and pamphlets for the use of this department.

(e) Obtain in like manner historical trophies, souvenirs and relics.

(f) Classify, edit, annotate, and publish from time to time such records as may be deemed expedient and proper, including messages of Governors, executive orders, State papers, military rosters of the Revolutionary, Mexican, Civil and European Wars.

(g) Diffuse knowledge in regard to the State's history.

(h) Prepare biennially an official register, giving the latest information of an official character in regard to the State, including a full list of Statehouse officers, legislators, judges and solicitors, members of Congress, county officials, etc., together with other pertinent items of information.

(i) Encourage the proper marking of battlefields, houses and other places celebrated in the history of the State.

(j) Encourage the study of Georgia history in our public schools.

(k) Assist in the observance of patriotic occasions.

(l) Assist and cooperate with the members of the Georgia Commission for the National Bicentennial Celebration in carrying out the lawful functions and programs of the commission.

(m) Plan and coordinate celebrations and observations of events and anniversaries having historic or special significance to this State.

(n) Stimulate historical research, especially in the prosecution of local histories.

(o) Foster sentiment looking to the better protection, classification and arrangement of records in the various courthouses of the State.

(p) Prepare a bibliography of Georgia, and to indicate, by title at least, every book written about Georgia or by Georgia authors.

(q) Collect biographical information in regard to all public officials and to keep same on file, in a classified arrangement, for convenient reference by investigators.

(Acts 1918, p. 137; 1931, pp. 7, 38; 1969, pp. 989, 990; 1980, p. 485, eff. March 20, 1980.)

40-801c Short title

This Chapter shall be known and may be cited as the "Georgia Records Act."

(Acts 1972, pp. 1267, 1268.)

40-802c Definitions

For the purpose of this Chapter:

(a) "Department" means the Department of Archives and History.

(b) "Records" means all documents, papers, letters, maps, books (except books in formally organized libraries), microfilm, magnetic tape, or other material regardless of physical form or characteristics made or received pursuant to law or ordinance or in performance of functions by any agency.

(c) "Agency" means any State office, department, division, board, bureau, commission, authority or other separate unit of State government created or established by law.

(d) "Georgia State Archives" means an establishment maintained by the department for the preservation of those records and other papers that have been determined by the department to have sufficient historical and other value to warrant their continued preservation by the State and have been accepted by the department for deposit in its custody.

(e) "Records center" means an establishment maintained by the department primarily for the storage, processing, servicing, and security of public records that must be retained for varying periods of time but need not be retained in an agency's office equipment or space.

(f) "Vital records" means any record vital to the resumption or continuation of operations, or both, to the re-creation of the legal and financial status of government in the State, or to the protection and fulfillment of obligations to citizens of the State.

(g) "Retention schedule" means a set of disposition instructions prescribing how long, where, and in what form a record series shall be kept;

(h) "Record series" means documents or records that are filed in a unified arrangement, having similar physical characteristics or relating to a similar function or activity;

(i) "Records management" means the application of management techniques to the creation, utilization, maintenance, retention, preservation and disposal of records undertaken to reduce costs and improve efficiency of record keeping. Records management includes management of filing and microfilming equipment and supplies; filing and information retrieval systems; files, correspondence, reports and forms management; historical documentation; micrographics; retention programming and vital records protection.

(j) "Court record" means all documents, papers, letters, maps, books (except books formally organized in libraries), microfilm, magnetic tape, or other material regardless of physical form or characteristics made or received pursuant to law or ordinance or in the necessary performance of any judicial function created or received by an official of the Supreme Court, Court of Appeals, and any superior, state, juvenile, probate, county or justice of the peace court, and includes records or the offices of the judge, clerk, prosecuting attorney, public defender, court reporter, or any employee of the court.

(Acts 1972, pp. 1267, 1268; 1973, pp. 691, 692; 1975, pp. 675, 676; 1978, pp. 1372, 1375, eff. April 3, 1978.)

40-803c State Records Committee; creation; membership; duties

(a) There is hereby created the State Records Committee, to be composed of the Governor, the Secretary of State, the Attorney General and the State Auditor, or their designated representatives. It shall be the duty of the committee to review, approve, disapprove, amend or modify retention schedules submitted by agency heads, school boards, county governments and municipal governments through the department for the disposition of records based on administrative, legal, fiscal or historical values. Such retention schedules, once approved, shall be authoritative, directive and have the force and effect of law. A retention schedule may be determined by three members of the committee. Retention schedules may be amended by the committee on change of program mission or legislative changes affecting the records. The Secretary of State shall serve as chairman of the committee and shall schedule meetings of the committee as required. Three members shall constitute a quorum. Each agency head has the right of appeal to the committee for actions taken under this section.

(b) Each court of this State may recommend to the State Records Committee and the Administrative Office of the Courts retention schedules for records of that court. The State Records Committee, with the concurrence of the Administrative Office of the Courts, shall adopt retention schedules for court records of each court. The destruction of court records by retention schedule shall not be construed as affecting the status of each court as a court of record.

(Acts 1972, pp. 1267, 1268; 1975, pp. 675, 676; 1978, pp. 1372, 1373; 1981, pp. 1422, 1424, eff. July 1, 1981.)

40-804c Duties of department

It shall be the duty of the department to:

(a) Establish and administer, under the direction of a State records management officer (who shall be employed under the rules and regulations of the State Merit System), a records management program;

(b) Develop and issue procedures, rules, and regulations establishing standards for efficient and economical management methods relating to the creation, maintenance, utilization, retention, preservation, and disposition of records, filing equipment, supplies, microfilming of records, and vital records program;

(c) Assist State agencies in implementing records programs by providing consultative services in records management, conducting surveys in order to recommend more efficient records management practices, and providing training for records management personnel;

(d) Operate a records center or centers which shall accept all records transferred to it through the operation of approved retention schedules, provide secure storage and reference service for the same and submit written notice to the applicable agency of intended destruction of records in accordance with approved retention schedules.

(Acts 1972, pp. 1267, 1269; 1975, pp. 675, 677.)

40-805c Duty of agencies

It shall be the duty of each agency to:

(a) Cause to be made and preserved records containing adequate and proper documentation of the organization, functions, policies, decisions, procedures, and essential transactions of the agency and designed to furnish the information necessary to protect the legal and financial rights of the Government and of persons directly affected by the agency's activities;

(b) Cooperate fully with the department in complying with the provisions of this Chapter;

(c) Establish and maintain an active and continuing program for the economical and efficient management of records and assist the department in the conduct of records management surveys;

(d) Implement records management procedures and regulations issued by the department;

(e) Submit to the department, in accordance with the rules and regulations of the department, a recommended retention schedule for each record series in its custody, except that schedules for common-type files may be established by the department. No records will be scheduled for permanent retention in an office. No records will be scheduled for retention any longer than is absolutely necessary in the performance of required functions. Records requiring retention for several years will be transferred to the records center for low-cost storage at the earliest possible date following creation.

(f) Establish necessary safeguards against the removal or loss of records and such further safeguards as may be required by regulations of the department. Such safeguards shall include notification to all officials and employees of the agency that no records in the custody of the agency are to be alienated or destroyed except in accordance with the provisions of this Chapter.

(g) Designate an agency records management officer who shall establish and operate a records management program.

(Acts 1972, pp. 1267, 1269; 1975, pp. 675, 677, 678; 1978, pp. 1372, 1374, eff. April 3, 1978.)

40-806c Construction of Chapter; confidential records

(a) Nothing in this Chapter shall be construed to divest agency heads of the authority to determine the nature and form of records required in the administration of their several departments. Notwithstanding this Section agency heads shall carry out provisions of section 40-805c.

(b) Any records designated confidential by law shall be so treated by the department in the maintenance, storage and disposition of such confidential records. These records shall be destroyed in such a manner that they cannot be read, interpreted, or reconstructed.

(Acts 1972, pp. 1267, 1270; 1975, pp. 675, 678.)

40-807c Disposal of records

(a) All records created or received in the performance of duty and paid for by public funds are deemed to be public property and shall constitute a record of public acts;

(b) The destruction of records shall occur only through the operation of an approved retention schedule. Such records shall not be placed in the custody of private individuals or institutions or semi-private organizations unless authorized by retention schedules;

(c) The alienation, alteration, theft or destruction of records by any person or persons in a manner not authorized by an applicable retention schedule is punishable as a misdemeanor;

(d) No person acting in compliance with the provisions of this Chapter shall be held personally liable.

(Acts 1972, pp. 1267, 1270; 1975, pp. 675, 679.)

40-808c Photostatic copies of records as primary evidence

Photostatic copies of records produced from microfilm and printout copies of computer records shall be received in any court of this State as primary evidence of the recitals contained therein.

(Acts 1972, pp. 1267, 1270.)

40-809c Certified copies

The department may make certified copies under seal of any records or any preservation duplicates transferred or deposited in the Georgia State Archives, or the records center, or may make reproductions of such records. Such certified copies or reproductions, when signed by the director of the department, shall have the same force and effect as if made by the agency from which the records were received. The department may establish and charge reasonable fees for such services.

(Acts 1972, pp. 1267, 1271.)

40-810c Title to records

(a) Title to any record transferred to the Georgia State Archives as authorized by this Chapter shall be vested in the department. The department shall not destroy any record transferred to it by an agency without consulting with the proper official of the transferring agency prior to submitting a retention schedule requesting such destruction to the State Records Committee. Access to records of Constitutional Officers shall be at the discretion of the Constitutional Officer who created, received, or maintained the records, but no limitation on access to such records shall extend more than 25 years after creation of the records.

(b) Title to any record transferred to the records center shall remain in the agency transferring such record to the records center.

(Acts 1972, pp. 1267, 1271; 1973, pp. 691, 692; 1975, pp. 675, 679.)

40-811c Applicability of Chapter to local governments

(a) The provisions of this Chapter apply to local governments, except as modified in this section.

(b) All records created or received in the performance of a public duty or paid for by public funds by a governing body are deemed to be public property and shall constitute a record of public acts.

(c) As used in this section, the term:

(1) "Governing body" means the governing body of any county, municipality, consolidated government, or school boards of this State.

(2) "Office or officer" means any county office or officer or any office or officer under jurisdiction of a governing body which maintains or is responsible for records.

(d) Prior to July 1, 1983, each office or officer shall recommend to the governing body a retention schedule. This schedule shall include an inventory of they type of records maintained and the length of time each type of record will be maintained in the office or in a record holding area. These retention periods will be based on the legal, fiscal, administrative, and historical needs for that record. Schedules previously approved by the State Records Committee will remain in effect until changed by the governing body.

(e) Prior to January 1, 1984, each governing body shall approve by resolution or ordinance a records management plan which shall include but is not limited to:

(1) The name of the person or title of officer who will coordinate and perform responsibilities of governing body under this Act.

(2) Each retention schedule approved by governing authority.

(3) Provisions for maintenance and security of the records.

(f) The Secretary of State through the Department of Archives and History shall coordinate all records management matters for purposes of this section. The department will provide local governments a list of common types of records maintained together with recommended retention period and will provide training and assistance as required. The Department of Archives and History will advise local governments of records of historical value which may be deposited in the State Archives. All other records will be maintained by the local government.

(g) Except as otherwise provided by law, ordinance, or policy adopted by the office or officer responsible for maintaining such records, all records shall be open to the public or the state or any agency thereof.

(Acts 1972, pp. 1267, 1271; 1973, pp. 691, 692; 1978, pp. 1372, 1375; 1981, pp. 1422, 1423, eff. July 1, 1981.)

40-812c Confidential, classified or restricted records; restrictions on access; lifting of restrictions

(a) This section applies only to those records (1) that are confidential, classified or restricted by Acts of the General Assembly, or may be declared to be confidential, classified or restricted by future Acts of the General Assembly, unless said future Acts specifically exempt these records from the provisions of this section; and (2) that have been, or are in the future, deposited in the Georgia State Archives or in other State-operated archival institutions because of their value for historical research;

(b) All restrictions on access to records covered by this section are hereby lifted and removed 75 years after the creation of the record;

(c) Restrictions on access to records covered by this section may be lifted and removed as early as 20 years after the creation of the record on unanimous approval in writing of the State Records Committee;

(d) Applications requesting that the State Records Committee review and consider lifting such restrictions may be made either by the director of the department or by the head of the agency that transferred the record to the Archives.

(Acts 1975, pp. 675, 680.)

40-813c Same; use for research purposes

(a) Records that are by law confidential, classified or restricted may be used for research purposes by private researchers providing that (1) the researcher is qualified to perform such research; (2) the research topic is designed to produce a study that would be of potential benefit to the State or its citizens; and (3) the researcher will agree in writing to protect the confidentiality of the information contained in the records. When the purpose of the confidentiality is to protect the rights of privacy of any person or persons who are named in the records the researcher must agree, in either his notes or in his finished study or in any manner, not to refer to said person in such a way that they can be identified. When the purpose of the confidentiality is to protect other information the researcher must agree not to divulge that information;

(b) The head of the agency that created the records (or his designee) shall determine whether or not the researcher and his research topic meets the qualifications set forth in subsection (a) above prior to accepting the signed agreement from the researcher and granting permission to use the confidential records;

(c) The use of such confidential records for research shall be considered a privilege and the agreement signed by the researcher shall be binding on him. Researchers who violate the confidentiality of these records shall be punishable in the same manner as would government employees or officials found guilty of this offense.

(Acts 1975, pp. 675, 680.)

40-814c Construction of certain laws and rules and regulations

(a) All laws or parts of laws prescribing how long or in what form records shall be kept are hereby repealed;

(b) Whenever laws or rules and regulations prescribed where a record series must be kept, the custodian of such records shall be considered in compliance with said laws, rules and regulations if he transfers said records to a local holding area, a records center, or the Georgia State Archives when he does so in accordance with an approved retention schedule.   (Acts 1975, pp. 675, 681.)

PUBLIC LIBRARIES
(Code of Georgia Annotated, 1982, s.32-2701 to 32-2709.)

32-2701 (1566) How libraries maintained
Any city may, through its properly constituted municipal authorities, raise by taxation, from year to year and permanently appropriate money for the purpose of establishing or erecting or maintaining a public library, or assisting in maintaining a public library. Any such sum or sums of money so appropriated shall be expended by and under the direction of the board of trustees of such public library elected by the city council of said city.
(Acts 1901, p. 52; 1904, p. 90.)

32-2702 (1567) Disbursements, how made
In any city in which an appropriation shall be made under or by virtue of the authority conferred by this Chapter, the money so appropriated shall be drawn from the treasury of said city on the warrant of said board of trustees of such public library elected by the city council of said city, and shall be paid out from time to time in the payment of salaries, purchase of books, and other necessary expenses of said library, and an itemized statement of the amounts so paid out shall be made annually to the mayor of said city, and by him submitted to the properly constituted authorities of said city.
(Acts 1901, p. 52; 1904, p. 90.)

32-2703 (1568) Donations
Said board of trustees are authorized to accept and receive donations, either in money, land, or other property for the purposes of erecting or assisting in the erection of suitable buildings for the use of said public library, for maintaining the same, or for assisting in maintaining the same.
(Acts 1901, p. 52; 1904, p. 90.)

32-2704 (1569) Duties of board of trustees
Said board of trustees shall exercise a strict and rigid supervision over said public library, and shall pass all necessary rules and regulations for the government and control of the same; shall elect a librarian and, if necessary, an assistant librarian, or designate some officer or officers to perform the duties of librarian or assistant librarian; and shall appoint and discharge the said officer or officers at pleasure.
(Acts 1901, p. 52; 1904, p. 90.)

32-2705 (1570) Powers of the city
The municipal government of any such city shall have authority to enter into a legal and binding agreement to accept and receive any donation offered by any person or persons on such terms as may be agreed upon between said person or persons and said municipal government, and such agreement so made shall be legal and binding upon said municipal government and its successors; and all agreements by said municipal government of said city to pay any sum or sums of money annually thereafter for the use of said public library shall be legal and binding on the said city; and any ordinance or ordinances carrying said agreement into effect shall have the force and effect of law and be binding on the said city during the time mentioned in said agreement and said ordinance.
(Acts 1901, p. 52.)

32-2706 Public libraries outside municipalities; authority to maintain

Political subdivisions, other than municipal corporations, are hereby authorized to establish and maintain public libraries for purposes of education, and to support the same by current revenue or by donations or bequests which they are authorized to receive for that purpose; and such political subdivisions may contract with each other and with such municipal corporations as may be already maintaining libraries, operated either by their own governing bodies or by boards of trustees or other officials, within the counties in which such municipal corporations are situated, or in adjoining counties, and may enter into cooperative agreements in the establishment and maintenance of such libraries upon such terms as may be agreed on between their respective governing bodies: Provided, however, that any such contract or cooperative agreement relating to a library maintained by a municipality, but operated by a board of trustees, or other officials, shall be made by the governing body of such political subdivision with the governing body of any such municipality and the board of trustees, or other officials through whom such library so maintained by such municipality is operated.

(Acts 1935, p. 409; 1937, p. 715.)

32-2707 Same; library board, its personnel and powers

Whenever, under the provisions of section 32-2706, the governing authorities of any political subdivision shall establish a public library therein, the county board of education shall, ex officio, constitute the library board: Provided, nevertheless, that in the establishment or maintenance of a public library or public library service by contract or cooperative agreement between said political subdivisions, the agreement between the respective governing authorities of said political subdivisions may provide that the library board of a political subdivision already maintaining a public library or public library service may constitute the library board, or said agreement may provide as to the constituency and method of selection of the library board, and such agreements shall be valid to that end; and the library board so constituted shall exercise the powers herein conferred upon library boards, subject to such terms not inconsistent with the general purposes herein provided for, as may be contained in such an agreement.

(Acts 1935, p. 409.)

32-2708 Same; supervision of libraries; branches and stations; contracts; librarian; employees

The library board, as constituted by section 32-2707, shall have general supervision of the public library established in such political subdivisions, and shall have power to make reasonable rules and regulations for the operation of the same. Said board may establish branches and stations wherever deemed advisable and carry on other forms of library extension service; they shall create the office of librarian and fix the term and compensation thereof, said office to be filled by a person with professional library training and experience; and shall determine the number and kind of other employees of the library, appointing and dismissing such employees upon recommendation of the librarian for just cause. Said board shall have power to contract within the limits of the funds available to them by appropriations, taxation, bequest, donation, or from other sources.

(Acts 1935, p. 409.)

32-2709 Same; reimbursement of travel expenses for members of regional and county library boards

Members of regional and county library boards may be entitled to receive reimbursement, at the same rate as State employees, for actual travel expenses incurred by them in carrying out their duties as members of such library boards. The statement for reimbursement of expenses shall be submitted for payment to the director of the library serving the respective regional or county library board. The funds necessary to carry out the provisions of this section shall come from local funds available to the regional or county library board for such purpose.

(Acts 1979, pp. 636, 637, eff. April 12, 1979.)

SCHOOL LIBRARIES
(Code of Georgia Annotated, 1982, s.32-613a.)

32-613a Instructional media
The amount of funds needed by a local unit of administration during a fiscal year for the maintenance, repair, and purchase of instructional media, including soft-covered as well as hard-covered text and library books and consumable as well as nonconsumable supplies, shall be determined by multiplying the number of certificated instructional units allotted to the local unit under sections 32-605a, 32-607a, 32-610a and 32-612a by a sum of money which shall not be less than $500. The State Board of Education shall have the authority to prescribe minimum requirements and standards for the purchase, distribution and use of such instructional media, and for the use of funds allotted under this section.

(Acts 1974, pp. 1045, 1055; 1975, pp. 539, 548; 1979, pp. 1279, 1280; 1980, p. 1413, eff. April 1, 1980.)

COUNTY LAW LIBRARIES
(Code of Georgia Annotated, 1982, s.23-3101 to 23-3110.)

23-3101 Board of trustees; creation; membership; chairman; quorum; treasurer
There is hereby created in each county in Georgia a board to be known as the Board of Trustees of the County Law Library, and hereafter referred to as the board. Said board shall consist of the senior judge of the superior court of the circuit in which said county is located, the judge of the probate court, the senior judge of the State court, if any, and two practicing attorneys of said county. Said practicing attorneys shall be selected by the other trustees and serve at their pleasure. All of said trustees shall serve without pay. The senior judge of the superior court shall be chairman of said board and a majority of the members of said board shall constitute a quorum for the purpose of transacting all business that may come before the board.

(Acts 1971, p. 180; 1973, p. 430.)

23-3102 Secretary-treasurer of board of trustees; librarian
There is hereby created an office to be known as secretary-treasurer of the board of trustees of the county law library in each such county, who shall be selected and appointed by the board and who shall serve at the pleasure of the board. The board may appoint one of its own members as secretary-treasurer or, in its discretion, may designate some other person to act as secretary-treasurer of the board. The secretary-treasurer of the board shall perform the duties provided for the treasurer in this Chapter.

The board of trustees may designate the judge of the probate court or a deputy clerk of the superior court of each such county to act as librarian, and any such official shall not receive any additional compensation for the performance of such duties. The board, however, in its discretion, may designate some other person to act as librarian and fix the compensation for such person.

(Acts 1971, p. 180; 1973, pp. 430, 431; 1976, p. 700, eff. March 24, 1976.)

23-3103. County law library fund.—The board shall have control of the funds provided for in this Chapter and all funds received shall be deposited in a special account to be known as the county law library fund. Said board shall have authority to expend the funds in accordance with provisions of this Chapter, and to invest any of the funds so received in any investments which are legal investments for fiduciaries in this State. (Acts 1971, pp. 180, 181.)

23-3104. Powers and duties of board of trustees.—The board of trustees hereby created is given the following powers and duties : To provide for the collection of all money provided for in this Chapter ; to select the books, reports, texts and periodicals ; to make all necessary rules and regulations governing the use of the library ; to keep records of all its meetings and proceedings ; and to exercise all other powers necessary for the proper administration of the provisions of this Chapter. (Acts 1971, pp. 180, 181.)

23-3105. Gifts of money or property.—The board may take by gift, grant, devise or bequest any money, real or personal property, or any other thing of value and hold or invest the same for the uses and purposes of the library. (Acts 1971, pp. 180, 181.)

23-3106 Court costs to be collected

For the purpose of providing funds for the purpose of purchasing law books, reports, texts and periodicals for such library, a sum not to exceed $2, in addition to all other legal costs, may be charged and collected in each suit, action or case, either civil or criminal, including, without limiting the generality of the foregoing, all adoptions, charters, certiorari, applications by personal representative for leave to sell or reinvest, trade name registrations, applications for change of name, and all other proceedings of civil or criminal or quasi-criminal nature, filed in the superior, State, probate and any other courts of record except recorder's or police courts. The amount of such additional costs to be charged and collected, if any, in each such case shall be fixed by the senior judge of the superior court of the circuit in which such county is located. Such additional costs shall not be charged and collected unless said senior judge shall first determine that a need exists for a law library in said county. The clerks of each and every such court in such counties in which such a law library shall be established shall collect such fees and remit same to the treasurer of the Board of Trustees of the County Law Library of the county in which said case was brought on the first day of each month. Where the costs in criminal cases are not collected, the costs herein provided for shall be paid from the fines and forfeitures fund of such court in which the case is filed before any other disbursement or distribution of such fines or forfeitures shall be made.

(Acts 1971, pp. 180, 181; 1973, pp. 430, 431; 1976, pp. 700, 701, eff. March 24, 1976.)

23-3107 Purposes for which money to be used

The money so paid into the hands of the treasurer of the Board of Trustees of the County Law Library herein provided shall be used for the following purposes: The purchase of law books, reports, texts and periodicals, supplies, desks, and equipment and for the maintenance, upkeep and operation of said law library, including the services of a librarian. All law books, reports, texts and periodicals purchased by the use of gifts and from the aforesaid funds shall become the property of the county.

(Acts 1971, pp. 180, 182; 1973, pp. 430, 432.)

23-3107.1 Maintenance of library

The board of county commissioners or other governing authority of such counties shall furnish necessary space, offices, lights, heat and water for the maintenance of such library.

(Acts 1976, pp. 700, 701, eff. March 24, 1976.)

23-3108. Bond of treasurer.—The treasurer of the board shall give a good and sufficient surety bond payable to the county in such an amount as may be determined by the board to faithfully account for all funds received and disbursed by him. The premium on said bond shall be paid out of the County Law Library Fund. (Acts 1971, pp. 180, 182.)

23-3109. Case defined.—A case, within the meaning of section 23-3106, shall mean and be construed as any matter which is docketed upon the official dockets of said courts and to which a number is assigned, whether such matter is contested or not. (Acts 1971, pp. 180, 182.)

23-3110. Ratification of prior actions, decisions, contracts, and purchases.—All actions, decisions, contracts, and purchases made by any board of trustees of a county law library or other person charged with the responsibility of operating or maintaining a county law library under any previously enacted law of this State are hereby ratified. (Acts 1971, pp. 180, 182.)

TAX EXEMPTION

(Code of Georgia Annotated, 1982, Constitution of the State of Georgia
of 1976, Art. VII, s.2-4604, Art. IX, s.2-6102, 2-6202.)

Georgia library laws are reprinted from CODE OF GEORGIA
ANNOTATED published by The Harrison Company, Norcross,
Georgia.

HAWAII

DEPARTMENT OF EDUCATION
(Hawaii Revised Statutes, 1982, s.26-12, 312-1 to 312-6.)

§26-12 **Department of education.** The department of education shall be headed by an executive board to be known as the board of education.

Under policies established by the board, the superintendent shall administer programs of education and public instruction throughout the State, including education at the preschool, primary and secondary school levels, adult education, school library services, health education and instruction (not including dental health treatment transferred to the department of health), and such other programs as may be established by law. The state librarian, under policies established by the board of education, shall be responsible for the administration of programs relating to public library services and transcribing services for the blind.

The functions and authority heretofore exercised by the department of public instruction (except dental health treatment transferred to the department of health), library of Hawaii, Hawaii county library, Maui county library, and the transcribing services program of the bureau of sight conservation and work with the blind, as heretofore constituted are transferred to the public library system established by this chapter.

The management contract between the board of supervisors of the county of Kauai and the Kauai public library association shall be terminated at the earliest time after November 25, 1959, permissible under the terms of the contract and the provisions of this paragraph shall constitute notice of termination, and the functions and authority heretofore exercised by the Kauai county library as heretofore constituted and the Kauai public library association over the public libraries in the county of Kauai shall thereupon be transferred to the public library system established by this chapter.

The management contracts between the trustees of the library of Hawaii and the Friends of the Library of Hawaii, and between the library of Hawaii and the Hilo library and reading room association, shall be terminated at the earliest time after November 25, 1959, permissible under the terms of the contracts, and the provisions of this paragraph shall constitute notice of termination.

Upon the termination of the contracts, the State or the counties shall not enter into any library management contracts with any private association; provided that in providing library services the board of education may enter into contracts approved by the governor for the use of lands, buildings, equipment, and facilities owned by any private association.

There shall be within the public library system a commission in each county to be known as the library advisory commission for the county which shall in each case sit in an advisory capacity to the board of education on matters relating to public library services in the respective county. Each commission shall consist of not less than seven and no more than eleven members. [L Sp 1959 2d, c 1, §18; am L 1965, c 175, §41(a); Supp, §14A-17; HRS §26-12; am L 1970, c 59, §1; am L 1981, c 150, §1]

§312-1 Duties of the board of education.

The board of education shall care for, manage, and control all property set apart, donated, loaned to, or in any manner acquired for the use of libraries; receive, care for, expend, and account for any money which may be received for the purpose of erecting buildings for libraries or for any other purposes of the libraries; collect, purchase, receive gifts of, and otherwise acquire all books and other publications proper for libraries, and arrange, classify, and catalogue the same; provide for their safekeeping; expend moneys appropriated by the legislature and otherwise acquired for the development, use, support, and maintenance of libraries; provide ways and means for placing libraries within reach of all residents throughout the State and particularly of all public and private school children; provide and maintain branch libraries, offices, or places for the distribution of books and periodicals throughout the State; make such contracts as may be necessary to carry into effect the general duties herein imposed; appoint such officers and employees as it deems necessary; and make rules for the management and use of libraries, and for the control of the property under its management. [L 1909, c 83, §2; RL 1925, §417; RL 1935, §801; RL 1945, §1912; RL 1955, §45-2; am L Sp 1959 2d, c 1, §18; HRS §312-1; am L 1981, c 150, §5]

§312-2 Powers of board; special fund.

The board of education may make such arrangements or contracts as are approved by the governor, with any county, city, association, society, person, or persons, for the purpose of benefiting the libraries and increasing their facilities and use; subject to section 26-12, enter into such arrangement or contract as is approved by the governor, with the Friends of the Library of Hawaii, for the purpose of obtaining the use of the books and property and income of the Friends of the Library of Hawaii; cooperate by exchange and otherwise with libraries now existing or hereafter to be formed; receive, use, manage, or invest moneys or other property, real, personal, or mixed which may be given, bequeathed, devised, or in any manner received from sources other than the legislature or any federal appropriation for any or all purposes of the libraries; deposit with the director of finance in a special fund all moneys donated to the board for library services; unless otherwise provided for by the terms and conditions of the donation, convert, at such time as the board may at its sole discretion determine, any or all donations of property, real, personal, or mixed, into money to be deposited into the special fund; expend the moneys in the special fund in accordance with the terms and conditions of each donation for the purposes of the libraries. The board shall be the trustee of the special fund and all moneys therein shall be deemed to have been appropriated to the use and for the purposes of the board in providing library services. Nothing in this section shall be construed to limit the powers and duties of the board hereinbefore expressed, or to empower the board to obligate the State financially in any sum which shall not have been appropriated by the legislature for the use of the board. [L 1909, c 83, §3; RL 1925, §418; RL 1935, §802; am L 1939, c 127, §1; RL 1945, §1913; am L 1953, c 171, §2; RL 1955, §45-3; am L Sp 1959 2d, c 1, §§14, 18; am L 1963, c 114, §1; HRS §312-2; am L 1981, c 150, §6]

§312-2.1 Appointment of state librarian; duties; salary. The state librarian shall be appointed by the board of education, shall be under the direction of the board, and shall be responsible for the operation, planning, programming, and budgeting of all community/school and public libraries within the State. Notwithstanding any other law to the contrary, the salary of the state librarian shall be set by the board of education and shall be the same as that of an assistant superintendent of education. [L 1969, c 127, §27; am L 1975, c 58, §16; am L 1979, c 59, §1; am L 1981, c 150, §7]

§312-3 Exchange of librarians. The board of education may contract for the exchange of librarians with librarians of any state, country, or territory in accordance with this section, except as otherwise provided in section 76-37. Local librarians so exchanged shall be paid their regular salaries out of the funds appropriated for personal services in the library budget for the library concerned. The qualifications of all librarians from any such state, country, or territory so exchanged shall be equal to those of the local librarians exchanged. In the selection of local librarians for exchange, preference shall be given to persons born in the State. The requirements of citizenship shall not apply to any librarian coming to the State from any foreign state, country, or territory under any such contract of exchange. All librarians so exchanged shall furnish their own transportation to and from the state, country, or territory with which exchanged.

No compensation shall be paid by the State to visiting exchange librarians; provided that in any case where the local exchanged librarian becomes incapacitated or, for any reason, leaves the exchanged position permanently, the library concerned may pay the visiting exchange librarian an amount not to exceed the salary rating of the local exchanged librarian, such an arrangement to continue until the end of the period of exchange or until such time as some satisfactory adjustment has been made. [L 1951, c 190, pt of §1; RL 1955, §45-30; HRS §312-3; am L 1981, c 150, §8]

§312-3.5 Wilful detention of books and other library materials; penalty. A person who wilfully and knowingly detains a book, newspaper, plate, picture, photograph, engraving, painting, drawing, map, magazine, document, letter, public record, microform, sound recording, audio visual materials in any format, magnetic or other tapes, artifacts, or other documentary (written or printed) materials belonging to any library or similar institution controlled by the State for seven days after the mailing date of a written notice forwarded to his last known address, from the librarian or designated representative, that such books or library materials are to be returned to the library or institution, shall be subject to a nominal charge established by the board of education.

A person detaining such books or library materials thirty days after the mailing of the written notice shall be subject to a charge commensurate with the replacement value of the books or library materials. [L 1979, c 117, §1; am L 1981, c 150, §9]

§312-4 Disposition of fines and related income. Income from the operation of libraries that are financially supported by the State shall be deposited with the director of finance to the credit of the general fund; provided that moneys or properties donated for library use and patrons' deposits shall be deposited and accounted for in accordance with regulations prescribed by the comptroller. [L 1961, c 184, §5; am L 1963, c 114, §1; Supp, §45-32]

§312-5 Annual report to the governor. Annually during the month of July but as of June 30 preceding, the board of education shall report to the governor the moneys received from all sources and expended for all purposes during the preceding year, and any other matters pertaining to the libraries which it may deem important, or the governor may require. [L 1909, c 83, §5; RL 1925, §420; RL 1935, §803; am L 1937, c 33, §1; RL 1945, §1914; RL 1955, §45-4; am L Sp 1959 2d, c 1, §18; HRS §312-5; am L 1981, c 150, §10]

§312-6 Bond memorial library. The public library operated and maintained in Kohala, North Kohala, county of Hawaii, formerly under the name of Kohala Public Library shall be designated and known as the "Bond Memorial Library". [L 1921, c 63, §1; RL 1925, §421; RL 1935, §804; RL 1945, §1915; am L 1951, c 190, pt of §1; RL 1955, §45-10; am L Sp 1959 2d, c 1, §18]

STATE PUBLICATIONS DISTRIBUTION CENTER
(Hawaii Revised Statutes, 1982, s.93-1 to 93-5, 93-11.)

§93-1 Establishment of state publications distribution center. There shall be established within the public library system and under the direction of the state librarian a state publications distribution center for depositing and distributing government publications and for promoting an orderly depository library system for state and county publications. [L 1965, c 175, pt of §2 (b); Supp, §13-20; HRS §93-1; am L 1981, c 150, §2]

§93-2 Definitions. (1) "State and county agency" includes every state, city and county and county office, officer, department, board, commission, and agency, whether in the legislative, executive, or judicial branch.

(2) "Publication" includes any document, compilation, journal, report, statute, regulation, ordinance issued in print by any state or county agency, and confidential publications which shall be deposited in accordance with security regulations to be determined by the issuing agency.

(3) "Print" includes all forms of printing and duplications, except administrative forms. [L 1965, c 175, pt of §2(b); Supp, §13-21]

§93-3 Deposit of publications. Every state and county agency shall immediately upon release of a publication, deposit fifteen copies with the state publications distribution center and one copy each with the state archives and the University of Hawaii. Additional copies of the publications shall be deposited with the publications distribution center upon request of the state librarian so long as copies are available.

The state librarian may enter into depository agreements with private and public educational, historical, or scientific institutions or other libraries, within or without the State in order to achieve the objectives sought under this part. [L 1965, c 175, pt of §2(b); Supp, §13-22; HRS §93-3; am L 1970, c 121, §1]

§93-4 Depository library system. The state librarian shall designate at least one government publications depository in each county and shall distribute to each depository one copy of each publication, as defined in this part. [L 1965, c 175, pt of §2(b); Supp, §13-23]

§93-5 Rules. The board of education may make such rules as are necessary to carry out the purposes of this part. [L 1965, c 175, pt of §2(b); Supp, §13-24; HRS §93-5; am L 1981, c 150, §3]

§93-11 Disposition of statutes and court reports. In addition to the copies of Hawaiian statutes and supreme court reports that may be disposed of by sale, exchange, or presentation to public officers for official use, not more than fifty copies of each volume may be presented to libraries of educational, historical, or scientific institutions or other libraries of a public or quasi-public nature in the State and elsewhere. [L 1907, c 16, §1; am L 1919, c 29, §1; RL 1925, §27; RL 1935, §28; RL 1945, §28; RL 1955, §13-2]

PUBLIC ARCHIVES
(Hawaii Revised Statutes, 1982, s.94-1 to 94-6, 92-29 to 92-31.)

§94-1 Duties of department. The department of accounting and general services shall collect all public archives; arrange, classify, and inventory the same; provide for their safe keeping; and compile and furnish information concerning them. The department may adopt and use a seal and may adopt, amend, or revise from time to time such rules and regulations as it may consider expedient for the conduct of its business. [L 1905, c 24, §2; RL 1945, §31; am L 1945, c 238, §1; RL 1955, §13-5; am L Sp 1959 2d, c 1, §12]

§94-2 Sale of duplicate government publications. The department of accounting and general services may determine and from time to time revise prices to be charged and collected by the department for the sale of duplicate publications in its possession. The funds realized under this section shall be paid into the treasury of the State as general fund realizations. [L 1953, c 160, §1; RL 1955, §13-7; am L Sp 1959 2d, c 1, §12]

§94-3 Disposal of government records generally. Each public officer having the care and custody of any government records shall submit to the state comptroller a list of records for disposal, which shall include the name of the office, department, or bureau, the subject of the records for disposal and the inclusive dates of the records. The comptroller shall determine the disposition of the records; stating whether such records should be retained by the office, department, or bureau; be transferred to the public archives, the University of Hawaii, the Hawaiian Historical Society, or other agency; or be destroyed. The comptroller shall have full power of disposal of all records submitted for such purpose. The records of all records disposed of, including lists submitted by the public officers, and the action taken by the comptroller, shall be kept on proper forms, specified by the comptroller, one copy of which shall be filed in the office, department or bureau where the records originated, one copy shall be filed in the office of the attorney general, and the original shall be filed in the public archives. [L 1949, c 65, §1; RL 1955, §7-8; am L 1957, c 46, §§1, 2 and c 152, §1; am L Sp 1959 2d, c 1, §12]

§94-4 Certificate to same. The comptroller of the State and the archivist or other officer performing the duties of archivist or custodian of the public archives are severally authorized and empowered to certify, as true and correct, copies or reproductions of any of the books, documents, papers, writings, or other records, or excerpts therefrom in their custody. Fees for copying, certification, and other services shall be prescribed by the comptroller in direct relation to the cost of the services.

The above fees shall not be charged where the work involved is required by any department or branch of the federal, state, or county governments. [L 1909, c 8, §2; RL 1925, §2603; am L 1932 2d, c 21, §1; RL 1935, §3842; RL 1945, §9890; am L 1945, c 109, §1; am L 1953, c 159, §1; RL 1955, §224-11; am L 1957, c 83, §1; am L Sp 1959 2d, c 1, §12]

§94-5 Disposal of examination records. All statutory boards or commissions authorized or empowered to hold examinations for candidates or applicants shall preserve all records of each examination, including, without prejudice to the generality of the foregoing, applications, questions, answers, and grades, until after the end of the legislative session following the examination. [L 1941, c 198, §1; RL 1945, §461; RL 1955, §7-9]

§94-6 Studies. Within ten days following the initiation of any study to be done on a contractual basis by the State or one of its political subdivisions, or any agency thereof, the initiating department or agency shall notify the State archivist of the initiation of the study in the form of notice prescribed by the archivist.

The archivist shall maintain a complete and current index of all studies so initiated and shall, at least semi-annually send current copies of this index to the governor, the mayors of the respective counties, the legislative reference bureau and the legislative auditor.

The archivist may at any time request that a copy of any study or portion of a study be deposited with the archives and this request shall be complied with by the department or agency initiating the study.

This section shall apply to all studies of whatever nature; provided, however that to the extent that the governor or mayor of any county initiating a study determines that compliance with any portion of this section would be contrary to the public interest they may waive compliance with respect to any study initiated under their jurisdiction. [L 1972, c 193, §1; am L 1973, c 198, §1]

§92-29 Reproduction of public records on films. Any public officer having the care and custody of any record, paper or document may cause the same to be photographed, microphotographed, or otherwise reproduced on film. The film shall be of durable material and the device used to reproduce the record, paper, or document on the film shall be one which accurately reproduces the original thereof in all details. [L 1945, c 26, pt of §1; RL 1955, §7-5]

§92-30 Film deemed original record. Such photograph, microphotograph, or reproduction on film shall be deemed to be an original record for all purposes, including introduction in evidence in all courts or administrative agencies. A transcript, exemplification, facsimile, or certified copy thereof shall, for all purposes recited herein, be deemed to be a transcript, exemplification, facsimile, or certified copy of the original record. [L 1945, c 26, pt of §1; RL 1955, §7-6]

§92-31 Disposition of original. Such photograph, microphotograph, or reproduction on film shall be placed in conveniently accessible files and provisions made for preserving, examining and using the same. Thereafter, such public officer, after having first received the written approval of the comptroller described in section 94-3, may cause such record, paper, or document to be destroyed. The comptroller may require, as a prerequisite to the granting of such approval, that a reproduction or print of such photograph, microphotograph, or reproduction on film, be delivered into the custody of the public archives for safekeeping. The comptroller may also require the delivery into the custody of another governmental department or agency or a research library of any such record, paper, or document proposed to be destroyed under the provisions of this section. [L 1945, c 26, pt of §1; RL 1955, §7-7; am L 1959, c 7, §1; am L Sp 1959 2d, c 1, §12]

SCHOOL LIBRARIES
(Hawaii Revised Statutes, 1982, s.296-1, 296-19, 297-40, 363.22.)

§296-1 Definitions. As used in chapters 296 to 302, the following terms have the following meanings unless the context indicates otherwise:

* * *

"Teacher" means a person whose duties in the educational system are primarily teaching or instruction of students or related activities centered primarily on students and who is in close and continuous contact with students and shall include, but not be limited to, classroom teachers, school librarians, counselors, registrars, and special education teachers. [L 1961, c 182, pt of §3(b); am L 1965, c 175, §3; Supp, §37-1; am L 1966, c 50, §3]

[§296-19] Public library system; board of education control. The board of education, through the state librarian, shall have direct control of the public library system, but not including school libraries. The board may adopt rules under chapter 91 for the purpose of this section. [L 1981, c 150, §4]

§297-40 Additional benefits to certain teachers. The department of education shall provide additional benefits to grade level chairmen, department heads, registrars, and librarians in schools. The department shall also provide additional benefits to teachers assigned to schools in areas designated as limited environment communities by the department. [L 1965, c 174, §1D; Supp, §38-35.5]

§362-22 Authorization. The department of education is authorized to make Nanaikapono school a model school within the meaning of this part. For this purpose, the department shall conduct a two week workshop for new teachers at Nanaikapono school prior to the beginning of the 1967-1968 school year for sensitivity training and cultural adjustment purposes. The department shall also design a community centered multipurpose library for public and school use at the proposed Nanakuli high school. [L 1967, c 299, §7]

MISCELLANEOUS PROVISIONS
(Hawaii Revised Statutes, 1982, s.298-26.)

§298-26 Unauthorized vehicles on school or public library grounds. Any unauthorized vehicle parked on school or public library grounds may be towed away at the owner's expense, or the owner or driver of the vehicle may be arrested by any police officer without warrant, on complaint of the principal, librarian or other person in charge of the school or library. Notwithstanding any provision to the contrary in the Penal Code or any other law, upon conviction thereof he shall be fined not more than $50. [L 1973, c 123, §2; am L 1979, c 138, §1]

Hawaii library laws are reprinted from HAWAII REVISED STATUTES.

IDAHO

STATE LIBRARY BOARD
(Idaho Code, 1982, s.33-2501 to 33-2504.)

33-2501. State library board — Membership. — The state library board which shall be maintained within the officer of the state board of education shall consist of the state superintendent of public instruction, as ex officio member, and three (3) members appointed by the state board of education, one (1) member for a term of one (1) year, one (1) member for a term of two (2) years, and one (1) member for a term of three (3) years. Thereafter the state board of education shall annually on the first Monday of July appoint one (1) member of said board to serve for a term of three (3) years. The state library board shall meet not less than twice each year, and the members thereof shall be compensated as provided by section 59-509(f), Idaho Code. The board shall elect its own officers and shall make and prescribe all necessary rules and regulations for the conduct of the public business hereby entrusted to its care. [1903, ch. 283, § 1; reen. R.C., § 672; reen. 1911, ch. 159, § 174, p. 550; reen. C.L. 38:288; C.S., § 1032; I.C.A., § 32-2001; am. 1953. ch. 38, § 1, p. 57; am. 1974, ch. 10, § 15, p. 49; am. 1980, ch. 247, § 27, p. 582.]

33-2502. Idaho state library — Cooperation with schools and libraries — Donations — Reports. — There shall be an Idaho State Library, with the responsibility to foster and promote library service in the state of Idaho, with the state librarian as its chief administrative officer. The

Idaho state library board shall have the management of the Idaho state library, and shall make such rules governing the use of the same, and of the books and property pertaining thereto, as it may deem necessary. Said board shall cause said books to be distributed throughout the state, and at suitable intervals change such distribution in such manner as to secure the use and enjoyment of said books to the people of the state. The board shall have power to employ a qualified librarian, graduate of an accredited library school, whose duties shall be defined by the said board. It shall cooperate with the management of public school libraries and other public libraries within the state, and adopt such means as shall promote their establishment. Said board may receive donations of money, books, or other property, real or personal, for the benefit of the Idaho state library, the title to which property shall vest in the state of Idaho, to be held and controlled by said board. Said board shall report biennially to the governor, with such recommendations as it may deem proper. [1903, p. 283, § 2, reen. R.C., § 673; am. 1911, ch. 159, § 175, p. 550; reen. C.L. 38:289; C.S., § 1033; I.C.A., § 32-2002; am. 1959, ch. 19, § 1, p. 40.]

33-2503. Accounts of board — Certification and payment of claims. — The secretary of said board shall keep a full report of the proceedings of said board, and accurate accounts of expenses incurred by it in carrying out the provisions of sections 33-2501 — 33-2503. The chairman of said board may issue certificates, countersigned by the secretary, for all claims, against said board, incurred in the management of said Idaho State Library, and in carrying out the objects of this chapter, which claims, when approved by the board of examiners, shall be paid by warrants drawn upon the fund in the state treasury provided for such purpose. [1903, p. 283, § 3; reen. R.C., § 674; reen. 1911, ch. 159, § 176, p. 551; C.S., § 1034; I.C.A., § 32-2003; am. 1959, ch. 19, § 2, p. 40.]

33-2504. Powers and duties of the Board. — In addition to the powers hereinbefore set out, the Idaho State Library Board shall have the following powers:

1. To accept, receive, administer, and expend, in accordance with the terms thereof, any moneys, materials or other aid granted, appropriated, or made available to Idaho by the United States, or any of its agencies, or by any other source, public or private, for library purposes. The Board is authorized to file any accounts required with reference to receiving and administering all such moneys, materials, and other aid.

2. To assist in the establishment and financing of a statewide program of regional public library service, which may be in cooperation with any taxing unit, or public or private agency.

3. To contract with other libraries or agencies, within or without the State

of Idaho, to render library services to people of the State of Idaho. The State Library Board shall have authority to reasonably compensate such other library unit or agency for the cost of the services it renders under any such contract. [I.C., § 33-2504, as added by 1965, ch. 252, § 1, p. 629.]

INTERSTATE LIBRARY COMPACT
(Idaho Code, 1982, s.33-25-5 to 33-2509.)

33-2505. Compact enacted. — The Interstate Library Compact is hereby enacted into law and entered into by this state with all states legally joining therein in the form substantially as follows:

INTERSTATE LIBRARY COMPACT
ARTICLE I. POLICY AND PURPOSE

Because the desire for the services provided by libraries transcends governmental boundaries and can most effectively be satisfied by giving such services to communities and people regardless of jurisdictional lines, it is the policy of the states party to this compact to cooperate and share their responsibilities; to authorize cooperation and sharing with respect to those types of library facilities and services which can be more economically or efficiently developed and maintained on a cooperative basis; and to authorize cooperation and sharing among localities, states and others in providing joint or cooperative library services in areas where the distribution of population or of existing and potential library resources make the provision of library service on an interstate basis the most effective way of providing adequate and efficient service.

ARTICLE II. DEFINITIONS

As used in this compact:

(a) "Public library agency" means any unit or agency of local or state government operating or having power to operate a library.

(b) "Private library agency" means any nongovernmental entity which operates or assumes a legal obligation to operate a library.

(c) "Library agreement" means a contract establishing an interstate library district pursuant to this compact or providing for the joint or cooperative furnishing of library services.

ARTICLE III. INTERSTATE LIBRARY DISTRICTS

(a) Any one or more public library agencies in a party state in cooperation with any public library agency or agencies in one or more other party states may establish and maintain an interstate library district. Subject to the provisions of this compact and any other laws of the party states which pursuant hereto remain applicable, such district may establish, maintain and operate some or all of the library facilities and services for the area concerned in accordance with the terms of a library agreement therefor. Any private library agency or agencies within an interstate library district may cooperate therewith, assume duties, responsibilities and obligations thereto, and receive benefits therefrom as provided in any library agreement to which such agency or agencies become party.

(b) Within an interstate library district, and as provided by a library agreement, the performance of library functions may be undertaken on a joint or cooperative basis or may be undertaken by means of one or more arrangements between or among public or private library agencies for the extension of library privileges to the use of facilities or services operated or rendered by one or more of the individual library agencies.

(c) If a library agreement provides for joint establishment, maintenance or operation of library facilities or services by an interstate library district, such district shall have power to do any one or more of the following in accordance with such library agreement:

1. Undertake, administer and participate in programs or arrangements for securing, lending or servicing books and other publications, any other materials suitable to be kept or made available by libraries, library equipment or for the dissemination of information about libraries, the value and significance of particular items therein, and the use thereof.

2. Accept for any of its purposes under this compact any and all donations, and grants of money, equipment, supplies, materials, and services (conditional or otherwise), from any state or the United States or any subdivision or agency thereof, or interstate agency, or from any institution, person, firm or corporation, and receive, utilize and dispose of the same.

3. Operate mobile library units or equipment for the purpose of rendering bookmobile service within the district.

4. Employ professional, technical, clerical and other personnel, and fix terms of employment, compensation and other appropriate benefits; and where desirable, provide for the in-service training of such personnel.

5. Sue and be sued in any court of competent jurisdiction.

6. Acquire, hold, and dispose of any real or personal property or any interest or interests therein as may be appropriate to the rendering of library service.

7. Construct, maintain and operate a library, including any appropriate branches thereof.

8. Do such other things as may be incidental to or appropriate for the carrying out of any of the foregoing powers.

ARTICLE IV. INTERSTATE LIBRARY DISTRICTS, GOVERNING BOARD

(a) An interstate library district which establishes, maintains or operates any facilities or services in its own right shall have a governing board which shall direct the affairs of the district and act for it in all matters relating to its business. Each participating public library agency in the district shall be represented on the governing board which shall be organized and conduct its business in accordance with provision therefor in the library agreement. But in no event shall a governing board meet less often than twice a year.

(b) Any private library agency or agencies party to a library agreement establishing an interstate library district may be represented on or advise with the governing board of the district in such manner as the library agreement may provide.

ARTICLE V. STATE LIBRARY AGENCY COOPERATION

Any two or more state library agencies of two or more of the party states may undertake and conduct joint or cooperative library programs, render joint or cooperative library services, and enter into and perform arrangements for the cooperative or joint acquisition. use, housing and disposition of items or collections of materials which, by reason of expense. rarity, specialized nature. or infrequency of demand therefor, would be appropriate for central collection and shared use. Any such programs, services or arrangements may include provision for the exercise on a cooperative or joint basis of any power exercisable by an interstate library district and an agreement embodying any such program, service or arrangement shall contain provisions covering the subjects detailed in Article VI, of this compact for interstate library agreements.

ARTICLE VI. LIBRARY AGREEMENTS

(a) In order to provide for any joint or cooperative undertaking pursuant to this compact, public and private library agencies may enter into library agreements. Any agreement executed pursuant to the provisions of this compact shall, as among the parties to the agreements:

1. Detail the specific nature of the services, programs, facilities, arrangements or properties to which it is applicable.

2. Provide for the allocation of costs, and other financial responsibilities.

3. Specify the respective rights, duties, obligations and liabilities of the parties.

4. Set forth the terms and conditions for duration, renewal, termination, abrogation, disposal of joint or common property, if any, and all other matters which may be appropriate to the proper effectuation and performance of the agreement.

(b) No public or private library agency shall undertake to exercise itself, or jointly with any other library agency, by means of a library agreement any power prohibited to such agency by the constitution or statutes of its state.

(c) No library agreement shall become effective until filed with the compact administrator of each state involved, and approved in accordance with Article VII of this compact.

ARTICLE VII. APPROVAL OF LIBRARY AGREEMENTS

(a) Every library agreement made pursuant to this compact shall, prior to and as a condition precedent to its entry into force, be submitted to the attorney general of each state in which a public library agency party thereto is situated, who shall determine whether the agreement is in proper form and compatible with the laws of his, state. The attorneys general shall approve any agreement submitted to them unless they shall find that it does not meet the conditions set forth herein and shall detail in writing addressed to the governing bodies of the public library agencies concerned the specific respects in which the proposed agreement fails to meet the requirements of law. Failure to disapprove an agreement submitted hereunder within ninety days of its submission shall constitute approval thereof.

(b) In the event that a library agreement made pursuant to this compact shall deal in whole or in part with the provision of services or facilities with regard to which an officer or agency of the state government has constitutional or statutory powers of control, the agreement shall, as a condition precedent to its entry into force, be submitted to the state officer or agency having such power of control and shall be approved or disapproved by him or it as to all matters within his or its jurisdiction in the same manner and subject to the same requirements governing the action of the attorneys general pursuant to paragraph (a) of this article. This requirement of submission and approval shall be in addition to and not in substitution for the requirement of submission to and approval by the attorneys general.

ARTICLE VIII. OTHER LAWS APPLICABLE

Nothing in this compact or in any library agreement shall be construed to supersede, alter or otherwise impair any obligation imposed on any library by otherwise applicable law, nor to authorize the transfer or disposition of any property held in trust by a library agency in a manner contrary to the terms of such trust.

ARTICLE IX. APPROPRIATIONS AND AID

(a) Any public library agency party to a library agreement may appropriate funds to the interstate library district established thereby in the same manner and to the same extent as to a library wholly maintained by it and, subject to the laws of the state in which such public library agency is situated, may pledge its credit in support of an interstate library district established by the agreement.

(b) Subject to the provisions of the library agreement pursuant to which it functions and the laws of the states in which such district is situated, an interstate library district may claim and receive any state and federal aid which may be available to library agencies.

ARTICLE X. COMPACT ADMINISTRATOR

Each state shall designate a compact administrator with whom copies of all library agreements to which his state or any public library agency thereof is party shall be filed. The administrator shall have such other powers as may be conferred upon him by the laws of his state and may consult and cooperate with the compact administrators of other party states and take such steps as may effectuate the purposes of this compact. If the laws of a party state so provide, such state may designate one or more deputy compact administrators in addition to its compact administrator.

ARTICLE XI. ENTRY INTO FORCE AND WITHDRAWAL

(a) This compact shall enter into force and effect immediately upon it [its] enactment into law by any two states. Thereafter, it shall enter into force and effect as to any other state upon the enactment thereof by such state.

(b) This compact shall continue in force with respect to a party state and remain binding upon such state until six months after such state has given notice to each other party state of the repeal thereof. Such withdrawal shall not be construed to relieve any party to a library agreement entered into pursuant to this compact from any obligation of that agreement prior to the end of its duration as provided therein.

ARTICLE XII. CONSTRUCTION AND SEVERABILITY

This compact shall be liberally construed so as to effectuate the purposes thereof. The provisions of this compact shall be severable and if any phrase, clause, sentence or provision of this compact is declared to be contrary to the constitution of any party state or of the United States or the applicability thereof to any government, agency, person or circumstance is held invalid, the validity of the remainder of this compact and the applicability thereof to any government, agency, person or circumstance shall not be affected thereby. If this compact shall be held contrary to the constitution of any state party thereto, the compact shall remain in full force and effect as to the remaining states and in full force and effect as to the state affected as to all severable matters. [I.C., § 33-2505, as added by 1965, ch. 252, § 1, p. 629.]

33-2506. Limitation on capital expenditures. — No taxing unit or public or private agency maintaining a library within this state shall be a party to a library agreement which provides for the construction or maintenance of a library pursuant to Article III, sub-division (c-7) of the compact, nor contribute to the capital financing thereof, except after compliance with any laws applicable to such taxing units or agencies relating to or governing capital outlays. [I.C., § 33-2506, as added by 1965, ch. 252, § 1, p. 629.]

33-2507. Definition. — As used in the compact, "state library agency", with reference to this state, means the Idaho State Library Board. [I.C., § 33-2507, as added by 1965, ch. 252, § 1, p. 629.]

33-2508. Designation of administrator. — The state librarian shall be the compact administrator pursuant to Article X of the compact. The State Library Board may appoint one or more deputy compact administrators pursuant to said Article. Every library agreement made pursuant to the compact shall, as a condition precedent to its entry into force, be submitted to the compact administrator for his recommendations and approval. [I.C., § 33-2508, as added by 1965, ch. 252, § 1, p. 629.]

33-2509. Withdrawal. — In the event of withdrawal from the compact the compact administrator shall send and receive any notices required by Article XI (b) of the compact. [I.C., § 33-2509, as added by 1965, ch. 252, § 1, p. 629.]

DISTRIBUTION OF PUBLIC DOCUMENTS
(Idaho Code, 1982, s.1-505, 1-508, 33-2510, 67-906, 67-5205, 67-5217, 67-5218.)

1-505. Distribution of reports. — The reporter shall have no pecuniary interest in the reports. The decisions of the said Supreme Court shall be prepared for publication, by the reporter, as rapidly as possible, and as soon as a sufficient number of decisions are prepared to fill a volume, such a volume shall be printed, and as many copies thereof as directed by the administrative director of the courts, shall be delivered to the state law librarian, who shall distribute them as follows: To the Librarian of Congress, three (3) copies; to the Idaho State Law Library, five (5) copies; to the University of Idaho, general library, two (2) copies; to the Idaho State University Library, one (1) copy; to the Boise State University Library, one (1) copy; to the College of Law of the University of Idaho, twelve (12) copies; to the Lewis-Clark State College, one (1) copy; to the library at the state penitentiary, one (1) copy; to each county prosecuting attorney, one (1) copy; to each magistrate, one (1) copy; to each district judge, one (1) copy; to each justice of the Supreme Court, one (1) copy; to the clerk of the Supreme Court, one (1) copy; to the attorney general five (5) copies; one (1) copy to the Department of Lands of Idaho; one (1) copy to the Public Utilities Commission of Idaho; one (1) copy to the Industrial Commission; one (1) copy to the Division of Public Works; one (1) copy to the Department of Insurance; one (1) copy to the Judiciary Committee of the Senate during sessions of the Legislature; one (1) copy to the Judiciary Committee of the House of Representatives during sessions of the Legislature; to each state and territory in the United States sending to this state copies of its printed court reports, one (1) copy for the use of the state library or law library thereof;

to each foreign state or country, sending to this state copies of its printed court reports, one (1) copy; to the governor, secretary of state, state treasurer, state auditor, superintendent of public instruction, each one (1) copy; and to other officers and institutions as directed by the administrative director of the courts; provided, that each public officer receiving a copy of any volume or volumes of said reports under the provisions of this section, shall take good care of the same, and shall upon retiring from office, turn the same over to his successor in office, provided further, that copies of any volume of such reports may be again issued to any of said officers, institutions, states or territories upon good and sufficient proof of loss of the copies sought to be replaced, presented to the administrative director of the courts, who may direct the librarian to furnish another copy of the volume so lost, in place thereof. [1903, p. 367, § 5; am. R.C., § 226; compiled & reen. C.L., § 226; C.S., § 203; am. 1925, ch. 7, § 1, p. 9; I.C.A., § 1-505; am. 1935, ch. 43, § 2, p. 79; am. 1939, ch. 28, § 1, p. 58; am. 1959, ch. 73, § 1, p. 165; am. 1969, ch. 122, § 1, p. 382; am. 1978, ch. 152, § 1, p. 334.]

1-508.   Receipt to printer — Record and receipt for reports distributed. — The librarian of the state law library shall give to the contracting printer a receipt for all copies of reports of said decisions delivered to him by such printer, and the librarian shall keep a correct record, in a book kept especially for that purpose, of all volumes received and distributed under the provisions of this chapter, and shall take a receipt for all copies of such reports distributed, and file and preserve the same. [1903, p. 367, § 8; am. R.C., § 229; reen. C.L., § 229; C.S., § 206; I.C.A., § 1-508; am. 1959, ch. 73, § 2, p. 165.]

33-2510.   State librarian — Depositary for public documents — Distribution. — It shall be the duty of the head of every agency, board, bureau, commission or department of the state of Idaho, including all state supported institutions of higher education in Idaho, to deposit with the librarian of the Idaho state library for use and distribution to the academic, regional public, special libraries of Idaho, the Library of Congress, and to others within the discretion of the state librarian twenty (20) copies of all documents, reports, surveys, monographs, serial publications, compilations, pamphlets, bulletins, leaflets, circulars, maps, charts or broadsides of a public nature which it prints, mimeographs or otherwise reproduces for public distribution. [1972, ch. 165, § 1, p. 413.]

67-906.   Distribution of session laws and journals. — (1) Immediately after the session laws are bound, they shall be delivered to the secretary of state, and the secretary of state shall distribute within thirty (30) days of receipt from printer as follows:
(a) To each department of government of this state, one (1) copy;
(b) To the library of congress, four (4), and to the state library, two (2) copies;

(c) To the senators and representatives in the United States congress representing Idaho, and to each of the justices of the Supreme Court of this state, and judges and magistrates of the district courts, one (1) copy;

(d) To each member of the legislature of the session when such session laws were adopted, one (1) copy;

(e) To the office of the attorney general, five (5) additional copies;

(f) To the legislature in sufficient number for one (1) copy for each standing committee of the house and senate;

(g) To the clerk of the district court of each county, sufficient copies of the session laws to supply one (1) copy for the board of county commissioners, and one (1) copy to each elected county officer and to the public defender;

(h) To Idaho state law library, five (5) copies;

(i) To each state and territory in the United States, one (1) copy for the use of the state law library;

(j) To each university or college law library sending to Idaho state law library copies of its law review, one (1) copy; and

(k) To the University of Idaho, College of Law library, thirty-two (32) copies.

(2) Immediately after the journals that are to be sold through the secretary of state's office are delivered to the secretary of state, the secretary of state shall offer such journals for sale to any person at the price fixed for such journals by the printing committee as provided in section 67-509, Idaho Code. Any moneys received by the secretary of state from the sale of journals shall be deposited in the general account in the state operating fund. [R.S., § 192; reen. R.C., § 96; compiled and reen. C.L., § 96; C.S., § 135; am. 1931, ch. 162, § 2, p. 274; I.C.A., § 65-805; am. 1935, ch. 43, § 1, p. 79; am. 1953, ch. 184, § 1, p. 295; am. 1972, ch. 231, § 3, p. 610; am. 1977, ch. 232, § 3, p. 687.]

67-5205. Publication of rules. — (a) Each agency shall compile, index and publish all effective rules adopted by such agency. Compilations shall be supplemented or revised as often as necessary and at least once every two (2) years.

(b) Compilations shall be made available upon request to officials of this state free of charge, and to other persons at prices fixed by each agency to cover mailing and publication cost.

(c) Each agency shall provide a complete set of rules, and furnish materials to keep the rules current, to the following libraries: Boise public library, Boise State University library, Burley public library, College of Idaho library, College of Southern Idaho library, Idaho Falls public library, Idaho State law library, Idaho State University library, Lewis-Clark State College library, North Idaho College library, Northwest Nazarene College library, Pocatello public library, Ricks College library, Salmon public library, Sandpoint public library, University of Idaho law library, and the University of Idaho library. These compilations of rules shall be maintained by the libraries for use by the public. The compilation maintained at the

Idaho State law library shall, along with the rules filed as required in section 67-5204, Idaho Code, constitute the official rules of the agency.

(d) Judicial notice shall be taken of rules filed and proposed as provided in this section.

(e) The word "publish" as used herein shall mean to bring before the public, to print or cause to be printed, to issue, to disseminate, to put into circulation, but shall not be construed to require publication in a newspaper. [1965, ch. 273, § 5, p. 701; am. 1980, ch. 78, § 1, p. 160.]

67-5217. Transmittal of rules for legislative action — Referral to appropriate legislative committee. — All rules heretofore or hereafter authorized or promulgated by any state agency, including all rules kept and maintained by the state law library, as provided in chapter 52, title 67, Idaho Code, shall be transmitted to the secretary of the senate and the chief clerk of the house of representatives by the law librarian of the state law library before the first day of the regular session of the legislature next following the promulgation or publication thereof. A statement, separate from the rules, shall be prepared by the promulgating agency and shall accompany each new rule or amendment to an existing rule adopted during the preceding year. The statement shall include: (a) the full text of the rule prepared so as to indicate words added or deleted from the presently effective text, if any; (b) an explanation of each change made and the effect thereof; (c) the date of adoption; (d) whether the rule was adopted as an emergency rule; and (e) whether hearings were held prior to adoption. The law librarian of the state law library shall similarly file during any regular session of the legislature all rules promulgated, and the required statement, between the first day of the session and adjournment sine die thereof. The secretary of the senate and the chief clerk of the house of representatives shall lay all such rules before the senate and house of representatives, respectively, and the same shall be referred to the respective standing committees in the same manner as bills are referred to the committees. [1969, ch. 48, § 1, p. 125; am. 1976, ch. 185, § 1, p. 671; am. 1980, ch. 212, § 3, p. 481.]

67-5218. Committee action. — By the forty-fifth day following transmission by the law librarian, the standing committee to which rules have been referred shall report to the membership of the body its findings and recommendations concerning its review of the rules. The report of the committee shall be printed in the journal. If the committee does not report by the forty-fifth day following transmission or prior to adjournment sine die if adjournment is more than twenty-one (21) but less than forty-five (45) days following transmission, such failure to report shall constitute legislative approval of the rules as submitted, except that no legislative approval shall be presumed if the legislature adjourns within twenty (20) days of the transmission, and the rules shall be transmitted by the law librarian to the next succeeding regular session, before the first day. If the committee to which any rule shall have been referred, or any member of the legislature, shall be of the opinion that such rule is violative of the legislative intent of the statute under which such rule was made, a concurrent resolution may be adopted rejecting, amending or modifying the same. Where an agency submits a rule or part of a rule which has been adopted or which has repealed or amended an already existing rule, the rejection or modification of the new rule by the legislature via concurrent resolution shall prevent the agency's intended action from remaining in effect beyond the date of the legislative action. It shall be the responsibility of the secretary of state to immediately notify the affected agency of the filing and effective date of any concurrent resolution enacted to amend, modify, or reject an agency rule and to transmit a copy of such concurrent resolution to the director of the agency for promulgation. The agency shall be responsible for implementing legislative intent as expressed in the concurrent resolution, including, as appropriate, the reinstatement of the prior rule, if any, in the case of legislative rejection of the new rule, or the incorporation of any legislative amendments to the new rule. The agency shall republish the rule in accordance with section 67-5205, Idaho Code, reflecting the action taken by the legislature and the effective date thereof. Every rule promulgated within the authority conferred by law, and in accordance with the provisions of chapter 52, title 67, Idaho Code, shall be in full force and effect until the same is rejected, amended or modified by the legislature. [am. 1981, ch. 243, § 1, p. 486.]

STATE LAW LIBRARY
(Idaho Code, 1982, s.4-101 to 4-105, 4-107.)

4-101. Establishment of a state law library.—A state law library for the use of the courts and members of the bar of this state is hereby established in the city of Boise. The Boise state law library shall be kept in the state capitol building or the Supreme Court and law library building, and is hereby also designated as the state depository for official publications received from other states and the federal government. [1925, ch. 86, § 1, p. 120; I. C. A., § 4-101; am. 1951, ch. 87, § 1, p. 157; am. 1959, ch. 73, § 3, p. 165; am. 1969, ch. 212, § 1, p. 614.]

4-102. State publication furnished law library.—A copy of each law, pamphlet or other publication hereafter made by or under authority of the state, or any of its agencies, shall be sent to the state law library. [1925, ch. 86, § 2, p. 120; I. C. A., § 4-102; am. 1951, ch. 87, § 2, p. 157.]

4-103. Control of the state law library.—The justices of the Supreme Court shall have the control and management of the state law library and shall make such rules and regulations respecting the same as they may deem best. They shall appoint librarians therefor and fix their compensation and the amount of bond required in case they deem bond should be given. Said justices may dispose of superfluous or duplicate publications or other property of said law library, by sale or otherwise as they may deem to be in the public interest. Any moneys so received shall be paid to the state treasurer and apportioned to the general fund. [1925, ch. 86, § 3, p. 120; I. C. A., § 4-103; am. 1951, ch. 87, § 3, p. 157.]

4-105. Disbursement of funds.—The justices of the Supreme Court shall have the management of all funds belonging to or appropriated for the use of the state law library, and expend and disburse the same for the benefit thereof, as, in their judgment may be best; and upon demand of said justices or any three of them, the state auditor shall draw his warrants upon the state treasurer to the extent of such sums as there may be in the treasurer's hands belonging to or appropriated for the use of said state law library. [1925, ch. 86, § 5, p. 120; am. 1927, ch. 187, § 2, p. 250; I. C. A., § 4-105; am. 1951, ch. 87, § 4, p. 157.]

4-107. Use and abuse of law library.—Any person may have access to and may use the books in the state law library under such restrictions as the justices of the Supreme Court may prescribe. Any person who shall violate any rule established for the management of the state law library may be denied the privileges thereof. Any person who shall wantonly mutilate or destroy any book or article of furniture, or any pamphlet or paper belonging to the state law library, shall be deemed guilty of a misdemeanor and shall be punished accordingly. Any person who fails to return to the state law library any book taken therefrom by him, within the time prescribed by the rules of said library, shall be liable to the librarian in three times its value to be recovered in a civil action; and if such person be an officer or employee of the state, the same shall be withheld from his salary. [1925, ch. 86, § 7, p. 120; I. C. A., § 4-107; am. 1951, ch. 87, § 5, p. 157.]

STATE HISTORICAL SOCIETY
(Idaho Code, 1982, s.67-4123 to 67-4129.)

67-4123. State historical society — Governed by board of trustees. — The Idaho State Historical Society, hereinafter referred to as the society, shall be governed by a board of trustees. The society and its board of trustees, shall, for the purposes of section 20, article IV, of the constitution of the state of Idaho, be within the office of the state board of education. The board shall be responsible for administering the powers and duties required to preserve and protect any historical record of the history and culture of Idaho. [1970, ch. 145, § 1, p. 438; am. 1974, ch. 10, § 18, p. 49.]

67-4124. Board of trustees — Qualifications, appointment and terms of members. — The board of trustees shall consist of five (5) members to be appointed by the state board of education. The members of the board shall be chosen with due regard to their knowledge, competence, experience and interest in the fields related to the preservation of the historical archives of Idaho. The state board of education shall consider geographic representation and population distribution when selecting board members. All appointees shall be chosen solely on the basis of their qualifications, and not more than three (3) members of the board shall belong to the same political party.

All members of the board of trustees shall serve for a specific term. Upon expiration of the terms of members serving on the board of trustees on the effective date [July 1, 1974] of this act, the board shall appoint one (1) member for a term of two (2) years, two (2) members for a term of four (4) years, and two (2) members for a term of six (6) years. Appointments thereafter, except appointments for the unexpired portion of a term, shall be for a term of six (6) years. [1970, ch. 145, § 2, p. 438; am. 1974, ch. 10, § 19, p. 49.]

67-4125. Board meetings — Officers — Quorum — Expenses. — The board shall hold such meetings as may be necessary for the orderly conduct of its business, with at least one (1) meeting in each calendar quarter, and from time to time on seventy-two (72) hours' notice of the chairman or of a majority of the members. At the first meeting of the board, and every two (2) years thereafter, the members of the board shall select a chairman and a vice-chairman. Three (3) members shall be necessary to constitute a quorum at any meeting and action of the majority of members present shall be the action of the board.

The members of the board of trustees of the society shall be compensated as provided by section 59-509(f), Idaho Code. [1970, ch. 145, § 3, p. 438; am. 1980, ch. 247, § 82, p. 582.]

67-4126. Powers and duties of board. — The board of trustees of the society shall have powers and duties as follows:

1. To appoint a director of the society as provided herein and advise him in the performance of his duties and formulate general policies affecting the society.

2. To encourage and promote interest in the history of Idaho and encourage membership in the society.

3. To collect for preservation and display artifacts and information illustrative of Idaho history, culture and society.

4. To print such publications and reports as may be deemed necessary.

5. To encourage creation of county historical societies and museums in the counties of Idaho.

6. To facilitate the use of Idaho records for official reference and historical research.

7. To accept from any state, county, or city, or any public official, any official books, records, documents, original papers, newspaper files, printed books, or portraits, not in current use. When such documents are so accepted, copies therefrom shall be made and certified under the seal of the society upon application of any person, which person shall pay for such copies reasonable fees established by the society.

8. To require that any state, county, or city, or any public official, deposit official books, records, documents, or original papers, not in current use, which are of definite historical importance, in the society for preservation and to provide methods whereby such materials, which have no significance, may be destroyed.

9. To establish such rules and regulations as may be necessary to discharge the duties of the society.

10. To employ such personnel as may be necessary for the administration of its duties in accordance with the standards prescribed by the personnel commission.

11. To have and use an official seal.

12. To delegate and provide subdelegation of any such authority.

13. To identify historic, architectural, archaeological, and cultural sites, buildings, or districts, and to coordinate activities of local historic preservation commissions. [1970, ch. 145, § 4, p. 438; am. 1974, ch. 234, § 1, p. 1596.]

67-4127. Director of the society appointed by board — Powers and duties. — A director of the society shall be appointed by the board of trustees, serve at the pleasure of the board, be qualified by reason of his education, training, experience and demonstrated ability to fill such position, and exercise the following powers and duties in addition to all other powers and duties inherent in the position or delegated to him or imposed upon him by the board:

1. To be a nonvoting member of the board of trustees and secretary thereto.

2. To be the administrative officer of the state historical society.

3. To prescribe such rules and regulations as may be necessary for the efficient operation of his office.

4. To serve as state historic preservation officer. [1970, ch. 145, § 5, p. 438; am. 1974, ch. 234, § 2, p. 1596.]

67-4128. Title to property vested in board. — All rights and title to property, real and personal, belonging to the historical society of the state of Idaho are hereby vested in the board of trustees and their successors. [1970, ch. 145, § 6, p. 438.]

67-4129. Board empowered to acquire and dispose of property. — The board of trustees of the society is empowered to acquire, by purchase or exchange, any property which in the judgment of the board is needful for the operation of the society, and to dispose of, by sale or exchange, any property which in the judgment of the board is not needful for the operation of the same. [1970, ch. 145, § 7, p. 438.]

PUBLIC RECORDS
(Idaho Code, 1982, s.67-5751, 67-5751a, 67-5752.)

67-5751. Records management. — The director of administration shall develop subject to the provisions of chapter 52, title 67, Idaho Code, rules and procedures pertaining to the management of all state records. "Records" shall mean; any document, book, paper, photograph, sound recording, or other material, regardless of physical form or characteristics, made or received pursuant to law or in connection with the transaction of official state business. Library and archive material made, acquired, or preserved solely for reference, exhibition, or historical purposes, extra copies of documents preserved only for convenience of reference, and stocks of publications and of processed documents are not included within the definition of records as used in this section.

The following rules and procedures shall be established:

(a) A rule pertaining to retention periods for all state records.

(b) A rule establishing a standard filing system for all state agencies.

(c) A rule prescribing conditions and procedures for destruction of state records.

(d) Procedures to ensure efficient utilization of manpower, building space, and supplies with regard to paper flow and forms usage.

(e) A rule pertaining to proper and efficient utilization of microfilming services. [I.C., § 67-5751, as added by 1974, ch. 34, § 2, p. 988.]

67-5751A. Historical records. — Upon the determination of the director of the department of administration that certain public records have no apparent official value but have historical value, those records shall be transferred to, and may constitute a part of, the collection of the state historical society. [I.C., § 67-5751A, as added by 1975, ch. 177, § 2, p. 482.]

67-5752. Records management manual. — The director of administration shall develop and distribute to all state agencies a record management manual containing all the rules and procedures developed for records management. Each state agency shall comply with rules and procedures promulgated. [I.C., § 67-5752, as added by 1974, ch. 34, § 2, p. 988.]

LEGISLATIVE COUNCIL
(Idaho Code, 1982, s.67-429.)

67-429. Powers and duties. — (1) It shall be the duty of the council to collect and compile information, to draft bills and to conduct research upon any subject which the legislature may authorize or direct or upon any subject which it may determine, provided that all activities of the council must be reasonably related to a legislative purpose. The legislature may make specific assignments to the council by a concurrent resolution approved by both houses. (2) The council may hold public hearings and it may authorize or direct any of its committees to hold public hearings on any matters within the jurisdiction of the council. (3) The council shall establish and maintain a legislative reference library. (4) For the purpose of conducting any study within the jurisdiction of the council, by resolution adopted by the affirmative vote of two thirds ($^2/_3$) of the entire membership of the council, the chairman of the council may subpoena witnesses, compel their attendance, take evidence and require the production of any books, papers, correspondence or other documents or records which the council deems relevant or material to any matter on which the council or any committee is conducting a study. (5) It shall be the duty of the council to superintend and administer the legislative space in the capitol building at all times, and to prepare such space when required for the sessions of the legislature, which shall include the provision of furniture and equipment. [1963, ch. 57, § 3, p. 222; am. 1967, ch. 365, § 3, p. 1054; am. 1977, ch. 306, § 1, p. 855.]

LIBRARY DISTRICTS
(Idaho Code, 1982, s.33-2701 to 33-2723.)

33-2701. Purpose and policy. — It is hereby declared to be the policy of the state of Idaho, as a part of the provisions for public education, to promote the establishment and development of free library service for all the people of Idaho. It is the purpose of this act to make more adequate provision for an informed electorate by integrating, extending, and adding to existing library services and resources in such manner that free local library service may be available to children in their formative years and to adults for their continuing education. [1963, ch. 188, § 1, p. 568.]

33-2702. Qualified elector. — Any person voting, or offering to vote, at an election to create a library district, add territory thereto, or elect trustees thereof, must be, at the time of the election, a resident of the area involved and an elector within the meaning of article 6, section 2 of the Constitution of the state of Idaho except that registration shall not be required. Each voter shall be required to execute an oath of election attesting his qualification, and file said oath with the board of election at the time he casts his ballot. [1963, ch. 188, § 2, p. 568; am. 1965, ch. 255, § 1, p. 648.]

33-2703. Library districts — Territory — Limitations. — A library district may be organized by vote of the qualified electors of the proposed district in an election called and held as provided by this chapter, with the following limitations:

a. The district may include incorporated or unincorporated territory or both, in one or more counties, but in any county in which the proposed district may lie it may include any of the area thereof except as may be excluded by this section, and as finally fixed and determined by the board of county commissioners.

b. The territory of the district shall be continuous, and no territory of an incorporated municipality shall be divided.

c. In the initial organization of the district, any governmental unit maintaining a tax-supported public library shall be excluded.

d. If, subsequent to the organization of a library district, any area thereof is annexed to a municipality which maintains a tax-supported library, such area shall cease to be a part of the library district and the board of trustees of said municipality shall so notify the board of county commissioners. [1963, ch. 188, § 3, p. 568; am. 1967, ch. 93, § 1, p. 198.]

33-2704. Petition — Verification. — A petition or petitions, signed by fifty (50) or more qualified electors residing in the proposed library district, giving the name of the proposed district, which shall include the words "free library," and describing the boundaries thereof and praying for the organization of the territory therein described as a free library, shall be filed with the clerk of the board of county commissioners of the county in which the proposed district is situate.

The petition or petitions shall be verified by at least one (1) qualified elector, which verification shall state that the affiant knows that all of the parties whose names are signed to the petition are qualified electors of the proposed district, and that their signatures to the petition were made in his presence. The verification may be made before any notary public. [1963, ch. 188, § 4, p. 568.]

33-2704A. Notice and public hearing.

a. When such petition or petitions are presented to the board of county commissioners and filed in the office of the clerk of such board, the board shall set the time for a hearing, which time shall be not less than three (3) nor more than six (6) weeks from the date of the presentation and filing of the petition. Notice of the time of hearing shall be published by said board once a week for two (2) weeks previous to the time set for the hearing, in a newspaper of general circulation within the county in which the proposed district is situated.

b. Said notice shall state that a library district is proposed to be organized, giving the proposed boundaries and name thereof, and that any resident elector or any taxpayer owning real property within the proposed boundaries of the proposed district may appear and be heard in regard to:

(1) the form of the petition;
(2) the genuineness of the signatures;
(3) the legality of the proceedings; and,
(4) any other matters in regard to the creation of the library district.

c. No later than five (5) days after the hearing, the board of county commissioners shall make an order thereon with or without modification, based upon the public hearing and their determination of whether such proposed library district would be in keeping with the declared public policy of the State of Idaho in regard to library districts as more particularly set forth in section 33-2701; and, shall accordingly fix the boundaries and certify the name of such proposed district in the order granting such petition. The boundaries so fixed shall be the boundaries of said district after its organization is completed as provided by this act. [I.C., § 33-2704A, as added by 1967, ch. 93, § 2, p. 198.]

33-2705. Conduct of election.

Upon the county commissioners having made the order referred to in subparagraph c, section 33-2704A, the clerk of the board of county commissioners shall cause to be published a notice of an election to be held for the purpose of determining whether or not the proposed library district shall be organized under the provisions of sections 33-2704 and 33-2704A. The date of this election shall be not later than sixty (60) days after the issuance of the above mentioned order. Whenever more than one petition is presented to the county commissioners calling for an election to create library districts, the first presented shall take precedence. Notice of said election shall be given, the election shall be conducted, and the returns thereof canvassed as provided for elections for the consolidation of school districts. The ballot shall contain the word "(Name) Library District — Yes" and "(Name) Library District — No," each followed by a box wherein the voter may express his choice by marking a cross "X." The board or boards of election shall make returns and certify the results to the boards of county commissioners within three (3) days after the election, and said board shall, within seven (7) days after the election, canvass the returns. If a majority of all votes cast be in the affirmative, the board shall enter an order declaring the library district established and designating its boundaries and name. [1963, ch. 188, § 5, p. 568; am. 1965, ch. 255, § 2, p. 648; am. 1967, ch. 93, § 3, p. 198.]

33-2706. Organization of library district embracing more than one county. — When the proposed library district embraces more than one county, the petition and procedure for praying for the organization of the district shall be carried forward in each such county as though that county were the only county affected. Each petition, however, shall designate the same county as the home county of the proposed district.

The board of county commissioners of said home county shall advise with the board of county commissioners in any other county affected to the end that the election shall be held in each county on the same day. The board of county commissioners in each county shall proceed in the conduct of the election as though the election were being held only in that county. After the canvass of the returns, the results in each other county shall be certified to the board of county commissioners of the home county, together with all ballots and tally sheets. Said board shall canvass all returns and certify the results of the election to the board of county commissioners of any other county affected. The proposal shall be deemed approved only if a majority of all votes cast in each county were cast in the affirmative. If this be the case, the board of county commissioners of the home county shall enter an order declaring the library district to be created, and defining its boundaries. A certified copy of said order shall be sent to the board of county commissioners of any other county affected, which shall enter such order in its minutes; and to the state library board. [1963, ch. 188, § 6, p. 27.]

33-2707. Addition of territory to a library district — Petitions and signatures — Election. — A county contiguous to a library district may become a part of said district by petition and election as herein, and hereinbefore, provided. The limitation of section 33-2703 shall be fully applicable.

A petition may arise as hereinbefore provided, in the county seeking to become a part of the library district. A true copy thereof shall be transmitted to the board of trustees of said district, and to the board of county commissioners of the home county of said district. The board of trustees of the library district may approve or disapprove such petition, and shall give notice of its decision to the board of county commissioners in each county affected.

When said notice carries the approval of the board of trustees of the district, the board of county commissioners in each county affected shall enter its order calling for an election on the question. Notice of the election shall be given, the election shall be conducted, and the returns thereof canvassed as provided in the case of the creation of a library district embracing more than one county. The ballot shall bear the question: "Shall _____ county become a part of the _____ library district ____ _____ Yes" and "Shall _____ county become a part of the _____ _____ library district _____ No," each followed by a box in which the voter may express his choice by marking a cross "X." The proposal shall be deemed approved only if the majority of the votes cast in the library district, and the majority of the votes cast in the county seeking to become a part thereof, are in the affirmative.

If the proposal has been approved by the majorities herein required, the board of county commissioners of the home county of the district shall enter its order amending the boundaries of the district, and a copy thereof shall be transmitted to the board of trustees of the library district, and to the board of county commissioners of the county in which the petition arose. Each such board shall enter said order in its record of proceedings. [1963, ch. 188, § 7, p. 568.]

33-2708. Existing tax-supported libraries may join library districts. — Any taxing district maintaining a tax-supported library under the provisions of law may have its area included in an established library district by majority vote of the qualified electors of such taxing district and of the established library district according to procedure set forth in section 33-2707 except that if the library district embrace territory in but one (1) county, all said proceedings shall be had in that county. In any election held for the purposes of this section, the area of not more than one (1) other taxing district may be added to the library district. [1963, ch. 188, § 8, p. 568.]

33-2709. Board of trustees — Selection — Number — Qualifications — Term — Oath — Appointment of first board. — Each library district shall be governed by a board of trustees of five (5) members elected or appointed as provided by law, who at the time of their selection and during their terms of office shall be qualified electors of the district and be representative of the several areas of the district. One (1) trustee shall be elected at each annual trustee election. The regular term of a trustee shall be for five (5) years, or until his successor has been elected and qualified. Within ten (10) days after his election or appointment a trustee shall qualify and assume the duties of his office as of the date of such qualification which shall be by taking the oath of office required of state officers, to be administered by one (1) of the present trustees or by a trustee retiring.

Following the initial establishment of a library district, the board of county commissioners of the home county within five (5) days shall appoint the members of the first board of trustees, who shall serve until the next annual election of trustees or until their successors are elected and qualified. Addition of new territory to an existing library district shall not be considered an initial establishment. Said first board of trustees shall be sworn by a member of the board of county commissioners of the home county of the district.

At its first meeting, and after each trustee election, the board shall organize and elect from its membership a chairman and such other officers as may be deemed necessary to conduct the affairs of the district.

Members of the board shall serve without salary but shall receive their actual and necessary expenses while engaged in business of the district. [1963, ch. 188, § 9, p. 568.]

33-2710. Board of trustees — Nomination and election. — The procedure for nomination and election of trustees of a library district shall be as provided for the nomination and election of trustees of a school district. This shall include notice requirements, conduct of election, qualifications of electors, provision for absentee voting, nominations, uniform date of election, and declaration and filling of vacancies. [I.C., § 33-2710, as added by 1980, ch. 231, § 2, p. 512.]

33-2710A. Board of trustees — One nomination — No election. — In any election for trustees if, after the expiration of the date for filing written nominations for the office of trustee, it appears that only one (1) qualified candidate has been nominated for each position to be filled, it shall not be necessary to hold an election, and the board of trustees shall within three (3) days after expiration of the date for filing written nominations declare such candidate elected as trustee, and the secretary shall immediately make and deliver to such person a certificate of election signed by him and bearing the seal of the district. The procedure set forth in this section shall not apply to any other library district election. [I.C., § 33-2710A, as added by 1980, ch. 232, § 1, p. 512.]

33-2711. Board of trustees — Meetings. — The regular meetings of the board of trustees shall be held once in each quarter, at such uniform day of such uniform month as the board of trustees shall determine at its annual meeting. Special or adjourned meetings may be held from time to time as the board may determine, but written notice thereof shall be given to the members at least two (2) days prior to the day of the meeting. A quorum shall consist of three (3) members, but a smaller number may adjourn. [1963, ch. 188, § 11, p. 568.]

33-2712. Powers and duties of the board of trustees. — The board of trustees of each library district shall have the following powers:

1. To make rules and regulations for its own government and that of the library or libraries under its control;

2. To establish and locate libraries, branch libraries or stations to serve the district and to provide suitable rooms, structures, facilities, furniture, apparatus and appliances necessary for the conduct thereof;

3. To acquire by purchase, devise, lease, or otherwise, and to own and hold real and personal property and to construct buildings for the use and purposes of the library district, and to sell, exchange or otherwise dispose of property real or personal, when no longer required by the district, and to insure the real and personal property of the district;

4. To accept gifts of real or personal property under such terms as may be a condition of the gift;

5. To purchase and distribute books, pamphlets, documents or publications;

6. To issue warrants in the manner specified for the issuance of warrants by school districts;

7. To invest any funds of the district in the manner specified for investment of funds by school districts, or in savings accounts insured by the federal deposit insurance corporation, to the extent of such insurance;

8. To pay necessary expenses of members of the library staff when on business of the district;

9. To exercise such other powers, not inconsistent with law, necessary for the effective use and management of the library. [1963, ch. 188, § 12, p. 568; am. 1965, ch. 255, § 3, p. 648.]

33-2713. Librarian and other employees. — The board of trustees of each library district shall appoint the chief librarian, who shall serve as the secretary of the board. With the recommendation of the chief librarian, the board shall employ such other persons as may be necessary in the administration of the affairs of the library district. The board may fix and pay their salaries and compensation, classify employees and adopt schedules of salaries; determine their number and prescribe their duties and discharge any librarian or other employee for cause. [1963, ch. 188, § 13, p. 568.]

33-2714. Taxes for the support of library district. — Any tax levied for library district purposes shall be a lien upon the property against which the tax is levied. The board of trustees shall determine and levy a tax in mills upon each dollar of assessed valuation of property within the district for the ensuing fiscal year as shall be required to satisfy all maturing bond, bond interest, and judgment obligations. For the maintenance and operation of the library district, the board of trustees may also levy upon the taxable property within the district a tax not to exceed three (3) mills. Said levies shall be certified to the clerk of the board of county commissioners of each county in which the district may lie, not later than the second Monday in September of each year. [1963, ch. 188, § 14, p. 568; am. 1965, ch. 255, § 6, p. 648; am. 1974, ch. 141, § 1, p. 1355.]

33-2715.   Treasurer. — The board of trustees of each library district shall appoint some qualified person in the library district, who may or may not be a member of the board of trustees, to act as treasurer of the library district. Such person shall, on taking office, give bond to the library district, with sureties approved by the board of trustees, in the amount of one thousand dollars ($1,000), which bond shall be paid for by the district, and shall be conditioned upon faithful performance of the duties of his office and his accounting for all moneys of the library district received by him or under his control. All moneys raised for the library district by taxation or received by the district from any other sources shall be paid over to him, and he shall disburse the funds of the district upon warrants drawn thereon by order of the board of trustees pursuant to vouchers approved by the board.

The treasurer shall deposit all moneys of the district in accordance with the Public Depository Law. [1963, ch. 188, § 15, p. 568.]

33-2716.   State treasurer trustee of library funds when required. — When the conditions of the grant or appropriation so require, the state treasurer shall serve as trustee of funds appropriated to the state from any appropriation made by the federal government, the state, or any other agency for providing and equalizing library service in Idaho. [1963, ch. 188, § 16, p. 568.]

33-2717.   Library districts — Public corporations. — Each library district shall be a public corporation, may sue and be sued in its corporate name and may contract and be contracted with. [1963, ch. 188, § 17, p. 568.]

33-2718.   Fiscal year — Annual reports — Audit. — The fiscal year of each library district shall commence on the first day of July of each year. The board of trustees of each library district shall annually, not later than the first day of September, file with the state library board a report of the operations of the district for the fiscal year just ended. The report shall be of such form and contain such information as the state library board may require, but in all cases must include a complete accounting of all financial transactions for the fiscal year being reported.

At intervals of not more than two (2) years the board of trustees of each library district shall cause to be made a full and complete audit of the books and accounts of the district, in form prescribed by the bureau of public accounts. Upon acceptance of the audit report by the board a copy thereof shall forthwith be filed with the bureau of public accounts, and a copy shall also be filed with the state library board. [1963, ch. 188, § 18, p. 568.]

33-2719.   Purchase and sale of library services — Contracts. — In lieu of establishing an independent library, the board of trustees may purchase specified library services by contract from any taxing unit, or public or private agency maintaining a library, providing that such unit or agency shall file an annual report with the board of trustees of the library district showing in detail the manner in which the funds of the library district have been spent.

The board of trustees of a library district may sell specified library services to any taxing unit, or public or private agency which agrees to make an acceptable annual appropriation for such services.

Any such purchase or sale of library services shall be under contract for a term of three years, which contract shall be automatically renewed at the end of said three-year period unless either party thereto gives notice not less than six months before the termination of any existing contract, of intention not to renew said contract. [1963, ch. 188, § 19, p. 568; am. 1965, ch. 255, § 4, p. 648.]

33-2720. Dissolution of library district. — A library district may be dissolved according to procedures followed in its original organization, but not earlier than five (5) years after the date of its establishment; provided, however, that a library district may be dissolved sooner if it has not received any ad valorem taxes for its operating budget or to satisfy any maturing bond, bond interest or judgment obligations during the district's first two (2) years of organization. If the library district embraces territory in more than one (1) county, an election for its dissolution shall be deemed approved only if a majority of the votes cast in each such county were cast in the affirmative. If, upon the canvass of ballots, it be determined that the proposition has been approved, the board of county commissioners of the home county shall enter its order to that effect and transmit a copy of said order to the board of county commissioners in any other county affected, and said order shall by them be made a matter of record. When any library district is dissolved, all unpaid taxes shall, when collected, revert to the general expense fund of the county where levied, and all property and assets of the library district shall be disposed of by the board of county commissioners of the home county. Receipts from the sale of assets shall be apportioned to the counties embraced in the library district in proportion to the assessed valuation of each which was included in the library district, and placed in the respective county general expense fund. [1963, ch. 188, § 20, p. 568; am. 1980, ch. 187, § 1, p. 414; am. 1981, ch. 305, § 1, p. 627.]

33-2721. Present library districts continued. — Any library district heretofore organized under any previous statute, now operating, is hereby confirmed and continued. Nothing herein contained shall affect the term of office of any trustee nor impair any contract, obligation or other act lawfully entered into under such statute. [1963, ch. 188, § 21, p. 568.]

33-2722. Alternate methods of organizing a library district. — An alternate method of organization of a library district may be initiated upon a petition or petitions, signed by resident electors equal in number to fifty-one per cent (51%) of those voting in the last gubernatorial election in the area involved.

Each petition shall be verified by an elector, which verification shall state that the affiant knows that all of the parties whose names are signed to the petition are electors of the proposed district and that their signatures to the petition were made in his presence. The verification may be made before any notary public.

Each petition shall give the name of the proposed district and describe the boundaries thereof.

On the filing with the clerk of the board of county commissioners of the county in which the proposed district is located, of such petition or petitions requesting the creation of a library district, the board of county commissioners shall thereupon by resolution declared [declare] that a petition to create a library district has been filed with the board and shall thereupon comply with subparagraphs a and b, section 33-2704A.

Upon the date fixed for the hearing the board of county commissioners shall canvass the petition or petitions for the purpose of determining that such petition or petitions have been signed by the required number of resident electors. The county commissioners shall make, after the hearing, a resolution in compliance with subparagraph c, section 33-2704A; such resolution shall be duly recorded and complete the creation of the district.

Within five (5) days from entry of the order creating a library district, the board of county commissioners shall appoint the members of the first board of trustees, who shall serve until the next annual election of trustees and until their successors are elected and qualified.

A library district established under this section shall in all succeeding matters function in accordance with provisions regarding the government of library districts as prescribed in this chapter. [I.C., § 33-2722, as added by 1965, ch. 255, § 5, p. 648; am. 1967, ch. 93, § 4, p. 198.]

33-2722A. Addition of a part of a county to an existing library district. — A part of a county which does not have a public or district library established under the provisions of law, but which is contiguous to an existing library district within said county, may become a part of said district by following the alternate method of organizing a library district provided in section 33-2722, Idaho Code.

The petition or petitions, to be signed by the resident electors of the area desiring to join the existing library district, shall state that the petitioners desire to have the described boundaries added to the "_____ Library District," and desire that the larger district formed thereby be known as the "_____ Library District."

A true copy of the petition shall be transmitted to the board of trustees of the library district which the petitioners seek to join. The board of trustees may approve or disapprove such petition, on the basis of concept, judgment on desirability of said expansion, and on proposed name. The trustees need not verify the names on the petition, but may for the purpose of entering the board's approval or disapproval assume that all signatures on the petition are valid.

The board of trustees shall give notice of its decision to the board of county commissioners. When said notice carries the approval of the board of trustees of the existing library district, the trustees shall forward the petitions to the clerk of the board of county commissioners, who shall verify the required signatures thereon, and shall file the petitions. Thereupon, the board of county commissioners shall proceed with the required hearing and resolution as outlined in sections 33-2722 and 33-2704A, Idaho Code.

In the order granting the petition and establishing the enlarged library district, the board of county commissioners shall amend the boundaries of the district to include the added territory, and shall certify the name of the enlarged district.

A copy of the said order shall be transmitted to the board of trustees of the library district, and to the Idaho state library board.

Such other notices as may be required by law shall be filed, including a legal description and map of altered boundaries to be filed with the state tax commission within ten (10) days of the effective date of the change.

Addition of new territory to an existing library district shall not be considered an initial establishment. The existing board of trustees shall continue to serve for the terms for which elected. When a vacancy occurs appointments shall be made as provided in section 33-2710, Idaho Code. [I.C., § 33-2722A, as added by 1973, ch. 102, § 2, p. 172.]

33-2722B. Adjustment of boundary lines of library districts. — When there are two (2) or more library districts, which have at least one (1) common boundary, established in one (1) county, the boards of trustees of said library districts, meeting together, may determine that it is in the best interest of library service in the county that the boundary lines be adjusted, as herein provided.

The boards of trustees shall jointly prepare a petition describing the boundaries of the existing library districts, the names of the existing library districts, and praying for the reorganization of the territory therein described as one (1) or more library districts to be known as the "_____ Library District or Districts" and with boundaries as set forth in the petition.

The petition shall be signed by all members of the boards of trustees of the library districts involved in the boundary adjustment.

The petition shall be forwarded to the clerk of the board of county commissioners, who shall verify the signatures of the trustees thereon, and shall file the petition. Thereupon, the board of county commissioners shall proceed with the hearing and resolution as outlined in section [sections] 33-2722 and 33-2704A, Idaho Code, for the organization of a library district.

In the order granting the petition and adjusting the boundaries, the board of county commissioners shall certify the new boundaries and the name of the district or districts.

A copy of the said order shall be transmitted to the board of trustees of the library districts involved, and to the Idaho state library board.

Such other notices as may be required by law shall be filed, including a legal description and map of altered boundaries to be filed with the state tax commission within ten (10) days of the effective date of the change.

Following the boundary adjustment, the board of county commissioners within five (5) days shall take action to reaffirm members of the board of trustees, or to appoint members of the board or boards, who may be chosen from the members of the boards initiating the boundary adjustment. These trustees shall serve until the next annual election of trustees or until their successors are elected and qualified. The board or boards of trustees shall be sworn by a member of the board of county commissioners.

If the property and assets of a library district become a matter of dispute, the state library board shall make the final decision as to their disposition, in accordance with procedures outlined in section 33-2720, Idaho Code. [I.C., § 33-2722B, as added by 1973, ch. 102, § 3, p. 172.]

33-2722C. Notice of filing of petition or petitions for organizing a library district, for adding to or adjusting boundaries of library districts — Confirmation of existing library districts. — When a petition or petitions are filed with the board of county commissioners requesting the creation of a library district, the addition of a part of a county to an existing library district, or the adjustment of boundary lines of library districts, as provided in chapter 27, title 33, Idaho Code, the sending of post card notices as outlined in section 31-863, Idaho Code, shall have no application. All existing library districts on the effective date of this act organized pursuant to chapter 27, title 33, Idaho Code, are hereby confirmed in organization and operation, notwithstanding that the county commissioners may not have caused post card notices to be sent as provided in section 31-863, Idaho Code. [I.C., § 33-2722C, as added by 1973, ch. 102, § 4, p. 172.]

33-2723. Bond election. — The purposes for which bonds may be issued shall be: To acquire, purchase, or improve a library site or sites; to build a library or libraries, or other building or buildings; to demolish or remove buildings; to add to, remodel or repair any existing building; to furnish and equip any building or buildings, including all facilities and appliances necessary to maintain and operate the buildings of the library; and to purchase motor vehicles for use as bookmobiles.

The library district may issue bonds in an amount not to exceed four-tenths percent (.4%) of the market value for assessment purposes of property within the district, less any aggregate outstanding indebtedness.

The board of trustees of any library district, upon approval of a majority thereof, may call a bond election on the question as to whether the board shall be empowered to issue negotiable coupon bonds of the district in an amount and for a period of time to be stated in the notice of election. The notice of bond election, the qualification of bond electors, the conduct of the election, the canvass of election and determination of the result of election, the issuance of bonds, the expenditure of bond proceeds and the repayment of the bonds shall all be determined and done in accordance with the laws of Idaho with respect to the authorization and issuance of bonds by school districts. [I.C., § 33-2723, as added by 1965, ch. 255, § 5, p. 648; am. 1980, ch. 350, § 16, p. 887.]

REGIONAL LIBRARY SYSTEMS
(Idaho Code, 1982, s.33-2609 to 33-2616.)

33-2609. Regional library systems — Purpose — Boundaries. — It is the purpose of this act to provide a method by which the library boards which govern Idaho's libraries, now or hereafter established in accordance with the Idaho Code, may contract to form regional library systems, in order to provide improved library and information services for residents of a multi-county region. The boundaries for library regions in Idaho shall be established by the Idaho state library board. [1974, ch. 74, § 1, p. 1156.]

33-2610. Definitions. — As used in this act, unless the context otherwise requires:

(a) "Library board" means the five (5) citizens appointed, or elected, to govern a public library, a school community library, or a library district, in accordance with chapters 26 and 27, title 33, Idaho Code.

(b) "Participating board" or "participating library" means a board or library or district which is cooperating and participating in a regional library system.

(c) "Region" means that geographic area, with boundaries established by the state library board, wherein library units are encouraged to work together.

(d) "Regional system" means two (2) or more library boards formally contracting a system approved by the state library board, officially designated as a regional library system under this act, and therein working together in specific efforts to extend and improve library services to their resident constituents.

(e) "System board" means the governing board comprised of representatives of library boards in a regional system, and which is authorized to direct and plan library service for a regional system to the extent and in the manner provided by this act. [1974, ch. 74, § 2, p. 1156.]

33-2611. Petition for establishment. — Any two (2) or more library boards may petition the state library board for the establishment of a regional system. Such petition shall be prepared in cooperation with the state librarian, on forms provided by the state library, and shall include but shall not be limited to the following information:

(a) A statement of purpose and an outline of the proposed program of the regional system.

(b) A list of the participating libraries, with a listing of the current tax levy and budget of each such participant; the names and addresses of the members of each library board, and a letter or resolution from each such board regarding participation in the regional system.

(c) A list of the counties in the geographic region as a whole, the number of persons who are within taxing districts supporting existing libraries, and the number of persons outside such districts but within a county in the region, and thus potentially eligible for service from the regional system being established.

(d) Proposed number of persons to be on the initial system board of directors.

(e) Proposed headquarters for the regional system, accompanied by a copy of a resolution by the governing authority for that library approving its designation as headquarters and, if a member of the staff of the headquarters is to be the administrator of the system, including approval of such designation.

The state library board shall consider any petition presented to it as provided in this act, and if it approves such petition it shall adopt a resolution officially designating such particular regional library system, describing the territory thereof, and designating the headquarters and the initial number of directors for the system board. [1974, ch. 74, § 3, p. 1156.]

33-2612.   System board of directors. — Each regional system shall be governed by a board of directors, to be selected by and from the governing boards of the participating libraries.

Initially, as the system is formed, each participating library shall be entitled to one (1) representative on the system board, and those libraries legally serving a population base of more than ten thousand (10,000) shall also be entitled to a second representative.

Within two (2) weeks after receiving notice of approval of a petition for establishment, as provided for under this act, the board of each participating library shall select its representative or representatives, and certify the names and addresses of such representatives to the state librarian.

As additional libraries, now or hereafter established, petition to join the system, the board shall not exceed twenty-five (25) in number. When the board members total twenty-five (25), or earlier with the unanimous agreement of the participating boards, the system board shall develop a plan for equitable rotation of trustees, while retaining representation from a library in each county. The designated headquarters for the system shall always have representation on the board.

At their first meeting the members of the system board shall divide themselves by lot into terms of one (1) to five (5) years. Thereafter, all vacancies shall be filled in the same manner as the original appointments, and appointments to complete an unexpired term shall be for the residue of the term only.

No member of any system board shall serve on the system board for more than five (5) consecutive years, and in no event shall service on the system board exceed the term of office of the incumbent on the governing board of the participating library which he represents.

The system board shall annually elect from its membership a chairman and such other officers as it may deem necessary to conduct the affairs of the system.

Members of the system board may receive from the regional system their actual and necessary expenses while engaged in business of said system. [1974, ch. 74, § 4, p. 1156.]

33-2613. Powers and duties of the system board. — The system board shall serve as a liaison agency between the participating libraries and their governing bodies and library boards. The system board shall make such bylaws, rules and regulations as may be necessary for its own government and that of the regional system, none of which shall deprive any participating library board of any of its powers or property.

The system board shall have the following powers and responsibilities, all of which relate to the functioning of the regional system and the management and control of its funds and property;

(a) To develop a long range plan of service for the regional system, and annually to submit to the state library board any changes in said long range plan, and a detailed plan of proposed system development and service for the following year.

(b) To provide improved library service for residents of the regional system, in cooperation with participating libraries, and to this end to purchase books and other library materials, supplies and equipment, for the system services, and to employ such personnel as the system board finds necessary.

(c) To set the administrator's hours and rate of compensation for regional system duties, and to delegate such administrative powers as the board deems in the best interest of the system.

(d) To enter into contracts to receive service from or to give service to other libraries, or agencies, within the state or interstate, and to file copies of such contracts with the state library board.

(e) To be a public corporation, as is provided for library districts, and to contract in the name of the "Board of directors of the _____ regional library system, Idaho" and in that name to sue and be sued and to take any action authorized by law.

(f) To acquire by purchase, lease, or otherwise, and to own and hold real and personal property and to construct buildings for the use of the regional system, and to sell, exchange or otherwise dispose of property real or personal when no longer required by the system, and to insure the real and personal property of the system.

(g) To have control of the expenditure of all funds of the regional system, to accept by gift or donation any funds and real or personal property under such terms as may be a condition of the gift.

(h) To exercise such other powers, not inconsistent with law, necessary for the effective use and management of the regional system. [1974, ch. 74, § 5, p. 1156.]

33-2614. Finance of regional systems — Budgets — Participating and nonparticipating units. — Each regional system may be financed by any combination of available funds, federal, state, local, public and/or private. Counties, cities and library districts are hereby authorized and empowered to join in the creation, development, operation and maintenance of regional systems, and to appropriate and allocate funds for the support of such systems. All funds collected or contributed for the support of each regional system shall be controlled and administered under the direction of the system board, following procedures outlined in the library district statutes, and as directed by the state library board.

(a) PARTICIPATING UNITS. Participating boards shall continue to control the funds appropriated or contributed for the support of the participating libraries, but may expend all or any part thereof for library services to be furnished by the regional system. Each participating board shall prepare its own annual budget as required by the Idaho Code, and said budget may include anticipated revenues or expenditures for regional system services. Tax levies made pursuant to each such budget shall be certified as provided by law.

(b) SYSTEM BUDGET. Each system board shall prepare a preliminary budget for the system for the coming year, and shall by the last day of October forward said budget to the boards of participating libraries. This budget shall be published, and a hearing held thereon before the last day of November.

(c) NON-PARTICIPATING AREAS. The system board shall also prepare a list of those areas within each county of the library region wherein public libraries, library districts, school-community libraries, or association libraries are not maintained as authorized in the Idaho Code. Such lists shall be forwarded to the state library board and to the board of county commissioners of each affected county. The system board shall include in its preliminary budget an estimate of the kinds of services which the system could provide to those areas without established libraries, and the cost of such services, and shall forward this to the appropriate boards of county commissioners. [1974, ch. 74, § 6, p. 1156.]

33-2615. Addition to or withdrawal from a regional system. — (1) After the establishment of a regional system as provided in this act, the board of any library which is not a part of the system, and which is within the boundaries of a library region as established by the Idaho state library board, may petition the state library board for addition to the regional system.

Petitions for addition shall be prepared and processed as provided in this act for initial petitions, except that prior approval in writing shall be obtained by the petitioning board from the regional system board, and shall be attached to the petition when it is submitted to the state library board.

(2) After the establishment of a regional system as provided in this act, a participating library board may petition the state library board for withdrawal from the system. A petition for withdrawal must be received by the state library board at least sixty (60) days before the end of the fiscal year of the system.

All assets of a participating library remain the property of that library, and if a unit withdraws from a system the disposal of the joint assets of the system shall be determined by the state library board, who shall give consideration to such items as the amount of funds raised from each unit of the system, and the ability of the units to make further use of such property or equipment for library purposes. [1974, ch. 74, § 7, p. 1156.]

33-2616. Administration of act by state library board. — The Idaho state library board shall administer the provisions of this act, and shall adopt such rules and regulations as are necessary for approval of regional system petitions, review and amendment of regional system plans and contracts, and such other matters as the state library board may deem advisable. [1974, ch. 74, § 8, p. 1156.]

MUNICIPAL LIBRARIES
(Idaho Code, 1982, s.33-2602 to 33-2608.)

33-2602. Cities may establish libraries — Tax levies. — The common council of every city and of every village of the state of Idaho shall have power to establish a public library and reading room, and for such purpose may annually levy and cause to be collected, as other taxes are, a tax not exceeding five (5) mills on the dollar of the taxable property of such city or village, to constitute a library fund, which shall be kept by the treasurer separate and apart from other moneys of the city or village, and be used exclusively for the purchase of books, periodicals, necessary furniture and fixtures, and whatever is required for the maintenance of such library and reading room, provided that every city and village shall have power to contract for specified library service with an existing library district and/or become part of an existing library district, by majority vote of the qualified electors of such city or village at an election to be called and conducted by the city or village council or other governing board thereof, such election to be called and held in accordance with the provisions of chapter 17, title 50, Idaho Code. [1901, p. 3, § 1; am. R.C., § 675; reen. 1911, ch. 159, § 177, p. 551; reen. C.L. 38:291; am. 1919, ch. 137, § 1, p. 433; C.S., § 1035; I.C.A., § 32-2101; am. 1945, ch. 100, § 1, p. 150; am. 1955, ch. 130, § 1, p. 268; am. 1963, ch. 121, § 1, p. 350.]

33-2603. Board of trustees — Appointment — Term of office — Vacancies — Compensation. — For the government of such library and reading room there shall be a board of five (5) library trustees appointed by the council of such city or village from among the citizens thereof at large, and not more than one member of the council of such city or village shall, at any time, be a member of said board. Such trustees shall hold their office for five (5) years from the date of appointment, and until their successors are appointed, but upon their first appointment they shall divide themselves at their first meeting, by lot, into five (5) classes: one member shall form the first class and shall serve for one (1) year from the date of appointment; one member shall form the second class and shall serve for two (2) years from the date of appointment; one member shall form the third class and shall serve for three (3) years from the date of appointment; one member shall form the fourth class and shall serve for four (4) years from the date of appointment; and one member shall form the fifth class and shall serve for five (5) years from the date of appointment. All vacancies shall be reported to the proper council within five (5) days by its trustees, and shall be filled by appointment in the same manner as appointments are originally made. Appointments to complete an unexpired term shall be for the residue of the term only. No compensation shall be paid or allowed to any trustee in any manner whatsoever. [1901, p. 3, § 3; reen. R.C., § 677; am. 1911, ch. 159, § 179. p. 552; reen. C.L. 38:293; C.S., § 1037; I.C.A., § 32-2103; am. 1959, ch. 19, § 3, p. 40.]

33-2604. Organization and powers of trustees. — Said trustees shall, immediately after their appointment, meet and organize by the election of one of their number president, and by the election of such other officers as they may deem necessary. They shall make and adopt such bylaws, rules and regulations for their own guidance and for the government of the library and reading room as may be expedient. They shall have the exclusive control of the expenditure of all moneys collected for the library fund, and the supervision, care, and custody of the room or buildings construed, leased or set apart for that purpose; and such money shall be drawn from the treasury by the proper officers, upon properly authenticated vouchers of the board of trustees, without otherwise being audited. They may, with the approval of the common council, lease and occupy, or purchase or erect on purchased ground, an appropriate building: provided, that no more than one-half (½) of the income in any one (1) year can be set apart in said year for such purchase of building. They may appoint a librarian and assistants, and prescribe rules for their conduct. [1901, p. 3, § 4; am. R.C., § 678; am. 1911, ch. 159, § 180, p. 553; reen. C.L. 38:294; C.S. § 1038; I.C.A., § 32-2104; am. 1959, ch. 19, § 4, p. 40.]

33-2605. Libraries to be free — Rules and regulations. — Every library and reading room established under sections 33-2602 — 33-2608 shall be forever free for the use of the inhabitants of the city, village, or school district where located, always subject to such reasonable rules and regulations as the library board may find necessary to adopt and publish in order to render the use of the library and reading room of the greatest benefit to the greatest number, and they may exclude and cut off from the use of said library and reading room any and all persons who shall wilfully violate such rules. [1901, p. 3, § 5: reen. R.C., § 679; reen. 1911, ch. 159, § 181, p. 553; reen. C.L. 38:295; C. S., § 1039; I.C.A., § 32-2105.]

33-2606. Reports of trustees. — Said board of trustees shall annually and no later than the first day of January of each year, file with the state library board in the office of the state librarian, a report of the operations of the library for the fiscal year just ended, stating the condition of their trust, the various sums of money received from the library fund and from all sources, and how much has been expended, the number of books and periodicals on hand, and the number added by purchase, gift, or otherwise during the year, the number lost or missing, the number of books loaned out, and the general character of such books, with such other statistics, information and suggestions as they may deem of general interest, and the state library board may require. [1901, p. 3, § 6; reen. R.C., § 680; am. 1911, ch. 159, § 182, p. 553; reen. C.L. 38:296; C.S., § 1040; I.C.A., § 32-2106; am. 1959, ch. 19, § 5, p. 40; am. 1981, ch. 85, § 1, p. 118.]

33-2607. Donations to library. — All persons desirous of making donations of money, personal property or real estate for the benefit of such library, shall have the right to vest the title to the same in the board of trustees created under this chapter, to be held and controlled by said board, when accepted according to the terms of the deed or gift, devise or bequest of such property; and as to such property the said board shall be held and considered to be the special trustees. [1901, p. 3, § 7; reen. R.C., § 681; am. 1911, ch. 159, § 183, p. 554; reen. C.L. 38:297; C.S., § 1041; I.C.A., § 32-2107; am. 1959, ch. 19, § 6, p. 40.]

33-2608. Taxes for existing libraries — Definitions. — In case a free subscription library has been established in any city or incorporated village, and duly incorporated and organized, the council may levy a tax for its support, as provided in sections 33-2602 — 33-2608, without change in the organization of such library association: provided, it becomes a free library. The sums so raised shall be duly paid to the officer duly authorized to receive the same, and shall be under the control of said library association: provided, that if at any time the said library association ceases to exist, or for any reason fails to provide a free circulating library as required by the provisions of this chapter, the books and other property accumulated from the proceeds of the levy herein authorized shall become the property of the city or village, and be subject to the control of the council as herein provided.

In this chapter, unless the context otherwise requires, "library" includes libraries with branches, loans, reference, traveling and reading room department, lectures and museums; "city" includes towns and villages; "council" means the legislative body of an incorporated city, town or village; "mayor" means the chief executive officer of an incorporated city, town or village. [1901, p. 3, § 8; am. R.C., § 682; am. 1911, ch. 159, § 184, p. 554; reen. C.L. 38:298; C.S., § 1042; I.C.A, § 32-2108.]

SCHOOL DISTRICT LIBRARIES
(Idaho Code, 1982, s.33-2601.)

33-2601. School-community libraries. — The board of trustees of any school district in which is situated no incorporated town or village having a population in excess of one thousand (1,000), and in which no public library is maintained under any other provision of law, shall, upon petition of twenty (20) or more school district electors, submit to the school district electors of the district the question whether there shall be a public library established by the district for the benefit of the citizens thereof.

The election on the question shall be held at the same time as the election of school district trustees, next following the filing of said petition, and notice shall be given, the election conducted, and the returns canvassed, as provided in sections 33-401 through 33-406, Idaho Code.

If a majority of the school district electors voting in said election vote in favor of the question, the board of trustees of the school district is authorized to levy annually thereafter, upon the assessed value of taxable property in the school district, a tax not to exceed three (3) mills for the purpose of establishing and maintaining such library and the procuring of suitable building or rooms therefor.

The board of trustees of any school district which establishes a public library under the provisions of this section shall perform the duties required of, and have the power and authority granted to, the council, commissioners, or board of trustees of any city or village under the provisions of law relating to library districts, and the treasurer of the school district shall serve as treasurer for said public library.

The board of trustees of the school district, serving as the board of trustees of the library, may contract for specified services with an existing library district or public library, and may submit to the school district electors of the district, at an election called and conducted as provided herein but without precedent petition, the question whether the public library established hereunder shall become a part of an existing library district organized under the provisions of law. [1963, ch. 13, § 96, p. 27; am. 1975, ch. 105, § 1, p. 215.]

SCHOOL LIBRARIES
(Idaho Code, 1982, s.33-512, s.33.1201, s.33.1212.)

33-512. Government of schools. — The board of trustees of each school district shall have the following powers and duties:

*   *   *

8. To equip and maintain a suitable library or libraries in the school or schools and to exclude therefrom, and from the schools, all books, tracts, papers, and catechisms of sectarian nature;

[1963, ch. 13, § 62, p. 27; am. 1972, ch. 9, § 1, p. 13; am. 1975, ch. 107, § 1, p. 218; am. 1980, ch. 198, § 1, p. 458.]

33-1201. Certificate required. — Every person who is employed to serve in any elementary or secondary school in the capacity of teacher, supervisor, administrator, education specialist, school nurse or school librarian shall be required to have and to hold a certificate issued under authority of the state board of education, valid for the service being rendered; except that the state board of education may authorize endorsement for use in Idaho, for not more than five (5) years, certificates valid in other states when the qualifications therefor are not lower than those required for an Idaho certificate.

No certificate shall be required of a student attending any teacher training institution, who shall serve as a practice teacher in a classroom under the supervision of a certificated teacher, and who is jointly assigned by such teacher-training institution and the governing board of a district or a public institution, and approved by the state board of education, to perform practice teaching in a non-salaried status. Those students attending a teacher-training institution of another state and who serve as a non-salaried practice teacher in an Idaho school district shall be registered by that school district and approved by the state board of education.

A student, while serving as a practice teacher under the supervision of a certificated teacher, shall be accorded the same liability insurance coverage by the school district being served as that accorded a certificated teacher in the same district, and shall comply with all rules and regulations of the school district or public institution while acting as such practice teacher. [1963, ch. 13, § 143, p. 27; am. 1975, ch. 45, § 1, p. 84.]

33-1212. Renewable contract. — During the third full year of continuous employment by the same school district, including any specially chartered district, each certificated employee named in subsection 13 of section 33-1001, Idaho Code, and each school nurse and school librarian shall be evaluated for a renewable contract and shall, upon having been offered a contract for the next ensuing year, having given notice of acceptance of renewal and upon signing a contract for a fourth full year, be placed on a renewable contract status with said school district, until the age of sixty-five (65) years is attained, and subject to the provisions included in this chapter.

Except as otherwise provided, each such certificated employee, school nurse, or school librarian shall have the right to automatic renewal of contract by giving notice, in writing, of acceptance of renewal. Such notice shall be given to the board of trustees of the school district then employing such person not later than the 1st day of May preceding the expiration of the

term of the current contract. Except as otherwise provided by this paragraph, the board of trustees shall notify each person entitled to be employed
on a renewable contract of the requirement that such person must give the
notice hereinabove and that failure so to do may be interpreted by the board
as a declination of the right to automatic renewal or the offer of another
contract. Such notification shall be made, in writing, not later than the 10th
day of April, in each year, except to those persons to whom the board, prior
to said date, has sent proposed contracts for the next ensuing year, or to
whom the board has given the notice required by section 33-1213, Idaho
Code.

Any contract automatically renewed under the provisions of this section
shall be for the same length of the term stated in the current contract and
at a salary no lower than that specified therein, to which shall be added such
increments as may be determined by the statutory or regulatory rights of
such employee by reason of training, or service, or both.

Nothing herein shall prevent the board of trustees from offering a renewed
contract increasing the salary of any certificated person, from reassigning
administrative or supervisory employees to classroom teaching duties with
appropriate reduction of salaries from pre-existing contracts.

Before a board of trustees can determine not to renew the contract of any
certificated person whose contract would otherwise be automatically
renewed, or to renew the contract of any such person at a reduced salary,
such person shall be entitled to a probationary period. This period of probation shall be preceded by a written notice from the board of trustees with
reasons for such probationary period and with provisions for adequate supervision and evaluation of the person's performance during the probationary
period. Such period of probation shall not affect the person's renewable
contract status. [1963, ch. 13, § 154, p. 27; am. 1973, ch. 126, § 2, p. 238; am.
1981, ch. 140, § 1, p. 242.]

COUNTY LAW LIBRARIES
(Idaho Code, 1982, s.31-825.)

31-825. Maintenance of county law library.—To contract to purchase and to purchase and provide for care by clerk of district court
of such law books and pamphlets as said commissioners may judge
from time to time necessary for use of the district court and the
county officials and bar of the county, and to provide for the care of all
such books and pamphlets as may be donated or loaned to the county
from time to time. [R. C., § 1917x, as added by 1917, ch. 135, § 1, p.
445; reen. C. L., § 1917y; C. S., § 3440; I. C. A., § 30-731.]

TAX EXEMPTION
(Idaho Code, 1982, State Constitution, Art. 7, s.4.)

§ 4. Public property exempt from taxation.—The property of the
United States, except when taxation thereof is authorized by the United

States, the state, counties, towns, cities, villages, school districts, and other municipal corporations and public libraries shall be exempt from taxation.

Idaho library laws are reprinted from the IDAHO CODE published by Bobbs-Merrill Co., Inc., Indianapolis, Indiana.

ILLINOIS

STATE LIBRARY
(Smith-Hurd Illinois Annotated Statutes, 1982,
Chap. 128, s.101-113, 118.121.)

101. Short title

§ 1. Short title. This Act shall be known and may be cited as "The State Library Act."

Laws 1939, p. 697, § 1. Amended by P.A. 77–1690, § 1, eff. Jan. 1, 1972.

102. Secretary of State to be librarian

§ 2. Secretary of State is State Librarian. The Secretary of State shall be the State Librarian of the State Library, shall have the direction and control thereof and he shall appoint a Director of the State Library and such other subordinate officers, personnel and other employees as may be necessary to carry out the provisions of this Act. He may make, amend and enforce such rules and regulations in relation to the care, arrangement and use of books, maps, charts, papers, furniture and other things belonging to the State Library as he may deem proper. Any rule or regulation made or amended hereunder shall be filed with the Office of Secretary of State.

Laws 1939, p. 697, § 2. Amended by P.A. 77–1690, § 1, eff. Jan. 1, 1972.

103. Declaration of policy—State Library

§ 3. Declaration of policy—State Library. It is the policy of the State of Illinois, to promote, support, implement and maintain library services on a State level for all State Officers, Offices, the General Assembly, the Judiciary and all State agencies, bodies and commissions, and to promote, support and implement library services on a statewide basis. It is the responsibility of government at all levels to promote, support, implement and maintain library services for the cultural, educational and economic development of the State of Illinois and of the inhabitants of the State of Illinois.

Laws 1939, p. 697, § 3, added by P.A. 77–1690, § 1, eff. Jan. 1, 1972.

104. Regional library districts

§ 4. Regional library districts. The State shall be divided into six regional library districts as follows:

District 1—Jo Daviess, Stevenson, Winnebago, Boone, McHenry, Lake, Carroll, Ogle, DeKalb, Whiteside, Lee, Rock Island, Henry, Bureau, LaSalle, Kendall, Stark, Putnam, Marshall, Grundy.

District 2—Kane, Cook, DuPage, Will.

District 3—Kankakee, Livingston, Iroquois, McLean, Ford, Vermilion, Champaign, DeWitt, Piatt, Macon, Christian, Shelby, Moultrie, Douglas, 'Edgar, Coles, Clark, Cumberland.

District 4—Mercer, Knox, Peoria, Woodford, Tazewell, Fulton, Warren, Henderson, Hancock, McDonough, Adams, Schuyler, Mason, Logan, Menard, Cass, Brown, Pike, Morgan, Sangamon, Scott, Greene, Calhoun, Jersey.

District 5—Macoupin, Montgomery, Madison, Bond, Fayette, Effingham, Jasper, Crawford, Lawrence, Richland, Clay, Marion, Clinton, St. Clair, Monroe, Washington, Jefferson, Perry, Randolph.

District 6—Jackson, Franklin, Wayne, Edwards, Wabash, White, Hamilton, Gallatin, Saline, Williamson, Union, Johnson, Pope, Hardin, Alexander, Pulaski, Massac.

Laws 1939, p. 697, § 3. Renumbered § 4 and amended by P.A. 77–1690, § 1, eff. Jan. 1, 1972.

105. State Library Advisory Committee

§ 5. State Library Advisory Committee. There is hereby created an Advisory Library Committee whose duty it shall be to make recommendations concerning the policies and management of the State Library.

The Committee shall consist of 19 persons appointed by the State Librarian, and he may take into consideration the recommendations of the Illinois Library Association and other similar organizations. The appointments shall consist of the following:

1—Educator in the library field;
1—Institutional Librarian;
1—Special Librarian;
2—School Librarians;
2—Academic Librarians;
6—Library Directors of Library Systems or Local Public Libraries; and
6—Citizens.

Additional persons may be made ex officio members of the Committee, but without voting powers.

The Director of the State Library shall serve as Secretary of the Committee but may vote only to break tie votes.

The Advisory Committee shall elect its own chairman and vice chairman, and committee members shall serve without compensation but may be reimbursed for expenses incurred as members of the committee.

Each committee member shall serve for a term of 3 years, or until his successor is appointed, and the State Librarian may stagger the terms. No person shall serve for more than 2 consecutive 3-year terms.

Laws 1939, p. 697, § 4. Renumbered § 5 and amended by P.A. 77–1690, § 1, eff. Jan. 1, 1972.

106. Responsibilities and duties of the Committee

§ 6. Responsibilities and duties of the Committee. The Advisory Committee has the responsibilities and duties to make recommendations to the State Librarian as follows:

(a) General policies of the State Library;

(b) Budget policies to the State Librarian as it pertains to the annual appropriations for the State Library;

(c) Such library standards for all public libraries required by federal law or regulation to administer federal aid;

(d) Policies of the State-funded library systems; and

(e) Policies of federally-funded library programs.

The committee may further assist in communicating the goals, plans, policies and work of the State Library to all governmental officials and the general public. Laws 1939, p. 697, § 6, added by P.A. 77–1690, § 1, eff. Jan. 1, 1972.

107. Purpose of the State Library

§ 7. Purpose of the State Library. The Illinois State Library shall:

(a) Maintain a library for State officials and employees of the State, especially of informational material pertaining to the phases of their work and to provide for them material for general reading and study.

(b) Establish and operate a Governmental Research Service of the Illinois State Library. This service shall make available printed and other materials that pertain to public and governmental affairs. State Officers, members of the General Assembly, members of their staffs, and other State employees shall have access to these materials.

(c) Maintain and provide research library services for all State agencies.

(d) Administer The Illinois Library System Act, as amended.

(e) Administer the law relating to Interstate Library Compacts.

(f) Function as a Research and Reference Center pursuant to The Illinois Library System Act, as amended.

(g) Promote and develop cooperative library network operating regionally or statewide for providing effective coordination of the library resources of public, academic, school, and special libraries, and to promote and develop information centers for improved supplemental library services for special library clientele served by each type of library or center.

(h) Administer grants of federal library funds pursuant to federal law and requirements.

(i) Be a supplementary source through the State-funded library systems for reading materials unavailable in the local libraries.

(j) Assist local libraries in their plans of cooperation for better work and library services in their communities and to loan them books and other library materials through the State-funded library systems in furtherance of this object.

(k) Be ready to help local groups in developing a program by which library service can be arranged for in rural communities and rural schools now without such service, and to develop standards for libraries.

(l) Be a clearing house, in an advisory capacity, for questions and problems pertaining to the administration and functioning of public and school libraries in Illinois and to publish booklets and pamphlets to implement this service.

(m) To seek the opinion of the Attorney General for legal questions pertaining to public libraries and their function as governmental agencies.

(n) Contract with any other library or library agency to carry out the purposes of the State Library.

(o) Collect, compile, preserve and publish public library statistical information.

(p) Compile and publish the annual report of local public libraries and library systems submitted to the State Librarian pursuant to law.

(q) Conduct and arrange for library training programs for library personnel, library directors and others involved in library services.

(r) Make and publish an annual report for each fiscal year.

(s) Review all rules of all State agencies adopted in compliance with the codification system prescribed by the Secretary of State. Such review shall be for the purposes and include all the powers and duties provided in Section 7 of "The Illinois Administrative Procedure Act", as now or hereafter amended. The State Library shall cooperate with the Legislative Information System to insure the accuracy of the text of the rules maintained pursuant to Section 5.08 of "An Act in relation to a Legislative Information System", as now or hereafter amended.

Laws 1939, p. 697, § 5, eff. July 13, 1939. Renumbered § 7 and amended by P.A. 77-1690, § 1, eff. Jan. 1, 1972. Amended by P.A. 79-1459, § 1, eff. Oct. 1, 1976; P.A. 81-1348, § 3, eff. July 16, 1980.

107.1. Governmental Research Service Advisory Committee

§ 7.1. Governmental Research Service Advisory Committee. There is created a Governmental Research Service Advisory Committee consisting of the Speaker of the House, the Minority Leader of the House, the President of the Senate, and the Minority Leader of the Senate or their designated representatives.

The Advisory Committee shall advise and consult with the Secretary of State concerning the policies and operation of this Governmental research service and the selection policies of materials to be acquired and maintained.

Laws 1939, p. 697, § 7.1, added by P.A. 79-1459, § 1, eff. Oct. 1, 1976.

108. Catalog

§ 8. Catalog. The State Librarian shall prepare a catalog containing information with respect to items in the State Library. Such catalog to be similar to those used in American libraries.

Laws 1939, p. 697, § 6. Renumbered § 8 and amended by P.A. 77-1690, § 1, eff. Jan. 1, 1972.

109. Ownership mark

§ 9. Ownership mark. The State Librarian shall cause each book in the State Library and those to be added to bear an ownership mark reading "Illinois State Library" and such other official marks as are commonly used in American libraries.

Laws 1939, p. 697, § 7. Renumbered § 9 and amended by P.A. 77-1690, § 1, eff. Jan. 1, 1972.

110. Users of the State Library

§ 10. Users of the State Library. Books, other reading materials and other library materials shall be loaned and library services shall be supplied to:

State Officers and Officials;

Members of the General Assembly;

State agencies, bodies and commissions;

State employees;

Urban and rural schools not having school library facilities or access to a State-funded library system;

Individuals living in communities without local library service and without access to a State-funded library system;

Local public libraries where such loans or services are not available or cannot be obtained as a State-funded library system and to other individuals and study groups at the discretion of the State Librarian.

Any individual, study group, school, library or community requesting books or other reading materials or other library materials from the State Library must fill in an application for this service, thereby becoming officially recorded as a registered borrower of the State Library.

Registrants not requesting reading materials for three consecutive years must renew their application before reading materials can be loaned to them.

Amended by P.A. 77-1597, § 1, eff. Sept. 21, 1971. Renumbered and amended by P.A. 77-1690,

§ 1, eff. Jan. 1, 1972. Amended by P.A. 77–2829, § 64, eff. Dec. 22, 1972; P.A. 78–255, § 61, eff. Oct. 1, 1973.

111. Registry of library materials

§ 11. Registry of library materials. A record shall be kept of all books or other items loaned by the Illinois State Library for such period and under such regulations as determined by the State Librarian.

Laws 1939, p. 697, § 9. Renumbered § 11 and amended by P.A. 77–1690, § 1, eff. Jan. 1, 1972.

112. Replacement of library materials

§ 12. Replacement of library materials. If any person fails to return any book or other item taken from the library within the time prescribed by the State Librarian, or injures the same, he shall be obliged to replace the said item, such replacement item to be in new condition.

Laws 1939, p. 697, § 10. Renumbered § 12 and amended by P.A. 77–1690, § 1, eff. Jan. 1, 1972.

113. Fines and recovery

§ 13. Fines and recovery. All fines and charges for any books or other items lost accruing under and by virtue of this Act, or for the violation of any of the rules adopted by the librarian, shall be recoverable in the name of the People of the State of Illinois in a civil action. In all such trials, the entries of the librarian, made as herebefore prescribed shall be evidence of the delivery of the book and of the date of such delivery; and it shall be his duty to carry the provisions of this Act into effect, and to sue for all injuries done to the library, and for all penalties under this Act.

Laws 1939, p. 697, § 11. Renumbered § 13 and amended by P.A. 77–1690, § 1, eff. Jan. 1, 1972; P.A. 79–1359, § 5, eff. Oct. 1, 1976.

118. Federal aid

§ 18. Federal aid. The Secretary of State and State Librarian is authorized and empowered to do all things necessary and proper to fully cooperate with the United States Commissioner of Education in the administering of any act heretofore, or hereafter enacted for the purpose of appropriation of funds for the payment of salaries, books, periodicals, library supplies, equipment, the construction of library buildings, for the maintenance of the expense of public library services, for interlibrary cooperation for library services to institutions operated or substantially supported by the State of Illinois, and for library services to the physically handicapped.

Laws 1939, p. 697, § 12. Renumbered § 18 and amended by P.A. 77–1690, § 1, eff. Jan. 1, 1972.

119. Reimbursement for services

§ 19. Reimbursement for services. When federal funds are expended to provide library services to local libraries pursuant to the Federal Library Services Act (Public Law 597—84th Congress) and reimbursement is received from such local libraries, the amount received as reimbursement shall be paid into the trust fund in the State Treasury from which such expenditure was made.

Laws 1939, p. 697, § 12a. Renumbered § 19 and amended by P.A. 77–1690, § 1, eff. Jan. 1, 1972.

120. Seal and authenticated copies

§ 20. Seal and authenticated copies. The State Librarian shall have an official seal which shall be used to authenticate all books or records in his custody that are not exempt from examination as confidential or protected by subsisting copyright. A fee of fifty cents per page shall be charged for each authenticated book or record, except there shall be no charge for the making or authentication of such copies or reproductions furnished to any department or agency of the State for official use. When any such copy or reproduction is authenticated by the official seal of the State Librarian, it shall be prima facie evidence of the correctness of such books and records and shall be received in evidence in the same manner and with like effect as the originals.

Laws 1939, p. 697, § 13. Renumbered § 20 and amended by P.A. 77–1690, § 1, eff. Jan. 1, 1972.

121. Publications and lists—Deposits by State agencies

§ 21. Publications and lists—Deposits by State agencies. (a) All State agencies shall provide and deposit with the Illinois State Library sufficient copies of all publications issued by such State agencies for its collection and for exchange purposes. The State Librarian shall by rule or regulation specify the number of copies required and the publications that must be deposited.

For the purposes of this section: (1) "State agencies" means every State office, officer, department, division, section, unit, service, bureau, board, commission, committee, and subdivision thereof of all branches of the State government and which agencies expend appropriations of State funds.

(2) "Publications" means any document, report, directory, bibliography, rule, regulation, newsletter, pamphlet, brochure, periodical or other printed material paid for in whole or in part by funds appropriated by the General Assembly or issued at the request of a State agency, excepting however, correspondence, inter-office memoranda, and confidential publications.

(3) "Printed material" means publications duplicated by any and all methods of duplication.

(b) The State Librarian shall from time to time publish a listing of the publications received by him under this Act.

Laws 1939, p. 697, § 18. Renumbered § 21 and amended by P.A. 77–1690, § 1, eff. Jan. 1, 1972.

STATE AID
(Smith-Hurd Illinois Annotated Statutes, 1982,
Chap. 81, s.111-1 to 126.)

111.1. Citation

§ 1.1. This Act shall be known and may be cited as The Illinois Library System Act.

Laws 1965, p. 3077, § 1.1, added by P.A. 76–645, § 1, eff. Aug. 5, 1969.

§ 111. Declaration of policy—State grants

Since the state has a financial responsibility in promoting public education, and since the public library is a vital agency serving all levels of the educational process, it is hereby declared to be the policy of the state to encourage the improvement of free public libraries. In keeping with this policy, provision is hereby made for a program of state grants designed to aid in the establishment and development of a network of public library systems covering the entire state. 1965, Aug. 17, Laws 1965, p. ——, H.B.No.563, § 1.

112. Definition

§ 2. The term "library system" as used in this Act means one or more tax-supported public libraries serving a minimum of 150,000 inhabitants or any area of not less than 4,000 square miles. A library system may consist of any of the following:

a) A cooperative library system in which 10 or more public libraries enter into a written agreement to provide any or all library services on a cooperative basis.

b) A consolidated library system in which 10 or more public libraries consolidate to form a single library.

c) A library system consisting of a single public library serving a city of over 500,000 population.

Amended by P.A. 81–1183, § 1, eff. Nov. 29, 1979.

§ 113. Administration of act—Rules and regulations

The State Librarian and his staff shall administer the provisions of this Act and shall prescribe such rules and regulations as are necessary to carry the provisions of this Act into effect.

The rules and regulations established by the State Librarian for the administration of this Act shall be designed to achieve the following standards and objectives:

a) Provide library service for every citizen in the state by extending library facilities to areas not now served.

b) Provide library materials for student needs at every educational level.

c) Provide adequate library materials to satisfy the reference and research needs of the people of this state.

d) Provide an adequate staff of professionally trained librarians for the state.

e) Provide an adequate stock of books and other materials sufficient in size and varied in kind and subject matter to satisfy the library needs of the people of this state.

f) Provide adequate library outlets and facilities convenient in time and place to serve the people of this state.

g) Encourage existing and new libraries to develop library systems serving a sufficiently large population to support adequate library service at reasonable cost.

h) Foster the economic and efficient utilization of public funds.

i) Promote the full utilization of local pride, responsibility, initiative and support of library service and at the same time employ state aid as a supplement to local support.

The Advisory Committee of the Illinois State Library shall confer with, advise and make recommendations to the State Librarian regarding any matter under this Act and particularly with reference to the formation of library systems. 1965, Aug. 17, Laws 1965, p. ——, H.B. No.563, § 3.

§ 114. Establishment—Manner

A public library system shall be established in the following manner: The formation of a library system shall first be approved by the boards of directors of the participating public libraries, followed by the election of a board of directors for the library system as provided in Sections 5 and 6 of this Act. An application for the formation of a library system shall then be submitted by the board of directors of the system to the State Librarian, together with a plan of service describing the specific purposes for which the system is formed and the means by which such purposes are to be accomplished. If it shall appear to the satisfaction of the State Librarian that the establishment of a library system will result in improved library service, he shall approve the application.

The State Librarian may grant conditional approval of an application proposing the formation of a library system serving a minimum of 50,000 inhabitants, but the plan of service must clearly indicate that the proposed system will meet either the population or area requirement as defined in Section 2 of this Act within a five-year period. 1965, Aug. 17, Laws 1965, p. ——, H.B.No.563, § 4.

115. Cooperative and consolidated library systems—Governing board

§ 5. Each public library system as provided in paragraphs "a" and "b" of Section 2 of this Act shall be governed by a board of directors numbering at least 5 and no more than 15 persons to be selected from the governing boards of the participating libraries. The number of directors, the manner of selection, the term of office and the provision for filling vacancies shall be determined by the governing boards of the participating libraries at a joint meeting called for that purpose. No director of any library system, however, shall be permitted to serve for more than 6 consecutive years. A director, upon serving 6 years, may again serve after an interim of at least 2 years.

The board of directors shall elect a president, secretary and treasurer. Before entering upon his duties, the treasurer shall be required to give a bond in an amount to be approved by the board, conditioned that he will safely keep and pay over upon the order of such board all funds received and held by him for the library system. The funds of the library system shall be deposited in a bank designated by the board of directors and shall be expended only under the direction of such board upon properly authenticated vouchers. The members of the board of directors of the library system shall serve without compensation but their actual and necessary expenses shall be a proper charge against the library fund.
Amended by P.A. 80–306, § 1, eff. Oct. 1, 1977.

§ 116. Libraries in cities over 500,000—Governing board

A public library system as provided in paragraph "c" of Section 2 of this Act shall be governed by the same board and officers that govern the existing public library of that area. The funds received from the state shall be expended only under the direction of such board upon properly authenticated vouchers. 1965, Aug. 17, Laws 1965, p. ——, H.B.No.563, § 6.

117. Powers of boards

§ 7. Each board of library directors of a system shall carry out the spirit and intent of this Act and, in addition to the other powers conferred by this Act, shall have the following powers:

1. To develop a plan of service for the library system to be submitted to the State Librarian.

2. To have the exclusive control of the expenditure of all moneys and funds held in the name of the library system.

3. To make and adopt such bylaws, rules and regulations for the government of the library system as necessary.

4. To purchase or lease ground and to construct, purchase or lease, and occupy an appropriate building or buildings for the use of the library system including but not limited to the power to purchase or lease either real or personal property for system purposes through contracts which provide for the consideration for such purchase or lease to be paid through installments at stated intervals during a certain period not to exceed 20 years together with interest at a rate not to exceed the interest rate specified in Section 2 of "An Act to authorize public corporations to issue bonds, other evidences of indebtedness and tax anticipation warrants subject to interest rate limitations set forth therein", approved May 26, 1970, as amended, on the unpaid

balance owing and to purchase real estate for system purposes upon a mortgage basis for up to 75% of the total consideration therefor, the remaining balance to be paid through installments at stated intervals for a period not to exceed 20 years together with interest at a rate not to exceed the interest rate specified in Section 2 of "An Act to authorize public corporations to issue bonds, other evidences of indebtedness and tax anticipation warrants subject to interest rate limitations set forth therein", approved May 26, 1970, as amended, on the unpaid balance owing, except that in the case of a library system consisting of a single public library serving a city of over 500,000 population, this power shall be governed by the provisions of Division 10 of Article 8 of the Illinois Municipal Code, as heretofore or hereafter amended.[2]

5. To appoint and to fix the compensation of a competent librarian, who shall have the authority to hire such other employees as may be necessary, to fix their compensation, and to remove such appointees, subject to the approval of the board. The board may also retain counsel and professional consultants, as needed.

6. To contract with any public or private corporation or entity for the purpose of providing or receiving library service or of performing any and all other acts necessary and proper to carry out the responsibilities and the provisions of this Act. This power includes, but is not limited to participation in interstate library compacts and library systems, and the expenditure of any federal or State funds made available to any county, municipality, township or to the State of Illinois for library purposes.

7. To amend or alter the plan of service for the library system subject to the approval of the State Librarian.

8. To accrue and accumulate funds in special reserve funds pursuant to the provisions of a plan to acquire realty, improved or unimproved, for library system purposes.

9. To be a body politic and corporate, to contract and to hold title to property by the name of the "Board of Directors of the .... Library System,......, Illinois", and in that name to sue and be sued and to take any action authorized by law.

10. To contract with other library systems for centralized purchasing and processing of library materials for public libraries.

11. To undertake programs for the purpose of encouraging the addition to the district of adjacent areas without local tax-supported library service, and to expend funds for this purpose.

12. To join the library system as a member in the Illinois Library Association and the American Library Association, non-profit, non-political, (501–C–3) associations, as designated by the federal Internal Revenue Service, having the purpose of library development and librarianship; to provide for the payment of annual membership dues, fees and assessments and act by, through and in the name of such instrumentality by providing and disseminating information and research services, employing personnel and doing any and all other acts for the purpose of improving library development.

Amended by Laws 1967, p. 2870, § 1; P.A. 76–592, § 1, eff. July 31, 1969; P.A. 76–645, § 1, eff. Aug. 5, 1969; P.A. 76–2111, § 1, eff. July 1, 1970; P.A. 77–1432, § 1, eff. Sept. 2, 1971; P.A. 79–989, § 2, eff. Oct. 1, 1975; P.A. 81–500, § 1, eff. Jan.1, 1980; P.A. 81–1071, § 2, eff. July 1, 1980; P.A. 81–1509, Art. I, § 52, eff. Sept. 26, 1980.

118. State grants

§ 8. There shall be a program of state grants within the limitations of funds appropriated by the Illinois General Assembly together with other funds made available by the Federal government or other sources for this purpose. This program of state grants shall be administered by the State Librarian in accordance with rules and regulations as provided in Section 3 of this Act, and shall include the following: (a) Annual equalization grants; (b) Establishment grants; (c) Annual per capita and area grants; (d) Annual grants to Research and Reference Centers; (e) Per capita grants to public libraries; and (f) Construction grants to public libraries.

An annual equalization grant shall be made to all public libraries for which the corporate authorities levy a tax for library purposes at a rate not less than .13% of the value of all the taxable property as equalized and assessed by the Department of Revenue, if the amount of tax revenue obtained from a rate of .13% produces less than $4.25 per capita. In such a case, the State Librarian is authorized to make an equalization grant equivalent to the difference between the amount obtained from a rate of .13% and an annual income of $4.25 per capita. No library shall continue to receive an equalization grant unless it is a member of a library system. If a library receiving an equalization grant reduces its tax levy below the amount levied at the time the original application is approved, it shall be ineligible to receive further equalization grants.

Notwithstanding any other provision in this Section:

(1) during fiscal year 1978 the levy required by the preceding paragraph shall be .12% and the amount of the equalization grant shall be $3.00 per capita, and during fiscal year 1979 and thereafter the levy required by the preceding paragraph shall be .13% and the equalization grant shall be $4.25 per capita; and

(2) libraries qualifying for equalization grants in fiscal year 1977 and fiscal year 1978 which are levying at less than the levy required under this Section on July 1, 1977, shall continue to receive equalization grants based on the .06%–$1.50 formula in effect prior to July 1, 1977 through fiscal year 1979 in order to allow such libraries to raise their levy to not less than .13%. If such libraries raise the levy to the levels required by Public Act 79–1472, they shall become eligible for grants based on the formula established by this Act.

Upon the approval of a library system by the State Librarian, one establishment grant shall be made in the amount of $25,000 to a system serving one county in whole or in part. For each additional county served in whole or in part, as it joins a system, an additional grant of $15,000 shall be made.

An annual per capita and area grant shall be made, upon application, to each library system approved by the State Librarian on the following basis:

(1) The sum of $1.00 per capita of the population of the area served plus

(2) The sum of $35 per square mile or fraction thereof of the area served.

The "area served" for the purposes of this Act means the area which the library system proposes to serve in the approved plan of service. In determining the population of the area served by the library system, the population shall be deemed to be that shown by the latest federal census for the political subdivisions in the area served.

In order to be eligible for a grant under this Section, the corporate authorities, in lieu of a tax levy at a particular rate, may provide from a source other than federal revenue sharing, an amount equivalent to the amount to be produced by that levy. Amended by P.A. 76–2585, § 1, eff. July 14, 1970; P.A. 77–1550, § 1, eff. Sept. 17, 1971; P.A. 78–754, § 1, eff. Oct. 1, 1973; P.A. 79–1471, § 1, eff. July 1, 1977; P.A. 79–1472, § 1, eff. July 1, 1977; P.A. 80–1031, § 19, eff. Sept. 22, 1977; P.A. 81–1509, Art. IV, § 77, eff. Sept. 26, 1980.

118.1. Eligibility for grants

§ 8.1. The State Librarian shall make grants annually under this Section to all qualified public libraries in the State from funds appropriated by the General Assembly. Such grants shall be in the amount of $1 per capita for the population of the area served by the respective public library. If the moneys appropriated for grants under this Section are not sufficient the State Librarian shall reduce the per capita amount of the grants so that the qualifying public libraries receive the same amount per capita.

To be eligible for grants under this Section, a public library must:

(1) Submit evidence satisfying the State Librarian that the public library has applied for federal revenue sharing funds to a unit of local government receiving such funds, if any, within the area served, and that such application has been acted upon by the respective unit of local government.

(2) Provide, as determined by the State Librarian, library services which either meet or show progress toward meeting the Illinois library standards, "Measures of Quality", established by the Illinois Library Association.

(3) Be a public library for which is levied a tax for library purposes at a rate not less than .13%.

Any other language in this Section to the contrary notwithstanding, grants under this Section 8.1 shall be made only upon application of the public library concerned, which applications shall be entirely voluntary and within the sole discretion of the public library concerned.

Notwithstanding the first paragraph of this Section, during fiscal year 1978, the amount of grants under this Section shall be .25 per capita, during fiscal year 1979 the amount of grants under this Section shall be $0.50 per capita, during fiscal year 1980 the amount of grants under this Section shall be $0.75 per capita, and during fiscal year 1981 and thereafter the amount of grants shall be $1 per capita.

In order to be eligible for a grant under this Section, the corporate authorities, in lieu of a tax levy at a particular rate, may provide from a source other than federal revenue sharing, an amount equivalent to the amount to be produced by that levy. Laws 1965, p. 660, § 8.1, added by P.A. 79–1472, § 1, eff. July 1, 1977.

119. Application to participate in library system—Approval

§ 9. The board of directors of any public library which is not participating in a library system may apply for membership in an already existing library system. If the application is approved by the governing board of such library system and the State Librarian, the library submitting the application shall become a participating library in such system and shall have the same rights, duties and privileges as other libraries participating therein. However, the board of library directors or trustees of any public library that is a member of any library system shall retain all powers specified by law.
Amended by P.A. 77–1432, § 1, eff. Sept. 2, 1971.

§ 120. Library systems receiving state aid—Information regarding service—Revocation of approval

Each library system receiving state aid shall furnish such information regarding its library service as the State Librarian may from time to time require. The State Librarian may revoke his approval of a library system if he finds that it does not conform to the plan of service or the regulations promulgated by the State Librarian; or in case of a conditional approval, if such library system does not fulfill the terms upon which conditional approval was based. In such a case a library system shall not thereafter be entitled to state aid until its plan of service is again approved by the State Librarian. 1965, Aug. 17, Laws 1965, p. ——, H.B.No.563, § 10.

121. Reduction of tax levy—Reduction of grants

§ 11. In the event that any library participating in a system reduces the amount of its annual public library tax levy to an amount which is less than the average amount levied for the 3 years immediately preceding the establishment of the system for non-capital expenditures, the annual per capita and area grants to which such library system would otherwise be entitled shall be reduced by 25%, until such time as it again levies an amount equal to that average.
Amended by Laws 1967, p. 2870, § 1, eff. Aug. 11, 1967.

122. Research and reference centers

§ 12. To encourage and to make available adequate library research and reference facilities for the residents of this state, the State Librarian shall designate the University of Illinois Library, the Chicago Public Library, Southern Illinois University Library and the Illinois State Library as Research and Reference Centers. The State Librarian may also designate libraries with special collections as Research and Reference Centers. Such designation shall be made subject to the approval of the governing authorities of the above named institutions. A committee composed of the head librarians of these four institutions and the Chairman of the Advisory Committee of the Illinois State Library shall be established to develop long range acquisition policies to strengthen the existing collections and to avoid unnecessary duplication. This committee shall determine the rules and regulations under which the Research and Reference Centers will be made available to the residents of this state. The

committee shall also have the authority to make recommendations to the State Librarian for the apportionment of the funds that are appropriated by the General Assembly for this specific purpose.
Amended by P.A. 77–1550, § 1, eff. Sept. 17, 1971.

123. Liquidation

§ 13. In the event that the board of directors of a library system determines to terminate the system and to cause liquidation thereof, the board of directors of the library system shall submit an application to the State Librarian together with a plan of liquidation describing the proposed liquidation and setting forth the plan of liquidating obligations of the system including but not limited to the obligations for pensions that may have been provided for employees of the system.

The State Librarian, upon receipt of the application, shall first determine if the area of service can be allocated to other adjoining systems, and whether the assets and liabilities of the system proposed to be liquidated can be assumed and absorbed by such adjoining systems.

If adjoining systems absorb the assets and assume the obligations of the liquidating system, the State Librarian shall approve of the amendments to the plans of service and amendments to the state grants to the systems succeeding to the liquidating system.

In the event, however, that a system must be liquidated, the plan of liquidation shall provide for the payment of all outstanding debts and may provide, in addition, that assets of intrinsic value only to libraries or of such historic value that such should remain in a library, then the plan of liquidation may provide for transfer of such items to the State Library of the State of Illinois. The State Library may itself transfer such items to other library systems or retain the items in its own collection.
Laws 1965, p. 3077, § 13, added by Laws 1967, p. 2428, § 1, eff. July 31, 1967.

124. Withdrawal from library system—Transfer from one library system to another

§ 14. In the event that the board of library directors or trustees of any public library determines to withdraw from a library system, the board of library directors or trustees shall submit an application to the library system for such withdrawal, and serve a copy thereof upon the State Librarian. Any such notice shall be filed on or before April 1st of any year, and shall be effective on or before June 30th of the next ensuing year.

In the event that the board of library directors or trustees of any public library determines to seek a transfer from one library system to another, the board of library directors or trustees shall submit an application to the library systems affected and serve a copy thereof upon the State Librarian. Any such notice shall be filed on or before April 1st of any year. The board of library directors or trustees of each affected system may consider the application, and in the event that each such boards approve the application, the State Librarian shall provide for the transfer as of the beginning of a fiscal year.
Laws 1965, p. 3077, § 14, added by P.A. 77–1433, § 1, eff. Sept. 2, 1971

125. Donations

§ 15. Any person wishing to make donations of money, personal property or real estate for the benefit of any library system may vest title to such property in the board of directors of such library system to be held and controlled by such board, when accepted, according to the terms of the deed, gift, devise or bequest of such property. The board shall be held and considered to be a special trustee of such donated property in accordance with the wishes of the donor, grantor or testator, and shall be accountable therefor.

The board may invest funds until utilized and interest earned shall be subject to the same limitations as the principal.
Laws 1965, p. 3077, § 15, added by P.A. 78–427, § 1, eff. Aug. 28, 1973.

126. Disposal of property

§ 16. When the board has determined to sell or otherwise dispose of real or personal property that it deems no longer necessary or useful for library purposes, such property may be disposed of as follows:

(1) Personal property having a unit value of $250 or less may be disposed of as the board may determine.

(2) Personal property having a unit value of more than $250 but less than $1,000 may be displayed at the library, and a public notice of its availability, the date and the terms of the proposed sale shall be posted.

(3) Personal property of any value may be donated or sold to any tax-supported library or to any other library system operating under the provisions of this Act under such terms or conditions, if any. as the board may determine.

(4) In all other cases, the board shall publish notice of the availability and location of the real or personal property, the date and terms of the proposed sale, giving such notice once each week for 2 successive weeks.

On the day of the sale, the board shall proceed with the sale and may sell such property for a price determined by the board, or, to the highest bidder. Where the board deems the bids inadequate, it may reject such bids and re-advertise the sale.

However, the various boards of public library directors, including boards of public libraries that are members of a system, and the Illinois State Library shall have the first right to purchase such property for library purposes by meeting terms or bids acceptable to the board.

Laws 1965, p. 3077, § 16, added by P.A. 79–850, § 1, eff. Sept. 9, 1975. Amended by P.A. 81–500, § 1, eff. Jan. 1, 1980.

INTERSTATE LIBRARY COMPACT
(Smith-Hurd Illinois Annotated Statutes, 1982,
Chap. 81, s.101-104.)

§ 101. Execution of compact

The interstate library compact is hereby enacted into law and entered into on behalf of this state with any state bordering on Illinois which legally joins therein in substantially the following form:

INTERSTATE LIBRARY COMPACT

The contracting states agree that:

ARTICLE I—PURPOSE

Because the desire for the services provided by public libraries transcends governmental boundaries and can be provided most effectively by giving such services to communities of people regardless of jurisdictional lines, it is the policy of the states who are parties to this compact to co-operate and share their responsibilities in providing joint and co-operative library services in areas where the distribution of population makes the provision of library service on an interstate basis the most effective way to provide adequate and efficient services.

ARTICLE II—PROCEDURE

The appropriate officials and agencies of the party states or any of their political subdivisions may, on behalf of said states or political subdivisions, enter into agreements for the co-operative or joint conduct of library services when they shall find that the executions of agreements to that end as provided herein will facilitate library services.

ARTICLE III—CONTENT

Any such agreement for the co-operative or joint establishment, operation or use of library services, facilities, personnel, equipment, materials or other items not excluded because of failure to enumerate shall, as among the parties of the agreement: (1) detail the specific nature of the services, facilities, properties or personnel to which it is applicable; (2) provide for the allocation of costs and other financial responsibilities; (3) specify the respective rights, duties, obligations and liabilities; (4) stipulate the terms and conditions for duration, renewal, termination, abrogation, disposal of joint or common property, if any, and all other matters which may be appropriate to the proper effectuation and performance of said agreement.

ARTICLE IV—CONFLICT OF LAWS

Nothing in this compact or in any agreement entered into hereunder shall be construed to supersede, alter, or otherwise impair any obligation imposed on any public library by otherwise applicable laws.

ARTICLE V—ADMINISTRATOR

Each state shall designate a compact administrator with whom copies of all agreements to which his state or any subdivision thereof is party shall be filed. The administrator shall have such powers as may be conferred upon him by the laws of his state and may consult and co-operate with the compact administrators of other party states and take such steps as may effectuate the purposes of this compact.

ARTICLE VI—EFFECTIVE DATE

This compact shall become operative immediately upon its enactment by any state or between it and any other contiguous state or states so enacting.

ARTICLE VII—RENUNCIATION

This compact shall continue in force and remain binding upon each party state until 6 months after any such state has given notice of repeal by the legislature. Such withdrawal shall not be construed to relieve any party to an agreement authorized by Articles II and III of the compact from the obligation of that agreement prior to the end of its stipulated period of duration.

ARTICLE VIII—SEVERABILITY; CONSTRUCTION

The provisions of this compact shall be severable. It is intended that the provisions of this compact be reasonably and liberally construed. 1961, Aug. 9, Laws 1961, p. 3042, § 1.

§ 102. Administrator

The Secretary of State, ex officio, shall be the compact administrator. The compact administrator shall receive copies of all agreements entered into by the state or its political subdivisions and other states or political subdivisions; consult with, advise and aid such governmental units in the formulation of such agreements; make such recommendations to the governor, legislature, governmental agencies and units as he deems desirable to effectuate the purposes of this compact and consult and co-operate with the compact administrators of other party states. 1961, Aug. 9, Laws 1961, p. 3042, § 2.

§ 103. Agreements

The compact administrator and the library board of any county, city, village or incorporated town, township, library district or library system are authorized and empowered to enter into agreements with other states or their political subdivisions pursuant to the compact. Such agreements as may be made pursuant to this compact on behalf of the state of Illinois shall be made by the compact administrator. Such agreements as may be made on behalf of a political subdivision shall be made after due notice to the compact administrator and consultation with him.
Amended by P.A. 76–593, eff. July 31, 1969.

§ 104. Enforcement

The agencies and officers of this state and its subdivisions shall enforce this compact and do all things appropriate to effect its purpose and intent which may be within their respective jurisdiction. 1961, Aug. 9, Laws 1961, p. 3042, § 4.

STATE HISTORICAL LIBRARY

(Smith-Hurd Illinois Annotated Statutes, 1982, Chap. 128, s.13, 15-20.)

§ 13. State Historical Library established

There is hereby established at the capital of the state a Historical Library, which shall be known as the "Illinois State Historical Library." 1889, May 25, Laws 1889, p. 199, § 1.

§ 15. Trustees—Appointment—No compensation

The Illinois State Historical Library shall be under the control and management of three trustees well versed in the history of the state, and qualified by habit and disposition to discharge the duties of their office, who shall be chosen and appointed by the Governor by and with the consent of the Senate, for the term of two years, and until their successors have been appointed and commissioned. The said trustees shall receive no compensation, for their services, except for their actual expenses while in the discharge of their official duties, to be paid upon itemized accounts approved by the Governor. 1889, May 25, Laws 1889, p. 199, § 3.

16. Powers of trustees

§ 4. These trustees may and they are hereby required to make all necessary rules, regulations and bylaws not inconsistent with law to carry into effect the purposes of this Act and to procure from time to time as may be possible and practicable, at reasonable cost, all books, pamphlets, manuscripts, monographs, writings, and other material of historical interest and useful to the historian bearing upon the political, physical, religious or social history of the State of Illinois from the earliest known period of time. The trustees may exchange any books, pamphlets, manuscripts, records or other material which such library may acquire that are of no historical interest or for any reason are of no value to it, with any other library, school or historical society. The trustees shall distribute volumes of the series known as the Illinois Historical Collections now in print, and to be printed, to all who may apply for same and who pay to the Illinois State Historical Library for such volumes an amount fixed by the trustees sufficient to cover the expenses of printing and distribution of each volume received by such applicants. However, the trustees shall have authority to furnish not to exceed 25 of each of the volumes of the Illinois Historical Collections, free of charge to each of the authors and editors of the collections or parts thereof; to furnish, as in their discretion they deem necessary or desirable, a reasonable number of each of the volumes of the Collections without charge to archives, libraries and similar institutions from which material has been drawn or assistance has been given in the preparation of such Collections, and to the officials thereof; to furnish, as in their discretion they deem necessary or desirable, a reasonable number of each of the volumes of the Collections without charge to the University of Illinois Library and to instructors and officials of that University, and to public libraries in the State of Illinois. The trustees may also make exchanges of Historical Collections with any other library, school or historical society, and to distribute volumes of collections for review purposes, without charge. All proceeds received by the Illinois State Historical Library from the sale of volumes of the series of the Illinois Historical Collections shall be paid into the General Revenue fund in the State treasury. The trustees also may obtain pursuant to the "Personnel Code" some person having the requisite qualifications as State Historian.
Amended by Laws 1955, p. 2230, § 1, eff. July 1, 1957; P.A. 78–378, § 1, eff. Oct. 1, 1973.

16.1. Microphotographing of past editions of newspapers—Copies

§ 5.1. The State Historian shall establish and supervise a program within the Illinois State Historical Library designed to preserve as historical records selected past editions of newspapers of this State. Such editions shall be microphotographed. The negatives of such microphotographs shall be stored in a place provided by the Illinois State Historical Library.

The State Historian shall determine on the basis of historical value the various newspaper edition files which shall be microphotographed and shall arrange a schedule for such microphotographing. The State Historian shall supervise the making of arrangements for acquiring access to past edition files with the editors or publishers of the various newspapers.

The method of microphotography to be employed in this program shall conform to the standards established pursuant to Section 17 of "The State Records Act", approved July 6, 1957.

Upon payment to the Illinois State Historical Library of the required fee, any person or organization shall be supplied with any prints requested to be made from the negatives of the microphotographs. The fee required shall be determined by the State Historian and shall be equal in amount to the cost incurred by the Illinois State Historical Library in supplying the requested prints.
Laws 1889, p. 199, § 5.1, added by Laws 1959, p. 2462, § 1, eff. July 24, 1959.

17. State Historical Society made a department of the State Historical Library

§ 6. That the Illinois State Historical Society, be, and the same is hereby declared a department of the Illinois State Historical Library, and the board of trustees of the said Illinois State Historical Library is hereby authorized to pay for the necessary stationery, postage and other like incidental expenses of the said Illinois State Historical Society, out of any fund the Legislature may appropriate to the said Illinois State Historical Library for such purposes; and also to pay the expenses of interviewing old settlers of the State of Illinois, examining county, church, school and the like records, at the discretion of the board of trustees of said Illinois State Historical Library, and the auditing of the accounts of which shall be subject to the approval of the Governor of the State of Illinois. A copy of each such audit shall be filed with the Governor and the Auditor General. And, provided, further, that all such material shall be the property of the said Illinois State Historical Library and shall be deposited among its archives for reference and safe keeping.

Amended by Laws 1961, p. 2729, § 1, eff. Aug. 3, 1961.

18. County may transfer original records to State Historical Library, etc.—Copies

§ 1. The county board of every county may, by order or resolution authorize and direct to be transferred to the Illinois State Historical Society, the Illinois State Historical Library, the State Archives or to the State University Library at Urbana, Illinois, or to any historical society duly incorporated and located within the county, such official papers, drawings, maps, writings and records of every description as may be deemed of historic interest or value, and as may be in the custody of any officer of such county. Accurate copies of the same when so transferred shall be substituted for the original when in the judgment of such county board the same may be deemed necessary.

Amended by Laws 1957, p. 1708, § 1; Laws 1961, p. 1419, § 1, eff. July 1, 1961.

19. Duty of officers having control of papers

§ 2. The officer having the custody of such papers, drawings, maps, writings and records shall permit search to be made at all reasonable hours and under his supervision for such as may be deemed of historic interest. Whenever so directed by the county board in the manner prescribed in the foregoing section such officer shall deliver the same to the trustee, directors or librarian or other officer of the library or society designated by such county board.

Amended by Laws 1961, p. 1419, § 1, eff. July 1, 1961.

20. Appropriations

§ 3. The county boards may make reasonable appropriations from their respective revenues for the purpose of carrying the provisions of this act into effect.

Amended by Laws 1961, p. 1419, § 1, eff. July 1, 1961.

STATE RECORDS ACT

(Smith-Hurd Illinois Annotated Statutes, 1982,
Chap. 116, s.43.4-43.28.)

43.4. Title

§ 1. This Act shall be known as "The State Records Act."

Laws 1957, p. 1687, § 1, eff. July 6, 1957.

43.5. Definitions

§ 2. For the purposes of this Act:

"Secretary" means Secretary of State.

"Record" or "records" means all books, papers, maps, photographs, or other official documentary materials, regardless of physical form or characteristics, made, produced, executed or received by any agency in the State in pursuance of state law or in connection with the transaction of public business and preserved or appropriate for preservation by that agency or its successor as evidence of the organization, function, policies, decisions, procedures, operations, or other activities of the State or of the State Government, or because of the informational data contained therein. Library and museum material made or acquired and preserved solely for reference or exhibition purposes, extra copies of documents preserved only for convenience of reference, and stocks of publications and of processed documents are not included within the definition of records as used in this Act.

"Agency" means all parts, boards, and commissions of the executive branch of the State government including but not limited to all departments established by the "Civil Administrative Code of Illinois," as heretofore or hereafter amended.

"Public Officer" or "public officers" means all officers of the executive branch of the State government, all officers created by the "Civil Administrative Code of Illinois," as heretofore or hereafter amended, and all other officers and heads, presidents, or chairmen of boards, commissions, and agencies of the State government.

"Commission" means the State Records Commission.

"Archivist" means the Secretary of State.

Laws 1957, p. 1687, § 2, eff. July 6, 1957.

43.6. Reports and records of obligation, receipt and use of public funds as public records

§ 3. Reports and records of the obligation, receipt and use of public funds of the State are public records available for inspection by the public. These records shall be kept at the official place of business of the State or at a designated place of business of the State. These records shall be available for public inspection during regular office hours except when in immediate use by persons exercising official duties which require the use of those records. The person in charge of such records may require a notice in writing to be submitted 24 hours prior to inspection and may require that such notice specify which records are to be inspected. Nothing in this section shall require the State to invade or assist in the invasion of any person's right to privacy. Nothing in this Section shall be construed to limit any right given by statute or rule of law with respect to the inspection of other types of records.

Warrants and vouchers in the keeping of the State Comptroller may be destroyed by him as authorized in "An Act in relation to the reproduction and destruction of records kept by the Comptroller", approved August 1, 1949, as now or hereafter amended.

Laws 1957, p. 1687, § 3. Amended by P.A. 77-1870, § 1, eff. Oct. 1, 1972; P.A. 79-139, § 2, eff. Oct. 1, 1975.

43.7. Right of access by public—Reproductions—Fees

§ 4. Any person shall have the right of access to any public records of the expenditure or receipt of public funds as defined in Section 3 for the purpose of obtaining copies of the same or of making photographs of the same while in the possession, custody and control of the lawful custodian thereof, or his authorized deputy. The photographing shall be done under the supervision of the lawful custodian of said records, who has the right to adopt and enforce reasonable rules governing such work. The work of photographing shall, when possible, be done in the room where the records, documents or instruments are kept. However, if in the judgment of the lawful custodian of the records, documents or instruments, it would be impossible or impracticable to perform the work in the room in which the records, documents or instruments are kept, the work shall be done in some other room or place as nearly adjacent as possible to the room where kept. Where the providing of a separate room or place is necessary, the expense of providing for the same shall be borne by the person or persons desiring to photograph the records, documents or instruments. The lawful custodian of the records, documents or instruments may charge the same fee for the services rendered by him or his assistant in supervising the photographing as may be charged for furnishing a certified copy or copies of the said record, document or instrument. In the event that the lawful custodian of said records shall deem it advisable in his judgment to furnish photographs of such public records, instruments or documents in lieu of allowing the same to be photographed, then in such event he may furnish photographs of such records and charge a fee of 35¢ per page when the page to be photographed does not exceed legal size and $1.00 per page when the page to be photographed exceeds legal size and where the fees and charges therefor are not otherwise fixed by law.

Laws 1957, p. 1687, § 4, eff. July 6, 1957.

43.8. State Archives Division—Creation

§ 5. The Secretary of State shall provide for a State Archives Division as a repository of State records. The State Archives may utilize space in the Archives Building or other buildings as may be necessary or appropriate for the purpose, in the opinion of the Secretary of State.

Laws 1957, p. 1687, § 5, eff. July 6, 1957.

43.9. Secretary of State to be State Archivist—Assistants

§ 6. The Secretary of State shall be the State Archivist and Records Administrator and he shall appoint such assistants, who shall be technically qualified and experienced in the control and management of archival materials and in records management practices and techniques, as are necessary to carry out his duties as State Archivist.

Laws 1957, p. 1687, § 6, eff. July 6, 1957.

43.10. Powers and duties of secretary—Public access to records

§ 7. The Secretary:

(1) whenever it appears to him to be in the public interest, may accept for deposit in the State Archives the records of any agency or of the Legislative or Judicial branches of the State government that are determined by him to have sufficient historical or other value to warrant the permanent preservation of such records by the State of Illinois;

(2) may accept for deposit in the State Archives official papers, drawings, maps, writings, and records of every description of counties, municipal corporations, political subdivisions and courts of this State, and records of the federal government pertaining to Illinois, when such materials are deemed by the Secretary to have sufficient historical or other value to warrant their continued preservation by the State of Illinois.

(3) whenever he deems it in the public interest, may accept for deposit in the State Archives motion picture films, still pictures, and sound recordings that are appropriate for preservation by the State government as evidence of its organization, functions and policies.

(4) shall be responsible for the custody, use, servicing and withdrawal of records transferred for deposit in the State Archives. The Secretary shall observe any rights, limitations, or restrictions imposed by law relating to the use of records, including the provisions of the Mental Health and Developmental Disabilities Confidentiality Act which limit access to certain records or which permit access to certain records only after the removal of all personally identifiable data. Access to restricted records shall be at the direction of the depositing State agency or, in the case of records deposited by the legislative or judicial branches of State government at the direction of the branch which deposited them, but no limitation on access to such records shall extend more than 75 years after the creation of the records, except as provided in the Mental Health and Developmental Disabilities Confidentiality Act. The Secretary shall not impose restrictions on the use of records that are defined by law as public records or as records open to public inspection;

(5) shall make provision for the preservation, arrangement, repair, and rehabilitation, duplication and reproduction, description, and exhibition of records deposited in the State Archives as may be needed or appropriate;

(6) shall make or reproduce and furnish upon demand authenticated or unauthenticated copies of any of the documents, photographic material or other records deposited in the State Archives, the public examination of which is not prohibited by statutory limitations or restrictions or protected by copyright. The Secretary shall charge a fee therefor in accordance with the schedule of fees in Section 10 of "An Act concerning fees and salaries, and to classify the several counties of this state with reference thereto," approved March 29, 1872, as amended, except that there shall be no charge for making or authentication of such copies or reproductions furnished to any department or agency of the State for official use. When any such copy or

reproduction is authenticated by the Great Seal of the State of Illinois and is certified by the Secretary, or in his name by his authorized representative, such copy or reproduction shall be admitted in evidence as if it were the original.

(7) any official of the State of Illinois may turn over to the Secretary of State, with his consent, for permanent preservation in the State Archives, any official books, records, documents, original papers, or files, not in current use in his office, taking a receipt therefor.

(8) shall require of all persons, firms, corporations or other legal entities who desire access to information not defined as public records or as records open to public inspection, but open to the public, as provided in this Act, an affidavit dated and signed by the person making the request or his representative, notarized by a notary public, and containing substantially the following:

"Application and Agreement for Release of Information

"The Secretary of State, State of Illinois, agrees to release the following described information subject to the following agreement:

"It is hereby agreed by _____, known as the User, that the information, lists, names and other material provided by the Office of the Secretary of State shall not be made available to other persons, firms, corporations or other legal entities. The User agrees that it shall preserve the confidentiality of any person or persons named in these records.

"The information contained shall not be exchanged with any other person, firm or corporation for other information or lists unless the identity of any person or persons named in these records has been removed. Such an act shall constitute a material breach of this agreement and all information previously received by the User shall be returned to the Office of the Secretary of State, State of Illinois.

"The user understands that any violation of this agreement is a Class A misdemeanor, punishable by imprisonment in a penal institution other than a penitentiary for not than one year or a fine not exceeding $1,000, or both.

"Description of information: _____

_____

Date	Date
Signature	Signature
User or his representative	by ___ Secretary of State, State of Illinois
User's name, if not above	Director Archives and Records Division
User's Address"	

A violation of the provisions of an agreement under this paragraph (8) is a Class A misdemeanor.

Laws 1957, p. 1687, § 7. Amended by P.A. 81–913, § 1, eff. Sept. 22, 1979.

43.11. Preservation of records

§ 8. The head of each agency shall cause to be made and preserved records containing adequate and proper documentation of the organization, functions, policies, decisions, procedures, and essential transactions of the agency designed to furnish information to protect the legal and financial rights of the state and of persons directly affected by the agency's activities.

This section shall not be construed to prevent the legal disposal of any records determined by the agency and by the Commission not to have sufficient value to warrant their continued preservation by the State or by the agency concerned. Laws 1957, p. 1687, § 8, eff. July 6, 1957.

43.12. Programs for efficient management of records

§ 9. The head of each agency shall establish, and maintain an active, continuing

program for the economical and efficient management of the records of the agency.
  Such program:
  (1) shall provide for effective controls over the creation, maintenance, and use of
records in the conduct of current business;
  (2) shall provide for cooperation with the Secretary in applying standards, procedures, and techniques to improve the management of records, promote the maintenance and security of records deemed appropriate for preservation, and facilitate the
segregation and disposal of records of temporary value;
  (3) shall provide for compliance with the provisions of this Act and the rules and
regulations issued thereunder.
Laws 1957, p. 1687, § 9, eff. July 6, 1957.

43.13. Transfer of agency records

  § 10. Whenever the head of an agency determines that substantial economies or
increased operating efficiency can be effected thereby, he may, subject to the
approval of the Secretary, provide for the storage, care, and servicing of records that
are appropriate therefor in a records center operated and maintained by the Secretary.
Laws 1957, p. 1687, § 10, eff. July 6, 1957.

43.14. Records not to be damaged or destroyed

  § 11. All records made or received by or under the authority of or coming into the
custody, control or possession of public officials of this State in the course of their
public duties are the property of the State and shall not be mutilated, destroyed,
transferred, removed or otherwise damaged or disposed of, in whole or in part except
as provided by law.
Laws 1957, p. 1687, § 11, eff. July 6, 1957.

43.15. Surveys of management and disposal practices

  § 12. The Secretary shall make continuing surveys of State records management
and disposal practices and obtain reports thereon from agencies.
Laws 1957, p. 1687, § 12, eff. July 6, 1957.

43.16. Improvement of management practices and security of records

  § 13. The Secretary, with due regard to the program activities of the agencies
concerned, shall make provision for the economical and efficient management of
records of State agencies by analyzing, developing, promoting, coordinating, and
promulgating standards, procedures, and techniques designed to improve the management of records, to insure the maintenance and security of records deemed appropriate for preservation, and to facilitate the segregation and disposal of records of
temporary value. The Secretary shall aid also in promoting the efficient and
economical utilization of space, equipment, and supplies needed for the purpose of
creating, maintaining, storing, and servicing records.
Laws 1957, p. 1687, § 13, eff. July 6, 1957.

43.17. Standards for retention

  § 14. The Secretary shall establish standards for the selective retention of records
of continuing value and assist agencies in applying such standards to records in their
custody.
Laws 1957, p. 1687, § 14, eff. July 6, 1957.

43.18. Records centers

  § 15. The Secretary shall establish, maintain, and operate records centers for the
storage, care, and servicing of records of State agencies pending their deposit in the
State Archives or the disposition of such records in any other manner authorized by
law. The Secretary may establish, maintain, and operate centralized microfilming
services for agencies.
Laws 1957, p. 1687, § 15, eff. July 6, 1957.

43.18a. System for protection and preservation of records—Establishment

§ 15a. The Secretary of State, and State Archivist, shall establish a system for the protection and preservation of essential State records necessary for the continuity of governmental functions in the event of an emergency arising from enemy action or natural disaster and for the reestablishment of State government thereafter.

Laws 1957, p. 1687, § 15a, added by Laws 1961, p. 3508, § 1, eff. Aug. 18, 1961.

43.18b. Records essential for emergency government operation—Determination

§ 15b. The Secretary shall:

(1) Determine what records are "essential" for emergency government operation through consultation with all branches of government, State agencies, and with the State Civil Defense Agency.

(2) Determine what records are "essential" for post-emergency government operations and provide for their protection and preservation.

(3) Establish the manner in which essential records for emergency and post-emergency government operations shall be preserved to insure emergency usability.

(4) Require every State agency to establish and maintain an essential records preservation program.

(5) Provide for security storage or relocation of essential State records in the event of an emergency arising from enemy attack or natural disaster.

Laws 1957, p. 1687, § 15b, added by Laws 1961, p. 3508, § 1, eff. Aug. 18, 1961.

43.19. State Records Commission—Membership—Meetings—Duties

§ 16. There is created the State Records Commission. The Commission shall consist of the following members: The Secretary of State, or his representative, who shall act as chairman; the State Historian, who shall serve as secretary; the State Treasurer, or his authorized representative; the Director of Administrative Services, or his authorized representative; the Attorney General, or his authorized representative; and the State Comptroller, or his authorized representative. The Commission shall meet whenever called by the chairman, who shall have no vote on matters considered by the Commission. It shall be the duty of the Commission to determine what records no longer have any administrative, legal, research, or historical value and should be destroyed or disposed of otherwise.

Laws 1957, p. 1687, § 16. Amended by P.A. 78–592, § 41, eff. Oct. 1, 1973; P.A. 80–57, § 19, eff. July 1, 1977.

43.20. Disposal and reproduction of records—Regulations

§ 17. Regardless of other authorization to the contrary, no record shall be disposed of by any agency of the State, unless approval of the State Records Commission is first obtained. The Commission shall issue regulations, not inconsistent with this Act, which shall be binding on all agencies. Such regulations shall establish procedures for compiling and submitting to the Commission lists and schedules of records proposed for disposal; procedures for the physical destruction or other disposition of records proposed for disposal; and standards for the reproduction of records by photography or microphotographic processes with the view to the disposal of the original records. Such standards shall relate to the quality of film used, preparation of the records for filming, proper identification matter on the records so that an individual document or series of documents can be located on the film with reasonable facility, and that the copies contain all significant record detail, to the end that the photographic or microphotographic copies will be adequate.

Such regulations shall also provide that the State archivist may retain any records which the Commission has authorized to be destroyed, where they have a historical value, and that the State archivist may deposit them in the State Library or State historical museum or with a historical society, museum or library.

Laws 1957, p. 1687, § 17. Amended by P.A. 76–1667, § 1, eff. Oct. 3, 1969.

43.21. Reports and schedules to be submitted by agency heads

§ 18. The head of each agency shall submit to the Commission, in accordance with the regulations of the Commission, lists or schedules of records in his custody that are not needed in the transaction of current business and that do not have sufficient administrative, legal or fiscal value to warrant their further preservation. The head of each agency also shall submit lists or schedules proposing the length of time each record series warrants retention for administrative, legal or fiscal purposes after it has been received by the agency.

Laws 1957, p. 1687, § 18, eff. July 6, 1957.

43.22. Disposition of reports and schedules

§ 19. All lists and schedules submitted to the Commission shall be referred to the Archivist who shall ascertain whether the records proposed for disposal have value to other agencies of the State or whether such records have research or historical value. The Archivist shall submit such lists and schedules with his recommendations in writing to the Commission; and the final disposition of such records shall be according to the orders of the Commission.

Laws 1957, p. 1687, § 19, eff. July 6, 1957.

43.23. Destruction of nonrecord materials

§ 20. Nonrecord materials or materials not included within the definition of records as contained in this Act may be destroyed at any time by the agency in possession of such materials without the prior approval of the Commission. The Commission may formulate advisory procedures and interpretation to guide in the disposition of nonrecord materials.

Laws 1957, p. 1687, § 20, eff. July 6, 1957.

43.24. Disposal of records—Consent of agency head

§ 21. The Archivist shall submit to the Commission, with his recommendations in writing, disposal lists of records that have been deposited in the State Archives as provided in subsections (1), (2), and (3) of Section 7 of this Act, after having determined that the records concerned do not have sufficient value to warrant their continued preservation by the State. However, any records deposited in the State Archives by any agency pursuant to the provisions of subsection (1) of Section 7 of this Act shall not be submitted to the Commission for disposal without the written consent of the head of such agency.

Laws 1957, p. 1687, § 21, eff. July 6, 1957.

43.25. Disposition of records of terminated state agency

§ 22. Upon the termination of any State agency whose function or functions have not been transferred to another agency, the records of such terminated agency shall be deposited in the State Archives. The Commission shall determine which records are of sufficient legal, historical, administrative, or fiscal value to warrant their continued preservation by the State. Records that are determined to be of insufficient value to warrant their continued preservation shall be disposed of as provided in Section 17 of this Act.

Laws 1957, p. 1687, § 22, eff. July 6, 1957.

43.26. Repeal—Saving clause

§ 23. "An Act creating the State Records Commission and defining its powers and duties," approved July 23, 1943, as amended, is repealed, but all orders heretofore issued by the State Records Commission created by said Act shall stand and continue to be in full force and effect.

Laws 1957, p. 1687, § 23, eff. July 6, 1957.

43.27. Penalty for violation

§ 24. Any officer or employee who violates the provisions of Section 3 of this Act is guilty of a Class B misdemeanor.

Laws 1957, p. 1687, § 24. Amended by P.A. 77–2221, § 1, eff. Jan. 1, 1973.

43.28. Partial invalidity

§ 25. The invalidity of any section or part or portion of this act shall not affect the validity of the remaining sections or parts thereof.
Laws 1957, p. 1687, § 25, eff. July 6, 1957.

LEGISLATIVE REFERENCE BUREAU

(Smith-Hurd Illinois Annotated Statutes, 1982,
Chap. 63, s.25-31.)

25. Establishment—Members—Ex officio members—Chairman

§ 1. There is established a joint Legislative Reference Bureau composed of 4 members of the Senate appointed by the President, 4 members of the House of Representatives appointed by the Speaker, and the members, ex officio, hereinafter provided. No more than 2 of the members appointed from each house may be of the same political party. Appointments shall be made in June of each odd-numbered year for terms beginning July 1 of that year. Appointments shall be in writing and filed with the Secretary of State as a public record. Vacancies shall be filled in the same manner as the original appointments. A vacancy is created when a member ceases to be a member of the house from which he was appointed.

The President of the Senate, the Speaker of the House of Representatives and the chairman of the Committee on Judiciary of the Senate and House of Representatives are, ex officio, members of the Legislative Reference Bureau.

During the month of July in each odd-numbered year, the bureau shall select from its membership a chairman and a vice chairman and shall prescribe its own rules of procedure.

Amended by Laws 1967, p. 2612, § 1; P.A. 78-4, § 13, eff. April 12, 1973.

26. Terms of office of members

§ 2. Those members serving on the reference bureau by virtue of being President of the Senate, Speaker of the House of Representatives or chairmen of committees of either house shall serve until their successors are chosen at the next General Assembly.

Amended by Laws 1967, p. 2612, § 1; P.A. 78-4, § 13, eff. April 12, 1973.

28. Secretary and employees—Compensation—Status

§ 4. The reference bureau shall appoint a secretary, who shall be the executive officer of the bureau, and such other agents and employees as may be necessary to carry out the provisions of this Act. The compensation of the executive secretary and of all other appointees shall be fixed by the bureau. Neither the secretary nor the other appointees shall be subject to the Personnel Code.

Amended by Laws 1965, p. 515, § 1; Laws 1967, p. 38, § 1, eff. March 8, 1967.

27. Meetings—Compensation and expenses

§ 3. The reference bureau shall meet as often as may be necessary to perform its duties and, in any event, shall meet at least once in each quarter. Seven members shall constitute a quorum, and a majority thereof shall have authority to act on any matter within the jurisdiction of the bureau. The members of the bureau shall receive no compensation for their services as members thereof, but shall be allowed their actual and necessary expenses incurred in the performance of their official duties.

Amended by Laws 1967, p. 2612, § 1, eff. Aug. 3, 1967.

29. Duties of bureau

§ 5. The reference bureau has the duties enumerated in Sections 5.01 through 5.06.

29.1. Establishment of bureau—Business hours—Collection and custody of laws, etc.

§ 5.01. To establish in the State Capitol a reference bureau, which shall be open daily, except Saturdays, Sundays and legal holidays, and at other times when the General Assembly is in session, in which shall be collected and kept, in such manner as to be readily accessible, such laws, reports, books, periodicals, documents, catalogues, check-lists, digests, summaries of the laws of other states upon current legislation, and such other printed or written matter as may aid the members of the General Assembly in the performance of their official duties.

Laws 1913, p. 391, § 5(a). Amended by Laws 1921, p. 471, § 1; Laws 1941, vol. 1, p. 818, § 1; Laws 1959, p. 164, § 1. Resectioned in part § 5.01 and amended by Laws 1965, p. 2527, § 1, eff. Aug. 4, 1965.

29.2. Service in regard to bills—Digests

§ 5.02. The reference bureau shall collect, catalogue, classify, index, completely digest, topically index, checklist and summarize all bills, memorials, resolutions and orders, as well as substitutes and amendments, and changes, if any, introduced in each branch of the General Assembly, as soon as practicable after they have been printed, and shall furnish, without cost, 2 copies of the digest indexed and topically indexed to each member of the General Assembly and 1 copy to each elected State officer in the executive department, and 40 copies of such digest to the Chief Clerk of the House of Representatives and 30 copies of such digest to the Secretary of the Senate for the use of the committee clerks and employees of the respective offices and 15 copies of such digest to the Legislative Council, and such number of digests as requested in writing by the President of the Senate, the Speaker of the House, the minority leader of the Senate, and the minority leader of the House, on Monday of each week during the session of the General Assembly. The reference bureau shall also furnish to each county clerk without cost one copy of such digest for each 100,000 inhabitants or fraction thereof in his county according to the last preceding federal decennial census. Upon receipt of an application therefor from any other person, signed by the applicant, accompanied by the payment of a fee of $55, the reference bureau shall furnish to the applicant a copy of each such digest for that calendar year issued after receipt of the application.

Laws 1913, p. 391, § 5(b). P.A. 81–1012, § 1, eff. Jan. 1, 1980.

29.3. Legal assistance legislators

§ 5.03. The reference bureau shall afford to any member of the General Assembly, upon his request, such legal assistance and information as may be practicable in the preparation of bills, memorials, resolutions, orders and amendments, alterations, changes thereto, and revisions and substitutes thereof, proposed to be introduced into the General Assembly by that member.

Laws 1913, p. 391, § 5(c). Amended by Laws 1921, p. 471, § 1; Laws 1941, vol. 1, p. 818, § 1; Laws 1959, p. 164, § 1. Resectioned in part § 5.01 and amended by Laws 1965, p. 2527, § 1, eff. Aug. 4, 1965.

29.4. Revision of laws

§ 5.04. The reference bureau shall, between sessions of the General Assembly, select such subjects and chapters of the statutory law as are considered most.in need of a revision and present to the next regular session of the General Assembly bills covering such revisions. In connection with such revisions, the reference bureau has full authority to recommend, and has the responsibility of recommending, the revision, simplification and rearrangement of existing statutory law and the elimination from such law of obsolete, superseded, duplicated and unconstitutional statutes or parts of statutes, but shall make no other changes in the substance of existing statutes. Any such revisions reported to the General Assembly may be accompanied by explanatory statements of changes in existing statutes or parts of statutes which such revisions, if enacted, would effect.

Laws 1913, p. 391, § 5(d). Amended by Laws 1921, p. 471, § 1; Laws 1941, vol. 1, p. 818, § 1; Laws 1959, p. 164, § 1. Resectioned in part § 5.04 and amended by Laws 1965, p. 2527, § 1, eff. Aug. 4, 1965.

29.5. Review of court decisions—Report

§ 5.05. The Legislative Reference Bureau shall review all reported decisions of Federal courts, the Illinois Supreme Court and the Illinois Appellate Court which affect the interpretation of the Illinois Constitution and statutes and shall report the results of its research to the General Assembly by October 1 of each year. Such report shall recommend any necessary technical corrections in the Illinois laws to comply with the decisions, and may point out where substantive issues arise, without making any judgment thereon.

Laws 1913, p. 391, § 5.05, added by P.A. 80–803, § 1, eff. Oct. 1, 1977. Amended by P.A. 81–1012, § 1, eff. Jan. 1, 1980.

29.6. Reorganization of executive branch—Revisory bills

§ 5.06. The reference bureau shall prepare bills for introduction to revise the existing statutory law to conform the statutes to any reorganization of the executive branch taking effect pursuant to executive order of the Governor under Article V, Section 11 of the Constitution and the Executive Reorganization Implementation Act. Such bills shall be prepared for introduction in the annual session of the General Assembly next occurring after a reorganization takes effect.

Laws 1913, p. 391, § 5.06, added by P.A. 81–984, § 14, eff. Sept. 22, 1979.

31. Co-operation of State library

§ 7. The Secretary of State, as librarian of the State library, shall cooperate with the reference bureau and shall make the facilities of the State library accessible, so far as practicable, for the use of the reference bureau, and may loan to the reference bureau any books, periodicals, documents, reports or other printed or written matter belonging to the State library.

Amended by Laws 1967, p. 2612, § 1, eff. Aug. 3, 1967.

DISTRIBUTION OF PUBLIC DOCUMENTS
(Smith-Hurd Illinois Annotated Statutes, 1982, Chap. 127, s.132.231.)

132.231. Session laws—Distribution

§ 31. Immediately upon receipt of the bound volumes of the session laws and of the journals of both Houses of the General Assembly, the Secretary of State shall make the following distribution:

(a) One copy of each to each State Officer, board, commission, institution and department, except judges of the Appellate Courts, and judges and associate judges of the Circuit Court;

(b) 10 copies to the law library of the Supreme Court; one copy each to the law libraries of the Appellate Courts and one copy to each of the County Law Libraries where same have been established. In those counties which do not have County Law Libraries, one copy to the Clerk of the Circuit Court;

(c) One copy of each to each county clerk;

(d) 10 Copies of each to the library of the University of Illinois;

(e) 3 Copies of each to the libraries of University of Illinois at Chicago Circle, Southern Illinois University at Carbondale, Southern Illinois University at Edwardsville, Northern Illinois University, Western Illinois University, Eastern Illinois University, Illinois State University at Normal, Chicago State College, Northeastern Illinois

State College, Chicago Kent College of Law, DePaul University, John Marshall Law School, Loyola University, Northwestern University, Roosevelt University and the University of Chicago;

(f) A number of copies sufficient for exchange purposes to the Legislative Reference Bureau and the University of Illinois College of Law library;

(g) A number of copies sufficient for public libraries in the State to the State library; and

(h) The remainder shall be retained for such distribution as the interests of the State may require to persons making application in writing or in person for any such publication.

Laws 1967, p. 313, § 31, eff. April 20, 1967. Amended by Laws 1967, p. 2209, § 1, eff. July 26, 1967; P.A. 78–386, § 1, eff. Aug. 28, 1973.

SUPREME COURT LIBRARY
(Smith-Hurd Illinois Annotated Statutes, 1982, Chap. 37, s.22.)

§ 22.   Librarian

The judges of the Supreme Court shall appoint a librarian for the Supreme Court Library, located at the State Capitol, and prescribe his duties and fix his compensation to be paid as other expenses of the Supreme Court are paid. Such librarian, before entering upon the duties of his office, shall give bond payable to the People of the State of Illinois in the penal sum of $5,000 with security to be approved by 2 judges of said court conditioned for the due preservation of the books belonging to the library, in his charge, and for the faithful performance of his duties as such librarian. As amended 1945, June 30, Laws 1945, p. 668, § 1; 1949, Aug. 2, Laws 1949, p. 712, § 1; 1955, July 7, Laws 1955, p. 1143, § 1; 1957, July 9, Laws 1957, p. 2221, § 1; 1961, May 5, Laws 1961, p. 468, § 1; 1965, May 25, Laws 1965, p. 766, § 1.

DISTRICT LIBRARIES
(Smith-Hurd Illinois Annotated Statutes, 1982,
Chap. 81, s.1001-1 to 1008-2, 1101.)

1001-1.   Short title

§ 1–1. This Act shall be known and may be cited as The Illinois Public Library District Act.

Laws 1967, p. 1684, § 1–1, eff. July 17, 1967.

1001-2.   Definitions

§ 1–2. For the purposes of this Act, unless the context indicated otherwise, the term "district" means a "library district" established hereunder and including a proposed "district", the term "library" means a "public library" including one privately endowed or tax-supported or one established hereunder, the term "Board" means the Board of Trustees created hereunder to administer this Act, the term "Trustee" means a Trustee elected or appointed hereunder, the term "judge" means any judge of any Circuit Court of this State assigned to hear any matter brought before him pursuant to this Act, the term "municipality" means a city, village or incorporated town, and the term "township" means a township part of a county under the township form of government.

Laws 1967, p. 1684, § 1–2. Amended by P.A. 76–1364, § 1, eff. Sept. 16, 1969.

1001–3. Establishment of districts and libraries

§ 1–3. Library districts may be established and libraries may be established, equipped and maintained by the Board pursuant to this Act, and every such library shall be forever free to the use of the residents of the district wherein it is located, subject however to such reasonable rules and regulations as the Board may adopt in order to render the use of the library of the greatest benefit to the greatest number of such residents.

Laws 1967, p. 1684, § 1–3, eff. July 17, 1967.

1001–4. Library districts established under prior laws—Members of board

§ 1–4. Any library district established or formed under any prior law, including those formed pursuant to "An Act authorizing the creation of public library districts", approved May 26, 1943, as amended, or, pursuant to "An Act in relation to the creation of public library districts", approved May 16, 1957, as amended, shall be deemed to have been established or formed pursuant to the provisions of this Act, notwithstanding the fact that any such library district does not meet all of the qualifications for the establishment or formation set forth in this Act, and shall be subject to the provisions of this Act. No further referendum need be held to authorize the levy of the annual public library tax up to the limitation of Section 3–1 of this Act.

The Trustees elected or appointed hereunder shall be the successors to the Trustees of districts established under any prior law repealed by this Act, and all right, title and interest in and to property of any type, and all rights and causes of action existing or vested in Trustees of districts created under any prior law, fully vests in the Trustees elected or appointed under the provisions of this Act.

Laws 1967, p. 1684, § 1–4. Amended by P.A. 81–1489, § 76, eff. Dec. 1, 1980.

1001–5. Board of trustees—Status—Name

§ 1–5. The Board of Trustees of each district shall be a body politic and corporate, by the name of "The Board of Library Trustees of the _____ _____ Public Library District, _____, Illinois", and in that name may enact ordinances and hold title to property, may sue and be sued in all courts and places where judicial proceedings are had, and take any action authorized by law.

Laws 1967, p. 1684, § 1–5, eff. July 17, 1967.

1001–6. Donation of property

§ 1–6. Any person desiring to make donations of money, personal property or real estate, for the benefit of any library, may vest title to the donation in the Board of Library Trustees of the district receiving the donation, to be held and controlled by such Trustees, when accepted, according to the terms of the deed, gift, devise or bequest of such donation. Such Board of Library Trustees shall be held and considered to be a special Trustee of such donated property.

Laws 1967, p. 1684, § 1–6, eff. July 17, 1967.

1001–7. Ordinances—Proof and determination of contents—Public inspection

§ 1–7. The contents of all district ordinances, the date of enactment or of publication or posting and the effective date, shall be determined from the records of the Secretary of the District, and may be proven by the certificate of the Secretary, under the seal of the district.

The Secretary shall maintain at a public place specified by ordinance, which may be the library operated by the district, certified copies of all ordinances and make such available for public inspection.

Laws 1967, p. 1684, § 1–7, eff. July 17, 1967.

1001–8. Ordinances—Numbering—Publication

§ 1–8. Ordinances shall be numbered serially and identified by such serial number and the date of enactment. Ordinances shall be posted, or published if so specified in this Act, within 20 days after enactment, and shall be effective on the day and date of such posting or publication.

Laws 1967, p. 1684, § 1–8, eff. July 17, 1967.

1001-9. Violations—Penalties

§ 1–9. Any Trustee as a Trustee or as an Officer who fails, neglects to discharge any duty imposed upon him by this Act, is guilty of a petty offense; and shall be fined not less than $25 nor more than $100 for each offense.

Any person who violates any ordinance of the district which provides for a penalty, is guilty of a petty offense and shall be fined not less than $25 nor more than $100 for each offense.

All actions for such violations shall be governed by and processed as in the case of violations of municipal ordinances.

All fines for violations of ordinances for injury to or for failure to return any book or material or personalty belonging to the library shall be paid into the library fund. All fines and penalties for the commission of injury upon the library or the grounds or other property thereof shall be paid into the fund of the public agency or body enforcing such ordinances.

Laws 1967, p. 1684, § 1–9. Amended by P.A. 76–1364, § 1, eff. Sept. 16, 1969; P.A. 77–2704, § 1, eff. Jan. 1, 1973.

1001-10. Membership in associations

§ 1–10. The corporate authorities of every public library may provide for joining the Illinois Library Association and the American Library Association, non-profit, non-political, (501–C–3) associations, as designated by the federal Internal Revenue Service, having the purpose of library development and librarianship. The corporate authorities of every public library may provide for the payment of annual membership dues, fees, and assessments to the Associations. The member public library may be active by, through and in the name of such instrumentality, may provide and disseminate information and research services, employ personnel, and do any and all other acts for the purpose for improving library development.

Laws 1967, p. 1684, § 1–10, added by P.A. 81–1071, § 3, eff. July 1, 1980.

1002-1. Authorization

§ 2–1. All or any portion of the territory within one or more counties may, pursuant to this Act, be organized and formed into a district for the purpose of levying a tax or taxes to pay for establishing, equipping, maintaining, and supporting a library or libraries, or for contracting for library services to be furnished to such district by any other library or libraries.

Laws 1967, p. 1684, § 2–1, eff. July 17, 1967.

1002-2. Petition to circuit court—Notice

§ 2–2. 100 or more of the voters of the proposed district may petition the Circuit Court of the county which contains all or a larger portion of the proposed district than any other county having territory therein, to cause the question to be submitted to the voters of the proposed district, whether the proposed territory shall be organized, formed and established as a public library district. The Petition shall contain a definite description of the boundaries of the territory to be embraced within the proposed district, the name of the proposed district, and the proposed tax rate limit for the proposed district if in excess of .15%, and shall petition the Circuit Court for the day and date of a hearing before a judge of said Circuit Court. Where the proposed territory encompasses the same territory as an existing city, village, incorporated town, township or county, the description of the district proposed may be by reference to such entity. The Circuit Court shall cause entry of an order setting forth the said day and date and naming the judge who will preside at the hearing.

The Petitioners, or some of them, shall publish notice of the time, date and place of the hearing upon the subject matter of the Petition, and name the judge assigned to hear the Petition. They shall also send notice of the hearing, by registered mail, to the President of the Board of Trustees or Board of Directors of each public library serving an area contiguous to or within the proposed library district boundaries.

Laws 1967, p. 1684, § 2–2. Amended by P.A. 77–1704, § 1, eff. July 1, 1972; P.A. 79–302, § 1, eff. Oct. 1, 1975; P.A. 80–405, § 1, eff. Oct. 1, 1977; P.A. 81–1489, § 76, eff. Dec. 1, 1980.

1002-3. Hearing on petition—Entry of final judgment

§ 2-3. At the hearing, the petitioners shall present proof of the Notice of the hearing and the Petition to the judge assigned to the matter. All persons residing within the proposed district shall have a reasonable opportunity to be heard touching upon the location and the boundaries of the proposed district and to make suggestions regarding the same.

The judge, after hearing the statements, evidence and suggestions of the petitioners and other persons appearing before him, shall, if he determines the petition is valid and sufficient according to law, enter a final judgment which shall:

(a) Fix and determine the limits and boundaries of the proposed district, and for that purpose and only to that extent, may alter and amend the petition;

(b) Cause a map to be prepared depicting: (1) the proposed district and indicating its limits and boundaries; (2) the limits and boundaries of any municipality or township affected thereby and as lie wholly or partially within the proposed district; (3) and the county lines of the counties affected;

(c) Designate the regular election at which the establishment question shall be submitted.

(d) Certify the proposition to the proper election officials for submission of the proposition at an election, in accordance with the general election law.

Laws 1967, p. 1684, § 2-3, eff. July 17, 1967. Amended by P.A. 79-1358, § 10, eff. Oct. 1, 1976; P.A. 79-1365, § 34, eff. Oct. 1, 1976; P.A. 81-1489, § 76, eff. Dec. 1, 1980.

1002-4. Submission of question of organization—Form of proposition

§ 2-4. At such designated election there shall be submitted to the voters of the proposed district, the question of organization and establishment of the proposed public library district.

Due notice of such election shall be given in the manner provided by the general election law and shall specify the purpose of the election and contain a map and description of the proposed district.

The proposition shall be substantially in the following form:

FOR the establishment of a public library district in all or part of .... County.	
AGAINST the establishment of a public library district in all or part of .... County.	

Laws 1967, p. 1684, § 2-4. Amended by P.A 81-1489, § 76, eff. Dec. 1, 1980.

1002-4.1. Tax rate limit—Ballots

§ 2-4.1. If no tax rate limit is specified in the ballot, the tax rate limit of the newly organized district shall be as set forth in Section 3-1 of this Act. If, however, the Petitioners pursuant to Section 2-2 of this Act specify a rate higher than the rate set forth in Section 3-1, the ballots shall be in substantially the following form:

FOR the establishment of a public library district in all or part of .... County, with a maximum annual public library tax rate established at . % of the value of all taxable property as equalized and assessed by the Department of Revenue.	
AGAINST the establishment of a public library district in all or part of .... County, with a maximum annual public library tax rate established at . % of the full value of all taxable property as equalized and assessed by the Department of Revenue.	

In no event shall said tax rate exceed the maximum tax rate set forth in Section 3–2 of this Act.

Laws 1967, p. 1684, § 2–4.1, added by P.A. 80–405, § 1, eff. Oct. 1, 1977. Amended by P.A. 81–1509, Art. IV, § 78, eff. Sept. 26, 1980.

1002–6. Results of election—Determination—Final order and decree

§ 2–6. The Election Authorities shall, within 10 days thereafter, file with the Circuit Court ordering the election, his certificate setting forth the results of the election in each precinct.

The question of establishment of a district shall be based upon the majority of votes cast on the question by the voters of the proposed territory determined as follows.

Where the proposed territory does not include a city, village or incorporated town or any portion thereof, then the majority of all the votes cast upon the question shall determine establishment.

Where the proposed territory does include a city, village or incorporated town or any portion thereof, then the votes cast shall be divided into two lots. The votes cast within such municipalities shall be counted together, and the votes cast outside of such municipalities shall be counted together, and the question must carry in each group in order to establish the district. Should there be 2 or more municipalities within the proposed territory, and the question of establishment carries in both groups as aforesaid, but, the votes cast in one municipality having its own tax-supported library are against establishment of the district, then the district shall have been established but the dissenting municipality with its own tax-supported library shall be excluded from the territory of the district.

Where the proposed territory includes a township having its own tax-supported library, and the question of establishment carries in all areas as aforesaid, such township votes on the question shall also be counted separately, and if the votes cast within such township with its own tax-supported library are against establishment, then the dissenting township shall be excluded from the territory of the district.

The judge assigned to the matter shall enter his final order and decree setting forth the results of the referendum based upon the certificate filed with him by the Election Authorities and such shall become a part of the records of such court. Where more than one county is involved in the referendum, a copy of the original petition, the order calling for the referendum and the order setting forth the results thereof shall be filed in the Circuit Court of each such county affected.

Laws 1967, p. 1684, § 2–6. Amended by P.A. 81–1489, § 76, eff. Dec. 1, 1980.

1002–7. Units of local government as all or part of district—Referendum

§ 2–7. A county, city, village, township, or incorporated town may become part of or all of a district as follows:

(1) No county, township or municipality which has a public tax-supported library may be included within the district at the time of the establishment of any district, unless the proposition of being included in the district is submitted to the voters of the county, township or municipality and is approved by a majority of those voting upon the proposition.

(2) At any time after the establishment, any county, township or municipality having its own public tax-supported library may become a part of the district, if the proposition is submitted to the voters thereof at a regular election, and the proposition is approved by a majority of those voting upon the proposition. In addition to the requirements of the general election law, the annexation provisions in this Act shall govern the petition requirements for a referendum for inclusion within an existing district.

(3) The electors of any county, township or municipality may cause the conversion thereof to a public library district by proceeding as follows: If a petition signed by not less than 100 voters or, in the case where there are 100 or fewer voters, then a majority thereof, residing within the county, township or municipality is filed with the clerk of such county, township or municipality and a copy thereof filed with the

existing board of library directors, such clerk shall certify the question of conversion to the proper election authorities who shall submit the question at a regular election in accordance with the general election law. In addition to the requirements of the general election law, the petition shall specify the new maximum tax rate if the rate is to be in excess of the existing ceiling or limitation of the library converted. Upon receipt of a certified copy of such petition, The Board of Library Directors shall within 10 days, file with the county, township or municipal clerk, as the case may be, an addendum to the petition setting forth: the establishment and history of the existing public library, the lawful ceiling on its public library tax levies, the geographic area or territory involved, and the identity of the county township or municipality involved.

The proposition shall be substantially in the following form:

FOR the conversion of the public library in the .... of ...., Illinois, to a public library district.	
AGAINST the conversion of the public library in the .... of ...., Illinois, to a public library district.	

If the petition specified a maximum tax rate in excess of the existing ceiling or limitation, the proposition shall be in substantially the following form:

FOR the conversion of the public library in the .... of ...., Illinois, to a public library district, with a maximum annual public library tax rate established at . % of the value of all taxable property as equalized and assessed by the Department of Revenue.	
AGAINST the conversion of the public library in the .... of ...., Illinois, to a public library district, with a maximum annual public library tax rate established at . % of the value of all taxable property as equalized and assessed by the Department of Revenue.	

Should the election results favor the conversion to a library district, The Board of Library Directors of the public library affected shall petition the Circuit Court of the County wherein the majority of the territory affected lies, for a final order to convert the public library to a library district, incorporating therein the election results and the addendum to the petition for the election. The Circuit Court upon finding the petition sufficient, shall enter its final order:

(a) Approving the conversion of the existing public library of such county, township or municipality to a public library district subject to this Act;

(b) Naming the district;

(c) Appointing the incumbent Library Directors, as Trustees of the district with the same terms each had as a Library Director;

(d) Fixing the boundary of the newly formed district, and, in the case of the conversion of a township library, deleting from the district all or part of any city, village or incorporated town within the township limits and having a tax-supported library and resulting in duplication of library tax levies;

(e) Specifying the ceiling or limitation upon the annual public library tax or any special tax which may be levied by the district thereafter based upon the existing ceilings or limitations and the obligation of the public library converted hereunder, or based upon the ceiling specified in the conversion petition and ballot, but in any case not to exceed the maximum specified in Section 3-2 of this Act;

(f) Specifying the first fiscal year of the newly formed district;

(g) Specifying the first year when appropriation and levy ordinances may be enacted by the newly formed district and requiring the Library Directors to cause an abatement of any annual public library tax levy for that same year, so that only one annual public library tax will be levied in that year;

(h) Specifying the effective date of the conversion and of the acquisition of the assets and assumption of the liabilities of the Board of Library Directors and of the public library affected by the conversion, by the Board of Library Trustees of the newly formed district; and

(i) Specifying the date when the newly formed district shall commence to render library service.

The Trustees of the newly formed district shall thereupon publish notice of that order and of its effect, and the order shall be effective not later than 30 days after the date of its entry. Library Directors of a library converted to a district shall serve out their respective terms. The Court which orders the conversion of a city library to a district shall appoint one Trustee to replace the 3 whose terms expire next after the conversion to a district and, if necessary, appoint 3 to succeed the following class of 3. The terms of those so appointed and of any incumbent directors shall expire on April 30 of the next even numbered year and a new board of Trustees shall then be elected as provided in Section 4–3 of this Article.

An existing bond issue shall not be affected by the conversion, and shall continue in full force and effect under the laws governing the bond issue.

(4) Whenever any county, township or municipality has been or shall be included by annexation or pursuant to an establishment election in a public library district organized hereunder, all of the assets and liabilities of its Board of Library Directors in connection with the operation of its library shall become the assets and liabilities of such public library district. The judge who entered the order for an election shall, within 30 days after the election, appoint an appraiser to determine the value of any tangible property thus acquired by the district as of the date of the formation of the district or as of inclusion within the district. The appraisal shall be filed with the Circuit Court and the County Collector of each county affected, and shall specify the amount by which the assets acquired exceeds any liabilities assumed by the district, the amount to be applied under Section 3–3 of this Act.

(5) The provisions of this Section relating to conversion to a public library district do not apply to a city of over 500,000 population.

Laws 1967, p. 1684, § 2–7. Amended by P.A. 76–959, § 1, eff. Aug. 26, 1969; P.A. 76–1795, § 1, eff. Oct. 9, 1969; P.A. 76–2112, § 1, eff. July 1, 1970; P.A. 77–1441, § 1, eff. Sept. 2, 1971; P.A. 80–405, § 1, eff. Oct. 1, 1977; P.A. 81–1490, § 14, eff. Dec. 1, 1980; P.A. 81–1509, Art. IV, § 78, eff. Sept. 26, 1980; P.A. 81–1550, Art. I, § 20, eff. Jan. 8, 1981.

1002–8. Contiguous territory—Annexation

§ 2–8. Territory outside of any district but contiguous thereto may be annexed in the manner following:

(1) Any territory which is not within the corporate limits of, but which is contiguous to a library district and which territory has no voters residing therein, or any such territory with voters residing therein, may be annexed to the district in the following manner: a written petition signed by the owners of record of all land within such territory, or if such territory is occupied, by the owners of record and by all voters residing therein, shall be filed with the district Secretary. The petition shall request annexation and shall state that no voters reside therein (or that all such voters residing therein join in the petition, whichever shall be the case) and shall be under oath. The Trustees shall then consider by a proposed ordinance the question of the annexation of the described territory. No referendum need be held.

(2) Whenever a municipality included entirely or partially within a district has annexed territory owned by the said municipality, or has lawfully annexed territory contiguous to the district, the district may annex such territory by the passage of an ordinance to the effect, describing the territory annexed, and reciting the annexation thereof by the municipality as well. No referendum need be held.

(3) Any library district by ordinance may annex contiguous territory dedicated for use as a street or highway under the jurisdiction of the Department of Transportation of the State of Illinois or a county or township highway department if no part of the annexed territory is within any other library district. No referendum need be held.

(4) Upon the written petition signed by the majority of the owners of record of land in any contiguous territory which is wholly bounded by two or more library districts, or two or more library districts and a river or a lake or the Illinois State boundary, or two or more library districts and property owned by the State of Illinois other than highway right-of-way, the specified territory may be annexed by one of the specified library districts by the passage of an ordinance providing therefor. The library district annexing the territory shall cause notice of the filing of such petition to be published once in a newspaper of general circulation within the territory to be annexed, not less than 10 days before passage of the annexation ordinance. The ordinance shall describe the territory to be annexed. No referendum need be held.

(5) Upon the filing of a petition with the Circuit Court of the county which contains all or a larger part of the territory of the district, signed by not less than 100 legal voters residing within any territory proposed to be annexed, or upon a petition of a library district seeking to annex such territory, the judge to whom the matter has been assigned shall, if he determines the petition to be in conformity with law, order the question to be submitted at an election in accordance with the general election law, and shall order the proposition certified to the proper election officials.

The order shall set forth the pertinent requirements as set forth in Section 2-3 of this Act.

Each voter within the territory proposed to be annexed and each voter within the district has the right to cast a ballot. If a majority of the votes cast upon the question by those voting in the territory proposed to be annexed and of those cast by those voting within the district is in favor of the proposition, the territory may be annexed; otherwise, the territory may not be annexed.

The proposition shall be in substantially the following form:

"Shall the .... (here describe the territory) be annexed to 'The .... Public Library District, ..., Illinois'?"	YES	
	NO	

The judge assigned to the matter shall enter his order setting forth the results of the referendum, and such order shall become a part of the records of such court. Where more than one county is involved in the referendum, a copy of the original petition, the order calling for the election, and the order setting forth the election results, shall be filed in the Circuit Court of each such county affected or involved.

(6) The proposition to annex any specific territory to a district shall not be submitted to the voters in any such territory sought to be annexed more often than once every 3 years.

(7) A copy of each ordinance of any library district annexing territory together with an accurate map of the territory annexed, shall be deposited with and recorded by the recorder of deeds, and filed with the County Clerk, of the County wherein the annexed territory is situated.

Laws 1967, p. 1684, § 2-8. Amended by P.A. 77-1442, § 1, eff. Sept. 2, 1971; P.A. 78-278, § 1, eff. Oct. 1, 1973; P.A. 79-605, § 1, eff. Aug. 27, 1975; P.A. 77-1441, § 1, eff. Sept. 2, 1971; P.A. 80-396, § 1, eff. Aug. 29, 1977; P.A. 81-1489, § 76, eff. Dec. 1, 1980.

1002-9. Disconnection from district

§ 2-9. A city, village, incorporated town or township, which has a public and tax-supported library established under the provisions of any statute, may be disconnected from a district as follows:

(1) Where a tax-supported public library is established in any city, village, incorporated town or township, lying wholly or partially within a library district, the Board

of Trustees of the affected public library district may enact an ordinance providing for disconnection of such entity, and for an appraisal setting forth the value of the tangible property of the district, the liabilities of the said district, and the excess of the liabilities over assets. Any excess liability shall be collected pursuant to Section 3–4 of this Act.

The said Board of Trustees shall provide for such disconnection and appraisal in any case where the disconnecting territory comprises less than 10% of the district, or the taxes from such territory amount to less than 10% of the library taxes collected annually.

(2) A referendum for disconnection shall be held upon the filing of a petition, signed by not less than 100 of the voters or, in the case where there are 100 or fewer voters, then a majority thereof, residing within any such city, village, incorporated town or township, addressed to and filed with the Secretary of the district.

Thereupon, the district shall certify the question to the proper election officials, who shall submit the proposition of disconnection to the voters at an election, and said referendum shall be held in accordance with the general election law. The proposition shall be substantially in the following form:

"Shall the .... of ...., in .... County, Illinois be disconnected from "The .... Public Library District, ..., Illinois'?"	YES	
	NO	

The majority of the votes cast upon the question of disconnection shall determine the matter.

Such proposition for disconnection from a district may not be submitted to the legal voters thereof oftener than once every 5 years.

(3) The district shall, upon enactment of a disconnection ordinance, or upon a referendum approving a disconnection, file with the Circuit Court of the county wherein the majority of the disconnecting territory lies, an appropriate Petition and a certified copy of the said ordinance, or the certificate of the results of the referendum. Such Petition shall request entry of an order of disconnection and the preparation of an appraisal setting forth the value of the tangible property of the district, the liabilities of the district, and the excess of liabilities over tangible assets or property. Notice shall be published by and within the disconnecting territory.

The judge assigned to the matter, shall, after a hearing upon the matter, enter his order revising the limits and boundaries of the district, and setting forth the liability, if any, yet to be retired and paid by the property owners of the disconnected territory. Such liability shall be collected pursuant to Section 3–4 of this Act.

(4) Expenses of a disconnection referendum, and all other costs and expenses shall be borne by the disconnecting territory.

(5) The Secretary shall record a certified copy of the disconnection order with the Recorder of Deeds and file the same with the County Clerk and the County Collector of each county affected.

Laws 1967, p. 1684, § 2–9. Amended by P.A. 76–606, § 1, eff. July 31, 1969; P.A. 81–1489, § 76, eff. Dec. 1, 1980.

1002–9.1. Disconnection by annexation to city, village or town

§ 2–9a. Any territory within a public library district that is or has been annexed to a city, village or incorporated town that maintains a public library is, by operation of law, disconnected from the public library district as of the January first next after such territory is annexed to the city, village or incorporated town, or in case any such territory has been so annexed prior to the effective date of this amendatory Act of 1969, as of January 1, 1970. Such disconnection by operation of law does not occur if, within 60 days after such annexation or after the effective date of this amendatory Act of 1969, whichever is later, the public library district files with the appropriate court a petition alleging that such disconnection will cause the territory remaining in the district to be noncontiguous or that the loss of assessed valuation by reason of

such disconnection will impair the ability of the district to render fully adequate library service to the territory remaining with the district. When such a petition is filed, the court shall set it for hearing. At such hearing, the district has the burden of proving the truth of the allegations in its petition. If there are any general obligation bonds of the public library district outstanding and unpaid at the time such territory is disconnected from the public library district by operation of this Section such territory shall remain liable for its proportionate share of such bonded indebtedness and the public library district may continue to levy and extend taxes upon the taxable property in such territory for the purpose of amortizing such bonds until such time as sufficient funds to retire such bonds have been collected.
Laws 1967, p. 1684, § 2–9a, added by P.A. 76–604, § 1, eff. July 31, 1969.

1002–10. Dissolution

§ 2–10. Dissolution of a district may be accomplished in the manner following:
25% but not less than 100 of the voters of a district may petition the Circuit Court of the county which contains all or a greater portion of the district than any other county having territory therein, to order the question of dissolution to be submitted to the voters of the district.

The judge assigned to the matter shall enter his order setting forth provisions similar to those as required for an establishment referendum, and the regular election at which the referendum for dissolution shall be held.

The proposition shall be in substantially the following form:

"Shall The . . . . Public Library District, ..., Illinois' lying in all or part of . . . . County, be dissolved?"	YES	
	NO	

The majority of the votes cast upon the question shall determine the matter.

The judge assigned to the matter shall enter his order and decree setting forth the results of the referendum and such order shall become a part of the records of such court. Where more than one county is involved in the referendum, a copy of the original petition and the original order calling for the referendum, and the order setting forth the results, shall be filed in the Circuit Court of each county affected or involved.

If the majority of the votes cast upon the question are in favor of dissolution, the Board shall proceed with dissolution of the district in compliance with the order of the Circuit Court and pursuant to Section 4–21 of this Act.

Such proposition for dissolution of a district may not be submitted to the voters thereof oftener than once every 5 years.
Laws 1967, p. 1684, § 2–10. Amended by P.A. 81–1489, § 76, eff. Dec. 1, 1980.

1002–11. Mergers of two or more districts

§ 2–11. Mergers of two or more districts contiguous to each other and having the same limitations upon the annual library taxes that may be levied may be accomplished in the manner following:

(1) The Board of Trustees of each district shall publish notice of its intent to adopt an ordinance for merger with another contiguous district. On the day and date specified in the said notice, the Board of Trustees may proceed to act upon and to enact the ordinance for merger. Enactment thereof must be by a ⅔ vote of all Trustees serving on the Board, and the ayes and nays shall be recorded.

(2) A referendum for a merger may be held at a regular election scheduled under the general election law if separate but identical petitions signed by 10% or 100 of the voters residing in the district, whichever is more, are filed with the secretary of each district affected by such election.

Thereupon, the secretary of each affected district shall certify the question of merger to the proper election authorities who shall submit the question at a regular election in accordance with the general election law. A separate referendum shall be held in each district affected and the results shall be reported by the election authority to the secretary of each district affected in accordance with the general election law. The proposition of merger shall be substantially in the following form:

| "Shall 'The .... Public Library District, of ...., Illinois', be merged with 'The | YES | |
| .... Public Library District of ...., ... Illinois'?" | NO | |

The combined majority of votes cast upon the question of merger shall determine the matter, and the question must carry in each of the districts affected.

Such proposition of merger may not be submitted to the legal voters of any district more often than once every 5 years.

(3) Each district shall, upon enactment of a merger ordinance and upon an election approving a merger, file, or the districts may file jointly, with the Circuit Court of the county wherein the majority of the merging territories lie, an appropriate petition. Such petition shall set forth: the merger ordinances or the certificate of the Secretary upon the question of merger; the establishment and history of the district; the lawful ceiling or limitation upon the annual public library tax levy; the territory of the district and a map thereof; the bond issues outstanding and the amount thereof as is due and the dates payments are due; and the petition shall request a date for a hearing thereon and the name of the judge appointed to preside.

The Circuit Court shall cause entry of its order setting forth the date of the hearing and naming the judge who will preside at the hearing. The Trustees of each district shall publish notice of the Petition and the time, date and place of the hearing, and shall post notice thereof at each library operated by each district. At the hearing, all residents of the effected districts shall have a reasonable opportunity to appear and present evidence touching upon the lawful ceiling, or limitations upon, or the duplications of, the library tax levies then in effect. The judge, upon hearing the petition and the evidence presented, and upon finding it sufficient shall enter his final judgment:

(a) Approving the merger of the districts petitioning for such;

(b) Naming the district;

(c) Appointing the incumbent Trustees as Trustees of the district with the same terms each had as a Trustee theretofore;

(d) Fixing the boundary of the district;

(e) Specifying the ceiling or limitation upon the annual public library tax which may be levied by the district thereafter based upon the existing ceilings or limitations of the affected districts;

(f) Specifying the effective date of the merger, such to be as of the ensuing July 1st after entry of the judgment.

(g) Specifying that the district formed by the merger has acquired the assets and has assumed the liabilities of the districts not herein excluded.

The Trustees shall thereupon publish Notice of the aforesaid Order and of its effect, and such Order shall be effective not later than 30 days after the date of its entry. No further referendum need be held on the question of merger or any part thereof made pursuant to this Section.

The Trustees of the merged districts shall serve out their respective terms, but, as the terms of such Trustees expire, successors shall be elected only in the case where it is necessary to preserve 7 Trustees to constitute the Board. Where one of the merged districts has appointed Trustees, the appointed Trustees shall continue until expiration of their terms, but all Trustees of a district formed by merger shall be elected until such time as appointment thereof is approved by the voters of the new district as provided in this Act.

An existing bond issue shall not be affected by such merger, but shall continue in full force and effect, and a special tax supporting the same shall continue to be levied upon the residents of the district originally approving the same. Nor shall the merger affect the levy of any other special tax pursuant to Sections 5–4 and 5–5 of this Act, but such shall continue in full force and effect, and such special taxes shall continue to be levied upon the residents of the district originally authorizing the same. Residents of the other district or districts involved in the merger shall not be especially taxed in these instances unless such special taxes are first approved by the voters in the same manner as in the case of the original voter approval as provided in Article 5 of this Act.

Laws 1967, p. 1684, § 2–11. Amended by P.A. 76–959, § 1, eff. Aug. 26, 1969; P.A. 79–1358, § 10, eff. Oct. 1, 1976; P.A. 79–1365, § 34, eff. Oct. 1, 1976; P.A. 81–1490, § 14, eff. Dec. 1, 1980.

1003–1. Tax levy for establishment, maintenance and support

§ 3–1. When a district has been organized and established under this Act, the Board, upon its formation and qualification of the Trustees to serve, may levy for the establishment, maintenance and support of a public library or libraries within the district or for contracting for library service, an annual public library tax not exceeding .15% of the value of all the taxable property within the district, as equalized and assessed by the Department of Revenue. If the annual public library tax rate of an established library was increased above .12% up to .20% as provided in this Act, the corporate authorities may then levy an amount that will require the extension of up to an additional .03% above the increased rate approved at the election. Any tax levied pursuant to Section 3–11 shall be disregarded in applying the provisions of this Section.

The corporate authorities may also levy an additional tax of .02% of the value of all the taxable property in the district, as equalized or assessed by the Department of Revenue, for the purchase of sites and buildings, for the construction and equipment of buildings, for the rental of buildings required for library purposes, and for maintenance, repairs and alterations of library buildings and equipment. In any year in which the corporate authorities propose to levy such additional .02% tax, the corporate authorities shall adopt a resolution determining to levy such tax. Within 15 days after the adoption of the resolution, it shall be published at least once in one or more newspapers published in the district, or if no newspaper is published therein, then in one or more newspapers with a general circulation within the district. In a district in which no newspaper is published, publication may instead be made by posting a notice in three prominent places within the district. If no petition is filed with the corporate authorities within 30 days after publication or posting of the resolution, the district shall then be authorized to levy the tax. However, if within the 30 day period, a petition is filed with the corporate authorities, signed by electors of the district equal in number to 10% or more of the total number of votes cast at the last preceding regular district election, asking that the question of levying such a .02% tax be submitted to the electors of the district, the question shall be certified to the proper election officials, who shall submit the question at an election in accordance with the general election law. The proposition shall be in substantially the following form: "Shall the corporate authorities of (name of district) be authorized to levy an additional tax of   % for the construction of buildings, provision of sites, etc., as determined by resolution of   , 19   ?". If a majority of votes cast upon the proposition are in favor thereof, the corporate authorities may levy the additional tax.

Laws 1967, p. 1684, § 3–1. Amended by P.A. 76–526, § 1, eff. July 28, 1969; P.A. 77–1540, § 1, eff. Aug. 17, 1971; P.A. 77–1793, § 1, eff. July 1, 1972; P.A. 77–2829, § 30, eff. Dec. 22, 1972; P.A. 78–255, § 61, eff. Oct. 1, 1973; P.A. 80–1152, § 2, eff. July 1, 1978; P.A. 80–1153, § 2, eff. July 1, 1978; P.A. 80–1364, § 34, eff. Aug. 13, 1978; P.A. 81–1489, § 76, eff. Dec. 1, 1980; P.A. 81–1509, Art. IV, § 78, eff. Sept. 26, 1980.

1003–1.1. Maximum tax levy

§ 3–1.1. If the petition and ballot so specify in the original establishment or conversion as set forth in Section 2–2 and 2–4.1 or 2–7 hereof, such district board may levy a tax in excess of the rate set forth in Section 3–1, not to exceed the rate specified in the establishment petition and ballot, but in any event not to exceed the rate set forth in Section 3–2 of this Act.

Laws 1967, p. 1684, § 3–1.1, added by P.A. 80–405, § 1, eff. Oct. 1, 1977.

1003–2. Increase of tax—Referendum

§ 3–2. Such annual public library tax may be increased to not exceed .40% if the voters of such district shall so determine and approve by a majority of those voting upon the question of such increase, at any regular election. Such question shall be submitted by the proper election officials pursuant to an ordinance, or pursuant to a petition served upon the Secretary and bearing not less than 100 signatures of voters residing within the district. The question shall be in substantially the following form:

"Shall the annual public library tax rate for 'The Public Library District, Illinois' be established at .40% of full, fair cash value instead of at .12%, the maximum rate otherwise applicable to the next taxes to be extended?"	YES	
	NO	

Voter approval of an increase under a prior law shall satisfy the requirements of this Section.

Laws 1967, p. 1684, § 3–2. Amended by P.A. 76–526, § 1, eff. July 28, 1969; P.A. 80–1153, § 2, eff. July 1, 1978; P.A. 81–1489, § 76, eff. Dec. 1, 1980.

1003–3. Procedure upon annexation or inclusion

§ 3–3. When the appraised net value of any library assets acquired by a district under an annexation or inclusion under this Act exceed the liabilities assumed and such is reported to the County Collector of the county involved, the collector shall credit such excess upon his books as a payment on any taxes thereafter levied by the district and extended against taxable property within the territory annexed or included and whose assets were so converted, in the proportion that the assessed value of all taxable property in such territory annexed or included bears to the assessed value of all taxable property within the library district involved. If the amount of such credit is less than the total tax extended against such taxable property, it shall be applied proportionately as to each taxpayer in abatement of his public library district tax.

This Section does not apply where the geographical territory of the acquiring district is identical to that of a city, village, incorporated town or township area acquired by the district in an annexation or inclusion.

Laws 1967, p. 1684, § 3–3. Amended by P.A. 77–1704, § 1, eff. July 1, 1972.

1003–4. Rights and liabilities of disconnected territory

§ 3–4. When any city, village or incorporated town or township has been disconnected from a district pursuant to the provisions of this Act and the court order providing for such disconnection also sets forth a continuing liability to be paid and retired by property owners of the disconnected territory, the County Collector of the county involved shall debit upon his books the taxes to be paid and thereafter levied by the district and extended against taxable property within the disconnected territory. The County Clerk shall continue to extend district library taxes upon the taxable property within the disconnected territory and the County Collector shall continue to collect district library taxes upon such taxable property within the disconnected territory until the excess liability has been paid and retired.

Until full and final payment of such liability, the said residents and property owners of the disconnected territory shall be entitled to full and free library service from the district, and upon full and final payment of such liability, such residents and property owners of the disconnected territory shall no longer be subject to any tax levies by the district, nor shall they thereafter have any right, title or interest in and to the assets and tangible property of the district affected by the disconnection.

Laws 1967, p. 1684, § 3–4.

1003–5. Status of library taxes—Districts in two or more counties—Expansion of district by annexation

§ 3–5. The library taxes provided for in this Act shall be in addition to all other taxes or tax rates authorized to be levied by the district or any other taxing authority lying wholly or partially within the district and they shall not be a part of the taxes making up any rate prescribed as a limitation on the amount of taxes such other taxing authority or the district may levy or collect, except that no library district tax for library purposes shall be levied within the district by any other taxing authority.

Where the corporate limits of any library district lie partly in 2 or more counties, the board shall ascertain the total amount of all taxable property lying within each county, as the property is assessed or equalized by the Department of Revenue for the current year, and shall certify the amount of taxable property in each county within the library district, to the county clerk of each county affected. Each county clerk shall then ascertain the rate per cent which, upon the total valuation of all property subject to taxation within that library district ascertained as provided in this Section, will produce a net amount not less than the total amount directed to be levied by the library district. The county clerk shall then certify the rate per cent under his hand and seal, and shall extend the library tax to be levied upon the books of the collector of taxes for his county against all taxable property within his county within the limits of such library district.

In addition, where the corporate limits of an existing library district are expanded by an annexation approved by the voters at a referendum, the added or annexed territory shall be subject to the library taxes provided for in this Act, as amended, to the same extent as territory within the district before the annexation.
Laws 1967, p. 1684, § 3–5. Amended by P.A. 76–804, § 1, eff. Aug. 18, 1969; P.A. 78–384, § 1, eff. Oct. 1, 1973; P.A. 81–1509, Art. IV, § 78, eff. Sept. 26, 1980.

1003–6. Levy and collection of taxes—Library fund

§ 3–6. The library taxes provided for in this Act shall be levied by the district, and collected in like manner with other general taxes by the county collector or collectors affected by the levy. The proceeds of all such taxes collected for district purposes, and all other moneys belonging to the district, shall be deposited with the Treasurer of the district and kept by him in separate funds. The Treasurer shall establish a library fund and one or more such separate funds as he deems necessary, but no part of any such fund or funds shall be expended by him except upon warrants certified to as correct by the librarian and approved by the Board.

Funds involved in accumulations as herein provided, or donations to the district, may be kept in separate and interest bearing accounts in any bank or bank in which public funds may be deposited, or invested as provided by law.

If a library district receives any payments or allocations of funds from the "Illinois Income Tax Act", as now or hereafter amended, the rate at which the library tax levied under this Article is extended shall be reduced by a rate which would produce an amount equal to the funds so received or by .03%, whichever is less.
Laws 1967, p. 1684, § 3–6. Amended by P.A. 77–1793, § 1, eff. July 1, 1972.

1003–7. Fiscal year

§ 3–7. The first fiscal year of any district shall close on June 30th following establishment thereof. Thereafter, the fiscal year of any district shall commence on July 1st and close on June 30th.
Laws 1967, p. 1684, § 3–7, eff. July 17, 1967.

1003–8. Tax to rebuild or restore library building

§ 3–8. If a library building is destroyed or seriously impaired by storm or fire or other casualty, the Board, in order to rebuild or restore any such library building thus destroyed or seriously impaired may levy an annual tax not exceeding .08333% of the value, as equalized or assessed by the Department of Local Governmental Affairs, on all the taxable property in the district and for not exceeding 10 successive years. This tax shall be levied and collected in like manner with other general taxes by the county collector or collectors affected by the levy and shall not be included in the aggregate amount of taxes limited by any provision of this Act.
Laws 1967, p. 1684, § 3–8, added by P.A. 79–414, § 1, eff. Aug. 14, 1975.

1003–9. Ordinance authorizing levy of tax—Submission to voters

§ 3–9. No public library district may levy the tax provided for in this Article unless it first adopts an ordinance authorizing the levy of such tax and orders such ordinance submitted to the voters of the public library district at an election and such ordinance is approved by a majority of such voters voting upon the question in accordance with the general election law. This Section does not apply to the tax authorized by Section 3–11.

Laws 1967, p. 1684, § 3–9, added by P.A. 79–414, § 1, eff. Aug. 14, 1975. Amended by P.A. 80–1153, § 2, eff. July 1, 1978; P.A. 81–1489, § 76, eff. Dec. 1, 1980.

1003–10. Amount of annual tax levy

§ 3–10. The Board shall not levy an annual tax which would produce revenues in excess of the difference between the actual cost of reconstruction of the building and insurance benefits paid to the Board as a result of the incurred physical loss.

Laws 1967, p. 1684, § 3–10, added by P.A. 79–414, § 1, eff. Aug. 14, 1975.

1003–11. Public library district working cash fund tax—Levy

§ 3–11. For the purpose of providing money to establish and replenish a library district working cash fund authorized by Section 4–17, the Board shall have the power to levy an annual tax not to exceed .05% of the value, as equalized or assessed by the Department of Revenue for the year in which each levy is made, on all taxable property in the district. The tax shall be levied and collected in like manner with other general taxes by the county collector or collectors affected by the levy but the collection of the tax shall not be anticipated by the issuance of any warrants drawn against the tax. The tax shall be known as the public library district working cash fund tax and shall be set apart in a special fund as prescribed in Section 4–17. Whenever a tax is first levied under this Section, any taxpayer in the district may, within 30 days after the levy is made, file with the Board a petition signed by not less than 10% or 1500, whichever is lesser, of the voters of the district requesting the submission of a proposition to the voters of the district at an election in accordance with the general election law. The Board shall certify the proposition to the proper election officials who shall submit the proposition at an election in accordance with the general election law. If a majority of the votes cast upon the proposition are in favor thereof the tax shall thereafter be authorized; if a majority of the votes cast upon the proposition are against the proposition the tax shall not be levied.

No public library district may levy a tax under this Section for more than 4 years, but the 4 years for which any such district elects to levy such tax need not be consecutive.

Laws 1967, p. 1684, § 3–11, added by P.A. 80–1153, § 2, eff. July 1, 1978. Amended by P.A. 81–1489, § 76, eff. Dec. 1, 1980; P.A. 81–1509, Art. IV, § 78, eff. Sept. 26, 1980.

1004–1. Initial appointment—Tenure—Election

§ 4–1. Within 60 days after the establishment of a library district, and if the district is wholly contained within a single county, the presiding officer of the county board with the advice and consent of the county board shall appoint the first board thereof, from a list of nominees submitted by the petitioners or persons appearing at the hearing. If however the district lies in more than one county, the first board shall be nominated in the manner herein provided but the appointment of the trustees shall be made by the members of the General Assembly whose legislative districts encompass any portion of the district. The trustees so appointed shall serve until their successors have been elected and qualified at the first election. The first such election shall be held at the regular election scheduled for Trustees of Public Library Districts under the general election law which occurs more than 4 months following the establishment election of the district.

Laws 1967, p. 1684, § 4–1. Amended by P.A. 76–1005, § 1, eff. Aug. 26, 1969; P.A. 77–687, § 1, eff. Aug. 9, 1971; P.A. 78–1128, § 36, eff. Oct 1, 1974; P.A. 79–327, § 1, eff. Oct. 1, 1975; P.A. 81–1490, § 14, eff. Dec. 1, 1980.

1004–2. Referendum for appointment of trustees—Results—Appointment and tenure

§ 4–2. If a petition signed by 100 or more voters residing within the district is filed with the Secretary of the District within the time provided by the general election law, the Secretary shall certify the question of changes from elected to appointed trustees to the proper election authorities who shall submit the question at the next regular election for Trustees of Public Library Districts in accordance with the general election law. If the district is wholly contained within a single county, the proposition shall be in substantially the following form: "Shall the trustees of 'The ..... Public Library District, ..., Illinois', hereafter be appointed by the presiding officer of the county board of ..... County, Illinois, with the advice and consent of the ..... County board?"

If the district lies in more than one county, the proposition shall be in substantially the following form: "Shall the Trustees of 'The ..... Public Library District, ..., Illinois', hereafter be appointed by the members of the General Assembly whose legislative districts encompass any portion of the above stated District?"

If a majority of the voters voting on the question vote in favor of the matter, the Trustees for such district shall thereafter be appointed for office by the appropriate appointing authority as named, and the appointed Board shall thereafter consist of 7 Trustees, but not more than 4 Trustees may be residents of the same municipality unless that municipality comprises the entire district.

Trustees who are incumbent, or elected at the time of such favorable vote, shall continue in office until the expiration of the term for which they are elected. As the terms of such elected Trustees expire, the appointing authority shall appoint their successors, except that 3 Trustees shall be appointed as the successor to the 2 Trustees whose terms expire immediately after such favorable vote for appointment of Trustees.

All such appointed Trustees, other than those appointed upon the establishment of the district, shall hold office for a term of 6 years from the 1st day in May of the year of their appointment.

Laws 1967, p. 1684, § 4–2. Amended by P.A. 76–959, § 1, eff. Aug. 26, 1969; P.A. 76–1005, § 1, eff. Aug. 26, 1969; P.A. 76–2113, § 1, eff. July 1, 1970; P.A. 77–687, § 1, eff. Aug. 9, 1971; P.A. 78–1128, § 36, eff. Oct. 1, 1974; P.A. 81–1490, § 14, eff. Dec. 1, 1980.

1004–3. Biennial elections and terms in other cases

§ 4–3. In all other cases, Trustees shall be elected biennially at the regular election scheduled for Trustees of Public Library Districts under the general election law, for 6-year terms, and 7 Trustees shall constitute a Board. Their terms shall be staggered. After the first election, the Trustees shall determine by lot, which Trustee shall serve for terms of 2, 4 and 6 years from the 1st Monday of the month next following the month of the election with 3 Trustees being selected for 6 year terms.

At each biennial election thereafter, the Trustees elected to succeed those whose terms have expired, shall hold office for the full term from the 1st Monday of the month next following the election and until their respective successors are elected and qualified.

Any district may provide by resolution of the Board that the term of its Trustees shall be 4 years. If the Board adopts such a resolution, then if 3 Trustees are to be elected at the next election or if 2 Trustees are to be elected at each of the next 2 elections, one of the Trustees elected at the first election, to be determined by lot at the first meeting after that election, shall serve a 2 year term.

Laws 1967, p. 1684, § 4–3. Amended by P.A. 76–959, § 1, eff. Aug. 26, 1969; P.A. 81–1180, § 2, eff. July 1, 1980; P.A. 81–1490, § 14, eff. Dec. 1, 1980.

1004–4. Nomination of candidates

§ 4–4. Nomination of candidates for election as Trustees shall be by petition, signed by at least 50 voters residing within the district, and filed with the Secretary of the district within the time provided by the general election law. No party name or affiliation may appear on such petition.

Laws 1967, p. 1684, § 4–4. Amended by P.A. 81–1490, § 14, eff. Dec. 1, 1980.

1004–5. Time and conduct of elections

§ 4–5. Elections of Trustees shall take place at the regular election scheduled for Trustees of Public Library Districts under the general election law.

Laws 1967, p. 1684, § 4–5. Amended by P.A. 81–1490, § 14, eff. Dec. 1, 1980.

1004–6. Names of candidates—Certification—Printing on ballot

§ 4–6. The names of all candidates for the office of Trustee shall be certified by the Secretary to the proper election authorities who shall conduct the election in accordance with the general election law. The ballot for such election shall not designate any political party, platform or political principle whatever.

Laws 1967, p. 1684, § 4–6. Amended by P.A. 81–1490, § 14, eff. Dec. 1, 1980.

1004–7. Vacancies

§ 4–7. Vacancies shall be declared in the office of Trustee by the Board when the elected or appointed Trustee declines or is unable to serve, or becomes a nonresident of the District or is convicted of a misdemeanor by failing, neglecting or refusing to discharge any duty imposed upon him by this Act, or who shall have failed to pay the library taxes levied by the District. Vacancies shall be filled by the remaining Trustees until the next regular election of Trustees, at which time a Trustee shall be elected to fill the vacancy for the unexpired term; however if such vacancy occurs with less than 28 months remaining in the term, or if the vacancy occurs less than 88 days before the next regularly scheduled election for this office, then the person appointed by the remaining trustees shall serve the remainder of the unexpired term and no election to fill the vacancy shall be held.

Laws 1967, p. 1684, § 4–7. Amended by P.A. 76–1005, § 1, eff. Aug. 26, 1969; P.A. 77–687, § 1, eff. Aug. 9, 1971; P.A. 81–1490, § 14, eff. Dec. 1, 1980; P.A. 81–1535, § 20, eff. Dec. 19, 1980.

1004–8. Compensation and expenses

§ 4–8. Trustees shall serve without compensation but shall be reimbursed for their actual and necessary expenses incurred in the performance of their duties from district funds.

Laws 1967, p. 1684, § 4–8, eff. July 17, 1967.

1004–9. Organization of board

§ 4–9. Within 60 days after their election or appointment, the incumbent and new Trustees shall meet to organize the Board.

The Secretary shall first certify the membership of the Board and Trustees duly elected or appointed and having taken their oath of office as prescribed by the Constitution shall be qualified to serve as Trustees under this Act. Upon establishment, the required oath shall be taken and subscribed before the County Clerk of the county containing all or a larger portion of the district or before the Judge entering the Order for the establishment referendum. In the case of a conversion, the required oath shall be taken and subscribed before the Judge entering the conversion order. The oath may also be taken and subscribed in all cases, before the Secretary of the district.

The Trustees shall then organize the Board, and elect from among its members, a President, a Treasurer, and a Secretary. The Secretary shall on or before the 1st day of July of each year file his certificate with the said County Clerk and with the Illinois State Librarian, listing the names and addresses of the Trustees and officers and their respective terms in office.

The first officers shall serve until the next regular election of Trustees, and thereafter, for 2-year terms, ending on the first Monday of the month following each regular election or until their successors are duly elected by the Board. A vacancy in any office shall be filled by the Board for the unexpired term.

Laws 1967, p. 1684, § 4–9. Amended by P.A. 76–1364, § 1, eff. Sept. 16, 1969; P.A. 77–1704, § 1, eff. July 1, 1972; P.A. 81–1490. § 14. eff. Dec. 1. 1980.

1004–10. Duties of officers

§ 4–10. The duties of the officers of the Board are as follows:

(1) The President shall preside over all meetings, and in his absence, a temporary chairman shall be elected by the Board. He shall not have nor exercise veto powers.

(2) The Treasurer shall keep and maintain accounts and records of the district during his term in office, indicating therein, a record of all receipts, disbursements and balances in any funds. His records shall be subject to audit by 2 other Trustees appointed by the President.

An audit shall be conducted each fiscal year, and a report filed with the Board not later than the 16th day of July each year, for the prior fiscal year. Such audit shall certify: (1) Cash on hand as of July 1st; (2) Cash in the Working Cash Fund as of July 1st, and the amounts outstanding and due to said Fund; (3) Total cash receipts from all sources; (4) Total disbursements; (5) Discrepancies; (6) Any other information deemed pertinent by the auditing Trustees.

Should a district have 10,000 or more residents within its territory, such audit shall be accompanied by the professional opinion of an accountant authorized to practice public accounting under the laws of this State, with respect to the financial status of the district and the accuracy of the audit, or, if an opinion cannot be expressed, a declaration that such accountant is unable to express such an opinion and an explanation of his reasons therefor.

The Treasurer shall give bond to the district to faithfully discharge the duties of his office and to account to the district for all district funds coming into his hands and which bond shall be in such amount and with such sureties as shall be approved by the Board. The minimum amount of the bond shall be based upon $\frac{1}{12}$ of the total annual library taxes collected by the District. Cost of any surety bond shall be borne by the District.

Any person or entity or public body or agency having district funds, property or records in their possession, shall, upon demand by any Trustee transfer and release all such to the Treasurer.

(3) The Secretary shall keep and maintain appropriate records for his term in office and shall include therein, a record of the minutes of all meetings, the names of those in attendance, the ordinances enacted, resolutions, rules and regulations adopted, and all other pertinent written matter as affect the operation of the district. The records shall be subject to an audit by 2 other Trustees appointed by the President and shall be conducted each fiscal year, and the audit report filed not later than the 31st day of July in each year. Such report shall certify as to the accuracy of the records of the Secretary, their completeness, and list the discrepancies, if any. The Secretary shall have the power to administer oaths and affirmations for the purposes of this Act.

(4) The Board shall take whatever action is deemed necessary to cure the discrepancies reported to it by any audit committee.

Laws 1967, p. 1684, § 4-10. Amended by P.A. 76-1364, § 1, eff. Sept. 16, 1969.

1004-11. Powers of board of trustees

§ 4-11. Each Board of Trustees of a District established pursuant to this Act, shall carry out the spirit and intent of this Act in establishing, supporting and maintaining a public library or libraries within the district and for providing library service, and, in addition to but without limiting other powers conferred by this Act, shall have the following powers:

(1) To enact ordinances and to make and adopt such bylaws, rules and resolutions for their own guidance and for the government of the library as may be expedient, and not inconsistent with this Act.

(2) To have the exclusive control of the expenditure of all moneys collected for the library and deposited to the credit of the library fund;

(3) To have exclusive control of the construction of any library building and of the supervision, care and custody of the grounds, rooms or buildings constructed, leased or set apart for that purpose;

(4) To purchase or lease real or personal property, and to construct an appropriate building or buildings for the use of the library or libraries established hereunder, using, at the board's option, contracts providing for all or part of the consideration to be paid through installments at stated intervals during a certain period not to exceed 10 years with interest at a rate not to exceed 7% on the unpaid balance, except that contracts for installment purchases of real estate shall provide for not more than 50%

of the total consideration to be repaid by installments;

(5) To remodel or reconstruct a building erected or purchased by the Board, when such building is in need thereof or is not adapted to its purposes and needs;

(6) To sell or otherwise dispose of real or personal property that it deems no longer necessary or useful for library purposes, and to lease to others any real property not immediately useful to the district but for which plans for ultimate use have been adopted;

(7) To appoint a competent librarian and necessary assistants and custodial employees, to fix their compensation, and to remove such appointees, and to retain counsel and professional consultants as needed;

(8) To contract with any tax-supported or privately endowed public library or library boards, or school library or school board, for the furnishing or receiving of library service, to participate in interstate library compacts and library systems, and to contract to supply library services and for the expenditure of any federal or State funds made available to any county, municipality, township or to the State of Illinois for library purposes;

(9) To join with the board or boards of one or more public libraries within this State, in maintaining libraries, or for the maintenance of a common library or common library services for the participants upon such terms and conditions as may be agreed upon by and between the participating library boards;

(10) To enter into contracts, and to take title to any property acquired by it for library purposes;

(11) To exclude from the use of the library, any person who willfully violates the rules prescribed by the Board;

(12) To extend the privileges and use of the library, to persons residing outside of the district, upon such terms and conditions as the Board may from time to time by its regulations prescribe, and to impose a non-resident fee for such services comparable to the cost paid by residents of the district;

(13) To provide for suitable civil or criminal penalties for persons committing injury upon the library or the grounds or other property thereof and for injury to or failure to return any book or material or personalty belonging to the library;

(14) To invest funds pursuant to "An Act relating to certain investments of public funds by public agencies", approved July 23, 1943, as amended;

(15) To exercise the power of eminent domain.

Laws 1967, p. 1684, § 4–11. Amended by P.A. 76–804, § 1, eff. Aug. 18, 1969; P.A. 79–989, § 3, eff. Oct. 1, 1975; P.A. 79–1061, § 3, eff. Oct. 1, 1975; P.A. 79–1454, § 36, eff. Aug. 31, 1976.

1004–12. Reports

§ 4–12. On or before the 1st day of September of each year, the Board shall prepare and file a written report for the past fiscal year. Such report shall include:

(a) The audit of the Treasurer and his records, accounts and funds;

(b) The audit of the Secretary and his records;

(c) A statement as to any change in the limits and boundaries of the district;

(d) A statement as to property of any type acquired by the district by purchase, devise, bequest, gift or otherwise;

(e) A statement as to the amount of accumulations and the reasons therefor;

(f) A statement as to any outstanding liabilities including those for bonds still outstanding;

(g) Any other pertinent information requested by the Illinois State Librarian.

Where dissolution of the district has been approved, the Board shall prepare a final report.

The Secretary shall file certified copies of the report on or before due date, with the Illinois State Librarian. He shall also file a copy thereof with the library or libraries operated by the district and make such available for public inspection.

Laws 1967, p. 1684, § 4–12, eff. July 17, 1967.

1004–13. Sale or disposition of property

§ 4–13. When the Board has determined to sell or otherwise dispose of real or personal property that it deems no longer necessary or useful for library purposes, such may be sold or disposed of at a public sale, as follows:

(1) Personal property having a value of less than $1,000 may be displayed at the library, and a public notice of its availability, the date and the terms of the proposed sale shall be posted.

(2) In all other cases, the Board shall publish notice of the availability and location of the real or personal property, the date and terms of the proposed sale, giving such notice once each week for 2 successive weeks.

On the day of the sale, the Board shall proceed with the sale and may sell such property for a price determined by the Board, or, to the highest bidder. Where the Board deems the bids inadequate, it may reject such bids and re-advertise the sale. Laws 1967, p. 1684, § 4–13, eff. July 17, 1967.

1004–14. Participation in maintenance of historical museum and library

§ 4–14. Whenever any historical society or other civic body or corporation, organized for the promotion of historical education, is maintaining a historical museum and library within the territory of a public library district organized under this Act, such public library district may participate in the maintenance of such historical museum and library upon such terms and conditions as may be mutually agreed upon by the Board of Trustees of such public library district and the governing board of such historical society or other civic body or corporation. Laws 1967, p. 1684, § 4–14, eff. July 17, 1967.

1004–15. Budget and appropriation ordinances

§ 4–15. The Board shall, within the first quarter of each fiscal year, and no later than the fourth Tuesday of September, prepare and enact a budget and appropriation ordinance pursuant to the provisions of "The Illinois Municipal Budget Law", as amended.

A certified copy of such ordinance shall be published once, and the Board shall then ascertain the total amount of the appropriation made for all purposes permitted by this Act, and the total amount of monies necessary to be raised therefor. Seven days or more after publication of the appropriation ordinance, the Board shall enact a levy ordinance incorporating the appropriation ordinance by reference, and shall levy not to exceed the total amount of such appropriation, taking into consideration monies to be raised from other than tax sources, upon all property subject to taxation within the district as that property is assessed and equalized for state and county purposes for that year.

The Secretary shall file, on or before the fourth Tuesday of September, a certified copy of such levy ordinance with the County Clerk of each county affected by the levy. Where more than one county is involved, the Secretary shall supply and certify under his hand and seal of the district such additional information as may be required by each County Clerk for his determination of the portion of the levy as required to be levied in his county.

The County Clerk shall ascertain the rate per cent which, upon the full, fair cash value of all property subject to taxation within the district, as that property is assessed or equalized by the Department of Revenue, will produce a net amount of not less than the total amount so directed to be levied and then add on for collection loss and costs. The County Clerk shall extend this tax in a separate column upon the books of the collector of state and county taxes within the district.

The Secretary shall also file on or before the fourth Tuesday of September, certified copies of the appropriation and levy ordinances with the library or libraries operated by the district and make such available to public inspection at all times. Laws 1967, p. 1684, § 4–15. Amended by P.A. 77–328, § 1, eff. July 22, 1971; P.A. 81–1509, Art. IV, § 78, eff. Sept. 26, 1980.

1004–17. Public library district working cash fund

§ 4–17. Any district may, by ordinance, create and maintain a working cash fund, for the sole purpose of enabling the district to have in its funds, at all times, sufficient money to meet demands thereon for ordinary and necessary and committed expenditures for library purposes.

Such working cash fund shall be known as the public library district working cash fund and may contain any amount deemed necessary by the Board to satisfy the purpose of the fund; provided, that the balance in the fund shall not at any time be allowed to exceed .2% of the full, fair cash value of all taxable property within the district, as equalized or assessed by the Department of Revenue for the year the fund was established or, if established after January 1, 1979, then for the year 1978. The money for such fund shall only accrue from the public library district working cash fund tax the Board is authorized to levy pursuant to Section 3–11.

Once the fund has been created, the proceeds shall be deposited in a special and separate fund, and may be carried over, from year to year without in any manner reducing or abating a future annual library tax levy. It shall be identified in the budget each year, but shall not be deemed as a current asset available for library purposes.

The proceeds of such fund may be transferred from the working cash fund to the general library fund, and disbursed therefrom in anticipation of the collection of taxes lawfully levied for general library purposes or in anticipation of such taxes, as by law now or hereafter enacted or amended, imposed by the General Assembly of the State of Illinois to replace revenue lost by units of local government and school districts as a result of the abolition of ad valorem personal property taxes, pursuant to Article IX, Section 5(c) of the Constitution of the State of Illinois. Such taxes when collected, and after payment of tax warrants, shall be drawn upon to reimburse the working cash fund.

Laws 1967, p. 1684, § 4–17. Amended by P.A. 78–1163, § 2, eff. Aug. 27, 1974; P.A. 80–1153, § 2, eff. July 1, 1978; P.A. 81–165, § 16, eff. Aug. 11, 1979; P.A. 81–924, § 2, eff. Jan. 1, 1980; P.A. 81–1509, Art. I, § 53, eff. Sept. 26, 1980; P.A. 81–1509, Art. IV, § 78, eff. Sept. 26, 1980.

1004–17.1. Abolition of working cash fund

§ 4–17.1. The Board may, by resolution, abolish a working cash fund established pursuant to Section 4–17 and direct the transfer of any balance in such fund, including any interest that has accrued, to the general library fund at the close of the fiscal year. However, if the Board abolishes a working cash fund under this provision, it shall not establish another working cash fund, unless establishment of the fund is approved by a majority of the voters of the district voting on the question at a referendum.

Laws 1967, p. 1684, § 4–17.1, added by P.A. 81–924, § 2, eff. Jan. 1, 1980.

1004–18. Warrants in anticipation of taxes

§ 4–18. When there is no money in the general fund to defray the necessary expenses of the district, and the Working Cash Fund has been drawn upon and depleted, the Board may cause warrants to be issued and drawn against and in anticipation of any taxes levied for the payment of the necessary expenses of the district, but only to the extent of 85% of the total amount of tax so levied. The warrants shall show upon their face that they are payable in numerical order of their issuance, solely from such taxes when collected, and shall be received by any county collector of taxes, in payment of the taxes against which they are issued, and such taxes shall be set apart and held for payment of such warrants.

Every such warrant shall bear interest payable only out of the taxes against which it is drawn, at a rate not exceeding 6% per annum from the date of its issuance until paid, or until notice shall be given by publication in a newspaper or otherwise, that the money for its payment is available and that such will be paid on presentation. Warrants not presented pursuant to such notice, shall after such due date, carry a lower rate of interest as specified, but not less than 3% and for only one year, and after such 1-year term, shall bear no interest thereafter.

Laws 1967, p. 1684, § 4–18. Amended by P.A. 81–165, § 16, eff. Aug. 11, 1979.

1004-19. Total indebtedness

§ 4-19. The total indebtedness incurred by the Board from time to time as is outstanding when aggregated with existing indebtedness may not exceed the debt limits prescribed by the Constitution.

Laws 1967, p. 1684, § 4-19, eff. July 17, 1967.

1004-20. Meetings—Quorum—Voting

§ 4-20. The Board shall call not less than 5 regular meetings each fiscal year, and shall each year by ordinance, specify the time, place, day and date thereof. Special meetings may be called by the President or the Secretary, or by any 4 Trustees, by written notice delivered the day immediately preceding the day of the special meeting, or by oral notice in the case of a stated emergency.

A quorum shall consist of 4 Trustees and a majority of those present shall determine the vote taken on any question unless a larger majority is specified in this Act.

All votes on any question shall be by ayes and nays and spread of record by the Secretary. Absentees and abstentions from voting shall be noted.

Laws 1967, p. 1684, § 4-20. Amended by P.A. 76-959, § 1, eff. Aug. 26, 1969.

1004-21. Procedure upon approval of dissolution of district

§ 4-21. Upon the favorable approval of dissolution of a district pursuant to Section 2-10 of this Act and the entry of the order of the Circuit Court, the Board shall continue in existence for the sole purpose of winding up its affairs and for disposition of district property. Trustees whose terms expire shall continue to serve until the Board dissolves. Personal property of intrinsic value only to libraries may be donated to other public libraries. All other property, real or personal, is to be sold pursuant to Section 4-13 hereof, and the proceeds thereof applied first to the debts of the district, and the balance, if any, paid to the County Collector. Where any such district lies in more than one county, then the said proceeds shall be equitably apportioned among the various counties affected, upon a ratio based upon the taxable property of the district within each such county.

The County Collectors shall thereupon credit the same on their books as a payment on behalf of the taxpayers of the dissolved district toward any other taxes levied by the County involved, and the said proceeds shall thereupon accrue to such county and the said proceeds shall abate the county tax levy for each county affected as to each taxpayer involved until the credit is used up or utilized and applied.

The Board shall then meet, prepare its final report and file the same, enact a dissolution ordinance and direct the filing of certified copies thereof with the County Clerk of each county affected and the Illinois State Librarian. The Board shall then dissolve.

Laws 1967, p. 1684, § 4-21, eff. July 17, 1967.

1005-1. Accumulation of funds—Proceedings of board—Notice

§ 5-1. Whenever the Board determines or resolves to erect a building to be used as a library, or to purchase a site for the same, or to purchase a building, or to repair, remodel or improve an existing library building, or to build an addition thereto, or to furnish necessary equipment therefor, or to accumulate a fund to accomplish any of such purposes, or to do any or all of these things, the Trustees may proceed as follows:

The Trustees shall cause a plan to be developed and prepared, and an estimate of the cost to be made. The Trustees may then determine the funds that will be available from accumulations and the amount to be raised from a bond issue, by annual certification, or by a mortgage. The Trustees shall then determine the term, not exceeding 20 years, over which they shall spread the collection of the costs of such plan, and shall make a record of their proceedings.

The Secretary shall thereupon post notice of these proceedings and of the meeting when the financing thereof shall be determined, and the notice shall specify the place where the plan and estimate are available for public inspection.

Laws 1967, p. 1684, § 5-1, eff. July 17, 1967.

1005-2. Bond—Issuance—Terms—Tax levy

§ 5-2. 30 days after the posting of the aforesaid notice, the Board may by ordinance provide that the bonds of the district be issued for the payment of the cost (so estimated as aforesaid) of erecting or constructing a building, or remodeling, repairing, improving an existing library building or the erection of an addition thereto, or purchasing a building, site or equipment, or any or all of these things. The ordinance shall also state the time or times when such bonds, and the interest thereon shall become payable. However, the whole of the principal of such bonds, and the interest thereon shall become payable within 20 years, and the interest on such bonds shall not exceed the rate of 7% per annum. The interest may be made payable at such times (annually or semiannually) as the ordinance may prescribe. Such ordinance shall be irrepealable by the Board, and shall make provision for the levy and collection annually of a special tax upon all of the taxable property within such district sufficient to meet the principal and interest of the bonds as they mature and collection loss and costs. Such tax shall be in addition to that otherwise authorized to be levied and collected for library purposes.

For the purpose of Article V of this Act, the acquisition of library material such as electronic data storage and retrieval facilities is considered to be in connection with the purchase or construction of a new library building or the expansion of an existing library building if the determination of the Board of Trustees to acquire such library materials is made within 5 years from the date that a new library building is purchased, or construction of a new library building or the expansion of an existing library building is completed.

Laws 1967, p. 1684, § 5-2. Amended by P.A. 76-533, § 1, eff. July 28, 1969; P.A. 79-483, § 1, eff. Oct. 1, 1975; P.A. 79-989, § 3, eff. Oct. 1, 1975; P.A. 79-1454, § 36, eff. Aug. 31, 1976.

1005-3. Referendum for issuance of bonds

§ 5-3. Bonds shall not be issued nor the special tax imposed until the proposition to issue such bonds has been submitted to and approved by a majority of the voters of said district voting upon the proposition at a regular election. The Board shall by ordinance designate the election at which the proposition is to be submitted and the amount of the bonds and their purpose. The Board shall certify the proposition to the proper election officials, who shall submit the question in accordance with the general election law.

The proposition to issue bonds shall be in substantially the following form:

"Shall the bonds of 'The .... Public Library District, ..., Illinois' in the amount of .... dollars ($) be issued for the purpose of ....?"	YES
(State one or more purposes authorized in Section 5-1 hereof.)	NO

When so authorized, such bonds shall be issued in the name of the district, signed by the President and Secretary, countersigned by the Treasurer, with the seal of the district affixed.

Laws 1967, p. 1684, § 5-3. Amended by P.A. 81-1489, § 76, eff. Dec. 1, 1980.

1005-4. Division of costs into parts without issuance of bonds—Ordinance

§ 5-4. If, however, the Board does not provide that the bonds of the district be issued, the Board shall divide the total cost of the plan into as many parts as the Trustees determine to spread the collection thereof, and shall by ordinance certify the amount of one of these parts each year during the term over which the Trustees have determined to spread the collection. Such ordinance shall be irrepealable by the Board.

The Board shall, in each succeeding annual appropriation ordinance, include an amount so certified and shall, for the amount so certified, either include such amount in the annual library tax levy, or, levy a special tax to pay the same, with the other library taxes for the district.

Laws 1967, p. 1684, § 5–4.

1005–5. Borrowing of money

§ 5–5. If the Trustees deem it best in order to provide and secure the necessary money to do any or all of the things they are authorized to do in this Article, they may at any time, borrow money and execute a mortgage on a library building or site for an amount not exceeding 75% of the value thereof as improved by the plan, and the money so obtained shall be used exclusively for the remodeling, repairing, or improving of the existing library building or for the building of an addition thereto or for the erection of a new library building or for the purchase of necessary equipment for such library, as provided in the plan. The Trustees shall determine and certify, by ordinance, the amount of the mortgage, and the amount of principal and interest to be retired each year for a specified number of years. The Board shall, in each succeeding annual appropriation ordinance, include the amount so certified and shall, for the amount so certified, include such amount in the annual library tax levy, or, levy a special tax to pay the same, with other library taxes for the district.

Laws 1967, p. 1684, § 5–5. Amended by P.A. 80–655, § 2, eff. Oct. 1, 1977; P.A. 81–1071, § 3, eff. July 1, 1980.

1005–6. Special tax levies—Requisites—Referendum

§ 5–6. No Board or district is authorized to levy the special tax provided for in Sections 5–4 and 5–5 of this Act unless the ordinance authorizing such special tax is submitted to and approved by a majority of the voters voting on the question, at an election.

Such special levy shall not exceed .0833% of the value, as equalized and assessed by the Department of Revenue in any one year, and shall be in addition to that otherwise authorized to be levied and collected for library purposes. Nor shall such be levied for more than the number of years into which the Trustees have divided the cost of the plan.

Submission of the special tax levy shall be authorized by an ordinance enacted by the Board, which shall designate the election at which the proposition is to be submitted, and designate the total amount of the cost of the project, the amount of the annual levy to be certified, and the number of years such levy is to be made. The Board shall certify the proposition to the proper election officials, who shall submit the proposition in accordance with the general election law.

The proposition of approval of the ordinance shall be substantially in the following form:

"Shall Ordinance # . . . . , dated . . . . , of 'The . . . . Public Library District, ... , Illinois' providing for a total expenditure of . . . . dollars ($) for * . . . . , and for the levy of a special annual tax in the amount of . . . . ($) for . . . . ( ) years be approved." (*State one or more purposes authorized in Sections 5–4 and 5–5 hereof.)	YES	
	NO	

Laws 1967, p. 1684, § 5–6. Amended by P.A. 77–1045, § 1, eff. Aug. 17, 1971; P.A. 81–1489, § 76, eff. Dec. 1, 1980; P.A. 81–1509, Art. IV, § 78, eff. Sept. 26, 1980.

1005–7. Special taxes supporting annual certification or mortgage and bond issue

§ 5–7. Upon approval by the voters of a bond issue, or of a special tax supporting an annual certification or a mortgage, the Secretary shall file certified copies of each ordinance and of the certificate of results of the canvass of the referendum on the question of the bond issue or on the question of the special tax for annual certification or the mortgage, with the County Clerk of each county affected thereby. The Secretary shall also certify under his hand and the seal of the district, and file with each County Clerk such other information as may be required by a County Clerk to determine the total amount of taxes to be extended along with collection loss and costs upon the taxable property within his county.

The special tax supporting a bond issue, and the special tax supporting an annual certification or a mortgage shall be levied, extended and collected each year, as in the case of other library taxes, until the debt involved has been paid and retired. Such special taxes shall not be included separately or together in the aggregate of tax levies otherwise limited by law, and shall be in addition to other taxes authorized by law. Nor shall such special taxes affect any appropriation made or to be made for the maintenance and support of the library or libraries operated by the Board.
Laws 1967, p. 1684, § 5–7. Amended by P.A. 81–1489, § 76, eff. Dec. 1, 1980.

1005–8. Construction or improvement—Investment of funds

§ 5–8. The Board shall determine when it will proceed with the construction of a building, or with the purchase of a site or building, or with the remodeling, repairing, or improving of an existing library building, or the building of an addition thereto, or with the purchase of necessary equipment, or any or all of these things. The Board may proceed at once or may determine to wait and allow funds to accumulate. If the Board determines to let funds accumulate, it shall invest the money as authorized by law, until the same is needed for any or all of the purposes enumerated aforesaid. The Board may contract to accomplish any or all of the purposes enumerated aforesaid, and shall apply the proceeds of any special tax as collected and the funds accumulated toward payment therefor.
Laws 1967, p. 1684, § 5–8, eff. July 17, 1967.

1005–9. Revision of plans—Adoption of new plans—Letting of contracts

§ 5–9. When the Trustees determine to commence the construction of the building or the remodeling, repairing or improving of an existing library building or the erection of an addition thereto, or the purchase of the necessary equipment for such library, they may then revise the plan therefor or adopt a new plan and provide estimates of the costs thereof, and shall advertise for bids for the construction of the building, or the remodeling, repairing or improving of an existing library building or the erection of an addition thereto, or the purchase of the necessary equipment for such library, and shall let the contract or contracts for the same to the lowest responsible bidder or bidders and shall require from such bidders, such security for the performance of the bids as the Board shall determine pursuant to law. The Trustees may let the contract or contracts to one or more bidders, as they shall determine.
Laws 1967, p. 1684, § 5–9, eff. July 17, 1967.

1005–10. Special reserve fund

§ 5–10. The Board may, by ordinance, establish a special reserve fund, and transfer thereto each year, the unexpended balances of the proceeds received annually from annual public library taxes not in excess of statutory limits, provided that the Board has resolved to develop and adopt a plan or plans pursuant to the provisions of this Article and that the Board provides in the annual appropriation ordinance for accumulation of such unexpended balances.
Laws 1967, p. 1684, § 5–10, eff. July 17, 1967.

1006–1. Conduct of elections by election clerk

§ 6–1. Elections and referenda herein provided are to be conducted at the time and in the manner provided by the general election law.

The general election law shall govern elections under this Act except that provisions relating to political parties shall not be applicable to elections under this Act, which shall be nonpartisan.
Laws 1967, p. 1684, § 6–1. Amended by P.A. 76–1364, § 1, eff. Sept. 16, 1969; P.A. 81–1489, § 76, eff. Dec. 1, 1980.

1006–15. Canvass of returns—Certificate of results

§ 6–15. The Election Clerk shall, together with 2 watchers, canvas the returns, and within 5 days, prepare a certificate of the results of the election, such being signed by the said Election Clerk and attested by the 2 watchers. The Election Clerk shall file such certificate with the County Clerk of each County affected by the election within 10 days after said election.

Laws 1967, p. 1684, § 6–15, eff. July 17, 1967.

1006–17. Tie-vote in election of trustees—Determination by lot—Vacancies

§ 6–17. Where a candidate for the office of Trustee should die before election day, and is nevertheless deemed as elected, another candidate on the ballot who receives the next highest vote as compared with those cast for the deceased candidate shall be deemed as elected. If there is no such other candidate, there shall be a vacancy.

Laws 1967, p. 1684, § 6–17. Amended by P.A. 81–1490, § 14, eff. Dec. 1, 1980.

1006–18. Tie-vote in election on proposition

§ 6–18. In the event of a tie-vote in an election on a proposition, the proposition shall fail.

Laws 1967, p. 1684, § 6–18, eff. July 17, 1967.

1006–19. Contests

§ 6–19. Any qualified voter in the district may contest such election of any person to the office of Trustee, or the announced results of a referendum within 30 days thereafter by commencing an appropriate action in the Circuit Court of the County which contains all or the larger portion of the district.

Laws 1967, p. 1684, § 6–19. Amended by P.A. 81–1490, § 14, eff. Dec. 1, 1980.

1006–20. Expenses and costs

§ 6–20. The court costs and legal costs incurred by the district involving an election contest shall be borne by the district unless otherwise specified in this Act, but the expenses incurred by any voter contesting any election shall not be an expense of the district.

Laws 1967, p. 1684, § 6–20. Amended by P.A. 81–1490, § 14, eff. Dec. 1, 1980.

1007–1. Manner of giving notice

§ 7–1. Notice of elections and referenda shall be given in the manner provided by the general election law.

Laws 1967, p. 1684, § 7–1. Amended by P.A. 76–1364, § 1, eff. Sept. 16, 1969; P.A. 81–1489, § 76, eff. Dec. 1, 1980.

1007–2. Contents of notice

§ 7–2. The notice of a referendum for establishment of, annexation to, inclusion within, disconnection from or dissolution of a district must include a map of the district, a legal description thereof and indicate county lines, and any territory sought to be annexed, included or disconnected.

Laws 1967, p. 1684, § 7–2. Amended by P.A. 81–1489, § 76, eff. Dec. 1, 1980.

1007–3. Copies of notices—Filing

§ 7–3. Copies of all notices must be filed by the Secretary, or in the case of an establishment election by the petitioners, with petitions for the proposed district to be formed under Section 2–2 of this Act, where a municipal library is affected, then with the mayor or president of all cities, villages or incorporated towns, and, where a township library is affected, with the supervisor of all townships, as lie entirely or partially within the district.

Copies of a notice of a petition filed with a Circuit Court for conversion of a public library to a library district shall be filed by the petitioners where a municipal library is affected, with the mayor or president of any municipality affected, where a township library is affected, then with the supervisor of the township affected, and where a county library is affected, then with the County Board affected.

Laws 1967, p. 1684, § 7–3. Amended by P.A. 76–1364, § 1, eff. Sept. 16, 1969; P.A. 81–1489, § 76, eff. Dec. 1, 1980.

1008–2. Saving clause

§ 8–2. Repeal of the aforesaid Act shall not abrogate any referendum held thereunder, but such shall be given full effect as if conducted under this Act. Nor shall the said repeal abrogate any bonds issued pursuant to the provisions of the said repealed law, but such bonds shall continue to be deemed as a valid bond issue and legally binding upon the district having sold the said bonds, and such district may continue to levy the taxes necessary and sufficient to pay the principal of and interest upon said bonds pursuant to the provisions of this Act.

Laws 1967, p. 1684, § 8–2, eff. July 17, 1967.

1101. Validation of levy ordinance

§ 1. If the board of a public library district subject to the "Illinois Public Library District Act" has, before the fourth Tuesday in September of 1975, passed and approved a levy ordinance in compliance with Section 4–15 of that Act and a certified copy of that ordinance was filed on or before December 31, 1975 with the county clerk of each county affected by the levy, the levy ordinance is valid and effective notwithstanding the filing with the county clerks was not accomplished on or before the fourth Tuesday in September of 1975.

P.A. 79–1413, § 1, eff. Aug. 19, 1976.

COUNTY LIBRARIES
(Smith-Hurd Illinois Annotated Statutes, 1982, Chap. 81, s.17-27a.)

§ 17.   Establishment, equipment and maintenance

Subject to the provisions of section 11 of this Act, every county board shall establish, equip and maintain a public county library service. 1919, June 28, Laws 1919, p. 736, § 1; 1943, May 25, Laws 1943, vol. 1, p. 854, § 1.

§ 18.   Contract with existing library to establish, equip and maintain library—Contents—Supervision

In performing this duty, the county board may, if it is deemed advisable, contract in writing, with an existing library or libraries in any county, to establish, equip and maintain a public county library service. The contract shall contain provisions requiring the contracting library or libraries to (a) establish, equip and maintain a county library; (b) establish, equip and maintain such branches and stations of the county library in the various parts of the county as may be deemed necessary by the county board; (c) acquire and circulate books, periodicals, pamphlets, musical scores and records, pictures, stereopticon slides, motion picture films and other educational material, (d) do all other things necessary to carry on an efficient public county library service; also such contract shall contain provisions specifying that one or more representatives of each party to the contract, may participate in and vote at all meetings in which matters relating to the library service, furnished under the contract, are considered.

The making and performance of any such contract shall be under the supervision of the county board. 1919, June 28, Laws 1919, p. 736, § 2; 1943, May 25, Laws 1943, vol. 1, p. 854, § 1; 1961, Aug. 10, Laws 1961, p. 3122, § 1.

19. County library board—Members—Appointment—Terms—Vacancy

§ 3. The public county library service except in counties where such a service is maintained by contract with an existing library or libraries, shall be under the direct supervision and control of a county library board. This board shall consist of five members, who shall be appointed by the presiding officer of the county board with the advice and consent of the county board. Of the first members to be appointed, one member shall be appointed for a term of one year, one for a term of two years, one for a term of three years, one for a term of four years, and another for a term of five years. Thereafter, upon the expiration of each of these terms, the members of the county library board shall be appointed for terms of five years each. A vacancy upon the county library board shall be filled for the unexpired portion of the term in like manner. In counties where the public county library service is maintained by contract with an existing library or libraries, the making and performance of any such contract shall be under the supervision of the county board.
Amended by P.A. 78–1128, § 34, eff. Oct. 1, 1974.

§ 20. Expenses of members

The members of the county library board shall serve without compensation but their actual and necessary expenses shall be a proper and legitimate charge against the library fund. 1919, June 28, Laws 1919, p. 736, § 4.

§ 21. Officers of board

Immediately after their appointment the members of the county library board shall elect a president and a secretary-treasurer from among their number. 1919, June 28, Laws 1919, p. 736, § 5.

22. County library board—Powers and duties

§ 6. The county library board shall (a) establish, equip and maintain a county library; (b) establish, equip and maintain branches and stations of the county library in the various parts of the county; (c) acquire and circulate books, periodicals, pamphlets, musical scores and records, pictures, stereopticon slides, motion picture films, and other educational material; (d) receive and administer devises, bequests and gifts of real and personal property; (e) appoint a county librarian and necessary assistants and employees, and fix their compensation; (f) make, alter and amend, from time to time, reasonable by-laws, rules and regulations for the operation of the public county library service; and (g) do all other things necessary to carry on an efficient public county library service.

In establishing, equipping and maintaining branches or stations of the county library, the county library board may, if deemed advisable, contract, in writing, with existing libraries to serve as such branches or stations.

Whenever a county library board which has been duly appointed may desire to erect a library building, or to purchase a building or a site, or both, for a library, or to accumulate a fund for either or both of these purposes, it shall proceed in the manner provided for the carrying out of similar purposes in "An Act in relation to free public libraries for cities, villages, incorporated towns and townships and to repeal Acts and parts of Acts therein named", approved July 12, 1965, as heretofore or hereafter amended.

Amended by Laws 1967, p. 995, § 1, eff. July 1, 1967.

23. Annual tax levy

§ 7. An annual tax of not to exceed .04%, or the rate limit in effect on July 1, 1967, whichever is greater, of the value, as equalized or assessed by the Department of Revenue, of all taxable property within each county which has established a public county library service may be assessed, levied and collected by that county in the manner provided for the assessment, levy and collection of other taxes for county purposes.

Such tax rate may be increased in excess of .04% but not in excess of .08% of the value, as equalized or assessed by the Department of Revenue under the following terms and conditions. Prior to the levy and collection of such a tax, the county board shall adopt a resolution authorizing the levy and collection of the tax at a rate not in excess of .08% of the value of all taxable property within the county as equalized or assessed by the Department of Revenue, and, within fifteen days after the adoption of such a resolution, it shall be published once in a newspaper published or having a general circulation in the county.

If no petition is filed in the office of the county clerk, as hereinafter provided in this Section, within 30 days after the publication of the resolution, or if all such petitions so filed are determined to be invalid or insufficient, the resolution shall be in effect. But, if within that 30 day period a petition is filed in the office of the county clerk, signed by electors numbering not less than 5% of the number of electors residing within the county, asking that the question of levying and collecting such tax be submitted to the electors of the county, the board shall certify that question to the proper election officials, who shall submit the question at an election in accordance with the general election law. If a majority of electors voting upon the question voted in favor of the levy and collection of the tax provided for, such county shall be authorized and empowered to levy and collect such tax annually, but if a majority of the electors voting upon the question are not in favor thereof, the resolution shall not take effect.

Such tax rate may be increased to not to exceed .20% of the value, as equalized or assessed by the Department of Revenue, if the voters in such county shall so determine by a majority of those voting upon the proposition at any regular election. The proposition shall be in substantially the following form:

| Shall the annual tax rate for county library purposes in .... County be increased from not to exceed (insert present maximum rate) to not to exceed .20% of the assessed value of all taxable property within the county? | YES | |
| | NO | |

Any such tax authorized by the voters shall not be included within any constitutional or statutory limitation for county purposes, but shall be excluded therefrom and be in addition thereto and in excess thereof. The foregoing limitations upon tax rates may be increased or decreased under the referendum provisions of the General Revenue Law of Illinois.

Amended by Laws 1967, p. 877, § 1; P.A. 77–1043, § 1, eff. Aug. 17, 1971; P.A. 79–1430, § 1, eff. Oct. 1, 1976; P.A. 81–1489, § 71, eff. Dec. 1, 1980; P.A. 81–1509, Art. IV, § 75, eff. Sept. 26, 1980.

§ 24. Proceeds of tax in separate fund—Custodian to give bond—Expenditures from library fund

In counties having a population of 25,000 or more, the proceeds of this tax shall be deposited in the treasury of the county in a separate library fund. In counties having a population of less than 25,000, the proceeds thereof, shall be paid over by the person charged with the collection thereof to the county library board and deposited by it in a fund to be known as the county library fund; and in counties of such population such library board shall require the treasurer of such board or such other person as may be designated as the custodian of the moneys paid over to such board to give a bond to be approved by it and in such amount, not less than $1,000 nor more than $10,000 as the board may determine, conditioned that he will safely keep and will pay over upon the order of such board all funds received and held by him for such board.

No part of this fund shall be expended except upon warrants certified to as correct by the county librarian and approved by the president of the county library board. In cases where the public county library service is maintained by contract with an existing library or libraries, no part of the library fund shall be expended except upon warrants certified to as correct by the librarian or two (2) members of the board of any such library and approved by the president of the board of trustees of any such library. 1919, June 28, Laws 1919, p. 736, § 8; 1933, June 9, Laws 1933, p. 700, § 1; 1943, May 25, Laws 1943, vol. 1, p. 854, § 1.

§ 25. Fiscal year

The fiscal year of any public county library service shall be co-extensive with the fiscal year of that county. 1919, June 28, Laws 1919, p. 736, § 9; 1943, May 25, Laws 1943, vol. 1, p. 854, § 1.

§ 26. County library board—Report—Contents—Filing

Within thirty days after the close of each fiscal year the county library board shall make a written report to the county board. In cases where a public county library service is maintained by contract with an existing library or libraries, a report shall be made to the county board at the same time by the librarian or the secretary or some other officer of the county library board of such library or libraries. A copy of each report shall be filed at the same time with the Illinois State library.

It shall contain (a), an itemized statement of the various sums of money received from the library fund, or from other sources; (b), an itemized statement of the objects and purposes to which those sums of money have been devoted; (c), a statement of the number of books and periodicals available for use, and the number thereof circulated during the fiscal year; (d), a statement of the real and personal property acquired by devise, bequest, purchase, gift or otherwise, during the fiscal year; (e), a statement of the number, location and character of the branches or stations of the public county library service, if any, established during the fiscal year; (f), a statement of the character of any other extensions of public county library service undertaken during the fiscal year; and (g), any other statistics or information that may be required by the county board. 1919, June 28, Laws 1919, p. 736, § 10; 1943, June 24, Laws 1943, vol. 1, p. 849, § 1; 1943, May 25, Laws 1943, vol. 1, p. 854, § 1; 1949, May 6, Laws 1949, p. 1078, § 1.

27. Referendum on establishment of county library service—Form of proposition

§ 11. None of the foregoing powers or duties shall be exercised, however, unless the question of establishing a public county library service shall have been submitted to the voters of the county, at a regular election, and unless a majority of the votes cast upon the question at any such election within the limits of the cities, villages and incorporated towns in the county and a majority of those cast upon the question outside the limits of such cities, villages or incorporated towns shall be in favor of the establishment of a public county library service.

This question shall not be submitted to the voters, however, unless there shall have been filed a petition therefor, signed by not less than one hundred legal voters of the county.

The proposition of establishing a public county library service shall be in substantially the following form: FOR the establishment of a public county library service. AGAINST the establishment of a public county library service.
Amended by P.A. 81–1489, § 71, eff. Dec. 1, 1980.

§ 27a. Inapplication to counties of 500,000 or more

This Act shall not apply to counties having a population of five hundred thousand or more. 1919, June 28, Laws 1919, p. 736, § 12, added 1943, May 25, Laws 1943, vol. 1, p. 854, § 1; 1943, May 25, Laws 1943, vol. 1, p. 858, § 1.

MUNICIPAL LIBRARIES
General Provisions
(Smith-Hurd Illinois Annotated Statutes, 1982,
Chap. 81, s.1-0.1 to 5-9,)

1-0.1. Short title and citation

§ 1–0.1. This Act shall be known and may be cited as The Illinois Local Library Act.
Laws 1965, p. 660, § 1–0.1, added by P.A. 77–15, § 1, eff. April 7, 1971.

1-1. Corporate authorities defined

§ 1–1. For the purposes of this Act the term "corporate authorities" means, as applied to cities, villages and incorporated towns, the corporate authorities as defined in Section 1–1–2 of the Illinois Municipal Code, and, as applied to townships, the Board of Auditors. The terms "board", "board of directors" or "board of library directors" means any Board of Library Directors of a city, village, incorporated town or township.
Amended by P.A. 77–15, § 1, eff. April 7, 1971.

§ 1—2. Establishment by corporate authorities or by voters

Public libraries may be established under this Act by cities by action of the corporate authorities and by villages, incorporated towns and townships by vote of the legal voters thereof in the manner provided in Article 2. 1965, July 12, Laws 1965, p. ——, H.B.No.956, § 1–2.

§ 1—3. Use—Rules and regulations

Every library established under this Act shall be forever free to the use of the inhabitants of the city, village, incorporated town or township where located, subject to such reasonable rules and regulations as the library board may adopt in order to render the use of the library of the greatest benefit to the greatest number. 1965, July 12, Laws 1965, p. ——, H.B.No.956, § 1-3.

§ 1—4. Libraries established under prior acts—Status

Any public library established under Division 48.1 of Article 11 of the "Illinois Municipal Code", approved May 29, 1961, as amended, or "An Act to authorize townships to establish and maintain free public libraries and reading rooms", approved March 7, 1872, as amended, shall be treated as libraries established under this Act and shall be subject to the provisions of this Act. 1965, July 12, Laws 1965, p. ——, H.B.No. 956, § 1-4.

1-5. Penalties

§ 1-5. The corporate authorities may provide for suitable penalties for persons committing injury upon a library or the grounds or other property thereof and for injury to or failure to return any library material belonging to the library. Amended by P.A. 78-426, § 1, eff. Aug. 28, 1973.

§ 1—6. Donations

Any person desiring to make donations of money, personal property or real estate for the benefit of any such library may vest the title to the money or real estate in the board of directors of such library to be held and controlled by such board, when accepted, according to the terms of the deed, gift, devise or bequest of such property. The board shall be held and considered to be a special trustee of such donated property. 1965, July 12, Laws 1965, p. ——, H.B.No.956, § 1-6.

§ 2—1. Establishment and maintenance in cities—Tax levy

The corporate authorities of any city may establish and maintain a public library for the use and benefit of the inhabitants of the city and may, subject to the limitations of Article 3, levy a tax for library purposes. 1965, July 12, Laws 1965, p. ——, H.B.No.956, § 2-1.

2-2. Elections for establishment and maintenance in towns, villages or townships

§ 2-2. When 50 legal voters of any incorporated town, village or township present a petition to the clerk thereof asking for the establishment and maintenance of a free public library in such incorporated town, village or township, the clerk shall certify the question of whether to establish and maintain a free public library to the proper election authorities who shall submit the question at a regular election in accordance with the general election law. Except in villages under the commission form of government, there shall be elected at such election, subject to the referendum, 7 persons as library directors, 2 to serve until the next election held in an odd-numbered year in the incorporated town, village or township, 2 to serve until the second such election after their election, and 3 to serve until the third such election after their election, the length of their respective terms to be so determined by designations thereof on the ballots, and until their successors are duly elected and qualified in accordance with the provisions of Article 4. In those incorporated towns, villages or townships, except villages under the commission form of government, where a free public library was established and directors elected before the effective date of the amendatory Act of 1967, 3 directors shall be elected at the next regular election for library directors.

The petition shall specify the maximum library tax rate, if the rate is to be in excess of .15%. In no case shall the rate specified in the petition be in excess of .40% of the value as equalized and assessed by the Department of Revenue. The proposition shall be in substantially the following form:

Shall a free public library be established and maintained in (name of incorporated town, village or township)?	YES	
	NO	

If the petition specified a maximum tax rate in excess of the statutory maximum tax rate of .15%, the proposition shall be in substantially the following form:

Shall a free public library be established and maintained in (name of incorporated town, village or township), with a maximum annual public library tax rate at . % of the value of all taxable property as equalized and assessed by the Department of Revenue?	YES	
	NO	

If the majority of all votes cast in the incorporated town, village or township on the proposition are in favor of a free public library, an annual tax may be levied for the establishment and maintenance of such library, subject to the limitations of Article 3.

Amended by Laws 1967, p. 3360, § 1; P.A. 80–406, § 1, eff. Oct. 1, 1977; P.A. 81–1490, § 13, eff. Dec. 1, 1980; P.A. 81–1509, Art. IV, § 74, eff. Sept. 26, 1980; P.A. 81–1550, Art. I, § 19, eff. Jan. 8, 1981.

2–3. Calling referenda in towns, villages, or townships

§ 2–3. Whenever the petition signed and filed with the clerk of an incorporated town, village or township requests the holding of a referendum for the purpose of voting upon the question of establishing and maintaining a free public library as provided in Section 2–2, or for voting upon the question of increasing or ceasing to levy the tax therefor as provided in Section 3–4, the clerk shall certify the Resolution and the proposition to the proper election officials, who shall submit the question at an election in such incorporated town, village or township in accordance with the general election law.
Amended by by P.A. 81–1489, § 70, eff. Dec. 1, 1980.

2–4. Commission form of government—Effect of change to or from on library directors

§ 2–4. In the event a village not under a commission form of government converts to a commission form of government or becomes a city, or a village or city under a commission form of government changes to a village or city not under a commission form of government, the incumbent board of library directors of the village or the city board of library directors of the city, as the case may be, shall thereupon become the library directors of the village or city, whichever is the form of the new municipal governmental organization, and shall serve as such until the term of office for which each had been elected or appointed expires, and until his successor has been elected or appointed according to law and has qualified for such office.

Thereafter, new or additional library directors shall be elected or appointed, or the number of directors reduced, so that the number of directors holding office at any one time shall conform as nearly as is practicable to the number of library directors required by law for the particular city or village as it is organized after changing its form or classification of municipal government.

The ceiling upon the annual public library tax existing prior to the conversion or change in form of municipal government and any special tax previously authorized by the electors shall be applicable after the conversion or change.

Any existing bond issue and the special tax therefor shall not be affected by such conversion or change and shall continue in full force and effect under the law governing such bond issue and special tax.

Laws 1965, p. 660, § 2–4, added by P.A. 76–1459, § 1, eff. Sept. 22, 1969.

2–5. Merger of libraries and board of directors—Assets and liabilities

§ 2–5. In the event the voters approve of a merger of 2 or more cities, or villages, or incorporated towns or townships, a merger of the affected public libraries shall also occur as follows:

Where the merger affects a city, village, incorporated town or township without a public library and one with a public library, then the existing board of library directors shall, upon the merger, exercise its powers and duties under this Act, as amended, over the merged territory, and this Act, as amended, shall govern the merged territory.

Where the merger affects 2 or more cities, villages, incorporated towns or townships, each with a public library, then the existing boards of library directors shall be merged into one new board, and the new board shall thereupon exercise its powers and duties under this Act, as amended, over the merged territory and this Act, as amended, shall govern the merged territory. Such board members shall serve out their respective terms, but as their respective terms expire, successors shall be elected or appointed, as the case may be, only in the case where it is necessary to provide a normal membership for a new board.

In every merger, the board whose territory is being expanded, or the board being merged, shall take such action as is necessary to effectuate the merger approved by the voters, and shall by resolution specify the effective date thereof. In addition, the new library board shall acquire the assets and assume the liabilities of the predecessor library board or boards.

Laws 1965, p. 660, § 2–5, added by P.A. 79–363, § 1, eff. Aug. 7, 1975.

2–6. Disestablishment—Election

§ 2–6. A public library established by any city, village or incorporated town under this Act may be disestablished if the library has no bonded indebtedness and the municipality is wholly included within a township which has a library established under this Act. Disestablishment may be effected in the following manner:

The corporate authorities of the municipality shall provide by resolution for the disestablishment of the library. Notice of the resolution shall be published on no less than 3 separate days in a newspaper having general circulation within the municipality at least 60 days prior to the date that the disestablishment is to be effective. The notice shall contain a statement that any legal voter of the municipality may within a specified period of time not less than 60 days file a petition signed by not less than 10% or 1500, whichever is less, of the voters of the municipality requesting the submission to a referendum of the question as to whether the library shall be disestablished.

Following publication of the notice, if a petition meeting the requirements described in the notice is filed, the proposition shall be certified to the proper election officials, who shall submit the proposition to the voters of the municipality at the next regular election in accordance with the general election law. The proposition shall be in substantially the following form:

Shall the .... library be disestablished?	YES	
	NO	

If a majority of the votes cast upon the proposition are in favor thereof, the library shall be disestablished. If less than a majority of the votes are in favor of the proposition, the disestablishment shall not occur. If no petition as prescribed herein is filed, the disestablishment shall take effect on the date provided in the resolution and set forth in the published notice.

If the disestablishment is authorized under this Section, the board of directors of the library shall immediately proceed to close up the business of the library. If a vacancy occurs on the board before all of the business affairs are completed, the vacancy shall not be filled except that if all positions become vacant, the corporate authorities of the incorporated town, village, or city concerned shall act as the board to close up the business of the library. In closing up the affairs of the library, the board shall sell all property and equipment of the library and pay all debts and obligations; however, if the board of directors of the township library concerned agrees to assume all debts and obligations of the library being disestablished, all remaining property and equipment may be transferred to the township library. Laws 1965, p. 660, § 2–6, added by P.A. 80–1448, § 1, eff. Jan. 1, 1979. Amended by P.A. 81–830, § 1, eff. Jan. 1, 1980; P.A. 81–1535, § 19, eff. Dec. 19, 1980.

3–1. Cities of less than 500,000—Tax rate—Election on increased rates—Additional tax levy

§ 3–1.. In any city of 500,000 or fewer inhabitants, the corporate authorities shall levy a tax for library purposes of not to exceed .15% of the value of all the taxable property in the city, as equalized or assessed by the Department of Revenue. If the annual public library tax rate of an established library was increased above .12% up to .20% as provided in this Act, the corporate authorities shall then levy up to an additional .03% above the increased rate approved at the election. If, however, the corporate authorities desire to increase the tax rate but not in excess of .40% of value for such purposes, the corporate authorities may, by ordinance, stating the tax rate desired, direct that a proposition be submitted to the voters of the city at any regular election. The proposition shall be in substantially the form prescribed in Section 3–3. If a majority of the votes cast upon the proposition are in favor thereof, the corporate authorities may thereafter levy annually a tax for library purposes at the authorized increased rate. Any tax levied pursuant to Section 3–9 shall be disregarded in applying the provisions of this Section.

The corporate authorities may also levy an additional tax of .02% of the value of all the taxable property in the city, as equalized or assessed by the Department of Revenue, for the purchase of sites and buildings, for the construction and equipment of buildings, for the rental of buildings required for library purposes, and for maintenance, repairs and alterations of library buildings and equipment. In any year in which the corporate authorities propose to levy such additional .02% tax, the corporate authorities shall adopt a resolution determining to levy such tax. Within 15 days after the adoption of the resolution, it shall be published at least once in one or more newspapers published in the city, or if no newspaper is published therein, then in one or more newspapers with a general circulation within the city. In a city in which no newspaper is published, publication may instead be made by posting a notice in three prominent places within the city. If no petition is filed with the corporate authorities within 30 days after publication or posting of the resolution, or if all petitions so filed are determined to be invalid or insufficient the city shall then be authorized to levy the tax. However, if within the 30 day period, a petition is filed with the corporate authorities, signed by electors of the city equal in number to 10% or more of the total number of votes cast for the municipal office viewing the greatest number of votes at the last preceding regular municipal election, asking that the question of levying such a .02% tax be submitted to the electors of the city, the question shall be submitted at an election. Notice of this referendum shall be given as provided by the general election laws of the state, and the referendum shall be held in all respects in accordance with those laws. The proposition shall be in substantially the following form: "Shall the corporate authorities of (name of city) be authorized to levy an additional tax of   % for the construction of buildings, provision of sites, etc., as determined by resolution of   , 19   ?". If a majority of votes cast upon the proposition are in favor thereof, the corporate authorities may levy the additional tax.

Amended by Laws 1967, p. 2717, § 1; P.A. 76–662, § 1, eff. Aug. 6, 1969; P.A. 76–2586, § 1, eff. July 14, 1978; P.A. 80–1152, § 1, eff. July 1, 1978; P.A. 80–1153, § 1, eff. July 1, 1978; P.A. 80–1364, § 33, eff. Aug. 13, 1978; P.A. 81–1489, § 70, eff. Dec. 1, 1980; P.A. 81–1509, Art. IV, § 74, eff. Sept. 26, 1980.

3–2. Cities over 500,000—Amount of tax

§ 3–2. The corporate authorities of any city of over 500,000 population may levy a tax for library maintenance and operation for the years 1970 and 1971 of not to exceed .10% and for the years thereafter of not to exceed .12% of the value of all taxable property in the city, as equalized or assessed by the Department of Revenue. The corporate authorities may also levy an additional tax of .02% of the value of all the taxable property in the city, as equalized or assessed by the Department of Revenue, for the purchase of sites and buildings, for the construction and equipment of buildings, for the rental of buildings required for library purposes, and for maintenance, repairs and alterations of library buildings and equipment. If, however, the corporate authorities desire to levy a tax for any year after 1971 in excess of .12% but not in excess of .20% of value for library maintenance and operation, the corporate authorities may, by ordinance, stating the tax rate desired, cause a proposition for an assent thereto to be submitted to the voters of the city at a general election to be held in November of even numbered years. The proposition shall be in substantially the form prescribed in Section 3–3. If a majority of the votes cast upon the proposition are in favor thereof, the corporate authorities may thereafter levy annually a tax for library maintenance and operation at the authorized increased rate. Any tax levied pursuant to Section 3–9 shall be disregarded in applying the provision of this Section.

Amended by P.A. 76–693, § 1, eff. Aug. 7, 1969; P.A. 77–1041, § 1, eff. Aug. 17, 1971; P.A. 80–1152, § 1, eff. July 1, 1978; P.A. 80–1153, § 1, eff. July 1, 1978; P.A. 80–1364, § 33, eff. Aug. 13, 1978; P.A. 81–1489, § 70, eff. Dec. 1, 1980; P.A. 81–1509, Art. IV, § 74, eff. Sept. 26, 1980.

3–3. Election for increase of tax

§ 3–3. The corporate authorities shall adopt an ordinance providing for submitting the question of increasing the library tax for maintenance and operation at such general election and the municipal clerk shall certify the proposition to the proper election officials, who shall submit the question at a general election in accordance with the general election law. The question shall be in substantially the following form:

| Shall the annual library tax for maintenance and operation in (insert name of city) be increased from (insert present tax) to (insert proposed tax)? | NO | |
| | YES | |

Amended by P.A. 76–693, § 1, eff. Aug. 7, 1969; P.A. 81–1489, § 70, eff. Dec. 1, 1980.

3–4. Tax levy in towns, villages or townships—Rate—Election on increase or termination of tax—Limitations

§ 3–4. When the electors of an incorporated town, village or township have voted to establish and maintain a public library as provided in Section 2–2, the corporate authorities of such incorporated town, village or township shall levy an annual tax for the establishment and maintenance of such library, not exceeding .15% of the value as equalized or assessed by the Department of Revenue. If the petition and ballots so specify in the original establishment as set forth in Section 2–2 of this Act, the corporate authorities may levy a tax in excess of 15%, not to exceed the rate specified in such establishment petition and ballot, but in any event not to exceed .40% of the value as equalized and assessed by the Department of Revenue. If the annual public library tax rate of an established library was increased above .12% up to .20% as provided in this Act, the corporate authorities shall then levy up to an additional .03% above the increased rate approved at the referendum. Such tax rate may be increased to not to exceed .40% of the value, as equalized or assessed by the Department of Revenue, or the tax shall no longer be levied, if the electors of such incorporated town, village or township shall so determine by referendum at any regular election. Such referendum shall be petitioned for in the manner as the referendum for the establishment and maintenance of the library. Any tax levied pursuant to Section 3–9 shall be disregarded in applying the provisions of this Section.

The corporate authorities may also levy an additional tax of .02% of the value of all the taxable property in the incorporated town, village or township, as equalized or assessed by the Department of Revenue, for the purchase of sites and buildings, for the construction and equipment of buildings, for the rental of buildings required for library purposes, and for maintenance, repairs and alterations of library buildings and equipment. In any year in which the corporate authorities propose to levy such additional .02% tax, the corporate authorities shall adopt a resolution determining to levy such tax. Within 15 days after the adoption of the resolution, it shall be published at least once in one or more newspapers published in the incorporated town, village or township, or if no newspaper is published therein, then in one or more newspapers with a general circulation therein. In an incorporated town, village or township in which no newspaper is published, publication may instead be made by posting a notice in three prominent places. If no petition is filed with the corporate authorities within 30 days after publication or posting of the resolution, the incorporated town, village or township shall then be authorized to levy the tax. However, if within the 30 day period, a petition is filed with the corporate authorities, signed by electors of the incorporated town, village or township equal in number to 10% or more of the total number of votes cast at the last preceding regular election of the incorporated town, village or township, asking that the question of levying such a .02% tax be submitted to the electors thereof, the question shall be submitted at a special or general election. Notice of this election shall be given as provided by the general election laws of this state in force at the time of the election, and the election shall be held in all respects in accordance with those laws. The ballot on which the proposition is submitted shall be in substantially the following form: "Shall the corporate authorities of (name of incorporated town, village or township) be authorized to levy an additional tax of   % for the construction of buildings, provision of sites, etc., as determined by resolution of, 19   ?". If a majority of votes cast upon the proposition are in favor thereof, the corporate authorities may levy the additional tax. Amended by Laws 1967, p. 996, § 1; Laws 1967, p. 2717, § 1; Laws 1968, p. 281, § 1, eff. July 1, 1969; P.A. 76–662, § 1, eff. Aug. 6, 1969; P.A. 76–2586, § 1, eff. July 14, 1970; P.A. 80–406, § 1, eff. Oct. 1, 1977; P.A. 80–1152, § 1, eff. July 1, 1978; P.A. 80–1153, § 1, eff. July 1, 1978; P.A. 80–1364, § 33, eff. Aug. 13, 1978; P.A. 81–1489, § 70, eff. Dec. 1, 1980; P.A. 81–1509, Art. IV, § 74, eff. Sept. 26, 1980.

3–5. Levy and collection of taxes—Disposition of proceeds

§ 3–5. The library taxes provided for in this Act shall be levied by the corporate authorities in the amounts determined by the board and collected in like manner with other general taxes of the city, village, incorporated town or township and the proceeds shall be deposited in a special fund, which shall be known as the library fund. In townships and in cities, villages and incorporated towns having a population of 50,000 or less the proceeds of any such tax shall be paid over by the officer charged with the collection thereof to the board of directors of the library. Expenditures from the library fund shall be under the direction of the board of library directors. Amended by Laws 1967, p. 2719, § 1; P.A. 76–662, § 1, eff. Aug. 6, 1969.

3–6. Library taxes—Status for limitation purposes

§ 3–6. The library taxes provided for in this Article are in addition to all other taxes or tax rates authorized to be levied by any city, incorporated town, village or township and shall not be a part of the taxes making up any rate prescribed as a limitation on the amount of taxes any city, incorporated town, village or township may levy.

Amended by Laws 1967, p. 2717, § 1, eff. Aug. 7, 1967.

3–7. Levy and collection by townships and municipalities

§ 3–7. Levy and collection by townships and by municipalities. (a) If a city, village or incorporated town which levies a tax under this Article is located in a county of less than 1,000,000 inhabitants and is situated wholly or partly in a township which levies a tax under this Article, such township may proceed as follows unless the authority to levy a library tax in the area which lies in both the municipality and the township has been determined under subsection (c). The township may cause an abatement in full of the township library tax on property subject to such tax as also lies within a city, village or incorporated town which also levies a library tax for the same year. However, such township may instead pay to such city, village or incorporated town the entire amount collected for such township from taxes levied under this Article on property subject to a tax which such city, village or incorporated town levies under this Article.

Whenever any city, village or incorporated town receives any payments from a township as provided in this Section, such city, village or incorporated town shall reduce and abate from the tax levied by the authority of this Article a rate which would produce an amount equal to the amount received from such township.

(b) If a city, village or incorporated town which levies a tax under this Article is located in a county of 1,000,000 or more inhabitants and is situated wholly or partly in a township which levies a tax under this Article, such township shall proceed as follows unless the authority to levy a library tax in the area which lies in both the municipality and the township has been determined under subsection (c). The township shall cause an abatement in full of the township library tax on property subject to such tax as also lies within a city, village or incorporated town which also levies a library tax for the same year. However, such city, village, or incorporated town shall, upon collection of its library tax on such property, pay ½ of the collections to the township for library purposes.

(c) If any part of a city, village or incorporated town which levies a tax under this Article is situated within a township which levies a tax under this Article, the corporate authorities of the municipality or township may cause the question of which such tax shall be applicable in that area which is situated in both the municipality and township to be submitted to the electors of such area at any regular election. The question shall be certified to the proper election officials, who shall submit the question at an election in accordance with the general election law.

The question shall be in substantially the following form:

Shall the area which lies in both (insert name of municipality) and (insert name of township) be subject to taxation for library purposes by (insert name of municipality) or by (insert name of township)?		
By (insert name of municipality)		
By (insert name of township)		

After such election, library taxes under this Article shall be levied and collected in such area only by the governmental unit which received the larger number of votes cast in such election.

(d) If a city, village, incorporated town or township which levies a tax under this Article is situated wholly or partly in a library district which levies a tax under "The Illinois Public Library District Act", such city, village, incorporated town or township shall pay to such library district the entire amount collected for such entity from library taxes levied under this Article upon taxable property within such library district.

Whenever any library district receives any payments from any city, village, incorporated town or township as provided in this Section, such library district shall reduce and abate from the library tax levied by the authority of "The Illinois Public Library District Act" on property which is subject to taxation for library purposes by both the district and the municipality or township a rate which would produce an amount equal to the amount received by such library district.

Amended by P.A. 76–1430, § 1, eff. Jan. 1, 1970; P.A. 76–2586, § 1, eff. July 14, 1970; P.A. 77–549, § 1, eff. July 31, 1971; P.A. 81–607, § 1, eff. Jan. 1, 1980; P.A. 81–1535, § 19, eff. Dec. 19, 1980.

3–8. Continuation of tax levy for merged libraries—Rate of tax

§ 3–8. In the event the voters approve of a merger of 2 or more cities, or villages, or incorporated towns or townships and the merger affects one or more public libraries the library taxes levied before such merger, shall continue to be levied and collected for library purposes. The ceiling on the annual tax for the maintenance of the public library resulting from the merger shall be at a rate not higher than any lawful rate authorized to be extended before the merger in any of the merged areas.

Laws 1965, p. 1402, § 3–8, added by P.A. 79–363, § 1, eff. Aug. 7, 1975.

3–9. Tax levy for local library working cash fund

§ 3–9. For the purpose of providing money to establish and replenish a local library working cash fund authorized by Section 4–13, corporate authorities shall have the power to levy, upon all the taxable property of a city, village, incorporated town or township, a tax not to exceed .05% of the value, as equalized or assessed by the Department of Revenue for the year in which the levy is made. The tax shall be levied and collected in like manner with other general taxes of the city, village, incorporated town or township but the collection of the tax shall not be anticipated by the issuance of any warrants drawn against the tax. The tax shall be known as the local library working cash fund tax and shall be set apart in a special fund as prescribed in Section 4–13. Whenever a tax is first levied under this Section, any taxpayer in the city, village, incorporated town or township may, within 30 days after the levy is made, file with the corporate authorities a petition signed by not less than 10% or 1500, whichever is lesser, of the voters of the city, village, incorporated town or township requesting the submission of a proposition to the voters of the city, village, incorporated town or township at an election in accordance with the general election law. The corporate authority shall certify the proposition to the proper election officials, who shall submit the proposition to the voters at an election in accordance with the general election law. If a majority of the votes cast upon the proposition are in favor thereof the tax shall thereafter be authorized; if a majority of the votes cast upon the proposition are against the proposition the tax shall not be levied.

No municipality or township may levy a tax under this Section for more than four years but the four years for which any municipality or township elects to levy such tax need not be consecutive.

Laws 1965, p. 1402, § 3–9, added by P.A. 80–1153, § 1, eff. July 1, 1978. Amended by P.A. 81 1489, § 70, eff. Dec. 1, 1980; P.A. 81–1509, Art. IV, § 74, eff. Sept. 26, 1980.

§ 4—1.   Board of directors in cities—Appointment

When the corporate authorities of a city establish a public library, the mayor shall, with the approval of the city council, appoint a board of 9 directors chosen from city residents with reference to their fitness for such office. Not more than one member of the city council shall be at any one time a member of the library board. 1965, July 12, Laws 1965, p. ——, H.B.No.956, § 4–1.

§ 4—1.1 Board of directors in cities—Tenure of initial members—Successors—Removal

The first library directors of a city shall hold office one-third for one year, one-third for 2 years, and one-third for 3 years, from the first of July following their appointment, and at their first regular meeting shall cast lots for the respective terms. Annually thereafter the mayor shall, before the first of July of each year, appoint as before 3 directors, to take the place of the retiring directors, who shall hold office for 3 years and until their successors are appointed. The mayor may remove any director in the manner provided in Section 3–11–1 of the Illinois Municipal Code. 1965, July 12, Laws 1965, p. ——, H.B.No.956, § 4–1.1.

4–2. Board of directors in villages under commission form of government

§ 4–2. In villages under the commission form of government, the village council at its first regular meeting following the election establishing a free public library, shall appoint a board of library directors of 6 members who are village residents, 2 to hold until the first regular meeting of the next succeeding fiscal year, 2 to hold for one year thereafter and 2 to hold for 2 years thereafter. The respective successors of the initial appointees shall be appointed for 6 year terms and shall serve until their successors are appointed and qualified.

Any board may provide by resolution that the term of its directors shall be 4 years. If the board adopts such a resolution, then at the time the next appointments are made, one director shall be appointed for a 2 year term.
Amended by Laws 1967, p. 1823, § 1; P.A. 81–1180, § 1, eff. July 1, 1980.

4–3. Board of directors in towns, other villages or townships—Election

§ 4–3. If a majority of the votes cast in any incorporated town or village (except a village under the commission form of government) or in any township conterminous' with a municipality on the proposition pursuant to Section 2–2 are in favor of a free public library, 7 persons who receive, for the respective terms designated on the ballot, the highest number of votes for library directors cast at such election shall constitute the board of library directors.
Amended by Laws 1967, p. 3360, § 1: P.A. 78–372, § 1, eff. Oct. 1, 1973; P.A. 81–1490, § 13, eff. Dec. 1, 1980.

4–3.1. Board of directors in towns, villages or townships—Terms

§ 4–3.1. As the terms of the library directors elected in any incorporated town or village expire, (except a village under the commission form of government) or in any township conterminous with a municipality their successors shall be elected in accordance with the general election law to hold their office for 6 years until their successors are elected and qualified.

Any board may provide by resolution that the term of its directors shall be 4 years. If the board adopts such a resolution, then if 3 directors are to be elected at the next election or if 2 directors are to be elected at each of the next 2 elections, one of the directors elected at the first election, to be determined by lot at the first meeting after that election, shall serve a 2 year term.
Amended by Laws 1967, p. 1823, § 1; P.A. 76–1459, § 1, eff. Sept. 22, 1969; P.A. 78–372, § 1, eff. Oct. 1, 1973; P.A. 80–1469, § 6, eff. Dec. 1, 1980; P.A. 81–1180, § 1, eff. July 1, 1980; P.A. 81–1490, § 13, eff. Dec. 1, 1980.

4–3.2. Board of directors in towns, other villages or townships—Election of successors

§ 4–3.2. As the terms of the library directors elected in any township (except a township conterminous with a municipality) expire at any time between October 1, 1973 and December 31, 1980, their successors shall be elected for terms of 4 years. Of the 7 directors elected in 1981, 4 shall be elected to serve terms of 4 years and 3 shall be elected to serve terms of 2 years. Nominating petitions for candidates for election in 1981, and the ballots at the 1981 election, shall specify the term of office. Directors elected in 1983 and thereafter shall serve for 4 years and until their successors are elected and have qualified.

Laws 1965, p. 1402, § 4–3.2, added by P.A. 78–372, § 1, eff. Oct. 1, 1973. Amended by P.A. 81–1489, § 70, eff. Dec. 1, 1980; P.A. 81–1535, § 19, eff. Dec. 19, 1980.

4–3.3.   Board of directors in towns, other villages or townships—Nomination—Ballots

§ 4–3.3.   Nominations for the position of library director including the first board of library directors shall be by petition, signed by at least 50 legal voters residing in the incorporated town or village (except a village under the commission form of government) or township coterminous with a municipality and filed with the clerk of such incorporated town, village, or township within the time prescribed by the general election law. Such clerk shall certify the candidates for library directors to the proper election authorities who shall conduct the election in accordance with the general election law. All candidates must be residents of the incorporated town, village or township involved. The ballots shall not designate any political party, platform or political principle.

Laws 1965, p. 1402, § 4–3.3, added by P.A. 78–372, § 1, eff. Oct. 1, 1973. Amended by P.A. 81–1490, § 13, eff. Dec. 1, 1980.

4–4.   Vacancies

§ 4.4.   Vacancies in the board of directors in a city, or a village under the commission form of government shall be reported to the mayor or president and be filled in like manner as original appointments.

If a vacancy occurs in the board of directors in any incorporated town or village (other than a village under the commission form of government) or in any township the vacancy may be filled by the remaining directors until the next regular library election at which library directors are scheduled to be elected under the consolidated schedule of elections in the general election law, at which election a director shall be elected to fill the vacancy. If there is a failure to appoint a library director or a failure to elect a library director, or if the person elected or appointed fails to qualify for office, the director may continue in office if available and qualified until his successor has been elected or appointed and qualified.

The board of directors may declare a vacancy where any person serving as a director is no longer a resident of the city, village, incorporated town or township, or where any person who has been elected or appointed and qualified, fails or neglects to serve as a board member. Absence without cause from all regular board meetings for a period of one year shall be a basis for declaring a vacancy.

Amended by P.A. 77–549, § 1, eff. July 31, 1971; P.A. 78–372, § 1, eff. Oct. 1, 1973; P.A. 80–1469, § 6, eff. Dec. 1, 1980.

§ 4—5.   Compensation

No director shall receive compensation as such.   1965, July 12, Laws 1965, p. ——, H.B.No.956, § 4–5.

4–6.   Organization—Meetings

§ 4–6.   Immediately after their election or appointment, the directors shall meet and organize by the election of one of their number president and by the election of such other officers as they may deem necessary and they shall further provide in the bylaws of the board as to the length of their term in office. The directors shall determine the time and place of all official meetings of the board at which any legal action may be taken and shall post notice thereof at the public library maintained by the board and at not less than one public place within the corporate confines of the area of library service one day in advance thereof.

Amended by Laws 1967, p. 2718, § 1, eff. Aug. 7, 1967.

4–7. Powers and duties

§ 4–7. Each board of library directors of a city, incorporated town, village or township shall carry out the spirit and intent of this Act in establishing and maintaining a public library and, in addition to other powers conferred by this Act, shall have the following powers:

1. To make and adopt such bylaws, rules and regulations, for their own guidance and for the government of the library as may be expedient, not inconsistent with this Act;

2. To have the exclusive control of the expenditure of all moneys collected for the library and deposited to the credit of the library fund;

3. To have the exclusive control of the construction of any library building and of the supervision, care and custody of the grounds, rooms or buildings constructed, leased or set apart for that purpose;

4. To purchase or lease real or personal property, and to construct an appropriate building or buildings for the use of the library, using, at the board's option, contracts providing for all or part of the consideration to be paid through installments at stated intervals during a certain period not to exceed 10 years with interest at a rate not to exceed 7% on the unpaid balance, except that contracts for installment purchases of real estate shall provide for not more than 50% of the total consideration to be repaid by installments;

5. To remodel or reconstruct a building erected or purchased by the board, when such building is not adapted to its purposes or needs;

6. To sell or otherwise dispose of any real or personal property that it deems no longer necessary or useful for library purposes, and to lease to others any real property not immediately useful but for which plans for ultimate use have been or will be adopted but the corporate authorities shall have the first right to purchase or lease except that in the case of the City of Chicago, this power shall be governed and limited by "An Act to authorize the Chicago public library to erect and maintain a public library on Dearborn Park in the city of Chicago, and to authorize the Soldiers' Home in Chicago to sell and dispose of its interest in the north one-quarter of the said park", approved June 2, 1891, as amended;

7. To appoint a competent librarian and necessary assistants, to fix their compensation, to remove such appointees, and to retain professional consultants as needed, but these powers are subject to Division 1 of Article 10 of the Illinois Municipal Code in municipalities in which that Division is in force;

8. To contract with any library association, school board, or any city, village, incorporated town, township, county, or district library board in the State of Illinois for furnishing or receiving library service including but not limited to contracts for such library service as participants in any library system formed pursuant to law and as participants in interstate library compacts, and to contract to supply library services and for the expenditure of any federal or State funds made available to any county, municipality, township or to the State of Illinois for library purposes;

9. To join with the board or boards of any one or more libraries of any city, incorporated town, village, township, county or district in maintaining libraries, or for the maintenance of a common library for such cities, incorporated towns, villages, townships, county or districts, upon such terms as may be agreed upon by and between the boards;

10. To enter into contracts and to take title to any property acquired by it for library purposes by the name and style of "The Board of Library Directors of the (city, village, incorporated town or township) of . . . ." and by that name to sue and be sued;

11. To exclude from the use of the library any person who wilfully violates the rules prescribed by the board;

12. To extend the privileges and use of the library to persons residing outside the city, incorporated town, village or township upon such terms and conditions as the board may from time to time by its regulations prescribe and to impose a nonresident fee for such privileges and uses comparable to the cost to residents of such entity;

13. To exercise the power of eminent domain subject to the prior approval of the corporate authorities under Sections 5–1 and 5–2 of this Act.

14. To join the public library as a member in the Illinois Library Association and the American Library Association, non-profit, non-political (501–C–3) associations, as designated by the federal Internal Revenue Service, having the purpose of library development and librarianship; to provide for the payment of annual membership dues, fees and assessments and act by, through and in the name of such instrumentality by providing and disseminating information and research services, employing personnel and doing any and all other acts for the purpose of improving library development.

Amended by Laws 1967, p. 3105, § 1; P.A. 76–803, § 1, eff. Aug. 18, 1969; P.A. 79–989, § 1, eff. Oct. 1, 1975; P.A. 79–1061, § 1, eff. Oct. 1, 1975; P.A. 79–1454, § 35, eff. Aug. 31, 1976; P.A. 81–1071, § 1, eff. July 1, 1980.

4–7.1. Additional powers and duties

§ 4–7.1. In addition to all other powers and authority now possessed by it, the board of library directors shall have the following powers:

(1) To lease from any public building commission created pursuant to the provisions of the Public Building Commission Act, as now or hereafter amended, any real or personal property for library purposes for a period of time not exceeding 20 years;

(2) To pay for the use of this leased property in accordance with the terms of the lease and with the provisions of the Public Building Commission Act, as now or hereafter amended;

(3) Such lease may be entered into without making a previous appropriation for the expense thereby incurred. However, if the board undertakes to pay all or any part of the costs of operating and maintaining the property of a public building commission as authorized in subparagraph (4) of this Section, such expenses of operation and maintenance shall be included in the annual budget of such board annually during the term of such undertaking;

(4) In addition, the board may undertake, either in the lease with a public building commission or by separate agreement or contract with a public building commission, to pay all or any part of the costs of maintaining and operating the property of a public building commission for any period of time not exceeding 40 years.

Laws 1965, p. 1402, § 4–7.1, added by P.A. 77–1232, § 1, eff. Aug. 24, 1971. Amended by P.A. 77–1980, § 1, eff. Oct. 1, 1972; P.A. 78–255, § 61, eff. Oct. 1, 1973.

§ 4—8. Cities over 500,000—Governing provisions for contracts and purchases

In cities of more than 500,000 population, the board of directors shall be governed by the provisions of Division 10 of Article 8 of the Illinois Municipal Code, as heretofore and hereafter amended, in relation to the letting of contracts and purchase orders in behalf of any library and the power, functions and authority of the purchasing agent, board of standardization and corporate authority in such cities. 1965, July 12, Laws 1965, p. ——, H.B.No.956, § 4–8.

4–9. Municipalities of less than 50,000—Bond of custodian of fund

§ 4–9. In townships and in cities, villages and incorporated towns having a population of 50,000 or less, the board of directors shall require the treasurer of such board or such other person as may be designated as the custodian of the moneys paid over to such board to give a bond to be approved by such board and in such amount, not less than 1/12 of the total annual library taxes collected, conditioned that he will safely keep and pay over upon the order of such board all funds received and held by him for such board of directors. Such board of library directors may designate the treasurer of the corporate authority, or the supervisor in the case of a township, as the custodian of the library fund, and the bond given by the treasurer or the supervisor shall satisfy the bond requirements of this section when properly endorsed. Amended by Laws 1967, p. 2719, § 1; P.A. 79–413, § 1, eff. Oct. 1, 1975.

4–10. Annual report

§ 4–10. Within 30 days after the expiration of each fiscal year of the city, incorporated town, village or township, the board of directors shall make a report of the condition of their trust on the last day of the fiscal year, to the city council, board of trustees or board of town auditors, as the case may be. This report shall be made in writing and shall be verified under oath by the secretary, or some other responsible officer of the board of directors. It shall contain (1) an itemized statement of the various sums of money received from the library fund and from other sources; (2) an itemized statement of the objects and purposes for which those sums of money have been expended; (3) a statement of the number of books and periodicals available for use, and the number and character thereof circulated; (4) a statement of the real and personal property acquired by devise, bequest, purchase, gift or otherwise; (5) a statement of the character of any extensions of library service which have been undertaken; (6) a statement of the financial requirements of the library for the ensuing fiscal year for inclusion in the appropriation of the corporate authority, and of the amount of money which, in the judgment of the board of library directors, it will be necessary to levy for library purposes in the next annual tax levy ordinance; (7) a statement as to the amount of accumulations and the reasons therefor; (8) a statement as to any outstanding liabilities including those for bonds still outstanding or amounts due for judgments, settlements, liability insurance, or for amounts due under a certificate of the board; (9) any other statistics, information and suggestions that may be of interest. A report shall also be filed, at the same time, with the Illinois State Library. The board of directors in a township shall also submit its appropriation and levy determinations to the Board of Auditors as provided in "The Illinois Municipal Budget Law", as amended.
Amended by Laws 1967, p. 2427, § 1; P.A. 76–527, § 1, eff. July 28, 1969; P.A. 77–15, § 1, eff. April 7, 1971.

4–11. Inclusion within public library district—Suspension of powers—Duties

§ 4–11. The powers granted boards of directors shall be suspended during any period that the city, incorporated town, village or township is included within any public library district established under "The Illinois Public Library District Act", as hereafter amended. However, such board shall exercise its powers as to any portion of a city, village, incorporated town or township which is not included within the district.

The board shall, under a court order or law, provide for payment of its liabilities, transfer of its assets to and continuation of library services by the library district within which has been wholly included, a city, or village, or incorporated town or township.
Amended by Laws 1967, p. 1820, § 1; P.A. 77–549, § 1, eff. July 31, 1971.

§ 4–12. Historical museum and library—Participation in maintenance

Whenever any historical society or other civic body or corporation, organized for the promotion of historical education, is maintaining a historical museum and library within the territory served by a public library subject to this Act, the board of directors of such public library may participate in the maintenance of such historical museum and library upon such terms and conditions as may be mutually agreed upon by the board of directors of such public library and the governing board of such historical society or other civic body or corporation. 1965, July 12, Laws

1965, p. ——, H.B.No.956, § 4–12, added 1965, Aug. 4, Laws 1965, p. ——, H.B.No.2191, § 1.

4–13. Local library working cash fund

§ 4–13. A Board of Library Directors may, by resolution, create and maintain a working cash fund, for the sole purpose of enabling the library board to have in its funds, at all times, sufficient money to meet demands thereon for ordinary and necessary and committed expenditures for library purposes.

Such working cash fund shall be known as the local library working cash fund and may contain any amount deemed necessary by the Board to satisfy the purpose of the fund; provided, that the balance in the fund shall not at any time be allowed to exceed .2% of the full, fair cash value of all taxable property within the corporate limits, as equalized or assessed by the Department of Revenue as of the year the fund is established or, if such fund is established after January 1, 1979, then for the year 1978. The money for such fund shall only accrue from the local library working cash fund tax authorized to be levied pursuant to Section 3–9.

Once the fund has been created, the proceeds shall be deposited in a special and separate fund, and may be carried over, from year to year without in any manner reducing or abating a future annual library tax levy. It shall be identified in the appropriation each year, but shall not be deemed as a current asset available for library purposes.

The proceeds of such fund may be transferred from the local library working cash fund to the general library fund, and disbursed therefrom in anticipation of the collection of taxes lawfully levied for general library purposes or in anticipation of such taxes, as by law now or hereafter enacted or amended, imposed by the General Assembly of the State of Illinois to replace revenue lost by units of local government and school districts as a result of the abolition of ad valorem personal property taxes, pursuant to Article IX, Section 5(c) of the Constitution of the State of Illinois. Such taxes when collected, and after payment of tax warrants, shall be drawn upon to reimburse the working cash fund.

Laws 1965, p. 1402, § 4–13, added by Laws 1967, p. 706, § 1. Amended by P.A. 78–1163, § 1, eff. Aug. 27, 1974; P.A. 80–1153, § 1, eff. July 1, 1978; P.A. 81–165, § 15, eff. Aug. 11, 1979; P.A. 81–924, § 1, eff. Jan. 1, 1980; P.A. 81–1509, Art. I, § 51, eff. Sept. 26, 1980; P.A. 81–1509, Art. IV, § 74, eff. Sept. 26, 1980.

4–13.1. Abolition of working cash fund—Transfer of balance—Approval of subsequent funds

§ 4–13.1. A Board of Library Directors may, by resolution, abolish a working cash fund established pursuant to Section 4–13 and direct the transfer of any balance in such fund, including any interest that has accrued, to the general library fund at the close of the fiscal year. However, if the board abolished a working cash fund under this provision, it shall not establish another working cash fund, unless establishment of the fund is approved by a majority of the voters of the city, village, incorporated town or township voting on the question at a referendum.

Laws 1965, p. 1402, § 4–13.1, added by P.A. 81–924, § 1, eff. Jan. 1, 1980.

4–14. Payment of judgments, settlements and liability insurance—Levy of additional taxes for payments

§ 4–14. A Board of Library Directors may, by resolution, provide for (a) the payment, in the manner provided for in Section 9–104 of the "Local Governmental and Governmental Employees Tort Immunity Act", of any judgment for which it is liable; (b) the making of payments to settle or compromise a claim or action against the board; and (c) the contracting and payment of premiums for insurance against loss or liability, as provided in Section 9–103 of the "Local Governmental and Governmental Employees Tort Immunity Act".

In addition, the board may include in the statement of financial requirements in its annual report to the corporate authorities the specific sums required to make the payments provided for in the first paragraph of this Section and the amount of any additional taxes it will be necessary to levy for those purposes. The corporate authorities may levy a tax for these purposes under Section 9–107 of the "Local Governmental and Governmental Employees Tort Immunity Act".

Laws 1965, p. 1402, § 4–13, added by P.A. 76–1908, § 1, eff. Oct. 10, 1969. Renumbered § 4–14 by P.A. 76–2110, § 1, eff. July 1, 1970.

4–15. Appropriations—Termination

§ 4–15. Appropriations for library purposes within the annual appropriation ordinance of the corporate authority, shall terminate with the close of the fiscal year of the library, except that any remaining balances shall be available for 60 days thereafter for the authorization of the payment of obligations incurred before the close of the fiscal year, and for an additional 30 days thereafter for payment of such prior incurred obligations, or for transfer of unexpended or unexpendable balances thereof to be accumulated under Sections 5–1 and 5–8 of this Act.

Laws 1965, p. 1402, § 4–15, added by P.A. 77–10, § 1, eff. July 1, 1971.

4–16. Sale or disposition of real or personal property

§ 4–16. When the board of directors has determined to sell or otherwise dispose of real or personal property that it deems no longer necessary or useful for library purposes, such may be sold or disposed of at a public sale, but the corporate authorities shall have the first right to purchase such property for public or corporate purposes by meeting bids acceptable to the board.

Public sales shall be conducted as follows:

1. Personal property having a value of less than $1,000 may be displayed at the library, and a public notice of its availability shall be posted at the library and at the office of the corporate authorities. Where there is no library building, then such notice may be posted at any other public building in the area.

2. In all other cases, the board shall publish notice of the availability and location of the real or personal property to be sold, a description thereof, the date of the sale, and the terms and conditions of the sale. Such notice shall be published once each week for 2 successive weeks in a newspaper circulated in the community.

On the day of the sale, the board shall proceed with the sale, and may sell property at a price determined by the board, or, to the highest bidder, whichever is greater. Where the board deems the bids inadequate, it may reject all bids and conduct another sale or sales in like manner as the original sale provided by this Section.

Laws 1965, p. 1402, § 4.16, added by P.A. 77–548, § 1, eff. July 31, 1971.

5–1. Sites, buildings and equipment—Purchase, erection, repair, remodeling, improvement—Procedure

§ 5–1. Whenever the board of directors of any public library organized under this Act determines to erect a building to be used as a library, or to purchase a site for the same, or to purchase a building, or to repair, remodel or improve an existing library building, or build an addition thereto, or to furnish necessary equipment therefor, or to acquire library materials such as books, periodicals, films, recordings and electronic data storage and retrieval facilities in connection with either the purchase or construction of a new library building or the expansion of an existing library building, or to accumulate a fund to accomplish any of such purposes, or to do any or all of these things, the directors may proceed as follows:

If a new building is to be erected, or an existing library building is to be remodeled, repaired, improved or an addition thereto erected, or necessary equipment is to be furnished, or any or all of these things are to be done, the board of directors shall cause a plan to be prepared and an estimate to be made of the cost. If a site or a building is to be purchased, the directors shall cause an estimate to be made of the cost of such site or building. The directors may then determine the funds that will be available from accumulations, and the amount to be raised from a bond issue, by annual certification, or by a mortgage. The directors shall further determine the term, not exceeding 20 years, over which they shall spread the collection of the cost of erecting a new building, or remodeling, repairing, improving an existing library building or erecting an addition thereto, or furnishing necessary equipment, or purchasing and improving a site or building, or the acquisition of library materials such as books, periodicals, recordings and electronic data storage and retrieval facilities in connection with either the purchase or construction of a new library building or the expansion of an existing library building, or any or all of these things.

For the purpose of Sections 5–1, 5–2, 5–3, 5–4 and 5–5 of this Act, the acquisition of library material such as books, periodicals, films, recordings and electronic data storage and retrieval facilities is considered to be in connection with the purchase or construction of a new library building or the expansion of an existing library building if the determination of the Board of Directors to acquire such library materials is made within 5 years from the date that a new library building is purchased, or construction of a new library building or the expansion of an existing library building is completed.

The board shall make a record of their proceedings and determinations and transmit a copy thereof to the corporate authorities for their consideration and approval.

Amended by Laws 1967, p. 3362, § 1; P.A. 77–1431, § 1, eff. Sept. 2, 1971.

5–2. Sites, buildings and equipment—Purchase, erection, repair, remodeling, improvement—Bonds

§ 5–2. If the corporate authorities approve the action of the library board under Section 5–1, they may, by ordinance, or by resolution in the case of a township, provide that the bonds of the city, village, incorporated town or township be issued for the payment of the cost (so estimated as aforesaid) of constructing a building, or remodeling, repairing, improving an existing library building or the erection of an addition thereto, or purchasing a building, site or equipment, or the acquisition of library materials such as books, periodicals, recordings and electronic data storage and retrieval facilities in connection with either the purchase or construction of a new library building or the expansion of an existing library building, or any or all of these things in which event the ordinance or resolution shall also state the time or times when such bonds, and the interest thereon shall become payable. However, the whole of the principal of such bonds and the interest thereon shall be payable within 20 years, and the interest on such bonds shall not exceed the rate of 7% per annum. The interest may be made payable at such times (annually or semi-annually) as the ordinance or resolution may prescribe. In case the corporate authorities provide for such payment by the issuance of bonds, they shall make provision at or before the issuance thereof, by ordinance or by resolution in the case of a township, which shall be irrepealable, for the levy and collection of a direct annual tax upon all the taxable property within such city, village, incorporated town or township sufficient to meet the principal and interest of the bonds as they mature, which tax shall be in addition to that otherwise authorized to be levied and collected for corporate purposes.

If, however, the corporate authorities do not provide that the bonds of the city, village, incorporated town or township be issued, but otherwise approve the action of the library board, then the library board shall divide the total cost of constructing and financing a building, or remodeling, repairing, improving an existing library building or the erection of an addition thereto, or purchasing and financing a building, site or equipment, or the acquisition of library materials such as books, periodicals, recordings and electronic data storage and retrieval facilities in connection with either the purchase or construction of a new library building or the expansion of an existing library building, or any or all of these things, into as many parts as the directors determine to spread the collection thereof, and shall certify the amount of one of these parts to the corporate authorities each year during the term over which the directors have determined to spread the collection. This action by the library board shall be irrepealable. The library board shall specify in its certificate the portion, if any, of the amount to be included in the annual appropriation and library tax levy, and the amount of the special tax required to pay the same as has been approved by the voters.

Amended by Laws 1967, p. 3362, § 1; P.A. 76–102, § 1, eff. May 21, 1969; P.A. 76–2423, § 1, eff. June 29, 1970; P.A. 77–1431, § 1, eff. Sept. 2, 1971; P.A. 79–989, § 1, eff. Oct. 1, 1975.

5–3. Sites, buildings and equipment—Purchase, erection, repair, remodeling, improvement—Levy and collection of taxes

§ 5–3. The corporate authorities on receiving the certificate of the board of library directors, as provided in Section 5–2, shall, in its next annual appropriation ordinance or resolution, include the amount so certified, and shall, for the amount so certified levy and collect a tax to pay such with the other general taxes of the city, village, incorporated town or township, and the proceeds of such tax shall be paid over by the officer charged with the collection thereof to the board of directors of such library in cities, villages and incorporated towns having a population of 50,000 inhabitants or less to be applied by such board of directors to the purpose for which such tax was levied. Such levy shall not exceed .0833% of the value, as equalized or assessed by the Department of Revenue, in any one year, and shall not be levied for more than the number of years into which the library board, in those cases where bonds are not issued as provided in Section 5–2, has divided the cost of constructing a building, or remodeling, repairing, improving an existing library building or the erection of an addition thereto, or purchasing a site, building or equipment, or to acquire library materials such as books, periodicals, films, recordings and electronic data storage and retrieval facilities in connection with either the purchase or construction of a new library building or the expansion of an existing library building, or any or all of these things. When collected as provided in this Section, the tax shall cease.

Amended by Laws 1967, p. 2719, § 1; Laws 1967, p. 3362, § 1; Laws 1968, p. 281, § 1, eff. July 1, 1969; P.A. 77–1042, § 1, eff. Aug. 17, 1971; P.A. 81–1509, Art. IV, § 74, eff. Sept. 26, 1980.

5–4. Sites, buildings and equipment—Purchase, erection, repair, remodeling, improvement—Commencement—Investment of funds—Contracts

§ 5–4. The library board shall determine when it will proceed with the construction of a building, or with the purchase of a site or building, or with the remodeling, repairing, or improving of an existing library building, or the building of an addition thereto, or with the purchase of necessary equipment, or the acquisition of library materials such as books, periodicals, recordings and electronic data storage and retrieval facilities in connection with either the purchase or construction of a new library building or the expansion of an existing library building, or any or all of these things. The board may proceed at once or may determine to wait and allow the fund to accumulate. If the board determines to let the fund accumulate, it shall invest the money in good interest paying securities, such as are authorized by law for the investment of trust funds, there to remain until the same is needed for any or all of the purposes enumerated aforesaid. The board may contract to accomplish any or all of the purposes enumerated aforesaid, and may apply the proceeds of the tax as collected, toward payment therefor.

Amended by Laws 1967, p. 3362, § 1, eff. Aug. 26, 1967.

5–5. Construction, repair or remodeling contracts—Procedure for awarding—Security

§ 5–5. When the directors determine to commence the construction of the building or the remodeling, repairing or improving of an existing library building or the erection of an addition thereto, the purchase of the necessary equipment for such library, or the acquisition of library materials such as books, periodicals, recordings and electronic data storage and retrieval facilities in connection with either the purchase or construction of a new library building or the expansion of an existing library building, they may then revise the plan therefor or adopt a new plan and provide estimates of the costs thereof, and shall advertise for bids for the construction of the building, or the remodeling, repairing or improving of an existing library building or the erection of an addition thereto, or the purchase of the necessary equipment for such library, or the acquisition of library materials such as books, periodicals, recordings and electronic data storage and retrieval facilities in connection with either the purchase or construction of a new library building or the expansion of an existing library building, and shall let the contract or contracts for the same to the lowest responsible bidder or bidders and may require from such bidders, such security for the performance of the bids as the board shall determine.

The directors may let the contract or contracts to one or more bidder, as they shall determine.
Amended by Laws 1967, p. 3362, § 1, eff. Aug. 26, 1967.

5–6. Mortgages—Execution—Retirement—Tax levies

If the directors deem it best, in order to provide and secure the necessary money to do any or all of the things they are authorized to do in and by this Article, they may with the approval of the corporate authorities at any time borrow money and execute a mortgage on an existing library building and site for an amount not exceeding 75% of the value thereof as improved, and the money so obtained shall be used exclusively for the remodeling, repairing or improving of such existing library building or building of an addition thereto or for the erection of a new library building or for purchase and improvement of a site or building adjoining or adjacent to the existing site and building or the purchase of necessary equipment for such library. The proceeds of any special tax levied under Section 5–3 may be applied in whole or in part in payment of any mortgage indebtedness so incurred. The levy of a tax hereunder for the purpose of meeting such mortgage and interest, or the principal and interest on bonds issued hereunder, or for the accumulation of a fund as hereinabove provided, shall not be included in the aggregate amount of taxes as limited by Division 3 of Article 8 of the Illinois Municipal Code nor shall it affect any appropriation made, or to be made, for the support of the library. This Section shall not apply to any city having over 500,000 inhabitants.
Amended by Laws 1967, p. 1821, § 1; P.A. 77–1431, § 1, eff. Sept. 2, 1971; P.A. 80–655, § 1, eff. Oct. 1, 1977; P.A. 81–1071, § 1, eff. July 1, 1980.

5–7. Tax levy—Referendum

§ 5–7. No city, village, township or incorporated town is authorized to levy the tax provided for in this Article unless it first adopts an ordinance, or resolution in the case of a township authorizing the levy of such tax, certifies to the proper election officials the proposition for the approval of such tax and such election officials submit the proposition to the voters of such city, village, township or incorporated town, as the case may be, at a regular election and such proposition is approved by a majority of such voters voting upon the question; the proposition shall state the tax, and the purpose thereof as established by the ordinance or resolution. However, in any city, village, township or incorporated town in which a majority of the voters voting upon the question have, subsequent to January 1, 1969, approved any such ordinance or resolution providing for the issuance of bonds pursuant to Section 5–2 of this Act at a coupon rate of less than 7% per annum, the corporate authorities of any such city, village, township or incorporated town are authorized to, and may, before January 1, 1972, issue such bonds, or any part thereof, so approved at a coupon rate that does not exceed 7% per annum and such corporate authorities are authorized to adopt an ordinance or resolution authorizing the levy of the tax provided for in this Article without submitting such ordinance or resolution to the voters of such city, village, township or incorporated town for approval.
Laws 1965, p. 1402, § 5–6. Resectioned § 5–7 and amended by Laws 1967, p. 1821, § 1. Amended by P.A. 76–2423, § 1, eff. June 29, 1970; P.A. 81–1489, § 70, eff. Dec. 1, 1980.

5–8. Accumulation of funds

§ 5–8. The library board of any public library organized under the provisions of this Act may accumulate and set apart, as reserve funds, for the purchase of sites and buildings, for the construction and equipment of buildings, for the rental and repair of buildings acquired for library purposes and for repairs and alterations of library buildings and equipment, the unexpended balances of the proceeds annually received from taxes not to excess of the statutory limits, provided the library board in its annual appropriation determination to the corporate authorities specifies that a specific fund is to be or is being accumulated for this purpose and has further resolved to develop and adopt a plan or plans pursuant to this Article.
Laws 1965, p. 1402, § 5–7. Renumbered § 5–8 and amended by Laws 1967, p. 1821, § 1; P.A. 76–527, § 1, eff. July 28, 1969.

5–9. Powers of board of directors of township libraries—Effect of this article

§ 5–9. Nothing in this Article 5 shall be construed as limiting or affecting in any way the powers of boards of directors of township libraries under "An Act to enable boards of directors of public libraries to borrow money for the erection or improvement of library buildings or to purchase library sites", approved May 18, 1905, as heretofore and hereafter amended.

Laws 1965, p. 1402, § 5–8. Renumbered § 5–9 and amended by Laws 1967, p. 1821, § 1, eff. July 20, 1967.

Township Library Buildings and Sites

(Smith-Hurd Illinois Annotated Statutes, 1982, Chap. 81, s.46–49, 52–54.)

46. Borrowing money for library purposes

§ 1. That for the purpose of erecting, repairing or improving library buildings or purchasing sites for library buildings, the directors of any township library, organized under the laws of this state, when thereunto authorized by majority of all the votes cast on the proposition at an election, may borrow money, and may issue bonds therefor, in the sums of not less than one hundred dollars ($100) bearing interest at a rate not exceeding six per centum per annum and for a term not to exceed twenty years: Provided, that the sum borrowed in any one year shall not exceed five per centum (including existing indebtedness) of the taxable property of the township, to be ascertained by the last assessment for state and county taxes previous to the incurring of such indebtedness. The proposition shall be submitted to the voters in accordance with the general election law upon the adoption of a resolution so requesting by the directors and certified to the proper election officials.

Amended by P.A. 81–1489, § 73, eff. Dec. 1, 1980.

§ 47. Bonds—Execution—Registration

All bonds authorized to be issued by virtue of the foregoing section before being so issued, negotiated and sold shall be signed by the president and secretary of such board of directors, and shall be registered, numbered and countersigned by the supervisor of the township wherein such library is located. Such registry shall be made in a book to be kept for that purpose; and in such register shall be first entered the record of the election authorizing the directors to borrow money, and then a description of the bonds issued by virtue of such authority as to number, date, to whom issued, amount, rate of interest and when due. 1905, May 18, Laws 1905, p. 313, § 2.

§ 48. Money delivered to supervisor

All moneys borrowed under the authority granted by this act shall be paid to the supervisor of the township wherein the bonds issued therefor are required to be registered, and upon receiving such moneys, the supervisor shall deliver the bond or bonds issued therefor, to the parties entitled to receive the same; and shall credit the sums received to the library fund of township issuing the bonds. The said supervisor of said township shall enter in the said bond register the exact amount received for each and every bond issued. And when any such bonds are paid, the supervisor shall cancel the same and shall enter in the said bond register against the record of such bonds, the words "Paid and canceled the _____ day of _____, A. D. _____," filling the blanks with the day, month and year corresponding with the date of such payment. 1905, May 18, Laws 1905, p. 313, § 3.

49. Election—Form of proposition

§ 4. The proposition shall be in substantially the following form: "For" or "Against" the proposition to issue the bonds of .... township to the amount of .... dollars due (here insert the times of payment, giving the amount falling due in each year, if the bonds mature at different dates), which bonds are to bear interest at the rate of .... per cent per annum, payable .... annually.

Amended by P.A. 81–1489, § 73, eff. Dec. 1, 1980; P.A. 81–1535, § 21, eff. Dec. 19, 1980.

52. Refunding bonds

§ 7. In all cases where any board of directors of any township library have issued or may hereafter issue bonds, or other evidence of indebtedness for money on account of any public library building, or for the improvement thereof, which remain outstanding and which are properly authorized by law, such board of directors may, upon the surrender of any such bonds or other evidence of indebtedness, or any number thereof, issue in place or in lieu thereof, or to take up the same to the holders or owners of the same, or to other persons for money with which to take up the same, new bonds or other evidences of the indebtedness in such form, of such amount, upon such time, not exceeding the term of twenty years, and drawing such rate of interest, not exceeding six per centum per annum, as may be determined upon, and such new bonds or other evidences of indebtedness so issued shall show that they are issued under this act. Provided, that the issue of such new bonds in lieu of such indebtedness must be authorized by the legal voters of such township voting at a referendum initiated as provided for in Section 1 of this act and conducted in accordance with the general election law: and, Provided, further, that such bonds or other evidence of indebtedness shall not be issued so as to increase the aggregate indebtedness of such township beyond five per centum of the value of the taxable property therein, to be ascertained by the last assessment for state and county taxes, prior to the issuing of such bonds or other evidences of indebtedness.

Amended by P.A. 81–1489, § 73, eff. Dec. 1, 1980.

§ 53.   Certificate for tax levy

The board of directors of the public library of any township, which shall have issued bonds pursuant to the provisions of this act, shall, on or before the first Tuesday in August, of each year, ascertain as near as practicable, the amount of money which must be raised by special taxation for the ensuing year, for the purpose of paying the interest upon such bonds and the principal thereof, as they shall respectively become due; and shall cause the same to be certified, under the hands of the president and secretary of such board of directors, and filed in the office of the county clerk of the county in which library is situated, on or before the second Monday in August of each year; which certificate may be substantially in the form following:

We hereby certify that the Board of Directors of the _____ Public Library have determined that they will require the sum of _____ dollars ($_____), to be levied as a special tax upon the taxable property of _____ Township, for the year A. D. _____, for the purpose of paying the bonds of said Township and the interest thereon.

Given under our hands, this _____ day of _____, A. D. _____.

Board of Directors of _____ Public Library.

_____ President.

_____ Secretary.

1905, May 18, Laws 1905, p. 313, § 8.

§ 54. Taxes—Computation by county clerk—Levy—Limitation

It shall be the duty of the county clerk when making out the tax books for the collector to compute each taxable person's taxes in such township upon the total amount of taxable property as equalized by the State Board of Equalization for that year, whether belonging to residents or non-residents, and also each and every tract of land assessed by the assessor, which lies in such township. Such computation shall be made so as to realize the amount of money required to be raised in such township, as shown and set forth in the certificate of tax levy, made out by the board of directors of such public library and filed with the said county clerk as required by the provisions of this act. The said county clerk shall cause each person's tax so computed to be set upon the tax books to be delivered to the collector for that year in a separate column, against each taxpayer's name, or parcel of taxable property, as it appears in said collector's books, to be collected in the same manner and at the same time and by the same persons as state and county taxes are collected. The computation of each person's tax and the levy made by the clerk, as aforesaid, shall be final and conclusive: Provided, that the rate shall be uniform and shall not exceed that required by the amount certified by the board of directors as aforesaid, together with the estimated cost of extending and collecting the same. 1905, May 18, Laws 1905, p. 313, § 9.

Libraries in Public Parks
(Smith-Hurd Illinois Annotated Statutes, 1982, Chap. 81, s.41.44.)

§ 41. Location within park—Condemnation

The corporate authorities of cities and park districts, or any board of park commissioners having the control or supervision of any public park or parks, are hereby authorized to permit any free public library, organized under the terms and provisions of an act entitled, "An act to encourage and promote the establishment of free public libraries in cities, villages and towns of this State," approved June 17, 1891, in force July 1, 1891, to erect and maintain, at its own expense, its library building within any public park now or hereafter under the control or supervision of such city, park district or board of park commissioners and to contract with any such free public library relative to the erection, maintenance and administration thereof. If any owner or owners of any lands or lots abutting or fronting on any such park, or adjacent thereto, or any other person or persons, have any right, easement, interest or property in such public park appurtenant to their lands or lots, or otherwise, which would be interfered with by the erection and maintenance of any free public library building, as hereinbefore provided, or any right to have such public park, or any part thereof, remain open and vacant and free from any buildings the corporate authorities of the city or park district or any board of park commissioners, having control of such park, may condemn the same in the manner prescribed in an act of the General Assembly entitled, "An Act to provide for the exercise of the right of eminent domain," approved April 10, 1872, in force July 1, 1872, and the amendments thereto. 1903, May 14, Laws 1903, p. 262, § 1.

§ 42.   Control and management

The directors, trustees or managers of any public library which shall erect its library building in or upon any public park, under the terms and provisions as aforesaid, shall, so long as said building is maintained as a free public library, control, direct and manage the affairs of such library, as heretofore, under the terms and provisions of an act entitled, "An Act to encourage and promote the establishment of free public libraries in cities, villages and towns of this State," approved June 17, 1891, in force July 1, 1891, and in all respects the same as though the said building was not erected in or upon a public park. 1903, May 14, Laws 1903, p. 262, § 2.

43. Submitting question to voters—Condemnation—Payment for property

§ 3.   In case the directors, trustees or managers of any free public library, or a majority of them, shall make request in writing, of the corporate authorities of such city, park district or board of park commissioners for permission to erect a free public library building in or upon any public park, under the control, supervision or jurisdiction of such city, park district or board of park commissioners designating the site desired and the general style and approximate cost of such building, it shall be the duty of the clerk or secretary thereof to certify the resolution and proposition of granting such request to the proper election officials who shall submit the proposition at an election in accordance with the general election law; and if a majority of the legal voters, voting upon such question at any such election shall favor the granting by said city, park district or board of park commissioners of the aforesaid request, then the said authorities or board of park commissioners shall authorize the erection of said building, as aforesaid, and if necessary proceed to condemn, as aforesaid, any right, easement or interest, belonging to such abutting property owners, which would be interfered with by the erection of said library building, and such city or park district shall have the power to pay for any right, easement or interest so condemned out of its general revenues.

Amended by P.A. 81–1489, § 72, eff. Dec. 1, 1980.

44. Corporate authorities of park district—Authority to permit erection of library building and contract in reference thereto

§ 3a. The corporate authorities of any park district whose limits are co-extensive with the limits of any city, village, or incorporated town lying wholly within any congressional township, in which there is established and maintained a free public library under "The Illinois Local Library Law" approved July 12, 1965, as heretofore or hereafter amended, or the corporate authorities of any such city, village, or incorporated town having the control or supervision of any public park or parks, may permit the board of library directors having control of such library or the board of trustees of a library district whose geographical area of service includes all or part of a public park or park district to erect and maintain in any public park of such park district, city, village, or incorporated town, a library building which shall be under the exclusive control and supervision of the board of library directors or library trustees, so long as such building is used as a free public library; and may contract with such board of library directors or library trustees relative to the erection and maintenance and administration thereof. Any portion of such building less than the whole which shall not from time to time be needed for library purposes, may be rented for public purposes only by the board of library directors or library trustees to or with the consent of such park district, city, village, or incorporated town.

Amended by Laws 1967, p. 2721, § 1; P.A. 79–1061, § 2, eff. Oct. 1, 1975.

Village Libraries Established by Gift
(Smith-Hurd Illinois Annotated Statutes, 1982,
Chap. 81, s.74-75.)

74. Tax authorized—Amount—Use of fund—Report to village board—Copy to be filed

§ 1. The corporate authorities of any village of 2,500 population or less, in which a free public library and gymnasium has been established by public and private, or public or private, grant or donation, absolutely or in trust, on land conveyed therefor to such village, where the management thereof has been vested by any such donor in a board of directors from time to time elected in accordance with "An Act in relation to free public libraries for cities, villages, incorporated towns and townships and to repeal Acts and parts of Acts therein named", approved July 12, 1965, as now or hereafter amended, or any board of trustees appointed by the president and board of trustees in accordance with the terms of any gift or grant, may levy a tax of not to exceed .15% of the value, as equalized or assessed by the Department of Revenue, on all the taxable property in such village, for the maintenance and operation of such library and gymnasium. Such tax shall be levied and collected with the general taxes of such village, and the proceeds shall be deposited in the treasury of such village to the credit of the library and gymnasium fund and kept separate and apart from other moneys of such village. Such fund shall be drawn upon by the proper officers of such library and gymnasium upon the properly authenticated vouchers of the library and gymnasium board, provided that no trustee shall receive compensation as such from such fund.

The board of directors shall make a report to the village board, and file a copy thereof with the Illinois State Library in accordance with Section 4–10 of "An Act in relation to free public libraries for cities, villages, incorporated towns and townships and to repeal Acts and parts of Acts therein named", approved July 12, 1965, as now or hereafter amended. Such taxes shall be in addition to the maximum of taxes permitted under Section 8–3–1 of the Illinois Municipal Code, as now or hereafter amended.

Amended by Laws 1967, p. 72, § 1; P.A. 77–1044, § 1, eff. Aug. 17, 1971; P.A. 81–1509, Art. IV, § 76, eff. Sept. 26, 1980.

75. Act to be submitted to voters

§ 2. This Act shall not become effective in any village to which it is applicable until the same shall first have been submitted to a vote of the electors of such village at a regular election. The proposition for the adoption of this Act shall be submitted to referendum upon the adoption of a resolution so directing by the corporate authorities and certified to the proper election officials in accordance with the general election law.

If a majority of those voting upon the proposition shall be for the adoption of this Act it shall thereafter be of full force and effect in such village, but if a majority be against the adoption of this Act, it shall not be again submitted to a vote until two years after the date of such referendum.

Amended by P.A. 81–1489, § 75, eff. Dec. 1, 1980.

Non-Tax Supported Village Libraries
(Smith-Hurd Illinois Annotated Statutes, 1982, Chap. 81, s.16c-16e.)

§ 16c.   Establishment—Donations

The board of trustees of any village shall have authority to establish and maintain a free, public library therein in any premises which may be available or which may be donated to such village for library purposes. The board may accept donations of such physical equipment as is suitable to the maintenance of a free, public library. 1939, July 20, Laws 1939, p. 700, § 1.

§ 16d.   Library commission—Compensation of members

The board of trustees shall appoint a library commission of three members who shall hold office at the pleasure of the board. Members of the commission shall receive no compensation but shall be reimbursed for expenses incurred in the performance of their duties. The commission shall conduct said library in accordance with rules adopted by it, shall employ such assistants as may be necessary and shall fix their compensation. 1939, July 20, Laws 1939, p. 700, § 2.

§ 16e.   Indebtedness—Taxes

Nothing herein contained shall be construed to confer on any village the authority to incur any indebtedness or to levy any additional taxes for the purpose of administering this Act. The powers herein contained are in addition to and not in limitation of any powers elsewhere granted to villages to establish and maintain free, public libraries. 1939, July 20, Laws 1939, p. 700, § 3.

INCORPORATED LIBRARIES
(Smith-Hurd Illinois Annotated Statutes, 1982, Chap. 81, s.32-35.)

§ 32.   Library founded by donation

Whenever property, real or personal, has heretofore been or shall hereafter be devised or bequeathed by last will and testament, or granted, conveyed or donated by deed or other instrument, to trustees to be applied by them to the foundation and establishment in any of the cities, villages and towns of this state of a free public library, it shall be lawful, when not otherwise provided in said will or other instrument of gift, for the acting trustees in any such case, in order to promote the better establishment, maintenance and management of such library, to cause to be formed a corporation under the provisions of this act, with the rights, powers and privileges hereinafter provided for. 1891, June 17, Laws 1891, p. 157, § 1.

§ 33. Statement for incorporation—Filing

Such acting trustees may make, sign and acknowledge before any officer authorized to take acknowledgments of deeds in this state, and file in the office of the Secretary of State a statement in writing, in which shall be set forth the intent of such trustees to form a corporation under this act; a copy of the will or other instrument by which endowment of said library has been provided; the name adopted for the proposed corporation (which shall not be the name of any other corporation already existing); the city, village or town in which the library and the principal place of business of the corporation will be located; the number of managers who may be denominated trustees, managers or directors of the corporation; and the names of the trustees, managers or directors who are to constitute the original board of such officers, and who shall hold until their successors respectively are elected and qualified, as in this act provided. 1891, June 17, Laws 1891, p. 157, § 2.

§ 34. Certificate of incorporation

Upon the filing in his office of such a statement as aforesaid the Secretary of State shall issue to the incorporators, under his hand and seal of state, a certificate, of which the aforesaid statement shall be a part, declaring that the organization of the corporation is perfected. The incorporators shall thereupon cause such certificate to be recorded in a proper record book for the purpose in the office of the recorder of deeds of the county in which the said library is to be located; and thereupon the corporation shall be deemed fully organized and may proceed to carry out its corporate purposes, and may receive by conveyance, from the trustees under said will, deed or other instrument of donation, the property provided by will or otherwise as aforesaid for the endowment of said library, and may hold the same in whatever form it may have been received or conveyed by said trustees until such form shall be changed by the action of the said corporation. 1891, June 17, Laws 1891, p. 157, § 3.

35. Powers of corporation—Members—Trustees—Exemption from taxation—Report to Governor

§ 4. Organizations formed under this act shall be bodies corporate and politic to be known under the names stated in the respective certificates or articles of incorporation; and by such corporate names they shall have and possess the ordinary rights and incidents of corporations, and shall be capable of taking, holding and disposing of real and personal estate for all purposes of their organization. The provisions of any will, deed or other instrument by which endowment is given to the library and accepted by the trustees, managers or directors shall, as to such endowment, be a part of the organic and fundamental law of such corporation.

The trustees, managers or directors of any such corporation shall compose its members, and shall not be less than 7 nor more than 25 in number; shall elect the officers of the corporation from their number; and shall have control and management of its affairs and property; may accept donations, and in their discretion hold the same in the form in which they are given, for all purposes of science, literature and as are germane to the object and purpose of the corporation. They may fill by election, vacancies occurring in their own number by death, incapacity, retirement or otherwise, and may make lawful by-laws for the management of the corporation and of the library, which by-laws shall set forth what officers there shall be of the corporation, and shall define and prescribe their respective duties. They may appoint and employ from time to time such agents and employees as they may deem necessary for the efficient administration and conduct of the library and other affairs of the corporation. Whenever any trustee, manager or director shall be elected to fill any vacancy, a certificate under the seal of the corporation, giving the name of the person elected, shall be recorded in the office of the recorder of deeds where the articles of incorporation are recorded.

Whenever, by the provisions of such will, deed or other instrument by which an endowment is created, the institution endowed is free and public, the library and other property of such corporation shall be forever exempt from taxation.

The trustees, managers or directors of such corporation shall, in the month of January in each year, cause to be made a report to the Secretary of State for the year ending on the preceding December 31 of the condition of the library and of the funds and other property of the corporation showing the assets and investments of such corporation in detail.

This report shall be made in writing and shall be verified under oath by the secretary, or by some other responsible officer of such corporation. It shall contain (1) an itemized statement of the various sums of money received from the library fund and from other sources; (2) an itemized statement of the objects and purposes for which those sums of money have been expended; (3) a statement of the number of books and periodicals available for use, and the number and character thereof circulated; (4) a statement of the real and personal property acquired by devise, bequest, purchase, gift or otherwise; (5) a statement of the character of any extensions of library service which have been undertaken; (6) any other statistics, information and suggestions that may be of interest. A report shall also be filed, at the same time, with the Illinois State Library.

Amended by P.A. 76–237, § 1, eff. July 1, 1969; P.A. 77–529, § 1, eff. July 31, 1971.

LIBRARY ASSOCIATIONS

(Smith-Hurd Illinois Annotated Statutes, 1982,
Chap. 81, s.28-29.)

§ 28. Library associations—Sale or lease of property to public libraries—Meeting—Notice

Whenever any library association organized under any law of this state, and owning any real or personal property in this state, shall desire to sell or lease the same, or any part thereof, absolutely or with conditions, to the board of directors of any free public library, organized under the laws of this state, such sale or lease may be made in the manner following, viz.: the directors of such association shall call a meeting of all the members, subscribers or stockholders thereof, to be held at the rooms of said library or office of the secretary of such association, written or printed notice of the time, place and object of such meeting, and of the terms and conditions of the proposed sale or lease being first mailed, at least thirty (30) days prior to the time of such meeting, to the address of each member, subscriber or stockholder whose place of residence is known to any of the officers or directors of such association, and by publishing such notice for at least thirty (30) consecutive days next preceding the time of such meeting, in some newspaper published and of general circulation in the county where the property of said association is situate. 1874, March 24, R.S.1874, p. 664, § 1.

§ 29. Vote—Manner of making conveyance, etc.

If the members, subscribers or stockholders representing the majority in amount of the stock of such association, shall vote, at such meeting, in favor of such sale or lease upon the terms or conditions specified in such notice, or, in case said association shall consist of two or more departments, if a majority of the members, subscribers or stockholders of each department shall vote at such meeting in favor of such sale or lease so specified, then the president and secretary shall cause a record of the proceedings of such meeting, verified by the oath of the president thereof, together with an affidavit of the service or publication of notice as herein required, to be filed in the office of the clerk of the circuit court of the county where the property of such association is situate; after which the president and secretary of the said association shall be and are hereby authorized and empowered to execute any and all necessary deeds, leases, bills of sale, or other instruments in writing, to carry out the object and intent of said vote; which, when duly executed, shall be sufficient to pass to the board of directors of such free public library all the legal and equitable title of said association in and to the real or personal property in said instrument described as therein set forth. 1874, March 24, R.S.1874, p. 664, § 2.

COUNTY LAW LIBRARIES
(Smith-Hurd Illinois Annotated Statutes, 1982, Chap. 81, s.81.)

81. Establishment—Use—Library fee

§ 1. The county board of any county may establish and maintain a county law library, to be located in any county building or public building at the county seat of government. The term "county building" includes premises leased by the county from a public building commission created pursuant to the Public Building Commission Act, approved July 5, 1955, as amended. After the effective date of this amendatory Act of 1976, the county board of any county may establish and maintain a county law library at the county seat of government and in addition such branch law libraries in other locations within that county as the county board deems necessary.

The facilities of such libraries shall be freely available to all licensed Illinois attorneys, judges and other public officers of such county, and to all members of the public, whenever the court house is open.

The expense of establishing and maintaining such libraries shall be borne by the county. To defray such expense, in any county having so established such a county law library or libraries, the clerk of all trial courts located at the county seat of government shall charge and collect a county law library fee of $2, and the county board may authorize a county law library fee of not to exceed $4 to be charged and collected by the clerks of all trial courts located in the county, such fee to be paid at the time of filing the first pleading, paper or other appearance filed by each party in all civil cases, but no additional fee shall be required if more than one party is represented in a single pleading, paper or other appearance.

Each such clerk shall commence such charges and collections upon receipt of written notice from the chairman of such county board that the board has acted under the provisions of this Act to establish and maintain such a law library.

Such fees shall be in addition to all other fees and charges of such clerks, and assessable as costs, and shall be remitted by such clerks monthly to the county treasurer, and retained by him in a special fund designated as the County Law Library Fund. Disbursements from such fund shall be by the county treasurer, on order of a majority of the judges of the circuit court of such county, except that in any county having a population of more than 500,000 inhabitants, the county board shall order disbursements from such fund and the presiding officer of the county board, with the advice and consent of the county board, may appoint a library committee of not less than 9 members, who, by majority vote, may recommend to such county board as to disbursements of such fund and the operation of such library. Such orders shall be pre-audited and such funds shall be audited by the county auditor, and report thereof rendered to the county board and to the judges.

Such fees shall not be charged in any criminal or quasi-criminal case, in any matter coming to any such clerk on change of venue, nor in any proceeding to review the decision of any administrative officer, agency or body.

Amended by P.A. 76–958, § 1, eff. Aug. 26, 1969; P.A. 77–1262, § 1, eff. Aug. 24, 1971; P.A. 78–1128, § 35, eff. Oct. 1, 1974; P.A. 79–1336, § 1, eff. Aug. 2, 1976; P.A. 81–629, § 1, eff. Jan. 1, 1980.

TAX EXEMPTION

(Smith-Hurd Illinois Annotated Statutes, 1982,
Chap. 120, s.500.7.)

Illinois library laws are reprinted from SMITH-HURD IL-LINOIS ANNOTATED STATUTES published by Burdette Smith Co., Chicago, Illinois and West Publishing Co., St. Paul, Minnesota.

INDIANA

STATE LIBRARY AND HISTORICAL DEPARTMENT

(Burns Annotated Indiana Statutes, 1982, s.4-23-7-1 to 4-23-7-5.4,
4-23-7.1 to 4-23-7.1-24, 4-23-7.1-32 to 4-23-7.1-38, 4-23-7.2-1 to
4-23-7.2-18, 4-23-8-1 to 4-23-8-3.)

4-23-7-1 [63-801]. Department created. — There is hereby created and established a department of the state government which shall be known as the Indiana library and historical department. [Acts 1925, ch. 58, § 1, p. 190.]

4-23-7-2 [63-802]. Board — Members, appointment, terms and certain powers. — The management and control of the Indiana library and historical department is hereby vested in a board which shall be known as the Indiana library and historical board, and which shall consist of five [5] members, who shall be appointed by the governor, as hereinafter provided. In the first instance, one [1] of such members shall be appointed for a term of one [1] year, one [1] member for a term of two [2] years, one [1] member for a term of three [3] years, and two [2] members for a term of four [4] years. Thereafter all members shall be appointed for terms of four [4] years. No person shall be appointed as a member of the Indiana library and historical board unless he is a citizen of high standing and probity and has a known and active interest in library or historical work. One [1] member of the library and historical board shall be appointed on recommendation of the state board of education, one [1] member shall be appointed on recommendation of the Indiana Library Trustee Association, one [1] member shall be appointed on recommendation of the Indiana Library Association, one [1] member shall be appointed on recommendation of the Indiana Historical Society, and one [1] member shall be selected and appointed by the governor. The members of the board shall serve without compensation, but shall be entitled to receive their actual expenses necessarily incurred in attending the meetings and transacting the business of the board, and in participating in such other activities as may be in the interest of the department. Any vacancy which may occur in the membership of the board for any cause shall be filled by appointment by the governor for the unexpired term, either on recommendation of the board, association or society hereinbefore authorized to make recommendations, or by selection by the governor, as hereinbefore provided. The board may prepare plans subject to the approval of the governor and advise with the proper officials in the construction of alterations and additions to the building and provide necessary equipment and furnishings within the appropriations of funds for these purposes. The board may receive and administer any state or federal aid which may become available for the improvement and development of library and historical services in Indiana. [Acts 1925, ch. 58, § 2, p. 190; 1947, ch. 327, § 1; 1967, ch. 38, § 1.]

4-23-7-2.1. Officers — Term — Executive secretary. — (a) The Indiana library and historical board shall elect one [1] of its members as president, another as secretary, and such other officers as it determines, each of whom shall hold office for a term of one [1] year.

(b) The board may designate the director of the state library or the director of the historical bureau as the executive secretary of the board with duties as prescribed by the board. [IC 4-23-7-2.1, as added by Acts 1981, P.L. 40, § 1.]

4-23-7-3 [63-803]. Divisions of department. — The Indiana library and historical department consists of two [2] divisions, the Indiana state library and the Indiana historical bureau. [Acts 1925, ch. 58, § 3, p. 190; 1947, ch. 327, § 2; 1981, P.L. 40, § 2.]

4-23-7-3.2. Apportionment of duties. — In perfecting the internal organization of the department, the board may so apportion the duties of the department and of the several divisions thereof that like services in the various divisions may be performed by the same employee or employees for the entire department. [IC 4-23-7-3.2, as added by Acts 1981, P.L. 40, § 3.]

4-23-7-3.5. Political contribution solicitation and required political activity prohibited. — No member of the library and historical board nor any director or other employee of the department shall directly or indirectly solicit subscription or contribution for any political party or political purpose, or be forced in any way to make such contribution, or be required to participate in any form of political activity. [IC 4-23-7-3.5, as added by Acts 1981, P.L. 40, § 4.]

4-23-7-5 [63-805]. Board — Rules and regulations. — Subject to the provisions of this act [4-23-7-1 — 4-23-7-5], the library and historical board shall formulate rules and regulations for the care, management and expansion of the library and historical department so that the department and its several divisions may at all times be operated according to the most approved standards of library and historical service. [Acts 1925, ch. 58, § 5, p. 190.]

4-23-7-5.2. Acceptance of gifts, bequests and devises — Limitation on liabilities. — The Indiana library and historical board may accept gifts, bequests, and devises of personal and real property for the maintenance, use, or benefit of the Indiana library and historical department under such terms and conditions and with such obligations, liabilities, and burdens as in the judgment of the board and the governor is in the best interest of the Indiana library and historical department; however, no obligation, liability, or burden shall be assumed that is in excess of appropriations made by law for the payment of such obligations, liabilities, and burdens. [IC 4-23-7-5.2, as added by Acts 1981, P.L. 40, § 5.]

4-23-7-5.4. Library and historical department fund established — Uses — Sale proceeds. — (a) The library and historical department fund is established as a dedicated fund to be administered by the Indiana library and historical board. The monies in the fund may be expended by the board exclusively for the maintenance, use, or benefit of the Indiana library and historical department.

(b) The proceeds from the sale of items as directed by law or by the Indiana library and historical board, from gifts of money or the proceeds from the sale of gifts donated to the fund, and from investment earnings from any portion of the fund, shall be deposited in the fund.

(c) All monies accruing in the fund are hereby appropriated continuously for the purposes specified in this section.

(d) No portion of the fund shall revert to the general fund of the state at the end of a fiscal year; however, if the fund is abolished, its contents shall revert to the general fund of the state. [IC 4-23-7-5.4, as added by Acts 1981, P.L. 40, § 6.]

4-23-7.1-1. Definitions. — As used in this chapter:

(1) "Agency" means any state administration, agency, authority, board,

bureau, commission, committee, council, department, division, institution, office, service, or other similar body of state government.

(2) "Board" means the Indiana library and historical board established by IC 4-23-7-2.

(3) "Department" means the Indiana library and historical department established by IC 4-23-7-1.

(4) "Director" means director of the Indiana state library.

(5) "Historical bureau" means the Indiana historical bureau established by IC 4-23-7-3.

(6) "State library" means the Indiana state library established by IC 4-23-7-3. [IC 4-23-7.1-1, as added by Acts 1981, P.L. 40, § 7.]

4-23-7.1-2. Execution of policies. — The state library is responsible for executing the policy of the state of Indiana:

(1) To develop and provide library service to state government, its branches, its departments and its officials and employees;

(2) To provide for the individual citizens of the state those specialized library services not generally appropriate, economical or available in other libraries of the state;

(3) To encourage and support the development of the library profession; and

(4) To strengthen services of all types of publicly and privately supported special, school, academic, and public libraries. [IC 4-23-7.1-2, as added by Acts 1981, P.L. 40, § 7.]

4-23-7.1-3. Library collection — Development and maintenance. — The state library shall maintain, develop and service a collection of books, periodicals, newspapers, maps, manuscripts, audiovisual materials, and other library materials for the purpose of:

(1) Meeting the informational, educational, and research needs of state government;

(2) Preserving and making available for use, materials bearing on the history of the state;

(3) Meeting the specialized library needs and interests of citizens of Indiana; and

(4) Supplementing the reference and materials resources of the libraries of the state. [IC 4-23-7.1-3, as added by Acts 1981, P.L. 40, § 7.]

4-23-7.1-4. Historical or library development programs. — The state library shall initiate or participate in plans or programs for historical or library development in Indiana that are considered appropriate by the Indiana library and historical board. [IC 4-23-7.1-4, as added by Acts 1981, P.L. 40, § 7.]

4-23-7.1-5. Interlibrary exchanges. — The state library shall develop plans and programs and participate in the operation of plans and programs that will encourage and facilitate the interlibrary exchange of services, information, and materials. [IC 4-23-7.1-5, as added by Acts 1981, P.L. 40, § 7.]

4-23-7.1-6. Library information publications — Distribution. — The state library shall prepare, collect, edit, publish, and distribute such information bulletins, periodicals, statistical compilations, catalogs, or other publications concerning:

(1) The Indiana State library or its collections, materials, or services;

(2) The organization, administration, and maintenance of libraries; or

(3) Libraries and librarianship;

as may be considered proper. [IC 4-23-7.1-6, as added by Acts 1981, P.L. 40, § 7.]

4-23-7.1-7. Information on library materials and services. — The state library shall inform and enlighten the citizens of Indiana as to the library materials and services of the state library which will meet the specialized needs and interests of the state's residents. [IC 4-23-7.1-7, as added by Acts 1981, P.L. 40, § 7.]

4-23-7.1-8. Library activity research — Studies of library community. — The state library shall conduct research in appropriate areas of library activity and survey and study the library community in Indiana, including all types of libraries, therein, on a continual basis for the purpose of:

(1) Collecting pertinent statistics and other information;

(2) Assessing the condition and capacity of existing library facilities, resources, and services;

(3) Defining the needs of society which are the responsibility of libraries to meet;

(4) Evaluating library performance in relation to these needs; and

(5) Preparing recommendations and plans which will develop and strengthen library service in Indiana. [IC 4-23-7.1-8, as added by Acts 1981, P.L. 40, § 7.]

4-23-7.1-9. Library profession and service development. — The state library shall encourage the development of the library profession and of library service in Indiana by planning or conducting, either independently or cooperatively, programs of:

(1) Recruiting to the profession;

(2) Education for librarianship;

(3) In-service training;

(4) Personnel classifications, evaluation, and utilization; and

(5) Postgraduate continuing education. [IC 4-23-7.1-9, as added by Acts 1981, P.L. 40, § 7.]

4-23-7.1-10. Assistance to other libraries. — The state library shall provide advice and assistance as to the organization, administration, and maintenance of libraries to any person responsible for a library, either publicly or privately supported, in the state. [IC 4-23-7.1-10, as added by Acts 1981, P.L. 40, § 7.]

4-23-7.1-11. Operating standards — Inspections. — The state library shall establish operating standards for libraries eligible to receive funds, either federal or state, under the provisions of any program for which the Indiana state library is the administrator, and inspect libraries eligible to receive funds or receiving such funds to ascertain whether or not the standards are being met. [IC 4-23-7.1-11, as added by Acts 1981, P.L. 40, § 7.]

4-23-7.1-12. Services and personnel for agency and other libraries. — The state library shall provide library personnel, services, materials, equipment, or facilities for other state agencies, for libraries in other state agencies or for other libraries in the state as may be considered appropriate. [IC 4-23-7.1-12, as added by Acts 1981, P.L. 40, § 7.]

4-23-7.1-13. Interstate and federal agreements. — The state library shall negotiate and enter into agreements with other states or the federal government, as may be permitted by law, for the resolution of common library problems or the provision of common library services. [IC 4-23-7.1-13, as added by Acts 1981, P.L. 40, § 7.]

4-23-7.1-14. Informational or statistical publications — Expenses. — The state library may compile and publish digests, reports and bulletins of purely informational or statistical character on any question which the board may deem to be of interest or value to the people of the state. Any expenses which may be incurred in the publication of any such digest, report or bulletin shall be defrayed out of the funds which may be appropriated for the use of the department or the state library. [IC 4-23-7.1-14, as added by Acts 1981, P.L. 40, § 7.]

4-23-7.1-15. Cooperation with educational institutions or others. — The state library may cooperate with any of the educational institutions of the state or other institutions, organizations, or individuals for the purpose of meeting its responsibilities in any manner and to any extent which may be approved by the board. [IC 4-23-7.1-15, as added by Acts 1981, P.L. 40, § 7.]

4-23-7.1-16. Copies of publications for historical bureau use — Other copies. — The state library shall retain copies of all reports, documents, bulletins, or other publications as may be necessary for its use or the use of the historical bureau, and the copies remaining shall be distributed and exchanged in such manner as may be prescribed by the board. [IC 4-23-7.1-16, as added by Acts 1981, P.L. 40, § 7.]

4-23-7.1-17. Sale or exchange of volumes and pamphlets — Use of proceeds. — The state library may sell or exchange any volumes or pamphlets it does not need. All money received from such sales or as payment for any books or documents that have been lost or mutilated shall be deposited in the state library publications fund. [IC 4-23-7.1-17, as added by Acts 1981, P.L. 40, § 7.]

4-23-7.1-18. Gifts. — The state library may receive gifts of money, books, or other property which shall be deposited in the state library publications fund and used or held in trust for the purpose or purposes given. [IC 4-23-7.1-18, as added by Acts 1981, P.L. 40, § 7.]

4-23-7.1-19. Transportation charges for library materials. — The state library may pay transportation charges one way on library materials sent to libraries and individuals. [IC 4-23-7.1-19, as added by Acts 1981, P.L. 40, § 7.]

4-23-7.1-20. Bookmobiles and other mobile library services. — The state library may establish, equip, maintain, and operate bookmobile or other mobile library services, and library service centers, offices, or other facilities in rented, leased, or state-owned quarters outside the Indiana state library and historical building. [IC 4-23-7.1-20, as added by Acts 1981, P.L. 40, § 7.]

4-23-7.1-21. Days and hours of operation. — The board shall determine the days and hours the library and its subdivisions will be open for public use; however, the provisions of the laws governing the length of the working day, the hours of public business, and the observance of legal holidays shall be observed. [IC 4-23-7.1-21, as added by Acts 1981, P.L. 40, § 7.]

4-23-7.1-22. Annual collection of library statistics — Duty of public officers to supply information. — The Indiana state library annually shall collect statistics of all libraries in Indiana. Each state, county, township, city, town, judicial, or other public officer having in his charge or custody or capable of supplying, or required to collect and compile the information which may be required by the library and historical department, or by the state library, shall supply such information promptly at the request of the department or of the state library, whether the request is oral or by letter or circular or by the filling out of blank forms provided for that purpose by the department or by the state library. [IC 4-23-7.1-22, as added by Acts 1981, P.L. 40, § 7.]

4-23-7.1-23.   Other powers and duties not excluded. — The enumeration of the specific powers and duties in this chapter does not exclude the state library from engaging in any other activity, not contrary to law, that the Indiana library and historical board may consider appropriate in the development of library service to state government, to the libraries and library profession of Indiana, and to the citizens of the state. [IC 4-23-7.1-23, as added by Acts 1981, P.L. 40, § 7.]

4-23-7.1-24.   Rules. — The board may promulgate rules, under IC 4-22-2 [4-22-2-1 — 4-22-2-12], to carry out the provisions and purpose of this chapter. [IC 4-23-7.1-24, as added by Acts 1981, P.L. 40, § 7.]

4-23-7.1-32.   Loans of books or other library materials. — Any book or other library material, unless restricted because of its value, physical condition, historical importance, demand, requirement for research or legal or contractual restriction, belonging to or in custody of the state library may be borrowed for use outside of the library by any resident of the state or any library in accordance with rules adopted by the Indiana library and historical board. [IC 4-23-7.1-32, as added by Acts 1981, P.L. 40, § 7.]

4-23-7.1-33.   Fines — Use of proceeds. — Rules for all loans including, at its discretion, the imposition of fines on borrowers for violation of the rules, shall be established by the board. All funds accruing from such fines shall be deposited in the state library publications fund. [IC 4-23-7.1-33, as added by Acts 1981, P.L. 40, § 7.]

4-23-7.1-34.   Injury or loss of books — Damages. — Any person injuring or losing a book, document, plaque, marker, or sign belonging to the department is liable for threefold damages, and if the book injured or lost be one [1] volume of a set he is liable for the whole set, but on paying for the same, he may take the broken set. All moneys received under this section shall be deposited in the state library publications fund. [IC 4-23-7.1-34, as added by Acts 1981, P.L. 40, § 7.]

4-23-7.1-35.   State library publications fund established — Uses — Sale proceeds. — (a) The state library publications fund is established as a dedicated fund to be administered by the state library. The monies in the fund may be expended by the director of the state library exclusively for the purchase of records of communication in any form or on any substance whatsoever and for the purchase of other library materials.

(b) The proceeds from the sale of items as directed by law or by the director of the state library, from gifts of money or the proceeds from the sale of gifts donated to the fund, from fines or other monetary penalties, and from investment earnings from any portion of the fund, shall be deposited in the state library publications fund.

(c) All monies accruing to the state library publications fund are hereby appropriated continuously for the purposes specified in this section.

(d) No portion of the fund shall revert to the general fund of the state at the end of a fiscal year; however, if the fund is abolished, its contents shall revert to the general fund of the state. [IC 4-23-7.1-35, as added by Acts 1981, P.L. 40, § 7.]

4-23-7.1-36. Organization of state library. — The state library shall be organized in such manner as determined by the director with the approval of the board. The duties of the state library established by law may be supplemented by the board according to its discretion. [IC 4-23-7.1-36, as added by Acts 1981, P.L. 40, § 7.]

4-23-7.1-37. Director — Appointment — Qualification — Removal. — (a) The board shall appoint a director to be the chief administrative officer of the state library.

(b) To qualify for the position of director, a person must:

(1) Be a graduate of a college or university of recognized standing;

(2) Have had special training in the technique and organization of library service;

(3) Possess such other qualifications as the board, in its discretion, may deem necessary.

(c) The director may be removed by the board at any time for cause. [IC 4-23-7.1-37, as added by Acts 1981, P.L. 40, § 7.]

4-23-7.1-38. Employees — Compensation of director. — (a) All state library employees, except the director, shall be selected by the director with the approval of the board and may be removed by the director for cause at any time with the approval of the board.

(b) In making selections for employment recognition shall be given to the fact that all certified librarians are under the Library Certification Act and that other staff personnel are under IC 4-15-2 [4-15-2-1 — 4-15-2-46].

(c) Any or all of the state library employees must have had such academic preparation and special training for the work which they are required to perform as may be prescribed in rules promulgated by the board.

(d) The board may provide that appointments may be made only after the applicant has successfully passed an examination given by the board or some person designated by the board.

(e) No employee of the state library may directly or indirectly solicit subscription or contribution for any political party or political purpose, or be forced in any way to make such contribution, or be required to participate in any form of political activity.

(f) The state budget agency shall fix the compensation of the director. The director shall fix the compensation of the employees of the state library with the approval of the board and the state budget agency. [IC 4-23-7.1-38, as added by Acts 1981, P.L. 40, § 7.]

4-23-7.2-1. Definitions. — As used in this chapter:

(1) "Agency" means any state administration, agency, authority, board, bureau, commission, committee, council, department, division, institution, office, service, or other similar body of state government.

(2) "Board" means the Indiana library and historical board established by IC 4-23-7-2.

(3) "Department" means the Indiana library and historical department established by IC 4-23-7-1.

(4) "Director" means director of the Indiana historical bureau.

(5) "Historical bureau" means the Indiana historical bureau established by IC 4-23-7-3.

(6) "Library" means the Indiana state library established by IC 4-23-7-3. [IC 4-23-7-2-1, as added by Acts 1981, P.L. 40, § 8.]

4-23-7.2-2. Duties. — It is the duty of the historical bureau to edit and publish documentary and other material relating to the history of the state of Indiana, and to promote the study of Indiana history in cooperation with the Indiana historical society, the county historical societies, and any other like organization, and to promote the development of the division of historic preservation of the department of natural resources. [IC 4-23-7.2-2, as added by Acts 1981, P.L. 40, § 8.]

4-23-7.2-3. General informational or statistical publications — Expenses. — The historical bureau may compile and publish digests, reports and bulletins of purely informational or statistical character on any question which the board may deem to be of interest or value to the people of the state. Any expenses which may be incurred in the publication of any such digest, report or bulletin shall be defrayed out of the funds which may be appropriated for the use of the department or the historical bureau. [IC 4-23-7.2-3, as added by Acts 1981, P.L. 40, § 8.]

4-23-7.2-4. Cooperation with educational institutions or others. — The historical bureau may cooperate with any of the educational institutions of the state or other institutions, organizations or individuals for the purpose of meeting its responsibilities in any manner and to any extent which may be approved by the board. [IC 4-23-7.2-4, as added by Acts 1981, P.L. 40, § 8.]

4-23-7.2-5. Publication expenses — Public printing contracts. — All expenses incurred in the preparation, compilation, printing, binding and publication of the volumes of source and other historical material issued by the historical bureau shall be defrayed out of funds at the disposal of the bureau which may be appropriated by law for that purpose, and shall be printed by the commission on public records, and under the terms of any contract which the state may have executed and entered into for public printing, and under the direction and supervision of the historical bureau. [IC 4-23-7.2-5, as added by Acts 1981, P.L. 40, § 8.]

4-23-7.2-6. Distribution of publications. — One [1] copy of each publication issued by the historical bureau shall be furnished to each public library in the state, and the board may furnish copies free of charge to such other persons, institutions or departments as in its judgment may be entitled thereto. The copies so remaining shall be sold by the bureau at a price which shall be fixed by the board. [IC 4-23-7.2-6, as added by Acts 1981, P.L. 40, § 8.]

4-23-7.2-7. Historical bureau publications and educational fund. — (a) The historical bureau publications and educational fund is established as a dedicated fund to be administered by the historical bureau. The monies in the fund may be expended by the director of the historical bureau exclusively for the publication of historical documents and other material to promote the study of Indiana history, and to inform the people of Indiana concerning the history of their state.

(b) The proceeds from the sale of items as directed by law or by the director of the historical bureau, from gifts of money or the proceeds from the sale of gifts donated to the fund, and from investment earnings from any portion of the fund, shall be deposited in the historical bureau publications fund.

(c) All monies accruing to the historical bureau publications fund are hereby appropriated continuously for the purposes specified in this section.

(d) No portion of the fund shall revert to the general fund of the state at the end of a fiscal year; however, if the fund is abolished, its contents shall revert to the general fund of the state. [IC 4-23-7.2-7, as added by Acts 1981, P.L. 40, § 8.]

4-23-7.2-8. Governors' portraits collection . —(a) The governors' portraits collection is placed in the custody of the Indiana historical bureau. The collection shall be permanently displayed in the statehouse under the supervision of the historical bureau which is charged with its care and maintenance.

(b) The director of the historical bureau shall inspect each painting in the collection at least twice annually in the company of one or more experts in the field of art conservation selected by him.

(c) After the inauguration of each governor the director of the historical bureau, with the concurrence of the governor, shall select and commission an artist to paint the governor's portrait.

(d) The historical bureau shall, from time to time, include in its budget requests the amount it deems necessary to provide for the proper care, maintenance and display of the governors' portraits collection, and the amount necessary to commission the painting of a portrait of each governor for the collection.

(e) In discharging his duties under this section the director of the historical bureau shall, as appropriate, make use of the cultural and technical resources of this state, including the department of natural resources and the department of administration. [IC 4-23-7.2-8, as added by Acts 1981, P.L. 40, § 8.]

4-23-7.2-9. Governors' portraits fund. — (a) The governors' portraits fund is established as a dedicated fund to be administered by the historical bureau. The monies in the fund may be expended by the director of the historical bureau exclusively for the preservation and exhibition of the state-owned portraits of former governors of Indiana.

(b) The proceeds from the sale of items as directed by law or by the director of the historical bureau, from gifts of money or the proceeds from the sale of gifts donated to the fund, and from investment earnings from any portion of the fund, shall be deposited in the governors' portraits fund.

(c) All monies accruing to the governors' portraits fund are hereby appropriated continuously for the purposes specified in this section.

(d) No portion of the fund shall revert to the general fund of the state at the end of a fiscal year; however, if the fund is abolished, its contents shall revert to the general fund of the state. [IC 4-23-7.2-9, as added by Acts 1981, P.L. 40, § 8.]

4-23-7.2-10. Sale of medallions and other commemorative items — Use of proceeds. — The historical bureau shall have custody of all unsold commemorative medallions and other items that were acquired for sale to the public by the Indiana historical commission, the Indiana sesquicentennial commission, or the Indiana American revolution bicentennial commission when that commission is abolished. These medallions and other commemorative items shall be offered for sale to the public at a price determined by the director of the historical bureau. The proceeds from the sale of such items shall be deposited in the governors' portraits fund. [IC 4-23-7.2-10, as added by Acts 1981, P.L. 40, § 8.]

4-23-7.2-11. Historical site markers — State format — Approval of historical accuracy. — (a) The historical bureau shall establish a program for marking historical sites in Indiana. As a part of this program, the historical bureau shall fix a state format for historical markers. No person may erect an historical marker in the state format without the approval of the historical bureau. All historical markers in the state format shall be provided by the historical bureau at the expense of the person desiring to erect the marker.

(b) No historical marker may be erected on a highway of the state highway system without the approval of the historical bureau as to its historical accuracy. This provision is in addition to any other requirement of law. [IC 4-23-7.2-11, as added by Acts 1981, P.L. 40, § 8.]

4-23-7.2-12. George Rogers Clark Day celebrations. — The historical bureau shall celebrate the memory of George Rogers Clark in a manner fitting each occasion of George Rogers Clark Day, every twenty-fifth day of February, established by IC 1-1-13-1. [IC 4-23-7.2-12, as added by Acts 1981, P.L. 40, § 8.]

4-23-7.2-13. Duty of public officials to supply information. — Each state, county, township, city, town, judicial, or other public officer having in his charge or custody or capable of supplying, or required to collect and compile the information which may be required by the historical bureau shall supply such information promptly at the request of the historical bureau, whether the request is oral or by letter or circular or by the filling out of blank forms provided for that purpose by the historical bureau. [IC 4-23-7.2-13, as added by Acts 1981, P.L. 40, § 8.]

4-23-7.2-14. Rules. — The board may promulgate rules, under IC 4-22-2 [4-22-2-1 — 4-22-2-12], to carry out the provisions and purpose of this chapter. [IC 4-23-7.2-14, as added by Acts 1981, P.L. 40, § 8.]

4-23-7.2-15. Organization of historical bureau. — The historical bureau shall be organized in such manner as determined by the director with the approval of the board. The duties of the historical bureau established by law may be supplemented by the board according to its discretion. [IC 4-23-7.2-15, as added by Acts 1981, P.L. 40, § 8.]

4-23-7.2-16. Director. — (a) The board shall appoint a director to be the chief administrative officer of the historical bureau.

(b) To qualify for the position of director, a person must:

(1) Be a graduate of a college or university of recognized standing;

(2) Have had special training in the nature, relative value and use of historical source material;

(3) Have had special training in the editing of historical publications; and

(4) Possess such other qualifications as the board, in its discretion, may deem necessary.

(c) The director may be removed by the board at any time for cause. [IC 4-23-7.2-16, as added by Acts 1981, P.L. 40, § 8.]

4-23-7.2-17. Employees — Compensation of director. — (a) All historical bureau employees, except the director, shall be selected by the director with the approval of the board and may be removed by the director for cause at any time with the approval of the board.

(b) Any or all of the historical bureau employees must have had such academic preparation and special training for the work which they are required to perform as may be prescribed in rules promulgated by the board.

(c) The board may provide that appointments may be made only after the applicant has successfully passed an examination given by the board or some person designated by the board.

(d) The state budget agency shall fix the compensation of the director. The director shall fix the compensation of the employees of the historical bureau, with the approval of the board and the state budget agency.

(e) No employee of the historical bureau may directly or indirectly solicit subscription or contribution for any political party or political purpose, or be forced in any way to make such contribution, or be required to participate in any form of political activity.

(f) All historical bureau employees are under IC 4-15-2 [4-15-2-1 — 4-15-2-46]. [IC 4-23-7.2-17, as added by Acts 1981, P.L. 40, § 8.]

4-23-7.2-18. Advisory committee. — The board may appoint an advisory committee of not to exceed nine [9] members, who shall consult and advise with the director of the historical bureau concerning the publication of historical material, the promotion of the interest of the historical societies of Indiana, and in the conduct of the historical work of the state generally. The committee so appointed shall serve without compensation. [IC 4-23-7.2-18, as added by Acts 1981, P.L. 40, § 8.]

4-23-8-1 [63-849]. Acceptance of gifts. — Express power and authority is hereby given to the Indiana library and historical board to accept gifts, bequests and devises of personal and real property for the maintenance, use or benefit of the Indiana library and historical department. [Acts 1939, ch. 116, § 1, p. 566.]

4-23-8-2 [63-850]. Terms of acceptance. — Said Indiana library and historical board may accept such gifts, bequests and devises as provided in section 1 [4-23-8-1] hereof, with such terms and conditions and with such obligations, liabilities and burdens as are imposed thereon when in the judgment of said board and with the approval of the governor it shall be determined that it is for the best interest of said department to do so: Provided, however, That no obligation, liability or burden shall be assumed on account thereof in excess of appropriations made by law and applicable to the payment of such obligations, liabilities and burdens. [Acts 1939, ch. 116, § 2, p. 566.]

4-23-8-3 [63-851]. Powers of board. — Any law to the contrary notwithstanding, any gift, bequest or devise received by said Indiana library and historical board, shall not be required to be covered into the general fund, but shall be administered by said board according to the terms of said gift, bequest or devise. [Acts 1939, ch. 116, § 3, p. 566.]

STATE AID

(Burns Annotated Indiana Statutes, 1982, s.4-23-7-28 to 4-23-7-29, 4-23-7.1-28 to 4-23-7.1-31.)

4-23-7-28. State aid for library districts. — (a) On or before June 15 of each year the state board of tax commissioners shall certify to the auditor of state the amounts to which each eligible public library district is entitled under this section. The board shall determine each district's entitlement by multiplying:

(1) The amount appropriated by the general assembly for the purposes of this section by

(2) A fraction, the numerator of which is the amount of the eligible public library districts' current certified operating fund budget, and the denominator of which is the total amount of the current certified operating fund budgets of all eligible public library districts in the state.

(b) To be eligible for payment under this section a public library district must be subject to the provisions of IC 20-13-1 [20-13-1-1 — 20-13-1-24] or IC 20-13-24 [20-13-24-1] and the district must submit to the board not later than May 1 of each year, its current operating fund budget and an application on a form provided by the board.

(c) The auditor of state shall issue the warrants under this section to the eligible public library districts not later than August 1 of each year.

(d) Any expenses incurred by the state board of tax commissioners in the distribution of funds under this section may not be charged against funds appropriated for the purposes of this section.

(e) The governing body of a public library district which receives funds under this section may appropriate the funds for any purpose for which the operating fund revenues of the district may be used. [IC 4-23-7-28, as added by Acts 1977, P.L. 43, § 1; 1978, P.L. 117, § 2.]

4-23-7-29. Distribution of funds to Indiana cooperative library services authority. — (a) After June 30 and before August 2 of each year, the Indiana library and historical board shall distribute to the Indiana cooperative library services authority funds appropriated by the general assembly for that purpose for the fiscal year in which the distribution is made.

(b) Any expenses incurred by the Indiana library and historical board in the distribution of funds under this section may not be charged against funds appropriated for the Indiana cooperative library services authority. [IC 4-23-7-29, as added by Acts 1978, P.L. 19, § 1.]

4-23-7.1-29. Funds for public library districts. — (a) On or before June 15 of each year the state board of tax commissioners shall certify to the auditor of state the amounts to which each eligible public library district is entitled under this section. The board of tax commissioners shall determine each district's entitlement by multiplying:

(1) The amount appropriated by the general assembly for the purposes of this section by

(2) A fraction, the numerator of which is the amount of the eligible public library districts' current certified operating fund budget, and the denominator of which is the total amount of the current certified operating fund budgets of all eligible public library districts in the state.

(b) To be eligible for payment under this section a public library district is subject to section 11 [4-23-7.1-11] of this chapter and must be subject to the provisions of IC 20-13-1 [20-13-1-1 — 20-13-1-24] or IC 20-13-24 [20-13-24-1] and the district must submit to the board of tax commissioners not later than May 1 of each year, its current operating fund budget and an application on a form provided by the board of tax commissioners.

(c) The auditor of state shall issue the warrants under this section to the eligible public library districts not later than August 1 of each year.

(d) Any expenses incurred by the state board of tax commissioners in the distribution of funds under this section may not be charged against funds appropriated for the purposes of this section.

(e) The governing body of a public library district which receives funds under this section may appropriate the funds for any purpose for which the operating fund revenues of the district may be used. [IC 4-23-7.1-29, as added by Acts 1981, P.L. 40, § 7.]

4-23-7.1-30. Distribution of funds to cooperative library services authority. — (a) After June 30 and before August 2 of each year, the Indiana library and historical board shall distribute to the Indiana cooperative library services authority funds appropriated by the general assembly for that purpose for the fiscal year in which the distribution is made.

(b) Any expenses incurred by the Indiana library and historical board in the distribution of funds under this section may not be charged against funds appropriated for the Indiana cooperative library services authority. [IC 4-23-7.1-30, as added by Acts 1981, P.L. 40, § 7.]

4-23-7.1-31. Distribution of funds to area library service authorities. — (a) After June 30 and before August 2 of each year, the Indiana library and historical board shall distribute to the area library services authorities funds appropriated by the general assembly for that purpose for the fiscal year in which the distribution is made.

(b) Any expenses incurred by the Indiana library and historical board in the distribution of funds under this section may not be charged against funds appropriated for the area library services authorities. [IC 4-23-7.1-31, as added by Acts 1981, P.L. 40, § 7.]

DISTRIBUTION OF PUBLIC DOCUMENTS
(Burns Annotated Indiana Statutes, 1982, s.4-23-7.1-25 to 4-23-7.1-28.)

4-23-7.1-25. State document depository system — Official file. — In order that all public documents of the state of Indiana shall be preserved and made available for use of the citizens of the state, the state library is designated as the depository library for Indiana documents. The state library shall maintain a complete collection of all Indiana public documents. This collection shall be the official file of Indiana state documents. The state

library shall establish a state document depository system by which copies
of all public documents published by the state which are of general interest
or use shall be deposited in designated depository libraries, and shall distribute to other libraries copies of those public documents published by the state
which are of greatest interest or use and for which a more general distribution is appropriate. [IC 4-23-7.1-25, as added by Acts 1981, P.L. 40, § 7.]

**4-23-7.1-26. Copies of agency publications furnished — Exemp-
tions from depository requirements.** — (a) Every state agency that issues
public documents shall furnish the state library fifty [50] copies of all
publications issued by them whether printed, mimeographed, or duplicated
in any way, which are not issued solely for use within the issuing office.
However, if the library requests, as many as twenty-five [25] additional
copies of each public document shall be supplied.

(b) If other provision is made by law for the distribution of the session
laws of the general assembly, the journals of the house and senate of the
general assembly, the supreme court and court of appeals reports or the
publications of the Indiana historical bureau, any of those for which distribution is provided for are exempted from the depository requirements of
subsection (a) of this section. However, two [2] copies of each document
exempted under this subsection from the general depository requirements
shall be deposited with the state library.

(c) Publications of the various schools, colleges, divisions, and departments of the state universities and their regional campuses are exempt from
the depository requirements of subsection (a) of this section, but two [2]
copies of each publication of these divisions shall be deposited in the state
library.

(d) Publications of state university presses, directives for internal administration, intraoffice and interoffice publications and forms are completely
exempt from all depository requirements. [IC 4-23-7.1-26, as added by Acts
1981, P.L. 40, § 7.]

**4-23-7.1-27. Disposition of state documents — Quarterly list of
documents — Document exchange system.** — The library shall:

(a) Keep at least two [2] copies of each Indiana state document as permanent reference copies.

(b) Send two [2] copies of each Indiana state document to the Library of
Congress excluding those where other provisions for distribution are made
by law.

(c) Designate the four [4] state university libraries and certain selected
Indiana public, school and college libraries in the several geographical sections of the state as secondary depository libraries to receive one [1] copy of
those Indiana state documents which are of general interest. Selection of
secondary depository libraries shall be made by the state library, based on
a determination that the libraries selected will keep the documents readily
accessible for use, and will render assistance for their use to qualified

patrons without charge.

(d) Prepare and issue quarterly, complete lists of state-issued documents, which were issued during the immediately preceding quarter. These lists shall be cumulated and printed annually, at the end of each calendar year. Copies of these lists shall be distributed by the state library to state departments and agencies, and to public and college libraries within the state.

(e) Set up a document exchange system with agencies in other states, in order that selected documents of various other states shall be available for use by the citizens of Indiana. [IC 4-23-7.1-27, as added by Acts 1981, P.L. 40, § 7.]

4-23-7.1-28. Documents from political subdivisions and public officials — Copying authorized. — (a) Each political subdivision of the state may deliver to the library ten [10] copies of every report, document, bulletin, or other publication published at the expense of the state or one or more of its political subdivisions.

(b) Any state, county, or other official of local government may turn over to the state library for permanent preservation, any books, records, documents, original papers, newspaper files, or printed books or materials not in current use in his office.

(c) The state library may make a copy, by photography or in any other way, of any official book, record, document, original paper, newspaper, or printed book or material in any county, city, or other public office for preservation in the state library. County, city, and other officials shall permit such copies to be made of the books, records, documents, and papers in their respective offices. [IC 4-23-7.1-28, as added by Acts 1981, P.L. 40, § 7.]

INTERSTATE LIBRARY COMPACT
(Burns Annotated Indiana Statutes, 1982, s.20-13-20-1 to 20-13-20-4.)

20-13-20-1 [41-1301]. Interstate library compact.—The interstate library compact is hereby enacted into law and entered into on behalf of this state with any state bordering on Indiana which legally joins therein in substantially the following form:

INTERSTATE LIBRARY COMPACT
The contracting states agree that:

ARTICLE 1—PURPOSE
Because the desire for the services provided by public libraries transcends governmental boundaries and can be provided most effectively by giving such services to communities of people regardless of jurisdictional lines, it is the policy of the states who are parties to this compact to cooperate and share their responsibilities in providing joint and cooperative library services in areas where the distribution of population makes the provision of library service on an

interstate basis the most effective way to provide adequate and efficient services.

ARTICLE 2—PROCEDURE

The appropriate officials and agencies of the party states or any of their political subdivisions may, on behalf of said states or political subdivisions enter into agreements for the cooperative or joint conduct of library services when they shall find that the executions of agreements to that end as provided herein will facilitate library services.

ARTICLE 3—CONTENT

Any such agreement for the cooperative or joint establishment, operation or use of library services, facilities, personnel, equipment, materials or other items not excluded because of failure to enumerate shall, as among the parties of the agreement: (1) detail the specific nature of the services, facilities, properties or personnel to which it is applicable; (2) provide for the allocation of costs and other financial responsibilities; (3) specify the respective rights, duties, obligations and liabilities; (4) stipulate the terms and conditions for duration, renewal, termination, abrogation, disposal of joint or common property, if any, and all other matters which may be appropriate to the proper effectuation and performance of said agreement.

ARTICLE 4—CONFLICT OF LAWS

Nothing in this compact or in any agreement entered into hereunder shall be construed to supersede, alter, or otherwise impair any obligation imposed on any public library by otherwise applicable laws.

ARTICLE 5—ADMINISTRATOR

Each state shall designate a compact administrator with whom copies of all agreements to which his state or any subdivision thereof is party shall be filed. The administrator shall have such powers as may be conferred upon him by the laws of his state and may consult and cooperate with the compact administrators of other party states and take such steps as may effectuate the purposes of this compact.

ARTICLE 6—EFFECTIVE DATE

This compact shall become operative immediately upon its enactment by any state or between it and any other contiguous state or states so enacting.

ARTICLE 7—RENUNCIATION

This compact shall continue in force and remain binding upon each party state until 6 months after any such state has given notice of repeal by the legislature. Such withdrawal shall not be construed to relieve any party to an agreement authorized by Articles 2 and 3 of the compact from the obligation of that agreement prior to the end of its stipulated period of duration.

ARTICLE 8—SEVERABILITY—CONSTRUCTION

The provisions of this compact shall be severable. It is intended that the provisions of this compact be reasonably and liberally construed. [Acts 1967, ch. 259, § 1, p. 740.]

20-13-20-2 [41-1302]. Compact administrator—Duties.—The director of the Indiana state library, ex officio, shall be the compact administrator. The compact administrator shall receive copies of all agreements entered into by the state or its political subdivisions and other states or political subdivisions; consult with, advise and aid such governmental units in the formulation of such agreements; make such recommendations to the governor, legislature, governmental agencies and units as he deems desirable to effectuate the purposes of this compact and consult and cooperate with the compact administrators of other party states. [Acts 1967, ch. 259, § 2, p. 740.]

20-13-20-3 [41-1303]. Agreements with other states—Notice to administrator.—The compact administrator and the chief executive of any political subdivision having a responsibility in law for a library, libraries, or library services may enter into agreements with other states or their political subdivisions pursuant to the compact. Such agreements as may be made pursuant to this compact on behalf of the state of Indiana shall be made by the compact administrator. Such agreements as may be made on behalf of a political subdivision shall be made after due notice to the compact administrator and consultation with him. [Acts 1967, ch. 259, § 3, p. 740.]

20-13-20-4 [41-1304]. Enforcement of compact.—The agencies and officers of this state and its subdivisions shall enforce this compact and do all things appropriate to effect its purpose and intent which may be within their respective jurisdiction. [Acts 1967, ch. 259, § 4, p. 740.]

CERTIFICATION OF LIBRARIES
(Burns Annotated Indiana Statutes, 1982, s.20-13-8-1 to 20-13-8-12.)

20-13-8-1 [41-801]. Indiana library certification board—Created—Personnel.—A board is hereby created which shall be known as the library certification board, which shall consist of the director of the state library and of two [2] additional members, who shall be appointed by the governor, as hereinafter provided. One [1] of the two [2] appointive members of the board shall be appointed on recommendation of the Indiana Library Association, and one [1] member shall be appointed on recommendation of the Indiana Library Trustees' Association. In the first instance, one [1] member shall be appointed for a term of two [2] years, and one [1] member shall be appointed for a term of four [4] years, and until their successors shall have been appointed and qualified.

Thereafter all appointive members shall be appointed for terms of four [4] years and until their successors shall have been appointed and qualified. No person shall be appointed as a member of the library certification board unless he is engaged in library work as a librarian or as a library trustee at the time of his appointment. Except as hereinafter otherwise provided, no librarian shall be appointed as a member of the library certification board unless he holds a certificate as provided in this act [20-13-8-1—20-13-8-12], but this provision shall not apply to the persons who are first appointed as members of the board. The governor may, at any time, remove any member of the board for misconduct, incapacity, or neglect of duty. Any vacancy which may occur in either of the appointive memberships of the board shall be filled by appointment by the governor for the unexpired term, either on recommendation of the board or association hereinbefore authorized to make recommendations, or by selection by the governor, as hereinbefore provided. The members of the board shall serve without compensation, but shall be entitled to receive their actual expenses necessarily incurred in attending the meetings and transacting the business of the board. The director of the state library shall be the executive secretary of the board and shall have the custody of the records, papers and effects of the board. The board shall organize by the election of one [1] of its members as president, who shall serve for a term of one [1] year. Two [2] members of the board shall constitute a quorum for the transaction of business. The board shall hold at least one [1] regular meeting each year, and such special meetings as may be determined by the board. [Acts 1941, ch. 195, § 1, p. 591.]

20-13-8-2 [41-802]. Duties. — The library certification board is hereby authorized and required:

(1) To prescribe and define grades of public library service and to prescribe the qualifications which persons shall possess who are employed in each of such grades of public library service, giving due consideration to the population served, the income and the salary schedule of each library.

(2) To make available the requirements for certification of all grades upon request and without charge to all prospective applicants.

(3) To examine candidates who apply for certificates qualifying them to secure employment in any designated grade or grades of public library service, and to issue certificates to such candidates as are found to be competent and who are eligible to apply for such examination;

(4) To issue certificates, without examination, to candidates who apply therefor, and who, by reason of their academic or technical training, and/or experience are found to be fit and suitable persons to certify;

(5) To prescribe and define what shall constitute a head librarian, and a head of any department or branch or professional assistant of a public library, for the purposes of this act [20-13-8-2—20-13-8-12]; and

(6) To adopt and promulgate such rules and regulations as the board may deem necessary and proper to carry out and administer the provisions of this act. [Acts 1941, ch. 195, § 2, p. 591.]

20-13-8-3 [41-803]. Appointment of librarians.—On and after the first day of January, 1942, and except as hereinafter otherwise provided, it shall be unlawful for the board of trustees, school board or any other governing body having the lawful charge of any public library, or any other library, supported in whole or in part by public funds, except school libraries and the libraries of educational institutions, to appoint as the head librarian, or as the head of any department or branch, or as professional assistant of any such library, any person who does not hold a certificate of a suitable and requisite grade, granted in accordance with the provisions of this act [20-13-8-1—20-13-8-12], and the rules and regulations of the library certification board issued thereunder. [Acts 1941, ch. 195, § 3, p. 591.]

20-13-8-4 [41-804]. Applications to board.—Any person who desires to be certified as a librarian in any designated division, grade, or type of public library service, and who possesses the qualifications which are prescribed in the rules and regulations of the library certification board as essential to enable such person to apply for an examination, shall apply to the board to be examined for a certificate in any grade or grades of public library service. The application shall be made on a blank form which shall be prescribed and furnished by the library certification board, shall be accompanied by a fee of not more than ten [$10.00] nor less than two dollars [$2.00], which shall be prescribed by the board, and, if found to be satisfactory, shall entitle such applicant to take the examination applied for in such application at a point within his own congressional district. [Acts 1941, ch. 195, § 4, p. 591.]

20-13-8-5 [41-805]. Licensing of applicants.—If, upon such examination, an applicant is found to be competent, he shall be granted a certificate of the suitable grade and class, which shall entitle such licensee to be appointed to and to hold in any public library contemplated in this act [20-13-8-1—20-13-8-12], any position, of the grade or class prescribed in such certificate. [Acts 1941, ch. 195, § 5, p. 591.]

20-13-8-6 [41-806]. Licensing without examination.—The library certification board may, by proper rules and regulations, provide for the issuance of certificates of any grade or class, without examination, to applicants who possess the requisite academic and professional training, experience and other qualifications necessary to satisfy the minimum qualifications prescribed in such rules and regulations for any such class or grade of public library service. [Acts 1941, ch. 195, § 6, p. 591.]

20-13-8-7 [41-807]. Fee for license without examination. — Any person who desires to be certified as a librarian in any designated division, grade, or type of public library service, without examination, and who possesses the qualifications which are prescribed in the rules and regulations of the library certification board as essential to enable such person to apply for a certificate, without examination, may apply to the board for a certificate in any grade or grades of public library service. The application shall be made on a blank form which shall be prescribed and supplied by the library certification board, shall be accompanied by a fee of two dollars [$2.00], and, if found to be satisfactory, shall entitle such applicant to a certificate in the grade or grades of public library service so applied for. [Acts 1941, ch. 195, § 7, p. 591.]

20-13-8-8 [41-808]. Who may apply.—Any person who is actively engaged or who expects to engage actively in any grade or class of public library service, and who is not a head librarian or the head of any department or branch of any public library, may apply for a certificate of any grade or class, either with or without an examination, and if found to be competent and qualified shall be granted the certificate so applied for, in the manner, and upon the payment of the same fees as hereinbefore provided for in this act [20-13-8-1—20-13-8-12]. [Acts 1941, ch. 195, § 8, p. 591.]

20-13-8-9 [41-809]. "Private library" defined.—Any person who is actively engaged or who expects to engage actively in any grade or class of private library service, or in the library service of any school or other educational institution, and whether such person is or expects to be a head librarian, or the head of any department or branch of any private library, or of the library of any school or other educational institution, or not, may apply for a certificate of any grade or class, either with or without an examination, and if found to be competent and qualified, shall be granted the certificate so applied for in the same manner and subject to the same conditions as are hereinbefore provided for the certification of librarians in public libraries. The term "private library" as used in this act [20-13-8-1—20-13-8-12] shall be construed to mean any library which is not supported by public funds. [Acts 1941, ch. 195, § 9, p. 591.]

20-13-8-10 [41-810]. Rules of board. — The library certification board is hereby authorized to adopt such rules and regulations as may be necessary for the reciprocal recognition of certificates for librarians issued by other states whose qualifications for library service are at least as high as the qualifications in this state, and to prevent unjust and arbitrary exclusions by other states of certified librarians who have complied with the requirements of the laws of this state. In order to effect this, the board shall give consideration to the recommendations of the American Library Association. [Acts 1941, ch. 195, § 10, p. 591.]

20-13-8-11 [41-811]. Life certificates.—Any person, who, when this act takes effect [July 8, 1941], is serving or is on leave of absence from his position, as head librarian, head of a department or professional assistant in any public library in the state of Indiana shall upon application and payment of the prescribed fee be awarded a life certificate of the grade issued for comparable positions throughout the state, which certificate shall have equal value for all purposes with any other certificate for that grade which the Indiana library certification board shall issue based upon examination, academic education, technical training, experience or any combination of these items. [Acts 1941, ch. 195, § 11, p. 591.]

20-13-8-12 [41-812]. Disposal of fees collected.—All fees collected under the provisions of this act [20-13-8-1—20-13-8-12] shall be covered into the state treasury and shall constitute a separate and distinct account of the general fund, which shall be known as the library certification account, and which shall be used to defray expenses incurred in the administration of this act. The balance in such account at the end of any fiscal year shall not revert to the general fund but shall be carried forward and be available for the fiscal year next succeeding. [Acts 1941, ch. 195, § 12, p. 591.]

LIBRARY SERVICES AUTHORITIES
(Burns Annotated Indiana Statutues, 1982, s.20-13-6-1 to 20-13-6-14.)

20-13-6-1 [41-1201]. Library services authority established. — It is the purpose of this chapter [20-13-6-1 — 20-13-6-14] to encourage the development and improvement of all types of library service and to promote the efficient use of finances, personnel, materials and properties by enabling governing authorities having library responsibilities to join together in a municipal corporation called a library services authority, which will provide such services and facilities as the governing authorities party to the establishment and support of the library services authority may determine. [Acts 1967, ch. 47, § 1, p. 77; 1977, P.L. 254, § 1, p. 1066.]

20-13-6-2 [41-1202]. Title. — This chapter [20-13-6-1 — 20-13-6-14] may be cited as the "Library Services Authority Act." [Acts 1967, ch. 47, § 2, p. 77; 1977, P.L. 254, § 2, p. 1066.]

20-13-6-3 [41-1203]. Definitions. — As used in this chapter [20-13-6-1 — 20-13-6-14]:

"Governing authority" means any governing body or governing or administrative officer of or for a municipal corporation, agency of state government, educational institution, association or other corporation, publicly or privately supported, having library responsibilities. The governing body or governing or administrative officer is that body or officer having the authority to negotiate and sign contracts, or pass resolutions, enact ordinances, issue executive orders, issue statements of participation or other official acts committing the corporation which the body or officer represents.

"Fiscal year" means the year beginning January 1, and ending December 31.

"Library" means a collection of a variety of books or other printed matter, audiovisual materials or other items in which knowledge is recorded; kept in a centralized place; for which a person who has knowledge of the materials, their arrangement, their use and of library skills is responsible; and which are for the use of individuals or groups in meeting their recreational, informational, educational, research or cultural needs.

"Library facilities" means buildings, bookmobiles, rooms or other definable and palpable structures or areas and the library materials and equipment contained therein which are used in the operation or provision of library services.

"Library responsibilities" means responsibility for the operation of a library or library facilities.

"Library services" means any or all of those activities in which libraries engage in the planning, managing, budgeting, financing, purchasing, staffing and evaluating of their libraries; in the selection, acquisition, processing and maintaining of their collections of materials and the related bibliographic records; and in the promotion, interpretation, servicing and use of their library materials and facilities.

"Municipal corporation" means any subdivision of the state of Indiana. [Acts 1967, ch. 47, § 3, p. 77; 1977, P.L. 254, § 3, p. 1066.]

20-13-6-4 [41-1204]. Library services authorities initiated — Details of authority — Attorney general to inspect agreement — Copy of agreement — Filing of agreement. — Whenever two [2] or more governing authorities, provided the number of private governing authorities does not equal or exceed the number of public governing authorities, have adopted by resolutions, ordinances, orders, statements of participation or other recorded acts, a joint agreement calling for the establishment of a library services authority under the provisions of this chapter [20-13-6-1 — 20-13-6-14], the library services authority specified is initiated.

Such joint agreement shall include the following details of the proposed library services authority: The name, to be given as _____ Library Services Authority; official address and county of location of the principal place of business; description of the library services to be provided; specification of the place and of the convening chairman who shall set the date and the time of the organizational meeting of the board of directors and who shall serve as temporary chairman; the names of the governing authorities signing the agreement, and thereby members of the library services authority; and the date of the agreement.

Upon the adoption of the joint agreement calling for the creation of the library services authority by two [2] or more of the governing authorities, the agreement shall be submitted to the attorney general of the state of Indiana who shall determine whether the agreement is in proper form and compatible with the laws of the state. The attorney general must approve any agreement submitted to him hereunder unless he finds that it is not legal, in which case he shall detail in writing addressed to each of the governing authorities adopting the agreement for the establishment of the library services authority the specific respects in which the proposed agreement fails to meet the requirements of law. Failure to disapprove an agreement submitted hereunder within thirty [30] days of its submission constitutes approval thereof.

The library services authority initiated by the joint agreement is legally established and the governing authorities originally signing the agreement are considered members of the library services authority when the attorney general has approved the agreement either by specific written approval or by the failure to indicate disapproval within the required time. A copy of the agreement and originally signed copies of the adopted resolutions, ordinances, orders, statements of participation or other recorded acts shall be filed with the Indiana state library within forty [40] days of the date of the submission of the agreement to the attorney general for his action. [Acts 1967, ch. 47, § 4, p. 77; 1977, P.L. 254, § 4, p. 1066.]

20-13-6-5 [41-1205]. Municipal corporation — Powers. — The library services authority herein created is a municipal corporation, and any power or powers, privileges or authority exercised or capable of being exercised by a public agency of this state except that of levying taxes may be exercised and employed by such library services authority established under this chapter [20-13-6-1 — 20-13-6-14]. [Acts 1967, ch. 47, § 5, p. 77; 1977, P.L. 254, § 5, p. 1066.]

20-13-6-6 [41-1206]. Board of directors. — (a) Within ten [10] days after the legal establishment of the library services authority, each governing authority which is a member shall appoint its representative or representatives to the board of directors of the library services authority. When there are fewer than four [4] libraries in the library services authority, each governing authority shall appoint four [4] directors to the board of directors; when there are more than three [3] but fewer than ten [10] libraries in the library services authority each governing authority shall appoint two [2] directors; when there are ten [10] or more libraries in the library services authority, each governing authority shall appoint one [1] director. A director may be a member of the governing authority, a librarian, or any other person who in the opinion of the governing authority will best serve the library interests of the governing authority.

Upon the expiration of the ten [10] days, the directors who have been appointed shall meet as specified in the joint agreement and determine by lot, in as nearly equal groups as possible, the one third [$^1/_3$] of the directors who shall have an initial term of one [1] year; the one third [$^1/_3$] who shall have an initial term of two [2] years; and the one third [$^1/_3$] who shall have an initial term of three [3] years. This determination shall be for the initial terms of office for all directors. After the initial term ends, all appointments to the board of directors shall be for three [3] years. Appointments to fill vacancies caused by death, resignation or otherwise shall be for the unexpired term only.

Upon the determination of the initial terms of office of the directors, an executive committee shall be elected for terms of one [1] year from the membership of the board of directors by vote on nominations from the floor. The executive committee shall consist of a president, a vice president, a secretary, a treasurer, and, if the total number of directors for the library service authority exceeds eight [8], three [3] members-at-large. The named offices shall have the duties and powers normally incumbent upon those offices.

(b) Within ten [10] days after the approval of a new membership under IC 20-13-6-9, the governing authority shall appoint as many directors as each of the other governing authorities has appointed. The initial terms of the new directors shall be determined by the executive committee so that as nearly as possible the terms of one-third [$^1/_3$] of the total board of directors shall end each year.

(c) If the addition of a new member increases the number of libraries in the library service authority such that each governing authority would appoint fewer representatives to the board of directors, the board of directors shall be reestablished as required under subsection (a) of this section.

Immediately after the organizational meeting of the board of directors, the board shall draft and adopt bylaws providing for the board's procedures and management not otherwise provided in this chapter [20-13-6-1 — 20-13-6-11]. [Acts 1967, ch. 47, § 6, p. 77; 1977, P.L. 254, § 6, p. 1066.]

20-13-6-6.2. Limitation on terms of executive committee members and of officers. — No director shall serve on the executive committee for more than four [4] consecutive terms or in the same office for more than two [2] consecutive terms.

Executive committee elections shall be held annually, in the manner prescribed by the bylaws of the library services authority. [IC 20-13-6-6.2, as added by Acts 1977, P.L. 254, § 7, p. 1066.]

20-13-6-7 [41-1207]. Amendments of agreement — Copy of record to be filed. — (a) Any detail or details of the joint agreement as specified in IC 20-13-6-4 may be changed upon the recommendation of the executive committee or petition of three [3] directors, and action by the board of directors, Provided That notice of the proposed change be sent to each governing authority which is a member of the library services authority at least sixty [60] days prior to the meeting at which the change is to be considered.

(b) Notwithstanding the notice requirement in subsection (a) of this section, the application of a new member may be considered at any time.

(c) Upon approval of the change of the joint agreement, a copy of the record of the action taken by the board of the library services authority shall be filed with the Indiana state library. [Acts 1967, ch. 47, § 7, p. 77; 1977, P.L. 254, § 8, p. 1066.]

20-13-6-8 [41-1208]. Board of directors — Duties — Meetings — Quorum — Executive committee — Meetings. — The board of directors of the library services authority shall be responsible for nominating and electing its officers and members of the executive committee; drafting and adopting bylaws for the conduct of business of the board and the executive committee; changing the address of the principal place of business of the authority; considering and acting upon recommendations of the executive committee in those matters specified in this section; and such other matters as may be appropriate.

The board of directors shall meet at least annually; special meetings may be called by the president or any three [3] directors. A majority of duly appointed members of the board shall constitute a quorum for the transaction of business and a concurrence of two thirds [$^2/_3$] of the members present is necessary to approve or to authorize any action.

The executive committee of the library services authority shall take full charge of, manage and conduct the business of the library services authority except that, unless otherwise properly delegated to the executive committee or administrative personnel in the bylaws, the board of directors must approve amendments to the joint agreement; budget; statements of policy; rules and regulations; development program and plans; appointment of or arrangement for the chief administrative officer; legal matters; purchases of property and equipment costing more than two thousand dollars [$2,000]; contracts for the purchase of services, materials, equipment, real or other property; sales of services or material other than those for which the library services authority was created; and the acceptance or release of members of the authority, and related matters.

In the discharge of its duties the executive committee shall meet at least quarterly; special meetings may be called by the president or any two [2] members of the committee. A majority of the committee members shall constitute a quorum for the transaction of business and a concurrence of a majority of the members of the committee shall be necessary to authorize any action.

Except for the election of officers and adoption or amendment of the bylaws, the bylaws may provide that any action required or permitted to be taken at any meeting of the board may be taken without a meeting if prior to such action a written consent to such action is signed by a majority of the duly appointed members of the board of directors. [Acts 1967, ch. 47, § 8, p. 77; 1977, P.L. 254, § 9, p. 1066.]

20-13-6-9 [41-1209]. New members in authority — Effect on board membership. — After the legal establishment of the library services authority as provided by this chapter [20-13-6-1 — 20-13-6-14], any governing authority may become a member of the library services authority after (a) approval by a majority of the board of directors, (b) adopting by resolution, ordinance, order, statement of participation or other recorded act the joint agreement as then in force, (c) providing for its pro rata share, if any, of the library services authority's budget for the fiscal year in which the applying library wishes to join the authority, and (d) meeting any and all conditions provided in the bylaws or in the rules and regulations: Provided, That if the governing authority is a private authority and its membership would create the same number or more private members than public members of the library services authority, then the membership shall not be affected until there are sufficient public members, after the admission of the applicant, to provide a majority of public members.

An originally signed copy of the joint agreement and adopting action shall be filed with the Indiana state library by the library services authority. [Acts 1967, ch. 47, § 9, p. 77; 1977, P.L. 254, § 10, p. 1066.]

20-13-6-10 [41-1210]. Powers of library services authority. — A library services authority has full power and authority to:

(a) Sue and be sued, plead and be impleaded.

(b) Establish or take charge of, manage, maintain and operate the library facilities and provide the library services specified in the joint agreement creating the library services authority.

(c) Employ and delegate duties and responsibilities to a chief administrative officer and such other employees as may be necessary for the performance of the authority's functions or to provide for such officer or other employees by contract with a library member of the authority, with another organization, institution or company, with an agency of government or with an individual; fix and pay their salaries and compensation; determine their number and prescribe their duties; and remove or discharge employees.

(d) Purchase supplies, materials and equipment to carry out the powers and duties of the board.

(e) Acquire and hold property, real or personal, by purchase, devise, lease, gift or otherwise, and sell, exchange, or otherwise dispose of property, real or personal, no longer needed for the purposes of the authority.

(f) Prepare and adopt a budget covering the anticipated expenditures for each fiscal year and enter into a contract with each member of the authority for the pro rata shares, if any, of the budget as provided in this chapter.

(g) Accept, receive and receipt for funds received from members of the library services authority, for federal or state funds, or for gift or other funds, budget the same and expend, without appropriation, the funds required in exercising the powers and discharging the duties of the authority. All funds received, unless specifically excepted by a condition or conditions, shall become the property of the library services authority.

(h) Adopt bylaws, administrative procedures, rules and regulations.

(i) Establish and maintain or participate in programs of employee benefits.

(j) Report annually to each governing authority which is a member of the library services authority on the budget and expenditures, services rendered, program, plans for development, and such other information as may be appropriate.

(k) Make and enter into all contracts and agreements necessary to the performance of the authority's duties and the execution of its powers under this chapter [20-13-6-1 — 20-13-6-14].

(l) Establish and collect reasonable rates and charges for services rendered to its members or others using the services of the authority.

(m) Invest excess funds in interest-bearing securities of the United States, or any security lawfully issued by any county, township, city or other municipal corporation of the state of Indiana, or to deposit such funds in any duly chartered national or state bank whose deposits are insured by any federal agency: Provided, however, That no deposits shall be made in excess of the amount of insurance protection afforded a member or investor of any such institution.

(n) Establish such special funds as may be necessary for the purpose of accumulating sufficient money over two [2] or more fiscal years for the purchase of specified real property or major equipment, or for the making of improvements to real property owned by the library services authority. Each such special fund shall be for a specific purpose and shall be named for that purpose. Any funds accumulated but not expended under this paragraph may be transferred and expended for any other legitimate purpose of the authority.

(o) Join and participate through its designated representative in the meetings and activities of state and national associations of a civic, educational, professional or governmental nature which have as their purpose the betterment and improvement of library operations. [Acts 1967, ch. 47, § 10, p. 77; 1977, P.L. 254, § 11, p. 1066.]

20-13-6-11 [41-1211]. Executive committee to prepare budget — Adoption by board — Tax levy. — The executive committee, annually shall prepare a budget for the operating expenditures of the library services authority and shall calculate the share of that budget to be charged to each governing authority according to the pro rata formula in its rules and regulations as authorized by the board of directors of the library services authority. Such budget shall be submitted to the board of directors for adoption. After adoption by the board, the appropriate pro rata charges, if any, shall be included in a contract submitted to each governing authority prior to May 1st of the year preceding the fiscal year of the budget for acceptance and inclusion in the budget of the governing authority.

Each governing authority which is a member of the library services authority and signs a contract for pro rata charges in the ensuing fiscal year shall provide the necessary funds with which to pay its contractual obligation under its contract with the library services authority. [Acts 1967, ch. 47, § 11, p. 77; 1977, P.L. 254, § 12, p. 1066.]

20-13-6-12 [41-1212]. Funds of authority—Bond of handlers—Records of authority as public records.—All funds coming into the possession of the library services authority shall be deposited, held, secured and expended in accordance with the general laws of the state relating to the handling of public funds. The handling and expenditure of these funds shall be subject to audit and supervision by the state board of accounts.

Any officer or employee of the library services authority who is authorized to receive or disburse or in any other way handle funds and securities of the authority shall give a corporate surety bond, in an amount specified in the rules and regulations, for the faithful performance of his duties and the proper accounting of all moneys and property which may come into his hands or under his control. The cost of such bond, including the cost of filing and recording, shall be paid out of funds of the library services authority.

The records of the library services authority shall be considered public records. [Acts 1967, ch. 47, § 12, p. 77.]

20-13-6-13 [41-1213]. Tax exemption.—All property owned by the library services authority and all revenues received by the authority shall be exempt from taxation in the state for any and all purposes. [Acts 1967, ch. 47, § 13, p. 77.]

20-13-6-14 [41-1214]. Withdrawal from authority—Procedure—Dissolution of authority — Requirements of dissolution. — Subject to making due provisions for the payment and performance of its obligations, any governing authority which is a member of the library services authority may withdraw from the authority by resolution, or ordinance, order, statement of separation, or other recorded act of that governing authority and upon notification to the library services authority prior to April 1st of the last fiscal year in which the library discontinuing membership is a member of the library services authority. Upon discontinuing membership in the library services authority the discontinuing member relinquishes its rights to any funds, supplies, materials, equipment, real or other property held by or belonging to the authority and in which the discontinuing member had a right by virtue of its membership, unless provision to the contrary is made by the official action of the board of directors. Upon the receipt of such notification and the satisfaction of all obligations by the withdrawing member, the board of directors shall officially note the withdrawal and shall file notice of the resulting change in the joint agreement with the Indiana state library and in the office of the recorder of the county in which the authority's principal place of business is located.

The library services authority shall be dissolved when the board of directors of the authority so vote, when such action is de facto by the notice of discontinuance of membership by the next to last remaining member or when the membership of the authority consists of a greater number of private governing authorities than public governing authorities. Upon the occurrence of any of these conditions, the board of directors shall dispose of the assets by division among the members at the time of dissolution and in the proportion and in the manner determined by the board of directors.

The dissolution shall not be in effect until all legal and fiscal obligations of the library services authority have been satisfied, and an official record of the dissolution is filed in the office of the recorder of the county in which the authority's principal place of business is located. Until such satisfaction of obligations has occurred and the record of dissolution has been filed, the final members of the authority shall continue to be members. [Acts 1967, ch. 47, § 14, p. 77.]

LIBRARY LEASING CORPORATIONS
(Burns Annotated Indiana Statutes, 1982, s.20-13-7-1 to 20-13-7-13.)

20-13-7-1 [41-1001]. Library buildings — Leasing authorized. — Any public library corporation organized and existing under IC 20-13-1 [20-13-1-1 — 20-13-1-24], or any school city, school town, school township or any other municipal or public corporation operating and maintaining a library or libraries (any such corporation being hereinafter referred to as a "library corporation") shall have the power to lease a library building or buildings for the use of such library corporation or of any joint or consolidated library corporation of which it is a part or to which it contributes: Provided, however, That no such contract of lease shall be entered into for a period of more than forty [40] years, nor unless there shall first be filed with the library board or boards of the library corporation a petition therefor signed by fifty [50] or more resident taxpayers of such library corporation and the library board shall have, after investigation, determined that a need exists for such library building or buildings and that such library corporation cannot provide the necessary funds to pay the cost or its proportionate share of the cost of the library building or buildings required to meet the present needs.

The term "library building" as used in this chapter shall be construed to mean any building used as a part of or in connection with the operation of libraries and shall include the site therefor, the equipment thereof and appurtenances thereto such as but not limited to, heating facilities, water supply, sewage disposal, landscaping, walks, drives and parking areas.

·If two [2] or more library corporations propose to enter into such a lease contract jointly, then joint meetings of the library boards of such corporations may be held but no action taken shall be binding on any such library corporation unless approved by its library board. Any lease contract executed by two [2] or more library corporations as joint lessees shall set out the amount of the aggregate lease rental to be paid by each, which may be as agreed upon, but there shall be no right of occupancy by any lessee unless the aggregate rental is paid as stipulated in the lease contract. All rights of joint lessees under the lease contract shall be in proportion to the amount of lease rental paid by each. [Acts 1959, ch. 69, § 1, p. 137; 1978, P.L. 118, § 1, p. —.]

20-13-7-2 [41-1002]. Purpose of corporation — Acquire site and erect library buildings — Nonprofit. — No library corporation or corporations shall enter into a contract of lease, under the provisions of this act, except with a corporation organized under the laws of the state of Indiana for the purpose solely of acquiring a site, erecting thereon a suitable library building or buildings, leasing the same to such library corporation or corporations, collecting the rentals therefor and applying the proceeds thereof in the manner herein provided. Such lessor corporation shall act entirely without profit to the corporation, its officers, directors and stockholders, but shall be entitled to the return of capital actually invested, plus sums sufficient to pay interest or dividends on outstanding securities or loans, and the cost of maintaining its corporation existence and keeping its property free of encumbrance. Upon receipt of any amount of lease rental by such lessor corporation over and above the amount necessary to meet incidental corporate expenses and to pay dividends or interest on corporate securities or loans, such excess funds shall be applied to the redemption and cancellation of its outstanding securities or loans as soon as may be done. [Acts 1959, ch. 69, § 2, p. 137; 1977, P.L. 250, § 7, p. 1042.]

20-13-7-3 [41-1003]. Contract of lease—Provisions.—All contracts of lease shall provide that such library corporation or corporations shall have an option to renew said lease for a further term, on like conditions, or to purchase the property covered by such contract of lease after six [6] years from the execution of the lease and prior to the expiration of the term of such contract of lease on such date or dates in each year as may be fixed therein, at a price equal to the amount required to enable the lessor corporation owning the same to liquidate by paying all indebtedness, with accrued and unpaid interest and to redeem and retire any stock at par, and the expenses and charges of liquidation. In no event, however, shall such purchase price exceed the capital actually invested in such property by such lessor corporation represented by outstanding securities or existing indebtedness plus the cost of transferring the property and liquidating the lessor corporation. The phrase "capital actually invested" as used in this act [20-13-7-1— 20-13-7-13] shall be construed to include, but not by way of limitation, the following amounts expended by the lessor corporation; organization and incorporation expenses, financing costs, carrying charges, legal fees, architects' fees, contractors' fees and reasonable costs and expenses incidental thereto. No such contract of lease shall provide, nor be construed to provide, that any such library corporation shall be under any obligation to purchase such leased library building or buildings, or under any obligation in respect to any creditors, shareholders or other security holders of the lessor corporation. [Acts 1959, ch. 69, § 3, p. 137.]

20-13-7-4 [41-1004]. Plans and specifications submitted to state agencies.—The lessor corporation proposing to build such a library building or buildings, including the necessary equipment and appurtenances thereof, shall submit to the lessee or lessees, prior to the execution of a contract of lease, plans, specifications and estimates for such building or buildings, and such plans and specifications shall be submitted to the state board of health, state fire marshal and such other agencies as may be designated by law to pass on plans and specifications for library buildings, and such plans and specifications shall be approved by such agencies in writing and the lessee or lessees prior to the execution of such contract of lease. [Acts 1959, ch. 69, § 4, p. 137.]

20-13-7-5 [41-1005]. Lease contract — Optional provisions. — Such contract of lease may provide that as a part of the lease rental for such library building or buildings the lessee or lessees shall agree to pay all taxes and assessments levied against or on account of the leased property, to maintain insurance thereon for the benefit of the lessor corporation and to assume all responsibilities for repair and alterations thereon or thereto during the term of such lease. [Acts 1959, ch. 69, § 5, p. 137.]

20-13-7-6 [41-1006]. Rental begins upon completion of building.— Such library corporation or corporations may, in anticipation of the acquisition of a site and the construction and erection of such library building or buildings, including the necessary equipment and appurtenances thereof, make and enter into a contract of lease with such lessor corporation prior to the actual acquisition of such site and the construction and erection of such building or buildings, but such contract of lease so entered into shall not provide for the payment of any lease rental by the lessee or lessees until the completion of such building or buildings ready for occupancy, at which time the stipulated lease rental may begin. The contractor shall be required to furnish to the lessor corporation a bond satisfactory to such corporation conditioned upon the final completion of such building or buildings within such a period as may be provided in the contract. [Acts 1959, ch. 69, § 6, p. 137.]

20-13-7-7 [41-1007]. Terms and conditions of proposed lease — Notice by publication — Hearing — Remonstrance — Appeal to state board of tax commissioners. — When the lessor corporation and the library corporation or corporations have agreed upon the terms and conditions of any lease proposed to be entered into pursuant to the terms and conditions of this chapter and before the final execution of such lease, a notice shall be given by publication to all persons interested of a hearing to be held before the library board, which hearing shall be on a day not earlier than ten [10] days after the publication of such notice. The notice of such hearing shall be published one [1] time in a newspaper of general circulation printed in the English language in the library corporation or in each library corporation if the proposed lease be a joint lease, or if no such paper be published therein, then in any newspaper of general circulation published in the county. Such notice shall name the day, place and hour of such hearing and shall set forth a brief summary of the principal terms of the lease agreed upon, including the location, name of the proposed lessor corporation and character of the property to be leased, the rental to be paid and the number of years the contract is to be in effect. The proposed lease, drawings, plans, specifications and estimates for such library building or buildings shall be available for inspection by the public during said ten [10] day period and at said meeting. All persons interested shall have a right to be heard at the time fixed, upon the necessity for the execution of such lease, and whether the rentals provided for therein to be paid to the lessor corporation is a fair and reasonable rental for the proposed building or buildings. Such hearing may be adjourned to a later date or dates, and following such hearing the library board may either authorize the execution of such lease as originally agreed upon or may make such modifications therein as may be agreed upon with such lessor corporation, but in no event shall the lease rentals as set out in the published notice be increased. The cost of the publication of the notice shall be borne by the lessor corporation.

In the event the execution of the lease as originally agreed upon, or as modified by agreement, is authorized by such library board, it shall give notice of the signing of said contract by publication one [1] time in a newspaper of general circulation printed in the English language in the library corporation or in each library corporation or one [1] of the same if the proposed lease be a joint lease, or if no such newspaper be published therein, then in any newspaper of general circulation published in the county. Fifty

[50] or more taxpayers in such library corporation or corporations who will be affected by the proposed lease and who may be of the opinion that no necessity exists for the execution of such lease, or that the proposed rental provided for therein is not a fair and reasonable rental, may file a petition in the office of the county auditor of the county in which such library corporation or corporations are located, within thirty [30] days after publication of notices of the execution of such lease, setting forth their objections thereto and facts showing that the execution of the lease is unnecessary or unwise, or that the lease rental is not fair and reasonable, as the case may be. Upon the filing of any such petition the county auditor shall immediately certify a copy thereof, together with such other data as may be necessary in order to present the questions involved, to the state board of tax commissioners, and upon the receipt of such certified petition and information, the state board of tax commissioners shall fix a time and place for the hearing of such matter which shall not be less than five [5] nor more than thirty [30] days thereafter, and said hearing shall be held in the library corporation or corporations, or in the county where such library corporations are located. Notice of the hearing shall be given by the state board of tax commissioners to the members of the library board and to the first ten [10] taxpayer-petitioners upon such petition by a letter signed by one [1] member of the state board of tax commissioners, and enclosed with full prepaid postage addressed to such persons at their usual place of residence, at least five [5] days before the date of such hearing. The decision of the state board of tax commissioners on such appeal, upon the necessity for the execution of said lease and as to whether the rental is fair and reasonable, shall be final. Any lease may be amended by the parties thereto by following the procedure herein provided for the execution of the original lease.

No action to contest the validity of the lease or any amendment thereto or to enjoin the performance of any of the terms and conditions of the lease or any amendment thereto shall be instituted at any time later than thirty [30] days after publication of notice of the execution of the lease or any amendment thereto by the library board of such library corporation or corporations; or if an appeal has been taken to the state board of tax commissioners, then within thirty [30] days after the decision of said board [Acts 1959, ch. 69, § 7, p. 137; 1978, P.L. 118, § 2, p. —.]

20-13-7-8 [41-1008]. Lessor to acquire fee simple title to land—Petition to sell land held by library corporation—Appraisers.—The lessor corporation shall acquire, own and hold in fee simple the land on which such building or buildings is to be erected. Any library corporation or corporations proposing to lease such library building or buildings, either alone or jointly with another library corporation, and owning the land on which it desires that such building or buildings be erected may and is hereby authorized to sell and transfer to the lessor corporation such land in fee simple. Before such sale may take place, the library board of the library corporation shall file a petition with the circuit court of such county in which the library corporation is located or with the judge thereof, if such court is in vacation requesting the appointment of three [3] disinterested freeholders of the library corporation as appraisers to determine the fair market value of such land. Upon their appointment, the three [3] appraisers shall proceed to fix the fair market value of such land and shall report the amount so fixed to the circuit court or the judge thereof within two [2] weeks from the date of their appointment. The library corporation may then sell such land to the lessor corporation for an amount not less than the amount so fixed as the fair market value by the three [3] appraisers, which amount shall be paid in cash upon delivery of the deed by the library corporation to the lessor corporation. [Acts 1959, ch. 69, § 8, p. 137.]

20-13-7-9 [41-1009]. Lessor corporation authorized to issue stock, bonds and other securities — Sale. — Any corporation qualifying as a lessor corporation under the provisions of this chapter shall have power, in furtherance of its corporate purposes, to issue stock, bonds and other securities and to sell the same. Mortgage bonds issued by such a lessor corporation which are a first lien on such leased property shall be considered legal and proper investments for state banks and trust companies, insurance companies and fiduciaries. Such bonds may be callable with or without premiums with accrued and unpaid interest thereon upon such notice as may be provided in the mortgage indenture.

All stocks, bonds and other securities issued by such lessor corporation shall be sold at not less than par value at public sale after advertisement once each week for two [2] weeks in two [2] newspapers of general circulation printed and published in the county in which such library building or buildings are located, and one [1] time in a newspaper of general circulation printed and published in the city of Indianapolis, the last of said publications to be seven [7] days prior to the date of sale. Said stocks, bonds, or securities shall be awarded by the board of directors of such lessor corporation on the date of sale to the highest bidder therefor. The highest bidder shall be determined by computing the total interest in case of bonds or like securities, or total dividends in case of preferred stock, from the date thereof to the date of maturity and deducting therefrom the premium bid, if any. Any premium received from the sale of said stocks, bonds or securities shall be used to retire as soon as possible said stocks, bonds or securities. If the stocks, bonds, or other securities are not sold on the date fixed for the sale thereof, then such sale may be continued from day to day until a satisfactory bid has been received. Provisions with reference to public sale shall not apply to the issuance of shares of common stock that do not bear dividends, and such shares may be issued for such consideration as may be determined.

The approval of the Indiana securities commission shall not be required in connection with the issuance and sale of any stock, bonds or other securities of [a] corporation. [Acts 1959, ch. 69, § 9, p. 137; 1978, P.L. 118, § 3, p. —.]

20-13-7-10 [41-1010]. General obligation bonds authorized. — Any library corporation availing itself of the provisions of this chapter shall have the power and authority to issue its general obligation bonds for the purpose of procuring funds to pay the cost of acquisition in the event such library corporation shall determine to exercise its option to purchase, which bonds shall be authorized, issued and sold in the manner now provided or which may hereafter be provided for the authorization, issuance and sale of bonds by such library corporation for library building purposes. [Acts 1959, ch. 69, § 10, p. 137; 1978, P.L. 118, § 4, p. —.]

20-13-7-11 [41-1011]. Special tax levy authorized to pay rental. — Any library corporation which shall execute a lease contract under the provisions of this act [20-13-7-1—20-13-7-13] shall annually levy a special tax in addition to other taxes authorized by law sufficient to produce each year the necessary funds with which to pay the lease rental stipulated to be paid by such library corporation in such lease contract. Such levy shall be reviewable by other bodies vested by law with such authority to ascertain that the levy is sufficient to raise the amount required to meet the rental of such lease contract. The first tax levy shall be made at the first annual tax levy period following the date of the execution of the aforesaid lease contract and said first annual levy shall be sufficient to pay the estimated amount of the first annual lease rental payment to be made under said lease; thereafter, the annual levies herein provided for shall be made. [Acts 1959, ch. 69, § 11, p. 137.]

20-13-7-12 [41-1012]. Lessor corporation exempt from certain taxes. — All property owned by a lessor corporation so contracting with such library corporation or corporations under the provisions of this act [20-13-7-1—20-13-7-13] and all stock and other securities including the interest or dividends thereon, issued by a lessor corporation shall be exempt from the state intangible tax and from all other state, county and other taxes, including the gross income tax, except however, inheritance taxes. The rental paid to a lessor corporation under the terms of such a contract of lease shall be exempt from the gross income tax. [Acts 1959, ch. 69, § 12, p. 137.]

20-13-7-13 [41-1013]. Act supplemental. — This act [20-13-7-1—20-13-7-13] is intended to be and shall be construed as being supplemental to all existing laws covering the acquisition, use and maintenance of library buildings by library corporations: Provided, That as to library buildings constructed, acquired, leased or purchased pursuant to the provisions of this act, it shall not be necessary to comply with the provisions of other laws concerning the acquisition, use and maintenance of library buildings by library corporations except as herein specifically required. [Acts 1959, ch. 69, § 13, p. 137.]

PUBLIC LIBRARY LAW OF 1947

(Burns Annotated Indiana Statutes, 1982, s.20-13-1-1 to 20-13-1-24,
20-13-11-1, 20-13-21-1 to 20-13-21-5.)

20-13-1-1 [41-901]. Policy of state concerning public libraries. — It is hereby declared to be the policy of the state, as a part of its provision for public education, to promote the establishment, maintenance, and development of public library service for each of its various subdivisions. Such public library service is to be provided by a library supported by public funds and operated for the benefit and free use of individuals and groups of all ages in the community in the meeting of their educational, informational, and recreational interests and needs. These interests and needs are met by the collection and organization of books and other library materials and the dissemination of the knowledge contained therein through reference, loan, and related services. It is the purpose of this act [20-13-1-1—20-13-1-24] to establish a unified law governing public libraries of the state which will promote efficiency and economy in the administration of such public supported libraries. [Acts 1947, ch. 321, § 1, p. 1273; 1965, ch. 115, § 1, p. 157.]

20-13-1-2 [41-902]. **Short title.**—This act may be cited as the "Public Library Law of 1947." [Acts 1947, ch. 321, § 2, p. 1273; 1965, ch. 115, § 2, p. 157.]

20-13-1-3 [41-903]. **Definitions.**—The following words and phrases as used in this act [20-13-1-1—20-13-1-24], unless a different meaning is plainly required by the context, shall have the following meanings:

"Library district" shall mean any municipal corporation, or combination thereof, organized under this act, or any existing library, or combination thereof, which subsequently shall come under the terms of this act.

"Existing library" shall mean any public library system in existence at the time of passage of this act [March 14, 1947] that is supported wholly or in part by public taxes and shall include any and all related libraries which are a part of such system and served by it.

"Public library system" shall mean all library services and all library properties within a total library service area and operated under the management and control of one [1] library board.

"Library board" shall mean the official governing body, known also as "board of trustees," of a public library system that is supported wholly or in part by public taxes.

"Municipal corporation" shall mean any civil city, town, county, township, or county contractual library.

"Town-township," for the purposes of this act, shall mean a combination of a civil city and/or town with a township or townships or a portion of a township not otherwise in a library district, for the purpose of creating a single library taxing district.

"County contractual library" shall mean a joining of that part of a county previously not taxed for public library service with a civil city, town, township, or town-township library for the purpose of providing by contract such library service to the previously unserved townships or portions of townships in said county, as provided for in this act. [Acts 1947, ch. 321, § 3, p. 1273; 1953, ch. 13, § 1, p. 38; 1965, ch. 115, § 3, p. 157; 1969, ch. 364, § 1, p. 1507.]

20-13-1-4 [41-904]. **Classification of libraries.**—In order to clarify the status of libraries with reference to the operation of this act [20-

13-1-1—20-13-1-24], and at the same time to provide for a maximum of local autonomy in matters of library administration, the following two [2] classes of libraries are hereby established:

Class I libraries: All libraries organized under the terms of this act and all existing libraries the boards of which file a resolution of conversion as provided by this act.

Class II libraries: All public libraries administered by boards of school trustees or boards of school commissioners; libraries having endowment funds in the total amount of at least five thousand dollars [$5,000], which endowment funds were created prior to the passage of this act [March 14, 1947]; township libraries organized prior to the passage of this act; libraries organized under laws which authorized no tax levies for the support thereof; and libraries in cities having a population of 100,000 or more as shown by the last preceding United States census and operating under chapter 79 of the Acts of 1937 [repealed]. Libraries in Class II are exempt from the compulsory provisions of this act and will continue to operate and function pursuant to the laws in effect at the time of and prior to the passage of this act, and shall continue to have the power and right to manage, operate, levy taxes, control the finances, and to perform all necessary acts as they can now do under existing laws, although the boards of trustees of such libraries may elect to have the powers and rights with respect to the management, control, financing, issuance of bonds and levy of taxes of and for said libraries as are contained and enumerated in this act. Such election is irrevocable. A copy of that portion of the board minutes showing passage of the resolution to elect the provisions of this act shall be filed with the Indiana state library. [Acts 1947, ch. 321, § 4, p. 1273; 1965, ch. 115, § 4, p. 157.]

20-13-1-5 [41-905]. Library districts—Public corporations—Name —Powers—Territory included.—All library districts in Indiana, organized or otherwise coming under the provisions of this act [20-13-1-1— 20-13-1-24], are hereby declared to be and are made public corporations for library purposes, separate and distinct from the civil or municipal corporations comprising such library districts, and shall be known and designated as _____ Public Library, as the case may be, and by such name may contract and be contracted with, sue and be sued in any court of competent jurisdiction, and shall constitute a separate and independent library taxing district.

Any resolution of establishment, conversion, transfer or merger after the enactment of this act shall specify and describe the territory included in said library district. After the recording of the resolution in the office of the county recorder and with the Indiana state library the specified and described territory shall be conclusively deemed to be a part of said library district.

In the case of any public library heretofore established or otherwise coming under this act, the territory of said library district shall be conclusively presumed to be the territory which includes the property against which a tax has been levied for library purposes in said library district for the two [2] years preceding the enactment of this act [March 14, 1947]. A certificate of the county auditor as to the property against which the tax for library purposes was levied shall constitute conclusive evidence as to the territory included in the library district.

When, however, the corporate limits of a civil town, civil township, civil city, or civil county and a library district established or otherwise coming under this act are coextensive, territory annexed by the civil town, civil township, civil city or civil county shall become part of the library district if said territory is not already part of another library district. If the territory of the library district is so increased, a statement specifying and describing the annexed territory shall be filed in the office of the county recorder and with the Indiana state library by the library annexing the territory and the specified and described territory shall be conclusively deemed to be a part of the library district. Conversely, any territory annexed by a civil town, civil township, civil city or civil county which territory also is already a part of an existing library district shall remain a part of its original library district unless and except it is mutually agreed by the libraries involved that the territory so annexed by the civil town, civil township, civil city or civil county shall be transferred to the principal library district serving the residents of the annexing town, township, city or county. A resolution signed by two thirds [⅔] of the members of the library boards shall be necessary to effect this transfer.

In the event that it should prove mutually advantageous for one public library district to surrender a part of its territory to another public library district, such transfer is hereby authorized provided that each library board passes a resolution signed by two thirds [⅔] of the members of each library board agreeing to the transfer of the territory identically specified and described in the two [2] resolutions. [Acts 1947, ch. 321, § 5, p. 1273; 1965, ch. 115, § 5, p. 157; 1967, ch. 123, § 1, p. 225.]

20-13-1-6 [41-906]. Libraries for municipal corporations not already taxed for libraries — Petitions — Remonstrances — Appointment of library board. — (a) The governing body (under IC 36-1-3-6) of a town, civil city or county, having a population of at least ten thousand [10,000], or the governing body of a town having a population of more than one thousand [1,000], which is located in a county having a population of more than one hundred thirty thousand [130,000] but less than one hundred thirty-eight thousand [138,000], not already taxed for public library purposes, may by written resolution, or upon petition signed by at least twenty percent [20%] of the registered voters of the appropriate town, civil city or county, not already taxed for public library purposes, such minimum percent to be based on the number of such voters of said municipal corporation voting at the last preceding general election, shall establish a free public library and create a library district for the residents of said municipal corporation under the name and style of _____ Public Library, unless a remonstrance against the same signed by as many registered voters of the municipal corporation as signed the petition shall be filed with the governing body of the municipal corporation.

(b) Upon the filing of any such petition with the governing body of the municipal corporation, the governing body shall within ten [10] days cause notice of that fact to be published in two [2] newspapers of general circulation in the county, one [1] of which is published in such town or city wherein the library is located, if any there be. And within ten [10] days after such publication any and every registered voter or group of registered voters shall have the right to sign and file with the governing body of such municipal corporation their remonstrance against the establishment of the library, stating therein that they are opposed to such establishment. At the first meeting of the governing body of the municipal corporation and not less than ten [10] days after such publication, the governing body shall proceed to consider the said petition and such remonstrance and determine whether or not registered voters of such municipal corporation have signed and presented the remonstrance equal to the number of such registered voters who signed and presented the petition for the same. And if at the meeting of the governing body it shall determine that a greater number of registered voters have signed the petition than the number who have signed a remonstrance against the establishment of the library district, the governing body shall by written resolution establish the library district mentioned effective as of the date of the adoption of the resolution. A copy of such resolution shall be recorded by the governing body, within five [5] days in the office of the county recorder in the county where such new library district is created and at the same time a copy also shall be filed with the Indiana state library, and notice shall be given by said governing body to all officials who have appointive powers under the provisions of this chapter to appoint members of the library board for such library, and such officials shall forthwith appoint the library board of the new library district.

(c) If, however, the governing body finds that a greater number of registered voters have signed a remonstrance against the establishment of the library district than the number who have signed the petition then the petition shall be dismissed and the governing body shall take no further action thereon except that a petition again may be presented one [1] year after the date on which the governing body dismissed the last previous petition.

(d) The library board of the library district established under provisions of this section shall have the powers and duties of library boards as set forth in this chapter. [Acts 1947, ch. 321, § 6; 1965, ch. 115, § 6; 1967, ch. 123, § 2; 1978, P.L. 114, § 1; 1982, P.L. 1, § 48.]

20-13-1-7 [41-907]. Conversion of Class II libraries to Class I—Resolution—Filing and notice to officials—Library board—Possession of property and funds.—Any Class II library may convert to Class I status at any time after the passage of this act [20-13-1-1—20-13-1-24] by passing the following resolution: _____ Public Library by action of its board of trustees (or library board) hereby resolves and elects to change its identity and become a library district under chapter 321 of the Acts of 1947, which act is known as the Public Library Law of 1947.

Before such resolution shall be effective under this act it shall be signed by not less than a majority of the members of the library board. The effective date of the conversion shall be the date on which a majority of the members of the library board have signed the resolution of conversion.

A copy of such resolution of conversion shall be recorded by said board within five [5] days in the office of the county recorder and at the same time a copy also shall be filed with the Indiana state library, and notice shall be given by the library board to all officials who have appointive powers under the provisions of this act and it shall be the duty of such officials forthwith to appoint a new library board for such library. Members of the old board shall remain as members of the new library board until a majority of the new library board has been appointed and such new appointees have qualified.

The filing of such resolution of conversion shall be deemed final and conclusive evidence that the library so converting is now and has always been a validly created and established public corporation as defined in section 5 [20-13-1-5] of this act: Provided, That any library which has previously filed a resolution of conversion under this act is hereby declared a legally organized library district entitled to enjoy all the rights and privileges granted to library districts by this act.

Upon the filing of the resolution and the appointment and qualification of the new library board as hereinafter provided, any existing tax levies shall continue under prior law until the next succeeding tax levying period at which time the tax provisions of this act shall become operative. The obligation of any political subdivision to levy and collect taxes for library purposes is not released by the resolution of conversion. Such resolution of conversion, once filed, is irrevocable. A library may not after converting to a Class I library revert to Class II.

Upon the taking effect of this act [March 14, 1947], the possession of property, equipment and records and any expendable funds held under any previous acts shall be lawfully possessed under the authority of this act. [Acts 1947, ch. 321, § 7, p. 1273; 1965, ch. 115, § 7, p. 157.]

20-13-1-7.5. Scope of a Class I county library district created prior to July 1, 1979 — Taxation. — (a) This section applies to any county in which there was on July 1, 1979, a class I library created or converted under IC 20-13-21 [20-13-21-1 — 20-13-21-5].

(b) The entire county is a single class I county library district under this chapter. Title to any real estate used for library purposes in the county, other than leased real estate, vests in the county library district. The taxing authority for the library district is vested in the library board appointed under section 8 [20-13-1-8] of this chapter and the tax rate adopted by the board under section 20 [20-13-1-20] of this chapter shall apply uniformly to the territory included in the county library district. [IC 20-13-1-7.5, as added by Acts 1979, P.L. 220, § 1; 1982, P.L. 1, § 49.]

20-13-1-8 [41-908]. Library boards — Membership — Tenure — Women members — Vacancies — Reappointment — Removal for cause — Vacancy by absence — No compensation. — The library board of a civil city, town, township, or county library district, organized or coming under the provisions of this act [20-13-1-1—20-13-1-24] by conversion shall be composed of resident citizens who have resided for at least two [2] years in the library district, except as provided hereinafter when there is a township or townships or portions of a township or townships contracting for service from such library district, and shall consist of the following members:

(a)   Three [3] members who shall be appointed by the judge of the circuit court of the county in which such library district is located, or if such district is located in more than one county, jointly by the judges of the circuit courts of the respective counties, one [1] of whom shall be appointed for one [1] year, one [1] for two [2] years and one [1] for three [3] years, and at least one [1] of whom shall be a woman.

(b)   Two [2] members who shall be appointed by the board of town trustees or common council of the civil city in the case of a town or city library, or by the township advisory board in the case of a township library, or by the board of county commissioners in the case of a county library, one [1] of whom shall be appointed for one [1] year and one [1] for two [2] years and at least one [1] of whom shall be a woman.

(c)   Two [2] members who shall be appointed by the school board, board of school trustees, or board of school commissioners, if any there be, and if such exist, of the school district in which the headquarters of the library district is located, one [1] of whom shall be appointed for a term of three [3] years and one [1] for four [4] years, at least one [1] of whom shall be a woman.

After the first appointments have been made all subsequent appointments shall be for a term of four [4] years. Appointments to fill vacancies created by death, resignation, or otherwise shall be for the unexpired term only. When there is a township or townships, or portions of a township or townships contracting for service from such library district, a judge of the circuit court may, in making his appointments, name a resident or residents of such township to such board: Provided, however, That such township appointee shall automatically cease to be a member of the library board if the township in which he resides fails to renew its contract for library service, and this authorization as to such representation shall not be construed to apply to, or in any way affect, the manner of appointment of members of a county library board.

Any member of a library board created under this act shall be eligible to reappointment for not more than three [3] consecutive terms; however, a member of a library board as of July 1, 1965, may be reappointed to not more than three [3] consecutive terms after that date. A board member may be removed at any time by the appointing authority, after public hearing, for any cause which interferes with the proper discharge of his duty as a member of such board or for cause which jeopardizes public confidence in the member. A vacancy shall occur whenever a member is absent from six [6] consecutive regular board meetings for any cause, other than illness, and the appointing authority shall be notified by the secretary of the board of the occurrence of such vacancy. All members of the board shall serve without compensation. No board member shall serve as a paid employee of the library. [Acts 1947, ch. 321, § 8, p. 1273; 1953, ch. 13, § 2, p. 38; 1965, ch. 115, § 8, p. 157; 1969, ch. 364, § 2, p. 1507.]

20-13-1-9   [41-909].   Certificates of appointment — Oath of office — Meetings of board — Officers — Bylaws — Quorum — Open meetings.

— The appointing authority shall issue to each appointee a signed certificate of appointment. Within ten [10] days after the receipt of the certificate of appointment, the appointee shall qualify for his office by taking an oath of office before any person authorized by law to administer the same to the effect that he will faithfully discharge his duties to the best of his ability, and shall file the certificate of appointment, with the oath endorsed thereon, with the records of the library, which shall be preserved as a public record.

Upon the creation of a new library, the board shall meet within ten [10] days after a majority of the appointees have qualified by taking an oath. The organizational meeting may be called by any two [2] appointees. The board shall elect from its members a president, a vice-president, and a secretary, and other officers as the board may deem necessary, and shall immediately draft and adopt bylaws for the board's procedure and management. Officers of the board shall be elected annually.

A majority of the members shall constitute a quorum for the transaction of business. The board shall meet at least monthly and at such times as may be necessary. Meetings may be called by the president or any two [2] board members. All meetings of the board, except necessary executive sessions, shall be open to the public. [Acts 1947, ch. 321, § 9, p. 1273; 1965, ch. 115, § 9; 1971, P.L. 341, § 1; 1973, P.L. 232, § 1; 1981, P.L. 205, § 1.]

20-13-1-10 [41-910]. **Extension of library service — Petition — Name — Notice — Remonstrance — Determination by commissioners — Recording — Library board created — Annual tax levy — Corporate title.** — The governing board of any library district may file with the board of county commissioners of the county a notice declaring consent to extend library service to the people of said county not already taxed for public library service on condition that that part of said county be organized as a library district for the purpose of contracting for such service with the library district filing the notice of consent. Upon receipt of this declaration of consent, such board of commissioners may or, upon petition of twenty per cent [20%] or more of the registered voters of each of at least two thirds [2/3] of all townships in the county not already taxed for public library purposes, such petition not overridden by remonstrance as hereinafter provided, shall establish by written resolution a library district, under the name and style of _____ County Contractual Public Library. This library so formed shall be for the purpose of joining with the library district filing the notice of consent in providing library service for the previously unserved townships of the county and the library district so served shall be called a county contractual library district. Upon the filing of any such petition of twenty per cent [20%] or more of the registered voters of such townships in the county, the county auditor shall within ten [10] days cause notice of that fact to be published in two [2] newspapers of general circulation in the county, one [1] of which is published in such town or city wherein the library is located, if any there be. And within ten [10] days after such publication any and every registered voter or group of registered voters shall have the right to sign and file with the county auditor their remonstrance against the establishment of the county contractual library, stating therein that they are opposed to such establishment. At the first meeting of the board of county commissioners and not less than ten [10] days after such publication, the board of commissioners shall consider said petition and such remonstrance and determine whether or not the total number of registered voters of such townships in said county not already taxed for public library purposes who had signed and presented a remonstrance is equal to the total number of such registered voters who signed and presented the petition for the same. And if the board of commissioners shall determine that a greater number of registered voters have signed the petition than the number who have signed a remonstrance against the establishment of the county contractual library, they shall by written resolution establish the county contractual library heretofore mentioned. The library board of the library district so established shall have the powers and duties of library boards as set forth in this act [20-13-1-1—20-13-1-24]. If, however, the board of county commissioners shall find that the number of remonstrances is greater, then the petition shall be dismissed and the board of county commissioners shall take no further action thereon except that a petition may again be presented one [1] year after the date on which the board of commissioners dismissed the last previous petition.

The board of county commissioners shall, within ten [10] days, cause a copy of the resolution establishing the county contractual library to be recorded in the office of the county recorder in the county where such new library district is created and a copy also to be sent to the Indiana state library, and to all officials whose duty it is under section 11 [20-13-1-11] of this act to appoint members of the library board of such library.

The library board thus created shall have the authority to make an appropriation and levy a tax, as provided for in this act, on taxable property in said county, including the property within any city or incorporated town in that part of the county not already taxed for public library purposes. The county treasurer shall collect and pay this sum to the treasurer of the newly created library district as a part of the library fund to be expended in the same manner as other library funds. Thereafter the library board shall make an annual tax levy and an annual appropriation for library purposes.

Any public library heretofore established under the provisions of this section, shall on and after July 1, 1965, operate under the name and style of _____ County Contractual Public Library. Such change of corporate title shall in no other way affect the organization, responsibilities, operation, or financial obligations of such heretofore established public library operating under the provisions of this section. [Acts 1947, ch. 321, § 10, p. 1273; 1955, ch. 12, § 1, p. 14; 1965, ch. 115, § 10, p. 157; 1967, ch. 123, § 3, p. 225.]

20-13-1-11 [41-911]. Library board—Appointment of members—Woman member—Tenure of office—Extension of service to county—Reappointments—Vacancies due to absences—No compensation.—If the board of county commissioners shall establish a county contractual public library as provided in section 10 [20-13-1-10] of this act, then within ten [10] days there shall be appointed as follows four [4] citizens who have resided for at least two [2] years in the county contractual library district:

(a)　Two [2] members who shall be appointed by the board of county commissioners of the county in which such library district is located, one [1] of whom shall be appointed for one [1] year and one [1] for three [3] years, and at least one [1] of whom shall be a woman; and

(b)　Two [2] members who shall be appointed by the county superintendent of schools, or if there be no county superintendent of schools, then by the county auditor of the county in which such library district is located, one [1] of whom shall be appointed for two [2] years, and one [1] for four [4] years, and at least one [1] of whom shall be a woman.

After the first appointments have been made all subsequent appointments shall be for a term of four [4] years. Appointments to fill vacancies created by death, resignation or otherwise shall be for the unexpired term only. The four [4] members so appointed, together with members of the board of the library district consenting to extend service, shall constitute a separate public library board and as such board shall exercise all powers and duties pertaining to library service to the county contractual district, and shall be known and designated as the board of trustees of _____ County Contractual Public Library. The members of the board of the library district extending service to the county shall continue as a separate board and continue to exercise all powers and duties pertaining to library service to the city or town.

Any member of a library board created under this act [20-13-1-1—20-13-1-24] shall be eligible to reappointment for not more than three [3] consecutive terms; however, a member of a library board as of July 1, 1965, may be reappointed to not more than three [3] consecutive terms after that date. A board member may be removed at any time by the appointing authority, after public hearing, for any cause which interferes with the proper discharge of his duty as a member of such board or for cause which jeopardizes public confidence in the member. A vacancy shall occur whenever a member is absent from six [6] consecutive regular board meetings for any cause, other than illness, and the appointing authority shall be notified by the secretary of the board of the occurrence of such vacancy. All members of the board shall serve without compensation. No board member shall serve as a paid employee of the library. [Acts 1947, ch. 321, § 11, p. 1273; 1963, ch. 129, § 1, p. 114; 1965, ch. 115, § 11, p. 157.]

20-13-1-12　[41-912]. Townships becoming part of library extended service district—Discontinuance of township library tax—County library district levy—Substitution automatic.—When a township, or townships, or part of township, is contracting with a library which is extending service to a county, or part of a county, or which inaugurates such service to a county, or part of a county, and when such library comes under the provisions of this act [20-13-1-1—20-13-1-24], then the separate tax levy of such township or townships for library purposes shall cease to be levied and such township or townships shall become a part of the county contractual library district, and the tax levy for such county library purposes shall be levied over such township or townships as part of the county contractual library district as provided for in this act. Likewise any township which ceases to levy a tax for public library purposes in any year shall become a part of its county library district or county contractual library district, if such exists, at the time the township levy is discontinued and the county library tax shall be levied over such townships. [Acts 1947, ch. 321, § 12, p. 1273; 1953, ch. 13, § 3, p. 38; 1965, ch. 115, § 12, p. 157; 1967, ch. 123, § 4, p. 225.]

20-13-1-13 [41-913]. Contracts for library service — Merger — Resolution — Recording — Change in tax levy — Merger dissolves board — Membership on board — Terms.

— (a) The library board of any library district operating under this chapter may enter into contract to receive service from any municipal corporation authorized to provide library services by contract. Said library board may also enter into contract to receive service from an established city, town, township, county or county contractual library district or may merge with such. Action to merge shall be by resolution signed by a two-thirds [²/₃] majority of the library board, which resolution shall authorize the library board making the same to give, devise in fee simple, sell or transfer all property belonging to the library which they represent to the library board of said library district under such terms and conditions as are set forth in the resolution. A copy of such resolution shall be filed with the county recorder and with the Indiana state library; on and after the filing of such resolution the tax levy of said library district shall provide for library service to the municipal corporation so merged and shall take the place of the previous separate tax levy of the municipal corporation for library purposes. When such merger is completed the library board of the library which has merged shall be considered dissolved. In the case of the merger of a city library district and a county library district, the city library district shall merge into the county library district.

(b) Notwithstanding any other laws, in the case of the merger of a city library district into a county library district, the city board and the county board shall be dissolved effective December 31 of the year of the merger. The newly created board shall take office January 1 and shall consist of the following members:

(1) Three [3] members who shall be appointed by the judge of the circuit court of the county in which the library district is located, or if such district is located in more than one county, jointly by the judges of the circuit courts of the respective counties, one [1] of whom shall be appointed for one [1] year, one [1] for two [2] years, and one [1] for three [3] years.

(2) Two [2] members who shall be appointed by the board of county commissioners of the county in which the library district is located, or if the district is located in more than one county, jointly by majority vote of the county commissioners from all of the counties involved, one [1] of whom shall be appointed for one [1] year and one [1] for two [2] years.

(3) Two [2] members who shall be appointed by the school board, board of school trustees, or board of school commissioners, if any there be, and if such exist, of the school district in which the headquarters of the library district is located, one [1] of whom shall be appointed for a term of three [3] years and one [1] for four [4] years.

After the initial appointments have been made, all subsequent appointments shall be for a term of four [4] years. Appointments to fill any vacancies shall be made for the unexpired term only. [Acts 1947, ch. 321, § 13, p. 1273; 1965, ch. 115, § 13; 1967, ch. 123, § 5; 1981, P.L. 206, § 1.]

20-13-1-14   [41-914].   Extended service to adjoining counties—Contracts—Tax levies.—The library board of a library district operating under this act [20-13-1-1—20-13-1-24] and extending service to the county in which it is located may extend service to an adjoining county or counties on a contractual basis to be agreed upon by such library board and the board of county commissioners of such adjoining county or counties. The contract shall set forth the manner and extent of service and the amount to be paid under the contract. The county commissioners of the county receiving such service shall agree to levy a tax sufficient to meet the amount agreed upon under the contract and the library extending such service shall be bound to expend funds received under the contract for services chargeable to the contract. Provided, however, That no such contract shall be made which applies to a municipal corporation in said adjoining county which is then levying a tax for public library purposes. [Acts 1947, ch. 321, § 14, p. 1273.]

20-13-1-15   [41-914a].   Library service furnished township — Tax levy — Limitation — Town-township unit — Prior actions legal. — The library board of any public library may furnish, or continue to furnish, service to any township, or any portion of a township not otherwise taxed for public library purposes, by agreement between the library board and township trustee, acting on the consent of the township advisory board. The township advisory board of a township receiving such service shall levy a tax upon all taxable property within the area to be served, except upon property otherwise taxed for library purposes, which tax shall be sufficient to meet the amount agreed to be paid for said service: Provided, however, That this rate shall not be less than nor more than the rate of taxation which a library board may fix under the provisions of this act [20-13-1-1—20-13-1-24]: Provided, however, That any library system which, while operating as a town-township unit, purported to convert to the terms of the "Public Library Law of 1947" as a town-township library, is hereby declared to be a town-township library under the terms of this act and shall hereafter operate as a town-township library district under the terms of this act. All actions heretofore taken on behalf of such library are hereby legalized and shall be considered to have been done pursuant to proper legal authority. [Acts 1947, ch. 321, § 14a, as added by Acts 1953, ch. 13, § 4, p. 38; 1955, ch. 12, § 2, p. 14; 1965, ch. 115, § 14, p. 157.]

20-13-1-16 [41-914b]. Proposal of merger — Petition — Notice — Remonstrance — Determination filed — Refiling after dismissal — Board membership — Woman member — Terms — Reappointment — Removal — Vacancy from absence — No compensation. — The board of any city, town, county, or county contractual library may file a proposal of merger with the township trustee and advisory board of the township or townships in which the library is located, or any other township. Such proposal shall state that said library is willing to combine with such township, townships or portions thereof, including towns or portions of towns not now being taxed for public library service to form a single town-township library district. On the receipt of such proposal the township trustee and advisory board may agree to such merger or upon petition of five per cent [5%] of the registered voters of the township, or portion of township, shall agree to such merger, unless a remonstrance against the same signed by as many registered voters of the township, or portion of the township, as have signed the petition shall be filed with the township trustee as hereinafter provided. Notice of the petition for acceptance of the proposal for merger shall be published within ten [10] days by the township trustee in a newspaper of general circulation in the township. Within ten [10] days after such publication any and every registered voter or group of registered voters shall have the right to sign and file with the township trustee and township advisory board their remonstrance against such acceptance of the proposal of merger. At the first meeting of the township advisory board and not less than ten [10] days after such publication, the advisory board shall consider said petition and such remonstrance and determine whether or not more registered voters of said township, or portion of a township, shall have signed the remonstrance than have signed the petition. If they determine that a greater number have signed the petition than have signed the remonstrance they shall agree to said merger, which shall become effective when record of said proposal and acceptance thereof shall be filed with the library board, the county recorder and the Indiana state library, such filing to be done within five [5] days. If, however, the township advisory board shall find that the number signing the remonstrance is greater, then the petition shall be dismissed and the township advisory board shall take no further action thereon except that a petition may again be presented one [1] year after the date on which the advisory board dismissed the last previous petition.

The library board of a town-township library district, organized under the provisions of this act [20-13-1-1—20-13-1-24], shall be composed of resident citizens who have resided for at least two [2] years in the library district, and shall consist of the following members:

(a) Three [3] members who shall be appointed by the judge of the circuit court of the county in which such library district is located, or if such district is located in more than one [1] county, jointly by the judges of the circuit courts of the respective counties, one [1] of whom shall be appointed for one [1] year, one [1] for two [2] years, and one [1] for three [3] years; and at least one [1] of whom shall be a woman.

(b) Two [2] members who shall be appointed by one or more of the following governing authorities as hereinafter provided: If (I) there is only one [1] town or civil city and one [1] township, one [1] member shall be appointed by the board of town trustees or the common council of the civil city for one [1] year and one [1] member shall be appointed by the township advisory board for two [2] years; or (II) if there is more than one [1] town or civil city or more than one [1] township then both appointments provided in this subsection shall be made by the board of county commissioners or if such district is located in more than one [1] county, jointly by the boards of county commissioners of the respective counties, one [1] for one [1] year and one [1] for two [2] years, at least one [1] of whom shall be a woman.

(c) Two [2] members who shall be appointed by the school board, board of school trustees or board of school commissioners, if any there be, and if such exist, of the school district in which the headquarters of the library district is located, one [1] of whom shall be appointed for a term of three [3] years and one [1] for four [4] years, at least one [1] of whom shall be a woman.

After the first appointments have been made all subsequent appointments shall be for a term of four [4] years. Appointments to fill vacancies created by death, resignation or otherwise shall be for the unexpired term only.

Any member of a library board created under this act shall be eligible to reappointment for not more than three [3] consecutive terms; however, a member of a library board as of July 1, 1965, may be appointed to not more than three [3] consecutive terms after that date. A board member may be removed at any time by the appointing authority, after public hearing, for any cause which interferes with the proper discharge of his duty as a member of such board or for cause which jeopardizes public confidence in the member. A vacancy shall occur whenever a member is absent from six [6] consecutive regular board meetings for any cause, other than illness, and the appointing authority shall be notified by the secretary of the board of the occurrence of such vacancy. All members of the board shall serve without compensation. No board member shall serve as a paid employee of the library. [Acts 1947, ch. 321, § 14b, as added by Acts 1953, ch. 13, § 5, p. 38; 1965, ch. 115, § 15, p. 157; 1967, ch. 123, § 6, p. 225.]

20-13-1-17 [41-915]. District library boards — Powers and duties.
— The library board of any library district organized under the provisions of this chapter shall manage and control all the affairs of the library. It shall have power to make all rules and regulations for the discharge of its responsibility. The library board shall have power, as such board:

(a) To take charge of, manage and conduct the library affairs of the library district, and to care for, manage and insure all property, real and personal, belonging to the library board of trustees.

(b) To establish and locate conveniently a sufficient number of libraries, branch libraries or stations to serve the library district, within the resources available, and to provide suitable rooms, structures, facilities, furniture, apparatus, and other articles and library appliances necessary for the thorough organization and efficient management of such libraries.

(c) To acquire by purchase, devise, lease or by condemnation or otherwise, and to own, and hold any land, real estate or interest therein and personal property for the uses and purposes of the library board.

(d) To sell, exchange, or otherwise dispose of property, both real and personal, no longer needed for library purposes.

(e) To accept gifts of realty or personalty and hold, use, mortgage, lease or sell such property as directed by the terms of the gift, bequest or devise when such action is in the interest of the library.

(f) To contract with other libraries or municipal corporations for the receipt or furnishing of library service.

(g) To provide for the purchase and loan of books and other media of communication, and for the dissemination of information to the citizens of the library district in any manner whatsoever.

(h) To issue, subject to the limitations of this chapter and subject to IC 6-1.1-20 [6-1.1-20-1 — 6-1.1-20-9], bonds for the purchase of realty and for the purchase or construction and equipment of structures with furniture, fixtures, supplies and personal property necessary for the efficient management of a library.

(i) To employ and discharge librarians, janitors, engineers and such other persons, employees and agents as may be necessary in the administration of the affairs of the library; to fix and pay their salaries and compensation; to classify them and adopt schedules of salaries; to determine their number and prescribe their duties; all with the advice and recommendations of the librarian as administrative head of the library; Provided, however, That appointments shall be made without regard to religious or political beliefs and with regard exclusively to merit and fitness and in conformity with IC 20-13-8 [20-13-8-1 — 20-13-8-12], and in conformity with other laws pertaining thereto.

(j) To issue, when necessary, warrants or tax anticipation bonds of not more than one [1] year's duration; and to borrow upon a temporary loan, upon the determination of the board so to do, any sum of money not to exceed fifty percent [50%] of the uncollected and anticipated taxes for the current year; to borrow money from other persons, firms, corporations, trust companies, banks and banking institutions; to issue, negotiate and sell negotiable notes and bonds of such library board and to levy, assess and collect, at the same time and in the same manner as other taxes of such library board are levied, assessed and collected, a special tax in addition to other taxes authorized by law to be levied sufficient to pay all yearly interest on the bonded and note indebtedness of such library board, and to provide a sinking fund for the liquidation of the principal thereof when it shall become due.

(k) To disburse according to law all moneys for all lawful library purposes, except that the purchase of books, magazines, pamphlets, films, filmstrips, microforms (microfilms), slides, transparencies, phonodiscs, phonotapes, models, art reproductions, and all other forms of library and audiovisual materials shall be exempt from the restrictions imposed by the law or laws governing public purchases.

(l) To establish a library improvement reserve fund, for the purpose of anticipating necessary future capital expenditures, and to accumulate moneys over a period of years in such fund for the purpose of financing such capital expenditures when they occur. The term "capital expenditures" as used in this chapter shall include the purchase of land, the purchase and construction of any building or structure, the construction of an addition or improvements to any existing structure, the purchase of equipment, and all repairs or replacements to buildings or equipment.

(m) To invest excess funds in interest-bearing securities of the United States, or any security lawfully issued by any county, township, city or other municipal corporation of the state of Indiana, or to deposit such funds in any duly chartered national or state bank whose deposits are insured by any federal agency: Provided, however, That no deposits shall be made in excess of the amount of insurance protection afforded a member or investor of any such institution.

(n) When the interests of the library require it, to authorize any member of the library board or any person in the employ of the library to be absent therefrom, and to pay out of its funds the necessary hotel and board bills and transportation expenses of such member or person while so absent in the interest of such library.

(o) To make, amend and repeal bylaws and rules for its procedure and for the government and management of the libraries of the corporation and to fix the time of meetings.

(p) To appropriate funds necessary to provide membership of the district in state and national associations of a civic, educational, professional or governmental nature which have as their purpose the betterment and improvement of library operations.

(q) The powers set forth in this section shall not be construed to limit the power and authority of such board to the powers herein expressly conferred or to restrict or modify any powers or authority granted by any other part of this chapter or any other law not in conflict with the provisions of this section. [Acts 1947, ch. 321, § 15, p. 1273; 1953, ch. 13, § 6, p. 38; 1965, ch. 115, § 17, p. 157; 1967, ch. 123, § 7, p. 225; 1977, P.L. 253, § 1, p. 1063; 1978, P.L. 115, § 1, p. 1096.]

20-13-1-18 [41-916]. **Administrative head of library—Selection by board—Qualifications—Compensation—Responsibility.**—The board shall select a librarian who shall be the administrative head of the library. The selection shall be in conformity with chapter 195 of the Acts of 1941 [20-13-8-1—20-13-8-12] and any subsequent amendments thereto and shall be made solely upon the basis of the candidate's training and proficiency in the science of library administration. The board shall fix the compensation of the librarian. The librarian, as the administrative head of the library, shall be solely responsible to the board for the operation and management of the library. [Acts 1947, ch. 321, § 16, p. 1273.]

20-13-1-19 [41-917]. **Free use of facilities — Fees and fines — Nonresidents.** — (a) When a library is maintained in whole or in part by public funds, the residents or property taxpayers of the municipal corporation or corporations taxed for the support of the library shall have the use of the facilities of the library without charge for library or related purposes. However, the library board may fix, establish and collect fees and rental charges, and may assess fines, penalties and damages for the loss of, injury to, or failure to return, any library property or material.

(b) For a reasonable fee, the library board of a library district which comes under this chapter may issue library cards to individuals who are residents of this state, who are not residents of the library district, and who apply for the cards. The reasonable fee or fees may be set by the library board on the basis of the various services to be rendered by the library to such individuals. [Acts 1947, ch. 321, § 17; 1978, P.L. 116, § 1; 1979, P.L. 221, § 1.]

20-13-1-20 [41-918]. Tax rate — Determined by library board — Certified to county auditor. — The library board shall determine and fix the rate of taxation of said library taxing district necessary for the proper operation of the library in amount of not less than five cents [$.05] or more than fifty-five cents [$.55] on each one hundred dollars [$100] of assessed value of taxable property. The library board shall certify the rate to the county auditor and the county auditor shall certify such tax rate to the county tax adjustment board in the same manner as other tax rates are certified.

If, however, the library board of any public library fails to give published notice to its taxpayers of its proposed budget and tax levy for the ensuing year at least twenty-one [21] days prior to the second Monday in September, or fails to finally adopt the budget and fix the tax levy at least two [2] days before the second Monday in September, then the last preceding annual appropriations made for any such public library shall be deemed to be continued and renewed for the ensuing year, and the last preceding annual tax levy continued; and, in such latter case, the treasurer of the library board shall report such continued tax levy to the county auditor, no later than two [2] days before the second Monday in September. [Acts 1947, ch. 321, § 18, p. 1273; 1955, ch. 12, § 3, p. 14; 1963, ch. 243, § 1, p. 360; 1965, ch. 115, § 18, p. 157; 1967, ch. 123, § 8, p. 225; 1969, ch. 364, § 3, p. 1507; 1971, P.L. 342, § 1, p. 1344; 1978, P.L. 117, § 1, p. 1100.]

20-13-1-20.1 [41-918a]. Appropriation of general revenue sharing funds to library board.—A county, township, city, or town may appropriate general revenue sharing funds which it receives under the State and Local Fiscal Assistance Act of 1972 [U.S.C., tit. 31, §§ 1221-1263] as amended, to a public library board organized under this chapter [20-13-1-1—20-13-1-24]. The local governmental unit shall make an appropriation to a public library board in the manner provided by law. Any general revenue sharing funds received by a public library board shall be deposited in any of the funds defined in IC 1971, 20-13-1-21 and the funds shall be budgeted and expended in the manner required by law. [IC 1971, 20-13-1-20.1, as added by Acts 1974, P. L. 101, § 1, p. 370.]

20-13-1-21   [41-919].   Use of tax funds — Treasurer's monthly report.—All money and securities of the library shall be kept in funds established by the library board as hereinafter provided:

(a)   All money collected from tax levies or securities now held or hereafter received, including, but not limited to, fees, fines, rentals or other revenues, shall, except as otherwise hereafter provided, be receipted into a fund to be known as the "library operating fund," which fund shall be budgeted and expended in the manner required by law.

(b)   All money received from the sale of bonds or other evidences of indebtedness for the purpose of construction, reconstruction or alteration of library buildings, except the premium and accrued interest thereon, shall be receipted into a fund to be known as the "construction fund." Such money so received shall be appropriated and expended solely for the purpose for which such indebtedness is created.

(c)   All money derived from the taxes levied for the purpose of retiring bonds or other evidence of indebtedness, together with any premium or accrued interest that may be received, shall be receipted into a fund to be known as the "bond and interest redemption fund." This fund shall be used for no other purpose than the payment of such indebtedness.

(d)   Money or securities kept in any library improvement reserve fund, established in accordance with the provisions of subsection (l) of section 15 [20-13-1-17] of this act, shall be kept in such fund and shall be appropriated and expended for the purposes therein provided.

(e)   Money or securities accepted and received by the library board as a gift, donation, endowment, bequest or trust may be set aside in a separate fund or funds, and shall be expended, without appropriation therefor, in accordance with and limited to the terms, conditions and purposes specified by the donor.

(f)   All moneys received in payment for library services or for library purchases made or to be made under the terms of a contract between two [2] or more libraries shall be receipted into a fund to be known as the "contractual service fund." Such money so received shall be expended solely for the purpose or purposes specified in said contract and shall be disbursed without further appropriation therefor. [Acts 1947, ch. 321, § 19, p. 1273; 1955, ch. 17, § 1, p. 34; 1967, ch. 123, § 9, p. 225.]

20-13-1-22.1.   Annual election of treasurer — Compensation — Duties and powers — Removal — Vacancy — Bond. — (a) The library board shall annually elect a treasurer of the library district who may be either a member of the library board or an employee of the library.

(b) Notwithstanding any other law, the library board may fix the rate of compensation for the services of the treasurer.

(c) The treasurer shall:

(1) Be the official custodian of all library funds;

(2) Keep the financial records of the library;

(3) Be responsible for the proper safeguarding and accounting for all library funds;

(4) Issue a receipt for moneys received by the library district;

(5) Deposit money belonging to the library district in accordance with the law governing the deposit of public funds;

(6) Except as otherwise provided by law, issue warrants which are approved by the library board in payment of expenses lawfully incurred in behalf of the library; and

(7) Make financial reports of library funds and present the reports to the library board as requested by the library board.

(d) The library board may prescribe the powers and duties of the treasurer consistent with the provisions of this chapter.

(e) The treasurer may be removed by the board at any regular or special meeting by a majority vote of the entire membership of the board.

(f) The board may elect a successor treasurer if a vacancy occurs in that office.

(g) The treasurer shall give a surety bond for the faithful performance of his duty and for the accurate accounting of all money coming into his custody. The bond shall be:

(1) Written by an insurance company licensed to do business in Indiana;

(2) For the term of office of the treasurer;

(3) In an amount determined by the library board;

(4) Paid for with the money from the library fund;

(5) Payable to the state of Indiana;

(6) Approved by the library board; and

(7) Deposited in the office of the recorder of the county in which the library district is located. [IC 20-13-1-22.1, as added by Acts 1981, P.L. 205, § 2.]

20-13-1-23 [41-920]. Bond issues — Authority — Purposes — Maximum issue — Sale — Status — Tax exempt — Use of funds from sale of bonds. — The board may, by resolution, authorize and issue bonds for any one or more of the following purposes:

(a) The acquisition or improvement of library sites.

(b) The acquisition, construction, extension, alteration or improvement of structures and equipment necessary for the proper operation of a library.

(c) To refund outstanding bonds and matured interest coupons, and issue and sell refunding bonds for that purpose.

The total bonds outstanding at any one [1] time shall not exceed two percent [2%] of the value of property taxable for library purposes or whatever the State Constitution allows, whichever is larger.

All bonds shall be advertised and sold by the board in compliance with IC 5-1-11 [5-1-11-1 — 5-1-11-7] at any interest rate. The bonds shall be payable at such times as the board shall fix in the authorizing resolution, but all shall be payable within a period not to exceed twenty [20] years from the date of issuance.

Bonds issued under the authority of this chapter shall not constitute a corporate obligation or indebtedness of any political subdivision in which the library is situated but shall constitute an indebtedness of the library taxing district only.

Bonds issued under the provisions of this chapter together with the interest thereon shall be tax exempt.

The board shall apply the proceeds from the sale of bonds only for the purpose for which the bonds were issued and to the extent necessary therefor, and any remaining balance shall be placed in a sinking fund for the payment of the bonds and the interest thereon. [Acts 1947, ch. 321, § 20, p. 1273; 1967, ch. 123, § 10; 1971, P.L. 343, § 1; 1981, P.L. 11, § 109.]

20-13-1-24 [41-921]. Future public libraries subject to act.—On and after the passage of this act [20-13-1-1—20-13-1-24] no public library shall be established in this state except under the provisions of this act. [Acts 1947, ch. 321, § 21, p. 1273.]

20-13-11-1 [41-911a]. Public library board—Appointment of additional members.—The public library boards of all county libraries accepting the provisions of the Library Law of 1947 [20-13-1-1—20-13-1-24] and now operating with public library boards composed of the members of the library board of the public library extending service to the county or to the county library district and four [4] additional members, two [2] to be appointed by the county commissioners and two [2] by the county superintendent of schools under the conditions and for the terms provided for such appointments in section 11 [20-13-1-11] of the Library Law of 1947, are hereby legalized and said libraries shall continue to operate as if such board had been regularly authorized by the Library Law of 1947 and all acts heretofore done by said board are to be considered as having been done by a regularly constituted library board of a public library. [Acts 1953, ch. 21, § 1, p. 84.]

20-13-21-1 [41-922]. Conversion of Class II libraries to Class I.—Any Class II library administered pursuant to chapter 321 of the Acts of 1947 [20-13-1-1—20-13-1-24], and the acts amendatory thereof, by a board of school trustees or school board of a consolidated school corporation created and organized pursuant to the provisions of chapter 123 of the Acts of 1947 [20-4-5-1—20-4-5-14], and the acts amendatory thereof, and which consolidated school corporation is composed of the territory located in a city of the second class and three [3] or more townships, may be converted to a library with all the attributes, rights, powers, and duties of a Class I library under said act by the adoption of a resolution of conversion by said board of school trustees or school board similar to the resolution provided in section seven [20-13-1-7] of said act. [Acts 1963, ch. 253, § 1, p. 382.]

20-13-21-2 [41-923]. Resolution—Recording and filing.—Upon the adoption of such resolution of conversion and the recording of the same in the office of the recorder of the county in which such consolidated school corporation is located, and the filing of the same with the state library said library shall be deemed so converted and shall be constituted a municipal corporation pursuant to chapter 321 of the Acts of 1947 [20-13-1-1—20-13-1-24], and the acts amendatory thereof, with a territory coterminous with the territory of such city of the second class. [Acts 1963, ch. 253, § 2, p. 382.]

20-13-21-3 [41-924]. Library board — Membership — Terms — Vacancies — Removal — Compensation. — Upon such conversion the library shall be governed and administered by a board composed of citizens who have resided for at least two [2] years in the library district and shall consist of two [2] members appointed by the mayor of the civil city and five [5] members appointed by the board of school trustees or school board of such consolidated school corporation, or a successor school corporation, if any. One [1] of the members appointed by the mayor shall be appointed for one [1] year and the other member shall be appointed for two [2] years. Of the members appointed by the board of school trustees or school board, one [1] shall be appointed for a term of one [1] year, two [2] for a term of three [3] years, and two [2] for a term of four [4] years. After the first appointments have been made, all subsequent appointments shall be for a term of four [4] years. It shall be lawful for the board of school trustees or school board to appoint one or more of their own members to membership on the library board. Terms of office shall commence as of July 1 next succeeding the respective dates of appointment and shall expire as of June 30 of the year of the ending of the term; Provided That interim members shall be appointed by the appointing authorities herein to serve from the date of conversion to the July 1 next succeeding the date of conversion. Appointments to fill vacancies created by death, resignation or otherwise shall be for the unexpired term only and any vacancies in membership of the library board shall be filled by the remaining membership, and the selection shall be made subject to the same qualifications and limitations that governed the selection of the member whose office is vacated.

Any member of a library board of a library converted under this act [20-13-21-1—20-13-21-5] shall be eligible to reappointment, but may be removed at any time by the appointing agency, after public hearing, for any cause which interferes with the proper discharge of his duty as a member of such board or for cause which jeopardizes public confidence in the member. A vacancy shall occur whenever a member is absent from six [6] consecutive regular board meetings for any cause, other than illness, and the appointing authority shall be notified by the secretary of the board of the occurrence of such vacancy. All members of the board shall serve without compensation. No board member shall serve as a paid employee of the library. [Acts 1963, ch. 253, § 3, p. 382.]

20-13-21-4 [41-925]. Certificate of appointment — Oath — Meetings — Officers — Quorum — Open meetings. — The appointing authority shall issue to each appointee a signed certificate of appointment. Within ten [10] days after the receipt of the certificate of appointment, the appointee shall qualify for his office by taking an oath of office before any person authorized by law to administer the same to the effect that he will faithfully discharge his duties to the best of his ability, and shall file the certificate of appointment, with the oath indorsed thereon, with the records of the library, which shall be preserved as a public record.

Upon the conversion of the library, the board shall meet upon the call of any two [2] appointees. The meeting shall be held within ten [10] days after all the appointees have qualified by taking the oath. The board shall elect from its members a president, a vice-president, a secretary, a treasurer, and such other officer or officers as the board may deem necessary. In the absence of the president the vice-president shall preside. A majority of the members shall constitute a quorum for the transaction of business. The board shall meet monthly and at such other times as may be necessary. All meetings of the board, except necessary executive sessions, shall be open to the public. [Acts 1963, ch. 253, § 4, p. 382.]

20-13-21-5 [41-926]. Powers and duties.—Upon the conversion of such library and the establishment of the library board as herein provided, said library and said library board shall have all of the rights and powers and shall perform all of the duties of a Class I library and the library board of a Class I library pursuant to the provisions of chapter 321 of the Acts of 1947 [20-13-1-1—20-13-1-24], and the acts amendatory thereof. [Acts 1963, ch. 253, § 5, p. 382.]

COUNTY LIBRARIES

(Burns Annotated Indiana Statutes, 1982, s.20-13-9-1 to 20-13-9-8,
20-13-10-1 to 20-13-10-6, 20-13-12-1 to 20-13-12-4.)

20-13-9-1 [41-510]. Free county library — Establishment — Library board. — The board of county commissioners of any county in which there is no free public tax supported library in any city or town may establish a county public library open and free to all the inhabitants of the county and levy a tax of not less than one tenth of a mill [$.0001] nor more than one mill [$.001] on the dollar [$1.00] on all taxable property assessed for taxation in such county; and on written petition of twenty-five [25] or more resident freeholders of each township in the county not already taxed for library purposes shall establish such library and levy such tax, unless a remonstrance against the same signed by as many or more resident freeholders of each such township as have signed said petition shall likewise be presented as hereinafter provided. Such petition shall be filed with the clerk of the circuit court and an attested copy of such petition shall be filed with (the clerk of the circuit court and an attested copy of such petition shall be filed with) the board of county commissioners. Thereupon notice of the filing shall be published by the auditor in two [2] newspapers published in said county, one [1] of which shall be published in the city or town wherein said library is petitioned for if any such newspaper there be, within ten [10] days after such petition has been filed. Any resident freeholder or freeholders may present and file with the auditor of said county a remonstrance or remonstrances stating that he or they are opposed to levying a tax and making an annual appropriation for said purpose of a public library. At the first meeting of the board of county commissioners and not less than ten [10] days after such publication, the board of commissioners shall consider the said petition and such remonstrances and determine whether or not resident freeholders of each township therein not already taxed for public purposes have signed and presented remonstrances equal to the number of such resident freeholders who signed and presented the petition for the same. And if they shall find that as many or more such resident freeholders have signed and filed remonstrances against the proposed public library as had signed and filed such petition then the proposed establishing of such county library shall be defeated and the board of commissioners shall take no further action in the matter. But if they shall find that the number of persons who signed and filed such petition was greater than the number of persons who signed and filed a remonstrance or remonstrances against the same then such board of commissioners shall establish a county public library in such city or town petitioned for, open and free to all the inhabitants of the county, and levy a tax of not less than one tenth of a mill [$.0001] nor more than one mill [$.001] on the dollar [$1.00] on all taxable property assessed for taxation in such county, and the auditor shall file a certified copy of the order levying such tax with the clerk of the circuit court. Within five [5] days after a tax for such library has been levied in such county, or such petition has been filed, the clerk of the circuit court of such county shall notify the judge of the circuit court, the county superintendent of schools and the board of county commissioners of such action. Within ten [10] days after these notices have been sent to such officials, the county commissioners shall appoint three [3] members, one [1] of whom shall be a woman, to the county public library board, the county superintendent of schools shall appoint three [3] members, one [1] of whom shall be a woman, and the judge of the circuit court shall appoint three [3] members, one [1] of whom shall be a woman. Of the appointment made by each official, one [1] shall be for a term of one [1] year, one [1] for [2] years, and one [1] for three [3] years. Not more than four [4] of the appointees shall reside in any one [1] township. The terms of office of all persons first appointed under this chapter [20-13-9-1—20-13-9-8] shall continue until January 15th following the date of their expiration as provided in this chapter and thereafter all appointments shall take effect on January 15th and shall be made for a term of three [3] years. All members of such public library board appointed as herein provided shall serve until their successors are appointed and qualified. The appointing officer or officers in making the appointment shall select persons of well known probity, integrity, business ability and experience and who are fitted for the character of the work they are to perform, and who shall have resided for a period of not less than one [1] year immediately preceding their appointment, in the county for which they are appointed, and who shall not be less than eighteen [18] years of age at the time of appointment, and who shall serve without compensation for service. In case of vacancy on such board from any cause it shall be the duty of the officer or board making such appointment to fill such vacancy occurring in the membership appointed by each respectively. [Acts 1917, ch. 45, § 1, p. 110; 1921, ch. 39, § 1, p. 107; 1927, ch. 220, § 1, p. 640; 1939, ch. 124, § 1, p. 642; 1973, P. L. 150, § 12, p. 768.]

20-13-9-2 [41-511]. Board members — Certificate — Oath. — All appointments to membership on the county library board shall be evidenced by certificates of appointment, duly signed by the officer or the clerk or secretary of the board making the appointment, and delivered to the appointee. Within ten [10] days after receiving such certificate such appointee shall qualify by taking an oath before some officer authorized to administer oaths that such appointee will faithfully discharge the duties as a member of the public library board to the best of his ability; and he shall file such certificate, with the oath indorsed thereon, with the clerk of the circuit court of the county in which such library is to be established. Such clerk shall thereupon make a record of such appointment and the term thereof. [Acts 1917, ch. 45, § 2, p. 110.]

20-13-9-3 [41-512]. **Organization — Powers — Duties — Funds. —**
The members appointed as in this act [20-13-9-1—20-13-9-8] provided, shall constitute and be known as the county library board. They shall meet within ten [10] days of their appointment and shall organize by electing a president, a vice-president, and a secretary. They shall have control and disbursement of the public funds for the use of the library from whatever source derived, and the custody and control of all the books and other property of every name and description, and shall have the power to purchase books, pamphlets, periodicals and other material and all necessary equipment, furniture and supplies, and direct all the affairs of such county public library; and such library board, in the name of the library, shall be empowered to receive donations, bequests and legacies, and to purchase, receive, sell and convey real estate and personal property for and on behalf of such library. They shall have the power to make and enforce rules for the management of such libraries as they may deem necessary, employ librarians, assistants, janitors and other employees, require official bonds, establish branches and deposit stations, issue or sell certificates or library cards to nonresidents, pay the expenses of delegates to library meetings, and do all things necessary to promote the interests of the library.

All county library money shall be held by the county treasurer and kept as a separate fund and deposited in the public depositories and all interest accruing thereon shall be credited to the library fund: Provided, That the library board may invest any gift, bequest, or devise in interest bearing securities. Such treasurer shall pay out library funds for library purposes only upon the warrant of the president of the library board, countersigned by the secretary thereof; and the president and secretary shall issue such warrant only upon itemized voucher which shall be accompanied by itemized bills, and which shall be certified as to correctness by the chairman of the finance committee of the library board and signed and sworn to by the librarian. The oath required may be administered by the secretary of the board and shall be administered without charge. The treasurer of such county shall be liable on his official bond for the faithful performance of the duties imposed upon him by this act.

In any county in which there now exists a county library fund, such fund shall become available for library purposes as soon as the county library board is organized as above required. [Acts 1917, ch. 45, § 3, p. 110.]

20-13-9-4 [41-513]. **City library — County aid. —** (a) Whenever the library board of any public library established in any city or incorporated town in this state shall file notice with the county council of any county of consent of such library board to make such library open and free to all the people of said county not already having free library privileges on the condition of the said county contributing to the support of such public library, such council may and upon petition of twenty-five [25] or more resident freeholders of each township in the county, not already taxed for public library purposes, shall make an annual appropriation and levy a tax of not less than one cent [1¢] nor more than ten cents [$.10] on each one hundred dollars [$100] of taxable property in the said county, including the property of any city or incorporated town in the county not already taxed for public library purposes, unless a remonstrance or remonstrances against the same signed by as many resident freeholders of each such township in the county as have signed the petition shall be filed with the county auditor as hereinafter stated.

(b) Upon the filing of any such petition of twenty-five [25] or more resident freeholders of each such township in the county, the county auditor shall cause notice of that fact to be published in two [2] newspapers of general circulation in the county, one [1] of which is published in such town or city wherein the library is located, if any there be. And within ten [10] days after such publication any and every resident freeholder or group of resident freeholders shall have the right to sign and file with the county auditor their remonstrance or remonstrances against giving such aid, stating therein that he or they are opposed to levying a tax and making an annual appropriation for said purposes of a public library.

(c) At the first meeting of the county council and not less than ten [10] days after such publication, the council shall proceed to consider and determine the matters thus presented as provided in section 1 [20-13-9-1] of this chapter. And if said council shall determine that a greater number of resident freeholders have signed the petition than the number who have signed a remonstrance or remonstrances against the levy of such tax and the making of such annual appropriation they shall thereupon make an annual appropriation and levy a tax as above provided and the county treasurer shall collect and pay the sum into the treasury of the city or town where such library is located to be held as part of the library fund and to be paid out in the same manner as other library funds. But if the county council shall not so find, then the petition or petitions shall be dismissed and the council shall take no further action.

(d) Said tax if imposed shall be continued so long as ten percent [10%] of the inhabitants of said county outside the limits of said city or town are found to be users of said library, or when less than ten percent [10%] of the inhabitants shall use the said library, the county council may, at its discretion, continue the tax herein specified. [Acts 1917, ch. 45, § 4, p. 110; 1921, ch. 39, § 2, p. 107; 1939, ch. 124, § 2, p. 642; 1981, P.L. 11, § 116.]

20-13-9-5 [41-514]. City library board — Members appointed by county commissioners—Number.—If the board of county commissioners shall levy a tax for library purposes as provided in section four [20-13-9-4] of this act, then such county commissioners shall within ten [10] days appoint two [2] persons, one [1] of whom shall be a woman, residing in some part of said county which is contributing a tax for the support of a county library, outside the limits of the city or town in which such library is located, not otherwise appointed, as members of

said public library board, who with the members of such city or town
public library board shall constitute a public library board for the
county from which they are appointed, and such appointment shall be
for a period of two [2] years, and the county superintendent of schools
likewise shall appoint two [2] such members with qualifications as above
provided for a period of one [1] year and three [3] years, respectively.
After the first appointment all appointments shall be made for a term
of two [2] years. The members so appointed shall have the same qualifications and equal authority with other members of the public library
board in the levying and expending of county taxes and in the maintaining of library service to the inhabitants of the county from which
they were appointed. [Acts 1917, ch. 45, § 5, p. 110; 1921, ch. 39, § 3,
p. 107; 1939, ch. 124, § 3, p. 642.]

20-13-9-6 [41-515]. Tax levy.—It shall be the duty of the county
library board as organized under any section of this act [20-13-9-1—
20-13-9-8], to determine annually the rate of taxation that shall
be necessary to establish, increase, equip and maintain the public library, and certify the same to the board of county commissioners, and
to the county auditor: Provided, That said levy shall not be less than
two tenths of a mill [$.0002] and not more than one mill [$.001] on
each dollar [$1.00] of all the taxable property assessed for taxation in
such county, city, town or township, as shown by the tax duplicate for
the year immediately preceding the fixing of such levy. When the levy
for such public library purposes shall be certified to the board of county
commissioners and the county auditor by the county library board, the
same shall be placed upon the tax duplicate of such county, and collected in like manner as other county taxes are levied and collected.
[Acts 1917, ch. 45, § 6, p. 110; 1921, ch. 39, § 4, p. 107.]

20-13-9-7 [41-516]. Combination of city and county libraries.—In
any county in this state in which there shall hereafter be established a
county library, the library board of any existing public library in any
incorporated town or city, or of any township or townships or any
combination thereof, may, with the consent of the county library board,
pay over to the county library board the income from any or all sources
on the condition that said county library board shall have full power in
management of and shall maintain such city or town or township library as a branch of the county library and that the inhabitants of
such city, town, township or townships shall have all the privileges of
said county library; and that such library shall remain a part of such
county library as long as ten per cent [10%] of the inhabitants of such
city, town, township or townships shall be users of the county library
through said branch. [Acts 1917, ch. 45, § 7, p. 110.]

20-13-9-8 [41-517]. Liability of commissioners and board.—If any
board of county commissioners or any board contributing to said library
shall fail or refuse to levy the library tax provided for herein, the
members of such board shall become jointly and severally liable for the
amount such levy would produce on the assessment of such county if
fully collected, and the same shall be recovered from them in suit by
any taxpayer of such county on behalf of the treasurer thereof, and

shall be included in the funds of such library in lieu of such law [levy]. [Acts 1917, ch. 45, § 8, p. 110.]

20-13-10-1 [41-501]. Establishment of county public libraries.—To establish and maintain a public library in each of the several counties, for the use of the inhabitants thereof, there shall be reserved ten per cent [10%] of the net proceeds [of the sale] of all lots within the town, where the county seat is situate, sold as the property of such county, and ten per cent [10%] upon all donations made to procure the location of such county seat; and the county commissioners shall make the necessary order for the collection and payment of the same. [1 R. S. 1852, ch. 63, § 1, p. 353.]

20-13-10-2 [41-502]. Annual appropriations.—The board of commissioners doing county business, may at their June session in each year, appropriate a sum not less than twenty [$20.00] nor more than seventy-five dollars [$75.00] for the purchase of books, maps and charts for such library, and the same shall be paid to the treasurer of the library, by the treasurer of the county, upon the certificate of the auditor thereof. [1 R. S. 1852, ch. 63, § 2, p. 353.]

20-13-10-3 [41-503]. Trustees—Duties.—The clerk, auditor, and recorder shall have the charge of such library, and are hereby constituted trustees for that purpose. They shall elect one [1] of their number treasurer, and a suitable person librarian, and shall prepare a proper room, with the necessary shelves, and cases, within some county office, or building when practicable, to place and safely keep such library. They shall cause all moneys appropriated or belonging to the library, to be expended in the purchase of books, charts and maps, and report to the board of county commissioners in June annually, the kind and number of books purchased, with the cost thereof. Each of said officers shall be liable on his official bond for the performance of duties herein required of him. [1 R. S. 1852, ch. 63, § 3, p. 353.]

20-13-10-4 [41-504]. Who may use books.—Every inhabitant of the county giving satisfactory evidence or security for the safekeeping and return of books, shall be entitled to take and use the same upon the proper application to the librarian. But no one [1] person shall at the same time have more than two [2] volumes of books, nor for a longer period than forty [40] days, without returning such books to the library. [1 R. S. 1852, ch. 63, § 4, p. 353.]

20-13-10-5 [41-505]. By-laws—Fines.—The trustees shall establish by-laws, and rules for the regulation of such library, and the same shall be placed at a conspicuous point in the library room, for the inspection of visiters [visitors]. All fines or forfeitures accruing from the violation of such by-laws shall be recoverable in an action before any court of competent jurisdiction in the name of the state of Indiana, for the use of such library; and the librarian shall be a competent witness in such action, and the entries made upon his books, in relation to such library, shall be prima facie evidence of the things therein charged. [1 R. S. 1852, ch. 63, § 5, p. 353.]

20-13-10-6   [41-506].   Duties of librarian.—The librarian shall make an entry in a proper book, of each book or map taken, the time thereof, by whom and when returned. He shall also keep a registry of the fines and penalties assessed, and collect the same by suit or otherwise. At the June session of the board of county commissioners in each year, he shall report the condition of such library, the books added, or lost, within the preceding year, and the value of the same. [1 R. S. 1852, ch. 63, § 6, p. 353.]

20-13-12-1   [41-520].   Transfer of books, documents, and library funds to Indiana Historical Society.—The books, documents and records constituting the county library of any county contemplated in this act [20-13-12-1—20-13-12-4], and the unexpended and unencumbered balance of the county library fund of any such county, may be transferred to the Indiana Historical Society, chartered by act of the general assembly, approved January 10, 1831, in the manner hereinafter prescribed in this act. [Acts 1931, ch. 62, § 1, p. 148.]

20-13-12-2   [41-521].   "County library" defined.—The term "county library" as used in this act [20-13-12-1—20-13-12-4] shall be construed to mean any county library which was established and which has been and is being operated, conducted, managed, financed and/or maintained under, pursuant to and in compliance with the provisions of any or either of the following enumerated acts:

Chapter 72 of the laws of the sixth general assembly; or

Chapter 36 of the special acts of the fifteenth general assembly; or

Chapter 11 of the local laws of the nineteenth general assembly; or

Chapter 148 of the local laws of the twenty-sixth general assembly; or

Chapter 128 of the local laws of the twenty-seventh general assembly; or

Chapter 178 of the local laws of the twenty-eighth general assembly; or

Chapter 71 of the acts of the forty-first general assembly. [Acts 1931, ch. 62, § 2, p. 148.]

20-13-12-3   [41-522].   Procedure for transfer.—The board of county commissioners, on recommendation of the library board of any county library contemplated in this act [20-13-12-1—20-13-12-4], may enter an order on the proper records of such board of county commissioners, transferring all right, title and possession in and to the books, documents and records constituting such county library to the said Indiana Historical Society. [Acts 1931, ch. 62, § 3, p. 148.]

20-13-12-4   [41-523].   Balance of library fund—Transfer.—If, at the time when the right, title and possession in and to the books, documents and records constituting such county library is transferred to the said Indiana Historical Society, there are any funds in the treasury of such county belonging to and constituting the fund of such county library, the board of commissioners of such county shall likewise enter an order that such fund shall be paid to the Indiana Historical Society and shall direct the treasurer of the board of trustees of such county library to draw his warrant for the full amount of the unexpended and unencumbered balance of such fund so remaining in the county treasury. Such warrant shall be drawn in favor of the Indiana Historical Society. The money so paid to the Indiana Historical Society shall be kept as a separate and distinct fund until expended and books and other material of historical value purchased either out of such fund or out of income derived from it shall be so labeled as to clearly indicate the source from which the purchase money is derived. [Acts 1931, ch. 62, § 4, p. 148.]

MUNICIPAL LIBRARIES
Cities and Towns
(Burns Annotated Indiana Statutes, 1982, s.20-13-2-1 to 20-13-2-13.)

20-13-2-1 [41-301]. Tax levy — Subscriptions. — The common council of any city or the town board of any incorporated town within this state desiring to establish, increase and maintain a public library in such city or town, open to and for the use and benefit of all the inhabitants thereof, may levy a tax annually of not to exceed one mill [$.001] on each dollar [$1.00] of all the taxable property assessed for taxation in such city or town; Provided, however, That the board of town trustees of any town having a population of less than five thousand [5,000], as shown by the last preceding United States census, may levy a tax annually of not to exceed two mills [$.002] on each dollar [$1.00] of all the taxable property assessed for taxation in such town, as shown by the tax duplicate for the year immediately preceding the fixing of such levy, which tax shall be placed on the tax duplicate of such city or town and collected in the same manner as other taxes are levied and collected, and such levy shall be certified to the auditor of the county. If the common council of such city, or the town board of such incorporated town do not make such levy they shall do so at the next ensuing levy, and annually thereafter, after taxpayers of such city or town raise by popular subscription for each of the two [2] years immediately following the date of the completion of such subscription, a sum of money equal to the amount that would be derived from a tax levy of the two tenths of a mill [$.0002] on each dollar [$1.00] of the taxable property assessed for taxation in such city or town, as shown by the tax duplicate immediately preceding the completion of such subscription: Provided, That no more than two per cent [2%] of the entire amount necessary to be subscribed shall be subscribed by any one [1] person, firm or corporation of such city or incorporated town. The amount of money so subscribed as herein provided, for library purposes, shall be made to fall due and be payable in eight [8] equal quarterly instalments. The first instalment shall become due and payable on the first Monday of the second month following the date of the completion and filing of such subscription, as hereinafter provided, and one [1] instalment shall become due and payable on the first Monday of each third month thereafter, till all of such subscription is paid. The subscriptions shall be collected by the public library board, hereby created, as hereinafter provided. [Acts 1901, ch. 55, § 1, p. 81; 1903, ch. 169, § 1, p. 301; 1945, ch. 40, § 1, p. 84.]

20-13-2-2 [41-302]. Subscription list. — The subscription list for

said money shall be filed with the clerk of the circuit court of the county
in which such city or incorporated town is located. The said clerk of the
court immediately thereafter shall notify the judge of the circuit court
of said county that such subscription has been filed, and he shall likewise notify the common council or town board and the board of school
trustees of such city or town proposing to establish a public library,
that said subscription has been filed. The original subscription list shall
be preserved by the clerk of the circuit court and by him placed in the
hands of the public library board, when the board shall have been appointed as hereinafter provided. [Acts 1901, ch. 55, § 2, p. 81.]

20-13-2-3 [41-303]. Examination of list — Library board — Tax. —
(a) Within ten [10] days after said judge of the circuit court shall have been
notified, as above provided, that such subscription list has been filed with
the clerk of the circuit court, if one has been filed to secure the levying of
such tax, or that the common council has certified to such clerk that the levy
as provided herein has been made, it shall be the duty of said judge to
examine such subscription list and if it be found that an amount of solvent
subscription has been made equal to the amount required by section 1
[20-13-2-1] of this chapter, then he shall order a copy of such subscription list
spread upon the records of said court, and he shall appoint three [3] persons,
residents of such city or town, as members of such public library board, one
[1] of whom he shall appoint for one [1] year, one [1] for two [2] years and
one [1] for three [3] years, from the date of their appointment, and after the
first appointment all appointments made by the judge of the court shall be
for a period of two [2] years; and all appointments so made by the judge of
the court shall be entered in the order books of said court.

(b) If the township advisory board of any township shall levy and collect
a tax for library purposes the total amount of which tax shall be greater than
the amount of tax collected by the town or city for said library purposes, and
pay the same into the treasury of the city or town where a library is located
and otherwise avail themselves of the provisions of this chapter as
hereinafter provided, then and in that event the judge, in appointing the
members of such public library board, at any time thereafter, may appoint
persons who are residents of such city or town or of such township outside
of such city or town.

(c) Within ten [10] days after the common council or the town board and
the board of school trustees shall have been notified, as in section 2
[20-13-2-2] of this chapter, each body shall appoint two [2] persons also
residents of such city or town, not otherwise appointed as members of such
board, who shall become members of such public library board. The members
so appointed by the common council or town board for the first appointment
under this chapter shall serve for a period of one [1] year, and after the first
appointment all appointments made by the common council or town boards
shall be for a period of two [2] years. The board of school trustees shall
appoint its members for a term of two [2] years, who may be from their own
board.

(d) If the township advisory board of any township shall levy and collect for library purposes five tenths of a mill [$.0005] on each dollar [$1.00] of all the taxable property assessed for taxation in said township, as shown by the tax duplicate for the year immediately preceding the fixing of such levy, exclusive of the property of such city or town already taxed for said library, and pay the same into the treasury of such city or town where such library is located, then in such case the township trustee shall, ex officio, be a member of such public library board, and the judge of the circuit court of the vicinity in which such township is located shall appoint one [1] person, a resident of said township, not otherwise appointed, as a member of said public library board, who shall become a member of such public library board, and such appointment by such judge shall be for a period of two [2] years, and all members of such public library board appointed as herein provided, shall serve until their successors are appointed and qualified: Provided, That women may be eligible to appointment as members of such library board and not less than three [3] of the members appointed shall be women.

(e) The judge, common council or town board, and the board of school trustees, in making the appointments, shall select persons of well known probity, integrity, business ability and experience, and who are fitted for the character of the work they are to perform and who shall have resided for a period of not less than two [2] years, immediately preceding their appointment in the city or town for which they are appointed, in the case of members appointed by the common council or town board and school trustees, and in the township in the case of the member appointed by the judge of the circuit court as hereinbefore provided and in the city, town or township in the case of the members appointed by the judge, and who shall not be less than eighteen [18] years of age at the time of appointment, and who shall serve without compensation for service.

(f) In case of vacancy on such board from any cause, it shall be the duty of said judge, common council or town board and board of school trustees to fill such vacancy occurring in the membership appointed by each respectively. [Acts 1901, ch. 55, § 3, p. 81; 1903, ch. 169, § 2, p. 301; 1911, ch. 241, § 1, p. 607; 1917, ch. 44, § 1, p. 108; 1921, ch. 192, § 1, p. 499; 1973, P.L. 150, § 11; 1981, P.L. 11, § 110.]

20-13-2-4 [41-304]. **Certificates — Oaths.** — All appointments to membership on the public library board shall be evidenced by certificates of appointment, duly signed by the judge as to members appointed by him, by the mayor or president of the town board and by the president of the board of school trustees as to members respectively appointed by them, which certificates of appointment shall be handed to or mailed to the address of the appointee. Within ten [10] days after receiving such certificates of appointment such appointees shall qualify by taking the oath of office before the clerk of the court that such appointee will faithfully discharge the duties as a member of the public library board to the best of his ability, and shall file such certificate, with the oath indorsed thereon, with the clerk of the circuit court of the county in which such library is to be established. [Acts 1901, ch. 55, § 4, p. 81; 1903, ch. 169, § 3, p. 301; 1921, ch. 192, § 2, p. 499.]

20-13-2-5 [41-305]. Organization of board.—Within five [5] days after all the members of such board shall have been appointed and qualified, they shall meet and organize by electing one [1] of their number president, one [1] vice-president and one [1] secretary, and shall select such committees or executive board as they may deem necessary to carry on the work of the board. [Acts 1901, ch. 55, § 5, p. 81.]

20-13-2-6 [41-306]. Powers of board — Public library board — Issuance, sale, and payment of bonds. — (a) The seven [7] members thus appointed shall constitute and be known as the public library board and shall have the control of the public library funds, and the custody and control of all the books and other property of every name and description, and shall have the power to direct all the affairs of such public library; and such public library board, in the name of the library, shall be empowered to receive donations, bequests and legacies, and to receive, acquire by purchase, or otherwise, and convey real estate, including both lands and buildings or parts thereof, for and on behalf of such library, and may construct and equip buildings, create a sinking fund, issue bonds, which sinking fund shall be created, and bonds issued, subject to to the approval of the city council or the town board, and provide for the retirement of said bonds and the payment of the interest accruing thereon, and shall be entitled to receive from the state library, copies of all documents and publications of the state available for distribution. They shall have the power to make and enforce rules for management of such libraries as they may deem necessary, and to employ librarians and assistants.

(b) Whenever the public library board has constructed or otherwise obtained a new building for library purposes, the public library board may sell and convey the building previously used and occupied for the public library, together with the land on which the same is situated; and the funds derived from such sale shall be under the control and disbursement of the public library board, for the use of the library, the same as other library funds.

(c) Subject to the approval of the city council or board of town trustees, the library board is hereby authorized and empowered to issue, negotiate and sell the bonds of such library board in such amounts and denominations as such library board may deem advisable, but in a face amount in the aggregate not in excess of one-half of one percent [½%] on the value of the taxable property of such city or town. Such bonds shall be known as "Public Library Bonds" and shall be payable at such places and at such times as such board may determine and as may be stated in the bonds, and they shall bear interest at any rate, payable annually or semiannually, as said board may determine, for which interest coupons may be attached to said bonds; and said bonds may be negotiated and delivered at any marketplace at not less than their par value. The full term for which such public library bonds shall run shall be fifteen [15] years from the date of issuance thereof, but said bonds may be issued in a series so that such portion thereof as said board may determine may be made to mature at the end of any year within such period, or such bonds may be issued so that one-fifteenth [1/15] thereof shall fall due at the end of each year and the portion so falling due, together with the interest thereon, shall, when due, be paid and canceled. Such bonds may be issued all at one [1] time or from time to time but no bonds issued under the authority of this chapter shall be delivered until the money therefor shall have been paid to the treasurer of the board issuing them and interest thereon shall begin to accrue at the time of such delivery.

(d) Preparatory to offering such bonds for sale by any such board, such board shall give notice for not less than three [3] weeks of the date fixed for the sale of such bonds, and in the notice give a brief description of the bonds and the mode of bidding and invite bids therefor. Such notice shall be given by advertisement once each week for three [3] successive weeks in one or more newspapers of general circulation published in the city in which such library is located, the last of which publications shall be at least one week before the date fixed for the sale of such bonds, or if no paper is published therein, then by such other means of advertising as such board may prescribe. The said board shall sell such bonds to the highest or best bidder, but shall have the right to reject any and all bids.

(e) The proceeds arising from all sales of bonds made in pursuance of this chapter shall be used only for the purposes or for one or more of the purposes hereinbefore mentioned as the purposes for which such bonds are authorized to be issued. The bonds issued under the provisions of this chapter shall not in any respect be a corporate obligation or indebtedness of the city or town in which such library board is located and acting, but shall be and constitute an indebtedness of the library board only. Such bonds and the interest thereon shall be payable only out of the funds of the library board, and such bonds shall so recite such terms upon their face together with the purposes for which they are issued. Such bonds, when issued, shall be exempt from taxation. When such bonds have been sold, the proceeds from such sale shall be held and disbursed as other library funds.

(f) Any sinking fund created in accordance with the provisions of this chapter may be accumulated over a period of years to provide for the construction of extensions of or additions to buildings in the future or to pay the bonds which are issued, together with the interest which may accrue thereon. No part of the sinking fund shall be used for any purpose other than the payment of bonds and the interest which will accrue thereon unless the use of any part of such fund will not affect the ability of the board to pay the bonds as they mature, together with the accrued interest. In providing for the issuance of bonds, the board shall compute the maximum amount which will be available each year from the tax levy herein authorized to apply on the payment of bonds and shall so issue the bonds that there will be sufficient funds on hand at maturity to redeem such bonds so falling due, together with the interest accruing thereon. [Acts 1901, ch. 55, § 6, p. 81;

1913, ch. 233, § 1, p. 657; 1927, ch. 178, § 1, p. 528; 1929, ch. 184, § 1, p. 595; 1981, P.L. 11, § 111.]

20-13-2-7 [41-307]. Assessment and collection of tax for library purposes. — (a) When such public library board shall have organized for the transaction of business, there shall be placed in its hands by the clerk of the circuit court, the original subscription list, if any has been made, for the procuring of the levy of the tax as herein provided, and it shall be the duty of such library board to collect quarterly all money subscribed, as the same becomes due, as provided for in section 1 [20-13-2-1] of this chapter, and pay the same into the treasury of such town or city, and to expend the same in the establishment, equipment, enlargement and management of a public library in the manner as provided for in section 8 [20-13-2-8] of this chapter which shall be open to and for the use and benefit of all the inhabitants of the city or town in which the same is located, and such library board may use such sum for the purchase of a building site and the erection of a library building and the creation of a sinking fund for the payment of any bonds which shall have been issued, or any other lawful purpose, as the board may decide.

(b) It shall be the duty of such library board to determine the rate of taxation that shall be necessary to establish, increase, equip and maintain the public library and pay any outstanding bonds and certify the same to the common council or town board and the county auditor: Provided, That said levy shall not exceed ten cents [$.10] on each one hundred dollars [$100] of all the taxable property assessed for taxation in such city or town as shown by the tax duplicate for the year immediately preceding the fixing of such levy. When the assessment for such public library purposes shall be certified to the common council or town board and the auditor, by the public library board, the same shall be placed on the tax duplicate of such county and city or town and collected in like manner as other taxes are levied and collected. [Acts 1901, ch. 55, § 7, p. 81; 1903, ch. 169, § 4, p. 301; 1927, ch. 178, § 2, p. 528; 1981, P.L. 11, § 112.]

20-13-2-8 [41-308]. Use of fund — Duty of treasurer. — The tax so levied as provided for in sections 1 [20-13-2-1] and 7 [20-13-2-7] of this chapter shall be held and kept as a separate fund by the fiscal officer (or county treasurer acting under IC 36-4-10-6) of such city or incorporated town for public library purposes, as herein provided, and he shall pay out the same for library purposes only upon the warrant of the president of the library board, countersigned by the secretary thereof. The fiscal officer (or county treasurer) shall be liable on his official bond for the faithful performance of the duties imposed upon him by this chapter. All library money held by him under this chapter shall be by him kept as a separate fund and deposited in the public depositories of such city or town, and all interest accruing thereon shall be credited to the library fund. [Acts 1901, ch. 55, § 8, p. 81; 1919, ch. 25, § 1, p. 61; 1981, P.L. 11, § 113.]

20-13-2-9 [41-309]. Use of library. — (a) When a public library shall have been established in any city or incorporated town in this state under this chapter, such library shall be open and free for the use and benefit of all the inhabitants of the township in which such library shall be located, provided the township advisory board of the township in which such library is located, shall levy and collect a tax of two cents [2¢] on each one hundred dollars [$100] of all the taxable property assessed for taxation in said township, as shown by the tax duplicate for the year immediately preceding the fixing of such levy, exclusive of the property of such city or town already taxed for said library, and collect and pay the same into the treasury of such city or town where such library is located, to be held in such treasury as a part of the public library fund.

(b) Said library shall remain open and free for the use and benefit of all the inhabitants of such township, so long as said tax as herein provided and specified shall be levied, collected and paid into the treasury of such city or town for the use of said library board for the purpose herein named. When the public library of any city or town is not so open and free for the use and benefit of the inhabitants of any township, by reason of such township failing to levy and collect the tax herein required, the public library board may issue and sell certificates or library cards to any person or family resident in such township at such annual fee as may be deemed by them to be a fair compensation for such privilege, and such library cards shall give to the purchaser thereof the same rights and privileges as the inhabitants of the city or incorporated town. [Acts 1901, ch. 55, § 9, p. 81; 1981, P.L. 11, § 114.]

20-13-2-10 [41-312]. Tender of library—Appointing board.—If any city or incorporated town in this state where a library of the value of an amount equal to the amount of money that would be derived from a tax levy of three tenths of a mill [$.0003] on each dollar [$1.00] of valuation of the taxable property within such city or town assessed for taxation, as shown by the preceding tax duplicate of said city or town, is already established and maintained under the existing laws of this state, and whenever the managing board of such library already so existing and maintained shall tender the ownership, custody and control of said library free of expense, to such public library board for the use and purpose of a public library, as contemplated by this act [20-13-2-1—20-13-2-13], which tender of custody and control thereof shall be evidenced by a certificate issued by the managing board thereof and filed in triplicate with the clerk of the circuit court of the county wherein said city or town is located, with the clerk of said city or town and the secretary of the board of school trustees, in the manner and form as prescribed in the certificates of popular subscription contained in section two [20-13-2-2] of this act, which certificate shall show the value of such library, a public library board shall be appointed (as) in the manner as set forth in this act, except such board shall be appointed only when the common council or town board have decided by a majority vote of the members thereof to accept such library and to levy annually and collect a tax as other taxes are levied and collected and not to exceed one mill [$.001] on each dollar [$1.00] of valuation of taxable property of such city or town, as herein specified. Said council or town board shall certify its said decision of acceptance, attested by the clerk of said city or town, and the mayor of such city or president of such town board, to the judge of the circuit court and the secretary of the said board of school trustees, whereupon said judge, city council or town board and board of school trustees shall proceed to appoint said public library board in the manner and form and to all intents and purposes as is done by the voluntary levy of such tax by the council or town board, or the popular subscriptions filed with the clerk of the court as hereinbefore provided. [Acts 1901, ch. 55, § 10, p. 81; 1903, ch. 169, § 5, p. 301.]

20-13-2-11   [41-313].   Removing members.—The judge of the circuit court, the common council or town board and the board of school trustees may at any time, for cause shown, remove any member of such library board that may have been appointed by each, respectively, and fill the vacancy occasioned thereby as provided for in section three [20-13-2-3] of this act. [Acts 1901, ch. 55, § 11, p. 81.]

20-13-2-12   [41-314].   Reports of treasurer. — The fiscal officer (or county treasurer acting under IC 36-4-10-6) of such city or incorporated town, operating libraries under this chapter, shall make and file with the common council or the town board thereof, not later than January 15 of each year, an itemized statement, under oath, of all the receipts and disbursements of such public library board for the year ending December 31, immediately preceding the making and filing of such report, and such report shall contain an itemized statement of the sources of all receipts, all disbursements made and the purpose for which the same were made, and such annual report shall be open to inspection of the citizens of such city or town, and also, the township in which such city or town is located, providing the township has complied with section 9 [20-13-2-9] of this chapter. [Acts 1901, ch. 55, § 12, p. 81; 1981, P.L. 11, § 115.]

20-13-2-13   [41-315].   Repeal—Limitation.—All laws and parts of laws in conflict with the provisions of this act [20-13-2-1—20-13-2-13] are hereby repealed: Provided, That this act shall not interfere with the maintenance or management of any existing library already established and operating under the laws of this state. [Acts 1901, ch. 55, § 13, p. 81.]

Township Libraries

(Burns Annotated Indiana Statutues, 1982, s.20-13-17-1, 20-13-17-2,
20-13-18-1.)

20-13-17-1   [41-603].   Township library tax.—The advisory board of any township desiring to establish and maintain a public library open to and for the free use of all the inhabitants thereof, may levy a tax annually of not more than one mill [$.001] on each dollar [$1.00] of taxable property assessed for taxation in such township. If the advisory board do [does] not make such levy, then, on the written petition of fifty [50] legal voters of any township filed with the county clerk not less than fifteen [15] days prior to a township election, the county board of election commissioners shall cause to be printed on the township ballots for such township' the words: "For a township library tax." "Yes." "No." If in the election a majority of the votes cast on said question shall be in the affirmative, the township trustee shall thereafter levy annually a tax of not less than five tenths of a mill [$.0005] nor more than one mill [$.001] on each dollar [$1.00] of the property taxable in said township for the establishment and support of a township library free to all inhabitants of such township, which tax shall be levied, assessed, collected and paid as other township taxes are levied, assessed, collected and paid: Provided, That after such library has been established such tax levy shall be discontinued when, under the above provision, the question of discontinuing such levy shall have been submitted to a vote and the majority of the votes cast on said question shall be in the negative: Provided further, That if there be located in said township a public library open to the use of all the inhabitants thereof, then the proceeds of said tax shall be paid to said public library. Be it further enacted, that in any township outside of cities in which there has been or may hereafter be established by private donations a library of the value of ten thousand dollars [$10,000] or more, including the real estate and buildings used for such library, for the use and benefit of all the inhabitants thereof, the township trustee of such township shall annually levy and collect not more than six cents [6c] on the hundred dollars [$100], upon the taxable property within the limits of such township, which shall be paid to the trustees of such library, and be applied by them to the purchase of books for said library and to the cost of the maintenance thereof, and said trustee may, with the consent of the board of commissioners of the county, when it shall become necessary to purchase additional ground for the extension or protection of library buildings already established by such private donation, annually levy and collect not more than five cents [5c] on the hundred dollars [$100] upon all taxable property of said township for not more than three [3] years successively, which shall be expended by said trustees in the purchase of said property and the erection and enlargement of library building thereon. [Acts 1899, ch. 103, § 7, p. 134; 1911, ch. 50, § 1, p. 73.]

20-13-17-2 [41-604]. Library board. — In any township where a free public library is established as above provided, there shall be established a township library board composed of the school township trustee and two [2] residents of the township, to be appointed by the judge of the circuit court (one [1] of whom shall be a woman). Of the first two [2] members of such board so appointed, one [1] shall be appointed for a term of two [2] years and one [1] for four [4] years, and thereafter the term of office shall be four [4] years. Such library board shall have control of the purchase of books and the management of such library, and shall serve without compensation. Said library shall be the property of the school township, and the school township trustee shall be responsible for the safe preservation of the same. Said board shall be entitled to the possession and custody of any books remaining in the old township library in such township; and such board shall be empowered to receive donations, bequests and legacies for and on behalf of such library, and shall be entitled to receive from the public library commission and state librarian copies of all documents of this state available for distribution. Two [2] or more adjacent townships may unite to establish and maintain a public library at the discretion of the advisory boards, and when two [2] or more townships have so united, the combined library boards appointed as herein specified or the board of the public library to which such money is paid as herein provided, shall control the library so established. [Acts 1899, ch. 103, § 8, p. 134; 1911, ch. 50, § 2, p. 73.]

20-13-18-1 [41-608]. Transfer of township library.—In any township in this state in which there has been or may hereafter be established by private donations a library of the value of one thousand dollars [$1,000], or more, for the use and benefit of all the inhabitants thereof, the board of commissioners of the county in which such township is situated, may, upon due proof thereof, by proper order entered upon its records, abolish the office of township librarian and require and order that the township library in the hands of the township trustee, or the librarian thereof (including all the books, papers, records, furniture and paraphernalia pertaining thereto), be turned over and transferred to the trustees or other managing officers of such library established as aforesaid. [Acts 1899, ch. 139, § 1, p. 228.]

SCHOOL DISTRICT LIBRARIES
(Burns Annotated Indiana Statutes, 1982, s.20-5-15-1 to 20-5-15-3, 20-13-26-1.)

20-5-15-1 [28-6137]. Libraries in cities and towns—Establishment authorized.—In all the cities and incorporated towns of this state the board of school trustees, board of school commissioners, or whatever board may be established by law to take charge of the public or common schools of said city or incorporated town, shall have power, if in their discretion, they deem it to the public interest, to establish a free public library in connection with the common schools of said city or incorporated town, and to make such rules and regulations for the care and protection and government of such library and for the care of the books provided therefor, and for the taking from and returning to said library of such books as the said board may deem necessary and proper; and to provide penalties for the violation thereof: Provided, That in any city or incorporated town where there is already established a library open to all the people, no tax shall be levied for the purpose herein named: Provided, further, That in all cities, having according to the last preceding United States census not less than four thousand [4,000] nor more than four thousand five hundred [4,500] population, in which there is a public library open to all the people already established under the library laws of this state, supported in whole or in part by taxation, such board of school trustees, board of school commissioners, or other board established by law to take charge of the public or common schools of said city or incorporated town, shall have the power, by and with the consent of the public library board in charge of such library already established, to take over, receive and take full charge of such established library, together with all the property, whether real, personal or mixed, and support, maintain and operate such library the same as if such library had been originally established by such board, and for the purpose of supporting, maintaining, increasing and operating such library, such board shall have the power and authority to receive gifts and donations, and shall have the same power of taxation as vested by law in the public library board from which such library was taken over and received. [Acts 1881, ch. 27, § 1, p. 47; 1883, ch. 82, § 1, p. 103; 1913, ch. 98, § 1, p. 269.]

20-5-15-2 [28-6138]. Tax levies—Gifts and devises.—Such board shall also have power to levy a tax of not exceeding one [1] mill on each dollar of taxable property assessed for taxation in such city in each year; which tax shall be placed on the tax duplicate of such city, and collected in the same manner as other taxes; and when said taxes are so collected, they shall be paid over to the said board for the support and maintenance of said public library. Such board shall have power, and it shall be its duty, to disburse said fund, and all revenues derived from gift or devise, in providing and fitting up suitable rooms for such library, in the purchase, care and binding of books therefor, and in the payment of salaries to a librarian and necessary assistants. [Acts 1881, ch. 27, § 2, p. 47; 1899, ch. 249, § 1, p. 561.]

20-5-15-3 [28-6139]. Acquisition, holding and sale of real estate authorized.—Any such city in which a free public library may be established in accordance with the terms of this act [20-5-15-1—20-5-15-3], may acquire by purchase, or take and hold by gift, grant or devise, any real estate necessary for, or which may be donated or devised for the benefit of such library, and all revenues arising therefrom, and the proceeds of the same, if sold, shall be devoted to the use of said library. [Acts 1881, ch. 27, § 3, p. 47.]

20-13-26-1 [28-1308]. Cities with population of 100,000 or more — Library building bonds — Limitation — Maturity — Interest — Notice. — (a) The common school corporation in each city of this state of one hundred thousand [100,000] or more inhabitants, according to the last preceding United States census, shall, in addition to all other powers granted it by law, have power to borrow money and issue its bonds therefor as hereinafter provided: Each such common school corporation is hereby authorized and empowered to issue and sell its bonds, in such amounts and denominations as the board of school commissioners thereof may deem advisable, but not a face amount in the aggregate in excess of five hundred thousand dollars [$500,000] principal, for the purpose of realizing money to be used in paying for the construction of a library building, or library buildings, for a main library or branch libraries, or both, and in paying for the equipping of such building or buildings and for the improvement of the grounds surrounding such buildings. Such bonds shall be known as "Library Building Bonds," and they shall bear interest at any rate, and the interest shall be paid semiannually.

(b) Such bonds shall be sold by the school city issuing them at not below par and shall mature not more than forty [40] years from their date. They may be issued all at one [1] time or from time to time, but, in no event, in an aggregate principal sum of more than five hundred thousand dollars [$500,000].

(c) No bond issued under the authority of this chapter shall be delivered until the money therefor shall have been paid to the treasurer of the school city issuing it and interest thereon shall begin to accrue at the time of such delivery.

(d) Preparatory to offering any such bonds for sale by any such school city, its board of school commissioners shall give notice for not less than three [3] weeks of the date fixed for the sale and in the notice give a brief description of the bonds and of the mode of bidding, and inviting bids. Such notice shall be by advertisement, one [1] time each week for three [3] successive weeks, in one [1] newspaper published in the city wherein the school corporation is located and in one [1] newspaper published in the city of New York, and by such other method of advertising, if any, as the board of school commissioners may prescribe.

(e) The said board shall sell the bonds to the highest and best bidder, reserving, however, in its advertisements and notices, the right to reject any and all bids. The proceeds arising from all sales of bonds, made in pursuance of this chapter, shall be kept in a separate fund to be known as the "Library Building Fund" and be used only for the purposes, or for some one or more of the purposes, hereinbefore referred to as objects for which such bonds are authorized to be issued. [Acts 1913, ch. 127, § 1, p. 318; 1981, P.L. 11, § 119.]

SCHOOL LIBRARIES
(Burns Annotated Indiana Statutes, 1982, s.20-1-1-6.)

20-1-1-6 [28-109]. Rules and regulations — Scope. — In addition to any other powers and duties prescribed by law, the state board of education shall adopt and promulgate such rules and regulations according to the provisions of IC 4-22-2 [4-22-2-1 — 4-22-2-12], as it may deem necessary and reasonable, concerning, but not limited to, the following matters:

*   *   *

(c) Media Centers, Libraries and Instructional Materials Centers.

(1) The establishment and maintenance of standards and guidelines for media centers, libraries, instructional materials centers, or any other area or system of areas in the school where a full range of information sources, associated equipment, and services from professional media staff are accessible to the school community, and

(2) The licensing of the professional employees manning these centers, libraries or areas.

1980, P.L. 143, § 1; 1981, P.L. 167, § 4.

LIBRARIES IN PARKS
(Burns Annotated Indiana Statutes, 1982, s.19-7-24-1, 19-7-24-2.)

19-7-24-1 [48-5810]. Libraries in parks.—It shall be lawful for the common councils or boards of trustees of all incorporated cities and towns in this state to authorize and permit the use of any public park in such cities or towns for the location and erection of city, county, town or township library buildings, and the use of such public park for such purpose shall not be considered as a vacation of such park nor as an abandonment thereof for the purposes for which the same was laid out or dedicated. [Acts 1903, ch. 197, § 1, p. 346.]

19-7-24-2 [48-5811]. Prior acts legalized—No vacation.—Prior actions of any of the common councils or boards of trustees of any of the incorporated cities or towns in this state in authorizing or permitting, by ordinance, the use of any of the public squares, spaces or parks in such cities or towns for the location and erection of said county, town or township library buildings be and the same are hereby ratified, confirmed, legalized and in all things made valid, and such action shall not be considered as a vacation of such square, space or park, nor as abandonment thereof for the purpose for which the same were laid out or dedicated. [Acts 1903, ch. 197, § 2, p. 346.]

ASSOCIATION AND
INCORPORATED LIBRARIES
(Burns Annotated Indiana Statutes, 1982, s.20-13-5-1 to 20-13-5-12, 20-13-4-1 to 20-13-4-8, 29-13-3-1 to 20-13-3-5.)

20-13-5-1 [41-101]. Establishment.—The inhabitants of any city, town, village or neighborhood in this state, or any part of them, whenever they have subscribed the sum of fifty dollars [$50.00] or upwards toward the establishment of a public library, may assemble themselves for the purpose of holding an election for directors. [1 R. S. 1852, ch. 64, § 1, p. 355.]

20-13-5-2 [41-102]. Chairman and clerk.—If two thirds [²⁄₃] of the subscribers are present, they may proceed to chose [choose], by voice, a chairman who shall preside at that meeting, and a clerk who shall keep a record of the same. [1 R. S. 1852, ch. 64, § 2, p. 355.]

20-13-5-3 [41-103]. Election of directors.—After a chairman and clerk are chosen, the shareholders may proceed to chose [choose], by ballot, seven [7] directors, and to agree upon a name by which their library shall be known, [and] the directors shall appoint one [1] of their number to be president at their meetings, who shall have no other than a casting vote. [1 R. S. 1852, ch. 64, § 3, p. 355.]

20-13-5-4 [41-104]. Statement.—A true statement of the proceedings of such meeting, including the amount subscribed and the number of subscribers present at their meeting, shall be sworn or affirmed to before some justice of the peace of the county, by the chairman or the clerk provided for by the second section [20-13-5-2] of this act, and filed in the recorder's office; and it shall be the duty of such justice to certify on such statement that it was sworn or affirmed to before him. [1 R. S. 1852, ch. 64, § 4, p. 355.]

20-13-5-5   [41-105].   Recording of statement.—The recorder of the county shall record the said statement in his book of record when required. [1 R. S. 1852, ch. 64, § 5, p. 355.]

20-13-5-6   [41-106].   Powers. — After such statement shall be duly recorded, the president and directors, and their successors forever, shall be a body corporate and politic, to be known by such name as is registered in the recorder's office; they shall be capable in law and equity to sue and be sued, plead and be impleaded, answer and be answered unto, defend and be defended, in any court or courts, or before any judge or judges, justice or justices, person or persons whatsoever, in all manner of suits, actions, plaints, pleas, causes, and demands whatever, in as effectual a manner as any other person or persons, body or bodies, corporate or politic, may or can do. [1 R. S. 1852, ch. 64, § 6, p. 355.]

20-13-5-7   [41-107].   Banking forbidden.—Nothing contained in this act [20-13-5-1—20-13-5-12] shall be so construed as to authorize any library company incorporated in this state, to issue notes or bills of credit payable to any person or persons on his or their order, or to bearer; nor to deal in any kind of bills of exchange, notes or due bills whatever. [1 R. S. 1852, ch. 64, § 7, p. 355.]

20-13-5-8   [41-108].   Directors, annual election.—Except the first election of directors, the annual election forever thereafter shall be held on the first Monday in January; but if any annual election should be omitted, the directors shall remain in power until the next annual election, and until successors shall be chosen. [1 R. S. 1852, ch. 64, § 8, p. 355.]

20-13-5-9   [41-109].   By-laws.—Such library or libraries shall be governed and regulated by such by-laws as may, from time to time, be made by the president and directors of the same, not inconsistent with the constitution and laws of this state, who shall have power to alter, amend, abolish, and renew, any such by-law or by-laws at pleasure. [1 R. S. 1852, ch. 64, § 9, p. 355.]

20-13-5-10   [41-110].   Seal — Assessments — Officers. — The president and directors shall have power to make a common seal, and the same to alter, break, change, or renew at pleasure, [and] they shall have power to levy a tax on the shareholders, provided such tax do [does] not exceed one dollar [$1.00] on each share in any one [1] year; nothing, however, in this act [20-13-5-1—20-13-5-12] shall be so construed as to prevent a majority of two thirds [2/3] of the shareholders, attending at their annual meeting, from increasing such tax to any sum not exceeding five dollars [$5.00] on each share in any one [1] year; they shall have power to appoint a treasurer and librarian, and the same to remove at pleasure. [1 R. S. 1852, ch. 64, § 10, p. 355.]

20-13-5-11 [41-111]. Quorum—Vacancies—Term.—A majority of the directors shall be necessary to form a quorum; they shall have power to fill vacancies that may happen in their own body; and the director or directors by them elected, shall serve until the next annual election thereafter, and until others are elected in their stead. [1 R. S. 1852, ch. 64, § 11, p. 355.]

20-13-5-12 [41-112]. Donations. — They shall have power to receive, by donation, any books, moneys, papers, lands, or any other thing or things, and such donation, or the income or the interest thereof, shall be applied to no other purpose than the true interest and objects of the library on which it was bestowed, according to the true intent and meaning of this act [20-13-5-1—20-13-5-12]. [1 R. S. 1852, ch. 64, § 12, p. 355.]

20-13-4-1 [41-113]. Stock.—All stock in such library association shall be deemed personal estate and shall be transferred in the manner and under the conditions prescribed by the by-laws of the same, and such stock shall be exempt from the levy of any state, county, township, or municipal tax, and shall not be liable to execution for the debts of the owners of the same. [Acts 1873, ch. 67, § 2, p. 176.]

20-13-4-2 [41-114]. Voting stock.—At all meetings of shareholders, each shareholder shall be entitled to one [1] vote for each share of stock held by him, and provision shall be made by the by-laws by which absent shareholders may vote by proxy. [Acts 1873, ch. 67, § 3, p. 176.]

20-13-4-3 [41-115]. Reading room and museum. — Library associations may make such provisions, as the board of directors may deem proper, for maintaining, in addition to the library, a reading room and museum. [Acts 1873, ch. 67, § 4, p. 176.]

20-13-4-4 [41-116]. Fines — Costs — Judgment without relief. — All fines and forfeitures, accruing from the violation of the by-laws and regulations made by the directors, shall be recoverable with costs in an action before any court of competent jurisdiction, and judgments for the same shall be collected without relief from valuation or appraisement laws. [Acts 1873, ch. 67, § 5, p. 176.]

20-13-4-5 [41-117]. Corporations may take stock.—Any mining or manufacturing company or other voluntary association within the state, shall have the power to subscribe to, and purchase stock in such library associations, and the provisions of all laws inconsistent with this section are hereby repealed. [Acts 1873, ch. 67, § 6, p. 176.]

20-13-4-6 [41-118]. Cities may take stock.—Any city incorporated under the laws of this state, may by the vote of two thirds [⅔] of the members of the common council thereof, subscribe to the stock of any public library association organized within its limits, and for the payment of such shares of stock, and the assessments on the same, may, from time to time, as the common council may think proper, annually levy, and collect, not more than two [2] mills on the dollar upon the taxable property within the limits of the city, which shall be paid into the city treasury and applied to the payment of such stock and assessments made thereon. [Acts 1873, ch. 67, § 7, p. 176.]

20-13-4-7 [41-119]. Stock as prizes.—The common council of such city shall have the power, in their discretion, to cause the distribution and transfer of shares of stock held by the city as prizes to the children of the public schools in the city, for good behavior and scholarship. [Acts 1873, ch. 67, § 8, p. 176.]

20-13-4-8 [41-120]. Dissolution—City to manage.—Upon the dissolution or forfeiture of the franchises of such library association, in which any city may have purchased stock, and is, at the time of such dissolution or forfeiture, the holder of one third [⅓] of the shares of the whole stock, the property of such association shall become the property of the city, for the free use and enjoyment of the inhabitants of such city, under regulations to be prescribed by the common council, and the common council shall thereafter control such library and shall have power to increase the same, and levy and apply the tax provided for in section seven [20-13-4-6] of this act, to the increase and expenses of such library. [Acts 1873, ch. 67, § 9, p. 176.]

20-13-3-1 [41-401]. Incorporation.—Whenever any number of persons, not less than seven [7], shall desire to associate themselves together for the purpose of establishing and maintaining a public library in any city or county in this state for the general benefit and advantage of all the inhabitants of such city or county, it shall be lawful for such persons to become incorporated under this act [20-13-3-1—20-13-3-5] in the manner hereinafter provided. [Acts 1881 (Spec. Sess.), ch. 84, § 1, p. 588.]

20-13-3-2 [41-402]. Instrument of association.—Whenever any persons shall desire to become incorporated under this act [20-13-3-1—20-13-3-5], for the purposes aforesaid, they shall, by an instrument in writing, set forth the objects of the association, the corporate name to be adopted, the names and places of residence of each of the incorporators, and a description of the corporate seal, and they shall also, in said instrument, provide the manner in which, in case of the death, resignation or removal for any cause of any of the original incorporators, their successors shall be selected, so that the number of the members of such incorporation shall never be less than the original number. They shall also provide in said instrument, what officers shall be elected by such corporation, and the time and manner of their election, and shall also provide therein generally in what manner the business of said corporation shall be conducted, which instrument shall be signed by all the proposed incorporators, and filed in the office of the recorder of the county in which such library or reading room is proposed to be established. [Acts 1881 (Spec. Sess.), ch. 84, § 2, p. 588.]

20-13-3-3 [41-403]. Recording — Powers — Exemption from taxation. — Upon the filing of such instrument in the proper recorder's office, it shall be the duty of the recorder to record the same in the miscellaneous records of such county, and from the time of the recording thereof as aforesaid, the said association and their successors shall be deemed and held a corporation, and shall have, possess and enjoy all the rights, powers and privileges given to corporations by common law, to sue and be sued, to borrow money and secure the payment of the same by notes and mortgages, bonds or deeds of trust, upon the person [personal] or real estate of such association, to purchase, rent, lease, hold, sell and convey real estate for the benefit of such corporation, and to erect and maintain suitable buildings for the purposes aforesaid, and for other objects properly connected therewith. Such corporation shall also have the right and power to receive and accept donations, either of money or real estate, either by gift or devise, and to hold, use, enjoy, mortgage, sell and convey the same for the benefit of such corporation, in the manner provided in the deed of gift or devise by which the same was received, and the real estate and personal property of any such corporation, which shall have established a public library for the purposes aforesaid, and shall have put the same into operation, shall be exempt from taxation for state, county and all municipal purposes, and shall remain exempt as aforesaid so long as the same is used exclusively for the general benefit of the inhabitants of the city or county in which such library may be located. [Acts 1881 (Spec. Sess.), ch. 84, § 3, p. 588.]

20-13-3-4 [41-404]. Gallery of art — Reading room — Park. — Whenever any such corporation shall be established, as in this act [20-13-3-1—20-13-3-5] provided, it shall be lawful, and such corporation shall have the power to establish and maintain, in connection with its library, a gallery of art and public reading rooms, and may also maintain, either in connection with its library building or separate therefrom, a public park. [Acts 1881 (Spec. Sess.), ch. 84, § 4, p. 588.]

20-13-3-5. Construction of act.—Nothing in this act [20-13-3-1—20-13-3-5] shall be so construed as to repeal any law now in force for the incorporation or regulation of public libraries. [Acts 1881 (Spec. Sess.), ch. 84, § 5, p. 588.]

COMMISSION ON PUBLIC RECORDS

(Burns Annotated Indiana Statutes, 1982, s.5-15-5.1 to 5-15-5.1-20.)

5-15-5.1-1. Definitions. — As used in this chapter:

"Commission" means the commission on public records created by this chapter.

"Record" means all documentation of the informational, communicative or decisionmaking processes of state government, its agencies and subdivisions made or received by any agency of state government or its employees in connection with the transaction of public business or government functions, which documentation is created, received, retained, maintained, or filed by that agency or its successors as evidence of its activities or because of the informational value of the data in the documentation, and which is generated on:

    (1) Paper or paper substitutes;

    (2) Photographic or chemically based media;

    (3) Magnetic or machine readable media; or

    (4) Any other materials, regardless of form or characteristics.

"Nonrecord materials" means all identical copies of forms, records, reference books, and exhibit materials which are made, or acquired, and preserved solely for reference use, exhibition purposes, or publication and which are not included within the definition of record.

"Personal records" means:

    (1) All documentary materials of a private or nonpublic character which do not relate to or have an effect upon the carrying out of the constitutional, statutory, or other official or ceremonial duties of a public official, including: diaries, journals, or other personal notes serving as the functional equivalent of a diary or journal which are not prepared or utilized for, or circulated or communicated in the course of, transacting government business; or

    (2) Materials relating to private political associations, and having no relation to or effect upon the carrying out of constitutional, statutory, or other official or ceremonial duties of a public official and are not deemed public records.

"Form" means every piece of paper, transparent plate, or film containing information, printed, generated, or reproduced by whatever means, with blank spaces left for the entry of additional information to be used in any transaction involving the state.

"Agency" means any state office, department, division, board, bureau, commission, authority, or other separate unit of state government established by the constitution, law, or by executive or legislative order.

"Public official" means an individual holding a state office created by the Constitution of Indiana, by act or resolution of the general assembly, or by the governor; all officers of the executive and administrative branch of state government; and all other officers, heads, presidents, or chairmen of agencies of state government.

"Indiana state archives" means the program maintained by the commission for the preservation of those records and other government papers that have been determined by the commission to have sufficient permanent values to warrant their continued preservation by the state.

"Forms management" means the program maintained by the commission to provide continuity of forms design procedures from the form's origin up to its completion as a record by determining the form's size, style and size of type; format; type of construction; number of plys [plies]; quality, weight and type of paper and carbon; and by determining the use of the form for data entry as well as the distribution.

"Information management" means the program maintained by the commission for the application of management techniques to the purchase, creation, utilization, maintenance, retention, preservation, and disposal of forms and records undertaken to improve efficiency and reduce costs of recordkeeping; including management of filing and microfilming equipment and supplies, filing and information retrieval systems, files, correspondence, reports and forms management, historical documentation, micrographic retention programming, and critical records protection.

"Record center" means a program maintained by the commission primarily for the storage, processing, retrieving, servicing, and security of government records that must be retained for varying periods of time but should not be maintained in an agency's office equipment or space.

"Critical records" means records necessary to resume or continue governmental operations, the reestablishing of the legal and financial responsibilities of government in the state, or to protect and fulfill governmental obligations to the citizens of the state.

"Retention schedule" means a set of instructions prescribing how long, where, and in what form a record series shall be kept.

"Records series" means documents or records that are filed in a unified arrangement, and having similar physical characteristics or relating to a similar function or activity.

"Records coordinator" means a person designated by an agency to serve as an information liaison person between the agency and the commission. [IC 5-15-5.1-1, as added by Acts 1979, P.L. 40, § 1.]

5-15-5.1-2. Application of chapter. — (a) This chapter applies to records:

(1) Open to the public and carrying no classification or restriction;
(2) Classified as restricted under IC 4-1-6 [4-1-6-1 — 4-1-6-9];
(3) Required to be kept confidential by federal law, rule, or regulation;
(4) Declared confidential by the general assembly; or
(5) Declared confidential by a rule or regulation promulgated under specific authority for confidential records granted to an agency by the general assembly.

(b) The provisions of this chapter do not apply to state supported colleges and universities and the department of revenue, but the commission may offer its services to them. However, the department of revenue shall submit retention schedules applying to its record series to the oversight committee on public records for approval.

(c) The provisions of this chapter shall in no way restrict the powers and duties of the state board of accounts as prescribed by IC 5-11 [5-11-1-1 — 5-11-18-2]. [IC 5-15-5.1-2, as added by Acts 1979, P.L. 40, § 1.]

5-15-5.1-3. Commission created — Seal — Services offered. — There is created the commission on public records to administer this chapter for the administrative and executive branches of state government. The commission shall adopt a seal which shall be the seal of the state of Indiana. The commission shall offer its services to the legislative and judicial branches of state government. [IC 5-15-5.1-3, as added by Acts 1979, P.L. 40, § 1.]

5-15-5.1-4. Director — Qualifications — Term — Removal — Staff — Salary. — (a) The governor shall appoint a director as the executive head of the commission. The director must be versed in the principles of information and forms management, archives, and the affairs and organization of state government. The director shall serve a term of four [4] years. However, the director may be removed for cause by the governor. It is the intent of the general assembly that the director be a person who is qualified by training and experience to administer the affairs of the commission and that his tenure of office is limited only by his ability and the proper performance of his duties.

(b) The director, subject to the approval of the governor and the state budget agency, shall appoint such staff as necessary to implement the provisions of this chapter.

(c) The salary of the director is subject to the approval of the governor and the state budget agency. Salaries of the staff are subject to the approval of the state personnel division and the state budget agency. The provisions of IC 4-15-2 [4-15-2-1 — 4-15-2-46] apply to the staff of the commission. [IC 5-15-5.1-4, as added by Acts 1979, P.L. 40, § 1.]

5-15-5.1-5. Duties of commission. — (a) Subject to approval by the oversight committee on public records created by section 18 [5-15-5.1-18] of this chapter, the commission shall:

(1) Establish a forms management program for state government including the design, typography, format, logo, data sequence, form analysis, form number, and agency file specifications.

(2) Establish a central state form numbering system and a central cross index filing system of all state forms, and shall standardize, consolidate and eliminate, wherever possible, forms used by state government.

(3) Approve, purchase, and provide photo-ready copy for all forms and printed materials to take advantage of competitive bidding, consolidated orders, and contract procurement and shall work towards more efficient, economical and timely procurement.

(4) Require that all forms be purchased through the commission.

(5) Establish a statewide records management program, prescribing the standards and procedures for recordmaking and recordkeeping; however, the investigative and criminal history records of the Indiana state police are exempted from this requirement.

(6) Establish coordinated utilization of all printing equipment and micrographics equipment in state government.

(7) Establish coordinated utilization of all copy machines and equipment in the executive and administrative branches. All requests for copy machines must be approved by the commission.

(8) Establish a centralized control over purchase of all paper and film storage equipment.

(9) Establish and operate a distribution center for the receipt, storage and distribution of all material printed for an agency.

(10) Establish and operate a statewide archival program to be called the Indiana state archives for the permanent government records of the state, provide consultant services for archival programs, conduct surveys, and provide training for records coordinators.

(11) Establish and operate a statewide record preservation laboratory.

(12) Prepare, develop, and implement record retention schedules.

(13) Establish and operate a central records center to be called the Indiana state records center which shall accept all records transferred to it, provide secure storage and reference service for the same, and submit written notice to the applicable agency of intended destruction of records in accordance with approved retention schedules.

(14) Demand, from any person or organization or body who has illegal possession of original state or local government records, those records, which shall be delivered to the commission.

(15) Have the authority to examine all forms and records housed or possessed by state agencies for the purpose of fulfilling the provisions of this chapter.

(16) In coordination with the data processing oversight commission created under IC 4-23-16 [4-23-16-1 — 4-23-16-11], establish standards to ensure the preservation of adequate and permanent computerized and auxiliary automated information records of the agencies of state government.

(b) In implementing a forms management program, the commission shall follow procedures and forms prescribed by the federal government. [IC 5-15-5.1-5, as added by Acts 1979, P.L. 40, § 1.]

5-15-5.1-6. State forms — Design, numbering, standardization, consolidation, elimination, evaluation. — The commission shall design, redesign, number, standardize, consolidate, or eliminate when obsolete, all forms used by state government, apply the definition of record to any governmental materials so questioned, and determine the nature of nonrecord materials housed or maintained by an agency. In performing these functions, the commission shall consult with each affected agency and shall consider each agency's statutory responsibilities, its relationships with federal or other governmental agencies and the requirements of state law. [IC 5-15-5.1-6, as added by Acts 1979, P.L. 40, § 1.]

5-15-5.1-7. State archives — Availability for public use — Furnishing copies of materials. — The commission shall make the archives of the state available for public use under supervised control at

reasonable hours. However, the commission shall weigh the need for preservation from deterioration or mutilation of original records in establishing
access use to such items. The commission shall furnish copies of archival
materials upon request, unless confidential by law or restricted by promulgated rule, and payment of such fees as may be required. [IC 5-15-5.1-7, as
added by Acts 1979, P.L. 40, § 1.]

**5-15-5.1-8. Central micrographics laboratory — Regulations —
Microfilming standards.** — The commission shall operate a central
micrographics laboratory. The oversight committee in coordination with the
Supreme Court shall promulgate regulations concerning quality standards
for microfilming documents that shall allow documents meeting those standards to be admissible in court. Such microfilming standards shall be
followed by all agencies of the administrative and executive branches of
state government. [IC 5-15-5.1-8, as added by Acts 1979, P.L. 40, § 1.]

**5-15-5.1-9. Transferred records — Effect of copies certified by
director.** — Copies of records transferred from the office of their origin to
the custody of the commission, when certified by the director or his designee,
under seal of the commission, shall have the same force and effect as if
certified by the original custodian. [IC 5-15-5.1-9, as added by Acts 1979,
P.L. 40, § 1.]

5-15-5.1-10. Duties of agencies. — Each agency shall:
(1) Make and preserve records containing adequate and proper documentation of the organization, functions, policies, decisions, procedures, and
essential transactions of the agency to protect the legal and financial rights
of the government and of persons directly affected by the agency's activities.
(2) Cooperate fully with the commission in implementing the provisions
of this chapter.
(3) Establish and maintain an active and continuing program for the
economical and efficient management of information and assist the commission in the conduct of information management surveys.
(4) Implement information management procedures and regulations
issued by the commission.
(5) Submit to the oversight committee, a recommended retention schedule
for each form and record series in its custody. However, retention schedules
for forms and record series common to more than one [1] agency may be
established by the oversight committee. Records may not be scheduled for
retention any longer than is necessary to perform required functions.
Records requiring retention for several years must be transferred to the
records center.
(6) Establish necessary safeguards against the removal, alteration, or loss
of records; safeguards shall include notification to all officials and employees
of the agency that records in the custody of the agency may not be alienated
or destroyed except in accordance with the provisions of this chapter.

(7) Designate an agency information coordinator, who shall assist the commission in the content requirements of the form design process and in the development of the agency's records retention schedules.

(8) Report to the commission before December 31 of each year those records which have been created or discontinued in the past year. [IC 5-15-5.1-10, as added by Acts 1979, P.L. 40, § 1.]

5-15-5.1-11. Title to records. — Title to any record transferred to the Indiana state archives as authorized by this chapter shall be vested in the commission. However, title to any record deposited in the Indiana state records center shall remain with the agency transferring that record. [IC 5-15-5.1-11, as added by Acts 1979, P.L. 40, § 1.]

5-15-5.1-12. Critical records program. — The commission shall establish and maintain a critical records program for the state of Indiana. It shall determine what records are essential to the continuity of state government operations and shall survey agency records to identify those records. The commission shall plan and implement a program for protection of critical records through dispersal, duplication, or secure vault storage of those records. [IC 5-15-5.1-12, as added by Acts 1979, P.L. 40, § 1.]

5-15-5.1-13. Confidential or restricted records — Disposition, destruction. — Records designated as confidential by law or restricted under IC 4-1-6 [4-1-6-1 — 4-1-6-9] shall be so treated by the commission in the maintenance, storage, transfer or other disposition of those records. Confidential or restricted records scheduled for destruction shall be destroyed in such a manner that they cannot be read, interpreted or reconstructed. [IC 5-15-5.1-13, as added by Acts 1979, P.L. 40, § 1.]

5-15-5.1-14. Unauthorized disposal of records prohibited. — A public official or agency may not mutilate, destroy, sell, loan, or otherwise dispose of any government record, except under a record retention schedule or with the written consent of the commission. [IC 5-15-5.1-14, as added by Acts 1979, P.L. 40, § 1.]

5-15-5.1-15. Delivery of records — Expiration of term of public official — Termination of state agency. — (a) A public official who has the custody of any records, excluding personal records, shall at the expiration of his term of office or appointment, deliver to his successor, or to the commission if there is no successor, all materials defined as records by this chapter.

(b) Upon the termination of a state agency whose functions have not been transferred to another agency, the records of the state agency shall be deposited with the commission. The commission shall determine which records are of sufficient legal, historical, administrative, research or fiscal value to warrant their continued preservation. Records that are determined to be of insufficient value to warrant continued preservation shall be disposed of or destroyed. [IC 5-15-5.1-15, as added by Acts 1979, P.L. 40, § 1.]

5-15-5.1-16. Agreements — Legislative branch — Supreme Court and Court of Appeals. — (a) The commission may enter into agreements with the legislative branch of government for transfer of the permanent records of that body not having current administrative value to the Indiana state archives.

(b) The commission may enter into agreements with the Indiana Supreme Court and Court of Appeals and their clerk for transfer of the permanent records of those bodies not having current administrative value to the state archives. [IC 5-15-5.1-16, as added by Acts 1979, P.L. 40, § 1.]

5-15-5.1-17. Preservation of official books, records, documents and papers — Authority of officials and commission. — (a) A state, county or other official is authorized and empowered, at his discretion, to turn over to the commission in accordance with the rules and regulations of the commission for permanent preservation, any official books, records, documents, original papers, newspaper files or printed books or materials not in current use in his office.

(b) The commission is authorized to make a copy, by photography or in any other way, of any official book, record, document, original paper, newspaper, or printed book or material in any county, city, or other public office for preservation in the state archives. County, city and other officials shall permit such copies to be made of the books, records, documents and papers in their respective offices. [IC 5-15-5.1-17, as added by Acts 1979, P.L. 40, § 1.]

5-15-5.1-18. Oversight committee on public records — Composition — Officers — Compensation. — (a) The oversight committee on public records consists ex officio of:

(1) The governor or his designee;

(2) The secretary of state or his designee;

(3) The state examiner of the state board of accounts or his designee;

(4) The director of the state library;

(5) The director of the historical bureau;

(6) The director of the commission on public records; and

(7) The commissioner of the department of administration or his designee.

(b) The oversight committee also consists of two [2] lay members appointed by the governor for a term of four [4] years. One [1] lay member shall be a professional journalist or be a member of an association related to journalism.

(c) The oversight committee shall elect one [1] of its members to be chairman. The director of the commission on public records shall be the secretary of the committee. The ex officio members of the oversight committee shall serve without compensation and shall receive no reimbursement for any expense which they may incur. Each lay member is entitled to reimbursement for traveling and other expenses as provided in the state travel policies and procedures, established by the department of administration and approved by the state budget agency and each lay member is entitled to the minimum salary per diem as provided in IC 4-10-11-2.1(b). [IC 5-15-5.1-18, as added by Acts 1979, P.L. 40, § 1.]

5-15-5.1-19. Duties of oversight committee — Master list of classified record series — Approval of record retention schedules. — (a) It is the duty of the oversight committee to:

(1) Function as the policy-making body for the commission; and

(2) Determine what records have no apparent official value but should be preserved for research, or other purposes; and

(3) Determine the status of records presently classified by statute or by promulgated rule or regulation based on statutory authority.

(b) The oversight committee shall maintain a master list of all record series classified as unrestricted, restricted, or confidential.

(c) The oversight committee has final approval of all record retention schedules. [IC 5-15-5.1-19, as added by Acts 1979, P.L. 40, § 1.]

5-15-5.1-20. Classification of restricted records — Establishment of standards for safeguarding personal information systems — Approval of form content — Regulations. — (a) The oversight committee, in the manner prescribed by IC 4-22-2 [4-22-2-1 — 4-22-2-12], may classify, as restricted, records containing private information, which are not already classified as confidential or public by statute or by promulgated rule or regulation based on statutory authority. The terms "restricted" and "private information" are as defined in IC 4-1-6-1.

(b) The oversight committee shall establish standards for safeguarding personal information systems which shall be followed by agencies maintaining such systems.

(c) The oversight committee shall approve the content of all forms which involve restricted and confidential records.

(d) The oversight committee may promulgate such regulations under IC 4-22-2 [4-22-2-1 — 4-22-2-12] as it deems necessary for the performance of its duties, consistent with the provisions of this chapter and other applicable laws of this state. [IC 5-15-5.1-20, as added by Acts 1979, P.L. 40, § 1.]

PROTECTION OF LIBRARY PROPERTY

(Burns Annotated Indiana Statutes, 1982, s.20-13-31-1 to 20-13-31-5.)

20-13-31-1 [41-1101]. Failure to return borrowed book or other publication—Notice—Penalty.—Whoever borrows from any library or gallery, museum, collection or exhibition, any book, newspaper, magazine, manuscript, pamphlet, publication, recording, film or other article belonging to or in the care of such library, gallery, museum, collection or exhibition, under any agreement to return the same, within a specified time, and thereafter fails to return such book, newspaper, magazine, manuscript, pamphlet, publication, recording, film or other article, shall be given written notice, which shall bear upon its face a copy of this section of this act [20-13-31-1—20-13-31-5], mailed or delivered in person to his last known address, to return such book, newspaper, magazine, manuscript, pamphlet, publication, recording, film or other article, within fifteen [15] days, and in the event that such person shall thereafter wilfully and knowingly fail to return such borrowed article within thirty [30] days, or shall fail to reimburse said library, gallery, museum, collection or exhibition for the value of such borrowed article, such person shall be guilty of a misdemeanor and upon conviction shall be liable to a fine of not more than fifty dollars [$50.00] or imprisonment for not more than ten [10] days. [Acts 1961, ch. 168, § 1, p. 372.]

20-13-31-2   [41-1102].   Stealing, selling, or receiving book or other publication—Penalty.—Any person who shall steal or unlawfully take or who shall sell or buy or receive, knowing the same to have been stolen, any book, pamphlet, document, newspaper, periodical, file card, map, chart, picture, portrait, engraving, statue, coin, medal, equipment, specimen, recording, film or other work of literature or object of art belonging to or in the care of a library, gallery, museum, collection, exhibition or belonging to or in the care of any department or office of the state or local government, or belonging to or in the care of a library, gallery, museum, collection or exhibition which belongs to any incorporated college or university or which belongs to any institution devoted to educational, scientific, literary, artistic, historical or charitable purposes shall be guilty of a misdemeanor and upon conviction shall be liable to a fine of not more than fifty dollars [$50.00] or imprisonment for not more than ten [10] days. [Acts 1961, ch. 168, § 2, p. 372.]

20-13-31-3   [41-1103].   Defacing book or other publication without making restitution—Penalty.—Any person who wilfully or maliciously writes upon, cuts, tears, defaces, disfigures, soils, obliterates, breaks or destroys any book, pamphlet, document, newspaper, periodical, file card, map, chart, picture, portrait, engraving, statue, coin, medal, equipment, specimen, recording, film or other work of literature or object of art belonging to or in the care of a library, gallery, museum, collection, exhibition or belonging to or in the care of any department or office of the state or local government, or belonging to or in the care of a library, gallery, museum, collection or exhibition which belongs to any incorporated college or university or which belongs to any institution devoted to educational, scientific, literary, artistic, historical or charitable purposes, without making restitution for the property damaged or destroyed to the owner or custodian shall be guilty of a misdemeanor and upon conviction shall be liable to a fine of not more than fifty dollars [$50.00] or imprisonment for not more than ten [10] days. [Acts 1961, ch. 168, § 3, p. 372.]

20-13-31-4   [41-1104].   Copies of this act to be publicly displayed.—Every library or gallery, museum, collection or exhibition, or any such institution belonging to any incorporated college or library or belonging to any incorporated institution devoted to educational, scientific, literary, artistic, historical or charitable purposes, whose books, newspapers, magazines, manuscripts, pamphlets, publications, recordings, films or other articles are covered by or protected by this act [20-13-31-1—20-13-31-5], shall post and display in at least two [2] public places within such institution or library a copy of this act so that it may be read by anyone going into, visiting or belonging to such institution and borrowing books or other material from such institution. [Acts 1961, ch. 168, § 4, p. 372.]

20-13-31-5 [41-1105]. Act supplemental.—The provisions of this act [20-13-31-1—20-13-31-5] are not intended as a substitute for or replacement of any penalties now provided by law, but shall be considered accumulative and in addition thereto. [Acts 1961, ch. 168, § 5, p. 372.]

TAX EXEMPTION
(Burns Annotated Indiana Statutes, 1982, s.6-1.1-10-5.)

Indiana library laws are reprinted from BURNS ANNOTATED INDIANA STATUTES published by Bobbs Merrill & Co., Indianapolis, Indiana.

IOWA

STATE LIBRARY DEPARTMENT
(Iowa Code Annotated, 1982, s.303A.1 to 303A.7.)

303A.1. Definitions

As used in this chapter, unless the context otherwise requires:

1. "Department" means the Iowa library department.

2. "Commission" means the state library commission.

Acts 1973 (65 G.A.) ch. 199, § 1.

303A.2. Library department

There is created the Iowa library department. The executive head of the department shall be the state librarian. The state librarian shall be appointed by the state library commission, with the approval of two-thirds of the members of the senate, and shall serve at the pleasure of the state library commission. The state librarian shall be a person upon whom a master's degree in library science has been conferred as a result of completing a program of study accredited by the American Library Association.

Acts 1973 (65 G.A.) ch. 199, § 2.

303A.3. Library commission

There is created a state library commission. The commission shall consist of the supreme court administrator, and four members appointed by the governor and serving four-year terms, one member of which shall be from the medical profession and three members selected at large, each based on their qualifications to serve as commission members. The appointed members of the commission shall be appointed for terms of one, two, three and four years and all subsequent appointments shall be for the full four-year term.

Members of the commission shall receive forty dollars per diem while engaged in their official duties. They shall be paid their actual and necessary travel and other official expenditures necessitated by their official duties.

The commission shall elect one of its members as chairman. It shall meet at such time and place as shall be specified by call of the chairman. At least one meeting shall be held bimonthly. All meetings shall be open to the public. Notice of each meeting shall be given in writing to each member at least three days in advance of the meeting. Three commissioners shall constitute a quorum for the transaction of business.

Acts 1973 (65 G.A.) ch. 199, § 3.

303A.4. Duties of commission

The state library commission shall:

1. Adopt and enforce rules necessary for the exercise of the powers and duties granted by this chapter and proper administration of the department.

2. Adopt rules providing penalties for injuring, defacing, destroying, or losing books or materials under the control of the commission. All fines, penalties, and forfeitures imposed by these rules may be recovered in an action in the name of the state and deposited in the general fund.

3. Develop and adopt plans to provide more adequate library service to all residents of the state.

4. Charge no fee for the use of libraries under its control or for the circulation of material from libraries, except where transportation costs are incurred in making materials available to users. The costs may be used as a basis for determining a fee to be charged to users.

5. Give advice and counsel to all public libraries in the state and to all political subdivisions which may propose to establish libraries.

6. Print lists and circulars of information and instruction as it deems necessary.

7. Continuously survey the needs of libraries throughout the state, and ascertain the requirements for additional libraries and for improving existing libraries to provide adequate service to all residents of the state.

8. Obtain from all public libraries reports showing the condition, growth, development and manner of conducting these libraries and at its discretion, obtain reports from other libraries in the state and make these facts known to the citizens of Iowa.

9. Encourage the implementation of the county library law, and of countywide library service through contracts with the boards of supervisors pursuant to chapter 378.

Acts 1973 (65 G.A.) ch. 199, § 4.

303A.5. Duties of state librarian

The state librarian shall:

1. Appoint the technical, professional, secretarial, and clerical staff necessary, within the limits of available funds, to accomplish the purposes of this chapter subject to the provisions of chapter 19A.

2. Act as secretary to the commission, keeping accurate records of the proceedings of the commission.

3. Keep accurate accounts of all financial transactions of the department.

4. Supervise all activities of the Iowa library department.

5. Provide technical assistance in organizing new libraries and improving those already established.

6. Perform such other library duties as may be assigned to him by the commission.

Acts 1973 (65 G.A.) ch. 199, § 5.

303A.6. Department divisions

The Iowa library department shall include but not be limited to the medical library division, the law library division, and the military library division.

1. The medical library division shall be headed by a medical librarian, appointed by the state librarian with the approval of the state library commission, subject to the provisions of chapter 19A. The medical librarian shall:

a. Operate the medical library division which shall always be available for free use by the residents of Iowa under such reasonable rules as the commission may adopt.

b. Give no preference to any school of medicine and shall secure books, periodicals, and pamphlets for every legally recognized school without discrimination.

c. Perform such other duties as may be imposed by law or prescribed by the rules of the commission.

2. The law library division shall be headed by a law librarian, appointed by the state librarian with the approval of the state library commission and the Iowa supreme court, subject to the provisions of chapter 19A. The law librarian shall:

a. Operate the law library division which shall be maintained in the capitol or elsewhere in rooms convenient to the supreme court and which shall always be available for free use by the residents of Iowa under such reasonable rules as the commission may adopt.

b. Maintain as an integral part of the law library reports of various boards and agencies and copies of bills, journals and other information relating to current or proposed legislation.

c. Arrange to make exchanges of all printed material published by the several states and the government of the United States.

d. Perform such other duties as may be imposed by law or by the rules of the commission.

3. The military library division shall be headed by the adjutant general. The adjutant general shall:

a. Operate the military library division which shall be maintained in the memorial hall at Camp Dodge and which shall be available for free use by the residents of Iowa under such reasonable rules as the commission may adopt.

b. Maintain as an integral part of the military library documents, reports, records, and books which describe the history of the national guard and individual Iowans who have served in the armed services.

c. Perform such other duties related to the military library as may be imposed by law or by rules of the commission.

Acts 1973 (65 G.A.) ch. 199, § 6. Amended by Acts 1975 (66 G.A.) ch. 6, §§ 5, 6, eff. Aug. 15, 1975.

303A.7. Money grants

The commission is authorized and empowered to receive, accept, and administer any money or moneys appropriated or granted to it, separate and apart from the general library fund, by the federal government or by any other public or private agencies.

The fund shall be administered by the commission, which shall frame bylaws and rules for the allocation and administration of this fund.

The fund shall be used to increase, improve, stimulate, and equalize library service to the people of the whole state, and for adult education and shall be allocated among the cities, counties, and regions of the state, taking into consideration local needs, area and population to be served, local interest as evidenced by local appropriations, and such other facts as may affect the state program of library service.

Any gift or grant from the federal government or other sources shall become a part of the fund, to be used as part of the state fund, or may be invested in such securities in which the state sinking fund may be invested as in the discretion of the commission may be deemed advisable, the income to be used for the promotion of libraries.

Acts 1973 (65 G.A.) ch. 199, § 7.

INTERSTATE LIBRARY COMPACT
(Iowa Code Annotated, 1982, s.303A.8 to 303A.11.)

303A.8. Library compact authorized

The state library commission is hereby authorized to enter into interstate library compacts on behalf of the state of Iowa with any state bordering on Iowa which legally joins therein in substantially the following form.

The contracting states agree that:

ARTICLE I—PURPOSE

Because the desire for the services provided by public libraries transcends governmental boundaries and can be provided most effectively by giving such services to communities of people regardless of jurisdictional lines, it is the policy of the states who are parties to this compact to co-operate and share their responsibilities in providing joint and co-operative library services in areas where the distribution of population makes the provision of library service on an interstate basis the most effective way to provide adequate and efficient services.

ARTICLE II—PROCEDURE

The appropriate state library officials and agencies having comparable powers with those of the Iowa library commission of the party states or any of their political subdivisions may, on behalf of said states or political subdivisions, enter into agreements for the co-operative or joint conduct of library services when they shall find that the executions of agreements to that end as provided herein will facilitate library services.

ARTICLE III—CONTENT

Any such agreement for the co-operative or joint establishment, operation or use of library services, facilities, personnel, equipment, materials or other items not excluded because of failure to enumerate shall, as among the parties of the agreement:

1. Detail the specific nature of the services, facilities, properties or personnel to which it is applicable;

2. Provide for the allocation of costs and other financial responsibilities;

3. Specify the respective rights, duties, obligations and liabilities;

4. Stipulate the terms and conditions for duration, renewal, termination, abrogation, disposal of joint or common property, if any, and all other matters which may be appropriate to the proper effectuation and performance of said agreement.

ARTICLE IV—CONFLICT OF LAWS

Nothing in this compact or in any agreement entered into hereunder shall alter, or otherwise impair any obligation imposed on any public library by otherwise applicable laws, or be constituted to supersede.

ARTICLE V—ADMINISTRATOR

Each state shall designate a compact administrator with whom copies of all agreements to which his state or any subdivision thereof is party shall be filed. The administrator shall have such powers as may be conferred upon him by the laws of his state and may consult and co-operate with the compact administrators of other party states and take such steps as may effectuate the purposes of this compact.

ARTICLE VI—EFFECTIVE DATE

This compact shall become operative when entered in by two or more entities having the powers enumerated herein.

ARTICLE VII—RENUNCIATION

This compact shall continue in force and remain binding upon each party state until six months after any such state has given notice of repeal by the legislature. Such withdrawal shall not be construed to relieve any party to an agreement authorized by Articles II and III of the compact from the obligation of that agreement prior to the end of its stipulated period of duration.

ARTICLE VIII—SEVERABILITY—CONSTRUCTION

The provisions of this compact shall be severable. It is intended that the provisions of this compact be reasonably and liberally construed.

Acts 1965 (61 G.A.) ch. 256, § 1. Amended by Acts 1973 (65 G.A.) ch. 199, § 14; Acts 1975 (66 G.A.) ch. 67, § 30, eff. Aug. 15, 1975.

303A.9. Administrator

The state librarian shall be the compact administrator. The compact administrator shall receive copies of all agreements entered into by the state or its political subdivisions and other states or political subdivisions; consult with, advise and aid such governmental units in the formulation of such agreements; make such recommendations to the governor, legislature, governmental agencies and units as he deems desirable to effectuate the purposes of this compact and consult and co-operate with the compact administrators of other party states.

Acts 1965 (61 G.A.) ch. 256, § 2. Amended by Acts 1973 (65 G.A.) ch. 199, § 15.

303A.10. Agreements

The compact administrator and the chief executive of any county, city, village, town or library board is hereby authorized and empowered to enter into agreements with other states or their political subdivisions pursuant to the compact. Such agreements as may be made pursuant to this compact on behalf of the state of Iowa shall be made by the compact administrator. Such agreements as may be made on behalf of a political subdivision shall be made after due notice to the compact administrator and consultation with him.

Acts 1965 (61 G.A.) ch. 256, § 3.

303A.11. Enforcement

The agencies and officers of this state and its subdivisions shall enforce this compact and do all things appropriate to effect its purpose and intent which may be within their respective jurisdiction.

Acts 1965 (61 G.A.) ch. 256, § 4.

DEPOSITORY LIBRARY CENTER

(Iowa Code Annotated, 1982, s.303A.21 to 303A.24.)

303A.21. Definitions

As used in this division unless the context otherwise requires:

1. "State agency" means a legislative, executive, or judicial office of the state and all

of its respective officers, departments, divisions, bureaus, boards, commissions, committees, and state institutions of higher education governed by the state board of regents.

2. "State publications" means all multiply produced publications, regardless of format which are produced by state agencies and supported by public funds, but does not include:

a. Correspondence and memoranda intended solely for internal use within the agency or between agencies.

b. Materials designated by law as being confidential.

c. Materials excluded from this definition by the commission through the adoption and enforcement of rules pursuant to section 303A.4, subsection 1.

3. "Depository library" means a library designated for the deposit of state publications under the provisions of this division.

Acts 1978 (67 G.A.) ch. 1105, § 1. Amended by Acts 1980 (68 G.A.) ch. 1092, § 1.

303A.22. Depository library center

There is created within the Iowa library department a depository library center. The state librarian shall appoint a depository librarian who shall administer the depository library center. The depository library center shall be the central agency for the collection and distribution of state publications to depository libraries.

Acts 1978 (67 G.A.) ch. 1105, § 2.

303A.23. Duties of the depository librarian

The depository librarian shall:

1. Enter into agreements according to rules promulgated by the depository librarian pursuant to chapter 17A with libraries for the deposit of state publications in the libraries. Rules shall provide for the classification of the libraries into depository libraries which, for a specified period of time, maintain either a full collection of state publications or a selected core of state publications. The state library commission and the state University of Iowa shall each permanently maintain two copies of each state publication. One copy shall not be removed from the library and the other copy may be loaned.

2. Adopt a classification scheme for state publications and establish a record of the number and manner of distribution.

3. Annually advise state agencies of the number of copies of each class of publication needed for distribution.

4. Prepare, publish, and distribute on a quarterly basis without charge to depository libraries, and upon the request of other libraries or by subscription, a list of state publications which list shall include a cumulated index. The depository library center established in section 303A.22 shall also prepare and publish decennial cumulative indexes.

5. Provide to the library of Congress two copies of each state publication collected.

Acts 1978 (67 G.A.) ch. 1105, § 3.

303A.24. Deposits by each state agency

Upon issuance of a state publication a state agency shall deposit with the depository library center at no cost to the center, seventy-five copies of the publication, or a lesser amount if specified by the depository librarian.

Acts 1978 (67 G.A.) ch. 1105, § 4.

DISTRIBUTION OF PUBLIC DOCUMENTS

(Iowa Code Annotated, 1982, s.18.84, 18.87, 18.89, 18.91,
18.92, 18.96, 18.97.)

18.84 Mailing lists

The superintendent shall require from officials or heads of departments mailing lists, or addressed labels or envelopes, for use in distribution of reports and documents. He shall revise such lists, eliminating duplications and adding thereto libraries, institutions, public officials, and persons having actual use for the material. He shall arrange such lists so as to reduce to the minimum the postage or other cost for delivery.

Formerly § 16.11, Code 1973. Renumbered as § 18.81 by code editor in 1974.

18.87 Libraries

The completed journals of the general assembly, and the official register shall be sent to each free public library in Iowa, the state library, the library commission, libraries at state institutions, and college libraries.

Formerly § 16.14, Code 1973. Renumbered as § 18.87 by code editor in 1974.

18.89 Congressional library

Two copies of each publication shall be sent to the library of Congress.

Formerly § 16.16, Code 1973. Renumbered as § 18.89 by code editor in 1974.

18.91 School libraries

The official register shall be distributed, in addition to the foregoing provisions to the school libraries.

Amended by Acts 1974 (65 G.A.) ch. 1172, § 14, eff. July 1, 1975.

18.92 General distribution

The superintendent may send additional copies of publications to other state officials, individuals, institutions, libraries, or societies that may make request therefor.

Formerly § 16.19, Code 1973. Renumbered as § 18.92 by code editor in 1974.

18.96 Distribution to colleges

Upon application, in writing, from the librarian or chief executive officer of any incorporated college in this state, the superintendent of printing shall, upon the approval of the director, forward to said applicant, without charge, bound volumes of the laws enacted.

Formerly § 16.23, Code 1973. Renumbered as § 18.96 by code editor in 1974.

18.97 Code—session laws

The superintendent of printing shall make free distribution of the Code, rules of civil procedure, rules of appellate procedure, supreme court rules, the Acts of each general assembly, and, upon request, the Iowa administrative code as follows:

1. To state law library for exchange purposes ....100 copies

2. To law library of state University of Iowa for exchange purposes .... 75 copies

3. To state historical department .... 5 copies

4. To state historical society .... 5 copies

*   *   *

17. To library of Congress and the library of the United States supreme court .... 1 copy
each

18. To library of the Iowa State University of science and technology and the libraries at the state University of Iowa and University of Northern Iowa .... 1 copy
each

19. To library of the United States department of justice .... 1 copy

20. To library of the judge advocate general, United States department of defense .... 1 copy

21. To library of the United States department of agriculture .... 1 copy

22. To library of the United States department of labor   1 copy

23. To legal staff, office of public debt, United States treasury department .... 1 copy

24. To library of the United States department of state   1 copy

25. To law library of the United States department of the interior .... 1 copy

26. To library of the United States department of internal revenue .... 1 copy

Acts 1977 (67 G.A.) ch. 40, § 2, eff. May 27, 1977.

STATE HISTORICAL DEPARTMENT
(Iowa Code Annotated, 1982, s.303.1 to 303.15.)

303.1. Establishment of department

There is established the Iowa state historical department which shall be governed by a state historical board consisting of twelve members, six of whom shall be appointed by the governor and six of whom shall be elected by the members of the state historical society established in section 303.4 of this chapter. The members appointed by the governor shall include one professionally qualified architectural historian, one historian, and one archaeologist. The members elected by the society shall include one resident of each congressional district.

The term of office for both elected and appointed members shall commence on July 1 of each year and shall be three years.

Acts 1974 (65 G.A.) ch. 1175, § 1. Amended by Acts 1975 (66 G.A.) ch. 162, § 1.

303.2. Officers—meetings

The state historical board shall annually elect a chairman and vice chairman from its membership, and the director of the division of historical museum and archives shall serve as secretary to the board. The board shall meet as often as deemed necessary, upon the call of the chairman and vice chairman, or at the request of a majority of the members of the board.

Members of the board shall be paid a forty-dollar per diem and shall be reimbursed for actual and necessary expenses while engaged in their official duties.

Acts 1974 (65 G.A.) ch. 1175, § 2.

303.3. Divisions of department

The Iowa state historical department shall consist of the division of historical museum and archives, located in Des Moines, the division of the state historical society, located in Iowa City, and the division of historic preservation.

Acts 1974 (65 G.A.) ch. 1175, § 2. Amended by Acts 1976 (66 G.A.) ch. 1158, § 5.

303.4. Membership in state historical society

The state historical board shall establish rules for membership of the general public in the state historical society, including rules relating to membership fees. Members shall be persons who indicate an interest in the history, progress, and development of the state and who pay the prescribed fee. The members of the state historical society may meet at least one time per year to further the understanding of the history of this state. The election of members of the state historical board, as provided in section 303.1, shall be by mailed ballot as provided in bylaws adopted by the society and approved by the state historical board. The society may elect officers and the director of the division of the state historical society shall serve as secretary to the society. The officers of the society shall not determine policy for the division of the state historical society but may perform functions to stimulate interest in the history of this state among the general public. The society may perform other activities related to history which are not contrary to the provisions of this chapter, subject to the approval of the board.

1. It is the intent of the general assembly that, as used in this chapter, "state historical society" means only the division of the Iowa state historical department, an agency solely of the state, which is denominated the division of the state historical society. It does not mean or include any private entity.

2. A corporation organized under the laws of this state shall not exercise any powers or duties exercisable by law by the Iowa state historical department and its divisions. If a corporation exercises or attempts to exercise these powers or duties, it shall be subject to an equitable suit for involuntary dissolution by any interested person.

3. Unless specifically designated otherwise, any gift, bequest, devise, endowment, or grant to or application for membership in the state historical society shall be presumed to be to or in the division of the state historical society of the Iowa state historical department.

Acts 1974 (65 G.A.) ch. 1175, § 4. Amended by Acts 1976 (66 G.A.) ch. 1158, § 10.

303.5. Powers and duties of the state historical board

The state historical board shall have the following powers and duties:

1. Establish policy for the division of historical museum and archives, the division of the state historical society, and the division of historic preservation, eliminating duplication of services whenever possible.

2. Appoint a director of the division of historical museum and archives, a director of the division of the state historical society, and a director of the division of historic preservation at annual salaries set by the general assembly. Directors of the divisions shall serve for

six-year terms and may be reappointed.

3. Control the historical building, the centennial building, and other properties and assign space.

4. Determine the scope of and authorize publications.

5. Make a biennial report to the governor and to the general assembly.

6. Co-ordinate activities of the department with federal, state, and local agencies.

7. Select sites for uniform historical markers.

8. Co-ordinate historic preservation matters.

9. Approve nominations to and removals from the state and national registers of historic places. The standards of the national register shall be adopted as the standards for the listing of historic property on the state register.

10. Approve the state preservation plan.

11. Acquire historic properties by gift, purchase, devise or bequest; preserve, restore, transfer and administer such properties; and charge reasonable admissions to such properties.

12. Promulgate rules and regulations for the effective and efficient operation of the department subject to the provisions of chapter 17A.

13. May periodically loan historical articles and artifacts, such as the silver tea service of General Grenville Dodge, owned or in the possession of the state of Iowa and on display or under the control of the state historical board for display at suitable locations within the state. A policy shall be determined and regulations adopted by the state historical board which establishes standards for the preservation, protection and security of the articles and artifacts. Suitable recognition of the loan shall be displayed and security safeguards, package, and freight shall be at the expense of the recipient of the loaned items.

14. May enter into agreements with the University of Northern Iowa, the state University of Iowa, Iowa State University of science and technology, or any accredited private institution as defined in section 261.9 to establish multicounty area research centers, which are in addition to but do not duplicate archives as defined in section 303.12. An area research center shall serve as the depository for the archives of counties and municipalities and for other unpublished original resource material of a given area to be designated in the agreement.

15. The division of the state historical society shall acquire on behalf of the state of Iowa title to the site known as Montauk governor's mansion. It is the recommendation of the general assembly that a nominal entrance fee be charged, as authorized by subsection 11, for Montauk governor's mansion, with all fees collected to be deposited in the general fund as required by section 303.9.

Acts 1974 (65 G.A.) ch. 1175, § 5. Added by Acts 1976 (66 G.A.) ch. 1158, §§ 3, 4.

303.6. Duties of the director of the division of historical museum and archives

The director of the division of historical museum and archives shall have the following powers and duties, under the direction of the board:

1. Administer the space in the historical building assigned to the department and maintain collections located in the building. Keep the building open for use by the public during hours prescribed by the board.

2. Administer the archives of the state as defined in section 303.12.

3. Collect, preserve, organize, arrange, and classify works of art, books, maps, charts, public documents, manuscripts, newspapers, and other objects and materials illustrative of the natural and political history of the territory and state and of the central west, and of the traditions and history of all prior occupants who settled in the region, including women and the various racial, religious and ethnic groups.

4. Collect memorials and mementos of the pioneers of Iowa and the soldiers of all wars

in which Iowa residents participated, including portraits, specimens of arms, clothing, army letters, commissions of officers and other military papers and documents.

5.   Exhibit objects illustrative of the history and prehistory archaeology of this state, to interpret that history, and to publish such matters as may be of value and interest to the public.

6.   Administer and care for and preserve the monuments, memorials, and works of art on the grounds and in the buildings at the seat of government, and report from time to time their condition and make recommendations to the proper officers or board.

7.   Employ necessary personnel under the provisions of chapter 19A.

8.   Report to the board as required.

9.   Perform such other duties as may be imposed by law or prescribed by the rules of the board.

Acts 1974 (65 G.A.) ch. 1175, § 6.

303.7. Duties of director of division of state historical society

The director of the division of the state historical society shall have the following powers and duties, under the direction of the board:

1.   Maintain a library of materials relating to the history of this state and illustrative of the progress and development of the state.

2.   Conduct historical studies and researches and issue publications.

3.   Disseminate a knowledge of the history of this state among the people of this state.

4.   Encourage and assist local, county, and regional organizations devoted to historical purposes and foster an understanding and appreciation of Iowa history among all units of government.

5.   Maintain artifacts of archaeological significance.

6.   Plan, develop and publicize a uniform system of marking state historical, archaeological, geological and legendary sites.

7.   Employ necessary personnel under the provisions of chapter 19A.

8.   Perform such other duties as may be imposed by law or prescribed by the rules of the board.

Acts 1974 (65 G.A.) ch. 1175, § 7.

303.8. Duties of the director of the division of historic preservation

The director of the division of historic preservation shall have the following powers and duties, under the direction of the board:

1.   Serve as the state historic preservation officer, certified by the governor in accordance with federal requirements.

2.   Identify and document historic properties, including those owned by the state, its instrumentalities and political subdivisions.

3.   Prepare and maintain the state register of historic places, including those listed on the national register of historic places.

4.   Prepare and annually update the state's preservation plan.

5.   Develop standards and criteria for the acquisition of historic properties and for the preservation, restoration, maintenance and operation of properties under the jurisdiction of the state historical board.

6.   Accept federal aid for historic preservation purposes.

7. Co-operate with federal, state and local government agencies in historic preservation matters.

8. Co-ordinate the activities of, and provide technical and financial assistance if federal funds are available, to local historic preservation commissions and private parties in accordance with the state plan and programs for historic preservation.

9. Stimulate public interest in historic preservation.

10. Pursue historical, architectural and archaeological research and development, which may include but shall not be limited to, continuing surveys, excavation, scientific recording, interpretation and publication of the historical, architectural, archaeological and cultural sites, buildings and structures in the state.

11. Employ necessary personnel under the provisions of chapter 19A.

Acts 1974 (65 G.A.) ch. 1175, § 8.

303.9. Funds received by state historical department

All funds received by the state historical department, including but not limited to gifts, endowments, funds from the sale of memberships in the state historical society and fees, except entrance fees for the Montauk governor's mansion, shall be credited to the account of the state historical department and are appropriated to the state historical department to be invested or used for programs and purposes under the authority of the state historical board.

Acts 1974 (65 G.A.) ch. 1175, § 9 Amended by Acts 1981 (69 G.A.) ch. 10, § 11.

303.10. Acceptance and use of money grants

All federal grants to and the federal receipts of the agencies receiving funds under this chapter are appropriated for the purpose set forth in the federal grants or receipts. Acts 1974 (65 G.A.) ch. 1175, § 10.

303.11. Gifts

The state historical board may accept gifts and bequests which shall be used in accordance with the desires of the donor if expressed. Funds contained in an endowment fund for either the department of history and archives or the state historical society existing on July 1, 1974 shall remain an endowment of either the division of historical museum and archives or the division of the state historical society. After July 1, 1974, gifts shall be accepted only on behalf of the state historical department. Funds in an endowment fund may be invested by the state historical board.

In instances where publication of a book is financed by the endowment fund, nothing in this chapter shall prevent the return of moneys from sales of the book to the endowment fund.

Acts 1974 (65 G.A.) ch. 1175, § 11.

303.12. Archives

Archives means those documents, books, papers, photographs, sound recordings, or similar material produced or received pursuant to law in connection with official government business, which no longer have administrative, legal, or fiscal value to the office having present custody of them, and which have been appraised by the director of the historical museum and archives as having sufficient historical, research, or informational value to warrant permanent preservation. The director of the division of historical museum and archives is the trustee and custodian of the archives of Iowa, except that archives do not include county or municipal archives unless they are voluntarily deposited with the director with the written consent of the director. The director shall prescribe rules for the systematic arrangement of archives as to the proper labeling to indicate the contents and order of filing and the archives must be so labeled before the archives may be transferred to the director's custody.

Acts 1974 (65 G.A.) ch. 1175, § 12. Amended by Acts 1977 (67 G.A.) ch. 98, § 1, eff. Jan. 1, 1978.

303.13. Transfer of archives

The several state, executive, and administrative departments, officers or offices, councils, boards, bureaus, and commissions, may transfer and deliver to the state historical department archives as defined in section 303.12 and as prescribed in the records management manual. Before transferring archives, the office of present custody shall file with the director a classified list of the archives being transferred made in such detail as the director shall prescribe. If the director, on receipt of the list, and after consultation with the chief executive of the office filing the classified list or with a representative designated by the executive, shall find that, according to the records management manual, certain classifications of the archives listed are not of sufficient historical, legal or administrative value of justify permanent preservation, the director shall not accept the material for deposit in the state archives.

Acts 1974 (65 G.A.) ch. 1175, § 13. Amended by Acts 1977 (67 G.A.) ch. 98, § 2, eff. Jan. 1, 1978.

303.14. Removal of original

After any archives have been received by the director, they shall not be removed from the director's custody without his consent except in obedience to a subpoena of a court of record or a written order of the state executive council.

The director shall not be required to preserve permanently vouchers, claims, canceled or redeemed state warrants, or duplicate warrant registers, respectively, of the state comptroller and the treasurer of state but may, after microfilming, destroy by burning of shredding any such warrants, having no historical value, that have been in the director's custody for a period of one year and likewise to destroy by burning or shredding any vouchers, claims and duplicate warrant registers which have been in the director's custody for a period of one year. A properly authenticated reproduction of any such microfilmed record shall be admissible in evidence in any court in this state.

Acts 1974 (65 G.A.) ch. 1175, § 14. Amended by Acts 1977 (67 G.A.) ch. 98, § 3, eff. Jan. 1, 1978.

303.15. Certified copies—fees

Upon request of any person, the director of the division of historical museum and archives or the director of the division of the state historical society shall make a certified copy of any document, manuscript, or record contained in the archives or in the custody of the division of the state historical society, and when a copy is properly authenticated it shall have the same legal effect as though certified by the officer from whose office it was obtained or by the secretary of state. The copy may be made in writing, or by any suitable photographic process. The director shall charge and collect for such copies the fees allowed by law to the official in whose office the document originates for such certified copies. The director shall charge a person requesting a search of census records for the purpose of determining genealogy the actual cost of performing the search.

Acts 1974 (65 G.A.) ch. 1175, § 15.

STATE RECORDS COMMISSION
(Iowa Code Annotated, 1982, s.304.1 to 304.17.)

304.1. Citation

This chapter shall be known and may be cited as the "Records Management Act."

Acts 1974 (65 G.A.) ch. 1176, § 1.

304.2. Definitions

As used in this chapter, unless the context otherwise requires:

1. "Record" means a document, book, paper, photograph, sound recording or other material, regardless of physical form or characteristics, made, produced, executed or received pursuant to law in connection with the transaction of official business of state government. "Record" does not include library and museum material made or acquired and preserved solely for reference or exhibition purposes, miscellaneous papers or correspondence without official significance, extra copies of documents preserved only for convenience of reference, and stocks of publications and processed documents.

2. "Agency" means any executive department, office, commission, board or other unit of state government except as otherwise provided by law.

3. "Commission" means the state records commission created by this chapter.

Acts 1974 (65 G.A.) ch. 1176, § 2. Amended by Acts 1977 (67 G.A.) ch. 98, § 4, eff. Jan. 1, 1978.

304.3. Commission created

There is created a state records commission. The commission shall consist of:
1. The secretary of state who shall act as chairman.
2. The director of the historical museum and archives.
3. The treasurer of state.
4. The state comptroller.
5. The court administrator of the judicial department.
6. The auditor of state or designee.
7. Director of the department of general services who shall act as secretary of the commission.

It is the duty of the commission to determine what records have no administrative, legal, fiscal, research or historical value and should be disposed of or destroyed. The decisions of the commission shall be made by a majority vote of the entire membership.

Acts 1974 (65 G.A.) ch. 1176, § 3. Amended by Acts 1976 (66 G.A.) ch. 1052, § 15; Acts 1977 (67 G.A.) ch. 48, § 28; Acts 1977 (67 G.A.) ch. 98, § 5, eff. Jan. 1, 1978.

304.4. Expenses

Members of the commission shall serve without compensation but may receive their actual expenses incurred in the performance of their duties.

Acts 1974 (65 G.A.) ch. 1176, § 4. Amended by Acts 1976 (66 G.A.) ch. 1052, § 16; Acts 1977 (67 G.A.) ch. 98, § 6, eff. Jan. 1, 1976.

304.5. Meetings

The commission shall have its offices at the seat of government but may hold meetings in other locations. It shall meet quarterly and at the call of the chairman.

Acts 1974 (65 G.A.) ch. 1176, § 5.

304.6. Powers

The primary agency responsible for providing administrative personnel and services for the commission shall be the department of general services. The purchase, rental or lease of equipment and supplies for record storage or preservation by agencies shall be subject to the approval of the commission except as otherwise provided by law. The commission shall review all record storage systems and installations of agencies subject to this chapter and recommend any changes necessary to assure maximum efficiency and economic use of equipment and procedures, including but not necessarily limited to, the type of equipment, methods and procedures for filing and retrieval of records and the location of equipment. The commission shall perform any act necessary and proper to carry out its duties.

Acts 1974 (65 G.A.) ch. 1176, § 6. Amended by Acts 1977 (67 G.A.) ch. 98, § 7, eff. Jan. 1, 1978.

304.7. Rules

The commission shall adopt rules in accordance with the provisions of chapter 17A which are necessary for the exercise of the powers and duties granted by this chapter. The rules shall provide for:

1. Procedures to promote the economical and efficient management of records and to insure the maintenance and security of records deemed appropriate for preservation.

2. Procedures and standards for the efficient and economical utilization of space, equipment, and supplies needed for the purpose of creating, maintaining, storing and servicing records.

3. Standards for the selective retention of records of continuing value.

4. Procedures for compiling and submitting to the commission lists and schedules of records proposed for disposal.

5. Procedures for the physical destruction of records proposed for disposal.

6. Standards for the reproduction of records.

In carrying out its duties under this chapter, the commission shall develop a records management manual within one year of July 1, 1974. The records management manual shall be made available to agencies subject to the provisions of this chapter and shall contain the rules and regulations required by this chapter, such other information as is necessary, and shall provided for implementing the provisions of this chapter. The commission may contract for services required to develop the records management manual. The records management manual shall be revised and updated periodically to reflect decisions made by the commission.

Acts 1974 (65 G.A.) ch. 1176, § 7.

304.8. Disposal prohibited

After July 1, 1975, no records shall be disposed of by any agency unless prior approval of the commission is obtained or has been previously granted or disposal is provided for in the records management manual.

Acts 1974 (65 G.A.) ch. 1176, § 8.

304.9. Lists of records

The head of each agency shall submit to the commission lists of the records in his custody. The head of each agency shall also submit a schedule proposing the length of time each record should be retained for administrative, legal or fiscal purposes.

Acts 1974 (65 G.A.) ch. 1176, § 9.

304.10. Director of historical museum and archives—duties

All lists and schedules submitted to the commission shall be referred to the director of the historical museum and archives, who shall determine whether the records proposed for disposal have value to other agencies of the state or have research or historical value. The director of the historical museum and archives shall submit the lists and schedules with his or her recommendations in writing to the commission and the final disposition of the records shall be according to the orders of the commission.

Acts 1974 (65 G.A.) ch. 1176, § 10. Amended by Acts 1977 (67 G.A.) ch. 98, § 8, eff. Jan. 10, 1978.

304.11. Termination of state agency

Upon the termination of any state agency whose functions have not been transferred to another agency, the records of the agency shall be disposed of according to the provisions of the state records management manual.

Acts 1974 (65 G.A.) ch. 1176, § 11. Amended by Acts 1977 (67 G.A.) ch. 98, § 9, eff. Jan. 1, 1978.

304.12. Emergency preparations

The commission shall establish a system for the protection and preservation of records essential for the continuity or establishment of governmental functions in the event of an emergency arising from enemy action or natural disaster. The commission shall:

1. Determine what records are essential for emergency government operations through consultation with all state agencies.

2. Determine what records are essential for postemergency government operations, and provide for their protection and preservation.

3. Establish the manner in which essential records for emergency and postemergency government operations shall be preserved to insure emergency use.

4. Provide for security storage or relocation of essential state records in the event of an emergency arising from enemy attack or natural disaster.

Acts 1974 (65 G.A.) ch. 1176, § 12.

304.13. Duplicates

The commission may make or cause to be made preservation duplicates of records and may designate as duplicates existing copies of initial state records. A preservation duplicate record shall be durable, accurate, complete and clear and shall be made by means designated by the commission.

A preservation duplicate record shall have the same force and effect for all purposes as the original record whether or not the original record is in existence. A transcript, exemplification or certified copy of a preservation duplicate record shall be deemed for all purposes to be a transcript, exemplification or certified copy of the original record.

The commission shall review all duplicating and microfilming systems and installations of agencies subject to this chapter and recommend any changes necessary to assure maximum efficiency and economic use of equipment and procedures, including but not necessarily limited to, the type of equipment, type of storage files, methods and procedures for keeping duplicate records and the location of equipment. The commission may establish centralized duplicating or microfilming facilities if it deems it in the best interest of the state. Agencies subject to this chapter shall consult with and receive approval of the commission prior to the purchase of any duplicating or microfilming equipment or files to be used for storage of records.

Acts 1974 (65 G.A.) ch. 1176, § 13.

304.14. Agency program

The head of each agency shall establish and maintain a program for the economical and efficient management of the records of the agency. The program shall:

1. Provide for effective controls over the creation, maintenance, and use of records in the conduct of current business.

2. Provide for co-operation with the secretary of the commission in applying standards, procedures, and techniques to improve the management of records, promote the maintenance and security of records deemed appropriate for preservation, and facilitate the segregation and disposal of records of temporary value.

3. Provide for compliance with the provisions of this chapter and the rules and regulations adopted by the commission.

Acts 1974 (65 G.A.) ch. 1176, § 14.

304.15. Records state property

All official records of this state are the property of the state and shall not be mutilated, destroyed, removed or disposed of, except as provided by law or by rule.

Acts 1974 (65 G.A.) ch. 1176, § 15.

304.16. Liability precluded

No member of the commission or head of an agency shall be held liable for damages or loss, or civil or criminal liability, because of the destruction of public records pursuant to the provisions of this chapter or any other law authorizing their destruction.

Acts 1974 (65 G.A.) ch. 1176, § 16.

304.17. Exemption—duty of department of transportation and board of regents

The state department of transportation and the agencies and institutions under the control of the state board of regents are exempt from the records management manual and the provisions of this chapter. However, the state department of transportation and the state board of regents shall adopt rules for their employees, agencies, and institutions which are consistent with the objectives of this chapter. The rules shall be approved by the state records commission and be subject to the provisions of chapter 17A.

Acts 1974 (65 G.A.) ch. 1176, § 17. Amended by Acts 1975 (66 G.A.) ch. 67, § 69, eff. Aug. 15, 1975; Acts 1980 (68 G.A.) ch. 1012, § 36.

REGIONAL LIBRARY SYSTEMS
(Iowa Code Annotated, 1982, s.303B.1 to 303B.9.)

303B.1. Purpose

There is established a regional library system for the purpose of providing supportive library services to existing public libraries and to individuals with no other access to public library service and to encourage local financial support of public library service in those localities where it is presently inadequate or nonexistent.

Acts 1973 (65 G.A.) ch. 200, § 1.

303B.2. Regional library trustees

The regional library system shall consist of seven regional boards of library trustees which shall serve respectively the seven geographic regions specified in this section. Each region shall be divided into geographic districts, which shall be drawn along county lines and which shall be represented on regional boards by trustees elected to the boards in the following numbers and from the following districts:

1. To the southwestern board, two from Pottawattamie county and one from each of the following five districts:

a. Harrison, Shelby and Audubon counties.

b. Guthrie, Cass and Adair counties.

c. Mills, Fremont and Page counties.

d. Montgomery, Adams, Union and Taylor counties.

e. Clarke, Lucas, Ringgold, Decatur and Wayne counties.

2. To the northwestern board, two from Woodbury county and one from each of the following five districts:

a. Lyon, Sioux and Osceola counties.

b. Dickinson, Emmet, Clay and Palo Alto counties.

c. O'Brien, Plymouth and Cherokee counties.

d. Buena Vista, Pocahontas, Ida, Sac and Calhoun counties.

e. Monona, Crawford and Carroll counties.

3. To the north central board, two from a district composed of Hancock, Cerro Gordo and Franklin counties; two from a district composed of Humboldt, Wright and Webster counties; and one from each of the following three districts:

a. Kossuth and Winnebago counties.

b. Hamilton and Hardin counties.

c. Worth, Mitchell and Floyd counties.

4. To the central board, four from a district composed of Polk and Marion counties, and one from each of the following three districts:

a. Greene, Dallas, Madison and Warren counties.

b. Boone and Story counties.

c. Marshall and Jasper counties.

5. To the southeastern board, two from Scott county and one from each of the following five districts:

a. Appanoose, Davis and Wapello counties.

b. Jefferson, Van Buren and Lee counties.

c. Monroe, Mahaska and Keokuk counties.

d. Henry and Des Moines counties.

e. Muscatine, Louisa and Washington counties.

6. To the east central board, three from a district composed of Linn and Jones counties; two from a district composed of Iowa, Johnson and Cedar counties; and one from each of the following two districts:

a. Tama, Benton and Poweshiek counties.

b. Jackson and Clinton counties.

7. To the northeastern board, two from Black Hawk county; two from a district composed of Delaware and Dubuque counties; and one from each of the following three districts:

a. Grundy, Butler and Bremer counties.

b. Howard, Winneshiek, Allamakee and Chickasaw counties.

c. Buchanan, Fayette and Clayton counties.

Acts 1973 (65 G.A.) ch. 200, § 2. Amended by Acts 1975 (66 G.A.) ch. 81, § 141.

303B.3. Election

A trustee of a regional board shall be elected without regard to political affiliation at the general election by the vote of the electors of his district from a list of nominees, the names of which have been taken from nomination papers filed in accordance with chapter 45 in all respects except that they shall be signed by not less than twenty-five eligible electors of the respective district. The election shall be administered by the commissioner who has jurisdiction under section 47.2.

Acts 1973 (65 G.A.) ch. 200, § 3. Amended by Acts 1974 (65 G.A.) ch. 1101, § 93, eff. April 26, 1974.

303B.4. Terms

Regional library trustees shall take office on the first day of January following the general election and shall serve terms of four years, except that trustees elected to the initial board in the year 1974 shall determine their respective terms by lot so that three members shall serve terms of two years and four members shall serve terms of four years. A vacancy shall be filled when it occurs not less than ninety days before the next general election by appointment by the regional board for the unexpired term. No trustee shall serve on a local library board or be employed by a library during his or her term of office as a regional library trustee.

Acts 1973 (65 G.A.) ch. 200, § 4. Amended by Acts 1975 (66 G.A.) ch. 81, § 142.

303B.5. Compensation

Regional trustees shall be reimbursed for the actual and necessary expenses incurred by them in the discharge of their duties, but shall receive no compensation for services.

Acts 1973 (65 G.A.) ch. 200, § 6.

303B.6. Powers and duties of regional trustees

Regional trustees may:

1. Receive and expend available local, state, federal and private funds.

2. Contract with libraries, library agencies, or individuals to improve **public** library service.

3. Provide direct public library service without charge in their respective **regions** for an initial period of four years to individuals who have no access to public library service.

4. Acquire land and construct or lease facilities to carry out the provisions of this chapter.

5. Provide technical assistance for the purchasing and processing of library materials.

6. Assist public library agencies in:

a. Providing reference and information services;

b. Providing interlibrary loan services;

c. Providing universal loan services for individuals;

d. Preparing budgets;

e. Maintaining library collections;

f. Preparing book lists and bibliographies;

g. Promoting library use by the public;

h. Planning and presenting public programs; and

i. Training library staff.

7. Provide resources and services to strengthen local public library services throughout the region by contracting to utilize the strengths of the seven existing public library agencies, one for each region, which are as follows: Council Bluffs public library; Sioux City public library; North Iowa library extension, incorporated; Des Moines public library; Davenport public library; Cedar Rapids public library; and Waterloo public library.

8. Supply statistical and descriptive information on its service program to the Iowa state traveling library or its successor.

Acts 1973 (65 G.A.) ch. 200, § 7.

303B.7. Regional administrator

A regional board shall appoint an administrator, who shall be a practicing librarian and who shall serve at the pleasure of the board. The administrator shall act as the executive secretary of the regional board and shall administer the public library system of the region in accordance with the objectives and policies adopted by the regional board.

Acts 1973 (65 G.A.) ch. 303, § 8.

303B.8. Administration of funds

Funds appropriated for the purpose of carrying out this chapter shall be distributed to regional boards by the board of trustees of the Iowa state traveling library or its successor on the basis of the population to be served by each regional board, but the funds shall, for the year commencing July 1, 1973, be allocated to regional boards on an equal basis. All funds appropriated for the regional library system shall be administered by the regional boards.

Acts 1973 (65 G.A.) ch. 200, § 9.

303B.9. Local financial support

A regional board shall have the authority to require as a condition for receiving services under section 303B.6 that a governmental subdivision maintain any tax levy for library maintenance purposes that is in effect on July 1, 1973. Commencing July 1, 1977, each city within its corporate boundaries and each county within the unincorporated area of the county shall levy a tax of at least six and three-fourths cents per thousand dollars of assessed value on the taxable property or at least the monetary equivalent thereof when all or a portion of the funds are obtained from a source other than taxation, for the purpose of providing financial support to the public library which provides library services within the respective jurisdictions.

Acts 1973 (65 G.A.) ch. 200, § 10. Amended by Acts 1975 (66 G.A.) ch. 67, § 67, eff. Aug. 15, 1975; Acts 1976 (66 G.A.) ch. 1160, § 2.

COUNTY LIBRARIES
(Iowa Code Annotated, 1982, s.358B.2 to 358B.18.)

358B.2   Library districts formed

A county library district may be established composed of one county or two or more adjacent counties and may include or exclude the entirety of a city partly within one of the counties.

Eligible electors residing within the proposed district in a number not less than five percent of those voting for president of the United States or governor, as the case may be, within said district at the last general election may petition the board of supervisors of the county or counties for the establishment of such county library district. Said petition shall clearly designate the area to be included in the district.

The board of supervisors of each county containing area within the proposed district shall submit the proposition to the qualified electors within their respective counties at any general or primary election provided said election occurs not less than forty days after the filing of the petition.

A county library district shall be established, if a majority of the electors voting on the proposition and residing outside of cities maintaining a free public library favor it.

The result of the election within cities maintaining a free public library shall be considered separately, and no city shall be included within the county library district unless a majority of its electors, voting on the proposition, favor its inclusion. In such cases the boundaries of an established district may vary from those of the proposed district.

After the establishment of a county library district other areas may be included by mutual agreement of the board of trustees of the county library district and the governing body of the area sought to be included.

Acts 1947 (52 G.A.) ch. 193, § 2; Amended by Acts 1949 (53 G.A.) ch. 163, § 3; Acts 1972 (64 G.A.) ch. 1088, § 298, eff. July 1, 1975; Acts 1973 (65 G.A.) ch. 136, § 376; Acts 1974 (65 G.A.) ch. 1087, § 32.

358B.3. Gifts

When a gift for library purposes is accepted by the county, its use for the county library may be enforced against the board of supervisors by the library board by an action of mandamus or by other proper action.

Amended by Acts 1981 (69 G.A.) ch. 117, § 1072.

358B.4 Library trustees

In any county or counties in which a library district has been established a board of library trustees, consisting of five, seven, or nine electors of the library district, shall be appointed by the board or boards of supervisors of the county or counties comprising such library district. Membership on the library board shall be apportioned between the rural and city areas of the district in proportion to the population in each of such areas. In the event the library district is composed of two or more counties, representation on said library board shall be equitably divided between or among said counties in proportion to the population in each of such counties.

Acts 1947 (52 G.A.) ch. 193, § 4. Amended by Acts 1974 (65 G.A.) ch. 1087, § 32.

358B.5 Terms

Of said trustees so appointed on boards to consist of nine members, three shall hold office for two years, three for four years, and three for six years; on boards to consist of seven members, two shall hold office for two years, two for four years, and three for six years; and on boards to consist of five members, one shall hold office for two years, two for four years, and two for six years, from the first day of July following their appointment in each case. At their first meeting they shall cast lots for their respective terms, reporting the result of such lot to the board of supervisors. All subsequent appointments, whatever the size of the board, shall be for terms of six years each. Vacancies shall be filled for unexpired terms by the governing body of the taxing unit of the district represented by the retiring member.

Acts 1947 (52 G.A.) ch. 193, § 5.

358B.6 Removal or absence of trustee

The board of library trustees may declare the office of a trustee vacant by his removal from the library district or his unexplained absence from six consecutive regular meetings.

Acts 1947 (52 G.A.) ch. 193, § 6.

358B.7 No compensation

Members of said board shall receive no compensation for their services.

Acts 1947 (52 G.A.) ch. 193, § 7.

358B.8 Powers

Said board of library trustees shall have and exercise the following powers:

1. To meet and organize by the election of one of their number as president of the board, and by the election of a secretary and such other officers as the board may deem necessary.

2. To have charge, and supervision of the public library, its appurtenances and fixtures, and rooms containing the same, directing and controlling all the affairs of such library.

3. To employ a librarian, such assistants and employees as may be necessary for the proper management of said library, and fix their compensation; but, prior to such employment, the compensation of such librarian, assistants, and employees shall be fixed for the term of employment by a majority of the members of said board voting in favor thereof.

4. To remove such librarian, assistants, or employees by a vote of two-thirds of such board for misdemeanor, incompetency, or inattention to the duties of such employment.

5. To select and make purchases of books, pamphlets, magazines, periodicals, papers, maps, journals, furniture, fixtures, stationery, and supplies for such library.

6. To authorize the use of such libraries by school corporations or by nonresidents of the area which is taxed to support such libraries and to fix charges therefor.

7. To make and adopt, amend, modify, or repeal bylaws, rules, and regulations, not inconsistent with law, for the care, use, government, and management of such library and the business of said board, fixing and enforcing penalties for the violation thereof.

8. To have exclusive control of the expenditures of all taxes levied for library purposes as provided by law, and of the expenditures of

all moneys available by gift or otherwise for the erection of library buildings, and of all other moneys belonging to the library fund, including fines and rentals collected under the rules of the board of trustees. Said board shall keep a record of its proceedings.

9. To accept gifts of any property, including trust funds; to take the title to said property in the name of said library; to execute deeds and bills of sale for the conveyance of said property; and to expend the funds received by them from such gifts, for the improvement of said library.

Acts 1947 (52 G.A.) ch. 193, § 8.

358B.9   Methods of service

Library service shall be accomplished by one or more of the following methods in whole or in part:

1. By the establishment of depositories of books or other educational materials to be loaned at stated times and places.

2. By the transportation of books and other educational materials by conveyances for lending the same at stated times and places.

3. By the establishment of branch libraries for lending books and other educational materials.

4. By contracting for library service with a free public library of any city.

Acts 1947 (52 G.A.) ch. 193, § 9; Amended by Acts 1949 (53 G.A.) ch. 163, §§ 4, 5; Acts 1972 (64 G.A.) ch. 1088, § 299, eff. July 1, 1975.

358B.10. Library fund

All moneys received and set apart for the maintenance of the library shall be deposited in the fund specified in section 331.425, subsection 10, and shall be kept by the treasurer separate from all other moneys, and paid out upon the orders of the board of trustees, signed by its president and secretary.

Provided that where a free public library is maintained jointly by two or more counties, the library trustees may elect a library treasurer therefor, and it shall be the duty of the city and county treasurers to pay over to said library treasurer any and all library taxes that may be collected by them monthly.

Such library treasurer shall be required to furnish a bond conditioned as provided by section 64.2 in such amount as agreed upon by the boards of supervisors and the cost thereof shall be paid by the counties.

Amended by Acts 1981 (69 G.A.) ch. 117, § 1073.

358B.11   Annual report

The board of trustees shall, immediately after the close of each fiscal year, make to the board of supervisors a report containing a statement of the condition of the library, the number of books added thereto, the number circulated, the number not returned or lost, the amount of fines collected, and the amount of money expended in the maintenance thereof during such year, together with such further information as it may deem important.

Acts 1947 (52 G.A.) ch. 193, § 11.

358B.12   Real estate acquired

In any county in which a free library has been established, the board of library trustees may purchase real estate in the name of the county for the location of library buildings and branch libraries, and for the purpose of enlarging the grounds thereof.

Acts 1947 (52 G.A.) ch. 193, § 12.   Amended by Acts 1970 (63 G.A.) ch. 1030, § 6.

358B.13.   Maintenance expense on proportionate basis

The maintenance of a county library shall be on a proportionate population basis whereby each taxing unit shall bear its share in proportion to its population as compared to the whole population of the county library district. The board of library trustees shall on or before January 10 of each year make an estimate of the amount it deems necessary for the maintenance of the county library and shall transmit the estimate in dollars to the boards of supervisors and to the city councils within the district. The entire rural area of each county in the library district shall be considered as a separate taxing unit. Each city which is a part of the county library district shall be considered as a separate taxing unit. The board of supervisors of each county and the council of each city composing a county library district shall make the necessary levies for library maintenance purposes subject to the levy limit in section 331.421, subsection 9.

Amended by Acts 1981 (69 G.A.) ch. 117, § 1074.

358B.14   Not applicable to contract service

The provisions of this chapter pertaining to the establishment of a county library district shall not apply to any area receiving library service from any city library, unless the petition for a county library district, in addition to the required signatures of electors, is signed by the governing body of the area receiving library service under contract.

Acts 1947 (52 G.A.) ch. 193, § 15; Amended by Acts 1949 (53 G.A.) ch. 163, § 9; Acts 1972 (64 G.A.) ch. 1088, § 301, eff. July 1, 1975.

358B.15   Existing contracts assumed

Whenever a county library district is established the board of trustees thereof shall assume all the obligations of the existing contracts made by cities, townships, school corporations or counties to receive library service from free public libraries.

Acts 1949 (53 G.A.) ch. 163, § 10.   Amended by Acts 1974 (65 G.A.) ch. 1087, § 32.

358B.16. Withdrawal of city from district

A city may withdraw from the county library district upon a majority vote in favor of withdrawal by the electorate of the city in an election held on a motion by the city council. The election shall be held simultaneously with a general or city election. Notice of a favorable vote to withdraw shall be sent by certified mail to the board of library trustees of the county library and the county auditor prior to January 10, and the withdrawal shall be effective on July 1.

Amended by Acts 1978 (67 G.A.) ch. 1126, § 1.

358B.17 Historical association

Whenever a local county historical association is formed in a county having a free public library, the trustees of the library may unite with the historical association and set apart the necessary room to care for articles which come into the possession of the association. The trustees may purchase necessary receptacles and materials for the preservation and protection of articles which are of a historical and educational nature and may pay for the same out of the library fund.

Added by Acts 1972 (64 G.A.) ch. 1088, § 303, eff. July 1, 1975.

358B.18. Contracts to use city library

1. A school corporation, township, or county library district may contract for the use by its residents of a city library, but if a contract is made by a county board of supervisors or township trustees, it may only be for the residents outside of cities. A contract by a county shall supersede all contracts by townships or school corporations within the county outside of cities.

2. a. Contracts shall provide to the rate of tax to be levied. They may, by mutual consent of the contracting parties, be terminated at any time. They may also be terminated by a majority of the voters represented by either of the contracting parties, voting on a proposition to terminate which shall be submitted by the governing body upon a written petition of qualified voters in a number not less than five percent of those who voted in the area for president of the United States or governor at the last general election.

b. The proposition may be submitted at any election provided by law which covers the area of the unit seeking to terminate the contract. The petition shall be presented to the governing body not less than forty days before the election at which the question is to be submitted.

3. The board of trustees of any township which has entered into a contract shall at the April meeting levy a tax not exceeding six and three-fourths cents per thousand dollars of assessed valuation on all taxable property in the township to create a fund to fulfill its obligation under the contract.

4. The board of supervisors, after it makes a contract, shall levy a tax as provided in section 331.421, subsection 10, to fulfill its obligation under the contract or under a contract of library trustees appointed under subsection 5.

5. a. Qualified electors of that part of any county outside of cities in a number of not less than twenty-five percent of those in the area who voted for president of the United States or governor at the last general election may petition the board of supervisors to

submit the proposition of requiring the board to provide library service for them and their area by contract as provided by this section.

b. The board of supervisors shall submit the proposition to the voters of the county residing outside of cities at the next election, primary or general, provided that the petition has been filed not less than forty days prior to the date of the election at which the question is to be submitted.

c. If a majority of those voting upon the proposition favors it, the board of supervisors shall within thirty days appoint a board of library trustees from residents of the petitioning area. Vacancies shall be filled by the board.

d. The board of trustees may contract with any library for library use or service for the benefit of the residents and area represented by it.

Amended by Acts 1981 (69 G.A.) ch. 117, § 1075.

MUNICIPAL LIBRARIES
(Iowa Code Annotated, 1982, s.392.5.)

392.5 Library board

A city library board of trustees functioning on the effective date of the city code shall continue to function in the same manner until altered or discontinued as provided in this section.

In order for the board to function in the same manner, the council shall retain all applicable ordinances, and shall adopt as ordinances all applicable state statutes repealed by 64 G.A., chapter 1088.

A library board may accept and control the expenditure of all gifts, devises, and bequests to the library.

A proposal to alter the composition, manner of selection, or charge of a library board, or to replace it with an alternate form of administrative agency, is subject to the approval of the voters of the city.

The proposal may be submitted to the voters at any city election by the council on its own motion. Upon receipt of a valid petition as defined in section 362.4, requesting that a proposal be submitted to the voters, the council shall submit the proposal at the next regular city election. A proposal submitted to the voters must describe with reasonable detail the action proposed.

If a majority of those voting approves the proposal, the city may proceed as proposed.

If a majority of those voting does not approve the proposal, the same or a similar proposal may not be submitted to the voters of the city for at least four years from the date of the election at which the proposal was defeated.

Acts 1972 (64 G.A.) ch. 1088, § 196, eff. July 1, 1972.

SCHOOL LIBRARIES
(Iowa Code Annotated, 1982, s.257.25, 273.6.)

257.25. Educational standards

In addition to the responsibilities of the state board of public instruction and the state superintendent of public instruction under other provisions of the Code, the state board of public instruction shall, except as otherwise provided in this section, establish standards for approving all public and nonpublic schools in Iowa offering instruction at any or all levels from the prekindergarten level through grade twelve. A nonpublic school which offers only a prekindergarten program may, but shall not be required to, seek and obtain approval under this chapter. A list of approved schools shall be maintained by the department of public instruction. The state board shall promulgate rules to require that a multicultural, nonsexist approach is used by school districts. The educational program shall be taught from a multicultural, nonsexist approach. The approval standards established by the state board shall delineate and be based upon the educational program described below:

*　　*　　*

9. To facilitate the implementation and economical operation of the educational program defined in subsections 4 and 6, each school offering any of grades seven through twelve, except a school which offers grades one through eight as an elementary school, shall have:

a. A qualified school media specialist who shall meet the certification and approval standards prescribed by the department of public instruction and adequate media center facilities as hereinafter defined.

(1) **School media specialist.** The media specialist may be employed on a part-time or full-time basis, or may devote only part time to media service activities, according to the needs of the school and the availability of media personnel, as determined by the local board. The state board shall recommend standards based upon the number of students in attendance, the nature of the academic curriculum, and other appropriate factors.

(2) **Organization and adequacy of collection.** The media center shall be organized as a resource center of instructional material for the entire educational program. The number and kind of library and reference books, periodicals, newspapers, pamphlets, information files, audio-visual materials, and other learning aids shall be adequate for the number of pupils and the needs of instruction in all courses.

Amended by Acts 1974 (65 G.A.) ch. 1168, § 1; Acts 1974 (65 G.A.) ch. 1172, § 21, eff. July 1, 1975; Acts 1975 (66 G.A.) ch. 79, §§ 2, 3; Acts 1975 (66 G.A.) ch. 153, § 1, eff. Aug. 15, 1975; Acts 1977 (67 G.A.) ch. 93, §§ 1, to 3; Acts 1978 (67 G.A.) ch. 1001, § 9; Acts 1978 (67 G.A.) ch. 1096, § 1; Acts 1980 (68 G.A.) ch. 1070, §§ 1, 2.

273.6. Media centers

1. The media centers required under section 273.2 shall contain:

a. A materials lending library, consisting of print and nonprint materials.

b. A professional library.

c. A curriculum laboratory, including textbooks and correlated print and audiovisual materials.

d. Capability for production of media-oriented instructional materials.

e. Qualified media personnel.

f. Appropriate physical facilities.

g. Other materials and equipment deemed necessary by the department.

2. Program plans submitted by the area education agency to the department of public instruction for approval by the state board of media centers under this subsection shall include all of the following:

a. Evidence that the services proposed are based upon an analysis of the needs of the local school districts in the area.

b. Description of the manner in which the services of the area education agency media center will be co-ordinated with other agencies and programs providing educational media.

c. Description of the means for delivery of circulation materials.

d. Evidence that the media center fulfills the requirements of subsection 1.

Acts 1974 (65 G.A.) ch. 1172, § 7, eff. July 1, 1974; Acts 1978 (67 G.A.) ch. 1095, § 8, eff. June 23, 1978.

MISCELLANEOUS PROVISIONS
(Iowa Code Annotated, 1982, s.427.1, 450.4, Constitution
Art. 9, 2nd, s.4.)

427.1 Exemptions

The following classes of property shall not be taxed:

* * *

8. **Libraries and art galleries.** All grounds and buildings used for public libraries, public art galleries, and libraries and art galleries owned and kept by private individuals, associations, or corporations, for public use and not for private profit. Code 1939, § 6944

450.4 Exemptions

The tax imposed by this chapter shall not be collected:

* * *

3. When the property passes to public libraries or public art galleries within this state, open to the use of the public and not operated for gain, or to hospitals within this state, or to trustees for such uses within this state, or to municipal corporations for purely public purposes. Codes 1939, 1935, 1931, § 7308.

§ 4. Payments for exemption from military duty and fines under penal laws—application to support of common schools and libraries

SEC. 4. The money which may have been or shall be paid by persons as an equivalent for exemption from military duty, and the clear proceeds of all fines collected in the several Counties for any breach of the penal laws, shall be exclusively applied, in the several Counties in which such money is paid, or fine collected, among the several school districts of said Counties, in proportion to the number of youths subject to enumeration in such districts, to the support of Common Schools, or the establishment of libraries, as the Board of Education shall, from time to time provide.

Iowa library laws are reprinted from IOWA CODE ANNOTATED published by West Publishing Co., St. Paul, Minnesota.

KANSAS

STATE LIBRARY

(Kansas Statutes Annotated, 1982, s.75-2534 to 75-2542,
75-2544 to 75-2546.)

75-2534. **Kansas state library in Topeka; composition; services; chief officer; application of sunset law.** (a) There shall be a state library which shall be designated as the Kansas state library which shall be located in Topeka. The state library shall consist of books, pamphlets, papers, pictures, maps, charts and documents of every description now belonging thereto, together with such others as may be acquired by gift, purchase, exchange or otherwise. The state library shall provide library and informational services to the judicial, legislative and executive branches of the state government and said library shall also provide extension services to all of the residents of the state. The chief officer of the state library shall be the state librarian.

(b) The provisions of the Kansas sunset law apply to the office of the state librarian and the Kansas state library provided for by this section, and such office and library are subject to abolition thereunder.

History: L. 1963, ch. 422, § 1; L. 1981, ch. 299, § 33; July 1.

75-2535. **State librarian; appointment; qualifications.** The state librarian shall be appointed by the governor with the consent of the senate. Any person appointed as the state librarian shall hold a graduate degree in library science and shall have not less than five years actual experience in library administration. The state librarian shall be within the unclassified service under the Kansas civil service act and shall hold office at the pleasure of the governor.

History: L. 1963, ch. 422, § 2; L. 1975, ch. 435, § 1; L. 1978, ch. 332, § 36; L. 1981, ch. 329, § 1; July 1.

75-2536. **State librarian; oath.** Before entering upon duties the state librarian shall take the oath of office prescribed by law for public officers.

History: L. 1963, ch. 422, § 3; L. 1967, ch. 434, § 59; July 1.

75-2537. **State librarian; duties, assistants, employees.** The state librarian shall have the complete management of the state library, including all extension library services. He or she shall employ a director of reference and such other employees as are required to administer the laws providing for the state library and reference services. Except as otherwise provided in this act, all employees of the state librarian shall be within the classified service under the Kansas civil service act.

History: K.S.A. 75-2537; L. 1978, ch. 332, § 37; July 1.

75-2538. **Same; exchanges with other states and governments.** The state librarian shall have the authority to procure from other states and governments of the United States and foreign countries, societies and institutions, their documents, laws, judicial decisions and publications by exchanging those of this state for them.

History: L. 1963, ch. 422, § 5; L. 1974, ch. 135, § 16; July 1, 1975.

75-2539. Same; duties of secretary of state. To enable the librarian to make these exchanges the secretary of state is hereby required to deliver to the librarian as soon as published, sufficient copies of all documents and publications to enable the librarian to supply such exchanges and to fill such other requests as are authorized by law.
History: L. 1963, ch. 422, § 6; L. 1974, ch. 135, § 17; July 1, 1975.

75-2540. Same; duplicate books, sets or temporary material; exchange, sale or loan; proceeds from sales. The librarian may exchange, sell or loan indefinitely, duplicate books, sets of works or other duplicate or temporary material and the proceeds from any such sales may be used for miscellaneous library purposes. Any proceeds from sales shall be deposited in the "duplicate book fund," which fund is hereby created; and any exchanges, sales or loans made hereunder shall be exempt from the provisions of K.S.A. 75-3739 to 75-3744, inclusive.
History: L. 1963, ch. 422, § 7; July 1.

75-2541. Same; labeling and cataloguing of books and material. The librarian shall cause each book, pamphlet and document received by the state library to be properly stamped with the words "Kansas state library" and to be classified and catalogued in accordance with approved library methods.
History: L. 1963, ch. 422, § 8; July 1.

75-2542. Same; rules and regulations for government of library and services; local library services. The state librarian shall adopt such rules for the government of the library and extension services and for the use of the books and other property thereof as he or she may deem necessary. Under such regulations, the State librarian may loan such books and materials as may be designated for that purpose to any library in the state, or to any community not having an established library, or to any organization or individual conforming to the conditions of said regulations; and such books and other material so loaned shall be changed at suitable intervals subject to such reasonable regulations as may be adopted by said librarian, and in such manner as to secure to the greatest practicable degree the use and enjoyment of such books and other materials to the people of the entire state.
The state librarian may establish area or branch offices and service centers of the state library for the purpose of facilitating local library service. The state librarian shall provide leadership and assistance in the organization and development of local library agencies through field visits, conferences, and institutes, and shall give advice and counsel to libraries, municipalities, organizations or individuals in details of library processes and of management, and may send a staff member to aid in organization or in improvement of library methods. The state librarian may help organize, set up standards for, and advise in the management of county and regional libraries, and may enter into contracts with municipalities and with library boards to effectively execute demonstration libraries or affiliated library systems, and may assume administrative responsibility and control of any contractual projects during any period when state or federal funds are being used to support such projects.
History: L. 1963, ch. 422, § 9; July 1.

75-2544. Same; transfer of powers, duties and jurisdiction from traveling libraries commission to state librarian; books and properties; traveling libraries commission abolished. All of the powers, duties, authority and jurisdiction vested in and imposed upon the traveling libraries commission under article 26 of chapter 75 of the General Statutes of 1949 and acts amendatory thereof are hereby transferred to and conferred upon the state librarian, and the state librarian is hereby authorized, empowered and directed to do all things necessary for the proper exercise thereof. On July 1, 1963, all books, papers, records and all other properties of the traveling libraries commission, including all motor vehicles, and any and all other properties purchased with state funds shall become and be the property of the state librarian and said librarian is hereby authorized to accept such properties for the use of the state library. The Kansas traveling libraries commission is hereby abolished.
History: L. 1963, ch. 422, § 12; July 1.

75-2546. Same; state library advisory commission; membership; officers; terms, duties; meetings; compensation and allowances. There is hereby established a state library advisory commission of seven (7) members, six (6) of whom shall be appointed by the governor. The chief justice of the supreme court shall be an ex officio member and chairman of the commission. The state librarian shall serve as secretary of said commission. One member shall be a representative librarian from the university of Kansas or Kansas state university and one member shall be a qualified member of the Kansas federation of women's clubs, such member to be appointed by the governor from a list of three candidates recommended by the federation. No member shall be appointed to more than two (2) consecutive terms. Of the members first appointed two shall be appointed for terms of one (1) year, two for terms of two (2) years, one for a term of three (3) years, and one for a term of four

(4) years. Terms of members shall expire on June 30 each year. As the terms of such appointive members expire, successors shall be appointed for terms of four (4) years. All appointed members shall be interested in promoting the establishment and developing of publicly supported free library services in the state and encouraging development of libraries of all types.

The state commission shall consult and advise with the state librarian from time to time and suggest or recommend to the governor and the state librarian such policies, management and services as will best promote and advance the use and usefulness of the state library and its extension services for the residents of the state. The commission shall elect a vice-chairman to preside at meetings in the absence of the chairman. Said commission shall hold quarterly meet-

ings and such other meetings as may be called by the secretary, and shall meet upon request of a majority of the members of the commission. Members of the state library advisory commission attending meetings of such commission, or attending a subcommittee meeting thereof authorized by such commission, shall be paid amounts provided in subsection (e) of K.S.A. 75-3223 and amendments thereto. Amounts paid under this section shall be paid from appropriations to the state library upon warrants of the director of accounts and reports issued pursuant to vouchers approved by the state librarian or a person or persons designated by him or her.

History: L. 1963, ch. 422, § 14; L. 1974, ch. 348, § 89; L. 1975, ch. 416, § 19; July 1.

STATE AID

(Kansas Statutes Annotated, 1982, s.75-2553 to 75-2564.)

75-2553. Grants-in-aid to libraries act; citation. This act may be cited as the state grants-in-aid to libraries act.

History: L. 1974, ch. 381, § 1; July 1.

75-2554. Grants-in-aid to libraries; definitions. As used in this act, unless the context clearly indicates a different meaning: (a) "Local public libraries" means (1) Kansas libraries operating under the provisions of K.S.A. 12-1215 to 12-1248, inclusive, and acts amendatory thereof and supplemental thereto, or (2) municipalities contracting with any library for the furnishing of library services to such municipality pursuant to K.S.A. 12-1230, and amendments thereto;

(b) "Regional libraries" means the regional systems of libraries heretofore organized and operating under authority of K.S.A. 75-2547 to 75-2552, inclusive;

(c) "State library" means the Kansas state library created and operating under authority of K.S.A. 75-2534; and "state librarian" means the chief officer thereof, appointed pursuant to K.S.A. 1978 Supp. 75-2535.

History: K.S.A. 75-2554; L. 1978, ch. 343, § 1; July 1.

75-2555. Same; grant-in-aid to libraries fund; apportionment and distribution to eligible libraries; computation. There is hereby established in the state treasury a grant-in-aid to libraries fund. All moneys transferred or credited to such fund shall be distributed as provided by the state grants-in-aid to libraries act, as amended. The state librarian shall annually apportion and direct the payment to each of the eligible libraries its pro rata share of the moneys in the grant-in-aid to libraries fund. The amount due each library shall be computed as follows: The total amount in the fund shall be distributed ⅔ to the eligible local public libraries on the basis that the population

lation of each of the eligible local districts bears to the total population of all eligible local public library districts in Kansas; and ⅓ of the total fund shall be distributed to each of the regional libraries in equal amounts to each such library.

History: L. 1974, ch. 381, § 3; L. 1974, ch. 382, § 1; L. 1981, ch. 330, § 1; April 6.

75-2556. Same; annual reports to state library of population and tax information; determination of amounts of and eligibility for aid; payment dates. (a) Annually, on or before December 1, each local public library shall report to the state library the total population residing within its district as determined from the latest population census figures as certified by the division of the budget. Such report shall also state:

(1) The amount produced by the local ad valorem tax levies for the current year expenses for such library;

(2) the amount of moneys received from the local ad valorem tax reduction fund for current year expenses for such library;

(3) the amount of moneys received from taxes levied upon motor vehicles under the provisions of article 51 of chapter 79 of the Kansas Statutes Annotated for current year expenses for such library;

(4) the amount of moneys received in the current year from collections of unpaid local ad valorem tax levies for prior year expenses for such library;

(5) the mill rate levied within the district during the previous year;

(6) the assessed taxable tangible property valuation within the district; and

(7) such other information as the state librarian shall require.

(b) Based upon such census figures the state librarian shall determine the amount each eligible local public library is to receive.

(c) No local public library shall be eligible for any state grants-in-aid if the total of:

(1) The amount produced by the local ad valorem tax levies for the current year expenses for such library;

(2) the amount of moneys received from the local ad valorem tax reduction fund for current year expenses for such library;

(3) the amount of moneys received from taxes levied upon motor vehicles under the provisions of article 51 of chapter 79 of the Kansas Statutes Annotated for current year expenses for such library; and

(4) the moneys received in the current year from collections of unpaid local ad valorem tax levies for prior year expenses for such library is less than the total amount produced from such sources for the same library for the previous year.

(d) Local public library districts in which the assessed valuation decreases shall remain eligible for state grants-in-aid so long as the ad valorem tax mill rate for the support of such library has not been reduced below the mill rate imposed for such purpose for the previous year.

(e) The distribution so determined shall be apportioned and paid on April 1 and June 1 of each year.

History: L. 1974, ch. 381, § 4; L. 1974, ch. 382, § 2; L. 1981, ch. 330, § 2; April 6.

75-2557. Same; certification by state librarian of amounts payable; duties of director of accounts and reports. Annually, on or before March 15, the state librarian shall certify to the director of accounts and reports the amounts payable for the current calendar year to each·of the libraries in the state as computed under the provisions of K.S.A. 1981 Supp. 75-2555, and amendments thereto. It.shall be. the duty of the director to draw warrants on such fund as specified by the state librarian upon claims properly submitted therefor. The director of accounts and reports shall notify the state treasurer and the state librarian of such action.

History: L. 1974, ch. 381, § 5; L. 1981, ch. 330, § 3; April 6.

75-2558. Same; limitations on expenditures from state aid funds; penalty. State funds distributed to a local public library or a regional library as grants-in-aid shall not be expended for construction or repair, debt reduction, utilities or capital outlay, other than for the purchase of books, periodicals and other circulating library materials or library service communications, but state funds so received by a local public library or a regional library shall be expended or encumbered as authorized during the calendar year received even though not included in any budget of expenditures for such year. Funds expended in violation of this section may thereafter be withheld from later state grants-in-aid to the local public library or the regional library even though such with-

holding be made in a different fiscal year.

History: L. 1974, ch. 381, § 6; L. 1975, ch. 436, § 1; April 25.

75-2559. Same; annual expenditure reports by libraries receiving grants-in-aid. Each local public library and each regional library receiving grants-in-aid under this act shall annually report to the state librarian the manner in which state grants-in-aid received were expended or are encumbered. Such report shall cover the period from January 1 to December 31 of the previous year and shall be filed with the state librarian on or before February 1 of each year.

History: L. 1974, ch. 381, § 7; L. 1974, ch. 382, § 3; L. 1981, ch. 330, § 4; April 6.

75-2560. Same; powers and duties of state librarian; withholding aid; notice of noncompliance with act to director of accounts and reports. The state librarian is hereby authorized to adopt such rules and regulations as may be necessary to properly administer this act. The state librarian shall review all reports submitted and is authorized to reject any report that he or she finds inaccurate. The state librarian is further authorized to withhold grants-in-aid to any library that fails to comply with this act or the rules and regulations of the state librarian. The state librarian shall apprise the director of accounts and reports of all failures of libraries to comply with the provisions of this act.

History: L. 1974, ch. 381, § 8; July 1.

75-2561. Same; budget requests of state librarian; reports of distributions and expenditures. The state librarian shall include in his or her annual budget request the estimated amount needed for the succeeding fiscal year for grants-in-aid to libraries of Kansas. This request shall be based on amounts requested by the libraries and amounts reasonably available for such purposes. The legislature may appropriate, credit or transfer funds to the grants-in-aid fund as deemed necessary. At the time of making such annual requests for funds, the state librarian shall report all apportionments and payments of moneys to libraries in accordance with this act during the preceding twelve-month period together with the manner such funds were expended or encumbered.

History: L. 1974, ch. 381, § 9; July 1.

75-2562. Same; acceptance of federal grants or funds by state librarian; distribution; plan by advisory commission; independent application for and receipt of federal funds; effect. The state librarian shall be vested with the authority to apply for and receive any grants or other funds for library purposes, from the federal government or any agency thereof and shall be authorized to enter into any agreement necessary on behalf of the state to receive such grants or funds. All amounts received under this section shall be deposited in the state treasury and shall be distributed in accordance with this act and appropriation acts of the legislature upon warrants of the director of accounts and reports issued pursuant to vouchers approved by the state librarian or a person or persons designated by the state librarian. Amounts distributed under this section shall be distributed by him or her. Amounts distributed under this section shall be distributed in accordance with any applicable requirements of federal statutes or other federal law, however, to the extent not prohibited by federal statutes or other federal law, such distributions shall be made from time to time in accordance with the formula prescribed in K.S.A. 75-2555. The library advisory commission established under K.S.A. 75-2546 and amendments thereto may adopt such plan as is required by federal statutes or other federal law relating to distribution of moneys under this section, and such plan shall be consistent with the requirements of this section to the extent authorized by federal statutes and other federal law. Vouchers approved by the state librarian under this section shall make distribution in accordance with any such plan and the requirements of this section. Nothing in this act shall be deemed to prohibit any local public library from making independent application to any federal agency for federal funds, and such applications by local public libraries are hereby authorized, and any federal funds received exclusively pursuant to such an application by a local public library may be expended without regard to the limitations of this act, and entitlements to grants-in-aid or federal moneys under this act shall not be reduced because of any funds so received.

History: L. 1974, ch. 381, § 10; L. 1974, ch. 382, § 4; July 1.

75-2563. Contracts for computerized information and cataloging services; cost

system; billing; receipts; deposit in computerized library services fund. The state librarian may contract with any state agency or institution, any board of trustees of a community junior college, any board of education of a school district, the governing authority of any nonpublic school or any public library or any regional system of cooperating libraries for computerized information and cataloging services. Such services may include computer generated catalogue cards and searches of bibliographic indices. The state librarian with the approval of the director of accounts and reports, shall maintain a cost system in accordance with generally accepted accounting principles. In determining cost rates for billing services, overhead expenses shall include but not be limited to light, heat, power, insurance, labor and depreciation. Billings shall include direct and indirect costs and shall be based on the foregoing cost accounting practices. All receipts for sales of goods and services shall be deposited in the computerized library services fund which is hereby created in the state treasury. The provisions of K.S.A. 75-4215 and any amendments thereto shall apply to the said fund to the extent not in conflict with this act.

History: L. 1976, ch. 362, § 1; July 1.

75-2564. Same; deposit of federal grants; expenditures. All amounts from any grants from the federal government in support of this act shall be deposited in the state treasury. All expenditures from the computerized library services fund or from any such federal grant shall be made in accordance with appropriation acts upon warrants of the director of accounts and reports issued pursuant to vouchers approved by the state librarian or by a person or persons designated by the state librarian.

REGIONAL LIBRARY SYSTEMS
(Kansas Statutes Annotated, 1982, s.75-2547 to 75-2552.)

75-2547. Regional system of cooperating libraries; purpose. The purpose of this act is for the state in cooperation with local libraries to provide adequate library services to all citizens of the state through the regional systems of cooperating libraries herein provided, by use of joint planning and financing of library services to improve existing service, to utilize such federal aid funds as may be available and to extend library service to persons not having the same at this time.

History: L. 1965, ch. 105, § 1; June 30.

75-2548. Same; definitions. As used in this act, unless the context otherwise requires:

(a) "Board" means the library board of any library established or operating under authority of the laws of Kansas.

(b) "Participating board" or "participating library" means a board or library or district that is cooperating and participating in a regional system of cooperating libraries.

(c) "Regional system of cooperating libraries" means two or more libraries cooperating in a system approved by the state commission and officially designated as a regional system of cooperating libraries under this act.

(d) "System board" means the governing board comprised of representatives of libraries in a regional system of cooperating libraries, and which is authorized by this act to direct and plan library service for a regional system to the extent and in the manner provided by this act.

(e) "Library" may include school, community junior college, college or university libraries to the extent authorized by rules and regulations of the state commission, but does not include law libraries.

(f) "State commission" means the state library advisory commission.

(g) "System librarian" means a person (not a state officer or employee) who has been certified by the state commission as being qualified by education or experience to perform duties as a librarian for a regional system of cooperating libraries, and who shall attend system board meetings but shall not be a voting member thereof.

History: L. 1965, ch. 105, § 2; L. 1968, ch. 214, § 1; March 26.

75-2549. Same; petition for establishment; contents. Any one or more boards, may petition the state commission for establishment of a regional system of cooperating libraries comprised of territory which includes one or more counties, except territory supporting a library regularly subject to a tax levy of one-fourth (¼) mill or more shall be excluded from the proposed regional system upon request of the governing body of the district making such levy. Such petition shall be prepared in cooperation with the state librarian on forms provided by him or her. Such petition may propose cooperative arrangements with institutions of higher learning. Such petition shall include but shall not be limited to the following information:

(a) A statement of purpose for establishment of the proposed system and an outline of the proposed program of the system.

(b) A list of the counties to be included in the proposed regional system of cooperating libraries and any exclusions therefrom.

(c) A list of the participating libraries within the proposed regional system of cooperating libraries, together with the names and addresses of the members of the board of each such library.

(d) Letters or resolutions from each of the boards of participating libraries indicating the interest and attitude of such board toward establishment of the regional system of cooperating libraries.

(e) A list of the current budgets of each participating library showing items for library material and personnel for each such budget.

(f) Indication of local support appropriate to the operation of the proposed regional system of cooperating libraries.

(g) The number of persons to be served by the system, showing those presently within the taxing districts supporting one of the participating libraries, and those persons not within such a district.

(h) Such other information as may be

requested by the state librarian.

History: L. 1965, ch. 105, § 3; June 30.

75-2549a. Same; constitute a body corporate and politic; powers and authority. Each regional system of cooperating libraries established under or governed by the provisions of this act shall constitute a body corporate and politic, possessing the usual powers of a corporation for public purposes and may contract, sue and be sued and acquire, hold and convey real and personal property in accordance with law.

History: L. 1968, ch. 214, § 2; March 26.

75-2549b. Same; certain regional systems of cooperating libraries validated. The following regional systems of cooperating libraries are hereby validated and established with names and territory, except territory excluded pursuant to law as specified by the state commission, as follows:

Northwest Kansas Library System, comprised of the counties of Trego, Gove, Logan, Wallace, Graham, Sheridan, Thomas, Sherman, Norton, Decatur, Rawlins, and Cheyenne.

Central Kansas Library System, comprised of the counties of Phillips, Rooks, Ellis, Rush, Pawnee, Smith, Osborne, Russell, Barton, Jewell, Mitchell, Lincoln, Ellsworth, Republic, Cloud, Ottawa, and Saline.

North Central Library System, comprised of the counties of Washington, Clay, Dickinson, Marion, Marshall, Riley, Pottawatomie, Geary, Wabaunsee, Morris, Chase, and Lyon.

Southeast Kansas Library System, comprised of the counties of Greenwood, Elk, Chautauqua, Coffey, Woodson, Wilson, Montgomery, Anderson, Allen, Neosho, Labette, Linn, Bourbon, Crawford, and Cherokee.

South Central Kansas Library System, comprised of the counties of Kiowa, Stafford, Pratt, Barber, Rice, McPherson, Reno, Harvey, Kingman, Harper, Sedgwick, Sumner, Butler, and Cowley.

Northeast Kansas Library System, comprised of the counties of Nemaha, Jackson, Shawnee, Osage, Brown, Doniphan, Atchison, Jefferson, Leavenworth, Wyandotte, Douglas, Johnson, Franklin, and Miami.

Southwest Kansas Library System, comprised of the counties of Greeley, Hamilton, Stanton, Morton, Wichita, Kearny, Grant, Stevens, Scott, Lane, Ness, Finney, Hodgeman, Gray, Ford, Haskell, Seward, Meade, Clark, Edwards, and Comanche.

History: L. 1968, ch. 214, § 4; March 26.

75-2550. Same; system board; membership; powers. The system board shall consist of one or more representatives selected by each of the boards participating in the regional system, and one or more representatives appointed by the governor to represent territory not within the district of participating library board but within the territory of the regional system of cooperating libraries. The petition provided for in K.S.A. 75-2549 may propose the number of representatives of each such board, but the determination thereof shall be made by the state commission when approving such petition. The state commission shall consider any petition presented to it as provided in this act and if it approves such petition it shall adopt a resolution officially designating such particular regional system of cooperating libraries and describing the territory thereof which shall include one or more counties but shall exclude the territory of any taxing district which regularly levies one-fourth (¼) or more mills of tax for the support of a public library upon the request of the governing body of the district making such levy. Any district so excluded may later petition to be added to and included in the regional system of cooperating libraries from which it was excluded and such petition shall be prepared and processed as other petitions provided for by this act. Additional counties may be added to the territory of any regional system of cooperating libraries upon petition by a library board located in such county and such a petition shall be prepared and processed as is provided in this act for initial petitions; except that the prior approval in writing of a petition under this sentence shall be obtained by the petitioning board from the regional board and attached to the petition when submitted to the state commission. Within two (2) weeks after receiving notice of approval of a petition provided for under this act the board of each participating library and the governor shall select the number of representatives determined by the state commission and shall certify the names and addresses of such representatives to the state librarian. The term of each such representative may be proposed in the petition provided under K.S.A. 75-2549, but shall not exceed four years, and the final determination of duration of terms shall be made by the state commission at the time of approval of the petition.

Any taxing district which regularly levies one-fourth mill or more of tax for the support of a public library, and which taxing district has been included in a regional system, may petition to be excluded from the regional system. Such petition shall be made and presented to the state commission. The state commission shall consider any such petition and if such taxing district meets the requirement for making such a petition and if excluding such taxing district from the regional system will do no manifest harm thereto, the state commission may enter its order excluding and detaching such taxing district from the regional system and making such adjustment to the organization of such regional system as may be appropriate to continue the operation of the regional system without interruption.

The system board shall have the authority and power to (1) operate a system of library service to and for participating libraries, (2) the system board may purchase service from a participating library for the benefit of the regional system of cooperating libraries, (3) the system board may contribute to or receive contribution from any participating library, and may receive and utilize any gift of funds or property donated to the regional system of cooperating libraries, (4) the system board may contract with any one or more participating libraries and the board of each participating library is hereby authorized to contract with the system board or with any one or more other boards, but any such contract shall provide that the same shall not take effect until approved by the state librarian, (5) the system board may contract with any other system board or any board, but any such contract shall provide that the same shall not take effect until approved by the state librarian, and (6) employ a system librarian and such other persons as the regional board may find convenient or necessary.

History: L. 1965, ch. 105, § 4; June 30.

75-2550a. Same; selection of an executive board; delegation of legal functions; exception. Subject to rules and regulations of the state commission, any system board may provide for the selection of an executive board to which it may delegate any or all of its legal functions except adoption of annual budget.

History: L. 1968, ch. 214, § 3; March 26.

75-2551. Same; finance. Federal funds for public library service made available to the state under legislation passed prior to or after the passage of this act, and which funds are administered by the state librarian or state commission, may be used in support of any one or more regional system of cooperating libraries within the provisions of such federal legislation. The use of funds of any regional system of cooperating libraries shall be established by the system board by contracts with boards of participating libraries, or otherwise.

Participating boards shall have the power and are hereby authorized to pay for services purchased from the system board.

Any funds appropriated by the legislature and administered by the state librarian for the promotion of library services may be used to pay all or part of the expenses and equipment of any regional system of cooperating libraries.

The system board shall be subject to the cash basis and budget laws of the state. The budget of the system board shall be prepared, adopted and published as provided by law and hearing shall be held thereon in the first week of the month of August of each year. The tax levy made pursuant to such budget shall be certified to the county clerks of each county in the territory of the regional system of cooperating libraries.

Each system board is hereby authorized to levy not in excess of one-half (½) mill of tax to be used for library purposes on all of the taxable property within the boundaries of such regional system of cooperating libraries that is not within a district supporting a library with funds of such district.

History: L. 1965, ch. 105, § 5; June 30.

75-2552. Same; establishment of standards by commission. The state commission shall adopt rules and regulations establishing standards for (1) approval of regional system petitions, (2) review and amendment of regional system plans, (3) certification of system librarians, and (4) such other matters as the state commission may deem advisable.

History: L. 1965, ch. 105, § 6; June 30.

DISTRIBUTION OF PUBLIC DOCUMENTS

(Kansas Statutes Annotated, 1982, s.2565 to 2568, 20-207 to 20-213, 75-704a, 75-1023, 75-3048b, 75-3048c.)

75-2565. Definitions. As used in this act, the following terms and phrases shall have the meanings respectively ascribed thereto in this section:

(a) "Publication" means any report, pamphlet, book or other materials provided by a state agency for use by the general public;

(b) "state agency" means any state office or officer, department, board, commission, institution, bureau, society or any agency, division or unit within any state office, department, board, commission or other state authority.

History: L. 1976, ch. 358, § 1; July 1.

75-2566. Establishment and operation of publication collection and depository system; duties of state agencies and the state librarian. (a) The state librarian is hereby authorized and directed to establish, operate and maintain a publication collection and depository system as provided in this act.

(b) Each state agency shall deposit with the Kansas state library copies of any publication issued by such state agency in such quantity as shall be specified by the state librarian.

(c) The state librarian shall forward two (2) copies of all such publications to the library of congress, one copy to the state historical society, one copy to the center for research libraries and one copy shall be retained permanently in the Kansas state library. Additional copies, as may be prescribed by rule and regulation, may be required for the depository system.

History: L. 1976, ch. 358, § 2; July 1.

75-2567. Same; powers and duties of state librarian; designation of libraries as complete or selective depositories. (a) The state librarian shall periodically publish and distribute to complete depository libraries, selective depository libraries, state agencies, state officers and members of the Kansas legislature, an official list of state publications with at least an annual cumulation. Said official list shall provide a record of each agency's publications and shall show, in addition, the author, title, major subject content and other appropriate catalogue information for any such publication. Annually each state agency shall furnish to the state library a complete list of their publications for the previous year which the state librarian shall use to maintain a permanent record of publications.

(b) To be designated as a complete depository library any Kansas resource library, regional public library, libraries in institutions of higher education or other libraries must contract with the state librarian agreeing at a minimum to provide adequate facilities for the storage and use of any such publication and to render reasonable service without charge to qualified patrons in the use of such publication and to maintain its full collection of such publications indefinitely subject to disposal upon approval by the state librarian. Any library designated as a complete depository shall receive one copy of every state publication deposited with the Kansas state library. Any library designated as a selective depository shall receive only copies of publications which such library requests.

History: L. 1976, ch. 358, § 3; July 1.

75-2568. Same; rules and regulations. The state librarian is hereby authorized to adopt rules and regulations necessary to implement and administer the provisions of this act.

History: L. 1976, ch. 358, § 4; July 1.

20-207. Delivery of court reports to state law librarian. The director of printing shall hereafter deliver the whole number of copies of reports of the supreme court and court of appeals required to be published to the state law librarian as soon as completed; and when the whole edition of any volume shall be so delivered, the librarian shall certify that fact to the secretary of state, who shall thereupon ascertain the amount due the director of printing therefor, and audit and certify the same to the director of accounts and reports for payment.

History: L. 1889, ch. 247, § 3; R.S. 1923, 20-207; L. 1974, ch. 135, § 5; L. 1976, ch. 147, § 3; Jan. 10, 1977.

20-208. Exchanges, distribution and sale of Kansas reports; preservation of proofs, matrices, plates, computer tapes and

impressions; use for computerized legal research. (a) When the reports of the decisions of the supreme court or court of appeals are delivered, the state law librarian shall use as many thereof as may be necessary to maintain reasonable and equitable exchanges of such reports for law books and other legal publications of the other states, territories, countries, societies and institutions, for use in the supreme court law library. As used herein, "Kansas reports" shall mean the reports of the decisions of the supreme court and court of appeals. The state law librarian shall distribute copies of the Kansas reports without charge, as follows:

(1) The supreme court, the court of appeals and the office of the attorney general shall receive the number of copies necessary to conduct the official business of such office, as certified to the state law librarian by the head or executive officer of the respective agencies;

(2) The office of each elected state official, other than those specifically provided for herein, shall receive one copy;

(3) The law library of the school of law of the university of Kansas shall receive thirty (30) copies to maintain its sets of Kansas reports and for exchange purposes, and the law library of the school of law of Washburn university of Topeka shall receive thirty (30) copies to maintain its sets of Kansas reports and for exchange purposes;

(4) The state library and the libraries of Emporia state university, Fort Hays state university, Pittsburg state university, Kansas state university, and Wichita state university shall receive two (2) copies to maintain its set of Kansas reports;

(5) The United States district court for the district of Kansas shall receive six (6) copies;

(6) The office of each judge of the district court shall each receive one copy;

(7) The state penitentiary at Lansing and the state industrial reformatory at Hutchinson shall each receive one copy for the use of inmates at such institutions and one copy for the use of the legal advisor at such institutions;

(8) The library of congress shall receive two (2) copies in order to complete the copyright of said reports;

(9) One copy shall be deposited with the appropriate office of the United States post office in order to obtain a postal permit for mailing such reports;

(10) A personal copy of the reports shall be presented to each justice of the supreme court, each judge of the court of appeals, the clerk of the supreme court, the supreme court reporter, and the judicial administrator of the district courts. Also, a personal copy shall be sent to any retired supreme court justice, judge of the court of appeals, district judge or associate district judge, if such retired judge or justice files with the clerk of the supreme court annually a certificate stating that he or she is not engaged in the active practice of law and is willing to accept judicial assignments; and

(11) The legislative coordinating council shall receive the number of copies necessary to conduct the official business of the legislative branch of government, as certified to the state law librarian by the legislative coordinating council.

(b) Except as otherwise specifically provided in paragraph (10) of subsection (a), all copies of the Kansas reports distributed pursuant to subsection (a) or purchased by any governmental agency or subdivision shall become the property of such office, agency or subdivision, which shall be accountable therefor, and the state law librarion whereby such corporation may utilize the services of equipment and personnel under the supervision of the director of printing for the purpose of converting reports of the Kansas supreme court and the Kansas court of appeals to machine readable form for use by such corporation in providing computerized legal research services, subject to protection of the state's copyright as to any purpose unnecessary for such computerized legal research.

History: L. 1909, ch. 117, § 1; R.S. 1923, 20-208; L. 1941, ch. 206, § 1; L. 1947, ch. 221, § 1; L. 1960, ch. 46, § 1; L. 1965, ch. 213, § 1; L. 1969, ch. 164, § 1; L. 1970, ch. 118, § 1; L. 1974, ch. 135, § 6; L. 1975, ch. 181, § 1; L. 1976, ch. 147, § 4; L. 1976, ch. 151, § 4; L. 1977, ch. 106, § 1; L. 1978, ch. 109, § 1; L. 1980, ch. 95, § 1; July 1.

20-208b. Distribution of supreme court reports to legislative coordinating council. The state law librarian shall provide the legislative coordinating council with the number of complete sets of available Kansas reports necessary to conduct the official business of the legislative branch of government, as certified to the state law librarian by the legislative coordinating council, without charge.

History: L. 1975, ch. 181, § 2; July 1.

20-209. Reports for new district judge and associate district judge positions; disposition. Whenever a new district judge or associate district judge position is created, the state law librarian shall provide a complete set of available Kansas reports to the clerk of the district court of the county of residence of the judge elected or appointed to such office. In the event any district or associate district judgeship is abolished, it shall be the duty of the clerk of such district court to return to the state law librarian all Kansas reports which were acquired by such court without charge under the provisions of this act or the acts of which this act is amendatory. Whenever a person is elected or appointed to succeed to the office of district judge or associate district judge, it shall be the duty of the clerk of the district court of the county where the person's predecessor in office kept the set of Kansas reports, accountable by such office, to deliver such reports to the person so elected or appointed.

History: L. 1911, ch. 161, § 1; R.S. 1923, 20-209; L. 1929, ch. 161, § 1; L. 1970, ch.

118, § 2; L. 1974, ch. 135, § 7; L. 1976, ch. 145, § 83; L. 1978, ch. 109, § 2; July 1.

20-210. **Replacement without charge, when.** The state law librarian is hereby authorized to replace without charge volumes of the Kansas reports which have been destroyed by fire, flood or other natural catastrophe, only if the same were originally delivered to and in the custody of an office or agency authorized to receive reports without charge pursuant to K.S.A. 20-208.

History: L. 1909, ch. 117, § 2; R.S. 1923, 20-210; L. 1947, ch. 221, § 2; L. 1970, ch. 118, § 3; L. 1974, ch. 135, § 8; July 1, 1975.

20-211. **Advance sheets; distribution and sale; subscription to advance sheets and permanent report; withholding opinions; removal of advance sheets from inventories upon publication of bound volume.** The state law librarian shall have authority to order advance sheets of the reports of the supreme court and court of appeals to be printed for distribution and temporary use until the reports themselves are issued. Upon such order it shall be the duty of the reporter, as soon as possible after they are filed, to prepare for publication, and of the director of printing immediately thereafter to print the syllabi and decisions of the court in the same form the permanent report will bear, but upon inexpensive paper and to be bound in paper. The number of copies of each issue shall be specified in the order. When issued they shall be delivered to the state law librarian, to be distributed in the manner provided in K.S.A. 20-208 for distributing copies of the Kansas reports, except that no copies of advance sheets shall be delivered to a law library for exchange purposes. The remaining copies shall be sold at the per copy price fixed by the supreme court under this section, plus the amount fixed by the supreme court under this section for the cost of postage and handling. Said librarian may sell subscriptions to the current advance sheets and permanent report together for the subscription price fixed by the supreme court under this section, plus the amount fixed by the supreme court under this section for the cost of any postage and handling, the same to be paid in advance and if any one person, firm, association or corporation shall subscribe for two hundred (200) or more copies of any bound volume and the advance sheets thereto, the state law librarian may sell subscriptions to such persons, firm, associations and corporations to the advance sheets and permanent report together for a reduced subscription price fixed by the supreme court under this section, plus the amount fixed by the supreme court under this section for the cost of postage and handling, the same to be paid in advance. Upon order of the court any opinion may be withheld from publication in the advance sheets until such time as it may designate. The increased prices provided for in this section shall apply to current reports and advance sheets commencing with volume 224, and subscriptions for earlier volumes and advance sheets, or purchases of advance sheets of earlier volumes, shall be at the rate prescribed by this section prior to this amendment. All copies of advance sheets distributed pursuant to this section or purchased by any governmental agency or subdivision may be removed from the inventory of such office, agency or subdivision upon publication of the volume of the Kansas reports for which such advance sheets were issued. The supreme court shall fix the per copy prices, subscription prices, and reduced subscription prices for advance sheets and permanent reports sold under this section to recover the costs of printing and binding such advance sheets and permanent reports and shall fix the amount to be charged in connection with the sale and distribution of such advance sheets and permanent reports under this section to cover the costs of postage and handling applicable thereto. The supreme court shall revise all such prices from time to time as necessary for the purposes of covering or recovering such costs.

History: L. 1909, ch. 117, § 3; R.S. 1923, 20-211; L. 1947, ch. 221, § 3; L. 1960, ch. 46, § 2; L. 1963, ch. 422, § 11; L. 1969, ch. 164, § 2; L. 1970, ch. 118, § 4; L. 1974, ch. 135, § 9; L. 1976, ch. 147, § 5; L. 1980, ch. 95, § 2; July 1.

20-212. **Sale of courts of appeals reports and Wyandotte constitutional convention proceedings.** The state law librarian is authorized and directed to sell the Kansas courts of appeals reports and proceedings and debates of the Wyandotte constitutional convention now in his hands at a cost of two dollars ($2) per volume, plus fifty cents (50¢) for postage and handling, to be paid in advance.

History: L. 1905, ch. 497, § 3; R.S. 1923, 20-212; L. 1970, ch. 118, § 5; L. 1974, ch. 135, § 10; July 1, 1975.

20-213. **Sale of reports; disposition of moneys; library report fee fund.** The state law librarian shall remit all moneys received by or for him from the sale of reports of the supreme court and from the sale of court of appeals reports to the state treasurer at least monthly. Upon receipt of any such remittance the state treasurer shall deposit the entire amount thereof in the state treasury and the same shall be credited to the library report fee fund. All expenditures from such fund shall be made in accordance with appropriation acts upon warrants of the director of accounts and reports issued pursuant to vouchers approved by the state law librarian or by a person or persons designated by him. The state law librarian may make expenditures from such fund for the purpose of paying the cost of transportation, handling and storage charges incurred by him in the sale, delivery and storage of said reports, including the cost of providing shelving for their storage, and for the purchase of library materials related to the subject of law and the rebinding of same, and for the purpose of reprinting volumes of said reports.

History: L. 1889, ch. 247, § 5; R.S. 1923, 20-213; L. 1947, ch. 221, § 4; L. 1970, ch. 118, § 6; L. 1973, ch. 309, § 12; L. 1974, ch. 135, § 11; July 1, 1975.

75-704a. Copies of written opinions filed with state librarian, in supreme court law library and in certain law school libraries; form; annual index. From and after the effective date of this act the attorney general shall file with the state librarian one (1) copy of each written opinion rendered after said effective date by or under the authority of the attorney general.

The librarian shall then cause each copy of such opinions to be properly stamped with the words "Kansas state library" and placed in the reference and readers' services division of the state library.

In like manner, one (1) copy of each such opinion rendered after the effective date of this act shall be filed in the supreme court law library and the law libraries of the university of Kansas school of law and Washburn university law school in the custody of the law librarian within thirty (30) days after such opinions are rendered.

*　　*　　*

History: L. 1973, ch. 344, § 1; L. 1974, ch. 135, § 14; L. 1976, ch. 372, § 2; May 8.

75-1023. Extra copies of certain publications; distribution; notification of secretary of historical society. Whenever the division of printing prints any of the publications of the state and of its societies and institutions, there shall be printed extra copies thereof as shall be necessary to deliver such number of copies thereof to the state historical society as the secretary of said society shall request but not exceeding thirty (30) copies, thirty-five (35) copies to the state library, to be used by said state historical society and said state library in making exchanges with other states, libraries, societies and institutions for similar publications, and two (2) copies thereof to each of the following named libraries, to wit:

The library of the university of Kansas, the library of Kansas state university of agriculture and applied science, the library of Wichita state university, the libraries of Fort Hays state university, Pittsburg state university and Emporia state university. In case any publication is issued in both bound and unbound form, bound copies shall be supplied. This section shall not apply to the reports of the supreme court of the state of Kansas, or to the statutes or session laws.

The director of printing shall notify the secretary of the state historical society of the printings of all publications so that said secretary may make proper requests for copies of such publications.

History: R.S. 1923, 75-1023; L. 1943, ch. 269, § 21; L. 1961, ch. 407, § 1; L. 1967, ch. 440, § 1; L. 1968, ch. 364, § 1; L. 1976, ch. 373, § 9; March 2.

75-3048a. Reports of state agencies; "publication" defined. As used in this act "publication" means any report or document which is intended to be made available to the public and which is originated by a state agency.

History: L. 1972, ch. 316, § 1; July 1.

75-3048b. Same; central duplicating to provide library with copies of certain publications. The central duplicating service of the department of administration shall make two additional copies of each publication that it reproduces in more than fifty (50) copies and shall deliver such additional copies to the state library for its use, except that no such additional copies shall be so made or delivered in the event that they are of a confidential class of material or if central duplicating is advised that they are of a confidential nature.

History: L. 1972, ch. 316, § 2; July 1.

75-3048c. Same; agency to provide library with copies of certain publications. Every state agency that prints or otherwise reproduces more than fifty (50) copies of any publication, except through the director of printing or the central duplicating service, shall make two additional copies of each publication it reproduces and shall deliver such additional copies to the state library for its use, unless the same are confidential.

History: L. 1972, ch. 316, § 3; July 1.

STATE HISTORICAL SOCIETY
(Kansas Statutes Annotated, 1982, s.75-2701 to 2705, 75-3148.)

75-2701. State historical society as trustee of state; board of directors; property; rules and regulations. The state historical society, heretofore organized under the incorporation laws of the state, shall be the trustee of the state, and as such shall faithfully expend and apply all money received from the state to the uses and purposes directed by law, and shall hold all its present

and future collections of property for the state, and shall not sell, mortgage, transfer or dispose of in any manner or remove from its building or buildings, except for temporary purposes, any article thereof, or part of the same, without authority of law: *Provided,* This shall not prevent the sale or exchange by the society of its publications, duplicate materials, or materials outside its fields of collection, that it may have or obtain. There shall continue to be a board of directors to consist of as many members as the society shall determine. The society may acquire property, real or personal, by gift, bequest or otherwise, in any amount, and upon such conditions as its executive committee may deem best for its interests. Any such property so acquired and any state-owned historic site, structure or property which has been placed by law under the jurisdiction and supervision of the society shall be administered by the society in the public interest, and the society is hereby authorized and directed to provide for the preservation thereof and to adopt such rules and regulations as are necessary for the proper use and enjoyment thereof.

History: L. 1879, ch. 167, § 1; R.S. 1923, 75-2701; L. 1957, ch. 444, § 1; L. 1971, ch. 271, § 1; April 21.

75-2702. General duties of society; rooms open for reception of citizens without fee; expenditures. It shall be the duty of the society to collect by gift, exchange or purchase books, maps, newspapers, pamphlets, periodicals, photographs, artifacts, relics, paintings, manuscripts and other papers and material illustrative of the history of Kansas in particular, and the west generally; to catalogue the collections of said society for the more convenient reference of all persons who may have occasion to consult the same; and to keep its collections arranged in suitable and convenient rooms, the rooms of the society to be open at all reasonable hours on business days and on Saturday mornings and during such other hours as may be prescribed by the secretary of administration for the reception of the citizens of this state who may wish to visit the same, without fee; to maintain museums in its buildings and in such other places as may be authorized; to inculcate through publications, museum extension services and other media a wider and fuller knowledge and appreciation of the history of Kansas and its significance, and specifically to publish a historical journal and such other historical materials as may from time to time be authorized by the appropriation of state funds for such publications and, because it is in the best interest of the state of Kansas and its historical heritage to encourage membership in the society, to make current issues of the historical journal available to members without charge during the terms of their memberships and also in its discretion to offer discounts to members who purchase earlier publications; to loan, in its discretion, for such periods and under such rules and restrictions as it may adopt, to libraries, educational institutions and other organizations such books, pamphlets, museum objects, or other materials that if lost or destroyed could easily and without much expense be replaced; to take an active interest in the preservation and use of noncurrent

public records of historical importance of counties, cities, villages, towns, school districts and other local governmental units; to cause to be bound, as necessary for their preservation, the unbound books, pamphlets, clippings and newspaper files in its possession. No expenditure shall be made under this act or expense incurred except in pursuance of specific appropriations therefor, and no officer of said society shall pledge the credit of the state in excess of such appropriation.

History: L. 1879, ch. 167, § 2; R.S. 1923, 75-2702; L. 1957, ch. 444, § 2; L. 1975, ch. 437, § 1; L. 1977, ch. 292, § 1; July 1.

75-2703. State publications for exchange purposes. To enable the society to augment its collections, by effecting exchanges with other societies and institutions, thirty (30) bound copies each of the several publications of the state, and of its societies and institutions, except the reports of the supreme court and the statutes and session laws, shall be and the same are hereby donated to said society as they shall be issued the same to be delivered to the society by the secretary of state or other officer having custody of the same—to include also for deposit in its collections one (1) set of all the publications of the state heretofore issued, including the supreme court reports, and six (6) sets of the general statutes and session laws.

History: R.S. 1923, 75-2703; L. 1943, ch. 269, § 24; L. 1957, ch. 444, § 3; April 13.

75-2704. Taking of documents or records from building; sale or exchange of materials. The secretary of the state historical society is hereby prohibited from permitting or allowing any of the files, documents or records of said society to be taken away from the building or buildings where its office and rooms are or shall be located: *Provided,* That this shall not prevent the removal of materials for temporary purposes, or the sale or exchange of materials as authorized in K.S.A. 75-2701 and 75-2702.

History: L. 1901, ch. 226, § 1; R. S. 1923, 75-2704; L. 1957, ch. 444, § 4; April 13.

75-2705. Certified copy of documents as evidence; fees, approval, disposition. (a) A copy of any file, document or record in the custody of said society, duly certified by the secretary of the state historical society or his or her authorized agent, may be received in evidence with the same effect as the original. To partially reimburse the state for the cost of such copies or services the secretary shall prescribe the fees, if any, to be paid for certified copies in amounts approved by the director of accounts and reports under K.S.A. 45-204 and the fees, if any, for search of the files or records when no certified copy is made.

(b) All moneys received under this section shall be remitted to the state treasurer at least monthly. Upon receipt of each such remittance, the state treasurer shall deposit the entire amount thereof in the state treasury and the same shall be credited to the state general fund.

History: K.S.A. 75-2705; L. 1978, ch. 347, § 19; July 1.

75-3148. Secretary; employees. The secretary of the state historical society is hereby authorized to appoint an assistant secretary, librarian, museum director, archaeologist, state archivist, and such other employees as may be necessary, within available appropriations, and all of such employees shall be within the classified service. The secretary of the state historical society shall be within the unclassified service.

History: K.S.A. 75-3148; L. 1978, ch. 332, § 41; July 1.

INTERLIBRARY COOPERATION
(Kansas Statutes Annotated, 1982, s.75-2575 to 75-2587.)

75-2575. Interlibrary cooperation and resource sharing; purpose of act. The purpose of this act is to provide for a more orderly process whereby all types of libraries in Kansas may participate in programs of interlibrary cooperation and resource sharing. It is deemed appropriate that there be a state-level coordinating authority for recommending statewide priorities for interlibrary cooperation and resource sharing among all of the various libraries in Kansas. Cooperative planning and priority recommendation by a state-level organization, which is broadly representative of all of the libraries in the state, can assure an efficient and comprehensive statewide development of library services.

History: L. 1981, ch. 319, § 1; July 1.

75-2576. Same; definitions. As used in this act, unless the context otherwise requires:

(a) "Board" means the Kansas library network board created by this act;

(b) "regional systems of cooperating libraries" means the regional systems of cooperating libraries created under authority of K.S.A. 75-2547 to 75-2552, inclusive, and amendments thereto;

(c) "systems librarians" means the chief officers of the regional systems of cooperating libraries;

(d) "public libraries" means libraries operated under the provisions of K.S.A. 12-1215 to 12-1248, inclusive, and amendments thereto;

(e) "public librarians" means the chief officers of the public libraries;

(f) "state library" means the Kansas state library created and operating under authority of K.S.A. 1981 Supp. 75-2534;

(g) "state librarian" means the chief officer thereof, appointed pursuant to K.S.A. 1981 Supp. 75-2535;

(h) "regents' librarians" means the chief officers of the libraries at institutions operated by the Kansas state board of regents;

(i) "school librarians" means the chief officers of libraries operated by unified school districts;

(j) "community college librarians" means chief officers of libraries operated by community colleges established pursuant to K.S.A. 71-1401 through 71-1420, inclusive, and amendments thereto;

(k) "private college librarians" means chief officers of libraries operated by accredited independent institutions as defined in K.S.A. 72-6107, and the chief officer of the library operated by Washburn university of Topeka;

(l) "special librarians" means the chief officers of all other publicly supported and private libraries, including special purpose libraries and archives located in Kansas;

(m) "library network" means an organization of types of libraries interconnected to achieve their common purposes through cooperative use of communications, computer technology, library and human resources.

History: L. 1981, ch. 319, § 2; July 1.

75-2577. Same; function of state library. One of the functions of the state library shall be to provide programs of interlibrary cooperation under the direction and supervision of the Kansas library network board.

History: L. 1981, ch. 319, § 3; July 1.

75-2578. Same; Kansas library network board; membership, appointment and ex officio; terms; vacancies. There is hereby created a Kansas library network board, hereinafter referred to as the board, which shall consist of 10 members:

(a) Seven of the members shall be professional librarians, one from each of seven types of librarians, and shall be selected from a list of three nominees submitted by each of the professional organizations representing the following types of librarians: (1) Public librarians; (2) school librarians; (3) regents' librarians; (4) community college librarians; (5) private college librarians; (6) regional library systems librarians; and (7) special librarians. It shall be the responsibility of the state librarian to collect the names of nominees from the professional organizations of the librarians and to transmit them to the governor.

(b) Three of the members shall be ex officio members and shall have voting powers. They shall be: (1) The executive officer of the board of regents or the designee of the executive officer; (2) the commissioner of education or the designee of the commissioner; and (3) the state librarian.

(c) The appointed members of the board shall hold their respective offices for a term of three years and until their successors are appointed and qualified except the first board shall hold their offices for terms as follows: From the group of seven librarians appointed pursuant to subsection (a): Two shall serve for a term of one year; two for a term of two years; and three for a term of three years. The governor in making the appointments shall designate the term for which each member is to serve. The appointed members of said board shall not serve more than two consecutive terms on the board.

(d) It shall be the duty of the governor to make appointments, as defined in subsection (a), to fill vacancies, as they occur, on the board. Any person appointed to fill an unexpired term shall serve to the end of the term and until a successor is appointed and qualified.

History: L. 1981, ch. 319, § 4; July 1.

75-2579. Same; board meetings and organization; compensation and expenses of members. The Kansas library network board shall hold regular meetings and such other meetings as may be called by the secretary, and shall meet upon request of a majority of the members of the board. On and after July 1, 1982, the board shall meet not more than quarterly. The board shall elect a chairperson to preside at the meetings. Members of the Kansas library network board attending meetings of such board, or attending a subcommittee meeting thereof authorized by such board, shall be paid amounts provided in subsection (e) of K.S.A. 75-3223 and amendments thereto. Amounts paid under this section shall be paid from appropriations to the state library upon warrants of the director of accounts and reports issued pursuant to vouchers approved by the state librarian or a person or persons designated by the state librarian.

History: L. 1981, ch. 319, § 5; July 1.

75-2580. Same; duties of board. The Kansas library network board shall:

(a) Recommend statewide priorities for interlibrary cooperation and resource sharing;

(b) develop and publish annually a state plan for library network activities;

(c) review and evaluate policies and activities of Kansas libraries which implement the state plan;

(d) encourage public awareness of the need for interlibrary cooperation and resource sharing;

(e) establish guidelines to carry out its activities.

History: L. 1981, ch. 319, § 6; July 1.

75-2581. Same; annual report by board. On or before November 1, 1981, and on or before November 1 of each year thereafter, the board shall forward to the governor, the president of the senate, the speaker of the house and the board of regents a report concerning interlibrary cooperation and resource sharing, as they expressly relate to the matters set forth in K.S.A. 1981 Supp. 75-2580. This report may also include comments on the funding and other needs of the state library, libraries under the control of the board of regents, public libraries, regional systems of cooperating libraries, community college libraries, public school libraries, private college libraries, the library of Washburn university of Topeka, and special libraries, as such funding and other needs relate to questions of interlibrary cooperation and resource sharing. The state librarian, the board of regents, and the department of education shall cooperate fully with the board in the preparation of this report.

History: L. 1981, ch. 319, § 7; July 1.

75-2582. Same; director of library network services; appointment; compensation. The board shall appoint a director of library network services. The director of library network services shall be in the unclassified service and shall receive such compensation as is recommended by the board and approved by the governor. The director of library network services shall serve following appointment at the pleasure of the board.

History: L. 1981, ch. 319, § 8; July 1.

75-2583. Same; duties of director of library network services. The director of library network services shall be responsible for the coordination of networking activities in accordance with the guidelines and procedures established by the board. Expenses incurred in operating this division shall be paid from appropriations for this division.

History: L. 1981, ch. 319, § 9; July 1.

75-2584. Same; staff assistance for board. The state librarian shall provide whatever staff assistance is required by the board.

History: L. 1981, ch. 319, § 10; July 1.

75-2585. Same; contracts for computerized services; state-level cooperative activities. The board may contract under K.S.A. 75-2563 when necessary and may make expenditures for state-level cooperative activities. Such expenditures may include federal funds awarded to the board for programs of interlibrary cooperation and resource sharing.

History: L. 1981, ch. 319, § 11; July 1.

75-2586. Same; budget request by board for network activities. The state librarian shall include in the annual budget request for the state library the amounts requested by the Kansas library network board for network activities.

History: L. 1981, ch. 319, § 12; July 1.

75-2587. Same; participation by unified school districts; costs. The board of education of any unified school district is hereby authorized to participate in the library network created by this act. Any costs involved in such participation shall be chargeable to the general fund of the school district.

History: L. 1981, ch. 319, § 13; July 1.

PUBLIC RECORDS

(Kansas Statutes Annotated, 1982, s.75-3501 to 75-3507, 75-3509 to 75-3511.)

75-3501. Records defined. For the purposes of this act: "Records" mean all documents, correspondence, original papers, maps, drawings, charts, indexes, plans, memoranda, sound recordings, microfilm, motion-picture or other photographic records, or other materials bearing upon the activities and functions of the department or agency or its officers or employees.

History: L. 1945, ch. 306, § 1; L. 1957, ch. 452, § 1; April 10.

75-3502. State records board; members, chairman, secretary. For the purpose of the permanent preservation of important state records and to provide an orderly method for the disposition of other state records, there is hereby created the state records board, consisting of the attorney general, state librarian, secretary of administration, secretary of the state historical society, or their designated representatives, the state archivist, and such ex officio members as are hereinafter provided. The attorney general shall be the chairman and the state archivist shall be the secretary of the board.

History: L. 1945, ch. 306, § 2; L. 1957, ch. 452, § 2; L. 1974, ch. 364, § 26; Jan. 13, 1975.

75-3502a. Same; attached to department of administration. The state records board created by K.S.A. 75-3502 is hereby attached to the department of administration, and from and after the effective date of this act shall be within the department of administration as a part thereof.

History: L. 1972, ch. 332, § 27; July 1.

75-3503. Same; ex officio members. The elective state officer, director, chairman, or other officer, the records of whose department or agency are being considered, or his or her designated representative, and the head of the specific division to which the records under consideration appertain shall be ex officio members of the board.

History: L. 1945, ch. 306, § 3; L. 1957, ch. 452, § 3; April 10.

75-3504. Same; authority to order disposition of records; establishment of disposal schedules; rules and regulations. The board shall pass upon the requests of the state departments or other agencies for the destruction or other disposition of records, and shall have power to order the destruction, reproduction, temporary or permanent retention, and disposition of the public records of any department or agency of the state, to establish records disposal schedules for the orderly retirement of records, and to adopt such other rules and regulations as they may deem necessary to accomplish the purposes of this act. Said disposal schedules shall be filed by the board with the revisor of statutes. Records so scheduled may be transferred to the state records center at regular intervals, in accordance with procedures to be established by the center, without further action by the board. In all its acts the board shall be specifically required to safeguard the legal, financial and historical interests of the state in such records.

History: L. 1945, ch. 306, § 4; L. 1957, ch. 452, § 4; L. 1965, ch. 506, § 39; June 30.

75-3505. Public officer defined. As used in this act, the term "public officer" means any officer, board, commission or agency of the state.

History: L. 1945, ch. 331, § 1; June 28.

75-3506. Reproduction of records on film. Any public officer of the state may cause any or all records, papers or documents kept by him or her to be photographed, microphotographed or reproduced on film. Such photographic film shall comply with federal standard No. 125a, dated April 24, 1958, or the latest revision thereof, issued pursuant to the federal property and administrative services act of 1949, as amended, and the device used to reproduce such records on such film shall be one which accurately reproduces the original thereof in all details.

History: L. 1945, ch. 331, § 2; L. 1972, ch. 41, § 4; Feb. 9.

75-3507. Same; evidence in courts or administrative agencies. Such photographs, microphotographs or photographic film shall be deemed to be an original record for all purposes, including introduction in evidence in all courts or administrative agencies. A transcript, exemplification or certified copy thereof shall, for all purposes recited herein, be deemed to be a transcript, exemplification, or certified copy of the original.

History: L. 1945, ch. 331, § 3; June 28.

75-3509. State records center; purpose; powers and duties of secretary of administration. There is hereby established, under the supervision and control of the department of administration, a state records center which shall serve as a depository for inactive records of state agencies and departments. The secretary of administration shall have authority to obtain a suitable building or buildings to be used as a records center, to employ personnel for the records center staff, and to supervise all operations of the center: *Provided,* No expenditures shall be made under this act or expense incurred except in pursuance of specific appropriations therefor.

History: L. 1957, ch. 459, § 1; L. 1959, ch. 341, § 1; June 30.

75-3510. **Same; receiving and disposition of records; "ultimate disposition" defined.** In accordance with records retention and disposal schedules established by the state records board in cooperation with the agencies and departments concerned, the records center shall receive, store, and ultimately dispose of, inactive and noncurrent records of state agencies and departments. Ultimate disposition shall be defined as

meaning destruction, reproduction followed by destruction, or, if a record shall be determined to have permanent value, transfer to the state archives or to another agency if deemed more appropriate. In cases where the agencies and departments are equipped to provide storage space, or where the transfer of records to the center is not practical for other reasons, such inactive records may be stored elsewhere and disposed of as the records board may direct.

History: L. 1957, ch. 459, § 2; April 8.

75-3511. **Same; availability of records in records center.** Records stored in the records center shall be available promptly when called for by the originating agencies or departments, but they shall not be used by others except with the approval of the originating department.

History: L. 1957, ch. 459, § 3; April 8.

REGIONAL LIBRARIES

(Kansas Statutes Annotated, 1982, s.12-1231 to 12-1235.)

12-1231. **Regional library; resolution; petition; election; board; certain cooperating township libraries to be maintained as regional libraries.** Any two (2) or more adjoining counties, or any two (2) or more adjoining townships, may establish and maintain a regional library as provided in this act. A proposition to establish and maintain a regional library may be submitted to the electors of each county or township proposing to participate therein, by resolution of the governing body thereof, and shall be submitted upon presentation of a petition signed by ten percent (10%) of the qualified electors of the county or township as determined upon the basis of the total vote cast for secretary of state at the last preceding general election. Such proposition shall be submitted at the first general election occurring after the passage of the resolution or the presentation of the petition, and if a majority of the votes cast in each county or township voting on the proposition shall be in the affirmative, the governing bodies of such counties or townships shall forthwith create a library board and proceed to establish a regional library. Any township library originally established under the authority of K.S.A. 80-804, which has been continuously maintained and operated and which is providing library services in the member townships on the effective date of this act shall be governed by and maintained in accordance with the provisions of K.S.A. 12-1231 to 12-1235, inclusive, and amendments thereto, as a regional library.

History: K.S.A. 12-1231; L 1980, ch. 66, § 1; April 26.

12-1232. **Same; appointment of board; terms; vacancies; eligibility.** The library board of a regional library shall consist of six (6) appointed members and, in addition thereto, the official head of each participating county or township shall be an ex officio member with the same powers as appointed members. Each county or township participating in a regional library shall be equally represented on the library board, but in case such uniform representation cannot be obtained because of the number of counties or townships participating, the governing body shall agree on a method of rotating representation among the participating counties or townships. The official head of each participating county or township, with the approval of the governing body thereof, shall appoint the members from such county or township.

Terms of all members of the library board of any township library previously established under the authority of K.S.A. 80-804 shall expire on the effective date of this act and successors to such members shall be appointed in the manner and for the terms prescribed in this section.

The members first appointed shall be appointed, one (1) for a term expiring the first April 30th following date of appointment, two (2) for terms expiring the second April 30th following date of appointment, one (1) for a term expiring the third April 30th following date of appointment, and two (2) for terms expiring the fourth April 30th following date of appointment. Upon the expiration of the terms of members first appointed, succeeding members shall be appointed in like manner for terms of four (4) years. Vacancies occasioned by removal from the county or township, resignation or otherwise, shall be filled by appointment for the unexpired term. Except for the ex officio members of the board, no person holding any office in a participating county or township shall be a member of the library board while holding such office, and no person who has been appointed for two (2) four-year terms to the library board shall be eli-

gible for further appointment to such board.
History: K.S.A. 12-1232; L. 1980, ch. 66, § 2; April 26.

12-1233. Same; powers and duties. Except as otherwise specifically provided herein, the powers and duties of regional library boards, the powers and duties of officers and members of such boards, and the manner and procedure by which such powers and duties are to be exercised, shall be as provided herein for library boards generally. [L. 1951, ch. 485, § 16; July 1.]

12-1234. Same; tax levies; allocation of costs. Each county or township participating in a regional library is authorized to, and shall annually levy a tax for the maintenance of such library in such sum as the library board shall determine within the limitations fixed by law. The costs of maintaining a regional library, other than a library originally established under the authority of K.S.A. 80-804, shall be allocated among the participating counties or townships in the proportion of their respective populations. Tax levies for the maintenance of libraries

originally established under the authority of K.S.A. 80-804 shall be made at a uniform rate in all townships participating in the maintenance of such libraries.
History: K.S.A. 12-1234; L. 1980, ch. 66, § 3; April 26.

12-1235. Same; withdrawal of county or township; election; division of property. After a county or township has participated in a regional library for not less than three (3) years, such county or township may vote to establish and maintain a separate library, and upon so voting shall be deemed to have withdrawn from the regional library. The withdrawal of a county or township from a regional library shall be effective on May first following the vote to establish a separate library. Upon the withdrawal of a participating county or township, such county or township shall be entitled to its fractional share (based upon the number of participating counties or townships) of the property and funds on hand and to be collected from levies made, of the regional library. Such division shall be made in cash or in property and in such proportions as the library board of the regional library shall determine. [L. 1951, ch. 485, § 18; July 1.]

LIBRARY DISTRICTS
(Kansas Statutes Annotated, 1982, s.12-1236 to 12-1248.)

12-1236. Establishment of library districts; petition; agreement to transfer city property to district, when; resolution; election, notice and conduct. Any one or more cities of the third class is hereby authorized to join with any one or more townships or portions of one or more townships in one or more counties in the creation of a library district, upon the presentation to the board of county commissioners, of the county in which such proposed library district is located, of a petition setting forth the boundaries of the proposed library district and requesting the formation of such library district. Such petition shall be signed by not less than ten percent (10%) of the qualified electors of said proposed district who reside outside the limits of the incorporated city, and a like petition signed by not less than ten percent (10%) of the qualified electors who reside within the corporate limits of a city of the third class within said proposed district. The sufficiency of such petition to be determined by the board of county commissioners, determined upon the basis of the total vote cast for secretary of state in the last preceding general election within said city of the third class and within the boundaries of said proposed district of the township or portions of townships comprised within the proposed boundaries of said library district; and in the event a portion of any township is within such proposed boundaries, the total vote cast for secretary of state in said township shall be used. If the city of the third class within the boundaries of said library district owns and is operating a library at the time said petitions are filed, said petitions shall be accompanied

by a copy of a resolution adopted by the governing body of said city of the third class within such district; such resolution shall state that said city of the third class agrees, upon the creation of the proposed library district, to convey, assign and transfer to said library district all books, equipment, moneys, endowment funds and all other assets of said city library, to and for the use of said proposed library district. The governing body of such city of the third class located within said library district is hereby authorized to adopt such a resolution, and upon the creation of said library district by the board of county commissioners the governing body of such city, in conformity with such resolution, is hereby authorized to make and execute the necessary assignments and conveyances to transfer to such library district all property and assets of said city library. The board of county commissioners of the county in which such proposed library district is located shall, at its next regular meeting following the filing of such petition, examine said petition and determine its sufficiency. If the board finds that said petition is regular and in due form, as herein provided, it shall cause to be submitted to the voters of such proposed district, at a special election called for the purpose of voting upon the question, the establishment and maintenance of a library by such proposed library district. A notice of such election shall be given by publication of such notice in a newspaper having general circulation within the boundaries of such proposed district. Said notice of election shall be published in two successive issues of such newspaper and such election shall be held within seven (7) days after the last publication of such notice. Such notice of election shall be signed by the board of county commissioners and such election shall be conducted by and under the supervision of the county clerk of said county in the manner provided by law for the conduct of general elections. The county clerk shall determine the number of voting precincts needed within such proposed district, at least one of which precincts shall be in the corporate limits of the third-class city in said proposed library district, and shall designate and appoint the election board, or boards, to serve at the voting precinct or precincts within such proposed library district. [L. 1965, ch. 145, § 1; L. 1969, ch. 78, § 1; July 1.]

12-1237. Same; election canvass; annual tax levy. The board of county commissioners shall, at its next meeting following the holding of such election, canvass the results of said election. If a majority of the votes cast at such election on such proposition shall be in the affirmative, the board of county commissioners shall forthwith establish such library district and such library district, through its governing body, is hereby authorized to and shall annually levy the tax for the maintenance of such library in such sum as the library board shall determine, within the limitations fixed by law. [L. 1965, ch. 145, § 2; June 30.]

12-1238. Same; election of directors; notice. Upon the establishment of such library district the county clerk of the county within which such library district is located, shall cause a publication notice to be published once each week for two consecutive weeks in a newspaper of general circulation in said library district, stating that a meeting of the qualified voters of said library district will be held at the time and place fixed in said notice, for the purpose of electing seven (7) directors to act as the governing body of said library district. The last publication of such notice shall be made not more than seven (7) days prior to the date fixed for the holding of said meeting. The costs of such publication shall be paid by the city of the third class located within said library district from the general funds of said city, or, from the library funds of said city. At the time and place fixed for the holding of said meeting the county clerk shall call such meeting to order and the electors of such district shall proceed to elect a chairman and a secretary for said meeting. Thereupon, the qualified voters shall proceed to elect, by ballot, seven (7) directors for said library district, one for a term expiring the first Tuesday in April of the year following the date of such election; two (2) for a term expiring the first Tuesday in April of the second year following the date of such election; two (2) for a term expiring the first Tuesday in April of the third year following the date of such election; and two (2) for a term expiring the first Tuesday in April of the fourth year following the date of such election. Upon the expiration of the terms of the first board of directors, their successors shall be elected in the manner provided for electing members of library boards. [L. 1965, ch. 145, § 3; June 30.]

12-1239. Same; annual meeting; time of. An annual meeting of the qualified voters of such library district shall be held on the first Tuesday in March of each year at 2 o'clock p. m. At the first annual meeting a majority of the qualified voters present may determine whether the subsequent annual meetings shall convene at 2 o'clock p. m. or at 7:30 o'clock p. m. Thereafter, said annual meeting shall convene at the time so determined, unless at a subsequent annual meeting a majority of the qualified voters present determine that the annual meeting shall convene at such later or earlier time, as the case may be. [L. 1965, ch. 145, § 4; June 30.]

12-1240. Same; notice of annual meeting. It shall be the duty of the board of directors to give notice of every annual meeting by causing a notice to be published once each week for two (2) consecutive weeks in a newspaper of general circulation in said library district. The last publication of such notice to be made not more than six (6) days prior to the date of holding the meeting. Such notice shall include the time and place of such meeting. [L. 1965, ch. 145, § 5; June 30.]

12-1241. Same; persons entitled to vote; officers of board; terms of directors; vacancies. Any person who shall have been in good faith a resident of said library district for thirty (30) days prior to the date of any district meeting or other election and who possesses the qualifications of a voter at a general election shall be entitled to vote at said meeting or at any bond election. Every library district so created shall be governed by a board of seven (7) directors who shall be qualified voters of such library district. The board of directors shall elect one of their number as chairman of said board and shall also elect from the members of said board a secretary and a treasurer and such other officers as they deem necessary. At each annual meeting, upon the expiration of the term of any director, his or her successor shall be elected for a term of four (4) years, expiring on the first Tuesday of April of the fourth year following his or her election. Vacancies in said board of directors accruing by death, removal, resignation or otherwise shall be filled for the unexpired term by appointment made by the chairman of said board, by and with the endorsement and approval of a majority of the remaining board members, and shall be for the unexpired term in like manner as the original elections. [L. 1965, ch. 145, § 6; June 30.]

12-1242. Same; powers of board of directors. The library board of a library established as herein provided shall constitute a body corporate and politic, possessing the usual powers of a corporation for public purposes under the name and style of: "library district No. _____, county of _____ state of Kansas." And under such name may contract, sue and be sued, acquire, hold and convey real and personal property in accordance with law. [L.1965, ch. 145, § 7; June 30.]

12-1243. Same; regular and special meetings. The library board shall fix the date and place of its regular meetings, and special meetings may be called by the chairman of said board, and shall be called by the chairman upon the written request of a majority of the board members. Written notice stating the time and place of any special meeting and the purpose for which called shall, unless waived, be given each member of the board at least two days in advance of such meeting, and no business other than that stated in the notice shall be transacted at such special meeting. [L. 1965, ch. 145, § 8; June 30.]

12-1244. Same; election on building, equipment and site; bonds. The board of directors of said library district shall have authority to call an election of said district for the purpose of building, erecting and equipping a library building and procuring a site therefor and may issue bonds of such district for the purpose of paying the costs of such building, equipment and site. Before issuing any bonds hereunder the question of such issuance shall be submitted to the qualified electors of such district. The election shall be called and held, and the bonds issued thereunder in accordance with the provisions of the general bond laws applicable thereto. [L. 1965, ch. 145, § 9; June 30.]

12-1245. Same; powers and duties. The directors of said library district shall have all of the powers and duties vested in library boards under the provisions of K.S.A. 12-1225. [L. 1965, ch. 145, § 10; June 30.]

12-1246. Same; bond of treasurer; records and reports. The treasurer of said library district shall give bond in an amount fixed and approved by the board of said library district for the safekeeping and due disbursement of all funds which may come into his or her hands as such treasurer. Said bond shall be filed with the county clerk of the county in which said district is located. Such treasurer shall keep an accurate record of all money and property received and disbursed by him or her and make a report thereof monthly to the library board, or, as often as said board may require. [L. 1965, ch. 145, § 11; June 30.]

12-1247. Same; annual tax levies, certification. The directors of said library district, as the governing body thereof, shall, in the same manner as required by law applying to other taxing units, annually levy a tax not to exceed one and one-half (1½) mills on each dollar assessed tangible valuation for the property of such library district, for the maintenance and support of a free public library, to be levied and collected in like manner with other taxes, which levy said library board shall cause to be certified on or before August 25th of each year to the county clerk who is hereby authorized and required to place the same on the tax rolls of said county to be collected by the treasurer of said county and to be paid over by him or her to the treasurer of such library district. [L. 1965, ch. 145, § 12; June 30.]

12-1248. Same; acceptance of grants. Such library district, after its creation and establishment as provided by this act, shall be vested with authority to apply for and receive any grants for library purposes or for the construction and maintenance of a library in said district, from the state or federal government, or any agency thereof, and shall be authorized to execute any agreements necessary, on behalf of said library district, to receive any such grants, all in the manner as is now or hereafter provided by law. [L. 1965, ch. 145, § 13; June 30.]

COUNTY AND MUNICIPAL LIBRARIES
(Kansas Statutes Annotated, 1982, s.12-1215 to 12-1230, 12-1249 to 12-1257.)

12-1215. Budgets and tax levies in certain cities; increase in levy; petition; election. (a) In the cities of Topeka, Salina and Hutchinson, Kansas, in which a free public library has been established as provided by law, in addition to the powers and duties conferred by law, the board of directors of the free public library shall prepare, publish and approve an annual budget for the maintenance and support of the free public library in the same manner as required by law applying to other taxing units and shall annually levy a tax not to exceed 2.5 mills on each dollar of the assessed tangible valuation of the property of such city for the maintenance and support of such free public library. Whenever the board of directors determines that the tax currently being levied by such board is insufficient to maintain and support the library and such board desires to increase the mill levy above the current levy, such board may adopt a resolution declaring it necessary to increase such annual levy in an amount which together with the amount of the current levy shall not exceed a total of four mills in any year.

(b) Whenever the board of directors of such free public library determines that the tax levy of four mills authorized by subsection (a) is insufficient to maintain and support the library, the board shall adopt a resolution declaring it necessary to increase the annual levy by an additional amount not to exceed ¼ mill in any one year up to a total amount which shall not exceed an amount equal to six mills in any year.

(c) Any such resolution adopted under subsection (a) or (b) shall state the total amount of the tax to be levied for library purposes and shall be published once each week for two consecutive weeks in the official city newspaper. Whereupon such annual levy in an amount not to exceed the amount stated in the resolution may be made for the ensuing budget year and each successive budget year unless a petition requesting an election upon the proposition to increase the tax levy in excess of the current tax levy, signed by electors equal in number to not less than 5% of the electors who voted at the last preceding regular city election, as shown by the poll books, is filed with the county election officer within 60 days following the date of the last publication of the resolution. In the event a valid petition is filed, no such increased levy shall be made without such proposition having been submitted to and having been approved by a majority of the electors voting at an election called and held thereon. All such elections shall be called and held in the manner prescribed for the calling and holding of elections upon the question of the issuance of bonds under the general bond law. Such taxes shall be levied and collected in like manner as other taxes, which levy the clerk of such board of directors shall certify, on or before August 25 of each year, to the county clerk who is hereby authorized and required to place the same on the tax roll of the county to be collected by the county treasurer and paid over by the county treasurer to the treasurer of such board of directors.

History: L. 1943, ch. 110, § 1; L. 1947, ch. 120, § 1; L. 1949, ch. 118, § 1; L. 1955, ch. 83, § 1; L. 1959, ch. 75, § 1; L. 1961, ch. 71, § 1; L. 1965, ch. 102, § 1; L. 1977, ch. 59, § 1; L. 1981, ch. 68, § 1; May 19.

12-1216. Same; tax levies separate from city and in addition to other levies; no city library levy. The tax levy provided in K. S. A. 12-1215, shall not be included in and shall not constitute a part of the tax levy of any city to which this act is applicable, and shall be in addition to all other levies authorized or limited by law and shall not be within or subject to any of the limitations prescribed by K. S. A. 1975 Supp. 79-1950 and 79-1951, or acts amendatory thereof or supplemental thereto. Whenever a tax levy is made under the provisions of this act the governing body of the city shall not make a levy for a library as provided in K. S. A. 1975 Supp. 79-1951. [L. 1947, ch. 120, § 2; L. 1949, ch. 118, § 2; L. 1955, ch. 83, § 2; June 30.]

12-1217. Maintenance and support of library; certain capital improvements or major equipment purchases. As used in this act, the words "maintenance and support" shall include the general and usual cost and expense of operating such free public library but shall not include the cost of erecting or equipping a public building therefor or the cost of a site for such building, except in any city having a population of more than 35,000 and not more than 150,000 where such free public library occupies a public building upon a site acquired therefor and which public building and site are free from any bonded indebtedness, then not to exceed 20% of any annual budget prepared, published and approved by the board of directors may be allocated to a special accruing fund for the cost of erecting and equipping any addition to, or branch of, such free public library and for the acquisition of any additional site required for the erection of any such addition, branch or parking facility for use by the patrons of such library. Expenses for major capital improvements or major equipment purchases to cover such matters as, but not limited to, major roof repair, new computerized circulation or security systems and bookmobile replacement may also be paid with funds from the special accruing fund.

History: L. 1947, ch. 120, § 3; L. 1968, ch. 101, § 1; L. 1981, ch. 69, § 1; July 1.

12-1218. City, county and township libraries; definitions. As used in this act unless the context requires a different meaning, the following words, terms and phrases shall have the meaning ascribed to them in this section:

(a) "Municipality" shall mean a county, township or incorporated city.

(b) "Governing body" shall mean the governing body of a city, the board of county commissioners of a county, and the township trustee, clerk and treasurer acting as the township board of a township.

(c) "Official head" shall mean the mayor of a city, the chairman of the board of county commissioners of the county, and the township trustee of a township.

(d) "Library" shall mean a library which serves the general public and is supported in whole or in part with tax money.

(e) "Regional library" shall mean a library maintained by two or more counties, or two or more townships.

(f) "Library board" shall mean the board of directors of a library. [L. 1951, ch. 485, § 1; July 1.]

12-1219. Establishment and maintenance; existing libraries. A municipality may establish and maintain a library in the manner provided in this act. Any library heretofore established and being maintained by a municipality shall be maintained in accordance with the provisions of this act, but this section shall not be construed as repealing any law not expressly repealed by this act. [L. 1951, ch. 485, § 2; July 1.]

12-1220. City, county and township libraries; election to establish; tax levy, use of proceeds; library fund established; territory of existing library excluded, when. The governing body of any municipality may by resolution, and shall, upon presentation of a petition signed by ten percent (10%) of the qualified electors of such municipality determined upon the basis of the total vote cast for the secretary of state at the last preceding general election, cause to be submitted to the voters of such municipality at the first local or general election thereafter, or if the petition so requires, at a special election called for that purpose, the question of the establishment and maintenance of a library by such municipality. If a majority of the votes cast at such election on such proposition shall be in the affirmative, the governing body shall forthwith establish such library and is hereby authorized to and shall annually levy a tax for the maintenance of such library in such sum as the library board shall determine within the limitations fixed. by law and to pay a portion of the principal and interest on bonds issued under the authority of K.S.A. 1979 Supp. 12-1774, and amendments thereto, by cities located in the county.

Such tax shall be levied and collected in like manner as other taxes of the municipality and, except for an amount to pay a portion of the principal and interest on bonds issued under the authority of K.S.A. 1979 Supp. 12-1774, and amendments thereto, by cities located in the county, shall be kept in a separate fund to be known as the library fund of such municipality. If the territory of the municipality includes another municipality which is then maintaining a library, the proposition to establish a library by the larger municipality shall not be voted upon by the residents of the included municipality, nor shall a levy to establish or maintain such library be assessed against property therein, unless the library board and governing body of the included municipality shall give notice in writing that they desire to participate in the library to be established and to pay the tax for the establishment and maintenance thereof as other parts of the municipality establishing such library.

History: K.S.A. 12-1220; L. 1979, ch. 52, § 40; July 1.

12-1221. County or township bonds for site, building and equipment; election. Any county or township which is maintaining, or has voted to establish a library may erect and equip a library building and procure a site therefor, and may issue the bonds of such county or township for the purpose of paying the cost of such building, equipment and site. Before issuing any bonds hereunder the question of such issuance shall be submitted to the qualified electors of the county or township and if a majority of those voting on the proposition shall vote in favor thereof, such bonds may be issued. A proposition to issue such bonds may be combined with the proposition to establish a library under the provisions of K. S. A. 12-1220. The election shall be called and held, and the bonds issued thereunder in accordance with the provisions of the general bond law. [L. 1951, ch. 485, § 4; July 1.]

12-1222. Board; appointment; terms; eligibility; vacancies; expenses. Upon the establishment of a library under this act the official head of a municipality shall appoint, with the approval of the governing body, a library board for such library. In the case of a county or township library five (5) members shall be appointed, one (1) for a term expiring the first April 30th following date of appointment, one (1) for a term expiring the second April 30th following date of appointment. one (1) for a term expiring the third April 30th following date of appointment, and two (2) for terms expiring the fourth April 30th following date of appointment. In the

case of a city library seven (7) members shall be appointed, one (1) for a term expiring the first April 30th following date of appointment. two (2) for terms expiring the second April 30th following date of appointment, two (2) for terms expiring the third April 30th following date of appointment, and two (2) for terms expiring the fourth April 30th following date of appointment: *Provided,* That in any city having a population of more than two hundred fifty thousand (250,000), the governing body of such city may, as an alternative to the membership hereinabove provided for, appoint ten (10) members to said city library board, which members shall, when first appointed, begin serving on May 1, 1975, and shall have terms as follows: Six (6) of such members first appointed shall serve for terms of four (4) years and four (4) of such members first appointed shall serve for terms of two (2) years; thereafter, upon the expiration of the terms, successors shall be appointed in each odd-numbered year to fill the vacancies created, and thereafter each member shall serve for a term of four (4) years. In addition to the appointed members of the board the official head of the municipality shall be ex officio a member of the library board with the same powers as appointed members, but no person holding any office in the municipality shall be appointed a member while holding such office.

Upon the expiration of the terms of members first appointed succeeding members shall be appointed in like manner for terms of four (4) years. Members of library boards holding office at the effective date of this act shall continue to hold their offices until April 30th following the expiration of the terms for which appointed, and on or before May 1st following the first expiration of a term a sufficient number shall be appointed by the official head of the municipality with the approval of the governing body for terms of four (4) years to constitute a library board of the number of members prescribed by this act.

All members appointed to a library board shall be residents of the municipality. Vacancies occasioned by removal from the municipality, resignation or otherwise, shall be filled by appointment for the unexpired term. No person who has been appointed for two (2) consecutive four-year terms to a library board shall be eligible for further appointment to such board until two (2) years after the expiration of the second term: *Provided,* That appointments made prior to the effective date of this act shall not be counted in determining eligibility for appointment hereunder. Members of library boards shall receive no compensation for their services as such but shall be allowed their actual and necessary expenses in attending meetings and in carrying out their duties as members. [L. 1951, ch. 485, § 5; L. 1975, ch. 62, § 1; Feb. 17.]

12-1223. Corporate status of board; powers. The library board of a library established under, or governed by the provisions of this act shall constitute a body corporate and politic, possessing the usual powers of a corporation for public purposes, under the name and style of "the board of directors of _____ (name of municipality) library" and under such name may contract, sue and be sued and acquire, hold and convey real and personal property in accordance with law. The acquisition or disposition of real property shall be subject to the approval of the governing body of the municipality. [L. 1951, ch. 485, § 6; July 1.]

12-1224. Officers of board; meetings; notice. The members of a library board shall, immediately after their appointment and annually thereafter, meet and organize by the election of a chairman, a secretary and a treasurer and such other officers as they may deem necessary. The board shall fix the date and place of its regular meetings and special meetings may be called by the chairman or upon written request of a majority of the members. Written notice, stating the time and place of any special meeting and the purpose for which called, shall, unless waived, be given each member of the board at least two (2) days in advance of such meeting, and no business other than that stated in the notice shall be transacted at such meeting. [L. 1951, ch. 485, § 7; July 1.]

12-1225. Powers and duties of board. Library boards shall have the following powers and duties: (a) To make and adopt rules and regulations for the administration of the library;

(b) with the approval of the governing body of the municipality, to purchase or lease a site or sites and to lease or erect a building or buildings for the use of the library;

(c) to acquire by purchase, gift or exchange, books, magazines, papers, printed materials, slides, pictures, films, projection equipment, phonograph records and other material and equipment deemed necessary by the board for the maintenance and extension of modern library service;

(d) to employ a librarian and such other employees as the board shall deem necessary and to remove them and to fix their compensation;

(e) to establish and maintain a library or libraries and traveling library service within the municipality or within any other municipality with which service contract arrangements have been made;

(f) to contract with other libraries established under the provisions of this act or with the governing body of a municipality not maintaining a public library for the furnishing of library service to the inhabitants of such municipality to the extent and upon such terms as may be agreed upon, and to contract with any school board to furnish library service to any school library or to use the library facilities of the public school to supplement the facilities of the public library;

(g) to receive, accept and administer any money appropriated or granted to it by the state or the federal government or any agency thereof for the purpose of aiding or providing library service;

(h) to receive and accept any gift or donation to the library and administer the same in accordance with any provisions thereof;

(i) to make annual reports to the state librarian and the governing body of the munici-

pality on or before January 31st of each year for the preceding calendar year, showing receipts and disbursements from all funds under its control, and showing such statistical information relating to library materials acquired and on hand, number of library users, library services available, and other information of general interest as said governing body may require;

(j) as to money received from sources other than a tax levy for library purposes, in its discretion, to place such money in a separate fund or funds, or to place the money in the fund to which the tax levy money is credited unless the grantor or donor shall direct how and for what purpose the money shall be handled and spent. [L. 1951, ch. 485, § 8; L. 1953, ch. 65, § 1; L. 1965, ch. 103, § 1; L. 1965, ch. 104, § 1; June 30.]

12-1226. Treasurer of board; bond; duties. The treasurer of the library board shall give bond, in an amount fixed by said board and approved by the governing body of the municipality, for the safekeeping and due disbursement of all funds that may come into his or her hands as such treasurer. Said bonds shall be filed with the clerk of the municipality. Except where otherwise provided by law, the treasurer of the municipality shall pay over to the treasurer of the library board all funds collected for the maintenance of the library, and the treasurer of the library board shall pay out said funds on orders of the board signed by the secretary and chairman thereof. Such treasurer shall keep an accurate record of all moneys received and disbursed by him or her and make a report thereof to the library board monthly, or as often as said board shall require. [L. 1951, ch. 485, § 9; July 1.]

12-1227. Use of library; rules and regulations. Every library established under, or governed by the provisions of this act shall be free to the use of the inhabitants of the municipality in which located, subject always to such reasonable rules and regulations as the library board may adopt, and said board may exclude from the use of said library any and all persons who shall willfully violate such rules. The library board may extend the use and privilege of such library to nonresidents of the municipality and may make exchanges of books with any other library upon such terms and conditions as said board may from time to time by its regulations prescribe. [L. 1951, ch. 485, § 10; July 1.]

12-1228. Penalties as to library property authorized. The governing body of a municipality maintaining a library shall have power to pass laws or ordinances imposing suitable penalties for the punishment of injury committed to library buildings or other property and for injury to or failure to return any book or other library material belonging to such library. [L. 1951, ch. 485, § 11; July 1.]

12-1229. Use of privately owned books or collections. The library board of any library may authorize any circulating library, reading matter or work of art belonging to private person, association or corporation, or loaned by any library or public institution, to be deposited in a library building, and to be drawn or used outside the library building only on payment of such fee or membership as the owner may require. Deposits of such material may be removed by the owner thereof at pleasure, and such material when deposited in the library shall be separately and distinctly marked and kept apart from similar material owned by the library, but all such material while so deposited or remaining in the library shall be subject to use without charge within the library by any person who is entitled to the use of such library. [L. 1951, ch. 485, § 12; July 1.]

12-1230. Contracts for library service; tax levy, use of proceeds. The governing body of any municipality not maintaining a library may contract with any library for the furnishing of library service to such municipality, and to pay the costs of such library service the municipality is hereby authorized to levy a tax in the amount authorized to be levied by such municipality for the establishment and maintenance of a library and, in the case of cities and counties, to pay a portion of the principal and interest on bonds issued under the authority of K.S.A. 1980 Supp. 12-1774, and amendments thereto, by cities located in the county.

History: K.S.A. 12-1230; L. 1980, ch. 65, § 1; July 1.

12-1249. Issuance of library bonds by certain counties between 6,600 and 7,300; duties of planning commission and governing board of city in which building to be located; election provisions. The board of county commissioners of any county having a population of more than six thousand six hundred (6,600) and less than seven thousand three hundred (7,300) and having an assessed tangible valuation of less than twenty-one million dollars ($21,000,000) and in which there is located a city of the second class which maintains a library is authorized to issue general obligation bonds of the county to acquire a site and construct a building to be used for library purposes in such second-class city. Before any such bonds are issued under authority of this act the governing body of such city shall request the recommendations of its library board as to the location and type of building needed to best serve the community, including the provision of such library materials as may be appropriate for use in connection with vocational or technical training. Upon receipt of recommendations from its library board the governing body of any such city shall transmit a copy thereof to the planning board of such city for its recommendations as to site location and accessibility. Such planning board shall promptly consider and act upon such recommendations by giving its advice thereon to the governing body of such city. Upon receipt of the recommendations of the planning board the governing body of such city shall by resolution duly adopted submit to the board of county commissioners of such county its findings as to the advisability of issuance of bonds under authority of this act and its recom-

mendations as to location, type of construction and such other recommendations as it may deem appropriate. Such resolution shall be transmitted to the board of county commissioners by such city and upon receipt thereof such board of county commissioners is authorized to issue general obligation bonds of the county in an amount not in excess of one percent (1%) of the assessed tangible valuation of the county: Provided, No bonds shall be issued under authority of this act until the same have been approved by the electors of such county at a special election called for the purpose or at a general election, and any such election shall be conducted and such bonds shall be issued in the manner prescribed in chapter 10 of Kansas Statutes Annotated. [L. 1965, ch. 208, § 1; June 30.]

12-1250. Same; cooperation between library board and county commissioners; use of library. Any board of county commissioners issuing bonds under authority of this act shall confer and advise with the library board of the second-class city involved in selection of an architect and in development of plans for such building. Upon completion of such building and acceptance thereof by the board of county commissioners, the same shall be made available for library purposes to be used by the library board of such city of the second class or any successor library board, or other authority offering public library services to all of the residents of such county. The library facilities and services offered in any library constructed under the provisions of this act shall be available to any persons authorized to use the same by the library board of such city. [L. 1965, ch. 208, § 2; June 30.]

12-1251. Same; gifts and assistance; federal aid. The board of county commissioners and the governing body of such city of the second class are authorized to receive any gifts, contributions or assistance for the use of any public library in such second-class city including any federal aid or assistance that is authorized by law. [L. 1965, ch. 208, § 3; June 30.]

12-1252. Acceptance of gifts for library purposes by cities and boards of education, or jointly; conditions. The board of education of any school district, or the governing body of any city, or the board of education of any school district jointly with the governing body of any city in such school district is hereby authorized to receive gifts of not to exceed five hundred thousand dollars ($500,-000) upon conditions provided in this act. Such a gift may be conditioned as follows:

(a) That the money given will be used only for the purpose of construction and furnishing of a library in a particular city or other place.

(b) That the board of education of the school district or the governing body of the city or both, as the case may be, shall by resolution contract and agree to pay the donor during his or her lifetime interest on the principal sum of such gift at such rate as the donor and the recipient may agree upon. The interest so agreed upon shall be paid by the school district or city, or both, in periodic semiannual payments in the same manner as interest on bonded indebtedness. Such interest may be paid by the school district or city, or both, from bond funds, or from special capital outlay funds, or if there are insufficient amounts in such funds, then from the general operating fund of the school district, or city, or both. The board of education of any school district making an agreement and receiving any gift under this act may make an annual tax levy on the taxable tangible property in the school district in an amount necessary to meet the interest requirements agreed upon in the resolution accepting such gift. Any tax levied under authority of this act shall not be subject to any tax levy limitation not specified in this act and expenditures for interest paid under authority hereof shall not be counted as operating expenses within the meaning of K. S. A. 1975 Supp. 72-7001 *et seq.* The aggregate amount of such periodic payments, using a standard annuity table, shall not at the time of the gift be estimated to exceed the principal amount of the gift.

(c) Such additional conditions as the donor and board of education or governing body, or both, may agree upon. [L. 1968, ch. 151, § 1; March 26.]

12-1253. Same; acceptance of gift; terms. Any gift offered under provisions of this act shall be accepted only by formal action by resolution in the case of a board of education or ordinance in the case of a city. Such resolution or ordinance shall cite this act as authority therefor and shall recite the terms of the gift and the conditions thereof. [L. 1968, ch. 151, § 2; March 26.]

12-1254. Library in cities between 120,-000 and 150,000; submission of proposition to levy tax for building fund; use of proceeds. In all cities having a population by the official state census of more than one hundred twenty thousand (120,000) and less than one hundred fifty thousand (150,000) in which a free public library has heretofore been established as provided by law, the board of directors of such free public library is hereby authorized and empowered to submit the question of making an annual tax levy of not to exceed one (1) mill for a period not to exceed five (5) years upon the taxable tangible property within such city for the purpose of creating a building fund to be used for the construction, reconstruction, additions to, furnishing and equipping of the building housing such free public library and of a building to house motor vehicles of such free public library and the architectural expense incidental thereto, to the electors of such city at an election called and held in the manner provided for the calling and holding of elections under the provisions of the general bond law, at the time fixed for the holding of the primary election in August. The amount of such levy and the period for which it will be made shall be stated in the notice and upon the ballot of such election. No tax levy shall be made under the provisions of this act without the question of the making of such levy having been submitted to and having received the approval of a majority of the electors of such city voting thereon at an election called and held for such purpose. All moneys derived from the tax levy authorized by this act shall be placed in a building fund to be used only for the purposes for which the tax levy was made. All tax levies authorized by this act shall be in addition to all other tax levies authorized by law and shall not be subject to any of the limitations prescribed by law, including K. S. A. 12-1215 and 12-1217 and any acts amendatory thereof or supplemental thereto. [L. 1970, ch. 73, § 1; March 11.]

12-1255. Libraries in cities between 120,000 and 150,000; investment of moneys in building fund. Such board of directors may invest any portion of the building fund which is not currently needed in investments authorized by K.S.A. 12-1675, and amendments thereto, in the manner prescribed therein or in direct short-term obligations of the United States government, the principal and interest whereof is guaranteed by the government of the United States. All interest received thereon on any such investment, shall upon receipt thereof be credited to the building fund.

History: K.S.A. 12-1255; L. 1977, ch. 54, § 7; July 1.

12-1256. Sale or lease of public park property to library board of township by certain third class cities; use of moneys; property to be used for library services. The governing body of any city of the third class having a population of more than two thousand three hundred (2,300) and located in a township having a population of more than three thousand (3,000) is hereby authorized to sell or lease any unimproved portion of any public park to the library board of the township in which such city is located on such terms as may be agreed upon between the governing body of such city and library board. Any funds derived from the sale or lease of such portion of a public park shall be placed in a special fund and used only for the care, maintenance and improvement of the park system in said third-class city. Said township library board may improve the area acquired for library purposes by constructing thereon a library building, and equipping the same, with funds acquired by gift, issuance of bonds, or tax funds. The city and township are hereby authorized to do all things necessary and proper to carry out the general objective of providing library facilities for both the city and township. [L. 1974, ch. 51, § 1; March 4.]

12-1257. Libraries in urban area counties; tax levy, use of proceeds; special fund established; issuance of bonds; territory of existing library excluded; adoption and publication of resolution; protest petition and election. The board of county commissioners of any county designated as an urban area under K.S.A. 19-2654, may, at the request of the county library board, make an annual levy of not to exceed one-half (½) mill upon all taxable tangible property within the county for the purpose of creating a special fund to be used for the acquisition of sites, and for the constructing, equipping, repairing, remodeling and furnishing of buildings for county library purposes and to pay a portion of the principal and interest on bonds issued under the authority of K.S.A. 1979 Supp. 12-1774, and amendments thereto, by cities located in the county. In addition to the tax levy authorized herein, the board of county commissioners, at the request of the county library board, may issue bonds of such county in an aggregate amount not exceeding one-half of one percent (½%) of the assessed tangible valuation of such county, the proceeds of which shall be placed in such special fund and may be used for the purposes herein enumerated. No tax levied under the authority of this act, either for the creation of said special fund or for the repayment of bonds issued hereunder, shall be assessed against property in any municipality in which a municipal library has been established and is being maintained.

Prior to the levying of a tax or the issuance of any bonds under the authority of this act, the board of county commissioners shall adopt a resolution authorizing and stating the purpose for the same. Such resolution shall be published once each week for two consecutive weeks in a newspaper of general circulation within the county. If, within sixty (60) days following the last publication of the resolution, a petition in opposition to the levy or the issuance of bonds, signed by not less than five percent (5%) of the qualified electors of the county, is filed with the county election officer, no such levy shall be made and no bonds shall be issued unless and until the same is approved by a majority of the qualified electors of the county voting thereon at a special election called and held for such purpose. Bonds issued under the authority of this act shall not be subject to or within any bonded debt limitation of the county prescribed by any other law of this state and shall not be considered or included in applying any other law limiting the bonded indebtedness of such county. Any such election shall be called, noticed and held in accordance with the provisions of K.S.A. 1979 Supp. 10-120, and amendments thereto. Any tax levy made under the authority of this act shall be in addition to all other tax levies authorized or limited by law and shall not be subject to or within the limitations upon the levy of taxes imposed by K.S.A. 79-5001 to 79-5016, inclusive, and amendments thereto.

No qualified elector of any municipality in which a municipal library has been established and is being maintained shall be entitled to vote at any election called and held under the provisions of this act, nor shall any such person's signature be considered valid on any petition provided for herein.

History: L. 1978, ch. 60, § 1; L. 1979, ch. 52, § 41; July 1.

SCHOOL DISTRICT LIBRARIES

(Kansas Statutes Annotated, 1982, s.72-1033, 72-1623, 72-1623a, 72-1626, 72-8115.)

72-1033. Control of school property; library services. The school board shall have control of the school-district property, including the school building or buildings, schoolgrounds and all buildings and structures erected thereon, all furniture, fittings, and equipment, such as books, maps, charts, and instructional apparatus. The school board may open the schoolhouse for public purpose, under such rules and regulations as the board shall adopt. The board may enter into contracts with public library boards to authorize such boards to use the library facilities of the school district to supplement the facilities of the public library; make such rules and regulations relating to such school libraries as they shall deem necessary; and appoint librarians.

History: L. 1861, ch. 76, art. 4, § 2; G.S. 1868, ch. 92, § 43; L. 1876, ch. 125, § 1; L. 1913, ch. 284, § 1; R.S. 1923, 72-1033; L. 1943, ch. 248, § 31; L. 1965, ch. 104, § 2; June 30.

72-1623. Powers and duties of board; libraries and certain cities. The board shall establish and maintain a system of free public schools for all children residing in the city school district and may make all necessary rules and regulations for the government and conduct of such schools, consistent with the laws of the state: *Provided,* The board of a city having a population of more than one hundred twenty thousand (120,000) and not more than two hundred thousand (200,000) may establish and maintain a public library and branch libraries, expenditures for which shall be paid from the general, building, and retirement funds in like manner to school expenditures:

* * *

History: L. 1951, ch. 395, § 37; L. 1955, ch. 316, § 1; L. 1957, ch. 385, § 1; June 29.

72-1623a. Libraries and library services; tax levy, use of proceeds; increase in levy; petition; election. (a) The board of education of a city of the first class which has established and is maintaining a public library and branch libraries as provided for in K.S.A. 72-1623, or of a unified or city unified school district wherein is included a disorganized district which had established and was maintaining a public library and branch libraries at the time of inclusion in the unified district, may levy annually, not to exceed 2.5 mills on each dollar of the assessed tangible valuation of the property of such district in addition to any levy otherwise authorized or by law provided, and the ad valorem receipts resulting therefrom may be in addition to any budget limitation otherwise provided for; and the funds derived from such tax levies shall be used for libraries and library services of the school district and for the purpose of paying a portion of the principal and interest on bonds issued by cities under the authority of K.S.A. 1980 Supp. 12-1774, and amendments thereto, for the financing of redevelopment projects upon property located within the school district.

(b) Whenever the board of education desires to increase the mill levy above 2.5 mills and such board shall determine that the current tax levy is insufficient to maintain and support the library, such board may adopt a resolution declaring it necessary to increase such annual levy in an amount which together with the current levy shall not exceed a total of four mills. Such resolution shall state the total amount of the tax to be levied for library purposes and shall be published once each week for three consecutive weeks in the official city newspaper. Whereupon such annual levy in an amount not to exceed the amount stated in the resolution may be made for the ensuing budget year and each successive budget year unless a petition requesting an election upon the proposition to increase the tax levy in excess of the current tax levy, signed by not less than 5% of the qualified electors who voted at the last preceding regular city election, as shown by the poll books, is filed with the county election officer within 60 days following the date of the last publication of the resolution. In the event a valid petition is filed, no such increased levy shall be made without such proposition having been submitted to and having been approved by a majority of the qualified electors voting at an election called and held thereon. All such elections shall be called and held in the manner prescribed for the calling and holding of elections upon the question of the issuance of bonds under the general bond law.

History: L. 1965, ch. 426, § 1; L. 1979, ch. 52, § 168; L. 1981, ch. 280, § 1; July 1.

72-1626. Sites, buildings, repairs and improvements; bonds; election; exception; limitations. Any board, upon determining that it is necessary to purchase or improve a school site or sites, to construct, equip, furnish, repair, remodel or make additions to any building or buildings used for school

purposes, may submit to the electors of the city school district the question of issuing general obligation bonds of the board for one or more of the above purposes, and upon the affirmative vote of the majority of those voting thereon, the board shall be authorized to issue such bonds: *Provided,* The board of any city which pursuant to law shall have established a public library may in like manner issue bonds for the purchase or improvement of a public library or branch library site, and the construction, equipping, remodeling, repairing, or making additions to a building used for library or branch library purposes.

The board shall adopt a resolution stating the purposes for which bonds are to be issued and the estimated amount thereof. A certified copy of such resolution, signed by the clerk and countersigned by the president, shall be sent to the mayor of the city whose duty it shall be to issue, within thirty (30) days, a proclamation for holding an election on the question of issuing such bonds, which election shall be called and held in accordance with the provisions of the general bond law. Any board may issue, without an election but with the written approval of the state superintendent of public instruction, bonds in an amount not exceeding five thousand dollars ($5,000) to pay for needed repairs on school buildings or equipment, but the aggregate amount of such bonds outstanding at any time shall not exceed ten thousand dollars ($10,000). The aggregate amount of bonds of a board outstanding at any time (exclusive of bonds specifically exempted from statutory limitations) shall not exceed six percent (6%) of the assessed valuation of tangible taxable property within the city school district.

History: L. 1951, ch. 395, § 40; L. 1957, ch. 386, § 1; June 29.

72-8115. Unified school districts operating public libraries. Whenever there is included in any unified district a disorganized district which had established and was maintaining as of January 1, 1965, a public library and branch libraries at the time of inclusion in said unified district, then said unified district may maintain and operate a public library and branch libraries and all statutes relating to the establishment, maintenance, and operation of a public library and branches and the issuing of bonds for the construction and equipping of such library and branch libraries shall apply to such unified district.

History: L. 1965, ch. 420, § 23; Feb. 23.

COUNTY LAW LIBRARIES

(Kansas Statutes Annotated, 1982, s.19-1308 to 19-1310,
19-1314 to 19-1325.)

19-1308. Registration of attorneys in certain counties; exceptions; fees. In all counties which now have or which may

hereafter have, a population of fifty thousand (50,000) or more and in all counties which may now or hereafter have a population of not more than forty thousand (40,000) and an assessed tangible valuation of more than ninety million dollars ($90,000,000), and in all counties which may now or hereafter have a population of not less than fifteen thousand (15,000) nor more than twenty-five thousand (25,000) and an assessed tangible valuation of not less than twenty-two million dollars ($22,000,000) nor more than twenty-eight million dollars ($28,000,000), and three (3) cities of the second class located therein, and in all counties in which there is located a city of the first class having a population of less than fifteen thousand (15,000) and having an assessed tangible valuation of more than twelve million dollars ($12,000,000), and in all counties having a population of more than twenty-four thousand (24,000) and less than twenty-eight thousand (28,000), and having an assessed tangible valuation of more than fifty million dollars ($50,000,000) and less than sixty million dollars ($60,000,000), and in all counties having a population of more than twelve thousand (12,000) and less than sixteen thousand (16,000) and in which there is located a city of the second class having a population of more than nine thousand (9,000), and in all counties which now have or which may hereafter have a population of not more than fifty thousand (50,000) in which there is located a city of the first class having a population of more than twenty-one thousand (21,000), and in all counties having a population of more than twenty thousand (20,000) and less than thirty thousand (30,000) in which there are located five (5) or more cities of the second class, and in all counties having a population of more than thirteen thousand (13,000) and less than seventeen thousand (17,000) and having an assessed valuation of more than fifty million dollars ($50,000,000) in which there are located two (2) cities of the second class, and in all counties having a population of more than twenty thousand (20,000) and not more than twenty-six thousand (26,000) and having an assessed valuation of tangible property of more than sixty million dollars ($60,000,000), as shown by the census returns of the county assessor for the preceding year; all practicing attorneys-at-law therein shall register annually with the clerk of the district court in a register which said clerk shall keep for that purpose. The clerk shall enter in such register, the name, age, place of residence, location of office, firm connection, if any, and the date of admission of every such attorney to the bar, and shall specify the date he was licensed to practice law in the state of Kansas. All attorneys-at-law living within such county, who appear in any court of said county, and all who maintain or work for, or are connected with any firm or individuals maintaining an office in such county, shall register within thirty (30) days from the taking effect of this act and on or before January 15, of each year thereafter: *Provided,* That this act only shall become effective when a majority of the members of the bar of any such county shall elect to come under the provisions of this act, and shall not apply to any county where there is located a law library maintained by the state of Kansas. Each attorney shall pay to the said clerk at the time of registering an annual registration fee of ten dollars ($10): *Provided, however,* That in counties having a population of more than one hundred eighty-five thousand (185,000) and not more than two hundred thousand (200,000), each attorney shall pay to the said clerk at the time of registering an annual registration fee of fifteen dollars ($15), except that in any such county the board of county commissioners shall pay the annual registration fee for the district attorney of such county and each of his assistant district attorneys and full-time deputy district attorneys, with such fees to be considered as expenses of the office of district attorney within the meaning of subsection (a) of K.S.A. 22a-106: *Provided further,* That in counties having a population of more than two hundred thousand (200,000) and not more than two hundred fifty thousand (250,000), each attorney shall pay to the said clerk at the time of registering an annual registration fee of fifteen dollars ($15): *Provided further,* That in counties having a population of more than two hundred fifty thousand (250,000), each attorney shall pay to the said clerk at the time of registering an annual registration fee of twenty-five dollars ($25): *Provided further,* That in counties having a population of more than fifty-five thousand (55,000) and less than one hundred thousand (100,000), each attorney shall pay the said clerk at the time of registering, an annual registration fee of fifteen dollars ($15), except that during the first five (5) years after admission to the practice of law, such fee shall be ten dollars ($10). In all such counties the clerk of the district court shall not file in his office in any matter or action, any pleading or other papers signed by an attorney who has not registered and who is required to register under this act and paid to said clerk said registration fee, and if any pleadings or other papers signed by an attorney who has not complied with the provisions of this act, are filed by said clerk through his mistake or neglect, then said pleadings or papers so filed shall be stricken from the files of said matter or cause on the order of the district judge before whom such cause is pending upon motion of the adverse party or motion of any registered attorney of said county.

History: L. 1919, ch. 178, § 1; L. 1920, ch. 32, § 1; R.S. 1923, 19-1308; L. 1925, ch. 133, § 1; L. 1938, ch. 40, § 1; L. 1943, ch. 136, § 1; L. 1945, ch. 164, § 1; L. 1951, ch. 221, § 1; L. 1953, ch. 145, § 1; L. 1957, ch. 163, § 1; L. 1961, ch. 132, § 1; L. 1963, ch. 167, § 1; L. 1974, ch. 117, § 1; July 1.

19-1309. Registration of attorneys in certain counties; use of registration fees for law library; trustees; treasurer; librarian; library fees as costs; compensation of librarian and expenditures. (a) The fees authorized by K.S.A. 19-1308 shall be used in the establishing and maintaining of a law library in each county in which the provisions of said statute have been made applicable, as provided therein. Except as otherwise provided in subsection (b), the judges of the district court ex officio, and two (2) members of the bar to be appointed by said judges for a term of two (2) years, shall be trustees of said library and shall have the management and control thereof, and shall use the fees paid by attorneys for registration, and all other sums donated or provided by law, for the purpose of establishing and maintaining a library in the county courthouse or other suitable place to be provided and maintained by the county commissioners of such county. In each such county, the judges of the district court, members of the bar who reside in such county and who have registered and paid the fee provided for in K.S.A. 19-1308, and all other county officials, shall have the right to use said library in accordance with the rules and regulations established by the trustees.

The clerk of the district court of each such county shall be ex officio treasurer of said library and safely keep the funds of said library and disburse them as the trustees, or a majority thereof, shall direct, and shall be liable on his or her official bond for any failure, refusal or neglect in performing his or her duties in said particulars.

(b) In counties having a population of more than two hundred fifty thousand (250,000), the trustees of said library shall be five (5) in number, two (2) of whom shall be judges of the district court, appointed by all of said judges, and three (3) of whom shall be members of the bar of said county, selected by the bar association of said county in the manner provided in its bylaws. In any such county, the trustees may release said board of county commissioners from the duty to maintain said library in the courthouse or other suitable place, and to establish and maintain said library in some suitable place not provided by the county commissioners, in which case the clerk of the district court shall appoint a deputy in addition to those otherwise provided by law, which said deputy shall act as custodian and librarian of said library, assist said clerk in the performance of the duties of treasurer thereof, perform such other duties not inconsistent with those herein enumerated as said clerk shall direct, and shall be paid a salary out of the county treasury, in equal monthly installments, of twenty-four hundred dollars ($2,400) per annum. Said trustees shall have the power to rescind said action at any time, in which case it shall become the duty of the county commissioners to establish the said library in the courthouse or any other place provided and maintained by the county. The clerk of the district court shall tax in all felony criminal cases and in all civil cases commenced pursuant to chapter 60 of the Kansas Statutes Annotated a library fee of two dollars ($2) and the clerk shall tax a fee of one dollar ($1) in all criminal misdemeanor cases and in all civil cases commenced pursuant to chapters 38, 59, or 65 of the Kansas Statutes Annotated for the benefit of the law library established in said county. Said fees shall be deducted from the required docket fee, except that in cases commenced pursuant to chapter 59 or 65 of the Kansas Statutes Annotated and cases commenced pursuant to the juvenile code such fee shall be taxed as additional court cost. All library fees shall be for the benefit and account of the law library established in said county.

(c) The clerk of the district court in any such county having a population of more than one hundred eighty-five thousand (185,000) and less than two hundred fifty thousand (250,000) shall tax in all criminal felony cases and in all civil cases pursuant to chapter 60 of the Kansas Statutes Annotated, a library fee of two dollars ($2), and the clerk shall tax a fee of one dollar ($1) in all criminal misdemeanor and civil cases filed pursuant to chapter 38, 59, or 61 of the Kansas Statutes Annotated. Such fees shall be deducted from the docket fee, except that in cases commenced pursuant to chapter 59 or 65 of the Kansas Statutes Annotated or cases commenced pursuant to the juvenile code such fee shall be taxed as additional court costs. All library fees shall be for the benefit and the account of the law library established in said county; and the board of trustees may pay the salary of said librarian in an amount established by such board, payable from funds of the library.

(d) The clerk of the district court of any county designated an urban area pursuant to K.S.A. 19-2654 is hereby authorized to appoint, by and with the advice and consent of the board of trustees of the law library of such county, a deputy who shall act as custodian and librarian of the law library of such county and shall assist the clerk in the performance of his or her duties as treasurer thereof. Said deputy also shall perform services with respect to legal aid referral assistance programs in such county and such other duties as may be assigned by the clerk of the district court, with the approval of the board of trustees of the law library of such county. Said deputy shall receive as compensation for his or her services an annual salary, payable from the general fund of such county in equal monthly installments, as is prescribed by the judges of the district court of such county, with the approval of the board of county commissioners of such county. The expenditure for the salary of such deputy may be paid during the budget year in which this act takes effect, even though the same was not included in the budget of expenditures for such year.

History: L. 1919, ch. 178, § 2; R.S. 1923, 19-1309; L. 1927, ch. 156, § 1; L. 1929, ch. 145, § 1; L. 1938, ch. 40, § 2; L. 1941, ch. 190, § 1; L. 1947, ch. 193, § 1; L. 1951, ch. 221, § 2; L. 1953, ch. 146, § 1; L. 1957, ch.

247, § 15; L. 1961, ch. 133, § 1; L. 1963, ch. 167, § 2; L. 1965, ch. 159, § 20; L. 1968, ch. 50, § 1; L. 1969, ch. 204, § 2; L. 1973, ch. 109, § 1; L. 1974, ch. 117, § 2; L. 1976, ch. 125, § 2; L. 1976, ch. 151, § 2; L. 1977, ch. 90, § 1; July 1.

19-1309a. Same; collection of library fees; liability of county and city. Except as otherwise authorized by law, the clerk of the district court in all counties where a law library is now or hereafter may be established shall tax in all civil cases commenced pursuant to chapter 60 of the Kansas Statutes Annotated, all felony criminal cases, and in all cases of appeals from any court, a library fee of one dollar ($1). In counties having a population of more than twenty thousand (20,000) and less than thirty thousand (30,000) in which there are located five or more cities of the second class, the said clerk shall tax in all such cases a fee of two dollars ($2). Said fees shall be deducted from the required docket fee, except that in actions commenced pursuant to chapter 59 or 65 of the Kansas Statutes Annotated and actions pursuant to the juvenile code such fee shall be taxed as additional court costs.

In criminal cases where the case is dismissed by the state, the county shall be liable for said library fee and where appeals from conviction in the municipal court are dismissed for want of prosecution, or by the defendant, the state or city shall collect said library fee, or upon failure to do so within ninety (90) days after said dismissal, the county in which the library is located or the city in which the municipal court is located from which said appeal is taken, as the case may be, shall be liable therefor.

History: L. 1927, ch. 156, § 2; L. 1957, ch. 163, § 2; L. 1976, ch. 145, § 63; L. 1977, ch. 105, § 6; July 1.

19-1309b. Same; collection of library fees in certain counties between 55,000 and 100,000. Except as otherwise provided by law, the clerks of all district courts established in counties having a population of more than fifty-five thousand (55,000) and less than one hundred thousand (100,000), where a law library is now or hereafter may be established, shall tax in all cases commenced pursuant to chapter 61 of the Kansas Statutes Annotated and in all misdemeanor criminal cases, a library fee of fifty cents (50¢). Said fees shall be deducted from the required docket fee, and when collected such fees shall be for the benefit and the account of the law library established in said county.

History: L. 1951, ch. 221, § 3; L. 1957, ch. 163, § 3; L. 1963, ch. 167, § 3; L. 1976, ch. 145, § 64; L. 1977, ch. 105, § 7; July 1.

19-1309c. Same; collection of library fees in certain counties. In all counties having a population of more than two hundred fifty thousand (250,000) the clerk of the district court shall tax a fee of one dollar ($1) as a library fee for each case or proceeding filed pursuant to chapter 59 or 65 of the Kansas Statutes Annotated. Said fees shall be taxed and collected as other costs in the case, and when collected, such fees shall be for the benefit and account of the law library established in said county. In all counties having a population of more than fifty-five thousand (55,000) and less than one hundred thousand (100,000), and where a law library is now or hereafter may be established, the clerk of the district court shall tax a fee of one dollar ($1) as a library fee for each petition filed to admit a will to probate and each petition for the administration of the estate of an intestate decedent or a ward. Said fee shall be taxed and collected as other costs in such proceeding, and when collected shall be covered into the county treasury for the benefit and account of the law library established in said county.

History: L. 1957, ch. 163, § 4; L. 1963, ch. 167, § 4; L. 1976, ch. 145, § 65; Jan. 10, 1977.

19-1310. Same; registrants exempt from license taxes. All attorneys registered under this act shall not be liable to pay any occupation tax or city license fees levied under the laws of this state by any municipality.

History: L. 1919, ch. 178, § 3; March 19; R.S. 1923, 19-1310.

19-1314. Law libraries in certain counties; registration of attorneys; election. In all counties that now have or may hereafter have a population of not less than thirty thousand (30,000) nor more than forty thousand (40,000) and an assessed tangible valuation of not less than seventy million dollars ($70,000,000) nor more than ninety million dollars ($90,000,000) and in all counties that now have or may hereafter have a population of not less than eleven thousand (11,000) and not more than fourteen thousand (14,000) and having an assessed taxable tangible valuation of not less than forty-five million dollars ($45,000,000) and not more than fifty-six million dollars ($56,000,000), and in all counties that now have or may hereafter have a population of not less than eight thousand five hundred (8,500) and not more than nine thousand five hundred (9,500) and having an assessed taxable tangible valuation of not less than thirty-four million dollars ($34,000,000) and not more than thirty-seven million dollars ($37,000,000), and in all counties having a population of not less than seven thousand (7,000) and not more than nine thousand (9,000) and having an assessed taxable tangible valuation of not less than forty-three million dollars ($43,000,000) and in all counties having a population of not less than twenty-five thousand (25,000) and not more than thirty thousand (30,000), all practicing attorneys at law therein shall register with the clerk of the district court in a register which said clerk shall keep for that purpose.

The clerk shall enter in such register the name, age, place of residence, location of office, firm connections, if any, the date of admission of every such attorney to the bar and shall specify the date he was licensed to practice law in the state of Kansas: *Provided,* This act shall not apply to or become effective in any such county until after a majority of the members of the bar of such county shall by resolution elect to come within the provisions, and shall not apply to any county where there is located a law library maintained by the state of Kansas.

History: L. 1957, ch. 194, § 1; L. 1959, ch. 130, § 1; L. 1961, ch. 134, § 1; L. 1963, ch. 168, § 1; June 30.

19-1315. Law libraries in certain counties; trustees, qualifications, powers; use of library; treasurer of fund; liability on bonds. After the members of the bar of any such county shall have elected to come within the provisions of this act, the judge or judges of the district court ex officio, and three (3) members of the bar of such county to be elected for a term of two (2) years by the members of the bar whose registration fees have been paid, shall be the trustees of a law library that may be acquired, established and maintained in such county under the provisions of this act and shall have the supervision, management and control thereof.

The judges of the district court, members of the bar who reside in said county and who have registered and paid the fees provided for herein, and all county officials in said county shall have the right to the use of such library in accordance with the rules and regulations established by the trustees.

The clerk of the district court shall be ex officio treasurer of said library fund and shall safely keep all funds paid to him or her under the provisions of this act, and disburse them as the trustees or a majority of them shall direct, and such clerk and the judge of the district court shall be liable on their respective official bonds for any failure, refusal or neglect in the performance of their respective duties as herein set forth.

History: L. 1957, ch. 194, § 2; L. 1976, ch. 125, § 3; L. 1976, ch. 151, § 3; Jan. 10, 1977.

19-1316. Same; registration; fee. All attorneys at law living within such county who appear as an attorney in any court in such county shall register with the clerk of such district court within thirty (30) days from the taking effect of this act, and on or before the fifteenth day of January in each year thereafter, and at the time of each such registration shall pay to the clerk of such court a fee of fifteen dollars ($15) to be known as a registration fee.

History: L. 1957, ch. 194, § 3; June 29.

19-1317. Same; collection of fees. The clerk of the district court shall tax as costs in

each case docketed in his or her court for all cases commenced pursuant to chapter 60 of the Kansas Statutes Annotated and in all felony criminal cases, a filing fee of two dollars ($2) and the clerk of the district court shall tax as costs in each, a case commenced pursuant to chapter 61 of the Kansas Statutes Annotated and each misdemeanor criminal case fee of one dollar ($1), such fees to be known as library fees. All such fees shall be deducted from the required docket fee and shall be for the use and account of said trustees. In all criminal cases that are dismissed in the district court or upon the motion of the county attorney or a city attorney or in which there is a verdict or judgment of not guilty, no filing fees shall be collected.

History: L. 1957, ch. 194, § 4; L. 1976, ch. 145, § 67; Jan. 10, 1977.

19-1318. Same; use of fees for law library; housing. All fees paid by the attorneys as a registration fee, and all other fees paid as a filing fee, and all sums donated, or provided by law, shall be used by said trustees for the purpose of acquiring, purchasing, establishing, maintaining, providing and operating a law library, such library to be kept and maintained in the courthouse in such county or other suitable place to be provided and maintained by the board of county commissioners of such county: *Provided,* In counties having a population of not less than twenty-six thousand (26,000) and not more than thirty thousand (30,000) such law library shall be located in any city in such county having a population of more than ten thousand (10,000), and the governing body of the city in which such library is located may provide suitable housing therefor.

History: L. 1957, ch. 194, § 5; L. 1963, ch. 168, § 2; June 30.

19-1319. County law libraries; establishment; election; registration; fees; filing pleadings signed by attorney; requirements. Any county of this state may establish a county law library, under the provisions of and subject to the qualifications of this act.

No county law library shall be established under the provisions of this act until a majority of the attorneys residing within such county and admitted to practice before the bar in Kansas shall elect to do so: *Provided,* That where a county law library has already been established pursuant to other statutory provisions, said library may come under the provisions of this act upon an affirmative vote of the majority of the board of trustees of said library. The results of the voting shall be filed with the county commissioners. The clerk of the district court shall at the request of the president of the county bar association provide for the mailing of ballots to all attorneys residing within the county, and for the tabulation of the results of such election. Such election shall be filed with the county commissioners: *Provided,* That this provision for the holding of an election shall not be construed as precluding any election in any other normally accepted manner.

After such election, all attorneys residing within such county shall register annually with the clerk of the district court in a register kept for that purpose. The clerk shall enter the name, place of residence, employment, location of office, and firm connection, if any, of such person. All of said attorneys shall register within thirty (30) days after an election has been made to provide for a county law library, and on or before January 15 of each year thereafter. All attorneys required to register shall pay to the clerk at the time of registering an annual registration fee of not less than ten dollars ($10). A registration fee in excess of ten dollars ($10) annually may be fixed by a majority of the attorneys registered under the provisions of this act. A schedule of current registration fees shall be filed with the clerk of the district court.

Whenever a law library shall have been established in any county, the clerk of the district court, or the clerk of any inferior court within such county, shall not file in his office in any matter or action, any pleading, or other papers signed by an attorney required to register under this act who has not so registered, and paid to the clerk of the district court the required registration fee. If any pleadings or other papers signed by an attorney who has not complied with the provisions of this act are filed by the clerk of any court within the county through his mistake or neglect, then said pleadings or papers so filed shall be stricken from the files on the order of the judge before whom such cause is pending upon motion of the adverse party or motion of any registered attorney of said county. The clerk of the district court shall keep a record of all those required to register under this act, and shall submit a copy thereof to all other clerks of any courts of countywide jurisdiction within said county.

History: L. 1967, ch. 137, § 1; L. 1968, ch. 306, § 1; July 1.

19-1320. County law libraries; board of trustees; use of fees and donations; use of library; treasurer, duties; custodian and librarian and assistants in certain counties; duties, compensation. All fees collected pursuant to K.S.A. 19-1319 shall be used to establish and maintain the county law library. A board of trustees consisting of the district judge or district judges of the district court and not less than two (2) attorneys who shall be elected for two (2) year terms by a majority of the attorneys residing in the county shall have the management and control of such library and shall use the fees paid for registration, and all other sums,

books, or library materials or equipment donated or provided by law, for the purpose of establishing and maintaining such library in the county courthouse or other suitable place to be provided and maintained by the county commissioners of such county. The district judge or district judges of the district court, members of the bar who reside in said county and who have registered and paid the fee provided for in K.S.A. 19-1319, judges of all other courts in the county and the county officials shall have the right to use the library in accordance with the rules and regulations established by the board of trustees.

The clerk of the district court of the county shall be treasurer of the library and shall safely keep the funds of such library and disburse them as the trustees, or a majority thereof, shall direct. The clerk shall be liable on an official bond for any failure, refusal or neglect in performing such duties.

The clerk of the district court of any county designated an urban area pursuant to K.S.A. 19-2654 wherein an election has been held to come under the provisions of this act is hereby authorized to appoint, by and with the advice and consent of the board of trustees of the law library of such county, a deputy, who shall act as custodian and librarian of the law library of such county and shall assist in the performance of the clerk's duties as treasurer thereof, and such assistants as are necessary to perform the duties of such deputy. Such deputy and assistants also shall perform services with respect to legal aid referral assistance programs in such county and such other duties as may be assigned by the clerk of the district court, with the approval of the board of trustees of the law library of the county. Such deputy and assistants shall receive as compensation for their services such annual salaries, payable from the general fund of such county in equal monthly installments, as are prescribed by the district judges of the district court of the county, with the approval of the board of county commissioners of the county.

History: L. 1967, ch. 137, § 2; L. 1968, ch. 306, § 2; L. 1974, ch. 118, § 1; L. 1975, ch. 159, § 1; L. 1976, ch. 125, § 1; L. 1976, ch. 151, § 1; Jan. 10, 1977.

19-1321. Same; maintenance of library; custodian and librarian; compensation. The trustees of any county law library may release the board of county commissioners from the duty to maintain said library in the courthouse or other suitable place, and may establish and maintain said library in some suitable place not provided by the county commissioners in which case a deputy clerk of the district court shall be appointed upon the approval thereof by said trustees, which deputy shall act as custodian and librarian of said library, assist said clerk in the performance of the duties of treasurer thereof, perform such other duties not inconsistent with those herein enumerated as said clerk shall direct, and shall be paid a salary by the trustees: *Provided, however,* That in all counties with a population in excess of one hundred thousand (100,000), the board of county commissioners shall pay out of the general fund an amount not in excess of two thousand seven hundred dollars ($2,700) annually to the said trustees, to be applied to the cost of operating said library as in the discretion of said trustees is determined most proper. Said sum shall be paid in equal monthly installments. The trustees shall have the power to rescind said action at any time, in which case it shall become the duty of the county commissioners to establish the said library in the courthouse or any other suitable place provided and maintained by the county.

History: L. 1967, ch. 137, § 3; April 22.

19-1322. Same; collection of library fees; liability of county. (a) Except as provided in subsection (b), the clerk of the district court shall tax in all cases commenced pursuant to chapter 60 of the Kansas Statutes Annotated and in all felony criminal cases a library fee of not less than $2 or more than $3 and shall tax in all other cases a library fee of not less than $.50 or more than $2, for the benefit and account of the law library in the county.

(b) In the judicial district comprising Sedgwick county, the clerk of the district court shall tax in all cases commenced pursuant to chapter 60 of the Kansas Statutes Annotated and in all felony criminal cases a library fee of not less than $2 or more than $5 and shall tax in all other cases a library fee of not less than $.50 or more than $4 for the benefit and account of the law library in the county.

(c) The fees provided for by subsection (a) shall be deducted from the docket fee.

(d) The fees provided for by subsection (b) shall be deducted from the docket fees only to the extent provided in subsection (a) and any excess fees shall be taxed as additional costs.

(e) In all cases commenced pursuant to chapter 38, 59 or 65 of the Kansas Statutes Annotated such fees shall be taxed as additional court costs.

(f) The trustees of each law library shall determine the fees to be charged within the limits above and shall file with the respective clerks the fees to be charged in that court.

(g) In all civil cases where the plaintiff settles with the defendant and as part of settlement the case is dismissed at the cost of the plaintiff or judgment is rendered against the plaintiff for costs but is not paid within 90 days after the entry of the judgment, the defendant shall be liable for the library fee. On motion in such case judgment may be rendered against the defendant for the library fee, and execution may issue on such judgment.

(h) In criminal cases where the case is dismissed by the state, the county shall be liable for the library fee. Where appeals from conviction in the city police court are dismissed for want of prosecution, or by the defendant, the state or city shall collect the library fee. Upon failure of the state or city to do so within 90 days after the dismissal, the county from which the appeal is taken shall be liable therefor.

History: L. 1967, ch. 137, § 4; L. 1976, ch. 145, § 69; L. 1981, ch. 117, § 1; July 1.

19-1323. County law libraries; use and investment of idle funds. The trustees may invest any idle funds in investments authorized by K.S.A. 1977 Supp. 12-1675, and amendments thereto, in the manner prescribed therein. The trustees may also direct that any funds collected may be used for any purpose consistent with the establishment and maintenance of a law library.

History: L. 1967, ch. 137, § 5; L. 1977, ch. 54, § 25; July 1.

19-1324. Same; branch library, when. Upon the election of a majority of the attorneys in any county, a branch of said library shall be established and maintained in a suitable place to be provided and maintained by the board of county commissioners. The provisions of this section shall be subject to all other provisions of this act.

History: L. 1967, ch. 137, § 6; April 22.

19-1325. Same; joint law library; establishment and maintenance. Upon the election of a majority of the attorneys in any county, with the mutual consent of a majority from any other county or counties, a joint law library may be established and maintained in any suitable place or places determined by a majority of said attorneys from each county so joining, and the boards of county commissioners of said counties shall provide and maintain a suitable place or places and such boards shall share equally in any expense. The provisions of this section shall be subject to all other provisions of this act, and shall be applied upon such terms and under such conditions as the trustees so elected may agree.

The trustees so elected shall determine which clerk of the district court shall act as treasurer.

No provisions of this act shall be construed to place the operation of any county law library established and maintained hereunder or under other enabling acts subject to any cash basis law of this state.

History: L. 1967, ch. 137, § 7; April 22.

KENTUCKY

DEPARTMENT FOR LIBRARIES AND ARCHIVES
(Kentucky Revised Statutes, 1982, s.171.125 to 171.221.)

171.125. Definitions for KRS 171.130 to 171.306. — As used in KRS 171.130 to 171.306, unless the context requires otherwise, "department" means the department of library and archives. (Enact. Acts 1962, ch. 106, Art. VIII, § 1; 1966, ch. 255, § 157; 1974, ch. 74, Art. VIII, B, § 1.)

171.130. Department for libraries and archives — Commissioner. — The department for libraries and archives is established. The department shall be headed by a commissioner whose title shall be state librarian who shall be appointed by and serve at the pleasure of the governor, and who shall have had technical training in the field of library science. (Enact. Acts 1954, ch. 41, § 1; 1962, ch. 106, Art. VIII, § 2; 1980, ch. 188, § 127, effective July 15, 1980; 1982, ch. 381, § 6, effective July 15, 1982.)

171.140. General powers and duties. — (1) The department shall give assistance and advice to all school, state institutional, free and public libraries, and to all communities in the state which propose to establish libraries, as to the best means of establishing and administering them, selecting and cataloging books, and other details of library management, and may send any of its members to aid in organizing such libraries or assist in the improvement of those already established.

(2) It may receive gifts which may be used or held for the purpose given, and may purchase and operate traveling libraries under such conditions and rules as it thinks necessary to protect the interests of the state and best increase the efficiency of its service to the public.

(3) The department may issue printed material, such as lists and circulars of information, and in the publication thereof may cooperate with other state library commissions and libraries, in order to secure the more economical administration of the work for which it was formed. It may conduct courses of library instruction and hold librarians' institutes in various parts of the state.

(4) The department shall perform such other service in behalf of public libraries as it considers for the best interests of the state. (2438c-4.)

171.145. Authority to provide library services for the blind and physically handicapped. — For the benefit of blind and physically handicapped readers of Kentucky, the department of library and archives may make available books and other reading matter in braille, talking books or any other medium of reading used by the blind and physically handicapped. To this end, the department is authorized to provide library services for the blind and physically handicapped of the Commonwealth through contract, agreement or otherwise with the Library of Congress or any regional library thereof. (Enact. Acts 1960, ch. 58; 1974, ch. 8, § 1; 1974, ch. 74, Art. VIII, B, § 1.)

171.150. Power to accept money appropriated and granted. — The department of libraries may accept and administer any money appropriated or granted to it, in addition to appropriations to it out of the general fund, for providing, improving and equalizing public library service, library service to state institutions, and cooperative systems of library service, including cooperative arrangements with public school, college, university and special libraries in Kentucky, by the federal government or by the state or any other agencies. (2438d-1: amend. Acts 1970, ch. 241, § 1.)

171.160. State treasurer to be trustee of funds — Disbursements. — (1) The state treasurer shall serve as trustee of funds apportioned to the state from any appropriations made by the federal government, the state or any other agency for providing and equalizing public library service in Kentucky.

(2) The executive department for finance and administration shall, on the requisition of the department, authorize the state treasurer to make disbursement from such funds to such libraries, cities, towns and counties for library service as have been approved and authorized to participate in the benefit of these funds under the terms of the federal acts, and for the payment of salaries and other authorized expenses out of the fund provided by the federal government. (2438d-2.)

171.170. Department to cooperate with federal government. — The department shall cooperate, as required by the acts of congress providing federal grants to states for library service, with the United States commissioner of eduction in the administration of the provisions of such acts, employ personnel and do all things necessary to entitle the state of Kentucky to receive the benefits thereof. (2438d-3.)

171.180. Reports and audits by local libraries and state officials. — All libraries, cities, towns, counties and school districts participating in or benefiting by the provisions of the federal grant for library service or receiving any service from the department, shall make such reports and audits as are required to the state treasurer, the department, and the United States commissioner of education. The state treasurer and department shall make such reports and audits as may be required by the federal government and the United States commissioner of education in respect to the expenditure of federal grants and progress of library service. (2438d-4.)

171.190. Merit system of employment to be used. — All appointments of personnel and the tenure thereof to the department and to such libraries, cities, towns, counties and school districts participating in or benefiting by the provisions of the federal grants for library service shall be based on merit without regard to political consideration. (2438d-5.)

171.200. Department to administer and maintain improved cooperative and integrated system of library service. — The department of libraries shall make and administer plans to lessen inequalities of opportunity for library service, for the maintenance of an improved cooperative and integrated system of library service throughout the state and for suitable cooperative arrangements between public library systems, school library systems, college and university libraries, special libraries, and other appropriate state agencies. (2438d-6: amend. Acts 1966, ch. 184, § 7; 1970, ch. 241, § 2.)

171.201. Public library service appropriations. — For grants to public libraries for promoting, aiding and equalizing public library service in Kentucky, there may be funds appropriated out of the general expenditure fund of the state treasury. (Enact. Acts 1952, ch. 114, §§ 1, 5; 1966, ch. 255, § 158; 1972, ch. 223, § 1; 1974, ch. 8, § 2.)

171.202. Administration of fund. — The state librarian shall administer the provisions of KRS 171.201 to 171.205. The secretary of the executive department for finance and administration shall approve expenditures of funds under these sections. (Enact. Acts 1952, ch. 114, § 2; 1954, ch. 41, § 2; 1962, ch. 106, Art. VIII, § 3.)

171.203. Expenditure of funds. — Any funds appropriated for the purpose of KRS 171.201 to 171.205 shall be expended for aiding in the establishment, extension and development of local public library facilities through the purchase, lease or repair of library books, equipment, furniture, buildings or bookmobiles and for such other methods and services as will best accomplish the purpose. Funds shall be paid out by the state treasurer on warrants drawn by the secretary of the executive department for finance and administration on order of the state librarian. (Enact. Acts 1952, ch. 114, § 3; 1962, ch. 106, Art. VIII, § 4; 1964, ch. 55, § 1; 1970, ch. 241, § 3.)

171.204.   Grants in aid to counties — Acceptance of federal funds. — To the extent of funds available, grants may be made to qualifying counties based on formulas and regulations designed by the department of libraries or provided as special grants for an approved program. The department of libraries may provide partial grants or loans for constructing county or district library buildings or for improving libraries and library services of all types, through such methods and services as will best accomplish this purpose, and may accept federal funds for these purposes. (Enact. Acts 1952, ch. 114, § 4; 1962, ch. 106, Art. VIII, § 5; 1964, ch. 55, § 2; 1970, ch. 241, § 4.)

171.205.   Legislative intent declared. — It is the intention of KRS 171.201 to 171.205 to add to the public library service given by local communities and not to relieve such communities of their responsibilities. (Enact. Acts 1952, ch. 114, § 6, effective June 19, 1952.)

171.210.   Federal laws — Department to give notice of acceptance of. — The department shall transmit to the United States commissioner of education official notice of acceptance of the provisions of acts of congress and legislative enactment pertaining to the matters specified herein. (2438d-7.)

171.215.   Department to purchase textbooks for use by nonpublic school pupils in grades one through twelve. — (1) The department of libraries shall purchase textbooks from publishers whose books have been adopted by the state textbook commission for distribution without cost to pupils attending grade one (1) through grade twelve (12) of the state's nonpublic schools which have been accredited by the state department of education.

(2) The chief school administrator of each eligible school may file a requisition with the state librarian for the books needed for the next ensuing school term. Textbooks eligible for distribution by grade level or subject shall conform to the schedule in use by the state board for elementary and secondary education for distribution to the public schools.

(3) The state librarian shall develop rules and regulations governing the purchase, requisition, distribution, assignment to students, care, use and return of textbooks, and a plan for permanently labeling the textbooks as the property of the department of libraries. The rules and regulations shall provide for the allocation of textbooks in a manner reflecting, and not to exceed the expressly limited appropriation to fund the allocation. The rules and regulations shall be developed in consultation with the department of education and shall conform, within statutory limits, to the rules and

regulations already established by the state board for elementary and secondary education.

(4) All textbooks purchased under the provisions of this section are the property of the state. Each school administrator obtaining books through the department of libraries is custodian of the books in his school. He shall issue the books to the students according to the rules and regulations formulated by the state librarian.

(5) Funds appropriated by the general assembly to the department of libraries for this purpose shall not be expended for any textbooks which present a particular religious philosophy and shall not be considered as or commingled with common school funds and shall be allocated each year to the nonpublic school students as provided by rule and regulation of the department of libraries to the extent allowed by the appropriation provided in Acts 1978, ch. 139, § 2. (Enact. Acts 1978, ch. 139, § 1, effective June 17, 1978.)

171.220. Contracts with government agencies for establishing local library service. — The department may enter into contracts with any local, state or federal governmental agency or authority for the purpose of enabling the establishment and maintenance of a local public library service. The contracting parties may establish such districts or units of library service as they may mutually agree upon. The library service within such districts shall be carried on according to plans approved by the state librarian. (2438d-8.)

171.221. Cooperative library services with other states. — The department of library and archives is empowered to enter into an agreement with any state for the purpose of providing cooperative library services. (Enact. Acts 1974, ch. 8, § 3; 1974, ch. 74, Art. VIII, B, § 1.)

CERTIFICATION OF LIBRARIANS
(Kentucky Revised Statutes, 1982, s.171.230 to 171.300.)

171.230. Application of KRS 171.240 to 171.300. — (1) The provisions of KRS 171.240 to 171.300 shall apply to public libraries.

(2) Public libraries are libraries which serve all citizens and which are supported in whole or in part with public funds. (4618-130f: amend. Acts 1972, ch. 223, § 2.)

171.240. Board for certification of librarians — Members — Terms — Meetings — Compensation. — (1) In the department for libraries and archives there shall be a state board for the certification of librarians, composed of the state librarian and five (5) members appointed by the governor from a list submitted by the board of directors of the Kentucky library association. Two members shall be full-time professional librarians in active public library work, two shall be public library trustees and one shall be a professional librarian from a department or school of library science in a state university.

(2) The term of office of each appointive member shall be four (4) years. The first appointive member of the board shall be appointed for terms beginning July 1, 1938; one for a term of one (1) year; one (1) for a term of two (2) years; one (1) for a term of three (3) years; and two (2) for terms of four (4) years. Vacancies shall be filled by appointment for the unexpired terms in the same manner as original appointments are made. The members shall receive twenty-five dollars ($25.00) per day for each meeting attended and reimbursement for actual and necessary expenses, incurred in attending meetings.

(3) The board shall hold at least one (1) meeting each year at a time fixed by the board, and such special meetings as may be determined by the board. A chairman and secretary shall be elected at each annual meeting to serve during the ensuing year. (4618-130b: amend. Acts 1954, ch. 41, § 3; 1966, ch. 82, § 1; 1972, ch. 223, § 3; 1974, ch. 74, Art. VIII, B, § 1; 1978, ch. 154, § 12, effective June 17, 1978; 1982, ch. 381, § 7, effective July 15, 1982.)

171.250. Certificates of librarianship — To whom granted. — (1) The board shall grant certificates of librarianship to applicants who are graduates of library schools approved by the board and shall grant certificates to other applicants when it has satisfied itself that the applicant is qualified for library work.

(2) The board may issue renewals, determine the positions for which certificates of librarianship shall be required, and may adopt rules and regulations for its own government and for carrying out the purposes of KRS 171.230 to 171.300.

(3) The board may issue certificates to qualified persons who are serving in libraries not supported from public funds.

(4) Librarians who were in service on May 31, 1938, and served one (1) year prior to such date shall be entitled to receive a life certificate in accordance with their qualifications, without examination, upon the payment of prescribed fee. (4618-130c, 4618-130d, 4618-130g: amend. Acts 1972, ch. 223, § 4.)

171.260. Certificate required. — No library coming under the provisions of KRS 171.230 to 171.300 shall have in its employ, in the position of librarian, or in any other full time professional library position, a person who does not hold a certificate of librarianship issued by the board. (4618-130e.)

171.270. Fee for certificate. — The board shall require a fee of not less than one dollar ($1.00) nor more than five dollars ($5.00) to be paid by each applicant for a librarian's certificate. (4618-130h.)

171.280. Librarian's certification fund. [Effective July 1, 1983.] — The revolving fund established by the joint budget resolution, consisting of all moneys collected under the provisions of KRS 171.230 to 171.300 shall be designated as the librarian's certification fund. All money credited to the fund shall be used for the support of the board for certification of librarians, and for the purposes of KRS 171.230 to 171.300. (4618-130j: amend. Acts 1982, ch. 450, § 73, effective July 1, 1983.)

171.290. Revocation of certificates — Notice. — In a proceeding to revoke a certificate of librarianship under the provisions of KRS 171.990(2), written notice of the proposed action shall be delivered in person, or forwarded by certified mail, return receipt requested to the holder of the certificate at his last known post-office address, stating the cause for the contemplated action together with a copy of the charges and appointing a time and a place for the hearing by the board. (4618-130K: amend. Acts 1974, ch. 315, § 20; 1980, ch. 114, § 28, effective July 15, 1980.)

171.300. Hearings to reconsider applications. — The board shall grant hearings for the purposes of reconsidering applications and awards if the applicant files with the board, within twenty (20) days of issuance of or refusal to issue a certificate, a petition for rehearing. The board's refusal to grant certificates may be reviewed and its issuance may be ordered by any court having jurisdiction. (4618-130*l*.)

LIBRARY SCIENCE SCHOLARSHIPS
(Kentucky Revised Statutes, 1982, s.171.303, 171.306.)

171.303. Library science scholarships — Applications — Awards. — (1) There is hereby established a library science scholarship fund.

(2) The state librarian may grant scholarships for study in library science at an institution within the Commonwealth which is accredited by the American library association or the southern association of colleges and secondary schools.

(3) The state librarian shall receive and consider all applications for scholarships for study in library science and may grant a scholarship to applicants who are residents of this Commonwealth and who are deemed by the state librarian to the qualified. The state librarian shall make a careful and full investigation of the ability, character and qualifications of each applicant and may personally examine each applicant. The state librarian shall, whenever possible, grant financial assistance to the applicants with the greatest financial need, provided such persons are found to possess such qualities as give reasonable assurance of their successfully completing the course of study made possible by the scholarship. (Enact. Acts 1962, ch. 106, Art. VIII, § 6; 1966, ch. 81, § 1.)

171.306. Obligations of scholarship recipient. — (1) To be eligible for a scholarship, an applicant shall contract in writing with the state librarian that he will, within six (6) months from the date he completes his term of study, accept employment with a library program approved by the state librarian for a period to be computed at the rate of one (1) year for each $1,000 received, or proportional time for less amounts.

(2) If the recipient of a scholarship fails to fulfill his obligations under the contract for a scholarship the entire amount of scholarship benefits received less credit for time actually employed in an approved program plus 6 percent interest thereon shall become due and payable.

(3) Upon recommendation of the state librarian, the attorney general shall institute proceedings for the purpose of recovering any amount due the Commonwealth under the provisions of this section.

(4) The state librarian may terminate employment of a scholarship recipient if the performance of the recipient is found to be unsatisfactory. In such a case, if the obligations of the recipient are not completely fulfilled they are canceled. (Enact. Acts 1962, ch. 106, Art. VIII, § 7; 1970, ch. 241, § 5.)

STATE ARCHIVES AND RECORDS
(Kentucky Revised Statutes, 1982, s.171.410 to 171.990.)

171.410. Definitions for KRS 171.410 to 171.740. — As used in KRS 171.410 to 171.740:

(1) "Records" means all books, papers, maps, photographs, cards, tapes, disks, recordings, and other documentary materials, regardless of physical form or characteristics, made or received by any agency of the state government in pursuance of the state law or in connection with the transaction of public business and preserved or appropriate for preservation by that agency or its legitimate successor as evidence of the organization, functions, policies, decisions, procedures, operations, or other activities of the government or because of the informational value of data contained therein.

(2) "Department" means the department for libraries and archives.

(3) "Commission" means the state archives and records commission.

(4) "Agency" means every state or local office, state department, division, bureau, board, commission and authority; every legislative board, commission, committee and officer; every county and city governing body, council, school district board, special district board, municipal corporation, and any board, department, commission, committee, subcommittee, ad hoc committee, council or agency thereof; and any other body which is created by state or local authority and which derives at least twenty-five percent (25%) of its funds from state or local authority. (Enact. Acts 1958, ch. 49, § 1; 1962, ch. 106, Art. V, § 2; 1966, ch. 255, § 159; 1970, ch. 92, § 32; 1974, ch. 74, Art. VIII, B, § 2; 1982, ch. 245, § 1, effective July 15, 1982.)

171.420. Archives and records commission. — The state archives and records commission, is hereby created and shall be a fifteen (15) member body constituted as follows: The state librarian, who shall be the chairman of the commission, secretary of the cabinet for education and humanities, the auditor of public accounts, the chief justice of the Supreme Court, the director of the legislative research commission, the attorney general, the director of the office for policy and management, one (1) member appointed by the governor from a list of three (3) persons submitted by the president of the University of Kentucky, one (1) member appointed by the governor from a list of three (3) persons submitted by the president of the Kentucky historical society, one (1) member appointed by the governor from a list of three (3) persons submitted by the president of the Kentucky library association, one (1) member appointed by the governor from a list of seven (7) persons with one (1) name submitted by each of the presidents of the state universities and colleges, and four (4) citizens-at-large. Vacancies shall be filled by the governor in the same manner as initial appointments are made. All members shall serve for a term of four (4) years, provided that one (1) of the initial appointments shall be for a term of four (4) years, one (1) for three (3) years, one (1) for two (2) years and one (1) for one (1) year. The commission shall advise the department for libraries and archives on matters relating to archives and records management. The commission shall have the authority to review and approve schedules for retention and destruction of records submitted by state and local agencies. In all cases, the commission shall determine question which relate to destruction of public records; their decision is binding on the parties concerned and final, except that the commission may reconsider or modify its actions upon the agreement of a simple majority of the membership present and voting. (Enact. Acts 1958, ch. 49, § 2; 1962, ch. 106, Art. V, § 3; 1970, ch. 92, §. 33; 1974, Art. II, § 9(2); 1974, ch. 257, § 5; 1976, ch. 242, § 1; 1978, ch. 384, § 120, effective June 17, 1978; 1982, ch. 245, § 2, effective July 15, 1982.)

171.430. Expenses of commission members. — Members of the commission shall serve without compensation other than actual expense of attending meetings of the commission or while in the performance of their official duties in connection with the business of the commission. (Enact. 1958, ch. 49, § 3, effective June 19, 1958.)

171.440. Commission meetings. — The commission shall meet in the city of Frankfort, but the commission may, by majority vote, hold special or regular meetings in other locations when the work of the commission would be facilitated thereby. The commission shall hold not less than four (4) meetings during each calendar year and may hold such special meetings as may be necessary to transact the business of the commission. All meetings shall be called by the chairman, or when requested in writing by any two (2) members of the commission. (Enact. Acts 1958, ch. 49, § 4; 1982, ch. 245, § 3, effective July 15, 1982.)

171.450. Department procedures and regulations. — (1) The department shall establish:

(a) Procedures for the compilation and submission to the department of lists and schedules of public records proposed for disposal;

(b) Procedures for the disposal or destruction of public records authorized for disposal or destruction;

(c) Standards for recording public records and for the reproduction of public records by photographic or microphotographic process;

(d) Procedures for collection and distribution by the central depository of all reports and publications, except the Kentucky Revised Statues editions, issued by any department, board, commission, officer or other agency of the commonwealth for general public distribution after July 1, 1958.

(2) The department shall enforce the provisions of KRS 171.410 to 171.740 by appropriate rules and regulations.

(3) The department shall make copies of such rules and regulations available to all officials affected by KRS 171.410 to 171.740 subject to the provisions of KRS Chapter 13.

(4) Such rules and regulations when approved by the department shall be binding on all state and local agencies, subject to the provisions of KRS Chapter 13. The department shall perform any acts deemed necessary, legal and proper to carry out the duties and responsibilities imposed upon it pursuant to the authority granted herein. (Enact. Acts 1958, ch. 49, § 5; 1970, ch. 92, § 34; 1982, ch. 245, § 4, effective July 15, 1982.)

171.460. Records management survey. — In order for proper planning to be accomplished, the department shall cause a records management survey to be conducted in accordance with the regulations issued by the department. (Enact. Acts 1958, ch. 49, § 6; 1970, ch. 92, § 35.)

171.470. Records management promotion — Reports. — The department is authorized to make continuing surveys of government records and records management and disposal practices and to obtain reports thereon from state and local agencies; to promote, in cooperation with the various state and local agencies, improved records management practices and controls in such agencies, including the central storage or disposition of records not needed by such agencies for their current use; and to report to the governor semiannually. The department shall submit a biennial report to the general assembly. (Enact. Acts 1958, ch. 49, § 7; 1970, ch. 92, §. 36.)

171.480. Buildings and facilities. — The secretary of the executive department for finance and administration, at the request of the commission, shall have authority to design, build, purchase, lease, maintain, operate, protect, and improve buildings or facilities, including a state archives and records center building, used for the storage of noncurrent records of state and local agencies. The department shall have custody and control of all such buildings and facilities and their contents. (Enact. Acts 1958, ch. 49, § 8; 1970, ch. 92, § 37.)

171.500. Central depository. — The department is hereby constituted the central depository for public records. It shall be the duty of all departments, boards, commissions, officers or other agencies of the Commonwealth to supply to the central depository copies of each of their reports and publications issued for general public distribution after July 1, 1958, in the number and in the manner prescribed by rule or regulation promulgated by the department pursuant to KRS 171.450. College, university, and public libraries may be constituted depository libraries by written order of the department. The central depository shall supply copies to such depository libraries in the number and in the manner prescribed by rule or regulation promulgated by the department pursuant to KRS 171.450. (Enact. Acts 1958, ch. 49, § 10; 1970, ch. 92, § 38.)

171.510. Advisory groups for commission. — The commission may from time to time appoint advisory groups to more effectively obtain the best professional thinking of the bar, historians, political scientists, accountants, genealogists, patriotic groups, and associations of public officials on the steps to be taken with regard to any particular group or type of records. (Enact. Acts 1958, ch. 49, § 11, effective June 19, 1958.)

171.520. Supervision of state and local agencies. — The department shall, with due regard to the program activities of the state and local agencies concerned, prescribe the policies and principles to be followed by state and local agencies in the conduct of their records management programs, and make provisions for the economical and efficient management of records by state and local agencies by analyzing, developing, promoting, and coordinating standards, procedures, and techniques designed to improve the management of records, to insure the maintenance and security of records deemed appropriate for preservation, and to facilitate the segregation and disposal of records of temporary value and by promoting the efficient and economical utilization of space, equipment, and supplies needed for the purpose of creating, maintaining, storing, and servicing records. (Enact. Acts. 1958, ch. 49, § 12; 1970, ch. 92, § 39.)

171.530. Retention and recovery of records. — The commission shall establish standards for the selective retention of records of continuing value, and the department shall assist state and local agencies in applying such standards to records in their custody. The department shall notify the head of any such agency of any actual, impending, or threatening unlawful removal, defacing, alteration, or destruction of records in the custody of such agency that has come to its attention, and initiate action through the agency head or attorney general for the recovery of such records as shall have been unlawfully removed and for such other redress as may be provided by law. (Enact. Acts 1958, ch. 49, § 13; 1970, ch. 92, § 40; 1982, ch. 245, § 5, effective July 15, 1982.)

171.540. Inspection of agency records. — The department is authorized to inspect or survey the records of any state or local agency, as well as to make surveys of records management and records disposal practices in such agencies, and shall be given full cooperation of officials and employes of agencies in such inspection and surveys; provided, that records, the use of which is restricted by or pursuant to law or for reasons of security or the public interest, shall be inspected or surveyed only in accordance with law, and the rules and regulations of the department. (Enact. Acts 1958, ch. 49, § 14; 1970, ch. 92, § 41.)

171.550. Processing and servicing records. — The department is authorized to establish an interim records center or centers for the storage, processsing, and servicing of records of state and local agencies pending their deposit in the state archives and records center or their disposition in any other manner authorized by law, and to establish, maintain and operate centralized microfilming, photostating, indexing, decontamination and lamination and any other records repair and rehabilitation services for state and local agencies. (Enact. Acts 1958, ch. 49, § 15; 1970, ch. 92, § 42.)

171.560. Transfer of records. — Subject to applicable provisions of law, the department shall promulgate rules and regulations governing the transfer of records from the custody of one (1) state or local agency to that of another. (Enact. Acts 1958, ch. 49, § 16; 1970, ch. 92, § 43.)

171.570. Extension of agency retention period. — The department may empower any state or local agency, upon the submission of evidence of the need therefor, to retain records for a longer period than that specified in any approved disposal schedule, or by law but the agency shall report all such actions to the commission at its next meeting for approval or disapproval. (Enact. Acts 1958, ch. 49, § 17; 1966, ch. 255, § 160; 1970, ch. 92, § 44.)

171.580. Historical records. — The department, whenever it appears to be in the public interest, is authorized:

(1) To accept for deposit in the state archives and records center the records of any state or local agency or of the general assembly that are determined by the department to have sufficient historical or other value to warrant their continued preservation;

(2) To direct and effect the transfer to the department of any records that have been in existence for more than fifty (50) years and that are determined by the department to have sufficient historical or other value to warrant their continued preservation, unless the head of the state or local agency which has custody of them certifies in writing to the department that they must be retained in his custody for use in the conduct of the regular current business of the said agency;

(3) To direct and effect, with the approval of the head of the originating agency, or its successor, if any, the transfer of records deposited, or approved

for deposit, in the state archives and records center to public or educational institutions for special research or exhibit purposes; providing that title to such records shall remain vested in the Commonwealth of Kentucky unless otherwise authorized by law, and provided further such records may be recalled after reasonable notice in writing;

(4) To direct and effect the transfer of materials from private sources authorized to be received by the state archives and records center by the provisions of KRS 171.620. (Enact. Acts 1958, ch. 49, § 18; 1970, ch. 92, § 45.)

171.590. Public nature of records in department's custody. — The department shall be responsible for the custody, use, and withdrawal of records transferred to it. All papers, books, and other records of any matters so transferred are public records and shall be open to inspection by any interested person subject to reasonable rules as to time and place of inspection established by the department; provided that whenever any records, the use of which is subject to statutory limitations and restrictions, are so transferred, the department shall enforce such limitations. Restrictions shall not remain in effect after the records have been in existence for fifty (50) years. (Enact. Acts 1958, ch. 49, § 19; 1970, ch. 92, § 46.)

171.600. Servicing records. — The department shall make provisions for the preservation, management, repair and rehabilitation, duplication and reproduction, description, and exhibition of records or related documentary material transferred to it as may be needful or appropriate, including the preparation and duplication of inventories, indexes, catalogs, and other finding aids or guides facilitating their use. (Enact. Acts 1958, ch. 49, § 20; 1970, ch. 92, § 47.)

171.610. Facilities for public inspection. — The department shall make such provision and maintain such facilities as it deems necessary or desirable for servicing records in its custody that are not exempt from examination by statutory provisions or other restrictions. (Enact. Acts 1958, ch. 49, § 21; 1970, ch. 92, § 48.)

171.620. Private documents of public interest. — The department is authorized, whenever it is deemed to be in the public interest, to accept for deposit:

(1) The papers and other historical materials of any governor of the Commonwealth of Kentucky, or of any other official or former official of the state or its subdivisions, and other papers relating to and contemporary with any governor or former governor of Kentucky, subject to restrictions agreeable to the department and the donor;

(2) Documents, including motion picture films, still pictures, sound recordings, maps, and papers, from private sources that are appropriate for preservation by the state government as evidence of its organization,

functions, policies, and transactions or those of its subdivisions. (Enact. Acts 1958, ch. 49, § 22; 1970, ch. 92, § 49.)

171.630.   Reproduction fee. — The department may charge a fee not in excess of 10 percent above the costs or expenses for 'making or authenticating copies or reproductions of materials transferred to its custody. All such fees shall be paid into a revolving fund for the continuation of such services on as self-sustaining a basis as possible. There shall be no charge for making or authenticating copies or reproductions of such materials for official use by the government of the commonwealth of Kentucky; provided, that reimbursement may be accepted to cover the cost of furnishing such copies or reproductions that could not otherwise be furnished. (Enact. Acts 1958, ch. 49, § 23; 1970, ch. 92, § 50.)

171.640.   Documentation of agency matters. — The head of each state or local agency shall cause to be made and preserved records containing adequate and proper documentation of the organizational functions, policies, decisions, procedures, and essential transactions of the agency and designed to furnish information necessary to protect the legal and financial rights of the government and of persons directly affected by the agency's activities. (Enact. Acts 1958, ch. 49, § 24.)

171.660.   Status and effect of authorized reproductions. — (1) Whenever the governor, lieutenant governor or any state agency or subdivision or the principal officer thereof, shall have, either in whole or in part, any records or papers photographed, photostated, microphotographed, microfilmed or filmed and preserved for record in accordance with rules and regulations promulgated by the department the original thereof may be disposed of or destroyed.

(2) Any such reproductions shall be deemed the originals of the records or papers for all purposes, and any facsimiles, certified copies or reproductions thereof, or any prints or enlargements of the reproductions shall be admissible as evidence in any court or proceeding of this Commonwealth, and shall be prima facie evidence of the facts set forth in and the contents of the original records or papers. (Enact. Acts 1958, ch. 49, § 26; 1970, ch. 92, § 51.)

171.670.   Destruction of records. — When there is a question whether a particular record of group of records should be destroyed, the commission shall have exclusive authority to decide whether or not the record or group of records are to be destroyed. (Enact. Acts 1958, ch. 49, § 27; 1962, ch. 106, Art. V, § 4; 1970, ch. 92, § 52; 1982, ch. 245, § 6, effective July 15, 1982.)

171.680.   Records management by agencies. — (1) The head of each state and local agency shall establish and maintain an active, continuing program for the economical and efficient management of the records of the agency.

(2) Such program shall provide for:

(a) Effective controls over the creation, maintenance, and use of records in the conduct of current business;

(b) Cooperation with the department in applying standards, procedures, and techniques designed to improve the management of records;

(c) Promotion of the maintenance and security of records deemed appropriate for preservation, and facilitation of the segregation and disposal of records of temporary value;

(d) Compliance with the provisions of KRS 171.410 to 171.740 and the rules and regulations of the department. (Enact. Acts 1958, ch. 49, § 28; 1970, ch. 92, § 53.)

171.690. Storage of agency records. — Whenever the head of a state or local agency determines that substantial economies or increased operating efficiency can be effected thereby, he shall provide for the storage, processing and servicing of records that are appropriate therefor in the records center maintained and operated by the department or, when approved by the department in such location maintained and operated by the head of such agency. (Enact. Acts 1958, ch. 49, § 29; 1970, ch. 92, § 54.)

171.700. Certification of records. — Any official who is authorized to certify to facts on the basis of records in his custody is authorized to certify to facts on the basis of records that have been transferred by him or his predecessors to the department, further provided, that any fee due any official of the state or its subdivision shall not be eliminated by KRS 171.410 to 171.740. (Enact. Acts 1958, ch. 49, § 30; 1970, ch. 92, § 55.)

171.710. Safeguarding agency records. — The head of each state and local agency shall establish such safeguards against removal or loss of records as he shall deem necessary and as may be required by rules and regulations issued under authority of KRS 171.410 to 171.740. Such safeguards shall include making it known to all officials and employes of the agency that no records are to be alienated or destroyed except in accordance with law, and calling their attention to the penalties provided by law for the unlawful removal or destruction of records. (Enact. Acts 1958, ch. 49, § 31, effective June 19, 1958.)

171.720. Agency recovery of records. — The head of each state and local agency shall notify the department of any actual, impending or threatened unlawful removal, defacing, alteration or destruction of records in the custody of the agency that shall come to his attention, and with the assistance of the department shall initiate action through the attorney general for recovery of such records as shall have been unlawfully removed and for such other redress as may be provided by law. (Enact. Acts 1958, ch. 49, § 32; 1970, ch. 92, § 56.)

171.730. Effect on public accounting and confidential nature of agency records. — Nothing in KRS 171.410 to 171.740 shall be construed as limiting the authority of the state auditor, or other officers charged with prescribing accounting systems, forms, or procedures or of lessening the responsibility of collecting and disbursing officers for rendering of their accounts for settlement. Nothing in KRS 171.410 to 171.740 shall be construed as changing, modifying or affecting the present law or laws concerning confidential records of any state agency and the use thereof. All such laws remain in full force and effect. (Enact. Acts 1958, ch. 49, § 33.)

171.740. General assembly records. — The Legislative Research Commission shall, unless otherwise directed by the senate or house of representatives obtain at the close of each session of the general assembly all of the noncurrent records of the general assembly and of each committee thereof and transfer them to the state archives and records center for preservation. (Enact. Acts 1958, ch. 49, § 34.)

171.990. Penalties. — (1) Any person or library board violating any of the provisions of KRS 171.240 to 171.300 shall be fined not less than ten nor more than one hundred dollars for each offense.

(2) The board for certification of librarians may revoke the certificate of any person violating any of the provisions of KRS 171.240 to 171.300, or any of the regulations as established by the board for certification.

(3) Any person knowingly violating the rules and regulations of the department pursuant to the provisions of KRS 171.450, 171.560, 171.670, 171.710, or 171.720 is guilty of a Class A misdemeanor and is also liable for damages or losses incurred by the Commonwealth. Any state employe who knowingly violates these provisions shall also be subject to dismissal from state employment upon a determination of fact, at a hearing, that a serious violation did occur. The employe's right to appeal to the state personnel board is not abridged or denied. In the event of an appeal, the decision of the state personnel board is final.

(4) State employes dismissed under the provision of subsection (3) of KRS 171.990 shall have the right to reapply for state employment in accordance with state personnel rules governing dismissal. Such individuals shall have the full rights and privileges accorded under applicable equal opportunity laws. (4618-130i, 4618-130k: amend. Acts 1972, ch. 223, § 5; 1982, ch. 245, § 7, effective July 15, 1982.)

STATE HISTORICAL SOCIETY

Kentucky Revised Statutes, 1982, s.171.311 to 171.340.)

171.311. Kentucky Historical Society. — The Kentucky Historical Society created by Acts 1880, ch. 244, shall have all the powers and liabilities of a corporation and there is hereby granted to the society the following charter:

I

The Kentucky Historical Society shall collect, maintain and preserve authentic records, information, facts and relics connected with the history of the Commonwealth and the genealogy of her peoples; and promote a wider appreciation of the American heritage, with particular emphasis on the advancement and dissemination of knowledge of the history of Kentucky. The society may receive and hold by donation or devise, real or personal property to any extent and may, by gift, loan, purchase or otherwise hold books, papers, documents, historical memorials, and any other articles suited to promote the objects of the society in the Old State Capitol Building but all such property shall be held in trust for the Commonwealth of Kentucky according to the terms of acceptance.

II

All American citizens, partnerships, corporations or associations who shall evidence their dedication to the promotion of the objects and purposes of the society may become active members thereof upon their approval under regulations prescribed by the executive committee, and the payment of annual dues in a sum determined by the executive committee. Any person possessing the qualifications for membership may become a life member on the payment of a sum determined by the executive committee. The executive committee may determine classes of memberships and establish respective rates of dues. Every member in good standing, including the authorized representative of an institutional member, shall have the right to vote in person or by proxy, hold office, and otherwise take part in the proceedings of the society. Membership may be terminated by resignation or nonpayment of dues.

III

The officers of the society shall be a chancellor, who shall be the Governor of the Commonwealth of Kentucky, a president, first, second and third vice-presidents, who shall be ex-officio members of the executive committee. All officers, except the chancellor, shall be elected for a term of one year at the annual meeting of the society in a manner provided by law, and the president shall be ineligible to succeed himself if he has been elected for two (2) successive terms.

IV

There is hereby created an executive committee which shall consist of sixteen members, the officers of the society and one person designated annually by the state archives and records commission. The sixteen (16) members of the executive committee shall be divided into four (4) equal classes, so arranged that the terms of one class shall expire at each annual meeting of the society. The class whose term expires shall be ineligible to succeed itself.

V

The executive committee shall execute all the powers and duties conferred on the society, except those expressly delegated to the officers. It shall adopt bylaws at any regular or special meeting. It shall supervise and direct the financial concerns of the society, approve an annual budget and provide for and fix the salaries of employes, subject to the approval of the department of personnel. It shall provide for reimbursement of travel expenses of employes and may provide for reimbursement of expenses of officers and members of the executive committee incurred in performing specific duties assigned to them. It shall appoint a director, who shall be the management officer of the society under the direction of the president and policies established by the executive committee, and an assistant director, who shall assume the duties of the director in his absence and perform such other duties as may be assigned to him by the director. It shall establish and prescribe the duties of such other positions as are necessary to operate the society, and all persons engaged to fill such positions shall be employed by the director, subject to the approval of the executive committee, which approval shall constitute exemption from KRS 18A.005 to 18A.200, and their work shall be under the director's supervision.

The committee shall provide for the publication or preservation of historical documents and manuscripts; publish an edition to be known as the "Register"; provide by contract, subject to the approval of the finance and administration cabinet, for all the printing, publication and distribution of reports, books and other publications calculated to promote and advance the historical interest of Kentucky and augment the society's various collections at all times. It shall supervise and direct the ordinary affairs of the society; appoint a nominating committee; and determine other necessary committees of which the president and the director of the society shall be ex-officio members. The committee shall cooperate with, provide assistance to and coordinate its functions with those of the state archives and records commission. It may designate honorary members of the society and it shall have the power to fill any vacancies until the next annual meeting, including those occurring within its own membership.

VI

The executive committee shall hold regular meetings in January, April, July and October. Matters to be determined and discussed at such meetings shall be furnished the director at least ten (10) days prior to such meetings in order that he may prepare and distribute an agenda to each member of the committee at least three (3) days before the meeting. Special meetings shall be held at the request of the president or any three (3) members of the committee, in which case the director shall give written notice together with the agenda of such meeting at least ten (10) days in advance. In an emergency, nine (9) members of the committee may waive the provision of notice.

VII

The regular annual meeting of the society shall be held in the Old State Capitol Building on the first Friday after the first Monday in November. The meeting shall be open to all members. Special meetings may be called in Frankfort or elsewhere by the president or a majority of the executive committee or by the director upon the written request of twenty (20) members of the society. Members shall have fifteen (15) days written notice of the time, place and object of the meeting.

VIII

Twenty-five (25) members shall constitute a quorum for the transaction of all business at any meeting of the society, and one-third of the membership of the executive committee shall constitute a quorum at their respective meetings.

IX

The Chancellor of the Society, at his discretion, may preside at any meeting of the society or the executive committee, or he may participate otherwise in any meetings.

X

The president of the society shall be the chief executive officer of the society and shall preside over meetings of the society or the executive committee in the absence of the chancellor or at his request. He shall recommend the appointment of all necessary or desirable committees and he shall name persons to comprise such committees, except the nominating committee.

XI

The vice-presidents of the society shall preside in the absence of their successive superiors in office at all meetings of the society and the executive committee. They shall attend all regular and special meetings of the society and the executive committee and endeavor to familiarize themselves with the conduct and operations of the affairs of the society. They shall aid and assist the president in the performance of his duties, counsel and advise the executive committee and endeavor at all times to advance and promote the public interest in the history of Kentucky and her people.

XII

Nominations to membership on the executive committee and to the offices of president, first vice-president, second vice-president and third vice-president shall be made by a nominating committee or by any member present at the regular annual meeting. The nominating committee shall consist of five (5) members, shall be appointed at the first regular meeting of the executive committee after the annual meeting of the society and shall consider candidates to fill vacancies in the executive committee and offices which will occur at the subsequent annual meeting. The nominating committee shall meet in the office of the society forty-five (45) days prior to the annual meeting and nominate candidates to fill vacancies on the executive committee and at least one (1) candidate for the office of president, first vice-president, second vice-president, and third vice-president, and file same with the president. Upon the call for the election of officers the president shall promptly report the nomination by the nominating committee together with all other nominations. When more than the required number of candidates have been nominated for membership on the executive committee or more than one (1) candidate for the offices to be filled, the president shall call for an election by the vote of those present, together with the number of votes cast by proxy, and a plurality of all votes cast shall be sufficient to elect. Where no vote count is required the president shall cast one (1) vote for each candidate and he or she shall be declared elected.

XIII

This charter may be amended by a two-thirds vote of the members present and voting at any regular meeting or at any special meeting of the society called for the purpose, provided that written notice containing the substance of the proposed amendments shall have been mailed to members not less than thirty (30) days in advance of such meeting and the same approved as an amendment by the first General Assembly, meeting after the action of the society. (Enact. Acts 1960, ch. 169, § 1; 1962, ch. 143; 1974, ch. 34, § 1; 1980, ch. 188, § 128, effective July 15, 1980; 1982, ch. 448, § 69, effective July 15, 1982.)

171.313. Duties as to information concerning Kentucky family cemeteries. — (1) In addition to the responsibilities set forth in KRS 171.311, the Kentucky Historical Society shall collect, maintain, preserve, categorize and cause to be published necessary information concerning Kentucky family cemeteries.

(2) The society shall prescribe rules and regulations necessary to carry out the purposes of this section. (Enact. Acts 1976, ch. 198, § 1.)

171.315. Headquarters of society — Priority for maintenance. — (1) The headquarters of the Kentucky Historical Society shall be located in the Old

State Capitol Building, and the said society shall control in all respects the manner in which the said capitol building and the space therein, shall be used. The said society shall exercise the same control over the Old State Capitol Building Annex, and the society shall use the said annex for such purposes of the society as it shall deem necessary and proper. The grounds around the Old State Capitol Building and its annex, such grounds being now bounded by Broadway, Clinton, and Lewis Streets, and adjoining the federal property occupied by the John C. Watts building, shall be subject to the control of the said society and be used by the society, for such purposes of the society as it shall deem necessary and proper. Major alterations or other changes concerning the said building, annex, or grounds shall be made under the authority of the executive committee of the Kentucky Historical Society and under the general supervision of the director who shall determine the nature and extent of any work to be done so as to protect the architectural integrity of the original structures. The maintenance and security of the said building, annex, and grounds shall be the responsibility of the executive department for finance and administration and shall be of highest priority among the other responsibilities of the state for capital construction, maintenance or security. At the direction of the executive committee, the director of the society may request the executive department for finance and administration to perform, or cause to be performed, any work he deems necessary for the proper preservation and protection of the properties. Such work will either be undertaken within no less than sixty (60) days from the date of notification to the executive department for finance and administration or, the secretary of said department shall show cause, in writing, to the executive committee and the director why such work was not undertaken.

(2) No part of, or interest in, the real property hereinabove specified shall be leased, sold, or otherwise disposed of under any circumstances. Said real property, including the building interiors, shall be maintained and preserved in a manner consistent with the best interests of the Commonwealth. (Enact. Acts 1954, ch. 40, § 1; 1968, ch. 186; 1974, ch. 74, Art. II, § 9(1); 1978, ch. 361, § 1, effective June 17, 1978.)

171.340. Old books and documents — Governor and fiscal courts may authorize delivery to society. — (1) The governor may assign to the Kentucky historical society for safekeeping any articles of historical interest belonging to the state.

(2) The county officers may turn over to the Kentucky historical society old books or documents in their offices suitable for preservation as archives of the state but no longer of use or value to the counties, in order that they may be properly preserved for future generations. No books or documents of any county shall be turned over to the society except upon the order of the fiscal court of the county. (2290a-2.)

DISTRIBUTION OF PUBLIC DOCUMENTS

(Kentucky Revised Statutes, 1982, s.57.290 to 57.370, 43.090.)

57.290. Legislative Research Commission to distribute public books. — The acts of the general assembly and the journals of each house shall, upon being printed, be delivered to the Legislative Research Commission, and distributed by it. The Commission shall prepare for each county a package containing the acts and journals, with a list of the persons entitled to receive them, and send one (1) package in the most inexpensive manner to the circuit clerk of each county, who shall distribute the books to those entitled to them. (2433, 2444: amend. Acts 1950, ch. 156, § 2; 1954, ch. 42, § 14.)

57.300. Acts of general assembly, who entitled to copies. — The following officers and libraries are entitled free of charge to copies of the acts of the general assembly, as they are published: members of the general assembly that passed the acts, the governor, the state treasurer, secretary of state, auditor of public accounts, justices and judges of the Court of Justice, Commonwealth's attorneys, and county attorneys, one (1) copy each; the attorney general, four (4) copies; the legislative research commission, for the use of the senate, five (5) copies, and for the use of the house of representatives, ten (10) copies; the state law library, nine (9) copies; the judge of each federal court for Kentucky, one (1) copy; the United States Court of Appeals at Cincinnati, one (1) copy; the Supreme Court of the United States, one (1) copy; the law library of each county, one (1) copy; the law library of the University of Kentucky, three (3) copies; the law library of the University of Louisville, three (3) copies; the Northern Kentucky University Chase Law School library, three (3) copies; the Library of Congress, five (5) copies; the Kentucky Historical Society, one (1) copy; the department of library and archives, two (2) copies; and each of the state universities in Kentucky, two (2) copies. (2421, 2422, 2426a, 2426b: amend. Acts 1944, ch. 150, § 1; 1954, ch. 42, § 15; 1968, ch. 152, § 23; 1976, ch. 62, § 53; 1982, ch. 316, § 2, effective July 15, 1982.)

57.310. House and senate journals, who entitled to copies of. — The following officers and libraries are entitled free of charge to copies of the journals of each house of the general assembly, as they are published: Each member of the general assembly, one (1) copy for the session in which he served; the law library of each county, one (1) copy; the governor and secretary of state, one (1) copy each; the state law library, two (2) copies; the legislative research commission, five (5) copies for the use of the senate and five (5) copies for the use of the house of representatives; the law library of the University of Kentucky, the law library of the University of Louisville, the Library of Congress, the Kentucky Historical Society, the department of library and archives, and each of the state universities in Kentucky, two (2) copies each. (2425, 2426a, 2426b: amend. Acts 1944, ch. 150, § 2; 1954, ch. 42, § 16; 1968, ch. 152, § 24; 1982, ch. 316, § 3, effective July 15, 1982.)

57.320. Purchase and distribution of bound volumes and advance sheets of opinions of Supreme Court and Court of Appeals. — The state law librarian, under direction of the Supreme Court, shall purchase bound volumes and advance sheets of the opinions of the Supreme Court and Court of Appeals and furnish them for the use of the Supreme Court, Court of Appeals, each county law library, and each judge of a circuit court. (2426, 2426a, 2426b: amend. Acts 1950, ch. 156, § 3; 1954, ch. 42, § 17; 1976 (Ex. Sess.), ch. 14, § 16, effective January 2, 1978.)

57.330. Acts of congress, who entitled to copies of. — Each member of the general assembly, each judge and each clerk of a state court, the attorney general, each commonwealth's attorney, each county attorney, the Legislative Research Commission, the Kentucky Historical Society and the state law library are each entitled, upon requesting it, to one (1) copy of the acts of congress sent to the state for distribution. (2428: amend. Acts 1954, ch. 42, § 18.)

57.340. Statutes, rules and compilation of administrative regulations, how furnished to circuit or district judges. — On a certificate from any circuit judge or district judge that he does not have a copy of the latest revision of the statutes and annotations thereto, rules of practice and procedure, or compilation of administrative regulations, or that his copy has been lost, mutilated or torn, the state law librarian shall furnish to the judge a copy of the publication needed and shall furnish from time to time supplements issued to these publications. The law librarian shall certify the cost of such books to the executive department for finance and administration, which shall issue its warrant on the state treasurer for the amount, payable out of funds appropriated for that purpose. (2432: amend. Acts 1954, ch. 42, § 19; 1956, ch. 236; 1968, ch. 152, § 25; 1974, ch. 74, Art. II, § 9(1); 1978, ch. 35, § 1, effective June 17, 1978.)

57.350. Burning of courthouse — Books replaced free of charge. — If any county courthouse containing the law library is destroyed by fire, the Legislative Research Commission shall, upon receipt of the affidavit of the county judge showing the loss, furnish to the county acts of the general assembly and journals of the house of representatives and senate, and the state law librarian shall furnish bound volumes of the opinions of the Court of Justice, if available. (2432a: amend. Acts 1950, ch. 156, § 4; 1954, ch. 42, § 20; 1976, ch. 62, § 54.)

57.360. Custody and care of public books. — Any public officer, except a member of the general assembly, who receives any books from the state shall hold them as public property and as an appendage to his office, and deliver them to his successor. Each officer shall take good care of the books delivered to him. (2423, 2424.)

57.370. State owned books to be marked for identification. — When deemed by the finance and administration cabinet to be desirable or necessary, consistent with all relevant factors concerning acquisition and use, all public books of the state shall be designated as public property by placing on the title page, "Property of the State of Kentucky," and the binder shall press those words on the cover. The words, "Property of the Commonwealth of Kentucky," may also be used for such purpose. Each officer who is charged with possession of books acquired under this chapter shall write or otherwise designate in or on each book the name of the office to which it belongs, if such books are to be retained permanently by such officer or his agency. (2427: amend. Acts 1966, ch. 129, § 1.)

43.090. Reports of audits and investigations — Implementation by agency of audit recommendation. — (1) Immediately upon completion of each audit and investigation, except those provided for in KRS 43.070, the auditor shall prepare a report of his findings and recommendations. He shall furnish one (1) copy of the report to the head of the agency to which the report pertains, one (1) copy to the governor, one (1) copy to the secretary of the finance and administration cabinet, one (1) copy to the legislative research commission and one (1) copy to the state librarian. The agency to which an auditor's draft report pertains shall respond in writing to any adverse or critical audit findings and to any recommendations contained in the draft report within fifteen (15) days of receipt of the draft report. The auditor shall distribute the agency's response to those entitled by this subsection to a copy of the audit report. Within sixty (60) days of the completion of the final audit report, the agency to which an auditor's report pertains shall notify the legislative research commission and the auditor of the audit recommendations it has implemented and of the audit recommendations it has not implemented. The agency shall state the reasons for its failure to implement any recommendation made in the final audit report. The auditor shall prepare and transmit to each member of the general assembly, by December 15 immediately preceding the convening of each regular session of the general assembly, a printed report of his activities, summarizing the findings and recommendations in his report on each audit or investigation made since the last preceding biennial report to the general assembly listing, by state agency, the audit recommendations that have not been implemented and the reason(s) given by state agencies for non-implementation, and presenting such other findings and recommendations as he sees fit to make. He shall file a copy of this report with the governor and five (5) copies with the state librarian. All audit reports shall be public documents to which taxpayers shall have access.

(2) The auditor shall, within a reasonable time after the examination of each county as provided in KRS 43.070, make a written report to the governor, the general assembly, the attorney general, the county officials' compensation board, the state librarian and to the fiscal court and county attorney of the county examined, calling attention in specific terms to any

mismanagement, misconduct, misapplication or illegal appropriation or extravagant use of money received or disbursed by any officer of the county examined. In addition, said report shall be sent to a newspaper having general circulation in the county examined and the letter of transmittal accompanying the report shall be published in said newspaper in accordance with the provisions of KRS Chapter 424. (1992b-59, 4618-135, 4636-4: amend. Acts 1942, ch. 139, §§ 1, 2; 1966, ch. 255, § 52; 1974, ch. 254, § 9; 1982, ch. 176, § 2, effective July 15, 1982.)

PUBLIC LIBRARY DISTRICTS
(Kentucky Revised Statutes, 1982, s. 173.450 to 173.800.)

173.450. Definitions for KRS 173.450 to 173.650. — (1) "District" means "public library district"; and

(2) "Board" means the board of trustees of a public library district. (Enact. Acts 1960, ch. 114, § 1; 1972, ch. 223, § 7.)

173.460. Public library district — Taxation — Purpose. — All of the territory in a county, or in two (2) or more counties contiguous to each other may be organized into a public library district for the purpose of levying a tax to pay for establishing, equipping, maintaining and administering libraries, or for contracting for library service from any existing library. (Enact. Acts 1960, ch. 114, § 2, effective June 16, 1960.)

173.470. Organization — Procedure — Special tax. — Districts shall be organized in the following manner:

(1) Upon the filing of a duly certified petition of one hundred (100) or more duly qualified voters in each county to be included within the territorial limits of the proposed district, the fiscal court of each county in the proposed district shall adopt a resolution submitting to the qualified voters of the county the question as to whether a public library district should be established for the area and a special ad valorem tax imposed for the maintenance and operation of the district, not to exceed twenty cents (20¢) on each one hundred dollars ($100) of the assessed valuation of all property in the district. A certified copy of the order of the fiscal court shall be filed with the county clerk at least sixty (60) days prior to the next regular election and thereupon the clerk shall cause the question to be placed before the voters.

(2) The question shall be in substantially the following form: "Are you in favor of establishing a public library district for (insert names of counties) which shall have the authority to impose a special ad valorem tax of (insert exact amount) on each one hundred dollars ($100) worth of property assessed for local taxation in the district for the maintenance and operation of the (insert name) public library district?"

(3) If a majority of those voting in each county on the question favor the establishment of a public library district it shall be so established and shall constitute and be a taxing district within the meaning of section 157 of the constitution of Kentucky.

(4) All special ad valorem taxes authorized by KRS 173.450 to 173.650 shall be collected in the same manner as are other county ad valorem taxes in each county affected and shall be turned over to the board as the governing body of the district. The special ad valorem tax shall be in addition to all other ad valorem taxes. (Enact. Acts 1960, ch. 114, § 3; 1962, ch. 71; 1964, ch. 55, § 4; 1978, ch. 384, § 296, effective June 17, 1978; 1982, ch. 360, § 52, effective July 15, 1982.)

173.480. Notice of organization — Duties of department for libraries and archives — Board membership. — Upon the creation of a district, the fiscal court of each county in the district shall at once notify the department for libraries and archives of the establishment of the district. The department for libraries and archives shall then recommend to the county judge/executive of each county in the district the names of suitable persons from that county to be appointed to the board. The department for libraries and archives recommending persons to the county judge/executive for appointment to the board shall recommend twice as many persons for each county as the county. is entitled to have members appointed, and the county judge/executive shall immediately, with the approval of the fiscal court, make his selection from those recommended. Where the district consists of one (1) county, the county judge/executive shall appoint five (5) persons from that county as members. The department for libraries and archives shall prescribe by regulation the number of board members when the district consists of more than one (1) county, provided that the board shall consist of not less than one (1) nor more than four (4) members from each county, each county having such number of members as the proportion of its population bears to the total population in the district, and that total membership of the board consists of not less than five (5) members. Where a county joins an already established district, the department for libraries and archives shall recommend to the county judge/executive of each county included in the new district twice as many persons for appointment to the board as the county is entitled to have appointed, and the county judge/executive shall select the members for his county from this list. The terms of the members of the counties composing the previously existing district shall expire immediately upon the organization of the new board. (Enact. Acts 1960, ch. 114, § 4, effective June 16, 1960; 1976 (Ex. Sess.), ch. 20, § 6, effective January 2, 1978; 1980, ch. 18, § 15, effective July 15, 1980; 1980, ch. 188, § 130, effective July 15, 1980.)

173.490. Terms of board members — Vacancies — Removal of members. — (1) One-third ($^1/_3$) of the persons first appointed to the board shall serve for a term of two (2) years, one-third ($^1/_3$) for a term of three (3) years and one-third ($^1/_3$) for a term of four (4) years. Where the board consists of a number of members not divisible by three (3), one-third ($^1/_3$) of the next higher number divisible by three (3), shall serve for a term of two (2) years, one-third ($^1/_3$) for a term of three (3) years and the remaining number shall serve for a term of four (4) years. Thereafter, as their terms expire, their successors shall be recommended and appointed in the same manner, but for a term of four (4) years each. Trustees may serve for two (2) consecutive terms after which they shall not succeed themselves, effective July 1, 1974, exclusive of present terms begun prior to that date. The members shall hold office until their respective successors are appointed and qualified. Absence of a trustee from four (4) regular monthly meetings of the board during any one (1) year of the trustee's term shall constitute automatic resignation from the board by the trustee.

(2) Any vacancy occurring in the terms of office of members shall be filled for the unexpired term by the county judge/executive, with the approval of the fiscal court, by appointment on recommendation of the department for libraries and archives of two (2) names for each vacancy from the county in which the vacancy occurred.

(3) A member of the board may be removed from office as provided by KRS 65.007. (Enact. Acts 1960, ch. 114, § 5; 1974, ch. 8, § 6; 1974, ch. 74, Art. VIII, B, § 1; 1980, ch. 18, § 16, effective July 15, 1980; 1982, ch. 245, § 10, effective July 15, 1982.)

173.500. Board constitutes body corporate — Name — Seal — Officers — Bond — Meetings — Quorum. — Each board shall be a body corporate under the name and style of " . . . Public Library District Board of Trustees." The members shall, as soon as possible after their appointment, adopt a seal and organize by electing a president, a secretary and a treasurer, each to serve for a term of two (2) years and until his successor is elected and qualified. The treasurer shall give bond to the Commonwealth for the faithful performance of his duties, in such sum and form and with such sureties as the board shall approve. The board shall meet on a regularly scheduled basis once each month. A majority of the board shall constitute a quorum. (Enact. Acts 1960, ch. 114, § 6; 1974, ch. 8, § 7.)

173.510. Expenses — Employment of relatives — Conflict of interest. — The members of the board shall not receive compensation for their services, but shall be reimbursed for their actual expenses necessarily incurred in the performance of their duties, upon vouchers duly approved by the board, signed by the secretary and countersigned by the president. No board shall newly employ as a member of its library staff any member of the board or any person related closer than a second cousin to any member of the board. No person is eligible to this office who is directly or indirectly interested in the sale to the library of books, magazines, supplies, equipment, materials, fire insurance, or services for which library funds are expended. (Enact. Acts 1960, ch. 114, § 7; 1982, ch. 245, § 14, effective July 15, 1982.)

173.520. Duties, powers of board — Approval by department. — (1) The board shall establish, equip and maintain libraries or contract with existing libraries for the furnishing of library service for the district and do all things necessary to provide efficient library service. No district shall establish a library unless the plans for the establishment, equipment and maintenance have been approved by the department for libraries and archives. No contract shall be made unless the libraries contracting to furnish service are libraries approved by the department for libraries and archives for this purpose.

(2) The district, as a body corporate, by and through the board may:

(a) Sue and be sued, complain and defend, purchase, or lease grounds, purchase, lease, occupy or erect appropriate buildings for the use of the district libraries and their branches, sell and convey real and personal property for and on behalf of the district, receive gifts of real and personal property for the use and benefit of the district, the same when accepted to be held and controlled by the board according to the terms of the deed, gift, devise or bequest of such property;

(b) Borrow money on the credit of the board in anticipation of the revenue to be derived from taxes levied by the district for the fiscal year in which the money is borrowed, and to pledge the taxes levied for the district for the payment of the principal and interest of the loan. The principal shall not exceed fifty percent (50%) of the anticipated revenue for the fiscal year in which the money is borrowed;

(c) Establish bylaws it deems necessary and expedient to define the duties of officers, assistants or employes and make all necessary rules and regulations governing libraries and library service within the district.

(3) The board in exercise of its powers shall be guided by the regulations and requirements of the department for libraries and archives.

(4) The powers set forth in this section shall not be construed to limit, restrict or modify any powers or authority granted by any other part of KRS 173.450 to 173.650 or any other law not in conflict with the provisions of this section. (Enact. Acts 1960, ch. 114, § 8, effective June 16, 1960; 1970, ch. 241, § 6; 1982, ch. 245, § 12, effective July 15, 1982.)

173.530. District librarian. — The board shall appoint a district librarian and such assistant librarians as it deems necessary. The district librarian shall be certified in accordance with the provisions of KRS 171.240 to 171.300. (Enact. Acts 1960, ch. 114, § 9, effective June 16, 1960.)

173.540. Duties of treasurer of board. — The treasurer of the board shall:

(1) Have the custody of all money, securities and obligations belonging to that district, and shall disburse money only for the uses and purposes of the district and in the manner prescribed by the bylaws on itemized vouchers allowed by the board, signed by the secretary and countersigned by the president;

(2) Keep a full and accurate account of all receipts and payments in the manner directed by the bylaws, and such other accounts as the board prescribes;

(3) Render statements of accounts of the several books, funds and property in his custody whenever required by the board;

(4) Have all accounts and records fully made up to the last day preceding the annual meeting, and present the same to the board at its annual meeting. (Enact. Acts 1960, ch. 114, § 10, effective June 16, 1960.)

173.550. Records to be kept open. — Every district established under KRS 173.450 to 173.650 shall at all reasonable times keep open for the inspection of the auditor of public accounts all of its records and books of accounts. (Enact. Acts 1960, ch. 114, § 11, effective June 16, 1960.)

173.560. Fiscal year. — The fiscal year of a district shall commence July 1st and close on June 30th. (Enact. Acts 1960, ch. 114, § 12, effective June 16, 1960.)

173.570. Report required — Contents. — Within sixty (60) days after the close of each fiscal year the board shall make a written report to the department of libraries. A copy of this report shall be filed with the county clerk of each county within the district. The report shall contain:

(1) An itemized statement of the various sums of money received for the district;

(2) An itemized statement of expenditures from the fund;

(3) A statement of the property acquired by devise, bequest, purchase, gift or otherwise during the fiscal year;

(4) A statement of the character of library service furnished to the district during the fiscal year; and

(5) Any other statistics or information requested by the department of libraries. (Enact. Acts 1960, ch. 114, § 13, effective June 16, 1960.)

173.580. Attorney — Compensation. — (1) The board may, in its discretion, employ or retain a regularly licensed attorney to advise them on all matters pertaining to their duties and shall have the discretion to delegate such authority to said attorney not forbidden by law. The attorney so employed or retained shall attend all meetings of the board, except executive sessions when the board does not desire his presence, whenever the board requests him to attend and shall advise the board on all legal matters on which he is requested to give advice.

(2) The board may fix the salary or compensation of the attorney provided for in subsection (1) of this section, in its discretion. (Enact. Acts 1960, ch. 114, § 14, effective June 16, 1960.)

173.600. Revenue bonds. — Public library districts may, in addition to all other methods provided by law, acquire, construct, and improve library facilities through the issuance of revenue bonds under the terms and provisions of KRS 58.010 to 58.140. (Enact. Acts 1960, ch. 114, § 16, effective June 16, 1960.)

173.610. Tax rate change prohibited except by vote of people — Procedure — Limitation. — (1) The special ad valorem tax rate for the maintenance and operation of a public library district provided for by KRS 173.470 may be increased or decreased by submission to the voters of the district at a general election and approved by a majority of the votes cast on the issue. The board or any one hundred (100) qualified voters residing within the district may file a duly certified copy of a resolution or petition with the clerk of each county within the district at least forty-five (45) days prior to the election and the clerk shall thereupon cause the question to be prepared to be presented to the voters in substantially the following form: "Are you in favor of increasing (or decreasing) from (insert amount) cents to (insert amount) cents on each one hundred dollars ($100) of the assessed valuation of all property in the (insert name of public library district) public library district the maximum tax which the district can impose for the maintenance and operation of (insert name of district) public library district?"

(2) Any increase provided for in subsection (1) or (3) of this section shall not exceed twenty cents (20¢) on each one hundred dollars ($100) of the assessed valuation of all property in the district.

(3) The special ad valorem tax rate for the maintenance and operation of a public library district provided for by KRS 173.470 may be increased or decreased by the procedure in KRS 173.790. (Enact. Acts 1960, ch. 114, § 17; 1972, ch. 223, § 8; 1982, ch. 360, § 53, effective July 15, 1982.)

173.620. Annexation — Procedure. — Counties outside of any existing district, and contiguous thereto, may be annexed to the district in the following manner:

(1) Upon filing with the fiscal court of a duly certified petition of one hundred (100) or more qualified voters residing within each county proposed to be annexed, the fiscal court of each county in the district and each county proposed to be annexed shall adopt a resolution submitting to the qualified voters of the county the question as to whether the territory should be annexed. A certified copy of the order of the fiscal court shall be filed with the county clerk at least sixty (60) days prior to the next general election and thereupon the county clerk shall cause the question to be placed before the voters.

(2) The question shall be in substantially the following form: "Are you in favor of annexing the following described territory (here describe the territory) to the (name district) public library district?"

(3) If the majority of those voting in each county on the question favor the annexation of the territory it shall be so annexed. (Enact. Acts 1960, ch. 114, § 18, effective June 16, 1960; 1982, ch. 360, § 54, effective July 15, 1982.)

173.630. Dissolution — Procedure. — A library district established pursuant to KRS 173.740 which has been in existence for at least three (3) years may be dissolved in the following manner:

(1) Upon filing of a duly certified petition of ten of ten percent (10%) or

more of the qualified voters in the district or one hundred (100) or more qualified voters in the district, whichever is more, the fiscal court of each county in the district shall adopt a resolution submitting to the qualified voters of the district the question as to whether the district shall be dissolved. A certified copy of the order of each fiscal court shall be filed with the county clerk at least ninety (90) days prior to the next regular election and thereupon the clerk shall cause the question to be placed before the voters.

(2) The question shall be in substantially the following form: "Are you in favor of dissolving the (insert name of district) public library district?"

(3) If a majority of those voting on the question within the district favor the dissolution such district shall thereupon be dissolved. (Enact. Acts 1960, ch. 114, § 19, effective June 16, 1960; 1978, ch. 384, § 297, effective June 17, 1978; 1982, ch. 245, § 17, effective July 15, 1982; 1982, ch. 360, § 55, effective July 15, 1982.)

173.640. Conduct of elections. — All elections authorized by KRS 173.450 to 173.650 shall be held and conducted in all respects under the general election laws obtaining in this Commonwealth at the time of the election. (Enact. Acts 1960, ch. 114, § 20, effective June 16, 1960.)

173.650. Certification of election results. — The results of the election in each county shall be certified by the county election commissioners to the county judge/executive in each county. When more than one (1) county is involved the county judges/executive shall certify the results in their respective counties to the county judge/executive of the county having the largest voting population. (Enact. Acts 1960, ch. 114, § 21, effective June 16, 1960; 1976 (Ex. Sess.), ch. 20, § 6, effective January 2, 1978.)

173.710. Definitions for KRS 173.710 to 173.810. — (1) "District" means "public library district";

(2) "Board" means the board of trustees of a public library district. (Enact. Acts 1964, ch. 92, § 1; 1972, ch. 223, § 9.)

173.715. County or counties may become library district. — All of the territory in a county, or in two (2) or more counties contiguous to each other may be organized into a public library district for the purpose of levying a tax to pay for establishing, equipping, maintaining and administering libraries, or for contracting for library service from any existing library. (Enact. Acts 1964, ch. 92, § 2.)

173.720. Organization of district — Procedure — Petition — Tax levy. — Districts shall be organized in the following manner:

(1) Upon the filing of a duly certified petition of fifty-one percent (51%) or more of the number of duly qualified voters who voted in the last general election in each county to be included within the territorial limits of the

proposed district, the fiscal court of each county in the proposed district shall adopt a resolution ordering the levy of a tax of not more than twenty cents (20¢) on each one hundred dollars ($100) worth of property assessed for local taxation. Such petition shall be filed with the fiscal court in each county in the proposed district not later than ninety (90) days after the date of the first signature on the petition. A certified copy of the order of the fiscal court shall be filed within thirty (30) days with the county clerk who will add the levy to the next annual tax bill of the county or counties concerned.

(2) The petition shall be in substantially the following form:

The following duly qualified voters of (insert name of county or counties) hereby petition the fiscal court of each county concerned to establish a public library district for (insert name of county or counties) which shall have the authority to impose a special ad valorem tax of (insert exact amount) on each one hundred dollars ($100) worth of property assessed for local taxation in the district for the maintenance and operation of the (insert name) public library district.

(3) The petition shall contain the following: The name and address of each petitioner and the date upon which he signed the petition.

(4) All special ad valorem taxes authorized by KRS 173.710 to 173.800 shall be collected in the same manner as are other county ad valorem taxes in each county affected and shall be turned over to the board as the governing body of the district. The special ad valorem tax shall be in addition to all other ad valorem taxes. (Enact. Acts 1964, ch. 92, § 3; 1978, ch. 384, § 298, effective June 17, 1978.)

173.725. Library board — Members, number, appointment. — (1) Upon the creation of a district, the fiscal court of each county in the district shall at once notify the department for libraries and archives of the establishment of the district. The department for libraries and archives shall then recommend to the county judge/executive of each county in the district the names of suitable persons from that county to be appointed to the board. The department for libraries and archives in recommending persons to the county judge/executive for appointment to the board shall recommend twice as many persons for each county as the county is entitled to have members appointed, and the county judge/executive shall immediately make his selection from those recommended. Where the district consists of one (1) county, the county judge/executive shall appoint five (5) persons from that county as members. The department for libraries and archives shall prescribe by regulation the number of board members when the district consists of more than one (1) county, provided that the board shall consist of not less than one (1) nor more than four (4) members from each county, each county having such number of members as the proportion of its population bears to the total population in the district, and that the total membership of the board consist of not less than five (5) members. Where a county joins an already established district, the department for libraries and archives shall recommend to the county judge/executive of each county included in the new district twice as many persons for appointment to the board as the county is entitled to have appointed, and the county judge/executive shall select the members for his county from this list. The terms of the members of the counties composing the previously existing district shall expire immediately upon the organization of the new board.

(2) In making recommendations and appointments under subsection (1) of this section and KRS 173.730, the department for libraries and archives and the county judge/executive shall attempt to assure, to the extent permitted by the county's entitlement to board members, that the board includes members from different geographical areas, and from both cities and unincorporated areas, of the county. (Enact. Acts 1964, ch. 92, § 4; 1976 (Ex. Sess.), ch. 20, § 6, effective January 2, 1978; 1980, ch. 18, § 17, effective July 15, 1980; 1980, ch. 167, § 3, effective July 15, 1980.)

173.730. Board members — Terms — Vacancies — Removal of board members. — (1) One-third ($^1/_3$) of the persons first appointed to the board shall serve for a term of two (2) years, one-third ($^1/_3$) for a term of three (3) years and one-third ($^1/_3$) for a term of four (4) years. Where the board consists of a number of members not divisible by three (3), one-third ($^1/_3$) of the next higher number divisible by three (3), shall serve for a term of two (2) years, one-third ($^1/_3$) for a term of three (3) years and the remaining number shall serve for a term of four (4) years. Thereafter, as their terms expire, their successors shall be recommended and appointed in the same manner, but for a term of four (4) years each. Trustees may serve for two (2) consecutive terms after which they shall not succeed themselves, effective July 1, 1974, exclusive of present terms begun prior to that date. The members shall hold office until their respective successors are appointed and qualified. Absence of a trustee from four (4) regular monthly meetings of the board during any one (1) year of the trustee's term shall constitute automatic resignation from the board by the trustee.

(2) Any vacancy occurring in the terms of office of members shall be filled for the unexpired term by the county judge/executive, with the approval of the fiscal court, by appointment on recommendation of the department for libraries and archives of two (2) names for each vacancy from the county in which the vacancy occurred.

(3) A member of the board may be removed from office as provided by KRS 65.007. (Enact. Acts 1964, ch. 92, § 5; 1974, ch. 8, § 8; 1974, ch. 74, Art. VIII, B, § 1; 1980, ch. 18, § 18, effective July 15, 1980; 1982, ch. 245, § 11, effective July 15, 1982.)

173.735. Corporate name — Seal — Officers — Treasurer's bond — Meetings — Quorum — Each board shall be a body corporate under the name and style of ". . . Public Library District Board of Trustees." The members shall, as soon as possible after their appointment, adopt a seal and organize by electing a president, a secretary and a treasurer, each to serve for a term of two (2) years and until his successor is elected and qualified. The treasurer shall give bond to the Commonwealth for the faithful performance of his duties, in such sum and form and with such sureties as the board shall approve. The board shall meet on a regularly scheduled basis once each month. A majority of the board shall constitute a quorum. (Enact. Acts 1964, ch. 92, § 6; 1974, ch. 8, § 9.)

173.740.   Expenses of board members — Employment of relatives — Conflict of interest. — The members of the board shall not receive compensation for their services, but shall be reimbursed for their actual expenses necessarily incurred in the performance of their duties, upon vouchers duly approved by the board, signed by the secretary and countersigned by the president. No board shall newly employ as a member of its library staff any member of the board or any person related closer than a second cousin to any member of the board. No person is eligible to this office who is directly or indirectly interested in the sale to the library of books, magazines, supplies, equipment, materials, fire insurance, or services for which library funds are expended. (Enact. Acts 1964, ch. 92, § 7; 1982, ch. 245, § 15, effective July 15, 1982.)

173.745.   Powers and duties of board. — (1) The board shall establish, equip and maintain libraries or contract with existing libraries for the furnishing of library service for the district and do all things necessary to provide efficient library service. No district shall establish a library unless the plans for the establishment, equipment and maintenance have been approved by the department for libraries and archives. No contract shall be made unless the libraries contracting to furnish service are libraries approved by the department for libraries and archives for this purpose.

(2) The district, as a body corporate, by and through the board may:

(a) Sue and be sued, complain and defend, purchase, or lease grounds, purchase, lease, occupy or erect appropriate buildings for the use of the district libraries and their branches, sell and convey real and personal property for and on behalf of the district, receive gifts of real and personal property for the use and benefit of the district, the same when accepted to be held and controlled by the board according to the terms of the deed, gift, devise or bequest of such property;

(b) Borrow money on the credit of the board in anticipation of the revenue to be derived from taxes levied by the district for the fiscal year in which the money is borrowed, and to pledge the taxes levied for the district for the payment of the principal and interest of the loan. The principal to be repaid annually shall not exceed fifty percent (50%) of the anticipated revenue for the fiscal year in which the money is borrowed.

(c) Establish bylaws it deems necessary and expedient to define the duties of officers, assistants or employes and make all necessary rules and regulations governing libraries and library service within the district.

(3) The board in exercise of its powers shall be guided by the regulations and requirements of the department for libraries and archives.

(4) The powers set forth in this section shall not be construed to limit,

restrict or modify any powers or authority granted by KRS 173.710 to 173.800 or any other law not in conflict with the provisions of this section. (Enact. Acts 1964, ch. 92, § 8; 1982, ch. 245, § 13, effective July 15, 1982.)

173.750. Librarians, appointment. — The board shall appoint a district librarian and such assistant librarians as it deems necessary. The district librarian shall be certified in accordance with the provisions of KRS 171.240 to 171.300. (Enact. Acts 1964, ch. 92, § 9.)

173.755. Treasurer of board, duties. — The treasurer of the board shall:

(1) Have the custody of all money, securities and obligations belonging to that district, and shall disburse money only for the uses and purposes of the district and in the manner prescribed by the bylaws on itemized vouchers allowed by the board, signed by the secretary and countersigned by the president;

(2) Keep a full and accurate account of all receipts and payments in the manner directed by the bylaws, and such other accounts as the board prescribes;

(3) Render statements of accounts of the several books, funds and property in his custody whenever required by the board;

(4) Have all accounts and records fully made up to the last day preceding the annual meeting, and present the same to the board at its annual meeting. (Enact. Acts 1964, ch. 92, § 10.)

173.760. Records open for state audit. — Every district established under KRS 173.710 to 173.800 shall at all reasonable times keep open for the inspection of the auditor of public accounts all of its records and books of accounts. (Enact. Acts 1964, ch. 92, § 11.)

173.765. Fiscal year. — The fiscal year of a district shall commence July 1 and close on June 30. (Enact. Acts 1964, ch. 92, § 12.)

173.770. Annual report. — Within sixty (60) days after the close of each fiscal year the board shall make a written report to the department of libraries. A copy of this report shall be filed with the county clerk of each county within the district. The report shall contain:

(1) An itemized statement of the various sums of money received for the district;

(2) An itemized statement of expenditures from the fund;

(3) A statement of the property acquired by devise, bequests, purchase, gift or otherwise during the fiscal year;

(4) A statement of the character of library service furnished to the district during the fiscal year; and

(5) Any other statistics or information requested by the department of libraries. (Enact. Acts 1964, ch. 92, § 13.)

173.775. Attorney for board, employment, authority. — (1) The board may, in its discretion, employ or retain a regularly licensed attorney to advise them on all matters pertaining to their duties and shall have the discretion to delegate such authority to said attorney not forbidden by law. The attorney so employed or retained shall attend all meetings of the board, except executive sessions when the board does not desire his presence, whenever the board requests him to attend and shall advise the board on all legal matters on which he is requested to give advice.

(2) The board may fix the salary or compensation of the attorney provided for in subsection (1) of this section, in its discretion. (Enact. Acts 1964, ch. 92, § 14.)

173.785. Revenue bonds may be issued. — Public library districts may, in addition to all other methods provided by law, acquire, construct, and improve library facilities through the issuance of revenue bonds under the terms and provisions of KRS 58.010 to 58.140. (Enact. Acts 1964, ch. 92, § 16.)

173.790. Increase or decrease in tax levy — Procedure. — (1) The special ad valorem tax rate for the maintenance and operation of a public library district provided for by KRS 173.710 to 173.800 shall not be increased or decreased unless a duly certified petition requesting an increase or decrease in the tax rate of a specifically stated amount is signed by fifty-one percent (51%) of the number of duly qualified voters voting at the last general election in each county in the district. Such petition shall be filed with the fiscal court in each county in the district not later than ninety (90) days after the date of the first signature. The fiscal court shall order the court to increase or decrease the ad valorem tax, as stated in the petition.

(a) The petition shall read, "The following duly qualified voters of (insert name of county or counties) hereby petition the fiscal court of each county concerned to increase (or decrease) the special ad valorem tax from (insert exact amount) to (insert exact amount) on each one hundred dollars ($100) worth of property assessed for local taxation in the district for the maintenance and operation of the (insert name) public library district."

(b) The petition shall contain the following: The name and address of each petitioner and the date upon which he signed the petition.

(2) Any increase provided for in subsection (1) of this section shall not exceed twenty cents (20¢) on each one hundred dollars ($100) of the assessed valuation of all property in the district.

(3) A petition requesting a decrease in the tax rate will not be considered of any legal effect if, at any time prior to the filing of such a petition for decrease, either:

(a) Contractual obligations have been assumed by pertinent contracting authorities in connection with said subject library, which contractual obligations would be adversely affected by any such decrease; or

(b) If, as of the time of filing of such a petition for decrease, the board of such district shall have arranged for the financing of a library in that district pursuant to a plan of financing involving a lease of that library to the board under which lease the board is not bound for more than one (1) year at a time without exercising an annual option to renew the lease and such lease remains effective and has not been terminated; or

(c) If less than three (3) years have passed since the certified copy of the order of the fiscal court ordering the levy of the tax was filed with the county clerk. (Enact. Acts 1964, ch. 92, § 17; 1970, ch. 241, § 7; 1972, ch. 223, § 10; 1978, ch. 384, § 299, effective June 17, 1978.)

173.795. Annexation of counties to district. — Counties outside of any existing district, and contiguous thereto, may be annexed to the district in the following manner:

(1) Upon filing with the fiscal court of a duly certified petition of fifty-one percent (51%) of the duly qualified voters voting at the last general election, the fiscal court of each county in the district and each county proposed to be annexed shall adopt a resolution annexing the territory to the district. A certified copy of the order of the fiscal court shall be filed with the county clerk within the next thirty (30) days.

(2) The petition shall be in substantially the following form: "The following duly qualified voters of (insert name of county or counties) petition their respective fiscal courts to annex the following described territory (here describe the territory) to the (name district) public library district with the authority to levy an ad valorem tax of (state exact amount) on each one hundred dollars ($100) worth of property subject to local taxation in the above stated territory." (Enact. Acts 1964, ch. 92, § 18.)

173.800. Dissolution of district, procedure. — A district may be dissolved in the following manner:

(1) Upon filing of a duly certified petition of fifty-one percent (51%) of the number of qualified voters who voted in the last general election in the district, the fiscal court of each county in the district shall adopt a resolution to dissolve a library district.

(2) The petition shall be in substantially the following form: "The following qualified voters in (insert name of county or counties) favor dissolving the (insert name of district) public library district." It shall be presented to the fiscal court within ninety (90) days after having been signed by the first petitioner.

(3) A certified copy of the order of the fiscal court shall be filed with the county clerk.

(4) The county clerk or clerks in the district will thereupon remove the tax levy from the tax bills of the property owners of the district and the district shall be dissolved.

(5) A petition for dissolution will not be considered of any legal effect if, at any time prior to the filing of such a petition for dissolution, either:

(a) Contractual obligations have been assumed by pertinent contracting parties in connection with said subject library, which contractual obligations would be adversely affected by any such dissolution; or

(b) If, as of the time of filing of such a petition for dissolution, the board of such district shall have arranged for the financing of a library in that district pursuant to a plan of financing involving a lease of that library to the board under which lease the board is not bound for more than one (1) year at a time without exercising an annual option to renew the lease and such lease remains effective and has not been terminated; or

(c) If less than three (3) years have passed since the certified copy of the order of the fiscal court ordering the levy of the tax was filed with the county clerk.

(6) After all contractual obligations, existing prior to the time of the attempted filing of such petition for dissolution, have been satisfied, then, at such time, a petition for dissolution may be effectively filed under this section, provided that other provisions of this section are complied with. (Enact. Acts 1964, ch. 92, § 19; 1966, ch. 154; 1970, ch. 241, § 8; 1972, ch. 223, § 11; 1978, ch. 384, § 300, effective June 17, 1978.)

REGIONAL, COUNTY AND MUNICIPAL LIBRARIES
(Kentucky Revised Statutes, 1982, s.173.300 to 173.410.)

173.300. Definitions for KRS 173.310 to 173.410. — As used in KRS 173.310 to 173.410, unless the context requires a different meaning:

(1) "Governmental unit" means any county or city; except a city of the first class and a county containing a city of the first class;

(2) "Legislative body" means the governing body of a governmental unit; and

(3) "Library" means a free public library supported in whole or in part with money derived from taxation, and governed by a board as provided for in KRS 173.340, excluding a city of the first class and a county containing a city of the first class. (Enact. Acts 1944, ch. 160, § 1.)

173.310. Methods by which library service may be provided — Appropriation or levy on establishment. — Any governmental unit may provide library service for its inhabitants according to any one (1) of the following methods:

(1) The legislative body on its own initiative may establish an independent library.

(2) Upon receipt of a petition signed by a number of taxpayers equal to five percent (5%) of the number of votes cast for officers in the last general election of such governmental unit, the legislative body shall submit the question to a vote at the next general election. If a majority of those voting on the question vote in favor of the proposition, the legislative body shall forthwith establish a library, except as provided in subsection (4) of this section.

(3) The legislative bodies of two (2) or more adjacent counties may on their own initiative, or upon a petition and vote in each county as provided in

subsection (2) above, or upon the initiative of some legislative bodies and petition and vote in others, join in establishing and maintaining a regional library, provided the aggregate assessed valuation of the property assessable for local taxation in such counties is a minimum of $10,000,000, and subject to the provisions of KRS 173.320.

(4) The legislative body of any governmental unit may on its own initiative contract to receive service from an existing nearby library, the library of a nearby institution of higher learning, the state department of libraries, or from a nearby library not owned by a governmental unit but which provides free service, each of these having reciprocal power to render the service. In the event of a petition and vote as provided by subsection (2), a legislative body shall have the privilege of providing library service by contract in lieu of establishing an independent library.

When any one (1) of the above methods has been complied with, the legislative bodies of the governing units shall at once make the necessary appropriation or levy to establish and maintain such library service annually and perpetually. (Enact. Acts 1944, ch. 160, § 2; 1960, ch. 61, § 1.)

173.320. Regional libraries. — The establishment of a regional library shall be by contract, in writing, by the legislative bodies of the counties. The expenses of the regional library shall be apportioned between the contracting parties concerned in proportion to the taxable property of each as shown by their respective assessments and as shall be agreed upon in the contract. The treasurer of one of the counties, as provided in the contract, shall have the custody of the funds for the regional library; and the treasurers of the other counties concerned shall transfer to him as collected all the moneys received for public library purposes and interest from library funds in their respective governmental units. The contract for a regional library shall continue in force for a period of five (5) years and no county shall be permitted to withdraw without the consent of all the other participating counties during the five (5) year period. If the legislative body of a county decides to withdraw from a regional library contract, it shall be entitled to a division of the property on the same basis as its contributions, such division being completed within six (6) months from the withdrawal date. If no unit withdraws, at the end of the five (5) year period, the contract shall continue in force for a like period. (Enact. Acts 1944, ch. 160, § 3.)

173.330. Contracts for library service. — A contract for library service made pursuant to subsection (4) of KRS 173.310 shall require the existing library to perform all the functions of a library within the governmental unit wanting service. Such contracts shall not be valid nor shall funds be obligated until the contracts are approved in writing by all the contracting parties and have been certified by the department of libraries as providing standard library service for the sum specified. Initial contracts shall be for two (2) years or longer, subject to renewal. The board of trustees of a regional library shall have the same power to contract for library service as is given to a legislative body in subsection (4) of KRS 173.310. (Enact. Acts 1944, ch. 160, § 4.)

173.340. Library board of trustees. — (1) The management and control of a library shall be vested in a board of trustees. In cities and counties the board shall consist of five (5) members except that in cities of the second class, it shall consist of seven (7) members. In the event a contract for library service is made pursuant to subsection (4) of KRS 173.310, the board may consist of equal representation from the contracting parties with the total membership not to exceed twelve (12). In a library region there shall be five (5) members except if the number of counties exceeds five (5) there shall be one (1) trustee from each county in the region.

(2) Within thirty (30) days after the establishment of a library has been authorized by any of the methods authorized by KRS 173.310, a library board shall be appointed. In cities the trustees shall be appointed by the mayor and in counties they shall be appointed by the county judge/executive. There shall be established a board of trustees in each regional library district for purposes of coordinating library programs and effecting economies and efficiencies of the member county library systems. In each regional library district the trustees shall be appointed by the joint action of the judges/executive of the respective counties or as may be agreed upon by contract. In any region in which there are four (4) or less counties, provision shall be made in the contract for rotation of members and an equitable adjustment of terms. If a region consists of an even number of counties, the trustees appointed by the judges/executive of the respective counties shall appoint an additional trustee whose term of office shall be four (4) years and whose successor shall be appointed by the trustees in office at the time of expiration of such term. Trustees shall be appointed from the governmental unit at large with special reference to their fitness for such office. Members of the board shall be appointed as follows: two (2) members for two (2) years, one (1) member for three (3) years, and two (2) members for four (4) years respectively, and thereafter trustees shall be appointed to serve four (4) years. Trustees may serve for two (2) consecutive terms after which they shall not succeed themselves, effective July 1, 1974, exclusive of present terms begun prior to that date. Vacancies shall be filled for the unexpired terms as soon as possible in the same manner as the original appointments. In the event that vacancies have existed for a period of at least six (6) months, the governor of the Commonwealth of Kentucky, upon the recommendation of the state librarian, may make such necessary appointments. Absence of a trustee from four (4) regular monthly meetings of the board during any one (1) year of the trustee's term shall constitute automatic resignation from the board by the trustee.

(3) A library trustee shall not receive a salary or other compensation for services as a trustee. Before entering upon the duties of his office, a trustee shall take oath that he will faithfully discharge his duties. No board shall employ as a member of its library staff any member of the board or any

person related closer than a second cousin to any member of the board. No person is eligible to this office who is directly or indirectly interested in the sale to the library of books, magazines, supplies, equipment, materials, fire insurance or services for which library funds are expended.

(4) A library trustee may be removed only by vote of the legislative body of the respective governmental unit from which he was appointed. (Enact. Acts 1944, ch. 160, § 5; 1970, ch. 109, § 1; 1974, ch. 8, § 4; 1976, ch. 367, § 2; 1982, ch. 245, § 9, effective July 15, 1982.)

173.350. Organization of board — Meetings — Powers and duties. — (1) The board of trustees shall constitute a corporate body with perpetual succession. Within ten (10) days after their appointment the appointive officer shall call a meeting of the library board to organize by the election of such officers as they deem necessary and meet on a regularly scheduled basis thereafter once each month. If the appointive officer does not call a meeting the trustees may do so on their own initiative.

(2) They shall adopt such bylaws, rules and regulations for their own guidance and for the government of the library as they deem expedient; have the supervision, care and custody of all property of the library including its quarters or buildings; employ a librarian and upon his recommendation employ such other assistants as may be necessary, all in accordance with the statutes relating to the certification of librarians and the rules and regulations adopted by the board pursuant thereto, and fix the compensation of libraries or assistants employed and remove them for cause; submit annually to the legislative body a budget containing estimates in detail of the amount of money necessary for the library for the ensuing year; allot funds for the purchase of books, periodicals, maps and supplies for the library; and do all other acts necessary for the orderly and efficient management and control of the library.

(3) They may accept such gifts of money or property for library purposes as they deem expedient; lease or purchase land for library buildings; lease, purchase or erect an appropriate building or buildings for library purposes and acquire such other property and equipment as may be needed therefor; and enter into contracts for library service with other library boards and as provided for in subsection (4) of KRS 173.310. (Enact. Acts 1944, ch. 160, § 6; 1974, ch. 8, § 5.)

173.360. Annual appropriations, amounts — Powers and duties of board as to funds. — (1) After the legislative body of a governmental unit has made provisions for library service according to any of the methods set forth in KRS 173.310, the legislative body shall appropriate money annually to furnish such service. In library regions it shall not be less than three cents (3¢), nor more than ten cents (10¢) on each one hundred dollars ($100) worth of property assessed for local taxation. In counties containing a city of the first class it shall be not more than fifteen cents (15¢) on each one hundred dollars ($100) worth of property assessed for local taxation. In all other governmental units it shall be not less than five cents (5¢) nor more than fifteen cents (15¢) on each one hundred dollars ($100) worth of property assessed for local taxation. In those instances where county library service has been established on the initiative of the fiscal court and when an appropriation of less than the minimum amount required by this subsection is proposed, the minimum amount of support for county library service may be determined annually through a mutual agreement of the county library board, the county fiscal court, and the state department of libraries. This agreement shall be reflected in the records of the legislative body of the governmental unit making the appropriation.

(2) All funds for the library shall be deposited monthly to the credit of the library board. These funds shall not be used for any but library purposes. The treasurer of the library board shall be required to execute bond with good and sufficient surety thereon for the faithful performance of his duties, the amount of the bond to be fixed by the board. If the bond has a corporate surety the premium shall be paid from the library fund. The board shall have exclusive control of expenditures, subject to an examination of accounts as may be required by the legislative body, and money shall be paid only upon vouchers approved by the board. The board shall not make expenditures or incur indebtedness in any year in excess of the amount of money appropriated and available for library purposes, except where a library board is the owner of real estate not used for library purposes, in which case they may borrow money secured solely by that property. Principal and interest on indebtedness on real estate owned by a library board not used for library purposes is not chargeable to the library funds derived from taxation. (Enact. Acts 1944, ch. 160, § 7; 1960, ch. 61, § 2; 1964, ch. 55, § 3.)

173.370. Annual reports. — At the close of its fiscal year the board of trustees of every library shall make a report to the legislative body of the governmental unit wherein the board serves, showing the condition of its trust during the year, the sums of money received for the library fund, the sums of money expended and the purposes of the expenditures, the number of books and bound periodicals on hand, the number added during the year, the number discarded, the number lent, and such other statistics and information and such suggestions as they deem of public interest. A report shall also be filed with the department of libraries at Frankfort, Kentucky, upon forms supplied by said department. (Enact. Acts 1944, ch. 160, § 8.)

173.380. Free use of libraries. — Every library established or maintained under KRS 173.300 to 173.390 shall be free for the use of the inhabitants of the governmental unit in which it is located, subject to such reasonable rules and regulations the trustees find necessary. (Enact. Acts 1944, ch. 160, § 9.)

173.390. Title to money and property. — The title to money or property given to or for the use or benefit of a library shall be vested in the board of trustees, to be used according to the terms of the gift. Should a library be closed or services discontinued, it shall be the duty of the governmental unit to hold all library property and funds received by gift in trust to be used for library purposes, unless the terms of the gift permit use for other purposes or unless such assets are transferred to a public library district pursuant to KRS 173.395. (Enact. Acts 1944, ch. 160, § 10; 1980, ch. 167, § 2, effective July 15, 1980.)

173.395. Consolidation of city library with public library district — Dissolution of city library tax levy — Transfer of assets. — (1) If a public library district is established under KRS 173.450 to 173.800, the legislative body of any city in such county that has established a library under KRS 173.310(1) or (2) may dissolve the city library for the purpose of consolidating library services in the public library district. Such dissolution shall have the effect of removing any tax levied under KRS 173.310 for the specific purpose of establishing and maintaining the city library.

(2) If a city library is dissolved pursuant to subsection (1) of this section, the city legislative body shall immediately file an order of dissolution with the official who is responsible for collecting any tax levied under KRS 173.310. The official shall thereupon remove any tax levied under KRS 173.310, for the specific purpose of establishing and maintaining the city library, from the tax bills of the property owners of the city.

(3) After the satisfaction of any existing contractual obligations assumed in connection with the dissolved library, the assets of the library shall be transferred to the public library district, unless the terms of a gift held in trust prohibit such transfer. (Enact. Acts 1980, ch. 167, § 1, effective July 15, 1980.)

173.400. Status of existing libraries and contracts. — Any free public library established after June 13, 1944 shall be established as provided in KRS 173.300 to 173.390. Every existing public library which has been heretofore established under provisions of state law except a city of the first class and a county containing a city of the first class shall be considered as operating under the authority of KRS 173.300 to 173.390. Every existing contract for library service shall continue until the contract be terminated or a library be established by the governmental unit for which the service was engaged. The provisions of KRS 173.300 to 173.390 shall be construed as superseding the provisions of any municipal charter in conflict therewith. (Enact. Acts 1944, ch. 160, § 11.)

LIBRARIES IN FIRST-CLASS CITIES
(Kentucky Revised Statutes, 1982, s.173.010 to 173.107.)

173.010. Public library in cities of first class — Arrangement with existing libraries — Provisions of contract. — (1) The mayor of any city of the first class, with the consent of the city legislative body, may contract with the governing authority of any library in the city, containing fifty thousand (50,000) or more volumes, for the purpose of making the library free and open to the public at reasonable times and under reasonable regulations to be determined by the governing authority of the library.

(2) The contract shall be for not over five (5) years and may be renewed. The contract shall provide that the uses, privileges and facilities of the library, subject to the reasonable regulation of its governing body, shall be equal and free to all persons; that it shall be nonsectarian; and that its reading rooms, and its circulating department shall be maintained free and open to the general public. (2801a-1.)

173.020. Tax for existing library — Report to mayor. — (1) Any city acting under the provisions of KRS 173.010 shall annually, in its annual ordinance fixing the tax rate, include a levy for library purposes not exceeding two cents (2¢) on each one hundred dollars ($100) worth of property assessed for taxation for city purposes. The amount levied annually shall be credited to the library fund of the city, and the revenue, as collected, shall be paid over to the governing authority of the library by the director of finance in regular weekly instalments.

(2) All money so received shall be used exclusively for conducting and maintaining the library for the public purposes mentioned in KRS 173.010. The governing authority of the library shall make a report to the mayor each September, showing statistics covering the attendance at and the use of the books of the library, the receipts and expenditures of all money handled by it during the year, and other information bearing upon the usefulness of the library to the public. (2801a-2.)

173.030. Establishment of free public library in cities of first class — Use of — Ordinances regarding conduct. — (1) Any city of the first class may, by ordinance, establish and maintain within its corporate limits a free public library, with circulating and reference departments and reading rooms, or any of them, for the use of the residents thereof, with such branches and stations as the board of trustees of the library think proper. All the uses and privileges of such library shall be free and equal to all residents of the city, subject only to the rules and regulations established by the board of trustees. The board may extend the privilege and use of the library to persons residing outside of the city, upon such terms and conditions as the board prescribes.

(2) The city legislative body may pass such ordinances as the board recommends providing for the punishment of persons injuring the library property and regulating the conduct of persons using the library. (2801b-1, 2801b-2, 2801b-8.)

173.040. Board of trustees — Officers and employes. — (1) As soon as practicable after the passage of the ordinance providing for a free public library, the mayor shall appoint twelve (12) trustees. The appointments shall be made for four (4) year terms except that the original appointees shall be so appointed that the terms of three (3) members shall expire each year. Each appointee must be, at the time of his appointment, a taxpayer and qualified voter in the city and must have resided therein for two (2) years prior to his appointment. The mayor shall continue to appoint all twelve (12) trustees unless the county judge/executive becomes authorized to appoint trustees under the provisions of KRS 173.105, after which the mayor shall appoint only the trustee positions not appointed by the county judge/executive. The trustees shall serve without compensation. The twelve (12) trustees, whether appointed under this subsection or under KRS 173.105, together with the mayor of the city, shall constitute the board of trustees of the free public library, and shall be a corporation with power to make such rules and regulations to govern itself and the property entrusted to its care as it deems proper. Absence of a trustee from four (4) regular monthly meetings of the board during any one (1) year of the trustee's term shall constitute automatic resignation from the board by the trustee.

(2) Vacancies in the office of trustee shall be reported by the board to the mayor, if the vacancy occurs in a trustee position filled by appointment of the mayor, or to the county judge/executive if the vacancy occurs in a trustee position which the county judge/executive has authority to fill under KRS 173.105. The vacancy shall be filled by the mayor if so authorized or the county judge/executive if so authorized under subsection (1) of this section and KRS 173.105, for the remainder of an unexpired term or for a full term if the vacancy results from the expiration of a term. The trustees shall, before entering upon the duties of office, make an oath or affirmation before a judicial officer that they will discharge their duties.

(3) At its first meeting and each year thereafter, the board shall select members of the board to serve as president and vice-president, and it may choose other necessary officers and employes, fix their duties and compensation, and remove them at pleasure. (2801b-3, 2801b-4: amend. Acts 1978, ch. 267, § 1, effective March 30, 1978; 1982, ch. 245, § 8, effective July 15, 1982.)

173.045. Retirement plan for employes. — The board of trustees of the free public libraries in cities of the first class, created or existing under the laws of Kentucky, which have not less than two (2) full time employes, may provide for their retirement with annuities; may adopt the American library association retirement plan or make such other provisions for retirement of its employes as the board deems proper, whether similar to the American library association retirement plan or otherwise. (Enact. Acts 1946, ch. 197, § 5.)

173.050. Powers of board of trustees. — (1) The board of trustees may, in its corporate name:

(a) Contract and be contracted with, sue and be sued, and have and use a corporate seal, which it may alter at pleasure;

(b) Acquire, by itself or jointly with the city in which the library is located, by gift, purchase or otherwise, and hold, in the same manner, real and personal property to the use of the public library, for the purpose for which it is dedicated;

(c) Use, manage and improve, sell and convey, rent or lease property, and erect suitable buildings.

(2) The board of trustees may mortgage any real or personal property owned by the library to secure any sums borrowed for making repairs or improvements, or paying off any indebtedness it may owe. The mortgage shall not exceed $1,000,000. (2801b-3, 2801b-7: amend. Acts 1946, ch. 197, § 1.)

173.060.   Meetings of board — Incurring of liabilities. — The board shall meet at least once each month for the transaction of its business. A majority of the board shall constitute a quorum, but no appropriation of money, except for ordinary or current expenditures, shall be made without the affirmative vote of a majority of its members. Except for the purpose of erecting the library building, the board of trustees shall not incur liabilities for any current year in excess of its annual income, including gifts and donations and unexpended balances from previous years. (2801b-4.)

173.065.   Fiscal year of library. — The fiscal year of the free public libraries in cities of the first class shall begin on the first day of July of each year and end on June 30 next following. (Enact. Acts 1946, ch. 197, § 4.)

173.070.   Appropriation for public library — Disposition of revenue — Report to legislative body. — (1) In order to provide funds for the establishment and maintenance of a library established as provided in KRS 173.030, the legislative body of a city of the first class shall annually appropriate from the general fund of the city such sum as in the judgment of the legislative body shall be reasonably necessary for such purposes. Moneys so appropriated shall be credited to the library fund of the city, and may be paid over to the board of trustees by the director of finance of such city in regular monthly instalments.

(2) The board shall make a report to the city legislative body each July, showing the use of the library for the fiscal year ending the last day of June preceding, the receipts and expenditures of all money handled by it during the year, and giving such other information as may promote the usefulness of the library to the public, or as is called for by the city legislative body. No portion of the property or fund held for library purposes under this section shall ever be applied to the support of any library not exclusively under the control of the board of trustees. (2801b-6: amend. Acts 1946, ch. 197, § 2; 1954, ch. 164, § 7.)

173.080.   Issuance of library bonds. — The board of trustees may, in its discretion, issue bonds in the sum of not over $1,000,000 for the purpose of making improvements or repairs, or paying off any indebtedness it may owe.

The bonds may be secured by any or all real or personal property owned by the library. The bonds shall be designated as "library bonds" and the board of trustees shall, by resolution, fix the date and maturity of the bonds, the rate of interest and form they shall bear, and where they shall be payable. The board shall determine when, at what price and how the bonds shall be sold. As the bonds are sold their proceeds shall be placed in some bank, but shall be kept in a separate account and shall be used only for the purpose for which the bonds were issued, provided however the expense and cost of floating the bonds may be paid therefrom. The rent received in any year from any real property belonging to the board of trustees shall be first applied to the payment of interest on bonds for such year, and next to the sinking fund requirements of the bond issue for such year, and the balance may be used for current operating expenses of the board of trustees. (2801b-9: amend. Acts 1946, ch. 197, § 3.)

173.090. City may guarantee library bonds. — (1) If bonds are issued as provided in KRS 173.030 to 173.100, the city in which the library is located may, by ordinance, guarantee the bonds, either as to principal or interest or both.

(2) When the ordinance guaranteeing the bonds is enacted by the city, the bonds shall be indorsed "guaranteed" and the name of the city attached and the guarantee shall be signed by the mayor and attested by the director of finance, and stamped with the proper seal of the city. (2801b-10.)

173.100. Deposit of library funds. — All money due the board shall be deposited in a bank, in the city, selected by the board, and funds shall be withdrawn from the bank only on order of the board by check of its treasurer countersigned by its president. (2801b-5.)

173.105. Contract with county — Support by county. — (1) The fiscal court of any county containing a population of over two hundred thousand (200,000) and a city of the first class, may contract with the board of trustees of the free public library of any such city for the purpose of granting to the residents and schools of such county the same privileges afforded by such library to residents and schools in the city.

(2) If the fiscal court enters into a contract pursuant to subsection (1) of this section, then the county judge/executive shall have the authority to appoint one-half (½) of the positions on the board of trustees of the free public library. Appointments shall be made for four (4) year terms. Each appointee must be at the time of his appointment a taxpayer and qualified voter in the county.

(3) The county judge/executive shall make the appointments authorized by subsection (2) of this section in the following manner. On March 31 of 1978 and March 31 of 1980, he shall appoint persons to fill two (2) of the vacancies which occur. On March 31 of 1979 and March 31 of 1981, he shall appoint a person to fill one (1) vacancy which occurs. He shall continue to make the appointments to these positions when a vacancy occurs or a term

expires, subject to subsection (4) of this section.

(4) If the contract between the fiscal court and a free public library terminates or ceases to be in effect, the county judge/executive shall no longer have the authority to appoint persons as trustees to the board of the free public library and the mayor may terminate the appointment of trustees appointed by the county judge/executive and appoint persons to fill their unexpired terms.

(5) The fiscal court may annually appropriate money out of the county treasury to the maintenance and support of the library.

(6) Money so appropriated by the fiscal court may be expended by the board of trustees of the free public library in the establishment of branch stations in the county outside the city of the first class, under regulations of the board of trustees. (2801c-1, 2801c-2: amend. Acts 1978, ch. 267, § 2, effective March 30, 1978.)

173.107. Library tax or appropriation not to be decreased when city becomes city of first class. — Any library established or maintained pursuant to the provisions of KRS 173.310 to 173.410 shall not, upon becoming a city of the first class or a county containing a city of the first class, have its tax levy or appropriation decreased except by the procedure in KRS 173.790. (Enact. Acts 1972, ch. 223, § 6.)

STATE ADVISORY COUNCIL
(Kentucky Revised Statutes, 1982, s.173.810.)

173.810. State advisory council on libraries — Membership — Duties — Compensation. — (1) The Kentucky state advisory council on libraries is hereby created and shall be composed of twenty-one (21) members, appointed by the governor for a term of four (4) years, except that of the twenty-one (21) members initially appointed, six (6) shall serve terms of four (4) years, five (5) shall serve terms of three (3) years, five (5) shall serve terms of two (2) years and five (5) shall serve terms of one (1) year. The governor of the Commonwealth of Kentucky shall appoint from this membership a chairman and co-chairman to serve for periods of two (2) years each. The council shall be attached to the cabinet for education and the arts for administrative purposes.

(2) Of the twenty-one (21) members, four (4) shall represent public libraries, two (2) shall represent school libraries, two (2) shall represent college or university libraries, two (2) shall represent special libraries, two (2) shall represent institutional libraries, two (2) shall represent the blind and physically handicapped and seven (7) members, at least one (1) of whom shall be representative of disadvantaged persons, shall represent library users.

(3) Vacancies shall be filled by the governor in the same manner as initial appointments are made.

(4) Members of the Kentucky state advisory council on libraries shall

receive twenty-five dollars ($25.00) per day for each meeting attended and shall be compensated for actual and necessary expenses.

(5) The council shall be the state advisory council on libraries for the purposes of section 3(8) of the Federal Library Services and Construction Act. (Enact. Acts 1976, ch. 367, § 1; 1978, ch. 154, § 14, effective June 17, 1978.)

URBAN LIBRARIES FUND
(Kentucky Revised Statutes, 1982, s.173.850 to 173.870.)

173.850. Definitions for KRS 173.860 and 173.870. — Unless the context otherwise requires:

(1) "State librarian" means the state librarian as defined in KRS 171.130;

(2) "Governmental unit" means any county or city or urban-county government or other agency or instrumentality which is authorized by Kentucky Revised Statutes to levy and collect taxes for public purposes; and

(3) "Qualifying library" means any free public library supported in whole or in part with money derived from taxation, and governed by a board as provided for in KRS 173.040, 173.340, 173.500 or 173.725, which is located in any county containing a city of the first or second class, or in any urban-county government. (Enact. Acts 1980, ch. 383, § 1, effective July 15, 1980.)

173.860. Urban libraries fund — Source of money. — There is hereby created the urban libraries fund for distribution to free public libraries in counties containing cities of the first or second class, or urban-county governments pursuant to the provisions of KRS 173.870. The fund shall consist of such sums as are appropriated by the general assembly, and any grants, gifts, legacies, devises or other funds or property from any available source, public or private. The receipt, control and expenditure of funds shall be subject to the general provisions of KRS Chapters 41 to 47, governing financial administration of state agencies. (Enact. Acts 1980, ch. 383, § 2, effective July 15, 1980.)

173.870. Allocation of fund. — The state librarian shall annually on September 1 cause the state treasurer to pay to each qualifying library out of the urban libraries fund, to the extent that funds are available, the sums computed as follows:

(1) The sum of twenty-five cents (25¢) for each resident of the county containing a qualifying library based on the then current census of such county supplied by the bureau of census, United States department of commerce; and

(2) The sum of ten thousand dollars ($10,000) for each one hundred thousand dollars ($100,000) which is appropriated for library purposes by any city, county, urban-county government or other governmental unit or

taxing authority supplying funds, excluding federal revenue sharing funds, to a free public library in such county. (Enact. Acts 1980, ch. 383, § 3, effective July 15, 1980.)

COUNTY LAW LIBRARIES
(Kentucky Revised Statutes, 1982, s.172.100 to 172.990.)

172.100. County law library — Location — Books. — (1) A county law library shall be established in each county seat and the fiscal court of each county shall designate sufficient room in the courthouse or in a building of good construction adjacent to the courthouse where such library shall be located and where the books of the library may be safely kept.

(2) The books of the county law library shall consist of all volumes belonging to the state heretofore sent to the various county officials directed by law to receive such books, and all volumes hereafter sent to such library by the state, and all books now owned or hereafter acquired by the county for the library. The counties may acquire books, maps, or other articles for the library by purchase, gift or devise. (2438c-8.)

172.110. Circuit clerk is librarian — Duties — Salary — Inventory. — (1) The circuit clerk shall be ex officio librarian of the county law library, and he shall see that county and state officials have access to the library at reasonable hours each day except Sunday and holidays. He shall receive a salary of not less than fifty dollars ($50.00) nor more than one hundred dollars ($100) per month for his services as librarian.

(2) He shall keep the library rooms in order, preserve, arrange and index all the books, charts, maps and furniture belonging in the library, and see that no books or other things are taken from the library rooms without a receipt being given therefor.

(3) He shall receipt for all books, maps and furniture placed in the library. The receipts shall be given to the state law librarian and preserved in his office at Frankfort.

(4) He shall take an inventory each December of all the books, maps, charts or other property in the library belonging to the state and report the inventory under oath to the state law librarian before January 1 of the following year. (2438c-8: amend. Acts 1954, ch. 42, § 22; 1956, ch. 142.)

172.120. Clerk to give inventories to successor — Receipt to predecessor — Liability for books lost. — (1) Each clerk shall turn over to his successor separate inventories of all books, stationery and other property in the library at the commencement of his term, and all property placed in the library during his term.

(2) Each clerk shall receipt to his predecessor for all books, stationery, and other property in the library at the time he takes charge, and shall be responsible upon his official bond for the value of all books lost from the library during his term of office. (2438c-9.)

172.130. Fiscal court members to be trustees — Appropriations. — The members of the fiscal court shall be trustees of the county law library and shall see that the circuit clerk properly discharges his duties as librarian. The fiscal court may appropriate money out of the county treasury to pay for legal textbooks and decisions of the courts of other states, and to replace decisions of the Court of Justice furnished by the state which have been lost, mutilated or destroyed. (2438c-10: amend. Acts 1976, ch. 62, § 91.)

172.140. Use of books — Removal from library — To be returned on request. — (1) Any person may use the books in the library, but the clerk shall not permit anyone to take the books out of the library, except that officials and attorneys at law may take the books to courtrooms to be used in the argument of cases there pending but not elsewhere.

(2) Any person who has in his possession any public book belonging to the state shall, upon request of the clerk having custody of the book, return it to the clerk. (2431, 2438c-11.)

172.150. Record of books taken from library — Liability for failure to return book — Action. — The clerk shall keep a record in which he shall charge each book to the person taking it from the library and he shall see that all books so taken are returned at the proper time. If any person fails to return a book taken out by him, he shall be liable for double the cost thereof and the clerk shall move for judgment in the name of the state against such person under the procedure set out in KRS 418.005 to 418.015 and CR 6.03(2). The state may have attachment without bond for all such books. (2438c-12, 2438c-13: amend. Acts 1962, ch. 210, § 24.)

172.160. State university and college libraries — Clerk may give material to. — The circuit clerk as county law librarian may give to the library of the University of Kentucky and to the libraries of the state universities and colleges, such noncurrent documents and reports and other library materials in his possession as are not needed by the county. (2438c-11a.)

172.170. County law library in certain counties containing city of second class. — (1) The provisions of KRS 172.100 to 172.160 shall not apply to any county containing a city of the second class which county has a law library that was acquired under the provisions of chapter 2 of the Acts of 1916. The fiscal court of such county may make such rules and regulations regarding the maintenance and operation of the library as the court deems proper and as are approved by the judge or judges of the circuit court of the county, and may employ a librarian at a salary not to exceed one hundred dollars ($100) per month, and pay said salary out of the general funds of the county. The library shall be for the use of the court officers and county officers of the county, and the fiscal court may provide for the use of the library by others than the court and county officers, on such terms as the fiscal court deems advisable and proper.

(2) All books belonging to the state heretofore or hereafter sent to the county officials directed by law to receive such books, all books sent to the library by the state, and all books now owned or hereafter acquired by the county for the library, shall constitute part of the library. The county may acquire books, maps or other articles for the library by purchase, gift or devise. (Enact. Acts 1946, ch. 168.)

172.180. Alternate method of financing library. — Any county may adopt the following method of financing the cost of operation and maintenance of the county law library, in lieu of the method set out in KRS 172.130 or 172.170:

(1) Upon petition of three-fourths (¾) of the duly licensed and practicing attorneys resident in the county addressed to the circuit judge of the county, to the effect that they, as officers of the various courts of the county, recognize the need of a more adequate county law library, there being attached to said petition an attested copy of a resolution of the fiscal court of the county endorsing the adoption of this optional method of financing the cost of operation and maintenance of the county law library, the circuit judge shall enter an order noting that said optional plan for the financing of the cost of operation and maintenance of the county law library has been adopted.

(2) The order shall set forth the name of each duly licensed and practicing attorney signing said petition, and the order book and page number containing the resolution of the fiscal court.

(3) The order shall direct the following:

(a) That upon receipt of the order by the clerks of said courts there shall be taxed as costs in all criminal actions, except examining trials and felony trials, thereafter instituted in said court the following fee, which shall be designated as county law library fee, in district court, a sum not to exceed fifty cents (50¢); in circuit and district courts, on all civil actions a sum not to exceed one dollar ($1.00); and

(b) That the circuit clerk shall at the end of each month pay all sums collected as county law library fees during the preceding month, to the trustees of the county law library, and the clerk shall make a full report with said payment, and receive a receipt for all payments. (Enact. Acts 1956, ch. 142, § 1; 1958, ch. 75, § 1; 1960, ch. 17; 1976 (Ex. Sess.), ch. 14, § 165, effective January 2, 1978; 1978, ch. 384, § 295, effective June 17, 1978.)

172.190. Library fund in county containing city of third or fourth class. — Upon adoption of the optional method of financing a county law library provided in KRS 172.180, the funds derived from the county law library fee shall be designated county law library fund, and said fund shall be under the sole and full control of the trustees of the county law library. (Enact. Acts 1956, ch. 142, § 2; 1958, ch. 75, § 2.)

172.200. Appointment of trustees — Powers — Duties — Limits on indebtedness — County not to be liable — Treasurer, duties. — (1) Upon the

adoption of this optional plan, in counties other than those containing a city
of the first class, the circuit judge shall appoint one (1) member of the
county's bar, and the members of the county's bar shall, by majority vote,
elect another of their number, which two (2) attorneys shall, with the county
attorney of the county, constitute and be designated as "Trustees, ...
County Law Library." In counties containing a city of the first class, the
chief circuit judge shall appoint one (1) member of the county's bar; the
members of the county's bar shall, by majority vote, elect another of their
number; the fiscal court shall appoint one (1) member and one (1) member
shall be appointed by the commonwealth's attorney, which four (4) attorneys
shall, with the county attorney of the county, constitute and be designated
as "Trustees, ... County Law Library."

(2) The trustees shall serve for a term of two (2) years or until their
successors are elected or qualified.

(3) The trustees shall be in charge of the county law library, and they shall
make purchases of the various state and federal case reports, textbooks,
legal encyclopedia, and all other books usually incident to or customarily
found in law libraries, or necessary to the protection of the rights of litigants,
and they shall cause same to be properly arranged in the county law library,
directing the ex officio librarian in the exercise of his duties.

(4) The trustees shall exercise their absolute discretion in the purchase of
books, pamphlets, periodicals, and other materials, and in the appointment
and compensation of personnel to assist the ex officio librarian in the
handling of materials and in the maintenance of the library, but the trustees
shall not contract for any such purchases and appointments so as to create
an indebtedness greater than the anticipated revenue for the following
eighteen (18) months, the anticipated revenue being based upon the
preceding eighteen (18) months' revenue, and any indebtedness of the
county law library fund shall not be considered in any way an indebtedness
of the county, but shall be an indebtedness of the county law library fund
only, and all creditors must look only to the county law library fund for
satisfaction of their indebtedness.

(5) The trustees shall designate one (1) of their number as treasurer and
he shall be accountable for the receipt, deposit, and disbursement of all sums
received for the operation of the county law library. He shall be bonded by
a corporate bond, the cost of which shall be paid out of the receipts of the
library fund. He shall deposit all sums received by him as treasurer in a
regular banking depository, and he shall pay for all purchases made by the
trustees by check or draft, keeping a true and accurate account of all sums
received and expended by him. He shall annually file a written report with
the circuit judge of the county showing all sums received by him, together
with the court from which they were received, and an itemized statement
of all expenditures made by him. The treasurer shall turn all funds over to
his successor, together with a full inventory of the county law library, and
together with a full and complete itemized statement of all outstanding
accounts. (Enact. Acts 1956, ch. 142, § 3; 1962, ch. 11; 1978, ch. 375, § 1,
effective June 17, 1978.)

172.990. Penalties. — (1) Any clerk who is delinquent in making the inventory required in subsection (4) of KRS 172.110 shall be fined five dollars ($5.00) for each month or part of month he is delinquent.

(2) Any person who violates subsection (2) of KRS 172.140 shall, in addition to his civil liability, be fined not exceeding fifty dollars ($50.00).

(3) Any clerk who knowingly permits any book of the laws of this state or reports of the Court of Justice to be taken from his office in such a manner that he cannot produce the book when called upon to do so, shall be fined not exceeding fifty dollars ($50.00). (2430, 2431, 2438c-8: amend. Acts 1976, ch. 62, § 92.)

TAX EXEMPTION

(Kentucky Revised Statutes, 1982, State Constitution s.170.)

Kentucky library laws are reprinted from KENTUCKY REVISED STATUTES published by The Bobbs Merrill Company Inc., Indianapolis, IN and The Michie Company, Charlottesville, VA.

LOUISIANA

STATE LIBRARY

(West's Louisiana Statutes Annotated, 1982, Title 25, s.1-17.)

§ 1. Establishment and location

There shall be a library known as the Louisiana State Library, domiciled in the parish of East Baton Rouge, Louisiana, and located in the city of Baton Rouge.

Amended by Acts 1950, No. 316, § 6.

§ 2. Board of commissioners; appointment, terms, and qualification of members; removal of members

There is created a board of commissioners of the Louisiana State Library, to be composed of five members appointed by the governor by and with the advice and consent of the senate, commissioned with overlapping terms. The first members of the board need not be confirmed by the senate but shall be appointed by the governor within thirty days after July 31, 1946, one for one year, one for two years, one for three years, one for four years, and one for five years. Their successors shall each be appointed as herein provided for five year terms, each member to serve until his successor is commissioned and qualified.

The members of the board shall serve without pay and shall not be removed except for cause shown during their terms of office.

Acts 1946, No. 102, §§ 2, 3.

§ 3. Selection of members of board

The members of the board of commissioners shall be selected without political consideration from the entire state, and at all times at least two members of the board shall be women.

Acts 1946, No. 102, § 3.

§ 4. Organization of board; meetings; quorum

Immediately upon the selection and appointment of the first board of commissioners, the members shall meet at Baton Rouge on the call of the secretary of the former Louisiana Library Commission and organize by electing a chairman, a vice-chairman, and an executive secretary; they shall also provide for quarterly meetings of the board and for special meetings on the call of the chairman or of any three members. A majority of the whole membership shall be required to constitute a quorum for the transaction of business, but the executive secretary and the chairman, acting jointly, will be authorized at all times to transact routine business. Acts 1946, No. 102, § 4.

§ 5. Executive secretary as chief librarian and director of library development; secretary of board of commissioners

The executive secretary shall be the chief librarian and chief executive officer of the Louisiana State Library as well as the director of library development and service throughout the state; he shall also be the secretary of the board of commissioners. Acts 1946, No. 102, § 5.

§ 6. Executive secretary; term of office; removal

The term of office of the executive secretary is five years, subject to removal for cause by the unanimous vote of the board of commissioners. Acts 1946, No. 102, § 6.

§ 7. Executive secretary; qualifications

The executive secretary shall possess the following qualifications: he or she shall be of good moral character and shall be a trained and experienced librarian holding a degree from some standard college or university. In addition, he must have completed the required course in a recognized or accredited school of library science and have had at least five years' experience as an administrative librarian or director of some state or public library serving a populated area of not less than fifty thousand inhabitants. Acts 1946, No. 102, § 7.

§ 8. Functions of board of commissioners; duties of executive secretary

The board of commissioners of the Louisiana State Library, through the executive secretary, shall plan and work toward a coordinated system of parish and regional libraries throughout the state so as to give and furnish every citizen and resident of the state free library service of the highest quality consistent with modern methods and as may be justified by financial and economic conditions.

The executive secretary shall endeavor to coordinate and integrate the library service so as to afford the schools, colleges, and universities the best free library service possible by means of interloan arrangements, book exchanges, and the like. Acts 1946, No. 102, § 8.

§ 9. Other functions, duties and powers of board

The board of commissioners may send any of its members to aid in the organization of public general libraries or to assist in the improvement of those already established. It may also receive gifts of books, money, or other property, which may be used or held in trust for the purpose or purposes given; may purchase and operate traveling libraries, and circulate such libraries within the state among communities, libraries, schools, colleges, universities, library associations, study clubs, and charitable and penal institutions, under such conditions and rules as the board may deem necessary to protect the interest of the state and best increase the efficiency of the service it is expected to render the public. It may publish lists and circulars of information, and may cooperate with other library commissions and libraries in the publication of documents, in order to secure the most economical administration of the work for which it was formed. It may conduct courses or schools of library instruction and hold library institutes in various parts of the state, and cooperate with others in such schools or institutes. It may also conduct a clearing house for periodicals for free gift to local libraries and shall perform such other service in behalf of public libraries as it may consider for the best interest of the state.

In connection with and under the supervision of each normal school in the state and the president of the state university the board may arrange for a course of lectures every year at each of the said normal schools and the state university on book selection, the use and care of books and the cataloging and administration of school libraries. It may cooperate with the state board of education in devising plans for the care of school libraries, in aiding teachers in school library administration, and in formulating rules and regulations governing the use of such libraries throughout the state. Such suggestions, rules, and regulations for school libraries are to be promulgated through the superintendent of public education. Acts 1920, No. 225, § 4.

§ 10. Supervision of public libraries; reports required

The executive secretary shall, from time to time when called upon, give supervisory service and advice to all parish, institutional, and public libraries in the state, except law libraries. He shall also require such libraries to file annually, and at such other times as he may deem necessary, reports giving such statistical and other information as he may require. These reports shall be filed with the Louisiana State Library on or before the thirty-first day of January of each year for the preceding calendar year. Acts 1946, No. 102, § 9.

§ 11. Reports to governor or legislature; duty of executive secretary to file

The executive secretary shall, at least thirty days before the regular session of the legislature, make a biennial report to the governor showing the progress and development of library service in the state and containing the statistical and other information thought desirable, or any that may be specially called for by the governor or the legislature. This report shall be printed and distributed at public expense in sufficient quantities to enable each member of the legislature and all public officials of the state to have copies when desired.

Acts 1946, No. 102, § 10.

§ 12. Travelling expenses of members; how paid

The necessary and actual travelling expenses incurred by the executive secretary or any members of the staff, acting under the authority and direction of the executive secretary, while on business for the Louisiana State Library, and all actual and necessary travelling expenses of the several members of the board of commissioners of the Louisiana State Library, shall be paid by the state from the funds appropriated and made available for the use, maintenance, and operation of the Louisiana State Library. Acts 1946, No. 102, § 12.

§ 13. Legislative reference library; organization and maintenance

The Louisiana State Library shall organize and maintain, for the use of the legislature and the state officials in particular, and for the public in general, a legislative reference library, at the State Capitol. This library shall be in charge of a trained and experienced librarian, working under the direction of the executive secretary, to give assistance to the legislators and state officials. Acts 1946, No. 102, § 14.

§ 14. State library as recipient of federal and state funds

A. The Louisiana State Library is named and designated as the proper state agency to accept, receive and administer any funds or moneys granted, furnished, provided, appropriated and dedicated or made available by the United States or any of its departments, commissions, boards, bureaus or agencies or by the state of Louisiana for the purpose of giving aid to libraries and providing educational library service for citizens in the state of Louisiana.

B. Any and all funds or moneys made available by the state of Louisiana for the purposes stated herein shall be received and administered by the assistant secretary of the office of the Louisiana State Library who is hereby vested with authority to establish rules, regulations, and restrictions not inconsistent with law for the distribution of said funds or moneys to the public libraries of the state and from time to time alter and amend the same. Amended by Acts 1977, No. 347, § 1, eff. July 10, 1977.

§ 15. Authority to do acts required by federal laws

The Louisiana State Library is authorized to file any and all applications and make any and all reports and keep and render any and all accounts required or specified by federal law or regulation with reference to securing, administering and using all such funds and moneys for said purposes in the state of Louisiana. Acts 1940, No. 56, § 2.

§ 16. Rendition of library services to blind persons

The Louisiana State Library may, with the approval of the federal government, enter into contractual agreements with surrounding states for library services to blind persons. Such agreements shall provide for the payment to the Louisiana State Library of their proportionate share of the total cost of the service by the states receiving the service under the agreement. The Louisiana State Library shall receive and retain all funds received, to be used to help defray the cost of the service in the foreign state.

Added by Acts 1956, No. 70, § 1.

§ 17. Anti-Communist Division

A. The Louisiana State Library shall organize, maintain and operate a special division of the library to be designated as "Anti-Communist Division" of the Louisiana State Library which will be in charge of a trained and experienced librarian.

B. The purpose of this special division will be to collect, maintain, lend, circulate and disseminate books, pamphlets, films, tapes, slides, congressional and other reports and studies and all other available materials which explain, discuss, espouse or disseminate information relative to the fundamental principles of the American form of government, free enterprise, capitalism, the American social and economic system, the philosophy, purposes, strategy, tactics, nature, effects, logistics and fallacies of communism in its goal of world domination, the evils of socialism, and the contrast between liberty under law and communism and socialism.

C. The anti-communist division shall arrange for the free loan of all such materials and distribution (including shipping costs) from this special collection to civic clubs, veterans' organizations, patriotic societies, bar associations, women's clubs, study groups, labor unions, chambers of commerce, schools, classes, libraries and other organizations and individuals in Louisiana for use in pro-American and anti-communist programs, instruction, study or reading.

Added by Acts 1962, No. 493, § 1.

INTERSTATE LIBRARY COMPACT
(West's Louisiana Statutes Annotated, 1982, Title 25, s.631-636.)

§ 631.   Interstate Library Compact; adoption

The Interstate Library Compact is hereby enacted into law and entered into by this state with all states legally joining therein in the form substantially as follows:

INTERSTATE LIBRARY COMPACT
Article I.   Policy and Purpose

Because the desire for the services provided by libraries transcends governmental boundaries and can most effectively be satisfied by giving such services to communities and people regardless of jurisdictional lines, it is the policy of the states party to this compact to cooperate and share their responsibilities; to authorize cooperation and sharing with respect to those types of library facilities and services which can be more economically or efficiently developed and maintained on a cooperative basis, and to authorize cooperation and sharing among localities, states and others in providing joint or cooperative library services in areas where the distribution of population or of existing and potential library resources make the provision of library service on an interstate basis the most effective way of providing adequate and efficient service.

Article II.   Definitions

As used in this compact:

(a) "Public library agency" means any unit or agency of local or state government operating or having power to operate a library.

(b) "Private library agency" means any nongovernmental entity which operates or assumes a legal obligation to operate a library.

(c) "Library agreement" means a contract establishing an interstate library district pursuant to this compact or providing for the joint or cooperative furnishing of library services.

Article III. Interstate Library Districts

(a) Any one or more public library agencies in a party state in cooperation with any public library agency or agencies in one or more other party states may establish and maintain an interstate library district. Subject to the provisions of this compact and any other laws of the party states which pursuant hereto remain applicable, such district may establish, maintain and operate some or all of the library facilities and services for the area concerned in accordance with the terms of a library agreement therefor. Any private library agency or agencies within an interstate library district may cooperate therewith, assume duties, responsibilities and obligations thereto, and receive benefits therefrom as provided in any library agreement to which such agency or agencies become party.

(b) Within an interstate library district, and as provided by a library agreement, the performance of library functions may be undertaken on a joint or cooperative basis or may be undertaken by means of one or more arrangements between or among public or private library agencies for the extension of library privileges to the use of facilities or services operated or rendered by one or more of the individual library agencies.

(c) If a library agreement provides for joint establishment, maintenance or operation of library facilities or services by an interstate library district, such district shall have power to do any one or more of the following in accordance with such library agreement:

1. Undertake, administer and participate in programs or arrangements for securing, lending or servicing of books and other publications, any other materials suitable to be kept or made available by libraries, library equipment or for the dissemination of information about libraries, the value and significance of particular items therein, and the use thereof.

2. Accept for any of its purposes under this compact any and all donations, and grants of money, equipment, supplies, materials and services (conditional or otherwise), from any state or the United States or any subdivision or agency thereof, or interstate agency, or from any institution, person, firm or corporation, and receive, utilize and dispose of the same.

3. Operate mobile library units or equipment for the purpose of rendering book-mobile service within the district.

4. Employ professional, technical, clerical and other personnel, and fix terms of employment, compensation and other appropriate benefits and, where desirable, provide for the in-service training of such personnel.

5. Sue and be sued in any court of competent jurisdiction.

6.   Acquire, hold and dispose of any real or personal property or any interest or interests therein as may be appropriate to the rendering of library service.

7.   Construct, maintain and operate a library, including any appropriate branches thereof.

8.   Do such other things as may be incidental to or appropriate for the carrying out of any of the foregoing powers.

Article IV.   Interstate Library Districts; Governing Board

(a) An interstate library district which establishes, maintains or operates any facilities or services in its own right shall have a governing board which shall direct the affairs of the district and act for it in all matters relating to its business. Each participating public library agency in the district shall be represented on the governing board, which shall be organized and conduct its business in accordance with provision therefor in the library agreement. But in no event shall a governing board meet less often than twice a year.

(b) Any private library agency or agencies party to a library agreement establishing an interstate library district may be represented on or advise with the governing board of the district in such manner as the library agreement may provide.

Article V.   State Library Agency Cooperation

Any two or more state library agencies of two or more of the party states may undertake and conduct joint or cooperative library programs, render joint or cooperative library services, and enter into and perform arrangements for the cooperative or joint acquisition, use, housing, and disposition of items or collections of materials which, by reason of expense, rarity, specialized nature or infrequency of demand therefor would be appropriate for central collection and shared use. Any such programs, services or arrangements may include provision for the exercise on a cooperative or joint basis of any power exercisable by an interstate library district and an agreement embodying any such program, service or arrangement shall contain provisions covering the subjects detailed in Article VI of this compact for interstate library agreements.

Article VI.   Library Agreement

(a) In order to provide for any joint or cooperative undertaking pursuant to this compact, public and private library agencies may enter into library agreements. Any agreement executed pursuant to the provisions of this compact shall, as among the parties to the agreement:

1 Detail the specific nature of the services, programs, facilities, arrangements or properties to which it is applicable.

2. Provide for the allocation of costs and other financial responsibilities.

3. Specify the respective rights, duties, obligations and liabilities of the parties.

4. Set forth the terms and conditions for duration, renewal, termination, abrogation, disposal of joint or common property, if any, and all other matters which may be appropriate to the proper effectuation and performance of the agreement.

(b) No public or private library agency shall undertake to exercise itself, or jointly with any other library agency, by means of a library agreement any power prohibited to such agency by the constitution, or statutes of its state.

(c) No library agreement shall become effective until filed with the compact administrator of each state involved and approved in accordance with Article VII of this compact.

Article VII.   Approval of Library Agreements

(a) Every library agreement made pursuant to this compact shall, prior to and as a condition precedent to its entry into force, be submitted to the attorney general of each state in which a public library agency party thereto is situated, who shall determine whether the agreement is in proper form and compatible with the laws of his state. The attorneys general shall approve any agreement submitted to them unless they find that it does not meet the conditions set forth herein, and they shall detail in writing addressed to the governing bodies of the public library agencies concerned the specific respects in which the proposed agreement fails to meet the requirements of law. Failure to disapprove an agreement submitted hereunder within ninety days of its submission shall constitute approval thereof.

(b) In the event a library agreement made pursuant to this compact deals in whole or in part with the provision of services or facilities with regard to which an officer or agency of the state government has constitutional or statutory powers of control, the agreement shall, as a condition precedent to its entry into force, be submitted to the state officer or agency having such power of control and shall be approved or disapproved by him or it as to all matters within his or its jurisdiction in the same manner and subject to the same requirements governing the action of the attorneys general pursuant to paragraph (a) of this article. This requirement of submission and approval shall be in addition to and not in substitution for the requirement of submission to and approval by the attorneys general.

Article VIII.   Other Laws Applicable

Nothing in this compact or in any library agreement shall be construed to supersede, alter or otherwise impair any obligation imposed on any library by otherwise applicable law, nor to authorize the transfer or disposition of any property held in trust by a library agency in a manner contrary to the terms of such trust.

Article IX.   Allocations and Aid

(a) Any public library agency party to a library agreement may allocate funds to the interstate library district established thereby in the same manner and to the same extent as to a library wholly maintained by it.

(b) Subject to the provisions of the library agreement pursuant to which it functions and the laws of the states in which such district is situated, an interstate library district may claim and receive any state and federal aid which may be available to library agencies.

Article X.   Compact Administrator

Each state shall designate a compact administrator with whom copies of all library agreements to which his state or any public library agency thereof is party shall be filed. The administrator shall have such other powers as may be conferred upon him by the laws of his state and may consult and cooperate with the compact administrators of other party states and take such steps as may effectuate the purposes of this compact. If the laws of a party state so provide, such state may designate one or more deputy compact administrators in addition to its compact administrator.

Article XI.   Entry into Force and Withdrawal

(a) This compact shall enter into force and effect immediately upon its enactment into law by any two states. Thereafter, it shall enter into force and effect as to any other state upon the enactment thereof by such state.

(b) This compact shall continue in force with respect to a party state and remain binding upon such state until six months after such state has given notice to each other party state of the repeal thereof. Such withdrawal shall not be construed to relieve any party to a library agreement entered into pursuant to this compact from any obligation of that agreement prior to the end of its duration as provided therein.

Article XII.   Construction and Severability

This compact shall be liberally construed so as to effectuate the purposes thereof. The provisions of this compact shall be severable, and if any phrase, clause, sentence or provision of this compact is declared to be contrary to the constitution of any party state or of the United States or the applicability thereof to any government, agency, person or circumstance is held invalid, the validity of the remainder of this compact and the applicability thereof to any government, agency, person or circumstance shall not be affected thereby. If this compact is held contrary to the constitution of any state party thereto, the compact shall remain in full force and effect as to the remaining states and in full force and effect as to the state affected as to all severable matters.

Added by Acts 1968, No. 216, § 1.

§ 632. Applicability

No parish, municipality or other political subdivision of this state shall be party to a library agreement which provides for the construction or maintenance of library pursuant to Article III, subdivision (c)7 of the compact, or pledge its credit in support of such a library, or contribute to the capital financing thereof, except after compliance with any laws applicable to such parishes, municipalities or other political subdivisions relating to or governing capital outlays and the pledging of credit.

Added by Acts 1968, No. 216, § 1.

§ 633. Louisiana State Library

As used in the compact, "state library agency," with reference to this state, means The Louisiana State Library.

Added by Acts 1968, No. 216, § 1.

§ 634. Interstate library district; state and federal aid

An interstate library district lying partly within this state may claim and be entitled to receive state aid in support of any of its functions to the same extent and in the same amount as such functions are eligible for support when carried on by entities wholly within this state. Subject to any applicable laws of this state, such a district also may apply for and be entitled to receive and expend any federal aid for which it may be eligible.

Added by Acts 1968, No. 216, § 1.

§ 635. State librarian; administrator

The state librarian shall be the compact administrator pursuant to Article X of the compact. The state librarian may appoint one or more deputy compact administrators pursuant to said article.

Added by Acts 1968, No. 216, § 1.

§ 636.   Withdrawal from compact

In the event of withdrawal from the compact the state librarian shall send and receive any notices required by Article XI(b) of the compact.

Added by Acts 1968, No. 216, § 1.

CERTIFICATION OF LIBRARIANS
(West's Louisiana Statutes Annotated, 1982, Title 25, s.222-223.)

§ 222.   State board of library examiners; creation; members, appointment and terms of office; duties; examinations of applicants; fee for examination and certificate

There is created a State Board of Library Examiners to be composed of three members, all of whom must be experienced and trained librarians, appointed and chosen by the Board of Commissioners of the Louisiana State Library for a term of four years who shall serve without pay. The members of the board shall meet and organize and elect one chairman and a secretary. The board of library examiners shall have authority to establish rules and regulations for its government and prescribe examinations, qualifications, conditions and requirements for those seeking certificates or permits to practice the profession of librarian. The board shall hold at least one examination a year for the purposes of examining applicants for certificates as librarians at the office of the Louisiana State Library in Baton Rouge and may hold other examinations at other places in the state as may suit the convenience of the board and the applicants.

All applicants for the certificates as librarian shall be required to deposit and pay to the Louisiana State Library a fee of five dollars; if the applicants are successful in the examination, they will be given a certificate by the board of examiners. All fees collected by the board shall be turned over by it to the Louisiana State Library to defray the incidental expenses for certificates, traveling expenses, stationery, postage, and the like.   Acts 1926, No. 36, §§ 12, 13.

§ 223.   Reports by board of examiners to state library

The board of library examiners shall report annually to the Louisiana State Library furnishing such statistical information as may be required by it.   Acts 1926, No. 36, § 13.

DISTRIBUTION OF PUBLIC DOCUMENTS

West's Louisiana Statutes Annotated, 1982, Title 25, s.121-125,
Title 24, s.173.)

§ 121. Policy

Freedom of access to public documents is a basic right of citizenship. Therefore, it is the policy of the state of Louisiana that state public documents shall be made available to the public. In order to obtain maximum efficient distribution and maximum availability of these documents, a depository system is hereby established.

Amended by Acts 1981, No. 906, § 1.

§ 121.1. Definitions

As used in this Chapter, the following terms shall have the following meanings unless the context clearly indicates otherwise:

(1) "Public document" means informational matter, for public distribution regardless of format, method of reproduction, source, or copyright, originating in or produced with the imprint of, by the authority of, or at the total or partial expense of, any state agency. Correspondence and inter-office or intra-office memoranda and records of an archival nature are excluded.

(2) "State agency" means an office, department, board, bureau, commission, council, institution, college or university, division, officer, or other person or group within the executive, judicial, or legislative branch of state government that is authorized to exercise or that exercises any of the functions of the government of the state of Louisiana.

(3) "Depository" means an institution which contracts with the state librarian to participate in the public document depository system.

Added by Acts 1981, No. 906, § 1.

§ 122. Establishment of depositories; administration of depository system; documents; rules and regulations

A. The state librarian shall be responsible for establishing a system of depositories for state public documents, and for the deposit and distribution of state public documents to the depositories.

B. The state librarian shall adopt and promulgate rules and regulations, and enter into agreements with depositories, as necessary to implement the provisions of this Chapter.

Amended by Acts 1981, No. 906, § 1.

§ 123. Recorder of documents; duties

A. The provisions of this Chapter shall be implemented and administered, under the supervision of the state librarian, by the recorder of documents, who shall be a graduate of an accredited school of library science.

B. Duties of the recorder of documents include:

(1) Preparation and distribution of the official bibliography of state documents.

(2) Prompt transmission of public documents received from state agencies to the depositories.

(3) Provision of bibliographical and practical assistance to the depositories in maintaining, developing, classifying, and utilizing their collections.

C. In addition, the recorder of documents may send copies of state documents to the office of state archives and to selected national and foreign libraries, including the Library of Congress.

Amended by Acts 1981, No. 906, § 1.

§ 124. Public documents of state agencies

A. Each state agency shall furnish to the recorder of documents, upon release, copies of public documents to meet the needs of the depository system.

B. Each state agency shall designate a liaison officer and shall notify the recorder of documents of the appointment.

C. The liaison officer shall submit semiannually to the recorder of documents a complete list of his agency's public documents.

D. The liaison officer shall insure the delivery of these documents as issued.

Amended by Acts 1981, No. 906, § 1.

§ 124.1. Depositories

A. Louisiana State Library and Louisiana State University Library at Baton Rouge are hereby designated complete public document depositories. Other Louisiana libraries may request complete public document depository status.

B. Libraries, including those in state agencies and other institutions, may contract with the state librarian to become depositories.

C. Each depository shall agree to make state documents accessible to the public, to render free service in their use, and to abide by the rules and regulations promulgated by the state librarian. Extended noncompliance with the contract provisions shall result in the loss of depository status.

Added by Acts 1981, No. 906, § 1.

§ 125. Documents to be supplied to law library of state university; exchanges

The secretary of state shall deliver to the law library of Louisiana State University and Agricultural and Mechanical College the following public documents, not later than ninety days after they are printed from time to time: one hundred copies of the acts of the legislature, fifty copies of the journals of each house of the legislature, and fifty copies of the proceedings of any constitutional convention.

In any contract which the Supreme Court may make for the printing of the supreme court reports, provision shall be made that the printer thereof shall deliver to the law library of Louisiana State University and Agricultural and Mechanical College without charge, fifty copies of each volume thereof within a reasonable time after printing.

The law library of the Louisiana State University and Agricultural and Mechanical College shall exchange the public documents enumerated in this Section for publications relating to government useful to students of public law and to public officials, and shall catalogue such material so as to make it serviceable to members of the legislature.

Acts 1916, No. 147, §§ 1, 2.

§ 173. Distribution of current acts and journals

A. In addition to the distribution authorized in R.S. 25:125, the secretary of state shall make the following distribution of the current acts and journals of the legislature:

* * *

(9) To the Louisiana State Library and to the Huey P. Long Memorial Library, three copies each of the acts and journals, for the use of those libraries; and to the Law Library of Louisiana at New Orleans, seventy copies of the acts to be used by it for library purposes and exchange purposes with state libraries of other states or other departments or agencies thereof;

Amended by Acts 1950, No. 367, § 1; Acts 1956, No. 360, § 1; Acts 1958, No. 285, § 1; Acts 1960, No. 17, § 1.

ARCHIVES AND RECORDS COMMISSION

(West's Louisiana Statutes Annotated, 1982, Title 44, s.404-429, Title 44, s.25.127.)

§ 404. Powers and duties

The commission shall; enforce the provisions of this Chapter; promulgate rules and regulations, not inconsistent with law establishing:

(a) procedures for the compiling and submitting to the archives and records service hereinafter created of lists and schedules of public records proposed for disposal.

(b) procedures for the disposal of public records authorized for disposal, and

(c) standards for the reproduction of public records by photographic or microphotographic process; publish the rules and regulations adopted under authority of this Chapter at least once in each biennium in the official journal, and make copies of such rules and regulations available to all officials concerned with this Chapter.

It is intended that such rules and regulations be worked out in cooperation with the various state agencies and the governing authorities of the various subdivisions of the state. Such rules and regulations when approved by the commission shall be binding on all the agencies of the state and its subdivisions. The director may employ such personnel, purchase such equipment, and provide such facilities as may be required in the execution of the powers and duties imposed upon the commission. The commission shall perform any acts deemed necessary, legal and proper to carry out the duties and responsibilities imposed upon it pursuant to the authority granted herein. Acts 1956, No. 337, § 4.

§ 405. Counsel

The attorney general and the various district attorneys in their respective districts shall represent the archives and records commission in all legal proceedings connected herewith. Acts 1956, No. 337, § 5.

§ 406. Archives and records service; director and associate; compensation

There is hereby created an archives and records service. A professionally qualified director and associate director of the archives and records service shall be appointed by the commission and may receive such compensation for their services as is determined and fixed by the commission. The director shall have overall administrative responsibility for the archives and records service. Acts 1956, No. 337, § 6.

§ 407. Records management; reports

The director of the archives and records service is authorized to make continuing surveys of government records and records management and disposal practices and obtain reports thereon from the state and local governmental agencies; to promote, in cooperation with the various state and local governmental agencies, improved records management practices and controls in such agencies, including the central storage or disposition of records not needed by such agencies for their current use; and to report to the legislature and to the governor from time to time on such activities. At least one such report shall be made in each biennium. Acts 1956, No. 337, § 7.

§ 408. Archives and records center building; custody and control

The director of the archives and records service shall have custody and control of a state archives and records center building and its contents, and through the Louisiana State Building Authority or its successors shall have authority to design, build, purchase, lease, maintain, operate, protect, and improve buildings or facilities used for the storage of non-current records of state and local agencies of Louisiana. Acts 1956, No. 337, § 8.

§ 409. Appointment of advisory groups

The director of the archives and records service may from time to time appoint advisory groups to more effectively obtain the best professional thinking of the bar, historians, political scientists, accountants, genealogists, patriotic groups, associations of public officials, et cetera, on the steps to be taken with regard to any particular group or type of records. Acts 1956, No. 337, § 9.

§ 410. Records management programs; policies and principles

The director of the archives and records service shall, with due regard to the program activities of the state and local agencies concerned, prescribe the policies and principles to be followed by state and local governmental agencies in the conduct of their records management programs, and make provision for the economical and efficient management of records by state and local governmental agencies: by analyzing, developing, promoting, and coordinating standards, procedures, and techniques, designed to improve the management of records, to insure the maintenance and security of records deemed appropriate for preservation, and to facilitate the segregation and disposal of records of temporary value; and by promoting the efficient and economical utilization of space, equipment, and supplies needed for the purpose of creating, maintaining, storing, and servicing records. Acts 1956, No. 337, § 10.

§ 411. Selective retention of records; actions for recovery of records

The director of the archives and records service shall establish standards for the selective retention of records of continuing value, and assist state and local agencies in applying such standards to records in their custody. He shall notify the head of any such agency of any actual, impending, or threatening unlawful removal, defacing, alteration, or destruction of records in the custody of such agency that shall come to his attention, and assist the head of such agency in initiating action through the attorney general for the recovery of such records as shall have been unlawfully removed and for such other redress as may be provided by law. Acts 1956, No. 337, § 11.

§ 412. Surveys and Inspections

The director of the archives and records service is authorized to inspect or survey the records of any state or local agency, as well as to make surveys of records management and records disposal practices in such agencies, and he shall be given full cooperation of officials and employees of agencies in such inspection and surveys; provided, that records, the use of which is restricted by or pursuant to law or for reasons of security or the public interest, shall be inspected or surveyed only in accordance with law, or the rules and regulations of the archives and records commission. Acts 1956, No. 337, § 12.

§ 413. Interim records centers; microfilming, photostating and repair

The director of the archives and records service is authorized to establish an interim records center or centers for the storage, processing, and servicing of records of state and local governmental agencies pending their deposit in the state archives and records center or their disposition in any other manner authorized by law; and to establish, maintain and operate centralized microfilming, photostating, indexing, decontamination and lamination and any other records repair and rehabilitation services for state and local agencies. Acts 1956, No. 337. § 13.

§ 414. Transfer of records

Subject to applicable provisions of law, the director of the archives and records service shall recommend and the archives and records commission promulgate rules and regulations governing the transfer of records from the custody of one agency of the state or its subdivisions to that of another. Acts 1956, No. 337, § 14.

§ 415. Retention of records for longer periods than scheduled

The director of the archives and records service may empower any state or local agency, upon the submission of evidence of the need therefor, to retain records for a longer period than that specified in any approved disposal schedule, or by law, but he shall report all such actions to the archives and records commission at its next meeting for approval or disapproval. Acts 1956, No. 337, § 15.

§ 416. Deposit of records of historical value; transfer of deposited records to public or educational institutions

The director of the archives and records service whenever it appears to him to be in the public interest is authorized: to accept for deposit in the state archives and records center the records of any state or local agency or of the legislature, that are determined by the director to have sufficient historical or other value to warrant their continued preservation by the state government of Louisiana; to direct and effect the transfer to the archives and records service of any records that have been in existence for more than fifty years and that are determined by the director to have sufficient historical or other value to warrant their continued preservation by the state, unless the head of the state or local agency which has custody of them certify in writing to the director that they must be retained in his custody for use in the conduct of the regular current business of the said agency; to direct and effect, with the approval of the head of the originating agency (or its successor, if any) the transfer of records deposited (or approved for deposit) in the state archives and records center to public or educational institutions for special research or exhibit purposes; provided that title to such records shall remain vested in the state of Louisiana unless otherwise authorized by law; and provided further such records may be recalled after reasonable notice in writing; to direct and effect the transfer of materials from private sources authorized to be received by the state archives and records center by the provisions of R.S. 44:420. Acts 1956, No. 337, § 16.

§ 417. Responsibility for custody, use and withdrawal of records

The director shall be responsible for the custody, use, and withdrawal of records transferred to him; provided that whenever any records, the use of which is subject to statutory limitation and restrictions are so transferred, then he shall enforce such limitations and restrictions shall not remain in force or effect after the records have been in existence for fifty years. Acts 1956, No. 337, § 17.

§ 418. Preservation, repair, exhibition of records; finding aids

The director shall make provisions for the preservation, management, repair and rehabilitation, duplication and reproduction, description, and exhibition of records or related documentary material transferred to him as may be needful or appropriate, including the preparation and duplication of inventories, indexes, catalogs, and other finding aids or guides facilitating their use. Acts 1956, No. 337, § 18.

§ 419. Servicing of records

The director shall make such provision and maintain such facilities as he deems necessary or desirable for servicing records in his custody that are not exempt from examination by statutory provisions or other restrictions. Acts 1956, No. 337, § 19.

§ 420. Deposit of papers and other historical materials of officials and individuals

The director is authorized, whenever he deems it to be in the public interest, to accept for deposit: the papers and other historical materials of any governor of the state of Louisiana, or of any other official or former official of the state and its subdivisions, and other papers relating to and contemporary with any governor or former governor of Louisiana, subject to restrictions agreeable to the archives and records commission and the donor; documents, including motion picture films, still pictures, sound recordings, maps, and papers, from private sources that are appropriate for preservation by the state government as evidence of its organization, functions, policies, and transactions or those of its subdivisions. Acts 1956, No. 337, § 20.

§ 421. Fees for copies or reproductions

The director may charge a fee not in excess of 10 per centum above the costs or expenses for making or authenticating copies or reproductions of materials transferred to his custody. All such fees shall be paid into a revolving fund for the continuation of such services on as selfsustaining a basis as possible. There shall be no charge for making or authenticating copies or reproductions of such materials for official use by the government of the state of Louisiana; provided, that reimbursement may be accepted to cover the cost of furnishing such copies or reproductions that could not otherwise be furnished. Acts 1956, No. 337, § 21.

§ 422. Agency heads to make and preserve records

The head of each agency of the state and its subdivisions shall cause to be made and preserved records containing adequate and proper documentation of the organization functions, policies, decisions, procedures, and essential transactions of the agency and designed to furnish information necessary to protect the legal and financial rights of the government and of persons directly affected by the agency's activities. Acts 1956, No. 337, § 22.

§ 423. Agency heads to maintain active records management programs

The head of each agency of the state and its subdivisions shall establish and maintain an active, continuing program for the economical and efficient management of the records of the agency. Such program shall provide for: effective controls over the creation, maintenance, and use of records in the conduct of current business; cooperation with the archives and records service in applying standards, procedures, and techniques designed to improve the management of records, promote the maintenance and security of records deemed appropriate for preservation, and facilitate the segregation and disposal of records of temporary value; compliance with the provisions of this Chapter and the rules and regulations of the archives and records commission. Acts 1956, No. 337, § 23.

§ 424. Use of records center by state and subdivisions

Whenever the head of an agency of the state or its subdivisions determines that substantial economics or increased operating efficiency can be effected thereby, he shall provide for the storage, processing and servicing of records that are appropriate therefor in the records center maintained and operated by the archives and records service or, when approved by the director in such location maintained and operated by the head of such agency. Acts 1956, No. 337, § 24.

§ 425. Certification to facts based on records transferred to archives

Any official who is authorized to certify to facts on the basis of records in his custody is authorized to certify to facts on the basis of records that have been transferred by him or his predecessors to the archives and records service, further provided, that any fee due any official of the state or its subdivisions shall not be eliminated by this Chapter. Acts 1956, No. 337, § 25.

§ 426. Safeguards against removal or loss of records

The head of each agency of the state or its subdivisions shall establish such safeguards against removal or loss of records as he shall deem necessary and as may be required by rules and regulations issued under authority of this Chapter. Such safeguards shall include making it known to all officials and employees of the agency that no records are to be alienated or destroyed except in accordance with law, and calling their attention to the penalties provided by law for the unlawful removal or destruction of records. Acts 1956, No. 337, § 26.

§ 427. Notification of actual or threatened unlawful removal or destruction

The head of each agency of the state or any of its subdivisions shall notify the director of the archives and records service of any actual, impending, or threatened unlawful removal, defacing, alteration or destruction of records in the custody of the agency that shall come to his attention and with the assistance of the director of the archives and records service shall initiate action through the attorney general for recovery. Acts 1956, No. 337, § 27.

§ 428. Authority of state auditor and others not limited

Nothing in this Chapter shall be construed as limiting the authority of the state auditor, or other officers charged with prescribing accounting systems, forms, or procedures or of lessening the responsibility of collecting and disbursing officers for rendering of their accounts for settlement. Acts 1956, No. 337, § 28.

§ 429. Transfer of non-current legislative records to archives

The secretary of the senate and the clerk of the house of representatives shall, unless otherwise directed by the senate or house of representatives obtain at the close of each session of the legislature all of the non-current records of the legislature and of each committee thereof and transfer them to the state archives and records center for preservation. Acts 1956, No. 337, § 29.

§ 127. State archives and records commission and state archives and records service merged and consolidated into the office of the secretary of state

A. In order to merge and consolidate into one department, under authority of Section 32 of Article III of the Constitution of 1921, the executive and administrative offices of the state of Louisiana whose duties and functions are of a similar nature or character, the State Archives and Records Commission and the State Archives and Records Service as created and provided for by the constitution and laws of Louisiana is hereby merged and consolidated into the office of the secretary of state, which hereafter shall exercise the administrative functions of the state now or hereafter authorized to be exercised by the constitution and laws in relation to the administration, management and operation of the functions, programs and facilities of the State Archives and Records Commission and the State Archives and Records Service.

B.   By authority of Section 32 of Article III of the Constitution of 1921, the State Archives and Records Commission and the State Archives and Records Service is hereby transferred to the secretary of state, and all of the functions, programs and operations of every kind of the State Archives and Records Commission and the State Archives and Records Service hereafter shall be exercised and performed by the secretary of state.

C.   Under the transfer of functions provided for by this section, any pending or unfinished business of the commission and service shall be taken over and be completed by the secretary of state with the same power and authority as was exercised by the commission and director of the State Archives and Records Service. The secretary of state shall be the successor in every way to the commission and service, and every act done in the exercise of such functions by the secretary of state shall be deemed to have the same force and effect under any provisions of the constitution and laws in effect on the effective date of this section, as if done by the office from which such functions are transferred.

D.   Whenever the commission or service is referred to or designated by the constitution or by any law or contract or other document, such reference or designation hereafter shall be deemed to apply to the secretary of state, and the legislature hereby specifically states that the provisions of this Section are in no way and to no extent intended to, nor shall they be construed in any manner which will impair the contractual obligations of the commission or service heretofore existing, or of the state of Louisiana.

E.   All books, papers, records, money, choses in action and other property heretofore possessed, controlled or used by the commission or service in the exercise of functions hereby transferred are hereby transferred to the secretary of state.

F.   All employees heretofore engaged in the performance of duties, in the State Archives and Records Service, in the exercise of functions transferred by this section to the secretary of state shall be transferred with such functions to the office of secretary of state to the full extent practicable to carry out the purposes of this Section and shall, so far as practicable, continue to perform the duties heretofore performed, subject to the state civil service law.

G.   The merger and consolidation of offices and functions herein provided shall be effective on and after January 1, 1973; provided, however, that to effect an orderly transfer of such offices and functions the following procedure shall be effected, to wit:

(1) Not later than September 15, 1972, the State Archives and Records Commission, together with the director of the State Archives and Records Service, herein merged and consolidated shall transmit to the governor, division of administration and the secretary of state such information as may be necessary to effect plans for such consolidation and merger of offices as may be prescribed by the commissioner of administration, including but not limited to the following: (a) a complete list of all personnel, their salaries and job descriptions; (b) a complete inventory of all furniture, fixtures and equipment of every kind and description whatsover; (c) all financial and bookkeeping records of the commission and service; (d) a summary of all floor space in state office buildings then being utilized.

(2) The secretary of state shall prepare and transmit to the governor and division of administration a "transition plan for consolidation" not later than November 1, 1972. This plan shall include a detailed procedure for the consolidation and merger of offices and functions, including the transfer and utilization of jobs, personnel, funds, office space and equipment, and such other information as the governor may require.

H.   All monies appropriated to, dedicated to or otherwise realized through any source whatsoever by the State Archives and Records Commission and the State Archives and Records Service herein being merged and consolidated, shall be, upon the effective date of consolidation, transferred to the secretary of state and thereafter the disbursement of and accountability for said funds shall be the responsibility of the secretary of state.

Added by Acts 1972, No. 691, § 1.

MUNICIPAL LIBRARIES
(West's Louisiana Statutes Annotated, 1982, Title 25, s.211-221.)

§ 211.   Establishment by parishes or municipalities

The governing authority of any parish or municipal corporation, the City of New Orleans and Parish of Orleans excepted, may of its own initiative create, establish, equip, maintain, operate and support a public library in such parish or municipality and shall create, establish, equip, maintain, operate and support such a public library when not less than twenty-five per cent of the duly qualified property taxpayers resident in such parish or municipality shall petition the governing authority thereof to establish such a public library for such parish or municipality. Provided that two or more parishes may join in the establishment of a public library to be supported and maintained by them jointly in the proportions as may be determined by the police juries of the respective parishes or other governing authority; and provided that a parish and one or more municipal corporations may jointly establish, maintain and operate a public library; and provided also one parish or municipality may contract with another parish or municipality to furnish library service upon such terms and conditions and for such considerations as the governing authorities concerned may stipulate and agree by written contract pursuant to ordinances duly passed by them.   Acts 1926, No. 36, § 1.

§ 212.   Ordinances creating library; place of establishment; branch libraries

A public library under this Part shall be created by an ordinance regularly passed and adopted by the police jury of the parish, or other governing authority thereof, and the municipal council or other governing authority of such municipality. All parish libraries shall be established at the parish seat and the municipal libraries within the corporate limits of the municipality so creating and establishing them. Provided that branch libraries may be established and maintained by either a parish or municipal library as the public demands require.   Acts 1926, No. 36, § 2.

§ 213.   Funds for acquiring site or construction of buildings; anticipation of revenues; bond issues; special tax

For the purpose of acquiring sites or erecting buildings thereon or additions thereto including furniture, fixtures and equipment for public libraries, the governing authority of the parish or municipality as the case may be, may either:

(1) Anticipate the revenues of the parish or municipality and issue bonds or certificates based thereon, as provided by law; or

(2) Issue negotiable bonds and thereafter levy and collect taxes to pay and retire the same, if so authorized by the vote of the property taxpayers voting at an election to be called and held for that purpose in the manner provided by law; or

(3) Levy a special tax, under the provisions of Article X, Section 10 of the Constitution of 1921, as amended.

Notwithstanding any other provision of law to the contrary, the St. Charles Parish Police Jury and the St. John the Baptist Parish Police Jury may authorize the St. Charles Parish library board and the St. John the Baptist Parish library board to use a portion of the millage dedicated to them for maintenance and support of the public library for any of the purposes set forth in this Section.

Amended by Acts 1954, No. 92, § 1; Acts 1974, No. 507, § 1.

§ 214. Board of control; members; appointment and terms of office

A. The governing authority of the municipality shall, in the ordinance creating a public library, name and appoint five citizens of the municipality as a board of control for such public library to serve for terms of one, two, three, four, and five years, the successors of whom shall each be appointed for a term of five years. The mayor of the municipality shall be ex officio, a member of the board of control of such public library, provided however that he shall have the right to designate another member of the governing authority of the municipality to serve in his place and stead on the board of control of such public library.

B. The governing authority of the parish shall, in the ordinance creating a public library, name and appoint, at its option, not less than five citizens nor more than seven citizens of the parish as a board of control for such parish library to serve for terms of one, two, three, four, and five years, the successors of whom shall each be appointed for a term of five years. The president of the police jury shall be ex officio, a member of the board of control for such public library, provided however that the president of the police jury shall have the right to designate another member of the governing authority of the parish to serve in his place and stead on the board of control of such public library.

C. The provisions of this Section shall not apply to the parish of Orleans. Amended by Acts 1978, No. 368, § 1.

§ 215. Duties and powers of board; employment of librarian, assistants, etc.

A. The board of control shall meet and organize immediately after their appointment and annually thereafter and elect a president, vice-president, secretary, and treasurer, whose duties shall be those customarily exercised by such officers. The board of control shall have authority to establish rules and regulations for its own government and that of the library not inconsistent with law; to elect and employ a librarian, and, upon the recommendation and approval of the latter, to employ assistant librarians and other employees and fix their salaries and compensation; provided that no contract of employment shall be made for a longer period than four years nor with any person as head librarian who has not been certified by the State Board of Library Examiners as provided in R.S. 25:222. The head librarian may be appointed or elected secretary of the board of control.

B. The administration of and accounting functions of the St. John the Baptist Parish Library Fund are hereby transferred from the St. John the Baptist Police Jury to the St. John the Baptist Parish Library Board of Control, effective February 1, 1979. Amended by Acts 1978, No. 229, § 1.

§ 216. Reports to Louisiana state library, persons required to make

The president of the board of control and the librarian of every public library established and maintained under this Part shall make annual reports to the Louisiana State Library giving such statistics and other information as may be required by it, such reports to be made at such time and on such blanks or forms as the Louisiana State Library may require and provide. The governing authority of the parish or municipality establishing the public library and creating the board of control may also require reports annually or quarterly or both of the board or its president.   Acts 1926, No. 36, § 6.

§ 217. Funds for maintenance and support; special taxes; libraries jointly established; sharing of expenses; payment for library service

The governing authority of a parish or municipality establishing a library under the provisions of this Part may, on its own initiative and shall, when requested by a petition of not less than twenty-five per cent of the duly qualified property taxpayers resident, submit to the property taxpayers a proposition to vote a special tax within the limitations as to millage and years, as provided by the constitution and laws of this state for the maintenance and support of such public library and its branches, which tax, if voted, shall be levied and assessed annually as authorized by the voters and collected and used exclusively for the support and maintenance of the public library. In all cases where a public library is jointly established and maintained, each parish and municipal corporation concerned shall contribute its pro rata or equitable share of the costs and expense and each shall be as nearly as possible equally represented on the board of control, the presiding officer of each governing authority being an ex-officio member thereof. Parishes or municipalities receiving library service from another parish or municipality may contract and pay for the same either out of general funds or out of special funds voted, levied and collected for the purpose, and the parish or municipality receiving such funds for such service shall use and expend the funds for library purposes only.   Acts 1926, No. 36, § 7.

§ 218. Costs of parish library, how borne; exclusion of municipalities within parish

The costs of establishing and maintaining a parish public library shall be borne by the entire parish including the incorporated towns therein and all taxes levied and assessed, whether general or special, for the establishment, support and maintenance of such parish public library shall be borne proportionately by all of the property of the parish including that within incorporated municipalities, unless in the ordinance creating the parish public library the municipality is expressly excluded because of its exemption from parochial taxation or because such municipality owns, maintains and operates its own public library, and in such cases will not be entitled to library service, except upon such terms and conditions as may be agreed upon as provided in R.S. 25:211. Nor shall the residents or taxpayers of such excluded municipality be counted in making up the number of petitioners required in R.S. 25:211 and 25:217.   Acts 1926, No. 36, § 8.

§ 219. Municipal libraries, consolidation with parish library; assumption of trusts, etc., by parish

Municipalities already owning and maintaining public libraries may consolidate the same with the parish public library, either the head library, if located in the parish seat, or a branch library, if located elsewhere in the parish, upon such terms and conditions as may be agreed upon between the governing authorities of the parish and municipality affected by ordinances regularly and legally passed and adopted evidencing such a merger and consolidation; provided that in all cases where the municipality has bound or obligated itself to maintain and support the public library, in order to keep inviolate any trust, gift or bequest for such purposes, the parish into which such municipal library is merged shall assume and become responsible for the faithful performance of the obligation and the execution of the trust assumed by the municipality.   Acts 1926, No. 36, § 9.

§ 220. Payment of maintenance costs and other expenses

The expenses or costs of maintenance of a public library established under this Part, including the salaries of librarian, assistants, and other employees as well as all other incidental expenses, shall be paid monthly by the governing authority establishing the library, upon the approval of such expenses and maintenance costs by the board of control of such library, out of the funds specially budgeted from the general fund for library purposes and, in default thereof, out of the special taxes voted, levied and collected by the governing authority for the library's support and maintenance. The board of control may delegate to the president or one of its members the duty of approving such monthly expenses and maintenance costs.

Amended by Acts 1958, No. 425, § 1.

§ 221. Gifts and contributions, acceptance by board of control

The board of control of every public library created and maintained under the provisions of this Part may receive and accept unconditional gifts, donations and contributions from individuals and corporations, but no gifts or donations conditionally made shall be accepted without the approval of the governing authority of the parish or municipality creating the public library. All moneys, property, and other things of value given or contributed to a public library shall be turned over to the treasurer of the board of control and shall be expended or invested by the librarian with the approval of the board of control.   Acts 1926, No. 36, § 11.

LAW LIBRARIES
General Provisions
(West's Louisiana Statutes Annotated, 1982, Title 25, s.261-262.)

§ 261.   Establishment and maintenance by parishes

The various parishes may respectively equip and maintain a law library for the use and benefit of the parish judges and officials.

Acts 1942, No. 237, § 1.

§ 262.   Certification by judge of books to be purchased or subscribed for

The judge or judges of the district court of the parish shall certify to the police jury desiring to purchase and maintain a law library for their parish, a list of the books or volumes or sets of books to be purchased or subscribed for; after this list has been certified the police jury shall be authorized to purchase or subscribe for the books or sets of books so certified.   Acts 1942, No. 237, § 2.

Law Library of Louisiana
(West's Louisiana Statutes Annotated, 1982, Title 25, s.91, 94, 95,
Title 43, s.22.)

§ 91.   Control and supervision

The Law Library of Louisiana domiciled in the Parish of Orleans and located in the Civil Courts Building in the City of New Orleans shall be under the direct control and supervision of the Supreme Court of Louisiana which is authorized, under such rules as it may adopt, to prescribe the necessary regulations concerning the maintenance, upkeep, and operation thereof, as well as necessary regulations and restrictions relative to the services to be rendered thereby.

Added by Acts 1954, No. 409, § 1.

§ 94.   Ownership of books

The books, periodicals, manuscripts or other papers in the possession of the Law Library of Louisiana or which may be subsequently acquired by it shall be the property of the state of Louisiana.

Added by Acts 1954, No. 409, § 1.

§ 95.   Appropriations

All appropriations made by the legislature to the Law Library of

Louisiana, whether general or special, shall be drawn on the warrant of the Chief Justice of the Supreme Court or any person designated by him.

Added by Acts 1954, No. 409, § 1.

§ 22. Sale of acts; price

The secretary of state shall retain and keep in the state archives at all times one printed copy and one microfilm copy of the acts of the legislature delivered to him under the provisions of R.S. 43:19, and, after making the distributions authorized by R.S. 24:173 and R.S. 25:125. The secretary of state shall collect from any person or public or private entity to which he distributes a copy or copies of the acts of the legislature, except any state agency or official of the state to which he is required by law to distribute copies including members of the legislature, a fee equal to the cost, plus ten percent of such cost, of printing and delivery thereof. The proceeds from collection of such fees shall be remitted by the secretary of state to the Supreme Court of Louisiana for the purchase of law books for the Law Library of Louisiana at New Orleans.

Amended by Acts 1977, No. 567, § 1, eff. July 15, 1977.

Louisiana State University Law Library

(West's Louisiana Statutes Annotated, 1982, Title 33, s.4682-4686.)

§ 4682. Preservation of duplicate file of transcripts of cases finally disposed of by Supreme Court; designation of Louisiana State University Law Library as depository

For the purpose of preserving a duplicate file of one of the triplicate copies of each transcript of appeal of cases finally disposed of by the Supreme Court, and for the further purpose of providing a duplicate file of each of the briefs lodged in the Supreme Court, the Louisiana State University Law Library is hereby designated as a depository to receive these documents from the clerk of the Supreme Court of Louisiana and to catalogue, index, file and preserve the documents.   Acts 1938, No. 167, § 1.

§ 4683. Same; delivery to depository of copy of brief and transcript; recall

The clerk of the supreme court is directed to deliver to the Law Library of the Louisiana State University, the depository designated in R.S. 13:4682, a copy of each brief filed in the supreme court, and to deliver to this depository a copy of the transcript when each case is finally disposed of by the supreme court. Any records so deposited may be recalled at pleasure by requisition of the chief justice, any associate justice or by the clerk of the supreme court. Acts 1938, No. 167, § 2.

§ 4684. Same; clerk to turn over duplicate copies to law library

The clerk of the supreme court is further directed to turn over to the Law Library of the Louisiana State University, a depository, any duplicate copies of each transcript and brief in the files of the supreme court and the depository shall catalogue, index and preserve the documents.   Acts 1938, No. 167, § 3.

§ 4685.   Construction of R.S. 13:4682 through 13:4685; intention

Nothing herein contained shall be so construed as to hamper the supreme court in the performance of its judicial functions, it being the sole purpose and intention of R.S. 13:4682 through 13:4685 to provide for the preservation of duplicate records no longer necessary for the business of the court.   Acts 1938, No. 167, § 4.

§ 4686.   Preservation of documents and records of the courts of appeal

The Louisiana State University Law Library is hereby designated as a depository to receive, catalog, index, file and preserve such documents, records and books as may be transmitted by the clerks of the several courts of appeal in accordance with the direction and orders of the respective courts. Added Acts 1960, No. 37, § 1.

Huey P. Long Memorial Law Library
(West's Louisiana Statutes Annotated, 1982, Title 25, s.61-67.)

§ 61.   Definitions
As used in this Part, the following terms shall have the following meanings:
   (1) "Board" means the Huey P. Long Memorial Law Library Board.
   (2) "Library" means the Huey P. Long Memorial Law Library.
Acts 1981, No. 730, § 1, eff. July 1, 1981.

§ 62.   Establishment, designation, and location
There shall be a library known as the Huey P. Long Memorial Law Library located in the state capitol building.
Acts 1981, No. 730. § 1, eff. July 1, 1981.

§ 63.   Administration
The library shall be administered through the state librarian in accordance with this Part and in accordance with the rules and regulations established by the Huey P. Long Memorial Law Library Board as authorized by this Part.
Acts 1981, No. 730, § 1, eff. July 1, 1981.

§ 64.   Primary use
The library shall be for the primary use of the Senate, the House of Representatives, the governor, and the attorney general, and their respective agencies and staffs.
Acts 1981, No. 730, § 1, eff. July 1, 1981.

§ 65.   Librarian and other library personnel
A. The state librarian shall employ a librarian who has been granted a master of library science degree from a college or university accredited by

the American Library Association and other personnel for the proper maintenance, upkeep, operation, and service of the library. All library personnel shall be in the classified state civil service.

B. Salaries of library personnel shall be funded through legislative appropriation to the office of the state library in the Department of Culture, Recreation and Tourism.

Acts 1981, No. 730, § 1, eff. July 1, 1981.

§ 66. Board; members, duties, authority

A. The Huey P. Long Memorial Law Library Board is hereby established. The board shall be composed of the attorney general, the president of the Senate, and the speaker of the House of Representatives, or their respective designees.

B. The board shall establish rules and regulations, not inconsistent with law, providing for the maintenance, upkeep, operation, and service of the library, including but not limited to, library acquisitions and hours of operation, and may from time to time alter and amend the same.

C. The board may accept donations to the library.

Acts 1981, No. 730, § 1, eff. July 1, 1981.

§ 67. Expenses of the library

Expenses of the library, other than for personnel, shall be incurred within the limits of funds provided by the Senate and the House of Representatives or otherwise made available to the board for such purposes.

Acts 1981, No. 730, § 1, eff. July 1, 1981.

UNION CATALOG OF LOUISIANA ITEMS

(West's Louisiana Statutes Annotated, 1982, Title 25, s.451-455.)

§ 451. Catalog established

There shall be established a Union Catalog of Louisiana Items (exclusive of state documents and state archives) to be found in all public libraries (state, parish and municipal) in the libraries of Louisiana State University and Agricultural and Mechanical College, in the libraries of the higher institutions of learning subject to the direct supervision of the state board of education, and in all other libraries which may be willing to participate.

Acts 1956, No. 361, § 1.

§ 452. Staff

The staff shall consist of an editor of the Union Catalog, who shall preferably be a graduate librarian with considerable cataloging experience, and necessary clerical assistants, to be appointed by the board of commissioners of the Louisiana State Library.

Acts 1956, No. 361, § 2.

§ 453. Boards to cooperate with libraries

The board of supervisors of Louisiana State University, the state board of education and the board of commissioners of the Louisiana State Library shall cooperate in establishing and setting up the Union Catalog of Louisiana Items. They shall cooperate with parish li-

braries and other public libraries, with all other libraries which may
be willing to participate, and with the Louisiana Library Association
and its Union Catalog Louisiana Items Committee, in this project.

Acts 1956, No. 361, § 3.

§ 454.   Domicile; maintenance and service

The established Union Catalog of Louisiana Items shall be housed
in the Louisiana State Library at Baton Rouge and shall be maintained and serviced by the board of commissioners of Louisiana State
Library.

Acts 1956, No. 361, § 4.

§ 455.   Main entry cards

The board of supervisors of Louisiana State University and Agricultural and Mechanical College, as to the university libraries, the
state board of education, as to the libraries of the higher institutions
of learning under its direction, the Louisiana State Library, all public
libraries (state, parish and municipal), and all other libraries which
may be willing to participate shall send to the Union Catalog of Louisiana Items, at the Louisiana State Library at Baton Rouge, one main
entry card for each Louisiana item added subsequently to each of
their respective libraries after the establishment of the Union Catalog.

Acts 1956, No. 361, § 5.

Louisiana library laws are reprinted from WEST'S LOU-
ISIANA STATUTES ANNOTATED published by West Publishing Co., St. Paul, Minnesota.

MAINE

STATE LIBRARY

(Maine Revised Statutes Annotated, 1982, Title 27, s.1-6,
31, 32, 34, 36-38.)

§ 1. Salary; duties

The Maine State Library shall be under the management and supervision of a State Librarian, as heretofore appointed, who shall make such rules and regulations as are necessary for the proper management of the library and the safety of its contents. The librarian shall receive such salary as shall be set by the Governor.

The librarian may employ, subject to the Personnel Law and the approval of the Commissioner of Educational and Cultural Services, a deputy state librarian, and such assistants as the business of the office may require.

1975, c. 771, § 290, eff. Jan. 4, 1977.

1. Library contents. The State Librarian shall procure and keep in the State Library the following:

A. Histories of this State, its counties and its towns;

B. Histories of all countries;

C. Family histories;

D. Works on the arts and sciences, with special reference to agriculture, forestry, fishing, manufacturers, shipbuilding and road making;

E. Maps, charts, plans, manuscripts and statistical and other publications relating to the financial, social, religious and educational condition of this State and then of the world as fast as the State furnishes the necessary means;

F. Full and complete sets of all the documents printed by the State; and

G. Full and complete sets of the reports of the towns, cities and counties of this State.

2. Exchanges. For the purpose of carrying out this section, the State Librarian may

conduct a system of exchanges with other libraries and institutions of learning.
1979, c. 541, § A, 185, eff. June 22, 1979.

§ 3.   Books lent

Under such rules and regulations as the State Librarian may prescribe, books and documents may be lent to any responsible resident of the State. Such rules and regulations may include the charge for overdue books and documents.

R.S.1954, c. 42, § 4. 1971, c. 127, § 1.

§ 4.   Responsibility for books borrowed

Any person or organization receiving the loan of any books, documents or other material from the Maine State Library shall be responsible for the full value thereof to the librarian, and in case of the loss of or damage to a volume belonging to a set, shall procure a new volume or be responsible for the value of the set. If any person or organization shall neglect or fail to return any books, documents or other material lent to them, or shall return the same in an injured or mutilated condition, after due demand and notice, the librarian may maintain a civil action against such person or organization for the full value thereof. Actions to enforce the liability mentioned in this section may be brought by the librarian in his own name in behalf of the State, and in case of his death or removal, the action shall be prosecuted by his successor.

R.S.1954, c. 42, § 6; 1961, c. 317, § 90.

§ 4–A. Revolving Fund

1. Fund created. There is established within the Maine State Library a revolving fund for use by the library to replace books, documents or other materials that are damaged, lost or unrecoverable for which a charge is made.

2. Price and rates. The State Librarian is authorized to fix the value of library items at current replacement costs plus a reasonable amount incurred in recovering these items.

3. Income. Income received from subsection 2 shall be credited to the revolving fund to be used as a continuing carrying account to carry out the purposes of subsection 1.
1981, c. 496.

§ 5.   Annual report

The State Librarian shall report to the Commissioner of Educational and Cultural Services annually the receipts and expenditures on account of the library, the number of acquisitions during the preceding year, specifying those obtained by purchase, donation and exchange and shall make in such report suggestions in relation to the improvement of the library.

R.S.1954, c. 42, § 14; 1955, c. 185, § 3. 1971, c. 610, § 14.

§ 6. Reports from counties, cities and towns

Town clerks of the several towns, city clerks of the several cities and treasurers of the several counties shall promptly transmit to the librarian of the Maine State Library copies of all printed reports of said towns, cities and counties, including all printed exhibits of town, city and county expenditures.

R.S.1954, c. 42, § 15.

§ 31. Library hours

The State Librarian shall keep the library open at least 35 hours per week. Neither the State Director of Public Improvements nor any of the state employees under his jurisdiction shall admit anyone to the library rooms out of library hours or permit any book to be taken therefrom without the consent of the librarian.

R.S.1954, c. 42, § 3; 1959, c. 363, § 33. 1973, c. 626, § 1.

§ 32. Historical research

As a part of the general duties of his office, the State Librarian shall maintain a section of historical research which shall have charge of all Maine historical work in the library and carry on research work relating to the history of the State.

R.S.1954, c. 42, § 7.

§ 34. Library extension

The State Librarian shall maintain a library development section which shall carry on such activities as are enumerated in sections 36 and 37.

R.S.1954, c. 42, § 9. 1971, c. 127, § 2; 1973, c. 626, § 2.

§ 36. Advice to local libraries; gifts; schools of library instruction

The Maine State Library shall give advice to all school, state, institutional and public libraries, and to all communities in the State which may propose to establish libraries, as to the best means of establishing and administering them, selecting and cataloging books and other details of library management, and may send its employees to aid in organizing such libraries or assist in the improvement of those already established. It shall formulate and present to the Legislature a plan for state-wide library development and it shall be designated as the agency for the administration of said plan and shall be granted the authority to administer said plan on behalf of the State. It may receive gifts

of money, books or other property which may be used or held
in trust for the purpose or purposes given. It may publish lists
and circulars of information and may cooperate with the libraries
and commissions of other states in the publication of documents
in order to secure the most economical administration of its
work. It may conduct courses or schools of library instruction
and hold librarians' institutes in various parts of the State, and
cooperate with others in such schools or institutes. It shall perform such other library service as it may consider for the best
interests of the citizens of the State.

R.S.1954, c. 42, § 11; 1955, c. 185, § 2. 1971, c. 480, § 7; 1973, c.
626, § 3.

§ 37.   Bookmobile service

In furtherance of, and in addition to, the powers given in
section 36, the State Librarian is authorized and empowered to
provide bookmobile service for residents of the State.

R.S.1954, c. 42, § 13. 1973, c. 626, § 4.

§ 38. Compliance with federal law

The State Librarian, with the approval of the Governor, may make any regulation
necessary to enable the State to comply with any law of the United States, heretofore or
hereafter enacted, intended to promote public library services. The Maine State Library
Bureau is the sole agency authorized to develop, submit and administer or supervise the
administration of any state plan required under such law. The Treasurer of State shall be
custodian of any money that may be allotted by the Federal Government for general public
library services.

1975, c. 771, § 291, eff. Jan. 4, 1977; 1981, c. 464, § 28, eff. June 16, 1981.

INTERSTATE LIBRARY COMPACT
(Maine Revised Statutes Annotated, 1982, Title 27, s.141-152,
181-186.)

§ 141.   Policy and purpose—Article I

Because the desire for the services provided by libraries
transcends governmental boundaries and can most effectively be
satisfied by giving such services to communities and people regardless of jurisdictional lines, it is the policy of the states party
to this compact to cooperate and share their responsibilities; to
authorize cooperation and sharing with respect to those types of
library facilities and services which can be more economically or
efficiently developed and maintained on a cooperative basis, and
to authorize cooperation and sharing among localities, states and
others in providing joint or cooperative library services in areas
where the distribution of population or of existing and potential
library resources make the provision of library service on an interstate basis the most effective way of providing adequate and

efficient service.

1963, c. 144.

§ 142. Definitions—Article II

As used in this compact:

"Public library agency" means any unit or agency of local or State Government operating or having power to operate a library.

"Private library agency" means any non-governmental entity which operates or assumes a legal obligation to operate a library.

"Library agreement" means a contract establishing an interstate library district pursuant to this compact or providing for the joint or cooperative furnishing of library services.

1963, c. 144.

§ 143. Interstate library districts—Article III

1. Interstate library districts. Any one or more public library agencies in a party state in cooperation with any public library agency or agencies in one or more other party states may establish and maintain an interstate library district. Subject to this compact and any other laws of the party states which pursuant hereto remain applicable, such district may establish, maintain and operate some or all of the library facilities and services for the area concerned in accordance with the terms of a library agreement therefor. Any private library agency or agencies within an interstate library district may cooperate therewith, assume duties, responsibilities and obligations thereto, and receive benefits therefrom as provided in any library agreement to which such agency or agencies become party.

2. Joint undertakings. Within an interstate library district, and as provided by a library agreement, the performance of library functions may be undertaken on a joint or cooperative basis or may be undertaken by means of one or more arrangements between or among public or private library agencies for the extension of library privileges to the use of facilities or services operated or rendered by one or more of the individual library agencies.

3. Powers. If a library agreement provides for joint establishment, maintenance or operation of library facilities or services by an interstate library district, such district shall have power to do any one or more of the following in accordance with such library agreement:

A.   Undertake, administer and participate in programs or arrangements for securing, lending or servicing of books and other publications, any other materials suitable to be kept or made available by libraries, library equipment or for the dissemination of information about libraries, the value and significance of particular items therein, and the use thereof;

B.   Accept for any of its purposes under this compact any and all donations, and grants of money, equipment, supplies, materials, and services, conditional or otherwise, from any state or the United States or any subdivision or agency thereof, or interstate agency, or from any institution, person, firm or corporation, and receive, utilize and dispose of the same;

C.   Operate mobile library units or equipment for the purpose of rendering bookmobile service within the district;

D.   Employ professional, technical, clerical and other personnel and fix terms of employment, compensation and other appropriate benefits; and where desirable, provide for the in-service training of such personnel;

E.   Sue and be sued in any court of competent jurisdiction;

F.   Acquire, hold and dispose of any real or personal property or any interest or interests therein as may be appropriate to the rendering of library service;

G.   Construct, maintain and operate a library, including any appropriate branches thereof;

H.   Do such other things as may be incidental to or appropriate for the carrying out of any of the foregoing powers.

1963, c. 144.

§ **144.**   —governing board—**Article IV**

1.   Governing board.   An interstate library district which establishes, maintains or operates any facilities or services in its own right shall have a governing board which shall direct the affairs of the district and act for it in all matters relating to its business. Each participating public library agency in the district shall be represented on the governing board which shall be organized and conduct its business in accordance with provision therefor in the library agreement. But in no event shall a governing board meet less often than twice a year.

2. Representation. Any private library agency or agencies party to a library agreement establishing an interstate library district may be represented on or advise with the governing board of the district in such manner as the library agreement may provide.

1963, c. 144.

§ 145. State library agency cooperation—Article V

Any 2 or more state library agencies of 2 or more of the party states may undertake and conduct joint or cooperative library programs, render joint or cooperative library services, and enter into and perform arrangements for the cooperative or joint acquisition, use, housing and disposition of items or collections of materials which, by reason of expense, rarity, specialized nature, or infrequency of demand therefor would be appropriate for central collection and shared use. Any such programs, services or arrangements may include provision for the exercise on a cooperative or joint basis of any power exercisable by an interstate library district and an agreement embodying any such program, service or arrangement shall contain provisions covering the subjects detailed in Article VI of this compact for interstate library agreements.

1963, c. 144.

§ 146. Library agreements—Article VI

1. Library agreements. In order to provide for any joint or cooperative undertaking pursuant to this compact, public and private library agencies may enter into library agreements. Any agreement executed pursuant to the provisions of this compact shall, as among the parties to the agreement:

A. Detail the specific nature of the services, programs, facilities, arrangements or properties to which it is applicable;

B. Provide for the allocation of costs and other financial responsibilities;

C. Specify the respective rights, duties, obligations and liabilities of the parties;

D. Set forth the terms and conditions for duration, renewal, termination, abrogation, disposal of joint or common property, if any, and all other matters which may be appropriate to the proper effectuation and performance of the agreement.

2. Prohibited powers. No public or private library agency shall undertake to exercise itself, or jointly with any other library agency, by means of a library agreement any power prohibited to such agency by the constitution or statutes of its state.

3.   Effective date of agreement. No library agreement shall become effective until filed with the compact administrator of each state involved, and approved in accordance with Article VII of this compact.

1963, c. 144.

§ 147.   Approval of library agreements—Article VII

1.   Approval of Attorney General. Every library agreement made pursuant to this compact shall, prior to and as a condition precedent to its entry into force, be submitted to the attorney general of each state in which a public library agency party thereto is situated, who shall determine whether the agreement is in proper form and compatible with the laws of his state. The attorneys general shall approve any agreement submitted to them unless they shall find that it does not meet the conditions set forth herein and shall detail in writing addressed to the governing bodies of the public library agencies concerned the specific respects in which the proposed agreement fails to meet the requirements of law.   Failure to disapprove an agreement submitted hereunder within 90 days of its submission shall constitute approval thereof.

2.   Approved by others. In the event that a library agreement made pursuant to this compact shall deal in whole or in part with the provision of services or facilities with regard to which an officer or agency of the State Government has constitutional or statutory powers of control, the agreement shall, as a condition precedent to its entry into force, be submitted to the state officer or agency having such power of control and shall be approved or disapproved by him or it as to all matters within his or its jurisdiction in the same manner and subject to the same requirements governing the action of the attorneys general pursuant to subsection 1 of this article.   This requirement of submission and approval shall be in addition to and not in substitution for the requirement of submission to and approval by the attorneys general.

1963, c. 144.

§ 148.   Other laws applicable—Article VIII

Nothing in this compact or in any library agreement shall be construed to supersede, alter or otherwise impair any obligation imposed on any library by otherwise applicable law, nor to authorize the transfer or disposition of any property held in trust by a library agency in a manner contrary to the terms of such trust.

1963, c. 144.

§ 149.   Appropriations and aid—Article IX

1.   Funds.   Any public library agency party to a library agreement may appropriate funds to the interstate library district established thereby in the same manner and to the same extent as to a library wholly maintained by it and, subject to the laws of the state in which such public library agency is situated, may pledge its credit in support of an interstate library district established by the agreement.

2.   State and federal aid.   Subject to the provisions of the library agreement pursuant to which it functions and the laws of the states in which such district is situated, an interstate library district may claim and receive any state and federal aid which may be available to library agencies.

1963, c. 144.

§ 150.   Compact administrator—Article X

Each state shall designate a compact administrator with whom copies of all library agreements to which his state or any public library agency thereof is party shall be filed. The administrator shall have such other powers as may be conferred upon him by the laws of his state and may consult and cooperate with the compact administrators of other party states and take such steps as may effectuate the purposes of this compact. If the laws of a party state so provide, such state may designate one or more deputy compact administrators in addition to its compact administrator.

1963, c. 144.

§ 151.   Entry into force and withdrawal—Article XI

1.   Force and effect.   This compact shall enter into force and effect immediately upon its enactment into law by any 2 states. Thereafter, it shall enter into force and effect as to any other state upon the enactment thereof by such state.

2.   Withdrawal.   This compact shall continue in force with respect to a party state and remain binding upon such state until 6 months after such state has given notice to each other party state of the repeal thereof. Such withdrawal shall not be construed to relieve any party to a library agreement entered into pursuant to this compact from any obligation of that agreement prior to the end of its duration as provided therein.

1963, c. 144.

§ 152.   Construction and severability—Article XII

This compact shall be liberally construed so as to effectuate the purposes thereof. The provisions of this compact shall be severable and if any phrase, clause, sentence or provision of this compact is declared to be contrary to the constitution of any party state or of the United States or the applicability thereof to any government, agency, person or circumstance is held invalid, the validity of the remainder of this compact and the applicability thereof to any government, agency, person or circumstance shall not be affected thereby. If this compact shall be held contrary to the constitution of any state party thereto, the compact shall remain in full force and effect as to the remaining states and in full force and effect as to the state affected as to all severable matters.

1963, c. 144.

§ 181.   Ratification

The Interstate Library Compact is enacted into law and entered into by this State with all states legally joining therein in the form substantially as provided in this chapter.

1963, c. 144.

§ 182.   Library agreements by municipalities

No municipality of this State shall be party to a library agreement which provides for the construction or maintenance of a library pursuant to Article III, subsection 3, paragraph G, of this compact, nor pledge its credit in support of such a library, or contribute to the capital financing thereof, except after compliance with any laws applicable to such municipalities relating to or governing capital outlays and the pledging of credit.

1963, c. 144.

§ 183.   State library agency

As used in the compact, "state library agency," with reference to this State, means the Maine State Library.

1963, c. 144.

§ 184.   Interstate library district

An interstate library district lying partly within this State may claim and be entitled to receive state aid in support of any of its functions to the same extent and in the same manner as such functions are eligible for support when carried on by entities wholly within this State. For the purposes of computing and apportioning state aid to an interstate library district, this State will consider what portion of the area which lies within this State as an independent entity for the performance of the aided function or functions and compute and apportion the aid accordingly. Subject to any applicable laws of this State, such a district may apply for and be entitled to receive any federal aid for which it may be eligible.

    1963, c. 144.

§ 185.   Compact administrator

    The State Librarian shall be the compact administrator pursuant to Article X of the compact. The deputy state librarian shall be deputy compact administrator pursuant to said article.

    1963, c. 144.

§ 186.   Renunciation

    In the event of withdrawal from the compact, the Governor shall send and receive any notices required by Article XI, subsection 2, of the compact.

    1963, c. 144.

DISTRIBUTION OF PUBLIC DOCUMENTS
(Maine Revised Statutes Annotated, 1982, Title 27, s.66, 69.)

§ 66.   Reports of departments and institutions

    The State Librarian shall distribute reports of the departments and institutions of the State and other books and documents published or purchased by the State in such manner as the law may direct. He may transmit one copy of each published report of each department of the State Government to each library in the State and to the libraries of other states and territories, and make such other and further distribution as in his judgment seems proper. He shall maintain a document room in which shall be stored all department reports and other publications of the State intended for distribution and shall keep an accurate account of all books and documents received.

    R.S.1954, c. 42, § 26.

§ 69.   Purchase and distribution of Maine histories

  1. Purchase. The State Librarian shall purchase at least 25 copies, and may purchase up to 200 copies, of every town history or other book concerning the history of this State that is published in Maine. He shall purchase, within these limits, the number of copies required to meet the distribution requirements of subsection 2.

  2. Distribution. The State Librarian shall retain sufficient copies of each history purchased under subsection 1 for the use of the State Library. The remaining copies shall be distributed without charge to all school, state, institutional and public libraries that request a copy. The State Librarian shall regularly publish and circulate to all these libraries a list of the histories available for distribution.

3. **Surplus.** The State Librarian may sell copies of each history that are not distributed under subsection 2. The State Librarian shall fix the price of sale at the retail price of the history. The Maine State Museum may sell these copies through its museum sales program, provided that the proceeds from the sale of these town histories shall not be used as required under section 89, and the complimentary publications required by that section shall not be required. All proceeds from the sales of these town histories shall be used to pay the costs of the distribution required under subsection 2, and any proceeds beyond these costs shall be used to meet the costs of purchase under subsection 1.

1977, c. 546, § 1.

STATE ARCHIVES
(Maine Revised Statutes Annotated, 1982, Title 5, s.91-97.)

§ 91.   Short title

This chapter shall be known and may be cited as the "Archives and Records Management Law."

1973, c. 625, § 16, eff. July 5, 1973.

§ 92.   Declaration of policy

The Legislature declares that it is the policy of the State to make the operations of State Government more efficient, more effective and more economical through current records management; and, to the end that the people may derive maximum benefit from a knowledge of state affairs, preserve its noncurrent records of permanent value for study and research.

1973, c. 625, § 16, eff. July 5, 1973.

§ 92-A.   Definitions

The following definitions are established for terms used in this chapter.

1. **Agency records.** "Agency records" means semicurrent records of government agencies to which they retain legal title, but that have been transferred to the custody of the Maine State Archives to effect economies and efficiency in their storage and use pending their ultimate disposition as authorized by law.

2. **Archives.** "Archives" means noncurrent government records that have been determined by the State Archivist to have sufficient value to warrant their continued preservation and that are in the physical and legal custody of the Maine State Archives.

3. **Record center.** "Record center" means facilities maintained by the State Archivist for the storage, security, servicing

and other processing of agency records that must be preserved for varying periods of time and need not be retained in office equipment and space.

1973, c. 625, § 16, eff. July 5, 1973.

§ 93. State Archivist

The Secretary of State shall appoint a State Archivist subject to review by the Joint Standing Committee on State Government and to confirmation by the Legislature. He shall be chosen without reference to party affiliation and solely on the ground of professional competence to perform the duties of his office. He shall hold office for a term of 6 years from the date of his appointment and until his successor has been appointed and qualified. The compensation of the State Archivist shall be fixed by the Governor.

This section shall not affect the term of the person holding office as State Archivist on October 1, 1977.

1973, c. 625, § 16, eff. July 5, 1973; 1975, c. 771, § 33, eff. Jan. 4, 1977; 1977, c. 674, § 2.

§ 94. Maine State Archives

The office of the State Archivist shall be a bureau within the Department of Secretary of State and shall be organized in the manner the State Archivist and the Secretary of State shall deem best suited to the accomplishment of the functions and purposes of this chapter. It shall be known as the Maine State Archives. The State Archivist shall be the official custodian of the archival resources of the State.

1973, c. 625, § 16, eff. July 5, 1973.

§ 95. Powers and duties of State Archivist

The State Archivist shall have the duties and powers established under the following provisions governing the creation, use, maintenance, retention, preservation and disposal of state records:

1. **Administration.** To administer the office of the State Archivist. In exercising his administration, the State Archivist shall formulate policies, establish organizational and operational procedures and exercise general supervision. He shall employ, with the approval of the Secretary of State subject to the Personnel Law, such assistants as may be necessary to carry out this chapter. The State Archivist shall adopt a seal for use in the official business of his office. He shall have custody and control of the facilities provided for the administration of this chapter;

2. Examination of public records. To have the right of reasonable access to and examination of all public records in Maine;

3. Rules and regulations. To promulgate such rules and regulations as are necessary to effectuate the purposes of this chapter. No restrictions or limitations shall be imposed on the use of records that are defined by law as public records or as records open to public inspection, unless necessary to protect and preserve them from deterioration, mutilation, loss or destruction. Restrictions or limitations imposed by law on the examination and use of records transferred to the archives under subsection 7, paragraph C and subsection 8 shall remain in effect until the records have been in existence for 50 years, unless removed or relaxed by the State Archivist with the concurrence in writing of the head of the agency from which the records were transferred or his successor in function, if any. The State Archivist shall promulgate rules and regulations governing the transfer of records from the custody of one agency to that of another subject to any applicable provision of law;

4. Acceptance of gifts and bequests. To accept gifts, bequests and endowments for purposes consistent with the objectives of this chapter. Such funds, if given as an endowment shall be invested in securities by the Treasurer of State according to the laws governing the investment of trust funds. All gifts, bequests and proceeds of invested endowment funds shall be used solely to carry out the purposes for which they were made;

5. Publication. To publish archival material, reports, bulletins and other publications which will promote the objectives of this chapter. He shall establish the price at which publications, photocopies and photoduplication services may be sold and delivered. The income received under this subsection and subsection 12 shall be credited to a special revenue account which shall be carried forward and expended by the agency for these purposes;

6. Biennial report. To report biennially to the Governor and Legislature facts and recommendations relating to the work and needs of his office;

7. Records management program. To establish and administer in the executive branch of State Government an active, continuing program for the economical and efficient management of state records. Upon request, the State Archivist shall assist and advise in the establishment of records management programs in the legislative and judicial branches of State Government and shall, as required by them, provide program services similar to those available to the executive branch. The State Archivist shall, with due regard for the functions of the agencies concerned:

A. Provide standards, procedures and techniques for effective management of records in the conduct of current business;

B. Recommend improvements in current records management practices, including the use of space, equipment and supplies employed in creating, maintaining, storing and servicing records;

C. Establish schedules, in consultation with the heads of state departments, under which each department shall retain state records of continuing value, and dispose, as provided by this chapter, of state records no longer possessing sufficient administrative, legal or fiscal value to warrant their further keeping for current business;

D. Obtain such reports from agencies as are required for the administration of the program;

The head of each agency shall establish and maintain an active, continuing program for the economical and efficient management of the records of the agency in compliance with the standards, procedures and regulations issued by the State Archivist.

8. Transfer of state records. To provide for the transfer to the archives of state records, disposed of under subsection 7, paragraph C, which have archival value;

9. Destruction of records. To authorize the destruction of the records of any state department which, in the opinion of the head of the department, are no longer of value to the department, and which, in the opinion of the State Archivist and the Archives Advisory Board, have no archival value to the State;

10. Transfer of public records. To receive all records transferred to the Maine State Archives under subsection 8 and to negotiate for the transfer of public records from the custody of any public official not governed by subsection 7. The State Archivist shall charge a fee sufficient to cover the cost of receiving and processing all transfers from the custody of any public official not governed by subsection 7. The fees collected shall be deposited in the General Fund. Any public officer in Maine is authorized to turn over to the State Archivist such public records legally in his custody as are not needed for the transaction of the current business of his office, whenever the State Archivist is willing and able to receive them. Whenever such transfer is made, the State Archivist shall transmit to the office from which the records are transferred a memorandum in which such records are described in terms sufficient to identify them, which shall be preserved in said office. Unless otherwise directed by law, the public records of any public office, commission or committee in the State shall, upon the termination of its existence or functions, be transferred to the custody of the State Archivist;

10–A. Records of Secretary of State. To preserve the records of the Secretary of State to the extent he deems desirable under the Constitution and the regulations of the State Archivist;

10–B. Permanent records of agency administration. To establish such standards concerning the establishment, maintenance and operation of state administered computerized and auxiliary automated information handling as may be necessary to insure the preservation of adequate and permanent records of the organization, functions, policies, procedures, decisions and essential transactions of the agencies of State Government;

10–C. Legislative records. The Secretary of the Senate and the Clerk of the House of Representatives shall obtain the noncurrent records of the Legislature and of each committee thereof at the close of each Legislature and transfer them to the Maine State Archives for preservation, subject to the orders of the Senate or the House, respectively;

11. Archives available for public use. To make archival material under his supervision available for public use at reasonable times. He shall carefully protect and preserve such materials from deterioration, mutilation, loss or destruction;

12. Copies. To furnish copies of archival material upon the request of any person, on payment in advance of such fees as may be required. Copies of public records transferred in pursuance of law from the office of their origin to the custody of the State Archivist, when certified by the State Archivist, under the seal of his office, shall have the same legal force and effect as if certified by their original custodian. A facsimile of the signature of the State Archivist imprinted by or at his direction upon any certificate issued by him shall have the same validity as his written signature;

13. **Photoreproduction and restoration.** To provide centralized photoreproduction and records preservation services for government agencies to the extent he deems advisable in his administration of the state program and facilities. Such services shall be furnished to such agencies at cost.

Fees collected under this subsection shall be deposited in the General Fund.

1981, c. 456, §§ A, 17, 18, eff. July 1, 1981.

§ 96. Archives Advisory Board

There shall be an Archives Advisory Board, the function of

which shall be to advise the State Archivist in his administration of this chapter and to perform such other duties as may be prescribed by law. The board shall consist of 9 persons especially interested in the history of the State appointed by the Governor as advisors for overlapping terms of 6 years. The 3 new advisors shall be first appointed one for one year, one for 3 years and one for 5 years. Their successors shall be appointed for terms of 6 years. Each advisor shall serve for the term of his appointment and thereafter until his successor is appointed and qualified. In case of the termination of an advisor's service during his term, the Governor shall appoint a successor for the unexpired term. Advisors shall serve without compensation, but shall receive their necessary expenses.

1973, c. 625, § 16, eff. July 5, 1973.

§ 97. Violation

Violation of any provision of this chapter or any rules and regulations issued under section 95, subsection 3, except those violations for which specific penalties are provided, is a Class E crime.

1973, c. 625, § 16, eff. July 5, 1973; 1977, c. 696, § 33, eff. March 31, 1978.

REGIONAL LIBRARY SYSTEMS
(Maine Revised Statutes Annotated, 1982, Title 27, s. 110-119.)

§ 110. Definitions

In this chapter, unless the context clearly requires a different meaning, the following words shall have the following meanings.

1. Appeals board. "Appeals board" means the Maine Library Commission acting, on request from interested citizens, as a board of review for decisions made concerning the State's library plan.

2. Area reference and resource center. "Area reference and resource center" means a large public, school or academic library designated by the Commissioner of Educational and Cultural Services and the State Librarian and receiving state aid for the purpose of making its resources and services available without charge to all residents of the district, of providing supplementary library services to local libraries within the district, of coordinating the services of all local libraries within the district which by contract become part of the library district.

3. Common borrower's card. "Common borrower's card" means a system of personal identification for the purpose of borrowing and returning books and other materials from any library that participates in the regional system.

4. District consultant. "District consultant" means one who acts as a general library consultant to one or more districts.

5. District council. "District council" means an advisory body representing a constituency of participating libraries within a geographical district.

1977, c. 125, § 1; 1981, c. 464, § 29, eff. June 16, 1981.

6. District plan. "District plan" in entirety means a statement describing the specific purposes for which the district is formed, the means and the agencies by which such purposes are to be accomplished, and an estimate of the funds necessary to their accomplishment; also the public agency which is to receive those funds.

7. Library district. "Library district" means a defined geographic area consisting of local libraries joined cooperatively to an area reference and resource center and a research center. Local libraries within the district may also be joined cooperatively with other types of libraries.

8. Local library board. "Local library board" means the body which has the authority to give administrative direction or advice to a library through its librarian.

9. Media center. "Media center" means any library utilizing print as well as extensive nonprint resources and materials.

10. Public library. "Public library" means a library freely open to all persons and receives its financial support from a municipality, private association, corporation or group. The above serves the informational, educational and recreational needs of all the residents of the area for which its governing body is responsible.

11. Regional library system. "Regional library system" means a network of library districts interrelated by formal or informal contract, for the purpose of organizing library resources and services for research, information and recreation to improve statewide library service and to serve collectively the entire population of the State.

12. Research center. "Research center" means any library designated as such by the Commissioner of Educational and Cultural Services and the State Librarian and receiving state aid for the purposes of making its major research collections, under such rules and regulations as are defined by its governing board and head librarian, available to the residents of the State.

1973, c. 626, § 6.

§ 111. Regional library development

1. Maine Library Commission. There shall be created within the Department of Educational and Cultural Services a library commission which shall be designated as the Maine Library Commission. It shall consist of 15 members appointed by the Governor. The library commission shall be broadly representative of the State's libraries and shall consist of a representative from public, school, academic, special, institutional and handicapped libraries, a trustee representative, one representative from each of the library districts as they are formed and 3 representatives from the State at large of whom one shall be representative of the disadvantaged.

The term of each appointed member shall be 5 years or until his successor is appointed and qualified. Of the members first appointed, 3 shall be for one year, 3 for 2 years, 3 for 3 years, 3 for 4 years and 3 for 5 years. Subsequent appointments shall be for the full term of 5 years. No members shall serve more than 2 successive terms. In the case of a vacancy other than the expiration of a term, the appointment of a successor shall be made in like manner for the balance of the term.

The commission shall meet at least 4 times a year. It shall elect a chairman for a term of 2 years and frame and modify bylaws for its internal organization and operation. The State Librarian shall serve as secretary to the commission. The members of the commission shall serve without compensation, but shall be reimbursed for expenses incurred in the performance of their duties.

1973, c. 626, § 6.

§ 112. —functions

The library commission shall:

1. Appointment of State Librarian. Give advice and make recommendations to the Commissioner of Educational and Cultural Services with regard to the appointment of the State Librarian;

2. Policies. Give advice and make recommendations to the Commissioner of Educational and Cultural Services with regard to: The policies and operations of the Maine State Library and the State's library program including minimum standards of library service, the apportionment of state aid to libraries, the designation of library districts and their boundaries, the designation of area reference and resource centers and the designation of research centers after full consideration of the advice of the district council;

3. Review. Act, on written request by any interested library, as an appeals board concerning decisions of the commissioner regarding the items in subsection 2. The written request for a hearing shall be filed within 30 days from the date of the decision.

1973, c. 626, § 6.

4. Federal program. Serve as the State Advisory Council on Libraries and in that capacity give advice and make recommendations to the Commissioner of Educational and Cultural Services with regard to the administration of federal funds, in accordance with the terms thereof, which may now or in the future become available for library purposes.

1977, c. 125, § 2.

§ 113. Library districts

Upon the advice of the Maine Library Commission, the State shall be divided into as many districts as the commissioner shall determine are required and shall establish or modify the geographical boundaries of each district.

1973, c. 626, § 6.

§ 114. District council

Each library district shall have an advisory council which shall be known as the district council.

1. Membership. The governing board of each library which has agreed to participate in the district system shall appoint a representative to the district council. The district council shall elect an executive board composed of 9 members and shall distribute this membership among librarians, trustees and lay members. The district executive board shall elect from its number the appropriate officers as needed. The district council shall meet at least twice a year.

2. Duties. The district council shall:

A. Serve as an advisory body for the districts.

B. Develop and evaluate a program of services in the district which will encourage cooperative activity among all types of libraries and media centers;

C. Provide liaison among the municipalities in the district;

D. Make recommendations to the Maine Library Commission which would in turn make recommendations to the commissioner regarding programs and services which would help to make libraries and media centers in the district accessible to all;

E. Assist in the development of a comprehensive district plan.
c. 125, §§ 3, 4; 1981, c. 464, § 30, eff. June 6, 1981.

F. Advise on the selection of an area reference and resource center and a research center for the district.
1973, c. 626, § 6.

§ 115. Area reference and resource centers

Each district shall be affiliated with an area reference and resource center which shall be designated by the commissioner, with the advice of the library commission.

1. Duties. The area reference and resource center may:

A. Provide a common borrower's card for member libraries;

B. Participate with the district consultant in planning and conducting workshops on community-library planning;

C. Provide office space and support services to the extent able to the district consultant;

D. Join with the district council in assigning priorities to implement the district plan;

E. Such other cooperative activities and services as member libraries may need or require.
1973, c. 626, § 6.

§ 116. Research centers

Research centers may be designated by the commissioner with the advice of the Library Commission.

1. Duties. The research center shall:

A. Provide for advanced research needs;

B. Act as a back-up collection for the specialized reference needs of the reference and resource centers;

C. Provide such other cooperative activities and services as member libraries may need or require.

1973, c. 626, § 6.

§ 117. District consultants

The State Librarian, with the advice of the district council, shall appoint a staff member, or contract with an area reference and resource center, to provide district consultant services to one or more districts as determined by the policies established by the commissioner.

1. Duties. The district consultant shall serve as secretary of the district council and further shall:

A. Serve as a professional consultant to libraries within the district or districts;

B. Study the needs of the district and make recommendations to the district council;

C. Coordinate services among libraries of all types;

D. Provide liaison between the district, other districts and the Maine State Library;

E. Encourage local initiative and commitment to regional cooperative library service;

F. Work with area reference and resource center staff members in planning area reference and interlibrary loan service; and

G. Help evolve a district plan of service.

1977, c. 125, §§ 5, 6; 1981, c. 464, §§ 31 to 33, eff. June 16, 1981.

§ 118. School libraries and media center

Any school library or media center in a community with no public library service, or serving communities with no public libraries, which agrees to offer service as a public library, is entitled to all the benefits accruing to a public library with the approval of the commissioner.

1973, c. 626, § 6.

§ 119. Distribution of appropriations

The Commissioner of Educational and Cultural Services, with the advice of the Maine Library Commission, is authorized to apportion funds appropriated by the Legislature for the support of regional library systems.

1977, c. 125, § 7; 1977, c. 564, § 100; 1977, c. 555, § 1; 1977, c. 690, § 15, eff. March 30, 1978.

MUNICIPAL LIBRARIES
(Maine Revised Statutes Annoated, 1982, Title 27, s-101-119.)

§ 101. Free public libraries established in towns

Any town may establish a free public library therein for the use of its inhabitants and provide suitable rooms therefor under such regulation for its government as the inhabitants from time to time prescribe, and may levy and assess a tax and make appropriation therefrom for the foundation and commencement of such library and for its maintenance and increase annually. Any town in which there is a public library may establish and maintain under the same general management and control such branches of the same as the convenience and wants of its citizens seem to demand.

R.S.1954, c. 42, § 29.

§ 102. Free public libraries established in village corporations

Any village corporation located in a town where no free library exists may establish a library within its limits for the free use of all its inhabitants and may levy and assess a corporate tax and make appropriation therefrom for its maintenance and increase annually. Village libraries established under this section shall be subject to all the duties and entitled to all the privileges prescribed by the laws relating to free public libraries in towns.

R.S.1954, c. 42, § 30.

§ 103. Free use of library in adjoining towns authorized

Any municipality may raise and appropriate annually a sum of money for the purpose of securing to its inhabitants free use of a library located in an adjoining municipality.

R.S.1954, c. 42, § 31; 1955, c. 185, § 12.

§ 104. Towns uniting for libraries

Two or more towns may unite in establishing and maintaining a free public library with branches thereof in each town for the free use of all the inhabitants of said towns and may each raise and make appropriation for that purpose annually. Such towns shall be subject to all duties and entitled to all the benefits prescribed by the laws relating to free libraries.

R.S.1954, c. 42, § 32.

§ 105. State aid for municipalities maintaining free public libraries

The officers of any municipality may certify to the State Librarian annually, before the first day of May, the amount of money appropriated and expended by said municipality during the preceding year for the benefit of a free public library established therein, or for the free use of a library in an adjoining town. Upon such certification the State Librarian, if satisfied with the quality of service performed by such library, shall approve for payment to such municipality an amount based on the following schedule:

On appropriations from $200 to $473, 10%;

On appropriations from $476 to $1,900, 7%;

On appropriations from $1,901 to $5,000, 4%.

No municipality shall receive annually less than $20 nor more than $200, except as otherwise provided. The state aid money must be spent for the purchase of books to be placed in said library.

If the appropriations of 2 or more towns for the use of the same library in an adjoining town amount to the sum of $200 or more, the State Librarian may make payment of state aid on the same basis and for the same purpose prescribed above. Such payment shall be made to the municipality where the library is situated.

R.S.1954, c. 42, § 33. 1955, c. 185, § 13.

§ 106. Libraries controlled by associations assisted by towns

Any town or city in which there is a library owned or controlled by a corporation or association or by trustees may levy and assess a tax and make appropriation therefrom annually to procure from such library the free use of its books for all the inhabitants of the town or city, under such restrictions and regulations as shall insure the safety and good usage of the books. Such library shall then be considered a free public library within the meaning of this chapter and said town or city shall be entitled to the benefits of section 105.

R.S.1954, c. 42, § 34; 1955, c. 185, § 14.

§ 107. Custody of public documents; list of books purchased

The officers of every free public library, on or before the first day of May of each year, shall send to the librarian of the State Library a report containing a list of all books and documents purchased with the state stipend for the preceding year. The aid from the State, provided by section 105, shall be withheld from any city, town or village corporation until the report required to be made shall have been received by the librarian of the State Library; and the same shall be withheld unless said report shall show that the laws and Maine Reports furnished by the State are kept constantly in said library for the free use and benefit of all the citizens.

R.S.1954, c. 42, § 35; 1955, c. 185, § 15.

§ 108. Donation of books and gifts for foundation of library

Whenever a municipality shall purchase books to aid in the establishment of a free public library, the State Librarian shall make a gift of money or new books to such library; the gift to equal 50% of the value of the books purchased by said municipality for said purpose, and in no instance to exceed $100.

R.S.1954, c. 42, § 36.

§ 109. Gifts and devises to towns

Any town, as such, may receive, hold and manage devises, bequests or gifts for the establishment, increase or maintenance of a public library therein; and may accept by vote of the legal voters thereof any land or land and buildings thereon, to be used as a public library or art gallery, or both combined. When any plantation is incorporated into a town such gifts and the proceeds thereof fully vest in such town.

R.S.1954, c. 42, § 37.

COUNTY LAW LIBRARIES
(Maine Revised Statutes Annotated, 1982, Title 4, s.191-198.)

§ 191. State Court Library Committee

There is created a State Court Library Committee consisting of 7 voting members, 2 of whom shall be members of the public, 2 of whom shall be members of the judiciary and 3 of whom shall be attorneys. The members shall be appointed by and serve at the pleasure of the Chief Justice of the Supreme Judicial Court. The Chief Justice shall designate the chairman. The State Law Librarian and the State Court Administrator shall be ex officio nonvoting members. A quorum shall consist of 4 of the voting members. The committee shall meet at least 4 times each year. Secretarial assistance shall be provided by the Administrative Office of the Courts.

1981, c. 510, § 1.

§ 192. Personnel

The State Court Administrator shall employ, subject to the approval of the State Court Library Committee, and shall supervise a professionally trained person, who shall be designated the State Court Library Supervisor. The supervisor shall have general supervision of the professional functions of all county law libraries, visit all libraries whenever necessary, meet with county law library committees, coordinate activities with the court administrator's offices, advise staff members of the clerks of courts and carry out any additional duties assigned by the State Court Library Committee.

The law libraries in locations without employees shall be maintained by the offices of the clerks of courts and the duties of each clerk's office shall be specified by the State Court Administrator, subject to the approval of the State Court Library Committee.

1981, c. 510, § 1.

§ 193. System of law libraries

There shall be a system of law libraries within the State, under the supervision of the State Court Library Committee. These libraries shall be arranged in a tier system according to the extent of potential use.

Tier I libraries shall be located in:
    Cumberland County, Portland; and
    Penobscot County, Bangor.

Tier II libraries shall be located in:
    Androscoggin County, Auburn;
    Aroostook County, Houlton; and
    Hancock County, Ellsworth.

Tier III libraries shall be located in:
    Franklin County, Farmington;
    Knox County, Rockland;
    Lincoln County, Wiscasset;
    Oxford County, South Paris;
    Sagadahoc County, Bath;
    Somerset County, Skowhegan;
    Washington County, Machias; and
    York County, Alfred.

Tier IV libraries shall be located in:
    Aroostook County, Caribou;
    Kennebec County, Augusta;
    Oxford County, Rumford;
    Piscataquis County, Dover-Foxcroft; and
    Waldo County, Belfast.

All funds appropriated by the Legislature for the use and benefit of the law libraries after the effective date of this chapter shall be paid to the Administrative Office of the Courts and shall be disbursed by that office under the direction of the State Court Library Committee for purchase of law books, legal literature and library equipment and necessary personnel. The committee shall allocate a specific amount of any appropriation for each tier, and each library within a specific tier shall receive an equal share of that amount.

The State Court Library Committee shall establish guidelines for each tier.

1981, c. 510, § 1.

§ 194. Duties of State Court Library Committee

The State Court Library Committee shall govern the county law library system. It shall formulate policy and exercise control and may delegate administrative policy.
1981, c. 510, § 1.

§ 195. County law libraries

There is created a County Law Library Committee, of not less than 3 nor more than 7 members, in each county in which a county law library is located. The members of the committee shall be appointed or elected by the county bar association, as its bylaws may provide. Membership on the committee need not be restricted to attorneys. The County Law Library Committee shall appoint a chairman, a treasurer and a clerk.
1981, c. 510, § 1.

§ 196. Duties, county committee

The County Law Library Committee shall establish local operating policies, such as, but not limited to, hours, circulation policies, smoking rules, access and photocopy privileges. Each county committee shall exercise supervision over the expenditures of private and nonstate funds, including endowments, and may use those funds to upgrade its county law library. Each County Law Library Committee, together with the State Court Library Committee, shall develop its basic collection within guidelines established by the State Court Library Committee. Each county committee, in consultation with the State Court Library Committee, shall determine new acquisitions. Each county committee shall determine space requirements, with the advice and assistance of the State Court Library Committee.

1981, c. 510, § 1.

§ 197. Duties of treasurer and clerk

The treasurer of each County Law Library Committee, under the direction of the County Law Library Committee, shall apply all private and nonstate moneys received, and all bequests and gifts, to form and operate a law library. The clerk shall keep an exact record of all the proceedings of the committee.

The treasurer shall, annually, before the last Wednesday in July, deposit in the office of the State Court Library Committee a statement of the funds received and expended by the treasurer during the preceding fiscal year.

1981, c. 510, § 1; 1981, c. 698, § 4, eff. April 16, 1982.

§ 198. Rules

The Supreme Judicial Court may promulgate rules to implement the purposes of this chapter.
1981, c. 510, § 1.

LAW AND LEGISLATIVE REFERENCE LIBRARY
(Maine Revised Statutes Annotated, 1982, Title 3, s.171, 173, 174.)

§ 171. Declaration of policy

The Legislature declares that it is the policy of the State to provide a law and legislative reference library adequate to the informational needs of the Legislature, other branches of State Government and the citizens of Maine.

1971, c. 480, § 1.

§ 173.   State Law Librarian; functions and duties

The State Law Librarian shall perform the following functions and duties:

1.   Legislative reference service.   Provide a comprehensive reference service on legislative problems for all members of the Legislature and its committees, equally and impartially, and to the limits of its staff and facilities.   Such reference services shall be available also to public officials and to citizens generally.

Collect, index and make available in the most suitable form information relative to governmental subjects which will aid the Legislature, other public officials and citizens to perform their duties in an enlightened manner.

2.   Law library.   Provide a law library for the use of all agencies of State Government, the judiciary, attorneys and citizens of Maine.

Give advice to county law libraries in all aspects of library management and cooperate with the judiciary and county law library associations in planning for their improvement.

3.   **Distribution, sale and exchange of law books.**   Copies of the Revised Statutes, supplements thereto and session laws shall be delivered by the printer to the State Law Librarian for distribution and sale.   The State Law Librarian shall fix the prices at which these items may be sold and delivered, and shall thereafter make sales at the prices fixed. All proceeds from such sales shall be deposited to the credit of the General Fund.

A.   A copy of all revisions of the statutes, and supplements thereto, and the session laws shall be sold at the established price to the following: Each free public library, college library, district attorney's office, county commissioner's court, sheriff's office, county treasurer's office, registry of deeds, registry of probate, office of a judge of probate and ex-Governor.   Two copies shall be sold at the established price to each municipality.

A copy of all revisions of the statutes, and supplements thereto, and the session laws shall be furnished to each county law library, each Justice of the Supreme Judicial and Superior Courts, the office of each clerk of courts, each District Court, the office of the Governor, the office of the Reporter of Decisions, the office of the Judge of the United States District Court for Maine, the office of the United States District Attorney for Maine, the Library of the United States Court of Appeals for the first circuit, the office of each Senator and Representative from Maine in the Congress of the United States, the office of the Secretary of the Senate and the office of the Clerk of the House.

The Legislature, state administrative departments, bureaus, agencies and commissions, and the Judicial Department, shall be sold or furnished copies necessary for legislative, administrative or judicial purposes under rules and regulations promulgated by the State Law Librarian.

Copies shall be sent, on an exchange basis, to the Library of Congress, secretary of the Maine State Bar Association, the Supreme Court Library of Canada and to each state or territorial library in the United States.

One copy of the laws passed by each session of the Legislature shall be given to each member thereof, the Secretary of the Senate, the Assistant Secretary of the Senate, the Clerk of the House and the Assistant Clerk of the House.

At any time prior to January 3, 1979, one copy of the latest unannotated revision of the statutes and any available supplement thereto shall be given to each member of the Legislature who has not previously received such a copy as a member of the Legislature which enacted the revision or a Legislature which met in regular session after the effective date of such revision of statutes.

On or after January 3, 1979, each member of the Legislature may, while holding office, purchase at the state price or obtain on loan under rules and regulations promulgated by the State Law Librarian, the latest annotated revision of the statutes and the current supplement thereto.

The remaining copies of the revisions of the statutes, and supplements thereto, and the session laws shall be held in the library for exchange or library use, except as otherwise provided by law.

B. A copy of the printed decisions of the Supreme Judicial Court, commonly called Maine Reports, and of the advance sheets, which are purchased by the State in accordance with Title 4, section 702, shall be distributed by the State Law Librarian to the following: Each county law library, each college library, each district attorney's office, each office of a judge of probate, each registry of probate, each office of a clerk of courts, each District Court, the office of each Senator and Representative from Maine in the Congress of the United States, each Justice and ex-Justice of the Supreme Judicial and Superior Courts, the office of the Governor, the office of the Judge of the United States District Court for Maine, the office of the United States District Attorney for Maine, the office of the Clerk of the United States District Court for Maine and the office of each Judge of the United States Court of Appeals for the first circuit.

Copies shall be sent, on an exchange basis, to the Library of Congress, secretary of the Maine State Bar Association, the Supreme Court Library of Canada, and to each state or territorial library in the United States.

Upon request of administrative officers thereof copies shall be placed in each state department or institution.

C. The State Law Librarian may, in his discretion, sell surplus copies of volumes entrusted to him or use them for exchange purposes to increase the usefulness of the library. Proceeds from all sales shall be deposited to the credit of the General Fund.

1981, c. 48, § 2.

§ 174. Administrative provisions

The State Law Librarian shall formulate policies for the operation of the Law and Legislative Reference Library and exercise general supervision. He shall promulgate any necessary rules and regulations governing the use of library property and admission to its quarters.

The State Law Librarian shall appoint, with the approval of the Legislative Council, a deputy law librarian for a term of 7 years from the date of his appointment and until his successor has been appointed and qualified, and employ such assistants as may be necessary to carry out this subchapter.

1979, c. 396, § 8, eff. June 11, 1979.

Maine library laws are reprinted from MAINE REVISED STATUTES ANNOTATED published by Equity Publishing Corp., Oxford, New Hampshire and West Publishing Co., St. Paul, Minnesota.

MARYLAND

STATE LIBRARY AGENCY

(The Annotated Code of Maryland, 1982, s.23-101 to 23-105, 23-201.)

§ 23-101. Findings and policy of State.

(a) *Findings.* — The General Assembly finds:

(1) That public library resources and services are essential components of the educational system; and

(2) That libraries stimulate awareness and understanding of critical social issues, and assist individuals in reaching their highest potential for self-development.

(b) *Policy.* — It is the policy of this State:

(1) To continue the orderly development and maintenance of library facilities and services throughout this State, in collaboration with the counties; and

(2) To develop coordinated programs and services among libraries and institutions to:

(i) Provide the widest possible access to the library and information resources of this State; and

(ii) Insure more effective and economical services to all library users. (An. Code 1957, art. 77, § 162; 1978, ch. 22, § 2.)

§ 23-102. Division of library development and services established.

There is a division of library development and services in the Department. The division is the central State library agency. (An. Code 1957, art. 77, § 164; 1978, ch. 22, § 2.)

§ 23-103. Staff of division.

(a) *Assistant superintendent for libraries — Position and appointment.* — The head of the division of library development and services is the assistant superintendent for libraries who is appointed by the State Board on the recommendation of the State Superintendent.

(b) *Same — Qualifications.* — The assistant superintendent for libraries shall:

(1) Hold an advanced degree in library and information service;

(2) Have administrative experience in libraries; and

(3) Have any other qualifications the State Superintendent considers necessary.

(c) *Other staff of division; compensation.* — (1) The division may employ the professional and clerical staff provided in the State budget.

(2) Each employee of the division is entitled to the salary provided in the State budget. (An. Code 1957, art. 77, §§ 164, 165; 1978, ch. 22, § 2.)

§ 23-104. Authority of State Board and State Superintendent.

(a) *In general.* — In addition to the other powers granted and duties imposed by this article, the State Board has the powers and duties set forth in this section.

(b) *General powers and duties.* — The State Board shall exercise general direction and control of library development in this State and may:

(1) Adopt rules and regulations necessary to administer this title;

(2) After considering the recommendations of the Advisory Council on Libraries, establish library policies and procedures for the statewide system of libraries;

(3) Consider the library needs of this State and recommend to the Governor and the General Assembly desirable legislation; and

(4) With the approval of the Governor, accept, administer, and spend any appropriation, gift, or grant for library purposes from the federal government or from any other person.

(c) *Certification of library personnel.* — In accordance with the bylaws, rules, and regulations of the State Board, the State Superintendent shall certificate professional library personnel.

(d) *Reports.* — Each year the State Board shall report to the Governor and the people of this State on the support, condition, progress, and needs of libraries.   (An. Code 1957, art. 77, §§ 163, 175; 1978, ch. 22, § 2.)

§ 23-105. Powers and duties of division.

(a) *In general.* — In addition to any other powers granted and duties imposed by this title, and subject to the authority of the State Board, the division of library development and services has the powers and duties set forth in this section.

(b) *General powers and duties.* — The division of library development and services shall:

(1) Provide leadership and guidance for the planning and coordinated development of library and information service in this state;

(2) Develop statewide public and school library services and networks, resource centers, and other arrangements to meet the library and information needs of this State;

(3) Provide professional and technical advice on improving library services in this State to:

(i) Public and school library officials;

(ii) State government agencies; and

(iii) Any other person;

(4) (i) Collect library statistics and other data;

(ii) Identify library needs and provide for needed research and studies of them; and

(iii) Publish and distribute findings in these areas; and

(iv) Coordinate library services with other information and education services and agencies;

(5) Administer federal and State funds appropriated to it by the State for library purposes;

(6) (i) Develop and recommend professional standards and policies for libraries; and

(ii) Establish requirements and procedures for the certification of librarians and library personnel;

(7) Provide:

(i) Specialized library service to the blind and other physically handicapped individuals in this State; and

(ii) Other desirable specialized library services;

(8) Encourage, advise, and assist in establishing, operating, and coordinating libraries at State institutions and agencies and administer the operation of library and information services for the department;

(9) Adopt guidelines for the administration of public libraries and recommend to the State Board rules and regulations to implement this title;

(10) Cooperate with national library agencies and those of any other state; and

(11) Perform any other duty necessary for its proper operation.

(An. Code 1957, art. 77, § 166; 1978, ch. 22, § 2.)

§ 23-201. State Library Resource Center.

(a) *Established.* — The Central Library of the Enoch Pratt Free Library system is the State Library Resource Center.

(b) *Purpose of Center.* — The State Library Resource Center shall provide and expand access to specialized library materials and services that are necessary for coordinated, efficient, and economical library services in this State. (An. Code 1957, art. 77, § 168; 1978, ch. 22, § 2.)

ADVISORY COUNCIL ON LIBRARIES
(The Annotated Code of Maryland, 1982, s.23-106.)

§ 23-106. Maryland Advisory Council on Libraries.

(a) *Established.* — There is a Maryland Advisory Council on Libraries.

(b) *Composition; term; vacancies; compensation.* — (1) The Advisory Council consists of 12 members, 7 of whom are appointed by the Governor. Each member is entitled to participate fully and equally in the activities of the Council.

(2) Each member shall:

(i) Be a resident of this State;

(ii) Be an individual of ability and integrity who is experienced in public or library affairs; and

(iii) Represent the interests of the citizens of this State in better library services.

(3) Of the appointed members:

(i) Five shall be selected from the public at large;

(ii) One shall be a professional librarian; and

(iii) One shall be a library trustee.

(4) The following officials serve ex officio and each may designate someone to serve in his place:

(i) The commissioner of higher education;

(ii) The President of the Board of Trustees of Enoch Pratt Free Library;

(iii) The President of the Maryland Library Association;

(iv) The Dean of the University of Maryland College of Library and Information Services; and

(v) The President of the Maryland Educational Media Organization.

(5) (i) Each appointed member serves for a term of 5 years and until a successor is appointed and qualifies. These terms are staggered as required by the terms of the members serving on July 1, 1978.

(ii) An appointed member may not serve more than two consecutive terms.

(iii) A member appointed to fill a vacancy in an unexpired term serves only for the remainder of that term and until a successor is appointed and qualifies.

(6) Each member of the Advisory Council:

(i) Serves without compensation; and

(ii) Is entitled to reimbursement for expenses in accordance with the Standard State Travel Regulations.

(c) *Chairman; officers; staff; meetings.* — (1) Each year:

(i) The Governor shall appoint a member of the Advisory Council as its chairman; and

(ii) The Advisory Council shall elect one of its members as its vice chairman.

(2) The assistant superintendent for libraries shall:
    (i) Serve as secretary to the Advisory Council;
    (ii) Record the proceedings of the Council; and
    (iii) Provide necessary staff services.

(3) The Advisory Council shall meet at least once a year at the times and places its chairman designates.

(4) Seven members of the Advisory Council are a quorum and at least 7 affirmative votes are required for any recommendation to:
    (i) The division of library services;
    (ii) The State Superintendent;
    (iii) The State Board; or
    (iv) The Governor.

(d) *Duties.* — The Advisory Council shall:
    (1) Gather information on the needs of libraries throughout this State;
    (2) Advise the division of library development and services, the State Superintendent, the State Board, and the Governor on library matters; and
    (3) Promote improvement of library services in this State.

(e) *Funds.* — The Advisory Council may be funded annually as provided in the budget of the division of library development and services. (An. Code 1957, art. 77, § 167; 1978, ch. 22, § 2; 1982, ch. 138.)

STATE AID

(The Annotated Code of Maryland, 1982, s.23-401 to 23-406.)

§ 23-401. Definitions.

(a) *In general.* — In this subtitle the following words have the meanings indicated.

(b) *Adjusted assessed valuation of real property.* — (1) "Adjusted assessed valuation of real property" means the most recent estimate by the Department of Assessments and Taxation before the State budget is submitted to the General Assembly, of the assessed value of real property for State purposes as of July 1 of the first completed fiscal year before the fiscal year for which the calculation of State library aid is made under this subtitle.

(2) If the Department of Assessments and Taxation estimates that real property in any county is assessed at other than 50 percent of market value, the assessed valuation of those categories of real property that are estimated to be assessed at other than 50 percent of market value, on the basis of surveys made under Article 81, § 232 (14) of the Code that are reported on or before November 1 of the first calendar year before the fiscal year for which the calculation is made, shall be adjusted to 50 percent. This adjustment does not apply to public utility operating property.
(1979, ch. 423, § 1.)

(c) *Capital expense.* — "Capital expense" means principal and interest payments, or current capital spending or accumulation for:
    (1) The purchase of land for libraries;
    (2) The purchase and construction of library buildings;

(3) Remodeling and adding to library buildings; and

(4) The purchase of equipment and furniture for these library buildings.

(d) *Net taxable income.* — "Net taxable income" means the amount certified by the State Comptroller for the second full calendar year before the fiscal year for which the calculation of State library aid is made under this subtitle, based on tax returns filed on or before July 1 after that calendar year.

(e) *Population.* — "Population" means population determined from figures available as of July 1 of the calendar year before the fiscal year for which the calculation is made, from:

(1) The latest decennial census; or

(2) Estimates prepared by the Department of Health and Mental Hygiene.

(f) *Real property.* — "Real property" includes:

(1) Land and improvements to land;

(2) Land and nonoperating property of railroads and public utilities; and

(3) Public utilities operating property classified as real property by the Department of Assessments and Taxation.

(g) *Wealth.* — "Wealth" means the sum of net taxable income and adjusted assessed valuation of real property.

(An. Code 1957, art. 77, § 176; 1978, ch. 22, § 2.)

§ 23-402. Program established.

(a) *In general.* — There is a county-State minimum library program for the support and growth of public libraries.

(b) *Expenses in which State shares.* — The State shall share in the current operating and capital expenses of the county public library systems that participate in the minimum library program. (An. Code 1957, art. 77, § 176; 1978, ch. 22, § 2.)

§ 23-403. State and counties to share cost.

(b) *Expenses in which State may share.* — (1) Each year, each county public library system that participates in the minimum library program shall be provided $5.67 for each resident of the county, to be used for operating and capital expenses. The State shall share in this amount.

(2) Any county may provide an amount greater than its share under the cooperative program, but the State may not share in the excess.

(1978, ch. 988; 1982, ch. 486.)

§ 23-404. Matching amounts; current and capital expenses.

(a) *County share.* — To be eligible for its State share of the minimum program, a county government shall levy an annual tax sufficient to provide an amount for library purposes equal to:

(1) The wealth of the county; times

(2) A uniform percentage, rounded to the third decimal place equal to:

(i) 60 percent of the total minimum program for current and capital expenses to be shared for all counties; divided by

(ii) The total wealth of all the counties.

(b) *State share.* — The State share of the minimum program for current and capital expenses for each county is the difference between the county share calculated under subsection (a) of this section and the minimum program for current and capital expenses to be shared under § 23-403 of this subtitle.

(c) *Limitation on capital expense.* — Not more than 20 percent of the county and State shares may be applied to capital expenses.

(d) *Source of funds for county share of capital expense.* — The county appropriation for capital expenses may include funds from any source except the State. (An. Code 1957, art. 77, § 176; 1978, ch. 22, § 2.)

§ 23-405. Payment and use of funds.

(a) *Payment.* — The State Superintendent shall authorize the payment of funds under this subtitle:

(1) To the board of library trustees of each county that has a board of trustees; or

(2) In each county that does not have a board of library trustees, to the county.

(b) *Administration of funds.* — (1) Current operating funds shall be administered by the county board of library trustees.

(2) Capital expense funds shall be administered by the county council, board of county commissioners, or Mayor and City Council of Baltimore City.

(c) *Use of funds.* — (1) The funds provided under this subtitle may be used only for library purposes.

(2) The State Superintendent shall require that these funds be used subject to any conditions specified by the appropriating agency or imposed under this subtitle. (An. Code 1957, art. 77, § 176; 1978, ch. 22, § 2.)

§ 23-406. Withholding by Comptroller.

The State Superintendent shall authorize the State Comptroller to withhold State funds from any county that fails:

(1) To appropriate the amount of its share of the minimum program; or

(2) To meet the requirements of the law or of the State Board for operating the county library. (An. Code 1957, art. 77, § 176; 1978, ch. 22, § 2.)

INTERSTATE LIBRARY COMPACT
(The Annotated Code of Maryland, 1982, s.25-301 to 25-303.)

§ 25-301. Execution of Compact.

The Interstate Library Compact is hereby enacted into law and entered into by this State with all states legally joining it, in the form substantially as it appears in §§ 25-302 and 25-303 of this subtitle. (An. Code 1957, art. 77, § 166A; 1978, ch. 22, § 2.)

§ 25-302. Implementation of Compact.

(a) *Compliance with laws applicable to political subdivisions.* — No political subdivision of this State shall be party to a library agreement which provides for the construction or maintenance of a library pursuant to Article III, subdivision (c-7) of the Compact, nor pledge its credit in support of such a library, or contribute to the capital financing thereof, except after compliance with any laws applicable to such political subdivisions relating to or governing capital outlays and the pledging of credit.

(b) *Meaning of "state library agency".* — As used in the Compact, "State library agency," with reference to this State, means the division of library development and services of the State Department of Education.

(c) *Interstate library districts.* — An interstate library district lying partly within this State may claim and be entitled to receive State aid in support of any of its functions to the same extent and in the same manner as such functions are eligible for support when carried on by entities wholly within this State. For the purposes of computing and apportioning State aid to an interstate library district, this State will consider that portion of the area which lies within this State as an independent entity for the performance of the aided function or functions and compute and apportion the aid accordingly. Subject to any applicable laws of this State, such a district also may apply for and be entitled to receive any federal aid for which it may be eligible.

(d) *Compact administrator and deputy administrators.* — The assistant superintendent for libraries shall be the compact administrator pursuant to Article X of the Compact. The State Board of Education on the recommendation of the State Superintendent of Schools may appoint one or more deputy compact administrators pursuant to said article.

(e) *Notices upon withdrawal.* — In the event of withdrawal from the Compact the Governor shall send and receive any notices required by Article XI (b) of the Compact. (An. Code 1957, art. 77, § 166A; 1978, ch. 22, § 2.)

§ 25-303. Text of Compact.

INTERSTATE LIBRARY COMPACT

Article I. Policy and Purpose

Because the desire for the services provided by libraries transcends governmental boundaries and can most effectively be satisfied by giving such services to communities and people regardless of jurisdictional lines, it is the policy of the states party to this Compact to cooperate and share their responsibilities; to authorize cooperation and sharing with respect to those types of library facilities and services which can be more economically or efficiently developed and maintained on a cooperative basis, and to authorize cooperation and sharing among localities, states and others in providing joint or cooperative library services in areas where the distribution of population or of existing and potential library resources make the provision of library service on an interstate basis the most effective way of providing adequate and efficient service.

Article II. Definitions

As used in this Compact:

(a) *"Public library agency"* means any unit or agency of local or State government operating or having power to operate a library.

(b) *"Private library agency"* means any nongovernmental entity which operates or assumes a legal obligation to operate a library.

(c) *"Library agreement"* means a contract establishing an interstate library district pursuant to this Compact or providing for the joint or cooperative furnishing of library services.

Article III. Interstate Library Districts

(a) Any one or more public library agencies in a party state in cooperation with any public library agency or agencies in one or more other party states may establish and maintain an interstate library district. Subject to the provisions of this Compact and any other laws of the party states which pursuant hereto remain applicable, such district may establish, maintain and operate some or all of the library facilities and services for the area concerned in accordance with the terms of a library agreement therefor. Any private library agency or agencies within an interstate library district may cooperate therewith, assume duties, responsibilities and obligations thereto, and receive benefits therefrom as provided in any library agreement to which such agency or agencies become party.

(b) Within an interstate library district, and as provided by a library agreement, the performance of library functions may be undertaken on a joint or cooperative basis or may be undertaken by means of one or more arrangements between or among public or private library agencies for the extension of library privileges to the use of facilities or services operated or rendered by one or more of the individual library agencies.

(c) If a library agreement provides for joint establishment, maintenance or operation of library facilities or services by an interstate library district, such district shall have power to do any one or more of the following in accordance with such library agreement:

(1) Undertake, administer and participate in programs or arrangements for securing, lending or servicing of books and other publications, any other materials suitable to be kept or made available by libraries, library equipment or for the dissemination of information about libraries, the value and significance of particular items therein, and the use thereof.

(2) Accept for any of its purposes under this Compact any and all donations, and grants of money, equipment, supplies, materials, and services, (conditional or otherwise), from any state or the United States or any subdivision or agency

thereof, or interstate agency, or from any institution, person, firm or corporation, and receive, utilize and dispose of the same.

(3) Operate mobile library units or equipment for the purpose of rendering bookmobile service within the district.

(4) Employ professional, technical, clerical, and other personnel, and fix terms of employment, compensation and other appropriate benefits; and where desirable, provide for the in-service training of such personnel.

(5) Sue and be sued in any court of competent jurisdiction.

(6) Acquire, hold, and dispose of any real or personal property or any interest or interests therein as may be appropriate to the rendering of library service.

(7) Construct, maintain and operate a library, including any appropriate branches thereof.

(8) Do such other things as may be incidental to or appropriate for the carrying out of any of the foregoing powers.

Article IV. Interstate Library Districts, Governing Board

(a) An interstate library district which establishes, maintains or operates any facilities or services in its own right shall have a governing board which shall direct the affairs of the district and act for it in all matters relating to its business. Each participating public library agency in the district shall be represented on the governing board which shall be organized and conduct its business in accordance with provision therefor in the library agreement. But in no event shall a governing board meet less often than twice a year.

(b) Any private library agency or agencies party to a library agreement establishing an interstate library district may be represented on or advise with the governing board of the district in such manner as the library agreement may provide.

Article V. State Library Agency Cooperation

Any two or more state library agencies of two or more of the party states may undertake and conduct joint or cooperative library programs, render joint or cooperative library services, and enter into and perform arrangements for the cooperative or joint acquisition, use, housing and disposition of items or collections of materials which, by reason of expense, rarity, specialized nature, or infrequency of demand therefor would be appropriate for central collection and shared use. Any such programs, services or arrangements may include provision for the exercise on a cooperative or joint basis of any power exercisable by an interstate library district and an agreement embodying any such program, service or arrangement shall contain provisions covering the subjects detailed in Article VI of this Compact for interstate library agreements.

Article VI. Library Agreements

(a) In order to provide for any joint or cooperative undertaking pursuant to this Compact, public and private library agencies may enter into library agreements. Any agreement executed pursuant to the provisions of this Compact shall, as among the parties to the agreement:

(1) Detail the specific nature of the services, programs, facilities, arrangements or properties to which it is applicable.

(2) Provide for the allocation of costs and other financial responsibilities.

(3) Specify the respective rights, duties, obligations and liabilities of the parties.

(4) Set forth the terms and conditions for duration, renewal, termination, abrogation, disposal of joint or common property, if any, and all other matters which may be appropriate to the proper effectuation and performance of the agreement.

(b) No public or private library agency shall undertake to exercise itself, or jointly with any other library agency, by means of a library agreement any power prohibited to such agency by the constitution or statutes of its state.

(c) No library agreement shall become effective until filed with the compact administrator of each state involved, and approved in accordance with Article VII of this Compact.

Article VII. Approval of Library Agreements

(a) Every library agreement made pursuant to this Compact shall, prior to and as a condition precedent to its entry into force, be submitted to the attorney general of each state in which a public library agency party thereto is situated, who shall determine whether the agreement is in proper form and compatible with the laws of his state. The attorneys general shall approve any agreement submitted to them unless they shall find that it does not meet the conditions set forth herein and shall detail in writing addressed to the governing bodies of the public library agencies concerned the specific respects in which the proposed agreement fails to meet the requirements of law. Failure to disapprove an agreement submitted hereunder within 90 days of its submission shall constitute approval thereof.

(b) In the event that a library agreement made pursuant to this Compact shall deal in whole or in part with the provision of services or facilities with regard to which an officer or agency of the state government has constitutional or statutory powers of control, the agreement shall, as a condition precedent to its entry into force, be submitted to the state officer or agency having such power of control and shall be approved or disapproved by him or it as to all matters within his or its jurisdiction in the same manner and subject to the same requirements governing the action of the attorneys general pursuant to paragraph (a) of this article. This requirement of submission and approval shall be in addition to and not in substitution for the requirement of submission to an approval by the attorneys general.

Article VIII. Other Laws Applicable

Nothing in this Compact or in any library agreement shall be construed to supersede, alter or otherwise impair any obligation imposed on any library by otherwise applicable law, nor to authorize the transfer or disposition of any property held in trust by a library agency in a manner contrary to the terms of such trust.

Article IX. Appropriations and Aid

(a) Any public library agency party to a library agreement may appropriate funds to the interstate library district established thereby in the same manner and to the same extent as to a library wholly maintained by it and, subject to the laws of the state in which such public library agency is situated, may pledge its credit in support of an interstate library district established by the agreement.

(b) Subject to the provisions of the library agreement pursuant to which it functions and the laws of the states in which such district is situated, an interstate library district may claim and receive any state and federal aid which may be available to library agencies.

Article X. Compact Administrator

Each state shall designate a compact administrator with whom copies of all library agreements to which his state or any public library agency thereof is party shall be filed. The administrator shall have such other powers as may be conferred upon him by the laws of his state and may consult and cooperate with the compact administrators of other party states and take such steps as may effectuate the purposes of this Compact. If the laws of a party state so provide, such state may designate one or more deputy compact administrators in addition to its compact administrator.

Article XI. Entry Into Force and Withdrawal

(a) This Compact shall enter into force and effect immediately upon its enactment into law by any two states. Thereafter, it shall enter into force and effect as to any other state upon the enactment thereof by such state.

(b) This Compact shall continue in force with respect to a party state and remain binding upon such state until six months after such state has given notice to each other party state of the repeal thereof. Such withdrawal shall not be construed to relieve any party to a library agreement entered into pursuant to this Compact from any obligation of that agreement prior to the end of its duration as provided therein.

Article XII. Construction and Severability

This Compact shall be liberally construed so as to effectuate the purposes thereof. The provisions of this Compact shall be severable and if any phrase, clause, sentence or provision of this Compact is declared to be contrary to the constitution of any party state or of the United States or the applicability thereof to any government, agency, person or circumstance is held invalid, the validity of the remainder of this Compact and the applicability thereof to any government, agency, person or circumstance shall not be affected thereby. If this Compact shall be held contrary to the constitution of any state party thereto, the Compact shall remain in full force and effect as to the remaining states and in full force and effect as to the state affected as to all severable matters. (An. Code 1957, art. 77, § 166B; 1978, ch. 22, § 2.)

REGIONAL RESOURCE CENTERS

(The Annotated Code of Maryland, 1982, s.23-202 to 23-205.)

§ 23-202. Regional resource centers.

(a) *Establishment.* — The boards of library trustees of at least three public library systems outside the standard metropolitan statistical areas defined by the United States Bureau of the Census may request the Department to establish and maintain a regional resource center.

(b) *Purpose of center.* — Each regional resource center shall provide, through mutual cooperation and coordination, books, information, and other material and service resources that an individual library cannot provide adequately by itself.

(c) *Standards for establishing; location of center.* — (1) A region to be served by a regional resource center shall have a population of at least 100,000.

(2) Subject to approval by the Department, the boards of library trustees of the participating library systems shall designate the library to serve as the resource center.

(3) If possible, the library selected as the regional resource center shall be:

(i) The strongest library in the region; and

(ii) Located so as to be of greatest service to the entire region.

(d) *Board of advisors.* — (1) There is a board of advisors for each regional resource center.

(2) The board of advisors consists of two individuals selected by the board of trustees of each participating library system to represent its library.

(3) The board of advisors for each regional resource center shall:

(i) Gather information on the resource needs of its region and this State;

(ii) Before State funds are distributed to it, make an annual report to the Department and the State Advisory Council on Libraries that evaluates and makes recommendations on the operation of the center;

(iii) Recommend to the board of trustees of the library designated as the regional resource center and to the Department policies and procedures for the development and use of the regional resource center;

(iv) Promote the use of the regional resource center;

(v) Recommend the purchase, condemnation, rental, use, sale, or conveyance of property for any purpose valid under this section; and

(vi) Recommend plans for the regional resource centers, which may include the use of facilities of participating libraries, additions to the facilities of participating libraries, or new facilities separate from the existing facilities of participating libraries.

(e) *Administration of center.* — (1) The head of each regional resource center is the administrator of the library designated as the center.

(2) The administrator shall operate the regional resource center under standards adopted by the Department.

(3) The policies and procedures of the regional resource center shall be:

(i) Recommended by the board of trustees of the library designated as the center; and

(ii) Approved by the board of advisors of the center.

(f) *Duties of regional resource centers.* — Each regional resource center shall:

(1) Make interlibrary loans of books and materials;

(2) Supply collections and exhibits of specialized materials;

(3) Provide consultant services;

(4) Organize inservice training for library staffs; and

(5) Develop and operate cooperative services among libraries. (An. Code 1957, art. 77, § 169; 1978, ch. 22, § 2.)

§ 23-203. Metropolitan cooperative service programs.

(a) *Authorized.* — The board of library trustees of any public library system that is not participating in a regional resource center may participate in a metropolitan cooperative service program.

(b) *Standards.* — Each metropolitan cooperative service program shall conform to standards adopted by the State Board.

(c) *Annual report.* — Each metropolitan cooperative service program shall make an annual report of its operations to the Department and the State Advisory Council on Libraries. (An. Code 1957, art. 77, § 169; 1978, ch. 22, § 2.)

§ 23-204. Evaluation of regional resource centers and metropolitan cooperative service programs.

The Department periodically shall evaluate the effectiveness of the services performed by each regional resource center and metropolitan cooperative service program and may request any reports and information necessary for this purpose. (An. Code 1957, art. 77, § 169; 1978, ch. 22, § 2.)

§ 23-205. Funding for programs.

(a) *Operating funds to be included in budget; review by Governor and General Assembly.* — Each year, the Department may include in its budget operating

funds for:
>   (1) The State Library Resource Center;
>   (2) Each regional resource center; and
>   (3) Each metropolitan cooperative service program.

(b) *Capital expenses.* — (1) The State shall pay all capital expenses for:
>   (i) The State Library Resource Center; and
>   (ii) Each regional resource center.

(2) Before any money is spent under this subsection, the appropriate board of library trustees shall:
>   (i) Have the project approved by the Department;
>   (ii) Through the Department, submit the request to the Department of State Planning for consideration under Article 88C, § 6 of the Code; and
>   (iii) Agree to reimburse the Department an amount the Department determines if the facility ceases to be used for a resource center or cooperative service program.

(c) *Payment of funds to resource centers and metropolitan cooperative service programs.* — (1) The Department shall:
>   (i) Disburse funds to the State and regional resource centers and metropolitan cooperative service programs; and
>   (ii) Require that these funds be used subject to any conditions specified by the appropriating agency or imposed under this subtitle.

(2) The Department may authorize the State Comptroller to withhold funds from any regional resource center or metropolitan cooperative service program that fails to meet the standards adopted by the Department. (An. Code 1957, art. 77, §§ 168, 169; 1978, ch. 22, § 2.)

COOPERATIVE LIBRARY CORPORATIONS
(The Annotated Code of Maryland, 1982, s.23-206.)

§ 23-206. Cooperative library corporations.

(a) *Formation.* — Any two or more boards of library trustees acting as incorporators under this section and the nonstock corporation laws may organize a cooperative library corporation to administer joint library projects in their counties.

(b) *Members.* — (1) The membership of the corporation consists of the members of each board of library trustees that signs the articles of incorporation.

(2) If each of the member boards agree, another county may become a member of the corporation.

(c) *Power to delegate.* — The member boards may delegate any of their intracounty powers and duties to the corporation to the extent necessary to enable it to carry out and administer joint library projects.

(d) *Retirement system for employees.* — Professional and clerical employees of a cooperative library corporation shall join the Teachers' Retirement System.

(e) *Corporation treated as a library.* — Each cooperative library corporation:

(1) Is entitled to use the library fund;

(2) Shall have the annual audit required for a library;

(3) Shall make the annual report required of a board of library trustees; and

(4) Is exempt from taxation under Article 81, § 9 (e) of the **Code**. (1979, ch. 65.)

DISTRIBUTION OF PUBLIC DOCUMENTS

(The Annotated Code of Maryland, 1982, s.23-2A-01 to 23-2A-05.)

§ 23-2A-01. Definitions.

As used in this subtitle:

(1) *State publication.* — "State publication" means informational materials produced, regardless of format, by the authority of, or at the total or partial expense of any State agency. It includes a publication sponsored by a State agency, issued in conjunction with, or under contract with the federal government, local units of government, private individuals, institutions, corporations, research firms or other entities. "State publication" does not include correspondence, interoffice and intraoffice memoranda, routine forms or other internal records. It also does not include publications of bicounty agencies which comply with this program as required in § 23-2A-05 of this article and it does not include any informational listing which any State statute provides shall be sold to members of the public for a fee.

(2) *State agency.* — "State agency" means any permanent or temporary State office, department, division or unit, bureau, board, commission, task force, authority, institution, State college or university, and any other unit of State government, whether executive, legislative, or judicial, and includes any subunits of State government.

(3) *Depository library.* — "Depository library" means a library designated for the receipt and maintenance of State publications. It includes but is not limited to:

(i) The State Library Resource Center;

(ii) The Maryland Department of Legislative Reference Library;

(iii) The Maryland Hall of Records;

(iv) The Maryland State Law Library;

(v) The McKeldin Library of the University of Maryland;

(vi) The Library of Congress; and

(vii) Any other library that the Commission on State Publications Depository and Distribution Program may designate as a depository library.

(4) *Program.* — "Program" means the State Publications Depository and Distribution Program.

(5) *Commission.* — "Commission" means the Commission on the State Publications Depository and Distribution Program. (1982, ch. 912.)

§ 23-2A-02. State Publications Depository and Distribution Program.

(a) *Created.* — There is created, as part of the State Library Resource Center at the Enoch Pratt Free Library, a State Publications Depository and Distribution Program.

(b) *Responsibilities.* — This Program is responsible for:

(1) The collection of State publications;

(2) The distribution of State publications to the depository libraries;

(3) The monthly issuance of a list of all State publications that have been received by the Center. This list shall be sent to all depository libraries and to others upon request and the center may provide for subscription services;

(4) Making determinations on exemptions of State publications from the depository requirements of this subtitle; and

(5) The implementation of rules and policies promulgated by the Commission on the State Publications Depository and Distribution Program.

(c) *Appointment of Administrator.* — The Administrator of the Program shall be appointed by the Director of the State Library Resource Center with the approval of the Commission on the State Publications Depository and Distribution Program.

(d) *Funding.* — Funding for the Program shall be provided in the aid to education budget of the State Board of Education in a program entitled State Publications Depository. (1982, ch. 912.)

§ 23-2A-03. Commission on the State Publications Depository and Distribution Program.

(a) *Commission established.* — There is established a Commission on the State Publications Depository and Distribution Program.

(b) *Commission membership.* — The Commission shall have 9 members appointed by the Governor as follows:

(1) 3 members representing depository libraries;

(2) 3 members representing State agencies; and

(3) 3 members from the general public.

(c) *Term of office.* — (1) Each member shall serve for a term of 4 years and until a successor is appointed and qualifies and may not serve more than 2 consecutive 4 year terms.

(2) These terms shall be staggered as required for the original appointments to the Commission.

(d) *Service without compensation; expense reimbursement.* — Each member of the Commission shall serve without compensation, but shall be reimbursed for expenses incurred while engaged in the performance of duties, in accordance with Standard Travel Regulations.

(e) *Election of officers; meetings.* — The Commission:

(1) Shall elect 1 of its members as its chair each year;

(2) May elect other officers as needed; and

(3) Shall meet at least quarterly.

(f) *Duties of Commission.* — The Commission shall:

(1) Promote the effective dissemination and the use of State publications;

(2) Provide for the granting of depository status to geographically dispersed libraries, other than those listed in § 23-2A-01 (3);

(3) Adopt rules and policies for the uniform identification, collection, distribution, accessibility, and retention of State publications;

(4) Advise the Program in implementing the purposes of this section;

(5) Provide for access to State publications; and

(6) Report to the Governor annually on the operations and effectiveness of the Program. (1982, ch. 912.)

§ 23-2A-04. Responsibilities of State agencies.

(a) *Designation of publications contact person by State agencies.* — Each State agency shall designate an agency publications contact person, and shall notify the Center of the designation.

(b) *State agencies to provide Center with agency publications.* — Each State agency shall furnish to the Center a sufficient quantity of each publication to meet the requirements of the depository system. (1982, ch. 912.)

§ 23-2A-05. Responsibilities of bicounty agencies.

(a) Each bicounty agency shall:

(1) Designate an agency publications contact person, and notify the Center of the designation;

(2) Furnish to the Center 1 copy of each publication to meet the requirements of the depository system;

(3) Furnish 1 copy each to a designated branch library within each county library system of the counties in which the bicounty agency operates;

(4) Or, in the alternative, furnish all copies to the Center for distribution as stated in this section. (1982, ch. 912.)

COUNTY LIBRARIES
(The Annotated Code of Maryland, 1982, s.23-301 to 23-307.)

§ 23-301. Authorized.

(a) *Establishment and support.* — The governing body of each county may establish, and appropriate an amount to support, a county public library system free from political influence.

(b) *Board of library trustees.* — Each county public library system shall be governed by a board of trustees. However, a charter county may:

(1) Establish a county library agency and grant it some or all of the powers of a board of trustees; or

(2) Have a board of library trustees, provide for the board's selection, and determine its powers. (An. Code 1957, art. 77, §§ 171, 172; 1978, ch. 22, § 2.)

§ 23-302. Special provisions for Baltimore City and Washington County.

(a) *Baltimore City.* — (1) The Mayor and City Council of Baltimore shall be governed by the requirements and regulations pertaining to the Enoch Pratt Free Library of Baltimore City as provided in Chapter 181 of the Acts of 1882 and any other laws applicable to the operation of public libraries.

(2) The powers and duties of the board of trustees of the Enoch Pratt Free Library are as provided in Chapter 181 of the Acts of 1882 and the charter and the articles of incorporation of the Enoch Pratt Free Library and other laws applicable to the board of trustees of the Enoch Pratt Free Library.

(b) *Washington County.* — (1) The County Commissioners of Washington County shall be governed by the requirements and regulations pertaining to the Washington County Free Library as provided in Chapter 511 of the Acts of 1898 and any other laws applicable to the operation of public libraries.

(2) The powers and duties of the board of trustees of the Washington County Free Library are as provided in Chapter 511 of the Acts of 1898 and the charter, articles of incorporation, and other laws applicable to the board of trustees of the Washington County Free Library. (An. Code 1957, art. 77, §§ 171, 173; 1978, ch. 22, § 2.)

§ 23-303. Boards of library trustees.

(a) *Composition.* — (1) Each board of library trustees consists of seven members appointed by the county governing body from nominees submitted by the board of library trustees.

(2) A board that existed before 1945 under a corporate charter may continue as constituted if:

(i) It has at least seven members;

(ii) The members are chosen on the basis of character, ability, and demonstrated interest in library matters; and

(iii) The members meet the qualifications required under subsection (b) of this section.

(b) *Qualifications.* — The members of the board shall be:

(1) Representative of the area the library serves; and

(2) Residents of the county that the library serves.

(c) *Term and vacancies.* — (1) Each member of a board serves for a term of 5 years and until a successor is appointed and qualifies. These terms are staggered as required by the terms of the members serving on the board as of July 1, 1978.

(2) A member may be reappointed but may not serve more than two consecutive terms.

(3) A member appointed to fill a vacancy in an unexpired term serves only for the remainder of that term and until a successor is appointed and qualifies.

(d) *Compensation.* — Each member of a board serves without compensation. (An. Code 1957, art. 77, § 172; 1978, ch. 22, § 2.)

§ 23-304. Officers; meetings; attendance.

(a) *Officers.* — Each year, each board of library trustees:

(1) Shall elect one of its members as its chairman; and

(2) May elect any other officer it requires.

(b) *Treasurer to be bonded.* — The treasurer of each board of library trustees shall be bonded adequately.

(c) *Meetings generally.* — Each board of library trustees may determine the time and place of its meetings and may adopt rules for the conduct of its meetings. However:

(1) Each board shall meet at least once every 3 months;

(2) Any final action of a board shall be taken at a public meeting; and

(3) The minutes of board meetings shall be open to the public.

(d) *Failure of member to attend meetings.* — (1) Any member of a board of library trustees who fails to attend at least half of the scheduled meetings of the board during any calendar year shall be considered to have resigned from the board.

(2) The chairman of the board of library trustees shall report the member's name and nonattendance to the county governing body by January 15 of the following year.

(3) The county governing body may reject the resignation if the member explains his nonattendance satisfactorily.

(4) The resignation is effective from the date of the final review by the county governing body, which shall be within 10 days after it receives the report from the chairman of the board of library trustees. The county governing body shall fill any resulting vacancy as provided in § 23-303 of this subtitle. (An. Code 1957, art. 77, §§ 172, 173; 1978, ch. 22, § 2.)

§ 23-305. Powers and duties of board.

(a) *In general.* — In addition to any other powers granted or duties imposed by this subtitle, each board of library trustees has the powers and duties set forth in this section.

(b) *Free service.* — Each board of library trustees:

(1) Shall establish and operate the library to provide free service to residents of the county in which it is located; and

(2) May permit persons outside of the county to use the library facilities on the terms and conditions it determines.

(c) *Management of library.* — Each board of library trustees may:

(1) Establish and operate libraries at any location in the county;

(2) Determine the policy of the library; and

(3) Adopt reasonable rules, regulations, and bylaws for the use of the library and the conduct of its business.

(d) *Fiscal matters.* — Each board of library trustees may:

(1) Advise in the preparation of, and approve, the library budget;

(2) Receive, account for, control, and supervise, under the rules and regulations of the county governing body, the spending of all public funds

received by the library; and

(3) Use the services of the fiscal agencies of the county governing body.

(e) *Audit and annual report.* — Each board of library trustees shall:

(1) Provide for an audit at least annually, by an accountant approved by the State Superintendent of its business and financial transactions and of the accounts of its treasurer;

(2) Make public the results of the annual audit; and

(3) Make an annual report to the county governing body and the State Superintendent on or before November 1 of each year that shows:

(i) The amounts of money received from the library fund and other sources;

(ii) The itemized expenses;

(iii) The number of books and periodicals the library has;

(iv) The results of the annual audit; and

(v) Any other information the Department requires.

(f) *Other powers.* — Each board of library trustees may:

(1) Accept any gift, grant, or appropriation for library purposes from any person under any appropriate terms and conditions;

(2) Own and dispose of these gifts, grants, and appropriations;

(3) Recommend to the county governing body the acquisition, use, or conveyance of property, for any purpose valid under this subtitle;

(4) Select the location of and approve plans for the erection of library buildings, subject to the approval of the county governing body;

(5) Make contracts for any library service with any person; and

(6) Do anything else necessary for the proper control and development of the library.

(An. Code 1957, art. 77, §§ 171, 173, 178, 179; 1978, ch. 22, § 2.)

§ 23-306. Library personnel.

(a) *Appointment of personnel.* — Each board of library trustees shall:

(1) Select and appoint a certificated professional librarian as director of the library; and

(2) On recommendation of the director, appoint any other necessary employees.

(b) *Personnel policies.* — Each board of library trustees:

(1) May adopt policies for staff classification, salaries, and benefits including vacation, sick leave, and hours of work; or

(2) Shall use the county personnel agency, if any, and request its advice in setting up personnel policies and procedures.

(c) *Qualifications of professional employees.* — Each appointee to the professional library staff shall hold a certificate or provisional certificate of library qualifications issued by the State Superintendent.

(d) *Dismissal of employees.* —(1) On written recommendation of the library director, each board of library trustees may suspend or dismiss any professional or clerical employee of any library under its jurisdiction for any of the following reasons:

    (i) Immorality;

    (ii) Misconduct in office;

    (iii) Insubordination;

    (iv) Incompetency; or

    (v) Willful neglect of duty.

(2) (i) Before removing an employee, the board shall send him a written copy of the charges against him and give him an opportunity to request a hearing within 10 days.

(ii) If the employee requests a hearing within the 10-day period the board promptly shall hold a hearing, but a hearing may not be set within 10 days after the board sends the employee a notice of the hearing. The employee shall have an opportunity to be heard publicly before the board in his own defense, in person or by counsel.

(3) If the board votes to remove the employee and:

    (i) The decision is unanimous, the decision of the board is final; or

    (ii) The decision is not unanimous, the employee may appeal to the State Superintendent.

(e) *Duties of library director.* — The director of each library shall:

(1) Act as the general executive officer of the library and manage its day-to-day operations under the policies approved by the board of library trustees;

(2) Prepare the annual budget of the library, and present it to the board for approval;

(3) Nominate for appointment all clerical and professional employees in the county library system; and

(4) Adopt reasonable rules and regulations for the use of the library system subject to approval by the board of library trustees. (An. Code 1957, art. 77, §§ 173-175; 1978, ch. 22, § 2.)

§ 23-307. Volunteer aides in public libraries.

The board of library trustees of any library may use volunteer aides. These volunteer aides may not replace library personnel but shall assist regular personnel in carrying out their duties. Each board of library trustees shall develop guidelines for the selection and use of volunteer aides in its library system. Volunteer aides shall be considered agents of the board of library trustees for the limited purpose of comprehensive liability insurance coverage. (An. Code 1957, art. 77, § 183; 1978, ch. 22, § 2.)

HALL OF RECORDS COMMISSION

(The Annotated Code of Maryland, 1982, Art. 54, s.1-13.)

§ 1. Membership; expenses.

There is hereby created as part of the Department of General Services a commission to be known as the Hall of Records Commission, which shall be composed of the Secretary of General Services, the State Comptroller, the State Treasurer, a member of the Senate, as appointed by the President of the Senate, a member of the House of Delegates, as appointed by the Speaker of the House, the Chief Judge of the Court of Appeals, the president of The Johns Hopkins University or his designated alternate, the president of the University of Maryland or his designated alternate, the president of St. John's College or his designated alternate, and the president of the Maryland Historical Society. The members of said Commission shall serve without compensation, but shall be reimbursed for expenses incurred while actually engaged in the performance of their duties in accordance with the standard travel regulations. (An. Code, 1951, art. 41, § 148; 1939, art. 41, § 123; 1935, ch. 18, § 87A; 1967, ch. 344, § 4; 1970, ch. 97, § 6; 1975, ch. 721, § 2; 1979, ch. 248.)

§ 2. Supervision and control of Hall of Records; Archivist and other employees; "Land Commissioner" to mean "Archivist."

(a) *Supervision and control of Hall of Records building.* — The Commission shall have supervision and control of the Hall of Records building and shall have authority to equip and furnish the said building and to preserve and repair the records, documents and archives placed under its supervision, the cost of same to be paid for out of any funds which may hereafter be appropriated for that purpose.

(b) *Archivist and other employees.* — The Commission shall appoint a competent, qualified person, to be known as Archivist, who shall have charge of the active management of the building and its contents; provided that the Commission shall allot and designate a portion of the building for the use of the Land Office. The Commission shall employ such assistants, clerks and other employees as may be necessary for the work of collecting, repairing, indexing, copying, filing and preserving the records, documents, papers, books and other data under the jurisdiction and supervision of the Commission. The Archivist, his assistants, clerks and other employees shall receive such salary or compensation as may be recommended by the Commission and provided in the budget.

(c) *Meaning of "Commissioner of the Land Office" or "Land Commissioner".* — The words "Commissioner of the Land Office" or "Land Commissioner" as used in this Code shall be construed to mean the Archivist appointed pursuant to subsection (b). (An. Code, 1951, art. 41, § 149; 1939, art. 41, § 124; 1935, ch. 18, § 87B; 1936, Sp. Sess., ch. 81; 1967, ch. 344, §§ 2, 4.)

§ 3. Collection of old records, documents, etc.; consolidated publications account; Archives Fund.

(c) (1) The Hall of Records Commission may accept the transfer of the inventory of the Archives of Maryland and funds relating thereto from the Maryland Historical Society. The State Comptroller shall maintain the transferred funds as a special fund, designated the Archives Fund to be used to:

(i) Prepare, edit, and publish future volumes of the Archives of Maryland series;

(ii) Reprint unavailable volumes of the Archives of Maryland; and

(iii) Receive moneys derived from the sale of or appropriated for publishing the Archives of Maryland.

(2) The Hall of Records Commission may request that the treasurer invest fund moneys only for the purposes specified in paragraph (1) of this subsection. (1981, ch. 119.)

§ 4. Seal; rules for governance; acquisitions by gift or purchase.

The Commission shall have power and authority to adopt a seal for its official use and business, to adopt rules for its own governance and to determine the type and character of records, documents, publications and other data which it will accept or receive for safekeeping.

The Commission shall have power to acquire by gift, or to purchase with any funds appropriated or given to it for that purpose, any records, documents, publications or other material which it may deem worthy of preservation. (An. Code, 1951, art. 41, § 151; 1939, art. 41, § 126; 1935, ch. 18, § 87D; 1967, ch. 344, § 4.)

§ 5. Transfer of certain papers, records and documents.

(a) *Papers, records and documents made prior to 1788.* — Papers, records and documents, now in the courthouses of this State, which were made prior to April 28th 1788, the date of the adoption of the Constitution of the United States by the State of Maryland, shall be transferred as soon as practicable after June 1, 1945, to the Hall of Records Commission, which is hereby made the official custodian of such papers, records and documents, with full power to certify the same as provided in § 7. Every clerk of court, register of wills, or other public official, now having custody of said papers, records and documents, is hereby directed to transfer the same to said Hall of Records Commission and upon making such transfer, every such clerk, register of wills or other official is hereby relieved from any duties or responsibilities in connection therewith.

(b) *Records, etc., formerly in custody of Commissioner of Land Office.* — The Hall of Records Commission shall also be the official custodian of all records of the court of chancery, including all ante-Revolution papers formerly in that office, and all other records, books, relics and memorials formerly in the custody of the Commissioner of the Land Office, except warrants, surveys, caveats, patents, and other records relating to proceedings for the issuance of patents. Copies of all items so transferred may be made and certified with the same effect as provided in subsection (a). (An. Code, 1951, art. 41, § 152; 1945, ch. 248; 1967, ch. 344, §§ 2, 4; 1968, ch. 43.)

§ 6. Custody of records of defunct State agencies, etc.

The records of all State agencies, boards and commissions which hereafter are

abolished or otherwise cease to function shall be transferred to the custody of
the Hall of Records Commission unless otherwise directed by law. (1956, ch. 79;
1967, ch. 344, § 4.)

§ 7. Officials authorized to turn over certain records.

*Every State, county, city, town or other public official in the State in custody
of public records or documents is hereby authorized and empowered, in his
discretion, to turn over to the Commission and deposit for preservation any
original papers, official books, records, documents, files, newspapers, printed
books, or portraits, not in current use in his office, and when so surrendered,
and accepted by the Commission, copies may be made and certified under the
seal of the Commission upon application of any person, which certification
shall have the same force and effect as if made by the officer originally in
charge of same, and the Commission shall charge for such copies the same fees
as such office is allowed by law to charge, which fees shall be accounted for and
paid into the State treasury.*

*Whenever any land records of any court have been turned over to the Com-
mission and deposited with it for preservation and so accepted by it, the Commission is hereby authorized and directed upon the written application of the
clerk of the circuit court for any county and with the written approval of a judge
of said court, to make photostatic or photographic reproductions of such land
records, the expense thereof to be borne by the Commission; and such
photostatic or photographic reproductions, when so made and certified under
the seal of the Commissioner, shall be deposited by the Commission in the
office of the clerk of the court making said application and said reproduced land
records when so deposited shall be entitled to the same legal force and effect
as the original land records from which such reproductions were made.*
(1982, ch. 820, § 1.)

§ 8. Destruction of certain records not accepted by Commission; lists thereof.

*If the Commission declines to accept any original papers, official books,
records, documents or files offered to it under the provisions of § 7, then their
custodian, with the written approval of the Commission, may destroy them.
After the records are destroyed, their custodian shall file with the Hall of
Records a list of all papers, books, documents and files destroyed and a certificate of destruction. These lists shall be retained in the custody of the Archivist
and shall be available at reasonable times to inspection by the members of the
public. This section does not authorize the destruction of (a) papers, books,
documents or files which have been designated for retention for a period of time
expressly prescribed by statute, (b) public records expressly required by statute
to be maintained permanently, except in those cases where the original record
has been photographed, photocopied, or microphotographed in accordance with
the provisions of § 11 of this article, if the copy or reproduction of the original
record is available upon request in the same manner as the original record, (c)*

permanent books of account, (d) the records of any court of record in this State, except as provided for in § 1-605 (d-3) and § 2-206 of the Courts Article of the Code, (e) the land records recorded by the respective clerks of the circuit court for the counties. Old records of which accurate transcriptions have been made and placed in use and the "housekeeping" records or the records of internal management of the offices of clerks of court and registers of wills may not be considered "records of a court" for the purpose of this section and §§ 9 and 10 and shall be subject to disposal as described above. However, the books, accounts, and records pertaining to the financial operations of any agency or department, officers, boards and commissions of the State of Maryland, and of all the clerks of courts, registers of wills, and all collectors of the State taxes of the State of Maryland, including the City of Baltimore, insofar as they affect the collection of State taxes, may not be destroyed until such time as the requirements of Article 40, §§ 61A to 61E, inclusive, relating to the audit of such books, accounts and records by the State Auditor, shall have been complied with.
(1982, ch. 820, § 1.)

§ 9. What constitute records under § 8.

For the purposes of § 8, the following types of material shall not be considered "records": printed books, magazines, newspapers and other library or museum materials made or acquired for reference or exhibition purposes, extra copies of documents preserved only for convenience of reference, stocks of publications, acceptances or refusals of invitations or engagements and other personal business of public officers. From time to time the Hall of Records Commission may further designate categories which may be included within the definition of "nonrecord material." And such nonrecord materials may be disposed of by the custodian when he shall deem them to be no longer necessary for the operation of his office. (An. Code, 1951, art. 41, § 155; 1949, ch. 755, § 127B; 1967, ch. 344, § 4; 1968, ch. 43.)

§ 10. Programs of record management; retention schedules; duties of Commission.

(a) *Programs and schedules.* — Each State agency shall develop a continuing program for the economical and efficient management of its records, including the establishment and/or revision of record retention schedules, in order to insure prompt and orderly disposal of records not required by the operations of the agency. Prior to becoming operative all such retention schedules shall receive the approval of the Hall of Records Commission. Schedules providing for the destruction of records also shall receive the written approval of the Commission.

(b) *Duties of Commission.* — It shall be the duty of the Hall of Records Commission to further the aforesaid program; to inspect the records and records management practices of all State agencies, boards and commissions; to review proposals for the purchase or rental of record equipment, storage space and services, including the microfilming and photocopying of records, and to make recommendations thereon to the Department of Budget and Procurement or to the Board of Public Works, as appropriate. (An. Code, 1951, art. 41, § 156; 1949, ch. 755, § 127C; 1953, ch. 436; 1967, ch. 344, § 4; 1978, ch. 24.)

§ 11. Photographs and other reproductions of records.

(a) *In general.* — Whenever any agency, department, board, or commission of the State of Maryland or of any county or incorporated municipality thereof shall have photographed, photocopied, or microphotographed all or any part of the records kept by it or under its control in a manner and on film or paper that complies with the standard of quality approved for permanent photographic records by the Hall of Records Commission, and whenever such photographs, photocopies, or microphotographs shall be placed in adequately accessible containers and provision made for preserving, examining, and using the same in a manner approved by the Hall of Records Commission, the head of such agency, department, board, or commission may, with the approval of the Archivist of the Hall of Records under the provisions of § 8, of this subtitle, cause the original records from which the photographs, photocopies, or microphotographs have been made, or any part thereof, to be disposed of as the law provides.

(b) *Effect of originals; admission in evidence.* — Photographs, photocopies, or microphotographs of any records photographed, photocopied, or microphotographed as herein provided shall have the same force and effect as the originals thereof would have had, and shall be treated as originals for the purpose of their admissibility in evidence. Certified or authenticated copies of such photographs, photocopies, or microphotographs or enlargements thereof shall be admitted in evidence equally with the original photographs, photocopies, or microphotographs. (An. Code, 1951, art. 41, § 157; 1949, ch. 518, § 127D; 1967, ch. 344, § 4; 1968, ch. 43.)

§ 12. Central depository for State real property records.

(a) The Commission shall be the official custodian, and central depository, for all deeds, title insurance policies and other pertinent records, current or noncurrent, relating to real property acquired by the State of Maryland. It is the duty of the Commission to maintain an indexed register of all deeds, title insurance policies and other pertinent records, with the authority to provide certified copies of such records to any interested person.

(b) The Commission may delegate the responsibility for the housing and care of original records relating to state-owned real property if such records are necessary for the daily operation of a State agency. A State agency requesting the delegation of such responsibility shall demonstrate to the Commission that such records will be adequately housed and maintained. If the Commission delegates responsibility for the care of records relating to state-owned real property, security microform copies of such records shall be deposited with the Hall of Records in lieu of the originals. (1977, ch. 597.)

§ 13. Forms management program.

(a) *Meaning of "form".* — For the purposes of this section, "form" means a document with a standard format for the systematic and repetitive collection, maintenance, or transmission of information.

(b) *Forms management plans required; forms management officer; provisions of plan.* — Each principal department headed by a secretary and each independent agency of the State government shall have a forms management plan to assure that the department or agency uses only those forms which are necessary for its effective or efficient operation.

(1) Each department and independent agency shall have a forms management officer, appointed from existing personnel, by the department or agency head, who shall devise and revise, as needed, the forms management plan, subject to the approval of the records management division of the Hall of Records Commission.

(2) Each plan shall provide for:

(i) An inventory of forms in current use;

(ii) A register of forms approved by the forms management officer;

(iii) Approval by the forms management officer of only those forms which are necessary for the effective or efficient operation of the department or agency; which ask for information necessary or relevant to the lawful purpose of the department or agency; which do not impose an undue burden on the persons completing them; which do not unnecessarily duplicate the other forms of the department or agency or the other forms of other departments or agencies; and which, to the greatest extent possible, are brief, plainly written, well designed, and easily completed;

(iv) Identification of the forms of the department or agency in accordance with a standard identification system to be devised or approved by the records management division of the Hall of Records Commission;

(v) The most economical system for the preparation, reproduction, and use of approved forms; and

(vi) The periodic review of all approved forms and the elimination of those which no longer meet the criteria set out in subparagraph (iii) of this paragraph.

(3) The forms management plan for a department or agency shall be administered by the forms management officer for that department or agency, subject to the provisions of subsection (e) of this section.

(c) *Use of approved forms required.* — After February 1, 1979, only forms approved by the forms management officer under the forms management plan and listed on the register of approved forms may be used by a department or agency.

(d) *Report on forms management activities.* — At the close of each fiscal year, beginning with the close of fiscal year 1979, each department or agency shall prepare a report on its forms management activities during the fiscal year which has just ended. This report shall be submitted to the records management division by July 31.

(e) *Copies of plans to be filed.* — Each department or agency shall file a copy of its forms management plan with the records management division of the Hall of Records Commission by August 1, 1978, and shall file a copy of any subsequent revision of its plan with the same division.

(f) *Duties of records management division of Commission.* — The records management division of the Hall of Records Commission shall:

(1) Assist each department and agency in the development and implementation of its forms management plan.

(2) Develop a standard identification system for the identification of forms.

(3) Assist each department and agency in coordinating its forms management plan with the plans of other departments and agencies.

(4) Review and approve those forms management plans which meet the provisions of paragraph (2) of subsection (b) of this section.

(5) Monitor the administration of each forms management plan to insure adherence to its provisions.

(6) Prepare, at the close of each fiscal year, beginning with the close of fiscal year 1979, a consolidated annual report on forms management activities in the fiscal year just ended. The consolidated report shall be based on the departmental and agency reports submitted to the division in accordance with subsection (d) of this section and shall be submitted to the Joint Budget and Audit Committee by September 1. (1978, ch. 981.)

LAW LIBRARIES
(The Annotated Code of Maryland, 1982, Art. 38, s.5.)

§ 5. Portion of fines and forfeited recognizances to go to law libraries.

(a) *Generally.* — One half of the fines imposed and recognizances forfeited to the circuit court for the several counties of the State shall be paid to the clerks of the respective courts, to be expended under the direction of the judge or judges of said courts, for the augmentation of the libraries of said courts. This section does not apply to Queen Anne's, Anne Arundel, Somerset, Howard and Talbot counties. The clerk shall retain a 5 percent commission on the fines and forfeitures collected. In Baltimore County, this section shall not apply to fines imposed in gambling cases.

(b) *In Harford County.* — In Harford County, in addition to the sums provided in subsection (a) the County Commissioners shall appropriate and pay to the clerk of the Circuit Court the sum of one thousand five hundred dollars ($1,500) and such additional sums as the Commissioners shall determine for the support and maintenance of the court library, including the necessary expenses for books and library equipment and the costs for the services of a librarian. This sum shall be expended under the direction of the judge of the Circuit Court for Harford County.

(c) *In Cecil County.* — In Cecil County, if in any year the payment to the court library of one half the fines imposed and recognizances forfeited plus attorney appearance fees as provided in § 7-204 of the Courts and Judicial Proceedings Article is less than $10,000 the County Commissioners shall pay to the clerk of the court, for the use of the library, whatever amount may be necessary to bring to $10,000 in the aggregate, the total amount to be paid to the library during that year under the provisions of this section, and in addition to the amount to be paid as aforesaid, the County Commissioners may, in their discretion, pay such sums over and above the $10,000 hereinabove provided for, as they consider reasonable for the proper maintenance of the library. All sums paid under the provisions of this section shall be expended under the direction of the judges of the Circuit Court for Cecil County.

(e) *In Kent County.* — Repealed by Acts 1978, ch. 552, § 1, effective July 1, 1978.

(1978, ch. 552, § 1; 1982, ch. 17, § 3; ch. 134; ch. 906, § 1.)

PROTECTION OF LIBRARY PROPERTY
(The Annotated Code of Maryland, 1982, s.23-308.)

§ 23-308. Theft or mutilation of books or other property.

(a) *Prohibited.* — A person may not unlawfully take, detain, mutilate, injure, or disfigure any book, map, picture, engraving, manuscript, or other property of any library.

(b) *Penalty.* — Any person who violates this section is guilty of a misdemeanor and on conviction is subject to a fine not exceeding $250, imprisonment not exceeding 3 months, or both. (An. Code 1957, art. 77, § 180; 1978, ch. 22, § 2.)

Maryland library laws are reprinted from THE ANNO-
TATED CODE OF MARYLAND published by The Michie
Co., Charlottesville, Virginia.

MASSACHUSETTS

STATE LIBRARY

(Massachusetts General Laws Annotated, 1982, Chap. 6, s.33-39A.)

§ 33. Composition; appointment; term; designated trustees; chairman; clerk; quorum

There shall be a board of trustees of the state library, consisting of the president of the senate, the speaker of the house of representatives and the state secretary, who shall be trustees ex-officiis, and four other persons appointed by the governor, of whom one shall be appointed annually for a four year term commencing June first of the year of appointment. An ex-officio member of the board may designate another person to serve in his place by notice in writing to the librarian. Any person so designated shall serve until such member ceases to be a member of the board ex-officio or until sooner removed by such member by notice in writing to the librarian stating the reasons for removal. The board shall elect from its membership a chairman to serve for a term of one year. The librarian shall serve as clerk to the board. Four members of the board, or their designees, shall constitute a quorum for the conduct of the official business of the board.

Amended by St.1977, c. 108, § 1.

§ 34. Powers and duties of trustees

Said trustees shall have the management and control of the state library and of the moneys appropriated therefor. They may sell or otherwise dispose of such books belonging to the library as they consider unsuitable for its purposes, and they may deposit any duplicate volumes for safe keeping and use in any town, city or college library in the commonwealth, upon such terms and conditions as they shall prescribe. They may make and enforce rules for the use of the library, and shall see that its rooms are properly prepared for the accommodation of persons permitted to use them. St.1910 c. 217 § 2.

§ 35. Librarian; compensation, etc.

The governor, with the advice and consent of the council, shall appoint a librarian of the state library, who shall hold office during their pleasure and the position of librarian shall be classified in accordance with section forty-five of chapter thirty and the salary shall be determined in accordance with section forty-six C of said chapter thirty.

Amended by St.1981, c. 699, § 2.

§ 35. Librarian; compensation, etc.

The governor, with the advice and consent of the council, shall appoint a librarian of the state library, who shall hold office during their pleasure and shall receive such salary as may be fixed by the trustees of said library with the approval of the governor and council.

St.1929 c. 277.

§ 36. Expenditures for state library; approval of accounts

The trustees of the state library may expend such sums annually as the general court may appropriate for permanent assistants and clerks, for books, maps, papers, periodicals and other material for the library and for binding the same and for incidental expenses including binding their report. All accounts for the maintenance of the state library shall be approved by the trustees thereof or by such person as may be designated for the purpose in a vote of said trustees who shall, nevertheless, remain responsible for such approval.

St.1925 c. 185.

§ 37. Trustees' annual report

The trustees of the state library shall keep records of their doings, and shall make an annual report thereof, with a list of books, maps and charts lost, missing or acquired during the preceding fiscal year, specifying those obtained by exchange, gift or purchase, and such suggestions for the improvement of the library as they may deem proper.

St.1910 c. 217 § 2.

§ 37A. Gifts in trust for state library

The said trustees may receive in trust for the commonwealth any gift or bequest of money or securities for any purpose incident to the uses of the state library, and shall forthwith transfer any money or securities so received to the state treasurer, who shall administer the same as provided by section sixteen of chapter ten.

St.1923 c. 376 § 1.

§ 38. Location; persons authorized to use

The state library shall be in the state house, and shall be kept open every day except Saturday, Sunday and legal holidays for the use of the governor, lieutenant governor, council, general court and such officers of the government and other persons as may be permitted to use it.

Amended by St.1973, c. 1043, § 1.

§ 39. Deposit of books, documents, etc., in state library

Unless otherwise provided, all books, maps, documents and other publications belonging to the commonwealth for public use, except such as by order of the respective departments of the government are retained in the chambers of the senate and the house of representatives or in the department of the state secretary, shall be deposited and suitably arranged in the library.

R.L.1902 c. 10 § 28.

§ 39A. Copies of reports of public authorities; deposit in state library; penalty

The chairman or chief executive officer of each independent public authority created by act of the general court shall deposit in the state library a copy of every report made by said independent public authority to the holders of its outstanding bonds, or to a trustee for the benefit of bond holders, and every other report required to be filed under the resolutions or trust indenture, or other document of similar import, pursuant to which said bonds were issued. Such copies shall be attested over the signature of the chairman or chief executive officer and the secretary or clerk of said public authority, and shall be deposited within thirty days of the time that the original reports are made to the persons entitled thereto. Any person wilfully violating the provisions hereof shall be punished by a fine not exceeding three thousand dollars or by imprisonment for not more than six months.

Added by St.1966, c. 259.

BOARD OF LIBRARY COMMISSIONERS

(Massachusetts General Laws Annotated, 1982, Chap. 78, s.14, 15, 19, 20.)

§ 14. Establishment of board; members; appointment; term; by-laws; reimbursement; officers; staff

There shall be a board of library commissioners for the commonwealth, in this section and in sections fifteen to thirty, inclusive, called the board, consisting of nine residents of the commonwealth appointed by the governor. Upon the expiration of the term of office of a member of the board, his successor shall be appointed for a term of five years.

No person shall be appointed to serve more than two consecutive terms. Prior service on the board for a period of less than three years resulting from an initial appointment or an appointment for the remainder of an unexpired term shall not be considered a full term. The board shall prepare and adopt by-laws for the conduct of its business. Said by-laws shall provide for the election of one of its members to be chairman of the board, establish the term of office, and provide for the ways and means for the election of other officers and their terms of office as deemed necessary by the board.

The members of the board shall be reimbursed for their necessary expenses incurred in the performance of their duties.

The board shall appoint a director and determine his duties and responsibilities and may at its discretion remove him. The board shall, upon recommendation of the director, appoint a deputy director and determine his duties and responsibilities and may at its discretion remove him. The director and the deputy director shall, subject to appropriation, receive such salary as the board may determine and such other perquisites as the board may approve. The director and the deputy director shall not be subject to the provisions of section nine A of chapter thirty or of chapter thirty-one.

Subject to appropriation and to the approval of the board the director shall appoint or release such professional and subprofessional staff as the functions, powers, and duties of the board shall require; provided, however, that the provisions of said section nine A of said chapter thirty and said chapter thirty-one shall not apply to any such appointment or release.

Amended by St.1952, c. 585, § 12; St.1977, c. 565, § 4.

§ 15. Duties relating to management and maintenance of libraries

The board of library commissioners shall advise the librarian or trustees of any free public library, and may on request advise the librarian or other person in charge of the library of any state or county institution, relative to the selection or cataloguing of books and any other matter pertaining to the maintenance or administration of such library.

Amended by St.1952, c. 585, § 13.

§ 19. Powers, duties and status of board

The board of library commissioners may expend such sums as may be appropriated for the extension and encouragement of library services within the commonwealth. The said board is hereby designated as the state agency to deal with the federal government with respect to federal grants which may be made available to the commonwealth for promoting library services, and to administer such state plans as may be approved as a condition of such grants. The board may contract with any other state agency, city or town, public or private library to provide improved library services in an area, or to secure such library services as may be agreed upon, which services may include, but need not be limited to, the lending of books and related library materials, the establishment of branch libraries, depositories or bookmobile service, and to co-operative purchasing and processing of books, recordings, films and related library materials. The board shall also represent the commonwealth in the receipt and disbursement of funds made available to the commonwealth from any private source for the promotion of library services. The state treasurer shall be the custodian of funds for this purpose received from the federal government or private services.

Amended by St.1952, c. 585, § 17; St.1960, c. 429, § 6.

§ 20. Librarians; appointment; examination; registration

The board may determine by examination or by such rules as it may establish the selection and appointment of supervising librarians and all other library workers who are paid wholly or in part, under the authority of said board, by the commonwealth. Such selection and appointment shall not be subject to chapter thirty-one.

In order to assist library trustees who seek advice from the board in securing qualified librarians and assistants, the board shall keep a registry of librarians which shall give due credit for experience and successful accomplishment as well as for formal examination.   St.1915, c. 106.

STATE AID
(Massachusetts General Laws Annotated, 1982, Chap. 78, s.19A-19E.)

§ 19A. State aid; determination

The state treasurer shall annually, on or before July first, pay from the General Fund to each city or town certified by the board of library commissioners to have met certain minimum standards of free public library service established by said board a sum of money for its free public library or libraries which shall be determined as follows:—

(1) To each town having a population of less than two thousand five hundred a sum equivalent to the amount appropriated by it for free public library service during the preceding year, but in no event

more than one thousand two hundred and fifty dollars;

(2) To each city and to each town having a population of two thousand five hundred or more, a sum not exceeding fifty cents for each resident therein; provided, that such city or town appropriates during the preceding year for its free public library service at least one thousand two hundred and fifty dollars.

No city or town which appropriates for its free public library service in any one year an amount less than six dollars per capita of population shall receive any money under this section, if such appropriation is below the average of its appropriation for free public library service for the four years immediately preceding.

If a city or town is eligible for state aid under this section, but gives approved free public library service only for a fraction of the year, the amount it shall receive shall be the amount computed hereunder multiplied by such fraction.

Added by St.1960, c. 760, § 1. Amended by St.1963, c. 672; St.1970, c. 636, §§ 1, 2; St.1980, c. 99, § 1.

§ 19B. State aid; annual reports by libraries; requisites for aid

The board of library commissioners, in setting up minimum standards of free public library service and in certifying such libraries for aid under section nineteen A shall require the filing of an annual report and shall require that such public libraries

(1) be open to all residents of the commonwealth,

(2) make no charge for normal library services,

(3) be kept open a minimum number of hours per week,

(4) employ a trained library worker,

(5) expend a reasonable portion of the library's total budget for books and periodicals,

(6) lend books to other libraries in the commonwealth and extend privileges to the holders of cards issued by other public libraries in the commonwealth on a reciprocal basis.

Added by St.1960, c. 760, § 1.

§ 19C. Regional public library service; annual appropriation

The board shall establish a comprehensive state-wide program of regional public library service, consisting of regional public library systems, which shall not exceed five. For such purpose there shall be an annual appropriation which the board shall apply in the following manner:

(1) Insofar as practicable the board shall enter into an arrangement or arrangements with such public library or libraries in each regional area as it may determine under the terms of which such library or libraries shall supply services or space, equipment, personnel, books, periodicals and other library materials to communities having fewer than twenty-five thousand inhabitants;

(2) Said board shall also designate such public library or libraries in each area or an additional such public library or libraries in the area to serve as a regional reference and research center or centers to meet the reference and research library needs of the residents of all the cities and towns in the area; the amount allocated for such reference and research service to be applied only to the cost of such reference and research books, periodicals and other library materials and to the cost of the personnel employed in such reference and research service;

(3) Any library system providing service under an approved plan shall be entitled to receive annually in state aid an amount per capita of its served population per square mile of the area served in accordance with the following schedule:—

Over 1,000 population	60 cents per capita
750–999 population	65 cents per capita
Under 750 population	80 cents per capita

(4) In addition to the sums provided in clause (3), the Boston public library, as the library of last recourse for reference and research services for the commonwealth, shall be entitled to receive in state aid the sum of ten cents for each resident in the commonwealth.

Added by St.1960, c. 760, § 1. Amended by St.1970, c. 636, § 3; St.1980, c. 99, §§ 2, 3; St.1981, c. 351, § 278.

§ 19D. Regional public library service; advisory council

For each regional area the board shall establish an advisory council which shall consist of the chief librarian or one trustee to be so designated by the board of trustees of each city or town in the regional area. Such advisory councils shall make suggestions and recommendations to the board of library commissioners concerning the regional public library systems.

Added by St.1960, c. 760, § 1. Amended by St.1970, c. 636, § 4.

§ 19E. Library media services; comprehensive statewide program; funds; standards

The board of library commissioners, hereinafter called the board, shall, subject to appropriation, establish a comprehensive statewide program for the improvement and development of library and media resources for all citizens. For the purposes of this section, "library media" shall mean print or nonprint resources, including but not limited to, books, periodicals, newspapers, pamphlets, serials, musical scores, manuscripts, sound recordings, tapes, films, filmstrips, transparencies, video tapes, microfilms, maps, art prints and realia. The term "library media center" shall be synonymous with the terms "public library", "school library", "school media center", "academic library", "state" or "county institution library" and "special library".

Such funds as may be appropriated shall be disbursed by the board for any or all of the following purposes:

(1) For the establishment and development of cooperation and coordination among library media centers, including in addition to the power to award grants to establish or expand interlibrary media center networks:

(a) the power to provide technical and support services, including consultative services;

(b) the power to acquire, rent, or contract for materials and resources;

(c) the power to provide staff at the service level;

(d) the power to participate in interstate library media services if such participation will increase the availability of library media.

(2) For demonstration grants for exemplary library media services, contingent upon the board conducting an evaluation of said services on a periodic basis.

[(3) Deleted by St.1977, c. 565, § 5.]

(4) For the establishment and development of library media centers in county and state institutions.

In making grants under this clause the board shall establish minimum standards for such library service which take into account:

(a) the type of institution;

(b) the size of the resident population;

(c) the availability of library media services to the institutional population;

(d) the qualifications of personnel for staffing of a library media center;

(e) the institution's commitment to annual budgetary support for library media services.

(5) For the establishment and development of services from library media centers of all types to the handicapped and disadvantaged including:

(*a*) the establishment and development of library media services and centers for persons whose native language is not English. The board shall establish standards for such services and centers;

(*b*) the development of library media services for the elderly, the unemployed, the poor, the functionally illiterate, and those persons who have cultural, social, or educational disadvantages that prevent them from using library media centers and services designed for persons without said disadvantages;

(*c*) the establishment and development of library media services for persons who are visually impaired, mentally, physically, or emotionally handicapped.

(6) To aid public library planning, reconstruction and construction.

The board shall adopt standards for the cities and towns receiving funds under this clause. In allocating funds under this clause the board shall take into account:

(*a*) local financial support for library media services;

(*b*) local financial support for a building program for a library media center;

(*c*) compliance with the standards established under this clause.

(7) To conduct, contract for, fund or publish studies relative to needs and services of library media centers of the commonwealth. The funding of such studies shall be for the purpose of advising the board in carrying out the provisions of this section. Such studies may include the testing and evaluation of findings by the board.

Added by St.1974, c. 764; St.1977, c. 565, § 5.

CERTIFICATION OF LIBRARIANS
(Massachusetts General Laws Annotated, 1982, Chap. 78, s.22-25, 27-32.)

§ 22. Authorization

The board of library commissioners shall certify, and issue certificates to, librarians. The board shall appoint an advisory committee of professional librarians practicing in the commonwealth to advise with it concerning certification.

Added by St.1948. c. 320. Amended by St.1952, c. 585, § 14.

§ 23. Board meetings; quorum

The board shall hold at least four regular meetings each year for the purpose of granting certificates. A quorum for said purpose shall consist of three members.

Added by St.1948, c. 320.

§ 24. Definitions

The following words and phrases used in sections twenty-two to thirty-one, inclusive, shall, unless the context otherwise requires, have the following meanings:—

"Board", the board of library commissioners.

"Professional librarian", a person qualified by education, training or study and experience to practice library work in a position requiring knowledge of books and library aims and techniques equivalent to that attained through graduation from a library school accredited by the American Library Association.

"Subprofessional librarian", a person in the opinion of the board qualified through an elementary knowledge of library techniques to engage in the necessary library routines involved in the acquiring and circulation of books but not qualified as a professional librarian.

Added by St.1948, c. 320. Amended by St.1952, c. 585, § 15.

§ 25. Rules and regulations

The board shall make such rules and regulations not inconsistent with law as are necessary and proper for the conduct of the process of certification, including issuance, renewal or revocation of certificates, and to provide for hearings in the case of applicants whose requests for certificates have been refused or whose certificates have been suspended or revoked, in cases where application for such hearing has been made to the board.

Added by St.1948, c. 320.

§ 27. Clerical assistance, etc., expenditures for

The board may expend, subject to appropriation, such sums for clerical assistance and incidentals as may be necessary for the proper performance of its work.

Added by St.1948, c. 320.

§ 28. Duties of board

The board shall:—

(1) Keep an official record of all its meetings or parts of meetings concerned with certification.

(2) Issue, suspend, revoke or renew certificates to properly qualified persons.

(3) Keep a roster showing the names and last-known business addresses of all persons holding certificates and furnish the information contained therein to the public on request.

(4) Furnish information as to the requirements for certification upon request and without charge to all prospective applicants.

(5) Hold examinations at least semi-annually if there are applicants for examination.

Added by St.1948, c. 320.

§ 29.   Librarians; qualifications

The board shall issue a certificate certifying as a professional librarian any person who requests certification upon a form prescribed by the board and who fulfills one or both of the following requirements:—

(1) Graduation from a library school accredited by the American Library Association or the passing of an examination which, with due consideration of education, professional training, practical experience and demonstrated ability, shall satisfy the board that the candidate has the qualifications required for the satisfactory practice of library work.

(2) The holding of an unexpired certificate issued by the proper authority in any state other than this commonwealth in which the requirements for certification are satisfactory to the board.

The board shall issue a certificate certifying as a sub-professional librarian any person who requests certification upon a form prescribed by the board and who, in the opinion of the board, is qualified to practice library work in a position not requiring the educational and other qualifications for certification as a professional librarian.

Added by St.1948, c. 320.

§ 30.   Fees

The board may fix fees for the issuance of certificates and for their renewal.

Added by St.1948, c. 320.

§ 31.   Status of existing librarians; certificates

Any person who, upon the effective date of this act, is employed in a position defined as that of professional librarian or subprofessional librarian in section twenty-four, shall be granted a certificate as a professional or subprofessional librarian, if he makes application within two years after such effective date.

Added by St.1948, c. 320.

§ 32.   Library staff members; leaves of absence for study or research

In a city or town which accepts this section the board of trustees of the public library or the city or town official possessing the appointive powers of such board may grant a leave of absence for study or research to any library staff member which would enable him to increase his professional ability, such leave to be for a period not exceeding one year at full or partial pay; provided, that prior to the granting of such leave said library staff member shall enter into a written agreement with said trustees or official that upon the termination of such leave he will return to service in the public library of such city or town for a period equal to twice the length of such leave and that, in default of completing such service, he will refund to the city or town an amount equal to such proportion of salary received by him while on leave as the amount of service not actually rendered as agreed bears to the whole amount of service agreed to be rendered.

Added by St.1964, c. 150.

INTERSTATE LIBRARY COMPACT
(Massachusetts General Laws Annotated, 1982, Chap. 78, s.1-1 to 1-6.)

§ 1-1. Form and contents

A compact is hereby entered into with such of the states of Connecticut, Rhode Island, Vermont, New Hampshire and Maine as may legally join therein, in substantially the following form:—

INTERSTATE LIBRARY COMPACT

ARTICLE I. POLICY AND PURPOSE

Because the desire for the services provided by libraries transcends governmental boundaries and can most effectively be satisfied by giving such services to communities and people regardless of jurisdictional lines, it is the policy of the states party to this compact to co-operate and share their responsibilities; to authorize co-operation and sharing with respect to those types of library facilities and services which can be more economically or efficiently developed and maintained on a co-operative basis, and to authorize co-operation and sharing among localities, states and others in providing joint or co-operative library services in areas where the distribution of population or of existing and potential library resources make the provision of library service on an interstate basis the most effective way of providing adequate and efficient service.

ARTICLE II. DEFINITIONS

As used in this compact:

(a) "Public library agency" means any unit or agency of local or state government operating or having power to operate a library.

(*b*) "Private library agency" means any non-governmental entity which operates or assumes a legal obligation to operate a library.

(*c*) "Library agreement" means a contract establishing an interstate library district pursuant to this compact or providing for the joint or co-operative furnishing of library services.

ARTICLE III. INTERSTATE LIBRARY DISTRICTS

(*a*) Any one *o*r more public library agencies in a party state in co-operation with any public library agency or agencies in one or more other party states may establish and maintain an interstate library district. Subject to the provisions of this compact and any other laws of the party states which pursuant hereto remain applicable, such district may establish, maintain and operate some or all of the library facilities and services for the area concerned in accordance with the terms of a library agreement therefor. Any private library agency or agencies within an interstate library district may co-operate therewith, assume duties, responsibilities and obligations thereto, and receive benefits therefrom as provided in any library agreement to which such agency or agencies become party.

(*b*) Within an interstate library district, and as provided by a library agreement, the performance of library functions may be undertaken on a joint or co-operative basis or may be undertaken by means of one or more arrangements between or among public or private library agencies for the extension of library privileges to the use of facilities or services operated or rendered by one or more of the individual library agencies.

(*c*) If a library agreement provides for joint establishment, maintenance or operation of library facilities or services by an interstate library district, such district shall have power to do any one or more of the following in accordance with such library agreement:

1. Undertake, administer and participate in programs or arrangements for securing, lending or servicing of books and other publications, any other materials suitable to be kept or made available by libraries, library equipment or for the dissemination of information about libraries, the value and significance of particular items therein, and the use thereof.

2. Accept for any of its purposes under this compact any and all donations, and grants of money, equipment, supplies, materials, and services (conditional or otherwise), from any state or the United States or any subdivision or agency thereof, or interstate agency, or from any institution, person, firm or corporation, and receive, utilize and dispose of the same.

3. Operate mobile library units or equipment for the purpose of rendering bookmobile service within the district.

4. Employ professional, technical, clerical and other personnel and fix terms of employment, compensation and other appropriate benefits; and where desirable, provide for the in-service training of such personnel.

5. Sue and be sued in any court of competent jurisdiction.

6. Acquire, hold and dispose of any real or personal property or any interest or interests therein as may be appropriate to the rendering of library service.

7. Construct, maintain and operate a library, including any appropriate branches thereof.

8. Do such other things as may be incidental to or appropriate for the carrying out of any of the foregoing powers.

ARTICLE IV. INTERSTATE LIBRARY DISTRICTS, GOVERNING BOARD

(a) An interstate library district which establishes, maintains or operates any facilities or services in its own right shall have a governing board which shall direct the affairs of the district and act for it in all matters relating to its business. Each participating public library agency in the district shall be represented on the governing board which shall be organized and conduct its business in accordance with provision therefor in the library agreement, but in no event shall a governing board meet less often than twice a year.

(b) Any private library agency or agencies party to a library agreement establishing an interstate library district may be represented on or advise with the governing board of the district in such manner as the library agreement may provide.

ARTICLE V. STATE LIBRARY AGENCY CO-OPERATION

Any two or more state library agencies of two or more of the party states may undertake and conduct joint or co-operative library programs, render joint or co-operative library services, and enter into and perform arrangements for the co-operative or joint acquisition, use, housing and disposition of items or collections of materials which, by reason of expense, rarity, specialized nature, or infrequency of demand therefor would be appropriate for central collection and shared use. Any such programs, services or arrangements may in-

clude provision for the exercise on a co-operative or joint basis of any
power exercisable by an interstate library district and an agreement
embodying any such program, service or arrangement shall contain
provisions covering the subjects detailed in Article VI of this compact
for interstate library agreements.

ARTICLE VI. LIBRARY AGREEMENTS

(a) In order to provide for any joint or co-operative undertaking
pursuant to this compact, public and private library agencies may enter into library agreements. Any agreement executed pursuant to
the provisions of this compact shall, as among the parties to the
agreement:

1. Detail the specific nature of the services, programs, facilities,
arrangements or properties to which it is applicable.

2. Provide for the allocation of costs and other financial responsibilities.

3. Specify the respective rights, duties, obligations and liabilities of the parties.

4. Set forth the terms and conditions for duration, renewal, termination, abrogation, disposal of joint or common property, if any,
and all other matters which may be appropriate to the proper effectuation and performance of the agreement.

(b) No public or private library agency shall undertake to exercise itself, or jointly with any other library agency, by means of a library agreement any power prohibited to such agency by the constitution or statutes of its state.

(c) No library agreement shall become effective until filed with
the compact administrator of each state involved, and approved in accordance with Article VII of this compact.

ARTICLE VII. APPROVAL OF LIBRARY AGREEMENTS

(a) Every library agreement made pursuant to this compact
shall, prior to and as a condition precedent to its entry into force, be
submitted to the attorney general of each state in which a public library agency party thereto is situated, who shall determine whether
the agreement is in proper form and compatible with the laws of his
state. The attorneys general shall approve any agreement submitted
to them unless they shall find that it does not meet the conditions set
forth herein and shall detail in writing addressed to the governing
bodies of the public library agencies concerned the specific respects in
which the proposed agreement fails to meet the requirements of law.

Failure to disapprove an agreement submitted hereunder within ninety days of its submission shall constitute approval thereof.

(b) In the event that a library agreement made pursuant to this compact shall deal in whole or in part with the provision of services or facilities with regard to which an officer or agency of the state government has constitutional or statutory powers of control, the agreement shall, as a condition precedent to its entry into force, be submitted to the state officer or agency having such power of control and shall be approved or disapproved by him or it as to all matters within his or its jurisdiction in the same manner and subject to the same requirements governing the action of the attorneys general pursuant to paragraph (a) of this article. This requirement of submission and approval shall be in addition to and not in substitution for the requirement of submission to and approval by the attorneys general.

ARTICLE VIII.   OTHER LAWS APPLICABLE

Nothing in this compact or in any library agreement shall be construed to supersede, alter or otherwise impair any obligation imposed on any library by otherwise applicable law, nor to authorize the transfer or disposition of any property held in trust by a library agency in a manner contrary to the terms of such trust.

ARTICLE IX.   APPROPRIATIONS AND AID

(a) Any public library agency party to a library agreement may appropriate funds to the interstate library district established thereby in the same manner and to the same extent as to a library wholly maintained by it and, subject to the laws of the state in which such public library agency is situated, may pledge its credit in support of an interstate library district established by the agreement.

(b) Subject to the provisions of the library agreement pursuant to which it functions and the laws of the states in which such district is situated, an interstate library district may claim and receive any state and federal aid which may be available to library agencies.

ARTICLE X.   COMPACT ADMINISTRATOR

Each state shall designate a compact administrator with whom copies of all library agreements to which his state or any public library agency thereof is party shall be filed. The administrator shall have such other powers as may be conferred upon him by the laws of his state and may consult and co-operate with the compact administrators of other party states and take such steps as may effectuate the purposes of this compact. If the laws of a party state so provide, such state may designate one or more deputy compact administrators in addition to its compact administrator.

ARTICLE XI. ENTRY INTO FORCE AND WITHDRAWAL

(*a*) This compact shall enter into force and effect immediately upon its enactment into law by any two states. Thereafter, it shall enter into force and effect as to any other state upon the enactment thereof by such state.

(*b*) This compact shall continue in force with respect to a party state and remain binding upon such state until six months after such state has given notice to each other party state of the repeal thereof. Such withdrawal shall not be construed to relieve any party to a library agreement entered into pursuant to this compact from any obligation of that agreement prior to the end of its duration as provided therein.

ARTICLE XII. CONSTRUCTION AND SEVERABILITY

This compact shall be liberally construed so as to effectuate the purposes thereof. The provisions of this compact shall be severable and if any phrase, clause, sentence or provision of this compact is declared to be contrary to the constitution of any party state or of the United States or the applicability thereof to any government, agency, person or circumstance is held invalid, the validity of the remainder of this compact and the applicability thereof to any government, agency, person or circumstance shall not be affected thereby. If this compact shall be held contrary to the constitution of any state party thereto, the compact shall remain in full force and effect as to the remaining states and in full force and effect as to the state affected as to all severable matters.

St.1963, c. 693, § 1.

§ 1-2. Political agency as party to library agreement; pre-requisites

No political subdivision of the commonwealth shall be a party to a library agreement which provides for the construction or maintenance of a library pursuant to Article III, paragraph (*c*) 7, of the compact, nor pledge its credit in support of such a library, or contribute to the capital financing thereof, except after compliance with any laws applicable to such political subdivision relating to or governing capital outlays and the pledging of credit.

St.1963, c. 693, § 2.

§ 1-3. State library agency defined

As used in this compact "state library agency", with reference to the commonwealth, means the board of library commissioners.

St.1963, c. 693, § 3.   Amended by St.1977, c. 565, § 7.

§ 1-4. State and federal aid

An interstate library district lying partly within the commonwealth may claim and be entitled to receive state aid in support of any of its functions to the same extent and in the same manner as such functions are eligible for support when carried on by entities wholly within this state. For the purpose of computing and apportioning state aid to an interstate library district, the commonwealth will consider that portion of the district which lies within the commonwealth as an independent entity for the performance of the aided function or functions and compute and apportion the aid accordingly. Subject to any applicable laws of this state, such a district also may apply for and be entitled to receive any federal aid for which it may be eligible.

St.1963, c. 693, § 4.

§ 1-5. Compact administrator

The governor, with the advice and consent of the council, shall appoint the compact administrator pursuant to Article X of the compact.

St.1963, c. 693, § 5.

§ 1-6. Withdrawal from compact; notice

In the event of withdrawal of the commonwealth from the compact the governor shall send and receive any notices required by Article XI of the compact.

St.1963, c. 693, § 6.

DISTRIBUTION OF PUBLIC DOCUMENTS
(Massachusetts General Laws Annotated, 1982, Chap. 5, s.3, 7,
10, 11, 17; Chap. 40, s.50.)

§ 3. Distribution of published laws

The state secretary shall determine the number of copies, not exceeding ten thousand, of said volume required to be printed each year and shall, immediately after their publication, distribute such copies as follows:

To the clerk of the senate, for the use of the senate, twelve;

To the counsel to the senate, twenty;

To the clerk of the house of representatives, for the use of the house, twenty-four;

To the counsel to the house of representatives, twenty;

To the legislative research bureau, four;

To each member of the general court, one; and upon written request of said member, an additional number, not exceeding ten;

To the state library, for use therein and for the purpose of exchange, one hundred;

To the governor, the lieutenant governor, the attorney general and his assistants, the senators and representatives in Congress from the commonwealth, the reporter of decisions, district attorneys, city and town clerks, county commissioners, county treasurers, registers of deeds, such free public libraries, academic and special libraries in the commonwealth as the state secretary may designate, county law libraries, all incorporated law libraries and branch libraries maintained by them, the justices of the supreme court of the United States, the judges and clerks of the United States circuit court of appeals and district court for the district of Massachusetts, all the justices and clerks of the various courts of the commonwealth, including masters in chancery, registers of deeds and probate, one each;

To such assistant clerks and assistant registers of deeds and probate, upon application in writing therefor, and a number sufficient to supply a copy for each courtroom where a session is held;

To the state secretary for distribution to such state departments, boards, commissions and agencies as in the opinion of the secretary require a copy for official use, an additional number not exceeding one hundred.

After making the foregoing distribution or making provision therefor, the state secretary may sell copies at such price per copy as shall be fixed by him in accordance with section one A.

Amended by St.1980, c. 281.

§ 7.   Distribution of printed copies of official reports

The state secretary shall furnish to each town of the commonwealth, to be preserved in a public place therein, one copy of each of such reports included in the public document series as the town clerk may apply for. He shall furnish one copy of each of said reports to such public and other libraries as may apply therefor. If the supervisor of public records shall report to the state secretary that such town is unable to make suitable provision for the care and use of the documents, he may discontinue sending them to such town. Each member of the general court and of the executive department, the clerk of each branch of the general court and each reporter assigned to either branch may, upon a written request signed by him and delivered to the state secretary, receive a copy of any such document. Ten copies shall be placed in the state library for the use of the library and for exchange.   St.1919 c. 350 § 24.

§ 10.   Printing and distribution of legislative journals

Such number of copies of the journals of the senate and of the house of representatives as the committees on rules thereof shall determine shall be printed annually under the direction of the respective clerks thereof; and, unless the general court shall otherwise order, two thousand copies of the lists of members and committees shall be printed annually under the joint direction of said clerks.

Copies of said journals shall, under the direction of said clerks, be distributed as follows:—one copy to each member of the general court, who requests the same in writing addressed to said clerks; one copy to each member of the executive department, who requests the same in writing addressed to said clerks; one copy to the clerk and assistant clerk of each branch of the general court and to each reporter who is entitled to the privileges of the reporters' gallery in either branch; and ten copies to the state library for use therein and for exchange. The state secretary shall send one copy of said journals to each member of the general court who requests the same as provided in this section. The state librarian shall send one copy of said journals to each free public library in the commonwealth which requests the same in writing.

Copies of the lists of members and committees shall, under the direction of said clerks, be distributed as follows:—one copy to each member of the general court, to each member of the executive department, to the clerk and assistant clerk of each branch of the general court and to each reporter who is entitled to the privileges of the reporters' gallery in either branch and ten copies to the state library for use therein and for exchange.

The remaining copies of the journals shall be turned over to the state secretary, and he shall sell copies at such price, not less than cost, as he shall fix.

The remaining copies of the lists of members and committees shall be distributed at the discretion of the clerks of the two branches, preference being given to the members of the general court and to state officers.

Two thousand copies of the governor's address to the general court shall be printed, of which fifteen hundred shall be for the general court and five hundred for the governor.

Amended by St.1939, c. 508, § 10; St.1945, c. 38, § 4; St.1968, c. 401; St. 1969, c. 150; St.1971, c. 226, §§ 1 to 3.

§ 11.   Printing and distribution of general court manual

The clerks of the two branches shall in every odd-numbered year prepare a manual for the general court, of which not more than ten thousand five hundred copies shall be printed under their direction. These copies shall be delivered to the state secretary and by him distributed, so far as the edition will permit, as follows:

To the clerk of each branch of the general court, fifty;

To the assistant clerk of each branch of the general court, thirty;

To the counsel to each branch of the general court, four;

To each member of the general court, five, and upon written application an additional number, not exceeding twenty;

To the governor, the lieutenant governor, and the members of the executive council, five each and, upon written application and additional number, not exceeding fifteen;

To the George Fingold Library, two hundred;

To the private secretary to the governor, the senators and representatives in congress from the commonwealth, the justices, clerks and registers of courts, such assistant clerks of courts as the state secretary may designate, the reporter of decisions, district attorneys, county commissioners, county treasurers, registers of deeds, medical examiners, sheriffs, city and town clerks, Harvard University and all incorporated colleges within the commonwealth, the Massachusetts Historical Society, the New England Historic Genealogical Society, the Boston Athenaeum, the American Antiquarian Society in Worcester, such free public libraries and branches thereof in the commonwealth as the state secretary may designate, and to such other free public libraries in the commonwealth making written application therefor, county law libraries, all incorporated law libraries in the commonwealth and branch libraries maintained by them, and to veteran organizations having headquarters in the state house, one, each;

To associate and special justices, assistant clerks of courts not otherwise provided for, and to reporters entitled to the privileges of the reporters' gallery in either branch of the general court, upon written application, one, each;

To the state secretary and his deputies, the state treasurer and his deputies, the state auditor and his deputies, the attorney-general and his assistants, the commissioner and associate commissioners of each state department, the director of each state division established by statute, the chairman of each state board and commission, and to each institution under the supervision of the state departments of correction, education, mental health, public health and public welfare, one, each;

To the state secretary for distribution not otherwise provided for, fifty;

Three hundred copies to the sergeant-at-arms to be reserved under the direction of the clerks of both branches for the use of the general court at its next annual session and three hundred copies for the use of the next succeeding general court.

After making the foregoing distribution or making provision therefor, the state secretary shall place copies of the manual on sale to the general public at a price not less than the cost thereof, as determined by the committees on rules of the senate and house of representatives. After December thirty-first of each even-numbered year copies of the manual remaining on hand may be distributed by the state secretary without charge.

Amended by St.1941, c. 329; St.1945, c. 538; St.1947, c. 295; St.1962, c. 170.

§ 17. Payment of delivery charges on documents

Delivery charges on documents forwarded to members of the general court and to free public libraries shall be prepaid by the commonwealth.

§ 50. Annual town report; copy to state library

One copy or more of the annual report and of any special report of a town shall annually, on or before the last day of May, be transmitted by the town clerk to the state library, and until such transmission the publications distributed by the commonwealth shall be withheld from the town.

Amended by St.1974, c. 268.

PUBLIC RECORDS
(Massachusetts General Laws Annotated, 1982, Chap. 30, s.42.)

§ 42. Records conservation board; composition; powers and duties; sale or destruction of records; records defined; inquiries from departments or agencies

The state librarian, the attorney general, the state comptroller, the commissioner of administration, the supervisor of public records and the chief of the archives division in the department of the state secretary, hereinafter called the archivist, or persons designated by them, shall act as a board, to be known as the records conservation board, of which board the archivist shall be secretary.

The board, after consultation with the executive head of any agency, executive office, department, board, commission, bureau, division or authority of the commonwealth or of any authority established by the general court to serve a public purpose or a person designated by such executive head may, either by its own motion or on the request of said executive head, sell or destroy, from time to time, all records in accordance with disposal schedules which shall have been submitted to said board and either approved or modified by said board or the board may authorize such sale or destruction. Until such action shall have been taken, all such records shall remain the property, as the case may be, of the commonwealth or an authority including an authority established by the general court to serve a public purpose.

The board shall have power to require all departments of the commonwealth to report to it what series of records they hold, to set standards for the management and preservation of such records, and to establish schedules for the destruction, in whole, or in part, and transfer to the archives or another appropriate division within the office of the state secretary, in whole, or in part, of records no longer needed for current business.

Nothing in this section shall affect judicial or legislative records, lessen the existing powers of the executive office for administration and finance, or compel any agency, executive office, department, board, commission, bureau, division or authority of the commonwealth or of any authority established by the general court to serve a public purpose to surrender records it deems of current use.

Records may be kept in the archives or in another appropriate division within the office of the state secretary, under reasonable restrictions as to access, for a reasonable length of time; provided, that such restrictions are in writing and accepted by the records conservation board at a meeting at which the attorney general, or his designee, is present. At least thirty days before selling or destroying any records so kept in the archives or another appropriate division within the office of the state secretary, the board may publish in a daily newspaper in Boston a notice of its intention to do so, containing a brief description of the articles to be sold or destroyed, and it shall give such other and further notice as it deems advisable to historical societies or persons interested in the matter.

The board may, before selling or destroying any particular records, books, vouchers or documents, give a public hearing to all persons interested, and ten days' notice of such hearing shall be given in a daily newspaper published in Boston.

The proceeds, if any, of a sale by the board of any records shall be paid to the state treasurer or to the treasurer of an authority, including an authority established by the general court to serve a public purpose, whose records were the subject of the sale.

As used in this section, the words "records" shall mean all books, papers, maps, photographs, recorded tapes, financial statements, statistical tabulations, or other documentary materials or data, regardless of physical form or characteristics, made or received by any officer or employee of any agency, executive office, department, board, commission, bureau, division or authority of the commonwealth or of any authority established by the general court to serve a public purpose.

Any agency, executive office, department, board, commission, bureau, division or authority of the commonwealth or of any authority established by the general court to serve a public purpose in doubt as to whether certain materials are records shall make inquiry thereof in writing to the records conservation board which shall determine the question.

Amended by St.1936, c. 359; St.1941, c. 450, § 1; St.1948, c. 21; St.1951, c. 397; St.1957, c. 477; St.1962, c. 427, § 2; St.1962, c. 757, § 60; St.1964, c. 131; St.1964, c. 726; St.1966, c. 219; St.1973, c. 1050, § 1A; St.1973, c. 1218; St.1976, c. 145, §§ 1, 2.

MUNICIPAL LIBRARIES
(Massachusetts General Laws Annotated, 1982, Chap. 78, s.7-13.)

§ 7. Establishment by cities and towns

A town may establish and maintain public libraries for its inhabitants under regulations prescribed by the city council or by the town, and may receive, hold and manage any gift, bequest or devise therefor. The city council of a city or the selectmen of a town may place in such library the books, reports and laws which may be received from the commonwealth.   R.L.1902, c. 38, § 6.

§ 8. Use of facilities by non-residents

Any free town public library may loan its books or other library material to any other such library or to citizens of other towns or non-residents, under such written conditions and regulations as may be made by the board of trustees or other authority having control of the library so loaning. Any town may raise money to pay the expenses of so borrowing books and other library material from the library of any other town.   St.1914, c. 118.

§ 9. Return of unwanted state publications

If the trustees of any town library shall vote not to keep or receive any of the books and reports which the state secretary is authorized to send thereto, the secretary, at the request of the supervisor of public records, may discontinue sending them. Any of said books and reports in the custody of any town library may be returned at its expense to the state library, or, with the sanction of the board of library commissioners, may otherwise be exchanged or disposed of.

Amended by St.1952, c. 585, § 10.

§ 10. Town libraries; selection of trustees and officers

A town which raises or appropriates money for the support of a free public library, or free public library and reading room, owned by the town, shall, unless the same has been acquired entirely or in part through some gift or bequest which contains other conditions or provisions for the election of its trustees, or for its care and management, which have been accepted by the town, elect by ballot at a meeting a board of trustees consisting of any number of persons, male or female, divisible by three, which the town determines to elect. When such board is first chosen, one third thereof shall be elected for one year, one third for two years and one third for three years, and thereafter one third shall be elected annually for a term of three years. The board shall, from its own number, annually choose a chairman and secretary and, if the town so votes, a treasurer, who shall give a bond similar to that given by the town treasurer, in an amount and with sureties to the satisfaction of the selectmen. Until the town otherwise directs the town treasurer shall act as treasurer of the board of trustees.

R.L.1902, c. 38, § 7.

§ 11. Board of trustees; powers and duties

The board shall have the custody and management of the library and reading room and of all property owned by the town relating thereto. All money raised or appropriated by the town for its support and maintenance shall be expended by the board, and all money or property which the town may receive by gift or bequest for said library and reading room shall be administered by the board in accordance with the provisions of such gift or bequest. The board of any library, for the purpose of improving the services of said library, may enter into an agreement with the board or boards of any neighboring library or libraries, to pay for services in common, such payments to be shared in accordance with terms of such agreement.

Amended by St.1952, c. 585, § 16.

§ 12. Annual report of trustees

The board shall make an annual report to the town of its receipts and expenditures and of the property in its custody, with a statement of any unexpended balance of money and of any gifts or bequests which it holds in behalf of the town, with its recommendations.

R.L.1902, c. 38, § 9.

§ 13. Applicability of sections relating to trustees

The three preceding sections shall not apply to library associations, nor to a library organized under a special act. R.L.1902, c. 38, § 10.

INCORPORATED LIBRARIES
(Massachusetts General Laws Annotated, 1982, Chap. 78, s.1,
Chap. 180, s.2.)

§ 1.   Existing corporations

Library corporations and associations which have been legally established shall continue to have all the powers and privileges and be subject to all the duties and restrictions attaching thereto.

R.L.1902 c. 38 § 1.

§ 2.   Purposes.
Such corporation may be formed for any civic, educational, charitable, benevolent or religious purpose; for the prosecution of any antiquarian, historical, literary, scientific, medical, artistic, monumental or musical purpose; for establishing and maintaining libraries; for supporting any missionary enterprise having for its object the dissemination of religious or educational instruction in foreign countries; for promoting temperance or morality in the commonwealth; for encouraging athletic exercises or yachting; for encouraging the raising of choice breeds of domestic animals and poultry; for the association and accommodation of societies of Free Masons, Odd Fellows, Knights of Pythias or other charitable or social bodies of a like character and purpose; for the establishment and maintenance of places for reading rooms, libraries or social meetings; for establishing boards of trade, chambers of commerce and bodies of like nature.   St. 1915 c. 213.

COUNTY LAW LIBRARIES
(Massachusetts General Laws Annotated, 1982, Chap. 78, s.2-6.)

§ 2.   Organization of county law libraries

Attorneys at law who have been admitted to practice in the courts of the commonwealth and who are resident in a county for which there is no law library association may organize, under chapter one hundred and eighty, by the name of the law library association for such county, and may adopt by-laws which shall be subject to the approval of the superior court.   R.L.1902, c. 38, § 2.

§ 3.   Use by residents of county

Inhabitants of the county shall, subject to the by-laws, have access to the library and the books therein.   R.L.1902, c. 38, § 3.

§ 4.   Source of funds

The treasurer of each county shall annually pay for the support of law libraries therein such sums as may be appropriated therefor by the general court, and the county commissioners shall include in the estimates required to be filed under the provisions of section twenty-eight of chapter thirty-five such sums as they may recommend for such law libraries. Sums so appropriated shall be applied to the purchase of books and maintenance of libraries for the use of courts and of citizens. In counties having any law library association the county commissioners shall secure from such association recommendations as to the amount deemed necessary for such maintenance.

Amended by St.1935, c. 202.   St.1913, c. 180.

§ 5.   Right to receive legislative documents

Each law library association shall be entitled to receive from the sergeant-at-arms, immediately after their publication, one copy of the volume of the legislative documents of the senate and house, the journal of the senate and the journal of the house.   R.L.1902, c. 38, § 5.

§ 6.   Right to receive other books and documents

All incorporated law libraries in the commonwealth shall be entitled to receive from the officers charged with the distribution of the same, copies of all books and documents to which the county law libraries are entitled by law, and one additional copy for each branch library maintained by them.   St.1904, c. 209.

SCHOOL LIBRARIES
(Massachusetts General Laws Annotated, 1982, Chap. 71, s.38H.)

§ 38H.   School librarian and school library supervisor or co-ordinator; tenure

Every school librarian and school library supervisor or co-ordinator appointed by a school committee shall acquire tenure in the school system of the city or town in which he is employed subject to the provisions of section forty-one, relating to tenure for teachers, and of sections forty-two and forty-three A, relating to dismissal, suspension and discharge and of appeals therefrom.

Added bv St.1965, c. 276.

PROTECTION OF LIBRARY PROPERTY
(Massachusetts General Laws Annotated, 1982, Chap. 266, s.99-100;
Chap. 272, s.41.)

§ 99.   Libraries; defacement of contents

Whoever wilfully, intentionally and without right, or wantonly and without cause, writes upon, injures, defaces, tears or destroys a book, plate, picture, engraving, map; newspaper, magazine, pamphlet, manuscript or statue which belongs to a law, city, town or other public or incorporated library shall be punished by a fine of not less than five nor more than fifty dollars or by imprisonment for not more than six months.

R.L.1902 c. 208 § 83.

§ 100. Libraries; wilful detention of books

Whoever wilfully, intentionally and without right, or wantonly and without cause detains a book, newspaper, magazine, pamphlet or manuscript which belongs to a law, city, town or other public or incorporated library for thirty days after a written notice to such person and to his parent or guardian, if he is a minor, from the librarian thereof, containing a copy of this section and sent by certified mail after the expiration of the time during which, by the regulations of such library, such book, newspaper, magazine, pamphlet or manuscript may be kept, shall be punished by a fine of not less than one nor more than twenty-five dollars.

Amended by St.1961, c. 316.

§ 41. Disturbance of libraries

Whoever wilfully disturbs persons assembled in a public library, or a reading room connected therewith, by making a noise or in any other manner during the time when such library or reading room is open to the public shall be punished as provided in the preceding section.

R.L.1902 c. 212 § 33.

Massachusetts library laws are reprinted from MASSACHU-SETTS GENERAL LAWS ANNOTATED published by West Publishing Co., St. Paul, Minnesota.

MICHIGAN

STATE LIBRARY

(Michigan Statutes Annotated, 1982, s.15.1541, 15.1544,
15.1545, 15.1546, 15.1549.)

§ 15.1541] State library; location, contents. SEC. 1. *The People of the State of Michigan enact,* That the state library shall be kept in the room in the capitol which it now occupies, unless some other provision shall be made by the legislature in reference thereto. It shall consist of the books, pamphlets, papers, pictures, maps, charts, and documents of every description now belonging to the same, together with all such others as it may acquire by gift, purchase, exchange or otherwise. The members of both houses of the legislature and the executive and judicial officers of the state shall at all times have free access thereto, under such rules and regulations as may be made for governing the library. (MCL §397.51; CL '29, §8022; CL '15, §1113; CL '97, §1763.)

§ 15.1544] State librarian; receipt for property, oath, bond. Sec. 4. The state librarian shall, before entering upon the duties of the office, file with the secretary of state his receipt for all property entrusted to him, take and subscribe the oath of office prescribed by the constitution and give a bond in the penal sum of ten thousand [10,000] dollars, with sureties to be approved by the secretary of state, conditioned for the safekeeping of such property as may be entrusted to his care. Said bond and receipt shall be filed in the office of the secretary of state, and they shall not be canceled, nor shall the sureties on said bond be released from their obligations thereon, until the receipt of the successor to the said librarian, for the property delivered over to him, shall have been obtained and payment for all deficiencies made. (MCL §397.54; CL '29, §8025; CL '15, §1116; CL '97, §1766.)

§ 15.1545 State library, depository, purpose.] Sec. 5. (1) The state library is designated as the depository library for state documents to preserve the public documents of this state and to make those documents available for use by the people of this state.

Collection of copies of public documents; permanent reference file.] (2) The state library shall maintain a complete collection of copies of public documents issued or published by the state as a permanent reference file.

State document depository system, establishment; designated depository libraries.] (3) The state library shall establish a state document depository system by which copies of public documents issued or published by the state shall be deposited in designated depository libraries. (MCL §397.55.)

§ 15.1546 Public documents furnished to state library; number; additional copies.] Sec. 6. (1) Each state official, state department, state board, state commission, and state agency which issues or publishes a public document shall furnish to the state library a minimum of 75 copies of each document issued in printed, mimeographed, or other duplicated form, which is not issued solely for use within the issuing agency. Additional copies of each public document shall be supplied upon the request of the state librarian.

Educational institution exemption; requirements.] (2) Publications of the various schools, colleges, divisions, and departments of the state universities and their regional campuses are exempt from the depository requirements of subsection (1), except that 2 copies of each publication shall be deposited in the state library.

Other exemptions.] (3) Publications of state university presses, directives for internal administration, intra-office and inter-office memoranda, forms, and correspondence are exempt from the depository requirements of this act. (MCL §397.56.)

§ 15.1549 State library, responsibilities.] Sec. 9. **[(1)]** The state ♦ **[library]** shall**[**:

(a) Keep at least 1 copy of each public document issued or published by the state and received from a state agency as a permanent reference copy.

(b)   Send 1 copy of each public document issued or published by the state and received from a state agency to the library of congress.

(c)   Designate state university libraries and certain selected Michigan public, school, and college libraries in the geographical regions of the state as depository libraries to receive 1 copy of public documents issued or published by the state and received from a state agency. Selection of depository libraries shall be made by the state library and shall be based on a determination that the libraries selected will keep the documents readily accessible for use, and will render assistance for their use to the people of this state without charge.

(d)   Prepare and issue quarterly, a complete list of public documents issued or published by the state during the immediately preceding quarter. The lists shall be cumulated and printed at the end of each calendar year. Copies shall be distributed by the state library to state departments, legislators, and to public and college libraries within the state.

(e)   Establish a document exchange system with agencies in other states to make available selected documents published by other states for use by the people of this state.]

Exchanges.]   **[(2) The state library may]** exchange the judicial decisions, statutes, journals, legislative and executive documents of Michigan, and other books placed in the care of the state ♦ **[library]** for the purpose of exchange, with the libraries of other states and the government of the United States, and of foreign countries, and with societies and institutions.

Sale or exchange of duplicates, use of proceeds.]   **[(3)]** The state ♦ **[library]** may sell or exchange duplicate volumes or sets of works not needed for use in the state library and apply the proceeds to the purchase of other books for the library. (MCL §397.59; CL '29, §8030; CL '15, §1121; CL '97, §1771.)

STATE BOARD FOR LIBRARIES
General Provisions
(Michigan Statutes Annotated, 1982, s.15.1565(1) to 15.1565(8).)

§ 15.1565(1)]   State board for libraries; members, term, appointment, vacancy, secretary, meetings, compensation and expenses, employes.   SEC. 1.   There is hereby created a state board for libraries, hereinafter called the board, which shall possess the powers and perform the duties hereinafter granted and imposed. The board shall consist of five [5] members, who shall be appointed by the governor by and with the advice and consent of the senate. The term of office of each member of the board shall be five [5] years: Provided, That of those first appointed under this act one [1] shall hold office for one [1] year, one [1] for two [2] years, one [1] for three [3] years, one [1] for four [4] years, and one [1] for five [5] years. Each member of the board shall hold office until the appointment and qualification of his successor. In case of vacancy in office other than by expiration of the term, the governor shall fill such office by appointment for the balance of the unexpired term. Immediately following the qualification of the new member each year the board shall elect from its membership a chairman and vice chairman. The state librarian shall be designated to act as secretary and his duties shall be prescribed by the board. Meetings of the board may be called by the chairman and shall be called on request of the majority of the members of the board. Such meetings may be held as often as necessary and at such place or places as may be designated in the call therefor: Provided, That approximately one [1] meeting shall be held each month and not fewer than ten [10] meetings shall be held in each year. The members of the board shall receive no compensation for their services, but each member and all officers and employes of the board shall be entitled to reasonable expenses while traveling in the performance of any of the duties hereby imposed. Such expenses of all board members and employes of the board and salaries of employes of the board shall be paid out of the state treasury in the same manner as the salaries and expenses of other state officers and employes are paid. (MCL §397.1.)

§ 15.1565(2)] Same; powers and duties. SEC. 2.   In addition to the other powers, duties and responsibilities in this act provided, the board (a) shall have general control and supervision of the state library; (b) may prepare and administer standards for certification for libraries and librarians; (c) shall inspect libraries which may be established or assisted under any legislative provision for state grants in aid to libraries; (d) shall assume immediate administrative responsibility and control over the establishment of regional libraries; (e) shall further the development of effective, state-wide school library service, encourage contractual and cooperative relations between school libraries and local, county, district, or regional libraries, and provide general advisory assistance; (f) may give advice and counsel to any public, school, state institutional, or other library within the state and to any community within the state which may propose to establish a library as to the best means of establishing and administering such library, selecting and cataloging books and other details of library management, may provide assistance by any of its employes in organizing such libraries or improving service given by them, and may aid in the establishment of libraries in any state institution; (g) shall be active in coordinating the library services of the states and in coordinating libraries with other educational agencies; (h) shall collect and preserve statistics, undertake research pertaining to libraries and make the resultant findings available to all public, school and institutional libraries within the state applying therefor; (i) may supply further advice and information to libraries in the state through field visits, conferences, institutes, correspondence, publications; and do any and all of the things it may reasonably be able to promote and advance library service in the state of Michigan. (MCL §397.2.)

§ 15.1565(3)] Same; control and direction of Michigan traveling libraries. SEC. 3.   Subject to the statutes of the state of Michigan, the board shall have general control over and direction of the "Michigan traveling libraries," may provide extension service and may prescribe rules and regulations under which selections of books may be loaned for a limited period to libraries and to communities in the state. (MCL §397.3.)

§ 15.1565(4)] Same; rules and regulations. SEC. 4. The board shall make and execute, modify and amend such rules and regulations not conflicting with the statutes governing the library as they may deem proper relative to the use and loans of books from the state library and also rules prescribing penalties and fines for any violation thereof, and shall determine all matters of policy in connection with the operation of the state library. (MCL §397.4.)

§ 15.1565(5)] State librarian; appointment, qualifications, term, compensation. SEC. 5. Upon the expiration of the term of the present librarian, the board shall appoint a state librarian, who shall have care and charge of the library and of the affairs pertaining thereto and shall perform such other duties as shall be prescribed by the board. The state librarian shall be a graduate of an accredited library school and shall have had at least four [4] years experience in library work in an administrative capacity: Provided, The foregoing restriction shall not prevent the board from reappointing the present incumbent at the expiration of her present term of office, if it shall see fit to do so. Such librarian shall hold office during the pleasure of the board. The salary of the state librarian shall be fixed by the board and shall be payable monthly out of the state treasury upon the warrant of the auditor general. (MCL §397.5.)

§ 15.1565(6)] Assistant state librarians; appointment, title, bond; general assistants and employes; compensation. SEC. 6. The board shall also be authorized on recommendation of the state librarian to appoint one assistant, who shall be known as the assistant state librarian, one assistant who shall be known as the assistant law librarian, and who shall have charge of the law library on filing a good and sufficient bond running to the state librarian, which shall be filed in the office of the secretary of state, and such other administrative and general assistants and employes as may be necessary for the care and management of the state library and the state law library and for carrying on and advancing the work of the board. The salaries of the assistant state librarian and of the assistant law librarian and of the other assistants and employes appointed by the board shall be fixed by it and shall be payable from the state treasury upon the presentation of a voucher certified to by the state librarian and drawn upon the warrant of the auditor general on any funds not otherwise appropriated. (MCL §397.6.)

§ 15.1565(7) Annual report; financial requirements, estimate.] SEC. 7. The board shall file an annual report with the governor of the state of Michigan covering the operations of the state library and the extension of library service throughout the state and containing such other information and recommendations as it may deem advisable or the governor shall request and shall from time to time and at least biennially prepare and file with the budget director or other proper officer of the state of Michigan an estimate of its financial requirements, together with such supporting information as may be necessary or advisable. (MCL §397.7.)

§ 15.1565(8)] Transfer of powers and duties of state board of library commissioners and state librarian. SEC. 8. Any and all powers and duties vested by any law of this state in the state board of library commissioners and the state librarian, except as conferred on the state librarian by the board, are hereby transferred to and vested in the state board for libraries.

When reference is made in any law of this state to the state board of library commissioners or the state librarian, such reference shall be deemed to be intended to be made to the state board for libraries created by section one [1] of this act. (MCL §397.8.)

State Library for the Blind
(Michigan Statutes Annotated, 1982, s.15.1566(1) to 15.1566(5).)

§ 15.1566(1) State library for the blind; jurisdiction.] SEC. 1. The state library for the blind, located at the employment institution for the blind at Saginaw, is hereby placed under the jurisdiction of the state board for libraries. (MCL §397.491.)

§ 15.1566(2) State board for libraries; powers.] SEC. 2. The state board for libraries shall have full power to administer this library, determine standards of operation, and make rules and regulations that will best serve both Braille and talking book readers. (MCL §397.492.)

§ 15.1566(3) Same; appropriation.] SEC. 3. The state board for libraries shall administer the appropriation for said library. (MCL §397.493.)

§ 15.1566(4) Same; library employees.] SEC. 4. The state board for libraries shall have full power to determine the qualifications of the personnel in said library and fill all vacancies, subject to the state civil service regulations. (MCL §397.494.)

§ 15.1566(5) Same; transfer of powers to.] SEC. 5. Any and all powers and duties vested by any law of this state in the state library for the blind are hereby transferred and vested in the state board for libraries. (MCL §397.495.)

STATE AID
(Michigan Statutes Annotated, 1982, s.15.1791(151) to 15.1791(175).)

§ 15.1791(151) Short title.] SEC. 1. This act shall be known and may be cited as the "state aid to public libraries act." (MCL §397.551.)

§ 15.1791(152) Definitions.] SEC. 2. As used in this act:
(a) "Local board" means the board of trustees or directors that

has, as its primary purpose, the supervision of a local public library, or that board contracting for library service, or if such a board does not exist, the legislative body of the local government which maintains the public library.

(b) "Local support" means funds from tax sources, gifts, endowments, penal fines, or other funds received from local sources, excluding state and federal aid as stated in this act.

(c) "Public library" means a library which is lawfully established for free public purposes by 1 or more counties, cities, townships, villages, school districts, or other local governments or a combination thereof, or by a general or local act, the entire interests of which belong to the general public. It does not include a special library such as a professional, technical, or school library.

(d) "Cooperative board" means the governing board of the cooperative library.

(e) "Cooperative library" means the library or service center designated by the cooperative board to execute services established by the cooperative plan and provided to libraries participating in the cooperative.

(f) "State board" means the state board of education. (MCL §397.552.)

§ 15.1791(153) Cooperative boards; establishment; number.] Sec. 3. Cooperative library boards representing local public libraries shall be established in accordance with this act and approved by the state board. The number of cooperative boards shall be determined by the state board in accordance with section 6. (MCL §397.553.)

§ 15.1791(154) Preliminary cooperative plan; contents.] Sec. 4. A preliminary cooperative plan for library services which sets forth a statement describing the specific services that will be rendered to those libraries participating in a cooperative library, the means and agencies by which the services will be rendered without duplication of existing resources and expertise, and the cooperative board that will receive funds and execute duties shall be developed by participating local public library boards. (MCL §397.554.)

§ 15.1791(155) Eligibility requirements.] Sec. 5. To be eligible for membership in a cooperative library, a local library shall:

(a) Maintain a minimum local support of 3/10 of a mill on state equalized valuation in the fiscal year before October 1 of the year before distribution.

(b) Participate in the development of cooperative library plans.

(c) Loan materials to other libraries participating in the cooperative library.

(d) Maintain an open door policy to the residents of the state, as provided by section 9 of article 8 of the state constitution of 1963. (MCL §397.555.)

§ 15.1791(156) Areas for inclusion; population.] Sec. 6. A cooperative library shall include those areas consisting of:

Two counties of 100,000 total.] (a) Two or more counties with a total population of at least 100,000.

One county plus portions of others.] (b) One county plus portions of other counties with a population of at least 100,000.

One county or portion thereof of 400,000.] (c) One county or portion thereof with a population of at least 400,000.

Portions of two counties with 350,000.] (d) Portions of 2 or more counties with a population of at least 350,000.

Counties or portions thereof with 50,000.] (e) Combinations of counties or portions of counties serving a population of at least 50,000, if the region served has a population of 35 or less per square mile.

Geosocioeconomic conditions; options of local board.] (f) The area covered by a cooperative library shall recognize the geosocioeconomic conditions within that area and regions established for governmental purposes throughout the state. A local board placed in a cooperative library shall have the option to petition the state board to be placed in a different cooperative library or to join with other local boards to form a cooperative library under this act. A local board serving an area adjoining more than 1 cooperative library shall have the option to determine the cooperative library in which it shall participate.

Certain system boards, designation as cooperative board, petition; expansion of certain cooperative boards; authority of expanded cooperative board; inclusion of certain communities.] (g) The system board of an existing library system serving over 1,000,000 population may petition the state board for designation as a cooperative board and the state board shall designate that system board, as already constituted, as the cooperative board. If a cooperative board is a county library board, the cooperative plan shall provide for expanding the cooperative board to represent proportionately the population served in any other county or counties within the area of the cooperative library. This expanded cooperative board shall have authority over those matters affecting the operation of the cooperative library except for the property, personnel, and governmental relationships of the county whose board was designated as the cooperative board, which matters shall continue to be the responsibility of that county library board. The state board shall include in the cooperative library serving over 1,000,000 population the communities presently served by the existing system and all other communities not in another cooperative library within counties represented by members on the expanded cooperative board other than the designated system board members. (MCL §397.556.)

§ 15.1791(157) Cooperative board; representation; membership; existing systems otherwise qualifying as cooperative libraries, continuation of numbers of members and relationships.] SEC. 7. A cooperative library board shall be representative of the participating libraries except as specifically provided in section 6. It shall consist of 9 members with the method of selection to be stated in the approved plan as provided in section 4. In the case of existing systems which otherwise qualify as cooperative libraries, the number of board members and their relationship to existing governmental units may continue if approved by a majority of the participating libraries and specified in the approved plan. (MCL §397.557.)

§ 15.1791(158) Same; powers and duties.] SEC. 8. The cooperative library board shall:

(a) Have powers which relate to the functioning of the cooperative library and the management and control of the cooperative library's funds and property.

(b) Select a chairperson.

(c) Be a body corporate and a juristic entity for social security and legal identity purposes.

(d) Establish, maintain, and operate cooperative services for public libraries in the cooperative library's area.

(e) Appoint a director or coordinator to administer the cooperative library, fix that person's compensation, and delegate those powers to that person as are in the best interest of the cooperative library, including the power to hire necessary employees.

(f) Purchase books, periodicals, library materials, equipment, and supplies for the cooperative services.

(g) Purchase sites, erect buildings, and lease suitable quarters, and have supervision and control of property of the cooperative library.

(h) Enter into contracts to receive service from or give service to libraries in the state, including public, school, academic, or special libraries, other cooperative libraries and political subdivisions of the state.

(i) Have exclusive control of expenditures for the cooperative library.

(j) Accept gifts and donations of property, real and personal, for the benefit of the cooperative library and for the purposes for which donated.

(k) Adopt bylaws and rules not inconsistent with this act for its own government and do those things necessary to carry out the purposes of this act. (MCL §397.558.)

§ 15.1791(159) Plan designating and describing responsibilities of cooperative library; contents; approval of original and modification; local libraries, restriction of jurisdiction of cooperative board.] SEC. 9. Following establishment of the cooperative library board, the board shall submit to the state board a plan which designates and describes the responsibilities of the cooperative library, provides for future selection of board membership, and gives notice of the cooperative board's meeting dates. The original plan and any substantial modification shall be approved by the state board. It is expressly understood the cooperative library board has no jurisdiction over the property or management of the local library. (MCL §397.559.)

§ 15.1791(160) Fiscal year of cooperative library; exception; deposit of funds.] SEC. 10. The fiscal year of the cooperative library is October 1 to September 30, except where the cooperative library must conform to the fiscal year fixed by another state law or local charter. The funds of the cooperative library shall be deposited in banks designated by the cooperative library board. (MCL §397.560.)

§ 15.1791(161) Eligibility for use of facilities and resources; availability of services; refusal of services, appeal to state board, withholding of funds.] SEC. 11. Following establishment of the cooperative library board, residents of the cooperative library's area are eligible to use the facilities and resources of the member libraries subject to the rules of the cooperative library plan, as long as the local area has provided for library service either through a local library or contractual arrangements. Services of the cooperative library, including those of participating libraries, are to be available at reasonable times and on an equal basis within the areas served to school children, individuals in public and nonpublic institutions of learning, and a student or resident within the area who is eligible under other provisions of this act. An applicant refused service may appeal to the state board which shall review the operation of the cooperative library and may withhold state aid funds until the services are granted. (MCL §397.561.)

§ 15.1791(162) Local board resolution to become participating library; procedure; rights, duties, privileges of participating library.] SEC. 12. Once a cooperative plan has been accepted by the state board, and a cooperative library board established, the board of a local library shall adopt a resolution requesting the local library become a participating library in the cooperative library. Duplicate copies of the resolution, certified by the clerk of the local board, shall be filed with the cooperative board. The cooperative board shall accept or show reason for denial of the request for membership within 60 days after filing. When the cooperative board has accepted the resolution, the resolution and the acceptance shall be indorsed and a copy filed with the state board. The participating library has the same rights, duties, and privileges as other libraries participating in that cooperative library. (MCL §397.562.)

§ 15.1791(163) State aid; rate.] SEC. 13. A cooperative library shall be granted continuing state aid act [sic] the rate of 50 cents per capita for its served population. (MCL §397.563.)

§ 15.1791(164) Services provided by cooperative board.] SEC. 14. The cooperative board shall provide, directly or through a written contract, services to member libraries within the cooperative library's area. The services, subject to standards approved by the state board, may include:
(a) A central pool or rotating book collection.
(b) In-service training.
(c) Book selection aids.
(d) Bibliographic services.
(e) Audio-visual services.
(f) Bookmobile service or other outlets to outlying areas.
(g) Publicity and public relations.
(h) Printing.
(i) A centralized purchasing operation.
(j) Centralized processing including cataloging and marking.
(k) Reference services.
(l) Delivery service. (MCL §397.564.)

§ 15.1791(165) Insufficiency of state aid; payments by member libraries; linking of cooperative headquarters to state library, provision of services.] Sec. 15. When the state aid grant is insufficient to provide all services, the member libraries may be required to pay for services in a priority order to be specified in the cooperative plan. Cooperative library headquarters shall be linked to the state library and may be required upon adequate funding to provide other services deemed essential to good public library service, and so designated by the state board. (MCL §397.565.)

§ 15.1791(166) Public libraries; state aid, 1977–78; conditions.] Sec. 16. (1) A public library shall receive 35 cents per capita from state aid during the fiscal year 1977–78 if in the prior year the library received local support equal to that required by this act.

Same; 1978–79.] (2) A public library shall receive 50 cents per capita from state aid during the fiscal year 1978–79 if in the prior year the library received local support equal to that required by this act, the library has not reduced its local support by an amount equal to, or larger than, the state aid from the previous year without the approval of the state board, and the library meets the minimum standards established by the state board and this act.

Public libraries belonging to cooperative libraries; 1977–78 additional grant; use of funds.] (3) A public library belonging to a cooperative library shall receive from state aid for the fiscal year 1977–78 an additional 15 cents per capita, all or a part of which must be used to pay for cooperative services from the cooperative board as provided by section 15 and the cooperative plan.

Same; years after 1977–78; areas with less than 75 persons per square mile.] (4) A public library belonging to a cooperative library shall receive from state aid each year after fiscal year 1977–78 an additional 50 cents per capita, all or part of which shall be used to pay for cooperative services from the cooperative board as provided by section 15 and the cooperative plan. When the cost of the cooperative library services has been paid, any remaining portion of the grant may be applied to local services under subsection (2). Each public library cooperative which qualifies under this act during fiscal year 1977–78 and following years shall receive an amount of $10.00 per square mile for the area which it serves if the area served has less than 75 people per square mile.

Public libraries which are county libraries serving population of 50,000 or less appointing certain persons as head librarians; reimbursement of portion of salaries; wage increases to present employees, payment; certification of amounts.] (5) A public library which is a county library serving a population of 50,000 or less which appoints to the office of head librarian a person with either a bachelor of arts or a bachelor of science degree from a college or university approved by an accrediting association of more than statewide standing, including or supplemented by 1 full year of training in a library school accredited by the American library association and with at least 4 years' experience in an administrative capacity in an approved library, shall be reimbursed for that portion of the salary not exceeding $400.00 for any 1 month of $4,800.00 in any 1 year, if the county library received during the last completed fiscal year before the year in which distribution is to be made, from the county or counties not less than $3,600.00 exclusive of money received from federal or state grants in aid to the library. Wage increases to present employees shall be paid equally by the state and local governments. Before September 6, December 6, March 6, and June 6 of the year of distribution, the county library board or the board's authorized agent shall certify to the state board the actual amount of the salary paid the head librarian during the 3-month period immediately preceding those months. (MCL §397.566.)

§ 15.1791(167) Certification requirements for personnel.] SEC. 17. A cooperative library and public library shall conform to certification requirements for personnel as established by the state board in order to qualify for state aid. (MCL §397.567.)

§ 15.1791(168) Application for state aid; certification.] SEC. 18. A cooperative library and public library desiring to participate in state aid shall apply before February 1 of each year of distribution. The applicant shall certify to the state board the amount of money received from each source during the last completed fiscal year before October 1 of the year of distribution. (MCL §397.568.)

§ 15.1791(169) Statement of amount to be distributed; vouchers, signature, delivery; warrants; time for distribution of aid.] SEC. 19. The state board shall prepare a statement of the amount to be distributed in accordance with this act. Vouchers for disbursement of state aid shall be signed by an authorized agent of the board and delivered to the department of management and budget, which shall draw up warrants on the department of treasury in favor of the fiscal agent of the cooperative or local board. State aid shall be distributed by September 30 of the year of distribution. (MCL §397.569.)

§ 15.1791(170) Deposit of funds; expenditures, review.] SEC. 20. A cooperative library or public library receiving state aid shall deposit the money in a separate fund. Expenditures from that fund are subject to review by the state board or its authorized representative. (MCL §397.570.)

§ 15.1791(171) Use of funds.] SEC. 21. State aid paid to a cooperative library or a public library may be used for any expenditure, including the cost of intersystem or intrasystem contracts. (MCL §397.571.)

§ 15.1791(172) Certain disputes, nonresolution on local level; hearing by state board; finality of decision.] SEC. 22. When there is a dispute concerning the cooperative library to which a public library shall belong, services rendered to member libraries, or the operations of a cooperative system which cannot be resolved on the local level, the state board may hear the case. The decision of the state board shall be final. (MCL §397.572.)

§ 15.1791(173) Guidelines for state board.] Sec. 23. The state board shall consider the following needs in carrying out its powers and duties:

(a) Library facilities shall be provided to residents of the area covered by a cooperative library without needless duplication of facilities, resources, or expertise.

(b) Establishment of a local library may be approved for state aid purposes where local conditions require an additional local library.

(c) Existing libraries and new libraries shall cooperate to provide adequate library services at a reasonable cost.

(d) Increased effort shall be made to provide residents the right to read with added emphasis on areas which normally cannot provide those services.

(e) Local responsibility, initiative, and support for library service shall be recognized and respected when provision is made for adequate local and cooperative library service. (MCL §397.573.)

§ 15.1791(174) Rules, promulgation.] Sec. 24. The state board may promulgate rules for administration of this act and for transition from Act No. 286 of the Public Acts of 1965, as amended, being sections 397.501 to 397.527 of the Michigan Compiled Laws, pursuant to Act No. 306 of the Public Acts of 1969, as amended, being sections 24.201 to 24.315 of the Michigan Compiled Laws. (MCL §397.574.)

§ 15.1791(175) Appropriations.] Sec. 25. There is appropriated for public libraries from the general fund of the state for the fiscal year ending September 30, 1977, and for each fiscal year thereafter, the sum necessary to fulfill the requirements of this act. The appropriation shall be distributed as provided in this act. (MCL §397.575.)

DISTRIBUTION OF PUBLIC DOCUMENTS

(Michigan Statutes Annotated, 1982, s.4.322, 4.339,
4.382, 4.411.)

§ 4.322 Public and local acts; free distribution; requisitions; sale; pamphlet compilations.] Sec. 2. There shall be published of the volume containing the public [and local] acts of each session of the legislature a sufficient number of copies to supply the following ◆ with 1 copy each: Libraries of all state [officers,] departments, boards, commissions and institutions; members of the legislature ◆ [who shall receive a complete set subsequent to the latest compiled laws for their personal property during each term for which elected;] senators and representatives of this state in congress; the secretary of state of the United States; the United States senate library and the library of congress; judges and clerks of circuit and district courts of the United States in this state; justices, clerks [and the reporter] of the supreme court, judges of the circuit courts, judges and clerks of the superior ◆ [, recorder's and municipal courts of this state;] all county officers; ◆ [to such supervisors, township clerks and justices of the peace as may file a requisition for same with the township clerk who shall file requisition for his township with his county clerk by January 31 of each year; clerks of in-.

corporated villages; clerks and justices of the peace of incorporated cities actually serving as such; the secretary of the senate; the clerk of the house of representatives, 36 copies imprinted "senate" and 114 copies imprinted "house of representatives" to be used as desk copies, to be delivered to the secretary of the senate and the clerk of the house of representatives respectively; public libraries, bar association libraries and county law libraries, county and county branch libraries. The county clerk shall file a requisition for all copies of public acts for the needs of his county, including county offices, townships, villages and cities within his county, with the secretary of state by February 15, of each year]. In addition to the foregoing, there may be published of said public [and local] acts such further number of copies as the secretary of state shall deem needful and 200 copies thereof shall be deposited in the state library for use in said library and for exchanges, and the remaining copies shall be deposited in the office of the secretary of state for sale and future distribution. The secretary of state is further authorized to publish and distribute at cost to all persons who shall require them, in pamphlet form, duly annotated and indexed, compilations of ◊ laws upon [particular] subjects. ◊ The auditor general shall publish and distribute all pamphlets of the general tax law or of all other laws relating to the revenues of the state ◆. (CL '48, § 24.2; CL '29, § 487; CL '15, § 821.)

§ 4.339 Publications; additional copies in discretion of state librarian.] SEC. 20. There shall be printed of all publications, reports and documents as provided in this act, such additional copies for use and exchanges by the state library as the state librarian may in his discretion deem necessary for such purpose ◆. (CL '48, § 24.20; CL '29, § 504; CL '15, § 838.)

§ 4.382] Same; copies to state librarian. SEC. 12. Such contractor shall, within sixty [60] days after receiving the final manuscripts of any volume from the reporter, deliver to the state librarian at Lansing, free of cost for publication or delivery, three hundred seventy-five [375] copies of the Michigan reports and twenty-five [25] copies of the advance sheets of Michigan reports, in good order and according to contract, to be distributed by the state librarian as authorized in writing from time to time by the justices of the supreme court. (CL '48, § 26.12; CL '29, § 534.)

§ 4.411] State librarian may exchange reports, sale; bond; money paid to state treasurer monthly; new edition. SEC. 7. The state librarian may exchange any of said reports for such other reports or law books as shall be approved by the chief justice of the supreme court, which reports or other books, procured by such exchange, shall be kept in the state library. After the publication of any volume under the provisions of this act the state librarian may sell the same at a price per volume not exceeding the actual cost to the state of publication thereof, to be determined by the board of state auditors, and twenty [20] per cent added thereto. The state librarian shall give a bond in the penal sum of five thousand [5,000] dollars to the state, conditioned for the faithful performance of the duties imposed by this act. He shall keep an account of all moneys received by him for said reports, and shall pay the same monthly to the state treasurer, who shall credit the same to the general fund. In case of sales to any one [1] person at one [1] time of twenty-five [25] volumes or over, the twenty [20] per cent aforesaid may be deducted from the selling price of such volumes. When the edition of any volume authorized to be sold by the state librarian shall be exhausted, a new edition of the same number of volumes shall be printed, bound, and sold, as provided in this act relative to the first [1st] edition. (CL '48, § 26.47; CL '29, § 543; CL '15, § 874; How § 7201; CL '97, § 229; CL '71, § 5657.)

STATE HISTORICAL COMMISSION
(Michigan Statutes Annotated, 1982, s.15.1801-15.1809.)

§ 15.1801] Historical commission; members, appointment, expenses. SEC. 1. There is hereby created a commission to be known as the Michigan historical commission. Said commission shall consist of 6 members, with the addition of the governor, ex-officio; said 6 members shall be appointed by the governor [by and with the advice and consent of the senate]. No member of said commission shall receive any compensation for his services, except actual and necessary expenses while attending the meetings or carrying out the purposes of said commission. (MCL §399.1; CL '29, §8114; CL '15, §10727.)

§ 15.1802] Same; terms of office. SEC. 2. The governor shall appoint the members of said commission for the following terms: One [1] for one [1] year, one [1] for two [2] years, one [1] for three [3] years, one [1] for four [4] years, one [1] for five [5] years, and one [1] for six [6] years, and thereafter one [1] member annually for a term of six [6] years until their successors shall have been appointed and qualified. (MCL §399.2; CL '29, §8115; CL '15, §10728.)

§ 15.1803] Same; meetings; organization; acceptance of property. SEC. 3. As soon as practicable after this act shall take effect, the said commission shall meet in the state capitol in Lansing, and shall organize by electing one of its members as president, and one as vice president, and shall appoint a secretary, and shall arrange a time and place of holding regular meetings of the commission, and for such special meetings as may be necessary. It shall take, as soon as practicable, necessary steps to receive and accept in the name of the state of Michigan, such of the property of the Michigan pioneer and historical society as the latter may convey to the state of Michigan, and shall take possession of the rooms in the capitol building now occupied by the said society, and may accept all gifts and bequests for the furtherance of its authorized purposes. (MCL §399.3; CL '29, §8116; CL '15, §10729.)

§ 15.1804] Same; duties. SEC. 4. It shall be the duty of said commission to collect, arrange and preserve historical material, including books, pamphlets, maps, charts, manuscripts, papers, copies of domestic and foreign records and archives, paintings, statuary, and other objects and material illustrative of and relating to the history of Michigan and the old northwest territory; to procure and preserve narratives of the early pioneers, their exploits, perils, privations and achievement; to collect material of every description relative to the history, language, literature, progress or decay of our Indian tribes; to collect, prepare and display in the museum of said commission objects indicative of the life, customs, dress and resources of the early residents of Michigan, and to publish source materials, and historical studies relative to and illustrative of the history of the state, including such historical materials and studies as may be furnished for that purpose by educational institutions and by the Michigan pioneer and historical society. The commission shall cooperate with and assist the Michigan pioneer and historical society and local historical societies in the state, and help to organize new local historical societies of similar nature and purpose. (MCL §399.4: CL '29, §8117; CL '15, §10730.)

§ 15.1805 **Historical records and papers; collection, preservation; local public institutions as depository; certified copies as evidence; disposal of valueless records.]** Sec. 5. The ◆ commission shall have power, and it is hereby made the duty of all public officials to assist in the performance of this power, to collect from the public offices in the state, including state, county, city, village, school and township offices, such records, files, documents, books and papers as are not in current use, and are of value, in the opinion of the commission; and it is hereby made the legal custodian of such records, files, documents, books and papers when collected and transferred to its possession. The commission shall provide for their preservation, classification, arranging and indexing, so that they may be made available for the use of the public. ◆ In counties where there is a public institution having a fireproof building and suitable arrangements for carefully keeping such publications, records, files, documents, [books and papers,] so that in the opinion of [the] commission they can be safely stored, the same or any part thereof may be left in the possession of such institution. A list thereof ◆ shall be furnished the commission and shall be kept of record in its office. A copy of the finding of the commission that such depository is a safe and a proper one in its opinion shall be made a part of the official records of [the] commission. Copies of all such papers, documents, files and records, when made and certified to by the secretary or archivist of [the] commission, shall be admitted in evidence in all courts, with the same effect as if certified to by the original custodian thereof.

Any record that is required to be kept by a public officer in the discharge of the duties imposed on him by law, or that is a writing required to be filed in a public office, or is a written memorial of a transaction of a public officer made in the discharge of his duty, shall be the property of the people of the state ◆, and may not be disposed of, mutilated or destroyed except as provided by law. [The provisions of this section shall not apply to bonds, bills, notes, interest coupons or other evidences of indebtedness issued by the state, county, multi-county, school, municipal agency, department, board, commission and institution of government.] The directing authority of each state, ◆ county, multi-county, school, ◆ municipal agency, department, board, commission and institution of government shall present to the ◆ commission a schedule governing disposal of, or a list or description of the papers, documents and other records which

[it] shall certify are useless and which have ceased to be of value to [the] governmental agency and to its duties to the public, whereupon the ♦ commission shall inspect the ♦ papers, documents and other records and shall requisition for transfer from [the] directing authority to ♦ [the] commission, such papers, documents and other records as [the] commission shall deem to be of value.

As soon as possible after the inspection by the ♦ commission and the transfer of records deemed to have value has been completed, the ♦ directing authority of [the] agency, department, board, commission and institution shall submit the schedule governing the disposal of, or the remainder of the list of such papers, documents and other records to the state administrative board, who shall approve or disapprove the disposal schedule or list and order the destruction of the valueless records accordingly. (MCL §399.5; CL '29, §8113; CL '15, §10731.)

§ 15.1806] Publication of material; payment of expenses.
SEC. 6.   It shall be the duty of said commission to prepare for publication the material referred to in section four [4] of this act. The volumes of said publication shall be issued in editions of not more than two thousand five hundred [2,500] copies, and contain not exceeding seven hundred fifty [750] pages each. They shall be printed and bound in substantial uniformity with the volumes issued by other historical societies and the several state departments. Said printing, together with such bulletins, including a historical quarterly journal such as is issued by other historical societies, and such reprints of books, maps, and articles as may be determined upon by the commission, shall be paid out of the appropriation hereby made. (MCL §399.6; CL '29, §8119; CL '15, §10732.)

§ 15.1807 Custodian of historical publications of state department, secretary of state; distribution or exchange of publications; free copies; appropriations; costs; price; credit and disposition of funds.] SEC. 7.   [(1)] The secretary of ♦ [state] shall be the custodian of the [historical] publications of the ♦ [department of state] and ♦ [may] distribute, ♦ exchange ♦ [, or both distribute and exchange the] publications with domestic and foreign states, governments, and institutions ♦ [.

(2)   The secretary of state] shall furnish 1 copy of each volume ♦ [of the journal, Michigan history, free of charge,] to each ♦ [cooperative] library, ♦ in ♦ [this state if] officially requested ♦ to do [so] by the officers ♦ [of the library.

(3)   The secretary of state] shall furnish to each member of the legislature ♦ 1 copy of each ♦ journal published during ♦ [the legislator's] term ♦ [, free of charge, if requested to do so by the legislator.

(4)   There is appropriated for the department of state for the fiscal year ending September 30, 1978, from the general fund of the state, to the Michigan heritage publications fund, the sum of $23,-000.00 or as much thereof as is necessary, for costs incurred by the journal, Michigan history, for printing, distributing, and promoting the journal. Except as provided in subsections (2) and (3), the secretary of state shall sell each copy of Michigan history at a price set

by the secretary of state. After September 30, 1978, printing, distribution, and promotion costs incurred by the journal shall be paid exclusively from the Michigan heritage publications fund.

(5) The secretary of state may raise or lower the selling price of Michigan history to reflect changes in printing, distribution, and promotion costs incurred by the journal.

(6)] The money ◆ [collected] from ◆ [the sale of Michigan history] shall be ◆ [credited to a revolving fund created by this act which is called the Michigan heritage publications fund. The money shall be used to pay the printing, distribution, and promotion costs of Michigan history. The money in the revolving fund at the close of the fiscal year shall remain in the revolving fund to be used to finance printing, distribution, and promotion costs of the publication]. (MCL §399.7; CL '29, §8120; CL '15, §10733.)

§ 15.1808 Historical commission; secretary, delegation of authority to; employees; salaries and expenses.] SEC. 8. The secretary of said commission shall act under the direction of the commission. The commission shall have power to appoint such other employees as shall be deemed necessary. [The commission may delegate to the secretary such authority as is necessary to carry out the provisions of this act.] The secretary and other employees shall receive such salaries as shall be appropriated by the legislature and also such traveling expenses as shall be necessary. (MCL §399.8; CL '29, §8121; CL '15, §10734.)

§ 15.1808(1) Same; rules and regulations.] SEC. 8A. The commission shall make rules and regulations necessary to carry out the provisions of this act pursuant to Act No. 88 of the Pub Acts of 1943, as amended, being sections 24.71 to 24.82, inclusive, of the Compiled Laws of 1948. (MCL §399.8a.)

§ 15.1809] Annual report; contents. SEC. 9. The said commission shall make annual reports on the first [1st] day of January of each year to the governor of the state, setting forth the character and extent of the work done under its supervision during the preceding year, and the amounts of money expended by it for the various purposes authorized by this act. (MCL §399.9; CL '29, §8122; CL '15, §10735.)

COOPERATIVE AGREEMENTS

(Michigan Statutes Annotated, 1982, s.15.1792(1), 15.1792(2).)

§ 15.1792(1) Cooperation and coordination in maintenance and operation of libraries; contracts with other libraries or political subdivisions; purpose.] SEC. 1. The officers, agency or other authority charged by law with the maintenance and operation of any library for general public use may enter into and perform contracts or arrangements with the officers, agency or other authority likewise charged in respect of any other such library ◆ for cooperation and coordination in the maintenance and operation of [the] libraries to ◆ [avoid] unnecessary duplication and at the same time [promote] the widest public use of books, manuscripts and other materials and facilities and [bring] about the supplementing of the 1 library by the other, which may include the accumulating of books, manuscripts and other materials and facilities, to whichever library belonging, of the same general nature or pertaining to the same general subject in such library as will best facilitate access thereto and promote the best use thereof by the members of the public desiring so to do.

[The] officers, agencies or other authorities ◆, jointly or severally, [may] enter into contracts or arrangements to make available to political subdivisions of the state, including school districts, otherwise authorized by law to maintain libraries, such library services and facilities as will promote the widest public use of books and avoid unnecessary duplication and expense. (MCL §397.471.)

§ 15.1792(2)   Same; libraries which may contract; use of libraries; budgeting expenditures; construction of act; authority of political subdivisions.]   SEC. 2.   Such contracts and arrangements may be made between and among any number of such libraries ◆. Any library supported in whole or in part by taxes or other public funds or competent in law to be so supported shall be eligible to be included in any such contract or arrangement by whatever authority such library may be maintained and operated. Residents of the territory subject to taxation for support of any library entering into any such contracts or arrangements shall have such rights and privileges in the use of the respective libraries entering into like contracts and arrangements as shall be provided therein. If the expenditures generally of such library shall by the law under which maintained and operated be subject to being budgeted and approved, any expenditure by such library required for carrying out any such contract or arrangement shall be likewise so subject.

The provisions hereof shall be broadly and liberally construed and applied and any provision in any contract or arrangement ◆ reasonably tending to effectuate in any part the intents and purposes hereof shall be deemed within the authority hereby granted. Any political subdivision of the state, including school districts, now or hereafter authorized by law to establish or maintain libraries or library services, ◆ [may] enter into contracts or arrangements for library services and facilities provided in section 1 and ◆ provide for the payments of obligations arising from such contracts or arrangements by resolution of the legislative body of the political subdivision or school district or in any other manner provided by law. (MCL §397.472.)

REGIONAL LIBRARIES
(Michigan Statutes Annotated, 1982, s.15.1781-15.1783,
15.1785-15.1788.)

§ 15.1781]   Regional libraries; plan for establishment and location.   SEC. 1.   The state [board for libraries] ◆ shall ◆ develop a plan for the establishment and location of regional libraries throughout the state based on a detailed survey of the needs of the various localities of the state. A region shall include 2 or more counties. (MCL §397.151.)

§ 15.1782   Referral to board of supervisors; adoption, rejection or alteration of plan.] SEC. 2.   On completion of the survey of any proposed region, ♦ [the proposal to establish a regional library shall be referred] to the boards of supervisors of all counties included in such proposed region. The boards of supervisors shall act upon such proposal by resolution, and the votes of a majority of [the members-elect] of [the] board of supervisors [in each] of the counties included in the proposed region shall be necessary for the adoption of such proposal. In case of the rejection of such proposal by the boards of supervisors of any of the counties included in such proposed region, ♦ [the] plan [may be altered] in accordance with such action in order to provide for a [regional library] in such section of the state. The vote of a majority of [the members-elect] of [the] board of supervisors in [each of] the counties in such altered region shall be necessary for the adoption of such proposal. (MCL §397.152.)

§ 15.1783]   Board of trustees; number, appointment, term, vacancies; compensation and expenses. SEC. 3.   Upon the adoption of the ♦ [regional library proposal], each board of supervisors shall name members to a library board, the members to be chosen from the citizens at large of each county with reference to their fitness for office. Not more than 1 member of the board of supervisors of each county shall be at any one time a member of said library board. Each county shall be entitled to 2 members on the regional library board, the members to be appointed for a term of 4 years each, except that the first members shall be appointed, 1 for 2 years and 1 for 4 years, or until their successors have been appointed ♦. In the case of only 2 counties joining in the regional library, the library board shall consist of not more than 4 members from each county, each for a term of 4 years, except that the first members shall be appointed, 2 for 2 years and 2 for 4 years, or until their successors have been appointed. Vacancies in the board of trustees shall be filled in like manner as the original appointments. Members of the board of trustees shall receive no compensation except their actual and necessary expenses. (MCL §397.153.)

§ 15.1785]   Board of trustees; powers. SEC. 5.   The board of trustees of each regional library so established shall have the following powers:

(a)   To establish, maintain and operate a public library for the region.

(b)   To appoint a [professionally qualified] librarian ♦, and the necessary assistants, and to fix their compensation. Said board shall also have the power to remove said librarian and other assistants.

(c)   To purchase books, periodicals, equipment and supplies.

(d)   To purchase sites and erect buildings, ♦ or to lease suitable quarters, and to have supervision and control of such property.

(e)   To borrow books from and lend books to other libraries.

(f)   To enter into contracts to receive service from or give service to libraries within or without the region and to give service to municipalities without the region which have no libraries.

(g)   To have exclusive control of the expenditure of all moneys collected to the credit of the library fund.

(h) To make such bylaws, rules and regulations not inconsistent with this act as may be expedient for their own government and that of the library. (MCL §397.155.)

§ 15.1786 Appropriations; basis; disbursement.] Sec. 6. Sums necessary for the establishment and operation of regional libraries shall be [provided] by the boards of supervisors of [each of] the counties included in such region [by an appropriation] from the general fund of the respective counties[, or by a tax levy for this purpose authorized by a vote of the qualified electors in each of the counties]. ◆ A budget [shall] be proposed annually by the board of trustees of the regional library to the boards of supervisors of the counties in the region. Upon approval of such budget by a majority of each of said boards of supervisors, the proposed budget shall be effective in all counties in the region. All appropriations shall be paid to the board of trustees and disbursed under its direction [by the county treasurer of the county designated by the regional library board as depository for the regional library fund]. (MCL §397.156.)

§ 15.1787] Cities over 5,000 having libraries, exemption. Sec. 7. Cities of a population of 5,000 or more, maintaining a public library, may be exempted from the provisions of this act on the filing with the state ◆ [board for libraries] of a request by the city legislative body based on action taken by them according to law ◆. Where any such city is included in any regional library proposal ◆ [the state board for libraries shall] notify each city so included in writing of the provisions of this section 15 days before the reference of any regional library proposal under the provisions of section 2. ◆ (MCL §397.157.)

§ 15.1788] Municipal libraries, transfer to regional libraries. Sec. 8. After the establishment of a regional library as provided for in this act, the township board, the legislative body of any city or village, the board of education of any school district or the board of supervisors of any municipality in the region, already maintaining a public, school or county library, may notify the board of trustees of the regional library that such township, city, village, school district or county library may be transferred to, leased to, or used by said board of trustees of the regional library under such terms as may mutually be agreed upon between the said board of trustees and the respective township boards, city or village legislative bodies, boards of education or boards of supervisors. (MCL §397.158.)

LIBRARY NETWORKS
(Michigan Statutes Annotated, 1982, s.15-1780(21)-15.1780(26).)

§ 15.1780(21) Short title.] Sec. 1. This act shall be known and may be cited as the "library network act of 1971". (MCL §397.131.)

§ 15.1780(22) Library network defined; administrative leadership.] SEC. 2. As used in this act "library network" means the connecting of the largest research libraries in the state for the express purpose of making their collections available to all citizens in the state through interlibrary loan. The state library shall assume administrative leadership in this network concept and shall designate participating libraries. (MCL §397.132.)

§ 15.1780(23) Maintenance of collection; electronic equipment connections; interlibrary loan agreements.] SEC. 3. A library shall maintain a collection of at least 1,000,000 volumes in order to be eligible for membership in the network. A library shall be connected to the state library by means of electronic equipment and shall agree to supply for interlibrary loan any volume in its collection, not in use, except rare volumes, reference works, books on reserve for course work, volumes of serials, fragile materials, and all other library materials which are not loaned under its regulations. (MCL §397.133.)

§ 15.1780(24) Interlibrary loan service; administration.] SEC. 4. The state library in Lansing shall administer the interlibrary loan service for the state. (MCL §397.134.)

§ 15.1780(25) Application for inclusion in network.] SEC. 5. A library meeting the requirements specified for inclusion in the network shall apply to the state board of education, indicating its compliance with the provisions of this act. (MCL §397.135.)

§ 15.1780(26) Rules.] SEC. 6. The state board of education may promulgate rules for administration of this act in accordance with and subject to Act No. 306 of the Public Acts of 1969, as amended, being sections 24.201 to 24.315 of the Compiled Laws of 1948. (MCL §397.136.)

DISTRICT LIBRARIES
(Michigan Statutes Annotated, 1982, s.15.1780(1)-15.1780(6)).)

§ 15.1780(1) District library; municipalities may unite to establish and operate; "municipalities" defined.] SEC. 1. Any municipality empowered by law to establish or maintain libraries or library services may cooperatively develop a plan and unite with any other municipality or municipalities for the establishment and operation of a district library.

The term "municipalities" as used in this act shall include cities, villages, school districts, townships and counties. (MCL §397.271.)

§ 15.1780(2) District library; submission of proposal to governing body of each municipality, vote, adoption.] SEC. 2. [(1)] The proposal to unite for the establishment and operation of [a] district library shall be submitted to the governing or legislative body of each municipality in [the] proposed district, and the vote of a majority of the members of each ◆ [of those bodies] shall be necessary for the adoption of [the] proposal.

Submission of proposal to people, vote, adoption.] [(2) If the governing or legislative body of a municipality submits the proposal for the establishment and operation of the district library to a vote of the people, a majority of those voting on the question in the municipality shall be necessary for the adoption of the proposal.]

(MCL §397.272.)

§ 15.1780(3)   Board of trustees; membership, term of office, vacancy, compensation and expenses, organization.]   SEC. 3. [(1)] Upon the adoption of the proposal for [a] district library, the governing or legislative body of each participating municipality shall choose from its ◆ [residents], with reference to their fitness for office, 2 members[, except if there are less than 4 participating municipalities, not less than 2 and not more than 4 members,] who shall compose the library board of trustees for terms of 4 years each. ◆ Of the members first appointed, 1 [or not more than 2, if the board consists of more than 2 members from each participating municipality,] shall be appointed for a term of 2 years and 1 [or not more than 2, if the board consists of more than 2 members from each participating municipality,] for a term of 4 years. [A member] shall serve until the appointment and qualification of ◆ [a successor. A vacancy] shall be filled in ◆ [a similar] manner for the unexpired term. ◆ [Each member] of the board shall serve without compensation. ◆ [The governing library board may pay to each member of the board the] actual and necessary expenses [which the member] incurred in the performance of official duties[, which shall conform to the per diem compensation of the local governing body and the schedule for reimbursement of expenses established annually by the legislature]. The members of the board shall select their own officers.

Submission of election to people, majority vote; membership; terms of office; nomination; election; vacancy.]   [(2) If the governing or legislative body of each participating municipality submits the proposal for the election of the members of the board of trustees of the district library to a vote of the people and a majority of those voting on the question in the proposed district vote in favor of the proposal, a board of 9 members shall be elected from the district at large. ● The 3 persons receiving the most votes shall receive 6 year terms, the 3 persons receiving the next highest number of votes shall receive 4 year terms, and the 3 remaining persons elected to the board shall receive 2 year terms. A member shall serve until a successor is elected and qualified. The term of office of an elected successor shall be 6 years, commencing on January 1 following the election. A nomination for a position on the board of trustees shall be by a petition signed by at least ½ of 1% of the qualified electors of the district and the election, other than the first election, shall be at the same time as the even year general November election. A vacancy shall be filled by the remaining members of the board until the next following even year general

November election at which a person shall be elected for the remainder of the term.]
(MCL §397.273.)

§ 15.1780(4) Powers.] SEC. 4. The board of trustees of each district library ♦ established shall have the following powers·

(a) To establish, maintain, and operate a public library for the district.

(b) To appoint a librarian, and the necessary assistants, and fix their compensation. [The] board ♦ [may] remove [the] librarian and other assistants.

(c) To purchase books, periodicals, equipment, and supplies.

(d) To purchase sites and erect buildings, ♦ to lease suitable quarters, [or to both erect building and lease quarters] and to have supervision and control of [the] property.

(e) To enter into [a contract] to receive service from or give service to [a library] within or without the district and to give service to municipalities [within or] without the district which [do not] have ♦ [a library].

(f) To have exclusive control of the expenditure of all money collected to the credit of the library fund.

(g) To make ♦ by-laws ♦ and regulations not inconsistent with this act as may be expedient for ♦ [the board's] own government and that of the library.
(MCL §397.274.)

§ 15.1780(4a) Municipalities constituting authority.] SEC. 4a. The municipalities which unite for the establishment and operation of a district library pursuant to section 2(2) of this act shall constitute an authority under section 6 of article 9 of the state constitution of 1963.
(MCL §397.274a.)

§ 15.1780(5) Appropriations; tax levies.] SEC. 5. The sums necessary for the establishment and operation of ♦ [a] district library shall be appropriated by the governing or legislative boards of the municipalities entering into the formation of the district library, or by a tax levy for this purpose authorized by a vote of the qualified electors in ♦ [a] participating municipality [or a vote of the qualified electors of the district established by the participating municipalities pursuant to section 2(2) of this act, if the proposed tax levy is submitted by the board of trustees of the district library]. If ♦ [a] municipality withdraws from the district library, ♦ [a] previously voted tax levy shall be continued for provision of public library support.
(MCL §397.275.)

§ 15.1780(6) Withdrawal of municipality; procedure; payment of share of assets.] SEC. 6. (1) Any municipality which has united with other municipalities in the establishment and operation of a district library under this act may withdraw therefrom upon a favorable vote by tne majority of those voting at the next regularly scheduled election of the withdrawing municipality.

(2)   The resolution shall state the effective date of the withdrawal of the municipality, which date shall be not less than 6 months from the date of the resolution. Notice of the resolution shall be published at least 10 days before its passage, in a newspaper of general circulation within the withdrawing municipality.

(3)   After passage of the resolution, duplicate certified copies of it shall be filed with the district library board for transmittal to the local boards of all other municipalities participating in the district library and with the state board of education.

(4)   The state board of education shall require the local board of the withdrawing municipality to furnish a plan for continuing public library service for all residents of the municipality after withdrawal from the district library.

(5)   The withdrawing municipality shall be entitled to receive its share of the net assets of the district library valued as of the date of withdrawal if it so desires. Payment of the withdrawing municipality's share shall be made within a reasonable period of time according to a plan approved by the state board of education. (MCL §397.276.)

COUNTY LIBRARIES

(Michigan Statutes Annotated, 1982, s.15-1701-15.1705.)

§ 15.1701   County library, establishment; contract for use of existing library; tax.]   SEC. 1.   The board of supervisors of any county shall have the power to establish a public library free for the use of the inhabitants of such county and they may contract for the use, for such purposes, of a public library already established within the county, with the body having control of such library, to furnish library service to the people of the county under such terms and conditions as may be stated in such contract. The amount agreed to be paid for such service under such contract and the amount which the board may appropriate for the purpose of establishing and maintaining a public library shall be a charge upon the county and the board may annually levy a tax ♦ [on] the taxable property of the county, to be levied and collected in like manner as other taxes in said county and paid to the county treasurer of said county and to be known as the library fund. (MCL §397.301; CL '29, §8084.)

§ 15.1702]   County library board; members, term, corporate body, powers.   SEC. 2.   For the purpose of administering the county library fund, there shall be a library board consisting of 5 members, to be appointed by the [county] board of ♦ [commissioners], for terms of 5 years each, except that the first members shall be appointed for 1, 2, 3, 4, and 5 years. [In a county with a population over 1,000,000, the superintendent of the intermediate school district serving the county shall be 1 of the 5 members of the library board during his or her term of office.]

The board shall be a body corporate and shall be authorized to contract for the leasing, construction, or maintenance of buildings or quarters, including the acquisition of sites, to house the county library service, and to do any other thing necessary for the conducting of the county library service, the cost thereof to be a charge against the county library fund. (MCL §397.302; CL '29, §8085.)

§ 15.1703   Contracts with existing libraries; supervision; employees.] Sec. 3.   In case a contract shall be made with an existing library, the county library fund shall be administered by the [county library board and such contract, and all services provided for thereunder, shall be supervised by the county library board; and all employees engaged in the execution and carrying out of such contract shall be county employees, except those furnished and employed by the library rendering such services in accordance with or fulfillment of such contract]. (MCL §397.303; CL '29, §8086.)

§ 15.1704   Payment of fund.] Sec. 4.   Said fund shall be paid by the county treasurer upon the order or warrants of said library board ♦. (MCL §397.304; CL '29, §8087.)

§ 15.1705   Contract for service to municipality; tax; effect of establishment of municipal library.] Sec. 5.   Any county possessing a county library or any board of trustees of a regional library may enter into a contract with one [1] or more counties, townships, villages, cities and/or other municipalities to secure to the residents of such municipality such library service as may be agreed upon, and the money received for the furnishing of such service shall be deposited to the credit of the library fund. Any municipality contracting for such library service shall have the power to levy a library tax in the same manner and amount as authorized in section one [1] hereof for the purpose of paying therefor. Any municipality contracting for such library service may at any time establish a public library free for the use of its inhabitants, whereupon its contract for said service may be continued or terminated on such terms as may be agreed upon between the parties thereto. (MCL §397.305.)

MUNICIPAL LIBRARIES
General Provisions
(Michigan Statutes Annotated, 1982, s.15.1661-15.1677.)

§ 15.1661]   City library; establishment, maintenance; library fund. Sec. 1.   *The People of the State of Michigan enact,* That the city council of each incorporated city shall have power to establish and maintain a public library and reading room, for the use and benefit of the inhabitants of such city, and may levy a tax of not to exceed one [1] mill on the dollar annually on all the taxable property in the city, such tax to be levied and collected in like manner with other general taxes of said city, and to be known as the "library fund." (MCL §397.201; CL '29, §8059; CL '15, §3431; How §5175; CL '97, §3449.)

§ 15.1662]   Board of directors [of city library; number,] appointment[, qualifications]. Sec. 2.   When any city council shall have decided to establish and maintain a public library and reading room under this act, the mayor of such city shall, with the approval of the city council, proceed to appoint a board of [five] [5] directors for the same, chosen from the citizens at large, with reference to their fitness for such office, and not more than one [1] member of the city council shall be at any one [1] time a member of said board. (MCL §397.202; CL '29, §0860; CL '15, §3432; How §5176; CL '97, §3450.)

§ 15.1663] **Same; [vacancy,] term, removal.** SEC. 3. ♦ [The offices of [members of] boards of directors heretofore appointed under this act, consisting of nine [9] members, are hereby declared vacant on July one [1], nineteen hundred thirty-two [1932], and a board of five [5] directors to succeed them or a board of directors of five [5] members for a library newly established hereunder shall be first appointed as follows: one [1] director shall be appointed for a term of five [5] years, one [1] director shall be appointed for a term of four [4] years, one [1] director shall be appointed for a term of three [3] years, one [1] director shall be appointed for a term of two [2] years, one [1] director shall be appointed for a term of one [1] year], and annually thereafter the mayor shall appoint ♦ [one [1] member of such board of directors for a term of five [5] years]. The mayor may, by and with the consent of the city council, remove any director for misconduct or neglect of duty. (MCL §397.203; CL '29, §8061; CL '15, §3433; How §5177; CL '97, §3451.)

§ 15.1664] **Same; vacancies, compensation.** SEC. 4. Vacancies in the board of directors occasioned by removals, resignation or otherwise, shall be reported to the city council, and be filled in like manner as original appointments, and no director shall receive compensation as such. (MCL §397.204; CL '29, §8062; CL '15, §3434; How §5178; CL '97, §3452.)

§ 15.1665] **Same; officers; powers and duties; library fund, accounting rules.** SEC. 5. Said directors shall, immediately after appointment, meet and organize, by the election of one [1] of their number president, and by the election of such other officers as they may deem necessary. They shall make and adopt such by-laws, rules, and regulations for their own guidance and for the government of the library and reading room, as may be expedient, not inconsistent with this act. They shall have the exclusive control of the expenditure of all moneys collected to the credit of the library fund, and of the construction of any library building, and of the supervision, care, and custody of the grounds, rooms, or buildings constructed, leased or set apart for that purpose: Provided, That all moneys received for such library shall be deposited in the treasury of said city to the credit of the library fund, and shall be kept separate and apart from other moneys of such city, and drawn upon by the proper officers of said city, upon the properly authenticated vouchers of the library board. Said board shall have power to purchase or lease grounds, to occupy, lease, or erect an appropriate building or buildings for the use of said library; shall have power to appoint a suitable librarian and necessary assistants, and fix their compensation; and shall also have power to remove such appointees; and shall, in general, carry out the spirit and intent of this act in establishing and maintaining a public library and reading room. (MCL §397.205; CL '29, §8063; CL '15, §3435; How §5179; CL '97, §3453.)

§ 15.1666]   Free use of library; regulations. Sec. 6.   Every library and reading room established under this act shall be forever free to the use of the inhabitants where located, always subject to such reasonable rules and regulations as the library board may adopt; and said board may exclude from the use of said library and reading room any and all persons who shall wilfully violate such rules. (MCL §397.206; CL '29, §8064; CL '15, §3436; How §5180; CL '97, §3454.)

§ 15.1667]   Board of directors; annual report, contents. Sec. 7.   The said board of directors shall make, at the end of each and every year from and after the organization of such library, a report to the city council, stating the condition of their trust at the date of such report, the various sums of money received from the library fund and from other sources, and how such moneys have been expended, and for what purposes; the number of books and periodicals on hand; the number added by purchase, gift, or otherwise during the year; the number lost or missing; the number of visitors attending; the number of books loaned out, and the general character and kind of such books, with such other statistics, information, and suggestions as they may deem of general interest. All such portions of said report as relate to the receipt and expenditure of money, as well as the number of books on hand, books lost or missing, and books purchased, shall be verified by affidavit. (MCL §397.207; CL '29, §8065; CL '15, §3437; How §5181; CL '97, §3455.)

§ 15.1668]   City library; injury, ordinances. Sec. 8.   The city council of said city shall have power to pass ordinances imposing suitable penalties for the punishment of persons committing injury upon such library, or the grounds or other property thereof, or for wilful injury to or failure to return any book belonging to such library. (MCL §397.208; CL '29, §8066; CL '15, §3438; How §5182; CL '97, §3456.)

§ 15.1669]   Same; donations. Sec. 9.   Any person desiring to make donations of money, personal property, or real estate for the benefit of such library, shall have the right to vest the title to [the] money or real estate so donated in the board of directors created under this act, to be held and controlled by such board, when accepted, according to the terms of the deed, gift, devise, or bequest of such property; and as to such property, the said board shall be held and considered to be special trustees. (MCL §397.209; CL '29, §8067; CL '15, §3439; How §5183; CL '97, §3457.)

§ 15.1670]   Village or township library; petition for tax; referendum; estimate of cost of maintenance; assessment. Sec. 10.   When fifty [50] voters of any incorporated village or township shall present a petition to the clerk of the village or township, asking that a tax may be levied for the establishment of a free public library in such village or township, and shall specify in their petition the rate of taxation, not to exceed one [1] mill on the dollar, such clerk shall, in the next legal notice of the regular annual election in such village or township, give notice that at such election every voter may

vote for a mill tax for a free public library, or against a mill tax for
a free public library, specifying in such notice the rate of taxation
mentioned in such petition; and if the majority of all the votes cast
in such village or township shall be for the tax for a free public
library, the tax specified in such notice shall be levied and collected
in like manner with other general taxes of said village or township,
and shall be known as the library fund, and when such free public
library shall have been established and a board of directors elected
and qualified, as hereinafter provided, it shall be the duty of such
board of directors on or before the first [1st] Monday of September
in each year, where it has been voted to establish a free public
library by a township, and on or before the second [2nd] Monday in
April, where it has been voted to establish a free public library by
an incorporated village, to prepare an estimate of the amount of
money necessary for the support and maintenance of such library
for the ensuing year, not exceeding one [1] mill on the dollar of the
taxable property of the village or township, and report such estimate
to the assessor of such village or the supervisors of such township for
assessment and collection, the same as other village or township
taxes, and the same shall be so assessed and collected; and the corporate authorities of any such villages or townships may exercise the
same powers conferred upon the corporate authorities of cities under
this act. (MCL §397.210; CL '29, §8068; CL '15, §3440; How §5184; CL
'97, §3458.)

§ 15.1671]   City library; referendum on tax for establishment, tax for maintenance. SEC. 10a. ♦ [If] 50 voters of
♦ [a] city ♦ present a petition to the clerk of the city, asking
that a tax ♦ be levied for the establishment of a free public
library in [that] city, and ♦ specify in ♦ [the] petition a
rate of taxation not to exceed 1 mill on the dollar, [the] clerk
shall in the next legal notice of the regular annual election
in [that] city, give notice that at [the regular annual] election
every voter may vote upon [the] proposition. ♦ [The] notice
shall specify the rate of taxation mentioned in [the] petition.
The form of the ballot shall be as follows:
     "For a mill tax for a free public library, Yes ☐
      For a mill tax for a free public library, No ☐"
If a majority of all votes cast in [the] city upon [the]
proposition ♦ [is] for the tax for a free public library, the
tax specified in [the] notice shall be levied and collected in ♦
[the same] manner ♦ [as] other general taxes of [that] city,
and shall be placed in a fund to be known as the library fund".
♦ When [the] free public library ♦ [has] been established
under this section, and a board of directors elected and qualified
as ♦ provided in section 11 ♦ [, the] board of directors on or
before the first Monday in September in each year ♦ [shall]
prepare an estimate of the amount of money necessary for the
support and maintenance of [the free public] library for the
ensuing year, not exceeding 1 mill on the dollar of the taxable
property of [the] city. ♦ [The board of directors shall] report
[the] estimate to the ♦ [legislative body] of [the] city. ♦ The
♦ [legislative body] shall cause to be raised by tax upon the

taxable property in the city [the amount of the estimate] in the same manner that other general taxes are raised in [the] city.
(MCL §397.210a.)

§ **15.1672** **Library board; establishment after vote to establish free public library.]** SEC. 11. ♦ [(1) Immediately] after ♦ [a] city ♦ [, a] village, or [a] township ♦ [has] voted to establish a free public library, [a library board shall be established by the] city, ♦ village ♦ [, or township as prescribed in subsections (3) and (4).]

Same; establishment in city, village, or township that has free public library.] [(2) A city, village, or township that has] a free public library and ♦ [if a] library board has [not] been elected, [including a city library and board of directors established under sections 1 to 10, the city, village, or township shall establish a library board as prescribed in subsections (3) and (4).]

Provisional library board; appointment.] [(3)] The legislative body of [a] city, ♦ village ♦ [, or township described in subsection (1) or (2) shall] appoint a ♦ provisional library board of ♦ [6 directors who shall] hold office until the ♦ next annual or biennial city or village election, or ♦ township election of a permanent library board.

Permanent library board; establishment, directors, election, procedures.] ♦ [(4) A] permanent library board [shall be established for a city, village, or township described in subsection (1) or (2) as follows:

(a)] In ♦ [a city or village] holding [an] annual ♦ [election,] 6 directors [shall be elected.] Two ♦ [directors] shall be elected for [a term of] 1 year; 2 for 2 years; and 2 for 3 years. ♦ [Each year] thereafter ♦, 2 directors ♦ shall ♦ [be elected] for ♦ [3-year terms.

(b)] In [a city] or [village that holds biennial] elections ♦, 6 directors [shall be elected.] Two ♦ [directors] shall be elected for [a term of] 2 years; 2 for 4 years; and 2 for 6 years. ♦ Biennially thereafter ♦, 2 directors ♦ shall ♦ [be elected] for [6-year terms.

(c) In a township holding elections for township officers every 4 years, 6 directors shall be elected for 4-year terms at the primary and general elections in 1984. A term of office shall not be shortened by the provisions of this subdivision. A director scheduled by this section before the effective date of this subdivision to be elected at a time other than 1984 shall not be elected on the date scheduled, but shall continue in office until a successor takes office pursuant to the election of 1984.

(d) The directors shall be nominated and elected on non-partisan ballots].

Director; term of office.] ♦ [(5) A director] shall hold office until ♦ [a successor is] elected and qualified.

Vacancies; filling.] ♦ [(6) A] library board ♦ [shall] fill ♦ [a] vacancy ♦ [in a directorship] by appointment of a person to hold ♦ office until the next election.

Powers.] [(7) A provisional or permanent library board has the powers prescribed in section 5.]

(MCL §397.211.)

§ 15.1673   Application of act.] SEC. 12.   Sections 10a and 11 ♦ [do] not apply to ♦ [a city,] village [, or township] maintaining a public library under ♦ [a] special act [or to a public library contained in the 1979 statement prepared by the state board for libraries pursuant to section 8 of Act No. 59 of the Public Acts of 1964, being section 397.38 of the Michigan Compiled Laws, except that an existing public library may, by petition, be organized under section 10a regardless of the library's original organization].

(MCL §397.212.)

§ 15.1674]   Joint municipal libraries; townships. SEC. 13. The people of any township adjacent to or adjoining any other township, any village or city, which supports a free public and circulating library and reading room under the provisions of this act, may be united thereunto for the same purpose under the following conditions. (MCL §397.213; CL '29, §8072; CL '15, §3444.)

§ 15.1675   Same; contract for use of municipal library by township, vote, term; tax.] SEC. 14.   Upon receipt of a petition signed by not less than ten [10] per cent of the electors in any township based on the highest vote cast at the last regular election for township officers of such township, addressed to the township board, requesting that a meeting be called of the electors in such township, to consider making a contract with any township, city or village supporting and maintaining a free public circulating library and reading room under this act, or under any special act, for the use of its privileges by the residents of such township, the township board shall call a meeting of the electors of [such] township by posting notices in at least five [5] public places within [such] township not less than ten [10] days previous to such meeting. At the meeting so called the electors present shall determine whether the township shall enter into a contract for the use of any free public circulating library and reading room in any township, city or village, as the case may be, and a tax levied for the purpose of paying for such use, in case the electors shall decide to enter into such contract: Provided, That the tax so levied shall in no case exceed one [1] mill upon the dollar of the assessed valuation of such township. If a majority of those present and voting shall be in favor of the township contracting for the use of a free public circulating library and reading room maintained in any township, city or village, the township board shall have power to enter into such contract and shall levy and collect the tax herein provided for, which tax when collected shall be placed in a fund to be known as the "library fund" and said tax shall be paid over by the township treasurer to the treasurer of the township, city or village in which said library is located, on the first [1st] day of January, February and March of each year, to be disbursed subject to the provisions of section five [5] of this act. The board of library commissioners of any township, city or village, supporting and maintaining a free public circulating library and reading room under this act, or under any special act, are hereby authorized and empowered to enter into a contract with any township to permit the residents of [such] township the full use of such library, upon terms and conditions to be agreed upon between such board of library commissioners and such township board: Provided, That ◆ such contract ◆ [shall be executed] for a ◆ term ◆ [of] three [3] years [and shall be automatically extended for an indefinite term thereafter and shall be terminable only on the giving of six [6] months' notice by either party thereto of the intent to terminate such contract]. (MCL §397.214; CL '29, §8073; CL '15, §3445.)

§ 15.1676] Same; right to user under contract. SEC. 16. The people of the said township uniting with another township, or with a village or city, shall, after they shall have paid their first taxes therefor, and thereafter while continuing so to do, have all rights in the use and benefits of said library that they would have had had they lived in the township where the same shall have been established, subject to uniform rules and regulations established by the board of library commissioners thereof. (MCL §397.216; CL '29, §8074; CL '15, §3446.)

§ 15.1677] Same; villages and cities. SEC. 17. The people of villages may join with townships, or townships with villages, or either with cities, by complying with similar provisions, as aforesaid in this act, and as amended, for the purpose of maintaining, supporting and receiving the benefits from a free public circulating library. (MCL §397.217; CL '29, §8074; CL '15, §3447.)

Library Commissions

(Michigan Statutes Annotated, 1982, s.15.1761-15.1765.)

§ 15.1761] Library commission; jurisdiction. SEC. 1. The territory over which the library commission in any city having a population of more than two hundred fifty thousand [250,000] shall conduct the activities to it by law confided, and to which shall apply charges and obligations heretofore or hereafter imposed for the purposes of any said commission, shall be coextensive with the boundaries of any said city and shall automatically change by and with any change in said boundaries. (MCL §397.401; CL '29, §8105.)

§ 15.1762] Same; annual budget. SEC. 2. The annual budget of any said commission shall be prepared in manner and time provided by the charter of any said city concerning the budget thereof and shall be submitted to and passed upon by the officers and boards of any said city as are the items in the budget thereof. (MCL §397.402; CL '29, §8106.)

§ 15.1763] Same; fiscal year. SEC. 3. The fiscal year of any said commission shall be identical with that of any said city. (MCL §397.403; CL '29, §8107.)

§ 15.1764]   Same; relations under local act.   SEC. 4.   The relation of officers or agencies of any said city to the affairs of any said commission growing out of any special or local act of the state legislature shall continue in officers or agencies of any said city on revision or amendment of said special or local act by the electors of any said city. (MCL §397.404; CL '29, §8108.)

§ 15.1765   Same; jurisdiction; payrolls and claims; certificates accompanying; audit, approval, submission to common council; provisions additional.]   SEC. 5.   All payrolls, bills, accounts and claims of every character against the library commission after having been duly audited and approved by [the] commission, the certificate of which audit and approval shall be endorsed thereon by the president or secretary of [the] commission or some member or other representative of [the] commission acting under authority conferred by [the] commission generally or specially, shall be transmitted to the city controller, who shall ◆ [endorse thereon] his approval or disapproval. When ◆ [so endorsed with approval] the controller shall draw his warrant or warrants on the city treasurer in payment therefor. No bill, account or claim shall be audited or approved by [the] commission unless the same shall be accompanied by a certificate of a representative of [the] commission who acted for [the] commission in making the purchase or contract or in taking the delivery or performance that he verily believes the services or property therein charged have been actually performed or delivered for [the] commission, that the sum or sums charged therefor are reasonable and just, and that to the best of his knowledge and belief no setoff exists, nor payment has been made on account thereof except such as are included ◆ or referred to in such account. A similar certificate shall be required upon all payrolls, [the] certificate to be made by the person under whose supervision the services charged have been rendered. ◆ The provisions hereof shall be in addition to any provisions covering the same matters in any general or local act or charter adopted pursuant to Act No. 279 of the Public Acts of 1909, as amended[, being sections 117.1 to 117.38 of the Compiled Laws of 1948]. (MCL §397.405.)

Employes' Retirement System
(Michigan Statutes Annotated, 1982, s.15.1771-15.1776.)

§ 15.1771]   Employes' retirement system; establishment. SEC. 1.   The legislative body of any incorporated city of two hundred fifty thousand [250,000] or more (hereinafter referred to for the purposes of this act as the local legislative body), where free public libraries have been or may hereafter be established is hereby authorized, upon the application and recommendation of the local library board or commission or body duly authorized by law to maintain free public libraries in such city (hereinafter referred to for the purposes of this act as the library board), to establish a system of retiring allowances for the employes of such libraries which system shall be based upon the principle that there shall be accumulated, year by year, a reserve fund sufficient to provide the agreed annuity at the time of retirement. Upon the establishment of such system, the local legislative body shall raise by taxation each year a sum which will provide an adequate reserve fund. (MCL §38.701; CL '29, §8109.)

§ 15.1772] Same; submission of plan to legislative body.

SEC. 2. It shall be the duty of said library board when it desires to establish a system of retiring allowances, to apply to the local legislative body and to submit to said local legislative body for its approval and adoption a detailed plan for such system which shall be based upon the following provisions and conditions:

Classes of employes. (a) It shall enumerate the classes of employes to be included in said system;

Retiring allowances. (b) It shall fix the amount of the annual retiring allowance, the number of years of service necessary to entitle an employe to a retiring allowance, the age at which an employe may be retired, the nature and extent of the physical or mental disability which shall entitle an employe to retire before reaching the age of retirement and the conditions upon which the age of retirement may be anticipated;

Retirement fund trustees. (c) It shall provide for a body to be known as the retiring fund trustees which shall consist of five [5] members. Two [2] members shall be elected by the staff; two [2] members shall be appointed by said local legislative body and the terms of office of said members shall be four [4] years except that when the system is first put into effect, the terms of office shall be so fixed that but one [1] member's term shall expire each year. The fifth [5th] member shall be ex-officio, the presiding officer of the said library board. Said trustees shall have charge of said retiring allowance fund and shall invest the same only in such securities as are legal for savings banks. Said trustees shall adopt such rules and by-laws as may be necessary, and not inconsistent with the constitution and laws of this state and the provisions of this act;

Certificate of actuary. (d) There shall be attached to such system as may be recommended, the certificate of a recognized and competent actuary stating that the system is actuarially sound, and the system shall provide for annual reports and valuations by such actuary to determine whether the fund is on a sound financial and actuarial basis. (MCL §38.702; CL '29, §8110.)

§ 15.1773] Same; approval of plan by legislative body; commencement.

SEC. 3. Upon the submission by said library board of a plan for a system of retiring allowances, the local legislative body shall take the same under consideration and shall then, in conference with said library board agree upon the details of said plan and if said plan so agreed upon differs from the one submitted, it shall, before adoption, be submitted to an actuary for report upon its financial and actuarial soundness and, if certified to be sound, may then be adopted. The plan shall then be put into operation at the beginning of the next fiscal year, unless an earlier date is agreed upon. (MCL §38.703; CL '29, §8111.)

§ 15.1774] Yearly assessment.

SEC. 4. When a system for retiring allowances has been agreed upon by the local legislative body and the library board and formally adopted by the former, then it shall be the duty of said local legislative body to raise by taxation each year, the sum found necessary to produce the retiring allowance fund required by the system adopted. (MCL §38.704; CL '29, §8112.)

§ 15.1775]   Reserve fund and annuities to be tax exempt.
Sec. 5.   When a system of retiring allowances is adopted under the
provisions of this act, the reserve fund thereby provided shall be free
from all state, county, township, city, village and school district
taxes and the annuities payable to the members of the staff shall
likewise be free from all such taxes. (MCL §38.705; CL '29, §8113.)

**§ 15.1776]   Retiring allowance plan for employes of cer-
tain public libraries.**   Sec. 6.   In lieu, however, of formulating any
plan under the foregoing sections of this act the library board and
the local legislative body may, by concurrent resolution, adopt and
put into effect for the employes of the library any plan which may
have been, or may hereafter be, adopted for the employes of the city.
(MCL §38.706.)

Consolidation of Township Libraries

(Michigan Statutes Annotated, 1982, s.15.1721-15.1728.)

§ 15.1721]   Consolidation of township libraries.   Sec. 1.
It shall hereafter be lawful for the township boards of adjoining
townships in the same county, by joint action of the respective township boards of such townships, by proceeding as hereinafter provided, to consolidate the libraries in each township into one library, and
to designate the site thereof. (MCL §397.351; CL '29, §8094.)

§ 15.1722]   Referendum; petition.   Sec. 2.   When the township board of each township having such libraries shall be presented
with a petition, signed by not less than twenty-five [25] per cent of
the resident freeholders of each of the respective townships, each
such township board shall forthwith adopt a resolution submitting
the question of consolidation of the libraries of the two townships to
the qualified electors of each township at any regular election or
special election duly called for that purpose. (MCL §397.352; CL '29,
§8095.)

§ 15.1723]   Same; form of ballot; conduct of election.   Sec.
3.   The election shall be by ballot in substantially the following
form:
   "Shall the township libraries of . . . . and
. . . . townships be consolidated?
   "Yes ☐
   "No ☐."
The election shall be conducted in every respect the same as other
special or general elections are conducted, and the results canvassed
and certified in like manner. (MCL §397.353; CL '29, §8096.)

**§ 15.1724]   Same; joint resolution of township boards can-
vassing returns.**   Sec. 4.   If the proposition shall be carried by a
majority of those voting at the election, in each township, and the
respective election boards shall so certify, the respective township
boards shall meet together in the township casting the largest vote
at such election and shall pass a joint resolution, which shall be
recorded in the minutes of the clerk of each board, canvassing the

returns of the elections, and shall formally consolidate the township libraries of the two townships. (MCL §397.354; CL '29, §8097.)

§ 15.1725] Site, designation. SEC. 5. Such resolution shall designate the site of the library, and if not able to agree by majority vote of the board members present and voting, the county commissioner of schools shall choose a site properly located and most advantageous to the townships. (MCL §397.355; CL '29, §8098.)

§ 15.1726] Maintenance. SEC. 6. The expense of maintenance for the ensuing year shall be estimated, and the expense apportioned between the two townships in proportion to their respective assessed valuations for the preceding year, and such tax certified by the clerk of each board to its respective supervisor. (MCL §397.356; CL '29, §8099.)

§ 15.1727] Control. SEC. 7. Said library when so consolidated shall be under the joint control of the township boards, and any matter upon which they can not agree shall be decided by the county commissioner of schools. Not more than two [2] joint meetings per year shall be held. (MCL §397.357; CL '29, §8100.)

§ 15.1728] Free public library. SEC. 8. After consolidation, the library may be formed into a free public library, with provisional board of directors in pursuance of the statute in such case made and provided, upon proper procedure for that purpose, jointly taken by the township boards of the townships consolidating. (MCL §397.358; CL '29, §8101.)

PENAL FINES

(Michigan Statutes Annotated, 1982, s.15.1793(1) to 15.1793(9).)

§ 15.1793(1) Definitions.] SEC. 1. As used in this act:
(a) "Public library" means a library, the whole interests of which belong to the general public, lawfully established for free public purposes by any 1 or more counties, cities, townships, villages, school districts or other local governments or any combination thereof, or by any general or local act, but shall not include a special library such as a professional or technical library or a school library.
(b) "Qualified public library" means any public library which is open to and available to the public at least 10 hours per week or any library which has a contract with a public library board to furnish library services to the public. (MCL §397.31.)

§ 15.1793(2) Apportionment of penal fines among libraries; method; basis for apportionment.] SEC. 2. The proceeds of all fines for any breach of the penal laws of this state when collected in any county and paid into the county treasury, together with all moneys heretofore collected and paid into the county treasury on account of such fines and not already apportioned, shall be apportioned by the county treasurer in accordance with the directions of the state board for libraries, as provided in section 8, before August 1 of each year among those public libraries and county libraries established under Act No. 138 of the Public Acts of 1917, as amended, being sections 397.301 to 397.305 of the Compiled Laws of 1948, or Act No. 250 of the Public Acts of 1931, as amended, being sections 397.151 to 397.158 of the Compiled Laws of 1948, or county library boards in each county entitled to such fines under this act on a per capita basis determined by the population of the governmental unit supporting the library according to the latest decennial or special federal census. (MCL §397.32.)

§ 15.1793(3)   County library board; appointment; receipt of moneys; membership, terms of office; contract for library services.]   SEC. 3.   In any county where there is no public library, or in any county within the boundaries of which there are municipalities which have not established public library service or which do not maintain public libraries, the county board of supervisors shall appoint a county library board to receive the per capita portion of penal fine moneys to be allocated for such areas. The county library board shall consist of 5 members appointed by the county board of supervisors for terms of 5 years each, except that the first members shall be appointed for 1, 2, 3, 4 and 5 years respectively. The board may contract with a qualified public library, within or without the county, to provide public library service for all residents of the county without legal access to a public library. (MCL §397.33.)

§ 15.1793(4)   Subsequent establishment of public library; effect; powers of county library board.]   SEC. 4.   If, after the appointment of the county library board, the board of supervisors votes to establish a public library as authorized by Act No. 138 of the Public Acts of 1917, as amended, then the county library board appointed under section 3 shall become the governing body of the county library. In addition to the powers and duties granted in Act No. 138 of the Public Acts of 1917, as amended, the county library board shall have all of the powers and duties granted to county library boards by this act. (MCL §397.34.)

§ 15.1793(5)   Municipality receiving library service under contract; municipality supporting more than one library.]   SEC. 5.   (1)   If any municipality within a county has not established a public library but is contracting for public library service with the governing body of a legally established public library, it is entitled to receive its per capita share of the penal fine moneys the same as if it had a legally established public library. The moneys shall be used for the provision of public library service for all residents of the municipality.

(2)   If any municipality within a county is supporting more than 1 public library, the penal fines shall be allocated to each public library in ratio to the tax support provided by the municipality to the respective public libraries. (MCL §397.35.)

§ 15.1793(6)   Application of funds; annual report.]   SEC. 6.   The penal fine moneys when received by the proper authorities shall be applied exclusively to the support of public libraries and to no other purpose except as provided in section 7. A report shall be made annually to the state board for libraries as to the receipt and expenditures of the penal fine moneys, and other public moneys, by the governing boards of the public libraries or by the county library boards. (MCL §397.36.)

§ 15.1793(7) Construction of Act.] Sec. 7. This act shall not be construed as affecting the provisions of sections 4845 and 4851 of Act No. 236 of the Public Acts of 1961, being sections 600.4845 and 600.4851 of the Compiled Laws of 1948. (MCL §397.37.)

§ 15.1793(8) Annual statement by state board for libraries.] Sec. 8. The state board for libraries, prior to July 15 of each year, shall transmit to the clerk and treasurer of each county a statement of the public libraries or the library boards established under section 3 in his county that are entitled to receive penal fines and the population served by each. (MCL §397.38.)

§ 15.1793(9) Rules and regulations.] Sec. 9. The state board for libraries may adopt such rules and regulations to carry out the provisions of this act as may be deemed expedient, in accordance with the provisions of Act No. 88 of the Public Acts of 1943, as amended, being sections 24.71 to 24.82 of the Compiled Laws of 1948, and subject to Act No. 197 of the Public Acts of 1952, as amended, being sections 24.101 to 24.110 of the Compiled Laws of 1948. (MCL §397.39.)

LIBRARY SITES AND BUILDINGS
Cities, Villages and School Districts
(Michigan Statutes Annotated, 1982, s.15.1681-15.1686, 15.1698(1) to 15.1698(3).)

§ 15.1681] Legislative bodies to provide sites and buildings; improvement of existing property; bonds, limitation. Sec. 1. The legislative body of any city, village or school district where free public libraries have been, or may hereafter be established, is hereby authorized upon the application of the local library board, or commission or body duly authorized by law to maintain free public libraries in such city, village or school district to borrow a sum of money upon the faith and credit of such city, village or school district not exceeding one-fourth of one [1/4 of 1] per centum of the assessed valuation of such city, village or school district to provide sites for, and for the erection thereon, of free public library buildings and for additions to and improvements of such sites and the buildings thereon now existing or hereafter acquired and to issue the bond or bonds of such city, village or school district therefor: Provided, That wherever library bonds have heretofore been issued or authorized said bonds shall be included in the limitation of one-fourth of one [1/4 of 1] per centum of the assessed valuation: And provided further, That such bonds hereafter issued shall be in addition to all other indebtedness which the city, village or school district is or may be authorized to incur for purposes other than library purposes. (MCL §397.241; CL '29, §8076.)

§ 15.1682 Bonds; form; contents; interest; maturity; execution; negotiation.] Sec. 2. [The] bonds shall be denominated "public library bonds of the city, village, or school district number of . . .," shall be regularly dated and numbered in the order of their issue, shall be for sums of not less than $100.00 each, shall bear interest [at a rate] not exceeding ♦ [the maximum rate permitted by Act No. 202 of the Public Acts of 1943, as amended, being sections 131.1 to 138.2 of the Michigan Compiled Laws,] shall be payable within such time from the date of issue [and shall be executed in such manner], as the local legislative body of [the] city, village, or school district may determine. ♦ [The] bonds shall not be negotiated at less than their par value. (MCL §397.242; CL '29, §8077.)

§ 15.1683] Same; approval of issue. SEC. 3. No bonds shall be issued under this act unless such issue has been approved by both the local legislative body and by that body to whom is entrusted the management of the local library system and upon such concurrent approval the legislative body of said city, village or school district shall thereupon proceed to issue and negotiate the sale of said bonds. (MCL §397.243; CL '29, §8078.)

§ 15.1684] Same; sinking fund for redemption; receipts from sale, disposition. SEC. 4. The local legislative body of such city, village or school district shall provide a sinking fund for the redemption of the bonds issued under the provisions of this act to which end it shall be its duty to raise by taxation, each year, upon the property assessed for city, village or school district purposes, such sum as shall be sufficient to make said sinking fund adequate at the maturity of the bonds, to pay the same and the moneys so raised shall be used for no other purpose. The principal realized from the sale of said bonds shall be deposited with the treasurer of said city, village or school district and credited to a public library fund for the purposes hereinbefore mentioned and shall be used for said purposes only. The premium and accrued interest of said bonds shall be credited to the sinking fund of said city, village or school district. (MCL §397.244; CL '29, §8079.)

§ 15.1685] Same; budget items for sinking fund and interest. SEC. 5. It shall be the duty of the local board entrusted with the management of the local library system, to include in its budget each year, an item of the amount necessary to be raised each year for the sinking fund and an item for the amount necessary to be raised each year for the interest on said bonds and said items shall be allowed by the local body or officer whose duty it is to determine the amount to be raised by taxation for said city, village or school district. Said items shall be in addition to the amount which may be annually raised by taxation for all other purposes. (MCL §397.245; CL '29, §8080.)

§ 15.1686 Same; library buildings or sites.] SEC. 6. Notwithstanding the provisions of this act, any city or village may borrow money and issue bonds for library buildings, additions thereto and/or sites therefor, in accordance with, and to the full extent authorized by its charter. (MCL §397.246.)

§ 15.1698(1) Repeal of local act; succession to library property.] Sec. 1. If the local act governing a city public library is repealed, the governing body of the city shall succeed to all title and interest in the real and personal property of the library. (MCL §397.231.)

§ 15.1698(2) Continuation of operation and maintenance.] Sec. 2. The governing body of the city may continue to operate and maintain the library in accordance with appropriate statutes of this state or the charter of that governmental unit. (MCL §397.232.)

§ 15.1698(3) Conveyance of property.] Sec. 3. The governing body of the city may convey the property of such library to the governing body of another governmental unit for use of the property for library purposes. (MCL §397.233.)

Townships and Villages

(Michigan Statutes Annotated, 1982, s.15.1711-1716.)

§ 15.1711] Issuance of library bonds by townships or villages; approval by electors. Sec. 1. The township board of any organized township and the village council, or board of trustees, of any incorporated village in the state of Michigan are hereby authorized and empowered, upon an application signed by not less than twenty-five [25] qualified electors of such township or incorporated village being first filed with the said township board, village council, or board of trustees, as the case may be, to borrow a sum of money, not exceeding one [1] per cent of the assessed valuation of such township, or incorporated village, on the faith and credit of such township, or incorporated village, and to issue the bond, or bonds of such township, or incorporated village, therefor; the money so borrowed to be used for the purpose of establishing a free public library, for purchasing a site for the same or constructing buildings thereon: Provided, That a majority of the voters of such township, or incorporated village, voting thereon at a township meeting, a general election, or at a special election called by the township board, or at a general or special election called by the village council, or board of trustees, for that purpose, shall vote in favor thereof. (MCL §397.321; CL '29, §8088.)

§ 15.1712] Same; referendum notice. Sec. 2. The question of issuing the bonds, provided for in section one [1] of this act, shall be submitted to the legal voters of such township, or incorporated village, by the township board, the village council or board of trustees, within thirty [30] days after the filing of the application mentioned in section one [1], giving due notice thereof by causing the date, place of voting and object of said election to be stated in written or printed notices to be posted in five [5] public places in such township, or incorporated village, at least ten [10] days before the time fixed by said board for such election, and by publishing the same in at least one [1] newspaper published in said township, or incorporated village, or if none be published in said township, or incorporated village, then in some newspaper published in the same county, which is circulated in such township or incorporated village, at least two [2] weeks before the time of such election. Such notice shall state the amount of money proposed to be raised by such bonding, and the purpose or purposes to which it shall be applied. (MCL §397.322; CL '29, §8089.)

§ 15.1713]   Same; form of ballot; conduct of election. SEC. 3. The vote upon such proposition shall be by printed ballot, and such ballots shall be in the following form:
"For the issuing of bonds to (Purpose) Yes ☐."
"For the issuing of bonds to (Purpose) No ☐."
The election shall be conducted and the votes canvassed in all respects, as in other township or village elections. (MCL §397.323; CL '29, §8090.)

§ 15.1714]   Same; terms, signature, negotiation; tax. SEC. 4. If at such election a majority of such qualified electors present thereat and voting upon said proposition shall vote in favor of such loan, such bonds shall be issued by the township board of the township or the village council or board of trustees of the village, as the case may be, in denominations not exceeding one thousand [1,000] dollars each, at a rate of interest not exceeding five [5] per centum per annum, and for a period not exceeding twenty-five [25] years, as the said township board, or the said common council, or board of trustees, by resolution, shall direct. Said bond, or bonds, issued by a township board, shall be signed by the members of the said township board and countersigned by the township treasurer, and when issued by a village council shall be signed by the president and clerk of said village and countersigned by the village treasurer. Said bond, or bonds, shall be negotiated by and under the direction of said township board, or common council, or board of trustees of incorporated village, to raise in each year by tax upon the taxable property of such township, or incorporated village, such sums of money as shall be sufficient to pay the amount of said bonds and the interest thereon, as the same shall become due. (MCL §397.324; CL '29, §8091.)

§ 15.1715]   Same; negotiation at less than par. SEC. 5. No bonds issued under and by virtue of this act shall be used or negotiated at less than their par value. (MCL §397.325; CL '29, §8092.)

§ 15.1716]   Declaration of necessity. SEC. 6. It is hereby declared that this act is immediately necessary for the public health, peace and safety. (MCL §397.326; CL '29, §8093.)

SCHOOL DISTRICT LIBRARIES

(Michigan Statutes Annotated, 1982, s.15-1691, 15-1692.)

§ 15.1691]   Boards of education; library, annual expense estimate. SEC. 1. Boards of education in cities where free public libraries are under control of such boards of education by reason of existing charters or otherwise, from and after the passage of this act are hereby authorized and empowered to include in their annual estimate a sum or sums sufficient to properly care for and defray the expense of maintenance and to purchase new books required for such libraries. (MCL §397.261; CL '29, §8081; CL '15, §5836.)

§ 15.1692] Same; issuance of bonds, maturity, approval by electors. SEC. 2. Boards of education in cities having the control of free public libraries by reason of existing charters or otherwise are hereby authorized and empowered to raise money, either by including the amount in their annual estimates, or to borrow same on the faith and credit of said school district, and to issue certificates or bonds to secure the payment of the sums borrowed; sufficient to purchase property for a site and to provide the money necessary to erect, equip and maintain buildings for a free public library and other educational uses: Provided, That when any bond issue shall be provided for under the terms of this act such bonds shall not be issued for a period of more than ten [10] years. No bonds provided for in this act shall be issued until issuance of same shall have been submitted to the electors of the district affected and approved by a majority of the electors voting thereon. (MCL §397.262; CL '29, §8082; CL '15, §5837.)

INCORPORATED AND ASSOCIATION LIBRARIES

(Michigan Statutes Annotated, 1982, s.21.321-21.325, 21.591, 15.741.)

§ 21.321] Incorporation of library; meeting, calling. SEC. 1. Any seven [7] or more proprietors of a library may form themselves into a corporation, under such corporate name as they may adopt, for the purpose of enlarging, regulating and using such library; and for that purpose any justice of the peace may, on the application of five [5] or more of the proprietors, issue his warrant to one of them, directing him to call a meeting of the proprietors at the time and place expressed in the warrant, for the purpose of forming such corporation, and such meeting shall be called by posting up a notice containing the substance of such warrant, in at least two [2] public places in the township where such library is kept, at least seven [7] days before the time of meeting.

(MCL § 450.691; CL '29, § 10176; CL '15, § 10683; How § 4407; CL '97, § 8164; CL '71, § 3146; CL '57, § 1782.)

§ 21.322] Same; proprietors, powers; certificate of proceedings, recording. SEC. 2. Any seven [7] or more of the proprietors of such library, met in pursuance of such notice, may choose a president, a clerk, a librarian, collector, treasurer, and such other officers as they may deem necessary; and they may also determine upon the mode of calling future meetings of the proprietors; and the proceedings of such first meeting, containing a specification of the corporate name adopted by such proprietors, shall be certified by the clerk of such corporation, and recorded by the county clerk of the county within which the same is formed, who shall be entitled to receive seventy-five [75] cents for recording the same.

(MCL § 450.692; CL '29, § 10177; CL '15, § 10684; How § 4408; CL '97, § 8165; CL '71, § 3147; CL '57, § 1783.)

§ 21.323] Powers of corporation; governing law. SEC. 3. When such proprietors shall be organized as a corporation in the manner hereinbefore provided, they shall have all the powers and privileges, and be subject to all the duties of a corporation, according to the provisions of chapter fifty-five [55], so far .as such provisions shall be applicable in such case, and not inconsistent with the provisions of this chapter.

(MCL § 450.693; CL '29, § 10178; CL '15, § 10685; How § 4409; CL '97, § 8166; CL '71, § 3148; CL '57, § 1784.)

§ 21.324] Bond of collector and treasurer. SEC. 4. The treasurer and collector shall give bond to such corporation, with sufficient sureties, to the satisfaction of the president, for the faithful discharge of their duties.

(MCL § 450.694; CL '29, § 10179; CL '15, § 10686; How § 4410; CL '97, § 8167; CL '71, § 3149; CL '57, § 1785.)

§ 21.325] Shares, assessment, transfer; holding of property. SEC. 5. The said proprietors may raise such sums of money by assessment on the shares as they shall judge necessary for the purpose of preserving, enlarging and using the library; and the shares may be transferred according to such regulations as they may prescribe, and such corporation may hold (and may acquire by gift, grant, bequest or devise) real and personal estate to any amount not exceeding (twenty-five thousand [25,000] dollars), in addition to the value of their books; (and may hold in trust property granted, bequeathed or devised as may be prescribed by the grantor or testator; and may be the beneficiaries of trusts created for their benefit).

(MCL § 450.695; CL '29, § 10180; CL '15, § 10687; How § 4411; CL '97, § 8168; CL '71, § 3150; CL '57, § 1786.)

§ 21.326 Organization of lyceums; powers.] SEC. 6. Any fifteen [15] or more persons, in any township or county within this state, who shall, by writing, associate for the purpose of mental improvement, and the promotion of education, may form themselves into a corporation by the name of "the lyceum of _____," (the name of the place where the meetings of the corporation are to be holden), by calling their first meeting and being organized in like manner as is provided in this chapter, in the case of library corporations, and every lyceum, upon becoming a corporation as aforesaid, shall have, during the pleasure of the legislature, all the like rights, powers and privileges, as the proprietors of such libraries, and may hold real

and personal estate, not exceeding six thousand [6,000] dollars.
(MCL § 450.696; CL '29, § 10181; CL '15, § 10688; How
§ 4412; CL '97, § 8169; CL '71, § 3151; CL '57, § 1787.)

§ 21.591] Libraries; maintenance, regulation. SEC. 11. All

societies or associations, organized as aforesaid, shall have the
right to keep and maintain libraries, and make all needful bylaws for the good government and regulation of the same.
(MCL § 454.11; CL '29, § 10272; CL '15, § 9805; How § 3934;
CL '97, § 7433; CL '71, § 2805; CL '57, § 1798.)

§ 15.1741] Privately owned library; conditions of sup-

port by public, limitation. SEC. 1. Any township, city or village
within this state, having within its limits a library that had been
open to the public upon the payment of dues, may appropriate not
to exceed one-half of one [1/2 of 1] mill on its assessed valuation for
the support of such library, and such sum or sums shall be raised by
taxation in the ordinary way: Provided, That any library so receiving support from any municipality shall be kept open for the convenience of the public not less than the afternoons and evenings of
three [3] days of each week, and the books therein shall be for the
free use of the public under such reasonable restrictions as such
library shall prescribe. (MCL §397.371; CL '29, §8102.)

COUNTY LAW LIBRARIES

(Michigan Statutes Annotated, 1982, s.27A.4851.)

§ 27A.4851 Same; credits to and expenditures from law library

funds; superior court of Grand Rapids; report of
county law librarian.]

SEC 4851

(1) In each county the county treasurer shall credit semiannually to a fund to be known as the "county law library fund,"
from the library fund, an amount as follows:

(a) In counties having a population of 250,000 or more,
but less than 1,000,000 inhabitants, the sum credited shall
not exceed $4,000.00 in any one year;

(b) In counties having a population of 50,000 or more,
but less than 250,000 inhabitants, the sum credited shall not
exceed $3,000.00 in any one year;

(c) In counties of 35,000 or more, but less than 50,000
inhabitants, the sum credited shall not exceed $2,000.00 in
any one year;

(d) In counties of 20,000 or more, but less than 35,000
inhabitants, the sum thus credited shall not exceed $1,500.00
in any one year;

(e) In counties of 10,000 or more, but less than 20,000
inhabitants, the sum credited shall not exceed $1,000.00 in
any one year; and

(f) In counties of less than 10,000 inhabitants, the sum
credited shall not exceed $750.00 in any one year.

(2) At no time shall the balance in such county law library

funds exceed the total of 2 annual allotments to such funds.

(3) All moneys so credited to the county law library fund shall be paid out by the county treasurer only upon the order of the circuit judge in multiple county circuits or upon the order of the presiding judge in single county circuits for the purpose of establishing, operating, and maintaining a law library for the use of the circuit and probate courts of such county and for the officers of such courts and persons having business in such courts.

(4) Beginning on the first day of January in each year, the clerk of the superior court of Grand Rapids shall credit the fines, penalties, and forfeitures paid for the violation of penal laws in said court to a fund to be designated as "the superior court law library fund," up to, but not exceeding the sum of $4,000.00 in any one year. All money so credited shall be paid out by the clerk of said court only upon order of the judge of the superior court, for the purpose of operating and maintaining a law library for the use of said court, for the officers of said court, and for the use of all other persons having business with said court. At no time shall the balance in such superior court law library fund exceed the total of 2 annual allotments to such fund.

(5) The county law librarian, or such other person as the circuit or presiding judge shall designate, shall make a detailed report on or before January 1 of each year of the sums expended for books for the county law library. Such report shall be filed with the county clerk.

(CL '48, § 600.4851.)

PHOTOSTATIC COPIES OF
LIBRARY MATERIALS

(Michigan Statutes Annotated, 1982, s.27A.2136.)

§ **27A.2136** Library book or paper; copy or photostat as evidence, fees; false certification, penalty.]

Sec 2136

(1) Any copy of the records, books or papers belonging to or in the custody of any public, college or university library, or of any incorporated library society, when accompanied by a sworn statement by the librarian or other officer or person in charge thereof, that the same is a true copy of the original record, book or paper in his custody, shall be admissible as evidence in all courts and proceedings in like manner and to the same extent as the original would be if produced.

(2) Any photostat copy of the records, books, papers or documents belonging to or in the custody of any public, college or university library, or of any incorporated library society, when accompanied by a sworn statement made by the librarian or other officer or person in charge thereof, stating that the copy is made under his supervision or that of a duly authorized representative, and that nothing has been done to alter or change the original, and that the same is a true photostat copy of the original record, book, paper, or document in his custody, shall be admissible as evidence in all courts and proceedings in like manner as the original would be if produced.

(3) For making and certifying such copies, a fee of 25 cents, and for making and certifying each photostat copy, a fee of $1.00,

may be charged and a further charge may be made of 10 cents per folio and 50 cents per photostat sheet for copies actually made.

(4) Anyone who shall certify falsely in regard to any of the foregoing copies shall be guilty of a felony and, upon conviction thereof in any court of competent jurisdiction, shall be subject to the same penalties provided by statute for perjury.

(CL '48, § 600.2136.)

PROTECTION OF LIBRARY PROPERTY
(Michigan Statutes Annotated, 1982, s.28.596.)

§ 28.596 Same; from libraries.] SEC. 364. Any person who shall procure, or take in any way from any public library or the library of any literary, scientific, historical or library society or association, whether incorporated or unincorporated, any book, pamphlet, map, chart, painting, picture, photograph, periodical, newspaper, magazine, manuscript or exhibit or any part thereof, with intent to convert the same to his own use, or with intent to defraud the owner thereof, or who having procured or taken any such book, pamphlet, map, chart, painting, picture, photograph, periodical, newspaper, magazine, manuscript or exhibit or any part thereof, shall thereafter convert the same to his own use or fraudulently deprive the owner thereof, shall be guilty of a misdemeanor. (C. L. '48, § 750.364.)

§ 28.623 Maliciously injuring or mutilating library books, etc.] SEC. 391. Any person who shall wilfully, maliciously or wantonly tear, deface or mutilate or write upon, or by other means injure or mar any book, pamphlet, map, chart, painting, picture, photograph, periodical, newspaper, magazine, manuscript or exhibit or any part thereof belonging to or loaned to any public library, or to the library of any literary, scientific, historical or library society or association, whether incorporated or unincorporated, shall be guilty of a misdemeanor. (C. L. '48, § 750.391.)

MISCELLANEOUS PROVISIONS
(Michigan Statutes Annotated, 1982, s.15.1751, 15.1752,
s.27A.4855, State Constitution Art. VIII; s.9.)

§ 15.1751] Donations. SEC. 1. Any board of education, library commission or other public corporation empowered to maintain a public library may receive and accept gifts and donations of property, real or personal, for the purpose of such library and shall hold, use and apply the property so received for the purposes set forth in the instrument of gift and in accordance with the provisions of such instrument and subject to the conditions and limitations, if any, therein expressed. (MCL §397.381; CL '29, §8103.)

§ 15.1752] Disposal of property not needed. SEC. 2. Whenever any property, real or personal, now or hereafter held and used for the purpose of a public library by any board of education, library commission or other public corporation shall, in the judgment of such corporation, be no longer needed for such purpose, such property may be sold and disposed of by such corporation unless such sale and disposal be inconsistent with the terms and conditions upon which such property was acquired, at such price and upon such terms and conditions as said corporation may deem proper, and the proceeds thereof shall by said corporation be used and applied for the purpose of such library. (MCL §397.382; CL '29, §8104.)

§ **27A.4845** Credit of fines, penalties and forfeitures; duties of county treasurer; real estate sold for breach of recognizance.]

SEC 4845
(1) The county treasurer shall credit all fines for the violation of the penal laws to the library fund and all other penalties to the general fund; and he shall account therefor to the board of supervisors annually. * * * (CL '48, § 600.4845.)

Sec. 9. The legislature shall provide by law for the establishment and support of public libraries which shall be available to all residents of the state under regulations adopted by the governing bodies thereof. All fines assessed and collected in the several counties, townships and cities for any breach of the penal laws shall be exclusively applied to the support of such public libraries, and county law libraries as provided by law.

TAX EXEMPTION
(Michigan Statutes Annotated, 1982, s.7.7, 7.9.)

Michigan library laws are reprinted from MICHIGAN STATUTES ANNOTATED published by Callaghan & Co., Chicago, Illinois.

MINNESOTA

STATE DEPARTMENT OF EDUCATION
(Minnesota Statutes Annotated, 1982, s.121.09.)

121.09. Administration; exceptions

The commissioner shall administer all laws and rules promulgated by the board relating to libraries and other public educational institutions, except such laws as may relate to the University of Minnesota and to the state universities and community colleges. Amended by Laws 1975, c. 321, § 2; Laws 1977, c. 305, § 40, eff. May 28, 1977.

STATE AID
(Minnesota Statutes Annotated, 1982, s.134.30-134.36.)

134.30. Definitions

Subdivision 1. As used in sections 134.30 to 134.35 and sections 134.351, 134.352, and 134.353, the terms defined in this section shall have the meanings ascribed to them.

Subd. 2. "Public library" means any library that provides free access to all residents of a city or county without discrimination, receives at least half of its financial support from public funds and is organized under the provisions of chapter 134 or section 375.33. It does not include libraries such as law, medical, school and academic libraries organized to serve a special group of persons, or libraries organized as a combination of a public library and another type of library.

Subd. 3. "Public library services" means services provided by or on behalf of a public library and does not include services for elementary schools, secondary schools or post-secondary educational institutions.

Subd. 4. "Regional public library system" means a multicounty public library service agency that provides free access to all residents of the region without discrimination, and is organized under the provisions of sections 134.12, 375.335, 471.59 or chapter 317.

Subd. 5. "Basic system services" means services offered by all regional public library systems either directly or by contract. These services shall include, but are not limited to, communication among participants, resource sharing, delivery of materials, reciprocal borrowing, and cooperative reference service.

Added by Laws 1978, c. 546, § 1.

Subd. 6. "Multi-county, multi-type library system" means a cooperative network composed of any combination of public libraries, regional public library systems, public school libraries, public or private college or university libraries and any other libraries which share services and resources within a multi-county area.
Amended by Laws 1979, c.-334, art. 9, §§ 1, 2.

134.31   State department of education;   library responsibilities

Subdivision 1. The state shall, as an integral part of its responsibility for public education, support the provision of library service for every citizen and the development of cooperative programs for the sharing of resources and services among all libraries.

Subd. 2. The department of education shall give advice and instruction to the managers of any public library or to any governing body maintaining a library or empowered to do so by law upon any matter pertaining to the organization, maintenance, or administration of libraries. The department may also give advice and instruction, as requested, to the managers of any library in a post-secondary educational institution. It shall assist, to the extent possible, in the establishment and organization of library service in those areas where adequate services do not exist, and may aid in improving previously established library services.

Subd. 3. The department may provide, for any library in the state, books, journals, audiovisual items, reference services or resource materials it deems appropriate and necessary and shall encourage the sharing of library resources and the development of interlibrary cooperation.

Subd. 4. The department shall collect statistics on the receipts, expenditures, services, and use of the regional public library systems and the public libraries of the state. It shall also collect statistics on all activities undertaken pursuant to sections

134.31 to 134.35. The department shall report its findings to the legislature prior to November 15 of each even numbered year, together with a statement of its expenditures relating to these activities and any other matters as it deems appropriate.

Added by Laws 1978, c. 546, § 2.

134.32   Grant authorization; types of grants

Subdivision 1. The department shall provide the grants specified in this section from any available state or federal funds.

Subd. 2. It shall provide establishment grants to regional public library systems which meet the requirements of section 134.33, to extend library services to additional counties.

Subd. 3. It shall provide regional library basic system support grants to regional public library systems which meet the requirements of section 134.34, to assist those systems in providing basic system services.

Subd. 4. It may provide special project grants to assist innovative and experimental library programs including, but not limited to, special services for American Indians and the Spanish-speaking, delivery of library materials to homebound persons, other extensions of library services to persons without access to libraries and projects to strengthen and improve library services.

Subd. 5. It may provide grants for interlibrary exchange of books, periodicals, resource material, reference information and the expenses incident to the sharing of library resources and materials, including planning, development and operating grants to multi-county, multi-type library systems.   Amended by Laws 1979, c. 334, art. 9, § 3.

Subd. 6. It may provide grants for the improvement of library services at welfare and corrections institutions and for library service for the blind and physically handicapped.

Subd. 7. Nothing within the provisions of this section shall be construed to allow state money to be used for the construction of library facilities.

Subd. 8. The state board shall promulgate rules consistent with sections 134.32 to 134.35 governing:

(a) Applications for these grants;

(b) Computation formulas for determining the amounts of establishment grants and regional library basic system support grants; and

(c) Eligibility criteria for grants.

Added by Laws 1978, c. 546, § 3.

134.33. Establishment grants

Subdivision 1. An establishment grant as described in section 134.32, subdivision 2, shall be made to any regional public library system for the first two state fiscal years after a board of county commissioners has contracted to join that system and has agreed that the county will provide the levels of support for public library service specified in this section. In the first year of participation, the county shall provide an amount of support equivalent to .3 mill times the adjusted assessed valuation of the taxable property of the county as determined by the equalization aid review committee for the second year preceding that calendar year or two-thirds of the per capita amount established under the provisions of section 134.34, subdivision 1, whichever amount is less. In the second year of participation and in each year thereafter, the county shall provide an amount of support equivalent to .4 mill times the adjusted assessed valuation of the taxable property of the county as determined by the equalization aid review committee for the second year preceding that calendar year or the per capita amount established under the provisions of section 134.34, subdivision 1, whichever is less. The minimum level of support shall be certified annually to the county by the department of education. In no event shall the department of education require any county to provide a higher level of support than the level of support specified in this section in order for a system to qualify for an establish-ment grant. This section shall not be construed to prohibit any county from providing a higher level of support for public libraries than the level of support specified in this section.   Amended by Laws 1979, c. 334, art. 9, § 4.

134.34. Regional library basic system support grants; requirements

Subdivision 1. A regional library basic system support grant shall be made to any regional public library system where there are at least three participating counties and where each participating city and county, except in the first year of participation as provided in section 134.33, is providing for public library service support the lesser of (a) an amount equivalent to .4 mill times the adjusted assessed valuation of the taxable property of that city or county, as determined by the equalization aid review committee for the second year preceding that calendar year or (b) a per capita amount calculated under the provisions of this subdivision. The per capita amount is established for calendar year 1980 as $3.00. In succeeding calendar years, the per capita amount shall be increased by a percentage equal to one-half of the percentage by which the total state adjusted assessed valuation of property as determined by the equalization aid review committee for the second year preceding that calendar year increases over that total adjusted assessed valuation for the third year preceding that calendar year. The minimum level of support shall be certified annually to the participating cities and counties by the department of education. A city which is a part of a regional public library system shall not be required to provide this level of support if the property of that city is already taxable by the county for the support of that regional public library system. In no event shall the department of education require any city or county to provide a higher level of support than the level of support specified in this section in order for a system to qualify for a regional library basic system support grant. This section shall not be construed to prohibit a city or county from providing a higher level of support for public libraries than the level of support specified in this section.

Subd. 2. Notwithstanding the provisions of section 134.33 and subdivision 1 of this section, after the second year of participation by a city or county, the dollar amount of the minimum level of support for that city or county shall not be required to increase by more than ten percent over the dollar amount of the minimum level of support required of it in the previous year. If a participating city or county which has been providing for public library service support in an amount equivalent to .67 mill times the assessed valuation of the taxable property of that city or county for the year preceding that calendar year would be required to increase the dollar amount of such support by more than ten percent to reach the equivalent of .4 mill times the adjusted assessed valuation of the taxable property of that participating city or county as determined by the equalization aid review committee for the second year preceding that calendar year or the per capita amount calculated under the provisions of subdivision 1, it shall only be required to increase the dollar amount of such support by ten percent per year until such time as it reaches an amount equivalent to .4 mill times the adjusted assessed valuation of that taxable property as determined by the equalization aid review committee for the second year preceding that calendar year or the per capita amount calculated under the provisions of subdivision 1.

Subd. 3. Regional library basic system support grants shall be made only to those regional public library systems officially designated by the state board of education as the appropriate agency to strengthen, improve and promote public library services in the participating areas. The state board of education shall designate no more than one such regional public library system located entirely within any single development region existing under sections 462.381 to 462.396 or chapter 473.

Subd. 4. A regional library basic system support grant shall not be made to a regional public library system for a participating city or county which decreases the dollar amount provided for support for operating purposes of public library service below the amount provided by it for the preceding year. This subdivision shall not apply to participating cities or counties where the adjusted assessed valuation of that city or county has decreased, if the dollar amount of the reduction in support is not greater than the dollar amount by which support would be decreased if the reduction in support were made in direct proportion to the decrease in adjusted assessed valuation.

Added by Laws 1978, c. 546, § 5.

Subd. 5. Maintenance of effort; exception. Notwithstanding subdivision 4, a regional library system support grant may be made in fiscal year 1983 to a regional public library system for a participating city or county which decreases the dollar amount provided by it for operating purposes of public library service below the amount provided by it for 1981 if the amount provided by the city or county in 1982 is not less than the amount provided by it in 1980. A regional library system support grant may be made in fiscal year 1984 to a regional public library system for a participating city or county which decreases the dollar amount provided by it for operating purposes of public library service below the amount provided by it for 1982, if the amount provided by the city or county in 1983 is not less than the amount provided by it in 1981. This subdivision shall not affect the eligibility of cities or counties to declare all or part of their library levies as special levies under the provisions of section 275.50, subdivision 5, clause (c).

Amended by Laws 1979, c. 334, art. 9, §§ 5, 6; Laws 1982, c. 548, art. 6, § 18, eff. March 23, 1982; Laws 1982, c. 576, § 1, eff. March 23, 1982.

134.35. Regional library basic system support grants; distribution formula

Subdivision 1. Grant application. Any regional public library system which qualifies according to the provisions of section 134.34 may apply for an annual grant for regional library basic system support. The amount of each grant for each fiscal year shall be calculated as provided in this section.

Subd. 2. Fifty-five percent of the available grant funds shall be distributed to provide all qualifying systems an equal amount per capita. Each system's allocation pursuant to this subdivision shall be based on the population it serves.

Subd. 3. Fifteen percent of the available grant funds shall be distributed to provide all qualifying systems an equal amount per square mile. Each system's allocation pursuant to this subdivision shall be based on the area it serves.

Subd. 4. The sum of $35,000 shall be paid to each system as a base grant for basic system services.

Subd. 5. After the allocations made pursuant to subdivisions 2, 3 and 4, any remaining available grant funds for basic system support shall be distributed to those regional public library systems which contain counties whose adjusted assessed valuations per capita were below the state average adjusted assessed valuation per capita for the second year preceding the fiscal year for which the grant is made. Each system's entitlement shall be calculated as follows:

(a) Subtract the adjusted assessed valuation per capita for each eligible county or participating portion of a county from the statewide average adjusted assessed valuation per capita;

(b) Multiply the difference obtained in clause (a) for each eligible county or participating portion of a county by the population of that eligible county or participating portion of a county;

(c) For each regional public library system, determine the sum of the results of the computation in clause (b) for all eligible counties or portions thereof in that system;

(d) Determine the sum of the result of the computation in clause (b) for all eligible counties or portions thereof in all regional public library systems in the state;

(e) For each system, divide the result of the computation in clause (c) by the result of the computation in clause (d) to obtain the allocation factor for that system;

(f) Multiply the allocation factor for each system as determined in clause (e) times the amount of the remaining grant funds to determine each system's dollar allocation pursuant to this subdivision.

Amended by Laws 1979, c. 334, art. 9, §§ 7, 8; Laws 1981, c. 358, art. 6, § 27.

134.351. Multi-county, multi-type library systems

Subdivision 1. Establishment. The state board of education, upon the advice of the advisory council to the office of public libraries and interlibrary cooperation, may approve the establishment of multi-county, multi-type library systems and the geographic boundaries of those systems.

Subd. 2. Services. Each multi-county, multi-type library system is encouraged to develop services including, but not limited to the following: referral of users, intrasystem reciprocal borrowing, cooperative collection development, cooperative reference services, staff development, research and development, cooperative storage facilities, publicity and community relations.

Subd. 3. Agreement. In order for a multi-county, multi-type library system to qualify for a planning, development or operating grant pursuant to sections 134.352 and 134.353, each participating library in the system shall adopt an organizational agreement providing for the following:

(a) Sharing of resources among all participating libraries;

(b) Long-range planning for cooperative programs;

(c) The development of a delivery system for services and programs;

(d) The development of a bibliographic data base; and

(e) A communications system among all cooperating libraries.

Subd. 4. Governance. In any area where the boundaries of a proposed multi-county, multi-type library system coincide with the boundaries of the regional library system, the regional library system board shall be designated as the governing board for the multi-county, multi-type library system. In any area where a proposed multi-county, multi-type library system encompasses more than one regional library system, the governing board of the multi-county, multi-type library system shall consist of nine members appointed by the cooperating regional library system boards from their own membership in proportion to the population served by each cooperating regional library system. In each multi-county, multi-type library system there shall be established an advisory committee consisting of two representatives of public libraries, two representatives of school media services, one representative of special libraries, one representative of public supported academic libraries, and one representative of private academic libraries. The advisory committee shall recommend needed policy to the system governing board.

Subd. 5. Property. All property given, granted, conveyed, donated, devised or bequeathed to, or otherwise acquired by any multi-county multi-type library system board shall vest in, and be held in the name of, the multi-county multi-type library system board. Any conveyance, grant, donation, devise, bequest, or gift made to, or in the name of, any multi-county multi-type library system shall be deemed to have been made directly to the multi-county multi-type library system board.

Subd. 6. Ratification. All property heretofore given, granted, conveyed, donated, devised, bequeathed to, or otherwise acquired by any multi-county multi-type library system board is hereby validated, ratified and confirmed as the property of the board.

Subd. 7. Reports. Each multi-county, multi-type system receiving a grant pursuant to section 134.352 or 134.353 shall provide an annual progress report to the department of education. The department shall report before November 15 of each year to the legislature on all projects funded under sections 134.352 and 134.353.

Added by Laws 1979, c. 334, art. 9, § 9. Amended by Laws 1981, c. 358, art. 6, §§ 28, 29, eff. June 2, 1981; Laws 1981, c. 358, art. 6, § 30.

134.352. Multi-county, multi-type library system; planning grants

The state board of education may award a one year planning grant to a multi-county, multi-type library system, to be available during the first year of operation of each system. In awarding a planning grant, the state board shall consider the extra costs incurred in systems located in sparsely populated and large geographic areas.

Added by Laws 1979, c. 334, art. 9, § 10.

134.353. Multi-county, multi-type library system development grant

The state board of education may provide development and operating grants to multi-

county, multi-type library systems in their second and subsequent years of operation. In awarding a development and operating grant, the state board shall consider the extra costs incurred in systems located in sparsely populated and large geographic regions.
Added by Laws 1979, c. 334, art. 9, § 11.

134.36. Rules

The state board of education shall promulgate rules as necessary for implementation of any provision of sections 134.30 to 134.353.
Amended by Laws 1981, c. 358, art. 6, § 31.

INTERSTATE LIBRARY COMPACT
(Minnesota Statutes Annotated, 1982, s.134.21-134.24.)

134.21 Interstate library compact

The interstate library compact is hereby enacted into law and entered into on behalf of this state with any state bordering on Minnesota which legally joins therein in substantially the following form:

INTERSTATE LIBRARY COMPACT

The contracting states agree that:

ARTICLE I
PURPOSE

Because the desire for the services provided by public libraries transcends governmental boundaries and can be provided most effectively by giving such services to communities of people regardless of jurisdictional lines, it is the policy of the states who are parties to this compact to cooperate and share their responsibilities in providing joint and cooperative library services in areas where the distribution of population makes the provision of library service on an interstate basis the most effective way to provide adequate and efficient services.

ARTICLE II
PROCEDURE

The appropriate officials and agencies of the party states or any of their political subdivisions may, on behalf of said states or political subdivisions, enter into agreements for the cooperative or joint conduct of library services when they shall find that the executions of agreements to that end as provided herein will facilitate library services.

ARTICLE III
CONTENT

Any such agreement for the cooperative or joint establishment, operation, or use of library services, facilities, personnel, equipment, materials, or other items not excluded because of failure to enumerate shall, as among the parties of the agreement: (1) Detail the specific nature of the services, facilities, properties, or personnel to which it is applicable; (2) provide for the allocation of costs and other financial responsibilities; (3) specify the respective rights, duties, obligations, and liabilities; (4) stipulate the terms and conditions for duration, renewal, termination, abrogation, disposal of joint or common property, if any, and all other matters which may be appropriate to the proper effectuation and performance of said agreement.

ARTICLE IV
CONFLICT OF LAWS

Nothing in this compact or in any agreement entered into hereunder shall be construed to supersede, alter, or otherwise impair any obligation imposed on any public library by otherwise applicable laws.

ARTICLE V
ADMINISTRATOR

Each state shall designate a compact administrator with whom copies of all agreements to which his state or any subdivision thereof is party shall be filed. The administrator shall have such powers as may be conferred upon him by the laws of his state and may consult and cooperate with the compact administrators of other party states and take such steps as may effectuate the purposes of this compact.

ARTICLE VI
EFFECTIVE DATE

This compact shall become operative immediately upon its enactment by any state or between it and any other contiguous state or states so enacting.

ARTICLE VII
RENUNCIATION

This compact shall continue in force and remain binding upon each party state until six months after any such state has given notice of repeal by the legislature. Such withdrawal shall not be construed to relieve any party to an agreement authorized by articles II and III of the compact from the obligation of that agreement prior to the end of its stipulated period of duration.

ARTICLE VIII

SEVERABILITY; CONSTRUCTION

The provisions of this compact shall be severable. It is intended that the provisions of this compact be reasonably and liberally construed.

Laws 1967, c. 4, § 1, eff. July 1, 1967.

134.22   Compact administrator

The state board of education shall designate an officer or employee of the state department of education as compact administrator. The compact administrator shall receive copies of all agreements entered into by the state or its political subdivisions and other states or political subdivisions; consult with, advise, and aid such governmental units in the formulation of such agreements; make such recommendations to the governor, legislature, and governmental agencies and units as he deems desirable to effectuate the purposes of this compact; and consult and cooperate with the compact administrators of other party states.

Laws 1967, c. 4, § 2, eff. July 1, 1967.

134.23   Agreements

The compact administrator and the governing body of any political subdivision of the state or the library board thereof operating a public library may enter into agreements with other states or their political subdivisions pursuant to the compact. Such agreements as may be made pursuant to this compact on behalf of the state of Minnesota shall be made by the compact administrator. Such agreements as may be made on behalf of a political subdivision shall be made after due notice to the compact administrator and consultation with him.

Laws 1967, c. 4, § 3, eff. July 1, 1967.

134.24   Enforcement of compact

The agencies and officers of this state and its political subdivisions shall enforce this compact and do all things appropriate to effect its purpose and intent which may be within their respective jurisdictions.

Laws 1967, c. 4, § 4, eff. July 1, 1967.

STATE LIBRARY
(Minnesota Statutes Annotated, 1982, s.480.09, 599.15.)

480.09 State library

Subdivision 1. The state library shall be maintained in the capitol and shall be under the supervision of the justices of the supreme court. Notwithstanding Minnesota Statutes, Section 16.02 or any other act inconsistent herewith or acts amendatory thereof or supplementary thereto, they shall direct the purchases of books, pamphlets, and documents therefor and the sales and exchanges therefrom upon such terms and conditions as they may deem just and proper. They may authorize the transfer of books and documents to the University of Minnesota or any department thereof, or to any state agency. They shall adopt rules for the government of the library and the management of its affairs, and prescribe penalties for the violation thereof.

Subd. 2. The justices of the supreme court shall appoint a state law librarian to serve at their pleasure. He shall give bond to the state in an amount not less than $2,000, to be approved by the chief justice, conditioned for the faithful performance of his official duties. Subject to the approval of the justices, he may appoint an assistant librarian who shall perform his duties when he is absent or disabled, and, subject to the approval of the justices, he may employ necessary assistants.

Subd. 3. The librarian shall

(1) have charge of the library rooms and property,

(2) under the direction of the justices attend to all purchases, exchanges, transfers, and sales,

(3) enforce the rules prescribed for the government of the library and the management of its affairs,

(4) collect all damages from injury to or retention of library property and all fines imposed for violation of the rules,

(5) effect exchanges of any books, documents, journals, maps, pamphlets, and reports delivered to the state library by any department, agency, or official of the state in accordance with the provisions of section 15.18,

(6) keep a detailed chronological record of all purchases, exchanges, transfers, and sales and of all additions to the library by gift, purchase, or exchange, respectively,

(7) keep an account of all amounts collected as damages or fines or from other sources, and of all expenditures.

Subd. 4. The records and accounts of the library shall be open to public inspection and shall be transferred to the successor of the librarian.

Subd. 5. All moneys collected shall be paid into the state treasury and shall be added to the current biennial appropriation for the library.

Amended by Laws 1982, c. 576, § 18, eff. March 23, 1982.

Subd. 6. All official publications of the United States and of other states and countries, which are received for the use of this state by any officer thereof, shall be sent to the state library forthwith.

Amended by Laws 1947, c. 365, § 4; Laws 1951, c. 3, § 1; Laws 1955, c. 89, § 1; Laws 1965, c. 45, § 67, eff. Feb. 28, 1965.

599.15 Copies of decisions, certified by librarian

Copies of judicial decisions contained in any of the law or equity reports in the state library, and of any other papers or documents contained in such library, certified by the state librarian, shall be received in evidence in like manner and with like effect as the originals. For making and certifying any such copy, the librarian shall be entitled to charge 15 cents a folio. St.1927, § 9858.

STATE ARCHIVES

(Minnesota Statutes Annotated, 1982, s.138.161, 138.17, 138.19-138.21, 138.225, 138.226)

138.161. State archives; establishment

State archives are hereby established and shall be administered by the Minnesota historical society.
Amended by Laws 1982, c. 573, § 2, eff. July 1, 1982.

138.17. Government records; administration

Subdivision 1. Destruction, preservation, reproduction of records; prima facie evidence. The attorney general, legislative auditor in the case of state records, state auditor in the case of local records, and director of the Minnesota historical society, hereinafter director, shall constitute the records disposition panel. The members of the panel shall have power by unanimous consent to direct the destruction or sale for salvage of government records determined to be no longer of any value, or to direct the disposition by gift to the Minnesota historical society or otherwise of government records determined to be valuable for preservation. The records disposition panel may by unanimous consent order any of those records to be reproduced by photographic or other means, and order that photographic or other reproductions be substituted for the originals of them. It may direct the destruction or sale for salvage or other disposition of the originals from which they were made. Photographic or other reproductions shall for all purposes be deemed the originals of the records reproduced when so ordered by the records disposition panel, and shall be admissible as evidence in all courts and in proceedings of every kind. A facsimile, exemplified or certified copy of a photographic or other reproduction, or an enlargement or reduction of it, shall have the same effect and weight as evidence as would a certified or exemplified copy of the original. The records disposition panel, by unanimous consent, may direct the storage of government records, except as herein provided, and direct the storage of photographic or other reproductions. Photographic or other reproductions substituted for original records shall be disposed of in accordance with the procedures provided for the original records. For the purposes of this chapter: (1) The term "government records" means state and local records, including all cards, correspondence, discs, maps, memoranda, microfilms, papers, photographs, recordings, reports, tapes, writings and other data, information or documentary material, regardless of physical form or characteristics, storage media or conditions of use, made or received by an officer or agency of the state and an officer or agency of a county, city, town, school district, municipal subdivision or corporation or other public authority or political entity within the state pursuant to state law or in connection with the transaction of public business by an officer or agency; (2) The term "state record" means a record of a department, office, officer, commission, commissioner, board or any other agency, however styled or designated, of the executive branch of state government; a record of the state legislature; a record of any court, whether of statewide or local jurisdiction; and any other record designated or treated as a state record under state law; (3) The term "local record" means a record of an agency of a county, city, town, school district, municipal subdivision or corporation or other public authority or political entity; (4) The term "records" excludes data and information that does not become part of an official transaction, library and museum material made or acquired and kept solely for reference or exhibit purposes, extra copies of documents kept only for convenience of reference and stock of publications and processed documents, and bonds, coupons, or other obligations or evidences of indebtedness, the destruction or other disposition of which is governed by other laws; (5) The term "state archives" means those records preserved or appropriate for preservation as evidence of the organization, functions, policies, decisions, procedures, operations or other activities of government or because of the value of the information contained in them, when determined to have sufficient historical or other value to warrant continued preservation by the state of Minnesota and accepted for inclusion in the collections of the Minnesota historical society.

Subd. 1a. Records inspection. Government records which a state agency, political subdivision, or statewide system lists on a records disposition application or records schedule, or on which archival assistance or advice is requested, may be inspected by state archives' employees if state archives gives prior notice. Employees of the archives shall have access to the records for the purpose of determining the historical or other continuing value of the records, regardless of the records' classification pursuant to chapter 13. Employees of the archives shall be liable to the penalties set forth for improper disclosure by them of private, confidential, nonpublic, or protected nonpublic data inspected for this purpose.

Subd. 1b. Transfer process. After July 1, 1982, all records deemed to be of continuing value and authorized for transfer to the archives by the records disposition panel shall be retained by the requesting agency or may be transferred to the archives in accordance with subdivision 1, notwithstanding the provisions of chapter 13. The responsible authority of the state agency, political subdivision, or statewide system transferring records to the archives shall notify the archivist or his designee with regard to the records transferred of the classification of the records pursuant to chapter 13.

Subd. 1c. Access to archives records. (a) All records transferred to the archives shall be accessible to the public unless the archives determines that the information:

(1) Was compiled for law enforcement purposes and disclosure would (i) materially impair the effectiveness of an ongoing investigation, criminal intelligence operation, or law enforcement proceeding; (ii) identify a confidential informant; (iii) reveal confidential investigative techniques or procedures, including criminal intelligence activity; or (iv) endanger the life of an individual;

(2) Is administrative or technical information, including software, operating protocols,

employee manuals, or other information, the disclosure of which would jeopardize the security of a record keeping system;

(3) Is proprietary information, including computer programs and software and other types of information manufactured or marketed by persons under exclusive legal right, owned by the agency or entrusted to it;

(4) Contains trade secrets or confidential commercial and financial information obtained, upon request, from a person;

(5) Is library, archival, or museum material contributed by private persons to the extent of any lawful limitation imposed upon the material; or

(6) Disclosure would constitute a clearly unwarranted invasion of personal privacy. Disclosure of an individually identifiable record does not constitute a clearly unwarranted invasion of personal privacy if the public interest in disclosure outweighs the privacy interest of the individual.

(b) The society may withhold access to state archives from any person who willfully mutilates, damages, or defaces archival records, or wrongfully removes them from state archives; provided that the society shall notify the person of the decision to withhold access, and the person may, within 30 days, appeal the decision to the executive council of the society.

(c) The state archivist shall notify any person from whom access is withheld pursuant to clause (a). The person may, within 30 days of the day the notice is sent, appeal the archivist's determination to the executive council of the society. The executive council shall, within 30 days of the filing of an appeal, issue a decision determining if the archivist has correctly applied the standards of clause (a). The decision of the executive council may be appealed to the district court of Ramsey County.

Subd. 2. Repealed by Laws 1971, c. 529, § 15, eff. May 26, 1971.

Subd. 3. University; state agricultural society; historical society. Laws 1971, Chapter 529, Sections 1 to 14 shall not apply to the public records of the University of Minnesota, the Minnesota State agriculture society, or the Minnesota historical society.

Subd. 4. State library. No public records of the Minnesota State Library shall be subject to the disposition or orders provided by Laws 1971, Chapter 529, except with the consent of the state librarian.

Subd. 5. Supreme court. No public records of the Supreme Court shall be subject to the disposition or orders provided by Laws 1971, Chapter 529, except with the consent of the court.

Subd. 6. Archivist; equipment; supplies. The Minnesota historical society shall employ a professional archivist, who shall be known as the state archivist, and other agents and personnel as are necessary to enable it to carry out its duties and powers. The archivist shall be appointed by the director of the society.

Subd. 7. Records management program. A records management program for the application of efficient and economical management methods to the creation, utilization, maintenance, retention, preservation, and disposal of official records shall be administered by the commissioner of administration. The state records center which stores and services state records not in state archives shall be administered by the commissioner of administration. The commissioner of administration is empowered to (1) establish standards, procedures, and techniques for effective management of government records, (2) make continuing surveys of paper work operations, and (3) recommend improvements in current records management practices including the use of space, equipment, and supplies employed in creating, maintaining, preserving and disposing of government records. It shall be the duty of the head of each state agency and the governing body of each county, municipality, and other subdivision of government to cooperate with the commissioner in conducting surveys and to establish and maintain an active, continuing program for the economical and efficient management of the records of each agency, county, municipality, or other subdivision of government. When requested by the commissioner, public officials shall assist in the preparation of an inclusive inventory of records in their custody, to which shall be attached a schedule, approved by the head of the governmental unit or agency having custody of the records establishing a time period for the retention or disposal of each series of records. When the schedule is unanimously approved by the records disposition panel, the head of the governmental unit or agency having custody of the records may dispose of the type of records listed in the schedule at a time and in a manner prescribed in the schedule for particular records which were created after the approval. A list of records disposed of pursuant to this subdivision shall be forwarded to the commissioner and the archivist by the head of the governmental unit or agency. The archivist shall maintain a list of all records destroyed.

Subd. 8. Emergency records preservation. In light of the danger of nuclear or natural disaster, the commissioner of administration shall establish and maintain a program for the selection and preservation of public records considered essential to the operation of government and to the protection of the rights and interests of persons, and shall make or cause to be made preservation duplicates or designate as preservation duplicates existing copies of such essential public records. Preservation duplicates shall be durable, accurate, complete, and clear, and such duplicates reproduced by photographic or other process which accurately reproduces and forms a durable medium for so reproducing the original shall have the same force and effect for all purposes as the original record whether the original record is in existence or not. A transcript, exemplification, or certified copy of such preservation duplicate shall be deemed for all purposes to be a transcript, exemplification, or certified copy of the original record. Such preservation duplicates shall be preserved in the place and manner of safekeeping prescribed by the commissioner.

Every county, municipality, or other subdivision of government may institute a program for the preservation of necessary documents essential to the continuity of government. Such a program shall first be submitted to the commissioner for his approval or disapproval and no such program shall be instituted until such approval is obtained.

Laws 1947, c. 547, § 5. Amended by Laws 1961, c. 175, §§ 3 to 8; Laws 1963, c. 695, §§ 2, 3; Laws 1971, c. 529, §§ 4 to 10, eff. May 26, 1971; Laws 1973, c. 32, §§ 2, 3; Laws 1973, c. 123, art. 5, § 7;

Laws 1974, c. 184, §§ 8, 9; Laws 1976, c. 324, § 22, eff. April 21, 1976; Laws 1978, c. 717, § 2.

Amended by Laws 1981, c. 311, § 39; Laws 1982, c. 545, § 24; Laws 1982 c. 573, §§ 3 to 8, eff. July 1, 1982.

138.19. Applications for orders of the panel

An officer, department, or agency of the state or an officer or agency of a county, city, town, school district, municipal subdivision or corporation, or other public authority or political entity shall apply in writing to the archivist for an order relating to the disposition of any government record. The records disposition panel shall consider and act upon applications and by unanimous consent make orders with respect to them.

Amended by Laws 1982, c. 573, § 9, eff. July 1, 1982.

138.20. Record of proceedings

The archivist shall keep a record of all orders authorizing the disposition of records. Orders shall be in writing and signed by the records disposition panel, and shall identify the records referred to in them. A certified copy of an order shall be admissible in evidence in any court or proceeding. The records shall be preserved in the office of the archivist and shall be open to public inspection. Proper records shall be kept by the archivist showing where records or reproductions of them have been stored, and also identifying any that have been ordered destroyed, sold for salvage or disposed of by gift or otherwise.

Amended by Laws 1982, c. 573, § 10, eff. July 1, 1982.

138.21. Storage space designated by panel

The Minnesota historical society may direct the storage of government records, including photographic or other reproductions which are state archives.

Amended by Laws 1982, c. 573, § 11, eff. July 1, 1982.

138.225. Prohibition against unauthorized disposal of records; penalty

Government records shall not be destroyed except by the authority of the records disposition panel. A person who intentionally and unlawfully removes, mutilates, destroys, conceals, alters, defaces or obliterates a record filed or deposited in a public office or with a public officer by authority of law or in state archives, or a public officer or employee who knowingly permits any other person to do any of the foregoing acts, is guilty of a misdemeanor.

Added by Laws 1982, c. 573, § 12, eff. July 1, 1982.

138.226. Replevin authority

The attorney general may replevin public records which have been unlawfully transferred or removed in violation of sections 15.17, subdivisions 2 and 3; 138.163; 138.17; and 138.21. The records shall be returned to the office of origin, or, in the case of state archives, to the society.

Added by Laws 1982, c. 573, § 13, eff. July 1, 1982.

DISTRIBUTION OF PUBLIC DOCUMENTS

(Minnesota Statutes Annotated, 1982, s.5.08, 137.04, 471.68, 648.39.)

5.08   Legislative manual

Subdivision 1. Preparation. The Secretary of State shall prepare, compile, edit, and distribute for use at each regular legislative session, a convenient manual, properly indexed, and containing: The Federal and State Constitutions; the acts of Congress relating to the organization of the territory and state; the rules of order and joint rules of the two houses, and lists of their members, committees and employees; the names of all state officials, whether elected or appointed, and of all persons holding office from this state under the national government, including postmasters appointed by the president; the places where the said several officials reside, and the annual compensation of each; and statistical and other information of the kind heretofore published in the legislative manuals.

Subd. 2. Distribution. 15,000 copies of the legislative manual shall be printed and distributed as follows:

(1) Up to 25 copies shall be available to each member of the legislature on request;

(2) 50 copies to the state historical society;

(3) 25 copies to the state university;

(4) 60 copies to the state library;

(5) Two copies each to the library of Congress, the Minnesota veterans home, the state universities, the state high schools, the public academies, seminaries, and colleges of the state, and the free public libraries of the state;

(6) One copy each to the state institutions not hereinbefore mentioned, the elective state officials, the appointed heads of departments, the officers and employees of the legislature, the justices of the supreme court, the judges of the district court, the senators and representatives in Congress from this state, and the county auditors;

(7) One copy to each public school, to be distributed through the superintendent of each school district; and

(8) The remainder may be disposed of as the secretary of state deems best.

Amended by Laws 1977, c. 455, § 67; Laws 1979, c. 333, § 59; Laws 1981, c. 356, § 252.

137.04 Library to get copies of state publications

The general library of the University of Minnesota is a depository of all books, pamphlets, maps, and other works published by or under the authority of the State of Minnesota.

Amended by Laws 1947, c. 365, § 3.

471.68 Distribution of publications by any county or city

Subdivision 1. Annual or biennial reports. When any county or city, or any department, agency, or official thereof issues for public distribution an annual or biennial report, copies thereof shall upon request be delivered immediately as follows:

One copy to each public library serving such local area of government for which said report is made; provided that in counties containing no county library, such report shall be delivered to the public library serving the most populous city in the county;

One copy to the Minnesota Historical Society;

One copy to the general library of the University of Minnesota.

Additonal copies may be delivered upon request.

Subd. 2. Appearing in newspaper. The publications enumerated in subdivision 1 shall not include publications appearing in newspapers.

Laws 1949, c. 438, §§ 1, 2. Amended by Laws 1973, c. 123, art. 5, § 7.

648.39. Minnesota statutes and session laws; sale and distribution

Subdivision 1. Free distribution. The revisor of statutes shall without charge distribute each edition of Minnesota Statutes, supplement to the Minnesota Statutes, and the Laws of Minnesota to the persons, officers, departments, agencies, or commissions listed in this subdivision. Prior to distribution of Minnesota Statutes, supplement to the Minnesota Statutes, or the Laws of Minnesota, the revisor of statutes shall inquire whether the full number of copies authorized by this subdivision are required for their work. Unless a smaller number is needed, each edition shall be distributed without charge as follows:

(a) 30 copies to the supreme court;

(b) 1 copy to each judge of a district court;

(c) 1 copy to the clerk of each district court for use in each courtroom of the district court of his county;

(d) 100 copies to the state law library;

(e) 100 copies to the law school of the University of Minnesota;

(f) 100 copies to the office of the attorney general;

(g) 10 copies each to the governor's office, the departments of agriculture, commerce, corrections, education, health, transportation, labor and industry, economic security, natural resources, public safety, public service, public welfare, and revenue, and the pollution control agency;

(h) 1 copy each to other state departments, agencies, boards, and commissions not specifically named in this subdivision;

(i) 1 copy to each member of the legislature;

(j) 100 copies for the use of the senate and 150 copies for the use of the house of representatives;

(k) 4 copies to the secretary of the senate;

(l) 4 copies to the chief clerk of the house of representatives;

(m) 1 copy to each judge, district attorney, clerk of court of the United States and the deputy clerk of each division of the United States district court in this state, the secretary of state of the United States, the library of congress, and the Minnesota historical society;

(n) 20 copies each to the department of administration, state auditor, and legislative auditor;

(o) 1 copy to each county library maintained pursuant to section 134.12 or 375.33, except in counties containing cities of the first class. If a county has not established a county library pursuant to section 134.12 or 375.33, the copy shall be provided to any public library in the county; and

(p) 50 copies to the revisor of statutes. Laws 1981, c. 356, § 370.

REGIONAL LIBRARIES
Minnesota Statutes Annotated, 1982, s.375.335.)

375.335 Regional libraries

Subdivision 1. Two or more contiguous counties, except counties one or more of which contain a city of the first class over 300,000 according to the 1960 United States census may, through action by their governing bodies under the provisions of Minnesota Statutes, Section 471.59, establish and maintain a regional library, even though any one or more of the counties may already have a county library with a library board; provided that in any such county already having a county library board, the approval of said library board shall also be required. Cities in any of the contracting counties having public libraries may join in the regional library by being parties to the agreement which establishes the regional library through action of their library boards, or as hereinafter provided in subdivision 3.

Subd. 2. The agreement establishing such regional library may provide for a library board to govern the organization having all the powers and duties of county library boards as provided in Minnesota Statutes, Section 375.33. Such regional library board may consist of as many members as the contracting parties deem necessary, appointed in such numbers and for such terms by each county board party to the contract as may be determined by the contracting parties, irrespective of the existence of one or more county library boards already in existence in the participating counties. In such participating counties, such portion of the proceeds of the county library tax authorized by Minnesota Statutes, Section 375.33, Subdivision 1, shall be used for the support of the regional library as the contracting agreement may provide.

Subd. 3. Where such regional library is established, any city located in any of the contracting counties which is excluded from the county tax supporting the regional library under the provisions of section 375.33, subdivision 1, may, upon recommendation of its library board and upon action by its governing body, be included in such county tax and become an integral part of the regional system. Such cities and any other cities in the participating counties, whether or not governed by home rule charter provisions, may levy taxes for the additional support of their local library services provided that said combined levies shall not exceed the statutory limit on the library levy. Any such local public library board or governing body may, at its option, continue to control such local library fund or pay all or part thereof into the regional library fund, to be used for the increase or improvement of library services in such city.

Subd. 4. Property. All property given, granted, conveyed, donated, devised or bequeathed to, or otherwise acquired by any regional library board or any regional public library system board however created shall vest in, and be held in the name of, the regional library board or regional public library system board. Any conveyance, grant, donation, devise, bequest, or gift made to, or in the name of, any regional library or public library system shall be deemed to have been made directly to the regional public library system board.

Subd. 5. Ratification. All property heretofore given, granted, conveyed, donated, devised, bequeathed to, or otherwise acquired by any regional library board or any regional public library system board however created is hereby validated, ratified and confirmed as the property of the board.

Subd. 6. Ratification. Any multicounty regional library heretofore created, and the agreements creating them, are hereby validated, ratified, and confirmed and the benefits of subdivisions 1 to 6 shall hereafter apply to these libraries.

Amended by Laws 1973, c. 123, art. 5, § 7; Laws 1981, c. 358, art. 6, §§ 34, 35, eff. June 2, 1981; Laws 1981, c. 358, art. 6, § 36.

COUNTY LIBRARIES
(Minnesota Statutes Annotated, 1982, s.375.33.)

375.33. Free county libraries

Subdivision 1. Creating, financing. The county board of any county may establish and maintain, at a location determined by the board, a public library for the free use of residents of the county, and may levy an annual tax upon all taxable property which is not already taxed for the support of any free public library and all taxable property which is situated outside of any city in which is situated a free public library. The proceeds of this tax shall be placed in the county library fund.

Subd. 2. Establishment; petition, election. If such county library be not otherwise established, upon petition of not less than 100 freeholders of the county, the county board shall submit the question of the establishment and maintenance of a free public library to the voters at the next county election. If a majority of the votes cast on such question be in the affirmative, the county board shall establish the library and shall levy annually a tax for its support.

Subd. 3. Contract with library board. If there be a free public library in the county, the county board may contract with the board of directors of such library for the use of such library by residents of the county, and may place the county library fund under the supervision of such library board, to be spent by such board for the extension of the free use of the library to residents of the county. If there be more than one such free public library in the county the county board may contract with one or all of such library boards for such free service if in its judgment advisable.

Subd. 4. Library board. If no free public library in the county is available for use as a central library of the county system, the county board shall appoint a library board of at least five directors. The term of office of these directors is three years, and each director shall hold office until his successor is appointed and qualifies. Of the directors first appointed, two shall hold office for three years, two for two years, and one for one year from the third Saturday of July following their appointment, as specified by the county board; and thereafter the directors shall be appointed for a term of three years. If more than five directors are appointed, terms shall be staggered as nearly as possible so no more than one-third of the membership terms expire each year. This board of directors shall have the powers and duties of a board of directors of any free public library in a city and shall be governed by the provisions of sections 134.09, 134.11 to 134.15.

Amended by Laws 1973, c. 123, art. 5, § 7; Laws 1973, c. 583, §§ 23, 24; Laws 1978, c. 624, § 1.

MUNICIPAL LIBRARIES
(Minnesota Statutes Annotated, 1982, s.134.07-134.16, 134.18, 134.19.)

134.07 Libraries, reading rooms; tax

Subdivision 1. The governing body of any city may establish and maintain a public library, a public reading room, or both, for the use of its inhabitants. By ordinance it may set apart for the benefit thereof any public property of the city. Except as provided in subdivision 2, in any statutory city and in any city of the second, third, or fourth class, the governing body thereof may levy an annual tax of not more than 2.6⅔ mills on the dollar, of all taxable property therein. The proceeds of any such tax shall be known as the library fund.

Subd. 2. The governing body of any city of the fourth class located in any county having over 7,000 and less than 9,000 inhabitants and over 70 full and fractional congressional townships, operating under a home rule charter, may levy an annual tax of not to exceed 1.6⅔ mills for such purposes, notwithstanding any limitation contained in its home rule charter.

Amended by Laws 1945, c. 319, § 1; Laws 1953, c. 434, § 1; Laws 1953, c. 686, § 1; Laws 1955, c. 120, § 1; Laws 1963, c. 144, § 1; Laws 1973, c. 123, art. 5, § 7; Laws 1973, c. 773, § 1.

134.08. When established by vote; existing libraries

If a library or reading-room is not otherwise established, the governing body of the municipality, upon the petition of 50 eligible voters, as defined in section 200.02, subdivision 25, of the municipality, shall submit the question of the establishment to the voters at the next municipal election. If two-thirds of the votes cast on the question are in the affirmative, the governing body shall establish the library or reading-room and levy a yearly tax for its support, within the limits fixed by section 134.07. All public libraries and reading-rooms heretofore established and now existing in cities are continued and all ordinances setting apart public property for their support are hereby confirmed. Nothing in sections 134.08 to 134.15 shall be construed as abridging any power or duty in respect to libraries conferred by any city charter.

Amended by Laws 1980, c. 609, art. 6, § 34, eff. April 25, 1980.

134.09 Directors; term; removal

Subdivision 1. When any such library or reading room is established, except in any city of the first class operating under a home rule charter, the mayor of the city or president of the statutory city, with the approval of the council, shall appoint a board of five, seven or nine directors, but not more than one of whom shall at any time be a member of such governing body, such appointments to be made prior to the first meeting of such library board after the end of the fiscal year. If nine are appointed, three shall hold office for one year, three for two years and three for three years. If seven members be appointed, three shall hold office for one year, two for two years, and two for three years; if five be appointed, two shall hold office for one year, two for two years, and one for three years. The number of directors on the board shall be determined by resolution or ordinance adopted by the council. All terms shall end with the fiscal year. Annually thereafter such mayor or president shall appoint for the term of three years and until their successors qualify a sufficient number of directors to fill the places of those whose term or terms expire.

Subd. 2. The mayor or president, by and with the consent of the council, may remove any director for misconduct or neglect.

Subd. 3. Terms of directors in office at the time Laws 1945, Chapter 46, takes effect shall expire at the end of the city's fiscal year current at the expiration of their terms as heretofore provided.

Subd. 4. Upon recommendation of a majority of any library board created under the provisions of subdivision 1, the governing body of such city may abolish such library board at the end of any fiscal year provided that such governing body shall simultaneously establish a successor library board of either five, seven or nine members by resolution or ordinance. In the event of such resolution or ordinance, the mayor, with the approval of the council, shall appoint a library board of the number of members as provided by said resolution or ordinance. If nine are appointed, three shall hold office for one year, three for two years and three for three years. If seven members be appointed, three shall hold office for one year, two for two years, and two for three years; if five be appointed, two shall hold office for one year, two for two years, and one for three years. Annually thereafter such mayor shall appoint for the term of three years and until their successors qualify a sufficient number of directors to fill the places of those whose term or terms expire. All terms shall end with the fiscal year.

Amended by Laws 1945, c. 46, §§ 1, 2; Laws 1961, c. 235, § 1; Laws 1973, c. 123, art. 5, § 7.

134.10 Vacancies; compensation

Vacancies in the board of directors shall be reported to the council and filled by like appointment for the unexpired term. Directors shall receive no compensation for their services as such.

St.1927, § 5664.

134.11 Organization of board; rules

Immediately after appointment, such board shall organize by electing one of its number as president and one as secretary, and from time to time it may appoint such other officers and employees as it deems necessary. The secretary, before entering upon his duties, shall give bond to the municipality in an amount fixed by the directors, conditioned for the faithful discharge of his official duties. The board shall adopt such bylaws and regulations for the government of the library and reading-room and for the conduct of its business as may be expedient and conformable to law. It shall have exclusive control of the expenditure of all moneys collected for or placed to the credit of the library fund, of the construction of library buildings, and of the grounds, rooms, and buildings provided for library purposes. All moneys received for such library shall be paid into the city treasury, credited to the library fund, kept separate from other moneys of the municipality, and paid out only upon itemized vouchers approved by the board. The board may lease rooms for library use, fix the compensation of employees, and remove any of them at pleasure. With the approval of the council, the board may purchase grounds and erect a library building thereon.

Amended by Laws 1973, c. 123, art. 5, § 7.

134.12 Benefits of library

Subdivision 1. Non-residents to receive. Any board of directors may admit to the benefits of its library persons not residing within the municipality under regulations and upon conditions as to payment and security prescribed by it.

Subd. 2. Loan of books, contracts. The board may contract with the county board of the county in which the library is situated or the county board of any adjacent county, or with the governing body of any neighboring town or city, to loan books of the library, either singly or in traveling libraries, to residents of the county, town, or city.

Subd. 3. Use of free public library; tax levy. Any such county board or governing body may contract with the board of directors of any free public library for the use of the library by the residents of the county, town, or city who do not have the use of a free library, upon the terms and conditions as those granted residents of the city where the library is located, and to pay such board of directors an annual amount therefor. Any such county board or governing body may establish a library fund by levying an annual tax upon all taxable property which is not already taxed for the support of any free public library and all taxable property which is situated outside of any city in which is situated a free public library.

Amended by Laws 1951, c. 217, § 1; Laws 1963, c. 144, § 2; Laws 1973, c. 123, art. 5, § 7; Laws 1973, c. 583, § 8.

134.13 Directors now in office; report; exceptions

The directors of any such library or reading room in office under existing laws shall so continue until the expiration of their terms, but their successors shall be appointed and vacancies filled under the provision of sections 134.08 to 134.15. At the first regular meeting of the board following the end of each fiscal year of a city, the board shall report to the governing body of the municipality all amounts received during the preceding year and the sources thereof, the amounts expended and for what purposes, the number of books on hand, the number purchased and loaned, and such other information as it deems advisable. A copy of such report shall be filed with the Library Division, State Department of Education. Nothing in this section shall apply to libraries in cities of the first class.

Amended by Laws 1945, c. 40, § 1; Laws 1973, c. 123, art. 5, § 7.

134.14 Title to property; free use

All property given, granted, conveyed, donated, devised, or bequeathed to, or otherwise acquired by, any municipality for a library or reading-room shall vest in, and be held in the name of, such municipality and any conveyance, grant, donation, devise, bequest, or gift made to, or in the name of, any public library or library board shall be deemed to have been made directly to such municipality. Every library and reading-room established under sections 134.08 to 134.15 shall be forever free to the use of the inhabitants of the municipality subject to such reasonable regulations as the directors may adopt.   St.1927, § 5668.

134.15 Gifts; contracts

With the consent of the governing body of any city, expressed by ordinance or resolution, and within the limitations of sections 134.08 to 134.15 as to the rate of taxation, the library board may accept any gift, grant, devise, or bequest made or offered by any person for library purposes, or for the establishment, enlargement, or maintenance of an art gallery or museum in connection with its library, and may carry out the conditions of such donation. The municipality in all such cases is authorized to acquire a site, levy a tax, and pledge itself by ordinance or resolution to a perpetual compliance with all the terms and conditions of the gift, grant, devise, or bequest so accepted.

Amended by Laws 1973, c. 123, art. 5, § 7.

134.16 Certain cities and towns to establish portable and circulating libraries

The board of supervisors of any town containing five or more governmental townships and having a total population of 15,000, including statutory cities therein which are not separated from the town for election and assessment purposes, may establish and maintain a portable circulating library for the education, benefit, and welfare of the people of the town.

For this purpose, the board may purchase and equip a motor vehicle and furnish a driver, a librarian, and such further clerical assistance as it shall deem reasonably necessary for the maintenance of such library, and the library board of such city is hereby authorized to cooperate with the town in the maintenance thereof and to loan books and periodicals to the town on such terms as it shall prescribe.

All expenditures made for the purposes of this section shall be within and not above the limitations now prescribed by law for the general fund of such town.

Amended by Laws 1973, c. 123, art. 5, § 7.

134.18 Privileges extended to counties and statutory cities

Any public library board in any city of the first class in this state, whether such board was created by and under the general laws or by special act of the legislature, may enter into arrangement with the authorities of the county within which it is located, or with the authorities of any adjoining county, or with the authorities of any statutory city within any such county, whereby the inhabitants of any such county or statutory city may secure the privileges of using the library and museums of any such library board and the authorities of any such county or statutory city are hereby authorized to defray the expenses any such arrangement may involve.

Amended by Laws 1973, c. 123, art. 5, § 7.

134.19   Tax for library board

There may be annually levied by, or for the benefit of, any public library board in any city of the first class in this state, whether such board was created by and under the general laws or by special act of the legislature, a tax of not to exceed one third of one mill upon each dollar of the property in such city, as the value of such property has been assessed and determined for the purposes of general taxation.

Amended by Laws 1973, c. 773, § 1.

SCHOOL DISTRICT LIBRARIES
(Minnesota Statutes Annotated, 1982, 134.03.)

134.03.   Tax levy

Subdivision 1. In cities of less than 2,000 inhabitants not levying a tax for public library purposes, the school board may maintain a public library for the use of all residents of the district and provide ample and suitable rooms for its use in the school buildings or the district.

Upon a library being so established in any such school district, whose library building has been erected with funds acquired by gift or donation, the school board is empowered to appoint a library board of nine members, of which each member of the school board shall be a member ex officio.

The remaining members of such library board shall be appointed by the school board, one of which remaining members shall hold office for one year, one for two years, and one for three years if the school board has only six members, from the first Saturday of September following their appointment, the term of office of each being specified in such appointment; annually thereafter, such school board shall appoint a member of the library board for the term of three years and until his successor shall qualify. Such school board may remove any member so appointed for misconduct or neglect. Vacancies in such board shall be filled by appointment for the unexpired term. Members of such board shall receive no compensation for their services as such.

Immediately after appointment, such board shall organize by electing one of its members as president and one as secretary and from time to time it may appoint such other officers and employees as it deems necessary. The secretary, before entering upon his duties, shall give bond to the school district in an amount fixed by the library board, conditioned for the faithful discharge of his official duties. The library board shall adopt such bylaws and regulations for the government of the library and reading-room and for the conduct of its business as may be expedient and conformable to law. It shall have exclusive control of the expenditures of all money collected for, or placed to the credit of, the library funds, and of the rooms and buildings provided for library purposes. All moneys received for such library fund shall be kept in the treasury of the school district, credited to the library fund, and be paid out only upon itemized vouchers approved by the library board. The library board may fix the compensation of employees and remove any of them at pleasure.

All books or other property given, granted, conveyed, donated, devised, or bequeathed to, or purchased by, such library shall vest in, and be held in the name of, such school district. Every library and reading-room established hereunder shall be free to the use of the inhabitants of the school district, subject to such reasonable regulations as the directors may adopt.

When so established, no such library shall be abandoned without a two-thirds majority vote of the electors cast at any annual or special school meeting called for the purpose.

Subd. 2. Notwithstanding subdivision 1, if the library building of a library established pursuant to this section has been erected with funds acquired by gift or donation, a school board may, if authorized by the vote of a majority of all members of the school board and the vote of a majority of all members of the governing body of the city, permanently transfer the responsibility for maintaining the library to the city.

Amended by Laws 1980, c. 609, art. 6, § 33, eff. April 25, 1980.

SCHOOL LIBRARIES
(Minnesota Statutes Annotated, 1982, s.134.01, 134.02, 134.04, 134.06.)

134.01 Maintenance

Every school district may provide library facilities as part of its school equipment according to the standards of the state board of education. St.1927, § 3015.

134.02 Funds

The school board of any district may vote sufficient funds for the maintenance of the school library, appoint a librarian, and make rules for the use and management of the library. St.1927, § 3016.

134.04 State department of education to furnish list of books

The state department of education shall from time to time prepare and amend a list of books suitable for school libraries, including dictionaries and other books of reference, histories and works of biography, literature, political economy, agriculture, travel, and science. St.1927, § 3018.

134.06 School and city libraries may combine

Any school board may contract with the board of any approved county or city library to become a branch of this public library and to receive therefrom library books suited to the needs of the pupils in the school and for the community according to the standards established in the rules of the state board of education. In the event of a contract between the school board and the public library board, the school board may place in the public library such books belonging to the school library as may be more useful in the public library for students and the community and the school board shall annually pay to the library board the school library book fund and the state library aid to which such school district is entitled. All books purchased by this public library from funds provided by the school district or state school library aid shall be selected from the state list for school libraries.

In the event of the making of such contract, a librarian shall be employed who meets the standards of the state board of education and the school board and the library board may jointly employ such librarian, who may spend her time partly in the school and partly in the library.

Amended by Laws 1973, c. 123, art. 5, § 7.

COUNTY LAW LIBRARIES
(Minnesota Statutes Annotated, 1982, s.140.34-140.40, 140.401, 140.421-140.423, 140.431, 140.44-140.47.)

140.34. Establishment of county law library

Any county may establish a county law library wherever sessions of court are required to be held by law upon the filing of an order by the judge of the county or county municipal court or by a judge of the judicial district in which the county is situated with the clerk of court of the county.
Amended by Laws 1982, c. 576, § 2, eff. March 23, 1982.

140.35. Who may use

Under proper regulations of the board of trustees the use of the library shall be free to the judges of the state, state officials, judges of the district, municipal, county, conciliation and probate courts of the county, city and county officials, members of the bar, and inhabitants of the county.
Amended by Laws 1982, c. 576, § 3, eff. March 23, 1982.

140.36. Board of trustees; composition

Subdivision 1. Trustees. The management of any library established shall be under a board of three, five or seven trustees, who shall serve without compensation.

A board of three trustees shall consist of:

(1) A judge of the district or county or county municipal court appointed by the chief judge of the judicial district.

(2) A member of the county board selected by it at its next regular meeting after the order establishing the library is filed and thereafter at the annual election of officers.

(3) One attorney admitted to the practice of law, residing in the county and selected by the county attorney.

When the board consists of five trustees, the additional members shall be a judge appointed by the chief judge of the judicial district and an additional attorney admitted to the practice of law, residing in the county and selected by the county attorney. When the board consists of seven trustees, the additional members shall be provided for in the bylaws.

Subd. 2. Membership changes. The bylaws shall state the procedure by which a board of trustees may increase or decrease its membership.

Subd. 3. Joint law library. Wherever a joint law library is established by order, or wherever two or more law libraries are maintained within one county, the board of trustees shall consist of a judge of the district or his designee, one judge from each county included in the order or from each district within a single county, or his designee, one member of the board of county commissioners from each county included in the order or from each district within a single county, to be selected by the county board at its annual election of officers, and one attorney admitted to the practice of law, residing in each county included in the order or in each district within a single county, to be selected by the county attorney of each county or district within the county.

Amended by Laws 1982, c. 576, § 4, eff. March 23, 1982.

140.37. Board of trustees, meetings; term of office

The trustees shall meet immediately after their selection and the board shall hold annual meetings thereafter. At each meeting it shall elect one of its members president and another member or the librarian secretary. The secretary shall act as the staff of the board and shall attend all meetings and prepare and distribute all agenda matters.

All members of the board of law library trustees shall hold office for a term to be set in the bylaws.

Amended by Laws 1982, c. 576, § 5, eff. March 23, 1982.

140.38. Bylaws and regulations; powers; title to remain in county

The board of trustees shall adopt bylaws and regulations for the conduct of its business and the government of the library and file them, along with all other records, minutes of meetings and other documents relating to the governance of the library with the clerk of the court.

It shall have powers necessary for the governance and maintenance of the library, including, but not limited to the power to:

(1) Amend its bylaws and regulations;

(2) On behalf of the county accept any gift, grant, devise, or bequest or the loan of books or property for the library, and carry out the conditions thereof;

(3) Purchase or lease books or library facilities with money from the county law library fund;

(4) Sell or exchange items of property of the library.

The title to the library and its property is in the county establishing the library.

Amended by Laws 1982, c. 576, § 6, eff. March 23, 1982.

140.39. Report to county auditor

The county auditor shall file with the board of trustees an annual report containing a detailed statement of the receipts and disbursements of the library for the preceding year. The board of trustees shall file an inventory with the county auditor showing the property belonging to the library or loaned or leased to the library.

Amended by Laws 1982, c. 576, § 7, eff. March 23, 1982.

140.40. Quarters

The county board shall provide suitable quarters within the courthouse for the use of the library, and shall also provide light, heat, janitor service and other necessary expenses of maintaining the library.

Amended by Laws 1982, c. 576, § 8, eff. March 23, 1982.

140.401. Librarian

In Hennepin and Ramsey Counties the board of trustees shall appoint a librarian and necessary assistants and clerical help, and fix their compensation. In all other counties, where a librarian is not employed by the county, the board of trustees may appoint a librarian and necessary assistants and clerical help and, with the approval of the county board, fix their compensation. In all counties where services cannot be provided by the Minnesota state law library, the board of trustees may contract with regional library systems for services.

Added by Laws 1982, c. 576, § 9, eff. March 23, 1982.

140.421.   Hennepin and Ramsey Counties; fees for law libraries

Subdivision 1.   Civil actions.   In Hennepin and Ramsey Counties, the district administrator or his designee shall collect in each civil suit, action or proceeding filed in the district, municipal and conciliation courts of the district, in the manner in which other fees are collected, a law library fee from:

(a) The plaintiff, petitioner or other person instituting the suit, action or proceeding, at the time of the filing of the first paper; and

(b) Each defendant, respondent, intervenor or other party who appears, either separately or jointly, to be collected at the time of the filing of the first paper by the defendant, respondent, intervenor or other party, or at the time when his appearance is entered in the case.

Subd. 2.   Probate proceedings.   The district administrator or his designee shall collect a law library fee from the petitioner instituting proceedings for supervised and unsupervised guardianship, conservatorship, descent, formal and informal probate, trusts and summary assignments at the time of the filing of the petition.   The disbursement shall be an item of expense of administration of the estate, entitling the petitioner to reimbursement out of the estate.

Subd. 3.   Setting fees.   The law library board of trustees shall, with the approval of the board of commissioners, set the amount of the law library fee in the district, probate, municipal and conciliation courts of the judicial district.   All law library fees shall be published in the state register.

Added by Laws 1982, c. 576, § 10, eff. March 23, 1982.

140.422.   Library fees collected in all other counties

Subdivision 1.   Civil fee assessment.   In counties other than Hennepin and Ramsey, the clerk of court shall collect in each civil suit, action or proceeding filed in the district, county or county municipal and conciliation courts of the county, in the manner in which other fees are collected, a law library fee from:

(a) The plaintiff, petitioner or other person instituting the suit, action or proceeding, at the time of the filing of the first paper; and

(b) Each defendant, respondent, intervenor or other party who appears, either separately or jointly, to be collected at the time of the filing of the first paper by the defendant, respondent, intervenor or other party, or at the time when his appearance is entered in the case.

Subd. 2.   Probate proceedings.   The judge of the probate court or the registrar of probate or the clerk of court shall collect a law library fee from the petitioner instituting proceedings for supervised and unsupervised guardianship, conservatorship, descent, formal and informal probate, trusts and summary assignments at the time of the filing of the petition.   The disbursement shall be an item of administration of the estate, entitling the petitioner to reimbursement out of the estate.

Subd. 3.   Criminal convictions; fee assessment.   The judge of district or county or county municipal court may, upon the recommendation of the board of trustees and by standing order, include in the costs or disbursements assessed against a defendant convicted in the district or county or county municipal court of the violation of any statute or municipal ordinance, in all criminal prosecutions in which, upon conviction, the defendant may be subject to the payment of the costs or disbursements in addition to a fine or other penalty a county law library fee.   The item of costs or disbursements may not be assessed for any offense committed prior to the establishment of the county law library.

Subd. 4.   Setting fees.   The law library board of trustees shall, with the approval of the board of commissioners, set the amount of the law library fee for civil and criminal matters in the district, county or county municipal and conciliation courts of the county. The fee shall be initially set on July 1, 1982.   Commencing with July 1, 1983, the law library fee shall be set every two years and shall remain in effect during that time. All law library fees shall be published in the state register.

Added by Laws 1982, c. 576, § 11, eff. March 23, 1982.

140.423. Limitations

The provisions of sections 140.421 and 140.422 shall not apply to actions or proceedings commenced by the state, the county or any municipality, to garnishment proceedings, to the filing of transcripts, to compensation awards, to proceedings under the Minnesota reciprocal enforcement of support act or to complaints in intervention in receivership proceedings.

Added by Laws 1982, c. 576, § 12, eff. March 23, 1982.

140.431. Taxable as costs

The law library fee is a cost in the action and taxable as such, and is to be allotted for the support of the library.

Added by Laws 1982, c. 576, § 13, eff. March 23, 1982.

140.44. Deposits with county treasurer; county auditor

These fees shall be paid to the county treasurer or county auditor, who shall give his receipt therefor. The county treasurer or county auditor may disburse these funds and any other money belonging to this board only at the direction of the board of trustees.

Amended by Laws 1982, c. 576, § 14, eff. March 23, 1982.

140.45. Existing libraries; joint law libraries

By July 1, 1983, all county law libraries shall come under the provisions of sections 140.34 to 140.46.

Two or more counties may unite in the establishment of a joint law library.

Amended by Laws 1982, c. 576, § 15, eff. March 23, 1982.

140.46. Annual appropriation by county board

The county board may in its discretion, provide for additional support and maintenance of the county law library out of county funds.

Amended by Laws 1982, c. 576, § 16, eff. March 23, 1982.

140.47. State law librarian to assist

The state law librarian, under the guidance of the supreme court, shall advise and assist in the operation and maintenance of the county law libraries.

Added by Laws 1982, c. 576, § 17, eff. March 23, 1982.

Minnesota library laws are reprinted from MINNESOTA STATUTES ANNOTATED published by West Publishing Co., St. Paul, Minnesota.

MISSISSIPPI

STATE LIBRARY
(Mississippi Code Annotated, 1982, s.39-1-1 to 39-1-35.)

§ 39–1–1. State library board.

The state library shall be under the supervision and control of a state library board, consisting of the governor of the state, the chief justice of the supreme court, the presiding justice of the other division of the supreme court, the attorney general of the state, and the state superintendent of public education. The governor shall be chairman of the board and in his absence the chief justice shall be acting chairman. Any three or more of the members of the board shall form a quorum for the transaction of business.

SOURCES: Codes, 1942, § 9037; Laws, 1940, ch. 135.

§ 39–1–3. Librarian.

There shall be a state librarian, to be elected as provided by the constitution, whose term of office shall be four years. He shall, before entering upon the discharge of the duties of his office, take the oath prescribed by section two hundred and sixty-eight of the constitution, and shall give bond with sufficient sureties, payable to the state, to be approved by the governor, in the penalty of five thousand dollars, and with such conditions as the board may prescribe. The bond shall be filed in the office of the secretary of state.

SOURCES: Codes, 1942, § 9038; Laws, 1940, ch. 135.

§ 39–1–5. Open hours.

The state library shall be open for the public Monday through

Friday of each week for eight hours each day. However, when the legislature is in session the state library shall remain open so long as either house is in session.

SOURCES: Codes, 1942, § 9039; Laws, 1940, ch. 135; 1958, ch. 483; 1964, ch. 542, § 8, eff from and after 10 days after passage (approved June 11, 1964).

§ 39-1-7. Assistant librarian.

The state librarian, with the approval of the governor, shall appoint a suitable and competent person to be assistant librarian. Said assistant shall have and possess all of the qualifications required by law of the state librarian, and shall have power and authority under the direction and supervision of the state librarian, to perform all the duties required of that officer, and shall be liable to all pains and penalties to which the state librarian is liable. The state librarian may discharge such assistant at pleasure and appoint another as aforesaid.

SOURCES: Codes, 1942, § 9040; Laws, 1940, ch. 135.

§ 39-1-9. Custody of property; arrangement.

The state librarian shall have charge of and faithfully keep and preserve all the books, maps, charts, astronomical instruments, manuscripts, and all other property of the state pertaining to the state library, or otherwise intrusted to his charge and shall assign and place the same in the proper alcoves and places for convenient access, examination and reference, and note the same in similar order in the catalogue or list, with all new receipts by exchange, purchase, or otherwise.

SOURCES: Codes, 1942, § 9041; Laws, 1940, ch. 135.

§ 39-1-11. Catalogue.

The state librarian shall from time to time, under the inspection and approval of the board, make out and keep a catalogue of the books, under the appropriate heads, alphabetically. As often as the board deems necessary he shall have one hundred copies of such catalogue printed for reference and distribution, and the convenience of persons desiring to examine the books in the library.

SOURCES: Codes, 1942, § 9042; Laws, 1940, ch. 135.

§ 39-1-13. Tables, chairs, etc., to be provided.

The state librarian shall, under the direction of the board, provide suitable tables, chairs, pens, ink and paper for the use of persons desiring to examine, take notes or copy from the books of the library, and shall attend, to hand them or place on the table, the books required.

SOURCES: Codes, 1942, § 9043; Laws, 1940, ch. 135.

§ 39–1–15. Care of library; privacy.

The state librarian shall at all times keep the rooms belonging to the library clean and properly ventilated, and, at the proper season, well warmed, and have them provided with tables, pen, ink, and paper, and so arranged for the examination and study of the books in the library that persons can make use of the same without interruption from transient visitors. He shall keep the main library room clean, properly ventilated and warmed.

SOURCES: Codes, 1942, § 9044; Laws, 1940, ch. 135.

§ 39–1–17. Board to supervise librarian.

The state librarian shall be under the supervision and control of the state library board.

SOURCES: Codes, 1942, § 9045; Laws, 1940, ch. 135.

§ 39–1–19. Regulations; return of borrowed books; penalties.

The board shall make all necessary by-laws and regulations for the government of the library, and for the accommodation and arrangement of the books, and concerning the taking of books out of the library, and may prescribe penalties for a violation thereof. A person taking any book from the library and not returning it when required shall be liable to pay double the value of the volume, or, if it be a volume of work consisting of several volumes, then double the value of the whole work. Penalties for a violation of the provisions of this chapter, or of the said by-laws and regulations, may be recovered by action in the name of the state, before any court having jurisdiction and such penalties shall be for the use of the library.

SOURCES: Codes, 1942, § 9046; Laws, 1940, ch. 135.

§ 39–1–21. Secretary of the board; records.

The state librarian shall be secretary of the board, and shall keep a record of all its proceedings. He shall keep and record an alphabetical list of all books purchased or acquired, with the prices of each, and the date of the acquisition. He shall also keep a blank book, in which he shall charge every person entitled to take books from the library with every book taken by him, and shall note therein the return of the same.

SOURCES: Codes, 1942, § 9047; Laws, 1940, ch. 135.

§ 39–1–23. Books, how taken from library.

A book belonging to the state library shall not be taken from the state capitol, except as provided by the board.

SOURCES: Codes, 1942, § 9048; Laws, 1940, ch. 135.

§ 39–1–25. Books taken by judges or officials.

Judges of the supreme court and state officers may take books from the library to the offices in the capitol, for the necessary examination of any subject, and shall return such book immediately after the necessary examination shall have been made.

SOURCES: Codes, 1942, § 9049; Laws, 1940, ch. 135.

§ 39–1–27. Books taken by attorneys.

Attorneys and solicitors of the supreme court may, on the written order of one of the judges thereof, be allowed, upon giving the proper receipt, to take the books necessary for use in a pending case to the supreme court room.

SOURCES: Codes, 1942, § 9050; Laws, 1940, ch. 135.

§ 39–1–29. Books taken by legislators.

Members of the legislature may take books for use in either house and in committees, upon signing the proper receipt and engagement to be responsible for the safe return of the same.

SOURCES: Codes, 1942, § 9051; Laws, 1940, ch. 135.

§ 39–1–31. Purchase of books.

Under the approval and direction of the board, the state librarian shall expend all appropriations made by the legislature and other moneys belonging to the library in the purchase of such books as the board may order, and shall, with the board's approval, upon the warrant of the auditor, draw any moneys from the treasury appropriated or belonging to the library for that purpose.

SOURCES: Codes, 1942, § 9052; Laws, 1940, ch. 135.

§ 39–1–33. Department reports deposited in library.

All state officers, departments, commissions and committees, bureaus and boards, issuing biennial, annual, or special reports of any nature, where such reports are printed, typewritten or mimeographed, shall deposit with the Mississippi state library, for general reference use in said library, at least two copies of each of such printed, typewritten or mimeographed reports. Such deposits to be made immediately after issuance of same.

The secretary of the senate and the clerk of the house shall, after the adjournment of each session of the legislature, deposit in the state library at least two copies of all special legislative committee reports, when such reports shall have been printed, typewritten or mimeographed.

The secretary of state shall, immediately after the passage of this section, give written notice to the head of each state department, committee, commission, bureau and board directing their attention to this section and the necessity of their compliance therewith.

SOURCES: Codes, 1942, § 9053; Laws, 1938, ch. 164.

§ 39–1–35. Legislative reference bureau.

There is hereby created a legislative reference bureau, for the use of the members of the legislature, the governor, and the various departments, institutions and agencies of this state, as well as for a limited service for such citizens of this state as may desire to avail themselves of its reference facilities. The legislative reference bureau shall be under the joint jurisdiction of the house management committee and the senate contingent expense committee of the legislature.

The purpose of the said legislative reference bureau shall be:

(a) To assist the legislature of this state in the proper performance of its constitutional functions by providing its members with impartial and accurate information and reports concerning the legislative problems which come before them, and by providing digests showing the practices of other states and of foreign nations in dealing with similar problems;

(b) To secure information for the legislators of this state by cooperating with the legislative reference services in other states, and with the interstate reference bureau maintained by the American legislators' association and by the council of state governments;

(c) To furnish the members of the legislature of this state, copies of the legislation of other states, uniform laws, model bills, textbooks on the preparation of legislative measures, and such other information and material as may be of value to them in the preparation of bills for introduction into the legislature of this state.

The legislative reference bureau shall have a director, who shall be hired jointly by the house management committee and the senate contingent expense committee, and the duties of the director shall be prescribed jointly by the house management committee and the senate contingent expense committee.

The legislative reference bureau shall be maintained out of the contingent funds of each house of the legislature, with an equal amount to be contributed by each house.

SOURCES: Laws, 1980, ch. 452, eff from and after July 1, 1980.

STATE LIBRARY COMMISSION
(Mississippi Code Annotated, 1982, s.39-3-101 to 39-3-111.)

§ 39–3–101. Mississippi Library Commission created; term of office.

There is hereby created a board of commissioners of the Mississippi Library Commission to be composed of five members appointed by the governor with overlapping terms, the members of the first board to be appointed one for one year, one for two years, one for three years, one for four years, one for five years, and their successors each to be appointed for five year terms, each member to serve until his successor is appointed. Two members shall be appointed by the governor from the state at large. Two members shall be appointed by the governor from a list of not less than six names submitted by the Mississippi library association, one of whom shall be a librarian who is a graduate of a library school accredited by the American Library Association and actively engaged in full time library work at the time of the appointment and one of whom shall be, at time of the appointment, a member of a legally organized board of trustees of a Mississippi free public library; and one member shall be the president of the Mississippi Federation of Women's Clubs, or a member of said federation recommended by her; and which federation member shall, when appointed, serve a full term as herein provided for members to serve under a staggered term basis, and the successor to the federation member shall be the president of the federation then serving, or a member of the federation recommended by her, when the term of the federation member shall expire; and after the appointment of a federation member to the board, and when her term as a member thereof shall expire, each succeeding member of the federation who becomes a member of the board shall serve a full term under the provisions of this article. Vacancies created by resignation shall be filled by appointment for the unexpired term.

SOURCES: Codes, 1942, § 6210-01; Laws, 1950, ch. 363, §§ 1, 2, eff from and after June 30, 1950.

§ 39–3–103. First meeting.

Within thirty days after the selection and appointment of the first board of commissioners the members shall meet at the headquarters of the Mississippi Library Commission in Jackson, Mississippi, and organize, setting up such policies as are deemed necessary and not inconsistent with this article. They shall elect annually from their membership a chairman and a secretary.

SOURCES: Codes, 1942, § 6210-02; Laws, 1950, ch. 363, § 3, eff from and after June 30, 1950.

§ 39-3-105.   Director to be elected; qualifications.

(1) The board of library commissioners shall elect a director whose term of office shall be for a period of four years, unless, for good cause shown, the board of library commissioners removes said director.

(2) The director shall be chosen outside the membership of the board of library commissioners, and shall be a trained, experienced librarian holding a degree from a college or university of recognized standing. The director shall have completed the required course covered in a school of library service accredited by the American Library Association and shall have had at least two years' experience as an administrative librarian or director of a state or public library. The director shall keep an accurate record of all accounts and financial transactions of the board, shall have charge of organizing new libraries and directing library development in the state, so as to give and furnish every citizen and resident of the state free library service of the highest quality consistent with modern methods and as may be justified by financial and economic conditions, and shall have all general administrative duties incident to carrying on the work of the Mississippi Library Commission. All necessary and actual traveling expense incurred by the members of the Mississippi Library Commission, and by the director or any member of the staff, acting under the authority and direction of the board of commissioners, while on business for the Mississippi Library Commission, shall be paid from the funds appropriated and made available for use, maintenance and operation of the Mississippi Library Commission. In addition to the director, the board of library commissioners may employ, upon recommendations of the director, such other persons as may be deemed necessary to carry out the purposes of this article.

SOURCES: Codes, 1942, § 6210-03; Laws, 1950, ch. 363, §§ 4, 5, eff from and after June 30, 1950.

§ 39-3-107.   Duties of commission.

The Mississippi Library Commission, when asked, shall give

advice to all schools, public and other libraries, and to all communities which may propose to establish them, as to the best means of establishing and maintaining such libraries, the selection of books, cataloging, and other details of library management. It may also purchase and operate traveling libraries, and circulate such traveling libraries within the state among communities, libraries, schools, colleges, universities, library associations, study clubs, charitable and penal institutions free of cost, except for transportation, and establish county and regional libraries and use any funds, separate and apart from the general library commission funds, which might come into its custody from any source, for such purpose, and for the purpose of establishing, stimulating, increasing, improving and equalizing library service in the various counties within the state, under such rules for safekeeping, preservation, care, handling of the books and allocation of the funds as may be fixed by the commission. It may publish such lists and circulars of information as it shall deem necessary, and it may also conduct a summer school of library instruction and a clearing house for periodicals for free gifts to local libraries. The commission shall each year obtain from all libraries in the state reports showing the condition, growth, development and manner of conducting such libraries together with such other facts and statistics regarding the same as may be deemed of public interest by the commission, and it shall be the duty of the board of the Mississippi Library Commission to make an annual report to the legislature of the facts of public interest and value in relation to the work of the commission.

SOURCES: Codes, 1930, § 5391; 1942, §§ 6210-04, 6213; Laws, 1926, ch. 180; 1940, ch. 143; 1950, ch. 363, § 6; 1970, ch. 358, § 1, ch. 359, § 1, eff from and after July 1, 1970.

§ 39–3–109. How funds drawn.

The board of commissioners of the Mississippi Library Commission may from time to time as needed draw an order signed by the director and the chairman in favor of any party to whom money is due stating in such order what the money is to be used for, and, upon presentation of such order, the state auditor shall draw his warrant upon the state treasurer for the amount therefor not to exceed the amount of the appropriation for the purposes of the Mississippi Library Commission.

SOURCES: Codes, 1942, § 6210-05; Laws, 1950, ch. 363, § 7, eff from and after June 30, 1950.

§ 39–3–111. Gifts, acceptance of.

The board of commissioners of the Mississippi Library Commission may accept in the name of the state gifts of money, real estate, books, periodicals, or other property for the purpose of promoting the work of the Mississippi Library Commission, and may accept and administer any funds which might be provided by the federal government for library purposes.

SOURCES: Codes, 1942, § 6210-06; Laws, 1950, ch. 363, § 8, eff from and after June 30, 1950.

INTERSTATE LIBRARY COMPACT
(Mississippi Code Annotated, 1982, s.39-3-201 to 39-3-211.)

§ 39-3-201. Entry into and contents of compact.

The Interstate Library Compact is hereby enacted into law and entered into by this state with all states legally joining therein in the form substantially as follows:

INTERSTATE LIBRARY COMPACT

Article I. Policy and Purpose

Because the desire for the services provided by libraries transcends governmental boundaries and can most effectively be satisfied by giving such services to communities and people regardless of jurisdictional lines, it is the policy of the states party to this compact to cooperate and share their responsibilities; to authorize cooperation and sharing with respect to those types of library facilities and services which can be more economically or efficiently developed and maintained on a cooperative basis, and to authorize cooperation and sharing among localities, states and others in providing joint or cooperative library services in areas where the distribution of population or of existing and potential library resources make the provision of library service on an interstate basis the most effective way of providing adequate and efficient service.

Article II. Definitions

As used in this compact:

(a) "Public library agency" means any unit or agency of local or state government operating or having power to operate a library.

(b) "Private library agency" means any nongovernmental entity which operates or assumes a legal obligation to operate a library.

(c) "Library agreement" means a contract establishing an interstate library district pursuant to this compact or providing for the joint or cooperative furnishing of library services.

Article III. Interstate Library Districts

(a) Any one or more public library agencies in a party state in cooperation with any public library agency or agencies in one or more other party states may establish and maintain an interstate library district. Subject to the provisions of this compact and any other laws of the party states which pursuant hereto remain applicable, such district may establish, maintain and operate some or all of the library facilities and services for the area concerned in accordance with the terms of a library agreement therefor. Any private library agency or agencies within an interstate library district may cooperate therewith, assume duties, responsibilities and obligations thereto, and receive benefits therefrom as provided in any library agreement to which such agency or agencies become party.

(b) Within an interstate library district, and as provided by a library agreement, the performance of library functions may be undertaken on a joint or cooperative basis or may be undertaken by means of one or more arrangements between or among public or private library agencies for the extension of library privileges to the use of facilities or services operated or rendered by one or more of the individual library agencies.

(c) If a library agreement provides for joint establishment, maintenance or operation of library facilities or services by an interstate library district, such district shall have power to do any one or more of the following in accordance with such library agreement:

1. Undertake, administer and participate in programs or arrangements for securing, lending or servicing of books and other publications, any other materials suitable to be kept or made available by libraries, library equipment or for the dissemination of information about libraries, the value and significance of particular items therein, and the use thereof.

2. Accept for any of its purposes under this compact any and all donations, and grants of money, equipment, supplies, materials, and services, (conditional or otherwise) from any state or the United States or any subdivision or agency thereof, or interstate agency, or from any institution, person, firm or corporation, and receive, utilize and dispose of the same.

3. Operate mobile library units or equipment for the purpose of rendering bookmobile service within the district.

4. Employ professional, technical, clerical, and other personnel, and fix terms of employment, compensation and other appropriate benefits; and where desirable, provide for the inservice training of such personnel.

5. Acquire, hold, and dispose of any real or personal property or any interest or interests therein as may be appropriate to the rendering of library service.

6. Construct, maintain and operate a library, including any appropriate branches thereof.

7. Do such other things as may be incidental to or appropriate for the carrying out of any of the foregoing powers.

Article IV. Interstate Library Districts, Governing Board

(a) An interstate library district which establishes, maintains or operates any facilities or services in its own right shall have a governing board which shall direct the affairs of the district and act for it in all matters relating to its business. Each participating public library agency in the district shall be represented on the governing board which shall be organized and conduct its business in accordance with provision therefor in the library agreement. But in no event shall a governing board meet less often than twice a year.

(b) Any private library agency or agencies party to a library agreement establishing an interstate library district may be represented on or advise with the governing board of the district in such manner as the library agreement may provide.

Article V. State Library Agency Cooperation

Any two or more state library agencies of two or more of the party states may undertake and conduct joint or cooperative library programs, render joint or cooperative library services, and enter into and perform arrangements for the cooperative or joint acquisition, use, housing and disposition of items or collections of materials which, by reason of expense, rarity, specialized nature, or infrequency of demand therefor would be appropriate for central collection and shared use. Any such programs, services or arrangements may include provision for the exercise on a cooperative or joint basis of any power exercisable by an interstate library district and an agreement embodying any such program, service or arrangement shall contain provisions covering the subjects detailed in Article VI of this compact for interstate library agreements.

Article VI. Library Agreement

(a) In order to provide for any joint or cooperative undertaking pursuant to this compact, public and private library agencies may enter into library agreements. Any agreement executed pursuant to the provisions of this compact shall, as among the parties to the agreement:

1. Detail the specific nature of the services, programs, facilities,

arrangements or properties to which it is applicable.

2. Provide for the allocation of costs and other financial responsibilities.

3. Specify the respective rights, duties, obligations and liabilities of the parties.

4. Set forth the terms and conditions for duration, renewal, termination, abrogation, disposal of joint or common property, if any, and all other matters which may be appropriate to the proper effectuation and performance of the agreement.

(b) No public or private library agency shall undertake to exercise itself, or jointly with any other library agency, by means of a library agreement any power prohibited to such agency by the constitution or statutes of its state.

(c) No library agreement shall become effective until filed with the compact administrator of each state involved, and approved in accordance with Article VII of this compact.

Article VII. Approval of Library Agreements

(a) Every library agreement made pursuant to this compact shall, prior to and as a condition precedent to its entry into force, be submitted to the attorney general of each state in which a public library agency party thereto is situated, who shall determine whether the agreement is in proper form and compatible with the laws of his state. The attorneys general shall approve any agreement submitted to them unless they shall find that it does not meet the conditions set forth herein and shall detail in writing addressed to the governing bodies of the public library agencies concerned the specific respects in which the proposed agreement fails to meet the requirements of law. Failure to disapprove an agreement submitted hereunder within ninety days of its submission shall constitute approval thereof.

(b) In the event that a library agreement made pursuant to this compact shall deal in whole or in part with the provision of services or facilities with regard to which an officer or agency of the state government has constitutional or statutory powers of control, the agreement shall, as a condition precedent to its entry into force, be submitted to the state officer or agency having such power of control and shall be approved or disapproved by him or it as to all matters within his or its jurisdiction in the same manner and subject to the same requirements governing the action of the attorneys general pursuant to paragraph (a) of this article. This requirement of submission and approval shall be in addition to and not in substitution for the requirement of submission to and approval by the attorneys general.

Article VIII. Other Laws Applicable

Nothing in this compact or in any library agreement shall be construed to supersede, alter or otherwise impair any obligation imposed on any library by otherwise applicable law, nor to authorize the transfer or disposition of any property held in trust by a library agency in a manner contrary to the terms of such trust.

Article IX. Appropriations and Aid

(a) Any public library agency party to a library agreement may appropriate funds to the interstate library district established thereby in the same manner and to the same extent as to a library wholly maintained by it and, subject to the laws of the state in which such public library agency is situated, may pledge its credit in support of an interstate library district established by the agreement.

(b) Subject to the provisions of the library agreement pursuant to which it functions and the laws of the states in which such district is situated, an interstate library district may claim and receive any state and federal aid which may be available to library agencies.

Article X. Compact Administrator

Each state shall designate a compact administrator with whom copies of all library agreements to which his state or any public library agency thereof is party shall be filed. The administrator shall have such other powers as may be conferred upon him by the laws of his state and may consult and cooperate with the compact administrators of other party states and take such steps as may effectuate the purposes of this compact. If the laws of a party state so provide, such state may designate one or more deputy compact administrators in addition to its compact administrator.

Article XI. Entry Into Force and Withdrawal

(a) This compact shall enter into force and effect immediately upon its enactment into law by any two states. Thereafter, it shall enter into force and effect as to any other state upon the enactment thereof by such state.

(b) This compact shall continue in force with respect to a party state and remain binding upon such state until six months after such state has given notice to each other party state of the repeal thereof. Such withdrawal shall not be construed to relieve any party to a library agreement entered into pursuant to this compact from any obligation of that agreement prior to the end of its duration as provided therein.

Article XII. Construction and Severability

This compact shall be liberally construed so as effectuate the purposes thereof. The provisions of this compact shall be severable and if any phrase, clause, sentence or provision of this compact is declared to be contrary to the constitution of any party state or of the United States or the applicability thereof to any government, agency, person or circumstance is held invalid, the validity of the remainder of this compact and the applicability thereof to any government, agency, person or circumstance shall not be affected thereby. If this compact shall be held contrary to the constitution of any state party thereto, the compact shall remain in full force and effect as to the remaining states and in full force and effect as to the state affected as to all severable matters.

SOURCES: Codes, 1942, § 6209-21; Laws, 1970, ch. 459, § 1, eff from and after passage (approved April 6, 1970).

§ 39-3-203. Agreements for construction or maintenance of interstate libraries; compliance with other governing laws.

No county, municipality, or other political subdivision of this state shall be party to a library agreement which provides for the construction or maintenance of a library pursuant to Article III, subdivision (c) 7 of the compact, nor pledge its credit in support of such a library, or contribute to the capital financing thereof, except after compliance with any laws applicable to such counties, municipalities, or other political subdivisions relating to or governing capital outlaws and the pledging of credit.

SOURCES: Codes, 1942, § 6209-22; Laws, 1970, ch. 459, § 2, eff from and after passage (approved April 6, 1970).

§ 39-3-205. State library agency defined.

As used in the compact, "state library agency" with reference to this state, means the Mississippi Library Commission.

SOURCES: Codes, 1942, § 6209-23; Laws, 1970, ch. 459, § 3, eff from and after passage (approved April 6, 1970).

§ 39-3-207. District partly within state; eligibility for state and federal aid.

An interstate library district lying partly within this state may claim and be entitled to receive state aid in support of any of its functions to the same extent and in the same manner as such functions are eligible for support when carried on by entities wholly within this state. For the purposes of computing and apportioning state aid to an interstate library district, this state will consider that portion of the area which lies within this state as an independent entity for the performance of the aided function or functions and compute and apportion the aid accordingly. Subject to any applicable laws of this state, such a district also may apply for and be entitled to receive any federal aid for which it may be eligible.

SOURCES: Codes, 1942, § 6209-24; Laws, 1970, ch. 459, § 4, eff from and after passage (approved April 6, 1970).

§ 39–3–209. Compact administrator and deputy administrators.

The director of the Mississippi Library Commission shall be the compact administrator pursuant to Article X of the compact. The director of the Mississippi Library Commission may appoint one or more deputy compact administrators pursuant to said article.

SOURCES: Codes, 1942, § 6209-25; Laws, 1970, ch. 459, § 5, eff from and after passage (approved April 6, 1970).

§ 39–3–211. Notices in event of withdrawal from compact.

In the event of withdrawal from the compact the governor shall send and receive any notices required by Article XI(b) of the compact.

SOURCES: Codes, 1942, § 6209-26; Laws, 1970, ch. 459, § 6, eff from and after passage (approved April 6, 1970).

DEPARTMENT OF ARCHIVES AND HISTORY
(Mississippi Code Annotated, 1982, s.39-5-1 to 39-5-11
39-8.)

§ 39–5–1. Department of archives and history—objects and purposes.

There shall be for the State of Mississippi a department of archives and history located in the state capitol in apartments set aside for its use by the governor. The objects and purposes of the department are the care and custody of official archives, the collecting of materials bearing upon the history of the state and of the territory included therein, from the earliest times, the editing of official records and other historical material, the diffusion of knowledge in reference to the history and resources of this state, the preparation and publication of annual reports, the encouragement of historical work and research and the performance of such other acts and requirements as may be enjoined by law.

SOURCES: Codes, 1906, § 1633; Hemingway's 1917, § 3447; 1930, § 3626; 1942, § 6180.

§ 39-5-3. Board of trustees to control department.

The department of archives and history shall be under the control of a board of nine trustees. The board shall have the power and authority to fill all vacancies occurring therein, whether by expiration of term of service or by death or resignation, but the names of all newly elected members shall be communicated to the next ensuing session of the state senate for confirmation, and in case it shall reject any of the said newly elected trustees it shall proceed forthwith to fill the vacancy or vacancies by an election. All trustees chosen to succeed the present members or their successors shall serve for a term of six years. The board of trustees shall hold at the state capitol at least one regular meeting during the year, and as many special meetings as may be necessary, and at said meetings five members shall constitute a quorum. The director of the department of archives and history, hereinafter provided, shall be secretary of the board. The trustees shall receive no compensation for their services other than the amount of their necessary expenses actually paid out while in attendance on the meetings of the board or the business of the department. The board is empowered to adopt rules for its own government and for the government of the department, to elect and fix the compensation of a director not to exceed the maximum set by the legislature, and other officials or employees, and to do and perform such other acts and things as may be necessary to carry out the true intent and purposes of this chapter.

SOURCES: Codes, 1906, § 1634; Hemingway's 1917, § 3448; 1930, § 3627; 1942, § 6181; Laws, 1960, ch. 237; 1966, ch. 445, § 16, eff from and after July 1, 1966.

§ 39-5-5. Additional powers and duties of department.

The duties and powers of the board of trustees of the department of archives and history shall include, in addition to other duties and powers granted or prescribed by law, the following:

(a) To determine the location of places of historical interest within the state;

(b) To make a survey of buildings of all types throughout the state which are in danger of destruction, without proper care, and which in the opinion of the board of trustees should be preserved for historical purposes;

(c) To contact the proper authorities of the United States national cemeteries and military parks to determine whether or not the record of Mississippi troops is adequately commemorated;

(d) To acquire, preserve, restore or operate any real or personal property deemed significant for historical, architectural, archeological or cultural reasons, to expend funds for such purposes, to enter into contracts or agreements with any agency of the United States or any person, firm, corporation or association for such purposes and to do any and all things which may be necessary or desirable to carry out such purposes;

(e) To participate with any agency of the United States, any other governmental agency or any person, firm, corporation, association or group in mutual or cooperative programs or projects within the duties and powers of the board of trustees; and

(f) To accept grants or donations of money or property, real or personal, from any agency of the United States, any other governmental agency or any person, firm, corporation, association or group. However, the board of trustees shall not be required, except by specific act of the legislature, to accept any property without its consent.

SOURCES: Laws, 1979, ch. 438, § 13, eff from and after February 1, 1980.

§ 39–5–7. Director of department—term of office—duties and powers.

The department of archives and history shall be under the immediate management and control of a director, to be elected by the board of trustees, whose term of office shall be six years, and until his successor is elected and qualified. He shall take an oath of office as do other state officials, and shall be commissioned in like manner. He shall have authority to adopt a seal for use in official business. He shall devote his time to the work of the department, using his best endeavor to develop and build it up, so as to carry out the design of its creation. He shall have the control and direction of the work and operations of the department, and shall preserve its collection, care for the official archives that may come into his custody, collect, as far as possible, all materials bearing upon the history of the state and the territory included therein from the earliest times, prepare the official registers hereinafter provided, and diffuse knowledge in reference to the history and resources of the state. The director of the department shall make a report of the expenses of the department to the legislature of the state as state officers.

SOURCES: Codes, 1906, § 1635; Hemingway's 1917, § 3449; 1930, § 3628; 1942, § 6182.

§ 39–5–9. Additional compensation for director.

The board of trustees of the department of archives and history is hereby authorized in its discretion to provide for the compensation of the director of said department in an amount not to exceed two thousand dollars ($2,000.00) per annum from any funds available to the department for that purpose, such compensation to be based on the performance of additional duties imposed by law on said director and to be supplemental to any other compensation heretofore authorized by law to be paid said director.

SOURCES: Codes, 1942, § 6182.5; Laws, 1968, ch. 427, § 1, eff from and after passage (approved August 6, 1968).

§ 39–5–11. State and county officials empowered to turn over all records to director not in current use.

Any state, county, municipal or other official is hereby authorized and empowered, in his discretion, to turn over to the department for permanent preservation therein, any official books, records, documents, original papers, newspaper files and printed books not in current use in their offices. When so surrendered copies therefrom shall be made and certified by the director upon the application of any person interested, which certification shall have all the force and effect as if made by the officer originally in the custody of them, and for which the same fees shall be charged, to be collected in advance.

SOURCES: Codes, 1906, § 1636; Hemingway's 1917, § 3450; 1930, § 3629; 1942, § 6183.

DISTRIBUTION OF PUBLIC DOCUMENTS
(Mississippi Code Annotated, 1982, s-1-1-11, 1-1-57, 1-5-7, 7-3-15, 7-3-19, 7-3-23.)

§ 1–1–11. Distribution of the Code of 1972.

The sets of the compilation of the Mississippi Code of 1972, so purchased by the state when received, shall be distributed by the secretary of state as follows:

* * *

One (1) set to each of the following:

* * *

and each county for the county library (an additional set for each of the last three (3) to be given in counties having two (2) judicial districts).

Two (2) sets to the department of archives and history; fifty (50) sets to the state library; two (2) sets to the Library of Congress; ten (10) sets to the University of Mississippi Law School; five (5) sets to the University of Mississippi; one (1) set each to the Mississippi School for the Deaf and the Mississippi School for the Blind; five (5) sets each to Mississippi State University, Mississippi

University for Women, University of Southern Mississippi, Delta State University, Alcorn State University, Jackson State University and Mississippi Valley State University; one (1) set to each of the state charitable institutions and state charity hospitals; two (2) sets to the supreme court judges' conference room. In furtherance of the state library's reciprocal program of code exchange with libraries of the several states, the secretary of state shall, at the direction and only upon the written request of the state librarian, make distribution to such librarian.

SOURCES: Laws, 1973, ch. 425, § 1; 1974, ch. 377; 1978, ch. 458, § 4; 1981, ch. 536, § 1, eff from and after passage (approved April 23, 1981.)

§ 1–1–57. Purchase and distribution of pocket part supplements and replacement bound volumes by secretary of state.

The secretary of state, upon approval thereof by the attorney general, is hereby authorized to purchase such numbers of sets of the pocket part supplements and the replacement volumes, including index replacement volumes, as may be required to maintain in a current status the sets of the code of 1972 authorized to be furnished under the provisions of section 1–1–11, Mississippi Code of 1972, and to distribute the same to the proper parties. In furtherance of the state library's reciprocal program of code exchange with libraries of the several states the secretary of state shall, at the direction and only upon the written request of the state librarian, make distribution to such libraries.

SOURCES: Laws, 1973, ch. 366, § 4; 1979, ch. 323, § 2, eff from and after passage (approved March 1, 1979).

§ 1–5–7. Acts and journals distributed.

The secretary of state shall distribute and transmit, free of cost, after the same have been printed and bound, the acts and journals of each session of the legislature, as follows: Two (2) copies of each to the executive of each state and territory of the United States, and to the governments of Canada and Mexico; and one (1) copy of each to the following officers and institutions: governor, lieutenant governor, secretary of state, auditor, treasurer, attorney general, public service commissioners, commissioner of corrections, warden of the penitentiary, superintendent of education, judges of the supreme, circuit and chancery courts; clerks of those courts, judge of county court, county attorney, and district attorneys; Mississippi State University, Mississippi University for Women, Alcorn State University, Mississippi College, Millsaps College, Memphis Law Library, at Memphis, Tennessee; University of Southern Mississippi, Delta State University, and each junior college located in the State of Mississippi; to the sheriff of each county, for the county library; and to each member of the legislature; and ten (10) copies of each to the University of Mississippi; and eight (8) copies of the acts and two (2) copies of the journals to the Library of Congress at Washington, D.C.

SOURCES: Laws, 1978, ch. 458, § 5, eff from and after January 1, 1980.

§ 7–3–15. "Mississippi Reports" distributed.

The secretary of state shall transmit, free of cost, one copy of each volume of "Mississippi Reports" to the sheriff of each county of the state, for the county library; one copy. of each volume thereof to each of the following educational institutions, to wit: Mississippi State University of Agriculture and Applied Science, Alcorn Agricultural and Mechanical College, Mississippi State College for Women, Mississippi College, Millsaps College, Delta State College and the University of Southern Mississippi; ten copies of each volume thereof to the University of Mississippi; and five copies of each volume to the library of congress at Washington, D. C.

The above provisions of this section shall be made in recognition of benefits received through receipt at depository libraries and elsewhere in the state of Mississippi of public documents of the United States under the provisions of federal law.

SOURCES: Codes, 1880, § 265; 1892, § 4093; 1906, § 4645; Hemingway's 1917, § 7483; 1930, § 6943; 1942, § 4203; Laws, 1936, 1st Ex. ch. 14; 1940, ch. 317.

§ 7–3–19. Books furnished University law school for exchange.

The dean of the law school of the University of Mississippi is hereby authorized and empowered, with the approval of the attorney general and secretary of state, to make requisitions to the secretary of state for the departmental reports and "Mississippi Reports" to exchange with other states for similar publications and make the same available in the law school library for the purpose of increasing its facilities.

The secretary of state is hereby authorized and empowered to furnish these publications upon requisition from the dean of the law school of the University of Mississippi.

SOURCES: Codes, 1942, § 4217; Laws, 1938, Ex. ch. 29.

§ 7–3–23. Acts of congress and other publications distributed.

The secretary of state shall, at the time of distributing the laws and journals, also transmit to the sheriff of each county, for the county library, one copy of the acts of congress, if there be so many remaining, and such other books, papers, maps, and documents as may be required by the legislature or governor to be distributed to the several counties.

SOURCES: Codes, 1857, ch. 6, art. 19; 1871, § 124; 1880, § 210; 1892, § 4096; 1906, § 4648; Hemingway's 1917, § 7486; 1930, § 6946; 1942, § 4206.

COUNTY, MUNICIPAL, REGIONAL LIBRARIES
(Mississppi Code Annotated, 1982, s.39-3-1 to 39-3-23.)

§ 39–3–1. Establishment of libraries by counties and municipalities.

It is hereby declared to be the policy of this state to allow and promote the establishment and development of free public library service throughout this state as a part of its provisions for public education.

The board of supervisors of any county in the State of Mississippi, or other governing bodies of the counties of this state, and municipalities and towns, through their governing bodies, may establish and maintain or aid in establishing and maintaining free public libraries for the use of the citizens of the respective counties, municipalities or towns, either separately or in connection with free public libraries already established therein. For said purpose said governing body may acquire the necessary real estate either by purchase, gift or donation and may erect the necessary buildings thereon.

SOURCES: Codes, 1942, § 6200; Laws, 1938, ch. 289.

§ 39–3–3. Funds for establishment and operation.

Where any library is established under this article, either by the county board of supervisors or the governing body of a municipality, the cost of purchasing land, erecting buildings, and equipping and maintaining such library may be paid for in whole or in part out of the general funds of the county or municipality if, in the opinion of the governing authority, said funds are adequate for that purpose, and, in the discretion of the governing authorities, a tax not exceeding one mill may be levied on all taxable property in the county or municipality for a period of not exceeding five years to raise money for the purposes of this section. No tax levies made under the provisions of this section shall be refunded under the "Homestead Exemption Act of 1946," sections 27–33–1 to 27–33–63, Mississippi Code of 1972.

SOURCES: Codes, 1942, § 6201; Laws, 1938, ch. 289; 1958, ch. 479.

§ 39–3–5. County library tax.

Any county which proposes to support or supports a public library may, by order of the board of supervisors of such county, in its discretion, levy not in excess of two mills tax on all taxable property within the county to be used for the support, upkeep and maintenance of any public library proposed to be supported or supported by said county and located therein, which levy shall be in addition to the maximum levy heretofore authorized to be levied by counties. However, those counties imposing such levy shall not receive homestead exemptions reimbursement for same.

SOURCES: Codes, 1942, § 6200-01; Laws, 1946, ch. 203; 1950, ch. 234, §§ 1, 2; 1952, ch. 206, §§ 1, 2; 1958, ch. 229, §§ 1, 2; 1962, ch. 258; 1968, ch. 383, § 1, eff from and after passage (approved August 7, 1968).

§ 39–3–7. Municipal library tax.

(1) Any municipality which supports a public library may, by order of the governing authorities of such municipality, in their discretion, levy a one mill tax on all taxable property within the municipality to be used for the support, upkeep and maintenance of any public library located in said municipality.

(2) The one mill levy herein authorized to be levied by the municipality shall be in addition to the maximum levy heretofore authorized to be levied by municipalities.

SOURCES: Codes, 1942, § 6200-01; Laws, 1946, ch. 203; 1950, ch. 234, §§ 1, 2; 1952, ch. 206, §§ 1, 2; 1958, ch. 229, §§ 1, 2; 1962, ch. 258; 1968, ch. 383, § 1, eff from and after passage (approved August 7, 1968).

§ 39–3–9. Regional libraries.

Two or more counties by action of their boards of supervisors may join in establishing and maintaining a regional library under the terms of a contract to which all of the participating counties agree. The expenses of the regional library shall be apportioned between or among the counties concerned on such basis as shall be agreed upon in the contract. The library building shall be located at a place in one of the counties to be agreed upon by the boards of supervisors of the various counties in the regional library district.

SOURCES: Codes, 1942, § 6202; Laws, 1938, ch. 289.

§ 39–3–11. Participation in regional or county libraries by existing libraries.

When a county or regional library shall have been established under this article, any municipality which is aiding in maintaining or supporting a public library, or which desires to aid in providing public library service for that portion of the county's residents which reside within the municipality, may participate in said county or regional library. This participation shall be on such terms as may be agreed upon among the governing body of the municipality, the board of trustees of the existing municipal library and the board of trustees of the county or regional library.

SOURCES: Codes, 1942, § 6203; Laws, 1938, ch. 289; 1962, ch. 335, § 1, eff from and after passage (approved May 22, 1962).

§ 39–3–13. Contract service.

The governing body of any municipality may contract with the board of trustees of any established library to receive the services of that established library.

The board of supervisors of any county in the state may, with the consent of the board of trustees of an established library, contract for library service from any established library.

The board of trustees of any regional library may contract for such region to receive library service from any established library. Such a contract shall contain such terms, agreements, conditions and financial arrangements as may be agreed upon between the board of trustees of the regional library and the board of trustees of the established library.

The board of trustees of any municipal library, or any group of municipal libraries, and the board of trustees of any county library, may, with the consent of the governing body of said municipality, or municipalities, and with the consent of the board of supervisors of said county, contract with each other or among themselves, to create, maintain and support a joint city-county library system. Such a contract shall contain such terms, agreements, and conditions as may be agreed upon by the board of trustees of the municipal library, or boards of trustees of the several municipalities, and by the board of trustees of the county library.

SOURCES: Codes, 1942, § 6204; Laws, 1938, ch. 289; 1944, ch. 200, § 1; 1962, ch. 335, § 2, eff from and after passage (approved May 22, 1962).

§ 39-3-15.   Board of trustees.

The management and control of a county or municipal library shall be vested in a board of five (5) trustees, who shall be appointed by the governing authorities of the county or municipality. The first appointments shall be for the terms of one (1), two (2), three (3), four (4) and five (5) years respectively, and thereafter, a trustee shall be appointed to serve five (5) years.

When five (5) or less counties support a regional library, the management and control of the regional library shall be vested in a board of five (5) trustees; if more than five (5) counties support a regional library, the board of trustees shall consist of as many members as the number of counties that support the library. The trustees shall be appointed by the governing authorities of the counties that support the library. In a regional library supported by less than five (5) counties, the distribution of the membership on the board of trustees shall be determined by agreement among the counties that support the library. In a regional library of five (5) counties or more, one (1) member of the board of trustees shall be appointed by the governing authority of each county supporting the regional library.

In the first appointments to the regional board of trustees five (5) members shall be appointed for terms of one (1), two (2), three (3), four (4) and five (5) years respectively, and any number of trustees above five (5) shall be appointed for terms of one (1) year. Thereafter, all trustees shall be appointed annually to serve five (5) years.

When five (5) or more counties join with a municipality with a population in excess of one hundred thousand (100,000), the management and control of this city-county regional library system shall be vested in a city-county regional library board composed as follows:

(a) Each county shall have one (1) trustee. A county shall have an additional trustee for each segment of population in excess of fifty thousand (50,000), or major fraction thereof. The population of a municipality that qualifies under (b) below will not be counted when applying this subsection (a).

(b) A municipality with a population in excess of one hundred thousand (100,000) and with a municipal levy for library support of at least one (1) mill, shall also have a trustee for each fifty thousand (50,000) population, or major fraction thereof.

The term of each trustee shall be for a period of five (5) years. Initial appointments to the city-county board shall be made in a manner determined by the counties and municipalities involved so that terms expire on a staggered basis.

The governing authorities of counties and municipalities joining
in a city-county regional library system may provide by contract
for the withdrawal from said system of any member on such terms
as may be agreed upon, including the manner of distribution of
book holdings and other personal property held or acquired by
any such district during the term of membership of any withdrawing member.

Vacancies on the board of trustees of a county, municipal,
regional or city-county regional library shall be filled for unexpired
terms in the same manner in which members of the board were
first appointed. No trustee shall receive a salary or other compensation for his service.

SOURCES: Laws, 1977, ch. 312, eff from and after passage (approved Febru-
     ary 24, 1977).

§ 39–3–17. Board of trustees—organization, powers and du-
ties.

The trustees, immediately after their appointment or election,
shall meet and organize by the election of such officers as they
deem necessary. They shall (1) adopt such by-laws, rules and
regulations for their own guidance and for the government of the
library as they deem expedient; (2) have the supervision, care, and
custody of all property of the library, including the rooms or
buildings constructed, leased or set apart therefor; (3) employ a
librarian, and upon his recommendation employ such other assistants as may be necessary, prescribe their duties, fix their compensation and remove them for a cause; (4) submit annually to the
governing body a budget containing estimates for the ensuing
year; (5) have exclusive control of the finances of the library; (6)
accept such gifts of money or property for library purposes as they
deem expedient; (7) on recommendation of librarian purchase
books, periodicals, maps, and supplies for the library; (8) and do
all other acts necessary for the orderly and efficient management
and control of the library. But no expenditure made or contracted
by the trustees shall be binding on any county or municipality so
as to require any payment in excess of funds made available for
library purposes under this article.

SOURCES: Codes, 1942, § 6206; Laws, 1938, ch. 289.

§ 39–3–19. Annual reports.

At the close of each year the board of trustees of every library
shall make a report to the governing body in the county or
municipality wherein the board serves, showing the condition of
their trust during the year, the sums of money received for the

library fund from taxes and other sources, the sums of money expended and the purposes of the expenditures, the number of books and periodicals on hand, the number added during the year, the number withdrawn, the number loaned out, and such other statistics and information and such suggestions as they deem of public interest. A copy of this report shall be filed in the state library commission.

SOURCES: Codes, 1942, § 6207; Laws, 1938, ch. 289.

§ 39–3–21. Free use of libraries.

Every library established or maintained under this article shall be free for the use of the residents of the territory included within the library district, subject to such reasonable rules and regulations as the trustees find necessary. The trustees may, however, charge a reasonable fee for the use of certain copies of popular fiction and non-fiction.

SOURCES: Codes, 1942, § 6208; Laws, 1938, ch. 289.

§ 39–3–23. Construction of article.

This article shall not be construed to abrogate the force of charter provisions or any local act governing existing public libraries. This chapter shall be construed as additional and supplemental to subsection (j) of section 19–5–93, Mississippi Code of 1972.

SOURCES: Codes, 1942, § 6209; Laws, 1938, ch. 289.

SCHOOL LIBRARIES
(Mississippi Code Annotated, 1982, s.37-55-1 to 37-55-5.)

§ 37–55–1. County library commission.

The county superintendent of education shall name two first grade teachers who, together with the county superintendent, shall constitute a county library commission. It shall be the duty of this commission to name a list of books suited for school libraries, and all books purchased under this chapter shall be selected from this list. It shall be the duty of this commission to make rules and regulations to govern and control the use of such libraries in the county, and the commission shall name a local manager of each library who shall make a report every year to the county commission of all books purchased during the year, of the money on hand at the time of the report, together with the amount expended for library purposes. The county superintendent shall keep a list of books purchased by the several libraries of his county and make a

library report to the state superintendent of education annually
with the county school report.

SOURCES: Codes, 1930, § 6787; 1942, § 6630; Laws, 1924, ch. 283; 1930, ch.
278; 1970, ch. 386, § 1, eff from and after July 1, 1970.

§ 37–55–3. Grants of aid to school libraries from school funds.

When any public free school in this state shall raise not less
than ten dollars by subscription or otherwise for a library for such
school, and shall furnish suitable bookcases with lock and key, the
superintendent of education of the county where such subscription
is raised may issue his certificate for a like amount not exceeding
twenty-five dollars in favor of such school, to be paid out of the
common school fund of that county. In no case shall the amount
given by the county in any one year exceed two hundred and fifty
dollars. No school shall receive a second donation from the school
fund for library purposes so long as there are any new applications
from schools that have not been supplied.

SOURCES: Codes, 1930, § 6786; 1942, § 6629; Laws, 1924, ch. 283; 1930, ch.
278.

§ 37–55–5. Appropriations by county boards of supervisors for support of libraries.

The board of supervisors of any county is authorized, in its
discretion, to appropriate a sum not to exceed three thousand
dollars per annum towards the support of public libraries, including circulating school libraries, in said county.

In counties where the enumeration of educable children is
shown by the most recent census to be 10,000 or more, the board
of supervisors may, in its discretion, appropriate an amount not to
exceed ten thousand dollars annually, towards the support of
public or school libraries.

SOURCES: Codes, 1930, § 6788; 1942, § 6631; Laws, 1930, ch. 278.

PROTECTION OF LIBRARY PROPERTY
(Mississippi Code Annotated, 1982, s.39-3-301 to 39-3-313.)

§ 39–3–301. Short title.

This article shall be known and may be cited as the "Mississippi
Library Materials Security Law."

SOURCES: Laws, 1978, ch. 418, § 1, eff from and after July 1, 1978.

§ 39–3–303. Unauthorized removal or wilful mutilation of library materials.

(1) It shall be unlawful for any person to remove library materi-

als, without authorization, from the premises wherein such materials are maintained or to retain possession of library materials without authorization.

(2) It shall be unlawful for any person to wilfully mutilate library materials.

SOURCES: Laws, 1978, ch. 418, § 2, eff from and after July 1, 1978.

§ 39–3–305. Definitions.

As used in this article the term:

(a) "Without authorization" means contrary to rules which set forth policies governing access to library materials and include eligibility for library patronage and lending procedures.

(b) "Library materials" means books, manuscripts, letters, newspapers, court records, films, microfilms, tape recordings, phonograph records, lithographs, prints, photographs or any other written or printed document, graphic material of any nature and other personal property which is the property or in the custody of or entrusted to a public or private library, museum, archives or other depository.

(c) "Mutilate" means, in addition to its commonly accepted definition, the wilfull removal or separation of constituent parts of an item of library materials causing library materials to be exposed to damage; or duplication without authorization.

SOURCES: Laws, 1978, ch. 418, § 3, eff from and after July 1, 1978.

§ 39–3–307. Applicability.

The provisions of this article shall apply to all libraries, museums, archives and other depositories operated by an agency, board, commission, department or officer of the State of Mississippi, by private persons, societies or organizations, or by agencies or officers of municipalities, counties, school and junior college districts or of any other political subdivisions of the State of Mississippi.

SOURCES: Laws, 1978, ch. 418, § 4, eff from and after July 1, 1978.

§ 39–3–309. Penalty.

Any person who violates the provisions of section 39–3–303 is guilty of a misdemeanor and shall be punished by a fine not to exceed five hundred dollars ($500.00) or by imprisonment in the county jail not to exceed six (6) months, or by both such fine and imprisonment.

SOURCES: Laws, 1978, ch. 418, § 5, eff from and after July 1, 1978.

§ 39–3–311. Relation with other criminal or civil proceedings.

The provisions of this article are supplemental to other criminal statutes. An acquital or conviction obtained under this article shall not be a bar to civil proceedings or actions arising from the same incident.

SOURCES: Laws, 1978, ch. 418, § 6, eff from and after July 1, 1978.

§ 39–3–313. Reasonable detention and questioning to determine whether offense was committed.

Any person employed by a library or any person charged with the supervision thereof with reason to believe that any person has committed or has attempted to commit any offense defined in section 39–3–303 of this article or if any person is believed to have concealed upon his person or within his belongings any library material, such person may be detained and questioned in a reasonable manner for the purpose of ascertaining whether or not such offense has been committed. Such detention and questioning shall not render such employee civilly liable for slander, false arrest, false imprisonment, malicious prosecution, unlawful detention or otherwise in any case where such library employee acts in good faith and in a reasonable manner.

SOURCES: Laws, 1978, ch. 418, § 7, eff from and after July 1, 1978.

Mississippi library laws are reprinted from MISSISSIPPI CODE ANNOTATED published by the Harrison Co., Atlanta, Georgia and Lawyers Co-operative Publishing Co., Rochester, New York.

MISSOURI

STATE LIBRARY COMMISSION
(Vernon's Annotated Missouri Statutes, 1982, s.181.011-181.051.)

181.011. State library commission, members, appointment. terms—officers

1. There is hereby created a state library commission to consist of six members. The governor shall appoint four of the members, with the advice and consent of the senate, one for one year, one for two years, one for three years, and one for four years. Thereafter the members appointed by the governor shall be appointed for terms of four years, except where filling a vacancy due to any cause other than expiration of term of office, in which event the appointment shall be for the remainder of the unexpired term. The members appointed by the governor shall be residents of the state of Missouri. The commissioner of education and the librarian of the state university shall be *ex officio* members of the commission.

2. The commission shall elect a president. In his absence any member may be chosen as president *pro tem*. The state librarian shall serve as secretary to the commission. (L.1955 p. 562 §§ 1, 2)

181.021.　Commission to manage state library—functions— report—receipt of gifts and federal funds

The Missouri state library shall be under the control of the state library commission and operated under rules and regulations promulgated by the commission. The commission shall:

(1) Direct the survey of services given by libraries which may be established or assisted under any law for state grants-in-aid to libraries.

(2) Further the coordination of library services furnished by the state with those of local libraries and other educational agencies.

(3) Publish an annual report showing conditions and progress of public library service in Missouri.

(4) Furnish information and counsel as to the best means of establishing and maintaining libraries, the selection of books, cataloging, and other details of library management; provide assistance in organizing libraries or improving service given by them and assist library services in state institutions.

(5) Receive and administer grants from the United States under any act of congress for public libraries, or other types of library service, and make rules and regulations in connection with such grants as may be necessary or required in the administration thereof.

(6) Receive gifts of money, books or other property which may be used or held in trust for the purposes given.

(7) Administer state grants-in-aid and encourage local support for the betterment of local library service and generally promote an effective state-wide public library system.

(8) Purchase library materials and circulate the material by all means necessary, including the use of bookmobiles, within the state among individuals, communities, libraries, schools, charitable and state institutions, state departments and other organizations approved by the state library commission.　(L.1955 p. 562 § 4)

181.025.　Deposit of federal funds in library service fund— how disbursed

All moneys received by the state from the United States under any act of congress for public library service purposes shall be deposited in the state treasury to the credit of the Library Service Fund, which is hereby created. Moneys in the library service fund shall be disbursed in accordance with requisitions of the state library commission.　(Added L.1957 p. 428 § 1)

181.033. Bookmobile service authorized

The state library may provide bookmobile service either from headquarters in Jefferson City or from area libraries or county, regional or city libraries or other types of extension service. (L. 1955 p. 562 § 6)

181.040. Headquarters

The headquarters of the state library shall be in Jefferson City in adequate and suitable quarters provided by the appropriate state agency. (L.1945 p. 1132 § 14735)

181.043. State librarian, appointment, duties, qualifications

The commission shall appoint a state librarian who shall administer the affairs of the Missouri state library under the rules and regulations of the commission and who shall serve at the pleasure of the commission. The state librarian shall be a graduate of an accredited college or university, and be graduated from an accredited library school, and must have library experience. He shall appoint the personnel in connection with the various activities of the state library, subject to the approval of the commission. (L.1955 p. 562 § 5)

181.047. Expenses of librarian and employees, how paid

All expenses of the state librarian and the other personnel of the state library shall be certified and paid in the same manner as expenses and personnel are paid in state departments or divisions. (L.1955 p. 562 § 6)

181.051. Compensation and expenses of members of commission

The members of the commission shall be reimbursed for traveling and other necessary expenses incurred in connection with their official duties; and in addition, the members of the commission, except the commissioner of education and the librarian of the state university, shall receive as compensation the sum of ten dollars for each day actually spent in attendance at commission meetings. Expenses shall be audited by the state auditor when approved by the president of the commission and the state librarian. All bills of the commission properly certified shall be paid as other bills of state departments and divisions are paid. (L.1955 p. 562 § 3)

STATE AID

(Vernon's Annotated Missouri Statutes, 1982, s.181.060, 181.065;
State Constitution, Art. 9, s.10.)

181.060.   State aid for public libraries—appropriation—allocation

1.   The general assembly may appropriate moneys for state aid to public libraries, which moneys shall be administered by the state librarian, under rules and regulations of the coordinating board for higher education.

2.   At least fifty percent of the moneys appropriated for state aid to public libraries shall be apportioned to all public libraries established and maintained under the provisions of the library laws or other laws of the state relating to libraries.   The allocation of the moneys shall be based on an equal per capita rate for the population of each city, village, town, township, school district, county or regional library district in which any library is or may be established, in proportion to the population according to the latest federal census of the cities, villages, towns, townships, school districts, county or regional library districts maintaining tax supported public libraries.   No grant shall be made to any public library if the rate of tax levied or the appropriation for the library should be decreased below the rate in force on December 31, 1946, or on the date of its establishment.   Grants shall be made to any public library if a public library tax of at least one mill has been voted in accordance with sections 182.010 to 182.460, RSMo, or as authorized in section 137.-030, RSMo, and is duly assessed and levied for the year preceding that in which the grant is made, or if the appropriation for the public library in any city of first class yields one dollar or more per capita for the previous year according to the population of the latest federal census.   Except that, no grant under this section shall be affected because of a reduction in the rate of levy which is required by the provisions of section 137.073, RSMo.

3.   The librarian of the tax supported library together with the treasurer of the library shall certify to the state librarian the annual tax income and rate of tax or the appropriation of the library on the date of the enactment of this law, and of the current year, and each year thereafter, and the state librarian shall certify to the commissioner of administration for his approval the amount to be paid to each library, and warrants shall be issued for the amount allocated and approved.

4.   The balance of the moneys shall be administered and supervised by the state librarian to provide establishment grants on a population basis to newly established county or regional libraries and equalization grants on a population basis to county or regional libraries in all districts in which a one mill or more tax does not yield a dollar per capita to the libraries.   A public library established by law after January 1, 1947, shall receive grants-in-aid only if serving five thousand or more population or if it was serving five thousand or more population at the time of establishment.   Newly established libraries and libraries in which a one mill tax does not yield a dollar per capita shall certify through the legally established board and the librarian of the library to the state librarian the fact of establishment, the rate of tax, the assessed valuation of the library district and the annual tax yield of the library.   The state librarian shall then certify to the commissioner of administration for his approval the amount of establishment grant or equalization grant to be paid to the libraries and warrants shall be issued for the amount allocated and approved.   The sum appropriated for state aid to public libraries shall be separate and apart from any and all appropriations made to the state library.

Amended by Laws 1981, p. 349, § 1.

181.065. State aid to public libraries for services to blind—amount, determined, how

1. In addition to moneys appropriated by the general assembly for state aid to public libraries as authorized in section 181.060, the general assembly may appropriate moneys to reimburse any public library in this state for its actual cost of furnishing library service to blind and physically handicapped citizens as defined in Public Law 89–522 (1966)[1] of this state, provided, however, that such library shall be designated by the Library of Congress as a regional library for service to the blind in order to qualify for payments hereunder.

2. The actual cost of furnishing library service to the blind and physically handicapped citizens as defined in Public Law 89–522 (1966) shall be determined annually by adding the total expenditures during the preceding year for salaries, books and supplies, rent, repairs, furnishings, heat, light, power, and administrative expense, except that no item of cost shall be included which is related to general library service and not to service for the blind and physically handicapped citizens as defined in Public Law 89–522 (1966).

3. The legally established board and the librarian in charge of such library shall certify to the state librarian annually the per capita cost of service to each blind person and physically handicapped citizens as defined in Public Law 89–522 (1966) served by the library during the fiscal year preceding the report and the number of blind and physically handicapped citizens as defined in Public Law 89–522 (1966) of this state served during such year, and the product of such per capita cost and the number of citizens of this state served during the year shall be the amount of reimbursement due the library for the year. The state librarian shall certify to the commissioner of administration for his approval the amount to be paid to any regional library and warrants shall be issued for the amount approved.

Amended by Laws 1972, p. 777, § 1; Laws 1974, p. 804, § 1.

§ 10. Free public libraries—declaration of policy—state aid to local public libraries

Section 10. It is hereby declared to be the policy of the state to promote the establishment and development of free public libraries and to accept the obligation of their support by the state and its subdivisions and municipalities in such manner as may be provided by law. When any such subdivision or municipality supports a free library, the general assembly shall grant aid to such public library in such manner and in such amounts as may be provided by law. (State Constitution, Art. 9, s.10.)

DISTRIBUTION OF PUBLIC DOCUMENTS

(Vernon's Annotated Missouri Statutes, 1982, s.181.100-181.140, (s.2.091, 3.130, 11.100.)

181.100. State publications defined

As used in sections 181.100 to 181.140, and sections 182.140 and 182.291, RSMo, "state publications" shall include all multiple-produced publications of state agencies, regardless of format or purpose, with the exception of correspondence and interoffice memoranda.

Laws 1976, p. 674, § 2.

181.110.   Publications of state officers, indexed list of to be published, distribution—depositories of publications, designation, request

The state library shall, under the direction of the coordinating board for higher education, publish monthly an official indexed list of all printed publications of all state offices, departments, divisions, boards and commissions, whether legislative, executive or judicial, and any subdivisions of each, including state-supported institutions of higher education.   The library shall also distribute such numbers of copies of such publications as it deems necessary to certain libraries, also designated by it, which shall serve as depositories for making available to the public such publications.   No publications shall be distributed to any libraries unless a request is made therefor.

Laws 1976, p. 674, § 3.

181.120.   Library to distribute publications, to whom

In addition to the distribution of the publications as aforesaid, the library shall distribute two copies of each publication to the state archives for preservation and two copies to the state historical society.

Laws 1976, p. 675, § 4.

181.130.   Depository agreements permitted, when

The state library may enter into depository agreements with public libraries and college and university libraries which meet standards for depository eligibility as approved by the state library.

Laws 1976, p. 675, § 5.

181.140.   State agencies to furnish copies of publications, to whom

Every state agency, as enumerated in section 181.100, shall, upon release, deposit with the state library sufficient copies of each of its publications to meet the purposes of sections 181.100 to 181.140, and sections 182.140 and 182.291, RSMo.

Laws 1976, p. 675, § 6.

2.091.   Bound journals, distributed how

The secretary of state shall deliver, upon request, one copy of the journal of each house to the secretary of the senate, the clerk of the house of representatives, the judge of any court of record, any member of either house of the general assembly, the head of any state department, bureau or state institution, the state university, the Missouri state historical society and any public library in the state, two copies of each to the law library association of St. Louis, and three copies of each to the library of congress at Washington, D. C.   The remaining copies shall be preserved, subject to the orders of the general assembly.   (Added L.1961 p. 462 § 1 (§ 2.095))

3.130.   Committee to determine number of copies—distribution

1.   Such number of copies of each volume of each edition of the re-

vised statutes of Missouri and annotations thereto and such number of the supplements or pocket parts thereto as may be necessary to meet the demand as determined by the committee shall be printed, bound and delivered to the revisor of statutes, who shall execute and file a receipt therefor with the director of revenue. The revisor of statutes shall distribute the copies without charge as follows:

(1) To each state department, and each division and bureau thereof, one copy;

(2) To each member of the general assembly at each general assembly, three copies;

(3) To each judge of the supreme court, the court of appeals and to each judge of the circuit courts, except municipal judges, one copy;

(4) To the probate divisions of the circuit courts of Jackson county, St. Louis county and the city of St. Louis, four additional copies each, and to the probate divisions of the circuit courts of those counties where the judge of the probate division sits in more than one city, one additional copy each;

(5) To the law library of the supreme court, ten copies;

(6) To the law libraries of each district of the court of appeals, six copies each;

(7) To the library of the United States Supreme Court, one copy;

(8) To the United States district courts and circuit court of appeals for Missouri, two copies each;

(9) To the state historical society, two copies;

(10) To the libraries of the state university at Columbia, at St. Louis, at Kansas City and at Rolla, three copies each;

(11) To the state colleges, Lincoln university, the junior colleges, Missouri western college and Missouri southern college, four copies each;

(12) To the public school library of St. Louis, two copies;

(13) To the Library of Congress, one copy;

(14) To the Mercantile Library of St. Louis, two copies;

(15) To each public library in the state, if requested, one copy;

(16) To the law libraries of St. Louis, St. Louis county, Kansas City and St. Joseph, three copies each;

(17) To the law schools of the state university, St. Louis university, and Washington university, three copies each;

(18) To the circuit clerk of each county of the state for distribution of one copy to each county officer, to be by him delivered to his successor in office, one copy;

(19) To the director of the committee on legislative research, such number of copies as may be required by such committee for the performance of its duties;

(20) To any county law library, when requested by the circuit clerk, two copies;

(21) To each county library, one copy, when requested;

(22) To any committee of the senate or house of representatives, as designated and requested by the accounts committee of the respective house.

2. The revisor of statutes shall also provide the librarians of the supreme court library, of the committee on legislative research, of the law schools of the state university such copies as may be necessary, not exceeding fifty-one each, to enable them to exchange the copies for like compilations or revisions of the statute laws of other states and territories.

Amended by Laws 1971, p. 82, § 1; Laws 1973, p. 85, § 1; Laws 1976, p. 594, effective May 12, 1976; Laws 1978, p. 714, § A (§ 1), effective Jan. 2, 1979.

11.100. Copies of certain publications to the university and school of mines

The secretary of state shall procure and furnish to the general library of the university of the state of Missouri and to the library of the school of mines two copies of each official report and publication issued by the state or any officer thereof; and so far as he is able to do so he shall procure and furnish to those libraries two copies of each and every printed report of any corporation organized under the laws of this state or which is authorized to do business therein. He shall also, from time to time, procure for the library of the school of mines copies of collated or revised statutes of the several states so far as it can be done by exchanging for the same copies of the revised statutes and session acts of the state of Missouri. (R.S.1939, § 10817, as amended L.1957 p. 726 § 1)

STATE HISTORICAL SOCIETY

(Vernon's Annotated Missouri Statutes, s. 183.010-183.030.)

183.010. Society made trustee for the state—powers—executive committee

1. The state historical society of Missouri, heretofore organized under the laws of this state, shall be the trustee of this state, and as such shall hold all its present and future collections and property for the state, and shall not mortgage or deed in trust any of its property or sell any of such property except by way of exchange for property of equal value or for reinvestment.

2. There shall continue to be an executive committee of said society, to consist of as many members as is or may be provided in the constitution of said society, and to have the same powers as the present executive committee. (R.S.1939 § 14902)

183.020. Society's duties

It shall be the duty of the society to collect books, maps and other papers and material for the study of history, especially of this state and of the middle west; to acquire narratives and records of the pioneers, to procure documents, manuscripts and portraits, and to gather all information calculated to exhibit faithfully the antiquities and the past and present condition, resources and progress of this state; to cause its collections to be properly bound and preserved; to conduct a library of historical reference, and to publish from time to time reports of its collections and such other matters as may tend to diffuse information relative to the history of this region; and to keep the rooms containing the collections of said society open at all reasonable hours on business days for the reception of the citizens of this state, without fee. (R.S.1939 § 14903)

183.030. **Executive committee to report—copies of state publications to society**

The executive committee of the society shall keep an accurate account of the expenditure of all money which may be appropriated for the purposes of the society, and report biennially to the governor a detailed statement of the expenditure. To enable the society to augment its collections by effecting exchanges with other societies and institutions, sixty bound copies each of the several publications of the state, and of its societies and institutions, except the reports of the supreme court and the court of appeals, shall be and the same are hereby donated to the society as they shall be issued, the same to be delivered to the society by the secretary of state or other officer having the custody of the same; to include, also, for deposit in its collections, one set of all the publications of the state, including those heretofore issued, so far as possible, not excepting the reports of the supreme court and of the court of appeals.
Amended by Laws 1973, p. 84, § 1.

LEGISLATIVE REFERENCE SERVICE
(Vernon's Annotated Missouri Statutes, 1982, s.23.030, 23.060-23.090.)

23.030. Legislative library—reference service

The legislative library room located on the third floor of the capitol building and in a northerly position between the senate chamber and the house chamber is set aside as a legislative library quarters under the direction and control of the committee on legislative research. Out of an appropriation made for that purpose, the committee on legislative research shall maintain a reference service which shall be available to the general assembly and the public. This service may include the following specific functions:

(1) Maintain a legislative library and purchase for the library any printed or written reference material relating to problems of the state or political subdivisions as would in the judgment of the committee aid the members of the general assembly;

(2) Secure and file copies of all bills, resolutions, amendments, memorials, reports of committees, journals and other documents printed by order of either house of the general assembly; and collect, catalogue and index material as soon as practicable after it has been printed;

(3) Keep an index or digest of the action on each bill, resolution, and memorial by either body of the general assembly and the governor, the digest to be printed and distributed at intervals the committee deems practicable. (R.S.1939, § 14743, as amended L.1943 p. 632; L.1957 p. 595 § 1)

23.060. Material available to whom—procuring information from other state agencies

The material, including books and other publications of the research library maintained by the committee is available to the members of the general assembly. All officers of the state, all departments, commissions and bureaus of the state and all persons connected therewith, the University of Missouri, the teachers' colleges and all agencies of the state which are supported in whole or in part by state funds shall give the committee, or its duly authorized representatives, complete access to their records and full information and all reasonable assistance in any matter of research or investigation which, in the judgment of the committee, requires recourse to them or to data within their knowledge or control; but this section does not compel the disclosure of any records or information which are declared to be privileged or confidential by any other law of this state, unless the committee is specifically authorized to procure the information by a joint resolution adopted by the general assembly. (R.S.1939, § 14744, as amended L.1943, p. 632; L.1957, p. 595 § 1)

23.070. Committee on legislative research, officers how selected—director, duties of—meetings, when held, quorum, number required for

The committee on legislative research shall meet within ten days after its creation and organize by selecting a chairman and a vice chairman, one of whom shall be a member of the senate and one of whom shall be a member of the house of representatives. The director shall serve as secretary to the committee on legislative research. He shall keep the records of the committee and be subject to the jurisdiction and order of the committee during the vacation or recess of the general assembly. The regular meeting place of the committee shall be in Jefferson City, Missouri, and after its inception and organization it shall regularly meet at least once every three months. A majority of the members of the committee shall constitute a quorum. Special meetings of the committee may be called at such time and place within the state as the chairman thereof designates.
Amended by Laws 1977, p. 130, § A.

23.080. Director, how employed, compensation, qualifications—other employees authorized—library, expenditures for authorized

1. The committee may regularly employ and fix the compensation of a director who is competent to assume administration of the necessary activities of the committee under the direction of the committee. The committee may also employ other attorneys, research assistants, clerks and other persons as it deems necessary within the limits of the appropriation made therefor to carry out the provisions of this chapter or to provide assistance for the members and committees of the general assembly. All employees of the committee shall be under the supervision of the director, and he shall, as directed by the committee, assign and supervise all work projects of the employees and keep all necessary personnel records for the employees.

2. The committee may provide necessary legal reports and other publications to be kept in the library of the committee and pay for same out

of any appropriations made to the committee. The secretary of state and the revisor of statutes shall furnish the librarian, without charge, the number of Missouri statutes and session laws as is desired by the committee to enable it to exchange the statutes and session laws for those of other states.

Amended by Laws 1977, p. 130, § A.

23.090. Legislative library and other space under control of committee on legislative research

The committee on legislative research has charge and control of the legislative library and all other space within the capitol assigned to it.
Amended by Laws 1977, p. 130, § A.

SUPREME COURT LIBRARY

(Vernon's Annotated Missouri Statutes, 1982, s.180.030-180.130.)

180.030. Term of office of librarian and assistant

The librarian and assistant librarian shall hold their offices during the pleasure of the supreme court, and the said court shall exercise a general care and superintendence over the library. (L.1945 p. 1129 § 14722)

180.040. Duty of librarian—secretary of state to deliver certain books and reports

The librarian shall have the custody, charge and safekeeping of all maps, charts and other things of every kind whatsoever, property belonging to the library, and shall take special care that none of them be lost or injured; and he shall cause the seal of the supreme court to be stamped on the outside of each volume. The secretary of state shall deliver to the librarian, as soon as received by him, one copy of the following books, viz.: The acts of each session of congress, acts of the several states and territories, the journals of the general assembly of this state, the journals of the general assemblies of the several states and territories, also one copy of the journals of each house of congress, and of all books, reports, state papers and documents ordered by congress or either house thereof to be distributed among the states, also, five copies of the acts of the general assembly of this state, which the librarian shall cause to be bound, if the same be not already done, and placed in the library. (R.S.1939 § 14714; L.1945 p. 1129)

180.050. Books to be replaced

Whenever any volumes in the supreme court library of the supreme court reports or of the court of appeals of this state, or of the revised statutes or session acts thereof, have become worn and defaced or unfit for use, the secretary of state, on the requisition of the supreme court librarian, shall exchange the volumes for others from the surplus volumes of the books in his possession.

Amended by Laws 1973, p. 84, § 1.

180.060. Librarian to care for miscellaneous books, maps and charts

The librarian shall cause all books, maps and charts now owned by the state, and such as may be hereafter acquired, to be appropriately arranged and kept in the rooms which are set apart for that purpose on the second floor of the supreme court building. He shall have the sole and entire control of said rooms, keep the keys of the same, and provide for the safekeeping of the books. (R.S.1939 § 14715; L.1945 p. 1129)

180.070. Librarian may procure books

When there shall be a want of continuity in any of the series of acts, journals or other books required to be placed in the library, it shall be the duty of the librarian to open a correspondence with the proper person, in order to obtain those which are wanting, and if they cannot otherwise be procured, he shall purchase the same and place them in the library. (R.S.1939 § 14716; L.1945 p. 1129)

180.080. Librarian may purchase, sell and exchange law books and reports

The librarian shall, under the direction of the judges of the supreme court, purchase such books as they may require, and place the same in the law library; and under the direction of such judges, he may sell or exchange any surplus or duplicate law books or reports. (L.1945 p. 1129 § 14717)

180.090. Necessary expenses allowed

All necessary expenses of stationery, lights, postage, fuel and keeping the library clean and in order, shall be allowed the librarian, and paid out of the general contingent fund. (L.1945 p. 1129 § 14720)

180.100. Comptroller to certify accounts

The comptroller shall certify the accounts of the librarian and assistant librarian and warrants shall be drawn on the treasury for the payment of the same. (L.1945 p. 1129 § 14719)

180.110. Who may take books from library

The library shall be open to the public and operated under the rules, orders and supervision of the supreme court of Missouri; but no book shall be taken from the library except by the state officers, members of the general assembly or the judges of the supreme court, or an attorney of the supreme court on an order of a judge of the supreme court; and no book shall be taken from the library in any case without it shall have been first charged to the person obtaining it, who shall also give his written receipt for the same. (L.1945 p. 1129 § 14721)

180.120. Supreme court library to exchange publications with other states

The supreme court library is hereby made and constituted the medium for exchange of the official publications of the various departments, institutions and bureaus of the state government, to be exchanged with the other states of the union for their official state publications, and the officials of this state in charge of said departments, institutions and bureaus, shall cause to be delivered to the supreme court library such number of copies of all their publications as is necessary to make such exchange, and for the use of the supreme court library. (L.1945 p. 1129 § 14724)

180.130. Fees for certain services—expenditures of fee revenues

The librarian may collect a reasonable fee for reproducing legal material. The librarian may make expenditures from these fees in order to secure legal material from other sources. A single expenditure from these fees shall not exceed twenty dollars. The aggregate of all expenditures from these fees during any fiscal year shall not exceed two hundred fifty dollars. Accurate records of all receipts and expenditures shall be maintained at all times. The balance of the fees shall be paid into the state treasury at least monthly.

Added by Laws 1982, p. ——, S.B.No.497, § A.

COOPERATIVE AGREEMENTS

(Vernon's Annotated Missouri Statutes, 1982, s.70.210-70.320.)

70.210. Definitions

As used in sections 70.210 to 70.320, the following terms mean:

(1) "**Governing body**", the board, body or persons in which the powers of a municipality or political subdivision are vested;

(2) "**Political subdivision**", counties, townships, cities, towns, villages, school, county library, city library, city-county library, road, drainage, sewer, levee and fire districts, soil and water conservation districts, watershed subdistricts, and any board of control of an art museum.

Amended by Laws 1955, p. 302, § 1; Laws 1961, p. 187, § 1; Laws 1963, p. 123, § 1; Laws 1967, p. 141, § 1.

70.220. Political subdivisions may cooperate with each other, with other states, the United States or private persons

Any municipality or political subdivision of this state, as herein defined, may contract and cooperate with any other municipality or political subdivision, or with an elective or appointive official thereof, or with a duly authorized agency of the United States, or of this state, or with other states or their municipalities or political subdivisions, or with any

private person, firm, association or corporation, for the planning, development, construction, acquisition or operation of any public improvement or facility, or for a common service; provided, that the subject and purposes of any such contract or cooperative action made and entered into by such municipality or political subdivision shall be within the scope of the powers of such municipality or political subdivision. If such contract or cooperative action shall be entered into between a municipality or political subdivision and an elective or appointive official of another municipality or political subdivision, said contract or cooperative action must be approved by the governing body of the unit of government in which such elective or appointive official resides.
Amended by Laws 1957, p. 248, § 1.

70.230. Procedure for exercising power

Any municipality may exercise the power referred to in section 70.220 by ordinance duly enacted, or, if a county, then by order of the county court duly made and entered, or if other political subdivision, then by resolution of its governing body or officers made and entered in its journal or minutes of proceedings, which shall provide the terms agreed upon by the contracting parties to such contract or cooperative action.   (L.1947 V. I p. 401 § 7403c)

70.240. Lands may be acquired—how

The parties to such contract or cooperative action or any of them, may acquire, by gift or purchase, or by the power of eminent domain exercised by one or more of the parties thereto in the same manner as now or hereafter provided for corporations created under the law of this state for public use, chapter 523, RSMo 1949, and amendments thereto, the lands necessary or useful for the joint use of the parties for the purposes provided in section 70.220, either within or without the corporate or territorial limits of one or more of the contracting parties, and shall have the power to hold or acquire said lands as tenants in common.   (L.1947 V. I p. 401 § 7403c)

70.250. Method of financing

Any such municipality or political subdivision may provide for the financing of its share or portion of the cost or expenses of such contract or cooperative action in a manner and by the same procedure for the financing by such municipality or political subdivision of the subject and purposes of said contract or cooperative action if acting alone and on its own behalf.   (L.1947 V. I p. 401 § 7403c)

70.260 Provisions which may be included in the joint contract

The joint contract may also provide for the establishment and selection of a joint board, commission, officer or officers to supervise, manage and have charge of such joint planning, development, construction, acquisition, operation or service and provide for the powers and duties, terms of office, compensation, if any, and other provisions relating to the members of such joint board, commission, officers or officer. Such contract may include and specify terms and provisions relative to the termination or cancellation by ordinance, order or resolution, as the case may be, of such contract or cooperative action and the notice, if any, to be given of such cancellation, provided that such cancellation termination shall not relieve any party participating in such contract or cooperative action from any obligation or liability for its share of the cost or expense incurred prior to the effective date of any such cancellation. (L.1947 V. I p. 401 § 7403c)

70.270. Sovereignty to be retained

Sovereignty shall be retained over any real property used under the terms of any contract or cooperative action within the jurisdiction and territorial limits of the municipality or political subdivision in which it is located, and to that extent shall be a limitation up on the contracting parties under the provisions of sections 70.210 to 70.320. (L.1947 V. I p. 401 § 7403e)

70.280. Office of facility taken over may be abolished and duties transferred

The governing body of any municipality or political subdivision shall have the power to abolish the office of the facility taken over by any other municipality or political subdivision, and the powers and duties thereof may be transferred to the officer who is to perform them under the terms of the contract or cooperative action. (L.1947 V. I p. 401 § 7403f)

70.290. Immunities and liabilities of officers

All officers acting under the authority of the municipality or political subdivision pursuant to such agreement or cooperative action under the provisions of sections 70.210 to 70.320 shall be deemed to be acting for a governmental purpose and shall enjoy all the immunities and shall be subject to the same liabilities which they would have within their own territorial limits. (L. 1947 V. I p. 401 § 7403g)

70.300. Execution of contracts

Whenever the contracting party is a political subdivision of this state, the execution of all contracts shall be authorized by a majority vote of the members of the governing body. Each contract shall be in writing and a copy filed in the office of the secretary of state and in the office of the recorder of deeds in the county in which each contracting municipality or political subdivision is situated. (L.1947 V. I p. 401 § 7403h)

70.310. Disbursement of funds

All money received pursuant to any such contract or cooperative action, under the provisions of sections 70.210 to 70.320, unless otherwise provided by law, shall be deposited in such fund or funds and disbursed in accordance with the provisions of such contract or cooperative action.   (L.1947 V. I p. 401 § 7403i)

70.320. Suits may be brought in circuit courts

Suits affecting any of the terms of any contract may be brought in the circuit court of the county in which any contracting municipality or political subdivision is located or in the circuit court of the county in which a party to the contract resides.   (L.1947 V. I p. 401 § 7403j)

COUNTY LIBRARY DISTRICTS

(Vernon's Annotated Missouri Statutes, 1982, s.182.010-182.080, 182.100-182.130.)

182.010.   County library districts—petition—tax levy—notice—elections —election to increase levy

1.   Whenever voters equal to five percent of the total vote cast for governor at the last election in any county, outside of the territory of all cities and towns in the county which at the time of election as hereinafter provided maintain and control free public and tax supported libraries pursuant to other provisions of this chapter except as provided in section 182.030, shall petition the county court in writing, asking that a county library district of the county, outside of the territory of all the aforesaid cities and towns, be established and be known as "...... county library district", and asking that an annual tax be levied for the purpose herein specified, and specifying in their petition a rate of taxation of not more than twenty-five cents for each one hundred dollars of assessed valuation, then the county court, if it finds the petition was signed by the requisite number of voters and verified in accordance with the provisions of section 126.040, RSMo, pertaining to initiative petitions, shall enter of record a brief recital of the petition, including a description of the proposed county library district, and of its finding; and shall order that the questions of the petition be submitted to the voters of the proposed county library district.   The order of court and the notice shall specify the name of the county and the rate of taxation mentioned in the petition.

2.   The question shall be submitted in substantially the following form:

Shall there be established a ...... county library district?

Shall there be a ...... tax for each one hundred dollars assessed valuation for a county library?

3.   In case the boundary limits of any city or town hereinabove mentioned are not the same as the boundary limits of the school district of the city or town, and the school district embraces territory outside the boundary limits of the city or town and within the boundary limits of the proposed county library district, then all voters, otherwise qualified and residing in the school district, but outside the limits of the city or town and within the limits of the proposed county library district, shall be eligible to vote on the proposition, and may cast a vote thereon at the designated polling place within the county.   The ballots shall be certified to county court as provided in section 179.020. RSMo.

4. In case the proposed tax is sought as an increased tax for the maintenance of a library already established hereunder, over a lesser tax rate theretofore voted and adopted, then such fact shall be recited in the petition and the notice of the submission of the question.

5. The question shall be submitted in substantially the following form: Shall there be a ..... tax increase over the present ..... tax for the county library?

6. If a majority of all the votes cast on the question are for the tax as submitted, the tax specified in the notice shall be levied and collected in the same manner as other county library taxes as provided in section 182.-020, and shall be known as and become a part of the "County Library Fund" to be administered as provided in section 182.020.
Amended by Laws 1969, p. 78, § 2; Laws 1974, p. 805, § 1; Laws 1978, p. 338, § 1.

182.015. County court may establish library district without vote, when —tax levy, submitted how

In addition to the provisions of section 182.010, the county court of any county of the state may establish by its order a county library district without a petition or submission to the voters as provided in section 182.010, provided such district conforms otherwise to the provisions of that section and does not include any part of a regional library system established pursuant to other provisions of this chapter. In the event a district is so established the county court shall propose an annual rate of taxation within the limitations prescribed by section 182.010, which proposal shall be submitted to a vote of the people in the same manner as though the district were formed under the provisions of that section.
Laws 1972, p. 778, § 1.

182.020. Levy and collection of tax—library fund—reconsideration of tax

1. If, from returns of the submission of the question, the majority of all the votes cast are in favor of establishing a county library district and for the tax for a free county library, the county court shall enter of record a brief recital of the returns and that there has been established "...... county library district", and thereafter such "...... county library district", shall be considered established; and the tax specified in the notice, subject to the provisions of this section, shall be levied and collected, from year to year.

2. The proceeds of the levy, together with all interest accruing on same, with library fines, collections, bequests and donations in money shall be deposited in the treasury of the county and be known as the "County Library Fund", and be kept separate and apart from other moneys of the county, and disbursed by the county treasurer only upon the proper authenticated warrants of the county library board.

3. The tax may be reconsidered whenever the voters of any county library district shall so determine by a majority vote on such questions after petition, order of the court, and notice of the election and of the purpose thereof, first having been made, filed, and given, as in the case of establishing such county library district. At least five years must elapse after the county library district has been established and a tax therefor has been levied before a question to reconsider the tax may be submitted.

4. As used in sections 182.010 to 182.120, the words "county court" shall be construed to mean the proper court or official in any county operating under a special charter.
Amended by Laws 1978, p. 339, § 1.

182.030.   Voters of municipal district may vote on establishing or inclusion in county district, when—effect

Whenever voters equal to five percent of the total vote cast for governor at the last election in an existing municipal library district within the geographical boundaries of a proposed or existing county library district shall petition in writing the county court to be included in the proposed or existing county library district, subject to the official approval of the existing county library board, the voters of the municipal library district shall be permitted to vote on the question for establishing or joining the county library district, and on the proposition for a tax levy for establishing and maintaining a free county library. If the question carries by a majority vote, the municipal library district shall become a part of the county library district at the beginning of the next fiscal year and the property within the municipal library district shall be liable to taxes levied for free county library purposes. If a majority of voters in the existing municipal library district oppose the county library district, the existing municipal library district shall continue.
Amended by Laws 1978, p. 339, § 1.

182.040.   City may become part of county library district—procedure—effect

After the establishment of a free county library district the legislative body of any incorporated city, town or village in the county which was excluded from the county library district because of the maintenance of a tax supported municipal library established and maintained pursuant to other provisions of this chapter, after approval of the proposed change by the trustees of the free county library district, may become a part of the free county library district by notifying the county court that the municipality desires to become a part of the free county library district at the beginning of the next fiscal year; and thereafter the municipality shall be liable for taxes levied for free county library purposes at the same rate as is levied for the free county library district in the county.
Amended by Laws 1974, p. 805, § 1.

182.050.   County library boards—appointment, removal, vacancies—nepotism forbidden

For the purpose of carrying into effect sections 182.010 to 182.120, in case a county libarry district is established and a free county library authorized as provided in section 182.010, within sixty days after the establishment of the county library district, there shall be created a county library board of trustees, of five members, none of whom shall be elected county officials. The members shall be appointed by the county court for terms of four years each, except that as to the members of the first board, two shall be appointed for one year, and one each shall be appointed for two years, three years, and four years, respectively, from the first day of July following their appointment; and annually thereafter before the first day of July the county court shall appoint successors. Vacancies in the board occasioned by removals, resignations or otherwise shall be reported to the county court and shall be filled in like manner as original appointments; except that if the vacancy is in an unexpired term, the appointment shall be made for only the unexpired portion of that term. No member of the board shall receive compensation as such. No person shall be employed by the board of library trustees or by the librarian who is related within the third degree by blood or by marriage to any trustee of the board.
Amended by Laws 1972, p. 777, § 1.

182.060.   Board to organize—rules and regulations—county librarian, appointment—annual reports

1.   The board of trustees, immediately after their appoint-

ment by the county court, shall meet and organize by the election of one of their number as president and by the election of such other officers as they may deem necessary; shall make and adopt such bylaws, rules and regulations for their own guidance as may be expedient, not inconsistent with law for the government of the library and in general shall carry out the spirit and intent of sections 182.010 to 182.120 in establishing and maintaining the free county library.

2. The board, in case such library district establishes its own free county library, shall appoint a qualified librarian who shall be the chief executive and administrative officer for the library district and shall serve at the pleasure of the board. On or before the second Monday in March of each year, the county librarian shall make a report to the board, stating the condition of the library and its services on the thiry-first day of December of the preceding year.

3. On or before the first day of April, the board of trustees shall make a report and send a copy to the county court and to the Missouri state library. (R.S.1939 § 14768; L.1955 p. 547 § 1)

182.070. General powers of district—seal

The county library district, as a body corporate, by and through the county library board of trustees, may sue and be sued, complain and defend, and make and use a common seal, purchase, or lease grounds, purchase, lease, occupy or erect an appropriate building for the use of the county library and branches thereof out of current funds if such funds are available above those necessary for normal operations or, as provided in section 182.105, and sell and convey real estate and personal property for and on behalf of the county library and branches thereof, receive gifts of real and personal property for the use and benefit of the county library and branch libraries thereof, the same when accepted to be held and controlled by the board of trustees, according to the terms of the deed, gift, devise or bequest of such property. (R.S.1939 § 14769; L.1955 p. 547 § 1)

182.080. Board may contract for library service—procedure

The county library board of trustees may contract with the body having control of a public library for assistance in the operation of a free county library under such terms and conditions as may be stated in the contract, or it may contract with the body having control of a public or a school library or any other library to furnish library service to the people of the county library district, under such terms and conditions as may be stated in the contract. The body having control of any library district may contract with any such county library board of trustees to provide library service to the people of the library district under such terms and conditions as may be stated in the contract. The county library board of trustees may contract with any other county library district under the terms outlined in sections 70.210 to 70.320, RSMo. In case a contract is made for services by any library, the contracting library boards of trustees shall advise and consult together with regard to the management and disbursement of funds, and other policies relating to the proper management of the library. (R.S.1939 § 14770; L.1955 p. 547 § 1)

182.100.   Tax for library building, election—duration, rate—building fund

1.   Whenever, in any county library district which has decided or shall hereafter decide to establish and maintain a free county library under the provisions of sections 182.010 to 182.120, the county library board of trustees, by written resolution entered of record, deems it necessary that free county library buildings be erected in the county and voters equal to five percent of the total vote cast for governor at the last election of any county library district shall petition the county court in writing asking that an annual tax be levied at and as an increased rate of taxation for the library buildings and specify in their petition a rate of taxation not to exceed two mills on the dollar annually, and not to be levied for more than ten years on all taxable property in such county library district, then the county court, if it finds the petition was signed by the requisite number of voters, shall enter of record a brief recital of the petition, and of its finding, and shall order that the question of the petition be submitted to the voters of the county library district at an election. The order of court and the notice shall specify the rate of taxation mentioned in the petition.

2.   The question shall be submitted in substantially the following form:

Shall there be a . . . . . . mill tax for the erection of a free county library building?

3.   If the majority of the voters of the county library district voting on said question vote in favor of the tax, the tax specified in the notice shall be levied and collected in like manner with other taxes of the county library district, and shall be known as the "County Library Building Fund", and shall be subject to the exclusive control of the county library board of trustees, and the fund shall be disbursed by the county treasurer only upon the properly authenticated warrants of the board and be used for expenses incident to the erection and furnishing of the library building. The fund hereby provided for the erection of free county library buildings in such county shall be in addition to the tax levied for the establishment and maintenance of such county library.
Amended by Laws 1978, p. 340, § 1.

182.105.   Issuance of bonds for building—limits—maturity—election—tax to pay

1.   The county library board in any county library district may provide for the purchase of ground and for the erection of public library buildings, and for the improvement of existing buildings, and may provide for the payment of the same by the issue of bonds or otherwise, subject to the conditions and limitations set forth in this section.

2.   No bonds shall be issued in an amount in excess of one percent of the value of taxable, tangible property in the county library district, as

shown by the last completed assessment for state and county purposes, nor shall such indebtedness be incurred unless it has been approved by the vote of two-thirds of the voters of the county library district voting on the question at a municipal election.

3. Before incurring any indebtedness as authorized in this section, the county library board shall provide for the collection of an annual tax on all taxable, tangible property in the county library district sufficient to pay the interest and principal of the indebtedness as they shall fall due and to retire the same within twenty years from the date contracted.

4. If, upon the returns from the election, which shall be certified to the county court, it appears that the question to incur or increase such indebtedness has been assented to by at least two-thirds of the voters voting on the question, the county court shall enter of record a brief recital of the returns and shall declare that the county library board may issue bonds of the county library district in a total amount not in excess of that authorized by the voters. The bonds shall be issued, payable to bearer and in denominations of not less than one hundred dollars, or some multiple thereof, payable in not more than twenty years from the date they bear, bearing interest from date at a rate not exceeding six percent per annum, payable semiannually, and with interest coupons attached to conform to the face thereof. All bonds shall be signed by the chairman of the county library board, attested by the signature of the secretary, and each bond shall have impressed thereon the corporate seal of the county library district.

Amended by Laws 1978, p. 340, § 1.

182.110. Librarians required to attend meetings—expenses

County librarians shall be required to attend state library meetings and district library institutes, the actual and necessary expenses incident thereto being a charge against the county library fund. (R.S.1939 § 14774; L.1955 p. 547 § 1)

182.120. Services accessible to all residents of county

The services of a free county library may be direct loan of books and other library materials, through branches, stations, or mobile units; but in all cases service shall be available to all residents of the county library district. (R.S.1939 § 14775; L. 1955 p. 547 § 1)

182.130. Certain areas excluded from county library districts (first class charter counties)

If, in any county of the first class having a charter form of government, any property located within the geographical boundaries of a county library district is now, or hereafter, included within the geographical boundaries of a school district having a free public library supported at least in part by taxation, the property now, or hereafter, included within the geographical boundaries of the school district shall be excluded from the county library district, and the excluded property shall only be subject to taxation for library purposes by the school district and shall no longer be subject to taxation for county library district purposes, provided that property which may henceforth be deannexed from such school district to another school district shall become part of the library district which serves the receiving school district.

Laws 1965, p. 312, § 4. Amended by Laws 1975, p. 223, § 1.

CONSOLIDATED LIBRARY DISTRICTS
(Vernon's Annotated Missouri Statutes, 1982, s.182.610-182.670.)

182.610.   County library districts may consolidate, when

Two or more county library districts having the same rate of taxation on assessed valuation of taxable property within each district may join in creating a consolidated public library district, which shall have the same rate of taxation as districts forming the consolidated public library district, shall have the powers and authority as set out in sections 182.-610 to 182.670, may perform any common function or service, including the purchase of land, and the purchase, construction and maintenance of buildings and any other property and may join in the common employment of any consolidated public library district officer, librarian or employee.

Added by Laws 1972, p. 779.

182.620.   Consolidation—resolution—election—form of ballot—transfer of property

1.   A consolidated public library district may be created by resolution, duly acted upon, by the governing boards of two or more county public library districts.   After the districts have each resolved to form a consolidated public library district, they shall apply to the county courts or county chief executive officers of the county districts served by the districts being consolidated.   Upon approval of the consolidation by the appropriate county courts or county executive officers, legal notice that the consolidated public library district has been created, and containing the names of the districts and members of the governing boards creating it, the names of the trustees of the consolidated public library district, the name of the consolidated public library district, the area to be served, the date of its creation and the location of its principal business office shall be published in newspapers of general circulation in the county districts to be served by the consolidated public library district.   Notice shall also be filed with the Missouri state library commission.

2.   Whenever five percent of the voters of each of any two or more county library districts sign a petition, and file it with their appropriate county courts or county executive officers requesting submission of the question of permitting the county library districts to create a consolidated public library district under section 182.610, the county courts or county executive officers shall submit the question to the voters at an election. The total vote for governor at the last general election before the filing of the petition whereat a governor was elected shall be used to determine the number of voters necessary to sign the petition.

3.   The question shall be submitted in substantially the following form:

Shall the ...... county public library district and the ...... county public library district be consolidated and the ...... public library district be created?

4.   If a majority of the voters voting on the question vote for the question in each of the counties taken separately, it shall be deemed to have been adopted, but if it fails to receive a majority in any one or more of the counties, it shall be deemed to have failed.   The board of election commissioners of each county shall canvass the certified abstracts and notify the presiding judge or county executive officer of each of the county courts of the results within twenty days of receipt of the certified abstracts.

5.   Within thirty days following the notification of the election authority of adoption of the question by a majority vote or within thirty

days following the adoption of the resolution, the taxing authorities and the boards of trustees of the county library districts affected shall take appropriate action transferring all title and interest in all property, both real and personal, in the name of the county public library district to the board of trustees of the consolidated public library district. Upon the transfer of such title and interest, the property shall become the property of and subject to the exclusive control of the consolidated public library district.

Added by Laws 1972, p. 779. Amended by Laws 1978, p. 343, § 1.

182.630. Consolidated district is body corporate and a political subdivision—corporate powers

A consolidated public library district is a body corporate and a political subdivision of the state of Missouri, and by and through its governing board of trustees may engage in and contract for every and all types of services, actions or endeavors, not contrary to law, necessary to the successful and efficient prosecution and continuation of the businesses and purposes for which it is created, including, but not limited to, the following:

(1) To have succession by its corporate name perpetually or for a period of time at the pleasure of the electorate of the counties it serves;

(2) To sue and be sued, complain and defend in any court of law or equity;

(3) To have a corporate seal which may be altered at the pleasure of the board and to use same by causing it or a facsimile thereof to be impressed or affixed or in any manner reproduced;

(4) To purchase, take, receive, lease, or otherwise acquire, by eminent domain or otherwise, own, hold, improve, use, sell, convey, lease, exchange, transfer and otherwise dispose of all or any part of its real or personal property, or any interest therein, or other assets wherever situated; and to hold for any period of time gifts of real and personal property for the use and benefit of it, the same to be accepted and controlled by the board of trustees, according to the terms of the deed, gift, devise or bequest of such property; to make contracts and guarantees and incur liability; to borrow money at rates of interest; to issue its bonds or other obligations;

(5) To elect or appoint directors, officers and agents of the district, define their duties and affix their compensation, to indemnify directors, officers and employees to the extent and in the manner permitted by law;

(6) To make and alter bylaws, not inconsistent with the laws of this state, for the administration and regulation of the affairs of the district, and to adopt emergency bylaws and exercise emergency powers as permitted by law;

(7) To invest all or any part of the funds of the district in obligations, redeemable at maturity at par, of the state of Missouri or any political subdivision thereof, or of the United States or of any wholly owned corporation of the United States, or certificates of deposit or time deposits of any financial institution if accompanied by a pledge of securities of the United States government or other political subdivision equal in value to the face amount of such securities of deposit; except that, no funds shall be invested in obligations which are to mature beyond the date that the funds are needed for purposes for which they were received by the consolidated public library district. Interest or earnings derived from the funds shall belong to the district and may be disbursed and expended for the same purposes and in the same manner as other funds belonging to the district;

(8) To authorize any employee, trustee, director or librarian of the board or of the district to attend national, regional or state conventions,

workshops or other meetings deemed by the board to be of interest to the district; and the board, in its discretion, may authorize the expenditure of funds of the district to reimburse the employee, trustee, officer or librarian for expenses incurred in attending such conventions, meetings or workshops;

(9) To retain or authorize the librarian to retain and employ accountants, bookkeeping services, architects, financial advisors, legal counsel, business managers, consultants or other persons offering specialized services on the conditions and for reasonable fees or compensation as the board may determine;

(10) To exercise the sole and exclusive control over all of the property and things of value owned or possessed by the district;

(11) To enter into contracts with any agency of the United States, of this state, or of any other state; or any city, municipal, school or public library districts or any political subdivisions of this state or of any other state, or with any college, university or educational institution, public or private, or any corporation, organization or association to render or to receive specific library services;

(12) To apply for and receive and otherwise expend and use any state aid which is appropriated by the general assembly of the state of Missouri, on such terms and conditions as shall be set forth and included in that legislation;

(13) To apply for and receive and otherwise expend and use any federal aid which is now or hereafter shall be appropriated by the Congress of the United States, on such terms and conditions as shall be set forth and included in that legislation.

Added by Laws 1972, p. 779.

182.640. Board of trustees—how appointed, ground for removal, vacancies how filled—librarian to be appointed

1. A consolidated public library district created under the provisions of sections 182.610 to 182.670 shall be governed by a board of trustees which shall consist of not less than eight trustees to be appointed by the county court or county executive officers of the counties participating in the consolidated public library district. The county court or county executive officers of each participating county shall appoint four trustees who are residents of that county, as representatives of its county. No appointed trustee shall be an elective official.

2. The trustees of the existing boards of a county public district shall remain as the representatives of their respective county and shall serve the remainder of their respective term as the governing board of a consolidated public library district. Upon expiration of their term the county court or county executive officer shall appoint a resident of the respective county for a four year term beginning the first day of July or until a successor shall be appointed.

3. Whenever any member of the board of trustees shall, without good cause, fail to attend six consecutive board meetings of the consolidated public library district or whenever any member of the board of trustees is deemed by the majority of the board of trustees to be guilty of conduct prejudicial to the good order and effective operation of the consolidated public library district, or whenever any member is deemed to be guilty of neglect of duty, then such member may be removed by resolution of the board of trustees duly acted upon, after specification of charge and hearing.

4. Vacancies in the board occasioned by removals, resignations, or otherwise shall be reported to the county courts or county executive officers and shall be filled in like manner as original appointments; except that, if the vacancy occurs during an unexpired term, the appoint-

ment shall be for only the unexpired portion of that term.

5. No person shall be employed by the board of library trustees or by the librarian who is related within the third degree by blood or by marriage to any trustee of the board.

6. Except as in sections 182.610 to 182.670 otherwise expressly provided, no trustee of a consolidated public library district shall receive any fee, salary, gratuity or other compensation or remuneration for acting as such; except that, the board of trustees may reimburse its members for actual and necessary expenses incurred in the performance of their duties.

7. The board of trustees shall have a president, secretary and a treasurer and such other officers as the board may select. All officers of the board shall be selected by the board. All officers of the board of trustees shall serve at the pleasure of the board, and shall not receive any salary, gratuity or other compensation or reimbursement for acting as such, except the treasurer, who may also serve as secretary.

8. The board shall provide for regularly scheduled meetings of the board to be held monthly; except that, the board shall not be required to meet more than ten times in any calendar year. The board shall make and adopt bylaws, rules and regulations governing the proceedings of the board, including bylaws prescribing the duties of each officer of the board of trustees. No bylaws, rules or regulations shall be contrary to, or inconsistent with, any provision of law.

9. A majority of the full board of trustees shall constitute a quorum for the transaction of business. The act of the majority of the trustees present at a meeting at which a quorum is present shall be the act of the board of trustees, except as hereinafter provided. The affirmative vote of a majority of the full board of trustees shall be required to enter into any contract, employ or dismiss the chief administrative officer of the district, effect a merger or consolidation or approve a budget.

10. The board of trustees of a consolidated public library district shall adopt policies for the government of the consolidated public library district that will carry out the spirit and intent of sections 182.610 to 182.670, and the board shall employ a duly qualified graduate librarian as the chief executive and administrative officer of the consolidated public library district charged with the duty of carrying out the policies adopted by the board. The librarian shall serve at the pleasure of the board. The librarian shall have the authority to employ professional library assistants and other employees to fill the positions that are created by the board. The assistants and employees may be dismissed by the librarian.

Added by Laws 1972, p. 779.

182.645. Fiscal year—budget—treasurer custodian of funds

1. The fiscal year for each consolidated public library district shall be July first to June thirtieth, and each year the librarian shall submit to the board of trustees a budget for the forthcoming fiscal year. The board shall approve the budget after making any changes therein that it deems necessary. The budget shall be approved on or before June thirtieth preceding the fiscal year for which the budget was prepared. The board on its own motion or at the request of the librarian, from time to time, may amend or modify the approved budget. A copy of the approved budget shall be filed with each county court or county executive office of the counties comprising the consolidated public library district, and with the state auditor.

2. The treasurer of the board of trustees of a consolidated public library district shall receive and be the custodian of all money belonging to the district from whatever source derived. All funds of the consolidated public library district derived from local taxation to be used

for normal operations of the district and received from the county collector, shall be kept in a consolidated library operating fund. All funds belonging to the district which are to be used for building purposes shall be kept in a consolidated library building fund; all funds derived from state aid or federal grants, other than land, building and furnishing grants, shall be kept in the consolidated library operating fund; and the board may establish any other funds that it deems necessary. The treasurer shall deposit all moneys belonging to the consolidated public library district in the depositaries that are selected by the board of trustees. The treasurer shall also be the custodian of all bonds or other securities belonging to the consolidated public library district.

3. Consolidated public library district moneys shall be disbursed by the treasurer by appropriate instrument of payment only upon due authorization of the consolidated public library district board of trustees and duly certified for payment by the president. The certification shall specify the amount to be paid, to whom payment is to be made and the purpose for which payment is being made. The board by resolution may direct that the signature of the president or treasurer be a facsimile signature in the manner provided by sections 105.272 to 105.278, RSMo.

4. No authorization or certification shall be made, and no instrument of payment issued for the payment of any consolidated public library district indebtedness unless there is sufficient money in the treasury and the proper fund for the payment of the indebtedness and be in the proper form.

5. The treasurer of the board of trustees shall submit to the board of trustees, at each regularly scheduled meeting of the board, an accounting reflecting receipt and disbursement of funds belonging to the consolidated public library district.
Added by Laws 1972, p. 779.

182.647. Bonds of employees—records and reports required

1. The treasurer, the librarian and other employees as designated by the board, before entering upon the discharge of their duties as such, shall enter into bond or bonds with a corporate surety to be approved by the board of trustees in such amount as may be fixed by the board, conditioned that they will render a faithful and just account of all money that comes into their hands, and otherwise perform the duties of their office according to law. The consolidated public library district shall pay the premium for the bond or bonds from its operating fund. A copy of such bond or bonds shall be filed with the treasurer of the board and clerk for each county included within the consolidated public library district. In case of a breach of the conditions of the bond or bonds the board or any taxpayer of the consolidated public library district may cause suit to be brought thereon. The suit shall be prosecuted in the name of the state of Missouri at the relation of and for use of the proper consolidated public library district.

2. The librarian, for and on behalf of the board, shall keep or cause to be kept financial records and accounts according to generally accepted accounting standards, and shall furnish to the board or any member thereof the financial records and accounts, or summaries thereof, that the board or any member thereof may request.

3. On or before the thirty-first day of August of each year, the librarian shall make a report to the board, stating the condition of the library and its services as of the thirtieth day of June of the preceding fiscal year. This report shall be accompanied by an audit conducted by an independent auditing firm. On or before the thirtieth day of September, the reports shall be submitted to the county courts and county executive officers and Missouri state library commission by the board of trustees of the consolidated public library district.
Added by Laws 1972, p. 779.

182.650.   Rate of tax—election to increase rate—form of ballot

1.   Whenever a consolidated public library district has been created it may levy a tax at a rate of not less than twenty cents on the one hundred dollars of assessed valuation of all taxable property in the districts to be served by the consolidated public library district; except that, any increase in the rate of taxation to be assessed shall, on resolution adopted by the board of trustees of the consolidated public library district, be submitted to the county court or county executive officers of the counties included within the district, to be submitted to the voters of the respective counties for approval.

2.   The county courts or county executive officers, after receipt of the resolution pursuant to the provisions of this section, shall order that the proposed increase in the rate of taxation be submitted to the voters of the consolidated public library district at an election.   The order of the court and the notice shall specify the name of the county and the rate of taxation mentioned in the petition.

3.   The question shall be submitted in substantially the following form: Shall there be a . . . . . . cent tax increase over the . . . . . . cent tax per hundred dollars assessed valuation for the . . . . . . consolidated public library district?

4.   If a majority of all the votes cast on the question shall be for the tax increase as submitted, the increased tax specified in the notice shall be levied and collected in like manner with other county taxes and shall be paid and forwarded to the treasurer of the board of trustees of the consolidated public library district by the county collector.

5.   If a majority of the votes cast on the question shall be against the tax rate as submitted, then the tax rate shall remain at the previously existing levy.

6.   Whenever in any consolidated public library district which has decided to establish and maintain a free library in any district served under the provisions of sections 182.610 to 182.670, the consolidated public library district board of trustees, by written resolution entered of record, deems it necessary that free library buildings be erected in the district, it shall notify the county court or chief executive in writing asking that an annual tax be levied at and as an increased rate of taxation for the library buildings and specify in its resolution an additional rate of taxation of . . . . cents on the hundred dollars annually, and not to be levied for more than ten years on all taxable property in such consolidated public library district, then the county court or county executive officer shall enter of record a brief recital of the resolution and shall order that the question be submitted to the voters of the consolidated public library district.   The order of the court or county executive officer and notice shall specify the rate of taxation mentioned in the resolution.

7.   The question shall be submitted in substantially the following form: Shall there be a . . . . . . cent tax for erection of library buildings?

8.   If the majority of the voters of the county library district voting on the question vote in favor of the tax, the tax specified in the notice shall be levied and collected in like manner with other taxes of the county, and delivered to the treasurer of the board of trustees of the consolidated public library district, and shall be subject to the exclusive control of the consolidated public library district board of trustees, and the fund shall be disbursed by the consolidated public library district treasurer only upon proper instrument of payment of the board, and be used for expenses incident to the erection and furnishing of the library buildings.   The levy herein providing for the erection of library buildings shall be in addition to the tax levied for the establishment and maintenance of the consolidated public library district.

Added by Laws 1972, p. 779.   Amended by Laws 1978, p. 344, § 1.

182.655. Board may purchase land and erect buildings—bonds issued, when—election

1. The board of trustees of the consolidated public library district may provide for the purchase of ground and for the erection of public library buildings, and for the improvement of existing buildings, and for the furnishing of said buildings and may provide for the payment of the same by the issue of bonds or otherwise, subject to the conditions and limitations set forth in this section.

2. No bonds shall be issued in an amount in excess of the constitutional limitations of the value of taxable, tangible property in the consolidated public library district, as shown by the last completed assessment for state and county purposes, nor shall such indebtedness be incurred unless it has been approved by the vote of the constitutionally required percentage of the voters of the consolidated public library district voting on the question at a municipal election. The ballot for approval shall state in boldfaced type the tax rate necessary to retire the bonds as nearly accurate as may be.

3. The boards of trustees shall provide for the collection of an annual tax on all taxable, tangible property in the consolidated public library district sufficient to pay the interest and principal of the indebtedness as they shall fall due and to retire the same within twenty years from the date contracted.

4. If, upon the returns from the election, which shall be certified to the board of trustees of the district, it appears that the question to incur indebtedness has been assented to by the constitutionally required percentage of the voters voting on the question, the board of trustees shall enter of record a brief recital of the returns and shall declare that the consolidated public library district board of trustees may issue bonds of the consolidated public library district in a total amount not in excess of that authorized by the voters. The board shall offer such bonds at public sale and shall provide such method as it may deem necessary for the advertisement of the sale of each issue of said bonds before the same are sold. The bonds shall be issued, payable to bearer and in denominations of not less than one hundred dollars, or some multiple thereof, payable in not more than twenty years from the date they bear, bearing interest from date at a rate not exceeding the rate allowable by law, payable semiannually, and with interest coupons attached to conform to the face thereof. All bonds shall be signed by the president of the board of trustees, attested by the signature of the treasurer, and each bond shall have impressed thereon the corporate seal of the consolidated public library district.

Added by Laws 1972, p. 779. Amended by Laws 1978, p. 345, § 1.

182.660. May incorporate other public library districts—petition, notice —transfer of property, when

1. Any consolidated public library district created under sections 182.610 to 182.670 may enlarge the area it serves by incorporating into it any county, city, municipal, school or public library district.

2. The board of trustees of a county, city, municipal, school or public library district may, by resolution duly acted upon, petition the board of trustees of a consolidated public library district to become a part of and be 1 included in such consolidated public library district. The petitioning district may be admitted into the consolidated public library district upon majority vote of the board of trustees of the consolidated public library district at the prevailing tax rate of the consolidated district. Notice of inclusion of the petitioning district into the consolidated public library district shall be given to the governing authority of the district so included in accordance with the notice provisions set out in section 182.620.

3. Whenever five percent of the voters of a county, city, municipal, school or public library district shall petition in writing the governing authority of the district to be included in the consolidated public library district and upon written approval by majority vote of the board of trustees of the consolidated public library district, it shall be the duty of the governing authority to submit the question to the voters of the petitioning district at an election.

4. Upon admission of any petitioning district by majority vote of the board of trustees of the consolidated public library district or upon majority approval of the voters of any such district for inclusion in the consolidated public library district, the taxing authority and governing authority of the district shall take appropriate action to transfer, within sixty days following the approval or election, all title and interest in all property both real and personal in the name of the district, to the board of trustees of the consolidated public library district. Upon the transfer of the title and interest in the property, it shall become a part of the consolidated public library district.

5. If the tax levy for the district admitted is not at the same rate as that of the consolidated public library district or if there is no tax levied in the district for the support of public libraries, then at the beginning of the next taxing period a tax or taxes shall be levied in the district admitted to conform to and be the same as that levied in the consolidated public library district.

Added by Laws 1972, p. 779. Amended by Laws 1978, p. 345, § 1.

182.670. Board to adopt rules and regulations—suspension of library privileges, when

1. The board of trustees of the consolidated public library district shall adopt reasonable rules and regulations governing the terms and privileges for the use of the library and its facilities and shall cause the same to be published, with amendments, and filed with the clerk of each county served by the consolidated public library district and shall have on file a copy thereof in all library facilities open to the public.

2. If any person or corporation using the facilities of the consolidated public library district shall violate any of the published rules or regulations adopted by the board, the board or the librarian of the consolidated public library district may suspend that person's or corporation's library privileges either temporarily or permanently, as the consolidated public library district shall deem to be in the best interests of the consolidated public library and of the people it serves.

Added by Laws 1972, p. 779.

MUNICIPAL LIBRARIES

(Vernon's Annotated Missouri Statutes, 1982, s.182.140-182.301,
182.410-182.460, 137.030.)

182.140. Petition for library tax—rate—election—library fund—increase in rate, procedure—reconsideration

1. Whenever voters equal to five percent of the total vote cast for governor at the last election in any city now or hereafter containing more than four thousand and less than six hundred thousand inhabitants petition the mayor, common council or other proper governing body in writing asking that an annual tax be levied for the establishment and maintenance of a free public library in the city, and specify in their petition a rate of taxation of not more than twenty-five cents for each one hundred dollars of assessed valuation on all the taxable property in the city, the governing body shall direct that the question be submitted to the voters of the city at an election. The order of the governing body and the notice shall

specify the name of the city and the rate of taxation mentioned in the petition.

2.   The question shall be submitted in substantially the following form: Shall there be a ...... cent tax for each one hundred dollars assessed valuation for a public library?

3.   If, from returns of the election, the majority of all the votes cast on the question are in favor of the tax, the governing body shall enter of record a brief recital of the returns and that there has been established a public library and thereafter the free public library shall be established, and shall be a body corporate, and known as such.

4.   The tax specified in the notice, subject to the provisions of this section, shall be levied and collected, from year to year, in like manner with other general taxes of the city. The proceeds of the levy, together with all interest accruing on same, with library fines, collections, bequests and donations in money shall be deposited in the city treasury and shall be known as the "City Library Fund", and shall be kept separate and apart from other moneys of the city, and disbursed by the proper city finance officer only upon properly authenticated warrants of the city library board of trustees.

5.   In case the proposed tax is sought as an increased tax for the maintenance of a free public library already established over a lesser tax rate theretofore voted and adopted, then such fact shall be recited in the petition and the notice of the election.

6.   The question shall be submitted in substantially the following form: Shall there be a ...... cent tax increase over the present .... tax for the public library?

7.   If a majority of all the votes cast on the question is for the tax submitted, the tax specified in the notice shall be levied and collected in like manner with other general taxes of the city, and shall be known as and become a part of the "City Library Fund," and be administered as provided in section 182.200.

8.   The tax may be reconsidered whenever the voters of the city determine by a majority vote given at an election.
Amended by Laws 1974, p. 805, § 1; Laws 1976, p. 672, § 1; Laws 1978, p. 341, § 1.

182.145.   Cities maintaining library prior to August 29, 1955, may levy tax for and maintain library

Any incorporated city having lawfully established a free public library prior to the effective date of section 182.140, and having had at that time authority to levy and collect a tax for the establishment and maintenance of the library, may levy and collect a tax for the maintenance of the library, and reduce or increase the tax in the manner provided in section 182.140.   (L. 1957 p. 461 § 1)

182.150.   Election on tax to establish and maintain library—procedure (cities over 600,000)

1.   In cities of six hundred thousand inhabitants or over when one hundred voters of the city, or the library board of any free public library heretofore established in the city, petition in writing the mayor and council, or the mayor and board of aldermen, of the city asking that an annual tax be levied for the establishment, maintenance, rehabilitation or extension of a free public library, or for the maintenance, rehabilitation or extension of a free public library therefore established in the city, and specify in their petition a rate of taxation not to exceed thirty cents for

each one hundred dollars assessed valuation of all taxable property in the city, the mayor and council, or mayor and board of aldermen, shall submit the question at an election.

2. The question shall be submitted in substantially the following form:

Shall there be a . . . . . . tax for each one hundred dollars valuation for a public library?

3. In case the proposed tax is sought as an increased tax for the maintenance, rehabilitation or extension of a library already established, over a lesser tax rate theretofore voted and adopted, then the fact shall be recited in the petition and the notice for the election.

4. The question shall be submitted in substantially the following form:

Shall there be a . . . . . . tax increase over the present . . . . tax per hundred dollars assessed valuation for the free public library?

5. If a majority of all the votes cast on the question is for the tax submitted, the tax specified in the notice shall be levied and collected in like manner with other general taxes of the city, and the proceeds of said tax shall be known as and become a part of the "Library Fund", to be administered as provided in section 182.440.

6. The tax shall cease or the tax rate thereof be decreased whenever the voters of the city determine by a majority vote on the question. The tax rate may be increased to but not to exceed the rate or limit as may be hereafter provided by law upon like petition, order of mayor and common council or board of aldermen, notice of election and the purpose thereof, and majority vote in favor of such increase as provided by this section to be made, given, filed and held as in the case of establishing the public library. Nothing contained in this section or done pursuant to its provisions shall be construed to waive or satisfy the duty of the general assembly under section 10 of article IX of the constitution of this state to grant aid to any free public library supported by the city, in such manner and in such amounts as may be provided by law. Any tax rate authorized hereunder may be levied in excess of the rates of taxation authorized by law for general municipal purposes, or for county purposes of the city of St. Louis, pursuant to section 11 of article X of the constitution of this state.

Amended by Laws 1969, p. 288, § 1; Laws 1974, p. 805, § 1; Laws 1978, p. 341, § 1.

182.170.   Trustees, number, appointment

When any city establishes and maintains a public library under sections 182.140 to 182.301, the mayor or other proper official of the city, with the approval of the legislative branch of the city government, shall proceed to appoint a library board of nine trustees, chosen from the citizens at large, with reference to their fitness for the office. No member of the city government shall be a member of the board. (R.S.1939 § 14753; L.1955 p. 555 § 1 (§ 182.160))

182.180.   Terms of office of trustees—removal

The trustees shall hold office, one-third for one year, one-third for two years and one-third for three years from the first of July following their appointment, and at their first regular meeting shall cast lots for the respective terms; and annually thereafter the mayor or other proper official, before the first of July of each year, shall appoint three trustees, who shall hold office for three years. The mayor or other proper official, by and with the consent of the legislative branch of the city government, may remove any trustee for misconduct or neglect of duty. (R.S.1939 § 14754; L.1955 p. 555 § 1 (§ 182.170))

182.190. Vacancies, how filled—three terms disqualifies—nepotism forbidden

Vacancies in the board of trustees, occasioned by removals, resignations or otherwise, shall be reported to the proper official and be filled in like manner as original appointments, except that if the vacancy is an unexpired term, the appointment shall be made for only the unexpired portion of that term. No member of the board shall serve for more than three successive full terms and shall not be eligible for further appointment to the board until two years after the expiration of the third term. No trustee shall receive compensation as such, and no person shall be employed by the board who is related either by blood or by marriage to any trustee of the board. (R.S.1939 § 14755; L.1955 p. 555 § 1 (§ 182.180))

182.200. Organization of board—general powers—rules and regulations—librarian—exchange services

1. The trustees, immediately after appointment, shall meet and organize by the election of one of their number as president, and by the election of such other officers as they may deem necessary.

2. They shall make and adopt such bylaws, rules and regulations for their own guidance, and for the government of the library, as may be expedient, and not inconsistent with sections 182.140 to 182.301.

3. They shall appoint a properly qualified librarian who shall be the chief executive and administrative officer for the library.

4. They shall have the exclusive control of the expenditure of all moneys collected to the credit of the library fund, and of the construction of any library building, and of the supervision, care and custody of the grounds, rooms or buildings constructed, leased, or set apart for that purpose. All moneys received for the library shall be deposited in the city treasury to the credit of the city library fund, and shall be kept separate and apart from other moneys of the city, and drawn upon by the proper officers of the city, upon the properly authenticated warrants of the library board.

5. The board, as a body corporate, may sue and be sued, com-

plain and defend, and make and use a common seal, purchase or lease grounds, purchase, lease, occupy or erect an appropriate building or buildings for the use of the public library and branches thereof, sell and convey real estate and personal property for and on behalf of the public library and branches thereof, receive gifts of real and personal property for the use and benefit of the public library and branch libraries thereof, the same when accepted to be held and controlled by the board of trustees, according to the terms of the deed, gift, devise or bequest of such property.

6. The board may extend the privileges and use of the library to nonresidents through agreements with other existing libraries allowing for exchanges of services, upon such terms and conditions as the boards of the libraries, from time to time, may prescribe. (R.S.1939 § 14756; L.1955 p. 555 § 1 (§ 182.190))

182.210. Annual report of librarian, contents, when submitted

The librarian shall make, within eight weeks after the end of the fiscal year of the library, an annual report to the board of trustees, stating the condition of the library and its services on the last day of the fiscal year, the various sums of money received from the library fund and from other sources, and how the moneys have been expended and for what purposes, and such other statistics, information and suggestions as may be of general interest. This report shall be transmitted by the board to the proper official and governing body of the city and a copy shall be transmitted at the same time to the Missouri state library. (R.S. 1939 § 14758; L.1955 p. 555 § 1 (§ 182.200))

182.230. Library free to public subject to regulations

Every library and reading room established under sections 182.140 to 182.301 shall be forever free to the use of the inhabitants of the city where located, always subject to such reasonable rules and regulations as the library board may adopt in order to render the use of the library and reading room of the greatest benefit to the greatest number. The board may exclude from the use of the library and reading room any and all persons who willfully violate such rules. The board may extend the privileges and use of the library and reading room to persons residing outside of the city in this state, upon such terms and conditions as the board, from time to time, by its regulations, may prescribe. (R. S.1939 § 14757; L.1955 p. 555 § 1 (§ 182.210))

182.240. Council may provide penalties for damage to property

The governing body of the city may pass ordinances imposing

suitable penalties for the punishment of persons committing injury upon the library or the grounds or other property thereof, and for injury to or failure to return any book belonging to the library. (R.S.1939 § 14759; L.1955 p. 555 § 1 (§ 182.220))

182.260. Library, building and maintenance, tax—duration—election—fund established—(cities 10,000 or over)

Whenever in any city which has decided or shall hereafter decide to establish and maintain a free public library under the provisions of sections 182.140 to 182.301, voters equal to five percent of the total vote cast for governor at the last election in the city in writing petition the proper authorities, asking that an annual tax be levied as an increased rate of taxation for the erection and maintenance of free public library buildings in the city, and specify in their petition a rate of taxation not to exceed two mills on the dollar annually, and not to be levied for more then ten years on all taxable property in the city, and the board of trustees of the free public library of the city deems it necessary that the library buildings be erected and properly maintained and refurbished, and so express its opinion by resolution, then the question shall be submitted at an election. The order of the governing body and the notice shall specify the name of the city and the rate of taxation mentioned in the petition. If a majority of the voters voting on the question vote in favor of the increased tax the tax specified in the notice shall be levied and collected in like manner with other general taxes of the city, and shall be known as the "Library Building, Maintenance and Refurbishing Fund". All funds received pursuant to this section shall be utilized by the board of trustees for erection of a library or for the normal maintenance, remodeling or refurbishing of any existing library under the control of the board.
Amended by Laws 1978, p. 342, § 1; Laws 1982, p. ——, S.B.No.495, § 1, effective April 30, 1982.

182.270. Plans—contracts for library building (cities 10,000 or over)

When it has been determined at the election to provide for the erection of a free public library building, the board of trustees shall proceed to have plans and specifications of a public library building prepared, shall take bids thereon for the construction of the building and shall let the contract therefor to the lowest and best responsible bidder, and shall require of such bidder securities for the performance of his bid. The board may let parts of the material or labor for the erection of the building to different bidders, as to it may seem best, and may reject any and all bids. (R.S.1939 § 14765; L.1955 p. 555 § 1 (§ 182.260))

182.280. Board may sell lands, when—exceptions (cities 10,000 or over)

Whenever the board of trustees of any public library acquires a lot or tract of land, and the board determines that it is not judicious to erect the library building upon the lot, the board may sell or exchange the lot and to use the proceeds of the sale or exchange for the purposes of a site for a library building, or for the erection of a library building, on any other land purchased or leased by or donated to the board and which it may deem suitable for the building. Sections 182.260, 182.270 and 182.280 shall not apply to cities under ten thousand inhabitants. (R.S. 1939 § 14766; L.1955 p. 555 § 1 (§ 182.270))

182.291. City-county library, how organized—board of trustees, duties—effect of merger on assets and liabilities—funds, how handled—budget required

1. After the establishment of a county library district as provided in section 182.010, the board of trustees of any city library within the county, which city has a population of more than four thousand and a library tax levy equal to that levied for the county library district, and which county library district has a population of under two hundred and fifty thousand, with the prior approval of the governing body of the city, may petition the county court to permit the organization of a city-county library to provide library service to the residents of the county by appropriate means from the city library.

2. After the county library board has been appointed as provided in section 182.050, the county library board may petition the county court to permit the organization of a city-county library which shall provide library service to the residents of the county by appropriate means from the city library. Within thirty days after receiving the petition the county court shall notify the county library board and the city library board of its decision by order of record. If the petition is approved the city-county library shall be deemed established; but if the petition is denied the parties may proceed as provided in sections 182.010 to 182.120.

3. The city-county library shall be under the control and supervision of a board of trustees of nine members. If the population of the county is larger than that of the city the county court shall appoint five members of the library board. If the population of the county is less than that of the city the county court shall appoint four members of the library board. If the population of the city is larger than that of the county the mayor of the city shall appoint five members to the library board. If the population of the city is less than that of the county the mayor shall appoint four members to the library board. The members shall serve a term of three years and until their successors are appointed and qualified in the same manner as their predecessors; except that the original members shall serve terms ranging from one to three years to be determined by the board at its first meeting. Immediately upon their appointment, the board shall organize as provided in section 182.060; and thereupon the city board shall cease to exist and shall turn over all property, books and records to the city-county board.

4. All unexpended funds of the preexisting separate city and county library districts shall be deposited by the custodians thereof with the city treasurer immediately upon the issuance of the county court approval of the petition.

5. For all tax purposes, including levies and adjustments thereof, the city library district shall become a part of the county library district at the beginning of the next fiscal year after the merger and the property within the city library district shall be treated as within the county library district for all such purposes; except, until the city library district shall become a part of the county library district the levy and collection

of taxes shall be made as though no merger had taken place, so that the levy and collection of taxes shall be without interruption, and during that period no change in the levy shall take place. The funds collected shall be turned over to the city treasurer immediately upon collection.

6. All of the real and personal property and all of the obligations of the preexisting separate city and county library districts shall, without further action, become the property and obligations of the merged city-county library district, which shall have an official name composed of the name of the city, followed by the name of the county and followed by the words "county library district".

7. The merged district, and the librarian, officials and board thereof, shall have all of the rights, powers, responsibilities, and privileges granted county library districts by the laws of the state of Missouri and shall be governed by such laws, as though the merged districts were a county library district, except:

(1) Where such laws are inconsistent with this section.

(2) The city treasurer shall be the custodian of all library funds, which shall be deposited by the city treasurer, in a depository selected and approved by the library board. The library funds shall be kept separate and apart from other moneys of the city and disbursed by the city treasurer only upon the proper authenticated warrants of the library board. Such funds shall be audited annually by the city in the same manner as other funds of the city are audited.

(3) The library board shall prepare a budget for each fiscal year and all expenditures shall conform to such budget. The budget shall be prepared and approved by the library board and made available to the members of the governing body of the city and the members of the county court sixty days before the beginning of each fiscal year, except the first budget of the merged district shall be prepared forthwith and so delivered after the merger.
Amended by Laws 1972, p. 778, § 1; Laws 1976, p. 672, § 1.

182.301. City or city-county library may contract for co-operative service

Any city library board or any city-county library board may contract for cooperative service with the body having control of a city library or school library or a county or other public library or any other library within the state under such terms or conditions as may be stated in the contract and the body having control of any library in the state may contract with city, city-county, county or public library in the state. (L.1955 p. 555 § 1 (§ 182.240))

182.410. Directors—appointment—number—board to be bi-partisan

When any incorporated city containing over three hundred thousand inhabitants shall have decided to establish and maintain a public library and reading room under this chapter, the mayor of such city shall, with the approval of the city council, proceed to appoint a board of nine directors for the same, chosen from the citizens at large, with reference to their fitness for such office; and no member of the municipal government shall be a member of said board; provided, that not more than five of such directors shall be members of the same political party. (R.S.1939 § 14777)

182.420. Term of directors—removal

Said directors shall hold office, one-third for one year, one-third for two years and one-third for three years, from the first of June following their appointment, and at their first regular meeting shall cast lots for their respective terms; and annually thereafter the mayor shall, before the first of June of each year, appoint, as before, three directors who shall hold office for three years, and until their successors are appointed. The mayor may, by and with the consent of the city council, remove any director for misconduct or neglect of duty. (R.S.1939 § 14778)

182.430. Vacancies, how filled—no compensation

Vacancies in the board of directors, occasioned by removals, resignation or otherwise, shall be reported to the mayor, and be filled in like manner as original appointments, and no director shall receive compensation as such. (R.S.1939 § 14779)

182.440. Duty of board—appointment of officers—powers

1. Said directors shall be known and styled in their corporate name as the board of directors of the public library, and in such name may exercise the powers herein granted.

2. They shall, immediately after appointment, meet and organize by the election of one of their number as president, and by the election of such other officers as they may deem necessary.

3. They shall make and adopt such bylaws, rules and regulations for their own guidance, and for the government of the library and reading room, as may be expedient, not inconsistent with this chapter.

4. They shall have the exclusive control of the expenditure of all moneys collected to the credit of the library fund, and of the construction of any library building, and of the supervision, care and custody of the grounds, rooms or buildings constructed, leased or set apart for that purpose; provided, that all moneys received for such library shall be deposited in the treasury of said city, to the credit of the library fund, and shall be kept separate and apart from other moneys of such city, and drawn upon by the proper officers of said city, upon the properly authenticated vouchers of the library board.

5. Said board shall have power to purchase, hold or lease

grounds, to occupy, lease or erect an appropriate building or buildings for the use of the said library, and to issue bonds, secured by deed of trust on any land of which they may be possessed, for the purpose of erecting library buildings, and for no other purpose; and all property by such board purchased, or otherwise obtained, shall vest in such board as a body corporate, and be held by it in trust.

6. They shall have power to appoint a suitable librarian and necessary assistants, and fix their compensation, and shall also have power to remove such appointees; and shall, in general, carry out the spirit and intent of this chapter in establishing and maintaining a public library and reading room. (R.S.1939 § 14780)

182.450. Board to make annual report—contents

The said board of directors shall make, on or before the second Monday in June, an annual report to the mayor, stating the condition of their trust on the first day of May of that year, the various sums of money received from the library fund and from other sources, and how such moneys have been expended and for what purposes; the number of books and periodicals on hand, the number added by purchase, gift or otherwise, during the year; the number and general character and kind of such books, with such other statistics, information and suggestions as they may deem of general interest. All such portions of said report as relate to the receipt and expenditure of money, as well as the number of books on hand, books lost or missing, and books purchased, shall be verified by affidavit. (R.S.1939 § 14781)

182.460. City to provide penalties

The said cities shall have power to pass ordinances imposing suitable penalties for the punishment of persons committing injury upon such library, or the grounds or other property thereof, and for injury to or failure to return any book belonging to such library. (R.S.1939 § 14782)

137.030. Levy for library purposes

1. Any county, or other political subdivision otherwise authorized by law to support and conduct a library, may levy for library purposes in addition to the limits prescribed in article X of the constitution a rate of taxation on all property subject to its taxing powers in an amount as now or hereafter prescribed by law; provided, that political subdivisions now having or hereafter having a population of not less than two hundred thousand inhabitants nor more than six hundred thousand inhabitants according to the last federal decennial census are authorized to levy for library purposes a rate which shall not exceed ten cents on the hundred dollars assessed valuation, annually, on all taxable property in such sub-

division and may, upon compliance with the provisions of subsection 2 of this section, levy an additional tax of not to exceed twenty cents the first year such tax is levied after September 28, 1979, twenty-one and one-half cents the second year such a tax is levied after September 28, 1979, twenty-three cents the third year such a tax is levied after September 28, 1979, and twenty-five cents the fourth year and each year thereafter in which such a tax is levied after September 28, 1979, for a total of not to exceed thirty-five cents on the hundred dollars assessed valuation, annually, on all taxable property in such subdivision.

2. In political subdivisions now having or hereafter having a population of not less than two hundred thousand inhabitants nor more than six hundred thousand inhabitants according to the last federal decennial census and levying the full tax of ten cents for library purposes provided for in subsection 1, the governing board or other governing body of the political subdivision may submit the question to the voters.

3. The question shall be submitted in substantially the following form: Shall the .... (name of governing board or other governing body) of .... (name of political subdivision) be authorized to levy a ... cent tax over the present ... cent tax for the free public library?

4. If a majority of all of the votes cast on the question is for the proposed grant of additional authority to levy tax, the governing board or other governing body of the political subdivision may thereafter annually levy a tax within the limitation of the authority granted, the tax to be collected in like manner with other taxes for the political subdivision.

5. Nothing contained in this section or done pursuant to its provisions shall be construed to waive or satisfy the duty of the general assembly, under section 10 of article IX of the constitution of this state, to grant aid to any free public library supported by the political subdivision, in such manner and in such amounts as may be provided by law. Any tax rate authorized hereunder may, pursuant to section 11(c) of article X of the constitution of this state, be levied in excess of the rates of taxation authorized by law for general municipal, county or school purposes of the political subdivision.

Amended by Laws 1971, p. 201, § 1; Laws 1972, p. 661, § 1; Laws 1978, p. 318, § 1; Laws 1979, p. 321, § 1; Laws 1982, p. ——, S.B.No.495, § 1, effective April 30, 1982.

MUNICIPAL LIBRARY DISTRICTS

(Vernon's Annotated Missouri Statutes, 1982, s.182.480-182.510.)

182.480. Municipal library districts created in cities—property subject to taxation

As of October 13, 1965, and any other provisions of law to the contrary notwithstanding, all of the area or territory included within the geographical boundaries of a city, including any area or territory which becomes a part of any city pursuant to any annexation pending on October 13, 1965, which maintains a free public library supported at least in part by taxation, shall be a "municipal library district" and shall have as its purpose the furnishing of free public library services to residents of the district, and the district shall be known as "The city of .... Municipal Library District", and each such district shall be a political subdivision of the state of Missouri and a body corporate with all the powers and rights of like or similar corporations, and as of the effective date of sections 182.130 and 182.480 to 182.510, all of the area or territory which is hereby included within a municipal library district shall be excluded from the boundaries of any existing county library district, and all of the taxable property located in the municipal library district shall only be subject to taxation by the municipal library district and shall hereafter not be subject to taxation by the county library dis-

trict; provided, however, that after October 13, 1965, any annexation by
a city having within its boundaries a municipal library district shall not
extend the boundaries of the municipal library district, and any annexed
areas shall remain in the county library district, and the taxable property in any such annexed areas shall only be subject to taxation by the
county library district and shall not be subject to taxation by the municipal library district; except, that in any county not having a county library any such annexation shall likewise extend the boundaries of any
existing municipal library district.

Laws 1965, p. 312, § 2, amended by Laws 1969, p. 290, § A.

182.490.   City library tax rate to be continued—construction of library laws

The current library tax rate being levied in any city in which there shall
be a municipal library district pursuant to the provisions hereof shall
continue to be levied by or for the benefit of the municipal library district, and all of the provisions of sections 182.010 to 182.460 shall apply
to the municipal library districts established by section 182.480, except
any such provision as may be inconsistent with, or repugnant to, the provisions of sections 182.480 to 182.510. Any reference to a city library
shall mean a municipal library district, and any reference to the area or
territory of a city shall mean the area or territory in a municipal library
district, it being the intention of the legislature that sections 182.010 to
182.460 as applied to the municipal library districts created by section
182.480 shall be construed in harmony with sections 182.480 to 182.510
as far as the same may be practicable.

Laws 1965, p. 312, § 3. Amended by Laws 1978, p. 343, § 1.

182.500.   Excluded property subject to taxation from payment of bonded indebtedness—alternative

All real property excluded from a county library district as provided
in sections 182.130 and 182.480 shall thereafter be subject to the levy
of taxes for the payment of any bonded indebtedness of the county library
district outstanding at the time of exclusion and for no other purpose;
provided, however, that any buildings and improvements thereafter erected or constructed on the excluded real property, and all machinery and
equipment thereafter installed or placed therein or thereon, and all tangible, personal property thereafter located therein or thereon shall not be
subject to the levy of any taxes of the county library district. In lieu of
the continuing taxation of the real property excluded from the county
library district, the governing body of the city in which the excluded
property is situated may pay to the county library district a sum equal
to that portion of the total bonded indebtedness of the county library
district that the assessed valuation of the excluded property bears to
the total assessed value of the county library district prior to the exclusion, after which payment the excluded property shall no longer be subject to any levy of taxes by the county library district. The funds paid
to the county library district shall be used for retiring the bonds of the
county library district.

Laws 1965, p. 312, § 5, amended by Laws 1969, p. 290, § A.

182.510.   Law not to prevent merger of city and county district

Nothing in sections 182.480 to 182.510 shall be construed so as to
prevent the merger of the city library and the county library district as
provided in section 182.040 or 182.291.

Laws 1965, p. 312, § 6, amended by Laws 1969, p. 290, § A; Laws 1971,
p. 96, § 1.

SCHOOL DISTRICT LIBRARIES
(Vernon's Annotated Missouri Statutes, 1982, s.164.081-164.111,
170.211,177.151.)

164.081. Levy of library building tax-vote required—rate and period of levy

The board of directors of any urban school district, in addition to other taxes it is authorized to levy for school purposes or library purposes, may levy a tax on all tangible taxable property subject to its taxing powers for the purchase of sites and for the erection, furnishing and maintenance of public library buildings and reading rooms, when authorized by approving vote of two-thirds of the voters of the district voting on the proposal as submitted by the board. The rate of the levy shall not exceed one and one-half cents on the one hundred dollars assessed valuation, and shall be submitted to be in effect annually for a period not in excess of five years, but nothing herein shall prevent the submission and approval of successive proposals for periods not in excess of five years each. Amended by Laws 1978, p. 332, § 1.

164.091. Notice of election

Whenever the board of directors, by resolution adopted by vote of not less than two-thirds of the members of the board, determines that the additional levy, at a rate and for a period fixed in the resolution, is necessary or desirable, they shall cause notice to be given that the proposed levy will be submitted. The notice shall state the proposed rate of levy and the period for which it is proposed to be levied annually. Amended by Laws 1978, p. 332, § 1.

164.101. Form of ballot

The question shall be submitted in substantially the following form:

Shall there be levied an additional tax at the rate of ...... cents on the one hundred dollars assessed valuation for a period of ...... years for library building purposes?

Amended by Laws 1978, p. 333, § 1.

164.111. Levy and collection of tax—library building fund

If two-thirds of the voters voting on the proposal vote in favor of the additional tax the result of the vote and the rate of taxation so voted and the period of years for which voted shall be certified by the secretary of the board to the clerk of the county court of the proper county who shall thereupon assess the amount at the rate returned on all tangible taxable property of the school district and the taxes shall be collected and paid over to the treasurer of the school district in like manner and with other general property taxes of the school district. The treasurer of the school district shall place the revenue derived from the tax in a separate fund to be known as the "Library Building Fund", which shall be subject to the exclusive control of the school board and shall be used for no purpose other than as stated in sections 164.081 to 164.111. The tax is in addition to the annual tax authorized to be levied under the provisions of section 137.030, RSMo. (L. 1963 p. 250 § 5–11)

170.211. Public library—powers of board in urban districts

1. The school board of any urban school district may establish and maintain a library and free reading room for the use of the school district, and may appropriate such sums as the board deems proper for the support of the library and reading room.

2. The school board may in the name of the school district accept, hold, invest and reinvest, use and disburse any donations, bequests or devises made to it for the benefit of the library or for library purposes in accordance with the terms of the donation, bequest or devise. (L.1963 p. 296 § 10–21)

177.151. Public auditorium—powers of board

The board may erect, construct and maintain, and use for all purposes connected with or incident to the work of the public schools or library or art gallery or museum, and let out to others for compensation, an auditorium or public hall suitable for public gatherings. The auditorium may be erected or constructed either in connection with the building devoted to the public library, art gallery or museum, or separate therefrom. The proceeds of rents over expenses shall be used for the purchase of books for the public library. (L.1963 p. 304 § 12—15)

SCHOOL LIBRARIES
(Vernon's Annotated Missouri Statutes, 1982, s.170.181-170.201.)

170.181. State school library board

A state school library board is created consisting of the state commissioner of education and four members appointed by the state board of education to serve for four years and until their successors are appointed. The state commissioner of education shall be ex officio chairman. (L.1963 p. 295 § 10–18)

170.191. Board to select lists of books for school libraries —contract with publishers—duty of commissioner of education

The state school library board shall select, classify and recommend a list of suitable books for school libraries, supplementary reading and school reference books. The list shall contain not less than forty suitable books to supplement the regular schoolroom work in each of the following lines: Reading, literature, history, geography and nature study, or practical agriculture. The list may be revised every two years by the board. The board shall enter into contract with the publishers of the selected books to furnish them, transportation charges prepaid, at the lowest possible costs to the districts. The state commissioner of education shall publish and distribute to the district clerks of the state a classified list of selected books, setting forth contract price of each. (L.1963 p. 295 § 10–19)

170.201. Boards may accept gifts for libraries—investment (six-director districts)

The board of any six-director district may accept and receive gifts and devises for the erection and endowment of libraries and for the purchase of books, and may invest the endowment fund upon the same security and in the same manner as required by section 7, article IX, of the Constitution of Missouri. (L. 1963 p. 296 § 10–20)

COUNTY LAW LIBRARIES

(Vernon's Annotated Missouri Statutes, 1982, s.514.440-514.480.)

514.440. Deposit required in civil actions—exemptions (first class counties)

The circuit judge or judges of the circuit court in any county of class one in this state, by rule of court, may require the attorney or attorneys for any party filing suit in the circuit court, at the time of filing the suit, to deposit with the clerk of the court a sum not to exceed five dollars in addition to all other deposits now or hereafter required by law or court rule, and no summons shall issue until the deposit has been made. Sections 514.440 to 514.460 shall not apply to actions sent to the county on change of venue or cases within the probate jurisdiction, cases filed under chapter 517, RSMo, procedures, cases filed under small claims procedures, applications for trial de novo, or to suits, civil or criminal, filed by the county or state or any city.

Amended by Laws 1955, p. 314, § 1; Laws 1977, p. 651, § 1; Laws 1978, p. 935, § A (§ 1), effective Jan. 2, 1979.

514.450. Fund paid to treasurer designated by circuit judge—use of fund for law library

On the first day of each month said circuit clerk shall pay the entire fund created by said deposits during the preceding month to the circuit judge or judges of the circuit court of the county in which such deposits were made, or to such person as is designated by local circuit court rule as treasurer of said fund, and said fund shall be applied and expended under the direction and order of the circuit judge or judges of the circuit court of any such county for the maintenance and upkeep of the law library maintained by the bar association in any such county, or such other law library in any such county as may be designated by the circuit judge or judges of the circuit court of any such county; provided, that the judge or judges of the circuit of any such county, and the officers of all courts of record of any such county, shall be entitled at all reasonable times to use the library to the support of which said funds are applied.

Amended by Laws 1978, p. 936, § A (§ 1), effective Jan. 2, 1979.

514.470. Law library fee, judge may require, exceptions (second, third & fourth class counties)

The circuit judge or judges of the circuit court in any county of the second, third or fourth class in this state may by rule of court require the attorney or attorneys for any party filing suit in the circuit court, at the time of filing the suit, to deposit with the clerk of the court a sum not to exceed five dollars in the circuit court in any county of the third and fourth class, not to exceed ten dollars in any county of the second class, except a county of the second class which is required by law to hold circuit court in more than one city, in addition to all other deposits now or hereafter required by law or court rule, and no summons shall issue until such deposit has been made. This law does not apply to actions sent to the county on change of venue or cases within the probate jurisdiction, cases filed under chapter 517, RSMo, procedures, cases filed under small claims procedures, applications for trial de novo, or to suits, civil or criminal, filed by the county or state or any city.

Amended by Laws 1953, p. 315, § 1; Laws 1957, p. 297, § 1; Laws 1961, p. 223, § 1; Laws 1967, p. 662, § 1; Laws 1971, p. 463, § 1; Laws 1977, p. 652, § 1; Laws 1978, p. 936, § A (§ 1), effective Jan. 2, 1979.

514.475. Law library fee (certain second class counties)

In all counties of the second class which are required by law to hold circuit court in two cities and a law library is maintained in each of said cities, the circuit judges of the circuit court may by rule of court require the attorney or attorneys for any party filing suit in the circuit court at the time of filing the suit to deposit with the clerk of the circuit court a sum not to exceed ten dollars, in addition to all other deposits now or hereafter required by law or court rule, and no summons shall issue until such deposit has been made. This law does not apply to actions sent to the county on a change of venue or cases within the probate jurisdiction, cases filed under chapter 517, RSMo, procedures, cases filed under small claims procedures, applications for trial de novo, or to suits, civil or criminal, filed by the county or state or any city.

Added by Laws 1971, p. 463, § 1 (§ 514.475(1)). Amended by Laws 1978, p. 936, § A (§ 1), effective Jan. 2, 1979.

514.480. Payment of fees monthly to circuit judges—maintenance of library

On the first day of each month each of said circuit clerks shall pay the entire fund created by said deposits during the preceding month to the circuit judge or judges of the circuit court of the county in which such deposits were made, or to such person as the circuit judge or judges of the circuit court of said county may designated by local circuit court rule as treasurer of said fund, and said fund shall be applied and expended under the direction and order of the circuit judge or judges of the circuit court of any such county for the maintenance and upkeep of the law library maintained by the bar association in any such county or in an adjoining county, or such other law library in any such county, or in an adjoining county, as may be designated by the circuit judge or judges of the circuit court of any such county, provided that the judge or judges of the circuit court of any such county, and the officers of all courts of record of any such county and all attorneys licensed to practice law in any such county shall be entitled at all reasonable times to use the library to the support of which said funds are applied.

Amended by Laws 1955, p. 312, § 1; Laws 1967, p. 654, § 1; Laws 1969, p. 565, § 1; Laws 1978, § A (§ 1), effective Jan. 2, 1979.

PRISON LIBRARIES
(Vernon's Annotated Missouri Statutes, 1982, s.216.565.)

216.565. Educational program—curricula for academic and vocational training—libraries—education department to cooperate

1. The director of the division of inmate education shall, immediately after the effective date of this chapter, plan and institute a long-range program and courses of instruction for the education of the inmates of all institutions under the control of the department. This educational program shall include:

* * * * * * * *

(3) The maintenance of adequate library facilities in each institution for the use and benefits of the inmates thereof. (L.1955 p. 318 § A [§ 49])

MISCELLANEOUS PROVISIONS
(Vernon's Annotated Missouri Statutes, 1982, s.182.800, 182.810; State Constitution, Art. 10, s.11.C.)

182.800. Free libraries—funds, investment of
The governing board of any free library district may invest funds of the district. The board may invest the funds in either open time deposits for ninety days or certificates of deposit in a depositary selected by the board, if the depositary has deposited securities under the provisions of sections 110.010 and 110.020, RSMo; or in bonds, redeemable at maturity at par, of the state of Missouri, of the United States, or of any wholly owned corporation of the United States; or in other short term obligations of the United States. No open time deposits shall be made or bonds purchased to mature beyond the date that the funds are needed for the purpose for which they were received by the district. Interest accruing from the investment of funds in such deposits or bonds shall be credited to the library district fund from which the money was invested. Laws 1971, p. 222, § 1.

182.810. Insurance for library boards
The library board or board of trustees of any library in the state supported in whole or in part by taxation may purchase and maintain insurance for members of the board, individually, against any liabilities incurred as board members.
Added by Laws 1982, p. ——, S.B.No.835, § 1.

§ 11(c). Increase of tax rate by popular vote
* * * * * and provided further, that any county or other political subdivision, when authorized by law and within the limits fixed by law, may levy a rate of taxation on all property subject to its taxing powers in

excess of the rates herein limited, for library, hospital, public health, recreation grounds and museum purposes.   Adopted Nov. 7, 1950.

Missouri library laws are reprinted from VERNON'S AN-NOTATED MISSOURI STATUTES published by Vernon Law Book Co., Kansas City, Missouri.

MONTANA

STATE LIBRARY COMMISSION
(Montana Code Annotated, 1982, s.22-1-101 to 22-1-103, 2-15-1511, 2-15-1514.)

22-1-101. State library commission established. A commission is hereby created to be known as the state library commission. This commission shall consist of the librarian of the university of Montana, the state superintendent of public instruction, ex officio member, and the three members to be appointed by the governor, who shall serve 1, 2, and 3 years respectively. As these terms expire, annually thereafter one person shall be appointed for a term of 3 years. The commission shall annually elect a chairman from its membership. The members of said commission shall receive no compensation for their services except their travel expenses, as provided for in 2-18-501 through 2-18-503.

History: En. Sec. 1, Ch. 184, L. 1929; re-en. Sec. 1575.1, R.C.M. 1935; amd. Sec. 1, Ch. 91, L. 1945; amd. Sec. 1, Ch. 55, L. 1961; amd. Sec. 1, Ch. 215, L. 1965; amd. Sec. 23, Ch. 439, L. 1975; R.C.M. 1947, 44-127.

22-1-102. Librarian and assistants. The commission shall employ as its executive officer a librarian, who is a graduate of an accredited library school and is not a member of the commission, for such compensation as the commission considers adequate. The executive officer shall perform the duties assigned by the commission and serve at the will of the commission. The commission may also employ such other assistants as are required for the performance of the commission's work. In addition to their salaries while on commission business, the librarian and assistants shall be allowed their travel expenses, as provided for in 2-18-501 through 2-18-503, as amended.

History: En. Sec. 2, Ch. 184, L. 1929; re-en. Sec. 1575.2, R.C.M. 1935; amd. Sec. 2, Ch. 91, L. 1945; amd. Sec. 2, Ch. 55, L. 1961; amd. Sec. 7, Ch. 453, L. 1977; R.C.M. 1947, 44-128.

22-1-103. State library commission — authority. The state library commission shall have the power to:

(1) give assistance and advice to all tax-supported or public libraries in the state and to all counties, cities, towns, or regions in the state which may

propose to establish libraries, as to the best means of establishing and improving such libraries;

(2) maintain and operate the state library and make provision for its housing;

(3) accept and expend in accordance with the terms thereof any grant of federal funds which may become available to the state for library purposes;

(4) make rules and establish standards for the administration of the state library and for the control, distribution, and lending of books and materials;

(5) serve as the agency of the state to accept and administer any state, federal, or private funds or property appropriated for or granted to it for library service or foster libraries in the state and establish regulations under which funds shall be disbursed;

(6) provide library services for the blind and physically handicapped;

(7) furnish, by contract or otherwise, library assistance and information services to state officials, state departments, and residents of those parts of the state inadequately serviced by libraries;

(8) act as a state board of professional standards and library examiners and develop standards for public libraries and adopt rules for the certification of librarians;

(9) designate areas for the establishment of federations of libraries and designate the headquarters library for such federations.

History: En. Sec. 2, Ch. 215, L. 1965; amd. Sec. 1, Ch. 357, L. 1974; R.C.M. 1947, 44-131(part).

2-15-1511. Agencies allocated to state board of education. The state historical society, the Montana arts council, and the state library commission are allocated to the state board of education for purposes of planning and coordination. Budget requests to the state for these agencies shall be included with the budget requests of the state board of education; however, the governance, management, and control of the respective agencies shall be vested respectively in the board of trustees of the state historical society, the Montana arts council, and the state library commission.

History: En. 82A-501.1 by Sec. 5, Ch. 51, L. 1974; R.C.M. 1947, 82A-501.1.

2-15-1514. State library commission. (1) There is a state library commission which is created in Title 22, chapter 1.

(2) The composition, method of appointment, terms of office, compensation, reimbursement, and qualifications of commission members remain as prescribed by law.

History: En. 82A-509 by Sec. 1, Ch. 272, L. 1971; amd. Sec. 9, Ch. 51, L. 1974; R.C.M. 1947, 82A-509.

STATE LIBRARY
(Montana Code Annotated, 1982, s.22-1-201, 22-1-11 to 22-1-18.)

22-1-201. State library authorized. The state library commission shall maintain and operate a state library to be located in Helena.

History: En. 44-126.1 by Sec. 1, Ch. 3, L. 1977; R.C.M. 1947, 44-126.1.

22-1-211. Definitions. As used in this part, the following definitions apply:

(1) "Print" includes all forms of printing and duplicating, regardless of

format or purpose, with the exception of correspondence and interoffice memoranda.

(2) "State publication" includes any document, compilation, journal, law, resolution, bluebook, statute, code, register, pamphlet, list, book, proceedings, report, memorandum, hearing, legislative bill, leaflet, order, regulation, directory, periodical, or magazine issued in print or purchased for distribution by the state, the legislature, constitutional officers, any state department, committee, or other state agency supported wholly or in part by state funds.

(3) "State agency" includes every state office, officer, department, division, bureau, board, commission, and agency of the state and, where applicable, all subdivisions of each.

History: En. Sec. 1, Ch. 261, L. 1967; R.C.M. 1947, 44-132.

22-1-212. Creation of distribution center. There is hereby created, as a division of the state library and under the direction of the state librarian, a state publications library distribution center. The center shall promote the establishment of an orderly depository library system. To this end the state library commission shall make such rules necessary to carry out the provisions of this part.

History: En. Sec. 2, Ch. 261, L. 1967; R.C.M. 1947, 44-133.

22-1-213. State agency publications to be deposited in state library — interlibrary loan — sale publications. Every state agency shall deposit upon release at least four copies of each of its state publications with the state library for record and depository purposes. Additional copies shall also be deposited in quantities certified to the agencies by the state library as required to meet the needs of the depository library system and to provide interlibrary loan service to those libraries without depository status. Additional copies of sale publications required by the state library shall be furnished only upon reimbursement to the state agency of the full cost of such sale publications, and the state library shall also reimburse any state agency for additional publications so required where the quantity desired will necessitate additional printing or other expense to such agency.

History: En. Sec. 3, Ch. 261, L. 1967; R.C.M. 1947, 44-134.

22-1-214. Depository libraries — eligibility. The center shall enter into depository contracts with any municipal or county free library, state college or state university library, the library of congress, the midwest interlibrary center, and other state libraries. The requirements for eligibility to contract as a depository library shall be established by the state library commission upon recommendations of the state librarian. The standards shall include and take into consideration the type of library, ability to preserve such publications and to make them available for public use, and also such geographical locations as will make the publications conveniently accessible to residents in all areas of the state.

History: En. Sec. 4, Ch. 261, L. 1967; R.C.M. 1947, 44-135.

22-1-215. Available publications. The center shall publish and distribute regularly to contracting depository libraries and other libraries upon

request a list of available state publications.
History: En. Sec. 5, Ch. 261, L. 1967; R.C.M. 1947, 44-136.

22-1-216. Current publications. Upon request by the center, issuing
state agencies shall furnish the center with a complete list of their current
state publications and a copy of their mailing and/or exchange lists.
History: En. Sec. 6, Ch. 261, L. 1967; R.C.M. 1947, 44-137.

22-1-217. No general public distribution. The center shall not
engage in general public distribution of either state publications or lists of
publications.
History: En. Sec. 7, Ch. 261, L. 1967; R.C.M. 1947, 44-138.

22-1-218. Exemptions. This part does not apply to officers of or affect
the duties concerning publications distributed by:
(1)   the state law library;
(2)   the secretary of state in connection with his duties under
2-15-401(13);
(3)   the code commissioner in connection with his duties under Title 1,
chapter 11, as amended; and
(4)   the legislative council in connection with its duties under 5-11-203, as
amended.
History: En. Sec. 8, Ch. 261, L. 1967; amd. Sec. 2, Ch. 3, L. 1977; R.C.M. 1947, 44-139; amd.
Sec. 11, Ch. 138, L. 1979.

INTERSTATE LIBRARY COMPACT
(Montana Code Annotated, 1982, s.22-1-601 to 22-1-602.)

22-1-601. Library compact. The Interstate Library Compact is
hereby approved, enacted into law, and entered into by the state of Montana,
which compact is in full as follows:

INTERSTATE LIBRARY COMPACT

Article I.   Policy and Purpose

Because the desire for the services provided by libraries transcends governmental boundaries and can most effectively be satisfied by giving such services to communities and people regardless of jurisdictional lines, it is the
policy of the states party to this compact to cooperate and share their
responsibilities; to authorize cooperation and sharing with respect to those
types of library facilities and services which can be more economically or efficiently developed and maintained on a cooperative basis; and to authorize
cooperation and sharing among localities, states, and others in providing joint
or cooperative library services in areas where the distribution of population
or of existing and potential library resources make the provision of library
service on an interstate basis the most effective way of providing adequate
and efficient service.

Article II. Definitions

As used in this compact:

(1) "public library agency" means any unit or agency of local or state government operating or having power to operate a library;

(2) "private library agency" means any nongovernmental entity which operates or assumes a legal obligation to operate a library;

(3) "library agreement" means a contract establishing an interstate library district pursuant to this compact or providing for the joint or cooperative furnishing of library services.

Article III. Interstate Library Districts

(1) Any one or more public library agencies in a party state in cooperation with any public library agency or agencies in one or more other party states may establish and maintain an interstate library district. Subject to the provisions of this compact and any other laws of the party states which pursuant hereto remain applicable, such district may establish, maintain, and operate some or all of the library facilities and services for the area concerned in accordance with the terms of a library agreement therefor. Any private library agency or agencies within an interstate library district may cooperate therewith, assume duties, responsibilities, and obligations thereto, and receive benefits therefrom as provided in any library agreement to which such agency or agencies become party.

(2) Within an interstate library district, and as provided by a library agreement, the performance of library functions may be undertaken on a joint or cooperative basis or may be undertaken by means of one or more arrangements between or among public or private library agencies for the extension of library privileges to the use of facilities or services operated or rendered by one or more of the individual library agencies.

(3) If a library agreement provides for joint establishment, maintenance, or operation of library facilities or services by an interstate library district, such district shall have power to do any one or more of the following in accordance with such library agreement:

(a) undertake, administer, and participate in programs or arrangements for:

(i) securing, lending, or servicing books and other publications, any other materials suitable to be kept or made available by libraries, or library equipment; or

(ii) for the dissemination of information about libraries, the value and significance of particular items therein, and the use thereof;

(b) accept for any of its purposes under this compact any and all donations and grants of money, equipment, supplies, materials, and services (conditional or otherwise) from any state or the United States or any subdivision or agency thereof or interstate agency or from any institution, person, firm, or corporation and receive, utilize, and dispose of the same;

(c) operate mobile library units or equipment for the purpose of rendering bookmobile service within the district;

(d) employ professional, technical, clerical, and other personnel and fix terms of employment, compensation, and other appropriate benefits; and where desirable, provide for the in-service training of such personnel;

(e)   sue and be sued in any court of competent jurisdiction;

(f)   acquire, hold, and dispose of any real or personal property or any interest or interests therein as may be appropriate to the rendering of library service;

(g)   construct, maintain, and operate a library, including any appropriate branches thereof;

(h)   do such other things as may be incidental to or appropriate for the carrying out of any of the foregoing powers.

Article IV.   Interstate Library Districts, Governing Board

(1)   An interstate library district which establishes, maintains, or operates any facilities or services in its own right shall have a governing board which shall direct the affairs of the district and act for it in all matters relating to its business. Each participating public library agency in the district shall be represented on the governing board which shall be organized and conduct its business in accordance with provision therefor in the library agreement. But in no event shall a governing board meet less often than twice a year.

(2)   Any private library agency or agencies party to a library agreement establishing an interstate library district may be represented on or advise with the governing board of the district in such manner as the library agreement may provide.

Article V.   State Library Agency Cooperation

Any two or more state library agencies of two or more of the party states may undertake and conduct joint or cooperative library programs, render joint or cooperative library services, and enter into and perform arrangements for the cooperative or joint acquisition, use, housing, and disposition of items or collections of materials which, by reason of expense, rarity, specialized nature, or infrequency of demand therefor would be appropriate for central collection and shared use. Any such programs, services, or arrangements may include provision for the exercise on a cooperative or joint basis of any power exercisable by an interstate library district, and an agreement embodying any such program, service, or arrangement shall contain provisions covering the subjects detailed in Article VI of this compact for interstate library agreements.

Article VI.   Library Agreements

(1)   In order to provide for any joint or cooperative undertaking pursuant to this compact, public and private library agencies may enter into library agreements. Any agreement executed pursuant to the provisions of this compact shall, as among the parties to the agreement:

(a)   detail the specific nature of the services, programs, facilities, arrangements, or properties to which it is applicable;

(b)   provide for the allocation of costs and other financial responsibilities;

(c) specify the respective rights, duties, obligations, and liabilities of the parties;

(d) set forth the terms and conditions for duration, renewal, termination, abrogation, disposal of joint or common property, if any, and all other matters which may be appropriate to the proper effectuation and performance of the agreement.

(2) No public or private library agency shall undertake to exercise, itself or jointly with any other library agency, by means of a library agreement, any power prohibited to such agency by the constitution or statutes of its state.

(3) No library agreement shall become effective until filed with the compact administrator of each state involved and approved in accordance with Article VII of this compact.

Article VII. Approval of Library Agreements

(1) Every library agreement made pursuant to this compact shall, prior to and as a condition precedent to its entry into force, be submitted to the attorney general of each state in which a public library agency party thereto is situated, who shall determine whether the agreement is in proper form and compatible with the laws of his state. The attorneys general shall approve any agreement submitted to them unless they shall find that it does not meet the conditions set forth herein and shall detail in writing addressed to the governing bodies of the public library agencies concerned the specific respects in which the proposed agreement fails to meet the requirements of law. Failure to disapprove an agreement submitted hereunder within 90 days of its submission shall constitute approval thereof.

(2) In the event that a library agreement made pursuant to this compact shall deal in whole or in part with the provision of services or facilities with regard to which an officer or agency of the state government has constitutional or statutory powers of control, the agreement shall, as a condition precedent to its entry into force, be submitted to the state officer or agency having such power of control and shall be approved or disapproved by him or it as to all matters within his or its jurisdiction in the same manner and subject to the same requirements governing the action of the attorneys general pursuant to paragraph (1) of this article. This requirement of submission and approval shall be in addition to and not in substitution for the requirement of submission to and approval by the attorneys general.

Article VIII. Other Laws Applicable

Nothing in this compact or in any library agreement shall be construed to supersede, alter, or otherwise impair any obligation imposed on any library by otherwise applicable law nor to authorize the transfer or disposition of any property held in trust by a library agency in a manner contrary to the terms of such trust.

Article IX. Appropriations and Aid

(1) Any public library agency party to a library agreement may appropri-

ate funds to the interstate library district established thereby in the same manner and to the same extent as to a library wholly maintained by it and, subject to the laws of the state in which such public library agency is situated, may pledge its credit in support of an interstate library district established by the agreement.

(2) Subject to the provisions of the library agreement pursuant to which it functions and the laws of the states in which such district is situated, an interstate library district may claim and receive any state and federal aid which may be available to library agencies.

Article X. Compact Administrator

Each state shall designate a compact administrator with whom copies of all library agreements to which his state or any public library agency thereof is party shall be filed. The administrator shall have such other powers as may be conferred upon him by the laws of his state and may consult and cooperate with the compact administrators of other party states and take such steps as may effectuate the purposes of this compact. If the laws of a party state so provide, such state may designate one or more deputy compact administrators in addition to its compact administrator.

Article XI. Entry into Force and Withdrawal

(1) This compact shall enter into force and effect immediately upon its enactment into law by any two states. Thereafter, it shall enter into force and effect as to any other state upon the enactment thereof by such state.

(2) This compact shall continue in force with respect to a party state and remain binding upon such state until 6 months after such state has given notice to each other party state of the repeal thereof. Such withdrawal shall not be construed to relieve any party to a library agreement entered into pursuant to this compact from any obligation of that agreement prior to the end of its duration as provided therein.

Article XII. Construction and Severability

This compact shall be liberally construed so as to effectuate the purposes thereof. The provisions of this compact shall be severable, and if any phrase, clause, sentence, or provision of this compact is declared to be contrary to the constitution of any party state or of the United States or the applicability thereof to any government, agency, person, or circumstance is held invalid, the validity of the remainder of this compact and the applicability thereof to any government, agency, person, or circumstance shall not be affected thereby. If this compact shall be held contrary to the constitution of any state party thereto, the compact shall remain in full force and effect as to the remaining states and in full force and effect as to the state affected as to all severable matters.

History: En. Sec. 1, Ch. 119, L. 1967; R.C.M. 1947, 44-601.

22-1-602. Executive officer of state library commission as administrator. The executive officer of the state library commission shall be the compact administrator of the Interstate Library Compact.

History: En. Sec. 2, Ch. 119, L. 1967; R.C.M. 1947, 44-602.

STATE LAW LIBRARY
(Montana Code Annotated, 1982, s.22-1-501 to 22-1-506.)

22-1-501. State law library created. The library heretofore known as a department of the state library of Montana and called "the law library" shall become a separate and distinct library designated the "state law library of the state of Montana". The collections of laws, decisions of courts, law reports, textbooks, legal periodicals, and miscellaneous books and journals together with pamphlets, papers, maps, charts, and manuscripts now in the law library in the capitol building or belonging to such law library or hereafter acquired by or donated to the law library shall constitute the library hereby established, and the title to all of the property constituting the same now or hereafter shall be in the state of Montana, subject to the custody and control of the library board established herein.

History: En. Sec. 1, Ch. 153, L. 1949; R.C.M. 1947, 44-401.

22-1-502. Location — control by board of trustees. The state law library of the state of Montana shall be located in Helena, Montana, and shall be in the immediate custody and subject to the control of a board of trustees consisting of the chief justice and the justices of the supreme court of the state of Montana.

History: En. Sec. 2, Ch. 153, L. 1949; amd. Sec. 1, Ch. 142, L. 1977; R.C.M. 1947, 44-402; amd. Sec. 1, Ch. 252, L. 1981.

22-1-503. Authority of board. The powers and duties of said board are as follows:

(1) to make rules, not inconsistent with law, for the government of the board and for the government and administration of the state law library, including rules designating when and for what periods of time the library shall be open to the public and the office hours of the library;

(2) to appoint a librarian and prescribe the duties of such librarian when not otherwise provided for by law;

(3) to sell or exchange duplicate copies of books and pay the moneys arising therefrom into the state law library fund;

(4) to see that the books and other properties of the library are maintained in good order and repair and are protected from theft or injury;

(5) to draw from the state treasury at any time when needed for the legitimate expenses in maintaining and operating the library and acquiring books, reports, journals, and other works and properties therefor, including complete sets of statutory laws and codified laws of the United States of America, of the several states of the union, and of other jurisdictions, any moneys in the fund and available for such purposes;

(6) to report as provided in 2-7-102;

(7) to establish such lawful relations and working arrangements with the library of congress of the United States, with the copyright office therein, and with the superintendent of documents of the United States as may be for the benefit and advantage of the state law library and promote the

acquisition of books and other works from such sources as may be useful to those resorting to the facilities of the state law library.

History: En. Sec. 3, Ch. 153, L. 1949; amd. Sec. 14, Ch. 93, L. 1969; R.C.M. 1947, 44-403.

22-1-504. Duties of librarian. The librarian shall develop and maintain an adequate collection and services to fulfill the needs of library users and shall establish procedures for the maintenance and control of the collection.

History: En. Sec. 5, Ch. 153, L. 1949; amd. Sec. 2, Ch. 142, L. 1977; R.C.M. 1947, 44-405(2).

22-1-505. Use of library. The state law library shall be maintained and operated for the use of the members of the supreme court, the members of the legislature, the several officers of the senate and of the house of representatives, for state officers and employees, for members of the bar of the supreme court of Montana, for members of the bar of supreme courts of other states while in attendance before the supreme court of Montana, and members of the general public agreeing to the rules established by the librarian.

History: En. Sec. 5, Ch. 153, L. 1949; amd. Sec. 2, Ch. 142, L. 1977; R.C.M. 1947, 44-405(1).

22-1-506. Liability for injury to books or failure to return. Every person who defaces, tears, or otherwise injures any book or other work or who fails to return any book taken by him is liable to the state in three times the value thereof if such book is not replaced by a new one or another book of identical title, in good order and condition; and no statute of limitations shall ever be effective against the claim of the state under this section.

History: En. Sec. 6, Ch. 153, L. 1949; R.C.M. 1947, 44-406.

STATE ARCHIVES

(Montana Code Annotated, 1982, s.22-3-201 to 22-3-203, 22-3-211, 22-3-212, 22-3-221.)

22-3-201. Public policy. The legislature declares that it is the public policy of the state of Montana that noncurrent records of permanent value to the state should be preserved and protected; that the operations of state government should be made more efficient, more effective, and more economical through current records management; and that to the end that the people may receive maximum benefit from a knowledge of state affairs, the state should preserve its noncurrent records of permanent value for study and research.

History: En. Sec. 1, Ch. 108, L. 1969; R.C.M. 1947, 82-3207.

22-3-202. Archives created — appointment, duties, and compensation of archivist. There is a state archives in the Montana historical society for the preservation of noncurrent records of permanent value to the state and for records management. The director of the Montana historical society shall appoint a state archivist, who serves at the pleasure of the director, define his duties, and fix his compensation with the approval of the board of trustees of the Montana historical society.

History: En. Sec. 2, Ch. 108, L. 1969; R.C.M. 1947, 82-3208.

22-3-203. Preservation of noncurrent records of permanent value. The state archivist shall preserve noncurrent records of permanent value. Upon request, he shall assist and advise in the establishment of records management programs in the executive, legislative, and judicial branches of state government with due regard to the functions of the officers and agencies involved.

History: En. Sec. 3, Ch. 108, L. 1969; amd. Sec. 1, Ch. 41, L. 1973; R.C.M. 1947, 82-3209.

22-3-211. Historic records network — creation — purpose. (1) The trustees of the Montana historical society shall establish and coordinate the administration of an historic records network.

(2) The staff of the society shall aid staff archivists and librarians at the university units in their work of acquiring, cataloguing, processing, microfilming, and preserving historic records.

History: En. 44-523.1 by Sec. 3, Ch. 366, L. 1977; R.C.M. 1947, 44-523.1.

22-3-212. Funding. The historic records network shall operate within the budgets of the historical society and the university system.

History: En. 44-523.2 by Sec. 4, Ch. 366, L. 1977; R.C.M. 1947, 44-523.2.

22-3-221. Storing and safekeeping of war records. The board of trustees of the Montana historical society is hereby authorized and directed to set apart a suitable room in the buildings under their jurisdiction for the storing and safekeeping of such archives, records, etc., of the grand army of the republic and the united Spanish war veterans, and said room shall be suitably furnished, and the librarian for the Montana historical society shall be custodian of said archives, records, etc.

History: En. Sec. 1, Ch. 32, L. 1913; amd. Sec. 2, Ch. 97, L. 1915; re-en. Sec. 321, R.C.M. 1921; amd. Sec. 1, Ch. 96, L. 1927; re-en. Sec. 321, R.C.M. 1935; amd. Sec. 3, Ch. 93, L. 1953; R.C.M. 1947, 82-2502.

STATE HISTORICAL SOCIETY
(Montana Code Annotated, 1982, s.22-3-101 to 22-3-112.)

22-3-101. Historical society. The historical society of Montana, originally organized under the provisions of an act of the legislative assembly of the territory of Montana entitled "An Act to Incorporate the Historical Society of Montana", approved February 2, 1865, and thereafter made to become the historical society of the state of Montana by an act approved March 4, 1891, entitled "An Act Concerning the Historical Society for the State of Montana and Making an Appropriation Therefor" and by "An Act to Perpetuate the Historical Society of the State of Montana", approved March 1, 1949, is hereby continued and perpetuated as the Montana historical society and as such constitutes an agency of state government for the use, learning, culture, and enjoyment of the citizens of the state and for the acquisition, preservation, and protection of historical records, art, archival, and museum objects, historical places, sites, and monuments and the custody, maintenance, and operation of the historical library, museums, art galleries, and historical places, sites, and monuments.

History: En. Sec. 1, Ch. 47, L. 1963; R.C.M. 1947, 44-516.

22-3-102.   Definitions. As used in this part, the following definitions apply:

(1)   "Society" means the Montana historical society and includes:

(a)   the historical library and its contents;

(b)   any museums and art galleries and their contents acquired by the trustees;

(c)   any historical places, sites, or monuments acquired or developed by the society;

(d)   any divisions, departments, and activities operated in conjunction with the historical library as are established by the trustees; and

(e)   any books, papers, maps, charts, manuscripts, photographs, writings, records, objects of history and art, paintings, engravings, relics, collections of artifacts and minerals, furniture, or fixtures acquired by the trustees.

(2)   "Trustees" means the board of trustees of the Montana historical society.

(3)   "Committee" means the executive committee of the board of trustees of the Montana historical society.

(4)   "Historic records" means manuscripts, papers, maps, charts, journals, diaries, photographs, business records, voice recordings, films, video tapes, or other records illustrative of the history of Montana in particular and generally of the region.

(5)   "Historic records network" means an agreement between the Montana historical society and the Montana university system to facilitate exchange and cooperation in the use, acquisition, and preservation of historic records.

History: En. Sec. 2, Ch. 47, L. 1963; amd. Sec. 5, Ch. 3, L. 1977; amd. Sec. 1, Ch. 366, L. 1977; R.C.M. 1947, 44-517.

22-3-103.   Historical library — independence from other libraries, museums, or galleries. (1) There is a historical library, to be maintained and operated by the Montana historical society.

(2)   The historical library and any historical museum administered by the society in accordance with the provisions of this part shall be independent of any other library, museum, or gallery owned, maintained, or operated by the state of Montana.

History: (1)En. 44-515.1 by Sec. 4, Ch. 3, L. 1977; Sec. 44-515.1, R.C.M. 1947; (2)En. Sec. 3, Ch. 47, L. 1963; amd. Sec. 6, Ch. 3, L. 1977; Sec. 44-518, R.C.M. 1947; R.C.M. 1947, 44-515.1, 44-518.

22-3-104.   Appointment and qualifications of board of trustees. (1) The government and administration of the society are vested in a board of 15 trustees appointed by the governor, by and with the consent of the senate. Three each of the original members of the board shall be appointed for 1-, 2-, 3-, 4-, and 5-year terms. An appointment to replace a member whose term has expired shall be for 5 years. An appointment to replace a member whose term has not expired shall be for the unexpired term.

(2)   Trustees shall be appointed because of their special interest in the

accomplishment of the purposes of the society, their fitness for discharging these duties, and their willingness to devote time and effort in the public interest. The governor, insofar as possible, shall appoint trustees from the various geographical areas of the state.

(3) Of the 15 trustees, at least one shall be a recognized historian and at least one shall be a recognized archeologist.

(4) The governor shall appoint these professionals to the board of trustees as vacancies occur.

History: (1)En. Sec. 4, Ch. 47, L. 1963; Sec. 44-519, R.C.M. 1947; (2) thru (4)En. Sec. 5, Ch. 47, L. 1963; amd. Sec. 7, Ch. 3, L. 1977; amd. Sec. 1, Ch. 520, L. 1977; Sec. 44-520, R.C.M. 1947; R.C.M. 1947, 44-519, 44-520.

22-3-105. Compensation and expenses of trustees. Each member of the board of trustees is entitled to be paid $25 for each day in which he is actually and necessarily engaged in the performance of board duties, and he is also entitled to be reimbursed for travel expenses, as provided for in 2-18-501 through 2-18-503, as amended, incurred while in the performance of board duties. Members who are full-time salaried officers or employees of this state or of any political subdivision of this state are not entitled to be compensated for their service as members but are entitled to be reimbursed for their travel expenses.

History: En. 82A-507 by Sec. 1, Ch. 272, L. 1971; amd. Sec. 7, Ch. 51, L. 1974; amd. Sec. 1, Ch. 203, L. 1975; amd. Sec. 23, Ch. 453, L. 1977; R.C.M. 1947, 82A-507(3); amd. Sec. 1, Ch. 3, L. 1979.

22-3-106. Executive committee. The trustees may select an executive committee of five trustees and delegate to the committee such functions in aid of the efficient administration of the affairs of the society as the trustees deem advisable.

History: En. Sec. 6, Ch. 47, L. 1963; R.C.M. 1947, 44-521.

22-3-107. Authority of board. The powers and duties of the trustees are as follows:

(1) to elect annually from among their number a president, a vice-president, and a secretary;

(2) to adopt bylaws for their own government and to make rules, not inconsistent with law, for the proper administration of the society in the interests of preserving the rich heritage of this state and its people;

(3) to appoint a director, fix his salary, and prescribe his duties and responsibilities;

(4) to create such classes of memberships in the society as they deem desirable, to determine the qualifications for any class of membership, and to set the fees to be paid for such memberships;

(5) to sell or exchange publications and other museum or art objects and use the money arising from such sales for the operation of the society and for the acquisition of historical materials and objects of art;

(6) to sell or exchange surplus or duplicate books, surplus museum or art objects or artifacts not pertinent to the region encompassed by the Montana historical society mission and to use the money arising from such sales exclusively for acquisitions of library, art, and museum artifacts;

(7) to see that the collections and properties of the society are maintained in good order and repair;

(8) to report to the governor and the legislature biennially. The report shall include a statement of all important transactions and acquisitions, with suggestions and recommendations for the better realization of the purposes of the society and the improvement of its collections and services.

(9) to accept, receive, and administer in the name of the society any gifts, donations, properties, securities, bequests, and legacies that may be made to the society. Moneys received by donation, gift, bequest, or legacy, unless otherwise provided by the donor, shall be deposited in the state treasury and used for the general operation of the society.

(10) to collect, assemble, preserve, and display, where appropriate, all obtainable books, pamphlets, maps, charts, manuscripts, journals, diaries. papers, business records, paintings, drawings, engravings, photographs, statuary, models, relics, and all other materials illustrative of the history of Montana in particular and generally of the Pacific Northwest, Northern Rocky Mountain, and Northern Great Plains regions and of the United States of America when pertinent;

(11) to procure from pioneers, early settlers, and others, narratives of the events relative to the early settlement of Montana, the Indian occupancy, Indian and other wars, overland travel and immigration to the territories of the west, and all other related documents of Montana's history, development, and society;

(12) to gather contemporary information, specimens, and all other materials which exhibit faithfully the distinctive historical and contemporary characteristics of the area with particular attention to Indian, military, and pioneer artifacts and implements;

(13) to collect and preserve such natural history objects as fossils, plants, minerals, and animals;

(14) to collect and preserve books, maps, manuscripts, and other materials as will tend to facilitate historical, scientific, and antiquarian research;

(15) to promote the study of Montana history by lectures and publications;

(16) to generally foster and encourage the fine arts and cultural activities in Montana;

(17) to receive for and on behalf of the state, by donation or otherwise, art objects of any kind and description and to exhibit and circulate such objects in Montana and elsewhere;

(18) to microfilm papers or documents in danger of disappearance or injury; and

(19) to coordinate the administration of the historic records network established in 22-3-211.

History: En. Sec. 8, Ch. 47, L. 1963; amd. Sec. 1, Ch. 204, L. 1975; amd. Sec. 2, Ch. 366, L. 1977; R.C.M. 1947, 44-523.

22-3-108. Function of director — employment of assistants. The director is fully responsible for the immediate direction, management, and control of the society, subject to the general programs and policies established by the trustees. The director may appoint and employ all assistants and employees required for the management of the historical society, subject to approval by the trustees.

History: En. Sec. 9, Ch. 47, L. 1963; R.C.M. 1947, 44-524.

22-3-109. Official seal. The design of the official seal of the society shall be substantially as follows: a central group representing a covered immigrant wagon drawn by two yoke of oxen, showing prairie in the foreground, mountains in the background, and directly beneath it the figures "1865". The seal shall be 2 inches in diameter and surrounded by the words, "Montana Historical Society Seal".

History: En. Sec. 10, Ch. 47, L. 1963; R.C.M. 1947, 44-525.

22-3-110. Decor of quarters. The offices, library, museums and galleries, and quarters for the activities of the society in the veterans' and pioneers' memorial building shall be decorated, fitted, furnished, and maintained in dignity and in harmony with the purposes of the society. All furniture and fittings for storage and the use of the library shall be, in design and function, adapted to the efficient and dignified operation and administration of the activities of the society.

History: En. Sec. 11, Ch. 47, L. 1963; R.C.M. 1947, 44-526.

22-3-111. Financing of society. The society may engage in such fund-raising drives and public contribution campaigns as will contribute to its continued development and support. It may produce, reproduce, sell, or exchange art objects, film, books, photographs, magazines, pamphlets, and museum objects which are appropriate and will bring credit to the society and to Montana. It may also receive fees, commissions, and royalties on the display and sale of arts and crafts. All profits, revenues, royalties, or fees received in any such manner shall be deposited in the state treasury and may not be used for any purposes other than the improvement, development, and operation of the society.

History: En. Sec. 12, Ch. 47, L. 1963; R.C.M. 1947, 44-527.

22-3-112. Cultural and aesthetic projects grants. (1) Any person, association, or representative of a governing unit seeking a grant for a cultural or aesthetic project from the income of the trust fund created in 15-35-108 must submit a grant proposal to the board of trustees of the Montana historical society by December 1 of the year preceding the convening of a legislative session.

(2)   The board of trustees of the Montana historical society shall present to the legislature by the 15th day of any legislative session a list of grant proposals to be made from the cultural and aesthetic projects account to any department, agency, board, commission, or other division of the state government or to any local government unit. These grant proposals shall be for the purpose of protecting works of art in the state capitol or other cultural and aesthetic projects.

(3)   The legislature must appropriate funds from this account before any grant is awarded.

(4)   The grant proposals approved by the legislature shall be administered by the Montana historical society.

History: En. Sec. 2, Ch. 653, L. 1979.

DISTRIBUTION OF PUBLIC DOCUMENTS
(Montana Code Annotated, 1982, s.1-11-301, 2-4-313, 5-11-203.)

1-11-301. Publication and sale of Montana Code Annotated — free distribution. (1) The legislative council with the advice of the code commissioner shall decide on the quantity, quality, style, format, and grade of all publications prior to having the code commissioner call for bids for the printing and binding and contract for their publication. The code commissioner shall follow the requirements of state law relating to contracts and bids, except as herein provided.

(2) The methods of sale to the public of the Montana Code Annotated and supplements or other subsequent and ancillary publications thereto may be included as an alternative specification and bid and as a part of a contract to be let by bids by the code commissioner.

(3) The sales price to the public shall be fixed by the legislative council but may not exceed the cost price plus 20%. All revenues generated from the sale of the Montana Code Annotated or ancillary publications shall be deposited in the revolving fund, from which fund appropriations may be made for the use of the office and facilities of the legislative council under this chapter.

(4) Sets of the Montana Code Annotated purchased by the state or local governmental agencies that are supported by public funds shall be for the cost price of the sets.

(5) (a) The Montana Code Annotated and supplements and other subsequent and ancillary publications except annotations shall be provided at no cost to the following:

(i) each library designated as a depository library under 22-1-214, one copy;

(ii) each library designated as a federation headquarters library under 22-1-402, one copy.

(b) The state law library in Helena shall be provided with four copies of the Montana Code Annotated and supplements including annotations and other subsequent and ancillary publications.

(c) The legislative council shall include in the cost price of the code the cost of providing the copies under this subsection.

History: En. 12-507 by Sec. 7, Ch. 419, L. 1975; amd. Sec. 5, Ch. 1, L. 1977; R.C.M. 1947, 12-507; amd. Sec. 3, Ch. 1, L. 1979; amd. Sec. 4, Ch. 265, L. 1979; amd. Sec. 1, Ch. 91, L. 1981.

2-4-313. Distribution, costs, and maintenance. (1) The secretary of state shall distribute copies of ARM and supplements or revisions thereto, with costs paid as provided in 2-4-312(2), to the following:

(a) attorney general, one copy;

(b) clerk of each court of record of this state, one copy;

(c) clerk of United States district court for the district of Montana, one copy;

(d) clerk of United States court of appeals for the ninth circuit, one copy;

(e) each county clerk of this state, for use of county officials and the public, one copy, which may be maintained in a public library in the county seat or in the county offices;

(f)   state law library, one copy;

(g)   state historical society, one copy;

(h)   each unit of the Montana university system, one copy;

(i)   law library of the university of Montana, one copy;

(j)   legislative council, three copies;

(k)   library of congress, one copy;

(l)   state library, one copy.

(2)   The secretary of state, clerk of each court of record in the state, clerk of each county in the state, and the librarians for the state law library and the university of Montana law library shall maintain a complete, current set of ARM, including supplements or revisions thereto. Such persons shall also maintain the register issues published during the preceding 2 years. The secretary of state shall also maintain a permanent set of the registers.

        *   *   *

History: En. Sec. 6, Ch. 2, Ex. L. 1971; amd. Sec. 11, Ch. 285, L. 1977; R.C.M. 1947, 82-4206(5) thru (8), (10), (11); amd. Sec. 11, Ch. 243, L. 1979.

5-11-203. Distribution of senate and house journals and session laws. (1) Immediately after the senate and house journals and the session laws are bound, the legislative council shall distribute them.

(2)   The council shall distribute the house and senate journals as follows:

(a)   to each county clerk, one copy of each for the use of the county;

(b)   to the Montana state library, 20 copies of each for the use of the library and distribution to depository libraries, of which 2 copies will be deposited with the state historical library for security purposes;

(c)   to the state law librarian, two copies of each for the use of the library and such additional copies as may be necessary for the purposes of exchange;

(d)   to the library of congress and each public officer as defined in 2-2-102, two copies of each; and

(e)   to each member of the legislature, the secretary of the senate, and the chief clerk of the house of representatives from the session at which the journals were adopted, one copy of each.

(3)   The council shall distribute the session laws as follows:

(a)   to each department of the executive branch of the United States; agency, commission, conference, or corporation established by the United States government; or any other subdivision thereof upon request and approval by the legislative council, one copy;

(b)   to the library of congress, eight copies;

(c)   to the state library, two copies;

(d)   to the state historical library, two copies;

(e)   to the state law librarian, four copies for the use of the library and such additional copies as may be required for exchange with libraries and institutions maintained by other states and territories and public libraries;

(f)   to the library of each custodial institution, one copy;

(g) to each Montana member of congress, each United States district judge in Montana, each of the judges of the state supreme and district courts, and each of the state officers as defined in 2-2-102(8), one copy;

(h) to each member of the legislature, the secretary of the senate, and the chief clerk of the house of representatives from the session at which the laws were adopted, one copy;

(i) to each of the community college districts of the state, as defined in 20-15-101, and each unit of the Montana university system, one copy;

(j) to each county clerk, three copies for the use of the county; and

(k) to each county attorney and to each clerk of a district court, one copy.

History: En. Sec. 1, Ch. 86, L. 1907; re-en. Sec. 155, Rev. C. 1907; amd. Sec. 1, Ch. 126, L. 1921; re-en. Sec. 135, R.C.M. 1921; amd. Sec. 1, Ch. 22, L. 1929; re-en. Sec. 135, R.C.M. 1935; amd. Sec. 1, Ch. 46, L. 1937; Sec. 82-2203, R.C.M. 1947; redes. 43-711.2 and amd. by Sec. 4, Ch. 96, L. 1973;

LIBRARY SYSTEMS

(Montana Code Annotated, 1982, s.22-1-401 to 22-1-405, 22-1-412, 22-1-413, 15-35-108.)

22-1-401. Policy. It is the policy of the legislature to encourage the most efficient delivery of library services to the people of Montana. To that end the state should be divided into regions within which libraries desiring to participate in the distribution of such state funding to libraries as may be available from time to time shall organize into library federations to pool resources and information and avoid duplication of effort.

History: En. Sec. 2, Ch. 215, L. 1965; amd. Sec. 1, Ch. 357, L. 1974; R.C.M. 1947, 44-131(part).

22-1-402. Library systems — definition. Library systems shall include library federations or library networks, as defined hereafter:

(1) (a) A library federation is a combination of libraries serving a multi-county, multicity, or city-county area within a federation area designated by the state library commission. Any other public library or town, city, or county within the federation area may participate in such a federation.

(b) Two or more cities, towns, counties, or a city and one or more counties may agree by contract to form such a federation by action of their respective governing bodies or duly created boards of library trustees, provided that one of the parties is or maintains a library which has been designated by the state library commission as a headquarters library for that federation area. The participating entities may retain such autonomy over their respective libraries as may be specified in the contract.

(c) The expense of providing library services for the library federation shall be based on funds received from the state or participating libraries as shall be agreed upon in the contract. The funds of the federation shall be maintained as a separate account as shall be provided in the contract. Participating libraries shall transfer semiannually to the account all money collected for the federation in their respective jurisdiction.

(d) A participating entity may withdraw from a federation according to the terms for withdrawal provided in the contract by the action of its governing body or by a majority of its qualified voters voting at a general or special election.

(2) A library network is an agreement between individual libraries or library systems, which may be intercity, intrastate, or interstate, for the exchange of information or to provide specific library services not provided in existing library federations.

History: En. Sec. 1, Ch. 132, L. 1939; amd. Sec. 2, Ch. 357, L. 1974; R.C.M. 1947, 44-212; amd. Sec. 1, Ch. 374, L. 1981.

22-1-403. Participation in the federation. (1) When a library federation shall have been established, the legislative body of any government unit in the designated library federation area may decide, with the concurrence of the board of trustees of its library if it is maintaining a library, to participate in the library federation. Each local entity may determine the amount of services it wishes to supply to fulfill the needs of its unit. After the necessary contract has been executed and beginning with the next fiscal year, the governmental unit shall participate in the library federation and its residents shall be entitled to the benefits of the library federation and property within its boundaries shall be subject to taxation for library federation purposes.

(2) The board of regents of higher education may contract with the government of any city or county, or the governments of both the city and the county, in which a unit of the Montana university system is located for the establishment and operation of joint library services. Any such contract which proposes the erection of a building shall be subject to the approval of the legislature. Any joint library services established pursuant to this section shall be operated and supported as provided in such contract and under this part.

History: En. Sec. 2, Ch. 132, L. 1939; amd. Sec. 1, Ch. 249, L. 1963; amd. Sec. 3, Ch. 357, L. 1974; R.C.M. 1947, 44-213.

22-1-404. Board of trustees — coordinator. (1) In a library federation there shall be a board of trustees with advisory powers only, the operation of the library federation having been specified by contract. The board of trustees of each participating library shall name one of their members to the federation advisory board of trustees, and each participating entity without a duly appointed library board shall name a layman to represent that entity on the library federation board of trustees.

(2) The librarian of the headquarters library shall serve as the coordinator of the federation and as a nonvoting member of the federation advisory board of trustees.

History: (1)En. Sec. 3, Ch. 132, L. 1939; amd. Sec. 10, Ch. 260, L. 1967; amd. Sec. 4, Ch. 357, L. 1974; Sec. 44-214, R.C.M. 1947; (2)En. Sec. 2, Ch. 215, L. 1965; amd. Sec. 1, Ch. 357, L. 1974; Sec. 44-131, R.C.M. 1947; R.C.M. 1947, 44-131(part), 44-214.

22-1-405. Boards of trustees — authority — resolution of disagreements. (1) The board of trustees of a library federation shall act as an advisor to the participating libraries and their boards of trustees.

(2) Control over the budgets and administrative policies of participating libraries shall remain in their boards of trustees as provided in 22-1-309.

(3) Any disagreement among participants in a library federation regarding the apportionment of funds or grants received from the state library commis-

sion shall be resolved by the state library commission.

History: En. 44-214.1 by Sec. 5, Ch. 357, L. 1974; R.C.M. 1947, 44-214.1.

22-1-412.   Purpose. It is the purpose of 22-1-412 and 22-1-413 to establish a program whereby state funds may be appropriated to the Montana state library commission to provide the benefits of quality public library service to all residents of Montana by developing and strengthening local public libraries through library federations as defined in 22-1-402.

History: En. 44-304 by Sec. 1, Ch. 416, L. 1975; R.C.M. 1947, 44-304; amd. Sec. 1, Ch. 373, L. 1981.

22-1-413.   Administration by Montana state library commission. The Montana state library commission shall receive and administer the appropriation for state funding to public library federations. The commission shall allocate such appropriation among such types of grant programs and shall allocate funds among federations according to such formulas for distribution as it shall establish from time to time by rules adopted pursuant to 22-1-103. Federations receiving state funds from the commission shall report semiannually to the commission concerning the progress of the various projects for which state funding was received, which reports shall contain an accounting for all state funds received.

History: En. 44-305 by Sec. 2, Ch. 416, L. 1975; R.C.M. 1947, 44-305; amd. Sec. 2, Ch. 373, L. 1981.

15-35-108.   *(Effective July 1, 1983)* **Disposal of severance taxes.** Severance taxes collected under the provisions of this chapter are allocated as follows:

(1)   To the trust fund created by Article IX, section 5, of the Montana constitution, 25% of total collections a year. After December 31, 1979, 50% of coal severance tax collections are allocated to this trust fund. The trust fund moneys shall be deposited in the fund established under 17-6-203(5) and invested by the board of investments as provided by law.

(2)   Coal severance tax collections remaining after allocation to the trust fund under subsection (1) are allocated in the following percentages of the remaining balance:

•   •   •

(h)   5% to the earmarked revenue fund to the credit of a trust fund for the purpose of parks acquisition or management, protection of works of art in the state capitol, and other cultural and aesthetic projects. Income from this trust fund shall be appropriated as follows:

(i) $\frac{1}{3}$ for protection of works of art in the state capitol and other cultural and aesthetic projects; and

(ii) $\frac{2}{3}$ for the acquisition of sites and areas described in 23-1-102 and the operation and maintenance of sites so acquired;

(i)   1% to the earmarked revenue fund to the credit of the state library commission for the purposes of providing basic library services for the residents of all counties through library federations and for payment of the costs of participating in regional and national networking;

History: En. 84-1309.1 by Sec. 2, Ch. 432, L. 1973; amd. Sec. 1, Ch. 250, L. 1974; amd. Sec. 4,

Ch. 501, L. 1975; amd. Sec. 3, Ch. 502, L. 1975; amd. and redes. 84-1319 by Sec. 8, Ch. 525, L. 1975; amd. Sec. 2, Ch. 156, L. 1977; amd. Sec. 1, Ch. 540, L. 1977; amd. Sec. 2, Ch. 549, L. 1977; R.C.M. 1947, 84-1319; amd. Sec. 1, Ch. 653, L. 1979; amd. Sec. 1, Ch. 694, L. 1979; amd. Sec. 1, Ch. 479, L. 1981; amd. Sec. 43, Ch. 505, L. 1981.

COUNTY AND MUNICIPAL LIBRARIES
(Montana Code Annotated, 1982, s.22-1-301 to 22-1-317.)

22-1-301. Definition. Wherever the word "city" is used in this part, it means city or town.

History: En. Sec. 11, Ch. 260, L. 1967; R.C.M. 1947, 44-227.

22-1-302. Purpose. It is the purpose of this part to encourage the establishment, adequate financing, and effective administration of free public libraries in this state to give the people of Montana the fullest opportunity to enrich and inform themselves through reading.

History: En. Sec. 1, Ch. 260, L. 1967; R.C.M. 1947, 44-218.

22-1-303. Creation of public library. A public library may be established in any county or city in any of the following ways:

(1) The governing body of any county or city desiring to establish and maintain a public library may pass and enter upon its minutes a resolution to the effect that a free public library is established under the provision of Montana laws relating to public libraries.

(2) By petition signed by not less than 10% of the resident taxpayers, whose names appear upon the last completed assessment roll of the city or county, being filed with the governing body requesting the establishment of a public library. The governing body of a city or county shall set a time of meeting at which they may by resolution establish a public library. The governing body shall give notice of the contemplated action in a newspaper of general circulation for 2 consecutive weeks giving therein the date and place of the meeting at which the contemplated action is proposed to be taken.

(3) (a) Upon a petition being filed with the governing body and signed by not less than 5% of the resident taxpayers of any city or county requesting an election, the governing body shall submit to a vote of the qualified electors thereof at the next general election the question of whether a free public library shall be established.

(b) If such a petition is submitted for a city, the petition must be signed by resident taxpayers of said city.

(c) If such a petition is submitted to the county commissioners of a county asking for the establishment of a county library, the petition must be signed by resident taxpayers of the county who reside outside the corporate limits of an incorporated city located in said county which may already have established a free public library for such city.

(d) If such petition specifically asks that a special election be called and such petition is signed by 35% of the resident freeholders affected by such petition, then the governing body shall, upon receipt of such petition, immediately set a date for a special election, which date shall be as soon as the procedures for establishing a special election will allow.

(e) If at such election a majority of the electors voting on the question vote in favor of the establishment of a library, the governing body shall immediately take the necessary steps to establish and maintain said library or to contract with any city or county for library service to be rendered to the inhabitants of such city or county.

History: En. Sec. 2, Ch. 260, L. 1967; amd. Sec. 1, Ch. 263, L. 1969; R.C.M. 1947, 44-219.

22-1-304. Tax levy — special library fund — bonds. (1) The governing body of any city or county which has established a public library may levy in the same manner and at the same time as other taxes are levied a special tax in the amount necessary to maintain adequate public library service, not to exceed 3 mills on the dollar, upon all property in such county which may be levied by the governing body of such county and not to exceed 4 ½ mills on the dollar upon all property in such city which may be levied by the governing body of such city.

(2) The proceeds of such tax shall constitute a separate fund called the public library fund and shall not be used for any purpose except those of the public library.

(3) No money shall be paid out of the public library fund by the treasurer of the city or county except by order or warrant of the board of library trustees.

(4) Bonds may be issued by the governing body in the manner prescribed by law for the erection and equipment of public library buildings and the purchase of land therefor.

History: En. Sec. 3, Ch. 260, L. 1967; R.C.M. 1947, 44-220.

22-1-305. Library depreciation reserve fund authorized. The governing body of any city or county or a combination of city and county in Montana may establish a library depreciation reserve fund for the replacement and acquisition of property, capital improvements, and equipment necessary to maintain and improve city, county, or city-county library services.

History: En. 44-229 by Sec. 1, Ch. 78, L. 1975; R.C.M. 1947, 44-229.

22-1-306. Moneys for library depreciation reserve fund. Moneys for the library depreciation reserve fund are those funds which have been allocated to the library in any year but which have not been expended by the end of the year. Such moneys include but are not limited to city or county or city-county appropriations, federal revenue sharing funds, and public and private grants.

History: En. 44-230 by Sec. 2, Ch. 78, L. 1975; R.C.M. 1947, 44-230.

22-1-307. Investment of fund. The moneys held in the library depreciation reserve fund may be invested as provided by law. All interest earned on the fund must be credited to the library depreciation reserve fund.

History: En. 44-231 by Sec. 3, Ch. 78, L. 1975; R.C.M. 1947, 44-231.

22-1-308. Public library — board of trustees. (1) Upon the establishment of a public library under the provisions of this part, the mayor, with the advice and consent of the city council or city commissioners, shall appoint a board of trustees for the city library and the chairman of the board of county commissioners, with the advice and consent of said board, shall appoint a board of trustees for the county library.

(2) The library board shall consist of five trustees. Not more than one member of the governing body shall be, at any one time, a member of such board.

(3) Trustees shall serve without compensation, but their actual and necessary expenses incurred in the performance of their official duties may be paid from library funds.

(4) Trustees shall hold their office for 5 years from the date of appointment and until their successors are appointed. Initially, appointments shall be made for 1-, 2-, 3-, 4-, and 5-year terms. Annually thereafter, there shall be appointed before July 1 of each year in the same manner as the original appointments for a 5-year term, a trustee to take the place of the retiring trustee. Trustees shall serve no more than two full terms in succession.

(5) Following such appointments, in July of each year, the trustees shall meet and elect a chairman and such other officers as they deem necessary, for 1-year terms. Vacancies in the board of trustees shall be filled for the unexpired term in the same manner as original appointments.

History: En. Sec. 4, Ch. 260, L. 1967; R.C.M. 1947, 44-221.

22-1-309. Trustees — powers and duties. The library board of trustees shall have exclusive control of the expenditure of the public library fund, of construction or lease of library buildings, and of the operation and care of the library. The library board of trustees of every public library shall:

(1) adopt bylaws and rules for its own transaction of business and for the government of the library, not inconsistent with law;

(2) establish and locate a central public library and may establish branches thereof at such places as are deemed necessary;

(3) have the power to contract, including the right to contract with regions, counties, cities, school districts, educational institutions, the state library, and other libraries, to give and receive library service, through the boards of such regions, counties, and cities and the district school boards, and to pay out or receive funds to pay costs of such contracts;

(4) have the power to acquire, by purchase, devise, lease or otherwise, and to own and hold real and personal property in the name of the city or county or both, as the case may be, for the use and purposes of the library and to sell, exchange or otherwise dispose of property real or personal, when no longer required by the library and to insure the real and personal property of the library;

(5) pay necessary expenses of members of the library staff when on business of the library;

(6) prepare an annual budget, indicating what support and maintenance of the public library will be required from public funds, for submission to the appropriate agency of the governing body. A separate budget request shall be submitted for new construction or for capital improvement of existing library property.

(7) make an annual report to the governing body of the city or county on

the condition and operation of the library, including a financial statement. The trustees shall also provide for the keeping of such records as shall be required by the Montana state library in its request for an annual report from the public libraries and shall submit such an annual report to the state library.

(8) have the power to accept gifts, grants, donations, devises, or bequests of property, real or personal, from whatever source and to expend or hold, work, and improve the same for the specific purpose of the gift, grant, donation, devise, or bequest. These gifts, grants, donations, devises, and bequests shall be kept separate from regular library funds and are not subject to reversion at the end of the fiscal year.

(9) exercise such other powers, not inconsistent with law, necessary for the effective use and management of the library.

History: Ap. p. Sec. 5, Ch. 260, L. 1967; Sec. 44-222, R.C.M. 1947; Ap. p. Sec. 1, Ch. 47, L. 1927; re-en. Sec. 5668.17, R.C.M. 1935; Sec. 11-1006, R.C.M. 1947; R.C.M. 1947, 11-1006(part), 44-222.

22-1-310. Chief librarian — personnel — compensation. The board of trustees of each library shall appoint and set the compensation of the chief librarian who shall serve as the secretary of the board and shall serve at the pleasure of the board. With the recommendation of the chief librarian, the board shall employ and discharge such other persons as may be necessary in the administration of the affairs of the library, fix and pay their salaries and compensation, and prescribe their duties.

History: En. Sec. 6, Ch. 260, L. 1967; R.C.M. 1947, 44-223.

22-1-311. Use of library — privileges. Every library established under the provisions of this part shall be free to the use of the inhabitants of the city or the county supporting such library. The board may exclude from the use of the library any and all persons who shall willfully violate the rules of the library. The board may extend the privileges and use of the library to persons residing outside of the city or county upon such terms and conditions as it may prescribe by its regulations.

History: En. Sec. 7, Ch. 260, L. 1967; R.C.M. 1947, 44-224.

22-1-312. Cooperation and merger. Library boards of trustees, boards of other educational institutions, library agencies, and local political subdivisions are hereby empowered to cooperate, merge, or combine in providing library service.

History: En. Sec. 8, Ch. 260, L. 1967; R.C.M. 1947, 44-225.

22-1-313. Existing tax-supported libraries — notification — exemption from county taxes. After the establishment of a county free library as provided in this part, the governing body of any city which has an existing tax-supported public library may notify the board of county commissioners that such city does not desire to be a part of the county library system. Such notification shall exempt the property in such city from liability for taxes for county library purposes.

History: En. Sec. 9, Ch. 260, L. 1967; R.C.M. 1947, 44-226.

22-1-314. Continued existence of all public libraries. All public libraries heretofore established shall continue in existence, subject to the changes in administration provided herein.

History: En. Sec. 12, Ch. 260, L. 1967; R.C.M. 1947, 44-228.

22-1-315. City library may assume functions of county library. (1) Instead of establishing a separate county free library, the board of county commissioners may enter into a contract with the board of library trustees or other authority in charge of the free public library of any incorporated city, and the board of library trustees or other authority in charge of such free public library is hereby authorized to make such a contract.

(2) Such contract may provide that the free public library of such incorporated city shall assume the functions of a county free library within the county with which such contract is made, and the board of county commissioners may agree to pay out of the county free library fund into the library fund of such incorporated city such sum as may be agreed upon.

(3) Either party to such contract may terminate the same by giving 6 months' notice of intention to do so.

History: En. Sec. 11, Ch. 45, L. 1915; re-en. Sec. 4573, R.C.M. 1921; re-en. Sec. 4573, R.C.M. 1935; R.C.M. 1947, 44-211.

22-1-316. Joint city-county library. (1) A county and any city or cities within the county, by action of their respective governing bodies, may join in establishing and maintaining a joint city-county library under the terms of a contract agreed upon by all parties.

(2) The expenses of a joint city-county library shall be apportioned between or among the county and cities on such a basis as shall be agreed upon in the contract.

(3) The governing body of any city or county entering into a contract may levy a special tax as provided in 22-1-304 for the establishment and operation of a joint city-county library.

(4) The treasurer of the county or of a participating city within the county, as shall be provided in the contract, shall have custody of the funds of the joint city-county library, and the other treasurers of the county or cities joining in the contract shall transfer quarterly to him all moneys collected for the joint city-county library.

(5) The contract shall provide for the disposition of property upon dissolution of the joint city-county library.

History: En. Sec. 1, Ch. 273, L. 1973; R.C.M. 1947, 44-219.1.

22-1-317. City-county library — board of trustees. (1) A joint city-county library shall be governed by a board of trustees composed of five members chosen as specified in the contract, with terms not to exceed 5 years.

(2) Trustees shall serve no more than two full terms in succession.

(3) Trustees shall serve without compensation, but their actual and necessary expenses incurred in the performance of their official duties may be paid from library funds.

(4) Trustees shall meet and elect a chairman and such other officers as they consider necessary for 1-year terms.

(5) The board of trustees shall have the same powers and duties as the board of trustees of a city library or a county library.

History: En. Sec. 2, Ch. 273, L. 1973; amd. Sec. 3, Ch. 3, L. 1977; R.C.M. 1947, 44-219.2.

Montana library laws are reprinted from MONTANA CODE ANNOTATED published by the Montana Legislative Council, Helana, Montana.

NEBRASKA

STATE LIBRARY

(Revised Statutes of Nebraska, 1982, s.51-101 to 51-105, 51-107 to 51-109.)

51-101. State Library; what constitutes. The books, pamphlets, maps and charts belonging to the state, now in the State Library, or which shall hereafter be added to the same, shall constitute the State Library.

> **Source:** Laws 1871, § 1, p. 52; R.S.1913, § 3777; C.S.1922, § 3170; C.S.1929, § 51-101.

51-102. State Library; librarian. The Clerk of the Supreme Court shall have the charge of the State Library, of which he shall be librarian.

> **Source:** Laws 1871, § 2, p. 52; R.S.1913, § 3778; C.S.1922, § 3171; C.S.1929, § 51-102.

51-103. State Library; directors; powers. The Judges of the Supreme Court shall constitute a board of directors of the State Library. They shall have power to make such rules as they may deem proper, not inconsistent with sections 51-101 to 51-112, for the regulation of the library under their direction, and may prescribe penalties for any violation thereof, which shall be collected in the same manner as for the nonreturn or injury of any books.

> **Source:** Laws 1871, §§ 3, 4, p. 52; R.S.1913, § 3779; C.S.1922, § 3172; C.S.1929, § 51-103.

51-104. Book register; entries. The librarian shall cause to be kept a register of all books issued and returned at the time they shall be so issued and returned. None of the books, except the laws, journals, and reports of this state, which may be taken from the library, shall be detained more than ten days, and all the books taken out by officers or members of the Legislature shall be returned at the close of the session.

Source: Laws 1871, § 6, p. 52; R.S.1913, § 3781; C.S.1922, § 3174; C.S.1929, § 51-104.

51-105. Books; injury or failure to return; penalty.   If any person injures or fails to return any book taken from the library, he shall forfeit and pay to the librarian for the use of the library, double the value of the book, or of the set to which it belongs, if a set is broken by its loss, to be recovered in an action in the name of the state. Before the Director of Administrative Services shall issue his warrant in favor of any person authorized to take books from the library, for the value of his services or amount of his salary, he shall be satisfied that such person has returned all books taken from the library, or settled for the same; otherwise he shall deduct all accounts for the detention or injury of such books.

Source: Laws 1871, § 7, p. 53; R.S.1913, § 3782; C.S.1922, § 3175; C.S.1929, § 51-105.

51-107. Books; labeling.   It shall be the duty of the librarian to cause each book to be labeled with a printed or stamped label containing the words Nebraska State Library, and also to write the same words on the thirtieth page of each volume.

Source: Laws 1871, § 12, p. 54; R.S.1913, § 3785; C.S.1922, § 3178; C.S.1929, § 51-107.

51-108. Books; sale, exchange, disposal; authorization.   The directors may authorize the sale, exchange, or disposal of any surplus, damaged, defective, obsolete, or duplicate books in the library and surplus or obsolete books, reports, or pamphlets which are for sale or distribution by the librarian.

Source: Laws 1871, § 13, p. 54; R.S.1913, § 3786; C.S.1922, § 3179; Laws 1929, c. 64, § 2, p. 241; C.S.1929, § 51-108; R.S.1943, § 51-108; Laws 1957, c. 222, § 1, p. 764.

51-109. Books; removal; penalty. If any person not authorized by the regulations made by the directors shall take a book from the library, either with or without the consent of the librarian, he shall be guilty of a Class V misdemeanor.

Source: Laws 1871, § 15, p. 54; R.S.1913, § 3788; C.S.1922, § 3181; Laws 1929, c. 64, § 3, p. 241; C.S.1929, § 51-109; R.S.1943, § 51-109; Laws 1977, LB 40, § 307.

STATE LIBRARY COMMISSION
(Revised Statutes of Nebraska, 1982, s.51-401 to 51-408, 51-410, 51-410.01.)

51-401. Nebraska Library Commission; members; term. A Nebraska Library Commission is hereby established composed of six members to be appointed by the Governor, one to serve one year, one for two years, one for three years, one for four years, and one for five years, and thereafter the Governor shall appoint a new member annually to serve for a term of three years and no person shall be appointed to more than two successive terms. The new member provided for by this section shall be appointed for an initial term of three years. The term of one of the three members whose term expires in 1981 shall expire in 1980. That member shall be selected by lot.

Source: Laws 1935, c. 115, § 1, p. 370; C.S.Supp.,1941, § 51-501; R.S.1943, § 51-401; Laws 1972, LB 1033, § 4; Laws 1979, LB 352, § 1.

51-402. Nebraska Library Commission; expenses; payment. The members of the Nebraska Library Commission shall serve without pay. They shall receive remuneration for traveling and actual expenses incurred while engaged in the business of the commission as provided in sections 84-306.01 to 84-306.05 for state employees. These expenses shall be paid out of the funds of the Nebraska Library Commission.

Source: Laws 1935, c. 115, § 2, p. 370; C.S.Supp., 1941, § 51-502; R.S.1943, § 51-402; Laws 1972, LB 1033, § 5; Laws 1981, LB 204, § 93.

51-403. Nebraska Library Commission; powers and duties; executive secretary; appointment; salary. The powers and duties of the Nebraska Library Commission shall be (1) to make rules and regulations not inconsistent with law for its government and operations, (2) to appoint a director, at a salary to be fixed by the commission, who shall be a technically trained, qualified, and experienced librarian, a graduate of an American Library Association accredited library school, to administer the work of the commission as hereinafter specified, (3) to require the director to execute an official bond to the State of Nebraska in the penal sum of three thousand dollars, (4) to authorize the director to employ such assistance as may be necessary to properly carry out the requirements of sections 51-401 to 51-410, (5) to be responsible for the statewide promotion, development, and coordination of library programs and services in accordance with nationally acceptable library standards, (6) to receive, as the legally designated state governmental agency, federal library funds which by federal law are to be dispersed within the state by a prescribed formula, (7) to accept and administer any gifts, bequests, and legacies which, in the opinion of the director and the commission, may be of value to it, and (8) to make a biennial report for the past two fiscal years to the Governor of its activities and the progress of its work on or before December 15 in each even-numbered year.

> **Source:**   Laws 1935, c. 115, § 3, p. 370; Laws 1937, c. 124, § 1, p. 435; C.S.Supp.,1941, § 51-503; R.S.1943, § 51-403; Laws 1945, c. 238, § 21, p. 713; Laws 1951, c. 311, § 3, p. 1066; Laws 1951, c. 171, § 1, p. 659; Laws 1953, c. 178, § 1, p. 562; Laws 1955, c. 231, § 10, p. 721; Laws 1961, c. 256, § 1, p. 750; Laws 1965, c. 315, § 1, p. 878; Laws 1972, LB 1033, § 6.

51-403.03.   Nebraska Library Commission; executive secretary; salary increase; when effective.   Section 51-403 shall be so interpreted as to effectuate its general purpose, to provide, in the public interest, adequate compensation as therein provided for the director of the Nebraska Library Commission; and to permit a change of such salary as soon as same may become operative under the Constitution of the State of Nebraska.

> **Source:**   Laws 1965, c. 315, § 2, p. 879; Laws 1972, LB 1033, § 7.

51-404.   Director; duties.   It shall be the duty of the director of the commission (1) to administer the work and activities of the commission, (2) to purchase books, periodicals, other library materials, and all necessary equipment and supplies for the commission, (3) to keep a catalog of all books, periodicals and other library materials belonging to the commission, (4) to keep a record of all books and property added to the library of the commission, and the cost thereof, (5) to keep a record of all books, periodicals and other library materials loaned by the commission and notify the borrowers of the expiration period of the loan, and (6) to keep fiscal and other operational records in accordance with state regulations.

> **Source:**   Laws 1935, c. 115, § 4, p. 371; C.S.Supp.,1941, § 51-504; R.S.1943, § 51-404; Laws 1972, LB 1033, § 8.

51-405.   Local libraries, organizations; entitled to privileges, when.   Any library, governmental agency, or any body of citizens or taxpayers organized for library purposes shall, upon complying with the rules prescribed by the Nebraska Library Commission, be entitled to the commission's services.

> **Source:**   Laws 1935, c. 115, § 5, p. 371; C.S.Supp.,1941, § 51-505; R.S.1943, § 51-405; Laws 1972, LB 1033, § 9.

51-406.   Books; loans to libraries.   Any books, collection of books or other property of the Nebraska Library Commission may be loaned to any library, under such rules for the safekeeping, preservation, care, handling and management of the same as may be fixed by the

Nebraska Library Commission.

> **Source:** Laws 1935, c. 115, § 6, p. 371; C.S.Supp.,1941, § 51-506; R.S.1943, § 51-406; Laws 1972, LB 1033, § 10.

51-407. Nebraska Library Commission; reports from all libraries required. The director shall each year obtain from all libraries in the state reports showing the conditions, growth, development and manner of conducting such libraries, together with such other facts and statistics regarding the same as may be deemed of public interest by the Nebraska Library Commission.

> **Source:** Laws 1935, c. 115, § 7, p. 371; C.S.Supp.,1941, § 51-507; R.S.1943, § 51-407; Laws 1972, LB 1033, § 11.

51-408. Nebraska Library Commission; assistance to local libraries. The director shall when asked give advice and instruction to all libraries or individuals and to all communities which may propose to establish libraries as to the best means for establishing, organizing and administering such libraries, selecting and cataloging books, and other duties of library management. The director shall, so far as possible, promote and assist by counsel and encouragement the formation of libraries where none exist, and the director may send one of his employees or assistants to aid in organizing new libraries or improving those already established.

> **Source:** Laws 1935, c. 115, § 8, p. 371; C.S.Supp.,1941, § 51-508; R.S.1943, § 51-408; Laws 1972, LB 1033, § 12.

51-410. Nebraska Library Commission; disbursements; power of director. The director may from time to time as needed draw a voucher signed by himself in favor of any party to whom money is due, stating in such voucher what the money is to be used for. Upon presentation of such order the Director of Administrative Services shall draw his warrant upon the State Treasurer for the amount thereof, not exceeding the amount of the appropriation for the purposes of the Nebraska Library Commission.

> **Source:** Laws 1935, c. 115, § 10, p. 372; C.S.Supp.,1941, § 51-510; R.S.1943, § 51-410; Laws 1972, LB 1033, § 14.

51-410.01. Nebraska Library Commission Cash Fund; created; how funded. There is hereby created a fund to be known as the Nebraska Library Commission Cash Fund, from which shall be appropriated such amounts as are available and as shall be considered incident to the administration of the Nebraska Library Commission. All funds received by the Nebraska Library Commission for services rendered shall be paid into the state treasury and the State Treasurer shall credit the money to the Nebraska Library Commission Cash Fund.

> **Source:** Laws 1975, LB 550, § 1.

STATE PUBLICATIONS CLEARINGHOUSE
(Revised Statutes of Nebraska, 1982, s.51-411 to 51-418.)

51-411. Terms, defined. As used in this act, unless the context otherwise requires:

(1) Print shall include all forms of printing and duplicating, regardless of format or purpose, with the exception of correspondence and interoffice memoranda;

(2) State publications shall include any multiply-produced publications printed or purchased for distribution, by the state, the Legislature, constitutional officers, any state department, committee or other state agency supported wholly or in part by state funds;

(3) State agency shall include every state office, officer, department, division, bureau, board, commission and agency of the state, and, where applicable, all subdivisions of each including state institutions of higher education, defined as all state-supported colleges, universities, junior colleges, and vocational technical colleges; and

(4) Governmental publications shall include any publications of associations, regional organizations, intergovernmental bodies, federal agencies, boards and commissions, or other publishers that may contribute supplementary materials to support the work of the state Legislature and state agencies.

Source: Laws 1972, LB 1284, § 1.

51-412. Nebraska Publications Clearinghouse; division of Nebraska Library Commission; created; duties. There is hereby created as a division of the Nebraska Library Commission, a Nebraska Publications Clearinghouse. The clearinghouse shall establish and operate a publications collection and depository system for the use of Nebraska citizens. To this end, the Nebraska Library Commission shall make such rules and regulations as shall be necessary to carry out the provisions of this act.

Source: Laws 1972, LB 1284, § 2.

51-413. State agencies; publications; filing with Nebraska Publications Clearinghouse. Every state agency head or his or her appointed records officer shall notify the Nebraska Publications Clearinghouse of his or her identity. The records officer shall upon release of a state publication deposit four copies and a short summary including author, title, and subject of each of its state publications with the Nebraska Publications Clearinghouse for record purposes. One of these copies shall be forwarded by the clearinghouse to the Nebraska Historical Society for archival purposes and one to the Library of Congress. Additional copies, including sale items, shall also be deposited in the Nebraska Publications Clearinghouse in quantities certified to the agencies by the clearinghouse as required to meet the needs of the Nebraska publications depository system, with the exception that the University of Nebraska Press shall only be required to deposit four copies of its publications.

Source: Laws 1972, LB 1284, § 3; Laws 1979, LB 322, § 80.

51-414. Depository contracts; standards; establish. The Nebraska Publications Clearinghouse may enter into depository contracts with any municipal, county, or regional public library, state college or state university library, and out-of-state research libraries. The requirements for eligibility to contract as a depository library shall be established by the Nebraska Publications Clearinghouse. The standards shall include and take into consideration the type of library, ability to preserve such publications and to make them available for public use, and also such geographical locations as will make the publications conveniently accessible to residents in all areas of the state.

Source: Laws 1972, LB 1284, § 4.

51-415. Official list of publications; publish; contents. The Nebraska Publications Clearinghouse shall publish and distribute regularly to contracting depository libraries, other libraries, state agencies and legislators, an official list of state publications with an annual cumulation. The official list shall provide a record of each agency's publishing and show author, agency, title and subject approaches.

Source: Laws 1972, LB 1284, § 5.

51-416. Current state publications; furnish. Upon request by the Nebraska Publications Clearinghouse, records officers of state agencies shall furnish the clearinghouse with a complete list of their current state publications.

Source: Laws 1972, LB 1284, § 6.

51-417. Distribution of state publications; restriction. The Nebraska Publications Clearinghouse shall not engage in general public distribution of either state publications or lists of publications. This act shall not affect the distribution of state publications distributed by state agencies except that the agencies must deposit in the Nebraska Publications Clearinghouse the number of copies of each of their state publications certified by the clearinghouse.

Source: Laws 1972, LB 1284, § 7.

51-418. Interlibrary loan service; provide. The Nebraska Publications Clearinghouse shall provide access to local, state, federal and other governmental publications to state agencies and legislators and through interlibrary loan service to citizens of the state.

Source: Laws 1972, LB 1284, § 8.

DISTRIBUTION OF PUBLIC DOCUMENTS

(Revised Statutes of Nebraska, 1982, s.49-502, 49-505 to 49-511, 49-617, 85-176, 85-177, 24-209, 24-212.)

49-502. Session laws and journals; distribution by county clerk; to judges, county officers, and members of Legislature. The county clerk shall distribute one copy of the session laws to the clerk of the district court for the use of the district court in all counties of the state except Lancaster and Douglas Counties, and in those counties one copy for each district judge in the county, to the county judge, the county attorney, and to the county law library. He shall also reserve one copy each of the laws and journals for himself and give one copy of each to every senator who was a member of the Legislature by which the laws were enacted, to each judge of the municipal court in the county, and to each associate county judge in the county.

Source: Laws 1972, LB 1032, § 253.

49-505. Distribution to public libraries. After the above distribution, the copies of laws and journals remaining in the hands of the county clerk may, upon their application, be distributed to the librarians of any public libraries within the county for whose support an annual tax is levied.

Source: Laws 1907, c. 78, § 5, p. 290; R.S.1913, § 3737; C.S.1922, § 3130; C.S.1929, § 49-505.

49-506. Laws, journals; distribution to state officers, boards and institutions; Nebraska Publications Clearinghouse; Law College, University of Nebraska; State Librarian; Revisor of Statutes. After all the requisitions before mentioned have been filled by the Secretary of State he shall deliver one copy of the laws and journal to each state officer, state institution, and state board, two copies to the Revisor of Statutes, and eight copies to the Nebraska Publications Clearinghouse. Distribution of copies to the library of the College of Law of the University of Nebraska shall be as provided in sections 85-176 and 85-177. The remaining copies shall be delivered to the State Librarian who shall use the same, so far as required for exchange purposes, in building up the State Library, and in the manner specified in sections 49-507 to 49-509.

Source: Laws 1907, c. 78, § 6, p. 290; R.S.1913, § 3738; C.S.1922, § 3131; C.S.1929, § 49-506; R.S.1943, § 49-506; Laws 1947, c. 185, § 4, p. 611; Laws 1961, c. 243, § 2, p. 725; Laws 1969, c. 413, § 1, p. 1419; Laws 1972, LB 1284, § 17.

49-507. Distribution by State Librarian. The librarian shall, upon the order of any Judge of the Supreme Court, issue one copy each of the laws and journals to the United States District Attorney, United States Marshal, the register and receiver of the United States land offices in the state, and to each United States Commissioner residing in the state.

Source: Laws 1907, c. 78, § 7, p. 291; R.S.1913, § 3739; C.S.1922, § 3132; C.S.1929, § 49-507.

49-508. Distribution to members of Legislature; duty of State Librarian. The new members of each Legislature shall be furnished by the State Librarian, at the commencement of the first session for which they are elected, with two copies of each of the laws and journals of the preceding session.

Source: Laws 1907, c. 78, § 8, p. 291; R.S.1913, § 3740; C.S.1922, § 3133; C.S.1929, § 49-508; R.S.1943, § 49-508; Laws 1975, LB 59, § 2; Laws 1980, LB 598, § 1.

49-509. Session laws and journals; sale by State Librarian; price; proceeds; disposition. Any remaining copies in the hands of the State Librarian shall be sold by him at a price of fifteen dollars for bound copies of the session laws and forty dollars for bound copies of the journal; *Provided*, the State Librarian is authorized to sell any copies of the session laws and journals, after two years have elapsed from date of publication, at a price of twenty-five cents per volume. The proceeds shall be turned into the General Fund of the state treasury. When there is no longer a demand for session laws and journals over two years old, the Supreme Court may authorize the State Librarian to make disposition of such session laws and journals in such manner as it deems proper.

Source: Laws 1907, c. 78, § 9, p. 291; R.S.1913, § 3741; Laws 1921, c. 213, § 5, p. 754; C.S.1922, § 3134; C.S.1929, § 49-509; R.S.1943, § 49-509; Laws 1945, c. 117, § 1, p. 390; Laws 1965, c. 307, § 1, p. 864; Laws 1971, LB 36, § 3; Laws 1973, LB 83, § 1.

49-510. Compiled or revised statutes; superseded; sale by State Librarian; price; disposition. The State Librarian is authorized to sell copies of any compilation or revision of the statutes of Nebraska, which have been superseded by a later official revision or compilation, at a price of one dollar per volume; *Provided*, that when there is no demand for such compilation or revision of the statutes of Nebraska that have been superseded, the Supreme Court may authorize the State Librarian to make disposition of such compilations or revisions in such manner as it deems proper.

Source: Laws 1945, c. 118, § 1, p. 391; Laws 1965, c. 307, § 2, p. 864.

49-511. Compiled or revised statutes; superseded; Secretary of State; deliver to State Librarian for sale. The Secretary of State is authorized and directed to turn over and deliver to the State Librarian any and all surplus copies of superseded revisions and compilations of the statutes of Nebraska now in his hands for sale and disposition as provided in section 49-510.

Source: Laws 1945, c. 118, § 2, p. 391.

49-617. Printing of statutes; distribution of copies. The Revisor of Statutes shall cause the statutes to be printed. The printer shall deliver all completed copies to the State Librarian. These copies shall be held and disposed of by such librarian as follows: Sixty copies to the Nebraska State Library to exchange for statutes of other states; five copies to the Nebraska State Library to keep for daily use; not to exceed twenty-five copies to the Nebraska Legislative Council for bill drafting and related services to the Legislature and executive state officers; not to exceed twenty copies to the Attorney General; twelve copies to the Tax Commissioner; eight copies to the Nebraska Publications Clearinghouse; six copies to the Public Service Commission; four copies to the Secretary of State; four copies to the Clerk of the Nebraska Legislature for use in his office and two copies to be maintained in the legislative chamber under control of the sergeant at arms; two copies each to the Governor of the state, the Chief Justice and each Judge of the Supreme Court, the Clerk of the Supreme Court, the Reporter of the Supreme Court, the Court Administrator, the Auditor of Public Accounts, the Commissioner of Labor, and the Revisor of Statutes; one copy each to the Secretary of State of the United States, the library of the Supreme Court of the United States, the Adjutant General, the Air National Guard, the Commissioner of Education, the State Treasurer, the Board of Educational Lands and Funds, the Director of Agriculture, the Director of Administrative Services, the Director of Aeronautics, the Department of Economic Development, the Director of the Public Employees Retirement Board, the Director of Health, the Director-State Engineer, the Director of Banking and Finance, the Director of Insurance, the Director of Motor Vehicles, the Director of Veterans' Affairs, the Director of Water Resources, the Director of Public Welfare, the Director of Public Institutions, the Director of Correctional Services, the Nebraska Emergency Operating Center, each judge of the Nebraska Workmen's Compensation Court, each judge of the Commission of Industrial Relations, the Nebraska Liquor Control Commission, the Nebraska Natural Resources Commission, the State Real Estate Commission, the secretary of the Game and Parks Commission, the Board of Pardons, each state institution under the Department of Public Institutions, each state institution under the State Department of Education, the State Surveyor, the Nebraska State Patrol, Puchasing Agent, State

Personnel Office, Nebraska Motor Vehicle Industry Licensing Board, Board of Trustees of the Nebraska State Colleges, each of the Nebraska State Colleges, each district judge of the State of Nebraska, each district county judge, each judge of a separate juvenile court, the Lieutenant Governor, each United States Senator from Nebraska, each United States Representative from Nebraska, each clerk of the district court for the use of the district court, the clerk of the Nebraska Workmen's Compensation Court, each associate county judge, each county attorney, each county public defender, and each county law library of the State of Nebraska, each judge of the municipal court, and the inmate library at all state penal and correctional institutions, and each member of the Legislature shall be entitled to two complete sets, and two complete sets of such volumes as are necessary to update previously issued volumes, but each member of the Legislature shall be entitled, on request, to a third complete set; *Provided*, copies of the statutes distributed without charge, as above listed, shall be the property of the state or governmental subdivision of the state and not the personal property of the particular person receiving a copy. Distribution of statutes to the library of the College of Law of the University of Nebraska shall be as provided in sections 85-176 and 85-177.

Source: Laws 1943, c. 115, § 17, p. 407; R.S.1943, § 49-617; Laws 1944, Spec.Sess., c. 3, § 5, p. 100; Laws 1947, c. 185, § 5, p. 612; Laws 1951, c. 345, § 1, p. 1132; Laws 1957, c. 210, § 3, p. 743; Laws 1961, c. 242, § 2, p. 722; Laws 1961, c. 243, § 3, p. 725; Laws 1961, c. 415, § 5, p. 1247; Laws 1961, c. 416, § 8, p. 1266; Laws 1963, c. 303, § 3, p. 898; Laws 1965, c. 305, § 1, p. 858; Laws 1967, c. 326, § 1, p. 865; Laws 1967, c. 325, § 1, p. 863; Laws 1971, LB 36, § 4; Laws 1972, LB 1174, § 1; Laws 1972, LB 1032, § 254; Laws 1972, LB 1284, § 18; Laws 1973, LB 1, § 5; Laws 1973, LB 572, § 1; Laws 1973, LB 563, § 4; Laws 1974, LB 595, § 1; Laws 1975, LB 59, § 4; Laws 1978, LB 168, § 1.

85-176. College of Law; state publications; number furnished free. The following publications of the State of Nebraska shall, as they are from time to time issued, be delivered by the respective officer having custody thereof to the library of the College of Law of the University of Nebraska:

(1) Fifteen copies of the Supreme Court Reports, two copies of the Legislative Journal, ten copies of the Session Laws, five copies of the opinions of the Attorney General, five copies of the Blue Book, and two copies each of the reports and recommendations of the Judicial Council and of the reports and recommendations of the Legislative Council;

(2) One copy each of the annual and biennial reports of the state officers who are required by law to make an annual or biennial report; and

(3) Statutes issued by the State Librarian shall be requisitioned by the librarian of the College of Law, allowing ten copies for the library of the College of Law, five copies for the Legal Aid Bureau and the editors and staff of the Nebraska Law Review, one copy each for every full-time member of the law faculty, and no more than fifteen copies for the university libraries, nonlaw faculty and administrative officers

of the university combined.

    Source: Laws 1947, c. 185, § 1, p. 610; Laws 1951, c. 345, § 2, p. 1133;
            Laws 1961, c. 243, § 4, p. 727.

    85-177. College of Law; state publications; additional copies; requisition. In order to enable the library of the College of Law to augment its collections, the librarian of the College of Law of the University of Nebraska is authorized to requisition from the respective officer having custody thereof up to one hundred copies of the following state publications: Supreme Court Reports, Legislative Journals, Session Laws, replacement volumes and supplements to the Revised Statutes, and opinions of the Attorney General.

    Source: Laws 1947, c. 185, § 2, p. 611; Laws 1951, c. 345, § 3, p. 1133;
            Laws 1961, c. 243, § 5, p. 727.

    24-209. Supreme Court Reports; printed volumes; disposition; price. The Supreme Court Reports shall be deposited in the State Library. Copies thereof shall be distributed by the librarian to each judge of the Supreme, district, and municipal courts, to each county court, to each county law library, to each state and territorial library, to each officer of the executive department of this state, to the Clerk of the Legislature, and to each judge of the United States District and Circuit Courts of this state; to the Nebraska Workmen's Compensation Court, two copies; to the Legislative Council, two copies; to the library of the College of Law of the University of Nebraska, as provided in sections 85-176 and 85-177; and to the Nebraska Publications Clearinghouse, eight copies. One complete set of Supreme Court Reports and one volume of all subsequent reports shall be furnished to each judge of a separate juvenile court by the State Librarian. The balance of such reports shall be sold as called for at such price as shall be prescribed by the Supreme Court. The Supreme Court shall also prescribe the price for microform copies of the reports. The money arising from such sales shall be paid into the General Fund of the state treasury.

    Source: Laws 1979, LB 377, § 1.

    24-212. Nebraska Reports; preparation and publication; copyright; disposition. It shall be the duty of the Reporter of the Supreme Court to prepare the opinions of said court for publication as fast as they are delivered to him or her, and when sufficient material is accumulated to form a volume of not less than nine hundred pages, he or she shall cause the same to be printed, and bound in a good and substantial manner, equal to Volume 50 of said Reports. He or she shall deliver one thousand copies of each volume to the State Librarian, and upon a presentation of proper vouchers to the Director of Administrative Services, he or she shall draw his or her warrant in payment thereof. The copyright of each volume shall be entered by said reporter for the benefit of the state, and all papers relating thereto shall be filed and recorded in the office of the Secretary of State. The title of the volume shall be Nebraska Reports, which, with the number of the volume, shall be printed on the back of each volume, and the reports of every case must show the name of the judge writing the opinion, the names of the judges concurring therein, and the names of the judges, if any, dissenting from said opinion. The reporter shall also edit and arrange for publication, in the Statutes of Nebraska, at such times as the Revisor of Statutes may request, annotations of the decisions of the Supreme Court of Nebraska and the federal courts and transmit them to the Revisor of Statutes. With the approval of the Supreme Court, the reporter may arrange for microform reproduction of the published reports and furnish them to the State Librarian for sale.

> **Source:** Laws 1879, § 19, p. 85; Laws 1901, c. 24, § 1, p. 329; R.S.1913, § 1146; C.S.1922, § 1075; Laws 1929, c. 84, § 1, p. 334; C.S.1929, § 27-212; R.S.1943, § 24-212; Laws 1967, c. 328, § 1, p. 868; Laws 1979, LB 377, § 2.

STATE HISTORICAL SOCIETY
(Revised Statutes of Nebraska, 1982, s.82-101 to 82-110.)

82-101. Nebraska State Historical Society; organization; building; purpose; acceptance of gifts; operation of historical sites and museums. The Nebraska State Historical Society shall be a state institution. Its headquarters building in Lincoln shall be used by the society as a museum and library building for the preservation, care, and exhibition of documents, books, newspapers, weapons, tools, pictures, relics, scientific specimens, farm and factory products, and all other collections pertaining to the history of the world, particularly to that of Nebraska and the West. It shall have the power to accept gifts, and to own, control and dispose of property, real and personal, with the consent of the Legislature. It shall, either alone or in cooperation with other agencies, operate historical sites and museums as agreed to with appropriate state agencies or as directed by the Governor and the Legislature.

> **Source:** Laws 1883, c. 95, § 1, p. 340; Laws 1907, c. 146, § 1, p. 458; R.S.1913, § 7166; C.S.1922, § 6817; C.S.1929, § 82-101; R.S.1943, § 82-101; Laws 1961, c. 438, § 1, p. 1356.

82-102. Nebraska State Historical Society; reports; contents. The president and secretary of the Nebraska State Historical Society shall make biennial reports to the Governor of its transactions. The report shall include the transactions and expenditures of the society, together with all historical addresses which have been read before the society during the preceding two years, or which furnish historical matter on data of the state and adjacent western regions.

> Source: Laws 1883, c. 95, § 2, p. 340; R.S.1913, § 7167; C.S.1922, § 6818; C.S.1929, § 82-102; R.S.1943, § 82-102; Laws 1955, c. 231, § 21, p. 728; Laws 1981, LB 545, § 38.

82-103. Nebraska State Historical Society; publications. The reports, addresses and papers mentioned in section 82-102 shall be published at the expense of the state and distributed as other similar official reports are distributed. The state and society shall decide upon a reasonable number of the published reports, which shall be furnished to the society for its use and distribution.

> Source: Laws 1883 c. 95, § 3, p. 341; R.S.1913, § 7168; C.S.1922, § 6819; C.S.1929, § 82-103.

82-104. Nebraska State Historical Society; public documents, records, relics; custodian. The Nebraska State Historical Society shall be the custodian of all public records, documents, relics, and other material which the society may consider to be of historic value or interest, and which may be in any of the offices or vaults of the several departments of the state, in any of the institutions which receive appropriations of money from the Legislature of Nebraska, or in any of the county courthouses, city halls, or other public buildings within the State of Nebraska.

> Source: Laws 1905, c. 157, § 1, p. 604; R.S.1913, § 7169; C.S.1922, § 6820; C.S.1929, § 82-104.

82-105. Nebraska State Historical Society; public documents, records, relics; obtaining possession; procedure. The Nebraska State Historical Society shall obtain possession of the historical material mentioned in section 82-104 whenever it is not in active use in any department, institution or building, or whenever it is liable to damage and destruction because of a lack of proper means to care for, or safe and adequate place to preserve it. The officer or board having the care and management of the department, institution or building shall consent in writing to the custody of the documents, records and materials by the society. The society shall prepare invoices and receipts in triplicate for the material turned over to the society, and shall deliver one copy to the Secretary of State, one copy to the officer or board turning over the material, and one copy shall be retained by the secretary of the society.

> Source: Laws 1905, c. 157, § 2, p. 604; R.S.1913, § 7170; C.S.1922, § 6821; C.S.1929, § 82-105; R.S.1943, § 82-105; Laws 1969, c. 810, § 1, p. 3047.

82-106. Nebraska State Historical Society; public documents,

records, relics; notice to be given. Every officer or board having control or management of any state department, institution or building shall notify the secretary of the Nebraska State Historical Society whenever any of the historical material mentioned in sections 82-104 and 82-105 shall be in his or their care.

Source: Laws 1905, c. 157, § 3, p. 605; R.S.1913, § 7171; C.S.1922, § 6822; C.S.1929, § 82-106.

82-107. Nebraska State Historical Society; public documents, records, relics; procedure after notice. Whenever the secretary of the Nebraska State Historical Society has received notice as provided for in section 82-106, the society shall, by its officers or employees, examine the material and remove and receipt for whatever material the society may deem to be of historic value. The society shall transport the material at its own cost to its museum, and shall catalog, arrange and display the material for the free use of the public.

Source: Laws 1905, c. 157, § 4, p. 605; R.S.1913, § 7172; C.S.1922, § 6823; C.S.1929, § 82-107.

82-108. Nebraska State Historical Society; documents and records; certified copies; fees. The secretary or curator of the Nebraska State Historical Society shall prepare certified copies of any record, document or other material, of which the society is the custodian, whenever application shall be made to the society. Such certified copies shall be received in courts and elsewhere as being of the same legal validity as similar copies prepared by the original custodian of the record, document or other material. The secretary or curator of the society shall be entitled to the same fees for making certified copies as the original custodian would be.

Source: Laws 1905, c. 157, § 5, p. 605; R.S.1913, § 7173; C.S.1922, § 6824; C.S.1929, § 82-108.

82-108.01. Nebraska State Historical Society; surplus, damaged, defective, and duplicate books and material; sell; exchange; destroy. The Nebraska State Historical Society is authorized to sell, exchange, destroy, or otherwise dispose of any surplus, damaged, defective, or duplicate books, or materials in its collections.

Source: Laws 1949, c. 289, § 1, p. 992.

82-108.02. Nebraska State Historical Society; funds from services rendered; Historical Society Fund; investment; deposit; disbursement. All funds received by the Nebraska State Historical Society for services rendered shall be transmitted to the State Treasurer and by him deposited in the state treasury to the credit of the Historical Society Fund which is hereby established. Funds to the credit of the Historical

Society Fund shall only be expended, as and when appropriated by the Legislature, by the Nebraska State Historical Society for the general purposes of such society. Any money in the Historical Society Fund available for investment shall be invested by the state investment officer pursuant to the provisions of sections 72-1237 to 72-1259.

Source: Laws 1961, c. 439, § 1, p. 1357; Laws 1969, c. 584, § 110, p. 2416.

82-109.   Nebraska State Historical Society; documents relating to General Land Office; agreement with United States Land Office. The Nebraska State Historical Society is authorized to enter into an agreement with the General Land Office at Washington, D. C., for the reception, preservation, organization and arrangement for public use of all documents relating to the former United States Land Offices in Nebraska that may be transferred from the custody of the General Land Office at Washington, D. C., to the custody of the society.

Source: Laws 1937, c. 196, § 1, p. 818; C.S.Supp.,1941, § 82-114.

82-110.   Documents relating to General Land Office; preservation and maintenance; federal authorities; free access. All documents obtained from the General Land Office at Washington, D. C., shall be preserved and maintained as a part of the public records of Nebraska by the Nebraska State Historical Society, and by all other persons in such manner as shall secure the chief objects of their use and preservation, their care, custody and service, under proper library regulations. The authorities of the United States shall have free access to such documents.

Source: Laws 1937, c. 196, § 2, p. 819; C.S.Supp.,1941, § 82-115.

RECORDS MANAGEMENT ACT
(Revised Statutes of Nebraska, 1982, s.84-1201 to 84-1204, 84-1206 to 84-1226.)

84-1201.   Legislative intent. The Legislature declares:

(1) That programs for the systematic and centrally-correlated management of state and local records will promote efficiency and economy in the day-to-day recordkeeping activities of state and local governments, and will facilitate and expedite governmental operations.

(2) That records containing information essential to the operations of government, and to the protection of the rights and interests of persons, must be safeguarded against the destructive effects of all forms of disaster and must be available as needed; wherefore it is necessary to adopt special provisions for the selection and preservation of essential state and local records, thereby insuring the protection and availability of such information.

Source: Laws 1961, c. 455, § 1, p. 1385.

84-1202. Terms, defined. As used in sections 84-1201 to 84-1226, unless the context otherwise requires:

(1) Agency shall mean any department, division, office, commission, court, board, or elected, appointed, or constitutional officer, except individual members of the Legislature, or any other unit or body, however designated, of the executive, judicial, and legislative branches of the state government or of the government of any local political subdivision;

(2) Agency head shall mean the chief or principal official or representative in any such agency, or the presiding judge of any court, by whatever title known; and when an agency consists of a single official, the agency and the agency head are one and the same;

(3) State agency shall mean an agency of the state government; and a local agency shall mean an agency of a local political subdivision;

(4) Local political subdivision shall mean any county, city, village, township, district, authority, or other public corporation or political entity, whether existing under charter or general law; except that a metropolitan class city or a district or other unit which by law is considered an integral part of the state government is not included in the term;

(5) Record shall mean any book, document, paper, photograph, microfilm, sound recording, magnetic storage medium, or other material regardless of physical form or characteristics, created or received pursuant to law, charter, ordinance or in connection with any other activity relating to or having an effect upon the transaction of public business;

(6) State record shall mean a record which normally is maintained within the custody or control of a state agency, or any other record which is designated or treated as a state record according to general law;

(7) Local record shall mean a record of a local political subdivision or of any agency thereof, unless designated or treated as a state record under general law;

(8) Essential record shall mean a state or local record which is within one or the other of the following categories, and which shall be preserved pursuant to sections 84-1201 to 84-1226:

(a) Category A. Records containing information necessary to the operations of government under all conditions, including a period of emergency created by a disaster; or

(b) Category B. Records not within Category A, but which contain information necessary to protect the rights and interests of persons, or to establish or affirm the powers and duties of state or local governments in the resumption of operations after a disaster;

(9) Preservation duplicate shall mean a copy of an essential record, which is used for the purpose of preserving the record pursuant to sections 84-1201 to 84-1226; and

(10) Disaster shall mean any occurrence of fire, flood, storm, earthquake, explosion, epidemic, riot, sabotage, or other conditions of extreme peril resulting in substantial injury or damage to persons or property within this state, whether such occurrence is caused by an act of nature or of man, including an enemy of the United States.

Source: Laws 1961, c. 455, § 2, p. 1385; Laws 1969, c. 841, § 1, p. 3167; Laws 1979, LB 559, § 1; Laws 1980, LB 747, § 1.

84-1203. Secretary of State; State Records Administrator; duties. The Secretary of State is hereby designated the State Records Administrator, hereinafter called the administrator. The administrator shall establish and administer, within and for state and local agencies, (1) a records management program which will apply efficient and economical methods to the creation, utilization, maintenance, retention, preservation, and disposal of state and local records, (2) a program for the selection and preservation of essential state and local records, (3) establish and maintain a depository for the storage and service of state records, and advise, assist, and govern by rules and regulations the establishment of similar programs in local political subdivisions in the state, and (4) establish and maintain a central microfilm agency for state records and advise, assist, and govern by rules and regulations the establishment of similar programs in state agencies and local political subdivisions in the State of Nebraska.

Source: Laws 1961, c. 455, § 3, p. 1387; Laws 1969, c. 841, § 2, p. 3169; Laws 1977, LB 520, § 1; Laws 1979, LB 559, § 2.

84-1204. State Records Board; established; members; duties; rules; adopt; meetings. A State Records Board, hereinafter called the board, is hereby established to advise and assist the administrator in the performance of the duties enjoined upon him or her by sections 84-1201 to 84-1226, and to perform such other functions and duties as sections 84-1201 to 84-1226 require. In addition to the administrator, the board shall consist of the Governor, the Attorney General, the Auditor of Public Accounts, the Chairman of the Judicial Council, the Clerk of the Legislature, the Director of Administrative Services, and the Director of the Nebraska State Historical Society, the state archivist, and the director of the records management program, who shall be appointed by the administrator with the approval of the board, or their personally-designated representatives. The administrator or his or her representative shall be chairman of the board, and the director of the records management program its secretary. Upon call by the administrator, the board shall convene periodically in accordance with its rules, or upon call by the administrator or his or her personally-designated representative.

Source: Laws 1961, c. 455, § 4, p. 1387; Laws 1969, c. 841, § 3, p. 3170; Laws 1979, LB 559, § 3.

84-1206. Administrator; duties. (1) With due regard for the functions of the agencies concerned, and with such guidance and assistance from the board as may be required, the administrator shall:

(a) Establish standards, procedures, and techniques for the effective management of public records;

(b) Make continuing surveys of paper work operations, and recommend improvements in current records management practices, including but not limited to the economical use of space, equipment, and supplies employed in creating, maintaining, storing, preserving, and servicing records;

(c) Establish standards for the preparation of schedules providing for the retention of records of continuing value, and for the prompt and orderly disposal of records no longer possessing sufficient administrative, legal, historical, or fiscal value to warrant their further retention; and

(d) Obtain from the agencies concerned such reports and other data as are required for the proper administration of the records management program including organizational charts of agencies concerned.

(2) The administrator shall establish standards for designating essential records, shall assist agencies in identifying essential records, and shall guide them in the establishment of programs for the preservation of essential records.

(3) The administrator may advise and assist members of the Legislature and other officials in the maintenance and disposition of their personal or political papers of public interest and may provide such other services as are available to state and local agencies, within the limitation of available funds.

Source: Laws 1961, c. 455, § 6, p. 1388; Laws 1969, c. 841, § 4, p. 3171; Laws 1976, LB 641, § 1; Laws 1980, LB 747, § 2.

84-1207. State executive head; duties. In accordance with general law, and with such rules and regulations as shall be promulgated by the administrator and the board as provided in section 84-1216, such head of any state agency, department, board, council, legislative or judicial branch, and political subdivision shall:

(1) Establish and maintain an active, continuing program for the efficient and economical management of the recordkeeping activities of the agency;

(2) Make and maintain records containing adequate and proper documentation of the organization, functions, policies, decisions, procedures, and essential transactions of the agency, designed to furnish information to protect the legal and financial rights of the state, and of persons directly affected by the agency's activities;

(3) Make, and submit to the administrator, schedules proposing the length of time each record series warrants retention for administra-

tive, legal, historical or fiscal purposes, after it has been made in or received by the agency, and lists of records in the custody or under the control of the agency which are not needed in the transaction of current business, and do not possess sufficient administrative, legal, historical or fiscal value to warrant their further retention;

(4) Inventory the records in the custody or under the control of the agency, and submit to the administrator a report thereon, containing such data as the administrator shall prescribe, and including his recommendations as to which if any such records should be determined to be essential records. He shall review his inventory and report periodically and, as necessary, shall revise his report so that it is current, accurate and complete; and

(5) Comply with the rules, regulations, standards and procedures issued and set up by the administrator and the board, and cooperate in the conduct of surveys made by the administrator pursuant to sections 84-1201 to 84-1226.

Source: Laws 1961, c. 455, § 7, p. 1389; Laws 1969, c. 841, § 5, p. 3171; Laws 1979, LB 559, § 4.

84-1207.01. Agency head; designate records officer; duties. In addition to the duties enumerated in section 84-1207, each state agency head shall designate a records officer from the management or professional level who shall be responsible for the overall coordination of records management activities within the agency.

Source: Laws 1976, LB 641, § 2.

84-1208. Administrator; preservation duplicates of essential records; process used; exception. (1) The administrator may make or cause to be made preservation duplicates of essential records, or may designate as preservation duplicates existing copies thereof. A preservation duplicate shall be durable, accurate, complete and clear, and if made by means of photography, microphotography, photocopying, film, microfilm, or similar processes, shall be prepared in conformity to standards prescribed and approved by the board.

(2) A preservation duplicate made by a photographic, photostatic, microfilm, microcard, miniature photographic or similar process, which accurately reproduces or forms a durable medium for so reproducing the original, shall have the same force and effect for all purposes as the original record, whether the original is in existence or not. A transcript, exemplification, or certified copy of such preservation duplicate shall for all purposes be deemed a transcript, exemplification or certified copy of the original record.

(3) No copy of an essential record shall be used as a preservation duplicate unless, under the general laws of the state, the copy has the same force and effect for all purposes as the original record.

Source: Laws 1961, c. 455, § 8, p. 1390.

84-1209. Administrator; storage of records and preservation duplicates. The administrator may establish storage facilities for essential records and preservation duplicates.

Source: Laws 1961, c. 455, § 9, p. 1390; Laws 1969, c. 841, § 6, p. 3172; Laws 1976, LB 641, § 3.

84-1210. Administrator; records; maintain; temporary removal; inspection. (1) The administrator shall properly maintain essential records and preservation duplicates stored by him.

(2) An essential record or preservation duplicate stored by the administrator may be removed by the regularly designated custodian for temporary use when necessary for the proper conduct of his office, and shall be returned to the administrator immediately after such use.

(3) When an essential record is stored by him, the administrator, upon the request of the regularly designated custodian thereof, shall provide for its inspection or for the making or certification of copies thereof, and such copies, when certified by the administrator, shall have the same force and effect for all purposes as if certified by the regularly designated custodian.

Source: Laws 1961, c. 455, § 10, p. 1391; Laws 1969, c. 841, § 7, p. 3173.

84-1211. Records; confidential; protection. (1) When an essential record is required by law to be treated in a confidential manner, the administrator, in effectuating the purposes of sections 84-1201 to 84-1226, shall protect its confidential nature, as well as that of any preservation duplicate or other copy thereof. Any hospital or medical record submitted to the administrator for microfilming or similar processing shall be made accessible in a manner consistent with the access permitted similar records under sections 83-109 and 83-1068.

(2) Nothing in this act shall be construed to affect the laws and regulations dealing with the dissemination, security, and privacy of criminal history information under Chapter 29, article 35.

Source: Laws 1961, c. 455, § 11, p. 1391; Laws 1969, c. 841, § 8, p. 3174; Laws 1979, LB 559, § 5.

84-1212. Program for selection and preservation of essential records; review, periodically. The administrator shall review periodically, and at least once each year, the program for the selection and preservation of essential records, including the classification thereof and the provisions for preservation duplicates and for the safeguarding of essential records and preservation duplicates to insure that the purposes of sections 84-1201 to 84-1226 are accomplished.

Source: Laws 1961, c. 455, § 12, p. 1392; Laws 1969, c. 841, § 9, p. 3174; Laws 1979, LB 559, § 6.

84-1212.01. Records retention and disposition schedule; review by state archivist; approval; review by administrator. (1) Each records retention and disposition schedule submitted to the administrator shall be reviewed by the state archivist of the Nebraska State Historical Society for purposes of selection of archival and historical material, and all such material shall be identified as such on the schedule. When the state archivist has determined that all archival and historical material has been properly identified and that no disposition, except by transfer to the state archives, has been recommended for such material, the state archivist shall approve such records retention and disposition schedule and return it to the administrator.

(2) The administrator shall review each records retention and disposition schedule submitted, and if the recommended retention periods and the recommended dispositions satisfy audit requirements and give proper recognition to administrative, legal, and fiscal value of the records listed therein, and if the records retention and disposition schedule has been approved by the state archivist, such records retention and disposition schedule shall be approved by the administrator.

Source: Laws 1976, LB 641, § 4.

84-1212.02. Records retention and disposition schedule; disposal of records pursuant to schedule; report. All state agency heads and all local agency heads are hereby authorized to dispose of the records of their agencies in accordance with records retention and disposition schedules which are applicable to their agencies if such schedules have been approved by the administrator pursuant to section 84-1212.01. Each agency head shall report any such records disposition to the administrator on forms provided by the administrator.

Source: Laws 1976, LB 641, § 5.

84-1213. Records; property of government; protected; willfully mutilate, destroy, transfer, remove, damage, or otherwise dispose of; violation; penalty. All records made or received by or under the authority of, or coming into the custody, control, or possession of agencies in any of the three branches of the state government, or of any local political subdivision, in the course of their public duties, are the property of the government concerned, and shall not be mutilated, destroyed, transferred, removed, damaged, or otherwise disposed of, in whole or in part, except as provided by law.

Any person who shall willfully mutilate, destroy, transfer, remove, damage, or otherwise dispose of such records or any part of such records, except as provided by law, and any person who shall retain and continue to hold the possession of any such records, or parts thereof, belonging to the state government or to any local political subdivision, and shall refuse to deliver up such records, or parts thereof, to the proper official under whose authority such records belong, upon demand being made by such officer or, in cases of a defunct office, to the succeeding agency or to the state archives of the Nebraska State Historical Society, shall be guilty of a Class III misdemeanor.

Source: Laws 1961, c. 455, § 13, p. 1392; Laws 1973, LB 224, § 15; Laws 1979, LB 559, § 7; Laws 1980, LB 747, § 3.

84-1213.01. Records; violation; prosecute. The State Records Administrator, or any official under whose authority such records belong, shall report to the proper county attorney any supposed violation of section 84-1213 that in its judgment warrants prosecution. It shall be the duty of the several county attorneys to investigate supposed violations of such section and to prosecute violations of such section.

Source: Laws 1973, LB 224, § 16.

84-1214. Agency; disposition of records; procedure. Whenever any agency desires to dispose of records which are not listed on an approved records retention and disposition schedule applicable to that agency, the agency head shall prepare and submit to the administrator, on forms provided by the administrator, a list of the records sought to be disposed of, and a request for approval of their disposition, which list and request shall be referred to the board for action at its next regular or special session. On consideration thereof, the board may approve such disposition thereof as may be legal and proper, or may refuse to approve any disposition, and the records as to which such determination has been made may thereupon be disposed of in accordance with the approval of the board.

Source: Laws 1961, c. 455, § 14, p. 1392; Laws 1969, c. 841, § 10, p. 3174; Laws 1976, LB 641, § 6.

84-1214.01. State archives; authority; duties. The state archives, a division of the State Historical Society, has the authority to acquire, in total or in part, any document, record or material, which has been submitted to the records board for disposition or transfer, when such material is determined to be of archival or historical significance by the state archivist or records board. The head of any agency shall certify in writing to the State Historical Society, the transfer of the custody of such material to the state archives. No agency shall dispose of, in any other manner except by transfer to the state archives, that material which has been appraised as archival or historical without the written consent of the state archivist and the records administrator. In any case where such material of archival or historical significance is determined to be in jeopardy of destruction or deterioration, and such material is not necessary to the conduct of daily business in the agency of origin, it shall be the prerogative of the state archivist to petition the State Records Administrator and the agency of origin, for the right to transfer such material into the safekeeping of the state

archives. It shall be the responsibility of the State Records Administrator to hear arguments for or against such petition and to determine
the results of such petition. The state archivist shall prepare invoices
and receipts in triplicate for materials acquired under the provisions
of this section, and shall deliver one copy to the State Records Administrator and one copy to the agency head from which the records are
obtained and retain one copy.

Source: Laws 1969, c. 841, § 11, p. 3175.

**84-1215.   Nonrecord material; destruction; procedure; personal and
political papers; preservation.** (1) If not otherwise prohibited by law,
nonrecord materials, not included within the definition of records as
contained in section 84-1202, may be destroyed at any time by the
agency in possession thereof, without the prior approval of the administrator or board. The administrator may formulate procedures and
interpretations to guide in the disposal of nonrecord materials, but
nothing therein shall be contrary to any provision of law relating to the
transfer of materials of historical value to the state archives of the
Nebraska State Historical Society.

(2) Members of the Legislature and other officials are encouraged
to offer their personal and political papers of public interest to the
state archives for preservation subject to any reasonable restrictions
concerning their use by other persons.

Source: Laws 1961, c. 455, § 15, p. 1393; Laws 1969, c. 841, § 12, p.
3176; Laws 1980, LB 747, § 4.

84-1216.   Administrator; rules and regulations; promulgate. The
administrator shall promulgate such rules and regulations as may be
necessary or proper to effectuate the purposes of sections 84-1201 to
84-1226. Those portions thereof which relate to functions specifically
delegated to the board shall be approved and concurred in by the
board.

Source: Laws 1961, c. 455, § 16, p. 1393; Laws 1979, LB 559, § 8.

84-1217.   Agencies; preservation of records; administrator; advise.
All provisions of the Records Management Act shall apply to all agencies as defined in subdivision (1) of section 84-1202 and the administrator shall advise and assist in the establishment of programs for
records management and for the selection and preservation of essential records of such branches, and, as required by such branches, shall
provide program services pursuant to the provisions of sections 84-
1201 to 84-1226.

Source: Laws 1961, c. 455, § 17, p. 1393; Laws 1969, c. 841, § 13, p.
3176; Laws 1979, LB 559, § 9.

84-1218. Political subdivisions; preservation of records; administrator; advise and assist; rules and regulations. The governing bodies of all local political subdivisions in this state, with the advice and assistance of the administrator and pursuant to the rules and regulations established by him, shall establish and maintain continuing programs to promote the principles of efficient records management for local records, and for the selection and preservation of essential local records, which programs, insofar as practicable, shall follow the patterns of the programs established for state records as provided in sections 84-1201 to 84-1226. Each such governing body shall promulgate such rules and regulations as are necessary or proper to effectuate and implement the programs so established, but nothing therein shall be in violation of the provisions of general law relating to the destruction of local records.

> **Source:** Laws 1961, c. 455, § 18, p. 1393; Laws 1969, c. 841, § 14, p. 3176; Laws 1979, LB 559, § 10.

84-1219. Administrator; biennial report; copies; furnish. The administrator shall prepare a biennial report on the status of programs established by him as provided in sections 84-1201 to 84-1226, and on the progress made during the preceding biennium in implementing and effectuating such programs. Copies of this report shall be furnished the Governor, the Speaker of the Legislature, and such other officials and agencies as the Governor or the board shall direct.

> **Source:** Laws 1961, c. 455, § 19, p. 1394; Laws 1979, LB 559, § 11.

84-1220. Act, how cited. Sections 84-1201 to 84-1226 shall be known and may be cited as the Records Management Act.

> **Source:** Laws 1961, c. 455, § 20, p. 1394; Laws 1979, LB 559, § 12.

84-1221. Revisor of Statutes; authority to substitute terms. Except within this act, the Revisor of Statutes shall substitute the term State Records Administrator for State Records Board wherever such term appears in the statutes.

> **Source:** Laws 1976, LB 641, § 7.

84-1222. Purchase of microfilm system or equipment; approval; property of State Records Administrator. After May 18, 1977, no state agency shall purchase any microfilm system or equipment prior to the approval of the State Records Administrator. The administrator shall not approve internal microfilm activities of any state agency unless such activities may not be feasibly provided by the central microfilming agency and are necessary to a particular operation within the state agency. Any equipment purchased under this section shall become the property of the State Records Administrator and shall be subject to the provisions of section 84-1223.

> **Source:** Laws 1977, LB 520, § 2; Laws 1979, LB 559, § 13.

84-1223. Micrographic production, processing, and viewing equipment; property of administrator; exception; credit. On May 19, 1979, all micrographic production, processing, and viewing equipment currently owned or subsequently acquired under the provisions of section 84-1222 by any state executive, judicial, or legislative agency, except the University of Nebraska or the state colleges, shall become the property of the State Records Administrator, regardless of the fund source from which the equipment was originally purchased. Appropriate credit, against future charges, shall be given to all agencies for the fair market value of all equipment accepted which had been purchased with federal funds or trust funds. Equipment purchased with funds from the Highway Cash Fund shall not be deemed to have been purchased with federal funds or trust funds.

Source: Laws 1977, LB 520, § 4; Laws 1979, LB 559, § 14; Laws 1980, LB 747, § 5.

84-1224. State Records Administrator; powers. The State Records Administrator shall:

(1) Be empowered to review the microfilm systems within every agency of the state;

(2) Be empowered to cause such systems to be merged with a central microfilm agency in the event that a cost analysis shows that economic advantage may be achieved;

(3) Be empowered to permit the establishment of microfilming services within any agency or department of the state if a potential economy or a substantial convenience for the state would result; and

(4) After July 1, 1978, be empowered to determine the operating locations of all micrographic equipment in his possession.

Source: Laws 1977, LB 520, § 4.

84-1225. State Records Administrator; micropublishing and computer output microfilm services; charges. The State Records Administrator shall provide for a system of charges for micropublishing services and computer output microfilm services rendered by the central microfilming agency to any other department or agency of the state when these charges are allocable to a particular project carried on by such microfilming agency. Such charges shall, as nearly as may be practical, reflect the actual cost of services provided by the central microfilming agency. On July 1, 1978, and thereafter the State Records Administrator shall extend this system of charges to include source document microfilming. The State Records Administrator shall extend this system of charges and user fees for all micrographic equipment which is the property of the administrator and which is used by any other state agency or department.

Source: Laws 1977, LB 520, § 5; Laws 1979, LB 559, § 15.

84-1226. Records Management Micrographics Services Revolving

Fund; created; credits; expenditures; rental. (1) There is hereby created a fund to be known as the Records Management Micrographics Services Revolving Fund. All charges received by the Secretary of State under section 84-1225 and legislative appropriations shall be credited to such fund. Whenever any micrographics equipment of any state agency, except the University of Nebraska or the state colleges, shall become surplus property and shall be sold pursuant to section 81-161.04, the proceeds from the sale of such equipment shall be deposited in the state treasury and shall be credited by the State Treasurer to the Records Management Micrographics Services Revolving Fund. Expenditures shall be made from such fund to finance the micropublishing services and the computer output microfilm services by the Secretary of State or his or her authorized agent in accordance with appropriations made by the Legislature and to receive and expend funds pursuant to section 84-1225 for the provision of source document microfilming and for procuring and replacing micrographic equipment provided to state agencies.

(2) By agreement between any state agency and the State Records Administrator, any state agency may be billed one full year's rental for equipment at the beginning of each fiscal year. The State Records Administrator may coordinate with the Director of Administrative Services to set up a separate subaccount within the fund for the purpose of accounting for micrographic equipment procurement and replacement.

Source: Laws 1977, LB 520, § 6; Laws 1979, LB 559, § 16.

COUNTY AND REGIONAL LIBRARIES
(Revised Statutes of Nebraska, 1982, s.51-301 to 51-305, 51-307 to 51-319.)

51-301. County and regional libraries; establishment. Notwithstanding any more general or special law respecting libraries, the county boards of the several counties, when authorized by a majority of the electors of any county residing outside cities, villages or townships at that time maintaining a public library by public tax, voting at a general election on the proposition hereinafter named, shall establish within their respective counties, county libraries in the manner and with the functions prescribed in sections 51-301 to 51-319; or two or more counties may cooperate to form a regional library in the same manner and with the same functions.

Source: Laws 1935, c. 114, § 1, p. 364; Laws 1941, c. 102, § 1, p. 420; C.S.Supp.,1941, § 51-401.

51-302. County and regional libraries; location. The county board of any county may establish at the county seat or some centrally located town a county library, or two or more counties may cooperate to form a regional library at a reasonably centrally located town or city for that part of such county or counties lying outside of incorporated cities and villages maintaining public libraries, and outside of townships maintaining township libraries, and for all such additional portions of such county or counties as may elect to become a part of, or to participate in, such county or regional library systems as hereinafter provided.

Source: Laws 1935, c. 114, § 2, p. 364; C.S.Supp.,1941, § 51-402.

51-303.   County and regional libraries; cities, villages, townships may join; township; discontinued; county; levy; tax.   After the establishment of a county or regional library as provided in sections 51-301 to 51-319, the board of trustees, city council or other governing authority of any incorporated city or village in the county or counties maintaining a public library, or the library board of any township library, may notify the county board or the commissioners of the regional library, that such city, village or township library desires to become a part of the county or regional library system, and thereafter such city, village or township library shall be a part thereof and its inhabitants shall be entitled to the benefits of such county or regional library, and the property within such city, village or township library shall be liable to taxes levied for county or regional library purposes; *Provided*, that when any county discontinues township organization the county shall assume the liability for taxes for the township library.

Source: Laws 1935, c. 114, § 3, p. 364; C.S.Supp.,1941, § 51-403; R.S.1943, § 51-303; Laws 1967, c. 120, § 3, p. 385.

51-304.   County and regional libraries; withdrawal by city, village, township libraries.   The board of trustees, city council or other governing authority of any incorporated city or town in the county or region, or the library board of any township library may at any time notify the county board or regional library commissioners that such city, village or township library no longer desires to be a part of the county library system, and thereafter such city, village or township library shall cease to participate in the benefits of such county or regional library, and the property situated in such city, village or township library shall not be liable for taxes levied to support or maintain county or regional library purposes.

Source: Laws 1935, c. 114, § 3, p. 365; C.S.Supp.,1941, § 51-403.

51-305.   County and regional libraries; withdrawal; notice of intention; publication.   The board of trustees, city council or other governing authority of any incorporated city or village, or the board of trustees of any township library, shall publish, at least once a week for two successive weeks prior either to giving or to withdrawing such notice, in a legal newspaper designated by said board of trustees, city council or library board, published in or of general circulation in such city, village or township, notice of such contemplated action, giving therein the date and the place of the meeting at which such contemplated action is proposed to be taken.

Source: Laws 1935, c. 114, § 3, p. 365; C.S.Supp.,1941, § 51-403.

51-307. County and regional librarian; term. Upon the establishment of a county or regional library the county board or regional library commission shall appoint a county or regional librarian who shall hold office for a term of four years, subject to prior removal for cause, after a hearing by said commission or commissioners.

Source: Laws 1935, c. 114, § 5, p. 366; C.S.Supp.,1941, § 51-405; R.S.1943, § 51-307; Laws 1971, LB 95, § 1.

51-308. County library; supervision; employees; powers of county board. The county library shall be under the general supervision of the county board, which shall have power to make general rules and regulations regarding the policy of the county library; to establish, upon the recommendation of the county librarian, branches and stations throughout the county and to locate said branches and stations in incorporated cities and villages wherever deemed advisable; to determine the number and kind of employees of such library; and to appoint and dismiss such employees upon the recommendation of the county librarian. Such employees shall not be removed except for cause, and in case any such removal be made upon the ground that the services of such employees are no longer required, such removed employee shall have the first right to be restored to such employment when such services are again required, but the county board may, at the time of appointing any employee, and upon the recommendation of the county librarian, enter into an agreement that such employee be employed for a definite time only.

Source: Laws 1935, c. 114, § 6, p. 366; C.S.Supp.,1941, § 51-406.

51-309. County library; employees; qualifications. All employees of the county library whose duties require special training in library work shall be graded in grades to be established by the county librarian, with the advice and approval of the director of the Nebraska Library Commission, according to the duties required of them, experience in library work, and other qualifications for the service required. Before appointment to a position in the graded service, the candidate must pass an examination appropriate to the position sought, satisfactory to the county librarian, and show a satisfactory experience in library work. Work in approved library schools or

libraries, or certificates issued by the state board for the certification
of librarians or board of library examiners, may be accepted by the
county librarian in lieu of such examination. The county librarian
may also accept as apprentices, without compensation, candidates
possessing personal qualifications satisfactory to him, and may dismiss the same at any time if in his judgment their work is not satisfactory to him.

Source: Laws 1935, c. 114, § 6, p. 366; C.S.Supp.,1941, § 51-406;
          R.S.1943, § 51-309; Laws 1972, LB 1033, § 1.

51-310.   Regional library; library commission; members; duties. The
regional library shall be under the general supervision of a regional
library commission which shall consist of not more than two commissioners from each of the county boards of the counties cooperating to
form the regional library. Such commissioners shall be designated by
their respective county boards. Their powers and duties and the general management and operation of the regional libraries shall be the
same as for the county libraries.

Source: Laws 1935, c. 114, § 6, p. 367; C.S.Supp.,1941, § 51-406.

51-311.   County or regional librarian; oath; bond.   The county or
regional librarian shall, prior to entering upon the duties of his office,
file with the county clerk or regional library commission the usual
oath of office and bond, conditioned upon the faithful performance of
his duties, with sufficient sureties approved by a judge of the county
court in the county or any one of the counties of which the librarian is
to be the county or regional librarian, in such sum as may be determined by the county board or boards, as the case may be.

Source: Laws 1935, c. 114, § 7, p. 367; C.S.Supp.,1941, § 51-407.

51-312.   County or regional librarian; duties.   The county or
regional librarian shall, subject to the general rules adopted by the
county board or regional library commission, build up and manage,
according to accepted principles of library management, a library for
the use of the people of the county or region, and shall determine
what books and other library equipment shall be purchased.

Source: Laws 1935, c. 114, § 7, p. 367; C.S.Supp.,1941, § 51-407.

51-313.   County or regional librarian; salary; expenses; payment. The
salary of each of the county librarians shall be paid by each of such
counties in equal monthly installments, at the same time and in the
same manner and out of the same fund as the salaries of the other
county officers are paid. The county or regional librarian and his or
her assistant shall be allowed actual and necessary traveling expenses
incurred on the business of the office, including mileage at the rate

provided in section 23-1112 for county officers and employees.

Source: Laws 1935, c. 114, § 7, p. 367; C.S.Supp.,1941, § 51-407; R.S.1943, § 51-313; Laws 1981, LB 204, § 91.

51-314. County and regional libraries; supervision; conventions. The county or regional libraries of the state shall be under the general supervision of the director of the Nebraska Library Commission, who shall from time to time, either personally or by one of his or her assistants, visit the county or regional libraries and inquire into their condition. The actual and necessary expenses of such visits shall be paid out of the Nebraska Library Commission Fund on the same basis as provided in sections 84-306.01 to 84-306.05 for state employees. The director of the Nebraska Library Commission may call a convention of county or regional librarians, to assemble at such time and place as he or she shall deem most convenient, for the discussion of questions pertaining to the supervision and administration of the county or regional libraries as shall properly be brought before it. It is hereby made the duty of all the county or regional librarians to attend and take part in the proceedings of such convention. The actual and necessary expenses of the county or regional librarians attending the convention shall be paid out of the county or regional library fund with reimbursement for mileage to be made at the rate provided in section 23-1112 for county officers and employees.

Source: Laws 1935, c. 114, § 8, p. 367; C.S.Supp.,1941, § 51-408; R.S.1943, § 51-314; Laws 1972, LB 1033, § 2; Laws 1981, LB 204, § 92.

51-315. County or regional librarian; annual report. The county or regional librarian shall, on or before July 31 in each year, report to the county or regional library commission and to the director of the Nebraska Library Commission on the condition of the county or regional library, for the year ending June 30 preceding. Such reports shall, in addition to other matters deemed expedient by the county or regional librarian, contain such statistical and other information as may be deemed desirable by the director. For this purpose the director may send to the several county librarians, instructions or question blanks in order to obtain the material for a comparative study of library conditions in the state.

Source: Laws 1935, c. 114, § 9, p. 368; C.S.Supp.,1941, § 51-409; R.S.1943, § 51-315; Laws 1972, LB 1033, § 3.

51-316. County or regional library; tax; budget; amount authorized. The county board or the regional library commissioners through their respective county boards shall, after a county or regional library has been established, when the annual budget statement has been adopted, annually levy, in the same manner and at the same time as other county taxes are levied and in addition to all other taxes, a tax in the amount required under the adopted budget statement to be received from taxation for the purpose of purchasing property for, establishing, and maintaining a county library, not to exceed seven cents on each one hundred dollars upon the actual value of all the taxable property in such county, except intangible property, outside of incorporated cities and villages maintaining public libraries, or a township maintaining a public library, and upon all property within incorporated cities, villages, or townships maintaining such a library, which have elected to become a part of such county library system as provided in sections 51-301 to 51-319.

> Source: Laws 1935, c. 114, § 10, p. 368; C.S.Supp.,1941, § 51-410; R.S.1943, § 51-316; Laws 1953, c. 287, § 66, p. 969; Laws 1971, LB 493, § 2; Laws 1979, LB 187, § 179.

51-317.   County or regional library; gifts and bequests; title; library tax; laws applicable.   The county board or the regional library commissioners are authorized to receive, on behalf of the county or region, any gift, bequest or devise for the county or regional library, or for any branch or subdivision thereof. The title to all property belonging to the county library shall be vested in the county, or that belonging to the regional library shall be vested in the regional library commission. All laws applicable to the collection of county taxes shall apply to the tax for library purposes levied in accordance with sections 51-301 to 51-319.

> **Source:**   Laws 1935, c. 114, § 10, p. 369; C.S.Supp.,1941, § 51-410.

51-318.   County or regional libraries; funds; control; disbursements. All funds of the county library, whether derived from taxation or otherwise, shall be in the custody of the county treasurer. All funds of the regional library, whether derived from taxation or otherwise, shall be in the custody of the treasurer of one of the counties forming the region when properly designated as custodian of funds by the regional library commission. They shall constitute a separate fund, called the county or regional library fund, as the case may be, and shall not be used for any purposes except those of the county or regional library. Each claim against the county library or regional library shall be authorized and approved by the county or regional librarian, or, in his absence from the county, by his designated deputy. It shall then be audited, allowed and paid in the same manner as are all other claims against the county.

> **Source:**   Laws 1935, c. 114, § 10, p. 369; C.S.Supp.,1941, § 51-410.

51-319.   County or regional libraries; disestablishment.   After a county library has been established it may be disestablished in the same manner as it was established, or after a regional library has been established it may be disestablished in the same manner as it was established.

> **Source:**   Laws 1935, c. 114, § 11, p. 369; C.S.Supp.,1941, § 51-411.

MUNICIPAL LIBRARIES
(Revised Statutes of Nebraska, 1982, s.51-201 to 51-219, 14-102, 15-230, 16-251, 17-967, 19-302.)

51-201. Municipal libraries; establishment; tax; amount authorized; library fund; county library, election required; discontinue; care; county. The city council of any city, the board of trustees of any incorporated village, the county board of any county, and the electors of any township at their annual town meeting shall have the power to establish a public library free for the use of the inhabitants of such city, village, county, or township. Any of those named may also contract for the use of a public library already established and may levy a tax of not more than ten and five-tenths cents on each one hundred dollars upon the actual value of all the taxable property in such city, village, township, or county, except intangible property, annually to be levied and collected in like manner as other taxes in such city, village, county, or township; *Provided*, that when any county discontinues township organization the county shall levy and collect a tax of not more than ten and five-tenths cents on each one hundred dollars for such public library. The amount collected from such levy shall be known as the library fund. When the county board makes a levy for a county library, it shall omit from the levy of the library tax all property within the limits of any city, village, or township in such county which already maintains a library by public tax. Before establishing a county library or levying a tax for a county library, the county board shall submit the question to the voters of the county and a majority of the voters voting thereon shall have authorized the establishment of such county library and the levying of the tax. Such questions shall be submitted at a general election only, and when so submitted and carried, it is hereby made the duty of the county board to include the county library in its next succeeding estimate and levy.

Source: Laws 1911, c. 73, § 1, p. 313; R.S.1913, § 3792; Laws 1919, c. 120, § 1, p. 285; C.S.1922, § 3185; C.S.1929, § 51-201; Laws 1931, c. 98, § 1, p. 267; C.S.Supp.,1941, § 51-201; R.S.1943, § 51-201; Laws 1951, c. 170, § 1, p. 657; Laws 1953, c. 287, § 65, p. 968; Laws 1957, c. 223, § 1, p. 765; Laws 1967, c. 120, § 2, p. 384; Laws 1971, LB 493, § 1; Laws 1979, LB 187, § 178.

51-202. City or village library; library board; members; elected or appointed; terms; vacancies, how filled. When any city council or village board shall have decided by ordinance to establish and maintain a public library and reading room under sections 51-201 to 51-219, a library board of five members shall be elected or appointed from the citizens at large, of which board neither the mayor nor any member of the city council or village board shall be a member. The members first elected or appointed shall hold their office, three for terms of four years, and two for terms of two years from the first day of July following their appointment or election, and their successors shall serve four-year terms; *Provided*, that the city council or village board may by ordinance make the terms of members of the library board for a period of two years.

At the election in 1974 and every fourth year thereafter, two members shall be elected or appointed for four-year terms. In 1976, and every fourth year thereafter, three members shall be elected or appointed for four-year terms. In cases of vacancies by resignation, removal, or otherwise, the city council or village board shall fill such vacancy for the unexpired term. Cities having home rule charters shall have the power to fix by ordinance the number of members and length of terms of members of such library boards. No member shall receive any pay or compensation for any services rendered as a member of the board.

The city council or village board shall by ordinance adopt the manner in which the library board of five members is to be chosen. If the city council or village board by ordinance provides for appointment of the members to the library board, such library board members shall be appointed by a majority vote of the members of the city council or village board. If the city council or village board adopts an ordinance to provide for the election of library board members at municipal elections in April, it shall follow the statutes governing municipal elections. If the municipal election is to be held in conjunction with the statewide primary, the election shall be held as provided in Chapter 32.

If the board members are to be elected, the city council or village board shall give public notice of such election after the adoption of such ordinance naming the offices to be filled, the length of terms, and the filing deadline for the placing of names of candidates on the ballot.

Source: Laws 1911, c. 73, § 2, p. 314; R.S.1913, § 3793; Laws 1919, c. 120, § 2, p. 286; Laws 1921, c. 233, § 1, p. 831; C.S.1922, § 3186; C.S.1929, § 51-202; R.S.1943, § 51-202; Laws 1961, c. 254, § 1, p. 748; Laws 1967, c. 329, § 1, p. 874; Laws 1972, LB 661, § 78; Laws 1973, LB 555, § 1; Laws 1981, LB 194, § 1.

51-203. County or township library; board; members; appointment; terms; vacancies; how filled. When the county board of any county or the electors of any township shall have voted to establish and maintain a public library, the county board of such county or the township board of such township shall appoint a library board of five members, no member of which shall be a member of the county or township board, one for a term of one year, one for a term of two years, one for a term of three years, one for a term of four years, and one for a term of five years, from the first day of July following their appointment; and thereafter the county or township board shall appoint annually one director to serve for a term of five years. Such county or township board shall have the power to fill for the unexpired term any vacancy which may occur in the county or township library board. No director shall receive any pay or compensation for any services rendered as a member of such board.

Source: Laws 1911, c. 73, § 3, p. 314; R.S.1913, § 3794; Laws 1919, c. 120, § 3, p. 287; C.S.1922, § 3187; C.S.1929, § 51-203.

51-204. Library board; organization; officers; quorum. The directors of any city, village, county, or township library shall immediately after their appointment meet and organize by electing from their number a president, secretary, and such other officers as may be necessary. Three members of a city or village library board, and three members of a county or township library board shall constitute a quorum for the transaction of business.

Source: Laws 1911, c. 73, § 4, p. 315; R.S.1913, § 3795; C.S.1922, § 3188; Laws 1923, c. 148, § 1, p. 363; Laws 1925, c. 38, § 1, p. 148; C.S.1929, § 51-204; Laws 1941, c. 103, § 1, p. 421; C.S.Supp.,1941, § 51-204.

51-205. Library board; rules and regulations. The library board shall have the power to make and adopt such by-laws, rules and regulations for its own guidance and for the government of the library and reading room as it may deem expedient, not inconsistent with sections 51-201 to 51-219.

Source: Laws 1911, c. 73, § 4, p. 315; R.S.1913, § 3795; C.S.1922, § 3188; Laws 1923, c. 148, § 1, p. 363; Laws 1925, c. 38, § 1, p. 149; C.S.1929, § 51-204; Laws 1941, c. 103, § 1, p. 421; C.S.Supp.,1941, § 51-204.

51-206. Library board; mortgages; release or renewal. The president shall have the power to release, upon full payment, any mortgage constituting a credit to the library fund and standing in the name of such library board. The signature of the president on any such release shall be authenticated by the secretary of the board. The president and secretary in like manner, upon resolution duly passed and adopted by the board, may renew any such mortgage.

Source: Laws 1925, c. 38, § 1, p. 149; C.S.1929, § 51-204; Laws 1941, c. 103, § 1, p. 421; C.S.Supp.,1941, § 51-204.

51-207. Library board; funds; buildings; custody and control. The library board shall have exclusive control of expenditures, of all money collected or donated to the credit of the library fund, of the renting and construction of any library building, and the supervision, care and custody of the grounds, rooms or buildings constructed, leased or set apart for that purpose.

Source: Laws 1911, c. 73, § 4, p. 315; R.S.1913, § 3795; C.S.1922, § 3188; Laws 1923, c. 148, § 1, p. 363; Laws 1925, c. 38, § 1, p. 149; C.S.1929, § 51-204; Laws 1941, c. 103, § 1, p. 421; C.S.Supp.,1941, § 51-204.

51-208. Library board; use of library for city or school purposes; contracts. The library board of any public library may contract with the city council of any city, with the trustees of any incorporated village, with the county board of the county in which such library is located or of any adjacent county, or with the directors of any school district, to furnish the use and privilege of its library to the inhabitants of such city, village, county, township or school district, to the extent and upon such terms as may be agreed upon.

> **Source:** Laws 1911, c. 73, § 4, p. 315; R.S.1913, § 3795; C.S.1922, § 3188; Laws 1923, c. 148, § 1, p. 363; Laws 1925, c. 38, § 1, p. 149; C.S.1929, § 51-204; Laws 1941, c. 103, § 1, p. 422; C.S.Supp.,1941, § 51-204.

51-209. Public library; funds; disbursements. All taxes levied or collected and all funds donated or in any way acquired for the erection, maintenance, or support of any public library shall be kept for the use of the library, separate and apart from all other funds of the city, village, county or township, and shall be drawn upon and paid out by the treasurer of such city, village, county or township upon vouchers signed by the president of the library board and authenticated by the secretary of such board, and shall not be used or disbursed for any other purpose or in any other manner.

> **Source:** Laws 1911, c. 73, § 5, p. 315; R.S.1913, § 3796; C.S.1922, § 3189; C.S.1929, § 51-205.

51-210. Library board; building sites; acquisition; procedure. Every library board created under the provisions of sections 51-201 to 51-219 shall have power to purchase or lease grounds, to exercise the power of eminent domain and to condemn real estate for the purpose of securing a site for a library building. The procedure to condemn property shall be exercised in the manner set forth in sections 76-704 to 76-724.

> **Source:** Laws 1911, c. 73, § 6, p. 316; R.S.1913, § 3797; Laws 1917, c. 86, § 1, p. 223; C.S.1922, § 3190; C.S.1929, § 51-206; R.S.1943, § 51-210; Laws 1951, c. 101, § 100, p. 494; Laws 1971, LB 560, § 1.

51-211. Library board; general powers. The library board shall have power to erect, lease, or occupy an appropriate building for the use of such library; to appoint a suitable librarian and assistants, to fix their compensation and to remove their appointees at pleasure. It shall have the power to establish regulations for the government of such library as may be deemed necessary for its preservation and to maintain its usefulness and efficiency. It shall have power to fix and impose, by general rules, penalties and forfeitures for trespasses upon or injury to the library grounds, rooms, books, or other property, or for failure to return any book, or for violation of any by-law or regulation; and shall have and exercise such power as may be necessary to carry out the spirit and intent of sections 51-201 to 51-219 in establishing and maintaining a public library and reading room.

Source: Laws 1911, c. 73, § 6, p. 316; R.S.1913, § 3797; Laws 1917, c. 86, § 1, p. 223; C.S.1922, § 3190; C.S.1929, § 51-206.

51-212. Public library; use and purpose. Every library and reading room supported by public tax shall be forever free to the use of the inhabitants of the city, village, county, or township maintaining such library, subject always to such reasonable regulations as the library board may adopt to render such library of the greatest use to the inhabitants of said city, village, county or township. The board may exclude from the use of the library and reading rooms any person who shall willfully violate or refuse to comply with rules and regulations established for the government thereof.

Source: Laws 1911, c. 73, § 7, p. 316; R.S.1913, § 3798; C.S.1922, § 3191; C.S.1929, § 51-207.

51-213. Library board; annual report; contents. The library board shall, on or before the second Monday in June in each year, make a report to the city council or village board or to the county or township board of the condition of its trust on June 1 of such year, showing all money received or expended; the number of books and periodicals on hand; newspapers and current literature subscribed for or donated to the reading room; the number of books and periodicals ordered by purchase, gift, or otherwise obtained during the year, and the number lost or missing; the number of and character of books loaned or issued, with such statistics, information and suggestions as it may deem of general interest, or as the city council, village, county or township board may require, which report shall be verified by affidavit of the proper officers of such board.

Source: Laws 1911, c. 73, § 8, p. 316; R.S.1913, § 3799; C.S.1922, § 3192; C.S.1929, § 51-208.

51-214. Rules and regulations; penalties; action to recover; disposition of funds collected. Penalties imposed or accruing by any by-law or regulation of the library board may be recovered in a civil action in county court, such action to be instituted in the name of the library board of the city, village, county or township. Money collected in such actions shall be forthwith placed in the treasury of the city, village, township or county to the credit of the city, village, township or county library fund.

> **Source:** Laws 1911, c. 73, § 9, p. 317; R.S.1913, § 3800; C.S.1922,
> § 3193; C.S.1929, § 51-209; R.S.1943, § 51-214; Laws 1972,
> LB 1032, § 256.

51-215. Public library; donations; library board may accept. Any person may make donation of money, lands or other property for the benefit of any public library. The title to property so donated may be made to and shall vest in the library board of such library and their successors in office, and the board shall thereby become the owners thereof in trust to the uses of the public library of the city, village, township or county.

> **Source:** Laws 1911, c. 73, § 10, p. 317; R.S.1913, § 3801; C.S.1922,
> § 3194; C.S.1929, § 51-210; Laws 1937, c. 123, § 1, p. 434;
> Laws 1941, c. 103, § 2, p. 422; C.S.Supp.,1941, § 51-210.

51-216. Real estate; sale and conveyance; conditions. The library board may, by resolution, direct the sale and conveyance of any real estate owned by the library board or by the public library, which is not used for library purposes, or of any real estate so donated or devised to said library board or to said public library upon such terms as the library board may deem best. Before any such sale is made the library board shall advertise such sale for three weeks in a legal newspaper published in the city, village, township or county in which the public library is situated, and such notice shall set out the time, place, terms, manner of sale, legal description of such real estate, and the right to reject any and all bids. If said bid or bids have not been rejected, then said real estate shall be sold to the highest bidder for cash, and the chairman of the library board, upon resolution of the library board directing him so to do, shall convey said real estate to the purchaser of said real estate upon his payment of his bid therefor; *Provided*, that if a remonstrance against such sale signed by thirty per cent of the electors of such city, village, township or county voting at the last regular city, village or county election be filed with the governing body of such city, village, township or county three or more days prior to the day set for sale, such property shall not then, nor within one year thereafter, be sold.

> **Source:** Laws 1937, c. 123, § 1, p. 434; Laws 1941, c. 103, § 2, p. 422;
> C.S.Supp.,1941, § 51-210.

51-217. Public library; use by school districts. Any school district may in its discretion at its annual meeting, by a majority vote, authorize the school board to contract for the use of a public library by the inhabitants of such district.

> **Source:** Laws 1911, c. 73, § 11, p. 317; R.S.1913, § 3802; C.S.1922,
> § 3195; C.S.1929, § 51-211.

51-218. Public library; property; exemption from execution and taxation. The property of any public library shall be exempt from execution and taxation, as is other public property.

Source: Laws 1911, c. 73, § 12, p. 317; R.S.1913, § 3803; C.S.1922, § 3196; C.S.1929, § 51-212.

51-219. Private and associate libraries; deposit and use; library board may accept; requirements. The library board shall have power to authorize any circulating library, reading matter, or work of art belonging to any private person, association or corporation, to be deposited in the public library rooms, to be drawn or used outside of the rooms only on payment of such fee or membership as the person, corporation or association owning the same may require. Deposits may be removed by the owner thereof at pleasure, but the books or other reading matter so deposited in the rooms of any such public library shall be separately and distinctly marked and kept upon shelves apart from the books of the public city or town library. Every such private or associate library or other property so deposited in any public library, while so placed or remaining, shall, without charge, be subject to use and reading within the library room by any person who is an inhabitant of such city or town and entitled to the use of the free library.

Source: Laws 1911, c. 73, § 13, p. 318; R.S.1913, § 3804; C.S.1922, § 3197; C.S.1929, § 51-213.

14-102. Metropolitan cities; additional powers. In addition to the powers granted in section 14-101, metropolitan cities, as therein defined, shall have power by ordinance:

*   *   *

Libraries, art galleries and museums.

(27) To establish and maintain public libraries, reading rooms, art galleries and museums, and to provide the necessary grounds or buildings therefor; to purchase books, papers, maps, manuscripts, works of art and objects of natural or of scientific curiosity, and instruction therefor; to receive donations and bequests of money or property for the same in trust or otherwise, and to pass necessary by-laws and regulations for the protection and government of the same. C.S.1929, § 14-102.

15-230. Public libraries; establishment; purchases; receive donations; by-laws and regulations. A primary city may establish, maintain, and operate public library facilities, purchase books, papers, maps and manuscripts therefor, receive donations and bequests of money or property for the same in trust or otherwise, and pass necessary by-laws and regulations for the protection and government of the same. Laws 1961, c. 36, § 2.

16-251. Libraries and museums; establishment; maintenance. The mayor and council of any city of the first class shall have power to establish and maintain public libraries, reading rooms, art galleries and museums, and to provide the necessary grounds or buildings therefor; to purchase the papers, books, maps, manuscripts and works of art, and objects of natural or scientific curiosity and instruction therefor; and to receive donations and bequests of money or property for the same in trust or otherwise. They may also pass necessary by-laws and regulations for the protection and government of the same. The ownership of the real and personal property of such library shall be in the city. C.S.1929, § 16-252.

17-967. Bonds; second-class city or village; municipal library; petition; election; issuance; interest; conditions; limitations; tax levy. Any city of the second class, or village, organized according to law, is hereby authorized to issue bonds in aid of improving municipal libraries of cities of the second class and villages, in an amount not exceeding seven-tenths of one per cent of the actual valuation of all the taxable property, except intangible property, as shown by the last assessment, within such city of the second class, or village, in the manner hereinafter directed, namely:

(1) A petition signed by not less than fifty freeholders of the city of the second class, or village, shall be presented to the city council of cities of the second class, or board of trustees of villages. Such petition shall set forth the nature of the work contemplated, the amount of bonds sought to be voted, the rate of interest, and the length of time such bonds shall run, which in no event shall be less than five years nor more than twenty years from the date thereof. The petitioners shall give bond, to be approved by the city council of cities of the second class, or board of trustees of villages, for the payment of the expenses of the election, in the event that the proposition shall fail to receive a majority of the votes cast at such election; and

(2) Upon the receipt of such petition the city council of cities of the second class, or board of trustees of villages shall give notice and call an election in the city of the second class, or village, as the case may be. Such notice, call, and election shall be governed by the laws regulating an election for voting bonds for such city or village; *Provided*, that when a proposition is submitted for the issuance of bonds for the acquisition of a site or the construction of a single building for the purpose of housing the municipal public library, in cities of the second class or villages, it shall be required, as a condition precedent to the issuance of such bonds, that a majority of the votes cast shall be in favor of such proposition. Bonds in such a city shall not be issued for such purpose in the aggregate to exceed one and four-tenths per cent of the actual valuation of all the taxable property in such a city, except intangible property, as shown by the last assessment within such city

of the second class.

Source: Laws 1967, c. 33, § 3, p. 154; Laws 1969, c. 51, § 60, p. 310; Laws 1971, LB 534, § 21; Laws 1979, LB 187, § 66.

19-1302. Sinking funds; purposes; tax to establish; amount of levy; when authorized. The local governing body of any city of the first or second class or any village, subject to all the limitations set forth in sections 19-1301 to 19-1304, shall have the power to levy a tax of not to exceed ten and five-tenths cents on each one hundred dollars in any one year upon the actual value of all the taxable property within such municipality, except intangible property, for a term of not to exceed ten years, in addition to the amount of tax which may be annually levied for the purposes of the adopted budget statement of such municipality, for the purpose of establishing a sinking fund for the construction, purchase, improvement, extension, original equipment, or repair, not including maintenance, of any one or more of the following public improvements, which shall include acquisition of any land incident to the making thereof: Municipal library; municipal auditorium or community house for social or recreational purposes; city or village hall; municipal public library, auditorium or community house in a single building; municipal swimming pool and appurtenances thereto; municipal jail; municipal building to house equipment or personnel of a fire department, together with firefighting equipment or apparatus; municipal park; municipal cemetery; municipal medical clinic building, together with furnishings and equipment; or municipal hospital; *Provided*, no such city or village shall be authorized to levy the tax or to establish the sinking fund, as hereinbefore provided, if, having bonded indebtedness, such city or village shall have been in default in the payment of interest thereon or principal thereof, for a period of ten years prior to the date of the passage of the resolution providing for the submission of the proposition for establishment of said sinking fund, as required in section 19-1303.

Source: Laws 1939, c. 12, § 2, p. 80; C.S.Supp.,1941, § 19-1302; R.S.1943, § 19-1302; Laws 1953, c. 287, § 35, p. 951; Laws 1961, c. 59, § 1, p. 217; Laws 1967, c. 95, § 1, p. 292; Laws 1969, c. 145, § 26, p. 669; Laws 1979, LB 187, § 80.

COUNTY LAW LIBRARIES
(Revised Statutes of Nebraska, 1982, s.51-220.)

51-220. Law library; establishment; maintenance; supervision. The county board may, when in its discretion it shall deem it advisable, provide by purchase or otherwise for the procuring and maintaining of a suitable law library for the use of the public. Such library shall be under the supervision of the judges of the district court of the county wherein the same is located.

Source: Laws 1911, c. 73, § 1, p. 319; R.S.1913, § 3805; C.S.1922, § 3198; C.S.1929, § 51-214; R.S.1943, § 51-220; Laws 1961, c. 255, § 1, p. 749.

SCHOOL LIBRARIES
(Revised Statutes of Nebraska, 1982, s.79-1313.)

79-1313. Public Grazing Fund; distribution by counties; use. The several county superintendents shall use the fund received from such apportionment to help support and maintain a county school library.

Source: Laws 1947, c. 300, § 2, p. 917; R.S.Supp.,1947, § 79-2014; Laws 1949, c. 266, § 1, p. 880; Laws 1949, c. 256, § 388, p. 822.

Nebraska library laws are reprinted from REVISED STAT-
UTES OF NEBRASKA published by the State of Nebraska.

NEVADA

STATE LIBRARY
(Nevada Revised Statutes, 1982, s.378.010 to 378.130.)

378.010 State librarian: Appointment; classified service; service at pleasure of governor; removal. The state librarian shall:
1. Be appointed by and be responsible to the governor, and he shall serve at the pleasure of the governor.
2. Be appointed on the basis of merit under the provisions of chapter 284 of NRS.
3. Be in the classified service, except for the purposes of removal.
[1:146:1951]—(NRS A 1960, 443)

378.020 Qualifications of state librarian. The state librarian shall:
1. Be a graduate of a library school accredited by the American Library Association; and
2. Have at least 2 years of library experience in an administrative capacity.
[3:146:1951]—(NRS A 1957, 13)

378.030 Compensation and expenses of state librarian. The state librarian shall:
1. Receive an annual salary which shall be fixed in accordance with the pay plan adopted under the provisions of chapter 284 of NRS.
2. Receive the per diem expense allowance and travel expenses as fixed by law.
[2:146:1951]

378.050 Biennial report. The state librarian shall submit a biennial report to the governor and the legislature of the condition, operation and functioning of the state library.
[Part 6:146:1951; A 1955, 900]

378.060 Library staff. The state librarian shall have such professional, nonprofessional, technical, clerical and operational staff as the execution of his duties and the maintenance and operation of the state library may require.

[4:146:1951]

378.070 Hours of state library. The state librarian shall have the power to designate the hours that the state library shall be open for the use of the public, but the state library shall be open for at least 5 days in each week and for at least 8 hours in each day with the exception of legal holidays.

[Part 6:146:1951; A 1955, 900]

378.080 Powers and duties of state librarian: Nevada state library.

1. The state librarian is responsible for the Nevada state library.

2. He shall:

(a) Administer the state library in accordance with law and good library practice.

(b) Withdraw from the library collection and dispose of any items no longer needed.

(c) Maintain the state library, including the selection, acquisition, circulation and custody of books, periodicals, pamphlets, films, recordings, papers and other materials and equipment.

(d) Maintain a comprehensive collection and reference service to meet reference needs of public officers, departments or agencies of the state, and other libraries and related agencies.

(e) Make and enforce regulations necessary for the administration, government and protection of the state library and all property belonging thereto.

(f) Issue official lists of publications of the state and other bibliographical and informational publications as appropriate.

3. He may:

(a) Borrow from, lend to, and exchange books and other library and informational materials with other libraries and related agencies.

(b) Accept, administer and distribute, in accordance with the terms thereof, any money, materials or other aid granted, appropriated or made available to the state library for library purposes by the United States or any of its agencies or by any other source, public or private.

[Part 6:146:1951; A 1955, 900]—(NRS A 1959, 176; 1969, 495; 1971, 286; 1973, 426, 1147; 1981, 995)

378.081 Powers and duties of state librarian: Statewide programs; contracts for library purposes.

1. The state librarian is responsible for the statewide program of development and coordination of library and informational services.

2. He shall:

(a) Collect, compile and publish statistics and information concerning the operation of libraries in the state.

(b) Carry out continuing studies and analyses of library problems.

(c) Maintain a clearinghouse of information, data and other materials in the field of library and informational services.

(d) Provide advice and technical assistance to public libraries, other libraries, agencies of the state, political subdivisions, planning groups and other agencies and organizations.

(e) Make available to public libraries advice and technical assistance with respect to programs of public relations.

(f) Assist and cooperate with other state agencies and officials, local governments, federal agencies and organizations in carrying out programs involving library and informational services.

(g) Encourage and assist the efforts of libraries and local governments to develop mutual and cooperative solutions to problems with respect to library and informational services.

(h) Administer such funds as may be made available by the legislature for improvement of public library services, interlibrary cooperation or for other library and information-transfer services.

(i) Subject to the approval of local governing bodies, designate certain libraries as resource center libraries and develop and encourage cooperative steps to link these centers with other libraries in a reference and information network.

3. He may contract with agencies, organizations, libraries, library schools, boards of education and universities, public and private, within or outside the state, for library services, facilities, research or any other related purposes.

(Added to NRS by 1981, 994)

378.083 Powers and duties of state librarien: Standards for public libraries; master plan. The state librarian shall develop:

1. Standards for public libraries which will serve as recommendations for those libraries with respect to services, resources, personnel and programs to provide sources of information to persons of all ages, including handicapped persons and disadvantaged persons, and encourage continuing education beyond the years of formal education. The standards must take into account the differences in size and resources among the public libraries of the state.

2. A statewide master plan for public libraries, including plans for levels of library services and resources, which is developed through a continuing process of planning in which representatives from public libraries throughout the state participate. The master plan must be designed to extend 5 years into the future and must be made current at least every 2 years.

(Added to NRS by 1981, 994)

378.085 Division for cooperative services: Creation; purposes; powers of state librarian; budget.

1. There is hereby created within the Nevada state library the division for cooperative services, which shall be administered by the state librarian.

2. The division may provide coordinated library services, which may relate to acquisition, cataloging, processing and delivery of library materials, to libraries, public agencies and institutions.

3. The state librarian may exercise those powers conferred upon him by law in carrying out the functions of the division.

4. Funds for operation and maintenance of the division of cooperative services shall be separately budgeted as a part of the appropriation for the support of the Nevada state library.

(Added to NRS by 1973, 1147)

378.090 State library gift fund. Any gift of money to the state library or to the State of Nevada for library purposes which the state librarian is authorized to accept must be deposited in the state treasury in a fund to be known as the state library gift fund. The state library gift fund is a continuing fund without reversion, and money in the fund must be used for library purposes only and expended in accordance with the terms of the gift.

[Part 6:146:1951; A 1955, 900] + [7:146:1951]—(NRS A 1979, 617)

378.100 State librarian authorized to accept federal money. The state librarian is authorized to accept and direct the disbursement of money appropriated by any act of Congress and apportioned to the state for library purposes. That federal money must be deposited in the state treasury for credit to the appropriate account of the state library.

[8a:146:1951; added 1953, 37]—(NRS A 1981, 260)

378.110 Disposition of library fines. Money collected by the state librarian from fines shall be deposited in the appropriated fund of the state library, and may be credited to those budgeted items as may be designated by the state librarian.

[8:146:1951]

378.120 Charges for photostatic copies of papers, documents; duplicate microfilm rolls.

1. The state librarian is authorized to collect and receive a charge from any person who shall request any photostatic copy, or photocopy print, of any paper or document from the state library. The amount of such charge shall be set by the state librarian but shall not exceed the cost of the photographic copying process for any specific paper or document.

2. Where any person requests a duplicate of a roll of microfilm belonging to the state library, the state library is entitled to a fee not exceeding $2 for each duplicate made in excess of the cost of the duplicate, and shall direct the processor making the duplicate to collect such fee for the state library. The money collected from such fees shall be deposited in the state treasurer's office and credited to the account of the state library. The receipts may be expended by the state library pursuant to the provisions of law authorizing budgeted expenditures of moneys not appropriated from the general fund by various state officers, departments, boards, agencies, commissions and institutions for specific fiscal years.

[8b:146:1951; added 1955, 75]—(NRS A 1963, 321)

378.130 Legislative appropriations. Funds to carry out the provisions of this chapter shall be provided by legislative appropriation from the general fund, and shall be paid out on claims as other claims against the state are paid. All claims shall be approved by the state librarian before they are paid.

[9:146:1951]

DISTRIBUTION OF PUBLIC DOCUMENTS

(Nevada Revised Statutes, 1982, s.345.010 to 345.023, 345.120.)

345.010 Distribution of Statutes of Nevada. Upon publication of the Statutes of Nevada, the director of the legislative counsel bureau shall distribute them as follows:

1. To each of the judges of the District Court of the United States

for the District of Nevada, one copy.
  2. To the supreme court law library, two copies.
  3. To each justice of the supreme court, clerk of the supreme court, district judge, county clerk, district attorney, justice of the peace and police judge in this state, one copy.
  4. To each public library in this state, one copy.
  5. To each library in the University of Nevada System, one copy.
  6. To the Nevada historical society, one copy.
  7. Upon request, to any state, county or municipal officer.
  [Part 1:3:1871; B § 2802; BH § 1801; C § 1951; RL § 2932; NCL § 5198] + [Part 1:104:1901; RL § 2934; NCL § 5200] + [2:104:1901; RL § 2935; NCL § 5201]—(NRS A 1965, 952; 1967, 86; 1973, 1409; 1975, 1396; 1977, 485; 1979, 23)

  345.020 Distribution of Nevada Reports. Upon receipt of copies of each volume of Nevada Reports from the superintendent of the state printing and records division of the department of general services, the director of the legislative counsel bureau shall distribute them as follows:
  1. To each of the judges of the District Court of the United States for the District of Nevada, one copy.
  2. The supreme court law library, two copies.
  3. To each justice of the supreme court, clerk of the supreme court, district judge, district attorney, county clerk, justice of the peace and police judge in this state, one copy.
  4. To each public library in this state, one copy.
  5. To each library in the University of Nevada System, one copy.
  6. To the Nevada historical society, one copy.
  7. Upon request, to any state, county or municipal officer.
  [9:187:1915; A 1955, 535]—(NRS A 1965, 952; 1967, 87; 1969, 1525; 1973, 1410, 1478; 1975, 1396; 1977, 485; 1979, 23)

  345.023 Distribution of Statutes of Nevada, Nevada Reports to supreme court law library for interchange use. The legislative counsel bureau shall distribute such additional copies of the Statutes of Nevada and of Nevada Reports to the supreme court law library as in the opinion of the director thereof may secure an interchange of appropriate works for such library.
  (Added to NRS by 1967, 87; A 1973, 1410)

  345.120 Biennial report, statistical abstract: Distribution free of charge. Each of the documents required by NRS 345.070, 345.090 and 345.100 shall be distributed without charge to:
  1. The governor.
  2. Each elected state officer.
  3. Each member of the legislature.
  4. Each state department or other agency of the executive branch.
  5. The clerk of each city and of each county.
  6. The legislative counsel bureau.
  7. Each public library in the state.
  8. Each library in the University of Nevada System.
  (Added to NRS by 1977, 568)

STATE PUBLICATIONS DISTRIBUTION CENTER
(Nevada Revised Statutes, 1982, s.378.150 to 378.210.)

378.150 Declaration of legislative intent. It is the intent of the legislature in enacting NRS 378.150 to 378.210, inclusive, that:

1. All state and local government publications be distributed to designated depository libraries for use by all inhabitants of the state; and

2. Designated depository libraries assume the responsibility for keeping such publications readily accessible for use and rendering assistance, without charge, to patrons using them.

(Added to NRS by 1971, 499)

378.160 Definitions. As used in NRS 378.150 to 378.210, inclusive:

1. "Print" means all forms of printing and duplicating other than by use of carbon paper.

2. "State agency" includes the legislature, constitutional officers or any department, division, bureau, board, commission or agency of the State of Nevada.

3. "State publication" includes any document issued in print by any state agency and which may legally be released for public distribution, but does not include:

(a) Nevada Revised Statutes;

(b) Nevada Reports;

(c) Bound volumes of the Statutes of Nevada;

(d) The Nevada Digest or Annotations to Nevada Revised Statutes prepared by the legislative counsel;

(e) Press items of the University of Nevada System which are not in the nature of public and other university items not designed for external distribution;

(f) Correspondence and intraoffice or interoffice communications which are not of vital interest to the public; or

(g) Publications from established agencies which are required by federal and state law to be distributed to depositories which duplicate those under NRS 378.200.

(Added to NRS by 1971, 499)

378.170 State publications distribution center: Creation; rules and regulations.

1. There is hereby created within the Nevada state library a state publications distribution center.

2. The state librarian may make such rules and regulations as may be necessary to carry out the purposes of the state publications distribution center.

(Added to NRS by 1971, 499)

378.180 State, local agencies to deposit copies of publications when issued.

1. Every state agency shall, upon release, deposit a specified number of copies of each of its state publications with the state publications distribution center to meet the needs of the depository library system and to provide interlibrary loan service to those libraries with-

out depository status. This distribution shall be required only if sufficient funds are appropriated for the printing of these materials.

2. For each item printed by the state printing and records division of the department of general services, 50 additional copies shall be authorized to be printed by the division, these to be collected by the state publications distribution center and distributed to public and university libraries within the state.

3. All city, county and regional agencies shall, upon release, deposit at least one copy of each of its publications with the state publications distribution center and a list of its publications for a calendar year.

(Added to NRS by 1971, 499; A 1973, 1472)

378.190 Depository agreements with other libraries; standards.

1. The state publications distribution center may enter into depository agreements with any city, county, district, regional, town or university library in this state.

2. The state librarian shall establish standards for eligibility as a depository library under subsection 1. Such standards may include and take into account:

(a) The type of library;

(b) Its ability to preserve such publications and to make them available for public use; and

(c) Its geographical location in order to assure that the publications are conveniently accessible to residents in all areas of the state.

(Added to NRS by 1971, 500)

378.200 Distribution of copies of state publications.

1. After receipt of any state publications, the state publications distribution center shall distribute copies of those publications as follows:

(a) One copy to the legislative counsel bureau;

(b) Two copies to the Library of Congress; and

(c) Two copies to each depository library in this state.

2. The center shall retain sufficient copies in the Nevada state library for preservation and use by the public. The remaining copies must be used for distribution in accordance with any agreements entered into with other states for the exchange of state publications, and for loaning services to those libraries without depository status.

(Added to NRS by 1971, 500; A 1973, 346; 1979, 182)

378.210 Publication, distribution of list of state publications. The state publications distribution center shall periodically publish, and, upon request, distribute to all state agencies and contracting depository libraries a list of state publications.

(Added to NRS by 1971, 500)

DIVISION OF ARCHIVES

(Nevada Revised Statutes, 1982, s.378.230 to 378.270.)

378.230 Division of archives: Creation; declaration of legislative intent.

1. The division of archives is hereby created in the Nevada state library. The division is administered by the state librarian.

2.   It is the intent of the legislature that the division, in carrying out its functions of preserving, maintaining and coordinating state, county and municipal archival material, follow accepted standards of archival practice to assure maximum accessibility for the general public.
(Added to NRS by 1979, 181)

378.240   Duties of state librarian.   The state librarian shall, within the limits of legislative appropriations:
1.   Maintain and properly equip safe and secure premises and vaults at the seat of government for the preservation and use of material deposited in the archives.
2.   Employ persons in the classified service of the state to preserve, index and aid in the use of material deposited in the archives.
3.   Give an appropriate receipt for material received by him for the archives.
4.   Make material deposited in the archives readily available for use.
5.   Receive into the archives any material when directed to do so by the state board of examiners.
(Added to NRS by 1979, 181)

378.250   Powers of state librarian.   The state librarian may:
1.   Receive into the archives any material from a state agency if he finds that it is of historical value.
2.   With the approval of the state board of examiners, return to the state agency from which it was received, material in the archives which he finds is not of historical value.
3.   Receive into the archives any material which has been directed to be deposited in the archives by an order or resolution of the governing body of a local governmental entity, if he finds that it is of historical value.
4.   With the approval of the state board of examiners, turn over to the Nevada historical society any material in the archives which he finds to be surplus, not properly in the archives, or appropriate to be kept in the custody of the Nevada historical society.
5.   Expend any gift of money he is authorized to accept for the purpose specified by the donor or, if no purpose is specified, in any manner which will further the purposes of the division of archives.
(Added to NRS by 1979, 181; A 1979, 625)

378.260   Agreement to maintain material of secretary of state in archives.   The state librarian may enter into an agreement with the secretary of state to keep in the archives any material of which the secretary of state is required by law to have custody and to preserve.
(Added to NRS by 1979, 181)

378.270   Duty of state librarian to furnish copy of material in archives; fee.   The state librarian shall furnish, on request, to any person who has paid the proper fees for it, a copy of any material in the archives, and may certify it if required. The state librarian may charge a reasonable fee for searching archives of the state, for producing copies of and for certifying copies of any material in the archives.
(Added to NRS by 1979, 181)

COUNTY, DISTRICT AND TOWN LIBRARIES
(Nevada Revised Statutes, 1982, s.379.002 to 379.060.)

379.002 Goal of public libraries, information centers. It is the goal of the state's publicly supported libraries and information centers to provide the resources and trained staff to meet the informational needs of all citizens.
(Added to NRS by 1981, 996)

379.003 Master plan for libraries. The governing body of every public library in this state shall develop, through a continuing process of planning, a master plan for the library or libraries for which it is responsible, including plans for levels of library services and resources, and shall submit the plan to the Nevada council on libraries. The master plan must be designed to extend 5 years into the future and must be made current at least every 2 years.
(Added to NRS by 1981, 996)

379.005 Definitions. As used in this chapter, unless the context otherwise requires:
1. "County library" means a library established pursuant to NRS 379.010.
2. "District library" means a library established pursuant to NRS 379.021.
3. "Public library" means a county, district, city or town library, a group of libraries which have entered into an interlocal agreement or any other library predominantly supported by public money.
4. "Town library" means a library existing pursuant to NRS 379.023.
(Added to NRS by 1967, 1058; A 1981, 996)

379.010 County library: Establishment; county library fund.
1. The board of county commissioners of each county may set apart a sum of money to be used in the establishment and maintenance of a public library in the county. Each year thereafter the board of county commissioners may set apart an amount of money for the purpose of operating and maintaining the library.
2. The fund so created is the county library fund.
[1:187:1925; A 1927, 84; 1943, 53; 1949, 110; 1955, 333]—(NRS A 1957, 20; 1967, 1060; 1981, 997)

379.020 County library trustees: Appointment; terms; vacancies; compensation; expenses; removal.
1. The board of county commissioners shall appoint five competent persons who are residents of the county to serve as county library trustees. Three trustees shall hold office for the terms of 1, 2 and 3 years respectively, and two trustees shall hold office for terms of 4 years. Annually thereafter, the board of county commissioners shall appoint one trustee who shall hold office for a term of 4 years, except that in those years in which the terms of two trustees expire, the board of county commissioners shall appoint two trustees for terms of 4 years. County library trustees shall hold office until their successors are

appointed and qualified.

2. No trustee may be appointed to hold office for more than two consecutive 4-year terms.

3. All vacancies which may occur at any time in the office of county library trustee must be filled by appointment by the board of county commissioners.

4. County library trustees serve without compensation, except that the board of county commissioners may provide for compensation in an amount of not more than $40 per meeting, with a total of not more than $80 per month, and may provide travel expenses and subsistence allowance for the members in the same amounts as are allowed for state officers and employees.

5. The board of county commissioners may remove any trustee who fails, without cause, to attend three successive meetings of the trustees.

[2:187:1925; A 1956, 214]—(NRS A 1959, 329; 1967, 1060; 1971, 133; 1981, 997)

379.021 County library districts: Procedure for formation; levy of taxes for maintenance.

1. Whenever in any county a petition or petitions praying for the formation of a county library district and the establishment of a public library therein setting forth the boundaries of the proposed library district, certified by the district judge of any judicial district as being signed by 10 percent of the taxpayers or by taxpayers representing 10 percent of the taxable property in the proposed county library district, as shown by the last-preceding assessment roll of the county, is presented to the board of county commissioners of the county in which the territory of the proposed county library district is situated, accompanied by an affidavit or affidavits of one or more of the signers thereof that the signatures thereto are genuine, the board of county commissioners shall, at their next regular meeting after the petition or petitions are so presented:

(a) Pass a resolution to the effect that a county library district with properly defined boundaries is to be established and cause to be published a notice thereof in a newspaper of general circulation within the district once a week for a period of 2 weeks; and

(b) Allow 30 days after the first publication of the notice during which all taxpayers of the district in which the district library is to be situated have the right to file protests with the county clerk.

2. If the aggregate of protests is less than 10 percent of the taxpayers voting in the last general election, the board of county commissioners shall order the creation of such county library district and the establishment of a public library therein and levy taxes in support and continued maintenance of such library in accordance with subsection 5.

3. If the aggregate of protests is more than 10 percent of the taxpayers voting in the last general election, the board of county commissioners shall:

(a) Proceed no further with reference to the establishment of a county library district without submitting the question to the voters; and

(b) Hold the election as soon as practicable and as nearly as may be in accordance with the general election laws of the state.

4. If the majority of votes cast at the election is against the establishment of the county library district, the question is lost and the

board of county commissioners shall proceed no further. If the majority of votes is in favor of the county library district, the board of county commissioners shall, within 10 days after such election, order the creation of the county library district and establishment of a public library therein.

5. Upon the creation of a county library district and establishment of a public library therein, the board of county commissioners shall, at the next time for levying taxes and in each year thereafter, at the time and in the manner other taxes are levied, levy a tax upon all taxable property in the county library district for the purpose of creating and maintaining a fund known as the library fund.

(Added to NRS by 1967, 1058; A 1981, 997)

379.022 District library trustees: Appointment; terms; vacancies; compensation; expenses; removal; additional trustees when service extended.

1. After ordering the creation of a county library district and the establishment of a public library therein as provided in NRS 379.021, the board of county commissioners shall appoint five competent persons who are residents of the county library district to serve as district library trustees.

2. The term of office of the trustees appointed pursuant to subsection 1 is as follows:

(a) Three persons must be appointed for terms of 2 years.

(b) Two persons must be appointed for terms of 4 years.

Thereafter the offices of district library trustees must be filled for terms of 4 years in the order in which the terms expire. No person may be appointed to hold office for more than two consecutive 4-year terms.

3. A vacancy in the office of district library trustee which occurs because of expiration of the term of office must be filled by appointment by the board of county commissioners for a term of 4 years. A vacancy which occurs other than by expiration of the term must be filled by appointment by the board of county commissioners for the unexpired term.

4. The board of district library trustees may provide for compensation of members of the board in an amount of not more than $40 per meeting, with a total of not more than $80 per month, and may provide travel expenses and subsistence allowances for the members in the same amounts as are allowed for state officers and employees.

5. The board of county commissioners may remove any district library trustee who fails, without cause, to attend three successive meetings of the trustees.

6. If the library trustees of any county library district have entered into a contract pursuant to NRS 379.060 with any city within the county, they may add to their number two additional library trustees who are appointed by the governing body of the city to represent the residents of the city. The terms of office of the two additional library trustees are 3 years or until the termination of the contract with the city for library services, if that termination occurs sooner. The additional library trustees have the same powers and duties as the trustees appointed pursuant to subsection 1.

(Added to NRS by 1967, 1059; A 1971, 133; 1981, 336, 998)

379.0225 District library trustees may propose issuance of general obligation bonds for library purposes.

1. The board of trustees of a county library district may propose

the issuance of general obligation bonds in an amount not to exceed 10 percent of the total last assessed valuation of the taxable property of the district for the purpose of acquiring, constructing or improving buildings and other real property to be used for library purposes.

2.   If the board desires the issuance of bonds, the proposal must be submitted to the general obligation bond commission of the county in which the district is situated, pursuant to the provisions of NRS 350.001 to 350.006, inclusive. If the commission approves the proposed issuance, the question of issuing the bonds must be submitted to the registered electors of the district in accordance with the provisions of NRS 350.020 to 350.070, inclusive. If a majority of the electors voting on the question favors the proposal, the board of county commissioners shall issue the bonds as general obligations of the county library district pursuant to the provisions of the Local Government Securities Law.

(Added to NRS by 1981, 996)

379.023   Town libraries: Maintenance; town library fund.

1.   Any free public library existing on July 1, 1967, which was established in an unincorporated town pursuant to the provisions of chapter 90, Statutes of Nevada 1895, or of NRS 379.070 to 379.120, inclusive, may be maintained pursuant to NRS 379.005 to 379.040, inclusive.

2.   So long as such library is so maintained, the board of county commissioners of the county in which such library exists shall each year, at the time and in the manner other taxes are levied, levy a tax upon all taxable property in such unincorporated town for the purpose of maintaining a fund to be known as the town library fund.

(Added to NRS by 1967, 1059; A 1981, 999)

379.025   Powers and duties of county, district, town or other public library trustees.

1.   The library trustees of any county, district, town or other public library, and their successors, shall:

(a) Establish, supervise and maintain a library.

(b) Appoint a librarian.

(c) Hold and possess the property and effects of the library in trust for the public.

(d) In the case of a county library, submit annual budgets to the board of county commissioners, containing detailed estimates of the amount of money necessary for the operation and management of the library for the next succeeding year.

(e) In the case of a district or town library, prepare annual budgets in accordance with NRS 354.470 to 354.626, inclusive.

(f) Establish bylaws and regulations for the management of the library and their own management.

(g) Manage all the property, real and personal, of the library.

(h) Acquire and hold real and personal property, by gift, purchase or bequest, for the library.

(i) Administer any trust declared or created for the library.

(j) Maintain or defend any action in reference to the property or affairs of the library.

2.   The library trustees may:

(a) Make purchases and secure rooms.

(b) Authorize the merger of a town or city library with a county library district.

(c) Do all acts necessary for the orderly and efficient management and control of the library.
(Added to NRS by 1959, 328; A 1967, 1060; 1969, 492; 1981, 999)

379.026 Library gift funds: Establishment; source; use; investment of moneys.
1. The library trustees of any county, district or town library are authorized to establish with the county treasurer, as custodian, a special fund, which fund shall be known as the county library gift fund, the .... district library gift fund, or the .... town library gift fund, as the case may be. The moneys in such fund shall be derived from all or any part of any gift, bequest or devise, including the interest thereon. Such fund shall be a separate and continuing fund and no moneys in such fund shall revert to the general fund of the county at any time.
2. The moneys in a library gift fund may be used for construction of new library buildings, capital improvements to library buildings, special library services, or other library purposes. No expenditure from a library gift fund shall be made until authorized by the library trustees.
3. The library trustees may invest or reinvest all or part of the moneys in the library gift fund in any investment authorized for city and county moneys under chapter 355 of NRS.
(Added to NRS by 1961, 354; A 1967, 1061)

379.027 Powers and duties of librarian. The librarian of any county, district or town library shall administer all functions of the library, employ assistants and carry out the policies established by the library trustees, and may recommend policies to the trustees.
(Added to NRS by 1959, 328; A 1967, 1061; 1981, 1000)

379.030 Payment of claims against library fund.
1. All claims for indebtedness incurred or created by the library trustees of any county, district or town library must:
(a) Be audited and approved by a majority of the library trustees;
(b) Be presented to and acted upon by the board of county commissioners; and
(c) Be paid out of the appropriate library fund in the same manner as claims against the county are presented, acted upon and paid.
2. In no case may any claim except for library and reading room purposes be allowed or paid out of the appropriate library fund.
3. Any money remaining in the county library fund on June 30 of any year reverts to the general fund of the county.
[3:187:1925; NCL § 5597]—(NRS A 1967, 1061; 1981, 1000)

379.040 Library to be free; trustees' regulations. The library and reading room of any county, district or town library shall forever be and remain free and accessible to the public, subject to such reasonable rules and regulations as the library trustees may adopt.
[4:187:1925; NCL § 5598]—(NRS A 1967, 1061)

379.050 Transfer of county library district property to new county library; merger of county library districts, city and town libraries.
1. Whenever a new county library shall be provided for in any county having a population of 15,000 or more persons, the library

trustees of any district library in the county previously established are authorized to transfer all books, funds, equipment or other property in the possession of such trustees to the new library upon the demand of the library trustees of the new library.

2. Whenever there are two or more county library districts in any county having a population of 15,000 or more persons, such districts may merge into one county library district upon approval of the library trustees of the merging districts.

3. Whenever there is a city or a town library located adjacent to a county library district, the city or town library may merge with the county library district upon approval of the library trustees of the merging library and district.

4. All expenses incurred in making such transfer or merger shall be paid out of the general fund of the new library.

[1:140:1929; A 1956, 213] + [2:140:1929; NCL § 5600]—(NRS A 1967, 1062; 1969, 493)

379.060 Extension of county, district library service: Contracts with counties, cities, towns and school districts.

1. The library trustees of any county or district library shall cooperate with and enter into contracts with the board of county commissioners of any other county, or with any city or town in any other county, or with any school district, when necessary to secure to the residents of such other county, or to the residents of such city or town in such other county, or to the pupils of the school district, the same privileges of the county or district library as are granted to or enjoyed by the residents of the county or county library district, or such privileges as may be agreed upon in the contract. The consideration agreed upon must be specified in the contract, and must be paid into the county or district library fund or a special fund for library purposes of the county providing the service.

2. Any contracting county, city, town or school district may terminate any such contract which may be entered into upon such terms as may be agreed upon by the parties thereto.

3. Any county, city or town wherein a library has been established may cooperate with and contract with the library trustees of any county, district or town library to obtain for the residents of such county, city or town an increase in library services or such privileges as may be agreed upon.

4. The library trustees of any county or district library may cooperate with and contract with the board of county commissioners of any other county, relative to any phase of library service.

5. Any county, city or town contracting for such library service may at any time establish a library for the use of its inhabitants, whereupon its contract for such service may be continued or terminated on such terms as may be agreed upon by the parties thereto.

6. The tax-levying body of any county, city or town contracting to receive such library services may budget for and levy a tax to meet the terms of the contract. The board of trustees of a school district may budget to meet the terms of the contract.

7. The library trustees of the county or district library providing such services may expend any amounts received in consideration of any such contract in addition to the amount budgeted for the county or district library.

[1:144:1945; A 1956, 213] + [2:144:1945; 1943 NCL § 5598.02] + [3:144:1945; 1943 NCL § 5598.03] + [4:144:1945; 1943 NCL § 5598.04]—(NRS A 1959, 279; 1961, 168; 1967, 1062; 1981, 1000)

CITY LIBRARIES

(Nevada Revised Statutes, 1982, s.379.070 to 379.120.)

379.070 City libraries: Establishment; maintenance. Any free public library which has been established in a city pursuant to chapter 90, Statutes of Nevada 1895, or any other law prior to July 1, 1967, or which is established after July 1, 1967, may be maintained and shall be governed by the provisions of NRS 379.070 to 379.120, inclusive.
[1:48:1956]—(NRS A 1967, 1063)

379.105 Governing authority of city library: City governing body or library trustees; powers and duties of governing authority.
1. The governing body of the city shall determine whether:
(a) To constitute itself the governing authority of the city library; or
(b) To appoint a board of trustees as such governing authority.
2. If library trustees are appointed, they and their successors shall:
(a) Establish, supervise and maintain a library.
(b) Appoint a librarian.
(c) Hold and possess the property and effects of the library in trust for the public.
(d) Submit annual budgets to the governing body of the city, containing detailed estimates of the amount of money necessary for the operation and management of the library for the next succeeding year.
(e) Establish bylaws and regulations for the management of the library and their own management.
(f) Manage all the property, real and personal, of the library.
(g) Acquire and hold real and personal property, by gift, purchase or bequest, for the library .
(h) Administer any trust declared or created for the library .
(i) Maintain or defend any action in reference to the property or affairs of the library.
3. If appointed, the library trustees may:
(a) Make purchases and secure rooms.
(b) Authorize the merger of a city library with a county library district.
(c) Do all acts necessary for the orderly and efficient management and control of the library.
4. The governing authority has all the powers and duties with respect to the city library that district library trustees have with respect to a district library.
(Added to NRS by 1959, 328; A 1965, 747; 1967, 1063; 1969, 493; 1981, 1001)

379.106 City library gift fund: Establishment; source; use; investment of money.
1. The governing authority of any city library is authorized to establish with the city treasurer, as custodian, a special fund, known as the "......................... city library gift fund." The moneys in such fund must be derived from all or any part of any gift, bequest or devise, including the interest thereon. The gift fund is a separate and continuing fund and no moneys in it revert to the general fund of the city at any time.

2. The moneys in a city library gift fund may be used for construction of new library buildings, capital improvements to library buildings, special library services, or other library purposes. No expenditure from a city library gift fund may be made until authorized by the governing authority.

3. The governing authority of a city library may invest or reinvest all or part of the moneys in the city library gift fund in any investment authorized for city and county moneys under chapter 355 of NRS.

(Added to NRS by 1961, 354; A 1967, 1064; 1981, 1002)

379.107 Powers and duties of librarian. The librarian of any city library shall administer all functions of the library, employ assistants and carry out the policies established by the governing authority, and may recommend policies to the governing authority.

(Added to NRS by 1959, 328; A 1967, 1064; 1981, 1002)

379.120 Library to be free; regulations. The library and reading room shall forever be and remain free and accessible to the people of the city, subject to such reasonable rules and regulations as the governing authority may adopt.

[6:48:1956]—(NRS A 1967, 1064)

REGIONAL LIBRARIES

(Nevada Revised Statutes, 1982, s.379.142 to 379.149.)

379.142 "Political subdivision" defined. As used in NRS 379.142 to 379.146, inclusive, "political subdivision" means county, city, town, or county library district, or legally established libraries therein.

(Added to NRS by 1959, 280; A 1965, 430)

379.143 Regional library: Establishment, maintenance by agreement; custody of funds.

1. Any two or more political subdivisions may join in establishing and maintaining a regional library through a written joint agreement of their governing bodies.

2. The agreement shall provide for the fair apportionment of expenses and that the treasurer or other fiscal officer of one of the participating political subdivisions shall be selected as treasurer of the regional library and shall have custody of the funds of the regional library.

(Added to NRS by 1959, 280)

379.144 Transfer of funds to regional library. The treasurer or other fiscal officer of the other participating political subdivisions shall transfer to the treasurer of the regional library all moneys collected for regional public library purposes in their respective political subdivisions, in accordance with a joint agreement.

(Added to NRS by 1959, 280; A 1965, 430)

379.145 Division of property on withdrawal. If one of the participating political subdivisions withdraws from the agreement, it is entitled to a division of the property of the regional library on the basis of its contribution.

(Added to NRS by 1959, 280)

379.146 Regional library board: Appointment; terms; number.
1. Each regional library shall be governed by a regional library board appointed in accordance with a method jointly agreed upon by the governing bodies of the participating political subdivisions, for a term of not more than 4 years.
2. The regional library board shall consist of not less than 5 nor more than 11 members.
(Added to NRS by 1959, 280)

379.147 "Library" defined. As used in NRS 379.1473 to 379.149, inclusive, "library" includes public libraries, school libraries where authorized by school districts, academic libraries, special libraries and the Nevada state library.
(Added to NRS by 1981, 726)

379.1473 Legislative declaration. The legislature declares:
1. That the state recognizes the desirability of supporting the extension of library services beyond the jurisdiction of any single library;
2. That the formation of a regional network of libraries is an effective means of providing services beyond local boundaries; and
3. That all public libraries in this state should be linked to regional networks to form a system of communications and provision of services which will encourage cooperation and maximum use of available resources.
(Added to NRS by 1981, 726)

379.1475 Agreement to form regional network of libraries.
1. The governing bodies of two or more libraries may enter into an agreement to form a regional network of libraries for the purpose of facilitating regional cooperation, improved communications and sharing of resources. The purposes of the regional network may be furthered by such activities as:
(a) Developing and operating interlibrary systems to improve access to dispersed library and information services.
(b) Applying new technologies for improved efficiency in the use and availability of resources.
(c) Improving access to advanced research which will help increase productivity and solve emerging problems of common concern.
2. An agreement to form a regional network of libraries is subject to the provisions of the Interlocal Cooperation Act.
(Added to NRS by 1981, 726)

379.148 Governing board of regional network of libraries: Members; organization; duties.
1. A regional network of libraries is governed by a board consisting of one representative from each participating entity.
2. The board shall:
(a) Elect its own officers.
(b) Establish rules for its own governance and bylaws for the operation of the regional network.
(c) Prepare an annual budget for the regional network.
(d) Develop, through a continuing process of planning, a master plan for the regional network of libraries for the provision of regional

services. The master plan must be designed to extend 5 years into the future and must be made current at least every 2 years.
(Added to NRS by 1981, 726)

379.1483 Governing board of regional network of libraries: Duty to establish policies, procedures to govern library programs and activities. The governing board of a regional network of libraries has primary responsibility for, and shall establish policies and procedures to govern, library programs and activities which extend beyond the jurisdiction of any single participating library. These programs and activities include but are not limited to libraries, interlibrary loans, development of data bases and utilization of new technologies for communication among libraries.
(Added to NRS by 1981, 727)

379.1485 Procedure for request by participating library for grant of money related to regional services.
1. Whenever a participating library seeks a grant of money related to regional services from the state, the Federal Government or another source, it must first submit the request to the governing board of the regional network for review.
2. After review, the governing board of the regional network shall forward the request to the granting agency along with its comments and suggestions for priority. If the request is for a state grant, the granting agency must consider the priority designated by the governing board.
3. The governing board may request and receive gifts or grants of money from the state, the Federal Government or another source for purposes of the regional network. Among requests for state grants, requests from the regional network have priority over requests from participating libraries.
(Added to NRS by 1981, 727)

379.149 Power of governing board of regional network of libraries to contract with state agencies. The governing board of a regional network of libraries may enter into contracts with state agencies for:
1. The administration of grants of money for library purposes; and
2. The provision of library services,
in the region served by the regional network.
(Added to NRS by 1981, 727)

SUPREME COURT LAW LIBRARY
(Nevada Revised Statutes, 1982, s.2.410 to 2.490.)

2.410 Supreme court law library: Supervision and control by supreme court; regulations governing operation. The supreme court law library shall be under the supervision and control of the supreme court, which may make and enforce such rules and regulations as may be necessary for the government, use and services of the library. Such rules or regulations shall assure that the library is accessible for public use and to users in all parts of the state.
(Added to NRS by 1973, 422)

2.420 Supreme court law library: Hours of use by public designated by supreme court. The justices of the supreme court may designate

the hours that the supreme court law library shall be open for the use of the public.
(Added to NRS by 1973, 423)

2.430 Law librarian, other personnel: Appointment; unclassified service; leaves of absence.
1. The supreme court may appoint a librarian, who shall serve at the pleasure of the supreme court.
2. The supreme court law librarian, with the approval of the supreme court, may employ such personnel as the execution of his duties and the maintenance and operation of the library may require.
3. All of the personnel of the supreme court law library are exempt from the provisions of chapter 284 of NRS, and are entitled to such leaves of absence as the supreme court prescribes.
(Added to NRS by 1973, 422)

2.440 Law librarian: Qualifications. The supreme court law librarian shall:
1. Be a graduate of a library school accredited by the American Library Association;
2. Have at least 2 years of library experience in an administrative capacity; and
3. Have at least 1 year of training in a law school or 2 years of experience as an employee in a law library.
(Added to NRS by 1973, 423)

2.450 Law librarian: Report to supreme court justices. The supreme court law librarian shall submit a biennial report to the justices of the supreme court concerning the condition, operation and functioning of the law library.
(Added to NRS by 1973, 423)

2.460 Purchase, exchange of publications authorized. The supreme court law librarian may purchase and exchange the Nevada Reports, Nevada Revised Statutes and supplements or any other compilation or code of Nevada laws, or any other book or periodical with other law libraries in the United States in return for their legal compilations, books or periodicals when, in the judgment of the supreme court law librarian, such exchange is in the best interests of the supreme court law library.
(Added to NRS by 1973, 423)

2.470 Charges for copying documents; disposition of receipts.
1. The supreme court law librarian may collect a charge from any person who requests any photostatic copy or photocopy print of any paper or document from the supreme court law library. The amount of such charge shall be set by the supreme court law librarian but shall not exceed the cost of the photographic copying process for any specific paper or document.
2. The money collected from such fees shall be deposited in the state treasurer's office and credited to the account of the supreme court law library. The receipts may be expended by the supreme court law library pursuant to the provisions of law authorizing budgeted expenditures of moneys not appropriated from the general fund by various state officers, departments, boards, agencies, commissions and

institutions for specific fiscal years.
(Added to NRS by 1973, 423)

2.480 Money for operation, maintenance; use of law library's account.
1. Funds for operation and maintenance of the supreme court law library must be provided by legislative appropriation from the general fund in the state treasury as a budgeted part of the appropriation for the support of the supreme court, and must be paid out on claims as other claims against the state are paid.
2. All unappropriated funds received by the supreme court law library shall be deposited in the supreme court law library's account and must be used for law library purposes.
(Added to NRS by 1973, 423; A 1981, 252)

2.490 Gifts: Deposit in law library gift fund; use. All gifts of money which the supreme court librarian is authorized to accept must be deposited in the state treasury in a fund to be known as the supreme court law library gift fund. The fund is a continuing fund without reversion, and money in the fund must be used for supreme court law library purposes only and expended in accordance with the terms of the gift.
(Added to NRS by 1973, 423; A 1979, 611)

COUNTY LAW LIBRARIES
(Nevada Revised Statutes, 1982, s.380.010 to 380.190.)

380.010 Law libraries: Establishment; government.
1. The board of county commissioners of any county may establish by ordinance a law library to be governed and managed by a board of law library trustees in accordance with the provisions of this chapter.
2. The board of county commissioners of any county with a population under 20,000 may establish by ordinance a law library to be governed and managed as prescribed by the board of county commissioners of that county. Such board may exercise or delegate the exercise of any power granted to a board of law library trustees under this chapter.
3. Any law library established pursuant to subsection 2 is subject to the provisions of NRS 380.065, 380.110 and 380.130 to 380.190, inclusive.
[Part 14:250:1913; 1919 RL p. 2709; NCL § 2263]—(NRS A 1969, 787; 1981, 1002)

380.020 Board of law library trustees: Members; appointments; terms.
1. Any law library established by ordinance as provided by subsection 1 of NRS 380.010 must be governed and managed by a board of law library trustees.
2. A board of law library trustees must consist of not less than five nor more than seven members. The district judge of the judicial district in which the county is situated or, if the district has more than one district judge, a maximum of three district judges designated by all the judges of the district from among their number, are ex officio trustees,

and the board of county commissioners shall appoint a sufficient number of trustees to complete the board, including at least two who are not attorneys at law.

3. Appointive members of the board must be appointed by the board of county commissioners at the first meeting of the board of county commissioners in each January, to serve for terms of 1 year.

[3:250:1913; 1919 RL p. 2707; NCL § 2252] + [4:250:1913; 1919 RL p. 2707; NCL § 2253]—(NRS A 1965, 223; 1969, 787; 1981, 1003)

380.030 Removal of trustee; vacancies. The board of law library trustees, by a majority vote of all the members recorded in the minutes with ayes and noes at length, may:

1. Remove any trustee who neglects to attend the meetings of the board, or who absents himself from such meetings.

2. Fill all vacancies that occur in the board from any cause, but the board must at all times include at least two persons who are not attorneys at law.

[Part 6:250:1913; 1919 RL p. 2708; NCL § 2255]—(NRS A 1981, 1003)

380.040 Seal. The board may adopt and use an official seal.

[Part 10:250:1913; 1919 RL p. 2708; NCL § 2259]

380.050 Officers and assistants: Selection; duties; salaries.

1. The members of the board of law library trustees shall appoint one of their number as president.

2. They shall elect a secretary who shall:

(a) Keep a full statement and account of all property, money, receipts and expenditures of the board.

(b) Keep a record and full minutes in writing of all proceedings of the board. The secretary may certify to such proceedings, or any part or portion thereof, under his hand, verified by the official seal adopted and provided by the board for that purpose.

3. The board of law library trustees, by a majority vote of all the members recorded in the minutes with ayes and noes at length, shall have power:

(a) To define the powers and prescribe the duties of any and all officers, determine the number, and elect all necessary subordinate officers and assistants.

(b) To remove, at its pleasure, any officer or assistant.

(c) To fix the salaries of the secretary and other subordinate officers and assistants.

[Part 6:250:1913; 1919 RL p. 2708; NCL § 2255] + [Part 10:250:1913; 1919 RL p. 2708; NCL § 2259]

380.060 Librarian: Appointment; salary. The board of law library trustees, by a majority vote of all the members recorded in the minutes with ayes and noes at length, shall have power:

1. To appoint a librarian.

2. To fix the salary of the librarian.

[Part 6:250:1913; 1919 RL p. 2708; NCL § 2255] + [Part 10:250:1913; 1919 RL p. 2708; NCL § 2259]

380.065 Librarian: Powers and duties. The librarian of any law library shall administer all functions of the library, employ assistants

and carry out the policies established by the governing body of the library, and may recommend policies to that governing body.
(Added to NRS by 1981, 1002)

380.070 Compensation of trustees. [Effective until January 3, 1983.] The office of trustee shall be honorary, without salary or other compensation.
[5:250:1913; 1919 RL p. 2707; NCL § 2254]—(NRS R 1981, 1360, effective January 3, 1983)

380.071 Compensation of trustees. [Effective January 7, 1985.] The office of trustee is honorary, without salary or other compensation.
(Added to NRS by 1981, 1360, effective January 7, 1985)

380.080 Meetings of board; quorum.
1. The board of law library trustees shall meet the 1st Tuesday of each month, and at such other times as the board may appoint, at a place to be appointed for that purpose.
2. A majority of all the members shall constitute a quorum for business.
[Part 10:250:1913; 1919 RL p. 2708; NCL § 2259]

380.090 Reports of board, secretary.
1. On or before the 1st Monday in December of each year, the board of law library trustees shall make an annual report to the board of county commissioners giving:
(a) The condition of the board's trust.
(b) A full statement of all the board's property and money received, whence derived, how used and how expended.
(c) The number of books, periodicals and other publications on hand.
(d) The number of books, periodicals and other publications added by purchase, gift or otherwise during the year.
(e) The number of books, periodicals and other publications lost or missing.
(f) Such other information as might be of interest.
2. At the same time, a financial report showing all receipts and disbursements of money shall also be made by the secretary. The report shall be duly verified by his oath.
[8:250:1913; 1919 RL p. 2708; NCL § 2257]

380.100 Powers of board. The board of law library trustees, by a majority vote of all its members, to be recorded in the minutes with ayes and noes at length, shall have power:
1. To make and enforce all rules, regulations and bylaws necessary for the administration, government and protection of the library, and all property belonging thereto, or which may be loaned, devised, bequeathed or donated to the same.
2. To purchase books, journals, publications and other personal property.
3. To contract with any existing law library association to make use of its library for the purpose of a public law library, under proper rules and regulations to be prescribed by the board, either by lease or such other contract as may best carry the purposes of this chapter into effect.

4. Generally to do all that may be necessary to carry into effect the provisions of this chapter.

[Part 6:250:1913; 1919 RL p. 2708; NCL § 2255]

380.110 Law library fund: Creation; source; use.

1. Any ordinance of a board of county commissioners establishing a law library under the provisions of this chapter must require that, from the fees received by the county clerk pursuant to chapter 19 of NRS, a sum established by the ordinance, not exceeding $15 in any case, must be allocated by the county clerk to a fund designated as the law library fund. These allocations may be made from the fees collected by the county clerk for the commencement in or removal to the district court of the county, of any civil action, proceeding or appeal, on filing the first paper therein, or from the fees collected by the county clerk for the appearance of any defendant, or any number of defendants, answering jointly or separately, or from both of such sources as may be determined by the ordinance.

2. All money so set aside must be paid by the county clerk to the county treasurer, who shall keep it separate in the law library fund.

3. The board of county commissioners may transfer from the county general fund to the law library fund such amounts as it determines are necessary for purposes of the law library.

4. Money in the law library fund must be:

(a) Expended for the purchase of law books, journals, periodicals and other publications.

(b) Expended for the establishment and maintenance of the law library.

(c) Drawn therefrom and used and applied only as provided in this chapter.

[Part 1:250:1913; A 1927, 74; NCL § 2250] + [2:250:1913; 1919 RL p. 2707; NCL § 2251]—(NRS A 1959, 264; 1981, 1003)

380.120 Payments from law library fund.

1. The board of law library trustees, by a majority vote of all its members, to be recorded in the minutes with ayes and noes at length, shall have power to order the drawing and payment, upon properly authenticated vouchers duly certified by the president and the secretary, of money from the law library fund, for any liability or expenditure authorized by law.

2. The orders and demands of the trustees, when duly made and authenticated as provided in subsection 1, shall be verified and audited by the county auditor and paid by the county treasurer from the law library fund, full entries and records being kept thereof as in other cases.

[Part 6:250:1913; 1919 RL p. 2708; NCL § 2255] + [7:250:1913; 1919 RL p. 2708; NCL § 2256]

380.130 Levy of special tax, use of general fund money to discharge law library indebtedness.

1. Whenever it shall appear to the board of county commissioners of any county having a law library that for any reason any debt incurred in the purchase and establishment of such library has not been fully paid or materially reduced with the funds provided by the provisions of NRS 380.110, within the period of 5 years immediately preceding, the board of county commissioners may, at the next annual tax

levy, levy a special tax upon all taxable property within the county, both real and personal, including the net proceeds of mines, sufficient to raise a sum which will discharge any such indebtedness, but no more. Such sum shall be placed in the law library fund in the county treasury and shall be used for the payment of such indebtedness and for no other purpose.

2. In lieu of the levy of a special tax as provided in subsection 1, the board of county commissioners of any county having a law library may, in the discretion of such board of county commissioners, transfer from the general funds of the county to the law library fund a sufficient sum of money to pay any debts incurred in the purchase and establishment and maintenance of such library, which has not been fully paid or materially reduced with the funds provided by the provisions of NRS 380.110, within the period of 5 years immediately preceding March 1, 1959.

[Part 1:250:1913; A 1927, 74; NCL § 2250]—(NRS A 1959, 264; 1969, 787)

380.140 Levy of special tax to replace uninsured law library destroyed by fire, other public calamity.

1. Subject to the provisions of subsection 2, whenever any law library established under the provisions of this chapter, being uninsured, shall have been destroyed by fire or by other public calamity, the board of county commissioners of the county in which such library was situated shall, at the next time that other tax levies are made, levy a special tax upon all taxable property, both real and personal, within the county, sufficient to raise a sum which will discharge any indebtedness owing for books so destroyed and a further sum sufficient to replace the library or to provide one substantially like it.

2. The sums so to be raised for such purposes shall not exceed in the aggregate the sum of $5,000 for any one law library.

3. The proceeds derived from such special tax levy shall be placed in the law library fund in the county treasury, and shall be drawn upon for the purpose herein authorized.

[15a:250:1913; added 1925, 50; NCL § 2265]—(NRS A 1969, 788)

380.150 Library room to be furnished by county commissioners.
The board of county commissioners shall provide a library room for the use of a law library established under the provisions of this chapter whenever such room may be demanded by a board of law library trustees of that county or as the need for such room may otherwise appear.

[9:250:1913; 1919 RL p. 2708; NCL § 2258]—(NRS A 1969, 788)

380.153 Primary legal books, materials to be made available in law library or public library.

1. The state librarian shall adopt by regulation a list of legal books and materials which are considered primary sources and which he has determined should be available in every county to the inhabitants of that county.

2. Each board of county commissioners shall ensure that all of the legal books and materials listed by the state librarian are available for use during normal business hours by the inhabitants of the county, in use during normal business hours by the inhabitants of the county, in either the law library or a public library. The place where they are

located must be plainly marked as an area accessible to the general public.

(Added to NRS by 1981, 1002)

380.155 Payment in advance for books, materials. The price for the purchase of books or library materials by subscription may be paid in advance of the receipt of such books or materials.

(Added to NRS by 1969, 1058)

380.160 Accessibility of law library to general public. The law library must be free to all inhabitants of the county. The board of law library trustees, or the board of county commissioners in a county having no board of law library trustees, may prescribe regulations imposing restrictions on the privilege of borrowing books and materials from the library but may not restrict the accessibility of the library to the general public.

[11:250:1913; 1919 RL p. 2709; NCL § 2260]—(NRS A 1969, 788; 1981, 1004)

380.170 Sales of state publications by director of legislative counsel bureau to law libraries. The director of the legislative counsel bureau is authorized to transmit to the county clerk of each county, for the use of the law library established therein pursuant to the provisions of this chapter:

1. A copy of each publication provided in NRS 345.050.

2. A copy of each volume of Nevada Reports and the Statutes of Nevada theretofore published.

The legislative counsel bureau shall charge and collect for such volumes the prices established pursuant to NRS 345.050.

[12:250:1913; 1919 RL p. 2709; NCL § 2261]—(NRS A 1965, 953; 1973, 1412)

380.180 Supreme court law librarian to furnish books. The supreme court law librarian shall distribute among the law libraries in this state established pursuant to the provisions of this chapter such duplicates of books as may be in the supreme court law library and not needed for the purposes of that library.

[13:250:1913; 1919 RL p. 2709; NCL § 2262]—(NRS A 1973, 427)

380.190 Discontinuance of law library: Procedure; disposition of books and money.

1. Whenever the board of county commissioners of any county in which a law library has been established pursuant to the provisions of this chapter desires to discontinue the law library, the board of county commissioners shall discontinue the law library by the enactment of an ordinance. The ordinance must provide for:

(a) The discontinuance of the law library.

(b) The transfer of the law library books to the chambers of the district judge or judges of the county or to other appropriate locations in the county.

(c) The keeping thereafter of such books in the judges' chambers or other locations.

(d) The transfer of all money in the law library fund to the county school district fund.

(e) The abolishment of the offices of law library trustees, if any.

2. After such an ordinance takes effect, the county clerk shall not set aside the fees provided for in NRS 380.110.

3. The discontinuance of a law library does not alter the duty of the board of county commissioners to provide, at a publicly accessible location, all legal books and materials which the state librarian has determined, pursuant to NRS 380.153, should be available in every county.

[15:250:1913; 1919 RL p. 2709; NCL § 2264]—(NRS A 1969, 788; 1981, 1004)

NEVADA COUNCIL ON LIBRARIES
(Nevada Revised Statutes, 1982, s.380A.011 to 380A.111.)

380A.011 Policy of state; purpose of chapter. It is the policy of this state to foster and further the establishment and proper maintenance of superior libraries and the acquisition of resources, facilities, professional staffs and auxiliary personnel fully to support such services. The purpose of this chapter is to provide the means for the overview and study of existing library facilities, resources and services and for the formulation of recommendations to strengthen and expand these components.
(Added to NRS by 1965, 331)

380A.021 "Council" defined. As used in this chapter, "council" means the Nevada council on libraries.
(Added to NRS by 1965, 332)

380A.031 Nevada council on libraries: Creation; number, appointment of members; responsibilities; recommendations. The Nevada council on libraries, consisting of six members appointed by the governor, is hereby created. The council is responsible to the governor and may make recommendations to the legislature of the State of Nevada.
(Added to NRS by 1965, 332; A 1977, 1212; 1981, 1005)

380A.041 Qualifications of council members.
1. The governor shall appoint:
(a) Two members who are librarians in active service.
(b) Two members who are trustees of legally established libraries or library systems.
(c) Two members who have an active and demonstrated interest, knowledge and understanding of libraries and library service.
2. A person may not serve as a member of the council for more than two consecutive terms.
(Added to NRS by 1965, 332; A 1977, 1212; 1981, 1005)

380A.051 Qualifications of library-affiliated members. Every library-affiliated member shall be a member in good standing of the Nevada Library Association and the American Library Association and file a certificate to this effect with the state librarian within 30 days after assuming office and annually thereafter for the duration of his term of office.
(Added to NRS by 1965, 332)

380A.061 Officers; records. The council shall elect a chairman and a vice chairman at the first meeting held after July 1 of each year. The state librarian shall serve as secretary of the council but is not entitled to a vote. The secretariat is the Nevada state library, where all files and records of the council must be maintained.

(Added to NRS by 1965, 332; A 1981, 1005)

380A.071 Meetings; salary, travel expenses of members.
1. The council shall meet at least twice each year and, within the limits of legislative appropriations, may hold additional meetings upon the call of the chairman.
2. Each member of the council is entitled to receive a salary of $60 for each day's attendance at a meeting of the council and the per diem allowance and travel expenses provided by law.
3. Payments must be made upon itemized and verified claims approved by the state librarian from money appropriated to the Nevada state library.

(Added to NRS by 1965, 332; A 1977, 1212; 1981, 1005, 1981)

380A.081 Powers and duties. The council shall have the duty and is directed to exercise the following powers:
1. Examine and overview the whole state of libraries, librarianship, library education, library resources, and all allied and cognate activities and prepare a record of its findings.
2. Require public libraries to provide necessary library statistics and reports and to make recommendations for the advancement of libraries.
3. Report biennially to the governor and legislature. The report shall be filed on or before January 1 of each odd-numbered year.
4. Publish any material pertaining to its work that it may order issued.
5. Review plans and applications submitted by libraries and political subdivisions for state grants-in-aid and make recommendations to the state librarian concerning approval.

(Added to NRS by 1965, 332)

380A.091 Cooperation with committees of Nevada Library Association, secretariat. The council shall carry on its work in cooperation with and in conjunction with the appropriate committees of the Nevada Library Association and with the secretariat. It shall not seek to limit the range and depth of library responsibilities and functions in any manner, but shall strive to extend these into any area of endeavor consistent with the needs of the citizens of the state.

(Added to NRS by 1965, 333)

380A.101 Deposit, expenditure of gifts of money. All gifts of money which the council is authorized to accept must be deposited in the state treasury in a nonreverting gift fund and expended in accordance with the budget laws of the State of Nevada upon properly itemized and verified claims approved by the state librarian and the council.

(Added to NRS by 1965, 333; A 1973, 1668; 1979, 617)

380A.111 Filing of reports, studies with Nevada state library. The council shall promptly file copies of any and all of its reports, studies,

documents and publications, regardless of form of issue, with the Nevada state library.
(Added to NRS by 1965, 333)

NEVADA LIBRARY ASSOCIATION
(Nevada Revised Statutes, 1982, s.82.650 to 82.690.)

82.650 Nevada Library Association: Nonprofit corporation; creation to promote library service and librarianship.
1. The Nevada Library Association shall be deemed a body corporate and politic.
2. The Nevada Library Association shall be a nonprofit corporation created to promote library service and librarianship in Nevada.
(Added to NRS by 1963, 219)

82.660 Powers of association. The Nevada Library Association, in its corporate capacity, shall have power:
1. To sue and be sued in any court having competent jurisdiction.
2. To make and use a common seal, and to alter the same at pleasure, but the use or nonuse of such a seal does not affect the legality of any instrument.
3. To acquire by purchase, bequest or donation, directly or indirectly, and to hold in perpetuity, sell and convey, and to mortgage such property real or personal, as may be deemed necessary by the proper authorities thereof to carry out the purposes of the association, and for the necessary uses, purposes and objects of the association, and to devise, lease and improve any real property held by or for the benefit of the corporation.
4. To elect or appoint, in accordance with the bylaws thereof, not less than three or more than 15 members of the association to serve as trustees, who shall have charge of all real and personal property belonging thereto, and transact all business relative thereto.
5. To be entitled to all the rights, privileges and immunities, usually had or enjoyed by such a corporation.
(Added to NRS by 1963, 219; A 1971, 1109)

82.670 Board of trustees: Selection; terms of office; vacancies.
1. The corporate powers of the association shall be vested in a board of trustees elected or appointed as provided in the bylaws of the corporation.
2. The trustees shall hold office until their successors are elected or appointed, and vacancies in such board of trustees shall be filled as provided in the bylaws.
(Added to NRS by 1963, 220)

82.680 Certificates of trustees' election, appointment recorded in office of secretary of state. Upon the election or appointment of trustees, a certificate of such election or appointment shall be executed by the person or persons making the appointment or the judges holding the election, duly acknowledged before a competent officer, and it shall be filed and recorded in the office of the secretary of state.
(Added to NRS by 1963, 220)

82.690 Disincorporation; proceeds granted to American Library Association. Whenever the Nevada Library Association shall disincorporate or disband, by its own act, the proceeds of all property, real or personal, shall, after paying all just charges or demands against the association, be granted to the American Library Association. The American Library Association shall use the proceeds for the improvement of libraries in the State of Nevada.

(Added to NRS by 1963, 220)

MISCELLANEOUS PROVISIONS
(Nevada Revised Statutes, 1982, s.379.150, 379.160, 285.240.)

379.150 Agreements with state librarian for improvement of library service. Any library operated under the provisions of this chapter may enter into agreements with the state librarian, where the objective of the agreements is the improvement of library service.

(Added to NRS by 1957, 341)

379.160 Willful detention, damage to public library property; penalties; liability of parents, guardians.

1. Any person who willfully detains any book, newspaper, magazine, pamphlet, manuscript, filmstrip or other property of any public library or reading room for more than 30 days after receipt of written notice demanding the return of any such article or property shall be punished by a fine of not more than $50.

2. Any person who willfully cuts, tears, defaces, breaks or injures any book, map, chart, picture, engraving, statute, coin, model, apparatus or other work of literature, art, mechanics or object of curiosity, deposited in any public library or reading room shall be punished by a fine of not more than $50.

3. The parent or guardian of a minor who willfully and maliciously commits any acts within the scope of subsection 1 or 2 shall be liable for all damages so caused by the minor.

(Added to NRS by 1957, 6; A 1965, 125; 1967, 563)

385.240 Approval of public school library books; actions subject to review of state board.

1. The superintendent of public instruction shall approve or disapprove lists of books for use in public school libraries, but such lists must not include books containing or including any story in prose or poetry the tendency of which would be to influence the minds of children in the formation of ideals not in harmony with truth and morality or the American way of life, or not in harmony with the Constitution and laws of the United States or of the State of Nevada.

2. Actions of the superintendent with respect to lists of books are subject to review and approval or disapproval by the state board.

[24:32:1956]—(NRS A 1979, 1570)

Nevada library laws are reprinted from NEVADA REVISED STATUTES published by the Nevada Statute Revision Commission.

NEW HAMPSHIRE

STATE LIBRARY

(New Hampshire Revised Statutes Annotated, 1982, s.201-A:1 to 201-A:10,
201A:12 to 201A:20.)

201-A: 1 State Library Established. There is hereby created a state library which shall be under the general control and supervision of a State Library Commission.

Source. 1943, 90: 1, par. 1. RSA 201: 1.
1963, 21: 1, eff. July 1, 1963.

201-A: 2 Services of the State Library. The state library shall provide the following library services and facilities for the benefit of the various branches of state government and for the people of the state.

I. LEGISLATIVE REFERENCE SERVICE. A reference service and collection of materials especially designed to provide such information as will aid the members of the general court to meet their legislative responsibilities.

II. LAW LIBRARY. A law library for the use of the justices of the supreme and superior courts and all other judicial officers of the state, and attorneys of New Hampshire.

III. GENERAL REFERENCE SERVICE. A collection of books and related materials necessary for an adequate reference service to provide for the needs of state and local officials and employees, educators and scholars, and the general public. This collection shall include:

(a) Materials especially relating to the work of the several departments;

(b) Books, manuscripts and other material concerning the state, including all the official publications of the state and its political subdivisions; and

(c) Books and related materials to supplement and reinforce the resources of public libraries and school libraries. [Amended 1981, 510: 6, eff. Aug. 28, 1981.]

IV. [Repealed. 1981, 499: 6, I, eff. Aug. 28, 1981.]

V. ADVISORY AND PLANNING ASSISTANCE. Promote and advance library service throughout the state and serve as the coordinator for a statewide system of libraries. It may supply professional advice and information on the management and operation of libraries through conferences, institutes, correspondence and publications and may organize and administer projects to demonstrate efficient and economical methods of improved service. It shall collect information about libraries; study library problems and make the findings known throughout the state.

VI. LIBRARY SERVICES TO THE HANDICAPPED AND ADVISORY SERVICE TO STATE INSTITUTIONS.

(a) Provide handicapped persons with talking books, large print books, and other federally funded services as provided under P.L. 91–600 as amended.

(b) Provide consultant services to the tax supported residential-treatment institutions of New Hampshire. Such services shall include, but not be limited to, the following:

(1) To render encouragement, advice and assistance for the establishment and operation of institutional libraries;

(2) To establish guidelines for institutional libraries;

(3) To make grants for developing library media services;

(4) To collect information on the nature, extent and quality of institutional library services and publish statistics on a regular basis;

(5) To promote the need for adequate institutional library service to the community at large;

(6) To promote inter-departmental cooperation and communication between institutional libraries;

(7) To promote cooperation between the public libraries, state agencies and institutional libraries; and

(8) To serve as a channel for informing institutions of federal and other library funding. [Added 1977, 241: 1. Amended 1981, 365: 1, eff. July 1, 1981.]

201-A: 3 Commission; Qualifications. The state library commission shall consist of 6 members of whom 5 shall be appointed by the governor with the advice and consent of the council and one as provided in RSA 201-A:6. No more than 3 of the appointed commissioners shall be of the same political party and one commissioner shall be a member of the New Hampshire bar.

Source. 1866, 4232: 1, 2. GS 7: 2, 3. 10: 2, 4. RL 15: 2, 4. 1943, 90: 1, par. 2. GL 7: 2, 3. PS 8: 2, 3, 4. 1917, 59: 1. PL RSA 201: 2. 1963, 21: 1, eff. July 1, 1963.

201-A: 4 —**Tenure.** The term of office of each appointive commissioner shall be 5 years and until his successor is appointed and qualified. In case of a vacancy other than by the expiration of the term, the appointment of a successor shall be made for the balance of the term.

Source. 1866, 4232: 1, 2. GS 7: 2, 3. 10: 3, 6. RL 15: 3, 6. 1943, 90: 1, par. 3. GL 7: 2, 3. PS 8: 2, 3. 1917, 59: 1. PL RSA 201: 3. 1963, 21: 1, eff. July 1, 1963.

201-A: 5 Removal. Any commissioner may be removed from office in accordance with the provisions of RSA 4:1.

Source. 1866, 4232: 1, 2. GS 7: 2, 3. 10: 7. RL 15: 7. 1943, 90: 1, par. 5. GL 7: 2, 3. PS 8: 2, 3. 1917, 59: 1. PL RSA 201: 5. 1963, 21: 1, eff. July 1, 1963.

201-A: 6 Member of the State Board of Education. In addition to the 5 appointive members of the state library commission the state board of education shall select one of its members to serve as a voting member on the commission.

Source. 1963, 21: 1, eff. July 1, 1963.

201-A: 7 —**Organization.** The commission shall adopt by-laws for its internal organization and operation. The state librarian shall serve as secretary to the commission and shall keep an accurate and complete record of all its meetings.

Source. 1866, 4232: 1, 2. GS 7: 2, 3. par. 6. RSA 201: 6. 1963, 21: 1, eff. July 1, GL 7: 2, 3. PS 8: 2, 3, 4. 1917, 59: 1. 1963. PL 10: 8, 14. RL 15: 8, 14. 1943, 90: 1,

201-A: 8 —**Compensation.** The appointive members of the commission shall serve without compensation but shall be reimbursed for their actual expenses incurred in the performance of their duties.

Source. 1866, 4232: 1, 2. GS 7: 2, 3. PL 10: 5. RL 15: 5. 1943, 90: 1, par. 4. GL 7: 2, 3. PS 8: 2, 3, 4. 1917, 59: 1. RSA 201: 4. 1963, 21: 1, eff. July 1, 1963.

201-A: 9 Powers and Duties. In addition to the other powers, duties and responsibilities provided by law, the commission shall:

I. Make all necessary rules and regulations for the proper control and administration of the state library;

II. Appoint a state librarian and, upon his or her recommendation, an assistant state librarian;

III. Preserve a sufficient number of copies of all official reports, documents, and records including those enumerated in RSA 20 and in RSA 505 to be deposited in the state library;

IV. Collect and analyze statistics and undertake research pertaining to libraries and make the resultant findings available to all public, school and institutional libraries within the state;

V. Publish and submit to the governor a biennial report of its activities and of the status and needs of the library as reported by the state librarian, including recommendations for improving library service;

VI. Issue a publication at least 4 times a year which shall contain general and specific information to improve library management. It shall be distributed under the direction of the commission.

Source. 1846, 343:2. 1862, 2588:1. 15:10, 22. 1943, 90:1, pars. 9, 13, 18. 1866, 4232:4. GS 7:5. GL 7:5. PS RSA 201:10, 15, 20. 1963, 21:1, eff. 8:11. 1917, 59:1. PL 10:11, 23. RL July 1, 1963.

201-A:10 Commission; Discretionary Authority. In addition to the duties imposed by law, the commission may, at its discretion:

I. Receive and accept at any time such sums of money as may be donated for the purpose of purchasing books or other supplies or facilities for the state library; and money so received shall be converted into a continuous fund or funds which shall not lapse; to be held by the state treasurer from which payments shall be made in accordance with the stipulations of the donor, upon warrant of the governor and council for such purposes as are approved by the commission;

II. Dispose by sale or exchange of all or any part of the surplus state publications deposited in the state library;

III. Act as custodians for the state of collections of books, pamphlets, maps, manuscripts and other materials, upon such terms and under such regulations as to them seem proper;

IV. [Repealed. 1981, 499:6, II, eff. Aug. 28, 1981.]

V. Enter, with the approval of the governor and council, into any agreement or compact with any other state or states, with the United States, and with library trustees and other agencies, public and private, for the purpose of developing, improving or operating library facilities and services on the basis of mutual advantages and thereby providing more efficient or economical library service;

VI. Issue booklets, bulletins, and other publications as will benefit the libraries of the state and increase the efficiency of the state library;

VII. Award scholarships to qualified persons to attend a graduate library school accredited by the American Library Association;

VIII. Establish, equip, and maintain branch offices when the library needs of the state will be better served;

IX. [Repealed. 1981, 499:6, III, eff. Aug. 28, 1981.]

X. Conduct and arrange for training programs for library personnel.

Source. 1895, 24:6. 1909, 39:1. 1917, RSA 201:13, 16, 22. 1957, 23:1. 1963, 59:1. PL 10:19, 20, 21. RL 15:18, 19, 21:1, eff. July 1, 1963. 20. 1943, 90:1, pars. 11, 14. 1947, 26:1.

201-A: 11   State Aid to Libraries or Groups of Libraries.
[Repealed 1981, 499: 6, IV, eff. Aug. 28, 1981.]

201-A: 12   Federal Grants.   The commission shall adopt rules, pursuant to RSA 541-A and after public hearing, and establish any advisory body, as may be required to comply with or interpret any federal law or regulation intended to promote library service.

Source.   1943, 90: 1, par. 20.   RSA
201: 23.   1963, 21: 1.   1981, 499: 3, eff.
Aug. 28, 1981.

201-A: 13   Acceptance of Funds.   The commission may receive, accept and administer any money granted by the federal government or other agencies, private or otherwise for providing, equalizing or strengthening a state-wide system of library service in New Hampshire. Any gift or grant from the federal government or other source as hereinbefore provided shall be deposited in the state treasury and credited to a special fund which shall be continuous and shall not lapse. Any moneys appropriated by the state for such purposes may be added to said fund and all moneys so deposited shall be paid out by the treasurer on a warrant of the governor and council for services approved by the commission which will improve and equalize library service in this state.

Source.   1947,   26: 1.   RSA   201: 22.
1963, 21: 1, eff. July 1, 1963.

201-A: 14   State Librarian, Qualifications and Tenure.   The state librarian shall be appointed to a 5-year term of office, and until his successor is appointed and qualified. He shall be a graduate of an accredited library school and shall have had at least 4 years' experience in a library in an administrative capacity. He may be removed by the commission after a hearing for reasonable cause. He shall be paid the annual salary prescribed by RSA 94: 1–4 as amended.

Source.   1917, 59: 1.   1921, 118: 1.   PL   90: 1, par. 8.   1953, 265: 1.   RSA 201: 8,
10: 12, 13, 14.   RL 15: 11, 12, 13.   1943,   9.   1963, 21: 1, eff. July 1, 1963.

201-A: 15   —Powers and Duties.   In addition to any other powers and duties which he may be delegated from time to time, the state librarian shall:

I. Serve as the executive and administrative office of the state libarary;

II. Recommend to the commission the appointment of an assistant state librarian;

III. Appoint all other employees of the state library subject to the regulations of the state personnel commission;

IV. Purchase books and related materials for the state library, subject to RSA 8: 25, III;

V. [Repealed. 1981, 499 : 6, V, eff. Aug. 28, 1981.]

VI. Operate a cataloging service for the benefit of the statewide development system. [Amended 1981, 499 : 5, eff. Aug. 28, 1981.]

201-A : 16 Assistant State Librarian; Qualifications and Tenure. The assistant state librarian shall be appointed to a 5-year term of office, and until his successor is appointed and qualified. He shall be a graduate of an accredited library school and shall have had such experience as will qualify him for the work. He may be removed by the commission after a hearing for reasonable cause. He shall be paid the annual salary prescribed by RSA 94 : 1–4 as amended.

Source. 1943, 90:1, par. 9. 1953, 265:1. RSA 201:10, 11. 1963, 21:1, eff. July 1, 1963.

201-A : 17 —Powers and Duties. In addition to any powers and duties which he may be delegated, he shall serve as the deputy to the state librarian and during the absence or disability of the state librarian perform all the duties of the office.

Source. 1943, 90:1, par. 9. RSA 201:10. 1963, 21:1, eff. July 1, 1963.

201-A : 18 Deposit of Official Reports and Publications.

I. Within 30 days after publication,

(1) the head of every state department and institution, every legislative commission and any commission operating under executive authority shall deliver to the state library 3 copies of all reports and all other publications issued under the authority of the state department or institution,

(2) the head of each state supported institution of learning, including the University of New Hampshire, shall deliver 2 copies of all reports and all other publications issued under the authority of the state department or institution,

(3) the county commissioners of each county shall forward to the state library 2 copies of the report of the county for the previous fiscal year,

(4) the clerk in each town and city shall forward to the state library 2 copies each, and to the library of the University of New Hampshire one copy each, of the city or town report for the previous fiscal year.

Source. 1891, 7:13. 1895, 3:3. 1907, 41:2. 1917, 59:1. PL 10:20, 21, 24, 25, 26. RL 15:19, 20, 23, 24, 25. 1943, 90:1, pars. 14, 15, 21, 22. RSA 201:16, 17, 24, 25. 1963, 21:1. 1973, 153:1, eff. July 21, 1973.

201-A : 19 Disposition of Fees, Fines and Exchange of Property. Any funds accruing to the state library from the sale or exchange of books, pamphlets, maps, manuscripts and other related material, or from fees and fines from lost or damaged property, shall be paid into the state treasury, and held in a continuous fund for the purchase of books and related materials for the state library.

Source. 1943, 90:1, par. 12. RSA 201:14. 1963, 21:1, eff. July 1, 1963.

201-A:20 Building and Facilities. The state library shall control all space in the state library building. The division of purchase and property shall maintain the state library building and grounds in suitable repair and condition for use by the state library.

Source. 1893, 11:1. 1895, 31:1. 1917, part 6:1, par. 17. RSA 201:19, 27. 1963, 59:1. PL 10:29, 48. 1939, 184:3. RL 21:1. 1973, 214:3, eff. Aug. 11, 1973. 15:28, 48. 1943, 90:1, par. 17. 1950, 5,

STATEWIDE LIBRARY DEVELOPMENT SYSTEM
(New Hampshire Revised Statutes Annotated, 1982, s.201-D:1 to 201-D:10.)

201-D:1 Definitions. In this chapter:

I. "Accredited library" means a member library which meets the standards of the highest category of affiliation, including providing specified services to other area libraries.

II. "Associate library" means a member library which meets the basic standards for affiliation.

III. "Certified library" means a member library which meets the standards for the middle category of affiliation, including providing specified services to nearby libraries.

IV. "Commission" means the state library commission established under RSA 201-A:1.

V. "Cooperative" means any joint effort by 2 or more libraries to improve library service.

VI. "Development system" means the statewide library development system, a network of public and other than public libraries cooperating in communities, regions and statewide to provide better library service.

VII. "Member library" means a public library which has been granted associate, certified, or accredited status by the commission.

VIII. "Public library" means a library which provides customary services, without charge, to all the residents of a town, city, or larger area.

IX. "Other than public library" means a school, college or university, medical, business or other special library.

Source. 1981, 499:2, eff. Aug. 28, 1981.

201-D:2 Member Libraries. There shall be 3 categories of member libraries: associate, certified, and accredited. The commission, through its rulemaking authority established under RSA 201-D:10, shall set affiliation standards for each category. The commission may establish subcategories. Any public library may become a member library by meeting the standards for any of the categories and following the application procedures set by the commission. Application for membership or change in status shall require the approval of the local library trustees. The commission may revoke the membership or change the category of any library which no longer meets the affiliation standards or which requests a change in status. Any affected library has the right to appeal a commission decision on membership.

Source. 1981, 499: 2, eff. Aug. 28, 1981.

201-D: 3 State Aid. Each member library shall receive an annual allocation of state funds to supplement the local appropriation and other income. Library cooperatives which include member libraries may receive state aid. The state aid shall be used only to support library services in member libraries and in cooperatives including member libraries. The amount of the allocation for each library shall be based on specified local expenditures for the library, and on its membership category. The commission shall set an allocation rate for each category, with progressively higher rates for certified and accredited libraries in recognition of service beyond their own towns or cities.

Source. 1981, 499: 2, eff. Aug. 28, 1981.

201-D: 4 State Services. The state library shall provide services to member libraries within the funds available and in keeping with the goal of efficient use of library resources in the state.

Source. 1981, 499: 2, eff. Aug. 28, 1981.

201-D: 5 State Library Staff. The state library shall employ consultants and other staff to promote the development system by working with library forums, cooperatives, and other groups which include member libraries.

Source. 1981, 499: 2, eff. Aug. 28, 1981.

201-D: 6 Regions and Areas. The state shall be divided into 4 or more library regions. Each region shall consist of one or more library areas. The commission shall set the number and boundaries of regions and areas. The goal of these decisions shall be to promote cooperative efforts and the most efficient use of local and state library resources.

Source. 1981, 499: 2, eff. Aug. 28, 1981.

201-D: 7 Library Forums. Each library area shall have a library forum consisting of one representative from each public library, at least one representative from each school district, and a representative of each other than public library which chooses to participate. The state library shall be represented on each forum.

Source. 1981, 499: 2, eff. Aug. 28, 1981.

201-D: 8 Selection of Representatives. The board of trustees of each public library, and the governing body of each other than public library, shall select its representative to the area library forum.

Source. 1981, 499: 2, eff. Aug. 28, 1981.

201-D: 9 Purposes. The purposes of the library forums are to:

I. Encourage information sharing between area libraries.

II. Promote cooperative planning and services among area libraries.

III. Provide liaison between area libraries and the state library.

IV. Communicate with the commission on local needs and state library services.

Source. 1981, 499: 2, eff. Aug. 28, 1981.

201-D: 10 Rulemaking. The commission shall adopt rules, pursuant to RSA 541-A and after public hearing, relative to:

I. Standards for the associate, certified and accredited categories, and for any subcategory, concerning any or all of the following:

    (a) Level of service;

    (b) Evaluation and planning;

    (c) Cooperation with other libraries;

    (d) Participation in the library forum and statewide programs;

    (e) Personnel qualifications;

    (f) Organization of materials; and

    (g) Physical facilities.

II. Allocation of state aid and other funds to individual libraries, cooperatives and other groups, and library areas. For state aid, this shall include setting the allocation rate for each membership category and the local library expenditures to be counted in applying the rate.

III. Requirements that member libraries adopt written policies concerning any or all of the following:

    (a) General objectives;

    (b) Organization of materials;

    (c) Materials selection and collection development;

    (d) Personnel;

    (e) Public relations; and

    (f) Cooperation with public school libraries.

IV. Reporting requirements for funded programs and services.

V. Number and boundaries of library areas.

VI. Democratic procedures for library forums.

Source. 1981, 499: 2, eff. Aug. 28, 1981.

INTERSTATE LIBRARY COMPACT

(New Hampshire Revised Statutes Annotated, 1982, s.201-B:1 to 201-B:6.)

201-B: 1 Compact Enacted. The Interstate Library Compact is hereby enacted into law and entered into by this state with all states legally joining therein in the form substantially as follows:

Article I

Policy and Purpose

Because the desire for the services provided by libraries transcends governmental boundaries and can most effectively be satisfied by giving such services to communities and people regardless of jurisdictional lines, it is the policy of the states party to this compact to cooperate and share their responsibilites; to authorize cooperation and sharing with respect to those types of library facilities and services which can be more economically or efficiently developed and maintained on a cooperative basis, and to authorize cooperation and sharing among localities, states and others in providing joint or cooperative library services in areas where the distribution of population or of existing and potential library resources make the provision of library service on an interstate basis the most effective way of providing adequate and efficient service.

Article II

Definitions

As used in this compact:

(a) "Public library agency" means any unit or agency of local or state government operating or having power to operate a library.

(b) "Private library agency" means any non-governmental entity which operates or assumes a legal obligation to operate a library.

(c) "Library agreement" means a contract establishing an interstate library district pursuant to this compact or providing for the joint or cooperative furnishing of library services.

Article III

Interstate Library Districts

(a) Any one or more public library agencies in a party state in cooperation with any public library agency or agencies in one or more other party states may establish and maintain an interstate library district. Subject to the provisions of this compact and any other laws of the party states which pursuant hereto remain applicable, such district may establish, maintain and operate some or all of the library facilities and services for the area concerned in accordance with the terms of a library agreement therefor. Any private library agency or agencies within an interstate library district may cooperate therewith, assume duties, responsibilities and obligations thereto, and receive benefits therefrom as provided in any library agreement to which such agency or agencies become party.

(b) Within an interstate library district, and as provided by a library agreement, the performance of library functions may be undertaken on a joint or cooperative basis or may be undertaken by means of one or more arrangements between or among public or private library agencies for the extension of library privileges to the use of facilities or services operated or rendered by one or more of the individual library agencies.

(c) If a library agreement provides for joint establishment, maintenance or operation of library facilities or services by an interstate library district, such district shall have power to do any one or more of the following in accordance with such library agreement:

1. Undertake, administer and participate in programs or arrangements for securing, lending or servicing of books and other publications, any other materials suitable to be kept or made available by libraries, library equipment or for the dissemination of information about libraries, the value and significance of particular items therein, and the use thereof.

2. Accept for any of its purposes under this compact any and all donations, and grants of money, equipment, supplies, materials, and services, (conditional or otherwise), from any state or the United States or any subdivision or agency thereof, or interstate agency, or from any institution, person, firm or corporation, and receive, utilize and dispose of the same.

3. Operate mobile library units or equipment for the purpose of rendering bookmobile service within the district.

4. Employ professional, technical, clerical and other personnel and fix terms of employment, compensation and other appropriate benefits; and where desirable, provide for the in-service training of such personnel.

5. Sue and be sued in any court of competent jurisdiction.

6. Acquire, hold, and dispose of any real or personal property or any interest or interests therein as may be appropriate to the rendering of library service.

7. Construct, maintain and operate a library, including any appropriate branches thereof.

8. Do such other things as may be incidental to or appropriate for the carrying out of any of the foregoing powers.

Article IV
Interstate Library Districts, Governing Board

(a) An interstate library district which establishes, maintains or operates any facilities or services in its own right shall have a governing board which shall direct the affairs of the district and act for it in all matters relating to its business. Each participating public library agency in the district shall be represented on the governing board which shall be organized and conduct its business in accordance with provision therefor in the library agreement. But in no event shall a governing board meet less often than twice a year.

(b) Any private library agency or agencies party to a library agreement establishing an interstate library district may be represented on or advise with the governing board of the district in such manner as the library agreement may provide.

Article V

State Library Agency Cooperation

Any 2 or more state library agencies of 2 or more of the party states may undertake and conduct joint or cooperative library programs, render joint or cooperative library services, and enter into and perform arrangements for the cooperative or joint acquisition, use, housing and disposition of items or collections of materials which, by reason of expense, rarity, specialized nature, or infrequency of demand therefor would be appropriate for central collection and shared use. Any such programs, services or arrangements may include provision for the exercise on a cooperative or joint basis of any power exercisable by an interstate library district and an agreement embodying any such program, service or arrangement shall contain provisions covering the subjects detailed in Article VI of this compact for interstate library agreements.

Article VI

Library Agreements

(a) In order to provide for any joint or cooperative undertaking pursuant to this compact, public and private library agencies may enter into library agreements. Any agreement executed pursuant to the provisions of this compact shall, as among the parties to the agreement:

1. Detail the specific nature of the services, programs, facilities, arrangements or properties to which it is applicable.

2. Provide for the allocation of costs and other financial responsibilities.

3. Specify the respective rights, duties, obligations and liabilities of the parties.

4. Set forth the terms and conditions for duration, renewal, termination, abrogation, disposal of joint or common property, if any, and all other matters which may be appropriate to the proper effectuation and performance of the agreement.

(b) No public or private library agency shall undertake to exercise itself, or jointly with any other library agency, by means of a library agreement any power prohibited to such agency by the constitution or statutes of its state.

(c) No library agreement shall become effective until filed with the compact administrator of each state involved, and approved in accordance with Article VII of this compact.

Article VII

Approval of Library Agreements

(a) Every library agreement made pursuant to this compact shall, prior to and as a condition precedent to its entry into force, be submitted to the attorney general of each state in which a public library agency party thereto is situated, who shall determine whether the agreement is in proper form and compatible with the laws of his state. The attorneys general shall approve any agreement submitted to them unless they shall find that it does not meet the conditions set forth herein and shall detail in writing addressed to the governing bodies of the public library agencies concerned the specific respects in which the proposed agreement fails to meet the requirements of law. Failure to disapprove an agreement submitted hereunder within 90 days of its submission shall constitute approval thereof.

(b) In the event that a library agreement made pursuant to this compact shall deal in whole or in part with the provision of services or facilities with regard to which an officer or agency of the state government has constitutional or statutory powers of control, the agreement shall, as a condition precedent to its entry into force, be submitted to the state officer or agency having such power of control and shall be approved or disapproved by him or it as to all matters within his or its jurisdiction in the same manner and subject to the same requirements governing the action of the attorneys general pursuant to paragraph (a) of this article. This requirement of submission and approval shall be in addition to and not in substitution for the requirement of submission to and approval by the attorneys general.

Article VIII

Other Laws Applicable

Nothing in this compact or in any library agreement shall be construed to supersede, alter or otherwise impair any obligation imposed on any library by otherwise applicable law, nor to authorize the transfer or disposition of any property held in trust by a library agency in a manner contrary to the terms of such trust.

Article IX

Appropriations and Aid

(a) Any public library agency party to a library agreement may appropriate funds to the interstate library district established thereby in the same manner and to the same extent as to a library wholly maintained by it and, subject to the laws of the state in which such public library agency is situated, may pledge its credit in support of an interstate library district established by the agreement.

(b) Subject to the provisions of the library agreement pursuant to which it functions and the laws of the states in which such district is situated, an interstate library district may claim and receive any state and federal aid which may be available to library agencies.

Article X

Compact Administrator

Each state shall designate a compact administrator with whom copies of all library ageements to which his state or any public library agency thereof is party shall be filed. The administrator shall have such other powers as may be conferred upon him by the laws of his state and may consult and cooperate with the compact administrators of other party states and take such steps as may effectuate the purposes of this compact. If the laws of a party state so provide, such state may designate one or more deputy compact administrators in addition to its compact administrator.

Article XI

Entry Into Force and Withdrawal

(a) This compact shall enter into force and effect immediately upon its enactment into law by any 2 states. Thereafter, it shall enter into force and effect as to any other state upon the enactment thereof by such state.

(b) This compact shall continue in force with respect to a party state and remain binding upon such state until 6 months after such state has given notice to each other party state of the repeal thereof. Such withdrawal shall not be construed to relieve any party to a library agreement entered into pursuant to this compact from any obligation of that agreement prior to the end of its duration as provided therein.

Article XII

Construction and Severability

This compact shall be liberally construed so as to effectuate the purposes thereof. The provisions of this compact shall be severable and if any phrase, clause, sentence or provision of this compact is declared to be contrary to the constitution of any party state or of the United States or the applicability thereof to any government, agency, person or circumstance is held invalid, the validity of the remainder of this compact and the applicability thereof to any government, agency, person or circumstance shall not be affected thereby. If this compact shall be held contrary to the constitution of any state party thereto, the compact shall remain in full force and effect as to the remaining states and in full force and effect as to the state affected as to all severable matters.

Source. 1963, 106:1, eff. July 23, 1963.

201-B:2 Limitation on Capital Expenditures. No city or town of this state shall be party to a library agreement which provides for the construction or maintenance of a library pursuant to Article III, subdivision (c-7) of the compact, nor pledge its credit in support of such a library, or contribute to the capital financing thereof, except after compliance with any laws applicable to such cities or towns relating to or governing capital outlays and the pledging of credit.

Source. 1963, 106:1, eff. July 23, 1963.

201-B:3 Definition. As used in the compact, "state library agency", with reference to this state, means the state library commission.

Source. 1963, 106:1, eff. July 23, 1963.

201-B:4 Eligibility for Aid. An interstate library district lying partly within this state may claim and be entitled to receive state aid in support of any of its functions to the same extent and in the same manner as such functions are eligible for support when carried on by entities wholly within this state. For the purposes of computing and apportioning state aid to an interstate library district, this state will consider that portion of the area which lies within this state as an independent entity for the performance of the aided function or functions and compute and apportion the aid accordingly. Subject to any applicable laws of this state, such a district also may apply for and be entitled to receive any federal aid for which it may be eligible.

Source. 1963, 106:1, eff. July 23, 1963.

201-B:5 Designation of Administrator. The state librarian shall be the compact administrator pursuant to Article X of the compact. The assistant state librarian shall be the deputy compact administrator pursuant to said Article.

Source. 1963, 106:1, eff. July 23, 1963.

201-B:6 Withdrawal. In the event of withdrawal from the compact the state librarian shall send and receive any notices required by Article XI(b) of the compact.

Source. 1963, 106:1, eff. July 23, 1963.

DISTRIBUTION OF PUBLIC DOCUMENTS
(New Hampshire Revised Statutes Annotated, 1982, s.20:3, 20:3-a,
20:3b, 20:4, 20:10 to 20:13, 20:16.)

20:3 Daily Journals. The clerks of the senate and house of representatives shall:

I. Cause to be printed in pamphlet form at the close of each legislative day twelve hundred copies of the daily journals of their respective body, and

II. Cause one copy of each to be distributed to each member of the general court before the beginning of the session on the next legislative day, and

III. Cause twenty-five copies of each to be delivered to the state library each day.

Source. RS 3:6. CS 3:6. 1857, 2009:1. GS 4:10. GL 4:10. 1879, 20:1. 1949, 128:2. RSA 20:3. 1969, 300:7. PS 5:9. 1919, 3:3. PL 5:3. RL 10:3. 1972, 60:76. 1975, 480:1, eff. July 1, 1976.

20: 3-a Permanent Journals. The clerks of the senate and house of representatives shall at the close of each legislative session:

I. Cause such numbers of copies of the permanent journals with indexes as the president of the senate and speaker of the house shall respectively direct to be printed and bound in paper and in hard cover.

II. Distribute copies without charge as follows:

(a) One hard cover copy each to the library of congress and the secretary of state;

(b) Six hard cover copies to the state library for its own use and for the use of the law library and the supreme court and 10 paper bound copies to the state library for its exchange program;

(c) As many hard cover copies and paper bound copies as requested by the president of the senate and the speaker of the house.

III. Sell all other copies of the journals, paper or hard cover, at prices to be established by the respective presiding officers of the senate and the house.

Source. 1975, 480: 2. 1979, 230: 1, eff.
Aug. 11, 1979.

20: 3-b Indexing by Law Librarian. As soon as possible after final adjournment of each session of the general court and in any case consistently with the schedule of performance set forth in contracts for printing and binding of the permanent journals of the general court, the law librarian shall prepare and furnish the clerk of each house with a complete index of the journal of his house.

Source. 1975, 480: 2, eff. July 1, 1976.

20: 4 Bills and Resolutions. The clerks of the senate and house of representatives may cause to be printed eleven hundred copies of every bill and joint resolution after its second reading, and shall cause one each of such copies to be distributed to each member of those bodies as soon as printed. Twenty-five copies of each shall be delivered to the state library.

Sources: 1869, 1: 7. GL 5: 7. 1891, 7: 9. PS 6: 8. 1919, 3: 4. PL 5: 4. RL 10: 4. 1949, 128: 3, eff. Apr. 6, 1949.

20: 10 Distribution of Records. The publications authorized under RSA 20: 9 shall be distributed as follows: one copy to each city and town in the state, one copy to such of the public libraries requesting them, fifty copies to the New Hampshire Historical Society, fifty copies to the state library and the remainder to be placed in the custody of the secretary of state, who is authorized to exchange the same for similar publications by other states.

Source. 1931, 28: 2. RL 10: 10. RSA
20: 10. 1973, 140: 1, eff. Jan. 1, 1974.

20: 11 Distribution of Acts, Resolves, etc. One copy of each publication provided for in RSA 20: 1, III, (b) ; 5; 6; and 7 shall be sent by the agency responsible for its issue, free of charge except as hereinafter provided, to each of the following officers and bodies: governor, each member of the council, each agency and institution of the state, state house press room, the justices and clerks of the supreme and superior courts, each free public library established under the laws of the state, the town clerk of each town, the library of Congress, and the state or territorial library of each state and territory in the United States. Provided, that in case any state or territory makes a charge to the New Hampshire state library for copies of its laws, the state librarian is hereby authorized to make the proper charge for copies of the laws of New Hampshire when forwarded to the state or territorial library of such state or territory. The agencies may make such further free distribution of such publications as they may deem wise, or as the governor and council may direct. Each member of the legislature shall be furnished one copy of the manual and of the paper bound session laws and one copy of each departmental and institutional report on application. However, each free public library and the town clerk of each town shall not be furnished a copy of the annual or biennial report of each state agency or institution.

Source. 1919, 3:9. 1925, 9:1. PL
5:10. 1931, 28:3. 1941, 22:1. RL 10:11.
RSA 20:11. 1973, 140:1. 1975, 464:6,
eff. June 20, 1975.

20:12 Distribution Discontinued. The secretary of state shall discontinue distribution of books or reports to any free public library when notified by its trustees that they have voted not to receive them.

SOURCES: 1933, 70:1. RL 10:12.

20:13 Disposition of Books and Reports. Books and reports furnished free by state agencies and institutions to any free public library may be disposed of at the best price obtainable, but only with the approval of the state librarian and of the secretary of state.

Source. 1933, 70:1. RL 10:13. 1943,
90:3. RSA 20:13. 1973, 140:1, eff.
Jan. 1, 1974.

20:16 Distribution of Revised Statutes Annotated.

I. Unless otherwise directed by the joint committee on legislative facilities, the director of legislative services is authorized to distribute official bound volumes of the Revised Statutes Annotated, replacement volumes thereof and periodic supplements thereto free of charge to each of the following: the clerk of the supreme court of the United States, each judge of the circuit court of the United States for this district, the district court of the United States for this district, the United States department of justice, the Library of Congress, the New Hampshire Historical Society, and a sufficient number of copies to the state library for its use and for distribution to each state or territorial library of the United States on an exchange basis. If any state or territory makes a charge to this state for copies of its laws such state or territory shall in a like manner be required to pay to the state library a price for copies of the Revised Statutes Annotated which shall be determined by the joint committee on legislative facilities.

Source. 1955, 231:3. 1970, 14:4. 1971,
300:1. 1973, 307:3. 1979, 380:3, eff.
June 23, 1979.

RECORDS MANAGEMENT AND ARCHIVES
(New Hampshire Revised Statutes Annotated, 1982, s.8-B:1 to 8-B:4, 8-B:7 to 8-B:17.)

8-B: 1 Declaration of Policy. The legislature declares that a program for the efficient and economical management of state and local records will promote economy and efficiency in the day-to-day record-keeping activities of the state government and will facilitate and expedite government operations. The legislature further declares that the interests of the state and of posterity require the establishment of archives in which may be preserved records, papers and documents having permanent and historical value.

SOURCE: 1961, 266: 1, eff. July 1, 1961.

8-B: 2 Short Title. This chapter shall be known as "Records Management and Archives Act."

SOURCE: 1961, 266: 1, eff. July 1, 1961.

8-B: 3 Division Established. There shall be a division of records management and archives in the department of state, under the executive direction of the state archivist.

Source. 1961, 266: 1. 1979, 256: 2, eff. July 1, 1979.

8-B: 4 Archivist. The secretary of state, with the approval of governor and council, shall appoint the state archivist who shall be an unclassified state employee. The state archivist shall have a minimum of a master's degree in library science or history and prior experience as an archivist or experience in a related field. The term of office for the state archivist shall be for 5 years. Any vacancy shall be filled for the unexpired term.

Source. 1961, 266: 1. 1977, 600: 63. 1979, 256: 3, eff. July 1, 1979.

8-B: 7 Definitions. As used in this chapter:

I. "Record" means document, book, paper, photograph, map, sound recording or other material, regardless of physical form or characteristics, made or received pursuant to law or in connection with the transaction of official business. Library and museum material made or acquired and preserved solely for library use or exhibition purposes, extra copies of documents preserved only for convenience or reference, and stocks of publications and of processed documents are not included within the definition of records as used herein, and are hereinafter designated "nonrecord materials".

II. "State record" means:

(1) A record of a department, office, commission, board or other agency, however designated, of the state government, or

(2) A record of the state legislature, or

(3) A record of any court of record, whether of statewide or local jurisdiction, or

(4) Any other record designated or treated as a state record under state law.

III. "Local record" means a record of county, city, town, district, authority or any public corporation or political entity whether organized and existing under charter or under general law unless the record is designated or treated as a state record under state law.

IV. "Agency" means any department, office, commission, board or other unit, however designated, or the executive branch of state government.

V. "Records center" means the depository of records and archives.

VI. "Archives" means that portion of the records center in which are kept records having permanent or historic values.

SOURCE: 1961, 266: 1, eff. July 1, 1961.

8-B: 8 Duties of State Archivist. The state archivist shall, with due regard for the functions of the agencies concerned, and subject to the approval of the secretary of state: [Amended 1979, 256: 5, eff. July 1, 1979.]

I. Establish standards, procedures, and techniques for effective management of records.

II. Make continuing surveys of paper work operations and recommend improvements in current records management practices including the use of space, equipment and supplies employed in creating, maintaining, storing and servicing records.

III. Establish standards for the preparation of schedules providing for the retention of state records of continuing value and for the prompt and orderly disposal of state records no longer possessing sufficient administrative, legal or fiscal value to warrant their further keeping.

IV. Establish standards and formulate procedures for the transfer of records having permanent and historical value to the archives.

V. Obtain reports from agencies as are required for the administration of the program.

SOURCE: 1961, 266: 1, eff. July 1, 1961.

8-B: 9 Records Center. The state archivist, subject to the supervision of the secretary of state, shall have charge of the records center. He shall, subject to the provisions of RSA 8-B: 17, promulgate rules governing the organization of the records center, transfer of records thereto, the indexing of materials therein, and the means of access and reference to such records and archives.

Source. 1961, 266: 1. 1979, 256: 6, eff. July 1, 1979.

8-B:10 Agency Heads. The head of each agency shall:

I. Establish and maintain an active, continuing program for the economical and efficient management of the records of the agency, consistently with the rules and regulations, and under the supervision, of the director.

II. Make and maintain records containing adequate and proper documentation of the organization, functions, policies, decisions, procedures and essential transactions of the agency designed to furnish information to protect the legal and financial rights of the state and of persons directly affected by the agency's activities.

III. Submit to the director, in accordance with the standards established by him, schedules proposing the length of time each state record series warrants retention for administrative, legal or fiscal purposes after it has been received by the agency. The head of each agency shall submit lists of state records in his custody that are of permanent and historical value to the state. He shall likewise submit lists of state records in his custody that are not needed in the transaction of current business and that do not have sufficient administrative, legal or fiscal value to warrant their further keeping.

IV. Cooperate with the director in the conduct of surveys made by him pursuant to the provisions of this chapter.

V. Comply with the rules, regulations, standards and procedures issued by the director.

Source: 1961, 266: 1, eff. July 1, 1961.

8-B:11 Construction of Chapter. Nothing herein shall be construed to divest agency heads of the authority to determine the nature and form of the records required in the administration of their several departments, or to compel the removal of records deemed necessary by them in the performance of their statutory duties. Any records made confidential by law shall be so treated in the records center.

Source: 1961, 266: 1, eff. July 1, 1961.

8-B:12 Local Records. The director shall accept for permanent storage in the state archives such local records as the municipal records board established under RSA 33-A: 4-a may require. Any material so stored may be withdrawn pursuant to rules promulgated by the municipal records board.

Source. 1961, 266: 1. 1977, 358: 5, eff. July 1, 1977.

8-B:13 Assistance to Legislative and Judicial Branches. Upon request, the director shall assist and advise in the establishment of records management programs in the legislative and judicial branches of state government and shall, as required by them, provide program services similar to those available to the executive branch of state government pursuant to the provisions of this chapter.

SOURCE: 1961, 266: 1, eff. July 1, 1961.

8-B: 14 Records not to be Damaged or Destroyed. All records made or received by or under the authority of or coming into the custody, control or possession of public officials of this state in the course of their public duties are the property of the state and shall not be mutilated, destroyed, transferred, removed or otherwise damaged or disposed of, in whole or in part, except as provided by law.

SOURCE: 1961, 266: 1, eff. July 1, 1961.

8-B: 15 Disposal of Records. Unless otherwise provided by law with respect to particular departments or particular records, records not having a permanent or historical value may be destroyed at the end of seven years from the making thereof; provided, however, that the rules and regulations of the director, as promulgated under section 17 may provide that designated records may be destroyed at an earlier period or require their retention for a longer period.

SOURCE: 1961, 266: 1, eff. July 1, 1961.

8-B: 16 Transfer of State Records. Subject to the limitations of the constitution, the secretary of state may transfer any of his records to the records center and he may transfer reports of state agencies to the state library.

Source. 1961, 266: 1.   1973, 20: 1.   1979, 256: 7, eff. July 1, 1979.

8-B: 17 Rules. The state archivist, under the supervision of the secretary of state, shall establish a manual of uniform rules necessary and proper to effectuate the purposes of this chapter. Such rules and any subsequent revisions, when approved by the governor and council, shall be binding upon all officers and employees of the state. Any rules promulgated pursuant to this section shall be in accordance with RSA 541-A.

Source. 1961, 266: 1.   1975, 145: 1. 1979, 256: 8, eff. July 1, 1979.

MUNICIPAL LIBRARIES
General Provisions
(New Hampshire Revised Statutes Annotated, 1982, s.202-A:1 to 202-A:8,
202-A:10 to 202-A:25.)

202-A: 1 Declaration of Policy. Mindful that, as the constitution declares, "knowledge and learning, generally diffused through a community" are "essential to the preservation of a free government" the legislature recognizes its duty to encourage the people of New Hampshire to extend their education during and beyond the years of formal education. To this end, it hereby declares that the public library is a valuable supplement to the formal system of free public education and as such deserves adequate financial support from government at all levels.

Source. 1963, 46: 1, eff. July 1, 1963.

202-A: 2 Definitions. As used in this chapter the following words shall be construed as follows unless the context clearly requires otherwise:

I. "Public library" shall mean every library which receives regular financial support, at least annually, from public or private sources and which provides regular and currently useful library service to the public without charge. The words may be construed to include reference and circulating libraries, reading rooms and museums regularly open to the public.

II. "Library trustees" shall mean the governing board of a public library.

Source. 891, 62:3, 4, 5. 1917, 59:1.
PL 10:50. RL 15:50. RSA 202:1. 1963, 46:1, eff. July 1, 1963.

202-A: 3 Establishment. Any town may establish a public library by majority vote at any duly warned town meeting. Any town may vote in the same manner to accept a public library which has been provided, in whole or in part, by private donation or bequest and may accept any bequest, devise or donation for the establishment, maintenance and support of such a library. The powers herein granted to a town may be exercised by a city by vote of the city council.

Source. 1963, 46:1, eff. July 1, 1963.

202-A: 4 Maintenance. Any city or town having a public library shall annually raise and appropriate a sum of money sufficient to provide and maintain adequate public library service therein or to supplement funds otherwise provided.

Source. 1895, 118:1–8. 1917, 59:1. 15:51. RSA 202:2. 1963, 46:1, eff.
PL 10:51. 1927, 82:2. 1933, 60:1. RL July 1, 1963.

202-A: 4-a Cooperatives. Any public library may join library cooperatives consisting of public libraries, or of public and other than public libraries including school, college and university, and special libraries. Towns are authorized to raise and appropriate sufficient money for participation in cooperatives.

Source. 1981, 499:4, eff. Aug. 28, 1981.

202-A: 4-b Contracts for Services. Any town may contract with another town or city, or with an institution or other organization, for any library service. If a town meeting votes to enter into such a contract, the town shall raise and appropriate sufficient money to carry out the contract.

Source. 1981, 499:4, eff. Aug. 28, 1981.

202-A: 5 Status. Every public library shall remain forever free to the use of every resident of the town wherein it is located.

Source. 1891, 62:3, 4, 5. 1917, 59:1.
PL 10:50. RL 15:50. RSA 202:1. 1963, 46:1, eff. July 1, 1963.

202-A: 6 Library Trustees; Election. The library trustees shall have the entire custody and management of the public library and of all the property of the town relating thereto, except trust funds held by the town. Any town having a public library shall, at a duly warned town meeting, elect a board of library trustees consisting of any number of persons divisible by 3 which the town may decide to elect. At the first election ⅓ of the trustees shall be elected for one year, ⅓ for 2 years and ⅓ for 3 years, or until their successors are elected and qualified. Thereafter each year ⅓ of the trustees shall be elected for a term of 3 years, each, and until their successors are elected and qualified.

Source. 1917, 59:1. PL 10:52. RL 15:55. RSA 202:6. 1963, 46:1, eff. July 1, 1963.

202-A: 7 —Special Provisions. In any town where a public library has been acquired by the town, in whole or in part, by donation or bequest containing other conditions or provisions for the election of its trustees or other governing board, which conditions have been agreed to by vote of the town and which conditions do not provide for a representative of the public, a special library trustee, to represent the public, shall be elected by the town for a 3-year term. Said special trustee shall act with the other trustees.

Source. 1963, 46:1, eff. July 1, 1963.

202-A: 8 City Trustees. The trustees of a public library in a city shall be elected as provided in the city charter. In case of trustees of a city library acquired by a city in whole or in part, by donation or bequest containing other conditions or provisions for the election or appointment of trustees, which conditions do not provide for a representative of the public on the board, the city council shall elect to said board a public trustee for a 3-year term.

Source. 1963, 46:1, eff. July 1, 1963.

202-A: 10 Library Trustees; Vacancies. Vacancies occurring on any board of library trustees in a town shall be filled as provided in RSA 669: 75. A vacancy occurring among the publicly elected members of the board of library trustees of a city library shall be filled by the city council or other appropriate appointing authority within 2 months of the notice by the remaining members of the board of trustees. The board of library trustees may recommend to the appointing authority names of persons for appointment to vacancies on expired terms.

Source. 1917, 59:1. PL 10:55. RL 15:58. RSA 202:9. 1963, 46:1. 1979, 410:19, eff. July 1, 1979.

Amendments—1979. Amended section generally.

202-A: 11 Powers and Duties. Except in those cities where other provision has been made by general or special act of the legislature, the library trustees of every public library in the state shall:

I. Adopt by-laws, rules and regulations for its own transaction of business and for the government of the library;

II. Prepare an annual budget indicating what support and maintenance of the free public library will be required out of public funds for submission to the appropriate agency of the municipality. A separate budget request shall be submitted for new construction, capital improvements of existing library property;

III. Expend all moneys raised and appropriated by the town or city for library purposes. All money received from fines and payments for lost or damaged books or for the support of a library in another city or town under contract to furnish library service to such town or city, shall be used for the purchase of books and shall be held in a non-lapsing separate fund and shall be in addition to the appropriation;

IV. Expend income from all trust funds for library purposes for the support and maintenance of the public library in said town or city in accordance with the conditions of each donation or bequest accepted by the town or city;

V. Appoint a librarian who shall not be a trustee and, in consultation with the librarian, all other employees of the library and determine their compensation and other terms of employment unless, in the cities, other provision is made in the city charter or ordinances.

Source. 1917, 59:1. 1919, 35:1. PL 15:59. 1943, 90:2. RSA 202:10. 1963, 10:56. 1927, 82:4. 1933, 60:3. RL 46:1, eff. July 1, 1963.

202-A:12 Annual Reports. Every library regularly open to the public, or to some portion of the public, with or without limitations, whether its ownership is vested in the town, in a corporation, in an organization association, or in individuals, shall make a written report to the town or city at the conclusion of each fiscal year of (a) all receipts from whatever sources, (b) all expenditures, (c) all property in the trustees' care and custody, including a statement and explanation of any unexpended balance of money they may have, (d) and any bequests or donations they may have received and are holding in behalf of the town, with such recommendations in reference to the same as they may deem necessary for the town to consider, (e) the total number of books and other materials and the number added by gift, purchase and otherwise; the number lost or withdrawn, (f) the number of borrowers and readers and a statement of the use of the property of the library in furthering the educational requirements of the municipality and such other information and suggestions as may seem desirable, (g) submit a similar report to the state librarian at such time and on such forms as the state library commission may require.

Source. 1917, 59:1. PL 10:57. RL 15:60. RSA 202:11. 1963, 46:1, eff. July 1, 1963.

202-A : 13 Discretionary Powers. The library trustees shall also have the following powers:

I. To authorize the payment from library funds for the necessary expenses of library staff members attending library courses and meetings for professional advancement;

II. To extend the privileges and use of the library to nonresidents upon such terms and conditions as they may prescribe;

III. To deposit library funds for the purchase of books and related materials with the state treasurer to secure economies through pooling of purchasing with the state library. Such funds so deposited shall be held by the state treasurer in a separate account to be paid out upon orders of the state library. The state library shall have no control over the selection of items to be purchased by public libraries.

Source. 1917, 59:1. 1919, 35:1. PL 15:59. 1943, 90:2. RSA 202:10. 1963, 10:56. 1927, 82:4. 1933, 60:3. RL 46:1, eff. July 1, 1963.

202-A : 14 Compensation of Trustees. No trustee of any public library shall receive any compensation for any services rendered as such trustee, unless compensation is stipulated in the terms of the bequest or gift establishing the library. Trustees may be reimbursed, however, for necessary travel expenses to attend professional meetings.

Source. 1933, 60:4. RL 15:61. RSA 202:12. 1963, 46:1, eff. July 1, 1963.

202-A : 15 Public Librarian; Qualification and Tenure. The librarian shall have education of sufficient breadth and depth to give leadership in the use of books and related materials. He shall be appointed by the board of library trustees for a term of office agreed to at the time of employment and until his successor is appointed and qualified.

Source. 1963, 46:1, eff. July 1, 1963.

202-A : 16 —Powers and Duties. In addition to any other duties which he may be delegated from time to time, the public librarian shall:

I. Serve as the administrative officer of the public library;

II. Recommend to the board of library trustees the appointment of all employees.

Source. 1963, 46:1, eff. July 1, 1963.

202-A : 17 Employees; Removal. No employee of a public library shall be discharged or removed from office except by the library trustees for malfeasance, misfeasance, or inefficiency in office, or incapacity or unfitness to perform his duties. Prior to the discharge or removal of any such employee, a statement of the grounds and reasons therefor shall be prepared by the library trustees, and signed by a majority of the board, and notice thereof shall be given to said employee not less than 15 days nor more than 30 days prior to the effective date of such discharge or removal. Upon receipt of said notice and within 30 days thereafter, but not otherwise, the employee may request a public hearing thereon. If such request is made, the library trustees shall hold a public hearing on such discharge or removal. Said hearing shall be held not more than 30 days after receipt of the request for the same, and if the trustees, upon due hearing, shall find good cause for discharge or removal of said employee, they shall order his or her discharge or removal from office. There shall be no change in salary of such employee during the proceedings for discharge or removal nor until the final effective date of the order for discharge or removal. The provisions of this section shall apply to the employees of any public library except in a case where said city or town has personnel rules and regulations which apply to said employees and which make provision for a public hearing in the case of such discharge or removal.

Source. 1955, 18:1. RSA 202:10-a. 1963, 46:1, eff. July 1, 1963.

202-A: 18 Discontinuance of Library. Any town now maintaining a public library established by expenditure of town funds may by majority vote at a regular town meeting discontinue said library. In case of such discontinuance the library property of the town may be loaned or disposed of by the library trustees, subject to the approval of the state library commission. The provisions of this section shall not apply in cases where a public library has been acquired by the town in whole or in part by donation or bequest.

Source. 1933, 60:2. RL 15:54. RSA 202:5. 1963, 46:1, eff. July 1, 1963.

202-A: 19 Defunct Libraries. When a public library in any town shall, as such, cease to function, all books or other property given by the state for the use of said library or purchased with state funds shall be returned to the state by the selectmen of said town, delivery to be made to the state library commission, who shall have the power to retain, sell, distribute, or otherwise dispose of such returned books or property as in its judgment seems wise.

Source. 1917, 59:1. PL 10:58. 1927, 82:5. RL 15:62. RSA 202:13. 1963, 46:1, eff. July 1, 1963.

202-A: 20 Custody of Publications. Any town clerk, board of selectmen, or others having custody of the books, pamphlets, and public documents that have been sent to the towns by the departments of state government may, with consent of the librarian, transfer these publications to the public library, upon condition that they be included in the catalogues of the library and be made accessible to the public.

SOURCES: 1913, 48:1. PL 10:60. RL 15:64. RSA 202:15. 1963, 46:1, eff. July 1, 1963.

202-A: 21 Penalties. Any town or library official violating any of the provisions of this chapter shall be guilty of a misdemeanor.

Source. 1917, 59:1. PL 10:61. RL 15:65. RSA 202:16. 1963, 46:1. 1973, 529:38, eff. at 11:59 P.M., Oct. 31, 1973.

202-A: 22 Custody and Control of Trust Funds. Trust funds given to towns and cities for the use of a public library shall be held in the custody and under the management of the trustees of trust funds. The entire income from such funds shall be paid over to the library trustees. Payment of such income shall be made by the trustees of trust funds to the library trustees as the same is received.

Source. 1917, 59:1. 1919, 35:1. PL 15:59. 1943, 90:2. RSA 202:10. 1963, 10:56. 1927, 82:4. 1933, 60:3. RL 46:1, eff. July 1, 1963.

202-A: 23 —Exceptions. Nothing in this chapter shall preclude the library trustees from receiving, investing and administering directly any trust funds and donations when so specified by the donor. Library trustees administering and investing such special funds shall be governed by the provisions of RSA 31:24, 25.

Source. 1963, 46:1, eff. July 1, 1963.

202-A: 24 Offenses Against Libraries. Any person who shall wilfully or maliciously deface, damage or destroy any property belonging to or in the care of any gallery or museum or any state, public, school, college, or other institutional library, shall be guilty of a misdemeanor. Any such person shall forfeit to or for the use of such library, gallery, or museum, 3 times the amount of the damage sustained, to be recovered in an action in the superior court.

Source. 1959, 60:1. RSA 572:42-a. 1973, 529:128; 532:11, eff. Nov. 1, 1973.

202-A: 25 Detaining Books. Any person who wilfully detains any book, newspaper, magazine, manuscript, pamphlet, publication, recording, film or other property belonging to or in the care of any gallery or museum of any state, public, school, college or other institutional library, may be given written notice to return it, which shall bear upon its face a copy of this section, mailed by certified mail to his last address or delivered by a person designated by the lawful custodian of such property; and if he shall thereafter wilfully and knowingly fail to return such property within 15 days after such notice, he shall be guilty of a violation.

Source. 1959, 60:1. RSA 572:42-b.
1973, 532:11, eff. Nov. 1, 1973.

Miscellaneous Provisions
(New Hampshire Revised Statutes Annotated, 1982, s.31:19.
41:20, 41:21.)

31:19 In General. Towns may take and hold in trust gifts, legacies and devises made to them for the establishment, maintenance and care of libraries, reading-rooms, schools and other educational facilities, parks, cemeteries and burial lots, the planting and care of shade and ornamental trees upon their highways and other public places, and for any other public purpose that is not foreign to their institution or incompatible with the objects of their organization.

SOURCES: GL 49:7; 50:3. PS 40:5. 1901, 83:1. 1907, 70:1. PL 42:18. 1941, 43:1. RL 51:19.

41:20 Reports on Public Libraries. He shall, within thirty days after the annual town meeting, report to the assistant state librarian the name of any public library within the city or town; the names and post-office addresses of all the officers of each; the town, person or persons in whom the ownership of said library is vested; for whom the use is provided; and the number of volumes owned by said library. He shall make like report of the names of officers elected or appointed at any other time, immediately after their election or appointment; and, if there is no public library within the town, he shall annually, within said time, notify the assistant state librarian of the fact.

SOURCES: 1893, 31:1. PL 47:5. 1933, 69:1. RL 59:5. 1943, 90:4, eff. March 30, 1943.

41:21 — Library Defined. For the purposes of this chapter, every library regularly open to the public, or to some portion of the public, with or without limitations, shall be considered a public library, whether its ownership is vested in the town, in a corporation, in an organized association, or in individuals.

SOURCES: 1893, 31:3. PL 47:7. RL 59:6.

New Hampshire library laws are reprinted from NEW HAMPSHIRE REVISED STATUTES ANNOTATED published by The Lawyers Cooperative Publishing Co., Rochester, New York and Equity Publishing Corp., Oxford, New Hampshire.

NEW JERSEY

DIVISION OF STATE LIBRARY, ARCHIVES AND HISTORY
General Provisions
New Jersey Statutes Annotated, 1982, s.18A:73-26 to 18A:73-43.)

18A:73–26. Division continued

The Division of the State Library, Archives and History in the State Department of Education is continued.
L.1969, c. 158, § 11, eff. Sept. 9, 1969.

18A:73–27. Assistant commissioner, council and personnel

The division shall consist of an assistant commissioner a director and an advisory council and such other personnel as the Commissioner of Education may deem necessary for the efficient administration thereof.
L.1969, c. 158, § 12, eff. Sept. 9, 1969. Amended by L.1977, c. 322, § 3, eff. Jan. 10, 1978.

18A:73–28. Advisory council

There shall be within the Division of the State Library, Archives and History an advisory council which shall be designated as the Advisory Council of the Division of the State Library, Archives and History. Such advisory council shall consist of 8 members. The commissioner shall serve as a member ex officio. The other 7 members shall be appointed by the Governor by and with the advice and consent of the Senate for a term of 5 years, beginning on July 1, and ending June 30, except as hereinafter provided. The 5 appointed members serving on the effective date of this act shall continue in office for the remainder of the respective terms for which they were appointed. The 2 additional members shall be appointed one for a term ending 4 years and one for a term ending 5 years from the June 30 following the effective date of this act. Each member shall serve until his successor has been appointed and qualified. In case of a vacancy, however, occurring, the successor shall be appointed in like manner for the unexpired term only. The State Librarian shall serve in the capacity of the secretary of the council. The council shall meet at least 4 times a year. It shall frame and modify by-laws for its own government, and elect its chairman and other officers. Any member of the advisory council may be removed from office by the Governor for cause, upon notice and opportunity to be heard.

L.1969, c. 158, § 13, eff. Sept. 9, 1969.

18A:73–29. Joint meetings

The Commissioner of Education may upon his own initiative, and must at the request of any 3 members of the Advisory Council of the Division of the State Library, Archives and History, call joint meetings from time to time of all of the members of the said advisory council and all the members of the Advisory Council of the Division of the State Museum to discuss the public services of such divisions, to promote the usefulness of the bureaus thereof, and to make recommendations for the improvement of their services.

L.1969, c. 158, § 14, eff. Sept. 9, 1969.

18A:73–30. Compensation and expenses

The members of the advisory council shall serve without compensation, but shall be reimbursed for necessary expenses incurred in the peformance of their duties under this act.

L.1969, c. 158, § 15, eff. Sept. 9, 1969.

18A:73–31. Functions of advisory council

The advisory council shall give advice and make recommendations to:

(a) The Commissioner of Education with regard to the appointment of the State Librarian;

(b) The Commissioner of Education and the State Librarian with regard to

(1) The policies and operations of the Division of the State Library, Archives and History and the State's library program;

(2) The adoption, amendment or rescission of such rules and regulations as may be necessary for the implementation of this act;

(3) Minimum standards of library service;

(4) The apportionment of State aid to libraries;

(5) Contractual arrangements for library services to which the State Department of Education is a party.

L.1969, c. 158, § 16, eff. Sept. 9, 1969.

18A:73–32. Assistant commissioner; state librarian; qualifications

The assistant commissioner for ~~director of~~ the division shall be the State Librarian. ~~The Commissioner of Education, subject to the approval of the State Board of Education, shall appoint the State Librarian and fix his compensation, subject to the provisions of Title 11, Civil Service of the Revised Statutes.~~

The assistant commissioner ~~State Librarian~~ shall be a graduate of an accredited university or college and shall, prior to his appointment, have graduated from a school of library service accredited by the American Library Association, and have had at least 4 years of library experience in a responsible administrative capacity.

L.1969, c. 158, § 17, eff. Sept. 9, 1969. Amended by L.1977, c. 322, § 4, eff. Jan. 10, 1978.

18A:73–33. Duties of state librarian as head of division

The State Librarian shall head the division and shall, with the approval and under the supervision of the Commissioner of Education:

(a) Direct and administer the work of the division;

(b) Administer all laws which are by their terms included under the jurisdiction of the division;

(c) Establish and organize the bureaus therein;

(d) Allocate the duties to be performed by the personnel of the State Library and the bureaus established within the library;

(e) Prescribe such rules and regulations, not inconsistent with law, as may be necessary to effectuate his powers and duties under this act;

(f) Prescribe minimum standards of service for libraries in the State of New Jersey as may be necessary to effectuate his powers under the law.
L.1969, c. 158, § 18, eff. Sept. 9, 1969.

18A:73–34. Appointment of staff and personnel; compensation; inclusion in classified service

The Commissioner of Education shall, with the advice of the State Librarian, appoint all professional staff in the division, and fix the compensation of all such persons thus appointed. He shall appoint such other personnel as he may consider necessary for the efficient performance of the work of the division and fix their compensation. All persons thus appointed shall be subject to the provisions of Title 11, Civil Service, of the Revised Statutes.[1]

L.1969, c. 158, § 19, eff. Sept. 9, 1969.

[1] Section 11:1–1 to 11:28–3.

18A:73–35. Duties and functions of division

The division shall:

(a) Maintain library resources and information services over a broad range of subjects which affect the educational, intellectual, cultural, economic and political life of the State;

(b) Provide special library services for the legislative, executive and judicial branches of State Government, supplemental library service for New Jersey libraries and citizens and direct library service for the handicapped:

(c) Purchase or otherwise acquire, and maintain a general collection of books, periodicals, newspapers, maps, slides, films and other library materials for the use of State and local governments, libraries, and the public generally; and exchange, discard, sell, or otherwise dispose of books and library materials as required within the purposes stated herein and all moneys to be secured from such sales shall be paid into the treasury to be used for the benefit of the State Library when appropriated to that purpose;

(d) Maintain as part of the State Library, a general reference service; a legislative reference service; a law library service; a documents depository service; an archival service for New Jersey materials; a records management service for State and local governments; a deposit and exchange service for library materials; an interlibrary loan service; an advisory service for public libraries, school libraries, libraries of institutions of higher education, industrial, commercial and other special libraries, State department and agency libraries, and the libraries the State maintains within the institutions carrying out its health, welfare and correctional programs; and a library service for the handicapped; and provide such other services as may be required by law;

(e) Preserve the records of the history of New Jersey through its official archives and other materials and promote interest and research in the history of the State;

(f) Co-ordinate a State-wide system of libraries in New Jersey, and administer State and Federal programs for the development of libraries, library facilities, library resources and library services in New Jersey, and require such reports as are necessary for the proper administration of its duties and for the gathering and publishing of annual and occasional statistics on libraries in the State;

(g) Promote and demonstrate library service throughout the State, and study library problems and needs in New Jersey and make the resultant findings known generally.

L.1969, c. 158, § 20, eff. Sept. 9, 1969.

18A:73-35.1 Purchase of library materials without advertising for bids

The State Librarian may, within the limits of funds appropriated or otherwise made available to the Division of the State Library, Archives and History, purchase the following without advertising for bids: library materials including books, periodicals, newspapers, documents, pamphlets, photographs, reproductions, microfilms, pictorial or graphic works, musical scores, maps, charts, globes, sound recordings, slides, films, filmstrips, video and magnetic tapes, other printed or published matter, and audiovisual and other materials of a similar nature and necessary binding or rebinding of library materials.

L.1980, c. 149, § 1, eff. Nov. 22, 1980.

18A:73-36. Publications from custodian of State House

The State Librarian shall annually receive from the custodian of the State House for reference use and for deposit and exchange purposes not less than 75 bound copies and not less than 75 unbound copies of all pamphlet laws, compilations and similar publications, published by or under the authority of this State or the Legislature thereof, or of which the State has become a purchaser, and 75 bound copies each of the journals of the Senate and the minutes of the General Assembly.

L.1969, c. 158, § 21, eff. Sept. 9, 1969.

18A:73-37. Informative materials accessible to legislature

The State Librarian shall collect and keep up to date and readily accessible to the Legislature, and to other persons within proper regulations, such materials as will furnish the fullest information practicable pertaining to current or proposed legislation or any legislative or administrative problems, and he shall prepare and submit digests of such informative materials upon the request of any member or committee of the Legislature.

L.1969, c. 158, § 22, eff. Sept. 9, 1969.

18A:73-38. Hours of state library

The State Library shall be kept open during the normal working hours of State Government and at all times during which the Legislature and the courts of this State and of the United States which sit at Trenton are in session, and at such other times as the State Librarian, with the approval of the Commissioner of Education, shall prescribe.

L.1969, c. 158, § 23, eff. Sept. 9, 1969.

18A:73-39. Application for and acceptance of funds, books and library facilities from federal government

Subject to approval by the State Board of Education, the Commissioner

of Education may apply for and accept on behalf of the State of New Jersey and, through the Division of the State Library, Archives and History, administer for the State, any funds, books and library facilities applicable to public or school library purposes, granted or provided by the Federal Government, or any agency or officer thereof, under or pursuant to any Federal Law heretofore or hereafter enacted authorizing grants to the States for such purposes or for similar purposes.
L.1969, c. 158, § 24, eff. Sept. 9, 1969

18A:73–40. Designation of state agency to carry out purpose of law

In the event that under or pursuant to any such Federal law it is required that a State agency be designated to carry out the purpose of such law, including the administration or suspension of administration of any plan or program pursuant thereto, the State Department of Education shall be the sole agency in this State for carrying out such purposes. The Governor is hereby authorized to make such designation, and the State Department of Education is hereby empowered to act as the sole agency in this State for carrying out such purposes.
L.1969, c. 158, § 25, eff. Sept. 9, 1969.

18A:73–41. Custody and use of federal funds granted

The State Treasurer shall receive and provide for the proper custody of any funds granted by the Federal Government for such public or school library purposes, under or pursuant to any Federal law. All moneys so received shall be used exclusively for the purposes of any such law. Such moneys shall be expended in the same manner as any funds of the State are expended, upon vouchers certified or approved by the Commissioner of Education or his duly authorized representative, as provided by law.
L.1969, c. 158, § 26, eff. Sept. 9, 1969.

18A:73–42. State librarian and personnel offices upon effective date continued

The State Librarian and the other personnel holding office, position or employment upon the effective date of this amendatory and supplemental act shall continue to hold the same according to their respective terms of office or conditions of employment.
L.1969, c. 158, § 27, eff. Sept. 9, 1969.

18A:73–43. Legislative joint committee; review of library and programs; recommendations

A joint committee of the Legislature shall be appointed which shall examine and review the library and its programs, particularly the legislative reference services, make recommendations for their development and improvement, and report to the Legislature.
L.1969, c. 158, § 28, eff. Sept. 9, 1969.

Miscellaneous Provisions

(New Jersey Statutes Annotated, 1982, s.1:2-9, 52:14-20, 52:14-25.1, 52:14-25.2, 52:36-1.)

1:2–9. Bills and joint resolutions not enacted or postponed; delivery to state librarian

The secretary of the senate and the clerk of the general assembly shall, immediately after the final action of both houses, deliver to the state librarian each and every bill and joint resolution lost upon its final passage, and they shall, at the close of each session of the legislature, also deliver to the state librarian all bills laid on the table and unacted upon, together with those indefinitely postponed or postponed to the next sitting of the legislature. L.1878, c. 153, § 10, p. 228 [C.S. p. 4902, § 10].

52:14-20. Editing and printing of official reports; duties of state librarian; approval of governor

The state librarian, subject to the approval of the governor, shall critically examine, edit and prepare appropriate indexes of all official reports presented by any official, institution, board, commission or department of the state, and determine what parts, if any, and the number of copies of such reports which shall be printed. No official report shall be printed unless so examined and edited by the state librarian and approved by the governor.

This section shall not apply to any report of any legislative committee or commission. L.1931, c. 162, §§ 1, 2, p. 304.

52:14-25.1 Annual or special reports; copies filed in state library

All State officers, departments and commissions or committees issuing annual reports or special reports required by law to be submitted to the Governor or to the Legislature of this State, where such reports are printed, mineographed or otherwise mechanically reproduced, shall file with the New Jersey State Library for general reference use in said library and for exchange purposes at least 75 copies of each of such printed, mimeographed or otherwise mechanically reproduced reports, and in those cases where such reports are made in typewritten form and not subsequently printed, mimeographed or otherwise mechanically reproduced shall file in the State Library for general reference use at least one each of such typewritten reports.

L.1967, c. 162, § 1, eff. July 25, 1967.

52:14-25.2 Publication other than annual or special reports; copies filed in state library

State officers, departments, commissions or committees issuing from time to time serial or other publications of a general informational character other than annual or special reports, where such publications are printed, mimeographed or otherwise mechanically reproduced for public distribution, shall file in the State Library for permanent reference use and for exchange purposes at least 75 copies of each of such publications, and in

those cases where such serials or other publications are not printed, mimeographed or otherwise mechanically reproduced but are
issued in typewritten form, shall file in the State Library for
general reference use at least one each of such typewritten publications.   L.1967, c. 162, § 2, eff. July 25, 1967.

52:36 – 1. Powers and duties of state purchasing department and commissioner

The state purchasing department shall have the supervision
and control of the printing of :   *   *   *

d. All such official reports and documents as the state librarian may require to be printed pursuant to section 52:14–20 of
this title.   L.1931, c. 180, §§ 2, 4, pp. 407, 408, suppl. to L.1895, c. 433,
p. 824.

STATE AID
(New Jersey Statutes Annotated, 1982, s.18:74-1 to 18:74-23.)

18A:74–1. Short title

This chapter shall be known as the "state library aid law."

Source: C. 18:24A–1 (L.1959, c. 177, § 1).

18A:74–2. Terms defined

For the purposes of this chapter, unless the context clearly requires a different meaning :

"Annual expenditure for library services" shall mean the
sum expended during the last completed fiscal year by a
municipality or county for library services as certified by
the governing body of the municipality or county to the
commissioner, excluding any sum paid to the municipality
or county under the provisions of this chapter.

"Area library" shall mean any library with which the
state contracts for specialized services to all residents of an
area specified in the contract.

"Equalized valuation" shall mean the equalized valuation
of the municipality as certified by the director of the state
division of taxation for the year preceding that in which the
calculation of state aid hereunder is made.

"Per capita" shall mean for each of the number of inhabitants of a municipality or county as shown by the latest
federal census effective in this state; provided that upon
application by a municipality or county to the commissioner, any special census of population taken by the United

States census bureau subsequent to its latest effective census shall determine such number of inhabitants.

"Research library center" shall mean the state library and any other library with which the state contracts to provide special services and research information throughout the state as specified in such contract.

Source: C. 18:24A–2 (L.1959, c. 177, § 2, amended L.1959, c. 178, § 1; L.1967 c. 28, § 1).

18A:74–3. Municipalities and counties supporting libraries

State funds shall be provided annually as follows:

a. Each municipality or county that supports, in whole or in part, library service from municipal or county tax sources pursuant to chapter 33 or 54 of Title 40 of the Revised Statutes shall qualify for one of the following:

(1) $0.25 per capita if its annual expenditure for library services is less than ⅕ mill per dollar upon the equalized valuation;

(2) $0.50 per capita if its annual expenditure for library services is more than ⅕ mill, but less than ¼ mill per dollar upon equalized valuation;

(3) $0.75 per capita if its annual expenditure for library services is more than ¼ mill, but less than ⅓ mill per dollar upon equalized valuation;

(4) $1.00 per capita if its annual expenditure for library services is more than ⅓ mill, but less than ½ mill per dollar upon equalized valuation;

(5) $1.25 per capita if its annual expenditure for library services is more than ½ mill per dollar upon equalized valuation;

provided, however, that payments hereunder to a municipality or county shall not be less than the amount which such municipality or county received in State library aid in the year preceding July 1, 1967, except that in no case shall payments under this section exceed one-half of the annual expenditure for library services by the municipality or the county, as the case may be.

b. For those municipalities which provide tax support for both a local library and a county library, the per capita aid provided for in subsection a. of this section shall be determined as follows: the total expenditure for library service pursuant to chapters 33 and 54 of Title 40 of the Revised Statutes shall be used to determine the scale of per capita aid. In counties in which the free county library has been reorganized pursuant to P.L.197__, c. ___ (now pending before the Legislature as Senate Bill No. 3068) the total payment shall be made to the municipality, in all other counties the ~~The~~ payment to the municipality and to the county, respectively, shall be apportioned in the same ratio as each expenditure bears to the total expenditure.

Amended by L.1977, c. 300, § 10, eff. Dec. 16, 1977.

18A:74–4. Area libraries

Every area library shall receive annually during the term of its contract with the state a base grant of $35,000.00 plus $0.20 per capita for each person residing in the area specified in such contract.

Source: C. 18:24A–8.2 (L.1967, c. 28, § 3).

18A:74—4.1 Optical scanner to convert printed materials into synthetic speech; availability for blind and visually impaired

The Commissioner of Education after consultation with the Commission for the Blind and Visually Impaired shall purchase and provide to designated area libraries or other public facilities accessible to the blind or visually impaired that may be appropriate an optical scanner, which converts printed materials into synthetic speech for the benefit of the blind and visually impaired. The commissioner shall provide for the training of personnel in the proper use of these devices.
L.1981, c. 225, § 1, eff. July 27, 1981.

18A:74–5.   Research library centers

Every research library center shall receive an annual grant of $100,000.00 with which to provide such special services and research information throughout the state as are specified in the contract, provided that the total of such grants to research library centers shall not exceed $400,000.00 in any one year.

Source: C. 18:24A–8.3 (L.1967, c. 28, § 4).

18A:74–6.   Emergency aid; incentive grant

There shall be appropriated annually the sum of $200,000.00 to be distributed by the commissioner upon the approval of the state board and in accordance with its rules and regulations to meet unforeseeable conditions in any municipality or county, and to encourage the formation and development of larger units of service pursuant to law. The amount of such emergency aid or incentive grant shall be payable by the state treasurer upon the certification of the commissioner and the warrant of the director of the division of budget and accounting.

Source: C. 18:24A–9 (L.1959, c. 177, § 9, amended L.1966, c. 255, § 2; L.1967, c. 28, § 5).

18A:74–7.   Determination of appropriation

On or before November 15 in each year, the commissioner shall estimate the amount necessary to be appropriated to carry out the provisions of this chapter for the succeeding fiscal year and shall determine for budget purposes the amount estimated to be payable to each of the counties and municipalities under this chapter for such succeeding year. The commissioner shall make such determination for budget purposes upon the basis of the annual appropriations for library purposes for the current calendar year.

On or before September 15 of each succeeding year, the commissioner shall make his final determination of the payments to be made under this chapter upon the basis of the annual expenditures for library purposes for the preceding calendar year.

Source: C. 18:24A–10 (L.1959, c. 177, § 10, amended L.1959, c. 178, § 4; L. 1967, c. 28, § 6).

18A:74–8. Payment of state aid

The sums payable as state aid, as finally determined by the commissioner, shall be payable on October 1 following the final determination in each such year. Payments shall be made by the state treasurer upon certificate of the commissioner and warrant of the director of the division of budget and accounting. Payment shall be made to the governing body of each municipality qualifying for aid under this chapter and to the treasurer of each county which supports a regional or county library system, and to the receiving officer designated by each research library center.

Source: 18:24A–11 (L.1959, c. 177, § 11, amended L.1959, c. 178, § 5; L.1962, c. 133, § 3; L.1967, c. 28, § 7).

18A:74–9. Application of benefits to library services

Benefits received pursuant to this chapter shall not be applied to any other purpose than library services maintained pursuant to chapters 33 and 54 of Title 40 of the Revised Statutes and pursuant to this chapter.

Source: C. 18:24A–11.1 (L.1967, c. 28, § 8).

18A:74–10. Compliance with regulations

In order to participate in any apportionment made according to the provisions of this chapter, municipalities and counties shall comply with the regulations and standards which have been, or which may be, prescribed by law or recommended by the advisory council of the division of the state library, archives and history, and approved by the state board for the operation and improvement of free public libraries to provide efficient and effective library services, to insure public benefit and convenience therefrom and to achieve the objects of this chapter.

Source: C. 18:24A–12 (L.1959, c. 177, § 12, amended L.1959, c. 178, § 6; L.1967, c. 28, § 9).

18A:74–11. Annual reports

On or before March 1 in each year each library receiving state aid according to the provisions of this chapter shall make and transmit a report to the state librarian of such information, based upon the records and statistics of the preceding calendar year, as the state librarian shall require.

Source: C. 18:24A–13 (L.1959, c. 177, § 13, amended L.1962, c. 133, § 4; L.1967, c. 28, § 10).

18A:74–12.   Enforcement of law and regulations

The commissioner is hereby empowered to withhold any form of state library aid from any municipality, county, or area library which does not comply with the provisions of chapters 33 and 54 of Title 40 of the Revised Statutes and chapter 132 of the laws of 1947 (C. 45:8A–1, et seq.) wherever applicable, or with any rules and regulations duly adopted pursuant to said statutes or this chapter, or which reduces its annual expenditures for library services pursuant to chapters 33 and 54 of Title 40 of the Revised Statutes below the average of those expenditures for normal, recurring, operating costs made during the three years previous to receipt of the first state aid under this chapter.

Source: C. 18:24A–13.1 (L.1967, c. 28, § 11).

18A:74–13.   Appropriation

There is hereby appropriated for the purposes of this chapter such sums as may be included therefor in any annual or supplemental appropriation. In the event the sums appropriated at any time are insufficient to carry out in full the provisions of this chapter, the commissioner, with the approval of the state board, shall allocate such sums on the basis of the method of allocation described in this chapter to the extent that he deems advisable and practicable. A sum not to exceed 1% of such total annual or supplemental appropriation for the purposes of this chapter may be allocated by the commissioner for the administrative costs thereof.

Source: C. 18:24A–14 (L.1959, c. 177, § 14, amended L.1967, c. 28, § 12).

18A:74–14.   Short title

This act shall be known as the "New Jersey Library Construction Incentive Act."
L.1973, c. 381, § 1, eff. July 1, 1973.

18A:74–15.   Public policy

It is hereby declared to be the public policy of the State of New Jersey to encourage, promote and support the extension of public library services by aiding in the construction and expansion of public library buildings.
L.1973, c. 381, § 2, eff. July 1, 1973.

18A:74–16.   Definitions

For the purposes of this act unless the context clearly indicates otherwise:

a. "Act" means the "New Jersey Library Construction Incentive Act."

b. "Area" means all or part of one or more political subdivisions of the State of New Jersey.

c. "Project," "construction project," "rehabilitation project," "expansion" or "acquisition," means a project which is eligible for a grant under regulations and standards promulgated under this act. When used alone, "project" means any construction, expansion, or rehabilitation project or acquisition.

d. "Public library" means a library that serves free of charges all residents of an area without discrimination and receives its financial support, in whole or in part, from public funds. "Public library" does not include any special-purpose library, such as a law, medical, school or academic library, which are organized to serve a special clientele or purpose.

e. "Authorized applicant" means a public library as defined in paragraph d. hereof.

f. "Eligible project costs" means costs incurred in a project approved by the Commissioner of Education, a portion of which may be reimbursed.

g. "Commissioner" means the Commissioner of Education of the State of New Jersey or his designated representative.

h. "Fiscal year" means the period between July 1 of any calendar year and June 30 of the next succeeding calendar year.
L.1973, c. 381, § 3, eff. July 1, 1973.

18A:74-17. Administration of act

The administration of this act shall be governed by rules and regulations, recommended by the Advisory Council of the Division of the State Library, Archives and History, and promulgated by the commissioner with the approval of the State Board of Education.
L.1973, c. 381, § 4, eff. July 1, 1973.

18A:74-18. Applications for grants; compliance with rules and regulations; approval

In order to participate in any grant made according to the provisions of this act, the applicant shall comply with the rules and regulations adopted as provided in section 4 of this act. Application for grants under this act shall be made to the commissioner on forms specified in said rules and regulations. Applications shall be approved by the commissioner in accordance with said rules and regulations. The commissioner is hereby empowered to withhold any grants from any public library which does not comply with said rules and regulations.
L.1973, c. 381, § 5, eff. July 1, 1973.

18A:74-19. Reimbursement of authorized applicant for portion of its eligible project costs

The State shall reimburse each authorized applicant whose application has been approved for a portion of its eligible project costs, determined in accordance with the rules and regulations promulgated pursuant to this act.
L.1973, c. 381, § 6, eff. July 1, 1973.

18A:74-20. Project costs eligible for grants

The following project costs shall be eligible for grants, at the discretion of the commissioner, when incurred after the date of project approval, or after such date as is indicated in paragraphs 3 and 5 of this section:

a. Construction of new buildings to be used for public library purposes.

b. Expansion, rehabilitation or acquisition of existing buildings to be used for public library purposes.

c. Expenses (other than interest and the carrying charge on bonds) related to the acquisition of land on which there is to be construction of new buildings or expansion of existing buildings to be used for public library purposes which are incurred within the 3 fiscal years preceding the fiscal year in which the project is approved by the commissioner, provided such expenses constitute an actual cost or a transfer of public funds in accordance with the usual procedures generally applicable to all State and local agencies and institutions.

d. Site grading and improvement of land on which buildings used for public library purposes are located or are to be located.

e. Architectural, engineering, consulting and inspection services related to the specific project for which application for financial assistance is made, provided the costs of such services are incurred within 3 fiscal years preceding the year in which the project is approved by the commissioner.

f. Expenses (other than interest and the carrying charges on bonds) related to the acquisition of existing buildings to be used for public library purposes, provided such expenses constitute an actual cost or a transfer of public funds in accordance with the usual procedures generally applicable to all State and local agencies and institutions.

g. Expenses relating to the acquisition and installation of initial equipment to be located in public library facilities, provided by a construction project, including all necessary building fixtures and utilities, office furniture and public library equipment, such as library shelving and filing equipment, card catalogs, cabinets, circulation desks, reading tables, study carrels, booklifts, elevators and information retrieval devices (but not books or other library materials).

L.1973, c. 381, § 7, eff. July 1, 1973.

18A:74-21. Accessibility and usability of projects by handicapped persons

The commissioner shall require that projects constructed with the use of State funds under this act shall, to the extent appropriate be accessible to and usable by handicapped persons.

L.1973, c. 381, § 8, eff. July 1, 1973.

18A:74-22. Use of facilities, equipment or land for purposes not authorized by act; credit to state

Whenever public library facilities, items of equipment or land to which the State has contributed funds under this act are not used for the purposes authorized by the act, the commissioner may require that the State be credited with its proportionate share of the fair market value of such facilities, equipment, or land. All moneys so credited shall be remitted to the Treasurer of the State of New Jersey. In no event, however, may the commissioner require that the State be so credited when such facilities, equipment or land have been used in excess of 20 years for the purposes authorized by this act.

L.1973, c. 381, § 9, eff. July 1, 1973.

18A:74-23. Costs of administration and supervision of act; limitation

All costs attributable to the administration and supervision of this act and the rules and regulations promulgated thereunder shall not exceed 8% of the total amount appropriated annually for the purposes of this act.

L.1973, c. 381, § 10, eff. July 1, 1973.

CERTIFICATION OF LIBRARIANS

(New Jersey Statutes Annotated, 1982, s.45:8A-1 to 45:8A-4.)

45:8A-1. Professional librarian's certificate

The State Board of Examiners shall, upon application, issue to any person a professional librarian's certificate to act as a professional librarian if he shall be a graduate from a library school accredited by the State Board of Education and shall meet such other requirements as shall be fixed by the State Board of Education for the issuance of such certificates except that the State Board of Examiners shall, upon application, issue such certificate to any person holding, at the time this act becomes effective, a professional office, or position, that requires for adequate performance the knowledge and techniques of library science as taught in accredited library schools, in any library within this State supported in whole or in part by public funds, except in a library under the charge and control of a board of education, provided such application is made within 3 years from the effective date of this act or in the case of a veteran of World War II, such a certificate shall be issued to any person holding such a professional office or position, who has held the same since November 1, 1957, provided application is made within 30 days of the enactment of this amendatory act.

L.1947, c. 132, p. 605, § 1. Amended by L.1956, c. 152, p. 622, § 2; L.1969, c. 83, § 1, eff. June 11, 1969.

45:8A-2. Rules and regulations; fee

The State Board of Education shall make and enforce rules and regulations for the granting of such certificates for the issuance of each of which a fee of not less than $5.00 shall be charged.

L.1947, c. 132, p. 605, § 2. Amended by L.1956, c. 152, p. 622, § 3.

45:8A-3. Public library officials may require certificate; persons already employed

The officer or body having charge and control of any library within this State supported in whole or in part by public funds, except a board of education, may, in its discretion, require, and any officer or body having charge and control of any such library serving any municipality or group of municipalities having a population of 10,000 inhabitants or over, except a board of education, shall require that any person hereafter employed in such library in any professional office or position, that requires for adequate performance the knowledge and techniques of library science as taught in accredited library schools, shall hold a professional librarian's certificate issued by the State Board of Examiners as provided in this act. No such officer or body shall terminate the employment of or refuse to continue the employment or re-employment of any person holding a professional office or position at the time this act becomes effective for the reason that such person is not the holder of any such certificate. L.1947, c. 132, p. 605, § 3. Amended by L.1956, c. 152, p. 623, § 4.

45:8A-4. School district employees not exempted from other requirements

Nothing in this act shall be construed to exempt any employee of any school district from obtaining any other certificate prescribed by the State Board of Education as a requirement for the holding of any office, position, or employment in the public schools.

L.1947, c. 132, p. 606, § 4.

DISTRIBUTION OF PUBLIC DOCUMENTS
(New Jersey Statutes Annotated, 1982, s.1:2-10, 2A:12-6, 38:25-10, 52:12-6, 52:14-24, 52:14-25, 52:27B-23.)

1:2-10. Distribution of bills and resolutions to free public libraries and historical societies

There shall be distributed, at the expense of the state, to each of the free public libraries and each of the incorporated historical societies in the counties of this state one copy of every bill and joint resolution of the legislature. L.1907, c. 154, § 1, p. 392 [C.S. p. 3098, § 7], as am. by L.1913, c. 40, § 2, p. 68 [1924 Suppl. § 115-7].

2A:12-6. Distribution of law reports

The administrative director of the courts is authorized to distribute or cause to be distributed any bound volumes of the New Jersey reports and the New Jersey superior court reports heretofore or hereafter published and delivered to him, as follows:

* * * * * * * *

ac. To the state university of New Jersey, for the library at Rutgers university, 2 copies; and the law schools, 5 copies each;

ad. To the law school of Seton Hall University, 5 copies;

ae. To Princeton university, 2 copies;

af. To the library of congress, 4 copies;

ag. To the New Jersey historical society, 1 copy;

ah. To every library provided by the board of chosen freeholders of any county at the courthouse in each county, 1 copy;

ai. To the library of every county bar association in this state, 1 copy;

aj. To each incorporated library association in this state which has a law library at the county seat of the county in which it is located, 1 copy.

The remaining copies of such reports shall be retained by the administrative director for the use of the state and for such further distribution as he may determine upon.   C. 2:19A-1 and 2 (L.1950, c. 330, p. 1103, §§ 1, 2).

38:25-10. Proceedings printed and bound; distribution

The adjutant general, shall in his discretion and under his direction, order such part of the proceedings as he shall approve, to be printed and bound. A printed and bound copy thereof shall be sent to each post and to each public library of this state together with seventy-five copies for exchange under the direction of the adjutant general. There shall also be sent one hundred advance, unbound copies of the annual report of the department commander and sundry officers for the use of the annual encampment.   L.1931, c. 86, § 1, p. 146.

52:12-6. Copies for public libraries and historical societies

There shall be distributed annually, at the expense of the state, one copy of the legislative manual to each of the free public libraries and each of the incorporated historical societies in the counties of this state.   L.1907, c. 154, § 1, p. 392 [C.S. p. 3098, § 7], as am. by L.1913, c. 40, § 2, p. 68 [1924 Suppl. § 115-7].

52:14-24. Binding and distribution of official reports

The custodian of the state house shall, under the direction and control of the state house commission, cause to be bound in plain and substantial binding so many of the printed copies of the various official reports and legislative documents as the state house commission shall direct, which bound copies shall be distributed by the custodian as follows:

a.   To the librarian of the congressional library at Washington, four copies.

b.   To the librarians of the theological seminaries at Princeton and New Brunswick, each one copy.

c.   To the state librarian, twenty copies.

d.   The remainder shall be distributed as the state house commission shall direct.   L.1931, c. 184, § 6. p. 415.

52:14-25. Distribution to public libraries and historical societies

There shall be distributed, at the expense of the state, to each of the free public libraries and to each of the incorporated historical societies in the counties of the state, one copy of every report, testimony, pamphlet or other publication printed or published by or under the direction of the state, or any officer thereof, and also one copy of any publication purchased by or under the direction of the state for distribution. L.1907, c. 154, § 1, p. 392 [C.S. p. 3098, § 7], as am. by L.1913, c. 40, § 2, p. 68 [1924 Suppl. § 115–7].

52:27B–23. Copies of budget message to be distributed

The commissioner shall cause copies of the budget message to be printed forthwith and a copy thereof shall be presented to each member of the Legislature, public libraries in the State and each newspaper in the State, and shall be available for distribution to any citizen on request. L.1944, c. 112. art. 3, p. 296, § 14.

PUBLIC RECORDS

(New Jersey Statutes Annotated, 1982, s.43:3-15 to 43:3-30.)

47:3–15. Short title

This act shall be known and cited as "Destruction of Public Records Law (1953)." L.1953, c. 410, p. 2061, § 1.

47:3–16. "Public records" and "bureau" defined

As used in this act, except where the context indicates otherwise, the words "public records" mean any paper, written or printed book, document or drawing, map or plan, photograph, microfilm, sound-recording or similar device, or any copy thereof which has been made or is required by law to be received for filing, indexing, or reproducing by any officer, commission, agency or authority of the State or of any political subdivision thereof, including subordinate boards thereof, or that has been received by any such officer, commission, agency or authority of the State or of any political subdivision thereof, including subordinate boards thereof, in connection with the transaction of public business and has been retained by such recipient or its successor as evidence of its activities or because of the information contained therein.

As used in this act the word "bureau" means the Bureau of Archives and History in the Department of Education. L.1953, c. 410, p. 2061, § 2.

47:3–17. Consent of bureau to disposition or destruction of public records or documents

No person shall destroy, sell or otherwise dispose of any public record, archives or printed public documents which are under his control or in his care or custody, whether or not they are in current use, without first having advised the Bureau of Archives and History in the Department of Education of their nature, and obtained the written consent of that bureau; which consent may be given by said bureau only if the same is in conformance with regulations governing the granting thereof which shall be made and promulgated by the State Records Committee established by section six of this act. L.1953, c. 410, p. 2062, § 3.

47:3–18. Classifications and categories

The bureau may from time to time establish specific classifications and categories for various types of the said "public records" and, in giving its consent as provided herein, may do so in a general and continuing manner according to the said classifications and categories. L.1953, c. 410, p. 2062, § 4.

47:3–19. Schedules

The bureau, in co-operation with the several State departments, commissions and agencies, shall make a study of the kind and character of public records in their control or custody and shall prepare proposed schedules for submission to the State Records Committee established by section six hereof for its approval and advise the said several departments, commissions and agencies of all applicable operative schedules. L.1953, c. 410, p. 2062, § 5.

47:3-20. State Records Committee; approval of schedule; regulations

No such schedule shall be operative unless approved by the State Records Committee which is hereby established in the State Department of Education and which shall consist of the State Treasurer, the Attorney-General, the State Auditor, the Director of the Division of Local Government in the Department of the Treasury, and the head of the Bureau of Archives and History in the Department of Education. Each member of the committee may designate in writing a representative to act in his place on said committee.

The State Records Committee shall have the powers and duties prescribed for it herein and shall make and promulgate such regulations, not inconsistent with law, as may be necessary to adequately effectuate such powers and duties. L.1953, c. 410, p. 2062, § 6.

47:3-21. Schedule; filing of copy; retention of original

Whenever any such schedule is approved by the committee, a copy thereof shall be filed with the State department, commission or agency involved and with the State Auditor, and the original approval shall be retained by the Bureau of Archives and History in the Department of Education. Thereupon, such schedule shall remain in force and effect and may be acted upon by the said department, commission or agency until superseded by a subsequent duly approved schedule. L.1953, c. 410, p. 2063, § 7.

47:3-22. Liability of officials and others for destruction of public records

No State official, or head of a State department, commission or other agency shall be held liable on his official bond, or in the way of damages for loss, or in any other manner, civil or criminal, because of the destruction of public records pursuant to the provisions of this act or any other law authorizing such destruction. L.1953, c. 410, p. 2063, § 8.

47:3-23. Cancelled bonds and other evidences of indebtedness; destruction

Whenever, under the laws of this State, there shall have been issued and sold by the State or by any municipality, county, or school district, bonds, coupons, or other evidences of indebtedness and such bonds, coupons and other evidences of indebtedness shall have been cancelled and redeemed by the State Treasurer, the State House Commission, or by any agency or authorized official of the State, or by any municipality, county, or school district issuing the same, it shall be lawful for the official or officials in charge of the issuance, redemption and cancellation of such bonds, coupons or other evidences of indebtedness to destroy the same upon the written consent of the bureau, subject to regulations which shall be made and promulgated by the State Records Committee established by section six hereof.

The said officials, in the same manner, may destroy any bonds, coupons or other evidences of indebtedness which have been printed and which remain unused, or any registered bonds which remain unused at the time the issue has completely matured. L.1953, c. 410, p. 2063, § 9.

47:3-24. Time for destruction or other disposition of bonds and other evidences of indebtedness

The bureau, subject to regulations which shall be made and promulgated by the State Records Committee established by section six hereof, may give its consent to the immediate destruction or other disposition of bonds, coupons or other evidences of indebtedness which have not been used, but shall not consent to the destruction or other disposition of temporary bonds unless they have been replaced by definitive bonds, and then, only after the expiration of a year from the date of such replacement, or to the destruction or other disposition of bonds, coupons or other evidences of indebtedness which have been issued, except after the expiration of a period of seven years from their cancellation or maturity dates. L.1953, c. 410, p. 2064, § 10.

47:3–25. Certificate of destruction; filing; evidence

Whenever bonds, coupons or other evidences of indebtedness are destroyed or otherwise disposed of under the provisions of this section, a certificate of destruction shall be prepared by the official having charge of such destruction or other disposition, setting forth the dates of issuances, the series and serial numbers and the face amounts of such bonds, coupons or other evidences of indebtedness.

Where the said certificates relate to State issues, they shall be filed in the office of the Secretary of State and where they relate to county or municipal issues, they shall be filed in the office of the chief financial officer of the county or municipality, as the case may be. Any such certificate or certified copy thereof shall be receivable in evidence in any court or proceeding as prima facie evidence of the destruction of such bonds, coupons or other evidences of indebtedness. L.1953, c. 410, p. 2064, § 11.

47:3–26. Photographing, microphotographing and microfilming of public records; destruction of originals; evidence

The Bureau of Archives and History in the Department of Education, with the approval of the State Records Committee established by section six hereof, shall formulate standards and procedures for the photographing, microphotographing and microfilming of public records and for the preservation, examination and use of such records, including the indexing and arrangement thereof, for convenient reference purposes.

Whenever any officer, commission, agency or authority of the State or of any political subdivision thereof, including subordinate boards thereof, shall have photographed, microphotographed or microfilmed all or any part of the public records, kept or required by law to be received and indexed in such manner as to conform with the standards and procedures, and such photographs, microphotographs or microfilms have been placed in conveniently accessible files and provision shall have been made for the preservation, examination and use of the same in conformity with the said standards and procedures, the original records from which the photographs, microphotographs or microfilms have been made, or any part thereof, may be destroyed or the records therein otherwise effectively obliterated; *provided*, the said bureau shall first have given its written consent to such destruction or other disposition.

In the event of any such destruction or other disposition of any public records under the provisions of this section, the photograph, microphotograph or microfilm, or a certified copy of said photograph, microphotograph or microfilm, shall be receivable in evidence in any court or proceeding and shall have the same force and effect as though the original public record had been there produced and proved. L.1953, c. 410, p. 2065, § 12.

47:3–27. Public records in private possession, bureau may demand

The bureau is empowered to demand and receive from any person any public record in private possession belonging to this State, or to any county, municipality or school district thereof. L.1953, c. 410, p. 2066, § 13.

47:3–28. Public records in private possession, person entitled to custody may demand

Any person who is entitled by law to the custody of public records shall demand the same from any person in whose possession they may be, and such records forthwith shall be delivered to the officer charged by law with their custody. L.1953, c. 410, p. 2066, § 14.

47:3–29. Removal, alteration or destruction of public records with malicious intent

Any person who ~~unlawfully keeps in his possession any public record, or alters, defaces, mutilates or destroys with malicious intent~~, without the consent of the person authorized to have custody thereof, removes an official record or paper from the files of any public agency or body, or who alters any map, plat, or other paper signed and approved by a public official without permission, or who alters, defaces, mutilates or destroys with malicious intent any public record shall be guilty of a high misdemeanor. L.1953, c. 410, p. 2066, § 15. Amended by L.1968, c. 465, § 1, eff. Feb. 21, 1969.

47:3–30. Rules and regulations

The bureau shall, with the approval of the State Records Committee established by section six hereof, make and promulgate rules and regulations for the effective administration of the laws relating to public records. L.1953, c. 410, p. 2066, § 16.

REGIONAL LIBRARIES
(New Jersey Statutes Annotated, 1982, s.40:33-13.3 to 40:33-13.18.)

40:33–13.3   Establishment by joint agreement

Any 2 or more counties may, by joint agreement adopted by similar resolutions of their boards of chosen freeholders, provide for the establishment and maintenance of a regional library for the use and benefit of the residents of the municipalities within said counties. L.1962, c. 134, § 1, eff. July 27, 1962.

40:33–13.4   Provisions of agreement

The regional library agreement shall provide for:

(a) the establishment and maintenance of a regional library upon the approval of such agreement by such counties as the agreement shall provide;

(b) a proposed initial budget for the regional library;

(c) the apportionment of the initial, annual and other appropriations for the regional library among the participating counties and the factor or factors upon which such apportionments shall be based;

(d) the withdrawal of any participating county from such agreement, the termination of the regional library and the apportionment of all assets and obligations of the regional library among the participating counties in the event of such withdrawal or termination;

(e) the number and initial terms of the members of the board of trustees of the regional library within the limits set forth in this act; and

(f) such other matters not inconsistent with the provisions of this act as may be necessary or desirable to accomplish the objectives of this act. L.1962, c. 134, § 2, eff. July 27, 1962.

40:33–13.5   Amendment of agreement; filing copy

The regional library agreement may, from time to time, be amended or supplemented by the adoption of similar resolutions by all the boards of chosen freeholders of the participating counties. A copy of the original regional library agreement, of any amendments or supplements thereto and of the resolutions approving such agreement, amendments or supplements shall be filed with the Commissioner of Education and with the Director of the Division of Local Government. L.1962, c. 134, § 3, eff. July 27, 1962.

40:33–13.6   Resolution; public inspection; publication

Upon the introduction of a resolution approving such agreement, or any amendment or supplement thereto, such resolutions, agreement, amendment, or supplement shall be and remain on file for public inspection in the office of the clerk of the board of chosen freeholders. Such resolution shall be published at least once 2 weeks or more before final consideration and passage in a newspaper published in the county or having a substantial circulation therein. L.1962, c. 134, § 4, eff. July 27, 1962.

40:33–13.7   Board of trustees; membership; appointment; vacancies; compensation

The regional library shall be under the management and control of a board of trustees to be designated as "the trustees of the .... (names of the participating counties) regional library" or by other appropriate designation. The board of trustees shall consist of 1, 2 or 3 members from each of the participating counties, as provided in the agreement. The trustees shall be appointed by the respective boards of chosen freeholders for 5-year terms ending on December 31. Vacancies shall be filled for the unexpired term only. No trustee shall be appointed to more than 2 consecutive 5-year terms. Trustees shall serve without compensation.

The initial terms of the trustees shall be so fixed in the joint library agreement to insure that no 2 terms of the trustees appointed from any one county shall expire in the same year, and, as nearly as may be, that the least possible number of terms of all the trustees shall expire in the same year. L.1962, c. 134, § 5, eff. July 27, 1962.

40:33-13.8 Organization of board; officers; term of office

The board of trustees shall organize annually and elect, from among its members, a president and vice-president. It shall also appoint a treasurer and secretary. The treasurer may be treasurer of one of the participating counties. All officers shall serve for 1 year and until their successors are elected. L.1962, c. 134, § 6, eff. July 27, 1962.

40:33-13.9 Board as body public and corporate; powers

The board of trustees shall be a body public and corporate and may:

(a) sue and be sued;

(b) adopt a corporate seal;

(c) hold in trust and manage all property of the regional library;

(d) acquire and dispose of any real and personal property, including books and all other library materials, by purchase, sale, gift, lease, bequest, device [1] or other similar manner for its corporate purposes;

(e) employ and fix the compensation of a library director, to whom it shall delegate the administrative responsibilities of the library, and such other professional librarians and other employees it deems necessary;

(f) adopt rules and regulations and do all things necessary for the proper establishment and operation of the library;

(g) contract with other counties, municipalities, library boards of trustees and other agencies for the furtherance of its purpose; and

(h) invest any funds in the same manner as the governing body of a municipality is authorized by law to invest moneys held by it. L.1962, c. 134, § 7, eff. July 27, 1962.

[1] Probably should read "devise".

40:33-13.10 Annual reports

The board of trustees shall make annual reports to the boards of chosen freeholders of the participating counties, to the governing bodies of such municipalities with which it has contractual arrangements to provide library services and to the boards of trustees of public libraries within such municipalities. L.1962, c. 134, § 8, eff. July 27, 1962.

40:33–13.11 Proposal of sum required for operation and expenses; objections; determination

The board of trustees shall annually, not later than November 1, propose to the boards of chosen freeholders of each of the participating counties the total sum required for the operation and other expenses of the library for the ensuing calendar year, including such sums proposed for the acquisition of lands or buildings or the improvement thereof, and that part of this total sum to be provided by each such county in accordance with the method of apportionment provided in the regional library agreement. If any board of chosen freeholders shall object to the amount or apportionment so proposed, the director thereof shall confer with the directors of the boards of chosen freeholders of the other participating counties and with the board of trustees. If, thereafter, any such director of a board of chosen freeholders shall object to such amount or apportionment, the matter shall be referred by said respective directors to their boards of chosen freeholders for determination. Such determination shall be made on the basis of fairness and equity, to promote the objectives of this act and the terms of the regional library agreement and to insure the public interest. L.1962, c. 134, § 9, eff. July 27, 1962.

40:33–13.12 Assessment and levy of taxes

Each board of chosen freeholders shall certify to its county board of taxation the sum to be provided by that county as certified or determined pursuant to section 8 of this act. The county board of taxation shall apportion such sum, in accordance with the provisions of section 54:4–49 of the Revised Statutes, among the municipalities within that county served by the regional library pursuant to the regional library agreement. The amounts thus apportioned shall be assessed, levied and collected in each such municipality in the same manner and at the same time as other county taxes are assessed, levied, and collected. Each such county shall pay over the sum so collected, in quarterly installments on February 15, May 15, August 15 and November 15 of each year, to the treasurer of the regional library. L.1962, c. 134, § 10, eff. July 27, 1962.

40:33–13.13 Duties of treasurer; annual audit

The treasurer of the board of trustees shall receive and hold, in behalf of the board, all funds of the library and shall pay out or transfer such funds, as directed by resolution of the board of trustees, by check signed by him and countersigned by the president of the board of trustees or other trustee or trustees designated by the board of trustees. The treasurer shall give adequate bond or bonds, conditioned for the faithful performance and discharge of his duties, payable to the board of trustees and to the participating counties, in an amount or amounts required by the board of trustees. All accounts and financial transactions of the regional library shall be audited annually by a registered municipal accountant of New Jersey and filed with the Director of the Division of Local Government on or before May 31. L.1962, c. 134, § 11, eff. July 27, 1962.

40:33–13.14 Agreements with municipalities not served by regional library

The board of trustees may enter into agreements with the governing body of any municipality which is not then served by the regional library to increase or improve the library services available to the residents of said municipality or to the residents of the municipalities then served by the regional library. Any such agreement shall specify the services to be rendered by the regional library and by the municipality and the amount and nature of payment of any consideration for such services. Any municipality may enter into such agreements with the board of trustees for periods of not more than 5 years and may renew such agreements for like periods.

No such agreement shall be concluded (a) without the approval of the boards of chosen freeholders of the counties participating in the regional library and, (b) in the event that the municipality maintains a municipal public library, without the approval of the board of trustees of such library. Such agreement may be amended and supplemented, from time to time, and a copy of such agreement, amendments and supplements, together with resolutions of the board of trustees approving such agreement, amendments and supplements, shall be filed with the Commissioner of Education and with the Director of the Division of Local Government. L.1962, c. 134, § 12, eff. July 27, 1962.

40:33–13.15 Disposition of revenues

Money paid to the regional library for lost or damaged books or other library materials, for use of "pay" or "rental" collections and for the sale of library books or other library property shall be held by the board of trustees and spent only for the purchase of books or other materials or for the replacement of library property.

Fines, nonresident fees and other miscellaneous revenue received by the regional library shall be turned over to the treasurers of the participating counties in proportionate shares as stipulated in the regional library agreement or in accordance with the apportionment of annual appropriations set forth therein. Each board of chosen freeholders of the participating counties may, by resolution, reappropriate the sums so received to the board of trustees, in addition to the other moneys appropriated for regional library purposes. L.1962, c. 134, § 13, eff. July 27, 1962.

40:33–13.16   County library commission; termination; assets and obligations

Upon the establishment of a regional library, the terms of office of all members of any county library commission of any participating county shall terminate. The assets and obligations of any such commission and of the county library under its supervision shall devolve upon such county, unless otherwise provided in the regional library agreement. L.1962, c. 132, § 14, eff. July 27, 1962.

40:33–13.17   Regional library as "public agency or organization" within Public Employees' Retirement Act

Any regional library established pursuant to this act shall be deemed a "public agency or organization" as that term is used in the Public Employees' Retirement Act (P.L.1954, c. 84) and as defined in section 71 of said Act. L.1962, c. 134, § 15, eff. July 27, 1962.

40:33–13.18   Withdrawal of participating county

If the board of chosen freeholders of any participating county shall determine by resolution to withdraw its participation in the support, maintenance and control of the regional library, it shall give notice thereof to the boards of chosen freeholders of other participating counties and to the board of trustees of the regional library. The directors of all boards of chosen freeholders participating in the regional library and the board of trustees shall confer as soon as practicable for the purpose of reaching an agreement among the participating counties as to the time and method of withdrawal by such county, the use of the library facilities thereafter, the adjustment, apportionment, accounting for, settlement, allowance and satisfaction of the rights and liabilities in or with respect to any property, obligations or other matters or things connected with said library and any other matters relating to the regional library. If said boards of chosen freeholders shall be unable to agree as to the terms and conditions of such withdrawal, the matter shall be referred by the board of chosen freeholders of the county which has adopted a resolution to withdraw to the Director of the Division of Local Government for determination on the basis of fairness and equity, the objectives of this act and the regional library agreement, and the public interest. Upon final approval of the resolution or determination by the Director of the Division of Local Government, the participation of the county in the support, maintenance and control in the regional library shall terminate in accordance with the terms of the withdrawal agreement or determination. L.1962, c. 134, § 16, eff. July 27, 1962.

COUNTY LIBRARIES

(New Jersey Statutes Annotated, 1982, s.44:33-1 to 44:33-13.2 n, 40:33-15 to 40:22-23.)

40:33–1. County library; establishment

The board of chosen freeholders of every county shall, in the manner hereinafter in this article provided, establish a free public library to be known as "the free county library". This library shall be established for such subdivisions of the county as do not maintain and control free public libraries, pursuant to the provisions of chapter 54 of this title (§ 40:54–1 et seq.).

Source. L.1920, c. 122, § 1, p. 257, as am. by L.1923, c. 107, § 1, p. 199 [1924 Suppl. § 48–*1750F(1)].

40:33–2. Referendum

No such library shall be established until assented to by the legal voters of the county at any election at which the question of the establishment thereof shall be submitted. In counties which have heretofore adopted the provisions of an act entitled "An act to provide for the establishment and maintenance of county free libraries," approved April seventh, one thousand nine hundred and twenty, the referendum election provided for herein need not be held and the provisions of this article shall apply to such counties. **Source.** L.1920, c. 122, § 2, p. 258 [1924 Suppl. § 48–*1750F(2)].

40:33–3. Petition for submission

At the request in writing of not less than three hundred qualified voters of the county, the board of chosen freeholders shall submit, at any general or special election, the question of the establishment of such library to the voters of the county for adoption or rejection.

Source. L.1920, c. 122, § 3, p. 258 [1924 Suppl. § 48–*1750F(3)].

40:33–4. Ballot; form and content

The board of chosen freeholders shall cause the question to be printed upon the ballots to be used at such election, in substantially the following form:

"To vote upon the public question printed below, if in favor thereof mark a cross (×) or plus (+) in the square at the left of the word YES, and if opposed thereto mark a cross (×) or plus (+) in the square at the left of the word NO.

☐ YES

☐ NO

"Shall the provisions of article 1 of chapter 33 of the title Municipalities and Counties of the Revised Statutes (§ 40:33–1 et seq.), providing for the establishment and maintenance of county free libraries, be adopted?"

Source. L.1920, c. 122, § 3, p. 258 [1924 Suppl. § 48–*1750F(3)].

40:33–5. Results canvassed and returned; vote required for adoption

The result of the election shall be returned and canvassed in the same manner and at the same time as other elections. If a majority of the votes cast on the question shall be in favor thereof the provisions of this article shall take effect in the county.

Source. L.1920, c. 122, § 3, p. 258 [1924 Suppl. § 48–*1750F(3)].

40:33–5.1 Establishment by resolution in counties under 150,000

The board of chosen freeholders of any county with a population of less than 150,000 which, on the effective date of this act, has not established a free county library pursuant to the provisions of article 1, chapter 33 of Title 40 of the Revised Statutes, may, by resolution, establish such a library for all the municipalities within the county. All libraries established pursuant to this act shall be governed by the provisions of article 1, chapter 33, Title 40 of the Revised Statutes insofar as they are not inconsistent with the provisions of this act. L.1963, c. 46, § 1, eff. May 25, 1963.

40:33-6. Arrangement for library; independently operated county library; plan for financing

Upon the adoption of the provisions of this article the board of chosen freeholders may contract with an existing library, or library board, within the county or the library commission of a county library already established and furnishing county library services in another county, for the establishment and maintenance of the county free library in accordance with the provisions of this article and subject to the rules and regulations of the board of chosen freeholders. No independently operated county library shall be established hereafter in any county unless a plan for the financing of the same, indicating the amount annually to be assessed, levied and collected in taxes for the establishment and thereafter for the maintenance, thereof, shall be submitted to, and shall be approved as sufficient by, the head of the bureau of public and school library services in the Division of the State Library, Archives and History in the Department of Education. As amended L.1950, c. 189, p. 423, § 1, eff. June 7, 1950.

40:33-7. Library commission; membership; term; vacancies; no compensation

a. Should the board of chosen freeholders governing body not enter into the contract provided for in section 40:33-6 of this Title, it shall within 60 days after this article becomes operative, appoint a commission to be known as "the county library commission." The commission shall consist of five members. On the first commission one member shall be appointed for 1 year; one for 2 years; one for 3 years; one for 4 years and one for 5 years, and thereafter all appointments shall be for terms of 5 years, except in the case of appointments to fill vacancies occurring other than by expiration of term, which vacancies shall be filled in the same manner as appointments are made, but for the unexpired terms only. The county library commission shall serve without compensation.

b. In addition to the members appointed pursuant to subsection a. above, the governing body may appoint two additional members for terms of 4 and 5 years respectively. Thereafter all future appointments shall be for terms of 5 years, except for vacancies which shall be filled for the unexpired terms only.
Amended by L.1981, c. 564, § 1, eff. Jan. 18, 1982.

40:33-8. Organization of commission; powers and duties; reports

The county library commission shall organize by the election of a chairman, and shall adopt rules and regulations for the establishment and maintenance of the county library. It shall employ a librarian, and such professional library assistants, if any, as may be required, who shall hold appropriate certificates issued by the State Board of Examiners and such other employees as it shall deem necessary for the performance of its functions. It may purchase such supplies and equipment and incur such expenses as it may deem necessary to carry out the provisions of this article, but shall not incur expenses or make purchases in any fiscal year from public funds in excess of the appropriation for county library purposes for that year. In addition to its other powers, it may accept gifts, devises, legacies and bequests of property, real and personal, and hold and use the property and income of the same in any manner, which is lawful and consistent with the purpose for which the commission is created, and with the provisions of the conveyance, will or other instrument in or under which such gift, devise, legacy or bequest is made and may dispose of the same subject to the same conditions. It shall make an annual report to the county board of freeholders. As amended L.1950, c. 189, p. 424, § 3, eff. June 7, 1950.

Source. L.1920, c. 122, § 6, p. 259, as am. by L.1922, c. 92, § 1, p. 169 [1924 Suppl. § 48–*1750F(6)].

40:33–8.1 Purchases not requiring advertisements for bids

The county library commission of any county or the board of trustees of any regional library established by 2 or more counties may, within the limits of funds appropriated or otherwise made available to the commission or board, purchase the following without advertising for bids therefor: (1) library materials including books, periodicals, newspapers, documents, pamphlets, photographs, reproductions, microforms, pictorial or graphic works, musical scores, maps, charts, globes, sound recordings, slides, films, filmstrips, video and magnetic tapes, other printed or published matter, and audiovisual and other materials of a similar nature; (2) necessary binding or rebinding of library materials; and (3) specialized library services.
L.1968, c. 227, § 1, eff. July 31, 1968.

40:33–9. Appropriations for establishment and maintenance; amount

Upon the adoption of the provisions of this article, the board of chosen freeholders shall determine a sum sufficient for the establishment and, annually thereafter, for the maintenance of the library. The sum so to be raised shall be certified by the board of chosen freeholders to the county board of taxation, which shall apportion such amount among the municipalities receiving the benefits of this article in accordance with the provisions of section 54:4–49 of the Revised Statutes. The sum so raised shall be not less than 1/15 of a mill per dollar on the "apportionment valuation," as defined in section 54:4–49 of the Revised Statutes, of the municipalities receiving the benefits of this article. The amount thus apportioned to each municipality shall be assessed, levied and collected in the same manner and at the same time as other county taxes are assessed, levied and collected therein. As amended L.1957, c. 14, p. 32, § 1, eff. April 3, 1957.

Source. L.1920, c. 122, § 7, p. 259, as am. by L.1923, c. 107, § 2, p. 199 [1924 Suppl. § 48–*1750F(7)].

40:33–10. Borrowing money in anticipation of library taxes; tax notes

The board of chosen freeholders may borrow money, in anticipation of the receipt of taxes levied for county library purposes, not in excess of the amount levied in any year for such purposes, and may issue notes therefor. Notes issued for this purpose shall be termed "county library tax anticipation notes" and shall be issued as other notes of the county are issued in anticipation of county taxes. The notes shall be paid on or before December thirty-first of the year in which and for which they are issued. They shall bear interest at a rate of not more than six per cent per annum and the interest and principal thereof shall be paid from the funds of the county library.

Source. L.1920, c. 122, § 7, p. 259, as am. by L.1923, c. 107, § 2, p. 199 [1924 Suppl. § 48–*1750F(7)].

40:33–11. Tax revenue notes or bonds for delinquent taxes

The board of chosen freeholders may issue tax revenue notes or tax revenue bonds for the county library tax which has become delinquent for the amount of such delinquent tax. Loans of this class shall be evidenced by the issue of "tax revenue notes" or "tax revenue bonds", and when issued shall be governed by the conditions set forth in sections 40:2–48 to 40:2–51 of this title, governing "tax revenue notes" or "tax revenue bonds".

Source. L.1920, c. 122, § 7, p. 259, as am. by L.1923, c. 107, § 2, p. 199 [1924 Suppl. § 48–*1750F(7)].

40:33–12. County treasurer custodian of library funds; payment of bills

The county treasurer shall be the custodian of the county library tax collected and of all other funds or moneys of the commission, and upon receipt of bills properly authorized by the commission, payment thereof shall be made if sufficient funds are on hand. As amended L.1950, c. 189, p. 424, § 4, eff. June 7, 1950.

Source. L.1920, c. 122, § 7, p. 259, as am. by L.1923, c. 107, § 2, p. 199 [1924 Suppl. § 48-*1750F(7)].

40:33-13.   Participation by municipalities

When any municipality, maintaining a public library and situte   in a county which has adopted a county library system under the provisions of this article, desires to participate in the benefits of this article, the governing body thereof, by resolution, may apply to the county library commission of such county to be included in the county library system, and the municipality shall be admitted to said county library system upon such terms and conditions as may be agreed upon by the governing body thereof and the county library commission of the county, not inconsistent with the provisions of this act ; *provided,* and so long as provision is made for assessing, levying and collecting within the municipality the special tax assessed, levied and collected in the other municipalities served by such county library system and thereafter such municipal public library shall continue to be operated as a municipal public library under its own governing board or body and shall be entitled to receive municipal appropriations notwithstanding its inclusion in the county library system and shall be entitled to receive from the county library system the same book loan, advisory, and other services as are received by the other municipalities within said system.   As amended L.1950, c. 189, p. 425, § 5, eff. June 7, 1950.

Source. L.1920, c. 122, § 8, p. 259 [1924 Suppl. § 48-*1750F(8)].

40:33-13.1   Contracts with other municipalities for additional library service

The governing body of any municipality which forms part of a county library system may, by resolution, contract with any other municipality which maintains a free public library, for the furnishing of additional library service to the inhabitants of the first municipality, and may appropriate annually for this purpose, such sum of money as may be agreed upon between the contracting parties, which sum shall be in addition to the amount raised annually in such municipality for the support of the county library system.   L.1951, c. 101, p. 506, § 1, eff. May 22, 1951.

40:33-13.2   Use of money received under contract

The governing body of such other municipality may, by resolution, enter into contract as provided in this act and all sums of money paid under such contract shall be appropriated and used for library purposes in accordance with the terms of said contract. L.1951, c. 101, p. 506, § 2, eff. May 22, 1951.

40:33–13.2b Agreements with respect to provision, leasing, use, operation or maintenance; payments on account

Said board of chosen freeholders and any county library commission, governing body of any municipality or board of trustees of any free public library in the county are hereby authorized and empowered to enter into agreements with respect to provision, leasing, use, operation or maintenance of all or any part of such real property, buildings or facilities, and for payments on account of any cost or expense or the use or services thereof, or the establishment or provision of such free county library or free county library services. Any such contract may be made with or without consideration and for an unspecified or unlimited period of time and on any terms and conditions therein set forth and shall be valid and binding on the parties thereto whether or not appropriation with respect thereto shall have been made prior to authorization or execution thereof. L.1966, c. 223, § 2, eff. Aug. 10, 1966.

40:33–13.2a Authority to acquire real property or other interest; maintaining facilities; bonds; ad valorem taxes

Notwithstanding the provisions of any other law, the board of chosen freeholders of any county is hereby authorized and empowered to acquire real property or any interest therein by purchase, condemnation, gift or otherwise, and to lease as lessor or as lessee, and to purchase, construct, reconstruct, enlarge, alter or improve, and to furnish and equip, and to operate and maintain, any buildings or facilities which are necessary or desirable in the judgment of said board for the purpose of establishing or providing a free county library or free county library services for the use of residents and inhabitants of the county, or jointly for such purpose and for any other county purpose or use, and to raise and appropriate moneys therefor in the same manner as moneys are raised and appropriated for other county purposes pursuant to the Local Budget Law, and to issue bonds or other obligations of the county for such purpose pursuant to

the Local Bond Law and to levy ad valorem taxes upon all the taxable **property** within the county for the payment of the principal **of and** interest on such bonds or other obligations without limitation **as** to rate or amount.   L.1966, c. 223, § 1, eff. Aug. 10, 1966.

40:33-13.2c Employee of county library system formerly employee of municipal free public library; classified service

Any former employee of a municipal free public library who has become an employee of a county library system pursuant to an agreement providing for the admission or merger of the municipal free public library to or into the county library system, shall be placed in the classified service of the civil service of the county, subject to individual entry qualifying examinations. Those employees so placed shall continue in the position in which employed at the time of the admission or merger and shall be subject to all provisions of Subtitle 3 of Title 11 (Civil Service) of the Revised Statutes.

As used in this act;

"Municipal free public library" means a free public library established pursuant to Article 1 of chapter 54 of Title 40 of the Revised Statutes by a municipality in which the provisions of Subtitle 3 of Title 11 (Civil Service) of the Revised Statutes have not been adopted;

"County library system" means a county library system established and organized pursuant to Article 1 of chapter 33 of Title 40 of the Revised Statutes in a county in which the provisions of Subtitle 3 of Title 11 (Civil Service) have been adopted.

L.1978, c. 23, § 1, eff. May 23, 1978.

40:33-13.2d Short title

This act shall be known and may be cited as the "County Library Reorganization Law."

L.1981, c. 489, § 1, eff. Jan. 12, 1982.

40:33-13.2e County library study commission; establishment; petition; members; chairman; reimbursement of expenses

The governing body of any county which has established a county library as provided in chapter 33 of Title 40 of the Revised Statutes may, by ordinance or resolution, as appropriate, establish a county library study commission to consider and make findings concerning the county library system. The governing body shall establish such a commission when it receives a petition calling for the creation of a county library study commission signed by 10% of the registered voters of the county.

a.   The commission shall be composed of nine members who shall be residents of the county and appointed by the governing body of the county.   Of the nine members, six shall be private citizens representing different municipalities in the county, none of whom shall be employed by any library within the county which is funded in whole or in part by county or municipal funds, and none of whom shall be a member of the governing body of the county or of any municipality therein.   Of the three remaining members, one shall be a member of the county library commission; one shall be a trustee of a public library of a municipality which is not a member of the county library system; and, one shall be a trustee of a public library of a municipality which is a member of the county library system.

b.   The county governing body shall designate the commission chairman from among the six private citizen members.

c.   Members of the commission shall serve without compensation, but shall be reimbursed, as hereinafter provided, by the county governing body for necessary expenses actually incurred in the performance of their duties under this act.

L.1981, c. 489, § 2, eff. Jan. 12, 1982.

40:33—13.2f County library commission; duties

It shall be the duty of the county library study commission to study the county library system, assess its needs, and evaluate its ability to provide library services to county residents. The library study commission may report and recommend that:

a. A referendum be held to submit to the voters of the county the question as to whether or not the county library system shall be reorganized to conform to one of the options set forth in sections 6, 7 and 8 of this act ;   or,

b. The county library system remain unchanged.

L.1981, c. 489, § 3, eff. Jan. 12, 1982.

40:33—13.2g Offices; expenses; payment; employees, consultants and clerical staff; report of findings and recommendations; referendum question on reorganization of system

a. The governing body of the county shall provide the county library study commission with such offices as may be necessary for the conduct of its business and shall make available such equipment and supplies as it may require.

b. All necessary expenses actually incurred by the county library study commission and its members shall be paid, upon certification of the chairman of the commission, by the county treasurer within the limits of funds appropriated by the county governing body for this purpose, subject to such fiscal procedures as may be established by the governing body.

c. The county library study commission may appoint such employees, consultants, and clerical staff as are necessary to carry out the provisions of this act within the limits of funds appropriated by the governing body of the county for this purpose, subject to such fiscal procedures as may be established by the governing body.

d. The county library study commission shall report its findings and recommendations to the county governing body within 1 calendar year following the date of its establishment and it shall be the responsibility of the governing body to make a copy of the commission's report available without cost to any member of the public requesting the same. If the county library study commission shall recommend the reorganization of the county library system as provided in section 8 of this act, the county clerk shall cause a referendum question conforming with the requirements of section 5 of this act to be placed on the ballot at the next general election occurring not less than 60 days following the clerk's receipt of notice of the commission's recommendations and the summary required to be prepared pursuant to section 5 of this act. If the commission recommends that a county library system be reorganized pursuant to sections 6 and 7 of this act, the county clerk shall cause a referendum question to appear only on the ballots in those municipalities to which the question is applicable at the next general election occurring not less than 60 days following the clerk's receipt of notice of the commission's recommendations.

L.1981, c. 489, § 4, eff. Jan. 12, 1982.

40:33—13.2h Question of reoragnization; form on ballot; publication of report; vote necessary

The question of the reorganization of the county library system shall be submitted to the voters in substantially the following form:

"Shall the county library system be reorganized pursuant to section ... of the "County Library Reorganization Law" (P.L.[1981] c. [489]) to implement the '............... Option,' as recommended by the .... County Library Study Commission?"

Not more than 45 days prior to the general election the county clerk shall cause to have published in a newspaper generally circulating in the county a summary of the commission's report prepared by the commission and a notice of the time and place at which copies of the commission's report may be obtained without cost by any member of the public requesting the same.

If at the election at which the question is submitted, a majority of all votes cast for and against adoption shall be cast in favor thereof, the question is adopted, and the date of the adoption shall be the effective date of reorganization of the county library system for the purposes of this act.
L.1981, c. 489, § 5, eff. Jan. 12, 1982.

40:33–13.2i Branch development option

The option for reorganization of the county library system provided in this section shall be known as the "Branch Development Option" and shall govern the county library system of any county whose voters have adopted it pursuant to section 5 of this act.

a. The county library commission shall establish a branch of the county library in each municipality; (1) which is a member of the county library system upon the effective date of the reorganization of the system; and (2) in which the municipal governing body adopts a resolution approving the establishment of a branch library. The county library commission may establish a joint branch library for two or more adjacent municipalities upon its determination that the library needs of such municipalities could best be served by a joint branch library, and upon the adoption by the governing bodies of all municipalities to be served thereby of joint resolutions, approving the establishment thereof. A branch library or a joint branch library established pursuant to this act shall conform to all standards promulgated by the Division of the State Library, Archives and History for branch libraries.

b. The county library commission shall assure that all branch or joint branch libraries agreed upon pursuant to subsection a. of this section are operating within 3 calendar years of the effective date of the reorganization of the county library system.

c. Any municipality which has agreed to the establishment of a branch library or joint branch library of the county library shall remain a member of the county library system for at least 5 years following the effective date of the reorganization of the county library system.

d. Any municipality which is a member of the county library system and whose governing body does not approve the establishment of a branch library or a joint branch library shall remain a member of the county library system until such time as it elects to withdraw from the system in the manner provided in chapter 33 of Title 40 of the Revised Statutes. The governing body of such a municipality may, by resolution, request that the county library establish a branch library or a joint branch library at any time following the effective date of the reorganization of the county library system, in the manner provided in subsection a.
L.1981, c. 489, § 6, eff. Jan. 12, 1982.

40:33–13.2j Service contract option

The option for reorganization of the county library system provided in this section shall be known as the "Service Contract Option" and shall govern the county library system of any county whose voters have adopted it pursuant to section 5 of this act.

a. The county library commission shall offer a contract to any of the municipalities identified by the county library study commission in its report to provide such municipalities with sufficient staff and materials to insure compliance with standards promulgated by the Division of the State Library, Archives and History for library service in those municipalities. Municipalities shall accept or reject such contracts by resolution of the governing body.

Any municipality which accepts a contract shall determine an appropriate geographic location within the municipality for the staff and materials provided by the county library.

b. Any municipality which rejects a contract pursuant to this section and is a member of the county library system shall remain a member of the sys-

tem until such time as it elects to withdraw from the system in the manner provided in chapter 33 of Title 40 of the Revised Statutes.
L.1981, c. 489, § 7, eff. Jan. 12, 1982.

40:33–13.2k Tax base sharing option

The option for reorganization of the county library system provided in this section shall be known as the "Tax Base Sharing Option," and shall be available only to any county in which revenues from the dedicated county library tax established pursuant to R.S. 40:33–9 or P.L.1977, c. 300 (C. 40:33–15 et seq.) have been derived from less than 75% of the total assessed property of the county in the calendar year prior to the establishment of the county library study commission. This option shall govern the county library system of any qualified county whose voters have adopted it pursuant to section 5 of this act.

a. The governing body of the county shall annually determine a sum sufficient to distribute among certain municipalities and the county according to the following formula:

$$A = CBS + CRS + LRS$$

where:

A is the total tax pool to be distributed;
CBS is the county base share and is determined as .0000666 X the apportionment valuation of the county;
CRS is the county residual share and is determined as [A–CBS] X .60; and,
LRS is the local residual share and is determined as [A–CBS] X .40.

The county base share (CBS) shall be appropriated to the county library which shall receive no funds from the library tax provided for in R.S. 40:33–9 or from the library tax established in P.L.1977, c. 300 (C. 40:33–15 et seq.). The local residual share (LRS) shall be distributed among those municipalities not members of the county library system on January 1, 1982. Each such municipality shall be apportioned an amount of those revenues in a proportion equal to the proportion which that municipality's apportionment valuation is of the apportionment valuation of all such municipalities. Any municipality receiving revenues from the tax base sharing option provided in this section shall appropriate those funds directly to the board of trustees of any library within its borders funded by the municipality in the calendar year prior to the reorganization of the county library system.

b. For each year following the reorganization of the county library system, the county library distribution (CBS + CRS) from the formula established in subsection a. of this section shall not be less than the appropriation made to the county library in the calendar year immediately prior to the reorganization of the county library system; provided, however, that in the first calendar year following the reorganization of the county library system, the county library shall receive an appropriation not less than an amount equal to the appropriation made to the county library in the calendar year preceding the reorganization of the system and not more than an amount equal to the prior year's appropriation plus 10% of that appropriation.

In each year following the reorganization of the county library system, the governing body of any municipality not a member of the county library system shall appropriate to any library in the municipality which was funded by the municipality prior to the reorganization of the county library system a sum of money not less than the average appropriation made to such libraries in the 3 years occurring immediately prior to the reorganization of the county library system. The governing body shall also provide any in-kind benefits or the cash equivalent thereof, which were provided to such libraries during that preceding period.

c. The county library shall receive State aid as provided in the "State Library Aid Law" (N.J.S. 18A:74–1 et seq.) based on expenditures from the

total appropriation from the tax base sharing option made to the county
library and the total resident population of the county. Any library located
within a municipality not a member of the county library system shall receive State aid as provided in the "State Library Aid Law" based on expenditures from the total appropriation made to the library from the municipality and from the portion of the local residual share received by the
municipality as provided in subsection a. of this section. Any municipality
which is a member of the county library system and which supports a library
shall receive State aid as provided in the "State Library Aid Law" based
on the total appropriation made by the municipality for library purposes.

    d. The county library shall make all of its patron services available to
all residents of the county. For the purpose of this act "patron services"
means services rendered by a library directly to patrons as distinguished from
those services rendered to other libraries. Patron services shall include circulation of library materials, reference assistance, and public programs.

    e. A municipality which maintains a municipal public library within the
county shall not dissolve its municipal public library for a period of 2 calendar years from the effective date of the reorganization of the county library
system.

    f. The county library commission may offer a service contract for library
services to any municipality within the county for any library services performed by the county library. Any such contracts shall conform to the contracts established in section 7 of this act.

    g. The county library study commission shall remain in existence for 1
calendar year after the effective date of such reorganization. It shall be
the responsibility of the commission to evaluate the tax base sharing option
and to determine if the appropriation for the county library system is sufficient to provide patron services to all residents of the county and that such
services are in compliance with standards promulgated by the Division of the
State Library, Archives and History for such libraries. The commission shall
make a report of its findings to the county governing body within 1 calendar
year of the reorganization of the county library system.
L.1981, c. 489, § 8, eff. Jan. 12, 1982.

40:33–13.2*l* County with tax base sharing option; exclusion of appropriations as county tax levy under Cap Law

    For the first 2 years following the reorganization of a county library system
pursuant to section 8 of this act, any appropriation made by the county governing body for library purposes shall not be included or considered a part
of the county tax levy under section 4 of P.L.1976, c. 68 (C. 40A:4–45.4). In
the third calendar year following the reorganization of the county library
system and every year thereafter any appropriation made by the county governing body for library purposes shall be considered a part of the county
tax levy for the purpose of calculating permissible expenditures.
L.1981, c. 489, § 9, eff. Jan. 12, 1982.

40:33–13.2m Evaluation of county library system after rejection by voters or after reorganization; time interval after election

    a. Except as provided in subsection c. of this section, the governing body
of any county which has rejected a question placed on the ballot pursuant
to section 5 of this act may, by ordinance or resolution, as appropriate, establish another county library study commission to evaluate the county library system. The governing body shall establish another commission when
it receives a petition signed by 10% of the registered voters of the county
calling for the creation of a county library study commission. Any such
commission shall be established and its membership appointed as provided
in section 2 of this act. The commission shall have the same powers and
responsibilities as established in sections 3 and 4 of this act.

    b. Except as provided in subsection c. of this section, the governing body of any county which has adopted any of the options provided in this act may, by ordinance or resolution, as appropriate, establish another county library study commission to evaluate the reorganized county library system. The governing body shall establish such a commission when it receives a petition signed by 10% of the registered voters of the county calling for the creation of a county library study commission. Any such commission shall be established and its members appointed as provided in section 2 of this act. The commission shall have the same powers and responsibilities as established in sections 3 and 4 of this act; except that, it may also recommend that any reorganized county library system be organized as provided in chapter 33 of Title 40 of the Revised Statutes. If the commission shall recommend the latter then the question to be submitted to the voters pursuant to section 5 of this act shall be in substantially the following form:

"Shall the county library system be reorganized pursuant to article 1 of chapter 33 of Title 40 of the Revised Statutes as recommended by .... County Library Study Commission."

c. No ordinance or resolution or petition establishing a county library study commission shall be valid and no question shall be submitted within 3 years of the date of any election at which the original question of adoption was submitted to the voters of the county.

L.1981, c. 489, § 10, eff. Jan. 12, 1982.

40:33-13.2n Rules and regulations

The Division of the State Library, Archives and History with the approval of the State Board of Education is authorized to promulgate, pursuant to the "Administrative Procedure Act," P.L.1968, c. 410 (C. 52:14B-1 et seq.), such rules and regulations as it deems necessary to effectuate the purposes of this act.

L.1981, c. 489, § 11, eff. Jan. 12, 1982.

40:33-15. Morris County; reorganization of free county library; resolution

Notwithstanding the provisions of any other law, the board of chosen freeholders of any county having a population of not less than 350,000 nor more than 450,000 according to the 1970 Federal census which has established a free county library under chapter 33 of Title 40 of the Revised Statutes may, by resolution to be effective January 1, 1978, reorganize the free county library pursuant to the provisions of this act in order to provide library services for the use of all residents and inhabitants of the county.

L.1977, c. 300, § 1, eff. Dec. 16, 1977.

40:33-16. Definitions

As used in this act:

a. "First level services" means services provided by a free county library which are coextensive with those provided by free public libraries established pursuant to chapter 54 of Title 40 of the Revised Statutes which may include but are not limited to over-the-counter borrowing, story-telling and bookmobile programs; and, in addition, the following services provided by the free county library to local libraries: material acquisition and processing, book allowances and book rental services.

b. "Second level services" means specialized services provided to all residents of a county by the free county library which supplement services provided by free public libraries and services provided by a free county library to all public libraries, school libraries, industrial, commercial and other special libraries in the county which are designed to assist and strengthen such libraries. Second level services shall include but not be limited to inter-library loan, in-library use of materials, reference and reading guidance, provision of photocopy at cost, compilation and publication of a union list of periodicals and the coordination of cooperative countywide services.

L.1977, c. 300, § 2, eff. Dec. 16, 1977.

40:33-17. County library commission; members

The "county library commission" in such counties shall consist of seven members. On or before the effective date of such reorganization, the board of chosen freeholders shall appoint the two additional members to the commission, for terms of 4 and 5 years respectively, who are residents of municipalities which only receive second level services from the county library, one of whom who has previously served as a trustee of a free public library. All future appointments to the commission shall be made for terms of 5 years, except for appointments to fill vacancies occurring on the commission which shall be filled for the unexpired term only. All future appointments shall be made in such a manner as to maintain at least one director, or his designee, from a municipal free public library or joint library which receives only second level services from the free county library, one member, or his designee, of the governing body of a municipality which receives only second level services from the free county library, a trustee of a municipal free library which receives only second level services from the free county library, and three members who are residents of municipalities which receive first level services from the free county library.

L.1977, c. 300, § 3, eff. Dec. 16, 1977.

40:33-18. Proposal of operational amount for ensuing calendar year

The county library commission in such counties shall annually, not later than November 1, propose to the board of chosen freeholders the total sum required for the operation of the library for the ensuing calendar year and identify that part of the total sum which will be used for second level services.
L.1977, c. 300, § 4, eff. Dec. 16, 1977.

40:33-19. First and second level services; annual determination of amount for maintenance; certification; apportionment; assessment, levy and collection; appropriation for second level services

Following the passage of a resolution to reorganize the free county library pursuant to the provisions of this act and annually thereafter, the board of chosen freeholders shall determine a sum sufficient for the maintenance of first and second level services at the county library. The sum to be raised for first level services shall be certified by the board of chosen freeholders to the county board of taxation, which shall apportion such amount among the municipalities receiving first level services.

The amount thus apportioned to each municipality for first level services shall be assessed, levied and collected in the same manner and at the same time as other county taxes are assessed, levied and collected therein. The sum to be raised and appropriated for second level services shall be raised and appropriated by the board of chosen freeholders in the same manner as moneys are raised and appropriated for other county purposes pursuant to the Local Budget Law (N.J.S. 40A:4-1 et seq.), provided, however, that such appropriation shall not be greater than the difference between the total State aid that the county library receives in the prebudget year pursuant to N.J.S. 18A:74-4 and the product of .0000718 multiplied by the net valuation on which county taxes are apportioned for the prebudget year.
L.1977, c. 300, § 5, eff. Dec. 16, 1977.

40:33-20. Municipalities; continuation of receipt of services from free county library; exceptions

Municipalities receiving benefits from the free county library prior to the adoption of a resolution by the board of chosen freeholders to reorganize the free county library pursuant to the provisions of this act shall continue to receive first and second level services from the free county library, except as provided below. On or before September 30 of the year following the reorganization of the free county library pursuant to the provisions of this act, the governing body of any municipality which maintains a free public library and receives first level services from the free county library may, by resolution, notify the county library commission of such county that it will withdraw from participation in the first level services of the free county library to be effective January 1 of the following year. On or before September 30 of the second year following the reorganization of the free county library pursuant to the provisions of this act, and every third year thereafter, the governing body of any municipality which maintains a free public library, receives first level services from the free county library and is in the first third of an alphabetical list of the municipalities in the county may, by resolution, notify the county library commission of such county that it will withdraw from participation in first level services of the free county library to be effective January 1 of the following year. On or before September 30 of the third year following the reorganization of the free county library pursuant to the provisions of this act, and every third year thereafter, the governing body of any municipality which maintains a free public library, receives first level services from the free county library and is in the second third of an alphabetical list of the municipalities in the county may, by resolution, notify the county library commission of such county that it will withdraw from participation in first level services of the free county library to be effective January 1 of the following year. On or before September 30 of the fourth year following the reorganization of the free county library pursuant to the provisions of this act, and every third year thereafter, the governing body of any municipality which maintains a free public library, receives first level services from the free county library and is in the remaining third of an alphabetical list of the municipalities in the county may, by resolution, notify the county library commission of such county that it will withdraw from participation in first level services of the free county library to be effective January 1 of the following year. The governing body of any municipality may, by resolution, on or before September 30 in any year, except as otherwise specifically provided hereinafter, notify the county library commission that it will receive and support first level services to be effective January 1 of the following year. In the event any municipality is a party to a joint library agreement pursuant to Article 2 of chapter 54 of Title 40 of the Revised Statutes in the year prior to the reorganization of the free county library, such notification may be given in the first 4 years following said reorganization only if the governing body of the other municipality party to such agreement consents thereto, or upon the condition that such agreement shall remain in force for the said 4 years. In the event that any municipality is a party to a contract for full library services with another municipality in the year prior to the reorganization of the free county library, such notification may be given in the first 4 years following said reorganization only if the governing body of the other municipality party to such agreement consents thereto, or if the municipality providing library services pursuant to the agreement is unwilling to renew the agreement for the next year for an amount less than 5% above the amount provided for in the current agreement.

L.1977, c. 300, § 6, eff. Dec. 16, 1977.

40:33-21. Report on effectiveness of second level services

Within 18 months following the reorganization of the free county library pursuant to this act, after consultation with all the libraries in the county, the county library commission shall submit a report to all the municipalities in the county which evaluates the effectiveness of the second level services provided by the free county library and indicates what action it will take to improve such services in the forthcoming year.

L.1977, c. 300, § 7, eff. Dec. 16, 1977.

40:33-22. Application of provisions on free county libraries

All free county libraries reorganized pursuant to the provisions of this act

shall be governed by the provisions of article 1, chapter 33, Title 40 of the Revised Statutes insofar as they are not inconsistent with the provisions of this act.
L.1977, c. 300, § 8, eff. Dec. 16, 1977.

40:33-23. Consideration of increase in county tax levy to fund second level services for purposes of calculating permissible expenditures

In the first year in which a free county library is reorganized pursuant to the provisions of this act, the amount which the county tax levy is increased to fund second level services provided by the county library shall not be considered as part of the county tax levy for the purposes of calculating permissible expenditures for that year pursuant to P.L.1976, c. 68 (C. 40A:4-45.1 et seq.), however the amount which the county tax levy is so increased in that first year shall be considered as part of the county tax levy for the purposes of calculating permissible expenditures pursuant to P.L.1976, c. 68, for the following year and every year thereafter.
L.1977, c. 300, § 9, eff. Dec. 16, 1977.

FEDERATION OF LIBRARIES
(New Jersey Statutes Annotated, 1982, s.40:9A-1 to 40:9A-4.)

40:9A–1. Federation of city-county libraries

Any county or counties, municipality or municipalities, or any combination thereof, operating libraries pursuant to chapters 33 or 54 of Title 40 of the Revised Statutes may, by contract or agreement, by and between the appropriate board or boards of chosen freeholders and the municipality or municipalities, establish and maintain a federation of their libraries for the purpose of providing such co-operative library services as shall be thereby agreed upon.   L.1956, c. 108, p. 492, § 1, as amended L.1959, c. 179, p. 725, § 1, eff. Dec. 1, 1959.

40:9A–2. Costs; management

Such contracts shall set forth the proportion of the cost each party thereto shall assume and specify all the details of the management of the joint undertakings, and any other matters that may be deemed necessary for insertion therein, and may be amended from time to time by the contracting parties.   L.1956, c. 108, p. 492, § 2.

40:9A–3. Interlibrary loan services; free use by residents

Such contracts shall provide for the establishment of interlibrary loan services among the federated libraries and the free use for reference purposes of the library resources in the federation by any resident of the area served by the participating municipalities and counties.   L.1956, c. 108, p. 493, § 3, as amended L.1959, c. 179, p. 725, § 2, eff. Dec. 1, 1959.

40:9A–4. Standards

The Commissioner of Education subject to the approval of the

State Board of Education shall formulate and promulgate standards for the said federations of libraries to insure the public convenience in the use of such library services. L.1956, c. 108, p. 493, § 4.

MUNICIPAL LIBRARIES
General Provisions
(New Jersey Statutes Annotated, 1982, s.49:54-1 to 49:54-29, 40:54-35.)

40:54-1. Establishment; chapter applicable to libraries established under other laws

Any municipality may, in the manner hereinafter provided, establish a free public library within its corporate limits.

Every library established under this chapter, and every free public library established pursuant to any general law shall be governed by the provisions of this chapter.

Source. L.1905, c. 150, §§ 1, 33, pp. 273, 285 [C.S. pp. 3116, 3123, §§ 65, 97].

40:54-2. Referendum

No such library shall be established in any municipality unless assented to by a majority of the legal voters of the municipality, at an election, general or special, at which the question of the adoption of this article shall be submitted to vote by direction of the governing body.

Source. L.1905, c. 150, § 2, p. 273 [C.S. p. 3116, § 66].

40:54-3. Referendum; notice

The municipal clerk shall cause public notice of such general or special election to be given by advertisement, signed by himself and set up in at least five public places in the municipality for at least ten days previous to the date of such election and published for the same period in two newspapers printed or circulating therein.

Source. L.1905, c. 150, § 2, p. 273 [C.S. p. 3116, § 66].

40:54-4. Ballot; form and content

The officer charged with the duty of preparing the ballots for such election shall cause the question to be submitted to be printed on the official ballots for such election in substantially the following form:

"To vote upon the public question printed below, if in favor thereof mark a cross ($\times$) or plus ($+$) in the square at the left of the word YES, and if opposed thereto mark a cross ($\times$) or plus ($+$) in the square at the left of the word NO.

"Shall a free public library be established in ....

☐ YES (name of municipality) pursuant to sections 40:54-1 to
        40:54-29 of the title Municipalities and Counties of the
☐ NO   Revised Statutes?"

Source. L.1905, c. 150, § 2, p. 273 [C.S. p. 3116, § 66].

40:54-5. Election returns

The election officers of the municipality shall make a true and
correct return of the result of such election in writing, under
their hands, and said statement shall be entered at large upon the
minutes of the governing body.

Source. L.1905, c. 150, § 2, p. 273 [C.S. p. 3116, § 66].

40:54-6. Vote required for adoption

If a majority of the votes so counted shall be in favor of a free
public library, the provisions of this article shall be deemed to
have been adopted.

Source. L.1905, c. 150, § 3, p. 274 [C.S. p. 3117, § 67].

40:54-7. Rejection of proposition; second election

Where any municipality shall vote against the establishment of
a free public library such vote shall not preclude the holding of
another election, general or special, to vote for or against the
adoption of the provisions of this article.

Source. L.1905, c. 150, § 2, p. 273 [C.S. p. 3116, § 66].

40:54-8. Tax levy; additional levy

The governing body or appropriate board of every municipality
governed by this article shall annually appropriate and raise by
taxation a sum equal to one-third of a mill on every dollar of
assessable property within such municipality.

Such additional sum, as in the judgment of such body or board
is necessary for the proper maintenance of a free public library,
may be appropriated and raised by taxation, annually. As
amended L.1944, c. 49, p. 107, § 1, eff. March 31, 1944.

Source. L.1905, c. 150, § 3, p. 274   1921, c. 191, § 1, p. 507 [1924 Suppl. §
[C.S. p. 3117, § 67]. L.1905, c. 150, § 4,   115-68].
p. 274 [C.S. p. 3117, § 68], as am. by L.

40:54-9. Trustees; number, appointment and term; alternates

Immediately upon the establishment by any municipality of a free public
library under this article, a board of trustees shall be formed to consist
of seven members, one of whom shall be the mayor or other chief executive officer of the municipality, one of the local superintendents of schools
or in the event that there be no such official, the principal with power of

supervision over the local school system, or in case such municipality shall have none of the school officials hereinbefore mentioned, then the president of the board of education, and five citizens to be appointed by the mayor or chief executive, at least four of whom shall be residents of the municipality. The appointments shall be for terms of 1, 2, 3, 4 and 5 years respectively, as they may be selected by the mayor or other chief executive officer, and, except in cities shall be made with the consent of the governing body. The mayor or other chief executive officer and the super-intendent of schools or the principal, as the case may be, serving as a member of the board, may, respectively, appoint an alternate to act in his place and stead with authority to attend all meetings of the board and, in his absence, to vote on all questions before the board.

Amended by L.1970, c. 143, § 1, eff. July 17, 1970.

40:54-10. Vacancies; how filled

Upon the expiration of the term of office of any trustee the mayor or other chief executive officer of the municipality shall appoint a citizen for a term of five years in the same manner as the original appointment was made. Vacancies occurring in the board of trustees shall be filled for the unexpired term only, in the same manner as the original appointments are made.

Source. L.1905, c. 150, § 5, p. 275 [C.S. p. 3117, § 69], as am. by L.1927, c. 290, § 1, p. 534, L.1928, c. 147, § 1, p. 298, L.1929, c. 225, § 1, p. 419.

40:54-11. Trustees; corporate name; organization; officers; certificate; recording and filing

The board of trustees shall be a body corporate under the name of "the trustees of the free public library of ...... (name of municipality)". It shall have corporate powers of succession, may sue and be sued, and adopt a corporate seal. It shall meet at a convenient time and place in the municipality within ten days after its appointment, and shall immediately proceed to organize by the election from its members of a president, treasurer, and secretary, who shall hold their offices for one year and until their successors are elected.

The members shall make and execute under their hands and seals a certificate setting forth their appointment and their organization and the names of the officers elected, such certificate to be acknowledged in the same manner as is required of conveyances of real estate, and recorded in the clerk's office of the county in which the municipality is located. They shall also send a certified copy of the certificate to the office of the secretary of state, at Trenton, to be there filed of record, but shall not be required to pay any fees for such recording and filing. The certificate, or copy thereof duly certified by the secretary of state or by the county clerk, shall be evidence in all courts and places of the incorporation of the board.

Source. L.1905, c. 150, § 6, p. 275 [C.S. p. 3117, § 70].

40:54–12. Trustees; powers; employees

The board shall hold in trust and manage all property of the library. It may rent rooms, or, when proper, construct buildings for the use of the library, purchase books, pamphlets, documents, papers and other reading matter, hire librarians, and other necessary personnel, and fix their compensation, make proper rules and regulations for the government of the library, and generally do all things necessary and proper for the establishment and maintenance of the free public library in the municipality. The board may also transfer to and receive from the deposit and exchange library service of the Bureau of Public and School Library Services, of the Division of the State Library, Archives and History, in the State Department of Education, books, magazines, prints, maps and other related library materials for the purpose of augmenting the interlibrary loan service. As amended L.1949, c. 98, p. 419, § 1, eff. May 11, 1949.

Source. L.1905, c. 150, § 6, p. 275 [C.S. p. 3117, § 70].

40:54–12.1 Purchases not requiring advertisements for bids

The board of trustees of the free public library of any municipality or of a joint free public library may, within the limits of funds appropriated or otherwise made available to the board, purchase the following without advertising for bids therefor: (1) library materials including books, periodicals, newspapers, documents, pamphlets, photographs, reproductions, microforms, pictorial or graphic works, musical scores, maps, charts, globes, sound recordings, slides, films, filmstrips, video and magnetic tapes, other printed or published matter, and audiovisual and other materials of a similar nature; (2) necessary binding or rebinding of library materials; and (3) specialized library services.
L.1968, c. 227, § 2, eff. July 31, 1968.

40:54–13. Trustees; treasurer; bond and duties

The treasurer of the board shall give bond in an amount to be fixed by the mayor in cities and by the governing body in municipalities other than cities, payable to the municipality by its corporate name, conditioned for the faithful performance and discharge of his duties. The board shall, by its treasurer, upon its warrant signed by its president, receive from the disbursing officer of the municipality the money raised therein for library purposes, as provided in section 40:54–8 of this title.

Source. L.1905, c. 150, § 6, p. 275 [C.S. p. 3117, § 70].

40:54–14. Trustees; compensation; limitation on amount of indebtedness

The trustees shall receive no compensation for their services, and shall not incur any expense or enter into any obligations to an amount in excess of the annual appropriation for library purposes and of the funds on hand.

Source. L.1905, c. 150, § 7, p. 276 [C.S. p. 3118, § 71].

40:54–15. Trustees; annual report

The board of trustees shall annually make a report of its transactions, accounts, and the state and condition of the library to the governing body of the municipality.

Source. L.1905, c. 150, § 8, p. 276 [C.S. p. 3118, § 72].

40:54–16. Appropriation for furnishing

Any municipality that shall establish a library under the provisions of this article, or that has heretofore established a free public library pursuant to law, and has purchased or shall purchase lands, and has erected or shall erect buildings thereon, or both, for the purposes of a free public library, and has made or shall make appropriations therefor under this article, may make additional appropriation for the equipment, furnishing and decorating of the library building in manner following: The board of trustees shall certify to the board or body having charge and control of the finances of the municipality the amount necessary for the equipment, furnishing and decorating of the library building, and thereupon such board or body may by resolution, at its discretion and with the approval of the mayor or other chief executive officer of the municipality, make appropriation of such money and authorize and empower the board of trustees of the free public library to expend such sum of money. Upon the passage of such resolution the board of trustees may enter into contracts for such equipment, furnishing and decorating, and expend money therefor to the amount of the appropriation.

Source. L.1905, c. 150, § 13, p. 279 [C.S. p. 3119, § 77], as am. by L.1921, c. 2, § 2, p. 14 [1924 Suppl. § 115–77].

40:54–17. Fines expended for library purposes

The board of trustees of the free public library may use and expend for library purposes all moneys received from library fines and shall account for such receipts and expenditure in the same manner as is required as to funds appropriated to the board of trustees by the governing body of the municipality.

Amended by L.1969, c. 295, § 1, eff. Jan. 16, 1970.

40:54–18. Use of money paid by library to municipal treasury

The governing body of any municipality may appropriate in the annual budget for the use of the free public library of such municipality a sum equal to the amount of the money paid into the general treasury by the free public library in the preceding fiscal year. The sum so appropriated shall be available for expenditure by the board of trustees of the free public library of the municipality for library purposes, shall be in addition to sums otherwise appropriated by law for library purposes and shall be controlled by the same laws as other budget appropriations.

Source. L.1922, c. 36, § 1, p. 70 [1924 Suppl. § *136–4300A(4)].

40:54–19. Devises and bequests to trustees

The board of trustees may receive, hold and manage any devise, bequest or donation heretofore made or hereafter to be made and given for the establishment, increase or maintenance of a free public library within the municipality.

Source. L.1905, c. 150, § 9, p. 276 [C.S. p. 3118, § 73].

40:54–19.1 Loan of funds received as gift or bequest

The board of trustees of the free public library may, upon the application of the governing body of the municipality, loan, upon "tax anticipation notes" or "bond anticipation notes" of the municipality, any funds heretofore or hereafter received, either by the board of trustees of the free public library or by the governing body, as a gift or bequest for free public library purposes and being held and managed by the board of trustees, or subject to their direction pursuant to the provisions of article one of chapter fifty-four of Title 40 of the Revised Statutes, pending the use thereof for the purposes for which the gift or bequest was made. L.1941, c. 67, p. 152, § 1, as amended L.1942, c. 139, p. 429, § 1, eff. May 6, 1942.

40:54–19.2 Strict compliance with law in making loans required

In the making of any loan authorized by the provisions of section one of this act the pertinent provisions of chapters one and two of Title 40 of the Revised Statutes shall, in all respects, be strictly complied with. L.1941, c. 67, p. 152, § 2, as amended L.1942, c. 139, p. 430, § 2, eff. May 6, 1942.

40:54–19.3 Investment of funds; regulation of bonds or securities

The board of trustees of the free public library may invest its funds in any interest-bearing obligations of the United States of America, or in interest-bearing bonds of the State of New Jersey, or any county or municipality of said state, or in any other securities authorized for investments by trustees under and in accordance with the provisions of article 2 of chapter 15 of Title 3A of the New Jersey Statutes, but the authorization to invest funds in any such obligations or bonds or securities shall be by resolution adopted by a majority vote of all the members of the board of trustees at any regular or special meeting of the board.

All such obligations or bonds or securities shall be registered in the official name of the board of trustees.

As used in this section invest means the buying and selling of authorized obligations, bonds and securities.

Amended by L.1968, c. 217, § 1, eff. July 24, 1968; L.1973, c. 344, § 1, eff. Dec. 27, 1973.

40:54–19.4 Custody of securities; report; minutes

When any obligations or bonds purchased by the board of trustees are received by the board, the treasurer of the board shall immediately record the receiving thereof in an appropriate manner and shall, unless otherwise previously directed by the board of trustees, promptly deliver the same to the clerk of the municipality for safe-keeping. At the next regular or special meeting after the receipt of such obligations or bonds, said treasurer shall present a written report to the board, setting forth the amounts of the obligations or bonds so received, and the dates, numbers and interest periods thereof and the date of delivery thereof to the clerk of the municipality. The secretary of the board of trustees shall record in the minutes of such regular or special meeting of the board the date of receipt of such obligations or bonds by the treasurer, the amounts, dates, numbers and interest periods thereof and the date on which they were delivered to the clerk of the municipality for safe-keeping. L.1942, c. 139, p. 430, § 4, supplementing L.1941, c. 67, eff. May 6, 1942.

40:54–19.5 Income from investments

All interest, income or profit which may be realized by the board of trustees from the investment, pursuant to this or any other act, of any such funds shall be added to the principal of such funds and be used for the same purpose or purposes for or toward which the principal gift or bequest was made until the purpose or purposes for or toward which such gift or bequest was made shall have been accomplished. L.1942, c. 139, p. 431, § 5, supplementing L.1941, c. 67, eff. May 6, 1942.

40:54–20. Gifts of works of art; acceptance and maintenance

Any free public library may accept gifts and bequests of paintings, statuary, ceramics and other art objects, and may care for and maintain them in accordance with the provisions of such gift or bequest.

Source. L.1906, c. 8, § 1, p. 20 [C.S. p. 3123, § 98], suppl. to L.1905, c. 150, p. 273.

40:54-21. Acceptance of conditional gifts generally

In any municipality in which there shall have been established a free public library pursuant to law, the governing body may, by resolution, accept gifts or bequests for the purpose of building a library building therein which may be made on condition that a sum not exceeding ten per cent of the amount of such gift or bequest be annually appropriated for the maintenance and support of such library, or which may be made on the above condition and on the further condition that the municipality to which such gift is made shall also provide a suitable site for the building. When any such conditional gift is accepted by any municipality such amount as may be required by the condition of the gift for the support and use of the library may be raised annually by taxation.

Source. L.1905, c. 150, § 23, p. 283 [C.S. p. 3122, § 87].

40:54-22. Custodian of gifts; expenditure

Any gift or bequest, when accepted by the governing body of the municipality, shall be received by the treasurer or other corresponding officer of the municipality and expended by and under the direction of the board of trustees of the free public library for the purposes for which the gift or bequest was made, in the same manner as other funds are expended by such board.

Source. L.1905, c. 150, § 26, p. 284 [C.S. p. 3122, § 90].

40:54-23. Municipalities may furnish site where buildings are offered; amount

When any person has offered or hereafter may offer to the board of trustees of the free public library of any municipality which shall hereafter establish a library under the provisions of this article or has heretofore established a free public library pursuant to law, or has offered or hereafter may offer to the council or other governing body of any such municipality, to provide or erect a building to be used as a free public library upon condition that the municipality, or the trustees of the free public library therein, or the council or governing body thereof, provide a site for the building, the council or other governing body of the municipality, by resolution adopted by the votes of a majority of all the members thereof, may appropriate for the purpose of purchasing a suitable site upon which to erect such library building, a sum of money not exceeding three mills in all municipalities except cities, and in cities a sum not exceeding three-fourths of one mill, on every dollar of assessable property according to the last preceding levy for the purposes of annual taxation therein.

Source. L.1905, c. 150, § 15, p. 280 [C.S. p. 3120, § ‚79], as am. by L.1916, c. 247, § 1, p. 513 [1924 Suppl. § 115-79]. L.1905, c. 150, § 24, p. 283 [C.S. p. 3122, § 88].

40:54–24. Purchase of site; title

At any time after the acceptance of any such last-mentioned gift the trustees of the free public library in any such municipality may purchase, at a cost not exceeding the amount appropriated therefor, a suitable site for the erection of a library building. The title of the real estate so purchased shall be taken in the name of the municipality. The use and control of the same shall be in the board of trustees of the free public library therein so long as it shall be used for free public library purposes.

Source. L.1905, c. 150, § 15, p. 280 [C.S. p. 3120, § 79], as am. by L.1916, c. 247, § 1, p. 513 [1924 Suppl. § 115–79]. L.1905, c. 150, § 25, p. 283 [C. S. p. 3122, § 89].

40:54–25. Lands and buildings; purchase and alteration; financing; title

When, in the judgment of the board of trustees of the free public library in any municipality that shall establish a library under the provisions of this article or has heretofore established a free public library pursuant to law, it is advisable to purchase lands or erect buildings thereon, or both, or to enlarge or alter any building already erected thereon, for the purpose of a free public library, the board may certify to the board or body having charge of the finances of such municipality the amount of money, in addition to such moneys as it may have on hand applicable to such purposes, necessary for the purpose of making such purchase of land, the erection of buildings or other improvements thereof, and shall also certify therewith the total amount of moneys and funds available for the purchase of lands or erection of buildings, and an estimated account of the amount necessary for the maintenance of the library for the balance of the then current year.

Thereupon the board, or body having charge of the finances of the municipality may by resolution, at its discretion ~~and with the approval of the mayor or other chief executive officer of the municipality,~~ and with the approval of the mayor or other chief executive officer of the municipality, authorize and empower the board of trustees of the free public library to expend such sums of money, in addition to the moneys belonging to it and not needed for the expenses of maintenance for the remainder of the then fiscal year, as to such common council, or such other body or board, may seem proper for such purposes, not to exceed, however, the amount certified by the board of trustees of the free public library.

Upon the passage of such resolution the board of trustees of the free public library shall be empowered and authorized, ~~with the consent of the mayor or other chief executive officer of such municipality,~~ with the consent of the mayor or other chief executive officer of such municipality, to purchase real estate, and to erect buildings and make improvements thereon, and to expend moneys therefor to the amount of such appropriation and surplus, but no lands shall be purchased for the purpose of erecting thereon a free public library building except with the concurrence of such common council, or such other body or board, expressed by resolution of such common council, or such other body or board with the approval of the mayor or other chief executive officer of the municipality. Any veto exercised by the mayor or other chief executive officer may be overridden by a ⅔ majority vote of the governing body of the municipality.

The title of any real estate so purchased shall be taken in the name of the municipality. The use and control of such real estate shall be in the board of trustees of the free public library so long as it shall be used for free public library purposes.

Amended by L.1971, c. 201, § 1, eff. June 9, 1971.

40:54-26.   Bond issues

Any municipality that shall hereafter establish a library under the provisions of this article or has heretofore established a free public library pursuant to law may create and issue bonds for the acquisition of lands, the acquisition and erection and improvement of buildings and appliances for library purposes and the equipment and furnishing of library buildings. Such bonds shall be issued pursuant to the provisions of article 1 of chapter 1 of this title (§ 40:1-1 et seq.).

Source. L.1905, c. 150, § 14, p. 279 [C.S. p. 3120, § 78], as am. by L.1921, c. 2, § 3, p. 15, L.1921, c. 161, § 1, p. 439 [1924 Suppl. § 115-78].

40:54-27.   Redemption of bonds

There shall be raised and levied annually by taxation in the municipality issuing such bonds a sum sufficient to pay the interest thereon and to redeem the part or proportion thereof maturing in the fiscal year for which such taxes are levied.

Source. L.1905, c. 150, § 17, p. 281 [C.S. p. 3121, § 81].

40:54-28.   Acquisition of lands by condemnation

When the board of trustees of the free public library in any municipality desire to acquire any lands, improved or unimproved, either in whole or in part, for the purposes of its building and library pursuant to the authority and power vested in it by section 40:54-25 of this title, and it cannot agree with the owner or owners of such lands, or with other persons interested therein, as to the amount of compensation to be paid therefor, proceedings shall be taken by said board to acquire such lands and ascertain the amount of compensation to be paid therefor, in the manner provided by the general laws for the condemnation and taking of lands for public use.

Source. L.1905, c. 150, § 12, p. 278 [C.S. p. 3119, § 76].

40:54-29.   Transfer of books to library

Any public board in any municipality wherein there is a free public library, or any department of the government of the municipality having under its control a library or collection of books useful for such public library, may transfer the control or property of said books to the trustees of a free public library established under this article for use therein. The board or department so transferring its books or library shall be relieved from further responsibility for the care or custody of or property in said books or library, and the board of trustees of the free public library shall hold and keep said books or library as if originally purchased by it.

Source. L.1905, c. 150, § 10, p. 277 [C.S. p. 3118, § 74].

40:54–35. Library funds

The governing body of any municipality may appropriate and raise such sum of money as in its judgment may be deemed necessary to aid libraries and reading rooms in serving any such municipality, whether such libraries or reading rooms be located in such municipality or in an adjoining municipality; provided, the person or corporation owning or controlling any library and reading room receiving and accepting such aid shall keep the same open free to the use of the public at such reasonable hours as meets the approval of the governing body of such municipality. As amended L.1938, c. 68, p. 179, § 1; L.1941, c. 199, p. 589, § 1; L.1943, c. 24, p. 58, § 1; L.1947, c. 219, p. 880, § 1; L.1956, c. 78, p. 165, § 1, eff. June 7, 1956.

Source. L.1918, c. 126, § 1, p. 290 [1924 Suppl. § *136–4300A(1)].

Joint Library Agreements
(New Jersey Statutes Annotated, 1982, s.40:54-29.1 to 40:54-29.25.)

40:54–29.1 Contracts with other municipalities for library service

The governing body of any municipality may, by resolution, contract with any other municipality which maintains a free public library, for the furnishing of library service to the inhabitants of the first municipality, and may appropriate annually for this purpose such sum of money as may be agreed upon between the contracting parties. L.1951, c. 102, p. 507, § 1, eff. May 22, 1951.

40:54–29.2 Use of moneys received under contracts

The governing body of such other municipality may, by resolution, enter into contract as provided in this act and all sums of money paid under such contract shall be appropriated and used for library purposes in accordance with the terms of said contract. L.1951, c. 102, p. 507, § 2, eff. May 22, 1951.

40:54–29.3   Support, maintenance and control of joint free public library

Any 2 or more municipalities may unite in the support, maintenance and control of a joint free public library for the use and benefit of the residents of such municipalities. L.1959, c. 155, p. 619, § 1, eff. Sept. 4, 1959.

40:54–29.4   Joint library agreement; contents

The governing bodies of such municipalities shall propose such an undertaking by a joint library agreement, which shall provide for the apportionment of annual and special appropriations therefor among such municipalities, for the initial annual appropriation for such library, for the abandonment or the continuance of such agreement in the event that it is not approved by all such municipalities as provided for in this act, and for such other matters as they shall determine. Such apportionment of appropriations may be based on the assessed valuations of the respective municipalities, their populations, or such factor or factors as the governing bodies shall agree. L.1959, c. 155, p. 619, § 2, eff. Sept. 4, 1959.

40:54–29.5   Filing of agreement and ordinance approving agreement; amendments

After the introduction of an ordinance approving such joint library agreement, which may be incorporated by reference therein, such agreement shall be and remain on file for public inspection in the municipal clerk's office from the time of introduction of such ordinance and such ordinance shall so state. A copy of such ordinance and of the joint library agreement shall be filed with the Commissioner of the Department of Education and the Director of the Division of Local Government. Subsequent amendments and supplements to such ordinance and agreement shall be filed in like manner. L.1959, c. 155, p. 619, § 3, eff. Sept. 4, 1959.

40:54–29.6   Notification of governing bodies after adoption of ordinance; submission of question to voters

After the adoption of such ordinance, each governing body shall notify each of the other governing bodies proposing to unite in the joint library of such adoption. After the adoption of such ordinances by all such governing bodies, the question of uniting in such undertaking shall be submitted to the legal voters of each such municipality at the next general election unless said election is less than 40 days after the adoption of such ordinances, in which event it shall be submitted at the next succeeding general election. L.1959, c. 155, p. 619, § 4, eff. Sept. 4, 1959.

40:54–29.7 Form of ballot

Such question shall be placed upon the official ballots in each of the participating municipalities in substantially the following form:

"Shall . . . (insert the name of one municipality) . . . unite with . . . (insert the name or names of the other municipality or municipalities) . . . in the support, maintenance and control of a joint free public library pursuant to chapter . . . (insert the chapter number of this act) . . . of the laws of 1959?"

L.1959, c. 155, p. 620, § 5, eff. Sept. 4, 1959.

40:54–29.8 Effect of majority approval

These municipalities in which at said election the question is approved by a majority of the legal votes cast in each, both for and against such question, shall, as of January 1 next following said election, unite in the support, maintenance and control of a joint free public library in accordance with such joint library agreement. Said municipalities shall not thereafter be required to participate in or support any county library system. L.1959, c. 155, p. 620, § 6, eff. Sept. 4, 1959.

40:54–29.9 Amendment of joint library agreement; approval by ordinance

The joint library agreement may be amended by agreement among the parties thereto but such amendments shall not become effective until approved in each of the participating municipalities by ordinance, which ordinances may incorporate such amendments by reference. L.1959, c. 155, p. 621, § 7, eff. Sept. 4, 1959.

40:54–29.10 Board of trustees of joint library; composition; terms of members; vacancies

The board of trustees of such joint library shall consist of (a) the mayor or other chief executive officer of each participating municipality; (b) the superintendent of schools of the local school district of each such municipality, or, if there be no such official, 1 of the principals in the local school system, selected by the mayor or other chief executive officer, or, if there be neither of such officials, the president of the board of education; and (c) 3 citizens to be appointed by the mayor or other chief executive officer of each such municipality, at least 2 of whom shall be residents of the municipality. The initial appointments of such citizen members shall be for terms of 3, 4 and 5 years, respectively, as they may be selected by the mayor or other chief executive officer. Thereafter, such citizen appointments shall be for terms of 5 years and until their successors are appointed and qualify. The original citizen appointments in any municipality having a free public library at the time for the formation of the joint library shall be made from among the appointed citizen members of the board of trustees of such library. Vacancies occurring on the board of trustees shall be filled for the unexpired term only. L.1959, c. 155, p. 621, § 8, eff. Sept. 4, 1959.

40:54–29.11   Termination of boards of trustees of free public libraries of participating municipalities; assets and obligations

Upon the formation of a joint free public library, the terms of office of the members of the board of trustees of any free public library of any participating municipality shall terminate. The assets and obligations of any such board of trustees shall devolve upon such municipality unless otherwise provided in the agreement. L.1959, c. 155, p. 621, § 9, eff. Sept. 4, 1959.

40:54–29.12   Board of trustees as body corporate; name

The board of trustees of the joint library shall be a body corporate under the name of "The trustees of the joint free public library of . . . (insert the names of the participating municipalities, or other appropriate designation). . . ." L.1959, c. 155, p. 622, § 10, eff. Sept. 4, 1959.

40:54–29.13   Powers and duties of board

The board of trustees shall be vested with authority to carry out the purposes of the joint library, in the manner provided for free public libraries governed pursuant to chapter 54 of Title 40 of the Revised Statutes. The powers and duties of boards of trustees of free public libraries governed by said chapter, not inconsistent herewith, are hereby conferred and imposed upon the board of trustes of such joint library and its trustees and officers. L.1959, c. 155, p. 622, § 11, eff. Sept. 4, 1959.

40:54–29.14   Disbursing officer

The board of trustees of the joint library shall designate the chief financial officer of 1 of the participating municipalities as the disbursing officer for such joint library. L.1959, c. 155, p. 622, § 12, eff. Sept. 4, 1959.

40:54–29.15 Employees

Employees of any free public library of any participating municipality at the time of the formation of the joint library shall, upon the formation thereof, become employees of the joint library without diminution in salary. L.1959, c. 155, p. 622, § 13, eff. Sept. 4, 1959.

40:54–29.16 Certification of sum needed for operation of joint library; apportionment

The board of trustees of the joint library shall, not later than December 1 of each year, certify to the respective municipalities the sum required for the operation of the joint library for the ensuing year and the share of such sum to be borne by each of the municipalities in accordance with the method of apportionment provided in the joint library agreement. If the governing body of any of the municipalities objects to the amount or apportionment so certified, it shall forthwith call a joint meeting of the governing bodies and the board of trustees for the purpose of adjusting and settling any differences. If the governing bodies of such municipalities cannot agree, the matter shall be referred to the Director of the Division of Local Government for determination. L.1959, c. 155, p. 622, § 14, eff. Sept. 4, 1959.

40:54–29.17 Appropriation by municipalities; payment to disbursing officer

Each municipality shall appropriate its proportionate share of the sum so certified or agreed upon or determined in its annual budget, shall raise the same by taxation, and shall pay over said share to the disbursing officer of the joint library at the times annual appropriations for other departments of the municipality are paid over. Operations under the budget and related matters shall be subject to and in accordance with rules of the local government board. L.1959, c. 155, p. 623, § 15, eff. Sept. 4, 1959.

40:54–29.18 Capital improvements; certification of sums needed; apportionment of costs

If the board of trustees shall determine that it is advisable to raise money for the acquisition of lands or a building or buildings or for the improvement of lands or for erecting, enlarging, repairing, altering, furnishing, decorating or equipping a building

or buildings or for other capital improvement for the purpose of
a joint free public library, it shall certify to the respective municipalities the sum or sums, in addition to such moneys as it
may have on hand applicable to such purposes, estimated to be
necessary for such purposes, and the share of such sum or sums
to be borne by each municipality in accordance with the method
of apportionment provided in the joint library agreement. If
the governing body of any of the municipalities objects to any
of said purposes or to the amount or apportionment of said sum
or sums, it shall forthwith call a joint meeting of the governing
bodies and board of trustees for the purpose of adjusting or settling any differences. If the governing bodies of such municipalities cannot agree, the matter shall be referred to the Director
of the Division of Local Government for determination. L.1959,
c. 155, p. 623, § 16, eff. Sept. 4, 1959.

40:54–29.19 Appropriation for capital improvements; borrowing

Each municipality, to provide for such capital improvement,
shall either:

(a) appropriate its proportionate share of the sum or sums for
the purposes certified or agreed upon or determined in the same
manner as other appropriations are made by it pursuant to the
Local Budget Law (R.S. 40:2–1 et seq.); or

(b) by ordinance appropriate such sum or sums for such purposes, pursuant to said ordinance borrow the sum or sums so
appropriated and secure the repayment of the sum or sums so
borrowed by the authorization and issuance of bonds or notes of
the municipality pursuant to and in the manner and within the
limitations prescribed by the Local Bond Law (R.S. 40:1–1 et
seq.). L.1959, c. 155, p. 623, § 17, eff. Sept. 4, 1959.

40:54–29.20 Consent to capital improvements; expenditures

The board of trustees shall be empowered and authorized, with
the consent of the governing bodies of the municipalities, to undertake the purpose or purposes for which such appropriation
for capital improvement was made and to expend moneys therefor to the amount of such appropriation, in addition to other
moneys available therefor. L.1959, c. 155, p. 624, § 18, eff. Sept.
4, 1959.

40:54–29.21 Title to realty

The title to any real estate acquired pursuant to any such appropriation shall be taken in the names of the municipalities as tenants in common, but the use and control thereof shall be in the board of trustees so long as such real estate is used for joint free public library purposes. L.1959, c. 155, p. 624, § 19, eff. Sept. 4, 1959.

40:54–29.22 Discontinuance of participation in joint library; notice; joint meeting of governing bodies

If the governing body of any municipality shall determine by ordinance to propose to discontinue its participation in the support, maintenance and control of the joint free public library, it shall give notice thereof to the governing body of each of the other participating municipalities and to the board of trustees. The said governing bodies and board of trustees shall hold a joint meeting as soon as practicable for the purpose of arriving at an agreement as to the method of such discontinuance, the use of the library facilities thereafter, the adjustment, apportionment, accounting for, settlement, allowance and satisfaction of the rights and liabilities in or with respect to any property, obligations or other matters or things connected with said library, and such other matters and things in connection therewith as such governing bodies shall determine. If said governing bodies shall be unable to agree, the matter shall be referred to the Director of the Division of Local Government for determination. L.1959, c. 155, p. 624, § 20, eff. Sept. 4, 1959.

40:54–29.23 Discontinuance; ordinance; filing; submission of question to voters

When such discontinuance has been agreed upon or determined and if the governing body of the municipality proposing such discontinuance shall determine to proceed therewith,

(a) such governing body shall introduce an ordinance authorizing and directing the submission to the legal voters the question whether said municipality shall discontinue participation in the joint library pursuant to said agreement or determination, which agreement or determination may be incorporated by reference in said ordinance provided said agreement or determination shall be and remain on file in the office of the municipal clerk for public inspection;

(b) if said ordinance shall be adopted, a copy thereof and of said agreement or determination shall be filed with the Director of the Division of Local Government and the Commissioner of the Department of Education; and

(c) the question of such discontinuance shall be submitted

to the legal voters of such municipality at the next general election to be held therein not less than 40 days after the adoption of said ordinance, and said agreement or determination shall remain on file in the office of the municipal clerk for public inspection pending such election. L.1959, c. 155, p. 625, § 21, eff. Sept. 4, 1959.

40:54-29.24   Discontinuance; form of ballot

Such question shall be placed upon the official ballots for such election in substantially the following form:

"Shall . . . (name of municipality submitting the question) . . . discontinue joint participation with . . . (name of the other participating municipality or municipalities) . . . in the support, maintenance and control of a joint free public library pursuant to chapter . . . (insert chapter number of this act) . . . of the laws of 1959?"

L.1959, c. 155, p. 625, § 22, eff. Sept. 4, 1959.

40:54-29.25   Discontinuance; effect of majority approval; participation in joint library by remaining municipalities

If at said election the question is approved in such municipality by a majority of the legal votes cast both for and against such question, the joint participation of said municipality in the support, maintenance and control of said joint free public library shall be discontinued in accordance with the agreement or determination. If more than 2 municipalities have united to participate in such joint free public library, the participation by the remaining municipalities shall continue, unless otherwise provided for in the discontinuance agreement or determination. L.1959, c. 155, p. 625, § 23, eff. Sept. 4, 1959.

Miscellaneous Provisions
(New Jersey Statutes Annotated, 1982, s.40:43-66.30, 40:60-10 to
40:60-13, 40:61-6, 40:171-188.1, 40:171-188.2.)

40:43-66.30. Library employees

Employees of a library of the consolidating municipality shall, after the date of consolidation, be library employees of the new municipality. L.1939, c. 343, p. 844, § 35.

40:60-10. Property of certain societies transferred in trust to municipality; purposes

Whenever any school society or religious organization of this state owns real or personal property and, owing to the establishment and existence of free schools and other public institutions, the society or organization finds it impossible or impracticable to continue in existence for the purposes for which it was created, desires to convey any such property to any municipality for the purpose of establishing free reading rooms, libraries or other institutions for the public benefit, such society or organization may convey the same to the municipality in trust for such purposes. L.1893. c. 287, preamble, p. 499 [C.S. p. 3510, § 218].

40:60–11. Acceptance of property in trust; appointment of trustees

The governing body of any municipality which is or shall be the beneficiary of such a trust may accept it for the purposes set forth in section 40:60–10 of this title and may appoint any number of trustees designated by the terms and under the conditions of the trust instrument. L.1893, c. 287, § 1, p. 500 [C.S. p. 3510, § 218].

40:60–12. Purchase of lands adjoining trust lands; bonds; use of income and proceeds

Any society or organization designated in section 40:60–10 of this title may sell to the municipality any lands owned by it and adjoining the lands conveyed in trust as provided in said section 40:60–10. The municipality may purchase such adjoining lands for the purposes aforesaid, and may issue bonds not to exceed ten thousand dollars in payment therefor; provided, that the interest accruing upon said bonds shall be used and devoted for the purpose of maintaining said trust and carrying out the purposes thereof. L.1893. c. 287, § 1, p. 500 [C.S. p. 3510, § 218].

40:60–13. Municipality not liable for misappropriation of funds

Nothing in sections 40:60–10 to 40:60–12 of this title contained shall be construed to make any municipality liable for the misappropriation of the funds created by the trust, nor to make good any diminution thereof resulting from the wrongful acts of its agents or any person appointed in conformity with the terms and conditions of the deed or instrument creating the trust. If, however, any agent or officer of the municipality is under bonds thereto, and upon default the municipality recovers from the sureties on the bond a sum sufficient to pay or make good the amount of misappropriation of the funds of the trust, the municipality shall make good the same out of the amount so received. No misappropriation of the funds aforesaid shall in anywise affect the trust. L.1893, c. 287, § 2, p. 500 [C.S. p. 3511, § 219].

40:61–6. Library, art gallery and museum in parks; site; control

A public library, art gallery, or museum, may be constructed or maintained in any public park or square in any municipality. The board or body having control of such park or square shall designate the part thereof upon which any such building may be constructed or maintained. The building shall be managed and controlled by the board or body charged with the care and maintenance thereof. L.1917, c. 152, Art. XXXVI, § 6, p. 453 [1924 Suppl. § *136-3606].

40:171–188.1. Procedure in dismissal of municipal librarians

1. Any person now holding the position or office of municipal librarian or of library assistant of any city of the second class of this state and not under the supervision and control of a public library board of trustees and not under civil service, and any other person who may hereafter be appointed to the position or office of municipal librarian or of library assistant in any such city, shall not be dismissed except for inefficiency, incapacity, conduct unbecoming a librarian or of library assistant, or other just cause, after written charge of the cause or causes shall have been preferred against him or her, signed by the person or persons making the same, and filed with the governing body in charge of the library or libraries in which such service is being rendered, and after the charges shall have been examined into, and found true in fact by said governing body, upon reasonable notice to the person charged, who may be represented by counsel at the hearing, which hearing is to be fair and impartial, notwithstanding that said librarian or library assistant may have been appointed for a fixed term: provided, however, that every such municipal librarian or library assistant now employed and intended to be granted tenure by this act shall possess at least ten years' continuous service or the minimum professional qualifications respecting education and experience as has been or may be established by the New Jersey Library Association; and provided, further, that subsequent appointments to these positions in filling vacancies or in the extension of library personnel shall likewise possess the said minimum professional qualifications as to education and experience as established by the New Jersey Library Association, subject to all of the provisions and requirements of an act entitled "An act regulating the employment, tenure and discharge of certain officers and employees of this state, and of the various counties and municipalities thereof, and providing for a civil service commission, and defining its powers and duties," approved April tenth, one thousand nine hundred and eight, and the acts amendatory thereof and supplementary thereto, the said laws applying to the employees of libraries in cities of the second class in the same way as if the said cities had adopted the provisions of the civil service laws by referendum vote. (L.1936, c. 92, § 1, p. 233.)

40:171–188.2. "Municipal librarian" defined

2. The term municipal librarian as used in this act shall be construed to mean and include librarian, manager of libraries, super-

intendent of libraries and director of libraries of all municipalities within the above classification. (L.1936, c. 92, § 2, p. 234.)

SCHOOL LIBRARIES
(New Jersey Statutes Annotated, 1982, s.18A:20-34.)

18A:20-34. Use of schoolhouse and grounds for various purposes

The board of education of any district may, pursuant to rules adopted by it, permit the use of any schoolhouse and rooms therein, and the grounds and other property of the district, when not in use for school purposes, for any of the following purposes:

* * * * *

b. Public library purposes or stations of public libraries;

L.1920, c. 342, § 1, p. 607 [1924 Suppl. § 185–86a], suppl. to L.1903 (2d Sp.Sess.). c. 1, p. 5.

COUNTY TEACHERS LIBRARIES
(New Jersey Statutes Annotated, 1982, s.18A:32-1, 18A-32-2.)

18A:32-1. Appropriation for establishment and maintenance

Whenever in any county there shall have been raised by subscription a sum of money not less than $100.00 for the establishment of a library of pedagogical books for the use of the teachers of the public schools, the director of the treasury shall, upon the order of the commissioner, draw his warrant on the state treasurer in favor of the county superintendent of the county for the sum of $100.00 for the benefit of such library. Annually thereafter there shall be paid on a like order a sum not less than $50.00 nor more than $100.00 upon condition that there shall have been raised by subscription a like sum for the maintenance of the library for the year.   Source: R.S. 18:5–22.

18A:32-2. Committee to select books and manage library

The county superintendent and three teachers of public schools in the county appointed by him shall constitute a committee to select and purchase books and apparatus for the library, and to make rules for the management, use, and safekeeping thereof.   Source: R.S. 18:13–121.

INCORPORATED LIBRARIES
(New Jersey Statutes Annotated, 1982, s.15:6-1 to 15:6-3.)

15:6-1. Abolition of capital stock by certain corporations

A corporation organized for educational, library or literary purposes under any general or special law of this state authorizing the issue of capital stock by the corporation, may, with the consent in writing of all its stockholders and the surrender by them in writing of all their voting and property rights as stockholders, abolish the capital stock of the corporation by a resolution of the trustees declaring:

a. That the capital stock is abolished and that the corporation shall no longer be a stock corporation; and

b. That the board of trustees then in office shall be a continuing and continuous board of trustees of the corporation, with power to enact by-laws, rules and regulations, elect officers, fill any vacancies in its membership and have all the powers, duties and rights conferred on the trustees of the corporation by its charter or certificate of incorporation, or any other law of this state.

A copy of the resolution, certified by the president and secretary under the corporate seal, and acknowledged or proved as in the case of deeds of real estate, together with the consent in writing of all its stockholders, and a statement certified by the secretary under the seal of the corporation, containing the names and post-office addresses of the trustees then in office, shall be filed and recorded in the office of the secretary of state. Upon the filing of such certificates the provisions of the resolution of the trustees shall take effect and such board of trustees shall have full power to exercise, maintain and perform all the powers, duties, rights, functions and purposes of the corporation or its stockholders, but such trustees may not divert the real or personal property of the corporation from the educational, library or literary uses to promote which the corporation was formed.

The certificate of the secretary of state that such copy of the resolution of trustees and consent of stockholders have been filed in his office, shall be taken and accepted as evidence of the change in the corporation in all courts and places.

No person shall be elected a trustee of the corporation who is not a citizen and resident of this state.   L.1904, c. 118, § 3, p. 245 [C.S. p. 4298, § 9].

15:6–2. Historical or library corporations; holding or conveying property; acting as trustee

Every corporation of this state organized for historical or library purposes under the provisions of any law, general, special or private, of this state, may take and hold by purchase, gift, devise, bequest or otherwise, for any historical or library purposes whatsoever, such real or personal property, or both, as such corporation may require, or as, in any manner, has been or may be vested in such corporation for any or all of such purposes, and may grant, bargain, sell or convey the same. Every such corporation may take and hold in trust for any historical or library purposes whatsoever such real or personal property, or both, as in any manner has been or may be given, granted, conveyed, bequeathed or devised to or otherwise vested in such corporation in trust for any of said purposes, and may grant, bargain, sell and convey property so held or to be held in trust for any such purposes, in accordance with the terms of the gift, grant, conveyance, bequest, devise or instrument creating such trust or trusts respectively. L.1910, c. 119, § 1, p. 199 [C.S. p. 4303, § 21].

15:6–3. Limitation on amount of property owned by private library

Any private library association or corporation of this state, organized or incorporated either under a general or special law of this state, may hold, receive, purchase or take by gift, grant or devise, or otherwise acquire or accept, any real property and any personal property for the purposes of said association or corporation, provided the total property owned by such association or corporation at the time of the acceptance thereof or the acquisition thereof, including the property then acquired or received, does not exceed in value the sum of five hundred thousand dollars. The amount of yearly income of such association or corporation shall not be limited. L.1934, c. 108, § 1, p. 297.

COUNTY LAW LIBRARIES
(New Jersey Statutes Annotated, 1982, s.2A:11-37, 40:33-14.)

2A:11–37. Librarian for county law library in first-class counties

The assignment judge of the superior court for a county of the first class, where no librarian has been appointed for the county law library, may designate a competent court officer, who shall, in addition to his other duties, attend the library, for which service the board may fix an additional compensation to be paid to such officer by the treasurer of the county.

40:33–14. Law library; maintenance; purchase of books; maximum expenditures to be fixed annually

The board of chosen freeholders may maintain at the courthouse a law library for the use of the courts held in the county, and for that purpose shall purchase such reports and statutes of the United States, the State of New Jersey and other States and countries and such textbooks as may be designated by the judge of the County Court or, in counties where there are 2 or more county judges, by a majority thereof. The amount so expended shall not exceed the sum fixed annually by the board of chosen freeholders. As amended L.1953, c. 37, p. 650, § 61; L.1954, c. 250, p. 917, § 1, eff. Dec. 13, 1954.

Source. L.1918, c. 185, § 1710, p. 620, as am. by L.1923, c. 100, § 1, p. 191 [1924 Suppl. § 48–*1710].

New Jersey library laws are reprinted from NEW JERSEY STATUTES ANNOTATED published by West Publishing Co., St. Paul, Minnesota and Soney and Sage Co., Newark, New Jersey.

NEW MEXICO

STATE LIBRARY COMMISSION
(New Mexico Statutes Annotated, 1982 s.18-2-1 to 18-2-7.1, 9-6-9.)

18-2-1. State library commission created.

There is created a "New Mexico state library commission," composed of five members, which shall have its headquarters at the state capitol. Four members of the commission shall be appointed by the governor from among resident citizens of the state interested in and informed with regard to library conditions, the appointees insofar as practicable to represent different sections of the state. Two of the members shall be originally appointed for a term of two years; one member shall be originally appointed for a term of four years; and one member shall be originally appointed for a term of six years. After the expiration of the original appointments, all appointments shall be for terms of six years. The fifth member of the commission shall be a member of the state board of education chosen by vote of the board's membership. The term of the fifth member shall be for so long as he serves on the state board of education, but not to exceed six years. At least one member of the commission shall be a professionally trained librarian. Members of the commission shall be entitled to per diem and mileage as provided in the Per Diem and Mileage Act [10-8-1 to 10-8-8 NMSA 1978] while engaged in the performance of their official duties for the commission.

History: Laws 1941, ch. 129, § 1; 1941 Comp., § 3-801; 1953 Comp., § 4-11-1; Laws 1961, ch. 126, § 1; 1975, ch. 34, § 1.

18-2-2. State library commission; duties.

The New Mexico state library commission shall provide advice, upon request, to the state librarian on:

A. matters germane to the powers and duties of the library division or the state library; and

B. any other matters related to libraries.

History: 1953 Comp., § 4-11-2, enacted by Laws 1977, ch. 246, § 9.

18-2-3. Library division; creation; director.

A. The "library division" is created within the office of cultural affairs.

B. Subject to the authority of the state cultural affairs officer, the administrative and executive head of the library division is the "state librarian." The state librarian shall be appointed by the state cultural affairs officer with the consent of the secretary of finance and administration.

History: 1953 Comp., § 4-11-3, enacted by Laws 1977, ch. 246, § 10; 1980, ch. 151, § 22.

18-2-4. Duties of the state librarian.

The state librarian shall:
A. administer the state library;
B. administer grants-in-aid and encourage local library service and generally promote an effective statewide library system;
C. make studies and surveys of public library needs;
D. supply advice and information to existing libraries and aid in the establishment of new libraries;
E. obtain each year, from all libraries in the state, reports showing the conditions, growth and development, together with such other facts and statistics regarding them as is of public interest;
F. cooperate with other educational services and governmental agencies of the state, and with library agencies of other states and with national library agencies;
G. cooperate with the administrative services division in preparing the budget for the state library;
H. administer the library extension service;
I. make rules and regulations necessary to administer the division and as provided by law; and to perform other duties as provided by law; and
J. establish and administer a library depository and distribution system for state documents and publications.

History: 1953 Comp., § 4-11-3.1, enacted by Laws 1961, ch. 126, § 4; 1977, ch. 246, § 11; 1978, ch. 140, § 1.

18-2-4. Duties of the state librarian.

Appropriations. — Laws 1981, ch. 59, §§ 1 through 5, appropriate $650,000 from the state general fund to the New Mexico state library for assisting local governments in providing their residents with books for public libraries, provide that the appropriation shall be distributed by warrants of the department of finance and administration upon certification by the state librarian as to the distribution and provide for the allocation of the money by the state librarian. The general purpose of the allocation is to provide to the various public libraries and the extension service of the state library with $.50 per capita for the purpose of purchasing books. The state librarian shall allocate the entire appropriation among the counties, each county to be allocated an amount equal to $.50 for each person in the county according to the population of the county as determined by the 1980 federal decennial census. The amount by which the appropriation exceeds this allocation shall revert to the general fund as soon as this allocation is made. The amount allocated to each county shall be distributed as follows: A. if there is no public library within the county, the total county allocation for that county shall be transferred to the New Mexico state library for purchasing books for its extension service; and B. the allocation made to each county in which there is a public library shall be further divided as follows: (1) each municipality containing a public library shall be allocated an amount equal to $.50 for each person in the municipality according to the population of the municipality as determined by the 1980 federal decennial census; and (2) the remainder of each county's allocation, after the allocation is made to public libraries within the municipalities in the county, shall be divided between these public libraries in that county in the New Mexico state library extension service on a formula to be devised by the state librarian and approved by the board of county commissioners and a governing board of each municipality in the county prior to distribution of remainder of that county's allocation. If the formula for the distribution of a county's allocation is not approved and the distribution made by the end of the seventieth fiscal year, that county's portion of the fund to be distributed shall revert to the general fund. All counties and municipalities owning and operating or funding public libraries in their counties and receiving funds under the act are prohibited from budgeting and spending for the library services and the purchase for books from funds other than those distributed by the act an amount less than budgeted for that item for the sixty-ninth fiscal year, for each of the seventieth, seventy-first and seventy-second fiscal years. It is the intent of the legislature that the funds provided by the act are to be used by local governments as supplemental funds for the purchase of books, and not in lieu of local funds. "Public library" means a library existing on January 1, 1981, which has been established by city or county ordinance or other legal resolution of establishment. Any funds distributed under the act may be used at any time during the seventieth through seventy-second fiscal years.

18-2-4.1. State publications; copies required.

A. Unless otherwise directed by the state librarian, every state agency shall deposit twenty-five copies of all its publications intended for public distribution, when issued, with the state library depository for depository and distribution purposes, excluding those publications issued strictly for internal use and those intended for public sale.

B. The state librarian shall determine the number of copies of regularly issued publications required to meet the needs of the various libraries in the state, and shall inform the affected agencies of the exact number of copies required.

History: 1953 Comp., § 4-11-3.2, enacted by Laws 1978, ch. 140, § 2.

18-2-5. State library administrative agency.

The library division of the office of cultural affairs is designated a state library administrative agency and is empowered to accept gifts or grants of any nature from federal, state, county, local or private agencies for the purpose of carrying on its work. Any grant of money so received shall be deposited in the state treasury to the credit of the library division and shall be used only for the purpose for which it is given or granted.

History: Laws 1941, ch. 129, § 3; 1941 Comp., § 3-804; 1953 Comp., § 4-11-4; Laws 1961, ch. 123, § 5; 1977, ch. 246, § 12; 1980, ch. 151, § 23.

18-2-6. Organization, officers.

The commission shall organize by electing a chairman and a vice chairman from its membership.

History: Laws 1941, ch. 129, § 4; 1941 Comp., § 3-805; 1953 Comp., § 4-11-5; Laws 1961, ch. 126, § 6; 1977, ch. 246, § 13.

18-2-7. Construction of provisions of act.

The provisions of this act shall not divest any state, county, municipal or other governing board or agency of its control and supervision of any library under its jurisdiction, except as the provisions of this act apply to the control and management of the state library. Specifically, nothing herein is intended to alter or amend the provisions of Sections 18-1-1 through 18-1-12 NMSA 1978.

History: Laws 1941, ch. 129, § 5; 1941 Comp., § 3-806; 1953 Comp., § 4-11-6; Laws 1961, ch. 126, § 7.

18-2-7.1. Distribution system; limitation.

The state library depository shall not engage in the direct distribution of state publications to the general public except in those cases where the state library does so in the course of operating as a library or a state extension service.

History: 1953 Comp., § 4-11-6.1, enacted by Laws 1978, ch. 140, § 3.

9-6-9. Creation of office.

The "office of cultural affairs" is created. The office shall consist of such divisions as are created by law or executive order, including but not limited to:
A. the administrative services division;
B. the arts division;
C. the library division;
D. the museum division; and
E. the international space hall of fame division.

History: Laws 1980, ch. 151, § 54.

FEDERAL GRANTS-IN-AID

(New Mexico Statutes Annotated, 1982, s.22-9-7 to 22-9-10, 22-9-12.)

22-9-7. Federal grant-in-aid funds; custody; deposit; disbursement.

The state treasurer is the trustee for all funds apportioned to the state under any act of congress and he is directed to enter into agreements with, and to comply with the rules and regulations of, such agencies of the federal government as are necessary to procure for the state grants of federal aid to education. Any funds received under any act of congress shall be held by the state treasurer in special funds designated in accordance with the purposes of the grant made and shall be paid out by him only on warrant of the secretary of finance and administration. Warrants shall be issued only upon voucher of the superintendent of public instruction for disbursements other than for rural library service. Disbursements made for rural library service shall be made only upon voucher issued by the state librarian.

History: Laws 1939, ch. 162, § 2; 1941 Comp.,
§ 55-519; 1953 Comp., § 73-6-32; Laws 1961, ch. 126,
§ 8; 1977, ch. 247, § 192.

22-9-8. State educational authorities for federal grant administration.

The superintendent of public instruction shall be the state educational authority to represent the state in administration of any funds received under any act of congress to authorize grants to states in aid of education other than grants for aid to rural library service and, as to such grants and funds received thereunder, the state librarian shall be the authority to represent the state in the administration of the funds.

History: Laws 1939, ch. 162, § 3; 1941 Comp.,
§ 55-520; 1953 Comp., § 73-6-33; Laws 1961, ch. 126,
§ 9.

22-9-9. Agencies for grants-in-aid; powers; duties.

Whenever, under any act of the congress of the United States, federal aid to education is made available to the states:

    *   *   *

B. the state librarian of this state is hereby authorized and directed to:
    (1) enter into any and all agreements with the proper federal agency or agencies necessary to procure for this state all benefits for rural or other library service which may be available under any such act of congress;
    (2) make and administer all plans which may be necessary to carry out any provisions of any such act of congress which offers aid to library service;
    (3) provide for and install an adequate system of auditing of the expenditure of funds to be received through the provisions of any such act of congress and to be apportioned to libraries and library services;
    (4) provide for an adequate system of reports to be made to him from libraries and library services; and
    (5) develop and provide a plan for apportioning any funds received for expenditure for library service which will provide for maintenance of a cooperative and integrated system of library service throughout the state, for suitable cooperative arrangements with school systems, cooperative agricultural extension services, and other appropriate agencies, and in such manner of apportioning as will effectively lessen inequalities of opportunity for library service.

History: Laws 1939, ch. 162, § 4; 1941 Comp.,
§ 55-521; 1953 Comp., § 73-6-34; Laws 1961, ch. 126,
§ 10; 1961, ch. 217, § 1; 1977, ch. 246, § 48.

22-9-10. Reports to federal agencies.

Whenever required by any act of congress authorizing federal aid to education or any

    *   *   *

B. the state librarian shall make reports with respect to expenditure of funds received and progress of library service in the form and containing information required by the appropriate federal agencies.

History: Laws 1939, ch. 162, § 5; 1941 Comp., § 55-522; 1953 Comp., § 73-6-35; Laws 1961, ch. 126, § 11.

CERTIFICATION OF LIBRARIANS

(New Mexico Statutes Annotated, 1982, s.18-2 to 18-2-18.)

18-2-8. Certification of librarians.

The state librarian is hereby authorized to issue certificates to librarians. He shall have authority to prescribe and hold examinations, or require submission of credentials to establish the qualifications of those seeking certificates as librarians, and to issue certificates of librarianship to qualified persons, in accordance with such reasonable rules and regulations as he may provide.

History: 1941 Comp., § 3-807, enacted by Laws 1947, ch. 91, § 1; 1953 Comp., § 4-11-7; Laws 1977, ch. 246, § 14.

18-2-9. Types of certificates.

The types of certificates issued by the state librarian shall be:
    A. permanent professional librarian;
    B. grade I librarian;
    C. grade II librarian; and
    D. temporary librarian.

History: 1953 Comp., § 4-11-8, enacted by Laws 1963, ch. 283, § 1; 1977, ch. 246, § 15.

18-2-10. Permanent professional certificate.

A permanent professional librarian's certificate shall be issued without examination to an applicant, otherwise qualified under the rules and regulations of the state librarian who is a graduate of a library school accredited by the American library association.

History: 1953 Comp., § 4-11-8.1, enacted by Laws 1963, ch. 283, § 2; 1977, ch. 246, § 16.

18-2-11. Grade I certificate.

A. A grade I librarian's certificate shall be issued to an applicant without examination when:

    (1) the applicant meets the minimum educational requirements established by the rules and regulations of the state librarian, which shall require completion of a minimum number of years of undergraduate work plus a minimum number of semester hours of library science courses in an institution accredited by its state department of education or a regional accrediting agency; and

    (2) the applicant demonstrates ability to perform the duties of a grade I librarian ably and efficiently.

B. A grade I librarian's certificate shall be issued by examination to an applicant who lacks the minimum educational requirements for a grade I certificate, and who:

    (1) demonstrates ability to perform the duties of a grade I librarian ably and efficiently; and

    (2) successfully passes the examination given by the state librarian for a grade I certificate.

History: 1953 Comp., § 4-11-8.2, enacted by Laws 1963, ch. 283, § 3; 1977, ch. 246, § 17.

18-2-12. Grade II certificate.

A. A grade II librarian's certificate shall be granted to an applicant without examination when the applicant is a graduate of a college or university accredited by its state department of education or a regional accrediting agency, and has a major in library science or has completed a minimum of twenty-one semester hours of library science courses beyond the requirements of a grade I certificate.

B. A grade II librarian's certificate shall be granted by examination to an applicant who lacks the educational requirements for a grade II certificate, and who:

(1) demonstrates ability to perform the duties of a grade II librarian ably and efficiently; and

(2) successfully passes the examination given by the state librarian for a grade II certificate.

History: 1953 Comp., § 4-11-8.3, enacted by Laws 1963, ch. 283, § 4; 1977, ch. 246, § 18.

18-2-13. Temporary certificates.

A. The state librarian shall issue a temporary certificate without examination to an applicant who is unqualified for any other type of librarian certificate when the state librarian receives written recommendation for the issuance of a temporary certificate for the applicant from the library board or governing body concerned which states that no qualified applicant is available for the position.

B. Temporary librarian's certificates shall be issued for all grades and are valid only for one year, but may be renewed or extended for one-year periods upon written recommendation from the library board or governing body concerned stating that no qualified applicant is available for the position.

History: 1953 Comp., § 4-11-8.4, enacted by Laws 1963, ch. 283, § 5; 1977, ch. 246, § 19.

18-2-14. [Applications; who may apply.]

Any person who is actively engaged in, or who expects to engage actively in library service may apply for a certificate, either with or without examination, and if found competent and qualified shall be granted the certificate so applied for, in the manner and upon the payment of the fees provided for in this act [18-2-8, 18-2-14, 18-2-17, 18-2-18 NMSA 1978].

History: 1941 Comp., § 3-809, enacted by Laws 1947, ch. 91, § 4; 1953 Comp., § 4-11-9.

18-2-15. Certificates required.

A. A permanent professional librarian's certificate is required for the chief librarian of any library:

(1) supported in whole or in part by public funds, and serving a municipality or other political subdivision having a population in excess of fifteen thousand persons as shown by the last federal decennial census; or

(2) of any state agency or state-supported institution.

B. A grade I librarian's certificate is required for the chief librarian of any library, supported in whole or in part by public funds, serving a municipality or other political subdivision having a population of at least three thousand, but not more than ten thousand persons, as shown by the last federal decennial census.

C. A grade II librarian's certificate is required for the chief librarian of any library, supported in whole or in part by public funds, serving a municipality or other political subdivision having a population of at least ten thousand and one, but not more than fifteen thousand persons, as shown by the last federal decennial census.

D. The provisions of this section do not apply to libraries of public schools or county law libraries.

History: 1953 Comp., § 4-11-10, enacted by Laws 1963, ch. 283, § 6.

18-2-16. Fees.

A. The fee for any certificate provided for in Section 18-2-9 NMSA 1978 may be prescribed by the state librarian, but the minimum fee for a certificate issued without examination shall be five dollars ($5.00) and the minimum fee for a certificate issued by examination shall be ten dollars ($10.00).

B. All fee money shall be deposited in the general fund.

History: 1953 Comp., § 4-11-11, enacted by Laws 1963, ch. 283, § 7; 1977, ch. 246, § 20.

18-2-17. [Libraries receiving public funds; compliance required.]

No public funds shall be paid to any library failing to comply with the provisions of this act [18-2-8, 18-2-14, 18-2-17, 18-2-18 NMSA 1978].

History: 1941 Comp., § 3-813, enacted by Laws 1947, ch. 91, § 8; 1953 Comp., § 4-11-13.

18-2-18. List of certificated librarians.

The library division of the office of cultural affairs shall issue annually a list of all persons holding librarians' certificates.

History: 1941 Comp., § 3-814, enacted by Laws 1947, ch. 91, § 9; 1953 Comp., § 4-11-14; Laws 1977, ch. 246, § 21; 1980, ch. 151, § 24.

INTERSTATE LIBRARY COMPACT

(New Mexico Statutes Annotated, 1982, s.18-2-19 to 18-2-22.)

18-2-19. Short title.

This act [18-2-19 to 18-2-22 NMSA 1978] may be cited as the "Interstate Library Compact Act."

History: 1953 Comp., § 4-11-15, enacted by Laws 1969, ch. 20, § 1.

18-2-20. Execution of compact.

The interstate library compact is hereby enacted into law and is entered into on behalf of this state with any state bordering on New Mexico which legally joins therein in substantially the following form:

INTERSTATE LIBRARY COMPACT

The contracting states agree that:

ARTICLE I—PURPOSE

Because the desire for the services provided by public libraries transcends governmental boundaries and can be provided most effectively by giving such services to communities of people regardless of jurisdictional lines, it is the policy of the states who are parties to this compact to cooperate and share their responsibilities in providing joint and cooperative library services in areas where the distribution of population makes the provision of library service on an interstate basis the most effective way to provide adequate and efficient services.

ARTICLE II—PROCEDURE

The appropriate officials and agencies of the party states or any of their political subdivisions may, on behalf of said states or political subdivisions, enter into agreements for the cooperative or joint conduct of library services when they shall find that the executions of agreements to that end as provided herein will facilitate library services.

ARTICLE III—CONTENT

Any such agreement for the cooperative or joint establishment, operation or use of library services, facilities, personnel, equipment, materials or other items not excluded because of failure to enumerate shall, as among the parties of the agreement: 1) detail the specific nature of the services, facilities, properties or personnel to which it is applicable; 2) provide for the allocation of costs and other financial responsibilities; 3) specify the respective rights, duties, obligations and liabilities; 4) stipulate the terms and conditions for duration, renewal, termination, abrogation, disposal of joint or common property, if any, and all other matters which may be appropriate to the proper effectuation and performance of said agreement.

ARTICLE IV—CONFLICT OF LAWS

Nothing in this compact or in any agreement entered into hereunder shall be construed to supersede, alter or otherwise impair any obligation imposed on any public library by otherwise applicable laws.

ARTICLE V—ADMINISTRATOR

Each state shall designate a compact administrator with whom copies of all agreements to which his state or any subdivision thereof is party shall be filed. The administrator shall have such powers as may be conferred upon him by the laws of his state and may consult and cooperate with the compact administrators of other party states and take such steps as may effectuate the purposes of this compact.

ARTICLE VI—EFFECTIVE DATE

This compact shall become operative immediately upon its enactment by any state or between it and any other contiguous state or states so enacting.

ARTICLE VII—RENUNCIATION

This compact shall continue in force and remain binding upon each party state until six months after any such state has given notice of repeal by the legislature. Such withdrawal shall not be construed to relieve any party to an agreement authorized by Articles II and III of the compact from the obligation of that agreement prior to the end of its stipulated period of duration.

ARTICLE VIII—SEVERABILITY

The provisions of this compact shall be severable. It is intended that the provisions of this compact be reasonably and liberally construed.

History: 1953 Comp., § 4-11-16, enacted by Laws 1969, ch. 20, § 2.

18-2-21. Compact administrator.

A. The state librarian, ex officio, is the compact administrator.

B. The compact administrator shall:

    (1) receive copies of all agreements entered into by the state or its political subdivisions and other states or political subdivisions;

    (2) consult with, advise and aid the state and its political subdivisions in the formulation of such agreements;

    (3) make recommendations to the governor, legislature, state agencies and departments and to the political subdivisions of the state, as he deems desirable to carry out the purposes of the interstate library compact; and

    (4) consult and cooperate with the compact administrators of other party states.

History: 1953 Comp., § 4-11-17, enacted by Laws 1969, ch. 20, § 3.

18-2-22. Agreements.

The compact administrator and the governing authority of any municipality or county may enter into agreements with other states or their political subdivisions pursuant to the interstate library compact. Such agreements made pursuant to the interstate library compact on behalf of the state shall be made by the compact administrator. Such agreements made on behalf of a political subdivision of the state shall be made after due notice to the compact administrator and after consultation with him.

History: 1953 Comp., § 4-11-18, enacted by Laws 1969, ch. 20, § 4.

SUPREME COURT LAW LIBRARY
(New Mexico Statutes Annotated, 1982, s.18-1-1 to 18-1-12.)

18-1-1. Board of trustees; membership.

There is hereby created a board of trustees, which shall consist of the chief justice and justices of the supreme court of the state of New Mexico, who shall have the management, control and supervision of the supreme court law library.

History: Laws 1915, ch. 47, § 1; C.S. 1929, § 133-101; 1941 Comp., § 3-701; 1953 Comp., § 4-10-1; Laws 1963, ch. 27, § 1.

18-1-2. Supreme court law library board of trustees; chairman and secretary.

The chief justice of the supreme court shall act as chairman of the board of trustees of the supreme court law library, and the clerk of the supreme court shall act as secretary for the board.

History: Laws 1915, ch. 47, § 2; C.S. 1929, § 133-102; Laws 1941, ch. 138, § 1; 1941 Comp., § 3-702; Laws 1949, ch. 97, § 1; 1951, ch. 158, § 1; 1953, ch. 133, § 1; 1953 Comp., § 4-10-2; Laws 1967, ch. 214, § 4.

18-1-3. Power to prescribe rules and regulations.

Said board of trustees shall have the right to prescribe such rules and regulations for the management and control of the supreme court law library, as in the judgment of said board may seem fit and proper for the safety, care and custody of the library, shelving, books, documents and archives therein, and for the convenience and accommodation of the patrons of such library.

History: Laws 1915, ch. 47, § 3; C.S. 1929, § 133-103; 1941 Comp., § 3-703; 1953 Comp., § 4-10-3; Laws 1963, ch. 27, § 2.

18-1-4. [Duties; purchase of books and management of affairs.]

Said board of trustees shall order and purchase all books for said library for which an appropriation shall have been made, and have full and complete management of all the financial affairs of said library.

History: Laws 1915, ch. 47, § 4; C.S. 1929, § 133-104; 1941 Comp., § 3-704; 1953 Comp., § 4-10-4.

18-1-5. Law library board; publishing opinions of supreme court.

In addition to other duties of the board of trustees of the supreme court law library provided by law, the board shall meet from time to time, select from opinions of the supreme court and designate to the clerk of the supreme court those which should be officially reported and published. The board shall also supervise, amend and correct all syllabi or headnotes for published opinions.

History: 1953 Comp., § 4-10-5, enacted by Laws 1966, ch. 28, § 16.

18-1-6. Payment of accounts.

The secretary of finance and administration shall draw warrants on the state treasurer in payment of all accounts which shall have been audited by said board of trustees, to the extent of the appropriations made for such purposes but for no more.

History: Laws 1915, ch. 47, § 5; C.S. 1929, § 133-105; 1941 Comp., § 3-706; 1953 Comp., § 4-10-6; Laws 1977, ch. 247, § 16.

18-1-7. Librarian; appointment by board; custody of property.

The supreme court law library shall be under the care and custody of a librarian, who shall be appointed by said board of trustees, and who shall hold office at the pleasure of said board of trustees. The librarian shall have the custody and charge of all books, archives, maps, charts, engravings and all other things properly belonging to the library, or directed to be deposited therein.

History: Laws 1915, ch. 47, § 6; C.S. 1929, § 133-106; 1941 Comp., § 3-707; 1953 Comp., § 4-10-7; Laws 1963, ch. 27, § 4.

18-1-8. [Bond of librarian; approval.]

The librarian, before taking office, shall give bond to the state of New Mexico in the sum of two thousand dollars [($2,000)], with sufficient surety or sureties, for the faithful performance of his or her duties, for the preservation and safe delivery of all property committed to his or her care, to his or her successor and for the faithful paying over of all moneys coming into his or her hands as librarian. Said bond shall be approved by the chief justice of the supreme court and be filed with the clerk of the supreme court of the state of New Mexico.

History: Laws 1915, ch. 47, § 7; C.S. 1929, § 133-107; 1941 Comp., § 3-708; 1953 Comp., § 4-10-8.

18-1-9. [Unauthorized removal of books or property; criminal liability of librarian.]

If the librarian shall permit or allow any person, not authorized by such rules and regulations as shall be prescribed by the board of trustees, to remove a book or other property from the library, he or she shall be deemed guilty of a misdemeanor, and subject to a fine of ten dollars [($10.00)] for every book or other article so removed.

History: Laws 1915, ch. 47, § 9; C.S. 1929, § 133-109; 1941 Comp., § 3-710; 1953 Comp., § 4-10-10.

18-1-10. [Unlawful removal of books or property; penalty.]

Any person not authorized by the rules and regulations of the board of trustees so to do, who shall take from the library any book or other property belonging thereto, either with or without the consent of the librarian, shall be deemed guilty of a misdemeanor and subject to a fine of ten dollars [($10.00)] for every book or other property so taken. Provided, that in case of a felonious taking of such book or property, the person guilty thereof shall be punished in the manner and to the extent now provided by law for the punishment of such felonies.

History: Laws 1915, ch. 47, § 10; C.S. 1929, § 133-110; 1941 Comp., § 3-711; 1953 Comp., § 4-10-11.

18-1-11. [Liability for injury to books or property.]

Any person injuring, defacing or destroying a book or other property belonging to the library shall forfeit twice the value thereof to be sued for and recovered by the state, and it shall be the duty of the librarian to promptly notify said board of trustees of any such offense.

History: Laws 1915, ch. 47, § 11; C.S. 1929, § 133-111; 1941 Comp., § 3-712; 1953 Comp., § 4-10-12.

18-1-12. Trade, barter and exchange of books and periodicals; powers of board of trustees.

The board of trustees of the supreme court law library, composed of the justices of the supreme court, is hereby authorized to trade, barter and exchange such books and periodicals as the said board of trustees may from time to time acquire, for books and periodicals of equal or similar value, whenever the books and periodicals which may be thus acquired by trade, barter and exchange will be useful to the supreme court law library in building or completing its files, and when in the judgment of the board of trustees such exchange is in the best interests of the said library.

History: Laws 1939, ch. 4, § 1; 1941 Comp., § 3-717; 1953 Comp., § 4-10-20; Laws 1963, ch. 27, § 11.

DISTRIBUTION OF PUBLIC DOCUMENTS

(New Mexico Statutes Annotated, 1982, s.34-4-1, 34-4-3, 14-4-4.)

34-4-1. Distribution of session laws.

A. The secretary of state shall transmit copies of the session laws without charge as follows:

   (1) one copy to each New Mexico supreme court justice;
   (2) one copy to each New Mexico court of appeals judge;
   (3) one copy to each New Mexico district court judge;
   (4) five copies to the New Mexico attorney general;
   (5) two copies to each New Mexico district attorney;
   (6) one copy to the board of county commissioners of each county;
   (7) copies to other state officers and agencies or additional copies to those listed above if the copies or additional copies are needed for governmental purposes and are not to replace lost volumes; and
   (8) copies to the supreme court law library as may be required for exchange of similar materials with officers and agencies of the federal government, other states, districts, territories or possessions of the United States.

B. Copies of session laws supplied to officers and agencies of this state remain the property of the state and shall be delivered to their successors.

C. Whenever it is necessary to replace a volume of the session laws, because of the loss of the original volume, the secretary of state shall charge the officer or agency the same price they would charge if it were sold to a private individual and the money from the sale shall be deposited in the fund it would be deposited in if it resulted from a sale to a private individual.

History: 1953 Comp., § 10-1-13, enacted by Laws 1973, ch. 248, § 1; 1978, ch. 130, § 2.

34-4-3. [Copies of reports of state officers, biennial budget and session laws transmitted to congressional library.]

The officer or employee of this state having charge of the publication of the public documents hereinafter mentioned shall transmit the same to the librarian of congress for the use of members of congress from New Mexico and others interested, if and when printed, as follows: 2 [two] copies each of the biennial budget, of the reports and official opinions of the attorney general of the state, and of all separate compilations of laws issued by state officers: 1 [one] copy each of the legislative journals and other documents published by order of the state legislature or either house thereof and of all reports, bulletins, circulars, pamphlets, maps, charts and other official publications of any executive department, office, commission, bureau, board or state institution now existing or hereafter authorized by law.

History: Laws 1937, ch. 171, § 2; 1941 Comp., § 12-115; 1953 Comp., § 10-1-15.

14-4-4. [Filing and distribution of publications and reports; official depository.]

Each agency issuing any publication, pamphlet, report, notice, proclamation or similar instrument shall immediately file five copies thereof with the records center. The records center shall deliver three copies to the state library which shall keep one copy available for public inspection during office hours. All other copies may be circulated. The state library is designated to be an official depository of all such publications, pamphlets, reports, notices, proclamations and similar instruments.

History: 1953 Comp., § 71-7-5, enacted by Laws 1967, ch. 275, § 5; 1969, ch. 92, § 3.

PUBLIC RECORDS ACT

(New Mexico Statutes Annotated, 1982, s.14-3-1 to 14-3-25.)

14-3-1. Short title.

This act [14-3-1 to 14-3-16, 14-3-18 NMSA 1978] may be cited as the "Public Records Act."

History: 1953 Comp., § 71-6-1, enacted by Laws 1959, ch. 245, § 1.

14-3-2. Definitions.

As used in the Public Records Act [14-3-1 to 14-3-16, 14-3-18 NMSA 1978]:

A. "commission" means the state commission of public records;

B. "administrator" means the state records administrator;

C. "public records" means all books, papers, maps, photographs or other documentary materials, regardless of physical form or characteristics, made or received by any agency in pursuance of law or in connection with the transaction of public business and preserved, or appropriate for preservation, by the agency or its legitimate successor as evidence of the organization, functions, policies, decisions, procedures, operations or other activities of the government, or because of the informational and historical value of data contained therein. Library or museum material of the state library, state institutions and state museums, extra copies of documents preserved only for convenience of reference and stocks of publications and processed documents are not included;

D. "agency" means any state agency, department, bureau, board, commission, institution or other organization of the state government, the territorial government and the Spanish and Mexican governments in New Mexico;

E. "records center" means the central records depository which is the principal state facility for the storage, disposal, allocation or use of noncurrent records of agencies, or materials obtained from other sources; and

F. "microphotography system" means all microphotography equipment, services and supplies.

History: 1953 Comp., § 71-6-2, enacted by Laws 1959, ch. 245, § 2; 1963, ch. 186, § 1; 1977, ch. 301, § 1.

14-3-3. State commission of public records; creation.

A. A "state commission of public records" is established consisting of:

(1) the secretary of state;

(2) the secretary of finance and administration;

(3) the state law librarian;

(4) the director of the museum of New Mexico;

(5) the state auditor;

(6) the attorney general; and

(7) a recognized, professionally trained historian in the field of New Mexico history, resident in New Mexico, appointed by the governor for a term of six years. Each member of the commission may designate an alternate to serve in his stead.

B. The commission shall elect one of its members to be chairman and another to be secretary. The members of the commission shall serve without compensation other than actual expenses of attending meetings of the commission or while in performance of their official duties in connection with the business of the commission.

C. The commission shall hold not less than four meetings during each calendar year and may hold special meetings as may be necessary to transact business of the commission. All meetings shall be called by the chairman or when requested in writing by any two members of the commission. Four members of the commission shall constitute a quorum.

D. The administrator shall attend all meetings of the commission.

History: 1953 Comp., § 71-6-3, enacted by Laws 1959, ch. 245, § 3; 1977, ch. 247, § 181.

14-3-4. Duties and powers of commission.

It shall be the duty of the commission to:

A. employ as state records administrator a competent, experienced person professionally trained as an archivist and records manager who shall serve at the pleasure of the commission. He need not be a resident of New Mexico at the time of his employment. His salary shall be fixed by the commission;

B. approve the biennial budget covering costs of the operations set forth in this act [14-3-1 to 14-3-16, 14-3-18 NMSA 1978], as prepared by the administrator for presentation to the state legislature;

C. decide, by majority vote, any disagreements between the administrator and any state officer regarding the disposition of records within the custody of said officer, such decisions to have the effect of law;

D. consider the recommendations of the administrator for the destruction of specifically reported records, and by unanimous vote either order or forbid such destruction;

E. approve in writing, or reject, the written terms and conditions of each proposed loan of documentary material to the records center, as agreed upon by the lender and the administrator;

F. adopt and publish rules and regulations to carry out the purposes of the Public Records Act [14-3-1 to 14-3-16, 14-3-18 NMSA 1978];

G. request any agency to designate a records liaison officer to cooperate with, assist and advise the administrator in the performance of his duties and to provide such other assistance and data as will enable the commission and administrator properly to carry out the purposes of the Public Records Act; and

H. prepare an annual report to the governor on the operations conducted under the terms of this act during the previous year, including a complete fiscal report on costs and effected savings, and cause same to be published.

History: 1953 Comp., § 71-6-4, enacted by Laws 1959, ch. 245, § 4.

14-3-5. Gifts, donations and loans.

The commission may receive from private sources, financial or other donations to assist in building, enlarging, maintaining or equipping a records center, or for the acquisition by purchase of documentary material, in accordance with plans made and agreed upon by the commission and the administrator. Funds thus received shall be administered by the commission separately from funds supplied by the state for the execution of this act [14-3-1 to 14-3-16, 14-3-18 NMSA 1978], but shall be audited by the state. Such funds shall not be subject to reversion to the general fund if unexpended at the close of the fiscal year. Although all material acquired by expenditure of such donated funds and all such donated material shall become the unqualified and unrestricted property of the state, permanent public acknowledgment of the names of the donors may in each case be made in an appropriate manner.

The commission may receive either as donations or loans from private sources, other state agencies, counties, municipalities, the federal government and other states or countries, documentary materials of any physical form or characteristics which are deemed to be of value to the state and the general public for historical reference or research purposes. Acceptance of both donations and loans shall be at the discretion of the commission upon advice of the administrator. Accepted donations shall become, without qualification or restriction, the property of the state of New Mexico. Loans shall be accepted only after a written agreement covering all terms and conditions of each loan shall have been signed by the lender and the administrator and approved by the commission.

History: 1953 Comp., § 71-6-5, enacted by Laws 1959, ch. 245, § 5.

14-3-6. Administrator; duties.

The administrator is the official custodian and trustee for the state of all public records and archives of whatever kind which are transferred to him from any public office of the state or from any other source. He shall have overall administrative responsibility for carrying out the purposes of the Public Records Act [14-3-1 to 14-3-16, 14-3-18 NMSA 1978], and may employ necessary personnel, purchase equipment and provide facilities as may be required in the execution of the powers conferred and duties imposed upon him. He shall keep the commission advised throughout the year of operations conducted and future operations projected, and shall report annually to the commission which records have been destroyed, transferred or otherwise processed during the year.

The administrator shall establish a records management program for the application of efficient and economical management methods to the creation, utilization, maintenance, retention, preservation and disposal of official records. It shall be the duty of the administrator, in cooperation with and with the approval of the department of finance and administration, to establish standards, procedures and techniques for effective management of public records, to make continuing surveys of paperwork operations, and to recommend improvements in current records management practices including the use of space, equipment and supplies employed in creating, maintaining and servicing records. It shall be the duty of the head of each state agency to cooperate with the administrator in conducting surveys and to establish and maintain an active, continuing program for the economical and efficient management of the agency's records.

The administrator shall establish records disposal schedules for the orderly retirement of records and adopt regulations necessary for the carrying out of the Public Records Act. Records disposal schedules shall be filed with the librarian of the supreme court library, and shall not become effective until thirty days after the date of filing. Records so scheduled may be transferred to the records center at regular intervals, in accordance with the regulations of the administrator.

History: 1953 Comp., § 71-6-6, enacted by Laws 1959, ch. 245, § 6; 1965, ch. 81, § 1.

14-3-7. Inspection and survey of public records.

The administrator is authorized to inspect or survey the records of any agency, and to make surveys of records management and records disposal practices in the various agencies, and he shall be given the full cooperation of officials and employees of the agencies in such inspections and surveys. Records, the use of which is restricted by or pursuant to law or for reasons of security or the public interest, may be inspected or surveyed by the administrator, subject to the same restrictions imposed upon employees of the agency holding the records.

History: 1953 Comp., § 71-6-7, enacted by Laws 1959, ch. 245, § 7.

14-3-8. Records center.

A records center is established in Santa Fe under the supervision and control of the administrator. The center, in accordance with the regulations established by the administrator and the commission, shall be the facility for the receipt, storage or disposition of all inactive and infrequently used records of present or former state agencies or former territorial agencies which at or after the effective date of this act may be in custody of any state agency or instrumentality, and which are not required by law to be kept elsewhere, or which are not ordered destroyed by the commission.

Records required to be confidential by law and which are stored in the center shall be available promptly when called for by the originating agency, but shall not be made available for public inspection except as provided by law. All other records retained by the center shall be open to the inspection of the general public, subject to reasonable rules and regulations prescribed by the administrator. Facilities for the use of these records in research by the public shall be provided in the center.

History: 1953 Comp., § 71-6-8, enacted by Laws 1959, ch. 245, § 8.

14-3-9. Disposition of public records.

Upon completion of an inspection or survey of the public records of any agency by the administrator, or at the request of the commission or the head of any agency, the administrator, attorney general and the agency official in charge of the records of that agency shall together make a determination as to whether:

    A. the records shall be retained in the custody of the agency;

    B. the records shall be transferred to the records center; or

    C. a recommendation for destruction of the records shall be made to the commission.

If it is determined that the records are to be transferred to the records center, they shall be within a reasonable time so transferred. A list of the records so transferred shall be retained in the files of the agency from which the records were transferred.

Public records in the custody of the administrator may be transferred or destroyed only upon order of the commission.

History: 1953 Comp., § 71-6-9, enacted by Laws 1959, ch. 245, § 9.

14-3-10. Disagreement as to value of records.

In the event the attorney general and the administrator determine that any records in the custody of a public officer including the administrator are of no legal, administrative or historical value, but the public officer having custody of the records or from whose office the records originated fails to agree with such determination or refuses to dispose of the records, the attorney general and the administrator may request the state commission of public records to make its determination as to whether the records should be disposed of in the interests of conservation of space, economy or safety.

History: 1953 Comp., § 71-6-10, enacted by Laws 1959, ch. 245, § 10.

14-3-11. Destruction of records.

If it is determined by the administrator, attorney general and agency head that destruction of records will be recommended, the administrator shall have prepared a list of records, together with a brief description of their nature, and shall place upon the agenda of the next meeting of the commission the matter of destruction of the records. The records may be stored in the center awaiting decision of the commission.

The commission's decision with reference to destruction of the records shall be entered on its minutes, together with the date of its order to destroy the records and a general description of the records which it orders to be destroyed. A copy of the commission's order shall be filed with the librarian of the supreme court library.

No public records shall be destroyed if the law prohibits their destruction.

History: 1953 Comp., § 71-6-11, enacted by Laws 1959, ch. 245, § 11; 1965, ch. 81, § 2.

14-3-12. Transfer of records upon termination of state agencies.

All public records of any agency, upon the termination of the existence and functions of that agency, shall be checked by the administrator and the attorney general and either transferred to the custody of another agency having a use for the records, or to the custody of the administrator at the center in accordance with the procedure of the Public Records Act [14-3-1 to 14-3-16, 14-3-18 NMSA 1978].

When an agency is terminated or reduced by the transfer of its powers and duties to another agency or to other agencies, its appropriate public records shall pass with the powers and duties so transferred.

History: 1953 Comp., § 71-6-12, enacted by Laws 1959, ch. 245, § 12.

14-3-13. Protection of records.

The administrator and every other custodian of public records shall carefully protect and preserve such records from deterioration, mutilation, loss or destruction and, whenever advisable, shall cause them to be properly repaired and renovated. All paper, ink and other materials used in public offices for the purposes of permanent records shall be of durable quality.

History: 1953 Comp., § 71-6-13, enacted by Laws 1959, ch. 245, § 13.

14-3-14. Advisory groups.

The commission upon recommendation of the administrator may from time to time appoint advisory groups to more effectively obtain the best professional thinking of the bar, historians, political scientists, librarians, accountants, genealogists, patriotic groups, associations of public officials and other groups, on the steps to be taken with regard to any particular group or type of records.

History: 1953 Comp., § 71-6-14, enacted by Laws
1959, ch. 245, § 14.

14-3-15. Reproduction on film; evidence; review, inventory and approval of systems.

A. Any public officer of the state or of any district or political subdivision may cause any public records, papers or documents kept by him to be photographed, microphotographed or reproduced on film.

B. The state records administrator shall review any proposed state agency microphotography system and shall advise and consult with the agency. The administrator has the authority to approve or disapprove the system of any state agency.

C. The microphotography system used pursuant to this section shall comply with the minimum standards approved by the New Mexico commission of public records. The microphotography system used to reproduce such records on film shall be one which accurately reproduces the original in all details.

D. The administrator shall establish and maintain an inventory of all microfilm equipment owned or leased by state agencies. The administrator is authorized to arrange the transfer of microphotography equipment from a state agency which does not use it, and which has released it, to a state agency needing such equipment for a current microphotography system.

E. Photographs, microphotographs or photographic film made pursuant to this section shall be deemed to be original records for all purposes, including introduction in evidence in all courts and administrative agencies. A transcript, exemplification or certified copy, for all purposes, shall be deemed to be a transcript, exemplification or certified copy of the original.

F. Whenever such photographs, microphotographs or reproductions on film are properly certified and are placed in conveniently accessible files, and provisions are made for preserving, examining and using them, any public officer may cause the original records from which the photographs or microphotographs have been made, or any part thereof, to be disposed of according to methods prescribed by Sections 14-3-9 through 14-3-11 NMSA 1978. Copies shall be certified by their custodian as true copies of the originals before the originals are destroyed or lost, and the certified copies shall have the same effect as the originals. Copies of public records transferred from the office of origin to the administrator, when certified by the administrator or his deputy, shall have the same legal effect as if certified by the original custodian of the records.

G. For the purposes of this section, "state agency" shall include the district courts.

History: 1953 Comp., § 71-6-15, enacted by Laws
1959, ch. 245, § 15; 1975, ch. 215, § 1; 1977, ch. 301, § 2.

14-3-16. Attorney general may replevin state records.

On behalf of the state and the administrator, the attorney general may replevin any papers, books, correspondence or other public records which were formerly part of the records or files of any public office in the territory or state of New Mexico, and which the state still has title to or interest in and which have passed out of the official custody of the state, its agencies or instrumentalities.

History: 1953 Comp., § 71-6-16, enacted by Laws
1959, ch. 245, § 16.

14-3-17. Approval of existing state agency systems.

Upon the effective date of this act, the state records administrator shall review any existing state agency microphotography system and, after consultation with the agency, shall approve, disapprove or require modification to the system. For the purposes of this section, "state agency" shall include the district courts. Upon disapproval, the agency shall cease to use the system. Modifications shall be completed within a period specified by the administrator.

History: 1953 Comp., § 71-6-17, enacted by Laws
1975, ch. 215, § 2.

14-3-18. County and municipal records.

The administrator may advise and assist county and municipal officials in the formulation of programs for the disposition of public records maintained in county and municipal offices.

History: 1953 Comp., § 71-6-17.1, enacted by Laws
1963, ch. 186, § 2; 1965, ch. 81, § 3.

14-3-19. Storage equipment, supplies and materials; microfilm services and supplies; purchase by state records commission for resale.

The state records commission may purchase for resale such storage boxes, forms, microfilm supplies necessary to the providing of microfilm services and other supplies and materials, as in its judgment are necessary to facilitate the various aspects of its programs. The commission may sell such items and services at a cost plus a five percent handling charge. All receipts from such sales shall go into the special revolving fund established by Laws 1961, Chapter 111, which is hereby continued. In addition to any moneys in the special revolving fund, there is hereby appropriated the sum of five hundred dollars ($500).

History: 1953 Comp., § 71-6-18, enacted by Laws
1968, ch. 14, § 1.

14-3-20. Interstate compacts; filing; index.

A. Each agency of this state and each political subdivision of the state entering into or administering an interstate compact or other intergovernmental agreement between or among states, subdivisions of this state and other states or between this state or any subdivision and the federal government, having the force of law and to which this state or any subdivision is a party, shall file with the supreme court librarian:

(1) a certified copy of the compact or agreement;

(2) a listing of all other jurisdictions party to the compact or agreement and the date on which each jurisdiction entered into participation;

(3) the status of each compact or agreement with respect to withdrawals of participating jurisdictions;

(4) citations to any act or resolution of the congress of the United States consenting to the compact or agreement; and

(5) any amendment, supplementary agreement or administrative rule or regulation having the force of law and implementing or modifying the compact or agreement.

B. The supreme court librarian shall index these documents and make them available for inspection upon request of any person during normal business hours.

C. The provisions of this section are in addition to other requirements of law for filing, publication or distribution.

D. No compact or agreement entered into after the effective date of this section shall become effective until filed as required in this section.

E. All compacts in force at the effective date of this section shall be filed as required by this section before July 1, 1964. The executive official in charge of any state agency or political subdivision which fails to file any compact or agreement required by this section to be filed is guilty of a misdemeanor.

History: 1953 Comp., § 71-6-19, enacted by Laws
1963, ch. 185, § 1.

14-3-21. [State publications; manuals of procedure; rules; reports; uniform style and form.]

The state records administrator shall develop and recommend to the state commission of public records uniform standards of style and format for the following:

A. manuals of procedure prepared and published by state agencies for the guidance of public officers and employees engaged in operations required for the efficient operation of state and local government, including but not limited to acquiring space, budgeting, accounting, purchasing, contracting, vouchering, printing, appointment and dismissal of employees and record maintenance;

B. manuals of procedure prepared and published by state agencies for the guidance of their own employees and for their own operations;

C. official rules and regulations and reprints of laws published by state agencies, excluding session laws published by the secretary of state; and

D. official reports of state agencies required by law, excluding the budget document presented to the legislature.

The state commission of public records, after consultation with the affected agencies, and with the approval of the governor, shall adopt and promulgate uniform standards of style and format for the above publications and a schedule of distribution for each class of publication which shall be binding upon all state agencies. "Agencies" means, for the purposes of this section, all state departments, bureaus, commissions, committees, institutions and boards, except those agencies of the legislative and judicial branches, and those educational institutions listed in Article 12, Section 11 of the New Mexico constitution.

History: 1953 Comp., § 71-6-20, enacted by Laws
1965, ch. 154, § 1.

14-3-22. Public policy on certain publications; state commission of public records duties.

A. It is the intent of the legislature and the public policy of this state to reduce unnecessary expense to the taxpayers of this state in connection with publications of state agencies designed primarily for the purpose of reporting to or the informing of the governor, the legislature, other state agencies or the political subdivisions of this state.

B. The state commission of public records shall develop and adopt regulations which shall be binding upon all state agencies. The regulations shall provide for uniform standards for those publications set forth in Subsection A of this section and shall include but be not limited to:

(1) a standard size format to accommodate paper of the most economical type available;

(2) prohibiting the use of expensive covers, binders and fasteners;

(3) prohibiting the use of photographs, art work and design, unless absolutely necessary for clarification of the report;

(4) limiting the use of color stock paper, where such color stock would be more expensive than the use of white paper; and

(5) requiring offset or mimeograph or other means of duplication when it cannot be demonstrated that printing of such publication would be equal to or less than the cost of offset, mimeograph or other means of duplication.

C. The state commission of public records shall maintain constant and continuing supervision of such publications by state agencies and shall report persistent violations of the regulations made pursuant to this act [this section] to the director of the department of finance and administration [secretary of finance and administration].

History: 1953 Comp., § 71-6-21, enacted by Laws
1977, ch. 209, § 1.

14-3-23. [Manuals of procedure; preparation by state agencies; review by state records administrator; publication.]

Each state agency which has an official duty to establish methods and procedures involved in the internal structure and operation of state government, including but not limited to acquiring space, budgeting, accounting, purchasing, contracting, vouchering, printing, appointment and dismissal of employees and record-keeping, shall prepare, within the means provided by current operating budgets, manuals of procedure for the guidance of public officers and employees engaged in such work. Such manual or manuals shall be reviewed and ordered published by the state records administrator and in accordance with uniform standards of style and format promulgated by the state commission of public records.

History: 1953 Comp., § 71-6-22, enacted by Laws 1963, ch. 154, § 3.

14-3-24. State publications for sale or issue by state agencies; listing by state records administrator.

The state records administrator shall maintain a file of all state publications which are for sale or issue by agencies of the state. He shall prepare and publish a list of all such publications which are current and effective. The list shall include such documents as books, manuals, pamphlets, bulletins, monographs and periodicals designed to instruct, inform or direct either the general public or public officers and employees. Correspondence and those documents developed by agencies for their own internal administration are excluded.

History: 1953 Comp., § 71-6-23, enacted by Laws 1967, ch. 275, § 8; 1977, ch. 301, § 3.

14-3-25. [Personal files, records and documents of elected state officials; placing in state archives by the state records administrator.]

The state records administrator may accept and place in the state archives the personal files, records and documents of elected state officials or of former elected state officials, subject to any reasonable restrictions, moratoriums and requirements concerning their use by other persons. Such restrictions, moratoriums and requirements made by the donor, however, shall not prevent the archivist of the state records center from having access to the files, records and documents for indexing and cataloguing purposes.

History: 1953 Comp., § 71-6-24, enacted by Laws 1967, ch. 275, § 9.

MUNICIPAL AND COUNTY LIBRARIES

(New Mexico Statutes Annotated, 1982, s.3-18-14, 4-36-1, 4-36-2, 4-49-6 to 4-49-8.)

3-18-14. Libraries; establishment; contract services; state publications; gifts and bequests.

A. A municipality may establish and maintain a free public library under proper regulation and may receive, hold and dispose of any gift, donation, devise or bequest that is made to the municipality for the purpose of establishing, increasing or improving.the library. The governing body may apply the use, profit, proceeds, interests and rents accruing from any such property in any manner that will best improve the library and its use.

B. After a public library is established, the secretary of state shall furnish to the public library a copy of any work subsequently published under his authority.

C. Any municipality establishing a public library may contract with the county, adjoining counties or the library division of the office of cultural affairs for the furnishing of library services. In the interest of establishing a county or regional library, a municipality may convey its library facilities to the county as part of a contract for furnishing library services to the inhabitants of the municipality by the county or regional library.

History: 1953 Comp., § 14-17-12, enacted by Laws 1965, ch. 300; 1977, ch. 246, § 45; 1980, ch. 151, § 1.

4-36-1. [County public library;] secretary of state to furnish publications.

After a public library is established, the secretary of state shall furnish to the public library a copy of any work published under his authority.

History: 1953 Comp., § 15-36-1.2, enacted by Laws 1965, ch. 87, § 2.

4-36-2. [Library services;] contract with other counties.

A. A county may:

(1) contract with one or more counties and with the library division of the office of cultural affairs for the furnishing of library services;

(2) contract for the establishment of a regional library serving more than one county; and

(3) appropriate money for the support of a regional library or library services.

B. Any regional library so established must first be approved by the state librarian.

History: 1953 Comp., § 15-36-1.3, enacted by Laws 1965, ch. 87, § 3; 1977, ch. 246, § 46; 1980, ch. 151, § 2.

4-49-6. Legislative declaration; necessary public buildings.

The legislature hereby declares that courthouses, jails, bridges, hospitals, public libraries, facilities for the holding of county fairs, cultural facilities, juvenile detention homes, athletic facilities and sewerage facilities are necessary public buildings.

History: 1953 Comp., § 15-49-6.1, enacted by Laws 1973, ch. 400, § 1; 1975, ch. 84, § 1; 1976, ch. 42, § 1; 1979, ch. 137, § 1.

4-49-7. General obligation bonds; authority to issue.

The boards of county commissioners may issue the general obligation bonds of such county, in any sum necessary, not greater than four percent, inclusive of all other bonded indebtedness, of the assessed value of the taxable property of the county, for the purpose of building courthouses, jails, bridges, hospitals, public libraries, facilities for the holding of county fairs, cultural facilities, juvenile detention homes, athletic facilities and sewerage facilities.

History: 1953 Comp., § 15-49-6.2, enacted by Laws 1973, ch. 400, § 2; 1975, ch. 84, § 2; 1976, ch. 42, § 2; 1979, ch. 137, § 2.

4-49-8. Election on bond question; petition; notice; election without petition.

Whenever a petition signed by not less than two hundred qualified electors of any county in this state shall be presented to the board of county commissioners, asking that a vote be taken on the question or proposition of building a courthouse, jail, bridge, hospital or public library, setting forth in general terms the object of such petition and the amount of bonds asked to be voted for, it shall be the duty of the board of county commissioners of such county to which said petition may be presented within ten days after the presentation, to call an election to be held within sixty days thereafter in such county, and shall give notice of such election by publication once a week for at least three consecutive weeks in any newspapers published in such county, which notices shall set forth the time and place of holding such election, the courthouse, jail, bridge, hospital or public library proposed to be built and which bonds are to be voted for. Except as provided herein, such elections shall be held and conducted in the same manner as general elections, including recount and contest, and the board of commissioners shall certify and declare on the records of such county the returns of such election. After the defeat of any proposition once voted for, a second special election upon any question or proposition under the provisions of this article shall not be held for a term of two years, unless a petition requesting another election, containing the names of qualified electors of said county equal to ten percent of the vote cast for governor in the last preceding election and otherwise conforming to the requirements of this section, shall be presented to the board of county commissioners; provided, however, that in no event shall more than two elections upon any proposition or question under this article be held in any term of two years. A bond election as above provided may also be called by the county commissioners, without any petition, after said commissioners have adopted a resolution calling such an election, which resolution shall set forth the object of the election and the amount of bonds to be issued.

History: Laws 1891, ch. 83, § 4; C.L. 1897, § 352; Code 1915, § 1159; C.S. 1929, § 33-3904; Laws 1937, ch. 52, § 1; 1941 Comp., § 15-4604; Laws 1947, ch. 20, § 3; 1951, ch. 83, § 3; 1953 Comp., § 15-49-7; Laws 1959, ch. 234, § 1.

LOTTERY

(New Mexico Statutes Annotated, 1982, s.30-19-6.)

30-19-6. Permissive lottery.

Nothing in this article [30-19-1 to 30-19-14 NMSA 1978] shall be construed to apply to any sale or drawing of any prize at any fair held in this state for the benefit of any church, public library or religious society situate or being in this state, or for charitable purposes when all the proceeds of such fair shall be expended in this state for the benefit of such church, public library, religious society or charitable purposes.

A lottery shall be operated for the benefit of the organization or charitable purpose only when the entire proceeds of the lottery go to the organization or charitable purpose and no part of such proceeds go [goes] to any individual member or employee thereof.

Nothing in this article shall be held to prohibit any bona fide motion picture theater from offering prizes of cash or merchandise for advertising purposes, in connection with such business, or for the purpose of stimulating business, whether or not any consideration other than a monetary consideration in excess of the regular price of admission is exacted for participation in drawings for prizes.

Nothing in this article shall be held to apply to any bona fide county fair, including fairs for more than one county, which shall have been held annually at the same location for at least two years and which shall offer prizes of livestock or poultry in connection with such fair when the proceeds of such drawings shall be used for the benefit of said fair.

History: 1953 Comp., § 40A-19-6, enacted by Laws 1963, ch. 303, § 19-6.

NEW YORK

STATE LIBRARY

(Consolidated Laws of New York Annotated, 1982, Education Law,
s.232, 245-252.)

§ 232. Departments and their government

The state library and state museum shall be departments of
the university, and the regents may establish such other departments and divisions therein as they shall deem useful in the discharge of their duties.

L.1947, c. 820, eff. July 1, 1947.

§ 245. State library, how constituted

All books, pamphlets, manuscripts, records, archives and
maps, and all other property appropriate to a general library, if
owned by the state and not placed in other custody by law, shall
be in charge of the regents and constitute the state library.

L.1947, c. 820, eff. July 1, 1947.

§ 246. State medical library

The state medical library shall be a part of the New York
state library under the same government and regulations and
shall be open for consultation to every citizen of the state at all

hours when the state library is open and shall be available for borrowing books to every accredited physician residing in the state of New York, who shall conform to the rules made by the regents for insuring proper protection and the largest usefulness to the people of the said medical library.

L.1947, c. 820, eff. July 1, 1947.

§ 247. State law library; legislative reference library

The state law library and the legislative reference library shall be parts of the New York state library under the same government and regulations and shall be open for consultation to every citizen of the state at all hours when the state library is open and the law library shall be available for borrowing books to every duly admitted attorney residing in the state of New York, who shall conform to the rules made by the regents for insuring proper protection and the largest usefulness to the people of the said law library.

L.1947, c. 820, eff. July 1, 1947.

§ 248. Manuscript and records "on file"

Manuscript or printed papers of the legislature, usually termed "on file," and which shall have been on file more than five years in custody of the senate and assembly clerks, and all public records of the state not placed in other custody by a specific law shall be part of the state library and shall be kept in rooms assigned and suitably arranged for that purpose by the trustees of public buildings. The regents shall cause such papers and records to be so classified and arranged that they can be easily found. No paper or record shall be removed from such files except on a resolution of the senate and assembly withdrawing them for a temporary purpose, and in case of such removal a description of the paper or record and the name of the person removing the same shall be entered in a book provided for that purpose, with the date of its delivery and return.

L.1947, c. 820, eff. July 1, 1947.

§ 249. State library, when open; use of books

The state library shall be kept open not less than eight hours every week day in the year except the legal holidays and such other days or occasions as determined by the commissioner of education, and members of the legislature, judges of the court of appeals, justices of the supreme court and heads of state departments may borrow from the library books for use in Albany, but shall be subject to such restrictions and penalties as may be pre-

scribed by the regents for the safety or greater usefulness of the
library.   Under such rules and conditions as the regents may
prescribe the state library may lend its books and printed material for a limited time to other individuals and institutions conforming to said rules and conditions.   Such service shall be free
to residents of this state as far as practicable but the regents
may, in their discretion, charge a proper fee to nonresidents or
for assistance of a personal nature or for other reason not properly an expense to the state, but which may be authorized for the
accommodation of users of the library.

L.1947, c. 820, eff. July 1, 1947.

§ 250.   Duplicate department

The regents shall have charge of the preparation, publication
and distribution, whether by sale, exchange or gift, of the colonial history, natural history and all other state publications not
otherwise assigned by law.   To guard against waste or destruction of state publications, and to provide for the completion of
sets to be permanently preserved in American and foreign libraries, the regents shall maintain a duplicate department to
which each state department, bureau, board or commission shall
send not less than five copies of each of its publications when issued, and after completing its distribution, any remaining copies
which it no longer requires.   The above, with any other publications not needed in the state library, shall be the duplicate department, and rules for sale, exchange or distribution from it
shall be fixed by the regents, who shall use all receipts from such
exchanges or sales for expenses and for increasing the state library.

L.1947, c. 820, eff. July 1, 1947.

§ 251.   Transfers from state officers

The librarian of any library owned by the state, or the officer
in charge of any state department, bureau, board, commission or
other office may, with the approval of the regents, transfer to
the permanent custody of the state library or museum any
books, papers, maps, manuscripts, specimens or other articles
which, because of being duplicates or for other reasons, will in
his judgment be more useful to the state in the state library or
museum than if retained in his keeping.

L.1947, c. 820, eff. July 1, 1947.

§ 252.   Other libraries owned by the state

The report of the state library to the legislature shall include
a statement of the total number of volumes or pamphlets, the

number added during the year, with a summary of operations and conditions, and any needed recommendation for safety or usefulness for each of the other libraries owned by the state, the custodian of which shall furnish such information or facilities for inspection as the regents may require for making this report. Each of these libraries shall be under the sole control now provided by law, but for the annual report of the total number of books owned by or bought each year by the state, it shall be considered as a branch of the state library and shall be entitled to any facilities for exchange of duplicates, inter-library loans or other privileges properly accorded to a branch.

L.1947, c. 820, eff. July 1, 1947.

LIBRARY EXTENSION SERVICE

(Consolidated Laws of New York Annotated, 1982, Education Law, s.213-216, 269-270.)

§ 213. Extension of educational facilities

1. The regents may extend to the people at large increased educational opportunities and facilities, stimulate interest therein, recommend methods, designate suitable teachers and lecturers, conduct examinations and grant credentials, and otherwise organize, aid and conduct such work. And the regents, and with their approval the commissioner of education, may buy, sell, exchange and receive by will, or other gift, or on deposit, books, pictures, statuary or other sculptered work, lantern slides, apparatus, maps, globes, films, sound films, kinescopes, photographic recordings and any article or collections pertaining to or useful in and to any of the departments, divisions, schools, institutions, associations or other agencies, or work, under their supervision, or control, or encouragement, and may lend or deposit any such articles in their custody or control, when or where in their judgment compensating educational usefulness will result therefrom; and may also, from time to time, enter into contracts desirable for carrying into effect the foregoing provisions.

2. In carrying out the provisions of subdivision one of this section, the regents may: a. Contract with institutions in the university, school districts, boards of cooperative educational services or other non-profit educational agencies for the acquisition from such institutions, school districts, boards or agencies and use of educational television facilities by educational television corporations established pursuant to the provisions of section two hundred thirty-six of this chapter. Such grants may be made upon such terms and conditions as the regents may prescribe.　　　　　　　　　L.1966, c. 404, eff. May 23, 1966.

§ 214.   Institutions in the university

The institutions of the university shall include all secondary and higher educational institutions which are now or may hereafter be incorporated in this state, and such other libraries, museums, institutions, schools, organizations and agencies for education as may be admitted to or incorporated by the university. The regents may exclude from such membership any institution failing to comply with law or with any rule of the university.

§ 215.   Visitation and reports

The regents, or the commissioner of education, or their representatives, may visit, examine into and inspect, any institution in the university and any school or institution under the educational supervision of the state, and may require, as often as desired, duly verified reports therefrom giving such information and in such form as the regents or the commissioner of education shall prescribe. For refusal or continued neglect on the part of any institution in the university to make any report required, or for violation of any law or any rule of the university, the regents may suspend the charter or any of the rights and privileges of such institution.

§ 216.   Charters

Under such name, with such number of trustees or other managers, and with such powers, privileges and duties, and subject to such limitations and restrictions in all respects as the regents may prescribe in conformity to law, they may, by an instrument under their seal and recorded in their office, incorporate any university, college, academy, library, museum, or other institution or association for the promotion of science, literature, art, history or other department of knowledge, or of education in any way, associations of teachers, students, graduates of educational institutions, and other associations whose approved purposes are, in whole or in part, of educational or cultural value deemed worthy of recognition and encouragement by the university. No institution or association which might be incorporated by the regents under this chapter shall, without their consent, be incorporated under any other general law. An institution or association which might be incorporated by the regents under this chapter may, with the consent of the commissioner of education, be formed under the business corporation law or pursuant to the membership corporations law if such consent of the commissioner of education is attached to its certificate of incorporation.

L.1947, c. 820; amended L.1963, c. 692, § 5, eff. Sept. 1, 1963.

§ 269. Library extension service

By such means, in such manner and upon such conditions as the regents may prescribe, they shall make provision for a library extension service for the promotion, organization and supervision of free libraries; for supplying information, advice, assistance or instruction on any matter pertaining to library methods or practice or to the establishment, equipment, organization or administration of libraries; for the acquisition, preparation and circulation of traveling libraries and other educational material; for aiding and encouraging study clubs; and for the employment of all suitable efforts to bring within the reach of all the people of the state, and awaken their desire for, increased opportunities and facilities for reading and study.

L.1947, c. 820; formerly § 270; renumbered 269, L.1950, c. 273, § 7, eff. April 1, 1950.

§ 270. Acceptance of surplus library books or property

The state education department is hereby authorized to cooperate with the United States commissioner of education, the war assets administration, and/or other federal officers and officials in the administration of any statute heretofore or hereafter enacted for the disposal of surplus library books or property, and to accept for and on behalf of the state of New York or its political subdivisions surplus library books or other property suitable and necessary to the operation of public and free libraries and for the improvement and extension of library service for New York state, and any funds, which may be made available to the state of New York by the federal government for these and related public library services.

L.1947, c. 820; formerly § 271; renumbered 270, L.1950, c. 273, § 7, eff. April 1, 1950.

STATE AID

(Consolidated Laws of New York Annotated, 1982, Education Law, s.271-273.)

§ 271. Apportionment of state aid to Indian libraries

Any Indian library chartered by the regents or in the absence of such library any tribal government contracting for service from a chartered and registered library or apporved [1] library system, shall be entitled to receive state aid during each calendar year consisting of the following amounts:

1. Twelve thousand dollars, and
2. The sum of twelve dollars per capita for persons residing on the reservation served by the Indian library or contract as shown by the latest federal census or certified by the New York state director of Indian services, and

3. The sum of one dollar per acre of area served by the Indian library or contract.

Such sums shall be paid to the Indian library board of trustees for the use of the Indian library, or in the absence of such a board, to the tribal government for a contract for library service. Nothing contained in this section shall be construed to diminish the funds, services or supplies provided to any Indian library by a library system as defined in section two hundred seventy-two of this article. Increases in appropriations for such purposes during a calendar year shall be pro rated.

Added L.1977, c. 476, § 13; amended L.1981, c. 718, § 3.

1 So in original. Probably should be "approved".

§ 272. Conditions under which library systems are entitled to state aid

1. Public library systems. a. The term "public library system" as used in this article means:

(1) A library established by one or more counties.

(2) A group of libraries serving an area including one or more counties in whole or in part.

(3) A library of a city containing one or more counties.

(4) A cooperative library system established pursuant to section two hundred fifty-five of this chapter, the plan of library service of any of which shall have been approved by the commissioner.

b. The "area served" by a public library system for the purposes of this article shall mean the area which the public library system proposes to serve in its approved plan of service. In determining the population of the area served by the public library system the population shall be deemed to be that shown by the latest federal census for the political subdivisions in the area served. Such population shall be certified in the same manner as provided by section fifty-four of the state finance law except that such population shall include the reservation and school Indian population and inmates of state institutions under the direction, supervision or control of the state department of correction, the state department of mental hygiene and the state department of social welfare. In the event that any of the political subdivisions receiving library service are included within a larger political subdivision which is a part of the public library system the population used for the purposes of computing state aid shall be the population of the larger political subdivision, provided however, that where any political subdivision within a larger political subdivision shall have taken an interim census since the last census taken of the larger political subdivision, the population of the larger political subdivision may be adjusted to reflect such interim census and, as so adjusted, may be used until the next census of such larger political subdivision. In the event that the area served is not coterminous with a political subdivision, the population of which is shown on such census, or the area in square miles of which is available from official sources. such population and area shall be determined, for the purpose of computation of state aid pursuant to section two hundred seventy-three by applying to the population and area in square miles of such political subdivision, the ratio which exists between the assessed valuation of the portion of such political subdivision included within the area served and the total assessed valuation of such political subdivision.

c. Members of a public library system shall be those public, free association, and Indian libraries located within the service area which have been admitted to membership prior to July first, nineteen hundred seventy-eight, or which apply for and are granted membership subsequent to that date with the approval of the commissioner. No public library system shall be subject to any loss of benefits under these provisions where such system has made reasonable effort to prevent the unapproved withdrawal of such library from the system and the system demonstrates, in a manner satisfactory to the commissioner, that the residents of the area encompassed by the withdrawing library will continue to benefit from the library services provided by the public library system.

d. "Approved plan" as used in this article means a plan of library service by a public library system approved by the commissioner subsequent to May first, nineteen hundred fifty-eight.

e. Approval shall not be given to a public library system unless it will serve at least two hundred thousand people or four thousand square miles of area, provided, however, that provisional approval may be given to a public library system which will serve at least fifty thousand persons provided the area served includes three or more political subdivisions and provided further that a satisfactory plan of expansion of service to be followed during the ensuing five-year period is adopted by such library system and approved by the commissioner.

f. The board of trustees of the public library system shall submit to the commissioner the plan of library service. Such plan shall be supported by such information as the commissioner may require in the form prescribed by him.

g. No such plan of library service shall be approved by the commissioner unless he finds that it provides for the residents of the area served thereby a method conforming to the regulations of the commissioner by which the participating libraries are obligated to permit the loan of books and material among members of the system for use on the same basis permitted by the library which owns or controls them.

h. The commissioner shall by regulation provide the standard of service with which such a public library system must comply. Such regulations shall, among other things, relate to the total book stock; the diversity of such book stock with respect to general subjects and type of literature, provided that such regulations shall not, directly or indirectly, prohibit the inclusion of a particular book, periodical or material or the works of a particular author or the expression of a particular point of view; annual additions to book stock; circulation of book stock; maintenance of catalogues; number and location of libraries or branch libraries; hours of operation and number and qualifications of personnel, necessary to enable a public library system to render adequate service. Such regulations may establish standards which differ on the basis of population; density of population; the actual valuation of the taxable property within the area served; the condition of library facilities in existence on April first, nineteen hundred fifty-seven; the amount raised by taxation by or for the area served; the relation of such amount to population and actual value of the property taxed; the relation of the amount of funds received by a public library sytem from local taxes to that derived from private contributions; or on such other basis as the commissioner finds necessary to provide for the equitable distribution of state aid.

i. Each public library system receiving state aid pursuant to this section and section two hundred seventy-three shall furnish such information regarding its library service as the commissioner may from time to time require to discharge his duties under such sections. The commissioner may at any time revoke his approval of a plan of library service if he finds that the public library system operating under such plan no longer conforms to the provisions of this section or the regulations promulgated by the commissioner hereunder; or, in the case of provisional approval, if such library system no longer conforms to the agreement, plans or conditions upon which such provisional approval was based. In such case a public library system shall not thereafter be entitled to state aid pursuant to this section or section two hundred seventy-three unless and until its plan of library service is again approved by the commissioner.

j. (1) In the event that the total sum raised by local taxation exclusive of capital expenditures for the support of a public library system and participating libraries in an annual period beginning January first, nineteen hundred seventy-nine, is less than ninety-five per centum of the average of the amounts raised for such purposes by local taxation for the two preceding calendar years, the state aid to which such library system would otherwise be entitled beginning April first, nineteen hundred eighty, shall be reduced by twenty-five per centum. However, state aid paid between April first, nineteen hundred seventy-eight and March thirty-first, nineteen hundred eighty, shall be reduced by twenty-five per centum only in the event such local support shall be less than the average of calendar years nineteen hundred sixty-four and nineteen hundred sixty-five. Such state aid shall likewise be reduced by twenty-five per centum in the event that the public library system shall refuse after reasonable notice to make provision for the expansion of the area served in accordance with the regulations of the commissioner.

(2) In the event that the total sum raised by local taxation, exclusive of capital expenditures, for the support of a central library of a public library system in an annual period beginning January first, nineteen hundred seventy-nine, is less than ninety-five per centum of the average of the amounts raised for such purposes by local taxation for the two preceding calendar years, the state aid to which such library system would otherwise be entitled for the development of its central library, beginning April first, nineteen hundred eighty, shall be reduced by twenty-five per centum. However, state aid paid between April first, nineteen hundred seventy-eight and March thirty-first, nineteen hundred eighty for such purpose, shall be reduced by twenty-five per centum only in the event such local support shall be less than the average of calendar years nineteen hundred sixty-four and nineteen hundred sixty-five.

k. In promulgating regulations and approving, rejecting or revoking plans of library service pursuant to this section, consideration shall be given to:

(1) The prevention of unreasonable discrimination among the persons served by such public library system.

(2) The need for rapid expansion of library facilities in areas not now served.

(3) The need of each public library system for the professional services of an adequate number of librarians having, in addition to general familiarity with literature, special training with respect to book selection and organization for library use.

(4) The need for a book stock sufficient in size and varied in kind and subject matter.

(5) The need for regular fresh additions to book stock.

(6) The need for adequate books, materials and facilities for research and information as well as for recreational reading.

(7) The need for libraries, branches, and other outlets convenient in location, and with adequate hours of service.

(8) The desirability for the integration of existing libraries and new libraries into systems serving a sufficiently large population to support adequate library service at a reasonable cost.

(9) The need for the economic and efficient utilization of public funds.

(10) The need for full utilization of local pride, responsibility, initiative and support of library service and the use of state aid in their stimulation but not as their substitute.

(11) The needs of special populations.

2. Reference and research library resources systems.

a. The term "reference and research library resources system" as used in this article means a duly chartered educational institution resulting from the association of a group of institutions of higher education, libraries, non-profit educational institutions, hospitals, and other institutions organized to improve reference and research library resources service. Such reference and research library resource systems may be registered upon meeting the standards set forth by the commissioner.

b. The "area served" by a reference and research library resources system for the purposes of this article shall include not less than seven hundred fifty thousand persons, as based upon the latest approved federal census, or not less than ten thousand square miles; and the defined area of service shall:

(1) Include more than one county; and

(2) Respect the integrity of the area of service of a public library system; and

(3) Constitute a service area effectively related to the availability of information resources and services and to the area of service of other reference and research library resources systems, as determined by the commissioner.

c. Membership in a reference and research library resources system.

(1) The membership shall include at least four chartered degree-granting institutions of higher education of the four year level whose libraries meet departmental standards.

(2) Membership shall also include either:

(i) at least one chartered degree-granting institution of higher education offering graduate programs for a masters degree whose library holds not less than two hundred seventy-five thousand volumes and currently receives not less than three thousand periodical titles, or

(ii) a public library which holds not less than four hundred thousand adult volumes and currently receives not less than one thousand five hundred periodical titles.

(3) The membership may also include approved public library systems which are within the region served by the reference and research library resources system.

(4) A reference and research library resources system may set its own minimum standards for membership consistent with regulations of the commissioner, except that;

(i) any chartered institution of higher education whose library meets the departmental standards shall be eligible for membership, and

(ii) any chartered institution of higher education whose library does not meet the departmental standards may not be eligible for membership unless it submits to the department a five-year plan for the realization of the standards, the plan bearing the signed approval of the head librarian, the president, and the academic dean of the institution, and

(iii) any hospital whose library meets the standards established by the regents in accordance with section two hundred fifty-four of this article shall be eligible for membership, and

(iv) any hospital whose library does not meet the standards established by the regents will not be eligible for membership unless it submits to the commissioner a five year plan for the realization of the standards, such plan bearing the signed approval of the head of the governing board of such hospital.

(5) The member institutions of each reference and research library resources system shall be broadly representative of the chartered educational agencies, nonprofit organizations, hospitals and other special libraries providing library service within the defined area of services of the system.

d. Plan of service.

(1) The reference and research library resources system shall submit a plan of service to the commissioner for approval, in a form to be prescribed by the commissioner to cover resources, needs, proposed program, budget, contractual agreements, and any other information which the commissioner may require.

(2) The plan of service must show the manner in which the reference and research library resources system will improve the library resources and services presently available in the area to the research community, including improved reader access.

(3) The plan of service shall indicate the manner in which the reference and research library resources system strengthens the library programs of its members and the manner in which the system program is related to appropriate regional programs in higher education.

(4) The plan of service shall identify the resources and needs of each hospital library, or a library serving hospitals in a rural area and show the manner in which the reference and research library resources system will assist each such library in meeting the regents' standards.

e. The commissioner shall by regulation establish the standard of service to be met by such a reference and research library resources system.

f. Each reference and research library resources system receiving state aid pursuant to this section and section two hundred seventy-three of this article shall furnish such information regarding its library service as the commissioner may from time to time require to discharge his duties under such sections. The commissioner may at any time revoke his approval of a plan of library service if he finds that the library system operating under such plan no longer conforms to the provisions of this section or the regulations promulgated by the commissioner hereunder. In such case a library system shall not thereafter be entitled to state aid pursuant to this section and section two hundred seventy-three of this article unless and until its plan of library service is again approved by the commissioner.

g. In promulgating regulations and approving, rejecting or revoking plans of library service pursuant to this section, consideration shall be given to:

(1) The prevention of unreasonable discrimination among the persons served by such library system;

(2) The need for regional resources of sufficient size and varied in kind and subject matter;

(3) The need for adequate books, materials (print and non-print) and facilities for research and information;

(4) The need for outlets convenient in time and place for the sharing of library materials;

(5) The need for the economic and efficient utilization of public funds;

(6) The need for full utilization of local responsibility, initiative and support of library service and the use of state aid in their stimulation but not as their substitute.

(7) The need for adequate books, materials, including both print and

non-print materials, and facilities for current medical information services to be provided each hospital in a rural area.

As amended L.1978, c. 787, §§ 6, 7; L.1981, c. 718, §§ 4–8.

1 So in original. Probably should be "system".

§ 273. Apportionment of state aid

1. Any public library system providing service under an approved plan during a calendar year shall be entitled to receive during that calendar year state aid consisting of the following amounts:

a. An annual grant of:

(1) Ten thousand dollars where the library system serves less than one county, or

(2) Twenty thousand dollars where the library system serves one entire county, or

(3) Where the library system serves more than one county the system shall be entitled to receive twenty-five thousand dollars for each entire county served and/or ten thousand dollars for each county, any part of which is served by the library system. If an entire county is served by two or more library systems, each of which serves a part thereof, each of such library systems shall be entitled to receive a grant of ten thousand dollars and in addition, a pro rata share of an additional sum of ten thousand dollars, such share to be computed in accordance with the ratio which the population of the area of the county served by such library system bears to the total population of the county, as determined under subdivision two of section two hundred seventy-two of this chapter.

b. In a library system which submits a plan for further development of its central library, which plan shall be approved by the commissioner in relation to standards for such central libraries, the amount of central library development aid shall be:

(1) twenty-one cents per capita of the population within the chartered area of service of such library system with a minimum amount of seventy-five thousand dollars, and

(2) an additional fifty thousand dollars to the library system for the purchase of books and materials including nonprint materials, as defined in regulations of the commissioner of education, for its central library. Such additional aid shall be payable on order and warrant of the comptroller on vouchers certified or approved by the commissioner in the manner provided by law. Ownership of library materials and equipment purchased with such central library aid provided by this paragraph b shall be vested in the public library system.

c. The sum of sixty-two cents per capita of population of the area served.

d. An amount equal to the amount by which expenditures by the library system for books, periodicals, binding and nonprint materials during the preceding calendar year exceeds forty cents per capita of population of the area served but the total apportionment pursuant to this paragraph d shall not exceed forty-six cents per capita of population served.

e. The sum of thirty-one dollars per square mile of area served by the library system in the case of library systems serving one county or less. Such sum of thirty-one dollars shall be increased by five dollars for each additional entire county served, provided, however, that no apportionment pursuant to this paragraph e shall exceed fifty-one dollars per square mile of area served. If an entire county is served by two or more library systems, each of which serves a part thereof, each of such library systems shall be entitled to receive, in addition to the aid computed in accordance with the foregoing provisions of this paragraph, a pro rata share of an increase of five dollars to be computed as follows: the sum resulting from the computation of five dollars per square mile of area served by the one of such library systems which would receive the largest amount of aid pursuant to this paragraph shall be pro rated among the library systems serving such county in accordance with the ratio which the population of the area served by each of such library systems bears to the population of the county as determined under subdivision two of section two hundred seventy-two of this chapter.

f. (1) Local sponsor incentive aid shall be paid annually as follows: the amount of sixty-five cents for every eleven dollars contributed by local sponsors to the approved public library systems and to registered public and free association libraries which are members of a public library system and which conform to regulations adopted by the commissioner, except that no library system shall receive a sum which is more than forty percent greater than the sum received in local sponsor incentive aid in nineteen hundred eighty and further provided that the aid shall be disbursed according to a plan agreed upon by the public library system board of trustees and the boards of trustees of a majority of the member libraries which shall provide that:

(i) at least forty percent of the total amount paid to any public library system under this provision shall be used by the system for system-wide services.

(ii) at least forty percent of the total amount paid to any public library system under this provision shall be distributed to its member public and free association libraries,

(2) A "local sponsor" shall mean any municipality, district or school district, as defined in the general municipal law, or any combination thereof.

(3) The local sponsor contribution shall be that amount other than funds allocated for capital expenditure or debt service received in any calendar year by a public library system or a public or free association library from such sponsor.

(4) Of the annual amount payable under this paragraph, fifty percent shall be paid on July fifteenth and fifty percent on November fifteenth in each year.

g. In addition to the sums provided in paragraphs a, b, c, d, e, f, h and i of this subdivision, the New York Public Library shall receive an amount equal to its actual expenditures for books, periodicals and binding for its research libraries which expenditures are not otherwise reimbursed or five hundred twenty-five thousand dollars whichever is less, and the additional sum of three million eight hundred fifty thousand dollars for the general support of such research libraries.

h. Each public library system which provides coordinated outreach services, as defined by regulations to be promulgated by the commissioner, to persons who are blind, physically handicapped, aged or confined in institutions, shall be entitled to receive forty thousand dollars annually, except that for the calendar year nineteen hundred eighty-one, this amount shall be twenty-nine thousand dollars.

i. In addition to any other sums provided for such purposes, the New York Public Library shall receive annually the additional sum of two hundred six thousand dollars for the program of the Schomburg center for research in black culture, and the additional sum of one hundred seven thousand dollars for the program of the library for the blind and physically handicapped.

j. In addition to any other sums provided to such library the sum of three hundred fifty thousand dollars shall be made available to the Brooklyn Public Library for its business library for each calendar year.

k. In addition to any other sums provided to such library the sum of fifty thousand dollars shall be made available to the Buffalo and Erie County Public Library for a continuity of service project approved by the commisioner for each calendar year.

l. In addition to any other sums provided to such library system the sum of thirty thousand dollars shall be made available to the Nassau library system for a continuity of service project approved by the commissioner for each calendar year.

m. Effective January first, nineteen hundred eighty-two, the minimum annual grant available to a library system under paragraphs a, c, d and e of this subdivision shall be five hundred thousand dollars.

2. Within the amounts appropriated therefor moneys paid out pursuant to this section shall be paid out of the state treasury on vouchers certified by the commissioner after audit by and upon the warrant of the comptroller.

3. The commissioner may waive the requirement that a public library system serve an entire county to earn the maximum annual grant under subparagraphs two and three of paragraph a of subdivision one of this section and paragraphs b, c, e and h of subdivision one of this section where he deems reasonable effort has been made by the system to encourage membership by all libraries in the county.

4. Reference and research library resources system. a. Any reference and research library resources system providing service under an approved plan during a calendar year shall be entitled to receive annual state aid consisting of an annual grant of one hundred fifty-five thousand dollars per system, but for the calendar year nineteen hundred eighty-one the amount of such aid shall be one hundred forty-five thousand six hundred fifty dollars. Such aid shall be paid on or before the first day of July in each year.

b. The commissioner of education is hereby authorized to expend up to three hundred fifty thousand dollars annually to contract with the New York Academy of Medicine, or such other agency or agencies as he may deem appropriate, to provide services to the reference and research library resources systems under the federal regional medical library program.

c. The commissioner of education is hereby authorized to expend up to four hundred ten thousand dollars annually to provide grants to reference and research library resources systems which provide services to member hospital libraries or libraries serving hospitals which are located in a rural area. For the purpose of this program, the commissioner shall define rural area on the basis of population, population density, and population characteristics. Such grants shall be determined on the basis of criteria to be developed by the commissioner including specific reference to plans to assist member hospital libraries or libraries serving hospitals in meeting the standards established by the regents in accordance with section two hundred fifty-four of this article, to provide integration of member hospital libraries or libraries serving hospitals into existing networks and to increase the number of member hospital libraries or libraries serving hospitals located in rural areas. Nothing contained herein shall preclude the awarding of such grants to a member hospital library or a library serving a hospital which is not located in a rural area in order to provide services to a hospital located in a rural area.

5. Coordinated collection development program for public and nonprofit independent colleges and universities.

a. Libraries of public and nonprofit independent colleges and universities are entitled to receive annual funding for a coordinated collection development grant if they meet the following conditions:

(1) Membership in a reference and research library resources system,

(2) Their resources are made available to the public, through full participation in the interlibrary loan and other resource sharing pro-

grams of the reference and research library resources system of which they are members, and

(3) They meet the requirements set forth in regulations adopted by the commissioner of education including but not confined to

(a) maintenance of effort,

(b) relationships between reference and research library resources systems' programs and the regional higher education master plan,

(c) submission of interlibrary loan statistics, and such other reports as may be required by the commissioner.

b. Public community colleges and nonprofit independent colleges and universities with libraries which meet the criteria of paragraph a of this subdivision are eligible for annual grants as follows:

(1) Four thousand dollars for each institution, except that in the fiscal year commencing April first, nineteen hundred eighty-one, this amount shall be two thousand dollars, and

(2) Forty-six cents for each full-time equivalent student enrolled in each qualifying institution, in the academic year completed prior to the state fiscal year except that in the fiscal year commencing April first, nineteen hundred eighty-one, this amount shall be twenty-three cents for each full-time equivalent student enrolled in the qualifying institution in the nineteen hundred seventy-nine—eighty academic year. For purposes of this section, a full-time equivalent shall be calculated as follows:

(i) one full-time undergraduate student shall be considered one full-time equivalent student;

(ii) one part-time undergraduate student shall be considered one-third of a full-time equivalent student;

(iii) one part-time graduate student shall be considered one full-time equivalent student; and

(iv) one full-time graduate student shall be considered one and one-half of a full-time equivalent student.

c. Funds for the support of this program shall be appropriated to the state education department, except that commencing with the fiscal year beginning April first, nineteen hundred eighty-two funds for the state-operated institutions of the state university of New York and the senior colleges of the city university of New York, shall be appropriated to the state university of New York out of any moneys in the state treasury in the general fund to the credit of the state purposes fund not otherwise appropriated, and funds shall be appropriated to the city university of New York out of any moneys in the state treasury in the general fund to the credit of the local assistance fund not otherwise appropriated, and shall be subject to the same distribution formula as provided in paragraph b of this subdivision. For the fiscal year commencing April first, nineteen hundred eighty-one the state education department shall make grants to the state university of New York and the city university of New York for the purposes of this subdivision, and such funds shall be distributed in accordance with the formula contained in paragraph b of this subdivision.   L.1981, c. 718, §§ 9, 10.

INTERSTATE LIBRARY DISTRICTS

(Consolidated Laws of New York Annotated, 1982, Education Law, s.293-297.)

§ 293.   Establishment of interstate library district

One or more incorporated public libraries of this state, by majority action of the board of trustees thereof, may enter into an agreement with one or more public library agencies in another state or states which have adopted the interstate library compact for the purpose of establishing and maintaining an interstate library district. For the purposes of this act, a cooperative library system established under article five of this chapter shall be deemed to be a public library.

Added L.1963, c. 787, § 2, eff. April 26, 1963.

§ 294. Appointment of members of governing board of interstate library district

(a) The board of trustees of each public library which is a party to an agreement establishing an interstate library district pursuant to section two hundred ninety-three of this article, shall appoint a member or members to represent such library on the governing board of such interstate library district. The number of such representatives shall be determined by the agreement establishing such interstate library district.

(b) The governing board of such interstate library district shall be a body corporate.

(c) Such governing board shall administer such interstate library district as provided in this act.

Added L.1963, c. 787, § 2, eff. April 26, 1963.

§ 295. Support of interstate library district

Any library, library system, county, city, village, town or school district of this state may provide funds, including funds received from local taxation for state aid for the support and operation of an interstate library district established as provided herein, in accordance with the terms of the agreement establishing the same provided that such agreement together with the plan of library service thereunder has been approved by the commissioner.

Added L.1963, c. 787, § 2, eff. April 26, 1963.

§ 296. Compact administrator

The commissioner of education shall be the administrator for the interstate library compact pursuant to article ten of the compact.

Added L.1963, c. 787, § 2, eff. April 26, 1963.

§ 297. Withdrawal

The commissioner of education is hereby designated as the official who is authorized to send and receive the notices provided in article eleven of the compact in the event of withdrawal of this state or any other state from the compact.

Added L.1963, c. 787, § 2, eff. April 26, 1963.

INTERSTATE LIBRARY COMPACT

Laws 1963, c. 787, § 1, eff. April 26, 1963, provided:

The interstate library compact is hereby enacted into law and entered into by this state with all states legally joining therein in the form substantially as follows:

ARTICLE I. POLICY AND PURPOSE

Because the desire for the services provided by the libraries transcends governmental boundaries and can most effectively be satisfied by giving such services to communities and people regardless of jurisdictional lines, it is the policy of the states party to this compact to cooperate and share their responsibilities; to authorize cooperation and sharing with respect to those types of library facilities and services which can be more economically or efficiently developed and maintained on a cooperative basis, and to authorize cooperation and sharing among localities, states and others in providing joint or cooperative library services in areas where the distribution of population or of existing and potential library resources make the provision of library service on an interstate basis the most effective way of providing adequate and efficient service.

ARTICLE II. DEFINITIONS

As used in this compact:

(a) "Public library agency" means any unit or agency of local or state government operating or having power to operate a library.

(b) "Private library agency" means any non-governmental entity which operates or assumes a legal obligation to operate a library.

(c) "Library agreement" means a contract establishing an interstate library district pursuant to this compact or providing for the joint or co-operative furnishing of library services.

ARTICLE III. INTERSTATE LIBRARY DISTRICTS

(a) Any one or more public library agencies in a party state in cooperation with any public library agency or agencies in one or more other party states may establish and maintain an interstate library district. Subject to the provisions of this compact and any other laws of the party states which pursuant hereto remain applicable, such district may establish, maintain and operate some or all of the library facilities and services for the area concerned in accordance with the terms of a library agreement therefor. Any private library agency or agencies within an interstate library district may cooperate therewith, assume duties, responsibilities and obligations thereto, and receive benefits therefrom as provided in any library agreement to which such agency or agencies become party.

(b) Within an interstate library district, and as provided by a library agreement, the performance of library functions may be undertaken on a joint or cooperative basis or may be undertaken by means of one or more arrangements between or among public or private library agencies for the extension of library privileges to the use of facilities or services operated or rendered by one or more of the individual library agencies.

(c) If a library agreement provides for joint establishment, maintenance or operation of library facilities or services by an interstate library district, such district shall have power to do any one or more of the following in accordance with such library agreement:

1. Undertake, administer and participate in programs or arrangements for securing, lending or servicing of

books and other publications, any other materials suitable to be kept or made available by libraries, library equipment or for the dissemination of information about libraries, the value and significance of particular items therein, and the use thereof.

2. Accept for any of its purposes under this compact any and all donations, and grants of money, equipment, supplies, materials, and services (conditional or otherwise), from any state or the United States or any subdivision or agency thereof, or interstate agency, or from any institution, person, firm or corporation, and receive, utilize and dispose of the same.

3. Operate mobile library units or equipment for the purpose of rendering bookmobile service within the district.

4. Employ professional, technical, clerical and other personnel and fix terms of employment, compensation and other appropriate benefits; and where desirable, provide for the in-service training of such personnel.

5. Sue and be sued in any court of competent jurisdiction.

6. Acquire, hold, and dispose of any real or personal property or any interest or interests therein as may be appropriate to the rendering of library service.

7. Construct, maintain and operate a library, including any appropriate branches thereof.

8. Do such other things as may be incidental to or appropriate for the carrying out of any of the foregoing powers.

ARTICLE IV. INTERSTATE LIBRARY DISTRICTS, GOVERNING BOARD

(a) An interstate library district which establishes, maintains or operates any facilities or services in its own right shall have a governing board which shall direct the affairs of the district and act for it in all matters relating to its business. Each participating public library agency in the district shall be represented on the governing board which

shall be organized and conduct its business in accordance with provision therefor in the library agreement. But in no event shall a governing board meet less often than twice a year.

(b) Any private library agency or agencies party to a library agreement establishing an interstate library district may be represented on or advise with the governing board of the district in such manner as the library agreement may provide.

ARTICLE V. STATE LIBRARY AGENCY COOPERATION

Any two or more state library agencies of two or more of the party states may undertake and conduct joint or cooperative library programs, render joint or cooperative library services, and enter into and perform arrangements for the cooperative or joint acquisition, use, housing and disposition of items or collections of materials which, by reason of expense, rarity, specialized nature, or infrequency of demand therefor, would be appropriate for central collection and shared use. Any such programs, services or arrangements may include provision for the exercise on a cooperative or joint basis of any power exercisable by an interstate library district and an agreement embodying any such program, service or arrangement shall contain provisions covering the subjects detailed in Article VI of this compact for interstate library agreements.

ARTICLE VI. LIBRARY AGREEMENTS

(a) In order to provide for any joint or cooperative undertaking pursuant to this compact, public and private library agencies may enter into library agreements. Any agreement executed pursuant to the provisions of this compact shall, as among the parties to the agreement:

1. Detail the specific nature of the services, programs, facilities, arrangements, or properties to which it is applicable.

2. Provide for the allocation of costs and other financial responsibilities.

3. Specify the respective rights, duties, obligations and liabilities of the parties.

4. Set forth the terms and conditions for duration, renewal, termination, abrogation, disposal of joint or common property, if any, and all other matters which may be appropriate to the proper effectuation and performance of the agreement.

(b) No public or private library agency shall undertake to exercise itself, or jointly with any other library agency, by means of a library agreement any power prohibited to such agency by the constitution or statutes of its state.

(c) No library agreement shall become effective until filed with the compact administrator of each state involved, and approved in accordance with Article VII of this compact.

ARTICLE VII. APPROVAL OF LIBRARY AGREEMENTS

(a) Every library agreement made pursuant to this compact shall, prior to and as a condition precedent to its entry into force, be submitted to the attorney general of each state in which a public library agency party thereto is situated, who shall determine whether the agreement is in proper form and compatible with the laws of his state and except that in the state of New York, such agreement shall be submitted to the counsel for the state education department for such determination. The attorneys general and such counsel shall approve any agreement submitted to them unless they shall find that it does not meet the conditions set forth herein and shall detail in writing addressed to the governing bodies of the public library agencies concerned the specific respects in which the proposed agreement fails to meet the requirements of law. Failure to disapprove an agreement submitted hereunder within ninety days of its submission shall constitute approval thereof.

(b) In the event that a library agreement made pursuant to this compact shall deal in whole or in part with the provision of services or facilities with regard to which an officer or agency of the state government has constitutional or statutory powers of control, the agreement shall, as a condition precedent to its entry into force, be submitted to the state officer or agency having such power of control and shall be approved or disapproved by him or it as to all matters within his or its jurisdiction in the same manner and subject to the same requirements governing the action of the attorneys general pursuant to paragraph (a) of this article. This requirement of submission and approval shall be in addition to and not in substitution for the requirement of submission to and approval by the attorneys general.

ARTICLE VIII. OTHER LAWS APPLICABLE

Nothing in this compact or in any library agreement shall be construed to supersede, alter or otherwise impair any obligation imposed on any library by otherwise applicable law, nor to authorize the transfer or disposition of any property held in trust by a library agency in a manner contrary to the terms of such trust.

ARTICLE IX. APPROPRIATIONS AND AID

(a) Any public library agency party to a library agreement may appropriate funds to the interstate library district established thereby in the same manner and to the same extent as to a library wholly maintained by it and, subject to the laws of the state in which such public library agency is situated, may pledge its credit in support of an interstate library district established by the agreement.

(b) Subject to the provisions of the library agreement pursuant to which it functions and the laws of the states in which such district is situated, an interstate library district may claim and receive any state and federal aid which may be available to it.

ARTICLE X. COMPACT ADMINISTRATOR

Each state shall designate a compact administrator with whom copies of all library agreements to which his state or any public library agency thereof is party shall be filed. The administrator shall have such other powers as may be conferred upon him by the laws of his state and may consult and cooperate with the compact administrators of other party states and take such steps as may effectuate the purposes of this compact. If the laws of a party state so provide, such state may designate one or more deputy compact administrators in addition to its compact administrator.

ARTICLE XI. ENTRY INTO FORCE AND WITHDRAWAL

(a) This compact shall enter into force and effect immediately upon its enactment into law by any two states. Thereafter, it shall enter into force and effect as to any other state upon the enactment thereof by such state.

(b) This compact shall continue in force with respect to a party state and remain binding upon such state until six months after such state has given notice to each other party state of the repeal thereof. Such withdrawal shall not be construed to relieve any party to a library agreement entered into pursuant to this compact from any obligation of that agreement prior to the end of its duration as provided therein.

ARTICLE XII. CONSTRUCTION AND SEVERABILITY

This compact shall be liberally construed so as to effectuate the purposes thereof. The provisions of this compact shall be severable and if any phrase, clause, sentence or provision of this compact is declared to be contrary to the constitution of any party state or of the United States or the applicability thereof to any government, agency, person or circumstance is held invalid, the validity of the remainder of this compact and the applicability thereof to any government, agency, person or circumstance shall not be affected thereby. If this compact shall be held contrary to the constitution of any state party thereto, the compact shall remain in full force and effect as to the remaining states and in full force and effect as to the state affected as to all severable matters.

DISTRIBUTION OF PUBLIC DOCUMENTS

(Consolidated Laws of New York Annotated, 1982, Legislative Law, s.47.)

§ 47. Officers and institutions entitled to receive bound volumes of journals, bills and documents

As soon as the journals, bills and documents are bound, the secretary of the senate and the clerk of the assembly respectively shall distribute them as follows:

1. To the legislative library, five copies of the journals and documents, and five copies of the bills;

2. To the New York state library, for incorporated colleges and universities in this state, for each state and territory, and for literary and scientific exchanges to be made by the New York state library, two hundred copies of the journals, one hundred copies of the documents, and five copies of the bills; As amended L.1955, c. 316, § 1, eff. Oct. 1, 1955.

3. To the executive chamber, one copy of the bills;

4. To the office of the secretary of state, one copy of the bills;

5. To the office of the attorney-general, one copy of the journals,

documents and bills. As amended L.1920, c. 64; L.1949, c. 20, eff. Feb. 21, 1949; L.1949, c. 230, § 12, eff. Dec. 31, 1949.

LEGISLATIVE LIBRARY

(Consolidated Laws of New York Annotated, 1982, Legislative Law, s.7-a.)

§ 7–a. Legislative library, librarian and assistants

There shall be a legislative library to be located in the state capitol in rooms assigned by the commissioner of general services, conveniently accessible to the members of both houses of legislature, and such library shall be open throughout the year.

Such library shall be suitably furnished, equipped and maintained under the direction of the legislative librarian, within the amount of any moneys available therefor by appropriation, subject to joint rules, if any, that may be adopted by the senate and assembly in relation thereto. There shall be, for such library, a legislative librarian and such assistant librarians and other employees as may be provided for in the legislative appropriation bill. Such librarian, assistant librarians and other employees shall be chosen by the temporary president of the senate and speaker of the assembly. One of the assistant librarians shall be assigned by the legislative librarian to have charge of the legislative correspondents' room in the capitol. The legislative librarian and assistant librarians heretofore chosen by the president of the senate and speaker of the assembly, and in office when this section as hereby amended takes effect, shall continue to serve until their successors shall be chosen. The salaries and compensation of the legislative librarian, assistant librarians and other employees shall be payable from moneys appropriated in the legislative appropriation bill. During a vacancy in the office of legislative librarian, the assistant librarian who shall have been longest in the service of the state as a legislative employee, shall be employed as acting legislative librarian with the powers and duties of such librarian, and shall receive during such period the compensation herein prescribed for the legislative librarian. Such librarian shall have charge of the legislative library, but the two houses of the legislature may, by joint rules, regulate the use of the library and prescibe the powers and duties of the legislative librarian and the assistant librarians.

As amended L.1962, c. 118, § 4; L.1974, c. 746, § 1.

DIVISIONS OF HISTORY AND PUBLIC RECORDS

(Consolidated Laws of New York Annotated, 1982, Education Law,
s.140-147.)

§ 140. Divisions of public records and history continued

The division of public records and the division of history in the education department, and the offices of supervisor of public records and state historian, as created and continued by chapter three hundred eighty of the laws of nineteen hundred eleven, are hereby continued as so constituted, with the powers and duties herein prescribed. Such divisions and officers and the employees thereof shall be subject to the same provisions of law and rules as the other divisions and employees of the education department.

L.1947, c. 820, eff. July 1, 1947.

§ 141. Functions of the division of history

It shall be the function of the division of history, subject to the regulations of the regents, to collect, collate, compile, edit and prepare for publication all official records, memoranda, statistics and data relative to the history of the colony and state of New York.

It shall also be the function of the division of history in collaboration with the division of public records, when authorized by the commissioner of education so to do, to collate, compile, edit and prepare for publication as above, the official records, archives or papers of any of the civil subdivisions of the state.

And it shall further be the function of the division of history to collate, compile, edit and prepare for publication as above such archives, records, letters and manuscripts, belonging to the state or any of its officers or departments, or to any historical or patriotic society or association chartered by the regents or by statute law, or any other archives, records, papers and manuscripts, as in the judgment of the state historian but by authority of the commissioner of education, it shall be deemed for the best interests of the state to publish, for the preservation of the state's history.

L.1947, c. 820, eff. July 1, 1947.

§ 142. Powers of regents in respect to public records and historical documents, et cetera

The education department, pursuant to the education law, shall have general and exclusive supervision, care, custody and control of all public records, books, pamphlets, documents, manuscripts, archives, maps and papers of any public office, body, board, institution or society now extinct, or hereafter becoming extinct, the supervision, care, custody and control of which are not already or shall not hereafter be otherwise provided for by law.

Such department shall take such action as may be necessary to put the records hereinabove specified, except as aforesaid, in the custody and condition contemplated by the various laws relating thereto and shall provide for their restoration and preservation, and cause copies thereof to be made whenever by reason of age, use, exposure or any casualty, such copies shall in their judgment be necessary. Whenever such copy is made, and after it has been compared with the original, it shall be certified by the official person, board or officer having the legal custody and control of said original, and shall thereafter be considered and accepted as evidence and, for all other purposes, the same as the original could be; provided that the original shall be thereafter cared for and preserved, the same as if no such copy had been

made, for such examination as may be directed by an order of
court in any action or proceeding in which the accuracy of the
copy is questioned.

The officers of any county, city, town or village or other political division of the state or of any institution or society created
under any law of the state may transfer to the regents with the
consent of the commissioner of education records, books, pamphlets, manuscripts, archives, maps, papers and other documents
which are not in general use, and it shall be the duty of the regents to receive the same and to provide for their custody and
preservation.

L.1947, c. 820; amended L.1952, c. 540, § 1, eff. April 5, 1952.

§ 143. General duties of supervisor of public records

The supervisor of public records shall examine into the condition of the records, books, pamphlets, documents, manuscripts,
archives, maps and papers kept, filed or recorded, or hereafter
to be kept, filed or recorded in the several public offices of the
counties, cities, towns, villages or other political divisions of the
state, and all other public records, books, pamphlets, documents,
manuscripts, archives, maps and papers heretofore or hereafter
required by law to be kept by any public body, board, institution
or society, created under any law of the state in said counties,
cities, towns, villages or other political divisions of the state, except where the same conflicts with the duties and offices of the
clerks of the counties of Kings and New York.

L.1947, c. 820, eff. July 1, 1947.

§ 144. Definition of public records

In construing the provisions of this chapter and other statutes, the words "public records" shall, unless a contrary intention clearly appears, mean any written or printed book or paper,
or map, which is the property of the state, or of any county, city,
town or village or part thereof, and in or on which any entry has
been made or is required to be made by law, or which any officer
or employee of the state or of a county, city, town or village has
received or is required to receive for filing.

All public records inscribed by public officials, other than
maps, shall be entered or recorded in durable ink on linen paper
durably made and well finished.

L.1947, c. 820, eff. July 1, 1947.

§ 145. Functions of the division of public records

It shall be the duty of the division of public records to take all necessary measures for the proper inscription, the retrieval, the care and the preservation of all public records in the various political divisions of the state, except as described in section one hundred forty-three.

The division of public records shall advise with and recommend to public officers hereinbefore described, as to the methods of inscribing, as to the materials used in, and as to the safety and preservation of all public records. The recommendations of the division of public records may be enforced by an order issued by a justice of the supreme court upon application of the commissioner of education, either with or without notice to the proper public officer, as such justice may require.

L.1947, c. 820, eff. July 1, 1947.

§ 146. Safeguarding of public records

Every person who has the custody of any public record books of a county, city, town or village shall, at its expense, cause them to be properly and substantially bound. He shall have any such books which may have been left incomplete, made up and completed from the files and usual memoranda, so far as practicable.

Officers or boards in charge of the affairs of counties, cities, towns and villages shall provide and maintain fireproof rooms, vaults, safes or other fire-resisting receptacles made of noncombustible materials, of ample size for the safe-keeping of the public records in their care, and shall furnish such rooms with fittings of only noncombustible material, the cost to be a charge against such county, city, town or village. All such records shall be kept in the buildings in which they are ordinarily used, and so arranged that they can be conveniently examined and referred to. Such records may be stored in such other fire resistant and otherwise suitable place as may be approved for such purpose by the commissioner of education. When not in use they shall be kept in the vaults, safes or other fire resisting receptacles provided for them; except that they may be removed from their regular place of use or storage for the purpose of repair, restoration or necessary reproduction.

L.1947, c. 820; amended L.1957, c. 522; L.1967, c. 253, eff. April 10, 1967.

§ 147. Destruction of public records

1. No officer of any county, city, town or village or other political division of the state shall destroy, sell or otherwise dispose of any public record, original or copied, or any archives, in his care or custody or under his control, and which are no longer in current use, without first having advised the commissioner of ed-

ucation of their nature and obtain[1] his consent.

2. The provisions of this section shall not apply to:

a. The records of any city with a population of one million or more, and the records of any county contained therein, so long as the destruction of the records of such city or county shall be carried out in accordance with the procedure prescribed by any existing law exclusively applicable to the destruction of the records of such city or county: If any such law shall be amended by local law after the first day of July, nineteen hundred fifty-one, the provisions of this section shall not apply to the destruction of such records if the procedures therefor established by such law, as amended by local law, shall be acceptable to the commissioner of education.

b. The records of any state department, division, board, bureau, commission or other agency.

c. The records of any court.

d. Any record required to be destroyed in the manner provided by section 63.10 of the local finance law.

e. The records of any public corporation which have not been retained for the longest minimum period of time required:

(1) by rules and regulations of the commissioner of education; or

(2) by any agency of the state so that it may properly carry out its assigned duties and responsibilities; or

(3) because of any provision of law.

3. Notwithstanding the provision of subdivision two of this section, the commissioner of education shall have power to consent to the disposition of records of a public corporation which have not been retained for the longest minimum period of time required by rules and regulations of the commissioner of education, by any agency of the state, or because of any provision of law, provided that such records have been photographed, micro-photographed, or reproduced on film, in accordance with section fifty-one-a of the general municipal law or section sixty-five-a of the public officers law.

L.1947, c. 820; amended L.1952, c. 540, § 2; L.1953, c. 566, eff. April 8, 1953.

PUBLIC AND ASSOCIATION LIBRARIES

(Consolidated Laws of New York Annotated, 1982, Education Law, s.253-268, 270.)

§ 253. Public and association libraries and museums

1. All provisions of this section and of sections two hundred fifty-four to two hundred seventy-one inclusive shall apply equal-

ly to libraries, museums, and to combined libraries and museums, and the word "library" shall be construed to mean reference and circulating libraries and reading rooms.

2. The term "public" library as used in this chapter shall be construed to mean a library, other than professional, technical or public school library, established for free public purposes by official action of a municipality or district or the legislature, where the whole interests belong to the public; the term "association" library shall be construed to mean a library established and controlled, in whole or in part, by a group of private individuals operating as an association, close corporation or as trustees under the provisions of a will or deed of trust; and the term "free" as applied to a library shall be construed to mean a library maintained for the benefit and free use on equal terms of all the people of the community in which the library is located.

L.1947, c. 820; amended L.1950, c. 273, § 1, eff. April 1, 1950.

3. The term "Indian library" shall be construed to mean a public library established by the tribal government of the Saint Regis Mohawk tribe, the Seneca Nations of Indians or the Tonawanda Seneca tribe and located on their respective reservations, to serve Indians residing on such reservations and any other persons designated by its board of trustees. As amended L.1977, c. 476, § 1.

1977 Amendment. Subd. 3. L. 1977, c. 476, § 1, eff. Aug. 1, 1977, added subd. 3.

§ 254. Standards of library service

The regents shall have power to fix standards of library service for every free association, public and hospital library or, with the advice of the appropriate tribal government and library board of trustees, Indian library which receives any portion of the moneys appropriated by the state to aid such libraries, or which is supported in whole or in part by tax levied by any municipality or district. In the case of a hospital library or a library serving a hospital, such standards shall be established in consultation with the commissioner of health. If any such library shall fail to comply with the regents requirements, such library shall not receive any portion of the moneys appropriated by the state for free, hospital or Indian libraries nor shall any tax be levied by any municipality or district for the support in whole or in part of such library.
As amended L.1977, c. 476, § 2; L.1981, c. 718, § 1.

§ 255. Establishment of a public library

1. By a majority vote at any election, or at a meeting of the electors duly held, any county, city, village, town, school district or other body authorized to levy and collect taxes; or by vote of its board of supervisors or other governing elective body any county, or by vote of its common council or by action of a board of estimate and apportionment or other proper authority any city, or by vote of its board of trustees any village, or by vote of

its town board any town, or any combination of such voting bodies, may individually or jointly authorize the establishment of a
public library with or without branches, and may appropriate
money raised by tax or otherwise to equip and maintain such library or libraries or to provide a building or rooms for its or
their use. Any such municipality or district may acquire real or
personal property for library purposes by gift, grant, devise, bequest or condemnation and may take, buy, sell, hold and transfer
either real or personal property for public library purposes.
Whenever twenty-five taxpayers shall so petition, the question of
providing library facilities shall be voted on at the next election
or meeting at which taxes may be voted, provided that due public
notice of the proposed action shall have been given. Whenever
the electors of a school district at a district meeting duly held
shall have authorized the establishment of a public library under
the provisions of this section, at such meeting or at any subsequent meeting duly held, they may determine by a majority of
the voters present and voting on the proposition to levy a tax to
be collected in installments for the purchase or condemnation of
a site and the erection thereon of a library building or the erection of a library building on land acquired otherwise than by
purchase or condemnation, or for the purchase of land and a
suitable building thereon and make necessary alterations and additions and equip such building for use as a library.

2. Upon the request of a majority of the members of the boards of
trustees of two or more libraries chartered by the regents, if it shall
appear to the satisfaction of the commissioner that the establishment
of a cooperative library system will result in improved and expanded
library service to the area and that the area is suitable for the establishment of such a cooperative library system, the commissioner may
call a joint meeting of the trustees of such libraries for the purpose
of determining whether a cooperative library system shall be established and electing a board of trustees of such cooperative library
system. If it shall appear to the commissioner that the area proposed
for the cooperative library system is not sufficient to warrant the
establishment of such system; that such area is not otherwise suitable
or that for sufficient other reason such cooperative library system
as proposed should not be established he shall disapprove such request.

a. Notice of such meeting shall be given by the commissioner
to each trustee by mail to his last known address at least five
days prior to such meeting. At such meeting the board of trustees of each library participating shall have five votes.

b. Such meeting shall be called to order by the person designated by the commissioner and shall thereupon organize by the
election of a chairman. At such meeting a resolution in substantially the following form shall be presented for the action of
the meeting: "Resolved that a cooperative library system be established consisting of the following libraries chartered by the
regents . . . (name libraries) for the purpose of expanding

and improving library service in the area served by the above named libraries."

c. If the resolution described above is adopted, then the meeting shall proceed to elect a board of trustees of such library system to consist of not less than five nor more than twenty-five members as determined by the meeting.

d. Within one month after taking office, the trustees-elect shall apply to the regents for a charter as a cooperative library system.

e. The board of trustees shall manage and control such cooperative library system and shall have all the powers of trustees of other educational institutions in the university as defined in this chapter. Such board shall elect a president, secretary and treasurer. Before entering upon his duties, such treasurer shall execute and file with the trustees an official undertaking in such sum and with such sureties as the board shall direct and approve. The treasurer need not be a member of such board. The funds of the cooperative library system shall be deposited in a bank or banks designated by the board of trustees and shall be expended only under the direction of such trustees upon properly authenticated vouchers.

f. The term of office of trustees shall be five years except that the members of the first board of trustees shall determine by lot the year in which the term of office of each trustee shall expire so that as nearly as possible the terms of one-fifth of the members of such board will expire annually. Thereafter, the successors of such trustees shall be elected annually by a meeting of the trustees of the participating libraries in the cooperative library system. No trustee shall hold office consecutively for more than two full terms. Such meeting shall be called by the secretary of the cooperative library system who shall give notice to all the trustees of participating libraries in the manner provided in subparagraph a of this subdivision for giving notice of the meeting to authorize the establishment of such cooperative library system.

g. A contract may be entered into between the board of trustees of a cooperative library system and the department under which the state library will provide services, facilities and staff to the cooperative library system upon terms agreed upon by and between the parties to such contract.

h. Nothing herein contained shall be deemed to deprive any participating library of its property.

i. The board of trustees of any library chartered by the regents which is not participating in a cooperative library system may adopt a resolution requesting that such library become a participating library in a cooperative library system. Duplicate copies of such resolution certified by the clerk of such board of trustees shall be filed with the board of trustees of the cooperative library system. If such board approve such resolution such approval shall be endorsed thereon and a copy thereof shall, be filed with the commissioner. Upon such resolution being approved by the commissioner such additional library shall become a participating library in such system and shall have the same rights, duties and privileges as other libraries participating therein.

j. The participating libraries in such library system shall be those libraries, members of the boards of trustees of which join in petitioning the commissioner to call the meeting for the establishment of the cooperative library system pursuant to this section, and who are named in the resolution voted upon by such meeting and in the charter of the library system.

k. The board of trustees of each public library system shall meet no fewer than six times a year.

3. Trustees of a reference and research library resources system shall have those powers set forth in section two hundred twenty-six of this article with respect to trustees of corporations chartered by the regents, and in addition shall have the following powers and duties:

a. The board of trustees of a reference and research library resources system shall include at least one representative of each constituent public library system, at least one representative of the member academic library with the largest collection, and at least two nonlibrarians from the research community served by the system.

b. The term of office of trustees shall be five years except that the members of the first board of trustees shall determine by lot the year in which the term of office of each trustee shall expire so that as nearly as possible the terms of one-fifth of the members of such board will expire annually. Thereafter, the successors of such trustees shall be elected annually by a meeting of the designated representatives of the member institutions participating in the reference and research library resources system. No trustee shall hold office consecutively for for more than two full terms. Such annual meeting shall be called by the secretary of the reference and research library resources system who shall give notice to all the participating libraries by mail at least five days prior to such meeting.

c. The board of trustees shall meet no fewer than six times a year.

4. By a majority vote of the tribal government of an Indian reservation, or upon the request of the tribal government of an Indian reservation, an Indian library may be established, with or without branches, and may make application to the state or other source for money to equip and maintain such library or libraries or to provide a building or rooms for its uses. Notwithstanding the provisions of section seven of the Indian law, the board of trustees of such library, on behalf of the tribal government, may acquire real or personal property for use by an Indian library by gift, grant, devise, bequest and may take, buy, sell, hold and transfer either real or personal property for the purposes of such library. No more than one Indian library may be established on a reservation and such library shall serve all inhabitants of that reservation. No such library shall be established on any reservation that has

fewer than three hundred permanent residents and one thousand acres of land.

5. The boards of trustees of any two, or more, public libraries, Indian libraries, reference and research library resources systems, cooperative library systems, or association libraries, as defined in this article, may pool surplus funds to be used for the purchase of certificates of deposit in any bank or trust company, provided that such certificate of deposit be secured by a pledge of obligations of the United States of America, or any obligation fully guaranteed or insured as to interest and principal by the United States of America acting through an agency, subdivision, department or division thereof, or obligations of the state of New York. Each participating public library, Indian library, reference and research library resources system, cooperative library system or association library shall be entitled to its pro-rata share of interest earned on such certificates in proportion to its contribution to the purchase price of such certificates.
As amended L.1975, c. 849, § 1; L.1977, c. 476, § 3; L.1978, c. 787, §§ 2–4; L.1981, c. 718, § 2.

§ 256. Contracts

1. Any authority named in section two hundred fifty-five may, individually or jointly with another municipal or district body or tribal government, grant money for the support of the cost of maintaining or the cost of any capital improvements to or expenditure for one or more: free association libraries, provided such libraries are registered by the regents; public libraries, provided such libraries are registered by the regents; and cooperative library systems approved by the commissioner; or may, individually or jointly with another municipal or district body or tribal government, contract with the trustees of a free association library registered by the regents, or with any municipal or district body having control of such a library, or with the trustees of the cooperative library system, or with the trustees of a public library registered by the regents to furnish library services to the people of the municipality, district or reservation for whose benefit the contract is made, under such terms and conditions as may be stated in such contract. The amount agreed to be paid for such services under such contract shall be a charge upon the municipal or district bodies or tribal government which agree to make the payment and shall be paid directly to the treasurer of the free association library, public library or of the cooperative library system.

2. When the municipality agreeing to make the payment or grant is a town in which there are one or more incorporated villages, which village or villages jointly with such town contract with the trustees of a cooperative library system, a free association library or with another municipal district or body having control of a public library whether or not such district or body is an incorporated village in such town, the amount appropriated by the town board in such town shall be a charge upon the taxable property of that part of the town outside of any such incorporated village.
As amended L.1972, c. 364, § 1; L.1977, c. 476, § 4; L.1980, c. 166, § 1.

§ 257. Acceptance of conditional gift

By majority vote at any election or at a meeting of the electors, duly held, any municipality or district or by three-fourths vote of its council any city, or any library or any designated branch thereof if so authorized by such vote of a municipality, district or council, or any combination of such voting bodies, may accept gifts, grants, devises or bequests for library purposes or for kindred affiliated educational, social and civic agencies on condition that a specified annual appropriation shall thereafter be made for the maintenance of a library or branches thereof, or of such kindred affiliated agencies, by the municipality or district or combination so authorizing such acceptance, or upon such other conditions as may be stipulated in the terms of the gift. Such acceptance when approved by the regents of the university under seal and recorded in its book of charters shall be a binding contract, and such municipality or district shall levy and collect yearly in the manner prescribed for other taxes the amount stipulated and shall maintain any so accepted gift, grant, devise or bequest intact and make good any impairment thereof, and shall comply with all other conditions set forth in the stated terms of the gift.

L.1947, c. 820; formerly § 259; renumbered 257, L.1950, c. 273, § 5, eff. April 1, 1950.

§ 258.　Closing of museum; admission fee during certain hours

The trustees of any institution supported under this chapter by public money, in whole or in part, may, so far as consistent with free use by the public at reasonable or specified hours, close any of its museum collections at certain other hours, for study, to meet the demands of special students or for exhibition purposes, and may charge an admission fee at such hours, provided that all receipts from such fees shall be paid into the treasury and be used for the maintenance or enlargement of the institution.

L.1947, c. 820; formerly § 260; renumbered 258, L.1950, c. 273, § 5, eff. April 1, 1950.

§ 259. Library taxes

1. Taxes, in addition to those otherwise authorized, may be voted for library purposes by any authority named in section two hundred fifty-five of this chapter and shall, unless otherwise directed by such vote, be considered as annual appropriations therefor until changed by further vote and shall be levied and collected yearly, or as directed, as are other general taxes. In the case of a school district the appropriation for library purposes shall be submitted to the voters of the district in a separate resolution and shall not be submitted as a part of the appropriation of the necessary funds to meet the estimated expenditures of the school district. All moneys received from taxes or other public sources for library purposes shall be kept as a separate library fund by the treasurer of the municipality or district making

the appropriation and shall be expended only under direction of the library trustees on properly authenticated vouchers, except that money received from taxes and other public sources for the support of a public library or a free association library or a cooperative library system shall be paid over to the treasurer of such library or cooperative library system upon the written demand of its trustees.

As amended L.1973, c. 200, § 1.

2.   In the case of a joint public library authorized to be established by two or more municipalities or districts pursuant to section two hundred fifty-five of this chapter, the governing bodies of the participating municipalities and districts shall enter into an agreement designating the treasurer of one of the participating municipalities or districts to be the treasurer of the joint public library.   The agreement shall be for a period of not less than one year nor more than five years and the state comptroller and the commissioner of education shall be notified in writing by the board of library trustees of such agreement and designation.

The municipality or district whose treasurer is designated to serve as treasurer of a joint public library may be compensated for the services rendered by such official to the library.   The amount to be paid for such services shall be determined by agreement between the governing body of the municipality or district and the board of library trustees, and shall be paid at least annually from the public library fund.

3.   The treasurer of a joint public library shall maintain the separate library fund required by subdivision one of this section and shall credit to such fund all moneys received.   The state aid apportioned to a joint public library, amounts appropriated by participants toward its support and all amounts received from other sources shall be paid to the library treasurer.   Appropriations for the library made by the participating municipalities or districts shall be paid in full to the library treasurer within sixty days after the beginning of the library fiscal year.

Disbursements for purposes of a joint public library shall be made by the treasurer in the manner prescribed in subdivision one of this section.

Within thirty days after the close of the fiscal year the treasurer shall make an annual report of the receipt and disbursement of library moneys to the board of library trustees and to the governing body of each of the participating municipalities or districts.

4.   Notwithstanding the provisions of subdivisions one and three of this section, the library trustees may by resolution establish a petty cash fund, in such amount as they shall determine, for any employee who has supervision of any library or

branch thereof. Expenditures from such fund may be made by
such employee in advance of audit by the library trustees, but
only after the submission of properly itemized and authenticated
vouchers for materials, supplies or services furnished to the library or branch thereof and upon terms calling for payment to
the vendor upon the delivery of any such materials or supplies
or the rendering of any such services. At each meeting of the
library trustees a list of all expenditures made from such fund
since the last meeting of the trustees, together with the vouchers
supporting such expenditures, shall be presented by such employee to the library trustees. The trustees shall direct the treasurer to reimburse such petty cash fund in an amount equal to
the total of such bills which the trustees shall so allow. Any of
such bills or any portion of such bills which the library trustees
shall refuse to allow shall be the personal liability of such employee and he shall promptly reimburse such petty cash fund in
the amount of such disallowances. If such reimbursement has
not been made by the time of the first payment of salary to such
employee after the action of the library trustees in disallowing
an amount so expended, such amount shall be withheld from such
salary payment to such employee and, if necessary, subsequent
salary payments and paid into such petty cash fund until an
amount so disallowed by the library trustees has been repaid in
full to the petty cash fund.

L.1947, c. 820; formerly § 261; renumbered 259, L.1950, c. 273,
§ 5; amended L.1955, c. 649; L.1958, c. 933, § 2; L.1959, c. 160,
§ 2; L.1961, c. 738, §§ 1, 2; L.1966, c. 378, eff. May 16, 1966.

§ 260. Trustees

1. Public libraries authorized to be established by action of the voters
or their representatives shall be managed by trustees who shall have all
the powers of trustees of other educational institutions of the university
as defined in this chapter; provided that the number of trustees of
county public libraries and Indian libraries shall not be less than five
nor more than eleven and that the number of trustees of other public
libraries shall not be less than five nor more than eleven. The number
of trustees of joint public libraries authorized to be established by two
or more municipalities or districts or any combination thereof shall be
not less than five nor more than twenty-five, as determined by agreement of the voting bodies empowered to authorize the establishment of
such libraries pursuant to subdivision one of section two hundred fifty-
five of this chapter and shall be set forth in the resolution authorizing
the establishment of such joint public library. Such resolution shall also
set forth the number of such trustees which each of the participating
municipalities or districts shall be entitled to elect or appoint, and the
terms of office of the first trustees as determined in accordance with
subdivision three of this section.

2. The trustees of public libraries authorized to be established by
cities shall be appointed by the mayor and confirmed by the common
council, in counties they shall be appointed by the county board of supervisors or other governing elective body, in villages they shall be appoint-

ed by the village board of trustees, in towns they shall be appointed by the town board, in school districts they shall be elected by the legal voters in the same manner as trustees are elected in the school district which established said library, and on Indian reservations they shall be elected at a general tribal election or otherwise designated by the chiefs or head men of an Indian tribe; that the first trustees shall determine by lot the year in which the term of office of each trustee shall expire and that a new trustee shall be elected or appointed annually to serve for five years. Notwithstanding the foregoing provisions of this subdivision, in any case where a town is a contributor to the support of any such public library in a village located within the town the appointment of trustees of such library who reside outside the village but within such town shall be subject to the approval of the town board of such town. The charter of any public library granted prior to April thirtieth, nineteen hundred and twenty-one, which provides for trustees, their terms of office and method of election or appointment in a manner differing from that hereinbefore provided, shall remain in full force and effect until the regents, upon application of the library trustees, shall amend the charter to conform to the provisions of law in effect when such amendment is made.

3. The trustees of a joint public library authorized to be established by two or more municipalities or districts or any combination thereof shall be appointed or elected by the body authorized by subdivision two of this section to elect or appoint trustees of public libraries authorized to be established by such municipality or district. The number of such trustees to be elected or appointed by each of the participating municipalities or districts shall be determined as provided in subdivision one of this section. The term of office of such trustees shall be five years except that the terms of the first trustees shall be so arranged that the terms of as nearly as possible to one-fifth of the members shall expire annually.

4. No person who is a member of any municipal council or board authorized by this section to appoint public library trustees in any municipality shall be eligible for the office of such public library trustee in such municipality.

5. The boards of trustees of public, free association and Indian libraries shall hold regular meetings at least quarterly, and such boards shall fix the day and hour for holding such meetings.

6. The board of trustees of a library system or a public or free association library chartered by the regents of the state of New York may determine to contribute annually a sum of money to assist the Library Trustees Foundation of New York State in fostering, encouraging and promoting the further development of library activities throughout the state and financing programs in this state which will assist in the dissemination of information leading to the improvement and extension of library services.

7. The board of trustees of a public library established and supported by a school district shall, in addition to powers conferred by this or

any other chapter, be authorized in its discretion to call, give notice of and conduct a special district meeting for the purpose of electing library trustees and of submitting initially a resolution in accordance with the provisions of subdivision one of section two hundred fifty-nine of this chapter. Such meeting shall be held prior to the first day of July but subsequent to the first day of April. Should the board of trustees of the library determine, in its discretion, not to notice and conduct such a meeting, then the election and budget vote will be noticed and conducted by the board of education of the school district as part of its annual meeting.

8. Candidates for the office of trustee of a public library established and supported by a school district shall be nominated by petition which shall meet the requirements of subdivision a of section two thousand eighteen of this chapter, except that such candidates shall be elected in the manner specified in subdivision b of such section except where a charter granted prior to April thirtieth, nineteen hundred seventy-one provides for a different procedure.

9. The board of trustees of a public library established and supported by a school district, in addition to any other powers conferred by this chapter, may, in its discretion, call, give notice of and conduct a special district meeting of the qualified voters of the school district for any proper library purpose, including the re-submission of a defeated library appropriation, at a time and place designated by said board of trustees, except as to those purposes set forth in subdivision seven of this section.

10. The board of trustees of a public library established and supported by a school district, in addition to any other powers conferred in this chapter, shall have the power to determine the necessity for construction of library facilities, to select a library site or sites, to select the architect, and to require that the board of education call, give notice of and conduct a special district meeting in accordance with the provisions of subdivision nine of this section for the purpose of designating and acquiring a site or sites and authorizing the issuance of obligations of the school district for acquisition and construction of library facilities, or either.

11. Whenever the board of trustees of a public library shall call, give notice of and conduct a special district meeting under subdivision seven or nine of this section, such meeting shall be established, noticed and conducted in the same manner and to the same extent as such meetings were theretofore established, noticed and conducted by the board of education of the school district, the board of trustees of the libraries making all the determinations and taking all action in respect thereto otherwise required of the board of education of the school district, except that the meeting need not, in the discretion of the board of trustees of the library, be held in separate election districts in those school districts where election districts have been established by the board of education. The board of registration shall meet as provided in section two thousand fourteen of this chapter and notice of the meeting shall be given in accordance with the provisions of sections two thousand four and two thousand seven of this chapter. The cost of all such meetings and registrations shall be a charge to the library.

Notwithstanding any other provision of law, prior to the discarding of used or surplus books or other such reading materials by trustees of a chartered public, cooperative or free association library which receives over ten thousand dollars in state aid, such trustees shall (i) offer to donate such books or materials which have no market value to a not-for-profit corporation or political subdivision located within the area of the library system or (ii) offer to sell such books or materials which do have a market value to the general public. The trustees shall retain any proceeds received from the sale of such books and materials for the purpose of maintaining and improving library service within the system.

As amended L.1970, c. 860; L.1971, c. 1085; L.1973, c. 691, § 1; L.1975, c. 442, § 1; L.1976, c. 327, §§ 1, 2; L.1977, c. 419, §§ 1–3; L.1977, c. 476, §§ 5–7; L.1977, c. 477, § 1; L.1978, c. 787, § 5; L.1979, c. 480, § 2.

§ 260–a. Meetings of board of trustees

Every meeting, including a special district meeting, of a board of trustees of a library system, cooperative library system, public library or free association library, including every committee meeting and subcommittee meeting of any such board of trustees in cities having a population of one million or more, which receives more than ten thousand dollars in state aid shall be open to the general public. Such meetings shall be held in conformity with and in pursuance to the provisions of article seven of the public officers law. Provided, however, and notwithstanding the provisions of subdivision one of section ninety-nine of the public officers law, public notice of the time and place of a meeting scheduled at least two weeks prior thereto shall be given to the public and news media at least one week before such meeting.

Added L.1979, c. 468, § 1; amended L.1980, c. 685, § 1.

§ 261. Incorporation

Within one month after taking office, the first board of trustees of any such public library or Indian library shall apply to the regents for a charter in accordance with the vote establishing the library.

As amended L.1977, c. 476, § 8.

§ 262. Use of public and Indian libraries

Every library established under section two hundred fifty-five of this chapter shall be forever free to the inhabitants of the municipality or district or Indian reservation, which establishes it, subject always to rules of the library trustees who shall have authority to exclude any person who wilfully violates such rules; and the trustees may, under such conditions as they think expedient, extend the privileges of the library to persons living outside such municipality or district or Indian reservation.

As amended L.1977, c. 476, § 9.

§ 263. Reports

Every library or museum, other than a school library, which enjoys any exemption from taxation or receives state aid or other privilege not usually accorded to business corporations shall make the report required by section two hundred fifteen of this chapter, and such report shall relieve the institution from making any report now required by statute or charter to be made to the legislature or to any department, court or other authority of the state. These reports shall be summarized and transmitted to the legislature by the regents with the annual reports of the university.

L.1947, c. 820; formerly § 265; renumbered 263, L.1950, c. 273, § 5, eff. April 1, 1950.

§ 264.   Injuries to property

Whoever intentionally injures, defaces or destroys any property belonging to or deposited in any incorporated library, reading-room, museum or other educational institution, shall be punished by imprisonment in a state prison for not more than three years, or in a county jail for not more than one year, or by a fine of not more than five hundred dollars, or by both such fine and imprisonment.

L.1947, c. 820; formerly § 266; renumbered 264, L.1950, c. 273, § 5, eff. April 1, 1950.

§ 265.   Detention

Whoever wilfully detains any book, newspaper, magazine, pamphlet, manuscript or other property belonging to any public or incorporated library, reading-room, museum or other educational institution, for thirty days after notice in writing to return the same, given after the expiration of the time which by the rules of such institution, such article or other property may be kept, shall be punished by a fine of not less than one nor more than twenty-five dollars, or by imprisonment in jail not exceeding six months, and the said notice shall bear on its face a copy of this section.

L.1947, c. 820; formerly § 267, renumbered 265, L.1950, c. 273, § 5, eff. April 1, 1950.

§ 265–a. Defense of lawful detention

In any action for false arrest, false imprisonment, unlawful detention, defamation of character, assault, trespass or invasion of civil rights brought by any person by reason of having been detained on or in the immediate vicinity of the premises of a public library for the purpose of investigation or questioning as to the ownership of any materials, it shall be a defense to such action that the person was detained in a reasonable manner and for not more than a reasonable time to permit such investigation or questioning by a peace officer or by the librarian in charge, his or her authorized employee or agent, and that such peace officer, librarian, employee or agent has reasonable grounds to believe that the person so detained was committing or attempting to commit larceny on such premises of such materials. As used in this section, "reasonable grounds" shall include, but not be limited to, knowledge that a person has concealed, unauthorized possession of material owned or belonging to the public library, and a "reasonable time" shall mean the time necessary to permit the person detained to make a statement or to refuse to make a statement, and the time necessary to examine employees and records of the public library relative to the ownership of the materials.
Added L.1982, c. 784, § 1.

§ 266. Transfer of libraries

By vote similar to that required by section two hundred fifty-five of this chapter any municipality or district or tribal government or combination of districts, or by action of its trustees at a meeting duly held any association library, incorporated or registered by the regents, may, when such vote or action has been duly approved by the regents, transfer, conditionally as provided in section two hundred fifty-seven of this chapter, or otherwise, the ownership and control of its library with all its property, real and personal, or any part thereof, to any municipality, or district, or institution providing for free library service; and the trustees or body making the transfer shall thereafter be relieved of all responsibility pertaining to property thus transferred.

As amended L.1975, c. 46, § 1; L.1977, c. 476, § 10.

§ 267. Local neglect

If the local authorities of any library supported wholly or in part by state money fail to provide for the support of such library and the public usefulness of its books, the regents shall in writing notify the trustees of said library what is necessary to meet the state's requirements, and on such notice all said library's rights to further grants of money or books from the state shall be suspended until the regents certify that the requirements have been met; and if said trustees shall refuse or neglect to comply with such requirements within sixty days after service of such notice, the regents may remove them from office and thereafter all books and other library property wholly or in part paid for from state moneys shall be under the full and direct control of the regents who, as shall seem best for public interests, may appoint new trustees to carry on the library, or may store it, or distribute its books to other libraries.

L.1947, c. 820; formerly § 269; renumbered 267, L.1950, c. 273, § 5, eff. April 1, 1950.

§ 268. Abolition

Any library established by public vote of any municipality or district, or by vote of the common council of any city, or by vote of the board of trustees of any village, or by action of school authorities, or by vote of the tribal government of an Indian reservation, or under section two hundred fifty-five of this chapter, may be abolished by majority vote at an election, or at a meeting of the electors duly held, provided that due public notice of the proposed action shall have been given, or by vote of such tribal government. If any such library is abolished, its property shall be used first to return to the regents, for the benefit of other free association or public or school libraries in that locality, the equivalent of such sums as it may have received from the state or from other sources as gifts for public use. After such return any remaining property may be used as directed in the vote abolishing the library, but if the entire library property does not exceed in value the amount of such gifts, it may be transferred to the regents for public use, and the trustees shall thereupon be free from further responsibility. No abolition of a public library shall be lawful until the regents grant a certificate that its assets have been properly distributed and its abolition completed in accordance with law.

As amended L.1977, c. 476, § 11.

§ 270. Acceptance of surplus library books or property

The state education department is hereby authorized to cooperate with the United States commissioner of education, the war assets administration, and/or other federal officers and officials in the administration of any statute heretofore or hereafter enacted for the disposal of surplus library books or property, and to accept for and on behalf of the state of New York or its political subdivisions surplus library books or other property suitable and necessary to the operation of public and free libraries and Indian libraries and for the improvement and extension of library service for New York state, and any funds, which may be made available to the state of New York by the federal government for these and related public and Indian library services.

As amended L.1977, c. 476, § 12.

CITY AND COUNTY LIBRARIES

(Consolidated Laws of New York Annotated, 1982, Unconsolidated Laws, s.6211-6227.)

§ 6211. Establishment of city and county public library; tax levy; appropriations; acquisition of property for library purposes; definitions

The governing body of any county is hereby authorized and empowered to establish a free public library, with or without branches, to be known as a city and county public library and to levy and raise by taxation and appropriate such sums as shall be necessary to establish, equip and maintain such library and branches, provide buildings and accommodations therefor, and provide the necessary salaries and expenses of a director, deputy directors, librarians, assistants and other employees, which said sums shall be charges upon the county. The levy, appropriation and use of such sums of money so raised are declared to be for the benefit of the county and are declared to be for a county purpose. Upon the establishment of a city and county public library, the county may acquire real or personal property for library purposes by gift, grant, devise, bequest, or pursuant to the provisions of the eminent domain procedure law, and may take, buy, sell, hold and transfer either real or personal property and administer the same for public library purposes.

The term "city library" as used herein shall mean any circulating library, reference library, or association library located within a city and organized under any general or special law, or created under or pursuant to the provisions of any will or deed of trust.

The term "county public library" shall mean any library having trustees appointed by the governing body of any county.

L.1953, c. 768, § 1; amended L.1977, c. 840, § 117.

§ 6212. Trustees; qualifications; appointment; terms of office

The trustees of any city and county public library, when established as aforesaid, shall consist of fifteen members appointed by the board of supervisors or other governing body of a county, all of whom shall be citizens of the United States, at least eight of whom shall be electors of the city and at least five of whom shall be electors of the county outside the city. The first board of trustees shall include among the fifteen members so appointed at least three members of the board of trustees of any county public library, in counties having a county public library, at least three members of the board of trustees of each city library, included in the consolidation. The first board of trustees shall take office upon appointment and shall hold office until the end of the second calendar year following the year of their appointment. The board of supervisors or other governing body of the county shall then appoint fifteen members of said board of trustees, three for a term of one calendar year, three for a term of two calendar years, three for a term of three calendar years, three for a term of four calendar years and three for a term of five calendar years. One trustee of each group of three shall be selected from a list of three nominees for that group named by the mayor of the city with the approval of the common council or other governing body of such city. Thereafter there shall be appointed annually by the board of supervisors or other governing body three trustees for a full term of five calendar years, one of whom shall be selected from a list of three nominees named by the mayor of the city with the approval of the common council or other governing body of such city. The board of supervisors or other governing body shall fill, for the unexpired term, any vacancy which occurs during a term of office without restriction except as to citizenship and residence requirements.

L.1953, c. 768, § 2.

§ 6213. Application for charter

Within one month after taking office, the first board of trustees of the city and county public library shall apply to the board of regents of the state of New York for a charter.

L.1953, c. 768, § 3.

§ 6214. Powers and duties of trustees

The fifteen trustees appointed as provided in section two shall serve without compensation and shall constitute a board

which, upon the granting of a charter by the board of regents
of the state of New York, shall be a body corporate, and shall
have all the powers and duties of trustees of other educational
institutions of the university of the state of New York, including
but not limited to the following exclusive powers and duties:

(a) To determine and cause to be carried out all policies and
principles pertaining to the operations and selection of library
material of such city and county public library, and, subject to
the provisions of section fifteen of this act, the exclusive power
and authority to appoint and remove employees of such city and
county public library, to fix and define their authority and duties,
and to fix their salaries within the limits of available appropriations, such employees to include a competent director and deputy
directors as provided in section fourteen of this act;

(b) To establish the headquarters of a city and county public
library and to establish such branches and book stations as may
be necessary and to provide one or more book trucks for the distribution of books, as they may deem desirable;

(c) To take and hold by gift, grant, devise or bequest in their
own right or in trust for any purpose comprised in the objects
of the corporation, any real or personal property, and to take
possession of, use, insure, protect and maintain any and all
property, real or personal, which may be conveyed or transferred to such city and county public library or to such trustees,
or placed under it or their jurisdiction;

(d) To buy, sell, mortgage, let or otherwise use or dispose of
the property of such city and county public library as they shall
deem for the best interests of such library, and to lend or deposit,
or to receive as a gift, or on loan or deposit, literary, or scientific
or other articles, collections or property pertaining to its work;

(e) To continue and to manage, operate, supervise and oversee
any library or libraries made a part of or placed under the jurisdiction of such city and county public library and to cause the
services performed by any such library or libraries to be continued;

(f) To assume and take over the supervision, direction and
management and the employment of all personnel of any library
or libraries made a part of or placed under the jurisdiction of a
city and county public library, subject only to the specific limitations hereinafter provided herein;

(g) Generally to do, perform and carry out all the necessary,
usual or customary acts and duties required by law and done and
performed by trustees of libraries in the state of New York;

(h) To meet and organize annually after its members are appointed, and elect from among its members a chairman, a vice-chairman, a secretary and an executive committee of five of its members, which committee, in intervals between meetings of the trustees, may transact such business as the trustees may authorize;

(i) To promulgate and enforce rules and regulations for the conduct of its business.

L.1953, c. 768, § 4.

§ 6215. Annual budget request; audit of appropriations

The board of trustees of any city and county public library shall submit annually a budget request to the comptroller or other fiscal officer of the county in such form and at such time as may be from time to time required by the comptroller or other fiscal officer. The appropriation of all moneys by the board of supervisors or other governing body of any county, its payment to, and its use and expenditure and accounting therefor by the city and county public library and the auditing thereof shall in all respects be subject to and governed by the provisions of the budget or fiscal laws applicable to such county and shall include the general power to examine and audit granted to the comptroller or other fiscal officer of the county and the comptroller or such officer shall report the results of any such audit to the board of supervisors or other governing body of the county.

L.1953, c. 768, § 5.

§ 6216. Contracts for county library service

The board of trustees of any city and county public library may contract with the trustees of any free library within the county registered, by the regents, or with any municipal or district body having control of such library, to furnish library privileges to the people of the county, under such terms and conditions as may be stated in such contract and within such amounts appropriated by the board of supervisors or other governing body and other available funds, as may be agreed upon by the contracting parties. The amount agreed to be paid for such privileges under such contract shall be a charge upon the county and shall be paid in the manner authorized by sections one and five of this act.

L.1953, c. 768, § 6.

§ 6217. Transfer of real and personal property of county

public library; dissolution of county library corporation; succession to devises, gifts or bequests

The trustees of any existing county public library are authorized and empowered to transfer to the county all its right, title and interest in and to any real and personal property used by such county public library; and upon the establishment of any city and county public library as aforesaid, and the assumption by it of all the liabilities, duties and obligations of such county public library, the trustees of such county public library are authorized and empowered to vote to dissolve the said library corporation, and to certify such vote to the board of regents of the state of New York; whereupon such county public library shall be considered as dissolved. Any devise, bequest, gift or grant contained in any will or other instrument, in trust or otherwise, made before or after the dissolution or intended for the benefit of such county public library shall inure to or for the benefit of the city and county public library, and so far as is necessary for that purpose the city and county public library shall be deemed to be the successor to the county public library; provided, however, that all such devises, bequests, gifts or grants shall be devoted by any city and county public library to the purposes intended by the testator, donor or grantor.

L.1953, c. 768, § 7.

§ 6218. Cancellation of contracts between city, and city library

Any city is hereby authorized and empowered by resolution to be adopted pursuant to the city charter to enter into an agreement or agreements with any city library cancelling and abrogating any contract between said parties, and assigning and transferring to such city library all its right, title and interest in any and all books, papers, documents, works of art and personal property of every name, nature and description covered by said contract, and any related lease or contract of occupancy may also be cancelled by agreement. Any city library is authorized and empowered by resolution to be adopted by the votes of a majority of its trustees, or if it has members, by a majority vote of such members, present in person or by proxy at a meeting of such members called for that purpose to enter into such agreements.

L.1953, c. 768, § 8.

§ 6219. Transfer of property rights and interest of city library to city and county public library for library purposes; terms and conditions

Any city library is authorized and empowered by resolution to be adopted by the votes of a majority of its trustees, or if it has members, by a vote of a majority of said members of those present in person or by proxy at a meeting of such members called for that purpose and notwithstanding the provisions of any general or special law, to convey, transfer and assign to any city and county public library all its right, title and interest in and to all its money and securities, and to convey and transfer to any county all its right, title and interest in and to all its real estate, books, papers, documents, music, works of art, and real and personal property of every name, nature and description, on condition that the governing board of any county authorizes the acceptance of such conveyances and transfers to the county and to the city and county public library and agrees, in consideration therefor, that such personal property and such land and buildings if so accepted by the county or the avails thereof, if the same shall be sold, shall be used by the county solely for the purposes of the city and county public library and that an annual appropriation shall be made by the county for the maintenance of library service within the city which service shall be at least equal to that then provided; and upon the further condition that the city and county public library undertakes to accept and administer the gifts and trust funds held by the city library and so conveyed to it for the purposes intended by the testator, donor or grantor of such gifts or trust funds and to discharge the debts, obligations and liabilities of the city library.

L.1953, c. 768, § 9.

§ 6220. Dissolution of city library; succession to gifts, devises or bequests

Upon the making and acceptance of such conveyance and transfer as aforesaid, and the certification of that fact to the board of regents of the state of New York, any city library shall be considered as dissolved. Any devise, bequest, gift or grant contained in any will or other instrument, in trust or otherwise, made before or after the dissolution or intended for the benefit of any city library shall inure to or for the benefit of the city and county public library, and so far as is necessary for that purpose the city and county public library shall be deemed to be the successor to any city library; provided, however, that all such devises, bequests, gifts or grants shall be devoted by the city and county public library to the purposes intended by the testator, donor or grantor.

L.1953, c. 768, § 10.

§ 6221. Conveyance, lease or transfer by city of branch library property to city and county library

Whenever the board of supervisors or other governing body of any county shall have established a city and county public library as provided herein, any city may, subject to the acceptance thereof by said board of supervisors or other governing body, without other authorization and notwithstanding any provisions of the charter of the city or other general or special law and for such consideration as may be agreed upon or without consideration convey or lease or transfer to a city and county public library or the county the whole or any part of the lands of the city used for branch library purposes, together with the buildings thereon and the furniture, fixtures and appurtenances thereof.

L.1953, c. 768, § 11.

§ 6222. Conveyance and transfer to city of devises and bequests to a library established under a will; acceptance and disposition by city

Notwithstanding the provisions of any general or special law, whenever the board of supervisors or other governing body of a county shall have established any city and county public library as provided herein,

(a) The trustees of any library established under a will are authorized to convey and transfer to the city all their right, title and interest in and to the money, securities, trust funds, real estate, books, papers, documents, music, works of art, phonograph records and real and personal property of every name, nature and description now used by or forming a part of such library. Upon making the conveyance and transfer as aforesaid such trustees shall be relieved of any and all further responsibility, liability or accountability in connection with their duties as trustees of such library.

(b) Any city is authorized and empowered by a resolution or resolutions to be adopted pursuant to the city charter to accept the aforesaid conveyance, transfer and assignment; to designate the city and county public library as trustee to administer the bequest made in any will creating a library and in furtherance thereof, (1) to transfer to the city and county public library charge and possession of all moneys, securities and trust funds transferred to the city by the trustees of any such library created under a will subject to the restrictions on the use thereof placed thereon by the will creating such library or by any other donor thereof; (2) to transfer to the county, but solely for the use of the city and county public library, all books, papers, documents, music, works of art, phonograph records and personal property of every name, nature and description received by said city from the trustees of any such library created by a will and (3) without other authorization and notwithstanding any provision of any city charter, and for such consideration as may be agreed upon, or without consideration, to convey and transfer to the county all its right, title and interest in and to the land and buildings occupied by such library created by a will, subject, however, to the acceptance of such transfer and conveyance by the board of supervisors or other governing body of the county; such land and buildings, if so accepted by the county, or the avails thereof, if the same shall be sold, shall be used by the county solely for the purposes of such city and county public library.

L.1953, c. 768, § 12.

§ 6223. Unexpended county appropriations

The unexpended balance of any appropriations made by any county to a county public library, any city library or any library created by a will for the year in which the consolidation provided by this act shall take place shall, upon such consolidation be deemed to have been made to the city and county public library and shall, subject to the provisions of sections four and five of this act, be available for the purposes of such city and county public library notwithstanding any contracts then in force between such county and any such city library.

L.1953, c. 768, § 13.

§ 6224. Director of library; appointment; term of office; duties

The board of trustees of any city and county public library is specifically authorized to appoint a director who shall be the chief librarian of such library and such deputy directors as may be determined by said board of trustees. Such deputy directors shall be authorized generally to act for and in the place of the director during his absence or inability to act, and shall have such other duties as may be defined by such board of trustees. The term of office of the director and of each deputy director shall be for a period of three years. The director shall be the administrative and executive officer of the library, and, subject to the supervision and control of the board of trustees of the library, shall perform the functions necessary to properly and efficiently conduct, manage and operate the said library in order to carry out the provisions of this act. The director shall be a citizen of the United States and he shall not be a member of the board.

The director, before entering upon the discharge of any of his official duties, shall take and file an official oath in the manner prescribed in section ten of the public officers law and shall also furnish an official undertaking in an amount, in such form and with such sureties, as shall be approved by the board of supervisors or other governing body of any county.

L.1953, c. 768, § 14.

§ **6225.** Employees; civil service status; transfer and removal

1. Findings and policy. Competitive examinations for appointments or employment in the operation of such libraries whose employees may not be under civil service laws, when and if consolidated into any city and county public library would be impractical in that such requirement of competitive tests would irreparably disorganize library service, interrupt continuous operation of such libraries, and place an undue financial burden on the county.

2. Notwithstanding any provision to the contrary contained in any general, special or local law, where employees affected, are not under civil service laws, when and if any city library and any library created by a will are consolidated into any city and county public library as provided herein, the latter shall continue to employ all employees of such libraries who shall then have been in the employ of such libraries or either of them for one year or more immediately prior to such consolidation and who shall be citizens or shall have filed declarations of intention to become citizens heretofore or within six months after such consolidation takes effect. The positions so held by such employees shall be in the non-competitive class of the civil service, and such employees shall continue to be employed in similar or corresponding positions and shall have the seniority theretofore held by them as among themselves. The personnel officer or similar authority of any county, however, after notice to any such employee of the reasons therefor, and after according such employee a hearing, must exclude him from further employment if he finds that he has failed to prosecute his application for citizenship in good faith and with due diligence. Not later than one year after such consolidation, the personnel or other similar officer of any county shall determine for what positions or class of positions competitive examinations have become feasible and shall thereupon reclassify the various positions with the approval of the state civil service commission. The then incumbents of such positions shall continue to hold their positions without further examination; provided, however, that all new positions

created after such consolidation and all vacancies occurring in positions already established shall be filled in accordance with the civil service law and rules. During the period between the date of such consolidation and the date of classification, no person employed pursuant to the provisions of this section shall be removed except as provided in subdivision two of section twenty-two of the civil service law [1] and in the case of veterans or exempt volunteer firemen, except as provided in subdivisions one and two of section twenty-two of the civil service law. The said board of trustees may, however, dispense with any unnecessary positions. It may transfer any employee from one position to another or change the title or designation of employment in accordance with civil service rules, with the approval of the personnel or similar officer of any county. The names of employees whose positions are so dispensed with shall be placed on a civil service preferred eligible list in the manner and subject to the provisions of section thirty-one of the civil service law, provided that their former positions or comparable positions are ultimately determined to be in the competitive class.

3. Upon such consolidation as aforesaid the permanent employees of any library who has civil service status shall be transferred to the city and county public library and shall retain their present civil service classification and status and shall be transferred without further examination or qualification. The board of trustees of any city and county public library may abolish unnecessary offices or positions. It may transfer employees from one position to another or change the title or designation of employment, in accordance with the civil service rules with the approval of the personnel officer or similar authority of any county.

L.1953, c. 768, § 15.

§ 6226. Purchases of supplies and services

All purchases made from appropriations by the board of supervisors or other governing body of any county, of supplies and services rendered by contract for said library, shall be made under the procedure provided by law for the making of purchases by the said county.

L.1953, c. 768, § 16.

§ 6227. Separability

If any part of this act or the application thereof to any person for any reason be adjudged by a court of competent jurisdiction to be unconstitutional or invalid, such judgment shall not

affect, impair or invalidate the remainder of this act, and the
application thereof to other persons or circumstances, but shall
be confined in its operation to the section or part of the act and
the persons and circumstances directly involved in the controversy in which such judgment shall have been rendered. It is
hereby declared the intent of the legislature that this act would
have been adopted had such invalid provision or application not
been included.

L.1953, c. 768, § 17.

TRUSTS FOR LIBRARIES

(Consolidated Laws of New York Annotated, 1982, General
Municipal Law, s.140-146.)

§ 140. Trusts for public parks, playgrounds, libraries and public buildings

It shall be lawful to grant and devise real estate, and to give and be-
queath personal property to trustees and their successors in trust, for the
purpose of creating, continuing and maintaining, according to the terms,
conditions and provisions of such grant, gift, devise or bequest, one or
more public parks, or public playgrounds, or a public library, or a public
building, or for the purpose of aiding and instructing children, or for
any one or more of such purposes, in any city, village or town of this
state. The number of such trustees shall not be less than three nor more
than nine. As amended L.1962, c. 850, eff. April 24, 1962.

§ 141. Trustees a corporation

Whenever any grant, gift, devise or bequest shall have been
made, under the provisions of this article, such trustees shall
thereupon become and be a body politic and corporate with the
name which shall have been specified by the donor in making
the donation, and with the number of trustees, within the foregoing limits, named by the donor; and such corporation shall
have full power to take and hold all property which shall have
been and also which shall thereafter be granted, given, devised
or bequeathed to it as aforesaid for said uses and purposes, and
shall possess the powers and be subject to the provisions and restrictions contained in general corporation law. If no name
shall have been specified by the donor as aforesaid, the name of
the corporation shall be such as the said trustees shall adopt,
certify and file in the county clerk's office of the county in which
the interested city, village or town is located. As amended
L.1910, c. 163, eff. April 25, 1910.

§ 142. Eligibility of trustees

In case of the death of a trustee or of his resignation, removal
from office, or inability to discharge the duties of his office, his

place shall be deemed to be vacant, and may be filled by the remaining trustees; and, in default of their so making an appointment within three months, the appointment to fill the vacancy shall be made by the supreme court, on the petition of any inhabitant of the interested city, village or town, and after due notice to the other trustees and to the mayor of the city, president of the village or supervisor of the town. Said trustees shall be subject to removal by said court for malfeasance or misfeasance in office, upon such notice and after trial in such manner as said court shall direct. As amended L.1910, c. 163, eff. April 25, 1910.

§ 143. Management and appropriation of property

Trustees created under the provisions of this article shall have the custody and management of all the property of such corporation, and shall appropriate the same, so far as the terms, provisions and conditions of the donations will permit, for the purpose of aiding and instructing children, or for providing suitable grounds for such a public park or parks and properly preparing, beautifying, embellishing and keeping up and maintaining the same, or for furnishing and supplying such library with a suitable and proper edifice, rooms, furniture, books, maps, magazines and whatever may be necessary to make, keep up and maintain a good and complete library, or for one or more of such purposes, and paying the expenses of the trust. Demising lands donated to the corporation and investing and keeping money invested at interest, and using the rents and interest therefrom for aiding and instructing children or for park purposes or library purposes, shall be deemed to be an appropriation of such property for said purposes. As amended L.1910, c. 163, eff. April 25, 1910.

§ 144. Parks, playgrounds and libraries to be free

All parks, playgrounds and libraries existing under this article shall be free and open to the public for use and enjoyment, subject only to such reasonable rules and regulations as the trustees from time to time shall adopt and promulgate. As amended L.1928, c. 435, § 2, eff. March 19, 1928.

§ 145. Subject to visitation of supreme court

All corporations existing under this article, together with their books and vouchers, shall be subject to the visitation and inspection of the justices of the supreme court, or of any person or persons who shall be appointed by the supreme court for that purpose; and it shall be the duty of the trustees or a majority of them, in the month of December in each year, to make and file in the office of the county clerk of the county in which the interested city, village or town is situate, a certificate under their hands. stating the names of the trustees and officers of such corporation, with an inventory of the property, effects and liabilities thereof, with an affidavit of the truth of such inventory and certificate. Said trustees shall be entitled to such compensation as said court shall fix. Said court shall also have power to control the discretion of said trustees in determining what property may be demised and for how long; also how much money may be invested and kept invested on interest to produce an income for the purpose of aiding and instructing children or to keep up and maintain the parks or libraries, or either of such purposes; and also in a summary way to determine the reasonableness of any rules and regulations, upon complaint of any inhabitant of the interested city, village or town, and upon notice to said trustees. As amended L.1910, c. 163, eff. April 25, 1910.

§ 146. Devises and bequests restricted

This article shall not be construed or held to authorize any devise or bequest whatever of more than one-half of the estate of the testator or testatrix over and above the payment of debts, liabilities and expenses, in case he or she shall leave a husband, wife, child, descendant, or parent him or her surviving. The validity of a devise or bequest for more than such one-half may be contested only by a surviving husband, wife, child, descendant or parent. As amended L.1933, c. 650, § 2; L.1947, c. 355, eff. March 25, 1947.

SCHOOL LIBRARIES

(Consolidated Laws of New York Annotated, 1982, Education Law, s.274-280, 414, State Constitution, Art. 11 s.3.)

§ 274. Use and care of school library

The school library shall be a part of the school equipment and shall be kept in the school building at all times. Such library shall be devoted to the exclusive use of the school, except as otherwise provided by the rules of the commissioner of education and except in a district where there is no free library, in which case such school library shall be a circulating library for the use of the residents of the district.

The commissioner of education shall prescribe rules regulating

1. The purchase, recording, safekeeping and loaning of books in school libraries, and the use of such books by pupils and teachers in the public schools.

2. The conditions under which books in a school library may be used by the public in a district in which a free library is situated.

3.   The management of school libraries and their use as circulating libraries by the residents of the district in which they are situated.

4.   The contents and submission of reports of school librarians, teachers and other school authorities as to school libraries.

L.1947, c. 820, eff. July 1, 1947.

§ 275.   Librarians of school libraries

In a school district maintaining an academic department or high school the board of education may employ, and fix the compensation of, a person to act as school librarian who may be engaged for all or a part of the time in performance of the duties of the position as may be directed by the said board. The person so employed, who may be the librarian of the free library, shall be possessed of the qualifications prescribed by the commissioner of education. In all other districts the trustees or board of education may appoint a competent person to act as librarian. In case of a failure of a city or union free school district maintaining an academic department or high school to employ a librarian as above provided, the teacher of English in such school shall be the librarian. In case of a failure to appoint a librarian in any other district, the teacher, or if there be more than one teacher the principal teacher, shall act as librarian. The trustees or board of education shall report to the commissioner of education the name and address of the person employed or appointed as librarian.

L.1947, c. 820, eff. July 1, 1947.

§ 276.   Existing rules continued in force

All existing provisions of law and rules established by the commissioner of education for the management of public school libraries shall hold good as to the management of such school libraries until altered by or in pursuance of law.

L.1947, c. 820, eff. July 1, 1947.

§ 277.   Authority to raise and receive money for school library

Each city and school district in the state is hereby authorized to raise moneys by tax in the same manner as other school moneys are raised, or to receive moneys by gift or devise, for starting, extending or caring for the school library.

L.1947, c. 820, eff. July 1, 1947.

§ 278.   Authority to transfer school library property to a free library

The board of education in any city or union free school district or the electors of any other district, by legal vote duly approved by the regents, may give to any free library any of the books or other public school library property not required in such school library, provided such free library is registered by the regents and situated in such city or district; and the school authorities or body making the transfer shall thereafter be relieved of all responsibility pertaining to the property so transferred.

L.1947, c. 820, eff. July 1, 1947.

§ 279. Fees

A fee of five dollars shall be paid for each public librarian's certificate or school librarian's certificate issued under part two of this article.

L.1947, c. 820; amended L.1959, c. 458, § 1, eff. April 16, 1959.

§ 280. Penalty for disobedience to library law, rules or orders

The commissioner of education is hereby authorized to withhold its share of public school moneys from any city or district which uses school library moneys for any other purpose than that for which they are provided, or for any wilful neglect or disobedience of the law or the rules or orders of said commissioner in the premises.

L.1947, c. 820, eff. July 1, 1947.

§ 414. Use of schoolhouse and grounds out of school hours

* * * * The trustees or board of education of each district may, subject to regulations adopted as above provided, permit the use of the schoolhouse and rooms therein, and the grounds and other property of the district, when not in use for school purposes, except as provided in subdivision seven hereof; for any of the following purposes:

* * *

2. For public library purposes, subject to the provisions of this chapter, or as stations of public libraries.

L.1962. c. 127, eff. March 13. 1962.

§ 3. [Common school, literature and the United States deposit funds.]

The capital of the common school fund, the capital of the literature fund, and the capital of the United States deposit fund shall be respectively preserved inviolate and the revenue of the said funds shall be applied to the support of common schools and libraries. Formerly § 3 of Art. 9, renumbered and amended by Constitutional Convention of 1938: approved by the people Nov. 8, 1938.

MISCELLANEOUS PROVISIONS

(Consolidated Laws of New York Annotated, 1982, Public
Officers Law, s.3, Correction Law, s.20, Retirement
and Social Security Law, s.32, Education Law, s.249a.)

§ 3. Qualifications for holding office

* * *

6. The provisions of this section requiring a person to be a resident of the political subdivision or municipal corporation of the state for which he shall be chosen or within which his official functions are required to be exercised, shall not apply to the appointment of trustees of a public village library, who reside outside the village in which such library is located.

L.1982, c. 70, § 2.

§ 20. Library

A library shall be provided in the department of correction containing the leading books on parole, probation and other correctional activities, together with reports and other documents on correlated topics of criminology and social work.

§ 32. Participation by certain New York city libraries

a. The boards of trustees of The New York Public Library, Astor, Lenox and Tilden Foundations, The Brooklyn Public Library and The Queens Borough Public Library, which organizations employ persons engaged in service to the public, by resolution legally adopted and approved by the comptroller, may elect to have their employees become eligible to participate in the retirement system. When such election is made by the board of trustees of any such library in pursuance of an agreement or plan concluded between it and the city of New York, for such of its employees whose salaries and compensation are paid from appropriations to such library by the city of New York in its budget, then such board of trustees shall also elect by separate resolution to have such of its employees, whose salaries and compensation for services are paid out of its own corporate funds, become eligible to participate in the retirement system.

b. Acceptance of the employees of such an employer for membership in the retirement system shall be optional with the comptroller. If he shall approve their participation, then such organization shall be treated as if it were a municipality that has approved the participation of its employees in the retirement system as provided in section thirty of this article. The comptroller shall determine the amounts of contribution payable by such libraries and their employees, and, in all other respects in so far as this article covering such a municipality is applicable, shall similarly treat all such employees.

c. When, as a condition of a contract or plan concluded with any one of such libraries, a number of whose employees are being paid from salaries and compensation for services out of appropriations as aforesaid, the city of New York obligates itself in any manner to pay or cause to be paid deficiency and normal contributions on account of such employees to the extent of, and not in excess of, a certain specified rate based on a fixed percentage of the payroll appropriated, then the comptroller shall have power to accept the participation of all the employees of such organization on the same terms and subject to the same limitations as provided for under both aforesaid resolutions. Such employees shall in all other respects participate in the retirement system as provided in section thirty-one of this article.

d.   Should there be a default in paying or causing to be paid pursuant to any contract or agreement with such employer the deficiency and normal contributions on account of the employees of any such library, whose salaries and compensation for services are paid out of funds appropriated by such city, or, if the amount of such contributions required to be paid by such city, pursuant to any contract or agreement made prior to the first participation of such employees, a copy of which shall have been filed with the comptroller, is, in the judgment of the comptroller, insufficient and inadequate to continue the membership of the employees of such employer in the retirement system because of the limit set in such contract, then such employer shall immediately be relieved and exonerated from any duty or obligation to any person whatsoever from making any contribution on account of any or all its employees. A certificate to such effect shall be sent to the employer and to the state superintendent of insurance. All members of the retirement system, who were employees of such employer at the time such certificate is issued, shall thereupon be entitled to discontinue membership as provided in section thirty-one of this article. Any such employer, however, within thirty days of the receipt of such certificate may notify the comptroller that it elects to continue the benefits of the retirement system for such of its employees whose salaries and compensation for services are paid out of its own corporate funds.

e.   Notwithstanding anything to the contrary, the retirement system shall not be liable for the payment of any pensions or other benefits on account of the officers and employees or pensioners of any employer under this section, for which reserves have not been previously created from funds contributed by such employer or its officers and employees for such benefits.

§ 249-a. Libraries of public institutions of higher education; access and use

The state university trustees and the board of higher education of

the city of New York are hereby authorized to establish such rules and regulations as may be necessary and appropriate to make provision for access and use by the residents of the state of the libraries and library facilities of the public institutions of higher education under their respective jurisdictions.
Added L.1974, c. 1048, § 1.

LAW LIBRARIES

(Consolidated Laws of New York Annotated, 1982, Judiciary Law, s.810-849.)

TAX EXEMPTION

(Consolidated Laws of New York Annotated, 1982, Real Property Tax Law, s.438.)

New York library laws are reprinted from CONSOLIDATED LAWS OF NEW YORK ANNOTATED published by Edward Thompson Co., Brooklyn, New York.

NORTH CAROLINA

STATE LIBRARY

(General Statutes of North Carolina, 1982, s.125-1, 125-2, 125-5 to
125-11.)

§ 125-1. State library agency.

The library agency of the State of North Carolina shall be the Department
of Cultural Resources. (1955, c. 505, s. 3; 1973, c. 476, s. 84.)

§ 125-2. Powers and duties of Department of Cultural Resources.

The Department of Cultural Resources shall have the following powers and
duties:

(1) To adopt a seal for use in official business.

(2) To make to the Governor a biennial report of its activities and needs,
including recommendations for improving its services to the State, to
be transmitted by the Governor to the General Assembly.

(3) To accept gifts, bequests and endowments for the purposes which fall
within the general legal powers and duties of the Department of
Cultural Resources. Unless otherwise specified by the donor or
legator, the Department of Cultural Resources may either expend
both the principal and interest of any gift or bequest or may invest
such sums in whole or in part, by and with the consent of the State
Treasurer, in securities in which sinking funds may be invested under
the provisions of G.S. 142-34.

(4) To purchase and maintain a general collection of books, periodicals,
newspapers, maps, films and audiovisual materials, and other materials for the use of the people of the State as a means for the general

1400

promotion of knowledge within the State. The scope of the Library's collections shall be determined by the Secretary of Cultural Resources upon consideration of the recommendation of the State Library Committee; and in making these decisions, the Secretary shall take into account the book collections of public libraries and college and university libraries throughout the State and the availability of such collections to the general public. All materials owned by the State Library shall be available for free circulation to public libraries and to all citizens of the State under rules and regulations fixed by the Librarian, except that the Librarian may restrict the circulation of books and other materials which, because they are rare or are used intensively in the Library for reference purposes or for other good reasons, should be retained in the Library at all times.

(5) To give assistance, advice and counsel to other State agencies maintaining special reference collections as to the best means of establishing and administering such libraries and collections, and to establish in the State Library a union catalogue of all books, pamphlets and other materials owned and used for reference purposes by all other State agencies in Raleigh and of all books, pamphlets and other materials maintained by public libraries in the State which are of interest to the people of the whole State. Where practical, the State Library may maintain a union catalogue of a part or all of the book collections in the Supreme Court Library, the North Carolina State College Library, and other libraries in the State for the use and convenience of patrons of the State Library.

(6) To fix reasonable penalties for damage to or failure to return any book, periodical or other material owned by the Department of Cultural Resources, or for violation of any rule or regulation concerning the use of books, periodicals, and other materials in the custody of the Department of Cultural Resources.

(7) To maintain at least two sets of the laws and journals of the General Assembly for the use of members of the General Assembly while in session. Before each session of the General Assembly the Librarian shall have these and other requested materials moved into the Senate and House chambers for the use of members of the General Assembly.

(8) To give assistance, advice and counsel to all libraries in the State, to all communities which may propose to establish libraries, and to all persons interested in public libraries, as to the best means of establishing and administering such libraries, as to the selection of books, cataloguing, maintenance and other details of library management.

(9) To enter into contracts with library agencies of other states for providing library service for the blind in this State and other states, provided adequate compensation is paid for such service and such contract is otherwise deemed advantageous to this State.

(10) To plan and coordinate cooperative programs between the various types of libraries within the State of North Carolina, and to coordinate State development with regional and national cooperative library programs. (1955, c. 505, s. 3; 1961, c. 1161; 1973, c. 476, s. 84; 1977, c. 645, s. 1.)

§ 125-5. Public libraries to report to Department of Cultural Resources.

Every public library in the State shall make an annual report to the Department of Cultural Resources in such form as may be prescribed by the Department. The term "public library" shall, for the purpose of this section, include subscription libraries, college and university libraries, legal association, medical association, Supreme Court, and other special libraries. (1955, c. 505, s. 3; 1973, c. 476, s. 84.)

§ 125-6. Librarian's seal.

It shall be the duty of the Secretary of State to furnish the State Librarian with a seal of office. The State Librarian is authorized to certify to the authenticity and genuineness of any document, paper, or extract from any document, paper, or book or other writing which may be on file in the Library. When a certificate is made under his hand and attested by his official seal, it shall be received as prima facie evidence of the correctness of the matter therein contained, and as such shall receive full faith and credit. (1955, c. 505, s. 3.)

§ 125-7. State policy as to public library service; annual appropriation therefor; administration of funds.

(a) It is hereby declared the policy of the State to promote the establishment and development of public library service throughout all sections of the State.

(b) For promoting, aiding, and equalizing public library service in North Carolina a sum shall annually be appropriated out of the moneys within the State treasury to be known as the Aid to Public Libraries Fund.

(c) The fund herein provided shall be administered by the Department of Cultural Resources, which shall frame bylaws, rules and regulations for the allocation and administration of such funds. The funds shall be used to improve, stimulate, increase and equalize public library service to the people of the whole State, shall be used for no other purpose, except as herein provided, and shall be allocated among the legally established municipal, county or regional libraries in the State taking into consideration local needs, area and population to be served, local interest and such other factors as may affect the State program of public library service.

(d) For the necessary expenses of administration, allocation, and supervision, a sum not to exceed seven percent (7%) of the annual appropriation may annually be used by the Department of Cultural Resources.

(e) The fund appropriated under this section shall be separate and apart from the appropriations of the Department of Cultural Resources, which appropriation shall not be affected by this section or the appropriation hereunder.

(f) Repealed by Session Laws 1973, c. 476, s. 84. (1955, c. 505, s. 3; 1973, c. 476, s. 84; 1979, c. 578.)

§ 125-8. Department of Cultural Resources authorized to accept and administer funds from federal government and other agencies.

The Department of Cultural Resources is hereby authorized and empowered to receive, accept and administer any money or moneys appropriated or granted to it, separate and apart from the appropriation by the State for the Department of Cultural Resources, for providing and equalizing public library service in North Carolina:

(1) By the federal government and,

(2) By any other agencies, private and/or otherwise.

The fund herein provided for shall be administered by the Department of Cultural Resources, which Department shall frame bylaws, rules and regulations for the allocation and administration of this fund. This fund shall be used to increase, improve, stimulate and equalize library service to people of the whole State, and shall be used for no other purpose whatsoever except as hereinafter provided, and shall be allocated among the counties of the State, taking into consideration local needs, area and population to be served, local interests as evidenced by local appropriations, and such other factors as may affect the State program of library service. Any gift or grant from the federal government or other sources shall become a part of said funds, to be used as part of the State fund, or may be invested as the Department of Cultural Resources may deem advisable, according to provisions of G.S. 125-5(5), the income to be used for the promotion of libraries as stated in this section. (1955, c. 505, s. 3; 1973, c. 476, s. 84.)

§ 125-9. Librarian certification.

The Secretary of Cultural Resources shall issue librarian certificates to public librarians under such reasonable rules and regulations as the Public Librarian Certification Commission may adopt. A complete record of the transaction of the Department in the issuance of librarian certificates shall be kept at all times in the office of the North Carolina State Library. (1955, c. 505, s. 3; 1973, c. 476, s. 53.)

§ 125-10. Temporary certificates for public librarians.

Upon the submission of satisfactory evidence that no qualified librarian is available for appointment as chief librarian, and upon written application by the Department of Cultural Resources for issuance of a temporary certificate to an unqualified person who is available for the position, a temporary certificate, valid for one year only, may be issued to such persons by the Public Librarian Certification Commission. (1955, c. 505, s. 3; 1973, c. 476, ss. 53, 84.)

§ 125-11. Failure to return books.

Any person who shall fail to return any book, periodical, or other material withdrawn by him from the Library shall be guilty of a misdemeanor punishable by a fine of not more than fifty dollars ($50.00) or imprisonment for not more than 30 days if he shall fail to return the borrowed material within 30 days after receiving a notice from the State Librarian that the material is overdue. The provisions of this section shall not be in effect unless a copy of this section is attached to the overdue notice by the State Librarian. (1955, c. 505, s. 3.)

STATE LIBRARY COMMITTEE
(General Statutes of North Carolina, 1982, s. 143B-90, 143B-91.)

§ 143B-90. State Library Committee — creation, powers and duties. — There is hereby created the State Library Committee of the Department of Cultural Resources. The State Library Committee shall have the following functions and duties:

(1) To advise the Secretary of the Department on matters relating to the operation and services of the State Library;

(2) To suggest programs to the Secretary of the Department to aid in the development of libraries statewide; and

(3) To advise the Secretary of Cultural Resources upon any matter the Secretary might refer to it. (1973, c. 476, s. 82.)

§ 143B-91. State Library Committee — members; selection; quorum; compensation. — The State Library Committee shall consist of seven members and shall be composed as follows: six members appointed by the Governor, and the duly elected and installed President of the North Carolina Library Association.

The initial members of the Committee shall be the current President of the North Carolina Library Association and the appointed members of the Library board of trustees who shall serve for a period equal to the remainder of their current terms on the Library board of trustees, two of whose appointments expire July 1, 1973; two of whose appointments expire July 1, 1975; and two of whose appointments expire July 1, 1977. At the end of the respective terms of office of the initial members, the appointments of all appointed members shall be for terms of six years and until their successors are appointed and qualify except in the case of the President of the North Carolina Library Association who shall be replaced biennially by his successor in office. Any appointment to fill a vacancy on the Committee created by the resignation, dismissal, death, or disability of a member shall be for the balance of the unexpired term.

The Governor shall have the power to remove any member of the Committee from office in accordance with the provisions of G.S. 143B-16 of the Executive Organization Act of 1973.

The Governor shall designate a member of the Committee to serve as chairman at his pleasure.

Members of the Committee shall receive per diem and necessary travel and subsistence expenses in accordance with the provisions of G.S. 138-5.

A majority of the Committee shall constitute a quorum for the transaction of business.

All clerical and other services required by the Committee shall be supplied by the Secretary of Cultural Resources. (1973, c. 476, s. 83.)

INTERSTATE LIBRARY COMPACT
(General Statutes of North Carolina, 1982, s.125-12 to 125-17.)

§ 125-12. Compact enacted into law; form.

The Interstate Library Compact is hereby enacted into law and entered into by this State with all states legally joining therein in the form substantially as follows:

INTERSTATE LIBRARY COMPACT.

ARTICLE 1. POLICY AND PURPOSE.

Because the desire for the services provided by libraries transcends governmental boundaries and can most effectively be satisfied by giving such services to communities and people regardless of jurisdictional lines, it is the policy of the states party to this Compact to cooperate and share their responsibilities; to authorize cooperation and sharing with respect to those types of library facilities and services which can be more economically or efficiently developed and maintained on a cooperative basis, and to authorize cooperation and sharing among localities, states and others in providing joint or cooperative library services in areas where the distribution of population or of existing and potential library resources make the provision of library service on an interstate basis the most effective way of providing adequate and efficient service.

ARTICLE II. DEFINITIONS.

As used in this Compact: (a) "Public library agency" means any unit or agency of local or state government operating or having power to operate a library.

(b) "Private library agency" means any nongovernmental entity which operates or assumes a legal obligation to operate a library.

(c) "Library agreement" means a contract establishing an interstate library district pursuant to this Compact or providing for the joint or cooperative furnishing of library services.

ARTICLE III. INTERSTATE LIBRARY DISTRICTS.

(a) Any one or more public library agencies in a party state in cooperation with any public library agency or agencies in one or more other party states may establish and maintain an interstate library district. Subject to the provisions of this Compact and any other laws of the party states which pursuant hereto remain applicable, such district may establish, maintain and operate some or all of the library facilities and services for the area concerned in accordance with the terms of a library agreement therefor. Any private library agency or agencies within an interstate library district may cooperate therewith, assume duties, responsibilities and obligations thereto, and receive benefits therefrom as provided in any library agreement to which such agency or agencies become party.

(b) Within an interstate library district, and as provided by a library agreement, the performance of library functions may be undertaken on a joint or cooperative basis or may be undertaken by means of one or more arrangements between or among public or private library agencies for the extension of library privileges to the use of facilities or services operated or rendered by one or more of the individual library agencies.

(c) If a library agreement provides for joint establishment, maintenance or operation of library facilities or services by an interstate library district, such district shall have power to do any one or more of the following in accordance with such library agreement:

    (1) Undertake, administer and participate in programs or arrangements for securing, lending or servicing of books and other publications, any other materials suitable to be kept or made available by libraries,

library equipment or for the dissemination of information about libraries, the value and significance of particular items therein, and the use thereof.

(2) Accept for any of its purposes under this Compact any and all donations, and grants of money, equipment, supplies, materials, and services, (conditional or otherwise), from any state or the United States or any subdivision or agency thereof, or interstate agency, or from any institution, person, firm or corporation, and receive, utilize and dispose of the same.

(3) Operate mobile library units or equipment for the purpose of rendering bookmobile service within the district.

(4) Employ professional, technical, clerical and other personnel, and fix terms of employment, compensation and other appropriate benefits; and where desirable, provide for the in-service training of such personnel.

(5) Sue and be sued in any court of competent jurisdiction.

(6) Acquire, hold, and dispose of any real or personal property or any interest or interests therein as may be appropriate to the rendering of library service.

(7) Construct, maintain and operate a library, including any appropriate branches thereof.

(8) Do such other things as may be incidental to or appropriate for the carrying out of any of the foregoing powers.

Article IV. Interstate Library Districts, Governing Board.

(a) An interstate library district which establishes, maintains or operates any facilities or services in its own right shall have a governing board which shall direct the affairs of the district and act for it in all matters relating to its business. Each participating public library agency in the district shall be represented on the governing board which shall be organized and conduct its business in accordance with provision therefor in the library agreement. But in no event shall a governing board meet less often than twice a year.

(b) Any private library agency or agencies party to a library agreement establishing an interstate library district may be represented on or advise with the governing board of the district in such manner as the library agreement may provide.

Article V. State Library Agency Cooperation.

Any two or more state library agencies of two or more of the party states may undertake and conduct joint or cooperative library programs, render joint or cooperative library services, and enter into and perform arrangements for the cooperative or joint acquisition, use, housing and disposition of items or collections of materials which, by reason of expense, rarity, specialized nature, or infrequency of demand therefor would be appropriate for central collection and shared use. Any such programs, services or arrangements may include provision for the exercise on a cooperative or joint basis of any power exercisable by an interstate library district and an agreement embodying any such program, service or arrangement shall contain provisions covering the subjects detailed in Article VI of this Compact for interstate library agreements.

Article VI. Library Agreements.

(a) In order to provide for any joint or cooperative undertaking pursuant to this Compact, public and private library agencies may enter into library agreements. Any agreement executed pursuant to the provisions of this Compact shall, as among the parties to the agreement:

    (1) Detail the specific nature of the services, programs, facilities, arrangements or properties to which it is applicable.

    (2) Provide for the allocation of costs and other financial responsibilities.

    (3) Specify the respective rights, duties, obligations and liabilities of the parties.

    (4) Set forth the terms and conditions for duration, renewal, termination, abrogation, disposal of joint or common property, if any, and all other matters which may be appropriate to the proper effectuation and performance of the agreement.

(b) No public or private library agency shall undertake to exercise itself, or jointly with any other library agency, by means of a library agreement any power prohibited to such agency by the constitution or statutes of its state.

(c) No library agreement shall become effective until filed with the Compact Administrator of each state involved, and approved in accordance with Article VII of this Compact.

Article VII. Approval of Library Agreements.

(a) Every library agreement made pursuant to this Compact shall, prior to and as a condition precedent to its entry into force, be submitted to the attorney general of each state in which a public library agency party thereto is situated, who shall determine whether the agreement is in proper form and compatible with the laws of his state. The attorneys general shall approve any agreement submitted to them unless they shall find that it does not meet the conditions set forth herein and shall detail in writing addressed to the governing bodies of the public library agencies concerned the specific respects in which the proposed agreement fails to meet the requirements of law. Failure to disapprove an agreement submitted hereunder within 90 days of its submission shall constitute approval thereof.

(b) In the event that a library agreement made pursuant to this Compact shall deal in whole or in part with the provision of services or facilities with regard to which an officer or agency of the state government has constitutional or statutory powers of control, the agreement shall, as a condition precedent to its entry into force, be submitted to the state officer or agency having such power of control and shall be approved or disapproved by him or it as to all matters within his or its jurisdiction in the same manner and subject to the same requirements governing the action of the attorneys general pursuant to subsection (a) of this Article. This requirement of submission and approval shall be in addition to and not in substitution for the requirement of submission to and approval by the attorneys general.

Article VIII. Other Laws Applicable.

Nothing in this Compact or in any library agreement shall be construed to supersede, alter or otherwise impair any obligation imposed on any library by otherwise applicable law, nor to authorize the transfer or disposition of any property held in trust by a library agency in a manner contrary to the terms of such trust.

ARTICLE IX. APPROPRIATIONS AND AID.

(a) Any public library agency party to a library agreement may appropriate funds to the interstate library district established thereby in the same manner and to the same extent as to a library wholly maintained by it and, subject to the laws of the state in which such public library agency is situated, may pledge its credit in support of an interstate library district established by the agreement.

(b) Subject to the provisions of the library agreement pursuant to which it functions and the laws of the states in which such district is situated, an interstate library district may claim and receive any state and federal aid which may be available to library agencies.

ARTICLE X. COMPACT ADMINISTRATOR.

Each state shall designate a Compact Administrator with whom copies of all library agreements to which his state or any public library agency thereof is party shall be filed. The Administrator shall have such other powers as may be conferred upon him by the laws of his state and may consult and cooperate with the compact administrators of other party states and take such steps as may effectuate the purposes of this Compact. If the laws of a party state so provide, such state may designate one or more deputy Compact administrators in addition to its Compact Administrator.

ARTICLE XI. ENTRY INTO FORCE AND WITHDRAWAL.

(a) This Compact shall enter into force and effect immediately upon its enactment into law by any two states. Thereafter, it shall enter into force and effect as to any other state upon the enactment thereof by such state.

(b) This Compact shall continue in force with respect to a party state and remain binding upon such state until six months after such state has given notice to each other party state of the repeal thereof. Such withdrawal shall not be construed to relieve any party to a library agreement entered into pursuant to this Compact from any obligation of that agreement prior to the end of its duration as provided therein.

ARTICLE XII. CONSTRUCTION AND SEVERABILITY.

This Compact shall be liberally construed so as to effectuate the purposes thereof. The provisions of this Compact shall be severable and if any phrase, clause, sentence or provision of this Compact is declared to be contrary to the constitution of any party state or of the United States or the applicability thereof to any government, agency, person or circumstance is held invalid, the validity of the remainder of this Compact and the applicability thereof to any government, agency, person or circumstance shall not be affected thereby. If this Compact shall be held contrary to the constitution of any state party thereto, the Compact shall remain in full force and effect as to the remaining states and in full force and effect as to the state affected as to all severable matters. (1967, c. 190, s. 1.)

§ 125-13. Political subdivisions to comply with laws governing capital outlay and pledging of credit.

No county, municipality, or other political subdivision of this State shall be party to a library agreement which provides for the construction or maintenance of a library pursuant to Article III, subdivision (c)(7) of the Compact, nor pledge its credit in support of such a library, or contribute to the capital financing thereof, except after compliance with any laws applicable to such counties, municipalities, or other political subdivisions relating to or governing capital outlays and the pledging of credit. (1967, c. 190, s. 2.)

§ 125-14. "State library agency" defined.

As used in the Compact, "state library agency," with reference to this State, means the Department of Cultural Resources. (1967, c. 190, s. 3; 1973, c. 476, s. 84.)

§ 125-15. State and federal aid to interstate library districts.

An interstate library district lying partly within this State may claim and be entitled to receive State aid in support of any of its functions to the same extent and in the same manner as such functions are eligible for support when carried on by entities wholly within this State. For the purposes of computing and apportioning State aid to an interstate library district, this State will consider that portion of the area which lies within this State as an independent entity for the performance of the aided function or functions and compute and apportion the aid accordingly. Subject to any applicable laws of this State, such a district also may apply for and be entitled to receive any federal aid for which it may be eligible. (1967, c. 190, s. 4.)

§ 125-16. Compact Administrator and deputies.

The State Librarian shall be the Compact Administrator pursuant to Article X of the Compact. The State Librarian may appoint one or more deputy Compact Administrators pursuant to said Article. (1967, c. 190, s. 5.)

§ 125-17. Withdrawal from Compact.

In the event of withdrawal from the Compact the Governor shall send and receive any notices required by Article XI(b) of the Compact. (1967, c. 190, s. 6.)

SUPREME COURT LIBRARY

(General Statutes of North Carolina, 1982, s.7A-12, 7A-13.)

§ 7A-12. Supreme Court marshal.

The Supreme Court may appoint a marshal to serve at its pleasure, and to perform such duties as it may assign. The marshal shall have the criminal and civil powers of a sheriff, and any additional powers necessary to execute the orders of the appellate division in any county of the State. His salary shall be fixed by the Administrative Officer, subject to the approval of the Supreme Court. The marshal may appoint such assistants, and at such salaries, as may be authorized by the Administrative Officer of the Courts. The Supreme Court, in its discretion, may appoint the Supreme Court librarian, or some other suitable employee of the court, to serve in the additional capacity of marshal. (1967, c. 108, s. 1.)

§ 7A-13. Supreme Court library; functions; librarian; library committee; seal of office.

(a) The Supreme Court shall appoint a librarian of the Supreme Court library, to serve at the pleasure of the court. The annual salary of the librarian shall be fixed by the Administrative Officer of the Courts, subject to the approval of the Supreme Court. The librarian may appoint assistants in numbers and at salaries to be fixed by the Administrative Officer of the Courts.

(b) The primary function of the Supreme Court library is to serve the appellate division of the General Court of Justice, but it may render service to the trial divisions of the General Court of Justice, to State agencies, and to the general public, under such regulations as the librarian, subject to the approval of the library committee, may promulgate.

(c) The library shall be maintained in the city of Raleigh, except that if the Court of Appeals sits regularly in locations other than the city of Raleigh, branch libraries may be established at such locations for the use of the Court of Appeals.

(d) The librarian shall promulgate rules and regulations for the use of the library, subject to the approval of a library committee, to be composed of two justices of the Supreme Court appointed by the Chief Justice, and one judge of the Court of Appeals appointed by the Chief Judge.

(e) The librarian may adopt a seal of office.

(f) The librarian may operate a copying service by means of which he may furnish certified or uncertified copies of all or portions of any document, paper, book, or other writing in the library that legally may be copied. When a certificate is made under his hand and attested by his official seal, it shall be received as prima facie evidence of the correctness of the matter therein contained, and as such shall receive full faith and credit. The fees for copies shall be approved by the library committee, and the fees so collected shall be administered in the same manner as the charges to litigants for the reproduction of appellate records and briefs. (1967, c. 108, s. 1.)

DISTRIBUTION OF PUBLIC DOCUMENTS
(General Statutes of North Carolina, 1982, s.147-50.)

§ 147-50. Publications of State officials and department heads furnished to certain institutions, agencies, etc. — Every State official and every head of a State department, institution or agency issuing any printed report, bulletin, map, or other publication, shall, on request, furnish copies of such reports, bulletins, maps or other publications to the following institutions in the number set out below:

University of North Carolina at Chapel Hill	25 copies;
University of North Carolina at Charlotte	2 copies;
University of North Carolina at Greensboro	2 copies;
North Carolina State University at Raliegh	2 copies;
East Carolina University at Greenville	2 copies;
Duke University	25 copies;
Wake Forest College	2 copies;
Davidson College	2 copies;
North Carolina Supreme Court Library	2 copies;

North Carolina Central University .... 5 copies;
Library of Congress .... 2 copies;
Department of Cultural Resources .... 5 copies;
Western Carolina University .... 2 copies;
Appalachian State University .... 2 copies;
University of North Carolina at Wilmington .... 2 copies;
North Carolina Agricultural and Technical State University .... 2 copies;
Legislative Library .... 2 copies;
and to governmental officials, agencies and departments and to other
educational institutions, in the discretion of the issuing official and subject to
the supply available, such number as may be requested: Provided that five sets
of all such reports, bulletins and publications heretofore issued, insofar as the
same are available and without necessitating reprinting, shall be furnished to
the North Carolina Central University. The provisions in this section shall not
be interpreted to include any of the appellate division reports or advance sheets
distributed by the Administrative Office of the Courts. (1941, c. 379, s. 5; 1955,
c. 505, s. 7; 1967, cc. 1038, 1065; 1969, c. 608, s. 1; c. 852, s. 3; 1973, c. 476, s.
84; c. 598; c. 731, s. 2; c. 776; 1977, c. 377.)

DEPARTMENT OF ARCHIVES AND HISTORY
(General Statutes of North Carolina, 1982, s.121-1 to 121-5.)

§ 121-1. Short title.

This Article shall be known as the North Carolina Archives and History Act.
(1973, c. 476, s. 48.)

§ 121-2. Definitions.

For the purposes of this Article:
  (1) "Agency" shall mean any State, county, or municipal office, depart-
      ment, division, board, commission or separate unit of government
      created or established by constitution or law.
  (2) "Commission" shall mean the North Carolina Historical Commission.
  (3) "Department" shall mean the Department of Cultural Resources of the
      State of North Carolina.
  (4) "Historic preservation" shall mean any activity reasonably related to
      the identification, research, conservation, protection, and restoration,
      maintenance, or operation of buildings, structures, objects, districts,
      areas, and sites significant in the history, architecture, archaeology,
      or culture of this State, its communities, or the nation.
  (5) "Historic property" or "historic properties" shall mean any building,
      structure, object, district, area, or site that is significant in the history,
      architecture, archaeology, or culture of this State, its communities, or
      the nation.
  (6) "North Carolina Museum of History" shall mean an establishment or
      establishments administered by the Department of Cultural
      Resources as the official State museum of history for the collection,
      preservation, and exhibition of artifacts and other materials that have
      been determined by the Department or by the Commission to have
      sufficient historical or other cultural value to warrant retention as
      evidence of the history and culture of the State and its subdivisions.
  (7) "North Carolina State Archives" shall mean an establishment or

establishments administered by the Department of Cultural
Resources as the State's official repository for the preservation of those
public records or other documentary materials that have been determined by the Department in accordance with rules, regulations, and
standards of the Historical Commission to have sufficient historical or
other value to warrant their continued preservation and have been
accepted by the Department for preservation in its custody.

(8) "Public record" or "public records" shall mean all documents, papers,
letters, maps, books, photographs, films, sound recordings, magnetic
or other tapes, electronic data processing records, artifacts, or other
documentary material, regardless of physical form or characteristics,
made or received pursuant to law or ordinance or in connection with
the transaction of official business by any agency.

(9) "Records center" or "records centers" shall mean an establishment or
establishments administered by the Department of Cultural
Resources primarily for the economical housing, processing, servicing,
microfilming or security of public records that must be retained for
varying periods of time but which need not be retained in an agency's
office equipment and space.

(10) "Secretary" shall mean the Secretary of Cultural Resources.

(11) "State historic site" or "state historic sites" shall mean a property or
properties acquired by the State and administered by the Department
of Cultural Resources because of its or their historical, archaeological,
architectural, or cultural value in depicting the heritage of the State.
(1973, c. 476, s. 48.)

§ 121-3. Name.

The archival and historical agency of the State of North Carolina shall be the
Department of Cultural Resources. (1945, c. 55; 1955, c. 543, s. 1; 1973, c. 476,
s. 48.)

§ 121-4. Powers and duties of the Department of Cultural Resources.

The Department of Cultural Resources shall have the following powers and
duties:

(1) To accept gifts, bequests, devises, and endowments for purposes which
fall within the general legal powers and duties of the Department.
Unless otherwise specified by the donor or legator, the Department
may either expend both the principal and interest of any gift or
bequests or may invest such funds in whole or in part, by and with the
consent of the State Treasurer.

(2) To conduct a records management program, including the operation of
a records center or centers and a centralized microfilming program, for
the benefit of all State agencies, and to give advice and assistance to
the public officials and agencies in matters pertaining to the
economical and efficient maintenance and preservation of public
records.

(3) To preserve and administer, in the North Carolina State Archives,
such public records as may be accepted into its custody, and to collect,
preserve, and administer private and unofficial historical records and
other documentary materials relating to the history of North Carolina

and the territory included therein from the earliest times. The Department shall carefully protect and preserve such materials, file them according to approved archival practices, and permit them, at reasonable times and under the supervision of the Department, to be inspected, examined, or copied: Provided, that any materials placed in the keeping of the Department under special terms or conditions restricting their use shall be made accessible only in accordance with such terms or conditions.

(4) To have materials on the history of North Carolina properly edited, published as other State printing, and distributed under the direction of the Department. The Department may charge a reasonable price for such publications and devote the revenue arising from such sales to the work of the Department.

(5) With the cooperation of the Department of Public Education, to develop, conduct, and assist in the coordination of a program for the better and more adequate teaching of State and local history in the public schools and the institutions of the community college system of North Carolina, including, as appropriate, the preparation and publication of suitable histories of all counties and of other appropriate materials, the distribution of such materials to the public schools and community college system for a reasonable charge, and the coordination of this program throughout the State.

(6) To maintain and administer the North Carolina Museum of History, to collect and preserve therein important historical and cultural materials, and according to approved museum practices to classify, accession, house, and when feasible exhibit such materials and make them available for study.

(7) To select suitable sites on property owned by the State of North Carolina, or any subdivision of the State, for the erection of historical markers calling attention to nearby historic sites and prepare appropriate inscriptions to be placed on such markers. The Department shall have all markers manufactured, and when completed, each marker shall be delivered to the Department of Transportation for payment and erection under the provisions of G.S. 136-42.2 and 136-42.3. The Secretary is authorized to appoint a highway historical marker advisory committee to approve all proposed highway historical markers and to establish criteria for carrying out this responsibility.

(8) In accordance with G.S. 121-9 of this Chapter, to acquire real and personal properties that have statewide historical, architectural, archaeological, or other cultural significance, by gift, purchase, devise, or bequest; to preserve and administer such properties; and, when necessary, to charge reasonable admission fees to such properties. In the acquisition of such property, the Department shall also have the authority to acquire nearby or adjacent property adjacent to properties having statewide significance deemed necessary for the proper use, administration, and protection of historic, architectural, archaeological, or cultural properties, or for the protection of the environment thereof.

(9) To administer and enforce reasonable rules adopted and promulgated by the Historical Commission for the regulation of the use by the public of such historical, architectural, archaeological, or cultural properties under its charge, which regulations, after having been posted in conspicuous places on and adjacent to such State properties and having been filed according to law, shall have the force and effect

of law and any violation of such regulations shall constitute a misdemeanor and shall be punishable by a fine of not more than fifty dollars ($50.00) or by imprisonment not to exceed 30 days.

(10) To coordinate the objectives of the state-created historical and commemorative commissions with the other policies, objectives, and programs of the Department of Cultural Resources.

(11) To organize and administer a junior historian program, in cooperation with the Department of Public Education, the public schools, and other agencies or organizations that may be concerned therein.

(12) With the approval of the Historical Commission, to dispose of any accessioned records, artifacts, and furnishings in the custody of the Department that are determined to have no further use or value for official or administrative purposes or for research and reference purposes.

(13) To promote and encourage throughout the State knowledge and appreciation of North Carolina history and heritage by encouraging the people of the State to engage in the preservation and care of archives, historical manuscripts, museum items, and other historical materials; the writing and publication of State and local histories of high standard; the display and interpretation of historical materials; the marking and preservation of historic, architectural, or archaeological structures and sites of great importance; the teaching of North Carolina and local history in the schools and colleges; the appropriate observance of events of importance to the State's history; the publicizing of the State's history through media of public information; and other activities in historical and allied fields. (Rev., ss. 4540, 4541; 1907, c. 714, s. 2; 1911, c. 211, s. 6; C. S., s. 6142; 1925, c. 275, s. 11; 1943, c. 237; 1945, c. 55; 1955, c. 543, s. 1; 1957, c. 330, s. 1; 1959, c. 68, s. 1; 1971, c. 345, s. 3; 1973, c. 476, s. 48; 1977, c. 464, s. 38.)

§ 121-5. Public records and archives.

(a) State Archival Agency Designated. — The Department of Cultural Resources shall be the official archival agency of the State of North Carolina with authority as provided throughout this Chapter and Chapter 132 of the General Statutes of North Carolina in relation to the public records of the State, counties, municipalities, and other subdivisions of government.

(b) Destruction of Records Regulated. — No person may destroy, sell, loan, or otherwise dispose of any public record without the consent of the Department of Cultural Resources. Whoever unlawfully removes a public record from the office where it is usually kept, or alters, mutilates, or destroys it shall be guilty of a misdemeanor and upon conviction fined at the discretion of the court.

When the custodian of any official State records certifies to the Department of Cultural Resources that such records have no further use or value for official and administrative purposes and when the Department certifies that such records appear to have no further use or value for research or reference, then such records may be destroyed or otherwise disposed of by the agency having custody of them.

When the custodian of any official records of any county, city, municipality, or other subdivision of government certifies to the Department that such records have no further use or value for official business and when the Department certifies that such records appear to have no further use or value for research or reference, then such records may be authorized by the governing body of said county, city, municipality, or other subdivision of government to be destroyed or otherwise disposed of by the agency having custody of them. A record of such certification and authorization shall be entered in the minutes of the governing body granting the authority.

The North Carolina Historical Commission is hereby authorized and empowered to make such orders, rules, and regulations as may be necessary and proper to carry into effect the provisions of this section. When any State, county, municipal, or other governmental records shall have been destroyed or otherwise disposed of in accordance with the procedure authorized in this subsection, any liability that the custodian of such records might incur for such destruction or other disposal shall cease and determine.

(c) Assistance to Public Officers. — The Department of Cultural Resources shall have the right to examine into the condition of public records and shall, subject to the availability of staff and funds, give advice and assistance to public officials and agencies in regard to preserving or disposing of the public records in their custody. When requested by the Department of Cultural Resources, public officials shall assist the Department in the preparation of an inclusive inventory of records in their custody, to which inventory shall be attached a schedule, approved by the head of the governmental unit or agency having custody of the records and the Department of Cultural Resources, establishing a time period for the retention or disposal of each series of records. So long as such approved schedule remains in effect, destruction or disposal of records in accordance with its provisions shall be deemed to have met the requirements of G.S. 121-5 (b).

The Department of Cultural Resources is hereby authorized and directed to conduct a program of inventorying, repairing, and microfilming in the counties for security purposes those official records of the several counties which the Department determines have permanent value, and of providing safe storage for microfilm copies of such records. Subject to the availability of funds, such program shall be extended to the records of permanent value of the cities, municipalities, and other subdivisions of government.

(d) Preservation of Permanently Valuable Records. — Public records certified by the Department of Cultural Resources as being of permanent value shall be preserved in the custody of the agency in which the records are normally kept or of the North Carolina State Archives. Any State, county, municipal, or other public official is hereby authorized and empowered to turn over to the Department of Cultural Resources any State, county, municipal, or other public records no longer in current official use, and the Department of Cultural Resources is authorized in its discretion to accept such records, and having done so shall provide for their administration and preservation in the North Carolina State Archives. When such records have been thus surrendered, photocopies, microfilms, typescripts, or other copies of them shall be made and certified under seal of the Department, upon application of any person, which certification shall have the same force and effect as if made by the official or agency by which the records were transferred to the Department of Cultural Resources; and the Department may charge reasonable fees for such copies. The Department may answer written inquiries for nonresidents of North Carolina and for such service charge a search and handling fee not to exceed five dollars ($5.00), the receipts from which fee shall be used to defray the cost of providing such service. (1907, c. 714, s. 5; C. S., s. 6145; 1939, c. 249; 1943, c. 237; 1945, c. 55; 1953, c. 224; 1955, c. 543, s. 1; 1959, c. 1162; 1973, c. 476, s. 48; 1979, c. 361; c. 801, s. 95.)

PUBLIC RECORDS

(General Statutes of North Carolina, 1982, s.132-1 to 132-9.)

§ 132-1. "Public records" defined.

"Public record" or "public records" shall mean all documents, papers, letters, maps, books, photographs, films, sound recordings, magnetic or other tapes, electronic data-processing records, artifacts, or other documentary material, regardless of physical form or characteristics, made or received pursuant to law or ordinance in connection with the transaction of public business by any agency of North Carolina government or its subdivisions. Agency of North Carolina government or its subdivisions shall mean and include every public office, public officer or official (State or local, elected or appointed), institution, board, commission, bureau, council, department, authority or other unit of government of the State or of any county, unit, special district or other political subdivision of government. (1935, c. 265, s. 1; 1975, c. 787, s. 1.)

§ 132-1.1. Confidential communications by legal counsel to public board or agency; not public records.

Public records, as defined in G.S. 132-1, shall not include written communications (and copies thereof) to any public board, council, commission or other governmental body of the State or of any county, municipality or other political subdivision or unit of government, made within the scope of the attorney-client relationship by any attorney-at-law serving any such governmental body, concerning any claim against or on behalf of the governmental body or the governmental entity for which such body acts, or concerning the prosecution, defense, settlement or litigation of any judicial action, or any administrative or other type of proceeding to which the governmental body is a party or by which it is or may be directly affected. Such written communication and copies thereof shall not be open to public inspection, examination or copying unless specifically made public by the governmental body receiving such written communications; provided, however, that such written communications and copies thereof shall become public records as defined in G.S. 132-1 three years from the date such communication was received by such public board, council, commission or other governmental body. (1975, c. 662.)

§ 132-2. Custodian designated.

The public official in charge of an office having public records shall be the custodian thereof. (1935, c. 265, s. 2.)

§ 132-3. Destruction of records regulated.

No public official may destroy, sell, loan, or otherwise dispose of any public record, except in accordance with G.S. 121-5, without the consent of the Department of Cultural Resources. Whoever unlawfully removes a public record from the office where it is usually kept, or alters, defaces, mutilates or destroys it shall be guilty of a misdemeanor and upon conviction fined not less than ten dollars ($10.00) nor more than five hundred dollars ($500.00). (1935, c. 265, s. 3; 1943, c. 237; 1953, c. 675, s. 17; 1957, c. 330, s. 2; 1973, c. 476, s. 48.)

§ 132-4. Disposition of records at end of official's term.

Whoever has the custody of any public records shall, at the expiration of his term of office, deliver to his successor, or, if there be none, to the Department of Cultural Resources, all records, books, writings, letters and documents kept or received by him in the transaction of his official business; and any such person who shall refuse or neglect for the space of 10 days after request made in writing by any citizen of the State to deliver as herein required such public records to the person authorized to receive them shall be guilty of a misdemeanor and upon conviction imprisoned for a term not exceeding two years or fined not exceeding one thousand dollars ($1,000) or both. (1935, c. 265, s. 4; 1943, c. 237; 1973, c. 476, s. 48; 1975, c. 696, s. 1.)

§ 132-5. Demanding custody.

Whoever is entitled to the custody of public records shall demand them from any person having illegal possession of them, who shall forthwith deliver the same to him. If the person who unlawfully possesses public records shall without just cause refuse or neglect for 10 days after a request made in writing by any citizen of the State to deliver such records to their lawful custodian, he shall be guilty of a misdemeanor and upon conviction imprisoned for a term not exceeding two years or fined not exceeding one thousand dollars ($1,000) or both. (1935, c. 265, s. 5; 1975, c. 696, s. 2.)

§ 132-5.1. Regaining custody; civil remedies.

(a) The Secretary of the Department of Cultural Resources or his designated representative or any public official who is the custodian of public records which are in the possession of a person or agency not authorized by the custodian or by law to possess such public records may petition the superior court in the county in which the person holding such records resides or in which the materials in issue, or any part thereof, are located for the return of such public records. The court may order such public records to be delivered to the petitioner upon finding that the materials in issue are public records and that such public records are in the possession of a person not authorized by the custodian of the public records or by law to possess such public records. If the order of delivery does not receive compliance, the petitioner may request that the court enforce such order through its contempt power and procedures.

(b) At any time after the filing of the petition set out in subsection (a) or contemporaneous with such filing, the public official seeking the return of the public records may by ex parte petition request the judge or the court in which the action was filed to grant one of the following provisional remedies:

    (1) An order directed at the sheriff commanding him to seize the materials which are the subject of the action and deliver the same to the court under the circumstances hereinafter set forth; or

    (2) A preliminary injunction preventing the sale, removal, disposal or destruction of or damage to such public records pending a final judgment by the court.

(c) The judge or court aforesaid shall issue an order of seizure or grant a preliminary injunction upon receipt of an affidavit from the petitioner which alleges that the materials at issue are public records and that unless one of said provisional remedies is granted, there is a danger that such materials shall be sold, secreted, removed out of the State or otherwise disposed of so as not to be forthcoming to answer the final judgment of the court respecting the same; or that such property may be destroyed or materially damaged or injured if not seized or if injunctive relief is not granted.

(d) The aforementioned order of seizure or preliminary injunction shall issue without notice to the respondent and without the posting of any bond or other security by the petitioner. (1975, c. 787, s. 2.)

§ 132-6. Inspection and examination of records.

Every person having custody of public records shall permit them to be inspected and examined at reasonable times and under his supervision by any person, and he shall furnish certified copies thereof on payment of fees as prescribed by law. (1935, c. 265, s. 6.)

§ 132-7. Keeping records in safe places; copying or repairing; certified copies.

Insofar as possible, custodians of public records shall keep them in fireproof safes, vaults, or rooms fitted with noncombustible materials and in such arrangement as to be easily accessible for convenient use. All public records should be kept in the buildings in which they are ordinarily used. Record books should be copied or repaired, renovated or rebound if worn, mutilated, damaged or difficult to read. Whenever any State, county, or municipal records are in need of repair, restoration, or rebinding, the head of such State agency, department, board, or commission, the board of county commissioners of such county, or the governing body of such municipality may authorize that the records in need of repair, restoration, or rebinding be removed from the building or office in which such records are ordinarily kept, for the length of time required to repair, restore, or rebind them. Any public official who causes a record book to be copied shall attest it and shall certify on oath that it is an accurate copy of the original book. The copy shall then have the force of the original. (1935, c. 265, s. 7; 1951, c. 294.)

§ 132-8. Assistance by and to Department of Cultural Resources.

The Department of Cultural Resources shall have the right to examine into the condition of public records and shall give advice and assistance to public officials in the solution of their problems of preserving, filing and making available the public records in their custody. When requested by the Department of Cultural Resources, public officials shall assist the Department in the preparation of an inclusive inventory of records in their custody, to which shall be attached a schedule, approved by the head of the governmental unit or agency having custody of the records and the Secretary of Cultural Resources, establishing a time period for the retention or disposal of each series of records. Upon the completion of the inventory and schedule, the Department of Cultural Resources shall (subject to the availability of necessary space, staff, and other facilities for such purposes) make available space in its Records Center for the filing of semicurrent records so scheduled and in its archives for noncurrent records of permanent value, and shall render such other assistance as needed, including the microfilming of records so scheduled. (1935, c. 265, s. 8; 1943, c. 237; 1959, c. 68, s. 2; 1973, c. 476, s. 48.)

§ 132-8.1. Records management program administered by Department of Cultural Resources; establishment of standards, procedures, etc.; surveys.

A records management program for the application of efficient and economical management methods to the creation, utilization, maintenance, retention, preservation, and disposal of official records shall be administered by the Department of Cultural Resources. It shall be the duty of that Department, in cooperation with and with the approval of the Department of Administration, to establish standards, procedures, and techniques for effective management of public records, to make continuing surveys of paper work operations, and to recommend improvements in current records management practices including the use of space, equipment, and supplies employed in creating, maintaining, and servicing records. It shall be the duty of the head of each State agency and the governing body of each county, municipality and other subdivision of government to cooperate with the Department of Cultural Resources in conducting surveys and to establish and maintain an active, continuing program for the economical and efficient management of the records of said agency, county, municipality, or other subdivision of government. (1961, c. 1041; 1973, c. 476, s. 48.)

§ 132-8.2. Selection and preservation of records considered essential; making or designation of preservation duplicates; force and effect of duplicates or copies thereof.

In cooperation with the head of each State agency and the governing body of each county, municipality, and other subdivision of government, the Department of Cultural Resources shall establish and maintain a program for the selection and preservation of public records considered essential to the operation of government and to the protection of the rights and interests of persons, and, within the limitations of funds available for the purpose, shall make or cause to be made preservation duplicates or designate as preservation duplicates existing copies of such essential public records. Preservation duplicates shall be durable, accurate, complete and clear, and such duplicates made by a photographic, photostatic, microfilm, micro card, miniature photographic, or other process which accurately reproduces and forms a durable medium for so reproducing the original shall have the same force and effect for all purposes as the original record whether the original record is in existence or not. A transcript, exemplification, or certified copy of such preservation duplicate shall be deemed for all purposes to be a transcript, exemplification, or certified copy of the original record. Such preservation duplicates shall be preserved in the place and manner of safekeeping prescribed by the Department of Cultural Resources. (1961, c. 1041; 1973, c. 476, s. 48.)

§ 132-9. Access to records.

Any person who is denied access to public records for purposes of inspection, examination or copying may apply to the appropriate division of the General Court of Justice for an order compelling disclosure, and the court shall have jurisdiction to issue such orders. (1935, c. 265, s. 9; 1975, c. 787, s. 3.)

PUBLIC LIBRARIAN CERTIFICATION COMMISSION
(General Statutes of North Carolina, 1982, s.143B-67 to 143B-70.)

§ **143B-67. Public Librarian Certification Commission — creation, powers and duties.** — There is hereby created the Public Librarian Certification Commission of the Department of Cultural Resources with the power and duty to adopt rules and regulations to be followed in the certification of public librarians.

The Commission shall adopt such rules and regulations consistent with the provisions of this Chapter. All rules and regulations consistent with the provisions of this Chapter heretofore adopted by the Library Certification Board shall remain in full force and effect unless and until repealed or superseded by action of the Public Librarian Certification Commission. All rules and regulations adopted by the Commission shall be enforced by the Department of Cultural Resources. (1973, c. 476, s. 49.)

§ **143B-68. Public Librarian Certification Commission — members; selection; quorum; compensation.** — The Public Librarian Certification Commission of the Department of Cultural Resources shall consist of five members as follows: (i) the chairman of the North Carolina Association of Library Trustees, (ii) the chairman of the public libraries section of the North Carolina Library Association, (iii) an individual named by the Governor upon the nomination of the North Carolina Library Association, (iv) the dean of a State or regionally accredited graduate school of librarianship in North Carolina appointed by the Governor and (v) one member at large appointed by the Governor.

The members shall serve four-year terms or while holding the appropriate chairmanships. Any appointment to fill a vacancy created by the resignation, dismissal, death or disability of a member shall be for the balance of the unexpired term.

The Governor shall have the power to remove any member of the Commission from office for misfeasance, malfeasance, and nonfeasance according to the provisions of G.S. 143B-13 of the Executive Organization Act of 1973.

The members of the Commission shall receive per diem, and necessary travel expenses in accordance with the provisions of G.S. 138-5.

A majority of the Commission shall constitute a quorum for the transaction of business.

All clerical and other services required by the Commission shall be supplied by the Secretary of the Department through the regular staff of the Department. (1973, c. 476, s. 50.)

§ **143B-69. Public Librarian Certification Commission — officers.** — The Public Librarian Certification Commission shall have a chairman and a vice-chairman. The chairman shall be designated by the Governor from among the members of the Commission to serve as chairman at his pleasure. The vice-chairman shall be elected by and from the members of the Commission and shall serve for a term of two years or until the expiration of his regularly appointed term. (1973, c. 476, s. 51.)

§ **143B-70. Public Librarian Certification Commission — regular and special meetings.** — The Public Librarian Certification Commission shall meet at least once in each quarter and may hold special meetings at any time and place within the State at the call of the chairman or upon the written request of at least three members. (1973, c. 476, s. 52.)

PUBLIC LIBRARIES

(General Statutes of North Carolina, 1982, s.153A-261 to 153A-271.)

§ 153A-261. Declaration of State policy. — The General Assembly recognizes that the availability of adequate, modern library services and facilities is in the general interest of the people of North Carolina and a proper concern of the State and of local governments. Therefore it is the policy of the State of North Carolina to promote the establishment and development of public library services throughout the State. (1973, c. 822, s. 1.)

§ 153A-262. Library materials defined. — For purposes of this Article, the phrase "library materials" includes, without limitation, books, plates, pictures, engravings, maps, magazines, pamphlets, newspapers, manuscripts, films, transparencies, microforms, recordings, or other specimens, works of literature, or objects of art, historical significance, or curiosity. (1953, c. 721; 1963, c. 945; 1971, c. 698, s. 3; 1973, c. 822, s. 1.)

§ 153A-263. Public library systems authorized. — A county or city may:
(1) Establish, operate, and support public library systems;
(2) Set apart lands and buildings for a public library system;
(3) Acquire real property for a public library system by gift, grant, purchase, lease, exercise of the power of eminent domain, or any other lawful method. If a library board of trustees is appointed, a county or city shall, before acquiring real property by purchase, lease, or exercise of the power of eminent domain, seek the recommendations of the board of trustees regarding the proposed acquisition;
(4) Provide, acquire, construct, equip, operate, and maintain buildings and other structures for a public library system;
(5) Acquire library materials by purchase, exchange, bequest, gift, or any other lawful method;
(6) Appropriate funds to carry out the provisions of this Article;
(7) Accept any gift, grant, lease, loan, exchange, bequest, or devise of real or personal property for a public library system. Devises, bequests, grants, and gifts may be accepted and held subject to any term or condition that may be imposed by the grantor or trustor, except that no county or city may accept or administer any term or condition that requires it to discriminate among its citizens on the basis of race, sex, or religion. (1953, c. 721; 1963, c. 945; 1971, c. 698, s. 3; 1973, c. 822, s. 1.)

§ 153A-264. Free library services. — If a county or city, pursuant to this Article, operates or makes contributions to the support of a library, any resident of the county or city, as the case may be, is entitled to the free use of the library. (1953, c. 721; 1963, c. 945; 1971, c. 698, s. 3; 1973, c. 822, s. 1.)

§ 153A-265. Library board of trustees. — The governing body of a county or city may appoint a library board of trustees. The governing body shall determine the number of members of the board of trustees (which may not be more than 12), the length of their terms, the manner of filling vacancies, and the amount, if any, of their compensation and allowances. The governing body may remove a trustee at any time for incapacity, unfitness, misconduct, or neglect of duty. (1953, c. 721; 1963, c. 945; 1971, c. 698, s. 1; 1973, c. 822, s. 1.)

§ 153A-266. **Powers and duties of trustees.** — If a board of trustees is appointed, it shall elect a chairman and may elect other officers. The governing body may delegate to the board of trustees any of the following powers:

(1) To formulate and adopt programs, policies, and regulations for the government of the library;

(2) To make recommendations to the governing body concerning the construction and improvement of buildings and other structures for the library system;

(3) To supervise and care for the facilities of the library system;

(4) To appoint a chief librarian or director of library services and, with his advice, to appoint other employees of the library system. If some other body or official is to appoint the chief librarian or director of library services, to advise that body or official concerning that appointment;

(5) To establish, a schedule of fines and charges for late return of, failure to return, damage to, and loss of library materials, and to take other measures to protect and regulate the use of such materials;

(6) To participate in preparing the annual budget of the library system;

(7) To extend the privileges and use of the library system to nonresidents of the county or city establishing or supporting the system, on any terms or conditions the board may prescribe.

(8) To otherwise advise the board of commissioners on library matters.

The board of trustees shall make an annual report on the operations of the library to the governing body of the county or city and shall make an annual report to the Department of Cultural Resources as required by G.S. 125-5. If no board of trustees is established, the governing body shall make the annual report to the Department. (1953, c. 721; 1963, c. 945; 1969, c. 488; 1971, c. 698, s. 3; 1973, c. 476, s. 84; c. 822, s. 1.)

§ 153A-267. **Qualifications of chief librarian; library employees.** — (a) To be eligible for appointment and service as chief administrative officer of a library system (whether designated chief librarian, director of library services, or some other title), a person must have a professional librarian certificate issued by the Secretary of Cultural Resources, pursuant to G.S. 125-9, under regulations for certification of public librarian as established by the North Carolina Public Librarian Certification Commission pursuant to the provisions of G.S. 143B-67.

(b) The employees of a county or city library system are, for all purposes, employees of the county or city, as the case may be. (1953, c. 721; 1963, c. 945; 1969, c. 488; 1971, c. 698, s. 3; 1973, c. 476, s. 53; c. 822, s. 1; 1975, c. 516.)

§ 153A-268. **Financing library systems.** — A county or city may appropriate for library purposes any funds not otherwise limited as to use by law. (1973, c. 822, s. 1.)

§ 153A-269. **Title to library property.** — The title to all property acquired by a county or city for library purposes shall be in the name of the county or city. If property is given, granted, devised, bequeathed, or otherwise conveyed to the board of trustees of a county or city library system, it shall be deemed to have been conveyed to the county or city and shall be held in the name of the county or city. (1953, c. 721; 1963, c. 945; 1971, c. 698, s. 3; 1973, c. 822, s. 1.)

§ 153A-270. **Joint libraries; contracts for library services.** — Two or more counties or cities or counties and cities may establish a joint library system or contract for library services, according to the procedures and provisions of Chapter 160A, Article 20, Part 1. (1953, c. 721; 1963, c. 945; 1971, c. 698, s. 3; 1973, c. 822, s. 1.)

§ 153A-271. Library systems operated under local acts brought under this Article. — If a county or city operates a library system pursuant to a local act, the governing body of the county or city may by ordinance provide that the library system is to be operated pursuant to this Article. (1973, c. 822, s. 1.)

SCHOOL LIBRARIES
(General Statutes of North Carolina, 1982, s.115-206.13, 115-206.14.)

§ 115-206.13. State Board of Education authorized to discontinue handling supplementary and library books.—The State Board of Education may discontinue the adoption of supplementary textbooks and, at the expiration of existing contracts, may discontinue the purchase, warehousing, and distribution of supplementary textbooks. The Board may also discontinue the purchase and resale of library books. Funds appropriated to the State Board of Education for supplementary textbooks shall be transferred to the State Nine Months School Fund for allotment to each school administrative unit, based on its average daily membership, for the purchase of supplementary textbooks, library books, periodicals, and other instructional materials. (1969, c. 519, s. 1.)

§ 115-206.14. Local boards of education to provide for local operation of the textbook program and the selection and procurement of other instructional materials.—(a) Local boards of education shall adopt rules and regulations not inconsistent with the policies of the State Board of Education concerning the local operation of the textbook program.

(b) Local boards of education shall adopt written policies concerning the procedures to be followed in its school administrative unit for the selection and procurement of supplementary textbooks, library books, periodicals, and other instructional materials needed for instructional purposes in the public schools of that unit. Supplementary books and other instructional materials shall neither displace nor be used to the exclusion of basic textbooks.

(c) Funds allocated by the State Board of Education or appropriated in the current expense or capital outlay budgets of the school administrative units, may be used for the above-stated purposes. (1969, c. 519, s. 1.)

PROTECTION OF LIBRARY PROPERTY
(General Statutes of North Carolina, 1982, s.14-398.)

§ 14-398. Theft or destruction of property of public libraries, museums, etc.

Any person who shall steal or unlawfully take or detain, or willfully or maliciously or wantonly write upon, cut, tear, deface, disfigure, soil, obliterate, break or destroy, or who shall sell or buy or receive, knowing the same to have been stolen, any book, document, newspaper, periodical, map, chart, picture, portrait, engraving, statue, coin, medal, apparauts, specimen, or other work of literature or object of art or curiosity deposited in a public library, gallery, museum, collection, fair or exhibition, or in any department or office of State or local government, or in a library, gallery, museum, collection, or exhibition, belonging to any incorporated college or university, or any incorporated institution devoted to educational, scientific, literary, artistic, historical or charitable purposes, shall, if the value of the property stolen, detained, sold, bought or received knowing same to have been stolen, or if the damage done by writing upon, cutting, tearing, defacing, disfiguring, soiling, obliterating, breaking or destroying any such property, shall not exceed fifty dollars ($50.00), be guilty of a misdemeanor and upon conviction shall be fined or imprisoned in the discretion of the court. If the value of the property stolen, detained, sold or received knowing same to have been stolen, or the amount of damage done in any of the ways or manners hereinabove set out, shall exceed the sum of fifty dollars ($50.00), the person committing same shall be punished as a Class H felon. (1935, c. 300; 1943, c. 543; 1979, c. 760, s. 5.)

North Carolina library laws are reprinted from GENERAL STATUTES OF NORTH CAROLINA published by The Michie Co., Charlottesville, Virginia.

NORTH DAKOTA

STATE LIBRARY COMMISSION

(North Dakota Century Code, 1982, s.54-24-01 to 54-24-03.1,
54-24-07 to 54-24-09.)

54-24-01. State library — State librarian appointed by director of institutions. The director of institutions shall appoint an executive officer to be known as the state librarian, who shall receive a salary within the amount appropriated for salaries by the legislative assembly. The state librarian shall have control of the work and shall be director of the state library.

Source: S.L. 1927, ch. 261, § 1; R.C. 1943, § 54-2401; S.L. 1979, ch. 550, § 7; 1981, ch. 535, § 15.

54-24-02. Library offices. The state library shall be furnished with adequate office room, with such suitable quarters as may be necessary for the proper shelving of the educational reference library, the books of the traveling libraries, and the legislative reference collection.

Source: S.L. 1907, ch. 243, § 8; 1909, ch. 156, § 8; C.L. 1913, § 1537; R.C. 1943, § 54-2402; S.L. 1979, ch. 550, § 8.

54-24-03. Powers and duties of state librarian. The state librarian shall:

1. Make rules and regulations according to which the business of the state library shall be done.
2. Provide and care for all books and library materials in all collections of the state library, general, reference, and special, and make all rules regarding the loaning and returning of library materials.
3. Employ qualified library personnel to care for all library procedures.
4. Make library materials available to libraries throughout the state, to individuals connected with departments of state, and to citizens of North Dakota who do not have adequate library facilities, under the rules and regulations of the state library.

5. Promote and assist by counsel and encouragement the formation of libraries and the improvement of those already established, in keeping with state and national standards, and be available to librarians and trustees of libraries in the state for assistance in organization, maintenance, or administration of the libraries.

6. Coordinate the efforts of librarianship throughout the state, advising and assisting the extension of qualified public libraries into centers of county or regional (multicounty) libraries.

7. Compile statistics of the free public libraries of North Dakota and their larger counterparts of county and regional libraries, and of the work done at the state library, and make a full biennial report to the state director of institutions and the governor.

8. Collect, maintain, and make available a reference and reading collection of books, slides, films, and other graphic materials such as will supplement and support the needs of all libraries in the state, either by direct loan or by consultation, and such as will form a reference source for the officers of the state in the performance of their duties.

9. Collect and maintain a collection of the publications of the departments and agencies of state government, including the enacted laws of this state, current session laws and journals.

10. Conduct, or arrange to have conducted, research into the conditions of library service in the state, and produce written plans for the development and betterment of such service.

11. Compile, or arrange to have compiled, union lists of resources of libraries throughout the state, and make such lists available for consultation.

12. Establish levels of certification for librarians of the state such as will meet the standards recommended by the American library association.

Source: S.L. 1907, ch. 243, § 5; 1909, ch. 156, § 5; C.L. 1913, § 1534; R.C. 1943, § 54-2403; S.L. 1965, ch. 352, § 8; 1979, ch. 550, § 9.

54-24-03.1. Acceptance of federal aid. The state library is hereby authorized to accept and to expend in accordance with the terms thereof any grant of federal funds which may become available to the state for library purposes. For the purpose of qualifying to receive such grants, the state library is authorized to make such applications and reports as may be required by the federal government as a condition thereto.

Source: S.L. 1949, ch. 320, § 1; R.C. 1943, 1957 Supp., § 54-24031; S.L. 1979, ch. 550, § 10.

54-24-07. Printing of state library — How paid. The printing of the report made by the state library to the legislative assembly, and all other printing coming within the purview of the library, shall be paid out of funds appropriated for that purpose by the legislative assembly.

Source: S.L. 1907, ch. 243, § 7; 1909, ch. 156, § 7; C.L. 1913, § 1536; R.C. 1943, § 54-2407; S.L. 1979, ch. 550, § 11.

54-24-08. Library contracts for library services. The state library is hereby authorized and empowered to cooperate with, and to contract with, cities, governmental subdivisions, and agencies of the state of North Dakota and other states of the United States, in the extension of library services.

Source: S.L. 1957, ch. 352, § 6; R.C. 1943, 1957 Supp., § 54-2408; S.L. 1967, ch. 389, § 1; 1979, ch. 550, § 12.

54-24-09. Distribution of certain state publications for certain libraries required. The state purchasing and printing agent shall arrange to deposit with the state library eight copies of all publications issued by all executive, legislative, and judicial agencies of state government intended for general public distribution. These publications shall be provided to the state library without charge. Should expense and limited supply of state publications, particularly audiovisual items, make strict compliance with the depository requirement impossible, the state library shall accept as many copies as an agency can afford to provide. However, no less than two copies shall be provided to the state library by each agency. State publications refer to any informational materials regardless of format, method of reproduction, or source, originating in or produced with the imprint of, by the authority of, or at the total or partial expense of, any state agency. The definition incorporates those publications that may or may not be financed by state funds but are released by private bodies such as research and consultant firms under contract with or supervision of any state agency. In circumstances not directly involving the state purchasing and printing agent, a state agency shall comply with the depository requirement by arranging with the necessary parties for the printing and deposit of eight copies of any state publication issued. State publications are specifically defined as public documents appearing as reports, directories, statistical compendiums, bibliographies, laws or bills, rules, regulations, newsletters, bulletins, state plans, brochures, periodicals, committee minutes, transcripts of public hearings, other printed matter, audio tapes, video tapes, films, filmstrips, or slides, but not those administrative or training materials used only within the issuing agency. As the document acquisition and distribution agency, the state library shall retain for its own use two copies of every state document received and transmit the remaining copies to the depository libraries. These shall be the libraries of the state historical board, the university of North Dakota, North Dakota state university, library of Congress, and two others to be designated by the state library. All nondepository North Dakota academic, public, and special libraries shall have the opportunity to receive state documents under an optional selection program developed by the state library. The state library shall catalog state publications and arrange for their conversion to microfilm and shall make available for distribution the same to the designated depository libraries.

Source: S.L. 1965, ch. 352, § 1; 1971, ch. 503, § 1; 1977, ch. 492, § 1; 1979, ch. 550, § 13.

STATE AID

(North Dakota Century Code, 1982, s.54-24.2-01 to 54.24.2-06.)

54-24.2-01. Eligibility. Public libraries eligible to receive financial aid under this chapter shall be limited to those public libraries that:

1. Apply to the state library for such financial aid.
2. Are established and operated in accordance with chapter 40-38.
3. Participate in the North Dakota network for knowledge interlibrary loan and information network.

Source: S.L. 1979, ch. 551, § 1.

54-24.2-02. Grant formula. Grants to eligible public libraries shall be in accordance with the following formula:
1. One dollar, or a percentage thereof, for each person residing in the city or county operating or providing financial support for the public library, as determined by the latest official federal census; and
2. Five dollars per square mile [259.00 hectares], or a percentage thereof, of land within the geographical boundaries of each county operating or providing financial support for a public library.

Source: S.L. 1979, ch. 551, § 2.

54-24.2-02.1. "Other public funds" defined. "Other public funds", as used in sections 54-24.2-03 and 54-24.2-05, means moneys appropriated for public library services by the governing body of the political subdivision providing public library services under chapter 40-38 in addition to the mill levy made for public library services.

Source: S.L. 1981, ch. 418, § 5.

54-24.2-03. Incentive for local funding. To provide for increased local funding, public libraries eligible to receive funds under section 54-24.2-02 shall have the funds allocated to them modified in accordance with the following formula:

Cities levying

8.00 or more mills	150 percent of allocation
6.00 — 7.99 mills	125 percent of allocation
4.00 — 5.99 mills	100 percent of allocation
3.00 — 3.99 mills	75 percent of allocation
2.00 — 2.99 mills	50 percent of allocation
1.00 — 1.99 mills	33 percent of allocation
0.01 — 0.99 mills	25 percent of allocation
0.00 — mills	0 percent of allocation

Counties levying

4.00 or more mills	150 percent of allocation
3.00 — 3.99 mills	125 percent of allocation
2.00 — 2.99 mills	100 percent of allocation
1.50 — 1.99 mills	75 percent of allocation
1.00 — 1.49 mills	50 percent of allocation
0.50 — 0.99 mills	33 percent of allocation
0.01 — 0.49 mills	25 percent of allocation
0.00 — mills	0 percent of allocation

The computation of mills shall be based upon the levy on the net assessed valuation and the mill levy equivalent of other public funds received and deposited in the library fund for the operation of the library by the governing body during the preceding fiscal year as certified by the auditor of the city or county operating the library.

Source: S.L. 1979, ch. 551, § 3.

54-24.2-04. Maintenance of local effort. No public library is eligible to receive any funds appropriated under this chapter during a fiscal year if the governing body has diminished the:
1. Mill levy on the taxable valuation below the average of the three preceding fiscal years; or
2. Appropriation for public library services below an amount equal to the revenue derived from the maximum mill levy for public library services authorized under section 40-38-02.

Source: S.L. 1979, ch. 551, § 4; 1981, ch. 418, § 6.

54-24.2-05. Limitations. For public libraries operated by cities, funds granted under this chapter shall not exceed thirty-three percent of the total expenditure of mill levy moneys and other public funds during the preceding year. For public libraries operated by counties, funds granted under this chapter shall not exceed the following percent of the total expenditure of mill levy moneys and other public funds during the preceding year:

less than $10,000	100 percent
$10,000 — $19,999	75 percent
$20,000 — $29,999	67 percent
$30,000 — $50,000	50 percent
over $50,000	33 percent

Source: S.L. 1979, ch. 551, § 5; 1981, ch. 418, § 7.

54-24.2-06. Use of funds — Reporting. Funds appropriated under this chapter may be expended by public libraries for the purchase of library materials, supplies and equipment, salaries of library staff, and services. No funds may be used for land acquisition, construction, or investment.

Each public library receiving funds under the chapter shall submit to the state library an annual report detailing the expenditures of these funds and all other funds expended by the library within the fiscal year. Such report shall be due within ninety days after the close of the fiscal year.

Source: S.L. 1979, ch. 551, § 6.

INTERSTATE LIBRARY COMPACT

(North Dakota Century Code, 1982, s.54-24.1-01 to 54-24.1-06.)

54-24.1-01. Interstate Library Compact. The Interstate Library Compact is hereby enacted into law and entered into by this state with all states legally joining therein in the form substantially as follows:

ARTICLE I — POLICY AND PURPOSE

Because the desire for the services provided by libraries transcends governmental boundaries and can most effectively be satisfied by giving such services to communities and people regardless of jurisdictional lines, it is the policy of the states party to this compact to cooperate and share their responsibilities; to authorize cooperation and sharing with respect to those types of library facilities and services which can be more economically or efficiently developed and maintained on a cooperative basis; and to authorize cooperation and sharing among localities, states, and others in providing joint or cooperative library services in areas where the distribution of population or of existing and potential library resources make the provision of library service on an interstate basis the most effective way of providing adequate and efficient service.

ARTICLE II — DEFINITIONS

As used in this compact:
1. "Library agreement" means a contract establishing an interstate library district pursuant to this compact or providing for the joint or cooperative furnishing of library services.
2. "Private library agency" means any nongovernmental entity which operates or assumes a legal obligation to operate a library.
3. "Public library agency" means any unit or agency of local or state government operating or having power to operate a library.

ARTICLE III — INTERSTATE LIBRARY DISTRICTS

1. Any one or more public library agencies in a party state in cooperation with any public library agency or agencies in one or more other party states may establish and maintain an interstate library district. Subject to the provisions of this compact and any other laws of the party states which pursuant hereto remain applicable, such district may establish, maintain, and operate some or all of the library facilities and services for the area concerned in accordance with the terms of a library agreement therefor. Any private library agency or agencies within an interstate library district may cooperate therewith, assume duties, responsibilities, and obligations thereto, and receive benefits therefrom as provided in any library agreement to which such agency or agencies become party.
2. Within an interstate library district, and as provided by a library agreement, the performance of library functions may be undertaken on a joint or cooperative basis or may be undertaken by means of one or more arrangements between or among public or private library agencies for the extension of library privileges to the use of facilities or services operated or rendered by one or more of the individual library agencies.
3. If a library agreement provides for joint establishment, maintenance, or operation of library facilities or services by an interstate library district, such district shall have power to do any one or more of the following in accordance with such library agreement:
   a. Undertake, administer, and participate in programs or arrangements for securing, lending, or servicing of books and other publications, any other materials suitable to be kept or made available

by libraries, library equipment or for the dissemination of information about libraries, the value and significance of particular items therein, and the use thereof.

b. Accept for any of its purposes under this compact any and all donations and grants of money, equipment, supplies, materials, and services. conditional or otherwise. from any state or the United States or any subdivision or agency thereof, or interstate agency, or from any institution, person, firm, or corporation, and receive, utilize, and dispose of the same.

c. Operate mobile library units or equipment for the purpose of rendering bookmobile service within the district.

d. Employ professional, technical, clerical, and other personnel, and fix terms of employment, compensation, and other appropriate benefits; and, where desirable, provide for the inservice training of such personnel.

e. Sue and be sued in any court of competent jurisdiction.

f. Acquire, hold, and dispose of any real or personal property or any interest or interests therein as may be appropriate to the rendering of library service.

g. Construct, maintain, and operate a library, including any appropriate branches thereof.

h. Do such other things as may be incidental to or appropriate for the carrying out of any of the foregoing powers.

ARTICLE IV — INTERSTATE LIBRARY DISTRICTS GOVERNING BOARD

1. An interstate library district which establishes, maintains, or operates any facilities or services in its own right shall have a governing board of not more than five members to be selected by the boards of the participating agencies which shall direct the affairs of the district and act for it in all matters relating to its business. Each participating public library agency in the district shall be represented on the governing board which shall be organized and conduct its business in accordance with provision therefor in the library agreement; but, in no event shall a governing board meet less often than twice a year.

2. Any private library agency or agencies party to a library agreement establishing an interstate library district may be represented on or advice with the governing board of the district in such manner as the library agreement may provide.

ARTICLE V — STATE LIBRARY AGENCY COOPERATION

Any two or more state library agencies of two or more of the party states may undertake and conduct joint or cooperative library programs, render joint or cooperative library services, and enter into and perform arrangements for the cooperative or joint acquisition, use, housing, and disposition of items or collections of materials which, by reason of expense, rarity, specialized nature, or infrequency of demand therefor would be appropriate for central collection and shared use. Any such programs, services, or arrangements may include provision for the exercise on a cooperative or joint basis of any power exercisable by an interstate library district and an agreement embodying any such program, service, or arrangement shall contain provisions covering the subjects detailed in Article VI of the compact for interstate library agreements.

ARTICLE VI — LIBRARY AGREEMENTS

1. In order to provide for any joint or cooperative undertaking pursuant to this compact, public and private library agencies may enter into library agreements. Any agreement executed pursuant to the provisions of this compact shall, as among the parties to the agreement:
   a. Detail the specific nature of the services, programs, facilities, arrangements, or properties to which it is applicable.
   b. Provide for the allocation of costs and other financial responsibilities.
   c. Specify the respective rights, duties, obligations, and liabilities of the parties.
   d. Set forth the terms and conditions for duration, renewal, termination, abrogation, disposal of joint or common property, if any, and all other matters which may be appropriate to the proper effectuation and performance of the agreement.
2. No public or private library agency shall undertake to exercise itself, or, jointly with any other library agency, by means of a library agreement, any power prohibited to such agency by the constitution or statutes of its state.
3. No library agreement shall become effective until filed with the compact administrator of each state involved, and approved in accordance with Article VII of this compact.

ARTICLE VII — APPROVAL OF LIBRARY AGREEMENTS

1. Every library agreement made pursuant to this compact shall, prior to and as a condition precedent to its entry into force, be submitted to the attorney general of each state in which a public library agency party thereto is situated, who shall determine whether the agreement is in proper form and compatible with the laws of his state. The attorneys general shall approve any agreement submitted to them unless they shall find that it does not meet the conditions set forth herein and shall detail in writing addressed to the governing bodies of the public library agencies concerned the specific respects in which the proposed agreement fails to meet the requirements of law. Failure to disapprove an agreement submitted hereunder within ninety days of its submission shall constitute approval thereof.
2. In the event that a library agreement made pursuant to this compact shall deal in whole or in part with the provision of services or facilities with regard to which an officer or agency of the state government has constitutional or statutory powers of control, the agreement shall, as a condition precedent to its entry into force, be submitted to the

state officer or agency having such power of control and shall be approved or disapproved by him or it as to all matters within his or its jurisdiction in the same manner and subject to the same requirements governing the action of the attorneys general pursuant to subsection 1. This requirement of submission and approval shall be in addition to and not in substitution for the requirement of submission to and approval by the attorneys general.

ARTICLE VIII — OTHER LAWS APPLICABLE

Nothing in this compact or in any library agreement shall be construed to supersede, alter, or otherwise impair any obligation imposed on any library by otherwise applicable law, nor to authorize the transfer or disposition of any property held in trust by a library agency in a manner contrary to the terms of such trust.

ARTICLE IX — APPROPRIATIONS AND AID

1. Any public library agency party to a library agreement may appropriate funds to the interstate library district established thereby in the same manner and to the same extent as to a library wholly maintained by it and, subject to the laws of the state in which such public library agency is situated, may pledge its credit in support of an interstate library district established by the agreement.
2. Subject to the provisions of the library agreement pursuant to which it functions and the laws of the states in which such district is situated, an interstate library district may claim and receive any state and federal aid which may be available to library agencies.

ARTICLE X — COMPACT ADMINISTRATOR

Each state shall designate a compact administrator with whom copies of all library agreements to which his state or any public library agency thereof is party shall be filed. The administrator shall have such other powers as may be conferred upon him by the laws of his state and may consult and cooperate with the compact administrators of other party states and take such steps as may effectuate the purposes of this compact. If the laws of a party state so provide, such state may designate one or more deputy compact administrators in addition to its compact administrator.

ARTICLE XI — ENTRY INTO FORCE AND WITHDRAWAL

1. This compact shall enter into force and effect immediately upon its enactment into law by any two states. Thereafter, it shall enter into force and effect as to any other state upon the enactment thereof by such state.
2. This compact shall continue in force with respect to a party state and remain binding upon such state until six months after such state has given notice to each other party state of the repeal thereof. Such withdrawal shall not be construed to relieve any party to a library agreement entered into pursuant to this compact from any obligation of that agreement prior to the end of its duration as provided therein.

ARTICLE XII — CONSTRUCTION AND SEVERABILITY

This compact shall be liberally construed so as to effectuate the purposes thereof. The provisions of this compact shall be severable and if any phrase, clause, sentence, or provision of this compact is declared to be contrary to the constitution of any party state or of the United States or the applicability thereof to any government, agency, person, or circumstance is held invalid, the validity of the remainder of this compact and applicability thereof to any government, agency, person, or circumstance shall not be affected thereby. If this compact shall be held contrary to the constitution of any state party thereto, the compact shall remain in full force and effect as to the remaining states and in full force and effect as to the state affected as to all severable matters.

Source: S.L. 1965, ch. 353, § 1.

54-24.1-02.   Must comply with state and local laws. No city, township, or county of this state shall be party to a library agreement which provides for the construction or maintenance of a library pursuant to subdivision g of subsection 3 of Article III of the compact, nor pledge its credit in support of such a library, or contribute to the capital financing thereof, except after compliance with any laws applicable to such cities, townships, or counties relating to or governing capital outlays and the pledging of credit.

Source: S.L. 1965, ch. 353, § 2.

54-24.1-03.   Definition. As used in the compact, "state library agency", with reference to this state, means the state library.

Source: S.L. 1965, ch. 353, § 3; 1979, ch. 550, § 14.

54-24.1-04.   Entitled to state aid. An interstate library district lying partly within this state may claim and be entitled to receive state aid in support of any of its functions to the same extent and in the same manner as such functions are eligible for support when carried on by entities wholly within this state. For the purposes of computing and apportioning state aid to an interstate library district, this state will consider that portion of the area which lies within this state as an independent entity for the performance of the aided function or functions and compute and apportion the aid accordingly. Subject to any applicable laws of this state, such a district also may apply for and be entitled to receive any federal aid for which it may be eligible.

Source: S.L. 1965, ch. 353, § 4.

54-24.1-05.   Interstate library compact director — Appointment — Deputy. The governor shall appoint an officer of this state who shall be the compact administrator pursuant to Article X of the compact. The governor shall also appoint one or more deputy compact administrators pursuant to said article.

Source: S.L. 1965, ch. 353, § 5.

54-24.1-06. Duties of governor in case of withdrawal. In the event of withdrawal from the compact the governor shall send and receive any notices required by subsection 1 of Article XI of the compact.

Source: S.L. 1965, ch. 353, § 6.

DISTRIBUTION OF PUBLIC DOCUMENTS
(North Dakota Century Code, 1982, s.46-04.02.)

46-04-02. State libraries entitled to receive copy of state laws.—The state libraries shall receive copies of the session laws, compilations, or codifications as follows:

1. The supreme court law library, five copies.
2. The law library of the state university, fifty copies.
3. The library in each state institution of higher education and junior college which receives state support, one copy.

Source: N.D.C.C.; S. L. 1961, ch. 294, § 1; 1971, ch. 451, § 1.

STATE HISTORICAL SOCIETY
(North Dakota Century, Code, 1982, s.55-01-01 to 55.01-03, 55-02-01 to 55.02.01.2.)

55-01-01. State historical board. There shall be a state historical society of North Dakota which will be under the supervision and control of the state historical board. The board shall consist of nine members who shall be appointed by the governor with the consent of the senate. Each member appointed to the board must be a citizen and resident of the state of North Dakota. Interim appointments may be made by the governor if the senate is not in session and such interim appointees may hold office until the senate has had an opportunity to confirm or reject such appointments. Appointments shall be for a term of three years from the first day of July to the thirtieth day of June of the third year or until a successor has been appointed and qualified except that the first appointments under this section shall be staggered so that the term of three members shall expire each year. Vacancies occurring other than by the expiration of an appointive term shall be filled by appointment for the remainder of the term only in the same manner as regular appointments. The board of directors shall select from its membership a president, vice president, and secretary to serve as officers of the board. The secretary of state, state engineer, state highway commissioner, state forester, state game and fish commissioner, director of the state library, and state treasurer shall be ex officio members of the board and shall take care that the interests of the state are protected.

Source: N.D.C.C.; S.L. 1981, ch. 91, § 47.

55-01-02. State historical board—Powers—Limitations.—The state historical board shall be authorized to:

1. Faithfully expend and apply all money received from the state, to the uses and purposes directed by law;

2. Hold all its present and future historical collections and property for the state;

3. Sell or exchange any duplicates of any article that the board may have or obtain;

4. Permit withdrawal from its collections and property of such articles as may be needed for exhibition purposes;

5. Permit the withdrawal of books and collections from the library and museum temporarily under such rules as the board may prescribe;

6. Select and appoint a superintendent to carry out the policies and directives of the board;

7. Acquire in behalf of the state of North Dakota, by lease, purchase, gift, or by the exercise of eminent domain, state monuments;

8. Set aside for monuments, such lands as are now owned by the state and not held or acquired for some other purpose;

9. Supervise, control, care for, maintain, and develop any such state monuments as trustees for the state;

10. Administer any such state monuments as an agent of the national park service, bureau of reclamation, corps of engineers, or any other division of federal, state, or local government; and

11. Cooperate with historical societies and associations duly organized under the laws of the state of North Dakota, and to provide the same with publications, pamphlets, and other documents of historical interest.

The secretary of the board shall have power to withdraw for temporary use such of the collections as shall be needed for the compilation and editing of the publications of the board. The board, however, shall not sell, mortgage, transfer, or dispose of any of its collections or property except as authorized by law, nor shall it, without authority of law, remove from the historical rooms in the capitol any article contained therein.

Source: N.D.C.C.; S. L. 1965, ch. 379,
§ 2; 1967, ch. 411, § 2.

55-01-03. Meetings—When held—Quorum—Compensation and expenses of members.—The state historical board shall meet at the call of the president not less than every three months and seven members shall constitute a quorum. The ex officio members shall receive no additional compensation for service upon the board but shall be paid their expenses when engaged in the discharge of their official duties as members of the commission, in the same manner and amounts as other state officers are paid, from funds available to the board.

Source: N.D.C.C.; S. L. 1965, ch. 379, § 3.

55-02-01. State historical board—Appointment of superintendent—Duties.—The board shall appoint a superintendent who shall act as chief administrative and executive officer in carrying out the policies and directives of the board and shall have charge of all employees and activities and shall perform such other duties as may be assigned to him by the board.

S. L. 1965, ch. 379, § 10.

55-02-01.1. Term of office—Vacancy—Salary and expenses—Bond.— The superintendent shall serve at the pleasure of the state historical board and until his successor is appointed and qualified. In case of vacancy by death, removal, resignation, or any other cause, the board shall fill the vacancy by appointment. The salary shall be determined by the board within the limits of legislative appropriation and the superintendent shall be entitled to compensation for his expenses incurred while in the discharge of his official duties, paid in the same manner and amounts as other state officials are paid, from funds available to the board. Before entering upon their duties, each shall furnish a bond in the penal sum of ten thousand dollars.   S. L. 1965, ch. 379, § 11.

55-02-01.2. Duties of the superintendent.—The superintendent shall:

1. Collect books, maps, charts, and other papers and materials illustrative of the history of this state in particular and of the west generally;

2. Obtain from the early pioneers narratives of their exploits, perils, and adventures;

3. Procure facts and statements relative to the history, progress, and decay of our Indian tribes so as to exhibit faithfully the antiquities and the past and present resources and conditions of this state;

4. Purchase books to supply deficiencies in the various departments of its collection, and especially reports on the legislation of other states, on railroads, and geological surveys and on educational and humane institutions for legislative reference, and such other books, maps, charts, and materials as will facilitate the investigation of historic, scientific, and literary subjects. The secretary of state shall furnish to the superintendent for reference and exchange purposes, as many copies as requested by the superintendent of every state publication;

5. Catalogue all of the collections of the board for the more convenient references of all persons who have occasion to consult the same. The state shall bind the unbound books, documents, manuscripts, and pamphlets, and especially newspaper files containing legal notices, in the possession of the board;

6. Prepare annually for publication four quarterly reports of its collections and such other matters relating to the transactions of the board as may be useful to the public. Such report shall be in such form and in such binding as the state historical board shall determine, and shall be printed by the state. The board shall have charge of the distribution and sale of such reports and shall account for the proceeds received therefrom to the state auditing board; and

7. Keep its rooms open at all reasonable hours on business days for the reception of the citizens of this state who may wish to visit the same, without fee.   S. L. 1965, ch. 379, § 12.

RECORDS MANAGEMENT

(North Dakota Century Code, 1982, s.54-46-01 to 54.46.13.)

54-46-01. Short title.—This chapter shall be known as the "Records Management Act." S. L. 1961, ch. 333, § 1.

54-46-02. Definitions.—As used in this chapter, unless the context or subject matter otherwise requires:

1. "Record" means document, book, paper, photograph, sound recording or other material, regardless of physical form or characteristics, made or received pursuant to law or in connection with the transaction of official business. Library and museum material made or acquired and preserved solely for reference or exhibition purposes, extra copies of documents preserved only for convenience of reference, and stocks of publications and of processed documents are not included within the definition of records as used in this chapter.

2. "State record" means:
   a. A record of a department, office, commission, board or other agency, however designated, of the state government;
   b. A record of the state legislature;
   c. A record of any court of record, whether of state-wide or local jurisdiction;
   d. Any other record designated or treated as a state record under state law.

3. "Agency" means any department, office, commission, board or other unit, however designated, of the executive branch of state government. S. L. 1961, ch. 333, § 3.

54-46-03. State records administrator.—The secretary of state is hereby designated the "state records administrator," hereinafter called the "administrator." The administrator shall establish and administer in the executive branch of state government a records management program, which will apply efficient and economical management methods to the creation, utilization, maintenance, retention, preservation and disposal of state records. S. L. 1961, ch. 333, § 4.

54-46-04. Duties of administrator.—The administrator shall, with due regard for the functions of the agencies concerned:

1. Establish standards, procedures, and techniques for effective management of records.

2. Make continuing surveys of paper work operations and recommend improvements in current records management practices including the use of space, equipment and supplies employed in creating, maintaining, storing and servicing records.

3. Establish standards for the preparation of schedules providing for the retention of state records of continuing value and for the prompt and orderly disposal of state records no longer possess-

ing sufficient administrative, legal or fiscal value to warrant their further keeping.

4. Obtain reports from agencies as are required for the administration of the program. S. L. 1961, ch. 333, § 5.

54-46-05. Duties of agency or department heads.—The head of each agency or department shall:

1. Establish and maintain an active, continuing program for the economical and efficient management of the records of the agency.

2. Make and maintain records containing adequate and proper documentation of the organization, functions, policies, decisions, procedures and essential transactions of the agency designed to furnish information to protect the legal and financial rights of the state and of persons directly affected by the agency's activities.

3. Submit to the administrator, in accordance with the standards established by him, schedules proposing the length of time each state record series warrants retention for administrative, legal or fiscal purposes after it has been received by the agency. The head of each agency also shall submit lists of state records in his custody that are not needed in the transaction of current business and that do not have sufficient administrative, legal or fiscal value to warrant their further keeping for disposal in conformity with the requirements of section 54-46-09.

4. Co-operate with the administrator in the conduct of surveys made by him pursuant to the provisions of this chapter.

5. Comply with the rules, regulations, standards and procedures issued by the administrator. S. L. 1961, ch. 333, § 6.

54-46-06. Assistance to legislative and judicial branches.—Upon request, the administrator shall assist and advise in the establishment of records managment programs in the legislative and judicial branches of state government and shall, as required by them, provide program services similar to those available to the executive branch of state government pursuant to the provisions of this chapter.

S. L. 1961, ch. 333, § 7.

54-46-07. Records not to be damaged or destroyed.—All records made or received by or under the authority of or coming into the custody, control or possession of public officials of this state in the course of their public duties are the property of the state and shall not be mutilated, destroyed, transferred, removed or otherwise damaged or disposed of, in whole or in part, except as provided by law.

S. L. 1961, ch. 333, § 8.

54-46-08. Disposal of records.—No type or class of record shall be destroyed or otherwise disposed of by any agency of the state, unless it is determined by the administrator, after consultation with the official or department head concerned, that the type or class of record has no further administrative, legal, fiscal, research or historical value.

S. L. 1961, ch. 333, § 9.

54-46-09. Destruction of nonrecord materials.—Nonrecord materials or materials not included within the definition of records as contained in this chapter may, if not otherwise prohibited by law, be destroyed at any time by the agency in possession of such materials without the prior approval of the administrator. The administrator may formulate procedures and interpretation to guide in the disposition of nonrecord materials.   S. L. 1961, ch. 333, § 10.

54-46-10. Rules and regulations.—The administrator shall promulgate such rules and regulations as are necessary or proper to effectuate the purposes of this chapter.   S. L. 1961, ch. 333, § 11.

54-46-11. Biennial report.—The administrator shall make a biennial report as prescribed by subsection 6 of section 54-06-04 to the governor and secretary of state. The report shall describe the status and progress of programs established pursuant to this chapter and shall include the recommendations of the administrator for improvements in the management of records in the state government.

Source: N.D.C.C.; S. L. 1961, ch. 333,
§ 12; 1963, ch. 346, § 68.

54-46-12. County records—Uniform system established by secretary of state.—On or before July 1, 1965, the secretary of state shall promulgate rules and regulations consistent with specific requirements of state law for a uniform system of cataloguing, reproducing, retaining, and disposing of county records. Upon promulgation of such rules and regulations all county offices, departments, and agencies shall be authorized to establish and maintain such uniform system as prescribed by the secretary of state. The secretary of state may, from time to time, revise such rules and regulations as he deems necessary.

Source: S. L. 1963, ch. 354, § 1.

54-46-13. Rules for destruction of certain state and county welfare records—Secretary of state to promulgate.—The secretary of state, in his capacity as state records administrator, shall promulgate rules and regulations for the destruction or disposal of state and county welfare case files pertaining to work relief and public assistance programs after such files have been closed for a minimum period of six years and shall also promulgate rules and regulations for the destruction or disposal of other state and county welfare records which are obsolete or have been duplicated. The secretary of state, prior to the promulgation of rules and regulations for the destruction of state and county welfare files and records, shall consult with the director of the state welfare board ir regard to the destruction of such files and records. The secretary of state may, from time to time, revise such rules and regulations after further consultation with the director of the state welfare board.

Source: S. L. 1965, ch. 189, § 2.

COUNTY AND MUNICIPAL LIBRARIES
(North Dakota Century Code, 1982, s.40-38-1 to 40-38-11.)

40-38-01. Public library and reading room — Establishment — Election. The governing body of any city or county upon petition of not less than fifty-one percent of the voters of the city or county as determined by the total number of votes cast at the last general election or upon a majority vote of the electors thereof shall establish and maintain public library service within its geographic limits by means of a public library and reading room or other public library service, either singly or in cooperation with the state library, or with one or more cities or counties, or by participation in an approved state plan for rendering public library service under the Library Services and Construction Act, 20 U.S.C. 351-358, and acts amendatory thereof. Such question shall be submitted to the electors upon resolution of the governing body or upon the petition of not less than twenty-five percent of that number of electors of the city or county that voted at the last general election, filed with the governing body not less than sixty days before the next regular election. Library service may be discontinued within any city or county by any of the methods by which library services may be established, except that once established, such service shall not be discontinued until after it has been in operation for at least five years from the date of establishment.

Source: N.D.C.C.; S.L. 1971, ch. 410, § 1;
1979, ch. 550, § 1.

40-38-02. Library fund — Levy — Kept separate — Exemption for municipality levying tax — Increasing levy.
1. For the purpose of establishing and maintaining public library service, the governing body of a municipality or county authorizing the same shall establish a library fund. The library fund shall consist of annually levying and causing to be collected as other taxes are collected, a municipal or county tax not to exceed four mills on the net taxable assessed valuation of property in the municipality and not to exceed two mills on the net taxable assessed valuation of property in the county, and any other moneys received for library purposes from federal, state, county, municipal, or private sources.
2. The city auditor or county treasurer shall keep the fund separate and apart from the other money of the county or municipality and promptly transmit all funds received pursuant to this section within thirty days of receipt to the board of directors. The funds may not revert to or be considered funds on hand by the governing body at the end of any fiscal year. The fund shall be used exclusively for the establishment and maintenance of public library service.
3. Whenever a tax for county library service is levied, any municipality already levying a tax for public library service under the provisions of this section or other provisions of law shall, upon written application to the county board of the county, be exempted from the county tax levy to the extent that the municipality making the application levies taxes for a library fund during the year for which the tax levy

is made. If the municipality has been totally exempted from participation in any prospective county library program, the phrase "not less than fifty-one percent of the voters of such municipality or county as determined by the total number of votes cast at the last general election" as stated in section 40-38-01 shall mean fifty-one percent of the total number of votes cast at the last general election in the county less the total number of votes cast at the last general election in the municipality. If an election on the question is held, the voters of any municipality so exempted from the county library tax shall not be entitled to vote on the establishment or discontinuance of the county library service.

4. Upon motion of the governing body or upon petition of not less than twenty-five percent of the voters in the last general election of any city, school district, township, or county, filed not less than sixty days before the next regular election, the governing body shall submit to the voters at the next regular election the question of whether the governing body shall increase the mill levy a specified amount for public library service above the mill levy limitation set out in this section. Upon approval by sixty percent of the voters voting in the election, the governing body shall increase the levy for public library service in the amount approved by the voters.

Source: N.D.C.C.; S.L. 1971, ch. 410, § 2;
1973, ch. 333, § 1; 1981, ch. 418, § 1.

40-38-03. Board of directors — Appointment — Term of office — No compensation — Filling vacancies — Organization. The governing body of a municipality which has established a public library and reading room, or the board of county commissioners for a county library, shall appoint a board of five directors who must be residents of the municipality or county, as the case may be, to govern such library and reading room. One member of the governing body of the municipality or designated representative shall be a member of the board of directors of a municipal library, and must be a resident of the municipality which establishes and maintains such municipal library; and one member of the board of county commissioners or designated representative shall be a member of the county board of directors. The terms of office of the members of the first board of directors shall be as follows: one member shall hold office for one year; two members shall hold office for two years; and two members shall hold office for three years. The members, at their first meeting, shall determine the length of their respective terms by lot. Thereafter, the number of directors required to fill expired terms shall be appointed each year, and each such director shall hold office for a term of three years from the first day of July in the year of his appointment and until his successor has been appointed. No member of such board shall serve for more than two consecutive terms, after which an interval of one year must elapse before the same member may be reappointed. All vacancies on the board of directors shall be reported by such board to the governing body of the municipality or the board of county commissioners, as the case may be, and shall be filled thereby. However, a member of any municipal board of directors of a public library and reading room who was appointed to such position by a school board prior to July 1, 1975, may serve upon such board for the residue of his unexpired term unless such position shall otherwise become vacant. Appointments made to fill unexpired terms shall be for the residue of the term only. No compensation shall be paid or allowed to a director. Immediately after the appointment of its members, the board of directors shall meet and organize by electing a president. The governing board of a municipality or county establishing public library service may, in lieu of appointing a library board, contract directly with a library board established by another governing body of a municipality or county for the purpose of extending public library service.

Source: N.D.C.C.; S.L. 1969, ch. 377, § 1; 1971, ch. 410, § 3; 1973, ch. 333, § 2; 1975, ch. 379, § 1.

40-38-04. General powers and duties of board of directors. The board of directors shall have the following powers and duties:

1. To make and adopt such bylaws, rules, and regulations relating to the duties of the officers of the board as may be expedient and not inconsistent with the provisions of this chapter.
2. To make and adopt such bylaws, rules, and regulations for the management of the library and reading room as are expedient and not inconsistent with the provisions of this chapter.
3. To control, exclusively, the expenditures of all moneys collected for or contributed to the library fund.
4. To have the supervision, care, and custody of the library property, and of the rooms or buildings constructed, leased, or set apart for use of library purposes.
5. To contract to furnish library service and to receive library service from other counties, school districts, and cities of the state of North Dakota and adjoining states, and the state library.
6. To employ qualified personnel to administer the public library and dispense library services.

Source: N.D.C.C.; S.L. 1973, ch. 333, § 3; 1975, ch. 379, § 2; 1975, ch. 380, § 1; 1979, ch. 550, § 2.

40-38-05. Board of directors may purchase, build, or lease building for library — Library building fund — Public hearing required. The board of directors, with the approval of the city or county governing body, may build, lease, lease-purchase, or purchase an appropriate building for a library and purchase a site therefor. Such lease, purchase, or contract shall not be valid without the approval of the governing body of the city or county. Prior to any actions on such proposals, the governing body shall hold a public hearing on the proposals. Notice of the hearing shall be published at least once, not less than six days prior to the hearing, in a newspaper of general circulation within the city or county. The governing body shall seek the advice and comment of the state library and the general public at the hearing. After such hearing, the governing body of a city or county may establish by resolution a library building fund for the purpose of construction, enlargement, or alteration of a building or for the purchase of an existing building to be used as a public library. The city auditor or county treasurer shall place in the library building fund all moneys for such purposes as may be appropriated by the governing body or received for such purposes from federal, state, county, city, or private sources. The library building fund shall not revert to the library general fund or the general fund of the city or county without authorization by formal resolution from both the library's board of directors and the governing body of the city or county.

Source: N.D.C.C.; S.L. 1973, ch. 333, § 4; 1979, ch. 550, § 3.

40-38-06. Vouchers — How drawn. The duly bonded secretary or treasurer of the board of directors may draw money from the library fund upon vouchers of the board of directors without any other audit.

Source: N.D.C.C.; S.L. 1981, ch. 418, § 2.

40-38-08. Donations — How accepted — Board of directors as trustee. All persons desirous of making donations of money, books, personal property, or real estate for the benefit of the library may vest the same in the board of directors. The board shall hold and control all property accepted for the use of the library and reading room as a special trustee.

Source: N.D.C.C.; S.L. 1981, ch. 418, § 3.

40-38-09. Annual report of board of directors — Contents — To whom made. The board of directors shall make a report on July first of each year to the governing body of the city or board of county commissioners, as the case may be, stating:
1. The condition of the library and property.
2. The various sums of money received from all sources.
3. How much money has been expended and for what purpose.
4. The number of books and periodicals on hand.
5. The number of books and periodicals added by purchase or gift during the year and the number thereof lost or loaned out.
6. The character and kind of books contained in the library.
7. Such other statistics, information, and suggestions as the board may deem of general interest or as may be required by the state library.
Copies of the report shall be filed with the governing body of the political subdivision and with the state library.

Source: N.D.C.C.; S.L. 1973, ch. 333, § 5; 1979, ch. 550, § 4.

40-38-10. Contributions by political subdivision to establishment of library without election authorized. To aid and facilitate the organization of library service, the governing body of any city where the population is less than two thousand five hundred may appropriate annually from its general fund, or from any other moneys received for library purposes from federal, state, and private sources, a sum not to exceed five dollars per capita for the purchase of books and periodicals to remain the property of the city and to be loaned to any local library for free public use. The governing body shall appoint a book committee of three which shall select the books and periodicals from standard and recommended lists furnished by the state library. The selection so made by such committee shall be submitted to the governing body for approval and purchase by such governing body, provided that the amount so expended for such books and periodicals shall be within the amount appropriated therefor. Books and periodicals purchased with this fund shall be properly stamped as belonging to the city. Such appropriation shall be made and books and periodicals purchased without submitting the same to vote as provided in section 40-38-02. As an alternative, the governing body may contract with a library operated by a city, county, school district, or the state library for the provision of public library service for the city.

Source: N.D.C.C.; S.L. 1973, ch. 333, § 6;
1979, ch. 550, § 5.

40-38-11. Joint public library services by cities and counties.

1. Upon compliance with section 40-38-01 for the establishment of public library services, public library services may be jointly provided through a written agreement between the governing bodies of any city or county or both to establish and maintain joint library services with one or more cities or counties or both.

2. A party shall be bound to an agreement entered into under subsection 1 for an initial five-year term and subsequent five-year terms unless it provides other parties to the agreement with notice of intent to withdraw from the agreement at least two years before the proposed date of withdrawal.

3. The parties to the agreement shall appoint a single joint library board to govern public library services covered by the agreement. The method of representation on the joint library board and the establishment of the initial board with staggered terms shall be determined in the agreement. Provided, the joint library board shall consist of an equal number of appointees from each party to the agreement and, in any case, shall consist of not less than five members nor more than eleven members. No member of the board shall serve for more than two consecutive three-year terms, after which an interval of one year must elapse before the same member may be reappointed.

4. The joint library board shall have all power and duties provided in sections 40-38-04 through 40-38-09.

5. A joint library fund shall be established for the public library services covered by the agreement. Each city or county represented in the agreement shall provide its pro rata share of funds for the services, as specified in the agreement, from the funds received under section 40-38-02.

6. The joint library board shall appoint, and may remove, a treasurer to administer the joint library fund. The treasurer may be a treasurer of one of the parties to the agreement or a member of the board or both. The city auditor and county treasurer of each city or county represented in the agreement and the state librarian shall promptly transmit all funds authorized under subsection 5 and chapter 54-24.2,

respectively, directly to the treasurer of the joint library board. The treasurer shall pay out moneys belonging to the joint library board only upon properly drawn vouchers, pursuant to order of the joint library board. The funds received by the treasurer shall not revert to or be considered funds on hand by any governmental unit furnishing the same, at the end of any biennium or fiscal year. The treasurer shall be bonded in such amount as may be specified by resolution adopted by the joint library board.

7. The agreement shall include provisions for the dissolution of the joint library board and distribution of assets in the event the agreement is terminated.

8. Joint libraries established and operated under this section are eligible to receive financial aid under chapter 54-24.2 to the extent that each city and county represented in the agreement would be eligible for the aid.

9. Agreements for public library services between cities or counties or both may be provided under this section or other provisions of this chapter and may not be provided under chapter 54-40 or other provisions of law.

10. After July 1, 1981, the establishment of joint library services pursuant to this section shall not be permitted unless approved by the electors of each individual city or county considering the question.

Source: N.D.C.C.; S.L. 1971, ch. 411, § 1; 1979, ch. 550, § 6; 1981, ch. 418, § 4.

MISCELLANEOUS PROVISIONS
(North Dakota Century Code, 1982, s.27-04-06, 27-04-07, 11-11-52, 26-24-09, 40-46-09, 57-15-49.)

27-04-06. Reporter's duties as to state law library.—The supreme court reporter, subject to the supervision and control of the supreme court, shall have the care and custody of the state law library and shall perform such duties in connection with the maintenance and operation of the same as the supreme court, by rule or regulation, may provide.

R. C. 1943. § 27-0406.

27-04-07. Reporter's duties as legislative reference librarian.—The supreme court reporter shall perform the duties of a legislative reference librarian and shall give information and assistance to the members of the legislative assembly in their legislative work. R. C. 1943, § 27-0407.

11-11-52. Board may provide room for historical society.—The board of county commissioners of any county, or the governing body of any municipal corporation, or the board of any public library in the state is hereby authorized and empowered to furnish a room or rooms in the county courthouse, in a municipal building, or in a public library building, as the case may be, for the use of the historical society of such county, and to furnish light and heat therefor. 1957 Supp., § 11-1152.

26-24-09. Commissioner to provide insurance on all public buildings.
—Upon application the commissioner shall provide for insurance against
loss by fire, lightning, inherent explosion, windstorm, cyclone, tornado
and hail, explosions, riot attending a strike, aircraft, smoke, and vehicles, all in the manner and subject to the restrictions of the standard
fire insurance policy and standard extended coverage endorsement, and
no other hazards, in the fund, on all buildings owned by the state, state
industries, and political subdivisions of the state, and the fixtures and
permanent contents in such buildings, to the extent of not to exceed
ninety percent of the full insurable value of such property, as such
value is determined by the commissioner and approved by the officer
or board having control of such property, or, in case of disagreement,
by approval through arbitration as hereinafter provided.

   *   *   *   *

    All public libraries owned by the state or the political subdivisions
of the state may, in addition to the coverage provided for in this
section, be covered against damage through vandalism. If such coverage cannot be extended to the public libraries situated within this
state, such libraries may contract for such coverage with private
insurance companies, provided that such coverage meets the recommendations of the insurance code of the American Library Association.

    Source: N.D.C.C.; S. L. 1963, ch. 229,
§ 2; 1965, ch. 352, § 3.

    **40-46-09. Who may be retired on pension — Amount paid to retiring
employee.** Any appointed full-time employee, who shall be a member of
a city employees' pension fund, including but not limited to librarians and
other employees of a public library, and full-time employees of a city recreation commission, of a city having an employees' pension fund who shall
have served two hundred forty months or more, whether or not consecutive,
as an employee and shall have reached the age of sixty years, or who, while
employed by such city, shall suffer permanent mental or physical disability
so that he is unable to discharge his duties, shall be entitled to be retired.
Upon retirement, he shall be paid out of the pension fund of such city a
monthly pension of not to exceed sixty percent of one-twelfth of his highest
three-year average annual earnings as provided for in the plan adopted
by the governing body of the city. If any member shall have served two
hundred forty months in such city employment but shall not have reached
the age of sixty years, he shall be entitled to retirement, but no pension
shall be paid while he lives until he reaches the age of sixty years.

    Source: N.D.C.C.; S.L. 1969, ch. 379, § 1;
1977, ch. 388, § 3.

    57-15-49. School district levy for school library fund.—The school
board of any school district, upon the passage of a resolution, may submit the question at the next regularly scheduled or special election in
the school district of providing for an annual levy of not in excess of two
mills for a school library fund. If the question submitted is approved

by a majority of the electors voting thereon, the school board shall proceed to make such levy, which levy shall be over and above any mill levy limitations provided by law. Upon approval of the levy for the school library fund, the school board shall create a school library fund and establish a budget for expenditures from such fund. The fund shall be kept separate and apart from other funds of the school district and shall be used exclusively for the maintenance of the school library services. Such levy may be discontinued upon the passage of a resolution by the school board, or if a petition signed by not less than twenty-five electors or five percent of the electors of the school district as indicated by the number of persons voting at the last school district election, whichever is greater, is presented to the school board, the question of discontinuance of the levy shall be submitted to the electors of the school district at any regular or special school district election. If a majority of the electors of the school district vote in favor of discontinuing the levy, such levy shall not be included in the next budget submitted by the school district.

Source: S. L. 1967, ch. 431, § 1.

North Dakota library laws are reprinted from the NORTH DAKOTA CENTURY CODE published by the Allen Smith Co., Indianapolis, Indiana.

OHIO

STATE LIBRARY BOARD

(Page's Ohio Revised Code, 1982, s.3375.01-3375.05.)

§ 3375.01 State library board.

A state library board is hereby created to be composed of five members to be appointed by the state board of education. One member shall be appointed each year for a term of five years. No one is eligible to membership on the state library board who is or has been for a year previous to his appointment a member of the state board of education. A member of the state library board shall not during his term of office be a member of the board of library trustees for any library in any subdivision in the state. Before entering on the duties of his appointment, each member shall subscribe to the official oath of office. All vacancies on the state library board shall be filled by the state board of education by appointment for the unexpired term. The members shall receive no compensation, but shall be paid their actual and necessary expenses incurred in the performance of their duties or in the conduct of authorized board business, within or without the state.

At its regular meeting next prior to the beginning of each fiscal biennium the state library board shall elect a president and vice-president each of whom shall serve for two years or until his successor is elected and qualified.

The state library board is responsible for the state library of Ohio and a statewide program of development and coordination of library services, and its powers include the following:

(A) Maintain the state library, holding custody of books, periodicals, pamphlets, films, recordings, papers, and other materials and equipment. The board may purchase or procure from an insurance company licensed to do business in this state policies of insurance insuring the members of the board and the officers, employees, and agents of the state library against liability on account of damage or injury to persons or property resulting from any act or omission of the board members, officers, employees, and agents of the state library in their official capacity.

(B) Accept, receive, administer, and expend, in

1449

accordance with the terms thereof, any moneys, materials, or other aid granted, appropriated, or made available to it for library purposes, by the United States, or any of its agencies, or by any other source, public or private;

(C) Administer such funds as the general assembly may make available to it for the improvement of public library services, interlibrary cooperation, or for other library purposes;

(D) Contract with other agencies, organizations, libraries, library schools, boards of education, universities, public and private, within or without the state, for library services, facilities, research, or any allied or related purpose;

(E) In accordance with Chapter 119. of the Revised Code, approve, disapprove, or modify resolutions for establishment of county district libraries, and approve, disapprove, or modify resolutions to determine the boundaries of such districts, along county lines or otherwise, and approve, disapprove, or modify resolutions to redefine boundaries, along county lines or otherwise, where questions subsequently arise as a result of school district consolidations;

(F) Upon consolidation of two or more school districts and in accordance with Chapter 119. of the Revised Code, to define and adjust the boundaries of the new public library district resulting from such consolidation and to resolve any disputes or questions pertaining to the boundaries, organization, and operation of the new library district;

(G) Upon application of one or more boards of library trustees and in accordance with Chapter 119. of the Revised Code, to amend, define, and adjust the boundaries of the library districts making such application and the boundaries of adjacent library districts. A library district boundary change made by the state library board pursuant to this division shall take effect sixty days after the day on which two certified copies of the boundary change order in final form are filed on the same date with the secretary of state and with the director of the legislative service commission unless a referendum petition is filed pursuant to section 3375.03 of the Revised Code.

(H) Certify its actions relating to boundaries authorized in this section, to boards of election, taxing authorities, the boards of trustees of libraries affected and other appropriate bodies;

(I) Encourage and assist the efforts of libraries and local governments to develop mutual and cooperative solutions to library service problems;

(J) Recommend to the governor and to the general assembly such changes in the law as will strengthen and improve library services and operations;

(K) In accordance with Chapter 119. of the Revised Code, adopt such rules as are necessary for the carrying out of any function imposed on it by law, and provide such rules as are necessary for its government and the government of its employees. The board may delegate to the state librarian the management and administration of any function imposed on it by law.

*HISTORY: 138 v H 847 (Eff 8-22-80); 139 v H 694. Eff 11-15-81.

§ 3375.02   State librarian.

The state library board shall appoint a state librarian, who shall be the secretary of said board, and under the direction and supervision of the board shall be the executive officer of the state library, with power to appoint and remove the employees thereof. The state librarian shall:

(A) Administer the state library and execute the policies of the board in accordance with law;

(B) Provide technical assistance and maintain a clearing house of information, data, and other materials in the field of library service, furnishing advice and assistance to the public libraries in the various subdivisions of the state, other libraries, state, local and regional agencies, planning groups and other appropriate agencies and organizations;

(C) Collect, compile, and publish statistics and information concerning the operation of libraries in the state;

(D) Carry out continuing studies and analyses of library problems;

(E) Assist and cooperate with other state agencies and officials, with organizations, with local governments and with federal agencies in carrying out programs involving library service;

(F) Maintain a comprehensive collection of official documents and publications of this state and a library collection and reference service to meet the reference and information needs of officers, departments, agencies of state government, and other libraries;

(G) Issue official lists of publications of the state, and other bibliographical and informational publications as appropriate;

(H) Withdraw books and materials from the collection and determine method of disposition of any items no longer needed.

The state librarian shall hold office during the pleasure of the board.

HISTORY: GC § 154-52; 109 v 105 (123); 120 v 475 (488); 122 v 166; 123 v 862 (906), § 3; 133 v S 262. Eff 11-25-69.

§ 3375.03   [Referendum against transfer of territory to another library district.]

Unless the transfer of certain library territory pursuant to division (G) of section 3375.01 of the Revised Code has been agreed to by the affected boards of library trustees, a referendum petition against the transfer of the territory to another library district, signed by qualified electors of the territory to be transferred and equal in number to at least ten per cent of such electors who voted in the last gubernatorial election may be filed with the library board of the territory's current library district within sixty days after certified copies of the boundary change order have been filed in final form with the secretary of state, and the order shall not become effective until after the outcome of the referendum procedure prescribed in this section.

Each part of a petition filed pursuant to this section shall contain a full and correct title of the petition, a brief summary of its purpose, and a statement by the person soliciting signatures for the petition, made under penalty of election falsification, certifying that, to the best of his knowledge and belief, each signature contained in the petition is that of the person whose name it purports to be, that each such person is an elector residing in the territory subject to transfer entitled to sign the petition, and that each such person signed the petition with knowledge of its contents. The petition may contain additional information that shall fairly and accurately present the question to prospective petition signers.

The form of a petition calling for a referendum and the statement of the circulator shall be substantially as follows:

"PETITION FOR REFERENDUM ON LIBRARY DISTRICT TRANSFER

A petition against the transfer of territory currently located in the .... library district and proposed for transfer by the state library board to the .... library district.

We, the undersigned, being electors residing in the area proposed to be transferred, equal in number to not less than ten per cent of the qualified electors in the area subject to transfer who voted at the last general election request the .... library board to submit the question of the transfer

of territory to the .... library district to the electors residing within the territory proposed to be transferred for approval or rejection at the next primary or general election.

Signature	Street Address or R.F.D.	Precinct	Date of Signing

....

....

STATEMENT OF CIRCULATOR

.... (name of circulator) .... declares under penalty of election falsification that he is an elector of the state of Ohio and resides at the address appearing below his signature hereto; that he is the circulator of the foregoing part petition containing ..... (number) .... signatures; that he witnessed the affixing of every signature; that all signers were to the best of his knowledge and belief qualified to sign; that every signature is to the best of his knowledge and belief the signature of the person whose signature it purports to be; and that such person signed the petition with knowledge of its contents.

....
(Signature of circulator)

....
(Address)

....
(City or village and zip code)

THE PENALTY FOR ELECTION FALSIFICATION IS IMPRISONMENT FOR NOT MORE THAN SIX MONTHS, A FINE OF NOT MORE THAN ONE THOUSAND DOLLARS, or BOTH."

The person presenting a referendum petition under this section shall be given a receipt containing the time of day and the date on which the petition is filed with the library board and noting the purpose of and the number of signatures on the petition. The secretary of the library board shall cause the board of elections of the county or counties in which the territory to be transferred is located to check the sufficiency of signatures on such petition, and if these are found to be sufficient, he shall present the petition to the library board at a meeting of the board, which shall occur not later than thirty days following the filing of the petition with the board. The board shall promptly certify the question to the board of elections of the county or counties in which the territory to be transferred is located for the purpose of having the proposal placed on the ballot within such territory at the next general or primary election occurring not less than sixty days after the certification.

The form of the ballot to be used at the election on the question of the transfer shall be as follows:

"Shall the territory .... (here insert its boundaries) which is currently within the .... (here insert the name of the current library district) library district be transferred to the

.... (here insert the name of the library district to which the territory is proposed to be transferred) library district?

.... for the transfer

.... against the transfer"

The persons qualified to vote on the question are the electors residing in the territory proposed to be transferred. The costs of an election held under this section shall be paid by the board of library trustees of the current library district of the territory to be transferred. The board of elections shall certify the result of the election to the state library board and to the library boards of the affected library district.

If a majority of electors voting on the question vote in favor of the transfer, the transfer shall take effect on the date of the certification of the election to the state library board. If a majority of the voters voting on the question do not vote for the transfer, the transfer shall not take place.

HISTORY: 138 v H 847. Eff 8-22-80.

§ **3375.04** Control and management of state library. (GC § 154-53)

The state library shall be under the control and management of the state library board. The board shall make and publish such rules and regulations for the operation and management of the library and for the use and location of the books and other property thereof as it deems necessary. The board may establish such divisions and departments within the library as it deems necessary, and shall determine the number of the employees therein.

HISTORY: GC § 154-53; 109 v 105 (125); 118 v 617; 122 v 166 (167); 123 v 862 (906), § 3. Eff 10-1-53.

§ **3375.05** Application for establishment of library stations, branches, or traveling library service. (GC § 154-53a)

The board of trustees of any public library receiving local tax support which desires to render public library service by means of branches, library stations, or traveling library service to the inhabitants of any school district, other than a school district situated within the territorial boundaries of the subdivision or district over which said board has jurisdiction of free public library service, may make application to the state library board, upon forms provided by said board, for the establishment of such service. Said application shall set forth the total number of people being served by said library on the date of said application; an inventory of the books owned by said library; the number of branches, library stations, and traveling library service maintained by said library on the date of said application; the number and classification of the employees of said library and such other information as the state library board deems pertinent. Such application shall be accompanied by a financial statement of the library making the application covering the two fiscal years next preceding the date of said application. Upon receipt of said application by the state library board, the state librarian, or an employee of the state library board designated by such librarian, shall visit the library making the application for the purpose of determining whether or not the establishment of branches, library stations, or traveling library service as requested in said application will promote better library service in the district covered by said application.

Upon the completion of such inspection, the librarian, or the person designated by the librarian to make such inspection, shall prepare a written report setting forth his recommendations pertaining to the establishment of the branches, stations, or traveling library service as set forth in the application. Such report shall be submitted to the state library board within ninety days after the receipt of such application by the state library board. Within thirty days after such report has been filed with the state library board, said board shall either approve or disapprove, in whole or in part, the establishment of branches, library stations, or traveling library service as requested in said application. The decision of the state library board shall be final. Within ten days after final action has been taken by the state library board, upon such application, the librarian shall notify in writing the board of trustees of the public library making such application of the decision of the state library board.

The state library board may withdraw its approval of library service rendered by any library to the inhabitants of a school district other than the school district in which the main library of such library is located. At least thirty days before the approval of such service may be withdrawn, the state library board shall give written notice to the board of trustees of the library rendering the service and the board of education of the school district to which such service is being rendered. Such notice shall set forth the reasons for the withdrawal of the approval of such service. If the board of trustees of the library rendering such service, or the board of education of a school district to which such service is being rendered, objects to the withdrawal of such approval it may, within twenty days of the receipt of such notice, request, in writing, the state library board to hold a hearing for the purpose of hearing protests to the withdrawal of such approval. Upon the receipt of such request, the state library board shall set the time and place of such hearing which shall be held within the territorial boundaries of the school district being served by the branch, station, or traveling library service whose continued operation is in question. Such hearing shall be held not less than thirty days after the receipt by the state library board of the request for such hearing. The state library board shall take no action on the withdrawal of approval of such service until after the holding of such hearing. The decision of the state library board shall be final.

HISTORY: GC § 154-53a; 122 v ¹⁶⁶ (167), § 1. Eff 10-1-53.

DISTRIBUTION OF PUBLIC DOCUMENTS
(Page's Ohio Revised Code, 1982, s.149.091, 149.1.)

[§ 149.09.1] § 149.091 Publication and distribution of session laws.

The secretary of state shall publish and distribute a maximum of nine hundred copies of the session laws in permanently bound form, either annually or biennially. The permanently bound volumes shall contain copies of all enrolled acts and joint resolutions, except appropriation laws, and shall contain a subject index and a table indicating Revised Code sections affected. The secretary of state shall cause to be printed in each volume his certificate that the laws, as assembled therein, are true copies of the original enrolled bills in his office.

The secretary of state shall distribute the permanently bound volumes of the session laws in the following manner:

(A) One hundred nine copies shall be forwarded to the legislative clerk of the house of representatives.

(B) Forty-three copies shall be forwarded to the clerk of the senate.

(C) One copy shall be forwarded to each county auditor.

(D) One copy shall be forwarded to each county law library.

(E) Seventy-five copies shall be forwarded to the Ohio supreme court.

(F) Two copies shall be forwarded to the division of the library of congress.

(G) Two copies shall be forwarded to the state library.

(H) Two copies shall be forwarded to the Ohio historical society.

(I) Thirteen copies shall be forwarded to the legislative service commission.

(J) Two hundred copies may be distributed, free of charge, to public officials.

(K) Remaining copies may be sold by the secretary of state at a price to be determined by the department of administrative services, but such selling price shall not exceed by ten per cent the cost of publication and distribution.

*HISTORY: 139 v H 694. Eff 11-15-81.

§ 149.11 Distribution of publications intended for general public use; schedules of record retention or destruction.

Any person or company, awarded a contract to print a report, pamphlet, document, or other publication intended for general public use and distribution for a department, division, bureau, board, or commission of the state government, shall print one hundred and fifty copies of such publication for delivery to the state library, subject to provisions of section 125.42 of the Revised Code.

Any department, division, bureau, board, or commission of the state government issuing a report, pamphlet, document, or other publication intended for general public use and distribution, which publication is reproduced by duplicating processes such as mimeograph, multigraph, planograph, rotaprint, or multilith, shall cause to be delivered to the state library one hundred fifty copies of such publication, subject to the provisions of section 125.42 of the Revised Code.

The state library board shall distribute the publications so received as follows:

(A) Retain two copies in the state library;

(B) Send two copies to the document division of the library of congress;

(C) Send one copy to the Ohio historical society and to each public or college library in the state designated by the state library board to be a depository for state publications. In designating which libraries shall be depositories, the board shall select those libraries which can best preserve such publications and which are so located geographically as will make the publications conveniently accessible to residents in all areas of the state;

(D) Send one copy to each state in exchange for like publications of such state.

All copies undistributed ninety days after receipt by the state library shall be returned to the issuing agency.

The provisions of this section shall not apply to any publication of the general assembly or to the publications described in sections 149.07, 149.08, 149.09, and 149.17 of the Revised Code, except that the secretary of state shall forward to the document division of the library of congress two copies of all journals, seven copies of laws in bound form as provided for in section 149.09 of the Revised Code, and seven copies of all appropriation laws in separate form.

HISTORY: GC § 2279-1; 113 v 298; 127 v 417, § 1. Eff 9-17-57.

§ 149.12 [Distribution of legislative publications to libraries.]

The state library board shall forward, free of charge, one copy of each legislative bulletin, daily house and senate journal, and summary of enactments published by the legislative service commission, to the following libraries:

(A) Each library within the state that has been designated by the state library board under section 149.11 of the Revised Code as a depository for state publications;

(B) In each county containing no library described in division (A) of this section, to a public library designated by the state library board to receive the journals, bulletins, and summaries described in this section. The state library board shall designate libraries that can best preserve the publications and are so located geographically that they can make the publications conveniently accessible to the residents of the county.

The state library board shall forward the daily house and senate journals once every week while the general assembly is in session and the legislative bulletin and summary of enactments as they are published.

Each library receiving publications under this section or under section 149.09 of the Revised Code shall make these publications accessible to the public.

HISTORY: 137 v S 205. Eff 3-15-79.

STATE RECORDS COMMISSION
(Page's Ohio Revised Code, 1982, s.149.31-149.44.)

§ 149.31 Archives administration.

(A) The Ohio historical society, in addition to its other functions, shall be the archives administration for the state and its political subdivisions.

It shall be the function of the archives administration to preserve archives, documents, and records of historical value which may come into its possession from public or private sources.

The archives administration shall evaluate, preserve, arrange, service, repair, or make other disposition, such as transfer to public libraries, county historical societies, state universities, or other public or quasi-public institutions, agencies, or corporations, of those public records of the state and its political subdivisions which may come into its possession under the provisions of this section. Such public records shall be transferred by written agreement only, and only to public or quasi-public institutions, agencies, or corporations capable of meeting accepted archival standards for housing and use.

The archives administration shall be headed by a trained archivist designated by the Ohio historical society, and shall make its services available to county, city, township, and school district records commissions upon request.

(B) The archives administration of the Ohio historical society may purchase or procure for itself, or authorize the board of trustees of an archival institution to purchase or procure from an insurance company licensed to do business in this state policies of insurance insuring the administration or the members of the board and their officers, employees, and agents against liability on account of damage or injury to persons and property resulting from any act or omission of the board members, officers, employees, and agents in their official capacity.

*HISTORY: 137 v H 403 (Eff 7-4-78); 138 v H 466. Eff 8-8-80.

§ 149.32 State records commission.

There is hereby created a "state records com- mission," to be composed of the superintendent of public instruction, the auditor of state, the attorney general, the secretary of state, the director of administrative services, and the director of the Ohio historical society, or their designated representatives. The archivist of the Ohio historical society shall be the secretary of the commission and shall advise the commission on the archival value of state records. The commission shall elect a chairman from its members and prescribe procedures for the compiling and submitting to the state records administrator of lists and schedules of records proposed for retention and disposal, procedures for the disposal of records authorized for disposal, and standards for the reproduction of records by photographic or microphotographic processes with a view to the disposal of the original records.

The functions of said commission shall be to review all applications for records disposal or transfer and all schedules of records retention and destruction as submitted by the state records administrator. The decision of the commission to approve, reject, or modify the applications or schedules shall be based upon the continuing administrative, legal, fiscal, or historical value of the records to the state or to its citizens.

The Ohio historical society shall be given a period of thirty days after the date of such review and before such records are otherwise disposed of to select for its custody such records as it may deem to be of continuing historical value. Records not so selected shall be disposed of in accordance with the procedures established by the state records commission.

The commission may revise, alter, approve, or reject any schedule and application or portion thereof and may designate transfer and disposal dates and methods of disposal of records when such are not specifically provided for by law. No records shall be retained, destroyed, or otherwise transferred in violation of any records schedule or application approved as provided in this section.

The commission shall make an annual report to the governor as prescribed by section 149.01 of the Revised Code.

HISTORY: GC § 1465-115; 121 v 268, § 2; 123 v 862 (932), § 3; 128 v 1021 (Eff 10-19-59); 131 v 173 (Eff 11-1-65); 135 v S 174. Eff 12-4-73.

§ 149.33   State records administrator.

The director of administrative services or his appointed representative is hereby designated the "state records administrator" and shall establish and administer a records management program as approved by the state records commission which will apply efficient and economical management methods to the creation, utilization, maintenance, retention, preservation, and disposition of state records.

HISTORY: 131 v 174 (Eff 11-1-65); 135 v S 174. Eff 12-4-73.

[§ 149.33.1] § 149.331 Duties of state records administrator.

The state records administrator shall, with due regard for the functions of the departments, offices, and institutions concerned:

(A) Establish and promulgate in consultation with the state archivist standards, procedures, and techniques for the effective management of state records;

(B) Make continuing surveys of record-keeping operations and recommend improvements in current records management practices including the use of space, equipment, and supplies employed in creating, maintaining, storing, and servicing records;

(C) Establish and operate such state records centers as may be authorized by appropriation and provide such related services as are deemed necessary for the preservation, screening, storage, and servicing of state records pending disposition;

(D) Submit to the state records commission applications for records disposal and schedules of record retention and destruction initiated by the said administrator or by any department, office, and institution;

(E) Submit to the state records commission at such times as deemed expedient, schedules designated "general schedules" proposing the disposal, after the lapse of specified periods of time, of records of specified form or character common to several or all agencies that either have accumulated or may accumulate in such agencies and that apparently will not, after the lapse of the periods specified, have sufficient administrative, legal, fiscal, or other value to warrant their further preservation by the state;

(F) Establish and maintain a records management training program for personnel involved in record-making and record-keeping functions of departments, offices, and institutions;

(G) Obtain reports from departments, offices, and institutions necessary for the effective administration of the program;

(H) Provide for the disposition of any remaining records of any state agency, board, or commission, whether in the executive, judicial, or legislative branch of government, that has terminated its operations.

HISTORY: 137 v H 844. Eff 8-16-78.

[§ 149.33.2] § 149.332   Records management programs in the legislative and judicial branches.

Upon request the state records administrator and state archivist shall assist and advise in the establishment of records management programs in the legislative and judicial branches of state government and shall, as required by them, provide program services similar to those available to the executive branch pursuant to section 149.33 of the Revised Code.

HISTORY: 131 v 175. Eff 11-1-65.

§ 149.34   Records management procedures for all state agencies.

The head of each department, office, institution, board, commission, or other state agency shall:

(A) Establish, maintain, and direct an active continuing program for the effective management of the records of the agency;

(B) Cooperate with the state records administrator in the conduct of surveys pursuant to section 149.331 [149.33.1] of the Revised Code;

(C) Submit to the state records administrator, in accordance with the standards and procedures established by him, schedules proposing the length of time each record series warrants retention for administrative, legal, or fiscal purposes after it has been received or created by the agency. The head of each agency also shall submit to the state records administrator applications for disposal of records in his custody that are not needed in the transaction of current business and are not otherwise scheduled for retention or destruction.

(D) Transfer to a state records center, in the manner prescribed by the state records commission and the state records administrator, those records of the agency that can be retained more efficiently and economically in such a center.

HISTORY: Bureau of Code Revision (Eff 10-1-53); 127 v 417 (418), § 1; 128 v 1021 (1022), § 1 (Eff 10-19-59); 131 v 175. Eff 11-1-65.

§ 149.35   Laws prohibiting destruction of records. (GC § 1465-117)

If any law prohibits the destruction of records, the state records commission shall not order their destruction or other disposition, and, if any law provides that records shall be kept for a specified period of time, the commission shall not order their destruction or other disposition prior to the expiration of such period.

HISTORY: GC § 1465-117; 121 v 268 (269), § 4. Eff 10-1-53.

[§ 149.35.1] § 149.351   Prohibition against destruction or damage of records.

All records as defined in section 149.40 of the Revised Code and required by section 121.21 of the Revised Code are the property of the agency concerned and shall not be removed, destroyed, mutilated, transferred, or otherwise damaged or disposed of, in whole or in part, except as provided by law or under the rules and regulations adopted by the state records commission provided for under sections 149.32 to 149.42, inclusive, of the Revised Code. Such records shall be delivered by outgoing officials and employees to their successors and shall not be otherwise removed, transferred, or destroyed unlawfully.

HISTORY: 131 v 175. Eff 11-1-65.

[§ 149.35.2] § 149.352 Replevin of public records unlawfully removed.

The attorney general may replevin any public records which have been unlawfully transferred or removed in violation of sections 149.31 to 149.44, inclusive, of the Revised Code or otherwise transferred or removed unlawfully. Such records shall be returned to the office of origin and safeguards shall be established to prevent further recurrence of unlawful transfer or removal.

HISTORY: 131 v 176. Eff 11-1-65.

§ 149.36 Authority not restricted.

The provisions of sections 149.31 to 149.42, inclusive, of the Revised Code shall not impair or restrict the authority given by other statutes over the creation of records, systems, forms, procedures, or the control over purchases of equipment by public offices.

HISTORY: GC § 1465-118; 121 v 268 (270), § 5; 128 v 1021 (1022), § 1. Eff 10-19-59.

§ 149.37 Permission to destroy records that have been copied.

The state records commission may order the destruction or other disposition, at any time, of any state record, document, plat, court file, paper, or instrument in writing that has been copied or reproduced in the manner and under the procedure prescribed in section 9.01 of the Revised Code. Before such order may be given by the commission and before such destruction or disposition of copied or reproduced records, the officer or person in charge, or the majority where there are more than one, of any office, court, commission, board, institution, department, or agency of the state shall request in the manner and form prescribed by the state records commission, that such permission be granted.

HISTORY: GC § 1465-119; 124 v 485 (486), § 1; 131 v 176. Eff 11-1-65.

§ 149.38 County records commission.

There is hereby created in each county a county records commission, composed of the president of the board of county commissioners as chairman, the prosecuting attorney, the auditor, the recorder, and the clerk of the court of common pleas. The commission shall appoint a secretary who may or may not be a member of the commission and who shall serve at the pleasure of the commission. The commission may employ an archivist to serve under its direction. The commission shall meet at least once every six months, and upon call of the chairman.

The functions of the commission shall be to provide rules for retention and disposal of records of the county and to review records disposal lists submitted by county offices. The disposal lists shall contain those records which have been microfilmed or no longer have administrative, legal, or fiscal value to the county or to the citizens thereof. Such records may be disposed of by the commission pursuant to the procedure outlined in this section.

When county records have been approved for disposal, a copy of such records list shall be sent to the bureau of inspection and supervision of public offices of the auditor of state. If the bureau disapproves the action by the county commission in whole or in part it shall so inform the commission within a period of sixty days and these records shall not be destroyed. Before public records are otherwise disposed of, the Ohio historical society shall be informed and given the opportunity for a period of sixty days to select for its custody or disposal such records as it considers to be of continuing historical value.

*HISTORY: 138 v H 466. Eff 8-8-80.

§ 149.39 City records commission.

There is hereby created in each municipal corporation a records commission composed of the chief executive or his appointed representative, as chairman, and the chief fiscal officer, the chief legal officer, and a citizen appointed by the chief executive. The commission shall appoint a secretary, who may or may not be a member of the commission and who shall serve at the pleasure of the commission. The commission may employ an archivist to serve under its direction. The commission shall meet at least once every six months, and upon call of the chairman.

The functions of the commission shall be to provide rules for retention and disposal of records of the municipal corporation and to review records disposal lists submitted by municipal offices. The disposal lists shall contain those records which have been microfilmed or no longer have administrative, legal, or fiscal value to the municipal corporation or to its citizens. Such records may be disposed of by the commission pursuant to the procedure outlined in this section.

When municipal records have been approved for disposal, a list of such records shall be sent to the bureau of inspection and supervision of public offices of the auditor of state. If the bureau disapproves of the action by the municipal commission, in whole or in part, it shall so inform the commission within a period of sixty days and these records shall not be destroyed. Before public records are otherwise disposed of, the Ohio historical society shall be informed and given the opportunity for a period of sixty days to select for its custody or disposal such public records as it considers to be of continuing historical value.

*HISTORY: 138 v H 466. Eff 8-8-80.

§ 149.40 Records and archives defined.

Any document, device, or item, regardless of physical form or characteristic, created or received by or coming under the jurisdiction of any public office of the state or its political subdivisions which serves to document the organization, functions, policies, decisions, procedures, operations, or other activities of the office, is a record within the meaning of sections 149.31 to 149.44, inclusive, of the Revised Code.

Any public record which is transferred to an archival institution pursuant to sections 149.31 to 149.44, inclusive, of the Revised Code because of the historical information contained therein shall be deemed to be an archive within the meaning of these sections.

HISTORY: GC § 154-59; 112 v 108; 128 v 1021 (1024), § 1 (Eff 10-19-59); 131 v 176. Eff 11-1-65.

§ 149.41 [School district records commission.]

There is hereby created in each county, city, and

exempted village school district a school district records commission, to be composed of the president, the treasurer of the board of education, and the superintendent of schools in each such district. The commission shall meet at least once every twelve months.

The function of the commission shall be to review records disposal lists submitted by any employee of the school district. The disposal lists shall contain those records which have been microfilmed or no longer have administrative, legal, or fiscal value to the school district or to the citizens thereof. Such records may be disposed of by the commission pursuant to the procedure outlined in this section.

When school district records have been approved for disposal, a list of such records shall be sent to the bureau of inspection and supervision of public offices of the auditor of state. If the bureau disapproves the action by the school district records commission, in whole or in part, it shall so inform the commission within a period of sixty days and these records shall not be destroyed. Before public records are otherwise disposed of, the Ohio historical society shall be informed and given the opportunity for a period of sixty days to select for its custody or disposal such public records as it considers to be of continuing historical value. The society may not review or select for its custody either of the following:

(A) Records containing personally identifiable information concerning any pupil attending a public school other than directory information, as defined in section 3319.321 [3319.32.1] of the Revised Code, without the written consent of the parent, guardian, or custodian of each such pupil who is less than eighteen years of age, or without the written consent of each such pupil who is eighteen years of age or older;

(B) Records the release of which would, according to the "Family Educational Rights and Privacy Act of 1974," 88 Stat. 571, 20 U.S.C. 1232g, disqualify a school or other educational institution from receiving federal funds.

HISTORY: 138 v H 1 (Eff 5-16-79); 138 v H 466. Eff 8-8-80.

§ 149.42 Township records commission.

There is hereby created in each township a township records commission, to be composed of the chairman of the board of township trustees, the clerk of the township, and the auditor of the county wherein the township is situated. The commission shall meet at least once every twelve months, and upon call of the chairman.

The function of the commission shall be to review records disposal lists submitted by township offices. The disposal lists shall contain those records which have been microfilmed or no longer have administrative, legal, or fiscal value to the township or to the citizens thereof. Such records may be disposed of by the commission pursuant to the procedure outlined in this section.

When township records have been approved for disposal, a list of such records shall be sent to the bureau of inspection and supervision of public offices of the auditor of state. If the bureau disapproves the action by the township records commission, in whole or in part, it shall so inform the commission within a period of sixty days and these records shall not be destroyed. Before public records are otherwise disposed of, the Ohio historical society shall be informed and given the opportunity for a period of sixty days to select for its custody or disposal such public records as it considers to be of continuing historical value.

HISTORY: 138 v H 466. Eff 8-8-80.

§ 149.43 Availability of public records.

(A) As used in this section:

(1) "Public record" means any record that is required to be kept by any governmental unit, including, but not limited to, state, county, city, village, township, and school district units, except medical records, records pertaining to adoption, probation, and parole proceedings, trial preparation records, confidential law enforcement investigatory records, and records the release of which is prohibited by state or federal law.

(2) "Confidential law enforcement investigatory record" means any record that pertains to a law enforcement matter of a criminal, quasi-criminal, civil, or administrative nature, but only to the extent that the release of the record would create a high probability of disclosure of any of the following:

(a) The identity of a suspect who has not been charged with the offense to which the record pertains, or of an information source or witness to whom confidentiality has been reasonably promised;

(b) Information provided by an information source or witness to whom confidentiality has been reasonably promised, which information would reasonably tend to disclose his identity;

(c) Specific confidential investigatory techniques or procedures or specific investigatory work product;

(d) Information that would endanger the life or physical safety of law enforcement personnel, a crime victim, a witness, or a confidential information source.

(3) "Medical record" means any document or combination of documents, except births, deaths, and the fact of admission to or discharge from a hospital, that pertains to the medical history, diagnosis, prognosis, or medical condition of a patient and that is generated and maintained in the process of medical treatment.

(4) "Trial preparation record" means any record that contains information that is specifically compiled in reasonable anticipation of, or in defense of, a civil or criminal action or proceeding, including the independent thought processes and personal trial preparation of an attorney.

(B) All public records shall be promptly prepared and made available to any member of the general public at all reasonable times for inspection. Upon request, a person responsible for public records shall make copies available at cost, within a reasonable period of time. In order to facilitate broader access to public records, governmental units shall maintain public records in such a manner that they can be made available for inspection in accordance with this division.

(C) Chapter 1347. of the Revised Code does not limit the provisions of this section.

HISTORY: 138 v S 62. Eff 1-18-80.

§ 149.44 Availability of records in centers and archival institutions.

Any state records center or archival institution established pursuant to sections 149.31 and 149.331 [149.33.1] of the Revised Code is an extension of the departments, offices, and institutions of the state and all state records transferred to records centers and archival institutions shall be available for use by the originating agencies and agencies or individuals so designated by the office of origin. The state records administrator and the state archivist shall establish regulations and procedures for the operation of state records centers and archival institutions respectively.

HISTORY: 131 v 631. Eff 11-1-65.

STATE LAW LIBRARY
(Page's Ohio Revised Code, 1982, s.2503.26-2503.28.)

§ 2503.26 Bond of law librarian. (GC § 1492)

Before entering upon the discharge of the duties of his office, the law librarian shall give bond to the state in the sum of five thousand dollars, with two or more sureties approved by the chief justice of the supreme court, conditioned for the faithful discharge of the duties of his office. Such bond with the approval of the chief justice and the oath of office indorsed thereon shall be deposited with the treasurer of state and kept in his office.

HISTORY: GC § 1492; RS § 423; S&S 250; S&C 635; 64 v 24, §§ 1, 2. Eff 10-1-53.

§ 2503.27 Duties of law librarian. (GC § 1493)

The law librarian shall make and deliver to his predecessor in office a receipt for the books and other property belonging to the law library which come into his possession. He separately shall specify in such receipt each book or set of books, and each article of property under his control, and file the receipt with the treasurer of state. Such librarian shall make further receipts for books or property purchased for or presented to such library and file them with the treasurer of state. On the death, resignation, or removal of such librarian, the books and other property of such library shall forthwith be delivered to his successor, and credit therefor entered on the receipts so filed. Such library shall be independent of the state library.

HISTORY: GC § 1493; RS § 423; S&S 250; S&C 635; 64 v 24, §§ 1, 2. Eff 10-1-53.

§ 2503.28 Librarian to have charge of law library. (GC § 1494)

The law librarian shall have charge of the law library, the rooms designated for the use of the court, with all property pertaining thereto, and perform such other services as the court directs.

HISTORY: GC § 1494; RS § 424; S&S 250; 64 v 24, §1. Eff 10-1-53.

REGIONAL LIBRARY DISTRICTS
(Page's Ohio Revised Code, 1982, s.3375.28-3375.31.)

§ 3375.28 Creation of regional library district. (GC § 7643-15)

The board of county commissioners of two or more contiguous counties may by joint resolution create a regional library district and may provide for the establishment, control, and maintenance in such district of a free public library.

Such district shall contain the territory of all school districts of such counties outside the territorial boundaries of a subdivision or district maintaining a free public library, including the territory of any such subdivision or district maintaining a free public library and petitioning to become a part of such regional library district pursuant to section 3375.29 of the Revised Code.

HISTORY: GC § 7643-15; 123 v 356 (357), § 1. Eff 10-1-53.

§ 3375.29 Resolution by taxing authority for inclusion in regional library district; transfer of title. (GC § 7643-16)

In any county comprising a part of a regional library district or in any county contiguous to such a county in which there has been created a regional library district, the taxing authority of any subdivision of the county, not included in said district and maintaining a free public library for the inhabitants thereof, may, upon request of the board of trustees of said free public library, adopt a resolution providing for the inclusion of said subdivision in the regional library district. Upon the adoption of such a resolution, the taxing authority and the board of trustees of the free public library shall take appropriate action transferring all title and interest in all property, both real and personal, in the name of said free public library to the board of library trustees of the regional library district. Upon the transfer of such title and interest in such property said subdivision shall become part of the regional library district.

HISTORY: GC § 7643-16; 123 v 356 (357), § 1. Eff 10-1-53.

§ 3375.30 Appointment, term, and compensation of board of library trustees of a regional library district. (GC § 7643-17)

In any two or more contiguous counties in which there has been created a regional library district, there shall be a board of library trustees consisting of seven members. Such trustees shall be qualified electors of the district. The first appointments to such board of library trustees shall be made by the boards of county commissioners of such counties in joint meeting. Thereafter each appointment to fill an expiring term shall be made by the board of county commissioners of a participating county in the rotating order represented by the alphabetical arrangement of the names of the counties. The term of office of said trustees shall be seven years, except that at the first appointment the terms must be such that one member retires each year. Any appointment made to fill a vacancy shall be made by the same body which appointed the trustee whose place has become vacant and shall be for his unexpired term. The members of such board of library trustees shall serve without compensation but shall be reimbursed for their actual and necessary expenses incurred in the performance of their duties. Such board of library trustees shall organize in accordance with section 3375.32 of the Revised Code. Such board of library trustees shall have the control and management of the regional district free public library and in exercise of such control and management shall be governed by sections 3375.33 to 3375.41, inclusive, and section 3375.19 of the Revised Code.

HISTORY: GC § 7643-17; 123 v 356 (357), § 1. Eff 10-1-53.

§ 3375.31 Tax levy by board of county commissioners for regional library district. (GC § 7643-18)

The board of library trustees of a regional library district may annually, during the month of May, certify to the boards of county commissioners of counties in such district the amount of revenue anticipated from all sources other than a tax levy on the taxable property of such district. The boards of county commissioners may annually levy a tax on the taxable property of such district situated within their respective counties, not to exceed one mill, for the purpose of providing funds for library operation pursuant to said certification.

HISTORY: GC § 7643-18; 123 v 356 (357), § 1. Eff 10-1-53.

COUNTY LIBRARY DISTRICTS
(Page's Ohio Revised Code, 1982, s.3375.19-3375.24, 3375.27, 3375.47.)

§ 3375.19 Creation of county library district.

In each county there may be created a county library district composed of all the local, exempted village, and city school districts in the county which are not within the territorial boundaries of an existing township, school district, municipal, county district, or county free public library, by one of the following methods:

(A) The board of county commissioners may initiate the creation of such a county library district by adopting a resolution providing for the submission of the question of creating a county library district to the electors of such proposed district. Such resolution shall define the territory to be included in such district by listing the school districts which will compose the proposed county library district.

(B) The board of county commissioners shall, upon receipt of a petition signed by no less than ten per cent, or five hundred, whichever is the lesser, of the qualified electors of the proposed county library district voting at the last general election, adopt a resolution providing for the submission of the question of creating a county library district to the electors of the proposed district. Such resolution shall define the territory to be included in such district by listing the school districts which will compose the proposed county library district.

Upon adoption of such a resolution authorized in either division (A) or (B) of this section the board of county commissioners shall cause a certified copy of it to be filed with the board of elections of the county prior to the fifteenth day of September. The board of elections shall submit the question of the creation of such county library district to the electors of the territory comprising such proposed district at the succeeding November election.

If a majority of the electors, voting on the question of creating such proposed district, vote in the affirmative such district shall be created.

HISTORY: GC § 7643-1; 109 v 351, § 1; 110 v 328; 114 v 54, § 1; 122 v 166 (178), § 1 (Eff 10-1-53); 129 v 1054, § 1. Eff 8-17-61.

§ 3375.20 Resolution by boards of library trustees requesting formation of county library district. (GC § 7643-1a)

In any county in which there is not in existence a county library district and in which all of the local, exempted village, and city school districts

in the county, in which there is not located a main library of a township, municipal, school district, association, or county free public library, are receiving approved service from one or more of such libraries, there may be created a county library district.

The boards of trustees of the library or libraries providing approved library service to the school districts in the county in which there is not located a main library of a township, municipal, school district, or county free public library may adopt a resolution requesting the formation of a county library district composed of all of the school districts being served by such library or libraries. Such resolution or resolutions shall set forth the school districts to be included in the proposed county library district and it shall be submitted to the taxing authority of the subdivision or subdivisions having jurisdiction over the library or libraries requesting the formation of such proposed library district.

Within thirty days after the receipt of such resolution by the taxing authority of a subdivision it shall either approve or disapprove the formation of the proposed county library district as set forth in said resolution. Within ten days after a taxing authority has either approved or disapproved the formation of a proposed county library district it shall notify the board of county commissioners of the county in which such proposed library is to be situated of its action.

If all of the taxing authorities to which such proposal has been submitted approve of the creation of such county library district, such district is created and the board of county commissioners shall immediately notify the boards of library trustees initiating such proposed county library district and the taxing authorities which approve the formation of such county library district that such county library district has been created.

Upon receipt of such notice from the board of county commissioners the boards of library trustees initiating such proposed county library district and the taxing authorities which approve the creation of such county library district shall take appropriate action transferring all title to the interest in all property, both real and personal, in the name of the public libraries under their jurisdiction to the board of trustees of the county library district.

For the purposes of this section the board of county commissioners is the taxing authority of an association library.

HISTORY: GC § 7643-1a; 114 v 54 (55), § 2; 115 v 210, § 1; 122 v 166 (179); 123 v 356, § 1. Eff 10-1-53.

[§ 3375.20.1] § 3375.201 Resolution for creation of county district library; submission to electors.

The taxing authority of a subdivision maintaining a free public library which is providing approved library service and whose board of library trustees therefor is qualified under section 3375.20 of the Revised Code to request the formation of a county library district shall, upon receipt of a petition signed by not less than ten per cent, or five hundred, whichever is the lesser, of the qualified electors of the subdivision voting at the last general election, adopt a resolution providing for the submission of the question, "Shall the free public library of the subdivision become a county district library?". The taxing authority shall cause a certified copy of it to be filed with the board of elections of the county prior to the fifteenth day of September. The board of elections shall submit the question of the creation of such county district library to the electors of the subdivision maintaining said free public library at the succeeding November election.

If a majority of the electors, voting on the question of creating such county district library, vote in the affirmative, the board of trustees of the library and the taxing authority of the subdivision shall establish a county library district in the manner prescribed in section 3375.20 of the Revised Code, by adopting and approving the resolutions so authorized.

HISTORY: 129 v. 1054 (1055), § 1. Eff 8-17-61.

§ 3375.21 Resolution for inclusion in county library district. (GC § 7643-1b)

In any county in which there has been created a county library district, the taxing authority of any subdivision of the county not included in said library district and maintaining a free public library for the inhabitants thereof may, upon request of the board of trustees of said free public library, adopt a resolution providing for the inclusion of said subdivision in said library district. Upon the adoption of such a resolution, the taxing authority of the subdivision and the board of trustees of the free public library shall take appropriate action transferring all title and interest in all property, both real and personal, in the name of said free public library to the board of trustees of the county library district. Upon the transfer of such title and interest in such property said subdivision shall become part of the county library district.

HISTORY: GC § 7643-1b; 122 v 166 (180), § 1. Eff 10-1-53.

[§ 3375.21.1] § 3375.211 Resolution for inclusion of subdivision; submission to electors.

The taxing authority of any subdivision maintaining a free public library for the inhabitants thereof and whose board of library trustees is qualified under section 3375.21 of the Revised Code to request inclusion of the subdivision in a county library district shall, upon receipt of a petition signed by not less than ten per cent, or five hundred, whichever is the lesser, of the qualified electors of the subdivision voting at the last general election, adopt a resolution providing for the submission of the question of the inclusion of said subdivision in such county library district

to the electors of the subdivision.

The taxing authority shall cause a certified copy of the resolution to be filed with the board of elections of the county prior to the fifteenth day of September. The board of elections shall submit the question of the inclusion of said subdivision in such county library district to the electors of the subdivision at the succeeding November election.

If a majority of the electors, voting on the question of including said subdivision in such county library district, vote in the affirmative, the taxing authority of the subdivision and the board of trustees of the free public library shall include the subdivision in the county library district in the manner prescribed in section 3375.20 of the Revised Code by adopting and approving the resolutions so authorized.

HISTORY: 129 v. 1054 (1055), § 1. Eff 8-17-61.

[§ 3375.21.2] § 3375.212 Consolidation; adoption of resolutions; submission to electors; duties of boards of library trustees.

The board of public library trustees of a county library district, appointed under section 3375.22 of the Revised Code, may consolidate with another subdivision in the county maintaining a free public library. Such consolidation may be accomplished by one of the following procedures:

(A) The board of public library trustees of the county library district may submit a resolution to the board of library trustees of such subdivision requesting such consolidation. The library trustees of the subdivision within thirty days of receipt of the resolution shall approve or reject such resolution; and, if approved shall forward the resolution together with a certification of its action to the taxing authority of said subdivision. Said taxing authority within thirty days of receipt of such resolution and certification shall approve or reject it and so notify the board of library trustees of the county district library and the board of county commissioners.

(B) Upon receipt of such resolution, under division (A) of this section the board of library trustees of the subdivision may request the taxing authority of the subdivision to adopt a resolution providing for the submission of the question of consolidation to the electors of the subdivision.

The taxing authority in turn shall adopt such a resolution and shall cause a certified copy of the resolution to be filed with the board of elections of the county prior to the fifteenth day of September. The board of elections shall submit the question to the electors of the subdivision at the succeeding November election.

(C) The board of county commissioners and the taxing authority of the subdivision, upon receipt of petitions signed by not less than ten per cent, or five hundred, whichever is the lesser, of the qualified electors in the county library district and not less than ten per cent, or five hundred, whichever is the lesser, of the qualified electors of the subdivision, voting at the last general election, shall adopt resolutions providing for the submission of the question of consolidation to the electors of the county library district and of the subdivision.

Each taxing authority in turn shall cause a certified copy of its resolution to be filed with the board of elections of the county prior to the fifteenth day of September. The board of elections shall submit the question of the consolidation of the county library district and the subdivision to the electors of the county library district and of the subdivision at the succeeding November election.

If under division (A) of this section the board of library trustees and the taxing authority of said subdivision approve the request for consolidation, or if under division (B) of this section a majority of the electors of the subdivision vote in favor of the consolidation, or if under division (C) of this section a majority of the electors of the county library district and a majority of the electors of the subdivision vote in favor of the consolidation, such consolidation shall take place. The taxing authority of the subdivision or the board of elections, whichever the case may be, shall notify the county commissioners and the respective library boards.

The board of library trustees of the county library district, the board of library trustees of the subdivision and their respective taxing authorities shall take appropriate action during the succeeding December, transferring all title and interest in all property, both real and personal, held in the names of said library boards to the board of trustees of the consolidated county library district, effective the second Monday of the succeeding January.

The board of library trustees of the county library district and the board of library trustees of the subdivision shall meet jointly on the second Monday of the succeeding January.

Acting as a board of the whole, the two boards shall become the interim board of library trustees of the consolidated county library district whose terms shall expire the second Monday of the second January succeeding the election at which the consolidation was approved. The board shall organize itself under section 3375.32 of the Revised Code and shall have the same powers, rights, and limitations in law as does a board of library trustees appointed under section 3375.22 of the Revised Code. In the event of a vacancy on the interim board the appointment shall be made by the same taxing authority which appointed the trustee whose place had become vacant and shall be only for the period in which the interim board is in existence.

At least thirty days prior to the second Monday of the second January succeeding the election at which the consolidation was approved, the board shall request the county commissioners and the judges of the court of common pleas to appoint a regular board of library trustees of seven members under the provisions of section 3375.22 of the Revised Code. The terms of said trustees shall commence on the second Monday of the January last referred to above. The control and management of such consolidated county library district shall continue to be under section 3375.22 of the Revised Code.

For the purposes of this section, whenever a county library district is consolidated with a subdivision other than a school district, the area comprising the school district in which the main library of said subdivision is located shall become a part of the county library district.

HISTORY: 129 v. 1054 (1055), § 1. Eff. 8-17-61.

[§ 3375.21.3] § 3375.213 Assets, liabilities, levies.

Whenever a county library district has been created, or enlarged, under sections 3375.20, 3375.201 [3375.20.1], 3375.21, 3375.211 [3375.-21.1], or 3375.212 [3375.21.2] of the Revised Code, all assets and liabilities of the former board of trustees of the library or libraries of the subdivisions which comprise said county library district shall become those of the county library district.

Any levies which the taxing authorities of such subdivision or of the former county library district have been authorized by the electors of the subdivision or of the former county library district to make for the payment of current expenses, interest, and retirement of bonds, or any other indebtedness of said boards of trustees shall thereafter be made upon the taxable property of all of the new or enlarged county library district and at such lesser rate as is necessary for the payment of such expenses, bonds, or indebtedness.

HISTORY: 129 v 1054 (1057), § 1. Eff 8-17-61.

§ 3375.22 Control and management of library in county library district; appointment of trustees.

In any county in which there has been created a county library district, the free public library of said district shall be under the control and management of a board of library trustees consisting of seven members. Such trustees shall be qualified electors of the library district or county. Three shall be appointed by the judges of the court of common pleas and four shall be appointed by the board of county commissioners of the county in which said district is situated. The term of office of said trustees shall be seven years, except that at the first appointment the terms of those appointed by the judges shall expire in two, four, and six years respectively, and the terms of those appointed by the board of county commissioners shall expire in one, three, five, and seven years respectively. Any appointment made to fill a vacancy shall be made by the same body which appointed the trustee whose place has become vacant and shall be for his unexpired term. The successor of any trustee of any county library district shall be appointed by the same board or officers which appointed his predecessor and all subsequent appointments shall be for seven years. The members of such board of library trustees shall serve without compensation but shall be reimbursed for their actual and necessary expenses incurred in the performance of their duties. Such board of library trustees shall organize in accordance with section 3375.32 of the Revised Code. Such board of library trustees shall have the control and management of the county district free public library and in the exercise of such control and management shall be governed by sections 3375.33 to 3375.41, inclusive, of the Revised Code.

HISTORY: GC § 7643-2; 109 v 351, § 2; 110 v 328; 114 v 54, § 3; 115 v 211; 122 v 166; 134 v H 786. Eff 6-13-72.

§ 3375.23 Tax levy by board of county commissioners for county library district. (GC § 7643-3)

The board of library trustees of a county library district may annually, during the month of May, certify to the board of county commissioners of the county in which such district is situated the amount of money required to maintain and operate the free public library during the ensuing year and the amount of revenue anticipated from all sources other than a tax levy on the taxable property of said district. The board of county commissioners may annually levy a tax on the taxable property of the district not to exceed one mill for the purpose of providing funds for library operation pursuant to said certification. The tax so levied shall be in addition to all other levies authorized by law.

HISTORY: GC § 7643-3; 109 v 351, § 3; 114 v 54 (56), § 4; 122 v 166 (181), § 1. Eff 10-1-53.

§ 3375.24 Issuance of notes and bonds; sale of real property.

The board of county commissioners of any county which has a county library district constitutes the taxing authority of such district and may issue notes and bonds of such district under sections 133.01 to 133.65, inclusive, of the Revised Code, for the acquisition of land and the construction of buildings and equipment of one or more buildings, but no notes or bonds shall be issued for such purpose except in accordance with the vote of the electors of such district. The proceeds of the sale of any former site, including land or buildings, or both, belonging to said district, may be applied to reduce the amount of the bonds ultimately issued to refund the notes issued under such section. All funds provided by the issue of county bonds or notes, or in any other manner, for the acquisition of property and the construction and equipment of library buildings shall be deposited in a special library fund, which shall be expended only on the order of the board of library trustees of the county library district, to be handled and disbursed in the same manner as other funds of the district. The title of all property so acquired shall be held by the board of library trustees of the county library district, and section 307.03 of the Revised Code shall not apply.

The title of all property acquired for use of the county library district which was held in the name of the county under former section 3375.26 of the Revised Code shall be held in the name of the board of library trustees of the county district library.

HISTORY: GC § 7643-11; 114 v 54 (58), § 8; 123 v 356 (357), § 1 (Eff 10-1-53); 129 v 1054 (1057), § 1. Eff 8-17-61.

§ 3375.27 Board of library trustees of a county library district may contract with other libraries. (GC § 7643-5)

The board of library trustees of a county library district may contract with the governing bodies of one or more libraries within the county, or within any contiguous county, and such gov-

erning bodies may enter into a contract for the free use of such libraries by the people of the county library district. If the board contracts for library service with more than one library, the county library district may be divided for such service. Such contract shall contain such provisions as shall best subserve the purpose of giving the people of the county library district the advantages of efficient library service. The board may contract to furnish library service to other county library districts, and the boards of such other county library districts may enter into such contract. The board of library trustees may contract with boards of education of school districts within its territory to provide school library service, the boards of education paying all or part of the expense thereof.

Contracts as provided in this section may be terminated by mutual agreement, or by either of the two contracting parties on giving six months' notice before the day upon which taxes upon real estate become a lien.

HISTORY: GC § 7643-5; 109 v 351 (352), § 5; 110 v 328 (330); 111 v 180. Eff 10-1-53.

§ 3375.47 Board of library examiners; term of office; duties. (CC § 7643-8)

The librarians of the two public libraries of largest circulation in the state, the state librarian, and two persons representing rural library work and chosen by the state library board constitute a state board of library examiners. The members chosen by the state library board shall serve for four years. The state board of library examiners shall examine applicants for the position of county district librarian. The members of the state board of library examiners shall receive no compensation but their necessary expenses shall be paid from the appropriation for the state library board on the warrant of that body. Such members may adopt rules and regulations for the government of the state board of library examiners and for carrying out this section. No person who has not received a certificate of qualification from the state board of library examiners shall be employed as librarian in charge of any county library district. The county librarian and his assistants shall be appointed and their salaries fixed by the board of trustees of the county library district, and shall also be allowed necessary traveling expenses incurred on the business of the library within the county, upon approval of the board of trustees of the county library district. In addition, the county librarian shall attend and take part in an annual state convention of county librarians, for which railroad expenses shall be allowed out of the county library district fund.

HISTORY: GC § 7643-8; 109 v 351 (353), § 8. Eff 10-1-53.

COUNTY LIBRARIES
(Page's Ohio Revised Code, 1982, s.3375.06-3375.08.)

§ 3375.06 County free public library; appointment of trustees. (GC § 2454-1)

In any county in which the board of county commissioners has accepted a gift or bequest, pursuant to volume 122, Ohio Laws, page 166, section 1 at "Sec. 2454," a county free public library shall be established for the use of all of

the inhabitants of the county. Such library shall be under the control and management of a board of library trustees consisting of six members. Such trustees shall be qualified electors of the county and shall be appointed by the court of common pleas of the county in which such library is situated. Not more than three of the members of such board of library trustees shall be of the same political party. They shall serve for a term of six years. All vacancies on such board of library trustees shall be filled by such court by appointment for the unexpired term. The members of such board of library trustees shall serve without compensation but shall be reimbursed for their actual and necessary expenses incurred in the performance of their official duties. The board of library trustees shall organize as provided by section 3375.32 of the Revised Code. Such board of library trustees shall have the control and management of the county free public library, and in the exercise of such control and management shall be governed by sections 3375.33 to 3375.41, inclusive, of the Revised Code. This section does not affect the term of any member of a board of library trustees of a county free public library appointed prior to September 4, 1947.

'HISTORY: GC § 2454-1; 122 v 166 (170), § 1. Eff 10-1-53.

§ 3375.07 Tax levy for maintenance of county free public library. (GC § 2454-2)

The board of county commissioners of any county in which there has been created a county free public library, pursuant to section 3375.06 of the Revised Code, may, at its June session each year, levy a tax not to exceed one mill on each dollar of taxable property in such county for the purpose of maintaining the library. The proceeds of such tax levy shall be paid over by the county treasurer to the treasurer of the board of trustees of the county free public library.

HISTORY: GC § 2454-2; 122 v 166 (171), § 1. Eff 10-1-53.

§ 3375.08 Board of county commissioners may transfer and lease property for library purposes. (GC § 2455)

The board of county commissioners may, by resolution, transfer, convey, or lease any property of the county, real or personal, suitable for public library purposes, to the board of trustees of any free public library rendering free public library service to all the inhabitants of the county, upon such terms as are agreed upon between the board of county commissioners and the board of library trustees of the library rendering such service.

HISTORY: GC § 2455; RS § 891a; 93 v 355; 98 v 194; 122 v 166 (171), § 1. Eff 10-1-53.

MUNICIPAL LIBRARIES
General Provisions
(Page's Ohio Revised Code, 1982, s.3375.12-3375.13.)

§ 3375.12 Erection, custody, and control of municipal free public libraries; appointment of trustees.

Except as provided in section 3375.13 of the Revised Code, the erection and equipment and the custody, control, and administration of free public libraries established by municipal corporations shall be vested in a board of library trustees composed of six members, not more than three of whom shall belong to the same political party. Such trustees shall be appointed by the mayor, to serve without compensation, for a term of four years. In the first instance three of such trustees shall be appointed for a term of two years, and three for a term of four years. Vacancies shall be filled by like appointment for the unexpired term. Such board shall organize in accordance with section 3375.32 of the Revised Code. In the exercise of its control and management of the municipal free public library, except as provided in section 3375.13 of the Revised Code, such board shall be governed by sections 3375.33 to 3375.41 of the Revised Code.

HISTORY: CC § 4004: RS § 1536-934; 96 v 91, § 218; 97 v 35, § 218; 107 v 612; 122 v 166; 136 v H 796. Eff 6-2-76.

[§ 3375.12.1] § 3375.121 Creation of municipal libraries.

(A) In any municipal corporation, not located in a county library district, which has a population of not less than twenty-five thousand, and within which there is not located a main library of a township, municipal, school district, association, or county free public library, a library district may be created by a resolution adopted by the legislative authority of such municipal corporation. No such resolution shall be adopted after one year from the effective date of this section. Upon the adoption of such resolution, any branches of an existing library which are located in such municipal corporation

shall become the property of the municipal library district created.

The municipal corporation and the board of trustees of the public library maintaining any existing branches in such municipal corporation shall forthwith take appropriate action transferring all title and interest in all property, both real and personal, located in such municipal corporation in the name of the library district maintaining such branches in such municipal corporation to the municipal corporation adopting the appropriate resolution. Upon transfer of such title and interest in such property they shall become a part of, and be operated by, the board of trustees appointed by the mayor.

(B) In any municipal corporation which has a population of less than twenty-five thousand and which has not less than one hundred thousand dollars available from a bequest for the establishment of a municipal library, the legislative authority of such municipal corporation may adopt, within one year after the effective date of this section, a resolution creating a library district. Upon the establishment of any such library, the board of trustees of any library operating a branch library in such municipal corporation shall not be required to transfer any property to the newly established library.

(C) The board of library trustees of any library created under this section shall be composed of six members. Such trustees shall be appointed by the mayor, to serve without compensation, for a term of four years. In the first instance three of such trustees shall be appointed for a term of two years, and three for a term of four years. Vacancies shall be filled by like appointment for the unexpired term. A library district created under this section shall be governed in accordance with and exercise such authority as provided for in sections 3375.32 to 3375.41 of the Revised Code.

(D) Any library district created under this section is eligible to participate in the proceeds of the classified property tax in accordance with section 5705.28 of the Revised Code.

HISTORY: 132 v H 494 (Eff 12-11-67); 137 v H 80. Eff 6-20-77.

§ 3375.13 Issuance of bonds; control of property vested in board of library trustees of municipal corporation; agreement with library organization. (GC § 4005-1)

In any municipal corporation where there is a library organization created by will or otherwise for the purpose of maintaining in perpetuity a public library, and such organization is endowed and owns and maintains a library, the board of library trustees mentioned in section 3375.12 of the Revised Code may request the taxing authority of the municipal corporation to submit to the electors the question of issuing bonds, in accordance with section 3375.43 of the Revised Code for the purpose of purchasing, erecting, constructing, enlarging, extending, or improving a building for library purposes, including a site therefor, and equipping and furnishing the same.

The acquisition of such improvement, including the maintenance and control of the building and property acquired, shall be vested in such board. Such board may enter into an agreement in writing with such library organization whereby said library organization may occupy all or a part of such building, and conduct, operate, and maintain therein a free public library, the period of each such agreement to be not less than ten nor more than twenty-five years. Such library organization shall administer, operate, and control such library in accordance with said agreement and in terms of the trust creating such organization, providing such library is free to all the inhabitants of the municipal corporation. Such board may enter into a similar agreement with any historical or other educational association whereby a part of said building may be used by such organization for the housing and displaying of its property and effects, providing the same is free to all the inhabitants of the municipal corporation.

HISTORY: GC § 4005-1; 107 v 612 (615); 115 v PtII 275, § 1. Eff 10-1-53. For a former analogous section, see GC § 4007.

Miscellaneous Provisions
(Page's Ohio Revised Code, 1982, s.715.13, 717.01, 719.01, 721.22, 735.27.)

§ 715.13 Public band concerts and libraries. (GC § 3620)

Any municipal corporation may establish, maintain, and regulate free public band concerts and maintain and regulate free public libraries established by the municipal corporation prior to September 4, 1947. Such municipal corporation may purchase books, papers, maps, and manuscripts for such libraries, receive donations and bequests of money or property for such libraries, in trust or otherwise, and provide for the rent and compensation for the use of any existing free public libraries established and managed by a private corporation or association organized for that purpose.

HISTORY: GC § 3620; Bates § 1536-100; 96 v 25, § 7-22; 97 v 508, § 7-22; 99 v 9, 7v; 100 v 53, § 7v; 122 v 166 (172), § 1. Eff 10-1-53. For an analogous section, see RS § 1692.

§ 717.01 Powers of municipal corporations.

Each municipal corporation may:

* * *

(K) Construct free public libraries and reading rooms, and free recreation centers;

'HISTORY: 136 v H 439. Eff 1-17-77.

§ 719.01 Appropriation of property by municipal corporations.

Any municipal corporation may appropriate, enter upon, and hold real estate within its corporate limits:

* * *

(H) For libraries, university sites, and grounds therefor;

HISTORY: GC § 3677; Bates §§ 1536-102, 1536-103; 96 v 26, § 9; 96 v 26, § 10; 97 v 333, § 10; 99 v 207, § 10; 101 v 15; 103 v 496; 111 v 47; 121 v 253 (263), § 14; 131 v 257. Eff 1-1-66.

§ 721.22 Transfer and lease of property by municipal corporation for library purposes. (GC § 3711)

A municipal corporation may, by ordinance, transfer, lease, or permit the use of any property, real or personal, suitable for library purposes, to the board of trustees of any free public library or any library association rendering free library service to the inhabitants of the municipal corporation, upon such lawful terms as are agreed upon between the municipal corporation and the trustees of such library or library association.

HISTORY: GC § 3711; Bates RS § 1536-124a; 97 v 125, § 1; 110 v 407 (408); 122 v 166 (172), § 1. Eff 10-1-53.

§ 735.27 Care, supervision, and management of public institutions in villages. (GC § 4356)

The legislative authority of a village shall provide by resolution or ordinance for the care, supervision, and management of all public parks, baths, libraries, market houses, crematories, sewage disposal plants, houses of refuge and correction, workhouses, infirmaries, hospitals, pesthouses, or any of such institutions owned, maintained, or established by such village. When the legislative authority determines to plat any of the streets it shall provide for the platting thereof.

HISTORY: GC § 4356; RS Bates § 1536-858; 96 v 85, § 204. Eff 10-1-53. Analogous to RS §§ 2031 et seq and 2084 et seq.

TOWNSHIP LIBRARIES
(Page's Ohio Revised Code, 1982, s.3375.09-3375.11.)

§ 3375.09 Tax levy by board of township trustees for maintenance of library. (GC § 3404)

In any township where a public library has been created by a vote of the electors thereof, prior to September 4, 1947, the board of township trustees may, annually, levy upon all the taxable property of such township a tax not exceeding one mill on the dollar valuation thereof to maintain such library and to procure suitable rooms therefor.

HISTORY: GC § 3404; RS § 1476; 70 v 244; 95 v 506; 97 v 26, 189; 122 v 166. Eff 10-1-53.

§ 3375.10 Control and management of township library; appointment of trustees. (GC § 3405)

In any township in which there has been established by a vote of the electors of such township, prior to September 4, 1947, a free public library, such library shall be under the control and management of a board of trustees consisting of three members to be appointed by the board of township trustees. Such members shall be qualified electors of the township. All vacancies on such board of trustees shall be filled by the board of township trustees by appointment. The members of such board of trustees shall serve without compensation. Such board of trustees shall organize in accordance with section 3375.32 of the Revised Code and shall have the control

and management of the township free public library. In the exercise of such control and management the board of trustees shall be governed by sections 3375.33 to 3375.41, inclusive, of the Revised Code. This section does not affect the term of any member of a board of library trustees of a township free public library appointed prior to September 4, 1947.

HISTORY: GC § 3405; RS § 1477; 70 v 244, § 2; 122 v 166. Eff 10-1-53.

§ 3375.11 Board of township trustees may transfer, convey, or lease property for library purposes. (GC § 3405-1)

The board of township trustees may, by resolution, transfer, convey, or lease any property of the township, real or personal, suitable for public library purposes to the board of trustees of any free public library rendering free public library service to the inhabitants of the township, upon such terms as are agreed upon between the board of township trustees and the board of trustees of the library rendering such service.

HISTORY: GC § 3405-1; 111 v 179; 122 v 166 (172), § 1. Eff 10-1-53.

SCHOOL DISTRICT LIBRARIES
(Page's Ohio Revised Code, 1982, s.3375.15-3375.18.)

§ 3375.15 School district public library; trustees.

In any school district in which a free public library has been established, by resolution adopted by the board of education of such school district, prior to September 4, 1947, such library shall be under the control and management of a board of library trustees consisting of seven members. No one is eligible to membership on such board of library trustees who is or has been for a year previous to his appointment a member of a board of education making such appointment. A majority of such trustees shall be qualified electors of the school district, but a minority may be qualified electors of the county who reside outside the school district, and all shall be appointed by the board of education of the school district. Such trustees shall serve for a term of seven years and without compensation. All vacancies on such board of library trustees shall be filled by the board of education by appointment for the unexpired term. Such board of library trustees shall organize in accordance with section 3375.32 of the Revised Code. Such board of library trustees shall have the control and management of the school district free public library and in the exercise of such control and management shall be governed by sections 3375.33 to 3375.41, inclusive, of the Revised Code. This section does not affect the term of any member of a board of library trustees of a school district free public library appointed prior to September 4, 1947.

HISTORY: GC § 4840-1; 122 v 166; 127 v 417; 128 v 80 (Eff 9-14-59); 132 v S 103. Eff 12-1-67.

§ 3375.16 Board of education may transfer, convey, or lease property for library purposes. (GC § 4840-2)

The board of education of any school district

may, by resolution, transfer, convey, or lease any property of the school district, real or personal, suitable for public library purposes to the board of trustees of any free public library rendering free public library service to the inhabitants of the school district, upon such terms as are agreed upon between the board of education and the board of trustees of the library rendering such service.

HISTORY: GC § 48-'0-2; 122 v 166 (173), § 1. Eff 10-1-53.

§ 3375.17 Tax levy by board of education for library purposes. (GC §§ 4840-3, 4840-4)

The board of library trustees of a school district free public library may annually, during the month of May, certify to the board of education of the school district the amount of money required to maintain and operate said library during the ensuing year and the amount of revenue anticipated from all sources other than a tax levy on the taxable property of said school district. The board of education may annually levy a tax on the taxable property of the school district, not to exceed one and one-half mills, for the purposes of providing funds for library operation pursuant to said certification. The tax so levied shall be in addition to all other levies authorized by law.

The proceeds of such tax levy shall be paid by the county treasurer to the treasurer of the board of library trustees.

HISTORY: GC §§ 4840-3, 4840-4; 122 v 166 (173, 174), § 1. Eff 10-1-53.

§ 3375.18 Building and operation of libraries by boards of education.

The board of education of any city, exempted village, or local school district may purchase, erect, construct, enlarge, improve, equip, and furnish buildings, and acquire real estate and interests in real estate therefor, for the purpose of rendering free [public] library service to the inhabitants of said school district, which library facilities shall be operated by the board of library trustees of such school district if a free public library was established by the board of education of such school district prior to September 4, 1947, or otherwise may be operated, under conveyance, lease, or otherwise, by the board of trustees of any free public library, library association, or corporation upon such terms as they may agree upon, provided, that the board of education of the school district finds and determines that such operation by such board of trustees will be beneficial to the school district and the residents thereof.

HISTORY: GC § 4840-5; 122 v 166 (174); 132 v S 161, § 1. Eff 7-20-67.

BOARDS OF LIBRARY TRUSTEES

(Page's Ohio Revised Code, 1982, s.3375.32-3375.46, 3375.63.)

§ 3375.32 Meeting of boards of library trustees; organization; election of clerk; bond. (GC § 7627)

Each board of library trustees appointed pursuant to sections 3375.06, 3375.10, 3375.12, 3375.15, 3375.22 and 3375.30, of the Revised Code shall meet in January of each year and organize by selecting from its membership a president, a vice-president, and a secretary who shall serve for a term of one year. At the same meeting each board shall elect and fix the compensation of a clerk, who may be a member of the board, and who shall serve for a term of one year. The clerk, before entering upon his duties, shall execute a bond in an amount and with surety to be approved by the board, payable to the board, and conditioned for the faithful performance of the official duties required of him.

HISTORY: GC § 7627; 122 v 166 (175), § 1. Eff 10-1-53. Not analogous to former GC § 7627 [106 v 492 (495)], repealed in 112 v 364 (385), § 21.

§ 3375.33 Boards of library trustees are bodies politic and corporate. (GC § 7628)

The boards of library trustees appointed pursuant to sections 3375.06, 3375.10, 3375.12, 3375.15, 3375.22, and 3375.30 of the Revised Code are bodies politic and corporate, and as such are capable of suing and being sued, contracting, acquiring, holding, possessing, and disposing of real and personal property, and of exercising such other powers and privileges as are conferred upon them by law.

HISTORY: GC § 7628; 122 v 166 (176), § 1. Eff 10-1-53. Not analogous to former GC § 7628 [RS § 3993], repealed in 112 v 364 (385), § 21.

§ 3375.34 Name of board of library trustees.

The board of trustees of a free public library, appointed pursuant to sections 3375.06, 3375.10, 3375.12, 3375.15, 3375.22, and 3375.30 of the Revised Code, shall designate the name under which it may acquire or convey property, contract, sue or be sued, or perform any other official act. If the board does not designate a name, the library shall be known as the .... public library, with the blank being filled in with the name of the subdivision which created the library.

*HISTORY: 138 v H 847. Eff 8-22-80.

§ 3375.35 Rules of procedure; annual report. (GC § 7630-1)

Each board of library trustees appointed pursuant to sections 3375.06, 3375.10, 3375.12, 3375.15, 3375.22, and 3375.30 of the Revised Code shall, in the exercise of the powers conferred upon it, be governed by this section. For the purpose of transacting any business a quorum is a majority of the full membership of the board. The purchase of any real property requires a two-thirds vote of the full membership of the board making such purchase. All conveyances of real property shall be executed by the president and the secretary of the board making such conveyance. No moneys credited to a free public library shall be paid out except on a check signed by the clerk of the board having jurisdiction over said moneys and the president, vice-president, or secretary of said board. Each board of library trustees shall, at the end of each fiscal year, transmit on forms provided by the state library board to the state librarian and officer or board which appointed said board of library trustees a report of the activities of said board of library trustees during said year. Such report shall include a complete financial statement showing the receipts and expenditures in detail of all library funds for the entire fiscal year made by such board of library trustees. No member of a board of library trustees shall have any pecuniary interest in any contract entered into by such board.

HISTORY: GC § 7630-1; 122 v 166 (177), § 1. Eff 10-1-53. Not analogous to former GC § 7630-1 [110 v 420], repealed in 112 v 364 (385), § 21.

§ 3375.36 Treasurer of library funds; deposits of moneys; monthly statement; financial statement.

The clerk of the board of library trustees of a free public library shall be the treasurer of the library funds. All moneys received by such clerk for library purposes shall be immediately placed by him in a depository designated by the board. Such clerk shall keep an account of the funds credited to said board upon such forms as are prescribed and approved by the bureau of inspection and supervision of public offices. Such clerk shall render a statement to the board monthly showing the revenues and receipts from whatever sources derived, the disbursements and the purposes for such disbursements, and the assets and liabilities of the board. At the end of each fiscal year the clerk shall submit to the board a complete financial statement showing the receipts and expenditures in detail for the entire fiscal year. The board of library trustees of a free public library may appoint a deputy clerk, for a term of one year, and may authorize such deputy to receive and disburse library funds. Such deputy, before entering upon his duties, shall execute a bond in an amount and with surety to be approved by the board, payable to the board, and conditioned for the faithful performance of the official duties required of him.

HISTORY: GC § 7627-1; 122 v 166 (175); 132 v H 205.
Eff 10-24-67.

§ 3375.37 Statement filed with county auditor. (GC § 7627-2)

Before giving the clerk of a board of library trustees of a free public library a warrant for funds due such board, the county auditor shall require the clerk to file with him a statement showing the amount of funds on hand, available for expenditure by said board, according to the books of the clerk and the books of the depository designated by the board. Such statement shall be in such form as is prescribed by the bureau of inspection and supervision of public offices, shall indicate that the clerk's books are in exact balance with the depository accounts, and shall be certified to by the clerk and proper officer of the depository.

HISTORY: GC § 7627-2; 122 v 166 (175), § 1. Eff 10-1-53.

§ 3375.38 Compliance with duties relating to moneys credited to board of library trustees. (GC § 7627-3)

All the duties required of the county auditor, county treasurer, or other officer or person relating to the moneys to the credit of or to be credited to a board of library trustees of a free public library shall be complied with by dealing with the clerk of such board.

HISTORY: GC § 7627-3; 122 v 166 (176), § 1. Eff 10-1-53.

§ 3375.39 Accounting by clerk; count and certificate. (GC § 7627-4)

At the expiration of the term of a clerk of a board of library trustees of a free public library or before such board approves the surety of any clerk, such board shall require the clerk to produce all money, bonds, or other securities in his hands, which then must be counted by the board, or a committee of the board, or by a representative of the bureau of inspection and supervision of public offices. A certificate setting forth the exact amount of such money, bonds, or other securities and signed by the representatives making such count shall be entered upon the records of the board and shall be prima-facie evidence that the amount stated in such certificate is actually in the treasury at that date.

HISTORY: GC § 7627-4; 122 v 166 (176), § 1. Eff 10-1-53.

§ 3375.40 Powers of boards of library trustees.

Each board of library trustees appointed pursuant to sections 3375.06, 3375.10, 3375.12, 3375.15, 3375.22, and 3375.30 of the Revised Code may:

(A) Hold title to and have the custody of all real and personal property of the free public library under its jurisdiction;

(B) Expend for library purposes, and in the exercise of the power enumerated in this section, all moneys, whether derived from unclassified property taxes or otherwise, credited to the free public library under its jurisdiction and generally do all things it considers necessary for the establishment, maintenance, and improvement of the public library under its jurisdiction;

(C) Purchase or lease buildings or parts of buildings and other real property and purchase or lease automobiles and other personal property necessary for the proper maintenance and operation of the free public libraries under its jurisdiction and pay the purchase price therefor in installments or otherwise;

(D) Purchase, lease, lease with an option to purchase, or erect buildings or parts of buildings to be used as main libraries, branch libraries, or library stations pursuant to section 3375.41 of the Revised Code;

(E) Establish and maintain a main library, branches, library stations, and traveling library service within the territorial boundaries of the subdivision or district over which it has jurisdiction of public library service;

(F) Establish and maintain branches, library stations, and traveling library service in any school district, outside the territorial boundaries of the subdivision or district over which it has jurisdiction of free public library service, upon application to and approval of the state library board, pursuant to section 3375.05 of the Revised Code; provided the board of trustees of any free public library maintaining branches, stations, or traveling-book service, outside the territorial boundaries of the subdivision or district over which it has jurisdiction of public library service, on September 4, 1947, may continue to maintain and operate such branches, stations, and traveling library service without the approval of the state library board;

(G) Appoint and fix the compensation of all of the employees of the free public library under its jurisdiction; pay the reasonable cost of tuition for any of its employees who enroll in a course of study the board considers essential to the duties of the employee or to the improvement of the employee's performance; and reimburse applicants for employment for any reasonable expenses they incur by appearing for a personal interview;

(H) Make and publish rules for the proper operation and management of the free public library under its jurisdiction, including rules pertaining to the provision of library services to individuals, corporations, or institutions that are not inhabitants of the county;

(I) Establish and maintain a museum in connection with and as an adjunct to the free public library under its jurisdiction;

(J) By the adoption of a resolution accept any bequest, gift, or endowment upon the conditions connected with such bequest, gift, or endowment; provided no such bequest, gift, or endowment shall be accepted by such board if the conditions thereof remove any portion of the free public library under its jurisdiction from the control of such board or if such conditions, in any manner, limit the free use of such library or any part thereof by the residents of the counties in which such library is located;

(K) At the end of any fiscal year by a two-thirds vote of its full membership set aside any unencumbered surplus remaining in the general fund of the library under its jurisdiction for the purpose of creating or increasing a special building and repair fund;

(L) Procure and pay all or part of the cost of group life, hospitalization, surgical, major medical, disability benefit, dental care, eye care, hearing aids, or prescription drug insurance, or a combination of any of the foregoing types of insurance or coverage, whether issued by an insurance company, hospital service association, or nonprofit medical or dental care corporation duly licensed by the state, covering its employees and in the case of hospitalization, surgical, major medical, dental care, eye care, hearing aids, or prescription drug insurance, also covering the dependents and spouses of such employees, and in the case of disability benefits, also covering spouses of such employees. With respect to life insurance, coverage for any employee shall not exceed the greater of the sum of ten thousand dollars or the annual salary of the employee, exclusive of any double indemnity clause that is a part of the policy.

(M) Pay reasonable dues and expenses for library trustees in library associations.

*HISTORY: 138 v H 847. Eff 8-22-80.

[§ 3375.40.1] § 3375.401 Authority to purchase liability insurance.

Each board of library trustees appointed pursuant to sections 1713.28, 3375.06, 3375.10, 3375.12, 3375.15, and 3375.22 of the Revised Code may procure policies of insurance insuring trustees, officers, and employees of the library against liability on account of damage or injury to persons and property, including liability on account of death by wrongful act, occasioned by the operation of a motor vehicle owned or operated by said library, and on account of damages or injury to persons or property resulting from any act or omission of such person in his official capacity as a trustee, officer, or employee of the library or resulting solely out of his membership on or employment by the library board. Whenever the board deems it necessary to procure such insurance, it shall adopt a resolution setting forth the necessity thereof, together with a statement of the estimated premium cost, and upon the adoption of the resolution the board may purchase such insurance. Premium for such insurance shall be paid from the current expense fund of the library. The amount of liability insurance carried on any motor vehicle operated by said public library may be distributed among more than one insurance company.

HISTORY: 125 v 235; 128 v 598 (Eff 11-9-59); 137 v S 116. Eff 11-11-77.

[§ 3375.40.2] § 3375.402 Authority to establish museums.

A library board may contract with a corporation not for profit organized to establish a museum for the use of the general public and located within the territory served by the library, to turn over to such corporation the museum physical assets of the library under such terms and conditions as the library board may deem proper. Such board may also loan books, periodicals, and similar matter belonging to the library to such corporation for use in its museum, and such library board may include in its annual budget a sum not to exceed fifteen thousand dollars, which sum it may pay to such corporation for the maintenance of such museum.

HISTORY: 126 v 1150, § 1. Eff 10-6-55.

§ 3375.41 Procedure for bidding and letting of contracts over five thousand dollars.

When a board of library trustees appointed pursuant to sections 3375.06, 3375.10, 3375.12, 3375.15, 3375.22, and 3375.30 of the Revised Code determines to construct, demolish, alter, repair, or reconstruct a library or make any improvements or repairs, the cost of which will exceed five thousand dollars, except in cases of urgent necessity or for the security and protection of library property, it shall proceed as follows:

(A) The board shall advertise for a period of four weeks for bids in some newspaper of general circulation in the district and if there are two such papers, the board shall advertise in both of them. If no newspaper has a general circulation in the district, the board shall advertise by posting such advertisement in three public places therein. Such advertisement shall be entered in full by the clerk on the record of proceedings of the board.

(B) The sealed bids shall be filed with the clerk by twelve noon of the last day stated in the advertisement.

(C) The bids shall be opened at the next meeting of the board, shall be publicly read by the clerk, and shall be entered in full on the records of the board; provided, that the board may by resolution provide for the public opening and reading of such bids by the clerk, immediately after the time for filing such bids has expired, at the usual place of meeting of the board, and for the tabulation of such bids and a report of such tabulation to the board at its next meeting.

(D) Each bid shall contain the name of every person interested therein, and shall meet the requirements of section 153.54 of the Revised Code.

(E) When both labor and materials are embraced in the work bid for, the board may require that each be separately stated in the bid, with the price thereof, or may require that bids be submitted without such separation.

(F) None but the lowest responsible bid shall be accepted. The board may reject all the bids or accept any bid for both labor and material for such improvement or repair which is the lowest in the aggregate.

(G) The contract shall be between the board and the bidders. The board shall pay the contract price for the work in cash at the times and in the amounts as provided by sections 153.12, 153.13, and 153.14 of the Revised Code.

(H) When two or more bids are equal, in whole or in part, and are lower than any others, either may be accepted, but in no case shall the work be divided between such bidders.

(I) When there is reason to believe there is collusion or combination among the bidders, the bids of those concerned in such collusion or combination shall be rejected.

*HISTORY: 138 v S 157. Eff 8-1-80.

[§ 3375.41.1] § 3375.411 Library-operated retirement systems.

A board of library trustees of a free public library, appointed pursuant to the provisions of sections 3375.06, 3375.08, 3375.12, 3375.15 and 3375.22 of the Revised Code, which has not less than seventy-five full-time employees, and which, prior to September 16, 1943, was providing for retirement of the employees of such library with annuities, insurance, or other provisions, under authority granted by former section 7889 of the General Code, may provide such retirement, insurance, or other provisions in the same manner authorized by former section 7889 of the General Code, as follows: the library board of such library which has appropriated and paid the board's portion provided in such system or plan, may continue to appropriate and pay the board's portion provided in such system or plan out of the funds received to the credit of such board by taxation or otherwise. Each employee of such library who is to be included in a system of retirement shall contribute to the retirement fund not less than four per cent per annum of his salary from the time of his eligibility to join the retirement system to the time of his retirement. If a group insurance plan is installed by any library, not less than fifty per cent of the cost of such insurance shall be borne by the employees included in such plan.

Provided, any employee whose employment by said library began on or after September 16, 1943, may exempt himself from inclusion in such retirement system, or withdraw from such retirement system. Upon such exemption or withdrawal, such person shall become a member of the public employees retirement system in accordance with sections 145.02, 145.03 and 145.-28 of the Revised Code respectively. All employees appointed for the first time on and after January 1, 1956, shall, for retirement purposes, be eligible only for membership in the public employees retirement system as provided in section 145.01 to 145.57, inclusive, of the Revised Code.

A library board which provides for the retirement of its employees with annuities, insurance, or other provisions under the authority granted by this section may, pursuant to a board resolution adopted within thirty days after the effective date of this section, terminate such retirement plan. Upon the effective date of such termination, which is specified in the resolution, each employee covered by such retirement plan shall become a member of the public employees retirement system.

HISTORY: 126 v 943 (Eff 10-6-55); 129 v 787 (Eff 1-10-61); 134 v H 165. Eff 6-29-72.

§ 3375.42 Contract for library service; tax levy.

The board of county commissioners of any county, the board of education of any school district, the legislative authority of any municipal corporation, or the board of township trustees of any township may contract with the board of library trustees of any public library, or with any private corporation or library association maintaining a free public library prior to September 4, 1947, situated within or without the taxing district, to furnish library service to all the inhabitants of said taxing district, notwithstanding the fact that such library is receiving proceeds from the classified property taxes collected within the county, and may levy a tax, or make an appropriation from its general fund or from federal funds, to be expended by such library in providing library service in said taxing district for any of the purposes specified in section 3375.40 of the Revised Code. The taxing authority may require an annual report in writing from such board of library trustees, private corporation, or library association. When a tax for library purposes has been so levied, at each semiannual collection of such tax the county auditor shall certify the amount collected to the proper officer of the taxing district who shall forthwith draw his warrant for such amount on the treasurer of such district payable to the proper officer of such library.

HISTORY: GC § 7632; RS § 3998-1; 96 v 8; 98 v 244; 110 v 407; 122 v 166; 125 v 235 (Eff 10-2-53); 129 v 1054 (Eff 8-17-61); 136 v S 257. Eff 11-28-75.

§ 3375.43 Submission of question; issuance and sale of bonds by subdivision for library purposes.

Any public library board of trustees charged with the title, custody, control; and maintenance of a public library in the state may request the taxing authority of the political subdivision to whose jurisdiction the board is subject to submit to the electors of such subdivision the question of issuing bonds for the purpose of purchasing, erecting, constructing, enlarging, extending, or improving a building for library purposes, including a site therefor, and equipping and furnishing the same. Such request shall be made by resolution adopted by the board,[;] the resolution shall declare the necessity of the issuance of such bonds and fix their amount and purpose, and shall further recite whether or not notes shall be issued in anticipation of the issuance of such bonds. A copy of the resolution shall be certified by the board to the taxing authority of the subdivision pursuant to section 5705.23 of the Revised Code. The submission to the electors of the question of the issuance of the bonds, the issuance, sale, characteristics, and requirements for the interest and retirement levies, and the method and means for payment of the bonds or notes, if notes are to be issued in anticipation of the issuance of the bonds, shall conform to Section II of Article XII, Ohio Constitution and sections 133.01 to 133.65 of the Revised Code, governing the issuance, sale, characteristics, and levies for, and method and means of payment of, bonds or notes issued by such subdivision pursuant to a vote of the electors. Such bonds or notes shall be sold and issued by the proper officer as is provided by law for the sale and issuance of bonds of the political subdivision to whose jurisdiction the board is subject. The indebtedness created by such bonds or notes constitutes a part of the indebtedness of such subdivision and is subject to the limitations imposed on the creation of indebtedness by such subdivision. The proceeds of the sale of such bonds shall be transferred by the fiscal officer of such subdivision to the board for the benefit of which the bonds were issued and shall be appropriated to and expended only for the purposes for which issued.

*HISTORY: 138 v H 847. Eff 8-22-80.

[§ 3375.43.1] § 3375.431 Issuance of bonds by board of education for libraries.

The board of education of a city, exempted village, or local school district, which does not have a board of library trustees established under section 3375.15 of the Revised Code may issue bonds in accordance with sections 133.01 to 133.65, inclusive, of the Revised Code, without regard to section 3375.43 of the Revised Code, for the purpose of purchasing, erecting, constructing, enlarging, improving, equipping, and furnishing library facilities and acquiring real estate and interests in real estate therefor, to be operated by the board of trustees of any free public library, library association, or corporation pursuant to section 3375.18 of the Revised Code.

HISTORY: 132 v S 161, § 1. Eff 7-20-67.

§ 3375.44 Payment of interest; retirement of bonds; annual levy. (GC § 4005-3)

After the issue of any notes or bonds under section 3375.43 of the Revised Code, the public library board of trustees on behalf of which said bonds are issued shall certify, on or before the first day of July in each year, to the taxing authority of the political subdivision to the jurisdiction of which such board is subject, a sufficient amount to pay the interest on and to retire at maturity such bonds or notes, and such taxing authority shall annually include in its budget the amount certified and required to pay the interest on and to retire such bonds or notes at maturity, and shall levy the necessary tax therefor.

Such board may appropriate and apply any moneys in its possession and control, which are available and unappropriated for other purposes, to the payment of the principal of and interest on such bonds or notes. Any moneys so to be applied shall be appropriated by resolution of the library board and transferred to the board or officers having charge of the retirement fund for such bonds to be applied to the payment of such bonds and for no other purposes. The interest and retirement charges to be levied in each year shall then be reduced by such amounts of money as are otherwise made available.

HISTORY: GC § 4005-3; 115 v PtII 275 (276), § 1. Eff 10-1-53. For an analogous section, see former GC § 4013.

§ 3375.45 Control and management of sinking or bond retirement fund. (GC § 4005-4)

When bonds are issued pursuant to section 3375.43 of the Revised Code, the board or officer of the political subdivision issuing such bonds having charge of the sinking fund or bond retirement fund of such subdivision shall have the control and management of all moneys and securities for the payment of interest on and for the redemption of the principal of such bonds, and shall exercise the same powers of control and

management thereof as for the management and control of the sinking or bond retirement fund for all bonds of such subdivision.

HISTORY: GC § 4005-4; 115 v PtII 275 (277), § 1. Eff 10-1-53. For analogous sections, see former GC §§ 4014, 4018.

§ 3375.46 Bureau of municipal research and information may be established. (GC § 7635)

Any board of library trustees of a school district may enter into an agreement with any municipal corporation located in such school district for the establishment of a bureau of municipal research and information. The agreement shall provide for the rendering of such services by and under the supervision and control of such board, and upon such terms, as are agreed upon between such board and municipal corporation.

HISTORY: GC § 7635; RS § 3998-2; 96 v 8; 100 v 16; 110 v 407 (408); 115 v PtII 275 (278), § 1; 122 v 533, § 1. Eff 10-1-53. Not analogous to former GC § 7635 [115 v PtII 275 (278)], repealed in 122 v 166 (181), § 2.

§ 3375.63 Eligibility for public library trustees.

No person shall be ineligible for membership on a board of public library trustees because of his employment by a school district or other political subdivision, provided that a majority of the members of each board of public library trustees shall be persons not employed by school districts or other political subdivisions.

HISTORY: 128 v 81, § 1. Eff 9-14-59.

METROPOLITAN LIBRARY SYSTEMS
(Page's Ohio Revised Code, 1982, s.3375.90-3375.93.)

§ 3375.90 [Agreement.]

Any four or more libraries within a metropolitan area, as defined by the state library board, with a population of two hundred fifty thousand or more may form a metropolitan library system by agreement in the manner set forth in this section.

(A) The libraries forming the system shall include two or more of the following types of libraries: academic, public, special, and school, including cooperative ventures established by two or more school districts. For the purposes of this section, such libraries may be serving the general public, public or private schools, colleges or universities, or a profession, occupation, or business.

An agreement for the formation of a metropolitan library system shall first be approved by the governing bodies of the participating libraries. For the purposes of this section, the governing body of a library means the board of trustees of a public library, or the board of education of a public school or school system if the library is a public school library, or otherwise the board of trustees or directors or other recognized governing board or committee of any private school, college, university, association or union, public or private, which provides, controls, or maintains a library which is intended to be a participating library.

(B) The agreement and an application for the formation of the metropolitan library system shall be submitted to the state library board in the form and in accordance with rules prescribed by the state library board, with a plan of service describing the specific purposes for which the system is formed and the means by which such purposes are to be accomplished.

(C) Upon approval of the application by the state library board and the making by that board or some other authority or authorities of a grant or grants for the system, the metropolitan library system shall become operable.

A metropolitan library system shall be governed by a board of trustees consisting of at least seven and no more than fifteen persons, to be selected from among the representatives of the participating libraries, duly appointed as such representatives by the governing bodies of the participating libraries.

The number of trustees, the manner of selection, the terms of office and the provisions for filling vacancies shall be determined by the agreement between the governing bodies of the participating libraries, and shall be set forth in the application submitted to the state library board. Nothing pertaining to the organization and operation of a metropolitan library system shall be construed to infringe upon the autonomy of any participating library or or of the governing body of any library.

HISTORY: 136 v S 257. Eff 11-28-75.

§ 3375.91 [Powers of board of trustees.]

The board of trustees of each metropolitan library system may:

(A) Develop plans of service and operation for the metropolitan library system and submit these to the state library board; and to each other granting authority if and when required by such authority;

(B) Receive grants, payments, bequests, and gifts and have exclusive control of the expenditure of all moneys held in the name of the metropolitan library system;

(C) Expend for library purposes, and in the exercise of the powers enumerated in this section, all moneys whether received as grants, payments, gifts, bequests, or otherwise, and generally do all things it determines necessary for the establishment, maintenance, and improvement of the metropolitan library system under its jurisdiction;

(D) Make and publish such bylaws and rules as may be necessary for its operation and for the government of the metropolitan library system;

(E) Purchase or lease vehicles and other personal property for the operation of the metropolitan library system;

(F) Purchase, erect, lease, or lease with an option to purchase, appropriate buildings or parts of buildings for use of the metropolitan library system;

(G) Hold title to and have the custody of all property, both real and personal, of the metropolitan library system;

(H) Appoint and fix the compensation of a director and necessary assistants who, subject to the approval of the state library board, shall have the same employment status as employees of public libraries;

(I) Elect and fix compensation of a clerk and a deputy clerk who shall serve for a term of one year;

(J) Enter into contracts with the governing body of any participating library organized under sections 1713.28, 3375.06, 3375.10, 3375.12, 3375.121 [3375.12.1], 3375.15, 3375.22, and 3375.30 of the Revised Code, the state library board, any granting authority, the board of county commissioners of any county, the board of education of any school district, the legislative authority of any municipal corporation, boards of township trustees, colleges, universities, or public or private agencies and corporations;

(K) Accept an application from any other library desiring to become a participating library in accordance with the agreement for the formation of the system, either as originally submitted to and approved by the state library board, or as amended by and with the agreement of all the participating libraries and the approval of the state library board.

HISTORY: 136 v S 257. Eff 11-28-75.

§ 3375.92 [Duties of clerk and deputy clerk.]

The clerk of the board of trustees of the metropolitan library system is the treasurer of the organization's funds. Before entering upon their duties, the clerk and the deputy clerk shall execute a bond in an amount and with surety to be approved by the board, and conditioned for the faithful performance of the official duties required of them.

All moneys received by the clerk shall be immediately placed by him in a depository designated by the board. The clerk shall keep an account of the funds credited to the board upon such forms as are prescribed and approved by the bureau of inspection and supervision of public offices.

The clerk shall render a monthly statement to the board showing the revenues and receipts from whatever sources derived, the disbursements and the purposes for such disbursements, and the assets and liabilities of the board. At the end of each fiscal year the clerk shall submit to the board and to the state library board and, if requested, to any granting authority, a complete financial statement showing the receipts and expenditures in detail for the entire fiscal year. Such financial records shall be open to public inspection at all reasonable times.

At the expiration of the term of the clerk or before the board of trustees approves the surety of any clerk, the board shall require the clerk to produce all moneys, bonds, or other securities in his hands, which then must be counted by the board, or a committee of the board, or by a representative of the bureau of inspection and supervision of public offices. A certificate setting forth the exact amount of such money, bonds, or other securities and signed by the representatives making such count shall be entered upon the records of the board and shall be prima-facie evidence that the amount stated in such certificate is actually in the treasury at that date.

HISTORY: 136 v S 257. Eff 11-28-75.

§ 3375.93 [Plan for dissolution.]

If the need for a metropolitan library system ceases to exist, the board of trustees may, by a two-thirds vote of its members, declare its intention to dissolve the organization and file with the state library board a plan for effecting such dissolution.

The plan shall state the means by which the participating libraries may record their approval or disapproval of such intended dissolution, and shall include a plan for the distribution of the assets of the metropolitan library system. If the metropolitan library system received more than fifty per cent of its total budget for the previous three years from grant funds provided by the state library board, the state library board shall make final determination of the distribution of the assets.

A participating library may withdraw from a metropolitan library system on the first day of July in any year, providing that notice of the withdrawal intention has been given at least eighteen months prior to the date of withdrawal. Whenever a withdrawal occurs or another library joins a metropolitan library system, an amended plan shall be submitted to the state library board for approval.

HISTORY: 136 v S 257. Eff 11-28-75.

AREA LIBRARY SERVICE

(Page's Ohio Revised Code, 1982, s.3375.70-3375.73, 3375.80-3375.82.)

§ 3375.70 Area library service organization.

Public libraries in two or more counties may form an "area library service organization" in the following manner:

(A) The formation of an area library service organization shall first be approved by the board of trustees of the participating public libraries, as provided in the rules and regulations of the state library board.

(B) An application for the formation of the area library service organization shall be submitted to the state library board in the form prescribed by the state library board, with a plan of service describing the specific purposes for which the organization is formed and the means by which such purposes are to be accomplished. The state library board shall approve or disapprove this application and plan of service in accordance with rules and regulations adopted under section 3375.82 of the Revised Code.

(C) Upon approval of the application by the state library board and the making of a grant or grants for the organization, the area library service organization shall become operable.

An area library service organization shall be governed by a board of trustees consisting of at least seven and no more than fifteen persons, to be selected from among the members of the boards of trustees of the participating public libraries.

The number of trustees, the manner of selection, the term of office and the provision for filling vacancies shall be determined by the governing boards of the participating libraries, and shall be set forth in the application submitted to the state library board. Nothing pertaining to the organization and operation of an area library service organization shall be construed to infringe upon the autonomy of any public library board of trustees.

HISTORY: 133 v S 262 (Eff 11-25-69); 134 v H 475. Eff 12-20-71.

§ 3375.71 Powers of board of trustees.

The board of trustees of each area library service organization may:

(A) Develop plans of service and operation for the area library service organization and submit these to the state library board;

(B) Receive grants, payments, bequests and gifts and have exclusive control of the expenditure of all moneys held in the name of the area library service organization;

(C) Expend for library purposes, and in the exercise of the powers enumerated in this section, all moneys whether received as grants, payments, gifts, bequests, or otherwise, and generally do all things it determines necessary for the establishment, maintenance, and improvement of the area library service organization under its jurisdiction;

(D) Make and publish such bylaws, rules, and regulations as may be necessary for its operation and for the government of the area library service organization;

(E) Purchase or lease vehicles and other personal property for the operation of the area library service organization;

(F) Purchase, erect, lease, or lease with an option to purchase, appropriate buildings or parts of buildings for use of the area library service organization;

(G) Hold title to and have the custody of all property, both real and personal, of the area library service organization;

(H) Appoint and fix the compensation of a director and necessary assistants who shall have the same employment status as employees of public libraries;

(I) Elect and fix compensation of a clerk and a deputy clerk who shall serve for a term of one year;

(J) Enter into contracts with the board of library trustees of any library organized under sections 3375.06, 3375.10, 3375.12, 3375.121 [3375.12.1], 3375.15, 3375.22, 3375.30, and 1713.28, of the Revised Code, the state library board, the board of county commissioners of any county, the board of education of any school district, the legislative authority of any municipal corporation, boards of township trustees, colleges,

universities, or public or private agencies and corporations.

HISTORY: 133 v S 262. Eff 11-25-69.

§ 3375.72 Management of funds.

The clerk of the board of trustees of the area library service organization is the treasurer of the organization's funds. Before entering upon their duties, the clerk and the deputy clerk shall execute a bond in an amount and with surety to be approved by the board, and conditioned for the faithful performance of the official duties required of them.

All moneys received by the clerk shall be immediately placed by him in a depository designated by the board. The clerk shall keep an account of the funds credited to the board upon such forms as are prescribed and approved by the bureau of inspection and supervision of public offices.

The clerk shall render a monthly statement to the board showing the revenues and receipts from whatever sources derived, the disbursements and the purposes for such disbursements, and the assets and liabilities of the board. At the end of each fiscal year the clerk shall submit to the board and to the state library board a complete financial statement showing the receipts and expenditures in detail for the entire fiscal year.

At the expiration of the term of the clerk or before such board approves the surety of any clerk, such board shall require the clerk to produce all moneys, bonds, or other securities in his hands, which then must be counted by the board, or a committee of the board, or by a representative of the bureau of inspection and supervision of public offices. A certificate setting forth the exact amount of such money, bonds, or other securities and signed by the representatives making such count shall be entered upon the records of the board and shall be prima-facie evidence that the amount stated in such certificate is actually in the treasury at that date.

HISTORY: 133 v S 262. Eff 11-25-69.

§ 3375.73 Dissolution; withdrawal.

If the need for an area library service organization ceases to exist, the board of trustees may, by a two-thirds vote of its members, declare its intention to dissolve the organization and file with the state library board a plan for effecting such dissolution.

The plan shall state the means by which the participating libraries may record their approval or disapproval of such intended dissolution, and shall include a plan for the distribution of the assets of the area library service organization. If the area library service organization received more than fifty per cent of its total budget for the previous three years from grant funds provided by the state library board, the state library board shall make final determination of the distribution of the assets.

A participating library may withdraw from an area library service organization on the first day of July in any year, providing that notice of the withdrawal intention has been given at least eighteen months prior to the date of withdrawal. Whenever a withdrawal occurs or another library joins an area library service organization, an amended plan shall be sub-

mitted to the state library board for approval.
HISTORY: 133 v S 262. Eff 11-25-69.

§ 3375.80 Resource centers.

To encourage and make available adequate library reference and research facilities, the state library board may designate certain libraries as resource centers and develop and encourage cooperative steps to link these centers with other libraries in a reference and information network. Such designation shall be made subject to the approval of the governing boards of the libraries. Grants may be made to these libraries and to other libraries which share their resources and facilities on an interlibrary basis.
HISTORY: 133 v S 262. Eff 11-25-69.

§ 3375.81 Essential library services support program.

A program of grants, to be known as the essential library services support program, is hereby established within the limitation of funds appropriated by the general assembly together with other funds made available by the federal government or other sources for this purpose. They shall include:

(A) Planning grants, to be paid to a public library or area library service organization;

(B) Establishment grants, to be paid to an area library service organization;

(C) Essential services operations grants, to be paid to an area library service organization;

(D) Reference services and interlibrary loan grants to be paid to a public library, university library, or other library participating in a reference and information network or similar program of interlibrary cooperation;

(E) Special program grants, to be paid to a public library, a metropolitan library system

organized under standards adopted under section 3375.82 of the Revised Code, or to an area library service organization.
HISTORY: 133 v S 262 (Eff 11-25-69); 134 v H 475. Eff 12-20-71.

§ 3375.82 Administration of grants.

The state library board shall administer all grants and shall provide for the expenditure of all funds appropriated for the essential library services support program. All grants shall be made under rules and regulations adopted by the state library board and under the terms of written agreements between the state library board and the recipient. Such rules and regulations shall be designed to:

(A) Ensure every resident of Ohio access to essential public library services;

(B) Provide adequate library materials to satisfy the reference and research needs of the people of this state;

(C) Assure and encourage local initiative and responsibility and support for library services;

(D) Encourage the formation of viable area library service organizations and library systems providing a full range of library services;

(E) Develop adequate standards for services, resources, and programs that will serve as a source of information and inspiration to persons of all ages, handicapped persons, disadvantaged persons, and will encourage continuing education beyond the years of formal education;

(F) Encourage adequate financing of public libraries from local sources with state aid to be furnished as a supplement to other library financial resources.
HISTORY: 133 v S 262. Eff 11-25-69.

INTERSTATE LIBRARY COMPACT

(Page's Ohio Revised Code, 1982, s.3375.83-3375.85.)

§ 3375.83 [Form of compact.]

The "interstate library compact" is hereby ratified, enacted into law, and entered into by the state of Ohio with all states legally joining therein in the form substantially as follows:

INTERSTATE LIBRARY COMPACT

Article I. Policy and Purpose.

Because the desire for the services provided by libraries transcends governmental boundaries and can most effectively be satisfied by giving such services to communities and people regardless of jurisdictional lines, it is the policy of the states party to this compact to cooperate and share their responsibilities; to authorize cooperation and sharing with respect to those types of library facilities and services which can be more economically or efficiently developed and maintained on a cooperative basis; and to authorize cooperation and sharing among localities, states, and others in providing joint or cooperative library services in areas where the distribution of population or of existing and potential library resources make the provision of library service on an interstate basis the most effective way of providing adequate and efficient service.

Article II. Definitions.

As used in this compact:

(A) "Public library agency" means any unit or agency of local or state government operating or having power to operate a library.

(B) "Private library agency" means any nongovernmental entity which operates or assumes a legal obligation to operate a library.

(C) "Library agreement" means a contract establishing an interstate library district pursuant to this compact or providing for the joint or cooperative furnishing of library services.

Article III. Interstate Library Districts.

(A) Any one or more public library agencies in a party state in cooperation with any public library agency or agencies in one or more other party states may establish and maintain an interstate library district. Subject to the provisions of this compact and any other laws of the party states which pursuant hereto remain applicable, such district may establish, maintain, and operate some or all of the library facilities and services for the area concerned in accordance with the terms of a library agreement therefor. Any private library agency or agencies within an interstate library district may cooperate therewith; assume duties, responsibilities, and obligations thereto; and receive benefits therefrom as provided in any library agreement to which such agency or agencies become party.

(B) Within an interstate library district, and as provided by a library agreement, the performance of library functions may be undertaken on a joint or cooperative basis or may be undertaken by means of one or more arrangements between or among public or private library agencies for the extension of library privileges to the use of facilities or services operated or rendered by one or more of the individual library agencies.

(C) If a library agreement provides for joint establishment, maintenance, or operation of library facilities or services by an interstate library district, such district shall have power to do any one or more of the following in accordance with such library agreement:

(1) Undertake, administer, and participate in programs or arrangements for securing, lending, or servicing of books and other publications, and other materials suitable to be kept or made available by libraries, library equipment, or for the dissemination of information about libraries, the value and significance of particular items therein and the use thereof;

(2) Accept for any of its purposes under this compact any and all donations and grants of money, equipment, supplies, materials, and services (conditional or otherwise), from any state or the United States or any subdivision or agency thereof, or interstate agency; or from any institution, person, firm, or corporation; and receive, utilize, and dispose of the same;

(3) Operate mobile library units or equipment for the purpose of rendering bookmobile service within the district;

(4) Employ professional, technical, clerical, and other personnel, and fix terms of employment, compensation, and other appropriate benefits; and where desirable, provide for the in-service training of such personnel;

(5) Sue and be sued in any court of competent jurisdiction;

(6) Acquire, hold, and dispose of any real or personal property or any interest or interests therein as may be appropriate to the rendering of library service;

(7) Construct, maintain, and operate a library, including any appropriate branches thereof;

(8) Do such other things as may be incidental to or appropriate for the carrying out of any of the foregoing powers.

Article IV. Interstate Library Districts, Governing Board.

(A) An interstate library district which establishes, maintains, or operates any facilities or services in its own right shall have a governing board which shall direct the affairs of the district and act for it in all matters relating to its business. Each participating public library agency in the district shall be represented on the governing board which shall be organized and conduct its business in accordance with provision therefor in the library agreement, but in no event shall a governing board meet less often than twice a year.

(B) Any private library agency or agencies party to a library agreement establishing an interstate library district may be represented on or advise with the governing board of the district in such manner as the library agreement may provide.

Article V. State Library Agency Cooperation.

Any two or more state library agencies of two or more of the party states may undertake and conduct joint or cooperative library programs, render joint or cooperative library services, and enter into and perform arrangements for the cooperative or joint acquisition, use, housing, and disposition of items or collections of materials which, by reason of expense, rarity, specialized nature, or infrequency of demand therefor, would be appropriate for central collection and shared use. Any such programs, services, or arrangements may include provision for the exercise on a cooperative or joint basis of any power exercisable by an interstate library district and an agreement embodying any such program, service, or arrangement shall contain provisions covering the subjects detailed in Article VI of this compact for interstate library agreement.

Article VI. Library Agreements.

(A) In order to provide for any joint or cooperative undertaking pursuant to this compact, public and private library agencies may enter into library agreements. Any agreement executed pursuant to the provisions of this compact shall, as among the parties to the agreement:

(1) Detail the specific nature of the services, programs, facilities, arrangements, or properties to which it is applicable;

(2) Provide for the allocation of costs and other financial responsibilities;

(3) Specify the respective rights, duties, obligations, and liabilities of the parties;

(4) Set forth the terms and conditions for duration, renewal, termination, abrogation, disposal of joint or common property, if any, and all other matters which may be appropriate to the proper effectuation and performance of the agreement.

(B) No public or private library agency shall undertake to exercise itself, or jointly with any other library agency, by means of a library agreement, any power prohibited to such agency by the constitution or statutes of its state.

(C) No library agreement shall become effective until filed with the compact administrator of each state involved and approved in accordance with Article VII of this compact.

Article VII. Approval of Library Agreements.

(A) Every library agreement made pursuant to this compact shall, prior to and as a condition precedent to its entry into force, be submitted to the attorney general of each state in which a public library agency party thereto is situated, who shall determine whether the agreement is in proper form and compatible with the laws of his state. The attorneys general shall approve any agreement submitted to them unless they shall find that it does not meet the conditions set forth herein and shall detail, in writing, addressed to the governing bodies of the public library agencies concerned, the specific respects in which the proposed agreement fails to meet the requirements of law. Failure to disapprove an agreement submitted hereunder within ninety days of its submission shall constitute approval thereof.

(B) In the event that a library agreement made pursuant to this compact shall deal in whole or in part with the provision of services or facilities with regard to which an officer or agency of the state government has constitutional or statutory powers of control, the agreement shall, as a condition precedent to its entry into force, be submitted to the state officer or agency having such power of control and shall be approved or disapproved by him or it as to all matters within his or its jurisdiction in the same manner and subject to the same requirements governing the action of the attorneys general pursuant to division (A) of this article. This requirement of submission and approval shall be in addition to and not in substitution for the requirement of submission to and approval by the attorneys general.

Article VIII. Other Laws Applicable.

Nothing in this compact or in any library agreement shall be construed to supersede, alter, or otherwise impair any obligation imposed on any library by otherwise applicable law, nor to authorize the transfer or disposition of any property held in trust by a library agency in a manner contrary to the terms of such trust.

Article IX. Appropriations and Aid.

(A) Any public library agency part to a library agreement may appropriate funds to the interstate library district established thereby in the same manner and to the same extent as to a library wholly maintained by it and, subject to the laws of the state in which such public library agency is situated, may pledge its credit in support of an interstate library district established by the agreement.

(B) Subject to the provisions of the library agreement pursuant to which it functions and the laws of the states in which such district is situated, an interstate library district may claim and receive any state and federal aid which may be available to library agencies.

Article X. Compact Administrator.

Each state shall designate a compact administrator with whom copies of all library agreements to which his state or any public library agency thereof is party shall be filed. The administrator shall have such other powers as may be conferred upon him by the laws of his state and may consult and cooperate with the compact administrators of other party states and take such steps as may effectuate the purposes of this compact. If the laws of a party state so provide, such state may designate one or more deputy compact administrators in addition to its compact administrator. The compact administrator and other persons performing official functions in connection with this compact shall be entitled to reimbursement for their actual and necessary expenses incurred in the performance of their duties or in the conduct of authorized business, within or without the state.

Article XI. Entry Into Force and Withdrawal.

(A) This compact shall enter into force and effect immediately upon its enactment into law by any two states. Thereafter, it shall enter into force and effect as to any other state upon the enactment thereof by such state.

(B) This compact shall continue in force with respect to a party state and remain binding upon such state until six months after such state has given notice to each other party state of the repeal thereof. Such withdrawal shall not be construed to relieve any party to a library agreement entered into pur-

suant to this compact from any obligation of that agreement prior to the end of its duration as provided therein.

Article XII. Construction and Severability.

This compact shall be liberally construed so as to effectuate the purposes thereof. The provisions of this compact shall be severable and if any phrase, clause, sentence, or provision of this compact is declared to be contrary to the constitution of any party state or of the United States, or the applicability thereof to any government, agency, person, or circumstance is held invalid, the validity of the remainder of this compact and the applicability thereof to any government, agency, person, or circumstance shall not be affected thereby. If this compact shall be held contrary to the constitution of any state party thereto, the compact shall remain in full force and effect as to the remaining states and in full force and effect as to the state affected as to all severable matters.

HISTORY: 136 v S 236. Eff 1-5-76.

§ 3375.84 [Definitions.]

As used in the interstate library compact:

(A) "State library agency," with reference to this state, means the state library board as designated in section 3375.01 of the Revised Code.

(B) "Compact administrator," with reference to this state, means the state librarian as designated in section 3375.02 of the Revised Code.

HISTORY: 136 v S 236. Eff 1-5-76.

§ 3375.85 [Aid to entities partly within state.]

An interstate library district lying partly within this state may claim and be entitled to receive appropriated state aid in support of any of its functions to the same extent and in the same manner as such functions are eligible for support when carried on by entities wholly within this state. For the purposes of computing and apportioning appropriated state aid to an interstate library district, this state will consider that portion of the area which lies within this state as an independent entity for the performance of the aided function or functions and compute and apportion the aid accordingly. Any library association that was organized and operated prior to January 1, 1968, and which pursuant to the authority granted in section 3375.83 of the Revised Code, has become part of an interstate library district shall be considered a library association under section 5705.28 of the Revised Code and entitled to participate in the proceeds of the classified property taxes and other public funds. Subject to any applicable laws of this state, such a district also may apply for and be entitled to receive any federal aid for which it may be eligible.

HISTORY: 136 v S 236. Eff 1-5-76.

LIBRARY TAX LEVIES
(Page's Ohio Revised Code, 1982, s.5705.06, 5705.19, 5705.23.)

§ 5705.06　Special levies without vote of the people within ten-mill limitation.　(GC § 5625-6)

The following special levies are hereby authorized without vote of the people:

(B) A levy for the library purposes of the subdivision, in accordance with the provisions of the Revised Code authorizing levies for such purposes, but only to the extent so authorized;

*　　*　　*

Each such special levy shall be within the ten-mill limitation and shall be subject to the control of the county budget commission, as provided by sections 5705.01 to 5705.47, inclusive, of the Revised Code.

Except for the special levies authorized in this section any authority granted by the Revised Code to levy a special tax within the ten-mill limitation for a current expense shall be construed as authority to provide for such expense by the general levy for current expenses.

HISTORY: GC § 5625-6; 112 v 391 (394), § 6; 115 v Pt.II 412 (413), § 1.

§ 5705.19 Resolution relative to tax levy in excess of ten-mill limitation.

The taxing authority of any subdivision at any time and in any year, by vote of two-thirds of all the members of the taxing authority, may declare by resolution and certify the resolution to the board of elections not less than seventy-five days before the election upon which it will be voted that the amount of taxes that may be raised within the ten-mill limitation will be insufficient to provide for the necessary requirements of the subdivision and that it is necessary to levy a tax in excess of that limitation for any of the following purposes:

* * *

(D) For a public library of, or supported by, a municipal corporation, township, school district, or county under whatever law organized or authorized to be supported;

HISTORY: 138 v S 274 (Eff 8-7-80); 138 v H 850 (Eff 8-7-80); 138 v H 873 (Eff 10-6-80); 138 v S 160 (Eff 10-31-80); 138 v H 1062 (Eff 3-23-81); 138 v H 268 (Eff 4-9-81); 139 v H 1 (Eff 8-5-81); 139 v H 694. Eff 11-15-81.

§ 5705.23 Resolution for special levy; submission to electors.

The board of library trustees of any county, municipal corporation, school district, or township public library by a vote of two-thirds of all its members may at any time declare by resolution that the amount of taxes which may be raised within the ten-mill limitation by levies on the current tax duplicate will be insufficient to provide an adequate amount for the necessary requirements of the public library, that it is necessary to levy a tax in excess of such limitation for current expenses of the public library or for the construction of any specific permanent improvement or class of improvements which the board of library trustees is authorized to make or acquire and which could be included in a single issue of bonds, and that the question of such additional tax levy shall be submitted by the taxing authority of the political subdivision to whose jurisdiction the board is subject, to the electors of the subdivision or, if the resolution so states, to the electors residing within the boundaries of the library district as defined by the state library board pursuant to section 3375.01 of the Revised Code, on the first Tuesday after the first Monday in June or at an election on another day to be specified in the resolution. No more than two elections shall be held under authority of this section in any one calendar year. Such resolution shall conform to section 5705.19 of the Revised Code, except that it shall specify the date of holding the election, which shall not be earlier than seventy-five days after the adoption and certification of the resolution to the taxing authority of the political subdivision to whose jurisdiction the

board is subject, and which shall be consistent with the requirements of section 3501.01 of the Revised Code. The resolution shall not include a levy on the current tax list and duplicate unless the election is to be held at or prior to the first Tuesday after the first Monday in November of the current tax year. Upon receipt of the resolution, the taxing authority of the political subdivision to whose jurisdiction the board is subject shall adopt a resolution providing for the submission of such additional tax levy to the electors of the subdivision or, if the resolution so states, to the electors residing within the boundaries of the library district as defined by the state library board pursuant to section 3375.01 of the Revised Code, on the date specified in the resolution of the board of library trustees. The resolution adopted by the taxing authority shall otherwise conform to the resolution certified to it by the board. The resolution of the taxing authority shall be certified to the board of elections of the proper county not less than seventy-five days before the date of such election. Such resolution shall go into immediate effect upon its passage and no publication of the same shall be necessary other than that provided in the notice of election. Section 5705.25 of the Revised Code shall govern the arrangements for the submission of such question and other matters concerning the election, to which that section refers, except that if the resolution so states, the question shall be submitted to the electors residing within the boundaries of the library district as defined by the state library board pursuant to section 3375.01 of the Revised Code and except that such election shall be held on the date specified in the resolution. If a majority of the electors voting on the question so submitted in an election vote in favor of such levy, the taxing authority may forthwith make the necessary levy within the subdivision or within the boundaries of the library district as defined by the state library board pursuant to section 3375.01 of the Revised Code at the additional rate in excess of the ten-mill limitation on the tax list, for the purpose stated in such resolutions. Such tax levy shall be included in the next annual tax budget that is certified to the county budget commission. The proceeds of any library levy in excess of the ten-mill limitation shall be used for purposes of said board in accordance with the law applicable to said board.

Notwithstanding sections 133.30 and 133.301 [133.30.1] of the Revised Code, after the approval of a levy on the current tax list and duplicate to provide an increase in current expenses, and prior to the time when the first tax collection from such levy can be made, the taxing authority at the request of the board of library trustees may anticipate a fraction of the proceeds of such levy and issue anticipation notes in an amount not exceeding fifty per cent of the total estimated proceeds of the levy to be collected during the first year of the levy.

After the approval of a levy to provide revenues for the construction or acquisitions of any specific permanent improvement or class of improvements and prior to the time when the first tax collection from such levy can be made, the taxing authority at the request of the board of library trustees may anticipate a fraction of the proceeds of such levy and issue anticipation notes in an amount not exceeding fifty per cent of the total estimated proceeds of the levy to be collected in each year over a period of five years after the issuance of such notes.

Such notes shall be sold as provided in sections 133.01 to 133.65 of the Revised Code. If such anticipation notes are issued, they shall mature serially and in substantially equal amounts during each year over a period not to exceed five years; and the amount necessary to pay the interest and principal as they mature shall be deemed appropriated for such purposes from such levy, and appropriations from such levy by the taxing authority shall be limited each year to the balance available in excess of such amount.

When a board of public library trustees of a county library district, appointed under section 3375.22 of the Revised Code, requests the submission of such special levy, the taxing authority shall submit the levy to the voters of the county library district only. For the purposes of this section, and of such board of library trustees only, the words "electors of the subdivision" as used in this section and in section 5705.25 of the Revised Code, means [sic] "electors of the county library district." Any levy approved by the electors of the county library district shall be made within the county library district only.

*HISTORY: 138 v H 847 (Eff 8-22-80); 138 v H 1062 (Eff 3-23-81); 139 v H 235. Eff 1-1-82.

LIBRARY TAX BUDGETS

(Page's Ohio Revised Code, 1982, s.5705.28, 5705.32, 5705.37.)

§ 5705.28 Adoption of tax budget; procedure for participation by public library trustees.

On or before the fifteenth day of July in each year, the taxing authority of each subdivision or other taxing unit shall adopt a tax budget for the next succeeding fiscal year. To assist in its preparation, the head of each department, board, commission, and district authority entitled to participate in any appropriation or revenue of a subdivision shall file with the taxing authority, or in the case of a municipal corporation, with its chief executive officer, before the first day of June in each year, an estimate of contemplated revenue and expenditures for the ensuing fiscal year, in such form as is prescribed by the taxing authority of the subdivision or by the bureau of supervision and inspection of public offices. The taxing authority shall include in its budget of expenditures the full amounts requested by district authorities, not to exceed the amount authorized by law, if such authorities may fix the amount of revenue they are to receive from the subdivision. In a municipal corporation in which a special levy for a municipal university has been authorized to be levied in excess of the ten-mill limitation, or is required by the charter of the municipal corporation, the taxing authority shall include an amount not less than the estimated yield of such levy, if such amount is requested by the board of directors of the municipal university.

The board of trustees of any public library, desiring to participate in the proceeds of classified property taxes collected in the county, shall adopt appropriate rules and regulations extending the benefits of the library service of such library to all the inhabitants of the county on equal terms, unless such library service is by law available to all such inhabitants, and shall certify a copy of such rules and regulations to the taxing authority with its estimate of contemplated revenue and expenditures. Where such rules and regulations have been so certified or where the adoption of such rules and regulations is not required, the taxing authority shall include in its budget of receipts such amounts as are specified by such board as contemplated revenue from classified property taxes, and in its budget of expenditures the full amounts requested therefrom by such board. No library association, incorporated or unincorporated, is entitled to participate in the proceeds of classified property taxes or other public funds unless such association was organized and operating prior to January 1, 1968.

HISTORY: GC § 5625-20; 112 v 391, § 20; 113 v 670; 115 v 590; 115 v PtII 412; 119 v 222; 122 v 166; 132 v H 177 (Eff 11-7-67); 133 v H 1. Eff 3-18-69.

§ 5705.32 Budget commission to adjust amounts required; revision of estimate; distribution; hearing.

The county budget commission shall adjust the estimated amounts required from the general property tax for each fund, as shown by such budgets, so as to bring the tax levies required therefor within the limitations specified in sections 5705.01 to 5705.47 of the Revised Code, for such levies, but no levy shall be reduced below a minimum fixed by law. The commission may revise and adjust the estimate of balances and receipts from all sources for each fund and shall determine the total appropriations that may be made therefrom. The commission shall fix the amount of proceeds of classified property taxes, collected within the county, to be distributed to each board of public library trustees that has qualified under section 5705.28 of the Revised Code for participation in the proceeds of such taxes. The commission shall base the amount for distribution on the needs of such library for the construction of new library buildings, parts of buildings, improvements, operation, maintenance, or other expenses. In determining the needs of each library board of trustees, and in calculating the amount to be distributed to any library board of trustees on the basis of its needs, the commission shall make no reduction in its allocation from the undivided classified property taxes on account of additional revenues realized by a library from increased taxes or service charges voted by its electorate, from revenues received through federal or state grants, projects, or programs, or from grants from private sources. Notwithstanding the fact that alternative methods of financing such needs are available, the commission shall fix the amount of proceeds of classified property taxes, collected within the county, to be distributed to each board of township park commissioners, the amount of proceeds of such taxes originating outside the limits of municipal corporations, to be distributed to the county, and the amount of proceeds of taxes originating within each municipal corporation, to be distributed to each municipal corporation and shall separately set forth the amount so fixed and determined in the "official certificate of estimated resources," as provided in section 5705.35 of the Revised Code, and separately certify such amount to the county auditor who shall be guided thereby in the distribution of the undivided classified property tax fund for and during the fiscal year. In determining such amounts, the commission shall be guided by the estimate of the auditor under section 5705.31 of the Revised Code as to the total amount of such undivided classified property taxes to be collected in the county during such fiscal year, and as to the shares thereof distributable to municipal corporations and the county, pursuant to section 5707.05 of the Revised Code.

Before the final determination of the amount to be allotted to each subdivision from any source, the commission shall permit representatives of each subdivision and of each board of public library trustees to appear before it to explain its financial needs.

If any public library receives and expends any funds allocated to it under this section for the construction of new library buildings or parts of buildings, such library shall be free and open to the inhabitants of the county in which it is located.

HISTORY: GC § 5625-24; 112 v 391(402), § 24; 115 v 591; 123 v 363; 124 v 441; 125 v 903(1040) (Eff 10-1-53); 137 v S 117. Eff 10-4-77.

§ 5705.37 Appeal to board of tax appeals; records of board of library trustees to be open to public inspection.

The taxing authority of any subdivision which is dissatisfied with any action of the budget commission may, through its fiscal officer, appeal to the board of tax appeals within thirty days after the receipt by such subdivision of the official certificate or notice of such action of said commission. In like manner, but through its clerk, the board of trustees of any public library of a subdivision whose fiscal officer is a member of the budget commission, or

any nonprofit corporation or library association maintaining a free public library which has adopted and certified rules and regulations under section 5705.28 of the Revised Code, may appeal to the board of tax appeals. The board of tax appeals shall forthwith consider the matter presented to the commission, and may modify any action of the commission with reference to the budget, the estimate of revenues and balances, or the fixing of tax rates. The finding of the board of tax appeals shall be substituted for the findings of the commission, and shall be certified to the tax commissioner, the commissioner of tax equalization, the county auditor, and the taxing authority of the subdivision affected, or to such board of public library trustees affected, as the action of such commission under sections 5705.01 to 5705.47 of the Revised Code.

This section does not give the board of tax appeals any authority to place any tax levy authorized by law within the ten-mill limitation outside of such limitation, nor to reduce any levy below any minimum fixed by law.

Any board of library trustees which receives funds under section 5707.05 of the Revised Code shall have its records open to public inspection at all reasonable times.

HISTORY: GC § 5625-28; 112 v 391, § 28; 115 v PtII 412; 120 v 30; 125 v 235 (Eff 10-2-53); 131 v 1318 (Eff 9-15-65); 136 v H 920. Eff 10-11-76.

SCHOOL LIBRARIES
(Page's Ohio Revised Code, 1982, s.3375.14.)

§ 3375.14 School libraries.

The board of education of any city, exempted village, or local school district may provide for the establishment, control, and maintenance of school libraries for the purpose of providing school library service to the pupils under its jurisdiction. Such board of education may contract with any public board, association, or other organization operating a public library in a community to furnish such school library service, the board of education paying all or such part of the expense thereof, including the salaries of school librarians, as compensation for the service rendered, as the two boards shall agree upon as terms of the contract, provided that nothing in

this section shall prevent such public board, association, or other organization operating a public library from providing classroom collections, operating bookmobiles, branches, or the main library of a public library, notwithstanding the fact that such branches or main library may be located within a school building.

Such board of education may purchase, erect, construct, enlarge, extend, or improve buildings for library purposes, including sites therefor, and equip and furnish such buildings.

HISTORY: GC § 4840; 120 v 475 (536); 128 v 598, § 1. Eff 11-9-59. Not analogous to former GC § 4840, repealed in 113 v 307 (412), § 234. For an analogous section, see former GC § 7631. RS § 3998-1; 96 v 8; 98 v 244, § 1; 104 v 225 (228); 110 v 407 (408); 115 v PtII 275 (278).

COUNTY LAW LIBRARIES
(Page's Ohio Revised Code, 1982, s.3375.48-3375.56.)

§ 3375.48 Compensation of law librarian.

The judges of the court of common pleas of any county in which there is a law library association which furnishes to all of the members of the Ohio general assembly, the county officers and the judges of the several courts in the county admission to its library and the use of its books free of charge, upon the appointment by the board of trustees of such association of a person to act as librarian thereof, or of a person to act as librarian and not more than two additional persons to act as assistant law librarians thereof, shall fix the compensation of such persons, which shall be paid from the county treasury. In counties where there is not more than one judge of the court of common pleas, the compensation to be

paid such librarian shall not exceed the sum of five hundred dollars per annum.

HISTORY: GC § 3054; RS § 2678; Bates § 1536-935; 70 v 162; 85 v 3; 91 v 207; 92 v 49; 94 v 237; 97 v 72; 127 v 25 (Eff 8-30-57); 136 v H 390. Eff 8-6-76.

§ 3375.49 Board of county commissioners shall provide for law library.

For the use of the law library referred to in section 3375.48 of the Revised Code, the board of county commissioners shall provide, at the expense of the county, suitable rooms with sufficient and suitable bookcases in the county courthouse or, if there are no suitable rooms in the courthouse, any other suitable rooms at the county seat with sufficient and suitable bookcases. The librarian or person in charge of the law library shall receive and safely keep in these rooms the law reports and other books furnished by the state for use of the court and bar. The board of county commissioners shall heat and light any such rooms. The books, computer communications console that is a means of access to a system of computerized legal research, microform materials and equipment, videotape materials and equipment, audio or visual materials and equipment, other materials and equipment utilized in conducting legal research, and furniture of the law library association that are owned by, and used exclusively in, the law library are exempt from taxation.

HISTORY: 138 v H 559 (Eff 1-15-81); 139 v S 114. Eff 10-27-81.

§ 3375.50 Allowance to law libraries from fines and penalties of municipal courts.

All moneys collected by a municipal corporation accruing from fines and penalties and from forfeited deposits, forfeited bail bonds, and forfeited recognizances taken for appearances, by a municipal court for offenses and misdemeanors brought for prosecution in the name of a municipal corporation under a penal ordinance thereof, where there is in force a state statute under which the offense might be prosecuted, or prosecuted in the name of the state, except a portion of such moneys, which plus all costs collected monthly in such state cases, equal the compensation allowed by the board of county commissioners to the judges of the municipal court, and prosecuting attorney of such court in state cases, shall be retained by the clerk of such municipal court, and paid by him forthwith, each month, to the board of trustees of the law library association in the county in which such municipal corporation is located. The sum so retained and paid by the clerk of said municipal court to the board of trustees of such law library association shall in no month be less than twenty-five per cent of the moneys arising from such fines and penalties and from forfeited deposits, bail bonds, and recognizances taken from appearances, in that month, without deducting the amount of the allowance of the board of county commissioners to said judge, clerk, and prosecuting attorney.

The total amount paid under this section in any one calendar year by the clerks of all municipal courts in any one county to the board of trustees of such law library association shall in no event exceed the following amounts:

(A) In counties having a population of fifty thousand or less, seventy-five hundred dollars and the maximum amount paid by any of such courts shall not exceed four thousand dollars in any calendar year.

(B) In counties having a population in excess of fifty thousand but not in excess of one hundred thousand, eight thousand dollars and the maximum amount paid by any of such courts shall not exceed five thousand five hundred dollars in any calendar year.

(C) In counties having a population in excess of one hundred thousand but not in excess of one hundred fifty thousand, ten thousand dollars and the maximum amount paid by any of such courts shall not exceed seven thousand dollars in any calendar year.

(D) In counties having a population of in excess of

one hundred fifty thousand, fifteen thousand dollars in any calendar year. The maximum amount to be paid by each such clerk shall be determined by the county auditor in December of each year for the next succeeding calendar year, and shall bear the same ratio to the total amount payable under this section from the clerks of all municipal courts in such county as the total fines, costs, and forfeitures received by the corresponding municipal court, bear to the total fines, costs, and forfeitures received by all the municipal courts in the county, as shown for the last complete year of actual receipts, on the latest available budgets of such municipal courts; and payments in the full amounts provided in this section shall be made monthly by each clerk in each calendar year until the maximum amount for such year has been paid. When such amount, so determined by the auditor, has been paid to the board of trustees of such law library association, then no further payments shall be required in that calendar year from the clerk of such court.

HISTORY: GC § 3056; RS § 2680; Bates § 1536-937; 69 v 165, § 2; 89 v 51; 91 v 296; 94 v 135; 101 v 295; 114 v 89; 118 v 483; 125 v 903; 128 v 51 (Eff 11-9-59); 136 v H 205. Eff 1-1-76.

§ 3375.51 Moneys collected by county judges paid to law library.

In each county fifty per cent of all moneys collected by judges of the county court of such county, accruing from fines, penalties, forfeited recognizances, and forfeited cash deposits, unless otherwise distributed by law, shall be paid to the board of trustees of the law library association of such county by the county treasurer, upon the voucher of the county auditor within thirty days after such moneys have been paid into the county treasury by such judges.

HISTORY: GC § 3056-1; 118 v 453 (454), § 1 (Eff 10-1-53); 129 v 582 (788). Eff 1-10-61.

§ 3375.52 Court of common pleas and probate court to pay fines and penalties to law library. (GC § 3056-2)

In each county of the state, all moneys arising from fines and penalties levied, and from cash deposits, bail bonds, and recognizances taken by the court of common pleas and the probate court of such county, which have been forfeited, on account of offenses and misdemeanors brought for prosecution in such courts in the name of the state, shall be retained and paid monthly by the clerk of such courts to the board of trustees of the law library association. The total sums so paid therefrom shall not exceed twelve hundred fifty dollars per annum, and when that amount has been paid to such board, in accordance with this section, then no further payments shall be required thereunder in that calendar year from the clerks of such respective courts.

HISTORY: GC § 3056-2; 118 v 453 (455), § 1. Eff 10-1-53.

§ 3375.53 Fines and penalties for violation of liquor control law and state traffic laws paid to law library. (GC § 3056-3)

In each county, fifty per cent of all moneys arising from fines and penalties and from forfeited deposits and forfeited bail bonds and recognizances taken for appearances on account of offenses brought for prosecution in any court in such county under Chapters 4301. and 4303. of the Revised Code and the state traffic laws shall be paid monthly by the treasurer of the county or municipal corporation to the board of trustees of the law library association in such county, but the sum so paid to such board by each treasurer shall not exceed twelve hundred dollars per annum under Chapters 4301. and 4303. of the Revised Code, and when that amount has been so paid to such board in accordance with this section, then no further payments shall be required thereunder in that calendar year from such treasurers.

HISTORY: GC § 3056-3; 118 v 453 (455), § 1; 125 v 903. Eff 10-1-53.

§ 3375.54 [Money used for lawbooks, computer communication facilities and equipment.]

The money that is paid to the board of trustees of a law library association under sections 3375.50 to 3375.53 of the Revised Code shall be expended in the support and operation of the law library association and in the purchase, lease, or rental of lawbooks, a computer communications console that is a means of access to a system of computerized legal research, microform materials and equipment, videotape materials and equipment, audio or visual materials and equipment, and other services, materials, and equipment that provide legal information or facilitate legal research.

*HISTORY: 138 v H 559. Eff 1-15-81.

§ 3375.55 Use of the law library.

Judges of the county court in the county and officers of the townships and municipal corporations therein shall have the same free use of the books of the law library receiving moneys under sections 3375.50 to 3375.53, inclusive, of the Revised Code, as the judges and county officers.

HISTORY: GC § 3057; RS § 2680; Bates § 1536-937; 69 v 165, § 2; 89 v 51; 91 v 296; 94 v 135 (Eff 10-1-53); 129 v 788. Eff 1-10-61.

§ 3375.56 Annual report by board of trustees of law library association; refund of excess. (GC § 3058)

On the first Monday of each year, the board of trustees of the law library association shall make a detailed statement to the county auditor, verified by the oath of the treasurer of the association, of the amount of the fines and penalties received under sections 3375.50 to 3375.53, inclusive, of the Revised Code, and of the money expended by the association.

If the total amount received under such sections during the preceding calendar year covered by such report exceeds the expenditures during the same period, the auditor shall certify such fact to the board which shall thereupon direct the treasurer of the association to refund proportionately to the treasurers of the political subdivisions from which such balance was received, not less than ninety per cent of any unencumbered balance on hand from the preceding year.

HISTORY: GC § 3058; RS § 2680; Bates § 1536-937; 69 v 165, § 2; 89 v 51; 91 v 296; 94 v 135; 118 v 453 (455), § I. Eff 10-1-53.

Ohio library laws are reprinted from PAGE'S OHIO REVISED CODE published by W. H. Anderson Co., Cincinnati, Ohio.

OKLAHOMA

DEPARTMENT OF LIBRARIES

(Oklahoma Statutes Annotated, 1982, Title 65,
s.1-101 to 3-115.)

§ 1–101. Short title

This Act shall be known as the Oklahoma Library Code.
Laws 1967, c. 45, § 1--101.

§ 1–102. Policy

It shall be the policy of the State of Oklahoma to promote, support, and implement the development and maintenance of adequate public and special library facilities and services throughout the State in whatever forms and by whatever means may be most beneficial and feasible. Adequate library services are deemed to be necessary to the cultural, educational and economic development of the State of Oklahoma and to the health, safety and welfare of its people, and to be the responsibility of government at all levels.
Laws 1967. c. 45, § 1–102.

§ 1–103. Purpose

It is the purpose of the Oklahoma Library Code to accomplish this policy by providing for:

(a) Creation of the Oklahoma Department of Libraries to discharge the responsibility and exercise the authority of the State of Oklahoma for adequate library facilities and services in and for State government and throughout the State.

(b) Establishment, development and operation of libraries and library systems throughout the State with the goal of providing adequate library services to all the people of the State.

(c) Financial support for libraries with guidelines for maximum economy and effectiveness in use of all funds.

(d) Cooperation with other State agencies, Federal agencies and private organizations in effecting the purposes of this Code.
Laws 1967, c. 45, § 1–103.

§ 1–104. Definitions

When used in this Code unless the context otherwise requires:

(a) The term "library system" shall mean a unified public library organization under single direction in an area of not less than one county.

(b) The term "public library" shall mean a library or library system that is freely open to all persons under identical conditions, and which is supported in whole or in part by public funds.

(c) The term "metropolitan library" shall mean a library system which is the public library for a county in which is located a city of at least two hundred fifty thousand population.

(d) The term "multi-county library" shall mean a library system which is the public library for a library district composed of two or more counties.

(e) The term "special library" shall mean any library, whether open to the general public or not, that is supported in whole or in part by public funds and which comes within one or more of the following categories:

(1) All libraries which are operated within or as an integral part of a publicly supported institution.

(2) All libraries that cater to a special clientele.

(3) All libraries that are concerned primarily with materials on a special subject.

Provided, however, that this definition shall not be construed to include libraries operated as a part of any university, college, school, museum, the Oklahoma Historical Society and county law libraries.

(f) The word "library" shall mean the contents as well as the building, equipment and facilities of the institution.

(g) The word "Department" shall mean the Oklahoma Department of Libraries, which shall be the official library and archival agency of the State.

(h) The word "Board" shall mean the Oklahoma Department of Libraries Board.

(i) The word "standards" shall mean the criteria pertaining to the scope and quality of library facilities, levels of financial support, adequacy and qualifications of personnel, organization and resources for service, areas of service and population to be served, and other factors deemed necessary to insure proper, economical and effective use of funds and resources in providing library facilities and services.

(j) The term "accreditation of libraries" shall mean the evaluation and rating of public libraries and library systems.

(k) The word "Director" shall mean the Director of the Department who shall be the State Librarian and the State Archivist.
Laws 1967, c. 45, § 1–104.

§ 2–101. Creation of Board

The Oklahoma Department of Libraries Board is hereby created. The Board shall consist of seven appointive members, and the Director, who shall be an ex-officio non-voting member. The Governor shall appoint, with the advice and consent of the Senate, one member from each Con-

gressional District created by Title 14, Chapter 1, Section 1, Oklahoma
Session Laws 1951 (14 O.S.1961 § 1), and one member-at-large. No
appointive member shall be a librarian in active practice. Appointments
shall be made on the basis of ability, sound understanding of the total
responsibilities and objectives of a state library agency and active interest in the attainment of these goals.
Laws 1967, c. 45, § 2–101.

§ 2–102. Membership of Board

The members appointed by the Governor shall be qualified electors of
the State and actual residents of the Congressional Districts from which
they are appointed. No member of the Board shall in any way be connected with the business of publishing or selling books, periodicals or
other forms of library materials, nor with the business of manufacturing
or selling library supplies or equipment. No member shall receive any
compensation for his service on the Board directly or indirectly; provided
that each appointive member may receive actual and necessary travel
expense and per diem as authorized by 74 O.S.1961, §§ 500.5–500.12,
as amended. Such reimbursements shall be made from funds appropriated to the Department on verified claims approved by the Secretary.
Laws 1967, c. 45, § 2–102.

§ 2–103. Terms of office

The term of office of each appointive member, except for initial appointments as herein specified, shall be six years, beginning July 1 of
the year of appointment or until his successor has been appointed and
qualified. The present State Library Board shall become members of
the Board of the Department and shall continue in office until their respective terms expire. The Governor shall appoint one member on or
before July 1 of each year; provided that he shall make the first appointments for the following terms in the years indicated: One member
for a term of one year, and one member for a term of two years in 1967;
one member for a term of two years, one member for a term of three
years and the member at large for a term of three years in 1968; one
member for a term of three years, and one member for a term of four
years in 1969. After the initial appointments, terms shall be for six
years. Any vacancy on the Board shall be filled for the remainder of
the term only and by the method of the original appointment. No
person who has served a full six-year term shall be appointed to succeed
himself. Members may be removed only for cause.
Laws 1967, c. 45, § 2–103.

§ 2–104. Officers

The Board shall elect a Chairman and Vice Chairman at the first
meeting held after July 1 of each year. The Director shall be the Secretary of the Board, and shall have custody of all files and records of the
Board.
Laws 1967, c. 45, § 2–104.

§ 2–105. Meetings

The Board shall meet at least once every three-month period. Additional meetings may be held upon call of the Chairman, Vice Chairman,
in the absence of the Chairman, or the Secretary. Four voting members
of the Board shall constitute a quorum. No question before the Board
shall be resolved without the concurrence of at least four members or
a majority of those members voting, whichever is the greater. Whenever circumstances require an immediate decision by the Board in the
course of intervals between Board meetings, the Secretary may request
the decision by mail or telegraph. The votes on these decisions must

be unanimous. The question and the vote on it shall be entered in minutes of the next meeting of the Board.
Laws 1967, c. 45, § 2–105.

§ 2–106. Powers and duties of the Board

The Oklahoma Department of Libraries Board shall be the supervisory and policymaking body of the Department and shall:

(a) Appoint the Director, who shall possess the qualifications specified by Section 3–103, and shall hold office at the pleasure of the Board;

(b) Formulate the general policies of the Oklahoma Department of Libraries, in consultation with the Director;

(c) Review and approve the budget requests for the Department;

(d) Formulate standards for public and special libraries in consultation with the Director and his staff, and with the Oklahoma Council on Libraries and the Oklahoma Library Association;

(e) Utilize such standards as guidelines in accreditation of public libraries and library systems, provided public libraries, other than those in a library system, shall be accredited only when requests for that purpose are made by resolutions of the elected city, town, or county governing bodies appropriating funds for their operation; provided further that any metropolitan or city-county library system may be accredited when requests for that purpose are made by resolution of its governing board;

(f) Utilize such standards and accreditation as guidelines in approval of apportionment of State funds or Federal funds such as may be administered by a state agency to public libraries, library systems and special libraries and their use of such funds;

(g) Serve as an appeal board in the execution of Title II, U.S.Public Law 88–269, including any amendments thereto, and any similar Federal legislative acts requiring such services;

(h) Approve the formation of library systems and designate areas for library districts;

(i) Maintain liaison with The Oklahoma Council on Libraries and the Oklahoma Library Association;

(j) Assist in communicating the goals, plans, budgets and work of the Department to executive, judicial and legislative officials, and to the public; and

(k) Adopt such rules and regulations as may be necessary to carry out the intent and purposes of this Act.
Laws 1967, c. 45, § 2–106.

§ 3–101. Creation of Department

The Oklahoma Department of Libraries is hereby created. The Department shall be the official library agency of the State and shall discharge the responsibilities and exercise the authority of the State with respect to all public and special libraries. The Department shall cooperate with other State agencies, local units of government, Federal agencies and private individuals and organizations with respect to library facilities and services, or any allied or related facilities and services. The Oklahoma State Library is hereby incorporated into and made a part of the Department, and all property, facilities, funds, services and powers of The Oklahoma State Library are hereby transferred to the Department. The Department shall be responsible for the receipt and administration of all State funds and such Federal funds as may be administered by a State agency, may receive and administer private and other funds, for libraries, library services or any allied or related services.

The Department shall have its headquarters and shall maintain The State Library in the State Capitol area, which library is hereby continued

as heretofore provided. Branches or offices of the Department may be established under such conditions and terms and in such locations within the State as are deemed necessary.
Laws 1967, c. 45, § 3–101.

§ 3–102. Department as official library of the State

The Department shall constitute the official library of the State of Oklahoma. The Department shall have custody of all books, documents, facsimiles, films, maps, manuscripts, pamphlets, papers, charts, archives, periodicals, records, and any other materials or objects now in its possession or that may be acquired. No department or institution of State government, except institutions of higher learning, museums and the Oklahoma Historical Society, shall establish a library without prior approval of and except in cooperation with the Department; provided that this provision is not to prevent a State agency from having the minimal necessary and frequently used office copies of reference works, catalogs, legal reports or technical publications required to conduct its daily operations.
Laws 1967, c. 45, § 3–102.

§ 3–103. Director and Assistant Director

The offices of Director and Assistant Director are hereby created. The Director shall be appointed by the Board on the basis of merit and appropriate experience, shall possess a library degree from a library school accredited by the American Library Association and shall serve at the pleasure of the Board. Upon entering upon the duties of the office, the Director shall file an official bond with the Secretary of State as provided by 74 O.S.1961, §§ 601–605, as amended, in the sum of Fifteen Thousand Dollars ($15,000.00) for the safekeeping of library property in his care. The Assistant Director shall be appointed by the Director, with the approval of the Board, and shall be subject to the same qualifications as herein specified for the Director. The Director shall be the State Librarian and the State Archivist, which offices are hereby created.
Laws 1967, c. 45, § 3–103.

§ 3–104. Duties of Director

The Director shall be the administrative, executive, directing and supervising official of the Department under the supervision of and in accordance with policies established by the Board. He shall:

(a) Approve all requisitions and claims;

(b) Prepare budgets;

(c) Prepare the staff organization and position classification with the approval of the Board;

(d) Employ or terminate employment of all personnel as provided by 74 O.S.1961, §§ 801–839, as amended; and

(e) Make all reports, maintain all records and execute all instruments required by law or regulation and perform all duties necessary to discharge the functions of the Department.

The Director shall be accountable and responsible to all proper State and Federal officials for the activities of the Department. He shall be the representative of the State in all matters pertaining to the duties and services of the Department, or any other library, archival, public documents, reference, research, records, information and information processing functions, including all allied or related services, of the State government, or in which the State may participate; provided that he may designate a staff member of the Department to act as his agent under such conditions as he may prescribe. The Director, or any staff member of the Department designated by him, shall receive travel expense and

per diem as provided by 74 O.S.1961, §§ 500.5–500.12, as amended, including necessary fees incurred in the exercise of his duties, or in attending conferences, institutes and meetings of library, reference, research, documentation and informational associations or bodies, or any allied or related groups.
Laws 1967, c. 45, § 3–104.

§ 3–105. Functions of Department

The departmental functions shall include but not be limited to library services, library research, library development, archival, records management and preservation, legislative reference, legal reference, general reference, library promotion and public information, informational, information processing and retrieval, government documents and any allied, cognate or related functions, and the Department shall be the authority of the State for these functions.

The Department is authorized and directed to discharge the State's responsibility for library service, including service to State government, to public and special libraries and library services, cooperation with and rendering of services to local units of government in the establishment and operation of local libraries and library systems, and the performance of all technical and other services necessary to the Department. The Department shall assist with and supervise the establishment and operation of libraries at all State institutions and agencies, except public schools and institutions of higher learning.
Laws 1967, c. 45, § 3–105.

§ 3–106. Creation of divisions authorized

There shall be created such divisions and sub-divisions of the Department as are deemed necessary to effect the purposes of this Code.
Laws 1967, c. 45, § 3–106.

§ 3–107. Appropriations, gifts, bequests or grants—Contracts—Libraries' Revolving Fund

The Department may receive and use appropriations, gifts, bequests or grants from any source, public or private, and may take such action as may be necessary to receive such funds. It may contract with other agencies, organizations, libraries, library schools or the agencies of other governments for library services, facilities, research or any allied or related purpose.

There is hereby created in the State Treasury a revolving fund for the Oklahoma Department of Libraries, to be designated the Oklahoma Department of Libraries' Revolving Fund. The fund shall be administered in accordance with the Revolving Fund Procedures Act. The Department is authorized to receive all money from departmental forfeitures, fees, sales of materials and services, payments for lost books and other receipts, and other miscellaneous sources, and all such income shall be deposited in such fund.
Laws 1967, c. 45, § 3–107. Amended by Laws 1978, c. 165, § 4, eff. Jan. 8, 1979.

§ 3–108. Participation in health insurance plans authorized

The Department may participate in an approved health insurance program for fulltime employees and use appropriated funds for said purpose, either for the exclusive benefits of its staff or jointly with other such programs.
Laws 1967, c. 45, § 3–108.

§ 3–109. Purchase, lease and disposal of real and personal property

The Department is authorized to purchase, lease or otherwise acquire

and hold title to and dispose of lands and buildings and other facilities, and materials, motor vehicles or other equipment, or to erect and equip buildings necessary in effecting the purposes of this Code.
Laws 1967, c. 45, § 3–109.

§ 3–110. Publications

The Department may compile, prepare and issue publications of any type related to and deemed necessary in effecting the purposes of this Code.
Laws 1967, c. 45, § 3–110.

§ 3–111. Standards for library equipment

The Department may prescribe standards for equipment and supplies purchased for its use and the use of units under its direction.
Laws 1967, c. 45, § 3–111.

§ 3–112. Petty cash fund

A petty cash fund of not more than Three Hundred Dollars ($300.00) is authorized. It shall be established and replenished by claims against appropriations. The fund may be used for postage due payments and for the purchase of minor items and services that cost less than Twenty-five Dollars ($25.00) each. Itemized receipts for all such purchases shall be secured and filed. The fund shall be audited by the State Auditor and Inspector as are other accounts of the Department.
Laws 1967, c. 45, § 3–112. Amended by Laws 1979, c. 30, § 112, emerg. eff. April 6, 1979.

§ 3–113. Postage

The Department is authorized to buy postage stamps and postal cards in an amount not to exceed Five Hundred Dollars ($500.00) for any one fiscal year for the purpose of pre-paying the postage for the return of information or statistical materials, field operations and other like purposes.
Laws 1967, c. 45, § 3–113.

§ 3–113.1 Publications Clearinghouse—Creation—Director—Rules and regulations

The Publications Clearinghouse is hereby created as a division of the Oklahoma Department of Libraries. The Publications Clearinghouse shall be directed by the Director of the Department of Libraries. The Director shall adopt rules and regulations necessary to implement the provisions of this act.
Added by Laws 1978, c. 165, § 1.

§ 3–113.2 Definitions

As used in this act:

1. "Agency" means any state office, officer, department, division or unit, bureau, board, commission, authority, institution, sub-state planning district, and agency of the state, and, where applicable, all subdivisions of each, including state institutions of higher education, defined as all state-supported colleges, universities, junior colleges and vocational-technical schools;

2. "Governmental publications" means any publication of associations, regional organizations, intergovernmental bodies, federal agencies, boards and commissions, or other publishers that may contribute supplementary materials to support the work of the State Legislature, state officers and state agencies;

3. "Print" means any form of printing and duplication, regardless of format or purpose, with the exception of correspondence and interoffice memoranda; and

4. "State publication" means any informational materials regardless of format, method of reproduction, or source, originating in or produced with the imprint of, by the authority of, or at the total or partial expense of, or purchased for distribution by, the state, the Legislature, constitutional officers, any state department, committee, sub-state planning district, or other state agency supported wholly or in part by state funds. The definition incorporates those publications that may or may not be financed by state funds but are released by private bodies such as research and consultant firms under a contract with and/or the supervision of any state agency; and specifically includes public documents appearing as reports, directories, statistical compendiums, bibliographies, laws or bills, rules, regulations, newsletters, bulletins, state plans, brochures, periodicals or magazines, committee minutes, transcripts of public hearings, journals, statutes, codes, pamphlets, lists, books, charts, maps, surveys, other printed matter, microfilm, microfiche and all sale items.

Added by Laws 1978, c. 165, § 2.

§ 3–113.3 Duties of Publications Clearinghouse

The Publications Clearinghouse shall have the following duties:

1. To establish an Oklahoma government publications depository library system for the use of the citizens of the State of Oklahoma;

2. To collect state publications from every state agency and to retain and preserve permanently a minimum of four copies of all such publications;

3. To enter into contracts with other libraries within the State of Oklahoma whereby the Publications Clearinghouse designates the contracting library to be a depository library for the Oklahoma Department of Libraries and agrees to distribute at least one copy of every state publication deposited with the Publications Clearinghouse to such depository library and the contracting library agrees to receive and maintain the full and complete collection of such publications and not to dispose of any such publication without prior approval of the Publications Clearinghouse, to provide adequate facilities for the storage and use of such publications and to provide free services to its patrons in the use of such publications;

4. To determine the necessity of and to make arrangements for the conversion of state publications to microfilm or microfiche and to establish a system to assure the availability of such microfilm or microfiche for distribution to designated depository libraries;

5. To prepare and publish official lists of all state publications and to distribute them to all contracting depository libraries, other libraries within the state, and every state agency, as required by the rules and regulations. The official lists shall include the name of the publishing agency, the name of the publisher, and the title and subject matter of each publication;

6. To determine the quantity of each publication of a state agency, in excess of twenty-five, required to meet the needs of the Publications Clearinghouse depository library system and to notify each agency of additional required quantity;

7. To distribute copies of all state publications including annual, semiannual or biennial reports as follows:

    a.   two copies to the United States Library of Congress,

    b.   one copy to the Archives Division of the Oklahoma Department of Libraries for preservation,

    c.   one copy to the Center for Research Libraries,

    d.   four copies for the collection of state publications within the Publications Clearinghouse,

    e.   one copy to each depository library, and

    f. one copy of each agency report to the Legislative Reference Division of the Oklahoma Department of Libraries;

    8. To receive and maintain, for exchange with the official libraries of each of the other states, territories and possessions of the United States, a minimum of fifty (50) copies of all state legal publications, including bar journals, official reports of decisions, codes, opinions, rules and regulations, and one hundred ten (110) copies of statute supplements and session laws;

    9. To aid in the maintenance of a law library within the Department to serve the state officers, agencies and members of the Oklahoma Legislature; and

    10. To compile and maintain a permanent record of all state publications caused to be published from and after April 10, 1978.

Added by Laws 1978, c. 165, § 3. Amended by Laws 1981, c. 272, § 15, eff. July 1, 1981.

§ 3–114. Deposit of state publications with Publications Clearinghouse—Failure to comply

    A. Every agency, authority, department, commission, board, institution, office or officer of the state, except institutions of higher education but specifically including any board of regents for higher education, who issue or publish, at state expense, regardless of form, any book, chart, document, facsimile, map, paper, periodical, report, serial, survey or any other type of publication, including statutes, statute supplements and session laws, shall immediately deposit a minimum of twenty-five (25) copies with the Publications Clearinghouse of the Department.

    B. Upon failure of an agency to comply with this section, the Publications Clearinghouse shall forward a written notice of such failure to the chief administrative officer of the agency; such notice shall state a reasonable time, not to exceed thirty (30) days, in which the agency shall fully comply. Further failure to comply shall be reported in writing to the Speaker of the House of Representatives, the President Pro Tempore of the Senate and the Attorney General. The Attorney General shall immediately institute mandamus proceedings to secure compliance by such agency.

Laws 1967, c. 45, § 3–114. Amended by Laws 1978, c. 165, § 5.

§ 3–115. Copies to other states, territories or possessions and The Library of Congress—Exchange agreements—Surplus publications

    The Publications Clearinghouse of the Department shall retain sufficient copies for use by the Department, and shall, pursuant to exchange agreements, send copies to the official library of each of the other states, territories and possessions of the United States and The Library of Congress, and may exchange copies for the publications of other governments or organizations and may send copies upon request to other bodies or persons. The Department may sell at the fair market value or otherwise dispose of any surplus publications and any receipts shall be deposited pursuant to Section 3–107 of this title.

Laws 1967, c. 45, § 3–115. Amended by Laws 1978, c. 165, § 6.

PUBLIC LIBRARY SYSTEMS

(Oklahoma Statutes Annotated, 1982, Title 65,
s.4-101 to 4-110.)

§ 4–101. Authority for establishment

    Counties, cities and towns are hereby authorized and empowered to join in creation, development, operation and maintenance of public library systems to serve multi-county districts, and to appropriate and allocate funds for the support of such systems. Such systems shall provide equitable library services to all persons in the district.

To insure the effective development of library service in all rural and urban areas, the creation and organization of library systems and the district to be served shall be subject to approval by the Oklahoma Department of Libraries Board in accordance with the provisions of Article X, Section 10A of the Oklahoma Constitution. After establishment, library systems shall be subject to accreditation by the Oklahoma Department of Libraries Board.

Parts of an adjacent county may be added to or included in multi-county systems if these additions are determined by agreement of the system board, the petitioning parties, and the Oklahoma Department of Libraries Board to be the most feasible way to provide public library services to such part of a county.

Special levies of any and all taxes authorized to be levied by counties, cities and towns under this and other Oklahoma Statutes as amended and the Oklahoma Constitution as amended are hereby authorized to be levied for support of library systems.

When any multi-county system is established under provisions of this act, existing public libraries in the district may be incorporated into the system under a unified administration by act of local governing bodies or vote of the people as provided in the procedure for establishment. Existing public libraries not incorporated into the system shall have the same relationship to the system as similar public libraries outside the district have to the local system and to other systems.

Laws 1967, c. 45, § 4–101.

§ 4–102. Procedure for establishment and termination

A library system may be created by resolution or ordinance approved by the Boards of County Commissioners and by the governing bodies of all cities or towns of two thousand or more according to the latest U. S. Census within the proposed district, or by the county seat town if no city or town within a county has a population of at least two thousand, subject to approval by the Oklahoma Department of Libraries Board. Such resolution and ordinances shall specify the type of system to be created, the district to be served, organization of the governing board of the system, proposed financing including agreement to call for a vote of the people as necessary for special tax levies, and shall constitute application for approval by the Oklahoma Department of Libraries Board when submitted to the Board.

A library system may be created upon initiative of the county, city and town governing bodies concerned, or upon presentation of petitions to the Board of County Commissioners of each county signed by not less than ten percent of the qualified electors of each county voting in the latest preceding general election. Upon receipt of such petitions, the Board of County Commissioners of each county shall forthwith call for a county-wide vote on the proposed library system.

When approval of the proposed system is granted by the Oklahoma Department of Libraries Board, the county, city and town governing bodies shall proceed with appointment of the system board and financing.

After approval of the Oklahoma Department of Libraries Board for creation of the system, the county, city and town governing bodies, or the governing board of the library system, may request demonstration library services by the Oklahoma Department of Libraries and/or a grant of funds for interim services before approval of special tax levies by the people of the district.

The Boards of County Commissioners and the governing bodies of cities and towns involved in creation of a library system, and the governing board of the library system, are authorized to enter into contracts and

agreements by and between such governing bodies and with other such li-
brary systems, special and school and college libraries, and the Oklahoma
Department of Libraries in effecting the purposes of this Article and other
Articles of this Code.

After a system has been created, another county or counties may be
added to the system by action of the governing bodies of the applicant
counties and cities as provided in the procedure for establishment.

Any library system created under the provisions of this Code may be
terminated, or a part thereof may withdraw and resulting special tax
levies shall be discontinued only by majority vote of qualified electors voting in an election called by petitions signed by not less than twenty percent of the qualified electors voting in the latest preceding general election
of the county or counties wishing to terminate or withdraw.

This provision for termination of all or a part of a library system shall
not prohibit the re-organization of any system, or the transfer of part of a
system to another system or the merging of systems, by act of the county,
city and town governing bodies with approval of the Oklahoma Department
of Libraries Board, provided that such changes do not result in termination of library service in any other area for which such service has been
approved.
Laws 1967, c. 45, § 4–102.

§ 4–103.   Governing   boards—Membership—Tenure—Qualifications—
            Compensation

(a) The Board of Trustees of a library system containing two or more
counties, herein defined as a multicounty library system, shall consist
of at least five (5) members. There shall be at least one member
from each county appointed by the board of county commissioners.
Additional members shall be appointed for each city within the system
with a population of two thousand (2,000) or more, with these appointments to be made by the governing body of the city. In addition, any
town with a population of at least one thousand (1,000), a distance of
at least thirty (30) miles from the next nearest town having a board
member, shall be entitled to a member, appointed by the governing board
of such town, for a term of three (3) years. In counties with no city
with a population of two thousand (2,000) or more, a member shall be
appointed by the governing body of the county seat city or town. Should
the board serving a multicounty unit result in fewer than five members,
additional board members shall be appointed on a proportional basis
agreed upon by the county governments involved.

(b) Initial appointments shall be distributed among one-, two- and
three-year terms, with one-third of the appointments to be made for
one (1) year, one-third to be made for two (2) years and one-third for
three (3) years. Subsequent appointments shall be for three-year terms,
except in the case of an appointment to fill a vacancy in the membership
of the system board, which appointment shall be for the remainder of
the unexpired term of the member where death, resignation or removal
has created the vacancy. No person shall serve more than two full
successive terms. All tenure of initial and future appointees shall expire
on June 30 of the designated year. A member of a system board once
qualified can thereafter be removed by the appointive authority during
his term of office only for misconduct or neglect of duty.

(c) Appointments to the system board shall be made on the basis of
ability, a sound understanding of the total responsibilities and objectives
of public libraries and an active interest in the attainment of these comprehensive goals. Appointive members shall be qualified electors and
bona fide residents of the counties from which they are appointed. No
member of the system board shall in any way be connected with the
business of publishing or selling books, periodicals or other forms of

library materials nor with the business of manufacturing or selling library supplies or equipment.

(d) All system board members shall serve thereon without compensation except actual and necessary travel expenses as authorized by the State Travel Reimbursement Act. Individual memberships for systems board members in state, regional, and national library associations and expenses incurred in attending conferences of these associations, board meetings and other library and library-related meetings may be paid from library funds upon proper authorization of the board.

Laws 1967, c. 45, § 4-103. Amended by Laws 1976, c. 45, § 1, emerg. eff. April 9, 1976.

§ 4-104. System board of trustees—Officers—Meetings—Quorum

The system board shall elect a chairman, vice chairman, and treasurer from the appointed members. The term of the officers shall be one year.

The system board shall meet as often as is required to transact necessary business and all meetings shall be open to the public, except for matters concerning personnel as set forth in 25 O.S.1961, §§ 201-202. It shall adopt rules for the transaction of business and keep a record of its functions and activities, which record shall be a public record.

A majority of the board membership shall constitute a quorum.

Laws 1967, c. 45, § 4-104.

§ 4-105. System board of trustees—Powers and duties

(a) Every system board created by this Code shall have all powers necessary or convenient for the accomplishment of the purpose and provisions hereof, including, in addition to others granted in this Article, the following powers:

(1) To operate and maintain a library system and to adopt such rules and regulations for the operation thereof as may be deemed necessary or expedient.

(2) To purchase, lease, or otherwise acquire land or buildings or portions of buildings for library purposes.

(3) To erect, maintain, and operate public library buildings at one or more places.

(4) To accept transfer of any existing public library or libraries by lease or other conveyance.

(5) To acquire, by purchase or otherwise, books and other personal property customarily used in the operation of public libraries including necessary motor vehicles.

(6) To sell and dispose of personal property acquired by purchase or any other means when by proper resolution the board finds that said property is not needed for library purposes.

(7) To acquire, accept, hold, and convey legal title to interest in real property in the name of the system board. Deeds or other conveyances of said interests in real property shall be executed for and on behalf of the system board by the chairman and shall be attested by the secretary upon proper resolution of the Board.

(8) To accept or decline donations tendered to the library system.

(9) To administer the expenditure of any funds which may become available for library purposes.

(10) To establish a schedule of fees to cover various services rendered and also to contract with other persons, including legal counsel and independent certified public or certified municipal accounting service, within the limits of its appropriations, and to incur necessary expenses. This subsection shall not be construed to preclude the use of the appropriate District Attorney or Assistant District Attorney for legal counsel and the State Auditor and Inspector for auditing services.

(11) To apply, contract for, receive and take advantage of any or all allocations of funds which may be available to the system board for library or library related purposes and services under the laws and regulations of the United States, the State of Oklahoma, or any other state, or any organization, agency, instrumentality or subdivision of these entities or undertake or contract for joint activities or programs with the United States, the State of Oklahoma or any other state, and any organization, agency, instrumentality, or subdivision of these entities pertaining to library or library related purposes or services; and to prepare and submit plans, specifications, reports or applications, to execute any agreements, to employ, fix duties and compensation of personnel, and to administer and direct any programs, plans or projects in connection with any of the foregoing.

(12) To do all other things necessary or desirable to carry out the purposes and provisions of this Code.

(b) It shall be the duty of the system board to prepare an annual budget which shall be filed on or before June 1 with the Boards of County Commissioners, The Oklahoma Department of Libraries, State Board of Equalization, and with cities and towns which participate in financial support of the system. The system board shall also submit an annual audit of its income and expenditures within ninety days following the close of the fiscal year to the Boards of County Commissioners, the Oklahoma Department of Libraries and with cities and towns which participate in financial support of the system.

(c) In the case of withdrawal of a county or abolishing of a library system, disposal of the assets, including capital equipment and other property of the library district, shall be made in the most equitable manner possible as determined by the Oklahoma Department of Libraries Board, who shall give consideration to such items as the original source of the property, the amount of funds raised from each county of the system, and the ability of the counties to make further use of such property or equipment for library purposes.

(d) Funds levied and collected pursuant to Article 10, Section 10–A of the Oklahoma Constitution shall be controlled and administered under the direction of the system board.

(e) Other funds contributed from Federal, State, county and city governments, and from any other source shall be deposited in the independent library account following such procedures as may be agreed upon by the contributing agency, the system board, and the Oklahoma Department of Libraries Board.

(f) Vouchers shall be drawn by such officers or employees as prescribed by the system board. Each designated officer or employee shall give a faithful performance bond approved by the system board in a sum determined by the board and sufficient in amount to equal the estimated largest sum of money which will be disbursed at any one time. Premiums for such bond may be paid from funds of the library system.

Laws 1967, c. 45, § 4–105. Amended by Laws 1979, c. 30, § 113, emerg. eff. April 6, 1979.

§ 4–106. Personnel

(a) The system board shall appoint a librarian of the library system on the basis of merit and experience. Such librarian shall be a graduate of a library school accredited by the American Library Association. The librarian shall be the administrative, executive and supervisory officer of the library and secretary to the system board. The librarian shall serve at the discretion of the system board.

(b) The librarian may appoint and remove staff members and other employees, subject to the approval of the system board.

(c) The librarian and staff shall receive actual and necessary travel expenses as set forth in 74 O.S.1961, §§ 500.5, 500.8—500.11 inclusive, or any amendments thereto, which expenses may be paid from the funds of the library system upon authorization of the board.

(d) The system board may establish or participate in employee retirement and health insurance programs either for the exclusive benefit of its staff or jointly and, in conjunction with city, county, State, or other retirement systems, may expend upon authorization of the board funds allocated by the board for such purposes.
Laws 1967, c. 45, § 4—106.

§ 4—107. Financing

Library systems are hereby authorized and empowered to receive and allocate funds for establishment, development and maintenance of library facilities and services through special library tax levies as hereinafter provided and other funds, including appropriations from city, town and county general funds, State and Federal grants-in-aid, and other public and private funds. All such funds received and appropriated may be used for library services throughout the library district.

(a) The governing boards of cities, towns, counties, and library systems established by vote of the people, as authorized, may submit to a vote of the people special tax levies of any tax or taxes which are or may be authorized for levying in and by cities, towns, counties and library system districts.

(b) The initial financing of any library system established under this Act shall be approved by the Oklahoma Department of Libraries Board.
Laws 1967, c. 45, § 4—107.

§ 4—108. Effect of Act on existing and new systems

(a) All library systems created after the effective date of this Act shall be created under the provisions of this Code.

(b) All library systems created before the effective date of this Code and financed under the provisions of Article X, Section 10A of the Oklahoma Constitution shall be deemed to be created under the provisions of this Act and shall within three years conform to the provisions of Section 4—103; provided, however, that this subsection (b) shall not apply to a library system organized and operating under the Metropolitan Library Act, Chapter 192 of 1965 Oklahoma Session Laws, or the Oklahoma City-County Library Act.
Laws 1967, c. 45, § 4—108.

§ 4—109. Metropolitan systems—Procedure for operating under this Code—Board of Trustees

(a) This Act shall not apply to a metropolitan system as defined by § 1–104(c) unless and until such metropolitan system shall elect to become subject to and operate under the provisions of this Code upon the adoption of resolutions for that purpose by the Library Commission of that metropolitan system, the Board of County Commissioners and the governing board of the largest city in the county. Such resolutions shall be filed with The Oklahoma Department of Libraries and when approved by The Oklahoma Department of Libraries Board, the metropolitan library system shall forthwith proceed to operate as provided by this Code.

(b) Any part of a county may be added to or included in a metropolitan system if said part of a county is within the official limits of a municipality included in such metropolitan system.

(c) The Board of Trustees of a library system containing at least one county but less than two counties, herein defined as a metropolitan library system, shall consist of eleven members. Six members shall be appointed by the mayor of the county seat city of the county served in its entirety, subject to approval of the governing body of the city. Three members shall be appointed by the Board of County Commissioners of the county served in its entirety. The mayor of the city and the Chairman of the Board of County Commissioners shall be ex-officio members of the Board of Trustees and shall be entitled to vote on all matters. Three additional non-voting members may be appointed by the Board of County Commissioners of any county served in part by such system; provided, however, this subsection (c) shall not apply to a metropolitan library system organized and operating under Chapter 192 of 1965 Oklahoma Session Laws or the Oklahoma City-County Library Act unless and until the three resolutions contemplated by subsection (a) of this section have been adopted and filed.

Laws 1967, c. 45, § 4–109.

§ 4–110. Grants-in-aid funds

All counties or cities not covered by this Code shall be considered in the allocation of State or Federal funds which now are or may hereafter become available for distribution.

Laws 1967, c. 45, § 4–110.

INTER-LOCAL AGREEMENTS
(Oklahoma Statutes Annotated, 1982, Title 65, s.5-101.)

§ 5–101. Inter-local agreements

In addition to the powers authorized by Chapter 189, Oklahoma Session Laws 1965, Sections 1–9, providing for inter-local cooperation among governmental agencies, libraries covered by this Code shall have the power to contract with private agencies under the same terms and conditions as stated in that Act.

Laws 1967, c. 45, § 5–101.

INTERSTATE LIBRARY COMPACT
(Oklahoma Statutes Annotated, 1982, Title 65,
s.6-101 to 6-106.)

§ 6–101. Text of compact

The Interstate Library Compact is hereby enacted into law and entered into by this State with all states legally joining herein in the form substantially as follows:

INTERSTATE LIBRARY COMPACT

Article I. Policy and Purpose

Because the desire for the services provided by libraries transcends governmental boundaries and can most effectively be satisfied by giving such services to communities and people regardless of jurisdictional lines, it is the policy of the states party to this compact to cooperate and share their responsibilities; to authorize cooperation and sharing with respect to those types of library facilities and services which can be more economically or efficiently developed and maintained on a cooperative basis, and to authorize cooperation and sharing among localities, states and others in providing joint or cooperative library services in areas where the distribution of population or of existing and potential library resources make the provision of library service on an interstate basis the most effective way of providing adequate and efficient service.

Article II. Definitions

As used in this compact:

(a) "Public library agency" means any unit or agency of local or state government operating or having power to operate a library.

(b) "Private library agency" means any nongovernmental entity which operates or assumes a legal obligation to operate a library.

(c) "Library agreement" means a contract establishing an interstate library district pursuant to this compact or providing for the joint or co-operative furnishing of library services.

Article III. Interstate Library Districts

(a) Any one or more public library agencies in a party state in coopera-tion with any public library agency or agencies in one or more other party states may establish and maintain an interstate library district. Subject to the provisions of this compact and any other laws of the party states which pursuant hereto remain applicable, such district may establish, maintain and operate some or all of the library facilities and services for the area concerned in accordance with the terms of a library agreement therefor. Any private library agency or agencies within an interstate library district may cooperate therewith, assume duties, responsibilities and obligations thereto, and receive benefits therefrom as provided in any library agree-ment to which such agency or agencies become party.

(b) Within an interstate library district, and as provided by a library agreement, the performance of library functions may be undertaken on a joint or cooperative basis or may be undertaken by means of one or more arrangements between or among public or private library agencies for the extension of library privileges to the use of facilities or services operated or rendered by one or more of the individual library agencies.

(c) If a library agreement provides for joint establishment, mainte-nance or operation of library facilities or services by an interstate library district, such district shall have power to do any one or more of the fol-lowing in accordance with such library agreement:

1. Undertake, administer and participate in programs or arrange-ments for securing, lending or servicing of books and other publications, any other materials suitable to be kept or made available by libraries, li-brary equipment or for the dissemination of information about libraries, the value and significance of particular items therein, and the use thereof.

2. Accept for any of its purposes under this compact any and all dona-tions, and grants of money, equipment, supplies, materials, and services (conditional or otherwise), from any state or the United States or any subdivision or agency thereof, or interstate agency, or from any institu-tion, person, firm or corporation, and receive, utilize and dispose of the same.

3. Operate mobile library units or equipment for the purpose of ren-dering bookmobile service within the district.

4. Employ professional, technical, clerical and other personnel, and fix terms of employment, compensation and other appropriate benefits; and where desirable, provide for the in-service training of such personnel.

5. Sue and be sued in any court of competent jurisdiction.

6. Acquire, hold, and dispose of any real or personal property or any interest or interests therein as may be appropriate to the rendering of li-brary service.

7. Construct, maintain and operate a library, including any appropriate branches thereof.

8. Do such other things as may be incidental to or appropriate for the carrying out of any of the foregoing powers.

Article IV. Interstate Library Districts, Governing Board

(a) An interstate library district which establishes, maintains or oper-ates any facilities or services in its own right shall have a governing board which shall direct the affairs of the district and act for it in all matters relating to its business. Each participating public library agency in the district shall be represented on the governing board which shall be organized and conduct its business in accordance with provision therefor in the library agreement. But in no event shall a governing board meet less often than twice a year.

(b) Any private library agency or agencies party to agreement establishing an interstate library district may be represented on or advise with the governing board of the district in such manner as the library agreement may provide.

Article V. State Library Agency Cooperation

Any two or more state library agencies of two or more of the party states may undertake and conduct joint or cooperative library programs, render joint or cooperative library services, and enter into and perform arrangements for the cooperative or joint acquisition, use, housing and disposition of items or collections of materials which, by reason of expense, rarity, specialized nature, or infrequency of demand therefor would be appropriate for central collection and shared use. Any such programs, services or arrangements may include provision for the exercise on a cooperative or joint basis of any power exercisable by an interstate library district and an agreement embodying any such program, service or arrangement shall contain provisions covering the subjects detailed in Article VI of this compact for interstate library agreements.

Article VI. Library Agreements

(a) In order to provide for any joint or cooperative undertaking pursuant to this compact, public and private library agencies may enter into library agreements. Any agreement executed pursuant to the provisions of this compact shall, as among the parties to the agreement:

1. Detail the specific nature of the services, programs, facilities, arrangements or properties to which it is applicable.

2. Provide for the allocation of costs and other financial responsibilities.

3. Specify the respective rights, duties, obligations and liabilities of the parties.

4. Set forth the terms and conditions for duration, renewal, termination, abrogation, disposal of joint or common property, if any, and all other matters which may be appropriate to the proper effectuation and performance of the agreement.

(b) No public or private library agency shall undertake to exercise itself or jointly with any other library agency, by means of a library agreement, any power prohibited to such agency by the constitution or statutes of its state.

(c) No library agreement shall become effective until filed with the compact administrator of each state involved, and approved in accordance with Article VII of this compact.

Article VII. Approval of Library Agreements

(a) Every library agreement made pursuant to this compact shall, prior to and as a condition precedent to its entry into force, be submitted to the attorney general of each state in which a public library agency party thereto is situated, who shall determine whether the agreement is a proper form and compatible with the laws of his state. The attorneys general shall approve any agreement submitted to them unless they shall find that it does not meet the conditions set forth herein and shall detail in writing addressed to the governing bodies of the public library agencies concerned the specific respects in which the proposed agreement fails to meet the requirements of law. Failure to disapprove an agreement submitted hereunder within ninety days of its submission shall constitute approval thereof.

(b) In the event that a library agreement made pursuant to this compact shall deal in whole or in part with the provision of services or facilities with regard to which an officer or agency of the state government has constitutional or statutory powers of control, the agreement shall, as a condition precedent to its entry into force, be submitted to the state officer or agency having such power of control and shall be approved or disapproved by him or it as to all matters within his or its jurisdiction in the same manner and subject to the same requirements governing the action of the attorneys general pursuant to paragraph (a) of this article. This requirement of submission and approval shall be in addition to and not in substitution for the requirement of submission to and approval by the attorneys general.

Article VIII. Other Laws Applicable

Nothing in this compact or in any library agreement shall be construed to supersede, alter or otherwise impair any obligation imposed on any library by otherwise applicable law, nor to authorize the transfer or disposition of any property held in trust by a library agency in a manner contrary to the terms of such trust.

Article IX. Appropriations and Aid

(a) Any public library agency party to a library agreement may appropriate funds to the interstate library district established thereby in the same manner and to the same extent as to a library wholly maintained by it and, subject to the laws of the state in which such public library agency is situated, may pledge its credit in support of an interstate library district established by the agreement.

(b) Subject to the provisions of the library agreement pursuant to which it functions and the laws of the states in which such district is situated, an interstate library district may claim and receive any state and federal aid which may be available to library agencies.

Article X. Compact Administrator

Each state shall designate a compact administrator with whom copies of all library agreements to which his state or any public library agency thereof is party shall be filed. The administrator shall have such other powers as may be conferred upon him by the laws of his state and may consult and cooperate with the compact administrators of other party states and take such steps as may effectuate the purposes of this compact. If the laws of a party state so provide, such state may designate one or more deputy compact administrators in addition to its compact administrators.

Article XI. Entry Into Force and Withdrawal

(a) This compact shall enter into force and effect immediately upon its enactment into law by any two states. Thereafter, it shall enter into force and effect as to any other state upon the enactment thereof by such state.

(b) This compact shall continue in force with respect to a party state and remain binding upon such state until six months after such state has given notice to each other party state of the repeal thereof. Such withdrawal shall not be construed to relieve any party to a library agreement entered into pursuant to this compact from any obligation of that agreement prior to the end of its duration as provided therein.

Article XII. Construction and Severability

This compact shall be liberally construed so as to effectuate the purposes thereof. The provisions of this compact shall be severable and if any phrase, clause, sentence or provision of this compact is declared to be contrary to the constitution of any party state or of the United States

or the applicability thereof to any government, agency, person or circumstance is held invalid, the validity of the remainder of this compact and the applicability thereof to any government, agency, person or circumstance shall not be affected thereby. If this compact shall be held contrary to the constitution of any state party thereto, the compact shall remain in full force and effect as to the remaining states and in full force and effect as to the state affected as to all severable matters.
Laws 1967, c. 45, § 6—101.

§ 6—102.   Compliance with applicable laws

No library system, county, city or town of this State shall be a party to a library agreement which provides for the construction or maintenance of a library pursuant to Article III, Subdivision (c) 7 of the compact, nor pledge its credit in support of such a library, or contribute to the capital financing thereof, except after compliance with any laws applicable to such library system, county, city or town relating to or governing capital outlays and the pledging of credit.
Laws 1967, c. 45, § 6—102.

§ 6—103.   State library agency

As used in the compact, "state library agency," with reference to this State, means the Oklahoma Department of Libraries.
Laws 1967, c. 45, § 6—103.

§ 6—104.   Districts lying partly within State

An interstate library district lying partly within this State may claim and be entitled to receive state aid in support of any of its functions to the same extent and in the same manner as such functions are eligible for support when carried on by entities wholly within this State. For the purposes of computing and apportioning state aid to an interstate library district, this State will consider that portion of the area which lies within this State as an independent entity for the performance of the aided function or functions and compute and apportion the aid accordingly. Subject to any applicable laws of this State, such a district also may apply for and be entitled to receive any federal aid for which it may be eligible.
Laws 1967, c. 45, § 6—104.

§ 6—105   Administrator

The Director of the Department of Libraries shall be the administrator pursuant to Article X of the compact. The Director shall appoint a deputy compact administrator pursuant to said article.
Laws 1967, c. 45, § 6—105.

§ 6—106.   Withdrawal from compact

In the event of withdrawal from the compact the Director shall send and receive any notices required by Article XI(b) of the compact.
Laws 1967, c. 45, § 6—106.

AUTOMATED DATA PROCESSING
(Oklahoma Statutes Annotated, 1982, Title 65, s.55-58.)

§ 55.   Automated data processing and information center

In order to expedite the management and organization of the vast and increasing resources of knowledge, to make it quickly available to our citizens, and to aid the functions of government, it shall be the policy of the State to foster the establishment and maintenance of a State Library Automated Data Processing and Information Center. Laws 1965, c. 253, § 1, emerg. eff. June 21, 1965.

§ 56. Subjects included in system

The Oklahoma State Library is hereby authorized and directed to establish at the earliest possible date an automated data processing and information retrieval system and a statewide information network. The system shall include these elements and operations as rapidly as circumstances permit:

(a) Legislative reference and research, including current legislative data.

(b) Circulation of books and other types of library holdings.

(c) Statistical information and reports of state institutions.

(d) Rules and regulations of state agencies.

(e) Laws of the state.

(f) Public documents of Oklahoma, the United States and other governments.

(g) Opinions of the Attorney General.

(h) General reference and research.

(i) Oklahoma information center.

(j) Legal reference and research.

(k) Archives and records of the state.

(l) Printed catalog of Oklahoma State Library Collections.

(m) Any other operation considered desirable, necessary or feasible.
Laws 1965, c. 253, § 2.

§ 57. Powers and duties of Librarian

The State Librarian is authorized to apply for and receive and to take advantage of any and all assistance, information, research, investigations, surveys, grants, appropriations, or allocations of funds made available for this or any related or allocated purposes from any source; to cooperate or undertake joint activities or programs with any organization or government, including their agencies or subdivisions, pertaining to the purposes of this act; to prepare and submit plans, reports, applications, specifications to appropriate agencies or bodies, to execute any agreements, to employ and fix the compensation and duties of personnel, and to administer and direct any programs, plans or projects in connection with any of the foregoing. Laws 1965, c. 253, § 3.

§ 58. Provisions cumulative

The provisions of this act are cumulative to existing laws. Laws 1965, c. 253, § 4.

LIBRARY SERVICE TO THE BLIND
(Oklahoma Statutes Annotated, 1982, Title 7, s.8.)

§ 8. Special library services to blind and physically handicapped persons

(a) See Title 74, State Officers and Employees, § 285(23) note.

(b) The State Plan for library services shall be amended in accordance with the Federal Library Services and Construction Act and applicable regulations to reflect the authority and duty of the Section of Services to the Blind of the Oklahoma Public Welfare Commission to provide special library services, including braille and recorded books, to blind and visually handicapped persons as provided by State law.

(c) On and after July 1, 1969, special library services for blind and physically handicapped adults, children, and students shall be provided by the Section of Services to the Blind of the Oklahoma Public Welfare Commission in accordance with the Federal Library Services and Construction Act, as amended, and applicable Federal regulations relating thereto; and consistent with applicable statutes and regulations, the library standards of the National Accreditation Council for Agencies Serving the Blind and Visually Handicapped shall be observed and followed in providing such special library services. The Oklahoma Public Welfare Commission shall, within the availability of State funds, annually make available for such special library services sufficient funds to earn the maximum available Federal funds under the Federal Library Services and Construction Act and appropriations made in pursuance thereof by Congress.

(d) All Federal requirements for interlibrary cooperation and consultation shall be observed; and entitlement of the Department of Libraries to receive Federal funds for library services or construction shall not be impaired by any State law prescribing the duties, responsibilities and functions of the Section of Services to the Blind.

Laws 1969, c. 290, § 2(b), (c) (d), emerg. eff. April 29, 1969.

DISTRIBUTION OF PUBLIC DOCUMENTS

(Oklahoma Statutes Annotated, 1982, Title 75, s.14.)

§ 14. Free copies of statutes and session laws

A. The following named officers shall be entitled to receive as soon as available from the state without cost one copy each of the printed volumes of the statutes and session laws of the state published or purchased by the Legislature, or under its authority, for distribution:

     *   *   *

11. Each library association organized in any county, city or town in this state for the benefit of the public.

B. Fifty-five (55) copies of each volume of statutes and session laws shall be furnished to the law library of the College of Law of the University of Oklahoma, five (5) copies of each volume shall be kept for use therein and fifty (50) copies for purposes of exchange.

C. Five (5) copies of each volume of statutes and session laws shall be placed in the Library of Oklahoma State University at Stillwater, Oklahoma, for use herein.

D. One hundred ten (110) copies of each volume of statutes and session laws shall be furnished to the Department of Libraries for use therein and for exchange purposes.

E. The Secretary of State may, in his discretion, furnish out of any copies of such laws on hand copies to other state officers than those mentioned herein for the use of their offices.

Amended by Laws 1976, c. 209, § 1; Laws 1978, c. 165, § 12.

ARCHIVES AND RECORDS COMMISSION

(Oklahoma Statutes Annotated, 1982, Title 74, s.564-576.)

§ 564. Creation—Personnel—Authority

There is hereby created the Archives and Records Commission, hereinafter referred to as the Commission, to be composed of one (1) member to be appointed by the Governor who shall serve as Chairman, the State Librarian as Vice Chairman and Secretary, the Lieutenant Governor, the State Auditor and Inspector and the State Treasurer as members. Any member may appoint and designate a subofficer or employee as his proxy for purposes of carrying on the duties of the Commission. The Commission shall have sole, entire and exclusive authority of the disposition for all public records and archives of state officers, departments, boards, commissions, agencies and institutions of this state. The authority herein granted shall not apply to records and archives of political subdivisions of the state. Amended by Laws 1978, c. 146, § 1; Laws 1979, c. 241, § 11, operative July 1, 1979.

§ 565. Unnecessary records and archives—Consultation with State Librarian—Application to Commission—Disposition

Every state officer and the heads of all departments, boards, commissions, agencies and institutions of the State of Oklahoma who have in their custody public records and archives deemed by them to be unnecessary for the transaction of the business of their offices shall consult with the State Librarian for the purpose of determining if such records and archives are desired for deposit in the archives division of the Oklahoma State Library. Upon certification by the State Librarian that such records and archives are or are not desired for such purpose, then such custodian shall, in conformity with such determination, apply to the Commission for authorization to destroy or transfer such records and archives to the Oklahoma State Library as hereinafter provided. Upon the filing of such application the Commission shall have authority to authorize or direct the disposition of such records and archives by any one or more of the following methods:

1. By destruction; provided that, the Commission shall not authorize destruction of records and archives less than five (5) years old except upon a showing of good cause by the agency or the Archives and Records Division of the Oklahoma Department of Libraries and a unanimous vote of the members of the Commission, or their designees, present.

2. By transfer to the custody and control of the Oklahoma State Library and there retained. The State Librarian may, in his discretion, microfilm such records and archives, especially if so doing would aid in the preservation of their contents.

3. By transfer to the Oklahoma State Library with authorization to the State Librarian to microfilm said records and archives and upon the completion of this process to destroy said records and archives in accordance with the order of the Commission.

Records and archives transferred to the Oklahoma State Library shall never be returned to their former custody except by order of the Commission and written consent of the State Librarian.
Amended by Laws 1978, c. 146, § 2.

§ 566. Assignment of employees for checking records and archives

The Commission is hereby given the authority to request any State officer or the head of any department, board, commission, agency or institution of the State of Oklahoma whose records and archives are being checked to furnish as many persons in the employ thereof, as in its discretion are necessary, to properly check and survey the records and archives of said State officer, department, board, commission, agency or institution. And it shall be the duty of any State officer, or the head of any department, board, commission, agency or institution to furnish the number of persons requested by the said Commission. Said employees so assigned to the Commission shall be under its direction and supervision in the performance of the functions set out by this Act. Laws 1947, p. 617, § 3.

§ 567.   Record of destroyed or transferred records or archives

A record shall be kept of the records and archives which are destroyed or transferred and it shall be in such form as prescribed by the Commission and shall disclose among other things the date and content of the records and archives destroyed, transferred, or micro-filmed. One (1) copy of said record shall be kept by the State Officer, department, board, commission, agency, or institution of the State of Oklahoma whose records have been destroyed or transferred. One (1) copy shall be filed with the Secretary of the State, and the original of such record shall be retained by the Secretary of the Commission, which record shall be certified as correct by the custodian of such records or archives. Laws 1947, p. 617, § 4.

§ 568.   Micro-film or micro-photograph film deemed original record—Exemplification or certified copy

Any micro-film or micro-photograph film of any original record or archives shall be deemed to be an original record or archive for all purposes and shall be admissible in evidence in all courts or administrative agencies the same as the originals. A facsimile exemplification or certified copy thereof shall for all purposes recited herein be deemed to be a description exemplification or certified copy of the original. Laws 1947, p. 617, § 5.

§ 569.   Records and archives on termination of functions of offices, etc.

All records and archives of any State officer or of any department, board, commission, agency or institution, shall upon the termination of the functions of that office, department, board, commission, or institution, be disposed of in accordance with the provisions of this Act. Laws 1947, p. 617, § 6.

§ 570.   Right of access to records and archives—Replevin for records or archives illegally removed

The Secretary of the Archives and Records Commission in person, or through a deputy authorized by him, shall have the right of access to all public records and archives of this State, except those records and archives classified as confidential by Act of the Legislature, with a view of securing their safety and preservation and determining their administrative or legal value. On behalf of the State of Oklahoma and the Oklahoma State Library the Attorney General may replevin any public records or archives illegally removed which were formerly part of the records or files of any public office of the Territory or of the State of Oklahoma. Laws 1947, p. 617, § 7.

§ 571. Equipment and supplies—Film library

The State Librarian shall acquire and maintain sufficient equipment and supplies to micro-film all records, archives and documents transferred to him for that purpose in conformity with the minimum standards of quality approved for permanent microfilming and photographing of records and archives by the National Bureau of Standards; and shall maintain a film library with a catalog system or index and adequate equipment to enable the various State officers, departments, boards, commissions, agencies and institutions to effectively use the micro-film service which is hereby established in the Oklahoma State Library. Laws 1947, p. 618, § 8.

§ 572. Examination of documents and records of state offices and agencies for preservation, destruction or microfilming—Privileged or confidential document or record

(a) The Secretary of the Archives and Records Commission is directed and authorized to begin not later than thirty (30) days after the effective date of this Resolution on examination of the documents, records, papers, and archives located in Oklahoma City, Oklahoma which belong to the agencies, authorities, boards, commissions, departments, institutions, instrumentalities, office, officers, officials, and societies of the State of Oklahoma, to determine (a) what part or parts of such documents, records, papers, and archives are to be preserved, (b) what part or parts of such documents, records, papers and archives are to be destroyed or sold as waste, and (c) what part or parts of such documents, records, papers, and archives are to be microfilmed and the original of such documents, records, papers, and archives destroyed or sold thereafter. The Secretary of the Archives and Records Commission is authorized to delegate his executive duties under this sub-section.

(b) No document, record, paper, or archive is to be withheld from examination by the Secretary of the Archives and Records Commission on the ground or grounds that the same is a privileged or confidential document, record, paper, or archive. If any statute or statutes of the State of Oklahoma as now enacted create any class of privileged or confidential document, record, paper, or archives and provide any penalty or penalties for disclosure of such document, record, paper, or archive it is the intent of the Legislature that such penalty or penalties not be applied in connection with any examination by the Secretary made for the purpose of compliance with this Resolution. In the event the Secretary examines a confidential or privileged document, record, paper, or archive he is forbidden to divulge or to disclose any information obtained from his examination. Laws 1953, p. 516, § 1.

§ 573. List of documents or records for disposition

The Secretary of the Archives and Records Commission is directed at such time as he completes the examination of each such agency, authority, board, commission, department, institution, instrumentality, office, officer, official, or society, to furnish to the appropriate head of each agency, authority, board, commission, department, institution, instrumentality, office, officer, official, or society with a listing which shows the type or class of the documents, records, papers, and archives which are to be: (a) retained, (b) destroyed, and (c) microfilmed. Laws 1953, p. 517, § 2.

§ 574. Delivery of documents or records for disposition— Refusal—Report of non-compliance—Filing

Within thirty (30) days after the head of each such agency, authority, board, commission, department, institution, instrumentality, office, officer, official, or society is furnished with such a listing by the Secretary of such documents, records, papers, and archives are to be delivered to the Secretary of the Archives and Records Commission for disposition as provided.

In the event delivery is refused of such documents, records, papers, and archives the Secretary of the Archives and Records Commission is directed not later than ten (10) days after the expiration of thirty (30) day period of compliance to report such non-compliance to the President Pro Tempore of the Senate, to the Speaker of the House of the Oklahoma Legislature, and to the Governor of the State of Oklahoma, setting forth in detail the extent of non-compliance and the reasons assigned therefor. In addition the Secretary is directed to file a copy of such report or reports of non-compliance with the Secretary of State of Oklahoma, and the same is to be a public record open for the inspection and information of the public. Laws 1953, p. 517, § 3.

§ 575. Delivery and preparation of documents and records for disposition—Moneys received

Upon the delivery to the Secretary of the Archives and Records Commission of the documents, records, papers, and archives, the Secretary is authorized and directed to prepare them for retention, microfilming, and destruction, in accordance with the terms of the Archives and Records Act. The Secretary is authorized and directed to deposit the money or monies received from the disposition of such documents, records, papers, and archives in the Official Depository Account Number 21 of the State Treasurer of Oklahoma. The money or monies so received is to be expended at the discretion of the Secretary in the advancement of this program. Laws 1953, p. 517, § 4.

§ 576. Definitions—Archives and Records Commission—Secretary—Dead storage files

As used in this Resolution unless the context otherwise requires:

1. Secretary of the Archives and Records Commission means and refers to that office created under the terms of Title 74 O.S. 1951, Section 564 and following, and to the powers, privileges, and duties assigned that office under such statutes.

2. The Archives and Records Commission means and refers to that Commission created under the terms of Title 74 O.S.1951, Section 564, and to the powers, privileges, and duties assigned such Commission under such statutes.

3. The phrase "dead storage files" refers to and includes all rooms, storehouses, warehouses, floor space, office space, files, filing cabinets, vaults, and other places in which are stored, kept, maintained, or otherwise held documents, papers, records, and archives not in actual use which belong to, or are in the custody of, any agency, authority, board, commission, department, institution, instrumentality, office, officer, official, or society of the State of Oklahoma. To be in actual usage such documents, papers, records, and archives must be in continual demand for immediate reference purposes, for actual use in the day-to-day work required of any agency, authority, board, commission, department, institution, instrumentality, office, officer, official, or society of the State of Oklahoma in their principal offices or places of business. Any documents, papers, records, and archives not in such continual usage are to be considered dead storage files. Laws 1953, p. 517, § 5.

PRESERVATION OF RECORDS
(Oklahoma Statutes Annotated, 1982, Title 67, s.151-166.)

§ 151. Name

This Act shall be known as the "Preservation of Essential Records Act." Laws 1961, p. 500, § 1.

§ 152. Declaration

The Legislature declares that records containing information essential to the operation of government and to the protection of the rights and interests of persons must be protected against the destructive effects of all forms of disaster and must be available when needed. It is necessary, therefore, to adopt special provisions for the selection and preservation of essential State and local records thereby providing for the protection and availability of such information. Laws 1961, p. 500, § 2.

§ 153. Definitions

As used in this Act.

(a) Disaster means any occurrence of fire, flood, storm, earthquake, explosion, epidemic, riot, sabotage or other condition of extreme peril resulting in substantial damage or injury to persons or property within this State, whether such occurrence is caused by an act of nature or man, including an enemy of the United States.

(b) Record means document, book, paper, photograph, microfilm, sound recording, or other material, regardless of physical form or characteristics, made or received pursuant to law or ordinance or in connection with the transaction of official business but does not include library and museum material made or received solely for reference or exhibition purposes.

(c) State record means:

(1) A record of department, office, commission, board, authority or other agency, however designated, of the State government; provided, however, the provisions of this Act shall not be applicable to, or binding upon, the State Department of Public Welfare or the Oklahoma Public Welfare Commission.

(2) A record of the State Legislature;

(3) A record of the Supreme Court, Court of Criminal Appeals or any other courts of record, whether of statewide or local jurisdiction; and

(4) Any other record designated or treated as a State record under the law of this State.

(d) Local record means a record of a county, city, town, village, township, district, authority or any public corporation or political entity whether organized and existing under charter or under general law unless the record is designated or treated as a State record under the law of this State.

(e) Preservation duplicate means a copy of an essential State record which is used for the purpose of preserving such State record pursuant to this Act. Laws 1961, p. 501, § 3.

§ 154. Essential records

State or local records which are within the following categories are essential records which shall be preserved pursuant to this Act:

Category A. Records containing information necessary to the operations of government in the emergency created by a disaster.

Category B. Records not within Category A but containing information necessary to protect the rights and interests of persons or to establish and affirm the powers and duties of governments in the resumption of operations after a disaster. Laws 1961, p. 501, § 4.

§ 155. Records Preservation Officer

The State Librarian, as The State Archivist, is hereby designated the Records Preservation Officer. The Records Preservation Officer shall establish and maintain a program for the selection and preservation of essential State records and shall, insofar as possible, advise in the establishment of programs for the selection and preservation of essential local records. Laws 1961, p. 501, § 5.

§ 156. Advisory committee

A Records Preservation Advisory Committee, hereinafter called the Committee, is hereby established to advise the Records Preservation Officer and to perform such other duties as this Act requires. The Committee shall be composed of the members of the Archives and Records Commission. The Committee may appoint qualified consultants to advise it on matters pertinent to its duties and such consultants shall be appointed for a specified term of service. The Records Preservation Officer shall be chairman, and the Committee shall adopt rules for the conduct of its business. The Committee and the consultants shall meet whenever called by the chairman. The members of the Advisory Committee and consultants shall serve without compensation but shall be reimbursed for their actual expenses incurred while performing their duties as members and consultants of the Committee. Laws 1961, p. 501, § 6.

§ 157. Rules and regulations

The Records Preservation Officer shall promulgate such rules and regulations concerning the selection and preservation of essential State records as are necessary or proper to effectuate the purpose of this Act. Laws 1961, p. 501, § 7.

§ 158. Inventory and report

The Records Preservation Officer shall select the State records which are essential and determine their category pursuant to this Act. In accordance with the rules and regulations promulgated by the Records Preservation Officer each person who has custody or control of State records shall (1) inventory the State records in his custody or control; (2) submit to the Records Preservation Officer a report thereon containing such information as the Records Preservation Officer directs and containing his recommendations as to which State records are essential; and (3) periodically review his inventory and his report and, if necessary, revise his report so that it is current, accurate and complete. Laws 1961, p. 502, § 8.

§ 159. Preservation duplicates

(a) The Records Preservation Officer may make or cause to be made preservation duplicates or may designate as preservation duplicates existing copies of essential State records. A preservation duplicate shall be durable, accurate, complete and clear and a preservation duplicate made by means of photography, microphotography, photocopying, file or microfilm shall be made in conformity with the standards prescribed therefor by the Records Preservation Officer.

(b) A preservation duplicate made by a photographic, photostatic, microfilm, micro-card, miniature photographic, or other process which accurately reproduces or forms a durable medium for so reproducing the original, shall have the same force and effect for all purposes as the original record whether the original record is in existence or not. A transcript, exemplification or certified copy of such preservation duplicate shall be deemed for all purposes to be a transcript, exemplification or certified copy of the original record.

(c) No copy of an essential State record shall be used as a preservation duplicate unless under the law of this State the copy has the same force and effect for all purposes as the original State record. Laws 1961, p. 502, § 9.

§ 160. Storage of records

(a) The Records Preservation Officer shall prescribe the place and manner of safekeeping of essential State records and preservation duplicates and may establish storage facilities therefor. The Records Preservation Officer may provide for storage outside the State.

(b) When in the opinion of the Records Preservation Officer the legally designated or customary location of an essential State record is such that the essential State record may be destroyed or unavailable in the event of a disaster caused by an enemy of the United States:

(1) The Records Preservation Officer shall store a preservation duplicate at another location and permit such State record to remain at its legally designated or customary location; or

(2) The Records Preservation Officer shall store such State record at a location other than its legally designated or customary location and deposit at the legally designated or customary location a preservation duplicate for use in lieu of the State record; or

(3) The Records Preservation Officer may store such State record at a location other than its legally designated or customary location without providing for a preservation duplicate upon a determination that it is impracticable to provide for a preservation duplicate and that the State record is not frequently used. Such determination shall be made by the Records Preservation Officer and the regularly designated custodian of such State record, but if they disagree, the determination shall be made by the Committee.

(c) The requirements of subsection (b) of this Section shall not prohibit the Records Preservation Officer from removing an essential State record or preservation duplicate from the legally designated or customary location of the State record if a disaster caused by an enemy of the United States or other disaster of a grave nature has occurred or is imminent. Laws 1961, p. 502, § 10.

§ 161. Maintenance and recall of essential State records—Inspection—Copies

(a) The Records Preservation Officer shall properly maintain essential State records and preservation duplicates stored by him.

(b) An essential State record or preservation duplicate stored by the Records Preservation Officer may be recalled by the regularly designated custodian of the State record for temporary use when necessary for the proper conduct of his office and shall be returned by such custodian to the Records Preservation Officer immediately after such use.

(c) When an essential State record is stored by the Records Preservation Officer, the Records Preservation Officer, upon request of the regularly designated custodian of the State record, shall provide for its inspection, or for the making or certification of copies thereof, and such copies when certified by the Records Preservation Officer shall have the same force and effect as if certified by the regularly designated custodian. Laws 1961, p. 502, § 11.

§ 162. Confidential records

When a State record is required by law to be treated in a confidential manner and is an essential State record, the Records

Preservation Officer, and his staff, in effectuating the purposes of the Act with respect to such State record, shall protect its confidential nature. Laws 1961, p. 503, § 12.

§ 163.   Review of program

The Records Preservation Officer shall review periodically but at least biennially the program for the selection and preservation of essential State records, including the classification of records and the provisions for preservation duplicates and for safekeeping of essential State records or preservation duplicates to ensure that the purposes of this Act are accomplished. Laws 1961, p. 503, § 13.

§ 164.   Program for selection and preservation of local records

The governing body of each county, city, town, village, township, district, authority, or any public corporation or political entity whether organized and existing under charter or under general law shall establish and maintain, with the advice of the Records Preservation Officer, a program for the selection and preservation of its essential local records. Such governing body shall, as far as practicable, follow the program established for the selection and preservation of essential State records. Such governing body shall report biennially to the Records Preservation Officer on the status and progress of its records preservation program. Laws 1961, p. 503, § 14.

§ 165.   Biennial report for Governor and Legislature

The Records Preservation Officer shall prepare a biennial report on the status and progress of the programs established under this Act for the selection and preservation of essential State records and essential local records and shall submit such a report to the Governor, the Legislature and the Committee. Laws 1961, p. 503, § 15.

§ 166.   Placing act into effect—Optional compliance

(a) The Records Preservation Officer shall place the provisions of this Act into effect with reasonable promptness conditioned only by the limitations of funds and staff available for this purpose.

(b) No department, office, commission, board, authority, or other agency, however designated, of the State government shall be subject to the provisions of this Act until such agency shall notify the Governor and the Records Preservation Officer in writing of its determination to comply with the Act's provisions; provided that such resolve may not be rescinded at a later date. Laws 1961, p. 503, § 16.

RECORDS MANAGEMENT

(Oklahoma Statutes Annotated, 1982, Title 67, s.201-214.)

§ 201. Name

This Act shall be known as the "Records Management Act." Laws 1961, p. 498, § 1.

§ 202. Declaration

The Legislature declares that programs for the efficient and economical management of State and local records will promote economy and efficiency in the day-to-day record-keeping activities of State and local governments and will facilitate and expedite government operations. Laws 1961, p. 498, § 2.

§ 203. Definitions

As used in this Act:

(a) "Record" means document, book, paper, photograph, sound recording or other material, regardless of physical form or characteristics, made or received pursuant to law or ordinance or in connection with the transaction of official business. Library and museum material made or acquired and preserved solely for reference or exhibition purposes, extra copies of documents preserved only for convenience of reference, and stocks of publications and of processed documents are not included within the definition of records as used in this Act.

(b) "State record" means:

(1) A record of a department, office, commission, board, authority or other agency, however designated, of the State government; provided, however, the provisions of this Act shall not be applicable to, or binding upon, the State Department of Public Welfare or the Oklahoma Public Welfare Commission.

(2) A record of the State Legislature.

(3) A record of the Supreme Court, the Court of Criminal Appeals or any other court of record, whether of statewide or local jurisdiction.

(4) Any other record designated or treated as a State record under State law.

(c) "Local record" means a record of a county, city, town, village, township, district, authority or any public corporation or political entity whether organized and existing under charter or under general law unless the record is designated or treated as a State record under State law.

(d) "Agency" means any department, office, commission, board, authority or other unit, however designated, of the State government; provided, however, the provisions of this Act shall not be applicable to, or binding upon, the State Department of Public Welfare or the Oklahoma Public Welfare Commission. Laws 1961, p. 498, § 3.

§ 204.   State Records Administrator

The State Librarian, as The State Archivist, is hereby designated the State Records Administrator, hereinafter called the Administrator. The Administrator shall establish and administer a records management program, which will apply efficient and economical management methods to the creation, utilization, maintenance, retention, preservation and disposal of State records. Laws 1961, p. 498, § 4.

§ 205.   Duties of Administrator

The Administrator shall, with due regard for the functions of the agencies concerned:

(a) Establish standards, procedures, and techniques for effective management of records.

(b) Make continuing surveys of paper work operations and recommend improvements in current records management practices including the use of space, equipment and supplies employed in creating, maintaining, storing and servicing records.

(c) Establish standards for the preparation of schedules providing for the retention of State records of continuing value and for the prompt and orderly disposal of State records no longer possessing sufficient administrative, legal or fiscal value to warrant their further keeping.

(d) Obtain reports from agencies as are required for the administration of the program. Laws 1961, p. 498, § 5.

§ 206.   Duties of agency heads

The head of each agency, except the Department of Public Welfare, shall:

(a) Establish and maintain an active, continuing program for the economical and efficient management of the records of the agency.

(b) Make and maintain records containing adequate and proper documentation of the organization, functions, policies, decisions, procedures and essential transactions of the agency designed to furnish information to protect the legal and financial rights of the State and of persons directly affected by the agency's activities.

(c) Submit to the Administrator, in accordance with the standards established by him, schedules proposing the length of time each State record series warrants retention for administrative, legal or fiscal purposes after it has been received by the agency. The head of each agency also shall submit lists of State records in his custody that are not needed in the transaction of current business and that do not have sufficient administrative, legal or fiscal value to warrant their further keeping for disposal in conformity with the requirements of Section 10 of this Act.

(d) Cooperate with the Administrator in the conduct of surveys made by him pursuant to the provisions of this Act.

(e) Comply with the rules, regulations, standards and procedures issued by the Administrator. Laws 1961, p. 499, § 6.

§ 207. Local records management

The governing body of each county, city, town, village, township, district, authority or any public corporation or political entity whether organized and existing under charter, or under general law shall promote the principles of efficient records management for local records. Such governing body shall, as far as practical, follow the program established for the management of State records. The Administrator shall, insofar as possible, upon the request of a governing body provide advice on the establishment of a local records management program. Laws 1961, p. 499, § 7.

§ 208. Records management program for legislative and judicial branches

Upon request, the Administrator shall advise and assist in the establishment of records management programs in the legislative and judicial branches of state government and shall, upon request, provide a program of services similar to those available to the executive branch of State government pursuant to the provisions of this Act. Laws 1961, p. 499, § 8.

§ 209. Prohibition on mutilation, destruction, etc. of records

All records made or received by or under the authority of or coming into the custody, control or possession of public officials of this State in the course of their public duties shall not be mutilated, destroyed, transferred, removed, altered or otherwise damaged or disposed of, in whole or in part, except as provided by law. Laws 1961, p. 499, § 9.

§ 210. Disposition of records

No record shall be destroyed or otherwise disposed of by any agency of the State, unless it is determined by the Administrator and the Archives and Records Commission that the record has no further administrative, legal, fiscal, research or historical value. This provision does not supersede 74 O.S.1951, §§ 564–571; 74 O.S.Supp.1959, §§ 572–576; and 19 O.S.1951, §§ 911–

918, 19 O.S.1959, §§ 157–159; 19 O.S.1959, §§ 232–234, and House Bills Nos. 659, 906 and 1016 enacted by the Twenty-eighth Legislature, but is cumulative to these laws. Laws 1961, p. 499, § 10.

§ 211.   Destruction of non-record materials

Non-record materials or materials not included within the definition of records as contained in this Act may, if not otherwise prohibited by law, be destroyed at any time by the agency in possession of such materials with the prior approval of the Administrator. The Administrator may formulate procedures and interpretation to guide in the disposition of non-record materials. Laws 1961, p. 499, § 11.

§ 212.   Rules and regulations

The Administrator shall promulgate such rules and regulations as are necessary or proper to effectuate the purposes of this Act, except that rules and regulations relating to the disposal of records pursuant to Section 10 of this Act shall be issued jointly by the Administrator and the Archives and Records Commission. Laws 1961, p. 499, § 12.

§ 213.   Biennial report to Governor

The Administrator shall make a biennial report to the Governor for transmission to the Legislature. The report shall describe the status and progress of programs established pursuant to this Act and shall include the recommendations of the Administrator for improvements in the management of records in the State government. Laws 1961, p. 500, § 13.

§ 214.   Personnel—Expenditure of funds—Contracts for records management—Bond

(a) ,When a State agency institutes a records management program under the provisions of this Act it is hereby authorized and directed to furnish the Administrator with as many persons in its employ as he considers necessary to carry on the program, and such employees shall be under his direction and supervision while performing the duties connected with the execution of the provisions of this Act, and the agency is furthermore authorized and directed to expend amounts from any funds under its control that the Administrator requests for the purpose of establishing and maintaining a records management program in the agency.

(b) In the furtherance of a records management program a State agency may con'ract, with the approval of the Administrator, with a reputable records management organization, having at least five years of experience in the techniques of records management operations, for the establishment of a records management program in the agency and may pay out sums for this purpose from any funds under its control. Such organization shall give a performance bond with good and sufficient sureties, payable to the State of Oklahoma, for a sum not less than the amount of the contract and the bond shall be approved by the Attorney General. All work performed under such contract shall be under the general direction and

supervision of the Administrator and shall have his written approval before any payments are made for such services.
Amended by Laws 1968, c. 67, § 2, emerg. eff. March 25, 1968.

STATE AGENCY RULES AND REGULATIONS
(Oklahoma Statutes Annotated, 1982, Title 75, s.251-256.)

§ 251. Filing of copies—Exceptions—Adoption of material by reference

(a) Every agency, including any authority, board, commission, department, instrumentality, office, or officer of the State of Oklahoma, that possesses rule-making powers shall file a certified original and one duplicate copy of all its rules or regulations in force and effect with the Secretary of State and a certified original and two duplicate copies with the State Librarian and Archivist on or before the effective date of this act. Thereafter, every such agency shall file similar copies of all new rules or regulations, and all amendments, revisions of existing rules and regulations, or revocations thereof, with the Secretary of State and with the State Librarian and Archivist within three days of their adoption, excluding holidays, Saturdays, and Sundays. The provisions of this act shall not apply to rules or regulations which (1) pertain to an agency's internal operation and organization only; (2) pertain to proclamations of the Governor; or (3) concern the internal management and operation only of an institution, including institutions of higher education. The filing of rules or regulations as required by this act does not dispense with the requirements of any other law necessary to make them effective.

(b) In order to avoid unnecessary expense, an agency may use the standards established by organizations and technical societies of recognized national standing by incorporating such standards in its rules by reference to the specific issue or issues of publications in which they are published, without reproduction of the standards in full, provided that such publications are readily available to the public for examination. If any such rule or regulation adopts by reference any standards which are published in any documents, pamphlets, publications, specifications, or other materials of any kind and which are not set forth fully in said rule or regulation, then two copies of such documents, pamphlets, publications, or other materials of any kind, certified by the adopting agency to be identical with that adopted in said rule or regulation, shall be filed with the State Librarian and Archivist and such adoption by reference shall not be valid until such copies are so filed; provided that nothing herein shall be construed to authorize any adoption by reference which could not have lawfully been adopted by reference prior to the effective date of this act. Laws 1961, p. 602, § 1.

§ 252.   Filing as condition of validity

Any rule or regulation, amendment, revision, or revocation of an existing rule or regulation made by an agency prior to the effective date of this act shall be void and of no effect unless filed as required by Section 1 of this act and, except to the extent otherwise provided in Section 3 of this act, any rule or regulation, amendment, revision, or revocation of an existing rule or regulation made by an agency after the effective date of this act shall be void and of no effect unless filed and published as required by Sections 1 and 5 of this act.   All provisions herein shall also apply to all agencies that may hereafter be created.   All courts, boards, commissions, agencies, authorities, instrumentalities, and officers of the State of Oklahoma shall take judicial or official notice of any rule or regulation, amendment, revision, or revocation of an existing rule or regulation duly filed, or duly filed and published under the provisions of this act. Laws 1961, p. 603, § 2.

§ 253.   Emergency rules and regulations

If an emergency situation arises and the preservation of the public peace, health, safety, welfare, or other compelling extraordinary circumstance requires that an emergency rule or regulation, amendment, revision, or revocation of an existing rule or regulation become effective without delay, an agency may adopt any such, provided the Governor shall first certify to this effect, and all such emergency adoptions shall be in force immediately, or on such date as specified therein, and the Governor shall immediately file copies of his certification and the emergency adoption with the Secretary of State and the State Librarian and Archivist as provided in Section 1 (a) of this act.   The Governor's certificate and the emergency adoption shall be published in accordance with the provisions of Section 5 of this act.   Executive orders of the Governor shall become effective upon the date specified therein or immediately upon issuance, and shall be published as required by Section 5 of this act. Laws 1961, p. 603, § 3.

§ 254.   Certified copies—Fees

The Secretary of State shall have authority to make and certify to the correctness of copies of any rule or regulation and any amendment, revision, or revocation thereof and to charge such fees as are allowed by law. Such certified copies shall have the same effect as the original for any purpose. Laws 1961, p. 603, § 4.

§ 255. Publication and distribution of The Oklahoma Gazette —Administrative rules and regulations

The State Librarian and Archivist is hereby authorized, directed, and empowered to publish The Oklahoma Gazette semimonthly and to publish therein and distribute copies of all rules and regulations adopted subsequently to the effective date hereof and all amendments or revisions of existing rules and regulations or revocations thereof adopted subsequently to the effective date hereof in the first number of The Oklahoma Gazette published after the date of receipt. No new rule or regulation nor any amendment, revision, or revocation of an existing rule and regulation shall be in effect until seven days, including holidays, Saturdays, and Sundays, have elapsed from the date of publication by the State Librarian and Archivist. The State Librarian and Archivist shall cause a copy of each such publication of a new rule or regulation or any amendment, revision, or revocation of an existing rule and regulation to be sent to every county clerk, court clerk, and county law library in the State of Oklahoma, to members of the legislature, and to such other appropriate agencies, libraries, and officials he may select; provided that he may charge nongovernmental and nonofficial recipients. The State Librarian and Archivist shall cause a copy of all rules and regulations, all new rules and regulations, and all amendments, re visions, or revocations of existing rules and regulations to be on file and available for public examination in the Oklahoma State Library during normal office hours. The county clerks, court clerks, and county law libraries shall also maintain files of these publications for public examination during normal office hours. The State Librarian and Archivist shall systematize the designations of rules and regulations and, in order to establish such system or to preserve uniformity of designations, he may change the title or numbering of any rule or regulation and any amendment, revision, or revocation thereof and as soon as possible thereafter he shall notify the agency concerned and the Secretary of State. Laws 1961, p. 603, § 5.

§ 256. Publication of Code of Oklahoma Rules and Regulations

(a) The Director of the Oklahoma Department of Libraries, as State Librarian and Archivist, is hereby authorized and empowered to furnish copies of all rules and regulations or any amendments, revisions, or revocations of existing rules and regulations, free of charge, to any publisher who agrees in writing to publish a Code of Oklahoma Rules and Regulations, and to publish cumulative supplements thereto not less often than once every two (2) years (the exact period to be specified in the agreement) during the period of time covered by the agreement; provided that after the first such agreement has been made and performed, subsequent agreements may be made and copies furnished of the publications of such supplements as are necessary to keep the code current. All such agreements shall provide that the publisher shall make such publications in such form and arrangement as shall be approved by the Director, and that the publisher shall furnish the Department with twelve (12) free copies of all such publications, and shall also furnish three (3) free copies of all such publications to the University of Oklahoma College of Law Library and one (1) free copy to the Oklahoma State University Library at Stillwater, Oklahoma. Failure of any such publisher to perform the terms of any such agreement as required therein shall terminate such agreement and such publisher shall be liable to the State Librarian and Archivist for the cost of all such copies furnished by him to such publisher, and all such costs recovered by the State Librarian and Archivist shall be paid into the State Library Fund.

(b) If at any time the State of Oklahoma should purchase copies of the Code of Oklahoma Rules and Regulations, or any supplements thereto, said publications shall be delivered to and distributed by the Secretary of State; provided that fifty (50) unmarked copies of the code or any supplements shall be purchased for and delivered to the Publications Clearinghouse of the Oklahoma Department of Libraries and become the property of the Oklahoma Department of Libraries for use of the library and for exchange by the Publications Clearinghouse for the administrative codes or other publications of the official libraries of other states, territories and possessions of the United States, as set out in Section 3 115 of Title 65 of the Oklahoma Statutes; and provided further that fifty (50) unmarked copies of each volume shall be purchased for and delivered to and become the property of the University of Oklahoma College of Law Library to be used for the exchange by the librarian of that library for the publications of other colleges or schools of law.
Amended by Laws 1978, c. 165, § 13.

STATE HISTORICAL SOCIETY
(Oklahoma Statutes Annotated, 1982, Title 53, s.1-3, 6-12, 16-19.)

§ 1.   Trustee of State for certain purposes—Board of directors

The Oklahoma Historical Society, shall faithfully expend and apply all money received from the State to the uses and purposes directed by law and shall hold all its present and future collections of property for the State, and shall not sell, mortgage or dispose of in any manner, or remove from the State University any article thereof or part of the same without authority of law: Provided, That this shall not prevent the sale or exchange of any duplicates that the society may have or obtain. There shall continue to be a board of directors of said society, to consist of as many members as the society shall determine, and who shall have the same powers as the present board of directors.
R.L.1910, § 4360.

§ 2.   Duties—Expenditures

It shall be the duty of the society to collect books, maps and other papers and materials illustrative of the history of Oklahoma in particular and the West generally; to procure from the early settlers narratives of events relative to the early settlement of Oklahoma and to the early explorations, Indian occupancy and overland travel in Oklahoma and Indian Territories and the West; to procure facts and statements relative to the history and conduct of our Indian tribes and to gather all information calculated to exhibit faithfully the antiquities and the past and present condition, resources and progress of the commonwealth; to purchase books to supply deficiencies in the various departments of its collections and to procure by gift and exchange such scientific and historical reports of the Legislatures of other States, of railroads, reports of geological and other scientific surveys, and such other books, maps, charts and other information as will facilitate the investigation of historical, scientific, social, educational and literary subjects and to cause them to be properly bound; to catalogue the collections of said society for the more convenient reference of all persons who may have occasion to consult the same; to prepare annually for publication a report of its collections and such other matters relating to its transactions as may be useful to the public; and to keep its collections arranged in suitable and convenient rooms, to be provided and furnished by the society as the board of directors may determine; the rooms of the society to be open at all reasonable hours on business days for the reception of the citizens of this commonwealth, who may wish to visit the same, without fee: Provided, that no expenditure shall be made under this Article, or expense incurred except in pursuance of specific appropriations therefor, and no officer of said society shall pledge the credit of the State in excess of such appropriation.

R.L.1910, § 4361.

§ 2A. Additional powers and duties—Historic Sites Revolving Fund—Vandalism—Penalties

(1). a. The Oklahoma Historical Society shall hereinafter have the authority to acquire by gift, devise, purchase or otherwise, absolutely or in trust, and to hold and, unless otherwise restricted by the terms of the gift or devise, to encumber, convey or otherwise dispose of any real property or real estate or other interest therein as may be necessary in carrying into effect the purpose of this act.

b. Authority is hereby granted to the Oklahoma Historical Society to enter into contracts and to execute all instruments necessary to fulfill its duties, respecting the protection, preservation, maintenance and/or operation of such historic buildings, sites and/or objects as it may select.

c. To correlate and preserve drawings, plans, photographs and other data of historic and archaeologic sites, buildings and objects.

d. To make surveys of historic and archaeologic sites, buildings and objects for the purpose of determining which possesses exceptional value as commemorating and/or relating to the history of Oklahoma.

e. Make necessary investigations and research in Oklahoma relating to particular sites, buildings or objects to obtain true and accurate historical and archaeological facts and information concerning the same.

f. Contract and make cooperative agreements with municipalities, corporations, associations and individuals, with proper bond where deemed ad-

visable to protect, preserve, maintain or operate any historic or archaeologic building, site, object or property used in connection therewith for
public use, regardless whether the title thereto is in the State of Oklahoma;
provided, that no contract or cooperative agreement shall be made or
entered into which will obligate the general fund of the State Treasury
unless or until the Legislature has appropriated sufficient monies for such
purpose.

g.   Restore, reconstruct, rehabilitate, preserve and maintain historic or
prehistoric sites, buildings, objects and properties of historical and archaeological significance and where deemed desirable establish and maintain museums in connection therewith.

h.   Operate and manage historic and archaeologic sites, buildings and
properties acquired under the provisions of this act, together with lands
and subordinate buildings for the benefit of the public, such authority
to include the power to charge reasonable visitation fes and grant concessions, leases or permits for the use of land, building space, roads or
trails when necessary or desirable either to accommodate the public or
to facilitate administration; provided that such concessions, leases or permits shall be granted only after competitive bids to the person making
the highest and best bid.

i.   When the Oklahoma Historical Society determines that it would be
administratively burdensome to restore, reconstruct, operate or maintain
any particular historic or archaeologic site, building or property donated
to the state, it may cause the same to be done by organizing a corporation for that purpose under the laws of the State of Oklahoma.

j.   Develop an education program and service for the purpose of making available to the public facts and information pertaining to Oklahoma
historic and archaeologic sites, buildings and property of state significance.
Reasonable charges may be made for the dissemination of any such facts
or information.

(2) No person shall wilfully or knowingly break, break off, crack, carve
upon, write, or otherwise mark upon, or in any manner damage, destroy,
mutilate, deface, mar or harm any historic or prehistoric site, building,
object, artifact or material in, around or upon any historic site owned,
operated, managed or under the control of the Oklahoma Historical Society, and any person violating any of the provisions hereof shall be
guilty of a misdemeanor and shall be punished by a fine of not to exceed
Two Hundred Dollars ($200.00) or by confinement in the county jail
for not to exceed thirty (30) days or by both such fine and confinement.
Amended by Laws 1973, c. 46, § 7, operative July 1, 1973.

§ 3.   Accounts and reports—Donation of state publications—
Duplication of publications

The board of directors shall keep a correct account of the expenditures of all money which may be appropriated in aid of the
society and report annually to the Governor a detailed statement
of such expenditure. To enable the society to augment its collections by effecting exchanges with other societies and institutions,
sixty bound copies each of the several publications of the State
and of its societies and institutions; except the reports of the
Supreme Court and the Criminal Court of Appeals, shall be, and
the same are hereby donated to said Oklahoma Historical Society as they shall be issued, the same to be delivered to the society

by the Secretary of State or other officer having custody of the same. The society shall not expend its resources in procuring duplicates of such publications as may be in the University library.

R.L.1910, § 4362.

§ 6. Board of directors—Membership—Powers

The Board of Directors of the Oklahoma Historical Society shall consist of not more than twenty-five members, also with the Governor as an ex-officio member, and shall have the same powers as now exist until changed according to the constitution and by-laws of said Society, or by Act of the Legislature: Provided, that the number of members of said board may be decreased by Act of the Legislature or by Act of said Society by amending its constitution. Laws 1935, p. 63, § 1.

§ 7. Duty of society—Expenditures from public fund limited to appropriation

It shall be the duty of said Society, through its board and agents, to collect or acquire books, newspapers, magazines, catalogues, maps, papers, records, reports, surveys, charts, pictures, photographs, paintings, relics, and such other matters and information as will facilitate the investigation of scientific, social, educational, economical, business, industrial, political and literary subjects and all historical matter, and to preserve the same by having such collections catalogued, indexed and bound for the convenient reference and study of persons who may have occasion to study, examine and consider same, and to prepare for publication reports and to publish matters relating to its transactions and research as may be useful to its membership and the citizens of the State and the public at large and to keep its collections and archives arranged in suitable, safe and convenient rooms in the Historical Building to be open at reasonable hours under reasonable regulations for the reception of the citizens of the State as may wish to visit and inspect same without fee or charge; Provided, that no expenditure out of the public funds shall be made or expense incurred to be borne by the State except in pursuance of specific appropriations theretofore made and no obligation shall be incurred in excess of such appropriations. Laws 1935, p. 63, § 2.

§ 8. Contributions, gifts and donations—Title to real estate— Leasing real estate—Custodians

The Oklahoma Historical Society may solicit and receive contributions, gifts, and donations to be held by it in trust under the terms and conditions imposed by the donors, and title to all real estate acquired, donated and granted to said Society shall be taken in the name of the State to be held for the use and benefit of the Oklahoma Historical Society under the conditions of such grants or donations, the Board of Directors of the Oklahoma Historical Society, through its officers or duly authorized agents to be manager of such real property with authorization to let and lease the same for a period not to exceed ten years, and where necessary employ a suitable custodian or custodians of such realty, with the proviso that no expense is to be incurred relative thereto except as is authorized by law and an appropriation theretofore made to meet same. Provided, further, that as to such realty as may consist of parks and places of historical interest with buildings thereon such custodian or caretaker may be employed by such board to be paid out of receipts from visitors or out of an appropriation theretofore specifically made for such purpose, and from donations theretofore pledged for such purpose and made to meet such expense, which is not to exceed such receipts or donations or such appropriation theretofore made for such purpose.   Laws 1935, p. 64, § 3.

§ 8.2   Title to locally owned historical or recreational site—Approval of funding

The title to any locally owned historic or recreational site or improvements thereon shall not be acquired by or conferred to the Oklahoma Historical Society to qualify for state funding without prior approval of both the Senate and the House of Representatives.
Laws 1982, c. 345, § 12, emerg. eff. June 2, 1982.

§ 9.   Accounts and reports of expenditures

The Board of Directors shall keep a correct account of the expenditures of all money which may be appropriated by the Legislature in aid of the Society and report annually to the Governor detailed statement of such expenditure, and also report to him a detailed expenditure of all donations, receipts and expenditures therefrom.   Laws 1935, p. 64, § 4.

§ 10.   Exchanges of duplicates

The Oklahoma Historical Society is authorized to make exchanges of duplicates held by it for matters of equal historical importance.   Laws 1935, p. 64, § 5.

§ 11.   Official seals, records and documents—Transfer to society

Any official of the State, or any sub-division thereof, having the custody of any seal, record, original paper or other document not required by laws of this State to be retained as a part of the record of such office shall transfer the same to the Oklahoma Historical Society to be held by it.   Laws 1935, p. 64, § 6.

§ 12. Certified copies of records, papers and documents— Fees for certificates

The Secretary, or in his absence the Chief Clerk, of the Historical Society is authorized to make certified copies of any and all records, papers or other documents, including excerpts and parts of all of any newspaper or file, and papers and archives held by said Society in trust for the United States Government, and such as may by him or her be certified and attested and the seal of the Historical Society affixed thereto, shall be received in evidence in all the Courts of this State and have the same force and effect as the original would when introduced in evidence; provided, that when such certificates are made for the United States Government, or any of its officers, to be used in evidence in behalf of the United States Government, or any of its agencies, such certificate shall be made without fee or charge, and the same as to the State of Oklahoma and its Agents, but in all other instances fees for such certificate shall be paid by the party applying therefor in such amount as allowed by law to the Secretary of State for such certification, and when such fee is not fixed by law it shall be a reasonable charge to be fixed by the Board of Directors of said Society. All fees so received shall be paid into the State depository in the State Treasury and held for the use and benefit of the Oklahoma Historical Society, provided, that no fee shall be charged for such certified copy when required in the transaction of the business of the State or the United States Government. Laws 1935, p. 64, § 7.

§ 16. Board of Directors

The Board of Directors of the Oklahoma Historical Society, consisting of not more than twenty-five (25) members, also with the Governor as an ex officio member, as now constituted, are hereby declared to be agents of the State of Oklahoma, and to hold as such directors until their successors are elected and qualified. Laws 1937, p. 99, § 1.

§ 17. Members of Oklahoma Historical Society

The members of said Society are hereby declared to be those who have heretofore become and are now members of said Society, and such others as may be admitted and elected as members thereof, in accordance with its constitution and by-laws, and are to continue as members thereof in accordance with the terms of said Constitution and by-laws as it may be amended in accordance with its terms or by Act of the Legislature.

Laws 1937, p. 99, § 2.

§ 18.   Oklahoma Historical Society as state agency—By-laws and rules and regulations—Acquisition of real property

The said Oklahoma Historical Society is hereby declared to be such organized agency of the State of Oklahoma and to have been such since the erection of the State of Oklahoma, with power to formulate and adopt rules and regulations by means of its constitution and by-laws, and resolutions for its government and regulation subject to the laws of the State, and have the power to acquire by purchase real property for the purposes for which it is created, when it has the funds on hand for such purposes, the title thereto to be taken in the name of the State for the use and benefit of the Oklahoma Historical Society as is authorized by law, and the Oklahoma Historical Society, through its Board of Directors.   Laws 1937, p. 100, § 3.

§ 19.   Historical Society Revolving Fund

There is hereby created in the State Treasury of the State of Oklahoma a Revolving Fund to be designated as the Historical Society Revolving Fund, which shall consist of all money appropriated to said fund and all money received by the Oklahoma Historical Society from membership, sales of publications, sales of merchandise to visitors, income from duplicating and microfilm services, contributions, gifts and endowments, excluding those gifts and endowments conditionally tendered, and other income derived from the operations of the Oklahoma Historical Society and from historic sites. The Oklahoma Historical Society is hereby authorized and directed to prepare for public distribution such historical data as may in its judgment meet the public demand; said Society shall determine the fee to be charged for each of the publications and such fee should be sufficient to cover the cost of preparing, publishing and marketing to the general public in the Historical Society Building.

Said revolving fund shall be a continuing fund not subject to fiscal year limitations and shall be under the control and management of the Oklahoma Historical Society and the disbursements therefrom shall be approved by the Society. Monies deposited in said revolving fund may be expended for the purpose of maintaining and operating the Oklahoma Historical Society functions and for operation of historic sites. Warrants for expenditures from this fund shall be drawn by the State Treasurer based on claims signed by the approving officer of the Society and approved for payment by the Director of State Finance.
Amended by Laws 1973, c. 46, § 8, operative July 1, 1973; Laws 1979, c. 287, § 18, emerg. eff. June 7, 1979.

CITY-COUNTY LIBRARIES
(Oklahoma Statutes Annotated, 1982, Title 65, s.151-161,
s.61, 81-83, State Constitution, Art. 10, s.10A.)

§ 151.   Short title

This act shall be known and may be cited as the Oklahoma City-County Library Act.   Laws 1961, p. 492, § 1.

§ 152. Policy and purpose

The purpose of this act is to foster and promote the establishment, maintenance and operation of city-county library systems in order to give all of the citizens of the counties affected hereby equal access to comprehensive library collections. It is the policy of the state to encourage the formation of such co-operative library systems to the end of avoiding unnecessary duplication in the maintenance and operation of public libraries and to stimulate the use of books and other library materials.

In order to make adequate library services available to the residents of the more densely populated counties of this state, to provide for the most efficient development of library facilities within such counties and to provide for each of such counties a city-county library system, there is hereby created in each of such counties which avails itself of the provisions of this act a City-County Library Commission, with the powers and duties set out in this act. Laws 1961, p. 492, § 2.

§ 153. Application

Any county of the state having within its boundaries a city having not less than one hundred thousand (100,000) population, according to the last or any succeeding Federal Decennial Census, is hereby authorized to avail itself of the provisions of this act and to combine its funds with the funds of such city to be expended for the purposes herein set forth. The board of county commissioners of any such county in this state is hereby authorized to contract with the governing body of any such city, as herein provided, for the establishment of a city-county library system. Laws 1961, p. 492, § 3.

§ 154. Library commission—Appointment—Tenure—Vacancies—Compensation

The City-County Library Commission shall consist of eleven members. Six of the members shall be appointed by the mayor of the city subject to approval of the governing body thereof. Three of the members shall be appointed by the board of county commissioners. The mayor of the city and the chairman of the board of county commissioners shall be ex officio members of the commission and shall be entitled to vote on all matters. The initial appointments by the city shall designate two members to serve a term of three years, two members to serve a term of two years, and two members to serve a term of one year. The initial appointments by the county shall designate one member to serve a term of three years, one member to serve a term of two years, and one member to serve a term of one year. Provided, that the terms of such initial appointees and the terms of all future appointees of both the city and county shall expire July 31st of that year in which they expire, regardless of the calendar date when such appointments are made. Subsequent appointments of either the city or the county shall be for three-year terms, except in the case of an appointment to fill a vacancy in the membership of the commission, which latter appointment shall be for the balance of the unexpired term of the member whose death, resignation, or removal has created the vacancy. A member of such commission once qualified can thereafter be removed during his term of office only for misconduct or neglect of duty and, if he requests a hearing before the governing body by which he was appointed, after such hearing has been held. All members of the commission shall serve thereon without compensation. Expenses which are incurred by members pursuant to prior specific authorization by the board of county commissioners and the governing body of the city shall be reimbursed, provided that expenses incurred for transportation, meals, and lodging shall be reimbursed only if incurred in connection with authorized travel outside the county. Laws 1961, p. 493, § 4.

§ 155. Officers—Meetings—Quorums—Contracts

The commission shall elect its chairman from the appointed members and fill such other offices as its bylaws may establish. The term of the chairman shall be one year. The commission shall hold at least one meeting each month and all meetings shall be open to the public. It shall adopt rules for the transaction of business and keep a record of its functions and activities, which record shall be a public record. Six commissioners shall constitute a quorum for the purpose of conducting business and exercising the powers of the commission. The commission may establish a schedule of fees to cover various services rendered and may also contract with other persons and agencies for such services as it may require, including private legal counsel and private auditing service, within the limits of its appropriations, and may incur necessary expenses, all subject to the approval of the governing body of the city and the board of county commissioners. The commission may contract for, receive, and utilize any grants or other financial assistance from the United States or from any other source, public or private, in furtherance of its functions; may incur necessary expenses in obtaining said grants and/or financial assistance, within the limits of its appropriations; and shall receive and disburse such grants and/or other financial assistance in such manner as may be agreed upon by the governing body of the city and board of county commissioners. Laws 1961, p. 493, § 5.

§ 156. Librarian—Qualifications—Staff—Other employees

The commission shall appoint a librarian of the city-county library system on the basis of merit and experience. Such librarian shall be a graduate of a library school accredited by the American Library Association. The librarian shall serve at the discretion of the commission. The librarian may appoint and remove staff members and other employees, subject to the approval of the commission. The appointment and compensation of the librarian, staff members and other employees shall all be subject to the approval of the governing body of the city and the board of county commissioners. Laws 1961, p. 493, § 6.

§ 157. Budget—Contributions—Expenditures

It shall be the duty of the commission to prepare an annual budget which shall be subject to the approval of the governing body of the city and the board of county commissioners.

Each county and city establishing a city-county library system, as herein provided, at the beginning of each fiscal year or as soon thereafter as may be practicable, shall agree upon the necessary contributions to be made by each for the establishment, operation and maintenance of the city-county library system, appropriate such funds as may be agreed upon, and combine said funds with funds from any other source. Periodically, as may be agreed upon, the city and county shall contribute their appropriated funds to a common fund upon claims therefor being filed by the commission with the governing body of the city and with the board of county commissioners. After approval of the claims, the contributions shall be made by warrants, issued by the appropriate officers and made payable to the city treasurer or county treasurer, as may be agreed upon by the city and county. Said common fund shall be maintained as a depository account with either the city treasurer or county treasurer, as may be agreed upon, and shall be disbursed upon vouchers drawn by such officer or employee of the commission as may be agreed upon by the city and county. Said vouchers shall be issued only in payment of claims which have been executed in the manner prescribed by law for claims against the county or the city and after such claims have been approved by the governing body of the city and the board of county commissioners, and before delivery to the payee, shall be registered with the city treasurer or county treasurer, as the case may be.

The officer or employee of the commission designated by the city and county to draw vouchers in payment of such claims shall be bonded in an amount as may be required by the city and county, but not less than Twenty Thousand Dollars ($20,000.00). The designated officer or employee shall be governed by the same statutory provisions relating to depository accounts as apply to county officials generally. Nothing contained herein shall be construed as exempting from the application of the general statutes relating to appropriations the funds contributed by the city and county to this common fund.

Income of the city-county library system from fines, fees, sales of personal property, and other miscellaneous sources, excluding income from sales of real property, shall not be considered general revenue of either the city or the county. It shall be deposited promptly with the city treasurer or the county treasurer, as the case may be, and shall be credited directly to the depository account of the commission without appropriation. Income from this source shall constitute a revolving fund which shall not be subject to fiscal limitations and which may be expended by the commission for the replacement or repair of books and other personal property other than motor vehicles.

In the event funds are made available for library purposes in the county, pursuant to the provisions of Section 10A of Article X of the Oklahoma Constitution, all or any part of the cost of establishing, maintaining and operating the city-county library system as set forth in the powers granted to the commission in Section 8 herein, and otherwise, may be paid with such funds, and the City-County Library Commission is authorized hereby to administer the expenditure of such funds in the same manner as herein provided for expenditure of funds appropriated from general revenue for library purposes. Laws 1961, p. 493, § 7.

§ 158. Library commission—General powers and duties

Every City-County Library Commission created by this act shall have all the powers necessary or convenient for the accomplishment of the purpose and provisions hereof, including in addition to others herein granted, the following powers, all of which shall be exercised subject to approval by the governing body of the city and the board of county commissioners:

(a) To establish a city-county library system and to adopt such rules and regulations for the operation thereof as may be deemed necessary or expedient.

(b) To purchase, lease, or otherwise acquire land or buildings or portions of buildings for library purposes.

(c) To erect, maintain, and operate public library buildings at one or more places in the county.

(d) To accept transfer of any existing public library or libraries by lease or other conveyance.

(e) To acquire by purchase or otherwise books and other personal property customarily used in the operation of public libraries, including necessary motor vehicles.

(f) To sell and dispose of personal property acquired by purchase or other means when by proper resolution the commission finds that said property is not needed for library purposes.

(g) To accept, hold, and convey legal title to interests in real property in the name "City-County Library Commission of County" which shall be its official name. Deeds or other conveyances of said interests in real property shall be executed for and on behalf of the commission by the chairman and shall be attested by the secretary, only after authorization by resolution of the governing body of the city and the board of county commissioners.

(h) To accept, or in its discretion to decline donations tendered to the city-county library system.

(i) To administer the expenditure of any funds which may become available for library purposes pursuant to the provisions of Section 10A, Article X of the Constitution of the State of Oklahoma. Laws 1961, p. 494, § 8.

§ 159. Other libraries—Contracts

The governing body of any other city or town in a county in which a city-county library system has been established is authorized to contract with the City-County Library Commission, subject to the approval of the governing body of the city and the board of county commissioners, to bring such other city or town into the city-county library system, upon such terms as may be mutually agreed upon, and for that purpose may lease to the City-County Library Commission any library facilities or property which such other city or town may own, may include in its annual budget appropriations for participation in the city-county library system, and shall pay over to the city-county library system funds so appropriated, which funds shall be combined with the funds of the city and county and expended in the same manner as herein provided for the expenditure of such funds. Laws 1961, p. 495, § 9.

§ 160. Employee retirement

If, pursuant to the provisions of Chapter 37 of Title 11 of the Oklahoma Statutes or of any statute supplemental thereto or of any charter provision of the city, a retirement system is established for the employees of the city, the employees of the city-county library system may be included in that retirement system on the same basis applicable to employees of the city, if the commission so recommends and the board of county commissioners and the governing body of the city approve. Nothing otherwise provided by law shall operate to prohibit the appropriation of county funds for the payment of the county's pro rata share of the contribution to be made to the retirement fund on behalf of the employees of the city-county library system. In the event funds become available for library purposes pursuant to the provisions of Section 10A of Article X of the Oklahoma Constitution, the entire contribution on behalf of the employees of the city-county library system may be paid from such funds. Laws 1961, p. 495, § 10.

§ 161. Act cumulative

This act is intended to be cumulative and in addition to any other law heretofore passed on libraries and shall not repeal any law on this subject. Laws 1961, p. 495, § 11.

§ 61. Excise board—Levy for county circulating library—Joint city and county library in certain cases

The excise board of any county in this state is hereby authorized to make an annual levy of not to exceed one-half of one mill on all taxable property of the county, which levy shall be in addition to all other levies authorized by law, for the purpose of providing funds to be used to establish, extend, operate, and maintain a county circulating library, and to employ help necessary in connection therewith. In any county of this state having a population of less than fifteen thousand (15,000) persons according to the last preceding Federal Decennial Census the excise board is authorized to make such levy for the purpose of providing funds to be used to establish, extend, operate, and maintain a joint county and city library. Provided, the said board of county commissioners shall have authority to use such funds in cooperation with any public library in said county when such cooperation will be advantageous for said county library.

Amended by Laws 1969, c. 207, § 1, emerg. eff. April 18, 1969.

§ 81. Governing bodies of cities—Authority to contract with county for library

The governing bodies of the cities of this State, are hereby empowered and authorized to enter into a contract with the County Commissioners of the county, in which such city is located, for the purpose of purchasing a site and erecting, maintaining, and operating a building thereon, to be used for Public Library, upon such terms or conditions as may be agreed upon between the two (2) contracting parties. Laws 1937, p. 167, § 1.

§ 82. County commissioners—Authority to contract with city for library

The County Commissioners of any county of the State, are hereby authorized to enter into a contract with the governing body of any city, county seat of such county, for the purpose of purchasing a site and the erecting, maintaining and operating a building thereon, to be used for a Public Library, on such terms and conditions as may be agreed upon by the parties thereto. Laws 1937, p. 167, § 2.

§ 83. Appropriation of funds for purchase, erection and maintenance of library

The County Commissioners and the governing body of any city entering into the above described contract, are hereby authorized to appropriate and pay out the necessary funds from the general funds of such county or city, respectively, for the purchase of a site and the erection and maintenance of such building thereon and to make appropriations for the purchase of books and circulation thereof in the county. Laws 1937, p. 167, § 3.

§ 10A. Tax levy for cooperative county libraries and joint city-county libraries

To provide funds for the purpose of establishing and maintaining or aiding in establishing and maintaining public libraries and library services, a special annual recurring ad valorem tax levy of not less than one (1) mill nor more than two (2) mills on the dollar of the assessed valuation of all taxable property in the county shall be levied when such levy is approved by a majority vote of the qualified electors of the county voting on the question at an election called for that purpose by the Board of County Commissioners, either upon its own initiative or upon petition initiated by not less than ten (10) per cent of the qualified electors of the county based on the total number of votes cast at the last general election for the county office receiving the highest number of votes at such an election. This special levy shall be in addition to all other levies and when authorized shall be made each fiscal year thereafter until such authority shall be cancelled by a majority vote of the qualified electors of the county voting on the question at an election called for that purpose by the Board of County Commissioners upon petition initiated by not less than twenty (20) per cent of the qualified electors of the county based on the total number of votes cast at the last general election for the county office receiving the highest number of votes at such an election.

In counties having a population of less than two hundred fifty thousand (250,000), according to the most recent Federal Decennial Census, the proceeds of such levy shall be used by the county only for such public libraries and library services as are in cooperation with one (1) or more other counties having such population of less than 250,000; and in counties having a population of more than two hundred fifty thousand (250,-000), according to the most recent Federal Decennial Census, the proceeds of such levy shall be used by the county only for joint city-county public libraries and library services. Nothing herein shall prohibit other levies for public libraries and library services or the use of other public funds for such purposes. All expenditures of the proceeds of such levies shall be made in accordance with laws heretofore or hereafter enacted concerning such libraries and library services. The provisions hereof shall be self-executing. Added State Question No. 392, Referendum Petition No. 127, adopted election July 26, 1960.

METROPOLITAN LIBRARIES
(Oklahoma Statutes Annotated, 1982, Title 65, s.551-561.)

§ 551. Short title
This act shall be known and may be cited as the "Metropolitan Library Act". Laws 1965, c. 192, § 1, emerg. eff. June 8, 1965.

§ 552. Applicability
This act shall apply to any joint city-county public libraries established and maintained under the provisions of Article X, Section 10A of the Oklahoma Constitution in any county having a population of five hundred thousand (500,000) or more according to the 1960 or any succeeding Federal Decennial Census, provided, that in counties with less than five hundred thousand (500,000) population, and having a joint city-county public library, such library may elect to come under the provisions of this act upon a majority vote of the City-County Library Commission.
Laws 1965, c. 192, § 2. Amended by Laws 1971, c. 77, § 1, emerg. eff. April 16, 1971.

§ 553. Purpose—Commission created
The purpose of this act is to foster and promote the establishment, maintenance and operation of city-county library systems in order to give all of the citizens of the counties affected hereby equal access to comprehensive library collections. It is the policy of the state to encourage the formation of such cooperative library systems to the end of avoiding unnecessary duplication in the maintenance and operation of public libraries and to stimulate the use of books and other library materials.

In order to make adequate library services available to the residents of the more densely populated counties of this state, to provide for the most efficient development of library facilities within such counties and to provide for each of such counties a city-county library system, there is hereby created in each of such counties which avails itself of the provisions of this act a Metropolitan Library Commission, with the powers and duties set out in this act. Laws 1965, c. 192, § 3.

§ 554. Membership—Tenure—Compensation—Secretary
A. In all cities with a population of four hundred thousand (400,000) or less, according to the latest Federal Decennial Census, the metropolitan library commission shall consist of eleven (11) members. Six of the members shall be appointed by the mayor of the county seat city, subject to approval of the governing body thereof. Three of the members shall be appointed by the board of county commissioners. The mayor of the county seat city and the chairman of the board of county commissioners shall be ex officio members of the commission and shall be entitled to vote on all matters. The initial appointments by the city shall designate two members to serve a term of three (3) years, two members to serve a term of two (2) years, and two members to serve a term of one (1) year. The initial appointments by the county shall designate one member to serve a term of three (3) years, one member to serve a term of two (2) years, and one member to serve a term of one (1) year. The terms of such initial appointees and the terms of all future appointees of both the

city and county shall expire July 31 of the year the term expires, regardless of the calendar date when such appointments are made. Subsequent appointments of either the city or the county shall be for three-year terms, except in the case of an appointment to fill a vacancy in the membership of the commission, which latter appointment shall be for the balance of the unexpired term of the member whose death, resignation, or removal has created the vacancy. A member of this commission, once qualified, can be removed during his term of office only for misconduct or neglect of duty and, if he requests a hearing before the governing body by which he was appointed, after such hearing has been held. All members of the commission shall serve without compensation and shall serve until their successors are appointed and confirmed. The librarian provided for in Section 556 of this title shall be the secretary of the metropolitan library commission and shall be a nonvoting member of the commission.

B. Beginning August 1, 1982, in all cities with a population of four hundred thousand (400,000) or more, according to the latest Federal Decennial Census, the metropolitan library commission shall consist of nineteen (19) members. Ten of the members shall be appointed by the mayor of the county seat city, subject to approval of the governing body thereof. One of the members shall be appointed by the board of county commissioners. The mayors of Midwest City, Oklahoma, Del City, Oklahoma, Edmond, Oklahoma, The Village, Oklahoma, Warr Acres, Oklahoma, and Bethany, Oklahoma, subject to the approval of the governing bodies thereof, shall each appoint one member to the commission. Of the initial appointments, the cities having larger populations according to the latest Federal Decennial Census shall appoint members for the longer terms provided in this section. The mayor of the county seat city and the chairman of the board of county commissioners shall be ex officio members of the commission and shall be entitled to vote on all matters. The terms of all members serving on the commission on July 1, 1982, shall expire July 31, 1982. All new appointees shall begin their term of office effective August 1, 1982. Of the new appointments by the county seat city, two members shall serve a term of three (3) years, three members shall serve a term of two (2) years, and five members shall serve a term of one (1) year. The new appointment by the board of county commissioners shall serve a term of three (3) years. Of the new appointments by the mayors of the six-named cities, two members shall serve a term of three (3) years, two members shall serve a term of two (2) years, and two members shall serve a term of one (1) year. The terms of such new appointees and the terms of all future appointees of both the county seat city, the six-named cities and the county shall expire July 31 of the year the term expires, regardless of the calendar date when such appointments are made. Subsequent appointments by either the county seat city, the mayors of the six-named cities or the county shall be for three-year terms, except in the case of an appointment to fill a vacancy in the membership of the commission, which latter appointment shall be for the balance of the unexpired term of the member whose death, resignation or removal has created the vacancy. A member of this commission, once qualified, can be removed during his term of office only for misconduct or neglect of duty and, if he requests a hearing before the governing body by which he was appointed, after such hearing has been held. All members of the commission shall serve without compensation and shall serve until their successors are appointed and confirmed. The librarian provided for in Section 556 of this title shall be the secretary of the metropolitan library commission and shall be a nonvoting member of the commission. Laws 1965, c. 192, § 4. Amended by Laws 1982, c. 66, § 1, operative July 1, 1982.

§ 555.   Officers—Meetings—Quorum—Contracts

The commission shall elect its chairman from the appointed members and fill such other offices as its bylaws may establish. The term of the chairman shall be one (1) year. The commission shall hold at least one meeting each month and all meetings shall be open to the public, except for matters concerning personnel. It shall adopt rules for the transaction of business and keep a record of its functions and activities, which record shall be a public record. For the purpose of conducting business and exercising the powers of the commission, in cities with a population of four hundred thousand (400,000) or less, six commissioners shall constitute a quorum and in cities with a population of four hundred thousand (400,000) or more, ten commissioners shall constitute a quorum. The commission may establish a schedule of fees to cover various services rendered and may also contract with other persons, agencies and any governmental unit for such services as it may require, including private legal counsel and private auditing service, within the limits of its appropriations, and may incur necessary expenses. The commission may contract for, receive, and utilize any grants or other financial assistance from the United States or from any other source, public or private, in furtherance of its functions; may incur necessary expenses in obtaining said grants or financial assistance, within the limits of its appropriations; and shall receive and disburse such grants or other financial assistance.
Laws 1965, c. 192, § 5. Amended by Laws 1982, c. 66, § 2, operative July 1, 1982.

§ 556.   Librarian

The commission shall appoint a librarian of the metropolitan library system on the basis of merit and experience. Such librarian shall be a graduate of a library school accredited by the American Library Association. The librarian shall serve at the discretion of the commission. The librarian may appoint and remove staff members and other employees, subject to the approval of the commission. Laws 1965, c. 192, § 6.

§ 557.   Annual budget and audit—Contributions—Allocation of income

It shall be the duty of the commission to prepare an annual budget which shall be subject to the general review of the governing body of the city and the Board of County Commissioners. The Metropolitan Library Commission shall submit an annual audit of its expenditures and income to the Board of County Commissioners and the governing board of the city. This audit shall be prepared by an independent accountant.

Each county and city establishing a city-county library system, as herein provided, at the beginning of each fiscal year or as soon thereafter as may be practicable, shall agree upon the necessary contributions to be made by each for the establishment, operation and maintenance of the city-county library system, appropriate such funds as may be agreed upon and combine said funds with funds from any source. Periodically, as may be agreed upon, the city and county shall contribute their appropriated funds to a common fund upon claims therefor being filed by the commission with the governing body of the city and with the Board of County Commissioners. After approval of the claims, the contributions shall be made by warrants issued by the appropriate officers and made payable to the city treasurer or county treasurer, as may be agreed upon by the city and county. Said common fund shall be maintained as a depository account. Vouchers shall be drawn by such officer or employee as prescribed by the Metropolitan Library Commission.

The officer or employee of the commission designated shall be bonded in an amount not less than Twenty Thousand Dollars ($20,000.00) the premiums for which shall be payable from the operating funds of the metropolitan library. The designated officer or employee shall be governed by the same statutory provisions relating to depository accounts as apply to county officials generally. Nothing contained herein shall be construed as exempting from the application of the general statutes relating to appropriations the funds contributed by the city and county to the common fund.

Income of the city-county library system from fines, fees, sales of personal property, and other miscellaneous sources, excluding income from sales of real property, shall not be considered general revenue of either the city or the county. It shall be deposited promptly directly to the depository account of the metropolitan library. Income from this source shall constitute a revolving fund which shall not be subject to fiscal limitations and which may be expended by the commission.

In the event funds are made available for library purposes in the county, pursuant to the provisions of Article X, Section 10A of the Oklahoma Constitution, all or any part of the cost of establishing, maintaining and operating the city-county library system as set forth in the powers granted to the commission in the succeeding section, and otherwise, may be paid with such funds, and the Metropolitan Library Commission is authorized hereby to administer the expenditure of such funds. Laws 1965, c. 192, § 7.

§ 558. Powers of commission

Every Metropolitan Library Commission created by this act shall have all powers necessary or convenient for the accomplishment of the purpose and provisions hereof, including, in addition to others herein granted, the following powers:

(a) To operate and maintain a city-county library system and to adopt such rules and regulations for the operation thereof as may be deemed necessary or expedient.

(b) To purchase, lease, or otherwise acquire land or buildings or portions of buildings for library purposes.

(c) To erect, maintain, and operate public library buildings at one or more places in the county.

(d) To accept transfer of any existing public library or libraries by lease or other conveyance.

(e) To acquire by purchase or otherwise, books and other personal property customarily used in the operation of public libraries including necessary motor vehicles.

(f) To sell and dispose of personal property acquired by purchase or other means when by proper resolution the commission finds that said property is not needed for library purposes.

(g) To accept, hold, and convey legal title to interests in real property in the name "Metropolitan Library Commission of _____ County" which shall be its official name. Deeds or other conveyances of said interests in real property shall be executed for and on behalf of the commission by the chairman and shall be attested by the secretary.

(h) To accept, or in its discretion to decline, donations tendered to the city-county library system.

(i) To administer the expenditure of any funds which may become available for library purposes pursuant to the provisions of Article X, Section 10A of the Constitution of the State of Oklahoma.

(j) To borrow on the credit of the commission for a period of time not to exceed one year.

(k) To do all other things necessary or desirable to carry out the purposes and provisions of this act. Laws 1965, c. 192, § 8.

§ 559. Bringing other cities and towns into system

The governing body of any other city or town in any county is authorized to contract with the Metropolitan Library Commission, to bring such other city or town into the city-county library system, upon such terms as may be mutually agreed upon, and for that purpose may lease to the Metropolitan Library Commission any library facilities or property which such other city or town may own, may include in its annual budget appropriations for participation in the city-county library system, and shall pay over to the city-county system funds so appropriated. Laws 1965, c. 192, § 9.

§ 560. Retirement system

If, pursuant to the provisions of Chapter 37 of Title 11 of the Oklahoma Statutes, or of any statute supplemental thereto or of any charter provision of the city, a retirement system is established for the employees of the city, the employees of the city-county library system may be included in that retirement system on the same basis applicable to employees of the city, if the commission so recommends and the governing body of the city approves. Nothing otherwise provided by law shall operate to prohibit the appropriation of county funds for the payment of the county's pro rata share of the contribution to be made to the retirement fund on behalf of the employees of the city-county library system. In the event funds become available for library purposes pursuant to the provisions of Article X, Section 10A, of the Oklahoma Constitution, the entire contribution on behalf of the employees of the city-county library system may be paid from such funds. The commission may act so as to cause its employees to be included in the state retirement system and from its funds make the contributions necessary therefor. The commission may, in lieu of participation in the above mentioned retirement systems, provide for the retirement of the employees of the city-county library system by the establishment of a self-insured trust, or by the purchase of annuity contracts or pension contracts from any insurance company authorized to do business in the State of Oklahoma.

Laws 1965, c. 192, § 10. Amended by Laws 1968, c. 196, § 1, emerg. eff. April 15, 1968.

§ 561. Act as cumulative

This act is intended to be cumulative and in addition to any other law heretofore passed on libraries and shall not repeal any law on this subject. Laws 1965, c. 192, § 11.

MUNICIPAL LIBRARIES
(Oklahoma Statutes Annotated, 1982, Title 11, s.31-101 to 31-108.)

§ 31-101. Establishment of municipal libraries—Financial statement and estimate

A municipal governing body may establish and maintain a public library for the use and benefit of the citizens of the municipality. The governing body may establish branch libraries in different parts of the municipality to accommodate the citizens of the municipality. After the establishment of a municipal public library, the municipal governing body shall include an item in its municipal financial statement and estimate of needs for the following fiscal year to maintain the public library.

Laws 1977, c. 256, § 31–101, eff. July 1, 1978.

§ 31-102. Library board of directors

The municipal governing body may, in its discretion and by ordinance, place the management and control of the public library under a library board of directors. The library board shall consist of five (5) directors, chosen by the municipal governing body from the citizens of the municipality with reference to their fitness for such office. No director shall receive compensation as such. The directors of the library board shall hold office for a term of five (5) years from the first day of May following their appointment, and their terms shall be staggered. At the first regular meeting of the board, the directors shall cast lots for respective terms of one (1) year, two (2) years, three (3) years, four (4) years and five (5) years; thereafter the terms of all directors shall be five (5) years. The municipal governing body may remove any director for misconduct or neglect of duty. Vacancies in the library board of directors shall be filled in the same manner as original appointments.

Laws 1977, c. 256, § 31–102, eff. July 1, 1978.

§ 31-103. Organization of library board

The library board, immediately after the appointment and qualification of its directors, shall meet and organize by electing one director as president, one director as secretary, and by electing such other officers as the board may deem necessary.

Laws 1977, c. 256, § 31–103, eff. July 1, 1978.

§ 31-104. Powers and duties of library board—Expenditures and receipts—Library fund—Personnel

The library board shall adopt rules and regulations for its own guidance and for the governance and operation of the municipal library, not inconsistent with this article, which shall be subject to the approval of the municipal governing body. The library board shall have control of the expenditure of all moneys collected and placed to the credit of the library fund, and of the construction of any library building, and of the supervision, care and custody of the grounds, rooms or buildings constructed, leased or set apart for the library. All money received by the board on account of the operation of the library, or otherwise, shall be paid by the board to the municipal treasurer, who shall deposit the same in a special account, separate and apart from other money in the municipal treasury, to be designated the "library fund". Such moneys shall be paid out only upon warrants authorized by the library board. The library board shall have authority to establish a petty cash fund, not to exceed the sum of One Hundred Dollars ($100.00) at any one time, for use in maintaining the library, which money shall be expended by the librarian on forms prescribed and authorized by the library board. The library board shall have authority to appoint, and remove, a suitable librarian and necessary assistants, and to fix their compensation, all of which shall be subject to the approval of the municipal governing body.

Laws 1977, c. 256, § 31–104, eff. July 1, 1978.

§ 31-105. Grounds and building

The library board shall have the power, with the approval of the municipal governing body, to purchase grounds and erect thereon a suitable building for the use of the municipal library and to suitably equip the same, and to lease rooms or buildings for the use of the library. The title to any grounds so purchased or leased, as well as any building thereon, shall be taken in the name of the municipality as grantee.

Laws 1977, c. 256, § 31–105, eff. July 1, 1978.

§ 31-106. Governing body may provide penalties

The municipal governing body may impose, by ordinance, suitable penalties for the punishment of persons committing injury upon the municipal library or other property thereof, and for injury to or failure to return any book belonging to the library.

Laws 1977, c. 256, § 31–106, eff. July 1, 1978.

§ 31-107. Donations

Any person desiring to make donations of money, personal or real property for the benefit of the municipal library, or for the establishment, maintenance or endowment of public lectures in connection with the library upon any subject designated by the donor in the field of literature, science and the arts (except that lectures in the interest of any political party, politics or sectarian religion are expressly prohibited) shall have the right to vest the title to such money or property in the municipality, to be held and controlled by the municipality, when accepted, according to the terms of the donation. The municipality shall be held and considered to be a special trustee as to such property or money donated.

Laws 1977, c. 256, § 31–107, eff. July 1, 1978.

§ 31-108. Annual report of board

The library board shall make, on or before the thirty-first day of July in each year, an annual report to the municipal governing body stating:

1. The condition of its trust on the thirtieth day of June of that year;

2. The various sums of money and property received from the library fund and other sources, and how such moneys have been expended and for what purposes;

3. The budget for the library for the next fiscal year;

4. Statistics on the general character and number of books and periodicals which:

a. are on hand;

b. are lost or missing;

c. have been added by purchase, gift or otherwise during the year; and

d. have been loaned out during the year;

5. The number of persons making use of the library during the year; and

6. Such other information, statistics and suggestions as it may deem of general interest.

Laws 1977, c. 256, § 31–108, eff. July 1, 1978.

LIBRARY INSURANCE
(Oklahoma Statutes Annotated, 1982, Title 65, s.181-185.)

§ 181. Insurance on vehicles operated by public libraries— Actions

When bookmobiles or other vehicles are operated by any state, multi-county or district, city-county or joint city-county, county, city, town or other public library, insurance may be purchased from the funds of such library for the purpose of paying damages to persons sustaining injuries or property damage proximately caused by the negligent operation of such vehicles. Such insurance may cover not only the vehicle but also the personal liability of the operator of the vehicle. The operation of said vehicles by such libraries is hereby declared to be a public governmental function. An action for damages may be brought against a library but the governmental immunity of such library shall be waived only to the extent of the amount of insurance purchased. The library shall be liable for negligence only while such insurance is in force, but in no case in an amount exceeding the limits of the coverage of any such insurance policy. No attempt shall be made in the trial of any action brought against the library to suggest the existence of any insurance which covers in whole or in part any judgment or award which may be rendered in favor of the plaintiff, and if the verdict rendered by the jury exceeds the limits of the applicable insurance, the court shall reduce the amount of said judgment or award to a sum equal to the applicable limits stated in the policy. Laws 1961, p. 496, § 1.

§ 182. Insurance against loss, destruction, theft of library property

Any library or libraries owned or operated by the state or any multi-county or district, city-county or joint city-county, county, city, town, or other public library or libraries, may purchase insurance from the funds of such libraries or entities for protection against loss, loss of use, destruction, theft, damages, or other casualties to the property belonging to or used by said libraries or library entities. The ownership and operation of such libraries is hereby declared to be a public governmental function. Laws 1961, p. 496, § 1.

§ 183. Act authorizing vehicle insurance unaffected

Nothing in this act shall affect, limit, modify, restrict, or supplant the provisions of House Bill 839, Twenty-eighth Legislature. Laws 1961, p. 496, § 2.

§ 184. Workmen's compensation insurance for library employees

From and after the effective date of this act, it shall be lawful to purchase Workmen's Compensation Insurance for all employees of City-County, Joint City-County, Cooperative County, and all other employees of public libraries authorized to be created under the Constitution and laws of Oklahoma. Laws 1965, c. 130, § 1, emerg. eff. May 24, 1965.

§ 185. Cost of premiums

The cost of premiums of such Workmen's Compensation Insurance shall be lawful expenditures, and shall be set up and estimated for budgetary purposes as are other governmental expenses. Laws 1965, c. 130, § 2.

AUDIOVISUAL MATERIALS
(Oklahoma Statutes Annotated, 1982, Title 70, s.12-101 to 12-108.)

§ 12-101. Program for audiovisual training

The State Board of Education shall have authority to formulate, establish and maintain and cause to be administered a program of audiovisual education for the public schools of the state. Laws 1971, c. 281, § 12-101, eff. July 2, 1971.

§ 12–102. Motion picture films—State depository

The State Board of Education shall have authority to select or cause to be selected motion picture films appropriate to the curriculum of the public schools of Oklahoma, and shall establish and maintain a state depository where all such films shall be kept for assignment. Certain special films may be designated by the State Board of Education to be circulated from the state depository to various schools.

Amended by Laws 1981, c. 353, § 4.

§ 12–103. Regional film libraries

The State Board of Education shall have authority to establish and maintain regional film libraries. It shall be the responsibility of such regional libraries to receive, maintain, keep a record of and circulate all films received from the state depository and to return such films to the state depository when there is no longer a need therefor in any of the schools served by the regional library or when directed to do so by the State Board of Education and to furnish films to county superintendents of schools and boards of school districts upon written requests therefor.

Amended by Laws 1981, c. 353, § 5.

§ 12–104. Local film library

Any county or school district or educational institution supported by tax funds may establish and maintain a local film library and shall have authority to expend local funds for such purpose. Monies expended by any county or school district, or by any educational institution supported by tax funds, for the purchase of projection and audio materials approved by the State Board of Education may be matched with state monies appropriated for such purpose, in amounts not to exceed the following: Any county, One Thousand Dollars ($1,000.00); any school district or tax-supported educational institution employing one (1) to fifty (50) teachers, One Thousand Dollars ($1,000.00); any school district or tax supported educational institution employing fifty-one (51) to two hundred fifty (250) teachers, Two Thousand Dollars ($2,000.00); and any school district or tax-supported educational institution employing more than two hundred fifty (250) teachers, Three Thousand Dollars ($3,000.00). Provided, monies received by a school district under the provisions of this section shall not be considered as a part of its chargeable income for State Aid purposes.

Laws 1971, c. 281, § 12–104, eff. July 2, 1971.

§ 12–105. Rules and regulations

The State Board of Education shall adopt and enforce such rules and regulations as may be necessary to make such program of audiovisual education effective.

Laws 1971, c. 281, § 12–105, eff. July 2, 1971.

§ 12–106.   Purchase or rent of motion picture projectors—
Film library

Pursuant to an estimate duly made and approved for such purpose, the county superintendent of schools of any county may:

1.   Purchase or rent motion picture projectors, either silent or sound; purchase or lease motion picture films for said machine or machines; and purchase attachments, film splicers, repair kits, cable, wire, and any and all equipment necessary for the successful operation of the visual education program in the schools of the county, with funds allotted to the office of the county superintendent of schools for such purposes.

2.   Take the projector or projectors, film and equipment into any and all schools of the county to show a visual education program of film or films at least once each month and collect travel expense therefor from funds allotted to the office of the county superintendent of schools for such purposes.

3.   Buy a film library and add new films or replacement films to said library from time to time with funds allotted to the office of county superintendent of schools for such purposes.

Laws 1971, c. 281, § 12–106, eff. July 2, 1971.

§ 12–107.   Board of education—Purchase or rent projec-
tors and supplies

Pursuant to an estimate duly made and approved for such purpose the board of education of any school district, or any two or more school districts in cooperation with each other, may purchase or rent moving picture projectors, either silent or sound; purchase attachments, film splicers or film repair equipment of all types, cable, wire or any and all equipment and materials deemed necessary by said board of education or boards of education for the successful operation and conduct of a visual education program in the schools of such district or districts.

Laws 1971, c. 281, § 12–107, eff. July 2, 1971.

§ 12–108.   Personnel to administer provisions of this article

The State Board of Education shall appoint, employ and fix the compensation and duties of necessary personnel, and shall incur necessary expenses, to administer and carry out the provisions of this article, and all such compensation and other expenses shall be paid from any funds appropriated to carry out the provisions of this article.

Laws 1971, c. 281, § 12–108, eff. July 2, 1971.

COUNTY LAW LIBRARIES

(Oklahoma Statutes Annotated, 1982, Title 20, s.1201-1217,
1219 to 1221, 1224 to 1226.)

§ 1201. Establishment—Free use

A county law library may be established in each county of this State.
The use of such county law library shall be free to the judges of the state,
to state officials, to all the judges of the district, to all county officials,
to the members of the bar, and to the inhabitants of the county, under
proper regulation.

Laws 1936, Ex.Sess., p. 27, § 2. Amended by Laws 1968, c. 138, § 1.

§ 1202. Quarterly transfer of money to Law Library Fund—Purchase of books and periodicals—Branch libraries

Unless the Board of Law Library Trustees shall direct that no disbursement be effected or that a lesser amount than herein provided be transferred, the court clerk shall, at the end of each quarter of every calendar
year, transfer to the Law Library Fund the sum equal to the number of
all noncriminal cases, except those on the small claims docket in an
amount of Six Hundred Dollars ($600.00) or less, which were filed in the
district court during the last preceding quarter and in which a cost
deposit was made, multiplied by Three Dollars and fifty cents ($3.50).

Said Law Library Fund shall be expended in the purchase of law books
and periodicals and in the establishment and maintenance of a law library at the county seat of said county at a suitable place provided by
the county commissioners of said county. The county commissioners and
the Board of Law Library Trustees, or either, may additionally provide a
place designated by the Board of Law Library Trustees elsewhere in the
county than the county seat and there establish a branch library of said
law library. Said law library or law library and branch law library shall
be governed and controlled and said Fund expended by the Board of Trustees hereinafter provided.

Laws 1936, Ex.Sess. p. 27, § 3. Amended by Laws 1972, c. 95, § 1,
operative April 1, 1972; Laws 1974, c. 126, § 1, emerg. eff. May 3,
1974; Laws 1975, c. 55, § 10, emerg. eff. April 9, 1975; Laws 1975, c.
293, § 8, emerg. eff. June 5, 1975; Laws 1976, c. 253, § 3, eff. Oct. 1,
1976; Laws 1979, c. 112, § 1, eff. July 1, 1979; Laws 1981, c. 242, § 2,
operative July 1, 1981.

§ 1203. Law Library Fund—Use

All money transferred to the Law Library Fund shall be paid by the
court clerk to the treasurer of the county in which the law library is
situated. The money shall be kept in a separate account to be known as
the "Law Library Fund". It shall be treated as a continuing fund. It
shall neither be diverted to any other account nor be used for any purpose
other than that specified in Section 1202 of Title 20 of the Oklahoma
Statutes.

Added by Laws 1972, c. 95, § 2, operative April 1, 1972.

§ 1204. Board of Law Library Trustees

The management of said library shall be under a Board of Law Library
Trustees, consisting of five (5) members, to be chosen in the manner
hereinafter provided, to-wit:

(a) In counties having two (2) or more District Judges, two (2) District Judges of the county, who shall be selected by the District Judges
of said county, in counties having only one (1) District Judge, such Dis-

trict Judge and the associate district judge of the county.

(b) The District Attorney for the district that includes the county in which the law library is located, or an assistant district attorney who is designated by the District Attorney.

(c) Two (2) members of the county bar association who shall be chosen by the members thereof.

The present members of the Board of Law Library Trustees shall remain in office until the expiration of their terms of office.
Laws 1936, Ex.Sess., p. 28, § 5. Amended by Laws 1968, c. 138, § 2.

§ 1205. Officers of Board of Law Library Trustees

The officers of said Board of Law Library Trustees shall consist of a president and secretary, who shall be elected by members of the Board.
Laws 1936, Ex.Sess., p. 28, § 6.

§ 1206. Terms of trustees

The four elective members of said Board of Trustees shall hold office for two years, except the members of the first Board, who shall be divided into two classes, with two trustees in each class, one class holding office for one year and the other class holding office for two years.

Immediately after the selection and election of said Trustees they shall be divided into said classes by lot.
Laws 1936, Ex.Sess., p. 28, § 7.

§ 1207. Trustees—Honorary office

The office of trustee shall be honorary, without salary or other compensation.
Laws 1936, Ex.Sess., p. 28, § 8.

§ 1208. Powers of Board of Law Library Trustees

Such Board of Trustees, by a majority vote of all their members, shall have power:

First: To make and enforce all rules, regulations and by-laws necessary for the administration, government and protection of such library, and all property belonging thereto, or that may be loaned, devised, bequeathed or donated to the same.

Second: To remove any trustee for just cause, and fill all vacancies that may from any cause occur on the Board.

Third: To define the powers and prescribe the duties of its officers, and to provide for the time and manner of their selection.

Fourth: To elect all necessary subordinate officers, including a librarian and such assistants as may be necessary, and to prescribe their duties and fix the salary of same, and at their pleasure remove any such officer or assistant.

Fifth: To purchase books, journals, publications, and other personal property, the title to which shall be in the county.

Sixth: To order the drawing and payment, upon properly authenticated vouchers, duly certified by the president and secretary, of money from the Law Library Fund, for any liability or expenditure herein authorized, and generally to do all that may be necessary to carry into effect the provisions of this Act.
Laws 1936, Ex.Sess., p. 28, § 9.

§ 1209. Claims, orders and demands—Filing—Payment—Contracts— Limitation

The claims, orders and demands of the trustees of any such law library when duly made and authenticated as above provided shall be filed with the county clerk and considered and disposed of by the treasurer of such

county out of the library fund, of which full entry and record shall be kept as in other cases. Provided that no contracts shall be entered into for any fiscal year in excess of the amount received the preceding fiscal year from such fund and such surplus as may remain on hand for such preceding year. Provided further that in order to determine said amount or limitation during the first year that this Act is made operative in any county the amount to be contracted for shall not exceed the fund or amount which would have been raised under this Act had it been in operation the year preceding the time it becomes effective.
Laws 1936, Ex.Sess., p. 29, § 10.

§ 1210. Reports—Filing

Text of section amended by Laws 1979, c. 112, § 2

The Board of Trustees, on August 1 each year, shall prepare the following reports, a copy of which shall be filed with the Administrative Director of the Courts and another copy with the State Auditor and Inspector:

1. A financial report showing the receipts and disbursements of money and the total amount in the fund at the end of the fiscal year, such report to be made on a form prescribed by the State Auditor and Inspector; and

2. An inventory report of all property, number of books, periodicals, and other publications on hand, the number added by purchase, gift or otherwise during the year, the number lost or missing, and such other information as is requested by the Administrative Director of the Courts.

The Administrative Director of the Courts may from time to time require additional reports to be made when such are deemed necessary in the discharge of his duties hereunder.
Laws 1936, Ex.Sess., p. 29, § 13. Amended by Laws 1968, c. 138, § 3; Laws 1972, c. 68, § 1, emerg. eff. March 28, 1972; Laws 1979, c. 112, § 2, eff. July 1, 1979.

§ 1211. Meetings of Board of Law Library Trustees

The Board of Trustees shall meet the third Friday of each month and at such other times as they may appoint, at a place to be appointed for that purpose; and a majority of all their number shall constitute a quorum for business.
Laws 1936, Ex.Sess., p. 29, § 12. Amended by Laws 1979, c. 112, § 3, eff. July 1, 1979.

§ 1212. Court reports—Legal publications—Delivery to library

Printed copies of Reports of the Supreme Court and of the Criminal Court of Appeals and other legal publications, now or hereafter furnished by law to district judges and other officers of counties availing themselves of the provisions of this Act, shall be delivered by said district judges and such county officers to the county law library, which shall be the custodian thereof.
Laws 1936, Ex.Sess., p. 29, § 13.

§ 1213. Acceptance of Act by resolution—Discontinuance

In order for this Act and the provisions thereof to apply and to be put in force and effect in any county, it shall be necessary for the governing board of the court fund of such county to adopt a resolution to that effect; and when such resolution shall be adopted, this Act shall be in full force and effect as to such county, provided that the Board of Library Trustees of such county created by this Act is hereby empowered at its discretion

to discontinue the operation of this Act in said county.
Laws 1936, Ex.Sess., p. 29, § 14.   Amended by Laws 1968, c. 138, § 4.

§ 1214.   Partial invalidity

If any section, paragraph, sentence or phrase of this Act shall be declared unconstitutional or void for any reason, by any court of final
jurisdiction, such decision shall not in any way invalidate or affect any
other section, paragraph, sentence or phrase of this Act, but the same
shall continue in full force and effect.
Laws 1936, Ex.Sess., p. 29, § 15.

§ 1215.   Transfer of moneys to court fund for purchases and maintenance

The Board of Law Library Trustees of any county Law Library in the
State of Oklahoma, by a majority vote, is hereby authorized to transfer
to the Court Fund of such county, from time to time, such unallocated
moneys in the Law Library Fund of the county as may be deemed unnecessary by said Board for the purchase of law books and periodicals
for said library, and for the proper maintenance thereof. The provisions
of this Act shall not apply to counties having a population in excess of
one hundred eighty-five thousand (185,000) according to the last preceding Federal Census.
Laws 1943, p. 80, § 1.

§ 1216.   Establishment, maintenance and operation of libraries au-
thorized by amendatory act

Libraries authorized to be established under the provisions of this Act
shall be established, maintained and operated in the manner now provided by §§ 812-825, inclusive, of 19 O.S.1951.[1]
Laws 1947, p. 214, § 2.

§ 1217.   Transfers from court fund to library fund

Whenever the provisions of this act have been put into effect in any
county, the court clerk of said county may transfer to the Law Library
Fund of said county a sum not to exceed Six Thousand Dollars ($6,000.-
00), upon the approval of the Board of Law Library Trustees, provided,
that on the date this act shall become operative in said county, there is a
surplus in the Court Fund of said county sufficient to leave a balance of
not less than Three Thousand Dollars ($3,000.00); and provided, that if
such transfer shall reduce the Court Fund of said county below Three
Thousand Dollars ($3,000.00) the sum transferred shall be reduced to an
amount sufficient to leave a balance of Three Thousand Dollars ($3,000.-
00) in the Court Fund of said county.
Laws 1947, p. 214, § 3.   Amended by Laws 1971, c. 176, § 1, emerg. eff.
May 28, 1971.

§ 1219.   Photographic or chemical reproduction apparatus—Rules

The Board of Law Library Trustees, in addition to the duties and authority now provided by law may acquire photographic or chemical reproduction apparatus for use in conjunction with the service now furnished the public in said Law Library. They are given the right to make
rules consistent herewith for the operation of said apparatus, and said
Law Library.
Laws 1957, p. 127, § 2.

§ 1220.   Counties in excess of 300,000 population—National Association
of Law Librarians—Dues—Conventions

In all counties of this State having a population in excess of three hundred thousand (300,000) according to the 1960 Federal Decennial Census or any subsequent Federal Decennial Census, the Board of Law Library Trustees in any county establishing a county law library, in addition to the duties and authority now provided by law, are hereby authorized, from the funds in its hands, to pay the annual dues of the librarian in the National Association of Law Librarians, and in addition thereto, the necessary expenses of such librarian in attending the annual conventions of such National Association of Law Librarians.

Laws 1963, c. 188, § 1, emerg. eff. June 10, 1963.

§ 1221. Court clerk as custodian—Duties

Unless otherwise provided by the Board of Trustees, the court clerk shall serve as custodian of the county law library. He shall make and maintain in his office a complete inventory of all the books, periodicals and other property of the law library; he shall make such reports as are required by the Board of Trustees and the Administrative Director of the courts; and he shall service the volumes of the county law library with current pocket parts and supplements.

Laws 1968, c. 138, § 5.

§ 1224. Transfer of surplus funds from Law Library Fund

On August 1 each year the Board of Trustees shall transmit to the Supreme Court for deposit in the State Judicial Fund all funds on deposit in the Law Library Fund in excess of twenty-five percent (25%) of the income to such Fund during the preceding fiscal year, the existing surplus on hand on the effective date of this act being excluded.

Added by Laws 1975, c. 55, § 11, emerg. eff. April 9, 1975. Amended by Laws 1979, c. 112, § 4, eff. July 1, 1979.

§ 1225. Enforcement of provisions

The State Auditor and Inspector shall enforce all of the provisions of this act and report any violations thereof to the Chief Justice, the President Pro Tempore of the Senate and the Speaker of the House.

Added by Laws 1975, c. 55, § 12, emerg. eff. April 9, 1975. Amended by Laws 1979, c. 30, § 85, emerg. eff. April 6, 1979.

§ 1226. Additional transfer of funds

At the request of the Board of Trustees of the law library, the presiding judge of an administrative district, subject to the approval of the Chief Justice of the Oklahoma Supreme Court, shall be authorized to approve a transfer of additional money other than the regular quarterly sums prescribed by Section 1202 of this title from the court fund of the county in which the law library is located, which additional transfer may not exceed the sum of Five Thousand Dollars ($5,000.00) per year in counties with a population of less than ten thousand (10,000), the sum of Seven Thousand Dollars ($7,000.00) per year in counties with a population of more than ten thousand (10,000) but less than thirty thousand (30,000), the sum of Nine Thousand Dollars ($9,000.00) per year in counties with a population of more than thirty thousand (30,000) but less than fifty-five thousand (55,000), or the sum of Ten Thousand Dollars ($10,000.00) per year in counties with a population of more than fifty-five thousand (55,000).

Laws 1975, c. 293, § 9, emerg. eff. June 5, 1975. Amended by Laws 1977, c. 105, § 1, emerg. eff. May 27, 1977; Laws 1979, c. 113, § 1, operative July 1, 1979; Laws 1981, c. 242, § 3, operative July 1, 1981.

REPRODUCTION OF PUBLIC RECORDS

(Oklahoma Statutes Annotated, 1982, Title 67, s.301-303.)

§ 301.   Photographing, microphotographing or filming of records— Standards—Preservation of original negatives

Any public officer of the state or any county, public trust, authority or agency, city, municipality, district or legal subdivision thereof, may cause any or all records, papers or documents kept by him to be photographed, microphotographed or reproduced on film. The custodian of the records may permit any record to be removed from his office for the purpose of photographic filming, and his responsibility for their care and return shall continue during the times of their removal from the area controlled by the custodian of the records during photographic processes. The custodian of the records shall, before delivering any records for photographing or microphotographing make a complete catalogue list of the records to be filmed and retain the same until the records are returned. He may require a bond, and shall require written receipt identifying each record removed from his custody. Such photographic film shall comply with the minimum standards of quality approved for permanent photographic records by the National Bureau of Standards and the device used to reproduce such records on such film shall accurately reproduce the original thereof in all details. Such photographs, microphotographs or photographic film shall be deemed to be original records for all purposes, including introduction in evidence in all courts or administrative agencies. A transcript, exemplification, or certified copy thereof, for all purposes recited herein, shall be deemed to be a transcript, exemplification, or certified copy of the original.

The original photographs, microphotographs or film shall be stored in a maximum security vault and only be removed therefrom for the purpose of making copies thereof as the custodian of the records may require or for replacement by a duplicate at not longer than twenty-year intervals as to all such records required to be kept for more than twenty (20) years. At the election of the custodian of the records, however, the master negative may, immediately upon being made, be deposited with the Division of Archives and Records of the Oklahoma Department of Libraries which shall retain it in a maximum security vault and furnish such copies thereof as may be required for the purposes of the custodian of the records. The cost of any photographic, microphotographic, or filming service requested by and furnished to a state agency or subdivision of government shall be paid to the Department of Libraries rendered on the basis of fee schedules established by the Archives and Records Commission.

A copy of such photographs, microphotographs or reproductions on film properly certified and catalogued shall be placed in conveniently accessible files and provisions made for preserving, examining and using the same, including reproduction of same. There shall be available for use by the public at least two devices for viewing, and at least one of said devices shall provide for reproducing the photographic records. Such copies shall be certified by their custodian as true copies of the originals, and the copies so certified shall have the same force and effect as the originals. A statement in writing describing the record and certifying it to be a true copy, and attached securely to the reproduction, will be deemed a sufficient certification. Any viewing devices in use at the time of the passage of this act   may continue to be used, although such device does not provide a reproducing system.

Laws 1968, c. 116, § 1, emerg. eff. April 1, 1968. Amended by Laws 1972, c. 209, § 1, emerg. eff. March 31, 1972.

§ 302. Instruments filed for record—Microfilming—Security copies— Sale of copies

The county clerk and ex officio registrar of deeds may record the instruments lawfully filed for record in his office by making and preserving microfilm thereof.

Whenever a system of microfilming is established at least two (2) microfilms shall be made of each recorded instrument which shall be kept separate, in order that they may not be subject to the same hazards. Additional copies of such microfilmed records may be produced by the public officer for sale to bonded abstractors of the county at a price not to exceed the cost of production plus twenty percent (20%).

The security copy of the microfilm may be deposited in a bank or other safe place.

Laws 1968, c. 116, § 2, emerg. eff. April 1, 1968.

§ 303. Court or judicial records

This Act shall not apply to any court or judicial records.

Laws 1968, c. 116, § 3, emerg. eff. April 1, 1968.

PROTECTION OF LIBRARY PROPERTY

(Oklahoma Statutes Annotated, 1982, Title 21, s.1785.)

§ 1785. Works of literature or art in public place, injuring

Every person who maliciously cuts, tears, disfigures, soils, obliterates, breaks or destroys any book, map, chart, picture, engraving, statue, coin, model, apparatus, specimen or other work of literature or art, or object of curiosity deposited in any public library, gallery, museum, collection, fair or exhibition, is punishable by imprisonment in the penitentiary for not exceeding three years, or in a county jail not exceeding one year. R.L. 1910, § 2790.

TAX EXEMPTION

(State Constitution, Art. 10, s.6.)

Oklahoma library laws are reprinted from OKLAHOMA STATUTES ANNOTATED published by West Publishing Co., St. Paul, Minnesota.

OREGON

STATE LIBRARY
(Oregon Revised Statutes, 1982, s.357.001-357.200.)

357.001 Legislative findings. The State of Oregon recognizes that:

(1) Libraries constitute a cultural, informational and educational resource essential to the people of this state.

(2) Library services should be available widely throughout the state to bring within convenient reach of the people appropriate opportunities for reading, study and free inquiry.

(3) Providing and supporting adequate library services is a proper and necessary function of government at all levels. [1975 c.476 §2]

357.003 Policy. It is the policy of the people of the State of Oregon:

(1) To promote the establishment, development and support of library services for all of the people of this state.

(2) To provide library services suitable to support informed decisions by the personnel of government.

(3) To encourage cooperation between units of government and between and among libraries and to encourage the joint exercise of powers where such cooperation or joint exercise will increase the extent of library services in a fair and equitable manner. [Formerly 357.705]

357.005 State Library duties; free book loans. (1) The State Library shall be the agency of government responsible for executing the functions as set forth in ORS 357.001 and 357.003.

(2) To carry out its duties under subsection (1) of this section, the State Library may:

(a) Promote adequate library services for all of the people of this state.

(b) Provide advice and assistance to libraries, to library boards, to units of local government empowered to establish libraries and to departments and agencies of state government in matters concerning the establishment, support, operation, improvement and coordination of libraries and library services, and the cooperation between libraries.

(c) Maintain and develop appropriate collections of library materials to supplement the collections and services of other libraries in the state and to meet the reference and research needs of the Legislative Assembly and of the state government by providing library services thereto.

(d) With the advice of the libraries of the state, provide a network whereby the library resources in this state are made available to all of the people of this state under reasonable conditions and subject to appropriate compensation to libraries providing library services to persons beyond their primary clientele.

(e) Provide for state participation in regional, national or international library networks and systems designed to increase the quality of library services for the people of this state.

(f) Provide for the people of this state specialized library services not generally available in other libraries in the state.

(g) Provide library services to the blind and physically handicapped in cooperation with the United States Library of Congress.

(h) Provide for in-service and continuing education programs for library personnel in the state.

(i) Expend such federal, state or private funds as may be available to the state to demonstrate, develop and support library services in accordance with long-range plans for statewide development and coordination of library services.

(j) Prescribe the conditions for use of state documents in depository libraries, and maintain a system of exchange of state documents with libraries outside this state.

(k) Issue a biennial report to the Governor and publish and distribute statistical data on libraries of this state useful in the conduct of the work of the State Library and in the development of effective library services throughout the state.

(L) Carry out other activities authorized by law for the development of library services for the people of this state.

(3) State Library books shall be loaned free of charge to the people of Oregon through existing libraries and to individuals upon proper guarantee, in cities, counties and regions without public libraries and in rural communities. However, the borrower shall pay the cost of returning the books to the State Library. [Formerly 357.080]

357.007 Location of State Library. Subject to ORS 276.004, the principal library of the State Library shall be in the state capitol mall area. Other quarters may also be obtained, leased, acquired or provided at other locations when necessary to carry out the functions of the State Library. [Formerly 357.060]

357.010 Trustees of State Library; confirmation; term; compensation and expenses; chairman; secretary. (1) The Governor shall appoint seven persons, who shall constitute the Trustees of the State Library. All appointments shall be for a term of four years beginning on July 1 of the year of appointment, except appointments to fill vacancies, which shall be made by the Governor for the unexpired term. Members shall be eligible for reappointment for only one additional term, but any person may be appointed

again to the board after an interval of one year. All appointments of members by the Governor are subject to confirmation by the Senate in the manner provided in ORS 171.562 and 171.565.

(2) A member is entitled to compensation and expenses as provided in ORS 292.495.

(3) The members shall elect a chairman who shall serve for one year commencing July 1. The State Librarian shall serve as secretary to the trustees. [Amended by 1955 c.41 §1; 1965 c.378 §6; 1969 c.314 §27; 1973 c.792 §12; 1975 c.476 §6]

357.015 Functions of trustees. The Trustees of the State Library shall be the policy-making body for the State Library and shall:

(1) Appoint the State Librarian who shall be a graduate of a library school accredited by the American Library Association or who possesses the equivalent in training and experience and who shall serve at the pleasure of the trustees. Except as otherwise provided by law, the trustees shall fix the compensation of the State Librarian.

(2) Formulate general policies for the State Library and, pursuant to ORS 183.310 to 183.550, adopt rules for its operation.

(3) Review and approve budget requests for the State Library.

(4) Adopt long-range plans for the statewide development and coordination of library service in consultation with libraries, state and local governments and the people of this state.

(5) At the beginning of each regular session of the Legislative Assembly, advise the Governor and the Legislative Assembly on new programs or legislation necessary for effective library service for the people of this state.

(6) Designate certain libraries within the state, including the library of every nationally accredited law school, as depository libraries for state publications.

(7) Have control of, use and administer the State Library Donation Fund for the benefit of the State Library, except that every gift, devise or bequest for a specific purpose shall be administered according to its terms. [Formerly 357.230]

357.031 Duties of trustees to enter into contracts and agreements. The Trustees of the State Library may:

(1) Enter into contracts with any person or governmental entity:

(a) To provide, extend, improve or coordinate library services; or

(b) To demonstrate appropriate programs of library services.

(2) Enter into library agreements pursuant to Article V of the Interstate Library

Compact (ORS 357.340).

(3) Establish, equip and maintain regional library service centers of the State Library outside the City of Salem when the library needs of the state will be better served. [1961 c.251 §2 (enacted in lieu of 357.030); 1965 c.354 §6; 1973 c.439 §10; 1975 c.476 §9]

357.035 Trustees as agency to apply for federal or private funds. Subject to the provisions of ORS 291.260 and 291.375, the Trustees of the State Library are designated as a state agency empowered to apply for federal or private funds and accept and enter into appropriate agreements for library purposes on behalf of the state or its political subdivisions or for any activity appropriate to the State Library on behalf of the state for the receipt of such funds from the Federal Government or its agencies or from any private source, and supervise the disbursement of such funds. [Formerly 357.220]

357.040 Authority of trustees over real and personal property acquired by gift; judicial proceedings. (1) The trustees of the State Library may acquire control and dispose of any and all real and personal property given to or for the benefit of the State Library by private donors, whether the gifts of the property are made to the State Library or to the trustees thereof or to the State of Oregon for the benefit of the library.

(2) The trustees may accept by assignment and hold mortgages upon real and personal property acquired by way of gift or arising out of transactions entered into in accord with the powers, duties and authority given by this section, ORS 357.015 (7) and 357.195 to the trustees.

(3) The trustees may institute, maintain and participate in suits, actions and other judicial proceedings in the name of the State of Oregon for the foreclosure of such mortgages or for the purpose of carrying into effect any and all of the powers, duties and authority now vested in or given by this section, ORS 357.015 (7) and 357.195 to the trustees. [Amended by 1975 c.476 §11]

357.050 Duties of State Librarian as secretary and administrator. The State Librarian shall:

(1) Serve as Secretary to the Trustees of the State Library and keep the official record of their actions.

(2) Be the chief administrative officer of the State Library in accordance with policies established by the trustees and the laws of this state. [Amended by 1961 c.251 §3; 1975 c.476 §12]

357.071 General duties of State Librarian. The State Librarian shall:

(1) Pursuant to the State Personnel Relations Law, appoint and fix the compensation of, and prescribe the working conditions for such staff as may be necessary to carry out the functions of the State Library.

(2) Make all reports, maintain all records and execute all instruments required by law or rule and perform all duties necessary to discharge the functions of the State Library.

(3) Assist local librarians and library boards in answering questions concerning the library laws. [1961 c.251 §5 (enacted in lieu of 357.070); 1971 c.185 §1; 1975 c.476 §13]

357.195 State Library Donation Fund. The interest, income, dividends or profits received on any property or funds of the State Library derived from gifts, legacies, devises, bequests or endowments shall be deposited with the State Treasurer and hereby are set apart and appropriated to the use, maintenance and support of the State Library, in like manner as the principal or corpus of each such gift or donation is set apart or appropriated. All such gifts or donations shall be placed by the State Treasurer to the credit of a separate fund, to be known as the State Library Donation Fund, and the State Treasurer shall credit monthly to such fund any interest or other income derived from the fund or the investing thereof. Claims against the fund shall be approved and warrants issued in the manner provided by law. [Formerly 357.270]

357.200 Miscellaneous Receipts Account. (1) The State Librarian shall deposit with the State Treasurer all moneys received for materials furnished and for services rendered, which moneys shall be deposited in the Miscellaneous Receipts Account for the State Library which may be used for books, pamphlets and periodicals, and for any other purpose authorized by law.

(2) The State Library may maintain a petty cash fund in compliance with ORS 293.180 in the amount of $200 from moneys in the Miscellaneous Receipts Account for the State Library. [Amended by 1953 c.136 §4; 1959 c.137 §1; 1961 c.172 §4; 1961 c.251 §7; 1975 c.476 §15]

STATE AID

(Oregon Revised Statutes, 1982, s.357.740-357.780.)

357.740 State grants to local units of government; purposes. The state shall provide financial assistance for public library service to public libraries established pursuant to law from funds specifically appropriated therefor by annual grants to units of local government. The grants shall be expended to:

(1) Broaden access to existing information resources by strengthening public libraries and encouraging cooperation among units of local government and among public, private, school and academic libraries;

(2) Extend public library services to persons not served by local public libraries; and

(3) Permit new services and new types of services as local need therefor is determined. [1977 c.291 §1]

357.750 Applications for grants; uses of grant moneys. Units of local government and counties may apply for annual establishment and development grants. The grants may be made from funds specifically appropriated therefor and are to be used to establish, develop or improve public library services. [1977 c.291 §2]

357.760 State library trustees to administer ORS 357.740 to 357.780. The Trustees of the State Library shall administer the provisions of ORS 357.740 to 357.780 and shall adopt rules governing the application for and granting of funds under ORS 357.740 to 357.780. [1977 c.291 §3]

357.770 Grant eligibility based on maintained local support. In order to be eligible for state financial assistance for any year for which assistance is sought, a unit of local government must not reduce its budgeted operating expenditures for public library service, exclusive of short-term special funding, in any fiscal year to less than the amount expended for the same purpose in the preceding fiscal year. [1977 c.291 §5]

357.780 Per capita grants for public library services. (1) Subject to subsection (2) of this section, the state shall distribute funds specifically appropriated by the Legislative Assembly for per capita grants for public library services in the following manner to assure the same population shall not be counted more than once:

(a) There shall be paid to each county that provides public library services to all persons in the county a per capita amount for each person residing in the county.

(b) Where public library services are provided by a unit of local government having jurisdiction in more than one county, there shall be paid to that unit a per capita amount for each person residing therein.

(c) Where public library services are not provided as described in paragraph (a) or (b) of this subsection, but by a unit of local government having jurisdiction less than county wide, there shall be paid to the unit a per capita amount for persons residing therein.

(d) Where public library services are provided both by a unit of local government within a county and by the county, there shall be paid to the unit a per capita amount for each person residing in the unit and to the county a per capita amount for each person residing outside the unit but within the county.

(e) Where public library services are provided both (a) by a unit of local government within a unit of local government having jurisdiction in more than one county and (b) by a unit of local government having jurisdiction in more than one county, there shall be paid to the smaller unit a per capita amount for each person residing in that unit and to the larger unit a per capita amount for each person residing outside the smaller unit but within the larger unit.

(2) If the moneys specifically appropriated for grants under this section are insufficient to make the full allocation for all grants, the grant to each eligible applicant shall be allocated according to the ratio that the total amount of funds available bears to the total amount that would be required to pay in full all grants. [1979 c.835 §2]

INTERSTATE LIBRARY COMPACT

(Oregon Revised Statutes, 1982, s.357.330-357.370.)

357.330 Definitions for ORS 357.330 to 357.370. As used in ORS 357.330 to 357.370, except where the context otherwise requires:

(1) "Compact" means the Interstate Library Compact.

(2) "Public library agency", with reference to this state, means the State Library or any local government unit authorized by ORS 357.410 to establish a public library, or any public library board. [1965 c.354 §1; 1975 c.476 §32]

357.340 Interstate Library Compact. The Interstate Library Compact hereby is enacted into law and entered into by this state with all states legally joining therein in the form substantially as follows:

POLICY AND PURPOSE

Because the desire for the services provided by libraries transcends governmental boundaries and can most effectively be satisfied by giving such services to communities and people regardless of jurisdictional lines, it is the policy of the states party to this compact to cooperate and share their responsibilities; to authorize cooperation and sharing with respect to those types of library facilities and services which can be more economically or efficiently developed and maintained on a cooperative basis; and to authorize cooperation and sharing among localities, states and others in providing joint or cooperative library services in areas where the distribution of population or of existing and potential library resources make the provision of library service on an interstate basis the most effective way of providing adequate and efficient service.

ARTICLE II

DEFINITIONS

As used in this compact:

(a) "Public library agency" means any unit or agency of local or state government operating or having power to operate a library.

(b) "Private library agency" means any nongovernmental entity which operates or assumes a legal obligation to operate a library.

(c) "Library agreement" means a contract establishing an interstate library district pursuant to this compact or providing for the joint or cooperative furnishing of library services.

ARTICLE III

INTERSTATE LIBRARY DISTRICTS

(a) Any one or more public library agencies in a party state in cooperation with any public library agency or agencies in one or more other party states may establish and maintain an interstate library district. Subject to the provisions of this compact and any other laws of the party states which pursuant hereto remain applicable, such district may establish, maintain and operate some or all of the library facilities and services for the area concerned in accordance with the terms of a library agreement therefor. Any private library agency or agencies within an interstate library district may cooperate therewith, assume duties, responsibilities and obligations thereto, and receive benefits therefrom as provided in any library agreement to which such agency or agencies become party.

(b) Within an interstate library district, and as provided by a library agreement, the performance of library functions may be undertaken on a joint or cooperative basis or may be undertaken by means of one or more arrangements between or among public or private library agencies for the extension of library privileges to the use of facilities or services operated or rendered by one or more of the individual library agencies.

(c) If a library agreement provides for joint establishment, maintenance or operation of library facilities or services by an interstate

library district, such district shall have power to do any one or more of the following in accordance with such library agreement:

1. Undertake, administer and participate in programs or arrangements for securing, lending or servicing books and other publications, any other materials suitable to be kept or made available by libraries, library equipment or for the dissemination of information about libraries, the value and significance of particular items therein, and the use thereof.

2. Accept for any of its purposes under this compact any and all donations, and grants of money, equipment, supplies, materials, and services, (conditional or otherwise), from any state or the United States or any subdivision or agency thereof, or interstate agency, or from any institution, person, firm or corporation, and receive, utilize and dispose of the same.

3. Operate mobile library units or equipment for the purpose of rendering bookmobile service within the district.

4. Employ professional, technical, clerical and other personnel, and fix terms of employment, compensation and other appropriate benefits; and where desirable, provide for the inservice training of such personnel.

5. Sue and be sued in any court of competent jurisdiction.

6. Acquire, hold, and dispose of any real or personal property or any interest or interests therein as may be appropriate to the rendering of library service.

7. Construct, maintain and operate a library, including any appropriate branches thereof.

8. Do such other things as may be incidental to or appropriate for the carrying out of any of the foregoing powers.

ARTICLE IV

INTERSTATE LIBRARY DISTRICTS, GOVERNING BOARD

(a) An interstate library district which establishes, maintains or operates any facilities or services in its own right shall have a governing board which shall direct the affairs of the district and act for it in all matters relating to its business. Each participating public library agency in the district shall be represented on the governing board which shall be organized and conduct its business in accordance with provision therefor in the library agreement. But in no event shall a governing board meet less often than twice a year.

(b) Any private library agency or agencies party to a library agreement establishing an interstate library district may be represented on or advise with the governing board of the district in such manner as the library agreement may provide.

ARTICLE V

STATE LIBRARY AGENCY COOPERATION

Any two or more state library agencies of two or more of the party states may undertake and conduct joint or cooperative library programs, render joint or cooperative library services, and enter into and perform arrangements for the cooperative or joint acquisition, use, housing and disposition of items or collections of materials which, by reason of expense, rarity, specialized nature, or infrequency of demand therefor would be appropriate for central collection and shared use. Any such programs, services or arrangements may include provision for the exercise on a cooperative or joint basis of any power exercisable by an interstate library district and an agreement embodying any such program, service or arrangement shall contain provisions covering the subjects detailed in Article VI of this compact for interstate library agreements.

ARTICLE VI

LIBRARY AGREEMENTS

(a) In order to provide for any joint or cooperative undertaking pursuant to this compact, public and private library agencies may enter into library agreements. Any agreement executed pursuant to the provisions of this compact shall, as among the parties to the agreement:

1. Detail the specific nature of the services, programs, facilities, arrangements or properties to which it is applicable.

2. Provide for the allocation of costs and other financial responsibilities.

3. Specify the respective rights, duties, obligations and liabilities of the parties.

4. Set forth the terms and conditions for duration, renewal, termination, abrogation, disposal of joint or common property, if any, and all other matters which may be appropriate to the proper effectuation and performance of the agreement.

(b) No public or private library agency shall undertake to exercise itself, or jointly with any other library agency, by means of a library agreement any power prohibited to such agency by the constitution or statutes of its state.

(c) No library agreement shall become effective until filed with the compact administrator of each state involved, and approved in accordance with Article VII of this compact.

ARTICLE VII

APPROVAL OF LIBRARY AGREEMENTS

(a) Every library agreement made pursuant to this compact shall, prior to and as a condition precedent to its entry into force, be submitted to the attorney general of each state in which a public library agency party thereto is situated, who shall determine whether the agreement is in proper form and compatible with the laws of his state. The attorneys general shall approve any agreement submitted to them unless they shall find that it does not meet the conditions set forth herein and shall detail in writing addressed to the governing bodies of the public library agencies concerned the specific respects in which the proposed agreement fails to meet the requirements of law. Failure to disapprove an agreement submitted hereunder within 90 days of its submission shall constitute approval thereof.

(b) In the event that a library agreement made pursuant to this compact shall deal in whole or in part with the provision of services or facilities with regard to which an officer or agency of the state government has constitutional or statutory powers of control, the agreement shall, as a condition precedent to its entry into force, be submitted to the state officer or agency having such power of control and shall be approved or disapproved by him or it as to all matters within his or its jurisdiction in the same manner and subject to the same requirements governing the action of the attorneys general pursuant to paragraph (a) of this article. This requirement of submission and approval shall be in addition to and not in substitution for the requirement of submission to and approval by the attorneys general.

ARTICLE VIII

OTHER LAWS APPLICABLE

Nothing in this compact or in any library agreement shall be construed to supersede, alter or otherwise impair any obligation imposed on any library by otherwise applicable law, nor to authorize the transfer or disposition of any property held in trust by a library agency in a manner contrary to the terms of such trust.

ARTICLE IX

APPROPRIATIONS AND AID

(a) Any public library agency party to a library agreement may appropriate funds to the interstate library district established thereby in the same manner and to the same extent as to a library wholly maintained by it and, subject to the laws of the state in which such public library agency is situated, may pledge its credit in support of an interstate library district established by the agreement.

(b) Subject to the provisions of the library

agreement pursuant to which it functions and the laws of the states in which such district is situated, an interstate library district may claim and receive any state and federal aid which may be available to library agencies.

ARTICLE X

COMPACT ADMINISTRATOR

Each state shall designate a compact administrator with whom copies of all library agreements to which his state or any public library agency thereof is party shall be filed. The administrator shall have such other powers as may be conferred upon him by the laws of his state and may consult and cooperate with the compact administrators of other party states and take such steps as may effectuate the purposes of this compact. If the laws of a party state so provide, such state may designate one or more deputy compact administrators in addition to its compact administrator.

ARTICLE XI

ENTRY INTO FORCE AND WITHDRAWAL

(a) This compact shall enter into force and effect immediately upon its enactment into law by any two states. Thereafter, it shall enter into force and effect as to any other state upon the enactment thereof by such state.

(b) This compact shall continue in force with respect to a party state and remain binding upon such state until six months after such state has given notice to each other party state of the repeal thereof. Such withdrawal shall not be construed to relieve any party to a library agreement entered into pursuant to this compact from any obligation of that agreement prior to the end of its duration as provided therein.

ARTICLE XII

CONSTRUCTION AND SEVERABILITY

This compact shall be liberally construed so as to effectuate the purposes thereof. The provisions of this compact shall be severable and if any phrase, clause, sentence or provision of this compact is declared to be contrary to the constitution of any party state or of the United States or the applicability thereof to any government, agency, person or circumstance is held invalid, the validity of the remainder of this compact and the applicability thereof to any government, agency, person or circumstance shall not be affected thereby. If this compact shall be held contrary to the constitution of any state party thereto, the compact shall remain in full force and effect as to the remaining states and in full force and effect as to the state affected as to all severable matters.

357.350 Library compact administrator; deputy; library agreements to be submitted to State Librarian. The State Librarian shall be the compact administrator pursuant to Article X of the compact. The State Librarian shall appoint one or more deputy compact administrators. Every library agreement made pursuant to Article VI of the compact shall, as a condition precedent to its entry into force, be submitted to the State Librarian for his recommendations. [1965 c.354 §3]

357.360 Compliance with laws on taxes and bonds required. No unit of local government or public library board shall be a party to a library agreement which provides for the construction or maintenance of a library pursuant to Article III, subdivision (c-7) of the compact, nor levy a tax or issue bonds to contribute to the construction or maintenance of such a library, except after compliance with any laws applicable to public libraries relating to or governing the levying of taxes or the issuance of bonds. [1965 c.354 §4; 1975 c.476 §33]

357.370 Duty of compact administrator upon withdrawal from compact. In the event of withdrawal from the compact the compact administrator shall send and receive any notices required by Article XI (b) of the compact. [1965 c.354 §5]

DISTRIBUTION OF PUBLIC DOCUMENTS
(Oregon Revised Statutes, 1982, s.182.070.)

182.070 Publications of state agencies to be furnished to State Librarian. (1) Unless a greater or lesser number is agreed upon by the State Librarian and the issuer of the publication, the State Printer or, in the event the State Printer is unable to furnish the number of copies of the publication, the person responsible for distribution of a publication issued by, or by authority of a state officer, agency or institution not under the control of the State Board of Higher Educa-

tion shall make available to the State Librarian for distribution and exchange purposes, 45 copies of all publications so issued in multiple form, other than interoffice memoranda or forms. The State Printer may withhold the prescribed number of copies from each printing order and forward them to the State Librarian. Cost of printing for all copies of a publication furnished to the State Librarian in compliance with this subsection shall be borne by the issuing agency.

(2) The term "publication," as used in this section, does not include:

(a) Oregon Revised Statutes or any edition thereof.

(b) Legislative bills, calendars and interim committee reports made available under ORS 171.206.

(c) Reports and publications of the Oregon Supreme Court, Oregon Court of Appeals and the Oregon Tax Court. [1953 c.527 §2; 1961 c.167 §21; 1979 c.215 §1]

STATE ARCHIVIST

(Oregon Revised Statutes, 1982, s.357.805-357.895,
170-407, 171-420-171.430.)

357.805 Definitions for ORS 357.805 to 357.895. As used in ORS 357.805 to 357.895, unless the context requires otherwise, "photocopy," "political subdivision," "public record," "public writing" and "state agency" are defined by ORS 192.005. [Formerly 358.005]

357.815 State Archivist; appointment; qualifications; assistants; compensation. The office of State Archivist hereby is created. It shall be under the control and supervision of the Secretary of State, who shall, subject to any applicable provisions of the State Personnel Relations Law, appoint and fix the compensation of the archivist and such assistants as may be necessary. No person who has not had at least five years' experience as an archivist shall be eligible for the office of State Archivist. [Formerly 358.010; 1973 c.439 §3]

357.825 Acquisition and custody of public records. The State Archivist may negotiate for, acquire and receive public records, writings and illustrative materials of value or interest for legal, administrative or research purposes. He is constituted official custodian of all such records, writings or materials deposited in, acquired for, or transferred upon his requisition to his custody for the state archives. [Formerly 358.020]

357.835 Transfer of noncurrent public records to State Archivist. (1) Except as otherwise provided by law, when the State Archivist has determined that noncurrent public records are stored under conditions where they are no longer available for use or which are dangerous to the safety and protection of the records, or where no safe storage is available, all such noncurrent public records or writings as the State Archivist may requisition as being of value or interest for the purposes mentioned in ORS 357.825 shall be transferred to his official custody. For the purposes of this subsection, "noncurrent public records or writings" are those which no longer are required to be retained for discharge of the duties of the official custodian thereof.

(2) If a state agency is abolished or ceases to operate, its public records and writings shall be transferred to the official custody of the State Archivist, except for records of functions transferred by law to other agencies and records needed for the liquidation of obligations or property of the agency. Records used in the liquidation of the agency shall be transferred to the State Archivist when the liquidation is completed.

(3) The Governor, the Secretary of State and the State Treasurer may deposit with the State Archivist for safekeeping in his official custody records of their offices that are used for historical rather than current administrative purposes. [Formerly 358.030]

357.845 Seal of State Archivist. The State Archivist shall have a seal which shall have the coat of arms of the state engraved in the center thereof, with the following inscription surrounding such coat of arms: "The State Archivist, State of Oregon." [Formerly 358.040]

357.855 Advice and assistance on public record problems. The State Archivist, without charge therefor, shall give advice and assistance on public record problems to any legislative, executive or judicial officer of this state or any political subdivision in this state. The State Archivist from time to time also shall give general advice and counsel on public record problems to all such officers. [Formerly 358.050]

357.865 Filing copy of public record with State Archivist; loss of original. (1) With the approval of the State Archivist, an original or duplicate photocopy or other copy of any public record or writing may be filed with the State Archivist by any of the public officers mentioned in ORS 357.855, or a political subdivision, for the purpose of insuring the preservation of such public record or writing.

(2) If the original public record or writing and any original photocopy in the possession of the public officer or political subdivision are lost, destroyed, mutilated or defaced, the photocopy or other copy filed with the State Archivist may be considered an original, with the same uses and effect as the original under ORS 192.050. In this event the State Archivist upon request shall return the photocopy or other copy to the public officer or his successor, or political subdivision, that filed it; or upon request may furnish the public officer or his successor, or political subdivision, a duplicate photocopy or other copy upon payment of

the cost thereof. [Formerly 358.060]

357.875 Access to public records; privileged information. The State Archivist shall be accorded, for the purposes of ORS 357.805 to 357.895, reasonable access to and may examine and receive any public records or writings whether or not they are subject to public inspection. He shall maintain inviolate any privileged or confidential information so acquired and any record or writing so defined by law. [Formerly 358.070]

357.885 Fees of State Archivist. The Secretary of State shall prescribe fees to be charged and collected by the State Archivist for copying and certifying public records or writings and for searching public records or writings in his official custody. All such fees received shall be deposited with the State Treasurer who shall receipt therefor. All such fees are continuously appropriated for the payment of expenses incurred by the Secretary of State in the administration of the office of the State Archivist. [Formerly 358.080; 1973 c.439 §11]

357.895 Rules and regulations. In accordance with ORS 183.310 to 183.550, the State Archivist shall issue rules and regulations to carry out his powers and duties under ORS 43.410, 192.005 to 192.170 and 357.805 to 357.895. [Formerly 358.090]

171.420 Classification and arrangement; delivery to State Archivist. The Legislative Administrator shall classify and arrange the legislative records delivered to him pursuant to ORS 171.415, in a manner that he considers best suited to carry out the efficient and economical utilization, maintenance, preservation and disposition of the records. The State Archivist shall assist him in the performance of this work. The Legislative Administrator shall deliver to the State Archivist all legislative records in his possession when such records have been classified and arranged. The State Archivist shall thereafter be official custodian of the records so delivered. [1961 c.150 §3; 1969 c.620 §11]

171.407 Sound recordings of legislative proceedings required; State Archivist to provide public access. (1) Sound record-

ings, produced on equipment selected by the Legislative Administration Committee for compatibility with equipment for reproduction by the State Archives, shall be made of every meeting of the Legislative Assembly and of every hearing and meeting of every standing, special and interim committee of the Legislative Assembly, or subcommittee thereof.

(2) The sound recordings required under subsection (1) of this section are part of the legislative records of the Legislative Assembly or committee and shall be subject to the provisions of ORS 171.410 to 171.430.

(3) Except as provided in ORS 171.425, the State Archivist shall not loan any sound recording required under subsection (1) of this section, but may arrange to have such recordings copied in an appropriate manner and may make a reasonable charge therefor. [1973 c.555 §1]

171.430 Disposal by certain committees; sound recordings by certain committees. (1) Except for legislative records borrowed under ORS 171.425 and except as provided in subsection (2) of this section, the Emergency Board, the Legislative Administration Committee, the Legislative Counsel Committee or the Joint Committee on Ways and Means may cause any legislative records in its possession to be destroyed or otherwise disposed of, if such legislative records are considered by such committee to be of no value to the state or the public and are no longer necessary under or pursuant to any statute requiring their creation or maintenance or affecting their use. However, such committee shall prior to destruction or disposal notify the State Archivist and transfer to his official custody any such legislative records that are requisitioned by the State Archivist, except those designated as confidential by statute or by rule or resolution of the Legislative Assembly or of such committee.

(2) The Emergency Board, the Legislative Administration Committee, the Legislative Counsel Committee and the Joint Committee on Ways and Means shall cause sound recordings of its hearings or meetings to be retained, or if not retained, to be delivered to the State Archivist. The archivist shall be official custodian of the sound recordings so delivered. [1961 c.150 §6; 1969 c.620 §13; 1973 c.555 §5]

PUBLIC RECORDS
(Oregon Revised Statutes, 1982, s.192.001-192-170.)

192.001 Policy concerning public records. (1) The Legislative Assembly finds that:

(a) The records of the state and its political subdivisions are so interrelated and interdependent, that the decision as to what records are retained or destroyed is a matter

of state-wide public policy.

(b) The interest and concern of citizens in public records recognizes no jurisdictional boundaries, and extends to such records wherever they may be found in Oregon.

(c) As local programs become increasingly intergovernmental, the state and its political subdivisions have a responsibility to insure orderly retention and destruction of all public records, whether current or noncurrent, and to insure the preservation of public records of value for administrative, legal and research purposes.

(2) The purpose of ORS 192.005 to 192.170 and 357.805 to 357.895 is to provide direction for the retention or destruction of public records in Oregon, and to assure the retention of records essential to meet the needs of the Legislative Assembly, the state, its political subdivisions and its citizens, in so far as the records affect the administration of government, legal rights and responsibilities, and the accumulation of information of value for research purposes of all kinds. All records not included in types described in this subsection shall be destroyed in accordance with the rules adopted by the Secretary of State. [1973 c.439 §1]

192.005 Definitions for ORS 192.005 to 192.170. As used in ORS 192.005 to 192.170, unless the context requires otherwise:

(1) "Archivist" means the State Archivist.

(2) "Photocopy" includes a photograph, microphotograph and any other reproduction on paper or film in any scale.

(3) "Photocopying" means the process of reproducing, in the form of a photocopy, a public record or writing.

(4) "Political subdivision" means a city, county, district or any other municipal or public corporation in this state.

(5) "Public record" means a document, book, paper, photograph, file, sound recording or other material, such as court files, mortgage and deed records, regardless of physical form or characteristics, made, received, filed or recorded in pursuance of law or in connection with the transaction of public business, whether or not confidential or restricted in use. "Public records" includes correspondence, public records made by photocopying and public writings, but does not include:

(a) Records of the Legislative Assembly, its committees, officers and employes.

(b) Library and museum materials made or acquired and preserved solely for reference or exhibition purposes.

(c) Extra copies of a document, preserved only for convenience of reference.

(d) A stock of publications.

(6) "Public writing" means a written act or record of an act of a sovereign authority, official body, tribunal or public officer of this state, whether legislative, judicial or executive.

(7) "State agency" means any state officer, department, board, commission or court created by the Constitution or statutes of this state. However, "state agency" does not include the Legislative Assembly or its committees, offi-

cers and employes. [1961 c.160 §2; 1965 c.302 §1]

192.015 Secretary of State as public records administrator. The Secretary of State is the public records administrator of this state, and it is his responsibility to obtain and maintain uniformity in the application, operation and interpretation of the public records laws. [1973 c.439 §2]

192.040 Making, filing and recording records by photocopying. A state agency or political subdivision making public records or receiving and filing or recording public records, may do such making or receiving and filing or recording by means of photocopying. Such photocopying shall, except for records which are treated as confidential pursuant to law, be made, assembled and indexed, in lieu of any other method provided by law, in such manner as the governing body of the state agency or political subdivision considers appropriate. [Amended by 1961 c.160 §5]

192.050 Photocopying records; evidentiary effect. A state agency or political subdivision may, with the approval of the proper budgetary authority, cause any public records in its official custody to be photocopied as in the case of original filings or recordings. Every such reproduction shall be deemed an original; and a transcript, exemplification or certified copy of any such reproduction shall be deemed a transcript, exemplification or certified copy, as the case may be, of the original. [Amended by 1961 c.160 §6]

192.060 Indexing and filing photocopied records. All photocopies made under ORS 192.040 and 192.050 shall be properly indexed and placed in conveniently accessible files. Each roll of microfilm shall be deemed a book or volume and shall be designated and numbered and provision shall be made for preserving, examining and using the same. [Amended by 1961 c.160 §7]

192.070 Duplicate rolls of microfilm required; delivery to State Archivist. A duplicate of every roll of microfilm of documents recorded pursuant to law and the indexes therefor shall be made and kept safely. The State Archivist upon request may, pursuant to ORS 357.865, accept for safekeeping the duplicate microfilm. [Amended by 1961 c.160 §8]

192.072 State Archivist performing microfilm services for political subdivision or state agency. (1) As used in this section:

(a) "Political subdivision" includes a city, county, district and any other municipal or public corporation in Oregon.

(b) "State agency" includes any state officer, department, board, commission or court, the Legislative Assembly, its committees, officers and employes.

(2) Upon request of a state agency or political subdivision, the State Archivist may perform microfilm services for the state agency or political subdivision. The cost of rendering the microfilm services shall be paid to the State Archivist by the state agency or political subdivision. The moneys received under this section shall be deposited with the State Treasurer who shall give a receipt therefor. All such moneys are continuously appropriated for the payment of expenses incurred by the Secretary of State in the administration of the office of the State Archivist. [1955 c.87 §1; 1961 c.172 §3; 1973 c.439 §8]

192.105 State Archivist authorization for public officials and political subdivisions to dispose of records; legislative records excepted. (1) Except as otherwise provided by law, the State Archivist may grant to public officials of the state or any political subdivision, as defined in ORS 192.072, specific or continuing authorization for the retention or disposition of public records which are in their custody, after the records have been in existence for a specified period of time. In granting such authorization, the State Archivist shall consider the value of the public records for legal, administrative or research purposes and shall establish rules for procedure for the retention or disposition of the public records.

(2) The State Archivist shall provide instructions and forms for obtaining authorization. Upon receipt of an authorization or upon the effective date of the applicable rule, the public official who has public records in his custody may destroy or otherwise dispose of those records that are older than the specified period of retention established by the authorization or rule. No record of accounts or financial affairs subject to audit shall be destroyed until released for destruction by the responsible auditor or his representative. If federal funds are involved, records retention requirements of the United States Government must be observed.

(3) Authorizations granted prior to January 1, 1978, by any state agency, the State Archivist, or any board of county commissioners, to state agencies, schools, school districts, soil and water conservation districts, or county officials and offices shall remain in effect until they are adopted or amended by the State Archivist.

(4) This section does not apply to legislative records, as defined in ORS 171.410. [1953 c.244 §1; 1961 c.160 §10; subsection (3) enacted as 1961 c.150 §5; 1971 c.508 §1; 1977 c.146 §1]

192.130 Disposition of valueless records in custody of State Archivist. If any public records of a state agency or political subdivision in the official custody of the State Archivist prove to be of insufficient value to warrant permanent preservation, the State Archivist may submit a statement or summary thereof to the state agency or governing body of the political subdivision, or successor agency or body, certifying the type and nature thereof and requesting approval of the destruction or other disposal thereof. Upon receipt of such approval, the State Archivist may destroy or otherwise dispose of the public records. If the state agency or political subdivision no longer exists and there is no successor agency or body, the State Archivist may, upon approval of the Attorney General, destroy or otherwise dispose of the records. [Amended by 1961 c.160 §12; 1971 c.508 §2]

.192.170 Disposition of materials without authorization. The destruction or other disposal of the following materials do not require specific authorization:

(1) Inquiries and requests from the public and answers thereto not required by law to be preserved or not required as evidence of a public or private legal right or liability.

(2) Public records which are duplicates by reason of their having been photocopied.

(3) Letters of transmittal and acknowledgment, advertising, announcements and correspondence or notes pertaining to reservations of accommodations or scheduling of personal visits or appearances. [Amended by 1961 c.160 §16; 1971 c.508 §3]

SUPREME COURT LIBRARY
(Oregon Revised Statutes, 1982, s.9.760-9.810.)

9.760 Supreme Court Library; copying services; fees. The Supreme Court Library shall be under the control of the Supreme Court. The court shall make all rules for the government, use and services of the library. The court may authorize the library to provide photographic or other copies of any of its materials, and to make reasonable charges for such copies or services at rates approved by the court. All sums collected shall be remitted monthly or oftener to the State Treasurer. [Amended by 1959 c.655 §1]

9.770 Librarian and assistants; compensation; bond; applicability of public employes' retirement and unemployment compensation laws. (1) The Supreme Court shall appoint the Librarian of the Supreme Court Library and such assistants as it deems necessary and shall fix the compensation of the librarian and assistants. The librarian shall give an undertaking to the state in the sum of $1,000, with one or more sufficient sureties, to be approved by a majority of the judges of the Supreme Court, to the effect that he will faithfully and impartially perform the duties of his office and safely keep and account for the public property committed to his custody.

(2) The Librarian of the Supreme Court Library shall not be considered an "employe" as the term is defined in the public employes' retirement laws and as such term is defined in the unemployment compensation laws. However, the Librarian of the Supreme Court Library may, at his option, for the purpose of becoming a member of the Public Employes' Retirement System, be considered an "employe" as the term is defined in the public employes' retirement laws. Such option may be exercised only at the end of the librarian's first six months of service. The option, once exercised by written notification directed to the Public Employes' Retirement Board, may not be revoked subsequently, except as may otherwise be provided by law. [Amended by 1959 c.655 §2]

9.780 Exchange of legal books and publications. The Librarian of the Supreme Court Library may send, free of charge, one copy of the codes, session laws and Supreme Court reports of this state as the same may be published, to each state and foreign country that exchanges, free of charge, its codes, ses-

sion laws and Supreme Court reports with this state. All legal books and publications received in exchange by the state shall be turned over to the Supreme Court Library.

9.790 Secretary of State furnishing librarian with copies for exchange. The Secretary of State shall, upon requisition of the Supreme Court, supply the Librarian of the Supreme Court Library with a sufficient number of copies of the codes, session laws and Supreme Court reports of this state, as the same may be published, to enable the librarian to carry out the provisions of ORS 9.780.

9.800 Sale of surplus codes and session laws. The Librarian of the Supreme Court Library may sell, at prices to be fixed by him with the approval of the Supreme Court, the unused sets of Oregon codes and session laws in the custody of the librarian which are not needed by him for the purpose of exchanging for the codes and session laws of other states and for other books.

9.810 Terms of sale; disposition of proceeds. The sales described in ORS 9.800 shall be for cash, and the proceeds shall be turned over by the librarian to the State Treasurer and become a part of the General Fund.

PUBLIC LIBRARIES

(Oregon Revised Statutes, 1982, s.357.216-357.286, 357.400-357.621.)

357.216 Definitions for ORS 357.216 to 357.286. As used in ORS 357.216 to 357.286, unless the context requires otherwise:

(1) "County governing body" means the county court or board of county commissioners of the county.

(2) "County" means the county in which the administrative office of the district is located.

(3) "District" means a library district formed under this Act.

(4) "District board" or "board" means the governing body of a district. [1981 c.226 §1]

357.221 District formation; petition requirements. (1) A library district may be created as provided in ORS 198.705 to 198.955 and 357.216 to 357.286.

(2) In addition to other required matters, a petition for formation of a district shall state the method of election of the board of the proposed district from among the methods described in ORS 357.241. [1981 c.226 §2]

357.226 District board members; appointment of librarian. (1) The officers of the district shall be a board of five members, to be elected by the registered voters of the district. The district board shall appoint a district librarian, who shall be the secretary

for the district.

(2) Any elector residing within the district shall be qualified to serve as a district board member. [1981 c.226 §3]

357.231 Number of board members, terms. (1) Five district board members shall be elected at the election for district formation. Nominating petitions shall be filed with the county governing body.

(2) If the effective date of the formation of the district occurs in an odd-numbered year, two district board members shall be elected for four-year terms and the other three district board members shall be elected for two-year terms. If the effective date of the formation occurs in an even-numbered year, two district board members shall be elected for three-year terms and the other three district board members shall be elected for one-year terms.

(3) Each district board member shall hold office until election and qualification of a successor. [1981 c.226 §4]

357.236 Election date for board members; procedure. (1) An election shall be held in the district, on the date fixed by ORS 255.335, at which a successor shall be elected for each of the members of the district board whose terms regularly expire on the following

June 30. If three board members are to be elected, the candidates receiving the first, second and third highest vote shall be elected. If two board members are to be elected, the candidates receiving the first and second highest vote shall be elected.

(2) Each district board member elected shall take an oath of office and shall hold office from July 1, next following election, for four years, and until a successor is elected and qualified. [1981 c.226 §5]

357.241 Method of electing board members. (1) The district board members may be elected in one of the following methods or a combination thereof:

(a) Elected by the qualified voters of zones as nearly equal in population as possible according to the latest federal census.

(b) Elected at large by position number by the qualified voters of the district.

(2) Candidates for election from zones shall be nominated by qualified voters of the zones. [1981 c.226 §6]

357.246 Zoning for board member elections; procedure. (1) If a petition signed by at least 1,000 qualified voters of the district or at least a number equal to 10 percent of the voters voting for the office of district board member at the last election for members of the district board, whichever is less, is presented to the board of such district requesting that the district be zoned for the purpose of nominating or electing one or more board members, the board shall submit the question to the qualified voters of the district at the next election of district board members for their approval or rejection. The question may also be presented to the voters of the district upon adoption of a resolution by the board. The petition or resolution shall describe the proposed boundaries of the zones and shall specify whether in filling each position on the board a qualified voter of the district shall be entitled to sign a petition of nomination or to vote for a candidate from any zone or only for a candidate from the zone in which the voter resides.

(2) If the qualified voters of the district approve the establishment of zones, board members shall continue to serve until their terms of office expire. As vacancies occur, positions to be filled by nomination or election by zone shall be filled by persons who reside within zones which are not represented on the board. If more than one zone is not represented on the board when a vacancy occurs, the zone entitled to elect a board member shall be decided by lot. [1981 c.226 §7]

357.251 Zone boundaries; changing method of electing board members. (1) The boundaries of zones established within a district, whether established upon formation of the district or thereafter, from which district

board members are to be nominated or elected shall be as nearly equal in population as is feasible according to the latest federal census and shall be adjusted by the district board to reflect boundary changes of the district.

(2) The method of nominating and electing board members may be changed to another method described in ORS 357.241 by submitting the question of such change to the qualified voters at the next election of district board members for their approval or rejection. The question shall be so submitted when a petition requesting the change and signed by at least 1,000 qualified voters of the district or at least a number equal to 10 percent of the voters voting for the office of director at the last election for members of the district board, whichever is less, is presented to the board or a resolution to submit the question to the voters is adopted by the board. The petition or resolution shall meet the requirements for a petition or resolution as set forth in ORS 357.246 (1). [1981 c.226 §8]

357.256 Board as district governing body; selection of president. (1) The district board shall be the governing body of the district and shall exercise all powers thereof.

(2) At its first meeting or as soon thereafter as may be practicable, the board shall choose one of its members as president. [1981 c.226 §9]

357.261 District as municipal corporation; powers. A district shall constitute a municipal corporation of this state, and a public body, corporate and politic, exercising public power. Every district shall have power:

(1) To have and use a common seal.

(2) To sue and be sued by its name.

(3) To make and accept any and all contracts, deeds, leases, releases and documents of any kind which, in the judgment of the board, are necessary or proper to the exercise of any power of the district, and to direct the payment of all lawful claims or demands.

(4) To assess, levy and collect taxes to pay the cost of acquiring sites for and constructing, reconstructing, altering, operating and maintaining a library or any lawful claims against the district, and the operating expenses of the district.

(5) To employ all necessary agents and assistants.

(6) To call, hold and conduct all elections, necessary or proper after the formation of the district.

(7) To enlarge the boundaries of the district as provided by ORS 198.705 to 198.955.

(8) Generally to do and perform any and all acts necessary and proper to the complete exercise and effect of any of its powers or the purposes for which it was formed.

(9) Whenever authorized by the voters, to issue general obligation bonds of the district. However, the aggregate amount of general obligation bonds issued and outstanding at any one time shall not exceed two and one-half percent of the true cash value of all taxable property of the district, computed in accordance with ORS 308.207.

(10) To exercise those powers granted to local government units for public libraries under ORS 357.410. [1981 c.226 §10]

357.266 Financing district activities; limitation on assessment. Each year the district board shall determine and fix the amount of money to be levied and raised by taxation, for the purposes of the district. The total amount in dollars and cents shall not exceed one-fourth of one percent (.0025) of the true cash value of all taxable property within the district computed in accordance with ORS 308.207. [1981 c.226 §11]

357.271 Sinking funds for acquisition of facilities; limitation on use of funds. The board, by resolution duly adopted, may establish sinking funds for the purpose of defraying the costs of acquiring land for library sites, and for acquiring or constructing buildings or facilities. A sinking fund may be created through the inclusion annually within the tax budget of the district of items representing the yearly instalments to be credited to the fund. The amount of these items shall be collected and credited to the proper fund in the same manner in which taxes levied or revenues derived for other purposes for the district are collected and credited. The balances to the credit of the funds need not be taken into consideration or deducted from budget estimates by the levying authority in preparing the annual budget of the district. None of the moneys in sinking funds shall be diverted or transferred to other funds, but if unexpended balances remain after disbursement of the funds for the purpose for which they were created, such balances, upon approval by resolution of the board, shall be transferred to the operation and maintenance fund of the district. [1981 c.226 §12]

357.276 Deposit of district funds; funds held by county treasurer; disbursement of funds. (1) The money of the district shall be deposited, in the discretion of the district board, either with the county treasurer of the county, in accordance with subsections (2) to (4) of this section, or in one or more banks or savings and loan associations to be designated by the board. Funds deposited in a bank or savings and loan association shall be withdrawn or paid out only upon proper order and warrant or check signed by the secretary and countersigned by the president of the district board. The board may by resolution designate a secretary pro tempore or a president pro tempore who may sign warrants or checks on behalf of the secretary and president, respectively.

(2) If district funds are deposited with the county treasurer, when the tax collector pays over to the county treasurer moneys collected for a district, the county treasurer shall keep the moneys in the county treasury as follows:

(a) The county treasurer shall place and keep in a fund called the operation and maintenance fund of the district (naming it) the moneys levied by the district board for that fund.

(b) The county treasurer shall place and keep in a fund called the construction fund of the district (naming it) the moneys levied by the board for construction, reconstruction and alteration.

(3) The county treasurer shall pay out moneys from the funds only upon the written order of the board, signed by the president and countersigned by the secretary. The order shall specify the name of the person to whom the money is to be paid and the fund from which it is to be paid, and shall state generally the purpose for which the payment is made. The order shall be entered in the minutes of the board.

(4) The county treasurer shall keep the order as a voucher, and shall keep a specific account of the county treasurer's receipts and disbursements of money for the district. [1981 c.226 §13]

357.281 District attorney to provide assistance; employment of special counsel. The district board may call upon the district attorney for the advice as to any district business. The district attorney shall give advice when called on therefor by the board. The board may at any time employ special counsel for any purpose. [1981 c.226 §14]

357.286 Retirement system for employes. A district may establish an employes retirement system as provided for rural fire protection districts under ORS 478.355 to 478.370. [1981 c.226 §15]

357.400 Definitions for ORS 357.400 to 357.621. As used in ORS 357.400 to 357.621:

(1) "Governing body" means the board, commission, council or other body which governs the local government unit.

(2) "Local government unit" means any city, county, library service district established under either ORS chapter 268 or 451, school district, community college district or a library district established under ORS 357.216 to 357.286.

(3) "Public library" or "public library system" means a public agency responsible for providing and making accessible to all residents of a local government unit library and

information services suitable to persons of all ages. [1955 c.432 §2; 1975 c.476 §16; 1981 c.226 §17]

357.410 Authority of local government units for public libraries. Any local government unit may:

(1) Establish, equip and maintain a public library.

(2) Contract with an established public library or with a private society or corporation owning and controlling a secular or nonsectarian library for the purpose of providing free use of the library for the residents of the local government unit, under such terms and conditions as may be agreed upon.

(3) Contract with one or more units of local government or library boards pursuant to ORS 190.003 to 190.620 to provide jointly a public library or public library service or share in the use of facilities, under such terms and conditions as may be agreed upon.

(4) Enter into an interstate library agreement pursuant to Article VI of the Interstate Library Compact (ORS 357.340).

(5) Contract with the Trustees of the State Library for assistance in establishing, improving or extending public library service.

(6) Levy annually and cause to be collected, as other general taxes are collected, a tax upon the taxable property in the local government unit to provide a library fund to be used exclusively to maintain such library.

(7) Levy and cause to be collected, as other taxes are collected, a special tax upon the taxable property in the local government unit, or contract bonded indebtedness under the provisions of ORS chapter 287 to provide a public library building fund to be used exclusively for the purchase of real property for public library purposes and for the erection and equipping of public library buildings including branch library buildings.

(8) Levy or impose such other taxes as may be authorized to the unit by city charter or the charter of a home-rule county. [Amended by 1955 c.432 §5; 1961 c.251 §8; 1965 c.354 §7; 1975 c.112 §1; 1975 c.476 §17]

357.417 Methods of establishing public library by local government unit. (1) A public library may be established by a local government unit by any of the following ways:

(a) The governing body may pass and enter upon its minutes a resolution or ordinance to the effect that a public library is established under the provisions of ORS 357.400 to 357.621.

(b) Upon petition signed by a number of registered voters equal to not less than five percent of the total number of votes cast within the boundaries of the local government unit for all candidates for Governor at the election at which a Governor was elected for a term of four years next preceding the filing of the petition, the governing body shall make and enter an order for an election requesting approval by the voters of the establishment and support of a public library.

(c) Upon its own motion, the governing body may make and enter an order for an election requesting approval by the voters of the establishment and support of a public library.

(2) Elections held under this section shall be held on a day specified in ORS 255.345. [Formerly 357.451; 1981 c.909 §10]

357.430 Methods of financing public library by local government unit. If a governing body acts under ORS 357.417 (1)(a) or (c), its order shall state the manner in which the local government unit proposes to finance the library, including the estimated amount of any annual tax levy necessary to provide for the library. If the governing body determines that financing may be had only through a serial levy to be submitted to the voters pursuant to ORS 357.525, the order shall so state. The notice of, time of and manner of election shall be governed by the applicable provisions of ORS chapter 310, ORS 255.005 to 255.035, 255.055 to 255.095 and 255.215 to 255.355. [Amended by 1955 c.432 §7; 1961 c.251 §9; 1975 c.476 §19]

357.435 Local government required to file plan with State Library; response; effect of advice or comment. Any local government unit acting under ORS 357.417 shall notify in writing the State Library of its plan for establishing a public library. The State Library shall respond in writing within 30 days, commenting on the plan for establishing the library and on its relationship to the long-range plans for the state-wide development and coordination of library services. The State Library's advice or comment is not binding upon the local government unit, and if no such advice or comment is received within 30 days of the request, the local government unit may act without further delay. [Formerly 357.640]

357.460 Appointment of county or city library board successors; vacancies; compensation; limitations. (1) No member of any public library board or the body appointing such board shall have any financial interest, either directly or indirectly, in any contract to which the library is a party, nor shall receive a salary or any payment for material or for services rendered the board.

(2) Board members may be reimbursed for expenses incurred in the performance of their duties. [Amended by 1975 c.112 §4; 1975 c.476 §22]

357.465 Regional public library board. (1) Each public library established under ORS 357.417 shall be governed by a library board unless some other method is specified in the charter, ordinance or resolution establishing the library.

(2) Upon resolution, ordinance or election pursuant to ORS 357.417, the governing body may appoint a library board. In the case of a city, such board shall consist of five members. In the case of a county or county service district, such board shall consist of five or seven members at the discretion of the governing body. In the case of a school district or community college district, such board shall consist of five, seven or more members at the discretion of the governing body.

(3) If the board will consist of five members, one member shall initially hold office for one year, one for two years, one for three years and two for four years, from July 1 in the year of their appointment. If the board will consist of seven members, one member shall initially hold office for one year, two for two years, two for three years, and two for four years, from July 1 in the year of their appointment. If the board will consist of more than seven members, the members first appointed shall hold office for such terms as will achieve the staggered term base established for smaller boards by this section. Succeeding appointees shall hold office for a term of four years from July 1 in the year of their appointment. At the expiration of the term of any member of such board, the governing body shall appoint a new member or may reappoint a member for a term of four years. If a vacancy occurs, the governing body shall appoint a new member for the unexpired term. No person shall hold appointment as a member for more than two full consecutive terms, but any person may be appointed again to the board after an interval of one year. [1955 c.432 §4; 1961 c.251 §12; 1975 c.476 §21]

357.470 Board organization; name of library. After appointment, the public library board shall meet and organize by the election of a chairman from among its members. The librarian shall serve as secretary to the board and keep the record of its actions. [Amended by 1955 c.432 §9; 1975 c.112 §5; 1975 c.476 §23]

357.490 Library board general powers. In the ordinance or resolution establishing the library, the governing body shall determine the library board's responsibility for:

(1) Appointment of the librarian and staff, fixing their compensation, determining their working conditions and prescribing their duties.

(2) Formulating rules and policies for the governance of the library.

(3) Preparing and submitting an annual budget request.

(4) Approving, or delegating to the librarian the responsibility for approving, all expenditures from the library fund or the public library building fund.

(5) Acceptance, use or expenditure of any real or personal property or funds donated to the library, or purchase, control or disposal of real and personal property necessary for the purposes of the library, except that each donation shall be administered in accordance with its terms, and all property or funds shall be held in the name of the governing body.

(6) Selection of sites for public library buildings or for location of library facilities.

(7) Entering into contracts.

(8) Such other activities as the governing body may assign. [Amended by 1955 c.432 §11; 1961 c.251 §15; 1965 c.354 §8; 1967 c.67 §19; 1975 c.112 §7; 1975 c.476 §24]

357.520 Annual report. Each public library established under ORS 357.417 shall make an annual report to the State Library and to the governing body on a form supplied by the State Library. [Amended by 1965 c.354 §9; 1975 c.476 §25]

357.525 Election to authorize serial levy by petition or order; notice. (1) Upon petition signed by a number of registered voters equal to not less than five percent of the total number of votes cast within the boundaries of the local government unit for all candidates for Governor at the election at which a Governor was elected for a term of four years next preceding the filing of the petition, or upon its own motion, the governing body shall make and enter an order for an election requesting approval by the voters of a serial levy for any of the purposes set forth in ORS 357.410, 357.417 or 357.490. The order shall state the purpose for which the funds are to be expended, the period during which the proposed taxes are to be levied and the amount to be levied each year, which amount shall be uniform throughout the period of levy, all according to the petition or motion.

(2) The notice of, time of and manner of election shall be governed by the applicable provisions of ORS chapter 310, 255.005 to 255.035, 255.055 to 255.095 and 255.215 to 255.355.

(3) Upon approval by a majority of the voters voting at such election, the taxing unit shall levy each year during the approved period the amount so approved. The tax levy proceeds shall be handled as provided by ORS 357.410 or 357.430, or as otherwise provided by law. [Formerly 357.455]

357.610 Conformity to ORS 357.400 to 357.621 by libraries organized prior to enactment of those statutes; effect on executed library contracts. (1) Libraries organized under Oregon laws prior to September 13, 1975, are continued, and may have their organizations changed so as to conform to ORS 357.001 to 357.200, 357.330, 357.360, 357.400 to 357.621, 357.975 and 357.990 by resolution of the governing body of the local government unit which established the library. The resolution shall outline the procedure necessary to be taken for such change.

(2) Nothing contained in ORS 357.001 to 357.200, 357.330, 357.360, 357.400 to 357.621, 357.975 and 357.990 shall affect nor change the terms of any library contract executed prior to September 13, 1975. However, by mutual consent, the parties to the contract may amend the contract so as to make it conform to all or any of the provisions of ORS 357.001 to 357.200, 357.330, 357.360, 357.400 to 357.621, 357.975 and 357.990. [Amended by 1975 c.476 §27]

357.621 Public hearings required prior to abolishing or withdrawing support from public library; notice of hearings. No governing body which has established a public library under the laws of this state shall abolish or withdraw support for such library without first holding at least two public hearings on the matter at least 90 days apart. The governing body shall give public notice of the public hearing in a newspaper of general circulation in the area for two successive weeks at least 30 days prior to the first hearing. [1975 c.476 §29 (enacted in lieu of 357.620)]

COUNTY LAW LIBRARIES
(Oregon Revised Statutes, 1982, s.9.820-9.850, 21.350.)

9.820   Law libraries in Multnomah County. In all counties containing more than 400,000 inhabitants, according to the latest federal decennial census, the county court or board of county commissioners may contract with any law library association or corporation owning and maintaining a law library in the county at or convenient to the courthouse, for the use of the library by the judges of the circuit and county courts, county commissioners, district attorney and all members of the bar, and shall, if the association permits the use of its library by all members of the bar without charge, pay therefor all library fees collected pursuant to ORS 21.350 (1) to the library association or corporation for the use of the library. [Amended by 1963 c.519 §1; 1965 c.619 §3]

9.830   Disposition of library fees in Multnomah County. On the first day of each month the county clerk making collections pursuant to ORS 21.350 (1) shall pay over to the library association or corporation contracted with pursuant to ORS 9.820 all the library fees collected for the preceding month, taking its receipt therefor. [Amended by 1965 c.619 §4]

Note: The amendments to 9.830 by section 78, chapter 3, Oregon Laws 1981 (special session), become operative January 1, 1983. See section 5, chapter 3, Oregon Laws 1981 (special session). 9.830, as amended, is set forth for the users' convenience.

9.830. The clerk of a court shall pay fees collected pursuant to ORS 21.350 (1) to the appropriate officer of the county within the first 10 days of the month following the month in which collected, for payment to the library association or corporation contracted with pursuant to ORS 9.820.

9.840   Law libraries in counties other than Multnomah County. The county court of any county containing not more than 400,000 inhabitants, according to the latest federal decennial census, may, after a resolution duly passed by the bar association of the county therefor has been filed with the county clerk, pass a resolution at a regular meeting of the county court, declaring that the county maintains and operates a law library as de-

scribed in ORS 21.350 (2), or that the county proposes, after the passing of the resolution by the county court, to establish, maintain and operate such a library, and reciting that the county has a population of not more than 400,000, according to the latest federal decennial census. Such resolution shall be authorization and direction to the county clerk to charge the fees prescribed in ORS 21.350 (1). [Amended by 1963 c.519 §2; 1965 c.619 §5]

Note: The amendments to 9.840 by section 79, chapter 3, Oregon Laws 1981 (special session), become operative January 1, 1983. See section 5, chapter 3, Oregon Laws 1981 (special session). 9.840, as amended, is set forth for the users' convenience.

9.840. The county court of any county containing not more than 400,000 inhabitants, according to the latest federal decennial census, may, after a resolution duly passed by the bar association of the county therefor has been filed with the county clerk, pass a resolution at a regular meeting of the county court, declaring that the county maintains and operates a law library as described in ORS 21.350 (2), or that the county proposes, after the passing of the resolution by the county court, to establish, maintain and operate such a library, and reciting that the county has a population of not more than 400,000, according to the latest federal decennial census. Such resolution shall be authorization and direction to the clerk of a court to collect the fees prescribed in ORS 21.350 (1). The clerk of a court shall pay fees so collected to the appropriate officer of the county within the first 10 days of the month following the month in which collected.

9.850   Disposition of library fees in counties other than Multnomah County. In all counties containing not more than 400,000 inhabitants, according to the latest federal decennial census, the county court may use such part of the law library fees collected pursuant to ORS 21.350 (1) as it deems desirable for the purpose of acquiring, maintaining or operating a law library at the county seat of the county, at such place as it may direct; but no part of the moneys received from such law library fees shall be used for any purpose other than acquiring, maintaining or operating such law library. [Amended by 1963 c.519 §3; 1965 c.619 §6]

21.350 Law library fees. (1) In counties containing more than 400,000 inhabitants, according to the latest federal decennial census, or when directed as provided in ORS 9.840, it shall be the duty of the county clerk to collect in each civil suit, action or proceeding filed in the circuit, district or county court a law library fee which shall be determined by the county court or board of county commissioners in an amount not greater than 40 percent of the filing fee provided by law. This fee shall be collected in the same manner as other fees are collected in the suit, action or proceeding, and is in addition to the other fees provided by law.

(2) The fee provided in subsection (1) of this section may be collected if the county owns and maintains, or hereafter may acquire, own or maintain under the provisions of ORS 9.840 and 9.850, a law library at the county seat, available at all reasonable times to the use of litigants, and permitted to be used by all attorneys at law duly admitted to practice in this state, without additional fees to such litigants or attorneys. [Formerly 21.140; 1973 c.381 §6]

Note: The amendments to 21.350 by section 77, chapter 3, Oregon Laws 1981 (special session), become operative January 1, 1983. See section 5, chapter 3, Oregon Laws 1981 (special session). 21.350, as amended, is set forth for the users' convenience.

21.350. (1) In counties containing more than 400,000 inhabitants, according to the latest federal decennial census, or when directed as provided in ORS 9.840, the clerk of the court shall collect in each civil suit, action or proceeding filed in the circuit, district or county court a law library fee determined by the county court or board of county commissioners in an amount not greater than 40 percent of the filing fee provided by law. This fee shall be collected in the same manner as other fees are collected in the suit, action or proceeding, and is in addition to the other fees provided by law.

(2) The fee provided in subsection (1) of this section may be collected if the county owns and maintains, or hereafter may acquire, own or maintain under the provisions of ORS 9.840 and 9.850, a law library at the county seat, available at all reasonable times to the use of litigants, and permitted to be used by all attorneys at law duly admitted to practice in this state, without additional fees to such litigants or attorneys.

PROTECTION OF LIBRARY PROPERTY

(Oregon Revised Statutes, 1982, s.357.975, 357.990.)

357.975 Wilful detention of library property. It shall be unlawful for any person wilfully or maliciously to detain any library materials belonging to a publicly supported library or privately supported school, academic or research library or incorporated library for 30 days after notice in writing from the librarian of such library, given after the expiration of time which by regulations of such library such materials may be kept. The notice shall bear upon its face a copy of this section and of ORS 357.990. [Formerly 357.830; 1975 c.476 §30]

357.990 Penalties. Violation of ORS 357.975 is punishable upon conviction by a fine of not less than $5 nor more than $25. Such conviction and payment of the fine shall not be construed to constitute payment for library material nor shall a person convicted under this section be thereby relieved of any obligation to return to the library such material. [Amended by 1971 c.743 §360; 1975 c.476 §31]

Oregon library laws are reprinted from OREGON REVISED STATUTES published by the Oregon Legislative Council Committee.

PENNSYLVANIA

STATE LIBRARY CODE
Definitions

(Purdon's Pennsylvania Statutes Annotated, 1982, Title 24,
s.4101-4102.)

§ 4101. Short title

This act shall be known and may be cited as "The Library Code".
1961, June 14, P.L. 324, Art. I, § 101.

§ 4102. Definitions

As used in this act—

(1) "Local Library." Any free, public, nonsectarian library, whether established and maintained by a municipality or by a private association, corporation or group, which serves the informational, educational and recreational needs of all the residents of the area for which its governing body is responsible, by providing free access (including free lending and reference services) to an organized and currently useful collection of printed items and other materials and to the services of a staff trained to recognize and provide for these needs.

(2) "County Library." Any local library or division of a local library, which derives income from the commissioners of the county for the express purpose of making its resources and services available without charge to all the residents of the county, and to bring direct library service to those county residents not served by other local libraries located within the same county. For the purposes of this act, a local library operating a distinct county division shall be considered as two agencies, namely, a local library and a county library which are merged or conjoined.

(3) "District Library Center." Any library designated as such by

the State Librarian and receiving State-aid for the purpose of making its resources and services available without charge to all the residents of the district, of providing supplementary library services to local libraries within the district, of coordinating the services of all local libraries within the district which by contract become part of the district library center system and of exchanging, providing or contracting for library services with other district library centers.

(4) "Regional Resource Center." Any library designated as such by the State Librarian and receiving State-aid for the purpose of acquiring major research collections and, under such rules and regulations as are promulgated by a board consisting of the head librarians of all regional resource centers and under the chairmanship of the State Librarian, making them available to the residents of the Commonwealth on a State-wide basis.

(5) "Library Trainee." Any employe of the State Library receiving on-the-job training in an institution of higher education, enrolled, or having an application for enrollment pending, as a candidate for a graduate degree in library service.

(6) "Municipality." Any county, city, borough, town, township or any school district of the second, third or fourth class, which establishes or maintains a local library.

(7) "Municipal Officers." The mayor and council of any city, the mayor and council of any borough or town, the commissioners or supervisors of any township, the commissioners of any county or the board of school directors of any school district of the second, third or fourth class. As amended 1982, April 27, P.L. 348, No. 96, § 1, effective in 60 days.

State Library

(Purdon's Pennsylvania Statutes Annotated, 1982, Title 24, s.4201-4211.)

§ 4201. State Library and State Librarian; powers and duties

The Department of Education shall have the power, and its duty shall be—
As amended 1982, May 4, P.L. 371, No. 105, § 1, imd. effective.

(1) To appoint a suitably qualified State Librarian as the person to exercise the powers and discharge the duties pursuant to this section.

(2) To control, direct, supervise and manage the State Library as an agency providing information and fostering continuing education in the state education program.

(3) To maintain, as part of the State Library, a law library.

(4) To receive copies of all publications of all agencies of the Commonwealth in order to maintain a definitive, organized collection of all such publications by the State Library and to provide for the distribution of such publications to other libraries. The State Librarian shall

also designate selected academic or public libraries within the Commonwealth to be State government document depository libraries under criteria and regulations approved by the Advisory Council on Library Development and, in the case of documents published pursuant to the act
of July 31, 1968 (Act No. 240), known as the "Commonwealth Documents Law," 1 by the Joint Committee on Documents.
As amended 1971, Dec. 1, P.L. 578, No. 150, § 1.

(5) To coordinate a State-wide system of local libraries and to counsel local libraries on minimum standards for number and quality of
library staff, resources of books and other materials, location of new
local libraries, hours and physical facilities. Nothing contained herein
shall restrict or limit public libraries in the selection of resources of
books and other material not determined from counselling.

(6) To give advice and counsel to all local libraries, district library
centers and regional resource centers and to all municipalities and
groups, which may propose to establish libraries, in the selection of
books, cataloguing and other details of library management and as to
the best means of establishing and administering such libraries.

(7) To inspect local libraries, district library centers and regional
resource centers and require reports in such manner as may be deemed
proper.

(8) To purchase and maintain a general collection of books, periodicals, newspapers, maps, slides, films and other library materials for the
use of State and local governments, libraries and the public generally.

(9) To make available all library materials of the State Library for
circulation to local libraries and to the public generally under rules and
regulations promulgated by the State Librarian, except that the State
Librarian may restrict the circulation of library materials which, because they are rare or are used intensively in the State Library for reference or other purposes, should be retained in the State Library at all
times.

(10) To promote and demonstrate library service throughout the
State.

(11) To collect, preserve and publish library statistics.

(12) To study library problems throughout the State and make the
resultant findings available to all libraries within the State applying
therefor.

(13) To certify library personnel in the following categories: Library Assistants having two years of college education in addition to in-
service library training; Provisional Librarians having a college degree
and introductory education in library service; and Professional Librarians having a college degree in addition to one or more academic years of
professional library education. The State Librarian may conduct examinations and promulgate rules and regulations providing for the cer-

tification of persons in the above categories based upon actual library experience as equivalent to the above minimum educational requirements: Provided, That this act shall not apply to clerks, typists, volunteer workers or other personnel, who do not need special library training: And provided further, That all library personnel employed at the effective date of this act shall be certified for the positions they then hold.

(14) To conduct and arrange for training programs for library personnel.

(15) Generally, to promulgate rules and regulations for the purpose of carrying out the powers and duties relating to libraries as are imposed by law: Provided, That such rules and regulations shall not, directly or indirectly, prohibit the inclusion of a particular book, periodical or material, the works of a particular author or the expression of a particular point of view. Such rules and regulations shall not take effect until approved by the Advisory Council on Library Development.

(16) Whenever necessary for the purpose of administering the library laws of the Commonwealth to act as arbiter in defining the direct service area of any library. 1961, June 14, P.L. 324, Art. II, § 201.

(17) To receive funds allocated to the State for library purposes by the Federal government or by private agencies and to administer such funds in library maintenance, improvement or extension programs consistent with Federal and State Library objectives.
Added 1967, Dec. 21, P.L. 887, No. 398, § 1.

(18) To promote, and support cooperation among the various types of libraries in Pennsylvania for the purpose of increasing the services and resources available through libraries, and to provide financial support for the development and maintenance of cooperative programs from funds appropriated to the State Library for the purpose of supporting interlibrary cooperative programs. It is the intent of this legislation to promote cooperation among types of libraries, not to decrease or supplant the existing financial support of any single type of library.
Added 1982, May 4, P.L. 371, No. 105, § 1, imd. effective.

§ 4202. Advisory Council on Library Development

The Advisory Council on Library Development is hereby created and placed in and made a part of the Department of Public Instruction. 1961, June 14, P.L. 324, Art. II, § 202.

§ 4203. Appointment, qualification, tenure

The Advisory Council on Library Development shall consist of twelve members who shall be appointed by the Governor, three of whom shall be trustees of local libraries, three of whom shall be professional librarians, and six of whom shall be laymen. The Superintendent of Public Instruction and the State Librarian shall be ex officio members of the council. The term of office of each member of the council shall be four years from the third Tuesday of January of the year in which he takes office, or until his successor has been appointed and has qualified, except that in the initial appointment of members of the council, four members shall be appointed for a term of one year, four members for a term of two years and four members for a term of three years. The members shall serve without compensation other than reimbursement for travel and other actual expenses incurred in the performance of their duties. The Governor shall designate one member as chairman of the council. The council shall meet at least four times a year at such times and places as it shall determine. 1961, June 14, P.L. 324, Art. II, § 203.

§ 4204. Powers and duties

The Advisory Council on Library Development shall have the power, and its duty shall be—

(1) To advise the Governor and the Superintendent of Public Instruction with regard to the appointment of the State Librarian.

(2) To give advice and make recommendations to the Governor, the Superintendent of Public Instruction and the State Librarian with respect to the general policies and operations of the State Library and the Commonwealth's library program.

(3) To constitute a board of appeal in regard to disputes arising from decisions of the State Librarian, which affect the amount of State-aid to a library or its eligibility for State-aid. In any such appeal, the ex officio members of the council shall not have voting rights and the vote of a majority of the duly appointed members of the council shall be determinative of the appeal.

(4) To aid in increasing public understanding of, and formulating plans for, furthering the purposes of this act.

(5) To promulgate rules and regulations for the approval of plans for the use of State funds. 1961, June 14, P.L. 324, Art. II, § 204.

(6) To approve or disapprove the library district designations and alignments which are recommended by the State Librarian. Added 1971, Dec. 1, P.L. 578, No. 150, § 2.

§ 4205. Library trainees

The Department of Public Instruction shall have authority to employ library trainees under the terms and conditions set forth in this act. During each calendar year the State Librarian may recommend from the list of persons qualified for employment as library trainees up to twenty-five persons. 1961, June 14, P.L. 324, Art. II, § 205.

§ 4206. Qualifications

To qualify for employment as a library trainee a person must—

(1) Be enrolled or have an application for enrollment pending in an

institution of higher learning as a candidate for a graduate degree in library service.

(2) Satisfactorily pass a competitive examination conducted by the Department of Public Instruction.

(3) Be otherwise qualified according to standards of qualifications for employment established for the State Library. 1961, June 14, P.L. 324, Art. II, § 206.

§ 4207. Selection

Competitive examinations for library trainees shall be held at such times and places, by such officials or citizens of the Commonwealth, as are designated by the rules and regulations of the Department of Public Instruction, and on such subjects as the State Librarian deems essential to qualify people for on-the-job training in the State Library. After each competitive examination, the Superintendent of Public Instruction shall furnish to the State Librarian a list of the persons qualified for employment as library trainees. 1961, June 14, P.L. 324, Art. II, § 207.

§ 4208. Contract of employment, compensation

Before commencing employment, a library trainee shall execute a contract of employment whereby he promises to perform services in the Commonwealth for a term twice the length of the period during which he will receive on-the-job training prior to being awarded a graduate degree in library service, and whereby, as an employe of the Commonwealth, he promises to perform continuous service for the Commonwealth during periods of the year when he is not receiving on-the-job training in an educational institution. In consideration of these promises, the Department of Public Instruction shall agree to employ such person so long as such person's services are necessary and valuable for the performance of the duties of the State Library, or so long as the person maintains an academic standing satisfactory to the proper authorities of the educational institution attended by such person, at a salary schedule established for the State Library. 1961, June 14, P.L. 324, Art. II, § 208.

§ 4209. Regional Library Resource Centers

The State Librarian shall designate four Regional Library Resource Centers to be located at the following places:

Free Library of Philadelphia,

Pennsylvania State Library,

Pennsylvania State University Library, and

Carnegie Library of Pittsburgh. 1961, June 14, P.L. 324, Art. II, § 209.

§ 4210. Powers and duties of Regional Library Resource Centers

Regional Library Resource Centers shall have the responsibility and power to acquire major research collections and, under rules and regulations as are promulgated by a board consisting of the head librarians of all Regional Library Resource Centers and under the chairmanship of the State Librarian, to make them available to the residents of the Commonwealth on a State-wide basis. 1961, June 14, P.L. 324, Art. II, § 210.

§ 4211. District Library Centers

The State Librarian, with the approval of the Advisory Council on Library Development, shall designate up to thirty libraries throughout the Commonwealth as District Library Centers which may include any local library, any State College library, the Pennsylvania State University library and any privately supported college or university library which may agree to serve as a District Library Center District. Library Centers shall have the power to contract with any city, borough, town, township, school district, county or board of trustees or managers of any local library, which wishes thereby to become part of the District Library Center system of such district. Any District Library Center shall have the power to provide direct library service to persons residing within the district, to provide supplementary library services to all local libraries within the district, and to exchange or provide services with other District Library Centers or contract for the provision of library services with other District Library Centers.
As amended 1971, Dec. 1, P.L. 578, No. 150, § 3.

State Aid

(Purdon's Pennsylvania Statutes Annotated, 1982, Title 24, s.4301-4304.)

§ 4301. System of State-aid for local libraries, county libraries, district library centers and regional library resource centers

A system of State-aid to assist in the support and maintenance of local libraries, county libraries, district library centers and regional library resource centers is hereby established. 1961, June 14, P.L. 324, Art. III, § 301.

§ 4302. Definitions

As used in this article—
(1) "Basic Standards." The basic standards are standards promulgated by the State Librarian and approved by the Advisory Council on Library Development, in compliance with sections 201(15) and 303, which must be achieved by a local library to qualify for the State-aid authorized by section 303(1) and (7) and by a branch library or a bookmobile to qualify for the State-aid authorized by section 303(7). The standards shall be those deemed essential to a library, branch or bookmobile for it to fulfill the definition of local library stated in section 102(1).
(2) "Direct Service Area." The municipality or municipalities to which the governing body of a library is responsible for extending all its

library services without charge.

(3) "Financial Effort." The sum expended annually by a local library for the establishment, operation and maintenance of library services which derives from local taxes, gifts, endowments and other local sources, as may be provided under rules and regulations adopted by the Advisory Council on Library Development, and which is used to determine eligibility for State-aid.

(4) "Financial Effort Equal to One-half Mill." The financial effort equal to one-half mill times the market value of taxable property, as determined by the State Tax Equalization Board, in the municipalities for which aid is claimed or in the direct service area of a local library, whichever is applicable.

(5) "Financial Effort Equal to One-quarter Mill." The financial effort equal to one-quarter mill times the market value of taxable property, as determined by the State Tax Equalization Board, in the municipalities for which aid is claimed or in the direct service area of a local library, whichever is applicable.

(6) "Minimum Standards." Standards promulgated by the State Librarian and approved by the Advisory Council on Library Development, in compliance with sections 201(15) and 303, which must be achieved by a local library or a library system to qualify for the incentive aid authorized by section 303(2).

(7) "Per Capita." Amounts determined on the basis of either the latest official United States Census report or the population upon which the 1979–1980 state aid payment was based, whichever is greater.

(8) "Surplus Financial Effort." The financial effort which is in excess of a financial effort equal to one-half mill on market value in the direct service area or two dollars ($2) per capita for each person residing in the direct service area of the local library, whichever is less.
As amended 1980, Dec. 9, P.L. 1125, No. 200, § 1, imd. effective.

§ 4303. State-aid

State-aid shall be paid when a library achieves the applicable standards determined by counselling with the State Librarian pursuant to the advice and recommendations of the Advisory Council on Library Development, or submits plans as set forth in section 304 of this act leading to the achievement of such standards, and makes a minimum financial effort as follows, except that no library receiving State-aid prior to and at time of the approval of this act shall receive less State-aid as a result of the provisions hereof notwithstanding that such library has not accepted the provisions of this act:

(1) Basic Aid to Local Libraries. Twenty-five percent (25%) of the Commonwealth's total annual appropriation for the system of state-aid established by section 301,[2] or a minimum of twenty-five cents (25¢) per capita for each person residing in the municipalities of the libraries which qualify for basic aid, shall be allocated as basic aid.

Any local library which makes a minimum financial effort equal to one-half mill, for the municipalities on behalf of which it applies for aid, or two dollars ($2) per capita for each person residing in those municipalities, whichever is less and achieves the basic standards, shall qualify for basic state-aid. Such aid shall not be less than twenty-five cents (25¢) for each person residing in the municipalities. However, when the allocation for basic aid exceeds the amount necessary to pay the minimum rate, the entire allocation shall be distributed at a per capita rate which shall be determined by dividing the allocation by the number of persons in the Commonwealth on behalf of which local libraries and library systems apply and qualify for basic aid: Provided, That in the first year in which a library applies for State-aid it shall qualify by making a minimum financial effort equal to one-quarter mill, or one dollar ($1) per capita for each person residing in the municipalities whichever is less.

In each of the succeeding five years, such library shall qualify for maximum State-aid only when it increases its financial effort by the following scale of percentages of the difference between the financial effort with which such library initially qualified for State-aid and a financial effort equal to one-half mill, or two dollars ($2) per capita for each person residing in the municipalities for which it applies for aid, whichever is less:

> 1st succeeding year—20 percent,
> 2nd succeeding year—40 percent,
> 3rd succeeding year—60 percent,
> 4th succeeding year—80 percent,
> 5th succeeding year—100 percent.

But where the increase in any year is less than the percentage specified above, the amount of State-aid shall be reduced by a percentage equal to one-fifth of the percentage which the difference between the required increase and the actual increase bears to the required increase multiplied by the number of years of participation in State-aid beyond the first year.

After the fifth succeeding year, a local library shall not be eligible for further State-aid unless it makes a financial effort equal to one-half mill for the municipalities on behalf of which it applies for aid, or two dollars ($2) per capita for each person residing in those municipalities, whichever is less.

(2) Incentive Aid to Local Libraries. Twenty-five percent (25%) of the Commonwealth's total annual appropriation for the system of State-aid established by section 301, or a minimum of twenty-five cents (25¢) per capita for each person residing in the direct service areas of the libraries which qualify for incentive aid, shall be allocated as incentive aid.

Any local library or library system which makes a minimum financial effort equal to one-half mill, or two dollars ($2) per capita for each person residing in its direct service area, whichever is less and fulfills the minimum standards for local libraries or the minimum standards for library systems, whichever is applicable, shall qualify for incentive aid, which shall be in addition to all other amounts of aid provided in this section. Each qualifying library or library system shall receive incentive aid up to fifty cents (50¢) for each one dollar ($1) of surplus financial effort but when fifty cents (50¢) per dollar of surplus financial effort is more than twenty-five cents (25¢) per capita the minimum incentive aid shall be per capita for each person residing in the direct service area. However, if after paying the minimum amount set forth in this subsection there is a balance in the allocation, the balance shall be prorated among the libraries and library systems which qualify for a larger amount of aid at the rate of fifty cents (50¢) for each one dollar ($1) of surplus financial effort rather than at the rate of twenty-five cents (25¢) per capita.

(3) County Libraries. Ten percent (10%) of the Commonwealth's total annual appropriation for the system of State-aid established by section 301 shall be allocated as aid to county libraries.

In the case of a county library of a second, second A, third, fourth, fifth, sixth, seventh or eighth class county, State-aid shall be given in an amount measured by the amount appropriated by the county government from county moneys, either from the General Fund or a special library tax or other sources, for the support and maintenance of the county library, and shall be determined as follows:

Class of County	Percentage of Aid Calculated on County Appropriation
2	15%
2A and 3	20%
4	25%
5	33%
6	50%
7	75%
8	125%

The amount to be paid by the Commonwealth for the maintenance of any county library that qualifies under this subsection shall, in any year, be not less than eight thousand dollars ($8,000), whenever the applicable percentage of aid calculated on the county government's appropriation amounts to more than eight thousand dollars ($8,000). If the applicable percentage of aid calculated on the county government's appropriation amounts to less than eight thousand dollars ($8,000), then the county shall receive such lesser amount. If the allocation for this category of aid is less than the total amount for which all county libraries qualify, the libraries shall be paid the minimum amount of eight thousand dollars ($8,000) or such lesser amount as may be necessary. After the minimum rates have been paid, a portion of the remaining allocation shall be transferred to the allocation for equal distribution grants in order to distribute five percent (5%) of the appropriation as equal distribution grants under subsection (7) of this section. Any portion not transferred shall then be prorated among the county libraries which qualify for more than the minimum rates. If the allocation is greater than the total amount of aid for which county libraries qualify, the balance shall be added to the amount of aid to be distributed under subsection (7) of this section. A report of the expenditure of such State moneys shall be made annually to the county government and the State Librarian in such form as may be required. County libraries may also apply for additional amounts of State-aid under subsections (1) and (2) above, and subsection (7) following.

Payment of aid to county libraries shall be made to the board of library directors in charge of each qualifying library.

(4) District Library Centers. Thirty percent (30%) of the Commonwealth's total annual appropriation for the system of State-aid established by section 301, or a minimum of twenty-five cents (25¢) per capita, shall be allocated as aid for district library centers.

Any library designated by the State Librarian to serve as a district library center shall qualify for an additional amount of State-aid. The rate of aid shall be determined by dividing the total amount allocated for district library centers by the total population of the State, but in no year shall that rate be less than twenty-five cents (25¢) per capita. The amount of aid to be paid each district library center shall be determined by multiplying the per capita rate by the number of persons residing in the district.

(5) Regional Library Resource Centers. Five percent (5%) of the Commonwealth's annual appropriation for the system of State-aid established by section 301 shall be allocated for aid to regional library resource centers.

Any library designated by the State Librarian to serve as a regional library resource center shall qualify for additional State-aid. The allocation shall be divided equally among the libraries so designated, but in no year shall the amount be less than one hundred thousand dollars ($100,000) per designated library.

(6) Equalization Aid. If a library qualifies for State-aid established

by section 301 with a financial effort of less than per capita for each person residing in the direct service area of such library, additional State-aid shall be given such library in an amount which shall equal the difference between the per capita value of one-half mill times the market value of taxable property, as determined by the State Tax Equalization Board, in the direct service area of such library and per capita for each person residing in its direct service area.

(7) Equal Distribution Grants to Local Libraries and Library Systems and Certain District Library Centers. After the amounts of aid have been paid as specified in the preceding subsections, five percent (5%) of the Commonwealth's annual appropriation for the system of State-aid established by section 301, and all funds transferred from the county library allocation after the county libraries have been paid the total amounts for which they qualify, shall be allocated as hereinafter provided: (i) five cents (5¢) per capita for each person presiding in the entire district for each district library center which has a population in its direct service area as a local or county library which is twelve percent (12%) or less of the population of the entire designated direct service area; (ii) the balance shall be allocated as equal grants to local libraries and library systems which qualify for aid under subsection (1). These grants shall be determined by dividing the total amount of money allocated by the number of local libraries, branch libraries and bookmobiles in the Commonwealth which achieve or exceed the applicable basic standards. Each library system shall receive an equal grant for each qualifying member local library, branch library and bookmobile. Each local library shall receive an equal grant for the central library and each qualifying branch library and bookmobile.

As amended 1968, June 24, P.L. 246, No. 116, § 1; 1971, Dec. 29, P.L. 656, No. 172, §§ 1, 2; 1980, Dec. 9, P.L. 1125, No. 200, § 2, imd. effective.

§ 4304. State Librarian to approve plans; District Library Center Cooperative Program; referendum

(a) Each library desiring to receive State-aid under this act shall submit to the State Librarian a plan for the use of the funds and no payments of State-aid shall be made until such plan is approved by the State Librarian in accordance with rules and regulations approved by the Advisory Council on Library Development. Subsequent changes and modifications in a library plan may be submitted at any time for approval by the State Librarian. Libraries qualifying for aid shall have five years to achieve applicable standards. Further extensions of time may be permitted with the approval of the State Librarian acting under regulations made by the advisory council.

(b) No State-aid shall be given to any library unless the local library board commits the library to participation in the District Library Center Cooperative Program including attendance at district meetings and the use of interlibrary loans and interlibrary references.

(c) If the local library board does not act to participate in the District Library Center Cooperative Program, upon petition of three per cent of the total number of persons voting in the last preceding general or municipal election, the question of participation shall be submitted to the qualified electors of the municipalities in the direct service area. The petition shall be circulated within and signed by a sufficient number of electors in the direct service area. The persons circulating the petition shall present it to the municipal officers who shall forward the petition to the county board of elections. The County Board of Elections shall, after determining that the petition contains a sufficient number of signatures, place the question of participation in the District Li-

brary Center Cooperative Program on the ballot in the municipalities
comprising the direct service area from which the petition was submitted. If a majority of the persons voting on the question vote in the affirmative, the local library board shall participate in the District Library
Center Cooperative Program.
As amended 1971, Dec. 1, P.L. 579, No. 150, § 3.

Municipal Libraries

(Purdon's Pennsylvania Statutes Annotated, 1982, Title 24,
s.4401-4427.)

§ 4401. Municipality empowered to make appropriations for library; taxation

The municipal officers of any municipality may make appropriations
out of current revenue of the municipality or out of moneys raised by the
levy of special taxes to establish and/or maintain a local library or to
maintain or aid in the maintenance of a local library established by deed,
gift, or testamentary provision, for the use of the residents of such municipality. The appropriations for maintenance shall not exceed a sum
equivalent to three mills on the dollar on all taxable property of the municipality annually. Special taxes for these purposes, not exceeding three
mills on the dollar, may be levied on the taxable property of the municipality or the same may be levied and collected with the general taxes:
Provided, That where a county levies a special tax for the support of a
public library, that tax shall not be levied upon residents of municipalities which appropriate funds or levy a tax for the support of a local library that is not a part of the county library district and is located within such municipality. The provisions of this section shall not be construed to limit appropriations made for library purposes to those made
from special tax levies. Wherever a special tax is levied, all income from
such tax shall be used for the support and maintenance of the local library.
As amended 1982, April 27, P.L. 348, No. 96, § 2, effective in 60 days.

§ 4402. Submission of question to voters

The municipal officers of any municipality may submit to the qualified
voters of such municipality at a special election to be held at the time of
the next general, municipal, or primary election occurring not less than
sixty days therefrom, the question of establishing, maintaining and/or aiding in maintaining a local library, and must submit such question, if petitioned for by three per centum of the number voting at the last preceding
general or municipal election. At such election, the question of establishing an annual tax at a certain rate not exceeding three mills on the dollar
on all taxable property of the municipality, shall be submitted.

In cases where such questions are submitted to the voters of a county,
they shall not be submitted to the voters residing in cities, boroughs,
towns, townships and school districts, in which there is then being maintained a local library that is not a part of the county library district
whether by the city, borough, town, township, school district or otherwise, unless the municipal officers or the board of trustees or managers
of any endowed library or association library in such municipality shall
have previous to such submission, signified their intent by ordinance or
resolution to become part of the county library district and to merge any
existing library in such municipal district with the county library, if the
same may be done legally. Any city, borough, town, township, school district or any board of trustees or managers of any endowed library or association library maintaining such a local library shall have the power to
contract with the county commissioners before the submission of such
questions upon the terms and conditions under which it will become a

part of such county library district. Title to the books and other property of said municipally supported library or other library shall remain in
the said municipality or with the board of trustees or managers, but the
books and other property shall be used by the county library in accordance with the terms of a written agreement between the county commissioners and the said municipal officers or board of trustees or managers
of any endowed library or association library: Provided, however, That
title to such books and other property may be transferred to the county
library district, if the same may be done legally.

But where a county library district is established and a municipality has
not joined in said establishment, it may, nevertheless, thereafter, join said
county library district, if the municipal officers or the board of trustees or
managers of any endowed library or association library in such municipality enter into an agreement with the county board of library directors to
merge its facilities with the county library in the manner herein provided.
As amended 1967, Dec. 14, P.L. 843, No. 366, § 1; 1982, April 27, P.L.
348, No. 96, § 3, effective in 60 days.

§ 4403. Tax-levying; restrictions as to county tax

If the majority of votes cast upon this question shall be in favor of establishing such tax rate, the municipal officers, at the first meeting following the official announcement of the results of such an election, shall take
the necessary steps to levy and collect the tax so levied and shall appoint
a board of library directors as provided in section 411 of this act. Said
board shall have exclusive control of the library so established and/or
maintained, and shall be governed as provided elsewhere in this act. In
the case of a county tax, no tax shall be levied on any property in cities,
boroughs, towns, townships or school districts, where local libraries are
being maintained by public tax funds and which have not elected up to
the time of such tax levy to join the county library district. 1961, June
14, P.L. 324, Art. IV, § 403.

§ 4404. Annual tax rate; levy and collection

The rate of tax so voted shall be an annual tax rate until another vote
is taken changing the same: Provided, That the municipal officers may increase said rate, the total tax rate not to exceed three mills on the dollar
on all taxable property of the municipality, without submitting the question to the voters. The tax shall be levied and collected in like manner as
other taxes in the municipality, and shall be in addition to all other taxes,
except where included within the general levy, and shall be used for no
other purpose than that of establishing and/or maintaining a local library.
The money so raised shall be under the exclusive control of the board of
library directors provided in section 411 of this act. 1961, June 14, P.L.
324, Art. IV, § 404.

§ 4405. Discontinuance of county library and tax in city, borough, town, township or school district

Wherever in a city, borough, town, township or school district, there has been or may be established and maintained a separate local library and there is at the time a county library in existence, three percentum of the number voting at the last preceding general or municipal election in said city, borough, town, township or school district, may petition the county commissioners to place on the ballot the question of whether or not such city, borough, town, township or school district, shall be a part of the county library district and be subject to levy and payment of any taxes levied for the purpose of maintaining or aiding in the maintenance of any county library. At the next general or municipal election occurring at least sixty days after the filing of the petition but not oftener than once in five years, such question shall be placed upon the ballots and submitted to the electors of the city, borough, town, township or school district, as provided by the election laws. If a majority of those voting on such questions vote in favor of the discontinuance of the county library and tax in said city, borough, town, township or school district, then such city, borough, town, township or school district, shall not thereafter be a part of the county library district and shall not be subject to the levy and payment of any taxes levied for the purpose of maintaining or aiding in the maintenance of any county library. 1961, June 14, P.L. 324, Art. IV, § 405.

§ 4406. Fund raised by popular subscription

If the residents of any municipality shall raise, by popular subscription, a sum equal to or exceeding the gross amount of a three mill tax on all taxable property in the municipality, and shall offer the sum so subscribed to the municipality for the purpose of establishing a local library, said sum shall be accepted by the municipal officers and shall be used for the sole purpose of establishing a local library provided not more than two percentum of the said sum shall be subscribed by one individual or organization. Said subscription may be made payable in four quarterly payments and shall be in such form as to be collectible by legal process if necessary. 1961, June 14, P.L. 324, Art. IV, § 406.

§ 4407. Control of popular subscription fund; maintenance tax

In case of the establishment of a local library under the provisions of section 406 of this act, the municipal officers shall immediately place the sum so subscribed under the control of a board of library directors appointed as provided in section 411 of this act, and proceed to levy and collect a tax at the annual rate of not less than one and one-half mills nor more than three mills, annually, on the dollar on all taxable property in the municipality for the purpose of maintaining the library so established. 1961, June 14, P.L. 324, Art. IV, § 407.

§ 4408. Joint action by municipalities

Two or more municipalities may unite in establishing and/or maintaining a local library under the terms of an agreement entered into between them. Said agreement shall be in writing and shall set forth the purpose, the terms as to support and control, and the conditions under which the agreement shall be altered or terminated. Said agreement shall not be valid until it has been accepted by a majority vote of the municipal officers of each of the municipalities agreeing thereto and signed by the proper officer of each of said municipalities. 1961, June 14, P.L. 324, Art. IV, § 408.

§ 4409. Municipality may contract for free library service

Any municipality may contract with the managers or owners of any existing local library for public library service to the residents of such municipality, whether said library is located in the same or in another municipality. Such contract shall be renewable as therein provided. 1961, June 14, P.L. 324, Art. IV, § 409.

§ 4410. Appropriation for contracted library service

The municipal officers of any municipality may make appropriations out of current revenue of the municipality or out of moneys raised by the levy of special taxes in an amount not to exceed three mills, annually, on the dollar on all taxable property in the municipality for the purpose specified in section 409 of this act. Whenever a special tax is levied, all income from such tax shall be used for the support and maintenance of the local library with which the municipal officers have entered into contract. 1961, June 14, P.L. 324, Art. IV, § 410.

§ 4411. Board of library directors, terms of members, vacancies

The affairs of all local libraries established after the effective date of this act and under the provisions of the preceding sections of this article shall be under the exclusive control of a board of library directors to be composed of not less than five nor more than seven members. The municipal officers shall appoint the members and fill any vacancies occurring from any cause: Provided, That where two or more municipalities contribute to the support and maintenance of a local library, they shall each appoint a number of members to serve on the board of library directors as is mutually agreed upon by the said municipalities, the total number not to exceed nine members: Provided further, That when a municipality maintains or aids in the maintenance of a local library established after the effective date of this act by deed, gift or testamentary provision or in any manner other than under the provisions of sections 401 to 406 of this act, it shall be sufficient if the municipal officers appoint the majority of the members of the board of library directors. The first appointees shall be appointed as nearly as may be one-third for one year, one-third for two years and one-third for three years. All appointments to fill the places of those whose terms expire shall be for a term of three years. Vacancies shall be filled for the unexpired terms. All members shall serve until their successors have been appointed. No member of the board shall receive any salary for his service as such.

In the case of a local library established by deed, gift or testamentary provision, or by any association, corporation or group, prior to the effective date of this act, this section shall not be construed to require the municipal officers of each municipality aiding in the maintenance of a local library to appoint more than two of the library directors of such local library. 1961, June 14, P.L. 324, Art. IV, § 411.

§ 4412. Organization of board, bond of treasurer

The board of library directors shall organize as soon as may be after appointment by electing a president, secretary and treasurer from its membership and such other officers and agents as the board may deem necessary. The treasurer shall give bond to the municipality with satisfactory surety in such amount as the board may determine. 1961, June 14, P.L. 324, Art. IV, § 412.

§ 4413. Library directors to control all funds

All moneys appropriated for the establishment and/or maintenance of a local library and all moneys, if any, received from other sources for its use, shall be under the exclusive control and shall be disbursed under the direction of the board of library directors. Such board of library directors shall have the power to contract with the board of directors of another library to establish a cooperative plan for improving library services.

The board of control of any library, established as specified in section 411 of this act, and of any library receiving municipal appropriations shall make a report, annually, to the proper municipal authorities, of the moneys received by such library from the municipality and the dispositions made thereof, and the accounts of the treasurer of said board shall be audited as in the case of other municipal expenditures. 1961, June 14, P.L. 324, Art. IV, § 413.

§ 4414. Annual reports

The annual report required by the last preceding section shall contain an itemized statement of all receipts from whatever source, and expenditures, and shall show the condition of the library and any branches thereof, the number of volumes, maps, pamphlets and other materials, the number added by purchase, gift or otherwise, the number lost or withdrawn, the number of registered borrowers and readers and a statement of the circulation of material, with such other information and suggestions as may seem desirable. A copy of each report made to the municipal officers shall be sent to the State Library in Harrisburg. 1961, June 14, P.L. 324, Art. IV, § 414.

§ 4415. Free use of library, rules and regulations

Every library, established and/or maintained under the provisions of this act, shall be free to the use of all the residents and taxpayers of the municipality, subject to such reasonable rules and regulations as the board of library directors may adopt, and the board may exclude from the use of the library any person who wilfully violates such rules. The board may extend the privileges of such library to persons residing outside the limits of such municipality upon such terms and conditions as the board may prescribe. 1961, June 14, P.L. 324, Art. IV, § 415.

§ 4416. Power to hold property; donations and gifts

It shall be lawful for any municipality or corporation, owning or managing a local library, to take and hold any property, real or personal, or both, for library purposes; and any person desiring to make donations of books, money, personal property or real estate for the benefit of a local library, whether established or maintained under the provisions of this act or not, may vest the title thereto in the municipality or the corporation having control of the affairs of said library, to be held and controlled by said municipality or corporation according to the terms of the deed, gift, devise or bequest; and, as to such property, the said municipality or corporation shall be held to be special trustee; but in the absence of restrictions by the terms of such donation, deed, gift, devise or bequest, the said property shall be controlled and administered by the board of library directors or by the corporation, as the case may be. 1961, June 14, P.L. 324, Art. IV, § 416.

§ 4417. Limitations of establishment of new libraries

Whenever there is in any municipality a local library which is open to the use of all the residents thereof and which meets the minimum standards recommended by the State Librarian as conditions for participation in State-aid, no new library shall be, there, established under the provisions of this act, but all public aid hereby authorized shall be given to such existing library to enable it to meet as far as possible the needs of such residents: Provided, however, That wherever there may have been on or before July 20, 1917, two or more such libraries receiving aid from the same municipality, the appropriation authorized by this act shall be divided between said libraries according to the terms of an agreement previously entered into between said libraries and approved by the State Librarian. 1961, June 14, P.L. 324, Art. IV, § 417.

§ 4418. Purchase, lease lands and buildings for library purposes

Any municipality is hereby authorized to purchase, set apart or lease lands and buildings, or parts of buildings already owned by it, or both, or to erect buildings, to be used for local library purposes, or to alter buildings already erected so as to make them suitable for such use, and it is hereby authorized to provide for the cost of the same as in the case of other buildings to be used for municipal purposes; and whenever, in any such municipality, a tax levy has been or may hereafter be authorized for the purpose of maintaining a local library therein as provided by this act, and, out of moneys raised from such levy, a surplus or excess has been or may hereafter be accumulated above the necessary cost of maintaining such library, it shall and may be lawful for the directors of such library to pay over such excess or surplus to the municipal officers of such municipality, to be used by them for any of the purposes provided in this section. 1961, June 14, P.L. 324, Art. IV, § 418.

§ 4419. Appropriation of private property

Any municipality may, by ordinance or resolution, purchase, enter upon and appropriate private property within its limits for the purpose of erecting or enlarging public library buildings. 1961, June 14, P.L. 324, Art. IV, § 419.

§ 4420. Board of viewers

Whenever any municipality shall appropriate private property for public library purposes and the municipality cannot agree with the owners thereof for the price to be paid therefor, or when, by reason of the absence or legal incapacity of the owner thereof, no such compensation can be agreed upon, the court of common pleas, or any judge thereof in vacation, on application thereto by petition, by the municipal authorities or any person interested, shall appoint a board of viewers for the assessment of damages caused by appropriations, as in such cases provided. 1961, June 14, P.L. 324, Art. IV, § 420.

§ 4421. Viewing proceedings

The proceedings before the viewers for the allowance of damages for property taken, injured or destroyed and the proceedings upon their report shall be as provided in other cases where such municipality appropriates private property for municipal purposes. 1961, June 14, P.L. 324, Art. IV, § 421.

§ 4422. Petition for submission of bond issue

If five percentum of the registered voters of any municipality shall petition the municipal officers to submit the question of executing a bonded indebtedness for purchasing grounds and/or erecting buildings for library purposes, the said officers must submit the question at the next ensuing election. 1961, June 14, P.L. 324, Art. IV, § 422.

§ 4423. Libraries exempt from tax; gifts exempt from collateral inheritance tax

Any building which shall be owned and occupied by a local library and the land on which it stands and that which is immediately and necessarily appurtenant thereto shall be exempt from all county, city, borough, town, township, school, bounty, poor or head taxes, notwithstanding the fact that some portion or portions of said building or land appurtenant may be yielding rentals to the corporation or association managing such library: Provided, That the net receipts of said corporation or association from rentals shall be used solely for the purpose of maintaining such library. All gifts, devises, grants or endowments made to such library, or to a national library, and for such purposes, shall be free from collateral inheritance tax; and any gifts, endowments or funds of such libraries, which are invested in interest-bearing securities, the income from which is used solely for the purpose of books or the maintenance of such libraries, shall be exempt from any State tax on money at interest. 1961, June 14, P.L. 324, Art. IV, § 423.

§ 4424. Existing agreements not affected

This act shall not in any way affect any agreement or agreements heretofore made by a municipality under any prior act relating to local libraries but all such agreements are hereby ratified and are to continue as binding contracts between the parties. 1961, June 14, P.L. 324, Art. IV, § 424.

§ 4425. Libraries to receive Commonwealth publications

The Department of Property and Supplies shall, as soon as practicable after publication, forward to those libraries designated by the State Librarian as State documents depository libraries, a copy of every publication of every department, board, commission or agency of the Commonwealth. The Department of Property and Supplies shall direct each such department, board, commission or agency to supply it with the number of copies, if any, of each publication remaining after regular distribution according to existing allocations, but in no case to exceed two hundred fifty copies, and upon receipt thereof shall notify the State Librarian who shall then designate the libraries to which the publication shall be forwarded. Any public library, school library, junior college or community college library, university library or historical society library in the Commonwealth shall be eligible to receive free copies of the publications. It shall be the privilege of the state to recall any or all of the said publications in the event of the loss of their own files by fire or other casualty.

The provisions of this section shall not apply to the distribution of documents published pursuant to the Commonwealth Documents Law. The State Librarian, with the approval of the Advisory Council on Library Development, shall make recommendations from time to time to the Joint Committee on Documents concerning criteria for the distribution to libraries of documents published pursuant to the Commonwealth Documents Law.
As amended 1971, Dec. 1, P.L. 580, No. 150, § 3.

§ 4426. Retention of library property after notice to return

Whoever retains any book, pamphlet, magazine, newspaper, manuscript, map or other property belonging in or to or on deposit with the State Library or any local library which is established or maintained under any law of this Commonwealth or the library of any university, college or educational institution chartered by the Commonwealth or the library of any public school or any branch reading room, deposit station or agency operated in connection therewith, for a period exceeding thirty days after such library has given written notice to return the same, shall, upon conviction in summary proceedings, be sentenced to pay a fine of not more than twenty-five dollars ($25) to be paid over by the magistrate imposing such fine to the library instituting the prosecution and costs of prosecution. Any person in default of payment of such fine and costs shall undergo imprisonment in the county jail for a period not exceeding ten days.

Such notice may be given by personal service upon the borrower or by the mailing of a letter, by first class mail, to the borrower's address on file with said library. The notice shall refer to this act and shall contain a demand that the property be returned.
As amended 1970, May 5, P.L. 330, No. 106, § 1.

§ 4427. Damaging library property

Anyone who shall willfully cut, mutilate, mark or otherwise injure any book, pamphlet, magazine, newspaper, manuscript, map or other property belonging in or to or on deposit with the State Library or any local library which is established or maintained under any law of this Commonwealth or the library of any university, college or educational institution chartered by the Commonwealth or the library of any public school or any branch reading room, deposit station or agency operated in connection therewith, shall be deemed to be guilty of a misdemeanor, and may be prosecuted for said offense before any court of competent jurisdiction and, upon conviction thereof, shall be liable to pay a fine of not more than twenty-five dollars ($25) and costs of prosecution or to undergo imprisonment in the county jail for a period not exceeding fifteen days, or both, at the discretion of the court, the said fine when collected to be for the use of the said library against which the aforesaid offense was committed. 1961, June 14, P.L. 324, Art. IV, § 427.

DISTRIBUTION OF PUBLIC DOCUMENTS
(Purdon's Pennsylvania Statutes Annotated, 1982, Title 71, s.1652.)

§ 1652. Libraries and associations to receive public documents

Every library, literary and scientific association, and historical society incorporated under the laws of this commonwealth, and owning a library of two thousand or more volumes, shall be entitled to receive one well bound volume of each of the executive and legislative documents hereafter published, and such other publications as are authorized by law to be printed by the state printer. 1883, June 1, P.L. 52, § 1.

COUNTY AND MUNICIPAL LIBRARIES
Miscellaneous Provisions
(Purdon's Pennsylvania Statutes Annotated, 1982, Title 16, s.2368, 2370, Title 52, s.1341-1345, 1371-1374, 23575, 38602-38605, 47809.)

§ 2368. Acquiring of Property

(a) Counties shall have power to take, by gift, purchase, by the issuance of bonds or otherwise, or acquire through condemnation proceedings, property for the purpose of erecting thereon public auditoriums, public libraries, public memorial buildings and monuments.

All proceedings for the condemnation of any property, under the provisions of this section, shall be in the manner and subject to the restrictions and procedure provided by law.

(b) Counties may appropriate money from the public funds or by issuance of bonds, in accordance with the Municipal Borrowing Law, for the erection on said property taken, purchased or acquired through condemnation proceedings, public auditoriums, public libraries, public memorial buildings and monuments. They may appropriate moneys for the operation and maintenance of such public auditoriums, public libraries, memorial buildings and monuments. 1955, Aug. 9, P.L. 323, § 2368.

§ 2370. Consent of City or Borough

No county shall acquire any property for, or erect any such public auditorium, library, memorial building or monument within the limits of any city or borough, except the county seat, without the consent of the corporate authorities of such city or borough. 1955, Aug. 9, P.L. 323, § 2369.

§ 1341. Powers

Whenever cities and counties of this Commonwealth are authorized to take, purchase, or acquire through condemnation proceedings property for the purpose of erecting thereon public auditoriums, libraries, memorial buildings, and monuments, and to appropriate money for the erection thereon of such buildings, and to provide for their operation and maintenance, such cities and counties shall have the power to jointly take, purchase, or acquire through condemnation proceedings such property as may be necessary for the purpose of erecting thereon such buildings; and jointly to erect the same; and shall have the power to appropriate money from the public funds or by issuance of bonds according to existing laws governing the issuance of such bonds, for the erection thereon of such buildings; and provide for their operation and maintenance jointly. 1925, April 27, P.L. 342, § 1.

§ 1342. Agreement as to site; tenancy in common; construction and maintenance

The county commissioners of such counties and the corporate authorities of such cities shall have the power and they are hereby authorized to agree upon a site within the limits of such cities and counties, and to acquire, own, and hold the same as tenants in common, and to erect thereon jointly public auditoriums, libraries, memorial buildings, or monuments. The county commissioners of such counties and the corporate authorities of such cities shall have full authority to erect upon the land thus obtained and held, the building or buildings agreed upon as hereinafter provided. 1925, April 27, P.L. 342, § 2.

§ 1343. Joint contract for construction; rentals

The county commissioners of such counties and the corporate authorities of such cities are authorized and empowered to enter into a joint contract or contracts, agreement or agreements, for the construction of such building or buildings and for the payment by each of them of the proportionate share of the cost of the construction, maintenance, and operation of such building or buildings, and for the use thereof, and in the case of public auditoriums for the rental to be charged thereof, and for the disposition for city and county purposes of any annual balance accruing from any rental derived from the use of such public auditorium. 1925, April 27, P.L. 342, § 3.

§ 1344. Erection on site acquired under existing law

Whenever under existing acts of Assembly of this Commonwealth any city or county has acquired, appropriated, or chosen, or shall acquire, appropriate, or choose a site for the erection of any public auditorium, library, memorial building, or monument, such city or county may agree with any other city or county with which under the provisions of this act it has the power jointly to erect such building, for the erection thereon of any such public auditorium, library, memorial building, or monument in accordance with the provisions of this act. 1925, April 27, P.L. 342, § 4.

§ 1345.   Condemnation; proportions in which land held

Whenever under the provisions of this act any city and county shall enter into an agreement for the acquisition through condemnation proceedings of property for the purpose of erecting thereon any public auditorium, library, memorial building, or monument, such property shall be acquired by such city and county in the proportion as may be designated by the said agreement between the said city and county under existing acts of Assembly empowering any city or county separately to acquire land for the purpose of erecting thereon public auditoriums, libraries, memorials, and monuments. 1925, April 27, P.L. 342, § 5.

§ 1371.   Power to acquire site

Cities shall have power to take, purchase, or acquire through condemnation proceedings, property for the purpose of erecting thereon public auditoriums, public libraries, public memorial buildings, and monuments. 1919, July 8, P.L. 783, § 1.

§ 1372.   Payment for property from public funds or by bond issue

Cities, by order of council or commissioners, shall have power to appropriate money, from the public funds or by issuance of bonds according to existing law governing the issuance of such bonds, for the erection, on said property taken, purchased, or acquired through condemnation proceedings, public auditoriums, public libraries, public memorial buildings, and monuments. Cities shall also have power to appropriate moneys for the operation and maintenance of such public auditoriums, public libraries, memorial buildings, and monuments. 1919, July 8, P.L. 783, § 2.

§ 1373.   Proceedings for assessment of damages

All proceedings for the assessment of damages for property taken under the provisions of this act shall be had in the same manner as is now provided by law for the taking of property for public improvements in such cities. 1919, July 8, P.L. 783, § 3.

§ 1374.   Property may be donated to library association; contributions for maintenance

Cities shall have power to donate ground thus acquired for a public library to any library association provided said association will furnish the funds for the erection of the library building, the plans of which are approved by the city, but only in such cases where the said library association is by its by-laws and charter compelled to put back into the property any surplus earnings from the operation of said library. Cities, by order of council or commissioners, may contribute from time to time towards the operating support of such library a sum not to exceed fifty per centum (50%) of the annual operating maintenance of said library. 1919, July 8, P.L. 783, § 4.

§ 23575. Retention of retirement rights by former city employees employed by certain free public libraries

(a) Any employe who has left or who shall hereafter leave the employ of any city of the second class to become an employe of any free public library located in any city of the second class and having in effect its own pension or retirement plan and who was a contributor to a retirement system in any city of the second class before leaving the city's employ may add to and retain his full membership rights under the retirement system of the city of the second class to which he contributed upon compliance with the provisions of this section.

(b) Any such employe as provided in subsection (a) shall receive full credit toward his retirement rights under the retirement system of the city of the second class if the following requirements are met.

(1) If the employe shall waive in writing and upon a form prescribed by the pension board in the city of the second class all rights and benefits under the retirement system of any free public library in any city of the second class.

(2) If the employe shall produce proof satisfactory to the pension board in the city of the second class that he was employed by the city of the second class and the number of years of his service prior to transfer.

(3) If the employe shall produce proof that he is employed with a free public library in a city of the second class which has its own retirement or pension plan and the number of years of his service.

(4) If the employe shall pay back in a lump sum or otherwise as may be determined by the pension board of the city of the second class all accumulated deductions withdrawn by him when he terminated his employ with the city of the second class, and if he shall pay into the retirement system of the city of the second class the difference, if any, in the amount he contributed as a member of the re-

tirement system of any free public library in any city of the second class and the amount he would have contributed based on his salary and age during such employment had he been an employe of any city of the second class: Provided, That if the amount contributed to the retirement system of the free public library was greater than the amount he would have contributed to the second class city retirement system, then the difference in amounts shall be credited to the employe's account towards the required back payments of withdrawn deductions or in lieu thereof as a credit towards future contributions in the retirement system of the city of the second class.

(5) If the officials in charge of the pension plan of the free public library shall forward to the pension board of the city of the second class all moneys contributed by the employe to the free public library pension plan, and if the officials of the free public library pension plan shall forward an amount equal to the amount, if any, which the city of the second class would have been required to pay towards an additional employe annuity had he been an employe of the second class city during a period corresponding to the period of his employment with the free public library based on his age and salary during such period.

(c) Upon the contributor accepting the provisions of this section and if the requirements of subsection (b) are satisfied the officials in charge of the free public library pension plan in a city of the second class shall deduct from the employe's salary the amount of contribution that the pension board of the city of the second class shall prescribe and shall forward to the pension board of the city of the second class on the first Monday of each month the amounts deducted.

(d) Any contributor desiring to accept the benefits of this section shall, if he is presently an employe of any free public library in any city of the second class which has its own retirement or pension plan, make application to the pension board of the city of the second class therefor within one year from the effective date of this act. Any contributor thereafter separating from the employment of any city of the second class to become an employe of any free public library in any city of the second class having its own retirement or pension plan and desiring to accept the provisions of this section shall make application to the pension board of the city of the second class within sixty days of such separation. 1915, May 28, P.L. 596, § 16, added 1955, July 27, P.L. 292, § 1.

§ 38602. Public auditoriums, libraries, memorials and monuments

Cities may take, purchase, or acquire, by any lawful means, or through condemnation proceedings, property for the purpose of erecting thereon public auditoriums, public libraries, public memorial buildings, and monuments. 1931, June 23, P.L. 932, art. XXXVI, § 3602; 1951, June 28, P.L. 662, § 36.

§ 38603. Payment of cost of erection and maintenance

Cities may appropriate money or issue bonds for the erection, on said property purchased or acquired through condemnation proceedings, public auditoriums, public libraries, public memorial buildings, and monuments. Cities may also appropriate moneys for the operation and maintenance of such public auditoriums, public libraries, memorial buildings, and monuments. 1931, June 23, P. L. 932, art. XXXVI, § 3603; 1951, June 28, P.L. 662, § 36.

§ 38604. Proceedings for assessment of damages

All proceedings for the assessment of damages for property taken for auditoriums, libraries, memorials and monuments shall be had in the manner provided by this act for property taken, injured or destroyed. 1931, June 23, P.L. 932, art. XXXVI, § 3604; 1951, June 28, P.L. 662, § 36.

§ 38605. Donation of land by city for library purposes; contributions toward maintenance

Cities may donate ground thus acquired for a public library to any library association provided said association will furnish the funds for the erection of the library building, the plans of which are approved by the city, but only in such cases where the said library association is by its by-laws and charter compelled to put back into the property and surplus earnings from the operation of said library. Cities may make appropriations towards the operating expense of such library. 1931, June 23, P.L. 932, art. XXXVI, § 3605; 1951, June 28, P.L. 662, § 36.

§ 47809. Removal of bodies to other cemeteries

Whenever any cemetery privately owned and in charge of no person, or any cemetery in charge of any religious society or church, has ceased to be used for interments, or has become so neglected as to become a public nuisance; or when such cemetery hinders the improvement and progressive interests of any borough, or is desired by the borough as a site for any free public library building, or for any other public purpose, the court of quarter sessions of the county, upon petition of the managers of such cemetery; or upon the petition of fifty residents in the vicinity in case such cemetery is not in charge of anyone, setting forth that the improvements and progressive interests of such borough are hampered and the welfare of such borough is injured; or upon the petition of such borough setting forth that such cemetery is desired by the borough for the erection thereon of a free public library building, or for use as a recreation place, or the opening, laying out or extension through said land of any street, or for any other public purpose; and after three successive weeks of advertisement in a newspaper of general circulation in the borough may direct the removal of the remains of the dead from such cemetery. 1966, Feb. 1, P.L. (1965) ——, No. 581, § 2809.

TAX EXEMPTION

(Purdon's Pennsylvania Statutes Annotated, Title 72, s.5020-204, 5453.202.)

§ 5020—204. Exemptions from taxation

The following property shall be exempt from all county, city, borough, town, township, road, poor and school tax, to wit:

* * * * * * * *

(k) All buildings owned and occupied by free, public, nonsectarian libraries, and the land on which they stand and that which is immediately and necessarily appurtenant thereto, notwithstanding the fact that some portion or portions of said building or lands appurtenant may be yielding rentals to the corporation or association managing such library: Provided, That the net receipts of such corporation or association from rentals shall be used solely for the purpose of maintaining the said library;

1943, May 3, P.L. 158, § 1.

§ 5453.202 Exemptions from taxation

(a) The following property shall be exempt from all county, borough, town, township, road, poor, county institution district and school (except in cities) tax, to wit:

* * * * * * * *

(11) All buildings owned and occupied by free public nonsectarian libraries and the land on which they stand and that which is immediately and necessarily appurtenant thereto, notwithstanding the fact that some portion or portions of said building or lands appurtenant may be yielding rentals to the corporation or association managing such library: Provided, That the net receipts of such corporation or association from rentals shall be used solely for the purpose of maintaining the said library.

1943, May 21, P.L. 571, art. II, § 202.

Pennsylvania library laws are reprinted from PURDON'S PENNSYLVANIA STATUTES ANNOTATED published by West Publishing Co., St. Paul, Minnesota, George T. Bisel Co., Philadelphia, Pennsylvania and Soney & Sage Co., Newark, New Jersey.

RHODE ISLAND

STATE LIBRARY
(General Laws of Rhode Island, 1982, s.29-1-1 to 29-1-12, 29-1-15.)

29-1-1. Library established — Librarian and record commissioner. — Within the department of state there shall be a state library and for the supervision of the state library the secretary of state shall appoint a state librarian qualified by training and experience who shall serve at the pleasure of the secretary of state. The state librarian shall carry out the duties required by chapters 1 to 3 inclusive, of this title. The state librarian shall continue to maintain and supervise the legislative reference bureau.   P.L. 1964. ch. 233, § 4.

29-1-2. Care of library — Preservation of books and documents. — The secretary of state shall have the care and custody of the state library, except the law library, and shall receive and preserve all books and documents which may be sent to or purchased for the same.
G.L. 1956, § 29-1-2.

29-1-3. Clerical assistance. — The general assembly shall annually appropriate such sums as it may deem necessary for clerical service in the state library, and the state librarian is hereby authorized and empowered to employ additional clerical assistance. The state controller shall draw his orders upon the general treasurer for the payment of all sums appropriated under the authority of this section, or so much thereof as may be from time to time required, upon the receipt by him of proper vouchers approved by the state librarian and the secretary of state.   G.L. 1956, § 29-1-3.

29-1-4. Annual report to general assembly. — The secretary of state shall annually at the January session make report to the general assembly of the condition of the library, and shall make such recommendations as he may deem advisable for the welfare thereof, and of the books purchased during the year preceding, and of the cost thereof.   G.L. 1956, § 29-1-4.

29-1-5. Exchange of publications with agencies outside state. — It shall be the duty of the state librarian to exchange with such nations, states, municipalities, institutions, and persons outside the state as may confer a corresponding benefit, copies of the laws, law reports, reports of departments and institutions, and all other books and pamphlets published by the state, and to distribute such publications to such other nations, states, municipalities, institutions, and persons outside the state as may by law be entitled to receive them. Nothing in this section shall be construed to prevent any department from distributing its own publications. Distributions to, or exchanges with, states shall be with the state libraries or the authorized exchange agencies of said states.   G.L. 1956, § 29-1-5.

29-1-6. Disposition of duplicates and surplus supplies. — The state librarian, with the consent of the secretary of state, is hereby authorized and empowered to sell, exchange, or destroy all duplicate books, pamphlets, or other surplus supplies, which, in his judgment, are not available for use in the state library. All sums received from said sales shall be turned over to the general treasurer of the state.   G.L. 1956, § 29-1-6.

29-1-7. Supply of state publications. — It shall be the duty of each state officer and director, upon the requisition of the state librarian, to supply the state library with a sufficient number of each publication issued from his department to enable him to carry into effect the provisions of chapters 1 and 2 of this title.
          G.L. 1956, § 29-1-7.

29-1-8. Distribution within state of state publications. — The state librarian shall distribute to the several libraries of the state, as may apply for them, copies of the laws, reports of departments and institutions, and all other books and pamphlets published by the state except such as are distributed by public law.   G.L. 1956, § 29-1-8.

29-1-9.   Exchange copies of state publications. — Copies of every volume published through the aid of the state shall upon requisition of the state librarian be transmitted to the state librarian for exchange with other libraries.   G.L. 1956, § 29-1-9

29-1-10.   Legislative reference bureau — Functions. — There shall be in the state library, under the direction of the state librarian, a legislative reference bureau which shall collect, arrange and place on file books, pamphlets, and other material relating to legislation, which shall prepare abstracts of laws in other states; and which shall present such other information as may be useful and necessary to the general assembly in the performance of its legislative duties.

G.L. 1956, § 29-1-10.

29-1-11.   Expense of legislative reference bureau. — The state librarian shall, with the approval of the secretary of state, employ such assistance and incur such expenses as may be necessary in the proper administration of the legislative reference bureau, and the general assembly shall annually appropriate such sum as it may deem necessary for said purpose.

The state controller is hereby authorized and directed to draw his orders upon the general treasurer for the payment of the amount appropriated, or so much thereof as may be from time to time required, upon receipt by him of proper vouchers approved by the state librarian and the secretary of state.   G.L. 1956, § 29-1-11.

29-1-12.   Appropriations for labor. — There shall be annually appropriated for labor in the state library, including cleaning, shifting and sorting books, such sums of money as the general assembly shall deem necessary; and the state controller is hereby authorized and directed to draw his orders upon the general treasurer for the payment of all sums appropriated under authority of this section, or so much thereof as may from time to time be required, upon receipt by him of proper vouchers approved by the state librarian and the secretary of state.   G.L. 1956, § 29-1-12.

29-1-15.   Cooperation with federal officials. — The secretary of state is hereby empowered to cooperate with the commissioner of education of the United States of America or any United States officer in carrying out the purposes of any and all acts of congress for the benefit of those library services including archives and records which are under his jurisdiction.   P.L. 1972, ch. 144, § 1.

DEPARTMENT OF STATE LIBRARY SERVICES
(General Laws of Rhode Island, 1982, s.29-3.1-1 to 29-3.1-11.)

29-3.1-1. Department established. — There shall be a department of state library services, control of which shall be vested in the director of state library services. Within the department of state library services there shall be such divisions as may be established from time to time by the director. The department of state library services is hereby empowered to cooperate with the commissioner of education of the United States of America in the carrying out of the purposes of any and all acts of congress for the benefit of library services within this state. The department of state library services is hereby designated as the agency for the administration of any plan or plans heretofore or hereafter formulated in conformity with said act or acts of congress and is authorized to administer any such plan or plans and to enter into such agreements with the commissioner of education of the United States of America as may be from time to time required under this chapter or said acts or acts of congress, and from time to time amend the same except any plan, or plans, or agreements, formulated or entered into or to be administered by the state board of education or the secretary of state. P.L. 1972, ch. 144, § 2.

29-3.1-2. Advisory board of library commissioners — Appointment of members. — There shall be an advisory board of library commissioners which shall consist of seven (7) members who shall be residents of this state, five (5) of whom shall be appointed by the governor as herein provided. In the first instance one (1) member shall be appointed to said board for a five (5) year term, one (1) member for a four (4) year term, one (1) member for a three (3) year term, one (1) member for a two (2) year term and one (1) member for a one (1) year term; said members to hold office until the first day of May in the years in which their respective terms end, and until their respective successors are appointed and qualified. Thereafter, in the month of April in each year, the governor shall appoint one (1) member of said board for a five (5) year term to succeed the member whose term will next expire, to hold office until the first day of May in the fifth year after his appointment and until his successor is appointed and qualified. The other two (2) members of the board shall be appointed in the following manner: The speaker of the house of representatives shall appoint one (1) member of said house to hold office during the term of his tenure in the house of representatives. The lieutenant governor shall appoint one (1) member of the senate to hold office during the term of his tenure in the senate. Any vacancies shall be filled by the appointing authority. At all times, at least two (2) members of said board shall be professional librarians, at least one (1) member of said board shall be a trustee of a public library in Rhode Island, and at least one (1) member of said board shall be an educator. The director of state library services shall serve as secretary of said board without vote. P.L. 1964, ch. 233, § 1.

29-3.1-3. Reimbursement of board members. — Members of the advisory board of library commissioners shall serve without compensation but shall be entitled to receive reimbursement for reasonable, actual and necessary expenses incurred in the performance of their duties. P.L. 1964, ch. 233, § 1.

29-3.1-4. Powers and duties of board. — The advisory board of library commissioners is hereby empowered:

(1) To review policies promulgated by the director of state library services and advise said director concerning such policies.

(2) To act as a board of appeal upon decisions as to either library services or library construction when such appeals are made by the library authorities affected to make a final judgment as to whether said decision shall stand or be reversed. In addition, said board may alter such decision when an appeal is made by the library authorities affected.

(3) To act as a board of review and appeal concerning library standards. Said board shall review and approve such standards as shall be promulgated by the director of state library services. Said board shall act as a board of appeal in hearing and making final judgment concerning interpretations of rules and regulations dealing with library standards upon request of the library authorities affected.

(4) To act as a board of review and appeal concerning certification. Said board shall review and approve such certification rules as shall be developed by the director of state library services. Said board shall act as a board of appeal in hearing and making final judgment concerning a decision of the director of state library services upon certification of any individual when so requested by the library authorities affected, individuals concerned and/or their representatives. It may also alter such decision.

(5) To serve as representatives of the people in securing a comprehensive program of free public library services in the state. P.L. 1964, ch. 233, § 1.

29-3.1-5. Director of state library services — Appointment and qualifications. — There shall be a director of state library services to be appointed by the governor with the advice and consent of the senate to serve at the pleasure of the governor. Said director shall hold a graduate degree in library science from an accredited library school or an undergraduate degree in library science from an accredited library school of library science and have five (5) years of experience in library administration or a graduate degree not in library science from an accredited university or college and have seven (7) years experience in library administration.

P.L. 1964, ch. 233, § 1.

29-3.1-6. Compensation of director. — The director of state library services shall be in the unclassified service of the state and shall receive such salary as the governor may determine.

P.L. 1964, ch. 233, § 1.

29-3.1-7. Duties of director. — The director of state library services shall be the executive and administrative officer in charge of the department of state library services. He shall also carry out the duties required of him by this chapter and by chapters 5 and 6 of this title. He shall also have the authority:

(1) To supervise and control the department of state library services.

(2) To promote and develop the department of state library services;

(3) To promote and develop library services throughout the state in co-operation with any and all other state or municipal libraries, public libraries, schools or other agencies wherever practical;

(4) To promote the establishment of cooperative library systems and the establishment of regional libraries as conditions within particular areas of the state may require;

(5) To make rules and regulations and establish standards of administration of the department of state library services and for the control, distribution and lending of books and materials to libraries, groups, or individuals;

(6) To make rules and regulations under which state or federal funds, which may now or hereafter be appropriated to further library development or use within the state, shall be granted to cities and towns or other agencies for improved library services (except that this provision shall not apply to appropriations made directly to any other agency or institution);

(7) To cooperate with the state department of education and the supervisor of school libraries in the development of statewide school library services;

(8) To give assistance, advice and counsel to all public libraries of any type within the state and to all communities or persons proposing to establish such libraries and to conduct courses and institutes in the approved methods of operation, selection of books, or other activities necessary to the proper administration of a library;

(9) To require that information and statistics necessary to the work of the state department of library services be collected, to publish findings and reports thereon, and to require careful and complete records to be kept of the condition and affairs of the department of state library services;

(10) To make an annual report concerning the activities of the department of state library services to the governor, as he may require;

(11) To develop standards for public libraries and to adopt rules and regulations for the certification of library positions and/or personnel, except that such rules and regulations shall provide that all library personnel employed on July 1, 1964 shall be automatically certified for the positions they then hold.   P.L. 1967, ch. 227, § 2.

29-3.1-8. Gifts, donations, and funds. — The director of state library services may accept donations of funds or property, real or personal, for the department of state library services or any of its divisions, and in his discretion, with the approval of the advisory board of library commissioners, shall hold the same in the form in which they were given for the purposes of the department of state library services, or disposes of them, with any financial benefits accruing to the department of state library services. The director of state library services shall be the authorized agent to accept, receive and administer any and all funds, moneys, or library materials granted, furnished, provided, appropriated and/or dedicated or made available by the United States of America or any of its departments, commissions, boards, bureaus, or agencies for library services in the state of Rhode Island other than funds, moneys or library materials granted, furnished, provided, appropriated and/or dedicated or made available directly to any agency or institution. The director of state library services shall turn over to the general treasurer for proper custody and safekeeping all such funds paid to the state from the federal treasury or other donating agency, and the general treasurer shall disburse such funds solely for the purpose provided by the original grantor upon orders drawn by the state controller upon receipt by him of duly authenticated vouchers. Any funds lost or diverted from the purposes for which paid by the United States of America shall be repaid by the state to the United States of America.

P.L. 1967, ch. 227, § 3.

29-3.1-9. Budget, appropriations and disbursements. — The director of state library services shall present a budget for all activities and maintenance of the department of state library services, including all necessary professional, semi-professional, clerical, janitorial, and other staff, for books, periodicals, maps, binding, micro-reproduction, supplies, equipment, etc., and for all necessary expenses incurred in the execution of the duties assigned to the department. The general assembly shall annually appropriate such sums as it may deem necessary for the department of state library services; and the state controller is hereby authorized and directed to draw his orders upon the general treasurer for the payment of said sums, or so much thereof as may be from time to time required, upon the receipt by him of duly authenticated vouchers.

P.L. 1964, ch. 233, § 1.

29-3.1-10. Staff. — The director of state library services is authorized and empowered to appoint all necessary professional and nonprofessional staff for the several divisions of the department. In appointing professional staff there shall be no qualifications restricting the appointment to residents of the state nor shall there be any qualifications regarding political party affiliation. The employees shall be in the unclassified service.   P.L. 1964, ch. 233, § 1.

29-3.1-11. Annual report. — The director of state library services shall annually make a report to the governor, who shall transmit the same to the general assembly at the January session, on the condition of the department of state library services at the end of the preceding fiscal year, on the activities of the department of state library services, and on the condition and state of the book collections and such other collections maintained by the department; and the director of state library services shall include therein such recommendations as he may deem advisable for the welfare of the department of state library services.   P.L. 1964, ch. 233, § 1.

STATE AID

(General Laws of Rhode Island, 1982, s.29-6-1 to 29-6-12.)

29-6-1. Statement of policy. — The general assembly hereby declares it to be the policy of this state that free public libraries are essential to the general enlightenment of citizens in a democracy;

that such free public libraries shall provide for the cultural, educational, informational and research needs of all citizens; that such free public libraries are an integral part of the educational system at all levels and a source for vocational information and continued learning following the period of formal education; and that it is the responsibility of government at all levels to provide adequate financial support for all such free public libraries. The general assembly further declares it to be the policy of this state to coordinate on a cooperative basis the resources of academic, free public, school and special libraries to meet the expanding needs of all citizens and that it is the responsibility of government at all levels to provide adequate financial support to coordinate library resources throughout the state for improved library services to all citizens.   P.L. 1967, ch. 227, § 5.

29-6-2. State aid to free public libraries. — The department of state library services shall cause to be paid annually to the city or town treasurers from general revenue appropriations made to the department for the use and benefit of free public libraries established and maintained in said cities or towns grants-in-aid of not less than thirty cents (30¢) per capita of the population in each of said cities and towns based on the latest decennial census by the United States census bureau.   P.L. 1976, ch. 226, § 1.

29-6-3. Grants-in-aid — Eligibility requirements. — To qualify for an annual grant-in-aid under § 29-6-2 of this chapter, a city or town shall

(A) Appropriate annually for the use and benefit of free public libraries therein either (1) an amount equal to the proposed state grant-in-aid to said city or town pursuant to § 29-6-2, or (2) an amount not less than the amount appropriated and expended by said city or town for the use and benefit of free public libraries therein for the fiscal year of said city or town next preceding the fiscal year of said city or town in which July 1, 1964 occurs, whichever amount shall be the greater;

(B) In the case of a city or town having more than one free public library therein, submit or cause to be submitted to the department of state library services a plan for the allotment or division of the proposed grant-in-aid to said city or town among the free public libraries in said city or town, said plan to be approved by the director of state library services; and

(C) Submit or cause to be submitted to the department of state library services evidence that the free public libraries in said city or town meet standards of service as set forth in regulations to be made by said director of state library services pursuant to the provisions of § 29-3.1-7 of the general laws.

The director of state library services with approval of the advisory board of library commissioners may in his discretion upon application and for cause shown authorize an annual grant-in-aid under § 29-6-2 of this chapter, or a portion thereof, to a city or town not fully meeting the requirements set forth in paragraphs (A), (B) and (C) above.

Decisions as to the eligibility of cities and towns for grants-in-aid under this chapter, and the amounts of such grants-in-aid, shall be made by the director of state library services.   P.L. 1964, ch. 233, § 3.

29-6-4. Library councils. — In cities or towns having more than one free public library therein, the boards of trustees or other governing bodies of said libraries in said city or town, may appoint an inter-library committee to include the principal librarian of each of said libraries and one other representative of each of said libraries, said inter-library committee to be known as a "Library council". Such a library council is hereby authorized to prepare and submit on behalf of a city or town the plan required by the provisions of § 29-6-3 for division of the proposed annual grant-in-aid to said city or town among the free public libraries therein. Such a library council may also serve as a means for promoting inter-library cooperation in said city or town, and is authorized to advise the free public libraries therein on all matters relating to cooperative or joint library services, and may make recommendations pertaining thereto.

P.L. 1964, ch. 233, § 3.

29-6-5. Cooperative library services. — Any city or town may enter into an agreement with another city or town, or more than one other to establish or maintain free public library service, or one or more aspects thereof to citizens therein, and such agreements for cooperative library service shall be valid when approved and accepted by the boards of trustees or other governing bodies of the libraries concerned, and by the respective city or town councils of the cities and towns parties to said agreement, and signed by the appropriate library officers and city or town officials thereunto authorized.

Like agreements for cooperative library service may be entered into by and between two (2) or more free public libraries, whether or not they are in the same city or town; provided, however, in the case of a free public library established or existing under the provisions of § 29-4-1 of the general laws, such agreement shall not be valid until it has been approved and accepted by the council of the city or town where said library is located.

Such agreements shall be reported to the department of state library services, and such appropriate and equitable adjustments in annual grants-in-aid under this chapter shall be made as the circumstances may require.

P.L. 1964, ch. 233, § 3.

29-6-6. State aid — Construction and capital improvements. — The department of state library services may cause to be paid to a city or town treasurer, or to any free public library in the state, such grant-in-aid for the construction and capital improvement of any free public library as the director of state library services may determine is necessary and desirable to provide better free library services to the public, which shall be paid in accordance with the following provisions:

(a) No such grant-in-aid shall be made unless the city or town receiving the same shall cause to be appropriated for the same purpose an amount from its own funds and not from any federal grant or other federal financial assistance equal to or more than the state grant-in-aid, (except, that any federal financial assistance allocated to a city or town under the state and local fiscal Assistance Act of 1972 (P.L. 92-512; 86 Stat. 919) shall be considered eligible for matching purposes), or unless funds from private sources are dedicated for the same purpose in an amount equal to or more than the state grant-in-aid, or unless the total of such city or town appropriation and such funds from private sources for the same purpose is equal to or more than the state grant-in-aid.

(b) The state grant-in-aid may be paid in installments over a period of years up to a maximum of twenty (20) years, beginning in the fiscal year during which the project is accepted by the department of state library services. Whenever a grant-in-aid is paid on the installment basis permitted herein, there shall be included in the state grant-in-aid the interest cost actually incurred by the city or town, or any free public library as a result of its having to borrow the state's portion of the total cost of the library project. The amount of this interest cost shall be computed on the actual interest cost paid by the city or town, or free public library less any applicable accrued interest, premiums and profits from investments, over the period of time elapsing between the date borrowed funds are made available and the date of the last installment payment of the state grant-in-aid. Interest cost incurred by the city or town, or any free public library as a result of having to borrow its portion of the total cost of the library project shall not be considered a part of the total cost of the project for the purposes of matching provided for in sub-paragraph (a) hereof. Nothing contained herein shall prohibit the department of state library services from accelerating the schedule of annual installments, or from paying the balance due of the state's grant-in-aid in a lump sum; provided, however, that the state grant-in-aid in any fiscal year shall include no less than one-twentieth ($^1/_{22}$) of the state's total reimbursable principal obligations.   P.L. 1974, ch. 117, § 1.

29-6-7. Interrelated library systems — Grants-in-aid. — In order for the department of state library services to coordinate on a cooperative basis library resources throughout the state to provide improved library services, the department is authorized to establish five (5) interrelated library systems, one (1) for the city of Providence and four (4) to be known as the northern, the western, the island and the south county interrelated library systems. Within each such system, other than the Providence system, the department shall designate a public library as the regional library center for such system, which library shall enter into an agreement with the department to administer the coordination of library resources within the system and to provide supplementary library and consulting services to libraries within the system and to residents of cities and towns within the system. Providence public library shall provide the coordination of library resources for the Providence system. Each regional library center so designated hereunder by the department shall be eligible for an annual grant-in-aid (in addition to any other grants-in-aid under the provisions of this chapter) not less than thirty thousand dollars ($30,000) base grant plus twenty-five cents (25¢) per capita of the population of the cities and towns served by it (other than the city or town where the same is located) based on the latest decennial census by the United States census bureau.   P.L. 1977, ch. 204, § 1.

29-6-7.1. Supplementary resource centers — Grants-in-aid. — The department of state library services is authorized to designate a library within each interrelated library system, as a supplementary resource center to coordinate school, public, academic and special library resources within the system in order to provide improved library services to students and other learners. Each such supplementary resource center shall enter into an agreement with the department to provide such services and shall receive a minimum grant of ten thousand dollars ($10,000) annually for its services as a supplementary resource center.   P.L. 1967, ch. 227, § 7.

29-6-7.2. Retirement of employees of the northern interrelated library system. — The administrator of the northern interrelated library system may elect to accept the provisions of chapter 21 of title 45 of the general laws entitled "Retirement of municipal employees," said acceptance to be forwarded to the retirement board by the administrator in the same manner as provided in § 45-21-4.

P.L. 1971, ch. 50, § 1.

29-6-8. Principal public library. — The department of state library services is hereby authorized to designate the Providence public library as the "principal public library" in the state, the collections and services of which are and will be used by and made available to other free public libraries in the state, by residents of cities and towns other than the city of Providence, and by regional library centers. Such principal public library shall be eligible for an annual grant-in-aid in addition to any other grants-in-aid under this chapter of not less than one hundred thousand dollars ($100,000), on condition that such principal public library so designated enter into an appropriate agreement with the department of state library services to act as such principal public library in accordance with regulations to be made by the director of state library services pursuant to the provisions of § 29-3.1-5 of the general laws.   P.L. 1964, ch. 233, § 3.

29-6-9. Special research centers. — The department of state library services is hereby authorized to designate certain other libraries, such as those at Brown University, the University of Rhode Island, Providence College, Bryant College, and Rhode Island College, as "special research centers," the special collections of which are available for research in particular fields of knowledge. A special research center so designated shall be eligible for an annual grant-in-aid in an amount to be determined by the director of state library services on condition that such special research center so designated enter into an appropriate agreement with the department of state library services to act as such special research center in accordance with regulations to be made by the director of state library services pursuant to the provisions of § 29-3.1-7 of the general laws.

P.L. 1977, ch. 205, § 1.

29-6-10. Appropriation authorization. — The general assembly shall annually appropriate such sums as it may deem necessary for the purpose of carrying into effect the provisions of §§ 29-6-2, 29-6-6, 29-6-7, 29-6-8, 29-6-9 and 29-6-12 of this chapter; and the state controller is hereby authorized and directed to draw his orders upon the general treasurer for the payment of said sums, or so much thereof as may from time to time be required, upon receipt by him of duly authenticated vouchers.   P.L. 1980, ch. 144, § 3.

29-6-11. Severability of provisions. — If any provision of § 29-1-1 or of chapter 3.1, 4 or 6 of this title, or the application thereof to any person or circumstances, is held invalid, the remainder of the act, and the application of such provision to other persons or circumstances, shall not be affected thereby.   P.L. 1964, ch. 233, § 6.

29-6-12. Rhode Island library film cooperative. — The department of state library services is hereby authorized to establish the Rhode Island Library Film Cooperative in order that public library film services may be coordinated on a cooperative basis. The department shall designate a public library as the public library film center, which said public library shall enter into an agreement with the department to administer public library film services for public libraries throughout the state. The Rhode Island public library so designated hereunder shall be eligible for an annual grant-in-aid, in addition to any grants-in-aid provided by this chapter, of not less than twenty-five thousand dollars ($25,000).   P.L. 1980, ch. 144, § 1.

INTERSTATE LIBRARY COMPACT
(General Laws of Rhode Island, 1982, s. 29-5-1 to 29-5-6.)

29-5-1. Compact. — The interstate library compact is hereby enacted into law and entered into by this state with all states legally joining therein in the form substantially as follows:

INTERSTATE LIBRARY COMPACT

ARTICLE I. Policy and Purpose

Because the desire for the services provided by libraries transcends governmental boundaries and can most effectively be satisfied by giving such services to communities and people regardless of jurisdictional lines, it is the policy of the states party to this compact to cooperate and share their responsibilities; to authorize cooperation and sharing with respect to those types of library facilities and services which can be more economically or efficiently developed and maintained on a cooperative basis, and to authorize cooperation and sharing among localities, states and others in providing joint or cooperative library services in areas where the distribution of population or of existing and potential library resources make the provision of library service on an interstate basis the most effective way of providing adequate and efficient service.

ARTICLE II. Definitions

As used in this compact:

(a) "Public library agency" means any unit or agency of local or state government operating or having power to operate a library.

(b) "Private library agency" means any non-governmental entity which operates or assumes a legal obligation to operate a library.

(c) "Library agreement" means a contract establishing an interstate library district pursuant to this compact or providing for the joint or cooperative furnishing of library services.

ARTICLE III. Interstate Library Districts

(a) Any one or more public library agencies in a party state in cooperation with any public library agency or agencies in one or more other party states may establish and maintain an interstate library district. Subject to the provisions of this compact and any other laws of the party states which pursuant hereto remain applicable, such district may establish, maintain and operate some or all of the library facilities and services for the area concerned in accordance with the terms of a library agreement therefor. Any private library agencies or agencies within an interstate library district may cooperate therewith, assume duties, responsibilities and obligations thereto, and receive benefits therefrom as provided in any library agreement to which such agency or agencies become party.

(b) Within an interstate library district, and as provided by a library agreement, the performance of library functions may be undertaken on a joint or cooperative basis or may be undertaken by means of one or more arrangements between or among public or private library agencies for the extension of library privileges to the use of facilities or services operated or rendered by one or more of the individual library agencies.

(c) If a library agreement provides for joint establishment, maintenance or operation of library facilities or services by an interstate library district, such district shall have power to do any one or more of the following in accordance with such library agreement:

1. Undertake, administer and participate in programs or arrangements for securing, lending or servicing of books and other

publications, any other materials suitable to be kept or made available by libraries, library equipment or for the dissemination of information about libraries, the value and significance of particular items therein, and the use thereof.

2. Accept for any of its purposes under this compact any and all donations, and grants of money, equipment, supplies, materials, and services, (conditional or otherwise), from any state or the United States or any subdivision or agency thereof, or interstate agency, or from any institution, person, firm or corporation, and receive, utilize and dispose of the same.

3. Operate mobile library units or equipment for the purpose of rendering bookmobile service within the district.

4. Employ professional, technical, clerical and other personnel and fix terms of employment, compensation and other appropriate benefits; and where desirable, provide for the in-service training of such personnel.

5. Sue and be sued in any court of competent jurisdiction.

6. Acquire, hold, and dispose of any real or personal property or any interest or interests therein as may be appropriate to the rendering of library service.

7. Construct, maintain and operate a library, including any appropriate branches thereof.

8. Do such other things as may be incidental to or appropriate for the carrying out of any of the foregoing powers.

ARTICLE IV. Interstate Library Districts, Governing Board

(a) An interstate library district which establishes, maintains or operates any facilities or services in its own right shall have a governing board which shall direct the affairs of the district and act for it in all matters relating to its business. Each participating public library agency in the district shall be represented on the governing board which shall be organized and conduct its business in accordance with provisions therefor in the library agreement. But in no event shall a governing board meet less often than twice a year.

(b) Any private library agency or agencies party to a library agreement establishing an interstate library district may be represented on or advise with the governing board of the district in such manner as the library agreement may provide.

ARTICLE V. State Library Agency Cooperation

Any two or more state library agencies of two or more of the party

states may undertake and conduct joint or cooperative library programs, render joint or cooperative library services, and enter into and
perform arrangements for the cooperative or joint acquisition, use,
housing and disposition of items or collections of materials which, by
reason of expense, rarity, specialized nature, or infrequency of
demand therefor would be appropriate for central collection and
shared use. Any such programs, services or arrangements may
include provision for the exercise on a cooperative or joint basis of any
power exercisable by an interstate library district and an agreement
embodying any such program, service or arrangement shall contain
provisions covering the subjects detailed in article VI of this compact
for interstate library.

ARTICLE VI. Library Agreements

(a) In order to provide for any joint or cooperative undertaking
pursuant to this compact, public and private library agencies may
enter into library agreements. Any agreement executed pursuant to
the provisions of this compact shall, as among the parties to the
agreement:

1. Detail the specific nature of the services, programs, facilities,
arrangements or properties to which it is applicable.

2. Provide for the allocation of costs and other financial
responsibilities.

3. Specify the respective rights, duties, obligations and liabilities
of the parties.

4. Set forth the terms and conditions for duration, renewal, termination, abrogation, disposal of joint or common property, if any,
and all other matters which may be appropriate to the proper
effectuation and performance of the agreement.

(b) No public or private library agency shall undertake to exercise
itself, or jointly with any other library agency, by means of a library
agreement any power prohibited to such agency by the constitution
or statutes of its state.

(c) No library agreement shall become effective until filed with the
compact administrator of each state involved, and approved in accordance with article VII of this compact.

ARTICLE VII. Approval of Library Agreements

(a) Every library agreement made pursuant to this compact shall,
prior to and as a condition precedent to its entry into force, be sub-

mitted to the attorney general of each state in which a public library agency party thereto is situated, who shall determine whether the agreement is in proper form and compatible with the laws of his state. The attorneys general shall approve any agreement submitted to them unless they shall find that it does not meet the conditions set forth herein and shall detail in writing addressed to the governing bodies of the public library agencies concerned the specific respects in which the proposed agreement fails to meet the requirements of law. Failure to disapprove an agreement submitted thereunder within ninety (90) days of its submission shall constitute approval thereof.

(b) In the event that a library agreement made pursuant to this compact shall deal in whole or in part with the provision of services or facilities with regard to which an officer or agency of the state government has constitutional or statutory powers of control, the agreement shall, as a condition precedent to its entry into force, be submitted to the state officer or agency having such power of control and shall be approved or disapproved by him or it as to all matters within his or its jurisdiction in the same manner and subject to the same requirements governing the action of the attorneys general pursuant to paragraph (a) of this article. This requirement of submission and approval shall be in addition to and not in substitution for the requirement of submission to an approval by the attorneys general.

ARTICLE VIII. Other Laws Applicable

Nothing in this compact or in any library agreement shall be construed to supersede, alter or otherwise impair any obligation imposed on any library by otherwise applicable law, nor to authorize the transfer or disposition of any property held in trust by a library agency in a manner contrary to the terms of such trust.

ARTICLE IX. Appropriations and Aid

(a) Any public library agency party to a library agreement may appropriate funds to the interstate library district established thereby in the same manner and to the same extent as to a library wholly maintained by it and, subject to the laws of the state in which such public library agency is situated, may pledge its credit in support of an interstate library district established by the agreement.

(b) Subject to the provisions of the library agreement pursuant to which it functions and the laws of the states in which such district is situated, an interstate library district may claim and receive any state and federal aid which may be available to library agencies.

ARTICLE X. Compact Administrator

Each state shall designate a compact administrator with whom copies of all library agreements to which his state or any public library agency thereof is party shall be filed. The administrator shall have such other powers as may be conferred upon him by the laws of his state and may consult and cooperate with the compact administrators of other party states and take such steps as may effectuate the purposes of this compact. If the laws of a party state so provide, such state may designate one or more deputy compact administrators in addition to its compact administrator.

ARTICLE XI. Entry into Force and Withdrawal

(a) This compact shall enter into force and effect immediately upon its enactment into law by any two (2) states. Thereafter, it shall enter into force and effect as to any other state upon the enactment thereof by such state.

(b) This compact shall continue in force with respect to a party state and remain binding upon such state until six (6) months after such state has given notice to each other party state of the repeal thereof. Such withdrawal shall not be construed to relieve any party to a library agreement entered into pursuant to this compact from any obligation of that agreement prior to the end of its duration as provided therein.

ARTICLE XII. Construction and Severability

This compact shall be liberally construed so as to effectuate the purposes thereof. The provisions of this compact shall be severable and if any phrase, clause, sentence or provision of this compact is declared to be contrary to the constitution of any party state or of the United States or the applicability thereof to any government, agency, person or circumstance is held invalid, the validity of the remainder of this compact and the applicability thereof to any government, agency, person or circumstance shall not be affected thereby. If this compact shall be held contrary to the constitution of any state party thereto, the compact shall remain in full force and effect as to the remaining states and in full force and effect as to the state affected as to all severable matters. P.L. 1963, ch. 22, § 1.

29-5-2. Compliance with local laws. — No city, town or library district of this state, hereinafter to be created, shall be party to a library agreement which provides for the construction or mainte-nance of a library pursuant to article III, subdivision (c-7) of the compact, nor pledge its credit in support of such a library, or contribute to the capital financing thereof, except after compliance with any laws applicable to such cities, towns or library districts hereinafter to be created relating to or governing capital outlays and the pledging of credit. P.L. 1963, ch. 22, § 1.

29-5-3. Definition. — As used in the compact, "state library agency" with reference to this state, means the director of the depart-ment of state library services or his designated agent.

P.L. 1972, ch. 144, § 4.

29-5-4. Appropriations. — An interstate library district lying partly within this state may claim and be entitled to receive state aid in support of any of its functions to the same extent and in the same manner as such functions are eligible for support when carried on by entities wholly within this state. For the purposes of computing and apportioning state aid to interstate library districts hereinafter to be created, this state will consider that portion of the area which lies within this state as an independent entity for the performance of the aided function or functions and compute and apportion the aid accord-ingly. Subject to any applicable laws of this state, such a district also may apply for and be entitled to receive any federal aid for which it may be eligible. P.L. 1963, ch. 22, § 1.

29-5-5. Compact administrator. — The director of the depart-ment of state library services shall be the compact administrator pursuant to article X of the compact. P.L. 1965, ch. 51, § 1.

29-5-6. Notices of withdrawal. — In the event of withdrawal from the compact the director of the department of state library ser-vices shall send and receive any notices required by article XI(b) of the compact. P.L. 1972, ch. 144, § 4.

HISTORICAL SOCIETY LIBRARIES
(General Laws of Rhode Island, 1982, s.29-2-1 to 29-2-6.)

29-2-1. Appropriations for Rhode Island historical society. — The general assembly shall annually appropriate such sum as it may deem necessary out of any money in the treasury not otherwise appropriated, to be expended by the state librarian for the purpose of caring for, preserving and cataloguing the property of the state in the keeping of the Rhode Island historical society, including such historical materials as may from time to time be transferred to the society from the state library collections by the state librarian, and for the purchase and binding of books relating to the history of the state and for copying and preserving the records of the several towns of the state, and the said state librarian, with the approval of the secretary of state, may pay said sum to said Rhode Island historical society for said purpose.   P.L. 1978, ch. 404, § 2.

29-2-2. Appropriations for Newport Historical Society. — The general assembly shall annually appropriate such sum as it may deem necessary, out of any money in the treasury not otherwise appropriated, to be expended by the state librarian for the purpose of caring for, preserving and cataloguing the property of the state in the keeping of the Newport Historical Society, and for the purchase and binding of books relating to the history of the state and for copying and preserving the records of the several towns of the state, and the said state librarian, with the approval of the secretary of state, may pay said sum to said Newport Historical Society for said purpose.
                                                    G.L. 1956, § 29-2-2.

29-2-3. Disbursement of appropriated funds. — The state controller is hereby authorized and directed to draw his orders upon the general treasurer for the payment of said sums or so much thereof as may be required upon receipt by him of proper vouchers approved by the state librarian and the secretary of state.   G.L. 1956, § 29-2-3.

29-2-4. Use of historical society libraries. — All books, periodicals and papers in the keeping of the Rhode Island historical society and the Newport Historical Society, shall at all reasonable times be open to the use of all the citizens of the state, under the same conditions pertaining to the members of the society as long as funds are provided under §§ 29-2-1, 29-2-2 and 29-2-3. P.L. 1978, ch. 404, § 2.

29-2-5. Reports on expenditures. — The Rhode Island historical society and the Newport historical society respectively shall place on file with the state librarian annual reports as to the manner in which the funds are expended, as long as funds are appropriated in accordance with §§ 29-2-1, 29-2-2 and 29-2-3. P.L. 1978, ch. 404, § 2.

29-2-6. Appropriations for purchase, microfilming, and binding of newspapers. — The general assembly shall annually appropriate such sum as it may deem necessary, to be expended by the said state librarian for the purchase of, microfilming and binding of newspapers published in this state; the copies to be received by the state librarian and to be deposited in the Rhode Island historical society in accordance with § 29-2-4; and the state controller is hereby authorized to draw his orders upon the general treasurer for such sum or sums, upon the receipt by him of vouchers approved by the state librarian and by the secretary of state.   P.L. 1978, ch. 404, § 2.

DISTRIBUTION OF PUBLIC DOCUMENTS
(General Laws of Rhode Island, 1982, s.43-2-5, 43-2-9.)

43-2-5.   Distribution of copies of proceedings. — The secretary of state shall, as soon as may be after the publication of the public laws, acts of a local and private nature and resolutions as provided in § 22-11-3.2 transmit one or more bound copies thereof to each of the following officers, libraries, or societies; one (1) copy each to the governor, lieutenant governor, justices of the supreme, superior, family and district courts, general treasurer, state controller, the director of each department, the chiefs of the divisions of public utilities, taxation, banking and insurance, the several town and city clerks, the several boards of canvassers and registration, the several probate courts where the clerk of such court is other than the town clerk, the several clerks of the supreme, superior, family and district courts, the reporter of opinions of the supreme court, the several sheriffs, the adjutant general, the state judge advocate general, the division of industrial inspection, the library of any accredited institution of higher education in the state of Rhode Island, Redwood Library and Athenaeum, the People's Library, Newport, Providence Athenaeum, Providence Public Library, Pawtucket Free Public Library, to any other incorporated library in the state or to any library in the state receiving state aid that may apply therefor, the Social Law Library at Boston, Massachusetts, the New York Public Library, in New York, the library of the Worcester County Bar Association, Massachusetts, the library of the John Hopkins University, Maryland, the library at Cornell University, New York, the law schools at Cambridge and Boston in Massachusetts, at New York and at Albany in New York, at New Haven in Connecticut, the library of the University of West Virginia, in West Virginia, the bar library in Chicago, in Illinois, the library of the law school of Georgetown University in Washington, D. C., the state libraries of the several states, the senate committees on judiciary, finance and corporations, the committees on judiciary, finance and corporations of the house of representatives, the legislative council and the house finance committee advisory staff, [each member of the general assembly, the associate justice of the supreme court of the United States assigned to the first circuit, each district judge of the United States for the district of Rhode Island, the United States district attorney for the district of Rhode Island, the United States marshal, the referee in bankruptcy for the district of Rhode Island, the clerk of the United States district court; four (4) copies to the secretary of state of the United States]; he shall also transmit two (2) copies each to the state library, the state law library, the attorney-general, each of the assistant attorneys-general, the Legal Aid Society of Rhode Island, the Rhode Island Historical Society, the Newport Historical Society, the warden's court at New Shoreham, and shall keep two (2) copies for the use of his office; which copies shall be by them transmitted to their respective successors in office, and the secretary of state shall retain the residue in his office for sale at the actual cost thereof, except as is hereinafter provided.

P. L. 1970, ch. 55, § 2; P. L. 1970, ch. 295, § 1.

43-2-9. Exchanges by secretary of state.—The secretary of state may in his discretion transmit copies of acts, resolutions and reports published by him to any state, territory, province or country which extends a similar privilege to the state library, and upon recommendation of the state librarian he shall send in exchange to a designated depository in such state, territory, province or country in accordance with the provisions of § 29-1-5, copies of acts, resolutions and reports published by him. The secretary of state may also transmit to any official receiving publications, in accordance with § 43-2-5, copies of publications issued under authority of the state, and in his custody, to replace volumes which have been mutilated or have become defective, upon receipt of the mutilated or defective volume in exchange therefor.

G. L. 1938, ch. 307, § 10.

MUNICIPAL LIBRARIES
(General Laws of Rhode Island, 1982, s.29-4-1 to 29-4-8.)

29-4-1. Founding by town or city of free public library. — The electors in any town qualified to vote upon any proposition to impose a tax, or for the expenditure of money in such town voting at any financial town meeting, or in the case of any city, the city council, may appropriate such sum or sums as they shall deem proper for the foundation therein of a free public library, with or without branches, for all the inhabitants thereof, and to provide suitable rooms, land, buildings and capital improvements for such library.

P.L. 1964, ch. 233, § 2.

29-4-2. Annual appropriations for library — Acceptance and management of donations. — Any town or city having established a free public library therein, in manner as aforesaid, may annually, by the majority vote of the electors of said town qualified as aforesaid and voting on the proposition, or by vote of the city council of said city, appropriate such sum or sums as they shall deem proper for the maintenance and increase of such library therein, and may take, receive, hold and manage any devise, bequest or donation for the establishment, maintenance or increase of a public library therein. Any such town or city may annually in like manner appropriate for the maintenance and increase of any free public library therein such sum or sums as may be deemed proper for the maintenance and increase of such free public library and, for land, buildings and capital improvements for such free public library.

P.L. 1964, ch. 233, § 2.

29-4-3. City or town appropriations for free public libraries. — Any town or city not owning a free public library may annually, by the majority vote of the electors of said town qualified as aforesaid and voting on the proposition, or by vote of the city council of said city, appropriate such sum or sums as they shall deem proper for the maintenance and increase of any free public library therein and for land, buildings and capital improvements for any such free public library therein.

P.L. 1964; ch. 233, § 2.

29-4-4. Gifts for free public libraries. — In case any library, or funds for the establishment thereof, may be offered to any city or town on the condition that said library shall be maintained as a free public library, the city council of any city, or town council of any town, is hereby authorized to accept such gift in behalf of the city or town.

P.L. 1964, ch. 233, § 2.

29-4-5. Appointment of board of trustees. — Whenever any city or town shall establish a free public library, or shall become possessed, as above provided, of any such library, the aforesaid city council or town council, as the case may be, shall proceed to elect a board of trustees, to consist of not less than three (3) members nor more than seven (7). As soon as possible after the election of the first board, the members thereof shall meet and be divided by lot into three (3) groups or classes, the terms of office of one (1) group expiring in one (1) year from the date of their election, those of another group in two (2) years, and those of the remaining group in three (3) years. With the expiration of the term of office of any member the vacancy shall be filled by the city council or town council, as the case may be, for the term of three (3) years. Vacancies occurring by resignation, removal, death, or otherwise, shall be filled as above for the unexpired term thereof.   P.L. 1964, ch. 233, § 2.

29-4-6. Powers and duties of trustees. — The aforesaid trustees shall take possession of said library, and shall thereafter be the legal guardians and custodians of the same. They shall provide suitable rooms for the library, arrange for the proper care of the same, choose one (1) or more competent persons as librarians and fix their compensation, and make all needful rules and regulations for the government of the library and the use of the books; provided, that no fee for the use of the books shall ever be exacted.   P.L. 1964, ch. 233, § 2.

29-4-7. Library funds. — All appropriations from the city or town and state, and the income of all funds belonging to the library, shall be subject to the exclusive control of the trustees, and the several city and town treasurers shall pay, within the limits of the appropriations and other library funds in their hands, all bills properly certified by the said trustees.   P.L. 1964, ch. 233, § 2.

29-4-8. Acceptance of gifts by trustees. — In case of any bequest, legacy or gift to, or in favor of, a public library, the trustees thereof are hereby authorized and empowered to accept the same in behalf of, and for the use of, the library, and their receipt shall be a full and sufficient discharge and release to any executor, administrator or other person authorized to make the payment thereof.   P.L. 1964, ch. 233, § 2.

SCHOOL LIBRARIES
(General Laws of Rhode Island, 1982, s.16-1-4, 16-1-5.)

16-1-4. Powers and duties of board.—The state board of education shall have power and shall be required:

*   *   *

(g) To recommend standards for school libraries and to provide school library services.   P. L. 1951, ch. 2752, § 9.

16-1-5. Duties of commissioner.—It shall be the duty of the commissioner of education:

*   *   *

(g) To exercise supervision over school libraries and library services. P. L. 1952, ch. 2975, § 2.

LAW LIBRARIES
(General Laws of Rhode Island, 1982, 29-3-1 to 29-3-4.)

29-3-1. Custody of law library — Use of books. — The supreme court shall have the custody of the law library, and shall be responsible for the care and keeping thereof, and shall permit no book to be taken therefrom, except for the use of the general assembly, or the justices of the supreme or superior courts, or upon the order of some one of said justices, or upon the order of some one of the standing masters in chancery; but any person may use the books within the library rooms. G.L. 1956, § 29-3-1.

29-3-2. Law librarian — Hours library open. — The supreme court shall appoint a librarian, who shall cause the library to be kept open daily, Sundays and holidays excepted, from nine o'clock in the forenoon until five o'clock in the afternoon, except during vacation of the courts, and on Saturdays, when it may be closed at three o'clock in the afternoon. G.L. 1956, § 29-3-2.

29-3-3. Reports and statutes from other states and United States. — The Secretary of state shall place in the law library, in the courthouse in Providence, all books of reports of judicial decisions and statutes which shall be received by him for this state from other states, and from the United States. G.L. 1956, § 29-3-3.

29-3-4. Appropriations for law library. — The general assembly shall annually appropriate such sum as it may deem necessary, to be expended under the direction of the justices of the supreme court, for the purchase of books and other literature, and binding the same, and for clerical assistance and incidental expenses for the state law library. G.L. 1956, § 29-3-4.

PROTECTION OF LIBRARY PROPERTY
(General Laws of Rhode Island, 1982, s.11-8-4, 11-41-14, 11-44-15.)

11-8-4. Breaking and entering business place, public building, or ship at night with felonious intent.—Every person who shall break and enter any bank, shop, office or warehouse, not adjoining to or occupied as a dwelling house, any meeting house, church, chapel, courthouse, town house, college, academy, schoolhouse, library or other building erected for public use or occupied for any public purpose or any ship or vessel, in the nighttime, with intent to commit murder, rape, robbery or larceny, shall be imprisoned not exceeding ten (10) years.

G. L. 1938, ch. 608, § 8.

11-41-14. Misappropriation of library property. — Every person who shall take or borrow from any public or reference library any book, pamphlet, periodical, paper, or other piece of property of said library, and who, upon neglect to return the same within the time required and specified in the by-laws, rules, or regulations of the library owning the property, has been notified by the librarian or other proper custodian of the property that the same is overdue, shall upon further neglect to return the same within two (2) months from the date of such notice, or upon neglect to pay the charges on the book, or other article, be guilty of a misdemeanor and shall be fined not more than ten dollars ($10.00), the same to be for the use of the library. A written or printed notice given personally or sent by mail to a last known or registered place of residence shall be considered a sufficient notice.

G. L. 1938, ch. 608, § 64.

11-44-15. Injury to library property.—Every person who wilfully and maliciously or wantonly and without cause writes upon, injures, defaces, tears, or destroys any book, pamphlet, plate, picture, engraving, statue, or other property belonging to any law, town, city, or other free public or reference library, or suffers such injury to be inflicted while said property is in his custody, shall be fined not more than twenty dollars ($20.00), the same to be for the use of the library.

G. L. 1938, ch. 608, § 63.

TAX EXEMPTION

(General Laws of Rhode Island, 1982, s.44-3-3.)

44-3-3. Property exempt.—The following property shall be exempt from taxation: *   *   *

(12) the property, real and personal, held for or by an incorporated library, society, or any free public library, or any free public library society, so far as said property shall be held exclusively for library purposes, or for the aid or support of the aged poor, or for the aid or support of poor friendless children, or for the aid or support of the poor generally, or for a hospital for the sick or disabled;

P. L. 1947, ch. 1920, § 1.

Rhode Island library laws are reprinted from GENERAL LAWS OF RHODE ISLAND published by Bobbs Merrill Co. Indianapolis, Indiana.

SOUTH CAROLINA

STATE LIBRARY
(Code of Laws of South Carolina, 1982, s.60-1-10 to 60-1-60,
State Constitution, Art. 17, s.1.)

§ 60–1–10. Name of State Public Library Association changed to South Carolina State Library.

The name of the State Public Library Association is hereby changed to the South Carolina State Library.

HISTORY: 1962 Code § 42-200; 1969 (56) 818.

§ 60–1–20. South Carolina State Library created; appointment and terms of board of directors; vacancies.

There is hereby created the South Carolina State Library which shall be governed by a board of directors consisting of seven members, one from each congressional district and one from the State at large. The members shall be appointed by the Governor for terms of five years and until their successors are appointed and qualify. All vacancies shall be filled in the manner of the original appointment for the unexpired term.

HISTORY: 1980 Act No. 317, § 1, eff March 4, 1980.

§ 60–1–30. Chairman and secretary of board; other officers and agents; compensation of board members.

The board of directors shall elect a chairman and secretary annually. The secretary, if possible, shall be an experienced librarian of administrative ability and shall be chosen either from within or without the board. Such other officers and agents as may be required may from time to time be chosen by the board. No member of the board shall receive compensation for services.

HISTORY: 1962 Code § 42-202; 1952 Code § 42-202; 1942 Code § 5500; 1932 Code § 5472; 1929 (36) 261; 1935 (39) 220.

§ 60–1–40. General duties of board.

It shall be the duty of the board of directors to create and improve public libraries over the entire State and devise and carry into effect methods by which public libraries may be extended to the rural districts of the State, and library service be provided for (A) inmates, patients or residents of penal institutions, reformatories, residential training schools, orphanages, or hospitals substantially supported by the State, and (B) students in residential schools for the handicapped, mentally retarded, hard of hearing, deaf, or other health-impaired persons who by reason thereof require special education, and departments of State government and for State government personnel requiring library services.

HISTORY: 1962 Code § 42-203; 1952 Code § 42-203; 1942 Code § 550; 1932 Code § 5472; 1929 (36) 261; 1935 (39) 220; 1967 (55) 1003; 1969 (56) 818.

§ 60–1–50. Powers of board.

The board of directors may:

(1) Receive funds derived from gifts to the Library or from any private or public source and administer and disburse such funds in such manner as may in its judgment best advance the objects above stated;

(2) Create districts of the State, having such area as the board may deem proper, for the purpose of facilitating the establishment and maintenance of public libraries;

(3) Allocate funds at its disposal between the districts so or otherwise created;

(4) Set standards for the library service rendered therein;

(5) Issue certificates to librarians or those desiring to become librarians in accordance with standards and under conditions prescribed by the board;

(6) Provide State government library services;

(7) Take such other action as may be deemed by it to be advisable or necessary to foster and encourage the establishment and maintenance of adequate library services to (A) inmates, patients, or residents of penal institutions, reformatories, residential training schools, orphanages, or hospitals substantially supported by the State, and (B) students in residential schools for the handicapped, mentally retarded, hard of hearing, deaf, or other health-impaired persons who by reason thereof require special education in public libraries within the State; and

(8) Make reasonable rules and regulations to carry out the intention of this chapter.

(9) Organize a system of complete and selective depository libraries in South Carolina for state publications to ensure that such publications are readily accessible to the citizens of the State.

HISTORY: 1982 Act No. 348, § 2, eff July 1, 1982.

§ 60–1–60. Public libraries and certain agencies shall furnish information to board.

All public libraries and agencies furnishing specialized library service to the persons listed in §§ 60–1–40 and 60–1–50 shall furnish the board with such statistics of conditions and growth as the board shall from time to time request.

HISTORY: 1962 Code § 42-205; 1952 Code § 42-205; 1942 Code § 5500; 1932 Code § 5472; 1929 (36) 261; 1935 (39) 220; 1967 (55) 1003.

§ 1. Qualifications of officers.—No person shall be elected or appointed to any office in this State unless he possess the qualifications of an elector: *Provided,* The provisions of this Section shall not apply to the offices of State Librarian and Departmental Clerks, to either of which offices any woman, a resident of the State two years, who has attained the age of twenty-one years, shall be eligible.

STATE DOCUMENTS DEPOSITORY
(Code of Laws of South Carolina, 1982, s.60-2-10 to 60-2-30.)

§ 60–2–10. Definitions.

The following words and phrases when used in this chapter, unless the context indicates otherwise, shall mean:

(a) "Complete depository" is a place, usually a library, that requests and receives at least one copy of all state publications;

(b) "Selective depository" is a place, usually a library, that requests and receives one copy of selected state publications;

(c) "Depository system" is a system in which copies of all state publications are deposited in one central depository or library for distribution to other designated depositories or libraries;

(d) "State publication" means any document, compilation, register, book, pamphlet, report, map, leaflet, order, regulation, directory, periodical, magazine or other similar written material excluding interoffice and intraoffice communications issued in print by the State, any state agency or department or any state-supported college or university for the use or regulation of any person; it shall also include those publications that may or may not be financed by state funds but are released by private bodies such as research and consultant firms under contract with or supervision of any state agency;

(e) "Print" means all forms of duplicating other than the use of carbon paper.

HISTORY: 1982 Act No. 348, § 1, eff July 1, 1982.

§ 60–2–20. State library as official state depository of all state publications.

Notwithstanding any other provision of law, the South Carolina State Library shall be the official state depository of all state publications, with the responsibility for organizing such publications and for providing bibliographic control over them and shall distribute state publications to all libraries participating in a depository system established by it.

The State Library shall also forward such publications to and receive such publications from out-of-state libraries, departments and agencies with whom the State Library has implemented an agreement to exchange such publications. The provisions of this section shall not affect the duties of either the Legislative Council or the Code Commissioner as provided for by law.

HISTORY: 1982 Act No. 348, § 1, eff July 1, 1982.

§ 60–2–30. Duties of state agencies, departments and state-supported colleges and universities.

All state agencies, departments and state-supported colleges and universities shall forward to the State Library at least fifteen copies of every state publication that such agency, department, college or university prints or causes to be printed within fifteen days after such printing. *Provided,* that additional state funds be used only in the publication and mailing of state publications, and not in their handling and storage. The State Librarian may waive the deposition of any agency publication if:

(1) The publication is of ephemeral value;

(2) Less than ten copies are to be printed; or

(3) The issuing agency requests a waiver.

Provided, the State Library shall make a report to the General Assembly by January 1, 1983, on the cost of compliance, to include, but not limited to, the cost of storage space, clerical and librarian help, mailing and handling, and new positions and additional space that may be required for the State Library and each of the depository libraries.

HISTORY: 1982 Act No. 348, § 1, eff July 1, 1982.

COUNTY LIBRARIES
(Code of Laws of South Carolina, 1982, s.4-9-35 to 4-9-39.)

§ 4–9–35. County public library systems; boards of trustees.

(A) Each county council shall prior to July 1, 1979, by ordinance establish within the county a county public library system, which ordinance shall be consistent with the provisions of this section; *provided,* however, notwithstanding any other provision of this chapter, the governing body of any county may by ordinance provide for the composition, function, duties, responsibilities, and operation of the county library system. County library systems created by such ordinances shall be deemed a continuing function of county government and shall not be subject to the provisions of § 4–9–50 except as state funds are specifically appropriated under other provisions of law.

(B) Each county public library system shall be controlled and managed by a board of trustees consisting of not fewer than seven nor more than eleven members appointed by the county council (council) for terms of four years and until successors are appointed and qualify except that of those members initially appointed one-half of such appointees less one shall be appointed for terms of two years only. Previous service on a county library board prior to the enactment of the county ordinance establishing the board shall not limit service on the board. Vacancies shall be filled in the manner of the original appointment for the unexpired term. To the extent feasible, members shall be appointed from all geographical areas of the county.

(C) The board shall annually elect a chairman, vice-chairman, secretary, treasurer and such other officers as it deems necessary. The board shall meet not less than four times each year and at other times as called by the chairman or upon the written request by a majority of the members.

HISTORY: 1978 Act No. 564 § 2, eff July 9, 1978.

§ 4–9–36. Duties of boards of trustees.

The board as provided for in § 4–9–35 shall be authorized to exercise powers as to the policies of the county library which shall not be inconsistent with the general policies established by the governing body of the county, and pursuant to that authority shall be empowered to:

(1) Employ a chief librarian whose qualifications and credentials shall meet the certification requirements of the State Library

Board, and who shall be responsible to the county library board for the administration of the program and the selection of library staff members required to carry out the functions of the library system.

(2) Purchase, lease, hold and dispose of real and personal property in the name of the county for the exclusive use of the county public library system. *Provided,* however, any such conveyance, lease or purchase of real property shall be by the county governing body in accordance with the provisions of §§ 4–9–10 et seq. and §§ 5–1–10 et seq., as amended.

(3) Acquire books and other library materials and provide for use thereof throughout the county.

(4) Accept donations of real property, services, books and other items suitable for use in the library system.

(5) Designate or mark equipment, rooms and buildings, and other library facilities to commemorate and identify gifts and donations made to the library system.

(6) Cooperate or enter into contracts or agreements with any public or private agency which results in improved services or the receipt of financial aid in carrying out the functions of the library system. *Provided,* however, such contracts and agreements shall be subject to approval by the governing body of the county.

(7) Enter into contracts or agreements with other counties to operate regional or joint libraries and related facilities. *Provided,* however, such contracts and agreements shall be subject to approval by the governing body of the county.

(8) Receive and expend grants, appropriations, gifts and donations from any private or public source for the operation, expansion or improvement of the library system.

(9) Take any actions deemed necessary and proper by the board to establish, equip, operate and maintain an effective library system within limits of approved appropriations of county council.

HISTORY: 1978 Act No. 564 § 2, eff July 9, 1978.

§ 4–9–37. Additional duties of boards of trustees.

In addition to the powers and duties prescribed in § 4–9–36 the board shall:

(a) Provide and make available to the residents of the county books and library materials and in the fulfillment of this function shall establish a headquarters library and may establish branches and subdivisions thereof in appropriate geographical areas of the county within the limits of available funds. The board may operate one or more bookmobiles over routes determined by the board.

(b) Adopt regulations necessary to insure effective operation, maintenance and security of the property of the library system. *Provided,* however, such regulations shall not be in conflict with policy or regulations established by the county governing body.

(c) Annually at a time designated by the county council submit to the council a budget for the ensuing fiscal year adequate to fund the operation and programs of the library system. Such budget shall list all funds which the board anticipates will be available for the operation of the library system. All funds appropriated, earned, granted or donated to the library system, including funds appropriated by the county council, shall be deposited and expended as provided for by the ordinance in each county establishing the library system. All funds appropriated, earned, granted or donated to the library system or any of its parts shall be used exclusively for library purposes. All financial procedures relating to the library system including audits shall conform to the procedures established by the county council.

(d) Annually file a detailed report of its operations and expenditures for the previous fiscal year with the county council.

HISTORY: 1978 Act No. 564 § 2, eff July 9, 1978.

§ 4–9–38. Status of donations for tax purposes; applicability of state laws.

All county public library systems established pursuant to § 4–9–35 are deemed to be educational agencies and gifts and donations of funds or property to such systems shall be deductible by the donors for tax purposes as provided by law for gifts and donations for tax purposes.

All state laws and regulations relating to county public library systems shall apply to library systems created pursuant to § 4–9–35.

All employees of a county public library system shall be subject to the provisions of item (7) of § 4–9–30.

HISTORY: 1978 Act No. 564 § 2, eff July 9, 1978.

§ 4–9–39. Funding of systems; transfer of assets of former libraries.

County public library systems shall be funded by annual appropriations by the county council including millage, if any, levied specifically for the county public library system plus aid provided by the state and federal governments and other sources. If any county council levies a tax specifically for the support of a county public library system, such tax shall apply to all persons and corporations subject to school taxes.

All assets and property, both real and personal, owned by any county library prior to the creation of a library system under § 4-9-35 shall be transferred to the county by the persons or entities owning title thereto; *provided,* however, that all such assets and property shall be used exclusively for library purposes.

HISTORY: 1978 Act No. 564 § 2, eff July 9, 1978.

DISTRIBUTION OF PUBLIC DOCUMENTS
(Code of Laws of South Carolina, 1982, s.11-25-640 to 11-25-680.)

§ 11–25–640. Persons entitled to receive copies of Acts and Joint Resolutions.

Copies of the Acts and Joint Resolutions shall be distributed as follows:

* * *

(13) To each professor and instructor at the law school of the University of South Carolina, one copy;

(14) To each of the chartered colleges of the State, one copy;

(15) To the library of the General Assembly, one hundred and fifty copies;

(16) To the University of South Carolina, two copies;

(17) To the Charleston library, two copies;

(18) To the governor of each state of the Union, for the use of the state, one copy;

(19) To the legislature of each state, one copy;

(20) To the legislative council of the province of Quebec, Canada, one copy;

(21) To each head of a department at Washington, for the use of his department, one copy;

(22) To the libraries of Harvard University, Princeton University, Yale University and the Universities of Alabama, Georgia, Gottingen, Heidelberg, North Carolina, the South and Virginia, one copy each;

(23) To the Athenaeum, Boston, and to the Athenaeum, Philadelphia, one copy each;

(24) To the committee of public records, London, one copy;

(25) To the London museum, one copy;

(26) To the British Museum, London, W. C. 1, one copy;

(27) To the King's Library, in Paris, one copy;

(28) To the royal library at Berlin, one copy;

(29) To the historical societies of South Carolina, Maryland,

New York, Pennsylvania and Virginia, each one copy;

(30) To each county attorney, one paperback copy;

(31) To each county solicitor; and

(32) To the judges of juvenile and domestic relations courts.

HISTORY: 1962 Code § 1-564; 1952, Code § 1-564; 1942 Code § 2109; 1932
Code § 2109; Civ. C. '22 § 73; Civ. C. '12 § 63; Civ. C. '02 § 60; G. S. 40; R.
S. 61; 1836 (6) 648; 1883 (18) 588; 1889 (20) 335; 1894 (21) 1076; 1897 (22)
458; 1902 (23) 964; 1936 (39) 1317, 1350, 1548; 1941 (42) 85; 1962 (52)
1731; 1967 (55) 719.

§ 11–25–650. Distribution of copies of publications to University of South Carolina Law Library.

The officials charged with distribution of such publications shall deliver to the law library of the University of South Carolina not later than thirty days after they are printed from time to time the following number of such publications in addition to those otherwise by law required to be delivered to said law library: Twenty-five copies of the Acts and Joint Resolutions of the General Assembly, twenty-five copies of the proceedings of any constitutional convention of this State, twenty-five copies of the Code, and forty-eight copies of the reports of the Supreme Court. The officials of the law library of the University of South Carolina shall exchange all or any part of such publications for publications relating to government useful to students of law and public officials and shall catalogue and arrange such material so as to make it serviceable to members of the General Assembly.

HISTORY: 1962 Code § 1-565; 1952 Code § 1-565; 1942 Code § 2109; 1932
Code § 2109; Civ. C. '22 § 73; Civ. C. '12 § 63; Civ. C. '02 § 60; G. S. 40; R.
S. 61; 1836 (6) 648; 1883 (18) 588; 1889 (20) 335; 1894 (21) 1076; 1897 (22)
458; 1902 (23) 964; 1936 (39) 1317, 1350, 1548; 1937 (40) 152; 1941 (42)
85.

§ 11–25–660. Distribution of copies of publications to State colleges and universities generally.

The State Librarian may furnish, upon request, copies of the Acts and Joint Resolutions and the permanent journals of the General Assembly to any recognized college or university in this State.

HISTORY: 1962 Code § 1-566; 1952 Code § 1-566; 1942 Code § 2109; 1932
Code § 2109; Civ. C. '22 § 73; Civ. C. '12 § 63; Civ. C. '02 § 60; G. S. 40; R.
S. 61; 1836 (6) 648; 1883 (18) 588; 1889 (20) 335; 1894 (21) 1076; 1897 (22)
458; 1902 (23) 964; 1936 (39) 1317, 1350, 1548; 1941 (42) 85.

§ 11–25–670. Distribution of copies of publications to College of Charleston.

The State Librarian shall include the College of Charleston

among the institutions of the State to which copies of the Acts and Joint Resolutions of the General Assembly, legislative journals and reports of State officers are directed to be sent annually.

HISTORY: 1962 Code § 1-567; 1952 Code § 1-567; 1942 Code § 2109; 1932 Code § 2109; Civ. C. '22 § 73; Civ. C. '12 § 63; Civ. C. '02 § 60; G. S. 40; R. S. 61; 1836 (6) 648; 1883 (18) 588; 1889 (20) 335; 1894 (21) 1076; 1897 (22) 458; 1902 (23) 964; 1936 (39) 1317, 1350, 1548; 1941 (42) 85.

§ 11–25–680. Distribution of copies of publications to Library of Congress.

The officials charged with the distribution shall annually forward by mail or otherwise, as they may deem expedient, the following number of such publications to the Library of Congress, Washington, D. C., to wit:

(1) Eight copies of the reports of the Supreme Court;

(2) Two copies of the journals and reports of the General Assembly; and

(3) Eight copies of the Acts and Joint Resolutions.

These provisions are made in recognition of benefits received through receipt at depository libraries and elsewhere in the State of public documents of the United States under the provisions of Federal laws.

HISTORY: 1962 Code § 1-568; 1952 Code § 1-568; 1942 Code § 2109; 1932 Code § 2109; Civ. C. '22 § 73; Civ. C. '12 § 63; Civ. C. '02 § 60; G. S. 40; R. S. 61; 1836 (6) 648; 1883 (18) 588; 1889 (20) 335; 1894 (21) 1076; 1897 (22) 458; 1902 (23) 964; 1936 (39) 1317, 1350, 1548; 1941 (42) 85.

SUPREME COURT LIBRARY
(Code of Laws of South Carolina, 1982, s.60-3-10, 60-3-20.)

§ 60–3–10. Care and custody of library; employment of departmental clerk to act as librarian.

The library of the Supreme Court shall be in the custody and care of the clerk of the court, who shall annually, with the consent and approval of the court, employ some suitable person, as a departmental clerk, to care for and attend in the library and perform such duties with reference thereto as may be prescribed by the court. The librarian so employed may be discharged by order of the court at any time and shall receive such compensation as may be provided by law.

Any woman who has attained the age of twenty-one years and has been a resident of this State for two years may be employed as such librarian.

HISTORY: 1962 Code § 42-51; 1952 Code § 42-51; 1942 Code § 16; 1932 Code § 16; Civ. P. '22 § 16; Civ. C. '12 § 3820; Civ. C. '02 § 2724; G. S. 2094; R. S. 2226; 1896 (22) 3; 1918 (30) 788.

§ 60–3–20.   Exchange of old or duplicate books.

The justices of the Supreme Court may, in their discretion, exchange old or duplicate editions of books in such library for other books, to be selected by the justices.

HISTORY: 1962 Code § 42-52; 1952 Code § 42-52; 1942 Code § 3202; 1932 Code § 3202; Civ. C. '22 § 899; Civ. C. '12 § 819; 1909 (26) 283.

SCHOOL LIBRARIES
(Code of Laws of South Carolina, 1982, 60-9-10 to 60-9-30, 59-3-10.)

§ 60–9–10.   Procedures for obtaining state and county aid; monies raised by public and private subscriptions.

Whenever the friends and patrons of a public school raise, from public subscription or otherwise, a sum not less than five dollars nor more than twenty-five dollars and deposit it with the county treasurer to the credit of their school district, the county board of education, through the county superintendent of education, shall credit such district with an equal amount, to be drawn from the county board fund or, if the county board fund has been exhausted, to be drawn from the general school fund of the county. The county superintendent shall then make application to the State Superintendent of Education for an amount equal to the sum raised, by private subscription or otherwise, and deposit it with the county treasurer. All the money resulting from private subscription or otherwise, from county funds, or from State funds shall be held in the county treasury to the credit of the school district and shall be paid out upon the warrant of the board of school district trustees, duly approved and countersigned by the county superintendent of education.

Nothing herein shall prevent other funds greater than those mentioned herein being raised by private subscription and applied by the county superintendent of education to the purposes herein set forth.

HISTORY: 1962 Code § 42-251; 1952 Code § 42-251; 1942 Code § 5498; 1932 Code § 5423; Civ. C. '22 § 2686; Civ. C. '12 § 1796; 1904 (24) 391; 1905 (24) 877; 1908 (25) 1024; 1913 (28) 190; 1914 (28) 752; 1919 (31) 150.

§ 60–9–20.   Disbursement of funds; list of books purchased.

The funds provided under § 60–9–10 shall be expended only for the establishment of a library, for the enlargement of a library or for the purchase of supplementary readers to be kept in the school library. Any free public school may participate in this fund but only once during a fiscal year. The trustees or teachers of any school receiving the benefits of this section and § 60–9–10 shall file, both with the county superintendent of education and with the State Superintendent of Education, a correct and legible list of the books purchased.

HISTORY: 1962 Code § 42-252; 1952 Code § 42-252; 1942 Code § 5499; 1932 Code § 5424; Civ. C. '22 § 2687; Civ. C. '12 § 1797; 1904 (24) 391; 1905 (24) 877; 1919 (31) 150.

§ 60–9–30. Duties of State Board of Education.

The State Board of Education shall select and publish a list of library books and also a list of supplementary readers and shall make all necessary rules and regulations concerning the use and care of libraries.

HISTORY: 1962 Code § 42-253; 1952 Code § 42-253; 1942 Code § 5499; 1932 Code § 5424; Civ. C. '22 § 2687; Civ. C. '12 § 1797; 1904 (24) 391; 1905 (24) 877; 1919 (31) 150.

§ 59–31–10. Library committee.

There shall be a library committee composed of the State Superintendent of Education, the director of the division of elementary education, the high school supervisor and four other members to be appointed by the State Superintendent of Education, two representing the elementary schools and two representing the high schools. All library books provided for under Article 3 of this chapter shall be selected from an approved list to be furnished the State Board of Education by the library committee.

HISTORY: 1962 Code § 21-454; 1952 Code § 21-454; 1942 Code § 5286; 1932 Code § 1549; 1937 (40) 206; 1939 (41) 1; 1945 (44) 266.

STATE ARCHIVES
(Code of Laws of South Carolina, 1982, s.60-11-10 to 60-11-90.)

§ 60–11–10. Short title.

This chapter may be cited as the Archives Act.

HISTORY: 1962 Code § 9-1; 1954 (48) 1752.

§ 60–11–20. Archives Department redesignated as Department of Archives and History.

The South Carolina Archives Department shall hereafter be styled as the South Carolina Department of Archives and History.

HISTORY: 1962 Code § 9-2; 1954 (48) 1752; 1967 (55) 211.

§ 60–11–30. Objects and purposes of Department.

The objects and purposes of the South Carolina Department of Archives and History shall be:

(1) The preservation and administration of those public records

formerly transferred to the custody of the Historical Commission
and those that may be transferred and accepted by the Department in the future;

(2) The collection, by purchase or otherwise, of the originals, or
transcripts, of public records in other states or counties relating to
South Carolina;

(3) The preservation and administration of the private records
formerly in the custody of the Historical Commission and those
that may be added by deposit, gift, or purchase in the future;

(4) The editing and publication of documents, treatises, etc.,
relating to the history of South Carolina;

(5) The stimulation of research, study, and other activity in the
field of South Carolina history, genealogy, and archaeology;

(6) The approval of the inscriptions for all historical markers or
other monuments erected on State highways or other State property;

(7) The improvement of standards for the making, care, and
administration of public records; and

(8) The performance of such acts and requirements as may be
enjoined by law.

HISTORY: 1962 Code § 9-3; 1954 (48) 1752; 1967 (55) 211.

§ 60–11–40. Department under control of Commission of Archives and History; membership and meetings of Commission; terms of office of members; vacancies.

(1) *Control and membership.*—The South Carolina Department
of Archives and History shall be under the control of the South
Carolina Commission of Archives and History, consisting of four
ex officio members and five non ex officio members selected and
appointed as hereinafter set out.

(2) *Ex officio members.*—The four ex officio members shall be
the heads, respectively, of the departments of history of the
University of South Carolina; The Citadel, the Military College of
South Carolina; Clemson University; and Winthrop College, the
South Carolina College for Women; and their successors in their
respective offices.

(3) *Non ex officio members.*—The five non ex officio members
shall be nominated, one by the South Carolina Historical Society,
one by the American Legion, Department of South Carolina, and
one by the South Carolina Historical Association, and appointed
by the Governor. Each shall serve for a term of five years. Two
members shall be appointed by the Governor with the advice and
consent of the Senate for terms of office to run concurrently with
the term of the Governor. In case of a vacancy it shall be filled for

the unexpired term in the same manner as the original appointment.

(4) *Meetings; quorum.*—The South Carolina Commission of Archives and History shall hold at the office of the Commission at least one regular meeting during the year and as many special meetings as may be necessary. Special meetings may be called by the chairman, or, in his absence, by the vice-chairman. Five members of the Commission shall constitute a quorum.

(5) *Expenses and per diem.*—All members of the Commission shall be reimbursed for expenses incurred in attending meetings and otherwise performing their duties under the direction of the Commission. The members who are not employed by the State shall receive the per diem paid by the State to members of boards and commissions during their attendance at meetings.

HISTORY: 1962 Code § 9-4; 1954 (48) 1752; 1967 (55) 211.

§ 60-11-50. Powers and duties of Commission.

The South Carolina Commission of Archives and History may:

(1) Elect its chairman and vice-chairman, who shall be chosen annually to serve during the fiscal year but who may serve for successive terms;

(2) Make rules and regulations for its own government and the administration of the Department;

(3) Elect an executive officer for the Department to be known as the Director;

(4) Appoint, on the recommendation of the Director, all other members of the staff;

(5) Adopt a seal for use in official departmental business;

(6) Control the expenditure in accordance with law of such public funds as may be appropriated to the Department;

(7) Accept gifts, bequests, and endowments for purposes consistent with the objectives of the Department;

(8) Make annual reports to the General Assembly of the receipts, disbursements, work, and needs of the Department; and

(9) Adopt policies designed to fulfill the duties and attain the objectives of the Department as established by law.

HISTORY: 1962 Code § 9-5; 1954 (48) 1752; 1967 (55) 211.

§ 60-11-60. Director of Department.

The active management and administration of the South Carolina Department of Archives and History shall be committed to the Director, who at the time of his election must have the qualifications of special training or experience in archival or historical work. The Director shall not do any additional work for pay. He shall furnish information free to the citizens of this State.

HISTORY: 1962 Code § 9-6; 1954 (48) 1752; 1967 (55) 211.

§ 60–11–70. Private records.

The Commission of Archives and History shall not solicit private records, but if its services are necessary to safeguard such records it may accept, either as a gift or deposit, collections offered by their legal owners or custodians. All such papers shall be open to inspection and examination for the purpose of research in like manner as are the public records. Neither the State nor the Commission of Archives and History shall be responsible for the loss of private records accepted on deposit.

HISTORY: 1962 Code § 9-12; 1954 (48) 1752; 1967 (55) 211.

§ 60–11–80. Commission shall publish information regarding public records; Director shall assist in preservation.

From time to time the Commission of Archives and History shall assembly and publish information regarding paper, ink, filing, binding, and any other matter that will be useful in improving the standards of making, caring for, and administering public records. Upon the request of any State or county official the Director shall examine the records in his custody and make recommendations regarding their preservation.

HISTORY: 1962 Code § 9-14; 1954 (48) 1752; 1967 (55) 211.

§ 60–11–90. State Archives Building.

The name of the State Archives Building shall be "The South Carolina Archives." It shall be occupied by the Commission of Archives and History and shall be operated by them in fulfilling the duties now assigned, or which may in the future be assigned, by the General Assembly. The Archives Building shall also provide space for the Confederate relics of the State.

HISTORY: 1962 Code § 9-13; 1954 (48) 1752; 1957 (50) 131; 1967 (55) 211.

PROTECTION OF LIBRARY PROPERTY
(Code of Laws of South Carolina, 1982, s. 16-13-331, 16-13-332.)

§ 16–13–331. Unauthorized removal or concealment of li-

brary property prohibited; penalty.

Whoever, without authority, with the intention of depriving the library or archive of the ownership of such property, willfully conceals a book or other library or archive property, while still on the premises of such library or archive, or willfully or without authority removes any book or other property from any library or archive or collection shall be deemed guilty of a misdemeanor and upon conviction shall be punished in accordance with the following: (1) by a fine of not more than six hundred dollars or imprisonment for not more than six months; *provided,* however, that if the value of the library or archive property is less than fifty dollars, the punishment shall be a fine of not more than one hundred dollars or imprisonment for not more than thirty days. Proof of the willful concealment of any book or other library or archive property while still on the premises of such library or archive shall be prima facie evidence of intent to commit larceny thereof.

HISTORY: 1980 Act No. 334, eff March 20, 1980.

§ 16–13–332. Library personnel exempt from liability for arrest of persons suspected of concealment or removal of library property.

A library or agent or employee of the library causing the arrest of any person pursuant to the provisions of § 16–13–331 shall not be held civilly liable for unlawful detention, slander, malicious prosecution, false imprisonment, false arrest, or assault and battery of the person so arrested, unless excessive or unreasonable force is used; whether such arrest takes place on the premises by such agent or employee; *provided* that, in causing the arrest of such person, the library or agent or employee of the library had at the time of such arrest probable cause to believe that the person committed willful concealment of books or other library property.

HISTORY: 1980 Act No. 334, eff March 20, 1980.

TAX EXEMPTION
(Code of Laws of South Carolina, 1982, State Constitution,
Art. 10, s.4.)

SOUTH DAKOTA

STATE LIBRARY OFFICE

(South Dakota Codified Laws, 1982, s.14-1-39 to 14-1-42, 14-1-44 to
14-1-51, 14-153-14-1-56, 14-1-53 to 14-1-62, 14-1-64, 14-1-65.)

14-1-39. Definition of terms. Terms used in this chapter, unless
the context otherwise plainly requires, shall mean:
(1) "Academic library," a library that supports the curriculum and
research needs of a college, university, or other post-secondary
educational institution;
(2) "Libraries," public, school, academic and special libraries when
all libraries are to be involved collectively;
(3) "Library materials," the various forms in which knowledge and
information are recorded;
(4) "Library service," the performance of all activities of a library
relating to the collection and organization of library materials
and to making the materials and information of a library available to a clientele;
(5) "Public library," any library that serves free of charge all residents of a chartered governmental unit, county, municipality,
township, or a combination of any of the above, and receives
its financial support in whole or in part from public funds;
(6) "School library," any library that supports the curriculum of
a school or a group of schools;
(7) "Special library," any library that supports the research needs
of an industry, governmental agency, or other noneducational
agency or institution; and,
(8) "State library agency," the state library office.

Source: SL 1975, ch 155, § 1.

1650

14-1-40. State policy on libraries. The policy of the state of South Dakota shall be that:

(1) Library services should be available widely throughout the state to bring within convenient reach of the people cultural, informational and educational resources essential to the improvement of their quality of life;

(2) The provision and support of library services should be a necessary function of government at all levels;

(3) The joint exercise of governmental powers under chapter 1-24 shall be encouraged where such action will increase the extent of library materials and services in a fair and equitable manner through cooperation between units of government and between and among libraries;

(4) Cooperation among and between libraries shall be encouraged and promoted by the state library agency; and

(5) Library services suitable to support informed decisions by the Legislature and the personnel of government shall be provided by the state library agency.

Source: SL 1975, ch 155, § 2.

14-1-41. Free use of all public libraries. The use by the public of all libraries established and maintained by the state, counties, townships, municipalities and chartered governmental units under the provisions of this code, subject to such reasonable rules and regulations as may be prescribed by the authorized commission or board in charge of such libraries shall be free except as otherwise expressly provided by law.

Source: SL 1975, ch 155, § 4.

14-1-42. State library office as official agency for library services. The state library office is the official agency of the state which is hereby charged with the extension and development of library services throughout the state.

Source: SL 1975, ch 155, § 3.

14-1-44. Execution of state library policy — Duties of library office. The state library office shall be responsible for executing the library policy of the state of South Dakota and shall:

(1) Promote adequate library service for all the people of the state;

(2) Supplement the services of libraries throughout the state;

(3) Increase the proficiency of library personnel through provision of in-service and continuing education programs for library personnel employed in the state;

(4) Provide for the citizens of the state specialized library services

and materials not generally appropriate, economical or available in other libraries of the state;

(5) Coordinate the libraries maintained by the executive department of state government within the governmental complex in Pierre;

(6) Establish and operate a state publications library distribution center; and

(7) Collect and publish annual statistical data of libraries in the state.

Source: SL 1975, ch 155, § 23.

14-1-45. Services to state government. The state library office shall provide library service to the Legislature and to the personnel of state government.

Source: SL 1975, ch 155, § 15.

14-1-46. Advice and assistance to libraries and governmental agencies. The state library office shall provide advice and assistance to libraries, library boards, units of local government empowered to establish libraries and to departments and agencies of state government in matters concerning the establishment, support, operation, improvement and coordination of libraries and library services, and in the cooperation between libraries.

Source: SL 1975, ch 155, § 16.

14-1-47. Collections maintained by state office. The state library office shall maintain appropriate collections of library materials to supplement the collections of other libraries in the state and to meet the research and informational needs of the Legislature and the employees of state government.

Source: SL 1975, ch 155, § 14.

14-1-48. Network to make library resources available to citizens. The state library office shall provide a network and system whereby the resources of libraries in this state are made available to the citizens of the state.

Source: SL 1975, ch 155, § 21.

14-1-49. State participation in interstate networks and systems. The state library office shall provide for state participation in regional, national, or international library networks and systems designed to increase the quality of library services for the citizens of the state.

Source: SL 1975, ch 155, § 18.

14-1-50. Services for visually and physically handicapped. The state library office shall provide for library services to the visually and physically handicapped.

Source: SL 1975, ch 155, § 20.

14-1-51. Libraries in penal and charitable institutions and special schools. The state library office shall establish, improve and supervise suitable libraries to be maintained by the state in the penal and charitable institutions and in the special schools supported in whole or in part by the state, with the consent and subject to such rules and regulations as may be made by the boards responsible for such institutions.

Source: SL 1975, ch 155, § 19.

14-1-53. Acceptance of gifts for library. The state library office may accept gifts of books, other library materials, money or property for the use of the state library.

Source: SL 1975, ch 155, § 13.

14-1-54. State office to receive federal and private funds — Purposes — Disbursement. The state library office may apply for federal or private funds and accept and enter into appropriate agreements for library purposes in the state or its political subdivisions or for any activity appropriate to a state library agency in behalf of the state for the receipt of such funds from the federal government or its agencies or any private source available, and supervise the disbursement of such funds.

Source: SL 1975, ch 155, § 17.

14-1-55. State library board created — Appointment and terms — Political affiliation. The Governor shall appoint a state library board that will perform all functions of the former state library commission. The board shall consist of seven members appointed by the Governor for four year terms. The members shall not be of all the same political party. The initial terms of the members of the board shall be set by the Governor in such a manner that no more than two members' terms expire in the same year. One member shall be the secretary of education and cultural affairs. The members shall represent, as nearly as practical, all geographic areas of the state.

Source: 1980, ch 21, §§ 4,5.

14-1-56. Office of state board. The state library board shall maintain its office in the state library at the capital of the state.

Source: SL 1975, ch 155, § 6.

14-1-59.   Supervisory and policy-making functions of board. The state library board shall be the supervisory and policy-making body of the state library office and shall:

(1)   Formulate general policies for the state library;

(2)   Make rules and regulations under which state library services and materials may be used by citizens and by libraries in the state, under which administration and execution of federal or private funds or programs that may be received by the state library may be carried out, and under which libraries of the state may have access to systems and networks provided outside the state by the state library;

(3)   Review and approve budget requests for the state library; and

(4)   Adopt a long-range plan for the state-wide coordination and development of library services.

Source: SL 1975, ch 155, § 12.

14-1-60.   General powers of board. The state library board may:

(1)   Contract, under such terms and conditions as may be suitable, with any person, any library, any state department, any unit of local government empowered to establish a library, or any library board to provide library services, to extend, improve or coordinate library services, or to demonstrate appropriate programs of library service;

(2)   Enter into library agreements pursuant to the interstate library compact;

(3)   Appoint any advisory councils it may deem necessary or may find are required for receipt of federal or private funds or programs; and

(4)   Accept gifts of library materials, money or property for the use of the state library.

Source: SL 1975, ch 155, § 24.

14-1-61.   Appointment and compensation of state librarian. The secretary of the department of education and cultural affairs shall appoint, subject to the approval of the Governor, the state librarian to serve at the pleasure of the secretary and shall fix the compensation of the state librarian as provided in § 4-7-10.1.

Source: 1979, ch 353, § 10.

14-1-62.   Professional qualifications of state librarian. The state librarian shall be a graduate of a library school accredited by the American Library Association and shall have experienced at least five years of professional employment in a public library or a state library agency and, in addition, at least two years of successful administrative employment in a public library or a state library agency.

Source: 1975, ch 155, § 10.

14-1-64. Administrative functions of state library board and state librarian. The state library board shall exercise the administrative function as defined in subdivision (12) of § 1-32-1 except for selecting, appointing, promoting, removing and managing personnel. The state librarian shall perform administrative functions in accordance with the general policies of the state library board.

Source: SL 1981, ch 163, § 2.

14-1-65. Audio-visual library services provided — Regulations — Fees. The state library board may promulgate reasonable rules to establish and collect fees for audio-visual library services. In determining these fees, the state library board shall consider the life expectancy of materials provided, replacement costs and means and costs to provide the services. Fees charged for services shall not exceed actual costs to provide them.

Source: SL 1981, ch 163, § 8.

DISTRIBUTION OF PUBLIC DOCUMENTS

(South Dakota Codified Laws, 1982, s.14-1A-1 to 14-1A-8, 2-3-12.)

14-1A-1. Definition of terms. Terms as used in this chapter, unless the context otherwise requires, mean:

(1) "Print," all forms of printing and duplicating, including audio-visual materials, regardless of format or purpose, with the exception of correspondence and interoffice memoranda;

(2) "State publication," any document, compilation, journal, law, resolution, bluebook, statute, code, register, pamphlet, list, microphotographic form, tape or disc recording, book, proceedings, report, memorandum, hearing, legislative bill, leaflet, order, regulation, directory, periodical or magazine published, issued, in print, or purchased for distribution, by the state, the Legislature, constitutional officers, any state department, committee or other state agency supported wholly or in part by public funds;

(3) "State agency," includes, but is not limited to, the Legislature, constitutional officers, and any department, division, bureau, board, commission, committee, or agency of the state of South Dakota;

(4) "Center," the state publications library distribution center.

Source: SL 1974, ch 150, § 1.

14-1A-2. Publications distribution center created — Purpose — Rules and regulations. There is hereby created as a section of the state library, and under the direction of the state librarian, a state publications library distribution center. The center shall promote the establishment of an orderly depository library system. To this end the state library board shall adopt rules and regulations necessary to carry out the provisions of this chapter.

Source: SL 1974, ch 150, § 2.

14-1A-3. Deposits of state agency publications and audio-visual materials. Every state agency shall upon release, deposit at least thirteen copies of each of its state publications, with the state library for record and depository system purposes, with the exception of audio-visual materials. At least two copies of audio-visual materials shall be deposited with the state library for record and depository system purposes.

Source: SL 1907, ch 185, § 2; RC 1919, § 14-1-17; SL 1969, ch 126; 1974, ch 150, § 3; § 9923; SDC 1939, § 29.0306; SDCL, 1982, ch 165, § 2.

14-1A-4. Publication lists and mailing lists to be furnished by state agencies. Upon request by the center, each issuing state agency shall furnish the center with a complete list of its current state publications and a copy of its mailing and exchange lists.

Source: SL 1974, ch 150, § 6.

14-1A-5. Institutions and libraries to receive copies of documents — Retention of permanent copies. The center shall assure that the university of South Dakota at Vermillion and the library of congress shall each receive two copies and that the center for research libraries at Chicago shall receive one copy of each document, with the exception of audio-visual materials. The university of South Dakota at Vermillion shall retain permanently at least one copy of each document distributed by the center for the purpose of historical research. Permanent retention may be encompassed through use of microforms.

Source: SL 1974, ch 150, § 4; 1976, ch 142; 1982, ch 165, § 1.

14-1A-6. Depository library contracts — Requirements. The center shall enter into depository contracts with any municipal or county free library, state college or state university library, the library of congress and the center for research libraries, and other state libraries. The requirements for eligibility to contract as a depository library shall be established by the state library board. The standards shall include and take into consideration the type of library, ability to preserve such publications and to make them available for public use, and also such geographical locations as will make the publications conveniently accessible to residents in all areas of the state.

Source: SL 1974, ch 150, § 4.

14-1A-7. Distribution of state publications list. The center shall publish and distribute regularly to contracting depository libraries and other libraries upon request a list of available state publications.

Source: SL 1974, ch 150, § 5.

14-1A-8. General public distribution prohibited. The center shall not engage in general public distribution of either state publications or lists of publications.

Source: SL 1974, ch 150, § 7.

2-13-12. Exchange copies of session laws for Supreme Court, legislative research council, and state library — Distribution to libraries. In addition to the distribution authorized by § 2-13-7, the bureau of administration shall deliver to the Supreme Court, the director of the legislative research council, and the state library commission, upon proper requisition from time to time, copies of the session laws which may be used in their discretion in exchange for the statutes, codes, or reports of other states, territories, or countries, or for textbooks or other works on law, for the purpose of completing and improving the Supreme Court and legislative reference libraries, for distribution to public and academic libraries in this state and for fulfilling the requirements of chapter 14-1A.

Source: SL 1913, ch 322; 1917, ch 343; RC 1919, § 5120; SDC 1939, § 55.0911; SL 1977, ch 24, § 10.

PUBLIC LIBRARIES
(South Dakota Codified Laws, 1982, s.14-2-27 to 14-2-50, 9-12-15, 9-38-5, 8-2-6.)

14-2-27. Definition of terms. Terms as used in this chapter, unless the context otherwise plainly requires, shall mean:
  (1) "Governing body," the commission, council or other elected body which governs a local governmental unit;
  (2) "Librarian," the chief administrative officer of a public library;
  (3) "Local governmental unit," any chartered governmental unit, county, or municipality, or two or more of them, if applicable, of the state of South Dakota;
  (4) "Public library," any library that serves free of charge all residents of a local governmental unit and receives its financial support in whole or in part from public funds made available by the governing body of that unit;
  (5) "Public library materials," the various forms in which knowledge, information, and humanity's cultural heritage are recorded that a public library might acquire, organize and make available to its clientele;

(6) "Public library services," the performance of all activities of a public library relating to the collection and organization of public library materials and to making those materials and the information contained in them available to its clientele.

Source: SL 1976, ch 143, § 1.

14-2-28. Existing libraries covered by chapter — Changes to effect compliance — Terms of previous contracts unaffected. Every existing public library shall be considered to be established under this chapter, and the public library board of trustees and the governing body of the local governmental unit in which the library is located shall make any changes necessary to effect compliance with the terms of this chapter. Nothing contained in this chapter shall affect nor change the terms of any library contract executed prior to July 1, 1976, but, by mutual consent, the parties to such contract may nevertheless amend such contract to make it conform to any or all of the provisions of this chapter.

Source: SL 1976, ch 143, § 24.

14-2-29. Optional methods of providing library service. Any governing body may provide public library services by either:
(1) Establishing a public library;
(2) Contracting with an established public library for extension of its services and loan of its materials to the citizens of the contracting local governmental unit; or
(3) Joining with one or more governing bodies under the provisions of chapter 1-24 to establish a joint public library.

Source: SL 1976, ch 143, § 2.

14-2-30. Resolution or ordinance to provide services. Any governing body may provide for public library services under one of the options offered in § 14-2-29 by passing and entering upon its minutes a resolution or ordinance to that effect.

Source: SL 1976, ch 143, § 3.

14-2-31. Services provided on approval by voters. A governing body shall provide for library services under one of the options offered in § 14-2-29 if a majority of its voters at any general election affirmatively answer the question: "Shall the (local governmental unit) provide public library services?"

Source: SL 1976, ch 143, § 5.

14-2-32. Petition to require referendum on library services — Referendum on motion of governing body. A governing body shall enter an order for the question as set forth in § 14-2-31 to be placed on the ballot at the next general election upon receipt of a petition signed by a number of registered voters equal to not less than five percent of the total number of votes cast within the boundaries of the local governmental unit for all candidates for Governor at the last certified gubernatorial election or may enter such order upon its own motion.

Source: SL 1976, ch 143, § 4.

14-2-33. County containing municipalities with libraries — Petition and election outside municipality only — Election of municipality to be included. When a county is the local governmental unit petitioned under the provision of § 14-2-32 and that county contains within its geographical boundaries one or more municipalities which provide and support public library services, then the petition shall be signed only by those people living outside of, and the election mandated in § 14-2-31 shall be held only outside of, the boundaries of such municipality or municipalities; provided, however, that by a resolution of the governing body of a municipality, such municipality may be included in the election and if a majority of both county and municipal voters, voting separately, vote to provide county library services then such municipal public library services shall cease and henceforth be provided the municipality by the county governmental unit.

Source: SL 1976, ch 143, § 6.

14-2-34. Services continued by chartered governmental units. Any local governmental unit which becomes a, or part of a, chartered governmental unit shall continue to provide public library services as provided by this chapter.

Source: SL 1976, ch 143, § 23.

14-2-35. Board of public library trustees — Appointment and terms of members. Any public library established under subdivision (1) of § 14-2-29 shall be governed by a board of public library trustees. The governing body shall appoint five competent citizens broadly representative of the population of the local governmental unit. One of the citizens shall be appointed for one year, two for two years, and two for three years and annually thereafter reappointments or new appointments shall be for a term of three years or to complete an unexpired term. In addition to the five appointees, the governing body may appoint one of its own members to serve as a full voting member of the public library board of trustees during that member's term of office.

Source: SL 1976, ch 143, § 10.

14-2-36. Contract with established library — Annual appointment of additional trustees — Number proportional to contributed funds. If a governing body contracts with an established public library under subdivision (2) of § 14-2-29, it may annually appoint additional members to the contracted public library board of public library trustees; provided, that the number of trustees appointed shall be in proportion to its part of the total funds made available during each year by both parties for the provision of public library services, for the purchase of public library materials, and for the provision and maintenance of public library quarters.

Source: SL 1921, ch 163, § 6; SDC 1939,
§ 12.2505; SDCL, § 14-3-4; SL 1976, ch 143,
§ 11.

14-2-37. Joint public library — Board of trustees — Proportional appointment. If one or more governing bodies join under the provision of chapter 1-24 to create a joint public library, the joint public library shall be governed by a board of public library trustees appointed respectively by each participating governing body in a number proportional to the funds provided by that governing body to the total of the joint public library's funds for the provision of public library services, for the purchase of public library materials, and for the provision and maintenance of public library quarters.

Source: SL 1959, ch 167, § 4; SDC Supp
1960, § 29.03A04; SDCL, § 14-2-2; SL 1976,
ch 143, § 12.

14-2-38. School board contracts for library services — Proportional appointment of trustees by board — Maximum number. A school board of any school district may contract with any board of public library or joint library trustees for provision of any or all school library services. If twenty per cent or more of the cost of providing these combined school and public library services shall be borne by the school district, then the school board may annually appoint additional members to the board of public library trustees in proportion to the school district's part of the total funds made available during each year by both parties for the combined school and public library services, for the purchase of school and public library materials, and for the provision and maintenance of quarters for the combined library; provided, however, that the school board shall not appoint more than seven members to the board.

Source: SL 1913, ch 217, § 7; 1915, ch   § 45.3103; SDCL, § 14-4-14; SL 1976, ch 143,
195, § 2; RC 1919, § 9935; SDC 1939,   § 22.

14-2-39. Per diem and expenses of trustees. Members of public library boards of trustees may receive per diem and expenses in the performance of their duties in amounts set by their respective governing bodies.

Source: 1976, ch 143, § 13.

14-2-40. Duties of trustees. Each board of public library trustees shall:

(1) Appoint a librarian to serve at the pleasure of the board;

(2) Adopt bylaws for the conduct of their business and adopt policies for the selection of public library materials, the governance of the library, and the use of public library services and materials;

(3) Prepare and submit an annual budget request to its governing body;

(4) Adopt a final annual budget within those funds certified to it as being appropriated in the annual budget of its governing body;

(5) Meet at least once during each quarter of the year;

(6) Prepare and submit an annual report to its governing body and to the South Dakota state library on such forms as may be provided by the state library.

Source: SL 1976, ch 143, § 14.

14-2-41. Powers of trustees. Each board of public library trustees may:

(1) Accept any gift, grant, devise or bequest made or offered by any person, private agency, agency of state government, the federal government or any of its agencies, for library purposes. Each donation shall be administered in accordance with its terms;

(2) Establish a special public library gift fund. The moneys in such fund shall be derived from all or any part of any gift, bequest or devise, including the interest thereon. Such gift fund shall be a separate and continuing fund and no moneys in such fund shall revert to the general fund of any local governmental unit;

(3) Enter into an interstate library agreement pursuant to § 14-7-12, Article VI;

(4) Establish a collection of public library materials to be loaned on a pay basis and make reasonable charge for use thereof;

(5) Enter into any contracts for the provision of or for the improvement of public library services.

Source: SL 1976, ch 143, § 15.

14-2-42. Duties of librarians. Each librarian shall:

(1) Serve as secretary to the board of public library trustees and keep all its records;

(2) Prepare such reports, budgets and other documents as are required by the board of public library trustees or are required of said board by its governing body;

(3) Appoint such staff as are necessary to operate the public library within its budgetary limitations. Library employees shall receive any employee benefits provided all employees of the local governing unit;

(4) Select and purchase all public library materials for use by the library in its provision of public library services within policies established by the board of public library trustees;

(5) Publish and enforce the policies of the board of public library trustees;

(6) Execute all contracts and agreements approved by the board of public library trustees;

(7) Keep an accurate account of the financial transactions of the public library; and

(8) Carry out any other activities authorized by law that the board of public library trustees consider appropriate in the development, improvement, and provision of public library services.

Source: SL 1976, ch 143, § 16.

14-2-43. Quarters for library — Location — Selection and approval. Each local governmental unit shall provide and maintain quarters for its public library. Such quarters shall be accessible to and conveniently located for all citizens of the area to be served and shall be selected by the board of public library trustees and approved by the governing body.

Source: SL 1976, ch 143, § 17.

14-2-44. Bond issuance for building construction — Use of municipal special assessment funds or county tax levies. A local governmental unit may issue bonds under the provisions of chapter 7-24 or 9-26 for the purpose of constructing a public library building. Funds or tax levies authorized by §§ 7-25-1 and 9-43-68 may be used for the construction of public library buildings.

Source: SL 1976, ch 143, § 18.

14-2-45. Long-term lease for building acquisitions — Maximum term — Property included — Rent payment sources. Any governing body or the board of trustees of a joint library with the permission of each of its participating governing bodies shall have the power to enter into a long-term lease, for a term not to exceed thirty years, with or without an option to renew or purchase, for the acquisition of public library buildings. The lease may be for real or personal property, or both, and may cover library building and site or building and contents only, with or without books, furniture or equipment and may provide for the erection of a public library building and equipping the same with furniture and books of such a public library upon a site owned by the local government unit or the joint library. A lease may be entered into for an existing building or for one to be erected in the future. Rent paid under the terms of a lease may be paid from the general fund of the local governmental unit or may be paid from any fund established for the purpose of providing public library services or the construction of a library.

Source: SL 1969, ch 128; SDCL Supp, §§ 14-2-11.1, 14-3-2.1, 14-4-2.1; SL 1976, ch 143, § 19.

14-2-46. Building funds — Appropriations — Continuation of previously established funds — Transfer of surplus to other funds. Any local governmental unit may establish a public library building fund and make appropriation to such fund. Any public library building funds established under previous law shall be continued and new appropriations may be made to them. If at any time a board of public library trustees ascertains that a building fund or a part thereof is not necessary, it may request its governing body to transfer all or any part of the fund to any other fund for the purpose of providing public library services or for purchase of public library materials and, upon receipt of such request, the governing body shall complete the requested transfer.

Source: SL 1976, ch 143, § 20.

14-2-47. Funds used for services — County tax levy — Public library fund. A governing body may use any funds, not otherwise restricted, available to it and a county may, in addition, levy a tax upon the taxable property of the local governmental unit not to exceed in any one year a rate of three mills for the provision of public library services, for the purchase of public library materials, and for the provision and maintenance of quarters for the public library. All such revenue shall be placed in a public library fund.

Source: SL 1978, ch 62, § 25.

14-2-48. County tax levy applied only outside municipalities using public funds. If a county is the local governmental unit taxing under the provisions of § 14-2-47 and that county contains within its geographical boundaries one or more municipalities which use public funds under those provisions, then the county library tax shall be levied only outside the boundaries of the municipality.

Source: SL 1978, ch 62, § 26.

14-2-49. Discard of old library materials — Marking — Disposition. Any public library may discard over-duplicated, outdated, inappropriate, or worn library materials; provided, that such materials shall be marked clearly with the words: "Discarded, _____ public library" wherever the property label of such library appears. Such discarded materials may be given to other libraries or to nonprofit agencies, destroyed, offered for public sale, or traded to a vendor for future library material purchasing credits.

Source: SL 1976, ch 143, § 21; 1977, ch 127.

14-2-50. Discontinuance of services by vote. Public library services provided for under this chapter may be discontinued only after a vote of the voters of the governmental unit in which the services are provided, taken in the manner prescribed in §§ 14-2-31 and 14-2-32.

Source: SL 1976, ch 143, § 7.

9-12-15. Power to maintain library. Every municipality shall have power to establish and maintain a municipal library, in the manner and subject to the conditions provided in chapter 14-2.

Source: SDC 1939, § 45.0201 (104); SL 1976, ch 143, § 26.

9-38-5. Libraries, museums and art galleries in parks. The governing body shall have authority to authorize the building and maintenance of public libraries, museums, and art galleries in any park. However, in cities of the first class, where a park board has been established according to law, such board shall be consulted by the governing body before action is taken authorizing any such building.

Source: SDC 1939, § 45.2522 as added by SL 1967, ch 222, § 2.

8-2-6. Township public library services. Each organized township in the state has power to provide for public library services, subject however to the same conditions as provided in chapter 14-2, and all provisions of such chapter, so far as reasonably adapted to townships, apply with reference to the establishment, management, and operation of such library services.

Source: SL 1976, ch 143, § 25.

COUNTY LAW LIBRARIES
(South Dakota Codified Laws, 1982, s.14-6-1 to 14-6-5.)

14-6-1. County lawbook and law library fee — Circuit court judges to order collection — Amount. Upon order of the presiding

judge of the circuit court made and filed in the office of the clerk of
courts of any county within the circuit of which such county is a part,
it shall be the duty of the clerk of courts of such county to collect
in each civil action, proceeding for judicial remedy and probate proceeding, except such as commenced by the state or county or municipality or school district therein, in the manner in which other fees
are collected therein and in addition thereto, as a county lawbook and
county law library fee, the sum of not to exceed one dollar in actions
commenced pursuant to chapter 15-39 and the sum of not to exceed
three dollars in all other civil actions, proceedings for judicial remedy
and probate proceedings, from the plaintiff or person instituting such
action or proceeding at the time of filing the first paper therein.

Source: SL 1968, ch 146; 1975, ch 161,
§ 6; 1976, ch 144.

14-6-2. Lawbook and law library fees taxable as costs. The
lawbook and law library fees provided for in § 14-6-1 shall be costs
in the case, and taxable as such.

Source: SL 1968, ch 146.

**14-6-3. Disposition of lawbook and library fees — County
lawbook and law library fund.** On the first day of each month, the
clerk of courts making collection of such lawbook and library fees shall
pay the same to the treasurer of the county taking his receipt therefor
and the county auditor shall keep such fees so remitted in a separate
revolving county lawbook and law library fund to be disbursed for
the purposes and in the manner provided in § 14-6-4.

Source: SL 1968, ch 146.

**14-6-4. Use of county lawbook and law library fund — Accept-
ance of gift, donations and bequests authorized.** Such fund shall
be used at the direction of the circuit judges and as by them deemed
necessary for the purchase of lawbooks and/or to pay the necessary
expenses of equipping and maintaining a law library in the courthouse
or other suitable place provided by the county, or other suitable place
outside the county in the circuit as directed by the circuit judges, and
in addition the county may appropriate additional amounts for such
purposes and may receive gifts, donations and bequests for such purposes.

Source: SL 1968, ch 146; 1973, ch 124.

14-6-5. Use of county law library. The use of the county law
library shall be open to all judges of courts of record, to all state officials, to all officials of the county wherein located, to members of the

state bar, and to the inhabitants of the county under such conditions as provided by the circuit judges.

Source: SL 1968, ch 146.

INTERSTATE LIBRARY COMPACT
(South Dakota Codified Laws, 1982, s.14-7-12 to 14-7-18).

14-7-12. Interstate library compact enacted — Text of compact. The interstate library compact is hereby enacted into law and entered into by this state with all states legally joining therein in a form substantially as follows:

INTERSTATE LIBRARY COMPACT

Article I. Policy and Purpose

Because the desire for the services provided by libraries transcends governmental boundaries and can most effectively be satisfied by giving such services to communities and people regardless of jurisdictional lines, it is the policy of the states party to this compact to cooperate and share their responsibilities; to authorize cooperation and sharing with respect to those types of library facilities and services which can be more economically or efficiently developed and maintained on a cooperative basis; and to authorize cooperation and sharing among localities, states and others in providing joint or cooperative library services in areas where the distribution of population or of existing and potential library resources make the provision of library service on an interstate basis the most effective way of providing adequate and efficient service.

Article II. Definitions

As used in this compact:

(a) "Public library agency" means any unit or agency of local or state government operating or having power to operate a library.

(b) "Private library agency" means any nongovernmental entity which operates or assumes a legal obligation to operate a library.

(c) "Library agreement" means a contract establishing an interstate library district pursuant to this compact or providing for the joint or cooperative furnishing of library services.

Article III. Interstate Library Districts

(a) Any one or more public library agencies in a party state in cooperation with any public library agency or agencies in one or more other party states may establish and maintain an interstate library district. Subject to the provisions of this compact and any other laws of the party states which pursuant hereto remain applicable, such district may establish, maintain and operate some or all of the library facilities and services for the area concerned in accordance with the terms of a library agreement therefor. Any private library agency or agencies within an interstate library district may cooperate therewith, assume duties, responsibilities and obligations thereto, and receive benefits therefrom as provided in any library agreement to which such agency or agencies become party.

(b) Within an interstate library district, and as provided by a library agreement, the performance of library functions may be undertaken on a joint or cooperative basis or may be undertaken by means of one or more arrangements between or among public or private library agencies for the extension of library privileges to the use of facilities or services operated or rendered by one or more of the individual library agencies.

(c) If a library agreement provides for joint establishment, maintenance or operation of library facilities or services by an interstate library district, such district shall have power to do any one or more of the following in accordance with such library agreement:

1. Undertake, administer and participate in programs or arrangements for securing, lending or servicing books and other publications, any other materials suitable to be kept or made available by libraries, library equipment or for the dissemination of information about libraries, the value and significance of particular items therein, and the use thereof.

2. Accept for any of its purposes under this compact any and all donations, and grants of money, equipment, supplies, materials and services, conditional or otherwise, from any state or the United States or any subdivision or agency thereof, or interstate agency, or from any institution, person, firm or corporation, and receive, utilize and dispose of the same.

3. Operate mobile library units or equipment for the purpose of rendering bookmobile service within the district.

4. Employ professional, technical, clerical and other personnel, and fix terms of employment, compensation and other appropriate benefits; and where desirable, provide for the in-service training of such personnel.

5. Sue and be sued in any court of competent jurisdiction.

6. Acquire, hold, and dispose of any real or personal property or any interest or interests therein as may be appropriate to the rendering of library service.

7. Construct, maintain and operate a library, including any appropriate branches thereof.

8. Do such other things as may be incidental to or appropriate for the carrying out of any of the foregoing powers.

Article IV. Interstate Library Districts, Governing Board

(a) An interstate library district which establishes, maintains or operates any facilities or services in its own right shall have a governing board which shall direct the affairs of the district and act for it in all matters relating to its business. Each participating public library agency in the district shall be represented on the governing board which shall be organized and conduct its business in accordance with provision therefor in the library agreement. But in no event shall a governing board meet less often than twice a year.

(b) Any private library agency or agencies party to a library agreement establishing an interstate library district may be represented on or advise with the governing board of the district in such manner as the library agreement may provide.

Article V. State Library Agency Cooperation

Any two or more state library agencies of two or more of the party states may undertake and conduct joint or cooperative library programs, render joint or cooperative library services, and enter into and perform arrangements for the cooperative or joint acquisition, use, housing and disposition of items or collections of materials which, by reason of expense, rarity, specialized nature, or infrequency of demand therefor would be appropriate for central collection and shared use. Any such programs, services or arrangements may include provision for the exercise on a cooperative or joint basis of any power exercisable by an interstate library district and an agreement embodying any such program, service or arrangement shall contain provisions covering the subjects detailed in Article VI of this compact for interstate library agreements.

Article VI. Library Agreements

(a) In order to provide for any joint or cooperative undertaking pursuant to this compact, public and private library agencies may enter into library agreements. Any agreement executed pursuant to the provisions of this compact shall, as among the parties to the agreement:

1. Detail the specific nature of the services, programs, facilities, arrangements or properties to which it is applicable.

2. Provide for the allocation of costs and other financial responsibilities.

3. Specify the respective rights, duties, obligations and liabilities of the parties.

4. Set forth the terms and conditions for duration, renewal, termination, abrogation, disposal of joint or common property, if any, and all other matters which may be appropriate to the proper effectuation and performance of the agreement.

(b)   No public or private library agency shall undertake to exercise itself, or jointly with any other library agency, by means of a library agreement any power prohibited to such agency by the constitution or statutes of its state.

(c)   No library agreement shall become effective until filed with the compact administrator of each state involved, and approved in accordance with Article VII of this compact.

Article VII. Approval of Library Agreements

(a)   Every library agreement made pursuant to this compact shall, prior to and as a condition precedent to its entry into force, be submitted to the attorney general of each state in which a public library agency party thereto is situated, who shall determine whether the agreement is in proper form and compatible with the laws of his state. The attorneys general shall approve any agreement submitted to them unless thay shall find that it does not meet the conditions set forth herein and shall detail in writing addressed to the governing bodies of the public library agencies concerned the specific respects in which the proposed agreement fails to meet the requirements of law. Failure to disapprove an agreement submitted hereunder within ninety days of its submission shall constitute approval thereof.

(b)   In the event that a library agreement made pursuant to this compact shall deal in whole or in part with the provision of services or facilities with regard to which an officer or agency of the state government has constitutional or statutory powers of control, the agreement shall, as a condition precedent to its entry into force, be submitted to the state officer or agency having such power of control and shall be approved or disapproved by him or it as to all matters within his or its jurisdiction in the same manner and subject to the same requirements governing the action of the attorneys general pursuant to paragraph (a) of this article. This requirement of submission and approval shall be in addition to and not in substitution for the requirement of submission to and approval by the attorneys general.

Article VIII. Other Laws Applicable

Nothing in this compact or in any library agreement shall be construed to supersede, alter or otherwise impair any obligation imposed on any library by otherwise applicable law, nor to authorize the transfer or disposition of any property held in trust by a library agency in a manner contrary to the terms of such trust.

Article IX. Appropriations and Aid

(a)   Any public library agency party to a library agreement may appropriate funds to the interstate library district established thereby in the same manner and to the same extent as to a library wholly maintained by it and, subject to the laws of the state in which such public library agency is situated, may pledge its credit in support of an interstate library district established by the agreement.

(b) Subject to the provisions of the library agreement pursuant to which it functions and the laws of the states in which such district is situated, an interstate library district may claim and receive any state and federal aid which may be available to library agencies.

Article X. Compact Administrator

Each state shall designate a compact administrator with whom copies of all library agreements to which his state or any public library agency thereof is party shall be filed. The administrator shall have such other powers as may be conferred upon him by the laws of his state and may consult and cooperate with the compact administrators of other party states and take such steps as may effectuate the purposes of this compact. If the laws of a party state so provide, such state may designate one or more deputy compact administrators in addition to its compact administrator.

Article XI. Entry Into Force and Withdrawal

(a) This compact shall enter into force and effect immediately upon its enactment into law. by any two states. Thereafter, it shall enter into force and effect as to any other state upon the enactment thereof by such state.

(b) This compact shall continue in force with respect to a party state and remain binding upon such state until six months after such state has given notice to each other party state of the repeal thereof. Such withdrawal shall not be construed to relieve any party to a library agreement entered into pursuant to this compact from any obligation of that agreement prior to the end of its duration as provided therein.

Article XII. Construction and Severability

This compact shall be liberally construed so as to effectuate the purposes thereof. The provisions of this compact shall be severable and if any phrase, clause, sentence or provision of this compact is declared to be contrary to the constitution of any party state or of the United States or the applicability thereof to any government, agency, person or circumstance is held invalid, the validity of the remainder of this compact and the applicability thereof to any government, agency, person or circumstance shall not be affected thereby. If this compact shall be held contrary to the constitution of any state party thereto, the compact shall remain in full force and effect as to the remaining states and in full force and effect as to the state affected as to all severable matters. **Source:** SL 1975, ch 158, § 1.

14-7-13. State librarian as compact administrator — Deputies.
The state librarian shall be the compact administrator pursuant to
Article X of this compact. The state librarian shall appoint one or
more deputy compact administrators.

Source: SL 1973, ch 125; SDCL Supp,
§ 14-7-2; SL 1975, ch 158, § 2.

14-7-14. Agreements submitted to state librarian for recommendations.
Every library agreement made pursuant to Article VI
of the compact shall, as a condition precedent to its entry into force,
be submitted to the state librarian for his recommendations.

Source: SL 1973, ch 125; SDCL Supp,
§ 14-7-5; SL 1975, ch 158, § 3.

14-7-15. Agreements to comply with tax levy and bond laws.
No public library of this state shall be party to a library agreement
which provides for the construction or maintenance of a library pursuant to Article III, subdivision (c) 7 of the compact, nor levy a tax or
issue bonds to contribute to the construction or maintenance of such
a library, except after compliance with any laws applicable to public
libraries relating to or governing the levying of taxes or the issuance
of bonds.

Source: SL 1975, ch 158, § 4.

14-7-16. State library office as "state library agency." As used
in the compact, "state library agency," with reference to this state,
means the state library office.

Source: SL 1975, ch 158, § 5.

14-7-17. Withdrawal notices. In the event of withdrawal from the
compact, the compact administrator shall send and receive any notices
required by Article XI (b) of the compact.

Source: SL 1975, ch 158, § 6.

14-7-18. Citation of chapter. This chapter may be cited as the
Interstate Library Compact.

Source: SL 1975, ch 158, § 7.

ARCHIVES RESOURCE CENTER
(South Dakota Codified Laws, 1982, s.1-18C-1 to 1-18C-13.)

1-18C-1. Definition of terms. Terms as used in this chapter, unless
the context otherwise requires, shall mean:
  (1) "State agency," any department, division, office, commission,

court, board, or any other unit or body, however designated, of the state government. The provisions of this chapter shall not extend to agencies of county and municipal government except in those instances when records of said agencies are in danger of deterioration, destruction, or loss and when the state archivist is willing and able to receive said records;

(2) "Agency head," the chief or principal official or representative in any such agency, or the presiding judge of any state court, by whatever title known;

(3) "Agency records," any book, document, paper, photograph, microfilm, sound recording, or other material, regardless of physical form or characteristics, made or received pursuant to law, charter, ordinance or other authority, in connection with the transaction of official business and which is normally maintained within the custody or control of a state agency;

(4) "Archival resources," those noncurrent state records which are no longer essential to the functioning of the agency of origin and which the state archivist determines to have permanent value for research, reference, or other usage appropriate to document the organization, function, policies, and transactions of state government.

Source: SL 1975, ch 24, § 1.

1-18C-2.   Center established within office of cultural preservation. There is hereby established in the office of cultural preservation an archives resource center. The center shall constitute one program within the office of cultural preservation in the department of education and cultural affairs.

Source: SL 1975, ch 24, §§ 2, 3.

1-18C-3.   State archivist — Appointment and compensation. The archives resource center shall be administered by a state archivist who shall be appointed by the secretary of the department of education and cultural affairs, subject to the Governor's approval, and shall serve at the pleasure of the secretary. Compensation for the state archivist, hereinafter called the archivist, shall be determined according to guidelines established by the bureau of personnel and within the limits of available appropriations.

Source: SL 1975, ch 24, § 3; 1979, ch 353, § 13.

1-18C-4.   Duty of archivist — Policies and procedures. It shall be the duty of the state archivist to administer the archives resource center. In exercising his administration, the archivist shall formulate policies, establish organizational and operational procedures, and exercise general supervision pursuant to the objectives and purposes of the archives resource center.

Source: SL 1975, ch 24, § 4.

1-18C-5. Archivist as official custodian of archival resources — Records. The archivist shall be the official custodian of the archival resources of the state, and it shall be his duty to assemble, preserve, and service the permanently valuable records of the state. It shall be his duty to receive all records transferred to the archives for permanent retention and to negotiate for the transfer of any records in the custody of a state agency. It shall be his responsibility to make the records in his custody available to serve the administrative and informational needs of state government and the people of the state of South Dakota.

Source: SL 1975, ch 24, § 5.

1-18C-6. Employment of additional personnel by secretary. Within limits of available appropriations and according to guidelines established by the bureau of personnel, the secretary of education and cultural affairs shall have authority to hire additional trained personnel in order to more efficiently index, catalog, and otherwise make accessible to state agencies and the public the permanently valuable records in the custody of the archives resource center.

Source: SL 1975, ch 24, § 11; 1979, ch 353, § 14.

1-18C-7. Acquisition of records submitted to records destruction board. The archivist shall have authority to acquire, in total or in part, any records, regardless of physical characteristics, which have been submitted to the records destruction board for final disposition when such material is determined to be of informational or historical significance by the archivist.

Source: SL 1975, ch 24, § 6.

1-18C-8. Receipts for archival resources acquired — Copies. The archivist shall prepare receipts for any archival resources acquired under provisions of this law, and shall deliver one copy to the state records manager and one copy to the agency head from which the records were obtained, and retain one or more copies for use in the archives resource center.

Source: SL 1975, ch 24, § 9.

1-18C-9. Safeguarding of restricted records. The archivist shall take all precautions necessary to ensure that records placed in his custody, the use of which is restricted by or pursuant to law or for reasons of security and the public interest, shall be inspected, surveyed, or otherwise used only in accordance with law and the rules and regulations imposed by the archivist in consultation with the agency of origin.

Source: SL 1975, ch 24, § 8.

1-18C-10. Availability of archival resources to public and state agencies — Protection and preservation. The archivist shall make archival resources under his supervision available to state agencies and to the public at reasonable times, subject to appropriate restrictions and regulations. He shall carefully protect and preserve such materials from deterioration, destruction, or loss through application of appropriate techniques for preserving archival and library materials.

Source: SL 1975, ch 24, § 11.

1-18C-11. Publications authorized — Price. The archivist shall have authority to publish archival material, reports, bulletins, and other publications which will further the objectives of the office of state archivist and the archives resource center. He shall, consistent with existing laws, establish the price at which publications may be sold or delivered.

Source: SL 1975, ch 24, § 12.

1-18C-12. Rules adoption. Any rules adopted by the state archivist shall be adopted in accordance with the provisions of chapter 1-26.

Source: SL 1975, ch 24, § 13.

1-18C-13. Annual report to cultural preservation office. The state archivist shall report annually to the office of cultural preservation any facts and recommendations relating to the work and needs of the archives resource center.

Source: SL 1975, ch 24, § 14.

PUBLIC RECORDS
(South Dakota Codified Laws, 1982, s.1-27-9 to 1-27-19.)

1-27-9. Records management programs — Definition of terms.
As used in §§ 1-27-9 to 1-27-18, inclusive:
(1) "State agency" or "agency" or "agencies" includes all state officers, boards, commissions, departments, institutions and agencies of state government.
(2) "Record" means document, book, paper, photograph, sound recording, or other material, regardless of physical form or

characteristics, made or received pursuant to law or ordinance or in connection with the transaction of official business. Library and museum material made or acquired and preserved solely for reference or exhibition purposes, extra copies of documents preserved only for convenience of reference, and stocks of publications and of processed documents are not included within the definition of records as used in §§ 1-27-9 to 1-27-18, inclusive.

(3) "State record" means:

    (a) A record of a department, office, commission, board or other agency, however designated, of the state government.

    (b) A record of the state Legislature.

    (c) A record of any court of record, whether of state-wide or local jurisdiction.

    (d) Any other record designated or treated as a state record under state law.

(4) "Local record" means a record of a county, city, town, township, district, authority or any public corporation or political entity whether organized and existing under charter or under general law, unless the record is designated or treated as a state record under state law.

Source: SL 1967, ch 253, § 1.

1-27-10. Records as property of state — Damage or disposal only as authorized by law.

All records made or received by, or under the authority of, or coming into the custody, control, or possession of public officials of this state in the course of their public duties, are the property of the state and shall not be mutilated, destroyed, transferred, removed, or otherwise damaged or disposed of, in whole or in part, except as provided by law.

Source: SL 1967, ch 253, § 6.

1-27-11. Board to supervise destruction of records — State records manager as ex officio member — Permission required for destruction.

There is hereby created a board consisting of the commissioner of administration, state auditor, attorney general, auditor-general, and state archivist to supervise and authorize the destruction of records. The state records manager shall also serve as an ex officio member in an advisory capacity only. No record shall be destroyed or otherwise disposed of by any agency of the state unless it is determined by majority vote of such board that the record has no further administrative, legal, fiscal, research or historical value.

Source: SL 1967, ch 253, § 7; 1975, ch 20; 1976, ch 19, § 2.

1-27-11.1. Direction and supervision of board by bureau of administration — Independent functions retained. The board created by § 1-27-11 shall be administered under the direction and supervision of the bureau of administration and the commissioner thereof, but shall retain the quasi-judicial, quasi-legislative, advisory, other nonadministrative and special budgetary functions (as defined in § 1-32-1) otherwise vested in it and shall exercise those functions independently of the commissioner of administration.

Source: SL 1974, ch 3, § 5 (a).

1-27-12. State records management program to be established. The commissioner of administration shall establish within the organizational structure of the bureau of administration a records management program, which will apply efficient and economical management methods to the creation, utilization, maintenance, retention, preservation and disposal of state records.

Source: SL 1967, ch 253, § 2.

1-27-13. Records management procedures proposed by state agencies. The head of each agency shall submit to the commissioner of administration, in accordance with the rules, regulations, standards, and procedures established by him, schedules proposing the length of time each state record series warrants retention for administrative, legal, or fiscal purposes after it has been received by the agency.

Source: SL 1967, ch 253, § 3.

1-27-14. Obsolete records listed by state agencies. The head of each agency, also, shall submit lists of state records in his custody that are not needed in the transaction of current business and that do not have sufficient administrative, legal or fiscal value to warrant further keeping for disposal in conformity with the requirements of § 1-27-11.

Source: SL 1967, ch 253, § 3.

1-27-14.1. Transfer of records by outgoing agency heads — Terminated agency records. Upon termination of employment with the state, each agency head shall transfer his records to his successor or to the archives resource center for appraisal and permanent retention, unless otherwise directed by law. The records of any state agency shall, upon termination of its existence or functions, be transferred to the custody of the archivist, unless otherwise directed by law.

Source: SL 1975, ch 24, § 7.

1-27-14.2. Transfer of jeopardized nonessential agency material to state archivist. In any case where material of actual or potential archival significance is determined by a state agency to be in jeopardy of destruction or deterioration, and such material is not essential to the conduct of daily business in the agency of origin, the agency head shall have authority to transfer said records to the physical and legal custody of the state archivist whenever the archivist is willing and able to receive them.

Source: SL 1975, ch 24, § 10.

1-27-14.3. Title to transferred records pending formal transfer. Records transferred to the physical custody of the archivist remain the legal property of the agency of origin, subject to all existing copyrights and statutory provisions regulating their usage, until such time as the agency head formally transfers legal title to the archivist.

Source: SL 1975, ch 24, § 8.

1-27-15. Destruction of nonrecord materials. Nonrecord material or materials not included within the definition of records as contained in § 1-27-9 may, if not otherwise prohibited by law, be destroyed at any time by the agency in possession of such materials without the prior approval of the commissioner of administration.

Source: SL 1967, ch 253, § 8.

1-27-16. Rules, standards and procedures. The commissioner of administration shall promulgate such rules, standards, and procedures as are necessary or proper to effectuate the purposes of §§ 1-27-9 to 1-27-18, inclusive, except that rules, standards, and procedures relating to disposal of records pursuant to § 1-27-11 shall be issued by the board created by § 1-27-11.

Source: SL 1967, ch 253, § 9; 1976, ch 18.

1-27-17. Legislative and judicial records management programs. Upon request, the commissioner of administration shall assist and advise in the establishment of records management programs in the legislative and judicial branches of state government and may, as required by them, provide program services similar to those available to the executive branch of state government pursuant to the provisions of §§ 1-27-9 to 1-27-16, inclusive.

Source: SL 1967, ch 253, § 5.

1-27-18. Local records management programs. The governing body of each county, city, town, township, district, authority or any public corporation or political entity, whether organized and existing under charter or under general law, shall promote the principles of efficient records management for local records. Such governing body may, as far as practical, follow the program established for the management of state records. The commissioner of administration may, upon the request of a governing body, provide advice and assistance in the establishment of a local records management program.

Source: SL 1967, ch 253, § 4.

1-27-19.   Annual meeting to authorize destruction of political subdivision records. The state record destruction board shall meet at least once each year and consider requests of all political subdivisions for the destruction of records and to authorize their destruction as in the case of state records.

Source: SDC Supp 1960, § 55.2012 as added by SL 1967, ch 254.

MISCELLANEOUS PROVISIONS
(South Dakota Codified Laws, 1982, 1-18B-2, 1-28-2, 16-1-14, 13-1-31.)

1-18B-2.   Preservation and publication of historical material by board — Activities authorized. In addition to the other duties imposed upon it by law, it shall be the duty of the board to collect, preserve, exhibit, and publish material for the study of history, especially the history of this and adjacent states; and to this end to explore the archaeology of the region; acquire documents and manuscripts; obtain narratives and records of pioneers; conduct a library of historical reference; maintain a gallery of historical portraiture, and an ethnological and historical museum; publish and otherwise diffuse information relating to the history of the region and, in general, encourage and develop within the state the study of history.

Source: SL 1974, ch 9, § 2.

1-28-2.   Annual agency reports — Period covered and time of filing — Distribution to libraries and Legislature — Misdemeanor. All state agencies shall make annual reports to the Governor. Such reports shall be made for the period ending June thirtieth and filed in duplicate as soon thereafter as possible, and not later than the thirtieth day of June of the following year. In addition fourteen copies shall be deposited with the state library commission for distribution under the provisions of chapter 14-1A. Copies shall be distributed to the Legislature or any member thereon upon request. A violation of this section is a Class 2 misdemeanor.   Source: SL 1980, ch 24, § 13.

16-1-14.   Supreme Court library—Publications included — Control by judges.—The Supreme Court library shall consist of all constitutions, statutes, session laws, court reports, digests, text-books and other legal publications now owned by the state and under the control of the judges of the Supreme Court, or which may hereafter be acquired by purchase, exchange, or otherwise.

The Supreme Court library shall be under the exclusive control and supervision of the judges of the Supreme Court who are hereby authorized to make such rules and regulations regarding its use as they may deem proper.

Source: SL 1907, ch 183, §§ 1, 2; RC 1919, § 5160; SDC 1939 & Supp 1960, § 32.0311.

13-1-31. School library supervision — No minimum expenditures. The state board of education shall have supervision over school libraries and shall adopt such rules as it deems necessary to govern them. The board may not require minimum library expenditures.

Source: SDC Supp 1960, § 15.0803 as added by SL 1967, ch 37, § 1; 1975, ch 128, § 10; 1980, ch 118.

South Dakota library laws are reprinted from SOUTH DAKOTA CODIFIED LAWS published by The Allen Smith Co., Indianapolis, Indiana.

TENNESSEE

STATE LIBRARY SYSTEM
General Provisions
(Tennessee Code Annotated, 1982, s.10-1-101 to 10-1-10.)

10-1-101. Division of public libraries and archives. — A division of public libraries and archives is hereby created within and administratively attached to the office of the secretary of state. The authority, powers, and duties formerly vested by law in the commissioner of the department of education shall be vested in the secretary of state and in the state library and archives management board, created by § 10-1-102, to be administered through and by the division of public libraries and archives. The division of public libraries and archives shall have transferred and attached to it:

(1) The office of state historian; and

(2) All historical and memorial commissions and associations created by act of the general assembly and expending public funds, for purposes of administration. [Acts 1959, ch. 9, § 12; 1975, ch. 143, § 2; T.C.A., § 10-101; Acts 1982 (Adj. S.), ch. 689, § 1.]

10-1-102. State library and archives management board. — There is hereby created the state library and archives management board. The board shall consist of the following five (5) members: the secretary of state, the state treasurer or his designee, the comptroller of the treasury or his designee, the commissioner of the department of education or his designee, and the commissioner of the department of finance and administration or his designee.

The secretary of state shall serve as chairman and chief administrative officer of the management board. The state librarian and archivist shall serve as executive secretary to the management board. The board shall adopt rules for the transaction of business and shall keep a record of all of its proceedings which record and proceedings shall be open to the public. The board shall: adopt by-laws to govern the conduct of its business, fix a number which shall constitute a quorum, provide for the calling of special meetings and otherwise establish orderly procedures for the conduct of its affairs. The board shall prepare such reports, statements and evidences of its operation as may be required by the governor or by the general assembly for submission to them at such time as they may require.

The management board shall meet quarterly, or more frequently, for the transaction of business. All meetings of this board shall be conducted in accordance with the provisions of chapter 44 of title 8. The management board shall serve as the chief policy-making body for the division of public libraries and archives on matters affecting the state libraries and archives system. The management board shall annually prepare and submit a budget request to the governor and to the general assembly and shall act as advocate for the budgetary needs of the division of public libraries and archives as reflected in such budget.

The secretary of state, acting through the state librarian and archivist and the division of public libraries and archives, shall take appropriate action to execute the rules, regulations, policies and programs adopted by the management board. [Acts 1951, ch. 197, §§ 1, 2 (Williams, §§ 2278.1, 2278.2); 1959, ch. 9, § 12; 1976 (Adj. S.), ch. 806, § 1(47); T.C.A. (orig. ed.), § 10-102; Acts 1982 (Adj. S.), ch. 689, § 2.]

10-1-103. State library system, of what it consists. — The state library system shall consist of the existing state library, archives, regional library for the blind and physically handicapped and library extension properties and services and such other properties and services as may from time to time be assigned to the division of public libraries and archives, excluding the law library of the state, which functions under the direction of the Supreme Court. [Acts 1951, ch. 197, § 2 (Williams, § 2278.3); impl. am. Acts 1959, ch. 9, § 12; Acts 1976 (Adj. S.), ch. 458, § 1; T.C.A. (orig. ed.), § 10-103.]

10-1-104. Functions of division. — The functions of the management board acting through the division of public libraries and archives shall include specifically the following:

(1) The collection and preservation of archival material and materials of historical, documentary and reference value, and such literary works or printed matter as may be considered by the division of special interest to the citizenship of Tennessee;

(2) The distribution and exchange of such publications of the state as may become available from time to time;

(3) The collection and distribution of reference material to state officials and employees and such public agencies as may be entitled thereto;

(4) The encouragement of library development throughout the state by means of advice, guidance, and library extension services, in the course of which the division is empowered to enter into local, regional or interstate

contracts with competent agencies in the furtherance of library services;

(5) Such other functions as may be designated and authorized from time to time or as may properly belong to the administration of an up-to-date library and archives for the state.

The enumeration of the specific items above shall not be deemed to exclude any other activities that the division may think proper to be handled by it and by the state librarian and archivist. [Acts 1951, ch. 197, § 2 (Williams, § 2278.4); impl. am. Acts 1959, ch. 9, § 12; T.C.A. (orig. ed.), § 10-104; Acts 1982 (Adj. S.), ch. 689, § 4.]

10-1-105. Administration of system — Custody of property — Circulation of books. — The management board acting through the division of public libraries and archives shall be responsible for the proper administration of this chapter and shall establish policies to govern the administration of the state library system. Such division shall have custody of and be responsible for the properties of the state library system, including such properties as may be assigned to it in the future. The management board shall establish such policies, rules, and regulations as may be deemed by it necessary to govern the use of such properties and the use and disposition of materials under its jurisdiction, including the circulation of books from the library. [Acts 1951, ch. 197, § 2 (Williams, § 2278.5); impl. am. Acts 1959, ch. 9, § 12; T.C.A. (orig. ed.), § 10-105; Acts 1982 (Adj. S.), ch. 689, § 5.]

10-1-106. Development of program — Budget. — The management board shall develop a state library program calculated to meet the needs of the state and the requirements of its citizens for such services. The management board shall annually prepare and submit to the governor and to the general assembly a budget consistent with such program and shall operate the state library system within the financial resources available. The management board shall take appropriate action each year to encourage adoption of its budget proposal. [Acts 1951, ch. 197, § 2 (Williams, § 2278.5); impl. am. Acts 1959, ch. 9, § 12; T.C.A. (orig. ed.), § 10-106; Acts 1982 (Adj. S.), ch. 689, § 6.]

10-1-107. Employment of necessary personnel. — In order effectively to carry on its program, the management board shall have authority to create such positions and make such employments as are deemed necessary to conduct the affairs of the library program and to expend funds for the special training and formal education of library personnel, provided such personnel shall agree to work in the state library system for at least two (2) years after the completion of said training and education. [Acts 1951, ch. 197, § 2 (Williams, § 2278.5); impl. am. Acts 1959, ch. 9, § 12; Acts 1965, ch. 223, § 1; T.C.A. (orig. ed.), § 10-107; Acts 1982 (Adj. S.), ch. 689, § 7.]

10-1-108. Cooperation with other agencies. — The management board shall have authority to call upon other state agencies for information, publications and related material needed to discharge its duties and may confer and cooperate with other agencies, whether federal, state or local, in order more effectively to carry out the program, it being the legislative intent that this chapter shall be broadly construed and applied in the interest of making the state library function to the best advantage of the citizenship of the state. [Acts 1951, ch. 197, § 3 (Williams, § 2278.7); impl. am. Acts 1959, ch. 9, § 12; T.C.A. (orig. ed.), § 10-110; Acts 1982 (Adj. S.), ch. 689, § 8.]

10-1-109. Administering funds and materials. — The management board is authorized to accept and administer funds or materials made available for library, archival, and historical purposes from public or private sources either by grant, bequest, donation or otherwise, and this may include any available grants from the federal government or cooperation with the federal government in the advancement of library activities when agreements to that effect are approved by the management board. [Acts 1951, ch. 197, § 4 (Williams, § 2278.8); impl. am. Acts 1959, ch. 9, § 12; T.C.A. (orig. ed.), § 10-111; Acts 1982 (Adj. S.), ch. 689, § 9.]

10-1-110. Physically handicapped — Blind. — The management board is authorized:

(a) To cooperate with the division for the blind and physically handicapped in the library of congress in planning and conducting a program of bringing free reading materials and related services and other library services to blind and physically handicapped residents of the state;

(b) To establish and implement eligibility and certification standards and rules and regulations for these services;

(c) To produce and distribute, and to contract with competent organizations and agencies for the production of and distribution of reading materials and related library services in the conduct of this program;

(d) To cooperate in making sound reproduction equipment and other reading equipment available to the blind and physically handicapped persons; and

(e) To establish and maintain local or regional centers as the library of congress may designate for the loan of reading materials, reproducers and other library materials to eligible readers in the state; provided, however, that nothing in this section shall be construed to interfere with or supersede the rules and regulations of the library of congress in the loan of library materials and reading equipment for blind and physically handicapped persons. [Acts 1976 (Adj. S.), ch. 458, § 2; T.C.A., § 10-114; Acts 1982 (Adj. S.), ch. 689, § 10.]

State Librarian and Archivist
(Tennessee Code Annotated, 1982, s.10-1-201 to 10-1-204, 10-1-301.)

10-1-201. Appointment — Duties and powers. — The management board shall have authority to appoint a state librarian and archivist to serve at the will of the management board for an indefinite term, who shall be subject to removal for cause. The person appointed as librarian and archivist shall be appointed without regard to political affiliation or place of previous residence.

He shall serve as chief administrative officer of the state library system and shall be responsible to the management board, shall attend all meetings of the state library and archives management board and shall have a voice but no vote in the proceedings. He shall have the power to make appointments to all subordinate positions which may be created by the management board and may dismiss or remove subordinate employees when he may deem that action for the best interests of the service, but only subject to approval of the management board. His personnel actions, however, shall conform with existing applicable civil service or other standardized state personnel procedures and regulations. He shall be responsible for the proper execution of policies as defined by the management board, shall carry out the management board's rules and regulations and shall submit such reports, estimates, documents, statements or other evidences pertaining to the operation of the library system as the management board, governor, or general assembly may require. [Acts 1951, ch. 197, § 2 (Williams, § 2278.6); impl. am. Acts 1959, ch. 9, § 12; T.C.A. (orig. ed.), § 10-108; Acts 1982 (Adj. S.), ch. 689, § 11.]

10-1-202. Authority to employ special consultants. — Subject to the direction and approval of the management board and within the limitation of funds available, the state librarian and archivist may engage the services of special consultants who are qualified in particular fields of library or archival administration, may make special investigations, studies and reports looking to the proper development of methods and procedures by means of which the state library service may be strengthened, extended, or made more efficient. The services of such consultants shall be rendered under a formal contract, stipulating, insofar as practicable, the services to be furnished, the cost thereof and the time within which such work shall be completed. Such contracts shall be approved in advance by the management board. [Acts 1951, ch. 197, § 2 (Williams, § 2278.6); impl. am. Acts 1959, ch. 9, § 12; T.C.A. (orig. ed.), § 10-109; Acts 1982 (Adj. S.), ch. 689, § 12.]

10-1-203. Preservation of records of soldiers and sailors serving in World War I. — The compilation of the records of the soldiers and sailors who served in World War I by enlistment from the state of Tennessee, compiled by Mrs. Rutledge Smith of Nashville, and a committee working under her supervision, consisting of separate volumes for each county, are declared to be public records of the state, and shall be carefully preserved by the state librarian and archivist as a part of the official records of this state, and copies thereof, duly certified by the state librarian and archivist, shall be receivable in evidence in all courts of competent jurisdiction in this state as to the truth of the facts therein recited. [Acts 1937, ch. 301, §§ 1, 3; mod. C. Supp. 1950, § 2287.1 (Williams, §§ 2287.1, 2287.3); impl. am. Acts 1951, ch. 197, § 2; T.C.A. (orig. ed.), § 10-112.]

10-1-204. Federal funds for library programs. — The state librarian and archivist, acting with the approval of the management board, is authorized and empowered to make agreements with the United States and its agencies in regard to the administration of library programs, and to accept federal funds upon such terms and conditions as may be required by act of congress or rules and regulations issued in accordance with such act; provided, however, state funds shall not be obligated for participation in any federal program unless the same are paid from current appropriations or operating funds. If required, the state treasurer shall give his receipt for such funds, make a special bond for the same, or keep special accounts of such funds. At the end of this or succeeding bienniums, such funds shall not become a part of the state's general fund but shall be expended only for such library purposes as may have been agreed upon. [Acts 1957, ch. 84, § 1; impl. am. Acts 1959, ch. 9, § 12; T.C.A., § 10-113; Acts 1982 (Adj. S.), ch. 689, § 13.]

10-1-301. General provisions. — (a) There is hereby created a commission of five (5) members to be known as the state library and archives advisory commission of Tennessee, with the members of said commission to be appointed by the governor. Such members shall be broadly representative of the grand divisions of the state, urban and rural libraries, librarians, trustees of libraries, patrons of libraries, library associations or professional librarian organizations. The term of each member shall be six (6) years except as to initial appointees, two (2) commissioners having been appointed for terms to expire June 30, 1984, two (2) having been appointed for terms to expire June 30, 1986 and one (1) having been appointed for a term to expire June 30, 1988. All subsequent appointments shall be for six (6) year terms expiring on June 30 of the appropriate year in each instance. Any vacancy shall be filled by the governor for the unexpired term.

(b) All members of said library commission shall serve without compensation but shall be reimbursed for all travel expenses in accordance with the provisions of the comprehensive travel regulations as promulgated by the department of finance and administration and approved by the attorney general.

(c) The commission shall meet and organize and elect a chairman from among its membership to serve for one (1) year. The commission shall adopt rules for the transaction of business and shall keep a record of all its proceedings which record and proceedings shall be open to the public. The commission shall adopt by-laws to govern the conduct of its business, fix a number which shall constitute a quorum, provide for the calling of special meetings and otherwise establish orderly procedures for the conduct of its affairs. The commission shall prepare such reports and statements as may be required by the management board.

(d) This commission shall meet annually or more frequently for the transaction of business. The chairman of the commission or a majority of its members may call a meeting, unless it shall adopt a contrary rule or by-laws.

(e) The state library and archives commission shall function as an advisory body to the state library and archives board who may implement the policies and programs of said commission affecting the state libraries and archives. [Acts 1982 (Adj. S.), ch. 689, § 3.]

REGIONAL LIBRARY BOARDS
(Tennessee Code Annotated, 1982, s.10-5-101 to 10-5-107.)

10-5-101. Agreements to create regional boards — Participation by municipalities. — Two (2) or more counties, which have qualified for participation in the state's multi-county regional library program and have been recognized as a region by the state library and archives management board, and have made the minimum local appropriation of funds as may now or hereafter be required by such management board are hereby empowered and authorized to execute contracts with each other to create a regional library board to administer and control the regional library services within the region. Each county shall be represented by two (2) members of the regional library board. The contract shall be authorized by a resolution of the legislative body of the county desiring to participate and the county executive shall execute the contract as authorized in the resolution, and such contract shall be attested by the county clerk. After the governing body of a county authorizes participation, municipalities within the county may participate in the regional library service so long as the county participates. Counties and municipalities may appropriate funds for this purpose. A single county, which is large enough to constitute a region and has been so recognized by the state library and archives management board, may also create a regional library board by executing a contract between the county and one (1) or more cities within the county. There shall be at least seven (7) board members apportioned among county and municipalities according to the ratio of population in each participating municipality and in the county outside the municipalities, based on the most recent federal census. [Acts 1955, ch. 88, § 1; 1961, ch. 73, § 1; impl. am. Acts 1978 (Adj. S.), ch. 934, §§ 7, 16, 22, 36; T.C.A., § 10-601; Acts 1982 (Adj. S.), ch. 689, § 14.]

10-5-102. Members of regional board. — At least one member shall be elected by the legislative body of each county in a multi-county region for a term of three (3) years in accordance with the contract between the counties and as provided in § 10-5-101. In accordance with the contract between the counties and as provided in § 10-5-101, the governing body of any municipality which contributes as much as one fourth (¼) of the public funds available for the operation of a joint city-county system may elect one (1) of the two (2) members representing that county for a term of three (3) years. If more than one municipality is entitled to elect a member, these municipalities shall alternate in electing one (1) member for a three-year term.

A member shall represent and reside in the county or municipality from which he was elected. In the event that a member removes his residence from the county or municipality from which he was elected, he shall thereby vacate his office. In the event of any vacancy in office a successor shall be elected for the unexpired term at the next meeting of the governing body of the county or city in which the vacancy occurred. No member shall be elected for more than two (2) successive terms. Every member of the regional library board who is not an active member of a county library board is hereby designated an ex officio member of such county board. A member of the regional library board may be an active member of a county library board. [Acts 1955, ch. 88, § 2; 1961, ch. 73, § 2; impl. am. Acts 1978, ch. 934, §§ 7, 36; T.C.A., § 10-602.]

10-5-103. Powers — Execution of contracts. — The regional library board shall have authority to execute contracts with the state library and archives management board, with the county library boards of the respective counties, with the municipal library boards, and any and all other agencies, for the purpose of administering a public library service within the region, and including contracts concerning funds and their expenditure as may be allocated by virtue of such contracts, to the same extent as any one of the counties which are parties to the agreement would be so authorized. [Acts 1955, ch. 88, § 3; impl. am. Acts 1959, ch. 9, § 12; T.C.A., § 10-603; Acts 1982 (Adj. S.), ch. 689, § 15.]

10-5-104. County and city appropriations — Reports by regional board. — The county legislative bodies and municipal governing bodies of counties and cities entering such contracts are hereby authorized to appropriate to the regional library board such funds as may be deemed necessary to supplement the funds received by that board through contract with the state library and archives management board. However, such funds shall be expended only for the library service for which the county or city contracted and for no other purpose. The regional library board shall make a detailed report of receipts and disbursements of all funds at the first regular meeting of the legislative body of every participating county and the governing body of every participating city after the close of the state's fiscal year. It shall make a similar report to the state library and archives management board. The treasurer of the board shall be bonded for an amount to be determined by the state library and archives management board. Bond premiums may be paid from state funds. [Acts 1955, ch. 88, § 4; impl. am. Acts 1959, ch. 9, § 12; impl. am. Acts 1978 (Adj. S.), ch. 934, §§ 7, 36; T.C.A., § 10-604; Acts 1982 (Adj. S.), ch. 689, § 16.]

10-5-105. Personnel — Salaries — Expenditures. — The board may employ such personnel as may be necessary provided that all persons regularly employed and salaries paid to such persons shall be in accordance with the terms of the contract between the board and the state library and archives management board. In no event shall the expenditure of funds for this or any other purpose exceed the allotments from the state library and archives management board, appropriations to the board by the county legislative bodies or municipal governing bodies for the fiscal year, income, and/or gifts on hand. [Acts 1955, ch. 88, § 5; impl. am. Acts 1959, ch. 9, § 12; impl. am. Acts 1978 (Adj. S.), ch. 934, §§ 7, 36; T.C.A., § 10-605; Acts 1982 (Adj. S.), ch. 689, § 17.]

10-5-106.   Donations — Lease of realty — Discontinuance. — The board is authorized to accept donations and bequests. It may lease such real estate as may be necessary for library purposes subject to the contracts between the state library and archives management board and the library boards of the participating counties. Every lease for more than one year shall contain a clause that its continuance shall be subject to necessary allotments from the state library and archives management board and the availability of other funds. In the event that the regional board is discontinued, the property administered by the board shall revert to the state library and archives management board and/or the several county or municipal library boards in accordance with the contracts between the regional board, state library and archives management board, and the county and municipal library boards. [Acts 1955, ch. 88, § 6; impl. am. Acts 1959, ch. 9, § 12; T.C.A., § 10-606; Acts 1982 (Adj. S.), ch. 689, § 18.]

10-5-107.   Boards not mandatory. — The formation and creation of such boards shall in no wise be considered or construed in any manner as mandatory upon any county by virtue of this chapter. [Acts 1955, ch. 88, § 7; T.C.A., § 10-607.]

INTERSTATE LIBRARY COMPACT
(Tennessee Code Annotated, 1982, s.10-6-101 to 10-6-106.)

10-6-101.   Enactment — Text. — The interstate library compact is hereby enacted into law and entered into by this state, with all states legally joining therein in the form substantially as follows:

INTERSTATE LIBRARY COMPACT

Article I. Policy and Purpose

Because the desire for the services provided by libraries transcends governmental boundaries and can most effectively be satisfied by giving such services to communities and people regardless of jurisdictional lines, it is the policy of the states party to this compact to cooperate and share their responsibilities; to authorize cooperation and sharing with respect to those types of library facilities and services which can be more economically or efficiently developed and maintained on a cooperative basis, and to authorize cooperation and sharing among localities, states and others in providing joint or cooperative library services in areas where the distribution of population or of existing and potential library resources makes the provision of library service on an interstate basis the most effective way of providing adequate and efficient service.

Article II. Definitions

As used in this compact:

(a) "Public library agency" means any unit or agency of local or state government operating or having power to operate a library.

(b) "Private library agency" means any nongovernmental entity which operates or assumes a legal obligation to operate a library.

(c) "Library agreement" means a contract establishing an interstate library district pursuant to this compact or providing for the joint or cooperative furnishing of library services.

Article III. Interstate Library Districts

(a) Any one or more public library agencies in a party state in cooperation with any public library agency or agencies in one or more other party states may establish and maintain an interstate library district. Subject to the provisions of this compact and any other laws of the party states which pursuant hereto remain applicable, such district may establish, maintain and operate some or all of the library facilities and services for the area concerned in accordance with the terms of a library agreement therefor. Any private library agency or agencies within an interstate library district may cooperate therewith, assume duties, responsibilities and obligations thereto, and receive benefits therefrom as provided in any library agreement to which such agency or agencies become party.

(b) Within an interstate library district, and as provided by a library agreement, the performance of library functions may be undertaken on a joint or cooperative basis or may be undertaken by means of one or more arrangements between or among public or private library agencies for the extension of library privileges to the use of facilities or services operated or rendered by one or more of the individual library agencies.

(c) If a library agreement provides for joint establishment, maintenance or operation of library or services by an interstate library district, such district shall have power to do any one or more of the following in accordance with such library agreement:

(1) Undertake, administer and participate in programs or arrangements for securing, lending or servicing of books and other publications, any other materials suitable to be kept or made available by libraries, library equipment or for the dissemination of information about libraries, the value and significance of particular items therein, and the use thereof.

(2) Accept for any of its purposes under this compact any and all donations, and grants of money, equipment, supplies, materials and services (conditional or otherwise) from any state of the United States or any subdivision or agency thereof, or interstate agency, or from any institution, person, firm or corporation and receive, utilize and dispose of the same.

(3) Operate mobile library units or equipment for the purpose of rendering bookmobile service within the district.

(4) Employ professional, technical, clerical and other personnel, and fix terms of employment, compensation and other appropriate benefits; and where desirable, provide for the in-service training of such personnel.

(5) Sue and be sued in any court of competent jurisdiction.

(6) Acquire, hold and dispose of any real or personal property or any interest or interests therein as may be appropriate to the rendering of library service.

(7) Construct, maintain and operate a library, including any appropriate branches thereof.

(8) Do such other things as may be incidental to or appropriate for the carrying out of any of the foregoing powers.

Article IV. Interstate Library Districts, Governing Board

(a) An interstate library district which establishes, maintains or operates any facilities or services in its own right shall have a governing board which shall direct the affairs of the district and act for it in all matters relating to its business. Each participating public library agency in the district shall be represented on the governing board which shall be organized and conduct its business in accordance with provision therefor in the library agreement. But in no event shall a governing board meet less often than twice a year.

(b) Any private library agency or agencies party to a library agreement establishing an interstate library district may be represented on or advise with the governing board of the district in such manner as the library agreement may provide.

Article V. State Library Agency Cooperation

Any two (2) or more state library agencies of two (2) or more of the party states may undertake and conduct joint or cooperative library programs, render joint or cooperative library services, and enter into and perform arrangements for the cooperative or joint acquisition, use, housing and disposition of items or collections of materials which, by reason of expense, rarity, specialized nature, or infrequency of demand therefor, would be appropriate for central collection and shared use. Any such programs, services or arrangements may include provision for the exercise on a cooperative or joint basis of any power exercisable by an interstate library district and an agreement embodying any such program, service or arrangement shall contain provisions covering the subjects detailed in article VI of this compact for interstate library agreements.

Article VI. Library Agreements

(a) In order to provide for any joint or cooperative undertaking pursuant to this compact, public and private library agencies may enter into library agreements. Any agreement executed pursuant to the provisions of this compact shall as among the parties to the agreement:

(1) Detail the specific nature of the services, programs, facilities, arrangements or properties to which it is applicable.

(2) Provide for the allocation of costs and other financial responsibilities.

(3) Specify the respective rights, duties, obligations and liabilities of the parties.

(4) Set forth the terms and conditions for duration, renewal, termination, abrogation, disposal of joint or common property, if any, and all other matters which may be appropriate to the proper effectuation and performance of the agreement.

(b) No public or private library agency shall undertake to exercise itself, or jointly with any other library agency, by means of a library agreement any power prohibited to such agency by the constitution or statutes of its state.

(c) No library agreement shall become effective until filed with the compact administrator of each state involved, and approved in accordance with article VII of this compact.

Article VII. Approval of Library Agreements

(a) Every library agreement made pursuant to this compact shall, prior to and as a condition precedent to its entry into force, be submitted to the attorney general of each state in which a public library agency party thereto is situated, who shall determine whether the agreement is in proper form and compatible with the laws of his state. The attorneys general shall approve any agreement submitted to them unless they shall find that it does not meet the conditions set forth herein and shall detail in writing, addressed to the governing bodies of the public library agencies, concerning the specific respects in which the proposed agreement fails to meet the requirements of law. Failure to disapprove an agreement submitted hereunder within ninety (90) days of its submission shall constitute approval thereof.

(b) In the event that a library agreement made pursuant to this compact shall deal in whole or in part with the provision of services or facilities with regard to which an officer or agency of the state government has constitutional or statutory powers of control, the agreement shall, as a condition precedent to its entry into force, be submitted to the state officer or agency having such power of control and shall be approved or disapproved by him or it as to all matters within his or its jurisdiction in the same manner and subject to the same requirements governing the action of the attorneys general pursuant to paragraph (a) of this article. This requirement of submission and approval shall be in addition to and not in substitution for the requirement of submission to and approval by the attorneys general.

Article VIII. Other Laws Applicable

Nothing in this compact or in any library agreement shall be construed to supersede, alter or otherwise impair any obligation imposed on any library by otherwise applicable law, nor to authorize the transfer or disposition of any property held in trust by a library agency in a manner contrary to the terms of such trust.

Article IX. Appropriations and Aid

(a) Any public library agency party to a library agreement may appropriate funds to the interstate library district established thereby in the same manner and to the same extent as to a library wholly maintained by it and, subject to the laws of the state in which such public library agency is situated, may pledge its credit in support of an interstate library district established by the agreement.

(b) Subject to the provisions of the library agreement pursuant to which it functions and the laws of the states in which such district is situated, an interstate library district may claim and receive any state and federal aid which may be available to library agencies.

Article X. Compact Administrator

Each state shall designate a compact administrator with whom copies of all library agreements to which his state or any public library agency thereof is party shall be filed. The administrator shall have such other powers as may be conferred upon him by the laws of his state and may consult and cooperate with the compact administrators of other party states and take such steps as may effectuate the purposes of this compact. If the laws of a party state so provide, such state may designate one or more deputy compact administrators in addition to its compact administrator.

Article XI. Entry into Force and Withdrawal

(a) This compact shall enter into force and effect immediately upon its enactment into law by any two (2) states. Thereafter, it shall enter into force and effect as to any other state upon the enactment thereof by such state.

(b) This compact shall continue in force with respect to a party state and remain binding upon such state until six (6) months after such state has given notice to each other party state of the repeal thereof. Such withdrawals shall not be construed to relieve any party to a library agreement entered into pursuant to this compact, from any obligation of that agreement prior to the end of its duration as provided therein.

Article XII. Construction and Severability

This compact shall be liberally construed so as to effectuate the purposes thereof. The provisions of this compact shall be severable and if any phrase, clause, sentence or provision of this compact is declared to be contrary to the constitution of any party state or of the United States or the applicability thereof to any government, agency, person or circumstance is held invalid, the validity of the remainder of this compact and the applicability thereof to any government, agency, person or circumstance shall not be affected thereby. If this compact shall be held contrary to the constitution of any state party thereto, the compact shall remain in full force and effect as to the state affected as to all severable matters. [Acts 1971, ch. 371, § 1; T.C.A., § 10-701.]

10-6-102. Construction of facilities — Compliance with law. — No municipality, county or library district of this state shall be a party to a library agreement which provides for the construction or maintenance of a library pursuant to article III, subdivision (c)(7) of the compact, nor pledge its credit in support of such a library, or contribute to the capital financing thereof, except after compliance with any laws applicable to such municipality, county or library district relating to or governing capital outlays and the pledging of credit. [Acts 1971, ch. 371, § 2; T.C.A., § 10-702.]

10-6-103. "State library agency" defined. — As used in the compact, "state library agency," with reference to this state, means the state library and archives. [Acts 1971, ch. 371, § 3; T.C.A., § 10-703.]

10-6-104. State aid to interstate library districts. — An interstate library district lying partly within this state may claim and be entitled to receive state aid in support of any of its functions to the same extent and in the same manner as such functions are eligible for support when carried on by entities wholly within this state. For the purposes of computing and apportioning state aid to an interstate library district, this state will consider that portion of the area which lies within this state as an independent entity for the performance of the aided function or functions and compute and apportion the aid accordingly. Subject to any applicable laws of this state, such a district also may apply for and be entitled to receive any federal aid for which it may be eligible. [Acts 1971, ch. 371, § 4; T.C.A., § 10-704.]

10-6-105. Compact administrator — Appointment — Deputies. — The governor of the state shall appoint the compact administrator pursuant to article X of the compact, and shall also appoint one or more deputy compact administrators, pursuant to said article. [Acts 1971, ch. 371, § 5; T.C.A., § 10-705.]

10-6-106. Notices upon withdrawal. — In the event of withdrawal from the compact, the governor shall send and receive any notices required by article XI(b) of the compact. [Acts 1971, ch. 371, § 6; T.C.A., § 10-706.]

PUBLIC RECORDS COMMISSION

(Tennessee Code Annotated, 1982, s.10-7-301 to 10-7-308.)

10-7-301. Definitions. — (a) "Section" and "Division" shall mean the records management division of the department of general services.

(b) "Public record(s)" or "state record(s)" shall mean all documents, papers, letters, maps, books, photographs, microfilms, electronic data processing files and output, films, sound recordings, or other material regardless of physical form or characteristics made or received pursuant to law or ordinance or in connection with the transaction of official business by any governmental agency.

(c) "Permanent records" shall mean those records which have permanent administrative, fiscal, historical or legal value.

(d) "Temporary records" shall mean material which can be disposed of in a short period of time as being without value in documenting the functions of an agency. Temporary records will be scheduled for disposal by requesting approval from the public records commission utilizing a records disposition authorization.

(e) "Working papers" shall mean those records created to serve as input for final reporting documents, including electronic data processed records, and/or computer output microfilm, and those records which become obsolete immediately after agency use or publication.

(f) "Agency" shall mean any department, division, board, bureau, commission, or other separate unit of government created or established by the constitution, by law or pursuant to law.

(g) "Disposition" shall mean preservation of the original records in whole or in part, preservation by photographic or other reproduction processes, or outright destruction of the records.

(h) "Records creation" shall mean the recording of information on paper, printed forms, punched cards, tape, disk, or any information transmitting media. It shall include preparation of forms, reports, state publications, and correspondence.

(i) "Records management" shall mean the application of management techniques to the creation, utilization, maintenance, retention, preservation, and disposal of records in order to reduce costs and improve efficiency of record-keeping. It shall include records retention schedule development, essential records protection, files management and information retrieval systems, microfilm information systems, correspondence and word processing management, records center, forms management, analysis, and design, and reports and publications management.

(j) "Records officer" shall mean an individual designated by an agency head to assume responsibility for implementation of the agency's records management program.

(k) "Essential records" shall mean any public records essential to the resumption or continuation of operations, to the re-creation of the legal and financial status of government in the state or to the protection and fulfillment of obligations to citizens of the state.

(l) "Records disposition authorization" shall mean the official document utilized by an agency head to request authority for the disposition of records. The public records commission shall determine and order the proper disposition of state records through the approval of records disposition authorizations. [Acts

1974 (Adj. S.), ch. 739, § 1; 1975, ch. 286, § 2; 1978 (Adj. S.), ch. 544, § 3; T.C.A., § 15-401; Acts 1981, ch. 364, § 3.]

10-7-302. Public records commission created — Duties. — A public records commission is hereby created to consist of the state treasurer, the comptroller of the treasury, the state librarian and archivist, the director of legal services for the general assembly, and the commissioner of general services as permanent members, any of whom may designate a deputy with a vote as his agent to represent him, the president of the Tennessee historical society as a nonvoting member, and, when required, one (1) temporary and nonvoting member as provided in § 10-7-303. It shall be the duty of the commission to determine and order proper disposition of state records. The commission shall direct the department of general services to initiate, through the records management division, by regulation or otherwise, any action it may consider necessary to accomplish more efficient control and regulation of records holdings and management in any agency. Such rules and regulations may authorize centralized microfilming for all departments, etc., or provide for other methods of reproduction for the more efficient disposition of state records. The commission shall elect its chairman and shall meet not less often than twice annually. Members shall be reimbursed for actual and necessary expenses when attending meetings, and those members who do not receive a fixed salary from the state also shall be paid a per diem of ten dollars ($10.00) for each day of actual meeting. All reimbursement for travel expenses shall be in accordance with the provisions of the comprehensive travel regulations as promulgated by the department of finance and administration and approved by the attorney general. [Acts 1974 (Adj. S.), ch. 739, § 2; 1975, ch. 286, § 2; 1976 (Adj. S.), ch. 806, § 1(58); 1977, ch. 89, § 24; T.C.A., § 15-402; Acts 1981, ch. 364, § 3; 1982 (Adj. S.), ch. 810, § 3.]

10-7-303. Records management division — Creation and disposition of records. — The records management division of the department of general services shall be the primary records management agency for state government, and as such shall direct the disposition of all records including electronic processed records and computer output microfilm records. The division shall cooperate with other agencies in the creation of records, forms, etc., which will eventually be subject to retention and/or disposition scheduling. Whenever the head of any state department, commission, board or other agency shall have certified that records created by his department, either permanent, temporary or working papers, as defined in § 10-7-301, have reached the end of the retention period established prior to the generation of such records, the public records commission shall then approve or disapprove by a majority vote, the disposition of such records in a manner specified in the rules and regulations of the commission and any disposition schedule already in effect may be voided or amended by a majority vote at any time by the commission, upon recommendation of a member of the commission or the head of the appropriate department, commission, board or other agency, in consultation with the staff of the records management division.

No record or records shall be scheduled for destruction without the unanimous approval of the voting members of the public records commission.

All records concerning private or public lands shall be forever preserved. This chapter shall not apply to legislative or judicial records except that upon the written request of the speaker of the senate, the speaker of the house of representatives, and the secretary of state as to legislative records and the attorney general as to judicial records, the commission may initiate and conduct a records disposition program limited to such records as may be designated in the said written request. For this purpose, a representative of the speaker of the senate, a representative of the speaker of the house of representatives, and a representative of the secretary of state or a representative of the attorney general shall serve as a nonvoting temporary member of the commission as may be appropriate when the disposition of legislative or judicial records is under consideration. [Acts 1974 (Adj. S.), ch. 739, § 3; 1975, ch. 286, § 2; 1977, ch. 38, § 2; T.C.A., § 15-403; Acts 1981, ch. 364, § 3.]

10-7-304. Records officer for each department or agency — Duties. — The head of each department, commission, board or agency shall designate a records officer, systems analyst, or records analyst, etc., who shall be an employee at the administrative level and who shall be instructed to cooperate with the staff of the records management section and the public records commission in carrying out the purposes of this chapter. It shall be the duty of the records officer to appear before the public records commission for the purpose of presenting on behalf of his department, commission, board or agency requests for disposition of records. [Acts 1974 (Adj. S.), ch. 739, § 4; T.C.A., § 15-404.]

10-7-305. Administrative officer and secretary — Duties. — The commissioner of general services shall be the administrative officer and secretary of the public records commission and act on its behalf and by its direction to make and enter into contracts and agreements with other departments, agencies, boards and commissions of state government as the commission may consider necessary, expedient or incidental to the performance of its duties under this chapter. [Acts 1974 (Adj. S.), ch. 739, § 5; 1975, ch. 286, § 2; T.C.A., § 15-405; Acts 1981, ch. 364, § 3.]

10-7-306. Rules and regulations of commission. — The commission shall issue rules and regulations which shall include such procedures as may be necessary to carry out the purposes of this chapter. Such rules and regulations shall provide but not be limited to:

(1) Procedures for the adoption of any record to be created by any department, board, commission or agency;

(2) Standards and procedures for the reproduction of records for security or for disposal of original records;

(3) Procedures for compiling and submitting to the division lists and schedules or records proposed for disposition;

(4) Procedures for the physical destruction or other disposition of records.

All rules and regulations must be approved by a majority of the voting members of the commission. The commissioner of general services as the administrative officer and secretary of the commission shall sign all rules and regulations on behalf of the commission.

The rules and regulations shall be issued and promulgated in accordance with chapter 5 of title 4. The commission need not formally meet to act under this section, but may adopt any rule, regulation, procedure or disposal with the written approval of all voting members. [Acts 1974 (Adj. S.), ch. 739, § 6; 1975, ch. 286, § 2; T.C.A., § 15-406; Acts 1981, ch. 364, § 3.]

10-7-307. Title to and destruction of records transferred to state archives. — Title to any record transferred to the state archives is vested in the state library and archives. The state librarian and archivist shall not destroy any record transferred to the state archives without advising the proper official of the transferring (or successor) agency prior to submitting a records disposition authorization to the public records commission, requesting such destruction authority. Concurrence or nonconcurrence of the proper official of the transferring (or successor) agency shall be noted on the submitted records disposition authorization. If there is no successor agency, the records disposition authorization shall be signed by the state librarian and archivist in lieu of the agency head. [Acts 1978 (Adj. S.), ch. 544, § 4; T.C.A., § 15-407.]

10-7-308. Title to records transferred to section. — Title to any record transferred to the section (records center) shall remain in the agency transferring such records to a state records center. [Acts 1978 (Adj. S.), ch. 544, § 4; T.C.A., § 15-408.]

CERTIFICATION OF LIBRARIANS
(Tennessee Code Annotated, 1982, s.10-2-101 to 10-2-107.)

10-2-101. Librarian certificates issued by board of education. — The state board of education is authorized to issue certificates to librarians. [Acts 1937, ch. 239, § 1; C. Supp. 1950, § 2305.1; T.C.A. (orig. ed.), § 10-201.]

10-2-102. Standards, rules and practices for issuance adopted by board of education. — The state board of education shall set up standards and shall adopt rules and practices, by which these librarians' certificates are to be issued. [Acts 1937, ch. 239, § 2; C. Supp. 1950, § 2305.2; Acts 1971, ch. 35, § 1; T.C.A. (orig. ed.), § 10-202.]

10-2-103. Librarians in public libraries certified by board of education. — The said state board of education shall pass upon the qualifications of persons applying for the position of librarian or professional library assistant in any library supported wholly or in part from public funds or in any state-supported library agency. [Acts 1937, ch. 239, § 4; C. Supp. 1950, § 2305.4; T.C.A. (orig. ed.), § 10-204.]

10-2-104. Librarians — Certificates required for appointment. — The governing boards of the libraries designated in § 10-2-103 shall be required to appoint to all vacant and new professional library positions falling under their respective jurisdictions only persons who prior to installation hold proper certificates as prescribed by the state board of education. [Acts 1937, ch. 239, § 5; C. Supp. 1950, § 2305.5; T.C.A. (orig. ed.), § 10-205.]

10-2-105. Professional librarians — Certifications provided. — The said state board of education shall provide for the certification of the following groups:

(1) All professional librarians and professional library assistants who are serving in libraries subject to this chapter;

(2) Professional librarians and professional library assistants who are serving in libraries not designated above in § 10-2-103, including librarians in other than publicly supported libraries. [Acts 1937, ch. 239, § 6; C. Supp. 1950, § 2305.6; T.C.A. (orig. ed.), § 10-206.]

10-2-106. Certificates from other states — Treatment. — The said state board of education may evaluate certificates issued by the proper authorities of other states requiring the certification of librarians and may accept such certificates in lieu of corresponding certificates in this state, or may issue or cause to be issued certificates in this state, to such persons holding such certificates from other states. [Acts 1937, ch. 239, § 7; C. Supp. 1950, § 2305.7; T.C.A. (orig. ed.), § 10-207.]

10-2-107. Application for certificates — Form — Fee. — The applications for library certificates under the provisions of this chapter shall be made to the commissioner of education in such manner and form as the state board of education may specify. The fee specified by the state board of education shall accompany each application and shall be deposited with the state treasurer to the credit of the state department of education. [Acts 1937, ch. 239, § 8; C. Supp. 1950, § 2305.8; T.C.A. (orig. ed.), § 10-208.]

DISTRIBUTION OF PUBLIC DOCUMENTS

(Tennessee Code Annotated, 1982, s. 12-6-102, 12-6-103,
12-6-107 to 12-6-114.)

12-6-102. General distribution of acts. — It is also the duty of the secretary of state to distribute the printed acts, upon written request received not later than February 1 of each year, as follows: to each executive officer and public service commissioner of the state, one (1) copy; to each judge and each clerk of the Supreme, Appeals, circuit and criminal courts, one (1) copy; to each chancellor, each clerk and master, one (1) copy; to each district attorney general and each assistant, one (1) copy; to the attorney general and each assistant, one (1) copy; to each clerk of the probate courts and each judge of the county or probate courts, and to each register and each trustee, one (1) copy; each of said copies to belong to the indicated office, and go to the successor of the incumbent; also to the order of the University of Tennessee, up to thirty (30) copies for the use of the University of Tennessee as a depository and for exchanges. And a copy of the printed acts shall be, upon written request received not later than February 1 of each year, delivered to every organized bar association in the state of Tennessee, provided such bar association maintains a law library and provided the name and address of such bar association shall be certified to the secretary of state by the county clerk of the county in which said association exists; and, provided, further, that should said association cease to function or to maintain a law library, all copies of said acts shall thereupon be turned over and delivered to the county clerk. Bound volumes of acts or resolutions may be made available to any person, firm, or corporation, requesting same in writing not later than February 1 of each year, at a cost of five dollars ($5.00) per volume. Any requests for acts or resolutions received later than February 1 of each year will be accepted subject to availability. This section and §§ 12-6-101, 12-6-103 shall not apply to Tennessee Code Annotated, any supplement thereto or replacement volume thereof, or any act enacting said Code. [Code 1858, § 30; Shan., § 42; Acts 1923, ch. 101, § 2; mod. Code 1932, § 70; Acts 1935, ch. 181, § 2; 1941, ch. 22, § 1; mod. C. Supp. 1950, § 70; modified; impl. am. Acts 1955, ch. 69, § 1; Acts 1961, ch. 290, § 1; modified; impl. am. Acts 1978 (Adj. S.), ch. 934, §§ 22, 36; T.C.A. (orig. ed.), § 12-602; Acts 1981, ch. 191, §§ 2-5.]

12-6-103. Acts and journals retained by secretary of state. — He shall also retain for the use of the executive and general assembly, unless a different number shall be prescribed by special law, fifty (50) copies of the acts and as many of the journals of each house, depositing three (3) copies of each in the state library. [Code 1858, § 31; Shan., § 43; mod. Code 1932, § 71; T.C.A. (orig. ed.), § 12-603.]

12-6-107. Libraries as depositories for documents. — The state library at Nashville, the library of the University of Tennessee, at Knoxville, the Cossitt Library at Memphis, and such other libraries as the governor may at any time name by executive order are designated depositories for state documents and for all publications issued by any official of the state. [Acts 1917, ch. 42, § 1; Shan. Supp., § 1387a7; Code 1932, § 2283; T.C.A. (orig. ed.), § 12-607; Acts 1981, ch. 191, § 7.]

12-6-108. Publications to be deposited. — The publications and documents referred to shall include:

(1) The acts and journals of the legislature, the reports of the Supreme Court, and such other courts as shall have their decisions reported by the attorney general and reporter of this state, or shall be required by any act

or resolution of the legislature;

(2) The periodical reports of officers of the state and any special reports that may from time to time be made by state officers or committees of the legislature or other committees provided for by law;

(3) Such other reports or statements as may be published under the authority of the state, or any official thereof. [Acts 1917, ch. 42, § 4; Shan. Supp., § 1387a11; Code 1932, § 2287; T.C.A. (orig. ed.), § 12-608.]

12-6-109. Notice of publications to secretary of state. — The person(s) in charge of the making of such documents and publications as are at any time issued by the state, or by any official(s) of the state, shall furnish a list of such documents and publications to the secretary of state. [Acts 1917, ch. 42, § 3; Shan. Supp., § 1387a10; Code 1932, § 2286; T.C.A. (orig. ed.), § 12-609; Acts 1981, ch. 191, § 8.]

12-6-110. Copies furnished to each depository and secretary of state. — At the expense of such department, agency, board or commission, the person in charge of the making of such documents and publications shall furnish two (2) copies directly to the librarian or person in charge of each of the depositories, and upon request two (2) copies to the secretary of state. [Acts 1917, ch. 42, § 2; Shan. Supp., § 1387a8; mod. Code 1932, § 2284; C. Supp. 1950, § 2284; T.C.A. (orig. ed.), § 12-610; Acts 1981, ch. 191, § 9.]

12-6-111. Exchange copies for university. — Upon request by the University of Tennessee, the person in charge of the making of such publications or the issuance of such documents shall furnish the university up to thirty (30) copies of each publication or document. [Acts 1935, ch. 181, § 3; C. Supp. 1950, § 2284; T.C.A. (orig. ed.), § 12-611; Acts 1981, ch. 191, § 10.]

12-6-112. Care of depository copies. — It shall be the duty of the librarian or other person in charge of each depository to give receipt for and carefully preserve all state documents and publications so received. One (1) of the two (2) copies shall be lendable on application, to the persons, if any, allowed to take other books from the library of the depository. The other copy shall not be allowed to be taken from the premises of the depository. [Acts 1917, ch. 42, § 2; Shan. Supp., § 1387a9; Code 1932, § 2285; T.C.A. (orig. ed.), § 12-612.]

12-6-113. Exchanges by state librarian. — The state librarian and archivist may, from time to time, procure from the general government, any foreign government, or from any state or territory within the United States, the public acts, and law and equity reports of such government, state or territory, by exchanging the public acts or reports of this state. [Code 1858, § 38 (deriv. Acts 1843-1844, ch. 135, § 2); impl. am. Priv. Acts 1859-1860, ch. 53, § 2; Acts 1879, ch. 31, §§ 1, 6; Shan., § 55; mod. Code 1932, § 79; impl. am. Acts 1951, ch. 197, § 1; T.C.A. (orig. ed.), § 12-613.]

12-6-114. Delivery of exchange copies. — Each person or persons in charge of making such documents and publications as provided in § 12-6-108(1) shall deliver upon request up to sixty (60) copies to the state librarian and archivist, to enable the librarian to make these exchanges. [Acts 1879, ch. 31, § 8; Shan., § 51; mod. Code 1932, § 80; impl. am. Acts 1951, ch. 197, § 1; T.C.A. (orig. ed.), § 12-614; Acts 1981, ch. 191, § 11.]

COUNTY AND MUNICIPAL LIBRARIES
(Tennessee Code Annotated, 1982, s.10-3-101 to 10-3-111.)

10-3-101. Establishment, maintenance and joint operation. — The legislative body of any county and/or the governing body of any incorporated city or town shall have the power to establish and maintair a free public library, or give support to any free public library already established therein, or contract with another library for library service for the use of the inhabitants of such county, city or town, or enter into contractual agreements with one or more counties or cities for joint operation of a free public library. [Acts 1963, ch. 370, § 1; impl. am. Acts 1978 (Adj. S.), ch. 934, §§ 7, 36; T.C.A., § 10-301.]

10-3-102. Taxes — Levy. — Upon the decision of such county legislative body and/or city governing body to establish, maintain or support a free public library, or to contract with another library for library service, or to contract with one or more counties or cities for joint operation of a free public library, it shall levy for the purpose a property tax, or shall use therefor funds raised by taxes for county or municipal purposes, such a library service being declared to be a county or municipal service.

If a portion of a county is already taxed for maintenance of a free public library, the county legislative body is empowered to levy a tax for a free library on all the property in the county, or the county legislative body may levy a tax on only the property of such portion of the county as is not already taxed for maintenance of a free public library. If a general county-wide tax levy is made for this purpose, the county trustee shall keep the funds raised thereby separate and apart from all other tax funds coming into his or her hands and shall make quarterly distribution of the same between the county library board and the governing body of the free public library of the city or cities within the limits of the county on the basis of the population enumerated by the most recent federal census. Subject to the last preceding sentence, funds raised under §§ 10-3-101 — 10-3-108 may be contributed toward the maintenance of any free public library maintained by a municipality in such county as provided in § 10-3-101. [Acts 1963, ch. 370, § 2; impl. am. Acts 1978 (Adj. S.), ch. 934, §§ 7, 36; T.C.A., § 10-302.]

10-3-103. Library board — Appointment — Terms. — Where a county legislative body and/or the governing body of a city or town, in lieu of giving support to a free public library already established, or of contracting with another library for library service, or of contracting with other counties and/or cities for joint operation of a free public library, establishes an independent free library of its own, it shall appoint a board of seven (7) members. Not more than one official each of the county and of the city governing bodies shall serve on this board. Said members shall serve without salary, three (3) for one (1) year, two (2) for two (2) years, and two (2) for three (3) years, and their successors for a term of three (3) years. Not more than five (5) of said members shall be of the same sex.

Where a county legislative body or city governing body elects to participate in joint operation of a public library maintained by the county and one or more cities within the county, the library board responsible for administering such joint library shall be appointed by one of the following methods:

(1) A library board of seven (7) members may be appointed by the county legislative body and city governing bodies which are parties to the agreement, the number appointed by each to be determined according to the ratio of population in each participating city and in the county outside the city or cities, based on the most recent federal census, provided that each shall appoint at least one member. Terms of office, qualifications of members, powers and duties of the board shall be in accordance with the provisions of §§ 10-3-101 — 10-3-108;

(2) A library board may be appointed in accordance with a contract as provided in § 5-113;

(3) In accordance with a private act. [Acts 1963, ch. 370, § 3; 1974 (Adj. S.), ch. 700, § 1; impl. am. Acts 1978 (Adj. S.), ch. 934, §§ 7, 36; T.C.A., § 10-303.]

10-3-104. Powers and duties of library board. — The members of the library board shall organize by electing officers and adopting bylaws and regulations. The board shall have the power to direct all the affairs of the library, including appointment of a librarian who shall direct the internal affairs of the library, and such assistants or employees as may be necessary. It may make and enforce rules and regulations and establish branches of travel service at its discretion. It may expend funds for the special training and formal education of library personnel, provided such personnel shall agree to work in the library for at least two (2) years after completion of said training and education. It may receive donations, devises and bequests to be used by it directly for library purposes. It may hold and convey realty and personal property and negotiate leases for and on behalf of such library. The library board shall furnish to the state library agency such statistics and information as may be required, and shall make annual reports to the county legislative body and/or city governing body. [Acts 1963, ch. 370, § 4; impl. am. Acts 1978 (Adj. S.), ch. 934, §§ 7, 36; T.C.A., § 10-304.]

10-3-105. Borrowing money to acquire library buildings and equipment. — A county legislative body and/or city governing body shall have power to borrow money for the purchase of realty and the erection or purchase of suitable buildings for the library and its branches and for their equipment. The title to such property may be vested in trust in said library board and their successors, who shall be responsible for expending as below such bond proceeds. [Acts 1963, ch. 370, § 5; impl. am. Acts 1978 (Adj. S.), ch. 934, §§ 7, 36; T.C.A., § 10-305.]

10-3-106. Tax funds held by county or city treasurer — Disbursement — Audit of accounts. — All county and/or city tax funds for library purposes, raised by bonds or taxation, shall be held by the county or city treasurer separate from other funds. Such funds may be disbursed when drawn upon by vouchers or orders authenticated by two (2) officers of the library board. All library accounts of every character shall be audited annually by or under the county legislative body and/or city governing body. [Acts 1963, ch. 370, § 6; impl. am. Acts 1978 (Adj. S.), ch. 934, §§ 7, 36; T.C.A., § 10-306.]

10-3-107. Libraries free to inhabitants — Extension of privileges to nonresidents. — Libraries so established or supported shall be free to the inhabitants. The board may extend the privileges and facilities of the library to persons residing outside the county or city upon such terms as it may deem proper. [Acts 1963, ch. 370, § 7; T.C.A., § 10-307.]

10-3-108. Penalties for loss of or injury to library property. — The library board shall have power to make and enforce rules providing penalties for loss of or injury to library property. [Acts 1963, ch. 370, § 8; T.C.A., § 10-308.]

10-3-109. Recreational facilities — County library board in counties of less than 3,500 population. — A county library board, appointed and functioning in accordance with the provisions of §§ 10-3-101 — 10-3-108, in all counties of Tennessee having a population of less than three thousand five hundred (3,500) according to the federal census of 1960 or any subsequent federal census, shall have, in addition to all other authority given to it, the authority to conduct such recreational facilities, in conjunction with the public library, as it deems necessary and beneficial, either with or without charge to patrons thereof, provided that any net proceeds from such recreational facilities be used solely for the capital improvement and operational expenses of the library and recreational facilities. [Acts 1961, ch. 222, § 1; T.C.A., § 10-309.]

10-3-110. Title to property acquired — Use of proceeds from activities. — The title to all property acquired by a library board operating hereunder shall be taken in the name of the county for the use and benefit of the public library and the proceeds from all activities conducted by the library board or from any disposition of its assets shall be taken in the name of the county for the use and benefit of the public library. [Acts 1961, ch. 222, § 2; T.C.A., § 10-310.]

10-3-111. Financial report of operations. — Such library board shall furnish a report to the county legislative body, at its first meeting of each fiscal year, setting forth its capital and operational receipts and expenditures for the preceding fiscal year. [Acts 1961, ch. 222, § 3; impl. am. Acts 1978 (Adj. S.), ch. 934, §§ 7, 36; T.C.A., § 10-311.]

LAW LIBRARIES
(Tennessee Code Annotated, 1982, s.10-4-101 to 10-4-104.)

10-4-101. State law library commission — Membership — Meetings — Travel expenses. — There is created a state law library commission composed of the chief justice of the Supreme Court, who shall serve as chairman, the presiding judge of the Court of Appeals, the attorney general and reporter, and two (2) other members appointed by the chief justice of the Supreme Court from the membership of the Supreme Court or the Court of Appeals or both. The members of the commission shall hold at least one meeting each year upon call of the chairman and they shall receive no compensation for their services as commissioners but they shall be reimbursed for their necessary travel expenses. [Acts 1965, ch. 103, § 2; T.C.A., § 10-515.]

10-4-102. Powers and duties of commission. — The state law library commission shall have full control and supervision of the existing state law libraries at Nashville, Knoxville, and Jackson. The commission's powers shall include but are not limited to the following: the power to employ necessary personnel, either full or part-time, and to fix their compensation; the power to purchase or otherwise acquire books, furniture, supplies and all other necessary equipment, including the power to dispose of by sale, exchange, gift, or otherwise, books and equipment whenever in the judgment of the commission it is deemed advisable; the power to make and enforce all necessary rules and regulations for the management and operation of said libraries; and the power to exchange the Tennessee Reports, the Tennessee Appeals Reports, Acts, and Codes for the reports, acts and codes of other jurisdictions, and the Tennessee Reports, the Tennessee Appeals Reports, Acts, and Codes available for exchange under present and future laws shall be at the disposal of the commission for such purpose. [Acts 1965, ch. 103, § 3; T.C.A., § 10-516.]

10-4-103. Expenditures within appropriation. — All expenditures made by the commission shall be within the limits of the amounts appropriated by the general assembly of the state of Tennessee; provided, however, that the commission shall have authority to allocate amounts necessary for the operation and maintenance of each library among the libraries as it deems to be in the best interest of each library, but within the limits of the entire appropriation. [Acts 1965, ch. 103, § 4; T.C.A., § 10-517.]

10-4-104. Secretary — Appointment — Duties. — The commission shall designate from time to time one (1) of its employees as secretary of said commission and such secretary shall prepare the minutes of the commission meetings and, under the direction and supervision of the commission, shall administer its finances, preparing the warrants for the payment of its obligations and recording all transactions in accordance with the laws and regulations governing state fiscal operations. [Acts 1965, ch. 103, § 5; T.C.A., § 10-518.]

UNIVERSITY OF TENNESSEE
(Tennessee Code Annotated, 1982, s.49-3321 to 49-3323.)

49-3321. Library endowment to meet terms of Carnegie grant. — In order to meet the conditions imposed by the late Andrew Carnegie, the state of Tennessee accepting same has provided an endowment fund for the university library of forty thousand dollars ($40,000), in a certificate of indebtedness of the state of Tennessee for the sum of forty thousand dollars ($40,000), bearing interest at the rate of five per cent (5%) per annum. [Acts 1909, ch. 180, § 3; Shan., § 373a7; mod. Code 1932, § 580.]

49-3322. Interest on library endowment. — In order to provide for the interest on this certificate of indebtedness, the board of trustees of the university is directed to set aside from any appropriation made to the support or equipment of said university at any biennial session of the general assembly the amount of four thousand dollars ($4,000), being at the rate of two thousand dollars ($2,000) per annum; and the amount thus set aside shall constitute the interest on the certificate of indebtedness for the biennial period. If at any future session the general assembly shall fail to make an appropriation for the support or equipment of the university, the board of trustees are empowered and directed to set aside from any other funds of said university not appropriated by the general assembly or the national congress for specific purposes the amount of four thousand dollars ($4,000), to represent the interest on said certificate of indebtedness for the period of two (2) years, for which no appropriation for support or equipment has been made, in which case they are directed to make a special report of the facts to the next session of the general assembly, to the end that provision for payment of the amount thus diverted may be included in its appropriation for the support or equipment of said university. [Acts 1909, ch. 180, § 4; Shan., § 373a8; Code 1932, § 581.]

49-3323. Library fund. — The interest provided for in §§ 49-3321 and 49-3322, together with any other gifts or income from endowment for the support of the library of the university, shall be regularly set aside by the board of trustees as a fund to be known as the "library fund," for the maintenance and development of the library of said university, and said fund shall not be used for any other purpose whatsoever, a separate account of said fund being kept on the books of the university showing the amounts and character of the disbursements made from it. An accounting for said fund shall be included in the biennial report to the governor and general assembly made by the board of trustees of the university. [Acts 1909, ch. 180, § 5; Shan., § 373a9; Code 1932, § 582.]

PENAL INSTITUTIONS
(Tennessee Code Annotated, 1982, s.4-6-144.)

4-6-144. Library region for penal and reformatory institutions. — There is created a library region to be composed of the penal and reformatory institutions under the control of the department of correction.

The library shall have a branch library at each of the penal and reformatory institutions.

A librarian shall be appointed who shall serve as a consultant in the state library and archives, public library section.

The commissioner of correction shall insure that penal and reformatory institutions shall comply with the requirements for libraries as provided in chapter 6 of title 10 of this Code, except for such provisions of any law, rule or regulation which conflicts with the primary penal and reformatory function of such institutions.

It is the legislative intent that the provisions of this section be implemented without any additional appropriation for the fiscal year 1975. [Acts 1974 (Adj. S.), ch. 764, §§ 1-5; T.C.A., § 4-656.]

Tennessee library laws are reprinted from TENNESSEE CODE ANNOTATED published by Bobbs-Merrill Co., Indianapolis, Indiana.

TEXAS

STATE LIBRARY AND ARCHIVES COMMISSION

(Vernon's Annotated Revised Civil Statutes of the State of
Texas, 1982, Art. 5434-5439, 5441-5443, 5445, 5446.)

Art. 5434.   [5600–5601] Organization

The Governor shall, by and with the advice and consent of the Senate,
appoint six (6) persons who shall constitute the Texas State Library and Archives
Commission. Appointments shall be made for a term of six (6) years.

Members of the Commission holding office at the time of passage of this Act
shall continue in office until the expiration of their present terms.

Upon the expiration of the terms of office of the two (2) members which
expire in 1953, the Governor shall, by, and with the advice of the Senate, appoint
three (3) persons as members of the Commission. The Governor shall designate
one (1) of the appointees to serve a term of two (2) years to expire concurrent
with the term of the present member of the Commission whose term of office
expires in 1955.

The other two (2) appointees shall serve for six (6) years.

Thereafter all appointments shall be for a six-year term, except that any
person appointed to fill a vacancy occurring prior to the expiration of the term for
which his predecessor was appointed shall be appointed only for the remainder of
such term.

The Commission shall be assigned suitable offices at the Capitol where they
shall hold at least one regular meeting annually, and as many special meetings as
may be necessary. Each such member while in attendance at said meetings shall
receive his actual expenses incurred in attending the meetings, and shall be paid a
per diem as set out in the General Appropriations Act.

Amended by Acts 1967, 60th Leg., p. 1755, ch. 661, § 1, eff. Aug. 28, 1967; Acts 1979, 66th
Leg., p. 856, ch. 382, § 2, eff. Aug. 27, 1979.

Art. 5434a. Application of Sunset Act

The Texas State Library and Archives Commission is subject to the Texas Sunset Act; and unless continued in existence as provided by that Act the commission is abolished effective September 1, 1983.

Added by Acts 1977, 65th Leg., p. 1843, ch. 735, § 2.082, eff. Aug. 29, 1977. Amended by Acts 1979, 66th Leg., p. 857, ch. 382, § 4, eff. Aug. 27, 1979.

Art. 5434b. Change of name

The name of the Texas Library and Historical Commission is changed to the Texas State Library and Archives Commission.

Acts 1979, 66th Leg., p. 856, ch. 382, § 1, eff. Aug. 27, 1979.

Art. 5435. [5599] Purpose; powers and duties of Commission; Director and Librarian

The appointed members of the Commission shall be responsible for the adoption of all policies, rules and regulations so as to aid and encourage libraries, collect materials relating to the history of Texas and the adjoining states, preserve, classify and publish the manuscript archives and such other matters as it may deem proper, diffuse knowledge in regard to the history of Texas, encourage historical work and research, mark historic sites and houses and secure their preservation, and aid those who are studying the problems to be dealt with by legislation. The Commission also is responsible for passing on the qualifications of persons wanting to become county librarians in this state and shall adopt rules necessary to administer this responsibility. The educational requirement for permanent certification as a county librarian is: (1) graduation from a library school accredited by the American Library Association if the Commission determines that the association has accreditation standards to ensure a high level of scholarship for students; or (2) graduation with a master's degree in library science from an institution of higher education accredited by an organization that the Commission determines has accreditation standards to ensure a high level of scholarship for students. The Commission shall appoint a Director and Librarian who shall perform all of the duties heretofore provided for the State Librarian, and all authority, rights and duties heretofore assigned by statute to the State Librarian are hereby transferred to and shall be performed by the Director and Librarian. He shall be the Executive and Administrative Officer of the Commission and shall discharge all administrative and executive functions of the Commission. He shall have had at least two years' training in library science or the equivalent thereof in library, teaching or research experience and shall have had at least two years of administrative experience in library, research or related fields. The Director and Librarian shall serve at the will of the Commission and shall give bond in the sum of Five Thousand Dollars ($5,000) for the proper care of the State Library and its equipment. He shall be allowed his actual expenses when travelling in the service of the Commission on his sworn account showing such expenses in detail. The Director and Librarian shall appoint, subject to the approval of the Commission, an Assistant State Librarian, a State Archivist, and such other assistants and employees as are necessary for the maintenance of the Library and Archives of the State of Texas.

Amended by Acts 1961, 57th Leg., p. 1064, ch. 476, § 1, eff. June 17, 1961; Acts 1981, 67th Leg., p. 2845, ch. 764, § 1, eff. Sept. 1, 1981.

Art. 5436. [5602–3] Powers and duties

(a) The Commission is authorized and empowered to purchase within the limits of the annual appropriation allowed by Act of the Legislature from time to time suitable books, pictures, etc., the same to be the property of the State. The Commission shall have power and authority to receive donations or gifts of money or property upon such terms and conditions as it may deem proper; provided, no financial liability is thereby entailed upon the State. It shall give advice to such persons as contemplate the establishment of public libraries, in regard to such matters as the maintenance cf public libraries, selection of books, cataloging and library management. The Commission shall conduct library institutes and encourage library associations.

(b) The Commission shall have the power and authority to transfer books and documents to other libraries which are supported by State appropriation when, in the opinion of the Commission, such transfer would be desirable for the benefit of the Texas State Library, and provided further that such transfer shall be permanent or temporary as may be decided by the Commission. The Commission shall have further power to exchange duplicate books and documents or to dispose of such books and documents to any public library, state or local, when such books and documents are no longer needed by the Texas State Library. No books or documents which constitute the archives of the Texas State Library shall ever be affected by this Act. Acts 1909, p. 122; Acts 1919, 2nd C.S., p. 152; Acts 1943, 48th Leg., p. 423, ch. 289, § 1.

(c) The commission is authorized to accept, receive, and administer federal funds made available by grant or loan or both to improve the public libraries of Texas.

(d) The commission may enter into contracts or agreements with the governing bodies and heads of the counties, cities, and towns of Texas to meet the terms prescribed by the United States and consistent with state law for the expenditure of federal funds for improving public libraries.

Subsecs. (c) and (d) added Acts 1965, 59th Leg., p. 1, ch. 1, § 2, eff. Feb. 4, 1965.

Art. 5436a. State plan for library services and library construction

The Texas State Library and Archives Commission is authorized to adopt a state plan for improving public library services and for public library construction. The plan shall include county and municipal libraries. The Texas State Library shall prepare the plan for the commission, and shall administer the plan adopted by the commission. Money to be used may include that available from local, state, and federal sources, and will be administered according to local, state, and federal requirements. The state plan shall include a procedure by which county and municipal libraries may apply for money under the state plan and a procedure for fair hearings for those applications that are refused money.

Acts 1965, 59th Leg., p. 1, ch. 1, § 1, eff. Feb. 1, 1965. Amended by Acts 1979, 66th Leg., p. 857, ch. 382, § 5, eff. Aug. 27, 1979.

Art. 5437. Seal

The style of the Library governed by the Commission shall be "Texas State Library." A circular seal of not less than one and one-half inches, and not more than two inches in diameter, bearing a star of five points, surrounded by two concentric circles, between which are printed the words, "Texas State Library," is hereby designated the official seal of said Library. Said seal shall be used in authentication of the official acts of the State Library. Acts 2nd C.S. 1919, p. 152.

Art. 5438. [5604-5] Custody of records

The custody and control of books, documents, newspapers, manuscripts, archives, relics, mementos, flags, works of art, etc., and the duty of collecting and preserving historical data, is under the control of the Commission. The gallery of the portraits of the Presidents of the Republic and the Governors of this State constitutes a part of the State Library. All books, pictures, documents, publications and manuscripts, received through gift, purchase or exchange, or on deposit, from any source, for the use of the State, shall constitute a part of the State Library, and shall be placed therein for the use of the public. Acts 1909, p. 122.

Art. 5438a. Historical relics

The Texas State Library and Archives Commission is hereby authorized in their discretion to place temporarily in the custody of the Daughters of the Republic of Texas and the United Daughters of the Confederacy, Texas Division, all or part of the historical relics belonging to the Texas State Library, under such conditions and terms of agreement as will insure the safekeeping of these relics in the Texas Museum.

Amended by Acts 1979, 66th Leg., p. 857, ch. 382, § 3, eff. Aug. 27, 1979.

Art. 5438c. Removal of relics

The Texas State Library and Archives Commission shall retain the right to remove these relics at any time they may see fit.

Amended by Acts 1979, 66th Leg., p. 857, ch. 382, § 6, eff. Aug. 27, 1979.

Art. 5438d. Admission fees; state property under control of Daughters of Confederacy and Daughters of Republic

The Daughters of the Confederacy, Texas Division, and the Daughters of the Republic of Texas, are hereby authorized to charge admission fees to the general public to visit State property under their custody and control except the Alamo, and such organizations are authorized to maintain and operate in any manner they deem appropriate concessions in State property under their custody and control. All money received from the admission charged and all profit obtained from the operation of concessions at each of the properties shall be held separately in trust by such organizations and shall be expended for the purpose of maintenance and repair of the State property and furnishings at the particular property at which the money was received. The admission fee to be charged the public shall be in the amount determined by such organizations as in their discretion they deem best for the interest of the State and the public. The operation of concessions shall be under the control of such organizations and they are authorized to operate such concessions themselves or to enter into necessary contracts with any other person, firm or corporation for the operation of concessions in any manner they deem necessary for the best interest of the State and public. Amended by Acts 1973, 63rd Leg., p. 1630, ch. 589, § 1, eff. June 15, 1973.

Art. 5439. [5606] Exchange of records

Any State, county or other official is hereby authorized in his discretion to turn over to the State Library for permanent preservation therein any official books, records, documents, original papers, maps, charts, newspaper files and printed books not in current use in his office, and the State Librarian shall receipt for the same. Acts 1909, p. 122; Acts 2nd C.S.1919, p. 152.

Art. 5439a. Photographic Reproductions as Public Records

When any State official has had photographic reproductions (as defined in Article 5441a) made of any public records (as defined in Article 5441a) in his office, even though such records be current, he may designate such photographic reproductions as original records for all legal purposes and may thereupon transfer the records which have been replaced by the photographic reproductions to the State Librarian, who shall receipt therefor. The State Librarian with the consent of the State Auditor may dispose of transferred records by further transfer or by destruction. Furthermore, when such photographic reproductions have been designated as original records, then copies thereof, in any form, may be introduced in evidence when properly certified or authenticated according to law. Added Acts 1947, 50th Leg., p. 945, ch. 403, § 2.

Art. 5441. [5606] Duties of Librarian

The duties of the State Librarian, acting under the direction of said Commission, shall be as follows:

1. He shall record the proceedings of the Commission, keep an accurate account of its financial transactions, and perform such other duties as said Commission may assign him; and he shall be authorized to approve the vouchers for all expenditures made in connection with the State Library.

2. He shall have charge of the State Library and all books, pictures, documents, newspapers, manuscripts, archives, relics, mementos, flags, etc., therein contained.

3. He shall endeavor to collect all manuscript records relating to the history of Texas in the hands of private individuals, and where the originals cannot be obtained he shall endeavor to procure authenticated copies. He shall be authorized to expend the money appropriated for the purchase of books relating to Texas, and he shall seek diligently to procure a copy of every book, pamphlet, map or

other printed matter giving valuable information concerning this State. He shall collect portraits or photographs of as many of the prominent men of Texas as possible. He shall endeavor to complete the files of the early Texas newspapers in the State Library and other publications of this state as seem necessary to preserve in the State Library an accurate record of the history of Texas.

Sec. 3 amended by Acts 1969, 61st Leg., p. 1931, ch. 643, § 1, eff. June 12, 1969.

4. He shall demand and receive from the officers of State departments having them in charge, all books, maps, papers, manuscripts, documents, memoranda and data not connected with or necessary to the current duties of said officers, relating to the history of Texas, and carefully classify, catalogue and preserve the same. The Attorney General shall decide as to the proper custody of such books, etc., whenever there is any disagreement as to the same.

5. He shall endeavor to procure from Mexico the original archives which have been removed from Texas and relate to the history and settlement thereof, and if he cannot procure the originals, he shall endeavor to procure authentic copies thereof. In like manner he shall procure the originals or authentic copies of manuscripts preserved in other archives beyond the limits of this State, in so far as said manuscripts relate to the history of Texas.

6. He shall preserve all historical relics, mementos, antiquities and works of art connected with and relating to the history of Texas, which may in any way come into his possession as State Librarian. He shall constantly endeavor to build up an historical museum worthy of the interesting and important history of this State.

7. He shall give careful attention to the proper classification, indexing and preserving of the official archives that are now or may hereafter come into his custody.

8. He shall make a biennial report to the Commission, to be by it transmitted to the Governor, to be accompanied by such historial papers and documents as he may deem of sufficient importance.

9. He shall ascertain the condition of all public libraries in this State and report the results to the Commission. He is authorized in his discretion to withhold from libraries refusing or neglecting to furnish their annual reports or such other information as he may request, public documents furnished the Commission for distribution, or interlibrary loans desired by such libraries. Id.; Acts 1909, p. 122.

Art. 5441a. Records Management Division

Establishment and maintenance; duties; qualifications of assistant

Section 1. The Texas State Library and Archives Commission is hereby authorized to establish and maintain in the State Library a records management division which (1) shall manage all public records of the state with the cooperation of the heads of the various departments and institutions in charge of such records and (2) shall also conduct a photographic laboratory for the purpose of making photographs, microphotographs, or reproductions on film, or to arrange for all or part of such work to be done by an established commercial agency which meets the specifications established by this Article for the proper accomplishment of the work. The assistant who shall be appointed by the Commission to head such division shall have had appropriate training and experience in the field of public records management.

Definitions

Sec. 2. For the purpose of this Article:

"Photographic reproduction" shall mean reproduction by an [1] photographic process, including that by microprint or by microphotography on film, including both negative and positive copies.

"Public Records" means document, book, paper, photograph, sound recording or other material, regardless of physical form or characteristics, made or received pursuant to law or ordinance or in connection with the transaction of official business. Library and museum material made or acquired and preserved solely for reference or exhibition purposes, extra copies of documents preserved only for convenience of reference, and stocks of publications and of processed documents are not included within the definition of records as used in the Article.

"Department or institution" shall mean any state department, institution, board or commission, whether executive, educational, judicial, or eleemosynary in character.

"Head of department or institution" shall mean the official or officials, whether appointive or elective, who has or have authority over the records of the department or institution involved.

"Local units of government" shall mean all local units of government, including cities, towns, counties, and districts.

[1] So in enrolled bill; should read "any".

Surveying, indexing, classification and destruction of records; duties of department heads pertaining to records

Sec. 3. With the cooperation of the heads of the various departments and institutions the public records of such departments and institutions shall be surveyed, indexed and classified under the direction of the records management division. Furthermore, with the approval of the State Director and Librarian the head of any department or institution may destroy any public records in his custody which, in his opinion have no further legal, administrative or historical value, provided, however, that he shall first file application to do so with the State Director and Librarian, describing in such application the original purposes and contents of such public records, and provided further, that the approval of the State Auditor shall also be required with regard to the destruction of public records of a fiscal or financial nature. The head of any department or institution shall (1) establish and maintain an active, continuing program for the economical and efficient management of the records of the agency; (2) make and maintain records containing adequate and proper documentation of the organization, functions, policies, decisions, procedures and essential transactions of the agency designed to furnish information to protect the legal and financial rights of the state and of persons directly affected by the agency's activities; and (3) submit to the Director, Records Management Division of the State Library, in accordance with the standards established by him, schedules proposing the length of time each state record series warrants retention for administrative, legal or fiscal purposes after it has been promulgated or received by the agency. The head of each department and institution also shall submit lists of public records in his custody that do not have sufficient administrative, legal or fiscal value to warrant their retention, for disposal in conformity with the requirements of this Section. The head of each department or institution shall act as, or shall appoint an employee of his department or institution performing other administrative duties to act as, a records administrator of the department or institution. Such records administrator shall comply with the rules, regulations, standards and procedures issued by the Director of the Records Management Division.

Photographic reproductions

Sec. 4. The State Director and Librarian, either on his own initiative or upon request of the head of any department or institution, may provide for the making of photographic reproductions of the public records of any department or institution, and such public records shall be open to the State Director and Librarian for such purpose; provided, however, that no such action shall be taken except with the consent of the head of such department or institution.

Quality and accuracy of photographic reproductions

Sec. 5. Any photographic reproduction made by microprint or by microphotography on film shall comply with the minimum standards of quality approved for permanent photographic records by the National Bureau of Standards, and the devices used to reproduce such public records shall be those which accurately reproduce the original thereof in all details.

Private or public use of photographic reproductions

Sec. 6. The State Director and Librarian is hereby authorized to make photographic reproductions for private and public use on the following basis: (1) For official use of departments and institutions no charge shall be made; (2) for the official use of local units of government charge shall be made on a cost basis; (3) for copies of public records for private use charge shall be at a rate to be fixed by the State Director and Librarian in keeping with standard commercial rates. All money received by the State Library in payment for charges for photographic reproduction shall be paid into the State Treasury.

Report of State Auditor; contents

Sec. 6a. The State Auditor, in the audit of the various agencies of the state, shall include the following information in his report:

(1) the degree to which the agency has complied with records disposal instructions and transfer agreements in order to reduce filing space and equipment required to house records;

(2) the date when records were last reviewed for transfer or disposal; and

(3) revisions required in scheduled transfer and disposal dates.

Amended by Acts 1963, 58th Leg., p. 435, ch. 154, § 1, eff. Aug. 23, 1963. Sec. 6a added by Acts 1965, 59th Leg., p. 605, ch. 299, § 1; Sec. 1 amended by Acts 1979, 66th Leg., p. 857, ch. 382, § 7, eff. Aug. 27, 1979.

Art. 5441b. Disposition of valueless records

Section 1. The State Librarian of the State of Texas is hereby authorized to transfer, destroy or otherwise dispose of any records of the State of Texas consigned by law to his custody that are more than ten (10) years old and which the State Librarian shall determine to be valueless, or of no further use, to the State of Texas as official records. Provided, however, none of such records shall be disposed of in any manner unless the State Comptroller, the State Auditor and the Attorney General of the State of Texas shall first have agreed with the State Librarian that the preservation of any such records are no longer necessary as evidence and will serve no useful purpose in the future efficient operation of the State Government. All such records disposed of, as agreed upon, shall be generally listed and referred to and such list shall be subscribed to by all of said Officials showing their consent to such disposition.

Sec. 2. Any such records which the Attorney General, State Comptroller, State Auditor and State Librarian, or any one or more of them deem necessary to preserve, may be so preserved by microfilming such records and such microfilm copies shall thereupon constitute original records for all legal purposes. Thereafter the originals of such records may be disposed of in such manner as such Officials may agree on; provided, however, that such microfilming shall be done only if funds are available for that purpose or are appropriated by the Legislature of the State of Texas for that purpose to cover the cost of such microfilming for the State of Texas.

Sec. 3. Any such records held to be no longer needed for the operation of the State Government or those replaced by microfilm copies may nevertheless be transferred to the Archives Division of the Texas State Library if the State Librarian deems them to be of historical value.

Acts 1959, 56th Leg., p. 1083, ch. 494, eff. June 1, 1959.

Art. 5441c. Destruction of worthless records

Section 1. State records have been allowed to accumulate over a period of years to the detriment of a well-organized records management program. It is necessary, therefore, to adopt special provisions for the selection of essential state records and the destruction of worthless material.

Sec. 2. The State Auditor, Board of Barber Examiners, Board of Control, Board of Cosmetology, Board of Medical Examiners, Board of Pardons and Paroles, Board of Regents of the State Teachers Colleges, Bureau of Labor Statistics, Comptroller, Court of Appeals for the Third Supreme Judicial District, Governor's Office, Health Department, Insurance Commission, Legislative Budget Board, Parks and Wildlife Commission, Railroad Commission, Real Estate Commission, Secretary of State, State Securities Board, Teacher Retirement System, Texas Education Agency, Texas State Library, Texas Water Commission, and the Treasury Department shall examine all books, papers, correspondence and records of any kind belonging to each respective agency, dated prior to 1952, which are stored with the Records Management Division.

Sec. 3. Each agency listed in Section 2 of this Act shall:

(1) classify and index its own records;

(2) furnish the Records Management Division of the State Library and Historical Commission a copy of the index in which they shall list the records to be preserved;

(3) name a retention period on records which are to be stored for a definite time; and

(4) request destruction of worthless records and material in compliance with Article 5441a, Revised Civil Statutes of Texas, 1925, as amended.

Acts 1965, 59th Leg., p. 1160, ch. 547, eff. Aug. 30, 1965. Sec. 2 amended by Acts 1981, 67th Leg., p. 791, ch. 291, § 65, eff. Sept. 1, 1981.

Art. 5441d. Preservation of Essential Records Act

Purpose

Section 1. The Legislature declares that records containing information essential to the operation of government and the protection of the rights and interests of persons must be protected against the destructive effects of all forms of disaster and must be available when needed. It is necessary, therefore, to adopt special provisions for the selection and preservation of essential state records to provide for the protection and availability of such information.

Short title

Sec. 2. This Act may be cited as the "Preservation of Essential Records Act."

Definitions

Sec. 3. In this Act, unless the context requires a different meaning:

(1) "essential record" means any written or graphic material made or received by any state agency in the conduct of the state's official business, which is filed or intended to be preserved permanently or for a definite period of time, as evidence of that business;

(2) "agency" means any state department, institution, board, or commission, whether executive, judicial, legislative, or eleemosynary in character;

(3) "departmental records supervisor" means the person or persons having authority over the records of the department involved;

(4) "disaster" means any occurrence of fire, flood, storm, earthquake, explosion, epidemic, riot, sabotage, or other condition of extreme peril resulting in substantial damage or injury to persons or property within this state, whether the occurrence is caused by an act of nature or man; and

(5) "preservation duplicate" means a copy of an essential record which is used for the purpose of preserving such state record.

Records Preservation Advisory Committee

Sec. 4. (a) A Records Preservation Advisory Committee is established to advise the Records Preservation Officer and to perform other duties as this Act requires. The committee is composed of the State Librarian, Secretary of State, State Auditor, State Comptroller, Attorney General, or their delegated agents, the Secretary of the Senate and the Chief Clerk of the House of Representatives, all of whom serve as ex officio members of the committee. The committee shall work with and is a part of the Records Management Division of the Texas State Library and Archives Commission.

(b) The State Librarian is the chairman of the committee.

(c) The committee shall:

(1) adopt rules for the conduct of its business;

(2) meet when called by the chairman, at least twice each year; and

(3) appoint consultants from time to time to obtain the best professional advice on the performance of its duties.

(d) The consultants shall serve without compensation, but shall be reimbursed for actual expenses incurred while performing their duties.

Records Preservation Officer

Sec. 5. The Director of the Records Management Division is also the Records Preservation Officer. The Records Preservation Officer shall establish and maintain such rules and regulations concerning the selection and preservation of essential state records as are necessary and proper to effectuate the purpose of this Act.

Bond

Sec. 6. The State Librarian and the Records Preservation Officer shall each execute and file with the Secretary of State a good and sufficient bond, payable to the State of Texas, in an amount consistent with his duties to be set by the committee and conditioned on the faithful performance of his duties.

Essential state records

Sec. 7. State records which are within the following categories are essential records which shall be preserved under this Act:

(1) Category A—Records containing information necessary to the operations of government in an emergency created by a disaster; and

(2) Category B—Records to protect the rights and interests of individuals, or to establish and affirm the powers and duties of government in the resumption of operations after a disaster.

Confidential records

Sec. 8. When a state record is required by law to be treated in a confidential manner the departmental records supervisor shall so indicate by labeling such record. The Records Preservation Officer and his staff shall protect the confidential nature of any record so labeled. Any employee who fails in this responsibility shall be dismissed from his duties and shall not be permitted to hold another state appointment.

Selection of records

Sec. 9. (a) Each agency shall select the state records which are essential to carrying out the work of its organization and shall determine the category of the record.

(b) In accordance with the rules and regulations promulgated by the Records Preservation Officer each departmental records supervisor shall:

(1) inventory the state records in his custody or control;

(2) submit to the Records Preservation Officer a report on the inventory containing, in addition to the information required by the rules and regulations, specific information showing which records are essential; and

(3) review periodically his inventory and his report and, if necessary, revise his report so that it is current, accurate and complete.

Preservation duplicates

Sec. 10. The Records Preservation Officer shall make, or cause to be made, preservation duplicates, or shall designate as preservation duplicates existing copies of essential state records. A preservation duplicate made by means of photography, microphotography, photocopying, or microfilm shall be made in conformity with the standards prescribed by the Records Preservation Officer, and which shall conform to the rules of the United States Bureau of Standards.

Use of duplicate

Sec. 11. A preservation duplicate made by a photographic, photostatic, microfilm, micro-card, miniature photographic, or other process which accurately reproduces or forms a durable medium for so reproducing the original, shall have the same force and effect for all purposes as the original record whether the original record is in existence or not. A transcript, exemplification or certified copy of such preservation duplicate shall be deemed for all purposes to be a transcript, exemplification or certified copy of the original record.

Record storage

Sec. 12. The Records Preservation Officer shall prescribe the place and manner of safekeeping of essential state records or preservation duplicates and shall establish storage facilities therefor. At least one copy of all essential records, together with a duplicate Seal of the State of Texas, shall be housed in the safest possible location and in facilities constructed to withstand blast, fire, water and other destructive forces. The storage facilities for the preservation duplicates, or the original record, must be in a place other than the legally designated or customary record storage location.

Removal from storage; temporary use

Sec. 13. The Records Preservation Officer shall properly maintain essential state records and preservation duplicates stored by him. An essential state record, or preservation duplicate, stored by the Records Preservation Officer shall be recalled by the regularly designated custodian of a state agency record for temporary use when necessary for the proper conduct of his office and shall be returned by such custodian to the Records Preservation Officer immediately after such use.

Removal from storage; inspection

Sec. 14. When an essential state record is stored by the Records Preservation Officer, the Records Preservation Officer, upon request of the regularly designated custodian of the state record, shall provide for its inspection, or for the making or certification of copies thereof and such copies when certified by the Records Preservation Officer shall have the same force and effect as if certified by the regularly designated custodian.

Program review

Sec. 15. The Records Preservation Officer and the committee shall at least once every two years review the entire program established by this Act.

Reports of compliance

Sec. 16. In the audit of the various state departments and agencies, the State Auditor shall report on the compliance of each state agency with all provisions of this Act.

Acts 1965, 59th Leg., p. 1161, ch. 548, eff. Aug. 30, 1965. Sec. 4(a) amended by Acts 1979, 66th Leg., p. 858, ch. 382, § 8, eff. Aug. 27, 1979.

Art. 5442a. State publications and depository libraries for state documents

Section 1. In this Act:

(1) "State publication" means printed matter that is produced in multiple copies by the authority of or at the total or partial expense of a state agency. The term includes publications sponsored by or purchased for distribution by a state agency and publications released by private institutions, such as research and consulting firms, under contract with a state agency, but does not include correspondence, interoffice memoranda, or routine forms.

(2) "State agency" means any state office, officer, department, division, bureau, board, commission, legislative committee, authority, institution, substate planning bureau, university system or institution of higher education as defined by Section 61.003, Texas Education Code, as amended, or any of their subdivisions.

(3) "Depository libraries" means the Texas State Library, the Texas Legislative Reference Library, the Library of Congress, the Center for Research Libraries, and other libraries that the Texas Library and Historical Commission designates as depository libraries.

Sec. 2. The Texas Library and Historical Commission shall adopt rules to establish procedures for the distribution of state publications to depository libraries and for the retention of those publications. The commission may contract with a depository library to receive all or a part of the state publications that are distributed.

Sec. 3. (a) Each state agency shall furnish to the Texas State Library its state publications in the quantity specified by the rules of the Texas Library and Historical Commission. The commission may not require more than 75 copies of a state publication.

(b) On the printing of or the awarding of a contract for the printing of a publication, a state agency shall arrange for the required number of copies to be deposited with the Texas State Library.

Sec. 4. The Texas State Library shall:

(1) acquire, organize, and retain the state publications;

(2) collect state publications and distribute them to depository libraries;

(3) establish a microform program for the preservation and management of state publications and make available state publications in microform to depository and other libraries at a reasonable cost;

(4) periodically issue a list of all state publications that it has received to all depository libraries and to other libraries on request;

(5) catalog, classify, and index all state publications that it has received and distribute the cataloging, classification, and indexing information to depository libraries and to other libraries on request; and

(6) ensure that state publications are fully represented in regional and national automated library networks.

Sec. 5. Each state agency shall designate one or more staff persons as the agency's publications contact person and shall notify the Texas State Library of the identity of each person selected. A state agency's contact person shall furnish to the Texas State Library each month a list of all of the agency's state publications that were produced during the preceding month.

Sec. 6. If a state agency's printing is done by contract, an account for the printing may not be approved and a warrant for the printing may not be issued unless the agency first furnishes to the State Board of Control a receipt from the state librarian for the publication or a written waiver from the state librarian exempting the publication from the requirements of this Act.

Sec. 7. The state librarian may specifically exempt a publication from the requirements of this Act.

Acts 1963, 58th Leg., p. 1133, ch. 438, eff. Aug. 31, 1963. Secs. 2 and 3 amended by Acts 1969, 61st Leg., p. 154, ch. 55, § 10, eff. Sept. 1, 1969; Sec. 2 amended by Acts 1979, 66th Leg., p. 858, ch. 382, § 9, eff. Aug. 27, 1979. Amended by Acts 1979, 66th Leg., p. 1775, ch. 720, § 2, eff. Aug. 27, 1979.

Art. 5442b.   Regional historical resource depositories

Definitions

Section 1. In this Act, unless the context requires a different meaning:

(1) "Commission" means the Texas State Library and Archives Commission.

(2) "Historical resource" means any book, publication, newspaper, manuscript, paper, document, memorandum, record, map, picture, photograph, microfilm, sound recording, or other material of historical interest or value.

(3) "Depository" means a regional historical resource depository authorized under this Act.

(4) "State Librarian" means the director and librarian of the Texas State Library.

Designation of regional depositories

Sec. 2. In order to provide for an orderly, uniform, state-wide system for the retention and preservation of historical resources on a manageable basis and under professional care in the region of origin or interest, the Texas State Library and Archives Commission is hereby authorized to designate to serve as a regional historical resources depository any institution which meets standards established by the commission in accordance with Section 3, Chapter 503, Acts of the 62nd Legislature, Regular Session, 1971 (Article 5442b, Vernon's Texas Civil Statutes).

Acceptance of gifts and donations

Sec. 2A. (a) To further implement the establishment of regional historical resource depositories, the commission is authorized, without obligation to the state or the general revenue fund, to accept, on behalf of the state, lands and buildings deemed by the commission as suitable for regional historical resource depositories, and to accept cash or property donations designated by the donors for the purpose of constructing libraries and regional depositories. For these purposes, the commission may enter into such agreements with donors as it may deem advisable for the acceptance, designation, and construction of such regional depositories or combined library and depository centers, but such agreements may not create any financial obligation on behalf of the state.

(b) Such regional libraries and depositories, when so accepted and designated by the commission, shall be subject to the applicable terms and provisions of this Act, except that they shall be owned by the state and under the direct control and supervision of the commission. The commission may provide for local staffing and maintenance, and may enter into any cooperative agreements it deems advisable with any city, county, state institution, or other governmental entity. The commission may accept gifts of furniture, equipment, maps, paintings, records, manuscripts, museum pieces, or any other historical resource for placement in the depositories upon conditions agreed upon between the commission and the donor of such a gift.

(c) If cash is donated and accepted by the commission for the building, maintenance, supplementing, expanding, or staffing of any such regional depository, or combined library and regional depository, the commission is authorized to keep such funds in a separate bank depository designated by the commission and to use such funds for the purposes designated by the donors. Also, if personal or real property is specifically donated to, and accepted by, the commission for the purpose of sale or lease to provide funds for any of the purposes of this Act, the proceeds received therefrom shall be deposited and used in the same manner as provided above for cash donations. In converting such donated property to cash, the commission may execute bills of sale, leases, or deeds in consideration of the payment to the commission by the purchasers or lessees of such donated property of the reasonable market value thereof as determined in writing by a licensed or professional appraiser. Such instruments of conveyance shall be authorized by written resolution of the commission and shall be signed by the chairman and attested to by the secretary.

(d) Subject to the terms of any donation given under this section, and unless otherwise provided by the donor, the commission, in acting for the state with respect to any donated property, shall have all of the applicable powers of trustees under the Texas Trust Act, as amended (Articles 7425b–1, et seq., Vernon's Texas Civil Statutes), with the state as beneficiary and owner of the remainder of such donated property. The commission shall annually report to the governor and the legislature all such donations, transactions, agreements, and special accounts, and same shall be subject to audit by the state auditor.

Area served; resource preservation, etc.

Sec. 3. The commission shall specify the geographical area of the state to be served by the designated depository and the methods of accessioning, cataloguing, housing, preserving, servicing, and caring for the historical resources which may be placed in the depository by or in the name of the commission.

Transfer or loan of resources

Sec. 4. (a) The commission may transfer to a depository historical resources which are under the custody and control of the commission.

(b) The commission may lend to a depository, for purposes of research or exhibit, and for such length of time and on such conditions as the commission may determine, historical resources which are under the custody and control of the commission.

(c) The commission may transfer historical resources placed by or in the name of the commission in a depository to another depository.

Offer, acceptance and loan of resources

Sec. 5. (a) County commissioners, other custodians of public records, and private parties may offer, and the Texas Library and Historical Commission [1] may accept, historical resources for preservation and retention in a depository.

(b) County commissioners, other custodians of public records, and private parties may lend historical resources to a depository for such length of time and on such conditions as the commission may prescribe.

[1] Name changed to Texas State Library and Archives Commission; see art. 5434b.

Removal of resources

Sec. 6. Nothing in this Act shall be construed so as to prevent the commission from removing historical resources placed by or in the name of the commission in depositories if the commission determines that such removal would insure the safety or availability of the historical resources.

Rules and regulations; notice and hearing; publication

Sec. 7. (a) Proposed initial rules and regulations necessary to the administration of the system of depositories shall be formulated by the State Librarian.

(b) These proposed rules and regulations shall be published in the official publication of the Texas State Library. Such publication shall include notice of a public hearing before the commission on the proposed rules and regulations to be held on a date certain not less than 30 nor more than 60 days following the date of such publication.

(c) Following the public hearing, the commission shall approve the proposed rules and regulations or return them to the State Librarian with recommendations for change. If the commission returns the proposed rules and regulations to the State Librarian, the State Librarian shall consider the recommendations for change and resubmit the proposed rules and regulations to the commission for its approval.

(d) Revised rules and regulations shall be adopted under the same procedure provided in this Act for the adoption of the initial rules and regulations.

Duties of state librarian

Sec. 8. The State Librarian shall supervise the system of depositories and shall promulgate the rules and regulations approved by the commission.

Appropriations

Sec. 9. The legislature may appropriate funds to the Texas State Library and Archives Commission sufficient for the purpose of carrying out the provisions of this Act.

Conflicting laws repealed

Sec. 10. All laws in conflict with the provisions of this Act are hereby repealed to the extent of such conflict.

Acts 1971, 62nd Leg., p. 1731, ch. 503, eff. Aug. 30, 1971. Sec. 2A added by Acts 1973, 63rd Leg., p. 254, ch. 122, § 1, eff. May 18, 1973; Sec. 1(1) amended by Acts 1979, 66th Leg., p. 858, ch. 382, § 10, eff. Aug. 27, 1979; Sec. 2 amended by Acts 1979, 66th Leg., p. 858, ch. 382, § 11, eff. Aug. 27, 1979; Acts 1979, 66th Leg., p. 1448, ch. 637, § 1, eff. Aug. 27, 1979; Sec. 5(a) amended by Acts 1979, 66th Leg., p. 1448, ch. 637, § 1, eff. Aug. 27, 1979; Sec. 9 amended by Acts 1979, 66th Leg., p. 858, ch. 382, § 12, eff. Aug. 27, 1979.

Art. 5442c. Maintenance and disposition of certain county records

Definitions

Section 1. In this Act:

(1) "County record" means any record required or authorized by law to be maintained in a county or precinct office or the office of district clerk.

(2) "Custodian" means the officer responsible for keeping a county record.

Records manual

Sec. 2. (a) The state librarian shall direct the staff of the regional historical resource depository program in the preparation of a county records manual.

Those preparing the manual shall consult with affected local officials and other interested persons.

(b) The manual shall list the various types of county records, state the minimum retention period prescribed by law for those records for which a minimum retention period is so prescribed, and prescribe a minimum retention period for all other county records except those subject to Section 8 of this Act. When the manual takes effect, those retention periods prescribed by it for county records for which no retention period is prescribed by law have the same effect as if they were prescribed by law.

(c) The manual also shall contain information to assist local officials in carrying out their functions under this Act, including model records schedules and implementation plans, and may prescribe rules consistent with this Act governing the disposition of obsolete county records.

(d) The manual has no legal effect until it is approved by a majority of the members of a review committee constituted as provided in Section 3 of this Act. The committee's approval is effective when a copy of the manual and a statement of its approval, signed and acknowledged by a majority of the members of the committee, is filed in the office of the Secretary of State.

(e) The state librarian may amend the manual from time to time. An amendment is effective when the state librarian files a certified copy of the amendment in the office of the Secretary of State, except that an amendment must first be approved by a review committee in the same manner as provided for approval of the original manual if it:

(1) prescribes a minimum retention period for a county record required by law to be kept and for which a minimum retention period is not prescribed by state law;

(2) changes a minimum retention period established by the manual; or

(3) changes the rules governing disposition of obsolete county records.

Review committee

Sec. 3. (a) A review committee required under this Act is composed of:

(1) the state librarian, who is chairman of the committee;

(2) the attorney general;

(3) a representative of the Texas Historical Commission, appointed by the commission; and

(4) one county clerk; one district clerk; one county judge or county commissioner; one county auditor; one county, district, or criminal district attorney; one county treasurer; one sheriff; and one county assessor-collector of taxes, each of whom shall be appointed by the state librarian.

(b) Except as provided in Subsection (d) of this section, an officer is eligible for appointment to the review committee under Subdivision (4), Subsection (a) of this section only if:

(1) he has been nominated by a petition signed by at least 50 other officers of the type nominated; or

(2) he has been nominated by an organization representing officers of the type nominated that has as members at least 50 of those officers.

(c) For the purposes of Subsection (b) of this section, county judges and commissioners are of the same type and county, district, and criminal district attorneys are of the same type.

(d) At least 30 days before making an appointment under Subdivision (4), Subsection (a) of this section, the state librarian shall cause to be published in the Texas Register a notice of his intention to make the appointment. If the state librarian does not receive a nomination for a particular type of officer meeting the requirements of Subsection (b) of this section before the 31st day after the notice is published, a nomination is not required.

(e) Service on a review committee by a public officer is an additional duty of his office.

(f) Members of the committee receive no compensation, but they are entitled to be paid their actual expenses incurred on committee business. The payment of the expenses of the attorney general and the representative of the Texas Historical Commission shall be paid from funds of the attorney general's office and the commission, respectively. The payment of the expenses of other members of the committee shall be from funds of the Texas State Library and Archives Commission.

(g) A review committee ceases to exist when it completes the work for which it was constituted unless it is sooner discharged by the state librarian.

Records schedule and implementation plan

Sec. 4. (a) A custodian of county records may prepare a records schedule applicable to his office and a plan for its implementation. On the request of the custodian, the state librarian and the staff of the regional historical resource depository program shall assist the custodian in this regard by furnishing him recommended model records schedules and implementation plans and other information.

(b) A records schedule, if prepared, shall contain an inventory of county records kept by the custodian. It shall prescribe a minimum retention period for each type of record. The retention period for each type of record must be at least as long as that prescribed by law or established in the county records manual.

(c) If a custodian prepares a records schedule, he shall also prepare an implementation plan that prescribes, in conformity with this Act, the manner and procedure for disposing of records no longer needed on the expiration of the applicable retention period.

(d) The records schedule and implementation plan take effect when the custodian files a certified copy of the schedule and plan in the office of the county clerk. A custodian may amend an existing schedule or plan. An amendment takes effect when the custodian files a certified copy of it in the office of the county clerk.

Disposition of obsolete records

Sec. 5. (a) When the retention period expires for a county record subject to an approved records schedule and implementation plan, and in the judgment of the custodian the record is no longer needed, he may dispose of the record in accordance with the implementation plan, the county records manual, and the provisions of this Act.

(b) No county record may be destroyed pursuant to an implementation plan unless at least 60 days before the day it is destroyed the custodian gives written notice to the state librarian of his intention to destroy the record. The notice must sufficiently describe the record to enable the state librarian to determine if it should be transferred to the state library for preservation in a regional historical resource depository. If the state librarian requests that a record be transferred, the custodian shall comply with the request. Otherwise, the record may be destroyed.

(c) County records may be destroyed only by the sale of them for recycling purposes or by shredding them or burning them. Regardless of the method used, adequate safeguards must be employed to insure that they do not remain in their original state and are no longer recognizable as county records.

(d) No later than the 10th day before records are destroyed, the custodian shall file and record with the county clerk a notice stating which records are to be destroyed, how they are to be destroyed, and the date they are to be destroyed. The same day the notice is filed, the county clerk shall post a copy of it in the

(e) Service on a review committee by a public officer is an additional duty of his office.

(f) Members of the committee receive no compensation, but they are entitled to be paid their actual expenses incurred on committee business. The payment of the expenses of the attorney general and the representative of the Texas Historical Commission shall be paid from funds of the attorney general's office and the commission, respectively. The payment of the expenses of other members of the committee shall be from funds of the Texas State Library and Archives Commission.

(g) A review committee ceases to exist when it completes the work for which it was constituted unless it is sooner discharged by the state librarian.

Records schedule and implementation plan

Sec. 4. (a) A custodian of county records may prepare a records schedule applicable to his office and a plan for its implementation. On the request of the custodian, the state librarian and the staff of the regional historical resource depository program shall assist the custodian in this regard by furnishing him recommended model records schedules and implementation plans and other information.

(b) A records schedule, if prepared, shall contain an inventory of county records kept by the custodian. It shall prescribe a minimum retention period for each type of record. The retention period for each type of record must be at least as long as that prescribed by law or established in the county records manual.

(c) If a custodian prepares a records schedule, he shall also prepare an implementation plan that prescribes, in conformity with this Act, the manner and procedure for disposing of records no longer needed on the expiration of the applicable retention period.

(d) The records schedule and implementation plan take effect when the custodian files a certified copy of the schedule and plan in the office of the county clerk. A custodian may amend an existing schedule or plan. An amendment takes effect when the custodian files a certified copy of it in the office of the county clerk.

Disposition of obsolete records

Sec. 5. (a) When the retention period expires for a county record subject to an approved records schedule and implementation plan, and in the judgment of the custodian the record is no longer needed, he may dispose of the record in accordance with the implementation plan, the county records manual, and the provisions of this Act.

(b) No county record may be destroyed pursuant to an implementation plan unless at least 60 days before the day it is destroyed the custodian gives written notice to the state librarian of his intention to destroy the record. The notice must sufficiently describe the record to enable the state librarian to determine if it should be transferred to the state library for preservation in a regional historical resource depository. If the state librarian requests that a record be transferred, the custodian shall comply with the request. Otherwise, the record may be destroyed.

(c) County records may be destroyed only by the sale of them for recycling purposes or by shredding them or burning them. Regardless of the method used, adequate safeguards must be employed to insure that they do not remain in their original state and are no longer recognizable as county records.

(d) No later than the 10th day before records are destroyed, the custodian shall file and record with the county clerk a notice stating which records are to be destroyed, how they are to be destroyed, and the date they are to be destroyed. The same day the notice is filed, the county clerk shall post a copy of it in the same manner that notices of meetings are posted under Chapter 271, Acts of the 60th Legislature, Regular Session, 1967, as amended (Article 6252-17, Vernon's Texas Civil Statutes).

(e) No person is civilly liable for the destruction of a record in accordance with this Act and an approved records schedule and implementation plan.

Transferral of records to state library

Sec. 6. (a) A custodian may transfer to the state library for preservation in a regional historical resource depository any county record that is not needed for administrative purposes.

(b) When a custodian transfers a county record to the state library under Subsection (a) of this section or under Subsection (b), Section 5 of this Act, the state librarian shall give the custodian a receipt for the record. The custodian is not required to make a microfilm or other copy of the record before transferring it.

(c) The state librarian may make certified copies of county records that have been transferred to the state library. Each certified copy shall state that it is a true and correct copy of the record in the state librarian's custody. A certified copy made under the authority of this subsection has the same force and effect for all purposes as a copy certified by the county clerk or other custodian as provided by law.

Microfilming of records

Sec. 7. This Act does not require the microfilming of county records, but an implementation plan may include provision for microfilming of records in accordance with other state law.

Sec. 8. This Act does not permit the establishment of a retention period for:

(1) any county record that affects the title to real property, other than a recorded lien that is no longer enforceable;

(2) a will;

(3) the minutes of a commissioners court; or

(4) the pleadings or any order, decree, or judgment, or any instrument incorporated by reference in an order, decree, or judgment, in a civil case in a court of record.

Acts 1977, 65th Leg., p. 1198, ch. 463, §§ 1 to 8, eff. Aug. 29, 1977. Sec. 3(f) amended by Acts 1979, 66th Leg., p. 859, ch. 382, § 13, eff. Aug. 27, 1979.

Art. 5443. Sale of archives

The Commission is authorized to sell copies of the Texas Archives, printed with funds appropriated for that purpose, at a price not to exceed twenty-five per cent above the cost of publishing, and all moneys received from such sale shall be paid into the State Treasury. One copy of each such volume may be distributed free to the Governor, the members of the Legislature, and to the libraries, indicated in the preceding article. Acts 1913, p. 281.

Art. 5445. Assistants

The Commission shall appoint an assistant librarian who shall rank as head of a department and who in the absence of the State Librarian may sign and certify accounts and documents in the same manner and with the same legal authority as the State Librarian. Said assistant shall give bond to the Governor in the sum of three thousand dollars and shall take the official oath. Other assistants in the State Library shall be appointed by the Commission and be divided into four grades: Heads of departments, library assistants, clerks and laborers. Heads of departments and library assistants shall be required to have technical library training; and heads of departments shall have had at least one year of experience in library work prior to appointment. Clerks shall be required to hold a diploma from a first class high school according to the standards of the State Board of Education or the University of Texas, or to present satisfactory evidence of educational training equal to that provided by such high school, and also to present satisfactory evidence of proficiency in stenography and typewriting or book-keeping. Laborers must present satisfactory evidence of education sufficient to do such elementary clerical work as shall be required of them. The archivist must present satisfactory evidence of one year's advanced work in American or Southwestern history in a standard college and of a fluent reading knowledge of Spanish and French; provided, that the archivist shall not be required to have technical library school training or any library experience. Acts 2nd C.S.1919, p. 151.

Art. 5446. [5609] Report to Governor

The Commission shall make a biennial report to the Governor, which shall include the biennial report of the State Librarian. Said report shall present a comprehensive view of the operation of the Commission in the discharge of the duties imposed by this title, shall present a review of the library conditions in this State, present an itemized statement of the expenditures of the Commission, make such recommendations as their experience shall suggest, and present careful estimates of the sums of money necessary for the carrying out of the provisions of this title. Said report shall be made and printed, and by the Governor laid before the Legislature as other departmental reports. Acts 1909, p. 122.

LEGISLATIVE REFERENCE LIBRARY
(Vernon's Annotated Revised Civil Statutes of the State of
Texas, 1982, Art. 5444a.)

Art. 5444a. Legislative reference library

Definitions

Section 1. In this Act, unless the context requires a different meaning,
(1) "library" means the legislative reference library;
(2) "board" means the legislative library board;
(3) "director" means the director of the legislative reference library.

Transfer of functions and duties

Sec. 2. The functions and duties now performed by the legislative reference section of the state library are transferred to the legislative reference library, which is established as an independent agency of the legislature.

Application of Sunset Act

Sec. 2a. The Legislative Reference Library is subject to the Texas Sunset Act; and unless continued in existence as provided by that Act the library is abolished, and this Act expires effective September 1, 1989.

Board; membership and expenses

Sec. 3. (a) The library is under the control of, and administered by, the legislative library board composed of the lieutenant governor, the speaker of the House of Representatives, the chairman of the Senate finance committee, the chairman of the appropriations committee of the House of Representatives, and one other member of the Senate and one other member of the House of Representatives, appointed by the president of the Senate and the speaker of the House of Representatives, respectively.

(b) Members of the legislative library board are not entitled to compensation for service on the board, but each member is entitled to reimbursement for actual and necessary expenses incurred in attending meetings and performing official duties, to be paid out of funds appropriated to the board.

Contents of library; aid to Legislature

Sec. 4. The library shall maintain for the use and information of the members of the legislature, the heads of state departments, and citizens of the state, a legislative reference library containing checklists and catalogues of current legislation in this and other states, catalogues of bills and resolutions presented in either House of the Legislature, checklists of public documents of the several states, including all reports issued by departments, agencies, boards, and commissions of this state, and digests of public laws of this and other states as may best be made available for legislative use. The director and employees of the library shall give any aid and assistance requested by members of the Legislature in researching and preparing bills and resolutions.

Director; appointment, term and salary; personnel

Sec. 5. The board shall appoint a director who shall serve for a period of one year from September 1st of each year, unless sooner discharged by said board for any reason. The salary of the director shall be fixed by the board. The director may, with the approval of the board, employ professional and clerical personnel at salaries fixed by the board.

Transfer of property; inventory

Sec. 6. All books, documents, files, records, equipment, and property of all kinds owned or used by the legislative reference section of the state library, and all facilities used for storage, are transferred to the library. The director and librarian of the state library and the director of the library and [1] shall sign a written agreement showing an inventory of all property to be transferred. When the agreement is signed, the comptroller of public accounts shall transfer to the library the property listed, enter the property in the inventory of the library, and delete the property from the inventory of the state library.

[1] Word "and" probably should be omitted.

Library or depository; disposition of legislative documents

Sec. 7. (a) The library is a depository library, as that term is defined by Section 2, Chapter 438, Acts of the 58th Legislature, 1963 (Article 5442a, Vernon's Texas Civil Statutes), and shall receive state documents and documents and publications from other states which are distributed by the state library, in the manner in which they were received by the legislative section of the state library.

(b) All printed daily legislative journals, bills, resolutions, and other legislative documents shall be delivered daily to the library, and at the close of each legislative session all daily journals, bills, and resolutions in the hands of the sergeant-at-arms of the House of Representatives and the Senate shall be delivered to the library to be disposed of at the discretion of the director.

Transfer of appropriations

Sec. 8. All money appropriated by the legislature to the state library and historical commission for the purpose of operating and administering the legislative reference section of the state library is transferred to the board to be used only for operating and administering the library.

Rules and regulations

Sec. 9. The board shall make all reasonable rules and regulations which are necessary to insure efficient operation of the library.

Acts 1969, 61st Leg., p. 154, ch. 55, eff. Sept. 1, 1969. Sec. 5 amended by Acts 1971, 62nd Leg., p. 1112, ch. 243, § 1, eff. May 17, 1971. Sec. 2a added by Acts 1977, 65th Leg., p. 1855, ch. 735, § 2.164, eff. Aug. 29, 1977.

STATE LAW LIBRARY
(Vernon's Annotated Revised Civil Statutes of the State of
Texas, 1982, Art. 5444b.)

Art. 5444b. State Law Library

Definitions

Section 1. In this Act, unless the context requires a different meaning:

(1) "Library" means the State Law Library.

(2) "Board" means the State Law Library Board.

(3) "Director" means the director of the State Law Library.

Transfer of functions and duties to library; status as state agency

Sec. 2. The functions and duties now performed by the library of the
Supreme Court under Article 1722, Revised Civil Statutes of Texas, 1925, are
transferred to the State Law Library, which is established as an independent
agency of the State.

Application of Sunset Act

Sec. 2a. The State Law Library is subject to the Texas Sunset Act; and
unless continued in existence as provided by that Act the library is abolished, and
this Act expires effective September 1, 1987.

Board; members or representatives; compensation

Sec. 3. (a) The library is under the control of, and administered by, the
State Law Library Board composed of the chief justice of the Supreme Court, the
presiding judge of the Court of Criminal Appeals, and the Attorney General.
Each member of the board may designate a personal representative to serve for
him.

(b) Members of the board or their designated representatives are not entitled
to compensation for service on the board, but each member or representative is
entitled to reimbursement for actual and necessary expenses incurred in attending
meetings and performing official duties, to be paid out of funds appropriated to
the board.

Legal reference facility; use

Sec. 4. The library shall maintain a legal reference facility to include the
statutes and case reports from the several states and legal journals and periodicals. The facility shall be maintained for the use and information of the members
and staff of the:

(1) Supreme Court;

(2) Court of Criminal Appeals;

(3) Attorney General's Department;

(4) commissions, agencies, and boards of the other branches of State government; and

(5) citizens of the State.

Director; staff personnel; salaries

Sec. 5. The board shall employ a director of the library and shall fix his
salary. The director shall be accountable only to the board and shall serve at the
pleasure of the board. The director may, with the approval of the board, employ
professional and clerical personnel at salaries fixed by the board.

Transfer of books, etc. to library

Sec. 6. All books, documents, files, records, equipment, and property of all kinds owned and used by the Supreme Court Library, the Court of Criminal Appeals library, and the Attorney General's library are transferred to the State Law Library.

State Law Library Fund; Appropriations; transfers to Fund; effect upon other law libraries

Sec. 7.   During the biennium ending August 31, 1973, the Comptroller of Public Accounts is hereby authorized and directed to set up an account to be known as the State Law Library Fund and is authorized and directed to transfer into such account from time to time moneys appropriated to the Supreme Court for the purpose of operating and administering the Supreme Court Library.   For the purpose of operating and administering the library for the Court of Criminal Appeals, the Comptroller is authorized and directed to transfer into such account from time to time such amounts as may be necessary for such court's appropriation for consumable supplies and materials or other designation for its library purposes.   For the purpose of operating and administering the library for the Attorney General, the Comptroller is authorized and directed to transfer into such account from time to time such amounts as may be necessary from the appropriation to the Attorney General's office for consumable supplies and materials or other designation for its library purposes.   Such transfers may be made on the direction of the Chief Justice of the Supreme Court, the Presiding Judge of the Court of Criminal Appeals, and the Attorney General, respectively.   Moneys in the State Law Library Fund may be expended by the board or its duly authorized representative for the purpose of maintaining, operating, and keeping up to date the State Law Library.   Moneys appropriated for use of the libraries of the Supreme Court, Court of Criminal Appeals, and the Attorney General's office during the present biennium shall not be affected by this Act.

Transfer of books, etc. to University of Texas Law School library

Sec. 8.   The library may transfer any books, papers, and publications located in and belonging to the library to the library of the Law School of The University of Texas.   The transfer may be made only on the unanimous vote of the members of the board.   By majority vote, the board may recall any books, papers, or publications transferred by authority of this section.

Rules and regulations

Sec. 9.   The board shall make all reasonable rules and regulations which are necessary to insure efficient operation of the library.

Acts 1971, 62nd Leg., p. 2359, ch. 722, eff. June 8, 1971. Sec. 2a added by Acts 1977, 65th Leg., p. 1852, ch. 735, § 2.141, eff. Aug. 29, 1977.

OTHER PUBLIC ARCHIVES
(Vernon's Annotated Revised Civil Statutes of the State of
Texas, 1982, Art. 254-260.)

Article 254.   [86] [66] [61]   Of State Department

The Secretary of State is authorized to take possession of rooms in the basement of the capitol for the use of the State Department and the better preservation of archives. Acts 1856, p. 3; G.L. vol. 4, p. 421.

Art. 255.   [87] [67] [62]   Archives of Republic

The entire archives of the Congress of the Republic of Texas, and of the several Legislatures of this State, arranged and filed according to law, together with the records, books and journals of said Congress and Legislatures, prepared in accordance with law, and heretofore, or hereafter, deposited in the office of the Secretary of State are declared to be archives of said office. Acts 1854, p. 113; Acts 1887, p. 47; G.L. vol. 3, p. 1557.

Art. 256. [88] [68] [63] Historical archives

All books, pictures, papers, maps, documents, manuscripts, memoranda and data which relate to the history of Texas as a province, colony, Republic or State, which have been or may be delivered to the State Librarian by the Secretary of State, Comptroller, Land Commissioner or by any head of any department, or by any person or officer, in pursuance of law, shall be deemed books and papers of the State Library and shall constitute a part of the archives of said State Library; and copies therefrom shall be made and certified by the State Librarian, or by the person serving as Archivist of the Texas State Library, upon application of any person interested, which certificate shall have the same force and effect as if made by the officer originally in custody of them. Acts 1907, p. 283; Acts 1943, 48th Leg., p. 267, ch. 165, § 1.

Art. 257. [89] [69] [64] Of Comptroller's office

All books, papers, records and archives, that were heretofore archives of the auditor's office, or of the office of the Commissioner of the Court of Claims, and which have heretofore, in pursuance of law, been delivered to the Comptroller, shall be deemed papers and records of the Comptroller's office, and shall constitute a part of the archives of his office. Acts 1858, p. 40; Acts 1860, p. 48; G.L. vol. 4, pp. 912, 1412.

Art. 258. [90] [70] [65] Other archives

All books, papers, records, rolls, documents, returns, reports, lists and all other papers that have been, are now, or that may be, required by law to be kept, filed or deposited in any office of the executive departments of this State, shall constitute a part of the archives of the offices in which the same are so kept, filed or deposited.

Art. 259. University archives

The librarian of the University of Texas and the archivist of the Department of History of said University are hereby authorized to make certified copies of all public records in the custody of the University of Texas, and said certified copies shall be valid in law and shall have the same force and effect for all purposes as if certified to by the county clerk or other custodian as now provided for by law. In making the certificate to the said certified copies, either by the librarian or by the archivist of the Department of History, the said officer shall certify that the foregoing is a true and correct copy of said document, and after signing the said certificate shall swear to the same before any officer authorized to take oaths under the laws of this State. Acts 1921, p. 94.

Art. 260.   Loan of archives

County Commissioners and other custodians of public records are hereby authorized, in their discretion, to lend to the Library of the University of Texas, for such length of time and on such conditions as they may determine, such parts of their archives and records as have become mainly of historical value, taking a receipt therefor from the librarian of such University; and the librarian of said University is hereby authorized to receipt for such records as may be transferred to the said Library, and to make copies thereof for historical study. Id.

LIBRARY SYSTEMS

(Vernon's Annotated Revised Civil Statutes of the State of
Texas, 1982, Art. 5446a.)

Art. 5446a.   Library Systems Act

CHAPTER A.   GENERAL PROVISIONS

Short title

Section 1.   This Act may be cited as the Library Systems Act.

Definitions

Sec. 2.   In this Act, unless the context requires a different definition:

(1) "public library" means a library operated by a single public agency or board that is freely open to all persons under identical conditions and receives its financial support in whole or in part from public funds;

(2) "Commission" means the Texas State Library and Archives Commission;

(3) "State Librarian" means the director and librarian of the Texas State Library;

(4) "library system" means two or more public libraries cooperating in a system approved by the Commission to improve library service and to make their resources accessible to all residents of the area which the member libraries collectively serve;

(5) "state library system" means a network of library systems, interrelated by contract, for the purpose of organizing library resources and services for research, information, and recreation to improve statewide library service and to serve collectively the entire population of the state;

(6) "major resource system" means a network of library systems attached to a major resource center, consisting of area libraries joined cooperatively to the major resource center and of community libraries joined cooperatively to area libraries or directly to the major resource center;

(7) "major resource center" means a large public library serving a population of 200,000 or more within 4,000 or more square miles, and designated as the central library of a major resource system for referral service from area libraries in the system, for cooperative service with other libraries in the system, and for

federated operations with other libraries in the system;

(8) "area library" means a medium-sized public library serving a population of 25,000 or more, which has been designated as an area library by the Commission and is a member of a library system interrelated to a major resource center;

(9) "community library" means a small public library serving a population of less than 25,000, which is a member of a library system interrelated to a major resource center;

(10) "contract" means a written agreement between two or more libraries to cooperate, consolidate, or receive one or more services;

(11) "standards" means the criteria established by the Commission which must be met before a library may be accredited and eligible for membership in a major resource system;

(12) "accreditation of libraries" means the evaluation and rating of public libraries and library systems using the standards as a basis;

(13) "governing body" means that body which has the power to authorize a library to join, participate in, or withdraw from a library system; and

(14) "library board" means the body which has the authority to give administrative direction or advisory counsel to a library or library system.

CHAPTER B. STATE LIBRARY SYSTEM

Establishment

Sec. 3. The Commission shall establish and develop a state library system.

Advisory board

Sec. 4. (a) The Commission shall appoint an advisory board of five librarians qualified by training, experience, and interest to advise the Commission on the policy to be followed in the application of the provisions of this Act.

(b) The term of office of a board member is three years, except that the initial members shall draw lots for terms, one to serve a one-year term, two to serve a two-year term, and two to serve a three-year term.

(c) The board shall meet at least once a year. Other meetings may be called by the Commission during the year.

(d) The members of the board shall serve without compensation, but shall be reimbursed their actual and necessary expenses incurred in the performance of their official duties.

(e) Vacancies shall be filled for the remainder of the unexpired term in the same manner as original appointments.

(f) No member may serve more than two consecutive terms.

Plan of service

Sec. 5. The State Librarian shall submit an initial plan for the establishment of the state library system and an annual plan for the development of the system for review by the advisory board and approval by the Commission.

CHAPTER C. MAJOR RESOURCE SYSTEM

Authority to establish

Sec. 6. The Commission may establish and develop major resource systems in conformity with the plan for a state library system as provided in Chapter B, Sec. 5 of this Act.

Membership in system

Sec. 7. (a) Eligibility for membership in the system is dependent on accreditation of the library by the Commission on the basis of standards established by the Commission.

(b) To meet population change, economic change, and changing service strengths of member libraries, a major resource system may be reorganized, merged with another system, or partially transferred to another system by the Commission with the approval of the majority of the appropriate governing bodies of the libraries comprising the system.

Operation and management

Sec. 8. (a) Governing bodies within a major resource system area may join in the development, operation, and maintenance of the system and appropriate and allocate funds for its support.

(b) Governing bodies of political subdivisions of the state may negotiate separately or collectively a contract with the governing bodies of member libraries of a major resource system for all library services or for those services defined in the contract.

(c) On petition of 10 percent of the qualified electors in the latest general election of a county, city, town, or village within the major resource system service area, the governing body of that political subdivision shall call an election to vote on the question of whether or not the political subdivision shall establish contractual relationships with the major resource system.

(d) The governing body of a major resource center and the Commission may enter into contracts and agreements with the governing bodies of other libraries, including but not limited to other public libraries, school libraries and media centers, academic libraries, technical information and research libraries, or systems of such libraries, to provide specialized resources and services to the major resource system in effecting the purposes of this Act.

Withdrawal from major resource system

Sec. 9. (a) The governing body of any political subdivision of the state may by resolution or ordinance withdraw from the system. Notice of withdrawal must be made not less than 90 days before the end of the major resource center fiscal year.

(b) The provision for termination of all or part of a major resource system does not prohibit revision of the system by the Commission, with the approval of the majority of the appropriate governing bodies, by reorganization, by transfer of part of the system, or by merger with other systems.

(c) The governing body of a public library which proposes to become a major resource center shall submit an initial plan of service for the major resource system to the State Librarian. Thereafter, the governing body of the major resource center shall submit an annual plan of system development, made in consultation with the advisory council, to the State Librarian.

Advisory council

Sec. 10. (a) An advisory council for each major resource system is established, consisting of six lay members representing the member libraries of the system.

(b) The governing body of each member library of the system shall elect or appoint a representative for the purpose of electing council members. The representatives shall meet following their selection and shall elect the initial council from their group. Thereafter, the representatives in an annual meeting shall elect members of their group to fill council vacancies arising due to expiration of terms of office. Other vacancies shall be filled for the unexpired term by the remaining members of the council. The major resource center shall always have one member on the council.

(c) The term of office of a council member is three years, except that the initial members shall draw lots for terms, two to serve a one-year term, two to serve a two-year term, and two to serve a three-year term. No individual may serve more than two consecutive terms.

(d) The council shall elect a chairman, vice chairman, and secretary.

(e) The council shall meet at least once a year. Other meetings may be held as often as is required to transact necessary business. A majority of the council membership constitutes a quorum. The council shall report business transacted at each meeting to all member libraries of the system.

(f) The members of the council shall serve without compensation, but shall be reimbursed their actual and necessary expenses incurred in the performance of their official duties.

(g) The council shall serve as a liaison agency between the member libraries and their governing bodies and library boards to:

(1) advise in the formulation of the annual plan for service to be offered by the system;

(2) recommend policies appropriate to services needed;

(3) evaluate services received;

(4) counsel with administrative personnel; and

(5) recommend functions and limitations of contracts between cooperating agencies.

(h) The functions of the advisory council in no way diminish the powers of local library boards.

CHAPTER D. CONSTITUENTS OF MAJOR RESOURCE SYSTEMS

Major resource center

Sec. 11. (a) The Commission may designate major resource centers. Designation shall be made from existing public libraries on the basis of criteria approved by the Commission and agreed to by the governing body of the library involved.

(b) The governing body of the library designated by the Commission as a major resource center may accept the designation by resolution or ordinance stating the type of service to be given and the area to be served.

(c) The Commission may revoke the designation of a major resource center which ceases to meet the criteria for a major resource center or which fails to comply with obligations stated in the resolution or ordinance agreements. The Commission shall provide a fair hearing on request of the major resource center.

(d) Funds allocated by governing bodies contracting with the major resource center and funds contributed from state grants-in-aid for the purposes of this Act shall be deposited with the governing body operating the major resource center following such procedures as may be agreed to by the contributing agency.

(e) The powers of the governing board of the major resource center in no way diminish the powers of local library boards.

Area library

Sec. 12. (a) The Commission may designate area libraries within each major resource system service area to serve the surrounding area with library services for which contracts are made with participating libraries. Area libraries may be designated only from existing public libraries and on the basis of criteria approved by the Commission and agreed to by the governing body of the library involved.

(b) The governing body of the library designated by the Commission as an area library may accept the designation by resolution or ordinance stating the type of service to be given and the area to be served.

(c) The Commission may revoke the designation of an area library which ceases to meet the criteria for an area library or fails to comply with obligations stated in the resolution or ordinance agreement. The Commission shall provide a fair hearing on request of the major resource center or area library.

(d) Funds allocated by governing bodies contracting with the area library and funds contributed from state grants-in-aid for the purposes of this Act shall be deposited with the governing body operating the area library following such procedures as may be agreed to by the contributing agency.

Community library

Sec. 13. (a) Community libraries accredited by the Commission are eligible for membership in a major resource system.

(b) A community library may join a system by resolution or ordinance of its governing body and execution of contracts for service.

(c) The Commission may terminate the membership of a community library in a system if the community library loses its accreditation by ceasing to meet the minimum standards established by the Commission or fails to comply with obligations stated in the resolution or ordinance agreement.

CHAPTER E. STATE GRANTS–IN–AID TO LIBRARIES

Establishment

Sec. 14. (a) A program of state grants within the limitations of funds appropriated by the Texas Legislature shall be established.

(b) The program of state grants shall include one or more of the following:

(1) system operation grants, to strengthen major resource system services to member libraries, including grants to reimburse other libraries for providing specialized services to major resource systems;

(2) incentive grants, to encourage libraries to join together into larger units of service in order to meet criteria for major resource system membership;

(3) establishment grants, to help establish libraries which will qualify for major resource system membership in communities without library service; and

(4) equalization grants, to help libraries in communities with relatively limited taxable resources to meet criteria for major resource system membership.

Rules and regulations

Sec. 15. (a) Proposed initial rules and regulations necessary to the administration of the program of state grants, including qualifications for major resource system membership, shall be formulated by the State Librarian with the advice of the advisory board.

(b) These proposed rules and regulations shall be published in the official publication of the Texas State Library. Such publication shall include notice of a public hearing before the Commission on the proposed rules and regulations to be held on a date certain not less than 30 nor more than 60 days following the date of such publication.

(c) Following the public hearing, the Commission shall approve the proposed rules and regulations or return them to the State Librarian with recommendations for change. If the Commission returns the proposed rules and regulations to the State Librarian with recommendations for change, the State Librarian shall consider the recommendations for change in consultation with the advisory board and resubmit the proposed rules and regulations to the Commission for its approval.

(d) Revised rules and regulations shall be adopted under the same procedure provided in this Chapter for the adoption of the initial rules and regulations.

Administration

Sec. 16. The State Librarian shall administer the program of state grants and shall promulgate the rules and regulations approved by the Commission.

Funding

Sec. 17. (a) The Commission may use funds appropriated by the Texas Legislature for personnel and other administrative expenses necessary to carry out the provisions of the Act.

(b) Libraries and library systems may use state grants for materials; for personnel, equipment, and administrative expenses; and for financing programs which enrich the services and materials offered a community by its public library.

(c) State grants may not be used for site acquisition, construction, or for acquisition of buildings, or for payment of past debts.

(d) State aid to any free tax-supported public library is a supplement to and not a replacement of local support.

(e) Exclusive of the expenditure of funds for administrative expenses as provided in Section 17(a) of this Act, all funds appropriated pursuant to Section 14 of this Act shall be apportioned among the major resource systems on the following basis:

Twenty-five percent of such funds shall be apportioned equally to the major resource systems and the remaining seventy-five percent shall be apportioned to them on a per capita basis determined by the last decennial census or the most recent official population estimate of the U.S. Department of Commerce, Bureau of the Census. This section takes effect September 1, 1979.

CHAPTER F. OTHER PROVISIONS

Severability

Sec. 18. If any provision of this Act or the application thereof to any person or circumstances is held invalid, such invalidity shall not affect other provisions or applications of the Act which can be given effect without the invalid provision or application, and to this end the provisions of this Act are declared to be severable.

Emergency clause

Sec. 19. The importance of this legislation and the crowded condition of the calendars in both houses create an emergency and an imperative public necessity that the Constitutional Rule requiring bills to be read on three several days in each house be suspended, and this Rule is hereby suspended.

Acts 1969, 61st Leg., p. 61, ch. 24, eff. Sept. 1, 1969; Sec. 7(b) amended Acts 1977, 65th Leg., p. 809, ch. 301, § 1, eff. Aug. 29, 1977; Sec. 9(b) amended by Acts 1977, 65th Leg., p. 809, ch. 301, § 2, eff. Aug. 29, 1977; Sec. 10(b) amended by Acts 1977, 65th Leg., p. 810, ch. 301, § 3, eff. Aug. 29, 1977; Sec. 17(c) amended by Acts 1977, 65th Leg., p. 810, ch. 301, § 4, eff. Aug. 29, 1977; Sec. 2(2) amended by Acts 1979, 66th Leg., p. 859, ch. 382, § 14, eff. Aug. 27, 1979; Sec. 17(e) amended by Acts 1979, 66th Leg., p. 1774, ch. 720, § 1, eff. Sept. 1, 1979.

COUNTY LIBRARIES
(Vernon's Annotated Revised Civil Statutes of the State of
Texas , 1982, Art. 1677-1681, 1683-1687, 1689-1696a.)

Article 1677. Authority to establish

The commissioners court of any county may establish, maintain, and operate within their respective counties, county free libraries in the manner and with the functions prescribed in this title. The said court shall also have the power and authority to establish in co-operation with another county or counties a joint free county library for the benefit of the co-operative counties. Acts 2nd C.S.1919, p. 219.

Art. 1678. Territory

The commissioners court of any county may establish county free libraries for that part of such county lying outside of the incorporated cities and towns already maintaining free public libraries and for such additional parts of such counties as may elect to become a part of or to participate in such county free library system. On their own initiative, or when petitioned to do so by a majority of the voters of that part of the county to be affected, said court shall proceed to establish and provide for the maintenance of such library according to the further provisions of this title. The county library shall be located at the county seat in the court house, unless more suitable quarters are available. Id.

Art. 1679. Tax for maintenance

The Commissioners Courts are hereby authorized to set aside annually from the General Tax Fund, or the Permanent Improvement Fund of the county, as the said Court may determine, sums for the maintaining of free county libraries and for the erection of permanent improvements and the securing of land for free county libraries, but not to exceed twelve cents (12¢) on the One Hundred Dollar ($100) valuation of all property in such county outside of all incorporated cities and towns already supporting a free public library, and upon all property within all incorporated cities and towns already supporting a free library, and upon all property within all incorporated cities and towns already supporting a free public library which have elected to become a part of such free library systems provided in Title 35 of the Revised Civil Statutes, for the purpose of maintaining county free libraries and for purchasing property therefor.

Acts 1959, 56th Leg., p. 282, ch. 158, § 1.

Art. 1680. Gifts and bequests

The commissioners court is authorized and empowered to receive on behalf of the county any gift, bequest, or devise for the county free library, or for any branch or subdivision thereof. The title to all property belonging to the county free library shall be vested in the county, but where the gifts or bequests shall be made for the benefit of any branch or branches of the county free library, such gifts or bequests shall be administered as designed by the donor. Id.

Art. 1681. Existing libraries

In any county where a farmers' county library has been established as provided by former laws the same shall continue to operate as a farmers' county library, unless a county free library shall be established as provided for in this title, in which case the former shall merge with and become a part of the latter. Id.

Art. 1683. County Librarian

Upon the establishment of a county free library the Commissioners Court shall biennially appoint a County Librarian who shall hold office for a term of two (2) years subject to removal for cause after a hearing by said Court. No person shall be eligible to the office of County Librarian unless prior to his appointment he has received from the Texas State Library and Archives Commission a certificate of qualification for office; and when any County Librarian has heretofore received a certificate of qualification for office from the Texas State Library and Archives Commission, and has served as County Librarian for any county in this State, said Librarian may be employed or reemployed by any county as Librarian without further examination and issuance of certificate from said Texas State Library and Archives Commission. The County Librarian shall, prior to entering upon the duties of his office, file with the County Clerk the official oath and make a bond upon the faithful performance of his duties with sufficient sureties approved by the County Judge of the county of which the Librarian is to be the County Librarian, in such sum as the Commissioners Court may determine.
Amended by Acts 1981, 67th Leg., p. 2845, ch. 764, § 1, eff. Sept. 1, 1981.

Art. 1684. Salary and expenses

The salary of the librarian and assistants shall be fixed by said court at the time they fix the salary of the appointive county officers. The county librarian and assistants shall be allowed actual and necessary traveling expenses incurred in the business of the library. Acts 2nd C.S.1919, p. 219.

Art. 1685. Duty of librarian

The librarian shall endeavor to give an equal and complete service to all parts of the county through branch libraries and deposit stations in schools and other locations where suitable quarters may be obtained, thus distributing printed matter, books, and other educational matter as quickly as circumstances will permit. The county librarian shall have the power to make rules and regulations for the county free library, to establish branches and stations throughout the county, to de-

termine the number and kind of employés of such library, and, with
the approval of the commissioners' court, to appoint and dismiss such
employés. The county librarian shall, subject to the general rules
adopted by the commissioners' court, build up and manage according
to accepted rules of library management, a library for the people of
the county and shall determine what books and other library equipment shall be purchased. Id.

Art. 1686. Report of librarian

The librarian of each county library shall, on or before the first
day of October in each year, report to the commissioners court and to
the State Librarian the operation of the county library during the
year ending August 31st preceding. Such report shall be made on
blanks furnished by the State Librarian, and shall contain a statement of the condition of the library, its operation during the year, and
such financial and book statistics as are kept in well regulated libraries. Id.

Art. 1687. Supervision of library

The county library shall be under the general supervision of the
commissioners court. Such libraries shall also be under the supervision of the State Librarian, who shall, from time to time, either
personally or by one of his assistants, visit the county free libraries
and inquire into their condition, advising with the librarians and said
court and rendering such assistance in all matters as he may be able
to give. Id.

Art. 1689. Funds for library

All funds of the county free library shall be in the custody of the
county treasurer, or other county official, who may discharge the duties
commonly delegated to the county treasurer. They shall constitute a
separate fund to be known as the county free library fund, and shall not
be used except for library purposes. The Commissioners Court may contract with privately-owned libraries which serve areas within the county
not adequately served by the county free library to provide county free
library services in such areas, and may require by such contract that such
library submit to such reasonable regulation as is required of governmental libraries. As amended Acts 1963, 58th Leg. p. 750, ch. 284, § 1.

Art. 1690. Joinder with city

After the establishment of a county free library the governing
body of any incorporated city or town in the county, maintaining a
free public library, may notify the commissioners court that such city
or town desires to become a part of the county free library system,
and thereafter such city or town shall be a part thereof, and its inhabitants shall be entitled to the benefits of such county free library,
and the property within such town or city shall be included in com-

puting the amount to be set aside as a fund for county free library purposes. Id.

Art. 1691. Contract with city

The commissioners court wherein a county free library has been established under the provisions of this title, shall have full power and authority to enter into contracts with any incorporated city or town maintaining a public free library, and such incorporated city or town shall through its governing body, have full power to enter into contracts with such county to secure to the residents of such incorporated city or town the same privileges of the county free library as are enjoyed by the residents of such county outside of such incorporated city or town, or such privileges as may be agreed upon in such contract, upon such consideration to be named in the contract as may be agreed upon, the same to be paid into the county library fund, and thereupon the residents of such incorporated city or town shall have the same privileges with regard to said county free library as are had by the residents of such county outside of such incorporated city or town, or such privileges as may be agreed upon by contract. Id.

Art. 1692. Withdrawal of city

The governing body of such incorporated city or town may at any time after two years notify the commissioners court that such city or town no longer desires to be a part of the county free library system and thereafter such city or town shall cease to participate in the benefits of such county free library system, and the property situated in said city or town shall no longer be assessed in computing the fund to be set aside for county free library purposes. The governing body of such city or town shall give the commissioners court six months notice and publish at least once a week for six successive weeks prior to either giving or withdrawing such notice in a county newspaper designated by the governing body, and circulated throughout such city or town, notice of such contemplated action, giving date and place of meeting at which such contemplated action is proposed to be taken. Id.

Art. 1693. Contract with another county

The commissioners court of any county, wherein a county free library has been established under the provisions of this title, shall have full power and authority to enter into contracts or agreements with the commissioners court of any other county to secure to the residents of such other county such privileges of such county free library as may, by such contract, be agreed upon, the same to be paid into the county free library fund, and thereupon the inhabitants of such other county shall have the privilege of such county free library as may by such contract be agreed upon; and the commissioners court shall have full power and authority to enter into a contract with the commissioners court of another county wherein a county free library has been established, under the provisions of this title and shall have power to provide for and to set aside a county free library fund, in the manner already set out, for the purpose of carrying out such contract. But the making of such contract shall not bar the commissioners court of such county from establishing a county free library therein, and upon the establishment of such county free library such contract may be terminated upon such terms as may be agreed upon by the parties thereto, or may continue for the term thereof. Id.

Art. 1694. Contract with established library

Instead of establishing a separate county free library, upon petition of a majority of the voters of the county, the commissioners court may contract for library privileges from some already established library. Such contract shall provide that such established library shall assume the functions of a county free library within the county with which the contract is made, including incorporated cities and towns therein, and shall also provide that the librarian of such established library shall hold or secure a county librarian's certificate from the Texas State Library and Archives Commission. Said court may contract to pay annually into the library fund of said established library such sum as may be agreed upon, to be paid out of the county library fund. Either party to such contract may terminate the same by giving six months notice of intention to do so. Property acquired under such contract shall be subject to division at the termination of the contract upon such terms as are specified in such contract.

Amended by Acts 1981, 67th Leg., p. 2845, ch. 764, § 1, eff. Sept. 1, 1981.

Art. 1695. Combined counties

Where found to be more practicable, two or more adjacent counties may join for the purposes of this law and establish and maintain a free library under the terms and provisions above set forth for the establishment and maintenance of a county free library. In such cases the combined counties shall have the same powers and be subject to the same liabilities as a single county as provided in this law. The commissioners courts of the counties which have combined for the establishment and maintenance of a free library shall operate jointly in the same manner as does the commissioners court of a single county in carrying out the provisions of this law. If any county desires to withdraw from such combination it shall be entitled to a division of property in such proportion as agreed upon in the terms of combination at the time such joint action was taken. Id.

Art. 1696. Termination of library

A county free library may be disestablished upon petition of a majority of the voters of that part of the county maintaining a county free library, asking that said library system be no longer maintained.

The commissioners court upon the termination of existing contracts shall call in all books and movable property of the defunct county free library, and have same inventoried and stored under lock and seal in some dry and suitable place in the county court house.   Id.

Art. 1696a.   Acquisition of land; construction, repair, equipment and improvement of buildings; bond issues; taxes

Section 1. The Commissioners Court of any county in this State is hereby authorized to acquire land for and to purchase, construct, repair, equip and improve buildings, and other permanent improvements to be used for county library purposes. Such building or buildings and other permanent improvements may be located in the county at such place or places as the Commissioners Court may determine. Payment for such buildings and repairs and improvements and other permanent improvements shall be made from the Constitutional Permanent Improvement Fund.

Sec. 2.   To pay the costs of acquiring land for and of purchasing, constructing, repairing, equipping and improving such buildings and other permanent improvements, the Commissioners Court is hereby authorized to issue negotiable bonds of the county and to levy and collect taxes in payment thereof, the issuance of such bonds and the levy and collection of taxes to be in accordance with the provisions of Chapter 1, Title 22, Revised Civil Statutes of Texas, 1925, as amended, governing the issuance of bonds by cities, towns, and/or counties in this State. Acts 1955, 54th Leg., p. 585. ch. 194.

MUNICIPAL LIBRARIES
(Vernon's Annotated Revised Civil Statutes of the State of
Texas, 1982, Art. 1015, 835m.)

Art. 1015. Other powers

The governing body shall also have power:

*   *   *

33. Libraries.—To establish a free library in such city or town; to adopt rules and regulations for the proper management thereof, and to appropriate such part of the revenues of such city or town for the management and increase of such free library as the municipal government of such city or town may determine.

Civ. St. Art. 853.

Art. 835m. Municipal libraries; fire stations; validation of bonds

Section 1. All bonds heretofore voted by any incorporated city or town, including home rule cities, for the purpose of enlarging and improving a municipally owned and operated library building or constructing a new municipal library building, either or both, and all proceedings relating thereto, are hereby in all things validated, ratified, approved, and confirmed, notwithstanding the fact that the election may not in all respects have been ordered and held in accordance with mandatory statutory provisions All bonds heretofore voted by any incorporated city or town, including home rule cities, for the purpose of constructing a fire station or a fire station and dormitory, either or both, and all proceedings relating thereto, are hereby in all things validated, ratified, approved, and confirmed, notwithstanding the fact that the election may not in all respects have been ordered and held in accordance with mandatory statutory provisions Such bonds, when approved by the Attorney-General of Texas and registered by the Comptroller of Public Accounts of Texas, and sold and delivered for not less than their par value plus accrued interest, shall be binding, legal, valid, and enforceable obligations of such city or town and shall be incontestable. Provided, however, that this Act shall apply only to such bonds which were authorized at an election or elections wherein a majority of the qualified property taxpaying voter: whose property had been duly rendered for taxation voted in favor of the issuance thereof.

Sec. 2. This Act shall not be construed as validating any such bonds or proceedings, the validity of which has been contested or attacked in any suit or litigation pending at the time this Act becomes effective. Acts 1953, 53rd Leg., p. 2, ch. 2.

COUNTY LAW LIBRARIES
(Vernon's Annotated Revised Civil Statutes of the State of
Texas, 1982, Art. 1702h.)

Art. 1702h.   County law libraries in all counties

Authority to establish

Section 1. The Commissioners Courts of all counties within this State shall have the power and authority, by first entering an order for that purpose, to provide for, maintain and establish a County Law Library.

Establishment on initiative of Commissioners Court; appropriations

Sec. 2. The Commissioners Court of any county may establish and provide for the maintenance of such County Law Library on its own initiative, and appropriate a sum not to exceed $20,000 to establish properly such library, and shall appropriate each year such sum as may be necessary to properly maintain and operate such County Law Library, which shall be established, maintained and operated at the county seat.

Sec. 2 amended by Acts 1977, 65th Leg., p. 270, ch. 131, § 1, eff. May 11, 1977.

Gifts and bequests

Sec. 3. The Commissioners Court of such county is hereby authorized and empowered to receive on behalf of such county any gift or bequest for such County Law Library. The title of all of such property shall be vested in the county. Where any gift or bequest is made with certain conditions, and accepted by the county, these conditions shall be administered as designated by the donor.

Costs; law library fund

Sec. 4. For the purpose of establishing County Law Libraries after the entry of such order, there shall be taxed, collected, and paid as other costs, a sum set by the Commissioners Court not to exceed $10 in each civil case, except suits for delinquent taxes, hereafter filed in every county or district court; provided, however, that in no event shall the county be liable for said costs in any case. Such costs shall be collected by the clerks of the respective courts in said counties and paid by said clerks to the County Treasurer to be kept by said Treasurer in a separate fund to be known as the "County Law Library Fund." Such fund shall not be used for any other purpose.

Sec. 4 amended by Acts 1977, 65th Leg., p. 270, ch. 131, § 1, eff. May 11, 1977.

Managing committee

Sec. 5. The Commissioners Court of such counties may vest the management of such library in a committee to be selected by the Bar Association of such county, but the acts of such committee shall be subject to the approval of the Commissioners Court.

Salaries

Sec. 6. The salary of the custodian or librarian and such other employees or assistants as may be necessary shall be fixed by the Commissioners Court and shall be paid out of the funds collected under this Act, or from appropriations made under this Act.

Administration of fund; space; rules

Sec. 7. Such fund shall be administered by the Commissioners Court, or under its direction, for the purchase and lease of library materials, the maintenance of the Law Library, and the acquisition of all furniture, shelving and equipment necessary thereto, in a place convenient and accessible to the Judges and litigants of such county. The Commissioners Court shall provide suitable space for housing the law library and may, with the advice of the committee referred to in Section 5 of this Act, use funds collected under this Act for the acquisition of such space. Priority in the use of such funds shall be given to providing books, periodicals, other library materials, and staff for the law library. The Commissioners Court of the counties affected by this Act shall make rules for the use of books in said library.

Sec. 7 amended by Acts 1979, 66th Leg., p. 234, ch. 121, § 1, eff. May 9, 1979.

Custody and use of funds; claims

Sec. 8. All funds for the County Law Library shall be in the custody of the County Treasurer of such county, or other official who may discharge the duties commonly delegated to county treasurers.

They shall constitute a separate fund and shall not be used for any other purpose than those of such County Law Library. Each claim against the County Law Library shall be acted upon and allowed or rejected in like manner as other claims against the county.

Partial invalidity

Sec. 9. If any section, paragraph, clause, phrase, sentence, or portion of this Act be held invalid or unconstitutional, such invalidity shall not affect the remainder thereof. Acts 1951, 52nd Leg., p. 777, ch. 429.

TAX EXEMPTION

(Vernon's Annotated Revised Civil Statutes of the State of
Texas, 1982, Art. 7150.)

Art. 7150. [7507] [5065] Exemption from taxation

The following property shall be exempt from taxation, to-wit:

* * *

8. Public libraries.—All public libraries and personal property belonging to the same. Acts 1907, p. 302.

EXEMPTION FROM FORCED SALE

(Vernon's Annotated Revised Civil Statutes of the State of
Texas, 1982, Art. 3838.)

Art. 3838. 3791, 2400, 2340 Public libraries

All public libraries shall be exempt from attachment, execution and every other specie of forced sale.

Texas library laws are reprinted from VERNON'S AN-
NOTATED REVISED CIVIL STATUTES OF THE STATE
OF TEXAS, published by the Vernon Law Book Co.,
Kansas City, Missouri.

UTAH

STATE LIBRARY

(Utah Code Annotated, 1982, s.37-4-1, 37-4-3, 37-4-4,
37-4-6 to 37-4-10.)

37-4-1. Division of state libraries created — Director — Appointment and qualifications — Functions and responsibilities of division. There is created within the department of community and economic development a division of state libraries. The director of the division of state libraries shall be appointed by the executive director of the department with the concurrence of the board. The director shall possess a degree from an institution approved by the American Library Association in library science and shall possess demonstrated administrative ability. The division shall function as the library authority for the state and is responsible for general library services, extension services, the preservation, distribution and exchange of state publications, legislative reference, and other services deemed proper for a state library.

History: C. 1953, 37-4-1, enacted by L. 1979, ch. 234, § 5.

37-4-3. State library board — Members — Appointment — Terms — Secretary of state as ex officio member — Expenses. There is established a state library board composed of nine members appointed to six-year terms of office by the governor with the advice and consent of the senate. The appointment shall be for six-year overlapping terms. The members may not serve more than two full consecutive terms. One member shall be appointed on recommendation from each of the following agencies: state department of public instruction, the law library board, the legislative council, and the state historical society board. Of the five remaining members at least two shall be appointed from rural areas.

The secretary of state shall be a member ex officio of the state library board. The board shall select its own chairman who shall serve for a period of two years. The director of the division of state libraries shall act as secretary to the board.

The members of the state library board shall serve without pay but their actual and necessary expenses incurred in the performance of their official duties shall be paid from state library funds.

History: L. 1957, ch. 68, § 3; 1963, ch. 58, § [1]; 1979, ch. 234, § 6.

37-4-4. State library board — Powers and duties. The state library board is the policy-making body for the division and has the following powers and duties pertaining to the operation of a state library and state library services:

(1)　Shall promote, develop and organize a state library and make provisions for its housing;

(2)　Shall promote and develop library services throughout the state in co-operation with any and all other state or municipal libraries, schools or other agencies wherever practical;

(3)　Shall promote the establishment of district, regional or multi-county libraries as conditions within particular areas of the state may require;

(4)　Shall have supervision of the books and materials of the state library and shall require careful and complete records of the condition and affairs of the state library to be kept;

(5)　Shall on the recommendation of the state director of libraries appoint and employ all professional, clerical or other help needed in the state library system, and shall determine standards for qualification and compensation;

(6)　Shall make rules and regulations and establish standards for the administration of the Utah state library, and for the control, distribution and lending of books and materials to those libraries, institutions, groups, or individuals entitled to the same through the provisions of this act;

(7)　Shall serve as the agency of the state for the administration of any state or federal funds which may now or in the future be appropriated to further library development within the state, and shall establish regulations under which such grants shall be made to individual libraries; except that this provision shall not apply to appropriations made directly to any other agency or institution;

(8)　Shall aid and provide general advisory assistance in the development of state-wide school library service and encourage contractual and co-operative relations between school and public libraries;

(9)　Shall give assistance, advice and counsel to all tax-supported libraries of any type within the state and to all communities or persons proposing to establish them and may conduct courses and institutes on the approved methods of operation, selection of books, or other activities necessary to the proper administration of a library;

(10)　Shall furnish or contract for the furnishing of library or information service to state officials, state departments or any groups that, in the opinion of the state director of libraries, warrants the furnishing of such services, particularly by and through the facilities of traveling libraries, to those parts of the state otherwise inadequately supplied by libraries; and where sufficient need exists and if the state director of libraries otherwise deems it advisable, may establish and maintain special departments in the state library to provide services for professional, occupational and other groups;

(11)　Shall administer a depository library, publications collection and bibliographic information system;

(12)　Shall require that information and statistics necessary to the work of the state library be collected, and that findings and reports thereon be published;

(13)　Shall make a biennial report concerning the activities of the state library to the governor, as he may require;

(14)　Shall develop standards for public libraries and rules and regulations for the certification of public librarians.

History: L. 1957, ch. 68, § 4; 1963, ch. 59, § [1]; 1979, ch. 141, § 9; 1979, ch. 234, § 7.

37-4-6. Director — Duties. The state director of libraries shall act as executive officer for the state library board and shall under their direction see that the responsibilities enumerated in section 37-4-4 above are carried out.

History: L. 1957, ch. 68, § 6; 1979, ch. 234, § 8.

37-4-7. Library — Co-operation — Bequests, gifts and endowments of money and property—Fees.—The Utah state library is hereby empowered:

1. To co-operate with other state or national libraries or library agencies;

37-4-8. Local libraries — Annual reports. All municipal, city, county and public school libraries shall submit their annual report to the state director of libraries on the condition and affairs of each respective library as required by the state library board.

History: L. 1957, ch. 68, § 8; 1979, ch. 234, § 9.

37-4-9. Nonpublic libraries — Contracts with. The state director of libraries, subject to the direction and approval of the state library board, shall have the power to contract with nonpublic libraries to receive library services from and otherwise co-ordinate the state library program with said libraries.

History: L. 1957, ch. 68, § 9; 1979, ch. 234, § 10.

37-4-10. Intentionally defacing, injuring, destroying or refusing to return property—Misdemeanor.—Whoever intentionally defaces, injures, or refuses to return on demand, or destroys any property belonging to the state library or loaned through its co-ordinating agencies or facilities, shall be guilty of a misdemeanor.

History: L. 1957, ch. 68, § 10.

STATE LAW LIBRARY
(Utah Code Annotated, 1982, s.37-1-1 to 37-1-12.)

37-1-1. Board of control.—The governor, the secretary of state and the justices of the Supreme Court shall constitute board of control of the state law library.

History: R. S. 1898 & C. L. 1907, § 1349; C. L. 1917, § 3699; R. S. 1933 & C. 1943, 51-1-1; L. 1957, ch. 67, § 1.

37-1-2. Open to public—Rules and regulations—Penalty.—The public shall have access to the state law library. The board of control may make such rules and regulations not inconsistent with the provisions of this chapter as it may deem proper for its use, and may prescribe and enforce penalties for any violation thereof, which shall be collected in the same manner as penalties for the nonreturn or injury of any book.

History: R. S. 1898 & C. L. 1907, § 1350; C. L. 1917, § 3700; R. S. 1933 & C. 1943, 51-1-2; L. 1957, ch. 67, § 1.

37-1-3. Withdrawing books—Limited rights.—Books may be taken from the state law library by the members and officers of the legislature, the officers of the executive departments and of the several boards and commissions of the state government, the justices of the Supreme Court and the judges of the district courts, but no other person shall be permitted to withdraw any book from the library.

History: R. S. 1898 & C. L. 1907, § 1351;
C. L. 1917, § 3701; R. S. 1933 & C. 1943,
51-1-3; L. 1957, ch. 67, § 1.

37-1-4. Time limit—Register of books withdrawn.—The state law librarian shall keep a register of all books issued and returned, showing to whom issued, by whom returned, and the time issued and returned. No book taken from the law library shall be detained more than ten days, except when taken for the use of officers and members of the legislature while it is in session, and all books so taken shall be returned at the close of the session.

History: R. S. 1898 & C. L. 1907, § 1352;
C. L. 1917, § 3702; R. S. 1933 & C. 1943,
51-1-4; L. 1957, ch. 67, § 1.

37-1-5. Injury to and failure to return books—Liability—Action.—If any person injures or fails to return any book taken from the law library, he shall pay to the law librarian for the use of the law library all loss or damage sustained thereby, including costs and reasonable attorneys' fees for collecting the same, to be recovered in an action in the name of the state, and it shall be the duty of the law librarian in behalf of the state to bring action for the collection of all damages so sustained and all penalties imposed.

History: R. S. 1898 & C. L. 1907, § 1353;
C. L. 1917, § 3703; R. S. 1933 & C. 1943,
51-1-5; L. 1957, ch. 67, § 1.

37-1-6. Annual report by law librarian.—On or before the 1st day of October in each year the law librarian shall report to the governor the condition of the law library, stating the number of volumes contained therein, the number purchased during the preceding year and the cost thereof, the number received by donation, the number injured or not returned, if any, and the amounts received in compensation therefor, and such suggestions and further information as may be deemed by him desirable.

History: R. S. 1898 & C. L. 1907, § 1354;
C. L. 1917, § 3704; R. S. 1933 & C. 1943,
51-1-6; L. 1957, ch. 67, § 1.

37-1-7. Catalogue—Rules to be posted.—The law librarian shall catalogue all books, pamphlets, maps, charts, globes, papers, apparatus and valuable specimens in the law library and shall post in some conspicuous place a copy of the rules and regulations of the law library. The catalogue shall be printed and distributed to the officers entitled to withdraw books from the law library.

History: R. S. 1898 & C. L. 1907, § 1355;
C. L. 1917, § 3705; R. S. 1933 & C. 1943,
51-1-7; L. 1957, ch. 67, § 1.

37-1-8. Books to be stamped and labeled.—The law librarian shall cause every book in the law library to be labeled with a printed or stamped label containing the words "Utah State Law Library," and shall cause the same words to be written or stamped on one or more pages of each volume.

History: R. S. 1898 & C. L. 1907, § 1356;
C. L. 1917, § 3706; R. S. 1933 & C. 1943,
51-1-8; L. 1957, ch. 67, § 1.

37-1-9. Sale and exchange of books.—The board of control of the law library may sell or exchange any surplus or duplicate sets of books in the law library and use the money arising from such sale in purchasing other books for the law library.

History: R. S. 1898 & C. L. 1907, § 1357;
C. L. 1917, § 3707; R. S. 1933 & C. 1943,
51-1-9; L. 1957, ch. 67, § 1.

37-1-10. Liability of law librarian.—If the law librarian permits any person not authorized by this chapter to take a book from the law library, he shall be liable to pay a fine of not less than $5 nor more than $50 for each book so taken.

History: R. S. 1898 & C. L. 1907, § 1358;
C. L. 1917, § 3708; R. S. 1933 & C. 1943,
51-1-10; L. 1957, ch. 67, § 1.

37-1-11. Wrongful withdrawal of books—Penalty.—If any person not authorized by this chapter takes a book from the library, either with or without the consent of the law librarian, or violates any of the provisions of this chapter, he shall be fined in any sum not less than $10 nor more than $50 for each book so taken.

History: R. S. 1898 & C. L. 1907, § 1359;
C. L. 1917, § 3709; R. S. 1933 & C. 1943,
51-1-11; L. 1957, ch. 67, § 1.

37-1-12. Disposition of fines and penalties.—All fines and penalties collected pursuant to the provisions of this chapter shall be paid into the state treasury for the benefit of the state law library.

History: R. S. 1898 & C. L. 1907, § 1358;
C. L. 1917, § 3708; R. S. 1933 & C. 1943,
51-1-12; L. 1957, ch. 67, § 1.

DIVISION OF STATE HISTORY
(Utah Code Annotated, 1982, s.63-18-2.1 to 63-18-6.)

63-18-2.1. Division of state history — Creation — Power and authority. There is created within the department of community and economic development a division of state history under the administration and general supervision of the executive director of the department and under the policy direction of the board of state history. The division of state history shall be the authority of the state for state history and is vested with such powers to perform such duties as are set forth in law.

History: L. 1967, ch. 175, § 67; 1969, ch.
199, § 41; 1979, ch. 234, § 17.

63-18-3.　Division of state history—Duties and objectives.—The duties
and objectives of the division of state history shall be the stimulation of
research, study, and activity in the field of Utah and related history; the
maintenance of a specialized history library; the marking and preservation of historic sites, areas, and remains; the collection, preservation, and
administration of historical records, and other relics relating to the history
of Utah; the editing and publication of historical records.

History: L. 1957, ch. 141, § 3; 1967,
ch. 175, § 69; 1969, ch. 212, § 30.

**63-18-4.　Board of state history—Members—Appointments—Terms—
Officers—Quorum—Expenses—Duty to establish policy.**—The governing
body of the division of state history and the Utah state historical society
shall be the board of state history consisting of eleven persons, ten of whom
shall be appointed by the governor with the advice and consent of the
senate. One member of the board shall be the secretary of state. The appointed members shall be appointed for terms of four years and shall
serve until their successors are appointed and qualified. The board shall
choose a president and a vice-president from its own members and shall
make rules and regulations for its own government and for the administration of the Utah state historical society and the division of state history.
Six members of the board shall constitute a quorum for the transaction of
business. Members of the board shall serve without compensation, but they
shall be allowed expenses incurred in the performance of their official
duties as provided for in respect to other state officials. Such expenses
shall be paid by the state treasurer on warrant of the department of
finance out of money in the treasury appropriated for that purpose.

The board shall establish policy to guide the division of state history in
carrying out its duties and objectives.

History: L. 1957, ch. 141, § 4; 1967,
ch. 175, § 70; 1969, ch. 199, § 42.

63-18-5.　Director of division of state history — Appointment. The chief
administrative officer of the division of state history shall be a director appointed
by the executive director of the department of community and economic development with the concurrence of the board. The director shall be experienced in
administration and qualified by education or training in the field of state history.

History: L. 1967, ch. 175, § 68; 1969, ch.
199, § 43; 1979, ch. 234, § 18.

**63-18-6.　Historical magazines, books, documents and microfilms—Pub-
lication and sale—Proceeds.**—The division of state history is authorized,
under the direction of the board of state history, to compile and publish an
historical magazine to be furnished to supporting members of the Utah
State Historical Society in accordance with membership subscriptions or to
be sold independently of membership, and to publish and sell other books,
documents, and microfilms at reasonable prices to be approved by the director of the division. Proceeds from such sales shall be retained in the treas-

ury of said society.

History: L. 1957, ch. 141, § 6; 1967, ch. 175, § 71; 1969, ch. 199, § 44.

DEPOSITORY LIBRARIES
(Utah Code Annotated, 1982, s.37-5-1 to 37-5-8.)

37-5-1. Definitions. As used in this act:

(1) "Commission" means the state library commission established under section 37-4-3.

(2) "Political subdivision" means any county, city, town, school district, public transit district, redevelopment agency, special improvement or taxing district.

(3) "State agency" means the state, any office, department, agency, authority, commission, board, institution, hospital, college, university or other instrumentality of the state.

(4) "State publication" means any blue book, book, compilation, directory, document, contract and grant report, hearing memorandum, journal, law, leaflet, legislative bill, list, magazine, map, minutes, monograph, order, ordinance, pamphlet, periodical, proceeding, public memorandum, resolution, register, regulation, report, statute, audiovisual material, microphotographic form and tape or disc recording regardless of format or method of reproduction, issued or published by any state agency or political subdivision for distribution, not including correspondence, internal confidential publications, office memoranda, university press publications, and publications of the state historical society.

History: L. 1979, ch. 141, § 1.

37-5-2. Commission to establish, operate and maintain. The commission shall establish, operate and maintain a publication collection, a bibliographic control system and depositories as provided in this act.

History: L. 1979, ch. 141, § 2.

37-5-3. Deposit of copies of publications with commission. (1) Each state agency shall deposit with the commission copies of each state publication issued by it in such number as shall be specified by the state librarian.

(2) Each political subdivision shall deposit with the commission two copies of each state publication issued by it.

(3) The commission shall forward two copies of each state publication deposited with it by a state agency to the Library of Congress, one copy to the state archivist, at least one copy to each depository library, and retain two copies.

(4) The commission shall forward one copy of each state publication deposited with it by a political subdivision to the state archivist and retain the other copy.

(5) Each state agency shall deposit with the commission two copies of audiovisual materials, and tape or disc recordings issued by it for bibliographic listing and retention in the state library collection. Materials not deemed by the commission to be of major public interest will be listed but no copies will be required for deposit.

History: L. 1979, ch. 141, § 3.

37-5-4. List of state agencies' state publications — Distribution. The commission shall publish a list of each state agency's state publications, which shall provide access by agency, author, title, subject and such other means as the commission may provide. The list shall be published periodically and distributed to depository libraries, state agencies, state officers, members of the legislature and other libraries selected by the commission, with at least an annual cumulation. Each state agency shall furnish the commission and the state archivist a complete list of its state publications for the previous year, annually.

History: L. 1979, ch. 141, § 4.

37-5-5.   Designation as depository library. Upon application, a library in this state may be designated as a complete or selective depository library by the commission.

History: L. 1979, ch. 141, § 5.

37-5-6.   Contract to provide facilities and service — Complete depository libraries — Selective depository libraries. To be designated as a depository library, a library must contract with the commission to provide adequate facilities for the storage and use of state publications, to render reasonable service without charge to patrons and reasonable access to state publications. A complete depository library shall receive at least one copy of all state publications issued by state

agencies. A selective depository library shall receive those state publications issued by state agencies pertinent to its selection profile and those specifically requested by the library.

History: L. 1979, ch. 141, § 6.

37-5-7.   Micrographics and other copying and transmission techniques. The commission may use micrographics or other copying or transmission techniques to meet the needs of the depository system.

History: L. 1979, ch. 141, § 7.

37-5-8.   Rules and regulations — Standards. The commission may adopt rules and regulations necessary to implement and administer the provisions of this act including standards which must be met by libraries to obtain and retain a designation as a depository library.

History: L. 1979, ch. 141, § 8.

COUNTY LIBRARIES
(Utah Code Annotated, 1982, s.37-3-1 to 37-3-11.)

37-3-1.   Tax for establishment and maintenance of public library — Library fund. County commissioners may establish and maintain a public library. For this purpose, counties may levy annually a tax not to exceed 3.75 mills on each dollar of assessed valuation on all taxable property in the county, outside of cities which maintain their own city libraries as authorized by chapter 2, Title 37, Utah Code Annotated 1953, as amended. Said tax shall be in addition to all taxes levied by counties and shall not be limited by levy limitation imposed on counties by law. However, if bonds are hereafter issued for purchasing a site, constructing a building, or furnishing the same, then taxes sufficient for the payment of such bonds and the interest thereon may be levied. Such taxes shall be levied and collected in the same manner as other general taxes of the county and shall constitute a fund to be known as the county library fund.

History: C. 1953, 37-3-1, enacted by L. 1963, ch. 57, § 1; L. 1975, ch. 110, § 3.

37-3-2. Library board of directors—Appointment—Membership—Payment of expenses.—Upon the establishment of a county public library under the provisions of this act, the county commissioners shall appoint a library board of five directors chosen from the citizens of the county with reference to their fitness for such office. One member of the county commission shall be a member of such board. Directors shall serve without compensation, but their actual and necessary expenses incurred in the performance of their official duties may be paid from library funds.

History: C. 1953, 37-3-2, enacted by L.
1963, ch. 57, § 1.

37-3-3. Library board of directors—Terms—Election of officers—Removal—Vacancies.—Directors shall be appointed for four-year terms, or until their successors are appointed. Initially, appointments shall be made for one-, two-, three-, and four-year terms, and one county commissioner for the term of his elected office. Annually thereafter, the county commissioners shall, before the first day of July of each year, appoint, for a four-year term, one director to take the place of the retiring director. Directors shall serve not more than two full terms in succession. Following such appointments, the directors shall meet and elect a chairman and such other officers, as they deem necessary, for one-year terms. The county commissioners may remove any director for misconduct or neglect of duty. Vacancies in the board of directors, occasioned by removals, resignations, or otherwise, shall be filled for the unexpired terms in the same manner as original appointments.

History: C. 1953, 37-3-3, enacted by L.
1963, ch. 57, § 1.

37-3-4. Library fund — Deposits and disbursements — General powers and authority of directors. The library board of directors may with the approval of the board of county commissioners have control of the expenditure of the library fund, of construction, lease or sale of library buildings and land, and of the operation and care of the library. All tax moneys received for such library shall be deposited in the county treasury to the credit of the library fund, and shall not be used for any purpose except that of the county library. Said funds shall be drawn upon by the authorized officers of the county upon presentation of the properly authenticated vouchers of the library board. All moneys collected by the library shall be deposited to the credit of the library fund. The board may with the approval of the governing body purchase, lease or sell land, and purchase, lease, erect or sell buildings, for the benefit of the library. The board shall be responsible for the maintenance and general care of the library and shall establish policies for its operation, and, in general, carry out the spirit and intent of the provisions of this chapter.

History: C. 1953, 37-3-4, enacted by L.
1963, ch. 57, § 1; L. 1975, ch. 110, § 4.

37-3-5. Directors to determine and certify amount of moneys necessary to provide library services—Levy of tax—Limit on levy.—The library board of directors shall furnish to the county commission, in writing, and amount of moneys necessary to establish, equip and maintain the library, and to provide library services during the next ensuing fiscal year and shall certify the same; the board of county commissioners may thereafter, at the time and in the manner of levying other taxes, impose such levy; provided, that such levy shall not exceed in any one year, three mills on each dollar of all of the taxable property of the county.

History: C. 1953, 37-3-5, enacted by L. 1963, ch. 57, § 1.

37-3-6. Rules and regulations—Use of library to be free subject to rules.—The library board of directors shall make and adopt rules and regulations, not inconsistent with law, for the governing of the library. Every library established under the provisions of this chapter shall be free to the use of the inhabitants of the area taxed for the support of said library, subject to the rules and regulations adopted by the board. The board may exclude from the use of the library any and all persons who shall willfully violate such rules. The board may extend the privileges and use of the library to persons residing outside of said area upon such terms and conditions as it may prescribe by its regulations.

History: C. 1953, 37-3-6, enacted by L. 1963, ch. 57, § 1.

37-3-7. Annual reports to county commission and Utah state library board. The library board of directors shall make an annual report to the county commission on the condition and operation of the library, including a financial statement. The directors shall also provide for the keeping of such records as shall be required by the Utah state library board in its request for an annual report from the public libraries, and shall submit such an annual report to the Utah state library board.

History: C. 1953, 37-3-7, enacted by L. 1963, ch. 57, § 1; L. 1979, ch. 234, § 4.

37-3-8. Directors to appoint librarian and other personnel.—The library board of directors shall appoint a competent person as librarian to have immediate charge of the library with such duties and compensation for his services as it shall fix and determine. The librarian shall act as the executive officer for the library board. The board shall appoint, upon the recommendation of the librarian, other personnel as needed.

History: C. 1953, 37-3-8, enacted by L. 1963, ch. 57, § 1.

37-3-9. Donations of money or property.—Any person desiring to make donations of money, personal property or real estate for the benefit of such library shall have the right to vest the title to the money, personal property or real estate so donated, in the board of directors thereof, to be held and controlled by such board, when accepted, according to the terms of the deed, gift, devise or bequest of such property; and as to such property the board shall be held and considered to be trustees.

History: C. 1953, 37-3-9, enacted by L. 1963, ch. 57, § 1.

37-3-10. Authority of boards, agencies and political subdivisions to co-operate, merge or consolidate.—Boards of directors of city libraries, boards of directors of county libraries, boards of education, governing boards of other educational institutions, library agencies, and local political subdivisions are hereby empowered to co-operate, merge, or consolidate in providing library services.

History: C. 1953, 37-3-10, enacted by L.
1963, ch. 57, § 1.

37-3-11. Library bonds—Issuance of previously voted bonds.—In each instance where an election has been heretofore held in any county in this state to authorize bonds of the county for the purpose of acquiring, improving and extending a public library for such county, including the acquisition of equipment, furnishings and books therefor, and it was specified in the proposition that such bonds are to be payable from ad valorem taxes to be levied on all taxable property in the county, and where such election has carried but none of the bonds so authorized has been issued, the bonds so authorized to be issued at any such election may be issued and shall be payable from taxes to be levied without limitation as to rate or amount on all taxable property in such county despite any provision of law to the contrary in effect at the time of such election. All such county library bonds so heretofore authorized but yet unissued, all such county library bond elections previously held and carried, and all proceedings in connection therewith heretofore adopted for the authorization of such bonds are hereby validated, ratified, approved and confirmed, and such bonds when issued in accordance with such election and proceedings shall be binding, legal, valid and enforceable obligations of the county issuing them in accordance with their terms.

History: L. 1965, ch. 31, § 1.

MUNICIPAL LIBRARIES
(Utah Code Annotated, 1982, s.37-2-1 to 37-2-10.)

37-2-1. Tax for establishment and maintenance of public library — Library fund. The governing body of cities may establish and maintain public libraries. For this purpose, cities may levy annually a tax not to exceed 3.75 mills on each dollar of assessed valuation on all taxable property within the city. Said tax shall be in addition to all taxes levied by said cities, and shall not be limited by levy limitation imposed on said cities by law. However, if bonds are hereafter issued for purchasing a site, constructing a building, or furnishing the same, then taxes sufficient for the payment of such bonds and the interest thereon may be levied. Such taxes shall be levied and collected in the same manner as other general taxes of the city, and shall constitute a fund to be known as the library fund.

History: C. 1953, 37-2-1, enacted by L.
1963, ch. 56, § 1; L. 1975, ch. 110, § 1.

37-2-2. Library board of directors—Appointment—Membership—Payment of expenses.—When the governing body in any city decides to establish and maintain a public library under the provisions of this act, it shall appoint a library board of directors, chosen from the citizens at large with reference to their fitness for such office. The board of directors shall consist of not less than five members and not more than nine members. Not more than one member of the governing body shall be, at any one time, a member of such board. Directors shall serve without compensation, but their actual and necessary expenses incurred in the performance of their official duties may be paid from library funds.

History: C. 1953, 37-2-2, enacted by L. 1963, ch. 56, § 1.

37-2-3. Library board of directors—Terms—Election of officers—Removal—Vacancies.—Directors shall be appointed for three-year terms, or until their successors are appointed. Initially, appointments shall be made for one- two- and three-year terms. Annually thereafter, the governing body shall, before the first day of July of each year, appoint for three-year terms directors to take the place of the retiring directors. Directors shall serve not more than two full terms in succession. Following such appointments, the directors shall meet and elect a chairman and such other officers, as they deem necessary, for one-year terms. The governing body may remove any director for misconduct or neglect of duty. Vacancies in the board of directors, occasioned by removals, resignations, or otherwise, shall be filled for the unexpired term in the same manner as original appointments.

History: C. 1953, 37-2-3, enacted by L. 1963, ch. 56, § 1.

37-2-4. Library fund — Deposits and disbursements — General powers and authority of board. The library board of directors may with the approval of the governing body have control of the expenditure of the library fund, of construction, lease or sale of library buildings and land, and of the operation and care of the library. All tax moneys received for such library shall be deposited in the city treasury to the credit of the library fund, and shall not be used for any purpose except that of the city library. Said fund shall be drawn upon by the authorized officers of the city, upon presentation of the properly authenticated vouchers of the library board. All moneys collected by the library shall be deposited to the credit of the library fund. The board may with the approval of the governing body purchase, lease or sell land, and purchase, lease, erect or sell buildings for the benefit of the library. The board shall be responsible for the maintenance and care of the library and shall establish policies for its operation, and, in general, carry out the spirit and intent of the provisions of this chapter.

History: C. 1953, 37-2-4, enacted by L. 1963, ch. 56, § 1; L. 1975, ch. 110, § 2.

37-2-5. Rules and regulations—Use of library to be free subject to rules. —The library board of directors shall make and adopt rules and regulations, not inconsistent with law, for the governing of the library. Every library established under the provisions of this chapter shall be free to the use of the inhabitants of the city where located, subject to the rules and regulations adopted by the board. The board may exclude from the use of the library any and all persons who shall willfully violate such rules. The board may extend the privileges and use of the library to persons residing outside of said city upon such terms and conditions as it may prescribe by its regulations.

History: C. 1953, 37-2-5, enacted by L. 1963, ch. 56, § 1.

37-2-6. Annual reports to governing body and Utah state library board. The library board of directors shall make an annual report to the governing body of the city on the condition and operation of the library, including a financial statement. The directors shall also provide for the keeping of records required by the Utah state library board in its request for an annual report from the public libraries, and shall submit such annual report to the board.

History: C. 1953, 37-2-6, enacted by L. 1963, ch. 56, § 1; L. 1979, ch. 234, § 3.

37-2-7. Directors to appoint librarian and other personnel.—The library board of directors shall appoint a competent person as librarian to have immediate charge of the library with such duties and compensation for his services as it shall fix and determine. The librarian shall act as the executive officer for the library board. The board shall appoint, upon the recommendation of the librarian, other personnel as needed.

History: C. 1953, 37-2-7, enacted by L. 1963, ch. 56, § 1.

37-2-8. Donations of money or property.—Any person desiring to make donations of money, personal property, or real estate for the benefit of such library shall have the right to vest the title to the money, personal property or real estate so donated, in the board of directors thereof, to be held and controlled by such board, when accepted, according to the terms of the deed, gift, devise or bequest of such property; and as to such property the board shall be held and considered to be trustees.

History: C. 1953, 37-2-8, enacted by L.   Compiler's Notes.
1963, ch. 56, § 1.

37-2-9. Authority of boards, agencies and political subdivisions to cooperate, merge or consolidate.—Boards of directors of city libraries, boards of directors of county libraries, boards of education, governing boards of other educational institutions, library agencies, and local political subdivisions are hereby empowered to co-operate, merge, or consolidate in providing library services.

History: C. 1953, 37-2-9, enacted by L. 1963, ch. 56, § 1.

37-2-10. Consolidation with county library.—When a city library consolidates with a county library, the city library board of directors shall convey all assets and trust funds to the county library board of directors and the city library shall cease operation.

History: C. 1953, 37-2-10, enacted by L. 1963, ch. 56, § 1.

SCHOOL LIBRARIES
(Utah Code Annotated, 1982, s.53-1-11, 53-2-14.)

53-1-11. State board of education and state superintendent, Utah agency — To formulate program. The state board of education and the state superintendent of public instruction as chief state school officer, are designated as the state educational authority, the state adult educational authority, and the state library administrative agency of the state of Utah, authorized to make and administer plans for distribution of funds allocated to the state of Utah under the provisions of said Federal Aid to Education Act of 1939 and said state board of education and state superintendent of public instruction, as the designated Utah agency to co-operate in the administration of said act in this state are directed to design and formulate a program to:

*   *   *

(9) Apportion to libraries and library services, and have an adequate system of reports from libraries or library services through such board of education and state superintendent of public instruction and shall make such report to the commissioner with respect to the expenditure of funds received through this act and the program of library service in such form and containing such information as the commissioner may require and shall prepare and file with the commissioner a plan for apportioning or disbursing the funds in such manner as will effectively lessen inequalities of opportunity to library service.

History: L. 1939, ch. 83, § 2; C. 1943,
75-1-11.

53-2-14. Public school libraries — Powers and duties of board. The state board of education shall promote the establishment and improvement of public school libraries, and shall provide for state-wide supervision of those libraries. It shall adopt standards, rules and regulations as may be necessary to provide adequate school library service. It is empowered and encouraged to co-operate with the Utah state library and other agencies in providing school library service.

History: R.S. 1898 & C.L. 1907, § 1763; L.
1911, ch. 67, § 1; 1915, ch. 109, § 1; C.L. 1917,
§ 4505; L. 1925, ch. 75, § 1; R.S. 1933 & C. 1943,
75-7-9; L. 1963, ch. 83, § 1.

LIBRARY FOR THE BLIND
(Utah Code Annotated, 1982, s.64-3-18.)

64-3-18. Utah division of services for the visually handicapped—Powers and duties.—Persons above the age of twenty-one years, capable of receiving beneficial instruction, but incapable on account of blindness or defective sight of receiving adequate instruction in the common schools, may in the discretion of the board of trustees, be admitted to the school and receive instruction. The state board of education shall be the governing board of the Utah division of services for the visually handicapped, hereinafter designated as the "division" and this division shall have general supervision of the blind of the state except as otherwise provided, shall prepare and maintain a register of the blind in the state which shall contain all such pertinent facts as the board may deem important. It may establish, equip and maintain such homes and workshops for the industrial training of the blind as it may deem necessary, furnish the needed materials and tools therefor and aid in the marketing of the products of their work. It may also provide a circulating library for the blind of the state and shall be authorized to become, instead of the state library commission, the agency for the state for supervision and administration of the books, sound reproduction recordings, musical scores, instructional texts, and other specialized materials for use by the blind received from or loaned by the Library of Congress.

The division shall also have authority to institute and supervise for the blind of the state recreational services, a sight conservation program, home teaching services, social case work, placement services, instruction facilities, and to employ personnel to carry out the provisions of this act. The division shall administer such rehabilitation activity for the visually handicapped as the governing board may assign to it.

History: L. 1909, ch. 79, § 6; C. L. 1917, § 430; L. 1921, ch. 6, § 1; R. S. 1933 & C. 1943, 85-3-18; L. 1947, ch. 127, § 1; 1949, ch. 87, § 1; 1963, ch. 158, § 1.

ARCHIVES AND RECORDS SERVICE
(Utah Code Annotated, 1982, s.63-2-59 to 63-2-89.)

63-2-59. Archives and records service and information practices — Short title of act. This act shall be known and may be cited as the "Archives and Records Service and Information Practices Act."

History: L. 1969, ch. 212, § 1; 1979, ch. 223, § 1.

63-2-60. Legislative intent. It is the intent of the legislature to create a central archives and records service within the department of ~~finance~~ administrative services to administer the archives and records-management programs of the state and apply efficient and economical management methods to the creation, utilization, maintenance, retention, preservation, and disposal of state records and documents.

It is also the intent of this act to establish fair information practices to ensure that the rights of persons are protected and that proper remedies are established to prevent abuse of personal information.

History: L. 1969, ch. 212, § 2; 1979, ch. 223, § 2; 1981, ch. 257, § 2.

63-2-61. Archives and records service — Definitions. As used in this act:
(1) "Public records" mean all written or printed books, papers, letters, docu-

ments, maps, plans, photographs, sound recordings, and other records made or received in pursuance of state law or in connection with the transaction of public business by the public offices, agencies, and institutions of the state and its counties, municipalities, and other subdivisions of government.

(2) "State agency" or "state agencies" mean any department, division, board, bureau, commission, council, institution, authority, or other unit, however designated, of the state.

(3) "Public offices" and "public officers" mean, respectively, the offices and officers of any court, department, division, board, commission, bureau, council, authority, institution or other agency of the state of Utah or any of its political subdivisions.

(4) "Public archives" mean the body of public records accumulated and preserved in an official custody for record purposes by any agency or its legal successor.

(5) "Archivist" means the state archivist and records administrator.

(6) "Print" includes all forms of duplicating other than by use of carbon paper.

(7) "State publication" or "publication" mean any document, compilation, journal, law, resolution, blue-book, statute, code, register, pamphlet, book, report, hearing, legislative bill, leaflet, order, regulation, directory, periodical, or magazine issued in print by the state, any officer of the state, the legislature, or any state agency.

(8) "Records committee" mean the state records committee.

(9) "Data on individuals" includes all records, files and processes which contain any data on any individual and which are kept or intended to be kept by state government on a permanent or semi-permanent basis, including, but not limited to, that data by which it is possible to identify with reasonable certainty the person to whom such information pertains.

(10) "Responsible authority" means any state office or state official established by law or executive order as the body responsible for the collection or use of any set of data on individuals or summary data.

(11) "Summary data" means statistical records and reports derived from data on individuals but in which individuals are not identified and from which neither their identities nor any other characteristic that could uniquely identify an individual is ascertainable.

(12) "Public data" means data on individuals collected and maintained by state government which, in the opinion of the state records committee, should be open to the public.

(13) "Confidential data" means data on individuals collected and maintained by state government which, in the opinion of the state records committee, should be available only to appropriate agencies for the use specified in subsection 63-2-85.3(2) and to others by express consent of the individual, but not to the individual himself.

(14) "Private data" means data on individuals collected and maintained by state government which, in the opinion of the state records committee, should be available only to the appropriate agencies for the uses specified in subsection 63-2-85.3(2), to others by the express consent of the individual, and to the individual himself or next of kin when information is needed to acquire benefits due a deceased person.

History: L. 1969, ch. 212, § 3; 1979, ch. 223, § 3.

63-2-62. Archives and records service created — Archivist and records administrator — Appointment — Qualifications. There is created in the department of ~~finance~~ administrative services a centralized archives and records service which shall administer the state's archives and records management programs, including storage of permanent records, central microfilming and document printing and distribution services. The ~~executive~~ director of the department of ~~finance shall be the ex officio archivist of the state and~~ administrative services, with the approval of the governor, shall ~~employ a qualified state~~ appoint an archivist and records administrator ~~to direct the archives and records service and who shall be selected under the competitive schedule of the state merit system~~ who is qualified by archival education, training, and experience to direct the division of archives and records.

History: L. 1969, ch. 212, § 4; 1981, ch. 257, § 3.

63-2-63. Powers and duties of archivist. (1) The archivist shall ~~be responsible, with the approval of the director of finance, for staffing and organizing~~ staff and organize the archives and records service to administer the following functions as provided by this ~~act~~ chapter.

~~(1)~~ (a) The Utah state archives~~.~~ ;

~~(2)~~ (b) A records management program~~.~~ ;

~~(3)~~ (c) Central microfilming services~~.~~ ; and

~~(4)~~ (d) Printing and distribution of official state documents.

(2) The executive director of ~~finance~~ administrative services may direct that other functions or services for which he or she is responsible be administered by the archives and records service.

History: L. 1969, ch. 212, § 5; 1981, ch. 257, § 4.

63-2-64. Archives and records service—Transfer of archives from public offices.—The archivist shall administer the Utah state archives. The archivist shall be the official custodian of all noncurrent public records of permanent and historic value which are not required by law to remain in the custody of the agency of origin. Unless otherwise directed by law, all public archives of any public office in the state shall, upon the termination of the existence and functions of that office, be transferred to the custody of the archivist.

History: L. 1969, ch. 212, § 6.

63-2-65. Archives and records service—Records declared property of state—Disposition.—All public records made or received by or under the authority of or coming into the custody, control or possession of public officials of this state in the course of their public duties are the property of the state and shall not be mutilated, destroyed, transferred, removed or otherwise damaged or disposed of, in whole or in part, except as provided by law.

History: L. 1969, ch. 212, § 7.

63-2-66. Archives and records service—Access—Certified copies.—The archivist shall keep the public archives in his custody in such arrangement and condition as to make them accessible for convenient use and shall permit them to be inspected, examined, abstracted or copied at reasonable times under his supervision by any person. He shall upon the demand of any person furnish certified copies thereof on payment in advance of reasonable fees as determined by the director of finance. Copies of public records transferred pursuant to law from the office of origin to the custody of the archivist when certified by the archivist under the seal of the Utah state archives shall have the same legal force and effect as if certified by their original custodian.

History: L. 1969, ch. 212, § 8.

63-2-67. Archives and records service — Records located in public offices—Right of archivist to inspect, to replevin.—The archivist, in person or through a deputy, shall have the right of reasonable access to and examination of all public archives in Utah, with a view to securing their safety and preservation. The attorney general, on behalf of the state of Utah or the archivist, may replevin any public records which are not adequately protected or cared for or which were formerly part of the records or files of any public office of the territory or state of Utah.

History: L. 1969, ch. 212, § 9.

63-2-68. State records committee created — Composition — Meetings — Executive secretary. There is hereby created a state records committee composed of the archivist, the state auditor, the director of the division of state history, the attorney general, and the ~~secretary of state of the state of Utah~~ lieutenant governor. The records committee shall meet at least once every quarter to review the policies and programs for the retention and disposal of state records. The archivist shall serve as executive secretary of the records committee.

History: L. 1969, ch. 212, § 10; 1975, ch. 194, § 12; 1981, ch. 257, § 5.

63-2-69. Archives and records service—Record of public offices—Disposition.—Every custodian of public records of the state of Utah who has in his or her custody public records deemed by the custodian to be unnecessary for the transaction of the business of said office shall consult through the office of the archivist with the records committee. The records committee shall determine whether the records in question are of administrative, legal, fiscal, research, or historical value. Those records unanimously determined to be of no administrative, legal, fiscal, research, or historical value shall be disposed of by such method as the records committee may specify. A list of all records so disposed of, together with a statement certifying compliance with this act, signed by members of the records committee, shall be filed and preserved in the office from which the records were drawn and in the files of each of the other officers who are signatories to the certificate. Records having future value may be transferred to the Utah state archives. Public records in the custody of the archivist may be disposed of upon a similar determination by the records committee and the head of the agency from which the records were received, or his legal successor.

History: L. 1969, ch. 212, § 11.

63-2-70. Archives and records service—Copies and reproductions of public records.—Any public officer may cause any or all records, papers, or documents kept by him to be photographed, microphotographed, or reproduced on film. Such photographic film shall comply with the minimum standards of quality approved for permanent photographic records by the National Bureau of Standards, and the device used to reproduce such records on such film shall be one which accurately reproduces the original thereon in all details. Such photographs, microphotographs, or photographic film shall be deemed to be original records for all purposes, including introduction in evidence in all courts or administrative agencies. A transcript, exemplification, or certified copy thereof shall, for all purposes recited herein, be deemed to be a transcript, exemplification, or certified copy of the original. Whenever such photographs, microphotographs, or reproductions on film properly certified shall be placed in conveniently accessible files and provisions made for preserving, examining, and using the same, any such public officer may cause the original records from which the photographs or microphotographs have been made, or any part thereof, to be disposed of according to methods prescribed by the provisions of this act. A microphotograph must be in duplicate before the original records are destroyed and one copy filed with the Utah state archives. Such copies shall be certified by their custodian as true copies of the originals before the originals are destroyed, and copies so certified shall have the same force and effect as the originals. An official chain of custody must be maintained.

History: L. 1969, ch. 212, § 12.

63-2-71. Use of materials to preserve public records. With a view to the preservation of public records, the ~~state purchasing agent~~ chief procurement officer and public officials shall consult with the archivist to assure that all paper, ink, and other materials used in public offices in the state for the purposes of permanent records shall be of durable quality.

History: L. 1969, ch. 212, § 13; 1981, ch. 257, § 6.

63-2-72. Archives and records service—Records of veterans buried in state—State military records.—It shall be the duty of the archivist to collect and maintain a record of all veterans of the United States Armed Forces who are buried in Utah and provide information which will aid in placing a headstone or marker at the head of any veteran's unmarked grave. The archivist shall collect and preserve all other military records pertaining to the state of Utah which are available to the Utah state archives.

History: L. 1969, ch. 212, § 14.

63-2-73. Archives and records service—Public records—Disposal by state agency without approval prohibited.—No public records shall be destroyed or otherwise disposed of by any state agency unless it is determined by the archivist and the records committee that the record has no further administrative, legal, fiscal, research, or historical value.

History: L. 1969, ch. 212, § 15.

63-2-74. Archives and records service—Nonrecord materials.—Nonrecord materials or materials not included within the definition of records as contained in this act may, if not otherwise prohibited by law, be destroyed at any time by the agency in possession of such materials without the prior approval of the archivist. The archivist may formulate procedures and interpretation to guide in the disposition of nonrecord materials.

History: L. 1969, ch. 212, § 16.

63-2-75. Archives and records service—Establishment of records-management program in executive branch.—The archivist shall establish and administer in the executive branch of state government a records-management program which will apply efficient and economical management methods to the creation, utilization, maintenance, retention, preservation, and disposal of state records.

History: L. 1969, ch. 212, § 17.

63-2-76. Archives and records service—Records-management program —Duties of archivist.—The archivist shall, with due regard for the function of the agencies concerned:

(1) Establish standards, procedures and techniques, for effective management of records.

(2) Make continuing surveys of paper-work operations and recommend improvements in current records-management practices including the use of space, equipment, and supplies employed in creating, maintaining, storing, and servicing records.

(3) Establish standards for the preparation of schedules providing for the retention of state records of continuing value and for the prompt and orderly disposal of state records no longer possessing sufficient administrative, historical, legal, or fiscal value to warrant their further keeping.

(4) Obtain reports from state agencies as are required for the administration of the program.

(5) Establish, maintain, and operate a records center for the storing, processing, and servicing of records for state agencies pending their deposit with the Utah state archives or their disposition in any other manner prescribed by law.

(6) Establish, maintain, and operate centralized microfilming services for state agencies. State agencies may operate their own microfilm services only where justified and with the approval of the archivist. Processing and developing of microfilm shall be provided by the central microfilm service unless otherwise justified and approved by the archivist. Microfilm services may also be provided to other public offices and reasonable charges made for such services.

(7) Establish a form control program to analyze and supervise use of forms by all state agencies.

(8) Establish a reports control and reports analysis program.

History: L. 1969, ch. 212, § 18.

63-2-77. Archives and records service—Records-management program —Duties of state agencies.—The head of each state agency shall:

(1) Establish and maintain an active, continuing program for the economical and efficient management of the records of the agency.

(2) Make and maintain records containing adequate and proper documentation of the organization, functions, policies, decisions, procedures, and essential transactions of the agency designed to furnish information to protect the legal and financial rights of the state and of persons directly affected by the agency's activities.

(3) Submit to the archivist, in accordance with the standards established by him, schedules proposing the length of time each state record series warrants retention for administrative, legal, or fiscal purposes after it has been created or received by the agency.

(4) Co-operate with the archivist in the conduct of surveys made by him pursuant to the provisions of this act.

(5) Comply with the rules, regulations, standards, and procedures issued by the archivist.

History: L. 1969, ch. 212, § 19.

63-2-78. Archives and records service—Other governing bodies to promote principles of efficient records management—Archivist to assist with local programs.—The governing body of each county, city, town, district, authority, or any public corporation, or political entity whether organized and existing under charter or under general law shall promote the principles of efficient records management for its records. Such governing body shall, as far as practicable, follow the program established for the management of records by state agencies. The archivist shall, upon the request of a local governing body, provide advice and assistance in the establishment of a local records-management program and shall provide services similar to those available to the executive branch of state government pursuant to the provisions of this act.

History: L. 1969, ch. 212, § 20.

63-2-79. Archives and records service—Records management—Archivist to assist legislative and judicial branches if requested.—Upon request, the archivist shall assist and advise the establishment of records-management programs in the legislative and judicial branches of state government and shall, as required by them, provide program services similar to those available to the executive branch of state government pursuant to the provisions of this act.

History: L. 1969, ch. 212, § 21.

63-2-80. Archives and records service—Purchases of filing and microfilm equipment—Approval and standards.—All purchases of filing equipment and microfilm equipment by state agencies must be approved by the archivist. The archivist shall issue standards for the purchase of all microfilm equipment and supplies by political subdivisions to ensure compatibility of such equipment with state equipment and record-keeping practices.

History: L. 1969, ch. 212, § 22.

63-2-81. Archives and records service—Distribution of state publications.—The archivist shall develop and administer a program to co-ordinate the distribution of all state publications. To facilitate the distribution of state publications, the archivist shall periodically publish lists of all state publications. All state agencies shall, upon request, supply information to the archivist for the preparation of such lists.

History: L. 1969, ch. 212, § 23.

63-2-82. Archives and records service—Publication and distribution of departmental administrative reports.—The archivist shall develop policies, practices and procedures for all state agencies for the format, size, quantity and quality for the publishing and distributing of departmental administrative reports.

History: L. 1969, ch. 212, § 24.

63-2-83. Archives and records service—Printing, storing and distributing session laws, house and senate journals, administrative reports and state code—Assistance to state library.—The archivist shall be charged with the printing, storing and distributing of session laws, the house and senate journals, administrative reports, also Utah Code Annotated when authorized by the legislature. He shall co-operate with the state library in the distribution of state publications to libraries in and out of the state.

History: L. 1969, ch. 212, § 25.

63-2-84. Charges for state publications. The executive director of finance administrative services shall determine the charge, if any, for the purchase of any state publications under control of the state archivist and shall remit daily to the state treasurer all moneys received from the sale of such publications.

History: L. 1969, ch. 212, § 26; 1981, ch. 257, § 7.

63-2-85. Archives and records service—Laws, resolutions and journals —To whom distributed—Statutory laws, purchase and distribution.—Immediately after the laws and resolutions of each session of the legislature have been engrossed and the journals approved the archivist must distribute them as follows:

(1) To each department of the government at Washington and of the government of this state, one copy.

(2) To the Library of Congress and the state law library, two copies each.

(3) To each of the states and territories, one copy.

(4) To the United States district judge for this state, to each of the judges of the supreme and district courts, and to each of the state officers of this state, one copy each.

(5) To each member of the legislature, the secretary of the senate, and the chief clerk of the house of representatives at the session at which such laws were adopted, one copy each.

(6) To each interim committee of the legislature, one copy each.

(7) To the incorporated universities and colleges of the state, one copy each.

(8) To the county clerk of each county, nine copies for the use of the county.

(9) To each county attorney, one copy and to each clerk of the district court, one copy for each division of the district court in his county.

(10) To each free public library in the state, one copy to be furnished on the application of the librarian.

The archivist shall also furnish to each member of the legislature of the state of Utah, and file copies with the Senate and the House without cost at the convening of each regular session, or as soon thereafter as may be convenient, a complete set of all the statutory laws of the state of Utah as are then in full force and effect, but once each has received such complete set, he shall only be entitled to receive such supplements and replacement parts as may be necessary to keep his set up-to-date. If a member is interrupted in his continuous service in his office, the archivist shall furnish a complete set of the laws of the state to such member, subsequently reassuming his office. The archivist is authorized and directed to purchase an adequate supply of the statutory laws of Utah for the purposes of this act, out of the funds made available by the legislature

History: L. 1969, ch. 212, § 27; 1973, ch. 197, § 10.

63-2-85.1. Archives and records service — Identification of authorities collecting or using data. The archivist is directed to identify responsible authorities in state government involved in the collection or use of data on individuals or summary data.

History: C. 1953, 63-2-85.1, enacted by L. 1979, ch. 223, § 4.

63-2-85.2. Archives and records service — Report on information practices — Contents. (1) On or before December 1 of each year, the archivist shall prepare a report or a revision of the previous year's report, on information practices for presentation to the legislature and to the governor. Summaries of the report shall be available to the public at a nominal cost. The report shall contain to the extent feasible, information including, but not limited to:

(a) A complete listing of all systems of confidential and private data on individuals which are kept by the state, a description of the kinds of information contained therein, and the reason that the data is kept;

(b) The title, name and address of the responsible authority for each system of confidential or private data on individuals;

(c) The policies and practices of the responsible authority and the secretary regarding data storage, duration of retention of data and disposal thereof;

(d) A description of the provisions for maintaining the integrity of the data pursuant to subsection 63-2-85.3(4);

(e) The procedures, pursuant to section 63-2-85.4, whereby an individual can:

(i) Be informed if he is the subject of any data on individuals in the system;

(ii) Gain access to that data; and

(iii) Contest the accuracy, completeness and pertinence of that data and necessity for retaining it; and

(f) Any recommendations concerning appropriate legislation.

(2) Each responsible authority shall furnish the archivist with the data set forth in subsection (1) at a time set by the archivist to enable preparation of that annual report.

History: C. 1953, 63-2-85.2, enacted by L. 1979, ch. 223, § 5.

63-2-85.3.   Rules and regulations. The executive director of administrative services, with the recommendation of the archivist shall promulgate rules and regulations in accordance with section 63-46-5 and 63-46-8. These rules and regulations shall apply only to state systems of data on individuals or summary data and shall provide for the implementation of the enforcement and administration of the following standards:

(1) Collection of data on individuals and establishment of related files of the data in state government shall be limited to that necessary for the administration and management of programs enacted by the legislature or by executive order.

(2) Data on individuals shall be under the jurisdiction of the responsible authority identified and designated by the archivist. The responsible authority shall document and file with the archivist the nature of all data on individuals collected and stored and the need for, and intended use of, the data and any other information required.

(3) The use of summary data under the jurisdiction of one or more responsible authorities shall be permitted, subject to the requirement that the data be summarized under the direction of, and by, that responsible authority. Requests for use of any data shall be in writing, stating the intended use.

(4) Appropriate safeguards shall be established in relation to the collection, storage, dissemination and use of data on individuals to assure that all data is accurate, complete and current. Emphasis shall be placed on the data security requirements of computerized files which are accessible directly by means of telecommunication, including security during transmission.

(5) Data on individuals shall be stored only so long as necessary to the administration of authorized programs as authorized by statute or by the state records committee.

History: C. 1953, 63-2-85.3, enacted by L. 1979, ch. 223, § 6; L. 1981, ch. 257, § 8.

63-2-85.4.   Archives and records service — Rights of individuals on whom data stored — Data in dispute, procedure. The rights of individuals on whom data is stored or is to be stored and the responsibilities of each responsible authority in regard to that data shall be as follows:

(1) The purposes for which the data on individuals is collected and used, or is to be collected and used, shall be filed in writing by the responsible authority with the archivist and shall be a matter of public record.

(2) An individual requested to supply confidential or private data shall be informed of the intended uses of that data.

(3) Any individual refusing to supply confidential or private data shall be informed by the requesting party of any known consequence arising from that refusal.

(4) No confidential or private data shall be used other than for the stated purposes nor shall it be disclosed to any person other than the individual to whom the data pertains, without express consent of that individual, except that next of kin may obtain information needed to acquire benefits due a deceased person.

(5) Upon request to the archivist, an individual shall be informed whether he is the subject of any data on individuals, informed of the content and meaning of that data, and shown the data without any charge. The archivist shall charge

an appropriate fee for any additional requests within a six-month period unless the requested information is in dispute.

(6) An individual shall have the right to contest the accuracy or completeness of any data on individuals about him. If that data is contested, the individual shall notify, in writing, the responsible authority of the nature of the disagreement. Within 30 days from that notice, the responsible authority shall either correct the data if it is found to be inaccurate or incomplete and notify past recipients of the inaccurate or incomplete data of the change, or shall notify the individual of his disagreement with the statement of contest. Any person aggrieved by the determination of that responsible authority may appeal that determination to the archivist and, if still dissatisfied, may bring appropriate action pursuant to section 63-46-9. Data in dispute shall not be disclosed except under conditions required by law or regulation and even then, only if the individual's statement of disagreement is included with the disclosed data.

History: C. 1953, 63-2-85.4, enacted by L. 1979, ch. 223, § 7.

63-2-87. Archives and records service — Violation of act a misdemeanor.

(1) Any person who violates any provision of this act shall be guilty of a class B misdemeanor.

(2) Any public employee who willfully violates any provision of this act or the rules and regulations promulgated pursuant thereto shall be subject to suspension without pay or discharge, after a hearing as provided by law.

History: L. 1969, ch. 212, § 29; 1979, ch. 223, § 8.

63-2-88. Archives and records service — Violation of act — Liability for damages — Injunction.

(1) Any responsible authority who violates any provision of this act shall be liable to any person, suffering damage as a result thereof, and the person damaged may bring an action against the state to recover any damages sustained, plus costs incurred and reasonable attorney fees.

(2) Any responsible authority who willfully violates any provision of this act shall, in addition to those remedies provided under subsection (1), be liable for exemplary damages of not less than $100 nor more than $1,000 for each violation.

(3) Any responsible authority which violates or proposes to violate the provisions of this act may be enjoined by any district court in this state. The court may make any order or judgment as may be necessary to prevent the use or employment by any person of such violations of this act.

History: C. 1953, 63-2-88, enacted by L. 1979, ch. 223, § 9.

63-2-89. Archives and records service — Exemptions from act.

No provisions of this act shall be deemed to apply to data on individuals relating to criminal investigations, nor shall they be construed to restrict or modify the rights heretofore existing of access to public records, or records more than 75 years old.

History: C. 1953, 63-2-89, enacted by L. 1979, ch. 223, § 10.

TAX EXEMPTION
(Utah Constitution, Art. 13, s.2.)

Utah library laws are reprinted from UTAH CODE AN-
NOTATED published by The Allen Smith Co., Indianapolis, Indiana.

VERMONT

DEPARTMENT OF LIBRARIES

(Vermont Statutes Annotated, 1982, Title 22, s.601-607.)

§ 601. Department established; supervision by board

There is established a department of libraries. The department of libraries shall be under the supervision and control of a board of libraries, referred to in this chapter as "the board." The board shall consist of seven members appointed by the governor with the advice and consent of the senate. At the time of appointment of the initial board one member shall be appointed for a term of one year, and two members for terms of two years, two for three years and two for four years. Thereafter, all appointments shall be for a term of four years. The governor may appoint a member to replace any member of the board who dies or resigns, to serve for the balance of the unexpired term of office. No person shall be appointed to the board for more than two full terms, consecutive or otherwise. In making appointments to the board the governor shall, as he finds feasible, consult with educational officials, librarians and library administrators, the Vermont Bar Association, or other segments of the population.—Added 1969, No. 226 (Adj. Sess.), § 4, eff. March 31, 1970.

§ 602. —Officers; meetings

The board shall elect annually a chairman and a vice-chairman. The chairman shall preside at meetings of the board; the vice-chairman shall preside in the absence of the chairman. The secretary shall record the votes and proceedings of the board.—Added 1969, No. 226 (Adj. Sess.), § 4, eff. March 31, 1970.

§ 603. Appointment of state librarian; powers and duties

(a) The governor shall appoint a state librarian after consultation with the board, and may remove him from office after consultation with the board. Any person appointed state librarian must be a professional librarian and must possess a degree in library science from an institution accredited by the American Library Association. The state librarian shall serve as the administrative head of the department of libraries, and shall serve as secretary to the board of libraries, but shall not be a member of the board.

(b) In his capacity as administrative head of the department of libraries the state librarian may appoint and engage employees subject to the provisions of chapter 13 of Title 3.

(c) The state librarian shall distribute, in accordance with sections 1152–1163 and 1191–1193a of Title 29, and other official lists maintained by the state librarian, the acts and resolves of the general assembly, the legislative directory, the Vermont Statutes Annotated, the Vermont key number digest, the journals of the senate and house of representatives, the Vermont reports and other official reports and documents. He shall maintain records of all documents which he distributes.—Added 1969, No. 226 (Adj. Sess.), § 4, eff. March 31, 1970.

§ 604. Books and materials

All books, documents, pictures, maps, pamphlets and other documentary material, and all films and film strips, belonging to the state and not placed by law in the custody of another department or agency of the state, shall constitute material of the department of libraries.—Added 1969, No. 226 (Adj. Sess.), § 4, eff. March 31, 1970.

§ 605. Duties and functions of the department of libraries

The duties and functions of the department of libraries shall be to provide, administer and maintain:

(1) A law library to serve the supreme court, the attorney general, other members of the judiciary, the legal profession, members of the legislature, officials of state government and the general public.

(2) A collection of state documents and of documents relating to other states, and local and federal governments. It shall arrange for and designate depositories of state documents which designation is to include Bailey library at the university of Vermont. The depart-

ment may acquire reports and documents published by federal agencies and by other states and countries, and may arrange for the exchange of official reports and publications with federal agencies, and with governmental agencies in other states and countries.

(3) An information and reference service to state government, including a comprehensive collection of current information relating to matters of public policy and topics pertinent to state government.

(4) A general library collection of a sufficient size and scope to reinforce and supplement the resources of local and regional libraries. All materials of the department of libraries shall be available for free circulation to all citizens, institutions and organizations under regulations of the state librarian except that the state librarian may restrict rare or reference-type materials to one location. The department shall arrange, classify and catalog all materials in its custody and provide for their safekeeping, and shall rebind books as needed. The department shall provide service to other libraries in the state, schools and individuals, and may provide service by mail or book wagon or otherwise.

(5) A service of advice and consultation to all libraries in the state, in order to assist them in realizing their potential. This service shall be provided at a regional level as well as at the state level. The department may provide centralized cataloging and other related technical services to libraries in the state to the extent feasible.

(6) All libraries in state correctional institutions and all state institutions for the treatment of the mentally ill and mentally handicapped.

(7) Reading materials for the blind and physically handicapped.
—Added 1969, No. 226 (Adj. Sess.), § 4, eff. March 31, 1970; amended 1971, No. 162 (Adj. Sess.), § 1.

§ 606. Other duties and functions

The department, in addition to the functions specified in the preceding section:

(1) Shall administer any grants-in-aid to libraries which may be available from state funds, and may prepare plans and applications to obtain federal aid monies which may be available.

(2) Shall compile and publish annual statistics covering all libraries in the state, including those maintained by the department of libraries.

(3) Shall provide consultative services to other libraries in the state, and shall encourage formation of central records of library holdings.

(4) Shall promote improved communications among libraries in the state as well as cooperative use of facilities.

(5) May provide facilities in cooperation with other libraries for storage of little used materials.

(6) May conduct seminars, workshops and other programs to increase the professional competence of librarians in the state.

(7) May receive and administer gifts of real and personal property accepted by the governor on behalf of the state under section 101 of Title 29.

(8) May dispose of by sale or exchange, or may discard, material which is obsolete or has ceased to be useful, because of its physical condition or otherwise. Any proceeds from the sale or disposition of materials shall be paid over to the state treasurer and credited to the account of the department for the purchase of library materials. Materials constituting public records or which are archival in nature may be disposed of only following thirty days' notice to the public records director.—Added 1969, No. 226 (Adj. Sess.), § 4, eff. March 31, 1970.

§ 607. Actions to recover books

The attorney general, at the request of the state librarian, shall institute appropriate legal proceedings in the name of the state for the recovery of books or materials of the department unlawfully taken or withheld by others.—Added 1969, No. 226 (Adj. Sess.), § 4, eff. March 31, 1970.

STATE AID
(Vermont Statutes Annotated, 1982, Title 22, s.631-635.)

§ 631. General provisions

On application by the board of trustees of a public library in a town, city or incorporated village not having a free public library owned and controlled by such town, city or village, the board of libraries may expend $100.00 of the moneys annually available for the purposes of this chapter, for books for such town, city or village, and shall select and purchase books for the purpose of establishing a free public library in that town, city or village.—Added 1969, No. 226 (Adj. Sess.), § 4, eff. March 31, 1970.

§ 632. Requirements

A town, city or incorporated village shall not be entitled to the benefits of section 631 of this title, unless such town, city or village has elected a board of library trustees as provided in chapter 3 of this title and has voted to instruct such trustees to make application therefor to the board of libraries and unless such trustees have provided, in a manner satisfactory to the board, for the care, custody and distribution of the books furnished under this subchapter.—Added 1969, No. 226 (Adj. Sess.), § 4, eff. March 31, 1970.

§ 633. —Appropriation by municipality

A town, city or incorporated village voting to instruct its board of library trustees to make application to the board of libraries under section 631 of this title, shall annually appropriate for the maintenance of its free public library a sum not less than $50.00, if its grand list is $10,000.00 or over, or a sum not less than $25.00, if its grand list is less than $10,000.00 and not less than $2,500.00, or a sum not less than $15.00 if its grand list is less than $2,500.00. The selectmen of such town or the trustees of such village shall annually, in the month of September, draw an order on the treasurer of the town or village, payable to such trustees, for the amount of such appropriation, without the town, city or village having voted such appropriation.—Added 1969, No. 226 (Adj. Sess.), § 4, eff. March 31, 1970.

§ 634. Aid to free public libraries

The board of libraries may assist free public or other nonprofit libraries which formulate and implement plans for the systematic and effective coordination of libraries and library services. Grants may be made in accordance with standards of the service, consistent with the Federal Library Services and Construction Act, chapter 16 of Title 20, United States code as amended.—Added 1969, No. 226 (Adj. Sess.), § 4, eff. March 31, 1970.

§ 635. —Requirements

If the board of trustees of a free public library, any part of whose books has been paid for with state funds, fails to provide for the safety and public usefulness of such books or fails to pay the annual appropriation in accordance with section 633 of this title, the board shall notify in writing the trustees of such library as to the requirements of the board in respect to such books. If such trustees neglect to comply with such requirements for sixty days after the serving of such notice, such books shall thereafter be under the full control of the board.—Added 1969, No. 226 (Adj. Sess.), § 4, eff. March 31, 1970.

INTERSTATE LIBRARY COMPACT
(Vermont Statutes Annotated, 1982, Title 22, s.21-32, 41-44.)

§ 21. Policy and purpose—Article I

Because the desire for the services provided by libraries transcends governmental boundaries and can most effectively be satisfied by giving such services to communities and people regardless of jurisdictional lines, it is the policy of the states party to this compact to cooperate and share their responsibilities; to authorize cooperation and sharing with respect to those types of library facilities and services which can be more economically or efficiently developed and maintained on a cooperative basis, and to authorize cooperation and sharing among localities, states and others in providing joint or cooperative library services in areas where the distribution of population or of existing and potential library resources make the provision of library service on an interstate basis the most effective way of providing adequate and efficient service.—1963, No. 119, § 2, eff. May 28, 1963.

§ 22. Definitions—Article II

As used in this compact:

(a) "Public library agency" means any unit or agency of local or state government operating or having power to operate a library.

(b) "Private library agency" means any non-governmental entity which operates or assumes a legal obligation to operate a library.

(c) "Library agreement" means a contract establishing an interstate library district pursuant to this compact or providing for the joint or cooperative furnishing of library services.—1963, No. 119, § 2, eff. May 28, 1963.

§ 23. Interstate library districts—Article III

(a) Any one or more public library agencies in a party state in cooperation with any public library agency or agencies in one or more other party states may establish and maintain an interstate library district. Subject to the provisions of this compact and any other laws of the party states which pursuant hereto remain applicable, such district may establish, maintain and operate some or all of the library facilities and services for the area concerned in accordance with the terms of a library agreement therefor. Any private library agency or agencies within an interstate library district may cooperate therewith, assume duties, responsibilities and obligations thereto, and receive benefits therefrom as provided in any library agreement to which such agency or agencies become party.

(b) Within an interstate library district, and as provided by a library agreement, the performance of library functions may be undertaken on a joint or cooperative basis or may be undertaken by means of one or more arrangements between or among public or private library agencies for the extension of library privileges to the use of facilities or services operated or rendered by one or more of the individual library agencies.

(c) If a library agreement provides for joint establishment, maintenance or operation of library facilities or services by an interstate library district, such district shall have power to do any one or more of the following in accordance with such library agreement:

1. Undertake, administer and participate in programs or arrangements for securing, lending or servicing of books and other publications, any other materials suitable to be kept or made available by libraries, library equipment or for the dissemination of information about libraries, the value and significance of particular items therein, and the use thereof.

2. Accept for any of its purposes under this compact any and all donations, and grants of money, equipment, supplies, materials, and services, (conditional or otherwise), from any state of the United States or any subdivision or agency thereof, or interstate agency, or from any institution, person, firm or corporation, and receive, utilize and dispose of the same.

3. Operate mobile library units or equipment for the purpose of rendering bookmobile service within the district.

4. Employ professional, technical, clerical and other personnel and fix terms of employment, compensation and other appropriate benefits; and where desirable, provide for the in-service training of such personnel.

5. Sue and be sued in any court of competent jurisdiction.

6. Acquire, hold, and dispose of any real or personal property or any interest or interests therein as may be appropriate to the rendering of library service.

7. Construct, maintain and operate a library, including any appropriate branches thereof.

Do such other things as may be incidental to or appropriate for the carrying out of any of the foregoing powers.—1963, No. 119, § 2, eff. May 28, 1963.

§ 24. Interstate library districts; governing board—Article IV

(a) An interstate library district which establishes, maintains or operates any facilities or services in its own right shall have a governing board which shall direct the affairs of the district and act for it in all matters relating to its business. Each participating public library agency in the district shall be represented on the governing board which shall be organized and conduct its business in accordance with provision therefor in the library agreement. But in no event shall a governing board meet less often than twice a year.

(b) Any private library agency or agencies party to a library agreement establishing an interstate library district may be represented on or advise with the governing board of the district in such manner as the library agreement may provide.—1963, No. 119, § 2, eff. May 28, 1963.

§ 25. State library agency cooperation—Article V

Any two or more state library agencies of two or more of the party states may undertake and conduct joint or cooperative library programs, render joint or cooperative library services, and enter into and perform arrangements for the cooperative or joint acquisition, use, housing and disposition of items or collections of materials which, by reason of expense, rarity, specialized nature, or infrequency of demand therefor would be appropriate for central collection and shared use. Any such programs, services or arrangements may include provision for the exercise on a cooperative or joint basis of any power exercisable by an interstate library district and an agreement embodying any such program, service or arrangement shall contain provisions covering the subjects detailed in article VI [section 26 of this title] of this compact for interstate library agreements.—1963, No. 119, § 2, eff. May 28, 1963.

§ 26. Library agreements—Article VI

(a) In order to provide for any joint or cooperative undertaking pursuant to this compact, public and private library agencies may enter into library agreements. Any agreement executed pursuant to the provisions of this compact shall, as among the parties to the agreement:

1. Detail the specific nature of the services, programs, facilities, arrangements or properties to which it is applicable.

2. Provide for the allocation of costs and other financial responsibilities.

3. Specify the respective rights, duties, obligations and liabilities of the parties.

4. Set forth the terms and conditions for duration, renewal, termination, abrogation, disposal of joint or common property, if any, and all other matters which may be appropriate to the proper effectuation and performance of the agreement.

(b) No public or private library agency shall undertake to exercise itself, or jointly with any other library agency, by means of a library agreement any power prohibited to such agency by the constitution or statutes of its state.

(c) No library agreement shall become effective until filed with the compact administrator of each state involved, and approved in accordance with article VII [section 27 of this title] of this compact. —1963, No. 119, § 2, eff. May 28, 1963.

§ 27. Approval of library agreements—Article VII

(a) Every library agreement made pursuant to this compact shall, prior to and as a condition precedent to its entry into force, be submitted to the attorney general of each state in which a public library agency party thereto is situated, who shall determine whether the agreement is in proper form and compatible with the laws of his state. The attorneys general shall approve any agreement submitted to them unless they shall find that it does not meet the conditions set forth herein and shall detail in writing addressed to the governing bodies of the public library agencies concerned the specific respects in which the proposed agreement fails to meet the requirements of law. Failure to disapprove an agreement submitted hereunder within 90 days of its submission shall constitute approval thereof.

(b) In the event that a library agreement made pursuant to this compact shall deal in whole or in part with the provisions of services or facilities with regard to which an officer or agency of the state government has constitutional or statutory powers of control, the agreement shall, as a condition precedent to its entry into force, be submitted to the state officer or agency having such power of control and shall be approved or disapproved by him or it as to all matters within his or its jurisdiction in the same manner and subject to the same requirements governing the action of the attorneys general pursuant to paragraph (a) of this article. This requirement of submission and approval shall be in addition to and not in substitution for the requirement of submission to and approval by the attorneys general.—1963, No. 119, § 2, eff. May 28, 1963.

§ 28. Other laws applicable—Article VIII

Nothing in this compact or in any library agreement shall be construed to supersede, alter or otherwise impair any obligation imposed on any library by otherwise applicable law, nor to authorize the transfer or disposition of any property held in trust by a library agency in a manner contrary to the terms of such trust.—1963, No. 119, § 2, eff. May 28, 1963.

§ 29. Appropriation and aid—Article IX

(a) Any public agency party to a library agreement may appropriate funds to the interstate library district established thereby in the same manner and to the same extent as to a library wholly maintained by it and, subject to the laws of the state in which such public library agency is situated, may pledge its credit in support of an interstate library district established by the agreement.

(b) Subject to the provisions of the library agreement pursuant to which it functions and the laws of the states in which such district is situated, an interstate library district may claim and receive any state and federal aid which may be available to library agencies. —1963, No. 119, § 2, eff. May 28, 1963.

§ 30. Compact administrator—Article X

Each state shall designate a compact administrator with whom copies of all library agreements to which his state or any public library agency thereof is party shall be filed. The administrator shall have such other powers as may be conferred upon him by the laws of his state and may consult and cooperate with the compact administrators of other party states and take such steps as may effectuate the purposes of this compact. If the laws of a party state so provide, such state may designate one or more deputy compact administrators in addition to its compact administrator.—1963, No. 119, § 2, eff. May 28, 1963.

§ 31. Entry into force and withdrawal—Article XI

(a) This compact shall enter into force and effect immediately upon its enactment into law by any two states. Thereafter, it shall enter into force and effect as to any other state upon the enactment thereof by such state.

(b) This compact shall continue in force with respect to a party state and remain binding upon such state until six months after such state has given notice to each other party state of the repeal thereof. Such withdrawal shall not be construed to relieve any party to a library agreement entered into pursuant to this compact from any obligation of that agreement prior to the end of its duration as provided therein.—1963, No. 119, § 2, eff. May 28, 1963.

§ 32. Construction and severability—Article XII

This compact shall be liberally construed so as to effectuate the purposes thereof. The provisions of this compact shall be severable and if any phrase, clause, sentence or provision of this compact is declared to be contrary to the constitution of any party state or of the United States or the applicability thereof to any government, agency, person or circumstance is held invalid, the validity of the remainder of this compact and the applicability thereof to any government, agency, person or circumstance shall not be affected thereby. If this compact shall be held contrary to the constitution of any state party thereto, the compact shall remain in full force and effect as to the remaining states and in full force and effect as to the state affected as to all severable matters.—1963, No. 119, § 2, eff. May 28, 1963.

§ 41. Town participation restricted

No town of this state may be a party to a library agreement which provides for the construction or maintenance of a library under article III, subdivision (c-7) [section 23(c)7 of this title] of the compact, nor pledge its credit in support of such a library, or contribute to the capital financing thereof, except after compliance with any laws applicable to towns relating to or governing capital outlays and the pledging of credit.—1963, No. 119, § 3, eff. May 28, 1963.

§ 42. State library agency defined

As used in the compact, "state library agency" with reference to this state, means, the department of libraries and any department of state government providing library services.—1963, No. 119, § 4, eff. May 28, 1963.

§ 43. Compact administrator, appointment

The governor shall appoint an officer of this state who shall be the compact administrator under article X [section 30 of this title] of this compact.—1963, No. 119, § 5, eff. May 28, 1963.

§ 44. Withdrawal, notices

In the event of withdrawal from the compact the governor shall send and receive any notices required by article XI(b) [section 31(b) of this title] of the compact.—1963, No. 119, § 6, eff. May 28, 1963.

DISTRIBUTION OF PUBLIC DOCUMENTS
(Vermont Statutes Annotated, 1982, Title 29, s.1152-1159,
1161-1163, 1192, 1193a, 1116.)

§ 1152. Duties of state librarian

The state librarian shall be charged with all deliveries of public documents made to him and he shall receipt therefor in duplicate to the purchasing director. Surplus copies shall be classified and stored by him.—Amended 1969, No. 226 (Adj. Sess.), § 5, eff. March 31, 1970.

§ 1153a. Legislative directory

The secretary of state shall at each biennial session of the legislature prepare a legislative directory containing appropriate matter. A sufficient number of copies of the same shall be printed by December 31 of each odd-numbered year and shall be delivered to the state librarian, who shall deliver one copy to each town and county clerk, each elective and appointive state officer, each member of the general assembly, the clerk of each state board, Castleton, Johnson and Lyndon state colleges, the university of Vermont and state agricultural college, Vermont technical college at Randolph, each high school and academy library in the state, to the secretary and assistant secretary of the senate, the clerk and assistant clerks of the house of representatives, 25 copies to the secretary of state and the remaining copies to the department of libraries. The state librarian may sell copies of the legislative directory to the general public and charge a reasonable price. The receipts from such sales shall be deposited in the general fund.—Added 1975, No. 246 (Adj. Sess.), § 1; amended 1981, No. 108, § 326.

§ 1154. —Distribution

The state librarian shall deliver on the second day of the session to the members of the general assembly who were not members of the last preceding general assembly, the clerk and assistant clerks of the house of representatives, the secretary and assistant secretary of the senate, one copy of the legislative directory prepared for the preceding session of the general assembly.—Amended 1969, No. 226 (Adj. Sess.), § 7, eff. March 31, 1970.

§ 1155. Report of state librarian

Annually, on or before June 1, the state librarian shall make a report to the purchasing director, showing the matters disclosed by such record since the time of making his last report, and in each even year, shall report to the governor in detail the number of volumes and pamphlets, the number distributed and the number on hand, and shall make recommendations relating to any shortage or wasteful surplus thereof.—Amended 1969, No. 226 (Adj. Sess.), § 8, eff. March 31, 1970.

§ 1156. Distribution of documents by state librarian

Immediately upon receipt of public documents, the state librarian shall cause the same to be distributed as hereinafter provided. The state librarian shall cause one hundred copies of each publication to be deposited in the state library, except when he determines that a lesser number is required.—Amended 1969, No. 226 (Adj. Sess.), § 9, eff. March 31, 1970.

§ 1157. —Copies for state officers

The state librarian shall deliver to a state officer as many copies of the report of such officer as he may require, upon requisition therefor showing the names and addresses of persons for whom such reports are intended.—Amended 1969, No. 226 (Adj. Sess.), § 10, eff. March 31, 1970.

§ 1158. —Acts and resolves; Vermont Statutes Annotated; distribution

(a) The state librarian shall deliver the acts and resolves as follows: to the secretary of state, six copies; to the clerk of the United States supreme court for the use of the court, one copy; to the governor's office and to the governor and lieutenant governor, one copy each; to the library of Congress, four copies; to each county clerk, three copies; one to each of the following officers and institutions: each department of the United States government and upon request to federal libraries, elective and appointive state officers, the clerk of each state board or commission, superintendent of each state institution, the library of the university of Vermont, the libraries of Castleton, Johnson and Lyndon state colleges, Vermont technical college, Middlebury college, Norwich university, St. Michaels college, senators and representatives of this state in Congress, members of the general assembly during the session at which such laws were adopted, the secretary and assistant secretary of the senate, clerk and assistant clerks of the house of representatives, the judges, attorney, marshall and clerk of the United States district court in this state, the judge of the second circuit United States court of appeals from Vermont, justices and ex-justices of the supreme court, superior judges, district court judges, the reporter of decisions, judges and registers of probate, sheriffs, state's attorneys, town clerks; one each, upon request and as the available supply permits, to assistant judges of the superior court, masters in chancery whose appointments have been properly certified to the secretary of state, justices of the peace, chairman of the legislative body of each municipality and town treasurers; one within the state, to the Vermont historical society, to each county or regional bar law library, and one copy to each state or territorial library or supreme court library, and foreign library which makes available to Vermont its comparable publication, provided that if any of these officials hold more than one of the offices named, that official shall be entitled to only one copy.

(b) The state librarian shall distribute the copies of Vermont Statutes Annotated and cumulative pocket part supplements thereto, when issued, as follows: one each to the governor, lieutenant governor, speaker of the house of representatives, the state treasurer, secretary of state, auditor of accounts, adjutant general, purchasing director, commissioner of taxes, sergeant at arms and the head of each administrative department; four copies to the attorney general; one to each town clerk, three to each county clerk;

one to each probate judge and two to the clerk of the supreme court; one to each ex-justice and justice of the supreme court, each superior judge, district judge, and state's attorney; two to the judge of the second circuit United States court of appeals from Vermont and four to the United States district judges for the district of Vermont. One copy shall be given to each state institution, each county or regional bar law library, each university, college and public library, as requested, and as many sets as are needed to effect exchange with state libraries and state law libraries. Such copies shall be kept for use in the offices of the officers and institutions mentioned. One copy shall be given to each member of the commission established by chapter 1 of Title 1 and counsel therefor, unless they are authorized to receive one in another capacity, and one to each of the fifteen members of the joint special committee on revision of the laws authorized by No. 86 of the Acts of 1959.—Amended 1969, No. 226 (Adj. Sess.), § 11, eff. March 31, 1970; 1971, No. 162 (Adj. Sess.), § 2.

§ 1159. —Sale of acts and resolves

Such further distribution may be made as the state librarian determines. The surplus copies may be sold at a price to be fixed by the purchasing director.—Amended 1969, No. 226 (Adj. Sess.), § 12, eff. March 31, 1970.

§ 1161. Distribution to schools

On request of the principal of any high school or academy the state librarian shall furnish such an institution with such state publications as in his opinion can be supplied without detriment to the state library.—Amended 1969, No. 226 (Adj. Sess.), § 13, eff. March 31, 1970.

§ 1162. Distribution to town and city clerks

The state librarian shall cause the books, pamphlets and documents that cannot be otherwise distributed more advantageously for the state, to be sent to the several town clerks. Each town clerk shall deliver the books, pamphlets or documents to the persons residing in their towns entitled to receive them.—Amended 1969, No. 226 (Adj. Sess.), § 14, eff. March 31, 1970.

§ 1163. Distribution to newspapers

The state librarian shall deliver to a person publishing a newspaper or magazine in this state, one copy each of the public documents requested which can be furnished without detriment

to the state library, provided that such person shall furnish free
to the state library the newspaper or magazine published by him.—
Amended 1969, No. 226 (Adj. Sess.), § 15, eff. March 31, 1970.

§ 1192. Distribution

The volumes and advance sheets of the Vermont Reports when
printed shall be delivered to the state librarian, or distributed
on his direction, to each of the following officers and institutions:
each county clerk for the use of the courts in his county, each
register of probate for the use of the probate court in his district,
each justice and ex-justice of the supreme court, each superior
judge, each district judge, the reporter of decisions, the attorney
general, each state's attorney, the United States district judges, the
clerk of the United States district court, the library of the
university of Vermont, the libraries of Castleton, Johnson and
Lyndon state colleges, Middlebury college, Norwich university,
St. Michael's college, Vermont technical college, each county or
regional bar law library, and each trustee of the state library. Of
each volume issued one volume shall be delivered to the law department of each state, territorial or district library, and to the library
of each province of the Dominion of Canada, sending similar publications to the library of this state, to the attorney general of the
United States, the Library of Congress, Library of Parliament of
the Dominion of Canada, the United States department of justice.
Such copies shall be kept for use in the offices of the officers or
institutions mentioned.—Amended 1969, No. 226 (Adj. Sess.), § 16,
eff. March 31, 1970; 1971, No. 162 (Adj. Sess.), § 3.

§ 1193a. Sale and exchange of surplus copies

The surplus volumes of Vermont reports, through volume 127,
shall be kept by the department of libraries for exchange and for
sale on the order of the state librarian, the price to be fixed by the
purchasing director.—Added 1975, No. 246 (Adj. Sess.), § 2.

§ 1116. Printing and distribution of public acts

During or after each session of the general assembly the secretary of state shall designate for publication, from time to time,
the public acts of the session which are of general interest. The
purchasing director shall cause the same to be printed in convenient
loose-leaf form and furnish them as soon as they are printed
and delivered, free of charge, to each member of the general
assembly and to the several town and city clerks for delivery as

follows: one to each town or city clerk, one to the chairman of each board of selectmen and president of a village, one to the chairman of each school board, and such number to the state librarian and secretary of state as each shall request.—Amended 1961, No. 30, eff. March 17, 1961.

GEOGRAPHIC NAMES
(Vermont Statutes Annotated, 1982, Title 10, s.151-154.)

§ 151. Terminology and spelling

(a) The state librarian is authorized to furnish for any federal or state publication the proper terminology and spelling of any geographic name in Vermont and may advise the United States post office department regarding the proper selection and spelling of the name of a Vermont post office or any railroad company regarding the use and spelling of the name of a Vermont station. The state librarian is authorized to function in collaboration with the United States board on geographic names and to conduct his operations similarly.

(b) The names used in the topographic maps of the state now being prepared by the United States geological survey in cooperation with the state shall be spelled in accordance with the recommendations of the state librarian.—Amended 1959, No. 329 (Adj. Sess.), § 45, eff. March 1, 1961.

§ 152. Authority to name roads and geographic locations

The board of libraries is hereby designated the state agency to name roads and geographic locations including but not limited to mountains, streams, lakes and ponds upon petition signed by not less than twenty-five interested persons or by petition of an administrative department of the state.—1961, No. 139, § 3, eff. May 24, 1961; amended 1969, No. 226 (Adj. Sess.), § 2, eff. March 31, 1970.

§ 153. Procedure

When the board receives a petition to act under section 152 of this title it shall give reasonable notice to each administrative department of the state having jurisdiction of the road or location to be named, and to each town in which the road or location lies of the time and place when it will hear all interested parties.—1961, No. 139, § 4, eff. May 24, 1961.

§ 154. Standards

The board in choosing names shall give preference to historical events, historic persons and flora and fauna native to Vermont, names characteristic to Vermont and its traditions and local place names where long usage has made them appropriate and useful. —1961, No. 139, § 5, eff. May 24, 1961.

STATE HISTORICAL SOCIETY
(Vermont Statutes Annotated, 1982, Title 22, s.281-285.)

§ 281. Members and trustees ex officio

The secretary of state, auditor of accounts and the state librarian, by virtue of their offices, shall be members of the Vermont Historical Society and of the board of trustees thereof.—Amended 1959, No. 80, § 1.

§ 282. Director

Subject to the final approval of the governor and with the approval of the board of trustees, the president of the society and the state librarian shall employ and determine the salary of the director of the society who shall have charge of the collections of the society and such historical objects, books and documents of the state as shall be placed therewith for use.—Amended 1959, No. 80, § 2.

§ 283. Expenditure of funds

The sums annually available for the society shall be expended by the director under the general supervision of the president for the purchase of books, pamphlets, manuscripts and museum items relating particularly to the history of Vermont and for such other historical material as may be deemed best, for the publication of its proceedings and other matters of historical importance, for the payment of the salary of the director and the salaries of other employees of the society, for procuring portraits of deceased governors and lieutenant governors not now possessed by the state and for binding and preserving documents and other property of the society.—Amended 1959, No. 80, § 3.

§ 284. Disposition of books, collections and property

If the society is ever dissolved, the books, collections and property thereof shall become the property of the state. Such society shall not sell or dispose of any part of its books or collections, except by way of exchange or to further the objects of the society and then only upon the vote of the board of trustees of the society. Any sale or disposal thereof contrary to the provisions of this section shall be void.—Amended 1959, No. 80, § 4.

§ 285. Classification of employees

Employees of the Vermont historical society shall be classified by the state classification system as if they were state employees and shall receive all general pay increases granted state employees.— Added 1967, No. 137, § 1; amended 1973, No. 37, § 4, eff. July 1, 1973.

PUBLIC RECORDS DIVISION
(Vermont Statutes Annotated, 1982, Title 22, s.451-457.)

§ 451. Composition of division

The public records division shall consist of the public records director and a public records advisory board.—Added 1959, No. 328 (Adj. Sess.), § 12.

§ 452. Public records director; appointment

The public records division of the agency of administration shall be headed by a public records director appointed by the governor, with the advice and consent of the senate.—Added 1959, No. 328 (Adj. Sess.), § 12; amended 1965, No. 125, § 8, eff. July 2, 1965.

§ 453. Duties of director

In addition to the duties otherwise assigned to him by law the director of public records may:

(1) Give aid, advice and information to all or any custodians of public records;

(2) Have access to all public records at all reasonable times;

(3) Receive gifts, aid or assistance, of any kind, from any source, public or private, for the purpose of housing, ordering, copying, preserving, editing or publishing, of public records;

(4) Recover public records not in the possession of their lawful custodians;

(5) Investigate all public offices in this state for the purpose of ascertaining the adequacy of protection of public records;

(6) Devise and advise as to the use of standard books or forms for the keeping of records, except such records as are otherwise regulated by law;

(7) Receive, with his consent, noncurrent records from any custodian who may desire to deliver the records;

(8) Copy, index, repair, edit or publish public records, or lists, inventories, guides, catalogues, or indices thereof;

(9) Cooperate with any federal agency for any of these ends;

(10) Adopt rules as may be necessary for the effectual preservation of all public records in this state, subject to the approval of the governor, including but not limited to the microfilming of all public records;

(11) Maintain a records center to hold little used departmental

records for later disposition;

(12) Administer a central microfilm program. Public records which are preserved on microfilm shall be taken and received in all courts, public offices, and official bodies as prima facie evidence.— Added 1959, No. 328 (Adj. Sess.), § 12; amended 1977, No. 32, § 1.

§ 454. Disposition of public records

A custodian of public records shall not destroy, give away, sell, discard or damage any record or records in his charge, unless specifically so authorized by law, without having first submitted to the public records director a list thereof, with accurate description. Within sixty days after receipt of the list and description, with an application for permission to destroy, cancel or dispose of the records, the public records director with the prior advice of the public records advisory board shall order the preservation, destruction, cancellation, or disposal thereof, in whole or in part, which order shall be duly recorded by the custodian, and shall be binding on him and his successors. Before approving a request for the destruction of any public record, the public records director, or the custodian of the record if the director approves, may make photographic copies of it and copies so made shall have the same force and effect for all purposes as the original record. Statutes concerning the retention of original materials shall be considered satisfied and no violation incurred when public records are officially microfilmed and stored and the original material destroyed pursuant to sections 453 and 457 of this title.—Amended 1979, No. 56, § 4.

§ 455. Penalties

A person who willfully destroys, gives away, sells, discards or damages the public records referred to in section 454 of this title, without having authority so to do, shall be fined at least $50.00 but not more than $1,000.00 for each offense.—Amended 1979, No. 56, § 5.

§ 456. Public records advisory board; composition

The public records advisory board shall consist of the secretary of state, director of the Vermont historical society, the auditor of accounts, ex officio, and two members appointed by the governor to represent municipal or public interests for terms of two years each. The secretary of state, ex officio, shall be the chairman of the board.—Added 1959, No. 328 (Adj. Sess.), § 12.

§ 457. Duties of Board

The public records advisory board shall advise the public records director concerning the preservation and disposal of public records and shall give prior advice to the director with regard to his orders to custodians of public records for the preservation, destruction, cancellation, or disposal thereof.—Amended 1979, No. 56, § 6.

MUNICIPAL LIBRARIES
(Vermont Statutes Annotated, 1982, Title 22, s.141-146.)

§ 141. Establishment and maintenance

A town or incorporated village may establish and maintain for the use of its inhabitants public libraries, with or without branches, which may render service to other towns and the inhabitants thereof upon terms to be agreed upon, and may annually contract with a library or library corporation to furnish books to its inhabitants free, and may appropriate money therefor, and may annually appropriate money for the maintenance, care, increase and support of a library held in trust for such town or incorporated village or the inhabitants thereof.

HISTORY

Source. V.S. 1947, § 4526. P.L. § 4428. G.L. § 1463. 1908, No. 52, § 21. P.S. § 1211. R. 1906, § 1119. 1898, No. 34, § 1. V.S. § 887. R.L. § 2738. 1867, No. 63, § 1.

§ 142. Appropriations

A town or incorporated village establishing and maintaining a library may appropriate for suitable rooms and buildings and for the foundation of such a library, a sum not exceeding $3.00 for each ratable poll in such town or village in the preceding year, and may also appropriate annually, for the maintenance, care and increase thereof, such sum of money as such town or village may vote at its annual meeting, and may receive, hold and manage a devise, bequest or gift for a public library.

HISTORY

Source. V.S. 1947, § 4527. P.L. § 4429. G.L. § 1464. 1908, No. 52, § 22. P.S. § 1212. V.S. § 888. 1894, No. 36. 1884, No. 65, § 1. R.L. § 2739. 1867, No. 63, § 2.

§ 143. Trustees

(a) A town or incorporated village which has established or shall establish a public library may elect at its annual meeting a board of five trustees who shall have full power to manage such public library and to receive, control and manage property which shall come into the hands of such town or village by gift, purchase, devise or bequest for the use and benefit of such library.

(b) At the meeting when such trustees are first chosen, they shall be elected for the following terms: one for one year, one for two years, one for three years, one for four years and one for five years, and until their respective successors are chosen. Annually thereafter such town or village shall elect one such trustee whose term of office shall be for five years from and including the date of such election.

HISTORY

Source. V.S. 1947, §§ 4528, 4529. P.L. §§ 4430, 4431. G.L. §§ 1465, 1466. 1917, No. 254, § 1428. 1908, No. 52, §§ 23, 24. P.S. §§ 1213, 1214. V.S. §§ 889, 890. 1892, No. 53, §§ 1, 2.

§ 144. —Annual report

Such trustees shall annually make a report to the annual meeting of the town or incorporated village of the condition of the library and of the management and expenditure of such moneys as have come into their hands.

HISTORY

Source. V.S. 1947, § 4530. P.L. § 4432. G.L. § 1467. 1908, No. 52, § 25. P.S. § 1215. R. 1906, § 1123. V.S. § 891. 1892, No. 53, § 3.

§ 145. When no trustee elected

When no trustees have been elected, moneys raised for a library shall be paid out by an agent to be appointed by the selectmen of a town, and trustees of an incorporated village or the mayor of a city.

HISTORY

Source. V.S. 1947, § 4531. P.L. § 4433. G.L. § 1468. 1908, No. 52, § 26. P.S. § 1216. R. 1906, § 1124. V.S. § 892. 1892, No. 53, § 4. R.L. § 2740. 1867, No. 63, § 3.

§ 146. Public documents and volumes

(a) When a town has established a public library, at an annual meeting, such town may vote to place in such library a copy of such documents and volumes theretofore received by such town for it or its town clerk's office, as it shall designate, and also a copy of such documents and volumes thereafter to be received from the state, except the Vermont Reports and other books and documents provided by law to be kept in the office of the town clerk, as it shall designate. Such books shall remain the property of the town, but their use shall be enjoyed by such library until such town votes otherwise.

(b) The state librarian shall deliver to a town public library that has been voted by its town the use of books owned by such town, such duplicate documents and volumes published or provided by the state, as can, in the judgment of the board of libraries, be delivered without prejudice to the department of libraries. Such documents and volumes shall be delivered on application stating what books have already been received from the town. Such documents and volumes shall remain the property of the state, but their use shall be enjoyed by such library, until the state librarian is directed by law to demand their return to the state library.

(c) When a public library exists in a town and is not established by it, such town may, at an annual meeting, by a two-thirds vote, make the provisions of subsection (a) in respect to use of books owned by the town, apply to such library; and, in case of such vote, the provisions of subsection (b) shall apply to such library the same as if it were established and maintained by such town.

HISTORY

Source. V.S. 1947, §§ 4532–4534. P.L. §§ 4434–4436. 1933, No. 156, § 3. 1933, No. 157, § 4167. G.L. §§ 1469–1471. 1908, No. 52, §§ 28–30. P.S. §§ 1218–1220. 1906, No. 97, § 1. V.S. §§ 894–896. 1894, No. 39, §§ 1–3.

INCORPORATED LIBRARIES
(Vermont Statutes Annotated, Title 22, s.101-110.)

§ 101. General authority

Trustees to whom real or personal property is devised, bequeathed, granted, conveyed or donated for the foundation and establishment of a free public library, may, unless otherwise provided by the devisor, grantor or donor of such property, in order to promote the better establishment, maintenance and management of such library, cause a corporation to be formed under the provisions of sections 102 and 103 of this title.

HISTORY

Source. V.S. 1947, § 4535. P.L. § 4437. G.L. § 1472. 1908, No. 52, § 15. P.S. § 1204. V.S. § 883. 1894, No. 38, § 1.

§ 102. Procedure

(a) The trustees may make, sign and acknowledge and file in the office of the secretary of state a statement in writing setting forth the intent of the trustees to form a corporation, a copy of the will or instrument by which the endowment of such library is provided, the name adopted for the corporation, which shall not be the name of a corporation already existing, and the name of the town or village in which such library and the principal place of business of such corporation will be located, the number of managers who may be denominated trustees, managers or directors of such corporation, and the names of the trustees, managers or directors who are to constitute the original board and who shall hold office until their successors are respectively elected and qualified as provided in section 106 of this title.

(b) The secretary of state shall forthwith, upon the finding of such statement, issue to the incorporators, under his hand and seal, a certificate of which such statement shall be a part, declaring that the organization of the corporation is perfected. The incorporators shall forthwith cause such certificate to be recorded in the office of the county clerk of the county in which such library is to be located; and thereupon the corporation shall be deemed fully organized and may proceed to carry out its corporate purposes and receive by conveyance from the trustees the property provided for the endowment of such library, and may hold the same in whatever form it may have been received or conveyed by such trustees, until such form shall be changed by action of such corporation.

HISTORY

Source. V.S. 1947, §§ 4536, 4537. P.L. §§ 4438, 4439. G.L. §§ 1473, 1474. 1908, No. 52, §§ 16, 17. P.S. §§ 1205, 1206. V.S. §§ 884, 885. 1894, No. 38, §§ 2, 3.

§ 103. Powers generally

An organization formed under the provisions of section 102 of this title shall be a body corporate and politic to be known by the name stated in its certificate. It shall have and possess the ordinary rights and incidents of a corporation, and shall be capable of taking, holding and disposing of real and personal estate for the purposes of its organization. The provisions of a will, deed or other instrument by which an endowment of a library is provided, and accepted by the trustees, managers or directors, shall, as to such endowment, be a part of the organic and fundamental law of such corporation.

HISTORY

Source. V.S. 1947, § 4538. P.L. § 4440. G.L. § 1475. 1908, No. 52, § 18. P.S. § 1207. V.S. § 886. 1894, No. 38, § 4.

§ 104. Trustees, managers or directors

The trustees, managers or directors of such corporation shall compose its members and shall not be more than nine nor less than five in number.

HISTORY

Source. V.S. 1947, § 4539. P.L. § 4441. 1923, No. 38. G.L. § 1476. 1908, No. 52, § 19. P.S. § 1208. V.S. § 886. 1894, No. 38, § 4.

§ 105. —General powers

Such trustees, managers or directors shall elect the officers of the corporation from their number and have the control and management of the affairs and property of the same, may accept donations and, in their discretion, hold the same in the form in which they are given for the purposes of science, literature and art germane to the objects and purposes of such corporation. They may, in their discretion, receive by loan, books, manuscripts, and works of art and hold or circulate the same under such conditions as the owners thereof may specify. The provisions of sections 3731 and 3732 of Title 13 shall apply to the injury and removal of such books, manuscripts and works of art.

HISTORY

Source. V.S. 1947, § 4539. P.L. § 4441. 1923, No. 38. G.L. § 1476. 1908, No. 52, § 19. P.S. § 1208. V.S. § 886. 1894, No. 38, § 4.

§ 106. —Vacancies

(a) They may fill by election vacancies occurring in their number.

(b) When a trustee, manager or director is elected to fill a vacancy, a certificate under the seal of the corporation, giving the name of the person elected, shall be recorded in the office of the county clerk where the articles of incorporation are recorded.— Amended 1963, No. 16, eff. March 20, 1963.

HISTORY

Source. V.S. 1947, §§ 4540, 4541. P.L. §§ 4442, 4443. 1923, No. 28. G.L. § 1476. 1908, No. 52, § 19. P.S. § 1208. V.S. § 886. 1894, No. 38, § 4.

§ 107. —Bylaws

They may make bylaws for the management of such corporation and library. The bylaws shall set forth the officers of the corporation and define and prescribe their respective duties.

HISTORY

Source. V.S. 1947, § 4540. P.L. § 4442. 1923, No. 28. G.L. § 1476. 1908, No. 52, § 19. P.S. § 1208. V.S. § 886. 1894, No. 38, § 4.

§ 108. —Employment of agents and employees

They may appoint and employ from time to time agents and employees, as they may deem necessary for the efficient administration and conduct of the library and all the affairs of such corporation.

HISTORY

Source. V.S. 1947, § 4541. P.L. § 4443. 1923, No. 28. G.L. § 1476. 1908, No. 52, § 19. P.S. § 1208. V.S. § 886. 1894, No. 38, § 4.

§ 109. Exemption from taxation

When the instrument providing the endowment declares that the institution shall be a free public library, such library and other property of the corporation shall be forever exempt from taxation.

HISTORY

Source. V.S. 1947, § 4542. P.L. § 4444. G.L. § 1477. 1908, No. 52, § 20. P.S. § 1209. V.S. § 886. 1894, No. 38, § 4.

§ 110. Merger

Two library corporations in the same town may, by a majority vote of the members of each of such corporations, at meetings thereof warned for that purpose, unite and assume the corporate name of either of such corporations.

HISTORY

Source. V.S. 1947, § 4543. P.L. § 4445. G.L. § 1478. 1908, No. 52, § 27. P.S. § 1217. V.S. § 893. R.L. § 2741. 1870, No. 22. 1869, No. 11.

COUNTY LAW LIBRARIES
(Vermont Statutes Annotated, 1982, Title 24, s.76.)

§ 76. County law library

Each county shall maintain a complete set of Vermont Reports including the digest thereof in the county clerk's office and in each probate office. The county may maintain in the courthouse or elsewhere such additional law books as in the opinion of the assistant judges are needful for the judges and officials having offices in the county.   1957, No. 85

LIBRARY SERVICE TO INSTITUTIONS
(Vermont Statutes Annotated, 1982, Title 28, s.6.)

§ 6. Supervision of libraries in state institutions

The free public library board shall provide and have the care and supervision of suitable libraries to be maintained in the penal and charitable institutions maintained by the state, subject to such rules and regulations as may be made by the commissioner of corrections.—1959, No. 329 (Adj. Sess.), § 46(a); amended 1967, No. 319 (Adj. Sess.), § 4, eff. March 22, 1968.

HISTORY

Source. 1951, No. 205, § 4. V.S. 1947, § 7983. P.L. § 8811. 1921, No. 65, § 5. G.L. § 7236. 1917, No. 58. 1917, No. 115, § 2. 1910, No. 235. P.S. § 6083. 1906, No. 191, §§ 1, 2, 4. V.S. § 5269. R.L. § 4426. 1872, No. 81, § 3. G.S. 123, § 17. 1854, No. 65.

TAX EXEMPTION
(Vermont Statutes Annotated, 1982, Title 32, s.3802.)

Vermont library laws are reprinted from VERMONT STATUTES ANNOTATED published by the State of Vermont.

VIRGINIA

STATE LIBRARY
(Code of Virginia, 1982, s.42.1-1 to 42.1-19, 42.1-30,
40.1-31, 2.1-45.)

§ 42.1-1. State Library. — The Virginia State Library shall be continued and shall be the library agency of the State, the archival agency of the Commonwealth, and the reference library at the seat of government. It shall have the following powers and duties:

(1) To make to the Governor and to members of the General Assembly an annual report of its receipts, expenditures, activities and needs, including recommendations for improving its services to the Commonwealth;

(2) To accept gifts, bequests and endowments for the purposes which fall within the general legal powers and duties of the State Library. Unless otherwise specified by the donor or legator, the Library may either expend both the principal and interest of any gift or bequest or may invest such sums as the Board deems advisable, with the consent of the State Treasurer, in securities in which sinking funds may be invested;

(3) To purchase and maintain a general collection of books, periodicals, newspapers, maps, films, audiovisual materials and other materials for the use of the people of the Commonwealth as a means for the promotion of knowledge within the Commonwealth. The scope of the Library's collections shall be determined by the Library Board on recommendation of the State Librarian, and, in making these decisions, the Board and Librarian shall take into account the book collections of public libraries and college and university libraries throughout the Commonwealth and the availability of such collections to the general public. The Board shall make available for circulation to libraries or to the public such of its materials as it deems advisable;

(4) To give assistance, advice and counsel to other agencies of the Commonwealth maintaining libraries and special reference collections as to the best means of establishing and administering such libraries and collections. It may establish in the State Library a union catalogue of all books, pamphlets and

other materials owned and used for reference purposes by all other agencies of the Commonwealth and of all books, pamphlets and other materials maintained by libraries in the Commonwealth which are of interest to the people of the whole Commonwealth;

(5) To fix reasonable penalties for damage to or failure to return any book, periodical or other material owned by the Library, or for violation of any rule or regulation concerning the use of books, periodicals, and other materials in the custody of the Library;

(6) To give direction, assistance and counsel to all libraries in the Commonwealth, to all communities which may propose to establish libraries, and to all persons interested in public libraries, as to means of establishment and administration of such libraries, selection of books, retrieval systems, cataloguing, maintenance, and other details of library management, and to conduct such inspections as are necessary;

(7) To engage in such activities in aid of city, county, town, regional and other public libraries as will serve to develop the library system of the Commonwealth;

(8) To administer and distribute State and federal library funds in accordance with law and its own regulations to the city, county, town and regional libraries of the Commonwealth; and

(9) To enter into contracts with other states or regions or districts for the purpose of providing cooperative library services. (Code 1950 (Repl. Vol. 1953), § 42-33; 1970, c. 606.)

§ 42.1-2. State Library under direction of Library Board; membership, chairman and vice-chairman; committees and advisory bodies.
— The State Library shall be directed by a board, consisting of nine members, to be appointed by the Governor, which shall be and remain a corporation under the style of "The Library Board," sometimes in this chapter called the Board. The Board shall meet and organize by electing from its number a chairman and vice-chairman. It shall have the power to appoint such committees and advisory bodies as it deems advisable. (Code 1950 (Repl. Vol. 1953), § 42-34; 1968, c. 122; 1970, c. 606.)

§ 42.1-3. Terms of office of members of Board; vacancies. — Within sixty days preceding July one of the year in which the terms of office respectively of the members of the Board expire by limitation the Governor shall appoint to fill the vacancies so occasioned qualified persons whose terms shall be for five years from the day on which that of their immediate predecessors expired; provided that of the three additional members to be appointed when this section as amended becomes effective, one shall be appointed for a term of four years, and his successor for a term of five years. Appointments to fill other vacancies shall be for the unexpired term.

No person shall be eligible to serve as a member of the Board for or during more than two successive terms. (Code 1950 (Repl. Vol. 1953), § 42-35; 1968, c. 122; 1970, c. 606.)

§ 42.1-4. Removal of member of Board. — The Governor may remove any member for misconduct, incapacity, or neglect of duty and he shall be the sole judge of the sufficiency of the cause for removal. He shall report every such removal at once to the General Assembly if it is in session, and if not at the beginning of the next session. (Code 1950 (Repl. Vol. 1953), § 42-36; 1970, c. 606.)

§ 42.1-5. Expenses of members of Board. — The members of the Board shall receive no compensation for their services as such; but reasonable expenses incurred as members of the Board in the discharge of their duties shall be paid out of the Library funds. (Code 1950 (Repl. Vol. 1953), § 42-37; 1970, c. 606.)

§ 42.1-6. Minutes and records of Board. — The Board shall keep minutes of all its proceedings, which shall be signed by the chairman and attested by the secretary, and a record of all receipts and disbursements, all of which shall be preserved as public records. (Code 1950 (Repl. Vol. 1953), § 42-38; 1970, c. 606.)

§ 42.1-7. Supervision of funds. — The Board shall make requests for appropriations of necessary funds and approve all expenditures of Library funds. Such expenditures shall be made as provided by law. (Code 1950 (Repl. Vol. 1953), § 42-39; 1970, c. 606.)

§ 42.1-8. Rules and regulations. — The Board shall make rules and regulations, not inconsistent with law, for the government and use of the State Library, and may by general or special regulation determine what books and other possessions of the Library may not be removed therefrom. (Code 1950 (Repl. Vol. 1953), § 42-41; 1970, c. 606.)

§ 42.1-9. When Library to be kept open. — The State Library shall be kept open for such days and hours each day as may be prescribed for other State agencies at the seat of government. But the Board may, in its discretion, prescribe additional hours in which the Library shall be kept open. (Code 1950 (Repl. Vol. 1953), § 42-43; 1970, c. 606.)

§ 42.1-10. Acquisition of books and other library matter. — The Library may from time to time acquire books and other library matter by gift, purchase, exchange or loan. And the Library shall cause to be procured, from time to time, as opportunity may offer, a copy of any book, pamphlet, manuscript, or other library material, relating to the history of Virginia, not now in the State Library, which can be obtained on reasonable terms. (Code 1950 (Repl. Vol. 1953), § 42-44; 1970, c. 606.)

§ 42.1-11. Editing and publishing State records and other special matter; list of publications. — The Board may edit, or cause to be edited, arranged and published, as the funds at its disposal permit, the State records now or hereafter deposited in the State Library and such other special matter as it deems of sufficient value.

The Board may cause to be printed any manuscript relating to the history of Virginia which has not been published, including such portions of the executive journals and letter books, and of the legislative papers, as the Board may deem proper, and shall cause the papers so to be printed to be arranged for that purpose and preserved for reference; and shall cause the records in the Library pertaining to the various wars in which the State has been engaged to be edited, arranged, and published so as to show the service of citizens of the State in such wars.

The Library may expend funds to list its publications in appropriate commercial listings. (Code 1950 (Repl. Vol. 1953), § 42-45; 1956, c. 169; 1970, c. 606.)

§ 42.1-12. Fees for copies made by Library staff. — The Library may, in its discretion, charge and collect such fees as it may deem reasonable for copies or extracts from any books, papers, records, documents or manuscripts in the Library, made by the Library staff, for persons applying for the same. The State Librarian shall keep an accurate account of all such fees and pay the same into the general fund of the State treasury. (Code 1950 (Repl. Vol. 1953), § 42-46; 1970, c. 606.)

§ 42.1-13. Appointment; terms of office or employment. — The Board shall appoint a librarian, to be known as the State Librarian, who shall serve at the pleasure of the Board. The Board shall appoint the principal assistant to the Librarian, and may approve the appointment of other employees. The terms of office and employment of such assistants and employees shall be subject to the personnel regulations of the Commonwealth. (Code 1950 (Repl. Vol. 1953), § 42-48; 1970, c. 606.)

§ 42.1-14. Compensation. — The State Librarian, assistants and employees shall be paid such salaries from appropriations out of the public treasury as are provided by law. (Code 1950 (Repl. Vol. 1953), § 42-49; 1970, c. 606.)

§ 42.1-15. Duties of State Librarian. — The State Librarian shall have charge of the State Library. He shall see that the Library is properly kept and that its contents are properly preserved and cared for.

He shall be secretary of the Board, and shall perform all duties belonging to that position. He shall keep a record of all proceedings of the Board and such financial records as are required by the Commonwealth. (Code 1950 (Repl. Vol. 1953), § 42-50; 1970, c. 606.)

§ 42.1-16. Bond of State Librarian. — The State Librarian shall give bond to the State in the sum of two thousand dollars, with sureties approved by the State Treasurer, subject to the approval of the Governor, for the faithful discharge of his duties and the delivery over to his successor of all the property of the State in his possession, which bond shall be recorded by the Secretary of the Commonwealth and deposited with the Comptroller. (Code 1950 (Repl. Vol. 1953), § 42-51; 1970, c. 606.)

§ 42.1-17. Cities and towns to furnish copies of official publications. — The mayor of each city and town in the Commonwealth shall send regularly at the time of publication to the State Library two copies of each of the official publications of such city or town, and also two copies of each publication of former years of which the supply has not been exhausted. Official publications for the purpose of this section shall embrace printed reports, in pamphlet or book form, of the officials of the city or town, printed volumes of ordinances and such other special publications as the city or town may authorize to be printed. (Code 1950 (Repl. Vol. 1953), § 42-52; 1970, c. 606.)

§ 42.1-18. Exchanges; donation, etc., of duplicate material. — The Library may arrange for the exchange of the Virginia publications with such states and institutions, the general government and other governments, societies and others, as it sees fit. Publications received on exchange are to become the property of the State Library, except statute and law books, which shall be placed in the Law Library. The Library may also, when deemed advantageous, donate, exchange or sell any or all duplicate material now or hereafter the property of the State Library, and other printed material not within the scope of its collections. The Librarian shall keep an accurate account of all such sales and pay the money arising therefrom into the general fund of the State treasury. (Code 1950 (Repl. Vol. 1953), § 42-56; 1970, c. 606.)

§ 42.1-19. Establishment of depository system; sending State publications to members. — The State Library shall establish a depository system and send to the members thereof copies of State publications furnished pursuant to § 2.1-467.2. (Code 1950 (Repl. Vol. 1953), § 42-57; 1970, c. 606; 1981, c. 234.)

§ 42.1-30. Virginia World War II History Commission abolished; duties transferred to State Librarian. — The Virginia World War II History Commission, heretofore created and existing, is hereby abolished and its duty of collecting, assembling, editing and publishing such information and material with respect to the contribution to World War II made by Virginia and Virginians as is most worthy of preservation shall hereafter be performed by the State Librarian. The Virginia World War II History Commission shall deliver to the State Librarian all material, records and information collected, assembled and compiled by it in the performance of its duties. (Code 1950 (Repl. Vol. 1953), § 42-64; 1970, c. 606.)

§ 42.1-31. Counties and cities may submit material. — Any county or city of the Commonwealth may assemble and submit to the State Librarian information and material relating to its contribution and that of its citizens to World War II, and the governing body of any county or city may appropriate for this purpose such funds as it deems necessary. (Code 1950 (Repl. Vol. 1953), § 42-65; 1970, c. 606.)

§ 2.1-45. Disposition of official correspondence. — The Governor preceding the end of his term of office shall have delivered to the State Library for safekeeping all correspondence of his office during his term; provided that this shall not apply to correspondence of a personal or private nature, the decision thereon to be made by the Governor. (Code 1950, § 2-40.1; 1966, c. 677.)

STATE AND FEDERAL AID
(Code of Virginia, 1982, s.42.1-46 to 42.1-58.)

§ 42.1-46. Library policy of the Commonwealth. — It is hereby declared to be the policy of the Commonwealth, as a part of its provision for public education, to promote the establishment and development of public library service throughout its various political subdivisions. (Code 1950 (Repl. Vol. 1953), § 42-23; 1970, c. 606.)

§ 42.1-47. Grants for development of library service. — In order to provide State aid in the development of public library service throughout the State, the Library Board, in this chapter sometimes called the Board, shall grant from such appropriations as are made for this purpose funds to provide library service. (Code 1950 (Repl. Vol. 1953), § 42-24; 1952, c. 494; 1970, c. 606.)

§ 42.1-48. Grants to improve standards. — In order to encourage the maintenance and development of proper standards, including personnel standards, and the combination of libraries or library systems into larger and more economical units of service, grants of State aid from funds available shall be made by the Board to any free public library or library system which qualifies under the standards set by the Board. The grants to each qualifying library or system in each fiscal year shall be as follows:

(a) Thirty-five cents of State aid for every dollar expended, or to be expended, exclusive of State and federal aid, by the political subdivision or subdivisions operating or participating in the library or system. The grant to any county or city shall not exceed one hundred fifty thousand dollars;

(b) A per capita grant based on the population of the area served and the number of participating counties or cities: Thirty cents per capita for the first six hundred thousand persons to a library or system serving one city or county, and an additional ten cents per capita for the first six hundred thousand persons for each additional city or county served. Libraries or systems serving a population in excess of six hundred thousand shall receive ten cents per capita for the excess; and

(c) A grant of ten dollars per square mile of area served to every library or library system, and an additional grant of twenty dollars per square mile of area served to every library system serving more than one city or county. (Code 1950 (Repl. Vol. 1953), § 42-26; 1952, c. 494; 1958, c. 513; 1960, c. 234; 1970, c. 606; 1978, c. 565.)

§ 42.1-49. Grants to municipal libraries. — Every qualifying municipal library serving an area containing less than five thousand population shall receive its proper share, but not less than four hundred dollars. (1970, c. 606.)

§ 42.1-50. Limitation of grants; proration of funds. — The total amount of grants under §§ 42.1-48 and 42.1-49 shall not exceed the amount expended, exclusive of State and federal aid, by the political subdivision or subdivisions operating the library. If the State appropriations provided for grants under §§ 42.1-48 and 42.1-49 are not sufficient to meet approved applications, the Library Board shall prorate the available funds in such manner that each application shall receive its proportionate share of each type of grant. Applications must be received prior to June one of each calendar year. (Code 1950 (Repl. Vol. 1953), § 42-25; 1952, c. 494; 1958, c. 426; 1970, c. 606.)

§ 42.1-51. Obligations of libraries and systems receiving aid. — The obligations of the various library systems and libraries receiving State aid, shall consist in establishing and maintaining an organization as approved by the Board; provided that personnel standards of such library systems and libraries shall conform to the provisions of chapter 11 (§ 54-261 et seq.) of Title 54 for the certification of librarians, and with rules and regulations prescribed by the State Board for the Certification of Librarians in accordance with such chapter. All books and bookmobiles purchased with State aid funds shall, if the Board so determines, become the property of the State Library in the case of any library system or library which does not meet its obligations as determined by the Board. (Code 1950 (Repl. Vol. 1953), § 42-27; 1952, c. 494; 1970, c. 606.)

§ 42.1-52. Standards of eligibility for aid; reports on operation of libraries; supervision of services. — The Board shall establish standards under which library systems and libraries shall be eligible for State aid and may require reports on the operation of all libraries receiving State aid.

As long as funds are available, grants shall be made to the various libraries, library systems or contracting libraries applying for State aid in the order in which they meet the standards established by the Board.

In the event that any library meets the standards of the State Library Board but is unable to conform to chapter 11 (§ 54-261 et seq.) of Title 54 of the Code relating to the employment of certified librarians, the Library Board may, under a contractual agreement with such library, provide professional supervision of its services and may grant State aid funds to it in reduced amounts under a uniform plan to be adopted by the State Library Board. (Code 1950 (Repl. Vol. 1953), § 42-28; 1960, c. 235; 1970, c. 606.)

§ 42.1-53. Expense of administration. — Not to exceed thirty percent per annum of appropriations may be used by the Board to defray the expense of administering the provisions of this chapter and to provide other public library extension functions. (Code 1950 (Repl. Vol. 1953), § 42-29; 1952, c. 494; 1970, c. 606.)

§ 42.1-54. Procedure for purchase of books, materials and equipment and payment on salaries. — All proposals for books, materials and equipment to be purchased with State aid funds and all proposals for aid in the payment of salaries of certified librarians shall be submitted for approval to the State Library by the libraries, library systems or contracting libraries applying for State aid, in form prescribed by the Board, and those approved may be ordered by the libraries, library systems or contracting libraries. Payments and disbursements from the funds appropriated for this purpose shall be made by the State Treasurer upon warrants of the Comptroller issued upon vouchers signed by the duly authorized representative of the library, library system or contracting library and approved by the duly authorized representative of the Board. Each voucher shall be accompanied by a certification by the duly authorized representative of such library, or library system that the books, materials or equipment have been received, or salaries paid, and that the same were approved by the State Library as hereinabove required. The Board shall act to obtain the best prices and most advantageous arrangements in securing all books, materials and equipment purchased through State aid. (Code 1950 (Repl. Vol. 1953), § 42-30; 1952, c. 494; 1956, c. 168; 1970, c. 606.)

§ 42.1-55. Free service available to all. — The service of books in library systems and libraries receiving State aid shall be free and shall be made available to all persons living in the county, region, or municipality. (Code 1950 (Repl. Vol. 1953), § 42-31; 1970, c. 606.)

§ 42.1-56. Meaning of term "books". — The term "books" as used in this chapter may be interpreted in the discretion of the Board to mean books, magazines, newspapers, appropriate audiovisual materials and other printed matter. (Code 1950 (Repl. Vol. 1953), § 42-32; 1952, c. 494; 1970, c. 606.)

§ 42.1-57. Authority of Library Board to accept and distribute federal funds. — The Library Board is empowered, subject to approval of the Governor, to accept grants of federal funds for libraries and to allocate such funds to libraries under any plan approved by the Board and the appropriate federal authorities. Such allocations shall not be subject to the restrictions of this chapter. (Code 1950 (Suppl.), § 42-32.1; 1964, c. 325; 1970, c. 606; 1972, c. 167.)

§ 42.1-58. Agreements providing for expenditure of federal and matching funds. — The Library Board and the cities and counties of the Commonwealth are authorized to enter into agreements providing for the supervision of the expenditure of federal funds allocated to such cities and counties and matching funds provided by such political subdivisions. Such agreement shall set forth the standards and conditions with respect to the expenditure of such funds. (Code 1950 (Suppl.), § 42-32.2; 1964, c. 324; 1970, c. 606.)

INTERSTATE LIBRARY COMPACT
(Code of Virginia, 1982, s.42.1-75.)

§ 42.1-75. Compact entered into and enacted into law. — The Interstate Library Compact is enacted into law and entered into by this State in the form substantially as follows:

The contracting states solemnly agree:

Article I

Policy and Purpose

Because the desire for the services provided by libraries transcends governmental boundaries and can most effectively be satisfied by giving such services to communities and people regardless of jurisdictional lines, it is the policy of the states party to this compact to cooperate and share their responsibilities; to authorize cooperation and sharing with respect to those types of library facilities and services which can be more economically or efficiently developed and maintained on a cooperative basis, and to authorize cooperation and sharing among localities, states and others in providing joint or cooperative library services in areas where the distribution of population or of existing and potential library resources make the provision of library service on an interstate basis the most effective way of providing adequate and efficient service.

Article II

Definitions

As used in this compact:

(a) *"Public library agency"* means any unit or agency of local or State government operating or having power to operate a library.

(b) *"Private library agency"* means any nongovernmental entity which operates or assumes a legal obligation to operate a library.

(c) *"Library agreement"* means a contract establishing an interstate library district pursuant to this compact or providing for the joint or cooperative furnishing of library services.

Article III

Interstate Library Districts

(a) Any one or more public library agencies in a party state in cooperation with any public library agency or agencies in one or more other party states may establish and maintain an interstate library district. Subject to the provisions of this compact and any other laws of the party states which pursuant hereto remain applicable, such district may establish, maintain and operate some or all of the library facilities and services for the area concerned in accordance with the terms of a library agreement therefor. Any private library agency or agencies within an interstate library district may cooperate therewith, assume duties, responsibilities and obligations thereto, and receive benefits therefrom as provided in any library agreement to which such agency or agencies become party.

(b) Within an interstate library district, and as provided by a library agreement, the performance of library functions may be undertaken on a joint or cooperative basis or may be undertaken by means of one or more arrangements between or among public or private library agencies for the extension of library privileges to the use of facilities or services operated or rendered by one or more of the individual library agencies.

(c) If a library agreement provides for joint establishment, maintenance or operation of library facilities or services by an interstate library district, such district shall have power to do any one or more of the following in accordance with such library agreement:

1. Undertake, administer and participate in programs or arrangements for securing, lending or servicing of books and other publications, any other materials suitable to be kept or made available by libraries, library equipment or for the dissemination of information about libraries, the value and significance of particular items therein, and the use thereof.

2. Accept for any of its purposes under this compact any and all donations, and grants of money, equipment, supplies, materials, and services, (conditional or otherwise), from any state or the United States or any subdivision or agency thereof, or interstate agency, or from any institution, person, firm or corporation, and receive, utilize and dispose of the same.

3. Operate mobile library units or equipment for the purpose of rendering bookmobile service within the district.

4. Employ professional, technical, clerical and other personnel and fix terms of employment, compensation and other appropriate benefits; and where desirable, provide for the in-service training of such personnel.

5. Sue and be sued in any court of competent jurisdiction.

6. Acquire, hold, and dispose of any real or personal property or any interest or interests therein as may be appropriate to the rendering of library service.

7. Construct, maintain and operate a library, including any appropriate branches thereof.

8. Do such other things as may be incidental to or appropriate for the carrying out of any of the foregoing powers.

Article IV

Interstate Library Districts, Governing Board

(a) An interstate library district which establishes, maintains or operates any facilities or services in its own right shall have a governing board which shall direct the affairs of the district and act for it in all matters relating to its business. Each participating public library agency in the district shall be represented on the governing board which shall be organized and conduct its business in accordance with provision therefor in the library agreement. But in no event shall a governing board meet less often than twice a year.

(b) Any private library agency or agencies party to a library agreement establishing an interstate library district may be represented on or advise with the governing board of the district in such manner as the library agreement may provide.

Article V

State Library Agency Cooperation

Any two or more state library agencies of two or more of the party states may undertake and conduct joint or cooperative library programs, render joint or cooperative library services, and enter into and perform arrangements for the cooperative or joint acquisition, use, housing and disposition of items or collections of materials which, by reason of expense, rarity, specialized nature, or infrequency of demand therefor would be appropriate for central collection and shared use. Any such programs, services or arrangements may include provision for the exercise on a cooperative or joint basis of any power exercisable by an interstate library district and an agreement embodying any such program, service or arrangement shall contain provisions covering the subjects detailed in Article VI of this compact for interstate library agreements.

Article VI

Library Agreements

(a) In order to provide for any joint or cooperative undertaking pursuant to this compact, public and private library agencies may enter into library agreements. Any agreement executed pursuant to the provisions of this compact shall, as among the parties to the agreement:

1. Detail the specific nature of the services, programs, facilities, arrangements or properties to which it is applicable.

2. Provide for the allocation of costs and other financial responsibilities.

3. Specify the respective rights, duties, obligations and liabilities of the parties.

4. Set forth the terms and conditions for duration, renewal, termination, abrogation, disposal of joint or common property, if any, and all other matters which may be appropriate to the proper effectuation and performance of the agreement.

(b) No public or private library agency shall undertake to exercise itself, or jointly with any other library agency, by means of a library agreement any power prohibited to such agency by the constitution or statutes of its state.

(c) No library agreement shall become effective until filed with the compact administrator of each state involved, and approved in accordance with Article VII of this compact.

Article VII

Approval of Library Agreements

(a) Every library agreement made pursuant to this compact shall, prior to and as a condition precedent to its entry into force, be submitted to the attorney general of each state in which a public library agency party thereto is situated, who shall determine whether the agreement is in proper form and compatible with the laws of his state. The attorneys general shall approve any agreement submitted to them unless they shall find that it does not meet the conditions set forth herein and shall detail in writing addressed to the governing bodies of the public library agencies concerned the specific respects in which the proposed agreement fails to meet the requirements of law. Failure to disapprove an agreement submitted hereunder within ninety days of its submission shall constitute approval thereof.

(b) In the event that a library agreement made pursuant to this compact shall deal in whole or in part with the provision of services or facilities with regard to which an officer or agency of the state government has constitutional or statutory powers of control, the agreement shall, as a condition precedent to its entry into force, be submitted to the state officer or agency having such power of control, and shall be approved or disapproved by him or it as to all matters within his or its jurisdiction in the same manner and subject to the same requirements governing the action of the attorneys general pursuant to paragraph (a) of this article. This requirement of submission and approval shall be in addition to and not in substitution for the requirement of submission to and approval by the attorneys general.

Article VIII

Other Laws Applicable

Nothing in this compact or in any library agreement shall be construed to supersede, alter or otherwise impair any obligation imposed on any library by otherwise applicable law, nor to authorize the transfer or disposition of any property held in trust by a library agency in a manner contrary to the terms of such trust.

Article IX

Appropriations and Aid

(a) Any public library agency party to a library agreement may appropriate funds to the interstate library district established thereby in the same manner and to the same extent as to a library wholly maintained by it and, subject to the laws of the state in which such public library agency is situated, may pledge its credit in support of an interstate library district established by the agreement.

(b) Subject to the provisions of the library agreement pursuant to which it functions and the laws of the states in which such district is situated, an interstate library district may claim and receive any state and federal aid which may be available to library agencies.

Article X

Compact Administrator

Each state shall designate a compact administrator with whom copies of all library agreements to which his state or any public library agency thereof is party shall be filed. The administrator shall have such other powers as may be conferred upon him by the laws of his state and may consult and cooperate with the compact administrators of other party states and take such steps as may effectuate the purposes of this compact. If the laws of a party state so provide, such state may designate one or more deputy compact administrators in addition to its compact administrator.

Article XI

Entry Into Force and Withdrawal

(a) This compact shall enter into force and effect immediately upon its enactment into law by any two states. Thereafter, it shall enter into force and effect as to any other state upon the enactment thereof by such state.

(b) This compact shall continue in force with respect to a party state and remain binding upon such state until six months after such state has given notice to each other party state of the repeal thereof. Such withdrawal shall not be construed to relieve any party to a library agreement entered into pursuant to this compact from any obligation of that agreement prior to the end of its duration as provided therein.

Article XII

Construction and Severability

This compact shall be liberally construed so as to effectuate the purposes thereof. The provisions of this compact shall be severable and if any phrase, clause, sentence or provision of this compact is declared to be contrary to the constitution of any party state or of the United States or the applicability thereof to any government, agency, person or circumstance is held invalid, the validity of the remainder of this compact and the applicability thereof to any government, agency, person or circumstance shall not be affected thereby. If this compact shall be held contrary to the constitution of any state party thereto, the compact shall remain in full force and effect as to the remaining states and in full force and effect as to the state affected as to all severable matters. (1970, c. 267.)

CERTIFICATION OF LIBRARIANS
(Code of Virginia, 1982, s.54-261, 54-262, 54-264, 54-268 to 54-272.

§ 54-261. Board for Certification of Librarians continued. — The State Board for the Certification of Librarians, referred to in this chapter as the Board, is continued. (1936, p. 113; Michie Code 1942, § 363; 1944, p. 256; 1946, p. 247.)

§ 54-262. Members and secretary of Board; terms. — The Board shall consist of two licensed librarians, to be appointed for five-year terms, and the State Librarian, who shall serve as secretary of the Board. (1936, p. 113; Michie Code 1942, § 363; 1944, p. 256; 1946, p. 247; 1981, c. 447.)

§ 54-264. Appointments from nominees of Virginia Library Association. — Each appointment on the Board may be made from a list of at least five names for each vacancy sent to the Governor, or to the Governor-elect, by the executive committee of the Virginia Library Association. The Governor shall notify the Association promptly of any vacancy other than by expiration and like nominations may be made for the filling of the vacancy. In no case shall the Governor be bound to make any appointment from among the nominees of the Association. (Michie Code 1942, § 363; 1944, p. 256; 1946, p. 248.)

§ 54-268. Granting librarians' licenses with or without examination.
— The Board shall grant librarians' licenses of appropriate grades without examination to applicants who are graduates of library schools accredited by the American Library Association for general library training, and it shall grant licenses of appropriate grades to other applicants when it has satisfied itself by examination or credentials that the applicant has attainments and abilities equivalent to those of a library school graduate and is qualified to carry on library work ably and efficiently; provided, that the Board may grant, in general emergency conditions, temporary or provisional certificates to applicants who have not met these requirements.

Any person not a graduate of a library school accredited by the American Library Association, but who has served as a librarian or a full-time professional assistant in any library to which this law applies for at least one year's continuous service or the equivalent thereof prior to July 1, 1937, shall be granted a librarian's license of appropriate grade without examination. (1936, p. 113; Michie Code 1942, § 363; 1944, p. 256; 1946, p. 248; 1974, c. 534.)

§ 54-269. Fees for certificates.
— The Board shall require a fee of one dollar to be paid by each applicant for a librarian's certificate. Money paid as fees shall be deposited with the State Treasurer. (1936, p. 114; Michie Code 1942, § 363; 1944, p. 257; 1946, p. 248.)

§ 54-270. Payment of expenses of Board.
— All necessary expenses of the Board shall be paid from the funds appropriated by the General Assembly to the State Library upon warrants drawn by the Comptroller upon the presentation of proper vouchers approved by the State Librarian. (1936, p. 114; Michie Code 1942, § 363; 1944, p. 257; 1946, p. 248.)

§ 54-271. License required to hold professional library position.
— No public library serving a political subdivision or subdivisions having over five thousand population and no library operated by the State or under its authority, including libraries of institutions of higher learning, shall have in its employ, in the position of librarian or in any other full-time professional library position, a person who does not hold a librarian's license issued by the Board.

A professional library position as used in this section is one that requires a knowledge of books and of library technique equivalent to that required for graduation from any accredited library school.

No public funds shall be paid to any library failing to comply with this chapter. (1936, p. 114; Michie Code 1942, § 363; 1944, p. 257; 1946, p. 249; 1974, c. 534.)

§ 54-272. Libraries exempted.
— Nothing in this chapter shall apply to the State Law Library or law libraries of counties and cities, or to libraries of public, elementary and high schools. (1936, p. 114; Michie Code 1942, § 363; 1944, p. 257; 1946, p. 249.)

PUBLIC RECORDS ACT

(Code of Virginia, 1982, s.42.1-76 to 42.1-91.)

§ 42.1-76. Legislative intent; title of chapter. — The General Assembly intends by this act to establish a single body of law applicable to all public officers and employees on the subject of public records management and preservation and to ensure that the procedures used to manage and preserve public records will be uniform throughout the State.

This chapter may be cited as the Virginia Public Records Act. (1976, c. 746.)

§ 42.1-77. Definitions. — As used in this chapter:

A. *"Agency"* shall mean all boards, commissions, departments, divisions, institutions, authorities, or parts thereof, of the Commonwealth or its political subdivisions and shall include the offices of constitutional officers.

B. *"Archival quality"* shall mean a quality of reproduction consistent with reproduction standards specified by the National Micrographics Association, American Standards Association or National Bureau of Standards.

C. *"Board"* shall mean the State Library Board.

D. *"Committee"* shall mean the State Public Records Advisory Committee.

E. *"Custodian"* shall mean the public official in charge of an office having public records.

F. *"State Librarian"* shall mean the State Librarian or his designated representative.

G. *"Public official"* shall mean all persons holding any office created by the Constitution of Virginia or by any act of the General Assembly, the Governor and all other officers of the executive branch of the State government, and all other officers, heads, presidents or chairmen of boards, commissions, departments, and agencies of the State government or its political subdivisions.

H. *"Public records"* shall mean all written books, papers, letters, documents, photographs, tapes, microfiche, microfilm, photostats, sound recordings, maps, other documentary materials or information in any recording medium regardless of physical form or characteristics, including data processing devices and computers, made or received in pursuance of law or in connection with the transaction of public business by any agency of the State government or its political subdivisions.

Nonrecord materials, meaning reference books and exhibit materials made or acquired and preserved solely for reference use or exhibition purposes, extra copies of documents preserved only for convenience or reference, and stocks of publications, shall not be included within the definition of public records as used in this chapter.

I. *"Archival records"* shall mean records of continuing and enduring value useful to the citizens of the Commonwealth and necessary to the administrative functions of public agencies in the conduct of those services and activities mandated by law. In appraisal of public records deemed archival, the terms "administrative," "legal," "fiscal," and "historical" shall be defined as:

1. *"Administrative value"*: Records shall be deemed of administrative value if they have utility in the operation of an agency.

2. *"Legal value"*: Records shall be deemed of legal value when they document actions taken in the protection and proving of legal or civil rights and obligations of individuals and agencies.

3. *"Fiscal value"*: Records shall be deemed of fiscal value so long as they are needed to document and verify financial authorizations, obligations and transactions.

4. *"Historical value"*: Records shall be deemed of historical value when they contain unique information, regardless of age, which provides understanding of some aspect of the government and promotes the development of an informed and enlightened citizenry. (1976, c. 746; 1977, c. 501; 1981, c. 637.)

§ 42.1-78. Confidentiality safeguarded. — Any records made confidential by law shall be so treated. Records which by law are required to be closed to the public shall not be deemed to be made open to the public under the provisions of this chapter and no provision of this chapter shall be construed to authorize or require the opening of any records ordered to be sealed by a court. (1976, c. 746; 1979, c. 110.)

§ 42.1-79. Records management function vested in Board; State Library to be official custodian; State Archivist. — The archival and records management function shall be vested in the State Library Board. The State Library shall be the official custodian and trustee for the State of all public records of whatever kind which are transferred to it from any public office of the State or any political subdivision thereof.

The State Library Board shall name a State Archivist who shall perform such functions as the State Library Board assigns. (1976, c. 746.)

§ 42.1-80. State Public Records Advisory Committee created; members; chairman and vice-chairman; compensation. — There is hereby created a State Public Records Advisory Committee. The Committee shall consist of ten members. The Committee membership shall include the Secretary of Administration and Finance, the State Librarian, the State Health Commissioner, the State Highway and Transportation Commissioner, the Director of the Division of Automated Data Processing, the Auditor of Public Accounts, the Executive Secretary of the Supreme Court, or their designated representatives and three members to be appointed by the Governor from the State at large. The gubernatorial appointments shall include two clerks of courts of record and a member of a local governing body. Those members appointed by the Governor shall remain members of the Committee for a term coincident with that of the Governor making the appointment, or until their successors shall be appointed and qualified. The Committee shall elect annually from its membership a chairman and vice-chairman. Members of the Committee shall receive no compensation for their services but shall be paid their reasonable and necessary expenses incurred in the performance of their duties. (1976, c. 746; 1977, c. 501.)

§ 42.1-81. Powers and responsibilities of Committee. — The Committee shall have responsibility for proposing to the State Library Board rules, regulations and standards, not inconsistent with law, for the purpose of establishing uniform guidelines for the management and preservation of public records throughout the State. The Committee shall have the power to appoint such subcommittees and advisory bodies as it deems advisable. The Committee shall be assisted in the execution of its responsibilities by the State Librarian. (1976, c. 746.)

§ 42.1-82. Duties and powers of Library Board. — The State Library Board shall with the advice of the Committee:

A. Issue regulations designed to facilitate the creation, preservation, storage, filing, microfilming, management and destruction of public records by all agencies. Such regulations shall establish procedures for records management containing recommendations for the retention, disposal or other disposition of public records; procedures for the physical destruction or other disposition of public records proposed for disposal; and standards for the reproduction of records by photocopy or microphotography processes with the view to the disposal of the original records. Such standards shall relate to the quality of film used, preparation of the records for filming, proper identification of the records so that any individual document or series of documents can be located on the film with reasonable facility and that the copies contain all significant record detail, to the end that the photographic or microphotographic copies shall be of archival quality.

B. Issue regulations specifying permissible qualities of paper, ink and other materials to be used by agencies for public record purposes. The Board shall determine the specifications for and shall select and make available to all agencies lists of approved papers, photographic materials, ink, typewriter ribbons, carbon papers, stamping pads or other writing devices for different classes of public records, and only those approved may be purchased for use in the making of such records, except that these regulations and specifications shall not apply to clerks of courts of record.

C. Provide assistance to agencies in determining what records no longer have administrative, legal, fiscal or historical value and should be destroyed or disposed of in another manner. Each public official having in his custody official records shall assist the Board in the preparation of an inventory of all public records in his custody and in preparing a suggested schedule for retention and disposition of such records. No land or personal property book shall be destroyed without having first offered it to the State Library for preservation.

All records created prior to the Constitution of nineteen hundred two that are declared archival may be transferred to the archives. (1976, c. 746; 1977, c. 501; 1981, c. 637.)

§ 42.1-83. Program for inventorying, scheduling, microfilming records; records of counties and cities; storage of records. — The State Library Board shall formulate and execute a program to inventory, schedule, and microfilm official records of counties and cities which it determines have permanent value and to provide safe storage for microfilm copies of such records, and to give advice and assistance to local officials in their programs for creating, preserving, filing and making available public records in their custody.

Any original records shall be either stored in the State Library or in the locality at the decision of the local officials responsible for maintaining public records. Any original records shall be returned to the locality upon the written demand of the local officials responsible for maintaining local public records. Microfilm shall be stored in the State Library but the use thereof shall be subject to the control of the local officials responsible for maintaining local public records. (1972, c. 555; 1976, c. 746.)

§ 42.1-84. Same; records of agencies and subdivisions not covered under § 42.1-83. — The State Library Board may formulate and execute a program of inventorying, repairing, and microfilming for security purposes the public records of the agencies and subdivisions not covered under the program established under § 42.1-83 which it determines have permanent value, and of providing safe storage of microfilm copies of such records. (1976, c. 746.)

§ 42.1-85. Duties of State Librarian; agencies to cooperate. — The State Librarian shall administer a records management program for the application of efficient and economical management methods to the creation, utilization, maintenance, retention, preservation, and disposal of public records consistent with rules, regulations or standards promulgated by the State Library Board, including operations of a records center or centers. It shall be the duty of the State Librarian to establish procedures and techniques for the effective management of public records, to make continuing surveys of paper work operations, and to recommend improvements in current records management practices, including the use of space, equipment, and supplies employed in creating, maintaining and servicing records.

It shall be the duty of any agency with public records to cooperate with the State Librarian in conducting surveys and to establish and maintain an active, continuing program for the economical and efficient management of the records of such agency. (1976, c. 746.)

§ 42.1-86. Program to select and preserve important records; availability to public; security copies. — In cooperation with the head of each agency, the State Librarian shall establish and maintain a program for the selection and preservation of public records considered essential to the operation of government and for the protection of the rights and interests of persons. He shall provide for preserving, classifying, arranging and indexing so that such records are made available to the public and shall make or cause to be made security copies or designate as security copies existing copies of such essential public records. Security copies shall be of archival quality and such copies made by photographic, photostatic, microfilm, microcard, miniature photographic, or other process which accurately reproduces and forms a durable medium and shall have the same force and effect for all purposes as the original record and shall be as admissible in evidence as the original record whether the original record is in existence or not. Such security copies shall be preserved in such place and manner of safekeeping as prescribed by the State Library Board and provided by the Governor. Those public records deemed unnecessary for the transaction of the business of any agency, yet deemed to be of administrative, legal, fiscal or historical value, may be transferred with the consent of the State Librarian to the custody of the State Library. No agency shall destroy, discard, sell or give away public records without first offering them to the State Library for preservation. (1976, c. 746; 1980, c. 365.)

§ 42.1-87. Where records kept; duties of agencies; repair, etc., of record books; agency heads not divested of certain authority. — Custodians of public records shall keep them in fireproof safes, vaults or in rooms designed to ensure proper preservation and in such arrangement as to be easily accessible. Current public records should be kept in the buildings in which they are ordinarily used. It shall be the duty of each agency to cooperate with the State Library in complying with rules and regulations promulgated by the Board. Each agency shall establish and maintain an active and continuing program for the economic and efficient management of records.

Record books should be copied or repaired, renovated or rebound if worn, mutilated, damaged or difficult to read. Whenever the public records of any public official are in need of repair, restoration or rebinding, a judge of the court of record or the head of such agency or political subdivision of the State may authorize that the records in need of repair be removed from the building or office in which such records are ordinarily kept, for the length of time necessary to repair, restore or rebind them, provided such restoration and rebinding preserves the records without loss or damage to them. Any public official who causes a record book to be copied shall attest it and shall certify an oath that it is an accurate copy of the original book. The copy shall then have the force of the original.

Nothing in this chapter shall be construed to divest agency heads of the authority to determine the nature and form of the records required in the administration of their several departments or to compel the removal of records deemed necessary by them in the performance of their statutory duty. (1976, c. 746.)

§ 42.1-88. Custodians to deliver all records at expiration of term; penalty for noncompliance. — Any custodian of any public records shall, at the expiration of his term of office, appointment or employment, deliver to his successor, or, if there be none, to the State Library, all books, writings, letters, documents, public records, or other information, recorded on any medium kept or received by him in the transaction of his official business; and any such person who shall refuse or neglect for a period of ten days after a request is made in writing by the successor or State Librarian to deliver the public records as herein required shall be guilty of a Class 3 misdemeanor. (1976, c. 746.)

§ 42.1-89. Petition and court order for return of public records not in authorized possession. — The State Librarian or his designated representative such as the State Archivist or any public official who is the custodian of public records in the possession of a person or agency not authorized by the custodian or by law to possess such public records shall petition the circuit court in the city or county in which the person holding such records resides or in which the materials in issue, or any part thereof, are located for the return of such records. The court shall order such public records be delivered to the petitioner upon finding that the materials in issue are public records and that such public records are in the possession of a person not authorized by the custodian of the public records or by law to possess such public records. If the order of delivery does not receive compliance, the plaintiff shall request that the court enforce such order through its contempt power and procedures. (1975, c. 180; 1976, c. 746.)

§ 42.1-90. Seizure of public records not in authorized possession. — A. At any time after the filing of the petition set out in § 42.1-89 or contemporaneous with such filing, the person seeking the return of the public records may by ex parte petition request the judge or the court in which the action was filed to issue an order directed at the sheriff or other proper officer, as the case may be, commanding him to seize the materials which are the subject of the action and deliver the same to the court under the circumstances hereinafter set forth.

B. The judge aforesaid shall issue an order of seizure upon receipt of an affidavit from the petitioner which alleges that the material at issue may be sold, secreted, removed out of this State or otherwise disposed of so as not to be forthcoming to answer the final judgment of the court respecting the same; or that such property may be destroyed or materially damaged or injured if permitted to remain out of the petitioner's possession.

C. The aforementioned order of seizure shall issue without notice to the respondent and without the posting of any bond or other security by the petitioner. (1975, c. 180; 1976, c. 746.)

§ 42.1-91. Development of disaster plan. — The State Library shall develop a plan to ensure preservation of public records in the event of disaster or emergency as defined in § 44-146.16. This plan shall be coordinated with the Office of Emergency Services and copies shall be distributed to all agency heads. The personnel of the Library shall be responsible for coordinating emergency recovery operations when public records are affected. (1981; c. 637.)

LAW LIBRARIES
(Code of Virginia, 1982, s.42.1-60 to 42.1-66, 42.1-70, 42.1-71.)

§ 42.1-60. State Law Library managed by Supreme Court. — There shall be a State Law Library at Richmond, with a branch thereof at Staunton, maintained as at present, which shall be managed by the Supreme Court. The Court shall appoint the librarian and other employees to hold office during the pleasure of the Court; provided, however, that the clerk at Staunton shall act as law librarian there without additional compensation therefor. (Code 1950 (Repl. Vol. 1953), § 42-13; 1970, c. 606; 1977, c. 397.)

§ 42.1-61. Books constituting Library. — The State Law Library shall consist of the books now in the law libraries at Richmond and Staunton, with such additions as may be made thereto. (Code 1950 (Repl. Vol. 1953), § 42-14; 1970, c. 606.)

§ 42.1-62. Additions to Library. — The Supreme Court shall, from time to time, make additions to the State Law Library by purchases, and may lease or purchase computer terminals for the purpose of retrieving available legal reference data, with funds at its disposal for these purposes, and may cause books to be transferred from one law library to another. All law books acquired by the State by gift, or by exchange, from the United States, or other states and countries, shall be placed in the Library. The Director of the Department of Purchases and Supply shall have placed in the State Law Library at Richmond, and in the branch thereof at Staunton, a copy of every law book required by §§ 2.1-257, 2.1-268, and 2.1-269. (Code 1950 (Repl. Vol. 1953), § 42-15; 1970, c. 606; 1977, c. 397.)

§ 42.1-63. Regulation of Library. — The Supreme Court shall have power to make and enforce such rules and orders for the regulation of the State Law Library, and the use thereof, as may to it seem proper. Such rules and orders may provide for the assessment and collection of fees for the use of computer research services other than for valid State uses; such fees shall be assessed in the amount necessary to cover the expenses of such services and those collected and hereby appropriated to the Court to be paid as part of the cost of maintaining such computer research capabilities. (Code 1950 (Repl. Vol. 1953), § 42-16; 1970, c. 606; 1977, c. 397.)

§ 42.1-64. Who may use Library. — The Governor and other State officers at the seat of government, the Reporter of the Supreme Court, members of the General Assembly, judges of courts, and practicing attorneys in good standing, and such other persons as the Supreme Court shall designate, shall have the use of the State Law Library, under such rules and regulations as the Court shall make. (Code 1950 (Repl. Vol. 1953), § 42-17; 1970, c. 606; 1977, c. 397.)

§ 42.1-65. Local law libraries in charge of circuit or corporation court clerks; computer research services. — A. If the members of the bar practicing in any county or city of the Commonwealth shall procure by voluntary contribution a law library of the value of five hundred dollars, at the least, for the use of the courts held in such county or city, and of the bar practicing therein, it shall be the duty of the circuit court of such county or city to require its clerk to take charge of the library so contributed and to keep the same in the courthouse or clerk's office building according to the rules prescribed by the bar and approved by the court.

B. If the members of the bars practicing in two or more adjoining counties or cities of the Commonwealth shall jointly procure by voluntary contribution a law library of the value of five hundred dollars, at the least, for the joint use of the courts held in such counties and cities, and of the bars practicing therein, it shall be the joint duty of the circuit courts of such counties and cities to require one of its clerks to take charge of the library so contributed and to keep the same in the most convenient courthouse or clerk's office building according to the rules jointly prescribed by the bars and jointly approved by the courts.

C. Such local and regional law libraries may purchase or lease computer terminals for the purpose of retrieving available legal reference data, and if so, the library rules shall provide for the assessment and collection of fees for the use of computer research services other than for official use of the courts, counties and cities serviced by such libraries, which fees shall be sufficient to cover the expenses of such services. Such libraries, pursuant to rules of the Supreme Court and at costs to such libraries, may have access to computer research services of the State Law Library. (Code 1950 (Repl. Vol. 1953), § 42-18; 1962, c. 515; 1970, c. 606; 1977, c. 397.)

§ 42.1-66. Circuit courts to enforce rules for government of such libraries. — The observance of the rules so prescribed and approved may be enforced by a circuit court sitting within the area served by the particular local or regional library by such summary process and judgment as shall be provided by such rules. (Code 1950 (Repl. Vol. 1953), § 42-19; 1962, c. 515; 1970, c. 606; 1977, c. 397.)

§ 42.1-70. Assessment for law library as part of costs in civil actions; contributions from bar associations. — Any county, city or town may, through its governing body, assess as part of the costs, incident to each civil action filed in the courts located within its boundaries a sum not in excess of two dollars. However, in the Counties of Wythe and Fairfax such sum shall not exceed three dollars.

The imposition of such assessment shall be by ordinance of the governing body, which ordinance may provide for different sums in circuit courts and district courts, and the assessment shall be collected by the clerk of the court in which the action is filed, and remitted to the treasurer of such county, city or town and held by such treasurer subject to disbursements by the governing body for the acquisition of law books, law periodicals and computer legal research services and equipment for the establishment, use and maintenance of a law library which shall be open for the use of the public. In addition to the acquisition of law books, law periodicals and computer legal research services and equipment, the disbursements may include compensation to be paid to librarians and other necessary staff for the maintenance of such library and acquisition of suitable quarters for such library. The compensation of such librarians and the necessary staff and the cost of suitable quarters for such library shall be fixed by the governing body and paid out of the fund created by the imposition of such assessment of cost. Such libraries, pursuant to rules of the Supreme Court and at costs to such libraries, may have access to com-

puter research services of the State Law Library. Disbursements may be made
to purchase or lease computer terminals for the purpose of retaining such
research services. The assessment provided for herein shall be in addition to
all other costs prescribed by law, but shall not apply to any action in which the
Commonwealth or any political subdivision thereof or the federal government
is a party and in which the costs are assessed against the Commonwealth,
political subdivision thereof, or federal government. The governing body is
authorized to accept contributions to the fund from any bar association.

Any such library established in the County of Wythe shall be located only
in a town which is the seat of the county government. (Code 1950 (Suppl.),
§ 42-19.4; 1964, c. 439; 1964, Ex. Sess., c. 26; 1966, c. 225; 1970, c. 606; 1972,
c. 343; 1977, c. 397; 1981, c. 48; 1982, c. 607; 1983, cc. 309, 355.)

**§ 42.1-71. Establishment of regional law libraries by governing
bodies.** — Any two or more adjoining counties or cities assessing costs as
provided in § 42.1-70 may jointly establish a regional law library, and each
such regional library shall be open to the public. (1977, c. 145.)

NETWORKING
(Code of Virginia, 1982, s.42.1-32.1 to 42.1-32.7.)

§ 42.1-32.1. Declaration of intent. — It is hereby declared to be the policy
of the Commonwealth, as part of its provision for public education, to promote
the cooperation and networking of all public, academic, special and school
libraries throughout the Commonwealth. It is the further intent of this article
that none of its provisions shall be construed to interfere with the autonomy
of the governing boards of institutions of higher education and the governing
boards of public, special and school libraries. (1983, c. 537.)

§ 42.1-32.2. Grants for establishment of library network. — In order to
assist in the development of library cooperation and a library network, the
Board shall grant from such appropriations as are made to it for this purpose,
funds to assist libraries in preparing for networking and in supporting a
library network. The Board shall seek the advice of the State Library Users
Advisory Council, as defined in § 42.1-32.7, to guide it in its allocation of such
grants and in the establishment of standards and priorities for the network.
(1983, c. 537.)

§ 42.1-32.3. Standards for networking. — Libraries receiving such aid, as
is provided by the Board for networking, shall be committed to the standards
and priorities established by the Board for interlibrary lending policies between network members, to cooperation in establishing collection development
policies and resource sharing for the greatest good of all library users, and to
the provision of comprehensive and cost-effective library services to the citizens of Virginia. (1983, c. 537.)

**§ 42.1-32.4. Computer programs and data bases property of the
Commonwealth.** — All computer programs and data bases created pursuant
to programs supported by grants made for networking shall be the property of
the Commonwealth and shall be made available to all libraries of the network
equally. (1983, c. 537.)

§ 42.1-32.5. Board to establish standards for grants. — The Board shall
establish standards under which a library shall be eligible for grants for
networking. (1983, c. 537.)

§ 42.1-32.6. Establishment and operation of communication centers and other networking services. — The Board may establish and operate or may contract for the establishment and operation of one or more automated communication centers and other networking services, based on a plan approved by the Board and the Governor after consultation with the Users Council. (1983, c. 537.)

§ 42.1-32.7. State Networking Users Advisory Council. — There is hereby created a State Networking Users Advisory Council, hereinafter referred to as the Council, which shall be composed of seven members, all librarians, to be appointed by the Governor for three-year terms. The State Networking Users Advisory Council shall advise the State Librarian and the Board in the development and direction of the network and its policies, standards, funding levels and requirements for use, after receiving the input of other libraries. The Council shall be appointed in such a way as to represent all classes of networking users in the statewide library community. The Council shall meet no less than twice annually. (1983, c. 537.)

LOCAL AND REGIONAL LIBRARIES
(Code of Virginia, 1982, s.42.1-33 to 42.1-45.)

§ 42.1-33. Power of local governments to establish and support libraries. — The governing body of any city, county or town shall have the power to establish a free public library for the use and benefit of its residents. The governing body shall provide sufficient support for the operation of the library by levying a tax therefor, either by special levy or as a fund of the general levy of the city, county or town. The word "support" as used in this chapter shall include but is not limited to, purchase of land for library buildings, purchase or erection of buildings for library purposes, purchase of library books, materials and equipment, compensation of library personnel, and all maintenance expenses for library property and equipment. Funds appropriated or contributed for public library purposes shall constitute a separate fund and shall not be used for any but public library purposes. (1970, c. 606.)

§ 42.1-34. Power of local governments to contract for library service. — Any city, town or county shall have the power to enter into contracts with adjacent cities, counties, towns, or state-supported institutions of higher learning to receive or to provide library service on such terms and conditions as shall be mutually acceptable, or they may contract for a library service with a library not owned by a public corporation but maintained for free public use. The board of trustees of a free public library may enter into contracts with county, city or town school boards and boards of school trustees to provide library service for schools. Any city or county governing body contracting for library service shall, as a part of such contract, have the power to appoint at least one member to the board of trustees or other governing body of the library contracting to provide such service. Any city or county thus contracting for library service shall be entitled to the rights and benefits of regional free library systems established in accordance with the provisions of § 42.1-37. The board of trustees or other governing body of any library established under the provisions of § 42.1-33 may also, with the approval of and on terms satisfactory to the State Library Board, extend its services to persons in adjacent areas of other states. (1970, c. 606.)

§ 42.1-35. Library boards generally. — The management and control of a free public library system shall be vested in a board of not less than five members or trustees. They shall be appointed by the governing body, chosen from the citizens at large with reference to their fitness for such office. One such member shall be appointed in the beginning for a term of one year, one member for a term of two years, one member for a term of three years, and two members for terms of four years; thereafter all five shall be appointed for terms of four years. The governing body of any county or city entitled to representation on a library board of a library system of another jurisdiction pursuant to § 42.1-34 shall appoint a member to serve for a term of four years, or until the contract is terminated, whichever is shorter. Vacancies shall be filled for unexpired terms as soon as possible in the manner in which members of the board are regularly chosen. A member shall not receive a salary or other compensation for services as a member but necessary expenses actually incurred shall be paid from the library fund; provided, however, the governing body of Fairfax County may pay members of its library board such compensation as it may deem proper. A member of a library board may be removed for misconduct or neglect of duty by the governing body making the appointment. The members shall adopt such bylaws, rules and regulations for their own guidance and for the government of the free public library system as may be expedient. They shall have control of the expenditures of all moneys credited to the library fund. The board shall have the right to accept donations and bequests of money, personal property, or real estate for the establishment and maintenance of such free public library systems or endowments for same. (1970, c. 606; 1974, c. 84.)

§ 42.1-36. Boards not mandatory. — The formation and creation of boards shall in nowise be considered or construed in any manner as mandatory upon any city or town with a manager, or upon any county with a county manager, county executive, urban county manager or urban county executive form of government or Chesterfield County, by virtue of this chapter. (1970, c. 606; 1978, c. 6.)

§ 42.1-37. Establishment of regional library system. — Two or more political subdivisions, (counties or cities), by action of their governing bodies, may join in establishing and maintaining a regional free library system under the terms of a contract between such political subdivisions; provided, that in the case of established county or city free library systems, the library boards shall agree to such action. (1970, c. 606.)

§ 42.1-38. Agreements to create regional boards. — Two or more political subdivisions (counties or cities) which have qualified for participation in the State's regional library program, have been recognized as a region by the State Library Board, and have made the minimum local appropriation of funds as may now or hereafter be recommended by the Board, are hereby empowered and authorized to execute contracts with each other to create a regional library board to administer and control the regional library services within the region. Each jurisdiction shall, as a part of such contract, have the power to appoint at least one member to the regional library board. (1970, c. 606.)

§ 42.1-39. Regional library boards generally. — The members of the board of a regional library system shall be appointed by the respective governing bodies represented. Such members shall in the beginning draw lots for expiration of terms, to provide for staggered terms of office, and thereafter the appointment shall be for a term of four years. Vacancies shall be filled for unexpired terms as soon as possible in the manner in which members are regularly chosen. No appointive member shall be eligible to serve more than two successive terms. A member shall not receive a salary or other compensation for services as member, but necessary expenses actually incurred shall be paid from the library fund. A regional board member may be removed for misconduct or neglect of duty by the governing body making the appointment. The board members shall elect officers and adopt such bylaws, rules and regulations for their own guidance and for the government of the regional free library system as may be expedient. They shall have control of the expenditure of all moneys credited to the regional free library fund. The regional board shall have the right to accept donations and bequests of money, personal property, or real estate for the establishment and maintenance of such regional free library system or endowments for same. (1970, c. 606.)

§ 42.1-40. **Power of regional library board to contract.** — The regional library board shall have authority to execute contracts with the State Library Board, with the library boards of the respective jurisdictions, and any and all other agencies for the purpose of administering a public library service within the region, including contracts concerning allocation and expenditure of funds, to the same extent as the library board of any one of the jurisdictions which are parties to the agreement would be so authorized. (1970, c. 606.)

§ 42.1-41. **Funds and expenses of regional library system.** — The expenses of the regional library system shall be apportioned among the participating political subdivisions on such basis as shall be agreed upon in the contract. The treasurer of the regional library board shall have the custody of the funds of the regional free library system; and the treasurers or other financial officers of the participating jurisdictions shall transfer quarterly to him all moneys collected or appropriated for this purpose in their respective jurisdictions. Such funds shall be expended only for the library service for which the county or city contracted and for no other purpose. The regional library board shall furnish a detailed report of receipts and disbursements of all funds at the regular meeting of the governing body of every participating jurisdiction after the close of the State's fiscal year. It shall make a similar report to the State Library. The treasurer of the board shall be bonded for an amount to be determined by the board. The board may authorize the treasurer to pay bond premiums from State aid library funds. (1970, c. 606.)

§ 42.1-42. **Withdrawal from regional library system.** — No county or city participating in a regional library system shall withdraw therefrom without two years' notice to the other participating counties and cities without the consent of such other participating political subdivisions. (1970, c. 606.)

§ 42.1-43. **Appropriation for free library or library service conducted by company, society or organization.** — The governing body of any county, city or town in which no free public library system as provided in this chapter shall have been established, may, in its discretion, appropriate such sums of money as to it seems proper for the support and maintenance of any free library or library service operated and conducted in such county, city or town by a company, society or association organized under the provisions of §§ 13.1-201 through 13.1-296. (1970, c. 606.)

§ 42.1-44. **Cooperative library system for Henrico and Chesterfield counties and city of Richmond.** — Notwithstanding the repeal of Title 42 of the Code of Virginia, §§ 42-12.1 to 42-12.5 of chapter 2.1 of former Title 42 are continued in effect and are incorporated into this title by reference. (1970, c. 606.)

§ 42.1-45. Transfer of properties, etc., of public free library to governing body of city in which it is situated. — The board of directors or trustees of any public free library established pursuant to chapter 13, Acts of Assembly, 1924, approved February 13, 1924, may lease, convey, or transfer any interest to its properties, real or personal, to the governing body of the political subdivision in which such library be situated in order that such library may become a part of the public library system of such city, subject to such restrictions and conditions as may be agreed to by such board of directors or trustees and such governing body. (1970, c. 367.)

DISTRIBUTION OF PUBLIC DOCUMENTS

(Code of Virginia, 1982, s.2.1-296, 2.1-297, 2.1-301, 2.1-302.)

§ 2.1-296. Agencies to furnish copies to State Library and Department of Purchases and Supply. — Every agency shall furnish two copies of each of its publications at the time of issue to the Virginia State Library and shall deliver one copy to the Department of Purchases and Supply at the same time. (Code 1950 (Suppl.), § 2-268.2; 1964, c. 303; 1966, c. 677.)

§ 2.1-297. State Librarian may acquire additional copies. — The State Librarian may require any agency to deliver to the State Library not exceeding one hundred additional copies of any publication delivered to him under § 2.1-296 of this chapter. (Code 1950 (Suppl.), § 2-268.3; 1964, c. 303; 1966, c. 677.)

§ 2.1-301. State Librarian to prepare and publish catalog. — On and after June twenty-sixth, nineteen hundred sixty-four, the State Librarian shall prepare, publish and make available a catalog of publications printed by State agencies. Such catalog shall be issued annually and each publication shall be indexed by subject, author and issuing agency. The date of publication of each listed publication shall be noted in the catalog together with information showing, in appropriate cases, that library copies only are available. To the extent such information is available, the catalog shall set forth the price charged, if any, of each publication and how and where the same may be obtained. (Code 1950 (Suppl.), § 2-268.7; 1964, c. 303; 1966, c. 677.)

§ 2.1-302. Distribution of catalog. — The catalog shall be made available without cost to persons indicating a continuing interest in such catalog. Copies sent out of State shall be on an exchange basis or at a price sufficient to equal the unit cost of printing and mailing; complimentary copies may be made available by the State Librarian. (Code 1950 (Suppl.), § 2-268.8; 1964, c. 303; 1966, c. 677.)

PROTECTION OF LIBRARY PROPERTY

(Code of Virginia, 1982, s.42.1-72 to 42.1-74.1.)

§ 42.1-72. Injuring or destroying books and other property of libraries. — Any person who willfully, maliciously or wantonly writes upon, injures, defaces, tears, cuts, mutilates, or destroys any book or other library property belonging to or in the custody of any public, county or regional library, the State Library, other repository of public records, museums or any library or collection belonging to or in the custody of any educational, eleemosynary, benevolent, hereditary, historical library or patriotic institution, organization or society, shall be guilty of a Class 1 misdemeanor. (Code 1950 (Repl. Vol. 1953), § 42-20; 1970, c. 606; 1975, c. 318.)

§ 42.1-73. Concealment of book or other property while on premises of library; removal of book or other property from library.

— Whoever, without authority, with the intention of converting to his own or another's use, wilfully conceals a book or other library property, while still on the premises of such library, or willfully or without authority removes any book or other property from any of the above libraries or collections shall be deemed guilty of larceny thereof, and upon conviction thereof shall be punished as provided by law. Proof of the willful concealment of such book or other library property while still on the premises of such library shall be prima facie evidence of intent to commit larceny thereof. (Code 1950 (Repl. Vol. 1953), § 42-21; 1970, c. 606; 1975, c. 318.)

§ 42.1-73.1. Exemption from liability for arrest of suspected person.

— A library or agent or employee of the library causing the arrest of any person pursuant to the provisions of § 42.1-73, shall not be held civilly liable for unlawful detention, slander, malicious prosecution, false imprisonment, false arrest, or assault and battery of the person so arrested, whether such arrest takes place on the premises of the library or after close pursuit from such premises by such agent or employee; provided that, in causing the arrest of such person, the library or agent or employee of the library had at the time of such arrest probable cause to believe that the person committed willful concealment of books or other library property. (1975, c. 318.)

§ 42.1-74. Failure to return book or other library property.

— Any person having in his possession any book or other property of any of the above libraries or collections, which he shall fail to return within thirty days after receiving notice in writing from the custodian, shall be guilty of a misdemeanor and punished according to law; provided, however, that if such book should be lost or destroyed, such person may, within thirty days after being so notified, pay to the custodian the value of such book, the value to be determined by the governing board having jurisdiction. (Code 1950 (Repl. Vol. 1953), § 42-22; 1970, c. 606.)

§ 42.1-74.1. "Book or other library property" defined.

— The terms "book or other library property" as used in this chapter shall include any book, plate, picture, photograph, engraving, painting, drawing, map, newspaper, magazine, pamphlet, broadside, manuscript, document, letter, public record, microform, sound recording, audiovisual materials in any format, magnetic or other tapes, electronic data processing records, artifacts, or other documentary, written, or printed material, regardless of physical form or characteristics, belonging to, on loan to, or otherwise in the custody of any library, museum, repository of public or other records institution as specified in § 42.1-72. (1975, c. 318.)

TAX EXEMPTION
(Code of Virginia, 1982, s.58-12.)

Virginia library laws are reprinted from CODE OF VIRGINIA published by The Michie Co., Charlottesville, Virginia.

WASHINGTON

STATE LIBRARY

(Revised Code of Washington Annotated, 1982,
s.27.04.010 to 27.04.090.)

27.04.010   Library created

There shall be a state library, and a state librarian as the chief executive officer in charge thereof.

Enacted by Laws 1943, ch. 207, § 1.

27.04.020   Library commission created—Terms, vacancies, travel expenses

A state library commission is hereby created which shall consist of the superintendent of public instruction, who shall be ex officio chairman of said commission and four commissioners appointed by the governor, one of whom shall be a library trustee at the time of appointment and one a certified librarian actually engaged in library work at the time of appointment. The first appointments shall be for terms of one, two, three and four years respectively, and thereafter one commissioner shall be appointed each year to serve for a four year term. Vacancies shall be filled by appointments for the unexpired terms. Each commissioner shall serve without salary or other compensation for his services, but shall be reimbursed for travel expenses incurred in the actual performance of their duties in accordance with RCW 43.03.050 and 43.03.060 as now existing or hereafter amended.

Enacted by Laws 1941, ch. 5, § 1. Amended by Laws 1961, ch. 45, § 1; Laws 1963, ch. 202, § 1; Laws 1967, ch. 198, § 1; Laws 1975–76, 2nd Ex.Sess., ch. 34, § 66, eff. July 1, 1976.

27.04.030 Duties of commission

The state library commission shall have charge and control of the state library. It shall appoint a state librarian, who shall hold office at the pleasure of the commission. It may make rules and regulations governing the administration of the library.

Enacted by Laws 1941, ch. 5, § 2. Amended by Laws 1943, ch. 207, § 2.

27.04.035 Duties of commission—Contracts for services to the blind

The state library commission shall have authority to contract with any public library in the state for that library to render library service to the blind throughout the state. The state library commission shall have authority to reasonably compensate such public library for the cost of the service it renders under such contract.

Added by Laws 1955, ch. 170, § 1.

27.04.037 Duties of commission—Deposit of copies of state publications

The state library commission, on recommendation of the state librarian, may provide by rule or regulation for deposit with the state library of up to three copies of any state publication, as defined in RCW 40.06.010 as now existing or hereafter amended, prepared by any state agency whenever fifteen or more copies are prepared for distribution.

Added by Laws 1977, Ex.Sess., ch. 232, § 7.

27.04.040 Library service to be expanded

In order to provide, expand, enlarge and equalize public library facilities and services and thereby promote and stimulate interest in reading throughout the entire state, the state library commission shall, from time to time, make studies and surveys of public library needs and adopt rules and regulations for the allocation of money to public libraries to be expended on vouchers approved by the commission.

Enacted by Laws 1945, ch. 232, § 1.

27.04.050   Duties of librarian

The state librarian is authorized, subject to any limitations and conditions imposed by the state library commission, to acquire by purchase, exchange, gift or otherwise library material, equipment and supplies and employ such assistance as is needed for the operation, growth and development of the library and to make rules and regulations governing the use of the library and the material therein.

Enacted by Laws 1943, ch. 207, § 3.

27.04.060   Commission may accept federal funds

The state library commission is hereby authorized to accept and to expend in accordance with the terms thereof any grant of federal funds which may become available to the state for library purposes. For the purpose of qualifying to receive such grants, the state library commission is authorized to make such applications and reports as may be required by the federal government as a condition thereto.

Enacted by Laws 1949, ch. 39, § 1.

27.04.070   Contracts to provide state agencies with library materials, supplies, equipment and personnel

The state library is authorized, subject to any limitations and conditions imposed by the state library commission, to contract with any agency of the state of Washington for the purpose of providing library materials, supplies, equipment and employing assistants as needed for the development, growth and operation of any library facilities or services of such agency.

Added by Laws 1967, ch. 67, § 1.

27.04.090   Depository for newspapers

The state library shall be the depository for newspapers published in the state of Washington, thus providing a central location for a valuable historical record for scholarly, personal, and commercial reference and circulation.

Added by Laws 1981, ch. 220, § 1.

WASHINGTON LIBRARY NETWORK

(Revised Code of Washington Annotated, 1982, s.27. 26.010,
27.26.020.)

27.26.010　Definitions

As used in this chapter, unless otherwise required by the context, the following definitions shall apply:

(1) "Washington library network computer system" means the communication facilities, computers, and peripheral computer devices supporting the automated library system developed by the state of Washington;

(2) "Network" means the Washington library network which is an organization of autonomous, geographically dispersed participants using the Washington library network computer system, telecommunications systems, interlibrary systems, and reference and referral systems;

(3) "Resources" are library materials which include but are not limited to print, nonprint (e.g., audiovisual, realia, etc.), and microform formats; network resources such as software, hardware, and equipment; electronic and magnetic records; data bases; communication technology; facilities; and human expertise;

(4) "Telecommunications" includes any point to point transmission, emission, or reception of signs, signals, writing, images, and sounds or intelligence of any nature by wire, radio, microwave radio, optical, or other electromagnetic system, including any intervening processing and storage serving a point to point system;

(5) "Interlibrary loan system" means the accepted procedures among libraries by which library materials are made available in some format to users of another library;

(6) "Reference and referral system" pertains to procedures among libraries whereby subject or fact-oriented queries may be referred to another institution when the answering resource or subject expertise is unavailable in the institution originally queried.

Added by Laws 1975–76, 2nd Ex.Sess., ch. 31, § 2.

27.26.020　Network established—Responsibility of state library commission and data processing authority

There is hereby established the Washington library network,

hereinafter called the network, which shall consist of the Washington library network computer system, telecommunications systems, interlibrary systems, and reference and referral systems.

Responsibility for the network shall reside with the Washington state library commission, except for certain automated data processing components as provided for and defined in chapter 43.105 RCW: *Provided,* That all components, systems and programs operated pursuant to this section shall be approved by the data processing authority created pursuant to chapter 43.105 RCW. The commission shall adopt and promulgate policies, rules, and regulations consistent with the purposes and provisions of this act pursuant to chapter 34.04 RCW, the administrative procedure act, except that nothing in this chapter shall abrogate the authority of a participating library, institution, or organization to establish its own policies for collection development and use of its library resources.

Added by Laws 1975–76, 2nd Ex.Sess., ch. 31, § 1.

CERTIFICATION OF LIBRARIANS
(Revised Code of Washington Annotated, 1982;
s.27.08.010, 27.08.045.)

27.08.010 State librarians' certification board created—Powers—Certificate fee—Expenses of board—Certified librarians required

(1) There is hereby created a state board for the certification of librarians, which shall consist of the state librarian, the executive officer of the department of librarianship of the University of Washington, and one other member to be appointed by the governor for a term of three years from a list of three persons nominated by the executive committee of the Washington library association. The members of the board shall serve without salary, shall have authority to establish rules and regulations for their own government and procedure, and shall prescribe and hold examinations to test the qualifications of those seeking certificates as librarians.

(2) The board shall grant librarians' certificates without examination to applicants who are graduates of library schools accredited by the American library association for general library training, and shall grant certificates to other applicants when it has satisfied itself by examination that the applicant has attainments and abilities equivalent to those of a library school graduate and is qualified to carry on library work ably and efficiently.

(3) Any person not a graduate of a library school accredited by the American library association, but who has served as a librarian or a full time professional assistant in any library in this state for at least one year or the equivalent thereof prior to midnight, June 12, 1935, shall be granted a librarian's certificate without examination, but such certificate shall be good only for the position specified therein, unless specifically extended by the board.

(4) The board shall require a fee of not less than one dollar nor more than five dollars to be paid by each applicant for a librarian's certificate. Money paid as fees shall be deposited with the state treasurer. All necessary expenses of the board shall be paid from funds appropriated by the legislature upon the presentation of proper vouchers approved by the board.

(5) After January 1, 1937, a library serving a community having over four thousand population shall not have in its employ, in the position of librarian or in any other full time professional library position, a person who does not hold a librarian's certificate issued by the board.

(6) A full time professional library position, as intended by this section, is one that requires, in the opinion of the state board for the certification of librarians, a knowledge of books and of library technique equivalent to that required for graduation from an accredited library school.

(7) The provisions in this section shall apply to every library serving a community having over four thousand population and to every library operated by the state or under its authority, including libraries of institutions of higher learning: *Provided,* That nothing in this section shall apply to the state law library or to county law libraries.

Enacted by Laws 1935, ch. 119, § 11. Amended by Laws 1973, ch. 106, § 12.

27.08.045 Funds for payment of expenses

The expenses provided for in RCW 27.08.010(4) for the state board for the certification of librarians shall be paid from any funds appropriated and available for the use of the state library commission.

Added by Laws 1955, ch. 295, § 1.

STATE LAW LIBRARY
(Revised Code of Washington Annotated, 1982,
s.27.20.030 to 27.20.050.)

27.20.030 Library part of judicial branch

The state law library shall be a part of the judicial branch of state government and shall be under the exclusive jurisdiction and control of the supreme court.

Added by Laws 1959, ch. 188, § 1.

27.20.040 State law librarian and assistants—Appointment, tenure, compensation

The supreme court shall appoint a state law librarian, who may be removed at its pleasure. The librarian shall receive such compensation only as shall be fixed by the court.

The court may also appoint and fix the salaries of such assistants and clerical personnel as may be required.

Added by Laws 1959, ch. 188, § 2.

27.20.050 Duties of law librarian

The duties of the state law librarian shall be as prescribed by statute and by rules of court.

Added by Laws 1959, ch. 188, § 3.

DISTRIBUTION OF PUBLIC DOCUMENTS
(Revised Code of Washington Annotated, 1982,
s.40.04.035 to 40.04.110.)

40.04.035 Temporary edition of session laws—Distribution and sale

The statute law committee, after each legislative session, shall furnish one temporary bound copy of each act as published under chapter 44.20 RCW to each member of the legislature at which such law was enacted, and to each state department or division thereof, commission, committee, board, and council, and to community colleges. Thirty-five copies shall be furnished to the senate and fifty copies to the house of representatives or such other number as may be requested. Two copies shall be furnished the administrator for the courts. One copy shall be furnished for each assistant attorney general; and one copy each to the Olympia representatives of the Associated Press and the United Press.

Each county auditor shall submit each year to the statute law committee a list of county officials requiring temporary session laws for official use only, and the auditor shall receive and distribute such copies to the county officials.

There shall be a charge of five dollars for each of the complete sets of such temporary publications when delivered to any person, firm, corporation, or institution excepting the persons and institutions named in this section. All moneys received from the sale of such temporary sets shall be transmitted to the state treasurer who shall deposit the same in the state treasury to the credit of the general fund.

[Added by Laws 1st Ex Sess 1982 ch 32 § 5.]

40.04.040 Permanent edition of session laws—Distribution, sale, exchange—Surplus copies, sale, price

Permanent session laws shall be distributed, sold and/or exchanged by the state law librarian as follows:

(1) Copies shall be given as follows: One to each United States senator and

representative in congress from this state; two to the Library of Congress; one to the United States supreme court library; three to the library of the circuit court of appeals of the ninth circuit; two to each United States district court room within this state; two to each office and branch office of the United States district attorneys in this state; one to each state official whose office is created by the Constitution; two each to the president of the senate, secretary of the senate, speaker of the house of representatives, and chief clerk of the house of representatives and such additional copies as they may request; fourteen copies to the code reviser; two copies to the state library; two copies to the law library of the University of Puget Sound law school; two copies to the law library of Gonzaga University law school; two copies to the law libraries of any accredited law schools as are hereafter established in this state; one copy to each state adult correctional institution; and one copy to each state mental institution.

(2) Copies, for official use only, shall be distributed as follows: Two copies to the governor; one each to the state historical society and the state bar association; and one copy to each prosecuting attorney.

Sufficient copies shall be furnished for the use of the supreme court, the court of appeals, the superior courts, and the state law library as from time to time are needed. Eight copies shall be distributed to the University of Washington law library; one copy each to the offices of the president and the board of regents of the University of Washington, the dean of the University of Washington school of law, and to the University of Washington library; one copy to the library of each of the regional universities and to The Evergreen State College; one copy to the president of the Washington State University and four copies to the Washington State University library. Six copies shall be sent to the King county law library, and one copy to each of the county law libraries organized pursuant to law; one copy to each public library in cities of the first class, and one copy to the municipal reference branch of the Seattle public library.

(3) Surplus copies of the session laws shall be sold and delivered by the state law librarian, in which case the price of the bound volumes shall be twenty dollars each. All moneys received from the sale of such bound volumes of session laws shall be paid into the state treasury for the general fund.

(4) The state law librarian is authorized to exchange bound copies of the session laws for similar laws or legal materials of other states, territories, and governments, and to make such other and further distribution of the bound volumes as in his judgment seems proper.
[Amended by Laws 1973 ch 33 § 1; Laws 1st Ex\Sess 1977 ch 169 § 94; Laws 1981 ch 162 § 1, effective May 14, 1981; Laws 1st Ex Sess 1982 ch 32 § 1.]

40.04.090 Legislative journals—Distribution, sale, exchange — Duties of law librarian

The house and senate journals shall be distributed and/or sold by the state law librarian as follows:

(1) Sets shall be distributed as follows: One set to each secretary and assistant secretary of the senate, chief clerk and assistant to the chief clerk of the house of representatives, and to each minute clerk and sergeant-at-arms of the two branches of the legislature of which they occupy the offices and positions mentioned. One to each official whose office is created by the Constitution, and one to each state department director; three copies to the University of Washington law library; two copies to the University of Washington library; one to the King county law library; one to the Washington State University library; one to the library of each of the regional universities and to The Evergreen State College; one to the law library of Gonzaga University law school; one to the law library of the University of Puget Sound law

school; one to the law libraries of any accredited law school as hereafter established in this state; and one to each free public library in the state which requests it.

(2) House and senate journals of the preceding regular session during an odd- or even-numbered year, and of any intervening special session, shall be provided for use of legislators in such numbers as directed by the chief clerk of the house of representatives and secretary of the senate; and sufficient sets shall be retained for the use of the state law library.

(3) Surplus sets of the house and senate journals shall be sold and delivered by the state law librarian, in which case the price shall be thirty-five dollars plus postage for those of the regular sessions during an odd- or even-numbered year, and at a price determined by the state printer to cover the cost of paper, printing, binding and postage for those of the special sessions, when separately bound, and the proceeds therefrom shall be paid to the state treasurer for the general fund.

(4) The state law librarian is authorized to exchange copies of the house and senate journals for similar journals of other states, territories, and/or governments, or for other legal materials, and to make such other and further distribution of them as in his judgment seems proper.
[Amended by Laws 1973 ch 33 § 2; Laws 1st Ex Sess 1977 ch 169 § 95; Laws 1980 ch 87 § 13; Laws 1st Ex Sess 1982 ch 32 § 2, effective July 10, 1982.]

40.04.100 Supreme court and court of appeals reports—Distribution, exchange—Duties of law librarian

The supreme court reports and the court of appeals reports shall be distributed by the state law librarian as follows:

(1) Each supreme court justice and court of appeals judge is entitled to receive one copy of each volume containing an opinion signed by him.

(2) The state law librarian shall retain such copies as are necessary of each for the benefit of the state law library, the supreme court and its subsidiary offices; and the court of appeals and its subsidiary offices; he shall provide one copy each for the official use of the attorney general and for each assistant attorney general maintaining his office in the attorney general's suite; three copies for the office of prosecuting attorney, in class A counties; two copies for such office in first class counties, and one copy for each other prosecuting attorney; one for each United States district court room and every superior court room in this state if regularly used by a judge of such courts; one copy for the use of each state department maintaining a separate office at the state capitol; one copy to the office of financial management, and one copy to the division of inheritance tax and escheats; one copy each to the United States supreme court, to the United States district attorney's offices at Seattle and Spokane, to the office of the United States attorney general, the library of the circuit court of appeals of the ninth circuit, the Seattle public library, the Tacoma public library, the Spokane public library, the University of Washington library, and the Washington State University library; three copies to the Library of Congress; and, for educational purposes, twelve copies to the University of Washington law library, two copies to the University of Puget Sound law library, and two copies to the Gonzaga University law school library and to such other accredited law school libraries as are hereafter established in this state; six copies to the King county law library; and one copy to each county law library organized pursuant to law in class AA counties, class A counties and in counties of the first, second and third class.

(3) The state law librarian is likewise authorized to exchange copies of the supreme court reports and the court of appeals reports for similar reports of other states, territories, and/or governments, or for other legal materials, and to make such other and further distribution as in his judgment seems proper.
[Amended by Laws 1973 ch 33 § 3; Laws 1979 ch 151 § 49, effective March 29, 1979.]

40.04.110 ———Purchase from publisher—Duties of supreme court, law librarian. On the publication of each volume of reports the supreme court must purchase for the use of the state, from the publisher to whom the contract is awarded, three hundred copies of each volume of supreme court and court of appeals reports, and such additional copies as the court may deem to be necessary, at the price named in the contract, and deliver the same to the law librarian of the state law library who shall distribute same as required by the provisions of RCW 40.04.100.

Amended by Laws 1971 ch 42 § 4,

STATE PUBLICATIONS DISTRIBUTION CENTER

(Revised Code of Washington Annotated 1982,
s.40.06.010 to 40.06.070.)

40.06.010 Definitions

As used in this chapter:

(1) "Print" includes all forms of reproducing multiple copies, with the exception of typewritten correspondence and interoffice memoranda.

(2) "State agency" includes every state office, officer, department, division, bureau, board, commission and agency of the state, and, where applicable, all subdivisions of each.

(3) "State publication" includes annual, biennial, and special reports, state periodicals and magazines, books, pamphlets, leaflets, and all other materials, other than news releases sent exclusively to the news media, typewritten correspondence and interoffice memoranda, issued in print by the state, the legislature, constitutional officers, or any state department, committee, or other state agency supported wholly or in part by state funds. [Amended by Laws 1st Ex Sess 1977 ch 232 § 8.]

40.06.020 Center created as division of state library—Depository library system—Rules and regulations

There is hereby created as a division of the state library, and under the direction of the state librarian, a state publications distribution center. The center shall utilize the depository library system to permit citizens economical and convenient access to state publications. To this end the state library commission shall make such rules and regulations as may be deemed necessary to carry out the provisions of this chapter. [Amended by Laws 1st Ex Sess 1977 ch 232 § 9.]

40.06.030 Deposits by state agencies—Exemptions

(1) Every state agency shall promptly deposit copies of each of its state publications with the state library in quantities as certified by the state librarian as required to meet the needs of the depository library system. Upon consent of the issuing state agency such state publications as are printed by the public printer shall be delivered directly to the center.

(2) In the interest of economy and efficiency, the state librarian may specifically or by general rule exempt a given state publication or class of publications from the requirements of this section in full or in part. [Amended by Laws 1st Ex Sess 1977 ch 232 § 10.]

40.06.040 Inter-library depository contracts

To provide economical public access to state publications, the center may enter into depository contracts with any free public library, The Evergreen

State College, regional university, or state university library, or, if needed, the library of any privately incorporated college or university in this state. The requirements for eligibility to contract as a depository library shall be established by the state library commission upon recommendations of the state librarian. The standards shall include and take into consideration the type of library, available housing and space for the publications, the number and qualifications of personnel, and availability for public use. The center may also contract with public, out-of-state libraries for the exchange of state and other publications on a reciprocal basis. Any state publication to be distributed to the public and the legislature shall be mailed at the lowest available postal rate.

[Amended by Laws 1st Ex Sess 1977 ch 169 § 96; Laws 1st Ex Sess 1977 ch 232 § 11; Reenacted by Laws 1981 ch 260 § 8, effective May 8, 1981.]

40.06.050 **Center to publish list and other printed matter.** The center shall publish and distribute regularly a list of available state publications, and may publish and distribute such other descriptive printed matter as will facilitate the distribution of state publications. Enacted Laws 1963 ch 233 § 5 p 1215.

40.06.060 **Agencies to furnish lists to center.** Upon request by the center, issuing state agencies shall furnish the center with a complete list of its current state publications and a copy of its mailing and/or exchange lists.

Enacted Laws 1963 ch 233 § 6 p 1215.

40.06.070 **Exemptions.** This chapter shall not apply to nor affect the duties concerning publications distributed by, or officers of:

(1) The state law library;

(2) The statute law committee and the code reviser; and

(3) The secretary of state in connection with his duties under RCW 44.20.030 and 44.20.040. Enacted Laws 1963 ch 233 § 7 p 1215.

INTERSTATE LIBRARY COMPACT

(Revised Code of Washington Annotated, 1982,
s.27.18.010 to 27.18.050.)

27.18.010 Definitions

As used in this chapter, except where the context otherwise requires:

(1) "Compact" means the interstate library compact.

(2) "Public library agency", with reference to this state, means the state library and any county or city library or any regional library, rural county library district library, or intercounty rural library district library.

(3) "State library agency", with reference to this state,

means the commissioners of the state library.

Added by Laws 1965, Ex.Sess., ch. 93, § 1.

27.18.020 Compact enacted—Provisions

The Interstate Library Compact hereby is enacted into law and entered into by this state with all states legally joining therein in the form substantially as follows:

INTERSTATE LIBRARY COMPACT

Article I. Policy and Purpose

Because the desire for the services provided by libraries transcends governmental boundaries and can most effectively be satisfied by giving such services to communities and people regardless of jurisdictional lines, it is the policy of the states party to this compact to cooperate and share their responsibilities; to authorize cooperation and sharing with respect to those types of library facilities and services which can be more economically or efficiently developed and maintained on a cooperative basis; and to authorize cooperation and sharing among localities, states and others in providing joint or cooperative library services in areas where the distribution of population or of existing and potential library resources make the provision of library service on an interstate basis the most effective way of providing adequate and efficient service.

Article II. Definitions

As used in this compact:

(a) "Public library agency" means any unit or agency of local or state government operating or having power to operate a library.

(b) "Private library agency" means any nongovernmental entity which operates or assumes a legal obligation to operate a library.

(c) "Library agreement" means a contract establishing an interstate library district pursuant to this compact or providing for the joint or cooperative furnishing of library services.

Article III. Interstate Library Districts

(a) Any one or more public library agencies in a party state in cooperation with any public library agency or agencies in one or more other party states may establish and maintain an interstate library district. Subject to the provisions of this compact and any other laws of the party states which pursuant hereto remain applicable, such district may establish, maintain and operate some or all of the library facilities and services for the area concerned in accordance with the terms of a library agreement therefor. Any private library agency or agencies within an interstate library district may cooperate therewith, assume duties, responsibilities and obligations thereto, and receive benefits therefrom as provided in any library agreement to which such agency or agencies become party.

(b) Within an interstate library district, and as provided by a library agreement, the performance of library functions may be undertaken on a joint or cooperative basis or may be undertaken by means of one or more arrangements between or among public or private library agencies for the extension of library privileges to the use of facilities or services operated or rendered by one or more of the individual library agencies.

(c) If a library agreement provides for joint establishment, maintenance or operation of library facilities or services by an interstate library district, such district shall have power to do any one or more of the following in accordance with such library agreement:

1. Undertake, administer and participate in programs or arrangements for securing, lending or servicing books and other publications, any other materials suitable to be kept or made available by libraries, library equipment or for the dissemination of information about libraries, the value and significance of particular items therein, and the use thereof.

2. Accept for any of its purposes under this compact any and all donations, and grants of money, equipment, supplies, materials, and services, (conditional or otherwise), from any state or the United States or any subdivision or agency thereof, or interstate agency, or from any institution, person, firm or corporation, and receive, utilize and dispose of the same.

3. Operate mobile library units or equipment for the purpose of rendering bookmobile service within the district.

4. Employ professional, technical, clerical and other personnel, and fix terms of employment, compensation and other appropriate benefits, and where desirable, provide for the inservice training of such personnel.

5. Sue and be sued in any court of competent jurisdiction.

6. Acquire, hold, and dispose of any real or personal property or any interest or interests therein as may be appropriate to the rendering of library service.

7. Construct, maintain and operate a library, including any appropriate branches thereof.

8. Do such other things as may be incidental to or appropriate for the carrying out of any of the foregoing powers.

Article IV. Interstate Library Districts, Governing Board

(a) An interstate library district which establishes, maintains or operates any facilities or services in its own right shall have a governing board which shall direct the affairs of the district and act for it in all matters relating to its business. Each participating public library agency in the district shall be represented on the governing board which shall be organized and conduct its business in accordance with provision therefor in the library agreement. But in no event shall a governing board meet less often than twice a year.

(b) Any private library agency or agencies party to a library agreement establishing an interstate library district may be represented on or advise with the governing board of the district in such manner as the library agreement may provide.

Article V. State Library Agency Cooperation

Any two or more state library agencies of two or more of the party states may undertake and conduct joint or cooperative library programs, render joint or cooperative library services, and enter into and perform arrangements for the cooperative or joint acquisition, use, housing and disposition of items or collections of materials which, by reason of expense, rarity, specialized nature, or infrequency of demand therefor would be appropriate for central collection and shared use. Any such programs, services or arrangements may include provision for the exercise on a cooperative or joint basis of any power exercisable by an interstate library district and an agreement embodying any such program, service or arrangement shall contain provisions covering the subjects detailed in Article VI of this compact for interstate library agreements.

Article VI. Library Agreements

(a) In order to provide for any joint or cooperative undertaking pursuant to this compact, public and private library agencies may enter into library agreements. Any agreement executed pursuant to the provisions of this compact shall, as among the parties to the agreement:

1. Detail the specific nature of the services, programs, facilities, arrangements or properties to which it is applicable.

2. Provide for the allocation of costs and other financial re-

sponsibilities.

3.   Specify the respective rights, duties, obligations and liabilities of the parties.

4.   Set forth the terms and conditions for duration, renewal, termination, abrogation, disposal of joint or common property, if any, and all other matters which may be appropriate to the proper effectuation and performance of the agreement.

(b) No public or private library agency shall undertake to exercise itself, or jointly with any other library agency, by means of a library agreement any power prohibited to such agency by the constitution or statutes of its state.

(c) No library agreement shall become effective until filed with the compact administrator of each state involved, and approved in accordance with Article VII of this compact.

Article VII.   Approval of Library Agreements

(a) Every library agreement made pursuant to this compact shall, prior to and as a condition precedent to its entry into force, be submitted to the attorney general of each state in which a public library agency party thereto is situated, who shall determine whether the agreement is in proper form and compatible with the laws of his state.   The attorneys general shall approve any agreement submitted to them unless they shall find that it does not meet the conditions set forth herein and shall detail in writing addressed to the governing bodies of the public library agencies concerned the specific respects in which the proposed agreement fails to meet the requirements of law. Failure to disapprove an agreement submitted hereunder within ninety days of its submission shall constitute approval thereof.

(b) In the event that a library agreement made pursuant to this compact shall deal in whole or in part with the provision of services or facilities with regard to which an officer or agency of the state government has constitutional or statutory powers of control, the agreement shall, as a condition precedent to its entry into force, be submitted to the state officer or agency having such power of control and shall be approved or disapproved by him or it as to all matters within his or its jurisdiction in the same manner and subject to the same requirements governing the action of the attorneys general pursuant to paragraph (a) of this article.   This requirement of submission and approval shall be in addition to and not in substitution for the requirement of submission to and approval by the attorneys general.

Article VIII.   Other Laws Applicable

Nothing in this compact or in any library agreement shall be construed to supersede, alter or otherwise impair any obligation imposed on any library by otherwise applicable law, nor to authorize the transfer or disposition of any property held in trust by a library agency in a manner contrary to the terms of such trust.

Article IX. Appropriations and Aid

(a) Any public library agency party to a library agreement may appropriate funds to the interstate library district established thereby in the same manner and to the same extent as to a library wholly maintained by it and, subject to the laws of the state in which such public library agency is situated, may pledge its credit in support of an interstate library district established by the agreement.

(b) Subject to the provisions of the library agreement pursuant to which it functions and the laws of the states in which such district is situated, an interstate library district may claim and receive any state and federal aid which may be available to library agencies.

Article X. Compact Administrator

Each state shall designate a compact administrator with whom copies of all library agreements to which his state or any public library agency thereof is party shall be filed. The administrator shall have such other powers as may be conferred upon him by the laws of his state and may consult and cooperate with the compact administrators of other party states and take such steps as may effectuate the purposes of this compact. If the laws of a party state so provide, such state may designate one or more deputy compact administrators in addition to its compact administrator.

Article XI. Entry Into Force and Withdrawal

(a) This compact shall enter into force and effect immediately upon its enactment into law by any two states. Thereafter, it shall enter into force and effect as to any other state upon the enactment thereof by such state.

(b) This compact shall continue in force with respect to a party state and remain binding upon such state until six months after such state has given notice to each other party state of the repeal thereof. Such withdrawal shall not be construed to relieve any party to a library agreement entered into pursuant to this compact from any obligation of that agreement prior to the end of its duration as provided therein.

Article XII.   Construction and Severability

This compact shall be liberally construed so as to effectuate the purposes thereof. The provisions of this compact shall be severable and if any phrase, clause, sentence or provision of this compact is declared to be contrary to the constitution of any party state or of the United States or the applicability thereof to any government, agency, person or circumstance is held invalid, the validity of the remainder of this compact and the applicability thereof to any government, agency, person or circumstance shall not be affected thereby. If this compact shall be held contrary to the constitution of any state party thereto, the compact shall remain in full force and effect as to the remaining states and in full force and effect as to the state affected as to all severable matters.

Added by Laws 1965, Ex.Sess., ch. 93, § 2.

27.18.030   Compact administrator — Deputies — Library agreements, submittal

The state librarian shall be the compact administrator pursuant to Article X of the compact. The state librarian shall appoint one or more deputy compact administrators. Every library agreement made pursuant to Article VI of the compact shall, as a condition precedent to its entry into force, be submitted to the state librarian for his recommendations.

Added by Laws 1965, Ex.Sess., ch. 93, § 3.

27.18.040   Compliance with tax and bonding laws enjoined

No regional library, county library, rural county library district library, intercounty rural library district library, or city library of this state shall be a party to a library agreement which provides for the construction or maintenance of a library pursuant to Article III, subdivision (c–7) of the compact, nor levy a tax or issue bonds to contribute to the construction or maintenance of such a library, except after compliance with any laws applicable to regional libraries, county libraries, rural county library district libraries, intercounty rural library district libraries, or city libraries relating to or governing the levying of taxes or the issuance of bonds.

Added by Laws 1965, Ex.Sess., ch. 93, § 4.

27.18.050   Withdrawal—Compact administrator to send and receive notices

In the event of withdrawal from the compact the compact administrator shall send and receive any notices required by Article XI(b) of the compact.

Added by Laws 1965, Ex.Sess., ch. 93, § 5.

DIVISION OF ARCHIVES AND RECORDS MANAGEMENT

(Revised Code of Washington Annotated, 1982, s.40.14.010 to 40.14.180, 40.10.010, 40.10.020.)

40.14.010 Definition and classification of public records

As used in this chapter, the term "public records" shall include any paper, correspondence, completed form, bound record book, photograph, film, sound recording, map drawing, machine-readable material, or other document, regardless of physical form or characteristics, and including such copies thereof, that have been made by or received by any agency of the state of Washington in connection with the transaction of public business, and legislative records as described in RCW 40.14.100.

For the purposes of this chapter, public records shall be classified as follows:

(1) Official public records shall include all original vouchers, receipts, and other documents necessary to isolate and prove the validity of every transaction relating to the receipt, use, and disposition of all public property and public income from all sources whatsoever; all agreements and contracts to which the state of Washington or any agency thereof may be a party; all fidelity, surety, and performance bonds; all claims filed against the state of Washington or any agency thereof; all records or documents required by law to be filed with or kept by any agency of the state of Washington; all legislative records as defined in RCW 40.14.100; and all other documents or records determined by the records committee, created in RCW 40.14.050, to be official public records.

(2) Office files and memoranda include such records as correspondence, exhibits, drawings, maps, completed forms, or documents not above defined and classified as official public records; duplicate copies of official public records filed with any agency of the state of Washington; documents and reports made for the internal administration of the office to which they pertain but not required by law to be filed or kept with such agency; and other documents or records as determined by the records committee to be office files and memoranda.

[Amended by Laws 1981 ch 32 § 4; Laws 1982 ch 36 § 3.]

40.14.020 Division of archives and records management—State archivist—Powers and duties—Duties of public officials

All public records shall be and remain the property of the state of Washington. They shall be delivered by outgoing officials and employees to their successors and shall be preserved, stored, transferred, destroyed or disposed of, and otherwise managed, only in accordance with the provisions of this chapter. In order to insure the proper management and safeguarding of public records, the division of archives and records management is established in the office of the secretary of state, and, under the administration of the state archivist, who shall have reasonable access to all public records, wherever kept, for purposes of information, surveying, or cataloguing, shall undertake the following functions, duties, and responsibilities:

(1) To manage the archives of the state of Washington;

(2) To centralize the archives of the state of Washington, to make them available for reference and scholarship, and to insure their proper preservation;

(3) To inspect, inventory, catalog, and arrange retention and transfer schedules on all record files of all state departments and other agencies of state government;

(4) To insure the maintenance and security of all state public records and to establish safeguards against unauthorized removal or destruction;

(5) To establish and operate such state record centers as may from time to time be authorized by appropriation, for the purpose of preserving, servicing, screening and protecting all state public records which must be preserved temporarily or permanently, but which need not be retained in office space and equipment;

(6) To gather and disseminate to. interested agencies information on all phases of records management and current practices, methods, procedures and devices for efficient and economical management of records;

(7) To operate a central microfilming bureau which will microfilm, at cost, records approved for filming by the head of the office of origin and the archivist: to approve microfilming projects undertaken by state departments and all other agencies of state government; and to maintain proper standards for this work;

(8) To maintain necessary facilities for the review of records approved for destruction and for their economical disposition by sale or burning; directly to supervise such destruction of public records as shall be authorized by the terms of this chapter.

[Amended by Laws 1981 ch 115 § 1, effective July 1, 1981.]

40.14.025   Division of archives and records management—Schedule of fees and charges—Archives and records management account

The secretary of state and the director of financial management shall jointly establish a schedule of fees and charges governing the services provided by the division of archives and records management to other state agencies, offices, departments, and other entities. The schedule shall be determined such that the fees and charges will provide the division with funds to meet its anticipated expenditures during any allotment period.

There is created the archives and records management account within the general fund, which shall consist of all fees and charges collected under this section. The account shall be appropriated exclusively for use by the secretary of state for the payment of costs and expenses incurred in the operation of the division of archives and records management.

[Added by Laws 1981 ch 115 § 4, effective May 8, 1981.]

40.14.030   Transfer to state archives—Certified copies, cost.

All public records, not required in the current operation of the office where they are made or kept, and all records of every agency, commission, committee, or any other activity of state government which may be abolished or discontinued, shall be transferred to the state archives so that the valuable historical records of the state may be centralized, made more widely available, and insured permanent preservation: *Provided,* That this section shall have no application to public records approved for destruction under the subsequent provisions of this chapter.

When so transferred, copies of the public records concerned shall be made and certified by the archivist, which certification shall have the same force and effect as though made by the officer originally in charge of them. Fees may be charged to cover the cost of reproduction. In turning over the archives of his office, the officer in charge thereof, or his successor, thereby loses none of his rights of access to them, without charge, whenever necessary.   Enacted Laws 1957 ch 246 § 3 p 965

40.14.040   Records officers—Designation—Powers and duties

Each department or other agency of the state government shall designate a records officer to supervise its records program and to represent the office in all contacts with the records committee, hereinafter created, and the division of archives and records management. The records officer shall:
(1) Coordinate all aspects of the records management program.
(2) Inventory, or manage the inventory, of all public records at least once during a biennium for disposition scheduling and transfer action, in accordance with procedures prescribed by the state archivist and state records committee: *Provided*, That essential records shall be inventoried and processed in accordance with chapter 40.10 RCW at least annually.
(3) Consult with any other personnel responsible for maintenance of specific records within his state organization regarding records retention and transfer recommendations.
(4) Analyze records inventory data, examine and compare divisional or unit inventories for duplication of records, and recommend to the state archivist and state records committee minimal retentions for all copies commensurate with legal, financial and administrative needs.
(5) Approve all records inventory and destruction requests which are submitted to the state records committee.
(6) Review established records retention schedules at least annually to insure that they are complete and current.
(7) Exercise internal control over the acquisition of filming and file equipment.
If a particular agency or department does not wish to transfer records at a time previously scheduled therefor, the records officer shall, within thirty days, notify the archivist and request a change in such previously set schedule, including his reasons therefor.
[Amended by Laws 1973 ch 54 § 3; Laws 1979 ch 151 § 51, effective March 29, 1979; Laws 1982 ch 36 § 4.]

40.14.050   Records committee—Composition, travel expenses, meetings, powers and duties—Retention schedules

There is created a committee, to be known as the records committee, composed of the archivist, an appointee of the state auditor, and an appointee of the attorney general. Committee members shall serve without additional salary, but shall be entitled to travel expenses incurred in accordance with RCW 43.03.050 and 43.03.060 as now existing or hereafter amended. Such expenses shall be paid from the appropriations made for operation of their respective departments or offices.

The records committee shall meet at least once every quarter or oftener as business dictates. Action by the committee shall be by majority vote and records shall be kept of all committee business.

It shall be the duty of the records committee to approve, modify or disapprove the recommendations on retention schedules of all files of public records and to act upon requests to destroy any public records: *Provided*, That any modification of a request or recommendation must be approved by the head of the agency originating the request or recommendation.

The division of archives and records management shall provide forms, approved by the records committee, upon which it shall prepare recommendations to the committee in cooperation with the records officer of the department or other agency whose records are involved. [Amended by Laws 2nd Ex Sess 1975–76 ch 34 § 83, effective July 1, 1976.]

40.14.060 Destruction, disposition of official public records or office files and memoranda—Record retention schedules

(1) Any destruction of official public records shall be pursuant to a schedule approved under RCW 40.14.050. Official public records shall not be destroyed unless:

(a) The records are six or more years old;

(b) The department of origin of the records has made a satisfactory showing to the state records committee that the retention of the records for a minimum of six years is both unnecessary and uneconomical, particularly if lesser federal retention periods for records generated by the state under federal programs have been established; or

(c) The originals of official public records less than six years old have been copied or reproduced by any photographic or other process approved by the state archivist which accurately reproduces or forms a durable medium for so reproducing the original.

(2) Any lesser term of retention than six years must have the additional approval of the director of financial management, the state auditor and the attorney general, except when records have federal retention guidelines the state records committee may adjust the retention period accordingly. An automatic reduction of retention periods from seven to six years for official public records on record retention schedules existing on June 10, 1982, shall not be made, but the same shall be reviewed individually by the state records committee for approval or disapproval of the change to a retention period of six years.

Recommendations for the destruction or disposition of office files and memoranda shall be submitted to the records committee upon approved forms prepared by the records officer of the agency concerned and the archivist. The committee shall determine the period of time that any office file or memorandum shall be preserved and may authorize the division of archives and records management to arrange for its destruction or disposition. [Amended by Laws 1973 ch 54 § 4; Laws 1979 ch 151 § 52, effective March 29, 1979; Laws 1982 ch 36 § 5.]

40.14.070 Destruction, disposition of local government records— Preservation for historical interest—Local records committee, duties—Record retention schedules

County, municipal, and other local government agencies may request authority to destroy noncurrent public records having no further administrative or legal value by submitting to the division of archives and records management lists of such records on forms prepared by the division. The archivist and the chief examiner of the division of municipal corporations of the office of the state auditor and a representative appointed by the attorney general shall constitute a committee, known as the local records committee, which shall review such lists and which may veto the destruction of any or all items contained therein.

A local government agency, as an alternative to submitting lists, may elect to establish a records control program based on recurring disposition schedules recommended by the agency to the local records committee. The schedules are to be submitted on forms provided by the division of archives and records management to the local records committee, which may either veto, approve, or amend the schedule. Approval of such schedule or amended schedule shall be by unanimous vote of the local records committee. Upon such approval, the schedule shall constitute authority for the local government agency to destroy the records listed thereon, after the required retention period, on a recurring basis until the schedule is either amended or revised by the committee.

Except as otherwise provided by law, no public records shall be destroyed until approved for destruction by the local records committee. Official public records shall not be destroyed unless:

(1) The records are six or more years old;

(2) The department of origin of the records has made a satisfactory showing to the state records committee that the retention of the records for a minimum of six years is both unnecessary and uneconomical, particularly where lesser federal retention periods for records generated by the state under federal programs have been established; or

(3) The originals of official public records less than six years old have been copied or reproduced by any photographic, photostatic, microfilm, miniature photographic, or other process approved by the state archivist which accurately reproduces or forms a durable medium for so reproducing the original.

An automatic reduction of retention periods from seven to six years for official public records on record retention schedules existing on June 10, 1982, shall not be made, but the same shall be reviewed individually by the local records committee for approval or disapproval of the change to a retention period of six years.

The state archivist may furnish appropriate information, suggestions, and guidelines to local government agencies for their assistance in the preparation of lists and schedules or any other matter relating to the retention, preservation, or destruction of records under this chapter. The local records committee may adopt appropriate regulations establishing procedures to be followed in such matters.

Records of county, municipal, or other local government agencies, designated by the archivist as of primarily historical interest, may be transferred to a recognized depository agency.

[Amended by Laws 1973 ch 54 § 5; Laws 1982 ch 36 § 6.]

40.14.080   Chapter not to affect other laws.

The provisions of this chapter shall not be construed as repealing or modifying any other acts or parts of acts authorizing the destruction of public records save for those specifically named in section 9 of this act; nor shall this chapter affect the provisions of RCW 40.04.020 requiring the deposit of all state publications in the state library.   Enacted Laws 1957 ch 246 § 8 p 968

40.14.100   Legislative records—Defined.

As used in RCW 40.14.010 and 40.14.100 through 40.14.180, unless the context requires otherwise, "legislative records" shall be defined as correspondence, amendments, reports, and minutes of meetings made by or submitted to legislative committees or subcommittees and transcripts or other records of hearings or supplementary written testimony or data thereof filed with committees or subcommittees in connection with the exercise of legislative or investigatory functions, but does not include the records of an official act of the legislature kept by the secretary of state, bills and their copies, published materials, digests, or multi-copied matter which are routinely retained and otherwise available at the state library or in a public repository, or reports or correspondence made or received by or in any way under the personal control of the individual members of the legislature.

Enacted Laws 1st Ex Sess 1971 ch 102 § 2

40.14.110 ———Contribution of papers by legislators and employees. Nothing in RCW 40.14.010 and 40.14.100 through 40.14.180 shall prohibit a legislator or legislative employee from contributing his personal papers to any private library, public library, or the state archives. The state archivist is authorized to receive papers of legislators and legislative employees and is directed to encourage the donation of such personal records to the state. The state archivist is authorized to establish such guidelines and procedures for the collection of personal papers and correspondence relating to the legislature as he sees fit. Legislators and legislative employees are encouraged to contribute their personal papers to the state for preservation.

Enacted Laws 1st Ex Sess 1971 ch 102 § 3

40.14.120 ———"Clerk", "secretary" defined. As used in RCW 40.14.010 and 40.14.100 through 40.14.180 "clerk" means clerk of the Washington state house of representatives and "secretary" means the secretary of the Washington state senate.

Enacted Laws 1st Ex Sess 1971 ch 102 § 4

40.14.130 ———Duties of legislative officials, employees and state archivist—Delivery of records—Custody—Availability. The legislative committee chairman, subcommittee chairman, committee member, or employed personnel of the state legislature having possession of legislative records that are not required for the regular performance of official duties shall, within ten days after the adjournment sine die of a regular or special session, deliver all such legislative records to the clerk of the house or the secretary of the senate.

The clerk of the house and the secretary of the senate are charged to include requirements and responsibilities for keeping committee minutes and records as part of their instructions to committee chairmen and employees.

The clerk or the secretary, with the assistance of the state archivist, shall classify and arrange the legislative records delivered to the clerk or secretary in a manner that he considers best suited to carry out the efficient and economical utilization, maintenance, preservation, and disposition of the records. The clerk or the secretary may deliver to the state archivist all legislative records in his possession when such records have been classified and arranged and are no longer needed by either house. The state archivist shall thereafter be custodian of the records so delivered, but shall deliver such records back to either the clerk or secretary upon his request.

The chairman, member, or employee of a legislative interim committee responsible for maintaining the legislative records of that committee shall, on a scheduled basis agreed upon by the

chairman, member, or employee of the legislative interim committee, deliver to the clerk or secretary all legislative records in
his possession, as long as such records are not required for the
regular performance of official duties. He shall also deliver to
the clerk or secretary all records of an interim committee within
ten days after the committee ceases to function.

Enacted Laws 1st Ex Sess 1971 ch 102 § 5

40.14.140 ———**Party caucuses to be advised—Information and instructions.** It shall be the duty of the clerk and the
secretary to advise the party caucuses in each house concerning
the necessity to keep public records. The state archivist or his
representative shall work with the clerk and secretary to provide information and instructions on the best method for keeping legislative records. Enacted Laws 1st Ex Sess 1971 ch 102 § 6

40.14.150 ———**Use for research.** Committee records
may be used by legislative employees for research at the discretion of the clerk or the secretary.

Enacted Laws 1st Ex Sess 1971 ch 102 § 7

40.14.160 ———**Rules for access to records.** The clerk or
the secretary shall, with advice of the state archivist, prescribe
rules for access to records more than three years old when such
records have been delivered to the state archives for preservation and maintenance. Enacted Laws 1st Ex Sess 1971 ch 102 § 8

40.14.170 ———**Sound recordings.** Any sound recording
of debate in the house or senate made by legislative employees
shall be preserved by the chief clerk of the house and by the secretary of the senate, respectively, for two years from the end of
the session at which made, and thereafter shall be transmitted
to the state archivist. The chief clerk and the secretary shall
catalogue or index the recordings in their custody according to a
uniform system, in order to allow easy access to the debate on
specific questions before either house, and shall make available
to any court of record, at the cost of reproduction, such portions
of the recordings as the court may request.

Enacted Laws 1st Ex Sess 1971 ch 102 § 9

40.14.180 ———**Construction—Confidentiality of bill
drafting records.** The provisions of RCW 40.14.010 and 40.14.100
through 40.14.180 shall not be construed as repealing or modifying any other acts or parts of acts authorizing the retention or
destruction of public records nor shall RCW 40.14.010 and 40.-
14.100 through 40.14.180 affect the provisions of RCW 40.04.020
requiring the deposit of all state publications in the state library
nor shall it affect the confidentiality of the bill drafting records
of the code reviser's office. Enacted Laws 1st Ex Sess 1971 ch 102 § 10

40.10.010 Essential records—Designation—List—Security and protection—Reproduction

In order to provide for the continuity and preservation of civil government, each elected and appointed officer of the state shall designate those public documents which are essential records of his office and needed in an emergency and for the reestablishment of normal operations after any such emergency. A list of such records shall be forwarded to the state archivist on forms prescribed by the state archivist. This list shall be reviewed at least annually by the elected or appointed officer to insure its completeness. Any changes or revisions following this review shall be forwarded to the state archivist. Each such elected and appointed officer of state government shall insure that the security of essential records of his office is by the most economical means commensurate with adequate protection. Protection of essential records may be by vaulting, planned or natural dispersal of copies, or any other method approved by the state archivist. Reproductions of essential records may be by photo copy, magnetic tape, microfilm or other method approved by the state archivist. Local government offices may coordinate the protection of their essential records with the state archivist as necessary to provide continuity of local government under emergency conditions.
[Amended by Laws 1973 ch 54 § 1; Laws 1982 ch 36 § 1.]

40.10.020 Essential records—Reproduction and storage—Coordination of protection program—Fees

The state archivist is authorized to reproduce those documents designated as essential records by the several elected and appointed officials of the state and local government by microfilm or other miniature photographic process and to assist and cooperate in the storage and safeguarding of such reproductions in such place as is recommended by the state archivist with the advice of the director of the department of emergency services. The state archivist shall coordinate the essential records protection program and shall carry out the provisions of the state emergency plan as they relate to the preservation of essential records. The state archivist is authorized to charge the several departments of the state and local government the actual cost incurred in reproducing, storing and safeguarding such documents: *Provided*, That nothing herein shall authorize the destruction of the originals of such documents after reproduction thereof.
[Amended by Laws 1973 ch 54 § 2; Laws 1982 ch 36 § 2.]

PUBLIC LIBRARIES
General Provisions
(Revised Code of Washington Annotated, 1982, s.27.12.010 to 27.12.030, 27.12.180 to 27.12.215, 27.12.240 to 27.12.320.)

27.12.010 Definitions

As used in this act, unless the context requires a different meaning:

(1) "Governmental unit" means any county, city, town, rural county library district or intercounty rural library district;

(2) "Legislative body" means the body authorized to determine the amount of taxes to be levied in a governmental unit; in rural county library districts and in intercounty rural library districts the legislative body shall be the board of library trustees of the district;

(3) "Library" means a free public library supported in whole or in part with money derived from taxation; and

(4) "Regional library" means a free public library maintained by two or more counties or other governmental units as provided in RCW 27.12.080; and

(5) "Rural county library district" means a library serving all the area of a county not included within the area of incorporated cities and towns: *Provided*, That any city or town with a population of one hundred thousand or less at the time of annexation may be included therein as provided in RCW 27.12.360 through 27.12.390; and

(6) "Intercounty rural library district" means a municipal corporation organized to provide library service for all areas outside of incorporated cities and towns within two or more counties: *Provided*, That any city or town with a population of one hundred thousand or less at the time of annexation may be included therein as provided in RCW 27.12.360 through 27.12.-390.

Enacted by Laws 1935, ch. 119, § 2. Amended by Laws 1941, ch. 65, § 1; Laws 1947, ch. 75, § 10; Laws 1965, ch. 122, § 1; Laws 1977, Ex. Sess., ch. 353, § 5; Laws 1981, ch. 26, § 1, eff. April 17, 1981.

27.12.020 Policy of state

It is hereby declared to be the policy of the state, as a part of its provision for public education, to promote the establishment and development of public library service throughout its various subdivisions.

Enacted by Laws 1935, ch. 119, § 1.

27.12.025 Authorization

Any governmental unit has power to establish and maintain a library, either by itself or in cooperation with one or more other governmental units.

Enacted by Laws 1935, ch. 119, § 3. Amended by Laws 1941, ch. 65, § 2.

27.12.030 Libraries, how established

A library may be established in any county, city, or town either (1) by its legislative body of its own initiative; or (2) upon the petition of one hundred taxpayers of such a governmental unit, the legislative body shall submit to a vote of the qualified electors thereof, at the next municipal or special election held therein (in the case of a city or town) or the next general election or special election held therein (in the case of a county), the question whether a library shall be established; and if a majority of the electors voting on the question vote in favor of the establishment of a library, the legislative body shall forthwith establish one.

Enacted by Laws 1935, ch. 119, § 4. Amended by Laws 1941, ch. 65, § 3; Laws 1965, ch. 122, § 2.

27.12.180   Contracts for library service

Instead of establishing or maintaining an independent library, the legislative body of any governmental unit authorized to maintain a library shall have power to contract to receive library service from an existing library, the board of trustees of which shall have reciprocal power to contract to render the service with the consent of the legislative body of its governmental unit. Such a contract shall require that the existing library perform all the functions of a library within the governmental unit wanting service. In like manner a legislative body may contract for library service from a library not owned by a public corporation but maintained for free public use: *Provided*, That such a library be subject to inspection by the state librarian and be certified by him as maintaining a proper standard. Any school district may contract for school library service from any existing library, such service to be paid for from funds available to the school district for library purposes.

Enacted by Laws 1935, ch. 119, § 7. Amended by Laws 1941, ch. 65, § 6.

27.12.190   Library trustees—Appointment, election, removal, compensation

The management and control of a library shall be vested in a board of either five or seven trustees as hereinafter in this section provided. In cities and towns five trustees shall be appointed by the mayor with the consent of the legislative body. In counties and rural county library districts five trustees shall be appointed by the board of county commissioners. In a regional library district a board of either five or seven trustees shall be appointed by the joint action of the legislative bodies concerned. In intercounty rural library districts a board of either five or seven trustees shall be appointed by the joint action of the boards of county commissioners of each of the counties included in a district. The first appointments for boards comprised of but five trustees shall be for terms of one, two, three, four, and five years respectively, and thereafter a trustee shall be appointed annually to serve for five years. The first appointments for boards comprised of seven trustees shall be for terms of one, two, three, four, five, six, and seven years respectively, and thereafter a trustee shall be appointed annually to serve for seven years. No person shall be appointed to any board of trustees for more than two consecutive terms. Vacancies shall be filled for unexpired terms as soon as possible in the manner in which members of the board are regularly chosen. A library trustee shall not receive a salary or other compensation for services as trustee, but necessary expenses actually incurred shall be paid from the library funds. A library trustee in the case of a city or town may be removed only by vote of the legislative body. A trustee of a county library or a rural county library district library may be removed for just cause by the county commissioners after a public hearing upon a written complaint stating the ground for removal, which complaint, with a notice of the time and place of hearing, shall have been served upon the trustee at least fifteen days before the hearing. A trustee of an intercounty rural library district may be removed by the joint action of the board of county commissioners of the counties involved in the same manner as provided herein for the removal of a trustee of a county library.

Enacted by Laws 1935, ch. 119, § 8. Amended by Laws 1939, ch. 108, § 1; Laws 1941, ch. 65, § 7; Laws 1947, ch. 75, § 12; Laws 1959, ch. 133, § 2; Laws 1965, ch. 122, § 3; Laws 1981, ch. 26, § 2, eff. April 17, 1981.

27.12.210 Library trustees—Organization—Bylaws—Powers and duties

The trustees, immediately after their appointment or election, shall meet and organize by the election of such officers as they deem necessary. They shall:

(1) Adopt such bylaws, rules, and regulations for their own guidance and for the government of the library as they deem expedient;

(2) Have the supervision, care, and custody of all property of the library, including the rooms or buildings constructed, leased, or set apart therefor;

(3) Employ a librarian, and upon his recommendation employ such other assistants as may be necessary, all in accordance with the provisions of RCW 27.08.010, prescribe their duties, fix their compensation, and remove them for cause;

(4) Submit annually to the legislative body a budget contain-

ing estimates in detail of the amount of money necessary for the library for the ensuing year; except that in a rural county library district the board of library trustees shall prepare its budget, certify the same and deliver it to the board of county commissioners in ample time for it to make the tax levies for the purpose of the district;

(5) Have exclusive control of the finances of the library;

(6) Accept such gifts of money or property for library purposes as they deem expedient;

(7) Lease or purchase land for library buildings;

(8) Lease, purchase, or erect an appropriate building or buildings for library purposes, and acquire such other property as may be needed therefor;

(9) Purchase books, periodicals, maps, and supplies for the library; and

(10) Do all other acts necessary for the orderly and efficient management and control of the library.

Enacted by Laws 1935, ch. 119, § 9. Amended by Laws 1941, ch. 65, § 8.

27.12.215 Job recruitment expenditures authorized

The trustees of a library or a library district have the authority to spend funds to recruit job candidates. The trustees have the authority to reimburse job candidates for reasonable and necessary travel expenses including transportation, subsistence, and lodging.

Added by Laws 1979, Ex.Sess., ch. 40, § 1.

27.12.240 Annual appropriations—Control of expenditures

After a library shall have been established or library service contracted for, the legislative body of the governmental unit for which the library was established or the service engaged, shall appropriate money annually for the support of the library. All funds for the library, whether derived from taxation or otherwise, shall be in the custody of the treasurer of the governmental unit, and shall be designated by him in some manner for identification, and shall not be used for any but library purposes. The board of trustees shall have the exclusive control of expenditures for library purposes subject to any examination of accounts required by the state and money shall be paid for library purposes only upon vouchers of the board of trustees, without further audit. The board shall not make expenditures or incur indebtedness in any year in excess of the amount of money appropriated and/or available for library purposes.

Enacted by Laws 1935, ch. 119, § 10. Amended by Laws 1939, ch. 108, § 3; Laws 1941, ch. 65, § 9; Laws 1965, ch. 122, § 4.

27.12.260   Annual report of trustees

At the close of each year the board of trustees of every library shall make a report to the legislative body of the governmental unit wherein the board serves, showing the condition of their trust during the year, the sums of money received for the library fund from taxes and other sources, the sums of money expended and the purposes of the expenditures, the number of books and periodicals on hand, the number added during the year, the number retired, the number loaned out, and such other statistics and information and such suggestions as they deem of public interest. A copy of this report shall be filed with the state librarian.

Enacted by Laws 1935, ch. 119, § 12.

27.12.270   Rules and regulations—Free use of libraries

Every library established or maintained under this act shall be free for the use of the inhabitants of the governmental unit in which it is located, subject to such reasonable rules and regulations as the trustees find necessary to assure the greatest benefit to the greatest number, except that the trustees may charge a reasonable fee for the use of certain duplicate copies of popular books.

Enacted by Laws 1935, ch. 119, § 13.

27.12.280   Use by nonresidents—Exchange of books

The board of trustees of a library, under such rules and regulations as it may deem necessary and upon such terms and conditions as may be agreed upon, may allow nonresidents of the governmental unit in which the library is situated to use the books thereof, and may make exchanges of books with any other library, either permanently or temporarily.

Enacted by Laws 1935, ch. 119, § 14.

27.12.285   Library services for Indian tribes

The legislature finds that it is necessary to give the several boards of library trustees in this state additional powers in order to effectuate the state's policy with regard to libraries as set forth in RCW 27.12.020. On and after March 27, 1975 the board of library trustees in any county of this state, in addition to any other powers and duties, is hereby authorized to provide library services to Indian tribes recognized as such by the federal government or to supplement any existing library services of such an Indian tribe. The power granted by this section shall extend beyond the geographic limits of the library district and the county or counties in which the district is located.

Added by Laws 1975, ch. 50, § 1, eff. March 27, 1975.

27.12.290 Violators may be excluded

A board of library trustees may exclude from the use of the library under its charge any person who wilfully and persistently violates any rule or regulation prescribed for the use of the library or its facilities or any person whose physical condition is deemed dangerous or offensive to other library users.

Enacted by Laws 1935, ch. 119, § 15.

27.12.300 Gifts—Title to property

The title to money or property given to or for the use or benefit of a library shall vest in the board of trustees, to be held and used according to the terms of the gift.

Enacted by Laws 1935, ch. 119, § 18.

27.12.305 Sale of library materials authorized—Disposition of proceeds

Any public library, including the state library created pursuant to chapter 27.04 RCW, shall have the authority to provide for the sale of library materials developed by the library staff for its use but which are of value to others such as book catalogs, books published by the library, indexes, films, slides, book lists, and similar materials.

The library commission, board of library trustees, or other governing authority charged with the direct control of a public library shall determine the prices and quantities of materials to be prepared and offered for sale. Prices shall be limited to the publishing and preparation costs, exclusive of staff salaries and overhead. Any moneys received from the sales of such materials shall be placed in the appropriate library fund.

Nothing in this section shall be construed to authorize any library to charge any resident for a library service nor to authorize any library to sell materials to a branch library or library which is part of a depository library system when such materials may be distributed free of cost to such library nor shall this section be construed to prevent, curtail, or inhibit any free distribution programs or exchange programs between libraries or between libraries and other agencies.

Added by Laws 1972, Ex.Sess., ch. 90, § 1.

27.12.310   Charter provisions superseded

Every existing free public library shall be considered as if established under this act , and the board of trustees and the legislative body of the governmental unit in which the library is located shall proceed forthwith to make such changes as may be necessary to effect compliance with the terms hereof; and every existing contract for library service shall continue in force and be subject to this act until the contract be terminated or a library be established by the governmental unit for which the service was engaged. The provisions of this act shall be construed as superseding the provisions of any municipal charter in conflict herewith.

Enacted by Laws 1935, ch. 119, § 19.

27.12.320   Dissolution—Disposition of property

A library established or maintained under this act (except a regional or a rural county library district library or an intercounty rural library district library) may be abolished only in pursuance of a vote of the electors of the governmental unit in which the library is located, taken in the manner prescribed in RCW 27.12.030 for a vote upon the establishment of a library. If a library of a city or town be abolished, the books and other printed or written matter belonging to it shall go to the library of the county whereof the municipality is a part, if there be a county library, but if not, then to the state library. If a library of a county or region be abolished, the books and other printed matter belonging to it shall go to the state library. All other library property shall be disposed of as the legislative body of the governmental unit shall direct.

After a rural county library district or an intercounty rural library district has been in operation for three or more years, it may be dissolved pursuant to a majority vote of all of the qualified electors residing outside of incorporated cities and towns voting upon a proposition for its dissolution, at a general election, which proposition may be placed upon the ballot at any such election whenever a petition by ten percent or more qualified voters residing outside of incorporated cities or towns within a rural county library district or an intercounty rural library district requesting such dissolution shall be filed with the board of trustees of such district not less than ninety days prior to the holding of any such election. If a rural county library district is dissolved, the books and other printed matter belonging to it shall go to the state library. All other library property shall be disposed of as the legislative body of the governmental unit shall direct. When an intercounty rural library district is dissolved, the books, funds and other property thereof shall be divided among the participating counties in the most equitable manner possible as determined by the state librarian, who shall give consideration to such items as the original source of property, the amount of funds raised from each county by the district, and the ability of the counties to make further use of such property or equipment for library purposes. Printed material which the state librarian finds will not be used by any of the participating counties for further library purposes shall be turned over to the state library.

Enacted by Laws 1935, ch. 119, § 20. Amended by Laws 1947, ch. 75, § 13; Laws 1965, ch. 122, § 5.

REGIONAL LIBRARIES
(Revised Code of Washington Annotated, 1982, s.27.12.080.)

27.12.080   Regional libraries

Two or more counties, or other governmental units, by action of their legislative bodies, may join in establishing and maintaining a regional library under the terms of a contract to which all will agree. The expenses of the regional library shall be apportioned between or among the contracting parties concerned on such basis as shall be agreed upon in the contract. The treasurer of one of the governmental units, as shall be provided in the contract, shall have the custody of the funds of the regional library; and the treasurers of the other governmental units concerned shall transfer quarterly to him all moneys collected for free public library purposes in their respective governmental units. If the legislative body of any governmental unit decides to withdraw from a regional library contract, the governmental unit withdrawing shall be entitled to a division of the property on the basis of its contributions.

Enacted by Laws 1935, ch. 119, § 5. Amended by Laws 1941, ch. 65, § 5.

LIBRARY DISTRICTS
Intercounty Rural Library Districts
(Revised Code of Washington Annotated, 1982, s.27.12.090 to
27.12.170.)

27.12.090   Intercounty rural library districts—Establishment—Procedure

Intercounty rural library districts may be established to provide throughout several counties free public library service similar to that provided within a single county by a rural county library district.

Enacted by Laws 1947, ch. 75, § 1.

27.12.100   Intercounty rural library districts—Establishment—Procedure

An intercounty rural library district shall be established by joint action of two or more counties proceeding by either of the following alternative methods:

(1) The boards of county commissioners of any two or more counties shall adopt identical resolutions proposing the formation of such a district to include all of the areas outside of incorporated cities or towns in such counties as may be designated in such resolutions. In lieu of such resolutions a petition of like purport signed by ten percent of the registered voters residing outside of incorporated cities or towns of a county, may be filed with the county auditor thereof, and shall have the same effect as a resolution. The proposition for the formation of the district as stated on the petition shall be prepared by the attorney general upon request of the state library commission. Action to initiate the formation of such a district shall become ineffective in any county if corresponding action is not completed within one year thereafter by each other county included in such proposal. The county auditor in each county shall check the validity of the signatures on the petition and shall certify to the board of county commissioners the sufficiency of the signatures. If each petition contains the signatures of ten percent of the registered voters residing outside the incorporated cities and towns of the county, each board of county commissioners shall pass a resolution calling an election for the purpose of submitting the question to the voters and setting the date of said election. When such action has been taken in each of the counties involved, notification shall be made by each board of county commissioners to the board of county commissioners of the county having the largest population according to the last federal cen-

sus, who shall give proper notification to each county auditor. At the next general or special election held in the respective counties there shall be submitted to the voters in the areas outside of incorporated cities and towns a question as to whether an intercounty rural library district shall be established as outlined in the resolutions or petitions. Notice of said election shall be given the county auditor pursuant to RCW 29.27.080. The county auditor shall provide for the printing of a separate ballot and shall provide for the distribution of ballots to the polling places pursuant to RCW 29.04.020. The county auditor shall instruct the election boards in split precincts. The respective county canvassing boards in each county to be included within the intercounty rural library district shall canvass the votes and certify the results to the county auditor pursuant to chapter 29.62; the result shall then be certified by each county auditor to the county auditor of the county having the largest population according to the last federal census. If a majority of the electors voting on the proposition in each of the counties affected shall vote in favor of such district it shall thereby become established, and the board of county commissioners of the county having the largest population according to the last federal census shall declare the intercounty rural library district established. If two or more of the counties affected are in an existing intercounty rural library district, then the electors in areas outside incorporated cities and towns in those counties shall vote as a unit and the electors in areas outside incorporated cities and towns in each of the other affected counties shall vote as separate units. If a majority of the electors voting on the proposition in the existing district and a majority of the voters in any of the other affected counties shall vote in favor of an expanded intercounty rural library district it shall thereby become established.

(2) The county commissioners of two or more counties meeting in joint session attended by a majority of the county commissioners of each county may, by majority vote of those present, order the establishment of an intercounty rural library district to include all of the area outside of incorporated cities and towns in as many of the counties represented at such joint meeting as shall be determined by resolution of such joint meeting. If two or more counties are in an existing intercounty rural library district, then a majority vote of all of the commissioners present from those counties voting as a unit, and a majority vote of the commissioners present from any other county shall cause the joint session to order the establishment of an expanded intercounty rural library district. No county, however,

shall be included in such district if a majority of its county commissioners vote against its inclusion in such district.

Enacted by Laws 1947, ch. 75, § 2. Amended by Laws 1961, ch. 82, § 1; Laws 1965, ch. 63, § 1.

27.12.110 Intercounty rural library districts—Expansion of existing districts

An existing rural county library district may be expanded into an intercounty rural library district or an established intercounty rural library district may be expanded to include additional counties by joint action of all counties included in the proposed expanded district taken in the same manner as prescribed for the initiation of an intercounty rural library district.

Enacted by Laws 1947, ch. 75, § 3.

27.12.120 Intercounty rural library districts—Assumption of property, assets, liabilities

All property, assets and liabilities of preexisting library districts within the area included in an intercounty rural library district shall pass to and be assumed by an intercounty rural library district: *Provided,* That where within any intercounty rural library district heretofore or hereafter organized under the provisions of this chapter a preexisting library district had incurred a bonded indebtedness which was outstanding at the time of the formation of the intercounty rural library district, such preexisting library district shall retain its corporate existence insofar as is necessary for the purpose until the bonded indebtedness outstanding against it on and after the effective date of said formation has been paid in full: *Provided further,* That a special election may be called by the board of trustees of the intercounty rural library district, to be held at the next general or special election held in the respective counties for the purpose of affording the voters residing within the area outside of the preexisting library district an opportunity to assume the obligation of the bonded indebtedness of the preexisting library district or the question may be submitted to the voters as a separate proposition at the election on the proposal for the formation of the intercounty rural library district.

Enacted by Laws 1947, ch. 75, § 4. Amended by Laws 1961, ch. 82, § 2.

27.12.130 Intercounty rural library districts—Board of trustees

Immediately following the establishment of an intercounty rural library district the boards of county commissioners of the counties affected shall jointly appoint a board of five or seven trustees for the district in accordance with RCW 27.12.190. The board of trustees shall appoint a librarian for the district.

Enacted by Laws 1947, ch. 75, § 5. Amended by Laws 1959, ch. 133, § 1.

27.12.140 Intercounty rural library districts—Name may be adopted

The board of trustees of an intercounty rural library district may adopt a name by which the district shall be known and under which it shall transact all of its business.

Enacted by Laws 1947, ch. 75, § 6.

27.12.150 Intercounty rural library districts—Tax levies

Funds for the establishment and maintenance of the library service of the district shall be provided by the boards of county commissioners of the respective counties by means of an annual tax levy on the property in the district of not more than fifty cents per thousand dollars of assessed value per year. The tax levy in the several counties shall be at a uniform rate and shall be based on a budget to be compiled by the board of trustees of the intercounty rural library district who shall determine the uniform tax rate necessary and certify their determination to the respective boards of county commissioners.

Excess levies authorized pursuant to RCW 27.12.222 and RCW 84.52.052 or 84.52.056 shall be at a uniform rate which uniform rate shall be determined by the board of trustees of the intercounty rural library district and certified to the respective boards of county commissioners.

Enacted by Laws 1947, ch. 75, § 7. Amended by Laws 1955, ch. 59, § 8; Laws 1973, 1st Ex.Sess., ch. 195, § 7, eff. Jan. 1, 1974.

27.12.160 Intercounty rural library districts—District treasurer

The board of trustees of an intercounty rural library district shall designate the county treasurer of one of the counties included in the district to act as treasurer for the district. All moneys raised for the district by taxation within the participating counties or received by the district from any other sources shall be paid over to him, and he shall disburse the funds of the district upon warrants drawn thereon by the auditor of the county to which he belongs pursuant to vouchers approved by the trustees of the district. Enacted by Laws 1947, ch. 75, § 8.

27.12.170 Intercounty rural library districts—Powers of board—Procedures

Except as otherwise specifically provided intercounty rural library districts and the trustees thereof shall have the same powers as are prescribed by RCW 27.12.040 through 27.12.070, for rural county library districts and shall follow the same procedures and be subject to the same limitations as are provided therein with respect to the contracting of indebtedness.

Enacted by Laws 1947, ch. 75, § 9.

Rural County Library Districts
(Revised Code of Washington Annotated, 1982, s.27.12.040 to 27.12.070.)

27.12.040 Rural library districts—Establishment

The procedure for the establishment of a rural county library district shall be as follows:

(1) Petitions signed by at least ten percent of the registered voters of the county, outside of the area of incorporated cities and towns, asking that the question, "Shall a rural county library district be established?" be submitted to a vote of the people, shall be filed with the board of county commissioners.

(2) The board of county commissioners, after having determined that the petitions were signed by the requisite number of qualified petitioners, shall place the proposition for the establishment of a rural county library district on the ballot for the vote of the people of the county, outside incorporated cities and towns, at the next succeeding general or special election.

(3) If a majority of those voting on the proposition vote in favor of the establishment of the rural county library district, the board of county commissioners shall forthwith declare it established.

Added by Laws 1955, ch. 59, § 4.

27.12.050 Rural library districts—Board of library trustees—Tax levies

After the board of county commissioners has declared a rural county library district established, it shall appoint a board of library trustees and provide funds for the establishment and maintenance of library service for the district by making a tax levy on the property in the district of not more than fifty cents per thousand dollars of assessed value per year sufficient for the library service as shown to be required by the budget submitted to the board of county commissioners by the board of library trustees, and by making a tax levy in such further amount as shall be authorized pursuant to RCW 27.12.222 or RCW 84.52.052 or 84.52.056. Such levies shall be a part of the general tax roll and shall be collected as a part of the general taxes against the property in the district.

Added by Laws 1955, ch. 59, § 5. Amended by Laws 1973, 1st Ex. Sess., ch. 195, § 5, eff. Jan. 1, 1974.

27.12.060 Rural library districts—Indebtedness—Coupon warrants

The board of library trustees of this district may contract indebtedness, and evidence it by issuing and selling, at par plus accrued interest, coupon warrants of the district in such form as the board of library trustees shall determine. Such warrants may be issued in advance of the tax levy. Such warrants, signed by the chairman and the secretary of the board of library trustees, shall be payable at such times as the board of library trustees shall provide not longer than six years from the date thereof.

The warrants shall be payable to bearer and shall have interest coupons attached providing for the payment of interest semiannually on the first day of January and of July. At the option of the district board, the aggregate amount of coupon warrants may include a sum sufficient to pay the annual interest for a period not exceeding one year from the issuing date of the coupon warrants and, in that event, such interest shall be taken from the proceeds of the sale of the coupon warrants and immediately placed in the coupon warrant fund of the district for payment of the interest coupons maturing during the first year of the coupon warrants. The issuance thereof shall be recorded in the office of the county treasurer in a book kept for that purpose. All district warrants of every kind shall outlaw and become void after six years from their maturity date but only if there is money in the proper fund available for their payment within such period.

A rural county library district shall be a public corporation with such powers as are necessary to carry out its functions and for taxation purposes shall have the power vested in municipal corporations for such purposes.

Added by Laws 1955, ch. 59, § 6. Amended by Laws 1980, ch. 100, § 1, eff. March 10, 1980.

27.12.070 Rural library districts—Limitation of indebtedness

At no time shall the total indebtedness of the district exceed an amount that could be raised by a one dollar per thousand dollars of assessed value levy on the then existing value of the taxable property of the district, as the term "value of the taxable property" as defined in RCW 39.36.015, except as provided in RCW 27.12.222 or RCW 84.52.052 or 84.52.056. The county treasurer of the county in which any rural county library district is created shall receive and disburse all district revenues and collect all taxes levied under this chapter.

Added by Laws 1955, ch. 59, § 7. Amended by Laws 1970, Ex.Sess., ch. 42, § 2, eff. Nov. 1, 1970; Laws 1973, 1st Ex.Sess., ch. 195, § 6, eff. Jan 1, 1974.

Capital Outlays and Bonds
(Revised Code of Washington Annotated, 1982, s.27.12.220, 27.12.222, 27.12.223, 84.52.052, 84.52.054, 84.52.063.)

27.12.220 Rural and intercounty districts—Budget for capital outlays—Accumulation of funds

The trustees of any rural county library district or any intercounty rural library district may include in the annual budget of such district an item for the accumulation during such year of a specified sum of money to be expended in a future year for the acquisition, enlargement or improvement of real or personal property for library purposes.

Enacted by Laws 1947, ch. 22, § 1.

27.12.222 Rural and intercounty districts—Bonds—Excess levies

In addition to the indebtedness authorized by RCW 27.12.150 and 27.12.070, rural county library districts and intercounty rural library districts may incur indebtedness for capital purposes to the full extent permitted by the Constitution and may issue general obligation bonds to pay therefor not to exceed an amount equal to one-half of one percent of the value of the taxable property within the district, as the term "value of the taxable property" is defined in RCW 39.36.015. Any such indebtedness shall be authorized by resolution of the board of library trustees, and the board of library trustees shall submit the question to the qualified electors of the district for their ratification or rejection whether or not such indebtedness shall be incurred and such bonds issued. Such proposition to be effective must be authorized by an affirmative vote of three-fifths of the electors within the district voting at a general or special election to be held for the purpose of authorizing such indebtedness and bond issue at which election the number of persons voting on the proposition shall constitute not less than forty percent of the total number of votes cast in such taxing district at the last preceding general election. If the voters shall so authorize, the district may levy annual taxes in excess of normal legal limitations to pay the principal and interest upon such bonds as they shall become due. The excess levies mentioned in this section or in RCW 84.52.052 or 84.52.056 may be made notwithstanding anything contained in RCW 27.12.050, 27.12.070 or 27.12.150 or any other statute pertaining to such library districts.

Added by Laws 1955, ch. 59, § 1. Amended by Laws 1970, Ex.Sess., ch. 42, § 3.

27.12.223　Bonds—Form—Sale—Security for deposit

Bonds authorized by RCW 27.12.222 shall be serial in form and maturity and numbered from one upward consecutively. Only bond No. 1 of any issue shall be of a denomination other than a multiple of one hundred dollars. The resolution authorizing the issuance of the bonds shall fix the rate of interest the bonds shall bear, and the place and date of payment of principal and interest. The bonds shall be signed by the chairman of the board of library trustees and attested by the secretary. Coupons in lieu of being signed may bear the facsimile signature of such officers. Bonds shall be sold in such manner as the board of library trustees deems for the best interests of the district. All such bonds shall be legal securities for any bank or trust company for deposit with the state treasurer or any county or city treasurer as security for deposits in lieu of a surety bond under any law relating to deposits of public moneys.

Added by Laws 1955, ch. 59, § 2. Amended by Laws 1969, Ex.Sess., ch. 232, § 4, eff. April 25, 1969; Laws 1970, Ex.Sess., ch. 56, § 6, eff. Feb. 23, 1970.

84.52.052　Excess levies authorized—When—Procedure

Text of section as amended by Laws 1982 ch. 123 § 19.

The limitations imposed by RCW 84.52.050 through 84.52.056, and RCW 84.52.043 shall not prevent the levy of additional taxes by any taxing district except school districts in which a larger levy is necessary in order to prevent the impairment of the obligation of contracts. Any county, metropolitan park district, park and recreation service area, park and recreation district, sewer district, water district, public hospital district, road district, rural county library district, island library district, intercounty rural library district, fire protection district, cemetery district, city, or town may levy taxes at a rate in excess of the rate specified in RCW 84.52.050 through 84.52.056 and RCW 84.52.043, or RCW 84.55.010 through 84.55.050, when authorized so to do by the electors of such county, metropolitan park district, park and recreation service area, park and recreation district, sewer district, water district, public hospital district, road district, rural county library district, island library district, intercounty rural library district, fire protection district, cemetery district, city, or town in the manner set forth in Article VII, Section 2(a) of the Constitution of this state, as amended by Amendment 64 and as thereafter amended, at a special or general election to be held in the year in which the levy is made.

A special election may be called and the time therefor fixed by the county legislative authority, or council, board of commissioners, or other governing body of any metropolitan park district, park and recreation service area, park and recreation district, sewer district, water district, public hospital district, road district, rural county library district, island library district, intercounty rural library district, fire protection district, cemetery district, city or town, by giving notice thereof by publication in the manner provided by law for giving notices of general elections, at which special election the proposition authorizing such excess levy shall be submitted in such form as to enable the voters favoring the proposition to vote "yes" and those opposed thereto to vote "no".
[Amended by Laws 1982 ch 123 § 19.]

84.52.054 Excess levies—Ballot contents—Eventual millage on tax rolls.

The additional tax provided for in subparagraph (a) of the seventeenth amendment to the state Constitution and specifically authorized by RCW 84.52.052 shall be set forth in terms of dollars on the ballot of the proposition to be submitted to the voters, together with an estimate of the millage that will be required to produce the dollar amount; and the county assessor, in spreading this tax upon the rolls, shall determine the eventual millage rate required to produce the amount of dollars so voted upon, regardless of the estimate of millage carried in said proposition.

Enacted Laws 1961 ch 15

84.52.063 Rural library district levies

A rural library district may impose a regular property tax levy in an amount equal to that which would be produced by a levy of fifty cents per thousand dollars of assessed value multiplied by an assessed valuation equal to one hundred percent of the true and fair value of the taxable property in the rural library district, as determined by the department of revenue's indicated county ratio: *Provided*, That when any county assessor shall find that the aggregate rate of levy on any property will exceed the limitation set forth in RCW 84.52.043 and RCW 84.52.050, as now or hereafter amended, before recomputing and establishing a consolidated levy in the manner set forth in RCW 84.52.010, the assessor shall first reduce the levy of any rural library district, by such amount as may be necessary, but the levy of any rural library district shall not be reduced to less than fifty cents per thousand dollars against the value of the taxable property, as determined by the county, prior to any further adjustments pursuant to RCW 84.52.010. For purposes of this section "regular property tax levy" shall mean a levy subject to the limitations provided for in Article VII, section 2 of the state Constitution and/or by statute. [Added by Laws 1st

Ex Sess 1970 ch 92 § 9, effective July 1, 1970; Amended by Laws 1st Ex Sess 1973 ch 195 § 150, effective April 25, 1973; Laws 1st Ex Sess 1973 ch 195 § 105, effective January 1, 1974.]

Local Improvement Districts

(Revised Code of Washington Annotated, 1982, s.27.14.010 to 27.14.050.)

27.14.010   Definitions

As used in this chapter:

"Library district" means a rural county library district, or intercounty rural library district.

Added by Laws 1961, ch. 162, § 1.

27.14.015   "Owner", "reputed owner"—Sufficiency of signatures

Whenever the terms "owner" or "reputed owner" of property are used in this chapter, such terms shall include the following:

(1) The signature of a record owner, as determined by the records of the county auditor, shall be sufficient without the signature of his or her spouse.

(2) In the case of mortgaged property, the signature of the mortgagor shall be sufficient.

(3) In the case of property purchased on contract, the signature of the contract purchaser, as shown by the records of the county auditor, shall be deemed sufficient.

(4) Any officer of a corporation owning land in the district duly authorized to execute deeds or encumbrances on behalf of the corporation may sign on behalf of such corporation, provided that there shall be attached to the petition a certified excerpt from the bylaws showing such authority.

(5) If any property in the district stands in the name of a deceased person or any person for whom a guardian has been appointed the signature of the executor, administrator or guardian, as the case may be, shall be equivalent to the signature of the owner of the property.

Added by Laws 1963, ch. 80, § 5.

27.14.020   Petition or resolution method authorized—Procedure—Assessments

In any instance where the acquisition of land, buildings or capital equipment, or the construction of library buildings are of special benefit to part or all of the lands in the district, the governing board of the library district shall have authority to include such lands in a local improvement district, and to levy special assessments under a mode of annual installments extending over a period not exceeding twenty years on all property specially benefited by any local improvement, on the basis of the special benefits to pay in whole or in part the damages or costs of any such improvements ordered in such library district. For the purposes of this chapter, the duties devolving upon the city treasurer under said laws are imposed upon the county treasurer serving the library district. Such local improvement districts may be initiated either by resolution of the governing board of the library district or by petition signed by the owners, according to the records of the office of the county auditor, of at least fifty-one percent of the area of the land within the local improvement district to be created excluding all federally owned or other nonassessable property.

In case the governing board of the library district shall desire to initiate the formation of a local improvement district by resolution, it shall first pass a resolution declaring its intention to order such improvement, setting forth the nature and territorial extent of such proposed improvement, designating the number of the proposed district, describing the boundaries thereof, stating the estimated cost and expenses of the improvement and the proportionate amount thereof which will be borne by the property within the proposed district, and fixing a date, time and place for a public hearing on the formation of the proposed district.

In case any such local improvement district shall be initiated by petition, such petition shall set forth the nature and territorial extent of such proposed improvement and the fact that the signers thereof are the owners according to the records of the county auditor of at least fifty-one percent of the area of land within the limits of the local improvement district to be created excluding all federally owned or other nonassessable property. Upon the filing of such petition with the secretary of the board of trustees of the library district, the board shall determine whether the same shall be sufficient, and the board's determination thereof shall be conclusive upon all persons. No person shall withdraw his name from said petition after the filing thereof with the secretary of the board of trustees. If the board shall find the petition to be sufficient, it shall proceed to adopt a resolution declaring its intention to order the improvement petitioned for, setting forth the nature and territorial extent of said improvement, designating the number of the proposed local districts describing the boundaries thereof, stating the estimated cost and expense of the improvement and the proportionate amount thereof which will be borne by the property within the

proposed local district, and fixing a date, time and place for a
public hearing on the formation of the proposed local district.

Added by Laws 1961, ch. 162, § 2. Amended by Laws 1963, ch. 80, §
1.

27.14.030   Resolution of intention—Publication—Notice to property owners

The resolution of intention, whether adopted on the initiative of
the board or pursuant to a petition of the property owners, shall
be published in at least two consecutive issues of a newspaper of
general circulation in the proposed local district, the date of the
first publication to be at least fifteen days prior to the date
fixed by such resolution for hearing before the board of library
trustees. Notice of the adoption of the resolution of intention
shall be given each owner or reputed owner of any lot, tract,
parcel of land or other property within the proposed improvement district by mailing said notice at least fifteen days before
the date fixed for the public hearing to the owner or reputed
owner of the property as shown on the tax rolls of the county
treasurer at the address shown thereon. The notice shall refer
to the resolution of intention and designate the proposed improvement district by number. Said notice shall also set forth
the nature of the proposed improvement, the total estimated
cost, the proportion of total cost to be borne by assessment, the
estimated amount of the cost and expense of such improvement
to be borne by the particular lot, tract or parcel, the date, time
and place of the hearing before the board of library trustees;
and in the case of improvements initiated by resolution, said notice shall also state that all persons desiring to object to the formation of the proposed district must file their written protests
with the secretary of the board of library trustees within three
weeks of the date said notice is mailed.

Added by Laws 1961, ch. 162, § 3. Amended by Laws 1963, ch. 80, §
2.

27.14.035   Hearing—Boundaries—Protests—Divestment of jurisdiction—Powers and duties pursuant to finding for formation

Whether the improvement is initiated by petition or resolution,
the board shall conduct a public hearing at the time and place
designated in the notice to property owners. At this hearing
the board shall hear objections from any person affected by the
formation of the local district and may make such changes in

the boundaries of the district or such modifications in plans for the proposed improvement as shall be deemed necessary: *Provided*, That the board may not change the boundaries of the district to include property not previously included therein without first passing a new resolution of intention and giving a new notice to property owners in the manner and form and within the time herein provided for the original notice.

After said hearing the board shall have jurisdiction to overrule protests and proceed with any such improvement initiated by petition or resolution: *Provided*, That the jurisdiction of the board to proceed with any improvement initiated by resolution shall be divested by protests filed with the secretary of the board pursuant to RCW 27.14.030, signed by the owners, according to the records of the county auditor, of at least forty percent of the area of land within the proposed local district, excluding all federally owned or other nonassessable property.

If the board finds that the district should be formed, they shall by resolution order the improvement, provide the general funds of the district to be applied thereto, adopt detailed plans of the local improvement district and declare the estimated cost thereof, acquire all necessary land therefor, pay all damages caused thereby, and commence in the name of the district such eminent domain proceedings and supplemental assessment or reassessment proceedings to pay all eminent domain awards as may be necessary to entitle the district to proceed with the work. The board shall proceed with the work and file with the county treasurer its roll levying special assessments in the amount to be paid by special assessment against the property situated within the local improvement district in proportion to the special benefits to be derived by the property therein from the improvement.

Added by Laws 1963, ch. 80, § 3.

27.14.040 Subsequent proceedings to be in accordance with sewer district law

All subsequent proceedings in connection with the local improvement, including but not limited to the levying, collection and enforcement of local improvement assessments, shall be in accordance with the provisions of law applicable to sewer district local improvement district improvements set forth in chapter 56.20 RCW, and references therein to the board of sewer commissioners and secretary of the board of sewer commissioners shall be deemed references to the governing board of the library district and secretary of the governing board of the library district.

Added by Laws 1961, ch. 162, § 4. Amended by Laws 1963, ch. 80, § 4.

27.14.050 Chapter may be used in conjunction with regional agreements

Library districts may use the provisions of this chapter for library district purposes alone or in conjunction with regional library agreements.

Added by Laws 1961, ch. 162, § 5.

ANNEXATIONS
(Revised Code of Washington Annotated, 1982, s.27.12.360 to 27.12.390.)

27.12.360 Annexation of city or town into rural county library district or intercounty rural library district—Initiation procedure

Any city or town with a population of one hundred thousand or less at the time of annexation may become a part of any rural county library district or intercounty rural library district lying contiguous thereto by annexation in the following manner: The inclusion of such a city or town may be initiated by the adoption of an ordinance by the legislative authority thereof stating its intent to join the library district and finding that the public interest will be served thereby. Before adoption, the ordinance shall be submitted to the library board of the city or town for its review and recommendations. If no library board exists in the city or town, the state librarian shall be notified of the proposed ordinance. If the board of trustees of the rural library district or intercounty rural library district concurs in the annexation, notification thereof shall be transmitted to the legislative authority or authorities of the counties in which the city or town is situated.

Added by Laws 1977, Ex.Sess., ch. 353, § 1. Amended by Laws 1981, ch. 26, § 3, eff. April 17, 1981.

27.12.370 Annexation of city or town into rural library district or intercounty rural library district—Special election procedure

The county legislative authority or authorities shall by resolution call a special election to be held in such city or town at the

next date provided in RCW 29.13.010 but not less than forty-five
days from the date of the declaration of such finding, and shall
cause notice of such election to be given as provided for in RCW
29.27.080.

The election on the annexation of the city or town into the library district shall be conducted by the auditor of the county or
counties in which the city or town is located in accordance with
the general election laws of the state and the results thereof
shall be canvassed by the canvassing board of the county or
counties. No person shall be entitled to vote at such election
unless he or she is registered to vote in said city or town for at
least thirty days preceding the date of the election. The ballot
proposition shall be in substantially the following form:

"Shall the city or town of .... be annexed to
and be a part of .... library district?
    YES ------------------------- ☐
    NO ------------------------- ☐"

If a majority of the persons voting on the proposition shall
vote in favor thereof, the city or town shall thereupon be annexed and shall be a part of such intercounty rural library district or rural library district.

Added by Laws 1977, Ex.Sess., ch. 353, § 2.

27.12.380 Annexation of city or town into rural county library district or intercounty rural library district—Withdrawal of annexed city or town

The legislative body of such a city or town which has annexed
to such a library district, may, by resolution, present to the voters of such city or town a proposition to withdraw from said rural county library district or intercounty rural library district at
any general election held at least three years following the annexation to the library district.

Added by Laws 1977, Ex.Sess., ch. 353, § 3.

27.12.390 Annexation of city or town into rural library district or intercounty rural library district—Tax levies

The annual tax levy authorized by RCW 27.12.050 and 27.12.-
150 shall be imposed throughout the library district, including
any city or town annexed thereto. Any city or town annexed to
a rural library district or intercounty rural library district shall

be entitled to levy up to three dollars and sixty cents per thousand dollars of assessed valuation less any regular levy made by such library district in the incorporated area, notwithstanding any other provision of law: *Provided,* That the limitations upon regular property taxes imposed by chapter 84.55 RCW shall apply.

Added by Laws 1977, Ex.Sess., ch. 353, § 4.

SCHOOL LIBRARIES
(Revised Code of Washington Annotated, 1982, s.27.16.010 to 27.10.060.)

27.16.010   Educational service district board may establish —Depository of instructional materials

The educational service district board of each educational service district may establish a circulating library and depository of instructional materials for the use and benefit of the pupils of the common schools of such educational service district.

Enacted by Laws 1909, ch. 97, § 1.   Amended by Laws 1955, ch. 163, § 1; Laws 1969, Ex.Sess., ch. 176, § 25, eff. April 25, 1969; Laws 1975, 1st Ex.Sess., ch. 275, § 39.

27.16.020   Tax levy for circulating school library fund— Deposit—Payments from fund

Each board of county commissioners may levy a tax not exceeding two and one-half cents per thousand dollars of assessed value for the support of the circulating library in its educational service district. The proceeds of the tax collected shall constitute the circulating school library fund for the payment of all bills created by the educational service district for the purchase of books and instructional materials and fixtures. The fund shall be deposited in the office of the county treasurer in which other educational service district funds are deposited, and shall be payable on order of the educational service district board.

Enacted by Laws 1909, ch. 97, § 2.   Amended by Laws 1955, ch. 163, § 2; Laws 1969, Ex.Sess., ch. 176, § 26, eff. April 25, 1969; Laws 1973, 1st Ex.Sess., ch. 195, § 8, eff. Jan. 1, 1974; Laws 1975, 1st Ex.Sess., ch. 275, § 40.

27.16.030   Allowance of bills

The educational service district board shall allow no bill or bills against said fund until it shall have been certified to be correct by the educational service district superintendent.

Enacted by Laws 1909, ch. 97, § 3.   Amended by Laws 1969, Ex.Sess., ch. 176, § 27, eff. April 25, 1969; Laws 1975, 1st Ex.Sess., ch. 275, § 41.

27.16.040 Purchase of books, instructional materials and fixtures

The educational service district shall purchase no books or instructional materials, or fixtures for the circulating library until there shall be to the credit of the circulating school library fund sufficient money to pay the purchase price thereof.

Enacted by Laws 1909, ch. 97, § 4. Amended by Laws 1955, ch. 163, § 3; Laws 1969, Ex.Sess., ch. 176, § 28, eff. April 25, 1969; Laws 1975, 1st Ex.Sess., ch. 275, § 42.

27.16.050 Disapproval of books by state educational officials

No book or instructional material shall be placed in an educational service district circulating library that has been disapproved by the state board of education or the superintendent of public instruction.

Enacted by Laws 1909, ch. 97, § 5. Amended by Laws 1955, ch. 163, § 4; Laws 1969, Ex.Sess., ch. 176, § 29, eff. April 25, 1969; Laws 1975, 1st Ex.Sess., ch. 275, § 43.

27.16.060 Duties of educational service district superintendent

The educational service district superintendent shall purchase the books and instructional materials and enforce such rules and regulations for their distribution, use, care, and preservation as he deems necessary.

Enacted by Laws 1909, ch. 97, § 6. Amended by Laws 1955, ch. 163, § 5; Laws 1969, Ex.Sess., ch. 176, § 30, eff. April 25, 1969; Laws 1975, 1st Ex.Sess., ch. 275, § 44.

COUNTY LAW LIBRARIES
(Revised Code of Washington Annotated, 1982, s.27.24.010 to 27.24.090.)

27.24.010 Establishment

In each county having a population of three hundred thousand or more there shall be a county law library, which shall be governed and maintained as hereinafter provided.

Enacted by Laws 1919, ch. 84, § 1.

27.24.020 Board of trustees—Composition—Terms

There shall be in every such county a board of law library trustees consisting of five members to be constituted as follows: The chairman of the board of county commissioners shall be ex officio a trustee, and the judges of the superior court of the county shall choose two of their number and two members of the bar of the county to be trustees. The term of office of a member of the board who is a judge shall be for as long as he continues to be a judge, and the term of a member who is from the bar shall be four years. Vacancies shall be filled as they occur and in the manner above directed. The office of trustee shall be without salary or other compensation. The board shall elect one of their number president and the librarian shall act as secretary. Meetings shall be held at least quarterly and as much oftener and at such times as may be prescribed by rule.

Enacted by Laws 1919, ch. 84, § 2.

27.24.030 Powers of board

The board of law library trustees shall have power:

(1) To make and enforce rules for their own procedure and for the government, care and use of the library, and for the guidance of employees.

(2) To remove any trustee, except an ex officio trustee, for neglect to attend the meetings of the board.

(3) To employ a librarian and assistants and to prescribe their duties, fix their compensation and remove them at will.

(4) To purchase books, periodicals and other property suitable for the library and to accept gifts and bequests of money and property for the library, and to sell property which is unsuitable or not needed for the library.

(5) To examine and approve for payment claims and demands payable out of the county law library fund.

Enacted by Laws 1919, ch. 84, § 3.

27.24.040 Annual report

The board of law library trustees shall, on or before the first Monday in September of each year, make a report to the board of county commissioners of their county giving the condition of their trust, with a full statement of all property received and how used, the number of books and other publications on hand, the number added by purchase, gift or otherwise during the preceding year, the number lost or missing, and such other information as may be of public interest, together with a financial report showing all receipts and disbursements of money.

Enacted by Laws 1919, ch. 84, § 4.

27.24.050 Library rooms and service

The board of county commissioners of each county to which this act [1] is applicable shall, upon demand by the board of law library trustees, provide a room suitable for the law library, adequately heated and lighted.

Enacted by Laws 1919, ch. 84, § 5.

27.24.060 Free use of library

The use of a county law library shall be free to the judges of the state and to state and county officials and to the inhabitants of the county. The board of law library trustees may prescribe uniform rules for the use of the library.

Enacted by Laws 1919, ch. 84, § 6.

27.24.062 Establishment of county and regional law libraries

In each county of the first, second, third, fourth, fifth, and sixth classes there shall be a county law library which shall be governed and maintained as hereinafter provided.

Two or more of such counties may, by agreement of the respective law library boards of trustees, create a regional law library and establish and maintain one principal law library at such location as the regional board of trustees may determine will best suit the needs of the users: *Provided, however,* That there shall be at all times a law library in such size as the board of trustees may determine necessary to be located at the courthouse where each superior court is located.

Enacted by Laws 1925, Ex.Sess., ch. 94, § 1. Amended by Laws 1933, ch. 167, § 1; Laws 1943, ch. 195, § 1; Laws 1971, Ex.Sess., ch. 141, § 1, eff. May 19, 1971.

27.24.063 Board of trustees for county and regional law libraries

There shall be in every such county a board of law library trustees consisting of five members to be constituted, as follows: Chairman of the board of county commissioners shall be ex officio trustee and the judges of the superior court of the county

shall choose one of their number, and the members of the county
bar association (or if there be no bar association, then the lawyers of said county) shall choose three of their number to be
trustees: *Provided, however,* That in the case of regional law libraries the board of trustees shall be one board of trustees
which shall be selected in the above manner and constituted as
follows: One superior court judge, one county commissioner
from each county and one lawyer from the county seat of each
county. The term of office of a member of the board who is a
judge, shall be for as long as he continues to be a judge, and the
term of a member who is from the bar shall be four years. Vacancies shall be filled as they occur and in the manner above directed. The office of trustee shall be without salary or other
compensation. The board shall elect one of their number president, and one as secretary, or if a librarian is appointed the librarian shall act as secretary. Meetings shall be held at least
once a year and as much oftener and at such times as may be
prescribed by rule.

Enacted by Laws 1933, ch. 167, § 3. Amended by Laws 1971, Ex.
Sess., ch. 141, § 2, eff. May 19, 1971.

27.24.064   Powers of board

The board of law library trustees shall have power:

(1) To make and enforce rules for their own procedure and
for the government, care and use of the library and for the guidance of employees.

(2) To remove any trustee, except an ex officio trustee, for
neglect to attend the meetings of the board.

(3) To employ a librarian and assistants if necessary, and to
prescribe their duties, fix their compensation and remove them at
will.

(4) To purchase books, periodicals and other property suitable for the library and to accept gifts and bequests of money
and property for the library and to sell property which is unsuitable or not needed for the library.

(5) To examine and approve for payment claims and demands
payable out of the county law library fund.

Enacted by Laws 1933, ch. 167, § 3.

27.24.065   Annual report

The board of law library trustees shall on or before the first
Monday of September of each year make a report to the board

of county commissioners of said county, giving the condition of their trust and a full statement of property received and how used, number of books and other publications on hand, the number added by purchase, gift or otherwise during the preceding year, the number lost or missing, and such other information as may be of public interest, together with a financial report of all receipts and disbursements of money.

Enacted by Laws 1933, ch. 167, § 3.

27.24.066   Library rooms and service

The board of county commissioners of each county to which this act   is applicable, shall upon demand by the board of law library trustees, provide a room suitable for the law library, adequately heated, lighted, and janitor service.

Enacted by Laws 1933, ch. 167, § 3.

27.24.067   Free use of library

The use of the county law library shall be free to the judges of the state, to state and county officials, and to members of the bar, and to such others as the board of trustees may by rule provide.

Enacted by Laws 1933, ch. 167, § 3.

27.24.068   Establishment of county law library—Trustee—Free use of library

In each county of the seventh and eighth class, there may be a county law library which shall be governed and maintained by the prosecuting attorney who shall also serve as trustee of such library without additional salary or other compensation.

The use of the county law library shall be free to the judges of the state, to state and county officials, and to members of the bar, and to such others as the prosecuting attorney may by rule provide.

Added by Laws 1975, ch. 37, § 1.

27.24.070   Additional filing fees

In each county pursuant to this chapter, the clerk of the superior court shall pay from each fee collected for the filing in his office of every new probate or civil matter, including appeals, the sum of seven dollars for the support of the law library in that county or the regional law library to which the county belongs, which shall be paid to the county treasurer to be credited to the county or regional law library fund: *Provided,* That upon a showing of need the seven dollar fee may be increased up to nine dollars upon the request of the law library board of trustees and with the approval of the county legislative body or bodies. There shall be paid from the filing fee paid by each person instituting an action, when the first paper is filed, to each justice of the peace in every civil action commenced in such court where the demand or value of the property in controversy is three hundred dollars or more, in addition to the other fees required by law the sum of three dollars as fees for the support of the law library in that county or for the regional law library which are to be taxed as part of costs in each case.

The justice of the peace shall pay such fees so collected to the county treasurer to be credited to the county or regional law library fund.

Enacted by Laws 1943, ch. 195, § 2. Amended by Laws 1953, ch. 249, § 1; Laws 1957, ch. 31, § 1; Laws 1961, ch. 304, § 9; Laws 1969, ch. 25, § 2; Laws 1971, Ex.Sess., ch. 141, § 3, eff. May 19, 1971; Laws 1979, ch. 126, § 1, eff. March 26, 1979.

27.24.090 Discontinuance of fees

The collection of the fees directed in RCW 27.24.070 shall be discontinued whenever the board of trustees of a county library or the prosecuting attorney, as the case may be, files with the county clerk and clerks of the justice courts a written resolution to the effect that the county library fund in its county is sufficient for all present needs, which resolution shall remain effective until it is later rescinded. Upon its rescission, the county clerk and clerks of the justice courts shall resume the collection of such fees.

Enacted by Laws 1925, Ex.Sess., ch. 94, § 3. Amended by Laws 1933, ch. 167, § 2; Laws 1953, ch. 249, § 3; Laws 1975, ch. 37, § 2.

PROTECTION OF LIBRARY PROPERTY
(Revised Code of Washington Annotated,1982, s.27.12.330-27.12.340.)

27.12.330 Penalty for injury to property

Whoever intentionally injures, defaces, or destroys any property belonging to or deposited in any public library, reading room, or other educational institution, shall be guilty of a misdemeanor.

Enacted by Laws 1935, ch. 119, § 16.

27.12.340 Penalty for wilfully retaining books

Whoever wilfully retains any book, newspaper, magazine, pamphlet, manuscript, or other property belonging in or to any public library, reading room, or other educational institution, for thirty days after notice in writing to return the same, given after the expiration of the time that by the rules of such institution such article or other property may be kept, shall be guilty of a misdemeanor.

Enacted Laws 1935 ch 119 § 17

TAX EXEMPTION

(Revised Code of Washington Annotated, 1982, s.84.36.040.)

Washington library laws are reprinted from the REVISED CODE OF WASHINGTON published by the Statute Law Committee of the State of Washington.

WEST VIRGINIA

STATE LIBRARY COMMISSION
(West Virginia Code Annotated, 1982, s.10-1-12 to 10-1-21.)

§ 10-1-12. State library commission.

There shall be a state library commission, known as the "West Virginia library commission," which shall consist of five members who shall be appointed by the governor, by and with the advice and consent of the senate, each for a term of four years. At least two members of the commission shall be women. No member of the commission shall receive compensation for services rendered, nor be engaged or interested in the publishing business.

The members of the commission in office on the date this Code takes effect shall, unless sooner removed, continue to serve until their respective terms expire and their successors have been appointed and have qualified. On or before the expiration of the terms for which said members are appointed, the governor shall appoint their successors. (1929, c. 5, § 1.)

§ 10-1-13. Same — Officers.

The officers of the commission shall be a chairman, elected from the members thereof, for a term of one year, and a secretary, who shall be a person trained in modern library methods, not a member of the commission. The secretary shall be appointed by the commission and shall serve at the will of the commission. The commission may establish headquarters or maintain its office at such point in the State as it may determine.

The secretary shall keep a record of the proceedings of the commission, have charge of its work in organizing new libraries and improving those already established, supervise the work of the traveling libraries, and in general perform such duties as may from time to time be assigned to him by the commission. (1929, c. 5, § 2.)

§ 10-1-14. Same — Powers and duties.

The commission shall give assistance, advice and counsel to all school, state-institutional, free and public libraries, and to all communities in the State which may propose to establish libraries, as to the best means of establishing and administering them, selecting and cataloging books, and other details of library management, and may send any of its members to aid in organizing such libraries or assist in the improvement of those already established.

It may also receive gifts of money, books, or other property which may be used or held for the purpose or purposes given; and may purchase and operate traveling libraries under such conditions and rules as the commission deems necessary to protect the interests of the State and best increase the efficiency of the service it is expected to render the public.

It may purchase suitable books for traveling libraries and distribute them as needed to those persons and places in the State without adequate public library service. It may collect books and other suitable library matter and distribute the same among state institutions desiring the same.

The commission may issue printed material, such as lists and circulars of information, and in the publication thereof may cooperate with other state library commissions and libraries, in order to secure the more economical administration of the work for which it was formed. It may conduct courses of library instruction and hold librarians' institutes in various parts of the State.

The commission shall perform such other service in behalf of public libraries as it may consider for the best interests of the State. (1929, c. 5, § 3.)

§ 10-1-15. Same — Disposition of monetary gifts.

If any sums of money are received by the commission as gifts, they shall be paid into the state treasury and used exclusively for carrying out the provisions of this article, and paying expenses of the commissioners. The commission shall expend no sums unless they are available by gift, appropriation or otherwise. (1929, c. 5, § 4.)

§ 10-1-16. Regional libraries and library areas — Establishment and location.

The West Virginia library commission is hereby authorized to develop a plan for the establishment and location of regional libraries, and library areas throughout the State, based on a detailed survey to be made by the commission of the needs of the various localities of the State. A region shall include two or more counties. (1939, c. 79.)

§ 10-1-17. Same — Referral of plan to county courts; action on; alteration of plan.

On completion of the survey of any proposed region, the executive secretary of the commission shall refer the proposal to the county courts of all the counties included in such proposed region. The county courts shall act upon such proposal by resolution, and the votes of a majority of each of the county courts of the counties included in the proposed region shall be necessary for the adoption of such proposal. In case of the rejection of such proposal by the county courts of any of the counties included in such proposed region, the library commission is hereby authorized to alter its plan in accordance with such action in order to provide for a region in such section of the State. The vote of a majority of each county court in the counties in such altered region shall be necessary for the adoption of such proposal. (1939, c. 79.)

§ 10-1-18. Same — Powers of West Virginia library commission.

The West Virginia library commission shall have the following powers for the establishment and maintenance of regional areas and regional libraries:

(a) To establish, maintain, and operate a public library for the region;

(b) To appoint a librarian and the necessary assistants, and to fix their compensation, such appointments to be based upon merit and efficiency as determined by the commission. The librarian shall hold a certificate from an approved school of library science and shall have had not less than three years of practical experience in library work. Said library commission shall also have the power to remove said librarian and other assistants;

(c) To purchase books, periodicals, equipment and supplies;

(d) To purchase sites and erect buildings, and/or to lease suitable quarters, and to have supervision and control of said property;

(e) To borrow books from and lend books to other libraries;

(f) To enter into contracts to receive service from or give service to libraries within or without the region and to give service to municipalities without the region which have no libraries, or to cooperate with and aid generally without such contracts, public school, institutional and other libraries;

(g) To make such bylaws, rules and regulations not inconsistent with this article as may be expedient for the government of such regional library areas and the regional libraries therein, and for the purpose of carrying out the provisions of this article;

(h) To accept for the State of West Virginia any appropriations of money that may hereafter be made out of the federal treasury by an act or acts of Congress and to disburse such funds for the purpose of carrying out the provisions of this article, in accordance with sections eleven and twelve [§§ 18-10-11, 18-10-12], article ten, chapter eighteen of the Code of one thousand nine hundred thirty-one, as amended. (1939, c. 79.)

§ 10-1-19. Same — Transfer of certain libraries to library commission.

After the establishment of a regional library area or regional library, as provided for in this article, the county court, legislative body of any city or town, the board of education of any county, or any other governing body of any political subdivision of this State, already maintaining a public, school or county library, may notify the West Virginia library commission and such county, city or town, or other subdivision library may be transferred to, leased to, or be used by said library commission for regional library purposes under such terms as may be mutually agreed upon between the said library commission and the respective county courts, legislative bodies of cities or towns, boards of education, or governing bodies of other political subdivisions. (1939, c. 79.)

§ 10-1-20. Aid to libraries by library commission.

The West Virginia library commission is hereby authorized and empowered to render such aid and assistance, financial, advisory and/or otherwise, to public, school, county, or regional libraries, whether established or maintained by said library commission or not, under such conditions and rules and regulations as the said commission deems necessary to further the interests of the State and best increase the efficiency of the service it is expected to render the public.

Having determined that the development and support of such libraries will further the education of the people of the State as a whole and will thereby aid in the discharge of the responsibility of the State to encourage and foster education, the West Virginia library commission is authorized and empowered to pay over and contribute to any board of library directors created and maintained pursuant to the provisions of this article or any special act of the legislature such sum or sums of money as may be available from funds included in appropriations made for the West Virginia library commission for such purpose. The amount of any such payment or contribution by the commission to any such local library board of directors shall be determined in accordance with rules and regulations promulgated by the commission. The library commission shall have authority to promulgate rules and regulations governing the manner in which such amount or amounts of money shall be accounted for and expended. (1939, c. 79; 1969, c. 113.)

§ 10-1-21. Collection and preservation of library data; surveys; employment of personnel; use of data.

The West Virginia library commission is hereby authorized and empowered to collect and preserve statistics and other data, concerning libraries of any sort located within this State; to make surveys relating to the needs or conditions of such libraries or the library conditions of any city, town, county, regional library area, or other subdivision of this State; and to publish the results and findings thereof in accordance with the provisions of section fourteen [§ 10-1-14] of this article. The commission may employ all necessary personnel for any of these purposes, such appointments to be based on merit and efficiency as determined by the commission. Such data, surveys and findings of the library commission shall be available to all school, public, institutional, regional and/or other libraries within this State, whether proposed or established. (1939, c. 79.)

ARCHIVES AND HISTORY DIVISION
(West Virginia Code Annotated, 1982, s.29-1-5 to 29.1-7a.)

§ 29-1-5. Archives and history division; director.

The purposes and duties of the archives and history division are to locate, survey, investigate, register, identify, excavate, preserve, protect, restore and recommend to the commissioner for acquisition historic, architectural, archaeological and cultural sites, structures, documents and objects worthy of preservation, relating to the state of West Virginia and the territory included therein from the earliest times to the present, upon its own initiative or in cooperation with any private or public society, organization or agency; to conduct a continuing survey and study throughout the state to determine the needs and priorities for the preservation, restoration and development of such sites, structures, documents and objects; to direct, protect, excavate, preserve, study, and develop such sites, structures, documents, and to operate and maintain a state library for the preservation of all public records, state papers, documents and reports of all three branches of state government including all boards, commissions, departments and agencies as well as any other private or public papers, books or documents of peculiar or historic interest or significance; to preserve and protect all battle or regimental flags borne by West Virginians and other memorabilia of historic interest; to designate appropriate monuments, tablets or markers, historic, architectural and scenic sites within the state and to arrange for the purchase, replacement, care of and maintenance of such monuments, tablets and markers and to formulate and prepare suitable copy for them; to operate and maintain a state museum; to cooperate with the state geological and economic surveys in the survey's archaeological work; to edit and publish a quarterly historical magazine devoted to the history, biography, bibliography and genealogy of West Virginia; and to perform such other duties as may be assigned to the division by the commissioner.

With the advice and consent of the archives and history commission, the commissioner shall appoint a director of the archives and history division, who shall have: (1) a bachelor's degree in one of the social sciences, or equivalent training and experience in the fields of West Virginia history, history, historic preservation, archaeology, or in records, library or archives management; or (2) three years' experience in administration in the fields of West Virginia history, history, historic preservation, archaeology, or in records, library or archives management. Notwithstanding these qualifications, the person serving as the state historian and archivist on the date of enactment of this article shall be eligible for appointment as the director of the archives and history division. The director of the archives and history division shall serve as the state historian and archivist.

With the approval of the commissioner, the director shall establish professional positions within the division. The director shall employ the personnel within these professional positions for the division.

The director may promulgate rules and regulations concerning the professional policies and functions of the archives and history division, subject to the approval of the archives and history commission. (1977, 1st Ex. Sess., c. 7.)

§ 29-1-6. Archives and history commission.

The West Virginia antiquities commission established by article twelve [§ 5-12-1 et seq.], chapter five of this Code shall continue in existence until the first day of July, one thousand nine hundred seventy-seven at which time it shall be abolished, and replaced by an archives and history commission which is hereby created and which shall be composed of nine appointed members.

The governor shall nominate, and by and with the advice and consent of the senate, appoint the members of the commission for staggered terms of three years. A person appointed to fill a vacancy shall be appointed only for the remainder of that term. Of the members of the archives and history commission first appointed, three shall be appointed for a term ending the thirtieth day of June, one thousand nine hundred seventy-eight, and three each for terms ending one and two years thereafter: Provided, that each person serving as a member of the West Virginia antiquities commission, for a term which has not expired on the effective date of this article, shall be appointed by the governor without senate confirmation to the archives and history commission, as one of the nine appointed members, for the term ending the thirtieth day of June in the year in which his term would expire as a member of the West Virginia antiquities commission.

No more than five of the appointed members may be of the same political party. Members of the commission shall be appointed so as to fairly represent both sexes, the ethnic and cultural diversity of the state and the geographic regions of the state. At least one of the appointed members shall be an archaeologist, one an architect and one an historian.

The commission shall elect one of its members chairman. It shall meet at such time as shall be specified by the chairman. Notice of each meeting shall be given to each member by the chairman at least five days in advance of the meeting. A majority of the members shall constitute a quorum for the transaction of business. The director of the archives and history division shall be an ex officio nonvoting member of the commission and shall serve as secretary. The director, or a majority of the members, may also call a meeting upon such notice as provided in this section.

Each member or ex officio member of the commission shall serve without compensation, but shall be reimbursed for all reasonable and necessary expenses actually incurred in the performance of his duties; except that in the event the expenses are paid, or are to be paid, by a third party, the member or ex officio member, as the case may be, shall not be reimbursed by the state.

In addition to the nine appointed members, the president of the state historical society and the president of the state historical association of college and university teachers shall serve as ex officio voting members of the archives and history commission. The director of the state geological and economic survey and the state historic preservation officer shall serve as ex officio nonvoting members of the archives and history division.

The commission shall have the following powers:

(1) To advise the commissioner and the director of the archives and history division concerning the accomplishment of the purposes of that division and to establish a state plan with respect thereto;

(2) To approve and distribute grants-in-aid and awards from federal and state funds relating to the purposes of the archives and history division;

(3) To request, accept or expend federal funds to accomplish the purposes of the archives and history division when federal law or regulations would prohibit the same by the commissioner or division director, but would permit the same to be done by the archives and history commission;

(4) To otherwise encourage and promote the purposes of the archives and history division;

(5) To approve rules and regulations concerning the professional policies and functions of the division as promulgated by the director of the archives and history division; and

(6) To advise and consent to the appointment of the director by the commissioner. (1965, c. 17; 1968, c. 5; 1977, 1st Ex. Sess., c. 7.)

§ 29-1-7. Protection of archaeological sites; penalties.

Archaeological sites and districts, identified as such by the archives and history division, on lands owned or leased by the state, or on private lands where investigation and development rights have been acquired by the state by lease or contract, shall not be disturbed, developed or destroyed except with permission of the commissioner.

Any person violating the provisions of this section shall be guilty of a misdemeanor, and, upon conviction thereof, shall be fined not more than five hundred dollars, or imprisoned in the county jail not more than six months, or both fined and imprisoned. (1965, c. 17; 1977, 1st Ex. Sess., c. 7.)

§ 29-1-7a. Reestablishment of division of archives and history.

After having conducted a performance and fiscal audit through its joint committee on government operations, pursuant to section nine, article ten, chapter four [§ 4-10-9] of this Code, the legislature hereby finds and declares that the division of archives and history should be continued and reestablished. Accordingly, notwithstanding the provisions of section four [§ 4-10-4], article ten, chapter four of this Code, the division of archives and history shall continue to exist until the first day of July, one thousand nine hundred eighty-six. (1980, c. 39.)

DISTRIBUTION OF PUBLIC DOCUMENTS
(West Virginia Code Annotated, 1982, s.4-1-19, 5A-3-31.)

§ 4-1-19. Distribution of acts of the legislature.

Free distribution of the acts and resolutions of each session of the legislature, and other matter directed by law to be published therewith, shall be made as follows by the clerk of the house of delegates: One copy to the judge of each court in this State; one copy each to the judge, clerk and district attorney of every United States district court of this State; one copy to every prosecuting attorney, sheriff, assessor, county superintendent of free schools, president of the county court, circuit clerk, county clerk and justices of the peace; five copies to the governor; six copies to the attorney general; two copies each to the secretary of state, auditor, state superintendent of free schools, treasurer and commissioner of agriculture; four copies to the public service commission; one copy to each executive department head, requesting the same; ten copies to the clerk of the senate, one for his own use, and the others to be kept in his office for the use of the senate; ten copies to each member of the legislature, one for his own use and others for distribution; ten copies to the college of law of West Virginia University; one copy to each public institution of the State; three copies to the librarian of Congress, one for the library and one for each house of Congress; one copy to each senator and representative in Congress from this State; one copy to each county law library; and one copy to each college and university in the State. The clerk shall retain ten copies in his own office, one for his own use and the others to be kept in his office for the use of the house.

All of the copies named in this section shall be sent by mail, express or otherwise as the clerk may deem best. The acts to which officers of a county may be entitled shall be forwarded to the clerk of the county court thereof and shall be delivered by him to the officers entitled to receive the same. Upon receipt of such acts by him, the clerk of the county court shall forward his receipt therefor to the clerk of the house of delegates specifying the number received, and he shall require each person receiving a copy of such acts from him to sign a receipt therefor in a book to be kept by him for that purpose. The remaining copies of the acts shall be in the custody of the division of purchases, department of finance and administration, and be sold and disposed of as provided in section thirty-one [§ 5A-3-31], article three, chapter five-A of this Code.

The clerk may cause a copy of such acts to be furnished to any officer, board, commission, institution or tribunal not named herein. (1967, c. 106.)

§ 5A-3-31. Custodian of reports and acts; delivery to state law librarian for distribution; sale.

The director shall be custodian of the West Virginia Reports after they are printed and bound and approved by the reporter, and of the acts of the legislature after they are printed and bound and approved by the clerk of the house of delegates. As soon as practicable after any new volume of such reports or acts has been delivered to the director, not including reprints of former volumes, he shall deliver to the state law librarian sufficient copies to enable him to make distribution thereof in the manner prescribed by sections five and six, article eight, chapter fifty-one [§§ 51-8-5 and 51-8-6] of this Code.

The director shall sell such copies of the reports and acts as remain after the distribution provided by law has been made at a price to be fixed by him with the approval of the commissioner, but in no case shall such price be less than the actual cost to the State of the publication thereof. The proceeds of such sales shall immediately be paid into the treasury. (1935, c. 76; 1961, c. 132.)

STATE AND COUNTY LAW LIBRARIES
(West Virginia Code Annotated, 1982, s.51-7-1 to 51-8-1.)

§ 51-8-1. West Virginia law library; control and management.

The State law library now in the city of Charleston shall be known as the "West Virginia law library," and shall be wholly under the control and management and in the custody of the supreme court of appeals. (Code 1849, c. 19, § 19; Code 1860, c. 19, § 19; 1921, c. 161, § 1; Code 1923, c. 15A, § 1.)

§ 51-8-2. Librarian; bond; assistants; compensation.

The supreme court of appeals, or the judges thereof in vacation, shall appoint a competent librarian to have immediate custody of the West Virginia law library under the direction of the court. Such librarian shall give bond in a penalty fixed by the court of not less than two nor more than five thousand dollars, with surety thereon, to be approved by the court, and conditioned as provided for official bonds. Such bond shall be deposited for safekeeping with the clerk of the court. The librarian shall be an officer of the court and shall hold his office and be removable at its pleasure. Vacancies in the office of librarian occurring during vacation of the court may be filled by appointment in writing made by the judges of the court, or any three of them. When, in the opinion of the court, other employees are needed for the proper protection and use of the library, it may employ such assistants as may be necessary for that purpose. The salary of the librarian and assistants shall be fixed by the court and shall be payable in monthly installments. (Code 1849, c. 19, §§ 20, 21; Code 1860, c. 19, §§ 20, 21; Code 1868, c. 15, § 3; 1872-3, c. 68; 1877, c. 14, § 1; 1882, c. 34, §§ 10, 11; 1891, c. 70, §§ 1, 2; 1921, c. 161, § 2; Code 1923, c. 15A, § 2; 1945, c. 43; 1949, c. 33; 1953, c. 53; 1958, c. 4; 1961, c. 22.)

§ 51-8-3. Rules and regulations governing use of library.

The library shall be open under such rules and regulations as the court may prescribe from time to time, and it shall be the duty of the court to adopt such rules and regulations and to cause them to be published, as other rules of the court are published. (Code 1849, c. 19, § 23; Code 1860, c. 19, § 23; Code 1868, c. 15, § 3; 1882, c. 34, § 10; 1891, c. 70, § 2; 1921, c. 161, § 3; Code 1923, c. 15A, § 2a.)

§ 51-8-4. Control of library by court; expenses.

The supreme court of appeals shall have the power and it shall be its duty, to purchase such new and additional books for the library as in its opinion shall be right and proper, and shall cause such exchanges or sales of books to be made as may be for the benefit of the library, and, in general, the court shall cause to be done and performed all things necessary and proper to keep the books of such library in good condition, and for that purpose may cause such catalogs to be made as may be necessary. All expenses necessarily incurred under the order of the court for the purposes of this article, including postage, freight and express charges, shall be paid out of appropriations for that purpose, under the order of the court. (1921, c. 161, § 6; Code 1923, c. 15A, § 2d.)

§ 51-8-5. Distribution of West Virginia reports.

The state law librarian shall have charge of and make distribution of the reports of the cases decided by the supreme court of appeals, after the same are printed and bound, and are approved by the reporter and the court. After any new volumes of such reports have been delivered to the librarian, not including reprints of former volumes, he shall distribute the volumes as follows: Five volumes to the governor; one volume to the president of the senate; one volume to the speaker of the house of delegates; twenty-five volumes to the attorney general; two volumes to each judge of the supreme court of appeals; one volume to each.clerk to the judges of the supreme court of appeals; one volume to the clerk of the supreme court of appeals; one volume to the judge of each judicial circuit for each county in such judicial circuit; one volume to each of the judges of courts of limited jurisdiction; one volume to each judge of the United States district courts in West Virginia; one volume to each prosecuting attorney in this State; three volumes to the public service commission; five volumes to the state road commissioner; three volumes to the State tax commissioner; five volumes to the library of Congress, Washington, District of Columbia; one volume to the director of legislative services; twenty volumes to the college of law of West Virginia University; one volume to the law library at Charles Town; one volume to the Ohio county law library at Wheeling; two volumes to the department of archives and history; one volume each to the auditor, commissioner of agriculture, state treasurer, secretary of state and state superintendent of free schools; and one volume to the head of subordinate executive departments, boards, commissions and agencies at the State capitol.

The state law librarian shall arrange, as far as possible, to exchange one volume of the West Virginia reports for a volume of the current reports of the court of last resort of each state, the District of Columbia and the territorial possessions of the United States. He may further arrange for the exchange of such volumes with law schools for law reviews, law bulletins, reports and other legal publications. All such law reviews, law bulletins, reports and other legal publications so received shall become the property of the State of West Virginia unless otherwise so designated, and shall be placed by the librarian and safely kept in the law library at the State capitol.

The supreme court of appeals, or a judge thereof in vacation of the court, may order the librarian to distribute volumes of the West Virginia reports to any university or college on written request therefor; and may order him to distribute additional volumes to any officer, judge, court, tribunal, prosecuting attorney, institution, library, board, commission or agency now entitled to one volume of such report, or any such agency hereafter created, upon written request therefor made to the court. Such volumes shall remain the property of the State of West Virginia and volumes so received by them shall be turned over to their successors in office.

The supreme court of appeals, or a judge thereof in vacation of the court, on written request therefor and as such court or judge deems best, may order the librarian to distribute reprints of old volumes of the reports as replacements when requested.

The librarian is charged with and it shall be his duty to retain and keep safely five volumes of the reports in the state law library, at Charleston.

All volumes of the reports distributed as herein provided shall be sent by the librarian by mail, express, freight or otherwise as he may deem best: Provided, that such reports so distributed shall contain a receipt which, on return to the librarian, shall be kept on file. (Code 1849, c. 19, §§ 4, 22; Code 1860, c. 19, §§ 4, 22; Code 1868, c. 15, § 6; 1872-3, c. 190, § 6; 1875, c. 65, § 6; 1882, c. 36, § 4; 1883, c. 46, § 4; 1890, c. 3, § 4; 1891, c. 70, § 2(10); 1915, c. 45, § 2(10); 1921, c. 161, § 5; Code 1923, c. 15A, § 2c; 1925, c. 3, § 2c; 1967, c. 43.)

§ 51-8-6. Exchange of acts of the legislature for acts of the legislatures of other states; distribution.

The librarian shall arrange as far as possible with each of the other states for the exchange of two copies of the acts of the West Virginia legislature for acts of the legislature of each state, one of which copies received from each state shall be deposited in the state law library at Charleston, one copy in the library of the college of law of West Virginia University, and the other copies if any, so received from any other state, to be disposed of as the supreme court of appeals shall direct.

The division of purchases, department of finance and administration, upon requisition of the librarian, shall, without cost, furnish such librarian with sufficient copies of the acts to make the exchanges provided for by this section. (Code 1849, c. 16, §§ 5-14; Code 1860, c. 16, §§ 5-14; 1864, Joint Resolution No. 12; 1865, c. 21, § 10; Code 1868, c. 13, § 1; 1882, c. 143, § 1; 1915, c. 54, § 1; Code 1923, c. 13, § 1; 1967, c. 106.)

§ 51-8-7. Accounts and reports of librarian.

The librarian shall keep full and complete account of all money transactions in connection with such library and of the receipt of all books therein, and shall perform such other duties in connection therewith as may be ordered by the court. The librarian shall make an annual report to the court within thirty days after the close of each fiscal year, in which he shall state the number of copies of reports and session acts received by him, and what disposition he made thereof, and also what money came into his hands, and from what sources, during the preceding fiscal year. (1921, c. 161, § 4; Code 1923, c. 15A, § 2b.)

§ 51-8-8. Authority to establish county law libraries; control of circuit judge; rules and regulations.

In addition to all other powers and duties now conferred by law upon the supreme court of appeals and the circuit courts, such courts are hereby authorized and empowered to establish county law libraries which shall be wholly under the control and management of the circuit judge, with the assistance of the circuit clerk. The supreme court of appeals may expend funds for the purchase of books or other expenses necessary to the operation of the county law library.

All county law libraries presently in existence shall be continued and kept current and the cost thereof, other than for provision of adequate space, shall be borne by the State and charged against the judicial accounts thereof. Such libraries shall be available for use by the public subject to such reasonable rules as may be adopted by the circuit judge. County commissions shall provide adequate space for such libraries. (1913, c. 35, § 1; Code 1923, c. 15A, § 3; 1975, c. 126.)

§ 51-8-9. Accounts and reports relating to county law libraries.

The administrative director of the supreme court of appeals, with the cooperation and assistance of each circuit clerk, shall keep full and complete account of all money transactions in connection with the various county law libraries and of the receipt of all books and other documents lodged in such libraries and shall perform such other duties in connection therewith as may be ordered by the supreme court of appeals. Such administrative director shall make an annual report to the supreme court of appeals within sixty days after the close of each fiscal year, in which he shall state the number of copies of reports, acts of the legislature and all other books and documents received by each county law library and the disposition made thereof. Such report shall also set forth what money came into his hands during the preceding fiscal year. (1913, c. 35, § 2; Code 1923, c. 15A, § 4; 1975, c. 126.)

INTERSTATE LIBRARY COMPACT
(West Virginia Code Annotated, 1982, s.10-1A-1 to 10-1A-6.)

§ 10-1A-1. Enactment of compact.

The "Interstate Library Compact" is hereby enacted into law and entered into by this State with all states legally joining therein in the form substantially as follows:

INTERSTATE LIBRARY COMPACT

Article I. Policy and Purpose.

Because the desire for the services provided by libraries transcends governmental boundaries and can most effectively be satisfied by giving such services to communities and people regardless of jurisdictional lines, it is the policy of the states party to this compact to cooperate and share their responsibilities; to authorize cooperation and sharing with respect to those types of library facilities and services which can be more economically or efficiently developed and maintained on a cooperative basis; and to authorize cooperation and sharing among localities, states and others in providing joint or cooperative library services in areas where the distribution of population or of existing and potential library resources make the provision of library service on an interstate basis the most effective way of providing adequate and efficient service.

Article II. Definitions.

As used in this compact:

(a) "Public library agency" means any unit or agency of local or state government operating or having power to operate a library.

(b) "Private library agency" means any nongovernmental entity which operates or assumes a legal obligation to operate a library.

(c) "Library agreement" means a contract establishing an interstate library district pursuant to this compact or providing for the joint or cooperative furnishing of library services.

Article III. Interstate Library Districts.

(a) Any one or more public library agencies in a party state in cooperation with any public library agency or agencies in one or more other party states may establish and maintain an interstate library district. Subject to the provisions of this compact and any other laws of the party states which pursuant hereto remain applicable, such district may establish, maintain and operate some or all of the library facilities and services for the area concerned in accordance with the terms of a library agreement therefor. Any private library agency or agencies within an interstate library district may cooperate therewith, assume duties, responsibilities and obligations thereto, and receive benefits therefrom as provided in any library agreement to which such agency or agencies become party.

(b) Within an interstate library district, and as provided by a library agreement, the performance of library functions may be undertaken on a joint or cooperative basis, or may be undertaken by means of one or more arrangements between or among public or private library agencies for the extension of library privileges or the use of facilities or services operated or rendered by one or more of the individual library agencies.

(c) If a library agreement provides for joint establishment, maintenance or operation of library facilities or services by an interstate library district, such district shall have power to do any one or more of the following in accordance with such library agreement:

(1) Undertake, administer and participate in programs or arrangements for securing, lending or servicing of books and other publications, any other materials suitable to be kept or made available by libraries, library equipment or for the dissemination of information about libraries, the value and significance of particular items therein and the use thereof;

(2) Accept for any of its purposes under this compact any and all donations and grants of money, equipment, supplies, materials and services (conditional or otherwise), from any state or the United States or any subdivision or agency thereof, or interstate agency or from any institution, person, firm or corporation, and receive, utilize and dispose of the same;

(3) Operate mobile library units or equipment for the purpose of rendering bookmobile service within the district;

(4) Employ professional, technical, clerical and other personnel, and fix terms of employment, compensation and other appropriate benefits; and where desirable, provide for the in-service training of such personnel;

(5) Sue and be sued in any court of competent jurisdiction;

(6) Acquire, hold and dispose of any real or personal property or any interest or interests therein as may be appropriate to the rendering of library service;

(7) Construct, maintain and operate a library, including any appropriate branches thereof;

(8) Do such other things as may be incidental to or appropriate for the carrying out of any of the foregoing powers.

Article IV. Interstate Library Districts, Governing Board.

(a) An interstate library district which establishes, maintains or operates any facilities or services in its own right shall have a governing board which shall direct the affairs of the district and act for it in all matters relating to its business. Each participating public library agency in the district shall be represented on the governing board which shall be organized and conduct its business in accordance with provision therefor in the library agreement. But in no event shall a governing board meet less often than twice a year.

(b) Any private library agency or agencies party to a library agreement establishing an interstate library district may be represented on or advise with the governing board of the district in such manner as the library agreement may provide.

Article V. State Library Agency Cooperation.

Any two or more state library agencies of two or more of the party states may undertake and conduct joint or cooperative library programs, render joint or cooperative library services, and enter into and perform arrangements for the cooperative or joint acquisition, use, housing and disposition of items or collections of materials which, by reason of expense, rarity, specialized nature or infrequency of demand therefor would be appropriate for central collection and shared use. Any such programs, services or arrangements may include provision for the exercise on a cooperative or joint basis of any power exercisable by an interstate library district and an agreement embodying any such program, service or arrangement shall contain provisions covering the subjects detailed in article VI of this compact for interstate library agreements.

Article VI. Library Agreements.

(a) In order to provide for any joint or cooperative undertaking pursuant to this compact, public and private library agencies may enter into library agreements. Any agreement executed pursuant to the provisions of this compact shall, as among the parties to the agreement:

(1) Detail the specific nature of the services, programs, facilities, arrangements or properties to which it is applicable;

(2) Provide for the allocation of costs and other financial responsibilities;

(3) Specify the respective rights, duties, obligations and liabilities of the parties;

(4) Set forth the terms and conditions for duration, renewal, termination, abrogation, disposal of joint or common property, if any, and all other matters which may be appropriate to the proper effectuation and performance of the agreement.

(b) No public or private library agency shall undertake to exercise itself, or jointly with any other library agency, by means of a library agreement any power prohibited to such agency by the constitution or statutes of its state.

(c) No library agreement shall become effective until filed with the compact administrator of each state involved and approved in accordance with article VII of this compact.

Article VII. Approval of Library Agreements.

(a) Every library agreement made pursuant to this compact shall, prior to and as a condition precedent to its entry into force, be submitted to the attorney general of each state in which a public library agency party thereto is situated, who shall determine whether the agreement is in proper form and compatible with the laws of his state. The attorneys general shall approve any agreement submitted to them unless they shall find that it does not meet the conditions set forth herein and shall detail in writing addressed to the governing bodies of the public library agencies concerned the specific respects in which the proposed agreement fails to meet the requirements of law. Failure to disapprove an agreement submitted hereunder within ninety days of its submission shall constitute approval thereof.

(b) In the event that a library agreement made pursuant to this compact shall deal in whole or in part with the provision of services or facilities with regard to which an officer or agency of the state government has constitutional or statutory powers of control, the agreement shall, as a condition precedent to its entry into force, be submitted to the state officer or agency having such power of control and shall be approved or disapproved by him or it as to all matters within his or its jurisdiction in the same manner and subject to the same requirements governing the action of the attorneys general pursuant to subsection (a) of this article. This requirement of submission and approval shall be in addition to and not in substitution for the requirement of submission to and approval by the attorneys general.

Article VIII. Other Laws Applicable.

Nothing in this compact or in any library agreement shall be construed to supersede, alter or otherwise impair any obligation imposed on any library by otherwise applicable law, nor to authorize the transfer or disposition of any property held in trust by a library agency in a manner contrary to the terms of such trust.

Article IX. Appropriations and Aid.

(a) Any public library agency party to a library agreement may appropriate funds to the interstate library district established thereby in the same manner and to the same extent as to a library wholly maintained by it and, subject to the laws of the state in which such public library agency is situated, may pledge its credit in support of an interstate library district established by the agreement.

(b) Subject to the provisions of the library agreement pursuant to which it functions and the laws of the states in which such district is situated, an interstate library district may claim and receive any state and federal aid which may be available to library agencies.

Article X. Compact Administrator.

Each state shall designate a compact administrator with whom copies of all library agreements to which his state or any public library agency thereof is party shall be filed. The administrator shall have such other powers as may be conferred upon him by the laws of his state and may consult and cooperate with the compact administrators of other party states and take such steps as may effectuate the purposes of this compact. If the laws of a party state so provide, such state may designate one or more deputy compact administrators in addition to its compact administrator.

Article XI. Appropriations and Aid.

(a) This compact shall enter into force and effect immediately upon its enactment into law by any two states. Thereafter, it shall enter into force and effect as to any other state upon the enactment thereof by such state.

(b) This compact shall continue in force with respect to a party state and remain binding upon such state until six months after such state has given notice to each other party state of the repeal thereof. Such withdrawal shall not be construed to relieve any party to a library agreement entered into pursuant to this compact from any obligation of that agreement prior to the end of its duration as provided therein.

Article XII. Construction and Severability.

This compact shall be liberally construed so as to effectuate the purposes thereof. The provisions of this compact shall be severable and if any phrase, clause, sentence or provision of this compact is declared to be contrary to the constitution of any party state or of the United States or the applicability thereof to any government, agency, person or circumstance is held invalid, the validity of the remainder of this compact and the applicability thereof to any government, agency, person or circumstance shall not be affected thereby. If this compact shall be held contrary to the constitution of any state party thereto, the compact shall remain in full force and effect as to the remaining states and in full force and effect as to the state affected as to all severable matters. (1972, c. 65.)

§ 10-1A-2. Restrictions relating to outlay of public funds.

No county, municipality or other political subdivision of this State shall be party to a library agreement which provides for the construction or maintenance of a library pursuant to article III, subsection (c), subdivision (7) of the compact, nor pledge its credit in support of such a library or contribute to the capital financing thereof, except after compliance with any laws applicable to such counties, municipalities or other political subdivisions of this State relating to or governing capital outlays and the pledging of credit. (1972, c. 65.)

§ 10-1A-3. State library agency defined.

As used in the compact, "state library agency," with reference to this State, means the West Virginia library commission as designated in section twelve [§ 10-1-12], article one of this chapter. (1972, c. 65.)

§ 10-1A-4. Interstate library districts; state and federal aid.

An interstate library district lying partly within this State may claim and be entitled to receive state aid in support of any of its functions to the same extent and in the same manner as such functions are eligible for support when carried on by entities wholly within this State. For the purposes of computing and apportioning state aid to an interstate library district, this State will consider

that portion of the area which lies within this State as an independent entity for
the performance of the aided function or functions and compute and apportion
the aid accordingly. Subject to any applicable laws of this State, such a district
also may apply for and be entitled to receive any federal aid for which it may
be eligible. (1972, c. 65.)

§ 10-1A-5. Compact administrator.

The governor shall appoint an officer or employee of this State who shall be
the compact administrator pursuant to article X of the compact. (1972, c. 65.)

§ 10-1A-6. Withdrawal.

In the event of withdrawal from the compact, the governor shall send and
receive any notices required by article XI, subsection (b) of the compact. (1972,
c. 65.)

PUBLIC LIBRARIES
(West Virginia Code Annotated, 1982, s.10-1-1 to 10-1-11a, 8-12-4.)

§ 10-1-1. "Public library" and "governing authority" defined.

The term "public library" as used in this article shall be construed to mean
a library maintained wholly or in part by any governing authority from funds
derived by taxation and the services of which are free to the public, except for
those charges for which provision may be made elsewhere in this article. The
term shall not, however, include special libraries, such as law, medical or other
professional libraries, or school libraries which are maintained primarily for
school purposes. The term "governing authority" shall be construed to mean
county court, county board of education or the governing body of any
municipality. (1915, c. 64, § 1; Code 1923, c. 47, § 50; 1945, c. 103, § 1; 1961, c.
112.)

§ 10-1-2. Power of governing authority to establish and maintain libraries; financing.

A governing authority either by itself or in cooperation with one or more other
such governing authorities, shall have the power to establish, equip and maintain
a public library, or to take over, maintain or support any public library already
established. Any library established, maintained or supported by a governing
authority may be financed either (1) by the appropriation from the general funds
of the governing authority of a sum sufficient for the purpose, or (2) by the
imposition of an excess levy for library purposes, in accordance with the
provisions of section sixteen [§ 11-8-16], article eight, chapter eleven of this Code.

Such sums as are appropriated hereunder may be transferred to the public
library board for deposit and disbursement as the public library board shall

direct. By such transfer the governing authority designates the public library board as its disbursing agent. (1915, c. 64, § 2; Code 1923, c. 47, § 51; 1945, c. 103, § 2; 1961, c. 112.)

§ 10-1-3. Regional library defined; apportionment of regional library expenses.

A regional library is a public library established and/or maintained by two or more counties, by action of their governing authorities, under the terms of a contract to which they all agree. The expenses of the regional library shall be apportioned between or among the counties concerned on such a basis as shall be agreed upon in the contract. (1945, c. 103, § 3; 1961, c. 112.)

§ 10-1-3a. Authority of regional library board to disburse funds.

The governing authorities which maintain a regional library may contribute the apportioned sum to the regional library board, such contributions to be deposited as the regional library board shall direct and to be disbursed by the officer designated by that board. By such contribution the governing authority designates the regional library board as its disbursing agent. (1961, c. 112.)

§ 10-1-4. Contract with existing public library.

The governing authority may, in lieu of supporting and maintaining its own public library, enter into a contract with an existing public library and make annual payments of money to such library, whose library materials and services shall be available without charge to all persons living within the area represented by such governing authority. Any school board may contract for school library service from an existing public library which shall agree to furnish books to a school or schools under the terms of the contract.

All money paid to a library under such a contract shall be expended solely for the maintenance and support of the library. (1945, c. 103, § 4; 1961, c. 112.)

§ 10-1-5. Board of library directors — Qualifications; term of office; vacancies; removal; no compensation.

Whenever a public library is established under this article the governing authority or authorities, shall appoint a board of five directors, chosen from the citizens at large of such governmental division or divisions, with reference to their fitness for such office, except that in a regional library the board of directors shall consist of not less than five nor more than ten members, with a minimum of one member from each county in the region, the total number of directors and the apportionment of directors by county to be determined by joint action of the governing authorities concerned. In either case directors shall hold office for five years from the first day of July following their appointment, and until their successors are appointed and qualified: Provided, that upon their first appointment under this article a proportionate number shall be appointed for one year, for two years, for three years, for four years and for five years; and thereafter all appointments shall be for terms of five years. Vacancies in the board shall be immediately reported by the board to the governing authority and filled by appointment in like manner, and, if an unexpired term, for the remainder of the term only. A director may be removed for just cause in the manner provided by the bylaws of the library board. No compensation shall be paid or allowed any director. (1915, c. 64, § 3; Code 1923, c. 47, § 52; 1945, c. 103, § 5; 1961, c. 112.)

§ 10-1-6. Same — Powers and duties.

The board of directors of each public library established or maintained under this article shall: (a) Immediately after appointment, meet and organize by electing one member as president and one as secretary, and such other officers as may be necessary. All officers shall hold office for one year and shall be eligible for reelection. (b) Adopt such bylaws, rules and regulations as are necessary for its own guidance and for the administration, supervision and protection of the library and all property belonging thereto as may not be inconsistent with the provisions of this article. (c) Supervise the expenditure of all money credited to the library fund. All money appropriated or collected for public library purposes shall be deposited in the treasury of the governing authority to the credit of the library fund, to be paid out on the certified requisition of the library board, in the manner provided by law for the disbursement of other funds of such governing authority, or shall be deposited as the library's board of directors shall direct and be disbursed by the officer designated by that board, such officer before entering upon his duties to give bond payable to and in an amount fixed by the board of directors of the library, conditioned for the faithful discharge of his official fiscal duties. The cost of such bond shall be paid from the library fund. The books, records and accounts of the library board shall be subject to audit and examination by the office of the state tax commissioner of West Virginia. (d) Lease or purchase and occupy suitable quarters, or erect upon ground secured through gift or purchase, an appropriate building for the use of such library; and have supervision, care, and custody of the grounds, rooms or buildings constructed, leased, or set apart for library purposes. (e) Employ a head librarian, and upon his recommendation employ such other assistants as may be necessary for the efficient operation of the library. (1915, c. 64, § 4; Code 1923, c. 47, § 53; 1945, c. 103, § 6; 1961, c. 112.)

§ 10-1-7. Free use of libraries.

Each library established or maintained by any governing authority shall be free for the use of all persons living within the area represented by such governing authority, except for those charges for which provision may be made elsewhere in this article. The use of the library is subject to reasonable rules and regulations adopted by the library board. The board may extend the privilege and use of the library to nonresidents upon such terms and conditions as it may prescribe.

The board may exclude from the use of the library under its charge any person who wilfully and persistently violates any rule or regulation prescribed for the use of the library or its facilities. (1915, c. 64, § 5; Code 1923, c. 47, § 54; 1945, c. 103, § 7; 1961, c. 112.)

§ 10-1-8. Annual report.

The board of directors shall make an annual report for the fiscal year ending June thirtieth to the governing authority or authorities appointing it, stating the conditions of the library property, the various sums of money received from the library fund, and all other sources, and how such money was expended, the number of books and periodicals on hand, the number added and withdrawn during the year, the number of books lent, the number of registered users of such library, with such other statistics, information and suggestions as may be deemed of general interest. A copy of this report shall be sent to the West Virginia library commission. (1915, c. 64, § 6; Code 1923, c. 47, § 55; 1945, c. 103, § 8; 1961, c. 112.)

§ 10-1-9. Library board to be a corporation; vesting of title to bequests or donations.

The board of directors of each public library shall be a corporation; and as such it may contract and be contracted with, sue and be sued, plead and be impleaded, and shall have and use a common seal.

The title to all bequests or donations of cash or other personal property or real estate for the benefit of such library shall be vested in the board of directors to be held in trust and controlled by such board according to the terms and for the purposes set forth in the deed, gift, devise or bequest: Provided, however, that the person making the bequest or donation of cash or other personal property or real estate for the benefit of such library shall have the right and privilege to vest the title thereto in a trustee, or trustees, of his own selection, and to provide for the selection of successor trustees, and to designate the manner in which said fund or property shall be invested and used. (1945, c. 103, § 9; 1947, c. 130; 1961, c. 112.)

§ 10-1-9a. Fees, service and rental charges; fines; sale of surplus or obsolete materials or equipment; deposit and disbursement of receipts.

The board of directors of a library established or maintained under this article may fix, establish, and collect such reasonable fees, service and rental charges as may be appropriate; may assess fines, penalties, damages, or replacement costs for the loss of, injury to, or failure to return any library property or material; and may sell surplus, duplicated, obsolete, or other unwanted materials or equipment belonging to the library. All moneys received from these or other sources in the course of the administration and operation of the library shall be deposited in the library fund and shall be disbursed by the board of directors in the manner prescribed elsewhere in this article. (1961, c. 112.)

§ 10-1-10. Injury to library property; penalty.

Any person who shall wilfully deface or injure any building or furniture, or deface, injure or destroy any picture, plate, map, engraving, newspaper, magazine, or book, or subject of art, or any other article belonging to a public library shall be guilty of a misdemeanor, and on conviction thereof shall be punished by a fine of not less than ten dollars, nor more than fifty dollars, or by imprisonment not exceeding six months. (1915, c. 64, § 8; Code 1923, c. 47, § 57; 1945, c. 103, § 10.)

§ 10-1-11. Wilful retention of library property.

Whoever wilfully retains any book, newspaper, magazine, pamphlet, manuscript, or other article belonging to any public library for thirty days after notice in writing to return the same, given after the expiration of the time that by the rules and regulations of the library such an article or other property may be kept, shall be liable for damages, to be recovered by said library board by appropriate proceedings before a justice of the peace; the recovery in each case to be paid to the proper office or custodian of the library fund: Provided, however, that the notice required hereby shall include a copy of this section. (1915, c. 64, § 9; Code 1923, c. 47, § 58; 1945, c. 103, § 11.)

§ 10-1-11a. Effect of article on existing laws.

Nothing in this article shall be construed to abolish or abridge any power or duty conferred upon any public library already established by virtue of any city or town charter or other special act, or to affect any existing local laws allowing or providing municipal aid to libraries. Any library now operating under any city or town charter or other special act has, however, the privilege of reorganizing under the provisions of this article.

All powers granted herein shall be considered to be conferred upon public libraries existing at the time of the passage of this act [February 21, 1961].

Any provision concerning the disbursement of funds including the designation of the depository of the library funds or of the library board's disbursing officer contained in this article may be adopted by a library board organized under the provisions of this article, notwithstanding any other provisions of law. (1945, c. 103, § 11a; 1961, c. 112.)

§ 8-12-5. General powers of every municipality and the governing body thereof.

In addition to the powers and authority granted by (i) the Constitution of this State, (ii) other provisions of this chapter, (iii) other general law, and (iv) any charter, and to the extent not inconsistent or in conflict with any of the foregoing except a special legislative charter, every municipality and the governing body thereof shall have plenary power and authority therein by ordinance or resolution, as the case may require, and by appropriate action based thereon:

* * *

(38) To establish, construct, acquire, maintain and operate a public library or museum or both for public use;

(39) To provide for the appointment and financial support of a library board in accordance with the provisions of article one [§ 10-1-1 et seq.], chapter ten of this Code; 1972, c. 77.)

SCHOOL LIBRARIES

(West Virginia Code Annotated, 1982, s.18-5-20.)

§ 18–5–20. School libraries; librarian.

The board may provide libraries for its schools and may purchase books, bookcases, and other things necessary therefor, and shall pay the cost of such libraries out of school funds of the county. In connection with any such school library, the board may employ a full-time librarian or may require one of the teachers at the school to serve as a part-time librarian. Any such full-time librarian or any such teacher-librarian, who holds a degree in library science based upon the successful completion of a full year of graduate work at an institution qualified and approved to offer such degree, and who holds a collegiate elementary, first-class high school, or other certificate of equal rank, shall be paid the same salary as is prescribed by law for teachers holding a master's degree.

The board shall have authority to employ during the vacation period a librarian for any school having a library of one hundred or more volumes, and to pay such librarian out of the school funds of the county an amount to be determined by the board. Any librarian so appointed shall keep the library open at least one day a week, at which time the patrons and pupils of the school may draw books from the library under such rules and regulations for the care and return thereof as the board may prescribe. (1908, c. 27, §§ 37, 38; 1919, c. 2, § 62; Code, 1923, c. 45, § 62; 1947, c. 83; 1949, c. 44.)

West Virginia library laws are reprinted from WEST VIRGINIA CODE ANNOTATED published by The Michie Co., Charlottesville, Virginia.

WISCONSIN

DIVISION FOR LIBRARY SERVICES

(West's Wisconsin Statutes Annotated, 1982, s.43.001-43.09.)

43.001 Definitions

In this chapter:

(1) "Division" means the division for library services.

(2) "State superintendent" means the state superintendent of public instruction.

(3) "Public library system" means a system established as either a federated public library system under s. 43.19 or a consolidated public library system under s. 43.21.

(4) "Municipality" means a city of the 2nd, 3rd or 4th class, village, town, county, tribal government or tribal association or a school district authorized to maintain a public library facility under s. 43.52. Notwithstanding its omission under this paragraph, a city of the 1st class may participate in a public library system under s. 43.19(3).

(5) "Network" means a formal or informal arrangement between libraries or other informational service organizations whereby materials, information and services are exchanged and made available to potential users.

History—
Subsec. (4) amended by—
    L.1979, c. 347, § 6, eff. July 1, 1980.
Subsec. (5) created by—
    L.1979, c. 347, § 6, eff. July 1, 1980.

43.03 General duties of state superintendent

The state superintendent shall:

(1) Promote, assist and plan the organization, development and improvement of school library media services to provide the resources needed for teaching and learning in the schools.

(2) Promote, assist, plan and coordinate the organization, development and improvement of public library services and public library systems to serve the needs of all citizens in the state.

(3)(a) Plan and coordinate school library media services with other library services and promote interlibrary cooperation and resource sharing between school library media programs and other libraries.

(b) Plan, coordinate, evaluate and set statewide priorities for the development of networks and intertype library cooperation among libraries in the state and by the libraries in the state with libraries and resource providers in other states, and promote interlibrary cooperation and resource sharing between local governments, public libraries and other libraries.

(c) Coordinate and promote the development of regional organizations for interlibrary cooperation and resource sharing among all types of libraries.

(d) Submit to the council on library and network development an annual report which describes the programs and policies carried out under pars. (a) to (c) in the preceding year and the programs and policies to be carried out under pars. (a) to (c) in the succeeding year.

(4) Plan and coordinate the provision of library services to groups with special needs, including institutional residents, the physically and mentally handicapped, the socially and economically disadvantaged and racial and ethnic minorities.

(5) Accept, on behalf of the state, grants from the federal government or any federal agency or gifts or grants from any other source to be used for the purposes designated under this chapter.

(6) Enter into an annual contract with the public library in a 1st class city for the provision of library services to physically handicapped persons, including the blind and visually handicapped, certified by competent authority as unable to read or use conventional printed materials as a result of physical limitations. For the purpose of this subsection, "competent authority" means any member of the medical or allied professions, and professional persons in the fields of public health, education, library service, rehabilitation, social work and public welfare.

(7) Contract for service with libraries and other resource providers in and outside of this state to serve as resources of specialized library materials and information not available in public libraries or the reference and loan library.

(8) Establish procedures necessary for the internal administrative operation of the division.

Source:
L.1979, c. 221, § 331, eff. April 30, 1980.
L.1979, c. 347, § 10, eff. July 1, 1980.

43.05   General duties of the division

The division shall:

(1) Coordinate and conduct continuing education programs for librarians of school library media programs, public libraries, public library systems and institutional library programs.

(2) Assist, as deemed appropriate by the division, in the recruitment of personnel for school library media programs, public libraries and public library systems.

(3) Provide professional and technical advisory, consulting and informational services to assist:

(a) School districts establishing, maintaining or expanding school library media programs and facilities;

(b) Public libraries and communities establishing, maintaining or expanding public libraries, public library systems and regional resource centers and their governing bodies;

(c) State agencies and officers; and

(d) Institutional library programs.

(4) Collect library statistics and conduct studies and surveys of library

needs throughout the state and report and publish the findings. The research shall be coordinated with statewide library planning.

(5) Ascertain which libraries in this state can suitably care for and advantageously use copies of the public documents printed at the expense of the state, including printing under ss. 35.28 and 35.29. The division shall designate the selected libraries as depositories of state documents and shall furnish lists of the depositories to the department of administration, to govern the distribution under s. 35.85(2)(b). All libraries designated as depositories for federal documents shall automatically be designated as depositories for state documents. The lists shall show, for each depository library, the number of copies of each printed state document it is to receive.

(6) Recommend and distribute standards for school library programs and facilities to school library media programs, standards for public libraries to public library governing bodies and standards for institutional library programs to governing bodies and administrators of institutional library programs and to heads of departments, as defined under s. 15.01(3), which administer institutional libraries.

(7) Establish standards for public library systems under s. 43.09(2).

(8) Establish standards for and issue certificates to public librarians under s. 43.09(1).

(9) Approve the establishment of public library systems under s. 43.13.

(10) Administer aids to public library systems under s. 43.24.

(11) Maintain a library to supplement the collections of public libraries, public library systems, regional resource centers and other types of libraries with specialized materials and information sources that are not appropriately held by such libraries, systems or centers and are not readily available from other resource providers, and to provide library lending services to state government.

(12) Assist the council on library and network development in the preparation of the descriptive and statistical report to be prepared by the council under s. 43.07(5).

(13) Carry out such other programs and policies as directed by the state superintendent.

Source:
L.1979, c. 347, § 12, eff. July 1, 1980.

43.07   Council on library and network development

The state superintendent and the division shall seek the advice of and consult with the council on library and network development in performing their duties in regard to library service. The state superintendent or the administrator of the division shall attend every meeting of the council. The council may initiate consultations with the department and the division. The council shall:

(1) Make recommendations to the division in regard to the development of standards for the certification of public librarians and standards for public library systems under s. 43.09.

(2) Advise the state superintendent in regard to the general policies and activities of the state's program for library development, interlibrary cooperation and network development.

(3) Advise the state superintendent in regard to the general policies and activities of the state's program for the development of school library media programs and facilities and the coordination of these programs with other library services.

(4) Hold an annual meeting for the purpose of discussing the report submitted by the state superintendent under s. 43.03(3)(d). Notice of the annual meeting shall be sent to appropriate libraries and audiovisual and informational services and library and audiovisual and informational service organizations. After the meeting, the council shall make recommendations to the state superintendent regarding the report.

(5) On or before July 1, 1980, and every 2nd year thereafter, transmit to the state superintendent a descriptive and statistical report on the condition

and progress of library services in the state and recommendations on how library services in the state may be improved. On or before September 1, 1980, and every 2nd year thereafter, the state superintendent shall transmit the report and recommendations to the governor and the legislature.

(6) Review that portion of the budget of the department of public instruction relating to library service. Recommendations of the council in regard to the budget shall be transmitted to the department at least 21 days before the department transmits its budget request to the governor, and shall accompany the department's budget request to the governor.

(7) Receive complaints, suggestions and inquiries regarding the programs and policies of the department of public instruction relating to library and network development, inquire into such complaints, suggestions and inquiries, and advise the state superintendent and the division on any action to be taken.

Source:
L.1979, c. 347, § 13, eff. July 1, 1980.

43.09   Certificates and standards

(1) Public librarians. The division shall issue certificates to public librarians and promulgate, under ch. 227, necessary standards for public librarians. The qualifications for public librarians shall be based on education, professional training and experience. Certificates already granted prior to December 17, 1971, shall remain in effect.

(2) Public library systems. (a) The division, by rule, shall promulgate necessary standards for public library systems. Such rules shall be consistent with s. 43.15 and shall be established in accordance with ch. 227, except that the division shall hold a public hearing prior to adoption of any proposed rule. In addition to the notice required under s. 227.021, the division shall endeavor to notify each public library of such public hearings. Standards for public library systems shall be based on the population served, adequacy of the buildings and physical facilities, the qualifications and number of personnel, book resources and other library materials, financial support and such other standards as the division finds necessary to ensure adequate library service.

(b) The division may provisionally approve, based on lesser standards than those set under par. (a), a newly established public library system for not more than 5 years. To be eligible for provisional approval, a system shall have a plan approved by the division which provides for compliance with the standards under par. (a) at the end of the period of provisional approval.

Source:
L.1971, c. 152, § 15, eff. Dec. 17, 1971.

PUBLIC LIBRARY SYSTEMS
(West's Wisconsin Statutes Annotated, 1982, s.43.11-43.22.)

43.11   County library planning committees

(1) Creation. Any county board may appoint a county library planning committee under this section. If a county board, in a county where all public library service is administered or coordinated by an existing library board, determines to appoint a committee under this section, the existing library board shall serve as the county library planning committee. The county board shall notify the division immediately upon appointment of the committee.

(2) **Organization.** (a) The county library planning committee shall be composed of not less than 7 nor more than 15 members. The residence of members shall reflect the population distribution within the county. The membership shall include representatives of existing public libraries in the county. One member only shall be a member of the county board. Appointments shall be for 3 years or until the committee's final report is accepted by the county board and the division, whichever occurs first.

(b) Annually, the committee shall select a chairman, vice chairman and secretary from its membership. The committee shall meet at least once every 3 months and more often on the call of the chairman or a majority of its members.

(3) **Duties.** (a) The committee shall investigate the potential of a public library system in the county and adjacent counties, and prepare a plan for the organization of a county or multicounty system. It shall conduct public hearings to which representatives of all libraries in the county shall be invited and shall cooperate with similar committees of adjoining counties for the purpose of planning multicounty public library systems.

(b) The committee's final report, including a plan for initial and long-range services and copies of any written agreements necessary to implement the proposed system, shall be filed with the county board and submitted to the division. Plans for multicounty systems shall include a method for allocating system board membership among library representatives and public members.

(4) **Dissolution.** The committee shall be dissolved either after 3 years or when its final report has been accepted both by the division and the county board, whichever occurs first.

Source:
L.1981, c. 20, § 711, eff. July 1, 1982.

43.13   Division review

(1) (a) No public library system may be established without the approval of the division. In reviewing final reports submitted by county library planning committees, the division shall consider, in addition to the standards set forth in s. 43.15, the proposed system territory, organization and financing, initial and long-range plans for library services, the role of existing multi-jurisdictional service programs in the territory and plans for cooperation with adjoining systems and with other kinds of libraries in the territory.

(b) If the division approves a final report, it shall report such approval to the appropriate county boards and county library planning committees. Upon acceptance by the county boards, the division shall certify to the appropriate county boards the establishment of the public library system proposed by the report, specifying the effective date of the establishment of the system.

(2) A public library system board may submit to the division a plan for the alteration in the territory included within the system or for a change in system organization from a federated to a consolidat-

ed system or vice versa. If the change proposed by the plan is approved, the division shall certify such fact to the system board, specifying the effective date of the change.

(3) The effective date of the establishment of a system under sub. (1) or of a change under sub. (2) shall be January 1 of the year specified by the division, except that the effective date of the establishment of a system approved prior to March 1, 1972, may be either January 1 or March 1, 1972.

(4) Any decision by the division under this section may be appealed to the state superintendent.

Source:

L.1971, c. 152, § 15, eff. Dec. 17, 1971.

43.15 Standards for public library systems

A public library system shall not be established unless it meets the requirements under this section.

(1) Population. The territory within the system shall:

(a) Contain at least one public library established under s. 43.52 in a city which, at the time of the system's establishment, has a population of more than 30,000. Any contractual arrangement existing on December 17, 1971, among a number of units of government whose territory consists of at least 3,500 square miles, and under which a multi-jurisdictional library service program is operated, which meets the requirements of this section other than the requirement for a city having a population of 30,000 or more shall be deemed to meet such requirement if it provides in the system plan for access by contract to the resources and services of a public library in a city having a population of 30,000 or more which is participating in a system.

(b) Have, at the time of its establishment, a population of 85,000 or more. Temporary certification shall be given to those systems which the 1970 census shows to have a population of at least 80,000. After January 1, 1981, no new system may be established, nor may a system be continued under temporary certification, containing territory having a total population of less than 85,000.

(2) Financial support. Each county proposed to be included within a system shall demonstrate, to the satisfaction of the division, its ability to comply with s. 43.24(2).

(3) Territory included. (a) A consolidated system shall consist of one county only. A federated system shall consist of one or more counties.

(b) No more than one system may be established within a single county. If the territory of a * * * municipality lies in 2 or more counties which are not in the same public library system, the municipal library board or, if no such board exists, the municipal governing body shall determine the system in which the city or village will participate.

(4) **Method of organization.** The system shall have a designated headquarters library and be organized as either of the following:

(a) A federated system in which the governing body of each included county, and those of its underlying * * * municipalities as have public libraries and are participating in the system, enter into written agreements for library services to be provided by the designated headquarters library or other system participants, except as provided in s. 43.64(2). The written agreements shall provide for each included county to furnish library service to residents of those * * * municipalities not maintaining a public library. A single-county public library system, whether federated or consolidated, may become part of a multicounty federated system by written agreement of the county board.

(b) A consolidated system in which the included county and its underlying * * * municipalities form a single library system, except as provided in s. 43.64(2). The county may for such purpose take over and acquire any library property by the consent of the authority controlling that property.

History—
Subsec. (3)(b) amended by—
L.1981, c. 197, § 1, eff. April 21, 1982.
Subsec. (4)(a) amended by—
L.1981, c. 197, § 1, eff. April 21, 1982.
Subsec. (4)(b) amended by—
L.1981, c. 197, § 1, eff. April 21, 1982.

43.17 Public library systems; general provisions

(1) **Board terms.** Every public library system shall be governed by a board appointed under s. 43.19 or 43.21. Upon the initial establishment of a board, the members shall be divided as nearly as possible into 3 equal groups to serve for terms expiring on January 1 of the 2nd, 3rd and 4th years, respectively, following their appointment. Thereafter, regular terms shall be for 3 years and shall commence on January 1. Vacancies shall be filled for the unexpired term in the same manner as regular appointments are made.

(2) **Board organization.** As soon as practicable after the initial establishment of a system, and thereafter in January of each year, the board shall organize by the election, from among its members, of a president and such other officers as it deems necessary.

(3) **Fiscal year.** The fiscal year of each federated public library system whose territory lies within 2 or more counties shall be the calendar year.

(4) **System administration.** Responsibility for administration of a public library system shall vest in a head librarian who shall be appointed by and directly responsible to the public library system board.

(5) **Annual report.** Annually, at the time required by the division, each public library system shall report to the division on its operations, expenditures and territory served during the preceding year, shall submit a plan describing the program for library service to be

carried out in the subsequent year and shall furnish such other information as the division requires.

(6) Cooperative services. A public library system may contract with another such system or with other libraries or resource centers to provide and receive library services.

(7) Existing employes. No person employed by a participating public library at the time of the establishment of a public library system shall lose, because of such establishment, any salary, fringe benefit or other employment rights in existence at that time.

(8) **Retirement.** If any employe of a participating * * * employer under the Wisconsin retirement * * * system becomes, by virtue of the establishment of a public library system, an employe of that library system, the library system shall become a participating * * * employer under the Wisconsin retirement * * * system.

(9) Contracts and bidding. All contracts for public construction, the estimated cost of which exceeds $1,000, made by a federated public library system whose territory lies within 2 or more counties shall be let by the public library system board to the lowest responsible bidder in accordance with s. 62.15(1) to (11) and (14). For purposes of this section, the system board possesses the powers conferred by s. 62.15 on the board of public works and the common council. All contracts made under this section shall be made in the name of the federated public library system and shall be executed by the system board president and such other board officer as the system board designates.

Source:
L.1971, c. 152, § 15, eff. Dec. 17, 1971.

43.18 Withdrawal and abolition

(1) **Withdrawal.** Not less than 3 years after affiliating with a public library system, a municipality may withdraw from the system by adoption of a resolution by a two-thirds vote of its governing body under pars. (a) and (b), if the resolution is adopted at least 6 months prior to the close of the system's fiscal year. The resolution shall become effective at the close of the system's fiscal year.

(a) With the approval of the governing body of each participating * * * municipality in the county, a county may withdraw from a federated public library system whose territory lies within 2 or more counties.

(b) A participating * * * municipality may withdraw from a federated public library system.

(2) Abolition. A county may abolish a public library system whose territory lies only within that county.

(3) Procedure. (a) Prior to taking any action under this section, the municipal governing body shall hold a public hearing on the proposed action and shall publish a class 1 notice, under ch. 985, of the hearing. Notice of the hearing also shall be given by registered mail not less than one week prior to the hearing to the governing body of every other municipality participating in the public library system, to the public library system board and to the division.

(b) A municipality withdrawing under this section from a public library system shall be responsible for its allocated share of the outstanding liabilities of the system on the effective date of its withdrawal.

(c) Upon taking final action under this section to withdraw from or abolish a public library system, a municipal governing body forthwith shall give notice, by registered mail, of the action taken to the governing body of every other municipality participating in the public library system, to the public library system board and to the division.

Source:

L.1971, c. 152, § 15, eff. Dec. 17, 1971.

43.19 Federated public library systems

(1) (a) In a federated public library system whose territory lies within a single county, the system board shall consist of 7 members appointed by the county board. At least 3 members of the system board, at the time of their appointment, shall be active voting members of library boards governing public libraries of participating municipalities, and at least one of these shall be a member of the library board governing the headquarters library. At least one but not more than 2 members of the county board shall be members of the system board at any one time.

(b) In a federated public library system whose territory lies within 2 or more counties, the system board shall consist of at least 15 and not more than 20 members appointed by the county boards, acting jointly. Appointments shall be in proportion to population as nearly as practical, but each county shall be represented by at least one member on the system board. Each county board may appoint one county board member to the system board, but if there are more than 5 counties, the total number of county board members shall not exceed 5 and county board representation shall be on a rotating basis. The library board governing the designated headquarters library shall have at least one member on the system board. The remaining system board members shall include such representatives of the library boards governing public libraries of participating municipalities and public members appointed from the counties at large as the county board determines.

(2) (a) A federated public library system whose territory lies within a single county shall be deemed an agency of the county. A

federated public library system whose territory lies within 2 or more counties shall be deemed a joint agency of those counties, but constitutes a separate legal entity for the following purposes: to have the exclusive custody and control of all system funds; to hold title to and dispose of property; to construct, enlarge and improve buildings; to make contracts; and to sue and be sued.

(b) A federated public library system board shall have the powers of a library board under ss. 43.58 to 43.62 with respect to system-wide functions and services. The local library boards shall retain responsibility for their public libraries in all other areas.

(3) Any county having a population of 500,000 or more and operating a library service program under s. 43.57 shall be paid state aid under s. 43.24 as if it were a federated public library system, if the library boards of the participating municipalities, acting jointly, file a plan describing the service program and proposed use and distribution of the state aid the program is expected to receive with the division and receive the division's approval. Such a program shall meet the standards promulgated under s. 43.09(2) and is subject to s. 43.17(5).

Source:
   L.1971, c. 152, § 15, eff. Dec. 17, 1971.

43.21   Consolidated public library systems

(1) In a consolidated public library system, the system board shall consist of 7 members appointed by the county board. In the initial appointment of a system board, at least 3 members of the system board, at the time of their appointment, shall be active voting members of library boards governing public libraries consolidated into the system. At least one but not more than 2 members of the county board shall be members of the system board at any one time.

(2) (a) A consolidated public library system shall be deemed an agency of the county by which created.

(b) A consolidated public library system board shall have the powers of a library board under ss. 43.58 to 43.62 and shall be responsible for the total program of public library service for the system territory.

(3) If it is consistent with the terms thereof, a gift, bequest, devise or endowment to a public library becoming part of a consolidated public library system may be taken over by the system board for general use of the system; otherwise, the system board shall maintain it for the benefit of the library to which given.

Source:
   L.1971, c. 152, § 15, eff. Dec. 17, 1971.

STATE AID

(West's Wisconsin Statutes Annotated, 1982, s.43.24.)

43.24 State aid

(1) Each public library system shall be paid state aid for the operation and maintenance of the system. The amount paid to each system shall be determined as follows:

(a) The total of the following shall be calculated for each system:

1. For each person residing in territory within the system, 50 cents.

2. For each square mile of territory within a system, $6 in a single-county system, $9 in a 2-county system, $12 in a 3-county system, $15 in a 4-county system and $18 in a system containing 5 or more counties.

3. An amount equal to 7% of the total operating expenditures for public library services in territory within the system from local and county sources in the calendar year immediately preceding the year for which aids are to be paid.

(b) The total amount for each system, determined under par. (a), shall be divided by the total amount, determined under par. (a), for all systems in the state.

(c) The ratio determined under par. (b) shall be multiplied by an amount equal to 11.25% of the total operating expenditures for public library services, in territories within all systems in the state, from local and county sources in the calendar year immediately preceding the calendar year for which aids are to be paid. The amount determined under this paragraph shall be the amount of aid paid to each system.

(2) (a) For a public library system to qualify for state aid under this section, the division shall find that a) the municipalities having territory within the system provided financial or other equivalent support for public library service during the preceding year in an amount which, when added to the state aid for which the system will be eligible, is adequate for the support and maintenance of public library service in the area in accordance with standards set under s. 43.09(2); and b) such support was at a level not lower than the average of the previous 3 years.

(b) For a public library system to maintain its eligibility for state aid under this section it must meet the service criteria specified under pars. (c) to (g).

(c) Each system shall provide the following services during the first year of operation:

1. Interloan of library materials among all participating libraries.

2. Reference and reference referral services from the headquarters library.

(d) Each system shall provide the following services by the end of the 2nd year of operation:

1. Complete library service as provided at the headquarters library or at the resource library if different from the headquarters li-

brary to any resident of the system on the same terms as the service is available to residents of the headquarters community.

2. The honoring of valid borrowers' cards of all public libraries in the system by all public libraries in the system.

(e) Each system shall provide the following services by the end of the 3rd year of operation:

1. In-service training for library personnel within the system.

2. Rapid and regular delivery and communication systems.

3. Service agreements with all adjacent library systems.

4. Professional consultant services to system libraries.

(f) A public library system shall by the end of the * * * 3rd year of its operation develop * * * agreements with other types of libraries in the system area, providing for appropriate sharing of library resources to benefit the clientele of all libraries.

(g) Each system shall engage in continuous planning with the division * * * and with libraries in the system area in regard to developing the library materials collection to meet the service needs * * * providing service to isolated, disadvantaged and handicapped residents, and furthering cooperative activities among all types of libraries in the system area.

(h) A public library system may regain its eligibility when it complies with pars. (c) to (g).

(3) Annually, the division shall review the reports and proposed service plans submitted by the public library systems under s. 43.17(5) for conformity with this chapter and such rules and standards as are applicable. Upon approval, the division shall certify to the department of administration * * * an estimated amount to which each system is entitled under this section * * *. Annually on or before December 1 of the year immediately preceding the year for which aids are to be paid, the department of administration

shall pay each system 75% of the certified estimated amount from the appropriation under s. 20.255(3)(d). The division shall, on or before the following April 30, certify to the department of administration the actual amount to which the system is entitled under this section. On or before July 1, the department of administration shall pay each system the difference between the amount paid on December 1 of the prior year and the certified actual amount of aid to which the system is entitled from the appropriation under s. 20.-255(3)(d). The division may reduce state aid payments when any system or any participant thereof fails to meet the requirements of sub. (2).

(4) The division shall assure through an annual audit and adjustment of aids, as necessary, that no more than 20% of the funds received by systems are used for administrative purposes.

(5) Any interest earned from the investment of state aid paid to each public library system under sub. (3) shall be allocated to the library system receiving the aid payments.

INTERSTATE LIBRARY COMPACT
(West's Wisconsin Statutes Annotated, 1982, Laws 1955, Chap. 496.)

Laws 1955, c. 496, effective July 1, 1955, provides:

Section 1. Execution of compact. The interstate library compact is hereby enacted into law and entered into on behalf of this state with any state bordering on Wisconsin which legally joins therein in substantially the following form:

INTERSTATE LIBRARY COMPACT

The contracting states agree that:

Article I—Purpose

Because the desire for the services provided by public libraries transcends governmental boundaries and can be provided most effectively by giving such services to communities of people regardless of jurisdictional lines, it is the policy of the states who are parties to this compact to co-operate and share their responsibilities in providing joint and co-operative library services in areas where the distribution of population makes the provision of library service on an interstate basis the most effective way to provide adequate and efficient services.

Article II—Procedure

The appropriate officials and agencies of the party states or any of their political subdivisions may, on behalf of said states or political subdivisions, enter into agreements for the co-operative or joint conduct of library services when they shall find that the executions of agreements to that end as provided herein will facilitate library services.

Article III—Content

Any such agreement for the co-operative or joint establishment, operation or use of library services, facilities, personnel, equipment, materials or other items not excluded because of failure to enumerate shall, as among the parties of the agreement: (1) detail the specific nature of the services, facilities, properties or personnel to which it is applicable; (2) provide for the allocation of costs and other financial responsibilities; (3) specify the respective rights, duties, obligations and liabilities; (4) stipulate the terms and conditions for duration, renewal, termination, abrogation, disposal of joint or common property, if any, and all other matters which may be appropriate to the proper effectuation and performance of said agreement.

Article IV—Conflict of laws

Nothing in this compact or in any agreement entered into hereunder shall be construed to supersede, alter, or otherwise impair any obligation imposed on any public library by otherwise applicable laws.

Article V—Administrator

Each state shall designate a compact administrator with whom copies of all agreements to which his state or any subdivision thereof is party shall be filed. The administrator shall have such powers as may be conferred upon him by the laws of his state and may consult and co-operate with the compact administrators of other party states and take such steps as may effectuate the purposes of this compact.

Article VI—Effective date

This compact shall become operative immediately upon its enactment by any state or between it and any other contiguous state or states so enacting.

Article VII—Renunciation

This compact shall continue in force and remain binding upon each party state until 6 months after any such state has given notice of repeal by the legislature. Such withdrawal shall not be construed to relieve any party to an agreement authorized by Articles II and III of the compact from the obligation of that agreement prior to the end of its stipulated period of duration.

Article VIII—Severability; Construction

The provisions of this compact shall be severable. It is intended that the provisions of this compact be reasonably and liberally construed.

Section 2. Administrator. The governor shall designate a state library official to be compact administrator. The compact administrator shall receive copies of all agreements entered into by the state or its political subdivisions and other states or political subdivisions; consult with, advise and aid such governmental units in the formulation of such agreements; make such recommendations to the governor, legislature, governmental agencies and units as he deems desirable to effectuate the purposes of this compact and consult and co-operate with the compact administrators of other party states.

Section 3. The compact administrator and the chief executive of any county, city, village or town is hereby authorized and empowered to enter into agreements with other states or their political subdivisions pursuant to the compact. Such agreements as may be made pursuant to this compact on behalf of the state of Wisconsin shall be made by the compact administrator. Such agreements as may be made on behalf of a political subdivision shall be made after due notice to the compact administrator and consultation with him.

Section 4. The agencies and officers of this state and its subdivisions shall enforce this compact and do all things appropriate to effect its purpose and intent which may be within their respective jurisdiction.

STATE HISTORICAL SOCIETY
(West's Wisconsin Statutes Annotated, 1982, s.44.01-44.11, 44.14.)

44.01   Historical society; corporate structure

(1) The historical society shall constitute a body politic and corporate by the name of "The State Historical Society of Wisconsin," and shall possess all the powers necessary to accomplish the objects and perform the duties prescribed by law. The historical society shall be an official agency and the trustee of the state.

(2) The historical society may adopt, and change, a seal, a constitution, bylaws and rules, and elect such officers as the constitution or bylaws prescribe. The composition and selection of the board of curators, and eligibility requirements for membership in the society shall be determined by the constitution and bylaws. There shall continue to be a board of curators for governing the historical society with powers substantially the same as at present.

(3) The governor, secretary of state and state treasurer shall be * * * members of the board of curators and shall * * * ensure that the interests of the state are protected.

(4) The historical society's acceptance of any benefits granted it by law shall be conclusively deemed its complete acquiescence in all laws enacted concerning the organization and operation of the society.

L.1971, c. 125, § 302, eff. Nov. 5, 1971.

44.015   Powers

The historical society may:

(1) Acquire any interest in real or personal property by gift, bequest or otherwise in any amount and may operate, manage, sell, rent or convey real estate acquired by gift, bequest, foreclosure or other means, upon such terms and conditions as the board of curators deems for its interests but may not sell, mortgage, transfer or dispose of in any manner or remove from its buildings, except for temporary purposes, any article therein without authority of law.

(2) Sell, exchange or otherwise dispose of duplicate books, periodicals or museum objects, or books, periodicals and museum objects outside its field of collection.

(3) Accept collections of private manuscripts, printed materials, tapes, films and artifacts, and it may enforce any and all reasonable restrictions on accessibility to the public, use or duplication of said collections which are agreed upon by the donor and the historical society.

(4) Take proper steps to promote the study of history by lectures, and diffuse and publish information relating to the description and history of the state.

Source:

L.1969, c. 276, § 294, eff. Dec. 28, 1969.
L.1977, c. 29, § 528, eff. July 1, 1977.

44.02 Historical society; duties

The historical society shall:

(1) Serve as trustee of the state in the preservation and care of all records, both printed and written, and all articles and other materials of historic interest and significance placed in its custody, and interest itself constructively as the agent of the state in the preservation and care of all similar materials wherever they may be.

(2) Collect by gift, exchange or purchase books, periodicals, pamphlets, records, tracts, manuscripts, maps, charts and other papers, artifacts, relics, paintings, photographs and other materials illustrative of the history of this state in particular and of the West generally.

(3) Conduct research in the history of Wisconsin in particular and of the West generally.

(4) Inculcate through publications, museum extension services and other media a wider and fuller knowledge and appreciation of the history of Wisconsin and its significance.

(5) Keep its main library and museum rooms open at all reasonable hours on business days for the reception of the citizens of this state who may wish to visit the same, without fee; except that the society may collect a fee for admission to historic sites or buildings acquired, leased or operated by the society elsewhere in the state, including areas within state parks or on other state-owned lands which incorporate historic buildings, restorations, museums or remains and which are operated by the society by agreement with the department of natural resources or other departments, or for lectures, pageants or similar special events, or for admission to defray the costs of special exhibits in its several buildings of documents, objects or other materials not part of the society's regular collections but brought in on loan from other sources for such special exhibitions. The society may also procure and sell or otherwise dispose of postcards, souvenirs

and other appropriate merchandise to help defray the costs of operating its several plants and projects.

(6) Thoroughly catalog the entire collections of said society for the more convenient reference of all persons who have occasion to consult the same.

(7) Loan, for such periods and under such rules and restrictions as it may adopt, to libraries, educational institutions and other organizations or to private individuals in good standing, such books, pamphlets, museum objects, or other materials that if lost or destroyed could easily and without much expense be replaced. No work on genealogy, no newspaper file, or book, map, chart, document, manuscript, pamphlet or other material whatsoever of a rare nature shall be permitted to be sent out from the library except on interlibrary loan to a research library under regulations safeguarding the materials during transit and while in use.

(8) Bind except when microfilmed the unbound books, documents, manuscripts, pamphlets, and especially newspaper files in its possession.

(9) Take an active interest in the preservation and use of the noncurrent public records of historical importance of counties, cities, villages, towns, school districts and other local governmental units.

(10) Conduct a research center in American history for the benefit of the students and faculty of the university of Wisconsin system as well as for members of the general public and to facilitate the further understanding by the general public of the significance of the American experiment.

(11) To work with the auxiliaries, affiliates and chapters established under s. 44.03 in the encouragement, stimulation and development of worth-while historical projects and undertakings at the county and local level.

(12)(a) Arrange and schedule the painting of the portrait of the governor * * * or any former governor.

(b) Establish a committee consisting of one member of a Wisconsin college or university art history department, a Wisconsin college or university art department, a member of the board of curators of the state historical society, a member of the arts board and the secretary of administration or his or her designee, that will select, subject to the approval of the governor, an artist to paint the portrait as provided under par. (a).

(c) Costs incurred under pars. (a) and (b) shall be charged to the appropriation under s. 20.245(1)(fb) up to a limit of $10,000 per portrait. Costs in excess of $10,000 per portrait may be charged to the appropriation under s. 20.245(1)(fb) only with the prior approval of the joint committee on finance

(d) Be the custodian of the official series of the painted portraits of the governors of Wisconsin and maintain the portraits in proper condition. No person may retouch, restore or alter any such portrait while the artist is alive, other than the artist or a person working under the artist's direction or authorization. The society may permit any or all of the portraits to be exhibited in such state buildings for such periods of time as it deems feasible.

(13) To faithfully expend and apply all money received to the fulfillment of its duties and purposes as directed by law.

(14) To hold all its present and future property for the state.

(15) To promote a wider appreciation of the American heritage with particular emphasis on the collection, advancement and dissemination of knowledge of the history of Wisconsin and of the West.

(16) To collect, embody, arrange and preserve in authentic form, a library of books, pamphlets, maps, charts, manuscripts, papers, paintings, statuary, and other materials illustrative of the history of the state.

(17) To preserve the memory of its early pioneers, and to obtain and preserve narratives of their exploits, perils, and adventures.

(18) To exhibit faithfully the antiquities, and the past and present condition, and resources of Wisconsin.

(20) Have authority to operate, maintain, acquire and develop outdoor historic sites related to the outdoor recreation program under s. 23.30.

(21) Serve as the principal historic preservation agency of the state and in that capacity carry out a program of preservation of historic properties as specified under s. 44.22.

(22) Acquire, maintain and operate historic properties representative of this state's rural and urban heritage.

Source:

L.1977, c. 26, § 26, eff. June 15, 1977.
L.1977, c. 29, §§ 529 to 531, eff. July 1, 1977.

44.03 Affiliated societies

(1) County or local historical societies without capital stock may be incorporated as affiliates of the historical society, to gather and preserve the books, documents and artifacts relating to the history of their region or locality. No fees shall be charged by any register of deeds for recording nor by the secretary of state for filing the articles of organization or its amendments, or for a certificate of incorporation of any such society, but the secretary of state shall not accept articles of incorporation under this section unless they are approved by

the board of curators of the historical society.

(2) State-wide, county or other patriotic or historical organizations, or chapters in this state may be incorporated as affiliates of the historical society under sub. (1) if their purposes and programs are similar to and consonant with those of the historical society and its affiliates, or if already incorporated, the organizations or chapters may apply to the board of curators for affiliation with the historical society. Upon incorporation under this section or acceptance of affiliation by the board of curators the applying organization shall as an affiliate accept the provisions and shall be entitled to all the benefits of this section. Any affiliated society shall be a member and entitled to one vote in any general meeting of the historical society. The board of curators may terminate the affiliation as an affiliate of the historical society under this section of any such organization by formal resolution, a copy of which shall be deposited with the secretary of state.

(3) Every affiliated society shall make a report of its work annually to the historical society, which, in its entirety or in part, may be included in the publications of the historical society, and upon application of any affiliated society the historical society may accept, in behalf of the state, custody of or title to the property, records and collections of the affiliated society or may assist in the disposal thereof. If any affiliated society becomes, in the opinion of the board of curators of the historical society, inactive or defunct, title to such property, records and collections not otherwise provided for in the grants of donors or in the articles of incorporation of the inactive and defunct society, shall vest in the historical society which shall take appropriate action in the public interest for the protection or disposal of such property, records and collections. Preference in disposition shall be given to historical or related organizations in the area or to whatever county or local governmental unit that has aided such affiliate financially.

(4) The historical society, for the purpose of establishing uniformity in organization and methods of work, may prepare and furnish uniform articles of organization and bylaws to any affiliated society, but the affiliate may adopt additional bylaws.

(5) The historical society may provide for annual or other meetings of officers or representatives of affiliated societies at times and places to be fixed by its director, or by such officers or representatives, and the proceedings of such meetings, or portions its director selects, may be included in its published reports. Each affiliated society shall receive a copy of each of the publications of the state society on the same terms as those granted to life members of the state society.

(6) Custody of public records of county, village, town, school district or other governmental units may be accepted by any affiliated society which has been designated a regional depository under s. 44.10, but title to these records shall remain with the historical society. In the event of the dissolution or incapacity of any affiliated society, it shall be obligatory on the last group of officers and members to notify the director of the historical society that the affiliated society can no longer retain custody of these records and to deliver them to a depository designated by the historical society.

Source:

L.1969, c. 276, §§ 296, 596, eff. Dec. 28, 1969.

44.04 School services

(1) The historical society, as part of its program as an educational institution, shall offer to the schools in this state such materials as it shall prepare or make available to facilitate the instruction in the history and civil government of Wisconsin required by s. 118.-01(1).

(2) To this end it may prepare, publish, issue, loan or circulate such magazines, books, aids, guides and other publications, such visual aids, special exhibits, and other teaching materials and aids as it, in consultation with the department of public instruction, deems advisable.

(3) It may make such charges as its board of curators shall establish as just and proper to defray in part the costs of this program.

Source:

L.1969, c. 276, § 596, eff. Dec. 28, 1969.

44.05 American history research center

(1) The historical society, in order to promote the wider understanding of the significance of the American heritage, shall encourage research in American history in general, and in the history of Wisconsin and the west particularly, through its American history research center and the other divisions of this agency, and interpret to the public the nature of the said heritage, and the role of state and local history in elucidating and facilitating the understanding of the American democracy, social, political, cultural and economic.

(2) The society, in pursuit of these goals, may be the beneficiary of bequests in any form, may undertake research projects, make grants-in-aid to students of particular topics germane to the purposes of the center, publicize the American story or parts thereof through publications of various types, exhibits, photographic or microphotographic reproductions, radio, pageantry and such other me-

dia as may best lend themselves to its work.

Source:

L.1967, c. 29, § 4, eff. May 18, 1967.
L.1969, c. 276, § 596, eff. Dec. 28, 1969.

44.06   Depository of public documents

(1) The historical society shall be the official public documents depository for the state. Three copies of all printed, mimeographed, or otherwise reproduced state publications, reports, releases and other matter published at the expense of the state shall be sent to the historical society by the department of administration in accordance with s 35.85(7). In those instances where a given publication is not distributed by the department of administration, 3 copies shall be sent to the historical society by the department, commission or agency of origin.

(2) The director of the historical society shall file with the department of administration, and may revise, lists of state, county, municipal, federal, or other agencies to which state public printing should be distributed in accordance with interstate or international comity, with or without exchange, as provided in s. 35.86, in order to maintain or enlarge the reference collections of the society and the state. The documents so specified shall be shipped to the addressees directly from the office of the department of administration, carriage charges payable by the state.

(3) The historical society shall keep available to other state agencies and to citizens of Wisconsin and other states its public document collections under such proper and reasonable regulations as may be deemed advisable.

(4) The historical society may loan such documents, except those of rare nature, to other state agencies for official use or on interlibrary loan to other reference libraries under such rules and regulations and for such period as may appear desirable.

(5) The historical society shall prepare a periodic checklist of public documents issued by the state, including all reports, circulars, bulletins and releases issued by the various state departments, boards, commissions and agencies and shall publish this list in such form and with such notes as to show the scope and purpose of such publication.

Source:

L.1969, c. 276, § 596, eff. Dec. 28, 1969.

44.07   Museum extension service

(1) The historical society, in conjunction with its museum program and in order to make its collections and the teaching values of

museum materials available on a state-wide basis and to stimulate more effective local museum techniques, may operate a museum extension service with or without the co-operation of other museums or its auxiliary societies.

(2) The said society may for such purpose lend to other museums, public libraries, art galleries, colleges, schools or other responsible institutions or organizations, under such rules and safeguards and for such period as it deems desirable, such items and objects from its collections as are not irreplaceable.

(3) The society may participate in co-operative or joint exhibits with other museums or auxiliary societies in this program, and may out of the appropriation in s. 20.245(1) extend financial assistance not to exceed $1,000 in the aggregate in any year to other museums or auxiliaries where and only where such aid is found necessary to enable such other museums or auxiliaries to participate in this program.

(4) Transportation charges and other minor costs of such extension exhibits may be charged the exhibitor.

Source:

L.1969, c. 276, § 596, eff. Dec. 28, 1969.

44.09   County, local and court records

The proper officer of any county, city, village, town, school district or other local governmental unit may offer, and the historical society may accept for preservation, title to such noncurrent records as in the historical society's judgment are of permanent historical value and which are no longer needed for administrative purposes by such local governmental unit. The proper officer of any court may offer, and the historical society may accept for preservation, on order of the judge of the court, title to such records as have been photographed or microphotographed or which have been on file for at least 75 years, and which are deemed by the historical society to be of permanent historical value.

Source:

L.1969, c. 276, § 297, eff. Dec. 28, 1969.

44.10   Regional depositories for records

(1) The historical society, through its board of curators, in its corporate capacity and as trustee of the state may enter into agreements with the university of Wisconsin system or such other public or quasi-public institutions, agencies or corporations as the board of curators of the society shall designate to serve as the regional records depository for a given area. Said agreements shall specify the area to

be served by the depository, and the methods of accessioning, cataloguing, care, housing, preservation and servicing of these and such other material as may be placed by the historical society or in the name of the historical society in such regional depositories under such agreements, it being the intent of this section to provide an orderly, uniform state-wide system for the retention and preservation of important court, county and local public records on a manageable basis and under proper professional care in the region of origin. Only where such arrangements cannot be accomplished may the said society transfer such records to the state archives. Said society shall compile and maintain for reference purposes as soon as may be convenient a union list of the records of county, city, village, town, school district, or other local governmental unit, or court, title to which is transferred to it under s. 44.09.

(2) The board of curators may establish county records depositories within the regions served by the regional depositories established in sub. (1). The board may enter into agreements with these county depositories similar to those provided above for regional depositories, and records may be loaned temporarily from regional depository to a county depository, title in all cases remaining in the state society. The union list of records of county, city, village, town, school district or other local governmental units, or court, provided in sub. (1) shall indicate such transfers or loans of records between depositories so as to show at all times the present location of each group of records.

Source:
L.1977, c. 26, § 27, eff. June 15, 1977.

44.11 Central depository library

The board of curators of the historical society shall have the same authority to participate in the formation and maintenance of a nonprofit-sharing corporation for the purpose of providing and operating a central library depository as is conferred upon the board of regents of the university of Wisconsin system under s. 36.11(12). Section 36.11(12) shall, so far as applicable, apply to the board of curators of the historical society and for the purposes of this section whenever the words "board of regents" appear in s. 36.11(12) they shall be deemed to mean "board of curators of the historical society".

Source:
L.1973, c. 335, § 13.

44.14 Central depository loan collection, federal documents

(1) It is the purpose of this section to establish a more economical system of handling federal documents in the state in such a way

as to effect savings of staff and space to the participating libraries, both state and local; to make such documents more available to more of the people, colleges and libraries of the state, in accordance with the purposes of the federal depository act of 1895 and the needs of the citizens of the state; and to make possible substantial economies in the publication costs of such documents at the federal level as well. To this end the state documents depository established by s. 44.06 may acquire and establish a central state depository and loan collection of federal documents for the benefit of the university of Wisconsin system, the state law library, the depository libraries and such other college and public libraries in this state as may desire to share in the benefits of this loan collection.

(2) The university of Wisconsin system and the public and other participating libraries, federal regulations permitting, may transfer outright or may loan indefinitely to this central depository any or all federal documents now in their possession which in their opinion are so little used for ready reference purposes as to make their retention unnecessary if copies are available on loan from the central depository loan collection.

(3) Documents so transferred may be used by the society to furnish participating libraries with items needed for their permanent reference collections, for the central loan collection, or for exchange, trade or sale in order to make more complete and useful the central loan collection established by this section.

(4) The board of curators may establish such rules governing the loan of books from the central depository loan collection and may make such charges to cover shipping costs as may be deemed necessary and advisable.

Source:

L.1977, c. 26, §§ 28, 29, eff. June 15, 1977.

COUNTY AND MUNICIPAL LIBRARIES
General Provisions
(West's Wisconsin Statutes, 1982, s.43.52-43.64.)

43.52   Municipal libraries

(1) Any municipality may establish, equip and maintain a public library, and may annually levy a tax or appropriate money to provide a library fund, to be used exclusively to maintain the public library; and may enact and enforce police regulations to govern the use, management and preservation thereof. After December 17, 1971, any municipality desiring to establish a new public library shall obtain a written opinion by the division regarding the feasibility and desirability of establishing the public library before final action is taken. The

division shall render its opinion within 30 days of the time the request is received.

(2) Every public library shall be free for the use of the inhabitants of the municipality by which it is established and maintained, subject to such reasonable regulations as the library board prescribes in order to render its use most beneficial to the greatest number. The library board may exclude from the use of the public library all persons who wilfully violate such regulations.

(3) Any school district which maintained and operated a public library facility prior to December 17, 1971, shall be considered a municipality for the purposes of this chapter.

Source:

L.1977, c. 418, § 286f, eff. May 19, 1978.

43.54 Municipal library board composition

(1) (a) Each public library established under s. 43.52 shall be administered by a library board composed in each city of the 2nd or 3rd class of 9 members, in each city of the 4th class or county of 7 members and in each village * * * town, tribal government or tribal association of 5 members. Members shall be residents of the municipality, except that not more than 2 members may be residents of towns adjacent to the municipality. Members shall be appointed by the mayor, county board chairman, village president * * *, town chairman or tribal chairman, respectively, with the approval of the municipal governing body. In school districts authorized to maintain public library facilities under s. 43.52, the library board shall be composed of 7 members appointed by the school board chairperson with the approval of the school board.

(b) Upon their first appointment, the members shall be divided as follows: the 9-member board into 3 equal classes, to serve 1, 2 and 3 years respectively; the 7-member board into 3 classes, 3 to serve for 3 years, 2 to serve for 2 years and 2 to serve for one year; the 5-member board into 3 classes, 2 to serve for 3 years, 2 to serve for 2 years and one to serve for one year, from July 1 in the year of their appointment in the case of cities, towns * * * villages and tribal governments or tribal associations and from January 1 following their appointment in the case of counties. Thereafter, each regular appointment shall be for a term of 3 years.

History—
Subsec. (1)(a) amended by—
L.1981, c. 197, § 3, eff. April 21, 1982.
Subsec. (1)(b) amended by—
L.1981, c. 197, § 3, eff. April 21, 1982.

(c) The appointing authority shall appoint as one of the members a school district administrator, or his representative, to represent the public school district or districts in which the public library is located. Not more than one member of the municipal governing body shall at any one time be a member of the library board.

(d) No compensation shall be paid to the members of a library board for their services, but they may be reimbursed for their actual and necessary expenses incurred in performing duties outside the municipality if so authorized by the library board.

(e) A majority of the membership of a library board constitutes a quorum, but any such board may, by regulation, provide that 3 or more members thereof shall constitute a quorum.

(2) As soon as practicable after the first appointments, at a date and place fixed by the appointing officer, and annually thereafter within 30 days after the time designated in this section for the beginning of terms, the members of the library board shall organize by the election, from among their number, of a president and such other officers as they deem necessary.

(3) In any city of the 2nd or 3rd class, the common council may, by a two-thirds vote, provide for the reduction of the number of appointive members of the library board to 7. Thereupon, whenever a term expires or a vacancy occurs, no appointment shall be made until the number of such members has been so reduced, whereupon the remaining members shall be by lot divided by the common council into 3 classes, 3 to serve for 3 years, 2 to serve for 2 years and 2 to serve for one year, respectively, from the date of such completed reduction, and thereafter each regular appointment shall be for a term of 3 years, from the succeeding July 1.

Source:

L.1971, c. 152, §§ 19, 20, eff. Dec. 17, 1971.

43.56 Joint library boards

Joint library boards may be created by any 2 or more municipalities by appropriate agreement of their governing bodies. When so created, such a joint board shall have all of the powers provided by s. 43.58 and other statutes relating to library boards for the purpose of operating the public libraries of the participating units of government. Without limitation because of enumeration, the agreements relating to the creation of joint library boards may cover subjects such as membership and length of terms of office of board members, and all other appropriate matters pertaining to the creation and operation of such a joint board.

Source:

L.1971, c. 152, § 19, eff. Dec. 17, 1971.

43.57 County system of libraries

(1) (a) The county board of any county having a population of 150,000 or more may, pursuant to ss. 43.52 to 43.64, establish and maintain a public library system for the county, and may for such purpose adopt, take over and acquire any libraries already established, by consent of the authorities controlling those libraries.

(b) The county board of any county having a population of 500,000 or more may, by contract with any municipality within the county, extend the jurisdiction of any existing library board therein and provide for the maintenance of a county system of libraries by that municipality.

(2) The clerk of each such county shall submit to the county board, at each annual November meeting, a report covering the preceding fiscal year, showing in detail the amount and proportion of the money expended by the county pursuant to sub. (1) in each village and city. The county board shall thereupon determine the proportionate amount to be raised and paid by each such municipality to reimburse the county for the amount so advanced. Within 10 days after such determination, the county clerk shall charge to each municipality and certify to its clerk the amounts due. Each municipality shall levy a tax sufficient to meet such charge and shall pay over to the county the amounts so certified in accordance with this subsection. The tax shall be deemed a county special tax for tax settlement purposes, but the city or village shall pay over to the county on or before March 22 in each year in cash the percentage of such tax actually collected. The percentage shall be determined by applying the ratio of collection of the entire tax roll of the city or village, excepting special assessments and taxes levied pursuant to * * * ss. 66.88 to 66.918, to the amount of the county special tax. If any city or village fails to so raise and pay over such money to the county, the county board may compel such payment.

History—
Subsec. (2) amended by—
L.1981, c. 282, § 47, eff. April 27, 1982.

43.58 Powers and duties

(1) The library board shall have exclusive control of the expenditure of all moneys collected, donated or appropriated for the library fund, and of the purchase of a site and the erection of the library building whenever authorized. The library board also shall have exclusive charge, control and custody of all lands, buildings, money or other property devised, bequeathed, given or granted to, or otherwise acquired or leased by, the municipality for library purposes.

(2) The library board shall audit and approve all vouchers for the expenditures of the public library and forward such vouchers or schedules covering the same, setting forth the names of claimants, the amounts of each claim and the purpose for which expended, to the municipal clerk or, in the case of a school district acting under s. 43.52, the school board clerk, with a statement thereon, signed by the library board secretary or other designee of the library board, that the expenditure has been incurred and that the library board has audited and approved the bill. The municipal or school board clerk shall thereupon draw an order upon the treasurer, and the same shall be paid as other municipal orders are paid as provided by s. 66.042 or, where appropriate, s. 120.54.

(3) Any person having a claim or demand against the munici-

pality growing out of any act or omission of the library board shall file with the library board a written statement thereof. If the claim or demand or any part thereof is disallowed, the claimant may bring an action against the municipality in the same manner that an action may be brought after the disallowance of a claim by the common council of a city under the general charter.

(4) The library board may appoint a librarian and such other assistants and employes as it deems necessary, and prescribe their duties and compensation.

(5) The library board may employ competent persons to deliver lectures upon scientific, literary, historical or educational subjects; and may cooperate with the university of Wisconsin system, vocational, technical and adult education schools, the historical society, the department of public instruction, cooperative educational service agencies, school board or other educational institutions to secure such lectures or to foster and encourage by other means the wider use of books and other resource, reference and educational materials upon scientific, historical, economic, literary, educational and other useful subjects.

(6) (a) Within 30 days after the conclusion of the fiscal year of the municipality in which the public library is located, the library board shall make a report to the division and to its municipal governing body. The report shall state the condition of the library board's trust and the various sums of money received for the use of the public library during the year, specifying separately the amounts received from appropriations, from the income of trust funds, from rentals and other revenues of the public library and from other sources. The report shall state separately the condition of the permanent trust funds in the library board's control, shall state in detail the disbursements on account of the public library during that fiscal year and shall contain an estimate of the needs of the public library for the next succeeding fiscal year.

(b) The report to the division shall include data concerning library materials, facilities, personnel, operations and such other information as the division requests.

Source:
L.1977, c. 26, § 25, eff. June 15, 1977.

43.60 Library extension and interchange

(1) The library board of any municipality may, by contract or upon such conditions and regulations as it prescribes, extend the use of the public library to nonresidents of the municipality, or exchange books either permanently or temporarily with any other library.

(2) The library board of any municipality may, by agreement with any other municipality, provide for the loaning of books from its public library, singly or in traveling libraries, to the residents of the other municipality. The other municipality may levy a tax and appropriate money annually to meet its obligations under the agreement.

(3) Whenever the annual sum appropriated by the other municipality pursuant to sub. (2) equals or exceeds one-sixth of the net annual income of the public library during the preceding fiscal year, the mayor, village president * * *, town or county chairman or tribal chairman of the other municipality, with the approval of the governing body thereof, shall appoint from among the residents of the municipality an additional member of the library board of the public library and, when such sum equals or exceeds one-third of the net annual income, 2 additional members, for a term of 3 years from the July 1 next succeeding such appointment, and thereafter for terms of 3 years. Whenever the appropriation made is less than the one-third specified, the office of one such additional member of the board and, if less than the one-sixth specified, the office of both shall be vacant from the July 1 next thereafter.

History—
Subsec. (3) amended by—
   L.1981, c. 197, § 4, eff. April 21, 1982.

43.62   Acquisition of property

(1) Any municipality may purchase or acquire one or more sites, erect one or more buildings and equip the same for a public library or any library already established; or may adopt, take over and acquire any library already established, by consent of the authorities controlling the same.

(2) All persons wishing to make donations of property for the benefit of a public library may vest the title thereto in the library board, to be held and controlled by the board, when accepted, according to the terms of the deed of gift, devise or bequest. As to such property the board shall be deemed special trustees.

(3) (a) If a gift, bequest, devise or endowment is made to any public library, the library board thereof may pay or transfer the gift, bequest, devise or endowment, or the proceeds thereof, to the treasurer of the municipality in which the public library is situated, may entrust any funds therefrom to a public depository under ch. 34 or may pay or transfer such gift, bequest, devise or endowment to any member of the library board to be selected by the library board and thereafter to be known as financial secretary. The financial secretary shall hold his office only during his membership on the library board and shall be elected annually at the same time and in the same manner as the other officers of the library board.

(b) If any such treasurer or financial secretary holds any property belonging to the public library, the library board shall require a bond from the treasurer or financial secretary to the library board in such sum, not less than double the amount of such property so held by him, and with such sureties as the library board requires. The bond shall be conditioned in substantially the same form as the ordinary bond required from the treasurer of the municipality, with the necessary changes.

(c) The treasurer or financial secretary shall make an annual report to the library board showing in detail the amount, investment, income and disbursements from the trust funds in his charge. Such report shall also be appended to the annual report of the library board under s. 43.58(6). The treasurer or financial secretary shall also send a copy of each annual report to the commissioner of banking.

(4) Any county may receive, by devise, bequest or gift, property for the purpose of establishing a public library for the county and may enter into an agreement to maintain a public library in consideration thereof, and shall be bound to faithfully perform such agreement. In such case the library board may properly administer the same.

(5) (a) In the case of a gift for a library building, the library board of the municipality shall have the exclusive right to select and contract for the purchase of a site therefor, at a cost not to exceed one-third of the gift. The library board shall report forthwith to the municipal governing body the amount required to pay for such site, and the municipal governing body shall thereupon by resolution include such sum in the next succeeding annual tax levy or provide for an issue of bonds in the required amount.

(b) Whenever the library board certifies to the municipal governing body that it is unable to acquire the site selected for a just and reasonable price and that a just and reasonable price for the site selected does not exceed the amount which may be legally expended therefor, the municipal governing body shall proceed to acquire such site by condemnation. If the compensation awarded in the condemnation proceedings exceeds one-third of the gift, the proceedings shall be valid if, within 60 days after the final award, the excess is provided for by private donation or otherwise. If the excess is not so provided for, the proceedings shall, upon motion, be dismissed with costs.

Source:

L.1971, c. 152, § 21, eff. Dec. 17, 1971.

43.64   County tax

(1) The county board of a county expending money for public library service to its inhabitants may levy a tax to provide funds for such service and shall include any amount of tax under this subsection in the amount of taxes determined to be levied under s. 70.62(1).

(2) Any city, town, village or school district in a county levying a tax for a county library under sub. (1) shall, upon written application to the county board of the county, be exempted from the tax levy, if the city, town, village or school district making the application expends for a library fund during the year for which the tax levy is made a sum at least equal to the sum which it would have to pay toward the county tax levy. For the purposes of this subsection, "library fund" means the funds raised by the city, town, village or school district by tax levy or appropriation under s. 43.52(1) or the funds expended by the city, town, village or school district under an agreement with another municipality under s. 43.60(2).

History—
Subsec. (2) amended by—
L.1981, c. 20, § 719, eff. July 31, 1981.

Cities-First Class
(West's Wisconsin Statutes Annotated, 1982, s.229.11-229.17.)

229.11   Milwaukee libraries and museums

Any city of the 1st class however incorporated may establish and maintain, for the free use of the inhabitants thereof, a public library or a public museum for the exhibition of objects in natural history, anthropology and history, either the several or any one of these specifically or either of such institutions; and may receive, hold and manage any devise, bequest, donation or loan for the establishment, increase or maintenance thereof, under such regulations and conditions as may be prescribed pursuant to law or agreed upon by and between the donors and said city.

Source:
L.1971, c. 152, § 27, eff. Dec. 17, 1971.

229.12   Board of trustees, constitution

(1) Each such institution shall be administered by a separate board of 10 trustees, consisting of:

(a) The president of the board of school directors and the city superintendent of schools.

(b) Seven members who shall be appointed by the mayor on the 3rd Tuesday in April. Three of the 7 members shall be selected from among the aldermen holding a 4-year term, and shall serve as such trustees during their aldermanic terms; and the other 4 shall be selected from among the residents and taxpayers of the city, for original terms of 1, 2, 3 and 4 years, respectively, commencing on May 1 next after their appointment, and for successive terms of 4 years each.

(c) One member who shall be a county board member residing in the county outside the city of the 1st class, who shall be appointed by the county executive and confirmed by the county board for a 4-

year term commencing on May 1 next after his appointment, and for successive terms of 4 years each.

(2) Said trustees shall take the official oath, and be subject to the restrictions, disabilities, liabilities, punishments and limitations prescribed by law as to aldermen in such city. They shall not receive any compensation for their services as such trustees; and shall not individually become or cause themselves to become interested, directly or indirectly, in any contract or job for the purchase of any matter pertaining to the institution in their charge, or of fuel, furniture, stationery or other things necessary for the increase and maintenance thereof.

Source:

L.1979, c. 110, § 36d, eff. March 1, 1980.

229.13 Board of trustees; annual meeting and general functions

(1) The annual meeting of the board of trustees of the public library shall be held on the 2nd Monday of May, and of the public museum on the 3rd Tuesday of May, in each year, at which meeting a president shall be chosen annually from their number.

(2) Each board shall have general care, control and supervision of the institution in its charge, its appurtenances, fixtures and furniture, and of the disbursements of all moneys belonging to the institutional funds, respectively. The trustees of the public library shall have charge of the selection and purchase of books, pamphlets, maps, and other matters pertaining to the library; and the trustees of the public museum shall have charge of the receipt, selection, arrangement and disposition of the specimens and objects pertaining to such museum. Each said board shall prescribe regulations for the management, care, and use of the institution, and adopt such measures as shall promote the public utility thereof, and may prescribe and enforce penalties for violations of such regulations.

(3) With the authorization of the common council, the board of trustees of the public library may contract with the county board under s. 43.57 for the provision of library services.

Source:

L.1971, c. 152, §§ 27, 36m, eff. Dec. 17, 1971.

229.14 Librarian, director and employes; curators

(1) At its first meeting the board of trustees shall elect by ballot a person of suitable learning, scientific attainments, ability and experience for librarian of the public library or director of the public museum respectively. Each shall be selected in accordance with and shall be subject to the usual laws, rules and regulations of the city

civil service commission. Each shall receive such compensation as shall be fixed by the board of trustees and shall be the secretary of the board.

(2) The board shall appoint and fix the compensation of such assistants and employes for the institution as they deem necessary and expedient.

(3) The board of the public museum may appoint an acting director whenever, in their discretion, the service of the museum shall require it, who shall also be acting secretary of the board and whose acts as such shall receive full credit.

(4) The board of the public museum may appoint as honorary curators persons who have manifested a special interest in the museum or some particular department thereof. Such curators shall perform such duties and have such privileges as may be prescribed in the regulations of the museum, but shall not receive any pecuniary compensation.

Source:
    L.1979, c. 110, § 36m, eff. March 1, 1980.

229.15   Library and museum funds; expenditures

(1) Public library and public museum funds appropriated to said institutions by the common council shall not be used or appropriated, directly or indirectly, for any purpose other than the maintenance and increase, payment of the salaries of the librarian or custodian and employes, purchase of fuel, supplies, furniture and fixtures, or incidental repairs of said institutions, respectively.

(2) All moneys appropriated for the purposes of said institutions shall be paid over to the city treasurer and credited to said funds, respectively. Each board of trustees shall provide for all necessary expenditures from each said fund, and all disbursements shall be made on orders of the president and secretary of the board, countersigned by the city comptroller; but, except as expressly provided otherwise, the board shall not in any one year expend or incur any liability for any sum in excess of the amount allocated to each such fund by the common council.

Source:
    L.1971, c. 152, § 27, eff. Dec. 17, 1971.

229.16   Donations and miscellaneous receipts

(1) All moneys, books, specimens and other property received by devise, bequest or gift for the purposes of said institutions shall, unless otherwise directed by the donor, be under the management and control of the board of trustees of each institution, respectively.

(2) All moneys derived from penalties for violations of the regulations of said institutions, or from any other source in the course of the administration thereof, including all moneys paid to the city upon any policy of insurance or other obligation or liability for or on account of loss or damage to property pertaining to the institutions, shall be credited to said institutional funds, respectively, and may be expended in the manner prescribed in s. 229.15(2), in addition to the annual tax.

Source:

L.1971, c. 152, §§ 27, 38, eff. Dec. 17, 1971.

229.17 Site, buildings and equipment

(1) The board of trustees of each such institution shall erect, purchase, hire or lease buildings, lots, rooms and furniture for the use and accommodation of the institution, and shall enlarge, improve and repair such buildings, rooms and furniture; but shall not erect, purchase, lease, or enlarge any building or lot without express authority of an ordinance or resolution of the common council. All deeds of conveyance and leases shall run to the city.

(2) The board of the public museum may enter into such agreements as it deems wise with the board of the public library for the use and occupation by such public library of such portion of any building erected for the purposes of said museum, upon such terms and for such time as may be agreed upon. Such agreement shall contain a provision for reasonable compensation to be paid for such use and occupation, which shall be paid into and credited to the museum fund.

(3) Whenever any board lawfully in charge of any public library in any city of the 1st class shall place and maintain in any school building in such city a branch library open to such school or to the public, and there shall be in such building any room suitable for said purposes which any board lawfully in charge of such building shall assign for such purpose, then such room shall be heated, lighted and cared for without cost to said library board.

Source:
L.1971, c. 152, § 27, eff. Dec. 17, 1971.

229.18 Accountability; reports

(1) Within 10 days after the appointment of a librarian or custodian or other salaried employes, the board of trustees of each such institution shall report to and file with the city comptroller a certified list of the persons so appointed, stating the salary allowed to each and the time or times fixed for the payment thereof.

(2) Immediately after any meeting of the board at which accounts and bills are allowed, the board shall furnish such comptroller with a list of all accounts and bills allowed at said meeting, stating the character of the materials or services for which the same were rendered.

(3) On or before the first day of March in each year, each such board, respectively, shall make a report to the common council, for the year ending with the December 31 next prior thereto, containing a statement of the condition of the institution, the number of books added to the library, the number of books circulated, the number of books lost or not returned, the articles added to the museums, and such other information and suggestions as they deem important, including also an account of the moneys credited to the institutional fund, and the expenditures therefrom during the year.

Source:
L.1971, c. 152, § 27, eff. Dec. 17, 1971.

SCHOOL LIBRARIES
(West's Wisconsin Statutes Annotated, 1982, s.43.70, 43.72.)

43.70   Common school fund

(1) No later than October 15 of each year, each school district administrator shall certify to the state superintendent, on forms provided by the state superintendent, a report of the total number of children between the ages of 4 and 20 years residing in his school district on the preceding June 30.

(2) Annually, within 40 days after December 1, the state superintendent shall ascertain the aggregate amount of all moneys received as income in the common school fund prior to that December 1 and shall apportion such amount to the school districts in proportion to the number of children resident therein between the ages of 4 and 20 years, as shown by the census report certified under sub. (1).

(3) Immediately upon making such apportionment, the state superintendent shall certify to the department of administration the amount that each school district is entitled to receive under this section and shall notify each school district administrator of the amount so certified for his or her school district. Within 15 days after receiving such certification, the department of administration shall issue its warrants upon which the state treasurer shall pay the amount apportioned forthwith to the proper school district treasurer. All moneys apportioned from the common school fund shall be expended for the purchase of library books and other instructional materials for school libraries, but not for public library facilities operated by school districts under s. 43.52, in accordance with rules prescribed by the state superintendent. Appropriate records of such purchases

shall be kept and necessary reports thereon shall be made to the state superintendent.

Source:
L.1977, c. 418, § 286t, eff. May 19, 1978.

43.72   Library exchanges

(1) School library books and other instructional material belonging to one school district may be loaned by the school board of the district to the school board of another school district for use in the school library of that school district, in consideration of school library books and other instructional material similarly loaned in exchange therefor.

(2) Any public library board and the school board of any school district in which a public library is maintained may make such exchanges and loans of books and other instructional material as are agreed upon by such boards for the purpose of increasing the efficiency of both libraries and insuring the best service to the schools and all citizens.

Source:
L.1971, c. 152, § 14, eff. Dec. 17, 1971.

STATE LIBRARY

(West's Wisconsin Statutes Annotated, 1982, s.257.01-257.07.)

257.01   State library; trustees

The justices of the supreme court and the attorney general or his representative shall be ex officio trustees of the state library, and shall have full power to make and enforce, by suitable penalties, such rules and regulations for the custody, superintendence, care and preservation of the books and other property contained in said library, and for the arrangement thereof as to said trustees shall seem necessary and proper.

Source:
L.1957, c. 528, § 15.
St. 1969, § 43.01.
L.1971, c. 152, § 7, eff. Dec. 17, 1971.

257.02   Differences with publishers of Wisconsin reports

The trustees of the state library may compromise the differences between the state and the publishers of the Wisconsin reports of the decisions of the supreme court as to the rights and duties of such publishers after the limitations for publishing such reports under their contracts have expired and may acquire for the state any stereotyped plates from which such reports are printed as they may deem advisable to acquire and may authorize the disposition or sale of same.

Source:
St.1969, § 43.015.
L.1971, c. 152, § 7, eff. Dec. 17, 1971.

257.03   State law librarian, assistant and clerical force

The board of trustees shall appoint a librarian, who shall serve under such conditions as shall be fixed by said board. He shall execute and file an official bond with good and sufficient surety in the sum of $10,000 to be approved by the trustees. Said board may also engage an assistant librarian and such clerical and expert assistance as shall be requisite in the proper care and maintenance of the library. The president of the board shall certify its appointments hereunder to the * * * department of administration, with amount of salary and the date of the commencement of the service of each appointee, and shall also notify him of the termination of such service. The pay of the librarian and other employes of the library shall be fixed by said board. The librarian shall be paid his actual and necessary travel expenses in attending the annual conference of the American Association of Law Libraries.

Source:
  L.1959, c. 659, § 79.
  St.1969, § 43.02.
  L.1971, c. 152, § 7, eff. Dec. 17, 1971.

257.04 Rules and regulations

* * * Said trustees shall provide by rules and regulations:

(1) That said library shall be kept open every day during the sessions of the supreme court and of the legislature, and on such other days and during such hours as they may direct, except Sundays.

(2) That books may be borrowed therefrom, under proper restrictions, by any state officer or member or officer of the legislature during the session thereof, or by any judge of the United States, upon written request, when holding court at Madison; but that no member of the legislature or officer thereof shall take more than 5 books at one time nor retain the same for more than 5 days, and that no book shall be taken out of the city of Madison.

(3) That attorneys and others shall be permitted to use, under proper restrictions, any books within said library.

(4) Such fines, penalties and forfeitures for any violation of the rules and regulations established by them for the management of said library and for the care and preservation of the books therein as to them shall seem necessary, and all such fines, penalties and forfeitures shall be sued for and collected before any court having jurisdiction of such action.

Source:
  L.1967, c. 29, § 1, eff. May 18, 1967.
  St.1969, § 47.03.
  L.1971, c. 152, § 7, eff. Dec. 17, 1971.

257.05 Catalog

The trustees may, whenever they deem it necessary, direct the catalog of said library or any part thereof to be printed.

Source:
  St.1969, § 43.04.
  L.1971, c. 152, § 7, eff. Dec. 17, 1971.

257.06 Duty of librarian

The librarian shall:

(1) Give his personal attention at the library during the hours it shall be directed to be kept open.

(2) Keep an account of all books or pamphlets added to the library by purchase or otherwise, and of all lost, destroyed, worn out or sold during his term, specifying dates, cost and values, and other material facts.

(3) Keep a full and accurate catalog of the library, noting all changes at the time when made; and whenever directed by the trustees, cause the same to be properly printed.

(4) Keep a true account of every book or pamphlet taken from the library, charging the same to the proper officer, with proper date and name of the person to whom delivered.

(5) Report to the presiding officer of each house, 5 days before the adjournment of each session of the legislature, the number of books taken out of the library by the members of each house and not returned, giving titles of

books, dates of taking, and names of members to whom charged. All sucn books shall be immediately returned.

(6) Sue for every fine, penalty or forfeiture incurred by violation of the rules and regulations prescribed by the trustees.

(7) To forward to the library of congress one copy of the supreme court reports and 2 copies of the legislative journals, laws and public documents published by authority of the state, and one copy of each of such publications and of the Blue Book to the several states and territories which practice like comity with this state, as soon as the same are received from the * * * department of administration. He may also effect exchanges of the statutes, laws and documents of this state with the libraries of foreign governments. His account for the expenses of transporting books sent or received by exchange or purchase, to be fixed by the * * * department of administration, shall be paid out of the state treasury, and charged to the proper appropriation for the law library.

(8) Perform all other duties prescribed by the trustees or by their rules and regulations or imposed by law.

(9) Said librarian shall also cause to be installed and maintained in said library, in the most scientific and improved manner, a card index and catalog of the books and material therein contained. The assistants necessary to carry out the purpose of this section shall be appointed in the manner provided by s. 257.03. Said librarian may attend the annual conferences of the American association of law libraries for the purpose of studying modern methods of law library administration.

(10) Subject to the approval of the trustees the librarian may sell or exchange duplicate books and pamphlets contained in the library.

Source:
L.1959, c. 659, §§ 77, 79.
L.1967, c. 29, § 1, eff. May 18, 1967.
St.1969, § 43.05.

L.1971, c. 152, §§ 7, 38, eff. Dec. 17, 1971.

257.07 Books to be delivered to

The acts of congress received from the general government shall be deposited in the state library and be distributed as the trustees shall direct. Every constitutional officer of the state who shall receive any volume of the laws, journals, reports or other documents of any other state or territory or of the United States, or any of the officers thereof, for the use of this state, shall promptly notify the state librarian as to the receipt thereof and shall deliver the same as the state librarian may direct.

Source:
St.1969, § 43.06.
L.1971, c. 152, § 7, eff. Dec. 17, 1971.

COUNTY LAW LIBRARIES
(West's Wisconsin Statutes Annotated, 1982, s.256.40, 256.41.)

256.40 Law library

Any circuit judge may, whenever he deems it desirable, purchase or direct the clerk of the circuit court for any county in his circuit to purchase law books and subscribe for the periodical reports of any of the courts of the several states or territories or of the United States, for any county in his circuit, provided the cost of such books and reports, including pocket parts and continuing services, shall not exceed $1,500 for any county in one year, unless the board of supervisors of such county authorizes the expenditure of a larger sum. Whenever·

such purchase or subscription is made such clerk shall have each volume of books received stamped or branded with the name of his county and take charge of the same for the use of the courts, judges, attorneys and officers thereof. The cost of such volumes shall be paid by the county treasurer upon the presentation to him of the accounts therefor, certified to by the clerk of the circuit court and the circuit judge.

L.1959, c. 416.

256.41 Law library; Milwaukee county

The county board of any county * * * having a population of 250,000 or more * * * may acquire by gift, purchase or otherwise, a law library and law books, and shall house the law library and additions in the courthouse or in suitable quarters elsewhere, and * * * may make, and enforce by suitable penalties, rules and regulations for the custody, care and preservation of the books and other property contained in said library. The county board * * * shall provide reasonable compensation for the law librarian and such assistants as * * * are necessary for the proper care and maintenance of * * * the library. * * * The librarian and assistants shall be appointed as the county board * * * determines, pursuant * * * to ss. 63.01 to 63.17. In such a county * * * the librarian shall perform all of the duties imposed by s. 256.40 upon the clerk of the circuit court and such clerk shall be free from all responsibility imposed by * * * that section. The purchase of additional law books, legal publications, periodicals and works of reference for * * * the library may be directed by each of the circuit judges of such county under s. 256.40. The library shall be kept open every day throughout the year * * *, except Sundays and holidays, * * * for such hours as * * * the county board * * * directs, but the county board may determine by ordinance that the library be closed on Saturdays. Attorneys and the general public shall be permitted to use the books in * * * the library in the building housing * * * the library under such rules and regulations as * * * the county board * * * adopts.

Source:
  L.1971, c. 111, eff. Nov. 7, 1971.

COUNCIL ON LIBRARY AND NETWORK DEVELOPMENT

(West's Wisconsin Statutes Annotated, 1982, s.15.377.)

15.377 Same; councils

*   *   *

(6) **Council on library and network development.** There is created in the department of public instruction a council on library and network development composed of 15 members. Eight of the members shall be library science, audiovisual and informational science professionals or members of governing bodies of libraries or resource centers and shall be representative of various types of libraries, information services and resource providers. Seven of the members shall be persons who are neither library science, audiovisual and informational science professionals, nor members of governing bodies of

libraries and resource centers. For the purposes of membership on the council, school boards and county, city, village and town governing bodies shall not be considered to be governing bodies of libraries or resource centers. The members of the council shall be appointed for staggered 3-year terms. The council shall meet 6 times annually and shall also meet on the call of the state superintendent, and may meet at other times on the call of the chairman or a majority of its members.

History—
Subsec. (6) created by—
L.1979, c. 347, § 4, eff. July 1, 1980.

MISCELLANEOUS PROVISIONS

(West's Wisconsin Statutes Annotated, 1982, s.43.27, 43.30.)

43.27   Distribution of materials from reference and loan collection to public library systems

The division for library services may disperse to public library systems, without charge, materials from the collection of the reference and loan library that the division determines are not appropriately held in the collection of the reference and loan library.

Source:
L.1979, c. 347, § 19, eff. July 1, 1980.

43.30   Public library circulation records

Records of any library which is in whole or in part supported by public funds, including the records of a public library system, indicating which of its documents or other materials have been loaned to or used by an identifiable individual may not be disclosed except to persons acting within the scope of their duties in the administration of the library or library system or persons authorized by the individual to inspect such records, or by order of a court of law.

Source:
L.1981, c. 335, § 15, eff. Jan. 1, 1983.

TAX EXEMPTION

(West's Wisconsin Statutes Annotated, 1982, s.70.11.)

Wisconsin library laws are reprinted from WEST'S WISCONSIN STATUTES ANNOTATED published by West Publishing Co., St. Paul, Minnesota.

WYOMING

STATE LIBRARY
AND
ARCHIVES, MUSEUMS AND HISTORICAL DEPARTMENT
(Wyoming Statutes Annotated, 1982, s.9-2-401 to 9-2-419.)

§ 9-2-401. Definitions.

(a)   As used in W.S. 9-2-401 through 9-2-425:

(i)   "Board" means the state library, archives, museums and historical board;

(ii)   "Department" means the state archives, museums and historical department;

(iii)   "Director" means the director of the department;

(iv)   "Political subdivision" means a county, municipality, special district or other local government entity;

(v)   "Public record" includes the original and all copies of any paper, correspondence, form, book, photograph, photostat, film, microfilm, sound recording, map, drawing or other document, regardless of physical form or characteristics, which have been made or received in transacting public business by the state, a political subdivision or an agency of the state. (Laws 1953, ch. 143, § 10; W.S. 1957, § 9-208; Laws 1959, ch. 77, § 1; 1973, ch. 86, § 1; W.S. 1977, §§ 9-3-960, 9-3-980, 9-3-987; Laws 1979, ch. 40, § 1; 1982, ch. 62, § 3.)

§ 9-2-402. State library, archives, museums and historical board; created; qualifications and appointment of membership; term; vacancies; expenses; quorum.

The state library, archives, museums and historical board is created to consist of nine (9) members. Seven (7) members shall be persons especially interested in and informed with regard to library conditions and interested in the history of the state. One (1) member from each appointment district provided by W.S. 9-1-218, and one (1) member at large shall be appointed by the governor. The attorney general shall be a member of the board. Appointments shall be made on a nonpartisan basis. Members shall be appointed for a six (6) year term. Vacancies shall be filled by the governor for any unexpired term. Members of the board shall receive no compensation, but shall be reimbursed under W.S. 9-3-102 and 9-3-103 for travel and per diem expenses incurred in the performance of their duties. A majority of the board constitutes a quorum. (Laws 1953, ch. 143, § 1; W.S. 1957, § 9-204; W.S. 1977, § 9-3-940; Laws 1982, ch. 62, § 3.)

§ 9-2-403. Same; powers and duties.

(a) The board has charge and supervision of the state library and of the department and shall:

(i) Elect its officers;

(ii) Make rules and regulations for its own government;

(iii) Adopt a seal for use in official business;

(iv) Approve selections of assistants appointed by the state librarian and the director;

(v) Approve budgets submitted by the department and library and control the expenditures of funds appropriated for and received by the library and the department;

(vi) Review all requests pertaining to historical projects in the state and submit its findings to the governor;

(vii) Accept gifts or grants of any nature from federal, state, county, local or private agencies or individuals for the purpose of carrying on its work;

(viii) Approve reports to the governor of the receipts, disbursements, work and needs of the state library and of the department;

(ix) Adopt policies and projects to fulfill the purposes of this act; and

(x) Stimulate research and the dissemination of information through publications by the state librarian and by the director. (Laws 1953, ch. 143, § 2; 1955, ch. 193, § 1; W.S. 1957, § 9-205; Laws 1973, ch. 215, § 1; W. S. 1977, § 9-3-941; Laws 1982, ch. 62, § 3.)

§ 9-2-404. State archives, museums and historical department created; director; appointment; term; qualifications; duties; official seal; powers; disposition of proceeds of sales; references to state archives and historical department.

(a) The state archives, museums and historical department is created and shall be in the charge of the director. The director shall be appointed by the board and shall hold office at the board's pleasure.

(b)   The director shall:
    (i)   Be a college graduate who has had work in social science and history or has educational and administrative experience satisfactory to the board;
    (ii)   Perform the duties of the state historian, state archivist and museum curator;
    (iii)   Have an official seal as director which shall be used to authenticate all official documents, instruments and official acts of the department.

(c)   The director may:
    (i)   Appoint necessary deputies, assistants and employees with the approval of the board;
    (ii)   Acquire by gift, devise, bequest, donation, purchase, lease or otherwise, money, books, manuscripts and other personal property of historical value. He shall hold and own the property in the name of the state and provide for its restoration, care and preservation;
    (iii)   Sell books, pamphlets, papers, pictures or other material produced by the department;
    (iv)   Operate sales desks, or contract under terms determined by the board with nonprofit and charitable corporations, to sell materials relevant to the interpretation of museums and historic sites;
    (v)   Do anything necessary to implement W.S. 9-2-404 through 9-2-416.

(d)   The proceeds received from sales authorized in subsection (c) of this section shall be deposited in the general fund of the state.

(e)   Any statute or legal or other document which refers to the state archives and historical department means the state archives, museums and historical department. (Laws 1953, ch. 143, §§ 10, 13 to 15; W.S. 1957, §§ 9-198, 9-208, 9-211, 9-212; Laws 1973, ch. 245, § 3; 1977, ch. 141, § 1; W.S. 1977, §§ 9-3-901, 9-3-960, 9-3-963, 9-3-964; Laws 1979, ch. 40, § 1; 1982, ch. 62, § 3.)

§ 9-2-405. Classifications of public records.

(a)   Public records shall be classified as follows:
    (i)   Official public records include:
        (A)   All original vouchers, receipts and other documents necessary to isolate and prove the validity of every transaction relating to the receipt, use and disposition of all public property and public income from all sources whatsoever;
        (B)   All agreements and contracts to which the state or any agency or political subdivision thereof is a party;
        (C)   All fidelity, surety and performance bonds in which the state is a beneficiary;
        (D)   All claims filed against the state or any agency or political subdivision thereof;
        (E)   All records or documents required by law to be filed with or kept by any agency of the state; and

(F)   All other documents or records determined by the records committee to be official public records.

(ii)   Office files and memoranda include:

(A)   All records, correspondence, exhibits, books, booklets, drawings, maps, blank forms or documents not defined and classified as official public records;

(B)   All duplicate copies of official public records filed with any agency of the state or political subdivision thereof;

(C)   All documents and reports made for the internal administration of the office to which they pertain but not required by law to be filed or kept with the agency; and

(D)   All other documents or records determined by the records committee to be office files and memoranda. (Laws 1959, ch. 77, § 1; W.S. 1957, § 9-212.1; W.S. 1977, § 9-3-980; Laws 1982, ch. 62, § 3.)

§ 9-2-406. Director; management of public records; administration of state archives; duties and responsibilities generally; establishment and operation of central microfilm division.

(a)   The director shall properly manage and safely keep all public records in his custody, and administer the state archives. He shall:

(i)   Manage the archives of the state;

(ii)   Centralize the archives of the state to make them available for reference and scholarship and to insure their proper preservation;

(iii)   Inspect, inventory, catalog and arrange retention and transfer schedules on all record files of all state departments and other agencies of state government;

(iv)   Maintain and secure all state public records and establish safeguards against unauthorized removal or destruction;

(v)   Establish and operate state record centers for preserving, servicing, screening and protecting all state public records which must be preserved temporarily or permanently, but which need not be retained in office space and equipment;

(vi)   Gather and disseminate to interested agencies information on all phases of records management and current practices, methods, procedures and devices for efficient and economical management of records;

(vii)   Establish and operate a central microfilm division in which all memoranda, writing, entry, print, representation or combination thereof, of any act, transaction, occurrence or event, may be microfilmed. The division shall microfilm public records approved for filming by the head of the office of origin and by the director, and shall establish standards for microfilming. All state departments, agencies and subdivisions of the state government and all counties, municipalities and political subdivisions thereof shall consult with the director prior to microfilming within the departments, agencies or political subdivisions and shall comply with the standards for all microfilming established by the central microfilm division. The central microfilm division may microfilm records which are required to be kept a specified length of time or permanently, or to be destroyed by specific methods or under specific supervision. When records are microfilmed, the microfilm may be substituted for the original documents and retained in lieu of the original documents and the original documents may be destroyed;

(viii)   Maintain necessary facilities for the review of records approved for destruction and their economical disposition by sale, shredding or burning, and supervise the destruction of public records. (Laws 1959, ch. 77, § 2; W.S. 1957, § 9-212.2; Laws 1963, ch. 117, § 11; W.S. 1977, § 9-3-981; Laws 1982, ch. 62, § 3.)

§ 9-2-407. Same; duties regarding public records in his custody; examination of records by public; furnishing of certified copies or photocopies; evidential value thereof; access to and examination of records.

(a)   The director shall collect, arrange and make available to the public at reasonable times in his office in original form, copies or microfilm copies or negatives, all records in his custody not restricted by law, including official records of the state and its political subdivisions, of the United States or of foreign nations. He is the legal custodian of all public records in the custody of the board.

(b)   The director shall furnish certified copies or photocopies of records in his custody on payment in advance of fees prescribed by the board. Copies of public records transferred pursuant to law from the office of their origin to the custody of the director when certified under seal by the director to be true, complete and correct have the same legal force and effect as evidence [as] if certified by their original custodian, and shall be admissible in all courts and before all tribunals the same as the originals thereof.

(c)   The director has the right of reasonable access to and may examine all public records in Wyoming. He shall examine into and report to the board on their condition. He shall require their custodians to put them in the custody and condition prescribed by law and to secure their custody, the recovery of records belonging to their offices, the delivery of records to their successors in office and the adoption of sound practices relative to the use of durable paper and ink, fireproof filing facilities and photographic processes for recording and copying. (Laws 1953, ch. 143, § 11; W.S. 1957, § 9-209; W.S. 1977, § 9-3-961; Laws 1982, ch. 62, § 3.)

§ 9-2-408. Transfer of public records to archives or other depository agency; transfer of records of

uncollectible accounts receivable to department; duties of department thereto.

(a) All public records, not required in the current operation of the office where they are made or kept, and all records of every public office of the state, agency, commission, committee or any other activity of the state or political subdivisions which are abolished or discontinued, shall be transferred to the state archives or to a recognized supplementary depository agency, selected by the board. Any public officer in Wyoming may deliver to the director for preservation and administration records in his custody if the director is willing and able to receive and care for them.

(b) All records of accounts receivable due to the state or any department or agency thereof, or to any political subdivision, or department or agency of a political subdivision of the state and considered to be uncollectible shall be transferred to the department if five (5) years past due and no collection activity or estate claim is in process. All those records shall be microfilmed and destroyed five (5) years after transfer. The microfilm constitutes the original or official copy of any records so destroyed. Each transmitting department or agency shall keep a list of the name and amount of each account record transferred to the department and shall provide a copy of the list to the state examiner, the department and the legislative service office audit division.

(c) The department shall:

(i) Furnish upon request from a transferring department or agency copies or information relating to the record of any account transferred to it;

(ii) Notify the state examiner and the legislative service office audit division of any requests by state agencies or departments for copies of or information relating to an account owing. (Laws 1959, ch. 77, § 3; W.S. 1957, § 9-212.3; Laws 1973, ch. 52, § 1; W.S. 1977, § 9-3-982; Laws 1982, ch. 62, § 3.)

§ 9-2-409. Designation of records officer by state departments or agencies; duties.

Each department or agency of the state government shall designate a records officer who shall supervise the departmental records program and who shall represent the office in all departmental matters before the records committee. The records officer and the director shall prepare transfer schedules for the transfer of public records to the records centers or to the archives. (Laws 1959, ch. 77, § 4; W.S. 1957, § 9-212.4; W.S. 1977, § 9-3-983; Laws 1982, ch. 62, § 3.)

§ 9-2-410. Records as property of state; delivery by outgoing officials and employees to successors; management and disposition thereof.

All public records are the property of the state. They shall be delivered by outgoing officials and employees to their successors and shall be preserved, stored, transferred, destroyed or disposed of, and otherwise managed, only in accordance with W.S. 9-2-405 through 9-2-413. (Laws 1959, ch. 77, § 5; W.S. 1957, § 9-212.5; W.S. 1977, § 9-3-984; Laws 1982, ch. 62, § 3.)

§ 9-2-411. Records committee created; composition; expenses; meetings; action by majority vote; duties as to retention and disposition of public records.

The records committee is created to be composed of the director or his deputy, who shall act as chairman and secretary of the committee, the attorney general or his appointee and the state examiner or his appointee. Committee members shall serve without additional salary, but shall be entitled to traveling expenses incurred incident to committee business. Expenses shall be paid from the appropriations made for operation of their respective departments or offices. The records committee shall meet upon call by the chairman at least once every quarter. Action by the committee shall be by majority vote and records shall be kept of all committee business. When the disposition of records is considered by the records committee, it shall ascertain the recommendations of the head of the department or the departmental records officer. The records committee shall approve, modify or disapprove the recommendations on retention schedules of all public records and act upon requests to destroy any public records. Any modification of a request or recommendation shall be approved by the head of the agency originating the request or recommendation. Upon written request of the department or agency head, the director shall furnish the film or a copy of the film to be retained by the department if deemed necessary or expedient by the records committee. The department shall provide forms, approved by the records committee, upon which it shall prepare recommendations to the committee in cooperation with the records officer of the department or other agency whose records are involved. (Laws 1959, ch. 77, § 6; W.S. 1957, § 9-212.6; W.S. 1977, § 9-3-985; Laws 1982, ch. 62, § 3.)

§ 9-2-412. Destruction or disposition of public records; procedure.

Public records of the state and political subdivisions shall be disposed of in accordance with W.S. 9-2-411. The records committee may approve a departmental written request upon proper and satisfactory showing that the retention of certain records for a minimum period of ten (10) years is unnecessary and uneconomical. Recommendations for the destruction or disposition of office files and memoranda shall be submitted to the records committee upon approved forms, prepared by the records officer of the agency concerned and the director. The committee shall determine the period of time that any office file or memorandum shall be preserved and may authorize the division of archives, records management and centralized microfilm to arrange for its destruction or disposition. (Laws 1959, ch. 77, § 7; W.S. 1957, § 9-212.7; Laws 1973, ch. 86, § 2; W.S. 1977, § 9-3-986; Laws 1982, ch. 62, § 3.)

§ 9-2-413. Reproduction of public records of political subdivisions; disposal of originals; consultation on reproductive processes; storage of official microfilm; availability for public inspection; limitation on reproduction of files by clerk of district court; inconsistent legislation.

(a)   Subject to this section and with the approval of the governing body of the political subdivision, any department, agency, board or individual of any political subdivision may record or copy by any microfilming, microphotographic, photographic, photostatic or other permanent reproductive device any public record which the department, agency, board or individual of the political subdivision records, keeps, retains, or is by law, rule or regulation required to record, keep or retain for a period of years or permanently. The microfilm, microphotograph, photograph, photostat or other permanent reproduction is deemed the original or official copy of the public record so reproduced for all purposes. If any department, agency, board or individual of any political subdivision is required to record any writing or document in books or on other forms, recording done directly onto microfilm, microphotograph or other permanent storage medium in lieu of the other required form of recordation constitutes compliance with the requirement. A master negative of microfilm or microphotographs shall be made whenever any process is used to reproduce public records with the intent of disposing of the original or copies of the original. The master negative shall be sent to the director. One (1) copy of all master negatives shall be retained by the governmental entity or officer having custody of the writings or papers thus recorded or copied as the official copy.

(b)   If any document is presented for recording or notation in public records the document shall, after recording, be returned to the party from whom it was received. If the party cannot be located or refuses to accept it, the document shall be disposed of in accordance with W.S. 9-2-411.

(c)   Prior to adopting any microfilming, microphotographic, photographic, photostatic or other reproductive process, the governing body of a political subdivision shall consult with the director. If any of the public records which are reproduced pursuant to this section are permanent records or, under the laws, rules or regulations in effect at the time of reproduction, are required to be transferred at a later date to any agency or department of the state, the particular microfilming, microphotographic, photographic, photostatic or other reproductive process shall be approved by the director as one which clearly and accurately makes copies that will last the time they are to be kept, or can be subsequently reproduced without distortions that substantially affect their legibility.

(d) If the original documents are disposed of as allowed by law, the set of official microfilm retained by the local governmental entity or official shall be stored in a safe place and protected from destruction. The official microfilm shall be available to the public for inspection in the same manner as the original documents would have been, and sufficient microfilm and microphotographic readers or other suitable devices shall be available to the public to permit inspection.

(e) The clerk of district court shall not microfilm, microphotograph, photograph, photostat or otherwise reproduce, for official record purposes, the files of any action or proceeding kept in his office until two (2) years have lapsed since the initial filing in the action or proceeding. The clerk of district court may make certified or other copies of documents in his office for individuals or officials.

(f) In recording, reproducing or copying any public records as authorized by this section and in disposing of the originals or copies, no restrictions or provisions of law regarding recording, reproducing or copying, or the disposition of originals or copies inconsistent with this section apply to the governmental entity or its officers, agents and employees. (Laws 1973, ch. 86, § 1; W.S. 1957, § 9-212.7:1; W.S. 1977, § 9-3-987; Laws 1982, ch. 62, § 3.)

§ 9-2-414. Director; powers and duties relative to museums and historical landmarks and sites.

(a) The director may:

(i) Assemble and collect archaeological and ethnological collections, relics of the history of the state and material illustrative of the natural history of the state, and works of art;

(ii) Preserve, repair and display in an orderly and educational manner the materials in the possession of the department;

(iii) Store and maintain these materials in the Wyoming state museum, the Wyoming state art gallery and other facilities.

(b) The director shall:

(i) Supervise and control museums established with approval of the board in state parks, public recreational grounds, public campgrounds, historic landmarks or historical sites of Wyoming;

(ii) Prepare and arrange all items, objects, furnishings and information in the museums;

(iii) Furnish and supervise employees in the museums;

(iv) Care for and maintain the interior of the museums;

(v) Prepare or approve all legends and historical information placed on historical landmarks and sites;

(vi) Provide all historical and interpretive material on approaches to and at historical landmarks and sites;

(vii) Supervise and approve in writing restorations, improvements, changes and alterations of historical landmarks and sites by the Wyoming recreation commission. (Laws 1953, ch. 143, § 12; W.S. 1957, §§ 9-210,

9-212.2; Laws 1959, ch. 77, § 2; 1963, ch. 117, § 11; 1969, ch. 12, § 1; W.S. 1977, §§ 9-3-962, 9-3-981; Laws 1982, ch. 62, § 3.)

§ 9-2-415. Same; duties relative to promotion of history of state and region.

(a) The director shall:

(i) Collect books, maps, charts, documents, manuscripts, other papers and any obtainable documentary material illustrative of the history and development of the state and region;

(ii) Collect, compile and publish data of the events which mark the progress of Wyoming from its earliest day to the present time, through the medium of a state historical periodical, to be published as and when the board directs;

(iii) Procure facts and statements relative to the history and ethnology of the Indian tribes and other inhabitants within the state;

(iv) File and carefully preserve all the historical data collected or obtained and arrange and classify it so it is readily accessible for disseminating historical or biographical information requested by the public;

(v) Accept and receive gifts;

(vi) Promote the founding and development of a state historical society and of county historical societies; and

(vii) Create and maintain local and statewide interest in the history of the state and region. (Laws 1953, ch. 143, § 13; W.S. 1957, § 9-211; W.S. 1977, § 9-3-963; Laws 1982, ch. 62, § 3.)

§ 9-2-416. Board; designated state agency to accept and administer funds or library materials from federal government; guidance of local library agencies participating in state plans for expenditure of same; extension and development of services; supervision of expenditures; state treasurer as custodian and disburser of federal funds.

(a) The board is the state agency to accept, receive and administer all funds, monies or library materials made available by the federal government for the improvement and development of public library services in the state.

(b) The state agency shall guide local library agencies participating in any state plan adopted by the board for the expenditure of any federal funds or materials. It may assure compliance with the policies and methods of administration adopted by the board pursuant to this section and under the state plan.

(c) The state agency is responsible for the extension and development of

library services throughout the state and shall supervise and superintend the
expenditures of monies provided for statewide library services and federal
funds allocated to the state for these purposes.

(d)   The state treasurer is custodian of all federal funds allocated to the state
for statewide library services and shall disburse the funds on the requisition
of the board subject to other provisions of law. (Laws 1959, ch. 26, §§ 1 to 4;
W. S. 1957, §§ 9-207.1 to 9-207.4; Laws 1974, ch. 16, § 2; W. S. 1977,
§§ 9-3-944 to 9-3-947; Laws 1982, ch. 62, § 3.)

§ 9-2-417. State librarian; appointment; qualifications; duties and responsibilities; appointment of necessary personnel; copies of state publications deposited with state library and university library; materials designed for use of state library to be deposited therein; exchange of session laws.

(a)   A state librarian shall be appointed by the board and shall hold office
during the pleasure of the board. The state librarian shall have:

(i)   Completed the required courses in a recognized or accredited library
school or shall have educational and library administrative experience
satisfactory to the board;

(ii)   Charge and custody of all materials belonging to the state library;

(iii)   Authority and responsibility to extend and develop public library
service throughout the state.

(b)   With the consent of the board, the state librarian may appoint necessary
deputies, assistants and employees.

(c)   Four (4) copies of each publication issued by a state officer, commission,
commissioner or board of a state institution shall be deposited with the state
library for its permanent file and one (1) copy shall be deposited with the
university library.

(d)   All officers and persons who receive any books, maps, charts or other
documents designed for the use of the state library or the department, shall
deposit the same immediately on receipt thereof with either the state librarian
or the director.

(e)   Upon request the state librarian shall send to the library of each state
and territory of the United States, free of expense, one (1) copy of the session
laws of this state in exchange for the laws of the requesting state or territory.
All the laws received in the exchange shall be deposited by the state librarian
in the law library of the state library and they become the property of this
state. (Laws 1941, ch. 84, §§ 2, 3; C.S. 1945, §§ 18-107, 18-108; Laws 1953, ch.
143, §§ 3 to 5, 15; 1955, ch. 193, § 4; 1957, ch. 146, § 1; W.S. 1957, §§ 9-7, 9-8,
9-198, 9-199, 9-200, 9-202; W.S. 1977, §§ 9-1-109, 9-1-110, 9-3-901, 9-3-902,
9-3-920, 9-3-922; Laws 1982, ch. 62, § 3.)

§ 9-2-418. Same; acquisition of books, materials, etc.; disposition of outdated and unused books; disposition of unused materials, supplies, etc., and promulgation of necessary rules by board.

(a)   With the approval of the board, the state librarian may:

(i)   Acquire books, materials, equipment and supplies which are necessary for the efficient operation of the state library;

(ii)   Sell outdated and unused books in the collection of the state library when the board deems the sale necessary due to limited shelf space;

(iii)   Regulate the hours during which the library is open for the use of educators, students and researchers. To accommodate these uses, he may stagger the working schedules of the library employees.

(b)   Prior to sale under subsection (a) of this section the department shall be given an opportunity to choose, without charge, books which have special historical value. After the department has had an opportunity to choose books it desires, any library in this state which is supported by public funds shall be given an opportunity to take, without charge, books it desires to add to its collection.

(c)   The board may dispose of unused materials, supplies or equipment belonging to the state library or the department in any manner provided by law.

(d)   The board may promulgate necessary rules and regulations to effectuate the purposes of this section. (Laws 1953, ch. 143, § 8; W.S. 1957, §§ 9-199.1 to 9-199.3, 9-203; Laws 1971, ch. 170, §§ 1 to 3; W.S. 1977, § 9-3-903 to 9-3-905, 9-3-923; Laws 1982, ch. 62, § 3.)

§ 9-2-419. Marking, defacing, removing or tampering with certain materials; penalty.

Any person marking, defacing, removing or tampering in any manner whatsoever with any property acquired under W.S. 9-2-403 through 9-2-418, by the director or board is guilty of a misdemeanor punishable by a fine of not more than one hundred dollars ($100.00). (Laws 1959, ch. 77, § 8; W.S. 1957, § 9-212.8; W.S. 1977, § 9-3-988; Laws 1982, ch. 62, § 3.)

INTERSTATE LIBRARY COMPACT
(Wyoming Statutes Annotated, 1982, s.9-2-420 to 9-2-425.)

§ 9-2-420. Interstate Library Compact; enactment; form.

The Interstate Library Compact is hereby enacted into law and entered into by this state with all states legally joining therein in the form substantially as follows:

INTERSTATE LIBRARY COMPACT

Article I

Because the desire for the services provided by libraries transcends governmental boundaries and can most effectively be satisfied by giving such services to communities and people regardless of jurisdictional lines, it is the policy of the states party to this compact to cooperate and share their responsibilities; to authorize cooperation and sharing with respect to those types of library facilities and services which can be more economically or efficiently developed and maintained on a cooperative basis, and to authorize cooperation and sharing among localities, states and others in providing joint or cooperative library services in areas where the distribution of population or of existing and potential library resources make the provision of library service on an interstate basis the most effective way of providing adequate and efficient service.

Article II

(a)   As used in this compact:

(i)   "Public library agency" means any unit or agency of local or state government operating or having power to operate a library;

(ii)   "Private library agency" means any nongovernmental entity which operates or assumes a legal obligation to operate a library;

(iii)   "Library agreement" means a contract establishing an interstate library district pursuant to this compact or providing for the joint or cooperative furnishing of library services.

Article III

(a)   Any one (1) or more public library agencies in a party state in cooperation with any public library agency or agencies in one (1) or more other party states may establish and maintain an interstate library district. Subject to the provisions of this compact and any other laws of the party states which pursuant hereto remain applicable, such district may establish, maintain and operate some or all of the library facilities and services for the area concerned in accordance with the terms of a library agreement therefor. Any private library agency or agencies within an interstate library district may cooperate therewith, assume duties, responsibilities and obligations thereto, and receive benefits therefrom as provided in any library agreement to which such agency or agencies become party.

(b)   Within an interstate library district, and as provided by a library agreement, the performance of library functions may be undertaken on a joint or cooperative basis or may be undertaken by means of one (1) or more arrangements between or among public or private library agencies for the extension of library privileges to the use of facilities or services operated or rendered by one (1) or more of the individual library agencies.

(c)   If a library agreement provides for joint establishment, maintenance or operation of library facilities or services by an interstate library district, such district shall have power to do any one (1) or more of the following in accordance with such library agreement:

(i)   Undertake, administer and participate in programs or arrangements for securing, lending or servicing of books and other publications, any other materials suitable to be kept or made available by libraries, library equipment or for the dissemination of information about libraries, the value and significance of particular items therein, and the use thereof;

(ii)   Accept for any of its purposes under this compact any and all donations, and grants of money, equipment, supplies, materials, and services, (conditional or otherwise), from any state or the United States or any subdivision or agency thereof, or interstate agency, or from any institution, person, firm or corporation, and receive, utilize and dispose of the same;

(iii)   Operate mobile library units or equipment for the purpose of rendering bookmobile service within the district;

(iv)   Employ professional, technical, clerical and other personnel, and fix terms of employment, compensation and other appropriate benefits; and where desirable, provide for the in-service training of such personnel;

(v)   Sue and be sued in any court of competent jurisdiction;

(vi)   Acquire, hold, and dispose of any real or personal property or any interest or interests therein as may be appropriate to the rendering of library service;

(vii)   Construct, maintain and operate a library, including any appropriate branches thereof;

(viii)   Do such other things as may be incidental to or appropriate for the carrying out of any of the foregoing powers.

Article IV

(a)   An interstate library district which establishes, maintains or operates any facilities or services in its own right shall have a governing board which shall direct the affairs of the district and act for it in all matters relating to its business. Each participating public library agency in the district shall be represented on the governing board which shall be organized and conduct its business in accordance with provision therefor in the library agreement. But in no event shall a governing board meet less often than twice a year.

(b)   Any private library agency or agencies party to a library agreement establishing an interstate library district may be represented on or advise with the governing board of the district in such manner as the library agreement may provide.

Article V

Any two (2) or more state library agencies of two (2) or more of the party states may undertake and conduct joint or cooperative library programs, render joint or cooperative library services, and enter into and perform arrangements for the cooperative or joint acquisition, use, housing and disposition of items or collections of materials which, by reason of expense, rarity, specialized nature, or infrequency of demand therefor would be appropriate for central collection and shared use. Any such programs, services or arrangements may include provision for the exercise on a cooperative or joint basis of any power exercisable by an interstate library district and an agreement embodying any such program, service or arrangement shall contain provisions covering the subjects detailed in article VI of this compact for interstate library agreements.

Article VI

(a)   In order to provide for any joint or cooperative undertaking pursuant to this compact, public and private library agencies may enter into library agreements. Any agreement executed pursuant to the provisions of this compact shall, as among the parties to the agreement:

(i)   Detail the specific nature of the services, programs, facilities, arrangements or properties to which it is applicable;

(ii)   Provide for the · allocation of costs and other financial responsibilities;

(iii)   Specify the respective rights, duties, obligations and liabilities of the parties;

(iv)   Set forth the terms and conditions for duration, renewal, termination, abrogation, disposal of joint or common property, if any, and all other matters which may be appropriate to the proper effectuation and performance of the agreement.

(b)   No public or private library agency shall undertake to exercise itself, or jointly with any other library agency, by means of a library agreement any power prohibited to such agency by the constitution or statutes of its state.

(c)   No library agreement shall become effective until filed with the compact administrator of each state involved, and approved in accordance with article VII of this compact.

Article VII

(a)   Every library agreement made pursuant to this compact shall, prior to and as a condition precedent to its entry into force, be submitted to the attorney general of each state in which a public library agency party thereto is situated, who shall determine whether the agreement is in proper form and compatible with the laws of his state. The attorneys general shall approve any agreement submitted to them unless they shall find that it does not meet the conditions set forth herein and shall detail in writing addressed to the governing bodies of the public library agencies concerned the specific respects in which the proposed agreement fails to meet the requirements of law. Failure to disapprove an agreement submitted hereunder within ninety (90) days of its submission shall constitute approval thereof.

(b)   In the event that a library agreement made pursuant to this compact shall deal in whole or in part with the provision of services or facilities with regard to which an officer or agency of the state government has constitutional or statutory powers of control, the agreement shall, as a condition precedent to its entry into force, be submitted to the state officer or agency having such power of control and shall be approved or disapproved by him or it as to all matters within his or its jurisdiction in the same manner and subject to the same requirements governing the action of the attorneys general pursuant to paragraph (a) of this article. This requirement of submission and approval shall be in addition to and not in substitution for the requirement of submission to and approval by the attorneys general.

Article VIII

Nothing in this compact or in any library agreement shall be construed to supersede, alter or otherwise impair any obligation imposed on any library by otherwise applicable law, nor to authorize the transfer or disposition of any property held in trust by a library agency in a manner contrary to the terms of such trust.

Article IX

(a)   Any public library agency party to a library agreement may appropriate funds to the interstate library district established thereby in the same manner and to the same extent as to a library wholly maintained by it and, subject to the laws of the state in which such public library agency is situated, may pledge its credit in support of an interstate library district established by the agreement.

(b)   Subject to the provisions of the library agreement pursuant to which it functions and the laws of the states in which such district is situated, an interstate library district may claim and receive any state and federal aid which may be available to library agencies.

Article X

Each state shall designate a compact administrator with whom copies of all library agreements to which his state or any public library agency thereof is party shall be filed. The administrator shall have such other powers as may be conferred upon him by the laws of his state and may consult and cooperate with the compact administrators of other party states and take such steps as may effectuate the purposes of this compact. If the laws of a party state so provide, such state may designate one (1) or more deputy compact administrators in addition to its compact administrator.

Article XI

(a) This compact shall enter into force and effect immediately upon its enactment into law by any two (2) states. Thereafter, it shall enter into force and effect as to any other state upon the enactment thereof by such state.

(b) This compact shall continue in force with respect to a party state and remain binding upon such state until six (6) months after such state has given notice to each other party state of the repeal thereof. Such withdrawal shall not be construed to relieve any party to a library agreement entered into pursuant to this compact from any obligation of that agreement prior to the end of its duration as provided therein.

Article XII

This compact shall be liberally construed so as to effectuate the purposes thereof. The provisions of this compact shall be severable and if any phrase, clause, sentence or provision of this compact is declared to be contrary to the constitution of any party state or of the United States or the applicability thereof to any government, agency, person or circumstance is held invalid, the validity of the remainder of this compact and the applicability thereof to any government, agency, person or circumstance shall not be affected thereby. If this compact shall be held contrary to the constitution of any state party thereto, the compact shall remain in full force and effect as to the remaining states and in full force and effect as to the state affected as to all severable matters. (Laws 1965, ch. 70, § 1; ch. 181, § 1; W.S. 1957, § 9-212.9; W.S. 1977, § 9-3-1001; Laws 1982, ch. 62, § 3.)

§ 9-2-421. Compliance with local laws prerequisite to entering into library agreement.

No city, town, county, school district or public district of any sort of this state shall be party to a library agreement which provides for the construction or maintenance of a library pursuant to article III, (c-7) [subsection (c)(vii)] of the Interstate Library Compact, nor pledge its credit in support of such a library, or contribute to the capital financing thereof, except after compliance with any laws applicable to such cities, towns, counties, school districts or public districts of any sort relating to or governing capital outlays and the pledging of credit. (Laws 1965, ch. 70, § 2; W.S. 1957, § 9-212.10; W.S. 1977, § 9-3-1002; Laws 1982, ch. 62, § 3.)

§ 9-2-422. "State library agency".

As used in the Interstate Library Compact, "state library agency", with reference to this state, means state library, archives and historical board [state library, archives, museums and historical board]. (Laws 1965, ch. 70, § 3; W.S. 1957, § 9-212.11; W.S. 1977, § 9-3-1003; Laws 1982, ch. 62, § 3.)

§ 9-2-423. State and federal aid to interstate library districts.

An interstate library district lying partly within this state may claim and be entitled to receive state aid in support of any of its functions to the same extent and in the same manner as such functions are eligible for support when carried on by entities wholly within this state. For the purpose of computing and apportioning state aid to an interstate library district, this state will consider that portion of the area which lies within this state as an independent entity for the performance of the aided function or functions and compute and apportion the aid accordingly. Subject to any applicable laws of this state, such a district also may apply for and be entitled to receive federal aid for which it may be eligible. (Laws 1965, ch. 70, § 4; W.S. 1957, § 9-212.12; W.S. 1977, § 9-3-1004; Laws 1982, ch. 62, § 3.)

§ 9-2-424. Appointment of compact administrator and deputy administrators.

The governor shall appoint an officer of this state who shall be the compact administrator pursuant to article X of the compact. The governor may also appoint one (1) or more deputy Interstate Library Compact administrators pursuant to article X. (Laws 1965, ch. 70, § 5; W.S. 1957, § 9-212.13; W.S. 1977, § 9-3-1005; Laws 1982, ch. 62, § 3.)

§ 9-2-425. Notice of withdrawal from compact.

In the event of withdrawal from the Interstate Library Compact the governor shall send and receive any notices required by article IX(b) of the compact. (Laws 1965, ch. 70, § 6; W.S. 1957, § 9-212.14; W.S. 1977, § 9-3-1006; Laws 1982, ch. 62, § 3.)

DISTRIBUTION OF PUBLIC DOCUMENTS
(Wyoming Statutes Annotated, 1982, s.5-2-401, 5-2-402.)

§ 5-2-401. Authority to contract for publication of reports.

The supreme court of the state of Wyoming is hereby vested with full and complete authority to arrange and contract for timely publication of its opinions from time to time, as may be required, and the legislature shall make adequate appropriation to defray the expenses thereof. (Laws 1961, ch. 35, § 1.)

§ 5-2-402. Distribution of copies of reports.

The books delivered to the librarian shall be used by him for the purpose of distribution as follows: one (1) copy of each volume shall be delivered to each justice of the supreme court, and to each district judge there shall be delivered as many copies as he has counties in his district, and to each state officer, said books to be labeled as the property of the state, and to be retained in the offices of said officials and by them delivered to their respective successors in office; one (1) copy shall be furnished to the library of the supreme court of the United States at Washington, one (1) copy to the office of the attorney general of the United States, and one (1) copy to the office of the United States district judge for the district of Wyoming. The remaining copies shall be used in exchange for the reports of other states and territories and governments as shall be determined upon by the justices of the supreme court, and a reasonable number shall be kept in the state law library. (Laws 1903, ch. 60, § 4; C.S. 1910, § 905; C.S. 1920, § 1134; Laws 1925, ch. 32, § 1; R.S. 1931, § 31-131; C.S. 1945, § 1-306; W.S. 1957, § 5-39.)

COUNTY LIBRARIES
(Wyoming Statutes Annotated, 1982, s.18-7-101 to 18-7-106.)

§ 18-7-101. Prerequisites to levy of tax for establishment and maintenance of library; payment of expenses.

When the board of county commissioners has received sufficient guarantees whether in the forms of conveyances or bonds of citizens, associations or corporations that a suitable place will be permanently furnished for the operation and use of a public library, it shall annually levy a tax of not more than two (2) mills on all taxable property in the county for the establishment and maintenance of a public library at the county seat of the county. Whenever suitable library quarters are acquired the county library board of directors may expend the taxes levied for the maintenance and operation of the county library and the county library system. (Laws 1886, ch. 10, § 1; R.S. 1887, § 684; R.S. 1899, § 1019; Laws 1901, ch. 72, § 1; 1907, ch. 45, § 1; C.S. 1910, § 1316; C.S. 1920, § 1563; R.S. 1931, § 29-901; C.S. 1945, § 26-601; Laws 1947, ch. 25, § 1; W.S. 1957, § 18-309; Laws 1961, ch. 32, § 1; 1967, ch. 160, § 1; 1977, ch. 124, § 1.)

§ 18-7-102. Manner of levying and collecting tax; library fund.

The county library tax shall be levied and collected as other county taxes and the money collected shall be set apart as the county library fund. Nothing herein shall be construed to authorize any levy in excess of those authorized by law. (Laws 1886, ch. 10, § 2; R.S. 1887, § 685; R.S. 1899, § 1020; Laws 1907, ch. 45, § 2; C.S. 1910, § 1317; C.S. 1920, § 1564; R.S. 1931, § 29-902; C.S. 1945, § 26-602; W.S. 1957, § 18-310; Laws 1961, ch. 32, § 2; 1977, ch. 124, § 1.)

§ 18-7-103. Library fund under control of board of directors;

appointment, powers, duties, terms of directors; manner of filling vacancies on board.

(a) The control, use and disposition of the county library fund is entrusted to the county library board of directors which shall budget and expend the fund for the maintenance and operation of the county library and county library system.

(b) The county library board of directors shall be appointed by the county commissioners and shall be composed of not less than three (3) and not more than five (5) competent and responsible residents who are representative of the entire county and who shall serve without compensation. Before entering upon his duties the treasurer of the county library board shall execute and deposit with the county commissioners a good and sufficient bond for the faithful performance of his duties in an amount required by the county commissioners. The bond shall be payable to the people of the state of Wyoming and be approved by the county commissioners. One (1) director shall be appointed for one (1) year, one (1) director (or two (2) if the board consists of four (4) or five (5) members) shall be appointed for two (2) years, and one (1) director (or two (2), if the board consists of five (5) directors) shall be appointed for three (3) years, each term to commence on July 1 following the appointment. Thereafter the county commissioners shall before July 1 of each year appoint a director or directors to replace the retiring director or directors for a term of three (3) years and until a successor is appointed. A director may be appointed for two (2) consecutive terms and shall not be eligible for reappointment until two (2) years after the expiration of his second term.

(c) The county commissioners may remove any director for misconduct or neglect of duty. Vacancies on the board of directors shall be filled by the county commissioners for the balance of the unexpired term created by the vacancy. (Laws 1886, ch. 10, § 3; R.S. 1887, § 686; Laws 1899, ch. 46, § 1; R.S. 1899, § 1021; Laws 1907, ch. 45, § 3; C.S. 1910, § 1318; C.S. 1920, § 1565; R.S. 1931,

§ 18-7-104. Authority of board to receive and dispose of property; appointment of librarian; library staff.

The library board of directors may receive and be responsible for real estate, money or other property to aid the establishment, maintenance or operation of the county library system. If received as a donation, they shall carefully observe as the trustee the conditions accompanying every such gift. When the board of directors determines it is in the best interests of the county library and in keeping with the purpose of the donor, it may with the approval of the board of county commissioners sell, exchange or otherwise dispose of such real estate or other property. The board of directors shall appoint a competent librarian who with the approval of the board of directors shall appoint a library staff. The duties and compensation of the staff shall be determined by the board. (Laws 1886, ch. 10, § 4; R.S. 1887, § 687; R.S. 1899, § 1022; Laws 1907, ch. 45, § 4; C.S. 1910, § 1319; C.S. 1920, § 1566; R.S. 1931, § 29-904; C.S. 1945, § 26-604; W.S. 1957, § 18-312; Laws 1961, ch. 32, § 4; 1965, ch. 23, § 1; 1977, ch. 124, § 1.)

§ 18-7-105. Organization of board; rules and regulations; filing of certificate of organization; incorporation; recovery of library materials; establishment of branch libraries; cooperative library service.

(a) Every library board of directors shall elect a chairman and other officers as necessary and shall prescribe rules and regulations for the establishment, organization, operation and use of the county library and library system. The board shall enforce such rules and regulations in any court of competent jurisdiction. As soon as the board is organized they shall file with the county clerk and with the secretary of state a certificate showing their organization, for which no filing fee or charge shall be paid.

(b) Upon filing of the certificate the board of directors is a body corporate, with power to sue and be sued under the name of "Board of Directors of the County Library of . . . . County," or the board by resolution filed as provided for filing of certificate of organization, may designate itself as "Board of Directors of Carnegie Public Library of . . . . County."

(c) No member of the board of directors is personally liable for any action or procedure of the board. The corporation has perpetual existence and it is not necessary to file any other or further certificate than that filed upon the original organization of the board of directors. Every library established and maintained under the provisions of W.S. 18-7-101 through 18-7-106 is free to all residents of the county on the condition that such persons comply with rules and regulations of the library as prescribed by the board of directors. Holders of library cards are responsible for all library materials borrowed on such cards. Whenever library materials are lost, destroyed or taken from the library and not returned the library board may institute proceedings in any court of competent jurisdiction to recover the materials or the value thereof. The library board may establish and maintain branch libraries, stations and other library services and facilities.

(d) Two (2) or more county library boards may contract to establish a federation of the libraries under their jurisdiction for the purpose of providing cooperative library services. Contracts shall be written, signed by the members of the contracting library boards and are binding upon the contracting library boards and their successors. The participating libraries may reserve the right to terminate the contracts by mutual agreement upon ninety (90) days written notice given to each contracting library board. (Laws 1886, ch. 10, § 5; R.S. 1887, § 688; R.S. 1899, § 1023; Laws 1907, ch. 45, § 5; C.S. 1910, § 1320; C.S. 1920, § 1567; Laws 1921, ch. 25, § 1; R.S. 1931, § 29-906; C.S. 1945, § 26-605; W.S. 1957, § 18-313; Laws 1961, ch. 32, § 5; 1965, ch. 23, § 2; 1977, ch. 124, § 1.)

§ 18-7-106. Directors to keep records and make annual report.

Each library board of directors shall keep a record of all its proceedings, file in the library all vouchers for expenditures, and after the close of the fiscal year submit an annual financial, statistical and operational report to the county commissioners and to the Wyoming state library. Whenever practical the annual report shall contain information and data requested or required by the county commissioners and the Wyoming state library. (Laws 1886, ch. 10, § 6; R.S. 1887, § 689; R.S. 1899, § 1024; Laws 1907, ch. 45, § 6; C.S. 1910, § 1321; C.S. 1920, § 1568; R.S. 1931, § 29-907; C.S. 1945, § 26-606; W.S. 1957, § 18-314; Laws 1961, ch. 32, § 6; 1977, ch. 124, § 1.)

COUNTY LAW LIBRARIES
(Wyoming Statutes Annotated, 1982, s.5-3-111.)

§ 5-3-111. County law library.

The board of county commissioners shall have the power to establish and maintain in their respective counties, a county law library, for the use and benefit of the judge of the district court and other citizens of the state and shall have the power to appropriate and set aside for the maintenance and support of said library, such moneys as it shall deem necessary or see fit. The district court of such county shall superintend and direct all expenditures made for said library, and shall have full power to make any rules and regulations, proper and necessary for the preservation, increase and use of the library, not inconsistent with law. (Laws 1919, ch. 84, §§ 1, 2; C.S. 1920, § 1569; R.S. 1931, § 29-908; C.S. 1945, § 1-520; W.S. 1957, § 5-51.)

TAX EXEMPTION
(Wyoming Statutes Annotated, 1982, s.39-1-201.)

Wyoming library laws are reprinted from WYOMING STATUTES ANNOTATED published by The Michie Co., Charlottesville, Virginia.

PART III
TERRITORIES
and
DEPENDENCIES

PUERTO RICO

CARNEGIE LIBRARY OF PUERTO RICO
(Laws of Puerto Rico Annotated, 1982, Title 18, s.931-936.)

§ 931. Carnegie Library — Supervision

The administration of the "Carnegie Library of Puerto Rico" shall be in charge of the Department of Education. — Nov. 22, 1917, No. 20, p. 234, § 2; 1950 Reorg. Plan No. 4, § 1, eff. July 1, 1950.

§ 932. — Librarian

The literary and technical management of the library, as well as the work and operation thereof, shall be in charge of the librarian or of the person who acts in his place, pursuant to rules and regulations issued by the Department of Education. — Nov. 22, 1917, No. 20, p. 234, § 3; 1950 Reorg. Plan No. 4, § 1, eff. July 1, 1950.

§ 933. — Rules governing use of books

The members of the Legislature, the heads of the Executive Departments of the Commonwealth Government, the justices of the Supreme Court and the judges of the Superior Courts and District Courts, and the prosecuting attorneys shall be entitled to the use of the books of the Carnegie Library, and to take them out of the said library for a period not exceeding thirty days; Provided, That the librarian or the person who acts in his stead, is hereby authorized to permit all responsible persons to draw books from the library and use them outside thereof, and to prescribe rules and regulations for the operation of the library in this respect. Those persons who fail to return the books within the period of time specified in the said rules and regulations shall be punished by fine to be determined by the Department of Education with the advice of the librarian. The proceeds of such fines shall be covered into the General Fund of the Commonwealth Treasury.

In no case shall books comprised in the following enumeration be permitted to be taken out of the library:

I. Incunabula.

II. Books printed in any country from 1457 to 1600.

III. Books printed in Spain from 1474 to 1650.

IV. Books printed in Puerto Rico from 1808 to 1840.

V. Copies of exhausted editions unless there is more than one copy of the same book in the library.

VI. Neither shall any person be permitted to take any book out of the library, if such person is suffering from any contagious disease or has in his home any other person suffering from such disease.

Upon the return of books taken from the library, pursuant to this section, they shall be immediately examined by some employee of the library so as to investigate whether or not there is any mutilation of the book; Provided, That wilful mutilation of books shall be punished by fine of not less than fifty dollars or by imprisonment for a term of not less than 20 days.

Books returned to the library shall be immediately disinfected by the most rapid, efficient and simple methods. — Nov. 22, 1917, No. 20, p. 234, § 5; 1950 Reorg. Plan No. 4. § 1; Const., art. I, § 1; July 24, 1952, No. 11, p. 30; May 16, 1958, No. 11, p. 13, § 1, eff. May 16, 1958.

§ 934. — Qualifications of librarian and assistant

To fill the vacancies that may occur in the positions of librarian and assistant librarian, either temporarily or permanently, the following qualifications shall be indispensable: (1) To have resided in Puerto Rico for at least two years prior to the date of appointment; (2) to have a knowledge of the Spanish and English languages, and (3) to have had at least two years' practice in modern library work; And provided, further, That the said positions of librarian or assistant librarian shall not be vacant for a longer period than six months if there are candidates qualified to fill the said office according to the provisions of sections 931–934 of this title. — Nov. 22, 1917, No. 20, p. 234, § 7, eff. Nov. 22, 1917.

§ 935. Circulating library — Organization

The sum of six thousand (6,000) dollars is hereby appropriated and placed at the disposal of the Board of Trustees of the Carnegie Library out of any available funds in the Commonwealth Treasury not otherwise appropriated, so that said Board may organize a circulating library. — Mar. 28, 1946, No. 222, p. 440, § 1; Const., art. I, § 1, eff. July 25, 1952.

§ 936. — Operation, equipment, rules

The Board of Trustees of the Carnegie Library is hereby authorized to place the circulating library in operation after the same is organized, and to purchase the equipment necessary therefor and prescribe adequate rules to carry out the provisions of sections 935–936 of this title. — Mar. 28, 1946, No. 222, p. 440, § 2, eff. 90 days after Mar. 28, 1946.

DISTRIBUTION OF PUBLIC DOCUMENTS

(Laws of Puerto Rico Annotated, 1982, Title 2, s.190,
Title 4, s.491.)

§ 190. Distribution of laws

Immediately after the laws, resolutions and other public documents are printed and bound, and within sixty days after the close of each session of the Legislature, the Secretary of State shall distribute the same as follows:

*   *   *   *   *   *   *   *

3. To the Library of Congress, and to the public and law libraries of Puerto Rico, two copies each;

*   *   *   *   *   *   *   *

6-A. To the Legislative Services Office of the Legislature, five (5) copies, and the same number of copies to the School of Law of the University of Puerto Rico.

Amended May 4, 1956, No. 17, p. 44, eff. May 4, 1956.

*   *   *   *   *   *   *   *

7. To the University of Puerto Rico, three copies, and to those literary and scientific institutions and to those nations and colonies with which an exchange of works may be established and which may be designated by the Secretary of State with the approval of the Council of Secretaries;   *   *   *

— Political Code, 1902, § 46; Apr. 13, 1916, No. 55, p. 109, § 1; Apr. 23, 1927, No. 23, p. 160, § 1; May 4, 1933, No. 39, p. 282, § 1; Apr. 14, 1936, No. 21, p. 204, § 1; Const., art. I, § 1; art. III, § 5; art. IX, § 4; July 24, 1952, Nos. 6, 11, pp. 10, 30, eff. July 25, 1952.

§ 491. —Distribution

The Secretary of the Supreme Court shall furnish a copy of the *"Decisiones de Puerto Rico"* (*Puerto Rico Reports*) of the new *"Puerto Rico Digest"* and of the fascicles of the *Puerto Rico Reports* to the following officials and entities:

(a) the Governor of Puerto Rico
(b) the members of the Legislature
(c) the Judges of the Supreme Court of Puerto Rico

(d) the Resident Commissioner of Puerto Rico in Washington

(e) the Government Secretaries

(f) to the Secretary of Justice for the use of the lawyers of said department, the district prosecuting attorneys, the Registrars of Property and any other officers that may be designated by said Secretary, two hundred copies

(g) The Secretaries and Sergeants at Arms of the Senate and of the House of Representatives

(h) the Secretary, the Compiler and Publisher and the Translations Office of the Supreme Court of Puerto Rico

(i) to the Office of Legislative Services of the Legislature, three copies

(j) to the Court Administration for the use of the judicial branch and of said office, two hundred fifty (250) copies.

(k) to the Office of the Commonwealth of Puerto Rico in Washington, D.C.

The Secretary of the Supreme Court shall also furnish a copy of the publications to which the above paragraph refers and of the *"Puerto Rico Reports"* to:

(a) the Supreme Court of the United States, three copies

(b) the Court of Appeals of the United States for the First Circuit

(c) the Judges of the United States District Court for the District of Puerto Rico

(d) the Referee in Bankruptcy of the United States District Court for the District of Puerto Rico.

There shall also be furnished a copy of the *"Puerto Rico Reports"* to the following officers:

(a) the governor of Puerto Rico

(b) the library of the Legislative Services Office of the Legislature, three copies

(c) the Judges of the Supreme Court and three copies to the Library of the Supreme Court

(d) the Resident Commissioner of Puerto Rico in Washington

(e) the Secretary, the Compiler and Publisher of Jurisprudence of the Supreme Court and to the head of the translations Office of the Supreme Court of Puerto Rico

(f) the Secretary of Justice, twenty (20) copies.

(g) to the Office of the Commonwealth of Puerto Rico in Washington, D.C.

The copies of the *Decisiones de Puerto Rico (Puerto Rico Reports)*, of the *Puerto Rico Reports* and of the new *Puerto Rico*

Digest which shall be furnished to the officers of the Government of Puerto Rico, shall be kept and delivered by them to their successors in office. The aforesaid provision shall not apply to the Governor, to the members of the Legislature and to the Judges of the Supreme Court of Puerto Rico.

The copies of the *Puerto Rico Reports*, fascicles of the *Puerto Rico Reports* and of the *Puerto Rico Digest* published in excess of the number which in conformity with the terms of this section are furnished to officers and to the agencies designated shall be kept in the Supreme Court for future use of the judiciary branch. The copies of the *Puerto Rico Reports* published in excess of the number which in conformity with the terms of this section which are furnished to the officers of entities designated, may be sent by the Supreme Court to courts of the United States or may be exchanged for similar publications.—Apr. 11, 1968, No. 19, p. 29, § 3, eff. Apr. 11, 1968; amended June 12, 1971, No. 28, p. 96, eff. June 12, 1971.

GENERAL ARCHIVES

(Laws of Puerto Rico Annotated, 1982, Title 3, s.1001-1013.)

§ 1001. Definitions

(a) Document—The word document shall include any paper, book, pamphlet, photograph, photostatic copy, film, microfilm, recording tape, map, drawing, plan, magnetic tape, record, video tape or any other material read by machine and any other informative material, regardless of its form or characteristics. Publications and bibliographical or museum material acquired for public viewing, consultation, or other related purposes, are not included in the definition of the word document.

(b) Public document—Any document which originates, or is kept or received, in any dependency of the Commonwealth, according to law or in relation to the management of public affairs, and which is to be permanently or temporarily preserved as evidence of transactions, or because of its administrative usefulness, or legal, fiscal, cultural or informative value, as the case may be, or which is to be destroyed because of its lack of permanent value or administrative, legal, fiscal, cultural or informative usefulness, and a copy of every publication issued by government dependencies. It shall also be understood that a public document is any document which is specifically declared as such by any law in effect or which is enacted in the future.

(*c*) Private document — Any document not included in the foregoing definition.

(*d*) Archives — The General Archives of Puerto Rico.

(e) Archivist — The General Archivist of Puerto Rico.

(f) Commonwealth — The Commonwealth of Puerto Rico, including its municipalities.

(g) Dependency—Shall include every department, agency or corporate entity, board, committee, body, bureau, office and every other government body of the three branches of the Commonwealth Government and the municipalities.

(h) Commission — The Archives Advisory Commission. — Dec. 8, 1955, No. 5, p. 78, § 3, eff. July 1, 1955.

(i) Program Administrator—The official designated by this chapter to administer and regulate the Public Documents Administration Program in his jurisdiction, and who is empowered to make special appointments of Documents Administrator, after consulting and receiving recommendations from the heads of the dependencies.

(j) Documents Administrator—The employee who is responsible for administering the Documents Administration Program in his respective dependency.

(k) Documents Administration—Is the planning, control, direction, organization, training, promotion and other administrative activities related to the creation, use and conservation of documents, as well as to their disposition.—Amended June 4, 1979, No. 63, p. 126, § 1, eff. June 4, 1979.

§ 1002. Public Documents Administration Program in the three branches of Government and the Office of the Controller

(a) The General Services Administrator or his authorized representative in the executive branch; public corporations and municipalities; the Chief Justice of the Supreme Court or his authorized representative in the judicial branch; the President of the Senate or his authorized representative; the Speaker of the House or his authorized representative; the Controller or his authorized representative are hereby authorized to administer the Public Documents Administration Program established pursuant to this chapter, in the dependencies under their jurisdictions, subject to what is hereinafter provided.

(b) Except as hereinafter provided regarding regulations on the periods for the conservation of documents of a fiscal nature or needed for checking and verifying accounts and fiscal operations, each Program Administrator must draft a set of rules and regulations for the dependencies under his jurisdiction that shall govern the Public Documents Administration Program, in which the provisions embodied in this section shall be set forth, and which, upon promulgation, shall have the force of law. The Program Administrators are hereby empowered to draft regulations to:

(1) Publish the specialized terms of each Program in each dependency and their scope, as defined by the dependency heads under its jurisdiction;

(2) publish lists of public documents which, because of their context, shall be deemed confidential and not subject to inspection by any citizen, and others; establish the method for their conservation and disposal. The Program Administrators must consult the heads of the dependencies under their jurisdiction when preparing this publication. The heads of dependencies shall be specific and brief when they consider these categories.

No document shall be deemed to be within these categories unless the Program Administrators have expressly defined it in their regulations, pursuant to the recommendations of the agency heads;

(3) draft substantive and procedural standards which must be followed in the filing systems of each dependency under their jurisdiction;

(4) establish standards, methods and techniques for the conservation of public documents;

(5) establish the qualifications for the Documents Administrators; their duties and responsibilities, the procedures for their designation and for the discharge of their duties;

(6) supervise the Documents Administrators with regard to their application of the standards established by the Program Administrators.

In order to do this, and to make sure the law and the regulations are complied with, the Program Administrators or their authorized representatives may supervise and inspect the systems as often as they deem necessary;

(7) any other matter concerning the Public Documents Administration Program must be regulated for the proper operation thereof;

(8) prior to the promulgation of the regulations provided herein, the Program Administrators shall consult and seek advice from the Executive Director of the Institute of Puerto Rican Culture for the purpose of achieving, to the extent it is possible, uniform criteria for the conservation of documents.

(c) The Program Administrators shall require that each head of a dependency under their jurisdiction complies with the following:

(1) Make an inventory of all the documents in their respective dependencies, except those going back to Spanish sovereignty and those that are more than fifty (50) years old, for which the pertinent action is provided elsewhere in this chapter.

After the inventory is made, each dependency head shall carefully inspect the documents in his dependency, classifying them according to their nature and character, into the following categories:

(A) Documents covered by Commonwealth legislation or contract with federal dependencies or other entities or individuals donating funds to public programs in the Island and which entail obligation to preserve them with no time limit or for a fixed time.

—These documents shall not be destroyed without express legal authorization or unless the head of the dependency has previously, with the approval of the administrator of the jurisdiction to which the dependency belongs, ascertained the uselessness of such documents both for public purposes as well as for purposes of individual interest.

The administrative officers designated in subsection (a) of this section shall periodically make recommendations to the Legislature on this type of documents, pointing out, whenever they deem it pertinent to do so, the advisability of reducing the preservation period fixed by law.

(B) Documents of a fiscal nature or necessary for the examination and verification of fiscal accounts and operations.— The preservation period for these documents shall be established through rules which the Secretary of the Treasury shall prepare in consultation with the Controller. In the promulgating of these regulations, the Secretary of the Treasury shall take into account the contracts with federal dependencies or other entities or individuals donating funds to public programs in Puerto Rico and which require, for audit purposes, the preservation of fiscal documents relating to the operation of the program to which the contribution is made.

(C) Documents not included in categories (A) and (B) which must be preserved either for a fixed time or indefinitely because they constitute evidence of title to public or private property or because of any lawful reason which justifies or necessitates their preservation.

(D) Documents not included in categories (A), (B) and (C), but which, because of their administrative usefulness due to their daily use in the operations of the dependency, or because of the information they contain, are necessary for substantiating important events of the past or for use as reference in mapping future operations and laying out patterns for programs.

The preservation period for these documents shall be fixed by the head of the dependency, with the approval of the administrator of the jurisdiction to which the dependency belongs.

(E) Documents which, not being included in categories (A), (B), (C) and (D), are ready to be destroyed or transferred to the Archives hereinafter established, subject to the approval of the administrator of the jurisdiction to which the dependency belongs.

(2) Submit a plan for the adequate conservation of documents within 6 months after the designation of their respective Documents Administrators, who shall be appointed no later than 2 months after the approval of this act.

(3) Submit within six (6) months after the approval of this act a plan for the prompt disposal of those documents that have lost their legal or fiscal administrative usefulness.

Program Administrators shall submit within 18 months after the approval of this act a report to the Legislature on the results obtained from the disposal plan ordered herein.

(d) Program Administrators shall require each dependency head in their jurisdiction to prepare annual lists for the disposal of documents in their respective dependencies, following the provisions of the preceding subsection (c). These lists shall include, at least, the following information:

(1) Title of the document.

(2) Description of the document, for the better identification of any whose title is not sufficiently explanatory.

(3) The length of time a document must be kept, pursuant to the provisions of paragraphs (A), (B), (C) and (D) of the preceding subsection (c).

(4) A list of those documents that, pursuant to the provisions of paragraphs (A), (B), (C), (D) and (E) of the preceding subsection (c), are to be destroyed or transferred to the Archives.

Each dependency head has the obligation to see that the reports required by the Program Administrators are prepared on time and that reference to said reports shall be made in the Annual Reports of his agency.

(e) As the Program Administrators or their authorized representatives begin to receive and approve the lists described in the preceding subsection (c), they must, in turn, send copies of these approved lists to the Archivist and shall refrain from taking any action until they receive notice from the Archivist as to whether he is interested in any of the documents on the list. The Archivist shall notify them within a maximum period of sixty (60) days. Documents thus claimed shall be transferred to the Archives and the Archivist shall issue a receipt to the transferring officials.

Those documents not claimed by the Archivist may be destroyed by the Documents Administrators after receiving an express authorization from the Program Administrator.

The Program Administrators may, by regulations, establish the methods of destroying the documents, but they must be methods that guarantee that the documents cannot be reproduced and which comply with environmental quality standards.

The Documents Administrators shall make a selection from the methods approved by the Program Administrator.

The useless documents, once destroyed in such a way as to render them unreproducible, may only be sold at public auction by the General Services Administrator. The income from these sales shall be covered into the General Fund of the Commonwealth Government.

Those papers which are not considered documents, as defined in this chapter, such as forms, publications and others which are going to be disposed of in large quantities, shall be considered surplus property and shall be disposed of as provided by the General Services Administrator in his Surplus Property Regulations.

Income received from the sale of this paper, if sold, shall be covered into the General Fund after reimbursing the General Services Administration for the expenses incurred.—Amended June 4, 1979, No. 63, p. 126, § 2, eff. June 4, 1979.

§ 1002a. Photographic reproduction of documents

(1) Program Administrators may authorize the heads of dependencies under their respective jurisdiction to reproduce through the process of microphotography, photocopy, miniature photographic reproduction or photographic copy, or any other method of electronic reproduction, any public documents under their custody which merit conservation because of their legal, fiscal, administrative, informational or historic value.

(2) The originals of the documents reproduced in accordance with the preceding paragraph may be destroyed pursuant to the provisions of this chapter and of the regulations promulgated hereunder.

(3) Reproductions by microphotography, photocopy, miniature photographic reproduction or other photographic copy, or any other method of electronic reproduction of said documents, shall be admitted as evidence and shall have the same value and effect as the originals, provided they are certified by the respective dependency heads in charge of their custody, or their authorized representatives, or by the General Archivist of Puerto Rico in those cases in which the documents have already been transferred to the General Archives of Puerto Rico.—Amended June 4, 1979, No. 63, p. 126, § 2, eff. June 4, 1979.

§ 1003. General Archives of the Commonwealth of Puerto Rico

The General Archives of the Commonwealth of Puerto Rico is hereby established. — Dec. 8, 1955, No. 5, p. 78, § 5, eff. July 1, 1955.

§ 1004. Archives as official depository of public and private documents

The Archives shall be the official depository of all public or private documents transferred to it under the provisions of this chapter. — Dec. 8, 1955, No. 5, p. 78, § 6, eff. July 1, 1955.

§ 1005. Archives attached to Institute of Puerto Rican Culture; supervision by Executive Director

The Archives shall be administratively attached to the Institute of Puerto Rican Culture and its operation shall be subject to the supervision of the Executive Director of the Institute of Puerto Rican Culture.—Amended June 4, 1979, No. 63, p. 126, § 3, eff. June 4, 1979.

§ 1006. General Archivist

The General Archivist, who shall be appointed by the Executive Director of the Institute of Puerto Rican Culture, shall be in charge of the direction of the Archives. The General Archivist's appointment shall be subject to the provisions of the Puerto Rico Public Service Personnel Act, sections 1301–1431 of this title.—Amended June 4, 1979, No. 63, p. 126, § 3, eff. June 4, 1979.

§ 1007. General Archives Advisory Committee

For the purpose of coordinating the Archives with the various government dependencies and formulating the general rules which are to govern the Archives, the Puerto Rico General Archives Advisory Committee is hereby established, composed of representatives of each of the Program Administrators. The Office of the Controller is excluded from this provision. The Executive Director of the Institute of Puerto Rican Culture or his authorized representative shall be the ex officio Chairman of the Committee. In addition to the Committee's regulations mentioned in the second paragraph of this section, this official shall establish the operating procedures of the General Archives Advisory Committee. If circumstances permit, he may require the Program Administrators to provide information, material, personnel, equipment and technical aid for the Committee's operation and for the establishment and enforcement of the general operating standards for the Archives, and he may increase the number of Committee members by a maximum of three (3) additional members, should they be needed for its operation. The Archivist shall be the Permanent Secretary of the Committee and shall preside over its meetings in the absence of the Chairman.

The Commission shall meet in regular session once a year and in special session as often as the Chairman of the Commission deems proper or as the members of the Commission so request. The Commission shall prepare a set of rules and regulations which shall fix, among other things, the procedure to be followed for the disposal of documents in the possession of the Archivist if same should turn out to be useless, to be duplicates, or to be devoid of historical interest; if they more properly belong in some other dependency of the Government; or, if for any other like reason, they no longer merit being preserved in the General Archives of Puerto Rico.— Amended June 4, 1979, No. 63, p. 126, § 3, eff. June 4, 1979.

§ 1008. Custody, preservation, and use of documents in Archives

The Archivist shall be responsible for the custody, preservation, and use of all the documents existing in the Archives. — Dec. 8, 1955, No. 5, p. 78, § 10, eff. July 1, 1955.

§ 1009. Transfer of documents to Archives

The Archivist shall be authorized to require the transfer of the following documents, subject to the availability of space in the Archives:

(a) All documents dating from the days of Spain sovereignty.

(b) All documents more than fifty (50) years old, exclusive of those preserved in the files of the Notarial Archives and in the Registries of Property.

(c) All public documents which have belonged to an agency no longer in existence, unless such documents have been transferred by law to another government dependency.

(d) All public documents, regardless of their antiquity, which, in the opinion of the Program Administrators, are deemed to have lost their administrative usefulness.

Provided, however, that the transfer to the Archives of the documents described in paragraphs (a) and (b) of this section shall not be made when the pertinent Administrator of the Public Documents Administration Program, as provided in section 1002a of this title, certifies in writing that the documents must remain in his custody for use in the current administration of the affairs of the dependencies under his jurisdiction.—Amended June 4, 1979, No. 63, p. 126, § 3, eff. June 4, 1979.

§ 1010. Documents and manuscripts acquired by purchase or donation

The Archivist may accept for transfer to the Archives those documents and manuscripts acquired from individuals by purchase or donation which he deems to be of sufficient worth to justify their preservation. — Dec. 8, 1955, No. 5, p. 78, § 12, eff July 1, 1955.

§ 1011. Documents found outside Puerto Rico

The Archivist shall take steps toward transferring to the Archives documents which are found outside Puerto Rico and which are of permanent interest with relation to the history of Puerto Rico; Provided, That in the event that it is impossible to obtain the original document, the same can be substituted by photostats, microfilms, reproductions, or any other copy or excerpt of the documents interested. — Dec. 8, 1955, No. 5, p. 78, § 13, eff. July 1, 1955.

§ 1012. Funds of Archives

The Archives shall have funds for:

(*a*) The preservation of documents and manuscripts by modern methods, such as: a vacuum fumigating chamber, a rolling press, bookbinding equipment, a photographic laboratory, and any other equipment necessary for such work.

(*b*) The arrangement of the documents and manuscripts deposited in the Archives, and the preparation of inventories and other guides or particularizations necessary for readily locating the said documents and manuscripts.

(*c*) The reproducing, publishing, and exhibiting of documents and manuscripts worthy thereof.

(*d*) Making the documents available for the use of Government employees and the general public, through the promulgation of rules for the purpose. — Dec. 8, 1955, No. 5, p. 78, § 14, eff. July 1, 1955.

§ 1013. General provisions

(a) Government offices shall send to the Puerto Rico Library and the Puerto Rican Collection of the University of Puerto Rico a copy or edition of each report, bulletin, magazine or book published by and disseminated within the Government.

(b) Reproductions of documents forming a part of the Archives which are made pursuant to the standards established by the Advisory Commission and certified by the Archivist, shall be admitted in evidence as though they were the originals.

(c) Upon accepting the donation of any document which is not of a public nature, the Institute of Puerto Rican Culture shall obtain from the donor a waiver of any author's rights the donor may be entitled to and, in the event that donor is a third person, shall take all suitable measures to avoid a copyright violation.

(d) The Archivist is duty bound and hereby authorized to certify and issue copies of those documents in his custody of which reproductions are impossible to obtain.

(e) The Archivist shall, for the certifying of documents, have his official seal, of which the courts shall take judicial notice.

(f) No document pertaining to any Commonwealth dependency shall be destroyed, transferred, donated, altered or disposed of unless it is done pursuant to the provisions of this chapter. Any person who commits one of these acts in connection with any public document shall be subject to the provisions of sections 4355, 4356 and 4357 of Title 33.

Any violation of the provisions of the regulations promulgated by the Program Administrators shall constitute a misdemeanor and, upon conviction, the person shall be punished by imprisonment not to exceed six (6) months or by a fine not to exceed five hundred (500) dollars, or by both penalties in the discretion of the Court.— Amended June 4, 1979, No. 63, p. 126, § 4, eff. June 4, 1979.

HISTORICAL ARCHIVES
(Laws of Puerto Rico Annotated, 1982, Title 18, s.944-951.)

§ 944. Historical Archive functions transferred to University

The functions of the Historical Archive of Puerto Rico are hereby transferred to the University of Puerto Rico. — June 20, 1919, No. 64, p. 389, § 1; 1950 Reorg. Plan No. 6, § 2, eff. July 1, 1950.

§ 945. — Preservation and classification of documents

This institution has for its object, and it shall be its duty, to keep, arrange, classify and catalog all documents belonging to the former Government and office of the Captain General of Puerto Rico and other governmental organizations which in 1898, by reason of the change of sovereignty, were reorganized or abolished, as well as all documents of a historical and political nature of the abolished Territorial Audiencia Court, and such other documents of like nature appertaining to the time of the Spanish régime, as may be found in the municipalities of the Commonwealth or in any other public archives, or which, being in the hands of private persons, may be acquired by the Government, either by donation

or with funds of the Commonwealth Treasury. — June 20, 1919,
No. 64, p. 398, § 2; Const., art. I, § 1, eff. July 25, 1952.

§ 946. — Indices

The indices of said archive shall be drafted in catalog form, but
with such details and notes that a single reading thereof will impart information to the Government and the public. — June 20,
1919, No. 64, p. 398, § 3, eff. 90 days after June 20, 1919.

§ 947. — Withdrawal of objects and papers

No book, pamphlet, document, record, diploma, degree, parch-
ment or paper (whether originals or copies) catalogued shall be
withdrawn from the place where the archive is located, except by
superior orders and upon taking all precautionary measures necessary for the security of the object or document and to guarantee
its return. — June 20, 1919, No. 64, p. 398, § 4; 1950 Reorg. Plan
No. 6. § 2, eff. July 1, 1950.

§ 948. — Certified copies of documents

The director of the archive is hereby authorized to issue and
certify copies of the documents in the archive to such persons as
may apply for the same, and these certificates, which shall bear
the seal of the archive, shall be admitted in evidence in the courts
of justice as in the case of original documents. Copies and certificates of documents requested by competent authorities for official
purposes exclusively shall be issued free of cost, but applications
made by private parties shall be issued upon payment of the fees
prescribed by law, payable in internal revenue stamps to be affixed
to said copies and certificates. A register shall be kept of all copies
and certificates issued, showing the name of the applicant, the
date of issue and whether or not fees were charged. — June 20,
1919, No. 64, p. 398, § 5; 1950 Reorg. Plan No. 6, § 2, eff. July 1,
1950.

§ 949. — Penalties

Any person or persons unduly withdrawing one or more documents from the archive, without proper written authorization,
shall be guilty of a misdemeanor, and upon conviction shall be punished by a fine of not less than one hundred (100) dollars or
imprisonment for not less than one year, or by both penalties.
— June 20, 1919, No. 64, p. 398, § 6; 1950 Reorg. Plan No. 6, § 2,
eff. July 1, 1950.

§ 950. — Municipal archives as source of materials

It shall be the duty of the director of the archive periodically
to investigate the archives of the municipalities of the Commonwealth and to transfer to the archive any document of a historical

or political nature which he may find therein, leaving a certified copy of the same. Such expenses as these trips, if necessary, shall occasion, shall be paid from funds of the Commonwealth Treasury, upon proper voucher therefor. — June 20, 1919, No. 64, p. 398, § 7; 1950 Reorg. Plan No. 6, § 2; Const., art. I, § 1, eff. July 25, 1952.

§ 951. — Historical compilation of annual events

It shall be the duty of the director to compile each year a chronicle of political, scientific, judicial, literary, religious, legislative, social and economical events worthy of record and of public importance occurring in Puerto Rico during each year. The manuscript containing said historical record shall be the property of the Commonwealth and be deposited in the Carnegie Library, and shall be prepared in such form that printed copies of the same may be published from time to time, whenever provision may have been made by the Legislative Assembly for such publication, such printed copies to be either distributed free of charge, or sold, as the Department of Education shall deem advisable, and in case of sale, the proceeds thereof shall be deposited in the Treasury of Puerto Rico. — Mar. 13, 1913, No. 76, p. 129, § 2; Nov. 22, 1917, No. 20, p. 234, § 1; Apr. 29, 1946, No. 486, p. 1452, § 2; 1950 Reorg. Plan No. 4, § 1; Const., art. I, § 1, eff. July 25, 1952.

MUNICIPAL LIBRARIES
(Laws of Puerto Rico Annotated, 1982, Title 18, s.969-975.)

§ 969. Municipal public libraries — Allotment of funds

The Secretary of the Treasury shall place at the disposal of any municipal government, in the manner prescribed by law, a sum equal to four (4) dollars for each dollar allotted for the establishing of a public library by said municipal government.

If said municipal government has in its possession, at the time of making such allotment, books or library equipment acquired by gift or otherwise, the Secretary of the Treasury, at the behest of the mayor, shall determine through appraisal the fair and reasonable value of said books and equipment and shall place at the disposal of said municipal government, in addition to the sum stated in the preceding paragraph, an amount equal to four (4) dollars for each dollar of said value.

Municipal governments shall use any sum placed at their disposal by the Secretary of the Treasury as provided in this section for the construction of buildings, reading matter and furniture of the said library. In the case of local cultural associations which through the proper undertaking bind themselves to put and do put their libraries to public use, the Secretary of the Treasury shall lend to said cultural associations, for the organization and operation of their libraries, the same proportional financial cooperation as is lent to municipal governments for the aforesaid purposes. — Amended June 30, 1961, No. 141, p. 311, § 1, eff. July 1, 1961.

§ 970. — Use of public buildings

The use of public buildings for the establishing of the said libraries is hereby authorized and ordered whenever the Secretary of Education, in consultation with the authority in charge of each pertinent building, so decides. In the case of a building belonging to a municipal government, the intervention of the Secretary of Education shall not be necessary if the decision is made by the municipality. — June 20, 1955, No. 86, p. 344, § 2, eff. June 20, 1955.

§ 971. — Supervision and recommendations of Secretary of Education

The Secretary of Education shall have charge of supervising the operation of the municipal libraries covered by the provisions of sections 969–973 of this title and shall make pertinent recommendations to the municipalities for the best selection of reading matter and equipment therefor. — June 20, 1955, No. 86, p. 344, § 3, eff. June 20, 1955.

§ 972. — Appropriations; reports to Legislative Assembly

For the year 1955–56 the sum of fifty thousand (50,000) dollars is hereby appropriated from any available funds in the Commonwealth Treasury not otherwise appropriated, for carrying out the purposes of sections 969–973 of this title; Provided, That in each succeeding year a like sum of fifty thousand (50,000) dollars shall be allotted to the Department of Education in the general budget of expenses of the Commonwealth of Puerto Rico, for the carrying out of the purposes of such sections.

The Secretary of Education shall report to the Legislature, during the regular sessions thereof, on the extent to which this plan for public libraries has been developed and put into operation, and shall make such recommendations as he deems pertinent with regard to additional funds required for the adequate functioning thereof. — June 20, 1955, No. 86, p. 344, § 4, eff. June 20, 1955.

§ 973. — Regulations

The Secretary of Education is hereby empowered to adopt such rules and regulations as may be necessary for the operation of sections 969–973 of this title, which rules and regulations shall have the force of law as soon as they are promulgated by the Secretary of State. — June 20, 1955, No. 86, p. 344, § 5, eff. June 20, 1955.

§ 974. Receipt of funds, books and library facilities from United States

The Department of Education of Puerto Rico is hereby authorized and empowered to request, accept, receive and administer, in behalf of the Commonwealth of Puerto Rico, any funds, books and library facilities or any other property that may be appropriated, supplied, donated or furnished by the Federal Government of the United States or any of its departments, commissions, boards, bureaus, agencies or officials, under the provisions of any federal law providing appropriations to the states, including the Commonwealth of Puerto Rico, for the purpose of establishing, improving, extending, aiding, or otherwise furthering the development of public or school library services.

When any federal law requires the designation of a commonwealth agency to administer any plan or program established thereunder to carry out its purposes, the Department of Education of Puerto Rico shall be the commonwealth agency for the purpose — May 19, 1958, No. 19, p. 23, § 1, eff. May 19, 1958.

§ 975. — Secretary of Treasury, duties as to library funds

The Secretary of the Treasury shall receive and keep all funds appropriated to the Commonwealth of Puerto Rico by the Federal Government of the United States, under any federal law, for the purposes mentioned in section 974 of this title. The Secretary of the Treasury of Puerto Rico is hereby authorized and directed to receive and make whatever provisions may be necessary for keeping such funds, as well as for making disbursements therefrom, in accordance with such procedure as may be applicable. — May 19, 1958, No. 19, p. 23, § 2, eff. May 19, 1958.

LAW LIBRARIES
(Laws of Puerto Rico Annotated, 1982, Title 4, s.773,
Title 3, s.119-121, Title 4, 305.)

§ 773. Powers

The Bar Association of Puerto Rico shall have power:

*   *   *

(j) To create a title insurance corporation which shall be subject to the provisions of the Insurance Code of Puerto Rico, Title 26. Eighty (80) per cent of the earnings from the operation of this undertaking shall be devoted by the Bar Association of Puerto Rico to the establishment of law libraries in the seats of the judicial districts of Puerto Rico. Said Libraries shall be open to the lawyers and the general public during working hours.

— Amended June 22, 1954, No. 76, p. 386, § 1,

eff. June 22, 1954; June 21, 1962, No. 73, p. —, § 1, eff. June 21, 1962.

§ 119. Law library of Department of Justice; initial appropriation

The sum of ten thousand (10,000) dollars is hereby appropriated during the fiscal year 1938–39, from any funds in the Treasury not otherwise appropriated, for the purchase of books and bookcases for the library of the Department of Justice of Puerto Rico, in the office of the Secretary of Justice. — Apr. 30, 1938, No. 55, p. 162, § 1; Const., art. I, § 1; July 24, 1952, No. 6, p. 10, eff. July 25, 1952.

§ 120. — Annual appropriation

The amount that shall be deemed necessary to carry out the purposes of sections 119–121 of this title shall be included in the general budget of expenses of the Government. — Apr. 30, 1938, No. 55, p. 162, § 2; May 10, 1943, No. 60, p. 142, § 1; Const., art. I, § 1, eff. July 25, 1952.

§ 121. — Caretaker of library, salary

There is also created by sections 119–121 of this title the position of caretaker of said library at a salary which shall be assigned him in the general budget of regular expenses for the support of the Government each year. — Apr. 30, 1938, No. 55, p. 162, § 3; Const., art. I, § 1, eff. July 25, 1952.

§ 305. Superior Court law libraries

The law libraries of each part of the Superior Court shall be under the control of the judges of the respective parts, who may permit the officers of the court and members of the bar to consult the books in such libraries, under such regulations as they may prescribe: *Provided*, That no book shall be taken out of any library except by a judge of the court. — Mar. 1, 1906, p. 102, § 2; July 24, 1952, No. 11, p. 30, eff. July 25, 1952.

Puerto Rico library laws are reprinted from LAWS OF PUERTO RICO ANNOTATED published by Equity Publishing Corp., Oxford, New Hampshire.

VIRGIN ISLANDS

PUBLIC LIBRARIES
(Virgin Islands Code Annotated, 1982, Title 17, s.321-325.)

§ 321. Supervision of public libraries; functions of Commissioner

(*a*) The Commissioner of Education shall administer and operate public libraries in the Virgin Islands, and shall be the custodian of all books, pamphlets, manuscripts, records, archives, maps, photographs, pictures, paintings, periodicals, films, slides, music, and all other similar property owned by the government of the Virgin Islands which has not been placed in other custody by law.

(*b*) The Commissioner—

(1) shall direct all publicly supported library service in the Virgin Islands so that it may respond to the growing needs of the cultural and educational advancement of the people of the Virgin Islands;

(2) shall organize, preserve, equip, and maintain special administrative and legislative reference collections for the several departments and agencies of the government;

(3) may prepare, print, and reproduce pamphlets, bibliographic catalogues, manuscripts, monographs, or any literary or scientific material necessary to be published in the interest of the government or the public welfare, pertaining to the history of the Virgin Islands, or of science and art in general;

(4) shall preserve, administer, classify and register such public papers, and documents of the government as are made available to the library;

(5) shall organize a filing system, distribute and exchange publications and objects of art and natural history with such other territories, states or countries as may wish to exchange such publications and objects; and

(6) in general, shall perform all functions and duties related to modern library administration and practice.

§ 322. Free services to public; reservation of certain materials

The services of the Department of Education with respect to public libraries shall be free. All books of general collection shall be circulated free of charge to all residents of the Virgin Islands. However, books, materials, and documents of reference and specialized collections shall be reserved for use within the libraries and shall be made available only to persons who qualify according to regulations prescribed by the Commissioner of Education.

§ 323. Acceptance of funds

The Virgin Islands Board of Education may accept contributions of funds from the United States Government and other sources for the purpose of maintaining and improving the public library service in the Virgin Islands.

§ 324. Rules and regulations

The Commissioner of Education shall issue rules and regulations governing opening hours, kind of equipment, fines, lending policy, and minimum qualifications of employees of the public libraries.

§ 325. Reports to Governor

The Commissioner of Education shall include in any regular report on the activities of the Department of Education, which may be required by the Governor under section 61 of Title 3, a report on the activities and needs of the public libraries.

INCORPORATED LIBRARIES
(Virgin Islands Code Annotated, 1982, Title 13, s.491.)

§ 491. Formation of nonprofit corporation; purposes; articles; filing

Three or more adult persons, who are bona fide residents of the Virgin Islands of the United States, and who desire to form a corporation for a college, seminary, church, library, or any other benevolent, fraternal, social, religious, educational, charitable or scientific association, whose chief business shall be in the Virgin Islands of the United States, shall make and subscribe written articles of incorporation in triplicate and acknowledge the same before any officer authorized to take the acknowledgement of deeds, and file one of said articles in the office of the Government Secretary, and another in the office of the clerk of the district court in the judicial division in which the principal place of business of the corporation is intended to be located, and retain the third in possession of the corporation, and each copy so filed shall be indexed by the officer with whom filed in a book kept by him for that purpose.

LAW LIBRARIES
(Virgin Islands Code Annotated, 1982, Title 4, s.442.)

§ 442. Law Library Fund

There is hereby created a Law Library Fund in the treasury of the Virgin Islands.

The annual license fees paid by practicing attorneys at law, as prescribed by section 303 of Title 27, and any gifts or contributions received by the Commissioner of Finance for the purposes of the fund, shall be paid by him into the Law Library Fund.

Payments shall be made from the Law Library Fund only for the purchase of books, periodicals, and other necessary expenses of the law libraries maintained by the district court in each judicial division upon vouchers approved by the judge of the district court. The clerk of the district court, as custodian of the law libraries of the court, shall keep them open during reasonable hours for the use of the court, the members of the bar, the members of the Legislature, officers and employees of the governments of the United States and the Virgin Islands, and the public.

Virgin Islands library laws are reprinted from VIRGIN ISLANDS CODE ANNOTATED published by the U.S. Government Printing Office, Washington, D.C.

Index

A

INDEX

M

P

R

S

U

Printed on 30-pound Glatfelter Reference,
a pH-neutral stock, and bound in
Holliston Record Buckram cloth
by Edwards Brothers, Inc.

120762